KU-186-284

PENGUIN REFERENCE BOOKS

The Penguin Pocket English Dictionary

Also published

A companion to ***The Penguin Pocket English Dictionary***

The Penguin English Thesaurus

The Penguin English Thesaurus is a unique volume designed to increase your command of the English language and build up your reserves of word power. It features:

* A comprehensive working vocabulary which takes modern needs and priorities into account
* Over 800 sections covering objects, activities and abstractions
* Related words, associations, figurative uses, idiomatic phrases and stylistic equivalents in both formal and colloquial language
* Full cross-referencing
* Expert input by compilers working within the system originally designed by Peter Mark Roget

Used as a vocabulary builder, for work purposes or for browsing, ***The Penguin English Thesaurus*** is the perfect portable and up-to-date companion to the English language.

The Penguin Pocket English Dictionary

PENGUIN BOOKS
in association with Longman Group Limited

Penguin Books Ltd, Harmondsworth, Middlesex, England
Viking Penguin Inc., 40 West 23rd Street, New York, New York 10010, U.S.A.
Penguin Books Australia Ltd, Ringwood, Victoria, Australia
Penguin Books Canada Limited, 2801 John Street, Markham, Ontario, Canada L3R 1B4
Penguin Books (N.Z.) Ltd, 182–190 Wairau Road, Auckland 10, New Zealand

This dictionary is based on the *Longman New Universal Dictionary (Longman Concise English Dictionary)* first published 1982 © G & C Merriam Company and Longman Group Limited.

This edition first published 1985
Reprinted 1985 (three times), 1986 (twice)

Copyright © Merriam-Webster Inc. and Longman Group Limited, 1985
ISBN 0 14 051.1393

All rights reserved

Printed and bound in Great Britain by
Cox & Wyman Ltd, Reading

Typeset in 7/7½pt. Videocomp. Times Roman

Except in the United States of America, this book is sold subject to the condition that it shall not, by way of trade or otherwise, be lent, re-sold, hired out, or otherwise circulated without the publisher's prior consent in any form of binding or cover other than that in which it is published and without a similar condition including this condition being imposed on the subsequent purchaser

Contents

How to use this Dictionary

1 Order of entries

1.1 Main entries

Alphabetical order of entry, letter by letter, applies to all main entries, whether they are single words, hyphenated words, or compounds consisting of two or more individual words.

Many words that share the same spelling have a different pronunciation or a different history, or are different in grammar. Such words are shown separately, with small numbers in front to distinguish them; see, for example, the entries at **lead**. These words are listed in historical order, according to when they first appeared in English.

1.2 Undefined words

Words whose meaning can easily be guessed, because they consist of a base form plus an added ending, are not given definitions. They follow the main entry and are shown in these ways:

a Where the undefined word is the same as the main entry, but has a different part of speech, it appears in full

b Where the main entry forms a stem to which an ending is added to form the undefined word, the stem is represented by ~, and the ending follows:
content *adj* . . . **~ment** *n*

c Where any part of the main entry forms the stem of an undefined word, the unchanged part is represented by – :
indifferent *adj* . . . **-ence** *n*

Occasionally no shortening of the undefined entry is possible, and it is given in full.

2 Alternative versions of words

Many words come in pairs, or even trios, that differ only in spelling (eg **judgment**, **judgement**), or in their ending (eg **consistency**, **consistence**), or even in the presence or absence of a complete word in a compound (eg **prime**, **prime number**). In this dictionary, common variant forms of a word are shown immediately after the main entry. When the variant is preceded by a comma, it is about as common as the main entry in current standard usage; when the variant is preceded by *also*, it is rather less common.

Variant spellings of the **-ize/-ise** type are shown in abbreviated form at the main entry:

real·ize, **-ise** *v*

This means that **realize** can also be spelt **realise**.

Variant forms that are entirely or partially restricted to British or American English are labelled *Br* or *NAm*:
jail, *Br also* **gaol** . . . *n* . . .
gaol . . . *v or n*, *chiefly Br* (to) jail

This means that the spelling **jail** is used everywhere in the English-speaking world, but British English also uses **gaol** (see 8.2).

3 Parts of speech

These are the various word classes to which the entries in this dictionary belong:

adj	adjective:	**energetic**
adv	adverb:	**happily**
conj	conjunction:	**but**
interj	interjection:	**hey**
n	noun:	**dynamite**
prep	preposition:	**for**
pron	pronoun:	**our**
trademark		**Hoover**
v	verb:	**agglomerate**

Sometimes two parts of speech are combined:

yelp . . . *v or n* (to utter) a sharp quick shrill cry

4 Inflections

The dictionary shows inflections only if they are irregular, and may therefore cause difficulty.

4.1 Nouns

Regular plurals of nouns (eg **cats, matches, spies**) are not shown. All other plurals (eg **louse**, **lice**; **sheep**, **sheep**) are given. Nouns that are always plurals are shown as follows:

environs . . . *n pl* . . .

Not all plural nouns always take a plural verb. This is shown as follows:

genetics *n pl but sing in constr* . . .
politics *n pl but sing or pl in constr* . . .

This means that one says 'Genetics is . . .' but one says either 'Politics is . . .' or 'Politics are . . .'

Some nouns in apparently singular form can take a plural verb:

police *n* . . . **2a** . . . **b** *pl in constr* policemen
crew *n sing or pl in constr* . . .

This means that one says 'Several police are . . .' but one says either 'The crew is . . .' or '. . . are . . .'

Some nouns are used with the same meaning in the plural. They are shown like this:

latitude . . . *n* . . . a region as marked by its latitude – often pl with sing. meaning

This means that one can say 'It's very hot at this latitude' or '. . . at these latitudes.'

4.2 Verbs

Regular verb forms (eg **halted**, **cadged**, **carrying**) are not shown. All other verb inflections (eg **ring**, **rang**, **rung**) are shown, including those for verbs which keep a final *-e* before inflections, and for verbs having alternative inflections.

Inflections are shown in the following order:

present: 1st, 2nd, and 3rd person singular; plural; present subjunctive; present participle; past: 1st, 2nd and 3rd person singular; plural; past subjunctive; past participle.

Only the irregular inflections are shown. Certain forms (eg the entire past tense, or the past tense and the past participle) are combined if they are identical. Thus in

run . . . *vb* **ran; run**

the entire past tense is **ran**, and the past participle is **run.**

4.3 Adjectives and adverbs

Adjectives and adverbs whose comparative and superlative are formed with **more** and **most**, or by adding **-(e)r** and **-(e)st** (eg **nicer, fastest, happier**), are not shown.

All other inflections (eg **good** . . . **better** . . . **best**) are shown.

4.4 Pronouns

Inflections of pronouns are entered at their alphabetical place and cross-referred to their main form:

[2]**her** *pron, objective case of* **she**

5 Capitalization

Some words, or meanings of words, can be used with or without a capital letter, and this is shown by the notes *often cap* and *often not cap*. In the case of compound words, the note specifies which parts are capitalized:

pop art *n, often cap P&A* . . .

6 How the meaning of words is shown

Sometimes, instead of giving a definition, the dictionary describes how a word is used:

[2]**after** *prep* . . . **3** – used to indicate the goal or purpose of an action (eg go *after* trout)

Trademarked terms are also treated in this way:

Hoover *trademark* – used for a vacuum cleaner

Most words, however, are given ordinary dictionary definitions, with one or more meanings.

6.1 The numbering of meanings

The main meanings of a word are numbered (**1**, **2**, **3**, etc) where there is more than one sense. Subdivisions of the senses are distinguished by lower-case letters, and further subdivisions by bracketed numbers.

When a definition is followed by a colon and two or more subsenses, this indicates that the meaning of the subsenses is covered by the introductory definition.

Sometimes an introductory definition is simply the common element shared by the following subsenses:

cheapen . . . *v* to make or become **a** cheap in price or value **b** lower in esteem **c** tawdry, vulgar, or inferior

This indicates that **cheapen** means 'to make or become cheap in price and value', 'to make or become lower in esteem', and 'to make or become tawdry, vulgar, or inferior'.

When two meanings of a word are very closely related, they are not separated off with numbers or letters, but run together, with the word *esp*, *specif*, *also*, or *broadly* between them to show the way in which they are related:

aggression . . . *n* . . . **2** attack, encroachment; *esp* unprovoked violation by one country of the territory of another

6.2 The order in which senses are shown

Those meanings that would be understood anywhere in the English-speaking world are shown first, in their historical order: the older senses before the newer. After these come the meanings whose usage is restricted in some way (eg because they are used in only one area, or have gone out of current use).

6.3 Brackets

Round brackets are used in four main ways in definitions:

They enclose the object of a verb:

[2]**contract** *v* . . . **2a** to catch (an illness)

They give extra information:

[3]**nap** *n* a hairy or downy surface (eg on a woven fabric)

They separate the parts of a combined definition that relate to different parts of speech:

cheep . . . *v or n* (to utter) a faint shrill sound characteristic of a young bird

They enclose optional wording:

afloat . . . *adj or adv* **1a** borne (as if) on the water or air

This indicates that **afloat** means both 'borne on the water or air' and 'borne as if on the water or air'.

7 Examples

Phrases illustrating a typical use of a word in context are used to clarify the definitions of some words, like **in** and **up.** These examples appear in round brackets.

8 Usage

Many words have peculiarities of usage that a dictionary must take account of. They may be restricted to a particular geographical area; they may be colloquial or slang, or felt to be 'incorrect'; they may have fallen out of use; and there may be limitations on the sort of context they can be used in.

This dictionary shows such restrictions in two different ways.

Words, or meanings, that are limited to a particular period or area are identified by an italic label. When an italic label comes between the main entry and the first definition it refers to all meanings of the word; otherwise, it applies to all subsenses of the number or letter it follows.

All other information on usage is given in a note at the end of a definition. When such a note applies to all or several meanings of a word, it follows the last definition, and is introduced by the word *USE*.

8.1 Words that are no longer in current use

The label *obs* for 'obsolete' means there is no evidence of use for a word or meaning since 1755.

The label *archaic* means that a word or meaning once in common use is found today only in special contexts, such as poetry or historical fiction.

Comparatively modern terms which have become old-fashioned are treated in a note:

matron . . . *n* . . . **3** a woman in charge of the nursing in a hospital – not now used technically
groovy . . . *adj* fashionably attractive or exciting – infml: no longer in vogue

8.2 Words that are not used throughout the English-speaking world

A word or sense limited in use to one or more of the countries of the English-speaking world is labelled accordingly:

tuxedo . . . *n, NAm* a dinner jacket

The label *Br* indicates that a word or meaning is used in Britain and also usually in the Commonwealth countries of Australasia. The label *NAm* indicates the use of a word or meaning in both the USA and Canada.

The label *dial* for 'dialect' indicates that a word or meaning belongs to the common local speech of several different places.

8.3 Words that suggest a particular style, attitude, or level of formality

Most English words can be generally used in both speech and writing, but some would be traditionally described as 'colloquial' or 'slang', and others, perhaps, as 'formal'.

The note '– infml' is used for words or senses that are characteristic of conversational speech and casual writing rather than of official or 'serious' speech or writing.

The note '– slang' is used for words or meanings usually found in contexts of extreme informality. Such words may be, or may have been until recently, used by a particular social group such as criminals or drug users. They often refer to topics that are thought of as risqué or 'low'.

The note '– fml', for 'formal', is used for words or meanings characteristic of written rather than spoken English, and particularly of official or academic writings.

Other notes describe the attitude or tone of the user of a word:

egghead . . . *n* an intellectual, highbrow – derog or humor
pass away *vi* . . . **2** to die – euph

8.4 Words that are not 'correct'

Many people would disapprove of the use of some of the words we have described as 'slang' or 'informal', and there are of course many contexts in which their use would be inappropriate; but there is a further distinct class of words that are generally felt to be 'incorrect'.

The note '– nonstandard' is used for words or meanings that are quite commonly used in English but are considered incorrect by many speakers.

Certain highly controversial words or meanings have the warning note '– disapproved of by some speakers'.

The note '– substandard' is used for words or meanings that are widely used but are not part of standard English.

8.5 The context in which a word can appear

Many words or meanings can be used only in certain contexts within a sentence: some verbs are used only in the passive; some words can appear only in the negative, along with **not**, **never**, etc; others are always used with particular prepositions or adverbs, or in certain fixed phrases. Such restrictions are shown in a note following a definition:

abide . . . *v* **1** to bear patiently; tolerate – used negatively
agree . . . *v* . . . **4** to give assent; accede – often + *to*

Sometimes a word that is commonly used with the main entry word in a sentence is printed in italic within the definition:

allude . . . *v* to make indirect or implicit reference *to*
[2]**altogether** *n the* nude – infml

This means that **allude** is almost always used in the phrase **allude to**, and that the noun **altogether** is almost always used with **the.**

9 Pronunciation

Pronunciation symbols, using the International Phonetic Alphabet, follow the headword and are enclosed within slash marks / /. The symbols used are as follows:

Consonants		***Vowels***	
symbol	*key word*	*symbol*	*key word*
b	*b*ack	æ	b*a*d
d	*d*ay	ɑː	p*al*m
ð	*th*en	ɑ̃ (French)	bl*anc*
ʤ	*j*ump	ɒ	p*o*t
f	*f*ew	aɪ	b*i*te
g	*g*ay	aʊ	n*ow*
h	*h*ot	aɪə	t*ire*
j	*y*et	aʊə	t*ower*
k	*k*ey	ɔː	c*augh*t
l	*l*ed	ɔɪ	b*oy*
m	su*m*	ɔɪə	empl*oyer*
n	su*n*	e	b*e*d
ŋ	su*ng*	eə	th*ere*
p	*p*en	eɪ	m*a*ke
r	*r*ed	eɪə	pl*ayer*
s	*s*oon	ə	*a*bout
ʃ	fi*sh*ing	əʊ	n*o*te
t	*t*ea	əʊə	l*ower*
tʃ	*ch*eer	ɜː	b*ir*d
θ	*th*ing	i	prett*y*
v	*v*iew	iː	sh*ee*p
w	*w*et	ɪ	sh*i*p
z	*z*ero	ɪə	h*ere*
ʒ	plea*s*ure	uː	b*oo*t
		ʊ	p*u*t
		ʊə	p*oor*
		ʌ	c*u*t

Certain additional special signs are also used:

/ˈ/ precedes the syllable on which main stress falls
/ˌ/ precedes the syllable on which secondary stress falls
/^{r}/ at the end of a word means that /r/ is pronounced when the next word begins with a vowel sound
/$\overset{\text{ɪ}}{\text{ə}}$/ means that either /ɪ/ or /ə/ may be used
/*ə*/ means that /ə/ may or may not be used

Variant pronunciations, which are to be taken as equally acceptable, are separated by a comma. Sometimes variant pronunciations are not shown in full; parts which are the same as the previous pronunciation are simply represented by a hyphen.

Pronunciations are not usually given for entries which are compounds of words listed individually, or which have the same pronunciation as the preceding entry. For some compounds and variants, only a stress pattern is shown: each syllable is represented by a dot, and stress marks show main and secondary stress.

Abbreviations used in this Dictionary

A

A ampere
abbr abbreviation
AD Anno Domini
adj adjective
adv adverb
am ante meridiem
apprec appreciative
approx approximate, approximately
arch archaic
attrib attributive
Austr Australian

B

BC before Christ
Br British
Btu British thermal unit

C

c centi-
c century
C Celsius, centigrade
Can Canadian
cap capital, capitalized
cgs centimetre-gram-second
cm centimetre
conj conjunction
constr construction
cwt hundredweight

D

derog derogatory
dial dialect
dr dram

E

E East, Eastern
eg for example
Eng English, England
esp especially
etc etcetera
euph euphemistic

F

F Fahrenheit
fem feminine
fl oz fluid ounce
fml formal
ft foot

G

gall gallon
gr grain

H

h hour
ha hectare
hp horsepower
humor humorous
Hz hertz

I

ie that is
imper imperative
in inch
Ind Indian
indic indicative
infin infinitive
infml informal
interj interjection
interrog interrogative

J

J joule
journ journalistic

K

k kilo-
kg kilogram
km kilometre

L

l litre
lat latitude
lb pound
long longitude

M

M metre
m milli-
M mega-
masc masculine
MHz megahertz
mi mile
Mid Eng Midlands
Mid US Mid United States
mil military
min minute
ml millilitre
mm millimetre
mph miles per hour
Mt Mount

N

n noun
N North, Northern
N Newton
NAm North American
naut nautical
neg negative
NZ New Zealand

O

obs obsolete
occas occasionally
orig original, originally
oz ounce

P

p pence
part participle
pass passive
perf perfect
phr(s) phrase(s)
pl plural
pm post meridiem
prep preposition
pres present
prob probably
pron pronoun
pt pint

Q

qr quarter
qt quart

R

RC Roman Catholic

S

s second
S South, Southern
SAfr South Africa, South African
sby somebody
Scot Scotland, Scottish
SI Système International d'Unités
sing singular
specif specifically
st stone
St Saint
sthg something
substand substandard

T

tech technical

U

UK United Kingdom
US United States
USA United States of America
usu usually

v verb
V volt
vulg vulgar

W

W watt
W West, Western
WI West Indian
WWI World War 1
WWII World War 2

Y

yd yard

[1]a /eɪ/ *n, pl* **a's, as** *often cap* **1a** (a graphic representation of or device for reproducing) the 1st letter of the English alphabet **b** a speech counterpart of written *a* **2** one designated *a*, esp as the 1st in order or class **3** a grade rating a student's work as superior

[2]a *indefinite article* **1** one – used before singular nouns when the referent is unspecified (e g *a* sheep) and before number collectives and some numbers (e g *a* great many) **2** the same (e g birds of *a* feather) **3a(1)** any (e g *a* bike has 2 wheels) **(2)** one single (e g can't see *a* thing) **b** one particular (e g health is *a* good thing) **c** – used before the gerund or infinitive of a verb to denote a period or occurrence of the activity concerned (e g *a* good cry) **4** – used before a proper name to denote (1) membership of a class (e g born *a* Romanov) (2) resemblance (e g *a* little Hitler) (3) one named but not otherwise known (e g *a* Dr Smith) **5** – used before a pair of items to be considered as a unit (e g *a* collar and tie) ***USE*** used before words or letter sequences with an initial consonant sound

[3]a *prep* **1** per **2** *chiefly dial* on, in, at ***USE*** used before words or letter sequences with an initial consonant sound

A /eɪ/ *n or adj* (a film that is) certified in Britain as suitable for all ages but requiring parental guidance for children under 14 – no longer used technically

A1 *adj* **1** *of a ship* having the highest possible classification of seaworthiness for insurance purposes **2** of the finest quality; first-rate

AA *n or adj* (a film that is) certified in Britain as suitable for people over 14 – no longer used technically

abacus /'æbəkəs/ *n, pl* **abaci, abacuses** **1** a slab that forms the uppermost part of the capital of a column **2** an instrument for performing calculations by sliding counters along rods or in grooves

[1]abandon /ə'bændən/ *v* **1** to give up completely, esp with the intention of never resuming or reclaiming **2** to leave, often in the face of danger **3** to forsake or desert (e g a responsibility) **4** to give (oneself) over *to* an emotion or activity – **~ment** *n*

abase /ə'beɪs/ *v* to bring lower in rank, office, prestige, or esteem – **~ment** *n*

abash /ə'bæʃ/ *v* to destroy the self-possession or self-confidence of; disconcert – usu pass

abate /ə'beɪt/ *v* **1** to put an end to; abolish **2** to reduce in amount, intensity, or degree; moderate **3** to decrease in force or intensity – **~ment** *n*

abattoir /'æbətwɑː/ *n* a slaughterhouse

abbess /'æbɪ̵s, 'æbes/ *n* the female superior of a convent of nuns

abbey /'æbi/ *n* **1** a religious community governed by an abbot or abbess **2** the buildings, esp the church, of a (former) monastery

abbot /'æbət/ *n* the superior of an abbey of monks

abbreviate /ə'briːvieɪt/ *v* to reduce to a shorter form – **-ation** *n*

ABC *n, pl* **ABC's, ABCs** **1** the alphabet **2** the first principles of a subject

abdicate /'æbdɪkeɪt/ *v* **1** to relinquish (e g sovereign power) formally **2** to renounce a throne, dignity, etc – **-cation** *n*

abdomen /'æbdəmən, æb'dəʊ-/ *n* **1** (the cavity of) the part of the body between the thorax and the pelvis that contains the liver, gut, etc **2** the rear part of the body behind the thorax in an insect, spider, etc – **-dominal** *adj*

abduct /æb'dʌkt, əb-/ *v* to carry off secretly or by force – **~ion** *n*

aberrant /æ'berənt/ *adj* **1** deviating from the right or normal way **2** diverging from the usual or natural type

aberration /ˌæbəˈreɪʃən/ *n* **1** being aberrant, esp with respect to a moral standard or normal state **2** (an instance of) unsoundness or disorder of the mind **3** a small periodic change of apparent position in celestial bodies due to the combined effect of the motion of light and the motion of the observer

abet /əˈbet/ *v* to give active encouragement or approval to – **~tor, ~ter** *n*

abeyance /əˈbeɪəns/ *n* temporary inactivity; suspension

abhor /əbˈhɔːʳ, æb-/ *v* **-rr-** to regard with extreme repugnance; loathe

abhorrent /əbˈhɒrənt/ *adj* **1** opposed, contrary *to* **2** causing horror; repugnant – **-rence** *n*

abide /əˈbaɪd/ *v* **abode, abided** **1** to bear patiently; tolerate – used negatively **2** to remain stable or fixed in a state **3** *archaic* to dwell **4** to comply with – usu + *by*

abiding /əˈbaɪdɪŋ/ *adj* enduring

ability /əˈbɪlʒti/ *n* **1a** being able; *esp* physical, mental, or legal power to perform **b** natural or acquired competence in doing; skill **2** a natural talent; aptitude – usu pl

abject /ˈæbdʒekt/ *adj* **1** showing utter hopelessness; wretched, miserable **2** despicable, degraded **3** very humble, esp to the point of servility – **~ly** *adv* – **~ion** *n*

abjure /əbˈdʒʊəʳ, æb-/ *v* to renounce on oath or reject formally (e g a claim, opinion, or allegiance) – **-ration** *n*

ablative /ˈæblətɪv/ *n* (a form in) a grammatical case expressing typically separation, source, cause, or instrument

ablaze /əˈbleɪz/ *adj or adv* **1** on fire **2** radiant with light or bright colour

able /ˈeɪbəl/ *adj* **1** having sufficient power, skill, resources, or qualifications *to* **2** marked by intelligence, knowledge, skill, or competence

able-bodied *adj* physically strong and healthy; fit

abnormal /æbˈnɔːməl/ *adj* deviating from the normal or average – **~ly** *adv* – **~ity** *n*

aboard /əˈbɔːd/ *adv or prep* **1** on, onto, or within (a ship, aircraft, train, or road vehicle) **2** alongside

abode /əˈbəʊd/ *n* a home, residence – fml

abolish /əˈbɒlɪʃ/ *v* to do away with (e g a law or custom) wholly; annul – **-ition** *n*

A-bomb /ˈeɪˌbɒm/ *n* an atom bomb

abominable /əˈbɒmʒnəbəl, -mənə-/ *adj* **1** worthy of or causing disgust or hatred; detestable **2** very disagreeable or unpleasant – esp in colloquial exaggeration – **-bly** *adv*

abominate /əˈbɒmʒneɪt/ *v* to hate or loathe intensely and unremittingly; abhor

abomination /əˌbɒmʒˈneɪʃən/ *n* **1** sthg abominable; *esp* a detestable or shameful action **2** extreme disgust and hatred; loathing

aboriginal /æbəˈrɪdʒʒnl/ *adj* **1** indigenous **2** of esp Australian aborigines

aborigine /ˌæbəˈrɪdʒʒni/ *n* **1** an indigenous inhabitant, esp as contrasted with an invading or colonizing people; *specif, often cap* a member of the indigenous people of Australia

abort /əˈbɔːt/ *v* **1** to expel a premature foetus **2** to fail to develop completely; shrink away **3** to induce the abortion of (a foetus) **4** to end prematurely – **~ion** *n* – **~ionist** *n*

abortive /əˈbɔːtɪv/ *adj* **1** fruitless, unsuccessful **2** imperfectly formed or developed – **~ly** *adv*

abound /əˈbaʊnd/ *v* **1** to be present in large numbers or in great quantity **2** to be amply supplied – + *in* **3** to be crowded or infested *with*

¹about /əˈbaʊt/ *adv* **1** round **2** in succession or rotation; alternately **3** approximately **4** almost **5** in the vicinity

²about *prep* **1** on every side of; surrounding **2a** in the vicinity of **b** on or near the person of **c** in the make-up of **d** at the command of **3a** engaged in **b** on the verge of – + *to* **4a** with regard to, concerning **b** intimately concerned with **5** over or in different parts of **6** *chiefly NAm* – used with the negative to express intention or determination

³about *adj* **1** moving from place to place; *specif* out of bed **2** in existence, evidence, or circulation

¹above /əˈbʌv/ *adv* **1a** in the sky overhead **b** in or to heaven **2a** in or to a higher place **b** higher on the same or an earlier page **c** upstairs **3** in or to a higher rank or number **4** upstage

[2]**above** *prep* **1** higher than the level of **2** over **3** beyond, transcending **4a** superior to (e g in rank) **b** too proud or honourable to stoop to **5** upstream from

[3]**above** *n, pl* **above** **1a** sthg (written) above **b** a person whose name is written above **2a** a higher authority **b** heaven

[4]**above** *adj* written higher on the same, or on a preceding, page

aboveboard /ə,bʌv'bɔːd, ə'bʌvbɔːd/ *adj* free from all traces of deceit or dishonesty

abracadabra /æbrəkə'dæbrə/ *n* a magical charm or incantation – used interjectionally as an accompaniment to conjuring tricks

abrade /ə'breɪd/ *v* to roughen, irritate, or wear away, esp by friction

abrasion /ə'breɪʒən/ *n* **1** a wearing, grinding, or rubbing away by friction **2** an abraded area of the skin or mucous membrane

[1]**abrasive** /ə'breɪsɪv, -zɪv/ *adj* tending to abrade; causing irritation – **~ly** *adv*

[2]**abrasive** *n* a substance (e g emery) that may be used for grinding away, smoothing, or polishing

abreast /ə'brest/ *adv or adj* **1** side by side and facing in the same direction **2** up-to-date in attainment or information

abridge /ə'brɪdʒ/ *v* **1** to reduce in scope; curtail **2** to shorten by omission of words without sacrifice of sense; condense – **-gment** *n*

abroad /ə'brɔːd/ *adv or adj* **1** over a wide area; widely **2** away from one's home; out of doors **3** beyond the boundaries of one's country **4** in wide circulation; about

abrogate /'æbrəgeɪt/ *v* to abolish by authoritative action; annul, repeal – **-gation** *n*

abrupt /ə'brʌpt/ *adj* **1** ending as if sharply cut off; truncated **2a** occurring without warning; unexpected **b** unceremoniously curt **c** marked by sudden changes in subject matter **3** rising or dropping sharply; steep – **~ly** *adv* – **~ness** *n*

abscess /'æbses/ *n* a pocket of pus surrounded by inflamed tissue

abscond /əb'skɒnd, æb-/ *v* to depart secretly, esp so as to evade retribution

absence /'æbsəns/ *n* **1** being absent **2** the period of time that one is absent **3** a lack

absence of mind *n* inattention to present surroundings or occurrences

[1]**absent** /'æbsənt/ *adj* **1** not present or attending; missing **2** not existing; lacking **3** preoccupied – **~ly** *adv*

[2]**absent** /əb'sent, æb-/ *v* to take or keep (oneself) away – usu + *from*

absentee /,æbsən'tiː/ *n* one who is absent or who absents him-/herself

absenteeism /,æbsən'tiːɪzəm/ *n* persistent and deliberate absence from work or duty

absent-minded /,æbsənt 'maɪndəd/ *adj* lost in thought and unaware of one's surroundings or actions; forgetful; *also* given to absence of mind

absinth, absinthe /'æbsɪnθ/ *n* a green liqueur flavoured with wormwood and aniseed

absolute /'æbsəluːt/ *adj* **1a** perfect **b** (relatively) pure or unmixed **c** outright, unmitigated **2** completely free from constitutional or other restraint **3** having no restriction, exception, or qualification **4** positive, unquestionable **5** being self-sufficient and free of external references or relationships – **~ness** *n*

absolutely /'æbsəluːtli, ,æbsə'luːtli/ *adv* totally, completely – often used to express emphatic agreement

absolute zero *n* the lowest temperature theoretically possible at which there is a complete absence of heat and which is equivalent to about –273.16°C or 0°K

absolution /,æbsə'luːʃən/ *n* the act of absolving; *specif* a declaration of forgiveness of sins pronounced by a priest

absolutism /'æbsəluːtɪzəm/ *n* (the theory favouring) government by an absolute ruler or authority

absolve /əb'zɒlv/ *v* **1** to set free *from* an obligation or the consequences of guilt **2** to declare (a sin) of (a person) forgiven by absolution

absorb /əb'sɔːb, əb'zɔːb/ *v* **1** to take

in and make part of an existing whole; incorporate **2a** to suck up or take up **b** to assimilate; take in **3** to engage or occupy wholly – **~ent** *adj*

absorbing /əb'sɔːbɪŋ, -'zɔː-/ *adj* engaging one's full attention; engrossing

absorption /əb'sɔːpʃən, -'zɔː/ *n* **1** absorbing or being absorbed **2** total involvement of the mind

abstain /əb'steɪn/ *v* **1** to refrain deliberately, and often with an effort of self-denial, *from* **2** to refrain from using one's vote

abstemious /əb'stiːmɪəs/ *adj* sparing, esp in eating or drinking; marked by abstinence – **~ly** *adv* – **~ness** *n*

abstention /əb'stenʃən/ *n* **1** abstaining – often + *from* **2** an instance of withholding a vote

abstinence /'æbstɨnəns/ *also* **abstinency** *n* **1** voluntary forbearance, esp from indulgence of appetite or from eating some foods – often + *from* **2** habitual abstaining from intoxicating beverages – esp in *total abstinence* – **-nent** *adj*

¹abstract /'æbstrækt/ *adj* **1a** detached from any specific instance or object **b** difficult to understand; abstruse **2** *of a noun* naming a quality, state, or action rather than a thing; not concrete **3** theoretical rather than practical **4** having little or no element of pictorial representation

²abstract /'æbstrækt/ *n* **1** a summary of points (e g of a piece of writing) **2** an abstract concept or state **3** an abstract composition or creation

³abstract /əb'strækt, æb-/ *v* **1** to remove, separate **2** to consider in the abstract **3** to make an abstract of; summarize **4** to draw away the attention of **5** to steal, purloin – euph

abstracted /əb'stræktɨd, æb-/ *adj* preoccupied, absentminded – **~ly** *adv*

abstraction /əb'strækʃən, æb-/ *n* **1** an abstract idea or term stripped of its concrete manifestations **2** absentmindedness **3** an abstract composition or creation

abstruse /əb'struːs, æb-/ *adj* difficult to understand; recondite – **~ly** *adv* – **~ness** *n*

¹absurd /əb'sɜːd, -'zɜːd/ *adj* **1** ridiculously unreasonable or incongruous; silly **2** lacking order or value; meaningless – **~ly** *adv* – **~ity** *n*

²absurd *n* *the* state or condition in which human beings exist in an irrational and meaningless universe, and in which their life has no meaning outside their own existence

abundance /ə'bʌndəns/ *n* **1** an ample quantity; a profusion **2** affluence, wealth

abundant /ə'bʌndənt/ *adj* **1a** marked by great plenty (e g of resources) **b** amply supplied *with*; abounding *in* **2** occurring in abundance – **~ly** *adv*

¹abuse /ə'bjuːz/ *v* **1** to attack in words; revile **2** to put to a wrong or improper use **3** to use so as to injure or damage; maltreat – **-sive** *adj*

²abuse /ə'bjuːs/ *n* **1** a corrupt practice or custom **2** improper use or treatment; misuse **3** vehemently expressed condemnation or disapproval **4** physical maltreatment

abut /ə'bʌt/ *v* **1** to border on; touch **2** to lean *on* for support

abysmal /ə'bɪzməl/ *adj* **1** deplorably great **2** immeasurably bad

abyss /ə'bɪs/ *n* **1** the infernal regions in old religions, thought of as a bottomless pit **2a** an immeasurably deep gulf **b** moral or emotional depths

¹academic /ˌækə'demɪk/ *also* **academical** *adj* **1a** of an institution of higher learning **b** scholarly **c** very learned but inexperienced in practical matters **2** conventional, formal **3** theoretical with no practical or useful bearing

²academic *n* a member (of the teaching staff) of an institution of higher learning

academician /əˌkædə'mɪʃən/ *n* a member of an academy for the advancement of science, art, or literature

academy /ə'kædəmi/ *n* **1** *cap* **a** the school for advanced education founded by Plato **b** the philosophical doctrines associated with Plato's Academy **2a** a secondary school; *esp* a private high school – now only in names **b** a college in which special subjects or skills are taught **3** a society of learned people organized to promote the arts or sciences

accede /ək'siːd, æk-/ *v* **1** to become a party (e g to a treaty) **2** to express approval or give consent, often in response to urging **3** to enter on an office or position; *esp* to become monarch ***USE*** usu + *to*

accelerate /ək'seləreɪt/ *v* **1** to bring about at an earlier time **2** to increase the speed of **3** to hasten the progress, development, or growth of **4** to move faster; gain speed **5** to increase more rapidly

acceleration /ək,selə'reɪʃən/ *n* (the rate of) change, specif increase, of velocity

accelerator /ək'seləreɪtəʳ/ *n* a pedal in a motor vehicle that controls the speed of the motor

[1]**accent** /'æksənt/ *n* **1** a distinctive pattern in inflection, tone, or choice of words, esp as characteristic of a regional or national area **2a** prominence given to 1 syllable over others by stress or a change in pitch **b** greater stress given to 1 musical note **c** rhythmically significant stress on the syllables of a verse **3a accent, accent mark** a mark added to a letter (e g in *à*, *ñ*, *ç*) to indicate how it should be pronounced **b** a symbol used to indicate musical stress **4** special concern or attention; emphasis

[2]**accent** /ək'sent/ *v* **1** to pronounce (a vowel, syllable, or word) with accent; stress **2** to make more prominent; emphasize

accentuate /ək'sentʃʊeɪt/ *v* to accent, emphasize – **-ation** *n*

accept /ək'sept/ *v* **1a** to agree to receive; *also* to agree to **b** to be able or designed to take or hold (sthg applied or inserted) **2** to give admittance or approval to **3a** to endure without protest; accommodate oneself to **b** to regard as proper, normal, or inevitable **c** to recognize as true, factual, or adequate **4** to undertake the responsibility of **5** to receive favourably sthg offered

acceptable /ək'septəbəl/ *adj* **1** capable or worthy of being accepted; satisfactory **2** welcome or pleasing to the receiver **3** tolerable – **-ability** *n* – **-bly** *adv*

acceptance /ək'septəns/ *n* **1** accepting, approval **2** acceptability **3** agreement to the act or offer of another so that the parties become legally bound

[1]**access** /'ækses, -səs/ *n* **1** freedom to approach, reach, or make use of sthg **2** a means (e g a doorway or channel) of access **3** the state of being readily reached or obtained

accessible /ək'sesəbəl/ *adj* **1** capable of being reached **2** of a form that can be readily grasped intellectually **3** able to be influenced – **-ibility** *n*

accession /ək'seʃən/ *n* **1** becoming joined **2** the act by which a nation becomes party to an agreement already in force **3a** an increase due to sthg added **b** acquisition of property by addition to existing property **4** the act of entering on a high office **5** assent, agreement – fml

[1]**accessory** /ək'sesəri/ *n* an inessential object or device that adds to the beauty, convenience, or effectiveness of sthg else

[2]**accessory** *adj* aiding or contributing in a secondary way; supplementary, subordinate

acciaccatura /ə,tʃækə'tʊərə/ *n* a discordant note sounded with or before a principal note or chord and immediately released

accident /'æksədənt/ *n* **1a** an event occurring by chance or arising from unknown causes **b** lack of intention or necessity; chance **2** an unexpected happening causing loss or injury **3** a nonessential property or condition of sthg

[1]**accidental** /,æksə'dentl/ *adj* **1** arising incidentally; nonessential **2a** occurring unexpectedly or by chance **b** happening without intent or through carelessness and often with unfortunate results – **~ly** *adv*

[2]**accidental** *n* **1** a nonessential property or condition **2** (a sign indicating) a note altered to sharp, flat, or natural and foreign to a key indicated by a key signature

accident-prone *adj* having personality traits that predispose to accidents

[1]**acclaim** /ə'kleɪm/ *v* **1** to applaud, praise **2** to hail or proclaim by acclamation

²acclaim *n* acclamation

acclamation /ˌækləˈmeɪʃən/ *n* **1** a loud expression of praise, goodwill, or assent **2** an overwhelming affirmative vote by cheers or applause rather than by ballot

acclimat·ize, -ise /əˈklaɪmətaɪz/ *v* to adapt to a new climate or situation – **-tization** *n*

accolade /ˈækəleɪd/ *n* **1** a mark of acknowledgment or honour; an award **2** an expression of strong praise

accommodate /əˈkɒmədeɪt/ *v* **1** to make fit or suitable *to* **2** to bring into agreement or concord; reconcile **3a** to give help to; oblige *with* **b** to provide with lodgings; house **4** to have or make adequate room for **5** to give consideration to; allow for

accommodating /əˈkɒmədeɪtɪŋ/ *adj* helpful, obliging – **~ly** *adv*

accommodation /əˌkɒməˈdeɪʃən/ *n* **1a** lodging, housing **b** space, premises **2a** sthg needed or desired for convenience; a facility **b** an adaptation, adjustment **c** a settlement, agreement **d** the (range of) automatic adjustment of the eye, esp by changes in the amount by which the lens bends light, for seeing at different distances

accompaniment /əˈkʌmpənimənt/ *n* **1** a subordinate instrumental or vocal part supporting or complementing a principal voice or instrument **2** an addition intended to give completeness; a complement

accompany /əˈkʌmpəni/ *v* **1** to go with as an escort or companion **2** to perform an accompaniment (to or for) **3a** to make an addition to; supplement *with* **b** *of a thing* to happen, exist, or be found with

accomplice /əˈkʌmplɪ̈s/ *n* sby who collaborates with another, esp in wrongdoing

accomplish /əˈkʌmplɪʃ/ *v* **1** to bring to a successful conclusion; achieve **2** to complete, cover (a measure of time or distance)

accomplished /əˈkʌmplɪʃt/ *adj* **1** fully effected; completed **2a** skilled, proficient **b** having many social accomplishments

accomplishment /əˈkʌmplɪʃmənt/ *n* **1** completion, fulfilment **2** an achievement **3** an acquired ability or esp social skill

¹accord /əˈkɔːd/ *v* **1** to grant, concede **2** to give, award **3** to be consistent *with*

²accord *n* **1a** accordance **b** a formal treaty of agreement **2** balanced relationship (e g of colours or sounds); harmony

accordance /əˈkɔːdəns/ *n* **1** agreement, conformity **2** the act of granting

accordingly /əˈkɔːdɪŋli/ *adv* **1** as suggested; appropriately **2** consequently, so

accordion /əˈkɔːdɪən/ *n* a portable keyboard wind instrument in which the wind is forced past free reeds by means of a hand-operated bellows

accost /əˈkɒst/ *v* **1** to approach and speak to, esp boldly or challengingly **2** *of a prostitute* to solicit

account /əˈkaʊnt/ *n* **1** a record of debits and credits relating to a particular item, person, or concern **2** a list of items of expenditure to be balanced against income – usu pl **3a** a periodically rendered calculation listing purchases and credits **b** business, patronage **4** a business arrangement whereby money is deposited in, and may be withdrawn from, a bank, building society, etc **5** a commission to carry out a particular business operation (e g an advertising campaign) given by one company to another **6** value, importance **7** profit, advantage **8** careful thought; consideration **9a** a statement explaining one's conduct **b** a statement of facts or events; a relation **10** hearsay, report – usu pl **11** a version, rendering

accountable /əˈkaʊntəbəl/ *adj* **1** responsible, answerable **2** explicable

accountancy /əˈkaʊntənsi/ *n* the profession or practice of accounting

accountant /əˈkaʊntənt/ *n* one who practises and is usu qualified in accounting

account for *v* to be or give an explanation for

accredit /əˈkredɪ̈t/ *v* **1a** to give official authorization to or approval of **b** to recognize or vouch for as conforming to a standard **2** to credit *with*, attribute *to*

accretion /ə'kriːʃən/ *n* **1a** an increase in size caused by natural growth or the external adhesion or addition of matter **b** sthg added or stuck extraneously **2** the growth of separate particles or parts (e g of a plant) into one

accrue /ə'kruː/ *v* **1** to come as a (periodic) increase or addition to sthg; arise as a growth or result **2** to collect, accumulate

accumulate /ə'kjuːmjʊleɪt/ *v* **1** to collect together gradually; amass **2** to increase in quantity or number

accumulation /ə,kjuːmjʊ'leɪʃən/ *n* **1** increase or growth caused by esp repeated or continuous addition; *specif* increase in capital from interest payments **2** sthg that has accumulated

accumulative /ə'kjuːmjʊlətɪv/ *adj* **1** cumulative **2** tending or given to accumulation, esp of money – **~ly** *adv*

accumulator /ə'kjuːmjʊleɪtə^r/ *n* **1** a part (e g in a computer) where numbers are added or stored **2** *Br* a rechargeable secondary electric cell; *also* a connected set of these **3** *Br* a bet whereby the winnings from one of a series of events are staked on the next event

accurate /'ækjərət/ *adj* **1** free from error, esp as the result of care **2** conforming precisely to truth or a measurable standard; exact – **-acy** *n* – **~ly** *adv*

accursed /ə'kɜːsɪ̈d, ə'kɜːst/ *adj* **1** under a curse; ill-fated **2** damnable, detestable – **~ly** *adv*

accusative *n* (a form (e g *me*) in) a grammatical case expressing the direct object of a verb or of some prepositions

accuse /ə'kjuːz/ *v* to charge with a fault or crime; blame – **-sation** *n* – **-singly** *adv*

accused /ə'kjuːzd/ *n, pl* **accused** *the* defendant in a criminal case

accustom /ə'kʌstəm/ *v* to make used *to* through use or experience; habituate

accustomed /ə'kʌstəmd/ *adj* **1** customary, habitual **2** in the habit of; used *to*

¹ace /eɪs/ *n* **1** a die face, playing card, or domino marked with 1 spot or pip; *also* the single spot or pip on any of these **2** (a point scored by) a shot, esp a service in tennis, that an opponent fails to touch **3** a combat pilot who has brought down at least 5 enemy aircraft **4** an expert or leading performer in a specified field

²ace *v* to score an ace against (an opponent)

³ace *adj* great, excellent – infml

acetate /'æsɪ̈teɪt/ *n* a salt or ester of acetic acid

acetic acid /ə,siːtɪk 'æsɪ̈d/ *n* a pungent liquid acid that is the major acid in vinegar

¹ache /eɪk/ *v* **1a** to suffer a usu dull persistent pain **b** to feel anguish or distress **2** to yearn, long

²ache *n* a usu dull persistent pain

achieve /ə'tʃiːv/ *v* **1** to carry out successfully; accomplish **2** to obtain by effort; win – **achievable** *adj*

achievement /ə'tʃiːvmənt/ *n* **1** successful completion; accomplishment **2** sthg accomplished, esp by resolve, persistence, or courage; a feat **3** performance in a test or academic course

Achilles' heel /ə,kɪliːz 'hiːl/ *n* a person's only vulnerable point

¹acid /'æsɪ̈d/ *adj* **1a** sour or sharp to the taste **b** sharp, biting, or sour in speech, manner, or disposition; caustic **2** of, like, containing, or being an acid; *specif* having a pH of less than 7

²acid *n* **1** a sour substance; *specif* any of various typically water-soluble and sour compounds having a pH of less than 7 that are capable of giving up a hydrogen ion to or accepting an unshared pair of electrons from a base to form a salt **2** LSD – infml

acidify /ə'sɪdɪ̈faɪ/ *v* to make or convert into (an) acid

acid test *n* a severe or crucial test (e g of value or suitability)

ack-ack /,æk 'æk/ *adj* antiaircraft

acknowledge /ək'nɒlɪdʒ/ *v* **1** to admit knowledge of; concede to be true or valid **2** to recognize the status or claims of **3a** to express gratitude or obligation for **b** to show recognition of (e g by smiling or nodding) **c** to confirm receipt of – **-gment** *n*

acme /'ækmi/ *n* the highest point or stage; *esp* a perfect representative of a specified class or thing

acne /'ækni/ *n* a skin disorder found esp among adolescents, characterized by inflammation of the skin glands and hair follicles and causing red pustules, esp on the face and neck

acorn /'eɪkɔːn/ *n* the nut of the oak, usu seated in a hard woody cup

[1]**acoustic** /ə'kuːstɪk/ *adj* of or being a musical instrument whose sound is not electronically modified – **~ally** *adv*

[2]**acoustic** *n* **1** *pl but sing in constr* the science of sound **2** the properties of a room, hall, etc that govern the quality of sound heard – usu pl with sing. meaning

acquaint /ə'kweɪnt/ *v* to make familiar *with*

acquaintance /ə'kweɪntəns/ *n* **1** personal knowledge; familiarity **2a** *sing or pl in constr* the people with whom one is acquainted **b** a person whom one knows but who is not a particularly close friend

acquiesce /,ækwi'es/ *v* to submit or comply tacitly or passively – often + *in* – **-escence** *n*

acquire /ə'kwaɪəʳ/ *v* **1** to gain or come into possession of, often by unspecified means; *also* to steal – euph **2** to gain as a new characteristic or ability, esp as a result of skill or hard work

acquisition /,ækwɪ̣'zɪʃən/ *n* **1** acquiring, gaining **2** sby or sthg acquired or gained, esp to one's advantage

acquisitive /ə'kwɪzɪ̣tɪv/ *adj* keen or tending to acquire and possess – **~ly** *adv* – **~ness** *n*

acquit /ə'kwɪt/ *v* **1** to free from responsibility or obligation; *specif* to declare not guilty **2** to conduct (oneself) in a specified, usu favourable, manner

acquittal /ə'kwɪtl/ *n* a judicial release from a criminal charge

acre /'eɪkəʳ/ *n* **1** *pl* lands, fields **2** a unit of area equal to 4840yd^2 (4046.86m^2) **3** *pl* great quantities – infml

acrid /'ækrɪ̣d/ *adj* **1** unpleasantly pungent in taste or smell **2** violently bitter in manner or language; acrimonious

acrimony /'ækrɪ̣məni/ *n* caustic sharpness of manner or language resulting from anger or ill nature – **-nious** *adj* – **-niously** *adv*

acrobat /'ækrəbæt/ *n* **1** one who performs gymnastic feats requiring skilful control of the body – **~ic** *adj* – **~ically** *adv*

acrobatics /,ækrə'bætɪks/ *n pl* **1** *sing or pl in constr* the art, performance, or activity of an acrobat **2** a spectacular performance involving great agility

acronym /'ækrənɪm/ *n* a word (e g *radar*) formed from the initial letters of other words

[1]**across** /ə'krɒs/ *adv* **1** from one side to the other crosswise **2** to or on the opposite side **3** so as to be understandable, acceptable, or successful

[2]**across** *prep* **1a** from one side to the other of **b** on the opposite side of **2** so as to intersect at an angle **3** into transitory contact with

acrostic /ə'krɒstɪk/ *n* **1** a composition, usu in verse, in which sets of letters (e g the first of each line) form a word or phrase **2** a series of words of equal length arranged to read the same horizontally or vertically

[1]**act** /ækt/ *n* **1** a thing done; a deed **2** a statute; *also* a decree, edict **3** the process of doing **4** *often cap* a formal record of sthg done or transacted **5a** any of the principal divisions of a play or opera **b** any of the successive parts or performances in an entertainment (e g a circus) **6** a display of affected behaviour; a pretence

[2]**act** *v* **1** to represent by action, esp on the stage **2** to feign, simulate **3** to play the part of (as if) in a play **4** to behave in a manner suitable to **5** to perform on the stage; engage in acting **6** to behave insincerely **7** to function or behave in a specified manner **8** to perform a specified function; serve *as* **9** to be a substitute or representative *for* **10** to produce an effect

[1]**acting** /'æktɪŋ/ *adj* holding a temporary rank or position

[2]**acting** *n* the art or practice of representing a character in a dramatic production

action /'ækʃən/ *n* **1** a civil legal proceeding **2** the process of acting or working, esp to produce alteration by force or through a natural agency **3** the mode of movement of the body **4** a voluntary act; a deed **5a** the state of functioning actively **b** practical, often militant, activity, often directed towards a political end **c** energetic activity; enterprise **6a** combat (e g in a war) **b** (the unfolding of) the events in a play or work of fiction **7** an operating mechanism (e g of a gun or piano); *also* the manner in which it operates **8** (*the* most) lively or productive activity – infml

action painting *n* abstract art in which spontaneous techniques (e g dribbling or smearing) are used to apply paint

activate /'æktɨveɪt/ *v* to make (more) active or reactive, esp in chemical or physical properties – **-ation** *n*

[1]**active** /'æktɪv/ *adj* **1** characterized by practical action rather than by contemplation or speculation **2** quick in physical movement; lively **3a** marked by or requiring vigorous activity **b** full of activity; busy **4** having practical operation or results; effective **5** *of a volcano* liable to erupt; not extinct **6** *of a verb form or voice* having as the subject the person or thing doing the action **7** of, in, or being full-time service, esp in the armed forces **8** capable of acting or reacting; activated – **~ly** *adv*

[2]**active** *n* **1** an active verb form **2** the active voice of a language

activity /æk'tɪvɨti/ *n* **1** the quality or state of being active **2** vigorous or energetic action; liveliness **3** a pursuit in which a person is active – usu pl

actor /'æktəʳ/, *fem* **actress** *n* one who represents a character in a dramatic production; *esp* one whose profession is acting

act out *v* **1** to represent in action **2** to translate into action

Acts *n pl but sing in constr* the fifth book of the New Testament narrating the beginnings of the Church

actual /'æktʃʊəl/ *adj* **1** existing in fact or reality; real **2** existing or occurring at the time; current

actuality /ˌæktʃʊ'ælɨti/ *n* an existing circumstance; a real fact – often pl

actually /'æktʃʊəli, -tʃəli/ *adv* **1** really; in fact **2** at the present moment **3** strange as it may seem; even

actuary /'æktʃʊəri/ *n* sby who calculates insurance risks and premiums – **-arial** *adj*

act up *v* **1** to behave in an unruly manner; play up **2** to give pain or trouble *USE* infml

acuity /ə'kjuːɨti/ *n* keenness of mental or physical perception – fml

acumen /'ækjʊmən, ə'kjuːmən/ *n* keenness and depth of discernment or discrimination, esp in practical matters

acupuncture /'ækjʊˌpʌŋktʃəʳ/ *n* an orig Chinese practice of puncturing the body at particular points with needles to cure disease, relieve pain, produce anaesthesia, etc

acute /ə'kjuːt/ *adj* **1** *of an angle* measuring less than 90° **2a** marked by keen discernment or intellectual perception, esp of subtle distinctions **b** responsive to slight impressions or stimuli **3** intensely felt or perceived **4** *esp of an illness* having a sudden severe onset and short course – contrasted with *chronic* **5** demanding urgent attention; severe **6** marked with, having the pronunciation indicated by, or being an accent mark written ´ – **~ly** *adv* – **~ness** *n*

ad /æd/ *n* an advertisement – infml

adage /'ædɪdʒ/ *n* a maxim or proverb that embodies a commonly accepted observation

[1]**adagio** /ə'dɑːdʒəʊ/ *adv or adj* in an easy slow graceful manner – used in music

[2]**adagio** *n, pl* **adagios** **1** a musical composition or movement in adagio tempo **2** ballet dancing, esp a pas de deux, involving difficult feats of balance

[1]**adamant** /'ædəmənt/ *n* a stone formerly believed to be of impenetrable hardness and sometimes identified with the diamond; *broadly* any very hard unbreakable substance

[2]**adamant** *adj* unshakable in determination; unyielding – **~ly** *adv*

Adam's apple *n* the projection in the front of the neck formed by the largest cartilage of the larynx

adapt /ə'dæpt/ *v* to make or become fit, often by modification

adaptation /ˌædəpˈteɪʃən/ *n* **1** adjustment to prevailing or changing conditions **2** a composition rewritten in a new form or for a different medium

adapter, adaptor /əˈdæptəʳ/ *n* **1** a device for converting a tool, piece of apparatus, etc to some new use **2** a plug or connector for joining several pieces of electrical apparatus to a single power point

add /æd/ *v* **1** to join so as to bring about an increase or improvement **2** to say or write further **3** to combine (numbers) into a single number – often + *up* **4a** to perform addition **b** to come together or unite by addition **5** to make or serve as an addition *to*

addendum /əˈdendəm/ *n, pl* **addenda** a supplement to a book – often pl with sing. meaning but sing. in constr

[1]**adder** /ˈædəʳ/ *n* the common European venomous viper or other ground-living viper

[2]**adder** *n* a device (e g in a computer) that performs addition

[1]**addict** /əˈdɪkt/ *v* **1** to devote or surrender (oneself) to sthg habitually or obsessively – usu pass **2** to cause (an animal or human) to become physiologically dependent upon a habit-forming drug – **~ion** *n* – **~ive** *adj*

[2]**addict** /ˈædɪkt/ *n* **1** one who is addicted to a drug **2** a devotee, fan

addition /əˈdɪʃən/ *n* **1** sthg or sby added, esp as an improvement **2** the act or process of adding, esp adding numbers

additional /əˈdɪʃənəl/ *adj* existing by way of addition; supplementary – **~ly** *adv*

additive /ædǰtɪv/ *n* a substance added to another in relatively small amounts to impart desirable properties or suppress undesirable ones

addle /ˈædl/ *v* **1** to throw into confusion **2** *of an egg* to become rotten **3** to become confused or muddled

[1]**address** /əˈdres/ *v* **1** to direct the efforts or attention of (oneself) **2a** to communicate directly **b** to speak or write directly to; *esp* to deliver a formal speech to **3** to mark directions for delivery on **4** to greet by a prescribed form **5** to take one's stance and adjust the club before hitting (a golf ball)

[2]**address** *n* **1** a formal communication; *esp* a prepared speech delivered to an audience **2** a place of residence (where a person or organization may be communicated with); *also* a detailed description of its location (e g on an envelope)

add up *v* **1** to amount *to* in total or substance **2** to come to the expected total **3** to be internally consistent; make sense

adept /ˈædept, əˈdept/ *adj or n* (being) a highly skilled expert *at* – **~ly** *adv*

adequate /ˈædɪkwǰt/ *adj* (barely) sufficient for a specific requirement – **~ly** *adv* – **-quacy** *n*

adhere /ədˈhɪəʳ/ *v* **1** to give continued support, observance, or loyalty **2** to hold or stick fast (as if) by glueing, suction, grasping, or fusing to cause to stick fast – **adherence** *n*

adherent /ədˈhɪərənt/ *n* a supporter of a leader, faction, etc

adhesion /ədˈhiːʒən/ *n* the action or state of adhering

[1]**adhesive** /ədˈhiːsɪv, -zɪv/ *adj* causing or prepared for sticking; sticky

[2]**adhesive** *n* an adhesive substance (e g glue or cement)

ad hoc /ˌæd ˈhɒk, -ˈhəʊk/ *adj or adv* with respect to the particular purpose at hand and without consideration of wider application

adieu /əˈdjuː/ *n, pl* **adieus, adieux** a farewell – often used interjectionally; usu poetic

ad infinitum /æd ɪnfǰˈnaɪtəm/ *adv or adj* without end or limit

adipose /ˈædǰpəʊs/ *adj* of animal fat; fatty

adjacent /əˈdʒeɪsənt/ *adj* having a common border; *broadly* neighbouring, nearby

adjective /ædʒɪktɪv/ *n* a word that modifies a noun or pronoun by describing a particular characteristic of it – **-tival** *adj* – **-tivally** *adv*

adjoin /əˈdʒɔɪn/ *v* to be next to or in contact with (one another)

adjourn /əˈdʒɜːn/ *v* to suspend (a session) until a later stated time – **~ment** *n*

adjudicate /əˈdʒuːdɪkeɪt/ *v* **1** to make a judicial decision on **2** to act as judge (e g in a competition) – -cation *n*

adjunct /'ædʒʌŋkt/ *n* **1** sthg joined to another thing as an incidental accompaniment but not essentially a part of it **2** a person, usu in a subordinate or temporary capacity, assisting another to perform some duty or service

adjure /ə'dʒʊəʳ/ *v* **1** to charge or command solemnly (as if) under oath or penalty of a curse **2** to entreat or advise earnestly *USE* fml

adjust /ə'dʒʌst/ *v* **1** to bring to a more satisfactory or conformable state by minor change or adaptation; regulate, correct, or modify **2** to determine the amount to be paid under an insurance policy in settlement of (a loss) **3** to adapt or conform oneself (e g to climate) – **~able** *adj* – **~ment** *n*

adjutant /'ædʒʊtənt/ *n* an officer who assists the commanding officer and is responsible for correspondence and for ensuring that his orders are carried out

ad-lib /,æd 'lɪb/ *v* **-bb-** to say (e g lines or a speech) spontaneously and without preparation; improvise – **ad-lib** *n, adj*

ad lib *adv* without restraint or limit

administer /əd'mɪnɨstəʳ/ *v* **1** to manage, supervise **2a** to mete out; dispense **b** to give or perform ritually **3** to perform the office of administrator; manage affairs – **-tration** *n*

administrative /əd'mɪnɨstrətɪv/ *adj* of (an) administration – **~ly** *adv*

administrator /əd'mɪnɨstreɪtəʳ/ *n* sby who administers esp business, school, or governmental affairs

admirable /'ædmərəbəl/ *adj* deserving the highest respect; excellent – **-bly** *adv*

admiral /'ædmərəl/ *n* the commander in chief of a navy

admiralty /'ædmərəlti/ *n* **1** *sing or pl in constr, cap* the executive department formerly having authority over naval affairs **2** the court having jurisdiction over maritime questions

admiration /,ædmɨ'reɪʃən/ *n* a feeling of delighted or astonished approval

admire /əd'maɪəʳ/ *v* to think highly of; express admiration for – sometimes sarcastically

admirer /əd'maɪərəʳ/ *n* a woman's suitor

admissible /əd'mɪsəbəl/ *adj, esp of legal evidence* capable of being allowed or conceded; permissible – **-bility** *n*

admission /əd'mɪʃən/ *n* **1** acknowledgment that a fact or allegation is true **2a** allowing or being allowed to enter sthg (e g a secret society) **b** a fee paid at or for admission

admit /əd'mɪt/ *v* **1a** to allow scope for; permit **b** to concede as true or valid **2** to allow to enter sthg (e g a place or fellowship) **3** to give entrance or access

admittance /əd'mɪtəns/ *n* **1** permission to enter a place **2** access, entrance

admittedly /əd'mɪtɨdli/ *adv* as must reluctantly be admitted

admixture /əd'mɪkstʃəʳ/ *n* an ingredient added by mixing, or the resulting mixture

admonish /əd'mɒnɪʃ/ *v* **1** to warn about remissness or error, esp gently **2** to give friendly earnest advice or encouragement to – **~ing** *adj* – **~ingly** *adv*

admonition /,ædmə'nɪʃən/ *n* (a) gentle friendly reproof, counsel, or warning – **-tory** *adj*

ad nauseam /,æd 'nɔːzɪəm, -iæm/ *adv* in an extremely tedious manner; enough to make one sick

ado /ə'duː/ *n* fussy bustling excitement, esp over trivia; to-do

adobe /ə'dəʊbi/ *n* **1** a building brick of sun-dried earth and straw **2** a heavy clay used in making adobe bricks

adolescent /ædə'lesənt/ *n* sby in the period of life between puberty and maturity – **-cence** *n*

adopt /ə'dɒpt/ *v* **1** to take by choice into a new relationship; *specif* to bring up voluntarily (a child of other parents) as one's own child **2** to take up and practise; take to oneself **3** to vote to accept **4** *of a constituency* to nominate as a Parliamentary candidate **5** *Br, of a local authority* to assume responsibility for the maintenance of (e g a road) – **~ion** *n*

adoptive /ə'dɒptɪv/ *adj* made or acquired by adoption

adorable /ə'dɔːrəbəl/ *adj* sweetly lovable; charming

adore /ə'dɔːʳ/ *v* **1** to worship or honour as a deity **2** to regard with reverent admiration and devotion **3** to like very much – infml – **adoration** *n*

adorn /ə'dɔːn/ *v* **1** to decorate, esp with ornaments **2** to add to the pleasantness or attractiveness of – **~ment** *n*

adrenalin, adrenaline /ə'drenəl$_{\text{ɪ}}$n/ *n* a hormone that stimulates the heart and causes constriction of blood vessels and relaxation of smooth muscle

adrift /ə'drɪft/ *adv or adj* **1** afloat without motive power or mooring and at the mercy of winds and currents **2** in or into a state of being unstuck or unfastened; loose – esp in *come adrift* **3** astray – infml

adroit /ə'drɔɪt/ *adj* **1** dexterous, nimble **2** marked by shrewdness, readiness, or resourcefulness in coping with difficulty or danger – **~ly** *adv* – **~ness** *n*

adsorb /əd'zɔːb/ *v* to become absorbed – **adsorption** *n*

[1]**adult** /'ædʌlt, ə'dʌlt/ *adj* **1** fully developed and mature; grown-up **2** of or befitting adults **3** suitable only for adults; *broadly* salacious, pornographic

[2]**adult** *n* a grown-up person or creature; *esp* a human being after an age specified by law (in Britain, 18)

adulterate /ə'dʌltəreɪt/ *v* to corrupt or make impure by the addition of a foreign or inferior substance

adulterer /ə'dʌltərəʳ/, *fem* **adulteress** *n* sby who has sex with someone other than his/her spouse – **adultery** *n* – **-terous** *adj*

[1]**advance** /əd'vɑːns/ *v* **1** to bring or move forwards in position or time **2** to accelerate the growth or progress of; further **3** to raise in rank; promote **4** to supply (money or goods) ahead of time or as a loan **5** to bring (an opinion or argument) forward for notice; propose **6** to go forwards; proceed **7** to make progress **8** to rise in rank, position, or importance

[2]**advance** *n* **1a** a moving forward **b** (a signal for) forward movement (of troops) **2a** progress in development; an improvement **b** advancement; promotion **3** a friendly or esp an amorous approach – usu pl **4** (a provision of) money or goods supplied before a return is received

[3]**advance** *adj* **1** made, sent, or provided ahead of time **2** going or situated ahead of others

advanced /əd'vɑːnst/ *adj* **1** far on in time or course **2** beyond the elementary; more developed

advancement /əd'vɑːnsmənt/ *n* **1a** (a) promotion or elevation to a higher rank or position **b** furtherance towards perfection or completeness **2** an advance of money or value

advantage /əd'vɑːntɪdʒ/ *n* **1** superiority of position or condition – often + *of* or *over* **2** a benefit, gain; *esp* one resulting from some course of action **3** (the score of) the first point won in tennis after deuce

advantageous /,ædvən'teɪdʒəs, ,ædvæn-/ *adj* furnishing an advantage; favourable – **~ly** *adv*

Advent /'ædvent/ *n* **1** the 4-week period before Christmas, observed by some Christians as a season of prayer and fasting **2** the coming of Christ to earth as a human being **3** *not cap* a coming into being; an arrival

adventitious /,ædvən'tɪʃəs, ,ædven-/ *adj* **1** coming accidentally or casually from another source; extraneous **2** occurring sporadically or in an unusual place – **~ly** *adv*

[1]**adventure** /əd'ventʃəʳ/ *n* **1** an undertaking involving danger, risks, uncertainty of outcome, or excitement **2** an enterprise involving financial risk – **-rous** *adj*

[2]**adventure** *v* **1** to hazard oneself; dare to go or enter **2** to take a risk

adventurer /əd'ventʃərəʳ/, *fem* **adventuress** *n* **1** sby who takes part in an adventure **2** sby who seeks wealth or position by unscrupulous means

adverb /'ædvɜːb/ *n* a word that modifies a verb, an adjective, another adverb, a preposition, a phrase, a clause, or a sentence, and that answers such questions as how?, when?, where?, etc – **~ial** *n, adj* – **~ially** *adv*

adversary /ˈædvəsəri/ *n* an enemy, opponent, or opposing faction

adverse /ˈædvɜːs/ *adj* **1** acting against or in a contrary direction **2** unfavourable – **~ly** *adv*

adversity /ədˈvɜːsɨti/ *n* a condition of suffering, affliction, or hardship

1advert /ədˈvɜːt/ *v* to make a (glancing) reference or refer casually *to* – fml

2advert /ˈædvɜːt/ *n, chiefly Br* an advertisement

advertise /ˈædvətaɪz/ *v* **1** to make publicly and generally known **2** to announce (e g an article for sale or a vacancy) publicly, esp in the press **3** to encourage sales or patronage (of), esp by emphasizing desirable qualities, or by description in the mass media **4** to seek *for* by means of advertising – **~r** *n*

advertisement /ədˈvɜːtɨsmənt/ *n* a notice published, broadcast, or displayed publicly to advertise a product, service, etc

advertising /ˈædvətaɪzɪŋ/ *n* **1** the action of calling sthg to the attention of the public, esp by paid announcements **2** advertisements **3** the profession of preparing advertisements for publication or broadcast

advice /ədˈvaɪs/ *n* **1** recommendation regarding a decision or course of conduct **2** communication, esp from a distance; intelligence – usu pl **3** an official notice concerning a business transaction

advisable /ədˈvaɪzəbəl/ *adj* fitting to be advised or done; prudent – **-sability** *n*

advise /ədˈvaɪz/ *v* **1a** to give advice (to) **b** to caution, warn **2** to give information or notice to; inform

advisory /ədˈvaɪzəri/ *adj* **1** having or exercising power to advise **2** containing or giving advice

advocacy /ˈædvəkəsi/ *n* **1** active support or pleading **2** the function of an advocate

1advocate /ˈædvəkeɪt/ *n* **1** a professional pleader before a tribunal or court **2** one who defends or supports a cause or proposal

2advocate /ˈædvəkɨt, -keɪt/ *v* to plead in favour of

adze /ædz/ *n* a tool that has the blade at right angles to the handle for cutting or shaping wood

aegis /ˈiːdʒɨs/ *n* sponsorship, backing

aeon, eon /ˈiːən/ *n* an immeasurably long period of time, *also* a geological unit of time equal to 1000 million years

aerate /ˈeəreɪt/ *v* **1** to combine, supply, charge, or impregnate with a gas, esp air, oxygen, or carbon dioxide **2** to make fizzy or effervescent – **-ation** *n*

1aerial /ˈeərɪəl/ *adj* **1a** of or occurring in the air or atmosphere **b** consisting of air **c** growing in the air rather than in the ground or water **d** operating overhead on elevated cables or rails **2** lacking substance; thin – **~ly** *adv*

2aerial *n* a conductor (e g a wire) or arrangement of conductors designed to radiate or receive radio waves

aerobatics /ˌeərəˈbætɪks/ *n pl but sing or pl in constr* the performance of feats (e g rolls) in an aircraft – **aerobatic** *adj*

aerodrome /ˈeərədrəʊm/ *n, chiefly Br* an airfield

aerodynamics /ˌeərəʊdaɪˈnæmɪks/ *n pl but sing or pl in constr* the dynamics of the motion of (solid bodies moving through) gases (e g air) – **aerodynamic** *adj* – **-ically** *adv*

aeronautics /ˌeərəˈnɔːtɪks/ *n pl but sing in constr* the art or science of flight – **-ic, -ical** *adj*

aeroplane /ˈeərəpleɪn/ *n, chiefly Br* an aircraft that is heavier than air, has nonrotating wings from which it derives its lift, and is mechanically propelled (e g by a propeller or jet engine)

aerosol /ˈeərəsɒl/ *n* (a container of) a substance dispersed from a pressurized container as a suspension of fine solid or liquid particles in gas – **aerosol** *v*

aerospace /ˈeərəspeɪs/ *n* **1** (a branch of physical science dealing with) the earth's atmosphere and the space beyond – **aerospace** *adj*

aesthete /ˈiːsθiːt/ *n* one who has or professes a developed sensitivity to the beautiful in art or nature

aesthetic /iːsˈθetɪk, es-/ *also* **aesthetical** *adj* **1a** of or dealing with aesthetics or the appreciation of the beautiful **b** artistic **2** having a developed sense of beauty – ~**ally** *adv*

aesthetics /iːs'θetɪks, es-/ *n pl but sing or pl in constr* a branch of philosophy dealing with the nature of the beautiful, with judgments concerning beauty and taste, and with theories of criticism in the arts

afar /ə'fɑːʳ/ *adv or n* (from, to, or at) a great distance

affable /'æfəbəl/ *adj* **1** being pleasant and relaxed in talking to others **2** characterized by ease and friendliness; benign – **-bility** *n* – **-bly** *adv*

affair /ə'feəʳ/ *n* **1a** *pl* commercial, professional, or public business or matters **b** a particular or personal concern **2a** a procedure, action, object, or occasion only vaguely specified **b** a social event; a party **3** *also* **affaire, affaire de coeur** a romantic or passionate attachment between 2 people who are not married to each other **4** a matter causing public anxiety, controversy, or scandal

[1]**affect** /ə'fekt/ *n* the conscious subjective aspect of an emotion considered apart from bodily changes

[2]**affect** /ə'fekt/ *v* **1** to be given to **2** to put on a pretence of (being); feign

[3]**affect** /ə'fekt/ *v* **1** to have a material effect on or produce an alteration in **2** to act on (e g a person or his/her mind or feelings) so as to effect a response

affectation /ˌæfek'teɪʃən/ *n* **1** an insincere display (e g of a quality not really possessed) **2** a deliberately assumed peculiarity of speech or conduct; an artificiality

affected /ə'fektɨ̵d/ *adj* **1** inclined, disposed *towards* – chiefly in *well-affected, ill-affected* **2a** given to affectation **b** assumed artificially or falsely; pretended – ~**ly** *adv* – ~**ness** *n*

affecting /ə'fektɪŋ/ *adj* evoking a strong emotional response; moving

[1]**affection** /ə'fekʃən/ *n* **1** emotion as compared with reason – often pl with sing. meaning **2** tender and lasting attachment; fondness

affectionate /ə'fekʃənɨ̵t/ *adj* **1** showing affection or warm regard; loving **2** proceeding from affection; tender – ~**ly** *adv*

affidavit /ˌæfɨ̵'deɪvɪt/ *n* a sworn written statement for use as judicial proof

affiliate /ə'fɪlieɪt/ *v* **1** to attach as a member or branch – + *to* or *with* **2** to connect or associate oneself *with* another, often in a dependent or subordinate position; combine

affinity /ə'fɪnɨ̵ti/ *n* **1** sympathy of thought or feeling **2** resemblance based on relationship or causal connection

affirm /ə'fɜːm/ *v* **1a** to confirm; make valid **b** to state positively **2** to assert (e g a judgment of a lower court) as valid; ratify **3** to testify by affirmation – ~**ation** *n*

[1]**affirmative** /ə'fɜːmətɪv/ *adj* **1** asserting or answering that the fact is so **2** favouring or supporting a proposition or motion – ~**ly** *adv*

[2]**affirmative** *n* **1** an expression (e g the word *yes*) of agreement or assent **2** an affirmative proposition

[1]**affix** /ə'fɪks/ *v* **1** to attach (physically); *esp* to add in writing **2** to impress (e g a seal)

[2]**affix** /'æfɪks/ *n* **1** an addition to the beginning or end of or an insertion in a word or root to produce a derivative word or inflectional form **2** an appendage

afflict /ə'flɪkt/ *v* **1** to distress so severely as to cause persistent suffering **2** to trouble

affliction /ə'flɪkʃən/ *n* **1** great suffering **2** a cause of persistent pain or distress

affluent /'æflʊənt/ *adj* **1** flowing in abundance **2** having a generously sufficient supply of material possessions; wealthy – **-ence** *n*

afford /ə'fɔːd/ *v* **1a** to be able to do or to bear without serious harm – esp + *can* **b** to be able to bear the cost of **2** to provide, supply

afforest /ə'fɒrɨ̵st/ *v* to establish or plant forest cover on – ~**ation** *n*

affray /ə'freɪ/ *n* a (public) brawl

affront /ə'frʌnt/ *v* to insult by openly insolent or disrespectful behaviour or language; give offence to

Afghan /'æfgæn/ *n* **1** a native or inhabitant of Afghanistan **2** the language of Afghanistan; Pashto **3** *not cap* a blanket or shawl of coloured wool knitted or crocheted in strips or squares **4 Afghan, Afghan hound** a tall hunting dog with a coat of silky thick hair

aficionado /ə,fɪʃjə'nɑːdəʊ/, *fem* **aficionada** *n, pl* **aficionados**, *fem* **aficionadas** a devotee, fan

afield /ə'fiːld/ *adv* **1** to, in, or on the field **2** (far) away from home; abroad **3** out of the way; astray

afloat /ə'fləʊt/ *adj or adv* **1a** borne (as if) on the water or air **b** at sea or on ship **2** free of debt **3** circulating about; rumoured **4** flooded with or submerged under water

afoot /ə'fʊt/ *adv or adj* **1** on foot **2** (in the process of) happening; astir

aforesaid /ə'fɔːsed/ *adj* previously mentioned

aforethought /ə'fɔːθɔːt/ *adj* premeditated, deliberate – fml; esp in *with malice aforethought*

afraid /ə'freɪd/ *adj* **1** filled with fear or apprehension **2** regretfully of the opinion – in apology for an utterance

afresh /ə'freʃ/ *adv* anew, again

African /'æfrɪkən/ *n or adj* (a native or inhabitant) of Africa

Afrikaans /,æfrɪ'kɑːns/ *n* a language of S Africa developed from 17th-c Dutch

Afrikaner /,æfrɪ'kɑːnəʳ/ *n* an Afrikaans-speaking S African of European, esp Dutch, descent

Afro /'æfrəʊ/ *n or adj, pl* **Afros** (a hairstyle) shaped into a round curly bushy mass

[1]**aft** /ɑːft/ *adv* near, towards, or in the stern of a ship or the tail of an aircraft

[2]**aft** *adj* rearward

[1]**after** /'ɑːftəʳ/ *adv* **1** behind **2** afterwards

[2]**after** *prep* **1** behind in place or order – used in yielding precedence or in asking for the next turn (e g *after* you with the map) **2a** following in time; later than **b** continuously succeeding **c** in view or in spite of (sthg preceding) **3** – used to indicate the goal or purpose of an action (e g go *after* trout) **4** so as to resemble: e g **a** in accordance with **b** in allusion to the name of **c** in the characteristic manner of **d** in imitation of **5** about, concerning

[3]**after** *conj* later than the time when

[4]**after** *adj* later, subsequent

after all *adv* **1** in spite of everything **2** it must be remembered

afterbirth /'ɑːftə bɜːθ/ *n* the placenta and foetal membranes expelled after delivery of a baby, young animal, etc

aftereffect /'ɑːftərɪ̗fekt/ *n* an effect that follows its cause after an interval of time

afterglow /'ɑːftəgləʊ/ *n* **1** a glow remaining (e g in the sky) where a light source has disappeared **2** a vestige of past splendour, success, or happy emotion

afterlife /'ɑːftəlaɪf/ *n* **1** an existence after death **2** a later period in one's life

aftermath /'ɑːftəmæθ/ *n* **1** a consequence, result **2** the period immediately following a usu ruinous event

afternoon /,ɑːftə'nuːn/ *n* the time between noon and sunset

afters /'ɑːftəz/ *n pl, Br* a dessert – infml

aftertaste /'ɑːftəteɪst/ *n* persistence of a flavour or impression

afterthought /'ɑːftəθɔːt/ *n* **1** an idea occurring later **2** sthg added later

afterwards /'ɑːftəwədz/ *adv* after that; subsequently, thereafter

again /ə'gen, ə'geɪn/ *adv* **1** so as to be as before **2** another time; once more **3** on the other hand **4** further; in addition

[1]**against** /ə'genst, ə'geɪnst/ *prep* **1a** in opposition or hostility to **b** unfavourable to **c** as a defence or protection from **2** compared or contrasted with **3a** in preparation or provision for **b** with respect to; towards **4** (in the direction of and) in contact with **5** in a direction opposite to the motion or course of; counter to **6** in exchange for

[2]**against** *adj* **1** opposed to a motion or measure **2** unfavourable to a specified degree; *esp* unfavourable to a win

agape /ə'geɪp/ *adj* **1** wide open; gaping **2** in a state of wonder

agate /'ægət, 'ægeɪt/ *n* a mineral used as a gem composed of quartz of various colours, often arranged in bands

[1]**age** /eɪdʒ/ *n* **1a** the length of time a

person has lived or a thing existed **b** the time of life at which some particular qualification, power, or capacity arises **c** a stage of life **2** a generation **3** a period of time dominated by a central figure or prominent feature **4** a division of geological time, usu shorter than an epoch **5** a long time – usu pl with sing. meaning; infml

[2]**age** *v* **aging, ageing 1** to become old; show the effects of increasing age **2** to become mellow or mature; ripen **3** to cause to seem old, esp prematurely **4** to bring to a state fit for use or to maturity

aged /'eɪdʒɨd; *sense 1b* eɪdʒd/ *adj* **1** grown old: e g **a** of an advanced age **b** having attained a specified age **2** typical of old age

ageless /'eɪdʒlɨs/ *adj* **1** never growing old or showing the effects of age **2** timeless, eternal – **~ness** *n*

agency /'eɪdʒənsi/ *n* **1** a power or force through which a result is achieved; instrumentality **2** the function or place of business of an agent or representative **3** an establishment that does business for another

agenda /ə'dʒendə/ *n* **1** a list of items to be discussed or business to be transacted (e g at a meeting) **2** a plan of procedure; a programme

agent /'eɪdʒənt/ *n* **1** sthg or sby that produces an effect or that acts or exerts power **2** a person who acts for or in the place of another by authority from him/her: e g **a** a business representative **b** one employed by or controlling an agency **3a** a representative of a government **b** a spy

agent provocateur /ɑːʒɒn prɒvɒkə'tɜːʳ/ *n, pl* **agents provocateurs** a person employed to incite suspected people to some open action that will make them liable to punishment

age of consent *n* the age at which one is legally competent to give consent; *specif* that at which a person, esp a female, may consent to sexual intercourse

[1]**agglomerate** /ə'glɒməreɪt/ *v* to (cause to) gather into a cluster or disorderly mass – **-ation** *n*

[2]**agglomerate** /ə'glomərəɪt/ *adj* gathered into a ball, mass, or cluster

[3]**agglomerate** /ə'glɒmərɨt/ *n* **1** a disorderly mass or collection **2** a rock composed of irregular volcanic fragments

aggrand·ize, -ise /ə'grændaɪz/ *v* **1** to give a false air of greatness to **2** to advance the power, position, etc of – **-izement** *n*

aggravate /'ægrəveɪt/ *v* **1** to make worse or more severe **2** to annoy, irritate – **-tion** *n*

[1]**aggregate** /'ægrɪgɨt/ *v* **1** to bring together into a mass or whole **2** to amount to (a specified total)

[2]**aggregate** *n* **1** a mass of loosely associated parts; an assemblage **2** the whole amount; the sum total

aggression /ə'greʃən/ *n* **1** a hostile attack; *esp* one made without just cause **2** attack, encroachment; *esp* unprovoked violation by one country of the territory of another **3** hostile, injurious, or destructive behaviour or outlook – **-ssor** *n*

aggressive /ə'gresɪv/ *adj* **1a** tending towards or practising aggression **b** ready to attack **2** forceful, dynamic – **~ly** *adv* – **~ness** *n*

aggrieved /ə'griːvd/ *adj* showing or expressing resentment; hurt

aggro /'ægroʊ/ *n, chiefly Br* **1** provocation, hostility **2** deliberate aggression or violence *USE* infml

aghast /ə'gɑːst/ *adj* suddenly struck with terror or amazement; shocked

agile /'ædʒaɪl/ *adj* **1** quick, easy, and graceful in movement **2** mentally quick and resourceful – **~ly** *adv* – **-ility** *n*

agitate /'ædʒɨteɪt/ *v* **1** to move, shake **2** to excite and often trouble the mind or feelings of; disturb **3** to work to arouse public feeling for or against a cause – **-tation** *n*

agitator /'ædʒɨteɪtəʳ/ *n* **1** sby who stirs up public feeling on controversial issues **2** a device or apparatus for stirring or shaking

aglow /ə'gləʊ/ *adj* radiant with warmth or excitement

[1]**agnostic** /æg'nɒstɪk/ *n* sby who holds the view that any ultimate reality is unknown and prob unknowable; *also* one who doubts the existence of God – **~ism** *n*

[2]**agnostic** *adj* of or being an agnostic or the beliefs of agnostics

ago /ə'gəʊ/ *adj or adv* earlier than now

agog /ə'gɒg/ *adj* full of intense anticipation or excitement; eager

agony /'ægəni/ *n* **1** intense and often prolonged pain or suffering of mind or body; anguish **2** the struggle that precedes death – **-nize** *v* – **-nized** *adj* – **-nizing** *adj*

agoraphobia /ˌægərə'fəʊbɪə/ *n* abnormal dread of being in open spaces – **-bic** *n, adj*

agrarian /ə'greərɪən/ *adj* **1** of or relating to (the tenure of) fields **2** (characteristic) of farmers or agricultural life or interests – **agrarian** *n*

agree /ə'griː/ *v* **1** to admit, concede – usu + a clause **2** to bring into harmony **3** *chiefly Br* to come to terms on, usu after discussion; accept by mutual consent **4** to give assent; accede – often + *to* **5a** to be of one mind – often + *with* **b** to decide together **6a** to correspond **b** to be consistent **7** to suit the health – + *with*

agreeable /ə'griːəbəl/ *adj* **1** to one's liking; pleasing **2** willing to agree or consent

agreement /ə'griːmənt/ *n* **1a** harmony of opinion or feeling **b** correspondence **2a** an arrangement laying down terms, conditions, etc **b** a treaty **3** (the language or document embodying) a legally binding contract

agriculture /'ægrɪˌkʌltʃəʳ/ *n* the theory and practice of cultivating and producing crops from the soil and of raising livestock – **-tural** *adj* – **-turally** *adv* – **-tur(al)ist** *n*

aground /ə'graʊnd/ *adv or adj* on or onto the shore or the bottom of a body of water

ah /ɑː/ *interj* – used to express delight, relief, regret, or contempt

ahead /ə'hed/ *adv or adj* **1a** in a forward direction **b** in front **2** in, into, or for the future **3** in or towards a better position

[1]**aid** /eɪd/ *v* **1** to give assistance to; help **2** to bring about the accomplishment of; facilitate

[2]**aid** *n* **1** help; assistance; *specif* tangible means of assistance (e g money or supplies) **2a** a helper **b** sthg that helps or supports; *specif* a hearing aid

aide /eɪd/ *n* **1** an aide-de-camp **2** *chiefly NAm* an assistant

aide-de-camp /eɪd də 'kɒm/ *n, pl* **aides-de-camp** an officer in the armed forces acting as a personal assistant to a senior officer

AIDS *n* acquired immune deficiency syndrome; an often fatal disease caused by a virus attacking cells that normally stimulate the production of antibodies to fight infection

ail /eɪl/ *v* **1** to give pain, discomfort, or trouble to **2** to be unwell

aileron /'eɪlərɒn/ *n* a movable control surface of an aircraft wing or a movable flap external to the wing at the trailing edge for giving a rolling motion and providing lateral control

ailment /'eɪlmənt/ *n* a bodily disorder or chronic disease

[1]**aim** /eɪm/ *v* **1** to direct a course; *specif* to point a weapon at an object **2** to channel one's efforts; aspire **3** to have the intention; mean **4** to direct or point (e g a weapon) at a target **5** to direct at or towards a specified goal; intend

[2]**aim** *n* **1a** the pointing of a weapon at a mark **b** the ability to hit a target **c** a weapon's accuracy or effectiveness **2** a clear intention or purpose – **~less** *adj*

[1]**air** /eəʳ/ *n* **1a** the mixture of invisible odourless tasteless gases, containing esp nitrogen and oxygen, that surrounds the earth **b** a light breeze **2a** empty unconfined space **b** nothingness **3a(1)** aircraft **(2)** aviation **b** the supposed medium of transmission of radio waves; *also* radio, television **4a** the appearance or bearing of a person; demeanour **b** *pl* an artificial or affected manner; haughtiness **c** outward appearance of a thing **d** a surrounding or pervading influence; an atmosphere **5** a tune, melody

[2]**air** *v* **1** to expose to the air for drying, freshening, etc; ventilate **2** to expose to public view or bring to public notice

air bed *n, chiefly Br* an inflatable mattress

air brick *n* a building brick or brick-sized metal box perforated to allow ventilation

airbus /'eəbʌs/ *n* a subsonic jet passenger aeroplane designed for short intercity flights

aircraft /'eəkrɑːft/ *n, pl* **aircraft** a weight-carrying structure that can travel through the air and is supported either by its own buoyancy or by the dynamic action of the air against its surfaces

aircraft carrier *n* a warship designed so that aircraft can be operated from it

aircraftman /'eəkrɑːftmən/ *n* (a person who holds) the lowest rank in the Royal Air Force

Airedale /'eədeɪl/ , **Airedale terrier** *n* any of a breed of large terriers with a hard wiry coat that is dark on the back and sides and tan elsewhere

airfield /'eəfiːld/ *n* an area of land maintained for the landing and takeoff of aircraft

air force /'eəfɔːs/ *n* the branch of a country's armed forces for air warfare

air gun *n* **1** a gun from which a projectile is propelled by compressed air **2** any of various hand tools that work by compressed air

air hostess *n* a stewardess on an airliner

airily /'eərʒli/ *adv* in an airy manner; jauntily, lightly

airing cupboard *n* a heated cupboard in which esp household linen is aired and kept dry

air lane *n* a path customarily followed by aeroplanes

airless /'eələs/ *adj* **1** still, windless **2** lacking fresh air; stuffy

airlift /'eə,lɪft/ *n* the transport of cargo or passengers by air, usu to an otherwise inaccessible area – **airlift** *v*

airline /'eəlaɪn/ *n* an organization that provides regular public air transport

air lock *n* **1** an airtight intermediate chamber (e g in a spacecraft or submerged caisson) which allows movement between 2 areas of different pressures or atmospheres **2** a stoppage of flow caused by air being in a part where liquid ought to circulate

airmail /'eəmeɪl/ *n* (the postal system using) mail transported by aircraft

air pocket *n* a region of down-flowing or rarefied air that causes an aircraft to drop suddenly

airport /'eəpɔːt/ *n* a fully-equipped airfield that is used as a base for the transport of passengers and cargo by air

air raid *n* an attack by armed aircraft on a surface target

airship /'eə,ʃɪp/ *n* a gas-filled lighter-than-air self-propelled aircraft that has a steering system

airspace /'eəspeɪs/ *n* the space lying above the earth or a certain area of land or water; *esp* the space lying above a nation and coming under its jurisdiction

airstrip /'eə,strɪp/ *n* a runway without airport facilities

airtight /'eətaɪt/ *adj* **1** impermeable to air **2** unassailable

airway /'eəweɪ/ *n* **1** a passage for air in a mine **2** a designated route along which aircraft fly

airy /'eəri/ *adj* **1a** not having solid foundation; illusory **b** showing lack of concern; flippant **2** being light and graceful in movement or manner **3** delicately thin in texture **4** open to the free circulation of air; breezy **5** high in the air; lofty – poetic

aisle /aɪl/ *n* **1** the side division of a church separated from the nave by columns or piers **2** *chiefly NAm* a gangway

ajar /ə'dʒɑː^r/ *adj or adv, esp of a door* slightly open

akimbo /ə'kɪmbəʊ/ *adj or adv* having the hands on the hips and the elbows turned outwards

akin /ə'kɪn/ *adj* **1** descended from a common ancestor **2** essentially similar, related, or compatible *USE* often + *to*

alabaster /'æləbɑːstə^r, -bæs-/ *n* a fine-textured usu white and translucent chalky stone often carved into ornaments

à la carte /,ælə 'kɑːt, ,ɑːlɑː-/ *adv or adj* according to a menu that prices each item separately

alacrity /ə'lækrʒti/ *n* promptness or cheerful readiness – fml

à la mode /,æ lə 'məʊd/ *adj* fashionable, stylish

[1]**alarm** /ə'lɑːm/ *n* **1** a signal (e g a loud noise or flashing light) that warns or alerts; *also* an automatic device that

alerts or rouses 2 the fear resulting from the sudden sensing of danger

[2]**alarm** *v* **1** to give warning to **2** to strike with fear

alas /əˈlæs/ *interj* – used to express unhappiness, pity, or disappointment

albatross /ˈælbətrɒs/ *n* any of various (very) large web-footed seabirds related to the petrels

albeit /ɔːlˈbiːᵊt/ *conj* even though – fml

albino /ælˈbiːnəʊ/ *n, pl* **albinos** a human being or other animal with a (congenital) lack of pigment resulting in a white or translucent skin, white or colourless hair, and eyes with a pink pupil

album /ˈælbəm/ *n* **1** a book with blank pages used for making a collection (e g of stamps or photographs) **2** a recording or collection of recordings issued on 1 or more long-playing gramophone records or cassettes

albumen /ˈælbjʊmᵊn/ *n* the white of an egg

alchemy /ˈælkəmi/ *n* **1** a medieval chemical science and philosophical doctrine aiming to achieve the transformation of the base metals into gold, a cure for disease, and immortality **2** the transformation of sthg common into sthg precious – **-mist** *n*

alcohol /ˈælkəhɒl/ *n* **1** a colourless volatile inflammable liquid that is the intoxicating agent in fermented and distilled drinks and is used also as a solvent **2** any of various organic compounds, specif derived from hydrocarbons, containing the hydroxyl group **3** intoxicating drink containing alcohol; *esp* spirits

alcoholic /ˌælkəˈhɒlɪk/ *adj* affected with alcoholism – **~ally** *adv* – **alcoholic** *n*

alcoholism /ˈælkəhɒlɪzəm/ *n* (a complex chronic psychological and nutritional disorder associated with) excessive and usu compulsive use of alcoholic drinks

alcove /ˈælkəʊv/ *n* **1a** a nook or recess off a larger room **2** a niche or arched opening (e g in a wall or hedge)

alder /ˈɔːldəʳ/ *n* any of a genus of trees or shrubs of the birch family that grow in moist ground

alderman /ˈɔːldəmən/ *n* **1** a person governing a kingdom, district, or shire as viceroy for an Anglo-Saxon king **2** a senior member of a county or borough council elected by the other councillors – not used officially in Britain after 1974

ale /eɪl/ *n* a malted and hopped alcoholic drink that is usually more bitter, stronger, and heavier than beer

[1]**alert** /əˈlɜːt/ *adj* **1** watchful, aware **2** active, brisk – **~ly** *adv* – **~ness** *n*

[2]**alert** *n* **1** an alarm or other signal that warns of danger (e g from hostile aircraft) **2** the danger period during which an alert is in effect

[3]**alert** *v* **1** to call to a state of readiness; warn **2** to cause to be aware (e g of a need or responsibility)

alfalfa /ælˈfælfə/ *n, NAm* lucerne

algebra /ˈældʒᵊbrə/ *n* a branch of mathematics in which letters, symbols, etc representing various entities are combined according to special rules of operation – **~ic(al)** *adj* – **~ically** *adv*

algorithm /ˈælgərɪðəm/ *n* a systematic procedure for solving a (mathematical) problem or accomplishing some end – **~ic** *adj*

[1]**alias** /ˈeɪlɪəs/ *adv* otherwise called or known as

[2]**alias** *n* an assumed name

alibi /ˈælᵊbaɪ/ *n* **1** (evidence supporting) the plea of having been elsewhere when a crime was committed **2** a plausible excuse, usu intended to avert blame or punishment

[1]**alien** /ˈeɪlɪən/ *adj* **1a** of or belonging to another person, place, or thing; strange **b** foreign **2** differing in nature or character, esp to the extent of being opposed – + *to*

[2]**alien** *n* **1** a person from another family, race, or nation; *also* an extraterrestrial being **2** a foreign-born resident who has not been naturalized; *broadly* a foreign-born citizen

alienate /ˈeɪlɪəneɪt/ *v* **1** to make hostile or indifferent, esp in cases where attachment formerly existed **2** to cause to be withdrawn or diverted

alienation /ˌeɪlɪəˈneɪʃən/ *n* (a feeling of) withdrawal from or apathy towards one's former attachments or whole social existence

[1]**alight** /ə'laɪt/ *v* **alighted** *also* **alit** 1 to come down from sthg: e g **a** to dismount **b** to disembark 2 to descend from the air and settle; land

[2]**alight** *adj* 1 animated, alive 2 *chiefly Br* on fire; ignited

align, aline /ə'laɪn/ *v* 1 to bring into proper relative position or state of adjustment; *specif* to bring three or more points into line 2 to join with others in a common cause – **~ment** *n*

[1]**alike** /ə'laɪk/ *adj* showing close resemblance without being identical

[2]**alike** *adv* in the same manner, form, or degree; equally

alimentary canal /ˌælʒ'mentəri/ *n* the tubular passage that extends from the mouth to the anus and functions in the digestion and absorption of food

alimony /'ælʒməni/ *n* 1 means of living; maintenance 2 *chiefly NAm* maintenance paid to a spouse during legal separation or after divorce

alive /ə'laɪv/ *adj* 1 having life 2 still in existence, force, or operation; active 3 realizing the existence of sthg; aware of sthg 4 marked by alertness 5 showing much activity or animation; swarming 6 of all those living – used as an intensive following the noun

alkali /'ælkəlaɪ/ *n, pl* **alkalies, alkalis** any of various chemical bases, esp a hydroxide or carbonate of an alkali metal – **~ne** *adj*

alkaloid /'ælkəlɔɪd/ *n* any of various plant derived substances often used as drugs (e g morphine)

[1]**all** /ɔːl/ *adj* 1a the whole amount or quantity of (e g awake *all* night) **b** as much as possible (e g say in *all* honesty) 2a every one of (more than 2) 3 the whole number or sum of (e g *all* cats like milk) 4 every (e g *all* manner of hardship) 5 any whatever (e g beyond *all* hope) 6a given to or displaying only (e g was *all* attention) **b** having or seeming to have (some physical feature) conspicuously or excessively (e g *all* thumbs)

[2]**all** *adv* 1 wholly, altogether (e g sitting *all* alone) 2 to a supreme degree – usu in combination (e g *all*-powerful) 3 for each side (e g a score of 3 *all*)

[3]**all** *pron, pl* **all** 1 the whole number, quantity, or amount (e g it was *all* we could afford) 2 everybody, everything (e g give up *all* for love)

[4]**all** *n* one's total resources (e g gave his *all* for the cause)

Allah /'ælə/ *n* God – used by Muslims or in reference to the Islamic religion

allay /ə'leɪ/ *v* 1 to reduce the severity of; alleviate 2 to make quiet; pacify

all clear *n* a signal that a danger has passed or that it is safe to proceed

allege /ə'ledʒ/ *v* to assert without proof or before proving – **-gation** *n*

allegedly /ə'ledʒʒdli/ *adv* according to allegation – used in reporting statements that have not been verified

allegiance /ə'liːdʒəns/ *n* 1 the obligation of a subject or citizen to his/her sovereign or government 2 dedication to or dutiful support of a person, group, or cause

allegory /'ælʒgəri/ *n* 1a the expression by means of symbolic figures and actions of truths or generalizations about human existence **b** an instance (e g Spenser's *Faery Queene*) of such expression 2 a symbolic representation; an emblem – **-rical** *adj* – **-rically** *adv*

allegretto /ˌælʒ'gretəʊ/ *adv or adj* faster than andante but not so fast as allegro – used in music

allegro /ə'legrəʊ/ *n, adv, or adj, pl* **allegros** (a musical composition or movement to be played) in a brisk lively manner

alleluia /ˌælʒ'luːjə/ *interj* – used as a joyous exclamation in praise of God

allergy /'ælədʒi/ *n* 1 exaggerated reaction by sneezing, itching, skin rashes, etc to substances that have no such effect on the average individual 2 a feeling of antipathy or aversion – infml – **-gic** *adj*

alleviate /ə'liːvieɪt/ *v* to relieve (a troublesome situation, state of mind, etc) – **-ation** *n*

[1]**alley** /'æli/ *n* 1 a bowling alley 2 a narrow back street or passageway between buildings

[2]**alley** *n* a playing marble (of superior quality)

all fours *n pl* hands and knees

alliance /ə'laɪəns/ *n* 1 a union of

families by marriage **2** a uniting of nations by formal treaty **3** a tie, connection

allied /'ælaɪd, ə'laɪd/ *adj* **1** in close association; united **2** joined in alliance by agreement or treaty **3a** related by resemblance or common properties; associated **b** related genetically **4** *cap* of the Allies

alligator /'æl\|geɪtə^r/ *n* **1** either of 2 crocodilians with broad heads that do not taper towards the snout **2** leather made from alligator hide

all-in *adj, chiefly Br* all-inclusive; *esp* including all costs

all in *adj* tired out; exhausted – infml

alliteration /əˌlɪtə'reɪʃən/ *n* the repetition of usu initial consonant sounds in neighbouring words or syllables (e g *thr*eatening *thr*ongs of *thr*eshers) – **-tive** *adj* – **-tively** *adv*

allocate /'æləkeɪt/ *v* **1a** to apportion and distribute (e g money or responsibility) in shares **b** to assign (sthg limited in supply) to as a share **2** to earmark, designate – **-tion** *n*

allot /ə'lɒt/ *v* to allocate

allotment /ə'lɒtmənt/ *n, Br* a small plot of land let out to an individual (e g by a town council) for cultivation

all-out *adj* using maximum effort and resources

all out *adv* with maximum determination and effort; flat out – chiefly in *go all out*

allover /ɔːl'əʊvə^r/ *adj* covering the whole extent or surface

all over *adv* **1** over the whole extent or surface **2** in every respect

allow /ə'laʊ/ *v* **1a(1)** to assign as a share or suitable amount (e g of time or money) **(2)** to grant as an allowance **b** to reckon as a deduction or an addition **2a** to admit as true or valid; acknowledge **b** to admit the possibility (of) **3a** to make it possible for; enable **b** to fail to prevent; let **4** to make allowance *for*

allowable /ə'laʊəbəl/ *adj* **1** permissible **2** assigned as an allowance – **-bly** *adv*

allowance /ə'laʊəns/ *n* **1a** a (limited) share or portion allotted or granted; a ration **b** a sum granted as a reimbursement or bounty or for expenses **2** a handicap (e g in a race) **3a** permission, sanction **b** acknowledgment **4** the taking into account of mitigating circumstances – often pl with sing. meaning

[1]**alloy** /'ælɔɪ/ *n* **1** a solid substance composed of a mixture of metals or a metal and a nonmetal thoroughly intermixed **2** a metal mixed with a more valuable metal **3** an addition that impairs or debases

[2]**alloy** *v* **1** to reduce the purity or value of by adding sthg **2** to mix so as to form an alloy **3a** to impair or debase by addition **b** to temper, moderate

all-purpose *adj* suited for many purposes or uses

[1]**all right** *adv* **1** well enough **2** beyond doubt; certainly

[2]**all right** *adj* **1** satisfactory, acceptable **2** safe, well **3** agreeable, pleasing – used as a generalized term of approval

[3]**all right** *interj* **1** – used for giving assent **2** – used in indignant or menacing response

all-round *adj* **1** competent in many fields **2** having general utility **3** encompassing all aspects; comprehensive – ~**er** *n*

all round *adv* **1** by, for, or to everyone present **2** in every respect

allspice /'ɔːlspaɪs/ *n* (a mildly pungent spice prepared from) the berry of a W Indian tree belonging to the myrtle family

all-time *adj* exceeding all others yet known

allude /ə'luːd/ *v* to make indirect or implicit reference *to*

[1]**allure** /ə'lʊə^r/ *v* to entice by charm or attraction

[2]**allure** *n* power of attraction or fascination; charm

allusion /ə'luːʒən/ *n* **1** alluding or hinting **2** (the use of) implied or indirect reference, esp in literature – **-sive** *adj* – **-sively** *adv*

alluvium /ə'luːviəm/ *n, pl* **alluviums, alluvia** clay, silt, or similar material deposited by running water – **-vial** *adj*

[1]**ally** /ə'laɪ/ *v* **1** to join, unite *with/to* **2** to relate *to* by resemblance or com-

mon properties **3** to form or enter into an alliance *with*

²ally /'ælaɪ/ *n* **1** a sovereign or state associated with another by treaty or league **2** a helper, auxiliary

alma mater /,ælmə 'mɑːtəʳ, 'meɪtəʳ/ *n* a school, college, or university which one has attended

almanac, almanack /'ɔːlmənæk/ *n* **1** a usu annual publication containing statistical, tabular, and general information **2** *chiefly Br* a publication containing astronomical and meteorological data arranged according to the days, weeks, and months of a given year

¹almighty /ɔːl'maɪti/ *adj* **1** *often cap* having absolute power over all **2** having relatively unlimited power **3** great in extent, seriousness, force, etc – infml

²almighty *adv* to a great degree; mighty – infml

Almighty *n* God – + *the*

almond /'ɑːmənd/ *n* (the edible oval nut of) a small tree of the rose family

almoner /'ɑːmənəʳ, 'æl-/ *n* **1** one who distributes alms **2** a social worker attached to a British hospital – not now used technically

almost /'ɔːlməʊst/ *adv* very nearly but not exactly or entirely

alms /ɑːmz/ *n sing or pl in constr* money, food, etc given to help the poor

almshouse /'ɑːmzhaʊs/ *n, Br* a privately endowed house in which a poor person can live

aloft /ə'lɒft/ *adv* **1** at or to a great height **2** at, on, or to the masthead or the upper rigging of a ship

alone /ə'ləʊn/ *adj or adv* **1** considered without reference to any other; *esp* unassisted **2** separated from others; isolated **3** exclusive of other factors **4** free from interference

¹along /ə'lɒŋ/ *prep* **1** in a line parallel with the length or direction of **2** in the course of (a route or journey) **3** in accordance with

²along *adv* **1** forward, on (e g move *along*) **2** as a necessary or pleasant addition; with one (e g bring the picnic *along*) **3** in company and simultaneously *with* (e g caught flu *along* with the others) **4** on hand, there (e g I'll be *along* soon) **5** also; in addition

¹alongside /ə,lɒŋ'saɪd/ *adv* along or at the side

²alongside, alongside of *prep* **1** side by side with; *specif* parallel to **2** concurrently with

¹aloof /ə'luːf/ *adv* at a distance; out of involvement

²aloof *adj* distant in interest or feeling; reserved, unsympathetic – **~ly** *adv* – **~ness** *n*

aloud /ə'laʊd/ *adv* with the speaking voice

alpaca /æl'pækə/ *n* **1** (the fine long woolly hair of) a type of domesticated llama found in Peru **2** a thin cloth made of or containing this wool

alpen horn /'ælpənhɔːn/ *n* a long straight wooden horn used, esp formerly, by Swiss herdsmen to call sheep and cattle

¹alpha /'ælfə/ *n* **1** the 1st letter of the Greek alphabet **2** sthg that is first; a beginning **3** – used to designate the chief or brightest star of a constellation

²alpha *adj* alphabetical

alphabet /'ælfəbet/ *n* a set of characters, esp letters, used to represent 1 or more languages, esp when arranged in a conventional order; *also* a system of signs and signals that can be used in place of letters – **~ical** *adj* – **~ically** *adv*

alpha particle *n* a positively charged nuclear particle identical with the nucleus of a helium atom ejected at high speed by some radioactive substances

alpine /'ælpaɪn/ *n* an (ornamental) plant native to alpine or northern parts of the northern hemisphere

Alpine *adj* **1** *often not cap* of, growing in, or resembling the Alps; *broadly* of or resembling any mountains **2** *often not cap* of or growing in the elevated slopes above the tree line **3** of or being competitive ski events comprising slalom and downhill racing

already /ɔːl'redi/ *adv* **1** no later than now or then; even by this or that time **2** before, previously

alright /,ɔːl'raɪt/ *adv, adj, or interj* all right – nonstandard

Alsatian /æl'seɪʃən/ *n* (any of) a breed of large intelligent dogs often used as guard dogs

also /'ɔːlsəʊ/ *adv* as an additional circumstance; besides

also-ran *n* **1** an entrant, esp a horse, that finishes outside the first 3 places in a race **2** a person of little importance

altar /'ɔːltəʳ/ *n* **1** a usu raised structure or place on which sacrifices are offered or incense is burnt in worship **2** a table on which the bread and wine used at communion are consecrated or which serves as a centre of worship or ritual

altarpiece /'ɔːltəpiːs/ *n* a work of art that decorates the space above and behind an altar

alter /'ɔːltəʳ/ *v* **1** to make different without changing into sthg else **2** to become different – **~able** *adj* – **~ation** *n*

altercation /,ɔːltə'keɪʃən/ *n* a heated quarrel; *also* quarrelling

alter ego /,æltər 'iːgəʊ, ɔːltəʳ/ *n* a second self; *esp* a trusted friend

[1]**alternate** /ɔːl'tɜːnɪ̣t/ *adj* **1** occurring or succeeding each other by turns **2** arranged one above or alongside the other **3** every other; every second – **~ly** *adv*

[2]**alternate** /'ɔːltəneɪt/ *v* **1** to interchange with sthg else in turn **2** *of 2 things* to occur or succeed each other by turns **3** to undergo or consist of repeated change from one thing to another – **-nation** *n*

alternating current *n* an electric current that reverses its direction at regularly recurring intervals

[1]**alternative** /ɔːl'tɜːnətɪv/ *adj* **1** affording a choice, esp between 2 mutually exclusive options **2** constituting an alternative – **~ly** *adv*

[2]**alternative** *n* **1** an opportunity or need for deciding between 2 or more possibilities **2** either of 2 possibilities between which a choice is to be made; *also* any of more than 2 such possibilities

alternator /'ɔːltəneɪtəʳ/ *n* an electric generator for producing alternating current

although /ɔːl'ðəʊ/ *conj* in spite of the fact or possibility that; though

altimeter /'æltɪmiːtəʳ/ *n* an instrument for measuring altitude

altitude /'æltɪ̣tjuːd/ *n* **1** the angular elevation of a celestial object above the horizon **2** the height of an object (e g an aircraft), esp above sea level

alto /'æltəʊ/ *n, pl* **altos** **1a** a countertenor **b** a contralto **2** the second highest part in 4-part harmony **3** a member of a family of instruments having a range between the treble or soprano and the tenor – **alto** *adj*

[1]**altogether** /,ɔːltə'geðəʳ/ *adv* **1** wholly, thoroughly **2** all told **3** in the main; on the whole **4** in every way

[2]**altogether** /,ɔːltə'geðə/ *n* *the* nude – infml

altruism /'æltrʊ-ɪzəm/ *n* unselfish regard for or devotion to the welfare of others – **altruist** *n* – **-istic** *adj* – **-istically** *adv*

aluminium /,æljʊ'mɪnɪəm, ,ælə-/ *n* a bluish silver-white malleable light metallic element with good electrical and thermal conductivity and resistance to oxidation

always /'ɔːlwɪ̣z, -weɪz/ *adv* **1a** at all times **b** in all cases **2** on every occasion; repeatedly **3** forever, perpetually **4** as a last resort; at any rate

am /m, əm; *strong* æm/ *pres 1 sing of* **be**

AM *adj* of or being a broadcasting or receiving system using amplitude modulation

amalgam /ə'mælgəm/ *n* a mixture of different elements

amalgamate /ə'mælgəmeɪt/ *v* to combine into a single body – **-ation** *n*

amass /ə'mæs/ *v* **1** to collect for oneself; accumulate **2** to bring together into a mass; gather

amateur /'æmətəʳ, -tʃʊəʳ, -tʃəʳ, ,æmə'tɜːʳ/ *n* **1** one who engages in a pursuit as a pastime rather than as a profession; *esp* a sportsman who has never competed for money **2** one who practises an art or science unskilfully; a dabbler – **amateur** *adj*

amatory /'æmətəri/ *adj* of or expressing sexual love

amaze /ə'meɪz/ *v* to fill with wonder; astound – **~ment** *n*

amazing /ə'meɪzɪŋ/ *adj* – used as a

generalized term of approval – ~ly *adv*

amazon /'æməzən/ *n, often cap* a tall strong athletic woman – ~**ian** *adj*

ambassador /æm'bæsədə'/ *n* **1** a top-ranking diplomat accredited to a foreign government or sovereign as a temporary or resident representative **2** a representative, messenger – ~**ship** *n* – ~**ial** *adj*

amber /'æmbə'/ *n* **1** a hard yellowish to brownish translucent fossil resin used chiefly for ornaments and jewellery **2** the colour of amber **3** a yellow traffic light meaning 'caution"

ambergris /'æmbəgri:s, -grıs/ *n* a waxy substance found floating in tropical waters, believed to originate in the intestines of the sperm whale, and used in perfumery as a fixative

ambidextrous /,æmbı'dekstrəs/ *adj* **1** able to use either hand with equal ease **2** unusually skilful; versatile **3** characterized by deceitfulness and double-dealing – ~**ly** *adv*

ambience, ambiance /'æmbıəns/ *n* a surrounding or pervading atmosphere; an environment, milieu

ambiguous /æm'bıgjʊəs/ *adj* **1** vague, indistinct, or difficult to classify **2** capable of 2 or more interpretations – -**guity** *n* – ~**ly** *adv* – ~**ness** *n*

ambition /æm'bıʃən/ *n* **1a** a strong desire for status, wealth, or power **b** a desire to achieve a particular end **2** an object of ambition

ambitious /æm'bıʃəs/ *adj* **1a** having, resulting from, or showing ambition **b** desirous *of*, aspiring **2** elaborate – ~**ly** *adv* – ~**ness** *n*

[1]**amble** /'æmbl/ *v* to move at an amble

[2]**amble** *n* **1** an easy gait **2** a leisurely stroll

ambrosia /æm'brəʊzıə/ *n* **1** the food of the Greek and Roman gods **2** sthg extremely pleasing to the taste or smell

ambulance /'æmbjʊləns/ *n* a vehicle equipped to transport the injured or ill

[1]**ambush** /'æmbʊʃ/ *v* to attack from an ambush; waylay

[2]**ambush** *n* the concealment of soldiers, police, etc in order to carry out a surprise attack from a hidden position

ameliorate /ə'mi:lıəreıt/ *v* to make or become better or more tolerable – -**ration** *n*

amen /ɑ:'men, eı-/ *interj* – used to express solemn confirmation (e g of an expression of faith) or hearty approval (e g of an assertion)

amenable /ə'mi:nəbəl/ *adj* **1** capable of submission (e g to judgment or test) **2** readily persuaded to yield or agree; tractable

amend /ə'mend/ *v* **1** to put right; *specif* to make corrections in (e g a text) **2** to change or modify for the better; improve

amendment /ə'mendmənt/ *n* **1** the act of amending, esp for the better **2** an alteration proposed or effected by amending

amends /ə'mendz/ *n pl but sing or pl in constr* compensation for a loss or injury; recompense

amenity /ə'mi:nʝti/ *n* **1** sthg (e g a public facility) conducive to material comfort – often pl **2** sthg (e g a conventional social gesture) conducive to ease of social intercourse – usu pl **3** pleasantness, esp of environment – fml

[1]**American** /ə'merıkən/ *n* **1** a N or S American Indian **2** a native or inhabitant of N or S America **3** a citizen of the USA **4** English as typically spoken and written in the USA

[2]**American** *adj* **1** (characteristic) of N or S America **2** (characteristic) of the USA **3** of the N and S American Indians

American Indian *n* a member of any of the indigenous peoples of N, S, or central America excluding the Eskimos

Americanism /ə'merʝkənızəm/ *n* **1** a characteristic feature (e g a custom or belief) of Americans or American culture **2** adherence or attachment to America, its culture, or its policies

amethyst /'æmʝθʝst/ *n* a semiprecious gemstone of clear purple or violet quartz

amiable /'eımıəbəl/ *adj* **1** (seeming) agreeable and well-intentioned; inoffensive **2** friendly, congenial – -**bility** *n* – -**bly** *adv*

amicable /'æmɪ̵kəbəl/ *adj* characterized by friendly goodwill; peaceable – **-bility** *n* – **-bly** *adv*

amid /ə'mɪd/ *prep* in or to the middle of – poetic

amidships /ə'mɪdʃɪps/ *adv* in or towards the middle part (of a ship)

amino acid /əˌmiːnəʊ 'æsɪ̵d, əˌmaɪ-/ *n* any of various organic acids containing an amino group and occurring esp in linear chains as the chief components of proteins

amiss /ə'mɪs/ *adv or adj* **1** astray **2** out of order; at fault **3** out of place in given circumstances – usu + a negative

amity /'æmɪ̵ti/ *n* friendship

ammeter /'æmɪtəʳ, 'æmˌmiːtəʳ/ *n* an instrument for measuring electric current in amperes

ammonia /ə'məʊnɪə/ *n* a pungent colourless gas that is a compound of nitrogen and hydrogen and is very soluble in water, forming an alkaline solution

ammonite /'æmənaɪt/ *n* a flat spiral fossil shell of a mollusc

ammunition /ˌæmjʊ'nɪʃən/ *n* **1** the projectiles, together with their propelling charges, used in the firing of guns; *also* bombs, grenades, etc containing explosives **2** material used to defend or attack a point of view

amnesia /æm'niːzɪə/ *n* a (pathological) loss of memory

amnesty /'æmnəsti/ *n* the act of pardoning a large group of individuals, esp for political offences

amoeba /ə'miːbə/ *n, pl* **amoebas, amoebae** any of various protozoans that are widely distributed in water and wet places – **-bic** *adj*

amok /ə'mɒk/, **amuck** *adv* **1** in a murderous frenzy; raging violently **2** out of hand *USE* chiefly in *run amok*

among /ə'mʌŋ/ *prep* **1** in or through the midst of; surrounded by **2** by or through the whole group of **3** in the number or class of **4** between – used for more than 2 (e g fight *among* themselves)

amoral /eɪ'mɒrəl, æ-/ *adj* **1** being neither moral nor immoral; *specif* lying outside the sphere of ethical judgments **2** having no understanding of, or unconcerned with, morals – **~ity** *n*

amorous /'æmərəs/ *adj* **1** of or relating to love **2** moved by or inclined to love or desire – **~ly** *adv* – **~ness** *n*

amorphous /ə'mɔːfəs/ *adj* **1** having no definite form; shapeless **2** without definite character; unclassifiable – **~ly** *adv* – **~ness** *n*

¹amount /ə'maʊnt/ *v* to be equal in number, quantity, or significance *to*

²amount *n* **1** the total quantity **2** the quantity at hand or under consideration

amour /ə'mʊəʳ/ *n* a love affair, esp when illicit

amp /æmp/ *n* an ampere *USE* infml

ampere /'æmpeəʳ/ *n* the basic unit of electrical current

ampersand /'æmpəsænd/ *n* a sign, typically &, standing for the word *and*

amphibian /æm'fɪbɪən/ *n* **1** an amphibious organism; *esp* a frog, toad, newt, or other member of a class of cold-blooded vertebrates intermediate in many characteristics between fishes and reptiles **2** an aeroplane, tank, etc adapted to operate on or from both land and water

amphibious /æm'fɪbɪəs/ *adj* **1** able to live both on land and in water **2a** relating to or adapted for both land and water **b** involving or trained for coordinated action of land, sea, and air forces organized for invasion

amphitheatre /'æmfɪ̵θɪətəʳ/ *n* **1** an oval or circular building with rising tiers of seats ranged about an open space **2a** a semicircular gallery in a theatre **b** a flat or gently sloping area surrounded by abrupt slopes **3** a place of public games or contests

amphora /'æmfərə/ *n, pl* **amphorae, amphoras** a 2-handled oval jar or vase with a narrow neck and base, orig used by the ancient Greeks and Romans for holding oil or wine

ample /'æmpəl/ *adj* **1** generous in size, scope, or capacity **2** abundant, plentiful – **-ply** *adv*

amplify /'æmplɪ̵faɪ/ *v* **1** to expand (e g a statement) by the use of detail, illustration, etc **2** to make larger or greater; increase **3** to increase the magnitude of (a signal or other input of power) **4** to expand *on* one's remarks or ideas – **-fication** *n*

amplitude /'æmplɨtjuːd/ *n* largeness of **a** dimensions **b** scope; abundance

ampoule /'æmpuːl/ *n* a hermetically sealed small bulbous glass vessel used esp to hold a sterile solution for hypodermic injection

amputate /'æmpjʊteɪt/ *v* to cut or lop off; *esp* to cut (e g a damaged or diseased limb) from the body – **-tation** *n*

amuck /ə'mʌk/ *adv* amok

amulet /'æmjʊlɨt, -let/ *n* a small object worn as a charm against evil

amuse /ə'mjuːz/ *v* **1** to entertain or occupy in a light or pleasant manner **2** to appeal to the sense of humour of

amusement /ə'mjuːzmənt/ *n* a means of entertaining or occupying; a pleasurable diversion

[1]**an** /ən; *strong* æn/ *indefinite article* **a** – used (1) before words with an initial vowel sound (2) frequently, esp formerly or in the USA, before words whose initial /h/ sound is often lost before the *an*

[2]**an, an'** *conj* and – infml

[3]**an** *prep* **a** – used under the same conditions as [1]**an**

anachronism /ə'nækrənɪzəm/ *n* **1** an error in chronology; *esp* a chronological misplacing of people, events, objects, or customs **2** sby who or sthg that seems chronologically out of place – **-nistic** *adj* – **-nistically** *adv*

anaconda /ˌænə'kɒndə/ *n* a large semiaquatic S American snake of the boa family that crushes its prey in its coils

anaemia /ə'nimiə/ *n* **1** a condition in which the blood is deficient in red blood cells, haemoglobin, etc **2** lack of vitality – **anaemic** *adj* – **-ically** *adv*

anaesthesia /ˌænɨs'θiːzɪə/ *n* loss of sensation, esp loss of sensation of pain, resulting either from injury or a disorder of the nerves or from the action of drugs – **-thetist** *n* – **-thetize** *v*

anaesthetic /ˌænɨs'θetɪk/ *n* a substance that produces anaesthesia, e g so that surgery can be carried out painlessly – **anaesthetic** *adj*

anagram /'ænəgræm/ *n* a word or phrase made by rearranging the letters of another

anal /'eɪnəl/ *adj* **1** of or situated near the anus **2** of or characterized by (typical of) the stage of sexual development during which the child is concerned esp with its faeces

analogue /'ænəlɒg/ *n* sthg analogous or parallel to sthg else

analogy /ə'nælədʒi/ *n* **1** inference from a parallel case **2** resemblance in some particulars; similarity **3** the tendency for new words or linguistic forms to be created in imitation of existing patterns – **-gous** *adj*

analyse /'ænəlaɪz/ *v* **1** to subject to analysis **2** to determine by analysis the constitution or structure of **3** to psychoanalyse

analysis /ə'nælɪsɪs/ *n, pl* **analyses** /-siːz/ **1a** examination and identification of the components of a whole **b** a statement of such an analysis **2** psychoanalysis – **-lytic, -lytical** *adj* – **-lytically** *adv*

analyst /'ænəlɨst/ *n* **1** a person who analyses or is skilled in analysis **2** a psychoanalyst

anarchism /'ænəkɪzəm/ *n* **1** a political theory holding all forms of governmental authority to be undesirable **2** the attacking of the established social order or laws; rebellion – **-chist** *n* – **-chistic** *adj* – **-chistically** *adv*

anarchy /'ænəki/ *n* **1a** absence of government **b** lawlessness; (political) disorder **c** a utopian society with complete freedom and no government **2** anarchism – **-chic, -chical** *adj* – **-chically** *adv*

anatomy /ə'nætəmi/ *n* **1** dissection **2** structural make-up, esp of (a part of) an organism **3** an analysis **4** the human body – **-ist** *n* – **-ical** *adj* – **-ically** *adv*

ancestor /'ænsəstəʳ, -ses-/, *fem* **ancestress** *n* **1a** one from whom a person is descended, usu more distant than a grandparent **b** a forefather **2** a progenitor of a more recent (species of) organism – **-tral** *adj*

ancestry /'ænsəstri, -ses-/ *n* a line of esp noble descent; a lineage

[1]**anchor** /'æŋkəʳ/ *n* **1** a usu metal device dropped to the bottom from a ship or boat to hold it in a particular

place 2 sby or sthg providing support and security; a mainstay 3 sthg that serves to hold an object firmly

[2]**anchor** *v* 1 to hold in place in the water by an anchor 2 to secure firmly; fix 3 to become fixed; settle

anchorage /'æŋkərɪdʒ/ *n* 1 a place (suitable) for vessels to anchor 2 a source of reassurance 3 sthg that provides a secure hold or attachment

anchorite /'æŋkəraɪt/ *fem* **anchoress, anchress** *n* one who lives in seclusion, usu for religious reasons

anchovy /'æntʃəvi/ *n* a common small Mediterranean fish resembling a herring and used esp in appetizers and as a garnish; *also* any of various small fish related to this

[1]**ancient** /'eɪnʃənt/ *adj* 1 having existed for many years 2 of (those living in) a remote period, specif that from the earliest known civilizations to the fall of the western Roman Empire in AD 476 3 old-fashioned, antique

[2]**ancient** *n* 1 sby who lived in ancient times 2 *pl the* members of a civilized, esp a classical, nation of antiquity

[1]**ancillary** /æn'sɪləri/ *adj* 1 subordinate, subsidiary 2 auxiliary, supplementary

[2]**ancillary** *n, Br* one who assists; a helper

and /ənd, ən, *strong* ænd/ *conj* 1 – used to join coordinate sentence elements of the same class or function expressing addition or combination (e g cold *and* tired) 2 – used, esp in Br speech, before the numbers 1–99 after the number 100; used also orig between tens and units 3 plus 4 – used to introduce a second clause expressing temporal sequence, consequence, contrast, or supplementary explanation 5 – used to join repeated words expressing continuation or progression (e g for miles *and* miles) 6 – used to join words expressing contrast of type or quality (e g fair, fat *and* forty) 7 – used instead of *to* to introduce an infinitive after *come, go, run, try, stop* (e g go *and* look)

andante /æn'dænti/ *n, adv, or adj* (a musical composition or movement to be played) moderately slow

android /'ændrɔɪd/ *n* an automaton externally indistinguishable from a human

anecdote /'ænɪkdəʊt/ *n* a usu short narrative about an interesting or amusing person or incident – **-dotal** *adj*

anemone /ə'neməni/ *n* 1 any of a large genus of plants of the buttercup family with lobed or divided leaves and showy flowers 2 a sea anemone

anew /ə'njuː/ *adv* 1 again, afresh 2 in a new form or way

angel /'eɪndʒəl/ *n* 1 a spiritual being, usu depicted as being winged, serving as God's intermediary or acting as a heavenly worshipper 2 an attendant spirit or guardian 3 a messenger, harbinger 4 a very kind or loving person, esp a woman or girl 5 a financial backer of a theatrical venture or other enterprise – chiefly infml – **~ic** *adj* – **~ically** *adv*

angelica /æn'dʒelɪkə/ *n* (the candied stalks, used esp as a decoration on cakes and desserts, of) a biennial plant of the carrot family

Angelus /'ændʒʃləs/ *n* (a bell rung to mark) a devotion of the Western church said at morning, noon, and evening to commemorate the Incarnation

[1]**anger** /'æŋgər/ *n* a strong feeling of displeasure and usu antagonism

[2]**anger** *v* to make or become angry

[1]**angle** /'æŋgəl/ *n* 1 a corner 2a the figure formed by 2 lines extending from the same point or by 2 surfaces diverging from the same line b a measure of the amount of turning necessary to bring one line of an angle to coincide with the other at all points 3a a precise viewpoint; an aspect b a special approach or technique for accomplishing an objective 4 a divergent course or position; a slant – esp in *at an angle*

[2]**angle** *v* 1 to place, move, or direct obliquely 2 to present (e g a news story) from a particular or prejudiced point of view; slant 3 to turn or proceed at an angle

[3]**angle** *v* to use artful means to attain an objective

Angle *n* a member of a Germanic people who invaded England along with the Saxons and Jutes in the 5th c AD

Anglican /'æŋglıkən/ *adj* of the body of churches including the established episcopal Church of England and churches of similar faith in communion with it – ~**ism** *n*

anglicism /'æŋglʒsızəm/ *n, often cap* **1** a characteristic feature of English occurring in another language **2** adherence or attachment to England, English culture, etc

angling /'æŋglıŋ/ *n* (the sport of) fishing with hook and line – **-gler** *n*

Anglo-American *n or adj* (a) N American, esp of the USA, of English origin or descent

Anglo-Indian *n* **1** a British person domiciled for a long time in India **2** a Eurasian of mixed British and Indian birth or descent

anglophile /'ængləfaıl, -gləʊ-/ *also* **anglophil** /-fıl/ *n, often cap* a foreigner who is greatly interested in and admires England and things English

anglophobe /'æŋgləfəʊb, -gləʊ-/ *n, often cap* a foreigner who is averse to England and things English

Anglo-Saxon /,æŋgləʊ'sæksən/ *n* **1** a member of the Germanic peoples who conquered England in the 5th c AD and formed the ruling group until the Norman conquest **2** sby of English, esp Anglo-Saxon, descent

angora /æŋ'gɔːrə/ *n* **1** the hair of the Angora rabbit or goat **2** a fabric or yarn made (in part) of Angora rabbit hair, used esp for knitting **3** *cap* an Angora cat, goat, or rabbit

Angora cat *n* a long-haired domestic cat

Angora goat *n* (any of) a breed of the domestic goat raised for its long silky hair which is the true mohair

Angora rabbit *n* a long-haired usu white domestic rabbit

angry /'æŋgri/ *adj* **1** feeling or showing anger **2** seeming to show or typify anger **3** painfully inflamed – **angrily** *adv*

angst /æŋst/ *n* anxiety and anguish, caused esp by considering the state of the world and the human condition

anguish /'æŋgwıʃ/ *n* extreme physical pain or mental distress – ~**ed** *adj*

angular /'æŋgjʊlə'/ *adj* **1a** having 1 or more angles **b** forming an angle; sharp-cornered **2a** stiff in character or manner; awkward **b** lean, bony – ~**ity** *n*

animadvert /,ænʒmæd'vɜːt/ *v* to comment critically or adversely *on* – fml – **-version** *n*

¹animal /'ænʒməl/ *n* **1** any of a kingdom of living things typically differing from plants in their capacity for spontaneous movement, esp in response to stimulation **2a** any of the lower animals as distinguished from human beings **b** a mammal – not in technical use **3** a person considered as a purely physical being; a creature

²animal *adj* **1** of or derived from animals **2** of the body as opposed to the mind or spirit – chiefly derog

¹animate /'ænʒmʒt/ *adj* **1** possessing life; alive **2** of animal life **3** lively

²animate /'ænʒmeıt/ *v* **1** to give spirit and support to; encourage **2** to give life or vigour to **3** to produce in the form of an animated cartoon

animation /,ænʒ'meıʃən/ *n* **1** vigorous liveliness **2** (the preparation of) an animated cartoon

animism /'ænʒmızəm/ *n* attributing conscious life, spirits, or souls to nature or natural objects or phenomena – **animist** *n, adj*

animosity /,ænʒ'mɒsʒti/ *n* powerful often active ill will or resentment

aniseed /'ænʒsiːd/ *n* a pepperminty seed used esp as a flavouring (e g in liqueurs)

ankle /'æŋkəl/ *n* the (region of the) joint between the foot and the leg; the tarsus

annals /'ænəlz/ *n pl* **1** a record of events, activities, etc, arranged in yearly sequence **2** historical records; chronicles

anneal /ə'niːl/ *v* to temper, toughen

¹annex /ə'neks, 'æneks/ *v* **1** to append **2** to take possession of; *esp* to incorporate (a country or other territory) within the domain of a state – ~**ation** *n*

²annex *chiefly Br* **annexe** /'æneks/ *n* **1** sthg, esp an addition to a document, annexed or appended **2** a separate or attached extra structure; *esp* a building providing extra accommodation

annihilate /ə'naɪəleɪt/ *v* **1** to destroy (almost) entirely **2** to defeat conclusively; rout – **-lation** *n*

anniversary /ˌænɪ̆'vɜːsəri/ *n* (the celebration of) a day marking the annual recurrence of the date of a notable event

anno Domini /ˌænəʊ 'dɒmɪni, -naɪ/ *adv, often cap A* – used to indicate that a year or century comes within the Christian era

annotate /'ænəteɪt/ *v* to provide (e g a literary work) with notes – **-tation** *n*

announce /ə'naʊns/ *v* **1** to make known publicly; proclaim **2a** to give notice of the arrival, presence, or readiness of **b** to indicate in advance; foretell **3** to give evidence of; indicate by action or appearance – **~r** *n* – **~ment** *n*

annoy /ə'nɔɪ/ *v* **1** to disturb or irritate, esp by repeated acts; vex – often pass + *with* or *at* **2** to harass **3** to be a source of annoyance – **~ance** *n*

[1]**annual** /'ænjʊəl/ *adj* **1** covering or lasting for the period of a year **2** occurring or performed once a year; yearly **3** *of a plant* completing the life cycle in 1 growing season – **~ly** *adv*

[2]**annual** *n* **1** a publication appearing yearly **2** sthg lasting 1 year or season; *specif* an annual plant

annuity /ə'njuːɪti/ *n* **1** an amount payable at a regular (e g yearly) interval **2** (a contract embodying) the right to receive or the obligation to pay an annuity

annul /ə'nʌl/ *v* **-ll-** **1** to reduce to nothing; obliterate, cancel **2** to declare (e g a marriage) legally invalid – **annulment** *n*

annular /'ænjʊlə'/ *adj* of or forming a ring

Annunciation /əˌnʌnsi'eɪʃən/ *n* (March 25 observed as a church festival commemorating) the announcement of the Incarnation to the Virgin Mary related in Luke 1:26–28

anode /'ænəʊd/ *n* **1** the electrode by which electrons leave a device and enter an external circuit; *specif* the negative terminal of a primary or secondary cell that is delivering current **2** a positive electrode used to accelerate electrons in an electron gun

anoint /ə'nɔɪnt/ *v* **1** to smear or rub with oil or a similar substance **2a** to apply oil to as a sacred rite, esp for consecration **b** to designate (as if) through the rite of anointment; consecrate – **~ment** *n*

anomalous /ə'nɒmələs/ *adj* **1** deviating from a general rule or standard; irregular, abnormal **2** incongruous – **~ly** *adv*

anomaly /ə'nɒməli/ *n* **1** the angular distance of a planet from its last perihelion **2** deviation from the common rule; an irregularity, incongruity **3** sthg anomalous

anon /ə'nɒn/ *adv, archaic* **1** soon, presently **2** at another time

anonymous /ə'nɒnɪ̆məs/ *adj* **1** having or giving no name **2** of unknown or unnamed origin or authorship **3** nondescript – **-mity** *n* – **~ly** *adv*

anorak /'ænəræk/ *n, chiefly Br* a short weatherproof coat with a hood

anorexia /ˌænə'reksɪə/ *n* (prolonged) loss of appetite; *specif* a pathological aversion to food – **~exic** *adj*

[1]**another** /ə'nʌðə'/ *adj* **1** being a different or distinct one **2** some other **3** being one additional (e g *another* baby) **4** patterned after (e g *another* Picasso)

[2]**another** *pron, pl* **others** **1** an additional one; one more **2** a different one

[1]**answer** /'ɑːnsə'/ *n* **1** a spoken or written reply to a question, remark, etc **2** an esp correct solution to a problem **3** a response or reaction **4** sby or sthg intended to be a close equivalent or rival of another

[2]**answer** *v* **1** to speak, write, or act in reply (to) **2a** to be responsible or accountable for **b** to make amends; atone for **3** to correspond *to* **4** to reply to in justification or explanation **5** to act in response to (a sound or other signal) **6** to offer a solution for; *esp* to solve

answerable /'ɑːnsərəbəl/ *adj* **1** responsible **2** capable of being answered or refuted – **-bly** *adv*

ant /ænt/ *n* any of a family of insects that live in large social groups having a complex organization and hierarchy

antacid /ænt'æsɪ̣d/ *adj* that corrects excessive acidity, esp in the stomach

antagonism /æn'tægənɪzəm/ *n* hostility or antipathy, esp when actively expressed

antagonist /æn'tægənɪ̣st/ *n* an opponent, adversary – **~ic** *adj* – **~ically** *adv*

antagon·ize, -ise /æn'tægənaɪz/ *v* to provoke the hostility of

antarctic /æn'tɑːktɪk/ *adj, often cap* of the South Pole or surrounding region

antarctic circle *n,* the parallel of latitude approx 66½° south of the equator that circumscribes the south polar region

anteater /'æntiːtə'/ *n* any of several mammals that feed (chiefly) on ants and termites

[1]**antecedent** /æntɪ̣'siːdənt/ *n* **1** a word, phrase, or clause functioning as a noun and referred to by a pronoun **2** a preceding thing, event, or circumstance **3** *pl* family origins; parentage

[2]**antecedent** *adj* **1** prior in time or order **2** causally or logically prior

antechamber /'æntɪ,tʃeɪmbə'/ *n* an anteroom

antedate /'æntɪdeɪt, ˌæntɪ'deɪt/ *v* **1** to attach or assign a date earlier than the true one to (e g a document), esp with intent to deceive **2** to precede in time

antediluvian /ˌæntɪdɪ̣'luːvɪən/ *adj* **1** of the period before the flood described in the Bible **2** completely out-of-date; antiquated

antelope /'æntɪ̣ləʊp/ *n* **1** any of various Old World ruminant mammals that are lighter and more graceful than the true oxen **2** leather made from antelope hide

ante meridiem /ˌæntɪ mə'rɪdɪəm, -dɪem/ *adj* being before noon – abbr *am*

antenatal /ˌæntɪ'neɪtl/ *adj* of or concerned with an unborn child, pregnancy, or a pregnant woman; prenatal

antenna /æn'tenə/ *n, pl* **antennae, antennas** **1** a movable segmented sense organ on the head of insects, crustaceans, etc **2** an aerial

anterior /æn'tɪərɪə'/ *adj* **1** before in time **2** situated before or towards the front

anthem /'ænθəm/ *n* **1** a piece of church music for voices usu set to a biblical text **2** a song or hymn of praise or gladness

anther /'ænθə'/ *n* the part of a stamen that contains and releases pollen

anthill /'ænt,hɪl/ *n* **1** a mound thrown up by ants digging their nest **2** a place (e g a city) that is overcrowded and constantly busy

anthology /æn'θɒlədʒi/ *n* a collection of selected (literary) passages or works

anthracite /'ænθrəsaɪt/ *n* a hard slow-burning coal containing little volatile matter

anthrax /'ænθræks/ *n* an often fatal infectious disease of warm-blooded animals (e g cattle, sheep, or human beings) caused by a spore-forming bacterium

anthropoid /'ænθrəpɔɪd/ *adj* resembling human beings or the anthropoid apes (e g in form or behaviour); apelike

anthropology /ˌænθrə'pɒlədʒi/ *n* the scientific study of human beings, esp in relation to physical characteristics, social relations and culture, and the origin and distribution of races – **-gist** *n* – **-gical** *adj* – **-gically** *adv*

anthropomorphism /ˌænθrəpə'mɔːfɪzəm/ *n* the ascribing of human behaviour, form, etc to what is not human (e g a god or animal) – **-phic** *adj*

antibiotic /ˌæntɪbaɪ'ɒtɪk/ *n* a substance produced by a microorganism and able in dilute solution to inhibit the growth of or kill another microorganism – **~ally** *adv*

antibody /'æntɪ,bɒdi/ *n* a protein that is produced by the body in response to a specific antigen and that counteracts its effects (e g by neutralizing toxins or grouping bacteria into clumps)

antic /'æntɪk/ *n* a ludicrous act or action; a caper – usu pl

anticipate /æn'tɪsɪ̣peɪt/ *v* **1** to give advance thought, discussion, or treatment to **2** to foresee and deal with in advance; forestall **3** to act before (another) often so as to thwart **4** to look forward to as certain; expect **5** to speak or write in knowledge or expectation of sthg due to happen – **-pation** *n*

anticlimax /ˌæntɪˈklaɪmæks/ *n* **1** (an instance of) the usu sudden and ludicrous descent in writing or speaking from a significant to a trivial idea **2** an event (e g at the end of a series) that is strikingly less important or exciting than expected

anticlockwise /ˌæntɪˈklɒkwaɪz/ *adj or adv* in a direction opposite to that in which the hands of a clock rotate when viewed from the front

anticyclone /ˌæntɪˈsaɪkləʊn/ *n* (a system of winds that rotates about) a centre of high atmospheric pressure

antidote /ˈæntɪdəʊt/ *n* **1** a remedy that counteracts the effects of poison **2** sthg that relieves or counteracts

antifreeze /ˈæntɪfriːz/ *n* a substance added to a liquid (e g the water in a car radiator) to lower its freezing point

antigen /ˈæntɪdʒən/ *n* a protein, carbohydrate, etc that stimulates the production of an antibody when introduced into the body

anti-hero /ˈæntɪˌhɪərəʊ/, *fem* **antiheroine** *n* a protagonist who lacks traditional heroic qualities (e g courage)

antiknock /ˌæntɪˈnɒk/ *n* a substance added to fuel to prevent knocking in an internal-combustion engine

antilogarithm /ˌæntɪˈlɒgərɪðəm/ *n* the number corresponding to a given logarithm

antimacassar /ˌæntɪməˈkæsəʳ/ *n* a usu protective cover put over the backs or arms of upholstered seats

antimatter /ˈæntɪˌmætəʳ/ *n* matter composed of antiparticles (e g antiprotons instead of protons, positrons instead of electrons, and antineutrons instead of neutrons)

antimony /ˈæntɨməni/ *n* a metal-like element used esp as a constituent of alloys

antipathy /ænˈtɪpəθi/ *n* a fixed aversion or dislike; a distaste – **-thetic** *adj*

antipersonnel /ˌæntɪpɜːsəˈnel/ *adj, of a weapon* (designed) for use against people

antipodes /ænˈtɪpədiːz/ *n pl the* region of the earth diametrically opposite; *specif, often cap* Australasia

[1]**antiquarian** /ˌæntɨˈkweərɪən/ *n* one who collects or studies antiquities

[2]**antiquarian** *adj* **1** of antiquarians or antiquities **2** *of books or prints* old (and rare)

antiquary /ˈæntɨkwəri/ *n* an antiquarian

antiquated /ˈæntɨkweɪtɨd/ *adj* **1** outmoded or discredited by reason of age; out-of-date **2** advanced in age

[1]**antique** /ænˈtiːk/ *adj* **1** belonging to or surviving from earlier, esp classical, times; ancient **2** old-fashioned **3** made in an earlier period and therefore valuable; *also* suggesting the style of an earlier period

[2]**antique** *n* **1** *the* ancient Greek or Roman style in art **2** a relic or object of ancient times **3** a work of art, piece of furniture, or decorative object made at an earlier period and sought by collectors

antiquity /ænˈtɪkwɨti/ *n* **1** ancient times; *esp* the period before the Middle Ages **2** the quality of being ancient **3** *pl* relics or monuments of ancient times

antirrhinum /ˌæntɨˈraɪnəm/ *n* any of a large genus of plants (e g the snapdragon or a related plant) with bright-coloured 2-lipped flowers

anti-Semitism /ˌæntɪ ˈsemɨtɪzəm/ *n* hostility towards Jews – **-Semitic** *adj* – **-Semite** *n*

[1]**antiseptic** /ˌæntɨˈseptɪk/ *adj* **1a** opposing sepsis (in living tissue), specif by arresting the growth of microorganisms, esp bacteria **b** of, acting or protecting like, or using an antiseptic **2a** scrupulously clean **b** extremely neat or orderly, esp to the point of being bare or uninteresting **3** impersonal, detached

[2]**antiseptic** *n* an antiseptic substance; *also* a germicide

antisocial /ˌæntɪˈsəʊʃəl/ *adj* **1** hostile or harmful to organized society **2a** averse to the society of others; unsociable **b** *Br* unsocial

antithesis /ænˈtɪθɨsɨs/ *n, pl* **antitheses** /-siːz/ **1a** a contrast of ideas expressed by a parallel arrangement of words (e g in 'action, not words") **b**

opposition, contrast **c** the direct opposite **2** the second stage of a reasoned argument, in contrast to the thesis

antler /'æntləʳ/ *n* (a branch of) the solid periodically shed horn of an animal of the deer family

antonym /'æntənɪm/ *n* a word having the opposite meaning

anus /'eɪnəs/ *n* the rear excretory opening of the alimentary canal

anvil /'ænvl̩/ *n* **1** a heavy, usu steel-faced, iron block on which metal is shaped **2** a bone in the inner ear

anxiety /æŋ'zaɪəti/ *n* **1a** apprehensive uneasiness of mind, usu over an impending or anticipated ill **b** a cause of anxiety **2** an abnormal overwhelming sense of apprehension and fear, often with doubt about one's capacity to cope with the threat

anxious /'æŋkʃəs/ *adj* **1** troubled, worried **2** causing anxiety; worrying **3** ardently or earnestly wishing *to* – **~ly** *adv*

¹any /'eni/ *adj* **1** one or some indiscriminately; whichever is chosen **2** one, some, or all; whatever: e g **a** of whatever number or quantity; being even the smallest number or quantity of (e g there's never *any* salt) **b** no matter how great (e g make *any* sacrifice) **c** no matter how ordinary or inadequate (e g *any* old card will do) **3** being an appreciable number, part, or amount of – not in positive statements (e g not for *any* length of time)

²any *pron, pl any* **1** any person; anybody **2a** any thing **b** any part, quantity, or number

³any *adv* to any extent or degree; at all

anybody /'eni,bɒdi, 'enibədi/ *pron* any person

anyhow /'enihaʊ/ *adv* **1** in a haphazard manner **2** anyway

anyroad /'enirəʊd/ *adv, Br* anyway – nonstandard

¹anything /'eniθɪŋ/ *pron* any thing whatever

²anything *adv* in any degree; at all

anyway /'eniweɪ/ *adv* **1** in any case, inevitably **2** – used when resuming a narrative (e g *anyway,* the moment we arrived ...)

¹anywhere /'eniweəʳ/ *adv* **1** in, at, or to any place **2** to any extent; at all **3** – used to indicate limits of variation (e g *anywhere* between here and London)

²anywhere *n* any place

aorta /eɪ'ɔːtə/ *n, pl* **aortas, aortae** the great artery that carries blood from the left side of the heart to be distributed by branch arteries throughout the body

apace /ə'peɪs/ *adv* at a quick pace; swiftly

apart /ə'pɑːt/ *adv* **1a** at a distance (from one another in space or time) **b** at a distance in character or opinions **2** so as to separate one from another **3** excluded from consideration **4** in or into 2 or more parts

apartheid /ə'pɑːtheɪt, -teɪt, -taɪt, -taɪd/ *n* racial segregation; *specif* a policy of segregation and discrimination against non-Europeans in the Republic of S Africa

apartment /ə'pɑːtmənt/ *n* **1** a single room in a building **2** a suite of rooms used for living quarters **3** *chiefly NAm* a flat

apathetic /,æpə'θetɪk/ *adj* **1** having or showing little or no feeling; spiritless **2** lacking interest or concern; indifferent – **~ally** *adv*

apathy /'æpəθi/ *n* **1** lack of feeling or emotion; impassiveness **2** lack of interest or concern; indifference

¹ape /eɪp/ *n* **1** a chimpanzee, gorilla, or any similar primate **2a** a mimic **b** a large uncouth person

²ape *v* to imitate closely but often clumsily and ineptly

aperitif /ə,perl̩'tiːf/ *n* an alcoholic drink taken before a meal to stimulate the appetite

aperture /'æpətʃəʳ/ *n* **1** an open space; a hole, gap **2** (the diameter of) the opening in an optical (photographic) system through which the light passes

apex /'eɪpeks/ *n, pl* **apexes, apices 1a** the uppermost peak; the vertex **b** the narrowed or pointed end; the tip **2** the highest or culminating point

aphelion /ə'fiːlɪən/ *n, pl* **aphelia** the point in the path of a planet, comet, etc that is farthest from the sun

aphid /'eɪfl̩d/ *n* a greenfly or related

small sluggish insect that sucks the juices of plants

aphorism /'æfərɪzəm/ *n* a concise pithy formulation of a truth; an adage

aphrodisiac /,æfrə'dɪziæk/ *n or adj* (a substance) that stimulates sexual desire

apiary /'eɪpɪəri/ *n* a place where (hives or colonies of) bees are kept, esp for their honey – **-rist** *n*

apiece /ə'piːs/ *adv* for each one; individually

apish /'eɪpɪʃ/ *adj* resembling an ape: e g **a** slavishly imitative **b** extremely silly or affected – **~ly** *adv* – **~ness** *n*

aplomb /ə'plɒm/ *n* complete composure or self-assurance; poise

apocalypse /ə'pɒkəlɪps/ *n* **1a** any of a number of early Jewish and Christian works, written esp under an assumed name, and characterized by symbolic imagery, which describe the establishment of God's kingdom **b** *cap* the Book of Revelation **2** sthg viewed as a prophetic revelation

apocalyptic /ə,pɒkə'lɪptɪk/ *also* **apocalyptical** *adj* **1** of or resembling an apocalypse **2** forecasting the ultimate destiny of the world; prophetic **3** foreboding imminent disaster; terrible – **~ally** *adv*

apocrypha /ə'pɒkrɟfə/ *n* **1** (a collection of) writings or statements of dubious authenticity **2** *sing or pl in constr, cap* books included in the Septuagint and Vulgate but excluded from the Jewish and Protestant canons of the Old Testament – usu + *the*

apocryphal /ə'pɒkrɟfəl/ *adj* **1** *often cap* of or resembling the Apocrypha **2** of doubtful authenticity

apogee /'æpədʒiː/ *n* **1** the point farthest from a planet or other celestial body reached by any object orbiting it **2** the farthest or highest point; the culmination

apologetic /ə,pɒlə'dʒetɪk/ *adj* **1a** offered in defence or vindication **b** offered by way of excuse or apology **2** regretfully acknowledging fault or failure; contrite – **~ally** *adv*

apolog·ize, -ise /ə'pɒlədʒaɪz/ *v* to make an apology

apology /ə'pɒlədʒi/ *n* **1** a excuse **2** an admission of error or discourtesy accompanied by an expression of regret **3** a poor substitute *for*

apoplectic /,æpə'plektɪk/ *adj* violently excited (e g from rage) – infml – **~ally** *adv*

apostle /ə'pɒsəl/ *n* **1** one sent on a mission; *esp* any of an authoritative New Testament group sent out to preach the gospel and made up esp of Jesus's original 12 disciples and Paul **2a** one who first advocates an important belief or system **b** an ardent supporter; an adherent

apostolic /,æpə'stɒlɪk/ *adj* **1** of an apostle or the New Testament apostles **2a** of the divine authority vested in the apostles held (e g by Roman Catholics, Anglicans, and Eastern Orthodox) to be handed down through the successive ordinations of bishops **b** of the pope as the successor to the apostolic authority vested in St Peter – **~ally** *adv*

apostrophe /ə'pɒstrəfi/ *n* a mark ' used to indicate the omission of letters or figures, the possessive case, or the plural of letters or figures

apothecary /ə'pɒθɟkəri/ *n, archaic or NAm* a pharmacist, chemist

appal /ə'pɔːl/ *v* **-ll-** to overcome with consternation, horror, or dismay

apparatus /,æpə'reɪtəs/ *n, pl* **apparatuses, apparatus** **1** (a piece of) equipment designed for a particular use, esp for a scientific operation **2** the administrative bureaucracy of an organization, esp a political party

apparel /ə'pærəl/ *n* **1** garments, clothing – chiefly fml **2** sthg that clothes or adorns – chiefly poetic – **apparel** *v*

apparent /ə'pærənt/ *adj* **1** easily seen or understood; plain, evident **2** seemingly real but not necessarily so **3** having an absolute right to succeed to a title or estate – **~ly** *adv*

apparition /,æpə'rɪʃən/ *n* **1a** an unusual or unexpected sight; a phenomenon **b** a ghostly figure **2** the act of becoming visible; appearance

¹appeal /ə'piːl/ *n* **1** a legal proceeding by which a case is brought to a higher court for review **2a(1)** an application (e g to a recognized authority) for corroboration, vindication, or decision (2) a call by members of the fielding side in cricket, esp by the bowler, for the umpire to decide whether a batsman is out **b** an earnest plea for aid or mercy; an entreaty **3** the power of arousing a sympathetic response; attraction

[2]**appeal** *v* **1** to take (a case) to a higher court **2a** to call on another for corroboration, vindication, or decision **b** to make an appeal in cricket **3** to make an earnest plea or request **4** to arouse a sympathetic response *USE* often + *to*

appealing /ə'piːlɪŋ/ *adj* **1** having appeal; pleasing **2** marked by earnest entreaty; imploring – **~ly** *adv*

appear /ə'pɪəʳ/ *v* **1a** to be or become visible **b** to arrive **2** to come formally before an authoritative body **3** to give the impression of being; seem **4** to come into public view

appearance /ə'pɪərəns/ *n* **1** the coming into court of a party in an action or his/her lawyer **2** a visit or attendance that is seen or noticed by others **3a** an outward aspect; a look **b** an external show; a semblance **c** *pl* an outward or superficial indication that hides the real situation

appease /ə'piːz/ *v* **1** to pacify, calm **2** to cause to subside; allay **3** to conciliate (esp an aggressor) by concessions – **~ment** *n*

appellation /ˌæpʒ̍'leɪʃən/ *n* an identifying name or title

append /ə'pend/ *v* to attach or add, esp as a supplement or appendix

appendage /ə'pendɪdʒ/ *n* sthg appended to sthg larger or more important

appendicitis /əˌpendʒ̍'saɪtʒ̍s/ *n* inflammation of the vermiform appendix

appendix /ə'pendɪks/ *n, pl* **appendixes, appendices** **1** a supplement (e g containing explanatory or statistical material), usu attached at the end of a piece of writing **2** the vermiform appendix or similar bodily outgrowth

appertain /ˌæpə'teɪn/ *v* to belong or be connected *to*

appetite /'æpʒ̍taɪt/ *n* **1** a desire to satisfy an internal bodily need; *esp* an (eager) desire to eat **2** a strong desire demanding satisfaction; an inclination

appet·izer, -iser /'æpʒ̍taɪzəʳ/ *n* a food or drink that stimulates the appetite and is usu served before a meal

appet·izing, -ising /'æpʒ̍taɪzɪŋ/ *adj* appealing to the appetite, esp in appearance or aroma – **~ly** *adv*

applaud /ə'plɔːd/ *v* to express approval (of), esp by clapping the hands

applause /ə'plɔːz/ *n* **1** approval publicly expressed (e g by clapping the hands) **2** praise

apple /'æpəl/ *n* **1** (the fleshy, edible, usu rounded, red, yellow, or green fruit of) a tree of the rose family **2** a fruit or other plant structure resembling an apple

appliance /ə'plaɪəns/ *n* an instrument or device designed for a particular use; *esp* a domestic machine or device powered by gas or electricity (e g a food mixer, vacuum cleaner, or cooker)

applicable /ə'plɪkəbəl, 'æplɪkəbəl/ *adj* appropriate

applicant /'æplɪkənt/ *n* one who applies

application /ˌæplɪ'keɪʃən/ *n* **1a** an act of applying **b** a use to which sthg is put **c** close attention; diligence **2** a request, petition **3** a lotion **4** capacity for practical use; relevance

applied /ə'plaɪd/ *adj* put to practical use; *esp* applying general principles to solve definite problems

appliqué /ə'pliːkeɪ/ *n* a cutout decoration fastened (e g by sewing) to a larger piece of material; *also* the decorative work formed in this manner – **appliqué** *v*

apply /ə'plaɪ/ *v* **1a** to bring to bear; put to use, esp for some practical purpose **b** to lay or spread on **2** to devote (e g oneself) with close attention or diligence – usu + *to* **3** to have relevance – usu + *to* **4** to make a request, esp in writing

appoint /ə'pɔɪnt/ *v* **1** to fix or name officially **2** to select for an office or position **3** to declare the disposition of (an estate) to sby

appointed /ə'pɔɪntʒ̍d/ *adj* equipped, furnished

appointment /ə'pɔɪntmənt/ *n* **1** an act of appointing; a designation **2** an office or position held by sby who has been appointed to it rather than voted into it **3** an arrangement for a meeting **4** *pl* equipment, furnishings

apportion /ə'pɔːʃən/ *v* to divide and share out in just proportion or according to a plan; allot – **~ment** *n*

apposite /'æpəzɨt/ *adj* highly pertinent or appropriate; apt

appraisal /ə'preɪzəl/ *n* an act or instance of appraising; *specif* a valuation of property by an authorized person

appraise /ə'preɪz/ *v* to evaluate the worth, significance, or status of; *esp* to give an expert judgment of the value or merit of – **appraiser** *n*

appreciable /ə'priːʃəbəl/ *adj* **1** capable of being perceived or measured **2** fairly large – **-bly** *adv*

appreciate /ə'priːʃieɪt/ *v* **1a** to understand the nature, worth, quality, or significance of **b** to recognize with gratitude; value or admire highly **2** to increase in value

appreciation /əˌpriːʃi'eɪʃən/ *n* **1a** sensitive awareness; *esp* recognition of aesthetic values **b** a judgment, evaluation; *esp* a favourable critical estimate **c** an expression of admiration, approval, or gratitude **2** an increase in value

apprehend /ˌæprɪ'hend/ *v* **1** to arrest, seize **2** to understand, perceive

apprehension /ˌæprɪ'henʃən/ *n* **1** the act or power of comprehending **2** arrest, seizure – used technically in Scottish law **3** anxiety or fear, esp of future evil; foreboding

apprehensive /ˌæprɪ'hensɪv/ *adj* viewing the future with anxiety, unease, or fear – often + *for* or *of* – **~ly** *adv*

[1]**apprentice** /ə'prentɨs/ *n* **1** one who is learning an art or trade **2** an inexperienced person; a novice

[2]**apprentice** *v* to set at work as an apprentice

apprise /ə'praɪz/ *v* to give notice to; tell – usu + *of*; fml

[1]**approach** /ə'prəʊtʃ/ *v* **1a** to draw closer (to) **b** to come very near to in quality, character, etc **2a** to make advances to, esp in order to create a desired result **b** to begin to consider or deal with

[2]**approach** *n* **1a** an act or instance of approaching **b** an approximation **2** a manner or method of doing sthg, esp for the first time **3** a means of access **4a** a golf shot from the fairway towards the green **b** (the steps taken on) the part of a tenpin bowling alley from which a bowler must deliver the ball **5** the final part of an aircraft flight before landing **6** an advance made to establish personal or business relations – usu pl

approachable /ə'prəʊtʃəbəl/ *adj* easy to meet or deal with

approbation /ˌæprə'beɪʃən/ *n* formal or official approval; sanction

[1]**appropriate** /ə'prəʊprieɪt/ *v* **1** to take exclusive possession of **2** to set apart (specif money) for a particular purpose or use **3** to take or make use of without authority or right

[2]**appropriate** /ə'prəʊprɪ-ɨt/ *adj* especially suitable or compatible; fitting – **~ly** *adv* – **~ness** *n*

appropriation /əˌprəʊpri'eɪʃən/ *n* sthg appropriated; *specif* money set aside by formal action for a particular use

approval /ə'pruːvəl/ *n* **1** a favourable opinion or judgment **2** formal or official permission

approve /ə'pruːv/ *v* **1** to have or express a favourable opinion (of) **2a** to accept as satisfactory **b** to give formal or official sanction to; ratify – **approvingly** *adv*

[1]**approximate** /ə'prɒksɨmɨt/ *adj* nearly correct or exact – **~ly** *adv*

[2]**approximate** /ə'prɒksɨmeɪt/ *v* **1** to bring or come near or close – often + *to* **2** to come near to; approach, esp in quality or number

apricot /'eɪprɨkɒt/ *n* **1** (the oval orange-coloured fruit of) a temperate-zone tree of the rose family closely related to the peach and plum **2** an orange pink colour

April /'eɪprɨl/ *n* the 4th month of the Gregorian calendar

April fool *n* the victim of a joke or trick played on April 1st

apron /'eɪprən/ *n* **1** a garment usu tied round the waist and used to protect clothing **2** sthg that suggests or resembles an apron in shape, position, or use **3** the part of a stage that projects in front of the curtain

apron strings *n pl* dominance, esp of a man by his mother or wife

[1]**apropos** /ˌæprəˈpəʊ/ *adv* **1** at an opportune time **2** by the way

[2]**apropos** *adj* both relevant and opportune

[3]**apropos** *prep* concerning; with regard to

apse /æps/ *n* a projecting part of a building (e g a church) that is usu semicircular or polygonal and vaulted

apt /æpt/ *adj* **1** ordinarily disposed; likely – usu + *to* **2** suited to a purpose; relevant – **~ly** *adv* – **~ness** *n*

aptitude /ˈæptɨtjuːd/ *n* **1** a natural ability; a talent, esp for learning **2** general fitness or suitability – usu + *for*

aqualung /ˈækwəlʌŋ/ *n* cylinders of compressed air, oxygen, etc carried on the back and connected to a face mask for breathing underwater

aquamarine /ˌækwəməˈriːn/ *n* **1** a transparent blue to green beryl used as a gemstone **2** a pale blue to light greenish blue colour

[1]**aquaplane** /ˈækwəpleɪn/ *n* a board towed behind a fast motorboat and ridden by sby standing on it

[2]**aquaplane** *v* **1** to ride on an aquaplane **2** *of a car* to go out of control by sliding on water lying on the surface of a wet road

aquarium /əˈkweəriəm/ *n, pl* **aquariums, aquaria** **1** a glass tank, artificial pond, etc in which living aquatic animals or plants are kept **2** an establishment where collections of living aquatic organisms are exhibited

Aquarius /əˈkweəriəs/ *n* (sby born under) the 11th sign of the zodiac in astrology, which is pictured as a man pouring water

[1]**aquatic** /əˈkwɒtɪk, -ˈkwæ-/ *adj* **1** growing, living in, or frequenting water **2** taking place in or on water – **~ally** *adv*

[2]**aquatic** *n pl but sing or pl in constr* water sports

aqueduct /ˈækwɨdʌkt/ *n* a conduit, esp an arched structure over a valley, for carrying water

aqueous /ˈeɪkwiəs, ˈækwiəs/ *adj* of, resembling, or made from, with, or by water – **~ly** *adv*

aquiline /ˈækwɨlaɪn/ *adj* **1** of or like an eagle **2** *of the human nose* hooked

Arab /ˈærəb/ *n* **1a** a member of a Semitic people orig of the Arabian peninsula and now widespread throughout the Middle East and N Africa **b** a member of an Arabic-speaking people **2** a typically intelligent, graceful, and swift horse of an Arabian stock – **~ian** *adj*

arabesque /ˌærəˈbesk/ *n* **1** a decorative design or style that combines natural motifs (e g flowers or foliage) to produce an intricate pattern **2** a posture in ballet in which the dancer is supported on one leg with one arm extended forwards and the other arm and leg backwards

[1]**Arabic** /ˈærəbɪk/ *adj* **1** (characteristic) of Arabia, Arabians, or the Arabs **2** of or being Arabic

[2]**Arabic** *n* a Semitic language, now the prevailing speech of Arabia, Jordan, Lebanon, Syria, Iraq, Egypt, and parts of N Africa

Arabic numeral *n, often not cap A* any of the number symbols 0, 1, 2, 3, 4, 5, 6, 7, 8, 9

arable /ˈærəbəl/ *n or adj* (land) being or fit to be farmed for crops

arachnid /əˈræknɪd/ *n pl* **-nids, -nidae** any of a class (e g spiders, mites, ticks, and scorpions) of arthropods whose bodies have 2 segments of which the front bears 4 pairs of legs

arbiter /ˈɑːbɨtəʳ/ *n* a person or agency with absolute power of judging and determining

arbitrary /ˈɑːbɨtrəri/ *adj* **1** depending on choice or discretion **2a** arising from unrestrained exercise of the will **b** selected at random and without reason – **-rily** *adv* – **-riness** *n*

arbitrate /ˈɑːbɨtreɪt/ *v* **1** to act as arbitrator **2** to act as arbiter upon **3** to submit for decision to an arbitrator – **-trator** *n* – **-tration** *n*

arboreal /ɑːˈbɔːriəl/ *adj* of, resembling, inhabiting, or frequenting a tree or trees

arboretum /ˌɑːbəˈriːtəm/ *n, pl* **arboretums, arboreta** /-tə/ a place where trees and shrubs are cultivated for study and display

arbour /ˈɑːbəʳ/ *n* a bower of (latticework covered with) shrubs, vines, or branches

[1]**arc** /ɑːk/ *n* **1** the apparent path described by a celestial body **2** sthg arched or curved

arcade /ɑːˈkeɪd/ *n* **1** a long arched gallery or building **2** a passageway or avenue (e g between shops)

Arcadia /ɑːˈkeɪdɪə/ *n* a usu idealized rural region or scene of simple pleasure and quiet

[1]**arch** /ɑːtʃ/ *n* **1** a typically curved structural member spanning an opening and resisting lateral or vertical pressure (e g of a wall) **2** sthg (e g the vaulted bony structure of the foot) resembling an arch in form or function **3** an archway

[2]**arch** *v* **1** to span or provide with an arch **2** to form or bend into an arch **3** to form an arch

[3]**arch** *adj* **1** principal, chief **2a** cleverly sly and alert **b** playfully saucy – **~ly** *adv*

archaeology /ˌɑːkiˈɒlədʒi/ *n* the scientific study of material remains (e g tools or dwellings) of past human life and activities – **-gical** *adj* – **-gically** *adv* – **-gist** *n*

archaic /ɑːˈkeɪ-ɪk/ *adj* **1** (characteristic) of an earlier or more primitive time; antiquated **2** no longer used in ordinary speech or writing – **~ally** *adv*

archaism /ɑːˈkeɪ-ɪzəm, ˈ----/ *n* **1** (an instance of) the use of archaic diction or style **2** sthg outmoded or old-fashioned

archangel /ɑːkˈeɪndʒəl, ˈ---/ *n* a chief angel

archbishop /ˌɑːtʃˈbɪʃəp/ *n* a bishop at the head of an ecclesiastical province, or one of equivalent honorary rank

archdeacon /ɑːtʃˈdiːkən/ *n* a clergyman having the duty of assisting a bishop, esp in administrative work

archduke /ɑːtʃˈdjuːk/ *n* a sovereign prince

archer /ˈɑːtʃəʳ/ *n* one who practises archery

archery /ˈɑːtʃəri/ *n* the art, practice, skill, or sport of shooting arrows from a bow

archetype /ˈɑːkɪtaɪp/ *n* **1** an original pattern or model; a prototype **2** a transcendent entity of which existing things are imperfect realizations – **-typal** *adj* – **-typical** *adj* – **-typically** *adv*

archipelago /ˌɑːkɪ̈ˈpeləgəʊ/ *n, pl* **-goes, -gos** (an expanse of water with) a group of scattered islands

architect /ˈɑːkɪ̈tekt/ *n* **1** sby who designs buildings and superintends their construction **2** sby who devises, plans, and achieves a difficult objective

architecture /ˈɑːkɪ̈tektʃəʳ/ *n* **1** the art, practice, or profession of designing and erecting buildings; *also* a method or style of building **2** product or work of architecture – **-tural** *adj* – **-turally** *adv*

architrave /ˈɑːkɪtreɪv/ *n* **1** the part of a structure resting immediately on the capital of the column **2** the moulded frame round a rectangular recess or opening (e g a door)

archway /ˈɑːtʃweɪ/ *n* (an arch over) a way or passage that runs beneath arches

arctic /ˈɑːktɪk/ *adj* **1** *often cap* of the N Pole or the surrounding region **2a** extremely cold; frigid **b** cold in temper or mood

arctic circle *n, often cap A&C* the parallel of latitude approx 66 ½ degrees north of the equator that circumscribes the north polar region

ardent /ˈɑːdənt/ *adj* characterized by warmth of feeling; eager, zealous – **~ly** *adv*

ardour /ˈɑːdəʳ/ *n* **1** (transitory) warmth of feeling **2** extreme vigour or intensity; zeal

arduous /ˈɑːdjʊəs/ *adj* **1** hard to accomplish or achieve; difficult, strenuous **2** hard to climb; steep – **~ly** *adv* – **~ness** *n*

are /əʳ; *strong* ɑːʳ/ *pres 2 sing or pres pl of* **be**

area /ˈeərɪə/ *n* **1** a level piece of ground **2** a particular extent of space or surface, or one serving a special function **3** the extent, range, or scope of a concept, operation, or activity; a field

arena /ə'riːnə/ *n* **1** (a building containing) an enclosed area used for public entertainment **2** a sphere of interest or activity; a scene

argon /'ɑːgɒn/ *n* a noble gaseous element found in the air and volcanic gases and used esp as a filler for vacuum tubes and electric light bulbs

argot /'ɑːgəʊ/ *n* a (more or less secret) vocabulary peculiar to a particular group

argue /'ɑːgjuː/ *v* **1** to give reasons for or against (sthg); reason, discuss **2** to contend or disagree in words **3** to give evidence of; indicate **4** to (try to) prove by giving reasons; maintain

argument /'ɑːgjʊmənt/ *n* **1** a reason given in proof or rebuttal **2a** the act or process of arguing; debate **b** a coherent series of reasons offered **c** a quarrel, disagreement **3** an abstract or summary, esp of a literary work

argumentative /,ɑːgjʊ'mentətɪv/ *adj* given to argument; disputatious – **~ly** *adv*

aria /'ɑːrɪə/ *n* an accompanied melody sung (e g in an opera) by 1 voice

arid /'ærɨd/ *adj* **1** excessively dry; *specif* having insufficient rainfall to support agriculture **2** lacking in interest and life – **~ity** *n* – **~ly** *adv*

Aries /'eəriːz, 'æri-iːz/ *n* (sby born under) the 1st sign of the zodiac in astrology, which is pictured as a ram

aright /ə'raɪt/ *adv* rightly, correctly

arise /ə'raɪz/ *v* **arose, arisen** /ə'rɪzən/ **1a** to originate from a source – often + *from* **b** to come into being or to attention **2** to get up, rise – chiefly fml

aristocracy /,ærɨ'stɒkrəsi/ *n* **1** (a state with) a government in which power is vested in a small privileged usu hereditary noble class **2** *sing or pl in constr* a (governing) usu hereditary nobility **3** *sing or pl in constr* the whole group of those believed to be superior (e g in wealth, rank, or intellect)

aristocrat /'ærɨstəkræt, ə'rɪ-/ *n* **1** a member of an aristocracy; *esp* a noble **2** one who has the bearing and viewpoint typical of the aristocracy – **~ic** *adj* – **~ically** *adv*

arithmetic /ə'rɪθmətɪk/ *n* **1** a branch of mathematics that deals with real numbers and calculations with them **2** computation, calculation – **~al** *adj* – **~ally** *adv*

ark /ɑːk/ *n* **1** a ship; *esp* (one like) the one built by Noah to escape the Flood **2a** the sacred chest representing to the Hebrews the presence of God among them **b** a repository for the scrolls of the Torah

[1]**arm** /ɑːm/ *n* **1** (the part between the shoulder and the wrist of) the human upper limb **2** sthg like or corresponding to an arm: e g **a** the forelimb of a vertebrate animal **b** a limb of an invertebrate animal **3** an inlet of water (e g from the sea) **4** might, authority **5** a support (e g on a chair) for the elbow and forearm **6** a sleeve **7** a functional division of a group or activity – **~less** *adj*

[2]**arm** *v* **1** to supply or equip with weapons **2** to provide with sthg that strengthens or protects **3** to equip for action or operation **4** to prepare oneself for struggle or resistance – **~ed** *adj*

[3]**arm** *n* **1a** a weapon; *esp* a firearm – usu pl **b** a combat branch (e g of an army) **2** *pl* the heraldic insignia of a group or body (e g a family or government) **3** *pl* **a** active hostilities **b** military service or profession

armada /ɑː'mɑːdə/ *n* a fleet of warships; *specif, cap* that sent against England by Spain in 1588

armadillo /,ɑːmə'dɪləʊ/ *n, pl* **-los** any of several burrowing chiefly nocturnal S American mammals with body and head encased in an armour of small bony plates

armament /'ɑːməmənt/ *n* **1** a military or naval force **2** the military strength, esp in arms and equipment, of a ship, fort, or combat unit, nation, etc **3** the process of preparing for war

armature /'ɑːmətʃə^r/ *n* **1** the central rotating part of an electric motor or generator **2** a framework on which a modeller in clay, wax, etc builds up his/her work

[1]**armchair** /ˈɑːmtʃeəʳ, -ˈ-/ *n* a chair with armrests

[2]**armchair** *adj* **1** remote from direct dealing with practical problems **2** sharing vicariously in another's experiences

armhole /ˈɑːmhəʊl/ *n* an opening for the arm in a garment

armistice /ˈɑːmɮstɮs/ *n* a temporary suspension of hostilities; a truce

armour /ˈɑːməʳ/ *n* **1a** a defensive covering for the body; *esp* a covering (e g of metal) worn in combat **b** a usu metallic protective covering (e g for a ship, fort, aircraft, or car) **2** armoured forces and vehicles (e g tanks)

armoured /ˈɑːməd/ *adj* consisting of or equipped with vehicles protected with armour plate

armourer /ˈɑːmərəʳ/ *n* **1** sby who makes or looks after armour or arms **2** sby who repairs, assembles, and tests firearms

armour plate *n* a defensive covering of hard metal plates for combat vehicles and vessels – **armour-plated** *adj*

armoury /ˈɑːməri/ *n* (a collection of or place for storing) arms and military equipment

armpit /ˈɑːmˌpɪt/ *n* the hollow beneath the junction of the arm and shoulder

army /ˈɑːmi/ *n* **1a** a large organized force for war on land **b** *often cap* the complete military organization of a nation for land warfare **2** a great multitude **3** a body of people organized to advance a cause

aroma /əˈrəʊmə/ *n* **1a** a distinctive and usu pleasant or savoury smell **b** the bouquet of a wine **2** a distinctive quality or atmosphere – **~tic** *adj* – **~tically** *adv*

arose /əˈrəʊz/ *past of* **arise**

[1]**around** /əˈraʊnd/ *adv, prep* **1** round **2** about

[2]**around** *adj* **1** about **2** in existence, evidence, or circulation

arouse /əˈraʊz/ *v* **1** to waken from sleep **2** to rouse to action; excite, esp sexually

arpeggio /ɑːˈpedʒiəʊ/ *n, pl* **arpeggios** (the sounding of) a chord whose notes are played in succession, not simultaneously

arraign /əˈreɪn/ *v* **1** to charge before a court **2** to accuse of wrong, inadequacy, or imperfection – **~ment** *n*

arrange /əˈreɪndʒ/ *v* **1** to put in order or into sequence or relationship **2** to make preparations (for); plan **3** to bring about an agreement concerning; settle **4** to adapt (a musical composition) by scoring for different voices or instruments

arrangement /əˈreɪndʒmənt/ *n* **1a** a preliminary measure; a preparation **b** an adaptation of a musical composition for different voices or instruments **c** an informal agreement or settlement, esp on personal, social, or political matters **2** sthg made by arranging constituents or things together

arrant /ˈærənt/ *adj* notoriously without moderation; extreme

[1]**array** /əˈreɪ/ *v* **1** to set or place in order; marshal **2** to dress or decorate, esp in splendid or impressive clothes; adorn

[2]**array** *n* **1** military order **2a** clothing, garments **b** rich or beautiful apparel; finery **3** an imposing group; a large number

[1]**arrest** /əˈrest/ *v* **1a** to bring to a stop **b** to make inactive **2** to seize, capture; *specif* to take or keep in custody by authority of law **3** to catch and fix or hold

[2]**arrest** *n* **1** the act of stopping **2** the taking or detaining of sby in custody by authority of law **3** a device for arresting motion

arrival /əˈraɪvəl/ *n* **1** the attainment of an end or state **2** sby or sthg that has arrived

arrive /əˈraɪv/ *v* **1** to reach a destination **2** to come **3** to achieve success

arrogant /ˈærəgənt/ *adj* aggressively conceited

arrogate /ˈærəgeɪt/ *v* to claim or seize without justification, on behalf of oneself or another

[1]**arrow** /ˈærəʊ/ *n* **1** a projectile shot from a bow, usu having a slender shaft, a pointed head, and feathers at the end **2** sthg shaped like an arrow; *esp* a mark to indicate direction

[2]**arrow** *v* to indicate with an arrow

arrowhead /ˈærəʊhed/ *n* **1** the

pointed front part of an arrow **2** sthg shaped like an arrowhead **3** any of several related (water) plants with leaves shaped like arrowheads

arrowroot /'ærəʊruːt/ *n* (a tropical American plant whose roots yield) a starch used esp as a thickening agent in cooking

arse /ɑːs/ *n* **1** the buttocks **2** the anus *USE* vulg

arsenal /'ɑːsənəl/ *n* **1** an establishment for the manufacture or storage of arms and military equipment; an armoury **2** a store, repertory

arsenic /'ɑːsənɪk/ *n* **1** a semimetallic steel-grey poisonous element – **arsenic, arsenical** *adj*

arson /'ɑːsən/ *n* the criminal act of setting fire to property in order to cause destruction – **~ist** *n*

[1]**art** /ɑːt/ *archaic pres 2 sing of* **be**

[2]**art** *n* **1** a skill acquired by experience, study, or observation **2** *pl* the humanities as contrasted with science **3a** the conscious use of skill and creative imagination, esp in the production of aesthetic objects; *also* works so produced **b** (any of the) fine arts or graphic arts

[3]**art** *adj* **1** composed, designed, or created with conscious artistry **2** designed for decorative purposes

arterial /ɑː'tɪərɪəl/ *adj* **1** of or (being the bright red blood) contained in an artery **2** of or being a main road

arteriosclerosis /ɑː'tɪəriəʊsklə'rəʊsɪ̣s/ *n* abnormal thickening and hardening of the arterial walls

artery /'ɑːtəri/ *n* **1** any of the branching elastic-walled blood vessels that carry blood from the heart to the lungs and through the body **2** an esp main channel (e g a river or road) of transport or communication

artesian well /ɑːˌtiːzɪən 'wel, -ʒən/ *n* a well by which water reaches the surface with little or no pumping

artful /'ɑːtfəl/ *adj* adroit in attaining an end, often by deceitful or indirect means; crafty – **~ly** *adv* – **~ness** *n*

arthritis /ɑː'θraɪtɪ̣s/ *n, pl* **arthritides** usu painful inflammation of 1 or more joints – **-tic** *adj, n*

arthropod /ɑː'θrəˌpod/ *n* any of a group of backboneless animals (e g insects, spiders, lobsters, etc) with a jointed body and hard outer skin

artichoke /'ɑːtɪ̣tʃəʊk/ *n* **1a** a tall composite plant like a thistle **b** the partly edible flower head of the artichoke, used as a vegetable **2 jerusalem artichoke** the edible tuber of a plant of the sunflower family

[1]**article** /'ɑːtɪ̣kəl/ *n* **1a(1)** a separate clause, item, provision, or point in a document **(2)** *pl* a written agreement specifying conditions of apprenticeship **b** a piece of nonfictional prose, usu forming an independent part of a magazine, newspaper, etc **2** an item of business; a matter **3** a word or affix (e g *a, an*, and *the*) used with nouns to give indefiniteness or definiteness **4a** a particular or separate object or thing, esp viewed as a member of a class of things **b** a thing of a particular and distinctive kind

[2]**article** *v* to bind by articles (e g of apprenticeship)

[1]**articulate** /ɑː'tɪkjʊlɪ̣t/ *adj* **1a** divided into syllables or words meaningfully arranged **b** having the power of speech **c** expressing oneself readily, clearly, or effectively; *also* expressed in this manner **2** jointed – **~ly** *adv* – **~ness** *n*

[2]**articulate** /ɑː'tɪkjʊleɪt/ *v* **1a** to utter distinctly **b** to give clear and effective utterance to **2** to unite with a joint **3** to utter articulate sounds **4** to become united or connected (as if) by a joint – **-lation** *n*

artifact, artefact /'ɑːtɪ̣fækt/ *n* a product of human workmanship; *esp* one characteristic of a (primitive) civilization

artifice /'ɑːtɪ̣fɪ̣s/ *n* **1** an artful device, expedient, or stratagem; a trick **2** clever or artful skill; ingenuity

artificer /ɑː'tɪfɪ̣səʳ/ *n* **1** a skilled or artistic worker or craftsman **2** a military or naval mechanic

artificial /ˌɑːtɪ̣'fɪʃəl/ *adj* **1** made by human skill and labour, often to a natural model; man-made **2a** lacking in natural quality; affected **b** imitation, sham – **~ly** *adv* – **~ity** *n*

artificial insemination *n* introduction of semen into the uterus or oviduct by other than natural means

artificial respiration *n* the rhythmic

forcing of air into and out of the lungs of sby whose breathing has stopped

artillery /ɑː'tɪləri/ *n* **1** large-calibre mounted firearms (e g guns, howitzers, missile launchers, etc) **2** *sing or pl in constr* a branch of an army armed with artillery

artisan /ˌɑːtɪ̇'zæn/ *n* **1** a skilled manual worker (e g a carpenter, plumber, or tailor) **2** a member of the urban proletariat

artist /'ɑːtɪ̇st/ *n* **1a** one who professes and practises an imaginative art **b** a person skilled in a fine art **2** a skilled performer; *specif* an artiste **3** one who is proficient in a specified and usu dubious activity; an expert – infml

artiste /ɑː'tiːst/ *n* a skilled public performer; *specif* a musical or theatrical entertainer

artistic /ɑː'tɪstɪk/ *adj* **1** concerning or characteristic of art or artists **2** showing imaginative skill in arrangement or execution – **~ally** *adv*

artistry /'ɑːtɪ̇stri/ *n* artistic quality or ability

artless /'ɑːtlɪ̇s/ *adj* **1** free from artificiality; natural **2** free from deceit, guile, or craftiness; sincerely simple – **~ly** *adv* – **~ness** *n*

art nouveau /ˌɑːh nuː'vəʊ/ *n, often cap A&N* a decorative style of late 19th-c origin, characterized esp by curved lines and plant motifs

arty /'ɑːti/ *adj* showily or pretentiously artistic – **artiness** *n*

[1]**as** /əz; *strong* æz/ *adv* **1** to the same degree or amount; equally **2** when considered in a specified form or relation – usu used before a preposition or participle (e g blind *as* opposed to stupid)

[2]**as** *conj* **1a** to the same degree that – usu used as a correlative after *as* or *so* to introduce a comparison or as a result **b** – used after *same* or *such* to introduce an example or comparison **c** – used after *so* to introduce the idea of purpose (e g hid so *as* to escape) in the way that –used before *so* to introduce a parallel **3** in accordance with what (e g late *as* usual) **4** while, when **5** regardless of the fact that; though (e g late *as* it was, I phoned her) **6** for the reason that; seeing (e g *as* it's wet, we'll stay at home)

[3]**as** *pron* **1** a fact that; and this (e g which, *as* history relates, was a bad king) **2** which also; and so (e g he's a doctor, *as* was his mother)

[4]**as** *prep* **1** like **2** in the capacity, character, role, or state of (e g works *as* an actor)

asbestos /əs'bestɒs, æs-/ *n* either of 2 minerals composed of thin flexible fibres, used to make noncombustible, nonconducting, or chemically resistant materials

ascend /ə'send/ *v* **1** to move or slope gradually upwards; rise **2a** to rise from a lower level or degree **b** to go back in time or in order of genealogical succession **3** to go or move up **4** to succeed to; begin to occupy – esp in *ascend the throne* – **~ancy** *n* – **~ant** *adj*

ascension /ə'senʃən/ *n* the act or process of ascending

Ascension Day *n* the Thursday 40 days after Easter observed in commemoration of Christ's ascension into Heaven

ascent /ə'sent/ *n* **1a** the act of going, climbing, or travelling up **b** a way up; an upward slope or path **2** an advance in social status or reputation; progress

ascertain /ˌæsə'teɪn/ *v* to find out or learn with certainty – **~able** *adj*

ascetic /ə'setɪk/ *also* **ascetical** *adj* **1** practising strict self-denial as a spiritual discipline **2** austere in appearance, manner, or attitude – **ascetic** *n* – **~ally** *adv* – **~ism** *n*

ascribe /ə'skraɪb/ *v* to refer or attribute something *to* a supposed cause or source

asexual /eɪ'sekʃʊəl, -'seksjʊəl/ *adj* **1** lacking sex (organs) **2** produced without sexual action or differentiation **3** without expression of or reference to sexual interest – **~ly** *adv* – **~ity** *n*

[1]**ash** /æʃ/ *n* (the tough elastic wood of) any of a genus of tall trees of the olive family

[2]**ash** *n* **1a** the solid residue left when material is thoroughly burned or oxidized **b** fine particles of mineral matter from a volcano **2** *pl* the remains of sthg destroyed by fire **3** *pl* the remains of a dead body after cremation or disintegration

ashamed /ə'ʃeɪmd/ *adj* **1** feeling shame, guilt, or disgrace **2** restrained by fear of shame – **~ly** *adv*

[1]**ashen** /'æʃən/ *adj* of or made from the wood of the ash tree

[2]**ashen** *adj* **1** consisting of or resembling ashes **2** deadly pale; blanched

ashore /ə'ʃɔːʳ/ *adv* on or to the shore

ashtray /'æʃtreɪ/ *n* a (small) receptacle for tobacco ash and cigar and cigarette ends

Ash Wednesday *n* the first day of Lent

Asian /'eɪʃən, 'eɪʒən/ *adj* (characteristic) of the continent of Asia or its people – **Asian** *n*

Asiatic /ˌeɪʃi'ætik, ˌeɪzi-, eɪʒi-/ *adv or n* Asian

[1]**aside** /ə'saɪd/ *adv or adj* **1** to or towards the side **2** out of the way **3** apart; in reserve **4** apart

[2]**aside** *n* **1** an utterance meant to be inaudible; *esp* an actor's speech supposedly not heard by other characters on stage **2** a digression

as if *conj* **1** as it would be if **2** as one would do if **3** that **4** – used in emphatic rejection of a notion (e g *as if* he would ever do a thing like that!)

asinine /'æsɮnaɪn/ *adj* stupid

ask /ɑːsk/ *v* **1a** to call on for an answer **b** to put a question about **c** to put or frame (a question) **2** to make a request of or for **3** to behave in such a way as to provoke (an unpleasant response) **4** to set as a price **5** to invite **6** to seek information

askance /ə'skɑːns/ *adv* with disapproval or distrust – esp in *look askance*

askew /ə'skjuː/ *adv or adj* awry

asking price *n* the price set by the seller

aslant /ə'slɑːnt/ *prep, adv, or adj* (over or across) in a slanting direction

asleep /ə'sliːp/ *adj* **1** in a state of sleep **2** dead – euph **3** lacking sensation; numb

as long as *conj* providing, while; so long as

asparagus /ə'spærəgəs/ *n* (any of a genus of Old World perennial plants of the lily family including) a tall plant widely cultivated for its edible young shoots

aspect /'æspekt/ *n* **1a** the position of planets or stars with respect to one another, held by astrologers to influence human affairs; *also* the apparent position (e g conjunction) of a body in the solar system with respect to the sun **b** a position facing a particular direction **2a** appearance to the eye or mind **b** a particular feature of a situation, plan, or point of view

aspen /'æspən/ *n* any of several poplars with leaves that flutter in the lightest wind

asperity /ə'sperɮti, æ-/ *n* **1** rigour, hardship **2** roughness of surface; unevenness **3** roughness of manner or temper; harshness

aspersion /ə'spɜːʃən, -ʒən/ *n* **1** a sprinkling with water, esp in religious ceremonies **2** an unwarranted doubt

asphalt /'æsfælt, 'æʃ-, -felt/ *n* **1** a brown to black bituminous substance found in natural beds and also obtained as a residue in petroleum or coal tar refining **2** an asphaltic composition used for surfacing roads and footpaths

asphyxia /əs'fɪksɪə, æs-/ *n* a lack of oxygen in the body, usu caused by interruption of breathing, and resulting in unconsciousness or death – **-xiate** *v*

aspic /'æspɪk/ *n* a clear savoury jelly (e g of fish or meat stock) used as a garnish or to make a meat, fish, etc mould

aspidistra /ˌæspɮ'dɪstrə/ *n* any of various Asiatic plants of the lily family with large leaves, often grown as house plants

[1]**aspirate** /'æspɮreɪt/ *v* to pronounce (a vowel, consonant, or word) with an *h*-sound

[2]**aspirate** /'æspɮrɮt/ *n* **1** (a character, esp *h*, representing) an independent /h/ sound **2** an aspirated consonant (e g the *p* of *pit*)

aspiration /ˌæspɪ'reɪʃən/ *n* **1** a strong desire to achieve sthg high or great **2** an object of such desire

aspire /ə'spaɪəʳ/ *v* to seek to attain or accomplish a particular goal – usu + *to*

aspirin /'æsprɮn/ *n, pl* **-rin, -rins** (a

tablet containing) a derivative of salicylic acid used for relief of pain and fever

[1]**ass** /æs/ *n* **1** the donkey or a similar long-eared hardy gregarious mammal related to and smaller than the horse **2** a stupid, obstinate, or perverse person or thing

[2]**ass** *n, chiefly NAm* the arse

assail /ə'seɪl/ *v* **1** to attack violently with blows or words **2** to prey on – **~ant** *n*

assassin /ə'sæsɨn/ *n* **1** *cap* any of a secret order of Muslims who at the time of the Crusades committed secret murders **2** a murderer; *esp* one who murders a politically important person, for money or from fanatical motives

assassinate /ə'sæsɨneɪt/ *v* to murder suddenly or secretly, usu for political reasons – **-ation** *n*

[1]**assault** /ə'sɔːlt/ *n* **1** a violent physical or verbal attack **2a** an attempt to do or immediate threat of doing unlawful personal violence **b** rape **3** an attempt to attack a fortification by a sudden rush

[2]**assault** *v* **1** to make an (indecent) assault on **2** to rape

assay /ə'seɪ/ *v* **1a** to analyse (e g an ore) for 1 or more valuable components **b** to judge the worth or quality of **2** to try, attempt – fml – **assay** *n*

assegai /'æsɨgaɪ/ *n* a slender iron-tipped hardwood spear used in southern Africa

assemblage /ə'semblɪdʒ/ *n* **1** a collection of people or things; a gathering **2** a three-dimensional collage made from scraps, junk, and odds and ends (e g of cloth, wood, or stone)

assemble /ə'sembəl/ *v* **1** to bring together (e g in a particular place or for a particular purpose) **2** to fit together the parts of **3** to gather together; convene

assembly /ə'sembli/ *n* **1** a company of people gathered for deliberation and legislation, entertainment, or worship **2** *cap* a legislative body **3a** an assemblage **b** assembling or being assembled **4** a bugle, drum, etc signal for troops to assemble or fall in **5** (a collection of parts assembled by) the fitting together of manufactured parts into a complete machine, structure, etc

[1]**assent** /ə'sent/ *v* to agree to sthg

[2]**assent** *n* acquiescence, agreement

assert /ə'sɜːt/ *v* **1** to state or declare positively and often forcefully **2** to demonstrate the existence of

assertion /ə'sɜːʃən/ *n* a declaration, affirmation

assertive /ə'sɜːtɪv/ *adj* characterized by bold assertion; dogmatic – **~ly** *adv* – **~ness** *n*

assess /ə'ses/ *v* **1a** to determine the rate or amount of (e g a tax) **b** to impose (e g a tax) according to an established rate **2** to make an official valuation of (property) for the purposes of taxation **3** to determine the importance, size, or value of – **~ment** *n*

assessor /ə'sesəʳ/ *n* **1** a specialist who advises a court **2** an official who assesses property for taxation **3** *chiefly Br* sby who investigates and values insurance claims

asset /'æset, 'æsɨt/ *n* **1a** *pl* the total property of a person, company, or institution; *esp* that part which can be used to pay debts **b** a single item of property **2** an advantage, resource **3** *pl* the items on a balance sheet showing the book value of property owned

asseverate /ə'sevəreɪt/ to affirm solemnly – fml – **-ation** *n*

assiduous /ə'sɪdjʊəs/ *adj* marked by careful unremitting attention or persistent application; sedulous – **~ly** *adv* – **-duity** *n*

assign /ə'saɪn/ *v* **1** to transfer (property) to another, esp in trust or for the benefit of creditors **2** to appoint to a post or duty **3** to fix authoritatively; specify, designate – **~able** *adj*

assignation /ˌæsɪg'neɪʃən/ *n* **1** the act of assigning; *also* the assignment made **2** a meeting, esp a secret one with a lover

assignment /ə'saɪnmənt/ *n* **1a** a position, post, or job to which one is assigned **b** a specified task or amount of work assigned by authority **2** (a document effecting) the legal transfer of property

assimilate /ə'sɪmɨleɪt/ *v* **1a** to take in or absorb into the system (as nourishment) **b** to absorb; *esp* to take into the mind and fully comprehend **2a** to make similar – usu + *to* or *with* **b** to absorb into a cultural tradition **3** to compare, liken – usu + *to* or *with* **4** to become assimilated – **-lation** *n*

assist /ə'sɪst/ *v* **1** to give support or aid **2** to be present as a spectator **3** to give support or aid to – **~ance** *n*

¹associate /ə'səʊʃieɪt, ə'səʊsi-/ *v* **1** to join as a friend, companion, or partner in business **2** to bring together in any of various ways (e g in memory, thought, or imagination) **3** to come together as partners, friends, or companions **4** to combine or join with other parts; unite *USE* often + *with*

²associate /ə'səʊʃiɨt, -ʃɨt/ *adj* **1** closely connected (e g in function or office) with another **2** having secondary or subordinate status

³associate /ə'səʊʃiɨt, -ʃɨt/ *n* **1** a fellow worker; partner, colleague **2** a companion, comrade **3** sthg closely connected with or usu accompanying another **4** one admitted to a subordinate degree of membership

association /ə,səʊsi'eɪʃən, ə,səʊʃi-/ *n* **1** an organization of people having a common interest; a society, league **2** sthg linked in memory, thought, or imagination with a thing or person **3** the formation of mental connections between sensations, ideas, memories, etc

assonance /'æsənəns/ *n* **1** resemblance of sound in words or syllables **2** repetition of esp only the vowel sounds (e g in *stony* and *holy*) or only the consonant sounds, as an alternative to rhyme **assonant** *adj*

assorted /ə'sɔːtɨd/ *adj* **1** consisting of various kinds **2** suited by nature, character, or design; matched

assortment /ə'sɔːtmənt/ *n* a collection of assorted things or people

assuage /ə'sweɪdʒ/ *v* to lessen the intensity of (pain, suffering, desire, etc); ease

assume /ə'sjuːm/ *v* **1a** to take to or upon oneself; undertake **b** to invest oneself formally with (an office or its symbols) **2** to seize, usurp **3** to pretend to have or be; feign **4** to take as granted or true; suppose – often + *that*

assumption /ə'sʌmpʃən/ *n* **1a** the taking up of a person into heaven **b** *cap* August 15 observed in commemoration of the assumption of the Virgin Mary **2** the act of laying claim to or taking possession of sthg **3a** the supposition that sthg is true **b** a fact or statement (e g a proposition, axiom, or postulate) taken for granted

assurance /ə'ʃʊərəns/ *n* **1a** a pledge, guarantee **b** *chiefly Br* (life) insurance **2a** the quality or state of being sure or certain; freedom from doubt **b** confidence of mind or manner; *also* excessive self-confidence; brashness **3** sthg that inspires or tends to inspire confidence

assure /ə'ʃʊəʳ/ *v* **1** to make safe; insure (esp life or safety) **2** to give confidence to; reassure **3** to inform positively **4** to guarantee the happening or attainment of; ensure

¹assured /ə'ʃʊəd, ə'ʃɔːd/ *adj* **1** characterized by self-confidence **2** satisfied as to the certainty or truth of a matter; convinced – **~ly** *adv*

²assured *n* an insured person

aster /'æstəʳ/ *n* **1** any of various chiefly autumn-blooming leafy-stemmed composite plants with often showy heads

asterisk /'æstərɪsk/ *n* a sign * used as a reference mark, esp to denote the omission of letters or words or to show that sthg is doubtful or absent

astern /ə'stɜːn/ *adv or adj* **1** behind the stern; to the rear **2** at or towards the stern of a ship **3** backwards

¹asteroid /'æstərɔɪd/ *n* any of thousands of small planets mostly between Mars and Jupiter

²asteroid *adj* **1** starlike **2** of or like a starfish

asthma /'æsmə/ *n* (an allergic condition marked by attacks of) laboured breathing with wheezing and usu coughing, gasping, and a sense of constriction in the chest – **~tic** *adj, n* – **~tically** *adv*

astir /ə'stɜːʳ/ *adj* **1** in a state of bustle or excitement **2** out of bed; up

astonish /ə'stɒnɪʃ/ *v* to strike with sudden wonder or surprise – **~ment** *n*

astound /ə'staʊnd/ *v* to fill with bewilderment and wonder

astrakhan /æstrə'kæn, -'kɑːn/ *n, often cap* **1** karakul of Russian origin **2** a woollen fabric with curled and looped pile

astray /ə'streɪ/ *adv or adj* **1** off the right path or route **2** in error; away from a proper or desirable course or development

[1]**astride** /ə'straɪd/ *adv* with the legs wide apart

[2]**astride** *prep* **1** on or above and with 1 leg on each side of **2** extending over or across; spanning

astringent /ə'strɪndʒənt/ *adj* **1** capable of making firm the soft tissues of the body; styptic **2** rigidly severe; austere – **-gency** *n* – **~ly** *adv*

astrolabe /'æstrəleɪb/ *n* an instrument used, before the invention of the sextant, to observe the position of celestial bodies

astrology /ə'strɒlədʒi/ *n* the art or practice of determining the supposed influences of the planets on human affairs – **-ger** *n* – **-gical** *adj* – **-gically** *adv*

astronaut /'æstrənɔːt/ *n* sby who travels beyond the earth's atmosphere

astronomical /,æstrə'nɒmɪkəl/, **astronomic** *adj* **1** of astronomy **2** enormously or inconceivably large – infml – **~ly** *adv*

astronomy /ə'strɒnəmi/ *n* a branch of science dealing with the celestial bodies – **-nomer** *n*

astrophysics /,æstrəʊ'fɪzɪks, ,æstrə-/ *n pl but sing or pl in constr* a branch of astronomy dealing with the physical and chemical constitution of the celestial bodies – **-ical** *adj* – **-icist** *n*

astute /ə'stjuːt/ *adj* shrewdly perspicacious – **~ly** *adv* – **~ness** *n*

asunder /ə'sʌndəʳ/ *adv or adj* **1** into parts **2** apart from each other in position

asylum /ə'saɪləm/ *n* **1** a place of retreat and security; a shelter **2a** the protection from the law or refuge afforded by an asylum **b** protection from arrest and being returned home given by a nation to political refugees **3** an institution for the care of the destitute or afflicted, esp the insane

asymmetric /,eɪsɪ̵'metrɪk, ,æ-/, **asymmetrical** *adj* not symmetrical – **~ally** *adv*

at /ət; *strong* æt/ *prep* **1** – used to indicate presence or occurrence in, on, or near a place imagined as a point (e g sick *at* heart) **2** – used to indicate the goal or direction of an action or motion (e g aim *at* the goal) **3a** – used to indicate occupation or employment (e g *at* tea) **b** when it comes to (an occupation or employment) (e g an expert *at* chess) **4** – used to indicate situation or condition (e g *at* risk) **5** in response to (e g shudder *at* the thought) **6** – used to indicate position on a scale (e g of cost, speed, or age) (e g *at* 80 mph) **7** – used to indicate position in time (e g *at* midday)

at all *adv* to the least extent or degree; under any circumstances

ate /et, eɪt/ *past of* eat

atheist /'eɪθiɪ̵st/ *n* a person who disbelieves in the existence of a deity – **atheism** *n*

athlete /'æθliːt/ *n* sby who is trained in, skilled in, or takes part in exercises, sports, etc that require physical strength, agility, or stamina

athlete's foot *n* ringworm of the feet

athletic /æθ'letɪk, əθ-/ *adj* **1** of athletes or athletics **2** characteristic of an athlete; *esp* vigorous, active

athletics /æθ'letɪks, əθ-/ *n pl but sing or pl in constr, Br* competitive walking, running, throwing, and jumping sports collectively

[1]**athwart** /ə'θwɔːt/ *adv* **1** across, esp in an oblique direction **2** in opposition to the right or expected course

[2]**athwart** *prep* **1** across **2** in opposition to

atlas /'ætləs/ *n* **1** *cap* one who bears a heavy burden **2** a bound collection of maps, charts, or tables **3** the first vertebra of the neck

atmosphere /'ætməsfɪəʳ/ *n* **1** a mass of gas enveloping a celestial body (e g a planet); *esp* all the air surrounding the earth **2** the air of a locality **3** a surrounding influence or environment **4** a dominant aesthetic or emotional effect or appeal

atmospheric /,ætməs'ferɪk/ *adj* **1** of, occurring in, or like the atmosphere **2**

having, marked by, or contributing aesthetic or emotional atmosphere

atmospherics /ˌætməsˈferɪks/ *n pl* (the electrical phenomena causing) audible disturbances produced in a radio receiver by electrical atmospheric phenomena (e g lightning)

atoll /ˈætɒl/ *n* a coral reef surrounding a lagoon

atom /ˈætəm/ *n* **1** any of the minute indivisible particles of which according to ancient materialism the universe is composed **2** a tiny particle; a bit **3** the smallest particle of an element that can exist either alone or in combination, consisting of various numbers of electrons, protons, and neutrons **4** nuclear power

atom bomb *n* a bomb whose violent explosive power is due to the sudden release of atomic energy derived from the splitting of the nuclei of plutonium, uranium, etc by neutrons in a very rapid chain reaction; *also* a hydrogen bomb

atomic /əˈtɒmɪk/ *adj* **1** of or concerned with atoms, atom bombs, or atomic energy **2** *of a chemical element* existing as separate atoms – **~ally** *adv*

atomic energy *n* energy liberated in an atom bomb, nuclear reactor, etc by changes in the nucleus of an atom

atomic pile *n* a nuclear reactor

atom·ize, -ise /ˈætəmaɪz/ *v* to break up a liquid into a fine mist or spray

atonal /eɪˈtəʊnl, æ-/ *adj* organized without reference to a musical key and using the notes of the chromatic scale impartially – **~ly** *adv* – **~ity** *n*

atone /əˈtəʊn/ *v* to supply satisfaction *for*; make amends *for* – **~ment** *n*

atrium /ˈætrɪəm, ˈeɪ-/ *n, pl* **atria** *also* **atriums** **1** an inner courtyard open to the sky (e g in a Roman house) **2** a chamber of the heart that receives blood from the veins and forces it into a ventricle or ventricles

atrocious /əˈtrəʊʃəs/ *adj* **1** extremely wicked or cruel; barbaric **2** of very poor quality – **-city** *n*

atrophy /ˈætrəfi/ *n* **1** (sometimes natural) decrease in size or wasting away of a body part or tissue **2** a wasting away or progressive decline; degeneration – **atrophy** *v*

attach /əˈtætʃ/ *v* **1** to seize by legal authority **2** to bring (oneself) into an association **3** to appoint to serve with an organization for special duties or for a temporary period **4** to fasten **5** to ascribe, attribute **6** to become attached; stick *USE* often + *to*

attaché /əˈtæʃeɪ/ *n* a technical expert on a diplomatic staff

attaché case *n* a small thin case used esp for carrying papers

attachment /əˈtætʃmənt/ *n* **1** a seizure by legal process **2a** fidelity – often + *to* **b** an affectionate regard **3** a device attached to a machine or implement **4** the physical connection by which one thing is attached to another

[1]attack /əˈtæk/ *v* **1** to set upon forcefully in order to damage, injure, or destroy **2** to take the initiative against in a game or contest **3** to assail with unfriendly or bitter words **4** to set to work on, esp vigorously **5** to make an attack

[2]attack *n* **1** the act of attacking; an assault **2** a belligerent or antagonistic action or verbal assault – often + *on* **3** the beginning of destructive action (e g by a chemical agent) **4** the setting to work on some undertaking **5** a fit of sickness or (recurrent) disease **6a** an attempt to score or to gain ground in a game **b** *sing or pl in constr* the attacking players in a team or the positions occupied by them; *specif* the bowlers in a cricket team

attain /əˈteɪn/ *v* **1** to reach as an end; achieve **2** to come or arrive by motion, growth, or effort – + *to* – **~able** *adj*

attainment /əˈteɪnmənt/ *n* sthg attained; an accomplishment

attar /ˈætəʳ/ *n* a fragrant essential oil (e g from rose petals); *also* a fragrance

[1]attempt /əˈtempt/ *v* to make an effort to do, accomplish, solve, or effect, esp without success

[2]attempt *n* **1** the act or an instance of attempting; *esp* an unsuccessful effort **2** an attack, assault – often + *on*

attend /əˈtend/ *v* **1** to take charge of; look after **2** to go or stay with as a companion, nurse, or servant **3** to be present with; accompany, escort **4** to be present at **5** to deal with **6** to apply the mind or pay attention; heed *USE* – often + *to*

attendance /ə'tendəns/ *n* **1** the number of people attending **2** the number of times a person attends, usu out of a possible maximum

[1]**attendant** /ə'tendənt/ *adj* accompanying or following as a consequence

[2]**attendant** *n* one who attends another to perform a service; *esp* an employee who waits on customers

attention /ə'tenʃən/ *n* **1** attending, esp through application of the mind to an object of sense or thought **2** consideration with a view to action **3a** an act of civility or courtesy, esp in courtship – usu pl **b** sympathetic consideration of the needs and wants of others **4** a formal position of readiness assumed by a soldier – usu as a command

attentive /ə'tentɪv/ *adj* **1** mindful, observant **2** solicitous **3** paying attentions (as if) in the role of a suitor – ~**ly** *adv* – ~**ness** *n*

[1]**attenuate** /ə'tenjʊeɪt/ *v* **1** to make thin **2** to lessen the amount, force, or value of; weaken **3** to become thin or fine; diminish

[2]**attenuate** /ə'tenjʊɨt, -eɪt/ *adj* tapering gradually

attest /ə'test/ *v* **1** to affirm to be true, authenticate **2** to be proof of; bear witness to **3** to put on oath **4** to bear witness, testify – often + *to*

attic /'ætɪk/ *n* a room or space immediately below the roof of a building

Attic *adj* (characteristic) of Attica or Athens

[1]**attire** /ə'taɪə[r]/ *v* to put garments on; dress, array; *esp* to clothe in fancy or rich garments

[2]**attire** *n* dress, clothes; *esp* splendid or decorative clothing

attitude /'ætɨtjuːd/ *n* **1** the arrangement of the parts of a body or figure; a posture **2** a feeling, emotion, or mental position with regard to a fact or state **3** a manner assumed for a specific purpose **4** a ballet position in which one leg is raised at the back and bent at the knee

attorney /ə'tɜːni/ *n* **1** sby with legal authority to act for another **2** *NAm* a lawyer

attorney general *n, pl* **attorneys general, attorney generals** *often cap A&G* the chief legal officer of a nation or state

attract /ə'trækt/ *v* **1** to pull to or towards oneself or itself **2** to draw by appeal to interest, emotion, or aesthetic sense **3** to possess or exercise the power of attracting sthg or sby – ~**ive** *adj*

attraction /ə'trækʃən/ *n* **1** a characteristic that elicits interest or admiration – usu pl **2** the action or power of drawing forth a response (e g interest or affection); an attractive quality **3** a force between unlike electric charges, unlike magnetic poles, etc, resisting separation **4** sthg that attracts or is intended to attract people by appealing to their desires and tastes

[1]**attribute** /'ætrɨbjuːt/ *n* **1** an inherent characteristic **2** an object closely associated with a usu specified person, thing, or office

[2]**attribute** /ə'trɪbjuːt/ *v* to reckon as originating in an indicated fashion – usu + *to* – **-table** *adj* – **-tion** *n*

attrition /ə'trɪʃən/ *n* **1** sorrow for one's sins arising from fear of punishment **2** the act of rubbing together; friction; *also* the act of wearing or grinding down by friction **3** the act of weakening or exhausting by constant harassment or abuse

attune /ə'tjuːn/ *v* to cause to become used or accustomed *to*

atypical /eɪ'tɪpɪkəl/ *adj* not typical; irregular – ~**ly** *adv*

aubergine /'əʊbəʒiːn/ **1** (the edible usu smooth dark purple ovoid fruit of) the eggplant **2** a deep reddish purple colour

auburn /'ɔːbən/ *adj or n* (of) a reddish brown colour

[1]**auction** /'ɔːkʃən/ *n* **1** a public sale of property to the highest bidder **2** the act or process of bidding in some card games

[2]**auction** *v* to sell at an auction – often + *off* – ~**eer** *n*

audacious /ɔː'deɪʃəs/ *adj* **1a** intrepidly daring; adventurous **b** recklessly bold; rash **2** insolent – **audacity** *n* – ~**ly** *adv*

audible /'ɔːdə̍bəl/ *adj* heard or capable of being heard – **-bility** *n* – **-bly** *adv*

audience /'ɔːdɪəns/ *n* **1a** a formal hearing or interview **b** an opportunity of being heard **2** *sing or pl in constr* a group of listeners or spectators

audio /'ɔːdi-əʊ/ *adj* **1** of or being acoustic, mechanical, or electrical frequencies corresponding to those of audible sound waves, approx 20 to 20,000Hz **2a** of sound or its reproduction, esp high-fidelity reproduction **b** relating to or used in the transmission or reception of sound – **audio** *n*

audiovisual /,ɔːdi-əʊ'vɪʒʊəl/ *adj* of (teaching methods using) both hearing and sight

[1]**audit** /'ɔːdə̍t/ *n* (the final report on) a formal or official examination and verification of an account book

[2]**audit** *v* to perform an audit on

[1]**audition** /ɔː'dɪʃən/ *n* **1** the act of hearing; *esp* a critical hearing **2** a trial performance to appraise an entertainer's abilities

[2]**audition** *v* **1** to test (e g for a part) in an audition **2** to give a trial performance – usu + *for*

auditorium /,ɔːdə̍'tɔːrɪəm/ *n, pl* **auditoria, auditoriums** the part of a public building where an audience sits

auditory /'ɔːdə̍təri/ *adj* of or experienced through hearing

au fait /,əʊ 'feɪ/ *adj* **1** fully competent; capable **2** fully informed; familiar *with*

auger /'ɔːgəʳ/ *n* a tool for boring holes in wood

aught /ɔːt/ *pron* all

augment /ɔːg'ment/ *v* to make or become greater, more numerous, larger, or more intense

[1]**augur** /'ɔːgəʳ/ *n* one held to foretell events by omens; a soothsayer; *specif* an official diviner of Ancient Rome

[2]**augur** *v* **1** to foretell or predict the future, esp from omens **2** to give promise of; presage

augury /'ɔːgjʊri/ *n* **1** predicting the future from omens or portents **2** an omen, portent

august /ɔː'gʌst/ *adj* marked by majestic dignity or grandeur – **~ly** *adv*

August /'ɔːgəst/ *n* the 8th month of the Gregorian calendar

auk /ɔːk/ *n* a puffin, guillemot, razorbill, or related short-necked diving seabird of the northern hemisphere

aunt /ɑːnt/ *n* **1a** the sister of one's father or mother **b** the wife of one's uncle **2** – often used as a term of affection for a woman who is a close friend of a young child or its parents

Aunt Sally /,ɑːnt 'sæli/ *n* **1** an effigy of a woman at which objects are thrown at a fair **2** *Br* an easy target of criticism or attack

au pair /,əʊ 'peəʳ/ *n* a foreign girl who does domestic work for a family in return for room and board and the opportunity to learn the language of the family

aura /'ɔːrə/ *n* **1** a distinctive atmosphere surrounding a given source **2** a luminous radiation; a nimbus

aural /'ɔːrəl/ *adj* of the ear or the sense of hearing – **~ly** *adv*

au revoir /,əʊ rə'vwɑːʳ, ,ɒ-/ *n* goodbye – often used interjectionally

auricle /'ɔːrɪkəl/ *n* **1** the projecting portion of the outer ear **2** an atrium of the heart – not now in technical use

aurora /ɔː'rɔːrə, ɒ-/ *n, pl* **auroras, aurorae** dawn

auspicious /ɔː'spɪʃəs/ *adj* **1** affording a favourable omen; propitious **2** attended by good omens; prosperous – **~ly** *adv*

Aussie /'ɒzi/ *n* an Australian – infml

austere /ɔː'stɪəʳ, ɒ-/ *adj* **1** stern and forbidding in appearance and manner **2** rigidly abstemious; self-denying **3** unadorned, simple – **~ly** *adv* – **-rity** *n*

Australasian /,ɒstrə'leɪʒən, -ʃən, ,ɔːstrə-/ *n or adj* (a native or inhabitant) of Australasia

[1]**Australian** /ɒ'streɪlɪən, ɔː-/ *n* **1** a native or inhabitant of Australia **2** the speech of the aboriginal inhabitants of Australia **3** English as spoken and written in Australia

[2]**Australian** *adj* **1** (characteristic) of Australia

authentic /ɔː'θentɪk/ *adj* **1** worthy of belief as conforming to fact or reality; trustworthy **2** not imaginary, false, or imitation; genuine – **~ally** *adv* – **~ity** *n*

authenticate /ɔːˈθentɪkeɪt/ *v* to (serve to) prove the authenticity of – **-ation** *n*

author /ˈɔːθəʳ/, *fem* **authoress** *n* **1a** the writer of a literary work **b** (the books written by) sby whose profession is writing **2** sby or sthg that originates or gives existence; a source

authoritarian /ɔːˌθɒrɨˈteərɪən/ *adj* of or favouring submission to authority rather than personal freedom

authoritative /ɔːˈθɒrɨtətɪv, ə-/ *adj* **1a** having or proceeding from authority; official **b** entitled to credit or acceptance; conclusive **2** dictatorial, peremptory – **~ly** *adv*

authority /ɔːˈθɒrɨti, ə-/ *n* **1a** a book, quotation, etc referred to for justification of one's opinions or actions **b** a conclusive statement or set of statements **c** an individual cited or appealed to as an expert **2a** power to require and receive submission; the right to expect obedience **b** power to influence or command **c** a right granted by sby in authority; authorization **3a** *pl the* people in command **b** persons in command; *specif* government **c** *often cap* a governmental administrative body **4a** grounds, warrant **b** convincing force; weight

author·ize, -ise /ˈɔːθəraɪz/ *v* **1** to empower **2** to sanction – **-ization** *n*

authorship /ˈɔːθəʃɪp/ *n* **1** the profession or activity of writing **2** the identity of the author of a literary work

autism /ˈɔːtɪzəm/ *n* a disorder of childhood development marked esp by inability to form relationships with other people – **-istic** *adj* – **-istically** *adv*

autobiography /ˌɔːtəbaɪˈɒgrəfi/ *n* the biography of a person written by him-/herself; *also* such writing considered as a genre – **-graphic** *adj* – **-graphically** *adv*

autocracy /ɔːˈtɒkrəsi/ *n* government by an autocrat

autocrat /ˈɔːtəkræt/ *n* **1** one who rules with unlimited power **2** a dictatorial person – **~ic** *adj* – **~ically** *adv*

autocue /ˈɔːtəʊˌkjuː/ *n* a device that enables a person (e g a newsreader) being televised to read a script without averting his/her eyes from the camera

[1]**autograph** /ˈɔːtəgrɑːf/ *n* an identifying mark, specif a person's signature, made by the individual him-/herself

[2]**autograph** *v* to write one's signature in or on

automate /ˈɔːtəmeɪt/ *v* **1** to operate by automation **2** to convert to largely automatic operation

[1]**automatic** /ˌɔːtəˈmætɪk/ *adj* **1a** acting or done spontaneously or unconsciously **b** resembling an automaton; mechanical **2** having a self-acting or self-regulating mechanism **3** *of a firearm* repeatedly ejecting the empty cartridge shell, introducing a new cartridge, and firing it – **~ally** *adv*

[2]**automatic** *n* an automatic machine or apparatus; *esp* an automatic firearm or vehicle

automation /ˌɔːtəˈmeɪʃən/ *n* **1** the technique of making an apparatus, process, or system operate automatically **2** automatic operation of an apparatus, process, or system by mechanical or electronic devices that take the place of human operators

automaton /ɔːˈtɒmətən/ *n, pl* **automatons, automata 1** a mechanism having its own power source; *also* a robot **2** a person who acts in a mechanical fashion

automobile /ˈɔːtəməbiːl/ *n, NAm* a motor car

autonomy /ɔːˈtɒnəmi/ *n* **1** self-determined freedom and esp moral independence **2** self-government; *esp* the degree of political independence possessed by a minority group, territorial division, etc – **-mous** *adj* – **-mously** *adv*

autopsy /ˈɔːtɒpsi/ *n* a postmortem examination

autumn /ˈɔːtəm/ *n* **1** the season between summer and winter, extending, in the northern hemisphere, from the September equinox to the December solstice **2** a period of maturity or the early stages of decline – **~al** *adj* – **~ally** *adv*

[1]**auxiliary** /ɔːg'zɪlɪəri, ɔːk-/ *adj* **1** subsidiary **2** being a verb (e g *be*, *do*, or *may*) used typically to express person, number, mood, voice, or tense, usu accompanying another verb **3** supplementary

[2]**auxiliary** *n* **1** an auxiliary person, group, or device **2** an auxiliary verb **3** a member of a foreign force serving a nation at war

[1]**avail** /ə'veɪl/ *v* to be of use or advantage (to)

[2]**avail** *n* benefit, use – chiefly after *of* or *to* and in negative contexts

available /ə'veɪləbəl/ *adj* **1** present or ready for immediate use **2** accessible, obtainable **3** qualified or willing to do sthg or to assume a responsibility – **-ability** *n* – **-ably** *adv*

[1]**avalanche** /'ævəlɑːnʃ/ *n* **1** a large mass of snow, rock, ice, etc falling rapidly down a mountain **2** a sudden overwhelming rush or accumulation of sthg

[2]**avalanche** *v* **1** to descend in an avalanche **2** to overwhelm, flood

[1]**avant-garde** /,ævɒŋ 'gɑːd/ *n* *the* group of people who create or apply new ideas and techniques in any field, esp the arts; *also* such a group that is extremist, bizarre, or arty and affected

[2]**avant-garde** *adj* of the avant-garde or artistic work that is new and experimental

avarice /'ævərɨs/ *n* excessive or insatiable desire for wealth or gain; cupidity – **-cious** *adj* – **-ciously** *adv*

avenge /ə'vendʒ/ *v* **1** to take vengeance on behalf of **2** to exact satisfaction for (a wrong) by punishing the wrongdoer – **~r** *n*

avenue /'ævɨnjuː/ *n* **1** a line of approach **2** a broad passageway bordered by trees **3** an often broad street or road

aver /ə'vɜːʳ/ *v* **-rr-** **1** to allege, assert **2** to declare positively – fml

[1]**average** /'ævərɪdʒ/ *n* **1** a single value representative of a set of other values; *esp* an arithmetic mean **2** a level (e g of intelligence) typical of a group, class, or series **3** a ratio expressing the average performance of a sports team or sportsman as a fraction of the number of opportunities for successful performance

[2]**average** *adj* **1** equalling an arithmetic mean **2a** about midway between extremes **b** not out of the ordinary; common

[3]**average** *v* **1** to be or come to an average **2** to do, get, or have on average or as an average sum or quantity **3** to find the arithmetic mean of **4** to bring towards the average **5** to have an average value of

averse /ə'vɜːs/ *adj* having an active feeling of repugnance or distaste – + *to* or *from*

aversion /ə'vɜːʃən/ *n* **1** a feeling of settled dislike for sthg; antipathy **2** *chiefly Br* an object of aversion; a cause of repugnance

avert /ə'vɜːt/ *v* **1** to turn away or aside (e g the eyes) in avoidance **2** to see coming and ward off; avoid, prevent

aviary /'eɪvɪəri/ *n* a place for keeping birds

aviation /,eɪvi'eɪʃən/ *n* **1** the operation of heavier-than-air aircraft **2** aircraft manufacture, development, and design

aviator /'eɪvieɪtəʳ/, *fem* **aviatrix** *n* the pilot of an aircraft

avid /'ævɨd/ *adj* urgently or greedily eager; keen *n* – **~ly** *adv* – **-ity** *n*

avocado /,ævə'kɑːdəʊ/ *n, pl* **-dos** *also* **-does** (a tropical American tree of the laurel family bearing) a pulpy green or purple pear-shaped edible fruit

avocation /,ævə'keɪʃən/ *n* a subordinate occupation pursued in addition to one's vocation, esp for enjoyment; a hobby

avocet /'ævəset/ *n* a black and white wading bird with webbed feet and a slender upward-curving bill

avoid /ə'vɔɪd/ *v* **1a** to keep away from; shun **b** to prevent the occurrence or effectiveness of **c** to refrain from **2** to make legally void – **~able** *adj* – **~ance** *n*

avoirdupois /,ævədə'pɔɪz, ,ævwɑːdjuː'pwɑː/, **avoirdupois weight** *n* the series of units of weight based on the pound of 16 ounces and the ounce of 16 drams

avow /ə'vaʊ/ *v* **1** to declare assuredly

2 to acknowledge openly, bluntly, and without shame – ~**al** *n*

avuncular /ə'vʌŋkjʊlə[r]/ *adj* **1** of an uncle **2** kindly, genial – ~**ly** *adv*

await /ə'weɪt/ *v* **1** to wait for **2** to be in store for

[1]**awake** /ə'weɪk/ *v* **awoke** *also* **awaked; awoken** **1** to emerge or arouse from sleep or a sleeplike state **2** to become conscious or aware of sthg – usu + *to* **3** to make active; stir up

[2]**awake** *adj* **1** roused (as if) from sleep **2** fully conscious; aware – usu + *to*

[1]**award** /ə'wɔːd/ *v* **1** to give by judicial decree **2** to confer or bestow as being deserved or needed

[2]**award** *n* **1** a final decision; *esp* the decision of arbitrators in a case submitted to them **2** sthg that is conferred or bestowed, esp on the basis of merit or need

aware /ə'weə[r]/ *adj* having or showing realization, perception, or knowledge; conscious – often + *of* – ~**ness** *n*

awash /ə'wɒʃ/ *adj* **1** covered with water; flooded **2** marked by an abundance

[1]**away** /ə'weɪ/ *adv* **1** on the way; along (e g get *away* early) **2** from here or there; hence, thence **3a** in a secure place or manner (e g locked *away*) **b** in another direction; aside (e g looked *away*) **4** out of existence; to an end (e g laze *away* an afternoon) **5** from one's possession (e g gave the car *away*) **6** on, uninterruptedly (e g chatted *away*)

[2]**away** *adj* **1** absent from a place; gone **2** distant (e g a town some way *away*) **3** played on an opponent's grounds

awe /ɔː/ *v or n* (to inspire with) an emotion compounded of dread, veneration, and wonder

awestruck /'ɔːstrʌk/ *also* **awestricken** *adj* filled with awe

[1]**awful** /'ɔːfəl/ *adj* **1** extremely disagreeable or objectionable **2** exceedingly great – used as an intensive; chiefly infml – ~**ly** *adv*

[2]**awful** *adv* very, extremely – nonstandard

awkward /'ɔːkwəd/ *adj* **1** lacking dexterity or skill, esp in the use of hands; clumsy **2** lacking ease or grace (e g of movement or expression) **3a** lacking social grace and assurance **b** causing embarrassment **4** poorly adapted for use or handling **5** requiring caution **6** deliberately thwarting or obstructive – ~**ly** *adv* – ~**ness** *n*

awl /ɔːl/ *n* a pointed instrument for marking surfaces or making small holes (e g in leather)

awning /'ɔːnɪŋ/ *n* **1** an often canvas rooflike cover, used to protect sthg (e g a shop window or a ship's deck) from sun or rain **2** a shelter resembling an awning

awoken /ə'wəʊkən/ *past part of* **awake**

awry /ə'raɪ/ *adv or adj* **1** in a turned or twisted position or direction; askew **2** out of the right or hoped-for course; amiss

[1]**axe** /æks/ *n* **1** a tool that has a cutting edge parallel to the handle and is used esp for felling trees and chopping and splitting wood **2** drastic reduction or removal (e g of personnel)

[2]**axe** *v* **1a** to hew, shape, dress, or trim with an axe **b** to chop, split, or sever with an axe **2** to remove abruptly (e g from employment or from a budget)

axiom /'æksɪəm/ *n* **1** a principle, rule, or maxim widely accepted on its intrinsic merit; a generally recognized truth **2a** a proposition regarded as a self-evident truth **b** a postulate – ~**atic** *adj* – ~**atically** *adv*

axis /'æksɨs/ *n, pl* **axes** **1** a straight line about which a body or a geometric figure rotates or may be supposed to rotate **2** a straight line with respect to which a body or figure is symmetrical **3** any of the reference lines of a coordinate system

axle /'æksəl/ *n* **1** a shaft on or with which a wheel revolves **2** a rod connecting a pair of wheels of a vehicle

axon /'æksɒn/ *n* a usu long projecting part of a nerve cell that usu conducts impulses away from the cell body

[1]**aye** /eɪ, aɪ/ *adv* ever, always

[2]**aye, aye, aye** *adv* yes – used as the correct reply to a naval order

azalea /ə'zeɪlɪə/ *n* any of a group of rhododendrons with funnel-shaped flowers and usu deciduous leaves

azimuth /'æzɨməθ/ *n* an arc of the horizon expressed as the clockwise angle measured between a fixed point (e g true N or true S) and the vertical circle passing through the centre of an object

azure /ˈæʒəʳ, ˈæʒjʊəʳ, ˈæzjʊəʳ/ *n* sky blue

B

b /biː/ *n, pl* **b's, bs** *often cap* **1a** (a graphic representation of or device for reproducing) the 2nd letter of the English alphabet **b** a speech counterpart of written *b* **2** one designated *b*, esp as the 2nd in order or class **3** a grade rating a student's work as good but short of excellent **4** sthg that is the supporting item of 2 things **5** – used euphemistically for any offensive word beginning with the letter *b*

baa /bɑː/ *v or n* (to make) the bleat of a sheep

babble /ˈbæbəl/ *v* **1a** to utter meaningless or unintelligible sounds **b** to talk foolishly; chatter **2** to make a continuous murmuring sound **3** to reveal by talk that is too free

babe /beɪb/ *n* **1** a naive inexperienced person **2a** an infant, baby – chiefly poetic **b** a girl, woman – slang; usu as a noun of address

Babel /ˈbeɪbəl/ *n, often not cap* **1** a confusion of sounds or voices **2** a scene of noise or confusion

baboon /bəˈbuːn/ *n* any of several large African and Asiatic primates having doglike muzzles and usu short tails

[1]**baby** /ˈbeɪbi/ *n* **1a(1)** an extremely young child; *esp* an infant **(2)** an unborn child **(3)** an extremely young animal **b** the youngest of a group **2** an infantile person **3** a person or thing for which one feels special responsibility or pride **4** a person; *esp* a girl, woman – slang; usu as a noun of address

[2]**baby** *adj* very small

[3]**baby** *v* to tend or indulge with often excessive or inappropriate care

baby-minder *n, chiefly Br* sby who minds babies or preschool children

baby-sit *v* to care for a child, usu for a short period while the parents are out – **~ter** *n*

baccarat /ˈbækərɑː/ *n* a three-handed card game usu associated with gambling

bacchanal /ˌbækəˈnæl, ˈbækənəl/ *n* **1a** a devotee of Bacchus, the Greek and Roman god of wine; *esp* one who takes part in a festival devoted to his riotous worship **b** a reveller **2** drunken revelry or carousal

baccy /ˈbæki/ *n, chiefly Br* tobacco – infml

bachelor /ˈbætʃələʳ/ *n* **1** a recipient of what is usu the lowest degree conferred by a college or university **2** an unmarried man **3** a male animal (e g a fur seal) without a mate during breeding time – **~hood** *n*

[1]**back** /bæk/ *n* **1a** the rear part of the human body, esp from the neck to the end of the spine **b** the corresponding part of a quadruped or other lower animal **2a** the side or surface behind the front or face; the rear part; *also* the farther or reverse side **b** sthg at or on the back for support **3** (the position of) a primarily defensive player in some games (e g soccer)

[2]**back** *adv* **1a(1)** to, towards, or at the rear **(2)** away (e g from the speaker) **b** in or into the past or nearer the beginning; ago **c** in or into a reclining position **d** in or into a delayed or retarded condition **2a** to, towards, or in a place from which sby or sthg came **b** to or towards a former state **c** in return or reply

[3]**back** *adj* **1a** at or in the back **b** distant from a central or main area; remote **2** being behindhand or in arrears **3** not current

[4]**back** *v* **1a** to support by material or moral assistance – often + *up* **b** to substantiate – often + *up* **c(1)** to countersign, endorse **(2)** to assume financial responsibility for **2** to cause to go back or in reverse **3a** to provide with a back **b** to be at the back of **4** to place a bet on (e g a horse) **5** to move backwards **6** *of the wind* to shift anticlockwise **7** to have the back in the direction of sthg

back bench *n* any of the benches in

Parliament on which rank and file members sit – usu pl – ~**er** *n*

backbite /ˈbækbaɪt/ *v* to say mean or spiteful things about (sby) – **-biting** *n*

backbone /ˈbækbəʊn/ *n* **1** the spinal column **2a** a chief mountain ridge, range, or system **b** the foundation or most substantial part of sthg **3** a firm and resolute character

backchat /ˈbæktʃæt/ *n, chiefly Br* impudent or argumentative talk made in reply, esp by a subordinate – infml

backcloth /ˈbæk-klɒθ/ *n, Br* **1** a painted cloth hung across the rear of a stage **2** a background or setting

backcomb /bæk-kəʊm/ *v* to comb (the hair) against the direction of growth starting with the short underlying hairs in order to produce a bouffant effect

backdate /ˌbækˈdeɪt/ *v* to apply (e g a pay rise) from a date in the past

back down *v* to retreat from a commitment or position

backdrop /ˈbækdrɒp/ *n* a backcloth

backer /ˈbækəʳ/ *n* **1** one who supports, esp financially **2** *Br* one who has placed a bet

[1]**backfire** /ˈbækfaɪəʳ/ *n* a premature explosion in the cylinder or an explosion in the exhaust system of an internal-combustion engine

[2]**backfire** /bækˈfaɪəʳ/ *v* **1** to make or undergo a backfire **2** to have the reverse of the desired or expected effect

backgammon /ˈbækgæmən/ *n* a board game played with dice and counters in which each player tries to move his/her counters along the board and at the same time to block or capture his/her opponent's counters

background /ˈbækgraʊnd/ *n* **1a** the scenery or ground behind sthg **b** the part of a painting or photograph that depicts what lies behind objects in the foreground **2** an inconspicuous position **3a** the conditions that form the setting within which sthg is experienced **b** information essential to the understanding of a problem or situation **c** the total of a person's experience, knowledge, and education

[1]**backhand** /ˈbækhænd/ *n* **1** a stroke in tennis, squash, etc made with the back of the hand turned in the direction of movement; *also* the side of the body on which this is made **2** handwriting whose strokes slant downwards from left to right

[2]**backhand** *adv* with a backhand

[3]**backhand** *v* to do, hit, or catch backhand

backhanded /ˌbækˈhændɪ̣d/ *adj* **1** using or made with a backhand **2** *of writing* being backhand **3** indirect, devious; *esp* sarcastic

backhander /ˈbækhændəʳ/ *n* **1** a backhanded blow or stroke **2** *Br* a backhanded remark **3** a bribe – infml

backing /ˈbækɪŋ/ *n* **1** sthg forming a back **2a** support, aid **b** endorsement

backlash /ˈbæklæʃ/ *n* **1** a sudden violent backward movement or reaction **2** a strong adverse reaction

backlog /ˈbæklɒg/ *n* **1** a reserve **2** an accumulation of tasks not performed, orders unfulfilled, or materials not processed

backmost /ˈbækməʊst/ *adj* farthest back

back number *n* sby or sthg that is out of date; *esp* an old issue of a periodical or newspaper

back out *v* to withdraw, esp from a commitment or contest

backpedal /ˌbækˈpedl/ *v* **1** to move backwards (e g in boxing) **2** to back down from or reverse a previous opinion or stand

backside /ˈbæksaɪd/ *n* the buttocks

backslide /ˈbækslaɪd/ *v* to lapse morally or in the practice of religion – **-slider** *n*

[1]**backstage** /bækˈsteɪdʒ/ *adv* **1** in or to a backstage area **2** in private, secretly

[2]**backstage** /ˈbæksteɪdʒ/ *adj* **1** of or occurring in the parts of a theatre that cannot be seen by the audience **2** of the inner working or operation (e g of an organization)

backstreet /ˈbækstriːt/ *adj* made, done, or acting illegally or surreptitiously

backstroke /ˈbækstrəʊk/ *n* a swimming stroke executed on the back

backtrack /ˈbæktræk/ *v* **1** to retrace

a path or course **2** to reverse a position or stand

backup /'bækʌp/ *n* **1** sby or sthg that serves as a substitute, auxiliary, or alternative **2** sby or sthg that gives support

back up *v* to support (sby), esp in argument or in playing a team game

backward /'bækwəd/ *adj* **1a** directed or turned backwards **b** done or executed backwards **2** retarded in development **3** of or occupying a fielding position in cricket behind the batsman's wicket – **~ly** *adv* – **~ness** *n*

backwards /'bækwədz/ *adv* **1** towards the back **2** with the back foremost **3** in a reverse direction; towards the beginning **4** perfectly; by heart **5** towards the past **6** towards a worse state

backwash /'bækwɒʃ/ *n* **1a** a backward movement in air, water, etc produced by a propelling force (e g the motion of oars) **b** the backward movement of a receding wave **2** a usu unwelcome consequence or by-product of an event; an aftermath

backwater /'bækwɔːtəʳ/ *n* **1** a stagnant pool or inlet kept filled by the opposing current of a river; *broadly* a body of water turned back in its course **2** a place or condition that is isolated or backward, esp intellectually

backwoods /'bækwʊdz/ *n, pl but sing or pl in constr* a remote or culturally backward area – usu + *the*

bacon /'beɪkən/ *n* (the meat cut from) the cured and often smoked side of a pig

bacteriology /bæk,tɪəri'ɒlədʒi/ *n* **1** a science that deals with bacteria **2** bacterial life and phenomena – **-ologist** *n*

bacterium /bæk'tɪəriəm/ *n, pl* **bacteria** a small, often disease-causing microorganism – **-rial** *adj*

[1]**bad** /bæd/ *adj* **worse; worst** **1a** failing to reach an acceptable standard; poor, inadequate **b** unfavourable **c** no longer acceptable, because of decay or disrepair **2a** morally objectionable **b** mischievous, disobedient **3** unskilful, incompetent – often + *at* **4** disagreeable, unpleasant **5a** injurious, harmful **b** worse than usual; severe **6** incorrect, faulty **7a** suffering pain or distress; unwell **b** unhealthy, diseased **8** sorry, unhappy **9** invalid, worthless **10** *of a debt* not recoverable – **~ness** *n* – **~ly** *adv*

[2]**bad** *n* an evil or unhappy state

bad blood *n* ill feeling; bitterness

bade /bæd, beɪd/ *past of* **bid**

badge /bædʒ/ *n* **1** a device or token, esp of membership in a society or group **2** a characteristic mark **3** an emblem awarded for a particular accomplishment

[1]**badger** /'bædʒəʳ/ *n* (the pelt or fur of) any of several sturdy burrowing nocturnal mammals widely distributed in the northern hemisphere

[2]**badger** *v* to harass or annoy persistently

badinage /'bædɪ̬nɑːʒ/ *n* playful repartee; banter

badminton /'bædmɪntən/ *n* a court game played with light long-handled rackets and a shuttle volleyed over a net

[1]**baffle** /'bæfl/ *v* to throw into puzzled confusion; perplex – **-ling** *adj* – **-lingly** *adv* – **~ment** *n*

[2]**baffle** *n* a structure that reduces the exchange of sound waves between the front and back of a loudspeaker

[1]**bag** /bæg/ *n* **1a** a usu flexible container for holding, storing, or carrying sthg **b** a handbag or shoulder bag **2** sthg resembling a bag; *esp* a sagging in cloth **3** spoils, loot **4** *pl chiefly Br* lots, masses – infml **5** a slovenly unattractive woman – slang **6** a way of life – slang

[2]**bag** *v* **1** to swell out; bulge **2** to hang loosely **3** to put into a bag **4a** to take (animals) as game **b** to get possession of, seize; *also* to steal

bagatelle /,bægə'tel/ *n* **1** a trifle; an unimportant matter **2** a game in which balls must be put into or through cups or arches at one end of an oblong table

baggage /'bægɪdʒ/ *n* **1** portable equipment, esp of a military force **2** superfluous or useless things, ideas, or practices **3** luggage, esp for travel by sea or air **4** a good-for-nothing woman; a pert girl – infml

baggy /'bægi/ *adj* loose, puffed out, or hanging like a bag

bags /bægz/ *n pl in constr* wide trousers

[1]**bail** /beɪl/ *n* **1** security deposited as a guarantee that sby temporarily freed from custody will return to stand trial **2** temporary release on bail **3** one who provides bail

[2]**bail** *v* **1** to deliver (property) in trust to another for a special purpose and for a limited period **2** to release on bail **3** to procure the release of (a person in custody) by giving bail – often + *out*

[3]**bail** *n* **1** either of the 2 crosspieces that lie on the stumps to form the wicket in cricket **2** *chiefly Br* a device for confining or separating animals

[4]**bail,** *Br also* **bale** *n* a container used to remove water from a boat

[5]**bail,** *Br also* **bale** *v* **1** to clear (water) from a boat by collecting in a bail, bucket etc and throwing over the side **2** to parachute from an aircraft *USE* usu + *out*

bailey /ˈbeɪli/ *n* (the space enclosed by) the outer wall of a castle or any of several walls surrounding the keep

Bailey bridge /ˈbeɪli/ *n* a prefabricated bridge built from interchangeable latticed steel panels

bailiff /ˈbeɪlɪf/ *n* **1** an official employed by a sheriff to serve writs, make arrests, etc **2** *chiefly Br* one who manages an estate or farm

bail out, *Br also* **bale out** *v* to help from a predicament; release from difficulty

bairn /beən/ *n, chiefly Scot & N Eng* a child

[1]**bait** /beɪt/ *v* **1** to provoke, tease, or exasperate with unjust, nagging, or persistent remarks **2** to harass (e g a chained animal) with dogs, usu for sport **3** to provide with bait

[2]**bait** *n* **1a** sthg used in luring, esp to a hook or trap **b** a poisonous material placed where it will be eaten by pests **2** a lure, temptation

baize /beɪz/ *n* a woollen cloth, resembling felt, used chiefly for covering and lining sthg (e g table tops or drawers)

bake /beɪk/ *v* **1** to dry or harden by subjecting to heat **2** to cook (food) by baking **3** to become baked **4** to become extremely hot – **~r** *n*

Bakelite /ˈbeɪkəlaɪt/ *trademark* – used for any of various synthetic resins and plastics

baker's dozen *n* thirteen

bakery /ˈbeɪkəri/ *n* a place for baking or selling baked goods, esp bread and cakes

baking powder *n* a powder that consists of a bicarbonate and an acid substance used in place of yeast as a raising agent in making scones, cakes, etc

baksheesh /ˈbækʃiːʃ/ *n* money given as a tip

balaclava /ˌbæləˈklɑːvə/, **balaclava helmet** *n, often cap B* a knitted pull-on hood that covers the ears, neck, and throat

balalaika /ˌbæleˈlaɪkə/ *n* a musical instrument of Russian origin, usu having 3 strings and a triangular body which is played by plucking

[1]**balance** /ˈbæləns/ *n* **1** an instrument for weighing **2** a counterbalancing weight, force, or influence **3** stability produced by even distribution of weight on each side of a vertical axis **4a** equilibrium between contrasting, opposing,, or interacting elements **b** equality between the totals of the 2 sides of an account **5** an aesthetically pleasing integration of elements **6** the ability to retain one's physical equilibrium **7** the weight or force of one side in excess of another **8a** (a statement of) the difference between credits and debits in an account **b** sthg left over; a remainder **c** an amount in excess, esp on the credit side of an account **9** mental and emotional steadiness

[2]**balance** *v* **1a(1)** to compute the difference between the debits and credits of (an account) **(2)** to pay the amount due on **b** to arrange so that one set of elements exactly equals another **2a** to counterbalance, offset **b** to equal or equalize in weight, number, or proportion **3** to compare the relative importance, value, force, or weight of; ponder **4** to bring to a state or position of balance **5** to become balanced or established in balance **6** to be an equal counterweight – often + *with*

balance of payments *n* the difference over a period of time between a country's payments to and receipts from abroad

balcony /'bælkəni/ *n* **1** a platform built out from the wall of a building and enclosed by a railing or low wall **2** a gallery inside a building (e g a theatre)

bald /bɔːld/ *adj* **1a** lacking a natural or usual covering (e g of hair, vegetation, or nap) **b** having little or no tread **2** unadorned, undisguised **3** *of an animal* marked with white, esp on the head or face – **~ness** *n*

balderdash /ˌbɔːldədæʃ/ *n* nonsense – often as a generalized expression of disagreement

[1]**bale** /beɪl/ *n* a large bundle of goods; *specif* a large closely pressed package of merchandise bound and usu wrapped for storage or transportation

[2]**bale** *n or v, Br* [4/5]**bail**

baleful /'beɪlfəl/ *adj* **1** deadly or pernicious in influence **2** gloomily threatening – **-fully** *adv*

bale out *v Br* bail out

balk, baulk /bɔːk, bɔːlk/ *v* **1** to stop short and refuse to continue **2** to refuse or turn down abruptly – usu + *at*

[1]**ball** /bɔːl/ *n* **1** a round or roundish body or mass: **a** a solid or hollow spherical or egg-shaped body used in a game or sport **b** a spherical or conical projectile; *also* projectiles used in firearms **c** the rounded slightly raised fleshy area at the base of a thumb or big toe **2** a delivery or play of the ball in cricket, baseball, etc **3** a game in which a ball is thrown, kicked, or struck; *specif, NAm* baseball **4a** a testis – usu pl; vulg **b** *pl* nonsense – often used interjectionally; vulg

[2]**ball** *v* **1** to form or gather into a ball **2** to have sexual intercourse (with) – vulg

[3]**ball** *n* **1** a large formal gathering for social dancing **2** a very pleasant experience; a good time – infml

ballad /'bæləd/ *n* **1** a narrative composition in rhythmic verse suitable for singing **2** a (slow, romantic or sentimental) popular, esp narrative, song

ballast /'bæləst/ *n* **1a** heavy material carried in a ship to improve stability **b** heavy material that is carried on a balloon or airship to steady it and can be jettisoned to control the rate of descent **2** sthg that gives stability, esp in character or conduct **3** gravel or broken stone laid in a bed for railway lines or the lower layer of roads

ball bearing *n* a bearing having minimal friction in which hardened steel balls roll easily in a groove between a shaft and a support; *also* any of the balls in such a bearing

ball cock *n* an automatic valve (e g in a cistern) controlled by the rise and fall of a float at the end of a lever

ballerina /ˌbælə'riːnə/ *n* a female, esp principal, ballet dancer

ballet /'bæleɪ/ *n* **1** (a group that performs) artistic dancing in which the graceful flowing movements are based on conventional positions and steps **2** a theatrical art form using ballet dancing, music, and scenery to convey a story, theme, or atmosphere

ballistics /bə'lɪstɪks/ *n pl but sing or pl in constr* **1** the science dealing with the motion of projectiles in flight **2** (the study of) the individual characteristics of and firing processes in a firearm or cartridge – **ballistic** *adj*

[1]**balloon** /bə'luːn/ *n* **1** an envelope filled with hot air or a gas lighter than air so as to rise and float in the atmosphere **2** an inflatable usu brightly coloured rubber bag used as a toy **3** a line enclosing words spoken or thought by a character, esp in a cartoon

[2]**balloon** *v* **1** to inflate, distend **2** to ascend or travel in a balloon **3** to swell or puff out; expand – often + *out* **4** to increase rapidly

[3]**balloon** *adj* relating to, resembling, or suggesting a balloon

ballooning /bə'luːnɪŋ/ *n* the act or sport of riding in a balloon – **-ist** *n*

[1]**ballot** /'bælət/ *n* **1** (a sheet of paper, or orig a small ball, used in) secret voting **2** the right to vote **3** the number of votes cast

[2]**ballot** *v* **1** to vote by ballot **2** to ask for a vote from

ballpoint /'bɔːlpɔɪnt/ *n* a pen having as the writing point a small rotating metal ball that inks itself by contact with an inner magazine

balls-up *n* a state of muddled confusion caused by a mistake – slang

balls up *v* to make or become badly muddled or confused – slang

ballyhoo /ˌbæliˈhuː/ *n* flamboyant, exaggerated, or sensational advertising or propaganda

balm /bɑːm/ *n* **1** an aromatic preparation (e g a healing ointment) **2** any of various aromatic plants of the mint family **3** sthg that soothes, relieves, or heals physically or emotionally

balmy /ˈbɑːmi/ *adj* **1a** having the qualities of balm; soothing **b** mild **2** barmy

balsa /ˈbɔːlsə/ *n* (the strong very light wood of) a tropical American tree

balsam /ˈbɔːlsəm/ *n* **1** (a preparation containing) an oily and resinous substance flowing from various plants **2a** any of several trees yielding balsam **b** any of a widely distributed genus of watery-juiced annual plants (e g touch-me-not) **3** sthg soothing

balustrade /ˌbæləˈstreɪd/ *n* a row of low pillars topped by a rail; *also* a usu low parapet or barrier

bamboo /ˌbæmˈbuː/ *n* any of various chiefly tropical giant grasses including some with strong hollow stems used for building, furniture, or utensils

bamboo curtain *n, often cap B&C* a political, military, and ideological barrier between China and the capitalist world

bamboozle /bæmˈbuːzəl/ *v* to deceive by trickery

[1]**ban** /bæn/ *v* to prohibit, esp by legal means or social pressure

[2]**ban** *n* **1** an ecclesiastical curse; excommunication **2** a legal or social prohibition

banal /bəˈnɑːl, bəˈnæl/ *adj* lacking originality, freshness, or novelty; trite, hackneyed – **~ity** *n*

banana /bəˈnɑːnə/ *n* (a tropical tree that bears) an elongated usu tapering fruit with soft pulpy flesh enclosed in a soft usu yellow rind that grows in bunches

banana republic *n* a small tropical country that is politically unstable and usu economically underdeveloped – derog

[1]**band** /bænd/ *n* **1** a strip or belt serving to join or hold things together **2** a ring of elastic **3** a more or less well-defined range of wavelengths, frequencies, or energies of light waves, radio waves, sound waves, etc **4** a narrow strip serving chiefly as decoration: e g **a** a narrow strip of material applied as trimming to an article of dress **b** *pl* 2 cloth strips sometimes worn at the front of the neck as part of clerical, legal, or academic dress **5** a strip distinguishable in some way (e g by colour, texture, or composition) **6** *Br* a group of pupils assessed as being of broadly similar ability

[2]**band** *v* **1** to fasten a band to or tie up with a band **2** *Br* to divide (pupils) into bands **3** to unite for a common purpose; confederate – often + *together*

[3]**band** *n sing or pl in constr* a group of people, animals, or things; *esp* a group of musicians organized for ensemble playing and using chiefly woodwind, brass, and percussion instruments

bandage /ˈbændɪdʒ/ *n* a strip of fabric used esp to dress and bind up wounds

bandanna, bandana /bænˈdænə/ *n* a large coloured and patterned handkerchief

bandit /ˈbændɨt/ *n, pl* **bandits** *also* **banditti** **1** an outlaw; *esp* a member of a band of marauders **2** a political terrorist – **~ry** *n*

bandoleer, bandolier /ˌbændəˈlɪəʳ/ *n* a cartridge belt usu worn over the shoulder and across the chest

bandsman /ˈbændzmən/ *n* a member of a musical band

bandstand /ˈbændstænd/ *n* a usu roofed stand or platform for a band to perform on outdoors

bandwagon /ˈbændˌwægən/ *n* a party, faction, or cause that attracts adherents by its timeliness, momentum, etc

[1]**bandy** /ˈbændi/ *v* **1** to exchange (words) in an argumentative, careless, or lighthearted manner **2** to use in a glib or offhand manner – often + *about*

[2]**bandy** *adj* **1** *of legs* bowed **2** bowlegged

bane /beɪn/ *n* **1** poison – esp in combination **2** a cause of death, ruin, or trouble – **~ful** *adj* – **~fully** *adv*

[1]**bang** /bæŋ/ *v* **1** to strike sharply; bump **2** to knock, beat, or strike hard,

often with a sharp noise **3** to have sexual intercourse with – vulg **4** to strike with a sharp noise or thump **5** to produce a sharp often explosive noise or noises

[2]**bang** *n* **1** a resounding blow; a thump **2** a sudden loud noise – often used interjectionally **3** an act of sexual intercourse – vulg

[3]**bang** *adv* **1** right, directly **2** exactly *USE* infml

[4]**bang** *n* a short squarely-cut fringe of hair – usu pl with sing. meaning

banger /ˈbæŋəʳ/ *n, Br* **1** a firework that explodes with a loud bang **2** a sausage **3** an old usu dilapidated car *USE* (*2&3*) infml

bangle /ˈbæŋgəl/ *n* a bracelet or anklet

bang-on *adj or adv, Br* just what is needed; first-rate – infml

banish /ˈbænɪʃ/ *v* **1** to require by authority to leave a place, esp a country **2** to dispel – **~ment** *n*

banister *also* **bannister** /ˈbænɪ̣stəʳ/ *n* a handrail with its upright supports guarding the edge of a staircase – often pl with sing. meaning

banjo /ˈbændʒəʊ/ *n, pl* **banjos** *also* **banjoes** a stringed instrument with a drumlike body that is strummed with the fingers

[1]**bank** /bæŋk/ *n* **1a** a mound, pile, or ridge (e g of earth or snow) **b** a piled up mass of cloud or fog **c** an undersea elevation rising esp from the continental shelf **2** the rising ground bordering a lake or river or forming the edge of a cut or hollow **3** the lateral inward tilt of a surface along a curve or of a vehicle when following a curved path

[2]**bank** *v* **1** to surround with a bank **2** to keep *up* to ensure slow burning **3** to build (a road or railway) with the outer edge of a curve higher than the inner **4** to rise in or form a bank – often + *up* **5** to incline an aircraft sideways when turning **6** to follow a curve or incline, specif in racing

[3]**bank** *n* **1** a bench for the rowers of a galley

[4]**bank** *n* **1** an establishment for the custody, loan, exchange, or issue of money and for the transmission of funds **2** a person conducting a gambling house or game; *specif* the banker in a game of cards **3** a supply of sthg held in reserve: e g **a** the money, chips, etc held by the bank or banker for use in a gambling game **b** the pool of pieces belonging to a game (e g dominoes) from which the players draw **4** a place where data, human organs, etc are held available for use when needed

[5]**bank** **1** to deposit (money) or have an account in a bank **2** to rely or count *on*

bankbook /ˈbæŋkbʊk/ *n* the depositor's book in which a bank enters a record of his/her account

[1]**banker** /ˈbæŋkəʳ/ *n* **1** one who engages in the business of banking **2** the player who keeps the bank in various games

banker's card *n, Br* a cheque card

bank holiday *n often cap B&H* a public holiday in the British Isles on which banks and most businesses are closed by law

banking /ˈbæŋkɪŋ/ *n* the business of a bank or a banker

[1]**bankrupt** /ˈbæŋkrʌpt/ *n* **1** an insolvent person whose estate is administered under the bankruptcy laws for the benefit of his/her creditors **2** one who is destitute of a usu specified quality or thing

[2]**bankrupt** *v* **1** to reduce to bankruptcy **2** to impoverish

[3]**bankrupt** *adj* **1** reduced to a state of financial ruin; *specif* legally declared a bankrupt **2a** broken, ruined **b** destitute – + *of* or *in* – **~cy** *n*

banner /ˈbænəʳ/ *n* **1** a usu square flag bearing heraldic arms; *broadly* a flag **2** a headline in large type running across a newspaper page **3** a strip of cloth on which a sign is painted **4** a name, slogan, or goal associated with a particular group or ideology – often + *under*

bannock /ˈbænək/ *n* a usu unleavened flat bread or biscuit made with oatmeal or barley meal

banns /bænz/ *n pl* the public announcement, esp in church, of a proposed marriage – chiefly in *publish/read the banns*

banquet /ˈbæŋkwɪ̣t/ *n, v* (to provide with or partake of) an elaborate ceremonial meal for numerous people often in honour of a person; (to have) a feast

banshee /bæn'ʃiː/ *n* a female spirit in Gaelic folklore whose wailing warns of approaching death in a household

bantam /'bæntəm/ *n* any of numerous small domestic fowl

bantamweight /'bæntəmweɪt/ *n* a boxer who weighs not more than 8st 6lb (about 53.5kg) if professional or more than 51kg (about 8st) but not more than 54kg (about 8st 7lb) if amateur

[1]**banter** /'bæntəʳ/ *v* to speak or act playfully or wittily

[2]**banter** *n* good-natured repartee; badinage

baptism /'bæptɪzəm/ *n* **1** the ritual use of water for purification, esp in the Christian sacrament of admission to the church **2** an act, experience, or ordeal by which one is purified, sanctified, initiated, or named – **~al** *adj* – **-tize** *v*

baptist /'bæptɨst/ *n* **1** one who baptizes **2** *cap* a member of a Protestant denomination which reserves baptism for full believers

[1]**bar** /bɑːʳ/ *n* **1** a straight piece (e g of wood or metal), that is longer than it is wide and has any of various uses (e g as a lever, support, barrier, or fastening) **2a** the extinction of a claim in law **b** an intangible or nonphysical impediment **c** a submerged or partly submerged bank (e g of sand) along a shore or in a river, often obstructing navigation **3a** the dock in a law court; *also* the railing that encloses the dock **b** *often cap* (1) *sing or pl in constr* the whole body of barristers (2) the profession of barrister **4a** a stripe or chevron **b** a strip of metal attached to a military medal to indicate an additional award of the medal **5a(1)** a counter at which food or esp alcoholic drinks are served (2) a room or establishment whose main feature is a bar for the serving of alcoholic drinks **b** a place where goods, esp a specified commodity, are sold or served across a counter **6** (a group of musical notes and rests that add up to a prescribed time value, bounded on each side on the staff by) a bar line **7** a small loop or crosspiece of oversewn threads used, esp on garments, as a fastening (e g for a hook), for joining, or for strengthening sthg

[2]**bar** *v* **1a** to fasten with a bar **b** to place bars across to prevent movement in, out, or through **2** to mark with stripes **3a** to shut in or out (as if) by bars **b** to set aside the possibility of; rule out **4a** to interpose legal objection to **b** to prevent, forbid

[3]**bar** *prep* except

[4]**bar** *adv, of odds in betting* being offered for all the unnamed competitors

[1]**barb** /bɑːb/ *n* **1a** a sharp projection extending backwards from the point of an arrow, fishhook, etc, and preventing easy extraction **b** a biting or pointedly critical remark or comment **2** any of the side branches of the shaft of a feather **3** a plant hair or bristle ending in a hook

[2]**barb** *v* to provide (e g an arrow) with a barb

barbarian /bɑː'beərɪən/ *adj* **1** of a land, culture, or people alien and usu believed to be inferior to and more savage than one's own **2** lacking refinement, learning, or artistic or literary culture – **barbarian** *n*

barbaric /bɑː'bærɪk/ *adj* **1** (characteristic) of barbarians; *esp* uncivilized **2** savage, barbarous – **-barize** *v* – **-barism** *n* – **~ally** *adv*

barbarity /bɑː'bærɨti/ *n* **1** barbarism **2** (an act or instance of) barbarous cruelty; inhumanity

barbarous /'bɑːbərəs/ *adj* **1** uncivilized **2** lacking culture or refinement **3** mercilessly harsh or cruel – **~ly** *adv*

[1]**barbecue** /'bɑːbɪkjuː/ *n* **1** a (portable) fireplace over which meat and fish are roasted **2** meat roasted over an open fire or barbecue pit **3** a social gathering, esp in the open air, at which barbecued food is served

[2]**barbecue** *v* to roast or grill on a rack over hot coals or on a revolving spit in front of or over a source of cooking heat, esp an open fire

barbed /bɑːbd/ *adj* **1** having barbs **2** characterized by pointed and biting criticism

barbed wire *n* twisted wires armed at intervals with sharp points

[1]**barbel** /'bɑːbəl/ *n* a European freshwater fish with 4 barbels on its upper jaw

[2]**barbel** *n* a slender tactile projecting organ on the lips of certain fishes (e g catfish) used in locating food

barber /'bɑːbəʳ/ *n* sby, esp a man, whose occupation is cutting and dressing men's hair and shaving

barber's pole *n* a red and white striped pole fixed to the front of a barber's shop

barbiturate /bɑː'bɪtʃʊrɪ̥t/ *n* any of several drugs that are used esp in the treatment of epilepsy and were formerly much used in sleeping pills

barcarole, barcarolle /,bɑːkə'rəʊl/ *n* (music imitating) a Venetian boat song with a beat suggesting a rowing rhythm

[1]**bard** /bɑːd/ *n* **1** sby, specif a Celtic poet-singer, who composed, sang, or recited verses on heroes and their deeds **2** a poet; *specif* one recognized or honoured at an eisteddfod **3** *cap* – used as an epithet for Shakespeare; + *the*

[2]**bard** *n* a strip of pork fat, bacon, etc for covering lean meat before roasting

[1]**bare** /beəʳ/ *adj* **1** lacking a natural, usual, or appropriate covering, esp clothing **2** open to view; exposed – often in *lay bare* **3a** unfurnished, empty **b** destitute *of* **4a** having nothing left over or added; scant, mere **b** undisguised, unadorned – ~**ness** *n*

[2]**bare** *v* to make or lay bare; uncover, reveal

bareback /'beəbæk/, **barebacked** *adv or adj* on the bare back of a horse without a saddle

barefaced /,beə'feɪst/ *adj* lacking scruples; shameless – ~**ly** *adv*

barely /'beəli/ *adv* **1** scarcely, hardly **2** in a meagre manner; scantily

[1]**bargain** /'bɑːgɪ̥n/ *n* **1** an agreement between parties concerning the terms of a transaction between them or the course of action each pursues in respect to the other **2** an advantageous purchase

[2]**bargain** *v* **1** to negotiate over the terms of a purchase, agreement, or contract **2** to come to terms; agree **3** to be prepared *for*

[1]**barge** /bɑːdʒ/ *n* **1a** a flat-bottomed boat used chiefly for the transport of goods on inland waterways or between ships and the shore **b** a flat-bottomed coastal sailing vessel with leeboards instead of a keel **2a** a large naval motorboat used by flag officers **b** an ornate carved vessel used on ceremonial occasions

[2]**barge** *v* **1** to move in a headlong or clumsy fashion **2** to intrude *in* or *into*

bargee /bɑː'dʒiː/ *n, Br* sby who works on a barge

baritone /'bærɪ̥təʊn/ *n* **1** (a person with) a male singing voice between bass and tenor **2** a member of a family of instruments having a range next below that of the tenor

barium /'beərɪəm/ *n* a soft bivalent metallic element of the alkaline-earth group

[1]**bark** /bɑːk/ *v* **1** to make (a sound similar to) the short loud cry characteristic of a dog **2** to speak or utter in a curt, loud, and usu angry tone; snap

[2]**bark** *n* **1** (a sound similar to) the sound made by a barking dog **2** a short sharp peremptory utterance

[3]**bark** *n* the tough exterior covering of a woody root or stem

[4]**bark** *v* to abrade the skin of

[5]**bark** *n* a boat – poetic

barley /'bɑːli/ *n* a widely cultivated cereal grass whose seed is used to make malt and in foods and stock feeds

barley wine *n* a strong ale

barman /'bɑːmən/, *fem* **barmaid** *n* one who serves drinks in a bar

bar mitzvah /,bɑː 'mɪtsvə/ *n, often cap B&M* (the initiatory ceremony of) a Jewish youth of 13 who assumes adult religious duties and responsibilities

barmy /'bɑːmi/ *adj* slightly mad; foolish – infml

barn /bɑːn/ *n* **1** a usu large farm building for storage, esp of feed, cereal products, etc **2** an unusually large and usu bare building

barnacle /'bɑːnəkəl/ *n* any of numerous marine crustaceans that are free-swimming as larvae but fixed to rocks or floating objects as adults

barn dance *n* a type of country dance, esp a round dance or a square dance with called instructions; *also* a social gathering for such dances

barnyard /'bɑːnjɑːd/ *n* a farmyard

barometer /bə'rɒmɨtəʳ/ *n* **1** an instrument for determining the pressure of the atmosphere and hence for assisting in predicting the weather or measuring the height of an ascent **2** sthg that serves to register fluctuations (e g in public opinion) – **-metric** *adj* – **-metrically** *adv*

baron /'bærən/ *n* **1** a lord of the realm **2a** a member of the lowest rank of the peerage in Britain **b** a European nobleman **3** a man of great power or influence in a specified field of activity **4** a joint of meat consisting of 2 loins or sirloins joined by the backbone – **~ial** *adj*

baroness /'bærənɨs/ *n* **1** the wife or widow of a baron **2** a woman having in her own right the rank of a baron

baronet /'bærənɨt, -net/ *n* the holder of a rank of honour below a baron and above a knight – **~cy** *n*

barony /'bærəni/ *n* the domain or rank of a baron

baroque /bə'rɒk, bə'rəʊk/ *adj* (typical) of a style of artistic expression prevalent esp in the 17th c that is marked by extravagant forms and elaborate and sometimes grotesque ornamentation

barque /bɑːk/ *n* a sailing vessel with the rearmost of usu 3 masts fore-and-aft rigged and the others square-rigged

[1]**barrack** /'bærək/ *n* **1** (a set or area of) buildings for lodging soldiers in garrison – often pl with sing. meaning but sing. or pl in constr **2** a large building characterized by extreme plainness or dreary uniformity with others – usu pl with sing. meaning but sing. or pl in constr

[2]**barrack** *v* to lodge in barracks

[3]**barrack** *v chiefly Br* to jeer, scoff (a)

barracuda /,bærə'kjuːdə/ *n, pl* **barracuda,** *esp for different types* **barracudas** any of several predatory fishes of warm seas that include excellent food fishes as well as forms regarded as poisonous

barrage /'bærɑːʒ/ *n* **1** a barrier, esp of intensive artillery fire, to hinder enemy action **2** a rapid series (e g of questions) – **barrage** *v*

barrel /'bærəl/ *n* **1** an approximately cylindrical vessel with bulging sides and flat ends constructed from wooden staves bound together with hoops; *also* any similar vessel **2** a drum or cylindrical part: e g **a** the discharging tube of a gun **b** the part of a fountain pen or pencil containing the ink or lead

barrel organ *n* a musical instrument consisting of a revolving cylinder studded with pegs that open a series of valves to admit air from a bellows to a set of pipes

barren /'bærən/ *adj* **1a** *of a female or mating* incapable of producing offspring **b** habitually failing to fruit **2** not productive; *esp* producing inferior or scanty vegetation **3** lacking, devoid *of* **4** lacking interest, information, or charm – **~ness** *n*

[1]**barricade** /'bærɨkeɪd, ,bærɨ'keɪd/ *v* **1** to block off, stop up, or defend with a barricade **2** to prevent access to by means of a barricade

[2]**barricade** *n* **1** an obstruction or rampart thrown up across a way or passage to check the advance of the enemy **2** a barrier, obstacle

barrier /'bærɪəʳ/ *n* **1** a material object (e g a stockade, fortress, or railing) or set of objects that separates, demarcates, or serves as a barricade **2** sthg immaterial that impedes or separates **3** a factor that tends to restrict the free movement, mingling, or interbreeding of individuals or populations

barring /'bɑːrɪŋ/ *prep* excepting

barrister /'bærɨstəʳ/ *n* a lawyer who has the right to plead as an advocate in an English or Welsh superior court

[1]**barrow** /'bærəʊ/ *n* a large mound of earth or stones over the remains of the dead; a tumulus

[2]**barrow** *n* a cart with a shallow box body, 2 wheels, and shafts for pushing it

[1]**barter** /'bɑːtəʳ/ *v* **1** to trade by

exchanging one commodity for another without the use of money **2** to part with unwisely or for an unworthy return – + *away*

[2]**barter** *n* the carrying on of trade by bartering

basalt /'bæsɔːlt, bə'sɔːlt/ *n* a dense to fine-grained dark igneous rock

[1]**base** /beɪs/ *n* **1a** the bottom of sthg; a foundation **b** the lower part of a wall, pier, or column considered as a separate architectural feature **c** that part of an organ by which it is attached to another structure nearer the centre of a living organism **2** a main ingredient **3** the fundamental part of sthg; a basis **4a** a centre from which a start is made in an activity or from which operations proceed **b** a line in a survey which serves as the origin for computations **c** the locality or installations on which a military force relies for supplies or from which it starts operations **d** the basis from which a word is derived **5a** the starting place or goal in various games **b** any of the stations at each of the 4 corners of the inner part of a baseball field to which a batter must run in turn in order to score a run **6** any of various typically water-soluble and acrid or brackish tasting chemical compounds that are capable of taking up a hydrogen ion from or donating an unshared pair of electrons to an acid to form a salt

[2]**base** *v* **1** to make, form, or serve as a base for **2** to use as a base or basis for; establish, found – usu + *on* or *upon*

[3]**base** *adj* constituting or serving as a base

[4]**base** *adj* **1** *of a metal* of comparatively low value and having relatively inferior properties (e g resistance to corrosion) **2** lacking higher values; degrading **3** of relatively little value – **~ly** *adv* – **~ness** *n*

baseball /'beɪsbɔːl/ *n* (the ball used in) a game played with a bat and ball between 2 teams of 9 players each on a large field centring on 4 bases arranged in a square that mark the course a batter must run to score

baseborn /'beɪsbɔːn/ *adj* of humble or illegitimate birth

baseline /'beɪslaɪn/ *n* the back line at each end of a court in tennis, badminton, etc

basement /'beɪsmənt/ *n* the part of a building that is wholly or partly below ground level

[1]**bash** /bæʃ/ *v* **1** to strike violently; *also* to injure or damage by striking; smash – often + *in* or *up* **2** to make a violent attack on *USE* infml

[2]**bash** *n* **1** a forceful blow **2** *chiefly Br* a try, attempt **3** a festive social gathering; a party *USE* infml

bashful /'bæʃfəl/ *adj* **1** socially shy or timid **2** characterized by, showing, or resulting from extreme sensitiveness or self-consciousness – **-fully** *adv* – **-fulness** *n*

[1]**basic** /'beɪsɪk, -zɪk/ *adj* **1** of or forming the base or essence; fundamental **2** constituting or serving as the minimum basis or starting point **3** of, containing, or having the character of a chemical base

[2]**basic** *n* sthg basic; a fundamental

BASIC *n* a high-level computer language for programming and interacting with a computer in a wide variety of applications

basil /'bæzəl/ *n* any of several plants of the mint family used as a kitchen herb

basilica /bə'zɪlɪkə, bə'sɪ-/ *n* **1** an oblong building used in ancient Rome as a place of assembly or as a lawcourt and usu ending in an apse **2** an early Christian church similar to a Roman basilica **3** a Roman Catholic church given certain ceremonial privileges

basin /'beɪsən/ *n* **1a** a round open usu metal or ceramic vessel with a greater width than depth and sides that slope or curve inwards to the base, used typically for holding water for washing **b** a bowl with a greater depth than width esp for holding, mixing, or cooking food **c** the contents of a basin **2a** a dock built in a tidal river or harbour **b** a (partly) enclosed water area, esp for ships **3a** a depression in the surface of the land or ocean floor **b** the region drained by a river and its tributaries

basis /'beɪsɨ̣s/ *n, pl* **bases** **1** a foundation **2** the principal component of sthg **3** a basic principle or way of proceeding

bask /bɑːsk/ *v* **1** to lie in, or expose oneself to, a pleasant warmth or atmosphere **2** to enjoy sby's favour or approval – usu + *in*

basket /'bɑːskʒ̍t/ *n* **1a** a rigid or semirigid receptacle made of interwoven material (e g osiers, cane, wood, or metal) **b** any of various lightweight usu wood containers **c** the contents of a basket **2** sthg that resembles a basket, esp in shape or use **3** a net open at the bottom and suspended from a metal ring that constitutes the goal in basketball **4** a collection, group

basketball /'bɑːskʒ̍tbɔːl/ *n* (the ball used in) an indoor court game between 2 teams of 5 players each who score by tossing a large ball through a raised basket

basketry /'bɑːskʒ̍tri/ *n* (the art or craft of making) baskets or objects woven like baskets

bas-relief /ˌbɑː rɪ'liːf, bæs-/ *n* sculptural relief in which the design projects very slightly from the surrounding surface

[1]**bass** /bæs/ *n, pl* **bass,** *esp for different types* **basses** any of numerous edible spiny-finned fishes

[2]**bass** /beɪs/ *adj* **1** deep or grave in tone **2a** of low pitch **b** of or having the range or part of a bass

[3]**bass** /beɪs/ *n* **1** the lowest part in 4-part harmony **2a** (a person with) the lowest adult male singing voice **b** a member of a family of instruments having the lowest range; *esp* a double bass or bass guitar

bass clef *n* a clef placing the F below middle C on the fourth line of the staff

basset /'bæsʒ̍t/ *n* (any of) a breed of short-legged hunting dogs with very long ears

bassoon /bə'suːn/ *n* a double-reed woodwind instrument with a usual range 2 octaves lower than the oboe

[1]**bastard** /'bæstəd, bɑː-/ *n* **1** an illegitimate child **2** sthg spurious, irregular, inferior, or of questionable origin **3a** an offensive or disagreeable person **b** a fellow of a usu specified type – infml

[2]**bastard** *adj* **1** illegitimate **2** of an inferior or less typical type, stock, or form **3** lacking genuineness or authority; false – **~ize** *v*

[1]**baste** /beɪst/ *v* to tack (fabric, etc)

[2]**baste** *v* to moisten (e g meat) at intervals with melted butter, dripping, etc during cooking, esp roasting

bastion /'bæstɪən/ *n* **1** a projecting part of a fortification **2** a fortified area or position **3** sthg considered a stronghold; a bulwark

[1]**bat** /bæt/ *n* **1** a stout solid stick; a club **2** a sharp blow; a stroke **3** a (wooden) implement used for hitting the ball in cricket, baseball, table tennis, etc **4a** a batsman **b** a turn at batting in cricket, baseball, etc

[2]**bat** *v* **1** to strike or hit (as if) with a bat **2** to strike a ball with a bat **3** to take one's turn at batting, esp in cricket – **batter** *n*

[3]**bat** *n* any of an order of nocturnal flying mammals with forelimbs modified to form wings

[4]**bat** *v* to blink, esp in surprise or emotion

batch /bætʃ/ *n* **1** the quantity baked at 1 time **2** the quantity of material produced at 1 operation or for use at 1 time **3** a group of people or things; a lot

[1]**bath** /bɑːθ/ *n* **1** a washing or soaking (e g in water or steam) of all or part of the body **2a** water used for bathing **b** a vessel for bathing in; *esp* one that is permanently fixed in a bathroom **c** (a vat, tank, etc holding) a specified type of liquid used for a special purpose (e g to keep samples at a constant temperature) **3a** a building containing an apartment or a series of rooms designed for bathing **b** a swimming pool – usu pl with sing. meaning but sing. or pl in constr **c** a spa ***USE*** (*3a&3c*) usu pl with sing. meaning

[2]**bath** *v, Br* **1** to give a bath to **2** to take a bath

bath chair *n, often cap B* a usu hooded wheelchair

[1]**bathe** /beɪð/ *v* **1** to wash or soak in a liquid (e g water) **2** to moisten **3** to apply water or a liquid medicament to **4** to suffuse, esp with light **5** to take a bath **6** to swim (e g in the sea or a river) for pleasure **7** to become immersed or absorbed

[2]**bathe** *n, Br* an act of bathing, esp in the sea

bathos /'beɪθɒs/ *n* **1** a sudden descent from the sublime to the commonplace or absurd; an anticlimax **2** exceptional commonplaceness; triteness

bathrobe /'bɑːθrəʊb/ *n* a loose usu absorbent robe worn before and after having a bath

bathroom /'bɑːθrʊm, -ruːm/ *n* **1** a room containing a bath or shower and usu a washbasin and toilet **2** a toilet – chiefly euph

bathyscaphe /'bæθɪ̬skeɪf, -skæf/ *n* a navigable submersible ship for deep-sea exploration

batik /'bætɪk/ *n* (a fabric or design printed by) an Indonesian method of hand-printing by coating with wax the parts to be left undyed

batman /'bætmən/ *n* a British officer's servant

baton /'bætɒn/ *n* **1** a cudgel, truncheon **2** a staff borne as a symbol of office **3** a wand with which a conductor directs a band or orchestra **4** a stick or hollow cylinder passed by each member of a relay team to the succeeding runner

bats /bæts/ *adj, chiefly Br* batty – infml

batsman /'bætsmən/ *n* sby who bats or is batting, esp in cricket

battalion /bə'tælɪən/ *n sing or pl in constr* **1** a large body of organized troops **2** a military unit composed of a headquarters and 2 or more companies **3** a large group

[1]**batten** /bætən/ *n* **1** a thin narrow strip of squared timber **2a** a thin strip of wood, plastic, etc inserted into a sail to keep it flat and taut **b** a slat used to secure the tarpaulins and hatch covers of a ship **3** a strip holding a row of floodlights

[2]**batten** *v* **1** to provide or fasten (e g hatches) with battens – often + *down* **2** to make oneself selfishly dependent *on* **3** to seize *on* (an excuse, argument, etc)

[1]**batter** /'bætəʳ/ *v* **1** to beat persistently or hard so as to bruise, shatter, or demolish **2** to wear or damage by hard usage or blows **3** to strike heavily and repeatedly; beat

[2]**batter** *n* a mixture that consists essentially of flour, egg, and milk or water and is thin enough to pour or drop from a spoon; *also* batter mixture when cooked

battering ram *n* an ancient military siege engine consisting of a large wooden beam with a head of iron used for beating down walls

battery /'bætəri/ *n* **1a** the act of battering **b** the unlawful application of any degree of force to a person without his/her consent **2** *sing or pl in constr* a tactical and administrative army artillery unit equivalent to an infantry company **3** one or more cells connected together to provide an electric current **4a** a number of similar articles, items, or devices arranged, connected, or used together; a set, series **b(1)** a large number of small cages in which egg-laying hens are kept **(2)** a series of cages or compartments for raising or fattening animals, esp poultry **c** an impressive or imposing group; an array **5** the position of readiness of a gun for firing

[1]**battle** /'bætl/ *n* **1** a general hostile encounter between armies, warships, aircraft, etc **2** a combat between 2 people **3** an extended contest, struggle, or controversy

[2]**battle** *v* **1** to engage in battle; fight against **2** to contend with full strength, craft, or resources; struggle **3** to force (e g one's way) by battling

battle-axe *n* a quarrelsome domineering woman

battle cruiser *n* a large heavily-armed warship faster than a battleship

battle royal *n, pl* **battles royal, battle royals** a violent struggle or heated dispute

battleship /'bætl,ʃɪp/ *n* the largest and most heavily armed and armoured type of warship

batty /'bæti/ *adj* mentally unstable; crazy – infml

bauble /'bɔːbəl/ *n* **1** a trinket or trifle **2** a jester's staff

baulk /bɔːk, bɔːlk/ *v or n, chiefly Br* (to) balk

bauxite /'bɔːksaɪt/ *n* the principal ore of aluminium

[1]**bawdy** /'bɔːdi/ *adj* boisterously or humorously indecent

[2]**bawdy** *n* suggestive, coarse, or obscene language

bawl /bɔːl/ *v* **1** to yell, bellow **2** to cry, wail

[1]**bay** /beɪ/ *n* **1** a horse with a bay-coloured body and black mane, tail, and points **2** a reddish brown colour

[2]**bay** *n* **1** any of several shrubs or trees resembling the laurel **2** an honorary garland or crown, esp of laurel, given for victory or excellence

[3]**bay** *n* **1** a division of a part of a building (e g the walls or roof) or of the whole building **2** a main division of a structure; *esp* a compartment in the fuselage of an aircraft

[4]**bay** *v* to bark with prolonged tones

[5]**bay** *n* the position of one unable to retreat and forced to face a foe or danger

[6]**bay** *n* (a land formation resembling) an inlet of a sea, lake, etc, usu smaller than a gulf

bay leaf *n* the leaf of the European laurel used dried in cooking

[1]**bayonet** /'beɪənɪ̥t, -net/ *n* a blade attached to the muzzle of a firearm and used in hand-to-hand combat

[2]**bayonet** *v* to stab or drive (as if) with a bayonet

bay window *n* a window or series of windows projecting outwards from the wall

bazaar /bə'zɑːʳ/ *n* **1** an (Oriental) market consisting of rows of shops or stalls selling miscellaneous goods **2** a fair for the sale of miscellaneous articles, esp for charitable purposes

bazooka /bə'zuːkə/ *n* an individual infantry antitank rocket launcher

be /bɪ; *strong* biː/ *v, pres 1 sing* **am;** *2 sing* **are;** *3 sing* **is;** *pl* **are;** *pres subjunctive* **be;** *pres part* **being;** *past 1&3 sing* **was;** *2 sing* **were;** *pl* **were;** *past subjunctive* **were;** *past part* **been** **1a** to equal in meaning; have the same connotation as (e g Venus *is* the evening star) **b** to represent, symbolize **c** to have identity with **d** to belong to the class of **e** to occupy a specified position in space (e g Dundee *is* in Scotland) **f** to take place at a specified time; occur (e g that concert *was* yesterday) **g** to have a specified qualification, destination, origin, occupation, function or purpose, cost or value, or standpoint **2** to have reality or actuality; exist **3** – used with the past participle of transitive verbs as a passive-voice auxiliary **4** – used as the auxiliary of the present participle in progressive tenses expressing continuous action or arrangement in advance **5** – used with *to* and an infinitive to express destiny, arrangement in advance, obligation or necessity, or possibility *USE* (*1*) used regularly as the linking verb of simple predication; used in the past subjunctive or often in the indicative to express unreal conditions; often in British English used of groups in the plural form

[1]**beach** /biːtʃ/ *n* a (gently sloping) seashore or lakeshore usu covered by sand or pebbles; *esp* the part of this between the high and low water marks

[2]**beach** *v* to run or drive ashore

beachcomber /'biːtʃˌkəʊməʳ/ *n* one who searches along a shore for useful or salable flotsam and jetsam; *esp* a white man on the islands of the S Pacific who earns a living by doing this

beachhead /'biːtʃhed/ *n* an area on a hostile shore occupied to secure further landing of troops and supplies

beacon /'biːkən/ *n* **1** a signal fire commonly on a hill, tower, or pole; *also, Br* a high conspicuous hill suitable for or used in the past for such a fire **2a** a signal mark used to guide shipping **b** a radio transmitter emitting signals for the guidance of aircraft **3** a source of light or inspiration

[1]**bead** /biːd/ *n* **1** a small ball (e g of wood or glass) pierced for threading on a string or wire **2** *pl* (a series of prayers and meditations made with) a rosary **3** a small ball-shaped body: e g **a** a drop of liquid **b** a small metal knob on a firearm used as a front sight **4** a projecting rim, band, or moulding

[2]**bead** *v* **1** to adorn or cover with beads or beading **2** to string together like beads **3** to form into a bead

beading /'biːdɪŋ/ *n* **1** material adorned with or consisting of beads **2a** a narrow moulding of rounded often semicircular cross section **b** a moulding that resembles a string of beads **3** a narrow openwork insertion or trimming (e g on lingerie)

beadle /ˈbiːdl/ *n* a minor parish official whose duties include ushering and preserving order at services

beady /ˈbiːdi/ *adj, esp of eyes* small, round, and shiny with interest or greed

beagle /ˈbiːgəl/ *n* (any of) a breed of small short-legged smooth-coated hounds

beak /biːk/ *n* **1** the bill of a bird; *also* any similar structure on another creature **2a** the pouring spout of a vessel **b** a projection suggesting the beak of a bird **3** the human nose – infml **4** *chiefly Br* **a** a magistrate – slang **b** a schoolmaster – slang

beaker /ˈbiːkəʳ/ *n* **1** a large drinking cup with a wide mouth; a mug **2** a cylindrical flat-bottomed vessel usu with a pouring lip that is used esp by chemists and pharmacists

be-all and end-all *n the* chief factor; *the* essential element – often derog

[1]**beam** /biːm/ *n* **1** a long piece of heavy often squared timber suitable for use in construction **b** the bar of a balance from which scales hang **c** any of the principal horizontal supporting members of a building or across a ship **d** the width of a ship at its widest part **2a** a ray or shaft of radiation, esp light **b** (the course indicated by) a radio signal transmitted continuously in one direction as an aircraft navigation aid **3** the width of the buttocks – infml

[2]**beam** *v* **1** to emit in beams or as a beam, esp of light **2** to aim (a broadcast) by directional aerials **3** to smile with joy

beam-ends *n pl, Br* buttocks – infml

bean /biːn/ *n* **1a** (the often edible seed of) any of various erect or climbing leguminous plants **b** a bean pod used when immature as a vegetable **c** (a plant producing) any of various seeds or fruits that resemble beans or bean pods **2a** a valueless item **b** the smallest possible amount of money *USE* (*2*) infml

[1]**bear** /beəʳ/ *n* **1** any of a family of large heavy mammals that have long shaggy hair and a short tail and feed largely on fruit and insects as well as on flesh **2** a surly, uncouth, or shambling person **3** one who sells securities or commodities in expectation of a fall in price

[2]**bear** *v* **bore; borne** *also* **born** **1a** to carry, transport – often in combination **b** to entertain mentally **c** to behave, conduct **d** to have or show as a feature **e** to give as testimony **2a** to give birth to **b** to produce as yield **c** to contain – often in combination **3a** to support the weight of **b** to accept the presence of; tolerate; *also* show patience *with* **c** to sustain, incur **d** to admit of; allow **4a** to become directed **b** to go or extend in a usu specified direction **5** to apply, have relevance **6** to support weight or strain

[1]**beard** /bɪəd/ *n* **1** the hair that grows on the lower part of a man's face, usu excluding the moustache **2** a hairy or bristly appendage or tuft (e g on a goat's chin)

[2]**beard** *v* to confront and oppose with boldness, resolution, and often effrontery; defy

bear down *v* **1** to overcome, overwhelm **2** to exert full strength and concentrated attention **3** *of a woman in childbirth* to exert concentrated downward pressure in an effort to expel the child from the womb **4** to come near threateningly – usu + *on* **5** to weigh heavily down *on*

bearer /ˈbeərəʳ/ *n* **1** a porter **2** a plant yielding fruit **3** a pallbearer **4** one holding an order for payment, esp a bank note or cheque

bear hug *n* a rough tight embrace

bearing /ˈbeərɪŋ/ *n* **1** the manner in which one bears or conducts oneself **2** the act, power, or time of bringing forth offspring or fruit **3a** an object, surface, or point that supports **b** a machine part in which another part turns or slides – often pl with sing. meaning **4a** the compass direction of one point (with respect to another) **b** a determination of position **c** *pl* comprehension of one's position, environment, or situation **d** a relation, connection, significance – usu + *on*

bear out *v* to confirm, substantiate

bearskin /ˈbeəˌskɪn/ *n* an article made

of the skin of a bear; *esp* a tall black military hat worn by the Brigade of Guards

bear up *v* **1** to support, encourage **2** to summon up courage, resolution, or strength

beast /biːst/ *n* **1a** an animal as distinguished from a plant **b** a 4-legged mammal as distinguished from human beings, lower vertebrates, and invertebrates **2** a contemptible person

[1]**beastly** /ˈbiːstli/ *adj* **1** bestial **2** abominable, disagreeable – **-liness** *n*

[2]**beastly** *adv* very – infml

[1]**beat** /biːt/ *v* **beat; beaten; beat 1** to strike repeatedly: **a** to hit repeatedly so as to inflict pain – often + *up* **b** to strike directly against (sthg) forcefully and repeatedly **c** to flap or thrash (at) vigorously **d** to strike at or range over (as if) in order to rouse game **e** to mix (esp food) by stirring; whip **f** to strike repeatedly in order to produce music or a signal **2a** to drive or force by blows **b** to pound into a powder, paste, or pulp **c** to make by repeated treading or driving over **d** to shape by beating; *esp* to flatten thin by blows **3** to overcome, defeat; *also* to surpass **4** to leave dispirited, irresolute, or hopeless **5** to act ahead of, usu so as to forestall – chiefly in *beat someone to it* **6** to bewilder, baffle – infml **7** to glare or strike with oppressive intensity **8a** to pulsate, throb **b** to sound on being struck **9** to progress with much difficulty; *specif, of a sailing vessel* to make way at sea against the wind by a series of alternate tacks across the wind

[2]**beat** *n* **1a** a single stroke or blow, esp in a series; *also* a pulsation, throb **b** a sound produced (as if) by beating **2a** (the rhythmic effect of) a metrical or rhythmic stress in poetry or music **b** the tempo indicated to a musical performer **3** an area or route regularly patrolled, esp by a policeman **4** a deadbeat – infml

[3]**beat** *adj* **1** of or being beatniks **2** exhausted – infml

[4]**beat** *n* a beatnik

beaten /ˈbiːtn/ *adj* **1** hammered into a desired shape **2** defeated

beater /ˈbiːtəʳ/ *n* **1a** any of various hand-held implements for whisking or beating **b** a rotary blade attached to an electric mixer **c** a stick for beating a gong **2** one who strikes bushes or other cover to rouse game

beatific /bɪəˈtɪfɪk/ *adj* **1** of, possessing, or imparting blessedness **2** having a blissful or benign appearance; saintly, angelic – **~ally** *adv*

beating /ˈbiːtɪŋ/ *n* **1** injury or damage inflicted by striking with repeated blows **2** a throbbing **3** a defeat

beatnik /ˈbiːtnɪk/ *n* a person, esp in the 1950s and 1960s, who rejected the moral attitudes of established society (e g by unconventional behaviour and dress)

beau /bəʊ/ *n, pl* **beaux, beaus 1** a lover **2** *archaic* a dandy

Beaujolais /ˈbəʊʒəleɪ/ *n* a chiefly red table wine made in southern Burgundy in France

beauteous /ˈbjuːtɪəs/ *adj, archaic* beautiful – **~ly** *adv*

beautician /bjuːˈtɪʃən/ *n* sby who gives beauty treatments

beautiful /ˈbjuːtʝfəl/ *adj* **1** having qualities of beauty; exciting aesthetic pleasure or keenly delighting the senses **2** generally pleasing; excellent – **~ly** *adv*

beautify /ˈbjuːtʝfaɪ/ *v* to make beautiful; embellish

beauty /ˈbjuːti/ *n* **1** the qualities in a person or thing that give pleasure to the senses or pleasurably exalt the mind or spirit; loveliness **2** a beautiful person or thing; *esp* a beautiful woman **3** a brilliant, extreme, or conspicuous example or instance **4** a particularly advantageous or excellent quality

beauty spot *n* a beautiful scenic area

[1]**beaver** /ˈbiːvəʳ/ *n* **1a** a large semiaquatic rodent mammal that has webbed hind feet, a broad flat tail, and builds dams and underwater lodges **b** the fur or pelt of the beaver **2** a heavy fabric of felted wool napped on both sides **3** an energetic hard-working person

[2]**beaver** *v* to work energetically

[3]**beaver** *n* **1** a piece of armour protecting the lower part of the face **2** a helmet visor

because /bɪˈkɒz, bɪˈkəz/ *conj* **1** for

the reason that; since **2** and the proof is that

beckon /'bekən/ *v* **1** to summon or signal, typically with a wave or nod **2** to appear inviting

become /bɪ'kʌm/ *v* **became** /bɪ'keɪm/; **become** **1** to come into existence **2** to come to be **3** to suit or be suitable to **4** to happen to – usu + *of*

becoming /bɪ'kʌmɪŋ/ *adj* suitable, fitting; *esp* attractively suitable – **~ly** *adv*

[1]**bed** /bed/ *n* **1a** a piece of furniture on or in which one may lie and sleep and which usu includes bedstead, mattress, and bedding **b** a place of sexual relations; *also* lovemaking **c** a place for sleeping or resting **d** sleep; *also* a time for sleeping **2** a flat or level surface: e g **a** (plants grown in) a plot of ground, esp in a garden, prepared for plants **b** the bottom of a body of water; *also* an area of sea or lake bottom supporting a heavy growth of a specified organism **3** a supporting surface or structure; *esp* the foundation that supports a road or railway **4** a stratum or layer of rock **5** a mass or heap resembling a bed; *esp* a heap on which sthg else is laid

[2]**bed** *v* **1a** to provide with a bed or bedding; settle in sleeping quarters **b** to go to bed with, usu for sexual intercourse **2a** to embed **b** to plant or arrange (garden plants, vegetable plants, etc) in beds – often + *out* **c** to base, establish **3** to lay flat or in a layer **4** to find or make sleeping accommodation **5** to form a layer

bedbug /'bedbʌg/ *n* a wingless blood-sucking bug that sometimes infests beds

bedclothes /'bedkləʊðz, -kləʊz/ *n pl* the covers (e g sheets and blankets) used on a bed

[1]**bedding** /'bedɪŋ/ *n* **1** bedclothes **2** a bottom layer; a foundation **3** material to provide a bed for livestock

[2]**bedding** *adj, of a plant* appropriate or adapted for culture in open-air beds

bedeck /bɪ'dek/ *v* to clothe with finery; deck out

bedevil /bɪ'devəl/ *v* **1** to possess (as if) with a devil; bewitch **2** to change for the worse; spoil, frustrate **3** to torment maliciously; harass – **~ment** *n*

bedfellow /'bed,feləʊ/ *n* **1** one who shares a bed **2** a close associate; an ally

bedlam /'bedləm/ *n* a place, scene, or state of uproar and confusion

bedouin /'bedʊɪn/ *n often cap* a nomadic Arab of the Arabian, Syrian, or N African deserts

bedpan /'bedpæn/ *n* a shallow vessel used by a person in bed for urination or defecation

bedpost /'bedpəʊst/ *n* a usu turned or carved post of a bedstead

bedraggled /bɪ'drægəld/ *adj* **1** left wet and limp (as if) by rain **2** soiled and stained (as if) by trailing in mud

bedridden /'bed,rɪdn/ *adj* confined (e g by illness) to bed

bedrock /'bedrɒk/ *n* **1** the solid rock underlying less compacted surface materials (e g soil) **2** the basis of sthg

[1]**bedroom** /'bedrʊm, -ruːm/ *n* a room furnished with a bed and intended primarily for sleeping

[2]**bedroom** *adj* dealing with, suggestive of, or inviting sexual relations

bedside manner *n* the manner with which a medical doctor deals with his/her patients

bed-sitter *n, Br* a single room serving as both bedroom and sitting room

bedspread /'bedspred/ *n* a usu ornamental cloth cover for a bed

bedstead /'bedsted/ *n* the framework of a bed

bee /biː/ *n* **1** a social 4-winged insect often kept in hives for the honey that it produces **2** a gathering of people for a usu specified purpose

beech /biːtʃ/ *n* (the wood of) any of a genus of hardwood deciduous trees with smooth grey bark and small edible triangular nuts

beech mast *n* the nuts of the beech (when lying on the ground)

[1]**beef** /biːf/ *n* **1** the flesh of a bullock, cow, or other adult domestic bovine animal **2** an ox, cow, or bull in a (nearly) full-grown state; *esp* a bullock or cow fattened for food **3** muscular flesh; brawn **4** a complaint – infml

[2]**beef** *v* **1** to add weight, strength, or

power to – usu + *up* **2** to complain – infml

beefeater /ˈbiːf,iːtəʳ/ *n* a yeoman of the guard – not used technically

beefy /ˈbiːfi/ *adj* **1** full of beef **2** brawny, powerful

beeline /ˈbiːlaɪn/ *n* a straight direct course

been /biːn, bɪn/ *past part of* **be;** *specif* paid a visit

beer /bɪəʳ/ *n* **1** an alcoholic drink brewed from fermented malt flavoured with hops **2** a carbonated nonalcoholic or fermented slightly alcoholic drink flavoured with roots or other plant parts

beeswax /ˈbiːzwæks/ *n* a yellowish plastic substance secreted by bees that is used by them for constructing honeycombs and is used as a wood polish

beet /biːt/ *n* any of various plants of the goosefoot family with a swollen root used as a vegetable, as a source of sugar, or for forage

[1]**beetle** /ˈbiːtl/ *n* **1** any of an order of insects that have 4 wings of which the front pair are modified into stiff coverings that protect the back pair at rest **2** a game in which the players attempt to be the first to complete a stylized drawing of a beetle in accordance with the throwing of a dice

[2]**beetle** *v Br* to move swiftly – infml

[3]**beetle** *n* a heavy wooden tool for hammering or ramming

beetroot /ˈbiːtruːt/ *n, pl* **beetroot, beetroots** *chiefly Br* a cultivated beet with a red edible root that is a common salad vegetable

befall /bɪˈfɔːl/ *v* **befell; befallen** to happen (to), esp as if by fate

befit /bɪˈfɪt/ *v* to be proper or becoming to – **~ting** *adj* – **~tingly** *adv*

[1]**before** /bɪˈfɔːʳ/ *adv* **1** so as to be in advance of others; ahead **2** earlier in time; previously

[2]**before** *prep* **1a** in front of **b** under the jurisdiction or consideration of **2** preceding in time; earlier than **3** in a higher or more important position than **4** under the onslaught of

[3]**before** *conj* **1** earlier than the time when **2** rather than

beforehand /bɪˈfɔːhænd/ *adv or adj* **1** in anticipation **2** ahead of time

befriend /bɪˈfrend/ *v* to become a friend of purposely; show kindness and understanding to

befuddle /bɪˈfʌdl/ *v* **1** to muddle or stupefy (as if) with drink **2** to confuse, perplex

beg /beg/ *v* **1** to ask for alms or charity **2** to ask earnestly (for); entreat **3a** to evade, sidestep **b** to assume as established or proved without justification **4** to ask permission – usu + an infinitive

beget /bɪˈget/ *v* **begot,** *archaic* **begat; begotten, begot** **1** to procreate as the father; sire **2** to produce as an effect; cause

[1]**beggar** /ˈbegəʳ/ *n* **1** one who lives by asking for gifts **2** a pauper **3** a person; *esp* a fellow – infml

[2]**beggar** *v* **1** to reduce to beggary **2** to exceed the resources or abilities of

beggarly /ˈbegəli/ *adj* **1** marked by extreme poverty **2** contemptibly mean, petty, or paltry – **-liness** *n*

beggary /ˈbegəri/ *n* poverty, penury

begin /bɪˈgɪn/ *v* **began** /bɪˈgæn/; **begun** /bɪˈgʌn/ **1a** to do the first part of an action; start **b** to undergo initial steps **2a** to come into existence; arise **b** to have a starting point **3** to call into being; found **4** to come first in

beginning /bɪˈgɪnɪŋ/ *n* **1** the point at which sthg begins; the start **2** the first part **3** the origin, source **4** a rudimentary stage or early period – usu pl

beg off *v* to ask to be released from sthg

begone /bɪˈgɒn/ *v* to go away; depart – usu in the infin or esp the imperative

begonia /bɪˈgəʊnɪə/ *n* any of a large genus of tropical plants that are widely cultivated as ornamental garden and house plants

begrudge /bɪˈgrʌdʒ/ *v* **1** to give or concede reluctantly **2** to envy the pleasure or enjoyment of

beguile /bɪˈgaɪl/ *v* **1** to deceive, hoodwink **2** to please or persuade by the use of deceit; charm – **-ling** *adj* – **-lingly** *adv* – **~ment** *n*

behalf /bɪˈhɑːf/ *n* representative interest – usu in *on someone's behalf*

behave /bɪˈheɪv/ *v* **1** to conduct (oneself) in a specified way **2** to conduct (oneself) properly

behaviour /bɪ'heɪvɪəʳ/ *n* **1a** anything that an organism does involving action and response to stimulation **b** the response of an individual, group, or species to its environment **2** the way in which sthg (e g a machine) functions – **~al** *adj*

behaviourism /bɪ'heɪvɪərɪzəm/ *n* a theory holding that the proper concern of psychology is the objective study of behaviour and that information derived from the subject's reports of his/her thoughts, feelings, etc is not admissible psychological evidence – **-rist** *n*

behead /bɪ'hed/ *v* to cut off the head of; decapitate

behest /bɪ'hest/ *n* an urgent prompting or insistent request

[1]**behind** /bɪ'haɪnd/ *adv* **1a** in the place, situation, or time that is being or has been departed from **b** in, to, or towards the back **2a** in a secondary or inferior position **b** unpaid, overdue **c** slow

[2]**behind** *prep* **1a(1)** at or to the back or rear of **(2)** remaining after (sby who has departed) **b** obscured by **2** – used to indicate backwardness, delay, or deficiency (e g he's always a long way *behind* the rest) **3a** in the background of **b** in a supporting position at the back of

[3]**behind** *n* the buttocks – slang

behindhand /bɪ'haɪndhænd/ *adj* **1** behind schedule; in arrears **2** lagging behind the times; backward

behold /bɪ'həʊld/ *v* **beheld** to see, observe – **~er** *n*

beholden /bɪ'həʊldn/ *adj* under obligation for a favour or gift; indebted *to*

behove /bɪ'həʊv/ *v* to be incumbent (on), or necessary, proper, or advantageous (for)

beige /beɪʒ/ *n* a yellowish grey colour

[1]**being** /'biːɪŋ/ *n* **1a** the quality or state of having existence **b** conscious existence; life **2** the qualities that constitute an existent thing; the essence; *esp* personality **3** a living thing; *esp* a person

belabour /bɪ'leɪbəʳ/ *v* **1** to work on or at to absurd lengths **2a** to beat soundly **b** to assail, attack

belated /bɪ'leɪtɪ̈d/ *adj* delayed beyond the usual time – **~ly** *adv*

[1]**belay** /bɪ'leɪ/ *v* **1** to secure or make fast (e g a rope) by turns round a support, post, etc **2** to stop **3** to secure (by or to) a rope **4** to stop; leave off – in the imper

[2]**belay** *n* **1** a method or act of belaying a rope or person in mountain climbing **2** (sthg to which is attached) a mountain climber's belayed rope

belch /beltʃ/ *v* **1** to expel gas suddenly from the stomach through the mouth **2** to erupt, explode, or detonate violently **3** to issue forth spasmodically; gush **4** to eject or emit violently

belfry /'belfri/ *n* (a room in which a bell is hung in) a bell tower, esp when associated with a church

belie /bɪ'laɪ/ *v* **belying** **1** to give a false impression of **2** to show (sthg) to be false

belief /bɪ̈'liːf/ *n* **1** trust or confidence in sby or sthg **2** sthg believed; *specif* a tenet or body of tenets held by a group **3** conviction of the truth of some statement or the reality of some being, thing, or phenomenon, esp when based on examination of evidence

believe /bɪ̈'liːv/ *v* **1a** to have a firm religious faith **b** to accept sthg trustfully and on faith **2** to have a firm conviction as to the reality or goodness of sthg **3** to consider to be true or honest **4** to hold as an opinion; think – **believable** *adj* – **believably** *adv* – **~r** *n*

Belisha beacon /bɪ̈ˌliːʃə 'biːkən/ *n* a flashing light in an amber globe mounted on a usu black and white striped pole that marks a zebra crossing

belittle /bɪ'lɪtl/ *v* to undermine the value of

[1]**bell** /bel/ *n* **1** a hollow metallic device that vibrates and gives forth a ringing sound when struck **2** *the* sound of a bell as a signal; *specif* one to mark the start of the last lap in a running or cycling race or the start or end of a round in boxing, wrestling, etc **3a** a bell rung to tell the hour **b** a half-hour

subdivision of a watch on shipboard indicated by the strokes of a bell **4** sthg bell-shaped: e g **a** the corolla of any of many flowers **b** the flared end of a wind instrument

[2]**bell** *v* **1** to provide with a bell **2** to make or take the form of a bell; flare

[3]**bell** *v, of a stag or hound* to make a resonant bellowing or baying sound

bell-bottoms *n pl* trousers with wide flaring bottoms

bellboy /ˈbelbɔɪ/ *n, chiefly NAm* a hotel page

belle /bel/ *n* a popular and attractive girl or woman

bellicose /ˈbelɪkəʊs/ *adj* disposed to or fond of quarrels or wars – **-cosity** *n*

belligerent /bəˈlɪdʒərənt/ *adj* **1** engaged in war **2** aggressive, hostile

bellow /ˈbeləʊ/ *v* **1** to make the loud deep hollow sound characteristic of a bull **2** to shout in a deep voice – **bellow** *n*

bellows /ˈbeləʊz/ *n, pl* **bellows** **1** a device that by alternate expansion and contraction supplies a current of air – often pl with sing. meaning **2** a pleated expandable part in a camera

[1]**belly** /ˈbeli/ *n* **1a** the undersurface of an animal's body **b** a cut of pork consisting of this part of the body **c** the stomach and associated organs **2** an internal cavity; the interior **3** a surface or object curved or rounded like a human belly

[2]**belly** *v* to swell, fill

[1]**bellyache** /ˈbeli-eɪk/ *n* colic

[2]**bellyache** *v* to complain whiningly or peevishly; find fault – infml

belly button *n* the navel – infml

bellyful /ˈbelifʊl/ *n* an excessive amount – infml

belly-land *v* to land an aircraft on its undersurface without the use of landing gear – **belly landing** *n*

belly laugh *n* a deep hearty laugh

belong /bɪˈlɒŋ/ *v* **1** to be in a proper situation (e g according to ability or social qualification), position, or place **2** to be attached or bound *to* by birth, allegiance, dependency, or membership **3** to be an attribute, part, or function of a person or thing **4** to be properly classified

belongings /bɪˈlɒŋɪŋz/ *n pl* (personal) possessions

beloved /bɪˈlʌvəd, bɪˈlʌvd/ *n or adj* (sby) dearly loved – usu in fml or religious contexts

[1]**below** /bɪˈləʊ/ *adv* **1** in, on, or to a lower place, floor, or deck; *specif* on earth or in or to Hades or hell **2** under **3** under the surface of the water or earth

[2]**below** *prep* **1** in or to a lower place than; under **2** inferior to (e g in rank) **3** not suitable to the rank of; beneath **4** covered by; underneath **5** downstream from **6** under

[3]**below** *n the* thing or matter written or discussed lower on the same page or on a following page

[1]**belt** /belt/ *n* **1** a strip of material worn round the waist or hips or over the shoulder for decoration or to hold sthg (e g clothing or a weapon) **2** an endless band of tough flexible material for transmitting motion and power or conveying materials **3** an area characterized by some distinctive feature (e g of culture, geology, or life forms); *esp* one suited to a specified crop

[2]**belt** *v* **1a** to encircle or fasten with a belt **b** to strap on **2a** to beat (as if) with a belt; thrash **b** to strike, hit – infml **3** to sing in a forceful manner or style – usu + *out*; infml **4** to move or act in a vigorous or violent manner – infml

[3]**belt** *n* a jarring blow; a whack – infml

belt up *v, Br* shut up – infml

bemoan /bɪˈməʊn/ *v* to express regret, displeasure, or deep grief over; lament

bench /bentʃ/ *n* **1a** a long usu backless seat (e g of wood or stone) for 2 or more people **b** a thwart in a boat **2** *often cap* **a** a judge's seat in court **b** the office of judge or magistrate **3** any of the long seats on which members sit in Parliament **4** a long worktable

benchmark /ˈbentʃmɑːk/ *n* **1** a point of reference (e g a mark on a permanent object indicating height above sea level) from which measurements may be made, esp in surveying **2** sthg that serves as a standard by which others may be measured

[1]**bend** /bend/ *n* any of various knots

for fastening one rope to another or to an object

[2]**bend** *v* **bent** **1** to force into or out of a curve or angle **2** to make submissive; subdue **3a** to cause to turn from a course; deflect **b** to guide or turn towards sthg; direct **4** to direct strenuously or with interest; apply **5** to alter or modify to make more acceptable, esp to oneself **6** to move or curve out of a straight line or position **7** to incline the body, esp in submission; bow **8** to yield, compromise

[3]**bend** *n* **1** bending or being bent **2** a curved part, esp of a road or stream **3** *pl but sing or pl in constr* pain or paralysis caused by the release of gas bubbles in body tissue occurring typically when a diver returns to the surface too quickly

[1]**beneath** /bɪ'niːθ/ *adv* **1** in or to a lower position; below **2** directly under; underneath

[2]**beneath** *prep* **1a** in or to a lower position than; below **b** directly under, esp so as to be close or touching **2** not suitable to; unworthy of **3** under the control, pressure, or influence of

Benedictine /,benɟ'dɪktiːn/ *n* **1** a monk or a nun of any of the congregations following the rule of St Benedict and devoted esp to scholarship **2** *often not cap* a brandy-based liqueur made orig by French Benedictine monks

benediction /,benɟ'dɪkʃən/ *n* **1** the invocation of a blessing; *esp* the short blessing with which public worship is concluded **2** *often cap* a Roman Catholic or Anglo-Catholic devotion including the exposition of the Host and the blessing of the people with it

benefactor /'benɟ,fæktəʳ/, *fem* **benefactress** *n* one who gives aid; *esp* one who makes a gift or bequest to a person, institution, etc – **-tion** *n*

beneficent /bɪ'nefɟsənt/ *adj* doing or producing good; *esp* performing acts of kindness and charity – **-cence** *n* – **~ly** *adv*

beneficial /,benɟ'fɪʃəl/ *adj* conferring benefits; conducive to personal or social well-being – **~ly** *adv*

beneficiary /,benɟ'fɪʃəri/ *n* one who benefits from sthg, esp the income or proceeds of a trust, will, or insurance policy

[1]**benefit** /'benɟfɪt/ *n* **1a** an advantage **b** good, welfare **2a** financial help in time of need (e g sickness, old age, or unemployment) **b** a payment or service provided for under an annuity, pension scheme, or insurance policy **3** an entertainment, game, or social event to raise funds for a person or cause

[2]**benefit** *v* **1** to be useful or profitable to **2** to receive benefit

benefit of the doubt *n* *the* assumption of innocence in the absence of complete proof of guilt

benevolent /bɟ'nevələnt/ *adj* having, showing, or motivated by a desire to do good – **-ence** *n*

benighted /bɪ'naɪtɟd/ *adj* intellectually, morally, or socially unenlightened – **~ly** *adv*

benign /bɪ'naɪn/ *adj* **1** gracious **2** mild **3** *of a tumour* not malignant – **~ly** *adv*

[1]**bent** /bent/ *adj* **1** changed from an original straight or even condition by bending; curved **2** set *on* (doing something) **3** *Br* homosexual – slang **4** *Br* corrupt; crooked – slang

[2]**bent** *n* **1** a strong inclination or interest; a bias **2** a special ability or talent

benzene /'benziːn, -'-/ *n* an inflammable poisonous liquid hydrocarbon used in the manufacture of organic chemical compounds and as a solvent

bequeath /bɪ'kwiːð, bɪ'kwiːθ/ *v* **1** to give or leave (sthg, esp personal property) by will **2** to transmit; hand down – **bequest** *n*

berate /bɪ'reɪt/ *v* to scold or condemn vehemently

bereave /bɟ'riːv/ *vt* **bereaved, bereft** to rob or deprive *of* sby or sthg held dear, esp through death – **~ment** *n*

bereaved /bɪ'riːvd/ *n or adj* (*the* person) suffering the death of a loved one

bereft /bɟ'reft/ *adj* **1** deprived or robbed *of*; completely without sthg **2** bereaved

beret /'bereɪ/ *n* a cap with a tight headband, a soft full flat top, and no peak

berk, burk /bɜːk/ *n, Br* a stupid person; a fool – slang

[1]**berry** /'beri/ *n* **1** a small, pulpy, and usu edible fruit (e g a strawberry or raspberry) **2** an egg of a fish or lobster

berserk /bɜː'sɜːk, bə-/ *adj* frenzied, esp with anger; crazed – usu in *go berserk*

[1]**berth** /bɜːθ/ *n* **1** safe distance for manoeuvring maintained between a ship and another object **2** an allotted place for a ship when at anchor or at a wharf **3** a place for sleeping (e g a bunk), esp on a ship or train **4** a job, post – infml

[2]**berth** *v* to dock

beryl /'berəl/ *n* a mineral that is a silicate of beryllium and aluminium, occurs as green, yellow, pink, or white crystals, and is used as a gemstone

beseech /bɪ'siːtʃ/ *v* **besought** **1** to beg for urgently or anxiously **2** to implore

besetting /bɪ'setɪŋ/ *adj* constantly causing temptation or difficulty; continuously present

beside /bɪ'saɪd/ *prep* **1a** by the side of **b** in comparison with **c** on a par with **2** besides

[1]**besides** /bɪ'saɪdz/ *adv* **1** as an additional factor or circumstance **2** moreover, furthermore

[2]**besides** *prep* **1** other than; unless we are to mention **2** as an additional circumstance to

besiege /bɪ'siːdʒ/ *v* **1** to surround with armed forces **2** to press with questions, requests, etc; importune

besmirch /bɪ'smɜːtʃ/ *v* to sully, soil

besotted /bɪ'sɒtəd/ *adj* **1** made dull or foolish, esp by infatuation **2** drunk, intoxicated

bespeak /bɪ'spiːk/ *v* **bespoke; bespoken** **1** to hire, engage, or claim beforehand **2** to indicate, signify *USE* fml

bespoke /bɪ'spəʊk/ *adj, Br* made-to-measure

[1]**best** /best/ *adj, superlative of* **good** **1** excelling all others (e g in ability, quality, integrity, or usefulness) **2** most productive of good **3** most, largest **4** reserved for special occasions

[2]**best** *adv, superlative of* **well** **1** in the best manner; to the best extent or degree **2** better

[3]**best** *n, pl* **best** **1** the best state or part **2** sby or sthg that is best **3** the greatest degree of good or excellence **4** one's maximum effort **5** best clothes **6** a winning majority

bestial /'bestɪəl/ *adj* marked by brutal or inhuman instincts or desires; *specif* sexually depraved – **~ly** *adv* – **~ity** *n*

bestir /bɪ'stɜːʳ/ *v* to stir up; rouse to action

best man *n* the principal attendant of a bridegroom at a wedding

bestow /bɪ'stəʊ/ *v* to present as a gift – usu + *on* or *upon* – **~al** *n*

bestrew /bɪ'struː/ *v* **bestrewed; bestrewed, bestrewn** to lie scattered over

bestride /bɪ'straɪd/ *v* **bestrode; bestridden** **1** to straddle **2** to tower over; dominate

best-seller *n* **1** sthg, esp a book, which has sold in very large numbers, usu over a given period **2** an author or performer whose works sell in very large numbers

[1]**bet** /bet/ *n* **1a** the act of risking a sum of money or other stake on the forecast outcome of a future event (e g a race or contest), esp in competition with a second party **b** a stake so risked **2** an opinion, belief **3** a plan of action; course – usu in *best bet*; infml

[2]**bet** *v* **bet** *also* **betted** **1** to stake as a bet – usu + *on* or *against* **2** to make a bet with (sby) **3** to be convinced that – infml

beta /'biːtə/ *n* **1a** the 2nd letter of the Greek alphabet **b** a second-class mark or grade **2** – used to designate the second brightest star of a constellation

beta particle *n* an electron or positron ejected from the nucleus of an atom during radioactive decay

betel nut /'biːtl/ *n* the astringent seed of the betel palm

bête noire /ˌbet 'nwɑːʳ/ *n, pl* **bêtes noires** a person or thing strongly detested

betide /bɪ'taɪd/ *v* to happen, esp as if by fate *USE* fml or poetic

betray /bɪ'treɪ/ *v* **1** to deceive, lead astray **2** to deliver to an enemy by treachery **3** to disappoint the hopes, expectation, or confidence of **4a** to be a sign of (sthg one would like to hide) **b** to disclose, deliberately or unintentionally, in violation of confidence – **~er** *n* – **~al** *n*

betroth /bɪ'trəʊð, bɪ'trəʊθ/ *v*. **betrothed, betrothing** to promise to marry or give in marriage – **~al** *n*

[1]**better** /'betəʳ/ *adj, comparative of* **good** *or of* **well** **1** improved in health; recovered **2** of greater quality, ability, integrity, usefulness, etc

[2]**better** *adv, comparative of* **well** **1** in a better manner; to a better extent or degree **2a** to a higher or greater degree **b** more wisely or usefully

[3]**better** *n* **1a** sthg better **b** one's superior, esp in merit or rank – usu pl **2** *the* advantage, victory

[4]**better** *v* **1** to make better: e g **a** to make more tolerable or acceptable **b** to make more complete or perfect **2** to surpass in excellence; excel – **~ment** *n*

[1]**between** /bɪ'twiːn/ *prep* **1a** through the common action of; jointly engaging **b** in shares to each of **2a** in or into the time, space, or interval that separates **b** in intermediate relation to **3a** from one to the other of **b** serving to connect or separate **4** in point of comparison of **5** taking together the total effect of; what with

[2]**between** *adv* in or into an intermediate space or interval

betwixt and between /bɪ'twɪkst ənd bɪ'twiːn/ *adv or adj* in a midway position; neither one thing nor the other

[1]**bevel** /'bevəl/ *n* the angle or slant that one surface or line makes with another when they are not at right angles

[2]**bevel** *v* **1** to cut or shape to a bevel **2** to incline, slant

beverage /'bevərɪdʒ/ *n* a liquid for drinking; *esp* one that is not water

bevy /'bevi/ *n* a group or collection, esp of girls

beware /bɪ'weəʳ/ *v* to be wary (of) – usu in imper and infin

bewilder /bɪ'wɪldəʳ/ *v* to perplex or confuse – **~ment** *n*

bewitch /bɪ'wɪtʃ/ *v* **1** to influence or affect by witchcraft **2** to enchant

[1]**beyond** /bɪ'jɒnd/ *adv* **1** on or to the farther side; farther **2** as an additional amount; besides

[2]**beyond** *prep* **1** on or to the farther side of; at a greater distance than **2a** out of the reach or sphere of **b** in a degree or amount surpassing **c** out of the comprehension of **3** besides **4** later than; past

[3]**beyond** *n* **1** sthg that lies beyond **2** sthg that lies outside the scope of ordinary experience; *specif* the hereafter

[1]**bias** /'baɪəs/ *n* **1** a line diagonal to the grain of a fabric, often used in the cutting of garments for smoother fit – usu + *the* **2a** a personal prejudice **b** a bent, tendency **3** (the property of shape or weight causing) the tendency in bowls for a bowl to take a curved path when rolled

[2]**bias** *v* **1** to give a prejudiced outlook to **2** to influence unfairly

bib /bɪb/ *n* **1** a covering (e g of cloth or plastic) placed over a child's front to protect his/her clothes **2** a small rectangular section of a garment (e g an apron or dungarees) extending above the waist

bible /'baɪbəl/ *n* **1a** *cap* the sacred book of Christians comprising the Old Testament and the New Testament **b** any book containing the sacred writings of a religion **2** an authoritative book – **-lical** *adj*

bibliography /ˌbɪbli'ɒgrəfi/ *n* a list of writings relating to a particular topic, written by a particular author, referred to in a text or consulted by the author in its production, etc – **-pher** *n*

bibulous /'bɪbjʊləs/ *adj* prone to alcoholic over-indulgence

bicarbonate /baɪ'kɑːbənl̩t, -neɪt/ *n* an acid carbonate; *esp* sodium bicarbonate used in baking or as a treatment for indigestion

bicentenary /ˌbaɪsen'tiːnəri/ *n or adj* (the celebration) of a 200th anniversary

biceps /'baɪseps/ *n* the large muscle at the front of the upper arm that bends the arm at the elbow when it contracts

bicker /'bɪkəʳ/ *v* to engage in petulant or petty argument

bicycle /'baɪsɪkəl/ *v or n* (to ride) a 2 wheeled pedal-driven vehicle with handlebars and a saddle – **bicyclist** *n*

[1]**bid** /bɪd/ *v* **bade, bid,** (*3*) **bid; bidden, bid** *also* **bade** **1a** to issue an order to; tell **b** to invite to come **2** to give expression to **3a** to offer (a price) for payment or acceptance (e g at an auction) **b** to make a bid of or in (a suit at cards) – **~der** *n*

[2]**bid** *n* **1a** the act of one who bids **b** a statement of what one will give or take for sthg; *esp* an offer of a price **2** an opportunity to bid **3** (an announcement of) the amount of tricks to be won, suit to be played in, etc in a card game **4** an attempt to win or achieve sthg

biddable /ˈbɪdəbl/ *adj* **1** easily led or controlled; docile **2** capable of being reasonably bid

bidding /ˈbɪdɪŋ/ *n* order, command

bide /baɪd/ *v* **bode, bided; bided** *archaic or dial* to remain awhile; stay

bidet /ˈbiːdeɪ/ *n* a bathroom fixture used esp for bathing the external genitals and the anus

biennial /baɪˈenɪəl/ *adj* **1** occurring every 2 years **2** *of a plant* fruiting and dying during the second year of growth – **~ly** *adv*

bier /bɪəʳ/ *n* a stand on which a corpse or coffin is placed; *also* a coffin together with its stand

biff /bɪf/ *n* a whack, blow – infml

bifocals /baɪˈfəʊkəlz/ *n pl* glasses with the upper and lower parts of the lenses ground to different prescriptions – **bifocal** *adj*

[1]**big** /bɪg/ *adj* **1** of great force **2a** large in bulk or extent, number or amount **b** large-scale **c** important in influence, standing, or wealth **3a** advanced in pregnancy **b** full to bursting; swelling **4** *of the voice* loud and resonant **5** older, grown-up **6** of great importance or significance **7a** pretentious, boastful **b** magnanimous, generous **8** popular – infml – **~ness** *n*

[2]**big** *adv* **1a** outstandingly **b** on a grand scale **2** pretentiously *USE* infml

bigamy /ˈbɪgəmi/ *n* the crime of going through a marriage ceremony with one person while legally married to another – **-mist** *n* – **-mous** *adj* – **-mously** *adv*

big bang theory *n* a theory in cosmology: the universe originated from the explosion of a single mass of material so that the components are still flying apart

big end *n* the end of an engine's connecting rod nearest the crankpin

big game *n* large animals hunted or fished for sport

bighead /ˈbɪghed/ *n* a conceited person – infml

big head *n* an exaggerated opinion of one's importance – infml

bigot /ˈbɪgət/ *n* one who is obstinately or intolerantly devoted to his/her own religion, opinion, etc – **~ed** *adj* – **~edly** *adv* – **~ry** *n*

big top *n* the main tent of a circus

bigwig /ˈbɪg,wɪg/ *n* an important person – infml

bike /baɪk/ *v or n* (to ride) **1** a bicycle **2** a motorcycle

bikini /bɪ̥ˈkiːni/ *n* a woman's brief 2-piece garment resembling bra and pants worn for swimming or sunbathing

bilateral /baɪˈlætərəl/ *adj* **1** having 2 sides **2** bipartite – **~ly** *adv*

bilberry /ˈbɪlbəri/ *n* (the bluish edible fruit of) a dwarf bushy European shrub of the heath family that grows on moorland

bile /baɪl/ *n* **1** a yellow or greenish fluid secreted by the liver into the intestines to aid the digestion of fats **2** inclination to anger – **bilious** *adj* – **biliousness** *n*

bilge /bɪldʒ/ *n* **1** the (space inside the) lowest usu rounded part of a ship's hull between the keel and the vertical sides **2** stale or worthless remarks or ideas – infml

bilingual /baɪˈlɪŋgwəl/ *adj* **1** of, containing, or expressed in 2 languages **2** using or able to use 2 languages with the fluency of a native speaker

[1]**bill** /bɪl/ *n* **1** (a mouthpart resembling) the jaws of a bird together with variously shaped and coloured horny coverings **2** a projection of land like a beak

[2]**bill** *v* to caress affectionately – chiefly in *bill and coo*

[3]**bill** *n* **1** a long staff with a hook-shaped blade used as a weapon up to the 18th c **2** a billhook

⁴bill *n* **1** a draft of a law presented to a legislature **2** (an itemized account of) charges due for goods or services **3a** a written or printed notice advertising an event of interest to the public (e g a theatrical entertainment) **b** an item (e g a film or play) in a programme entertainment

⁵bill *v* **1** to submit a bill of charges to **2a** to advertise, esp by posters or placards **b** to arrange for the presentation of as part of a programme

billboard /ˈbɪlbɔːd/ *n* an advertising hoarding

¹billet /ˈbɪlɪ̈t/ *n* **1a** an official order directing that a member of a military force be provided with board and lodging (e g in a private home) **b** quarters assigned (as if) by a billet **2** a position, job

²billet *n* **1** a small thick piece of wood (e g for firewood) **2** a usu small bar of iron, steel, etc **3** a Romanesque architectural moulding or ornamentation consisting of raised short cylinders or square pieces placed at regular intervals

billhook /ˈbɪlhʊk/ *n* a tool for pruning that has a blade with a hooked point

billiards /ˈbɪljədz/ *n pl but sing in constr* any of several games played on an oblong table by driving small balls against one another or into pockets with a cue; *specif* one with 3 balls in which scores are made by causing a cue ball to hit 2 object balls in succession – **billiard** *adj*

billion /ˈbɪljən/ *n* **1** *Br* a million millions (10^{12}) **2** *NAm* a thousand millions (10^{9}) **3** an indefinitely large number – often pl with sing. meaning – **~th** *adj, n, pron, adv*

¹billow /ˈbɪləʊ/ *n* **1** a great wave, esp in the open sea **2** a rolling swirling mass (e g of flame or smoke) – **~y** *adj*

²billow *v* to (cause to) rise, roll, bulge, or swell out (as if) in billows

¹billy /ˈbɪli/, **billy club** *n*, *NAm* a truncheon

²billy, *chiefly Austr* **billycan** *n* a metal can with an arched handle and a lid, used for outdoor cooking

billy goat *n* a male goat – infml

bimonthly /baɪˈmʌnθli/ *adj or adv* (occurring) every 2 months or twice a month

¹bin /bɪn/ *n* **1** a container used for storage (e g of flour, grain, bread, or coal) **2** a partitioned case or stand for storing and aging bottles of wine **3** *Br* a wastepaper basket, dustbin, or similar container for rubbish **4** *Br* a mental hospital – *infml*

binary /ˈbaɪnəri/ *adj* **1** consisting of or marked by 2 things or parts **2a** of, being, or belonging to a system of numbers having 2 as its base

¹bind /baɪnd/ *v* **bound** **1a** to make secure by tying (e g with cord) or tying together **b** to put under a (legal) obligation **2** to wrap round with sthg (e g cloth) so as to enclose or cover **3** to encircle, gird **4** to cause to stick together **5** to cause to be attached (e g by gratitude or affection) **6** to form a cohesive mass **7** to jam **8** to complain – infml

²bind *n* a nuisance, bore – infml

binder /ˈbaɪndəʳ/ *n* **1** a person who binds books **2** a usu detachable cover (e g for holding sheets of paper) **3** sthg (e g tar or cement) that produces or promotes cohesion in loosely assembled substances

¹binding /ˈbaɪndɪŋ/ *n* a material or device used to bind: e g **a** a covering that fastens the leaves of a book **b** a narrow strip of fabric used to finish raw edges

²binding *adj* imposing an obligation

bind over *v* to impose a specific legal obligation on

bindweed /ˈbaɪndwiːd/ *n* any of various twining plants with usu large showy trumpet-shaped flowers

binge /bɪndʒ/ *n* an unrestrained indulgence in sthg, esp drink – infml

¹bingo /ˈbɪŋgəʊ/ *interj* **1** – used to express the suddenness or unexpectedness of an event **2** – used as an exclamation to show that one has won a game of bingo

²bingo *n* a game of chance played with cards having numbered squares corresponding to numbers drawn at random and won by covering or marking off all or a predetermined number of such squares

binnacle /ˈbɪnəkəl/ *n* a case, stand, etc containing a ship's compass

binocular /bɪˈnɒkjʊləʳ/ *adj* of, using, or adapted to the use of both eyes

binoculars /bɪˈnɒkjʊləz, baɪ-/ *n pl,* field glasses or opera glasses

biochemistry /ˌbaɪəʊˈkemɪ̈stri/ *n* chemistry that deals with the chemical compounds and processes occurring in organisms

biodegradable /ˌbaɪəʊdɪˈgreɪdəbəl/ *adj* capable of being broken down, esp into simpler harmless products, by the action of living beings (e g micro-organisms)

biography /baɪˈɒgrəfi/ *n* **1** a usu written account of a person's life **2** biographical writing as a literary genre – **-phic, -phical** *adj* – **-phically** *adv* – **-pher** *n*

biology /baɪˈɒlədʒi/ *n* a science that deals with the structure, function, development, distribution, and life processes of living organisms – **-gical** *adj* – **-gically** *adv* – **-gist** *n*

bionic /baɪˈɒnɪk/ *adj* having exceptional abilities or powers – infml

biosphere /ˈbaɪəsfɪəʳ/ *n* the part of the world in which life exists

bipartisan /baɪpɑːtɪ̈ˈzæn/ *adj* of or involving 2 parties

bipartite /baɪˈpɑːtaɪt/ *adj* **1** being in 2 parts **2** *of a treaty, contract, etc between 2 parties* **a** having 2 correspondent parts, one for each party **b** affecting both parties in the same way

biped /ˈbaɪped/ *n* a 2-footed animal

biplane /ˈbaɪpleɪn/ *n* an aeroplane with 2 pairs of wings placed one above and usu slightly forward of the other

[1]**birch** /bɜːtʃ/ *n* **1** (the hard pale close-grained wood of) any of a genus of deciduous usu short-lived trees or shrubs typically having a layered outer bark that peels readily **2** a birch rod or bundle of twigs for flogging

[2]**birch** *v* to whip (as if) with a birch

bird /bɜːd/ *n* **1** any of a class of warm-blooded vertebrates with the body more or less completely covered with feathers and the forelimbs modified as wings **2a** a (peculiar) fellow – chiefly infml **b** *chiefly Br* a girl – infml **3** a hissing or jeering expressive of disapproval or derision – chiefly in *give somebody the bird/get the bird*; infml **4** *Br* a spell of imprisonment – slang

birdie /ˈbɜːdi/ *n* **1** a (little) bird – used esp by or to children **2** a golf score of 1 stroke less than par on a hole

bird's-eye view *n* **1** an aerial view **2** a brief and general summary

Biro /ˈbaɪərəʊ/ *trademark* – used for a ballpoint pen

birth /bɜːθ/ *n* **1** the act or process of bringing forth young from within the body **2** being born, esp at a particular time or place **3** (noble) lineage or extraction **4** a beginning, start

birth control *n* contraception

birthday /ˈbɜːθdeɪ/ *n* **1a** the day of a person's birth **b** a day of origin **2** an anniversary of a birth

birthright /ˈbɜːθraɪt/ *n* sthg (e g a privilege or possession) to which a person is entitled by birth

biscuit /ˈbɪskɪ̈t/ *n* **1** earthenware or porcelain after the first firing and before glazing **2** a light yellowish brown colour **3** *Br* any of several variously-shaped small usu unleavened thin dry crisp bakery products that may be sweet or savoury **4** *NAm* a soft cake or bread (e g a scone) made without yeast

bisect /baɪˈsekt/ *v* **1** to divide into 2 (equal) parts **2** to cross, intersect – **~ion** *n*

bisexual /baɪˈsekʃʊəl/ *adj* **1** possessing characteristics of both sexes **2** sexually attracted to both sexes – **~ity** *n* – **~ly** *adv*

bishop /ˈbɪʃəp/ *n* **1** a clergyman ranking above a priest, having authority to ordain and confirm, and typically governing a diocese **2** either of 2 chess pieces of each colour allowed to move diagonally across any number of consecutive unoccupied squares

bismuth /ˈbɪzməθ/ *n* a heavy metallic element

bison /ˈbaɪsən/ *n, pl* **bison 1** a large shaggy-maned European bovine mammal that is now nearly extinct **2** the American buffalo

bisque /bɪsk/ *n* a thick cream soup (e g of shellfish or game)

bistro /ˈbiːstrəʊ/ *n* a small bar, restaurant, or tavern

[1]**bit** /bɪt/ *n* **1** a bar of metal or occas rubber attached to the bridle and

inserted in the mouth of a horse **2** the biting, boring, or cutting edge or part of a tool

[2]**bit** *n* **1a** a small piece or quantity of anything (e g food) **b(1)** a usu specified small coin **(2)** a money unit worth ⅛ of a US dollar **c** a part, section **2** sthg small or unimportant of its kind: e g **a** a brief period; a while **b** an indefinite usu small degree, extent, or amount **3** all the items, situations, or activities appropriate to a given style, role, etc **4** a young woman – slang

[3]**bit** *n* a unit of computer information equivalent to the result of a choice between 2 alternatives (e g *on* or *off*)

[1]**bitch** /bɪtʃ/ *n* **1** the female of the dog or similar flesh-eating animals **2** a malicious, spiteful, and domineering woman

[2]**bitch** *v* to complain – infml

bitchy /ˈbɪtʃi/ *adj* characterized by malicious, spiteful, or arrogant behaviour – **bitchily** *adv* – **bitchiness** *n*

[1]**bite** /baɪt/ *v* **bit; bitten** *also* **bit** **1a** to seize or sever with teeth or jaws **b** to sting with a fang or other specialized part **2** *of a weapon or tool* to cut, pierce **3** to cause sharp pain or stinging discomfort **4** to take strong hold of; grip **5** *of fish* to take a bait

[2]**bite** *n* **1** the amount of food taken with 1 bite; *also* a snack **2** a wound made by biting **3** the hold or grip by which friction is created or purchase is obtained **4** a sharp incisive quality or effect

biting /ˈbaɪtɪŋ/ *adj* sharp, cutting – **~ly** *adv*

[1]**bitter** /ˈbɪtəʳ/ *adj* **1a** being or inducing an acrid, astringent, or disagreeable taste similar to that of quinine that is one of the 4 basic taste sensations **b** distressing, galling **2a** intense, severe **b** very cold **c** cynical; full of ill-will – **~ly** *adv* – **~ness** *n*

[2]**bitter** *n* **1** *pl but sing or pl in constr* a usu alcoholic solution of bitter and often aromatic plant products used esp in preparing mixed drinks or as a mild tonic **2** *Br* a very dry beer heavily flavoured with hops

bittern /ˈbɪtən/ *n* any of various small or medium-sized herons with a characteristic booming cry

bittersweet /ˌbɪtəˈswiːt/ *n* a rambling poisonous nightshade with purple-and-yellow flowers

bitty /ˈbɪti/ *adj* scrappy, disjointed – **-tiness** *n*

bitumen /ˈbɪtʃʊmɪ̣n/ *n* any of various mixtures of hydrocarbons (e g tar) that occur naturally or as residues after heating petroleum, coal, etc – **-minous** *adj*

bivalent /baɪˈveɪlənt/ *adj* having a valency of 2

bivalve /ˈbaɪvælv/ *n or adj* (a mollusc) having a shell composed of 2 valves

biweekly /baɪˈwiːkli/ *n, adj, or adv* (a publication) issued or occurring **a** every 2 weeks **b** twice a week

bizarre /bɪ̣ˈzɑːʳ/ *adj* **1** odd, extravagant, eccentric **2** involving sensational contrasts or incongruities – **~ly** *adv*

blab /blæb/ *v* to talk indiscreetly or thoughtlessly

blabber /ˈblæbəʳ/ *v* **1** to babble **2** to say indiscreetly

[1]**black** /blæk/ *adj* **1a** of the colour black **b** very dark in colour **2** *often cap* **a** having dark pigmentation; *esp* of the Negro race **b** of black people or culture **3** having or reflecting little or no light **4** *of coffee* served without milk or cream **5** thoroughly sinister or evil **6** very dismal or disastrous **7** characterized by grim, distorted, or grotesque humour **8** bought, sold, or operating illegally and esp in violation of official economic regulations – **~ness** *n*

[2]**black** *n* **1** the colour of least lightness that belongs to objects that neither reflect nor transmit light **2** sthg black; *esp* black clothing **3** one who belongs wholly or partly to a dark-skinned race; *esp* a Negro **4** (the player playing) the dark-coloured pieces in a board game (e g chess) for 2 players **5** the condition of being financially in credit or solvent or of making a profit – usu + *in the*

[3]**black** *v chiefly Br* to declare (e g a business or industry) subject to boycott by trade-union members

Black and Tan *n* a member of the Royal Irish Constabulary resisting the armed movement for Irish independence in 1921

black-and-white *adj* **1** reproducing visual images in tones of grey rather than in colours **2** evaluating things as either all good or all bad

black and white *n* writing, print

blackball /ˈblækbɔːl/ *v* **1** to vote against (esp a candidate for membership of a club) **2** to ostracize

black belt *n* (one who has) a rating of expert in judo, karate, etc

blackberry /ˈblækbəri/ *n* (the usu black seedy edible fruit of) any of various prickly shrubs of the rose family

blackbird /ˈblækbɜːd/ *n* a common Old World thrush the male of which is black with an orange beak and eye rim

blackboard /ˈblækbɔːd/ *n* a hard smooth usu dark surface for writing or drawing on with chalk

black box *n* **1** a usu electronic device, esp one that can be plugged in or removed as a unit, whose internal mechanism is hidden from or mysterious to the user **2** a flight recorder

blackcurrant /ˈblæk,kʌrənt/ *n* (the small black edible fruit of) a widely cultivated European currant

black death *n, often cap B&D* a form of plague epidemic in Europe and Asia in the 14th c

blacken /ˈblækən/ *v* **1** to make dark or black **2** to defame, sully

blackguard /ˈblægəd/ *n* a coarse or unscrupulous person; a scoundrel – now often humor

blackhead /ˈblækhed/ *n* a small usu dark-coloured oily plug blocking the duct of a sebaceous gland, esp on the face

black hole *n* a celestial body, prob formed from a collapsed star, with a very high density and an intense gravitational field, from which no radiation can escape

black ice *n, Br* transparent slippery ice (e g on a road)

blacking /ˈblækɪŋ/ *n* a paste, polish, etc applied to an object to make it black

blackleg /ˈblækleg/ *n, chiefly Br* a worker hostile to trade unionism or acting in opposition to union policies

blacklist /ˈblæk,lɪst/ *n, v* (to put on) a list of people or organizations who are disapproved of or are to be punished or boycotted

black magic *n* magic performed with the aim of harming or killing sby or sthg

blackmail /ˈblækmeɪl/ *v* to extort or obtain money by threats, esp of exposure of secrets that would lead to loss of reputation, prosecution, etc – **blackmail** *n* – **~er** *n*

Black Maria /,blæk məˈraɪə/ *n* an enclosed motor vehicle used by police to carry prisoners

black market *n* illicit trade in commodities or currencies in violation of official regulations (e g rationing) – **~eer** *n*

blackout /ˈblækaʊt/ *n* **1** a period of darkness enforced as a precaution against air raids, or caused by a failure of electrical power **2** a temporary loss or dulling of vision, consciousness, or memory **3** a usu temporary loss of radio signal (e g during the reentry of a spacecraft)

black out *v* **1** to faint **2** to suppress, esp by censorship

black pudding *n, chiefly Br* a very dark sausage made from suet and a large proportion of pig's blood

black sheep *n* a disreputable member of a respectable group, family, etc

Blackshirt /ˈblækʃɜːt/ *n* a member of a fascist organization having a black shirt as part of its uniform

blacksmith /ˈblæk,smɪθ/ *n* one who works iron, esp at a forge

black spot *n, Br* a stretch of road on which accidents occur frequently

blackthorn /ˈblækθɔːn/ *n* a European spiny shrub of the rose family with hard wood and small white flowers

black-tie *adj* characterized by or requiring the wearing of semiformal evening dress by men including a dinner jacket and a black bow tie

bladder /ˈblædəʳ/ *n* **1a** a membranous sac in animals that serves as the receptacle of a liquid or contains gas; *esp* the urinary bladder **2** a bag filled with a liquid or gas (e g the air-filled rubber one inside a football)

blade /bleɪd/ *n* **1** (the flat expanded part, as distinguished from the stalk, of) a leaf, esp of a grass, cereal, etc **2a** the broad flattened part of an oar, paddle, bat, etc **b** an arm of a screw propeller, electric fan, steam turbine, etc **c** the broad flat or concave part of a machine (e g a bulldozer) that comes into contact with material to be moved **3a** the cutting part of a knife, razor, etc **b** the runner of an ice skate **4** *archaic* a dashing lively man – now usu humor

[1]**blame** /bleɪm/ *v* **1** to find fault with; hold responsible for **2** to place responsibility for (sthg reprehensible) – + *on*

[2]**blame** *n* **1** an expression of disapproval or reproach **2** responsibility for sthg reprehensible – **~worthy** *adj* – **~worthiness** *n*

blanch /blɑːntʃ/ *v* **1** to take the colour out of **2** to scald or parboil (e g almonds or food for freezing) in water or steam

blancmange /blə'mɒnʒ, -'mɒndʒ/ *n* a usu sweetened and flavoured dessert made from cornflour and milk

bland /blænd/ *adj* **1a** smooth, soothing **b** unperturbed **2a** not irritating or stimulating; mild **b** dull, insipid – **~ly** *adv* – **~ness** *n*

[1]**blank** /blæŋk/ *adj* **1a** dazed; taken aback **b** expressionless **2a** lacking interest, variety, or change **b** free from writing; not filled in **3** absolute, unqualified **4** having a plain or unbroken surface where an opening is usual – **~ly** *adv* – **~ness** *n*

[2]**blank** *n* **1** an empty space **2a** a void **b** a vacant or uneventful period **3** a piece of material prepared to be made into sthg (e g a key or coin) by a further operation **4** a cartridge loaded with powder but no bullet

[3]**blank** *v* **1** to make blank – usu + *out* **2** to block – usu + *off*

[1]**blanket** /'blæŋkɪ̇t/ *n* **1** a large thick usu rectangular piece of fabric (e g woven from wool or acrylic yarn) used esp as a bed covering or a similar piece of fabric used as a body covering (e g for a horse) **2** a thick covering or layer

[2]**blanket** *v* to cover (as if) with a blanket

[3]**blanket** *adj* applicable in all instances or to all members of a group or class

blank verse *n* unrhymed verse, esp in iambic pentameters

blare /bleəʳ/ *v* **1** to emit loud and harsh sound **2** to proclaim loudly or sensationally

blarney /'blɑːni/ *n* **1** smooth wheedling talk **2** nonsense

blasé /'blɑːzeɪ/ *adj* indifferent to pleasure or excitement as a result of excessive indulgence or enjoyment; *also* sophisticated

blaspheme /blæs'fiːm/ *v* to speak of or address (God or sthg sacred) with impiety – **~r, -my** *n* – **-mous** *adj* – **-mously** *adv*

[1]**blast** /blɑːst/ *n* **1** a violent gust of wind **2** the sound produced by air blown through a wind instrument or whistle **3** a stream of air or gas forced through a hole **4** (a violent wave of increased atmospheric pressure followed by a wave of decreased atmospheric pressure produced in the vicinity of) an explosion or violent detonation **5** the utterance of the word *blast* as a curse

[2]**blast** *v* **1** to injure (as if) by the action of wind; blight **2** to shatter, remove, or open (as if) with an explosive **3** to apply a forced draught to **4** to denounce vigorously **5** to curse, damn **6** to hit vigorously and effectively – **~ed** *adj*

[3]**blast** *interj, Br* – used to express annoyance; slang

blast furnace *n* a furnace, esp for converting iron ore into iron, in which combustion is forced by a current of air under pressure

blast off *v, esp of rocket-propelled missiles and vehicles* to take off – **blast-off** *n*

blatant /'bleɪtənt/ *adj* completely obvious, conspicuous, or obtrusive, esp in a crass or offensive manner – **~ly** *adv*

[1]**blaze** /bleɪz/ *n* **1a** an intensely burning flame or sudden fire **b** intense direct light, often accompanied by heat **2** a sudden outburst **3** *pl* hell – usu as an interjection or as a generalized term of abuse – **-zing** *adj*

[2]**blaze** *v* **1a** to burn intensely **b** to flare up **2** to be conspicuously brilliant or

resplendent **3** to shoot rapidly and repeatedly

[3]**blaze** *n* **1** a broad white mark on the face of an animal, esp a horse **2** a trail marker; *esp* a mark made on a tree by cutting off a piece of the bark

[4]**blaze** *v* to lead or pioneer in (some direction or activity) – chiefly in *blaze the trail*

blazer /ˈbleɪzəʳ/ *n* a jacket, esp with patch pockets, that is for casual wear or is part of a school uniform

[1]**bleach** /bliːtʃ/ *v* **1** to remove colour or stains from **2** to make whiter or lighter, esp by physical or chemical removal of colour

[2]**bleach** *n* a chemical preparation used in bleaching

bleak /bliːk/ *adj* **1** barren and windswept **2** cold, raw **3a** lacking in warmth or kindness **b** not hopeful or encouraging **c** severely simple or austere

bleary /ˈblɪəri/ *adj* **1** *of the eyes or vision* dull or dimmed, esp from fatigue or sleep **2** poorly outlined or defined – **blearily** *adv* – **bleariness** *n*

bleat /bliːt/ *v* **1** to make (a sound like) the cry characteristic of a sheep or goat **2** to talk complainingly or with a whine

[1]**bleed** /bliːd/ *v* **bled 1** to emit or lose blood **2** to feel anguish, pain, or sympathy **3** to lose some constituent (e g sap or dye) by exuding it or by diffusion **4** to extort money from **5** to extract or drain the vitality or lifeblood from

bleeding /ˈbliːdɪŋ/ *adj or adv* bloody – slang

[1]**bleep** /bliːp/ *n* a short high-pitched sound (e g from electronic equipment)

[2]**bleep** *v* to replace (recorded words) with a bleep or other sound – usu + *out*

blemish /ˈblemɪʃ/ *vt or n* (to spoil the perfection of by) a noticeable imperfection

blench /blentʃ/ *v* to draw back or flinch from lack of courage

[1]**blend** /blend/ *v* **blended** *also* **blent 1** to mix; *esp* to combine or associate so that the separate constituents cannot be distinguished **2** to produce a harmonious effect

[2]**blend** *n* **1** an act or product of blending **2** a word (e g *brunch*) produced by combining other words or parts of words

blender /ˈblendəʳ/ *n* an electric appliance for grinding or mixing; *specif* a liquidizer

bless /bles/ *v* **blessed** *also* **blest 1** to hallow or consecrate, esp by making the sign of the cross **2** to invoke divine care for **3a** to praise, glorify **b** to speak gratefully of **4** to confer prosperity or happiness on **5** – used in exclamations chiefly to express mild or good-humoured surprise

blessed /ˈblesɨd/ *adj* **1** *often cap* holy; venerated **2** – used as an intensive – **~ly** *adv* – **~ness** *n*

blessing /ˈblesɪŋ/ *n* **1a** the invocation of God's favour upon a person **b** approval **2** sthg conducive to happiness or welfare

blew /bluː/ *past of* **blow**

[1]**blight** /blaɪt/ *n* **1** (an organism that causes) a disease or injury of plants resulting in withering, cessation of growth, and death of parts without rotting **2** sthg that impairs, frustrates, or destroys **3** a condition of disorder or decay

[2]**blight** *v* **1** to affect (e g a plant) with blight **2** to impair, frustrate

blighter /ˈblaɪtəʳ/ *n, chiefly Br* a fellow; *esp* one held in low esteem – infml

blimey /ˈblaɪmi/ *interj, chiefly Br* – used for expressing surprise; slang

[1]**blind** /blaɪnd/ *adj* **1** unable to see; sightless **2a** unable or unwilling to discern or judge **b** not based on reason, evidence, or knowledge **3** without sight or knowledge of anything that could serve for guidance beforehand **4** performed solely by the use of instruments within an aircraft **5** hidden from sight; concealed **6** having only 1 opening or outlet – **~ly** *adv* – **~ness** *n*

[2]**blind** *v* **1** to make blind **2** to rob of judgment or discernment **3** to dazzle

[3]**blind** *n* **1** sthg to keep out light: e g **a** *chiefly Br* an awning **b** a flexible screen (e g a strip of cloth) usu mounted on a roller for covering a window **2** a cover, subterfuge

[4]**blind** *adv* **1** to the point of insensibility – usu in *blind drunk* **2** without seeing outside an aircraft

blind alley *n* a fruitless or mistaken course or direction

blind date *n* a date between people who have not previously met

blindfold /ˈblaɪndfəʊld/ *v or n* **1** (to cover the eyes of with) a piece of material (e g a bandage) for covering the eyes to prevent sight **2** (to hinder from seeing or esp understanding with) sthg that obscures vision or mental awareness

blindman's buff /ˌblaɪndmænz ˈbʌf/ *n* a group game in which a blindfolded player tries to catch and identify another player

blind spot *n* **1a** the point in the retina where the optic nerve enters that is not sensitive to light **b** a part of a visual field that cannot be seen or inspected **2** an area in which one lacks knowledge, understanding, or discrimination

[1]**blink** /blɪŋk/ *v* **1** to close and open the eyes involuntarily **2** to shine intermittently **3a** to wink *at* **b** to look with surprise or dismay *at*

[2]**blink** *n* **1** a glimmer, sparkle **2** a usu involuntary shutting and opening of the eye

blinking /ˈblɪŋkɪŋ/ *adj or adv, Br* bloody – euph

blip /blɪp/ *n* an image on a radar screen

bliss /blɪs/ *n* **1** complete happiness **2** paradise, heaven – **~ful** *adj* – **~fully** *adv* – **~fulness** *n*

blister /ˈblɪstəʳ/ *n* **1** a raised part of the outer skin containing watery liquid **2** an enclosed raised spot (e g in paint) resembling a blister **3** a disease of plants marked by large swollen patches on the leaves

blithe /blaɪð/ *adj* **1** lighthearted, merry, cheerful **2** casual, heedless – **~ly** *adv*

blitz /blɪts/ *v or n* **1** (to make) an intensive aerial bombardment **2** (to mount) an intensive nonmilitary campaign – chiefly journ

blizzard /ˈblɪzəd/ *n* **1** a long severe snowstorm **2** an intensely strong cold wind filled with fine snow **3** an overwhelming rush or deluge

bloated /ˈbləʊtɪ̣d/ *adj* **1** unpleasantly swollen **2** much larger than is warranted

bloater /ˈbləʊtəʳ/ *n* a large herring or mackerel lightly salted and briefly smoked

blob /blɒb/ *n* **1** a small drop of liquid or of sthg viscous or thick **2** sthg ill-defined or amorphous

bloc /blɒk/ *n* a (temporary) combination of individuals, parties, or nations for a common purpose

[1]**block** /blɒk/ *n* **1** a mould or form on which articles are shaped or displayed **2** a rectangular building unit that is larger than a brick **3** a wooden or plastic building toy that is usu provided in sets **4** the metal casting that contains the cylinders of an internal-combustion engine **5** a head – slang **6** an obstacle **7** a wooden or metal case enclosing 1 or more pulleys **8** (a ballet shoe with) a solid toe on which a dancer can stand on points **9** a part of a building or set of buildings devoted to a particular use **10** *chiefly NAm* (the distance along 1 side of) a usu rectangular space (e g in a town) enclosed by streets and usu occupied by buildings **11** a piece of engraved or etched material (e g wood or metal) from which impressions are printed

[2]**block** *v* **1a** to hinder the passage, progress, or accomplishment of (as if) by interposing an obstruction **b** to shut off from view **c** to obstruct or interfere usu legitimately with (e g an opponent) in various games or sports **d** to prevent normal functioning of **2** to arrange (e g a school timetable) in long continuous periods – **~age** *n*

blockade /blɒˈkeɪd/ *n* the surrounding or blocking of a particular enemy area to prevent passage of people or supplies – **blockade** *v*

block and tackle *n* an arrangement of pulley blocks with associated rope or cable for hoisting or hauling

blockbuster /ˈblɒkˌbʌstəʳ/ *n* **1** a huge high-explosive demolition bomb **2** sby or sthg particularly outstanding or effective *USE* infml

blockhouse /ˈblɒkhaʊs/ *n* **1** a building made of heavy timbers with loopholes for firing through, observation, etc, formerly used as a fort **2** an observation post built to withstand heat, blast, radiation, etc

block in *v* to sketch the outlines of, in a design

bloke /bləʊk/ *n, chiefly Br* a man – infml

[1]**blond** /blɒnd/ *adj* **1a** (having hair) of a flaxen, golden, light auburn, or pale yellowish brown colour **b** of a pale white or rosy white colour **2** of a light colour

[2]**blond** *n* **1** sby with blond hair and often a light complexion and blue or grey eyes **2** a light yellowish brown to dark greyish yellow colour

blonde /blɒnd/ *n or adj* (a) blond – used esp for or in relation to women

[1]**blood** /blʌd/ *n* **1a** the usu red fluid that circulates in the heart, arteries, capillaries, and veins of a vertebrate animal, carrying nourishment and oxygen to, and bringing away waste products from, all parts of the body **b** a comparable fluid of an invertebrate animal **2a** human lineage; *esp* the royal lineage **b** kinship **3** temper, passion **4** *archaic* a dashing lively esp young man; a rake – now usu humor

[2]**blood** *v* **1** to stain or wet with blood; *esp* to mark the face of (an inexperienced fox hunter) with the blood of the fox **2** to give an initiating experience to (sby new to a particular field of activity)

bloodbath /ˈblʌdbɑːθ/ *n* a great slaughter; a massacre

bloodcurdling /ˈblʌd,kɜːdlɪŋ/ *adj* arousing horror

blood heat *n* a temperature approximating to that of the human body; about 37°C or 98°F

bloodhound /ˈblʌdhaʊnd/ *n* **1** a large powerful hound of European origin remarkable for its acuteness of smell and poor sight **2** a person (e g a detective) who is keen in pursuing or tracking sby or sthg down

bloodless /ˈblʌdlʒs/ *adj* **1** deficient in or free from blood **2** not accompanied by the shedding of blood **3** lacking in spirit, vitality, or human feeling – **~ly** *adv* – **~ness** *n*

bloodletting /ˈblʌd,letɪŋ/ *n* bloodshed

blood pressure *n* pressure that is exerted by the blood on the walls of the blood vessels, esp arteries, and that varies with the age and health of the individual

bloodshed /ˈblʌdʃed/ *n* the taking of life

bloodshot /ˈblʌdʃɒt/ *adj, of an eye* having the white part tinged with red

blood sport *n* a field sport (e g fox hunting or beagling) in which animals are killed

bloodstain /ˈblʌdsteɪn/ *n* a discoloration caused by blood – **bloodstained** *adj*

bloodsucker /ˈblʌd,sʌkəʳ/ *n* a person who extorts sthg, esp money, from another

bloodthirsty /ˈblʌd,θɜːsti/ *adj* eager for bloodshed – **-tily** *adv* – **-tiness** *n*

bloody /ˈblʌdi/ *adj* **1** smeared, stained with, or containing blood **2** accompanied by or involving bloodshed **3a** murderous, bloodthirsty **b** merciless, cruel **4** – used as an intensive; slang – **bloodily** *adv* – **bloodiness** *n*

Bloody Mary /,blʌdi ˈmeəri/ *n* a cocktail consisting chiefly of vodka and tomato juice

bloody-minded *adj* deliberately obstructive or unhelpful – **~ness** *n*

[1]**bloom** /bluːm/ *n* **1a** a flower **b** the flowering state **2** a time of beauty, freshness, and vigour **3a** a delicate powdery coating on some fruits and leaves **b** cloudiness on a film of varnish or lacquer **4** a rosy or healthy appearance

[2]**bloom** *v* **1** to produce or yield flowers **2a** to flourish **b** to reach maturity; blossom

bloomer /ˈbluːməʳ/ *n* a stupid blunder – infml

bloomers /ˈbluːməz/ *n pl* a woman's undergarment with full loose legs gathered at the knee

blooming /ˈblʊmɪŋ, ˈbluːmɪŋ/ *adj, chiefly Br* – used as a generalized intensive

[1]**blossom** /ˈblɒsəm/ *n* **1a** the flower of a plant **b** the mass of bloom on a single plant **2** a high point or stage of development

[2]**blossom** *vi* **1** to bloom **2** to come into one's own; develop

[1]**blot** /blɒt/ *n* **1** a soiling or disfiguring mark; a spot **2** a mark of reproach; a blemish

[2]**blot** *v* **1** to spot, stain, or spatter with a discolouring substance **2** to dry or remove with an absorbing agent (e g blotting paper)

blotch /blɒtʃ/ *n* **1** an imperfection, blemish **2** an irregular spot or mark (e g of colour or ink) – **~y** *adj*

blotter /ˈblɒtəʳ/ *n* a piece of blotting paper

blotting paper *n* a spongy unsized paper used to absorb ink

blotto /ˈblɒtəʊ/ *adj, Br* extremely drunk – slang

blouse /blaʊz/ *n* a usu loose-fitting woman's upper garment that resembles a shirt or smock

[1]**blow** /bləʊ/ *v* **blew; blown** **1** *of air* to move with speed or force **2** to act on with a current of gas or vapour **3** to make a sound by blowing **4a** to pant **b** *of a whale* to eject moisture-laden air from the lungs through the blowhole **5** *of an electric fuse* to melt when overloaded **6a** to shatter, burst, or destroy by explosion **b** *of a tyre* to lose the contained air through a spontaneous puncture – usu + *out* **7** to produce or shape by the action of blown or injected air **8** to damn, disregard – infml **9** to squander (money or an advantage) – slang **10** to leave hurriedly – slang

[2]**blow** *n* **1** an instance of (the wind) blowing **2** a walk or other outing in the fresh air – infml

[3]**blow** *v* **blew; blown** to cause (e g flowers or blossom) to open out, usu just before dropping

[4]**blow** *n* **1** a hard stroke delivered with a part of the body or with an instrument **2** *pl* a hostile or aggressive state – esp in *come to blows* **3** a shock or misfortune

blow-by-blow *adj* minutely detailed

blower /ˈbləʊəʳ/ *n* **1** a device for producing a current of air or gas **2** *Br the* telephone – infml

blowfly /ˈbləʊflaɪ/ *n* any of various 2-winged flies that deposit their eggs or maggots esp on meat or in wounds

blowhole /ˈbləʊhəʊl/ *n* **1** a nostril in the top of the head of a whale, porpoise, or dolphin **2** a hole in the ice to which aquatic mammals (e g seals) come to breathe

blow in *v* to arrive casually or unexpectedly – infml

blowlamp /ˈbləʊlæmp/ *n* a small portable burner that produces an intense flame and has a pressurized fuel tank

blowout /ˈbləʊaʊt/ *n* **1** a large meal –infml **2** a bursting of a container (e g a tyre) by pressure of the contents on a weak spot **3** an uncontrolled eruption of an oil or gas well

blow out *v, of an oil or gas well* to erupt out of control

blowpipe /ˈbləʊpaɪp/ *n* **1** a small tube for blowing air, oxygen, etc into a flame to direct and increase the heat **2** a tube for propelling a projectile (e g a dart) by blowing

blowsy, blowzy /ˈblaʊzi/ *adj, esp of a woman* slovenly in appearance and usu fat

blowup /ˈbləʊ-ʌp/ *n* **1** an outburst of temper **2** a photographic enlargement

blow up *v* **1** to explode or be exploded **2** to build up or exaggerate to an unreasonable extent **3** to fill up with a gas, esp air **4** to make a photographic enlargement of **5** to become violently angry **6** to come into being; arise

blowy /ˈbləʊi/ *adj* windy

[1]**blubber** /ˈblʌbəʳ/ *n* the fat of large marine mammals, esp whales

[2]**blubber** *v* to weep noisily – infml

[1]**bludgeon** /ˈblʌdʒən/ *n* a short club used as a weapon

[2]**bludgeon** *v* to overcome by aggressive argument

[1]**blue** /bluː/ *adj* **1** of the colour blue **2** discoloured through cold, anger, bruising, or fear **3** low in spirits **4** Conservative **5a** obscene, pornographic **b** off-colour, risqué – **~ness** *n* – **bluish** *adj*

[2]**blue** *n* **1** a colour whose hue is that of the clear sky and lies between green and violet in the spectrum **2** a blue preparation used to whiten clothes in laundering **3a** the sky **b** the far distance **4** any of numerous small chiefly blue butterflies **5** *often cap, Br* a usu notional award given to sby who has

played in a sporting contest between Oxford and Cambridge universities; *also* sby who has been given such an award

[3]**blue** *v, Br* to spend lavishly and wastefully – infml

blue baby *n* a baby with a bluish tint, usu from a congenital heart defect

bluebell /'bluːbel/ *n* **1** the wild hyacinth **2** *chiefly Scot* the harebell

blueberry /'bluːbəri/ *n* (the edible blue or blackish berry of) any of several shrubs of the heath family

blue blood *n* high or noble birth

bluebottle /'bluːˌbɒtl/ *n* any of several blowflies of which the abdomen or the whole body is iridescent blue, that make a loud buzzing noise in flight

blue chip *n* a stock issue of high investment quality that enjoys public confidence in its worth and stability

blue-collar *adj* of or being the class of manual wage-earning employees

blueprint /'bluːˌprɪnt/ *n* **1** a photographic print in white on a bright blue ground, used esp for copying maps and plans **2** a detailed programme of action

blues /bluːz/ *n* **1** *sing or pl in constr* low spirits; melancholy – + *the* **2** (a song in) a melancholy style of music characterized by flattened thirds or sevenths where a major interval would be expected in the melody and harmony

bluestocking /'bluː ˌstɒkɪŋ/ *n* a woman with intellectual or literary interests – derog

[1]**bluff** /blʌf/ *adj* **1** rising steeply with a broad, flat, or rounded front **2** good-naturedly frank and outspoken – **~ly** *adv* – **~ness** *n*

[2]**bluff** *v* to deceive by pretence or an outward appearance of strength, confidence, etc

[1]**blunder** /'blʌndəʳ/ *v* **1** to move unsteadily or confusedly **2** to make a blunder – **~er** *n*

[2]**blunder** *n* a gross error or mistake resulting from stupidity, ignorance, or carelessness

blunderbuss /'blʌndəbʌs/ *n* an obsolete short firearm with a large bore and usu a flaring muzzle

[1]**blunt** /blʌnt/ *adj* **1** having an edge or point that is not sharp **2a** aggressively outspoken **b** direct, straightforward – **~ness** *n* – **~ly** *adv*

[2]**blunt** *v* to make less sharp or definite

[1]**blur** /blɜːʳ/ *n* **1** a smear or stain **2** sthg vague or indistinct

[2]**blur** *v* **1** to obscure or blemish by smearing **2** to become vague, indistinct, or confused

blurb /blɜːb/ *n* a short publicity notice, esp on a book cover

blurt out /ˌblɜːt 'aʊt/ *v* to utter abruptly and impulsively

[1]**blush** /blʌʃ/ *v* to become red in the face, esp from shame, modesty, or embarrassment – **~ingly** *adv*

[2]**blush** *n* **1** a reddening of the face, from shame, embarrassment, etc **2** a red or rosy tint

[1]**bluster** /'blʌstəʳ/ *v* to talk or act in a noisily self-assertive or boastful manner

[2]**bluster** *n* **1** a violent blowing **2** loudly boastful or threatening talk – **~ous, ~y** *adj*

BO *n* a disagreeable smell, esp of stale perspiration, given off by a person's body

boa /'bəʊə/ *n* **1** a large snake (e g the boa constrictor, anaconda, or python) that crushes its prey **2** a long fluffy scarf of fur, feathers, or delicate fabric

boar /bɔːʳ/ *n* **1a** an uncastrated male pig **b** the male of any of several mammals (e g a guinea pig or badger) **2** the Old World wild pig from which most domestic pigs derive

[1]**board** /bɔːd/ *n* **1a** a usu long thin narrow piece of sawn timber **b** *pl the* stage **2** daily meals, esp when provided in return for payment **3** *sing or pl in constr* **a** a group of people having managerial, supervisory, or investigatory powers **b** an official body **4** a flat usu rectangular piece of material designed or marked for a special purpose (e g for playing chess, ludo, backgammon, etc or for use as a blackboard or surfboard) **5** any of various wood pulps or composition materials formed into stiff flat rectangular sheets (e g cardboard)

[2]**board** *v* **1** to come up against or alongside (a ship), usu to attack **2** to go aboard (e g a ship, train, aircraft, or

bus) **3** to cover with boards – + *over* or *up* **4** to take one's meals, usu as a paying customer

boarder /ˈbɔːdəʳ/ *n* **1** a lodger **2** a resident pupil at a boarding school

boardinghouse /ˈbɔːdɪŋhaʊs/ *n* a lodging house that supplies meals

boarding school *n* a school at which meals and lodging are provided

boardroom /ˈbɔːdrʊm, -ruːm/ *n* a room in which board meetings are held

boast /bəʊst/ *v* **1** to praise oneself **2** to speak of or assert with excessive pride – **boast** *n* – **boaster** *n* – **~ful** *adj*

[1]**boat** /bəʊt/ *n* **1** a usu small ship **2** a boat-shaped utensil or dish

[2]**boat** *v* to use a boat, esp for recreation

boater /ˈbəʊtəʳ/ *n* a stiff straw hat with a shallow flat crown and a brim

boathook /ˈbəʊthʊk/ *n* a pole with a hook at one end, used esp for fending off or holding boats alongside

boatswain, bosun /ˈbəʊsən/ *n* a petty officer or warrant officer responsible for the supervision of all work done on deck and for routine maintenance of the ship's structure

[1]**bob** /bɒb/ *v* **1** to move down and up briefly or repeatedly **2** to curtsy briefly **3** to try to seize a suspended or floating object with the teeth

[2]**bob** *n* **1** a short quick down-and-up motion **2** (a method of bell ringing using) a modification of the order in change ringing

[3]**bob** *n* **1a** a knot or twist (e g of ribbons or hair) **b** a haircut for a woman or girl in which the hair hangs loose just above the shoulders **2** a float **3** *pl* a small insignificant item – in *bits and bobs*

[4]**bob** *v* to cut (hair) shorter; crop

[5]**bob** *n, pl* **bob** *Br* a shilling; *also* the sum of 5 new pence – infml

bobbin /ˈbɒbɪ̣n/ *n* a cylinder or spindle on which yarn or thread is wound (e g for use in spinning, sewing, or lacemaking)

bobsleigh /ˈbɒbsleɪ/ *n* a large usu metal sledge for 2 or 4 people used in racing

bod /bɒd/ *n* a person – infml

bode /bəʊd/ *v* to augur, presage

bodice /ˈbɒdɪ̣s/ *n* the part of a dress that is above the waist

bodily /ˈbɒdɪ̣li/ *adv* **1** in the flesh, in person **2** as a whole; altogether

bodkin /ˈbɒdkɪ̣n/ *n* a blunt thick needle with a large eye used to draw tape or ribbon through a loop or hem

body /ˈbɒdi/ *n* **1a(1)** the organized physical substance of a living animal or plant **(2)** a corpse **b** a human being; a person **2** the main, central, or principal part: e g **a** the main part of a plant or animal body, esp as distinguished from limbs and head **b** the part of a vehicle on or in which the load is placed **3** the part of a garment covering the body or trunk **4a** a mass of matter distinct from other masses **b** sthg that embodies or gives concrete reality to a thing; *specif* a material object in physical space **5** *sing or pl in constr* a group of people or things: e g **a** a fighting unit **b** a group of individuals organized for some purpose **6a** compactness or firmness of texture **b** comparative richness of flavour in wine – **bodily** *adj*

bodyguard /ˈbɒdigɑːd/ *n* an escort whose duty it is to protect a person from bodily harm

body politic *n* a group of people under a single government

bodywork /ˈbɒdiwɜːk/ *n* the structure or form of a vehicle body

Boer /ˈbəʊəʳ, bɔːʳ, bʊəʳ/ *n* a S African of Dutch descent

boffin /ˈbɒfɪ̣n/ *n, chiefly Br* a scientific or technical expert – infml

bog /bɒg/ *n* **1** (an area of) wet spongy poorly-drained ground **2** *Br* a toilet – slang – **~gy** *adj*

bog down *v* to cause to sink (as if) into a bog; impede

bogey, bogie /ˈbəʊgi/ *n* **1** a monstrous imaginary figure used to frighten children **2** a golf score of 1 stroke over par on a hole

boggle /ˈbɒgəl/ *v* **1** to be startled or amazed **2** to hesitate because of doubt, fear, or scruples

bogie, bogey /ˈbəʊgi/ *n* a swivelling framework with 1 or more pairs of wheels to carry and guide one end of a railway vehicle

bogus /'bəʊgəs/ *adj* spurious, sham

Bohemian /bəʊ'hiːmɪən, bə-/ *n* **1a** a native or inhabitant of Bohemia **b** the group of Czech dialects used in Bohemia **2** a person (e g a writer or artist) living an unconventional life

[1]**boil** /bɔɪl/ *n* a localized pus-filled swelling of the skin resulting from infection in a skin gland

[2]**boil** *v* **1a** *of a fluid* to change into (bubbles of) a vapour when heated **b** to come to the boiling point **2** to bubble or foam violently; churn **3** to be excited or stirred **4** to subject to the action of a boiling liquid (e g in cooking)

[3]**boil** *n* the boiling point

boil down *v* **1** to condense or summarize **2** to amount *to*

boiler /'bɔɪlə[r]/ *n* **1** a vessel used for boiling **2** the part of a steam generator in which water is converted into steam under pressure **3** a tank in which water is heated or hot water is stored

boiler suit *n, chiefly Br* a one-piece outer garment combining shirt and trousers, worn chiefly to protect clothing

boiling point *n* **1** the point at which a liquid boils **2** the point at which a person loses his/her self-control

boil over *v* **1** to overflow as a result of boiling **2** to lose one's temper

boisterous /'bɔɪstərəs/ *adj* **1** noisily and cheerfully rough **2** stormy, wild – **~ly** *adv* – **~ness** *n*

[1]**bold** /bəʊld/ *adj* **1** showing or requiring a fearless adventurous spirit **2** impudent, presumptuous **3** standing out prominently; conspicuous – **~ly** *adv* – **~ness** *n*

[2]**bold** *n* boldface

boldface /'bəʊldfeɪs/ *n* (printing in) the thickened form of a typeface used to give prominence or emphasis

bole /bəʊl/ *n* the trunk of a tree

bolero /bə'leərəʊ; *sense 2* 'bɒlərəʊ/ *n, pl* **boleros** **1** (music for) a type of Spanish dance **2** a loose waist-length jacket open at the front

boll /bəʊl/ *n* the seed pod of cotton or similar plants

bollard /'bɒləd/ *n* **1** a post on a wharf or on a ship's deck round which to fasten mooring lines **2** *Br* a short post (e g on a kerb or traffic island) to guide vehicles or forbid access

bollock /'bɒlək/ *n, Br* **1** a testicle – usu pl **2** *pl* nonsense – often used interjectionally *USE* vulg

Bolshevik /'bɒlʃɪ̣vɪk/ *n, pl* **Bolsheviks** *also* **Bolsheviki** **1** a member of the more radical wing of the Russian Social Democratic party that seized power in Russia in 1917 **2** a communist – derog – **-vism** *n*

[1]**bolster** /'bəʊlstə[r]/ *n* **1** a long pillow or cushion placed across the head of a bed, usu under other pillows **2** a structural part (e g in machinery) that eliminates friction or provides support

[2]**bolster** *v* to give support to; reinforce

[1]**bolt** /bəʊlt/ *n* **1a** a short stout usu blunt-headed arrow shot from a crossbow **b** a thunderbolt **2a** a sliding bar or rod used to fasten a door **b** the part of a lock that is shot or withdrawn by the key **3** a roll of cloth or wallpaper of a standard length **4a** a metal rod or pin for fastening objects together **b** a screw-bolt with a head suitable for turning with a spanner **5** a rod or bar that closes the breech of a breech-loading firearm

[2]**bolt** *v* **1** to move rapidly; dash **2a** to dart off or away; flee **b** to break away from control **3** to produce seed prematurely **4** to swallow (e g food) hastily or without chewing

[3]**bolt** *adv* in a rigidly erect position

[4]**bolt** *n* a dash, run

[5]**bolt** *v* to sift (e g flour)

bolt-hole *n* **1** a hole into which an animal runs for safety **2** a means of rapid escape or place of refuge

[1]**bomb** /bɒm/ *n* **1a** any of several explosive or incendiary devices usu dropped from aircraft and detonated by impact **b** nuclear weapons – + *the* **2** a rounded mass of lava exploded from a volcano **3** *Br* a large sum of money – infml **4** *NAm* a failure, flop – infml

[2]**bomb** *v* **1** to attack with bombs; bombard **2** to fail; fall flat – infml

bombard /bɒm'bɑːd/ *v* **1** to attack with heavy artillery or with bombers **2** to attack vigorously or persistently (e g with questions)

bombardier /ˌbɒmbə'dɪə[r]/ *n* **1** a non-commissioned officer in the British artillery 2 a US bomber-crew member who aims and releases the bombs

bombast /'bɒmbæst/ *n* pretentious inflated speech or writing – ~**ic** *adj* – ~**ically** *adv*

bomber /'bɒməʳ/ *n* **1** an aircraft designed for bombing **2** sby who throws or places bombs

bombshell /'bɒmʃel/ *n* sby or sthg that has a stunning or devastating effect

bona fide /ˌbəʊnə 'faɪdi/ *adj* genuine, sincere

bonanza /bə'nænzə, bəʊ-/ *n* sthg (unexpectedly) considered valuable, profitable, or rewarding

bonbon /'bɒnbɒn/ *n* a sweet; *specif* a fondant

¹bond /bɒnd/ *n* **1** sthg (e g a fetter) that binds or restrains **2** a binding agreement **3** an adhesive or cementing material **4** sthg that unites or binds **5a** a legally enforceable agreement to pay **b** a certificate of intention to pay the holder a specified sum, with or without other interest, on a specified date **6** the system of overlapping bricks in a wall **7** the state of imported goods retained by customs authorities until duties are paid **8** a strong durable paper, now used esp for writing and typing

²bond *v* **1** to overlap (e g bricks) for solidity of construction **2** to put (goods) in bond until duties and taxes are paid **3** to cause to stick firmly

bondage /'bɒndɪdʒ/ *n* **1** the tenure or service of a villein, serf, or slave **2a** slavery, serfdom **b** a form of sexual gratification involving the physical restraint of one partner

bonded /'bɒndɪ̣d/ *adj* **1** used for or being goods in bond **2** composed of 2 or more layers of fabric held together by an adhesive

¹bone /bəʊn/ *n* **1a** (the material that makes up) any of the hard body structures of which the adult skeleton of most vertebrate animals is chiefly composed **b** (a structure made of) ivory or another hard substance resembling bone **2** *the* essential or basic part or level; *the* core **3** *pl* the core of one's being **4** a subject or matter of dispute **5a** *pl* thin bars of bone, ivory, or wood held in pairs between the fingers and used to produce musical rhythms **b** a strip of whalebone or steel used to stiffen a corset or dress **c** *pl* dice – ~**less** *adj*

²bone *v* **1** to remove the bones from **2** to stiffen (a garment) with bones **3** to try to find out about, esp hurriedly; revise – usu + *up* – ~**d** *adj*

³bone *adv* absolutely, utterly – chiefly in *bone dry, bone idle*

bone china *n* a type of translucent and durable white porcelain made from a mixture of bone ash and kaolin

bone meal *n* fertilizer or feed made of crushed or ground bone

bonfire /'bɒnfaɪəʳ/ *n* a large fire built in the open air

¹bongo /'bɒŋgəʊ/ *n* any of 3 large striped antelopes of tropical Africa

²bongo *n, pl* **bongos** *also* **bongoes** either of a pair of small tuned drums played with the hands

bonhomie /'bɒnəmi/ *n* good-natured friendliness

bonkers /'bɒŋkəz/ *adj, chiefly Br* mad, crazy – infml

bonnet /'bɒnɪ̣t/ *n* **1** a cloth or straw hat tied under the chin, now worn chiefly by children **2** *Br* the hinged metal covering over the engine of a motor vehicle

bonny /'bɒni/ *adj, chiefly Br* attractive, comely – **bonnily** *adv*

bonsai /bɒn'saɪ/ *n* (the art of growing) a potted plant dwarfed by special methods of culture

bonus /'bəʊnəs/ *n* **1** sthg given in addition to what is usual or strictly due **2** money or an equivalent given in addition to an employee's usual pay

bony, boney /'bəʊni/ *adj* **1** consisting of or resembling bone **2** having large or prominent bones **3** skinny, scrawny

¹boo /buː/ *interj* – used to express contempt or disapproval or to startle or frighten

²boo *n, pl* **boos** a shout of disapproval or contempt

³boo *v* to show scorn or disapproval (of) by uttering 'boo''

¹boob /buːb/ *n* **1** a stupid mistake; a blunder – infml **2** a breast – slang

[2]**boob** *v* to make a stupid mistake – infml

[1]**booby** /'bu:bi/ *n* **1** an awkward foolish person **2** any of several small gannets of tropical seas **3** the poorest performer in a group

[2]**booby** *n* a breast – vulg

booby prize /'bu:bi praɪz/ *n* an award for the poorest performance in a contest

booby trap *n* **1** a trap for the unwary or unsuspecting **2** a harmless-looking object concealing an explosive device that is set to explode by remote control or if touched

[1]**book** /bʊk/ *n* **1a** a set of written, printed, or blank sheets bound together into a volume **b** a long written or printed literary composition **c** a major division of a treatise or literary work **d** a record of business transactions – usu pl **2** the bets registered by a bookmaker

[2]**book** *v* **1a** to reserve or make arrangements for in advance **b** *chiefly Br* to register in a hotel **2a** to take the name of with a view to prosecution **b** to enter the name of (a player) in a book for a violation of the rules usu involving foul play – used with reference to a rugby or soccer player – **~able** *adj* – **~ing** *n*

[3]**book** *adj* **1** derived from books; theoretical **2** shown by books of account

bookcase /'bʊk-keɪs/ *n* a piece of furniture consisting of a set of shelves to hold books

bookend /'bʊkend/ *n* a support placed at the end of a row of books

bookish /'bʊkɪʃ/ *adj* **1** relying on theoretical knowledge rather than practical experience **2** literary as opposed to colloquial – **~ly** *adv* – **~ness** *n*

bookkeeper *n* sby who records the financial dealings of a business – **-ping** *n*

bookmaker /'bʊk,meɪkəʳ/ *n* sby who determines odds and receives and pays off bets

bookmark /'bʊkmɑ:k/ *n* sthg used to mark a place in a book

bookstall /'bʊkstɔ:l/ *n* a stall where books, magazines, and newspapers are sold

bookworm /'bʊkwɜ:m/ *n* a person unusually fond of reading and study

[1]**boom** /bu:m/ *n* **1** a spar at the foot of the mainsail in fore-and-aft rig that is attached at its fore end to the mast **2** a long movable arm used to manipulate a microphone **3** a barrier across a river or enclosing an area of water to keep logs together; *also* the enclosed logs **4** a cable or line of spars extended across a river or the mouth of a harbour as a barrier to navigation

[2]**boom** *v* **1** to make a deep hollow sound or cry **2** to experience a rapid increase in activity or importance

[3]**boom** /bu:m/ *n* **1** a booming sound or cry **2a** a rapid growth or increase in a specified area **b** a rapid widespread expansion of economic activity

boomerang /'bu:məræŋ/ *n* **1** a bent piece of wood shaped so that it returns to its thrower and used by Australian aborigines as a hunting weapon **2** an act or utterance that backfires on its originator

[1]**boon** /bu:n/ *n* **1** a benefit or favour, esp when given in answer to a request **2** a timely benefit; a blessing

[2]**boon** *adj* close, intimate, and convivial – esp in *boon companion*

boor /bʊəʳ, bɔ:ʳ/ *n* a coarse, ill-mannered, or insensitive person – **~ish** *adj* – **~ishly** *adv* – **~ishness** *n*

[1]**boost** /bu:st/ *v* **1** to push or shove up from below **2** to increase, raise **3** to encourage, promote **4** to raise the voltage of or across (an electric circuit)

[2]**boost** *n* **1** a push upwards **2** an increase in amount **3** an act that promotes or encourages

booster /'bu:stəʳ/ *n* **1** an auxiliary engine which assists (e g at take-off) by providing a large thrust for a short time **2** a supplementary dose of a medicament

[1]**boot** /bu:t/ *n* **1** a high stout shoe; *also* a shoe for certain sports (e g football) **2** a blow or kick delivered (as if) by a booted foot **3** *Br* the major luggage compartment of a motor car **4** summary discharge or dismissal – slang; chiefly in *give/get the boot*

[2]**boot** *v* to kick

bootee, bootie /'bu:ti:, bu:'ti:/ *n* **1** a

short boot 2 an infant's sock worn in place of a shoe

booth /buːð/ *n* **1** a stall or stand for the sale or exhibition of goods **2** a small enclosure affording privacy (e g for telephoning, dining, etc)

bootleg /ˈbuːtleg/ *v, chiefly NAm* to manufacture, sell, or transport for sale (esp alcoholic drink) contrary to law – **-legger** *n*

booty /ˈbuːti/ *n* **1** plunder taken (e g in war) **2** a rich gain or prize

[1]**booze** /buːz/ *v* to drink intoxicating liquor to excess – slang

[2]**booze** *n* intoxicating drink *USE* slang

boozer /ˈbuːzəʳ/ *n* **1** a public house **2** sby who boozes – slang

[1]**bop** /bɒp/ *v or n* (to strike with) a blow (e g of the fist) – infml

[2]**bop** *n* jazz characterized by unusual chord structures, syncopated rhythm, and harmonic complexity and innovation

[3]**bop** *v* to dance (e g in a disco) in a casual and unrestricted manner, esp to popular music – infml

borage /ˈbɒrɪdʒ/ *n* a coarse hairy blue-flowered European herb

Bordeaux /bɔːˈdəʊ/ *n* a red or white wine of the Bordeaux region of France

[1]**border** /ˈbɔːdəʳ/ *n* **1** an outer part or edge **2** a boundary, frontier **3** a narrow bed of planted ground (e g beside a path) **4** an ornamental design at the edge of sthg (e g printed matter, fabric, or a rug)

[2]**border** *v* **1** to put a border on **2** to adjoin at the edge or boundary

borderline /ˈbɔːdəlaɪn/ *adj* **1** verging on one or other place or state without being definitely assignable to either **2** not quite meeting accepted standards (e g of morality or good taste)

[1]**bore** /bɔːʳ/ *v* **1** to make a hole with a rotary tool **2** to drill a mine or well – **~r** *n*

[2]**bore** *n* **1** a hole made (as if) by boring **2** a barrel (e g of a gun) **3a** the interior diameter of a tube **b** the diameter of an engine cylinder

[3]**bore** *past of* **bear**

[4]**bore** *n* a tidal flood that moves swiftly as a steep-fronted wave in a channel, estuary, etc

[5]**bore** *n* a tedious person or thing

[6]**bore** *v* to weary by being dull or monotonous – **~dom** *n*

born /bɔːn/ *adj* **1a** brought into existence (as if) by birth **b** by birth; native **2** having a specified character or situation from birth

borne /bɔːn/ *past part of* **bear**

borough /ˈbʌrə/ *n* a British urban constituency; *also* a similar political unit in the USA

borrow /ˈbɒrəʊ/ *v* **1** to take or receive with the intention of returning **2a** to appropriate for one's own use **b** to copy or imitate – **~er** *n* – **~ing** *n*

borscht /bɔːʃt/ *n* beetroot soup, served hot or cold usu with sour cream

borstal /ˈbɔːstl/ *n, often cap, Br* a penal institution for young offenders

borzoi /ˈbɔːzɔɪ/ *n* any of a breed of large long-haired dogs developed in Russia, esp for pursuing wolves

bosh /bɒʃ/ *n* nonsense – infml

[1]**bosom** /ˈbʊzəm/ *n* **1** the front of the human chest; *esp* the female breasts **2a** the breast considered as the centre of secret thoughts and emotions **b** close relationship

[2]**bosom** *adj* close, intimate

bosomy /ˈbʊzəmi/ *adj* having large breasts

[1]**boss** /bɒs/ *n* **1** a protuberant part or body **2** a raised ornamentation **3** a carved ornament concealing the intersection of the ribs of a vault or panelled ceiling

[2]**boss** *n* **1** one who exercises control or authority; *specif* one who directs or supervises workers **2** a politician who controls a party organization (e g in the USA)

[3]**boss** *v* to order – often + *'about* or *around* *USE* infml

boss-eyed *adj, Br* having a squint; cross-eyed – infml

bossy /ˈbɒsi/ *adj* domineering, dictatorial – infml – **bossiness** *n*

bosun /ˈbəʊsən/ *n* a boatswain

botany /ˈbɒtəni/ *n* **1** a branch of biology dealing with plant life **2** the properties and life phenomena exhibited by a plant, plant type, or plant group – **-anist** *n* – **-anic, -anical** *adj* – **-anize** *v*

[1]**botch** /bɒtʃ/ *v* **1** to repair, patch, or assemble in a makeshift or inept way **2** to foul up hopelessly; bungle *USE* infml

[2]**botch** *n* **1** sthg botched; a mess **2** a clumsy patchwork *USE* infml

[1]**both** /bəʊθ/ *adj* being the 2; affecting or involving the one as well as the other

[2]**both** *pron pl in constr* the one as well as the other

[3]**both** *conj* – used to indicate and stress the inclusion of each of 2 or more things specified by coordinated words or word groups

[1]**bother** /ˈbɒðəʳ/ *v* **1** to cause to be troubled or perplexed **2a** to annoy or inconvenience **b** – used as a mild interjection of annoyance **3** to take pains; take the trouble

[2]**bother** *n* **1** (a cause of) mild discomfort, annoyance, or worry **2** unnecessary fussing **3** a minor disturbance – ~**some** *adj*

[1]**bottle** /ˈbɒtl/ *n* **1a** a rigid or semirigid container, esp for liquids, usu of glass or plastic, with a comparatively narrow neck or mouth **b** the contents of a bottle **2a** intoxicating drink – slang **b** bottled milk used to feed infants **3** *Br* nerve; guts – slang

[2]**bottle** *v* **1** to put into a bottle **2** *Br* to preserve (e g fruit) by storage in glass jars

bottle-feed *v* to feed (e g an infant) by means of a bottle

bottle green *adj or n* very dark green

bottleneck /ˈbɒtlnek/ *n* **1a** a narrow stretch of road **b** a point or situation where free movement or progress is held up **2** a style of guitar playing using an object (e g a metal bar or the neck of a bottle) pressed against the strings to produce the effect of one note sliding into another

bottle up *v* to confine, restrain

[1]**bottom** /ˈbɒtəm/ *n* **1a** the underside of sthg **b** a surface on which sthg rests **c** the buttocks, rump **2** the ground below a body of water **3** the part of a ship's hull lying below the water **4a** the lowest, deepest, or farthest part or place **b** the lowest or last place in order of precedence **c** the transmission gear of a motor vehicle giving lowest speed of travel **d** the lower part of a two-piece garment – often pl with sing. meaning

[2]**bottom** *v* to reach the bottom – usu + *out*

bottom drawer *n, Br* a young woman's collection of clothes and esp household articles, kept in anticipation of her marriage

bottomless /ˈbɒtəmlǥs/ *adj* **1** extremely deep **2** boundless, unlimited

botulism /ˈbɒtʃʊlɪzəm/ *n* acute often fatal bacterial food poisoning

boudoir /ˈbuːdwɑːʳ/ *n* a woman's dressing room, bedroom, or private sitting room

bouffant /ˈbuːfɒŋ/ *adj* puffed out

bough /baʊ/ *n* a (main) branch of a tree

bought /bɔːt/ *past of* **buy**

bouillon /ˈbuːjɒn/ *n* a thin clear soup made usu from lean beef

boulder /ˈbəʊldəʳ/ *n* a large stone or mass of rock

boulevard /ˈbuːlvɑːd/ *n* a broad avenue, usu lined by trees

[1]**bounce** /baʊns/ *v* **1** to cause to rebound **2** to return (a cheque) as not good because of lack of funds in the payer's account – infml

[2]**bounce** *n* **1a** a sudden leap or bound **b** a rebound **2** verve, liveliness – **bouncy** *adj* – **-cily** *adv* – **-ciness** *n*

bounce back *v* to recover quickly from a blow or defeat

bouncer /ˈbaʊnsəʳ/ *n* **1** a man employed in a public place to restrain or remove disorderly people **2** a fast intimidatory short-pitched delivery of a cricket ball that passes or hits the batsman at above chest height after bouncing

bouncing /ˈbaʊnsɪŋ/ *adj* enjoying good health; robust

[1]**bound** /baʊnd/ *adj* going or intending to go

[2]**bound** *n* **1** a limiting line; a boundary **2** sthg that limits or restrains *USE* usu pl with sing. meaning

[3]**bound** *v* **1** to set limits to **2** to form the boundary of *USE* usu pass

[4]**bound** *adj* **1a** confined **b** certain, sure *to* **2** placed under legal or moral obligation

[5]**bound** *n* **1** a leap, jump **2** a bounce

[6]**bound** *v* **1** to move by leaping **2** to rebound, bounce

boundary /'baʊndəri/ *n* **1** sthg, esp a dividing line, that indicates or fixes a limit or extent **2a** the marked limits of a cricket field **b** (the score of 4 or 6 made by) a stroke in cricket that sends the ball over the boundary

bounder /'baʊndəʳ/ *n* a cad – not now in vogue

boundless /'baʊndlɪ̵s/ *adj* limitless – **~ly** *adv* – **~ness** *n*

bounteous /'baʊntɪəs/ *adj* giving or given freely – **~ly** *adv* – **~ness** *n*

bountiful /'baʊntɪfəl/ *adj* **1** generous, liberal **2** abundant, plentiful – **~ly** *adv*

bounty /'baʊnti/ *n* **1** generosity **2** sthg given generously **3** a financial inducement or reward, esp when offered by a government for some act or service

bouquet /bəʊ'keɪ, buː-/ *n* **1** a bunch of flowers fastened together **2** a distinctive and characteristic fragrance (e g of wine)

bouquet garni /ˌbuːkeɪ 'gɑːni/ *n* a small bunch of herbs (e g thyme, parsley, and a bay leaf) for use in flavouring stews and soups

bourbon /'bʊəbən, 'bɔː-/ *n* **1** *cap* a member of a royal dynasty who ruled in France, Spain, etc **2** a whisky distilled from a mash made up of not less than 51 per cent maize plus malt and rye

[1]**bourgeois** /'bʊəʒwɑː/ *n, pl* **bourgeois** **1** a middle-class person **2** one whose behaviour and views are influenced by bourgeois values or interests

[2]**bourgeois** *adj* **1** middle-class **2** marked by a narrow-minded concern for material interests and respectability **3** capitalist

bourgeoisie /ˌbʊəʒwɑː'ziː/ *n sing or pl in constr* the middle class

bout /baʊt/ *n* **1** a spell of activity **2** an athletic match (e g of boxing) **3** an outbreak or attack of illness, fever, etc

boutique /buː'tiːk/ *n* a small fashionable shop selling specialized goods

bouzouki *also* **bousouki** /bʊ'zuːki/ *n* a long-necked Greek stringed instrument that resembles a mandolin

bovine /'bəʊvaɪn/ *adj* **1** of oxen or cows **2** like an ox or cow (e g in being slow, stolid, or dull)

[1]**bow** /baʊ/ *v* **1** to submit, yield **2** to bend the head, body, or knee in respect, submission, or greeting – **~ed** *adj*

[2]**bow** /baʊ/ *n* a bending of the head or body in respect, submission, or greeting

[3]**bow** /bəʊ/ *n* **1** a bend, arch **2** a strip of wood, fibreglass, etc held bent by a strong cord and used to shoot an arrow **3** an often ornamental slipknot (e g for tying a shoelace) **4** (a stroke made with) a resilient wooden rod with horsehairs stretched from end to end, used in playing an instrument of the viol or violin family

[4]**bow** /bəʊ/ *v* **1** to (cause to) bend into a curve **2** to play (a stringed instrument) with a bow

[5]**bow** /baʊ/ *n* **1** the forward part of a ship – often pl with sing. meaning **2** the rower in the front end of a boat

bowdler·ize, -ise /'baʊdləraɪz/ *v* to remove unseemly or offensive passages from a book

bowels /'baʊəlz/ *n* **1** the gut, intestines **2** the innermost parts

[1]**bower** /'baʊəʳ/ *n* **1** an attractive dwelling or retreat **2** a (garden) shelter made with tree boughs or vines twisted together **3** a boudoir – poetic

[2]**bower** *n* a ship's principal anchor carried in the bows

[1]**bowl** /bəʊl/ *n* **1** any of various round hollow vessels used esp for holding liquids or food or for mixing food **2** the contents of a bowl **3a** the hollow of a spoon or tobacco pipe **b** the receptacle of a toilet **4a** a bowl-shaped geographical region or formation **b** *NAm* a bowl-shaped structure; *esp* a sports stadium – **~ful** *n*

[2]**bowl** *n* **1** a ball used in bowls that is weighted or shaped to give it a bias **2** *pl but sing in constr* a game played typically outdoors on a green, in which bowls are rolled at a target jack in an attempt to bring them nearer to it than the opponent's bowls

[3]**bowl** *v* **1** to play or roll a ball in bowls or bowling **2a** to play as a bowler in cricket **b** to deliver (a ball) to a batsman in cricket **c** to dismiss (a batsman

in cricket) by breaking the wicket – used with reference to a bowled ball or a bowler **3** to travel in a vehicle smoothly and rapidly – often + *along*

bowlegged /bəʊ'legɨ̣d, -'legd/ *adj* having legs that are bowed outwards at the knees

[1]**bowler** /'bəʊlə^r/ *n* the person who bowls in a team sport; *specif* a member of the fielding side who bowls (as a specialist) the ball in cricket

[2]**bowler, bowler hat** *n* a stiff felt hat with a rounded crown and a narrow brim

bowline /'bəʊlɨ̣n/ *n* **1** a rope attached to a sail to keep its windward edge taut and at a steady angle to the wind **2** a knot used to form a non-slipping loop at the end of a rope

bowling /'bəʊlɪŋ/ *n* any of several games in which balls are rolled at 1 or more objects

bowl over *v* **1** to strike with a swiftly moving object **2** to overwhelm with surprise

bow out *v* to retire, withdraw

bowsprit /'bəʊsprɪt/ *n* a spar projecting forwards from the bow of a ship

bow window /ˌbəʊ 'wɪndəʊ/ *n* a curved bay window

[1]**box** /bɔks/ *n* any of several evergreen shrubs or small trees used esp for hedges

[2]**box** *n* **1a** a rigid container having 4 sides, a bottom, and usu a cover **b** the contents of a box **2a** a small compartment (e g for a group of spectators in a theatre) **b(1)** the penalty area **(2)** the penalty box **3a** a shield to protect the genitals, worn esp by batsmen and wicketkeepers in cricket **b** a structure that contains a telephone for use by members of a specified organization **4** a small simple sheltering or enclosing structure **5** *Br* a gift given to tradesmen at Christmas **6** *Br* television; *specif* a television set – + *the*; infml

[3]**box** *v* **1** to enclose (as if) in a box – + *in* or *up* **2** to hem in (e g an opponent in soccer) – usu + *in*

[4]**box** **1** to slap (e g the ears) with the hand **2** to engage in boxing

Box and Cox /ˌbɒks ən 'kɒks/ *adv or adj, Br* alternating; in turn

[1]**boxer** /'bɒksə^r/ *n* one who engages in the sport of boxing

[2]**boxer** *n* a compact medium-sized short-haired dog of a breed originating in Germany

Boxer *n* a member of a Chinese secret society which was opposed to foreign influence in China and whose rebellion was suppressed in 1900

boxing /'bɒksɪŋ/ *n* the art of attack and defence with the fists practised as a sport

Boxing Day *n* December 26, observed as a public holiday in Britain (apart from Scotland), on which service workers (e g postmen) were traditionally given Christmas boxes

box number *n* the number of a box or pigeon hole at a newspaper or post office where arrangements are made for replies to advertisements or other mail to be sent

box office *n* **1** an office (e g in a theatre) where tickets of admission are sold **2** sthg that enhances ticket sales

[1]**boy** /bɔɪ/ *n* **1a** a male child from birth to puberty **b** a son **c** an immature male; a youth **d** a boyfriend **2** a fellow, person **3** a male servant – sometimes taken to be offensive – **~hood** *n* – **~ish** *adj* – **~ishly** *adv* – **~ishness** *n*

[2]**boy** *interj, chiefly NAm* – used to express excitement or surprise

boycott /'bɔɪkɒt/ *v* to refuse to have dealings with (e g a person, shop, or organization), usu to express disapproval or to force acceptance of certain conditions – **boycott** *n*

boyfriend /'bɔɪfrend/ *n* **1** a frequent or regular male companion of a girl or woman **2** a male lover

bra /brɑː/ *n, pl* **bras** a woman's closely fitting undergarment with cups for supporting the breasts

[1]**brace** /breɪs/ *n* **1** two of a kind; a pair **2** sthg (e g a clasp) that connects or fastens **3** a crank-shaped instrument for turning a drilling bit **4a** a diagonal piece of structural material that serves to strengthen **b** a rope attached to a yard on a ship that swings the yard horizontally to trim the sail **c** *pl* straps worn over the shoulders to hold up trousers **d** an appliance for supporting

a weak leg or other body part **e** a dental fitting worn to correct irregular teeth **5a** a mark { or } used to connect words or items to be considered together **b** (this mark connecting) 2 or more musical staves the parts of which are to be performed simultaneously

[2]**brace** *v* **1a** to prepare for use by making taut **b** to prepare, steel **2** to provide or support with a brace

bracelet /ˈbreɪslɨt/ *n* **1** an ornamental band or chain worn round the wrist **2** *pl* handcuffs – infml

bracing /ˈbreɪsɪŋ/ *adj* refreshing, invigorating

bracken /ˈbrækən/ *n* a common large coarse fern of esp moorland

[1]**bracket** /ˈbrækɨt/ *n* **1** an overhanging projecting fixture or member that is designed to support a vertical load or strengthen an angle **2a** a parenthesis **b** either of a pair of marks [ ] used in writing and printing to enclose matter **c** an angle bracket **3** (the distance between) a pair of shots fired usu in front of and beyond a target to aid in range-finding **4** any of a graded series of income groups

[2]**bracket** *v* **1** to place (as if) within brackets **2** to put in the same category; associate – usu + *together* **3a** to get a range by firing in front of and behind (a target) **b** to establish a margin on either side of (e g an estimation)

brackish /ˈbrækɪʃ/ *adj* slightly salty – **~ness** *n*

bract /brækt/ *n* a usu small leaf near a flower or floral axis

bradawl /ˈbrædɔːl/ *n* an awl; *esp* one used by a woodworker

[1]**brag** /bræg/ *n* a card game resembling poker

[2]**brag** *v* to talk or assert boastfully

braggart /ˈbrægət/ *n* a loud arrogant boaster

Brahman /ˈbrɑːmən/ *n* **1a** a Hindu of the highest caste traditionally assigned to the priesthood **b** the impersonal ground of all being in Hinduism **2** any of an Indian breed of humped cattle; *also* a large vigorous heat-resistant and tick-resistant animal developed in the USA by interbreeding Indian cattle

[1]**braid** /breɪd/ *v* **1** *chiefly NAm* to plait **2** to ornament, esp with ribbon or braid

[2]**braid** *n* **1** a narrow piece of fabric, esp plaited cord or ribbon, used for trimming **2** *chiefly NAm* a length of plaited hair

braille /breɪl/ *n, often cap* a system of writing or printing for the blind that uses characters made up of raised dots

[1]**brain** /breɪn/ *n* **1a** the portion of the vertebrate central nervous system enclosed within the skull, that constitutes the organ of thought and neural coordination **b** a nervous centre in invertebrates comparable in position and function to the vertebrate brain **2a** intellectual endowment; intelligence – often pl with sing. meaning **b(1)** a very intelligent or intellectual person **(2)** the chief planner of an organization or enterprise – usu pl with sing. meaning but sing. in constr

[2]**brain** *v* **1** to kill by smashing the skull **2** to hit hard on the head – infml

brainchild /ˈbreɪntʃaɪld/ *n* a product of one's creative imagination

brain drain *n* *the* loss of highly qualified workers and professionals through emigration

brainless /ˈbreɪnlɨs/ *adj* stupid, foolish – **~ly** *adv*

brainstorm /ˈbreɪnstɔːm/ *n* **1** a fit of insanity **2** *chiefly NAm* a sudden good idea

brain wave *n* **1** a rhythmic fluctuation of voltage between parts of the brain **2** a sudden bright idea

brainy /ˈbreɪni/ *adj* intelligent, clever – infml – **braininess** *n*

braise /breɪz/ *v* to cook (e g meat) slowly by first sautéing in hot fat and then simmering gently in a closed container

[1]**brake** /breɪk/ *n* **1** a device for arresting usu rotary motion, esp by friction **2** sthg that slows down or stops movement or activity

[2]**brake** *v* to slow or stop by a brake

[3]**brake** *n* an estate car

bramble /ˈbræmbəl/ *n* a rough prickly shrub, esp a blackberry

bran /bræn/ *n* the broken husk of cereal grain separated from the flour or meal by sifting

[1]**branch** /braːntʃ/ *n* **1** a secondary shoot or stem (e g a bough) arising from a main axis (e g of a tree) **2a** a tributary **b** a side road or way **3** a distinct part of a complex whole: e g **a** a division of a family descending from a particular ancestor **b** a distinct area of knowledge **c** a division or separate part of an organization

[2]**branch** *v* **1** to put forth branches **2** to spring out (e g from a main stem)

[1]**brand** /brænd/ *n* **1** a charred piece of wood **2a** a mark made by burning with a hot iron, or with a stamp or stencil, to identify manufacture or quality or to designate ownership (e g of cattle) **b** a mark formerly put on criminals with a hot iron **3a** a class of goods identified by name as the product of a single firm or manufacturer **b** a characteristic or distinctive kind **4** a sword – poetic

[2]**brand** *v* **1** to mark with a brand **2** to stigmatize **3** to impress indelibly

brandish /ˈbrændɪʃ/ *v* to shake or wave (e g a weapon) menacingly or ostentatiously

brand-new *adj* conspicuously new and unused

brandy /ˈbrændi/ *n* a spirit distilled from wine or fermented fruit juice

brash /bræʃ/ *adj* **1** impetuous, rash **2** uninhibitedly energetic or demonstrative **3** aggressively self-assertive; impudent

brass /braːs/ *n* **1** an alloy of copper and zinc **2** *sing or pl in constr* the brass instruments of an orchestra or band **3** brazen self-assurance **4 brass, brass hats** *sing or pl in constr* senior military personnel **5** *chiefly N Eng* money *USE* (*3, 4, & 5*) infml

brass band *n* a band consisting (chiefly) of brass and percussion instruments

brassiere /ˈbræzjəʳ/ *n* a bra – fml

brass tacks *n pl* details of immediate practical importance – esp in *get down to brass tacks*

brassy /ˈbraːsi/ *adj* **1** shamelessly bold; brazen **2** resembling brass, esp in colour

brat /bræt/ *n* an (ill-mannered) child

bravado /brəˈvaːdəʊ/ *n* blustering swaggering conduct

[1]**brave** /breɪv/ *adj* **1** courageous, fearless **2** excellent, splendid – **~ly** *adv* – **~ry** *n*

[2]**brave** *v* to face or endure with courage

[3]**brave** *n* a N American Indian warrior

[1]**bravo** /braːˈvəʊ/ *n, pl* **bravos, bravoes** a villain, desperado; *esp* a hired assassin

[2]**bravo** /ˈbraːvəʊ/ *n, pl* **bravos** a shout of approval – often used interjectionally in applauding a performance

[1]**brawl** /ˈbrɔːl/ *v* **1** to quarrel or fight noisily **2** *of water* to make a loud confused bubbling sound

[2]**brawl** *n* a noisy quarrel or fight

brawn /brɔːn/ *n* **1a** strong muscles **b** muscular strength **2** pork trimmings, esp the meat from a pig's head, boiled, chopped, and pressed into a mould

brawny /ˈbrɔːni/ *adj* muscular, strong – **-niness** *n*

[1]**bray** /breɪ/ *v* **1** to utter the loud harsh cry characteristic of a donkey **2** to utter or play loudly, harshly, or discordantly – **bray** *n*

[2]**bray** *v* to crush or grind finely

[1]**brazen** /ˈbreɪzən/ *adj* **1** resembling or made of brass **2** sounding harsh and loud like struck brass **3** contemptuously bold

[2]**brazen** *v* to face with defiance or impudence – esp in *brazen it out*

[1]**brazier** /ˈbreɪzjəʳ, ˈbreɪʒəʳ/ *n* one who works in brass

[2]**brazier** *n* a receptacle or stand for holding burning coals

[1]**breach** /briːtʃ/ *n* **1** infraction or violation (e g of a law, obligation, or standard) **2** a gap (e g in a wall) made by battering **3** a break in customarily friendly relations

[2]**breach** *v* **1** to make a breach in **2** to break, violate

[1]**bread** /bred/ *n* **1** a food consisting essentially of flour or meal which is baked and usu leavened, esp with yeast **2** food, sustenance **3a** livelihood **b** money – slang

[2]**bread** *v* to cover with breadcrumbs

breadcrumb /ˈbredkrʌm/ *n* a small fragment of bread

breadline /ˈbredlaɪn/ *n* **1** *Br* the level of income required for subsistence **2**

chiefly NAm a queue of people waiting to receive food given in charity

breadth /bredθ, bretθ/ *n* **1** distance from side to side **2a** sthg of full width **b** a wide expanse **3** liberality of views or taste

breadwinner /'bredwɪnəʳ/ *n* one whose wages are a family's livelihood

[1]**break** /breɪk/ *v* **broke; broken** **1a** to separate into parts with suddenness or violence **b** to come apart or split into pieces; burst, shatter **2** to violate, transgress **3a** to force a way through or into **b** to escape with sudden forceful effort – often + *out* or *away* **c** to make a sudden dash **4** to make or effect by cutting or forcing through **5** to disrupt the order or compactness of **6a** to defeat utterly; destroy **b** to give way in disorderly retreat **c** to crush the spirit of **d(1)** to train (an animal, esp a horse) for the service of human beings **(2)** to inure, accustom **e(1)** to exhaust in health, strength, or capacity **(2)** to fail in health, strength, or control **7a** to ruin financially **b** to reduce in rank **8a** to reduce the force or intensity of **b** to cause failure and discontinuance of (a strike) by measures outside bargaining processes **9** to exceed, surpass **10** to ruin the prospects of **11a** to stop or interrupt **b** to destroy the uniformity of **12a** to end a relationship, agreement, etc *with* **b** to cause to discontinue a habit **13a** to come to pass; occur **b** to make known; tell **14a** to solve or crack (a code or cipher system) **b** to demonstrate the falsity of (an alibi) **15** to split into smaller units, parts, or processes; divide – often + *up* or *down* **16** to become inoperative because of damage, wear, or strain **17** to open the operating mechanism of (a gun) **18** to separate after a clinch in boxing **19** *of a wave* to curl over and disintegrate in surf or foam **20** *of weather* to change suddenly, esp after a fine spell **21** *esp of a ball bowled in cricket* to change direction of forward travel on bouncing **22** *of a voice* to alter sharply in tone, pitch, or intensity; *esp* to shift abruptly from one register to another **23** to interrupt one's activity for a brief period **24** to make the opening shot of a game of snooker, billiards, or pool **25** *of cream* to separate during churning into liquid and fat

[2]**break** *n* **1** an act or action of breaking **2a** a condition produced (as if) by breaking; a gap **b** a rupture in previously good relations **3** the action or act of breaking in, out, or forth **4** a dash, rush **5a** a change or interruption in a continuous process or trend **b** a respite from work or duty; *specif* a daily pause for play and refreshment at school **c** a planned interruption in a radio or television programme **6a** the opening shot in a game of snooker, billiards, or pool **b** a slow ball bowled in cricket that deviates in a specified direction on bouncing **c** the act or an instance of breaking an opponent's service in tennis **d** a sequence of successful shots or strokes (e g in snooker) **7** a notable variation in pitch, intensity, or tone in the voice **8a** the point where one musical register changes to another **b** a short ornamental passage inserted between phrases in jazz **9a** a stroke of esp good luck **b** an opportunity, chance

breakage /'breɪkɪdʒ/ *n* **1** sthg broken – usu pl **2** allowance for things broken (e g in transit)

[1]**breakaway** /'breɪkəweɪ/ *n* a breaking away (e g from a group or tradition); a withdrawing

[2]**breakaway** *adj* **1** favouring independence from an association; withdrawing **2** *chiefly NAm* made to break or bend easily

breakdown /'breɪkdaʊn/ *n* **1** a failure to function **2** a physical, mental, or nervous collapse **3** failure to progress or have effect **4** a division into categories; a classification **5** an account in which the transactions are recorded under various categories

break down *v* **1a** to divide into (simpler) parts or categories **b** to undergo decomposition **2** to take apart, esp for storage or shipment **3** to become inoperative through breakage or wear **4** to lose one's composure completely

[1]**breaker** /'breɪkəʳ/ *n* a wave breaking into foam

[2]**breaker** *n* a small water cask

break-even *adj or n* (of or being) the point at which profit equals loss

breakfast /ˈbrekfəst/ *n* (food prepared for) the first meal of the day, esp when taken in the morning

break in *v* **1** to enter a house or building by force **2a** to interrupt a conversation **b** to intrude **3** to accustom to a certain activity **4** to use or wear until comfortable or working properly

breakneck /ˈbreɪknek/ *adj* extremely dangerous

break out *v* **1** to become affected with a skin eruption **2** to develop or emerge with suddenness and force **3** to escape **4** to take from shipboard stowage ready for use **5** to unfurl (a flag) at the mast

breakthrough /ˈbreɪkθruː/ *n* **1** an act or point of breaking through an obstruction **2** an attack that penetrates enemy lines **3** a sudden advance, esp in knowledge or technique

breakup /ˈbreɪkʌp/ *n* **1** a dissolution, disruption **2** a division into smaller units **3** *chiefly Can* the spring thaw

break up *v* **1** to disrupt the continuity of **2** to decompose **3** to come or bring to an end **4a** to break into pieces (e g for salvage); scrap **b** to crumble **5** to (cause to) lose morale or composure; *also* to give way to laughter **6** *Br, of a school* to disband for the holidays

breakwater /ˈbreɪk,wɔːtəʳ/ *n* an offshore structure (e g a wall) used to protect a harbour or beach from the force of waves

bream /briːm/ *n, pl* **bream,** *esp for different types* **breams** any of various European freshwater fishes related to the carps and minnows

¹breast /brest/ *n* **1** either of 2 milk-producing organs situated on the front of the chest in the human female and some other mammals **2** the fore part of the body between the neck and the abdomen **3** sthg (e g a swelling or curve) resembling a breast **4** the seat of emotion and thought; the bosom – fml

²breast *v* **1** to contend with resolutely; confront **2** to meet, lean, or thrust against with the breast or front **3** *chiefly Br* to climb, ascend

breastbone /ˈbrestbəʊn/ *n* the sternum

breast-feed *v* to feed (a baby) with the milk from the breast rather than a bottle

breastplate /ˈbrestpleɪt/ *n* a metal plate worn as defensive armour for the chest

breaststroke /ˈbrest-strəʊk/ *n* a swimming stroke executed on the front by thrusting the arms forwards while kicking outwards and backwards with the legs, then sweeping the arms backwards

breath /breθ/ *n* **1** a slight indication; a suggestion **2a** breathing **b** opportunity or time to breathe; respite **3** spirit, animation

breathalyse *also* **breathalyze** /ˈbreθəl-aɪz/ *v* to test (e g a driver) for the level of alcohol in exhaled breath

breathalyser *also* **breathalyzer** /ˈbreθəl-aɪzəʳ/ *n* a device used to test the alcohol content in the blood of a motorist, usu consisting of a plastic bag into which the subject blows through crystals which turn green if the alcohol level is too high

breathe /briːð/ *v* **1a** to draw air into and expel it from the lungs **b** to send *out* by exhaling **2** to live **3a** to pause and rest before continuing **b** to allow (e g a horse) to rest after exertion **4** *of wine* to be exposed to the beneficial effects of air after being kept in an airtight container (e g a bottle) **5** to utter, express

breather /ˈbriːðəʳ/ *n* **1** a small vent in an otherwise airtight enclosure (e g a crankcase) **2** a break in activity for rest or relief – infml

breathing space *n* a pause in a period of activity, esp for rest

breathless /ˈbreθlɪ̥s/ *adj* **1** not breathing; *esp* holding one's breath due to excitement or suspense **2a** gasping; out of breath **b** gripping, intense – **~ly** *adv* – **~ness** *n*

breathtaking /ˈbreθ,teɪkɪŋ/ *adj* making one breathless; exciting, thrilling – **~ly** *adv*

breathy /ˈbreθi/ *adj* characterized or accompanied by the audible passage of breath – **breathily** *adv* – **breathiness** *n*

breech /briːtʃ/ *n* **1** the buttocks **2** the part of a firearm at the rear of the barrel

breeches /ˈbrɪtʃɪ̵z/ *n pl* **1** knee-length trousers, usu closely fastened at the lower edges **2** jodhpurs that are baggy at the thigh and close fitting and fastened with buttons from the knee to the ankle

breeches buoy *n* a seat in the form of a pair of canvas breeches hung from a life buoy running on a rope leading to a place of safety for use in rescue at sea

[1]**breed** /briːd/ *v* **bred** **1** to rear; bring up **2** to produce, engender **3** to propagate (plants or animals) sexually and usu under controlled conditions – ~**er** *n*

[2]**breed** *n* **1** a group of animals or plants, often specially selected, visibly similar in most characteristics **2** race, lineage **3** class, kind

breeding /ˈbriːdɪŋ/ *n* **1** ancestry **2** behaviour; *esp* that showing good manners **3** the sexual propagation of plants or animals

[1]**breeze** /briːz/ *n* **1** a light gentle wind **2** a slight disturbance or quarrel – infml **3** *chiefly NAm* sthg easily done; a cinch – infml

[2]**breeze** *v* **1** to come *in* or *into*, or move *along*, swiftly and airily **2** to make progress quickly and easily – infml

breeze-block *n* a rectangular building block made of coke ash mixed with sand and cement

breezy /ˈbriːzi/ *adj* **1** windy, fresh **2** brisk, lively **3** off-hand, airy – **breezily** *adv* – **breeziness** *n*

brethren /ˈbreðrɪ̵n/ *pl of* **brother** – chiefly in fml address or in referring to the members of a profession, society, or sect

breve /briːv/ *n* a note equal in time value to 2 semibreves or 4 minims

brevity /ˈbrevɪ̵ti/ *n* **1** shortness of duration; the quality of being brief **2** expression in few words; conciseness

[1]**brew** /bruː/ *v* **1** to prepare (e g beer or ale) by steeping, boiling, and fermentation or by infusion and fermentation **2a** to contrive, plot – often + *up* **b** to be in the process of formation – often + *up* **3** to prepare (e g tea) by infusion in hot water

[2]**brew** *n* **1** a brewed beverage **2a** an amount brewed at once **b** the quality of what is brewed

brewery /ˈbruːəri/ *n* an establishment in which beer or ale is brewed

[1]**briar** /ˈbraɪəʳ/ *n* a plant with a prickly stem (e g a blackberry)

[2]**briar** *n* **1** a plant of the heather family; a brier **2** a tobacco pipe made from the root of a brier

[1]**bribe** /braɪb/ *v* to induce or influence (as if) by a bribe – ~**ry** *n*

[2]**bribe** *n* sthg, esp money, given or promised to influence the judgment or conduct of a person

bric-a-brac /ˈbrɪk əˌbræk/ *n* miscellaneous small articles, usu of ornamental or sentimental value; curios

[1]**brick** /brɪk/ *n* **1** a usu rectangular unit for building or paving purposes, typically about 8in × 3¾in × 2¼in made of moist clay hardened by heat **2** a rectangular compressed mass (e g of ice cream) **3** a reliable stout-hearted person; a stalwart – infml

[2]**brick** *v* to close, face, or pave with bricks – usu + *up*

brickbat /ˈbrɪkbæt/ *n* **1** a fragment of a hard material (e g a brick); *esp* one used as a missile **2** a critical remark

bride /braɪd/ *n* a woman at the time of her wedding – **-dal** *adj*

bridegroom /ˈbraɪdgruːm, -grʊm/ *n* a man at the time of his wedding

bridesmaid /ˈbraɪdzmeɪd/ *n* an unmarried girl or woman who attends a bride

[1]**bridge** /brɪdʒ/ *n* **1a** a structure spanning a depression or obstacle and supporting a roadway, railway, canal, or path **b** a time, place, or means of connection or transition **2a** the upper bony part of the nose **b** an arch serving to raise the strings of a musical instrument **c** a raised platform on a ship from which it is directed **d** the support for a billiards or snooker cue formed esp by the hand **3a** sthg (e g a partial denture permanently attached to adjacent natural teeth) that fills a gap

[2]**bridge** *v* to make a bridge over or across; *also* to cross (e g a river) by a bridge

[3]**bridge** *n* any of various card games for

usu 4 players in 2 partnerships in which players bid for the right to name a trump suit, and in which the hand of the declarer's partner is exposed and played by the declarer

bridgehead /ˈbrɪdʒhed/ *n* an advanced position (to be) seized in hostile territory as a foothold for further advance

[1]**bridle** /ˈbraɪdl/ *n* a framework of leather straps buckled together round the head of a draught or riding animal, including the bit and reins, used to direct and control it

[2]**bridle** *v* **1** to restrain or control (as if) with a bridle **2** to show hostility or resentment (e g because of an affront), esp by drawing back the head and chin

bridle path *n* a track or right of way suitable for horseback riding

Brie /briː/ *n* a large round cream-coloured soft cheese

[1]**brief** /briːf/ *adj* **1** short in duration or extent **2** in few words; concise – **~ly** *adv*

[2]**brief** *n* **1a** a statement of a client's case drawn up for the instruction of counsel **b** a case, or piece of employment, given to a barrister **c** a set of instructions outlining what is required, and usu setting limits to one's powers (e g in negotiating) **2** *pl* short close-fitting pants

[3]**brief** *v* **1** to provide with final instructions or necessary information **2** *Br* to retain (a barrister) as legal counsel – **~ing** *n*

briefcase /ˈbriːfkeɪs/ *n* a flat rectangular case for carrying papers or books

[1]**brier, briar** /ˈbraɪəʳ/ *n* a plant with a thorny, prickly stem

[2]**brier, briar** *n* a S European plant of the heather family with a root used for making pipes

[1]**brig** /brɪg/ *n* a 2-masted square-rigged sailing vessel

[2]**brig** *n* a prison in the US Navy

brigade /brɪˈgeɪd/ *n* **1** a large section of an army usu composed of a headquarters, several fighting units (e g infantry battalions or armoured regiments), and supporting units **2** an organized or uniformed group of people (e g firemen)

brigadier /ˌbrɪgəˈdɪəʳ/ *n* an officer commanding a brigade in the British army

brigand /ˈbrɪgənd/ *n* one who lives by plunder, usu as a member of a group; a bandit – **~age** *n*

brigantine /ˈbrɪgəntiːn/ *n* a 2-masted square-rigged sailing vessel differing from a brig in not carrying a square mainsail

bright /braɪt/ *adj* **1a** radiating or reflecting light; shining **b** radiant with happiness **2** *of a colour* of high saturation or brilliance **3a** intelligent, clever **b** lively, charming **c** promising, talented – **~ly** *adv* – **~ness** *n*

brighten /ˈbraɪtn/ *v* to make or become bright or brighter – often + *up*

brilliant /ˈbrɪlɪənt/ *adj* **1** very bright; glittering **2** of high quality; good – infml – **-liance, -liancy** *n*

[1]**brim** /brɪm/ *n* **1** the edge or rim of a hollow vessel, a natural depression, or a cavity **2** the projecting rim of a hat

[2]**brim** *v* to be full

brimstone /ˈbrɪmstəʊn, -stən/ *n* sulphur

brindled /brɪndəld/ *adj* having obscure dark streaks or flecks on a grey or tawny ground

brine /braɪn/ *n* water (almost) saturated with common salt

bring /brɪŋ/ *v* **brought 1a** to convey (sthg) to a place or person; come with or cause to come **b** to cause to achieve a particular condition **2a** to cause to occur, lead to **b** to offer, present **3** to prefer (a charge or legal case) **4** to sell for (a price)

bring down *v* **1** to cause to fall or come down **2** to kill by shooting **3** to reduce

bring forth *v* **1** to give birth to; produce **2** to offer, present

bring forward *v* **1** to produce to view; introduce **2** to carry (a total) forward (e g to the top of the next page)

bring in *v* **1** to produce as profit or return **2** to introduce **3** to pronounce (a verdict) in court **4** to earn

bring off *v* to carry to a successful conclusion; achieve, accomplish

bring on *v* **1** to cause to appear or occur **2** to improve, help

bring out *v* **1** to make clear **2a** to publish **b** to introduce (a young woman) formally to society **3** to utter **4** to cause (sby) to be afflicted with a rash, spots, etc – usu + *in* **5** to encourage to be less reticent – esp in *bring somebody out of him-/herself* **6** *chiefly Br* to instruct or cause (workers) to go on strike

bring round *v* **1** to cause to adopt a particular opinion or course of action; persuade **2** to restore to consciousness; revive

bring up *v* **1** to educate, rear **2** to cause to stop suddenly **3** to bring to attention; introduce **4** to vomit

brink /brɪŋk/ *n* **1** an edge; *esp* the edge at the top of a steep place **2** *the* verge, onset

brisk /brɪsk/ *adj* **1** keenly alert; lively **2** fresh, invigorating **3** energetic, quick – **~ly** *adv* – **~ness** *n*

brisket /ˈbrɪskɪ̈t/ *n* a joint of beef cut from the breast

[1]**bristle** /ˈbrɪsəl/ *n* a short stiff coarse hair or filament

[2]**bristle** *v* **1** to rise and stand stiffly erect **2** to take on an aggressive attitude or appearance (e g in response to a slight) **3** to be filled or thickly covered (*with* sthg suggestive of bristles)

bristly /ˈbrɪsli/ *adj* **1** thickly covered with bristles **2** tending to bristle easily; belligerent

bristols /ˈbrɪstəlz/ *n pl, Br* breasts – vulg

Brit /brɪt/ *n* a British person – infml

British /ˈbrɪtɪʃ/ *n* **1** *pl in constr* the people of Britain **2** *chiefly NAm* English as typically spoken and written in Britain – **British** *adj*

Briton /ˈbrɪtən/ *n* **1** a member of any of the peoples inhabiting Britain before the Anglo-Saxon invasions **2** a native, inhabitant, or subject of Britain

brittle /ˈbrɪtl/ *adj* **1** easily broken or cracked; frail **2** easily hurt or offended; sensitive **3** sharp, tense

[1]**broach** /brəʊtʃ/ *n* any of various pointed or tapered tools: e g **a** a tool for tapping casks **b** a spit for roasting meat

[2]**broach** *v* **1** to open up or break into (e g a bottle or stock of sthg) and start to use **2** to open up (a subject) for discussion

[1]**broad** /brɔːd/ *adj* **1** having ample extent from side to side **2** extending far and wide; spacious **3** open, full – esp in *broad daylight* **4** marked by lack of restraint or delicacy; coarse **5** liberal, tolerant **6** relating to the main points; general **7** dialectal, esp in pronunciation – **~ly** *adv* – **~ness** *n*

[2]**broad** *n* **1** the broad part **2** *often cap, Br* a large area of fresh water formed by the broadening of a river – usu pl; used chiefly with reference to such formations found in E Anglia **3** *chiefly NAm* a woman – slang

broad bean *n* (the large flat edible seed of) a widely cultivated Old World leguminous plant

[1]**broadcast** /ˈbrɔːdkɑːst/ *adj* cast or scattered in all directions

[2]**broadcast** *n* **1** the act of transmitting by radio or television **2** a single radio or television programme

[3]**broadcast** *v* **1** to scatter or sow (seed) broadcast **2** to make widely known **3** to transmit as a broadcast, esp for widespread reception **4** to speak or perform on a broadcast programme – **~er** *n* – **~ing** *n*

broaden /ˈbrɔːdn/ *v* to make or become broad

broadloom /ˈbrɔːdluːm/ *n or adj* (a carpet) woven on a wide loom

broad-minded *adj* tolerant of varied views, unconventional behaviour, etc; liberal – **~ly** *adv* – **~ness** *n*

broadsheet /ˈbrɔːdʃiːt/ *n* a large sheet of paper printed on 1 side only; *also* sthg (e g an advertisement) printed on a broadsheet

[1]**broadside** /ˈbrɔːdsaɪd/ *n* **1** a broadsheet **2a** (the simultaneous firing of) all the guns on 1 side of a ship **b** a forceful verbal or written attack

[2]**broadside** *adv* with the broader side towards a given object or point

broadsword /ˈbrɔːdsɔːd/ *n* a sword for cutting rather than thrusting

brocade /brəˈkeɪd/ *n* a rich (silk) fabric woven with raised patterns

broccoli /ˈbrɒkəli/ *n* a branching form of cauliflower whose young shoots are used for food

brochure /ˈbrəʊʃəʳ, -ʃʊəʳ/ *n* a small pamphlet

[1]**brogue** /brəʊg/ *n* a stout walking shoe characterized by decorative punched holes on the uppers

[2]**brogue** *n* a dialect or regional pronunciation; *esp* an Irish accent

broil /brɔɪl/ *v* **1** to cook by direct exposure to radiant heat (e g over a fire); *specif, NAm* to grill **2** to become extremely hot

[1]**broke** /brəʊk/ *past of* **break**

[2]**broke** *adj* penniless – infml

broken /ˈbrəʊkən/ *adj* **1** violently separated into parts; shattered **2a** having undergone or been subjected to fracture **b** *of a land surface* irregular, interrupted, or full of obstacles **c** not fulfilled; violated **d** discontinuous, interrupted **3a** made weak or infirm **b** subdued completely; crushed **c** not working; defective **4** affected by separation or divorce – **~ly** *adv* – **~ness** *n*

broker /ˈbrəʊkəʳ/ *n* an intermediary; *specif* an agent who negotiates contracts of purchase and sale (e g of securities)

brolly /ˈbrɒli/ *n, chiefly Br* an umbrella – infml

bromine /ˈbrəʊmiːn/ *n* a nonmetallic element, usu occurring as a deep red corrosive toxic liquid

bronchitis /brɒŋˈkaɪtɨs/ *n* (a disease marked by) acute or chronic inflammation of the tubes of the lungs accompanied by a cough and catarrh – **-tic** *adj*

bronco /ˈbrɒŋkəʊ/ *n, pl* **broncos** an unbroken or imperfectly broken horse of western N America

brontosaurus /ˌbrɒntəˈsɔːrəs/ *n* any of various large 4-legged and prob plant-eating dinosaurs – no longer used technically

[1]**bronze** /brɒnz/ *v* to make brown or tanned

[2]**bronze** *n* **1** any of various copper-base alloys; *esp* one containing tin **2** a sculpture or artefact made of bronze **3** a yellowish-brown colour **4 bronze, bronze medal** an award for coming third in a competition

Bronze Age *n* the period of human culture characterized by the use of bronze or copper tools and weapons

brooch /brəʊtʃ/ *n* an ornament worn on clothing and fastened by means of a pin

[1]**brood** /bruːd/ *n* **1** young birds, insects, etc hatched or cared for at one time **2** the children in one family – humor

[2]**brood** *v* **1** *of a bird* to sit on eggs in order to hatch them **2a** to dwell gloomily *on*; worry *over* or *about* **b** to be in a state of depression – **~er** *n*

[3]**brood** *adj* kept for breeding

broody /ˈbruːdi/ *adj* **1** *of fowl* ready to brood eggs **2** contemplative; moody **3** *of a woman* feeling a strong desire or urge to be a mother – infml – **-dily** *adv* – **-diness** *n*

[1]**brook** /brʊk/ *v* to tolerate; stand for

[2]**brook** *n* a usu small freshwater stream

broom /bruːm, brʊm/ *n* **1** any of various leguminous shrubs with long slender branches, small leaves, and usu showy yellow flowers **2** a long-handled brush, *esp* one made of a bundle of twigs

broomstick /ˈbruːmˌstɪk, ˈbrʊm-/ *n* the long thin handle of a broom

broth /brɒθ/ *n* (a thin soup made from) stock

brothel /ˈbrɒθəl/ *n* a house of prostitution

brother /ˈbrʌðəʳ/ *n, pl* **brothers,** (*3, 4, & 5*) **brothers** *also* **brethren** **1** a male having the same parents as another person; *also* a half brother or stepbrother **2** a kinsman **3** a fellow member **4** one, esp a male, who is related to another by a common tie or interest **5** a member of a men's religious order who is not in holy orders

brotherhood /ˈbrʌðəhʊd/ *n* **1** being brothers **2a** an association (e g a religious body) for a particular purpose **b** (an idea of) fellowship between all human beings

brother-in-law *n,* **1** the brother of one's spouse **2** the husband of one's sister

brought /brɔːt/ *past of* **bring**

brow /braʊ/ *n* **1a** an eyebrow **b** the forehead **2** the top or edge of a hill, cliff, etc

browbeat /ˈbraʊbiːt/ *v* **browbeat; browbeaten** to intimidate, coerce, or bully by a persistently threatening or dominating manner

[1]**brown** /braʊn/ *adj* **1** of the colour brown; *esp* of dark or tanned complexion **2** (made with ingredients that are) partially or wholly unrefined or unpolished – **~ish** *adj*

[2]**brown** *n* any of a range of dark colours between red and yellow in hue

[3]**brown** *v* to make or become brown (e g by sautéing)

brownie /'braʊni/ *n* **1 brownie guide, brownie** a member of the most junior section of the (British) Guide movement for girls aged from 7 to 10 **2** *chiefly NAm* a small square or rectangle of rich chocolate cake containing nuts

brown study *n* a state of serious absorption or abstraction; a reverie

[1]**browse** /braʊz/ *n* a period of time spent browsing

[2]**browse** *v* **1** *of animals* to nibble at leaves, grass, or other vegetation **2** to read or search idly *through* a book or a mass of things (e g in a shop), in the hope of finding sthg interesting

brucellosis /ˌbruːsl̩'ləʊsl̩s/ *n* a serious long-lasting disease, esp of human beings and cattle, caused by a bacterium

[1]**bruise** /bruːz/ *v* **1** to inflict a bruise on **2** to crush (e g leaves or berries) by pounding **3** to wound, injure; *esp* to inflict psychological hurt on

[2]**bruise** *n* **1** an injury involving rupture of small blood vessels and discoloration without a break in the skin; *also* a similar plant injury **2** an injury to the feelings

bruiser /'bruːzəʳ/ *n* a large burly man; *specif* a prizefighter

brunch /brʌntʃ/ *n* a meal, usu taken in the middle of the morning, that combines a late breakfast and an early lunch

brunette, *NAm also* **brunet** /bruː'net/ *n or adj* (sby, esp a young adult woman,) having dark hair and usu a relatively dark complexion

brunt /brʌnt/ *n* the principal force or stress (e g of an attack) – esp in *bear the brunt of*

[1]**brush** /brʌʃ/ *n* scrub vegetation

[2]**brush** *n* **1** an implement composed of bristles set into a firm piece of material and used for grooming hair, painting, sweeping, etc **2** a bushy tail, esp of a fox **3** an act of brushing **4** a quick light touch or momentary contact in passing

[3]**brush** *v* **1a** to apply a brush to **b** to apply with a brush **2** to remove with sweeping strokes (e g of a brush) – usu + *away* or *off* **3** to pass lightly over or across **4** to move lightly, heedlessly, or rudely – usu + *by* or *past*

[4]**brush** *n* a brief encounter or skirmish

brush-off *n* a quietly curt or disdainful dismissal; a rebuff – infml

brush up *v* **1** to tidy one's clothes, hair, etc **2** to renew one's skill in; refresh one's memory of – **brush-up** *n*

brusque /bruːsk, brʊsk/ *adj* abrupt to the point of rudeness in manner or speech – **~ly** *adv* – **~ness** *n*

brussels sprout /ˌbrʌsəlz 'spraʊt/ *n, often cap B* (any of the many edible small green buds that grow on the stem of) a plant of the cabbage family

brutal /'bruːtl/ *adj* **1** grossly ruthless or unfeeling **2** cruel, cold-blooded **3** harsh, severe **4** unpleasantly accurate and incisive – **-tality** *n* – **-tally** *adv*

[1]**brute** /bruːt/ *adj* **1** characteristic of an animal in quality, action, or instinct: e g **a** cruel, savage **b** not working by reason; mindless **2** purely physical

[2]**brute** *n* **1** a beast **2** a brutal person – **brutish** *adj* – **brutishly** *adv*

[1]**bubble** /'bʌbəl/ *v* **1** to form or produce bubbles **2** to make a sound like the bubbles rising in liquid **3** to be highly excited or overflowing (with a feeling)

[2]**bubble** *n* **1a** a usu small body of gas within a liquid or solid **b** a thin spherical usu transparent film of liquid inflated with air or vapour **2** sthg that lacks firmness or reality; *specif* an unreliable or speculative scheme **3** a sound like that of bubbling

bubble and squeak *n, chiefly Br* a dish consisting of usu leftover potato, cabbage, and sometimes meat, fried together

[1]**bubbly** /'bʌbli/ *adj* **1** full of bubbles **2**

overflowing with good spirits or liveliness; vivacious

[2]**bubbly** *n* champagne; *broadly* any sparkling wine – infml

bubonic plague /bjʊˌbɒnɪk ˈpleɪg/ *n* plague characterized by swellings in the groin and armpits

buccaneer /ˌbʌkəˈnɪəʳ/ *n* **1** a pirate esp in the W Indies in the 17th c **2** an unscrupulous adventurer, esp in politics or business

[1]**buck** /bʌk/ *n* **1a** a male animal, esp a male deer, antelope, rabbit, rat, etc **b** an antelope **2** a dashing fellow; a dandy **3** *NAm* a dollar – slang

[2]**buck** *v* **1** *of a horse or mule* to spring into the air with the back curved and come down with the forelegs stiff and the head lowered **2** to fail to comply with; run counter to

[3]**buck** *n the* responsibility – esp in *pass the buck*

bucked /bʌkt/ *adj* pleased, encouraged

bucket /ˈbʌkɨt/ *n* **1** a large open container used esp for carrying liquids **2** the scoop of an excavating machine **3** *pl* large quantities – infml

[1]**buckle** /ˈbʌkəl/ *n* a fastening consisting of a rigid rim, usu with a hinged pin, used to join together 2 loose ends (e g of a belt or strap) or for ornament

[2]**buckle** *v* **1** to fasten with a buckle **2** to bend, give way, or crumple

buckle down *v* to apply oneself vigorously

buckshee /ˌbʌkˈʃiː/ *adj or adv, Br* without charge; free – slang

buckshot /ˈbʌkʃɒt/ *n* a coarse lead shot used esp for shooting large animals

buckskin /ˈbʌkˌskɪn/ *n* a soft pliable usu suede-finished leather

bucktooth /bʌkˈtuːθ/ *n* a large projecting front tooth

buck up *v* **1** to become encouraged **2** to hurry up

buckwheat /ˈbʌkwiːt/ *n* **1** any of a genus of plants of the dock family that have pinkish white flowers and triangular seeds **2** the seed of a buckwheat, used as a cereal grain

bucolic /bjʊˈkɒlɪk/ *adj* **1** of shepherds or herdsmen; pastoral **2** (typical) of rural life – **~ally** *adv*

[1]**bud** /bʌd/ *n* **1** a small protuberance on the stem of a plant that may develop into a flower, leaf, or shoot **2** sthg not yet mature or fully developed: e g **a** an incompletely opened flower **b** an outgrowth of an organism that becomes a new individual

[2]**bud** *v* **1** *of a plant* to put forth buds **2** to reproduce asexually by forming and developing buds **3** to graft a bud into (a plant of another kind), usu in order to propagate a desired variety

Buddhism /ˈbʊdɪzəm/ *n* an eastern religion growing out of the teaching of Gautama Buddha that one can be liberated from the suffering inherent in life by mental and moral self-purification – **Buddhist** *n or adj*

budding /ˈbʌdɪŋ/ *adj* being in an early and usu promising stage of development

buddy /ˈbʌdi/ *n, chiefly NAm* **1** a companion, partner **2** mate – used in address *USE* infml

budge /bʌdʒ/ *v* **1** to (cause to) move or shift **2** to (force or cause to) change an opinion or yield

budgerigar /ˈbʌdʒərigaːʳ/ *n* a small Australian bird that belongs to the same family as the parrots and is often kept in captivity

[1]**budget** /ˈbʌdʒɨt/ *n* **1** a statement of a financial position for a definite period of time (e g for the following year), that is based on estimates of expenditures and proposals for financing them **2** a plan of how money will be spent or allocated **3** the amount of money available for, required for, or assigned to a particular purpose – **~ary** *adj*

[2]**budget** *v* to plan or provide for the use of (e g money, time, or manpower) in detail

[1]**buff** /bʌf/ *n* **1** *the* bare skin – chiefly in *in the buff* **2** (a) pale yellowish brown **3** a device (e g a stick or pad) with a soft absorbent surface used for polishing sthg **4** one who has a keen interest in and wide knowledge of a specified subject; an enthusiast

[2]**buff** *v* to polish, shine *up*

buffalo /ˈbʌfələʊ/ *n* **1 buffalo, water buffalo** an often domesticated Asian ox **2** a large N American wild ox with short horns, heavy forequarters, and a large muscular hump

[1]**buffer** /ˈbʌfəʳ/ *n* an (ineffectual) fellow – chiefly in *old buffer*; infml

[2]**buffer** *n* **1** a spring-loaded metal disc on a railway vehicle or at the end of a railway track **2** a device that serves to protect sthg, or to cushion against shock **3** a person who shields another, esp from annoying routine matters

[3]**buffer** *v* to lessen the shock of; cushion

buffer state *n* a small neutral state lying between 2 larger potentially rival powers

[1]**buffet** /ˈbʌfɪ̣t/ *n* **1** a blow, esp with the hand **2** sthg that strikes with telling force

[2]**buffet** *v* **1** to strike sharply, esp with the hand; cuff **2** to strike repeatedly; batter **3** to use roughly; treat unpleasantly

[3]**buffet** /ˈbʊfeɪ/ *n* **1** a meal set out on tables or a sideboard for diners to help themselves **2** *chiefly Br* a self-service restaurant or snack bar

buffoon /bəˈfuːn/ *n* **1** a ludicrous figure; a clown **2** a rough and noisy fool – **~ery** *n*

[1]**bug** /bʌg/ *n* **1** any of several insects commonly considered obnoxious; *esp* a bedbug **2** an unexpected defect or imperfection **3** a disease-producing germ; *also* a disease caused by it – not used technically **4** a concealed listening device **5** a temporary enthusiasm; a craze – infml

[2]**bug** *v* **1** to plant a concealed listening device in **2** to bother, annoy – infml

bugbear /ˈbʌgbeəʳ/ *n* an object or (persistent) source of fear, concern, or difficulty

[1]**bugger** /ˈbʌgəʳ/ *n* **1** a sodomite **2** a (worthless or contemptible) person, esp male **3** *Br* a cause of annoyance or difficulty *USE* (*except 1*) vulg

[2]**bugger** *v* **1** to practise sodomy on **2** – used interjectionally to express contempt or annoyance **3** to damage or ruin – often + *up* **4** to fool *around* or *about* *USE* (*except 1*) vulg

buggery /ˈbʌgəri/ *n* sodomy

buggy /bʌgi/ *n* a light one-horse carriage

[1]**bugle** /ˈbjuːgəl/ *n* a European annual plant of the mint family that has spikes of blue flowers

[2]**bugle** *n* a valveless brass instrument that is used esp for military calls

[1]**build** /bɪld/ *v* **built** **1** to construct by putting together materials gradually into a composite whole **2** to develop according to a systematic plan, by a definite process, or on a particular base **3a** to increase in intensity **b** to develop in extent – **~er** *n*

[2]**build** *n* the physical proportions of a person or animal; *esp* a person's figure of a usu specified type

build in *v* to construct or develop as an integral part

building /ˈbɪldɪŋ/ *n* **1** a permanent structure (e g a school or house) usu having walls and a roof **2** the art, business, or act of assembling materials into a structure

building society *n* any of various British organizations in which the public can invest money, and which advance money for house purchase

buildup /ˈbɪld-ʌp/ *n* praise or publicity, esp given in advance

build up *v* **1** to accumulate or develop appreciably **2** to promote the esteem of; praise

bulb /bʌlb/ *n* **1a** a short stem base of a plant (e g the lily, onion, or hyacinth), with 1 or more buds enclosed in overlapping membranous or fleshy leaves, that is formed underground as a resting stage in the plant's development **b** a tuber, corm, or other fleshy structure resembling a bulb in appearance **c** a plant having or developing from a bulb **2** a glass globe containing a filament that produces light when electricity is passed through it – **~ous** *adj*

[1]**bulge** /bʌldʒ/ *n* **1** a swelling or convex curve on a surface, usu caused by pressure from within or below **2** a sudden and usu temporary expansion (e g in population) – **bulgy** *adj* – **bulgily** *adv* – **bulginess** *n*

[2]**bulge** *v* to jut out; swell

[1]**bulk** /bʌlk/ *n* **1a** spatial dimension; also volume **b** roughage **2** voluminous or ponderous mass – often used with reference to the shape or size of a corpulent person **3** the main or greater part *of*

²bulk *v* **1** to cause to swell or to be thicker or fuller; pad – often + *out* **2** to gather into a mass **3** to appear as a factor; loom

³bulk *adj* (of materials) in bulk

bulkhead /ˈbʌlkhed/ *n* a partition or wall separating compartments (e g in an aircraft or ship)

bulky /ˈbʌlki/ *adj* **1** having too much bulk; *esp* unwieldy **2** corpulent – chiefly euph – **-kily** *adv* – **-kiness** *n*

¹bull /bʊl/ *n* **1a** an adult male bovine animal **b** an adult male elephant, whale, or other large animal **2** one who buys securities or commodities in expectation of a price rise or who acts to effect such a rise **3** a bull's eye – **~ish** *adj*

²bull *n* a papal edict on a subject of major importance

³bull *n* **1** empty boastful talk; nonsense **2** *Br* unnecessary or irksome fatigues or discipline, esp in the armed forces *USE* slang

bulldog /ˈbʊldɒg/ *n* **1** a thickset muscular short-haired dog of an English breed that has widely separated forelegs and a short neck **2** a proctor's attendant at Oxford or Cambridge

bulldoze /ˈbʊldəʊz/ *v* **1** to move, clear, gouge out, or level off with a bulldozer **2** to force insensitively or ruthlessly

bulldozer /ˈbʊldəʊzəʳ/ *n* a tractor-driven machine with a broad blunt horizontal blade that is used for clearing land, building roads, etc

bullet /ˈbʊl̩ɪt/ *n* a small round or elongated missile designed to be fired from a firearm; *broadly* a cartridge – **~proof** *adj*

bulletin /ˈbʊlətl̩ɪn/ *n* a brief public notice; *specif* a brief news item

bullfight /ˈbʊlfaɪt/ *n* a spectacle (in an arena) in which bulls are ceremonially excited, fought with, and killed, for public entertainment – **~ing** *n* – **~er** *n*

bullfinch /ˈbʊl,fɪntʃ/ *n* a European finch, the male of which has a rosy red breast and throat

bullfrog /ˈbʊlfrɒg/ *n* a heavy-bodied deep-voiced frog

bullion /ˈbʊljən/ *n* gold or silver (in bars) that has not been minted

bullock /ˈbʊlək/ *n* a young or castrated bull

bullring /ˈbʊl,rɪŋ/ *n* an arena for bullfights

bull's-eye *n* **1** a small thick disc of glass inserted (e g in a ship's deck) to let in light **2** a very hard round usu peppermint sweet **3a** (a shot that hits) the centre of a target **b** sthg that precisely attains a desired end

¹bully /ˈbʊli/ *n* **1** a browbeating person; *esp* one habitually cruel to others weaker than him-/herself **2** a hired ruffian

²bully *v* to treat abusively; intimidate

³bully, bully-off *v or n* (to perform) a procedure for starting play in a hockey match in which 2 opposing players face each other and alternately strike the ground and the opponent's stick 3 times before attempting to gain possession of the ball

bulrush /ˈbʊlrʌʃ/ *n* **1** any of a genus of annual or perennial sedges **2** the papyrus – used in the Bible **3** *Br* either of 2 varieties of reed

bulwark /ˈbʊlwək/ *n* **1a** a solid wall-like structure raised for defence; a rampart **b** a breakwater, seawall **2** a strong support or protection **3** the side of a ship above the upper deck – usu pl with sing. meaning

¹bum /bʌm/ *n* the buttocks – slang

²bum *v* **1** to spend time idly and often travelling casually – usu + *around*; slang **2** to obtain by begging; cadge – slang

³bum *n, NAm* **1** a vagrant, tramp **2** an incompetent worthless person *USE* slang

⁴bum *adj, chiefly NAm* **1** inferior, worthless **2** disabled *USE* slang

bumble /ˈbʌmbəl/ *v* **1** to speak in a faltering manner **2** to proceed unsteadily; stumble – often + *along*

bumblebee /ˈbʌmbəlbiː/ *n* any of numerous large robust hairy bees

bumf, bumph /bʌmf/ *n* **1** toilet paper – slang **2** (boring or unnecessary) paperwork

bummer /ˈbʌməʳ/ *n* an unpleasant experience (e g a bad reaction to a hallucinogenic drug) – infml

¹bump /bʌmp/ *v* **1** to knock against sthg with a forceful jolt – often + *into* **2** to meet, esp by chance

²bump *n* **1** a sudden forceful blow or jolt **2** a rounded projection from a surface; *esp* a swelling of tissue **3** a thrusting of the hips forwards in an erotic manner **4** *pl the* act of holding a child by his/her arms and legs and swinging him/her into the air and back to the ground

¹bumper /ˈbʌmpəʳ/ *n* a brimming cup or glass

²bumper *adj* unusually large

³bumper *n* a metal or rubber bar, usu at either end of a motor vehicle, for absorbing shock or minimizing damage in collision

bumpkin /ˈbʌmpkɨn/ *n* an awkward and unsophisticated rustic

bump off *v* to murder – slang

bumptious /ˈbʌmpʃəs/ *adj* self-assertive in a presumptuous, obtuse, and often noisy manner – **~ly** *adv* – **~ness** *n*

bumpy /ˈbʌmpi/ *adj* **1** having or covered with bumps; uneven **2** marked by jolts – **-pily** *adv* – **-piness** *n*

bun /bʌn/ *n* **1** any of various usu sweet and round small rolls or cakes that may contain added ingredients (e g currants or spice) **2** a usu tight knot of hair worn esp on the back of the head

¹bunch /bʌntʃ/ *n* **1** a compact group formed by a number of things of the same kind, esp when growing or held together; a cluster **2** *sing or pl in constr* the main group (e g of cyclists) in a race **3** *pl, Br* a style in which the hair is divided into 2 lengths and tied, usu one on each side of the head **4** *sing or pl in constr* a group of people – infml

²bunch *v* to form (into) a group or cluster – often + *up*

¹bundle /ˈbʌndl/ *n* **1a** a collection of things held loosely together **b** a package **c** a collection, conglomerate **2** a great deal; mass **3** a sizable sum of money – slang

²bundle *v* **1** to make into a bundle or package **2** to hustle or hurry unceremoniously **3** to hastily deposit or stuff *into* a suitcase, box, drawer, etc

¹bung /bʌŋ/ *n* the stopper of a cask; *broadly* sthg used to plug an opening

²bung *v* **1** to plug, block, or close (as if) with a bung – often + *up* **2** *chiefly Br* to throw, toss – infml

bungalow /ˈbʌŋgələʊ/ *n* a usu detached or semidetached 1-storied house

bungle /ˈbʌŋgəl/ *v* to perform clumsily; mishandle, botch – **~r** *n*

bunion /ˈbʌnjən/ *n* an inflamed swelling at the side of the foot on the first joint of the big toe

¹bunk /bʌŋk/ *n* a built-in bed (e g on a ship) that is often one of a tier of berths

²bunk *v* to sleep or bed *down*, esp in a makeshift bed

³bunk *n* nonsense, humbug

¹bunker /ˈbʌŋkəʳ/ *n* **1** a bin or compartment for storage; *esp* one on a ship for storing fuel **2a** a fortified chamber mostly below ground **b** a golf course hazard that is an area of sand-covered bare ground with 1 or more embankments

bunkum /ˈbʌŋkəm/ *n* insincere or foolish talk; nonsense

bunny /ˈbʌni/ *n* a rabbit – usu used by or to children

Bunsen burner /ˌbʌnsən ˈbɜːnəʳ/ *n* a gas burner in which air is mixed with the gas to produce an intensely hot blue flame

¹bunting /ˈbʌntɪŋ/ *n* any of various birds that have short strong beaks and are related to the finches

²bunting *n* (flags or decorations made of) a lightweight loosely woven fabric

¹buoy /bɔɪ/ *n* a distinctively shaped and marked float moored to the bottom **a** as a navigational aid to mark a channel or hazard **b** for mooring a ship

²buoy *v* **1** to mark (as if) by a buoy **2a** to keep afloat **b** to support, sustain **3** to raise the spirits of *USE* (*2 & 3*) usu + *up* – **~ancy** *n* – **~ant** *adj* – **~antly** *adv*

burble /ˈbɜːbəl/ *v* **1** to make a bubbling sound; gurgle **2** to babble, prattle

¹burden /ˈbɜːdən/ *n* **1a** sthg that is carried; a load **b** a duty, responsibility

2 sthg oppressive or wearisome; an encumbrance

[2]**burden** *v* to load, oppress

[3]**burden** *n* **1** a chorus, refrain **2** a central topic; a theme

burdensome /ˈbɜːdənsəm/ *adj* oppressive – ~**ness** *n*

burdock /ˈbɜːdɒk/ *n* any of a genus of coarse composite plants bearing prickly spherical flower heads

bureau /ˈbjʊərəʊ/ *n, pl* **bureaus** *also* **bureaux 1a** a specialized administrative unit; *esp* a government department **b** an establishment for exchanging information, making contacts, or coordinating activities **2** *Br* a writing desk; *esp* one with drawers and a sloping top

bureaucracy /bjʊˈrɒkrəsi, bjʊə-/ *n* government characterized by specialization of functions, adherence to fixed rules, and a hierarchy of authority; *also* the body of appointed government officials

bureaucrat /ˈbjʊərəkræt/ *n* a government official who follows a rigid routine – ~**ic** *adj* – ~**ically** *adv*

burgeon /ˈbɜːdʒən/ *v* **1** to send forth new growth (e g buds or branches) **2** to grow and expand rapidly

burgh /ˈbʌrə/ *n* a borough; *specif* a town in Scotland that has a charter – ~**er** *n*

burglar /ˈbɜːgləʳ/ *n* sby who unlawfully enters a building (e g to steal) – ~**y** *n* – **burgle** *v*

Burgundy /ˈbɜːgəndi/ *n* a red or white table wine from the Burgundy region of France

burial /ˈberɪəl/ *n* the act, process, or ceremony of burying esp a dead body

burlesque /bɜːˈlesk/ *n* **1** a literary or dramatic work that uses exaggeration or imitation to ridicule **2** mockery, usu by caricature **3** a US stage show usu consisting of short turns, comic sketches, and striptease acts

burly /ˈbɜːli/ *adj* strongly and heavily built – **-liness** *n*

[1]**burn** /bɜːn/ *n, chiefly Scot* a small stream

[2]**burn** *v* **burnt, burned 1a** to consume fuel and give off heat, light, and gases **b** to undergo combustion **c** to destroy by fire **d** to use as fuel **2a** *of the ears or face* to become very red and feel uncomfortably hot **b** to produce or undergo a painfully stinging or smarting sensation **c** to be filled *with*; experience sthg strongly **3a** to injure or damage by exposure to fire, heat, radiation, caustic chemicals, or electricity **b** to execute by burning **c** to char or scorch by exposing to fire or heat

[3]**burn** *n* **1** injury or damage resulting (as if) from burning **2** a burned area **3** a burning sensation

burner /ˈbɜːnəʳ/ *n* the part of a fuel-burning device (e g a stove or furnace) where the flame is produced

burning /ˈbɜːnɪŋ/ *adj* **1a** on fire **b** ardent, intense **2a** affecting (as if) with heat **b** resembling that produced by a burn **3** of fundamental importance; urgent

burnish /ˈbɜːnɪʃ/ *v* to make shiny or lustrous, esp by rubbing; polish

burnous /bɜːˈnuːs/ *n* a hooded cloak traditionally worn by Arabs

burnt-out *adj* exhausted or worn out by too much activity or use

burn up *v* to drive along extremely fast – infml

burp /bɜːp/ *v* to (cause to) belch – infml

burr, bur /bɜːʳ/ *n* **1** a rough or prickly fruit or seed that sticks or clings **2** a thin rough edge left after cutting or shaping metal, plastic, etc **3** the pronunciation of /r/ in a W country or Northumberland accent

[1]**burrow** /ˈbʌrəʊ/ *n* a hole or excavation in the ground made by a rabbit, fox, etc for shelter and habitation

[2]**burrow** *v* **1a** to make a burrow **b** to progress (as if) by digging **2** to make a motion suggestive of burrowing; snuggle, nestle **3** to make a search as if by digging

bursar /ˈbɜːsəʳ/ *n* an officer (e g of a monastery or college) in charge of funds

bursary /ˈbɜːsəri/ *n* **1** a bursar's office **2** a grant of money to a needy student

[1]**burst** /bɜːst/ *v* **burst 1** to break open, apart, or into pieces, usu from impact or because of pressure from within **2a** to give way from an excess of emotion **b** to give vent suddenly to a repressed

emotion **3a** to emerge or spring suddenly **b** to launch, plunge **4** to be filled to breaking point or to the point of overflowing

[2]**burst** *n* **1** an explosion, eruption **2** a sharp temporary increase (of speed, energy, etc) **3** a volley of shots

burst out *v* **1** to begin suddenly **2** to exclaim suddenly

bury /'beri/ *v* **1** to dispose of by depositing (as if) in the earth; *esp* to (ceremonially) dispose of a dead body thus **2** to conceal, hide **3** to put completely out of mind **4** to submerge, engross – usu + *in*

[1]**bus** /bʌs/ *n* a large motor-driven passenger vehicle operating usu according to a timetable along a fixed route

[2]**bus** *v* to transport by bus; *specif, chiefly NAm* to transport (children) by bus to a school in another district where the pupils are of a different race, in order to create integrated classes

busby /'bʌzbi/ *n* **1** a military full-dress fur hat worn esp by hussars **2** the bearskin worn by the Brigade of Guards – not used technically

[1]**bush** /bʊʃ/ *n* **1a** a (low densely branched) shrub **b** a close thicket of shrubs **2** a large uncleared or sparsely settled area (e g in Africa or Australia), usu scrub-covered or forested **3** a bushy tuft or mass

[2]**bush** *v* to extend like or resemble a bush

bush baby *n* a member of either of 2 genera of small active nocturnal tree-dwelling African primates

bushed /bʊʃt/ *adj* **1** perplexed, confused **2** tired, exhausted – infml

bushel /'bʊʃəl/ *n* **1** any of various units of dry capacity **2** a container holding a bushel

bush telegraph *n* the rapid unofficial communication of news, rumours, etc by word of mouth

bushy /'bʊʃi/ *adj* **1** full of or overgrown with bushes **2** growing thickly or densely – **bushiness** *n*

business /'bɪzn̩ɪs/ *n* **1a** a role, function **b** an immediate task or objective **2a** a usu commercial or mercantile activity engaged in as a means of livelihood **b** one's regular employment, profession, or trade **c** a commercial or industrial enterprise; *also* such enterprises **d** economic transactions or dealings **3** an affair, matter **4** movement or action performed by an actor **5a** personal concern **b** proper motive; justifying right **6** serious activity – **~man,** – **~woman** *n*

businesslike /'bɪzn̩ɪs-laɪk/ *adj* **1** (briskly) efficient **2** serious, purposeful

busk /bʌsk/ *v* to sing or play an instrument in the street (e g outside a theatre) in order to earn money – **~er** *n*

busman's holiday *n* a holiday spent doing one's usual work

bus-stop *n* a place, usu marked by a standardized sign, where people may board and alight from buses

[1]**bust** /bʌst/ *n* **1** a sculpture of the upper part of the human figure including the head, neck, and usu shoulders **2** the upper part of the human torso between neck and waist; *esp* the (size of the) breasts of a woman

[2]**bust** *v* **busted** *also* **bust** **1a** to break, smash; *also* to make inoperative **b** to bring to an end; break up – often + *up* **c** to burst **d** to break down **2a** to arrest **b** to raid **3** to lose a game or turn by exceeding a limit (e g the count of 21 in pontoon)

[3]**bust** *adj* **1** broken – chiefly infml **2** bankrupt – chiefly in *go bust*; infml

[1]**bustle** /'bʌsəl/ *v* to move briskly and often ostentatiously

[2]**bustle** *n* noisy and energetic activity

[3]**bustle** *n* a pad or framework worn to expand and support fullness at the back of a woman's skirt

bust-up *n* **1** a breaking up or apart **2** a quarrel *USE* infml

[1]**busy** /'bɪzi/ *adj* **1** engaged in action; occupied **2** full of activity; bustling **3** foolishly or intrusively active; meddlesome **4** full of detail – **busily** *adv* – **busyness** *n*

[2]**busy** *v* to make (esp oneself) busy; occupy

busybody /'bɪzi,bɒdi/ *n* an officious or inquisitive person

[1]**but** /bət; *strong* bʌt/ *conj* **1a** were it not **b** without the necessary accompaniment that – used after a negative **2a** on the contrary; on the other hand – used to join coordinate sentence

elements of the same class or function expressing contrast **b** and nevertheless; and yet

²but *prep* **1a** with the exception of; barring **b** other than **c** not counting **2** *Scot* without, lacking

³but *adv* **1** only, merely **2** to the contrary **3** – used for emphasis **4** *NE Eng & Aust* however, though

butane /ˈbjuːteɪn/ *n* an inflammable gas used esp as a fuel (e g in cigarette lighters)

butch /bʊtʃ/ *adj* aggressively masculine in appearance – used, often disparagingly, of both women and (esp homosexual) men

¹butcher /ˈbʊtʃəʳ/ *n* **1** sby who slaughters animals or deals in meat **2** sby who kills ruthlessly or brutally

²butcher *v* **1** to slaughter and prepare for market **2** to kill in a barbarous manner **3** to spoil, ruin – **~y** *n*

butler /ˈbʌtləʳ/ *n* **1** a manservant in charge of the wines and spirits **2** the chief male servant of a household

¹butt /bʌt/ *n* a blow or thrust, usu with the head or horns – **butt** *v*

²butt *n* **1a** a target **b** *pl* a range, specif for archery or rifle practice **c** a low mound, wall, etc from behind which sportsmen shoot at game birds **2** an object of abuse or ridicule; a victim

³butt *v* to abut – usu + *against* or *onto*

⁴butt *n* **1** the end of a plant or tree nearest the roots **2** the thicker or handle end of a tool or weapon **3** the unsmoked remnant of a cigar or cigarette

⁵butt *n* a large cask, esp for wine, beer, or water

butter /ˈbʌtəʳ/ *n* **1** a pale yellow solid emulsion made by churning milk or cream and used as food **2** any of various food spreads made with or having the consistency of butter

butter bean *n* a large flat usu dried bean

buttercup /ˈbʌtəkʌp/ *n* any of many plants with usu bright yellow flowers that commonly grow in fields and as weeds

butterfingers /ˈbʌtəˌfɪŋgəz/ *n* sby clumsy and bad at catching – infml

butterfly /ˈbʌtəflaɪ/ *n* **1** any of numerous slender-bodied day-flying insects with large broad often brightly coloured wings **2** a swimming stroke executed on the front by moving both arms together forwards out of the water and then sweeping them back through the water **3** *pl* a feeling of sickness caused esp by nervous tension – infml

buttermilk /ˈbʌtəmɪlk/ *n* **1** the liquid left after butter has been churned from milk or cream **2** cultured milk made by the addition of suitable bacteria to milk

butterscotch /ˈbʌtəskɒtʃ/ *n* (the flavour of) a brittle toffee made from brown sugar, syrup, butter, and water

butter up *v* to charm with lavish flattery; cajole – infml

¹buttery /ˈbʌtəri/ *n* a room (e g in a college) in which food and drink are served or sold

²buttery /ˈbʌtəri/ *adj* similar to or containing butter

butt in *v* **1** to intrude or interrupt

buttock /ˈbʌtək/ *n* the back of a hip that forms one of the 2 fleshy parts on which a person sits

¹button /ˈbʌtn/ *n* **1** a small knob or disc secured to an article (e g of clothing) and used as a fastener by passing it through a buttonhole or loop **2** an immature whole mushroom **3** a guard on the tip of a fencing foil

²button *v* to close or fasten (as if) with buttons – often + *up*

¹buttonhole /ˈbʌtnhəʊl/ *n* **1** a slit or loop through which a button is passed **2** *chiefly Br* a flower worn in a buttonhole or pinned to the lapel

²buttonhole *v* to detain in conversation

buttress /ˈbʌtrɪ̥s/ *n* **1** a structure built against a wall or building to provide support or reinforcement **2** a projecting part of a mountain **3** sthg that supports or strengthens

buxom /ˈbʌksəm/ *adj* attractively or healthily plump; *specif* full-bosomed

¹buy /baɪ/ *v* **bought** **1** to purchase **2** to obtain, often by some sacrifice **3** to bribe, hire **4** to believe, accept – slang

²buy *n* an act of buying; a purchase

buyer /ˈbaɪəʳ/ *n* one who selects and

buys stock to be sold in an esp large shop

buyer's market *n* a market in which supply exceeds demand, buyers have a wide range of choice, and prices tend to be low

buy off *v* to make a payment to in order to avoid some undesired course of action (e g prosecution)

buy out *v* **1** to purchase the share or interest of **2** to free (e g from military service) by payment – usu + *of*

buy up *v* **1** to purchase a controlling interest in (e g a company), esp by acquiring shares **2** to buy the entire available supply of

[1]**buzz** /bʌz/ *v* **1** to make a low continuous vibratory sound like that of a bee **2** to be filled with a confused murmur **3** to fly over or close to in order to threaten or warn **4** to summon or signal with a buzzer

[2]**buzz** *n* **1** a persistent vibratory sound **2a** a confused murmur or flurry of activity **b** rumour, gossip **3** a telephone call – infml **4** a pleasant stimulation; a kick – infml

buzzard /'bʌzəd/ *n* **1** a common large European hawk with soaring flight **2** *chiefly NAm* a (large) bird of prey (e g the turkey buzzard)

buzzer /'bʌzəʳ/ *n* an electric signalling device that makes a buzzing sound

buzz off *v* to go away quickly

[1]**by** /baɪ/ *prep* **1a** in proximity to; near **b** on the person or in the possession of **2a** through (the medium of); via **c** up to and then beyond; past **3a** in the circumstances of; during (e g slept *by* day) **b** not later than (e g home *by* dark) **4a(1)** through the instrumentality or use of (e g *by* bus) **(2)** through the action or creation of (e g a song *by* Wolf) **b(1)** sired by **(2)** with the participation of (the other parent) (e g a son *by* an earlier marriage) **5** with the witness or sanction of **6a** in conformity with (e g done *by* the rules) **b** in terms of (e g paid *by* the dozen) **c** from the evidence of (e g judge *by* appearances) **7** with respect to **8** to the amount or extent of **9** in successive units or increments of **10** – used in division as the inverse of *into,* in multiplication, and in measurements **11** *chiefly Scot* in comparison with; beside

[2]**by** *adv* **1a** close at hand; near **b** at or to another's home (e g *by* sometime) **2** past **3** aside, away; *esp* in or into reserve

by and by *adv* soon

by and large *adv* on the whole, in general

[1]**bye, by** /baɪ/ *n* **1** the passage to the next round of a tournament allowed to a competitor without an opponent **2** a run scored in cricket off a ball that passes the batsman without striking the bat or body

[2]**bye, by** *interj* – used to express farewell

by-election *also* **bye-election** *n* a special election to fill a vacancy

bygone /'baɪgɒn/ *adj* earlier, past; *esp* outmoded

bylaw, bye law /'baɪlɔː/ *n* a local or secondary law or regulation

by-line *n* **1** a secondary line; a sideline **2** the author's name printed with a newspaper or magazine article

[1]**bypass** /'baɪpɑːs/ *n* a road built so that through traffic can avoid a town centre

[2]**bypass** *v* to neglect or ignore, usu intentionally; circumvent

by-product *n* sthg produced (e g in manufacturing) in addition to a principal product

byre /baɪəʳ/ *n, dial* a cow shed

bystander /'baɪ,stændəʳ/ *n* one present but not involved in a situation or event

byte /baɪt/ *n* a string of adjacent binary digits that is processed by a computer as a unit; *esp* one that is 8 bits long

byway /'baɪweɪ/ *n* **1** a little-used road **2** a secondary or little known aspect

byword /'baɪwɜːd/ *n* (the name of) sby or sthg taken as representing some usu bad quality

C

c /siː/ *n, pl* **c's, cs** **1** the 3rd letter of the English alphabet **2** the keynote of a C-major scale **3** a grade rating a student's work as fair or mediocre in quality **4** one hundred

cab /kæb/ *n* **1** a taxi **2** the part of a locomotive, lorry, crane, etc that houses the driver and operating controls

cabal /kə'bæl/ *v or n* (to unite in or form) a clandestine or unofficial faction, esp in political intrigue

cabaret /'kæbəreɪ/ *n* a stage show or series of acts provided at a nightclub, restaurant, etc

cabbage /'kæbɪdʒ/ *n* **1** a cultivated plant that has a short stem and a dense globular head of usu green leaves used as a vegetable **2a** one who has lost control of his/her esp mental and physical faculties as the result of illness or accident **b** an inactive and apathetic person *USE* (*2*) infml

cabby, cabbie /'kæbi/ *n* a taxi driver

caber /'keɪbəʳ/ *n* a roughly trimmed tree trunk that is tossed for distance in a Scottish sport

cabin /'kæbɪ̇n/ *n* **1a** a room or compartment on a ship or boat for passengers or crew **b** a compartment in an aircraft for cargo, crew, or passengers **2** a small usu single-storied dwelling of simple construction

cabin boy *n* a boy employed as a servant on board a ship

cabin cruiser *n* a private motorboat with living accommodation

cabinet /'kæbɪ̇nɪ̇t, 'kæbnɪ̇t/ *n* **1a** a case for storing or displaying articles **b** an upright case housing a radio or television set **2** *sing or pl in constr, often cap* a body of advisers of a head of state, who formulate government policy – **cabinet** *adj*

[1]**cable** /'keɪbəl/ *n* **1** a strong thick (wire) rope **2** an assembly of electrical conductors insulated from each other and surrounded by a sheath **3** a telegram **4** a nautical unit of length equal to about **a** *Br* 185m (202yd) **b** *NAm* 219m (240yd)

[2]**cable** *v* to communicate by means of a telegram

cable car *n* a carriage made to be moved on a cable railway or along an overhead cable

cable railway *n* a railway along which the carriages are pulled by an endless cable operated by a stationary motor

cable stitch *n* a knitting stitch that produces a twisted rope-like pattern

caboodle /kə'buːdl/ *n* a collection, lot – infml

cache /kæʃ/ *n* a hiding place, esp for provisions or weapons

cachet /'kæʃeɪ/ *n* (a characteristic feature or quality conferring) prestige

cackle /'kækəl/ *v* **1** to make the sharp broken noise or cry characteristic of a hen, esp after laying **2** to laugh in a way suggestive of a hen's cackle **3** to chatter – **cackle** *n* – **cackler** *n*

cacophony /kə'kɒfəni/ *n* harsh or discordant sound; dissonance – **-onous** *adj*

cactus /'kæktəs/ *n, pl* **cacti, cactuses** any of a family of plants that have fleshy stems and scaly or spiny branches instead of leaves and are found esp in dry areas (e g deserts)

cad /kæd/ *n* an unscrupulous or dishonourable man – derog; not now in vogue – **~dish** *adj*

cadaver /kə'deɪvəʳ, kə'dæ-/ *n* a corpse, usu intended for dissection

cadaverous /kə'dævərəs/ *adj* **1** (suggestive) of a corpse **2** unhealthily pale or thin

caddie, caddy /'kædi/ *n* one who assists a golfer, esp by carrying clubs

cadence /'keɪdəns/ *n* **1** a falling inflection of the voice **2** a concluding strain; *specif* a musical chord sequence giving the sense of harmonic completion **3** the modulated and rhythmic recurrence of a sound

cadenza /kə'denzə/ *n* a technically showy sometimes improvised solo passage in a concerto

cadet /kə'det/ *n* **1** a younger brother or son; a younger branch of a family **2** sby receiving basic military or police training

cadge /kædʒ/ *v* to get (sthg) by asking and usu imposing on sby's hospitality or good nature – infml – **cadger** *n*

cadmium /'kædmɪəm/ *n* a bluish-white soft toxic bivalent metallic element used esp in platings and bearing metals

cadre /'keɪdə, 'kɑːdə, -drə/ *n* **1** a permanent nucleus of an esp military organization, capable of rapid expansion if necessary **2** (a member of) a group of activists working for the Communist party cause

Caerphilly /kə'fɪli, keə-, kɑː-/ *n* a mild white moist cheese

caesura /sɪ'zjʊərə/ *n, pl* **caesuras, caesurae** a break or pause in usu the middle of a line of verse

café /'kæfeɪ/ *n* a small restaurant serving snacks, tea, coffee etc

cafeteria /ˌkæfɪ'tɪərɪə/ *n* a restaurant in which the customers serve themselves or are served at a counter and take the food to tables to eat

caffeine /'kæfiːn/ *n* an alkaloid found esp in tea and coffee that acts as a stimulant and diuretic

caftan, kaftan /'kæftæn/ *n* a long loose garment traditionally worn by Arabs

[1]**cage** /keɪdʒ/ *n* **1** a box or enclosure of open construction for animals **2** a barred cell or fenced area for prisoners **3** a framework serving as a support

[2]**cage** *v* to put or keep (as if) in a cage

cagey *also* **cagy** /'keɪdʒi/ *adj* **1** hesitant about committing oneself **2** wary of being trapped or deceived; shrewd *USE* infml – **cagily** *adv* – **caginess** *n*

cagoule /kə'guːl/ *n* a long waterproof anorak

cairn /keən/ *n* a pile of stones built as a memorial or landmark

caisson /'keɪsən, kə'suːn/ *n* **1** a chest or wagon for artillery ammunition **2** a watertight chamber used for construction work under water or as a foundation

cajole /kə'dʒəʊl/ *v* to persuade or deceive with deliberate flattery, esp in the face of reluctance

[1]**cake** /keɪk/ *n* **1** (a shaped mass of) any of various sweet baked foods made from a basic mixture of flour and sugar, usu with fat, eggs, and a raising agent **2** a block of compressed or congealed matter

[2]**cake** *v* to encrust

calamity /kə'læmɪ̣ti/ *n* **1** a state of deep distress caused by misfortune or loss **2** an extremely grave event; a disaster

calcify /'kælsɪ̣faɪ/ *v* to make or become hardened by deposition of calcium salts, esp calcium carbonate

calcium /'kælsɪəm/ *n* a silver-white bivalent metallic element that occurs only in combination

calculate /'kælkjʊleɪt, -kjə-/ *v* **1** to determine by mathematical processes **2** to forecast consequences **3** to count, rely – + *on* or *upon*

calculating /'kælkjʊleɪtɪŋ, -kjə-/ *adj* marked by shrewd consideration of self-interest; scheming

calculation /ˌkælkjʊ'leɪʃən, -kjə-/ *n* **1** (the result of) the process or an act of calculating **2** studied care in planning, esp to promote self-interest

calculator /'kælkjʊleɪtəʳ, -kjə-/ *n* an electronic or mechanical machine for performing mathematical operations

calculus /'kælkjʊləs, -kjə-/ *n, pl* **calculi** *also* **calculuses** the mathematical methods comprising differential and integral calculus

caldron /'kɔːldrən/ *n* a cauldron

calendar /'kæləndəʳ/ *n* **1** a system for fixing the beginning, length, and divisions of the civil year and arranging days and longer divisions of time (e g weeks and months) in a definite order **2** a usu printed display of the days of 1 year **3** a chronological list of events or activities

calends, kalends /'kæləndz/ *n pl but sing or pl in constr* the first day of the ancient Roman month

[1]**calf** /kɑːf/ *n, pl* **calves** *also* **calfs,** (*2*) **calfs** **1a** the young of the domestic cow or a closely related mammal (e g

a bison) **b** the young of some large animals (e g the elephant and whale) **2** calfskin – **calve** *v*

[2]**calf** *n, pl* **calves** the fleshy back part of the leg below the knee

calfskin /'kɑːfˌskɪn/ *n* a high-quality leather made from the skin of a calf

calibrate /'kæləˌbreɪt/ *v* to determine the correct reading of (an arbitrary or inaccurate scale or instrument) by comparison with a standard – **-ation** *n*

calibre, *NAm chiefly* **caliber** /'kæləbəʳ/ *n* **1** the diameter of a round body (e g a bullet or other projectile) or a hollow cylinder (e g a gun barrel) **2a** degree of mental capacity or moral quality **b** degree of excellence or importance

calico /'kælɪkəʊ/ *n* white unprinted cotton cloth of medium weight, orig imported from India

caliph /'keɪlɪf/ *n* an Islamic leader claiming descent from Mohammad

[1]**call** /kɔːl/ *v* **1a** to speak loudly or distinctly so as to be heard at a distance **b** to utter or announce in a loud distinct voice – often + *out* **c** *of an animal* to utter a characteristic note or cry **2a** to command or request to come or be present **b** to summon to a particular activity, employment, or office **3** to rouse from sleep **4** to make a brief visit – often + *in* or *by* **5** to (try to) get into communication by telephone – often + *up* **6a** to make a demand in bridge for (a card or suit) **b** to require (a player) to show the hand in poker by making an equal bet **7** to speak of or address by a specified name; give a name to **8a** to regard or characterize as a certain kind; consider **b** to consider for purposes of an estimate or for convenience **9** to predict, guess

[2]**call** *n* **1a** calling with the voice **b** the cry of an animal (e g a bird); *also* an imitation of an animal's cry made to attract the animal **2a** a request or command to come or assemble **b** a summons or signal on a drum, bugle, or pipe **3a** a divine vocation or stronger inner prompting **b** the attraction or appeal of a particular activity or place **4a** a demand, request **b** need, justification **5** a short usu formal visit **6** calling in a card game **7** telephoning **8** a direction or a succession of directions for a square dance rhythmically called to the dancers – ~**er** *n*

call box *n* a public telephone box

call girl *n* a prostitute who accepts appointments by telephone

calligraphy /kə'lɪgrəfi/ *n* (beautiful or elegant) handwriting – **-pher, -phist** *n*

calling /'kɔːlɪŋ/ *n* **1** a strong inner impulse towards a particular course of action, esp when accompanied by conviction of divine influence **2** a vocation, profession

call off *v* **1** to draw away; divert **2** to cancel

callous /'kæləs/ *adj* **1** hardened and thickened **2** unfeeling; *esp* unsympathetic – ~**ly** *adv* – ~**ness** *n*

call out *v* **1** to summon into action **2** to challenge to a duel **3** to order a strike of

callow /'kæləʊ/ *adj* lacking adult attitudes; immature

call sign *n* the combination of letters or letters and numbers assigned to an operator, activity, or station for identification of a radio broadcast

call-up *n* an order to report for military service

call up *v* **1** to bring to mind; evoke **2** to summon together or collect (e g for a united effort) **3** to summon for active military duty

callus /'kæləs/ *n* **1** a hard thickened area on skin or bark **2** soft tissue that forms over a cut plant surface

[1]**calm** /kɑːm/ *n* **1a** the absence of winds or rough water; stillness **b** a state in which the wind has a speed of less than 1km/h (about ⅝mph) **2** a state of repose free from agitation

[2]**calm** *adj* **1** marked by calm; still **2** free from agitation or excitement

[3]**calm** *v* to make or become calm

calorie *also* **calory** /'kæləri/ *n* **1a** the quantity of heat required to raise the temperature of 1g of water by 1°C under standard conditions **b** a kilocalorie; *also* an equivalent unit expressing the energy-producing value of food when oxidized **2** an amount of food having an energy-producing value of 1 kilocalorie

calumniate /kəˈlʌmni-eɪt/ *v* to slander – fml

calumny /ˈkæləmni/ *n* (the act of uttering) a false charge maliciously calculated to damage another's reputation

calvary /ˈkælvəri/ *n* **1** an open-air representation of the crucifixion of Christ **2** an experience of intense mental suffering

calves /kɑːvz/ *pl of* **calf**

Calvinism /ˈkælvɪ̣nɪzəm/ *n* the theological system of Calvin and his followers, marked by emphasis on the sovereignty of God and esp by the doctrine of predestination – **-ist** *adj, n*

calypso /kəˈlɪpsəʊ/ *n* an improvised ballad, usu satirizing current events, in a style originating in the W Indies

calyx /ˈkeɪlɪks, ˈkælɪks/ *n, pl* **calyxes, calyces** the outer usu green or leafy part of a flower or floret, consisting of sepals

cam /kæm/ *n* a mechanical device (e g a wheel attached to an axis at a point other than its centre) that transforms circular motion into intermittent or back-and-forth motion

camaraderie /ˌkæməˈrædəri/ *n* friendly good humour amongst comrades

¹camber /ˈkæmbəʳ/ *v* to curve upwards in the middle

²camber *n* **1** a slight convexity or arching (e g of a beam or road) **2** an arrangement of the wheels of a motor vehicle so as to be closer together at the bottom than at the top

cambium /ˈkæmbɪəm/ *n* a thin layer of cells between the xylem and phloem of most plants that divides to form more xylem and phloem

cambric /ˈkæmbrɪk/ *n* a fine thin white linen or cotton fabric

came /keɪm/ *past of* **come**

camel /ˈkæməl/ *n* **1** either of 2 large ruminants used as draught and saddle animals in (African and Asian) desert regions: **a** the 1-humped Arabian camel **b** the 2-humped Bactrian camel **2** a float used to lift submerged ships **3** a light yellowish brown colour

camel hair *n* cloth, usu of a light tan colour with a soft silky texture, made from the hair of a camel or a mixture of this and wool

camellia *also* **camelia** /kəˈmiːlɪə/ *n* an ornamental greenhouse shrub with glossy evergreen leaves and roselike flowers

Camembert /ˈkæməmbeəʳ/ *n* a round thin-rinded soft rich cheese

cameo /ˈkæmi-əʊ/ *n* **1a** a gem cut in relief in one layer with another contrasting layer serving as background **b** a small medallion with a profiled head in relief **2** a usu brief part in literature or film that reveals or highlights character, plot, or scene **3** a small dramatic role often played by a well-known actor

camera /ˈkæmərə/ *n* a lightproof box having an aperture, and esp a lens, for recording the image of an object on a light-sensitive material: e g **a** one containing photographic film for producing a permanent record **b** one containing a device which converts the image into an electrical signal (e g for television transmission)

camiknickers /ˈkæmiˌnɪkəz/ *n pl in constr, Br* a one-piece close-fitting undergarment worn by women, that combines a camisole and knickers

camisole /ˈkæmɪ̣səʊl/ *n* a short bodice worn as an undergarment by women

camomile /ˈkæməmaɪl/ *n* a plant whose flower heads are often used in herbal remedies

camouflage /ˈkæməflɑːʒ/ *n* **1** the disguising of esp military equipment or installations with nets, paint, etc **2** concealment by means of disguise

¹camp /kæmp/ *n* **1a** a temporary shelter (e g a tent) or group of shelters **b** a new settlement (e g in a lumbering or mining region) **2** *sing or pl in constr* a group of people engaged in promoting or defending a theory or position **3** a place where troops are housed or trained

²camp *v* **1** to pitch or occupy a camp **2** to live temporarily in a camp or outdoors – **~er** *n*

³camp *adj* **1** exaggeratedly effeminate **2** deliberately and outrageously artificial, affected, or inappropriate, esp to the point of tastelessness ***USE*** infml

[4]**camp** *v* to behave in a camp style, manner, etc – usu + *up*; infml

campaign /kæm'peɪn/ *n* **1** a connected series of military operations forming a distinct phase of a war **2** a connected series of operations designed to bring about a particular result – **campaign** *v* – **~er** *n*

campanology /,kæmpə'nɒlədʒi/ *n* the art of bell ringing – **-gist** *n*

camp bed *n* a small collapsible bed, usu of fabric stretched over a frame

camphor /'kæmfəʳ/ *n* a tough gummy volatile fragrant compound obtained esp from the wood and bark of an evergreen tree and used as a liniment and insect repellent – **~ated** *adj*

campus /'kæmpəs/ *n* the grounds and buildings of a geographically self-contained university

camshaft /'kæmʃɑːft/ *n* a shaft to which a cam is fastened

[1]**can** /kən; *strong* kæn/ *verbal auxiliary, pres sing & pl* **can**; *past* **could** **1a** know how to **b** be physically or mentally able to **c** may perhaps – chiefly in questions **d** be logically inferred or supposed to – chiefly in negatives **e** be permitted by conscience or feeling to **f** be inherently able or designed to **g** be logically able to **h** be enabled by law, agreement, or custom to **2** have permission to – used interchangeably with *may* **3** will – used in questions with the force of a request

[2]**can** /kæn/ *n* **1** a usu cylindrical receptacle: **a** a vessel for holding liquids **b** a tin; *esp* a tin containing a beverage (e g beer) **2** *NAm the* toilet – infml

[3]**can** /kæn/ *v* **1** to pack or preserve in a tin **2** *chiefly NAm* to put a stop or end to – slang

Canadian /kə'neɪdɪən/ *n or adj* (a native or inhabitant) of Canada

canal /kə'næl/ *n* **1** a tubular anatomical channel **2** an artificial waterway for navigation, drainage, or irrigation

canal·ize, -ise /'kænəlaɪz/ *v* to direct into (preferred) channels

canapé /'kænəpeɪ/ *n* an appetizer consisting of a piece of bread, biscuit, etc, topped with a savoury spread

canary /kə'neəri/ *n* a small usu green to yellow finch of the Canary islands, widely kept as a cage bird

canasta /kə'næstə/ *n* **1** a form of rummy usu for 4 players using 2 full packs plus jokers **2** a combination of 7 cards of the same rank in canasta

cancan /'kænkæn/ *n* a dance performed by women, characterized by high kicking usu while holding up the front of a full ruffled skirt

[1]**cancel** /'kænsəl/ *v* **1** to mark or strike out for deletion **2a** to make void; countermand, annul **b** to bring to nothingness; destroy **c** to match in force or effect; counterbalance – usu + *out* **3** to call off, usu without intending to reschedule to a later time **4** to deface (a stamp), usu with a set of parallel lines, so as to invalidate reuse

cancellation /,kænsə'leɪʃən/ *n* **1** sthg cancelled, esp a seat in an aircraft, theatre performance, etc **2** a mark made to cancel sthg (e g a postage stamp)

cancer /'kænsəʳ/ *n* **1** *cap* (sby born under) the 4th zodiacal constellation, pictured as a crab **2** (a condition marked by) a malignant tumour of potentially unlimited growth **3** a source of evil or anguish – **~ous** *adj* – **~ously** *adv*

candelabrum /,kænd̮ɪ'lɑːbrəm/ *n, pl* **candelabra** *also* **candelabrums** a branched candlestick or lamp with several lights

candid /'kænd̮ɪd/ *adj* **1** indicating or suggesting complete sincerity **2** disposed to criticize severely; blunt – **~ly** *adv*

candidate /'kænd̮ɪd̮ɪt/ *n* **1** one who is nominated or qualified for, or aspires to an office, membership, or award **2** one who is taking an examination **3** sthg suitable for a specified action or process – **-ature** *n*

candle /'kændl/ *n* a usu long slender cylindrical mass of tallow or wax enclosing a wick that is burnt to give light

Candlemas /'kændlməs/ *n* February 2 observed as a church festival in commemoration of the presentation of Christ in the temple and the purification of the Virgin Mary

candlestick /'kændl,stɪk/ *n* a holder with a socket for a candle

candlewick /'kændl,wɪk/ *n* a very

thick soft cotton yarn; *also* fabric with a raised tufted pattern, used esp for bedspreads

candour, *NAm chiefly* **candor** /'kændəʳ/ *n* unreserved and candid expression; forthrightness

[1]**candy** /'kændi/ *n* **1** crystallized sugar formed by boiling down sugar syrup **2** *chiefly NAm* a sweet

[2]**candy** *v* to encrust or glaze (e g fruit or fruit peel) with sugar

candy floss *n* a light fluffy mass of spun sugar, usu wound round a stick as a sweet

[1]**cane** /keɪn/ *n* **1a** a hollow or pithy usu flexible jointed stem (e g of bamboo) **b** an elongated flowering or fruiting stem (e g of a raspberry) **c** any of various tall woody grasses or reeds; *esp* sugarcane **2a** a walking stick made of cane **b** (*the* use of) a cane or rod for flogging **c** a length of split cane for use in basketry

[2]**cane** *v* to beat with a cane; *broadly* to punish

[1]**canine** /'keɪnaɪn/ *adj* of or resembling a dog or (members of) the dog family

[2]**canine** *n* any of the 4 conical pointed teeth each of which lies between an incisor and the first premolar on each side of both the top and bottom jaws

canister *also* **cannister** /'kænɨstəʳ/ *n* **1** a small usu metal box or tin for holding a dry product (e g tea or shot) **2** encased shot for close-range antipersonnel artillery fire

[1]**canker** /'kæŋkəʳ/ *n* **1a** an area of local tissue death in a plant **b** any of various inflammatory animal diseases **2** a source of corruption or debasement – **~ous** *adj*

[2]**canker** *v* **1** to corrupt with evil intentions **2** to become infested with canker

cannabis /'kænəbɨs/ *n* the dried flowering spikes of the female hemp plant, sometimes smoked in cigarettes for their intoxicating effect

cannelloni /ˌkænɨ'ləʊni/ *n* large tubular rolls of pasta (filled with meat, cheese, etc)

cannibal /'kænɨbəl/ *n* **1** a human being who eats human flesh **2** an animal that eats its own kind – **~ism** *n* – **~istic** *adj*

cannibal·ize, ise /'kænɨbəlaɪz/ *v* to dismantle a machine to provide spare parts for others

[1]**cannon** /'kænən/ *n, pl* **cannons, cannon** **1** a usu large gun mounted on a carriage **2** an automatic shell-firing gun mounted esp in an aircraft

[2]**cannon** *n, Br* a shot in billiards in which the cue ball strikes each of 2 object balls

[3]**cannon** *v* **1** to collide – usu + *into* **2** to collide with and be deflected *off* sthg

cannonball /'kænənbɔːl/ *n* a round solid missile made for firing from an old type of cannon

cannot /'kænət, -nɒt/ can not

canny /'kæni/ *adj* **1** cautious and shrewd; *specif* thrifty **2** *Scot & NE Eng* careful, steady **3** *NE Eng* agreeable, comely – **cannily** *adv*

canoe /kə'nuː/ *n* **1** a long light narrow boat with sharp ends and curved sides usu propelled by paddling **2** *chiefly Br* a kayak

[1]**canon** /'kænən/ *n* **1** the series of prayers forming the unvarying part of the Mass **2a** an authoritative list of books accepted as Holy Scripture **b** the authentic works of a writer **3** an accepted principle, rule, or criterion **4** a musical composition for 2 or more voice parts in which the melody is repeated by the successively entering voices

[2]**canon** *n* a clergyman belonging to the chapter of a cathedral or collegiate church

canon·ize, -ise /'kænənaɪz/ *v* to recognize officially as a saint

[1]**canopy** /'kænəpi/ *n* **1a** a cloth covering suspended over a bed **b** an awning, marquee **2** an ornamental rooflike structure **3a** the transparent enclosure over an aircraft cockpit **b** the lifting or supporting surface of a parachute

canst /kənst; *strong* kænst/ *archaic pres 2 sing of* **can**

[1]**cant** /kænt/ *n* an oblique or slanting surface; a slope

[2]**cant** *v* **1** to set at an angle; tip or tilt up or over **2** to pitch to one side; lean

[3]**cant** *n* **1** jargon; *specif* the argot of the underworld **2** a set or stock phrase **3** the insincere expression of platitudes or sentiments, esp those suggesting piety

can't /kɑːnt/ can not

cantaloup /'kæntəluːp/ *n* a melon with a hard rough rind and reddish orange flesh

cantankerous /kæn'tæŋkərəs/ *adj* ill-natured, quarrelsome – **~ly** *adv* – **~ness** *n*

cantata /kæn'tɑːtə/ *n* a usu religious choral composition comprising choruses, solos, recitatives, and interludes

canteen /kæn'tiːn/ *n* **1** a dining hall **2** a partitioned chest or box for holding cutlery **3** a usu cloth-covered flask carried by a soldier, traveller, etc and containing a liquid, esp drinking water

[1]**canter** /'kæntəʳ/ *v* to progress or ride at a canter

[2]**canter** *n* **1** a 3-beat gait of a horse, resembling but smoother and slower than the gallop **2** a brisk ride

cantilever /'kæntɨ̬,liːvəʳ/ *n* a projecting beam or member supported at only 1 end: e g **a** a bracket-shaped member supporting a balcony or a cornice **b** either of the 2 beams or trusses that when joined directly or by a suspended connecting member form a span of a cantilever bridge

canto /'kæntəʊ/ *n, pl* **cantos** a major division of a long poem

cantor /'kæntəʳ, -tɔːʳ/ *n* a singer who leads liturgical music (e g in a synagogue)

canvas *also* **canvass** /'kænvəs/ *n* **1** a firm closely woven cloth usu of linen, hemp, or cotton used for clothing, sails, tents etc **2** a set of sails; sail **3** a cloth surface suitable for painting on in oils; *also* the painting on such a surface **4** a coarse cloth so woven as to form regular meshes as a basis for embroidery or tapestry **5** the floor of a boxing or wrestling ring

canvass /'kænvəs/ *v* to seek orders or votes; solicit

canyon, cañon /'kænjən/ *n* a deep valley or gorge

[1]**cap** /kæp/ *n* **1a** a soft usu flat head covering with a peak and no brim **b** (one who has gained) selection for an esp national team; *also* a cap awarded as a mark of this **2a** a usu unyielding overlying rock or soil layer **b** (a patch of distinctively coloured feathers on) the top of a bird's head **3** sthg that serves as a cover or protection, esp for the end or top of an object **4** the uppermost part; the top **5** a small container holding an explosive charge (e g for a toy pistol or for priming the charge in a firearm) **6** *Br* a Dutch cap

[2]**cap** *v* to follow with sthg more noticeable or significant; outdo

capability /,keɪpə'bɪlɨ̬ti/ *n* **1** being capable **2** the capacity for an indicated use or development; potential

capable /'keɪpəbəl/ *adj* **1** susceptible **2** having the attributes or traits required to perform a specified deed or action **3** able *USE* (*except 3*) + *of* – **-bly** *adv*

capacious /kə'peɪʃəs/ *adj* able to hold a great deal – **~ly** *adv* – **~ness** *n*

capacitance /kə'pæsɨ̬təns/ *n* **1** the ability of a conductor or system of conductors and insulators to store electric charge **2** the measure of capacitance equal to the ratio of the charge induced to the potential difference

capacity /kə'pæsɨ̬ti/ *n* **1a** the ability to accommodate or deal with sthg **b** an ability to contain **c** the maximum amount that can be contained or produced **2** legal competence or power **3a** ability, calibre **b** potential **4** a position or role assigned or assumed

[1]**cape** /keɪp/ *n* a peninsula or similar land projection jutting out into water

[2]**cape** *n* a sleeveless outer (part of a) garment that fits closely at the neck and hangs loosely from the shoulders

[1]**caper** /'keɪpəʳ/ *n* a greenish flower bud or young berry pickled and used as a seasoning, garnish, etc

[2]**caper** *v* to leap about in a carefree way; prance

[3]**caper** *n* **1** a joyful leap **2** a high-spirited escapade; a prank **3** an illegal enterprise; a crime

[1]**capillary** /kə'pɪləri/ *adj* **1** resembling

a hair, esp in slender elongated form **2** *of a tube, passage, etc* having a very fine bore

²capillary *n* a capillary tube; *esp* any of the smallest blood vessels connecting arteries with veins and forming networks throughout the body

¹capital /ˈkæpɨtl/ *adj* **1a** punishable by death **b** involving execution **2** *of a letter* of or conforming to the series (e g A, B, C rather than a, b, c) used to begin sentences or proper names **3a** of the greatest importance or influence **b** being the seat of government **4** excellent – not now in vogue

²capital *n* **1a** (the value of) a stock of accumulated goods, esp at a particular time and in contrast to income received during a particular period **b** accumulated possessions calculated to bring in income **c** *sing or pl in constr* people holding capital **d** a sum of money saved **2** an esp initial capital letter **3** a city serving as a seat of government

³capital *n* the top part or piece of an architectural column

capital assets *n pl* tangible or intangible long-term assets

capitalism /ˈkæpɨtlɪzəm/ *n* an economic system characterized by private ownership and control of the means of production, distribution, and exchange and by the profit motive

capitalist /ˈkæpɨtlɨst/, **capitalistic** *adj* **1** owning capital **2** practising, advocating, or marked by capitalism – **capitalist** *n*

capital·ize, -ise *v* **1** to write in capital letters **2** to convert assets into capital **3** to gain by turning sthg to advantage – usu + *on*

capitol /ˈkæpɨtl/ *n* **1** a building in which a US legislative body meets **2** *cap* the building in which Congress meets at Washington

capitulate /kəˈpɪtʃʊleɪt/ *v* **1** to surrender, often after negotiation of terms **2** to cease resisting; acquiesce – **-tion** *n*

capon /ˈkeɪpən/ *n* a castrated male chicken

caprice /kəˈpriːs/ *n* **1** a sudden and seemingly unmotivated change of mind **2** a disposition to change one's mind impulsively

capricious /kəˈprɪʃəs/ *adj* apt to change suddenly or unpredictably – **~ly** *adv* – **~ness** *n*

Capricorn /ˈkæprɪkɔːn/ *n* (sby born under) the 10th zodiacal constellation, pictured as a creature resembling a goat with the tail of a fish

capsicum /ˈkæpsɪkəm/ *n* a sweet pepper

capsize /kæpˈsaɪz/ *v* to (cause to) overturn

capstan /ˈkæpstən/ *n* **1** a mechanical device consisting of an upright drum round which a rope, hawser, etc is fastened, used for moving or raising heavy weights **2** a rotating shaft that drives tape at a constant speed in a tape recorder

capsule /ˈkæpsjuːl/ *n* **1** a closed plant receptacle containing spores or seeds **2** a usu gelatin shell enclosing a drug for swallowing **3** a detachable pressurized compartment, esp in a spacecraft or aircraft, containing crew and controls; *also* a spacecraft **4** a covering that encloses the top of a bottle, esp of wine, and protects the cork

¹captain /ˈkæptɨn/ *n* **1a** a middle-ranking military or naval officer **b** an officer in charge of a ship **c** a pilot of a civil aircraft **2** a distinguished military leader **3** a leader of a team, esp a sports team **4** a dominant figure **5** *Br* the head boy or girl at a school

caption /ˈkæpʃən/ *n* **1** a heading or title, esp of an article or document **2** a comment or description accompanying a pictorial illustration **3** a film subtitle

captivate /ˈkæptɨveɪt/ *v* to fascinate or charm irresistibly – **-ation** *n*

captive /ˈkæptɪv/ *adj* **1a** taken and held as prisoner, esp by an enemy in war **b** kept within bounds **2** in a situation that makes departure or inattention difficult – **captive** *n* – **-vity** *n*

captor /ˈkæptəʳ/ *n* one who or that which holds another captive

capture /ˈkæptʃəʳ/ *v* **1** to take captive; win, gain **2** to preserve in a relatively permanent form **3** to remove (e g a chess piece) from the playing board according to the rules of a game – **capture** *n*

car /kɑːʳ/ *n* **1a** a railway carriage; *esp*

one used for a specific purpose **b** a motor car **2** the passenger compartment of an airship or balloon **3** *NAm* the cage of a lift

carafe /'kærəf, kə'ræf, -'rɑːf/ *n* a (glass) bottle used to hold water or wine, esp at table

caramel /'kærəməl/ *n* **1** a brittle brown somewhat bitter substance obtained by heating sugar and used as a colouring and flavouring agent **2** a chewy usu quite soft caramel-flavoured toffee

carapace /'kærəpeɪs/ *n* a hard case over the back of a turtle, crab, etc

carat /'kærət/ *n* **1** a unit of weight for precious stones equal to 200mg **2** *NAm chiefly* **karat** a unit of fineness for gold equal to $\frac{1}{24}$ part of pure gold in an alloy

caravan /'kærəvæn/ *n* **1a** *sing or pl in constr* a company of travellers on a journey through desert or hostile regions; *also* a train of pack animals **b** a group of vehicles travelling together **2** *Br* a covered vehicle designed to be towed by a motor car or horse and to serve as a dwelling when parked

caraway /'kærəweɪ/ *n* a usu white-flowered aromatic plant with pungent seeds used as a flavouring

carbohydrate /ˌkɑːbəʊ'haɪdreɪt, -drɪ̤t/ *n* any of various compounds of carbon, hydrogen, and oxygen (e g sugars, starches, and celluloses) formed by green plants and constituting a major class of energy-providing animal foods

carbon /'kɑːbən/ *n* **1** a nonmetallic element occurring as diamond, graphite, charcoal, coke, etc and as a constituent of coal, petroleum, carbonates (e g limestone), and organic compounds **2a** a sheet of carbon paper **b** a copy (e g of a letter) made with carbon paper – **~ize** *v*

carbonate /'kɑːbəneɪt/ *n* a salt or ester containing a metal and carbon and oxygen

carbonated /'kɑːbəneɪtɪ̤d/ *adj* made fizzy by having carbon dioxide gas added

carbon dioxide *n* a heavy colourless gas that is formed esp by the combustion and decomposition of organic substances and is absorbed from the air by plants in photosynthesis

carboniferous /ˌkɑːbə'nɪfərəs/ *adj* producing or containing carbon or coal

carbon monoxide *n* a colourless odourless very toxic gas formed as a product of the incomplete combustion of carbon

carbon paper *n* thin paper coated on one side with a dark pigment used to make copies of letters, etc by pressure

carbuncle /'kɑːbʌŋkəl/ *n* **1** a red gemstone, usu a garnet, cut in a domed shape without facets **2** a painful local inflammation of the skin and deeper tissues with multiple openings for the discharge of pus

carburettor /ˌkɑːbə'retəʳ, -bjʊ-/ *n* a device for supplying an internal combustion engine with vaporized fuel mixed with air in an explosive mixture

carcass /'kɑːkəs/ *n* a dead body; *esp* the dressed body of a meat animal

carcinogen /kɑː'sɪnədʒɪ̤n/ *n* sthg (e g a chemical compound) that causes cancer

card /kɑːd/ *n* **1** a playing card **2** *pl but sing or pl in constr* a game played with cards **3** a valuable asset or right for use in negotiations **4** a flat stiff usu small and rectangular piece of paper or thin cardboard: e g **a** a postcard **b** a visiting card **c** a programme; *esp* one for a sporting event **d** a greeting card **5** *pl, Br* the National Insurance and other papers of an employee, held by his/her employer

cardamom /'kɑːdəməm/ *n* an E Indian plant with aromatic seeds used as a spice or condiment

[1]**cardboard** /'kɑːdbɔːd/ *n* material of similar composition to paper but thicker and stiffer

[2]**cardboard** *adj* **1** made (as if) of cardboard **2** unreal, insubstantial

card-carrying *adj* being a fully paid-up member, esp of the Communist party

cardiac /'kɑːdiæk/ *adj* of, situated near, or acting on the heart

cardigan /'kɑːdɪgən/ *n* a knitted garment for the upper body that opens down the front and is usu fastened with buttons

[1]**cardinal** /'kɑːdənəl/ *adj* of primary importance; fundamental

[2]**cardinal** *n* a member of a body of high officials of the Roman Catholic church whose powers include the election of a new pope

cardinal number *n* a number (e g 1, 2, 3) that is used in simple counting and that indicates how many elements there are in a collection

cardsharp, cardsharper /'kɑːdʃɑːp/ *n* one who habitually cheats at cards

[1]**care** /keəʳ/ *n* **1** a cause for anxiety **2** close attention; effort **3** change, supervision; *specif, Br* guardianship and supervision of children by a local authority

[2]**care** *v* **1** to feel interest or concern – often + *about* **2** to give care – often + *for* **3** to have a liking or taste *for*

[1]**career** /kə'rɪəʳ/ *n* a field of employment in which one expects to remain; *esp* such a field which requires special qualifications and training

[2]**career** *v* to move swiftly in an uncontrolled fashion

carefree /'keəfriː/ *adj* free from anxiety or responsibility

careful /'keəfəl/ *adj* **1** exercising or taking care **2a** marked by attentive concern **b** cautious, prudent – often + *to* and an infinitive – **~ly** *adv* – **~ness** *n*

careless /'keələs/ *adj* **1** not taking care **2a** negligent, slovenly **b** unstudied, spontaneous **3a** free from care; untroubled **b** indifferent, unconcerned – **~ly** *adv* – **~ness** *n*

[1]**caress** /kə'res/ *n* **1** a kiss **2** a caressing touch or stroke

[2]**caress** *v* **1** to touch or stroke lightly and lovingly **2** to touch or affect gently or soothingly

caretaker /'keəteɪkəʳ/ *n* **1** one who takes care of the house or land of an owner, esp during his/her absence **2** one who keeps clean a large and/or public building (e g a school or office), looks after the heating system, and carries out minor repairs **3** sby or sthg temporarily installed in office

careworn /'keə,wɔːn/ *adj* showing the effects of grief or anxiety

cargo /'kɑːgəʊ/ *n* the goods conveyed in a ship, aircraft, or vehicle; freight

caribou /'kærɪ̵buː/ *n* any of several large N American deer

caricature /'kærɪkətʃəʳ, -tʃʊəʳ/ *n* **1** exaggeration of features or characteristics, often to a ludicrous or grotesque degree **2** a comic or satirical representation, esp in literature or art, that has the qualities of caricature – **caricature** *v*

caries /'keəriz/ *n, pl* **caries** progressive decay of a tooth or sometimes a bone, caused by microorganisms – **-ious** *adj*

carillon /'kærɪ̵ljən, kə'rɪ-/ *n* a set of bells sounded by hammers controlled from a keyboard

Carmelite /'kɑːmɪ̵laɪt/ *n* a member of the Roman Catholic mendicant Order of Our Lady of Mount Carmel founded in the 12th c

carmine /'kɑːmɪ̵n, -maɪn/ *n* a vivid red (pigment)

carnage /'kɑːnɪdʒ/ *n* great slaughter (e g in battle)

carnal /'kɑːnl/ *adj* **1** given to or marked by physical and esp sexual pleasures and appetites **2** temporal, worldly – **~ly** *adv* – **~ity** *n*

carnation /kɑː'neɪʃən/ *n* **1** light red or pink **2** any of numerous cultivated usu double-flowered pinks

carnival /'kɑːnɪ̵vəl/ *n* **1** an instance of merrymaking or feasting **2** an exhibition or organized programme of entertainment; a festival

carnivore /'kɑːnɪ̵vɔːʳ/ *n* a flesh-eating animal – **-rous** *adj*

[1]**carol** /'kærəl/ *n* a Christmas song or hymn

[2]**carol** *v* to sing (joyfully)

carotid /kə'rɒtɪ̵d/ *adj or n* (of or being) the chief artery or pair of arteries that supply the head with blood

carouse /kə'raʊz/ *v* **1** to drink alcoholic beverages heavily or freely **2** to take part in a drinking bout – **carouse, carousal** *n*

[1]**carp** /kɑːp/ *v* to find fault or complain querulously and often unnecessarily – infml; usu + *at*

[2]**carp** *n* a large soft-finned freshwater fish often farmed for food

carpel /'kɑːpəl/ *n* any of the structures of a flowering plant that constitute the female (innermost) part of a flower and usu consist of an ovary, style, and stigma

carpenter /ˈkɑːpɪ̣ntəʳ/ *n* a woodworker; *esp* one who builds or repairs large-scale structural woodwork – **~try** *n*

[1]**carpet** /ˈkɑːpɪ̣t/ *n* a heavy woven or felted material used as a floor covering; *also* a floor covering made of this fabric

[2]**carpet** *v* **1** to cover (as if) with a carpet **2** to reprimand – infml

carpetbag /ˈkɑːpɪ̣tbæg/ *n* a bag made of carpet fabric, common in the 19th c

carport /ˈkɑːpɔːt/ *n* a usu open-sided shelter for cars

carriage /ˈkærɪdʒ/ *n* **1** the manner of bearing the body; posture **2** (the price or cost of) carrying **3** a wheeled vehicle; *esp* a horse-drawn passenger-carrying vehicle designed for private use **4** a movable part of a machine that supports some other part **5** a railway passenger vehicle; a coach

carriageway /ˈkærɪdʒweɪ/ *n* the part of a road used by traffic

carrier /ˈkærɪəʳ/ *n* **1** an individual or organization that contracts to transport goods, messages, etc **2** a container for carrying **3** a bearer and transmitter of something that causes a disease; *esp* one who is immune to the disease **4** a radio or electrical wave of relatively high frequency that can be modulated by a signal (e g representing sound or vision information), esp in order to transmit that signal **5** an aircraft carrier

carrier bag *n* a bag of plastic or thick paper used for carrying goods, esp shopping

carrier pigeon *n* a homing pigeon (used to carry messages)

carrion /ˈkærɪən/ *n* dead and putrefying flesh

carrot /ˈkærət/ *n* **1** (a biennial plant with) a usu orange spindle-shaped root eaten as a vegetable **2** a promised and often illusory reward or advantage

carroty /ˈkærəti/ *adj* bright orange-red in colour

[1]**carry** /ˈkæri/ *v* **1** to support and move (a load); transport **2** to convey, conduct **3** to lead or influence by appeal to the emotions **4** to transfer from one place to another; *esp* to transfer (a digit corresponding to a multiple of 10) to the next higher power of 10 in addition **5a** to bear on or within oneself **b** to have as a mark, attribute, or property **6** to have as a consequence, esp in law; involve **7** to hold (e g one's person) in a specified manner **8** to keep in stock for sale **9** to maintain through financial support or personal effort **10** to extend or prolong in space, time, or degree **11** to gain victory for **12a** to broadcast or publish **b** to reach or penetrate to a distance **c** to convey itself to a reader or audience **13** to perform with sufficient ability to make up for the poor performance of (e g a partner or teammate)

[2]**carry** *n* the range of a gun or projectile

carrycot /ˈkærikɒt/ *n, chiefly Br* a small lightweight boxlike bed, usu with 2 handles, in which a baby can be carried

carry forward *v* to transfer (e g a total) to the succeeding column, page, or book relating to the same account

carry off *v* **1** to cause the death of **2** to perform easily or successfully **3** to gain possession or control of; capture

carry-on *n* an instance of rowdy, excited, or improper behaviour; a to-do – infml

carry on *v* **1** to conduct, manage **2** to behave in a rowdy, excited, or improper manner **3** to continue one's course or activity, esp in spite of obstacles or discouragement **4** to flirt; *also* to have a love affair – usu + *with*

carryout /ˈkæri-aʊt/ *n, chiefly Scot* (an item of) food or esp alcoholic drink bought to be consumed off the premises

carry out *v* **1** to put into execution **2** to bring to a successful conclusion; complete, accomplish

carry over *v* to persist from one stage or sphere of activity to another

carry through *v* carry out

[1]**cart** /kɑːt/ *n* **1** a heavy 2-wheeled or 4-wheeled vehicle used for transport-

ing bulky or heavy loads (e g goods or animal feed) **2** a lightweight 2-wheeled vehicle drawn by a horse or pony **3** a small wheeled vehicle

[2]**cart** *v* to take or drag away without ceremony or by force – infml; usu + *off*

cartel /kaː'tel/ *n* a combination of independent commercial enterprises designed to limit competition

cartilage /'kaːtəlɪdʒ/ *n* a translucent elastic tissue that is mostly converted into bone in adult higher vertebrates – **-ginous** *adj*

cartography /kaː'tɒgrəfi/ *n* map making – **-pher** *n*

carton /'kaːtn/ *n* a box or container made of plastic, cardboard, etc

cartoon /kaː'tuːn/ *n* **1** a preparatory design, drawing, or painting (e g for a fresco) **2a** a satirical drawing commenting on public and usu political matters **b** a series of drawings (e g in a magazine) telling a story **3** a film using animated drawings – **~ist** *n*

cartridge /'kaːtrɪdʒ/ *n* **1** a tube of metal, paper, etc containing a complete charge, a primer, and often the bullet or shot for a firearm **2** the part of the arm of a record player holding the stylus and the mechanism that converts movements of the stylus into electrical signals

[1]**cartwheel** /'kaːt-wiːl/ *n* a sideways handspring with arms and legs extended – **cartwheel** *v*

carve /kaːv/ *v* **1** to cut so as to shape **2** to make or acquire (a career, reputation, etc) through one's own efforts – often + *out* **3** to cut (food, esp meat) into pieces or slices

carving /'kaːvɪŋ/ *n* a carved object or design

caryatid /,kæri'ætɪ̣d/ *n, pl* **caryatids, caryatides** a draped female figure used as a column

cascade /kæ'skeɪd/ *n* **1** a steep usu small fall of water; *esp* one of a series of such falls **2a** sthg arranged in a series or in a succession of stages so that each stage derives from or acts on the product of the preceding stage **b** an arrangement of fabric (e g lace) that falls in a wavy line **3** sthg falling or rushing forth in profusion – **cascade** *v*

[1]**case** /keɪs/ *n* **1** a situation (requiring investigation or action) **2** an (inflectional) form of a noun, pronoun, or adjective indicating its grammatical relation to other words **3a** a suit or action that reaches a court of law **b(1)** the evidence supporting a conclusion **(2)** an argument; *esp* one that is convincing **4a** an instance of disease or injury; *also* a patient suffering from a specific illness **b** an example **5** a peculiar person; a character – infml

[2]**case** *n* **1** a box or receptacle for holding sthg: e g **a** a glass-panelled box for the display of specimens (e g in a museum) **b** a suitcase **2** an outer covering (e g of a book)

[3]**case** *v* to inspect or study (e g a house), esp with intent to rob – slang

casework /'keɪswɜːk/ *n* social work involving direct consideration of the problems of individual people or families – **~er** *n*

[1]**cash** /kæʃ/ *n* **1** ready money **2** money or its equivalent paid promptly at the time of purchase

[2]**cash** *v* **1** to pay or obtain cash for **2** to lead and win a bridge trick with (the highest remaining card of a suit)

cash-and-carry *adj* sold for cash and collected by the purchaser

cash crop *n* a crop (e g cotton or sugar beet) produced for sale rather than for use by the grower

cashew /'kæʃuː, kə'ʃuː/ *n* an edible kidney-shaped nut produced by a tropical American tree

[1]**cashier** /kæ'ʃɪəʳ/ *v* to dismiss, usu dishonourably, esp from service in the armed forces

[2]**cashier** *n* **1** one employed to receive cash from customers, esp in a shop **2** one who collects and records payments (e g in a bank)

cash in *v* **1** to convert into cash **2** to exploit a financial or other advantage – usu + *on*

cashmere /'kæʃmɪəʳ/ *n* fine wool from the undercoat of the Kashmir goat

cash register *n* a machine that has a drawer for cash and is used to record and display the amount of each purchase and the money received

casing /ˈkeɪsɪŋ/ *n* sthg that encases; material for encasing

casino /kəˈsiːnəʊ/ *n, pl* **casinos** a building or room used for gambling

cask /kɑːsk/ *n* a barrel-shaped container, usu for holding liquids

casket /ˈkɑːskɪ̈t/ *n* **1** a small usu ornamental chest or box (e g for jewels) **2** *NAm* a coffin

[1]**casserole** /ˈkæsərəʊl/ *n* **1** a heatproof dish with a cover in which food may be baked and served **2** the savoury food cooked and served in a casserole

cassette, casette /kəˈset/ *n* **1** a lightproof container for holding film or plates that can be inserted into a camera **2** a small case containing magnetic tape that can be inserted into a tape recorder

cassock /ˈkæsək/ *n* an ankle-length garment worn by the Roman Catholic and Anglican clergy or by laymen assisting in services

[1]**cast** /kɑːst/ *v* **cast** **1a** to cause to move (as if) by throwing **b** to place as if by throwing **c** to deposit (a vote) formally **d(1)** to throw off or away **(2)** to shed, moult **(3)** *of an animal* to give birth to (prematurely) **2** to calculate (a horoscope) by means of astrology **3a** to arrange into a suitable form or order **b** to assign a part for (e g a play) or to (e g an actor) **4** to shape (e g metal or plastic) by pouring into a mould when molten **5** to throw out a line and lure with a fishing rod **6** to look round; seek – + *about* or *around*

[2]**cast** *n* **1** a throw of a (fishing) line or net **2** *sing or pl in constr* the set of performers in a dramatic production **3** a slight squint in the eye **4a** a reproduction (e g of a statue) formed by casting **b** an impression taken from an object with a molten or plastic substance **c** a plaster covering and support for a broken bone **5** a tinge, suggestion **6** the excrement of an earthworm

castaway /ˈkɑːstəweɪ/ *n* a person who is cast adrift or ashore as a result of a shipwreck or as a punishment

caste /kɑːst/ *n* **1** any of the hereditary social groups in Hinduism that restrict the occupations of their members and their association with members of other castes **2** a social class; *also* the prestige conferred by this

castellated /ˈkæstɪ̈leɪtɪ̈d/ *adj* having battlements like a castle

caster sugar /ˈkɑːstəˌʃʊgəʳ/ *n* finely granulated white sugar

castigate /ˈkæstɪ̈geɪt/ *v* to punish or reprimand severely – fml – **-gation** *n*

casting /ˈkɑːstɪŋ/ *n* **1** sthg cast in a mould **2** sthg cast out or off

cast-iron *adj* **1** capable of withstanding great strain; strong, unyielding **2** impossible to disprove or falsify

cast iron *n* a hard brittle alloy of iron, carbon, and silicon cast in a mould

[1]**castle** /ˈkɑːsəl/ *n* **1** a large fortified building or set of buildings **2** a stronghold **3** a rook in chess

[2]**castle** *v* to move (a chess king) 2 squares towards a rook and then place the rook on the square on the other side of the king

castoff /ˈkɑːstɒf/ *n* **1** a cast-off article (e g of clothing) – usu pl **2** an estimate of the space that will be required for a given amount of text when printed

cast-off *adj* thrown away or discarded, esp because outgrown or no longer wanted – **castoff** *n*

cast off *v* **1** to unfasten or untie (a boat or line) **2a** to remove (a stitch or stitches) from a knitting needle in such a way as to prevent unravelling **b** to finish a knitted article by casting off all the stitches **3** to get rid of; discard

cast on *v* to place (a stitch or stitches) on a knitting needle for beginning or enlarging a knitted article

castor, caster /kɑːstəʳ/ *n* **1** a small wheel set in a swivel mounting on the base of a piece of furniture, machinery, etc **2** a container with a perforated top for sprinkling powdered or granulated foods, esp sugar

castor oil *n* a pale viscous oil from the beans of a tropical Old World plant, used esp as a purgative

castrate /kæˈstreɪt/ *v* **1a** to remove the testes of; geld **b** to remove the ovaries of; spay **2** to deprive of vitality or vigour; emasculate – **-tration** *n*

casual /ˈkæʒʊəl/ *adj* **1** subject to,

resulting from, or occurring by chance **2a** occurring without regularity; occasional **b** employed for irregular periods **3a** feeling or showing little concern; nonchalant **b** informal, natural; *also* designed for informal wear – **~ly** *adv* – **~ness** *n*

casualty /ˈkæʒʊəlti/ *n* **1** a member of a military force killed or wounded in action **2** a person or thing injured, lost, or destroyed

¹cat /kæt/ *n* **1a** a small domesticated flesh-eating mammal kept as a pet or for catching rats and mice **b** any of a family of carnivores that includes the domestic cat, lion, tiger, leopard, jaguar, cougar, lynx, and cheetah **2** a malicious woman **3** a cat-o'-nine-tails **4** a (male) person – slang

²cat *n* a catamaran – infml

cataclysm /ˈkætəklɪzəm/ *n* **1** a flood, deluge **2** a violent geological change of the earth's surface **3** a momentous event marked by violent upheaval and destruction – **~ic** *adj*

catacomb /ˈkætəkuːm/ *n* **1** a galleried subterranean cemetery with recesses for tombs **2** an underground passageway or group of passageways; a labyrinth *USE* often pl with sing. meaning

catalogue, *NAm chiefly* **catalog** /ˈkætəlɒg/ **1** (a pamphlet or book containing) a complete list of items arranged systematically with descriptive details **2** a list, series – **catalogue** *v*

catalyst /ˈkætl-ɪ̣st/ *n* **1** a substance that changes, esp increases, the rate of a chemical reaction but itself remains chemically unchanged **2** sby or sthg whose action inspires further and usu more important events – **-lytic** *adj* – **-lysis** *n*

catamaran /ˈkætəməræn/ *n* **1** a raft made of logs or pieces of wood lashed together **2** a boat with twin hulls side by side

cat-and-mouse *adj* consisting of continuous chasing and near captures and escapes

¹catapult /ˈkætəpʌlt, -pʊlt/ *n* **1** an ancient military device for hurling missiles **2** *Br* a Y-shaped stick with a piece of elastic material fixed between the 2 prongs, used for shooting small objects (e g stones)

²catapult *v* **1** to throw or launch (a missile) by means of a catapult **2** to (cause to) move suddenly or abruptly

cataract /ˈkætərækt/ *n* **1** clouding of (the enclosing membrane of) the lens of the eye; *also* the clouded area **2** steep rapids in a river; *also* a waterfall

catarrh /kəˈtɑːʳ/ *n* (the mucus resulting from) inflammation of a mucous membrane, esp in the human nose and air passages – **~al** *adj*

catastrophe /kəˈtæstrəfi/ *n* a momentous, tragic, and unexpected event of extreme gravity – **-phic** *adj* – **-phically** *adv*

cat burglar *n, Br* a burglar who enters buildings by climbing up walls, drainpipes, etc

catcall /ˈkæt-kɔːl/ *n* a loud or raucous cry expressing disapproval

¹catch /kætʃ/ *v* **caught** **1a** to capture or seize, esp after pursuit **b** to discover unexpectedly; surprise **c** to become entangled, fastened, or stuck **2a** to seize; *esp* to intercept and keep hold of (a moving object), esp in the hands **b** to dismiss (a batsman in cricket) by catching the ball after it has been hit and before it has touched the ground **3a** to contract; become infected with **b** to hit, strike **c** to receive the force or impact of **4** to attract, arrest **5** to take or get quickly or for a moment **6** to be in time for **7** to grasp with the senses or the mind **8** *of a fire* to start to burn

²catch *n* **1** sthg caught; *esp* the total quantity caught at one time **2** a game in which a ball is thrown and caught **3** sthg that retains or fastens **4** an often humorous or coarse round for 3 or more voices **5** a concealed difficulty; a snag **6** an eligible marriage partner – infml

catching /ˈkætʃɪŋ/ *adj* **1** infectious, contagious **2** alluring, attractive

catchment area /ˈkætʃmənt/ *n* **1** the area from which a lake, reservoir, etc gets its rainwater **2** a geographical area from which people are drawn to attend a particular school, hospital, etc

catch on *v* **1** to become popular **2** to understand, learn – often + *to*; infml

catch out *v* to expose or detect in wrongdoing or error – usu passive

catchpenny /ˈkætʃpeni/ *n or adj* (sthg) worthless but designed to appear attractive, esp by being showy – derog

catchphrase /ˈkætʃfreɪz/ *n* an arresting phrase that enjoys short-lived popularity

catch up *v* **1** to act or move fast enough to draw level *with* **2** to acquaint oneself or deal with sthg belatedly – + *on* or *with*

catchword /ˈkætʃwɜːd/ *n* a word or expression associated with some school of thought or political movement; a slogan

catchy /ˈkætʃi/ *adj* **1** tending to attract the interest or attention **2** easy to remember and reproduce – **catchily** *adv*

catechism /ˈkætʃ̩ˌkɪzəm/ *n* **1** a summary of religious doctrine, often in the form of questions and answers **2** a set of formal questions put as a test – **catechist** *n*

categorical /ˌkætʃ̩ˈgɒrɪkəl/ *also* **categoric** *adj* absolute, unqualified – **~ly** *adv*

category /ˈkæt̩gəri/ *n* **1** a general or fundamental form or class of terms, things, or ideas (e g in philosophy) **2** a division within a system of classification – **-orize** *v*

cater /ˈkeɪtəʳ/ *v* **1** to provide and serve a supply of usu prepared food **2** to supply what is required or desired – usu + *for* or *to* – **~er** *n*

caterpillar /ˈkætəˌpɪləʳ/ *n* a wormlike larva, specif of a butterfly or moth

caterwaul /ˈkætəwɔːl/ *v* to cry noisily – **caterwaul** *n*

catfish /ˈkætˌfɪʃ/ *n* any of numerous large-headed fishes with long barbels

catgut /ˈkætgʌt/ *n* a tough cord usu made from sheep intestines and used esp for the strings of musical instruments and tennis rackets and for surgical sutures

catharsis /kəˈθɑːs̩s/ *n, pl* **catharses** **1** purification or purgation of the emotions through drama **2** the process of bringing repressed ideas and feelings to consciousness and expressing them, esp during psychoanalysis – **-artic** *adj*

cathedral /kəˈθiːdrəl/ *n* a church that is the official seat of a bishop

catherine wheel /ˈkæθər̩n ˌwiːl/ *n, often cap C* a firework in the form of a wheel that spins as it burns

catheter /ˈkæθ̩təʳ/ *n* a tubular device for insertion into a hollow body part (e g a blood vessel), usu to inject or draw off fluids or to keep a passage open

cathode /ˈkæθəʊd/ *n* the electrode by which electrons leave an external circuit and enter a device; *specif* the positive terminal of a primary cell or of a storage battery that is delivering current

cathode-ray tube *n* a vacuum tube in which a beam of electrons is projected onto a fluorescent screen to provide a visual display (e g a television picture)

catholic /ˈkæθəlɪk/ *adj* **1** comprehensive, universal; *esp* broad in sympathies or tastes **2** *cap* **a** of or forming the entire body of worshippers that constitutes the Christian church **b** of or forming the ancient undivided Christian church or a church claiming historical continuity from it; *specif* Roman Catholic

catkin /ˈkætkɪn/ *n* a hanging spike-shaped densely crowded group of flowers without petals (e g in a willow)

catnap /ˈkætnæp/ *n* a brief period of sleep, esp during the day

cat-o'-nine-tails *n, pl* **cat-o'-nine-tails** a whip made of usu 9 knotted cords fastened to a handle

cat's cradle *n* a game in which a string looped in a pattern on the fingers of one person's hands is transferred to the hands of another so as to form a different figure

cat's-eye *also* **catzeye** *n, pl* **cat's-eyes** a small reflector set in a road, usu in a line with others, to reflect vehicle headlights

cat's-paw *n, pl* **cat's-paws** **1** a light breeze that ruffles the surface of water in irregular patches **2** sby used by another as a tool or dupe

catsuit /ˈkætsuːt, -sjuːt/ *n* a tightly

fitting 1-piece garment combining top and trousers

cattle /'kætl/ *n, pl* bovine animals kept on a farm, ranch, etc

cattle grid *n, Br* a shallow ditch in a road covered by parallel bars spaced far enough apart to prevent livestock from crossing

catty /'kæti/ *adj* slyly spiteful; malicious – **cattiness** *n* – **cattily** *adv*

catwalk /'kætwɔːk/ *n* **1** a narrow walkway (e g round a machine) **2** a narrow stage in the centre of a room on which fashion shows are held

caucus /'kɔːkəs/ *n* a closed political meeting to decide on policy, select candidates, etc

caught /kɔːt/ *past of* **catch**

caul /kɔːl/ *n* **1** the large fatty fold of membrane covering the intestines **2** the inner foetal membrane of higher vertebrates, esp when covering the head at birth

cauldron /'kɔːldrən/ *n* a large open metal pot for cooking over an open fire

cauliflower /'kɒlɪˌflaʊəʳ/ *n* (a plant closely related to the cabbage with) a compact head of usu white undeveloped flowers eaten as a vegetable

caulk, calk /kɔːk/ *v* to stop up and make watertight (e g the seams of a boat, cracks in wood, etc) by filling with a waterproof material

causal /'kɔːzəl/ *adj* **1** expressing or indicating cause; causative **2** of or being a cause – **~ly** *adv*

¹cause /kɔːz/ *n* **1a** sby or sthg that brings about an effect **b** a reason for an action or condition; a motive **2** a ground for legal action **3** a principle or movement worth defending or supporting

²cause *v* to serve as the cause or occasion of

'cause /kəz/ *conj* because – nonstandard

cause célèbre /ˌkəʊz seɪ'lebrə, ˌkɔːz-/ *n, pl* **causes célèbres** **1** a legal case that excites widespread interest **2** a notorious incident or episode

causeway /'kɔːzweɪ/ *n* a raised road or path, esp across wet ground or water

caustic /'kɔːstɪk, 'kɒstɪk/ *adj* **1** capable of destroying or eating away by chemical action; corrosive **2** incisive, biting

cauter·ize, -ise /'kɔːtəraɪz/ to sear or burn (e g a wound) with a hot iron or caustic chemical, esp to get rid of infection

¹caution /'kɔːʃən/ *n* **1** a warning, admonishment; *specif* an official warning given to sby who has committed a minor offence **2** prudent forethought intended to minimize risk; care **3** sby or sthg that causes astonishment or amusement – infml

²caution *v* **1a** to advise caution to; warn; *specif* to warn (sby under arrest) that his/her words will be recorded and may be used in evidence **b** to admonish, reprove; *specif* to give an official warning to **2** *of a soccer referee* to book

cautious /'kɔːʃəs/ *adj* careful, prudent – **~ly** *adv* – **~ness** *n*

cavalcade /ˌkævəl'keɪd, 'kævəlkeɪd/ *n* **1** a procession; *esp* one of riders or carriages **2** a dramatic sequence or procession; a series

¹cavalier /ˌkævə'lɪəʳ/ *n* **1** a gallant gentleman of former times; *esp* one in attendance on a lady **2** *cap* an adherent of Charles I of England, esp during the Civil War

²cavalier *adj* **1** debonair **2** given to or characterized by offhand dismissal of important matters

cavalry /'kævəlri/ *n, sing or pl in constr* **1** a branch of an army consisting of mounted troops **2** a branch of a modern army consisting of armoured vehicles – **~man** *n*

¹cave /keɪv/ *n* a natural chamber (e g underground or in the side of a hill or cliff) having a usu horizontal opening on the surface

²cave /kɑː'viː/ *interj, Br* – used as a warning call among schoolchildren, esp at public school

caveat emptor /ˌkæviæt 'emptɔː, ˌkeɪ-/ *n* the principle in commerce which states that without a guarantee the buyer takes the risk of quality upon him-/herself

cave in *v* **1** to fall in or collapse **2** to cease to resist; submit – **cave-in** *n*

caveman /'keɪvmæn/ *n* **1** a cave dweller, esp of the Stone Age **2** a man

who acts in a rough primitive manner, esp towards women
cavern /ˈkævən/ *n* a large usu underground chamber or cave
caviar, caviare /ˈkæviɑːʳ/ *n* salted fish (esp sturgeon) roe usu considered a delicacy
cavil /ˈkævəl/ *v* to raise trivial and frivolous objections – **~ler** *n*
cavity /ˈkævɪ̵ti/ *n* an empty or hollowed-out space within a mass; *specif* a decaying hollow in a tooth
cavort /kəˈvɔːt/ *v* **1** to prance **2** to engage in extravagant behaviour
cavy /ˈkeɪvi/ *n* a guinea pig or related short-tailed S American rodent
caw /kɔː/ *v* to utter (a sound like) the harsh raucous cry of the crow
cayenne pepper /ˌkeɪen ˈpepəʳ/ *n* a pungent red condiment consisting of the ground dried pods and seeds of hot peppers
cease *v* /siːs/ to bring to an end; terminate, discontinue – **cease** *n*
cease-fire *n* (a military order for) a cessation of firing or of active hostilities
ceaseless /ˈsiːslɪ̵s/ *adj* continuing endlessly; constant – **~ly** *adv*
cedar /ˈsiːdəʳ/ *n* (the fragrant wood of) any of a genus of usu tall evergreen coniferous trees of the pine family
cede /siːd/ *v* to yield or surrender (e g territory), usu by treaty
cedilla /sɪ̵ˈdɪlə/ *n* a mark ¸ placed under a letter (e g ç in French) to indicate an alteration or modification of its usual phonetic value (e g in the French *façade*)
ceiling /ˈsiːlɪŋ/ *n* **1** the overhead inside surface of a room **2** the height above the ground of the base of the lowest layer of clouds **3** an upper usu prescribed limit
celandine /ˈseləndaɪn/ *n* **1** *also* **greater celandine** a yellow-flowered biennial plant of the poppy family **2** *also* **lesser celandine** a common yellow-flowered European perennial plant of the buttercup family
celebrant /ˈselɪ̵brənt/ *n* the priest officiating at the Eucharist
celebrate /ˈselɪ̵breɪt/ *v* **1** to perform (a sacrament or solemn ceremony) publicly and with appropriate rites **2a** to mark (a holy day or feast day) ceremonially **b** to mark (a special occasion) with festivities or suspension of routine activities – **-ation** *n* – **-atory** *adj*
celebrated /ˈselɪ̵breɪtɪ̵d/ *adj* widely known and often referred to
celebrity /sɪ̵ˈlebrɪ̵ti/ *n* **1** the state of being famous **2** a well-known and widely acclaimed person
celerity /sɪ̵ˈlerɪ̵ti/ *n* rapidity of motion or action – fml
celery /ˈseləri/ *n* a European plant of the carrot family with leafstalks eaten cold or hot as a vegetable
celestial /sɪ̵ˈlestɪəl/ *adj* **1** of or suggesting heaven or divinity; divine **2** of or in the sky or visible heavens
celibate /ˈselɪ̵bɪ̵t/ *n* one who is unmarried and does not have sexual intercourse, esp because of a religious vow – **-bacy** *n*
cell /sel/ *n* **1** a 1-room dwelling occupied esp by a hermit **2** a small room for a prisoner, monk, etc **3** a small compartment (e g in a honeycomb), receptacle, cavity (e g one containing seeds in a plant ovary), or bounded space **4** the smallest structural unit of living matter consisting of nuclear and cytoplasmic material bounded by a membrane and capable of functioning either alone or with others in all fundamental life processes **5** a vessel (e g a cup or jar) containing electrodes and an electrolyte either for generating electricity by chemical action or for use in electrolysis **6** the primary unit of a political, esp Communist, organization
[1]**cellar** /ˈseləʳ/ *n* **1** an underground room; *esp* one used for storage **2** an individual's stock of wine
cello /ˈtʃeləʊ/ *n, pl* **cellos** a large stringed instrument of the violin family tuned an octave below the viola – **cellist** *n*
cellophane /ˈseləfeɪn/ *n* regenerated cellulose in the form of thin transparent sheets, used esp for wrapping goods
cellular /ˈseljʊləʳ/ *adj* **1** of, relating to, or consisting of cells **2** containing cavities; porous
celluloid /ˈseljʊlɔɪd/ *n* film for the cinema; *also* film as a medium
Celluloid *trademark* – used for a

tough inflammable plastic composed essentially of cellulose nitrate and camphor

cellulose /'seljʊləʊs/ *n* **1** a sugar made up of glucose units that constitutes the chief part of plant cell walls, occurs naturally in cotton, kapok, etc, and is the raw material of many manufactured goods (e g paper, rayon, and cellophane) **2** paint or lacquer of which the main constituent is cellulose nitrate or acetate

Celsius /'selsɪəs/ *adj* relating to, conforming to, or being a scale of temperature on which water freezes at 0° and boils at 100° under standard conditions

[1]**Celtic** /'keltɪk/ *adj* (characteristic) of the Celts or their languages

[2]**Celtic** *n* a branch of Indo-European languages comprising Welsh, Cornish, Breton, Irish, Scots Gaelic, and Manx, which is now confined to Brittany and parts of the British Isles

[1]**cement** /sɪ̥'ment/ *n* **1** a powder consisting of ground alumina, silica, lime, iron oxide, and magnesia burnt in a kiln, that is used as the binding agent in mortar and concrete **2** a substance (e g a glue or adhesive) used for sticking objects together **3** sthg serving to unite firmly **4** concrete – not used technically

[2]**cement** *v* **1** to unite or make firm (as if) by the application of cement **2** to overlay with concrete

cemetery /'semɪ̥tri/ *n* a burial ground; *esp* one not in a churchyard

cenotaph /'senətɑːf/ *n* a tomb or monument erected in honour of a person or group of people whose remains are elsewhere; *specif, cap* that standing in Whitehall in London in memory of the dead of WWs I and II

[1]**censor** /'sensəʳ/ *n* an official who examines publications, films, letters, etc and has the power to suppress objectionable (e g obscene or libellous) matter – **~ship** *n* – **~ious** *adj* – **censor** *v*

censure /'senʃəʳ/ *n* **1** a judgment involving condemnation **2** the act of blaming or condemning sternly **3** an official reprimand – **censure** *v*

census /'sensəs/ *n* **1** a periodic counting of the population and gathering of related statistics (e g age, sex, or social class) carried out by government **2** a usu official count or tally

cent /sent/ *n* (a coin or note representing) a unit worth $^1/_{100}$ of the basic money unit of certain countries (e g the American dollar)

centaur /'sentɔːʳ/ *n* any of a race of mythological creatures having the head, arms, and upper body of a man, and the lower body and back legs of a horse

centenarian /ˌsentɪ̥'neərɪən/ *n* sby who is (more than) 100 years old

centenary /sen'tiːnəri/ *n* (the celebration of) a 100th anniversary

centigrade /'sentɪ̥greɪd/ *adj* Celsius

centigram /'sentɪ̥græm/ *n* one hundredth of a gram

centime /'sɒntiːm/ *n* (a note or coin representing) a unit worth $^1/_{100}$ of the basic money unit of certain French-speaking countries (e g Algeria, Belgium, France)

centimetre /'sentɪ̥ˌmiːtəʳ/ *n* one hundredth of a metre (about 0.4in)

centipede /'sentɪ̥piːd/ *n* any of a class of many-segmented arthropods with each segment bearing 1 pair of legs

central /'sentrəl/ *adj* **1** containing or constituting a centre **2** of primary importance; principal **3** at, in, or near the centre **4** having overall power or control **5** of, originating in, or comprising the central nervous system – **~ly** *adv* – **~ize** *v*

central heating *n* a system of heating whereby heat is produced at a central source (e g a boiler) and carried by pipes to radiators or air vents throughout a building (e g a house or office block)

central nervous system *n* the part of the nervous system which in vertebrates consists of the brain and spinal cord and which coordinates the activity of the entire nervous system

[1]**centre,** *NAm chiefly* **center** /'sentəʳ/ *n* **1** the point round which a circle or sphere is described; *broadly* the centre of symmetry **2a** a place, esp a collection of buildings, round which a usu specified activity is concentrated **b** sby or sthg round which interest is concentrated **c** a source from which

sthg originates **d** a region of concentrated population **3** the middle part (e g of a stage) **4** *often cap* a group, party, etc holding moderate political views **5** a player occupying a middle position in the forward line of a team (e g in football or hockey) **6** a temporary wooden framework on which an arch is supported during construction

[2]**centre,** *NAm chiefly* **center** *v* **1** to place, fix, or move in, into, or at a centre or central area **2** to gather to a centre; concentrate **3** to adjust (e g lenses) so that the axes coincide

centreboard /'sentəbɔːd/ *n* a retractable keel used esp in small yachts

centre-forward *n* (the position of) a player in hockey, soccer, etc positioned in the middle of the forward line

centre of gravity *n* the point at which the entire weight of a body may be considered as concentrated so that if supported at this point the body would remain in equilibrium in any position

centrifugal /,sentrɪ'fjuːgəl/ *adj* proceeding or acting in a direction away from a centre or axis

centripetal /sen'trɪpʒtl/ *adj* **1** proceeding or acting in a direction towards a centre or axis **2** tending towards centralization; unifying

centurion /,sen'tʃʊərɪən/ *n* an officer commanding a Roman century

century /'sentʃəri/ *n* **1** a subdivision of the ancient Roman legion orig consisting of 100 men **2** a group, sequence, or series of 100 like things; *specif* 100 runs made by a cricketer in 1 innings **3** a period of 100 years; *esp* any of the 100-year periods reckoned forwards or backwards from the conventional date of the birth of Christ

ceramic /sʒ'ræmɪk/ *adj* of or relating to pots and pottery

cereal /'sɪərɪəl/ *n* **1** (a grass or other plant yielding) grain suitable for food **2** a food made from grain and usu eaten with milk and sugar at breakfast

cerebellum /,serʒ'beləm/ *n, pl* **cerebellums, cerebella** a large part of the back of the brain which projects outwards and is concerned esp with coordinating muscles and maintaining equilibrium

cerebral /'serʒbrəl/ *adj* **1** of the brain or the intellect **2a** appealing to the intellect **b** primarily intellectual in nature – **~ly** *adv*

ceremonial /,serʒ'məʊniəl/ *n* **1** a usu prescribed system of formalities or rituals **2** (a book containing) the order of service in the Roman Catholic church

ceremony /'serʒməni/ *n* **1** a formal act or series of acts prescribed by ritual, protocol, or convention **2** (observance of) established procedures of civility or politeness – **-nial** *adj* – **-nious** *adj*

cerise /sə'riːz/ *n or adj* (a) light purplish red

cert /sɜːt/ *n, Br* a certainty; *esp* a horse that is sure to win a race – infml

[1]**certain** /'sɜːtn/ *adj* **1a** of a particular but unspecified character, quantity, or degree **b** named but not known **2a** established beyond doubt or question; definite **b** unerring, dependable **3a** inevitable **b** incapable of failing; sure – + infinitive **4** assured in mind or action – **~ly** *adv*

certainty /'sɜːtnti/ *n* **1** sthg certain **2** the quality or state of being certain

[1]**certificate** /sə'tɪfɪkət/ *n* a document containing a certified statement; *esp* one declaring the status or qualifications of the holder

[2]**certificate** /sə'tɪfɪkeɪt/ *v* to testify to with a certificate – **-ation** *n*

certify /'sɜːtʒfaɪ/ *v* **1a** to declare officially as being true or as meeting a standard **b** to declare officially the insanity of **2** to certificate, license **3** to guarantee the payment or value of (a cheque) by endorsing on the front – **-fiable** *adj* – **-fiably** *adv*

certitude /'sɜːtʒtjuːd/ *n* the state of being or feeling certain

cerulean /sʒ'ruːlɪən/ *adj* deep sky blue in colour

cervix /'sɜːvɪks/ *n, pl* **cervices, cervixes** the narrow outer end of the uterus – **-ical** *adj*

cessation /se'seɪʃən/ *n* a temporary or final stop; an ending

cesspit /'sespɪt/ *n* **1** a pit for the

disposal of refuse (e g sewage) **2** a corrupt or squalid place

cetacean /sɪ'teɪʃən/ *n* any of an order of aquatic, mostly marine, mammals that includes the whales, dolphins, and porpoises – **cetacean** *adj*

cha-cha /'tʃɑː tʃɑː/ **cha-cha-cha** *n* (a piece of music for performing) a fast rhythmic ballroom dance of Latin American origin

chafe /tʃeɪf/ *v* **1** to feel irritation or discontent; fret **2** to warm (part of the body) by rubbing **3** to rub so as to wear away or make sore

[1]**chaff** /tʃɑːf, tʃæf/ *n* **1** the seed coverings and other debris separated from the seed in threshing grain **2** worthless matter – esp in *separate the wheat from the chaff* **3** chopped straw, hay, etc used for animal feed

[2]**chaff** *n* light jesting talk; banter

[3]**chaff** *v* to tease good-naturedly

chaffinch /'tʃæˌfɪntʃ/ *n* a European finch with a reddish breast, a bluish head, and white wing bars

chagrin /ʃægrɪn/ *v or n* (to subject to) mental distress caused by humiliation, disappointment, or failure

[1]**chain** /tʃeɪn/ *n* **1a** a series of usu metal links or rings connected to or fitted into one another and used for various purposes (e g support or restraint) **b** a unit of length equal to 66ft (about 20.12m) **2** sthg that confines, restrains, or secures – usu pl **3a** a series of linked or connected things **b** a group of associated establishments (e g shops or hotels) under the same ownership

[2]**chain** *v* to fasten, restrict, or confine (as if) with a chain – often + *up* or *down*

chain gang *n, sing or pl in constr* a gang of convicts chained together, usu while doing hard labour outside prison

chain mail *n* flexible armour of interlinked metal rings

chain reaction *n* **1** a series of events so related to each other that each one initiates the next **2** a self-sustaining chemical or nuclear reaction yielding energy or products that cause further reactions of the same kind

chain saw *n* a portable power saw that has teeth linked together to form a continuous revolving chain

chain store *n* any of several usu retail shops under the same ownership and selling the same lines of goods

[1]**chair** /tʃeəʳ/ *n* **1** a seat for 1 person, usu having 4 legs and a back and sometimes arms **2a** an office or position of authority or dignity; *specif* a professorship **b** a chairman **3** a sedan chair

[2]**chair** *v* **1** to install in office **2** to preside as chairman of **3** *chiefly Br* to carry shoulder-high in acclaim

chair lift *n* a ski lift with seats for passengers

chairman /'tʃeəmən/, *fem* **chairlady, chairwoman** *n* **1** one who presides over or heads a meeting, committee, organization, or board of directors **2** a radio or television presenter; *esp* one who coordinates unscripted or diverse material – **~ship** *n*

chaise /ʃeɪz/ *n* a light carriage, usu having 2 wheels and a folding top

chaise longue /ˌʃeɪz 'lɒŋg/ *n, pl* **chaise longues** *also* **chaises longues** a low sofa with only 1 armrest, on which one may recline

chalet /'ʃæleɪ/ *n* **1** a usu wooden house or hut with a steeply sloping roof and widely overhanging eaves, common esp in Switzerland **2** a small house or hut used esp for temporary accommodation (e g at a holiday camp)

chalice /'tʃælɪ̣s/ *n* a drinking cup or goblet; *esp* one used to hold the wine at communion

[1]**chalk** /tʃɔːk/ *n* **1** a soft white, grey, or buff limestone composed chiefly of the shells of small marine organisms **2** a short stick of chalk or chalky material used esp for writing and drawing – **~y** *adj*

[2]**chalk** *v* to set down or add up (as if) with chalk – usu + *up*

chalk up *v* **1** to ascribe, credit; *specif* to charge to sby's account **2** to attain, achieve

[1]**challenge** /'tʃælɪ̣ndʒ/ *v* **1** to order to halt and prove identity **2** to dispute, esp as being unjust, invalid, or outmoded; impugn **3a** to defy boldly; dare **b** to call out to duel, combat, or

competition **4** to stimulate by testing the skill of (sby or sthg) – ~**r** *n*

[2]**challenge** *n* **1a** a command given by a sentry, watchman, etc to halt and prove identity **b** a questioning of right or validity **2a** a summons that is threatening or provocative; *specif* a call to a duel **b** an invitation to compete **3** (sthg having) the quality of being demanding or stimulating

[1]**chamber** /'tʃeɪmbəʳ/ *n* **1** a natural or artificial enclosed space or cavity **2** a room **a(1)** where a judge hears private cases – usu pl with sing. meaning **(2)** *pl* used by a group of barristers **b** with an official or state function **3** (a hall used by) a legislative or judicial body; *esp* either of 2 houses of a legislature **4** the part of a gun that holds the charge or cartridge

chamberlain /'tʃeɪmbəlɪ̯n/ *n* **1** a chief officer of a royal or noble household **2** a treasurer (e g of a corporation)

chambermaid /'tʃeɪmbəmeɪd/ *n* a maid who cleans bedrooms and makes beds (e g in a hotel)

chamber music *n* music written for a small group of instruments

chamber pot *n* a bowl-shaped receptacle for urine and faeces, used chiefly in the bedroom

chameleon /kə'miːlɪən/ *n* **1** any of a group of Old World lizards with a long tongue, a prehensile tail, and the ability to change the colour of the skin **2** sby or sthg changeable; *specif* a fickle person

chamois /'ʃæmwɑː, 'ʃæmi/ *n, pl* **chamois** *also* **chamoix** **1** a small goatlike antelope of Europe and the Caucasus **2** a soft pliant leather prepared from the skin of the chamois or sheep, used esp as a cloth for polishing

[1]**champ** /tʃæmp/ *v* **1** to make biting or gnashing movements **2** to eat noisily **3** to show impatience or eagerness – usu in *champ at the bit*

[2]**champ** *n* a champion – infml

champagne /ʃæm'peɪn/ *n* a white sparkling wine made in the old province of Champagne in France

[1]**champion** /'tʃæmpɪən/ *n* **1** a militant supporter of, or fighter for, a cause or person **2** one who shows marked superiority; *specif* the winner of a competitive event

[2]**champion** *v* to protect or fight for as a champion

[3]**champion** *adj, chiefly N Eng* superb, splendid

championship /'tʃæmpɪənʃɪp/ *n* a contest held to determine a champion

[1]**chance** /tʃɑːns/ *n* **1** the incalculable (assumed) element in existence; that which determines unaccountable happenings **2** a situation favouring some purpose; an opportunity **3a** the possibility of a specified or favourable outcome in an uncertain situation **b** *pl* the more likely indications **4** a risk – **chance** *adj*

[2]**chance** *v* **1** to take place or come about by chance; happen **2** to come or light *on* or *upon* by chance **3** to accept the hazard of; risk

chancel /'tʃɑːnsəl/ *n* the part of a church containing the altar and seats for the clergy and choir

chancellery, **chancellory** /'tʃɑːnsələri/ *n* **1** the position or department of a chancellor **2** the office or staff of an embassy or consulate

chancellor /'tʃɑːnsələʳ/ *n* **1** the Lord Chancellor **2** the titular head of a British university **3** a usu lay legal officer of an Anglican diocese **4** the chief minister of state in some European countries

chancery /'tʃɑːnsəri/ *n* **1 Chancery Division, Chancery** a division of the High Court having jurisdiction over causes in equity **2** a record office for public archives or those of ecclesiastical, legal, or diplomatic proceedings **3** a chancellor's court, office, etc

chancy /'tʃɑːnsi/ *adj* uncertain in outcome or prospect; risky – **-ciness** *n*

chandelier /ˌʃændə'lɪəʳ/ *n* a branched often ornate lighting fixture suspended from a ceiling

[1]**change** /tʃeɪndʒ/ *v* **1a** to make or become different **b** to exchange, reverse – often + *over* or *round* **2a** to replace with another **b** to move from one to another **c** to exchange for an equivalent sum or comparable item **d** to put on fresh clothes or covering **3**

to go from one vehicle of a public transport system to another **4** *of the (male) voice* to shift to a lower register; break **5** to undergo transformation, transition, or conversion

[2]**change** *n* **1a** a (marked) alteration **b** a substitution **2** an alternative set, esp of clothes **3a** money returned when a payment exceeds the amount due **b** coins of low denominations **4** an order in which a set of bells is struck in change ringing

changeable /ˈtʃeɪndʒəbəl/ *adj* **1** able or apt to vary **2** capable of being altered or exchanged **3** fickle – **-bly** *adv* – **~ness** *n*

changeling /ˈtʃeɪndʒlɪŋ/ *n* a child secretly exchanged for another in infancy; *specif* an elf-child left in place of a human child by fairies

change of life *n the* menopause

change-over *n* a conversion to a different system or function

[1]**channel** /ˈtʃænl/ *n* **1a** the bed where a stream of water runs **b** the deeper part of a river, harbour, or strait **c** a narrow region of sea between 2 land masses **d** a path along which information passes or can be stored (e g on a recording tape) **e** a course or direction of thought, action, or communication – often pl with sing. meaning **f** a television station **2** a usu tubular passage, esp for liquids **3** a long gutter, groove, or furrow

[2]**channel** *v* to convey into or through a channel; direct

chant /tʃɑːnt/ *n* **1** (the music or performance of) a repetitive melody used for liturgical singing in which as many syllables are assigned to each note as required **2** a rhythmic monotonous utterance or song – **chant** *v*

chanticleer /ˈtʃæntɪ̣klɪəʳ/ *n* – used as a poetic name of the domestic cock

chaos /ˈkeɪ-ɒs/ *n* **1** *often cap* the confused unorganized state of primordial matter before the creation of distinct forms **2** a state of utter confusion – **chaotic** *adj* – **chaotically** *adv*

[1]**chap** /tʃæp/ *n* a man, fellow – infml

[2]**chap** *v* to (cause to) open in slits or cracks

[3]**chap** *n* a crack in the skin caused by exposure to wind or cold

[4]**chap** *n* (the fleshy covering of) a jaw

[1]**chapel** /ˈtʃæpəl/ *n* **1a** a place of worship serving a residence, institution, or a Christian group other than an established church **b** a room or bay in a church for prayer or minor religious services **2** a chapel service or assembly **3** *sing or pl in constr* the members of a trade union, esp in a printing office

[2]**chapel** *adj* belonging to a Nonconformist church

chaperone, chaperon /ˈʃæpərəʊn/ *n* an older woman who accompanies a younger woman on social occasions to guard against impropriety

chaplain /ˈtʃæplɪ̣n/ *n* a clergyman officially attached to a branch of the armed forces, an institution, or a family or court – **~cy** *n*

chaplet /ˈtʃæplɪ̣t/ *n* **1** a wreath to be worn on the head **2a** a string of beads **b** a part of a rosary comprising 5 decades

chaps /tʃæps/ *n pl* leather leggings worn over the trousers, esp by N American ranch hands

chapter /ˈtʃæptəʳ/ *n* **1a** a major division of a book **b** sthg resembling a chapter in being a significant specified unit **2** (a regular meeting of) the canons of a cathedral or collegiate church, or the members of a religious house **3** a local branch of a society or fraternity

[1]**char, charr** /tʃɑːʳ/ *n* any of a genus of small-scaled trouts

[2]**char** *v* **1** to convert to charcoal or carbon, usu by heat; burn **2** to burn slightly; scorch

[3]**char** *v or n* (to work as) a cleaning woman

[4]**char, cha** *n, Br* tea – infml

character /ˈkærɪ̣ktəʳ/ *n* **1a** a distinctive mark, usu in the form of a stylized graphic device **b** a graphic symbol (e g a hieroglyph or alphabet letter) used in writing or printing **2** (any of) qualities that make up and distinguish the individual **3a** a person, esp one marked by notable or conspicuous traits **b** any of the people portrayed in a novel, film, play, etc **4** (good) reputation **5** moral strength; integrity

[1]**characteristic** /ˌkærɪ̣ktəˈrɪstɪk/ *adj* serving to reveal and distinguish the

individual character; typical – ~**ally** *adv*

[2]**characteristic** *n* a distinguishing trait, quality, or property

character·ize, -ise *v* **1** to describe the character of **2** to be a characteristic of – **-ization** *n*

charade /ʃə'rɑːd/ *n* **1** *pl* a game in which one team acts out each syllable of a word or phrase while the other tries to guess it **2** a ridiculous pretence

charcoal /'tʃɑːkəʊl/ *n* **1** a dark or black porous carbon prepared by partly burning vegetable or animal substances (e g wood or bone) **2** fine charcoal used in pencil form for drawing

[1]**charge** /tʃɑːdʒ/ *v* **1a** to load or fill to capacity **b(1)** to restore the active materials in (a storage battery) by the passage of a direct current in the opposite direction to that of discharge **(2)** to give an electric charge to **c** to fill with (passionate) emotion, feeling, etc **2** to command or exhort with right or authority **3** to blame or accuse **4** to rush violently at; attack; *also* to rush into (an opponent), usu illegally, in soccer, basketball, etc **5a** to fix or ask as fee or payment **b** to ask payment of (a person) **c** to record (an item) as an expense, debt, obligation, or liability

[2]**charge** *n* **1** the quantity that an apparatus is intended to receive and fitted to hold; *esp* the quantity of explosive for a gun or cannon **2a** power, force **b** a definite quantity of electricity; *esp* the charge that a storage battery is capable of yielding **3a** an obligation, requirement **b** control, supervision **c** sby or sthg committed to the care of another **4** the price demanded or paid for sthg **5** an accusation, indictment, or statement of complaint **6** a violent rush forwards (e g in attack)

chargé d'affaires /ˌʃɑːʒeɪ dæ'feəʳ/ *n, pl* **chargés d'affaires** a diplomatic representative inferior in rank to an ambassador

[1]**charger** /'tʃɑːdʒəʳ/ *n* a large flat meat dish

[2]**charger** *n* a horse for battle or parade

chariot /'tʃærɪət/ *n* **1** a light 4-wheeled pleasure or state carriage **2** a 2-wheeled horse-drawn vehicle of ancient times used in warfare and racing – ~**eer** *n*

charisma /kə'rɪzmə/ *n* the special magnetic appeal, charm, or power of an individual (e g a political leader) that inspires popular loyalty and enthusiasm – ~**tic** *adj* – ~**tically** *adv*

charitable /'tʃærl̩təbl/ *adj* **1a** liberal in giving to the poor; generous **b** of or giving charity **2** merciful or kind in judging others; lenient – **-bly** *adv*

charity /'tʃærl̩ti/ *n* **1** benevolent goodwill towards or love of humanity **2a** kindly generosity and helpfulness, esp towards the needy or suffering; *also* aid given to those in need **b** an institution engaged in relief of the poor, sick, etc **3a** a gift for public benevolent purposes **b** an institution (e g a hospital) funded by such a gift **4** lenient judgment of others

charlatan /'ʃɑːlətn/ *n* **1** a quack doctor **2** one who pretends, usu ostentatiously, to have special knowledge or ability; a fraud

Charleston /'tʃɑːlstən/ *v or n* (to dance) a lively ballroom dance in which the heels are swung sharply outwards on each step

[1]**charm** /tʃɑːm/ *n* **1** an incantation **2** sthg worn to ward off evil or to ensure good fortune **3a** a quality that fascinates, allures, or delights **b** *pl* physical graces or attractions, esp of a woman **4** a small ornament worn on a bracelet or chain

[2]**charm** *v* **1a** to affect (as if) by magic; bewitch **b** to soothe or delight by compelling attraction **2** to control (esp a snake) by the use of rituals (e g the playing of music) – ~**ing** *adj* – ~**ingly** *adv* – ~**er** *n*

[1]**chart** /tʃɑːt/ *n* **1a** an outline map showing the geographical distribution of sthg (e g climatic or magnetic variations) **b** a navigator's map **2a** a sheet giving information in the form of a table; *esp, pl the* list of best-selling popular gramophone records (produced weekly) **b** a graph **c** a schematic, usu large, diagram

[2]**chart** *v* **1** to make a chart of **2** to lay *out* a plan for

[1]**charter** /'tʃɑːtəʳ/ *n* **1** a document that creates and defines the rights of a city, educational institution, or company **2** a constitution **3** a special privilege, immunity, or exemption **4** a total or partial lease of a ship, aeroplane, etc for a particular use or group of people

[2]**charter** *v* **1a** to establish or grant by charter **b** to certify as qualified **2** to hire or lease for usu exclusive and temporary use

charwoman /'tʃɑːˌwʊmən/ *n* a cleaning woman

chary /'tʃeəri/ *adj* **1** cautious; *esp* wary of taking risks **2** slow to grant or accept – **charily** *adv*

[1]**chase** /tʃeɪs/ *v* **1a** to follow rapidly or persistently; pursue **b** to rush, hasten **2** to cause to depart or flee; drive **3** *chiefly Br* to investigate (a matter) or contact (a person, company, etc) in order to obtain information or (hasten) results – usu + *up*

[2]**chase** *n* **1a** chasing, pursuit **b** *the* hunting of wild animals **2** sthg pursued; a quarry **3** a tract of unenclosed land set aside for the breeding of animals for hunting and fishing **4** a steeplechase

[3]**chase** *v* to ornament (metal) by indenting with a hammer and tools that have no cutting edge – **~r** *n*

[4]**chase** *n* a groove cut in a surface for a pipe, wire, etc

chaser /'tʃeɪsəʳ/ *n* **1** a glass or swallow of a mild drink (e g beer) taken after spirits; *also* a drink of spirits taken after a mild drink (e g beer) **2** a horse for steeplechases

chasm /'kæzəm/ *n* **1** a deep cleft in the earth **2** an apparently unbridgeable gap

chassis /'ʃæsi/ *n, pl* **chassis** **1** a supporting framework for the body of a vehicle (e g a car) **2** the frame on which the electrical parts of a radio, television, etc are mounted

chaste /tʃeɪst/ *adj* **1** abstaining from (unlawful or immoral) sexual intercourse; celibate **2** pure in thought and act; modest **3** severely simple in design or execution; austere – **~ly** *adv* – **~ness** *n* – **chastity** *n*

chasten /'tʃeɪsən/ *v* **1** to correct by punishment or suffering; discipline **2** to subdue, restrain

chastise /tʃæ'staɪz/ *v* **1** to inflict punishment on, esp by whipping **2** to subject to severe reproof or criticism – **~ment** *n*

[1]**chat** /tʃæt/ *v* to talk in an informal or familiar manner

[2]**chat** *n* (an instance of) light familiar talk; *esp* (a) conversation

chattel /'tʃætl/ *n* an item of personal property – usu in *goods and chattels*

chatter /'tʃætəʳ/ *v* **1** to talk idly, incessantly, or fast; jabber **2a** *esp of teeth* to click repeatedly or uncontrollably (e g from cold) **b** *of a cutting tool (e g a drill)* to vibrate rapidly while cutting – **~er** *n* – **chatter** *n*

chatterbox /'tʃætəbɒks/ *n* one who engages in much idle talk – infml

chatty /'tʃæti/ *adj* **1** fond of chatting; talkative **2** having the style and manner of light familiar conversation

chat up *v* to engage (sby) in friendly conversation for an ulterior motive, esp with amorous intent – infml

chauffeur /'ʃəʊfəʳ, ʃəʊ'fɜːʳ/ *n* a person employed to drive a private passenger-carrying motor vehicle, esp a car

chauvinism /'ʃəʊvɪ̥nɪzəm/ *n* **1** blind attachment to one's group, cause, or country **2** unquestioning belief in the superiority of one's own (male) sex – **-ist** *n, adj* – **-istic** *adj* – **-istically** *adv*

cheap /tʃiːp/ *adj* **1a** (relatively) low in price **b** charging a low price **2** gained with little effort; *esp* gained by contemptible means **3a** of inferior quality or worth; tawdry, sleazy **b** contemptible because of lack of any fine or redeeming qualities – **~ly** *adv* – **~ness** *n*

cheapen /'tʃiːpən/ *v* to make or become **a** cheap in price or value **b** lower in esteem **c** tawdry, vulgar, or inferior

[1]**cheap-jack** *n* sby, esp a pedlar, who sells cheap wares

[2]**cheap-jack** *adj* **1** inferior, cheap, or worthless **2** characterized by unscrupulous opportunism

[1]**cheat** /tʃiːt/ *n* **1** a fraudulent deception; a fraud **2** one who cheats; a pretender, deceiver

[2]**cheat** *v* **1a** to practise fraud or deception **b** to violate rules dishonestly (e g at cards or in an exam) **2** to be sexually unfaithful – usu + *on* **3** to defeat the purpose or blunt the effects of

[1]**check** /tʃek/ *n* **1** exposure of a chess king to an attack from which it must be protected or moved to safety – often used interjectionally **2** a sudden stoppage of a forward course or progress; an arrest **3** one who or that which arrests, limits, or restrains; a restraint **4** a criterion **5** an inspection, examination, test, or verification **6a** (a square in) a pattern of squares (of alternating colours) **b** a fabric woven or printed with such a design **7** *NAm* a cheque **8a** *chiefly NAm* a ticket or token showing ownership or identity **b** *NAm* a bill, esp for food and drink in a restaurant

[2]**check** *v* **1** to put (a chess opponent's king) in check **2a** to slow or bring to a stop; brake **b** to block the progress of **3** to restrain or diminish the action or force of **4a** to compare with a source, original, or authority; verify **b** to inspect for satisfactory condition, accuracy, safety, or performance – sometimes + *out* or *over* **c** *chiefly NAm* to correspond point for point; tally – often + *out* **5** to note or mark with a tick – often + *off* **6** *chiefly NAm* to leave or accept for safekeeping in a cloakroom or left-luggage office – often + *in*

checkers /'tʃekəz/ *n pl but sing in constr, NAm* the game of draughts

check in *v* to report one's presence or arrival; *esp* to arrive and register at a hotel or airport

checkmate *v* **1** to thwart or counter completely **2** to check (a chess opponent's king) so that escape is impossible

checkout /'tʃek-aʊt/ *n* a cash desk equipped with a cash register in a self-service shop

check out *v* to complete the formalities for leaving, esp at a hotel

checkup *n* a (routine) general medical examination

Cheddar /'tʃedəʳ/ *n* a hard smooth-textured cheese with a flavour that ranges from mild to strong as the cheese matures

cheek /tʃiːk/ *n* **1** the fleshy side of the face below the eye and above and to the side of the mouth **2** either of 2 paired facing parts (e g the jaws of a vice) **3** insolent boldness; impudence **4** a buttock – infml

cheeky /'tʃiːki/ *adj* impudent, insolent – **cheekily** *adv* – **cheekiness** *n*

cheep /tʃiːp/ *v or n* (to utter) a faint shrill sound characteristic of a young bird

[1]**cheer** /'tʃɪəʳ/ *n* **1** happiness, gaiety **2** sthg that gladdens **3** a shout of applause or encouragement

[2]**cheer** *v* **1a** to instil with hope or courage; comfort **b** to make glad or happy – usu + *up* **2** to urge *on*, encourage, or applaud esp by shouts

cheerful /'tʃɪəfəl/ *adj* **1a** full of good spirits; merry **b** ungrudging **2** conducive to good cheer; likely to dispel gloom – **~ly** *adv* – **~ness** *n*

cheerio /ˌtʃɪəri'əʊ/ *interj, chiefly Br* – used to express farewell

cheers /tʃɪəz/ *interj* – used as a toast and sometimes as an informal farewell or expression of thanks

cheery /'tʃɪəri/ *adj* marked by or causing good spirits; cheerful – **cheerily** *adv* – **cheeriness** *n*

[1]**cheese** /tʃiːz/ *n* **1** (an often cylindrical cake of) a food consisting of coagulated, compressed, and usu ripened milk curds **2** a fruit preserve with the consistency of cream cheese

[2]**cheese** *n* an important person; a boss – slang; chiefly in *big cheese*

cheesecake /'tʃiːzkeɪk/ *n* **1** a baked or refrigerated dessert consisting of a soft filling, usu containing cheese, in a biscuit or pastry case **2** titillating photography of women

cheesecloth /'tʃiːzklɒθ/ *n* a very fine unsized cotton gauze

cheeseparing /'tʃiːzpeərɪŋ/ *n* miserly or petty economizing; stinginess

cheetah /'tʃiːtə/ *n* a long-legged spotted swift-moving African cat

chef /ʃef/ *n* a skilled cook; *esp* the chief cook in a restaurant or hotel

[1]**chemical** /'kemɪkəl/ *adj* **1** of, used in, or produced by chemistry **2** acting, operated, or produced by chemicals – **~ly** *adv*

[2]**chemical** *n* a substance (e g an

element or chemical compound) obtained by a chemical process or used for producing a chemical effect

chemise /ʃə'miːz/ *n* **1** a woman's one-piece undergarment **2** a usu loose straight-hanging dress

chemist /'kemɨst/ *n* **1** one who is trained in chemistry **2** *Br* (a pharmacist, esp in) a retail shop where medicines and miscellaneous articles (e g cosmetics and films) are sold

chemistry /'kemɨstri/ *n* **1** a science that deals with the composition, structure, and properties of substances and of the transformations they undergo **2a** the composition and chemical properties of a substance **b** chemical processes and phenomena (e g of an organism)

chemotherapy /ˌkiːməʊ'θerəpi, ˌkeməʊ-/ *n* the use of chemical agents in the treatment or control of disease

cheque /tʃek/ *n, chiefly Br* a written order for a bank to pay money as instructed; *also* a printed form on which such an order is usually written

cheque card *n* a card issued to guarantee that the holder's cheques up to a specific amount will be honoured by the issuing bank

chequer, *chiefly NAm* **checker** /'tʃekəʳ/ *v* **1** to mark with different colours or shades; *esp* to mark with squares of (2) alternating colours **2** to vary with contrasting elements or situations *USE* usu in past part

cherish /'tʃerɪʃ/ *v* **1a** to hold dear; feel or show affection for **b** to keep or cultivate with care and affection; nurture **2** to keep in the mind deeply and with affection

cheroot /ʃə'ruːt/ *n* a cigar cut square at both ends

cherry /'tʃeri/ *n* **1** (the wood or small pale yellow to deep red or blackish fruit of) any of numerous trees and shrubs of the rose family, often cultivated for their fruit or ornamental flowers **2** light red

cherub /'tʃerəb/ *n, pl* **cherubs,** (*1*) **cherubim** **1** a biblical attendant of God or of a holy place, often represented as a being with large wings, a human head, and an animal body **2a** a beautiful usu winged child in painting and sculpture **b** an innocent-looking usu chubby and pretty person – **~ic** *adj* – **~ically** *adv*

chess /tʃes/ *n* a game for 2 players each of whom moves his/her 16 chessmen according to fixed rules across a chessboard and tries to checkmate his/her opponent's king

chessman /'tʃesmæn, -mən/ *n, pl* **chessmen** any of the pieces used by each side in playing chess

chest /tʃest/ *n* **1a** a box with a lid used esp for the safekeeping of belongings **b** a usu small cupboard used esp for storing medicines or first-aid supplies **2** the part of the body enclosed by the ribs and breastbone

chesterfield /'tʃestəfiːld/ *n* a heavily padded usu leather sofa

[1]**chestnut** /'tʃesnʌt/ *n* **1** (the nut or wood of) a tree or shrub of the beech family **2** reddish brown **3** a horse chestnut **4** a chestnut-coloured animal, specif a horse **5** an often repeated joke or story; *broadly* anything repeated excessively

[2]**chestnut** *adj* of the colour chestnut

chevalier /ˌʃevə'lɪəʳ/ *n* a member of certain orders of merit (e g the French Legion of Honour)

chevron /'ʃevrən/ *n* a figure, pattern, or object having the shape of an (inverted) V; *esp* a sleeve badge that usu consists of 1 or more chevron-shaped stripes and indicates the wearer's rank

chew /tʃuː/ *v* to crush, grind, or gnaw (esp food) (as if) with the teeth

Chianti /ki'ænti/ *n* a dry (red) Italian table wine

chiaroscuro /kiˌɑːrə'skʊərəʊ/ *n* **1** pictorial representation in terms of light and shade **2** the arrangement or treatment of light and shade in a painting

chic /ʃiːk/ *adj or n* (having or showing) elegance and sophistication, esp of dress or manner – **~ly** *adv*

chicanery /ʃɪ'keɪnəri/ *n* **1** deception by the use of fallacious or irrelevant arguments **2** a piece of sharp practice or legal trickery

chichi /'ʃiːʃi/ *adj or n* **1** showy, frilly, or elaborate (ornamentation) **2**

unnecessarily elaborate or affected (behaviour, style, etc)

chick /tʃɪk/ *n* **1** a young bird; *esp* a (newly hatched) chicken **2** a young woman – slang

[1]**chicken** /ˈtʃɪkɪ̣n/ *n* **1** the common domestic fowl, esp when young; *also* its flesh used as food **2** a young person – chiefly in *he/she is no chicken* – slang

[2]**chicken** *adj* scared – infml

chicken feed *n* a small and insignificant amount, esp of money – infml

chickenhearted /ˌtʃɪkɪ̣nˈhɑːtɪ̣d/ *adj* timid, cowardly – **~ness** *n*

chicken out *v* to lose one's nerve – infml

chicken pox *n* an infectious virus disease, esp of children, that is marked by mild fever and a rash of small blisters

chick-pea /tʃɪk piː/ *n* (the hard edible seed of) an Asiatic leguminous plant

chickweed /ˈtʃɪkwiːd/ *n* any of various low-growing small-leaved plants of the pink family that occur commonly as weeds

chicory /ˈtʃɪkəri/ *n* a usu blue-flowered European perennial composite plant widely grown for its edible thick roots and as a salad plant; *also* the ground roasted root used as a coffee additive

chide /tʃaɪd/ *v* **chid, chided; chid, chidden, chided** to rebuke (sby) angrily; scold

[1]**chief** /tʃiːf/ *n* the head of a body of people or an organization; a leader

[2]**chief** *adj* **1** accorded highest rank or office **2** of greatest importance or influence

chiefly /ˈtʃiːfli/ *adv* **1** most importantly; principally, especially **2** for the most part; mostly, mainly

chief of staff *n* the senior officer of an armed forces staff that serves a commander

chieftain /ˈtʃiːftɪ̣n/ *n* a chief, esp of a band, tribe, or clan

chiffchaff /ˈtʃɪfˌtʃæf/ *n* a small greyish European warbler

chiffon /ˈʃɪfɒn/ *n* a sheer (silk) fabric

chiffonier /ˌʃɪfɒˈnɪeɪ/ *n* a high narrow chest of drawers

chignon /ʃɪnjɒn/ *n* a usu large smooth knot of hair worn esp at the nape of the neck

Chihuahua /tʃɪ̣ˈwɑːwə/ *n* a very small round-headed large-eared dog of Mexican origin

chilblain /ˈtʃɪlbleɪn/ *n* an inflammatory sore, esp on the feet or hands, caused by exposure to cold

child /tʃaɪld/ *n, pl* **children** /ˈtʃɪldrən/ **1** an unborn or recently born person **2a** a young person, esp between infancy and youth **b** sby under the age of 14 – used in English law **3a** a son or daughter **b** a descendant **4** one strongly influenced by another or by a place or state of affairs **5** a product, result

childbirth /ˈtʃaɪldbɜːθ/ *n* parturition

childhood /ˈtʃaɪldhʊd/ *n* **1** the state or period of being a child **2** an early period in the development of sthg

childish /ˈtʃaɪldɪʃ/ *adj* **1** of or befitting a child or childhood **2** marked by or suggestive of immaturity – **~ly** *adv* – **~ness** *n*

childlike /ˈtʃaɪldlaɪk/ *adj* marked by innocence and trust

child's play *n* an extremely simple task or act

[1]**chill** /tʃɪl/ *v* **1a** to make cold or chilly **b** to make (esp food or drink) cool, esp without freezing **2** to affect as if with cold; dispirit

[2]**chill** *adj* chilly

[3]**chill** *n* **1** a cold **2** a moderate but disagreeable degree of cold **3** coldness of manner

chilli, chili /ˈtʃɪli/ *n* the pod of a hot pepper used either whole or ground as a pungent condiment

chilly /ˈtʃɪli/ *adj* **1** noticeably (unpleasantly) cold **2** lacking warmth of feeling; distant, unfriendly **3** tending to arouse fear or apprehension – **chilliness** *n*

[1]**chime** /tʃaɪm/ *n* (the sound of) a set of bells or other objects producing a similar sound – often pl with sing. meaning

[2]**chime** *v* **1** to cause to chime **2** to signal or indicate by chiming **3** to be or act in accord

chime in *v* **1** to break into a conversation or discussion, esp in order to express an opinion **2** to combine harmoniously – often + *with*

chimera /kaɪ'mɪərə/ *n* **1** a mythological monster with a lion's head, a goat's body and a serpent's tail **2** an illusion or fabrication of the mind; *also* an imaginary terror – **-rical** *adj*

chimney /'tʃɪmni/ *n* **1** a flue or flues for carrying off smoke; *esp* the part of such a structure extending above a roof **2** a structure through which smoke and gases (e g from a furnace or steam engine) are discharged **3** a tube, usu of glass, placed round a flame (e g of an oil lamp) to serve as a shield

chimney breast *n* the wall that encloses a chimney and projects into a room

chimney pot *n* a usu earthenware pipe at the top of a chimney

chimney stack *n* **1** a masonry, brickwork, etc chimney rising above a roof and usu containing several flues **2** a tall chimney, typically of circular section, serving a factory, power station, etc

chimney sweep *n* one whose occupation is cleaning soot from chimney flues

chimpanzee /,tʃɪmpæn'ziː, -pən-/ *n* a tree-dwelling anthropoid ape of equatorial Africa that is smaller and less fierce than the gorilla

chin /tʃɪn/ *n* the lower portion of the face lying below the lower lip; the lower jaw

china /'tʃaɪnə/ *n* **1** porcelain; *also* vitreous porcelain ware (e g dishes and vases) for domestic use **2** crockery **3** *chiefly Br* bone china

china clay *n* kaolin

chinaman /'tʃaɪnəmən/ *n* **1** a delivery by a left-handed bowler in cricket that is an off break as viewed by a right-handed batsman **2** *cap* a native of China – derog

chinchilla /tʃɪn'tʃɪlə/ *n* **1** (the soft pearly-grey fur of) a S American rodent the size of a large squirrel **2** (any of) a breed of domestic rabbit with long white or greyish fur; *also* (any of) a breed of cat with similar fur

Chinese /tʃaɪ'niːz/ *n, pl* **Chinese** **1** a native or inhabitant of China **2** a group of related Sino-Tibetan tone languages used by the people of China; *specif* Mandarin – **Chinese** *adj*

[1]**chink** /tʃɪŋk/ *n* **1** a small slit or fissure **2** a means of evasion or escape; a loophole

[2]**chink** *n* a short sharp sound

chinless /'tʃɪnlɨs/ *adj* lacking firmness of purpose; ineffectual – infml

chintz /tʃɪnts/ *n* a (glazed) printed plain-weave fabric, usu of cotton

chin-wag *n* a conversation, chat – infml

[1]**chip** /tʃɪp/ *n* **1** a small usu thin and flat piece (e g of wood or stone) cut, struck, or flaked off **2** a counter used as a token for money in gambling games **3** a flaw left after a chip is removed **4** (the small piece of semiconductor, esp silicon, on which is constructed) an integrated circuit **5a** *chiefly Br* a strip of potato fried in deep fat **b** *NAm & Austr* a potato crisp

[2]**chip** *v* **-pp-** **1a** to cut or hew with an edged tool **b** to cut or break a fragment from **2** to kick or hit a ball, pass, etc in a short high arc

chipboard /'tʃɪpbɔːd/ *n* an artificial board made from compressed wood chips

chip in *v* **1** to contribute **2** to interrupt or add a comment to a conversation between other people

chipmunk /'tʃɪpmʌŋk/ *n* any of numerous small striped American squirrels

Chippendale /'tʃɪpəndeɪl/ *adj or n* (of or being) an 18th-c English furniture style characterized by graceful outline and fine ornamentation

chippy /'tʃɪpi/ *n* **1** a carpenter **2** *Br* a shop selling fish and chips *USE* infml

chiropody /ʃɨ'rɒpədi, kɨ-/ *n* the care and treatment of the human foot in health and disease – **-dist** *n*

chirp /tʃɜːp/ *v or n* (to make or speak in a tone resembling) the characteristic short shrill sound of a small bird or insect

chirpy /'tʃɜːpi/ *adj* lively, cheerful – infml – **chirpily** *adv* – **chirpiness** *n*

[1]**chisel** /'tʃɪzəl/ *n* a metal tool with a cutting edge at the end of a blade used in dressing, shaping, or working wood, stone, metal, etc

[2]**chisel** *v* **1** to cut or work (as if) with a chisel **2** to trick, cheat, or obtain (sthg) by cheating – slang – **~ler** *n*

[1]**chit** /tʃɪt/ *n* an immature often disrespectful young woman

[2]**chit** *n* a small slip of paper with writing on it; *esp* an order for goods

chitchat /ˈtʃɪt-tʃæt/ *v or n* **-tt-** (to make) small talk; gossip – infml

chivalrous /ˈʃɪvəlrəs/ *adj* **1** having the characteristics (e g valour or gallantry) of a knight **2a** honourable, generous **b** graciously courteous and considerate, esp to women – **~ly** *adv*

chivalry /ˈʃɪvəlri/ *n* **1** the system, spirit, or customs of medieval knighthood **2** the qualities (e g courage, integrity, and consideration) of an ideal knight; chivalrous conduct

chive /tʃaɪv/ *n* a perennial plant related to the onion and used esp to flavour and garnish food – usu pl with sing. meaning

chivvy, chivy /ˈtʃɪvi/ *v* **1** to harass **2** to rouse to activity – usu + *up* or *along*

chloride /ˈklɔːraɪd/ *n* a compound of chlorine with another element or radical; *esp* a salt or ester of hydrochloric acid

chlorine /ˈklɔːriːn/ *n* a highly reactive element that is isolated as a pungent heavy greenish yellow gas

chloroform /ˈklɒrəfɔːm/ *v or n* (to anaesthetize with) a colourless volatile liquid used esp as a solvent and formerly as a general anaesthetic

chlorophyll /ˈklɒːrəfɪl/ *n* the green colouring matter found in the stems and leaves of plants

[1]**chock** /tʃɒk/ *n* a wedge or block placed under a door, barrel, wheel, etc to prevent movement

[2]**chock** *v* to raise or support on blocks

[3]**chock** *adv* as closely or as completely as possible

chock-a-block /ˌtʃɒk əˈblɒk/ *adj or adv* tightly packed; in a very crowded condition

chocolate /ˈtʃɒkl̩ɪ̈t/ *n* **1** a paste, powder, or solid block of food prepared from (sweetened or flavoured) ground roasted cacao seeds **2** a beverage made by mixing chocolate with usu hot water or milk **3** a sweet made or coated with chocolate **4** a dark brown colour

[1]**choice** /tʃɔɪs/ *n* **1** the act of choosing; selection **2** the power of choosing; an option **3** sby or sthg chosen **4** a sufficient number and variety to choose among

[2]**choice** *adj* **1** selected with care; well chosen **2** of high quality – **~ly** *adv* – **~ness** *n*

choir /ˈkwaɪəʳ/ *n* **1** *sing or pl in constr* an organized company of singers **2** the part of a church occupied by the singers or the clergy; *specif* the part of the chancel between the sanctuary and the nave

choirboy /ˈkwaɪəbɔɪ/ *n* a boy singer in a (church) choir

[1]**choke** /tʃəʊk/ *v* **1** to check the normal breathing esp by compressing or obstructing the windpipe **2a** to stop or suppress expression of or by; silence – often + *back* or *down* **b** to become obstructed or checked **c** to become speechless or incapacitated, esp from strong emotion – usu + *up* **3a** to restrain the growth or activity of **b** to obstruct by filling up or clogging; jam

[2]**choke** *n* sthg that obstructs passage or flow: e g **a** a valve in the carburettor of a petrol engine for controlling the amount of air in a fuel air mixture **b** a narrowing towards the muzzle in the bore of a gun

[3]**choke** *n* the fibrous (inedible) central part of a globe artichoke

choker /ˈtʃəʊkəʳ/ *n* a short necklace or decorative band that fits closely round the throat

cholera /ˈkɒlərə/ *n* an often fatal infectious epidemic disease caused by a bacterium and marked by severe gastrointestinal disorders

choleric /ˈkɒlərɪk/ *adj* **1** easily moved to (excessive) anger; irascible **2** angry, irate *USE* fml – **~ally** *adv*

cholesterol /kəˈlestərɒl/ *n* a substance present in animal and plant cells that is a possible factor in artery and heart disease

choose /tʃuːz/ *v* **chose; chosen 1a** to select freely and after consideration **b** to decide on; *esp* to elect **2a** to decide **b** to wish

choosy, choosey /'tʃu:zi/ *adj* fastidiously selective

[1]**chop** /tʃɒp/ *v* **-pp-** **1a** to cut into or sever, usu by a blow or repeated blows of a sharp instrument **b** to cut into pieces – often + *up* **2** to make a quick stroke or repeated strokes (as if) with a sharp instrument

[2]**chop** *n* **1** a forceful blow (as if) with an axe **2** a small cut of meat often including part of a rib **3** an uneven motion of the sea, esp when wind and tide are opposed **4** abrupt removal; *esp the* sack – infml

[3]**chop** *n* (a licence validated by) a seal or official stamp such as was formerly used in China or India

chopper /'tʃɒpəʳ/ *n* **1** a short-handled axe or cleaver **2** a helicopter – infml

choppy /'tʃɒpi/ *adj, of the sea or other expanse of water* rough with small waves – **choppiness** *n*

chopstick /'tʃɒp-stɪk/ *n* either of 2 slender sticks held between thumb and fingers, used chiefly in oriental countries to lift food to the mouth

chopsuey /tʃɒp'su:i/ *n* a Chinese dish of shredded meat or chicken with bean sprouts and other vegetables, usu served with rice

choral /'kɔ:rəl/ *adj* accompanied with or designed for singing (by a choir)

chorale *also* **choral** /kɒ'rɑ:l/ *n* (music composed for) a usu German traditional hymn or psalm for singing in church

[1]**chord** /kɔ:d/ *n* a combination of notes sounded together

[2]**chord** *n* **1** a strand-like anatomical structure **2** a straight line joining 2 points on a curve **3** an individual emotion or disposition

chore /tʃɔ:ʳ/ *n* **1** a routine task or job **2** a difficult or disagreeable task

choreography /,kɒri'ɒgrəfi, ,kɔ:-/ *n* the composition and arrangement of a ballet or other dance for the stage – **-grapher** *n*

chorister /'kɒrɪstəʳ/ *n* a singer in a choir; *specif* a choirboy

chortle /'tʃɔ:tl/ *v* to laugh or chuckle, esp in satisfaction or exultation

chorus /'kɔ:rəs/ *n* **1** a character (e g in Elizabethan drama) or group of singers and dancers (e g in Greek drama) who comment on the action **2** *sing or pl in constr* **a** a body of singers who sing the choral parts of a work (e g in opera) **b** a group of dancers and singers supporting the featured players in a musical or revue **3** a part of a song or hymn recurring at intervals **4** sthg performed, sung, or uttered simultaneously by a number of people or animals

chose /tʃəuz/ *past of* **choose**

chosen /'tʃəuzən/ *adj* selected or marked for favour or special privilege

chowder /'tʃaudəʳ/ *n* a thick (clam or other seafood) soup or stew

chow mein /tʃau 'meɪn/ *n* a Chinese dish of fried noodles usu mixed with shredded meat or poultry and vegetables

Christ /kraɪst/ *n* the Messiah; Jesus

christen /'krɪsən/ *v* **1a** to baptize **b** to name esp at baptism **2** to name or dedicate (e g a ship or bell) by a ceremony suggestive of baptism **3** to use for the first time – infml – **~ing** *n*

Christendom /'krɪsəndəm/ *n* the community of people or nations professing Christianity

[1]**Christian** /'krɪstʃən, -tɪən/ *n* **1a** an adherent of Christianity **b** a member of a Christian denomination, esp by baptism **2** a good or kind person regardless of religion

[2]**Christian** *adj* **1** of or consistent with Christianity or Christians **2** commendably decent or generous

Christianity /,krɪsti'ænḷti/ *n* **1** the religion based on the life and teachings of Jesus Christ and the Bible **2** conformity to (a branch of) the Christian religion

Christian name *n* **1** a name given at christening (or confirmation) **2** a forename

Christian Science *n* a religion founded by Mary Baker Eddy in 1866 that includes a practice of spiritual healing

Christmas /'krɪsməs/ *n* **1** a festival of the western Christian churches on December 25 that commemorates the birth of Christ and is usu observed as a public holiday **2 Christmas, Christmastide** the festival season from

Christmas Eve till the Epiphany (January 6)

chromatic /krəʊ'mætɪk, krə-/ *adj* **1a** of colour sensation or (intensity of) colour **b** highly coloured **2a** *of a scale* having an interval of a semitone between each note **b** characterized by frequent use of intervals or notes outside the diatonic scale – **~ally** *adv*

chrome /krəʊm/ *n* **1** (a pigment formed from) chromium **2** (sthg with) a plating of chromium

chromium /'krəʊmɪəm/ *n* a blue-white metallic element found naturally only in combination and used esp in alloys and in electroplating

chromosome /'krəʊməsəʊm/ *n* any of the gene-carrying bodies that contain DNA and protein and are found in the cell nucleus

chronic /'krɒnɪk/ *adj* **1** *esp of an illness* marked by long duration or frequent recurrence **2a** always present or encountered; *esp* constantly troubling **b** habitual, persistent **3** *Br* bad, terrible – infml – **~ally** *adv*

[1]**chronicle** /'krɒnɪkəl/ *n* **1** a usu continuous and detailed historical account of events arranged chronologically without analysis or interpretation **2** a narrative

[2]**chronicle** *v* **1** to record (as if) in a chronicle **2** to list, describe – **~r** *n*

chronology /krə'nɒlədʒi/ *n* (a method for) setting past events in order of occurrence – **-gical** *adj*

chronometer /krə'nɒmɪ̣tə^r/ *n* an instrument for measuring time

chrysalis /'krɪsəlɪ̣s/ *n, pl* **chrysalides, chrysalises** **1** (the case enclosing) a pupa, esp of a butterfly or moth **2** a sheltered state or stage of being or growth

chrysanthemum /krɪ'sænθɪ̣məm, -'zæn-/ *n* any of various (cultivated) composite plants with brightly coloured often double flower heads

chubby /'tʃʌbi/ *adj* of large proportions; plump – **chubbiness** *n*

[1]**chuck** /tʃʌk/ *n* – used as a term of endearment

[2]**chuck** *v* **1** to pat, tap **2a** to toss, throw **b** to discard – often + *out* or *away* **3** to leave; give up – often + *in* or *up* *USE* (*except 1*) infml

[3]**chuck** *n* **1** a pat or nudge under the chin **2** a throw – infml

[4]**chuck** *n* **1** a cut of beef that includes most of the neck and the area about the shoulder blade **2** a device for holding a workpiece (e g for turning on a lathe) or tool (e g in a drill)

chuckle /'tʃʌkl/ *v* to laugh inwardly or quietly – **chuckle** *n*

chuck out *v* to eject (a person) from a place or an office; dismiss – infml

chug /tʃʌg/ *v or n* (to move or go with) a usu repetitive dull explosive sound made (as if) by a labouring engine

[1]**chum** /tʃʌm/ *n* a close friend; a mate – infml; no longer in vogue

[2]**chum** *v* to form a friendship, esp a close one – usu + *(up) with*; no longer in vogue

chump /tʃʌmp/ *n* **1** a cut of meat taken from between the loin and hindleg **2** a fool, duffer – infml

chunk /tʃʌŋk/ *n* **1** a lump; *esp* one of a firm or hard material (e g wood) **2** a (large) quantity – infml

chunky /'tʃʌŋki/ *adj* **1** stocky **2** *of materials, clothes, etc* thick and heavy

church /tʃɜːtʃ/ *n* **1** a building for public (Christian) worship; *esp* a place of worship used by an established church **2** *often cap* institutionalized religion; *esp* the established Christian religion of a country **3** *cap* a body or organization of religious believers: e g **a** the whole body of Christians **b** a denomination **c** a congregation **4** an occasion for public worship **5** the clerical profession

churchwarden /tʃɜːtʃ'wɔːdən/ *n* either of 2 lay parish officers in Anglican churches with responsibility esp for parish property and alms

churchyard /'tʃɜːtʃjɑːd/ *n* an enclosed piece of ground surrounding a church; *esp* one used as a burial ground

churl /tʃɜːl/ *n* **1a** a rude ill-bred person **b** a mean morose person **2** *archaic* a rustic, countryman

churlish /'tʃɜːlɪʃ/ *adj* **1** lacking refinement or sensitivity **2** rudely uncooperative; surly – **~ly** *adv* – **~ness** *n*

[1]**churn** /tʃɜːn/ *n* **1** a vessel used in

making butter in which milk or cream is agitated to separate the oily globules from the watery medium **2** *Br* a large metal container for transporting milk

[2]**churn** *v* **1** to agitate (milk or cream) in a churn in order to make butter **2** to produce or be in violent motion

churn out *v* to produce prolifically and mechanically, usu without great concern for quality – chiefly infml

chute /ʃuːt/ *n* **1** a waterfall, rapid, etc **2** an inclined plane, channel, or passage down which things may pass **3** a parachute – infml

chutney /ˈtʃʌtni/ *n* a thick condiment or relish of Indian origin that contains fruits, sugar, vinegar, and spices

cicada /sɨ̥ˈkɑːdə/ *n* any of a family of insects that have large transparent wings and whose males produce a shrill singing noise

cider, cyder /ˈsaɪdəʳ/ *n* an alcoholic drink made from apples

cigar /sɪˈgɑːʳ/ *n* a small roll of tobacco leaf for smoking

cigarette, *NAm also* **cigaret** /ˌsɪgəˈret/ *n* a narrow cylinder of tobacco enclosed in paper for smoking

[1]**cinch** /sɪntʃ/ *n* **1** a task performed with ease **2** sthg certain to happen

[2]**cinch** *v* to make certain of; assure

cinder /ˈsɪndəʳ/ *n* **1** a fragment of ash **2** a piece of partly burned material (e g coal) that will burn further but will not flame

cinema /ˈsɪnɨ̥mə/ *n* **1a** films considered esp as an art form, entertainment, or industry – usu + *the* **b** the art or technique of making films **2** a theatre where films are shown – **~tic** *adj*

cinematography /ˌsɪnɨ̥məˈtɒgrəfi/ *n* the art or science of cinema photography – **-phic** *adj*

cinnamon /ˈsɪnəmən/ *n* **1** (any of several trees of the laurel family with) an aromatic bark used as a spice **2** a light yellowish brown colour

cinquefoil /ˈsɪŋkfɔɪl, sæŋk-/ *n* **1** any of a genus of plants of the rose family with 5-lobed leaves **2** a design enclosed by 5 joined arcs arranged in a circle

circa /ˈsɜːkə/ *prep* at, in, or of approximately – used esp with dates

circadian /sɜːˈkeɪdɪən/ *adj* being, having, characterized by, or occurring in approximately day-long periods or cycles (e g of biological activity or function)

[1]**circle** /ˈsɜːkəl/ *n* **1a** a closed plane curve every point of which is equidistant from a fixed point within the curve **b** the plane surface bounded by such a curve **2** sthg in the form of (an arc of) a circle **3** a balcony or tier of seats in a theatre **4** cycle, round **5** *sing or pl in constr* a group of people sharing a common interest, activity, or leader

[2]**circle** *v* **1** to enclose or move (as if) in a circle **2** to move or revolve round

circlet /ˈsɜːklɨ̥t/ *n* a little circle; *esp* a circular ornament

circuit /ˈsɜːkɨ̥t/ *n* **1** a closed loop encompassing an area **2a** a course round a periphery **b** a racetrack **3** a regular tour (e g by a judge) round an assigned area or territory **4a** the complete path of an electric current, usu including the source of energy **b** an array of electrical components connected so as to allow the passage of current **5a** an association or league of similar groups **b** a chain of theatres at which productions are presented successively

circuitous /sɜːˈkjuːɨ̥təs/ *adj* indirect in route or method; roundabout – **~ly** *adv*

[1]**circular** /ˈsɜːkjʊləʳ/ *adj* **1** having the form of a circle **2** moving in or describing a circle or spiral **3** marked by the fallacy of assuming sthg which is to be demonstrated **4** marked by or moving in a cycle **5** intended for circulation – **~ity** *n* – **~ly** *adv*

[2]**circular** *n* a paper (e g a leaflet or advertisement) intended for wide distribution

circulate /ˈsɜːkjʊleɪt/ *v* **1** to move in a circle, circuit, or orbit; *esp* to follow a course that returns to the starting point **2a** to flow without obstruction **b** to become well known or widespread **c** to go from group to group at a social gathering **d** to come into the hands of readers; *specif* to become sold or distributed **3** to cause to circulate

circulation /ˌsɜːkjʊˈleɪʃən/ *n* **1** a flow **2** orderly movement through a circuit; *esp* the movement of blood through the vessels of the body induced by the pumping action of the heart **3a** passage or transmission from person to person or place to place; *esp* the interchange of currency **b** the average number of copies (e g of a newspaper) of a publication sold over a given period

circumcise /ˈsɜːkəmsaɪz/ *v* to cut off the foreskin of (a male) or the clitoris of (a female) – **-ision** *n*

circumference /səˈkʌmfərəns/ *n* **1** the perimeter of a circle **2** the external boundary or surface of a figure or object – **-ential** *adj*

circumflex /ˈsɜːkəmfleks/ *n* an accent mark ˆ, ˜, or ¯ used in various languages to mark length, contraction, or a particular vowel quality – **circumflex** *adj*

circumlocution /ˌsɜːkəmləˈkjuːʃən/ *n* **1** the use of an unnecessarily large number of words to express an idea **2** evasive speech – **-tory** *adj*

circumnavigate /ˌsɜːkəmˈnævɨgeɪt/ *v* to go round; *esp* to travel completely round (the earth), esp by sea – **-gation** *n*

circumscribe /ˈsɜːkəmskraɪb/ *v* **1** to surround by a physical or imaginary line **2** to restrict the range or activity of definitely and clearly

circumspect /ˈsɜːkəmspekt/ *adj* careful to consider all circumstances and possible consequences; prudent – **~ly** *adv* – **~ion** *n*

circumstance /ˈsɜːkəmstæns, -stəns/ *n* **1** a condition or event that accompanies, causes, or determines another; *also* the sum of such conditions or events **2a** a state of affairs; an occurrence – often pl with sing. meaning **b** *pl* situation with regard to material or financial welfare **3** attendant formalities and ceremony

circumstantial /ˌsɜːkəmˈstænʃəl/ *adj* **1** belonging to, consisting in, or dependent on circumstances **2** pertinent but not essential; incidental – **~ly** *adv*

circumvent /ˌsɜːkəmˈvent/ *v* to check or evade, esp by ingenuity or stratagem – **~ion** *n*

circus /ˈsɜːkəs/ *n* **1a** a large circular or oval stadium used esp for sports contests or spectacles **b** a public spectacle **2a** (the usu covered arena housing) an entertainment in which a variety of performers (e g acrobats and clowns) and performing animals are involved in a series of unrelated acts **b** an activity suggestive of a circus (e g in being a busy scene of noisy or frivolous action) **3** *Br* a road junction in a town partly surrounded by a circle of buildings – usu in proper names

cirque /sɜːk/ *n* a deep steep-walled basin on a mountain

cirrhosis /sɨˈrəʊsɨs/ *n* hardening of the liver

cirrus /ˈsɪrəs/ *n, pl* **cirri** **1** a slender usu flexible (invertebrate) animal appendage **2** a wispy white cloud formation usu of minute ice crystals formed at high altitudes

cissy /ˈsɪsi/ *n, Br* **1** an effeminate boy or man **2** a cowardly person *USE* infml

cistern /ˈsɪstən/ *n* an artificial reservoir for storing liquids, esp water

citadel /ˈsɪtədl, -del/ *n* **1** a fortress; *esp* one that commands a city **2** a stronghold

citation /saɪˈteɪʃən/ *n* **1a** an act of citing or quoting **b** a quotation **2** a mention; *specif* specific reference in a military dispatch to meritorious conduct

cite /saɪt/ *v* **1** to call upon to appear before a court **2** to quote by way of example, authority, precedent, or proof **3** to refer to or name; *esp* to mention formally in commendation or praise

citizen /ˈsɪtɨzən/ *n* **1** an inhabitant of a city or town; *esp* a freeman **2** a (native or naturalized) member of a state – **~ship** *n*

citizenry /ˈsɪtɨzənri/ *n sing or pl in constr* the whole body of citizens

citric acid /ˌsɪtrɪk ˈæsɨd/ *n* an acid occurring in lemons, limes, etc and used as a flavouring

citron /ˈsɪtrən/ *n* **1** a (tree that bears) fruit like the lemon but larger and with a thicker rind **2** the preserved rind of the citron, used esp in cakes and puddings

citrus /ˈsɪtrəs/ *n* any of several shrubs

or trees with edible thick-rinded juicy fruit (e g the orange or lemon) – **citrus** *adj*

city /'sɪti/ *n* **1a** a large town **b** an incorporated British town that has a cathedral or has had civic status conferred on it **c** a usu large chartered municipality in the USA **2** a city-state **3a** *the* financial and commercial area of London **b** *cap, sing or pl in constr the* influential financial interests of the British economy

city-state *n* an autonomous state consisting of a city and surrounding territory

civic /'sɪvɪk/ *adj* of a citizen, a city, or citizenship

civics /'sɪvɪks/ *n pl but sing or pl in constr* a social science dealing with the rights and duties of citizens

civil /'sɪvəl/ *adj* **1** of citizens **2** adequately courteous and polite; not rude **3** relating to private rights as distinct from criminal proceedings **4** of or involving the general public as distinguished from special (e g military or religious) affairs

civil defence *n, often cap C&D* protective measures organized by and for civilians against hostile attack, esp from the air, or natural disaster

civilian /sɟ'vɪlɪən/ *n* one who is not in the army, navy, air force, or other uniformed public body

civility /sɟ'vɪlɟti/ *n* **1** courtesy, politeness **2** a polite act or expression – usu pl

civilization *n* **1** a relatively high level of development of culture and technology **2** the culture characteristic of a time or place

civil·ize, -ise *v* **1** to cause cultural development, esp along Western or modern lines **2** to educate, refine – **~d** *adj*

civil law *n, often cap C&L* **1** the body of private law developed from Roman law as distinct from common law **2** the law established by a nation or state for its own jurisdiction (e g as distinct from international law) **3** the law of private rights

civil liberty *n* a right or freedom of the individual citizen in relation to the state (e g freedom of speech); *also* such rights or freedoms considered collectively

civil rights *n pl* civil liberties; *esp* those of status equality between races or groups

civil servant *n* a member of a civil service

civil service *n sing or pl in constr* the administrative service of a government or international agency, exclusive of the armed forces

civil war *n* a war between opposing groups of citizens of the same country

[1]**clack** /klæk/ *v* **1** to clatter – infml **2** to make an abrupt striking sound or sounds **3** to cause to make a clatter

[2]**clack** *n* **1** rapid continuous talk; chatter – infml **2** a sound of clacking

clad /klæd/ *adj* being covered or clothed

[1]**claim** /kleɪm/ *v* **1a** to ask for, esp as a right **b** to require, demand **c** to take; account for **2** to take as the rightful owner **3** to assert in the face of possible contradiction; maintain

[2]**claim** *n* **1** a demand for sthg (believed to be) due **2a** a right or title to sthg **b** an assertion open to challenge **3** sthg claimed; *esp* a tract of land staked out

claimant /'kleɪmənt/ *n* one who asserts a right or entitlement

clairvoyance /kleə'vɔɪəns/ *n* **1** the power or faculty of discerning objects not apparent to the physical senses **2** the ability to perceive matters beyond the range of ordinary perception – **-ant** *n, adj*

clam /klæm/ *n* **1** any of numerous edible marine molluscs (e g a scallop) living in sand or mud **2** a freshwater mussel

clamber /'klæmbəʳ/ *v* to climb awkwardly or with difficulty – **clamber** *n*

clammy /'klæmi/ *adj* being damp, clinging, and usu cool – **-mily** *adv* – **-miness** *n*

clamour /'klæməʳ/ *v or n* **1** (to engage in) noisy shouting **2** (to make) a loud continuous noise **3** (to make) insistent public expression (e g of support or protest)

[1]**clamp** /klæmp/ *n* **1** a device that holds or compresses 2 or more parts

firmly together **2** a heap of wooden sticks or bricks for burning, firing, etc

[2]**clamp** *v* **1** to fasten (as if) with a clamp **2** to hold tightly

clamp down *v* to impose restrictions; *also* to make restrictions more stringent

clam up *v* to become silent – infml

clan /klæn/ *n* **1a** a (Highland Scots) Celtic group of households descended from a common ancestor **b** a group of people related by family **2** a usu close-knit group united by a common interest or common characteristics

clandestine /klæn'destɨn/ *adj* held in or conducted with secrecy; surreptitious – **~ly** *adv* – **~ness** *n*

clang /klæŋ/ *v* **1** to make a loud metallic ringing sound **2** *esp of a crane or goose* to utter a harsh cry **3** to cause to clang – **clang** *n*

clanger /'klæŋəʳ/ *n, Br* a blunder – infml

clank /'klæŋk/ *n* a sharp brief metallic sound

clannish /'klænɪʃ/ *adj* tending to associate only with a select group of similar background, status, or interests – **~ly** *adv* – **~ness** *n*

[1]**clap** /klæp/ *v* **1** to strike (e g 2 flat hard surfaces) together so as to produce a loud sharp noise **2a** to strike (the hands) together repeatedly, usu in applause **b** to applaud **3** to strike with the flat of the hand in a friendly way **4** to place, put, or set, esp energetically – infml

[2]**clap** *n* **1** a loud sharp noise, specif of thunder **2** a friendly slap **3** the sound of clapping hands; *esp* applause

[3]**clap** *n* venereal disease; *esp* gonorrhoea – slang

clapped out *adj, chiefly Br, esp of machinery* (old and) worn-out; liable to break down irreparably – infml

clapper /'klæpəʳ/ *n* the tongue of a bell

clapper-board *n* a hinged board containing identifying details of the scene to be filmed that is held before the camera and banged together to mark the beginning and end of each take

claptrap /'klæptræp/ *n* pretentious nonsense; rubbish – infml

claret /'klærɨt/ *n* **1** a dry red Bordeaux **2** a dark purplish red colour

clarify /'klærɨfaɪ/ *v* **1** to make (e g a liquid) clear or pure, usu by freeing from suspended matter **2** to make free from confusion **3** to make understandable – **-ification** *n*

clarinet /,klærɨ'net/ *n* a single-reed woodwind instrument with a usual range from D below middle C upwards for 3½ octaves – **~(t)ist** *n*

[1]**clarion** /'klærɪən/ *n* (the sound of) a medieval trumpet

[2]**clarion** *adj* brilliantly clear

clarity /'klærɨti/ *n* the quality or state of being clear

[1]**clash** /klæʃ/ *v* **1** to make a clash **2a** to come into conflict **b** to form a displeasing combination; not match

[2]**clash** *n* **1** a noisy usu metallic sound of collision **2a** a hostile encounter **b** a sharp conflict

[1]**clasp** /klɑːsp/ *n* **1** a device for holding objects or parts of sthg together **2** a holding or enveloping (as if) with the hands or arms

[2]**clasp** *v* **1** to fasten (as if) with a clasp **2** to enclose and hold with the arms; *specif* to embrace **3** to seize (as if) with the hand; grasp

[1]**class** /klɑːs/ *n* **1a** *sing or pl in constr* a group sharing the same economic or social status in a society consisting of several groups with differing statuses – often pl with sing. meaning **b** the system of differentiating society by classes **c** high quality; elegance **2** *sing or pl in constr* a body of students meeting regularly to study the same subject **3** a group, set, or kind sharing common attributes **4a** a division or rating based on grade or quality **b** *Br* a level of university honours degree awarded to a student according to merit

[2]**class** *v* to classify

class-conscious *adj* **1** actively aware of one's common status with others in a particular class **2** taking part in class war – **~ness** *n*

[1]**classic** /'klæsɪk/ *adj* **1a** of recognized value or merit; serving as a standard of excellence **b** both traditional and enduring **2** classical **3a** authoritative, definitive **b** being an example that

shows clearly the characteristics of some group of things or occurrences

[2]**classic** *n* **1a** a literary work of ancient Greece or Rome **b** *pl* Greek and Latin literature, history, and philosophy considered as an academic subject **2a** (the author of) a work of lasting excellence **b** an authoritative source **3** a classic example; archetype **4** an important long-established sporting event; *specif, Br* any of 5 flat races for horses (e g the Epsom Derby)

classical /'klæsɪkəl/ *adj* **1** standard, classic **2** of the (literature, art, architecture, or ideals of the) ancient Greek and Roman world **3** of or being music in the educated European tradition that includes such forms as chamber music, opera, and symphony as distinguished from folk, popular music, or jazz **4a** both authoritative and traditional **b** of or being systems or methods that constitute an accepted although not necessarily modern approach to a subject – **~ly** *adv* – **~ity** *n*

classicism /'klæsɨsɪzəm/ *n* **1a** the principles or style embodied in classical literature, art, or architecture **b** a classical idiom or expression **2** adherence to traditional standards (e g of simplicity, restraint, and proportion) that are considered to have universal and lasting worth – **-icist** *n*

classification /ˌklæsɨfɨ'keɪʃən/ *n* **1** classifying **2a** systematic arrangement in groups according to established criteria; *specif* taxonomy **b** a class, category

classified /'klæsɨfaɪd/ *adj* withheld from general circulation for reasons of national security

classify /'klæsɨfaɪ/ *v* **1** to arrange in classes **2** to assign to a category

classless /'klɑːslɨs/ *adj* **1** free from class distinction **2** belonging to no particular social class – **~ness** *n*

classmate /'klɑːsmeɪt/ *n* a member of the same class in a school or college

classroom /'klɑːs-rʊm, -ruːm/ *n* a room where classes meet

classy /'klɑːsi/ *adj* elegant, stylish – infml

[1]**clatter** /'klætəʳ/ *v* **1** to make a clatter **2** to move or go with a clatter **3** to cause to clatter

[2]**clatter** *n* **1** a rattling sound (e g of hard bodies striking together) **2** a commotion

clause /klɔːz/ **1** a distinct article or condition in a formal document **2** a phrase containing a subject and predicate capable of functioning either in isolation or as part of a sentence

claustrophobia /ˌklɔːstrə'fəʊbɪə, ˌklɒ-/ *n* abnormal dread of being in closed or confined spaces – **-phobic** *n, adj*

clavichord /'klævɨkɔːd/ *n* an early usu rectangular keyboard instrument

clavicle /'klævɪkəl/ *n* a bone of the vertebrate shoulder typically linking the shoulder blade and breastbone; the collarbone

[1]**claw** /klɔː/ *n* **1** (a part resembling or limb having) a sharp usu slender curved nail on an animal's toe **2** any of the pincerlike organs on the end of some limbs of a lobster, scorpion, or similar arthropod **3** sthg (e g the forked end of a claw hammer) resembling a claw

[2]**claw** *v* to rake, seize, dig, pull, or make (as if) with claws

clay /kleɪ/ *n* **1a** (soil composed chiefly of) an earthy material that is soft when moist but hard when fired and is used for making brick, tile, and pottery **b** thick and clinging earth or mud **2a** a substance that resembles clay and is used for modelling **b** the human body as distinguished from the spirit – **~ey** *adj*

claymore /'kleɪmɔːʳ/ *n* a large single-edged broadsword formerly used by Scottish Highlanders

clay pigeon *n* a saucer-shaped object usu made of baked clay and hurled into the air as a target for shooting at with a shotgun

[1]**clean** /kliːn/ *adj* **1** (relatively) free from dirt or pollution **2** unadulterated, pure **3a** free from illegal, immoral, or disreputable activities or characteristics **b** observing the rules; fair **4** thorough, complete **5** relatively free from error or blemish; clear; *specif* legible **6a** characterized by clarity, precision, or deftness **b** not

jagged; smooth – ~**ness** *n* – ~**ly** *adv*

[2]**clean** *adv* **1a** so as to leave clean **b** in a clean manner **2** all the way; completely

[3]**clean** *v* **1** to make clean – often + *up* **2a** to strip, empty **b** to deprive of money or possessions – often + *out*; infml **3** to undergo cleaning

[4]**clean** *n* an act of cleaning away dirt

clean-cut *adj* **1** sharply defined **2** of wholesome appearance

cleaner /'kliːnəʳ/ *n* **1** sby whose occupation is cleaning rooms or clothes **2** a substance, implement, or machine for cleaning

cleanliness /'klenlinɨs/ *n* fastidiousness in keeping things or one's person clean – **cleanly** *adj*

cleanse /klenz/ *v* to clean

cleanser /'klenzəʳ/ *n* a preparation (e g a scouring powder or skin cream) used for cleaning

clean-shaven *adj* with the hair, specif of the beard and moustache, shaved off

clean up *v* to make a large esp sweeping gain (e g in business or gambling)

[1]**clear** /klɪəʳ/ *adj* **1a** bright, luminous **b** free from cloud, mist, haze, or dust **c** untroubled, serene **2** clean, pure: e g **a** free from blemishes **b** easily seen through; transparent **3a** easily heard **b** easily visible; plain **c** free from obscurity or ambiguity; easily understood **4a** capable of sharp discernment; keen **b** free from doubt; sure **5** free from guilt **6a** net **b** unqualified, absolute **c** free from obstruction or entanglement **d** full – ~**ness** *n* – ~**ly** *adv*

[2]**clear** *adv* **1** clearly **2** *chiefly NAm* all the way

[3]**clear** *v* **1a** to make transparent or translucent **b** to free from unwanted material – often + *out* **2a** to free from accusation or blame; vindicate **b** to certify as trustworthy **3a** to rid (the throat) of phlegm; *also* to make a rasping noise in (the throat) **b** to erase accumulated totals or stored data from (e g a calculator or computer memory) **4** to authorize or cause to be authorized **5a** to free from financial obligation **b(1)** to settle, discharge **(2)** to deal with until finished or settled **c** to gain without deduction **d** to put or pass through a clearinghouse **6a** to get rid of; remove – often + *off, up*, or *away* **b** to kick or pass (the ball) away from the goal as a defensive measure in soccer **7** to go over without touching **8a** to become clear – often + *up* **b** to go away; vanish – sometimes + *off, out,* or *away*

clearance /'klɪərəns/ *n* **1a** an authorization **b** a sale to clear out stock **c** the removal of buildings, people, etc from the space they previously occupied **d** a clearing of the ball in soccer **2** the distance by which one object clears another, or the clear space between them

clear-cut *adj* **1** sharply outlined; distinct **2** free from ambiguity or uncertainty

clearheaded /ˌklɪə'hedɨd/ *adj* **1** not confused; sensible, rational **2** having no illusions about a state of affairs; realistic

clearing /'klɪərɪŋ/ *n* an area of land cleared of wood and brush

clearinghouse /'klɪərɪŋhaʊs/ *n* an establishment maintained by banks for settling mutual claims and accounts

clear-sighted *adj* clearheaded; *esp* having perceptive insight – ~**ly** *adv* – ~**ness** *n*

clear up *v* **1** to tidy up **2** to explain

clearway /'klɪəweɪ/ *n, Br* a road on which vehicles may stop only in an emergency

cleavage /'kliːvɪdʒ/ *n* **1** (a) division **2** (the space between) a woman's breasts, esp when exposed by a low-cut garment

[1]**cleave** /kliːv/ *v* **cleaved, clove** to stick firmly and closely or loyally and steadfastly – usu + *to*

[2]**cleave** *v* **cleaved** *also* **cleft, clove; cleaved** *also* **cleft, cloven** to divide or pass through (as if) by a cutting blow; split, esp along the grain

cleaver /'kliːvəʳ/ *n* a butcher's implement for cutting animal carcasses into joints or pieces

clef /klef/ *n* a sign placed on a musical staff to indicate the pitch represented by the notes following it

cleft /kleft/ *n* **1** a space or opening

made by splitting; a fissure **2** a usu V-shaped indented formation; a hollow between ridges or protuberances

cleft palate *n* a congenital fissure of the roof of the mouth

clematis /klə'meɪtǰs, 'klemətǰs/ *n* a usu climbing or scrambling plant of the buttercup family with 3 leaflets on each leaf and usu white, pink, or purple flowers

clemency /'klemənsi/ *n* disposition to be merciful, esp to moderate the severity of punishment due

clement /'klemənt/ *adj* **1** inclined to be merciful; lenient **2** *of weather* pleasantly mild – **~ly** *adv*

clench /klentʃ/ *v* **1** to clinch **2** to hold fast; clutch **3** to set or close tightly

clerestory /'klɪə,stɔːri/ *n* the part of an outside wall of a room or building that rises above an adjoining roof

clergy /'klɜːdʒi/ *n sing or pl in constr* a group performing pastoral or liturgical functions in an organized religion, esp a Christian church

clergyman /'klɜːdʒimən/ *n* an ordained minister

¹clerical /'klerɪkəl/ *adj* **1** (characteristic) of the clergy or a clergyman **2** of a clerk or office worker

²clerical *n* **1** a clergyman **2** *pl* clerical clothes

¹clerk /klɑːk/ *n* sby whose occupation is keeping records or accounts or doing general office work

²clerk *v* to act or work as a clerk

clever /'klevəʳ/ *adj* **1a** skilful or adroit *with* the hands or body; nimble **b** mentally quick and resourceful; intelligent **2** marked by wit or ingenuity; *also* thus marked but lacking depth or soundness – **~ly** *adv* – **~ness** *n*

clever-dick *n, Br* a know-all – infml

cliché /'kliːʃeɪ/ *n* **1** a hackneyed phrase or expression; *also* the idea expressed by it **2** a hackneyed theme or situation – **~d** *adj*

¹click /klɪk/ *n* **1** a slight sharp sound **2** a sharp speech sound in some languages made by the sudden inrush of air at the release of an obstruction or narrowing in the mouth

²click *v* **1** to strike, move, or produce with a click **2** to operate with or make a click **3a** to strike up an immediately warm friendship, esp with sby of the opposite sex **b** to succeed **c** *Br* to cause sudden insight or recognition – sometimes in *click into place* *USE* (3) infml

client /'klaɪənt/ *n* **1** sby who engages or receives the advice or services of a professional person or organization **2** a customer

clientele /,kliːən'tel/ *n sing or pl in constr* a body of clients

cliff /klɪf/ *n* a very steep high face of rock, earth, ice, etc

cliff-hanger *n* **1** an adventure serial or melodrama, usu presented in instalments each ending in suspense **2** a contest or situation whose outcome is in doubt to the very end

climacteric /klaɪ'mæktərɪk/ *n* **1** a major turning point or critical stage; *specif* one supposed to occur at intervals of 7 years **2** the menopause; *also* a corresponding period in the male during which sexual activity and competence are reduced – **climacteric** *adj*

climactic /klaɪ'mæktɪk/ *adj* of or being a climax

climate /'klaɪmǰt/ *n* **1** (a region of the earth having a specified) average course or condition of the weather over a period of years as shown by temperature, wind, rain, etc **2** the prevailing state of affairs or feelings of a group or period; a milieu – **-atic** *adj*

climatology /,klaɪmə'tɒlədʒi/ *n* a branch of meteorology dealing with climates

¹climax /'klaɪmæks/ *n* **1** the highest point; a culmination **2** the point of highest dramatic tension or a major turning point in some action (e g of a play) **3** an orgasm

²climax *v* to come to a climax

climb /klaɪm/ *v* **1a** to go gradually upwards; rise **b** to slope upwards **2a** to go *up, down*, etc on a more or less vertical surface using the hands to grasp or give support **b** *of a plant* to ascend in growth (e g by twining) **3** to get *into* or *out of* clothing, usu with some haste or effort **4** to go upwards on or along, to the top of, or over **5** to draw or pull oneself up, over, or to the top of, by using hands and feet **6** to grow up or over – ~**er** *n*

climb down *v* to back down – **climb-down** *n*

clinch /klɪntʃ/ *v* **1** to turn over or flatten the protruding pointed end of (e g a driven nail) **2** to fasten in this way **3** to hold an opponent (e g in boxing) at close quarters – **clinch** *n*

clincher /ˈklɪntʃəʳ/ *n* a decisive fact, argument, act, or remark

cling /klɪŋ/ *v* **clung 1a** to stick as if glued firmly **b** to hold (on) tightly or tenaciously **2a** to have a strong emotional attachment or dependence **b** *esp of a smell* to linger

clinic /ˈklɪnɪk/ *n* **1** a meeting held by an expert or person in authority, to which people bring problems for discussion and resolution **2a** a facility (e g of a hospital) for the diagnosis and treatment of outpatients **b** a usu private hospital

clinical /ˈklɪnɪkəl/ *adj* detached; unemotional – ~**ly** *adv*

[1]**clink** /klɪŋk/ *v* to (cause to) give out a slight sharp short metallic sound – **clink** *n*

[2]**clink** *n* prison – slang

clinker /ˈklɪŋkəʳ/ *n* stony matter fused by fire; slag

[1]**clip** /klɪp/ *v* to clasp or fasten with a clip

[2]**clip** *n* **1** any of various devices that grip, clasp, or hold **2** (a device to hold cartridges for charging) a magazine from which ammunition is fed into the chamber of a firearm **3** a piece of jewellery held in position by a spring clip

[3]**clip** *v* **1a** to cut (off) (as if) with shears **b** to excise **2** to abbreviate in speech or writing **3** to hit with a glancing blow; *also* to hit smartly – infml

[4]**clip** *n* **1a** the product of (a single) shearing (e g of sheep) **b** a section of filmed material **2a** an act of clipping **b** the manner in which sthg is clipped **3** a sharp blow **4** a rapid rate of motion *USE* (*3&4*) infml

clipboard /ˈklɪpbɔːd/ *n* a small writing board with a spring clip for holding papers

clipper /ˈklɪpəʳ/ *n* **1** an implement for cutting or trimming hair or nails – usu pl with sing. meaning **2** a fast sailing ship, esp with long slender lines, a sharply raked bow, and a large sail area

clippie /ˈklɪpi/ *n, Br* a female bus conductor – infml

clipping /ˈklɪpɪŋ/ *n* a (newspaper) cutting

clique /kliːk/ *n sing or pl in constr* a highly exclusive and often aloof group of people held together by common interests, views, etc – ~**y, cliquish** *adj* – **cliquishness** *n*

clitoris /ˈklɪtərɪ̣s/ *n* a small erectile organ at the front or top part of the vulva that is a centre of sexual sensation in females

cloaca /kləʊˈeɪkə/ *n, pl* **cloacae** a conduit for sewage

[1]**cloak** /kləʊk/ *n* **1** a sleeveless outer garment that usu fastens at the neck and hangs loosely from the shoulders **2** sthg that conceals; a pretence, disguise

[2]**cloak** *v* to cover or hide (as if) with a cloak

cloak-and-dagger *adj* dealing in or suggestive of melodramatic intrigue and action usu involving espionage

cloakroom /ˈkləʊkrʊm, -ruːm/ *n* **1** a room in which outdoor clothing or luggage may be left during one's stay **2** *chiefly Br* a room with a toilet – euph

[1]**clobber** /ˈklɒbəʳ/ *n, Br* gear, paraphernalia; *esp* clothes worn for a usu specified purpose or function – infml

[2]**clobber** *v* **1** to hit with force **2** to defeat overwhelmingly *USE* infml

cloche /klɒʃ/ *n* **1** a translucent cover used for protecting outdoor plants **2** a woman's usu soft close-fitting hat with a deeply rounded crown and narrow brim

[1]**clock** /klɒk/ *n* **1** a device other than a watch for indicating or measuring time **2** a recording or metering device with a dial and indicator attached to a mechanism **3** *Br* a face – slang

[2]**clock** *v* **1a** to register on a mechanical recording device **b** *Br* to attain a time, speed, etc, of – often + *up*; infml **2** to hit – infml

[3]**clock** *n* an ornamental pattern on the outside ankle or side of a stocking or sock

clock in *v* to record the time of one's arrival or commencement of work by punching a card in a time clock

clock out *v* to record the time of one's departure or stopping of work by punching a card in a time clock

clock-watcher *n* a person (e g a worker) who keeps close watch on the passage of time in order not to work a single moment longer than he/she has to – **-watching** *n*

clockwise /ˈklɒk-waɪz/ *adj, adv* in the direction in which the hands of a clock rotate as viewed from in front

clockwork /ˈklɒk-wɜːk/ *n* machinery that operates in a manner similar to that of a mechanical clock; *specif* machinery powered by a coiled spring

clod /klɒd/ *n* **1** a lump or mass, esp of earth or clay **2** an oaf, dolt **3** a gristly cut of beef taken from the neck

clodhopper /ˈklɒdhɒpəʳ/ *n* **1** an awkward, boorish person – infml **2** a large heavy shoe – chiefly humor

[1]**clog** /klɒg/ *n* a shoe, sandal, or overshoe with a thick typically wooden sole

[2]**clog** *v* **1** to obstruct so as to hinder motion in or through **2** to block or become blocked *up*

cloister /ˈklɔɪstəʳ/ *n* **1** a monastic establishment **2** a covered passage on the side of an open court, usu having one side walled and the other an open arcade

[1]**clone** /kləʊn/ *n* an individual that is asexually produced and is therefore identical to its parent – **clone** *v*

clop /klɒp/ *n* a sound made (as if) by a hoof or shoe against a hard surface

[1]**close** /kləʊz/ *v* **1a** to move so as to bar passage **b** to deny access to **c** to suspend or stop the operations of; *also* to discontinue or dispose of (a business) permanently – often + *down* **2a** to bring to an end **b** to conclude discussion or negotiation about; *also* to bring to agreement or settlement **3** to bring or bind together the parts or edges of **4a** to contract, swing, or slide so as to leave no opening **b** to cease operation; *specif, Br* to stop broadcasting – usu + *down* **5** to draw near, esp in order to fight – usu + *with* **6** to come to an end

[2]**close** /kləʊz/ *n* a conclusion or end in time or existence

[3]**close** /kləʊs/ *n* **1** a road closed at one end **2** *Br* the precinct of a cathedral

[4]**close** /kləʊs/ *adj* **1** having no openings; closed **2** confined, cramped **3** restricted, closed **4** secretive, reticent **5** strict, rigorous **6** hot and stuffy **7** having little space between items or units; compact, dense **8** very short or near to the surface **9** near; *esp* adjacent **10** intimate, familiar **11a** searching, minute **b** faithful to an original **12** evenly contested or having a (nearly) even score – **~ly** *adv* – **~ness** *n*

[5]**close** /kləʊs/ *adv* in or into a close position or manner; near

close call *n* a narrow escape

close-cropped *adj* clipped short

closed /kləʊzd/ *adj* **1a** not open **b** enclosed **2** forming a self-contained unit allowing no additions **3a** confined to a few **b** rigidly excluding outside influence

closed circuit *n* a television installation in which the signal is transmitted by wire to a limited number of receivers, usu in 1 location

closedown /ˈkləʊzdaʊn/ *n* the act or result of closing down; *esp* the end of a period of broadcasting

closed shop *n* an establishment which employs only union members

close in *v* **1** to gather in close all round with an oppressing effect **2** to approach from various directions to close quarters, esp for an attack or arrest **3** to grow dark

close-knit /ˌkləʊs ˈnɪt/ *adj* bound together by close ties

close season /ˈkləʊs ˌsiːzən/ *n, Br* a period during which it is illegal to kill or catch certain game or fish

[1]**closet** /ˈklɒzɟt/ *n* **1** a small or private room **2** *chiefly NAm* a cupboard

[2]**closet** *v* **1** to shut (oneself) up (as if) in a closet **2** to take into a closet for a secret interview

close-up /ˈkləʊs ʌp/ *n* **1** a photograph or film shot taken at close range **2** a view or examination of sthg from a small distance away

closure /ˈkləʊʒəʳ/ *n* **1** closing or

being closed **2** the ending of a side's innings in cricket by declaration **3** the closing of debate in a legislative body, esp by calling for a vote

[1]**clot** /klɒt/ *n* **1a** a roundish viscous lump formed by coagulation of a portion of liquid (e g cream) **b** a coagulated mass produced by clotting of blood **2** *Br* a stupid person – infml

[2]**clot** *v* to form clots

cloth /klɒθ/ *n* **1** a pliable material made usu by weaving, felting, or knitting natural or synthetic fibres and filaments **2** a piece of cloth adapted for a particular purpose **3** (the distinctive dress of) a profession or calling distinguished by its dress; *specif* *the* clergy

clothe /kləʊð/ *v* **clothed, clad** to cover (as if) with clothing; dress

clothes /kləʊðz, kləʊz/ *n pl* **1** articles of material (e g cloth) worn to cover the body, for warmth, protection, or decoration **2** bedclothes

clotheshorse /ˈkləʊðzhɔːs,ˈkləʊz-/ *n* a frame on which to hang clothes, esp for drying or airing indoors

clothing /ˈkləʊðɪŋ/ *n* clothes

[1]**cloud** /klaʊd/ *n* **1a** a visible mass of particles of water or ice at a usu great height in the air **b** a light filmy, puffy, or billowy mass seeming to float in the air **2** any of many masses of opaque matter in interstellar space **3** a great crowd or multitude; a swarm, esp of insects **4** sthg that obscures or blemishes

[2]**cloud** *v* **1** to grow cloudy – usu + *over* or *up* **2a** *of facial features* to become troubled, apprehensive, etc **b** to become blurred, dubious, or ominous **3a** to envelop or obscure (as if) with a cloud **b** to make opaque or murky by condensation, smoke, etc **4** to make unclear or confused **5** to taint, sully **6** to cast gloom over

cloudburst /ˈklaʊdbɜːst/ *n* a sudden very heavy fall of rain

cloud nine *n* a feeling of extreme well-being or elation – usu + *on*; infml

cloudy /ˈklaʊdi/ *adj* **1** (having a sky) overcast with clouds **2** not clear or transparent – **cloudiness** *n*

[1]**clout** /klaʊt/ *n* **1** a blow or lusty hit with the hand, cricket bat, etc **2** influence; *esp* effective political power *USE* infml

[2]**clout** *v* to hit forcefully – infml

[1]**clove** /kləʊv/ *n* any of the small bulbs (e g in garlic) developed as parts of a larger bulb

[2]**clove** *past of* **cleave**

[3]**clove** *n* (a tree of the myrtle family that bears) a flower bud that is used dried as a spice

clove hitch *n* a knot used to secure a rope temporarily to a spar or another rope

cloven /ˈkləʊvən/ *past part of* **cleave**

clover /ˈkləʊvəʳ/ *n* any of a genus of leguminous plants having leaves with 3 leaflets and flowers in dense heads

clown /klaʊn/ *n* **1** a jester in an entertainment (e g a play); *specif* a grotesquely dressed comedy performer in a circus **2** one who habitually plays the buffoon; a joker – **clown** *v*

cloy /klɔɪ/ *v* to (cause) surfeit with an excess, usu of sthg orig pleasing

[1]**club** /klʌb/ *n* **1a** a heavy stick thicker at one end than the other and used as a hand weapon **b** a stick or bat used to hit a ball in golf and other games **2a** a playing card marked with 1 or more black figures in the shape of a cloverleaf **b** *pl but sing or pl in constr* the suit comprising cards identified by this figure **3** *sing or pl in constr* **a** an association of people for a specified object, usu jointly supported and meeting periodically **b** an often exclusive association of people that has premises available as a congenial place of retreat or temporary residence or for dining at **c** a group of people who agree to make regular payments or purchases in order to secure some advantage **d** a nightclub

[2]**club** *v* **1** to beat or strike (as if) with a club **2** to combine to share a common expense or object – usu + *together*

clubfoot /ˌklʌbˈfʊt/ *n* a misshapen foot twisted out of position from birth – **~ed** *adj*

[1]**cluck** /klʌk/ *v* **1** to make or call with a cluck **2** to express fussy interest or concern – usu + *over*; infml

²cluck *n* the characteristic guttural sound made by a hen

clue /kluː/ *n* sthg that guides via intricate procedure to the solution of a problem

clueless /ˈkluːlᵻs/ *adj, Br* hopelessly ignorant or lacking in sense – infml

¹clump /klʌmp/ *n* **1** a compact group of things of the same kind, esp trees or bushes; a cluster **2** a compact mass **3** a heavy tramping sound

²clump *v* **1** to tread clumsily and noisily **2** to arrange in or (cause to) form clumps

clumsy /ˈklʌmzi/ *adj* **1a** awkward and ungraceful in movement or action **b** lacking tact or subtlety **2** awkwardly or poorly made; unwieldy – **clumsily** *adv* – **clumsiness** *n*

clung /klʌŋ/ *past of* **cling**

¹cluster /ˈklʌstəʳ/ *n* **1** a compact group formed by a number of similar things or people; a bunch **2** a group of faint stars or galaxies that appear close together and have common properties (e g distance and motion)

²cluster *v* to grow or assemble in or collect into a cluster

¹clutch /klʌtʃ/ *v* **1** to grasp or hold (as if) with the hand or claws, esp tightly or suddenly **2** to seek to grasp and hold – often + *at*

²clutch *n* **1** (the claws or a hand in) the act of grasping or seizing firmly **2** (a lever or pedal operating) a coupling used to connect and **3** a paper tape on which a certain type of telegraphic receiving disconnect a driving and a driven part of a mechanism

³clutch *n* a nest of eggs or a brood of chicks; *broadly* a group, bunch

¹clutter /ˈklʌtəʳ/ *v* to fill or cover with scattered or disordered things – often + *up*

²clutter *n* **1** a crowded or confused mass or collection **2** scattered or disordered material

¹coach /kəʊtʃ/ *n* **1a** a large usu closed four-wheeled carriage **b** a railway carriage **c** a usu single-deck bus used esp for long-distance or charter work **2a** a private tutor **b** sby who instructs or trains a performer, sportsman, etc

²coach *v* **1** to train intensively by instruction, demonstration, and practice **2** to act as coach to

coachman /ˈkəʊtʃmən/ *n* a man who drives or whose business is to drive a coach or carriage

coagulate /kəʊˈægjʊleɪt/ *v* to (cause to) become viscous or thickened into a coherent mass; curdle, clot – **-lation** *n* – **-lant** *adj*

coal /kəʊl/ *n* **1** a piece of glowing, burning, or burnt carbonized material (e g partly burnt wood) **2** a (small piece or broken up quantity of) black or blackish solid combustible mineral consisting chiefly of carbonized vegetable matter and widely used as a natural fuel

coalesce /ˌkəʊəˈles/ *v* to unite into a whole; fuse – **coalescence** *n*

coalhole /ˈkəʊlhəʊl/ *n* a hole, chute, or compartment for receiving coal

coalition /ˌkəʊəˈlɪʃən/ *n* **1a** an act of coalescing; a union **b** a body formed by the union of orig distinct elements **2** *sing or pl in constr* a temporary alliance (e g of political parties) for joint action (e g to form a government)

coarse /kɔːs/ *adj* **1** of ordinary or inferior quality or value; common **2a(1)** composed of relatively large particles **(2)** rough in texture or tone **b** adjusted or designed for heavy, fast, or less delicate work **c** not precise or detailed with respect to adjustment or discrimination **3** crude or unrefined in taste, manners, or language – **~ly** *adv* – **~ness** *n*

coarse fish *n, chiefly Br* any freshwater fish not belonging to the salmon family

coarsen /ˈkɔːsən/ *v* to make or become coarse

¹coast /kəʊst/ *n* the land near a shore; the seashore – **~al** *adj*

²coast *v* **1** to sail along the shore (of) **2a** to slide, glide, etc downhill by the force of gravity **b** to move along (as if) without further application of driving power **c** to proceed easily without special application of effort or concern

coaster /ˈkəʊstəʳ/ *n* **1** a small vessel trading from port to port along a coast **2a** a tray or stand, esp of silver, for a decanter **b** a small mat used, esp under a drinks glass, to protect a surface

coastguard /ˈkəʊstgɑːd/ *n* (a member of) a force responsible for maintaining lookout posts round the coast of the UK for mounting rescues at sea, preventing smuggling, etc

[1]**coat** /kəʊt/ *n* **1** an outer garment that has sleeves and usu opens the full length of the centre front **2** the external covering of an animal **3** a protective layer; a coating

[2]**coat** *v* to cover or spread with a protective or enclosing layer

coating /ˈkəʊtɪŋ/ *n* a layer of one substance covering another

coat of arms *n* a set of distinctive heraldic shapes or representations, usu depicted on a shield, that is the central part of a heraldic achievement

coax /kəʊks/ *v* **1** to influence or gently urge by caresses or flattery; wheedle **2** to manipulate with great perseverance and skill towards a desired condition – ~**ingly** *adv*

[1]**cob** /kɒb/ *n* **1** a male swan **2** a corncob **3** (any of) a breed of short-legged stocky horses **4** *Br* a small rounded usu crusty loaf

[2]**cob** *n* a building material used chiefly in SW England and consisting of natural clay or chalk mixed with straw or hair as a binder; *also* a house built of cob

cobalt /ˈkəʊbɔːlt/ *n* a tough silver-white magnetic metallic element

cobber /ˈkɒbəʳ/ *n, Austr* a man's male friend; a mate – infml

[1]**cobble** /ˈkɒbəl/ *v* **1** to repair (esp shoes); *also* to make (esp shoes) **2** to make or assemble roughly or hastily – usu + *together*

[2]**cobble** *n* a naturally rounded stone of a size suitable for paving a street

cobbler /ˈkɒbləʳ/ *n* **1** a mender or maker of leather goods, esp shoes **2** *pl, Br* nonsense, rubbish – often used interjectionally; infml

cobra /ˈkɒbrə, ˈkəʊ-/ *n* any of several venomous Asiatic and African snakes that have grooved fangs and when excited expand the skin of the neck into a hood

cobweb /ˈkɒbweb/ *n* **1** (a) spider's web **2** a single thread spun by a spider

cocaine /kəʊˈkeɪn/ *n* an alkaloid that is obtained from coca leaves, has been used as a local anaesthetic, and is a common drug of abuse that can result in psychological dependence

cochineal /ˌkɒtʃɪˈniːl/ *n* a red dyestuff consisting of the dried bodies of female cochineal insects, used esp as a colouring agent for food

cochlea /ˈkɒklɪə/ *n, pl* **cochleas, cochleae** a coiled part of the inner ear of higher vertebrates that is filled with liquid through which sound waves are transmitted to the auditory nerve

[1]**cock** /kɒk/ *n* **1a** the (adult) male of various birds, specif the domestic fowl **b** the male of fish, crabs, lobsters, and other aquatic animals **2** a device (e g a tap or valve) for regulating the flow of a liquid **3** the hammer of a firearm or its position when cocked ready for firing **4** *Br* – used as a term of infml address to a man **5** the penis – vulg **6** *Br* nonsense, rubbish – slang

[2]**cock** *v* **1a** to draw back and set the hammer of (a firearm) for firing **b** to draw or bend back in preparation for throwing or hitting **2a** to set erect **b** to turn, tip, or tilt, usu to one side **3** to turn up (e g the brim of a hat)

[3]**cock** *n* a small pile (e g of hay)

cockade /kɒˈkeɪd/ *n* an ornament (e g a rosette or knot of ribbon) worn on the hat as a badge

cock-a-hoop /ˌkɒk ə ˈhuːp/ *adj* triumphantly boastful; exulting – infml

cockatoo /ˌkɒkəˈtuː/ *n* any of numerous large noisy usu showy and crested chiefly Australasian parrots

cockchafer /ˈkɒktʃeɪfəʳ/ *n* a large European beetle destructive to vegetation

cockcrow /ˈkɒk-krəʊ/ *n* dawn

cocked hat *n* a hat with brim turned up at 3 places to give a 3-cornered shape

cockerel /ˈkɒkərəl/ *n* a young male domestic fowl

cocker spaniel /ˌkɒkə ˈspænɪəl/ *n* a small spaniel with long ears and silky coat

cockeyed /ˌkɒkˈaɪd/ *adj* **1** having a squint **2a** askew, awry **b** somewhat foolish or mad *USE* infml

cockle /ˈkɒkəl/ *n* (the ribbed shell of) a (common edible) bivalve mollusc

cockleshell /ˈkɒkəlʃel/ *n* **1** the shell

of a cockle, scallop, or similar mollusc **2** a light flimsy boat

cockney /ˈkɒkni/ *n* **1** a native of London and now esp of the E End of London **2** the dialect of (the E End of) London

cockpit /ˈkɒk,pɪt/ *n* **1** a pit or enclosure for cockfights **2a** a recess below deck level from which a small vessel (e g a yacht) is steered **b** a space in the fuselage of an aeroplane for the pilot (and crew) **c** the driver's compartment in a racing or sports car

cockroach /ˈkɒk-rəʊtʃ/ *n* any of numerous omnivorous usu dark brown chiefly nocturnal insects that include some that are domestic pests

cocksure /,kɒkˈʃʊəʳ, -ˈʃɔːʳ/ *adj* cocky – infml

cocktail /ˈkɒkteɪl/ *n* **1a** a drink of mixed spirits or of spirits mixed with flavourings **b** sthg resembling or suggesting such a drink; *esp* a mixture of diverse elements **2a** an appetizer of tomato juice, shellfish, etc **b** a dish of finely chopped mixed fruits

cocky /ˈkɒki/ *adj* marked by overconfidence or presumptuousness – infml

cocoa /ˈkəʊkəʊ/ *n* **1** the cacao tree **2a** powdered ground roasted cacao seeds from which some fat has been removed **b** a beverage made by mixing cocoa with usu hot milk

coconut *also* **cocoanut** /ˈkəʊkənʌt/ *n* the large oval fruit of the coconut palm whose outer fibrous husk yields coir and whose nut contains thick edible meat and a thick sweet milk

coconut shy *n* a stall at a funfair where one throws balls at coconuts on stands

[1]**cocoon** /kəˈkuːn/ *n* **1** (an animal's protective covering similar to) a (silk) envelope which an insect larva forms about itself and in which it passes the pupa stage **2** a (protective) covering like a cocoon (e g for an aeroplane in storage) **3** a sheltered or insulated state of existence

[2]**cocoon** *v* to wrap or envelop, esp tightly, (as if) in a cocoon

[1]**cod** /kɒd/ *n, pl* **cod** (the flesh of) a soft-finned N Atlantic food fish or related Pacific fish

[2]**cod** *n, Br* nonsense – slang

coda /ˈkəʊdə/ *n* **1** a concluding musical section that is formally distinct from the main structure **2** sthg that serves to round out or conclude sthg, esp a literary or dramatic work, and that has an interest of its own

coddle /ˈkɒdl/ *v* **1** to cook (esp eggs) slowly in a liquid just below the boiling point **2** to treat with extreme care; pamper

[1]**code** /kəʊd/ *n* **1** a systematic body of laws, esp with statutory force **2** a system of principles or maxims **3a** a system of signals for communication **b** a system of symbols used to represent assigned and often secret meanings

[2]**code** *v* to put into the form or symbols of a code

codeine /ˈkəʊdiːn/ *n* a derivative of morphine that is weaker in action than morphine and is given orally to relieve pain and coughing

codger /ˈkɒdʒəʳ/ *n* an old and mildly eccentric man – esp in *old codger*; infml

codicil /ˈkəʊdɪ̣sɪl/ *n* **1** a modifying clause added to a will **2** an appendix, supplement

codify /ˈkəʊdɪ̣faɪ/ *v* **1** to reduce to a code **2** to express in a systematic form – **-fication** *n*

codpiece /ˈkɒdpiːs/ *n* a flap or bag concealing an opening in the front of men's breeches, esp in the 15th and 16th c

codswallop /ˈkɒdzwɒləp/ *n, chiefly Br* nonsense – slang

coed /,kəʊˈed/ a coeducational school

coeducation /,kəʊedʒʊˈkeɪʃən/ *n* the education of students of both sexes at the same institution – **~al** *adj*

coefficient /,kəʊɪ̣ˈfɪʃənt/ *n* **1** any of the factors, esp variable quantities, that are multiplied together in a mathematical product considered in relation to a usu specified factor **2** a number that serves as a measure of some property or characteristic (e g of a device or process)

coelacanth /ˈsiːləkænθ/ *n* any of a family of mostly extinct fishes

coelenterate /siːˈlentəreɪt, -rət/ *n* any of a phylum of invertebrate animals including the corals, sea anemones, and jellyfishes

coerce /kəʊ'ɜːs/ *v* **1** to compel to an act or choice – often + *into* **2** to enforce or bring about by force or threat – **-cion** *n* – **-cive** *adj* – **-cively** *adv*

coexist /ˌkəʊɪg'zɪst/ *v* **1** to exist together or at the same time **2** to live in peace with each other – **~ence** *n* – **~ent** *adj*

coffee /'kɒfi/ *n* **1** a beverage made from the roasted seeds of a coffee tree; *also* these seeds either green or roasted **2** a cup of coffee **3** a time when coffee is drunk

coffee-table *adj, of a publication* being outsize and lavishly produced (e g with extensive use of full-colour illustrations) as if for display on a coffee table

coffer /'kɒfəʳ/ *n* **1** a chest, box; *esp* a strongbox **2** a treasury, exchequer; *broadly* a store of wealth – usu pl with sing. meaning **3** a recessed decorative panel in a vault, ceiling, etc

coffin /'kɒfɪn/ *n* **1** a box or chest for the burial of a corpse **2** the horny body forming the hoof of a horse's foot

¹cog /kɒg/ *n* **1** a tooth on the rim of a wheel or gear **2** a subordinate person or part

²cog *v* to direct the fall of (dice) fraudulently

cogent /'kəʊdʒənt/ *adj* appealing forcibly to the mind or reason; convincing – **-ency** *n* – **~ly** *adv*

cogitate /'kɒdʒɪteɪt/ *v* to ponder, usu intently and objectively; meditate on – **-ation** *n*

cognac /'kɒnjæk/ *n* a French brandy, specif one from the departments of Charente and Charente-Maritime distilled from white wine

¹cognate /'kɒgneɪt/ *adj* **1** related by blood, esp on the mother's side **2** of the same or similar nature

²cognate *n* sthg (e g a word) having the same origin as another

cognition /kɒg'nɪʃən/ *n* (a product of) the act or process of knowing that involves the processing of sensory information and includes perception, awareness, and judgment – **-ive** *adj* – **-ively** *adv*

cogn·izant, -isant /'kɒgnɪzənt/ *adj* having special or certain knowledge, often from firsthand sources – fml or technical

cohabit /ˌkəʊ'hæbɪt/ *v* to live or exist together, specif as if husband and wife – **~ation** *n*

cohere /kəʊ'hɪəʳ/ *v* **1** to hold together firmly as parts of the same mass; *broadly* to stick, adhere **2a** to become united in ideas or interests **b** to be logically or aesthetically consistent

coherent /kəʊ'hɪərənt/ *adj* **1** having the quality of cohering **2a** logically consistent **b** showing a unity of thought or purpose – **~ly** *adv* – **-ence, -ency** *n*

cohesion /kəʊ'hiːʒən/ *n* the act or process of cohering – **-ive** *adj* – **-ively** *adv*

cohort /'kəʊhɔːt/ *n* **1a** a group of soldiers; *esp, sing or pl in constr* a division of a Roman legion **b** a band, group **2** *chiefly NAm* a companion, accomplice

coiffure /kwɒ'fjʊəʳ/ *n* a hairstyle – **-fured** *adj*

¹coil /kɔɪl/ *v* **1** to wind into rings or spirals **2** to move in a circular, spiral, or winding course **3** to form or lie in a coil

²coil *n* **1a** (a length of rope, cable, etc gathered into) a series of loops; a spiral **b** a single loop of a coil **2** a number of turns of wire, esp in spiral form, usu for electromagnetic effect or for providing electrical resistance **3** a series of connected pipes in rows, layers, or windings

¹coin /kɔɪn/ *n* **1** a usu thin round piece of metal issued as money **2** metal money

²coin *v* **1a** to make (a coin), esp by stamping; mint **b** to convert (metal) into coins **2** to create, invent **3** to make or earn (money) rapidly and in large quantity – often in *coin it* – **~er** *n*

coinage /'kɔɪnɪdʒ/ *n* **1** coining or (a large number of) coins **2** sthg (e g a word) made up or invented

coincide /ˌkəʊɪn'saɪd/ *v* **1** to occupy the same place in space or time **2** to correspond in nature, character, function, or position **3** to be in accord or agreement; concur – **-dent** *adj*

coincidence /kəʊ'ɪnsɪdəns/ *n* **1** the act or condition of coinciding; a correspondence 2 (an example of) the chance occurrence at the same time or place of 2 or more events that appear to be related or similar – -ental *adj* – -entally *adv*

coir /kɔɪəʳ/ *n* a stiff coarse fibre from the husk of a coconut

coitus /'kɔɪtəs, 'kəʊɪtəs/ *n* the natural conveying of semen to the female reproductive tract; *broadly* sexual intercourse – **coital** *adj*

coitus interruptus /ˌkɔɪtəs ɪntə'rʌptəs/ *n* coitus which is purposely interrupted in order to prevent ejaculation of sperm into the vagina

¹coke /kəʊk/ *n* a solid porous fuel that remains after gases have been driven from coal by heating

²coke *n* cocaine – slang

col /kɒl/ *n* a depression or pass in a mountain ridge or range

cola *also* **kola** /'kəʊlə/ *n* a carbonated soft drink flavoured with extract from coca leaves, kola nut, sugar, caramel, and acid and aromatic substances

colander /'kʌləndəʳ, 'kɒ-/ *n* a perforated bowl-shaped utensil for washing or draining food

¹cold /kəʊld/ *adj* **1** having a low temperature, often below some normal temperature or below that compatible with human comfort **2a** marked by lack of warm feeling; unemotional; *also* unfriendly **b** marked by deliberation or calculation **3a** previously cooked but served cold **b** not (sufficiently) hot or heated **c** made cold **4a** depressing, cheerless **b** producing a sensation of cold; chilling **c** cool **5a** dead **b** unconscious **6a** retaining only faint scents, traces, or clues **b** far from a goal, object, or solution sought **7** presented or regarded in a straightforward way; impersonal **8** unprepared **9** intense yet without the usual outward effects – ~**ly** *adv* – ~**ness** *n*

²cold *n* **1a** a condition of low temperature **b** cold weather **2** bodily sensation produced by relative lack of heat; chill **3** a bodily disorder popularly associated with chilling; *specif* an inflamation of the mucous membranes of the nose, throat, etc **4** a state of neglect or deprivation – esp in *come/bring in out of the cold*

³cold *adv* with utter finality; absolutely

cold-blooded *adj* **1a** done or acting without consideration or compunction; ruthless **b** concerned only with the facts; emotionless **2** having a body temperature not internally regulated but approximating to that of the environment

cold cream *n* a thick oily often perfumed cream for cleansing and soothing the skin of the neck, face, etc

cold shoulder *n* intentionally cold or unsympathetic treatment – usu + *the*

cold war *n* a conflict carried on by methods short of military action

coleslaw /'kəʊlslɔː/ *n* a salad of raw sliced or chopped white cabbage

coley /'kəʊli/ *n, pl* **coley,** *esp for different types* **coleys** *Br* an important N Atlantic food fish closely related to the cod

colic /'kɒlɪk/ *n* a paroxysm of abdominal pain localized in the intestines or other hollow organ and caused by spasm, obstruction, or twisting – ~**ky** *adj*

collaborate /kə'læbəreɪt/ *v* **1** to work together or with another (e g in an intellectual endeavour) **2** to cooperate with an enemy of one's country – -**ration** *n* – -**rator** *n*

collage /'kɒlɑːʒ/ *n* **1** an (abstract) composition made of pieces of paper, wood, cloth, etc fixed to a surface **2** an assembly of diverse fragments

¹collapse /kə'læps/ *v* **1** to break down completely; disintegrate **2** to fall in or give way abruptly and completely (e g through compression) **3** to lose force, value, or effect suddenly **4** to break down in energy, stamina, or self-control through exhaustion or disease; *esp* to fall helpless or unconscious **5** to fold down into a more compact shape **6** to cause to collapse

²collapse *n* **1a** an (extreme) breakdown in energy, strength, or self-control **b** an airless state of (part of) a lung **2** the act or an instance of collapsing

¹collar /'kɒləʳ/ *n* **1a** a band that serves to finish or decorate the neckline of a garment; *esp* one that is turned over **b**

a band fitted about the neck of an animal **c** a part of the harness of draught animals that fits over the shoulders and takes the strain when a load is drawn **d** a protective or supportive device worn round the neck **2** any of various animal structures or markings similar to a collar in appearance or form **3** a cut of bacon from the neck of a pig

[2]**collar** *v* **1** to seize by the collar or neck; *broadly* to apprehend **2** to buttonhole *USE* infml

collarbone /'kɒləbəʊn/ *n* the clavicle

collate /kə'leɪt/ *v* **1** to collect and compare carefully in order to verify and often to integrate or arrange in order **2** to assemble in proper order – **-ation** *n*

[1]**collateral** /kə'lætərəl/ *adj* **1** accompanying as secondary or subordinate **2** belonging to the same ancestral stock but not in a direct line of descent – usu contrasted with *lineal* **3** parallel or corresponding in position, time, or significance **4** of or being collateral

[2]**collateral** *n* **1** a collateral relative **2** property pledged by a borrower to protect the interests of the lender

colleague /'kɒliːg/ *n* a fellow worker, esp in a profession

[1]**collect** /'kɒlɪkt/ *n* a short prayer; *specif, often cap* one preceding the Epistle read at Communion

[2]**collect** /kə'lekt/ *v* **1a** to bring together into 1 body or place; *specif* to assemble a collection of **b** to gather or exact from a number of sources **2** to accumulate, gather **3** to claim as due and receive possession or payment of **5** to provide transport or escort for **6** *chiefly Br* to gain, obtain **7** to come together in a band, group, or mass; gather **8a** to assemble a collection **b** to receive payment

collected /kə'lektɨd/ *adj* exhibiting calmness and composure – **~ly** *adv*

collection /kə'lekʃən/ *n* sthg collected; *esp* an accumulation of objects gathered for study, comparison, or exhibition

[1]**collective** /kə'lektɪv/ *adj* **1** denoting a number of individuals considered as 1 group **2** of, made, or held in common by a group of individuals **3** collectivized – **~ly** *adv*

[2]**collective** *n* **1** *sing or pl in constr* a collective body; a group **2** a cooperative organization; *specif* a collective farm

collective bargaining *n* negotiation between an employer and union representatives usu on wages, hours, and working conditions

collectivism /kə'lektɨvɪzəm/ *n* a political or economic theory advocating collective control, esp over production and distribution

collectiv·ize, -ise /kə'lektɨvaɪz/ *v* to organize under collective control

collector /kə'lektə[r]/ *n* **1a** an official who collects funds, esp money **b** one who makes a collection **2** a region in a transistor that collects charge carriers

colleen /'kɒliːn, kɒ'liːn/ *n* **1** an Irish girl **2** *Irish* a girl

college /'kɒlɪdʒ/ *n* **1** a building used for an educational or religious purpose **2a** a self-governing endowed constituent body of a university offering instruction and often living quarters but not granting degrees **b** an institution offering vocational or technical instruction **3** an organized body of people engaged in a common pursuit **4** *chiefly Br* a public school or private secondary school; *also* a state school for older pupils *USE* (except 1) sing. or pl in constr

collegiate /kə'liːdʒɪət/ *adj* of or comprising a college

collide /kə'laɪd/ *v* **1** to come together forcibly **2** to come into conflict

collie /'kɒli/ *n* a large dog of any of several varieties of a breed developed in Scotland, esp for use in herding sheep and cattle

collier /'kɒlɪə[r]/ *n* **1** a coal miner **2** a ship for transporting coal

colliery /'kɒljəri/ *n* a coal mine and its associated buildings

collision /kə'lɪʒən/ *n* an act or instance of colliding; a clash

colloquial /kə'ləʊkwɪəl/ *adj* used in, characteristic of, or using the style of familiar and informal conversation; conversational – **~ism** *n* – **~ly** *adv*

collude /kə'luːd/ *v* to conspire, plot – **-lusion** *n*

collywobbles /ˈkɒliwɒbəlz/ *n pl* **1** stomachache **2** qualms, butterflies *USE* + *the*; infml

cologne /kəˈləʊn/ *n* toilet water

[1]**colon** /ˈkəʊlɒn, -lən/ *n, pl* **colons, cola** the part of the large intestine that lies in front of the rectum

[2]**colon** *n, pl* **colons, cola** **1** a punctuation mark : used chiefly to direct attention to matter that follows, to introduce the words of a speaker (e g in a play), in various references (e g in John 4:10), and, esp in NAm, between the parts of an expression of time in hours and minutes **2** the sign : used in a ratio where it is usu read as 'to'' (e g in 4:1), or in phonetic transcription (e g in iː) where it signals a change in length and in vowel quality

colonel /ˈkɜːnəl/ *n* an officer of middle rank in the army or American air force

Colonel Blimp /ˌkɜːnəl ˈblɪmp/ *n* a pompous person with out-of-date or ultraconservative views; *broadly* a reactionary

[1]**colonial** /kəˈləʊnɪəl/ *adj* **1** (characteristic) of a colony **2** *often cap* made or prevailing in America before 1776 **3** possessing or composed of colonies

[2]**colonial** *n* a member or inhabitant of a (British Crown) colony

colonialism /kəˈləʊnɪəlɪzəm/ *n* (a policy based on) control by a state over a dependent area or people – **-ist** *n, adj*

colonist /ˈkɒlənɪ̵st/ *n* **1** a member or inhabitant of a colony **2** one who colonizes or settles in a new country

colony /ˈkɒləni/ *n* **1** a body of settlers living in a new territory but subject to control by the parent state; *also* their territory **2** (the area occupied by) a group of individuals with common interests living close together **3** a group of people segregated from the general public – **-nize** *v*

Colorado beetle /ˌkɒlərɑːdəʊ ˈbiːtl/ *n* a black-and-yellow striped beetle that feeds on the leaves of the potato

coloration, *Br also* **colouration** /ˌkʌləˈreɪʃən/ *n* **1** colouring, complexion **2** use or choice of colours (e g by an artist) **3** an arrangement or range of colours

coloratura /ˌkɒlərəˈtʊərə/ *n* (a singer who uses) elaborate embellishment in vocal music

colossal /kəˈlɒsəl/ *adj* of or like a colossus; *esp* of very great size or degree – **~ly** *adv*

colossus /kəˈlɒsəs/ *n, pl* **colossuses, colossi** **1** a statue of gigantic size **2** sby or sthg remarkably preeminent

colostrum /kəˈlɒstrəm/ *n* the milk that is secreted for a few days after giving birth and is characterized by high protein and antibody content

[1]**colour** /ˈkʌləʳ/ *n* **1** a hue, esp as opposed to black, white, or grey **2** an identifying badge, pennant, or flag (e g of a ship or regiment) **3** character, nature **4** the use or combination of colours (e g by painters) **5** vitality, interest **6** a pigment **7** tonal quality in music **8** skin pigmentation other than white, characteristic of race **9** *Br* the award made to a regular member of a team

[2]**colour** *v* **1a** to give colour to **b** to change the colour of **2** to change as if by dyeing or painting: e g **a** to misrepresent, distort **b** to influence, affect **3** to take on or impart colour; *specif* to blush

colour-blind *adj* (partially) unable to distinguish 1 or more colours – **colour blindness** *n*

[1]**coloured** /ˈkʌləd/ *adj* **1** having colour **2** marked by exaggeration or bias **3a** of a race other than the white; *esp* black **b** *often cap* of mixed race – esp of S Africans of mixed descent

[2]**coloured** *n often cap* a coloured person

colourfast /ˈkʌləfɑːst/ *adj* having colour that will not fade or run – **~ness** *n*

colourful /ˈkʌləfəl/ *adj* **1** having striking colours **2** full of variety or interest – **~ly** *adv* – **~ness** *n*

colouring /ˈkʌlərɪŋ/ **1a** (the effect produced by combining or) applying colours **b** sthg that produces colour **c(1)** natural colour **(2)** complexion **2** an influence, bias **3** a timbre, quality

colourless /ˈkʌləlɪ̵s/ *adj* lacking colour: e g **a** pallid **b** dull, uninteresting – **~ly** *adv* – **~ness** *n*

colt /kəʊlt/ *n* a young male horse that

is either sexually immature or has not attained an arbitrarily designated age

coltish /ˈkəʊltɪʃ/ *adj* **1** frisky, playful **2** of or resembling a colt – **~ly** *adv* – **~ness** *n*

columbine /ˈkɒləmbaɪn/ *n* any of a genus of plants of the buttercup family with showy spurred flowers

column /ˈkɒləm/ *n* **1a** a vertical arrangement of items or a vertical section of printing on a page **b** a special and usu regular feature in a newspaper or periodical **2** a pillar that usu consists of a round shaft, a capital, and a base **3** sthg resembling a column in form, position, or function **4** a long narrow formation of soldiers, vehicles, etc in rows – **~ar** *adj*

columnist /ˈkɒləmɟst, -ləmnɟst/ *n* one who writes a newspaper or magazine column

coma /ˈkəʊmə/ *n* a state of deep unconsciousness caused by disease, injury, etc

comatose /ˈkəʊmətəʊs/ *adj* characterized by lethargy and sluggishness; torpid

¹comb /kəʊm/ *n* **1a** a toothed instrument used esp for adjusting, cleaning, or confining hair **b** a structure resembling such a comb; *esp* any of several toothed devices used in handling or ordering textile fibres **2** a fleshy crest on the head of a domestic fowl or a related bird **3** a honeycomb

²comb *v* **1** to draw a comb through for the purpose of arranging or cleaning **2** to pass across with a scraping or raking action **3** to search or examine systematically **4** to use with a combing action **5** *of a wave* to roll over or break into foam

¹combat /ˈkɒmbæt, kəmˈbæt/ *v* **1** to fight with; battle **2** to struggle against; *esp* to strive to reduce or eliminate

²combat /ˈkɒmbæt/ *n* **1** a fight or contest between individuals or groups **2** a conflict, controversy **3** active fighting in a war

combatant /ˈkɒmbətənt/ *n* a person, nation, etc that is (ready to be) an active participant in combat

combative /ˈkɒmbətɪv/ *adj* marked by eagerness to fight or contend – **~ly** *adv*

combination /ˌkɒmbɟˈneɪʃən/ *n* **1a** a result or product of combining **b** a group of people working as a team **2** *pl* any of various 1-piece undergarments for the upper and lower parts of the body and legs **3** a (process of) combining, esp to form a chemical compound

¹combine /kəmˈbaɪn/ *v* **1a** to bring into such close relationship as to obscure individual characters; merge **b** to (cause to) unite into a chemical compound **2** to cause to mix together **3** to possess in combination **4** to become one **5** to act together

²combine /ˈkɒmbaɪn/ *n* **1** a combination of people or organizations, esp in industry or commerce, to further their interests **2 combine, combine harvester** a harvesting machine that cuts, threshes, and cleans grain while moving over a field

combo /ˈkɒmbəʊ/ *n* a usu small jazz or dance band

combustible /kəmˈbʌstɟbəl/ *adj* **1** capable of (easily) being set on fire **2** easily excited

combustion /kəmˈbʌstʃən/ *n* a chemical reaction, esp an oxidation, in which light and heat are evolved

¹come /kʌm/ *v* **came; come 1a** to move towards sthg nearer, esp towards the speaker; approach **b** to move or journey nearer, esp towards or with the speaker, with a specified purpose **c(1)** to reach a specified position in a progression **(2)** to arrive, appear, occur **d(1)** to approach, reach, or fulfil a specified condition – often + *to* **(2)** – used with a following infinitive to express arrival at a condition or chance occurrence **2a** to happen, esp by chance **b(1)** to extend, reach **(2)** to amount **c** to originate, arise, or be the result *of* **d** to fall within the specified limits, scope, or jurisdiction **e** to issue *from* **f** to be available or turn out, usu as specified **g** to be or belong in a specified place or relation; *also* take place **3** to become; *esp* to reach a culminating state **4** to experience orgasm – infml **5a** to move nearer by traversing **b** to reach some state after traversing **6** to take on the aspect of; play the role of – infml

[2]**come** *interj* – used to express encouragement or to urge reconsideration

comeback /ˈkʌmbæk/ *n* **1a** a means of redress **b** a retrospective criticism of a decision **2** a return to a former state or condition **3** a sharp or witty reply; a retort – infml

Comecon /ˈkɒmikɒn/ *n* an economic organization formed in 1949 by the countries of the Soviet bloc to coordinate their economies, and promote mutual aid

comedian /kəˈmiːdɪən/, *fem* **comedienne** /kə,miːdiˈen/ *n* **1** an actor who plays comic roles **2** one, esp a professional entertainer, who aims to be amusing

comedown /ˈkʌmdaʊn/ *n* a striking descent in rank or dignity – infml

comedy /ˈkɒmɪ̈di/ *n* **1a** a drama of light and amusing character, typically with a happy ending **b** (a work in) the genre of (dramatic) literature dealing with comic or serious subjects in a light or satirical manner **2** a ludicrous or farcical event or series of events **3** the comic aspect of sthg

come-hither *adj* sexually inviting

comely /ˈkʌmli/ *adj* of pleasing appearance; not plain – **comeliness** *n*

come-on *n* **1** *chiefly NAm* an attraction or enticement (e g in sales promotion) to induce an action **2** an instance of sexually provocative enticement – infml

comet /ˈkɒmɪ̈t/ *n* a celestial body that follows a usu highly elliptical orbit round the sun and consists of an indistinct head usu surrounding a bright nucleus, often with a long tail which points away from the sun

come to *v* to recover consciousness

come-uppance /kʌmˈʌpəns/ *n* a deserved rebuke or penalty

[1]**comfort** /ˈkʌmfət/ *n* **1** (sby or sthg that provides) consolation or encouragement in time of trouble or worry **2** contented well-being

[2]**comfort** *v* **1** to cheer up **2** to ease the grief or trouble of; console – ~**er** *n*

comfortable /ˈkʌmftəbəl, ˈkʌmfət-/ *adj* **1a** providing or enjoying contentment and security **b** providing or enjoying physical comfort **2a** causing no worry or doubt **b** free from stress or tension – **-bly** *adv*

comfrey /ˈkʌmfri/ *n* any of a genus of (tall) plants of the borage family whose coarse hairy leaves are much used in herbal medicine

[1]**comic** /ˈkɒmɪk/ *adj* **1** of or marked by comedy **2** causing laughter or amusement; funny

[2]**comic** *n* **1** a comedian **2** a magazine consisting mainly of strip-cartoon stories

comical /ˈkɒmɪkəl/ *adj* being of a kind to excite laughter, esp because of a startlingly or unexpectedly humorous impact – ~**ly** *adv*

comic strip *n* a cartoon story

[1]**coming** /ˈkʌmɪŋ/ *n* an act or instance of arriving

[2]**coming** *adj* **1** immediately due in sequence or development; next **2** gaining in importance; up-and-coming

comma /ˈkɒmə/ *n* **1** a punctuation mark , used esp as a mark of separation within the sentence **2** a butterfly with a silvery comma-shaped mark on the underside of the hind wing

[1]**command** /kəˈmɑːnd/ *v* **1** to direct authoritatively; order **2a** to have at one's immediate disposal **b** to be able to ask for and receive **c** to overlook or dominate (as if) from a strategic position **d** to have military command of as senior officer **3** to be commander; be supreme

[2]**command** *n* **1** an order given **2a** the ability or power to control; the mastery **b** the authority or right to command **c** facility in use **3** *sing or pl in constr* the unit, personnel, etc under a commander

[3]**command** *adj* done on command or request

commandant /,kɒmənˈdænt/ *n* a commanding officer

commandeer /,kɒmənˈdɪə^r/ *v* **1** to seize for military purposes **2** to take arbitrary or forcible possession of

commander /kəˈmɑːndə^r/ *n* a middle-ranking officer in the navy; *also* an officer of any rank who is in charge of a group of soldiers

commander-in-chief *n* one who is in supreme command of an armed force

commanding /kəˈmɑːndɪŋ/ *adj* **1**

having command; being in charge **2** dominating or having priority **3** deserving or expecting respect and obedience

commandment /kəˈmɑːndmənt/ *n* sthg commanded; *specif* any of the biblical Ten Commandments

commando /kəˈmɑːndəʊ/ *n* (a member of) a usu small military unit for surprise raids

commedia dell'arte /kəˌmeɪdɪə deˈlɑːhti/ *n* Italian comedy of the 16th–18th c, improvised from standardized situations and stock characters

commemorate /kəˈmeməreɪt/ *v* **1** to call to formal remembrance **2** to mark by some ceremony or observation; observe **3** to serve as a memorial of – **-ration** *n* – **-rative** *adj*

commence /kəˈmens/ *v* to start, begin – fml – **~ment** *n*

commend /kəˈmend/ *v* **1** to entrust for care or preservation **2** to recommend as worthy of confidence or notice – **~able** *adj* – **~ably** *adv*

commendation /ˌkɒmənˈdeɪʃən/ *n* sthg (e g a formal citation) that commends

commensurate /kəˈmenʃərɪ̈t/ *adj* **1** (approximately) equal in measure or extent; coextensive **2** corresponding in size, extent, amount, or degree; proportionate

[1]**comment** /ˈkɒment/ *n* **1** a note explaining or criticizing the meaning of a piece of writing **2a** an observation or remark expressing an opinion or attitude **b** a judgment expressed indirectly

[2]**comment** *v* to explain or interpret sthg by comment; *broadly* to make a comment

commentary /ˈkɒməntəri/ *n* **1** a systematic series of explanations or interpretations (e g of a piece of writing) **2** a series of spoken remarks and comments used as a broadcast description of some event

commentate /ˈkɒmənteɪt/ *v* to give a broadcast commentary – **-tator** *n*

commerce /ˈkɒmɜːs/ *n* the exchange or buying and selling of commodities, esp on a large scale

[1]**commercial** /kəˈmɜːʃəl/ *adj* **1a(1)** engaged in work designed for the market **(2)** (characteristic) of commerce **(3)** having or being a good financial prospect **b** producing work to a standard determined only by market criteria **2a** viewed with regard to profit **b** designed for a large market **3** supported by advertisers – **~ize** *v*

[2]**commercial** *n* an advertisement broadcast on radio or television

commercial traveller *n, Br* a sales representative

commie /ˈkɒmi/ *n* a communist – chiefly derog

commiserate /kəˈmizəreɪt/ *v* to feel or express sympathy *with* sby

commissar /ˈkɒmɪ̈sɑːʳ, --ˈ-/ *n* **1** a Communist party official assigned to a military unit to teach party principles and ideals **2** the head of a government department in the USSR until 1946

commissariat /ˌkɒmɪ̈ˈseərɪət/ *n* **1** the department of an army that organizes food supplies **2** a government department in the USSR until 1946

[1]**commission** /kəˈmɪʃən/ *n* **1a** a formal warrant granting various powers **b** (a certificate conferring) military rank above a certain level **2** an authorization or command to act in a prescribed manner or to perform prescribed acts; a charge **3** authority to act as agent for another; *also* sthg to be done by an agent **4a** *sing or pl in constr* a group of people directed to perform some duty **b** *often cap* a government agency **5** an act of committing sthg **6** a fee, esp a percentage, paid to an agent or employee for transacting a piece of business or performing a service

[2]**commission** *v* **1a** to confer a formal commission on **b** to order, appoint, or assign to perform a task or function **2** to put (a ship) in commission

commissionaire /kəˌmɪʃəˈneəʳ/ *n, chiefly Br* a uniformed attendant at a cinema, theatre, office, etc

commissioner /kəˈmɪʃənəʳ/ *n* **1** a member or the head of a commission **2** the government representative in a district, province, etc

commit /kəˈmɪt/ *v* **1a** to entrust **b** to place in a prison or mental institution **c** to transfer, consign **2** to carry out (a crime, sin, etc) **3a** to obligate, bind **b**

to assign to some particular course or use

commitment /kə'mɪtmənt/ *n* **1** an act of committing to a charge or trust; *esp* a consignment to an institution **2a** an agreement or pledge to do sthg in the future **b** sthg pledged **c** loyalty to a system of thought or action

committal /kə'mɪtl/ *n* commitment or consignment (e g to prison or the grave)

committee /kə'mɪti/ *n sing or pl in constr* a body of people delegated **a** to report on, investigate, etc some matter **b** to organize or administrate a society, event, etc

commode /kə'məʊd/ *n* **1** a low chest of drawers **2** a boxlike structure or chair with a removable seat covering a chamber pot

commodious /kə'məʊdɪəs/ *adj* comfortably or conveniently spacious; roomy – fml – **~ly** *adv*

commodity /kə'mɒdʒti/ *n* **1** sthg useful or valuable **2a** a product possessing utility; sthg that can be bought and sold **b** an article of trade or commerce, esp when delivered for shipment

commodore /'kɒmədɔːʳ/ *n* **1** a middle-ranking officer in the navy **2** the senior captain of a merchant shipping line **3** the chief officer of a yacht club

[1]**common** /'kɒmən/ *adj* **1** of the community at large; public **2** belonging to or shared by 2 or more individuals or by all members of a group **3a** occurring or appearing frequently; familiar **b** of the familiar kind **4a** widespread, general **b** characterized by a lack of privilege or special status **5** lacking refinement – **~ness** *n* – **~ly** *adv*

[2]**common** *n* **1** *pl but sing or pl in constr, often cap* **a** the political group or estate made up of commoners **b** the House of Commons **2** a piece of land open to use by all: e g **a** undivided land used esp for pasture **b** a more or less treeless expanse of undeveloped land available for recreation **3a** a religious service suitable for any of various festivals **b** the ordinary of the Mass **4** *Br* common sense – slang

commoner /'kɒmənəʳ/ *n* a member of the common people; sby not of noble rank

common-law *adj* **1** of the common law **2** recognized in law without formal marriage

common law *n* the body of uncodified English law that forms the basis of the English legal system

common market *n* an economic unit formed to remove trade barriers among its members; *specif, often cap C&M the* European economic community

[1]**commonplace** /'kɒmənpleɪs/ *n* **1** an obvious or trite observation **2** sthg taken for granted

[2]**commonplace** *adj* routinely found; ordinary, unremarkable

common room *n* a room or set of rooms in a school, college, etc for the recreational use of the staff or students

common sense *n* sound and prudent (but often unsophisticated) judgment

commonwealth /'kɒmənwelθ/ *n* **1** a political unit: e g **a** one founded on law and united by agreement of the people for the common good **b** one in which supreme authority is vested in the people **2** *cap* the English state from 1649 to 1660 **3** a state of the USA **4** *cap* a federal union of states – used officially of Australia **5** *often cap* a loose association of autonomous states under a common allegiance; *specif* an association consisting of Britain and states that were formerly British colonies

commotion /kə'məʊʃən/ *n* **1** a state of civil unrest or insurrection **2** a disturbance, tumult **3** noisy confusion and bustle

communal /'kɒmjʊnəl/ *adj* **1** of a commune or communes **2** of a community **3** shared

[1]**commune** /kə'mjuːn/ *v* **1** to receive Communion **2** to communicate intimately

[2]**commune** /'kɒmjuːn/ *n* **1** the smallest administrative district of many (European) countries **2** *sing or pl in constr* an often rural community of unrelated individuals or families organized on a communal basis

communicable /kə'mjuːnɪkəbəl/

adj, esp of a disease transmittable – **-bly** *adv*

communicant *n* **1** a church member who receives or is entitled to receive Communion **2** an informant

communicate /kəˈmjuːnɪ̈keɪt/ *v* **1** to convey knowledge of or information about; make known **2** to receive Communion **3** to transmit information, thought, or feeling so that it is satisfactorily received or understood **4** to give access to each other; connect

communication /kəˌmjuːnɪ̈ˈkeɪʃən/ *n* **1** a verbal or written message **2** (the use of a common system of symbols, signs, behaviour, etc for the) exchange of information **3** *pl* a system (e g of telephones) for communicating **4** *pl but sing or pl in constr* techniques for the effective transmission of information, ideas, etc

communication cord *n, Br* a device (e g a chain or handle) in a railway carriage that may be pulled in an emergency to sound an alarm

communicative /kəˈmjuːnɪ̈kətɪv/ *adj* **1** tending to communicate; talkative **2** of communication

communion /kəˈmjuːnɪən/ *n* **1a** *often cap* the religious service celebrating the Eucharist in Protestant churches **b** the act of receiving the Eucharist **2** intimate fellowship or rapport **3** a body of Christians having a common faith and discipline

communiqué /kəˈmjuːnɪ̈keɪ/ *n* a bulletin

communism /ˈkɒmjʊnɪzəm/ *n* **1a** a theory advocating elimination of private property **b** a system in which goods are held in common and are available to all as needed **2** *cap* **a** a doctrine based on revolutionary Marxian socialism and Marxism-Leninism that is the official ideology of the USSR **b** a totalitarian system of government in which a single party controls state-owned means of production – **-ist** *n* – **-istic** *adj*

community /kəˈmjuːnɪ̈ti/ *n* **1** *sing or pl in constr* **a** a group of people living in a particular area **b** a group of individuals or a body of people or nations with some common characteristic **2** society in general **3a** joint ownership or participation **b** common character; likeness **c** social ties; fellowship **d** the state or condition of living in a society

community home *n, Br* a local-authority centre for housing juvenile offenders and deprived children

commutation /ˌkɒmjʊˈteɪʃən/ *n* **1** a replacement; *specif* a substitution of one form of payment or charge for another **2** an act or process of commuting **3** the process of converting an alternating current to a direct current – **-tative** *adj*

commutator /ˈkɒmjʊteɪtəʳ/ *n* a device for reversing the direction of an electric current; *esp* a device on a motor or generator that converts alternating current to direct current

commute /kəˈmjuːt/ *v* **1** to convert (e g a payment) into another form **2** to exchange (a penalty) for another less severe **3** to travel back and forth regularly (e g between home and work) – **-muter** *n*

[1]**compact** /kəmˈpækt/ *adj* **1** having parts or units closely packed or joined **2** succinct, terse **3** occupying a small volume because of efficient use of space – **~ly** *adv* – **~ness** *n* – **~ed** *adj*

[2]**compact** *v* **1a** to knit or draw together; combine, consolidate **b** to press together; compress **2** to make up by connecting or combining; compose

[3]**compact** /ˈkɒmpækt/ *n* **1** a small slim case for face powder **2** a medium-sized US motor car

[4]**compact** /ˈkɒmpækt/ *n* an agreement, contract

companion /kɒmˈpænɪən/ *n* one who accompanies another; a comrade – **~ship** *n*

companionable /kəmˈpænjənəbəl/ *adj* marked by, conducive to, or suggestive of companionship; sociable

companionway /kəmˈpænɪənweɪ/ *n* a ship's stairway from one deck to another

company /ˈkʌmpəni/ *n* **1a** friendly association with another; fellowship **b** companions, associates **c** *sing or pl in constr* visitors, guests **2** *sing or pl in* *constr* **a** a group of people or things **b** a unit of soldiers composed usu of a headquarters and 2 or more platoons **c** an organization of musical or dramatic performers **d** the officers and men of a ship **3** *sing or pl in constr* an association of people for carrying on a commercial or industrial enterprise

comparable /'kɒmpərəbəl/ *adj* **1** capable of or suitable for comparison **2** approximately equivalent; similar – **-bly** *adv*

comparative /kəm'pærətɪv/ *adj* **1** considered as if in comparison to sthg else as a standard; relative **2** characterized by the systematic comparison of phenomena – **~ly** *adv*

¹compare /kəm'peəʳ/ *v* **1** to represent as similar; liken **2** to examine the character or qualities of, esp in order to discover resemblances or differences **3** to bear being compared **4** to be equal or alike – + *with*

²compare *n* comparison

comparison /kəm'pærḷsən/ *n* **1a** the representing of one thing or person as similar to or like another **b** an examination of 2 or more items to establish similarities and dissimilarities **2** identity or similarity of features

compartment /kəm'pɑːtmənt/ *n* **1** any of the parts into which an enclosed space is divided **2** a separate division or section – **~alize** *v*

¹compass /'kʌmpəs/ *v* **1** to encompass **2** to travel entirely round *USE* fml

²compass *n* **1a** a boundary, circumference **b** range, scope **2a** an instrument that indicates directions, typically by means of a freely-turning needle pointing to magnetic north **b** an instrument for drawing circles or transferring measurements that consists of 2 legs joined at 1 end by a pivot – usu pl with sing. meaning

compassion /kəm'pæʃən/ *n* sympathetic consciousness of others' distress together with a desire to alleviate it – **~ate** *adj* – **~ately** *adv*

compatible /kəm'pætəbəl/ *adj* capable of existing together in harmony – **-bility** *n* – **-bly** *adv*

compatriot /kəm'pætrɪət/ *n* a fellow countryman

compel /kəm'pel/ *v* **1** to drive or force irresistibly *to* do sthg **2** to cause to occur by overwhelming pressure – **compelling** *adj* – **compellingly** *adv*

compendious /kəm'pendɪəs/ *adj* comprehensive but relatively brief – **~ly** *adv*

compendium /kəm'pendɪəm/ *n, pl* **compendiums, compendia** **1** a brief summary of a larger work or of a field of knowledge; an abstract **2** a collection of indoor games and puzzles

compensate /'kɒmpənseɪt/ *v* **1** to have an equal and opposite effect to; counterbalance **2** to make amends to, esp by appropriate payment **3** to supply an equivalent *for* – **-sation** *n* – **-satory** *adj*

compere /'kɒmpeəʳ/ *n, Br* the presenter of a radio or television programme, esp a light entertainment programme – **compere** *v*

compete /kəm'piːt/ *v* to strive consciously or unconsciously for an objective; *also* to be in a state of rivalry

competence /'kɒmpḷtəns/ *also* **competency** *n* **1** the quality or state of being competent **2** a sufficiency of means for the necessities and conveniences of life – fml

competent /'kɒmpḷtənt/ *adj* **1a** having requisite or adequate ability **b** showing clear signs of production by a competent agent (e g a workman or writer) **2** legally qualified – **~ly** *adv*

competition /ˌkɒmpḷ'tɪʃən/ *n* **1** the act or process of competing; rivalry **2** a usu organized test of comparative skill, performance, etc; *also, sing or pl in constr* the others competing with one – **-itive** *adj* – **-itively** *adv* – **-itiveness** *n*

competitor /kəm'petḷtəʳ/ *n* sby who or sthg that competes; a rival

compilation /ˌkɒmpḷ'leɪʃən/ *n* sthg compiled

compile /kəm'paɪl/ *v* **1** to collect into 1 work **2** to compose out of materials from other documents

complacency /kəm'pleɪsənsi/ *n* self-satisfaction accompanied by unawareness of actual dangers or failings – **complacent** *adj* – **complacently** *adv*

complain /kəm'pleɪn/ *v* **1** to express feelings of discontent **2** to make a formal accusation or charge – ~**ing** *adj* – ~**ingly** *adv*

complaint /kəm'pleɪnt/ *n* **1** an expression of discontent **2a** sthg that is the cause or subject of protest or outcry **b** a bodily ailment or disease

complaisant /kəm'pleɪzənt/ *adj* **1** marked by an inclination to please or comply **2** tending to consent to others' wishes – ~**ly** *adv*

¹complement /'kɒmplɨmənt/ *n* **1** sthg that fills up or completes **2** the quantity required to make sthg complete; *specif* a (ships) company **3** either of 2 mutually completing parts; a counterpart

²complement /'kɒmplɨment/ *v* to be complementary to

complementary /,kɒmplɨ'mentəri/ *adj* **1** serving to fill out or complete **2** mutually supplying each other's lack **3** of or constituting either of a pair of contrasting colours that produce a neutral colour when combined

¹complete /kəm'pliːt/ *adj* **1** having all necessary parts, elements, or steps **2** whole or concluded **3** thoroughly competent; highly proficient **4a** fully carried out; thorough **b** total, absolute – ~**ness** *n*

²complete *v* **1** to bring to an end; *esp* to bring to a perfected state **2a** to make whole or perfect **b** to mark the end of **c** to execute, fulfil – ~**ly** *adv* – **-tion** *n*

¹complex /'kɒmpleks/ *adj* **1** composed of 2 or (many) more parts **2** hard to separate, analyse, or solve – ~**ity** *n*

²complex *n* **1** a whole made up of complicated or interrelated parts **2** a group of repressed related desires and memories that usu adversely affects personality and behaviour

complexion /kəm'plekʃən/ *n* **1** the appearance of the skin, esp of the face **2** overall aspect or character

compliance /kəm'plaɪəns/ *n* **1** the act or process of complying (readily) with the wishes of others **2** a disposition to yield to others

complicate /'kɒmplɨkeɪt/ *v* **1** to combine, esp in an involved or inextricable manner **2** to make complex or difficult

complicated /'kɒmplɨkeɪtɨd/ *adj* **1** consisting of parts intricately combined **2** difficult to analyse, understand, or explain – ~**ly** *adv* – ~**ness** *n*

complication /,kɒmplɨ'keɪʃən/ *n* **1a** intricacy, complexity **b** an instance of making difficult, involved, or intricate **c** a complex or intricate feature or element **d** a factor or issue that occurs unexpectedly and changes existing plans, methods, or attitudes – often pl **2** a secondary disease or condition developing in the course of a primary disease

complicity /kəm'plɪsɨti/ *n* (an instance of) association or participation (as if) in a wrongful act

¹compliment /'kɒmplɨmənt/ *n* **1** an expression of esteem, affection, or admiration; *esp* a flattering remark **2** *pl* best wishes; regards

²compliment /'kɒmplɨment/ *v* **1** to pay a compliment to **2** to present with a token of esteem

complimentary /,kɒmplɨ'mentəri/ *adj* **1** expressing or containing a compliment **2** given free as a courtesy or favour

comply /kəm'plaɪ/ *v* to conform or adapt one's actions to another's wishes or to a rule – **-liant** *adj*

¹component /kəm'pəʊnənt/ *n* a constituent part; an ingredient

²component *adj* serving or helping to constitute; constituent

compose /kəm'pəʊz/ *v* **1a** to form by putting together **b** to form the substance of; make up – chiefly passive **2a** to create by mental or artistic labour; produce **b** to formulate and write (a piece of music) **3** to free from agitation; calm, settle

composer /kəm'pəʊzəʳ/ *n* a person who writes music

¹composite /'kɒmpəzɨt/ *adj* **1** made up of distinct parts **2** combining the typical or essential characteristics of individuals making up a group

²composite *n* sthg composite; a compound

composition /,kɒmpə'zɪʃən/ *n* **1** the act or process of composing; *specif* arrangement into proper proportion or relation and esp into artistic form **2** the factors or parts which go to make sthg; *also* the way in which the factors or parts make up the whole **3** a product of mixing or combining various elements or ingredients **4** an intellectual creation: e g **a** a piece of writing; *esp* a school essay **b** a written piece of music, esp of considerable size and complexity

compositor /kəm'pɒzɪtəʳ/ *n* sby who sets type

compost /'kɒmpɒst/ *n* a mixture of decayed organic matter used for fertilizing and conditioning land

composure /kəm'pəʊʒəʳ/ *n* calmness or repose, esp of mind, bearing, or appearance

compote /'kɒmpəʊt/ *n* a dessert of fruit cooked in syrup and usu served cold

[1]**compound** /kəm'paʊnd/ *v* **1** to put together (parts) so as to form a whole; combine **2** to form by combining parts **3** to add to; augment **4** to become joined in a compound

[2]**compound** /'kɒmpaʊnd/ *adj* **1** composed of or resulting from union of (many similar) separate elements, ingredients, or parts **2** involving or used in a combination

[3]**compound** /'kɒmpaʊnd/ *n* **1** a word consisting of components that are words, combining forms, or affixes (e g *houseboat, anthropology*) **2** sthg formed by a union of elements or parts; *specif* a distinct substance formed by combination of chemical elements in fixed proportion by weight

[4]**compound** *n* a fenced or walled-in area containing a group of buildings, esp residences

compound eye *n* an arthropod eye consisting of a number of separate visual units

compound fracture *n* a bone fracture produced in such a way as to form an open wound

compound interest *n* interest computed on the original principal plus accumulated interest

comprehend /,kɒmprɪ'hend/ *v* **1** to grasp the nature, significance, or meaning of; understand **2** to include – fml – **-hensible** *adj* – **-hensibility** *n*

comprehension /,kɒmprɪ'henʃən/ *n* **1a** grasping with the intellect; understanding **b** knowledge gained by comprehending **c** the capacity for understanding fully **2** a school exercise testing understanding of a passage

[1]**comprehensive** /,kɒmprɪ'hensɪv/ *adj* **1** covering completely or broadly; inclusive **2** having or exhibiting wide mental grasp **3** *chiefly Br* of or being the principle of educating in 1 unified school nearly all children above the age of 11 from a given area regardless of ability – **~ly** *adv* – **~ness** *n*

[2]**comprehensive** *n, Br* a comprehensive school

[1]**compress** /kəm'pres/ *v* **1** to press or squeeze together **2** to reduce in size or volume as if by squeezing **3** to be compressed – **~ible** *adj* – **~ibility** *n* – **~ion** *n*

[2]**compress** /'kɒmpres/ *n* a pad pressed on a body part (e g to ease the pain and swelling of a bruise)

compressor /kɒm'presəʳ/ *n* a machine for compressing gases

comprise /kəm'praɪz/ *v* **1** to include, contain **2** to be made up of **3** to make up, constitute

[1]**compromise** /'kɒmprəmaɪz/ *n* **1a** the settling of differences through arbitration or through consent reached by mutual concessions **b** a settlement reached by compromise **c** sthg blending qualities of 2 different things **2** a concession to sthg disreputable or prejudicial

[2]**compromise** *v* **1** to adjust or settle by mutual concessions **2** to expose to discredit or scandal **3** to come to agreement by mutual concession

compulsion /kəm'pʌlʃən/ *n* **1a** compelling or being compelled **b** a force or agency that compels **2** a strong impulse to perform an irrational act

compulsive /kəm'pʌlsɪv/ *adj* of, caused by, like, or suffering from a psychological compulsion or obsession – **~ly** *adv* – **~ness** *n*

compulsory /kəm'pʌlsəri/ *adj* **1** mandatory, enforced **2** involving compulsion or obligation; coercive – **-rily** *adv*

compunction /kəm'pʌŋkʃən/ *n* **1** anxiety arising from awareness of guilt; remorse **2** a twinge of misgiving; a scruple

computation /,kɒmpjʊ'teɪʃən/ *n* **1** the use or operation of a computer **2**

(a system of) calculating; *also* the amount calculated

compute /kəm'pjuːt/ *v* **1** to determine, esp by mathematical means; *also* to determine or calculate by means of a computer **2** to make calculation; reckon **3** to use a computer

computer /kəm'pjuːtəʳ/ *n* a programmable electronic device that can store, retrieve, and process data

comrade /'kɒmrɪ̈d, -reɪd/ *n* **1a** an intimate friend or associate; a companion **b** a fellow soldier **2** a communist – **~ship** *n*

[1]**con** /kɒn/ *v* to conduct or direct the steering of (e g a ship) – **con** *n*

[2]**con** *adv* on the negative side; in opposition

[3]**con** *n* (sby holding) the opposing or negative position

[4]**con** *v* **1** to swindle, trick **2** to persuade, cajole *USE* slang

[5]**con** *n* a convict – slang

[6]**con** *prep* with – used in music

concave /ˌkɒn'keɪv, kən-/ *adj* hollowed or rounded inwards like the inside of a bowl – **-cavity** *n*

conceal /kən'siːl/ *v* **1** to prevent disclosure or recognition of **2** to place out of sight – **~ment** *n*

concede /kən'siːd/ *v* **1** to grant as a right or privilege **2a** to accept as true, valid, or accurate **b** to acknowledge grudgingly or hesitantly **3** to allow involuntarily – chiefly journ **4** to make concession; yield

conceit /kən'siːt/ *n* **1** excessively high opinion of oneself **2a** a fanciful idea **b** an elaborate, unusual, and cleverly expressed figure of speech – **~ed** *adj*

conceivable /kən'siːvəbəl/ *adj* capable of being conceived; imaginable – **-bly** *adv*

conceive /kənsiːv/ *v* **1** to become pregnant (with) **2a** to cause to originate in one's mind **b** to form a conception of; evolve mentally; visualize **3** to be of the opinion – fml

[1]**concentrate** /'kɒnsəntreɪt/ *v* **1a** to bring or direct towards a common centre or objective; focus **b** to gather into 1 body, mass, or force **2a** to make less dilute **b** to express or exhibit in condensed form **3** to draw towards or meet in a common centre **4** to gather, collect **5** to concentrate one's powers, efforts, or attention

[2]**concentrate** *n* sthg concentrated; *esp* a feed for animals rich in digestible nutrients

concentration /ˌkɒnsən'treɪʃən/ *n* **1** direction of attention to a single object **2** a concentrated mass or thing **3** the relative content of a (chemical) component; strength

concentration camp *n* a camp where political prisoners, refugees, etc are confined; *esp* any of the Nazi camps for the internment or mass execution of (Jewish) prisoners during WW II

concentric /kən'sentrɪk/ *adj* having a common centre

concept /'kɒnsept/ *n* **1** sthg conceived in the mind; a thought, notion **2** a generic idea abstracted from particular instances – **~ual** *adj* – **~ually** *adv* – **~ualize** *v*

conception /kən'sepʃən/ *n* **1** conceiving or being conceived **2** a general idea; a concept **3** the originating of sthg in the mind

[1]**concern** /kən'sɜːn/ *v* **1** to relate to; be about **2** to have an influence on; involve; *also* to be the business or affair of **3** to be a care, trouble, or distress to **4** to engage, occupy

[2]**concern** *n* **1** sthg that relates or belongs to one **2** matter for consideration **3** marked interest or regard, usu arising through a personal tie or relationship **4** a business or manufacturing organization or establishment – **~ed** *adj* – **~edly** *adv*

concerning /kən'sɜːnɪŋ/ *prep* relating to; with reference to

concert /'kɒnsət/ *n* **1** an instance of working together; an agreement – esp in *in concert (with)* **2** a public performance of music or dancing; *esp* a performance, usu by a group of musicians, that is made up of several individual compositions

concerted /kən'sɜːtɪ̈d/ *adj* **1a** planned or done together; combined **b** performed in unison **2** arranged in parts for several voices or instruments – **~ly** *adv*

concert grand *n* a grand piano of the largest size for concerts

[1]**concertina** /ˌkɒnsə'tiːnə/ *n* a small

hexagonal musical instrument of the accordion family

[2]**concertina** *v, Br* to become compressed in the manner of a concertina being closed, esp as a result of a crash

concerto /kən'tʃɜːtəʊ/ *n, pl* **concerti, concertos** a piece for 1 or more soloists and orchestra, usu with 3 contrasting movements

concert pitch *n* a tuning standard of usu 440 Hz for A above middle C

concession /kən'seʃən/ *n* **1** the act or an instance of conceding **2** a grant of land, property, or a right made, esp by a government, in return for services or for a particular use **3** a reduction of demands or standards made esp to accommodate shortcomings

conch /kɒntʃ, kɒŋk/ *n, pl* **conches** (the spiral shell of) any of various large marine snails

conciliate /kən'sɪlieɪt/ *v* **1** to reconcile **2** to appease – **-tion** *n* – **-tory** *adj*

concise /kən'saɪs/ *adj* marked by brevity of expression or statement; free from all elaboration and superfluous detail – **~ly** *adv* – **~ness, ~ision** *n*

conclude /kən'kluːd/ *v* **1** to bring to an end, esp in a particular way or with a particular action **2a** to arrive at as a logically necessary inference **b** to decide **c** to come to an agreement on; effect **3** to end – **-clusion** *n*

conclusive /kən'kluːsɪv/ *adj* putting an end to debate or question, esp by reason of irrefutability – **~ly** *adv*

concoct /kən'kɒkt/ *v* to prepare (e g a meal, story, etc) by combining diverse ingredients – **~ion** *n*

concord /'kɒŋkɔːd/ *n* **1a** a state of agreement; harmony **b** a harmonious combination of simultaneously heard notes **2** a treaty, covenant

concordance /kən'kɔːdəns/ *n* **1** an alphabetical index of the principal words in a book or an author's works, with their immediate contexts **2** agreement

concordat /kɒn'kɔːdæt/ *n* a compact, covenant; *specif* one between a pope and a sovereign or government

[1]**concrete** /'kɒŋkriːt/ *adj* **1a** characterized by or belonging to immediate experience of actual things or events **b** specific, particular **c** real, tangible – **~ly** *adv* – **~ness** *n*

[2]**concrete** *n* a hard strong building material made by mixing a cementing material (e g portland cement) and a mineral aggregate (e g sand and gravel) with sufficient water to cause the cement to set and bind the entire mass

[3]**concrete** *v* **1** to form into a solid mass; solidify **2** to cover with, form of, or set in concrete

concubine /'kɒŋkjʊbaɪn/ *n* a woman who lives with a man as his wife; a mistress; *esp* a woman who lives with a man in addition to his lawful wife or wives

concur /kən'kɜːʳ/ *v* **1** to happen together; coincide **2** to act together to a common end or single effect **3** to express agreement – **~rence** *n*

concurrent /kən'kʌrənt/ *adj* **1a** meeting or intersecting in a point **b** running parallel **2** operating or occurring at the same time – **~ly** *adv*

concuss /kən'kʌs/ *v* to affect with concussion

concussion /kən'kʌʃən/ *n* a jarring injury to the brain often resulting in unconciousness caused by a hard blow

condemn /kən'dem/ *v* **1** to declare to be utterly reprehensible, wrong, or evil, usu after considering evidence **2a** to prescribe punishment for; *specif* to sentence to death **b** to sentence, doom **3** to declare unfit for use or consumption – **~ation** *n*

condemned cell *n* a prison cell for people condemned to death

condensation /ˌkɒnden'seɪʃən/ *n* **1** a change to a denser form (e g from vapour to liquid) **2** a product of condensing; *specif* an abridgment of a literary work

condense /kən'dens/ *v* to make denser or more compact; *esp* to subject to or to undergo condensation

condenser /kən'densəʳ/ *n* **1** an apparatus for condensing gas or vapour **2** a device for storing electrical charge – now used chiefly in the motor trade

condescend /ˌkɒndɪ'send/ *v* to waive the privileges of rank; *broadly* to descend to less formal or dignified action or speech – **-cension** *n*

condiment /'kɒndʒmənt/ *n* sthg used to enhance the flavour of food; *esp* seasoning

[1]**condition** /kən'dɪʃən/ *n* **1** sthg essential to the appearance or occurrence of sthg else; a prerequisite **2** a favourable or unfavourable state of sthg **3a** a state of being **b** a usu defective state of health or appearance **c** a state of physical fitness or readiness for use **d** *pl* attendant circumstances

[2]**condition** *v* **1** to put into a proper or desired state for work or use **2** to give a certain condition to **3a** to adapt to a surrounding culture **b** to modify so that an act or response previously associated with one stimulus becomes associated with another

conditional /kən'dɪʃənəl/ *adj* **1** subject to, implying, or dependent on a condition **2** expressing, containing, or implying a supposition – **~ly** *adv*

condole /kən'dəʊl/ *v* to express sympathetic sorrow

condolence /kən'dəʊləns/ *n* (an expression of) sympathy with another in sorrow

condom /'kɒndəm/ *n* a sheath, usu of rubber, worn over the penis (e g to prevent conception or venereal infection during sexual intercourse)

condone /kən'dəʊn/ *v* to pardon or overlook voluntarily; tacitly accept; *esp* to treat as if harmless or of no importance

condor /'kɒndɔːʳ/ *n* a very large vulture of the high Andes with bare head and neck

[1]**conduct** /'kɒndʌkt/ *n* **1** the act, manner, or process of carrying on; management **2** a mode or standard of personal behaviour, esp as based on moral principles

[2]**conduct** /kɒn'dʌkt/ *v* **1** to bring (as if) by leading; guide **2** to carry on or out, usu from a position of command or control **3** to convey in a channel, pipe, etc **4** to behave in a specified manner **5** to direct the performance or execution of (e g a musical work or group of musicians) **6** to act as leader or director, esp of an orchestra **7** to have the property of transmitting (heat, sound, electricity, etc)

conduction /kən'dʌkʃən/ *n* **1** the act of conducting or conveying **2** the transmission of an electrical impulse through (nerve) tissue – **-tive** *adj*

conductor /kən'dʌktəʳ/ *n* **1** a collector of fares on a public conveyance, esp a bus **2** one who directs the performance of musicians **3** a substance or body capable of transmitting electricity, heat, sound, etc

conduit /'kɒndɪt, -djʊʒt, -dwɪt/ *n* **1** a channel through which sthg (e g a fluid) is conveyed **2** a pipe, tube, or tile for protecting electric wires or cables

cone /kəʊn/ *n* **1** a mass of overlapping woody scales that, esp in trees of the pine family, are arranged on an axis and bear seeds between them; *broadly* any of several similar flower or fruit clusters **2a** a solid generated by rotating a right-angled triangle about a side other than its hypotenuse **b** a solid figure tapering evenly to a point from a circular base **3** any of the relatively short light receptors in the retina of vertebrates that are sensitive to bright light and function in colour vision **b** a crisp cone-shaped wafer for holding a portion of ice cream

confection /kən'fekʃən/ *n* a fancy or rich dish (e g a cream cake or preserve) or sweetmeat

confectioner /kən'fekʃənəʳ/ *n* a manufacturer of or dealer in confectionery

confectionery /kən'fekʃənəri/ *n* **1** confections, sweets **2** the confectioner's art, business, or shop

confederacy /kən'fedərəsi/ *n* **1** a league or compact for mutual support or common action; an alliance **2** an unlawful association; a conspiracy **3** a league or alliance for common action; *esp, cap* the 11 states withdrawing from the USA in 1860 and 1861 – **-ate** *n, adj*

confer /kən'fɜːʳ/ *v* **1** to bestow (as if) from a position of superiority **2** to come together to compare views or take counsel; consult – **~ment** *n*

conference /'kɒnfərəns/ *n* **1a** a usu formal interchange of views; a consultation **b** a meeting of 2 or more people for the discussion of matters of common concern **2** a representative assembly or administrative organization of a denomination, organization, association, etc

confess /kən'fes/ *v* **1** to make known (e g sthg wrong or damaging to oneself); admit **2a** to acknowledge (one's sins or the state of one's conscience) to God or a priest **b** to hear a confession **3** to declare faith in or adherence to

confession /kən'feʃən/ *n* **1** a disclosure of one's sins **2** a statement of what is confessed: e g **a** a written acknowledgment of guilt by a party accused of an offence **b** a formal statement of religious beliefs **3** an organized religious body having a common creed

confessional /kən'feʃənəl/ *n* **1** a place where a priest hears confessions **2** *the* practice of confessing to a priest

confetti /kən'feti/ *n* small bits of brightly coloured paper meant to be thrown (e g at weddings)

confide /kən'faɪd/ *v* **1** to show confidence *in* by imparting secrets **2** to tell confidentially

confidence /'kɒnfɨ̣dəns/ *n* **1** faith, trust **2** a feeling or consciousness of one's powers being sufficient, or of reliance on one's circumstances **3** the quality or state of being certain **4a** a relationship of trust or intimacy **b** reliance on another's discretion **5** sthg said in confidence; a secret

confidence trick *n* a swindle performed by a person who pretends to be sthg that he/she is not

confident /'kɒnfɨ̣dənt/ *adj* **1** characterized by assurance; *esp* self-reliant **2** full of conviction; certain – **~ly** *adv*

confidential /,kɒnfɨ̣'denʃəl/ *adj* **1** private, secret **2** marked by intimacy or willingness to confide – **~ity** *n* – **~ly** *adv*

configuration /kən,fɪgjʊ'reɪʃən/ *n* **1** (relative) arrangement of parts **2** sthg (e g a figure, contour, pattern, or apparatus) produced by such arrangement

[1]**confine** /kən'faɪn/ *v* **1** to keep within limits; restrict **2a** to shut up; imprison **b** to keep indoors or in bed, esp just before childbirth – usu passive

[2]**confine** /'kɒnfaɪn/ *n* **1** bounds, borders **2** outlying parts; limits *USE* usu pl with sing. meaning

confinement /kən'faɪnmənt/ *n* confining or being confined, esp in childbirth

confirm /kən'fɜːm/ *v* **1** to make firm or firmer; strengthen **2** to give approval to; ratify **3** to administer the rite of confirmation to **4** to make certain of; remove doubt about by authoritative act or indisputable fact – **~ation** *n*

confirmed /kən'fɜːmd/ *adj* **1a** made firm; strengthened **b** being so fixed in habit as to be unlikely to change **2** having received the rite of confirmation

confiscate /'kɒnfɨ̣skeɪt/ *v* to seize (as if) by authority – **-cation** *n* – **-catory** *adj*

conflagration /,kɒnflə'greɪʃən/ *n* a (large disastrous) fire

[1]**conflict** /'kɒnflɪkt/ *n* **1** a sharp disagreement or clash (e g between divergent ideas, interests, or people) **2** (distress caused by) mental struggle resulting from incompatible impulses **3** a hostile encounter (e g a fight, battle, or war)

[2]**conflict** /kən'flɪkt/ *v* to be in opposition (to another or each other); disagree

confluence /'kɒnflʊəns/ *n* **1** a coming or flowing together; a meeting or gathering at 1 point **2** the (place of) union of 2 or more streams

conform /kən'fɔːm/ *v* **1** to give the same shape, outline, or contour to; bring into harmony or accord **2** to be similar or identical **3** to be obedient or compliant; *esp* to adapt oneself to prevailing standards or customs – **~ist** *adj, n* – **~ism** *n*

conformity /kən'fɔːmɨ̣ti/ *n* **1** correspondence in form, manner, or character; agreement **2** an act or instance of conforming **3** action in accordance with a specified standard or authority; obedience

confound /kən'faʊnd/ *v* **1** to refute **2** to damn – used as a mild interjection of annoyance **3** to throw into confusion or perplexity

confounded /kən'faʊndɨ̣d/ *adj* damned

confront /kən'frʌnt/ *v* **1** to face, esp in challenge; oppose **2a** to cause to meet; bring face to face *with* **b** to be faced with – **~ation** *n*

confuse /kən'fjuːz/ *v* **1a** to make embarrassed; abash **b** to disturb or muddle in mind or purpose **2a** to make indistinct; blur **b** to mix indiscriminately; jumble **c** to fail to differentiate from another often similar or related thing – **~d** *adj* – **~dly** *adv* – **-fusing** *adj* – **-fusingly** *adv*

confusion /kən'fjuːʒən/ *n* **1** an instance of confusing or being confused **2** (a) disorder, muddle

conga /'kɒŋgə/ *n* **1** a dance involving 3 steps followed by a kick and performed by a group, usu in single file **2** a tall narrow bass drum beaten with the hands

congeal /kən'dʒiːl/ *v* **1** to bring from a fluid to a solid state (as if) by cold; to coagulate **2** to make rigid, inflexible, or immobile **3** to become congealed

congenial /kən'dʒiːnɪəl/ *adj* **1** existing or associated together harmoniously – often + *with* **2** pleasant; *esp* agreeably suited to one's nature, tastes, or outlook – **~ly** *adv*

congenital /kən'dʒenɪ̥tl/ *adj* **1a** existing at or dating from birth **b** constituting an essential characteristic; inherent **2** being such by nature – **~ly** *adv*

congest /kən'dʒest/ *v* **1** to cause an excessive fullness of the blood vessels of (e g an organ) **2** to clog – **~ion** *n*

¹conglomerate /kən'glɒmərɪ̥t/ *adj* made up of parts from various sources or of various kinds

²conglomerate /kən'glɒməreɪt/ *v* **1** to accumulate **2** to gather into a mass or coherent whole

³conglomerate /kən'glɒmərɪ̥t/ *n* **1** a composite mixture; *specif* (a) rock composed of variously-sized rounded fragments in a cement **2** a widely diversified business company

conglomeration /kən,glɒmə'reɪʃən/ *n* a mixed coherent mass

congratulate /kən'grætʃuleɪt/ *v* to express pleasure to (a person) on account of success or good fortune – **-lation** *n* – **-latory** *adj*

congregate /'kɒŋgrɪ̥geɪt/ *v* to (cause to) gather together

congregation /,kɒŋgrɪ̥'geɪʃən/ *n* **1** an assembly of people; *esp* such an assembly for religious worship **2** a religious community; *esp* an organized body of believers in a particular locality – **~al** *adj*

congress /'kɒŋgres/ *n* **1** a formal meeting of delegates for discussion and usu action on some question **2** the supreme legislative body of a nation; *esp, cap* that of the USA **3** an association, usu made up of delegates from constituent organizations **4** the act or action of coming together and meeting – fml

congressman /'kɒŋgresmən/ *fem* **congresswoman** *n* a member of a congress

congruent /'kɒŋgruənt/ *adj* **1** in harmony or correspondent; appropriate **2** being exactly the same in size and shape – **~ly** *adv* – **-ence, -uity** *n* – **-uous** *adj*

conical /'kɒnɪkəl/, **conic** *adj* of or resembling a cone – **~ally** *adv*

conifer /'kəunɪ̥fəʳ, 'kɒ-/ *n* any of an order of mostly evergreen cone-bearing trees and shrubs including pines, cypresses, and yews – **~ous** *adj*

¹conjecture /kən'dʒektʃəʳ/ *n* **1** the drawing of conclusions from inadequate evidence **2** a conclusion reached by surmise or guesswork – **-tural** *adj*

²conjecture *v* **1** to arrive at by conjecture **2** to make conjectures as to

conjugal /'kɒndʒugəl/ *adj* of the married state or married people and their relationship

conjugate /'kɒndʒugeɪt/ *v* **1** to give in prescribed order the various inflectional forms of (a verb) **2** to become joined together

conjugation /,kɒndʒu'geɪʃən/ *n* (a diagrammatic arrangement of) the inflectional forms of a verb

conjunction /kən'dʒʌŋkʃən/ *n* **1** joining together; being joined together **2** occurrence together in time or space; concurrence **3** the apparent meeting or passing of 2 or more celestial bodies **4** a word (e g *and* or *when*) that joins together sentences, clauses, phrases, or words

conjunctiva /kən'dʒʌŋktɪvə,

kɒndʒʌŋk'taɪvə/ *n, pl* **conjunctivas, conjunctivae** the mucous membrane that lines the inner surface of the eyelids and is continued over part of the eyeball

conjunctivitis /kən,dʒʌŋktɪv'aɪtʝs/ *n* inflamation of the conjunctiva

conjure /'kʌndʒə'/ *v* **1a** to summon by invocation or by uttering a spell, charm, etc **b(1)** to affect or effect (as if) by magical powers **(2)** to imagine, contrive – often + *up* **2** to make use of magical powers **3** to use a conjurer's tricks – **-rer, -ror** *n*

[1]**conk** /kɒŋk/ *n* (a punch on) the nose – infml

[2]**conk** *v* **1** to break down; *esp* to stall **2** to faint *USE* usu + *out*; infml

conker /'kɒŋkə'/ *n* **1** *pl but sing in constr* a British game in which each player in turn swings a conker on a string to try to break one held on its string by his/her opponent **2** the large seed of the horse chestnut, esp as used in playing conkers

connect /kə'nekt/ *v* **1** to join or fasten together, usu by some intervening thing **2** to place or establish in relationship **3** to be or become joined **4** to make a successful hit or shot – **~ed** *adj* – **~ion, connexion** *n*

connecting rod *n* a rod that transmits power from a part of a machine in reciprocating motion (e g a piston) to another that is rotating (e g a crankshaft)

conning tower /'kɒnɪŋ ,taʊə'/ *n* a raised observation tower and usu entrance on the deck of a submarine

connive /kə'naɪv/ *v* **1** to pretend ignorance of or fail to take action against sthg one ought to oppose **2a** to be indulgent or in secret sympathy **b** to cooperate secretly or have a secret understanding; conspire *USE* often + *at* – **-vance** *n*

connoisseur /,kɒnə'sɜː'/ *n* **1** an expert judge in matters of taste or appreciation (e g of art) **2** one who enjoys with discrimination and appreciation of subtleties

connote /kə'nəʊt/ *v* **1** to convey in addition to exact explicit meaning **2** to be associated with or inseparable from as a consequence or accompaniment **3** to imply or indicate as a logically essential attribute of sthg denoted – **-tation** *n*

connubial /kə'njuːbɪəl/ *adj* conjugal

conquer /'kɒŋkə'/ *v* **1** to acquire or overcome by force of arms; subjugate **2** to gain mastery over **3** to be victorious – **~or** *n*

conquest /'kɒŋkwest/ *n* **1** conquering **2a** sthg conquered; *esp* territory appropriated in war – often pl **b** a person who has been won over, esp by love or sexual attraction

conquistador /kɒn'kwɪstədɔː'/ *n, pl* **-dores, -dors** one who conquers; *specif* any of the Spanish conquerors of America

conscience /'kɒnʃəns/ *n* **1** the consciousness of the moral quality of one's own conduct or intentions, together with a feeling of obligation to refrain from doing wrong **2** conformity to the dictates of conscience; conscientiousness

conscientious /,kɒnʃi'enʃəs/ *adj* **1** governed by or conforming to the dictates of conscience; scrupulous **2** meticulous or careful, esp in one's work; *also* hard-working – **~ly** *adv* – **~ness** *n*

conscientious objector *n* one who refuses to serve in the armed forces or bear arms, esp on moral or religious grounds – **conscientious objection** *n*

[1]**conscious** /'kɒnʃəs/ *adj* **1** perceiving with a degree of controlled thought or observation **2** personally felt **3** capable of or marked by thought, will, intention, or perception **4** having mental faculties undulled by sleep, faintness, or stupor; awake **5** done or acting with critical awareness **6** marked by awareness of or concern for sthg specified – **~ness** *n* – **~ly** *adv*

[2]**conscious** *n* consciousness – used in Freudian psychology

[1]**conscript** /'kɒnskrɪpt/ *n or adj* (sby) conscripted

[2]**conscript** /kən'skrɪpt/ *v* to enlist compulsorily, esp for military service – **~ion** *n*

consecrate /'kɒnsʝkreɪt/ *v* **1** to ordain to a religious office, esp that of bishop **2a** to make or declare sacred by a solemn ceremony **b** to prepare (bread and wine used at communion) to be received as Christ's body and blood **c** to devote to a purpose with deep solemnity or dedication **3** to make inviolable or venerable – **-ration** *n*

consecutive /kən'sekjʊtiv/ *adj* following one after the other in order without gaps – **~ly** *adv*

consensus /kən'sensəs/ *n* **1** general agreement; unanimity **2** the judgment arrived at by most of those concerned

[1]**consent** /kən'sent/ *v* to give assent or approval; agree *to*

[2]**consent** *n* compliance in or approval of what is done or proposed by another; acquiescence

consequence /'kɒnsɪ̵kwəns/ *n* **1** sthg produced by a cause or necessarily following from a set of conditions **2** a conclusion arrived at by reasoning **3a** importance in terms of power to produce an effect; moment **b** social importance

consequent /'kɒnsɪ̵kwənt/ *adj* following as a result or effect

consequential /,kɒnsɪ̵'kwenʃəl/ *adj* **1** consequent **2** of the nature of a secondary result; indirect **3** having significant consequences; important

consequently /'kɒnsɪ̵kwəntli/ *adv* as a result; in view of the foregoing

conservancy /kən'sɜːvənsi/ *n* **1** conservation **2** (an area protected by) an organization with powers to conserve and protect the environment

conservation /,kɒnsə'veɪʃən/ *n* careful preservation and protection, esp of a natural resource, the quality of the environment, or plant or animal species, to prevent exploitation, destruction, etc

conservatism /kən'sɜːvətɪzəm/ *n* **1** (a political philosophy based on) the disposition to preserve what is established **2** *cap* the principles and policies of a Conservative party **3** the tendency to prefer an existing situation to change

[1]**conservative** /kən'sɜːvətɪv/ *adj* **1a** of or being a philosophy of conservatism; traditional **b** *cap* advocating conservatism; *specif* of or constituting a British political party associated with support of established institutions and opposed to radical change **2a** moderate, cautious **b** marked by or relating to traditional norms of taste, elegance, style, or manners – **-tively** *adv*

[2]**conservative** *n* **1** *cap* a supporter of a Conservative party **2** one who keeps to traditional methods or views

conservatory /kən'sɜːvətəri/ *n* a greenhouse, usu forming a room of a house, for growing or displaying ornamental plants

[1]**conserve** /kən'sɜːv/ *v* **1a** to keep in a state of safety or wholeness **b** to avoid wasteful or destructive use of **2** to preserve, esp with sugar **3** to maintain (mass, energy, momentum, etc) constant during a process of chemical or physical change

[2]**conserve** /'kɒnsɜːv/ *n* a preserve of fruit boiled with sugar that is used like jam

consider /kən'sɪdəʳ/ *v* **1** to think about with care or caution **2** to gaze on steadily or reflectively **3** to think of as specified; regard as being **4** to have as an opinion **5** to reflect, deliberate

considerable /kən'sɪdərəbəl/ *adj* **1** worth consideration; significant **2** large in extent or degree – **-bly** *adv*

considerate /kən'sɪdərɪ̵t/ *adj* marked by or given to consideration of the rights and feelings of others – **~ly** *adv* – **~ness** *n*

consideration /kən,sɪdə'reɪʃən/ *n* **1** continuous and careful thought **2a** sthg considered as a basis for thought or action; a reason **b** a taking into account **3** thoughtful and sympathetic or solicitous regard

considered /kən'sɪdəd/ *adj* matured by extended thought

[1]**considering** /kən'sɪdərɪŋ/ *prep* taking into account

[2]**considering** *conj* in view of the fact that

consign /kən'saɪn/ *v* **1** to give over to another's care **2** to give, transfer, or deliver into the hands or control of another; *also* to assign *to* sthg as a destination or end

consignee /,kɒnsaɪ'niː, -sɪ̵-/ *n* one to whom sthg is consigned

consignment /kən'saɪnmənt/ *n* sthg consigned, esp in a single shipment

consist /kən'sɪst/ *v* **1** to lie, reside *in* **2** to be made up or composed *of*

consistency /kən'sɪstənsi/ *also* **con-**

sistence *n* **1** internal constancy of constitution or character; persistenness **2** degree of resistance of **a** a liquid to movement **b** a soft solid to deformation **3a** agreement or harmony of parts or features to one another or a whole; *specif* ability to be asserted together without contradiction **b** harmony of conduct or practice with past performance or stated intent

consistent /kən'sɪstənt/ *adj* marked by harmonious regularity or steady continuity; free from irregularity, variation, or contradiction – **~ly** *adv*

[1]**console** /kən'səʊl/ *v* to alleviate the grief or sense of loss of – **-lation** *n* – **-latory** *adj*

[2]**console** /'kɒnsəʊl/ *n* **1** a carved bracket projecting from a wall to support a shelf or cornice **2** the desk containing the keyboards, stops, etc of an organ **3** a control panel; *also* a cabinet in which a control panel is mounted **4** a cabinet (e g for a radio or television set) designed to rest directly on the floor

consolidate /kən'sɒlɨdeɪt/ *v* **1** to join together into 1 whole; unite **2** to make firm or secure; strengthen **3** to form into a compact mass **4** to become consolidated; *specif* to merge – **-dation** *n*

consommé /kən'sɒmeɪ, 'kɒnsəmeɪ/ *n* a thin clear meat soup made from meat broth

consonance /'kɒnsənəns/ *n* **1** an agreeable combination of musical notes in harmony **2** harmony or agreement among components – fml

[1]**consonant** /'kɒnsənənt/ *n* (a letter or other symbol representing) any of a class of speech sounds (e g /p/, /g/, /n/, /l/, /s/, /r/) characterized by constriction or closure at 1 or more points in the breath channel

[2]**consonant** *adj* **1** marked by musical consonances **2** in agreement or harmony; free from elements making for discord – fml

[1]**consort** /'kɒnsɔːt/ *n* **1** an associate **2** a spouse

[2]**consort** *n* **1** a group of musicians performing esp early music **2** a set of musical instruments (e g viols or recorders) of the same family played together

[3]**consort** /kən'sɔːt/ *v* **1** to keep company *with* **2** to accord, harmonize *with* *USE* fml

consortium /kən'sɔːtɪəm/ *n, pl* **consortia** *also* **consortiums** a business or banking agreement or combination

conspicuous /kən'spɪkjʊəs/ *adj* **1** obvious to the eye or mind **2** attracting attention; striking – **~ly** *adv* – **~ness** *n*

conspiracy /kən'spɪrəsi/ *n* **1** (the offence of) conspiring together **2a** an agreement among conspirators **b** *sing or pl in constr* a group of conspirators

conspire /kən'spaɪəʳ/ *v* **1a** to join in a plot **b** to scheme **2** to act together – **-rator** *n* – **-ratorial** *adj* – **-ratorially** *adv*

constable /'kʌnstəbəl/ *n* **1** a high officer of a medieval royal or noble household **2** the warden or governor of a royal castle or a fortified town **3** *Br* a policeman; *specif* one ranking below sergeant

constabulary /kən'stæbjʊləri/ *n sing or pl in constr* **1** the police force of a district or country **2** an armed police force organized on military lines

constancy /'kɒnstənsi/ *n* **1** fidelity, loyalty **2** freedom from change

[1]**constant** /'kɒnstənt/ *adj* **1** marked by steadfast resolution or faithfulness; exhibiting constancy of mind or attachment **2** invariable, uniform **3** continually occurring or recurring; regular – **~ly** *adv*

[2]**constant** *n* sthg invariable or unchanging: e g **a** a number that has a fixed value in a given situation or universally or that is characteristic of some substance or instrument **b** a number that is assumed not to change value in a given mathematical discussion **c** a term in logic with a fixed designation

constellation /,kɒnstɨ'leɪʃən/ *n* **1** any of many arbitrary configurations of stars supposed to fill the outlines of usu mythical figures **2** a cluster, group, or configuration; *esp* a large or impressive one

consternation /,kɒnstə'neɪʃən/ *n*

amazed dismay that hinders or throws into confusion

constipate /'kɒnstȷ̀peɪt/ *v* to cause constipation in

constipation /,kɒnstȷ̀'peɪʃən/ *n* **1** abnormally delayed or infrequent passage of faeces **2** impairment or a blocking of proper functioning

constituency /kən'stɪtʃʊənsi/ *n* (the residents in) an electoral district

[1]**constituent** /kən'stɪtʃʊənt/ *n* **1** an essential part; a component **2** a resident in a constituency

[2]**constituent** /kən'stɪtʃʊənt/ *adj* **1** serving to form, compose, or make up a unit or whole; component **2** having the power to frame or amend a constitution

constitute /'kɒnstȷ̀tju:t/ *v* **1** to appoint to an often specified office, function, or dignity **2** to establish; set up: e g **a** to establish formally **b** to give legal form to **3** to form, make, be

constitution /,kɒnstȷ̀'tju:ʃən/ *n* **1** the act of establishing, making, or setting up **2a** the physical and mental structure of an individual **b** the factors or parts which go to make sthg; composition; *also* the way in which these parts or factors make up the whole **3** the way in which a state or society is organized **4** (a document embodying) the fundamental principles and laws of a nation, state, or social group

[1]**constitutional** /,kɒnstȷ̀'tju:ʃənəl/ *adj* **1** relating to, inherent in, or affecting the constitution of body or mind **2** being in accordance with or authorized by the constitution of a state or society **3** regulated according to a constitution **4** of a constitution – **~ly** *adv*

[2]**constitutional** *n* a walk taken for one's health

constrain /kən'streɪn/ *v* **1** to force by imposed stricture or limitation **2** to force or produce in an unnatural or strained manner **3** to hold within narrow confines; *also* to clasp tightly – **~t** *n*

constrict /kən'strɪkt/ *v* **1a** to make narrow **b** to compress, squeeze **2** to set or keep within limits – **~ion** *n* – **~ive** *adj*

[1]**construct** /kən'strʌkt/ *v* **1** to make or form by combining parts; build **2** to set in logical order – **~ion** *n* – **~or** *n* – **~ional** *adj*

[2]**construct** /'kɒnstrʌkt/ *n* sthg constructed, esp mentally

constructive /kən'strʌktɪv/ *adj* **1** (judicially) implied rather than explicit **2** of or involved in construction **3** suggesting improvement or development – **~ly** *adv* – **~ness** *n*

construe /kən'stru:/ *v* **1** to analyse the syntax of (e g a sentence or sentence part) **2** to understand or explain the sense or intention of **3** to construe a sentence or sentence part, esp in connection with translating

consubstantiation /,kɒnsəbstænʃi'eɪʃən/ *n* (the Anglican doctrine of) the actual presence and combination of the body and blood of Christ with the bread and wine used at Communion

consul /'kɒnsəl/ *n* **1a** either of 2 elected chief magistrates of the Roman republic **b** any of 3 chief magistrates of France from 1799 to 1804 **2** an official appointed by a government to reside in a foreign country to look after the (commercial) interests of citizens of the appointing country – **~ar** *adj* – **~ship** *n*

consulate /'kɒnsjʊlȷ̀t/ *n* **1** a government by consuls **2** the residence, office, or jurisdiction of a consul

consult /kən'sʌlt/ *v* **1** to ask the advice or opinion of **2** to refer to **3** to deliberate together; confer **4** to serve as a consultant – **~ation** *n* – **~ative** *adj*

consultant /kən'sʌltənt/ *n* **1** one who consults sby or sthg **2** an expert who gives professional advice or services **3** the most senior grade of British hospital doctor, usu having direct clinical responsibility for hospital patients – **-ancy** *n*

consulting /kən'sʌltɪŋ/ *adj* **1** providing professional or expert advice **2** of a (medical) consultation or consultant

consume /kən'sju:m/ *v* **1** to do away with completely; destroy **2a** to spend wastefully; squander **b** to use or use up **3** to eat or drink, esp in great quantity or eagerly **4** to engage fully;

engross **5** to waste or burn away; perish

consumer /kən'sjuːmə'/ *n* a customer for goods or services

¹consummate /kən'sʌmḷt, 'kɒnsʊmḷt/ *adj* **1** extremely skilled and accomplished **2** of the highest degree

²consummate /'kɒnsəmeɪt/ *v* to make (a marriage) complete by sexual intercourse

consumption /kən'sʌmpʃən/ *n* **1** the act or process of consuming **2** the making use of economic goods for the satisfaction of wants or in the process of production, resulting chiefly in their destruction, deterioration, or transformation **3** (a progressive wasting of the body, esp from) lung tuberculosis

consumptive /kən'sʌmptɪv/ *adj* of or affected with consumption (of the lungs) – **consumptive** *n*

¹contact /'kɒntækt/ *n* **1a** (an instance of) touching **b** (a part made to form) the junction of 2 electrical conductors through which a current passes **2a** association, relationship **b** connection, communication **c** the act of establishing communication with sby or observing or receiving a significant signal from a person or object **3** one serving as a carrier or source

²contact *v* **1** to bring into contact **2a** to enter or be in contact with; join **b** to get in communication with

³contact *adj* maintaining, involving, or activated or caused by contact

contact lens *n* a thin lens designed to fit over the cornea of the eye, esp for the correction of a visual defect

contagion /kən'teɪdʒən/ *n* **1** the transmission of a disease by (indirect) contact **2** corrupting influence or contact

contagious /kən'teɪdʒəs/ *adj* **1** communicable by contact; catching **2** exciting similar emotions or conduct in others – **~ly** *adv* – **~ness** *n*

contain /kən'teɪn/ *v* **1** to keep within limits; hold back or hold down: e g **a** to restrain, control **b** to check, halt **c** to prevent (an enemy, opponent, etc) from advancing or attacking **2a** to have within; hold **b** to comprise, include

container /kən'teɪnə'/ *n* **1** a receptacle **2** a metal packing case, standardized for mechanical handling, usu forming a single lorry or rail-wagon load – **~ize** *v*

contaminate /kən'tæmḷneɪt/ *v* **1a** to soil, stain, or infect by contact or association **b** to make inferior or impure by adding sthg **2** to make unfit for use by the introduction of unwholesome or undesirable elements – **-nation** *n*

contemplate /'kɒntəmpleɪt/ *v* **1** to view or consider with continued attention; meditate on **2** to have in view as contingent or probable or as an end or intention – **-lation** *n* – **-lative** *adj*

contemporaneous /kən,tempə'reɪnɪəs/ *adj* contemporary – **~ly** *adv*

¹contemporary /kən'tempərəri, -pəri/ *adj* **1** happening, existing, living, or coming into being during the same period of time **2** marked by characteristics of the present period; modern

²contemporary *n* sby or sthg contemporary with another; *specif* one of about the same age as another

contempt /kən'tempt/ *n* **1a** the act of despising; the state of mind of one who despises **b** lack of respect or reverence for sthg **2** the state of being despised **3** obstruction of the administration of justice in court; *esp* wilful disobedience to or open disrespect of a court – **~ible** *adj* – **~ibly** *adv*

contemptuous /kən'temptʃʊəs/ *adj* manifesting, feeling, or expressing contempt – **~ly** *adv*

contend /kən'tend/ *v* **1** to strive or vie in contest or rivalry or against difficulties **2** to strive in debate; argue **3** to maintain, assert – **-tention** *n* – **~er** *n*

¹content /kən'tent/ *adj* happy, satisfied – **~ment** *n* – **~ed** *adj*

²content /kən'tent/ *v* **1** to appease the desires of; satisfy **2** to limit (oneself) in requirements, desires, or actions – usu + *with*

³content /'kɒntent/ *n* freedom from care or discomfort; satisfaction

⁴content /'kɒntent/ *n* **1a** that which is contained – usu pl with sing. meaning **b** *pl* the topics or matter treated in a written work **2a** the substance, gist **b**

the events, physical detail, and information in a work of art **3** the matter dealt with in a field of study **4** the amount of specified material contained; proportion

contentious /kən'tenʃəs/ *adj* **1** exhibiting an often perverse and wearisome tendency to quarrels and disputes **2** likely to cause strife – **~ly** *adv* – **~ness** *n* – **-tion** *n*

[1]**contest** /kən'test/ *v* **1** to make the subject of dispute, contention, or legal proceedings **2** to strive, vie – **~ant** *n*

[2]**contest** /'kɒntest/ *n* **1** a struggle for superiority or victory **2** a competitive event; a competition; *esp* one adjudicated by a panel of specially chosen judges

context /'kɒntekst/ *n* **1** the parts surrounding a written or spoken word or passage that can throw light on its meaning **2** the interrelated conditions in which sthg exists or occurs – **~ual** *adj* – **~ually** *adv*

contiguous /kən'tɪgjʊəs/ *adj* **1** in actual contact; touching along a boundary or at a point **2** next or near in time or sequence – **-guity** *n* – **~ly** *adv*

continence /'kɒntɮnəns/ *n* **1** self-restraint from yielding to impulse or desire **2** ability to refrain from a bodily activity; the state of being continent

[1]**continent** /'kɒntɮnənt/ *adj* **1** exercising continence **2** not suffering from incontinence of the urine or faeces

[2]**continent** *n* **1** any of the (7) great divisions of land on the globe **2** *cap the* continent of Europe as distinguished from the British Isles

continental shelf *n* the gently sloping part of the ocean floor that borders a continent and ends in a steeper slope to the ocean depths

contingency /kən'tɪndʒənsi/ *n* **1** an event that may occur; *esp* an undesirable one **2** an event that is liable to accompany another event

[1]**contingent** /kən'tɪndʒənt/ *adj* **1** happening by chance or unforeseen causes **2** dependent *on* or conditioned by sthg else **3** not logically necessary; *esp* empirical – **~ly** *adv*

[2]**contingent** *n* a quota or share, esp of people supplied from or representative of an area, group, or military force

continual /kən'tɪnjʊəl/ *adj* **1** continuing indefinitely without interruption **2** recurring in steady rapid succession – **~ly** *adv*

continue /kən'tɪnjuː/ *v* **1** to maintain (a condition, course, or action) without interruption; carry on **2** to remain in existence; endure **3** to remain in a place or condition; stay **4** to resume (an activity) after interruption **5** to cause to continue **6** to say further – **-uation** *n* – **-uance** *n*

continuity /ˌkɒntɮ'njuːɮti/ *n* **1a** uninterrupted connection, succession, or union **b** persistence without essential change **c** uninterrupted duration in time **2** sthg that has, displays, or provides continuity: e g **a** a script or scenario in the performing arts; *esp* one giving the details of the sequence of individual shots **b** speech or music used to link parts of an entertainment, esp a radio or television programme

continuous /kən'tɪnjʊəs/ *adj* marked by uninterrupted extension in space, time, or sequence – **~ly** *adv*

continuum /kən'tɪnjʊəm/ *n, pl* **continua, continuums** **1** sthg (e g duration or extension) absolutely continuous and homogeneous that can be described only by reference to sthg else (e g numbers) **2a** sthg in which a fundamental common character is discernible amid a series of imperceptible or indefinite variations **b** an uninterrupted ordered sequence

contort /kən'tɔːt/ *v* to twist in a violent manner; deform – **~ion** *n*

contortionist /kən'tɔːʃənɮst/ *n* **1** an acrobat who specializes in unnatural body postures **2** one who extricates him-/herself from a dilemma by complicated but doubtful arguments

[1]**contour** /'kɒntʊəʳ/ *n* **1** (a line representing) an outline, esp of a curving or irregular figure **2 contour, contour line** a line (e g on a map) connecting points of equal elevation or height

[2]**contour** *v* **1a** to shape the contour of **b** to shape or construct so as to fit contours

contraband /'kɒntrəbænd/ *n* goods or merchandise whose import, export, or possession is forbidden; *also* smuggled goods – **contraband** *adj*

contrabass /ˌkɒntrəˈbeɪs/ *n* a double bass

contraceptive /ˌkɒntrəˈseptɪv/ *n* a method or device used in preventing conception – **-tion** *n* – **-tive** *adj*

[1]**contract** /ˈkɒntrækt/ *n* **1a** (a document containing) a legally binding agreement between 2 or more people or parties **b** a betrothal **2** an undertaking to win a specified number of tricks in bridge

[2]**contract** /kənˈtrækt/ *v* **1** to undertake by contract **2a** to catch (an illness) **b** to incur as an obligation **3** to knit, wrinkle **4** to reduce to a smaller size (as if) by squeezing or forcing together **5** to shorten (e g a word) **6** to make a contract **7** to draw together so as to become smaller or shorter

contract bridge *n* a form of bridge in which tricks made in excess of the contract do not count towards game bonuses

contractile /kənˈtræktaɪl/ *adj* having the power or property of contracting

contraction /kənˈtrækʃən/ *n* **1** the shortening and thickening of a muscle (fibre) **2** (a form produced by) shortening of a word, syllable, or word group

contractor /kənˈtræktəʳ/ *n* one who contracts to perform work, esp building work, or to provide supplies, usu on a large scale

contract out *v* to agree to exclusion (of) from a particular scheme

contractual /kənˈtræktʃʊəl/ *adj* of or constituting a contract – **contractually** *adv*

contradict /ˌkɒntrəˈdɪkt/ *v* **1** to state the contrary of (a statement or speaker) **2** to deny the truthfulness of (a statement or speaker) – **~ion** *n* – **~ory** *adj*

contralto /kənˈtræltəʊ/ *n* **1** (a person with) the lowest female singing voice **2** the part sung by a contralto

contraption /kənˈtræpʃən/ *n* a newfangled or complicated device; a gadget

contrapuntal /ˌkɒntrəˈpuntl/ *adj* of counterpoint – **~ly** *adv*

contrariwise /kənˈtreəriwaɪz/ *adv* conversely; vice versa

[1]**contrary** /ˈkɒntrəri/ *n* **1** a fact or condition incompatible with another **2** either of a pair of opposites **3** either of 2 terms (e g true and false) that cannot both simultaneously be said to be true of the same subject

[2]**contrary** /ˈkɒntrəri, *sense* 4 kənˈtreəri/ *adj* **1** completely different or opposed **2** opposite in position, direction, or nature **3** *of wind or weather* unfavourable **4** obstinately self-willed; inclined to oppose the wishes of others – **-arily** *adv* – **-ariness** *n*

[1]**contrast** /ˈkɒntrɑːst/ *n* **1a** juxtaposition of dissimilar elements (e g colour, tone, or emotion) in a work of art **b** degree of difference between the lightest and darkest parts of a painting, photograph, television picture, etc **2** comparison of similar objects to set off their dissimilar qualities **3** a person or thing against which another may be contrasted

[2]**contrast** /kənˈtrɑːst/ *v* **1** to exhibit contrast **2** to put in contrast **3** to compare in respect to differences

contravene /ˌkɒntrəˈviːn/ *v* to go or act contrary to – **-vention** *n*

contribute /kənˈtrɪbjuːt/ *v* **1** to give in common with others **2** to supply (e g an article) for a publication **3** to help bring about an end or result – **-bution** *n*

[1]**contributory** /kənˈtrɪbjʊtəri/ *adj* **1** contributing to a common fund or enterprise **2** of or forming a contribution **3** financed by contributions; *specif, of an insurance or pension plan* contributed to by both employers and employees

[2]**contributory** *n* sby liable in British law to contribute towards meeting the debts of a bankrupt company

contrite /ˈkəntraɪt/ *adj* **1** grieving and penitent for sin or shortcoming **2** showing contrition – **~ly** *adv*

contrition /kənˈtrɪʃən/ *n* sorrow for one's sins, arising esp from the love of God rather than fear of punishment

contrive /kənˈtraɪv/ *v* **1a** to devise, plan **b** to create in an inventive or resourceful manner **2** to bring about; manage – **-vance** *n*

contrived /kənˈtraɪvd/ *adj* unnatural and forced

[1]**control** /kən'trəʊl/ *v* **1** to check, test, or verify **2a** to exercise restraining or directing influence over **b** to have power over; rule – **~ler** *n* – **~lable** *adj* – **~lably** *adv*

[2]**control** *n* **1** power to control, direct, or command **2a** (an organism, culture, etc used in) an experiment in which the procedure or agent under test in a parallel experiment is omitted and which is used as a standard of comparison in judging experimental effects **b** a mechanism used to regulate or guide the operation of a machine, apparatus, or system – often pl **c** an organization that directs a space flight

controversy /'kɒntrəvɜːsi, kən'trɒvəsi/ *n* (a) debate or dispute, esp in public or in the media – **-sial** *adj* – **-sially** *adv*

contuse /kən'tjuːz/ *v* to bruise (tissue) – **-sion** *n*

conundrum /kə'nʌndrəm/ *n* **1** a riddle; *esp* one whose answer is or involves a pun **2** an intricate and difficult problem

conurbation /ˌkɒnɜː'beɪʃən/ *n* a grouping of several previously separate towns to form 1 large community

convalesce /ˌkonvə'les/ *v* to recover gradually after sickness or weakness – **~nce** *n* – **~nt** *adj, n*

convection /kən'vekʃən/ *n* (the transfer of heat by) the circulatory motion that occurs in a gas or liquid at a nonuniform temperature owing to the variation of density with temperature

convector /kən'vektəʳ/ *n* a heating unit from which heated air circulates by convection

convene *v* /kən'viːn/ **1** to come together in a body **2** to summon before a tribunal **3** to cause to assemble – **~r, -enor** *n*

convenience /kən'viːnɪəns/ *n* **1** fitness or suitability **2** an appliance, device, or service conducive to comfort **3** a suitable time; an opportunity **4** personal comfort or advantage **5** *Br* a public toilet

convenient /kən'viːnɪənt/ *adj* **1** suited to personal comfort or to easy use **2** suited to a particular situation **3** near at hand; easily accessible – **~ly** *adv*

convent /'kɒnvənt/ *n* a local community or house of a religious order or congregation; *esp* an establishment of nuns

convention /kən'venʃən/ *n* **1** an agreement or contract, esp between states or parties **2** a generally agreed (social) principle or practice **3** an assembly **4a** an established artistic technique or practice **b** an agreed system of bidding or playing that conveys information between partners in bridge or another card game

conventional /kən'venʃənəl/ *adj* **1a** conforming to or sanctioned by convention **b** lacking originality or individuality **2** *of warfare* not using atom or hydrogen bombs – **~ly** *adv* – **~ize** *v*

converge /kən'vɜːdʒ/ *v* **1** to move together towards a common point; meet **2** to come together in a common interest or focus – **~nt** *adj* – **~nce** *n*

conversant /kən'vɜːsənt/ *adj* having knowledge or experience; familiar *with*

conversation /ˌkɒnvə'seɪʃən/ *n* **1** (an instance of) informal verbal exchange of feelings, opinions, or ideas **2** an exchange similar to conversation; *esp* real-time interaction with a computer, esp through a keyboard – **~al** *adj* – **~ally** *adv* – **~alist** *n*

[1]**converse** /kən'vɜːs/ *v* to exchange thoughts and opinions in speech; talk

[2]**converse** /'kɒnvɜːs/ *n* conversation – fml

[3]**converse** /'kɒnvɜːs/ *adj* reversed in order, relation, or action; opposite – **~ly** *adv*

[4]**converse** /'kɒnvɜːs/ *n* sthg converse to another; *esp* a proposition in logic in which the subject and predicate terms have been interchanged

[1]**convert** /kən'vɜːt/ *v* **1a** to win over from one persuasion or party to another **b** to win over to a particular religion or sect **2a** to alter the physical or chemical nature or properties of, esp in manufacturing **b** to change from one form or function to another; *esp* to make (structural) alterations to

(a building or part of a building) **c** to exchange for an equivalent **3** to gain extra points for a try in rugby by kicking the ball between the uprights of the goal above the cross-bar – **-version** *n*

[2]**convert** /ˈkɒnvɜːt/ *n* a person who has experienced an esp religious conversion

[1]**convertible** /kənˈvɜːtəbəl/ *adj* **1** capable of being converted **2** *of a motor vehicle* having a top that may be lowered or removed **3** capable of being exchanged for a specified equivalent (e g another currency) – **-bility** *n*

[2]**convertible** *n* a convertible motor car

convex /ˌkɒnˈveks, kən-/ *adj* curved or rounded outwards like the outside of a bowl – **~ity** *n* – **~ly** *adv*

convey /kənˈveɪ/ *v* **1** to take or carry from one place to another **2** to impart or communicate (e g feelings or ideas) **3** to transmit, transfer; *specif* to transfer (property or the rights to property) to another – **~er, ~or** *n*

conveyance /kənˈveɪəns/ *n* **1** a document by which rights to property are transferred **2** a means of transport; a vehicle

conveyancing /kənˈveɪənsɪŋ/ *n* the act or business of transferring rights to property

[1]**convict** /kənˈvɪkt/ *v* **1** to find or prove to be guilty **2** to convince of error or sinfulness

[2]**convict** /ˈkɒnvɪkt/ *n* a person serving a (long-term) prison sentence

conviction /kənˈvɪkʃən/ *n* **1** convicting or being convicted, esp in judicial proceedings **2a** a strong persuasion or belief **b** the state of being convinced

convince /kənˈvɪns/ *v* to cause to believe; persuade – **~d** *adj*

convincing /kənˈvɪnsɪŋ/ *adj* having the power to overcome doubt or disbelief; plausible – **~ly** *adv*

convivial /kənˈvɪvɪəl/ *adj* relating to or fond of eating, drinking, and good company – **~ly** *adv* – **~ity** *n*

convocation /ˌkɒnvəˈkeɪʃən/ *n* **1** an assembly of people called together: e g **a** either of the 2 provincial assemblies of bishops and representative clergy of the Church of England **b** a ceremonial assembly of graduates of a college or university **2** the act of calling together

convoke /kənˈvəʊk/ *v* to call together to a formal meeting

convolution /ˌkɒnvəˈluːʃən/ *n* sthg intricate or complicated – **-ted** *adj*

convolvulus /kənˈvɒlvjʊləs/ *n, pl* **convolvuluses, convolvuli** any of a genus of usu twining plants (e g bindweed)

[1]**convoy** /ˈkɒnvɔɪ/ *v* to accompany or escort, esp for protection

[2]**convoy** *n* **1** convoying or being convoyed **2** *sing or pl in constr* a group of ships, military vehicles, etc moving together, esp with a protective escort; *also* such an escort

convulse /kənˈvʌls/ *v* **1** to shake or agitate violently, esp (as if) with irregular spasms **2** to cause to laugh helplessly – **-sion** *n* – **-sive** *adj* – **-sively** *adv*

cony, coney /ˈkəʊni/ *n* a rabbit; *also* its fur, esp when prepared to imitate some other fur

coo /kuː/ *v* **1** to make (a sound similar to) the low soft cry characteristic of a dove or pigeon **2** to talk lovingly or appreciatively – **coo** *n*

[1]**cook** /kʊk/ *n* sby who prepares food for eating

[2]**cook** *v* **1** to prepare food for eating, esp by subjection to heat **2** to undergo the process of being cooked **3** to subject to the action of heat or fire

cooker /ˈkʊkəʳ/ *n* **1** an apparatus, appliance, etc for cooking; *esp* one typically consisting of an oven, hot plates or rings, and a grill fixed in position **2** a variety, esp of fruit, not usu eaten raw

cookery /ˈkʊkəri/ *n* the art or practice of cooking

cookie /ˈkʊki/ *n* **1a** *Scot* a plain bun **b** *NAm* a sweet flat or slightly leavened biscuit **2** *chiefly NAm* a person, esp of a specified type – infml

[1]**cool** /kuːl/ *adj* **1** moderately cold; lacking in warmth **2a** dispassionately calm and self-controlled **b** lacking friendliness or enthusiasm **c** of or being an understated, restrained, and melodic style of jazz **3** bringing or suggesting relief from heat **4** showing sophistication by a restrained or

detached manner 5 – used as an intensive; infml 6 very good; excellent – slang – ~**ish** *adj* – ~**ly** *adv* – ~**ness** *n*

[2]**cool** *v* 1 to become cool; lose heat or warmth 2 to lose enthusiasm or passion 3 to make cool; impart a feeling of coolness to – often + *off* or *down* 4 to moderate the excitement, force, or activity of

[3]**cool** *n* 1 a cool atmosphere or place 2 poise, composure – infml

[4]**cool** *adv* in a casual and nonchalant manner – infml

coolant /'kuːlənt/ *n* a liquid or gas used in cooling, esp in an engine

coolie /'kuːli/ *n* an unskilled labourer or porter, usu in or from the Far East, hired for low or subsistence wages

[1]**coop** /kuːp/ *n* 1 a cage or small enclosure or building, esp for housing poultry 2 a confined space

[2]**coop** *v* 1 to confine in a restricted space – usu + *up* 2 to place or keep in a coop – often + *up*

co-op /'kəʊ-op/ *n* a cooperative

cooper /'kuːpəʳ/ *n* a maker or repairer of barrels, casks, etc

cooperate /kəʊ'ɒpəreɪt/ *v* to act or work with others for a common purpose – **-ation** *n* – **-ative** *adj*

cooperative /kəʊ'ɒpərətɪv/ *n* an enterprise (e g a shop) or organization (e g a society) owned by and operated for the benefit of those using its services

co-opt /,kəʊ 'opt/ *v* 1 to choose or elect as a member; *specif, of a committee* to draft onto itself as an additional member 2 to gain the participation or services of; assimilate

[1]**coordinate** /kəʊ'ɔːdɪ̣nɪ̣t/ *adj* 1 equal in rank, quality, or significance 2 relating to or marked by coordination – ~**ly** *adv*

[2]**coordinate** *n* 1 any of a set of numbers used in specifying the location of a point on a line, on a surface, or in space 2 *pl* outer garments, usu separates, in harmonizing colours, materials, and pattern

[3]**coordinate** /kəʊ'ɔːdɪ̣neɪt/ *v* 1 to combine in a common action; harmonize 2 to be or become coordinate, esp so as to act together harmoniously – **-ation** *n* – **-ative** *adj* – **-ator** *n*

coot /kuːt/ *n* 1 any of various slaty-black water birds of the rail family that somewhat resemble ducks 2 a foolish person – infml

[1]**cop** /kɒp/ *v* to get hold of; catch; *specif, Br* to arrest – slang

[2]**cop** *n, Br* a capture, arrest – esp in *a fair cop*; slang

[3]**cop** *n* a policeman – infml

[1]**cope** /kəʊp/ *n* a long ecclesiastical vestment resembling a cape, worn on special occasions (e g processions)

[2]**cope** *v* to supply or cover with a cope or coping

[3]**cope** *v* to deal with a problem or task effectively – usu + *with*

copier /'kɒpɪəʳ/ *n* a machine for making copies, esp by photocopying or xeroxing

co-pilot *n* a qualified aircraft pilot who assists or relieves the pilot but is not in command

coping /'kəʊpɪŋ/ *n* the final, usu sloping, course of brick, stone, etc on the top of a wall

copious /'kəʊpɪəs/ *adj* 1 plentiful, lavish 2 profuse in words or expression – ~**ly** *adv* – ~**ness** *n*

cop out *v* to avoid an unwanted responsibility or commitment – infml – **cop-out** *n*

[1]**copper** /'kɒpəʳ/ *n* 1 a common reddish metallic element that is ductile and malleable and one of the best conductors of heat and electricity 2 a coin or token made of copper or bronze and usu of low value 3 any of various small butterflies with usu copper-coloured wings 4 *chiefly Br* a large metal vessel used, esp formerly, for boiling clothes – **copper,** ~**y** *adj*

[2]**copper** *n* a policeman – infml

copperplate /'kɒpəpleɪt/ *n* handwriting modelled on engravings in copper and marked by lines of sharply contrasting thickness; *broadly* formal and ornate handwriting

coppersmith /'kɒpəsmɪθ/ *n* sby who works in, or produces articles of, copper

coppice /'kɒpɪ̣s/ *n* a thicket, grove, etc of small trees

copra /'kɒprə/ *n* dried coconut meat yielding coconut oil

copulate /'kɒpjʊleɪt/ *v* to engage in sexual intercourse – **-lation** *n*

[1]**copy** /'kɒpi/ *n* **1** an imitation, transcript, or reproduction of an original work **2** any of a series of esp mechanical reproductions of an original impression **3** (newsworthy) material ready to be printed

[2]**copy** *v* **1** to make a copy (of) **2** to model oneself on **3** to undergo copying

copybook /'kɒpibʊk/ *n* a book formerly used in teaching writing and containing models for imitation

copy-book *adj, Br* completely correct; proper

copycat /'kɒpikæt/ *n* one who slavishly imitates the behaviour or practices of another – used chiefly by children

copyright /'kɒpiraɪt/ *v or n* (to secure) the exclusive legal right to reproduce, publish, and sell a literary, musical, or artistic work

copywriter /'kɒpiraɪtə^r/ *n* a writer of advertising or publicity copy

coquetry /'kɒkʒtri/ *n* flirtatious behaviour or attitude

coquette /kəʊ'ket/ *n* a woman who tries to gain the attention and admiration of men without sincere affection – **coquettish** *adj*

coracle /'kɒrəkəl/ *n* a small (nearly) circular boat of a traditional Welsh or Irish design made by covering a wicker frame with waterproof material

coral /'kɒrəl/ *n* **1** (the hard esp red deposit produced as a skeleton chiefly by) a colony of smart marine animals **2** a piece of (red) coral **3a** a bright reddish mass of ovaries (e g of a lobster or scallop) **b** deep orange-pink – **coral** *adj*

cor anglais /,kɔːr 'ɒŋgleɪ/ *n* a double-reed woodwind instrument similar to, and with a range a fifth lower than, the oboe

corbel /'kɔːbəl/ *n* a projection from a wall which supports a weight; *esp* one stepped upwards and outwards from a vertical surface

[1]**cord** /kɔːd/ *n* **1** (a length of) long thin flexible material consisting of several strands (e g of thread or yarn) woven or twisted together **2** a moral, spiritual, or emotional bond **3** an electric flex **4** a unit of cut wood usu equal to 128ft^3 (about 3.63m^3); *also* a stack containing this amount of wood **5a** a rib like a cord on a textile **b(1)** a fabric made with such ribs **(2)** *pl* trousers made of corduroy

[2]**cord** *v* to provide, bind, or connect with a cord

[1]**cordial** /'kɔːdɪəl/ *adj* **1** warmly and genially affable **2** sincerely or deeply felt – **~ity** *n* – **~ly** *adv*

[2]**cordial** /'kɔːdɪəl/ *n* **1** a stimulating medicine **2** a nonalcoholic sweetened fruit drink; a fruit syrup

[1]**cordon** /'kɔːdən/ *n* **1a** *sing or pl in constr* a line of troops, police, etc enclosing an area **b** a line or ring of people or objects **2** a plant, esp a fruit-tree, trained to a single stem by pruning off all side shoots

[2]**cordon** *v* to form a protective or restrictive cordon round – often + *off*

cordon bleu /,kɔːdɒŋ 'blɜː/ *adj or n* (typical of or being) sby with great skill or distinction in (classical French) cookery

corduroy /'kɔːdərɔɪ/ *n* a durable usu cotton pile fabric with lengthways ribs

[1]**core** /kɔː^r/ *n* **1** a central or interior part, usu distinct from an enveloping part: e g **a** the usu inedible central part of an apple, pineapple, etc **b** the portion of a foundry mould that shapes the interior of a hollow casting **c** a cylindrical portion removed from a mass for inspection; *specif* such a portion of rock got by boring **d** a piece of ferromagnetic material (e g iron) serving to concentrate and intensify the magnetic field resulting from a current in a surrounding coil **e** the central part of a planet, esp the earth **f** a subject which is central in a course of studies **2** the essential, basic, or central part (e g of an individual, class, or entity)

[2]**core** *v* to remove a core from

co-respondent /,kəʊ rʒ'spɒndənt/ *n* a person claimed to have committed adultery with the respondent in a divorce case

corgi /'kɔːgi/ *n, pl* **corgis** (any of) either of 2 varieties of short-legged long-backed dogs with fox-like heads, orig developed in Wales

coriander /ˌkɒriˈændəʳ/ *n* (the aromatic ripened dried fruits used for flavouring of) an Old World plant of the carrot family

Corinthian /kəˈrɪnθɪən/ *adj* **1** (characteristic) of (inhabitants of) Corinth **2** of the lightest and most ornate of the 3 Greek orders of architecture characterized esp by a bell-shaped capital decorated with acanthus leaves

[1]**cork** /kɔːk/ *n* **1a** the elastic tough outer tissue of the cork oak used esp for stoppers and insulation **b** a layer of similar tissue in other plants **2** a usu cork stopper, esp for a bottle **3** an angling float

[2]**cork** *v* to fit or close with a cork

[1]**corkscrew** /ˈkɔːkskruː/ *n* an implement for removing corks from bottles, typically consisting of a pointed spiral piece of metal attached to a handle

[2]**corkscrew** *v* **1** to twist into a spiral **2** to move in a winding course

[3]**corkscrew** *adj* spiral

corm /kɔːm/ *n* a rounded thick underground plant stem base with buds and scaly leaves

cormorant /ˈkɔːmərənt/ *n* a common dark-coloured web-footed European seabird with a long neck, hooked bill, and white throat and cheeks; *also* any of several related seabirds

[1]**corn** /kɔːn/ *n* **1** a small hard seed **2** (the seeds of) the important cereal crop of a particular region (e g wheat and barley in Britain) **3** sweet corn, maize **4** sthg corny – infml

[2]**corn** *v* to preserve or season with salt or brine

[3]**corn** *n* a local hardening and thickening of skin (e g on the top of a toe)

corncob /ˈkɔːnkɒb/ *n* **1** the axis on which the edible kernels of sweet corn are arranged **2** an ear of sweet corn

cornea /ˈkɔːnɪə/ *n* the hard transparent part of the coat of the eyeball that covers the iris and pupil – ~l *adj*

cornelian /kɔːˈniːlɪən/ *n* a hard reddish gem stone

[1]**corner** /ˈkɔːnəʳ/ *n* **1a** the point where converging lines, edges, or sides meet; an angle **b** the place of intersection of 2 streets or roads **c** a piece designed to form, mark, or protect a corner (e g of a book) **2** the angular space between meeting lines, edges, or borders: e g **a** the area of a playing field or court near the intersection of the sideline and the goal line or baseline **b** any of the 4 angles of a boxing ring; *esp* that in which a boxer rests between rounds **3** *sing or pl in constr* a contestant's group of supporters, adherents, etc **4** a corner kick; *also* a corner hit **5a** a private, secret, or remote place **b** a difficult or embarrassing situation; a position from which escape or retreat is difficult **6** control or ownership of enough of the available supply of a commodity or security to permit manipulation of esp the price **7** a point at which significant change occurs – often in *turn a corner*

[2]**corner** *v* **1a** to drive into a corner **b** to catch and hold the attention of, esp so as to force into conversation **2** to get a corner on **3** to turn a corner

cornerstone /ˈkɔːnəstəʊn/ *n* **1** a block of stone forming a part of a corner or angle in a wall; *specif* a foundation stone **2** the most basic element; a foundation

cornet /ˈkɔːnɨt/ *n* **1** a valved brass instrument resembling a trumpet but with a shorter tube and less brilliant tone **2** sthg shaped like a cone: e g **a** a piece of paper twisted for use as a container **b** an ice cream cone

cornflakes /ˈkɔːnfleɪks/ *n pl* toasted flakes of maize eaten as a breakfast cereal

cornflour /ˈkɔːnflaʊəʳ/ *n* a finely ground flour made from maize, rice, etc and used esp as a thickening agent in cooking

cornflower /ˈkɔːnflaʊəʳ/ *n* a usu bright-blue-flowered European composite (garden) plant

cornice /ˈkɔːnɨs/ *n* **1a** the ornamental projecting piece that forms the top edge of a building, pillar, etc **b** an ornamental plaster moulding between wall and ceiling **2** a decorative band of metal or wood used to conceal curtain fixtures **3** an overhanging mass of snow, ice, etc on a mountain

[1]**Cornish** /ˈkɔːnɪʃ/ *adj* (characteristic) of Cornwall

[2]**Cornish** *n* the ancient Celtic language of Cornwall

cornucopia /ˌkɔːnjʊˈkəʊpɪə/ *n* **1** a goat's horn overflowing with fruit and corn used to symbolize abundance **2** an inexhaustible store; an abundance **3** a vessel shaped like a horn or cone

corny /'kɔːni/ *adj* **1** tiresomely simple and sentimental; trite **2** hackneyed – infml

corolla /kə'rɒlə/ *n* the petals of a flower constituting the inner floral envelope

corollary /kə'rɒləri/ *n* **1** a direct conclusion from a proved proposition **2** sthg that naturally follows or accompanies

corona /kə'rəʊnə/ *n* **1a** a usu coloured circle of usu diffracted light seen round and close to a luminous celestial body (e g the sun or moon) **b** the tenuous outermost part of the atmosphere of the sun and other stars appearing as a halo round the moon's black disc during a total eclipse of the sun **2** a long straight-sided cigar with a roundly blunt sealed mouth end

[1]**coronary** /'kɒrənəri/ *adj* (of or being the arteries or veins) of the heart

[2]**coronary** *n* coronary thrombosis

coronary thrombosis *n* the blocking of a coronary artery of the heart by a blood clot, usu causing death of heart muscle tissue

coronation /,kɒrə'neɪʃən/ *n* the act or ceremony of investing a sovereign or his/her consort with the royal crown

coroner /'kɒrənəʳ/ *n* a public officer whose principal duty is to inquire into the cause of any death which there is reason to suppose might not be due to natural causes

coronet /'kɒrənɟt/ *n* **1** a small crown **2** an ornamental wreath or band for the head

[1]**corporal** /'kɔːpərəl/ *adj* of or affecting the body

[2]**corporal** *n* a low-ranking non-commissioned officer in the army or British air force

corporate /'kɔːpərɟt/ *adj* **1a** incorporated **b** of a company **2** of or formed into a unified body of individuals – **~ly** *adv*

corporation /,kɔːpə'reɪʃən/ *n* **1** *sing or pl in constr* the municipal authorities of a town or city **2** a body made up of more than 1 person which is formed and authorized by law to act as a single person with its own legal identity, rights, and duties **3** an association of employers and employees or of members of a profession in a corporate state **4** a potbelly – humor

corps /kɔːʳ/ *n, pl* **corps** **1** *sing or pl in constr* an army unit usu consisting of 2 or more divisions (organized for a particular purpose) **2** any of various associations of people united for some common purpose

corps de ballet /,kɔː də 'bæleɪ/ *n, pl* **corps de ballet** the ensemble of a ballet company

corpse /kɔːps/ *n* a dead (human) body

corpuscle /'kɔːpəsəl, kɔː'pʌ-/ *n* **1** a minute particle **2** a living (blood) cell

[1]**corral** /kɒ'rɑːl, kə-/ *n* **1** a pen or enclosure for confining livestock **2** an enclosure made with wagons for defence of an encampment

[2]**corral** *v* **1** to enclose in a corral **2** to arrange (wagons) so as to form a corral

[1]**correct** /kə'rekt/ *v* **1** to alter or adjust so as to counteract some imperfection or failing **2a** to punish (e g a child) with a view to reforming or improving **b** to point out the faults of – **~ion** *n* – **~ive** *adj, n*

[2]**correct** *adj* **1** conforming to an approved or conventional standard **2** true, right – **~ly** *adv* – **~ness** *n*

correlate /'kɒrɟleɪt/ *v* to have a mutual or reciprocal relationship; correspond – **-ation** *n* – **-ative** *adj*

correspond /,kɒrɟ'spɒnd/ *v* **1a** to be in conformity or agreement; suit, match – usu + *to* or *with* **b** to be equivalent or parallel **2** to communicate *with* a person by exchange of letters – **~ence** *n*

[1]**correspondent** /,kɒrɟ'spɒndənt/ *adj* **1** corresponding **2** fitting, conforming *USE* + *with* or *to*

[2]**correspondent** *n* **1** one who communicates with another by letter **2** one who has regular commercial relations with another **3** one who contributes news or comment to a publication or radio or television network

corresponding /,kɒrɟ'spɒndɪŋ/ *adj*

1a agreeing in some respect (e g kind, degree, position, or function) **b** related, accompanying **2** participating at a distance and by post – ~**ly** *adv*

corridor /'kɒrɨdɔːʳ/ *n,* **1** a passage (e g in a hotel or railway carriage) onto which compartments or rooms open **2** a usu narrow passageway or route: e g **a** a narrow strip of land through foreign-held territory **3** a strip of land that by geographical characteristics is distinct from its surroundings

corrie /'kɒri/ *n, chiefly Scot* a steep-sided bowl-like valley in the side of a mountain; a cwm, cirque

corrigendum /,kɒrɨ'dʒendəm/ *n, pl* **corrigenda** an error in a printed work, shown with its correction on a separate sheet

corroborate /kə'rɒbəreɪt/ *v* to support with evidence or authority; make more certain – **-rator** *n* – **-rative** *adj* – **-ration** *n*

corrode /kə'rəʊd/ *v* **1** to eat or wear (esp metal) away gradually, esp by chemical action **2** to weaken or destroy (as if) by corrosion **3** to undergo corroding – **-rosion** *n* – **-rosive** *adj* – **-rosively** *adv*

corrugate /'kɒrəgeɪt/ *v* to shape or become shaped into alternating ridges and grooves; furrow – **-tion** *n*

[1]**corrupt** /kə'rʌpt/ *v* **1a** to change from good to bad in morals, manners, or actions; *also* to influence by bribery **b** to degrade with unsound principles or moral values **2** to alter from the original or correct form or version **3** to become corrupt – ~**ible** *adj* – ~**ibility** *n*

[2]**corrupt** *adj* **1a** morally degenerate and perverted **b** characterized by bribery **2** having been vitiated by mistakes or changes – ~**ly** *adv* – ~**ness** *n*

corruption /kə'rʌpʃən/ *n* **1** impairment of integrity, virtue, or moral principle **2** decay, decomposition **3** inducement by bribery to do wrong **4** a departure from what is pure or correct

corsair /'kɔːseəʳ/ *n* a pirate; *esp* a privateer of the Barbary coast

[1]**corset** /'kɔːsɨt/ *n* a boned supporting undergarment for women, extending from beneath the bust to below the hips, and designed to give shape to the figure; *also* a similar garment worn by men and women, esp in cases of injury

[2]**corset** *v* to restrict closely

cortege, cortège /kɔː'teɪʒ/ *n* a funeral procession

cortex /'kɔːteks/ *n, pl* **cortices, cortexes** **1** the outer part of the kidney, adrenal gland, a hair, etc; *esp* the outer layer of grey matter of the brain **2** the layer of tissue between the inner vascular tissue and the outer epidermal tissue of a green plant

coruscate /'kɒrəskeɪt/ *v* to sparkle, flash

corvette /kɔː'vet/ *n* **1** a small sailing warship with a flush deck **2** a small highly manoeuvrable armed escort ship

[1]**cos** /kəz/ *conj* because – used in writing to represent a casual or childish pronunciation

[2]**cos** /kɒz/, **cos lettuce** *n* a long-leaved variety of lettuce

cosh /kɒʃ/ *v or n, chiefly Br* (to strike with) a short heavy rod often enclosed in a softer material and used as a hand weapon

cosine /'kəʊsaɪn/ *n* the trigonometric function that for an acute angle in a right-angled triangle is the ratio between the side adjacent to the angle and the hypotenuse

[1]**cosmetic** /kɒz'metɪk/ *n* a cosmetic preparation for external use

[2]**cosmetic** *adj* of or intended to improve beauty (e g of the hair or complexion); *broadly* intended to improve the outward appearance – ~**ian** *n*

cosmic /'kɒzmɪk/ *also* **cosmical** *adj* **1** of the universe in contrast to the earth alone **2** great in extent, intensity, or comprehensiveness – ~**ally** *adv*

cosmic ray *n* a stream of highly energetic radiation reaching the earth's atmosphere from space – usu pl with sing. meaning

cosmology /kɒz'mɒlədʒi/ *n* **1** a theoretical account of the nature of the universe **2** astronomy dealing with the origin, structure, and space-time relationships of the universe

cosmonaut /'kɒzmənɔːt/ *n* a usu Soviet astronaut

[1]**cosmopolitan** /ˌkɒzmə'pɒlɪtn/ *adj* **1** having worldwide rather than provincial scope or bearing **2** marked by a sophistication that comes from wide and often international experience **3** composed of people, constituents, or elements from many parts of the world

[2]**cosmopolitan** *n* a cosmopolitan person

cosmos /'kɒzmɒs/ *n* **1** an orderly universe **2** a complex and orderly system that is complete in itself **3** any of a genus of tropical American composite plants grown for their yellow or red flower heads

cosset /'kɒsɪt/ *v* to treat as a pet; pamper

[1]**cost** /kɒst/ *n* **1a** the price paid or charged for sthg **b** the expenditure (e g of effort or sacrifice) made to achieve an object **2** the loss or penalty incurred in gaining sthg **3** *pl* expenses incurred in litigation

[2]**cost** *v* **1** to require a specified expenditure **2** to require the specified effort, suffering, or loss **3** to cause to pay, suffer, or lose **4** to estimate or set the cost of

co-star /'kəʊ stɑːʳ/ *n* a star who has equal billing with another leading performer in a film or play – **co-star** *v*

costermonger /'kɒstəmʌŋgəʳ/ *n, Br* a seller of articles, esp fruit or vegetables, from a street barrow or stall

costly /'kɒstli/ *adj* **1** valuable, expensive **2** made at great expense or with considerable sacrifice – **-liness** *n*

[1]**costume** /'kɒstjʊm/ *n* **1** a distinctive fashion in coiffure, jewellery, and apparel of a period, country, class, or group **2** a set of garments suitable for a specified occasion, activity, or season **3** a set of garments belonging to a specific time, place, or character, worn in order to assume a particular role (e g in a play or at a fancy-dress party)

[2]**costume** *v* **1** to provide with a costume **2** to design costumes for

[3]**costume** *adj* characterized by the use of costumes

[1]**cosy** /'kəʊzi/ *adj* **1** enjoying or affording warmth and ease; snug **2a** marked by the intimacy of the family or a close group **b** self-satisfied, complacent – **cosily** *adv* – **cosiness** *n*

[2]**cosy** *n* a covering, esp for a teapot, designed to keep the contents hot

[1]**cot** /kɒt/ *n* a small house; a cottage – poetic

[2]**cot** *n* **1** a lightweight bedstead **2** a small bed with high enclosing sides, esp for a child

cotangent /kəʊ'tændʒənt/ *n* the trigonometric function that is the reciprocal of the tangent

cottage /'kɒtɪdʒ/ *n* a small house, esp in the country

cottage cheese *n* a soft white bland cheese made from the curds of skimmed milk

cottage pie *n* a shepherd's pie esp made with minced beef

[1]**cotton** /'kɒtn/ *n* **1** (a plant producing or grown for) a soft usu white fibrous substance composed of the hairs surrounding the seeds of various tropical plants of the mallow family **2a** fabric made of cotton **b** yarn spun from cotton

[2]**cotton** *v* to come to understand; catch on – usu + *on* or *onto*; infml

cotton wool *n* raw cotton; *esp* cotton pressed into sheets used esp for lining, cleaning, or as a surgical dressing

cotyledon /ˌkɒtɪ'liːdn/ *n* the first leaf or either of the first pair or whorl of leaves developed by the embryo of a seed plant

[1]**couch** /kaʊtʃ/ *v* **1** to phrase in a specified manner **2** *of an animal* to lie down to sleep; *also* to lie in ambush

[2]**couch** *n* **1** a piece of furniture for sitting or lying on **a** with a back and usu armrests **b** with a low back and raised head-end **2** a long upholstered seat with a headrest for patients to lie on during medical examination or psychoanalysis **3** the den of an animal (e g an otter)

couchette /kuː'ʃet/ *n* a seat in a railway-carriage compartment that converts into a bunk

couch grass /'kuːtʃ ˌgrɑːs, kaʊtʃ/ *n* any of several grasses that spread rapidly by long creeping underground stems and are difficult to eradicate

cougar /'kuːgəʳ/ *n, chiefly NAm* a puma

cough /kɒf/ *v* **1** to expel air from the lungs suddenly with an explosive noise **2** to make a noise like that of coughing – **cough** *n*

cough up *v* to produce or hand over (esp money or information) unwillingly

could /kəd; *strong* kʊd/ *verbal auxiliary* **1** *past of* **can** – used in the past, in the past conditional, as an alternative to *can* suggesting less force or certainty, as a polite form in the present, as an alternative to *might* expressing purpose in the past, and as an alternative to *ought* or *should* **2** feel impelled to

[1]**council** /'kaʊnsəl/ *n sing or pl in constr* an elected or appointed body with administrative, legislative, or advisory powers; *esp* a locally-elected body having power over a parish, district, county, etc

[2]**council** *adj, Br* provided, maintained, or operated by local government

councillor, *NAm also* **councilor** /'kaʊnsələʳ/ *n* a member of a council – ~**ship** *n*

[1]**counsel** /'kaʊnsəl/ *n* **1** advice; consultation **2** thoughts or intentions – chiefly in *keep one's own counsel* **3a** a barrister engaged in the trial of a case in court **b** a lawyer appointed to advise a client

[2]**counsel** *v* to advise

counsellor /'kaʊnsələʳ/ *n* **1** an adviser **2** *NAm* a lawyer; *specif* a counsel

[1]**count** /kaʊnt/ *v* **1a** to reckon by units so as to find the total number of units involved – often + *up* **b** to name the numbers in order **c** to include in a tallying and reckoning **2** to include or exclude (as if) by counting **3** to rely *on* or *upon* sby or sthg **4** to have value or significance – ~**able** *adj*

[2]**count** *n* **1** a total obtained by counting **2a** an allegation in an indictment **b** a specific point under consideration; an issue **3** the total number of individual things in a given unit or sample **4** the calling out of the seconds from 1 to 10 when a boxer has been knocked down during which he must rise or be defeated

[3]**count** *n* a European nobleman corresponding in rank to a British earl

countdown /'kaʊntdaʊn/ *n* a continuous counting backwards to zero of the time remaining before an event, esp the launching of a space vehicle

[1]**countenance** /'kaʊntɪ̬nəns/ *n* **1** composure **2** a face; *esp* the face as an indication of mood, emotion, or character

[2]**countenance** *v* to extend approval or support to – fml

[1]**counter** /'kaʊntəʳ/ *n* **1** a small disc of metal, plastic, etc used in counting or in games **2** sthg of value in bargaining; an asset **3** a level surface (e g a table) over which transactions are conducted or food is served or on which goods are displayed

[2]**counter** *v* **1** to nullify the effects of; offset **2** to meet attacks or arguments with defensive or retaliatory steps

[3]**counter** *adv* in an opposite, contrary, or wrong direction

[4]**counter** *n* **1** the contrary, opposite **2** an overhanging stern of a vessel **3a** the (blow resulting from the) making of an attack while parrying (e g in boxing or fencing) **b** an agency or force that offsets; a check

[5]**counter** *adj* **1** marked by or tending towards an opposite direction or effect **2** showing opposition, hostility, or antipathy

counteract /,kaʊntə'rækt/ *v* to lessen or neutralize the usu ill effects of by an opposing action – ~**ion** *n*

counterattack /'kaʊntərə'tæk/ *v* to make an attack (against) in reply to an enemy's attack – **counterattack** *n*

counterbalance /,kaʊntə'bæləns/ *v* to oppose or balance with an equal weight or force – **counterbalance** *n*

counterclockwise /,kaʊntə'klɒkwaɪz/ *adj or adv, chiefly NAm* anticlockwise

counterespionage /,kaʊntər'espɪənɑːʒ, -nɪdʒ/ *n* espionage directed towards detecting and thwarting enemy espionage

[1]**counterfeit** /'kaʊntəfɪt/ *v* to imitate or copy (sthg) closely, esp with intent to deceive or defraud – ~**er** *n*

[2]**counterfeit** *adj* **1** made in imitation

of sthg else with intent to deceive or defraud **2** insincere, feigned

[3]**counterfeit** *n* a forgery

counterfoil /'kaʊntəfɔɪl/ *n* a detachable part of a cheque, ticket, etc usu kept as a record or receipt

counterintelligence /ˌkaʊntərɪn'telɪ̣dʒəns/ *n* organized activity of an intelligence service designed to block an enemy's sources of information

countermand /ˌkaʊntə'mɑːnd, '---/ *v* **1** to revoke (a command) by a contrary order **2** to order back (e g troops) by a superseding contrary order

countermeasure /'kaʊntəmeʒə^r/ *n* a measure designed to counter another action or state of affairs

counteroffensive /ˌkaʊntərə'fensɪv/ *n* a military offensive undertaken from a previously defensive position

counterpane /'kaʊntəpeɪn/ *n* a bedspread

counterpart /'kaʊntəpɑːt/ *n* **1** sthg that completes; a complement **2** one having the same function or characteristics as another; an equivalent, duplicate

[1]**counterpoint** /'kaʊntəpɔɪnt/ *n* **1a** one or more independent melodies added above or below a given melody **b** the combination of 2 or more independent melodies into a single harmonic texture **2** (use of) contrast or interplay of elements in a work of art

[2]**counterpoint** *v* to set off or emphasize by contrast or juxtaposition

counterrevolution /ˌkaʊntərevə'luːʃən/ *n* a revolution directed towards overthrowing the system established by a previous revolution – **~ary** *n, adj*

[1]**countersign** /'kaʊntəsaɪn/ *n* a password or secret signal given by one wishing to pass a guard

[2]**countersign** *v* to add one's signature to (a document) as a witness of another signature

countersink /'kaʊntəsɪŋk/ *v* **countersunk** to set the head of (e g a screw) below or level with the surface

countertenor /'kaʊntətenə^r/ *n* (a person with) an adult male singing voice higher than tenor

countess /'kaʊntɪ̣s/ *n* **1** the wife or widow of an earl or count **2** a woman having in her own right the rank of an earl or count

countinghouse /'kaʊntɪŋhaʊs/ *n* a building, room, or office used for keeping account books and transacting business

countless /'kaʊntlɪ̣s/ *adj* too numerous to be counted; innumerable

countrified *also* **countryfied** /'kʌntrifaɪd/ *adj* **1** rural, rustic **2** unsophisticated

country /'kʌntri/ *n* **1** an indefinite usu extended expanse of land; a region **2a** the land of a person's birth, residence, or citizenship **b** a political state or nation or its territory **3** *sing or pl in constr* **a** *the* populace **b** *the* electorate **4** rural as opposed to urban areas

country dance *n* any of various native or folk dances for several pairs of dancers typically arranged in square or circular figures or in 2 long rows facing a partner

countryman /'kʌntrimən/ *n* **1** a compatriot **2** one living in the country or having country ways

country music *n* music derived from or imitating the folk style of the southern USA or the Western cowboy

country seat *n* a mansion or estate in the country that is the hereditary property of 1 family

countryside /'kʌntrisaɪd/ *n* a rural area

[1]**county** /'kaʊnti/ *n* any of the territorial divisions of Britain and Ireland constituting the chief units for administrative, judicial, and political purposes; *also* a local government unit in various countries (e g the USA)

[2]**county** *adj* characteristic of or belonging to the English landed gentry

county borough *n* a borough which until 1974 had the local-government powers of a county

county court *n, often cap 1st C* a local civil court in England which is presided over by a judge and deals with relatively minor claims

coup /kuː/ *n* **1** a brilliant, sudden, and usu highly successful stroke or act **2 coup, coup d'état** an overthrowing of a government, esp by a small group

coupe /kuːp/ *n* (a cold dessert of fruit

and ice cream served in) a small goblet-shaped dish

coupé /ˈkuːpeɪ/ , **coupe** /kuːp/ *n* **1** a 4-wheeled horse-drawn carriage for 2 passengers with an outside seat for the driver **2** a closed 2-door motor car for usu 2 people

¹couple /ˈkʌpəl/ *v* **1** to unite or link **2** to fasten together; connect **3** to copulate

²couple *n* **1** *sing or pl in constr* 2 people paired together; *esp* a married or engaged couple **2a** 2 things considered together; a pair **b** an indefinite small number; a few – infml **3** 2 equal and opposite forces that act along parallel lines and cause rotation

³couple *adj* two

couplet /ˈkʌplɪ̈t/ *n* a unit of 2 successive, usu rhyming, lines of verse

coupling /ˈkʌplɪŋ/ *n* a device that serves to connect the ends of adjacent parts or objects

coupon /ˈkuːpɒn/ *n* **1** a detachable ticket or certificate that entitles the holder to sthg **2** a voucher given with a purchase that can be exchanged for goods **3** a part of a printed advertisement to be cut off for use as an order form or enquiry form **4** a printed entry form for a competition, esp the football pools

courage /ˈkʌrɪdʒ/ *n* mental or moral strength to confront danger, fear, etc; bravery – **-ageous** *adj* – **-ageously** *adv*

courgette /kʊəˈʒet/ *n* (the plant that bears) a variety of small vegetable marrow cooked and eaten as a vegetable

courier /ˈkʊrɪəʳ/ *n* **1a** a member of a diplomatic service who carries state or embassy papers **b** one who carries secret information, contraband, etc **2** a tourist guide employed by a travel agency

¹course /kɔːs/ *n* **1** the moving in a path from point to point **2** the path over which sthg moves: e g **a** a racecourse **b** the direction of travel, usu measured as a clockwise angle from north **c** a golf course **3a** usual procedure or normal action **b** progression through a series of acts or events or a development or period **4a** a series of educational activities relating to a subject, esp when constituting a curriculum **b** a particular medical treatment administered over a designated period **5** a part of a meal served at one time **6** a continuous horizontal layer of brick or masonry throughout a wall

²course *v* **1** to hunt or pursue (e g hares) with dogs that follow by sight **2** *of a liquid* to run or pass rapidly (as if) along an indicated path

¹court /kɔːt/ *n* **1a** the residence or establishment of a dignitary, esp a sovereign **b** *sing or pl in constr* the sovereign and his officers and advisers who are the governing power **c** a reception held by a sovereign **2a** a manor house or large building (e g a block of flats) surrounded by usu enclosed grounds – archaic except in proper names **b** a space enclosed wholly or partly by a building **c** (a division of) a rectangular space walled or marked off for playing lawn tennis, squash, basketball, etc **d** a yard surrounded by houses, with only 1 opening onto a street **3a** (a session of) an official assembly for the transaction of judicial business **b** *sing or pl in constr* judicial officers in session

²court *v* **1** to act so as to invite or provoke **2a** to seek the affections of; woo **b** *of a man and woman* to be involved in a relationship that may lead to marriage **c** *of an animal* to perform actions to attract (a mate) **3** to seek to win the favour of

courteous /ˈkɜːtɪəs/ *adj* showing respect and consideration for others – **~ly** *adv* – **~ness** *n*

courtesan /ˌkɔːtɪ̈ˈzæn/ *n* a prostitute with a courtly, wealthy, or upper-class clientele

¹courtesy /ˈkɜːtɪ̈si/ *n* courteous behaviour; a courteous act

²courtesy *adj* granted, provided, or performed by way of courtesy

courtier /ˈkɔːtɪəʳ/ *n* one in attendance at a royal court

courtly /ˈkɔːtli/ *adj* of a quality befitting the court; elegant, refined – **-liness** *n*

¹court-martial *n* (a trial by) a court of commissioned officers that tries members of the armed forces

[2]**court-martial** *v* to try by court-martial

courtship /kɔːt-ʃɪp/ *n* the act, process, or period of courting

courtyard /'kɔːtjɑːd/ *n* an open court or enclosure adjacent to a building

cousin /'kʌzən/ *n* **1** a child of one's uncle or aunt **2** a relative descended from one's grandparent or more remote ancestor in a different line

couture /kuː'tjʊəʳ/ *n* the business of designing and making fashionable women's clothing; *also* the designers and establishments engaged in this business – **couturier** *n*

[1]**cove** /kəʊv/ *n* **1** a small sheltered area; *esp* an inlet or bay **2** a concave moulding, esp at the point where a wall meets a ceiling or floor

[2]**cove** *n, Br* a man, fellow – slang; no longer in vogue

coven /'kʌvən/ *n sing or pl in constr* an assembly or band of witches

covenant /'kʌvənənt/ *n* **1** a solemn agreement **2** a written promise

Coventry /'kʌvəntri, 'kɒv-/ *n* a state of social exclusion – chiefly in *send to Coventry*

[1]**cover** /'kʌvəʳ/ *v* **1a** to guard from attack **b** to have within the range of one's guns **c** to insure **d** to make sufficient provision for (a demand or charge) by means of a reserve or deposit **2a** to hide from sight or knowledge; conceal – usu + *up* **b** to lie or spread over; envelop **3** to lay or spread sthg over **4** to extend thickly or conspicuously over the surface of **5** to include, consider, or take in **6a** to have as one's territory or field of activity **b** to report news about **7** to pass over; traverse **8** to conceal sthg illicit, blameworthy, or embarrassing from notice – usu + *up* **9** to act as a substitute or replacement during an absence – chiefly in *cover for someone*

[2]**cover** *n* **1a** natural shelter for an animal **b(1)** a position affording shelter from attack **(2)** (the protection offered by) a force supporting a military operation **2** sthg that is placed over or about another thing e g **a** a lid, top **b** (the front or back part of) a binding or jacket of a book **c** a cloth (e g a blanket) used on a bed **d** sthg (e g vegetation or snow) that covers the ground **e** the extent to which clouds obscure the sky **3a** sthg that conceals or obscures **b** a masking device; a pretext **4** an envelope or wrapper for postal use **5a** cover-point, extra cover, or a cricket fielding position between them **b** *pl the* fielding positions in cricket that lie between point and mid-off

coverage /'kʌvərɪdʒ/ *n* **1** the act or fact of covering **2** inclusion within the scope of discussion or reporting **3** the total range of risks covered by the terms of an insurance contract

cover charge *n* a charge (e g for service) made by a restaurant or nightclub in addition to the charge for food and drink

[1]**covering** /'kʌvərɪŋ/ *n* sthg that covers or conceals

[2]**covering** *adj* containing an explanation of an accompanying item

coverlet /'kʌvəl͡ɪt/ *n* a bedspread

cover note *n, Br* a provisional insurance document providing cover between acceptance of a risk and issue of a full policy

cover-point *n* a fielding position in cricket further from the batsman than point and situated between mid-off and point

[1]**covert** /'kʌvət/ *adj* not openly shown; secret – **~ly** *adv*

[2]**covert** *n* **1** a hiding place; a shelter **2** a thicket affording cover for game

covet /'kʌv͡ɪt/ *v* to desire what belongs to another

covetous /'kʌv͡ɪtəs/ *adj* showing an inordinate desire for esp another's wealth or possessions – **~ly** *adv* – **~ness** *n*

[1]**cow** /kaʊ/ *n* **1** the mature female of cattle or of any animal the male of which is called *bull* **2** a domestic bovine animal regardless of sex or age **3** a woman; *esp* one who is unpleasant

[2]**cow** *v* to intimidate with threats or a show of strength

coward /'kaʊəd/ *n* one who lacks courage or resolve – **~ly** *adj* – **~ice** *n* – **~liness** *n*

cowbell /'kəʊbel/ *n* a bell hung round the neck of a cow

cowboy /'kaʊbɔɪ/ *n* **1** a cattle ranch

hand in N America **2** one who employs irregular or unscrupulous methods, esp in business

cower /'kaʊəʳ/ *v* to crouch down or shrink away (e g in fear) from sthg menacing

cowhand /'kaʊhænd/ *n* a cowherd or cowboy

cowl /kaʊl/ *n* **1a** a hood or long hooded cloak, esp of a monk **b** a draped neckline on a garment resembling a folded-down hood **2** a chimney covering designed to improve ventilation

cowling /'kaʊlɪŋ/ *n* a removable metal covering over an engine, esp in an aircraft

cowpat /'kaʊpæt/ *n* a small heap of cow dung

cowpox /'kaʊpɒks/ *n* a mild disease of the cow that when communicated to humans gives protection against smallpox

cowrie, cowry /'kaʊri/ a rounded often glossy and brightly coloured sea shell with a long thin opening, formerly used as money in parts of Africa and Asia

cowslip /'kaʊ,slɪp/ *n* a common European plant of the primrose family with fragrant yellow or purplish flowers

cox /kɒks/ *v* to steer esp a rowing boat – **cox** *n*

coxcomb /'kɒkskəʊm/ *n* a conceited foolish person; a fop

coy /kɔɪ/ *adj* **1a** (affectedly) shy **b** provocatively playful or coquettish **2** showing reluctance to make a definite commitment or face unpleasant facts – **~ly** *adv* – **~ness** *n*

coyote /'kɔɪəʊt, kɔɪ'əʊti/ *n* a small N American wolf

coypu /'kɔɪpuː/ *n* a S American aquatic rodent with webbed feet now commonly found in E Anglia

[1]**crab** /kræb/ *n* **1** any of numerous chiefly marine crustaceans usu with the front pair of limbs modified as grasping pincers and a short broad flattened carapace; *also* the flesh of this cooked and eaten as food **2** *pl* infestation with crab lice

[2]**crab** *v* to cause to move sideways or in an indirect or diagonal manner

[3]**crab** *v* **1** to make sullen; sour **2** to carp, grouse

[4]**crab** *n* an ill-tempered person – infml

crab apple *n* (a tree that bears) a small usu wild sour apple

crabbed /'kræbɪ̣d/ *adj* **1** morose, peevish **2** difficult to read or understand – **~ly** *adv* – **~ness** *n*

crabwise /'kræbwaɪz/ *adv* **1** sideways **2** in a sidling or cautiously indirect manner

[1]**crack** /kræk/ *v* **1** to make a sudden sharp explosive noise **2** to break or split (apart) esp so that fissures appear **3** to lose control or effectiveness under pressure – often + *up* **4a** *esp of hydrocarbons* to break up into simpler chemical compounds when heated, usu with a catalyst **b** to produce (e g petrol) by cracking **5** to tell (a joke) **6a** to puzzle out and expose, solve, or reveal the mystery of **b** to break into **7** to open (e g a can or bottle) for drinking – infml

[2]**crack** *n* **1** a sudden sharp loud noise **2** a narrow break or opening; a chink, fissure **3** a sharp resounding blow **4** a witty remark; a quip – infml **5** an attempt, try *at* – infml

[3]**crack** *adj* of superior quality or ability

crack down *v* to take regulatory or disciplinary action – usu + *on*

cracked /krækt/ *adj* **1** marked by harshness, dissonance, or failure to sustain a tone **2** mentally disordered; crazy – infml

cracker /'krækəʳ/ *n* **1** a brightly coloured paper and cardboard tube that makes an explosive crack when pulled sharply apart and usu contains a toy, paper hat, or other party item **2** *pl* a tool for cracking nuts **3** a thin often savoury biscuit **4** *Br* an outstandingly attractive girl or woman – infml

crackers /'krækəz/ *adj, chiefly Br* mad, crazy – infml

[1]**crackle** /'krækəl/ *v* to crush or crack with a snapping sound

[2]**crackle** *n* **1** the noise of repeated small cracks or reports **2** a network of fine cracks on an otherwise smooth surface

crackling /'kræklɪŋ/ *n* the crisp skin of roast meat, esp pork

crackpot /ˈkrækpɒt/ *n* sby with eccentric ideas; a crank – infml

¹cradle /ˈkreɪdl/ *n* **1a** a baby's bed or cot, usu on rockers **b** a framework of wood or metal used as a support, scaffold, etc **2a** the earliest period of life; infancy **b** a place of origin

²cradle *v* **1** to place or keep (as if) in a cradle **2** to shelter or hold protectively

¹craft /krɑːft/ *n* **1** skill in planning, making, or executing; dexterity – often in combination **2** an activity or trade requiring manual dexterity or artistic skill; *broadly* a trade, profession **3** skill in deceiving to gain an end **4a** a (small) boat **b** an aircraft **c** a spacecraft

²craft *v* to make (as if) using skill and dexterity

craftsman /ˈkrɑːftsmən/ *n* **1** a workman who practises a skilled trade or handicraft **2** one who displays a high degree of manual dexterity or artistic skill – **~ship** *n*

crafty /ˈkrɑːfti/ *adj* showing subtlety and guile – **craftily** *adv* – **craftiness** *n*

crag /kræg/ *n* a steep rugged rock or cliff

craggy /ˈkrægi/ *adj* rough, rugged

cram /kræm/ *v* **1** to pack tight; jam **2** to thrust forcefully **3** to study hastily and intensively for an examination **4** to eat greedily or until uncomfortably full – infml

¹cramp /kræmp/ *n* **1** a painful involuntary spasmodic contraction of a muscle **2** *pl* severe abdominal pain

²cramp *n* **1** a usu metal device bent at the ends and used to hold timbers or blocks of stone together **2** a clamp

³cramp *v* **1a** to confine, restrain **b** to restrain from free expression – esp in *cramp someone's style* **2** to fasten or hold with a clamp

crampon /ˈkræmpən/ *n* a metal frame with downward- and forward-pointing spikes that is fixed to the sole of a boot for climbing slopes of ice or hard snow

cranberry /ˈkrænbəri/ *n* any of various plants of the heath family; *also* the red acid berry of such plants used in making sauces and jellies

¹crane /kreɪn/ *n* **1** any of a family of tall wading birds **2** a machine for moving heavy weights by means of a projecting swinging arm or a hoisting apparatus supported on an overhead track

²crane *v* to stretch one's neck, esp in order to see better

crane fly *n* any of numerous long-legged slender two-winged flies that resemble large mosquitoes but do not bite

cranium /ˈkreɪnɪəm/ *n, pl* **craniums, crania** the skull; *specif* the part that encloses the brain – **-ial** *adj* – **-ially** *adv*

¹crank /kræŋk/ *n* **1** a part of an axle or shaft bent at right angles by which reciprocating motion is changed into circular motion or vice versa **2** an eccentric person; *also* one who is excessively enthusiastic or fastidious about sthg

²crank *v* **1** to move or operate (as if) by a crank **2** to start by use of a crank – often + *up*

crankshaft /ˈkræŋkʃɑːft/ *n* a shaft driven by or driving a crank

cranky /ˈkræŋki/ *adj* **1** *of machinery* working erratically; unpredictable **2** eccentric, mad

cranny /ˈkræni/ *n* a small crack or slit; a chink – **-nied** *adj*

crap /kræp/ *n* **1a** excrement **b** an act of defecation **2** nonsense, rubbish – slang; sometimes used as an interjection *USE* (*1*) vulg

¹crash /kræʃ/ *v* **1a** to break violently and noisily; smash **b** to damage (an aircraft) in landing **c** to damage (a vehicle) by collision **2a** to make a crashing noise **b** to force one's way with loud crashing noises **3** to enter without invitation or payment – infml **4** to spend the night in a (makeshift) place; go to sleep – sometimes + *out*; slang **5** *esp of a computer system or program* to become (suddenly) completely inoperative

²crash *n* **1** a loud noise (e g of things smashing) **2** a breaking to pieces (as if) by collision; *also* an instance of crashing **3** a sudden decline or failure (e g of a business)

³crash *adj* designed to achieve an

intended result in the shortest possible time

crash helmet *n* a helmet that is worn (e g by motorcyclists) to protect the head in the event of an accident

crashing /ˈkræʃɪŋ/ *adj* utter, absolute

crass /kræs/ *adj* **1** insensitive, coarse **2** deplorably great; complete – **~ly** *adv* – **~ness** *n*

¹crate /kreɪt/ *n* a usu wooden framework or box for holding goods (e g fruit, bottles, etc), esp during transit

²crate *v* to pack in a crate

crater /ˈkreɪtəʳ/ *n* **1** a hole in the ground made (as if) by an explosion **2** a jar or vase with a wide mouth used in classical antiquity for mixing wine and water

cravat /krəˈvæt/ *n* a decorative band or scarf worn round the neck, esp by men

crave /kreɪv/ *v* **1** to have a strong or urgent desire for **2** to ask for earnestly; beg – fml – **-ving** *n*

craven /ˈkreɪvən/ *adj* completely lacking in courage; cowardly – **cravenness** *n* – **cravenly** *adv*

¹crawl /krɔːl/ *v* **1** to move slowly in a prone position (as if) without the use of limbs **2** to move or progress slowly or laboriously **3** to be alive or swarming (as if) with creeping things **4** to behave in a servile manner – infml

²crawl *n* **1a** crawling **b** slow or laborious motion **2** the fastest swimming stroke, executed lying on the front and consisting of alternating overarm strokes combined with kicks with the legs

crayfish /ˈkreɪˌfɪʃ/ *n* any of numerous usu freshwater crustaceans resembling the lobster but usu much smaller

crayon /ˈkreɪən, -ɒn/ *v or n* (to draw or colour with) a stick of coloured chalk or wax used for writing or drawing

¹craze /kreɪz/ *v* **1** to produce minute cracks on the surface or glaze of **2** to make (as if) insane

²craze *n* **1** an exaggerated and often short-lived enthusiasm; a fad **2** fine cracks in a surface or coating of glaze, enamel, etc

crazy /ˈkreɪzi/ *adj* **1** mad, insane **2** impractical, eccentric **3** extremely enthusiastic *about*; very fond – **-zily** *adv* – **-ziness** *n*

crazy paving *n, Br* a paved surface made up of irregularly shaped paving stones

creak /kriːk/ *v or n* (to make) a prolonged grating or squeaking noise

¹cream /kriːm/ *n* **1** the yellowish part of milk that forms a surface layer when milk is allowed to stand **2a** a food (e g a sauce or cake filling) prepared with or resembling cream in consistency, richness, etc **b** a biscuit, chocolate, etc filled with (a soft preparation resembling) whipped cream **c** sthg with the consistency of thick cream; *esp* a usu emulsified medicinal or cosmetic preparation **3** the choicest part **4** a pale yellowish white colour – **creamy** *adj* – **~iness** *n*

²cream *v* **1** to take away (the choicest part) – usu + *off* **2** to break into a creamy froth **3** to form a surface layer of or like cream **4** *NAm* to defeat completely

cream cheese *n* a mild white soft unripened cheese made from whole milk enriched with cream

cream of tartar *n* a white powder used esp in baking powder

¹crease /kriːs/ *n* **1** a line or mark made (as if) by folding a pliable substance **2a** an area surrounding the goal in lacrosse, hockey, etc into which an attacking player may not precede the ball or puck **b** the bowling crease, popping crease, or return crease of a cricket pitch

²crease *v* **1** to make a crease in or on; wrinkle **2** *chiefly Br* to cause much amusement to – often + *up*

create /kriˈeɪt/ *v* **1** to bring into existence **2a** to invest with a new form, office, or rank **b** to produce, cause **3** to design, invent **4** to make a loud fuss about sthg – infml – **-tively** *adv* – **-tiveness** *n* – **-tivity** *n*

creation /kriˈeɪʃən/ *n* **1** *often cap* the act of bringing the world into ordered existence **2** sthg created: e g **a** creatures singly or collectively **b** an original work of art **c** a product of some minor art or craft (e g dressmaking or cookery) showing unusual flair or imagination – often derog – **-tive** *adj*

creator /kri'eɪtəʳ/ *n* a person who creates, usu by bringing sthg new or original into being; *esp, cap* God

creature /'kriːtʃəʳ/ *n* **1** a lower animal **2a** an animate being; *esp* a non-human one **b** a human being; a person **3** one who is the servile dependant or tool of another

crèche /kreʃ/ *n* **1** a representation of the Nativity scene **2** *chiefly Br* a centre where children under school age are looked after while their parents are at work

credence /'kriːdəns/ *n* acceptance of sthg as true or real

credible /'kredɨbəl/ *adj* offering reasonable grounds for belief – **-ibility** *n* – **-bly** *adv*

[1]**credit** /'kredɨt/ *n* **1a** the balance in a person's favour in an account **b** a sum loaned by a bank to be repaid with interest **c** time given for payment for goods or services provided but not immediately paid for **2** credence **3** influence derived from enjoying the confidence of others; standing **4** a source of honour or repute **5** acknowledgment, approval **6** an acknowledgment of a contributor by name that appears at the beginning or end of a film or television programme **7a** recognition that a student has fulfilled a course requirement **b** the passing of an examination at a level well above the minimum though not with distinction

[2]**credit** *v* **1** to believe **2** to place to the credit of **3** to ascribe some usu favourable characteristic to – + *with*

creditable /'kredɨtəbəl/ *adj* **1** worthy of esteem or praise **2** *NAm* capable of being attributed *to* – **-bly** *adv*

credit card *n* a card provided by a bank, agency, or business allowing the holder to obtain goods and services on credit

creditor /'kredɨtəʳ/ *n* one to whom a debt is owed

credo /'kriːdəʊ, 'kreɪ-/ *n, pl* **credos** **1** a creed **2** *cap* a musical setting of the creed in a sung mass

credulity /krɪ'djuːlɨti/ *n* undue willingness to believe; gullibility – **-lous** *adj* – **-lously** *adv* – **-lousness** *n*

creed /kriːd/ *n* **1** a brief statement of religious belief; *esp* such a statement said or sung as part of Christian worship **2** a set of fundamental beliefs

creek /kriːk/ *n* **1** *chiefly Br* a small narrow inlet of a lake, sea, etc **2** *chiefly NAm & Austr* a brook

[1]**creep** /kriːp/ *v* **crept** **1** to move along with the body prone and close to the ground **2a** to go very slowly **b** to go timidly or cautiously so as to escape notice **3a** to crawl **b** *of a plant* to spread or grow over a surface by clinging with tendrils, roots, etc or rooting at intervals

[2]**creep** *n* **1** a movement of or like creeping **2** *Br* an obnoxious or ingratiatingly servile person – infml

creeper /'kriːpəʳ/ *n* **1** a creeping plant **2** a bird (e g a tree creeper) that creeps about on trees or bushes

creepy /'kriːpi/ *adj* producing a sensation of shivery apprehension – **creepily** *adv* – **creepiness** *n*

creepy-crawly *n, Br* a small creeping or scuttling creature (e g a spider) – infml

cremate /krɨ'meɪt/ *v* to reduce (a dead body) to ashes by burning – **cremation** *n*

crematorium /ˌkremə'tɔːrɪəm/ *n, pl* **crematoriums, crematoria** a place where cremation is carried out

crème de menthe /ˌkrem də 'mɒnθ/ *n* a sweet green or white mint-flavoured liqueur

Creole /'kriːəʊl/ *n* **1** a person of European descent in the W Indies or Spanish America **2** a person of mixed French or Spanish and Negro descent **3** *not cap* a language based on 2 or more languages that serves as the native language of its speakers

creosote /'kriːəsəʊt/ *n* a brownish oily liquid obtained from tar and used esp as a wood preservative – **creosote** *v*

crepe, crêpe /kreɪp/ *n* **1** a light crinkled fabric **2** a thin pancake

crepe paper *n* thin paper with a crinkled or puckered texture

crept /krept/ *past of* **creep**

crepuscular /krɪ'pʌskjʊləʳ/ *adj* of or resembling twilight

[1]**crescendo** /krɨ'ʃendəʊ/ *n* a gradual increase; *esp* a gradual increase in volume in a musical passage

²crescendo *adv or adj* with an increase in volume – used in music

crescent /'kresənt, 'krez-/ *n* **1** the figure of the moon at any stage between new moon and first quarter or last quarter and the succeeding new moon **2** sthg shaped like a crescent and consisting of a concave and a convex curve

cress /kres/ *n* any of numerous plants of the mustard family that have mildly pungent leaves and are used in salads and as a garnish

crest /krest/ *n* **1a** a showy tuft or projection on the head of an animal, esp a bird **b** the plume, emblem, etc worn on a knight's helmet **c** coat of arms – not used technically in heraldry **2** the ridge or top, esp of a wave, roof, or mountain **3** *the* climax, culmination – **~ed** *adj*

crestfallen /'krest,fɔːlən/ *adj* disheartened, dejected

cretaceous /krɪ'teɪʃəs/ *adj* **1** resembling or containing chalk **2** *cap* of or being the last period of the Mesozoic era

cretin /'kretɨn/ *n* sby physically stunted and mentally retarded as the result of a glandular deficiency; *broadly* an imbecile, idiot

crevasse /krɨ'væs/ *n* a deep fissure, esp in a glacier

crevice /'krevɨs/ *n* a narrow opening resulting from a split or crack

¹crew /kruː/ *chiefly Br past of* **crow**

²crew *n sing or pl in constr* **1** a company of men working on 1 job or under 1 foreman **2a** the personnel of a ship or boat (excluding the captain and officers) **b** the people who man an aircraft in flight **3** a number of people temporarily associated – infml

crew cut *n* a very short bristly haircut, esp for a man

¹crib /krɪb/ *n* **1** a manger for feeding animals **2** a cradle **3** cribbage **4** a literal translation; *esp* one used surreptitiously by students

²crib *v* to pilfer, steal; *esp* to copy from the work of another

cribbage /'krɪbɪdʒ/ *n* a card game for 2 to 4 players each attempting to form various counting combinations of cards

¹crick /krɪk/ *n* a painful spasmodic condition of the muscles of the neck, back, etc

²crick *v* to cause a crick in

¹cricket /'krɪkɨt/ *n* a leaping insect noted for the chirping sounds produced by the male

²cricket *n* a game played with a bat and ball on a large field with 2 wickets near its centre by 2 sides of 11 players each – **~er** *n*

crime /kraɪm/ *n* **1** (a) violation of law **2** a grave offence, esp against morality **3** criminal activity **4** sthg deplorable, foolish, or disgraceful – infml

¹criminal /'krɪmɨnəl/ *adj* **1** involving or being a crime **2** relating to crime or its punishment **3** guilty of crime **4** disgraceful, deplorable – infml – **~ly** *adv*

²criminal *n* one who has committed or been convicted of a crime

criminology /,krɪmɨ'nɒlədʒi/ *n* the study of crime, criminals, and penal treatment – **-gist** *n*

crimp /krɪmp/ *v* **1** to make wavy, or curly **2** to pinch or press together in order to seal or join

crimson /'krɪmzən/ *adj or n* (a) deep purplish red

cringe /krɪndʒ/ *v* **1** to shrink or wince, esp in fear or servility **2** to behave with fawning self-abasement

¹crinkle /'krɪŋkəl/ *v* to wrinkle

²crinkle *n* a wrinkle – **-kly** *adj*

crinoline /'krɪnəlɨn/ *n* (a padded or hooped petticoat supporting) a full skirt as worn by women in the 19th c

¹cripple /'krɪpəl/ *n* a lame or partly disabled person or animal

²cripple *v* **1** to make a cripple; lame **2** to deprive of strength, efficiency, wholeness, or capability for service

crisis /'kraɪsɨs/ *n, pl* **crises** **1** the turning point for better or worse in an acute disease (e g pneumonia) **2** an unstable or crucial time or situation; *esp* a turning point

¹crisp /krɪsp/ *adj* **1a** easily crumbled; brittle **b** desirably firm and fresh **c** newly made or prepared **2** sharp, clean-cut, and clear **3** decisive, sharp **4** *of weather* briskly cold; fresh; *esp* frosty – **~ly** *adv* – **~ness** *n*

²crisp *n, chiefly Br* a thin slice of (flavoured or salted) fried potato, usu eaten cold

[1]**crisscross** /ˈkrɪskrɒs/ *adj or n* (marked or characterized by) criss-crossing or a crisscrossed pattern

[2]**crisscross** *v* **1** to mark with intersecting lines **2** to pass back and forth through or over

criterion /kraɪˈtɪərɪən/ *n, pl* **criteria** a standard on which a judgment or decision may be based

critic /ˈkrɪtɪk/ *n* **1** one who evaluates works of art, literature, or music, esp as a profession **2** one who tends to judge harshly or to be over-critical of minor faults

critical /ˈkrɪtɪkəl/ *adj* **1a** inclined to criticize severely and unfavourably **b** involving careful judgment or judicious evaluation **2a** of a measurement, point, etc at which some phenomenon undergoes a marked change **b** crucial, decisive **c** being in or approaching a state of crisis **3** *of a nuclear reactor* sustaining an energy-producing chain reaction – **~ly** *adv*

criticism /ˈkrɪtɪ̱sɪzəm/ *n* **1** criticizing, usu unfavourably **2** the art or act of analysing and evaluating esp the fine arts, literature, or literary documents

critic·ize, -ise /ˈkrɪtɪ̱saɪz/ *v* **1** to judge the merits or faults of **2** to stress the faults of

critique /krɪˈtiːk/ *n* a critical estimate or discussion (e g an article or essay)

[1]**croak** /krəʊk/ *v* **1** to utter (gloomily) in a hoarse raucous voice **2** to die – slang

[2]**croak** *n* a deep hoarse cry characteristic of a frog or toad

[1]**crochet** /ˈkrəʊʃeɪ/ *n* crocheted work

[2]**crochet** *v* to form (e g a garment or design) by drawing a single continuous yarn or thread into a pattern of interlocked loops using a hooked needle

[1]**crock** /krɒk/ *n* **1** a thick earthenware pot or jar **2** a piece of broken earthenware used esp to cover the bottom of a flowerpot

[2]**crock** *n* **1** an old (broken-down) vehicle **2** an (elderly) disabled person

crockery /ˈkrɒkəri/ *n* earthenware or china tableware, esp for everyday domestic use

crocodile /ˈkrɒkədaɪl/ *n* **1** any of several tropical or subtropical large voracious thick-skinned long-bodied aquatic reptiles **2** (leather prepared from) the skin of a crocodile **3** a line of people (e g schoolchildren) walking in pairs

crocodile tears *n pl* false or affected tears; hypocritical sorrow

crocus /ˈkrəʊkəs/ *n, pl* **crocuses** any of a large genus of usu early-flowering plants of the iris family bearing a single usu brightly-coloured long-tubed flower

croft /krɒft/ *n* a small farm on often poor land, esp in Scotland, worked by a tenant – **~er** *n*

croissant /ˈkrwɑːsɒŋ/ *n* a usu flaky rich crescent-shaped roll of bread or yeast- leavened pastry

crone /krəʊn/ *n* a withered old woman

crony /ˈkrəʊni/ *n* a close friend, esp of long standing; a chum – infml; often derog

crook /krʊk/ *n* **1** a shepherd's staff **2** a bend, curve **3** a person given to criminal practices; a thief, swindler – infml

crooked /ˈkrʊkɪ̱d/ *adj* **1** having a crook or curve; bent **2** not morally straightforward; dishonest – **~ly** *adv* – **~ness** *n*

croon /kruːn/ *v* to sing usu sentimental popular songs in a low or soft voice

[1]**crop** /krɒp/ *n* **1** (the stock or handle of) a riding whip **2** a pouched enlargement of the gullet of many birds in which food is stored and prepared for digestion **3** a short haircut **4** (the total production of) a plant or animal product that can be grown and harvested extensively

[2]**crop** *v* **1a** to harvest **b** to cut short; trim **2** to grow as or to cause (land) to bear a crop

cropper /ˈkrɒpəʳ/ *n* **1** a severe fall **2** a sudden or complete disaster *USE* chiefly in *come a cropper*; infml

crop up *v* to happen or appear unexpectedly or casually – infml

croquet /ˈkrəʊkeɪ, -ki/ *n* a game in which wooden balls are driven by mallets through a series of hoops set out on a lawn

croquette /krəʊ'ket/ *n* a small (rounded) piece of minced meat, vegetable, etc coated with egg and breadcrumbs and fried in deep fat

[1]**cross** /krɒs/ *n* **1a** an upright stake with a transverse beam used, esp by the ancient Romans, for execution **b** *often cap* the cross on which Jesus was crucified; *also* the Crucifixion **2** an affliction, trial **3** a design of an upright bar intersected by a horizontal one used esp as a Christian emblem **4** a monument surmounted by a cross **5** a mark formed by 2 intersecting lines crossing at their midpoints that is used as a signature, to mark a position, to indicate that sthg is incorrect, or to indicate a kiss in a letter **6** sby who or sthg that combines characteristics of 2 different types or individuals **7** a hook delivered over the opponent's lead in boxing **8** crossing the ball in soccer

[2]**cross** *v* **1** to make the sign of the cross on or over **2a** to intersect **b** to move, pass, or extend across sthg – usu + *over* **3** to run counter to; oppose **4** to go across **5** to draw 2 parallel lines across (a cheque) so that it can only be paid directly into a bank account **6** to kick or pass (the ball) across the field in soccer, specif from the wing into the goal area **7** *of letters, travellers, etc* to meet and pass **8** to interbreed, hybridize

[3]**cross** *adj* **1** lying or moving across **2** mutually opposed **3** involving mutual interchange; reciprocal **4a** irritable, grumpy **b** angry, annoyed **5** crossbred, hybrid – **~ly** *adv* – **~ness** *n*

crossbar /'krɒsbɑːʳ/ *n* a transverse bar (e g between goalposts)

crossbow /'krɒsbəʊ/ *n* a short bow mounted crosswise near the end of a wooden stock and used to fire bolts and stones

[1]**crossbreed** /'krɒsbriːd/ *v* to hybridize or cross (esp 2 varieties or breeds of the same species) – **crossbreed** *n*

cross-check *v* to check (information) for validity or accuracy by reference to more than 1 source

[1]**cross-country** *adj* proceeding over countryside and not by roads – **cross-country** *adv*

[2]**cross-country** *n* cross-country running, horse riding, etc

crosscurrent /'krɒskʌrənt/ *n* a conflicting tendency – usu pl

cross-examine *v* to question closely (esp a witness in a law court) in order to check answers or elicit new information – **-ination** *n* – **-iner** *n*

cross-eyed *adj* having a squint towards the nose

cross-fertilize *v* **1** to fertilize with pollen or sperm from a different individual **2** to interreact, esp in a productive or useful manner – **-lization** *n*

crossfire /'krɒsfaɪəʳ/ *n* **1** firing from 2 or more points in crossing directions **2** rapid or heated interchange

cross-grained *adj* **1** having the grain or fibres running transversely or irregularly **2** difficult to deal with; intractable

crossing /'krɒsɪŋ/ *n* **1** a place or structure (e g on a street or over a river or railway) where pedestrians or vehicles may cross **2** a place where railway lines, roads, etc cross each other

crosspiece /krɒspiːs/ *n* a horizontal part (e g of a structure)

crossply /'krɒsplaɪ/ *n or adj* (a tyre) with the cords arranged crosswise to strengthen the tread

cross-refer *v* **1** to direct (a reader) from one page or entry (e g in a book) to another **2** to refer from (a secondary entry) to a main entry – **-reference** *n*

cross-section *n* **1** (a drawing of) a surface made by cutting across sthg, esp at right angles to its length **2** a representative sample

cross-stitch *n* (needlework using) a stitch in the shape of an X formed by crossing one stitch over another

cross-talk *n* rapid exchange of repartee (e g between comedians)

crosswise /'krɒs,waɪz/ *adv* so as to cross sthg; across

crotch /krɒtʃ/ *n* **1** an angle formed where 2 branches separate off from a tree trunk **2** the angle between the inner thighs where they meet the human body

crotchet /'krɒtʃɨt/ *n* a musical note

with the time value of half a minim or 2 quavers

crotchety /ˈkrɒtʃɪ̣ti/ *adj* bad-tempered – infml

crouch /kraʊtʃ/ *v* to lower the body by bending the legs – **crouch** *n*

croup /kruːp/ *n* a spasmodic laryngitis, esp of infants, marked by periods of difficult breathing and a hoarse cough – **croupy** *adj*

croupier /ˈkruːpɪəʳ/ *n* an employee of a gambling casino who collects and pays out bets at the gaming tables

crouton /ˈkruːtɒn/ *n* a small cube of crisp toasted or fried bread served with soup or used as a garnish

[1]**crow** /krəʊ/ *n* **1** the carrion or hooded crow or a related large usu entirely glossy black bird **2** a crowbar

[2]**crow** *v* **crowed,** (*1*) **crowed** *also* **crew** **1** to make the loud shrill cry characteristic of a cock **2** *esp of an infant* to utter sounds of happiness or pleasure **3** to exult gloatingly, esp over another's misfortune

[3]**crow** *n* **1** the characteristic cry of the cock **2** a triumphant cry

crowbar /ˈkrəʊbɑːʳ/ *n* an iron or steel bar for use as a lever that is wedge-shaped at the working end

[1]**crowd** /kraʊd/ *v* **1a** to collect in numbers; throng **b** to force or thrust into a small space **2** to hoist more (sail) than usual for greater speed – usu + *on* **3** to press close to; jostle

[2]**crowd** *n sing or pl in constr* **1** a large number of people gathered together without order; a throng **2** people in general – + *the* **3** a large number of things close together and in disorder

crowded /ˈkraʊdɪ̣d/ **1** filled with numerous people, things, or events **2** pressed or forced into a small space – **~ness** *n*

[1]**crown** /kraʊn/ *n* **1** a reward of victory or mark of honour; *esp* the title representing the championship in a sport **2** a (gold and jewel-encrusted) headdress worn as a symbol of sovereignty **3a** the topmost part of the skull or head **b** the summit of a slope, mountain, etc **c** the upper part of the foliage of a tree or shrub **d** the part of a hat or cap that covers the crown of the head **e** (an artificial substitute for) the part of a tooth visible outside the gum **4** *often cap* the sovereign as head of state; *also* sovereignty **5** the high point or culmination **6** a British coin worth 25 pence (formerly 5 shillings)

[2]**crown** *v* **1** to invest with a crown **2** to surmount, top **3** to bring to a successful conclusion **4** to put an artificial crown on (a tooth)

Crown Court *n* a local criminal court in England and Wales having jurisdiction over serious offences

crown prince *n* an heir apparent to a crown or throne

crown princess *n* **1** the wife of a crown prince **2** a female heir apparent or heir presumptive to a crown or throne

crow's nest *n* a partly enclosed high lookout platform (e g on a ship's mast)

crucial /ˈkruːʃəl/ *adj* **1** essential to the resolving of a crisis; decisive **2** of the greatest importance or significance – **~ly** *adv*

crucible /ˈkruːsɪ̣bl/ *n* **1** a vessel for melting a substance at a very high temperature **2** a severe test

crucifix /ˈkruːsɪ̣fiks/ *n* a representation of Christ on the cross

crucifixion /ˌkruːsɪ̣ˈfikʃən/ *n cap the* crucifying of Christ

crucify /ˈkruːsɪ̣faɪ/ *v* to execute by nailing or binding the hands and feet to a cross and leaving to die

[1]**crude** /kruːd/ *adj* **1** existing in a natural state and unaltered by processing **2** vulgar, gross **3** rough or inexpert in plan or execution – **~ly** *adv* – **~ness, crudity** *n*

[2]**crude** *n* a substance, esp petroleum, in its natural unprocessed state

cruel /ˈkruːəl/ *adj* **1** liking to inflict pain or suffering; pitiless **2** causing suffering; painful – **~ly** *adv* – **~ness** *n*

cruelty /ˈkruːəlti/ *n* **1** being cruel **2** (an instance of) cruel behaviour

cruet /ˈkruːɪ̣t/ *n* a small container (e g a pot, shaker or jug) for holding a condiment, esp salt, pepper, oil, vinegar, or mustard, at table

[1]**cruise** /kruːz/ *v* **1** to travel by sea for pleasure **2** to go about or patrol the streets without any definite destina-

tion **3a** *of an aircraft* to fly at the most efficient operating speed **b** *of a vehicle* to travel at an economical speed that can be maintained for a long distance **4** to make progress easily **5** to search (e g in public places) for an esp homosexual partner – slang

cruiser /'kruːzəʳ/ *n* **1** a cabin cruiser **2** a large fast lightly armoured warship

crumb /krʌm/ *n* **1** a small fragment, esp of bread **2** a small amount **3** (loose crumbly soil or other material resembling) the soft part of bread inside the crust **4** a worthless person – slang

¹crumble /'krʌmbl/ *v* to break or fall into small pieces; disintegrate – often + *away* – **-ly** *adj*

²crumble *n* a dessert of stewed fruit topped with a crumbly mixture of fat, flour, and sugar

crummy, crumby /'krʌmi/ *adj* **1** miserable, filthy **2** of poor quality; worthless *USE* slang

crumpet /'krʌmpɪ̈t/ *n* **1** a small round cake made from an unsweetened leavened batter that is cooked on a griddle and usu toasted before serving **2** *Br* women collectively as sexual objects – slang

crumple /'krʌmpl/ *v* **1** to press, bend, or crush out of shape **2** to collapse – often + *up*

¹crunch /krʌntʃ/ *v* **1** to chew or bite (sthg) with a noisy crushing sound **2** to make (one's way) with a crushing sound – **crunchy** *adj*

²crunch *n* **1** an act or sound of crunching **2** *the* critical or decisive situation or moment – infml

crusade /kruː'seɪd/ *n* **1** *cap* any of the medieval Christian military expeditions to win the Holy Land from the Muslims **2** a reforming enterprise undertaken with zeal and enthusiasm – **crusade** *v*

¹crush /krʌʃ/ *v* **1** to alter or destroy by pressure or compression **2** to subdue, overwhelm **3** to crowd, push

²crush *n* **1** a crowding together, esp of many people **2** (the object of) an intense usu brief infatuation – infml

crust /krʌst/ *n* **1** the hardened exterior of bread **2** the pastry cover of a pie **3a** the outer rocky layer of the earth **b** a deposit built up on the inside of a wine bottle during long aging

crustacean /krʌ'steɪʃən/ *n, pl* **crustaceans, crustacea** any of a large class of mostly aquatic arthropods including the lobsters, crabs and woodlice

crusty /'krʌsti/ *adj* **1** having a hard well-baked crust **2** surly, uncivil – **-tily** *adv* – **-tiness** *n*

crutch /krʌtʃ/ *n* **1a** a staff of wood or metal typically fitting under the armpit to support a disabled person in walking **b** a prop, stay **2** the crotch of an animal or human **3** the part of a garment that covers the human crotch

crux /krʌks/ *n, pl* **cruxes** *also* **cruces** **1** a puzzling or difficult problem **2** an essential or decisive point

¹cry /kraɪ/ *v* **1** to call loudly; shout (e g in fear or pain) **2** to weep, sob **3** *of a bird or animal* to utter a characteristic sound or call **4** to require or suggest strongly a remedy – usu + *out for*; infml

²cry *n* **1** an inarticulate utterance of distress, rage, pain, etc **2** a loud shout **3** a watchword, slogan **4** a general public demand or complaint **5** a spell of weeping **6** the characteristic sound or call of an animal or bird **7** pursuit – in *in full cry*

crying /'kraɪ-ɪŋ/ *adj* calling for notice

cry off *v* to withdraw; back out

crypt /krɪpt/ *n* a chamber (e g a vault) wholly or partly underground; *esp* a vault under the main floor of a church

cryptic /'krɪptɪk/ *adj* **1** intended to be obscure or mysterious **2** making use of cipher or code – **~ally** *adv*

cryptogram /'krɪptəgræm/ *n* a communication in cipher or code

cryptography /krɪp'tɒgrafi/ *n* **1** secret writing; cryptic symbolization **2** the preparation of cryptograms, ciphers, or codes – **-pher** *n* – **-phic** *adj* – **-phically** *adv*

crystal /'krɪstl/ *n* **1** a chemical substance in a form that has a regularly repeating internal arrangement of atoms and often regularly arranged external plane faces **2** (an object made of) a clear colourless glass of superior quality **3** sthg resembling crystal in transparency and colourlessness – ~line *adj* – ~lize *v*

crystal gazing *n* the attempt to predict future events, esp without adequate data – **crystal gazer** *n*

cub /kʌb/ *n* **1** the young of a flesh-eating mammal (e g a bear or lion) **2** an inexperienced newspaper reporter

¹cube /kjuːb/ *n* **1a** the regular solid of 6 equal square sides **b** a block of anything so shaped **2** the product got by multiplying together 3 equal numbers

²cube *v* **1** to raise to the third power **2** to cut into cubes

cubic /'kjuːbɪk/ *adj* **1** cube-shaped **2** three-dimensional **3** being the volume of a cube whose edge is a specified unit

cubicle /'kjuːbɪkəl/ *n* a small partitioned space or compartment

cubism /'kjuːbɪzəm/ *n* a 20th-c art movement that stresses abstract form, esp by displaying several aspects of the same object simultaneously – **cubist** *n*

cubit /'kjuːbɟt/ *n* any of various ancient units of length based on the length of the forearm from the elbow to the tip of the middle finger

¹cuckoo /'kʊkuː/ *n, pl* **cuckoos** **1** (any of a large family of birds including) a greyish brown European bird that lays its eggs in the nests of other birds which hatch them and rear the offspring **2** the characteristic call of the cuckoo

²cuckoo *adj* deficient in sense or intelligence; silly – infml

cuckoo spit *n* (a frothy secretion exuded on plants by the larva of) a small insect

cucumber /'kjuːkʌmbəʳ/ *n* (a climbing plant with) a long green edible fruit cultivated as a garden vegetable and eaten esp in salads

cud /kʌd/ *n* food brought up into the mouth by a ruminating animal from its first stomach to be chewed again

cuddle /'kʌdl/ *v* to hold close for warmth or comfort or in affection – **cuddle** *n*

cudgel /'kʌdʒəl/ *n* a short heavy club

¹cue /kjuː/ *n* **1** a signal to a performer to begin a specific speech or action **2** sthg serving a comparable purpose; a hint

²cue *n* a leather-tipped tapering rod for striking the ball in billiards, snooker, etc

¹cuff /kʌf/ *n* a fold or band at the end of a sleeve which encircles the wrist

²cuff *v* to strike, esp (as if) with the palm of the hand

³cuff *n* a blow with the hand, esp when open; a slap

cuff link *n* a usu ornamental device consisting of 2 linked parts used to fasten a shirt cuff

cuirass /kwɪ'ræs/ *n* a piece of armour consisting of a (joined backplate and) breastplate

cuisine /kwɪ'ziːn/ *n* a manner of preparing or cooking food; *also* the food prepared

cul-de-sac /'kʌl dɟ ˌsæk, 'kʊl/ *n, pl* **culs-de-sac** *also* **cul-de-sacs** a street, usu residential, closed at 1 end

culinary /'kʌlɟnəri/ *adj* of the kitchen or cookery

cull /kʌl/ *v* **1** to select from a group; choose **2** to identify and remove the rejects from (a flock, herd, etc) **3** to control the size of a population of (animals) by killing a limited number

culminate /'kʌlmɟneɪt/ *v* to reach the highest or a decisive point – often + *in* – **-ation** *n*

culottes /kjuː'lɒts/ *n pl* short trousers having the appearance of a skirt and worn by women

culpable /'kʌlpəbəl/ *adj* meriting condemnation or blame – **-bility** *n* – **-bly** *adv*

culprit /'kʌlprɟt/ *n* one guilty of a crime or a fault

cult /kʌlt/ *n* **1a** a system of religious beliefs and ritual **b** a religion regarded as unorthodox or spurious **2** great devotion, often regarded as a fad, to a person, idea, or thing

cultivate /'kʌltɟveɪt/ *v* **1** to prepare or use (land, soil, etc) for the growing of crops; *also* to break up the soil about (growing plants) **2a** to foster the growth of (a plant or crop) **b** to improve by labour, care, or study; refine **3** to further, encourage – **-vation** *n*

cultivated /'kʌltɟveɪtɟd/ *adj* refined, educated
cultivator /'kʌltɟveɪtəʳ/ *n* an implement to break up the soil (while crops are growing)
[1]**culture** /'kʌltʃəʳ/ *n* **1** enlightenment and excellence of taste acquired by intellectual and aesthetic training **2a** the socially transmitted pattern of human behaviour that includes thought, speech, action, institutions, and man-made objects **b** the customary beliefs, social forms, etc of a racial, religious, or social group **3** (a product of) the cultivation of living cells, tissue, viruses, etc in prepared nutrient media – **-ral** *adj* – **-rally** *adv*
[2]**culture** *v* **1** to cultivate **2** to grow (bacteria, viruses, etc) in a culture
cultured /'kʌltʃəd/ *adj* cultivated
culvert /'kʌlvət/ *n* a construction that allows water to pass over or under an obstacle (e g a road or canal)
cumbersome /'kʌmbəsəm/ *adj* unwieldy because of heaviness and bulk
cumin /'kʌmɟn, 'kju:mɟn/ *n* a plant cultivated for its aromatic seeds used as a flavouring
cummerbund /'kʌməbʌnd/ *n* a broad waistsash worn esp with men's formal evening wear
cumulative /'kju:mjʊlətɪv/ *adj* **1a** made up of accumulated parts **b** increasing by successive additions **2** formed by adding new material of the same kind – **~ly** *adv*
cumulonimbus /ˌkju:mjʊləʊ'nɪmbəs/ *n* a cumulus cloud formation often in the shape of an anvil, extending to great heights and characteristic of thunderstorm conditions
cumulus /'kju:mjʊləs/ *n, pl* **cumuli** a massive cloud formation with a flat base and rounded outlines often piled up like a mountain
cuneiform /'kju:nifɔ:m, 'kju:niɟfɔ:m/ *adj* **1** wedge-shaped **2** composed of or written in the wedge-shaped characters used in ancient Assyrian, Babylonian, and Persian inscriptions
[1]**cunning** /'kʌnɪŋ/ *adj* **1** dexterous, ingenious **2** devious, crafty – **~ly** *adv*
[2]**cunning** *n* craft, slyness
cunt /kʌnt/ *n* **1** the female genitals **2** sexual intercourse – used by men **3** *Br* an unpleasant person *USE* vulg
cup /kʌp/ *n* **1** a small open drinking vessel that is usu bowl-shaped and has a handle on 1 side **2** the consecrated wine of the Communion **3** (a competition or championship with) an ornamental usu metal cup offered as a prize **4** sthg resembling a cup **5** either of 2 parts of a garment, esp a bra, that are shaped to fit over the breasts **6** any of various usu alcoholic and cold drinks made from mixed ingredients
cupboard /'kʌbəd/ *n* a shelved recess or freestanding piece of furniture with doors, for storage of utensils, food, clothes, etc
cupboard love *n* insincere love professed for the sake of gain
Cupid /'kju:pɟd/ *n* **1** the Roman god of erotic love **2** *not cap* a representation of Cupid as a winged naked boy often holding a bow and arrow
cupidity /kjʊ'pɪdɟti/ *n* inordinate desire for wealth; avarice, greed
cupola /'kju:pələ/ *n* a small domed structure built on top of a roof
cuppa /'kʊpə/ *n, chiefly Br* a cup of tea – infml
cup-tie *n* a match in a knockout competition for a cup
cur /kɜ:ʳ/ *n* **1** a mongrel or inferior dog **2** a surly or cowardly fellow
curate /'kjʊərɟt/ *n* a clergyman serving as assistant (e g to a rector) in a parish – **-acy** *n*
curator /kjʊ'reɪtəʳ/ *n* sby in charge of a place of exhibition (e g a museum or zoo) – **~ship** *n*
[1]**curb** /kɜ:b/ *n* **1a** a chain or strap that is used to restrain a horse and is attached to the sides of the bit and passes below the lower jaw **b** a bit used esp with a curb chain or strap, usu in a double bridle **2** a check, restraint **3** an edge or margin that strengthens or confines
[2]**curb** *v* to check, control
curd /kɜ:d/ *n* **1** the thick part of coagulated milk used as a food or made into cheese **2** a rich thick fruit preserve made with eggs, sugar, and butter
curdle /'kɜ:dl/ *v* **1** to form curds (in);

specif to separate into solid curds and liquid **2** to spoil, sour

[1]**cure** /kjʊəʳ/ *n* **1** spiritual or pastoral charge **2** (a drug, treatment, etc that gives) relief or esp recovery from a disease **3** sthg that corrects a harmful or troublesome situation; a remedy **4** a process or method of curing

[2]**cure** *v* **1a** to restore to health, soundness, or normality **b** to bring about recovery from **2a** to rectify **b** to free (sby) from sthg objectionable or harmful **3** to prepare by chemical or physical processing; *esp* to preserve (meat, fish, etc) by salting, drying, smoking, etc – **-rable** *adj*

cure-all *n* a remedy for all ills; a panacea

curfew /ˈkɜːfjuː/ *n* **1** a regulation imposed esp during times of civil disturbance, requiring people to withdraw from the streets by a stated time **2** a signal (e g the sounding of a bell) announcing the beginning of a time of curfew

Curia /ˈkjʊərɪə/ *n* the administration and governmental apparatus of the Roman Catholic church

curio /ˈkjʊərɪəʊ/ *n* sthg considered novel, rare, or bizarre

curiosity /ˌkjʊəriˈɒsəti/ *n* **1** inquisitiveness; nosiness **2** a strange, interesting, or rare object, custom, etc

curious /ˈkjʊərɪəs/ *adj* **1** eager to investigate and learn **2** inquisitive, nosy **3** strange, novel, or odd – **~ly** *adv*

[1]**curl** /kɜːl/ *v* **1a** to grow in coils or spirals **b** to form curls or twists **2** to move or progress in curves or spirals

[2]**curl** *n* **1** a curled lock of hair **2** sthg with a spiral or winding form; a coil **3** a (plant disease marked by the) rolling or curling of leaves

curler /ˈkɜːləʳ/ *n* a small cylinder on which hair is wound for curling

curlew /ˈkɜːljuː/ *n* any of various largely brownish (migratory) wading birds with long legs and a long slender down-curved bill

curling /ˈkɜːlɪŋ/ *n* a game in which 2 teams, of 4 players each, slide heavy round flat-bottomed stones over ice towards a target circle marked on the ice

curly /ˈkɜːli/ *adj* tending to curl; having curls – **curliness** *n*

curmudgeon /kəˈmʌdʒən, kɜː-/ *n* a crusty ill-tempered (old) man

currant /ˈkʌrənt/ *n* **1** a small seedless type of dried grape used in cookery **2** a redcurrant, blackcurrant, or similar acid edible fruit

currency /ˈkʌrənsi/ *n* **1** (the state of being in) general use, acceptance, or prevalence **2** sthg (e g coins and bank notes) that is in circulation as a medium of exchange

[1]**current** /ˈkʌrənt/ *adj* **1** occurring in or belonging to the present time **2** used as a medium of exchange **3** generally accepted, used, or practised at the moment – **~ly** *adv*

[2]**current** *n* **1a** the part of a body of gas or liquid that moves continuously in a certain direction **b** the swiftest part of a stream **c** a (tidal) movement of lake, sea, or ocean water **2** a flow of electric charge; *also* the rate of such flow

current account *n, chiefly Br* a bank account against which cheques may be drawn and on which interest is usu not payable

curriculum /kəˈrɪkjʊləm/ *n, pl* **curricula** the courses offered by an educational institution or followed by an individual or group

curriculum vitae /kəˌrɪkjʊləm ˈvaɪtiː, ˈviːtaɪ/ *n, pl* **curricula vitae** a summary of sby's career and qualifications, esp as relevant to a job application

[1]**curry** /ˈkʌri/ *v* to dress tanned leather

[2]**curry** *also* **currie** *n* a food or dish seasoned with a mixture of spices or curry powder

[3]**curry** *v* to flavour or cook with curry powder or sauce

curry powder *n* a condiment consisting of several pungent ground spices (e g cayenne pepper, fenugreek, and turmeric)

[1]**curse** /kɜːs/ *n* **1** an utterance (of a deity) or a request (to a deity) that invokes harm or injury **2** an evil or misfortune that comes (as if) in response to cursing or as retribution **3** a cause of misfortune **4** menstruation – + *the*; infml

[2]**curse** *v* **1** to call upon divine or super-

natural power to cause harm or injury to 2 to use profanely insolent language against 3 to bring great evil upon; afflict

cursed *also* **curst** /'kɜːsɨ̞d/ *adj* under or deserving a curse – ~**ly** *adv*

cursive /'kɜːsɪv/ *adj* written in flowing, usu slanted, strokes with the characters joined in each word – ~**ly** *adv*

cursory /'kɜːsəri/ *adj* rapid and often superficial; hasty – -**rily** *adv*

curt /kɜːt/ *adj* marked by rude or peremptory shortness; brusque – ~**ly** *adv* – ~**ness** *n*

curtail /kɜː'teɪl/ *v* to cut short, limit – ~**ment** *n*

curtain /'kɜːtɨ̞ŋ/ *n* **1** a hanging fabric screen (at a window) that can usu be drawn back **2** a device or agency that conceals or acts as a barrier **3** an exterior wall that carries no load **4a** the movable screen separating the stage from the auditorium of a theatre **b** the ascent or opening (e g at the beginning of a play) of a stage curtain; *also* its descent or closing **c** *pl* the end; *esp* death – infml

curtain call *n* an appearance by a performer after the final curtain of a play in response to the applause of the audience

curtsy, curtsey /'kɜːtsi/ *n* an act of respect, made by a woman, performed by bending at the knees and bowing the head – **curtsy** *v*

curvaceous, curvacious /kɜː'veɪʃəs/ *adj, of a woman* having an attractively well-developed figure

curvature /'kɜːvətʃəʳ/ *n* **1** (a measure or amount of) curving or being curved **2** an abnormal curving (e g of the spine)

¹**curve** /kɜːv/ *v* to have or make a turn, change, or deviation from a straight line without sharp breaks or angularity

²**curve** *n* **1** a curving line or surface **2** sthg curved (e g a curving line of the human body) **3** a representation on a graph of a varying quantity (e g speed, force, or weight)

¹**cushion** /'kʊʃən/ *n* **1** a soft pillow or padded bag; *esp* one used for sitting, reclining, or kneeling on **2** a bodily part resembling a pad **3** a pad of springy rubber along the inside of the rim of a billiard table off which balls bounce **4** sthg serving to mitigate the effects of disturbances or disorders

²**cushion** *v* **1** to mitigate the effects of **2** to protect against force or shock

cushy /'kʊʃi/ *adj* entailing little hardship or effort; easy – infml – **cushiness** *n*

cusp /kʌsp/ *n* a point, apex: e g **a** either horn of a crescent moon **b** a pointed projection formed by or arising from the intersection of 2 arcs or foils **c** a point on the grinding surface of a tooth

¹**cuss** /kʌs/ *n* **1** a curse **2** a fellow *USE* infml

²**cuss** *v* to curse – infml

cussed /'kʌsɨ̞d/ *adj* **1** cursed **2** obstinate, cantankerous *USE* infml – ~**ly** *adv* – ~**ness** *n*

custard /'kʌstəd/ *n* **1** a semisolid usu sweetened and often baked mixture made with milk and eggs **2** a sweet sauce made with milk and eggs or a commercial preparation of coloured cornflour

custodian /kʌ'stəʊdɪən/ *n* the curator of a public building – ~**ship** *n*

custody /'kʌstədi/ *n* **1a** the state of being cared for or guarded **b** imprisonment, detention **2** the act or right of caring for a minor, esp when granted by a court of law; guardianship – -**dial** *adj*

¹**custom** /'kʌstəm/ *n* **1a** an established socially accepted practice **b** the usual practice of an individual **c** the usages that regulate social life **2a** *pl* duties or tolls imposed on imports or exports **b** *pl but sing or pl in constr* the agency, establishment, or procedure for collecting such customs **3** business patronage

²**custom** *adj, chiefly NAm* made or performed according to personal order

customary /'kʌstəməri/ *adj* established by or according to custom; usual – -**rily** *adv*

customer /'kʌstəməʳ/ *n* **1** one who purchases a commodity or service **2** an individual, usu having some specified distinctive trait

¹**cut** /kʌt/ *v* -**tt**-; **cut** **1a** to penetrate (as if) with an edged instrument **b** to hurt

the feelings of **2a** to trim, pare **b** to shorten by omissions **c** to reduce in amount **3a** to mow or reap **b(1)** to divide into parts with an edged instrument **(2)** to fell, hew **c** to make a stroke with a whip, sword, etc **4a** to divide into segments **b** to intersect, cross **c** to break, interrupt **d** to divide (a pack of cards) into 2 portions **5a** to refuse to recognize (an acquaintance) **b** to stop (a motor) by opening a switch **c** to terminate the filming of (a scene in a film) **6a** to make or give shape to (as if) with an edged tool **b** to record sounds on (a gramophone record) **c** to make an abrupt transition from one sound or image to another in film, radio, or television **7a** to perform, make **b** to give the appearance or impression of **8a** to stop, cease – infml **b** to absent oneself from (e g a class) – infml

[2]**cut** *n* **1a** a (slice cut from a) piece from a meat carcass or a fish **b** a share **2a** a canal, channel, or inlet made by excavation or worn by natural action **b(1)** an opening made with an edged instrument **(2)** a gash, wound **c** a passage cut as a roadway **3a** a gesture or expression that hurts the feelings **b** a stroke or blow with the edge of sthg sharp **c** a lash (as if) with a whip **d** the act of reducing or removing a part **e** (the result of) a cutting of playing cards **4** an attacking stroke in cricket played with the bat held horizontally and sending the ball on the off side **5** an abrupt transition from one sound or image to another in film, radio, or television **6a** the shape and style in which a thing is cut, formed, or made **b** a pattern, type **c** a haircut

cut-and-dried *adj* completely decided; not open to further discussion

cutback /'kʌtbæk/ *n* a reduction

cute /kjuːt/ *adj* attractive or pretty, esp in a dainty or delicate way – infml – **~ly** *adv* – **~ness** *n*

cut glass *n* glass ornamented with patterns cut into its surface by an abrasive wheel and then polished

cuticle /'kjuːtɪkəl/ *n* a skin or outer covering: e g **a** the (dead or horny) epidermis of an animal **b** a thin fatty film on the external surface of many higher plants

cutlass *also* **cutlas** /'kʌtləs/ *n* a short curved sword, esp as used formerly by sailors

cutler /'kʌtləʳ/ *n* one who deals in, makes, or repairs cutlery

cutlery /'kʌtləri/ *n* edged or cutting tools; *esp* implements (e g knives, forks, and spoons) for cutting and eating food

cutlet /'kʌtlʒ̍t/ *n* **1** (a flat mass of minced food in the shape of) a small slice of meat from the neck of lamb, mutton, or veal **2** a cross-sectional slice from between the head and centre of a large fish

cutout /'kʌtaʊt/ *n* a device that is automatically switched off by an excessive electric current

cut out *adj* naturally fitted or suited

cut-price *adj* selling or sold at a discount

cutter /'kʌtəʳ/ *n* **1** one whose work is cutting or involves cutting (e g of cloth or film) **2a** a ship's boat for carrying stores or passengers **b** a fore-and-aft rigged sailing boat with a single mast and 2 foresails **c** a small armed boat in the US coastguard

[1]**cutthroat** /'kʌtθrəʊt/ *n* a murderous thug

[2]**cutthroat** *adj* **1** murderous, cruel **2** ruthless, unprincipled

[1]**cutting** /'kʌtɪŋ/ *n* **1** a part of a plant stem, leaf, root, etc capable of developing into a new plant **2** *chiefly Br* an excavation or cut, esp through high ground, for a canal, road, etc **3** *chiefly Br* an item cut out of a publication

[2]**cutting** *adj* **1** designed for cutting; sharp, edged **2** *of wind* marked by sharp piercing cold **3** likely to wound the feelings of another; *esp* sarcastic – **~ly** *adv*

cuttlefish /'kʌtl,fɪʃ/ *n* a 10-armed marine animal differing from the related squids in having a hard internal shell

cut up *adj* deeply distressed; grieved – infml

cwm /kuːm/ *n* a cirque

cyanide /'saɪənaɪd/ *n* an extremely poisonous chemical with a smell of bitter almonds

cybernetics /,saɪbə'netɪks/ *n pl but*

sing or pl in constr the comparative study of the automatic control systems formed by the nervous system and brain and by mechanical-electrical communication systems – **-ic** *adj* – **-ically** *adv*

cyclamate /'saɪkləmeɪt/ *n* a synthetic compound used, esp formerly, as an artificial sweetener

[1]**cycle** /'saɪkəl/ *n* **1a** (the time needed to complete) a series of related events happening in a regularly repeated order **b** one complete performance of a periodic process (e g a vibration or electrical oscillation) **2** a group of poems, plays, novels, or songs on a central theme **3** a bicycle, motorcycle, tricycle, etc

[2]**cycle** *v* to ride a bicycle – **-list** *n*

cyclic /'sɪklɪk, 'saɪklɪk/, **cyclical** *adj* **1** of or belonging to a cycle **2** of or containing a ring of atoms – **~ally** *adv*

cyclone /'saɪkləʊn/ *n* a storm or system of winds that rotates about a centre of low atmospheric pressure, advances at high speeds, and often brings abundant rain

cyclopedia, cyclopaedia /ˌsaɪklə'piːdɪə/ *n* an encyclopedia

cygnet /'sɪgnɨt/ *n* a young swan

cylinder /'sɪlɨndəʳ/ *n* **1a** a surface traced by a straight line moving in a circle or other closed curve round and parallel to a fixed straight line **b** a hollow or solid object with the shape of a cylinder and a circular cross-section **2a** the piston chamber in an engine **b** any of various rotating parts (e g in printing presses) – **-drical** *adj*

cymbal /'sɪmbəl/ *n* a concave brass plate that produces a clashing tone when struck with a drumstick or against another cymbal – **~ist** *n*

cynic /'sɪnɪk/ *n* **1** *cap* an adherent of an ancient Greek school of philosophers who held that virtue is the highest good and that its essence lies in mastery over one's desires and wants **2** one who sarcastically doubts the existence of human sincerity or of any motive other than self-interest; *broadly* a pessimist – **~al** *adj* – **~ism** *n* – **~ally** *adv*

cynosure /'sɪnəzjʊəʳ/ *n* a centre of attraction or attention

cypher /'saɪfəʳ/ *v or n, chiefly Br* (to) cipher

cypress /'saɪprɨs/ *n* (the wood of) any of a genus of evergreen trees with aromatic overlapping leaves resembling scales

Cyrillic /sɨ'rɪlɪk/ *adj* of or constituting an alphabet used for writing various Slavic languages (e g Russian)

cyst /sɪst/ *n* a closed sac (e g of watery liquid or gas) with a distinct membrane, developing (abnormally) in a plant or animal

cystitis /sɪ'staɪtɨs/ *n* inflammation of the urinary bladder

cytology /saɪ'tɒlədʒi/ *n* the biology of (the structure, function, multiplication, pathology, etc of) cells – **-gist** *n*

cytoplasm /'saɪtəplæzəm/ *n* the substance within a plant or animal cell excluding the nucleus – **~ic** *adj*

czar, tsar /zɑːʳ/ *n* a former ruler of Russia

Czech /tʃek/ *n* **1** a native or inhabitant of Czechoslovakia; *specif* a Slav of W Czechoslovakia **2** the Slavonic language of the Czechs – **Czech** *adj*

D

d /diː/ *n, pl* **d's, ds** *often cap* **1** (a graphic representation of or device for reproducing) the 4th letter of the English alphabet **2** five hundred **3** the 2nd note of a C-major scale **4** one designated *d*, esp as the 4th in order or class, or as a mark of lesser quality than *a, b*, or *c*

[1]**dab** /dæb/ *n* **1** a sudden feeble blow or thrust; a poke **2** a gentle touch or stroke (e g with a sponge); a pat

[2]**dab** *v* **1** to touch lightly, and usu repeatedly; pat **2** to apply lightly or irregularly; daub

[3]**dab** *n* **1** a daub, patch **2** *pl, Br* fingerprints – infml

[4]**dab** *n* a flatfish; *esp* any of several flounders

dabble /ˈdæbəl/ *v* **1** to paddle, splash, or play (as if) in water **2** to work or concern oneself superficially **3** to wet slightly or intermittently by dipping in a liquid

dabchick /ˈdæb,tʃɪk/ *n* any of several small grebes

dachshund /ˈdækshʊnd, -sənd/ *n* (any of) a breed of dogs of German origin with a long body, short legs, and long drooping ears

dad /dæd/ *n* a father – infml

daddy longlegs *n, pl* **daddy longlegs** a crane fly

dado /ˈdeɪdəʊ/ *n, pl* **dadoes** **1** the part of a pedestal between the base and the cornice **2** the lower part of an interior wall when specially decorated or faced; *also* the decoration adorning this part of a wall

daemon /ˈdiːmən/ *n* **1** an attendant power or spirit **2** a supernatural being of Greek mythology **3** a demon – **~ic** *adj* – **~ically** *adv*

daffodil /ˈdæfədɪl/ *n* any of various plants with flowers that have a large typically yellow corona elongated into a trumpet shape

daft /dɑːft/ *adj* **1** silly, foolish **2** *chiefly Br* fanatically enthusiastic *USE* infml – **~ly** *adv* – **~ness** *n*

dagger /ˈdægəʳ/ *n* a short sharp pointed weapon for stabbing

dahlia /ˈdeɪlɪə/ *n* any of an American genus of composite (garden) plants with showy flower heads and roots that form tubers

[1]**daily** /ˈdeɪli/ *adj* **1a** occurring, made, or acted on every day **b** *of a newspaper* issued every weekday **c** of or providing for every day **2** covering the period of or based on a day

[2]**daily** *adv* every day; every weekday

[3]**daily** *n* **1** a newspaper published daily from Monday to Saturday **2** *Br* a charwoman who works on a daily basis

[1]**dainty** /ˈdeɪnti/ *n* a delicacy

[2]**dainty** *adj* **1** attractively prepared and served **2** delicately beautiful **3a** fastidious **b** showing avoidance of anything rough – **-tily** *adv* – **-tiness** *n*

daiquiri /daɪˈkɪəri, ˈdækɪ̣ri/ *n* a cocktail made of rum, lime juice, and sugar

dairy /ˈdeəri/ *n* **1** a room, building, etc where milk is processed and butter or cheese is made **2** farming concerned with the production of milk, butter, and cheese **3** an establishment for the sale or distribution of milk and milk products – **~ing** *n*

dairyman /ˈdeərimən/, *fem* **dairymaid** *n* one who operates or works for a dairy (farm)

dais /ˈdeɪɪ̣s, deɪs/ *n* a raised platform; *esp* one at the end of a hall

daisy /ˈdeɪzi/ *n* a usu white composite plant with a yellow disc and well-developed ray flowers in its flower head

Dalai Lama /ˌdælaɪ ˈlɑːmə/ *n* the spiritual head of Tibetan Buddhism

dally /ˈdæli/ *v* **1a** to act playfully; *esp* to flirt **b** to deal lightly; toy **2** to waste time; dawdle – **dalliance** *n*

dalmatian /dælˈmeɪʃən/ *n, often cap* (any of) a breed of medium-sized dogs with a white short-haired coat with black or brown spots

[1]dam /dæm/ *n* a female parent – used esp with reference to domestic animals

[2]dam *n* a barrier preventing the flow of a fluid; *esp* a barrier across a watercourse

[3]dam *v* to stop up; block

[1]damage /'dæmɪdʒ/ *n* **1** loss or harm resulting from injury to person, property, or reputation **2** *pl* compensation in money imposed by law for loss or injury **3** expense, cost – infml

[2]damage *v* to cause damage to

damask /'dæməsk/ *n* **1** a reversible lustrous fabric (e g of linen, cotton, or silk) having a plain background woven with patterns **2** greyish red

dame /deɪm/ *n* **1a** the wife or daughter of a lord **b** a female member of an order of knighthood – used as a title preceding the Christian name **2a** an elderly woman; *specif* a comic one in pantomime played usu by a male actor **b** *chiefly NAm* a woman – infml

[1]damn /dæm/ *v* **1** to condemn to a punishment or fate; *esp* to condemn to hell **2** to condemn as a failure by public criticism **3** to bring ruin on **4** to curse – often used as an interjection to express annoyance

[2]damn *n* **1** the utterance of the word *damn* as a curse **2** the slightest bit – chiefly in negative phrases

[3]damn *adj or adv* – used as an intensive

damnation /dæm'neɪʃən/ *n* damning or being damned

damning /'dæmɪŋ/ *adj* causing or leading to condemnation or ruin

[1]damp /dæmp/ *n* moisture, humidity

[2]damp, dampen *v* **1a** to diminish the activity or intensity of – often + *down* **b** to reduce progressively the vibration or oscillation of (e g sound waves) **2** to make damp

[3]damp *adj* slightly or moderately wet – **~ly** *adv*

damper /'dæmpə^{r}/ *n* **1a** a valve or plate (e g in the flue of a furnace) for regulating the draught **b** a small felted block which prevents or stops the vibration of a piano string **c** a device (e g a shock absorber) designed to bring a mechanism to rest with minimum oscillation **2** a dulling or deadening influence

damsel /'dæmzəl/ *n, archaic* a young woman; a girl

damson /'dæmzən/ *n* (the small acid purple fruit of) an Asiatic plum

[1]dance /dɑːns/ *v* **1** to engage in or perform a dance **2** to move quickly up and down or about – **dancer** *n*

[2]dance *n* **1** (an act or instance or the art of) a series of rhythmic and patterned bodily movements usu performed to music **2** a social gathering for dancing **3** a piece of music for dancing to

dandelion /'dændɪlaɪən/ *n* any of a genus of yellow-flowered composite plants including one that occurs virtually worldwide as a weed

dandle /'dændl/ *v* to move (e g a baby) up and down in one's arms or on one's knee in affectionate play

dandruff /'dændrəf, -drʌf/ *n* a scurf that comes off the scalp in small white or greyish scales

dandy /'dændi/ *n* a man who gives exaggerated attention to dress and demeanour

danger /'deɪndʒə^{r}/ *n* **1** exposure to the possibility of injury, pain, or loss **2** a case or cause of danger – **~ous** *adj* – **~ously** *adv*

dangle /'dæŋgəl/ *v* to hang or swing loosely

[1]Danish /'deɪnɪʃ/ *adj* (characteristic) of Denmark

[2]Danish *n* the Germanic language of the people of Denmark

Danish pastry *n* (a piece of) confectionery made from a rich yeast dough with a sweet filling

dank /dæŋk/ *adj* unpleasantly moist or wet – **~ness** *n*

dapper /'dæpə^{r}/ *adj, esp of a small man* neat and spruce

Darby and Joan /,dɑːbi ən 'dʒəʊn/ *n* a happily married elderly couple

[1]dare /deə^{r}/ *v* **dared,** *archaic* **durst** **1** to have sufficient courage or impudence (to) **2a** to challenge to perform an action, esp as a proof of courage **b** to confront boldly; defy

[2]dare *n* a challenge to a bold act

daredevil /'deədevəl/ *n or adj* (sby) recklessly bold

[1]daring /'deərɪŋ/ *adj* adventurously bold in action or thought

[2]daring *n* venturesome boldness

[1]dark /dɑːk/ *adj* **1** (partially) devoid of light **2a** (partially) black **b** *of a colour* of (very) low lightness **3a** arising from or showing evil traits or desires; evil **b** dismal, sad **c** lacking knowledge or culture **4** not fair; swarthy – **~ly** *adv* – **~ness** *n*

[2]dark *n* a place or time of little or no light; night, nightfall

Dark Ages *n pl* the period from about AD 476 to about 1000

darken /ˈdɑːkən/ *v* to make or become dark or darker

dark horse *n* sby or sthg (e g a contestant) little known, but with a potential much greater than the evidence would suggest

darkroom /ˈdaːkruːm, -rʊm/ *n* a room for handling and processing light-sensitive photographic materials

[1]darling /ˈdɑːlɪŋ/ *n* **1a** a dearly loved person **b** a dear **2** a favourite

[2]darling *adj* **1** dearly loved; favourite **2** charming – used esp by women

[1]darn /dɑːn/ *v* to mend (sthg) with interlacing stitches woven across a hole or worn part

[2]darn *n* a place that has been darned

[3]darn *v* to damn

[4]darn *adj or adv* damned

[1]dart /dɑːt/ *n* **1a** a small projectile with a pointed shaft at one end and flights of feather, plastic, etc at the other **b** *pl but sing in constr* a game in which darts are thrown at a dartboard **2** sthg with a slender pointed shaft or outline; *specif* a stitched tapering fold put in a garment to shape it to the figure **3** a quick movement; a dash

[2]dart *v* to move suddenly or rapidly

dartboard /ˈdɑːtbɔːd/ *n* a circular target used in darts that is divided, usu by wire, into different scoring areas

[1]dash /dæʃ/ *v* **1** to move with sudden speed **2a** to strike or knock violently **b** to break by striking or knocking **3** to destroy, ruin **4** *Br* to damn – euph

[2]dash *n* **1** (the sound produced by) a sudden burst or splash **2a** a stroke of a pen **b** a punctuation mark – used esp to indicate a break in the thought or structure of a sentence **3** a small but significant addition **4** liveliness of style and action; panache **5** a sudden onset, rush, or attempt **6** a signal (e g a flash or audible tone) of relatively long duration that is one of the 2 fundamental units of Morse code

dashboard /ˈdæʃbɔːd/ *n* a panel extending across a motor car, aeroplane, etc below the windscreen and usu containing dials and controls

dashing /ˈdæʃɪŋ/ *adj* **1** vigorous, spirited **2** smart in dress and manners – **~ly** *adv*

data /ˈdeɪtə, ˈdɑːtə/ *n pl but sing or pl in constr* factual information (e g measurements or statistics) used as a basis for reasoning, discussion, or calculation

data processing *n* the conversion (e g by computer) of crude information into usable or storable form

[1]date /deɪt/ *n* (the oblong edible fruit of) a tall palm

[2]date *n* **1** the time reckoned in days or larger units at which an event occurs **2** the period of time to which sthg belongs **3a** an appointment for a specified time; *esp* a social engagement between 2 people of opposite sex – infml **b** *NAm* a person of the opposite sex with whom one has a date – infml

[3]date *v* **1** to determine or record the date of **2a** to have been in existence – usu + *from* **b** to become old-fashioned **3** to mark with characteristics typical of a particular period **4** *chiefly NAm* to make or have a date with (a person of the opposite sex) – infml – **datable, dateable** *adj*

dated /ˈdeɪt̬ɪd/ *adj* out-of-date, old-fashioned

dateline /ˈdeɪtlaɪn/ *n* **1** a line in a written document or publication giving the date and place of composition or issue **2** an arbitrary line east and west of which the date differs by 1 calendar day

dative /ˈdeɪtɪv/ *n* (a form in) a grammatical case expressing typically the indirect object of a verb, the object of some prepositions, or a possessor – **dative** *adj*

[1]daub /dɔːb/ *v* **1** to coat with a dirty substance **2** to paint without much skill

[2]daub *n* **1** sthg daubed on; a smear **2** a crude picture

daughter /ˈdɔːtəʳ/ *n* **1a** a human female having the relation of child to parent **b** a female descendant – often pl **2a** a human female having a specified origin, loyalties, etc **b** sthg considered as a daughter

daughter-in-law *n, pl* **daughters-in-law** the wife of one's son

daunt /dɔːnt/ *v* to lessen the courage of; inspire awe in

dauphin /ˈdəʊfɪ̆n/ *n, often cap* the eldest son of a king of France

davit /ˈdævɪ̆t, ˈdeɪ-/ *n* any of 2 or more projecting arms on a vessel used esp for lowering boats

dawdle /ˈdɔːdl/ *v* **1** to spend time idly **2** to move lackadaisically – **~r** *n*

[1]**dawn** /dɔːn/ *v* **1** to begin to grow light as the sun rises **2** to begin to be perceived or understood

[2]**dawn** *n* **1** the first appearance of light in the morning **2** a first appearance; a beginning

day /deɪ/ *n* **1** the time of light when the sun is above the horizon between one night and the next **2** the time required by a celestial body, specif the earth, to turn once on its axis **3** the solar day of 24 hours beginning at midnight **4** a specified day or date **5** a specified time or period **6** the time established by usage or law for work, school, or business

daybreak /ˈdeɪbreɪk/ *n* dawn

daydream /ˈdeɪdriːm/ *v or n* (to have) a visionary, usu wish-fulfilling, creation of the waking imagination – **~er** *n*

daylight /ˈdeɪlaɪt/ *n* **1** dawn **2** knowledge or understanding of sthg that has been obscure **3** *pl* mental soundness or stability; wits – infml

day-return *n, Br* a ticket sold for a return journey on the same day and usu at a reduced rate if used outside rush hours

day-to-day *adj* **1** taking place, made, or done in the course of successive days **2** providing for a day at a time with little thought for the future

daze /deɪz/ *v* to stupefy, esp by a blow; stun – **daze** *n* – **~dly** *adv*

dazzle /ˈdæzəl/ *v* **1** to overpower or temporarily blind (the sight) with light **2** to impress deeply, overpower, or confound with brilliance – **dazzle** *n*

D day *n* a day set for launching an operation; *specif* June 6, 1944, on which the Allies began the invasion of France in WW II

DDT *n* a synthetic insecticide that tends to accumulate in food chains and is poisonous to many vertebrates

deacon /ˈdiːkən/ *n* **1** a clergyman ranking below a priest and, in the Anglican and Roman Catholic churches, usu a candidate for ordination as priest **2** any of a group of laymen with administrative and sometimes spiritual duties in various Protestant churches

[1]**dead** /ded/ *adj* **1** deprived of life; having died **2a(1)** having the appearance of death; deathly **(2)** lacking power to move, feel, or respond; numb **b** grown cold; extinguished **3** inanimate, inert **4a** no longer having power or effect, interest or significance **b** no longer used; obsolete **c** lacking in activity **d** lacking elasticity or springiness **5a** absolutely uniform **b** exact **c** abrupt **d** complete, absolute – **~ness** *n*

[2]**dead** *n* **1** *pl in constr* dead people or animals **2** the time of greatest quiet or inactivity

[3]**dead** *adv* **1** absolutely, utterly **2** suddenly and completely **3** directly, exactly **4** *Br* very, extremely – infml

deaden /ˈdedn/ *v* **1** to deprive of liveliness, brilliance, sensation, or force **2** to make (e g a wall) impervious to sound

dead heat *n* an inconclusive finish to a race or other contest, in which the fastest time, highest total, etc is achieved by more than one competitor

dead letter *n* a law that has lost its force without being formally abolished

deadline /ˈdedlaɪn/ *n* a date or time before which sthg (e g the presentation of copy for publication) must be done

deadlock /ˈdedlɒk/ *n* **1** inaction or neutralization resulting from the opposition of equally powerful and uncompromising people or factions; a standstill **2** a tied score

[1]**deadly** /ˈdedli/ *adj* **1** capable of producing death **2a** implacable **b** unerring **c** marked by determination or extreme seriousness **3** lacking animation; dull **4** intense, extreme – **-liness** *n*

[2]**deadly** *adv* **1** suggesting death **2** extremely

deadly nightshade *n* a European poisonous nightshade that has dull purple flowers and black berries

dead man's handle *n, Br* a handle that requires constant pressure to allow operation (e g of a train or tram)

deadpan /ˈdedpæn/ *adj* impassive, expressionless

dead reckoning *n* the calculation without celestial observations of the position of a ship or aircraft, from the record of the courses followed, the distance travelled, etc

deadweight /ˈded,weɪt/ *n* **1** the unrelieved weight of an inert mass **2** a ship's total weight including cargo, fuel, stores, crew, and passengers

deaf /def/ *adj* **1** (partially) lacking the sense of hearing **2** unwilling to hear or listen *to*; not to be persuaded – **~ness** *n*

deafen /ˈdefən/ *v* to make deaf

deaf-mute *n or adj* (one who is) deaf and dumb

[1]**deal** /diːl/ *n* **1** a usu large or indefinite quantity or degree; a lot **2** the act or right of distributing cards to players in a card game; *also* the hand dealt to a player

[2]**deal** *v* **dealt** /delt/ **1** to distribute the cards in a card game **2** to concern oneself or itself **3a** to trade **b** to sell or distribute sthg as a business **4** to take action with regard to sby or sthg – **~er** *n*

[3]**deal** *n* **1** a transaction **2** treatment received **3** an arrangement for mutual advantage

[4]**deal** *n* (a sawn piece of) fir or pine timber

dealing /ˈdiːlɪŋ/ *n* **1** *pl* friendly or business interactions **2** a method of business; a manner of conduct

dean /diːn/ *n* **1** the head of a cathedral chapter or of part of a diocese – often used as a title **2** the head of a university division, faculty, or school

deanery /ˈdiːnəri/ *n* the office, jurisdiction, or official residence of a clerical dean

[1]**dear** /dɪəʳ/ *adj* **1** highly valued; much loved – often used in address **2** expensive **3** heartfelt – **~ness** *n* – **~ly** *adv*

[2]**dear** *n* **1a** a loved one; a sweetheart **b** – used as a familiar or affectionate form of address **2** a lovable person

[3]**dear** *interj* – used typically to express annoyance or dismay

dearth /dɜːθ/ *n* an inadequate supply; a scarcity

death /deθ/ *n* **1** a permanent cessation of all vital functions; the end of life **2** the cause or occasion of loss of life **3** *cap* death personified, usu represented as a skeleton with a scythe **4** the state of being dead **5** extinction, disappearance

deathblow /ˈdeθbləʊ/ *n* a destructive or killing stroke or event

deathless /ˈdeθlɪ̣s/ *adj* immortal, imperishable – **~ly** *adv*

death's-head *n* a human skull symbolic of death

death trap *n* a potentially lethal structure or place

deathwatch /ˈdeθwɒtʃ/ *n* **1** a vigil kept with the dead or dying **2 deathwatch beetle, deathwatch** a small wood-boring beetle common in old buildings

debacle /deɪˈbɑːkəl, dɪ-/ *n* **1** a violent disruption (e g of an army); a rout **2** a complete failure; a fiasco

debar /dɪˈbɑːʳ/ *v* to bar or ban *from* having, doing, or undergoing sthg

debase /dɪˈbeɪs/ *v* **1** to lower in status, esteem, quality, or character **2** to reduce the intrinsic value of (a coin) by increasing the content of low-value metal – **~ment** *n*

[1]**debate** /dɪˈbeɪt/ *n* the usu formal discussion of a motion **a** in parliament **b** between 2 opposing sides

[2]**debate** *v* **1** to argue about **2** to consider – **-table** *adj* – **~r** *n*

[1]**debauch** /dɪˈbɔːtʃ/ *v* **1** to lead away from virtue or excellence **2** to make excessively intemperate or sensual

[2]**debauch** *n* an orgy

debauchery /dɪˈbɔːtʃəri/ *n* excessive

indulgence in the pleasures of the flesh

debenture /dɪ'bentʃəʳ/ *n, Br* a loan secured on the assets of a company in respect of which the company must pay a fixed interest before any dividends are paid to its own shareholders

debilitate /dɪ'bɪlɟteɪt/ *v* to impair the strength of; enfeeble – **debility** *n*

[1]**debit** /'debɟt/ *n* **1** a record of money owed **2** a charge against a bank account

[2]**debit** *v* to charge to the debit of

debonair /,debə'neəʳ/ *adj* **1** suave, urbane **2** lighthearted, nonchalant

debouch /dɪ'baʊtʃ/ *v* to emerge or issue, esp from a narrow place into a wider place

debris /'debri, 'deɪ-/ *n* **1** the remains of sthg broken down or destroyed **2a** an accumulation of fragments of rock **b** accumulated rubbish or waste

debt /det/ *n* **1** a state of owing **2** sthg owed; an obligation

debtor /'detəʳ/ *n* one who owes a debt

debut /'deɪbjuː, 'debjuː/ *n* **1** a first public appearance **2** a formal entrance into society

debutante /'debjʊtɑːnt/ *n* a young woman making her formal entrance into society

decade /'dekeɪd/ *n* **1** a period of 10 years **2** a division of the rosary containing 10 Hail Marys

decadence /'dekədəns/ *n* **1** the gratification of ones desires, whims, etc in an excessive or unrestrained manner **2** a (period of) decline in moral or cultural standards – **-ent** *adj* – **-ently** *adv*

decamp /dɪ'kæmp/ *v* **1** to break up a camp **2** to depart suddenly; abscond

decant /dɪ'kænt/ *v* to pour from one vessel into another, esp without disturbing the sediment – **~er** *n*

decapitate /dɪ'kæpɟteɪt/ *v* to cut off the head of – **-tation** *n*

decathlon /dɪ'kæθlɒn/ *n* a men's athletic contest in which each competitor competes in 10 running, jumping, and throwing events

[1]**decay** /dɪ'keɪ/ *v* **1** to decline from a sound or prosperous condition **2** to decrease gradually in quantity, activity, or force; *specif* to undergo radioactive decay **3** to decline in health, strength, or vigour **4** to undergo decomposition

[2]**decay** *n* **1** a gradual decline in strength, soundness, prosperity, or quality **2** a wasting or wearing away; ruin **3** (a product of) rot; *specif* decomposition of organic matter chiefly by bacteria in the presence of oxygen **4** decrease in quantity, activity, or force; *esp* spontaneous disintegration of an atom or particle usu with the emission of radiation

decease /dɪ'siːs/ *n* death – fml – **~d** *adj, n*

deceit /dɪ'siːt/ *n* **1** the act or practice of deceiving; deception **2** the quality of being deceitful

deceitful /dɪ'siːtfəl/ *adj* having a tendency or disposition to deceive: **a** not honest **b** deceptive, misleading – **~ly** *adv* – **~ness** *n*

deceive /dɪ'siːv/ *v* to cause to accept as true or valid what is false or invalid; delude – **deceiver** *n*

decelerate /,diː'seləreɪt/ *v* to (cause to) move at decreasing speed – **-ation** *n*

December /dɪ'sembəʳ/ *n* the 12th month of the Gregorian calendar

decent /'diːsənt/ *adj* **1** conforming to standards of propriety, good taste, or morality; *specif* clothed according to standards of propriety **2** adequate, tolerable **3** *chiefly Br* obliging, considerate – infml – **decency** *n* – **~ly** *adv*

decentral·ize, -ise /diː'sentrəlaɪz/ *v* to shift governmental powers from central to regional or local authorities – **-ization** *n*

deception /dɪ'sepʃən/ *n* **1** deceiving or being deceived **2** sthg that deceives; a trick

deceptive /dɪ'septɪv/ *adj* tending or having power to deceive; misleading – **~ly** *adv* – **~ness** *n*

decibel /de'sɟbel/ *n* a unit for expressing the intensity of sounds on a scale from zero for the average least perceptible sound to about 130 for the average pain level

decide /dɪ'saɪd/ *v* **1** to arrive at a solution that ends uncertainty or dispute about **2** to bring to a definitive end **3** to make a choice or judgment

decided /dɪˈsaɪdɪ̣d/ *adj* **1** unquestionable **2** free from doubt or hesitation – **~ly** *adv*

deciduous /dɪˈsɪdʒʊəs/ *adj* (having parts) that fall off or are shed seasonally or at a particular stage in development

[1]**decimal** /ˈdesɪ̣məl/ *adj* **1** numbered or proceeding by tens: **a** based on the number 10 **b** subdivided into units which are tenths, hundredths, etc of another unit **2** using a decimal system (e g of coinage) – **~ly** *adv*

[2]**decimal, decimal fraction** *n* a fraction that is expressed as a sum of integral multiples of powers of $^1/_{10}$ by writing a dot followed by 1 digit for the number of tenths, 1 digit for the number of hundredths, and so on (e g 0.25 = $^{25}/_{100}$)

decimal·ize, -ise *v* to convert (currency, weights and measures, etc) to a decimal system

decimal point *n* the dot at the left of a decimal fraction

decimate /ˈdesɪ̣meɪt/ *v* **1** to kill every tenth man of (e g mutinous soldiers) **2** to destroy a large part of – **-mation** *n*

decipher /dɪˈsaɪfəʳ/ *v* **1** to decode **2** to make out the meaning of despite obscurity

decision /dɪˈsɪʒən/ *n* **1a** deciding **b** a conclusion arrived at after consideration **2** a report of a conclusion **3** promptness and firmness in deciding

decisive /dɪˈsaɪsɪv/ *adj* **1** conclusive, final **2** firm, resolute **3** unmistakable, unquestionable – **~ly** *adv* – **~ness** *n*

[1]**deck** /dek/ *n* **1** a platform in a ship serving usu as a structural element and forming the floor for its compartments **2a** a level or floor of a bus with more than 1 floor **b** the part of a record player or tape recorder on which the record or tape is mounted when being played **3** *NAm* a pack of playing cards **4** *the* ground – infml; chiefly in *hit the deck*

[2]**deck** *v* to array, decorate – often + *out*

deck chair *n* an adjustable folding chair made of canvas stretched over a wooden frame

deckhand /ˈdekhænd/ *n* a seaman who performs manual duties

declaim /dɪˈkleɪm/ *v* to speak rhetorically, pompously, or bombastically – **declamation** *n* – **declamatory** *adj*

declaration /ˌdekləˈreɪʃən/ *n* **1** sthg declared **2** a document containing such a declaration

declare /dɪˈkleəʳ/ *v* **1** to make known formally or explicitly **2** to make evident; show **3** to state emphatically; affirm **4** to make a full statement of (one's taxable or dutiable income or property) **5** *of a captain or team* to announce one's decision to end one's side's innings in cricket before all the batsmen are out – **declarable** *adj* – **declaratory** *adj*

declination /ˌdeklɪ̣ˈneɪʃən/ *n* **1** angular distance (e g of a star) N or S from the celestial equator **2** the angle between a compass needle and the geographical meridian, equal to the difference between magnetic and true north

[1]**decline** /dɪˈklaɪn/ *v* **1** to slope or bend down **2a** *of a celestial body* to sink towards setting **b** to draw towards a close; wane **3a** to refuse to undertake, engage in, or comply with **b** to refuse courteously

[2]**decline** *n* **1a** a gradual physical or mental decay **b** a change to a lower state or level **2** the period during which sthg is approaching its end **3** a downward slope

decode /ˌdiːˈkəʊd/ *v* to convert (a coded message) into intelligible language

decolon·ize, -ise /ˌdiːˈkɒlənaɪz/ *v* to free from colonial status; grant self-government

decompose /ˌdiːkəmˈpəʊz/ *v* to undergo chemical breakdown; decay, rot – **-position** *n*

decompress /ˌdiːkəmˈpres/ *v* to release from pressure or compression – **~ion** *n*

decontaminate /ˌdiːkənˈtæmɪ̣neɪt/ *v* to rid of (radioactive) contamination – **-nation** *n*

decor, décor /ˈdeɪkɔːʳ/ *n* the style and layout of interior decoration and furnishings

decorate /'dekəreɪt/ *v* **1a** to add sthg ornamental to **b** to apply new coverings of paint, wallpaper, etc to the interior or exterior surfaces of **2** to award a mark of honour to – **-ation** *n*

decorative /'dekərətɪv/ *adj* purely ornamental rather than functional – **~ly** *adv*

decorator /'dekəreɪtəʳ/ *n* one who designs or executes interior decoration and furnishings

decorous /'dekərəs/ *adj* marked by propriety and good taste; correct – **~ly** *adv*

decorum /dɨ'kɔːrəm/ *n* propriety and good taste in conduct or appearance

decoy /'diːkɔɪ/ *n* **1** a pond into which wild fowl are lured for capture **2** sthg used to lure or lead another into a trap **3** sby or sthg used to distract or divert the attention (e g of an enemy) – **decoy** *v*

[1]**decrease** /dɪ'kriːs/ *v* to (cause to) grow progressively less (e g in size, amount, number, or intensity)

[2]**decrease** *n* **1** the process of decreasing **2** the amount by which sthg decreases

[1]**decree** /dɪ'kriː/ *n* **1** an order usu having legal force **2** a judicial decision, esp in an equity, probate, or divorce court

[2]**decree** *v* to command or impose by decree

decree nisi /dɪ,kriː 'naɪsaɪ, 'niːsi/ *n* a provisional decree of divorce that is made absolute after a fixed period unless cause to the contrary is shown

decrepit /dɪ'krepɨt/ *adj* **1** wasted and weakened e g by old age **2a** worn-out **b** fallen into ruin or disrepair – **~ude** *n*

decry /dɪ'kraɪ/ *v* to express strong disapproval of

dedicate /'dedɨkeɪt/ *v* **1** to consecrate **2a** to set apart to a definite use **b** to assign permanently to a goal or way of life **3** to inscribe or address (a book, song, etc) to somebody or something as a mark of esteem or affection

dedicated /'dedɨkeɪtɨd/ *adj* **1** devoted to a cause, ideal, or purpose; zealous **2** given over to a particular purpose – **~ly** *adv*

dedication /,dedɨ'keɪʃən/ *n* **1** a devoting or setting aside for a particular, specif religious, purpose **2** a phrase or sentence that dedicates **3** self-sacrificing devotion

deduce /dɪ'djuːs/ *v* to infer from a general principle – **-ducible** *adj* – **-duction** *n* – **-ductive** *adj*

deduct /dɪ'dʌkt/ *v* to subtract (an amount) from a total – **~ible** *adj* – **~ion** *n*

deed /diːd/ *n* **1** an illustrious act or action; a feat, exploit **2** the act of performing **3** a signed (and sealed) written document containing some legal transfer, bargain, or contract

deem /diːm/ *v* to judge, consider – fml

[1]**deep** /diːp/ *adj* **1a** extending far downwards **b** (extending) far from the surface of the body **c** extending well back from a front surface **d** near the outer limits of the playing area **2** having a specified extension in an implied direction **3a** difficult to understand **b** capable of profound thought **c** engrossed, involved **d** intense, extreme **4a** *of a colour* high in saturation and low in lightness **b** having a low musical pitch or pitch range – **~ly** *adv* – **~ness** *n*

[2]**deep** *adv* **1a(1)** to a great depth **(2)** deep to a specified degree – usu in combination **b** well within the boundaries **2** far on; late **3** in a deep position

[3]**deep** *n* **1** a vast or immeasurable extent; an abyss **2** *the* sea

deepen /'diːpən/ *v* to make or become deeper or more profound

deep-freeze *v* to freeze or store (e g food) in a freezer

deep freeze *n* a freezer

deep-fry *v* to fry (food) by complete immersion in hot fat or oil

deep-rooted *adj* firmly established

deep-seated *adj* **1** situated far below the surface **2** firmly established

deer /dɪəʳ/ *n, pl* **deer** *also* **deers** any of several ruminant mammals of which most of the males and some of the females bear antlers

deerstalker /'dɪəstɔːkəʳ/ *n* a close-fitting hat with peaks at the front and the back and flaps that may be folded down as coverings for ears

deface /dɪ'feɪs/ *v* to mar the external appearance of – **~ment** *n*

[1]**de facto** /dɪ 'fæktəʊ, deɪ-/ *adv* in reality; actually

[2]**de facto** *adj* existing in fact; effective

defame /dɪ'feɪm/ *v* to injure the reputation of by libel or slander – **defamatory** *adj* – **defamation** *n*

[1]**default** /dɪ'fɔːlt/ *n* failure to act, pay, appear, or compete

[2]**default** *v* to fail to meet an esp financial obligation – **~er** *n*

[1]**defeat** /dɪ'fiːt/ *v* **1a** to nullify **b** to frustrate **2** to win victory over

[2]**defeat** *n* **1** an overthrow, esp of an army in battle **2** the loss of a contest

defeatism /dɪ'fiːtɪzəm/ *n* acceptance of or resignation to defeat – **-ist** *n*

defecate, *Br also* **defaecate** /'defɪ̇keɪt/ *v* to discharge (esp faeces) from the bowels – **-cation** *n*

[1]**defect** /'diːfekt/ *n* an imperfection that impairs worth or usefulness – **~ive** *n*

[2]**defect** /dɪ'fekt/ *v* to desert a cause or party, often in order to espouse another – **~or** *n* – **~ion** *n*

defence, *NAm chiefly* **defense** /dɪ'fens/ *n* **1** the act or action of defending **2a** a means or method of defending; *also, pl* a defensive structure **b** an argument in support or justification **c** a defendant's denial, answer, or strategy **3** *sing or pl in constr* **a** a defending party or group (e g in a court of law) **b** defensive players, acts, or moves in a game or sport **4** the military resources of a country – **~less** *adj*

defend /dɪ'fend/ *v* **1a** to protect from attack **b** to maintain by argument in the face of opposition or criticism **2a** to play or be in defence **b** to attempt to prevent an opponent from scoring (e g a goal) **3** to act as legal representative in court for

defendant /dɪ'fendənt/ *n* a person, company, etc against whom a criminal charge or civil claim is made

defensible /dɪ'fensɪ̇bl/ *adj* capable of being defended – **-bly** *adv*

[1]**defensive** /dɪ'fensɪv/ *adj* **1** serving to defend **2a** disposed to ward off expected criticism or critical inquiry **b** of or relating to the attempt to keep an opponent from scoring

[1]**defer** /dɪ'fɜːʳ/ *v* to delay; put off – **~ment** *n*

[2]**defer** *v* to submit *to* another's opinion, usu through deference or respect

deference /'defərəns/ *n* respect and esteem due a superior or an elder – **-ential** *adj* – **-entially** *adv*

defiance /dɪ'faɪəns/ *n* a disposition to resist; contempt of opposition – **defiant** *adj* – **defiantly** *adv*

deficient /dɪ'fɪʃənt/ *adj* **1** lacking in some necessary quality or element **2** not up to a normal standard or complement – **~ly** *adv* – **-iency** *n*

deficit /'defɪ̇sɪ̇t/ *n* **1** a deficiency in amount or quality **2** an excess of expenditure over revenue

[1]**defile** /dɪ'faɪl/ *v* to make unclean or (sexually) impure – **~r** *n* – **~ment** *n*

[2]**defile** *v* to march off in a file

[3]**defile** *n* a narrow passage or gorge

define /dɪ'faɪn/ *v* **1** to fix or mark the limits of; demarcate **2a** to be the essential quality or qualities of; identify **b** to set forth the meaning of

definite /'defɪ̇nɪ̇t, 'defənɪ̇t/ *adj* **1** having distinct or certain limits **2a** free of all ambiguity, uncertainty, or obscurity **b** unquestionable, decided **3** designating an identified or immediately identifiable person or thing – **~ly** *adv*

definition /ˌdefɪ̇'nɪʃən/ *n* **1** a word or phrase expressing the essential nature of a person, word, or thing; a meaning **2a** the action or power of making definite and clear **b(1)** distinctness of outline or detail (e g in a photograph) **(2)** clarity, esp of musical sound in reproduction

definitive /dɪ'fɪnɪ̇tɪv/ *adj* **1** authoritative and apparently exhaustive **2** *of a postage stamp* issued as one of the normal stamps of the country or territory of use – **~ly** *adv*

deflate /ˌdiː'fleɪt, dɪ-/ *v* **1** to release air or gas from **2a** to reduce in size or importance **b** to reduce in self-confidence or self-importance, esp suddenly **3** to reduce (a price level) or cause (the availability of credit or the economy) to contract

deflation /dɪ'fleɪʃən, ˌdi-/ *n* **1** a contraction in the volume of available money and credit, and thus in the economy, esp as a result of government policy **2** a decline in the general level of prices

deflect /dɪ'flekt/ *v* to turn from a straight course or fixed direction

deflection, *Br also* **deflexion** /dɪ'flekʃən/ *n* (the amount or degree of) deflecting

deflower /ˌdiː'flaʊəʳ, dɪ-/ *v* to deprive of virginity; ravish

deform /dɪ'fɔːm/ *v* **1** to spoil the form or appearance of **2** to make hideous or monstrous **3** to alter the shape of by stress – **~ation** *n*

deformity /dɪ'fɔːmɪ̥ti/ *n* a physical blemish or distortion; a disfigurement

defraud /dɪ'frɔːd/ *v* to cheat of sthg

defray /dɪ'freɪ/ *v* to provide for the payment of

defrost /ˌdiː'frɒst/ *v* **1** to thaw out, esp from a deep-frozen state **2** to free from ice – **~er** *n*

deft /deft/ *adj* marked by facility and skill – **~ly** *adv* – **~ness** *n*

defunct /dɪ'fʌŋkt/ *adj* no longer existing or in use; *esp* dead

defuse /ˌdiː'fjuːz/ *v* **1** to remove the fuse from (a mine, bomb, etc) **2** to make less harmful, potent, or tense

defy /dɪ'faɪ/ *v* **1** to challenge to do sthg considered impossible; dare **2** to show no fear of nor respect for **3** to resist attempts at

[1]**degenerate** /dɪ'dʒenərɪ̥t/ *n* sthg or esp sby degenerate; *esp* one showing signs of reversion to an earlier cultural or evolutionary stage

[2]**degenerate** /dɪ'dʒenəreɪt/ *v* **1** to pass from a higher to a lower type or condition; deteriorate **2** to sink into a low intellectual or moral state **3** to decline from a former thriving or healthy condition – **-ration** *n* – **-rative** *adj* – **-racy** *n*

degrade /dɪ'greɪd/ *v* **1a** to demote **b** to impair with respect to some physical property **2** to bring to low esteem or into disrepute – **-dation** *n*

degree /dɪ'griː/ *n* **1** a step or stage in a process, course, or order of classification **2a** the extent or measure of an action, condition, or relation **b** a legal measure of guilt or negligence **c** a positive and esp considerable amount **3** the civil condition or status of a person **4** an academic title conferred: **a** on students in recognition of proficiency **b** honorarily **5** a division or interval of a scale of measurement; *specif* any of various units for measuring temperature **6** a 360th part of the circumference of a circle

dehuman·ize, -ise /ˌdiː'hjuːmənaɪz/ *v* to divest of human qualities

dehydrate /ˌdiː'haɪdreɪt/ *v* to remove (bound) water from (a chemical compound, foods, etc) – **~d** *adj* – **-dration** *n*

deify /'diːɪ̥faɪ, 'deɪ-/ *v* to make a god or an object of worship of – **deification** *n*

deign /deɪn/ *v* to condescend to give or offer

deity /'diːɪ̥ti, 'deɪ-/ *n* **1** *cap the* Supreme Being; God **2** a god or goddess

déjà vu /ˌdeɪʒɑː 'vuː/ *n* **1** the illusion of remembering scenes and events when they are experienced for the first time **2** sthg excessively or unpleasantly familiar

dejected /dɪ'dʒektɪ̥d/ *adj* cast down in spirits; depressed – **~ly** *adv*

dejection /dɪ'dʒekʃən/ *n* lowness of spirits

de jure /diː 'dʒʊəri/ *adv or adj* by (full legal) right

[1]**delay** /dɪ'leɪ/ *n* **1** delaying or (an instance of) being delayed **2** the time during which sthg is delayed

[2]**delay** *v* **1a** to postpone **b** to move or act slowly **2a** to pause momentarily **b** to stop, detain, or hinder for a time

delectable /dɪ'lektəbəl/ *adj* **1** highly pleasing; delightful **2** delicious – **-bly** *adv* – **-tation** *n*

[1]**delegate** /'delɪ̥gɪ̥t/ *n* a person delegated to act for another; *esp* a representative to a conference

[2]**delegate** /'delɪ̥geɪt/ *v* **1** to assign responsibility or authority **2** to appoint as one's representative

delegation /ˌdelɪ̥'geɪʃən/ *n sing or pl in constr* a group of people chosen to represent others

delete /dɪ'liːt/ *v* to eliminate, esp by

blotting out, cutting out, or erasing – **-tion** *n*

deleterious /ˌdelə̇ˈtɪərɪəs/ *adj* harmful, detrimental – fml – **~ly** *adv*

delft /delft/ *n* tin-glazed Dutch earthenware with usu blue and white decoration

¹**deliberate** /dɪˈlɪbərə̇t/ *adj* **1** of or resulting from careful and thorough consideration **2** characterized by awareness of the consequences **3** slow, unhurried – **~ly** *adv* – **~ness** *n*

²**deliberate** /dɪˈlɪbəreɪt/ *v* to ponder issues and decisions carefully – **-ative** *adj*

deliberation /dɪˌlɪbəˈreɪʃən/ *n* **1** deliberating or being deliberate **2** a discussion and consideration of pros and cons

delicacy /ˈdelɪkəsi/ *n* **1** sthg pleasing to eat that is considered rare or luxurious **2** the quality or state of being dainty **3** frailty, fragility **4** precise and refined perception or discrimination **5** refined sensibility in feeling or conduct

delicate /ˈdelɪkə̇t/ *adj* **1** pleasing to the senses in a subtle way; dainty, charming **2a** marked by keen sensitivity or subtle discrimination **b** fastidious, squeamish **3** marked by extreme precision or sensitivity **4** calling for or involving meticulously careful treatment **5a** very finely made **b(1)** fragile **(2)** weak, sickly **c** marked by or requiring tact – **~ly** *adv*

delicatessen /ˌdelɪkəˈtesən/ *n* **1** *pl in constr* (delicacies and foreign) foods ready for eating (e g cooked meats) **2** a shop where delicatessen are sold

delicious /dɪˈlɪʃəs/ *adj* **1** affording great pleasure; delightful **2** highly pleasing to one of the bodily senses, esp of taste or smell – **~ly** *adv* – **~ness** *n*

¹**delight** /dɪˈlaɪt/ *n* **1** great pleasure or satisfaction; joy **2** sthg that gives great pleasure

²**delight** *v* to take great pleasure *in* doing sthg

delightful /dɪˈlaɪtfəl/ *adj* highly pleasing – **~ly** *adv*

delineate /dɪˈlɪnieɪt/ *v* **1** to show by drawing lines in the shape of **2** to describe in usu sharp or vivid detail – **-ation** *n*

delinquency /dɪˈlɪŋkwənsi/ *n* (the practice of engaging in) antisocial or illegal conduct – used esp when emphasis is placed on maladjustment rather than criminal intent – **-quent** *n*

delinquent /dɪˈlɪŋkwənt/ *adj* **1** guilty of wrongdoing or of neglect of duty **2** marked by delinquency

delirium /dɪˈlɪərɪəm/ *n* **1** confusion, frenzy, disordered speech, hallucinations, etc occurring as a (temporary) mental disturbance **2** frenzied excitement – **-rious** *adj* – **-riously** *adv*

delirium tremens /dɪˌlɪərɪəm ˈtremenz/ *n* a violent delirium with tremors induced by chronic alcoholism

deliver /dɪˈlɪvəʳ/ *v* **1** to set free **2** to hand over **3a** to aid in the birth of **b** to give birth to **4** to utter **5** to aim or guide (e g a blow) to an intended target or destination **6** to produce the promised, desired, or expected results – infml

deliverance /dɪˈlɪvərəns/ *n* liberation, rescue

delivery /dɪˈlɪvəri/ *n* **1** handing over **2a** a physical or legal transfer **b** sthg delivered at 1 time or in 1 unit **3** the act of giving birth **4** the manner or style of uttering in speech or song **5** the act or manner or an instance of sending forth, throwing, or bowling

dell /del/ *n* a small secluded hollow or valley, esp in a forest

delouse /ˌdiːˈlaʊs/ *v* to remove lice from

Delphic /ˈdelfɪk/, **Delphian** *adj* **1** of ancient Delphi or its oracle **2a** ambiguous **b** obscure, enigmatic

delphinium /delˈfɪnɪəm/ *n* any of a genus of plants of the buttercup family with deeply cut leaves and flowers in showy spikes

delta /ˈdeltə/ *n* **1** the 4th letter of the Greek alphabet **2** a triangular deposit (e g of silt) at the mouth of a river

delta wing *n* an approximately triangular aircraft wing with a (nearly) straight rearmost edge

delude /dɪˈluːd/ *v* to mislead the mind or judgment of; deceive, trick

¹**deluge** /ˈdeljuːdʒ/ *n* **1a** a great flood; *specif, cap the* Flood recorded in the Old Testament (Gen 6:8) **b** a drench-

ing fall of rain 2 an overwhelming amount or number

[2]**deluge** *v* **1** to overflow with water; inundate **2** to overwhelm, swamp

delusion /dɪ'luːʒən/ *n* (a mental state characterized by) a false belief (about the self or others) that persists despite the facts and occurs esp in psychotic states – **-sive** *adj*

de luxe /dl̥ 'lʌks/ *adj* notably luxurious or elegant

delve /delv/ *v* **1** to dig or work (as if) with a spade **2** to make a careful or detailed search for information

demagogue, *NAm also* **demagog** /'deməgɒg/ *n* **1** a leader of the common people in ancient times **2** an agitator who makes use of popular prejudices in order to gain power – **~ry** *n* – **-gogic** *adj* – **-gogically** *adv*

[1]**demand** /dɪ'mɑːnd/ *n* **1** demanding or asking, esp with authority; a claim **2a** an expressed desire for ownership or use **b** willingness and ability to purchase a commodity or service **c** the quantity of a commodity or service wanted at a specified price and time **3** a desire or need *for*; the state of being sought after

[2]**demand** *v* **1** to make a demand; ask **2** to call for urgently, abruptly, or insistently

demanding /dɪ'mɑːndɪŋ/ *adj* exacting

demarcate /'diːmɑːkeɪt/ *v* **1** to mark the limits of **2** to set apart; separate – **-tion** *n*

demean /dɪ'miːn/ *v* to degrade, debase

demeanour, *NAm chiefly* **demeanor** /dɪ'miːnəʳ/ *n* behaviour towards others; outward manner

demented /dɪ'mentl̥d/ *adj* insane; *also* crazy – **~ly** *adv*

demerara sugar /ˌdeməˌreərə 'ʃʊgəʳ/ *n* brown crystallized unrefined cane sugar from the W Indies

demerit /diː'merl̥t/ *n* a quality that deserves blame or lacks merit; a fault, defect

demesne /dɪ'meɪn, dɪ'miːn/ *n* **1** land actually occupied by the owner and not held by tenants **2a** the land attached to a mansion **b** landed property; an estate

demigod /'demigɒd/, *fem* **demigoddess** *n* **1** a mythological superhuman being with less power than a god **2** an offspring of a union between a mortal and a god

demise /dɪ'maɪz/ *n* **1** the conveyance of an estate or transfer of sovereignty by will or lease **2a** death – technical, euph, or humor **b** a cessation of existence or activity – fml or humor

demist /ˌdiː'mɪst/ *v* to remove mist from (e g a car windscreen) – **~er** *n*

demo /'deməʊ/ *n* a (political) demonstration

demobil·ize, -ise /ˌdiː'məʊbl̥laɪz/ *v* to discharge from military service – **-ization** *n*

democracy /dɪ'mɒkrəsi/ *n* **1a** government by the people **b** (a political unit with) a government in which the supreme power is exercised by the people directly or indirectly through a system of representation usu involving free elections **2** the absence of class distinctions or privileges

democrat /'deməkræt/ *n* **1a** an adherent of democracy **b** one who practises social equality **2** *cap* a member of the Democratic party of the USA

democratic /ˌdemə'krætɪk/ *adj* **1** of or favouring democracy or social equality **2** *often cap* of or constituting a political party of the USA associated with policies of social reform and internationalism – **~ally** *adv* – **-ratization** *n*

demography /dɪ'mɒgrəfi/ *n* the statistical study of human populations, esp with reference to size and density, distribution, and vital statistics – **-pher** *n* – **-phic** *adj*

demolish /dɪ'mɒlɪʃ/ *v* **1** to destroy, smash, or tear down **2** to eat up – infml – **~er** *n* – **-ition** *n*

demon /'diːmən/ *n* **1** an evil spirit **2** one who has unusual drive or effectiveness – **~ic** *adj* – **~ically** *adv*

demonstrate /'demənstreɪt/ *v* **1** to show clearly **2** to illustrate and explain, esp with many examples **3** to show or prove the application, value, or efficiency of to a prospective buyer **4** to take part in a (political) demonstration – **-tion** *n* – **-strable** *adj*

demonstrative /dɪmɒnstrətɪv/ *adj* given to or marked by display of feeling

demonstrator /ˈdemənstreɪtəʳ/ *n* **1** a junior staff member who demonstrates experiments in a university science department **2** sby who participates in a demonstration

demoral·ize, -ise /dɪˈmɒrəlaɪz/ *v* to discourage; dispirit

demote /di'məʊt/ *v* to reduce to a lower grade or rank – **-tion** *n*

demur /dɪˈmɜːʳ/ *v* to take exception; (mildly) object

demure /dɪˈmjʊəʳ/ *adj* **1** reserved, modest **2** affectedly modest, reserved, or serious; coy – **~ly** *adv* – **~ness** *n*

den /den/ *n* **1** the lair of a wild, usu predatory, animal **2** a centre of secret, esp unlawful, activity **3** a comfortable usu secluded room

denial /dɪˈnaɪəl/ *n* **1** a refusal to satisfy a request or desire **2a** a refusal to admit the truth or reality (e g of a statement or charge) **b** an assertion that an allegation is false **3** a refusal to acknowledge sby or sthg; a disavowal

denier /ˈdiːnɪəʳ, ˈdenɪəʳ/ *n* a unit of fineness for silk, rayon, or nylon yarn

denigrate /ˈden̩greɪt/ *v* **1** to cast aspersions on; defame **2** to belittle – **-gration** *n* – **-gratory** *adj*

denim /ˈden̩m/ *n* **1** a firm durable twilled usu blue cotton fabric used esp for jeans **2** *pl* denim trousers; *esp* blue jeans

denizen /ˈden̩zən/ *n* **1** an inhabitant **2** a naturalized plant or animal

denomination /dɪˌnɒm̩ˈneɪʃən/ *n* **1** a religious organization or sect **2** a grade or degree in a series of values or sizes (e g of money)

denominator /dɪˈnɒm̩neɪtəʳ/ *n* the part of a vulgar fraction that is below the line and that in fractions with 1 as the numerator indicates into how many parts the unit is divided

denote /dɪˈnəʊt/ *v* **1** to indicate **2** to be a sign or mark for **3** to mean – **denotation** *n*

denouement /deɪˈnuːmɑ̃/ *n* **1** the resolution of the main complication in a literary work **2** the outcome of a complex sequence of events

denounce /dɪˈnaʊns/ *v* **1** to condemn, esp publicly, as deserving censure or punishment **2** to inform against; accuse

dense /dens/ *adj* **1** marked by high density, compactness, or crowding together of parts **2** sluggish of mind; stupid **3** demanding concentration to follow or comprehend – **~ly** *adv* – **~ness** *n*

density /ˈdens̩ti/ *n* **1** the mass of a substance or distribution of a quantity per unit of volume or space **2** the degree of opaqueness of sthg translucent

dent /dent/ *n* **1** a depression or hollow made by a blow or by pressure **2** an adverse effect – **dent** *v*

dental /ˈdentl/ *adj* of the teeth or dentistry

dentifrice /ˈdent̩fr̩s/ *n* a powder, paste, or liquid for cleaning the teeth

dentine /ˈdentiːn/ *n* a calcium-containing material, similar to but harder and denser than bone, of which the principal mass of a tooth is composed

dentist /ˈdent̩st/ *n* one who treats diseases, injuries, etc of the teeth, and mouth and who makes and inserts false teeth – **~ry** *n*

denture /ˈdentʃəʳ/ *n* an artificial replacement for 1 or more teeth; *esp, pl* a set of false teeth

denude /dɪˈnjuːd/ *v* **1a** to strip of all covering **b** to lay bare by erosion **2** to remove an important possession or quality from; strip

denunciation /dɪˌnʌnsiˈeɪʃən/ *n* a (public) condemnation

deny /dɪˈnaɪ/ *v* **1** to declare to be untrue or invalid; refuse to accept **2a** to give a negative answer to **b** to refuse to grant **3** to restrain (oneself) from self-indulgence

deodorant /diːˈəʊdərənt/ *n* a preparation that destroys or masks unpleasant smells – **-orize** *v*

depart /dɪˈpɑːt/ *v* **1** to leave; go away (from) **2** to turn aside; deviate *from* – **~ed** *adj* – **~ure** *n*

department /dɪˈpɑːtmənt/ *n* **1a** a division of an institution or business that provides a specified service or deals with a specified subject **b** a major administrative subdivision (e g in France) **c** a section of a large store **2** a distinct sphere (e g of activity or thought) – infml – **~al** *adj*

depend /dɪ'pend/ *v* **1** to be determined by or based on some condition or action **2a** to place reliance or trust **b** to be dependent, esp for financial support *USE* (*1&2*) + *on* or *upon*

dependable /dɪ'pendəbəl/ *adj* reliable – **-bly** *adv* – **-bility** *n*

dependant, *NAm chiefly* **dependent** /dɪ'pendənt/ *n* a person who relies on another for esp financial support

dependence *also* **dependance** /dɪ'pendəns/ *n* **1** being influenced by or subject to another **2** reliance, trust **3** psychological need for a drug after a period of use; habituation

dependency /dɪ'pendənsi/ *n* a territorial unit under the jurisdiction of a nation but not formally annexed to it

dependent /dɪ'pendənt/ *adj* **1** determined or conditioned by another; contingent **2** relying on another for support **3** subject to another's jurisdiction *USE* (*1&2*) + *on* or *upon*

depict /dɪ'pɪkt/ *v* **1** to represent by a picture **2** to describe – **depiction** *n*

deplete /dɪ'pliːt/ *v* to reduce in amount by using up; exhaust, esp of strength or resources – **depletion** *n*

deplore /dɪ'plɔːʳ/ *v* to regret or disapprove of strongly – **-rable** *adj* – **-rably** *adv*

deploy /dɪ'plɔɪ/ *v* **1** to spread out (e g troops or ships), esp in battle formation **2** to utilize or arrange as if deploying troops – **~ment** *n*

depopulate /ˌdiː'pɒpjʊleɪt/ *v* to greatly reduce the population of – **-lation** *n*

¹deport /dɪ'pɔːt/ *v* to expel (e g an alien or convicted criminal) legally from a country – **~ation** *n*

²deport *v* to behave or conduct (oneself) in a specified manner – fml

deportment /dɪ'pɔːtmənt/ *n* **1** the manner in which one stands, sits, or walks; posture **2** behaviour, conduct

depose /dɪ'pəʊz/ *v* **1** to remove from a position of authority (e g a throne) **2** to testify under oath or by affidavit

¹deposit /dɪ'pɒzɟt/ *v* **1** to place, esp for safekeeping or as a pledge; *esp* to put in a bank **2** to lay down; place – **~or** *n*

²deposit *n* **1** depositing or being deposited **2a** money deposited in a bank **b** money given as a pledge or down payment **3** a depository **4** sthg laid down; *esp* (an accumulation of) matter deposited by a natural process

deposit account *n, chiefly Br* an account (e g in a bank) on which interest is usu payable and from which withdrawals can be made usu only by prior arrangement

deposition /ˌdepə'zɪʃən/ *n* **1** removal from a position of authority **2** a (written and sworn) statement presented as evidence

depository /dɪ'pɒzɟtəri/ *n* a place where sthg is deposited, esp for safekeeping

depot /'depəʊ/ *n* **1** a place for the reception and training of military recruits; a regimental headquarters **2a** a place for storing goods **b** a store, depository **3** *Br* an area (e g a garage) in which buses or trains are stored, esp for maintenance

deprave /dɪ'preɪv/ *v* to corrupt morally; pervert – **depravation** *n*

depravity /dɪ'prævɟti/ *n* (an instance of) moral corruption

deprecate /'deprɟkeɪt/ *v* to express disapproval of, esp mildly or regretfully – **-catingly** *adv* – **-cation** *n*

deprecatory /'deprɟkeɪtəri/ *adj* **1** apologetic **2** disapproving

depreciate /dɪ'priːʃieɪt/ *v* to lessen in value – **-atory** *adj* – **depreciation** *n*

depress /dɪ'pres/ *v* **1** to push or press down **2** to lessen the activity or strength of **3** to sadden, dispirit – **depressing** *adj* – **depressingly** *adv* – **depressed** *adj*

depression /dɪ'preʃən/ *n* **1a** a pressing down; a lowering **b** (a mental disorder marked by inactivity, difficulty in thinking and concentration, and esp by) sadness or dejection **2** a depressed place or part; a hollow **3** an area of low pressure in a weather system **4** a period of low general economic activity marked esp by rising levels of unemployment

deprivation /ˌdeprɨˈveɪʃən/ *n* **1** an act of depriving; a loss **2** being deprived; privation

deprive /dɪˈpraɪv/ *v* **1** to take sthg away from **2** to withhold sthg from *USE* + *of*

deprived /dɪˈpraɪvd/ *adj* lacking the necessities of life or a good environment

depth /depθ/ *n* **1a** a part that is far from the outside or surface **b(1)** a profound or intense state (e g of thought or feeling) **(2)** the worst, most intensive, or severest part **2a** the perpendicular measurement downwards from a surface **b** the distance from front to back **3** the degree of intensity *USE* (*1*) often pl with sing. meaning

depth charge *n* an explosive projectile for use underwater, esp against submarines

deputation /ˌdepjʊˈteɪʃən/ *n sing or pl in constr* a group of people appointed to represent others

depute /dɪˈpjuːt/ *v* to delegate

deputy /ˈdepjʊti/ *n* **1** a person (e g a second-in-command) appointed as a substitute with power to act for another **2** a member of the lower house of some legislative assemblies – **-tize** *v*

derail /ˌdiːˈreɪl, dɪ-/ *v* to cause (e g a train) to leave the rails – **~ment** *n*

derange /dɪˈreɪndʒ/ *v* to disturb the operation or functions of – **~ment** *n*

derby /ˈdɑːbi/ *n* **1** *cap* a flat race for 3-year-old horses over 1½mi (about 2.9km) held annually at Epsom in England **2** a usu informal race or contest for a specified category of contestant **3** a sporting match against a major local rival **4** *chiefly NAm* a bowler hat

¹**derelict** /ˈderɨlɪkt/ *adj* left to decay

²**derelict** *n* **1** sthg voluntarily abandoned; *specif* a ship abandoned on the high seas **2** a down-and-out

dereliction /ˌderɨˈlɪkʃən/ *n* **1** (intentional) abandonment or being abandoned **2a** conscious neglect **b** a fault, shortcoming

deride /dɪˈraɪd/ *v* to mock, scorn – **derision** *n* – **derisive** *adj* – **derisively** *adv*

derisory /dɪˈraɪsəri/ *adj* worthy of derision; ridiculous; *specif* contemptibly small – **-rily** *adv*

derivative /dɪˈrɪvətɪv/ *adj* made up of derived elements; not original – **derivative** *n*

derive /dɪˈraɪv/ *v* **1** to obtain or receive, esp *from* a specified source **2** to infer, deduce *from* – **-vation** *n*

dermatitis /ˌdɜːməˈtaɪtɨs/ *n* a disease or inflammation of the skin

dermatology /ˌdɜːməˈtɒlədʒi/ *n* a branch of medicine dealing with (diseases of) the skin – **-ogist** *n*

derogatory /dɪˈrɒgətəri/ *adj* expressing a low opinion; disparaging – **-rily** *adv*

derrick /ˈderɪk/ *n* **1** a hoisting apparatus employing a tackle rigged at the end of a beam **2** a framework over an oil well or similar hole, for supporting drilling tackle

derring-do /ˌderɪŋ ˈduː/ *n* daring action

derv /dɜːv/ *n* fuel oil for diesel engines

dervish /ˈdɜːvɪʃ/ *n* a member of a Muslim religious order noted for devotional exercises (e g bodily movements leading to a trance)

desalinate /ˌdiːˈsælɨneɪt/ *v* to remove salt from (esp sea water)

descant /ˈdeskænt/ *n* a counterpoint superimposed on a simple melody and usu sung by some or all of the sopranos

descend /dɪˈsend/ *v* **1** to pass from a higher to a lower level **2** to pass by inheritance **3** to incline, lead, or extend downwards **4** to come down or make a sudden attack – usu + *on* or *upon* **5** to sink in status or dignity; stoop

descendant, *NAm also* **descendent** /dɪˈsendənt/ *n* sby or sthg descended or deriving from another

descended /dɪˈsendɨd/ *adj* having as an ancestor; sprung *from*

descent /dɪˈsent/ *n* **1** the act or process of descending **2** a downward step (e g in status or value) **3a** derivation from an ancestor **b** a transmission from a usu earlier source; a derivation **4** a downward inclination; a slope

describe /dɪ'skraɪb/ *v* **1** to give an account of in words **2** to trace the outline of

description /dɪ'skrɪpʃən/ *n* **1** an account **2** kind, sort – **-tive** *adj* – **-tively** *adv* – **-tiveness** *n*

descry /dɪ'skraɪ/ *v* to notice or see, esp at a distance – fml

desecrate /'desɪkreɪt/ *v* to violate the sanctity of; profane – **-cration** *n*

desegregate /diː'segrɪ̣geɪt/ *v* to eliminate (racial) segregation in – **-ation** *n*

desensit·ize, -ise /diː'sensɪ̣taɪz/ *v* to cause to become less sensitive. or insensitive

[1]**desert** /'dezət/ *n* (a desolate region like) a dry barren region incapable of supporting much life

[2]**desert** /dɪ'zɜːt/ *n* deserved reward or punishment – usu pl with sing. meaning

[3]**desert** *v* **1** to quit one's post, (military) service, etc without leave or justification **2** to abandon or forsake, esp in time of need – **deserter** *n* – **desertion** *n*

Desert /'dezət/ *trademark* – used for an ankle-high laced suede boot with a rubber sole

deserve /dɪ'zɜːv/ *v* to be worthy of or suitable for (some recompense or treatment) – **~dly** *adv* – **deserving** *adj*

deshabille /,deɪzæ'biːl, ,dɪsæ'biːl/ , **déshabillé** /,deɪzæ'biːeɪ/ *n* the state of being only partially or carelessly dressed

desiccate /'desɪ̣keɪt/ *v* **1** to dry up **2** to preserve (a food) by drying to dehydrate – **-cant** *n* – **-ation** *n*

[1]**design** /dɪ'zaɪn/ *v* **1** to conceive and plan out in the mind **2a** to draw the plans for **b** to create or execute according to a plan; devise – **~er** *n*

[2]**design** *n* **1** a mental plan or scheme **2** *pl* dishonest, hostile, or acquisitive intent – + *on* **3** (the act of producing) a drawing, plan, or pattern showing the details of how sthg is to be constructed **4** the arrangement of the elements of a work of art or article **5** a decorative pattern

[1]**designate** /'dezɪgneɪt/ *adj* chosen for an office but not yet installed

[2]**designate** *v* **1** to indicate **2** to call by a distinctive name or title **3** to nominate for a specified purpose, office, or duty – **-nation** *n*

designing /dɪ'zaɪnɪŋ/ *adj* crafty, scheming

desirable /dɪ'zaɪərəbəl/ *adj* **1** causing (sexual) desire; attractive **2** worth seeking or doing as advantageous, beneficial, or wise – **-bility** *n* – **-bly** *adv*

[1]**desire** /dɪ'zaɪəʳ/ *v* **1** to long or hope for **2** to express a wish for; request **3** to wish to have sexual relations with – **desirous** *adj*

[2]**desire** *n* **1** a conscious impulse towards something promising enjoyment or satisfaction **2** a (sexual) longing or craving

desist /dɪ'zɪst, dɪ'sɪst/ *v* to cease to proceed or act – fml

desk /desk/ *n* **1a** a table with a sloping or horizontal surface and often drawers and compartments, that is designed esp for writing and reading **b** a music stand **2** a division of an organization specializing in a usu specified phase of activity

desolate /'dezələt/ *adj* **1** deserted, uninhabited **2** forsaken, forlorn **3** barren, lifeless – **~ly** *adv* – **-lation** *n*

[1]**despair** /dɪ'speəʳ/ *v* to lose all hope or confidence

[2]**despair** *n* **1** utter loss of hope **2** a cause of hopelessness

despatch /dɪ'spætʃ/ *v or n* (to) dispatch

desperado /,despə'rɑːdəʊ/ *n* a bold, reckless, or violent person, esp a criminal

desperate /'despərɪ̣t/ *adj* **1** being (almost) beyond hope **2a** reckless because of despair **b** undertaken as a last resort **3** suffering extreme need or anxiety – **~ly** *adv* – **-ation** *n*

despicable /dɪ'spɪkəbəl, 'despɪ-/ *adj* morally contemptible – **-bly** *adv*

despise /dɪ'spaɪz/ *v* **1** to regard with contempt or distaste **2** to regard as negligible or worthless

despite /dɪ'spaɪt/ *prep* notwithstanding; in spite of

despondent /dɪ'spɒndənt/ *adj* feeling extreme discouragement or dejection – **~ly** *adv* – **-dency** *n*

despot /'despɒt, -ət/ *n* **1** a ruler with

absolute power **2** a person exercising power abusively or tyrannically – **~ic** *adj* – **~ically** *adv* – **~ism** *n*

dessert /dɪ'zɜːt/ *n* a usu sweet course or dish served at the end of a meal

dessertspoon /dɪ'zɜːtspuːn/ *n* a spoon intermediate in size between a teaspoon and a tablespoon and used for eating dessert

destination /ˌdestʲ̣'neɪʃən/ *n* a place which is set for the end of a journey or to which sthg is sent

destine /'destɪn/ *v* **1** to designate or dedicate in advance **2** to direct or set apart for a specified purpose or goal

destiny /'destʲ̣ni/ *n* **1** the power or agency held to determine the course of events **2** sthg to which a person or thing is destined; fortune **3** a predetermined course of events

destitute /'destʲ̣tjuːt/ *adj* **1** lacking sthg necessary or desirable – + *of* **2** lacking the basic necessities of life; extremely poor – **-tution** *n*

destroy /dɪ'strɔɪ/ *v* **1** to demolish, ruin **2** to put an end to; kill

destroyer /dɪ'strɔɪəʳ/ *n* a fast multi-purpose warship smaller than a cruiser

destruction /dɪ'strʌkʃən/ *n* **1** destroying or being destroyed **2** a cause of ruin or downfall

destructive /dɪ'strʌktɪv/ *adj* **1** causing destruction **2** designed or tending to destroy; negative – **~ly** *adv* – **~ness** *n*

desultory /'desəltəri, 'dez-/ *adj* passing aimlessly from one subject or activity to another – **-rily** *adv*

detach /dɪ'tætʃ/ *v* to separate, esp from a larger mass and usu without causing damage – **~able** *adj*

detached /dɪ'tætʃt/ *adj* **1** standing by itself; *specif* not sharing any wall with another building **2** free from prejudice or emotional involvement; aloof – **~ly** *adv*

detachment /dɪ'tætʃmənt/ *n* **1** a detaching, separation **2** *sing or pl in constr* a body of troops, ships, etc separated from the main body for a special mission **3** freedom from bias

¹detail /'diːteɪl/ *n* **1** a small and subordinate part; *specif* part of a work of art considered or reproduced in isolation **2** an individual relevant part or fact – usu pl **3** *sing or pl in constr* a small military detachment selected for a particular task

²detail *v* **1** to report in detail **2** to assign to a particular task or place

detain /dɪ'teɪn/ *v* **1** to hold or retain (as if) in custody **2** to delay; hold back

detainee /ˌdiːteɪ'niː/ *n* a person held in custody, esp for political reasons

detect /dɪ'tekt/ *v* to discover the existence or presence of – **detector** *n* – **~ive** *adj*

detective /dɪ'tektɪv/ *n* a policeman or other person engaged in investigating crimes, detecting lawbreakers, or getting information that is not readily accessible

détente /'deɪtɒnt, deɪ'tɒnt/ *n* a relaxation of strained relations (e g between ideologically opposed nations)

detention /dɪ'tenʃən/ *n* **1** detaining or being detained, esp in custody **2** the keeping in of a pupil after school hours as a punishment

deter /dɪ'tɜːʳ/ *v* to discourage or prevent from acting

detergent /dɪ'tɜːdʒənt/ *n* a cleansing agent (e g washing-up liquid)

deteriorate /dɪ'tɪərɪəreɪt/ *v* to grow or make or worse – **-ration** *n*

determinant /dɪ'tɜːmɪnənt/ *n* sthg that determines, fixes, or conditions

determination /dɪˌtɜːmʲ̣'neɪʃən/ *n* **1** firm intention **2** the ability to make and act on firm decisions; resoluteness

determine /dɪ'tɜːmʲ̣n/ *v* **1** to settle, decide **2a** to fix beforehand **b** to regulate **3** to ascertain the intent, nature, or scope of

determined /dɪ'tɜːmʲ̣nd/ *adj* **1** decided, resolved **2** firm, resolute

determinism /dɪ'tɜːmɪnɪzəm/ *n* **1** a doctrine that all phenomena are determined by preceding occurrences **2** a belief in predestination

deterrent /dɪ'terənt/ *n* sthg that deters; *esp* a (nuclear) weapon that is held in readiness by one nation or alliance in order to deter another from attacking – **-rence** *n*

detest /dɪ'test/ *v* to feel intense dislike for; loathe – **~able** *adj* – **~ably** *adv* – **~ation** *n*

detonate /'detəneɪt/ *v* to (cause to)

explode with sudden violence – -nation *n*

detonator /'detəneɪtəʳ/ *n* a device used for detonating a high explosive

detour /'diːtʊəʳ/ *n* a deviation from a course or procedure; *specif* a way that is an alternative to a shorter or planned route – **detour** *v*

detract /dɪ'trækt/ *v* to take away something desirable *from* – **~ion** *n*

detractor /dɪ'træktəʳ/ *n* one who belittles sby or his/her ideas or beliefs

detriment /'detrɪ̣mənt/ *n* (a cause of) injury or damage – **~al** *adj* – **~ally** *adv*

detritus /dɪ'traɪtəs/ *n, pl* **detritus** debris caused by disintegration

deuce /djuːs/ *n* **1** a playing card or the face of a dice representing the number 2 **2** a tie in a game (e g tennis) after which a side must score 2 consecutive clear points to win **3a** the devil, the dickens – formerly used as an interjection or intensive

devalue /diː'væljuː/ *v* **1** to reduce the exchange value of (money) **2** to lessen the value or reputation of – **-uation** *n*

devastate /'devəsteɪt/ *v* **1** to reduce to ruin; lay waste **2** to have a shattering effect on; overwhelm – **-station** *n*

develop /dɪ'veləp/ *v* **1a** to show signs of **b** to subject (exposed photograph material) esp to chemicals, in order to produce a visible image **2** to bring out the possibilities of **3a** to promote the growth of **b** to make more available or usable **4** to acquire gradually **5a** to go through a process of natural growth, differentiation, or evolution by successive changes **b** to evolve; *broadly* to grow

developer /dɪ'veləpəʳ/ *n* **1** a chemical used to develop exposed photographic materials **2** sby who buys land and builds and sells houses on it

development /dɪ'veləpmənt/ *n* **1** the act, process, or result of developing; *esp* economic growth **2** being developed

deviant /'diːvɪənt/ *adj* deviating, esp from a norm

deviate /'diːvieɪt/ *v* to stray, esp from a topic, principle, or accepted norm or from a straight course

deviation /ˌdiːvi'eɪʃən/ *n* **1** deflection of a compass needle caused by local magnetic influences **2** the difference between a value in a frequency distribution and a fixed number **3** departure from an established party line

device /dɪ'vaɪs/ *n* **1a** sthg elaborate or intricate in design **b** sthg (e g a figure of speech or a dramatic convention) designed to achieve a particular artistic effect **c** a piece of equipment or a mechanism designed for a special purpose or function **2** *pl* desire, will

devil /'devəl/ *n* **1** *often cap* the supreme spirit of evil in Jewish and Christian belief **2** a malignant spirit **3** an extremely cruel or wicked person **4** a high-spirited, reckless, or energetic person **5a** a person of the specified type **b** sthg provoking, difficult, or trying – **~ish** *adj* – **~ishly** *adv* – **~ry** *n*

devilment /'devəlment/ *n* wild mischief

devil's advocate *n* **1** the Roman Catholic official who presents the possible objections to claims to canonization **2** a person who champions the less accepted or approved cause, esp for the sake of argument

devious /'diːvɪəs/ *adj* **1** deviating from a straight or usual course **2** not straightforward or wholly sincere – **~ly** *adv* – **~ness** *n*

devise /dɪ'vaɪz/ *v* **1** to formulate in the mind; invent **2** to give or leave (real property) by will

devoid /dɪ'vɔɪd/ *adj* not having or using; lacking – + *of*

devolution /ˌdiːvə'luːʃən/ *n* **1** the passage of rights, property, etc to a successor **2** the surrender of functions and powers to regional authorities by a central government

devolve /dɪ'vɒlv/ *v* **1** to pass by transmission or succession **2** to fall or be passed, usu as an obligation or responsibility *USE* + *on*

devote /dɪ'vəʊt/ *v* **1** to set apart for a special purpose; dedicate *to* **2** to give (oneself) over wholly *to*

devoted /dɪ'vəʊtɪ̣d/ *adj* loyally attached – **~ly** *adv*

devotee /ˌdevəˈtiː/ *n* a keen follower or supporter; an enthusiast

devotion /dɪˈvəʊʃən/ *n* **1** a special act of prayer – usu pl **2a** devoting or being devoted **b** ardent love, affection, or dedication

devour /dɪˈvaʊəʳ/ *v* **1** to eat up greedily or ravenously **2** to swallow up; consume **3** to take in eagerly through the mind or senses

devout /dɪˈvaʊt/ *adj* devoted to religion; pious – **~ly** *adv* – **~ness** *n*

dew /djuː/ *n* moisture that condenses on the surfaces of cool bodies, esp at night – **dewy** *adj* – **dewily** *adv* – **dewiness** *n*

dewlap /ˈdjuːlæp/ *n* a hanging fold of skin under the neck of an animal (e g a cow)

dexterous, dextrous /ˈdekstərəs/ *adj* **1** skilful with the hands **2** mentally adroit – **~ly** *adv* – **-rity** *n*

dextrose /ˈdekstrəʊz, -strəʊs/ *n* the form of glucose found in fruit and honey

dhoti /ˈdəʊti/ *n, pl* **dhotis** a loincloth worn by Hindu men

dhow /daʊ/ *n* an Arab boat, usu having a large 4-sided sail, a long overhanging bow and a high poop

diabetes /ˌdaɪəˈbiːtiːz, -tɨs/ *n* any of various abnormal conditions characterized by an excess of sugar in the blood – **-betic** *adj*

diabolic /ˌdaɪəˈbɒlɪk/ *adj* **1** (characteristic) of the devil; fiendish **2** dreadful, appalling – **~ally** *adv*

diadem /ˈdaɪədem/ *n* a crown; *specif* a headband worn as a badge of royalty

diagnosis /ˌdaɪəgˈnəʊsɨs/ *n, pl* **diagnoses** **1** the art or act of identifying a disease from its signs and symptoms **2** (a statement resulting from) the investigation of the cause or nature of a problem or phenomenon – **-nostic** *adj* – **-nose** *v*

diagonal /daɪˈægənəl/ *adj* **1** joining 2 nonadjacent angles of a polygon or polyhedron **2** running in an oblique direction from a reference line (e g the vertical) – **~ly** *adv*

diagram /ˈdaɪəgræm/ *n* **1** a line drawing made for mathematical or scientific purposes **2** a drawing or design that shows the arrangement and relations (e g of parts) – **~matic** *adj*

[1]**dial** /ˈdaɪəl/ *n* **1** the graduated face of a timepiece **2a** a face on which some measurement is registered, usu by means of numbers and a pointer **b** a disc-shaped control on an electrical or mechanical device **3** *Br* a person's face – slang

[2]**dial** *v* to make a call on the telephone

dialect /ˈdaɪəlekt/ *n* a regional, social, or subordinate variety of a language, usu differing distinctively from the standard or original language – **~al** *adj*

dialectic /ˌdaɪəˈlektɪk/ *n* a systematic reasoning, exposition, or argument that juxtaposes opposed or contradictory ideas and usu seeks to resolve their conflict – **~al adj** – **~ally adv** – **~ian n**

dialogue, *NAm also* **dialog** /ˈdaɪəlɒg/ *n* **1a** a conversation between 2 people or between a person and sthg else (e g a computer) **b** an exchange of ideas and opinions **2** the conversational element of literary or dramatic composition

diameter /daɪˈæmɨtəʳ/ *n* the length of a straight line through the centre of an object (e g a circle)

[1]**diamond** /ˈdaɪəmənd/ *n* **1** a (piece of) very hard crystalline carbon that is highly valued as a precious stone, esp when flawless and transparent, and is used industrially as an abrasive and in rock drills **2** a square or rhombus orientated so that the diagonals are horizontal and vertical **3a** a playing card marked with 1 or more red diamond-shaped figures **b** *pl but sing or pl in constr* the suit comprising cards identified by this figure

[2]**diamond** *adj* of, marking, or being a 60th or 75th anniversary

diaper /ˈdaɪəpəʳ/ *n, chiefly NAm* a nappy

diaphanous /daɪˈæfənəs/ *adj* so fine as to be almost transparent

diaphragm /ˈdaɪəfræm/ *n* **1** the partition separating the chest and abdominal cavities in mammals **2** a device that limits the aperture of a lens or optical system **3** a thin flexible disc that is free to vibrate (e g in an earphone) **4** a Dutch cap

diarist /'daɪərɪ̥st/ *n* one who keeps a diary

diarrhoea /ˌdaɪə'rɪə/ *n* abnormally frequent intestinal evacuations with more or less fluid faeces

diary /'daɪəri/ *n* **1** (a book containing) a daily record of personal experiences or observations **2** *chiefly Br* a book with dates marked in which memoranda can be noted

Diaspora /daɪ'æspərə/ *n* (the settling, or area of settlement, of) Jews outside Palestine or modern Israel

diatom /'daɪətɒm/ *n* any of a class of minute single-celled plants with hard shell-like skeletons

diatonic /ˌdaɪə'tonɪk/ *adj* of a musical scale of 8 notes to the octave

diatribe /'daɪətraɪb/ *n* a (lengthy) piece of bitter and abusive criticism

¹dibble /'dɪbl/ *n* a small pointed hand implement used to make holes in the ground for plants, seeds, or bulbs

²dibble *v* **1** to plant with a dibble **2** to make holes in (soil) (as if) with a dibble

¹dice /daɪs/ *n, pl* **dice** **1a** a small cube that is marked on each face with from 1 to 6 spots so that spots on opposite faces total 7 and that is used to determine arbitrary values in various games **b** a gambling game played with dice **2** a small square piece (e g of food)

²dice *v* **1** to cut (e g food) into small cubes **2** to take a chance

dicey /'daɪsi/ *adj* risky, unpredictable – infml

dichotomy /daɪ'kɒtəmi/ *n* a division into 2 esp mutually exclusive or contradictory groups

dickens /'dɪkɪ̥nz/ *n* devil, deuce – used as an interjection or intensive

dicker /'dɪkəʳ/ *v* **1** to bargain, haggle **2** to hesitate, dither

dicky /'dɪki/ *adj, Br* in a weak or unsound condition – infml

¹dictate /dɪk'teɪt/ *v* **1** to speak or read for a person to transcribe or for a machine to record **2** to impose, pronounce, or specify with authority – **-tation** *n*

²dictate /'dɪkteɪt/ *n* **1** an authoritative rule, prescription, or command **2** a ruling principle – usu pl

dictator /dɪk'teɪtəʳ/ *n* an absolute ruler; *esp* one who has seized power unconstitutionally and uses it oppressively – **~ial** *adj*

dictatorship /dɪk'teɪtəʃɪp/ *n* **1** total or absolute control; leadership, rule **2** a state or form of government where absolute power is concentrated in one person or a small clique

diction /'dɪkʃən/ *n* **1** choice of words, esp with regard to correctness or clearness **2** pronunciation and enunciation of words in speaking or singing

dictionary /'dɪkʃənəri/ *n* **1** a reference book containing the meanings of words or terms often together with information about their pronunciations, etymologies, etc **2** a reference book giving for words of one language equivalents in another

dictum /'dɪktəm/ *n, pl* **dicta** *also* **dictums** an authoritative statement on some topic; a pronouncement

did /dɪd/ *past of* **do**

didactic /daɪ'dæktɪk/ *adj* **1** intended to teach sthg, esp a moral lesson **2** having a tendency to teach in an authoritarian manner – **~ally** *adv*

diddle /dɪdl/ *v* to cheat, swindle – infml

didst /dɪdst/ *archaic past 2 sing of* **do**

¹die /daɪ/ *v* **dying** **1** to stop living; suffer the end of physical life **2** to pass out of existence, cease **3** to long keenly or desperately

²die *n* any of various tools or devices for giving a desired shape, form, or finish to a material or for impressing an object or material

die-hard *n or adj* (one) strongly resisting change

diesel engine /'diːzəl ˌendʒɪ̥n/ *n* an internal-combustion engine in which fuel is ignited by air compressed to a sufficiently high temperature

diet /'daɪət/ *n* **1** the food and drink habitually taken by a group, animal, or individual **2** the kind and amount of food prescribed for a person or animal for a special purpose (e g losing weight) – **dietary** *adj*

²diet *n* any of various national or provincial legislatures

differ /ˈdɪfəʳ/ *v* **1** to be unlike; be distinct *from* **2** to disagree

difference /ˈdifərəns/ *n* **1a** unlikeness between 2 or more people or things **b** the degree or amount by which things differ **2** a disagreement, dispute; dissension **3** a significant change in or effect on a situation

different /ˈdɪfərənt/ *adj* **1** partly or totally unlike; dissimilar – + *from*, chiefly Br *to*, or chiefly NAm *than* **2a** distinct **b** various **c** another **3** unusual, special – **~ly** *adv*

[1]**differential** /ˌdɪfəˈrenʃəl/ *adj* **1a** of or constituting a difference **b** based on or resulting from a differential **c** functioning or proceeding differently or at a different rate **2** of or involving a differential or differentiation **3** of quantitative differences

[2]**differential** *n* **1** the amount of a difference between comparable individuals or classes; *specif* the amount by which the remuneration of distinct types of worker differs **2** (a case covering) a differential gear

differential calculus *n* a branch of mathematics dealing chiefly with the rate of change of functions with respect to their variables

differential gear *n* an arrangement of gears in a vehicle that allows one of the wheels imparting motion to turn (e g in going round a corner) faster than the other

differentiate /ˌdɪfəˈrenʃieɪt/ *v* **1** to obtain the mathematical derivative of **2** to mark or show a difference in **3** to express the specific difference of – **-ation** *n*

difficult /ˈdɪfɪkəlt/ *adj* **1** hard to do, make, carry out, or understand **2a** hard to deal with, manage, or please **b** puzzling

difficulty /ˈdɪfɪkəlti/ *n* **1** being difficult **2** an obstacle or impediment **3** a cause of (financial) trouble or embarrassment – usu pl with sing. meaning

diffident /ˈdɪfɨdənt/ *adj* **1** lacking in self-confidence **2** reserved, unassertive – **~ly** *adv* – **-dence** *n*

diffract /dɪˈfrækt/ *v* to cause a beam of light to become a set of light and dark or coloured bands in passing by the edge of an opaque body, through narrow slits, etc – **~ion** *n*

[1]**diffuse** /dɪˈfjuːs/ *adj* **1** not concentrated or localized; scattered **2** lacking conciseness; verbose – **~ly** *adv* – **~ness** *n*

[2]**diffuse** /dɪˈfjuːz/ *v* **1** to spread out freely in all directions **2** to break up and distribute (incident light) by reflection – **-fusion** *n*

[1]**dig** /dɪg/ *v* **1** to break up, turn, or loosen earth with an implement **2** to bring to the surface (as if) by digging; unearth **3** to hollow out by removing earth; excavate **4** to drive down into; thrust **5** to poke, prod **6** to understand, appreciate – slang – **~ger** *n*

[2]**dig** *n* **1a** a thrust, poke **b** a cutting or snide remark **2** an archaeological excavation (site) **3** *pl, chiefly Br* lodgings

[1]**digest** /daɪˈdʒest, dɨ-/ *n* **1** a systematic compilation of laws **2** a shortened version (e g of a book)

[2]**digest** *v* **1** to convert (food) into a form the body can use **2** to assimilate mentally **3** to compress into a short summary – **~ible** *adj* – **~ibility** *n*

digestion /daɪˈdʒestʃən, dɨ-/ *n* the process or power of digesting sthg, esp food

digestive /daɪˈdʒestɪv/ *adj* of, causing, or promoting digestion

digit /ˈdɪdʒɨt/ *n* **1a** any of the Arabic numerals from 1 to 9, usu also including 0 **b** any of the elements that combine to form numbers in a system other than the decimal system **2** a finger or toe – **~al** *adj*

dignify /ˈdɪgnɨfaɪ/ *v* to confer dignity or distinction on – **-fied** *adj*

dignitary /ˈdɪgnɨtəri/ *n* a person of high rank or holding a position of dignity or honour

dignity /ˈdɪgnɨti/ *n* **1** being worthy, honoured, or esteemed **2** high rank, office, or position **3** stillness of manner; gravity

digress /daɪˈgres/ *v* to turn aside, esp from the main subject in writing or speaking – **~ion** *n* – **~ive** *adj*

dike /daɪk/ *n* a dyke

dilapidated /dɨˈlæpɨdeɪtɨd/ *adj* decayed or fallen into partial ruin, esp through neglect or misuse – **-dation** *n*

dilate /daɪˈleɪt/ **1** to comment at length *on* or *upon* **2** to become wide – **-lation** *n*

dilatory /ˈdɪlətəri/ *adj* **1** tending or intended to cause delay **2** slow, tardy

dilemma /dʒ̍ˈlemə, daɪ-/ *n* a situation involving choice between 2 equally unsatisfactory alternatives

dilettante /ˌdɪlʒ̍ˈtænti/ *n, pl* **dilettanti** a person with a superficial interest in an art or a branch of knowledge

diligent /ˈdɪlʒ̍dʒənt/ *adj* showing steady application and effort – **~ly** *adv* – **-gence** *n*

dill /dɪl/ *n* a European plant with aromatic foliage and seeds, both of which are used in flavouring foods (e g pickles)

dillydally /ˈdɪlidæli/ *v* to waste time by loitering; dawdle – infml

[1]**dilute** /daɪˈluːt/ *v* **1** to make thinner or more liquid by adding another liquid **2** to diminish the strength or brilliance of by adding more liquid, light, etc – **-tion** *n*

[2]**dilute** *adj* weak, diluted

[1]**dim** /dɪm/ *adj* **1** giving out a weak or insufficient light **2a** seen or seeing indistinctly **b** characterized by an unfavourable or pessimistic attitude – esp in *take a dim view of* **3** lacking intelligence; stupid – infml – **~ly** *adv* – **~ness** *n*

[2]**dim** *v* to make or become dim

dime /daɪm/ *n* a coin worth $^1/_{10}$ of a US dollar

dimension /daɪˈmenʃən, dʒ̍-/ *n* **1a** (the size of) extension in 1 or all directions **b** the range over which sthg extends; the scope – usu pl with sing. meaning **c** an aspect **2** any of the fundamental quantities, specif mass, length, and time, which combine to make a derived unit – usu pl – **~al** *adj*

diminish /dʒ̍ˈmɪnɪʃ/ *n* **1** to become gradually less; dwindle **2** to lessen the reputation of; belittle – **-nution** *n*

diminished /dɪˈmɪnɪʃt/ *adj, of a musical interval* made a semitone less than perfect or minor

diminuendo /dɪˌmɪnjʊˈendəʊ/ *n, adv, or adj, pl* **diminuendos** (a musical passage played) with a decrease in volume

diminutive /dʒ̍ˈmɪnjʊtɪv/ *adj* **1** indicating small size and sometimes lovableness or triviality – used in connection with affixes and words formed with them (e g *duckling*), with clipped forms (e g *Jim*), and with altered forms (e g *Peggy*) **2** exceptionally small; tiny – **~ly** *adv* – **~ness** *n*

dimple /ˈdɪmpl/ *n* **1** a slight natural indentation in the cheek or another part of the human body **2** a depression or indentation on a surface

dimwit /ˈdɪmˌwɪt/ *n* a stupid or mentally slow person – infml – **dim-witted** *adj*

din /dɪn/ *n* a loud continued discordant noise

dine /daɪn/ *v* to eat dinner – **diner** *n*

[1]**dingdong** /ˈdɪŋdɒŋ/ *n* **1** the ringing sound produced by repeated strokes, esp on a bell **2** a rapid heated exchange of words or blows – infml

[2]**dingdong** *adj* **1** of or resembling the sound of a bell **2** with the advantage (e g in an argument or race) passing continually back and forth from one participant, side, etc to the other – infml

dinghy /ˈdɪŋgi/ *n* **1** a small boat often carried on a ship and used esp as a lifeboat or to transport passengers to and from shore **2** a small open sailing boat

dingo /ˈdɪŋgəʊ/ *n, pl* **dingoes** a wild dog of Australia

dingy /ˈdɪŋdʒi/ *adj* **1** dirty, discoloured **2** shabby, squalid – **dingily** *adv* – **dinginess** *n*

dinner /ˈdɪnəʳ/ *n* **1** (the food eaten for) the principal meal of the day taken either in the evening or at midday **2** a formal evening meal or banquet

dinner jacket *n* a usu black jacket for men's semiformal evening wear

dinosaur /ˈdaɪnəsɔːʳ/ *n* **1** any of a group of extinct, typically very large flesh- or plant-eating reptiles, most of which lived on the land **2** something that is unwieldy and outdated

diocese /ˈdaɪəsʒ̍s/ *n* the area under the jurisdiction of a bishop – **-cesan** *adj*

diode /ˈdaɪəʊd/ *n* **1** a electronic valve having only an anode and a cathode **2**

a semiconductor device having only 2 terminals

[1]**dip** /dɪp/ *v* **1a(1)** to plunge or immerse in a liquid (e g in order to moisten or dye) **(2)** to plunge into a liquid and quickly emerge **b(1)** to immerse sthg in a processing liquid or finishing material **(2)** to immerse a sheep in an antiseptic or parasite-killing solution **2a** to lower and then raise again **b** to drop down or decrease suddenly **3** to reach inside or below sthg, esp so as to take out part of the contents – usu + *in* or *into* **4** to lower (the beam of a vehicle's headlights) so as to reduce glare **5** to incline downwards from the plane of the horizon

[2]**dip** *n* **1** a brief bathe for sport or exercise **2** a sharp downward course; a drop **3** a hollow, depression **4a** a sauce or soft mixture into which food is dipped before being eaten **b** a liquid preparation into which an object or animal may be dipped (e g for cleaning or disinfecting)

diphtheria /dɪf'θɪərɪə, dɪp-/ *n* an acute infectious disease marked by the formation of a false membrane in the throat, causing difficulty in breathing

diphthong /'dɪfθɒŋ, 'dɪp-/ *n* a gliding monosyllabic vowel sound (e g /oy/ in *toy*) that starts at or near the articulatory position for one vowel and moves to or towards the position of another

diploma /dʒ̩'pləʊmə/ *n* **1** a document conferring some honour or privilege **2** (a certificate of) a qualification, usu in a more specialized subject or at a lower level than a degree

diplomacy /dʒ̩'pləʊməsi/ *n* **1** the art and practice of conducting international relations **2** skill and tact in handling affairs – **-mat** *n* – **-matic** *adj* – **-matically** *adv*

dipper /'dɪpəʳ/ *n* **1** sthg (e g a long-handled cup) used for dipping **2** a bird that habitually feeds walking underwater in streams or shallow rivers

dipsomania /ˌdɪpsə'meɪnɪə/ *n* an uncontrollable craving for alcoholic drinks – **~c** *n*

dipstick /'dɪpˌstɪk/ *n* a graduated rod for measuring the depth of a liquid (e g the oil in a car's engine)

dire /daɪəʳ/ *adj* **1** dreadful, awful **2** warning of disaster; ominous **3** desperately urgent

[1]**direct** /dʒ̩'rekt, daɪ-/ *v* **1** to address or aim a remark **2** to cause to turn, move, point, or follow a straight course **3** to show or point out the way for **4a** to supervise **b** to order or instruct with authority **c** to produce a play **d** *NAm* to conduct an orchestra

[2]**direct** *adj* **1** going from one point to another in time or space without deviation or interruption; straight **2** stemming immediately from a source, cause, or reason **3** frank, straightforward **4a** operating without an intervening agency **b** effected by the action of the people or the electorate and not by representatives **5** consisting of or reproducing the exact words of a speaker or writer – **~ness** *n*

[3]**direct** *adv* **1** from point to point without deviation; by the shortest way **2** without an intervening agency or stage

direct current *n* an electric current flowing in 1 direction only

direction /dʒ̩'rekʃən, daɪ-/ *n* **1** guidance or supervision of action **2a** the act, art, or technique of directing an orchestra, film, or theatrical production **b** a word, phrase, or sign indicating the appropriate tempo, mood, or intensity of a passage or movement in music **3** *pl* explicit instructions on how to do sthg or get to a place **4a** the line or course along which sby or sthg moves or is aimed **b** the point towards which sby or sthg faces **5a** a tendency, trend **b** a guiding or motivating purpose

directional /dʒ̩'rekʃənəl/ *adj* **1a** of or indicating direction in space **b** of or being a device that operates more efficiently in one direction than in others **2** relating to direction or guidance, esp of thought or effort

[1]**directive** /dʒ̩'rektɪv, daɪ-/ *adj* **1** serving to direct, guide, or influence **2** serving to provide a direction

[2]**directive** *n* an authoritative instruction issued by a high-level body or official

[1]**directly** /dǰ'rektli, daɪ-/ *adv* **1** in a direct manner **2a** without delay; immediately **b** soon, shortly

[2]**directly** *conj* immediately after; as soon as – infml

direct object *n* a grammatical object representing the primary goal or the result of the action of its verb (e g *me* in 'he hit me'' and *house* in 'we built a house'')

director /dǰ'rektəʳ, daɪ-/ *n* **1** the head of an organized group or administrative unit **2** a member of a governing board entrusted with the overall direction of a company **3** sby who has responsibility for supervising the artistic and technical aspects of a film or play – ~**ship** *n*

directory /dǰ'rektəri, daɪ-/ *n* an alphabetical or classified list (e g of names, addresses, telephone numbers, etc)

dirge /dɜːdʒ/ *n* **1** a song or hymn of grief or lamentation, esp intended to accompany funeral or memorial rites **2** a slow mournful piece of music

[1]**dirigible** /'dɪrǰdʒəbəl, dǰ'rɪ-/ *adj* capable of being steered

[2]**dirigible** *n* an airship

dirk /dɜːk/ *n* a long straight-bladed dagger, used esp by Scottish Highlanders

dirndl /'dɜːndl/ *n* a full skirt with a tight waistband

dirt /dɜːt/ *n* **1a** a filthy or soiling substance (e g mud or grime) **b** sby or sthg worthless or contemptible **2** soil **3a** obscene or pornographic speech or writing **b** scandalous or malicious gossip

dirty /'dɜːti/ *adj* **1a** not clean or pure **b** causing sby or sthg to become soiled or covered with dirt **2a** base, sordid **b** unsportsmanlike, unfair **c** low, despicable **3a** indecent, obscene **b** sexually illicit **4** *of weather* rough, stormy **5** *of colour* not clear and bright; dull – **dirtily** *adv*

disability /ˌdɪsə'bɪlǰti/ *n* **1a** inability to do sthg (e g pursue an occupation) because of physical or mental impairment **b** a handicap **2** a legal disqualification

disable /dɪs'eɪbəl/ *v* **1** to deprive of legal right, qualification, or capacity **2** to cripple – ~**ment** *n*

disadvantage /ˌdɪsəd'vɑːntɪdʒ/ *n* **1** an unfavourable, inferior, or prejudicial situation **2** a handicap

disaffected /ˌdɪsə'fektǰd/ *adj* discontented and resentful, esp towards authority – **-tion** *n*

disagree /ˌdɪsə'griː/ *v* **1** to be unlike or at variance **2** to differ in opinion – usu + *with* **3** to have a bad effect – usu + *with* – ~**ment** *n*

disagreeable /ˌdɪsə'griːəbəl/ *adj* **1** unpleasant, objectionable **2** peevish, ill-tempered – ~**ness** *n* – **-ably** *adv*

disappear /ˌdɪsə'pɪəʳ/ *v* **1** to pass from view suddenly or gradually **2** to cease to be or to be known **3** to leave or depart, esp secretly – infml – ~**ance** *n*

disappoint /ˌdɪsə'pɔɪnt/ *v* to fail to meet the expectation or hope of; *also* to sadden by so doing – ~**ed** *adj* – ~**edly** *adv* – ~**ing** *adj* – ~**ingly** *adv* – ~**ment** *n*

disapprobation /ˌdɪsæprə'beɪʃən/ *n* disapproval – fml

disapprove /ˌdɪsə'pruːv/ *v* to have or express an unfavourable opinion *of* – **-proval** *n* – **-provingly** *adv*

disarm /dɪs'ɑːm/ *v* **1a** to deprive of a weapon or weapons **b** to make (e g a bomb) harmless, esp by removing a fuse or warhead **2** to reduce or abolish weapons and armed forces **3** to dispel the hostility or suspicion of – ~**ament** *n*

disarray /ˌdɪsə'reɪ/ *n* a lack of order or sequence; disorder

disassociate /ˌdɪsə'seʊʃieɪt, -sieɪt/ *v* to dissociate

disaster /dɪ'zɑːstəʳ/ *n* **1** a sudden event bringing great damage, loss, or destruction **2** a failure – **-trous** *adj* – **-trously** *adv*

disavow /ˌdɪsə'vaʊ/ *v* to deny knowledge of or responsibility for; repudiate – fml – ~**al** *n*

disband /dɪs'bænd/ *v* to (cause to) break up and separate; disperse – ~**ment** *n*

disbar /dɪs'bɑːʳ/ *v* to deprive (a barrister) of the right to practise; expel from the bar – ~**ment** *n*

disbelief /ˌdɪsbǰ'liːf/ *n* mental rejection of sthg as untrue

disbelieve /ˌdɪsbǰ'liːv/ *v* to reject or withhold belief (in) – **-liever** *n*

disburse /dɪs'bɜːs/ *v* to pay out, esp from a fund – **~ment** *n*

disc, *NAm chiefly* **disk** /dɪsk/ *n* **1** a thin flat circular object **2** any of various round flat anatomical structures; *esp* any of the cartilaginous discs between the spinal vertebrae **3** a gramophone record **4** a magnetic disc used for the storage of computer data

discard /dɪs'kɑːd/ *v* to get rid of as useless or superfluous

discern /di'sɜːn/ *v* **1** to detect with one of the senses, esp vision **2** to perceive or recognize mentally – **~ible** *adj* – **~ibly** *adv* – **~ment** *n*

discerning /dɪ'sɜːnɪŋ/ *adj* showing insight and understanding; discriminating

¹discharge /dɪs'tʃɑːdʒ/ *v* **1a** to unload **b** to release from an obligation **2a** to shoot **b** to release from custody or care **c** to send or pour out; emit **3a** to dismiss from employment or service **b** to fulfil (e g a debt or obligation) by performing an appropriate action **4** to remove an electric charge from or reduce the electric charge of

²discharge *n* **1** the relieving of an obligation, accusation, or penalty **2** the act of discharging or unloading **3** legal release from confinement; *also* an acquittal **4** a flowing or pouring out **5** release or dismissal, esp from an office or employment **6** the conversion of the chemical energy of a battery into electrical energy

disciple /dɪ'saɪpəl/ *n* one who assists in spreading another's doctrines; *esp* any of Christ's 12 appointed followers – **~ship** *n*

disciplinarian /,dɪsɪ̣plɪ̣'neərɪən/ *n* one who enforces or advocates (strict) discipline or order

¹discipline /'dɪsɪ̣plɪ̣n/ *n* **1** a field of study **2** training of the mind and character designed to produce obedience and self-control **3** punishment, chastisement **4** order obtained by enforcing obedience (e g in a school or army) – **-plinary** *adj*

²discipline *v* **1** to punish or penalize for the sake of discipline **2** to train by instruction and exercise, esp in obedience and self-control **3** to bring (a group) under control

disc jockey *n* one who introduces records of popular usu contemporary music (e g on a radio programme or at a discotheque)

disclaim /dɪs'kleɪm/ *v* **1** to renounce a legal claim to **2** to deny, disavow

disclaimer /dɪs'kleɪməʳ/ *n* **1** a denial of legal responsibility **2** a denial, repudiation

disclose /dɪs'kləʊz/ *v* **1** to expose to view **2** to reveal to public knowledge

disclosure /dɪs'kləʊʒəʳ/ *n* **1** (an instance of) disclosing; an exposure **2** sthg disclosed; a revelation

disco /'dɪskəʊ/ *n, pl* **discos** **1** a collection of popular records together with the equipment for playing them **2** a discotheque – infml

discolour /dɪs'kʌləʳ/ *v* to (cause to) change colour for the worse; stain – **discoloration** *n*

discomfit /dɪs'kʌmfɪ̣t/ *v* **1** to frustrate the plans of; thwart **2** to cause perplexity and embarrassment to; disconcert – **~ure** *n*

¹discomfort /dɪs'kʌmfət/ *v* to make uncomfortable or uneasy

²discomfort *n* (sthg causing) mental or physical unease

discompose /,dɪskəm'pəʊz/ *v* to destroy the composure of – fml – **-posure** *n*

disconcert /,dɪskən'sɜːt/ *v* to disturb the composure of; fluster – **~ingly** *adv*

disconnect /,dɪskə'nekt/ *v* to cut off (e g an electricity supply)

disconnected /,dɪskə'nektɪ̣d/ *adj* disjointed, incoherent – **~ly** *adv* – **-nection** *n*

disconsolate /dɪs'kɒnsəlɪ̣t/ *adj* dejected, downcast – **~ly** *adv*

discontent /,dɪskən'tent/ *n* **1** lack of contentment; dissatisfaction **2** one who is discontented; a malcontent – **~ed** *adj* – **~edly** *adv* – **discontent** *v*

discontinue /,dɪskən'tɪnjuː/ *v* to cease, stop; *specif* to cease production of – **-tinuance** *n*

discontinuous /,dɪskən'tɪnjʊəs/ *adj* lacking sequence, coherence, or continuity – **~ly** *adv* – **-tinuity** *n*

discord /'dɪskɔːd/ *n* **1** lack of agreement or harmony; conflict **2** a harsh unpleasant combination of sounds – ~**ant** *adj* – ~**antly** *adv* – ~**ance** *n*

discotheque /'dɪskətek/ *n* a night-club for dancing to usu recorded music

[1]**discount** /'dɪskaʊnt/ *n* **1** a reduction in the price of goods, accorded esp to special or trade customers **2** a reduction in the amount due on a bill of exchange, debt, etc when paid promptly or before the specified date

[2]**discount** /'dɪskaʊnt; *sense 2* dɪs'kaʊnt/ *v* **1a** to make a deduction from, usu for cash or prompt payment **b** to sell or offer for sale at a discount **2a** to leave out of account as unimportant, unreliable, or irrelevant **b** to underestimate the importance of

discountenance /dɪs'kaʊntɪ̣nəns/ *v* **1** to abash, disconcert **2** to discourage by showing disapproval – fml

discourage /dɪs'kʌrɪdʒ/ *v* **1** to deprive of confidence; dishearten **2a** to hinder, deter *from* **b** to attempt to prevent, esp by showing disapproval – **-agingly** *adv* – ~**ment** *n*

[1]**discourse** /'dɪskɔːs/ *n* **1** a talk, conversation **2** (orderly expression of ideas in) a formal speech or piece of writing

[2]**discourse** /'dɪskɔːs, -'-/ *v* **1** to express one's ideas in speech or writing **2** to talk, converse *USE* usu + *on* or *upon*

discourteous /dɪs'kɜːtɪəs/ *adj* rude, impolite – ~**ly** *adv* – ~**ness** *n*

discourtesy /dɪs'kɜːtəsi/ *n* (an instance of) rudeness; (an) incivility

discover /dɪs'kʌvəʳ/ *v* **1** to obtain sight or knowledge of for the first time **2** to make known or visible – fml – ~**able** *adj* – ~**er** *n* – ~**y** *n*

[1]**discredit** /dɪs'kredɪ̣t/ *v* **1** to refuse to accept as true or accurate **2** to cast doubt on the accuracy, authority, or reputation of

[2]**discredit** *n* **1** (sby or sthg causing) loss of credit or reputation **2** loss of belief or confidence; doubt

discreditable /dɪs'kredɪ̣təbəl/ *adj* bringing discredit or disgrace – **-bly** *adv*

discreet /dɪ'skriːt/ *adj* **1** capable of maintaining a prudent silence **2** unpretentious, modest – ~**ly** *adv*

discrete /dɪ'skriːt/ *adj* **1** individually distinct **2** consisting of distinct or unconnected elements – ~**ly** *adv* – ~**ness** *n*

discretion /dɪ'skreʃən/ *n* **1** the ability to make responsible decisions **2a** individual choice or judgment **b** power of free decision within legal bounds – in *age of discretion* – ~**ary** *adj*

discriminate /dɪ'skrɪmɪ̣neɪt/ *v* **1a** to make a distinction *between* **b** to show good judgment or discernment **2** to treat sby differently and esp unfavourably on the grounds of race, sex, religion, etc

discrimination /dɪˌskrɪmɪ̣'neɪʃən/ *n* **1** discernment and good judgment, esp in matters of taste **2** prejudicial treatment (e g on the grounds of race or sex)

discriminatory /dɪ'skrɪmɪ̣nətəri/ *adj* showing esp unfavourable discrimination

discursive /dɪ'skɜːsɪv/ *adj* **1** passing usu unmethodically from one topic to another; digressive **2** proceeding by logical argument or reason – ~**ly** *adv* – ~**ness** *n*

discus /'dɪskəs/ *n, pl* **discuses** (the athletic field event involving the throwing of) a solid disc, between 180mm and 219mm (about 7 to 9in) in diameter, that is thicker in the centre than at the edge

discuss /dɪ'skʌs/ *v* to consider or examine (a topic) in speech or writing – ~**ion** *n*

disdain /dɪs'deɪn/ *n* contempt for sthg regarded as worthless or insignificant; scorn – **disdain** *v*

disdainful /dɪs'deɪnfəl/ *adj* feeling or showing disdain – ~**ly** *adv*

disease /dɪ'ziːz/ *n* **1** a condition of (a part of) a living animal or plant body that impairs the performance of a vital function; (a) sickness, malady **2** a harmful or corrupt development, situation, condition, etc – ~**d** *adj*

disembark /ˌdɪsɪ̣m'bɑːk/ *v* to (cause to) alight from a ship, plane, etc – ~**ation** *n*

disembowel /ˌdɪsɪm'baʊəl/ *v* to remove the bowels or entrails of; eviscerate

disembroil /ˌdɪsɪ̣m'brɔɪl/ *v* to free

from a confused or entangled state or situation

disenchant /ˌdɪsɪnˈtʃɑːnt/ *v* to rid of an illusion – **~ment** *n*

disencumber /ˌdɪsɪ̣nˈkʌmbəʳ/ *v* to free from an burden or impediment

disengage /ˌdɪsɪ̣ŋˈgeɪdʒ/ *v* to detach or release (oneself) *specif, esp of troops* to withdraw – **~ment** *n*

disentangle /ˌdɪsɪ̣nˈtæŋgəl/ *v* to (cause to) become free from entanglements: unravel – **~ment** *n*

disestablish /ˌdɪsɪ̣ˈstæblɪʃ/ *v* to deprive (esp a national church) of established status – **~ment** *n*

disfavour /dɪsˈfeɪvəʳ/ *n* **1** disapproval, dislike **2** the state of being disapproved of

disfigure /dɪsˈfɪgəʳ/ *v* to spoil the appearance or quality of; mar – **~ment** *n*

disfranchise /dɪsˈfræntʃaɪz/ *v* to deprive of the right to select an elected representative – **~ment** *n*

disgorge /dɪsˈgɔːdʒ/ *v* **1** to discharge the contents of with force; *specif* to vomit **2** to give up on request or under pressure

¹disgrace /dɪsˈgreɪs/ *v* **1** to bring reproach or shame to **2** to cause to lose favour or standing

²disgrace *n* **1a** loss of favour, honour, or respect; shame **b** the state of being out of favour **2** sby or sthg shameful

disgraceful /dɪsˈgreɪsfəl/ *adj* shameful, shocking – **~ly** *adv*

disgruntled /dɪsˈgrʌntld/ *adj* aggrieved and dissatisfied

¹disguise /dɪsˈgaɪz/ *v* **1** to change the appearance or nature of in order to conceal identity **2** to hide the true state or character of

²disguise *n* **1** (the use of) sthg (e g clothing) to conceal one's identity **2** an outward appearance that misrepresents the true nature of sthg

disgust /dɪsˈgʌst, dɪz-/ *n* strong aversion aroused by sby or sthg physically or morally distasteful – **disgust** *v*

¹dish /dɪʃ/ *n* **1a** a shallow open often circular or oval vessel used esp for holding or serving food; *broadly* any vessel from which food is eaten or served **b** *pl the* utensils and tableware used in preparing, serving, and eating a meal **2** a type of food prepared in a particular way **3a** a directional aerial, esp for receiving radio or television transmissions or microwaves, having a concave usu parabolic reflector **b** a hollow or depression **4** an attractive person – infml

²dish *v* **1** to make concave like a dish **2** *chiefly Br* to ruin or spoil (e g a person or his/her hopes) – infml

dishabille /ˌdɪsəˈbiːl/ *n* deshabille

disharmony /dɪsˈhɑːməni/ *n* lack of harmony; discord – **-monious** *adj*

dishcloth /ˈdɪʃklɒθ/ *n* a cloth for washing or drying dishes

dishearten /dɪsˈhɑːtn/ *v* to cause to lose enthusiasm or morale; discourage – **~ment** *n*

dishevelled, *NAm chiefly* **disheveled** /dɪˈʃevəld/ *adj, esp of a person's hair or appearance* unkempt, untidy

dishonest /dɪsˈɒnɪ̣st/ *adj* not honest, truthful, or sincere – **~ly** *adv* – **~y** *n*

dishonour /dɪsˈɒnəʳ/ *n* **1** (sby or sthg causing) loss of honour or reputation **2** a state of shame or disgrace – **dishonour** *v* – **~able** *adj* – **~ably** *adv*

dish out *v* to give or distribute freely – infml

dish up *v* **1** to put (a meal, food, etc) onto dishes; serve **2** to produce or present (e g facts) – infml

dishwasher /ˈdɪʃwɒʃəʳ/ *n* a person or electrical machine that washes dishes

dishy /ˈdɪʃi/ *adj, chiefly Br, of a person* attractive – infml

disillusion /ˌdɪsɪ̣ˈluːʒən/ *v* to reveal the usu unpleasant truth (e g about sby or sthg admired) to; disenchant – **disillusion, ~ment** *n*

disincentive /ˌdɪsɪnˈsentɪv/ *n* sthg that discourages action or effort; a deterrent

disinclined /ˌdɪsɪnˈklaɪnd/ *adj* unwilling – **-clination** *n*

disinfect /ˌdɪsɪ̣nˈfekt/ *v* to cleanse of infection, esp by destroying harmful microorganisms – **~ion** *n*

disinfectant /ˌdɪsɪ̣nˈfektənt/ *n* a chemical that destroys harmful microorganisms

disingenuous /ˌdɪsɪnˈdʒenjʊəs/ *adj*

insincere; *also* falsely frank or naive in manner – ~**ly** *adv* – ~**ness** *n*

disinherit /ˌdɪsɪ̣n'herɪ̣t/ *v* to deprive (an heir) of the right to inherit – ~**ance** *n*

disintegrate /dɪs'ɪntɪ̣greɪt/ *v* **1** to break into fragments or constituent elements **2** to lose unity or cohesion – **-gration** *n*

disinter /ˌdɪsɪn'tɜːʳ/ *v* **1** to remove from a grave or tomb **2** to bring to light; unearth – ~**ment** *n*

disinterested /dɪs'ɪntrɪ̣stɪ̣d/ *adj* **1** uninterested – disapproved of by some speakers **2** free from selfish motive or interest; impartial – ~**ly** *adv* – ~**ness** *n*

disjointed /dɪs'dʒɔɪntɪ̣d/ *adj* lacking orderly sequence; incoherent – ~**ly** *adv* – ~**ness** *n*

¹**dislike** /dɪs'laɪk/ *v* to regard with dislike

²**dislike** /ˌdɪs'laɪk/ *n* (an object of) a feeling of aversion or disapproval

dislocate /'dɪsləkeɪt/ *v* **1** to put out of place; *esp* to displace (e g a bone or joint) **2** to put (plans, machinery, etc) out of order – **-cation** *n*

dislodge /dɪs'lɒdʒ/ *v* to force out of or remove from a fixed or entrenched position – ~**ment** *n*

disloyal /dɪs'lɔɪəl/ *adj* untrue to obligations or ties; unfaithful – ~**ly** *adv* – ~**ty** *n*

dismal /'dɪzməl/ *adj* causing or expressing gloom or sadness – ~**ly** *adv*

dismantle /dɪs'mæntl/ *v* to take to pieces

dismay /dɪs'meɪ/ *v or n* (to fill with) sudden consternation or apprehension

dismember /dɪs'membəʳ/ *v* **1** to cut or tear off the limbs or members of **2** to divide up (e g a territory) into parts – ~**ment** *n*

dismiss /dɪs'mɪs/ *v* **1** to remove or send away, esp from employment or service **2** to put out of one's mind; reject as unworthy of serious consideration **3** to refuse a further hearing to (e g a court case) **4** to bowl out (a batsman or side) in cricket – ~**al** *n*

dismount /dɪs'maʊnt/ *v* **1** to alight from a horse, bicycle, etc **2** to remove from a mounting

disobedient /ˌdɪsə'biːdɪənt, ˌdɪsəʊ-/ *adj* refusing or failing to obey – ~**ly** *adv* – **-ience** *n*

disobey /ˌdɪsə'beɪ, ˌdɪsəʊ-/ *v* to fail to obey

disorder /dɪs'ɔːdəʳ/ *n* **1** lack of order; confusion **2** breach of the peace or public order **3** an abnormal physical or mental condition; an ailment – **disorder** *v*

disorderly /dɪs'ɔːdəli/ *adj* **1a** untidy, disarranged **b** unruly, violent **2** offensive to public order – **-liness** *n*

disorgan·ize, -ise /dɪs'ɔːgənaɪz/ *v* to throw into disorder or confusion – **-ization** *n*

disorientate /dɪs'ɔːrɪənteɪt/ *v* to confuse – **-tation** *n*

disown /dɪs'əʊn/ *v* **1** to refuse to acknowledge as one's own **2** to repudiate any connection with

disparage /dɪ'spærɪdʒ/ *v* to speak slightingly of; belittle – **-agingly** *adv* – ~**ment** *n*

disparate /'dɪspərɪ̣t/ *adj* markedly distinct in quality or character – ~**ly** *adv*

disparity /dɪ'spærɪ̣ti/ *n* (a) difference or inequality

dispassionate /dɪs'pæʃənɪ̣t/ *adj* not influenced by strong feeling; *esp* calm, impartial – ~**ly** *adv* – ~**ness** *n*

¹**dispatch** /dɪ'spætʃ/ *v* **1** to send off or away promptly, esp on some task **2** to get through or carry out quickly **3** to kill, esp with quick efficiency – euph

²**dispatch** *n* **1** an important diplomatic or military message **2** a news item sent into a newspaper by a correspondent **3** promptness and efficiency

dispel /dɪ'spel/ *v* to drive away; disperse

dispensable /dɪ'spensəbəl/ *adj* inessential

dispensary /dɪ'spensəri/ *n* a part of a hospital or chemist's shop where drugs, medical supplies, etc are dispensed

dispensation /ˌdɪspən'seɪʃən, -pen-/ *n* **1** a usu specified religious system, esp considered as controlling human affairs during a particular period **2a** an exemption from a law, vow, etc; *specif* permission to disregard or break a rule of Roman Catholic church law **b** a formal authorization

dispense /dɪ'spens/ *v* **1a** to deal out, distribute **b** to administer (e g law or justice) **2** to prepare and give out (drugs, medicine, etc on prescription) **3** to do without – usu + *with* – **dispenser** *n*

disperse /dɪ'spɜːs/ *v* **1** to break up in random fashion; scatter **2** to evaporate or vanish – **dispersal** *n* – **dispersion** *n*

dispirit /dɪ'spɪrɪt/ *v* to dishearten, discourage

displace /dɪs'pleɪs/ *v* **1a** to remove from or force out of the usual or proper place **b** to remove from office **2** to take the place of (e g an atom) in a chemical reaction

displacement /dɪs'pleɪsmənt/ *n* **1** the volume or weight of a fluid (e g water) displaced by a body (e g a ship) of equal weight floating in it **2** the difference between the initial position of a body and any later position

[1]**display** /dɪ'spleɪ/ *v* **1** to expose to view; show **2** to exhibit, esp ostentatiously

[2]**display** *n* **1a** a presentation or exhibition of sthg in open view **b** an esp ostentatious show or demonstration **c** an eye-catching arrangement of sthg (e g goods for sale) **2** a pattern of behaviour exhibited esp by male birds in the breeding season

displease /dɪs'pliːz/ *v* to cause annoyance or displeasure (to)

displeasure /dɪs'pleʒəʳ/ *n* disapproval, annoyance

disposable /dɪs'pəʊzəbl/ *adj* **1** available for use; *specif* remaining after deduction of taxes **2** designed to be used once and then thrown away

disposal /dɪ'spəʊzəl/ *n* **1a** orderly arrangement or distribution **b** bestowal **c** the act or action of getting rid of sthg; *specif* the destruction or conversion of waste matter **2** the power or right to use freely

dispose /dɪ'spəʊz/ *v* **1** to incline *to* **2** to put in place; arrange **3** to cause to have a specified attitude *towards* **4** to settle a matter finally; *also* get rid *of*

disposition /ˌdɪspə'zɪʃən/ *n* **1a** final arrangement; settlement **b** orderly arrangement **2a** natural temperament **b** a tendency, inclination

dispossess /ˌdɪspə'zes/ *v* to deprive of possession or occupancy – **~ed** *adj* – **~ion** *n*

disproportion /ˌdɪsprə'pɔːʃən/ *n* (a) lack of proportion, symmetry, or proper relation

disproportionate /ˌdɪsprə'pɔːʃənɪ̣t/ *adj* out of proportion – **~ly** *adv*

disprove /dɪs'pruːv/ *v* to prove to be false; refute

disputant /'dɪspjʊtənt, dɪ'spjuːtənt/ *n* one engaged in a dispute

[1]**dispute** /dɪ'spjuːt/ *v* **1a** to discuss angrily **b** to call into question **2a** to struggle against; resist **b** to struggle over; contest – **disputation** *n* – **disputable** *adj* – **disputably** *adv*

[2]**dispute** /dɪ'spjuːt, 'dɪspjuːt/ *n* **1** controversy, debate **2** a quarrel, disagreement

disqualification /ˌdɪskwɒlɪ̣fɪ̣'keɪʃən/ *n* **1** disqualifying or being disqualified **2** sthg that disqualifies

disqualify /dɪs'kwɒlɪ̣faɪ/ *v* **1** to make or declare unfit or unsuitable to do sthg **2** to declare ineligible (e g for a prize) because of violation of the rules

disquiet /dɪs'kwaɪət/ *v or n* (to cause) anxiety or worry

disregard /ˌdɪsrɪ'gɑːd/ *v* **1** to pay no attention to **2** to treat as not worthy of regard or notice – **disregard** *n*

disrepair /ˌdɪsrɪ'peəʳ/ *n* the state of being in need of repair

disreputable /dɪs'repjʊtəbəl/ *adj* **1** having a bad reputation; not respectable **2** dirty or untidy in appearance – **~ness** *n* – **-tably** *adv*

disrepute /ˌdɪsrɪ'pjuːt/ *n* lack of good reputation or respectability

disrespect /ˌdɪsrɪ'spekt/ *n* lack of respect or politeness – **~ful** *adj* – **~fully** *adv*

disrobe /dɪs'rəʊb/ *v* to take off (esp ceremonial outer) clothing – fml or humor

disrupt /dɪs'rʌpt/ *v* **1** to throw into disorder **2** to interrupt the continuity of – **~ion** *n* – **~ive** *adj* – **~ively** *adv*

dissatisfy /dɪ'sætɪ̣sfaɪ, dɪs'sæ-/ *v* to make displeased, discontented, or disappointed – **-faction** *n*

dissect /dɪˈsekt, daɪ-/ *v* **1** to cut (e g an animal or plant) into pieces, esp for scientific examination **2** to analyse and interpret in detail – **~ion** *n*

dissemble /dɪˈsembəl/ *v* to conceal facts, intentions, or feelings under some pretence – **~r** *n*

disseminate /dɪˈsemɪ̣neɪt/ *v* to spread about freely or widely – **-nation** *n*

dissension /dɪˈsenʃən/ *n* disagreement in opinion; discord

[1]**dissent** /dɪˈsent/ *v* **1** to withhold assent **2** to differ in opinion; *specif* to reject the doctrines of an established church

[2]**dissent** *n* religious or political nonconformity

Dissenter /dɪˈsentəʳ/ *n* an English Nonconformist

dissertation /ˌdɪsəˈteɪʃən/ *n* a long detailed treatment of a subject; *specif* one submitted for a (higher) degree

disservice /dɪˈsɜːvɪ̣s, dɪsˈsɜː-/ *n* an action or deed which works to sby's disadvantage

dissident /ˈdɪsɪ̣dənt/ *n or adj* (sby) disagreeing strongly or rebelliously with an established opinion, group, government, etc – **-dence** *n*

dissimilar /dɪˈsɪmɪ̣ləʳ, dɪsˈsɪ-/ *adj* not similar; unlike – **~ly** *adv* – **~ity** *n*

dissimulate /dɪˈsɪmjʊleɪt/ *v* to dissemble – **-lation** *n*

dissipate /ˈdɪsɪ̣peɪt/ *v* **1** to cause to disappear or scatter; dispel **2** to spend or use up (money, energy, etc) aimlessly or foolishly – **-pation** *n*

dissipated /ˈdɪsɪ̣peɪtɪ̣d/ *adj* dissolute

dissociate /dɪˈsəʊʃieɪt, -sieɪt/ *v* to separate from association or union with sby or sthg else; disconnect – **-ation** *n*

dissolute /ˈdɪsəluːt/ *adj* loose in morals; debauched – **~ly** *adv* – **~ness** *n*

dissolution /ˌdɪsəˈluːʃən/ *n* **1** the termination of an association, union, etc **2** the breaking up or dispersal of a group, assembly, etc

dissolve /dɪˈzɒlv/ *v* **1a** to terminate officially **b** to cause to break up; dismiss **2a** to pass into solution **b** to melt, liquefy **3** to fade away; disperse **4** to fade out (one film or television scene) while fading in another

dissonance /ˈdɪsənəns/ *n* **1** a combination of discordant sounds **2** lack of agreement **3** (the sound produced by playing) an unresolved musical note or chord – **-nant** *adj* – **-nantly** *adv*

dissuade /dɪˈsweɪd/ *v* to deter or discourage *from* a course of action by persuasion – **-suasion** *n*

distaff /ˈdɪstɑːf/ *n* **1** a staff for holding the flax, wool, etc in spinning **2** woman's work or domain

distal /ˈdɪstəl/ *adj, esp of an anatomical part* far from the centre or point of attachment or origin; terminal – **~ly** *adv*

[1]**distance** /ˈdɪstəns/ *n* **1a** (the amount of) separation in space or time between 2 points or things **b** a distant point or place **2a** remoteness in space **b** reserve, coldness **c** difference, disparity

[2]**distance** *v* to place or keep physically or mentally at a distance

distant /ˈdɪstənt/ *adj* **1a** separated in space or time by a specified distance **b** far-off or remote in space or time **2** not closely related **3** different in kind **4** reserved, aloof **5** coming from or going to a remote place – **~ly** *adv*

distaste /dɪsˈteɪst/ *n* (a) dislike, aversion

distasteful /dɪsˈteɪstfəl/ *adj* showing or causing distaste; offensive – **~ly** *adv* – **~ness** *n*

[1]**distemper** /dɪˈstempəʳ/ *n* any of various animal diseases; *esp* a highly infectious virus disease of dogs

[2]**distemper** *n* **1** a method of painting in which pigments are mixed with white or yolk of egg or size, esp for mural decoration **2** the paint used in the distemper process; *broadly* any of numerous water-based paints for general, esp household, use – **distemper** *v*

distend /dɪˈstend/ *v* to (cause to) swell from internal pressure – **-tension** *n*

distil /dɪˈstɪl/ *v* **1** to subject to or transform by heating and condensing the resulting vapour **2a** to obtain or separate *out* or *off* (as if) by distilling **b** to obtain spirits by distilling the products of fermentation **c** to extract the essence of (e g an idea or subject) – ~**lation** *n*

distiller /dɪ'stɪlə^r/ *n* a person or company that makes alcohol, esp spirits, by distilling

distinct /dɪ'stɪŋkt/ *adj* **1** different, separate *from* **2** readily perceptible to the senses or mind; clear – ~**ly** *adv* – ~**ness** *n*

distinction /dɪ'stɪŋkʃən/ *n* **1** a difference made or marked; a contrast **2** a distinguishing quality or mark **3a** outstanding merit, quality, or worth **b** special honour or recognition

distinctive /dɪ'stɪŋktɪv/ *adj* clearly marking sby or sthg as different from others; characteristic – ~**ly** *adv* – ~**ness** *n*

distinguish /dɪ'stɪŋgwɪʃ/ *v* **1a** to mark or recognize as separate or different – often + *from* **b** to recognize the difference *between* **c** to make (oneself) outstanding or noteworthy **d** to mark as different; characterize **2** to discern; make out – ~**able** *adj*

distinguished /dɪ'stɪŋgwɪʃt/ *adj* **1** marked by eminence, distinction, or excellence **2** dignified in manner, bearing, or appearance

distort /dɪ'stɔːt/ *v* **1** to alter the true meaning of; misrepresent **2** to cause to take on an unnatural or abnormal shape – ~**ion** *n*

distract /dɪ'strækt/ *v* to draw (e g one's attention) to a different object

distraction /dɪ'strækʃən/ *n* **1** extreme agitation or mental confusion **2** sthg that distracts; *esp* an amusement

distraught /dɪ'strɔːt/ *adj* mentally agitated; frantic

distress /dɪ'stres/ *n* **1** mental or physical anguish **2** a state of danger or desperate need – **distress** *v*

distribute /dɪ'strɪbjuːt/ *v* **1** to divide among several or many **2a** to disperse or scatter over an area **b** to give out, deliver – **-bution** *n* – **-butional** *adj*

distributive /dɪ'strɪbjʊtɪv/ *adj* of distributing esp goods and services

distributor /dɪ'strɪbjʊtə^r/ *n* **1** sby employed to manage the distribution of goods **2** an apparatus for directing current to the various sparking plugs of an internal-combustion engine

district /'dɪstrɪkt/ *n* **1** a territorial division made esp for administrative purposes **2** an area or region with a specified character or feature

distrust /dɪs'trʌst/ *v or n* (to view with) suspicion or lack of trust – ~**ful** *adj* – ~**fully** *adv*

disturb /dɪ'stɜːb/ *v* **1a** to break in upon; interrupt **b** to alter the position or arrangement of **2a** to destroy the peace of mind or composure of **b** to throw into disorder **c** to put to inconvenience – ~**ance** *n*

disturbed /dɪ'stɜːbd/ *adj* having or showing symptoms of emotional or mental instability

disunite /,dɪsjʊ'naɪt/ *v* to divide, separate

disuse /dɪs'juːs/ *n* the state of no longer being used – ~**d** *adj*

¹**ditch** /dɪtʃ/ *n* a long narrow excavation dug in the earth for defence, drainage, irrigation, etc

²**ditch** *v* **1** to make a forced landing of (an aircraft) on water **2** to get rid of; abandon

¹**dither** /'dɪðə^r/ *v* to act nervously or indecisively; vacillate

²**dither** *n* a state of indecision or nervous excitement

ditto /'dɪtəʊ/ *n* **1** a thing mentioned previously or above; the same – used to avoid repeating a word **2** *also* **ditto mark** a mark ,, or " used as a sign indicating repetition usu of a word directly above in a previous line

ditty /'dɪti/ *n* a short simple song

diuretic /,daɪjʊ'retɪk/ *n or adj* (a drug) acting to increase the flow of urine

diurnal /daɪ'ɜːnəl/ *adj* **1** having a daily cycle **2a** occurring during the day or daily **b** opening during the day and closing at night **c** active during the day – ~**ly** *adv*

divan /dɪ'væn/ *n* **1** a council chamber in some Muslim countries, esp Turkey **2a** a long low couch, usu without arms or back, placed against a wall **b** a bed of a similar style without a head or foot board

¹**dive** /daɪv/ *v* **1a** to plunge into water headfirst **b** to submerge **2a** to descend or fall steeply **b** to plunge one's hand quickly *into* **3** to lunge or dash headlong

²**dive** *n* **1a(1)** a headlong plunge into water; *esp* one executed in a pre-

scribed manner (2) submerging (e g by a submarine) **b** a sharp decline **2** a disreputable bar, club, etc – informal

diver /ˈdaɪvəʳ/ *n* **1** a person who works or explores underwater for long periods, either carrying a supply of air or having it sent from the surface **2** any of various diving birds

diverge /daɪˈvɜːdʒ/ *v* **1a** to move in different directions from a common point **b** to differ in character, form, or opinion – often + *from* **2** to turn aside from a path or course – often + *from* – **-gence, -gency** *n* – **-gent** *adj*

divers /ˈdaɪvəz/ *adj, archaic* various

diverse /daɪˈvɜːs/ *adj* **1** different, unlike **2** varied, assorted – **~ly** *adv*

diversify /daɪˈvɜːsɨ̣faɪ/ *v* **1** to make diverse; vary **2** to engage in varied business operations in order to reduce risk

diversity /daɪˈvɜːsɨ̣ti, dɨ̣-/ *n* **1** the condition of being different or having differences **2** a variety, assortment

divert /daɪˈvɜːt, dɨ̣-/ *v* **1a** to turn aside from one course or use to another **b** to distract **2** to entertain, amuse – **diversion** *n* – **diversionary** *adj*

divertimento /dɪˌvɜːtɨ̣ˈmentəʊ/ *n, pl* **divertimenti** an instrumental chamber work in several movements and usu light in character

divest /daɪˈvest/ *v* **1** to rid or free oneself *of* **2** to take away (e g property or vested rights)

¹divide /dɨ̣ˈvaɪd/ *v* **1** to separate into 2 or more parts, categories, divisions, etc **2** to give out in shares; distribute **3a** to cause to be separate; serve as a boundary between **b** to separate into opposing sides or parties **4** to determine how many times a number contains another number by means of a mathematical operation – **divisible** *adj*

²divide *n* **1** a watershed **2** a point or line of division

dividend /ˈdɪvɨ̣dənd, -dend/ *n* **1** (a pro rata share in) the part of a company's profits payable to shareholders **2** a reward, benefit **3** a number to be divided by another

divination /ˌdɪvɨ̣ˈneɪʃən/ *n* **1** the art or practice that seeks to foresee the future or discover hidden knowledge (e g by using supernatural powers) **2** (an instance of) unusual insight or perception

¹divine /dɨ̣ˈvaɪn/ *adj* **1a** of, being, or proceeding directly from God or a god **b** devoted to the worship of God or a god; sacred **2** delightful, superb – infml – **~ly** *adv*

²divine *n* a clergyman; *esp* one skilled in theology

³divine *v* **1** to discover, perceive, or foresee intuitively or by supernatural means **2** to discover or locate (e g water or minerals) by means of a divining rod – **diviner** *n*

divining rod *n* a forked rod (e g a twig) believed to dip downwards when held over ground concealing water or minerals

divinity /dɨ̣ˈvɪnɨ̣ti/ *n* **1** the quality or state of being divine **2** a male or female deity **3** theology

division /dɨ̣ˈvɪʒən/ *n* **1** dividing or being divided **2** any of the parts or sections into which a whole is divided **3** *sing or pl in constr* a military unit having the necessary tactical and administrative services to act independently **4** an administrative or operating unit of an organization **5** a group of organisms forming part of a larger group **6** a competitive class or category (e g of a soccer league) **7** sthg that divides, separates, or marks off **8** disagreement, disunity **9** the physical separation into different lobbies of the members of a parliamentary body voting for and against a question **10** the mathematical operation of dividing one number by another

divisive /dɨ̣ˈvaɪsɪv/ *adj* tending to cause disunity or dissension – **~ly** *adv* – **~ness** *n*

divisor /dɪˈvaɪzəʳ/ *n* the number by which another number or quantity is divided

divorce /dɨ̣ˈvɔːs/ *v* **1a** to end marriage with (one's spouse) by divorce **b** to dissolve the marriage between **2** to end the relationship or union of; separate – usu + *from* – **divorce** *n*

divot /ˈdɪvət/ *n* a piece of turf dug out in making a golf shot

divulge /daɪˈvʌldʒ, dɨ̣-/ *v* to make

known (e g a confidence or secret); reveal – ~**nce** *n*

dixieland /'dıksilænd/ *n* traditional jazz

[1]**dizzy** /'dızi/ *adj* **1** experiencing a whirling sensation in the head with a tendency to lose balance **2** causing or feeling giddiness or mental confusion **3** foolish, silly – infml – **dizzily** *adv* – **dizziness** *n*

[2]**dizzy** *v* to make dizzy; bewilder

DJ /'diː ˌdʒeı/ *n* **1** a disc jockey **2** a dinner jacket

djellaba *also* **djellabah, jellaba** /dʒə'lɑːbə, 'dʒeləbə/ *n* a long loose outer garment with full sleeves and a hood, traditionally worn by Arabs

DNA *n* any of various acids that are found esp in cell nuclei, are constructed of a double helix and are responsible for transmitting genetic information

[1]**do** /duː/ *v* **does** /dəz; *strong* dʌz/; **did** /dıd/; **done** /dʌn/ **1a** to carry out the task of; effect, perform (e g *do* some washing) **b** to act, behave (e g *do* as I say) **2** to put into a specified condition (e g *do* him to death) **3** to have as a function (e g what's that book *doing* on the floor?) **4** to cause, impart (e g sleep will *do* you good) **5** to bring to an esp unwanted conclusion; finish – used esp in the past participle (e g that's *done* it) **6a** to fare; get along (e g *do* well at school) **b** to carry on business or affairs; manage (e g we can *do* without you) **7** to be in progress; happen (e g there's nothing *doing*) **8** to provide or have available (e g they *do* teas here) **9** to bring into existence; produce (e g *did* a portrait of his mother) **10** to put on; perform (e g *do* a Shakespearean comedy) **11** to come to or make an end; finish – used in the past participle; (e g have you *done* with the newspaper?) **12** to suffice, serve (e g half of that will *do*) **13** to be fitting; conform to custom or propriety (e g won't *do* to be late) **14a** to put in order, arrange, clean (e g *do* the garden) **b** to cook (e g likes her steak well *done*) **15** to perform the appropriate professional service or services for (e g the barber will *do* you now) **16a** to work at, esp as a course of study or occupation (e g *do* classics) **b** to solve; work out (e g *do* a sum) **17** to travel at a (maximum) speed of (e g *do* 70 on the motorway) **18** to serve out, esp as a prison sentence (e g *did* 3 years) **19** to suffice, suit (e g that will *do* nicely) **20** – used as a substitute verb to avoid repetition (e g if you must make a noise; *do* it elsewhere) **21** – used to form present and past tenses expressing emphasis (e g *do* be quiet) **22a** *chiefly Br* to arrest, convict – slang (e g get *done* for theft) **b** to treat unfairly; *esp* to cheat, deprive (e g *did* him out of his inheritance) – infml **c** to rob – slang (e g *do* a shop)

[2]**do** *n*, **1** sthg one ought to do – usu pl **2** *chiefly Br* a festive party or occasion – infml

[3]**do, doh** /dəʊ/ *n* the 1st note of the diatonic scale in solmization

docile /'dəʊsaıl/ *adj* easily led or managed; tractable – ~**lity** *n*

[1]**dock** /dɒk/ *n* any of a genus of coarse weeds whose leaves are used to alleviate nettle stings

[2]**dock** *v* **1** to cut (e g a tail) short **2** to make a deduction from (e g wages) **3** to take away (a specified amount) from

[3]**dock** *n* **1** a usu artificially enclosed body of water in a port or harbour, where a ship can moor (e g for repair work to be carried out) **2** *pl the* total number of such enclosures in a harbour, together with wharves, sheds, etc

[4]**dock** *v* **1** to come or go into dock **2** *of spacecraft* to join together while in space

[5]**dock** *n* the prisoner's enclosure in a criminal court

docker /'dɒkəʳ/ *n* sby employed in loading and unloading ships, barges, etc

[1]**docket** /'dɒkɨt/ *n* **1** a label attached to goods bearing identification or instructions **2** (a copy of) a receipt

[2]**docket** *v* to put an identifying statement or label on

dockyard /'dɒkjɑːd/ *n* a place or enclosure in which ships are built or repaired

[1]**doctor** /'dɒktəʳ/ *n* **1** a holder of the highest level of academic degree conferred by a university **2** one qualified

to practise medicine; a physician or surgeon **3** sby skilled in repairing or treating a usu specified type of machine, vehicle, etc

[2]**doctor** *v* **1a** to give medical treatment to **b** to repair, mend **2a** to adapt or modify for a desired end **b** to alter in a dishonest way **3** to castrate or spay – euph

doctrinaire /ˌdɒktrɪ̈ˈneəʳ/ *n or adj* (one) concerned with abstract theory to the exclusion of practical considerations – chiefly derog

doctrine /ˈdɑktrɪ̈n/ *n* **1** sthg that is taught **2** a principle or the body of principles in a branch of knowledge or system of belief – **-inal** *adj*

[1]**document** /ˈdɒkjʊmənt/ *n* an original or official paper that gives information about or proof of sthg – **~ary** *adj*

[2]**document** /ˈdɒkjʊment/ *v* **1** to provide documentary evidence of **2** to support with factual evidence, references, etc **3** to provide (a ship) with papers required by law recording ownership, cargo, etc

documentary /ˌdɒkjʊˈmentəri/ *n* a broadcast or film that presents a factual account of a person or topic using a variety of techniques (e g narrative and interview)

[1]**dodder** /ˈdɒdəʳ/ *n* any of a genus of leafless plants of the bindweed family that are wholly parasitic on other plants

[2]**dodder** *v* **1** to tremble or shake from weakness or age **2** to walk feebly and unsteadily – **~er** *n*, **~ing** *adj*

doddle /ˈdɒdl/ *n, chiefly Br* a very easy task – infml

[1]**dodge** /ˈdɒdʒ/ *v* **1** to shift position suddenly (e g to avoid a blow or a pursuer) **2** to evade (e g a duty) usu by trickery

[2]**dodge** *n* **1** a sudden movement to avoid sthg **2** a clever device to evade or trick

dodgem /ˈdɒdʒəm/, **dodgem car** *n, Br* any of a number of small electric cars designed to be steered about and bumped into one another as a fun-fair amusement

dodgy /ˈdɒdʒi/ *adj, chiefly Br* **1** shady, dishonest **2** risky, dangerous **3** liable to collapse, fail, or break down

dodo /ˈdəʊdəʊ/ *n* an extinct heavy flightless bird that formerly lived on the island of Mauritius

doe /dəʊ/ *n* the adult female fallow deer; *broadly* the adult female of any of various mammals (e g the rabbit) or birds (e g the guinea fowl) of which the male is called a buck

doer /ˈduːəʳ/ *n* one who takes action or participates actively in sthg, rather than theorizing

does /dəz; *strong* dʌz/ *pres 3rd sing of* **do**

doff /dɒf/ *v* to take off (one's hat) in greeting or as a sign of respect

[1]**dog** /dɒg/ *n* **1a** a 4-legged flesh-eating domesticated mammal occurring in a great variety of breeds and prob descended from the common wolf **b** any of a family of carnivores to which the dog belongs **c** a male dog **2** any of various usu simple mechanical devices for holding, fastening, etc that consist of a spike, rod, or bar **3** *chiefly NAm* sthg inferior of its kind **4** an esp worthless man or fellow **5** *pl* ruin

[2]**dog** *v* to pursue closely like a dog; hound

[3]**dog** *adj* male

dog collar *n* a narrow collar without points worn by clergymen – infml

dog days *n pl* the hottest days in the year

dog-eared *adj* worn, shabby

dog-eat-dog *adj* marked by ruthless self-interest; cutthroat

dogfight *n* **1** a viciously fought contest **2** a fight between aircraft, usu at close quarters

dogfish /ˈdɒgˌfɪʃ/ *n* any of various small sharks

dogged /ˈdɒgɪ̈d/ *adj* stubbornly determined – **~ly** *adv* – **~ness** *n*

doggerel /ˈdɒgərəl/ *n* (an example of) verse that is loosely styled and irregular in measure, esp for comic effect

doggo /ˈdɒgəʊ/ *adv, Br* in hiding and without moving – infml; chiefly in *lie doggo*

doghouse /ˈdɒghaʊs/ *n* a dog kennel

dogleg /ˈdɒgleg/ *n* **1** a sharp bend (e g in a road) **2** an angled fairway on a golf course

dogma /ˈdɒgmə/ *n* **1** an authoritative tenet or principle **2** a doctrine or body of doctrines formally and authoritatively stated by a church **3** a point of view or tenet put forth as authoritative without adequate grounds – chiefly derog – **~tic** *adj* – **~tically** *adv* – **~tism** *n*

do-gooder *n* an earnest often naive and ineffectual humanitarian or reformer

dog paddle *n* an elementary form of swimming (e g for learners) in which the arms paddle and the legs kick

dogsbody /ˈdɒgzˌbɒdi/ *n, chiefly Br* a person who carries out routine or menial work – infml

dog-tired *adj* extremely tired – infml

doh /dəʊ/ *n* the note of do

doily, doyley, doyly /ˈdɔɪli/ *n* a small decorative mat, esp of paper, often placed under cakes on a plate or stand

do in *v* **1** to kill **2** to wear out, exhaust *USE* infml

doing /ˈduːɪŋ/ *n* **1** the act or result of performing; action (e g this must be your *doing*) **2** effort, exertion (e g that will take a great deal of *doing*) **3** *pl* things that are done or that occur; activities

doings /ˈduːɪŋz/ *n, chiefly Br* a small object, esp one whose name is forgotten or not known – infml

doldrums /ˈdɒldrəmz/ *n pl* **1** a depressed state of mind; *the* blues **2** an equatorial ocean region where calms, squalls, and light shifting winds prevail **3** a state of stagnation or slump

dole /dəʊl/ *n* **1** a distribution of food, money, or clothing to the needy **2** *the* government unemployment benefit

doleful /ˈdəʊlfəl/ *adj* sad, mournful – **~ly** *adv* – **~ness** *n*

dole out *v* to give, distribute, or deliver, esp in small portions

doll /dɒl/ *n* **1** a small-scale figure of a human being used esp as a child's toy **2a** a (pretty but often silly) young woman – infml **b** an attractive person – slang

dollar /ˈdɒləʳ/ *n* (a coin or note representing) the basic money unit of the USA, Canada, Australia, etc

¹dollop /ˈdɒləp/ *n* a soft shapeless blob; *esp* a serving of mushy or semiliquid food

²dollop *v* to serve *out* carelessly or clumsily

doll's house *n* a child's small-scale toy house

doll up *v* to dress prettily or showily – infml

¹dolly /ˈdɒli/ *n* **1** a doll – used chiefly by or to children **2** a wooden-pronged instrument for beating and stirring clothes while washing them in a tub **3a** a platform on a roller or on wheels or castors for moving heavy objects **b** a wheeled platform for a film or television camera

²dolly *v* to move a film or television camera on a dolly towards or away from a subject – usu + *in* or *out*

dolly bird *n, chiefly Br* a pretty young woman, esp one who is a slavish follower of fashion and not regarded as intelligent

dolmen /ˈdɒlmen, -mḷn/ *n* a prehistoric monument consisting of 2 or more upright stones supporting a horizontal slab

dolorous /ˈdɒlərəs/ *adj* causing or expressing misery or grief – **~ly** *adv*

dolphin /ˈdɒlfḷn/ *n* **1** any of various small toothed whales with the snout elongated into a beak to varying extents **2** a spar or buoy for mooring boats

dolt /dəʊlt/ *n* an extremely dull or stupid person – **~ish** *adj* – **~ishly** *adv*

domain /dəˈmeɪn/ *n* **1** a territory over which control is exercised **2** a sphere of influence or activity

¹dome /dəʊm/ *n* a (nearly) hemispherical roof or vault – **~d** *adj*

²dome *v* to cover with or form into a dome

Domesday Book /ˈduːmzdeɪ bʊk/ *n* a record of a survey of English lands made by order of William I about 1086

¹domestic /dəˈmestɪk/ *adj* **1** of or devoted to the home or the family **2** of one's own or some particular country; not foreign **3a** living near or about the habitations of human beings **b** tame; *also* bred by human beings for some specific purpose (e g food, hunting, etc) – ~**ally** *adv*

²**domestic** *n* a household servant

domesticate /də'mestɨkeɪt/ *v* **1** to bring (an animal or species) under human control for some specific purpose (e g for carrying loads, hunting, food, etc) **2** to cause to be fond of or adapted to household duties or pleasures – **-cation** *n*

domesticity /,dəumes'tɪsɨti/ *n* (devotion to) home or family life

¹**domicile** /'dɒmɨsaɪl/ *also* **domicil** /-sɪl/ *n* a home; *esp* a person's permanent and principal home for legal purposes

²**domicile** *v* to establish in or provide with a domicile

domiciliary /,dɒmɨ'sɪlɪəri/ *adj* **1** of or being a domicile **2** taking place or attending in the home

¹**dominant** /'dɒmɨnənt/ *adj* **1** commanding, controlling, or prevailing over all others **2** overlooking and commanding from a superior height **3** being the one of a pair of (genes determining) contrasting inherited characteristics that predominates – **-nance** *n*

²**dominant** *n* the fifth note of a diatonic scale

dominate /'dɒmɨneɪt/ *v* **1** to exert controlling influence or power over **2** to overlook from a superior height **3** to occupy a commanding or preeminent position in **4** to have or exert mastery or control – **-nation** *n*

domineer /,dɒmɨ'nɪəʳ/ *v* to exercise arbitrary or overbearing control

Dominican /də'mɪnɪkən/ *n or adj* (a member) of a preaching order of mendicant friars founded by St Dominic in 1215

dominion /də'mɪnɪən/ *n* **1** the power or right to rule; sovereignty **2** absolute ownership **3** *often cap* a self-governing nation of the Commonwealth other than the United Kingdom

domino /'dɒmɨnəu/ *n, pl* **dominoes, dominos 1a** a long loose hooded cloak worn with a mask as a masquerade costume **b** a half mask worn with a masquerade costume **2a** a flat rectangular block whose face is divided into 2 equal parts that are blank or bear from 1 to usu 6 dots arranged as on dice faces **b** *pl but usu sing in constr* any of several games played with a set of usu 28 dominoes

¹**don** /dɒn/ *n* **1** a Spanish nobleman or gentleman – used as a title preceding the Christian name **2** a head, tutor, or fellow in a college of Oxford or Cambridge university; *broadly* a university teacher

²**don** *v* to put on (clothes, etc)

donate /dəu'neɪt/ *v* to make a gift (of), esp to a public or charitable cause – **-ion** *n*

¹**done** /dʌn/ **1** *past part of* **do** **2** *chiefly dial & NAm past of* **do**

²**done** *adj* **1** socially conventional or accepted (e g it's not *done* to eat peas off your knife) **2** arrived at or brought to an end; completed **3** physically exhausted; spent **4** no longer involved; through (e g I'm *done* with the Army) **5** doomed to failure, defeat, or death **6** cooked sufficiently **7** arrested, imprisoned – slang

³**done** *interj* – used in acceptance of a bet or transaction

donjon /'dɒndʒən, 'dʌn-/ *n* a massive inner tower in a medieval castle

Don Juan /,dɒn 'hwɑːn, -'wɑːn, -'dʒuːən/ *n* a promiscuous man; *broadly* a lady-killer

donkey /'dɒŋki/ *n* **1** the domestic ass **2** a stupid or obstinate person

donkey jacket *n* a thick hip-length hard-wearing jacket, usu blue and with a strip of (imitation) leather across the shoulders

donkey's years *n pl, chiefly Br* a very long time – infml

donkeywork /'dɒŋkiwɜːk/ *n* hard, monotonous, and routine work – infml

donnish /'dɒnɪʃ/ *adj* pedantic – ~**ly** *adv*

donor /'dəunəʳ/ *n* **1** a person who gives, donates, or presents **2** sby used as a source of biological material

doodle /'duːdl/ *v or n* (to make) an aimless scribble or sketch

¹**doom** /duːm/ *n* **1** God's judgment of the world **2a** an (unhappy) destiny **b** unavoidable death or destruction; *also* environmental catastrophe – often in combination

[2]**doom** *v* to destine, esp to failure or destruction

doomsday /ˈduːmzdeɪ/ *n, often cap* judgment day; *broadly* some remote point in the future

door /dɔːʳ/ *n* **1** a usu swinging or sliding barrier by which an entry is closed and opened; *also* a similar part of a piece of furniture **2** a doorway **3** a means of access

doorkeeper /ˈdɔːkiːpəʳ/ *n* a person who guards the main door to a building and lets people in and out

doorman /ˈdɔːmən/ *n* a (uniformed) person who tends the entrance to a hotel, theatre, etc and assists people (e g in calling taxis)

doormat /ˈdɔːmæt/ *n* **1** a mat (e g of bristles) placed before or inside a door for wiping dirt from the shoes **2** a person who submits to bullying and indignities – infml

doornail /ˈdɔːneɪl/ *n* a large-headed nail formerly used for the strengthening or decoration of doors – chiefly in *dead as a doornail*

doorstep /ˈdɔːstep/ *n* **1** a step in front of an outer door **2** *Br* a very thick slice of bread – infml

doorway /ˈdɔːweɪ/ *n* an entrance into a building or room that is closed by means of a door

[1]**dope** /dəʊp/ *n* **1** a coating (e g a cellulose varnish) applied to a surface or fabric (e g of an aeroplane or balloon) to improve strength, impermeability, or tautness **2** absorbent or adsorbent material used in various manufacturing processes (e g the making of dynamite) **3a** marijuana, opium, or another drug **b** a preparation given illegally to a racing horse, greyhound, etc to make it run faster or slower **4** a stupid person – infml **5** information, esp from a reliable source – infml

[2]**dope** *v* to treat or affect with dope; *esp* to give a narcotic to

dopey, dopy /ˈdəʊpi/ *adj* **1** dulled, doped, or stupefied (e g by drugs, alcohol, or sleep) **2** dull, stupid

Doppler effect /ˈdɒplər ɪˌfekt/ *n* a change in the apparent frequency of sound, light, or other waves when there is relative motion between the source and the observer

[1]**Doric** /ˈdɒrɪk/ *adj* **1** (characteristic) of the Dorians or their language **2** of the oldest and simplest of the 3 Greek orders of architecture

[2]**Doric** *n* a broad rustic dialect of English, esp a Scots one

dormant /ˈdɔːmənt/ *adj* **1** marked by a suspension of activity: e g **a** temporarily devoid of external activity **b** temporarily in abeyance **2** (appearing to be) asleep or inactive, esp throughout winter – **-ancy** *n*

dormer /ˈdɔːməʳ/ *n* a window set vertically in a structure projecting through a sloping roof

dormitory /ˈdɔːmɪ̣təri/ *n* **1** a large room containing a number of beds **2** a residential community from which the inhabitants commute to their places of employment

dormouse /ˈdɔːmaʊs/ *n* any of numerous small Old World rodents having a long bushy tail

dorsal /ˈdɔːsəl/ *adj* relating to or situated near or on the back or top surface esp of an animal or aircraft or of any of its parts

dose /dəʊs/ *n* **1** the measured quantity of medicine to be taken at one time **2** a part of an experience to which one is exposed **3** an infection with a venereal disease – slang

[2]**dose** *v* to give a dose, esp of medicine, to

doss /dɒs/ *n, chiefly Br* **1** a crude or makeshift bed, esp one in a cheap lodging house **2** a short sleep *USE* slang

doss down *v, chiefly Br* to sleep or bed down in a makeshift bed – infml

dosser /ˈdɒsəʳ/ *n, chiefly Br* a down-and-out

dossier /ˈdɒsieɪ/ *n* a file of papers containing a detailed report or information

dost /dʌst/ *archaic pres 2 sing of* **do**

[1]**dot** /dɒt/ *n* **1** a small spot; a speck **2a(1)** a small point made with a pointed instrument **(2)** a small round mark used in spelling or punctuation **b(1)** a point after a note or rest in music indicating lengthening of the time value by one half **(2)** a point over or under a note indicating that it is to

be played staccato **3** a precise point, esp in time **4** a signal (e g a flash or audible tone) of relatively short duration that is one of the 2 fundamental units of Morse code

[2]**dot** *v* **1** to mark with a dot **2** to intersperse with dots or objects scattered at random

dotage /ˈdəʊtɪdʒ/ *n* a state or period of senile mental decay resulting in feeblemindedness

doth /dʌθ/ *archaic pres 3 sing of* **do**

dotty /ˈdɒti/ *adj* **1** crazy, mad **2** pleasantly eccentric or absurd *USE* infml – **dottiness** *n* – **dottily** *adv*

[1]**double** /ˈdʌbəl/ *adj* **1** twofold, dual **2** consisting of 2, usu combined, similar members or parts **3** being twice as great or as many **4** marked by duplicity; deceitful **5** folded in 2 **6** of twofold or extra size, strength, or value

[2]**double** *n* **1** a double amount; *esp* a double measure of spirits **2a** a living person who closely resembles another living person **b** a ghostly counterpart of a living person **c(1)** an understudy **(2)** one who resembles an actor and takes his/her place in scenes calling for special skills **3** a sharp turn or twist **4a** a bet in which the winnings and stake from a first race are bet on a second race **b** two wins in or on horse races, esp in a single day's racing **5** an act of doubling in a card game **6** the outermost narrow ring on a dartboard counting double the stated score; *also* a throw in darts that lands there

[3]**double** *adv* **1** to twice the extent or amount **2** two together

[4]**double** *v* **1a** to increase by adding an equal amount **b** to make a call in bridge that increases the value of tricks won or lost on (an opponent's bid) **2a** to make into 2 thicknesses; fold **b** to clench **c** to cause to stoop or bend over – usu + *up* or *over* **3** to become twice as much or as many **4** to turn back on one's course – usu + *back* **5** to become bent or folded, usu in the middle – usu + *up* or *over* **6** to serve an additional purpose – usu + *as*

double-barrelled /ˌ--ˈ--/ *adj* **1** *of a firearm* having 2 barrels **2** having a double purpose **3** *of a surname* having 2 parts

double bass /ˌdʌbəl ˈbeɪs/ *n* the largest instrument in the violin family tuned a fifth below the cello

double-breasted *adj* having a front fastening with one half of the front overlapping the other and usu a double row of buttons and a single row of buttonholes

double cream *n* thick heavy cream suitable for whipping

double-cross *v or n* (to deceive by) an act of betraying or cheating – **double-crosser** *n*

double-decker *n* sthg that has 2 decks, levels, or layers; *esp* a bus with seats on 2 floors

double dutch *n, often cap 2nd D* unintelligible or nonsensical speech or writing; gibberish – infml

double-edged *adj* having 2 purposes or possible interpretations; *specif, of a remark* seeming innocent, but capable of a malicious interpretation

double-jointed *adj* having or being a joint that permits an exceptional degree of flexibility of the parts joined

double-park *v* to park beside a row of vehicles already parked parallel to the kerb

double-quick *adj* very quick

doubles /ˈdʌbəlz/ *n* a game between 2 pairs of players

doublet /ˈdʌblɪ̈t/ *n* **1** a man's close-fitting jacket, with or without sleeves, worn in Europe, esp in the 15th to 17th c **2** two thrown dice showing the same number on the upper face

double take *n* a delayed reaction to a surprising or significant situation – esp in *do a double take*

double-talk *n* involved and often deliberately ambiguous language – **double-talk** *v* – **double-talker** *n*

doubloon /dʌˈbluːn/ *n* a former gold coin of Spain and Spanish America

doubly /ˈdʌbli/ *adv* **1** to twice the degree **2** in 2 ways

[1]**doubt** /daʊt/ *v* **1** to be in doubt about **2a** to lack confidence in; distrust **b** to consider unlikely – ~**er** *n*

[2]**doubt** *n* **1** (a state of) uncertainty of belief or opinion **2** a lack of confi-

dence; distrust **3** an inclination not to believe or accept; a reservation

doubtful /ˈdaʊtfəl/ *adj* **1** causing doubt; open to question **2a** lacking a definite opinion; hesitant **b** uncertain in outcome; not settled **3** of questionable worth, honesty, or validity – ~**ly** *adv*

doubtless /ˈdaʊtlɨs/ *adv* **1** without doubt **2** probably

douche /duːʃ/ *n* (a device for giving) a jet or current of fluid, directed against a part or into a cavity of the body, esp the vagina

dough /dəʊ/ *n* **1** a mixture that consists essentially of flour or meal and milk, water, or another liquid and is stiff enough to knead or roll **2** money – slang

doughnut /ˈdəʊnʌt/ *n* a small round or ring-shaped cake that is often made with a yeast dough, filled with jam, and deep-fried

doughty /ˈdaʊti/ *adj* valiant, bold – poetic

doughy /ˈdəʊi/ *adj* unhealthily pale; pasty

do up *v* **1** to repair, restore **2** to wrap up **3** to fasten (clothing or its fastenings) together **4** to make more beautiful or attractive – infml

dour /dʊəʳ/ *adj* **1** stern, harsh **2** gloomy, sullen – ~**ly** *adv*

douse, dowse /daʊs/ *v* **1** to plunge into or drench with water **2** to extinguish (e g lights)

dove /dʌv/ *n* **1** any of various (smaller and slenderer) types of pigeon **2** an advocate of negotiation and compromise; *esp* an opponent of war – usu contrasted with *hawk*

[1]**dovetail** /ˈdʌvteɪl/ *n* a tenon like a dove's tail and the mortise into which it fits to form a joint

[2]**dovetail** *v* **1** to join (as if) by means of dovetails **2** to fit skilfully together to form a whole

dowager /ˈdaʊɨdʒəʳ/ *n* **1** a widow holding property or a title received from her deceased husband **2** a dignified elderly woman

dowdy /ˈdaʊdi/ *adj* **1** not neat or smart in appearance **2** old-fashioned, frumpy – **-dily** *adv* – **-diness** *n*

[1]**dowel** /ˈdaʊəl/ *n* a usu metal or wooden pin fitting into holes in adjacent pieces to preserve their relative positions; *also* rods of wood or metal for sawing into such pins

[2]**dowel** *v* to fasten by dowels

[1]**down** /daʊn/ *n* (a region of) undulating treeless usu chalk uplands, esp in S England – usu pl with sing. meaning

[2]**down** *adv* **1a** at or towards a relatively low level (e g *down* into the cellar) **b** downwards from the surface of the earth or water **c** below the horizon **d** downstream **e** in or into a lying or sitting position (e g lie *down*) **f** to or on the ground, surface, or bottom (e g telephone wires are *down*) **g** so as to conceal a particular surface (e g turned it face *down*) **h** downstairs **2** on the spot 2; *esp* as an initial payment (e g paid £10 *down*) **3a(1)** in or into a relatively low condition or status (e g family has come *down* in the world) – sometimes used interjectionally to express opposition (e g *down* with the oppressors!) **(2)** to prison – often + *go* or *send* **b(1)** in or into a state of relatively low intensity or activity (e g calm *down*) **(2)** into a slower pace or lower gear (e g changed *down* into second) **c** lower in amount, price, figure, or rank (e g prices are *down*) **d** behind an opponent (e g we're 3 points *down*) **4a** so as to be known, recognized, or recorded, esp on paper (e g scribbled it *down*; you're *down* to speak next) **b** so as to be firmly held in position (e g stick *down* the flap of the envelope **c** to the moment of catching or discovering (e g track the criminal *down*) **5** in a direction conventionally the opposite of up: e g **a** to leeward **b** in or towards the south **c** *chiefly Br* away from the capital of a country or from a university city **6** downwards **7a** to a concentrated state (e g got his report *down* to 3 pages) **b** so as to be flattened, reduced, eroded, or diluted (e g heels worn *down*) **c** completely from top to bottom (e g hose the car *down*)

[3]**down** *adj* **1** directed or going downwards (e g the *down* escalator) **2a** depressed, dejected **b** ill (e g *down* with flu) **3** having been finished or dealt with (e g eight *down* and two to go) **4** with the rudder to windward –

used with reference to a ship's helm **5** *chiefly Br* bound in a direction regarded as down; *esp* travelling away from a large town, esp London

4down *prep* **1a** down along, round, through, towards, in, into, or on **b** at the bottom of (e g the bathroom is *down* those stairs) **2** *Br* down to; to (e g going *down* the shops) – nonstandard

5down *n* a grudge, prejudice – often in *have a down on*

6down *v* **1** to cause to go or come down **2** to drink down; swallow quickly – infml **3** to defeat – infml

7down *n* a covering of soft fluffy feathers

down-and-out *n or adj* (sby) destitute or impoverished

1downbeat /'daʊnbiːt/ *n* the principally accented (e g the first) note of a bar of music

2downbeat *adj* **1** pessimistic, gloomy **2** relaxed, informal

downcast /'daʊnkɑːst/ *adj* **1** dejected, depressed **2** directed downwards

downer /'daʊnəʳ/ *n* a depressing experience or situation – infml

downfall /'daʊnfɔːl/ *n* **1** (a cause of) a sudden fall (e g from high rank or power) **2** an often heavy fall of rain or esp snow

downgrade /'daʊngreɪd, daʊn'greɪd/ *v* **1** to lower in rank, value, or importance **2** to alter the status of (a job) so as to lower the rate of pay

downhearted /,daʊn'hɑːtɨd/ *adj* downcast, dejected – **~ly** *adv*

1downhill /'daʊn,hɪl/ *n* a skiing race downhill against time

2downhill /,daʊn'hɪl/ *adv* **1** towards the bottom of a hill **2** towards a lower or inferior state or level – in *go downhill*

3downhill /,daʊn'hɪl/ *adj* sloping downhill

Downing Street /'daʊnɪŋ striːt/ *n* the British government; *also* (a spokesman for) the British prime minister

down payment *n* a deposit paid at the time of purchase or delivery

downpour /'daʊnpɔːʳ/ *n* a heavy fall of rain

1downright /'daʊnraɪt/ *adv* thoroughly, outright

2downright *adj* **1** absolute, thorough **2** plain, blunt

Down's syndrome /'daʊnz ,sɪndrəʊm/ *n* a form of congenital mental deficiency in which a child is born with slanting eyes, a broad short skull, and broad hands with short fingers; mongolism

downstage /daʊn'steɪdʒ/ *adv or adj* at the front of a theatrical stage; *also* towards the audience or camera

1downstairs /,daʊn'steəz/ *adv* down the stairs; on or to a lower floor

2downstairs *adj* situated on the main, lower, or ground floor of a building

3downstairs *n, pl* **downstairs** the lower floor of a building

downstream /,daʊn'striːm/ *adv or adj* in the direction of the flow of a stream

down-to-earth *adj* practical, realistic

downtrodden /'daʊn,trɒdn/ *adj* oppressed by those in power

downward /'daʊnwəd/ *adj* **1** moving or extending downwards (e g the *downward* path) **2** descending to a lower pitch **3** descending from a head, origin, or source

downwards /'daʊnwədz/ *adv* **1a** from a higher to a lower place or level; in the opposite direction from up **b** downstream **c** so as to conceal a particular surface (e g turned it face *downwards*) **2a** from a higher to a lower condition **b** going down in amount, price, figure, or rank **3** from an earlier time **4** from an ancestor or predecessor

downwind /,daʊn'wɪnd/ *adv or adj* in the direction that the wind is blowing

downy /'daʊni/ *adj* **1** resembling or covered in down **2** made of down

dowry /'daʊəri/ *n* the money, goods, or estate that a woman brings to her husband in marriage

1dowse /daʊs/ *v* to douse

2dowse /daʊz/ *v* to search for hidden water or minerals with a divining rod – **~r** *n* – **dowsing** *n*

dowsing rod /'daʊzɪŋ ,rɒd/ *n* a divining rod

doyen /'dɔɪən/, *fem* **doyenne** /dɔɪ'en/

n the senior or most experienced member of a body or group

doze /dəʊz/ *v* **1** to sleep lightly **2** to fall into a light sleep – usu + *off* – **doze** *n*

dozen /'dʌzən/ *n, pl* **dozens, dozen 1** a group of 12 **2** an indefinitely large number – usu pl with sing. meaning – **dozen** *adj*

dozy /'dəʊzi/ *adj* **1** drowsy, sleepy **2** *chiefly Br* stupid and slow-witted – infml – **-zily** *adv* – **-ziness** *n*

drab /dræb/ *adj* **1** of a dull brown colour **2** dull, cheerless – **~ly** *adv* – **~ness** *n*

drachma /'drækmə/ *n* the standard unit of currency of Greece

draconian /drə'kəʊnɪən/, **draconic** *adj, often cap, esp of a law* extremely severe; drastic

[1]**draft** /drɑːft/ *n* **1** the act, result, or plan of drawing out or sketching: e g **a** a construction plan **b** a preliminary sketch, outline, or version **2a** a group of individuals selected for a particular job **b** (the group of individuals resulting from) the selecting of certain animals from a herd or flock **3a** an order for the payment of money drawn by one person or bank on another **b** (an instance of) drawing from or making demands on sthg **4** *chiefly NAm* conscription – usu + *the*

[2]**draft** *adj, esp of livestock* chosen from a group

[3]**draft** *v* **1** to draw the preliminary sketch, version, or plan of **2** *NAm* to conscript for military service

draftsman /'drɑːftsmən/ *n* sby who draws up legal documents or other writings

[1]**drag** /dræg/ *n* **1** a device for dragging under water to search for objects **2** sthg that retards motion, action, or progress; a burden **3a** a drawing along or over a surface with effort or pressure **b** motion effected with slowness or difficulty **c** a drawing into the mouth of pipe, cigarette, or cigar smoke – infml **4a** woman's clothing worn by a man – slang; often in *in drag* **b** clothing – slang **5** a dull or boring person or experience – slang

[2]**drag** *v* **1a** to draw slowly or heavily; haul **b** to cause to move with painful or undue slowness or difficulty **2a** to search (a body of water) with a drag **b** to catch with a dragnet or trawl **3** to bring by force or compulsion – infml **4** to hang or lag behind **5** to trail along on the ground **6** to move or proceed laboriously or tediously – infml **7** to draw tobacco smoke into the mouth – usu + *on*; infml

[3]**drag** *adj* of drag racing

dragnet /'drægnet/ *n* **1** a net drawn along the bottom of a body of water or the ground to catch fish or small game **2** a network of measures for apprehension (e g of criminals)

dragon /'drægən/ *n* **1** a mythical winged and clawed monster, often breathing fire **2** a fierce, combative, or very strict person

dragonfly /'drægənflaɪ/ *n* any of various long slender-bodied often brightly coloured insects that have a fine network of veins in their wings and often live near water

[1]**dragoon** /drə'guːn/ *n* a member of a European military unit formerly composed of mounted infantrymen armed with carbines

[2]**dragoon** *v* **1** to reduce to subjection by harsh use of troops **2** to (attempt to) force into submission by persecution

[1]**drain** /dreɪn/ *v* **1a** to draw off (liquid) gradually or completely **b** to exhaust physically or emotionally **2a** to make gradually dry **b** to carry away the surface water of **c** to deplete or empty (as if) by drawing off gradually **d** to empty by drinking the contents of **3** to flow off gradually **4** to become gradually dry

[2]**drain** *n* **1** a means (e g a pipe) by which usu liquid matter is drained away **2** a gradual outflow or withdrawal **3** sthg that causes depletion; a burden

drainage /'dreɪnɪdʒ/ *n* **1a** draining **b** sthg drained off **2** a system of drains

drainpipe /'draɪnpaɪp/ *n* a pipe that carries waste, liquid sewage, excess water, etc away from a building

drainpipe trousers, drainpipes *n pl* tight trousers with narrow legs

drake /dreɪk/ *n* a male duck

dram /dræm/ *n* **1** a unit of mass equal to $^1/_{16}$oz avoirdupois (about 1.77g) **2**

chiefly Scot a tot of spirits, usu whisky

drama /'drɑːmə/ *n* **1** a composition in verse or prose intended to portray life or character or to tell a story through action and dialogue; *specif* a play **2** dramatic art, literature, or affairs **3** a situation or set of events having the qualities of a drama – **~tize** *v*

dramatic /drə'mætɪk/ *adj* **1** of drama **2a** suitable to or characteristic of drama; vivid **b** striking in appearance or effect – **~ally** *adv*

dramatics /drə'mætɪks/ *n pl* **1** *sing or pl in constr* the study or practice of theatrical arts (e g acting and stagecraft) **2** dramatic behaviour; *esp* an exaggerated display of emotion

dramatis personae /ˌdræmətʲs pɜː'səʊnaɪ/ *n pl* (a list of) the characters or actors in a play

dramatist /'dræmətʲst/ *n* a playwright

drank /dræŋk/ *past of* **drink**

[1]**drape** /dreɪp/ *v* **1** to cover or decorate (as if) with folds of cloth **2** to hang or stretch loosely or carelessly **3** to arrange in flowing lines or folds

[2]**drape** *n* a piece of drapery; *esp, chiefly NAm* a curtain

draper /'dreɪpəʳ/ *n, chiefly Br* a dealer in cloth and sometimes also in clothing, haberdashery, and soft furnishings

drapery /'dreɪpəri/ *n* **1a** (a piece of) cloth or clothing arranged or hung gracefully, esp in loose folds **b** cloth or textile fabrics used esp for clothing or soft furnishings **2** *Br* the trade of a draper

drastic /'dræstɪk/ *adj* radical in effect or action; severe – **~ally** *adv*

drat /dræt/ *v* to damn – euph; used as a mild oath

[1]**draught** /drɑːft/ *n* **1** a team of animals together with what they draw **2** the act or an instance of drinking; *also* the portion drunk in such an act **3** the act of drawing (e g from a cask); *also* a quantity of liquid so drawn **4** the depth of water a ship requires to float in, esp when loaded **5** a current of air in a closed-in space

[2]**draught** *adj* **1** used for drawing loads **2** served from the barrel or cask

draughtboard /'drɑːftbɔːd/ *n* a chessboard

draughts /drɑːfts/ *n pl but sing or pl in constr, Br* a game for 2 players each of whom moves his/her usu 12 draughtsmen according to fixed rules across a chessboard usu using only the black squares

draughtsman /drɑːftsmən/ *n* **1a** an artist skilled in drawing **b** *fem* **draughtswoman** sby who draws plans and sketches (e g of machinery or structures) **2** *Br* a disc-shaped piece used in draughts

draughty /'drɑːfti/ *adj* having a cold draught blowing through

[1]**draw** /drɔː/ *v* **drawn** **1** to pull, haul **2** to cause to go in a certain direction **3a** to attract **b** to bring in, gather, or derive from a specified source **c** to bring on oneself; provoke **d** to bring out by way of response; elicit **4** to inhale **5a** to bring or pull out, esp with effort **b** to disembowel **c** to cause (blood) to flow **6a** to accumulate, gain **b** to take (money) from a place of deposit – often + *out* **c** to use in making a cash demand **d** to receive regularly, esp from a particular source **7a** to take (cards) from a dealer or pack **b** to receive or take at random **8** to strike (a ball) so as to impart a curved motion or backspin **9** to produce a likeness of (e g by making lines on a surface); portray, delineate **10** to formulate or arrive at by reasoning **11** to pull together and close (e g curtains) **12** to stretch or shape (esp metal) by pulling through dies; *also* to produce (e g a wire) thus **13** to come or go steadily or gradually **14** to advance as far as a specified position **15a** to pull back a bowstring **b** to bring out a weapon **16** to produce or allow a draught **17** to sketch **18** to finish a competition or contest without either side winning **19** to obtain resources (e g of information) **20** *chiefly NAm* to suck in sthg, esp tobacco smoke – usu + *on*

[2]**draw** *n* **1a** a sucking pull on sthg held between the lips **b** *the* removing of a handgun from its holster in order to shoot **2** a drawing of lots; a raffle **3** a contest left undecided; a tie **4** sthg that draws public attention or patron-

age **5** the usu random assignment of starting positions in a competition, esp a competitive sport

drawback /ˈdrɔːbæk/ *n* an objectionable feature; a disadvantage

draw back *v* to avoid an issue or commitment; retreat

drawbridge /ˈdrɔːˌbrɪdʒ/ *n* a bridge made to be raised up, let down, or drawn aside so as to permit or hinder passage

drawer /drɔːʳ/ *n* **1** one who draws a bill of exchange or order for payment or makes a promissory note **2** an open-topped box in a piece of furniture which to open and close slides back and forth in its frame **3** *pl* an undergarment for the lower body – now usu humor

drawing /ˈdrɔːɪŋ/ *n* **1** the art or technique of representing an object, figure, or plan by means of lines **2** sthg drawn or subject to drawing: e g **a** an amount drawn from a fund **b** a representation formed by drawing

drawing pin *n, Br* a pin with a broad flat head for fastening esp sheets of paper to boards

drawing room *n* **1** a formal reception room **2** a living room – fml

¹drawl /drɔːl/ *v* to speak or utter slowly and often affectedly, with vowels greatly prolonged

²drawl *n* a drawling manner of speaking

draw on *v* **1** to approach **2** to cause; bring on **3** to put on

draw out *v* **1** to remove, extract **2** to extend beyond a minimum in time; prolong **3** to cause to speak freely

drawstring /ˈdrɔːˌstrɪŋ/ *n* a string or tape threaded through fabric, which when pulled closes an opening (e g of a bag) or gathers material (e g of curtains or clothes)

draw up *v* **1** to bring (e g troops) into array **2** to draft **3** to straighten (oneself) to an erect posture, esp as an assertion of dignity or resentment **4** to bring or come to a halt

¹dray /dreɪ/ *n* a strong low cart or wagon without sides, used esp by brewers

²dray, drey a squirrel's nest

¹dread /dred/ *v* **1** to fear greatly **2** to be extremely apprehensive about

²dread *n* (the object of) great fear, uneasiness, or apprehension

³dread *adj* causing or inspiring dread

dreadful /ˈdredfəl/ *adj* **1** inspiring dread; causing great and oppressive fear **2a** extremely unpleasant or shocking **b** very disagreeable (e g through dullness or poor quality) **3** extreme – **~ness** *n* – **~ly** *adv*

¹dream /driːm/ *n* **1** a series of thoughts, images, or emotions occurring during sleep **2** sthg notable for its beauty, excellence, or enjoyable quality **3** a strongly desired goal; an ambition; *also* a realization of an ambition – often used attributively

²dream *v* **dreamed, dreamt** **1** to have a dream (of) **2** to indulge in daydreams or fantasies **3** to consider as a possibility; imagine **4** to pass (time) in reverie or inaction – usu + *away*

dreamboat /ˈdriːmbəʊt/ *n* a highly attractive person of the opposite sex – infml; no longer in vogue

dreamy /ˈdriːmi/ *adj* **1** pleasantly abstracted from immediate reality **2** given to dreaming or fantasy **3a** suggestive of a dream in vague or visionary quality **b** delightful, pleasing; *esp, of a man* sexually attractive – infml – **-mily** *adv* – **-miness** *n*

dreary /ˈdrɪəri/ *adj* causing feelings of cheerlessness or gloom; dull – **-arily** *adv* – **-ariness** *n*

¹dredge /dredʒ/ *n* **1** an oblong frame with an attached net for gathering fish, shellfish, etc from the bottom of the sea, a river, etc **2** a machine for removing earth, mud, etc usu by buckets on an endless chain or suction tube

²dredge *v* **1a** to dig, gather, or pull out with a dredge – often + *up* or *out* **b** to deepen (e g a waterway) with a dredging machine **2** to bring to light by thorough searching – usu + *up*; infml **3** to use a dredge

³dredge *v* to coat (e g food) by sprinkling (e g with flour)

dredger /ˈdredʒəʳ/ *n* a barge with an apparatus for dredging harbours, waterways, etc

¹drench /drentʃ/ *n* a poisonous or medicinal drink, esp put down the throat of an animal

²drench *v* **1** to administer a drench to

(an animal) **2** to make thoroughly wet (e g with falling water or by immersion); saturate

[1]**dress** /dres/ *v* **1a** to put clothes on **b** to provide with clothing **2** to add decorative details or accessories to; embellish **3** to prepare for use or service; *esp* to prepare (e g a chicken) for cooking or eating **4a** to apply dressings or medicaments to (e g a wound) **b(1)** to arrange (the hair) **(2)** to groom and curry (an animal) **c** to kill and prepare for market **d** to cultivate, esp by applying manure or fertilizer **e** to finish the surface of (e g timber, stone, or textiles) **f** to arrange goods on a display in (e g a shop window) **5a** to put on clothing **b** to put on or wear formal, elaborate, or fancy clothes **6** *of a man* to have one's genitals lying on a specified side of the trouser crutch

[2]**dress** *n* **1** utilitarian or ornamental covering for the human body; *esp* clothing suitable for a particular purpose or occasion **2** a 1-piece outer garment including both top and skirt usu for a woman or girl **3** covering, adornment, or appearance appropriate or peculiar to a specified time

[3]**dress** *adj* of, being, or suitable for an occasion requiring or permitting formal dress

dressage /ˈdresɑːʒ/ *n* the execution by a trained horse of precise movements in response to its rider

dress circle *n* the first or lowest curved tier of seats in a theatre

dress down *v* to reprove severely – **dressing-down** *n*

[1]**dresser** /ˈdresəʳ/ *n* a piece of kitchen furniture resembling a sideboard with a high back and having compartments and shelves for holding dishes and cooking utensils

[2]**dresser** *n* a person who looks after stage costumes and helps actors to dress

dressing /ˈdresɪŋ/ *n* **1** a seasoning, sauce, or stuffing **2** material applied to cover a wound, sore, etc **3** manure or compost to improve the growth of plants

dressing gown *n* a loose robe worn esp over nightclothes or when not fully dressed

dressing table *n* a table usu fitted with drawers and a mirror for use while dressing and grooming oneself

dress rehearsal *n* **1** a full rehearsal of a play in costume and with stage props shortly before the first performance **2** a full-scale practice

dressy /ˈdresi/ *adj* **1** showy in dress or appearance **2** *of clothes* stylish, smart

drew /druː/ *past of* **draw**

[1]**dribble** /ˈdrɪbəl/ *v* **1** to fall or flow in drops or in a thin intermittent stream; trickle **2** to let saliva trickle from the mouth; drool **3** to come or issue in piecemeal or disconnected fashion **4** to propel (a ball or puck) by successive slight taps or bounces with hand, foot, or stick **5** to proceed by dribbling

[2]**dribble** *n* **1** a small trickling stream or flow **2** a tiny or insignificant bit or quantity **3** an act or instance of dribbling

drier *also* **dryer** /ˈdraɪəʳ/ *n* any of various machines for drying sthg (e g the hair or clothes)

[1]**drift** /drɪft/ *n* **1a** a mass of sand, snow, etc deposited (as if) by wind or water **b** rock debris deposited by natural wind, water, etc; *specif* a deposit of clay, sand, gravel, and boulders transported by (running water from) a glacier **2** a general underlying tendency or meaning, esp of what is spoken or written **3** the motion or action of drifting: e g **a** a ship's deviation from its course caused by currents **b** a slow-moving ocean current **c** an easy, moderate, more or less steady flow along a spatial course **d** a gradual shift in attitude, opinion, or emotion **e** an aimless course, with no attempt at direction or control **4** a nearly horizontal mine passage on or parallel to a vein or rock stratum

[2]**drift** *v* **1a** to become driven or carried along by a current of water or air **b** to move or float smoothly and effortlessly **2a** to move in a random or casual way **b** to become carried along aimlessly **3** to pile up under the force of wind or water **4** to pile up in a drift

drifter /ˈdrɪftəʳ/ *n* **1** sby or sthg that travels or moves about aimlessly **2** a coastal fishing boat equipped with drift nets

driftwood /ˈdrɪftwʊd/ *n* wood cast up on a shore or beach

[1]**drill** /drɪl/ *v* **1a** to bore or drive a hole in (as if) by the piercing action of a drill **b** to make (e g a hole) by piercing action **2a** to instruct and exercise by repeating **b** to train or exercise in military drill

[2]**drill** *n* **1** (a device or machine for rotating) a tool with an edged or pointed end for making a hole in a solid substance by revolving or by a succession of blows **2** training in marching and the manual of arms **3** a physical or mental exercise aimed at improving facility and skill by regular practice **4** a marine snail that bores through oyster shells and eats the flesh **5** *chiefly Br* the approved or correct procedure for accomplishing sthg efficiently – infml

[3]**drill** *n* **1a** a shallow furrow into which seed is sown **b** a row of seed sown in such a furrow **2** a planting implement that makes holes or furrows, drops in the seed and sometimes fertilizer, and covers them with earth

[4]**drill** *v* to sow (seeds) by dropping along a shallow furrow

[5]**drill** *n* a durable cotton fabric in twill weave

drily /ˈdraɪli/ *adv* dryly

[1]**drink** /drɪŋk/ *v* **drank; drunk, drank** **1a** to swallow (a liquid); *also* to swallow the liquid contents of (e g a cup) **b** to take in or suck up; absorb **c** to take in or receive avidly – usu + *in* **2** to join in (a toast) **3** to take liquid into the mouth for swallowing **4** to drink alcoholic beverages, esp habitually or to excess

[2]**drink** *n* **1a** liquid suitable for swallowing **b** alcoholic drink **2** a draught or portion of liquid for drinking **3** excessive consumption of alcoholic beverages **4** *the* ocean; *broadly* any large body of water – + *the*; infml

drinkable /ˈdrɪŋkəbl/ *adj* suitable or safe for drinking

drinker /ˈdrɪŋkəʳ/ *n* one who drinks alcoholic beverages to excess

[1]**drip** /drɪp/ *v* **1a** to let fall drops of moisture or liquid **b** to overflow (as if) with moisture **2** to fall or let fall (as if) in drops

[2]**drip** *n* **1a** the action or sound of falling in drops **b** liquid that falls, overflows, or is forced out in drops **2** a projection for throwing off rainwater **3** a device for the administration of a liquid at a slow rate, esp into a vein **4** a dull or inconsequential person – infml

[1]**drip-dry** *v* to dry with few or no wrinkles when hung dripping wet

[2]**drip-dry** *adj* made of a washable fabric that drip-dries

dripping /ˈdrɪpɪŋ/ *n* the fat that runs out from meat during roasting

[1]**drive** /draɪv/ *v* **drove** /drəʊv/; **driven** /ˈdrɪvən/ **1a** to set in motion by physical force **b** to force into position by blows **c** to repulse or cause to go by force, authority, or influence **d** to set or keep in motion or operation **2a** to control and direct the course of (a vehicle or draught animal) **b** to convey or transport in a vehicle **3** to carry on or through energetically **4a** to exert inescapable or persuasive pressure on; force **b** to compel to undergo or suffer a change (e g in situation, awareness, or emotional state) **c** to urge relentlessly to continuous exertion **5** to cause (e g game or cattle) to move in a desired direction **6a** to propel (an object of play) swiftly **b** to play a drive in cricket at (a ball) or at the bowling of (a bowler) **7** to rush or dash rapidly or with force against an obstruction **8** to imply as an ultimate meaning or conclusion – + *at*

[2]**drive** *n* **1** a trip in a carriage or motor vehicle **2** a private road giving access from a public way to a building on private land **3** a (military) offensive, aggressive, or expansionist move **4** a strong systematic group effort; a campaign **5a** a motivating instinctual need or acquired desire **b** great zeal in pursuing one's ends **6a** the means for giving motion to a machine (part) **b** the means by or position from which the movement of a motor vehicle is controlled or directed **7** the act or an instance of driving an object of play; *esp* an attacking cricket stroke played conventionally with a straight bat and designed to send the ball in front of the batsman's wicket

drive-in *adj or n* (being) a place (e g a bank, cinema, or restaurant) that people can use while remaining in their cars

[1]**drivel** /ˈdrɪvəl/ *v* **1** to let saliva dribble from the mouth or mucus run from the nose **2** to talk stupidly and childishly or carelessly

[2]**drivel** *n* foolish or childish nonsense

driver /ˈdraɪvəʳ/ *n* **1** a coachman **2** the operator of a motor vehicle **3** a golf club with a wooden head used in hitting the ball long distances, esp off the tee

driving /ˈdraɪvɪŋ/ *adj* **1** that communicates force **2a** having great force **b** acting with vigour; energetic

[1]**drizzle** /ˈdrɪzəl/ *v* to rain in very small drops or very lightly – **drizzle** *n* – **drizzly** *adj*

drogue /drəʊg/ *n* **1** a small parachute for stabilizing or decelerating sthg or for pulling a larger parachute out of stowage **2** a sea anchor shaped like a drogue

droll /drəʊl/ *adj* humorous, whimsical, or odd – **drolly** *adv* – **~ness** *n*

drollery /ˈdrəʊləri/ *n* the act or an instance of jesting or droll behaviour

dromedary /ˈdrʌmədəri, ˈdrɒm-/ *n* a (1-humped) camel bred esp for riding

[1]**drone** /drəʊn/ *n* **1** the male of a bee (e g the honeybee) that has no sting and gathers no honey **2** sby who lives off others **3** a remotely-controlled pilotless aircraft, missile, or ship

[2]**drone** *v* **1** to make a sustained deep murmuring or buzzing sound **2** to talk in a persistently monotonous tone

[3]**drone** *n* **1** any of the usu 3 pipes on a bagpipe that sound fixed continuous notes **2** a droning sound **3** an unvarying sustained bass note

drool /druːl/ *v* **1** to secrete saliva in anticipation of food **2** to make a foolishly effusive show of pleasure **3** to express sentimentally or effusively

[1]**droop** /druːp/ *v* **1** to (let) hang or incline downwards **2** to become depressed or weakened; languish

[2]**droop** *n* the condition or appearance of drooping

[1]**drop** /drɒp/ *n* **1a(1)** the quantity of fluid that falls in 1 spherical mass **(2)** *pl* a dose of medicine measured by drops **b** a minute quantity **2a** an ornament that hangs from a piece of jewellery (e g an earring) **b** a small globular often medicated sweet or lozenge **3a** the act or an instance of dropping; a fall **b** a decline in quantity or quality **4** the distance from a higher to a lower level or through which sthg drops **5** sthg that drops, hangs, or falls: e g **a** an unframed piece of cloth stage scenery **b** a hinged platform on a gallows **6** a small quantity of drink, esp alcohol; *broadly* an alcoholic drink – infml **7** (a secret place used for the deposit and collection of) letters or stolen or illegal goods – slang

[2]**drop** *v* **1** to fall in drops **2a(1)** to fall, esp unexpectedly or suddenly **(2)** to descend from one level to another **b** to fall in a state of collapse or death **3a** to cease to be of concern; lapse **b** to become less **4** to let fall; cause to fall **5a** to lower from one level or position to another **b** to cause to lessen or decrease; reduce **6** to set down from a ship or vehicle; unload; *also* to airdrop **7a** to give up (e g an idea) **b** to leave incomplete; cease **c** to break off an association or connection with; *also* to leave out of a team or group **8a** to utter or mention in a casual way **b** to send through the post **9** to lose – infml

dropkick /ˈdrɒp,kɪk/ *n* a kick made (e g in rugby) by dropping a football to the ground and kicking it at the moment it starts to rebound – **drop-kick** *v*

drop-off *n* a marked dwindling or decline

drop off *v* **1** to fall asleep **2** to decline, slump

dropout *n* **1** one who rejects or withdraws from participation in conventional society **2** a student who fails to complete or withdraws from a course, usu of higher education **3** a dropkick awarded to the defending team in rugby (e g after an unconverted try)

drop out *v* **1** to withdraw from participation **2** to make a dropout in rugby

dropper /ˈdrɒpəʳ/ *n* a short usu glass tube fitted with a rubber bulb and used to measure or administer liquids by drops

droppings /ˈdrɒpɪŋz/ *n pl* animal dung

dropsy /ˈdrɒpsi/ *n* abnormal accumulation of liquid in the body tissues causing painful swelling – **-sical** *adj*

dross /drɒs/ *n* waste, rubbish, or foreign matter; impurities

drought /draʊt/ *n* **1** a prolonged period of dryness **2** a prolonged shortage of sthg

¹drove /drəʊv/ *n* **1** a group of animals driven or moving in a body **2** a crowd of people moving or acting together

²drove *past of* **drive**

drover /ˈdrəʊvəʳ/ *n* one who drives cattle or sheep

drown /draʊn/ *v* **1a** to suffocate by submergence, esp in water **b** to wet thoroughly; drench **2** to engage (oneself) deeply and strenuously **3** to blot out (a sound) by making a loud noise **4** to destroy (e g a sensation or an idea) as if by drowning

drowse /draʊz/ *v* to doze – **drowse** *n*

drowsy /ˈdraʊzi/ *adj* **1a** sleepy **b** tending to induce sleepiness **c** indolent, lethargic **2** giving the appearance of peaceful inactivity – **-sily** *adv* – **-siness** *n*

drub /drʌb/ *v* **1** to beat severely **2** to defeat decisively

drudge /drʌdʒ/ *v* to do hard, menial, routine, or monotonous work – **drudge** *n* – **~ry** *n*

¹drug /drʌg/ *n* **1** a substance used as (or in the preparation of) a medication **2** a substance that causes addiction or habituation

²drug *v* **1** to administer a drug to **2** to lull or stupefy (as if) with a drug

drugstore /ˈdrʌgstɔːʳ/ *n, chiefly NAm* a chemist's shop; *esp* one that also sells sweets, magazines, and refreshments

druid /ˈdruːɪ̈d/, *fem* **druidess** *n, often cap* a member of a pre-Christian Celtic order of priests associated with a mistletoe cult

¹drum /drʌm/ *n* **1** a percussion instrument usu consisting of a hollow cylinder with a drumhead stretched over each end, that is beaten with a stick or a pair of sticks in playing **2** the tympanic membrane of the ear **3** the sound made by striking a drum; *also* any similar sound **4** a cylindrical container; *specif* a large usu metal container for liquids

²drum *v* **1** to beat a drum **2** to make a succession of strokes, taps, or vibrations that produce drumlike sounds **3** to throb or sound rhythmically **4** to summon or enlist (as if) by beating a drum **5** to instil (an idea or lesson) by constant repetition – usu + *into* or *out of* **6** to strike or tap repeatedly **7** to produce (rhythmic sounds) by such action

drumhead /ˈdrʌmhed/ *n* the material stretched over the end of a drum

drummer /ˈdrʌməʳ/ *n* one who plays a drum

drum out *v* to dismiss in disgrace; expel

drumstick /ˈdrʌm,stɪk/ *n* **1** a stick for beating a drum **2** the part of a fowl's leg below the thigh when cooked as food

drum up *v* **1** to bring about by persistent effort **2** to invent, originate

¹drunk /drʌŋk/ *past part of* **drink**

²drunk *adj* **1** under the influence of alcohol **2** dominated by an intense feeling

drunkard /ˈdrʌŋkəd/ *n* a person who is habitually drunk

drunken /ˈdrʌŋkən/ *adj* **1** drunk **2a** given to habitual excessive use of alcohol **b** of, characterized by, or resulting from alcoholic intoxication – **~ly** *adv* – **~ness** *n*

¹dry /draɪ/ *adj* **1a** (relatively) free from a liquid, esp water **b** not in or under water **c** lacking precipitation or humidity **2a** characterized by exhaustion of a supply of water or liquid **b** devoid of natural moisture; *also* thirsty **c** no longer sticky or damp **d** *of a mammal* not giving milk **e** lacking freshness; stale **3** not shedding or accompanied by tears **4** prohibiting the manufacture or distribution of alcoholic beverages **5** lacking sweetness **6** functioning without lubrication **7** built or constructed without a process which requires water **8a** not showing or communicating warmth, enthusiasm, or feeling; impassive **b** uninteresting **c** lacking embellishment, bias, or emotional concern; plain **9** not yielding what is expected or desired; unproductive **10** marked by a matter-of-fact, ironic, or terse manner of expression – **~ly, drily** *adv* – **~ness** *n*

[2]**dry** *v* to make or become dry – often + *out*

dryad /ˈdraɪæd/ *n* a nymph of the woods in Greek mythology

dry-clean *v* to subject to or undergo dry cleaning – **~er** *n*

dry-cleaning *n* **1** the cleaning of fabrics or garments with organic solvents and without water **2** that which is dry-cleaned

dry dock *n* a dock from which the water can be pumped to allow ships to be repaired

dry ice *n* solidified carbon dioxide

dry out *v* to undergo treatment for alcoholism or drug addiction

dry rot *n* (a fungus causing) a decay of seasoned timber in which the cellulose of wood is consumed leaving a soft skeleton which is readily reduced to powder

dry-shod *adj* having or keeping dry shoes or feet

dry up *v* **1** to disappear or cease to yield (as if) by evaporation, draining, or the cutting off of a source of supply **2** to wither or die through gradual loss of vitality **3** to wipe dry dishes, cutlery, etc by hand after they have been washed **4** to stop talking; shut up – infml **5** to cause to dry up

dt's /ˌdiː ˈtiːz/ *n pl, often cap D&T* delirium tremens

dual /ˈdjuːəl/ *adj* **1** consisting of 2 (like) parts or elements **2** having a double character or nature

dual carriageway *n, chiefly Br* a road that has traffic travelling in opposite directions separated by a central reservation

[1]**dub** /dʌb/ *v* **1** to confer knighthood on **2** to call by a descriptive name or epithet; nickname

[2]**dub** *v* **1** to make alterations to the original sound track of (a film): e g **a** to provide with a sound track in which the voices are not those of the actors on the screen **b** to provide with a sound track in a new language **2** to transpose (a previous recording) to a new record **3** *chiefly Br* to mix (a recording)

dubbin /ˈdʌbɨn/ *n* a dressing of oil and tallow for leather – **dubbin** *v*

dubious /ˈdjuːbɪəs/ *adj* **1** giving rise to doubt; uncertain **2** unsettled in opinion; undecided **3** of uncertain outcome **4** of questionable value, quality, or origin – **~ly** *adv* – **~ness** *n*

ducal /ˈdjuːkəl/ *adj* of or relating to a duke or duchy

ducat /ˈdʌkət/ *n* a usu gold coin formerly used in many European countries

duchess /ˈdʌtʃɨs/ *n* **1** the wife or widow of a duke **2** a woman having in her own right the rank of a duke

duchy /ˈdʌtʃi/ *n* a dukedom

[1]**duck** /dʌk/ *n* **1a** any of various swimming birds in which the neck and legs are short, the bill is often broad and flat, and the sexes are almost always different from each other in plumage **b** the flesh of any of these birds used as food **2** a female duck **3** *chiefly Br* dear – often pl with sing. meaning but sing. in constr; infml

[2]**duck** *v* **1** to plunge (something) under the surface of water **2** to move or lower the head or body suddenly, esp as a bow or to avoid being hit **3** to avoid, evade (a duty, question, or responsibility) – **duck** *n*

[3]**duck** *n* a durable closely woven usu cotton fabric

[4]**duck** *n* a score of nought, esp in cricket

duckling /ˈdʌklɪŋ/ *n* a young duck

duckweed /ˈdʌkwiːd/ *n* any of several small free-floating stemless plants that often cover large areas of the surface of still water

[1]**duct** /dʌkt/ *n* **1** a bodily tube or vessel, esp when carrying the secretion of a gland **2** a pipe, tube, or channel that conveys a substance **3** a continuous tube in plant tissue

ductile /ˈdʌktaɪl/ *adj* **1** capable of being easily fashioned into a new form **2** *of metals* capable of being drawn out or hammered thin **3** easily led or influenced; tractable – infml – **-tility** *n*

[1]**dud** /dʌd/ *n* **1** a bomb, missile, etc that fails to explode **2** *pl* personal

belongings; *esp* clothes **3** a failure **4** a counterfeit, fake *USE* (*2, 3, & 4*) infml

²dud *adj* valueless – infml

dudgeon /ˈdʌdʒən/ *n* indignation, resentment – esp in *in high dudgeon*

¹due /djuː/ *adj* **1** owed or owing as a debt **2a** owed or owing as a natural or moral right (e g got his *due* reward) **b** appropriate (e g after *due* consideration) **3a** (capable of) satisfying a need, obligation, or duty **b** regular, lawful (e g *due* proof of loss) **4** ascribable – + *to* **5** payable **6** required or expected in the prearranged or normal course of events (e g *due* to arrive soon)

²due *n* sthg due or owed: e g **a** sthg esp nonmaterial that rightfully belongs to one **b** *pl* fees, charges

³due *adv* directly, exactly – used before points of the compass

¹duel /ˈdjuːəl/ *n* **1** a formal combat with weapons fought between 2 people in the presence of witnesses in order to settle a quarrel **2** a conflict between usu evenly matched antagonistic people, ideas, or forces

²duel *v* to fight a duel

duenna /djuːˈenə/ *n* **1** an older woman serving as governess and companion to the younger ladies in a Spanish or Portuguese family **2** a chaperone

duet /djuːˈet/ *n* a (musical) composition for 2 performers

duffel bag, duffle bag /ˈdʌfəl/ *n* a fabric bag, usu closed with a drawstring

duffel coat, duffle coat *n* a usu thigh or knee-length coat with a hood and fastened with toggles

duffer /ˈdʌfəʳ/ *n* an incompetent, ineffectual, or clumsy person

¹dug /dʌg/ *past of* **dig**

²dug *n* an udder; *also* a teat – usu used with reference to animals

dugong /ˈduːgɒŋ/ *n* an aquatic plant-eating mammal related to the manatee

dugout /ˈdʌgaʊt/ *n* **1** a boat made by hollowing out a large log **2** a shelter dug in the ground or in a hillside, esp for troops

duke /djuːk/ *n* **1** a sovereign ruler of a European duchy **2** a nobleman of the highest hereditary rank; *esp* a member of the highest rank of the British peerage – **~dom** *n*

dulcimer /ˈdʌlsɪ̣məʳ/ *n* a stringed instrument having strings of graduated length stretched over a sounding board and played with light hammers

¹dull /dʌl/ *adj* **1** mentally slow; stupid **2a** slow in perception or sensibility; insensible **b** lacking zest or vivacity; listless **3** lacking sharpness of cutting edge or point; blunt **4** not resonant or ringing **5** cloudy, overcast **6** boring, uninteresting – **~y** *adv* – **~ness** *n*

²dull *v* to make or become dull

dullard /ˈdʌləd/ *n* a stupid or insensitive person

duly /ˈdjuːli/ *adv* in a due manner, time, or degree; properly

dumb /dʌm/ *adj* **1** (temporarily) devoid of the power of speech **2** not expressed in uttered words **3** not willing to speak **4** stupid – **~ly** *adv* – **~ness** *n*

dumbfound, dumfound /dʌmˈfaʊnd/ *v* to strike (as if dumb) with amazement

dumb waiter *n* **1** a movable table or stand often with revolving shelves for holding food or dishes **2** a small lift for conveying food and dishes (e g from the kitchen to the dining area of a restaurant)

dumdum /ˈdʌmdʌm/ *n* a bullet that expands on impact and inflicts a severe wound

¹dummy /ˈdʌmi/ *n* **1** the exposed hand in bridge played by the declarer in addition to his/her own hand; *also* the player whose hand is a dummy **2** an imitation or copy of sthg used to reproduce some of the attributes of the original; e g **a** *chiefly Br* a rubber teat given to babies to suck in order to soothe them **b** a large puppet in usu human form, used by a ventriloquist **c** a model of the human body, esp the torso, used for fitting or displaying clothes **3** a person or corporation that seems to act independently but is in reality acting for or at the direction of another **5** an instance of dummying an opponent in sports **6** a dull or stupid person – infml

²dummy *adj* resembling or being a

dummy: e g **a** sham, artificial **b** existing in name only; fictitious

[3]**dummy** *v* to deceive an opponent (e g in rugby or soccer) by pretending to pass or release the ball while still retaining possession of it

dummy run *n* a rehearsal; trial run

[1]**dump** /dʌmp/ *v* **1a** to unload or let fall in a heap or mass **b** to get rid of unceremoniously or irresponsibly; abandon **2** to sell in quantity at a very low price; *specif* to sell abroad at less than the market price at home

[2]**dump** *n* **1a** an accumulation of discarded materials (e g refuse) **b** a place where such materials are dumped **2** a quantity of esp military reserve materials accumulated in 1 place **3** a disorderly, slovenly, or dilapidated place – infml

dumpling /ˈdʌmplɪŋ/ *n* **1** a small usu rounded mass of leavened dough cooked by boiling or steaming often in stew **2** a short round person – humor

dumps /dʌmps/ *n pl* a gloomy state of mind; despondency – esp in *in the dumps*; infml

dumpy /ˈdʌmpi/ *adj* short and thick in build; squat – **-piness** *n*

[1]**dun** /dʌn/ *adj* **1** of the colour dun **2** *of a horse* having a greyish or light brownish colour

[2]**dun** *n* **1** a dun horse **2** a slightly brownish dark grey colour

[3]**dun** *v* to make persistent demands upon for payment

[4]**dun** *n* an urgent request; *esp* a demand for payment

dunce /dʌns/ *n* a dull or stupid person

dunderhead /ˈdʌndəhed/ *n* a dunce, blockhead

dune /djuːn/ *n* a hill or ridge of sand piled up by the wind

dung /dʌŋ/ *n* the excrement of an animal

dungarees /ˌdʌŋgəˈriːz/ *n pl* a 1-piece outer garment consisting of trousers and a bib with shoulder straps fastened at the back

dungeon /ˈdʌndʒən/ *n* a dark usu underground prison or vault, esp in a castle

dunk /dʌŋk/ *v* to dip (e g a piece of bread) into liquid (e g soup) before eating

duo /ˈdjuːəʊ/ *n, pl* **duos** a pair (of performers); *also* a piece (e g of music) written for 2 players

duodecimal /ˌdjuːəʊˈdesɪməl, ˌdjuːə-/ *adj* proceeding by or based on the number of 12

duodenum /ˌdjuːəˈdiːnəm/ *n, pl* **duodena, duodenums** the first part of the small intestine – **-nal** *adj*

[1]**dupe** /djuːp/ *n* one who is easily deceived or cheated

[2]**dupe** *v* to make a dupe of; deceive

[1]**duplicate** /ˈdjuːplɨkɨt/ *adj* **1a** consisting of or existing in 2 corresponding or identical parts or examples **b** being the same as another **2** being a card game, specif bridge, in which different players play identical hands in order to compare scores

[2]**duplicate** *n* **1** either of 2 things that exactly resemble each other; *specif* an equally valid copy of a legal document **2** a copy

[3]**duplicate** /ˈdjuːplɨkeɪt/ *v* to make an exact copy of – **-cation** *n*

duplicator /ˈdjuːplɨkeɪtəʳ/ *n* a machine for making copies, esp by means other than photocopying or xeroxing

duplicity /djuːˈplɪsɨti/ *n* malicious deception in thought, speech, or action

durable /ˈdjʊərəbəl/ *adj* able to exist or be used for a long time without significant deterioration – **-bly** *adv* – **-bility** *n*

duration /djʊˈreɪʃən/ *n* **1** a continuing in time **2** the time during which sthg exists or lasts

durbar /ˈdɜːbɑːʳ/ *n* a reception held in former times by an Indian prince or a British governor or viceroy in India

duress /djʊˈres/ *n* **1** forcible restraint or restriction **2** compulsion by threat, violence, or imprisonment

Durex /ˈdjʊəreks/ *trademark* – used for a condom

during /ˈdjʊərɪŋ/ *prep* **1** throughout the whole duration of **2** at some point in the course of

dusk /dʌsk/ *n* (the darker part of) twilight

dusky /ˈdʌski/ *adj* **1** somewhat dark

in colour; *esp* dark-skinned **2** shadowy, gloomy – **-kiness** *n*

[1]**dust** /dʌst/ *n* **1** fine dry particles of any solid matter, esp earth; *specif* the fine particles of waste that settle esp on household surfaces **2** the particles into which sthg, esp the human body, disintegrates or decays **3** sthg worthless **4** the surface of the ground **5a** a cloud of dust **b** confusion, disturbance – esp in *kick up/raise a dust* – **~less** *adj*

[2]**dust** *v* **1** to make free of dust (e g by wiping or beating) **2** to prepare to use again – usu + *down* or *off* **3a** to sprinkle with fine particles **b** to sprinkle in the form of dust **4** *of a bird* to work dust into the feathers **5** to remove dust (e g from household articles), esp by wiping or brushing

dustbin /ˈdʌstˌbɪn/ *n, Br* a container for holding household refuse until collection

dust bowl *n* a region that suffers from prolonged droughts and dust storms

dustcart /ˈdʌstkɑːt/ *n, Br* a vehicle for collecting household waste

duster /ˈdʌstəʳ/ *n* sthg that removes dust; *specif* a cloth for removing dust from household articles

dust jacket *n* a removable outer paper cover for a book

dustman /ˈdʌstmən/ *n, Br* one employed to remove household refuse

dustpan /ˈdʌstpæn/ *n* a shovel-like utensil with a handle into which household dust and litter is swept

dustsheet /ˈdʌstˌʃiːt/ *n* a large sheet (e g of cloth) used as a cover to protect sthg, esp furniture, from dust

dust-up *n* a quarrel, row – infml

dusty /ˈdʌsti/ *adj* **1** covered with or full of dust **2** consisting of dust; powdery **3** resembling dust, esp in consistency or colour **4** lacking vitality; dry

[1]**dutch** /dʌtʃ/ *adv, often cap* with each person paying for him-/herself

[2]**dutch** *n, Br* one's wife – slang

Dutch /dʌtʃ/ *n* **1** the Germanic language of the Netherlands **2** *pl in constr* the people of the Netherlands

Dutch auction *n* an auction in which the auctioneer gradually reduces the bidding price until a bid is received

Dutch barn *n* a large barn with open sides used esp for storage of hay

Dutch cap *n* a moulded cap, usu of thin rubber, that fits over the cervix to act as a contraceptive barrier

Dutch courage *n* courage produced by drink rather than inherent resolution

Dutch elm disease *n* a fatal disease of elms caused by a fungus, spread from tree to tree by a beetle

Dutch uncle *n* one who admonishes sternly and bluntly

dutiable /ˈdjuːtɪəbl/ *adj* subject to a duty

dutiful /ˈdjuːtɪfəl/ *adj* **1** filled with or motivated by a sense of duty **2** proceeding from or expressive of a sense of duty – **~ly** *adv*

duty /djuːti/ *n* **1** conduct due to parents and superiors; respect **2a** tasks, conduct, service, or functions that arise from one's position, job, or moral obligations **b** assigned (military) service or business **3a** a moral or legal obligation **b** the force of moral obligation **4** a tax, esp on imports

duty-free *adj* exempted from duty

duvet /ˈduːveɪ/ *n* a large quilt filled with insulating material (e g down, feathers, or acrylic fibre), usu placed inside a removable fabric cover and used in place of bedclothes

[1]**dwarf** /dwɔːf/ *n, pl* **dwarfs, dwarves** **1** a person of unusually small stature **2** an animal or plant much below normal size **3** a small manlike creature in esp Norse and Germanic mythology who was skilled as a craftsman

[2]**dwarf** *v* **1** to stunt the growth of **2** to cause to appear smaller

dwell /dwel/ *v* **dwelt, dwelled** **1** to remain for a time **2** to keep the attention directed, esp in speech or writing; linger – + *on* or *upon* **3** to live as a resident; reside – fml

dwelling /ˈdwelɪŋ/ *n* a place (e g a house or flat) in which people live – fml or humor

dwindle /ˈdwɪndl/ *v* to become steadily less in quantity; shrink, diminish

[1]**dye** /daɪ/ *n* a soluble or insoluble colouring matter

[2]**dye** *v* to impart a new and often per-

manent colour to, esp by dipping in a dye – **dyer** *n*

dyed-in-the-wool *adj* thoroughgoing, uncompromising

dying *pres part of* **die**

dyke, dike /daɪk/ *n* **1** a bank, usu of earth, constructed to control or confine water **2** *dial Br* a wall or fence of turf or stone

¹dynamic /daɪˈnæmɪk, dʒ-/ *adj* **1a** of physical force or energy in motion **b** of dynamics **2a** marked by continuous activity or change **b** energetic, forceful – **~ally** *adv* – **-ism** *n*

dynamics /daɪˈnæmɪks/ *n pl but sing or pl in constr* **1** a branch of mechanics that deals with forces and their relation to the motion of bodies **2** a pattern of change or growth **3** variation and contrast in force or intensity (e g in music)

¹dynamite /ˈdaɪnəmaɪt/ *n* **1** a blasting explosive that is made of nitroglycerine absorbed in a porous material **2** sby or sthg that has explosive force or effect – infml

dynamo /ˈdaɪnəməʊ/ *n, pl* **dynamos** **1** a machine by which mechanical energy is converted into electrical energy; *specif* such a device that produces direct current (e g in a motor car) **2** a forceful energetic person

dynasty /ˈdɪnəsti/ *n* a succession of hereditary rulers; *also* the time during which such a dynasty rules – **-tic** *adj*

dysentery /ˈdɪsəntəri/ *n* any of several infectious diseases characterized by severe diarrhoea, usu with passing of mucus and blood

dyslexia /dɪsˈleksɪə/ *n* a failure in children to learn to read and write – **-lexic** *adj*

dyspepsia /dɪsˈpepsɪə, -ˈpepʃə/ *n* indigestion – **-peptic** *adj, n*

E

e /iː/ *n, pl* **e's, es** *often cap* **1a** (a graphic representation of or device for reproducing) the 5th letter of the English alphabet **b** a speech counterpart of written *e* **2** the 3rd note of a C-major scale **3** one designated *e* (e g the 5th in order or class) **4** a mark rating a student's work as poor or failing

[1]**each** /iːtʃ/ *adj* being one of 2 or more distinct individuals considered separately and often forming a group

[2]**each** *pron* each one

[3]**each** *adv* to or for each; apiece

each other *pron* each of 2 or more in reciprocal action or relation – not used as subject of a clause (e g wore *each other's* shirts)

each way *adj or adv, Br, of a bet* backing a horse, dog, etc to finish in the first two, three, or four in a race as well as to win

eager /ˈiːgəʳ/ *adj* marked by keen, enthusiastic, or impatient desire or interest – **~ly** *adv* – **~ness** *n*

eagle /ˈiːgəl/ *n* **1** any of various large birds of prey noted for their strength, size, gracefulness, keenness of vision, and powers of flight **2** any of various emblematic or symbolic representations of an eagle: e g **a** the standard of the ancient Romans **b** the seal or standard of a nation (e g the USA) having an eagle as emblem **3** a golf score for 1 hole of 2 strokes less than par

eagle-eyed *adj* **1** having very good eyesight **2** looking very keenly at sthg **3** good at noticing details; observant

[1]**ear** /ɪəʳ/ *n* **1** (the external part of) the characteristic vertebrate organ of hearing and equilibrium **2** the sense or act of hearing **3** sthg resembling an ear in shape or position; *esp* a projecting part (e g a lug or handle) **4a** sympathetic attention **b** *pl* notice, awareness

[2]**ear** *n* the fruiting spike of a cereal, including both the seeds and protective structures

earache /ˈɪəreɪk/ *n* an ache or pain in the ear

eardrum /ˈɪədrʌm/ *n* a thin membrane separating the outer ear from the middle ear and transmitting sound to the organs of heavily

earful /ˈɪəfəl/ *n* **1** an outpouring of news or gossip **2** a sharp verbal reprimand ***USE*** infml

earl /ɜːl/ *n* a member of the British peerage ranking below a marquess and above a viscount – **~dom** *n*

earlobe /ˈɪələʊb/ *n* the pendent part of the ear of humans or of some fowls

[1]**early** /ˈɜːli/ *adv* **1** at or near the beginning of a period of time, a development, or a series **2** before the usual or proper time

[2]**early** *adj* **1a** of or occurring near the beginning of a period of time, a development, or a series **b(1)** distant in past time **(2)** primitive **2a** occurring before the usual time **b** occurring in the near future **c** maturing or producing sooner than related forms – **-liness** *n*

[1]**earmark** /ˈɪəmɑːk/ *n* **1** a mark of identification on the ear of an animal **2** a distinguishing or identifying characteristic

[2]**earmark** *v* **1** to mark (livestock) with an earmark **2** to designate (e g funds) for a specific use or owner

earn /ɜːn/ *v* **1** to receive (e g money) as return for effort, esp for work done or services rendered **2** to bring in as income **3a** to gain or deserve because of one's behaviour or qualities **b** to make worthy of or obtain for – **~er** *n*

[1]**earnest** /ˈɜːnɪ̈st/. *n* a serious and intent mental state – esp in *in earnest*

[2]**earnest** *adj* determined and serious – **~ly** *adv* – **~ness** *n*

[3]**earnest** *n* **1** sthg of value, esp money,

given by a buyer to a seller to seal a bargain **2** a token of what is to come; a pledge

earnings /ˈɜːnɪŋz/ *n pl* money earned; *esp* gross revenue

earphone /ˈɪəfəʊn/ *n* a device that converts electrical energy into sound waves and is worn over or inserted into the ear

earring /ˈɪə,rɪŋ/ *n* an ornament for the ear that is attached to the earlobe

earshot /ˈɪəʃɒt/ *n* the range within which sthg, esp the unaided voice, may be heard

¹earth /ɜːθ/ *n* **1** soil **2** the sphere of mortal or worldly existence as distinguished from spheres of spiritual life **3a** areas of land as distinguished from sea and air **b** the solid ground **4** *often cap* the planet on which we live that is third in order from the sun **5** the people of the planet earth **6** the lair of a fox, badger, etc **7** *chiefly Br* an electrical connection to earth

²earth *v* **1** to drive (e g a fox) to hiding in its earth **2** to draw soil about (plants) – usu + *up* **3** *chiefly Br* to connect electrically with earth

earthbound /ˈɜːθbaʊnd/ *adj* **1a** restricted to the earth **b** heading or directed towards the planet earth **2a** bound by worldly interests; lacking spiritual quality **b** pedestrian, unimaginative

earthen /ˈɜːðən, ˈɜːθən/ *adj* made of earth or baked clay

earthenware /ˈɜːθənweəʳ, -ðən/ *n* ceramic ware made of slightly porous opaque clay fired at a low temperature

earthly /ˈɜːθli/ *adj* **1a** characteristic of or belonging to this earth **b** relating to human beings' actual life on this earth; worldly **2** possible – usu + neg or interrog

earthquake /ˈɜːθkweɪk/ *n* a (repeated) usu violent earth tremor caused by volcanic action or processes within the earth's crust

earthshaking /ˈɜːθʃeɪkɪŋ/ *adj* having tremendous importance or a widespread often violent effect – chiefly infml – **~ly** *adv*

earthworm /ˈɜːθwɜːm/ *n* any of numerous widely distributed worms that live in the soil

earthy /ˈɜːθi/ *adj* **1** consisting of, resembling, or suggesting earth **2** crude, coarse – **-thiness** *n*

earwig /ˈɪə,wɪg/ *n* any of numerous insects that have slender many-jointed antennae and a pair of appendages resembling forceps

¹ease /iːz/ *n* **1** being comfortable: e g **a** freedom from pain, discomfort, or anxiety **b** freedom from labour or difficulty **c** freedom from embarrassment or constraint; naturalness **2** facility, effortlessness **3** easing or being eased

²ease *v* **1** to free from sthg that pains, disquiets, or burdens – + *of* **2** to alleviate **3** to lessen the pressure or tension of, esp by slackening, lifting, or shifting **4** to make less difficult **5** to manoeuvre gently or carefully in a specified way **6** to decrease in activity, intensity, or severity – often + *off* or *up* **7** to manoeuvre oneself gently or carefully

easel /ˈiːzəl/ *n* a frame for supporting sthg (e g an artist's canvas)

easily /ˈiːzəli/ *adv* **1** without difficulty **2** without doubt; by far

¹east /iːst/ *adj or adv* towards, at, belonging to, or coming from the east

²east *n* **1** (the compass point corresponding to) the direction 90° to the right of north that is the general direction of sunrise **2a** *often cap* regions or countries lying to the east of a specified or implied point of orientation **b** *cap* regions lying to the east of Europe **3** the altar end of a church **4** sby (e g a bridge player) occupying a position designated east

Easter /ˈiːstəʳ/ *n* a feast that commemorates Christ's resurrection and is observed on the first Sunday after the first full moon following March 21

Easter egg *n* a (chocolate or painted and hard-boiled) egg given as a present and eaten at Easter

¹easterly /ˈiːstəli/ *adj or adv* east

²easterly *n* a wind from the east

eastern /ˈiːstən/ *adj* **1** *often cap* (characteristic) of a region conventionally designated east **2** east **3** **Eastern, Eastern Orthodox** of the

Russian or Greek Orthodox churches

[1]**easy** /ˈiːzi/ *adj* **1** causing or involving little difficulty or discomfort **2a** not severe; lenient **b** readily prevailed on; compliant: e g (**1**) not difficult to deceive or take advantage of (**2**) readily persuaded to have sexual relations – infml **3a** plentiful in supply at low or declining interest rates **b** less in demand and usu lower in price **4a** marked by peace and comfort **b** not hurried or strenuous **c** free from pain, annoyance, or anxiety **5** marked by social ease **6** not burdensome or difficult **7** marked by ready facility and freedom from constraint **8** *chiefly Br* not having marked preferences on a particular issue – infml – **easiness** *n*

[2]**easy** *adv* **1** easily **2** without undue speed or excitement; slowly, cautiously

easy chair *n* a large usu upholstered armchair designed for comfort and relaxation

easygoing /ˌiːziˈgəʊɪŋ/ *adj* taking life easily: e g **a** placid and tolerant **b** indolent and careless

eat /iːt/ *v* **ate; eaten** **1** to take in through the mouth and swallow as food **2** to consume gradually; corrode **3** to vex, bother – infml **4** to take food or a meal

eats /iːts/ *n pl* food – infml

eau de cologne /ˌəʊ də kəˈləʊn/ *n, pl* **eaux de cologne** toilet water

eaves /iːvz/ *n pl* the lower border of a roof that overhangs the wall

eavesdrop /ˈiːvzdrɒp/ *v* to listen secretly to what is said in private – **-dropper** *n*

[1]**ebb** /eb/, **ebb tide** *n* **1** the flowing out of the tide towards the sea **2** a point or condition of decline

[2]**ebb** *v* **1** *of tidal water* to recede from the flood state **2** to decline from a higher to a lower level or from a better to a worse state

[1]**ebony** /ˈebəni/ *n* (any of various tropical trees that yield) a hard heavy black wood

[2]**ebony** *adj* **1** made of or resembling ebony **2** black, dark – usu apprec

ebullience /ɪˈbʌlɪəns, ɪˈbʊ-/, **ebulliency** *n* the quality of being full of liveliness and enthusiasm; exuberance – **-ient** *adj* – **-iently** *adv*

[1]**eccentric** /ɪkˈsentrɪk/ *adj* **1** deviating from established convention; odd **2a** deviating from a circular path **b** located elsewhere than at the geometrical centre; *also* having the axis or support so located – **~ally** *adv* – **~ity** *n*

[2]**eccentric** *n* an eccentric person

ecclesiastical /ɪˌkliːziˈæstikəl/ *adj* of a church or religion

echelon /ˈeɪʃəlɒn, ˈeʃ-/ *n* **1** an arrangement of units (e g of troops or ships) resembling a series of steps **2** a particular division of a headquarters or supply organization in warfare **3** any of a series of levels or grades (e g of authority or responsibility) in some organized field of activity

echinoderm /ɪˈkaɪnəʊdɜːm/ *n* any of a phylum of radially symmetrical marine animals consisting of the starfishes, sea urchins, and related forms

[1]**echo** /ˈekəʊ/ *n, pl* **echoes** **1** the repetition of a sound caused by the reflection of sound waves **2** sby or sthg that repeats or imitates another **3** a repercussion, result **4** a soft repetition of a musical phrase

[2]**echo** *v* **1** to resound with echoes **2** to produce an echo **3** to repeat, imitate

éclair /ɪˈkleəʳ, eɪ-/ *n* a small light oblong cake that is split and filled with cream and usu topped with (chocolate) icing

[1]**eclectic** *adj* **1** selecting or using elements from various doctrines, methods, or styles **2** composed of elements drawn from various sources – **~ally** *adv* – **~ism** *n*

[2]**eclectic** *n* one who uses an eclectic method or approach

[1]**eclipse** /ɪˈklɪps/ *n* **1a** the total or partial obscuring of one celestial body by another **b** passage into the shadow of a celestial body **2** a falling into obscurity or decay; a decline

[2]**eclipse** *v* to cause an eclipse of: e g **a** to obscure, darken **b** to surpass

ecliptic /ɪˈklɪptɪk/ *n* the plane of the earth's orbit extended to meet the celestial sphere – **ecliptic** *adj*

ecology /ɪˈkɒlədʒi/ *n* (a science concerned with) the interrelationship of living organisms and their environments – -gist *n* – -gical *adj*

economic /ˌekəˈnɒmɪk, iː-/ *adj* **1** of economics **2** of or based on the production, distribution, and consumption of goods and services **3** of an economy **4** having practical or industrial significance or uses; affecting material resources **5** profitable

economical /ˌekəˈnɒmɪkəl, ˌiː-/ *adj* thrifty – ~**ly** *adv*

economics /ˌekəˈnɒmɪks, ˌiː-/ *n pl but sing or pl in constr* **1** a social science concerned chiefly with the production, distribution, and consumption of goods and services **2** economic aspect or significance – -**mist** *n*

econom·ize, -ise /ɪˈkɒnəmaɪz/ *v* to be frugal – often + *on*

economy /ɪˈkɒnəmi/ *n* **1** thrifty and efficient use of material resources; frugality in expenditure; *also* an instance or means of economizing **2** efficient and sparing use of nonmaterial resources (e g effort, language, or motion) **3** the structure of economic life in a country, area, or period; *specif* an economic system

ecosystem /ˈiːkəʊˌsɪstɨm/ *n* a complex consisting of a community and its environment functioning as a reasonably self-sustaining ecological unit in nature

ecru /ˈekruː, eɪ-/ *adj or n* (of) a pale fawn colour

ecstasy /ˈekstəsi/ *n* **1** a state of very strong feeling, esp of joy or happiness **2** a (mystic or prophetic) trance

ecstatic /ɪkˈstætɪk, ek-/ *adj* subject to, causing, or in a state of ecstasy – ~**ally** *adv*

ecumenical, oecumenical /ˌiːkjʊˈmenɪkəl/ *adj* promoting worldwide Christian unity or cooperation

eczema /ˈeksɨmə/ *n* an inflammatory condition of the skin characterized by itching and oozing blisters

Edam /ˈiːdæm/ *n* a yellow mild cheese of Dutch origin usu made in flattened balls coated with red wax

[1]**eddy** /ˈedi/ *n* **1** a current of water or air running contrary to the main current; *esp* a small whirlpool **2** sthg (e g smoke or fog) moving in the manner of an eddy or whirlpool

[2]**eddy** *v* to (cause to) move in or like an eddy

Eden /ˈiːdn/ *n* **1** the garden where, according to the account in Genesis, Adam and Eve lived before the Fall **2** paradise

[1]**edge** /edʒ/ *n* **1a** the cutting side of a blade **b** the (degree of) sharpness of a blade **c** penetrating power; keenness **2a** the line where an object or area begins or ends; a border **b** the narrow part adjacent to a border; the brink, verge **c** a point that marks a beginning or transition; a threshold – esp in *on the edge of* **d** a favourable margin; an advantage **3** a line where 2 planes or 2 plane faces of a solid body meet or cross

[2]**edge** *v* **1** to give or supply an edge to **2** to move or force gradually in a specified way **3** to incline (a ski) sideways so that 1 edge cuts into the snow **4** to hit (a ball) or the bowling of (a bowler) in cricket with the edge of the bat

edgeways /ˈedʒweɪz/, **edgewise** *adv* with the edge foremost; sideways

edging /ˈedʒɪŋ/ *n* sthg that forms an edge or border

edgy /ˈedʒi/ *adj* tense, irritable; on edge – **edgily** *adv*

edible /ˈedɨbəl/ *adj* fit to be eaten as food – **edibility** *n* – ~**s** *n*

edict /ˈiːdɪkt/ *n* **1** an official public decree **2** the order or command of an authority

edification /ˌedɨfɨˈkeɪʃən/ *n* the improvement of character or the mind – fml

edifice /ˈedɨfɨs/ *n* **1** a building; *esp* a large or massive structure **2** a large abstract structure or organization

edify /ˈedɨfaɪ/ *v* to instruct and improve, esp in moral and spiritual knowledge

edit /ˈedɨt/ *v* **1a** to prepare an edition of **b** to assemble (e g a film or tape recording) by deleting, inserting, and rearranging material **c** to alter or adapt (e g written or spoken words), esp to make consistent with a particular standard or purpose **2** to direct the publication of **3** to delete – usu + *out*

edition /ɪˈdɪʃən/ *n* **1a** the form in which a text is published **b** the whole number of copies published at one time **c** the issue of a newspaper or periodical for a specified time or place **2** the whole number of articles of one style put out at one time **3** a copy, version

editor /ˈedʒtəʳ/ *n* **1** one who edits written material, films, etc, esp as an occupation **2** a person responsible for the editorial policy and content of a (section of a) newspaper or periodical – **~ship** *n*

[1]**editorial** /ˌedʒˈtɔːrɪəl/ *adj* of or written by an editor – **~ly** *adv*

[2]**editorial** *n* a newspaper or magazine article that gives the opinions of the editors or publishers

educate /ˈedjʊkeɪt/ *v* **1** to provide schooling for **2** to develop mentally or morally, esp by instruction **3** to train or improve (faculties, judgment, skills, etc) – **-ator** *n*

education /ˌedjʊˈkeɪʃən/ *n* **1** educating or being educated **2** the field of study that deals with methods of teaching and learning – **~al** *adj* – **~ally** *adv*

educe /ɪˈdjuːs/ *v* **1** to elicit, develop **2** to arrive at through a consideration of the facts or evidence; infer *USE* fml

eel /iːl/ *n* any of numerous long snakelike fishes with a smooth slimy skin and no pelvic fins

eerie *also* **eery** /ˈɪəri/ *adj* frighteningly strange or gloomy; weird – **eerily** *adv* – **eeriness** *n*

efface /ɪˈfeɪs/ *v* **1** to eliminate or make indistinct (as if) by wearing away a surface; obliterate **2** to make (oneself) modestly or shyly inconspicuous – **~ment** *n*

[1]**effect** /ɪˈfekt/ *n* **1a** the result of a cause or agent **b** the result of purpose or intention **2** the basic meaning; intent – esp in *to that effect* **3** power to bring about a result; efficacy **4** *pl* personal movable property; goods **5a** a distinctive impression on the human senses **b** the creation of an often false desired impression **c** sthg designed to produce a distinctive or desired impression – often pl **6** the quality or state of being operative; operation **7** an experimental scientific phenomenon named usu after its discoverer

[2]**effect** /əˈfekt/ *v* **1** to bring about, often by surmounting obstacles; accomplish **2** to put into effect; carry out

effective /ɪˈfektɪv/ *adj* **1a** producing a decided, decisive, or desired effect **b** impressive, striking **2** ready for service or action **3** actual, real **4** being in effect; operative – **~ly** *adv* – **~ness** *n*

effectual /ɪˈfektʃʊəl/ *adj* producing or able to produce a desired effect; adequate, effective – **~ness** *n* – **~ly** *adv*

effeminate /ʒˈfemʒnʒt/ *adj* **1** *of a man* having qualities usu thought of as feminine; not manly in appearance or manner **2** marked by an unbecoming delicacy or lack of vigour – **~ly** *adv* – **-acy** *n*

effervesce /ˌefəˈves/ *v* **1** *of a liquid* to bubble, hiss, and foam as gas escapes **2** to show liveliness or exhilaration – **-vescence** *n* – **-vescent** *adj* – **-vescently** *adv*

effete /ɪˈfiːt/ *adj* **1** worn out; exhausted **2** marked by weakness or decadent overrefinement – **~ness** *n*

efficacious /ˌefʒˈkeɪʃəs/ *adj* having the power to produce a desired effect – **~ly** *adv* – **-acy** *n* – **~ness** *n*

efficient /ɪˈfɪʃənt/ *adj* **1** *of a person* able and practical; briskly competent **2** productive of desired effects, esp with minimum waste – **~ly** *adv* – **-ency** *n*

effigy /ˈefʒdʒi/ *n* an image or representation, esp of a person; *specif* a crude figure representing a hated person

[1]**effluent** /ˈeflʊənt/ *adj* flowing out; emanating

[2]**effluent** *n* sthg that flows out: e g **a** an outflowing branch of a main stream or lake **b** smoke, liquid industrial refuse, sewage, etc discharged into the environment, esp when causing pollution

effort /ˈefət/ *n* **1** conscious exertion of physical or mental power **2** a serious attempt; a try **3** sthg produced by exertion or trying **4** the force applied (e g to a simple machine) as distinguished from the force exerted against the load

effrontery /ɪˈfrʌntəri/ *n* the quality of being shamelessly bold; insolence

effusion /ɪ'fjuːʒən/ *n* **1** unrestrained expression of words or feelings **2** the escape of a fluid from a containing vessel; *also* the fluid that escapes

effusive /ɪ'fjuːsɪv/ *adj* unduly emotionally demonstrative; gushing – **~ly** *adv* – **~ness** *n*

egalitarian /ɪ,gælɪ̣'teərɪən/ *adj* marked by or advocating egalitarianism – **egalitarian** *n* – **~ism** *n*

¹egg /eg/ *v* to incite to action – usu + *on*

²egg *n* **1a** the hard-shelled reproductive body produced by a bird; *esp* that produced by domestic poultry and used as a food **b** an animal reproductive body consisting of an ovum together with its nutritive and protective envelopes that is capable of developing into a new individual **c** an ovum **2** sthg resembling an egg in shape

eggcup /'egkʌp/ *n* a small cup without a handle used for holding a boiled egg

egghead /'eghed/ *n* an intellectual, highbrow – derog or humor

eggnog /'egnɒg/ *n* a drink consisting of eggs beaten up with sugar, milk or cream, and often spirits (e g rum or brandy)

eggplant /'egplɑːnt/ *n* a widely cultivated plant of the nightshade family; *also, chiefly NAm* its fruit, the aubergine

¹eggshell /'egʃel/ *n* the hard exterior covering of an egg

²eggshell *adj* **1** *esp of china* thin and fragile **2** *esp of paint* having a slight sheen

ego /'iːgəʊ, 'egəʊ/ *n* **1** the self, esp as contrasted with another self or the world **2** self-esteem **3** the one of the 3 divisions of the mind in psychoanalytic theory that serves as the organized conscious mediator between the person and reality, esp in the perception of and adaptation to reality

egocentric /,iːgəʊ'sentrɪk, ,e-/ *adj* limited in outlook or concern to one's own activities or needs; self-centred, selfish – **~ally** *adv* – **~ity** *n*

egoism /'iːgəʊɪzəm, 'e-/ *n* **1** (conduct based on) a doctrine that individual self-interest is or should be the foundation of morality **2** egotism – **-ist** *n* – **-istic** *adj* – **-istical** *adj* – **-istically** *adv*

egotism /'egətɪzəm, 'iː-/ *n* **1** the practice of talking about oneself too much **2** an extreme sense of self-importance – **-ist** *n* – **-istic** *adj* – **-istical** *adj* – **-istically** *adv*

egregious /ɪ'griːdʒəs/ *adj* conspicuously or shockingly bad; flagrant – fml – **~ly** *adv*

egress /'iːgres/ *n* **1** going or coming out; *specif* the emergence of a celestial object from eclipse, transit, etc **2** a place or means of going out; an exit – fml

¹Egyptian /ɪ'dʒɪpʃən/ *adj* (characteristic) of Egypt

²Egyptian *n* **1** a native or inhabitant of Egypt **2** the Afro-Asiatic language of the ancient Egyptians to about the 3rd C AD

eiderdown /'aɪdədaʊn/ *n* **1** the down of the eider duck **2** a thick warm quilt filled with eiderdown or other insulating material

eider duck *n* any of several large northern sea ducks having fine soft down

eight /eɪt/ *n* **1** the number 8 **2** the eighth in a set or series **3** sthg having 8 parts or members or a denomination of 8; *esp* (the crew of) an 8-person racing boat – **eighth** *adj, n, pron, adv*

eighteen /eɪ'tiːn/ *n* the number 18 – **~th** *adj, n, pron, adv*

18 *n or adj* (a film that is) certified in Britain as suitable only for people over 18

eighty /'eɪti/ *n* **1** the number 80 **2** *pl* the numbers 80 to 89; *specif* a range of temperatures, ages, or dates within a century characterized by those numbers – **eightieth** *adj, n, pron, adv*

eisteddfod /aɪ'stedfəd/ *n, pl* **eisteddfods, eisteddfodau** a Welsh-language competitive festival of the arts, esp music and poetry

¹either /'aɪðəʳ/ *adj* **1** being the one and the other of 2 (e g flowers blooming on *either* side of the path) **2** being the one or the other of 2 (e g take *either* road)

²either *pron* the one or the other (e g could be happy with *either* of them)

³either *conj* – used before 2 or more

sentence elements of the same class or function joined usu by *or* to indicate that what immediately follows is the first of 2 or more alternatives (e g *either* sink or swim)

[4]**either** *adv* for that matter, likewise – used for emphasis after a negative or implied negation (e g not wise or handsome *either*)

[1]**ejaculate** /ɪ'dʒækjʊleɪt/ *v* **1** to eject (semen) in orgasm **2** to utter suddenly and vehemently – fml – **-lation** *n*

eject /ɪ'dʒekt/ *v* **1** to drive out, esp by physical force **2** to evict from property **3** to escape from an aircraft by using the ejector seat – **~ion, ~or** *n*

ejector seat /ɪ'dʒektə siːt/ *n* an emergency escape seat that propels an occupant out and away from an aircraft by means of an explosive charge

eke out /ˌiːk 'aʊt/ *v* **1a** to make up for the deficiencies of; supplement **b** to make (a supply) last by economy **2** to make (e g a living) by laborious or precarious means

[1]**elaborate** /ɪ'læbərət/ *adj* **1** planned or carried out with great care and attention to detail **2** marked by complexity, wealth of detail, or ornateness; intricate – **~ly** *adv* – **~ness** *n*

[2]**elaborate** /ɪ'læbəreɪt/ *v* to work out or go into in detail; develop – often + *on* – **-tion** *n*

elapse /ɪ'læps/ *v, of a period of time* to pass by

[1]**elastic** /ɪ'læstɪk/ *adj* **1** buoyant, resilient **2** capable of being easily stretched or expanded and resuming its former shape **3** capable of ready change; flexible, adaptable – **~ity** *n*

[2]**elastic** /ɪ'læstɪk/ *n* **1** an elastic fabric usu made of yarns containing rubber **2** easily stretched rubber, usu prepared in cords, strings, or bands

elastic band *n, Br* a rubber band

elate /ɪ'leɪt/ *v* to fill with joy or pride; put in high spirits – **~d** *adj* **-tion** *n*

[1]**elbow** /'elbəʊ/ *n* **1** the joint between the human forearm and upper arm **2** the part of a garment that covers the elbow

[2]**elbow** *v* to push or shove aside (as if) with the elbow; jostle

elbow grease *n* hard physical effort – infml

elbowroom /'elbəʊrʊm, -ruːm/ *n* adequate space or scope for movement, work, or operation

[1]**elder** /'eldəʳ/ *n* any of several shrubs or small trees of the honeysuckle family

[2]**elder** *adj* of earlier birth or greater age, esp than another related person or thing

[3]**elder** *n* **1** one who is older; a senior **2** one having authority by virtue of age and experience **3** an official of the early church or of a Presbyterian congregation

elderly /'eldəli/ *adj* rather old

eldest /'eldɪ̣st/ *adj* of the greatest age or seniority; oldest

[1]**elect** /ɪ'lekt/ *adj* **1** chosen for salvation through divine mercy **2** chosen for office or position but not yet installed

[2]**elect** *v* **1** to select by vote for an office, position, or membership **2** to choose, decide – fml – **~ion** *n*

electioneer /ɪˌlekʃə'nɪəʳ/ *v* to work for a candidate or party in an election – **~ing** *n*

elective /ɪ'lektɪv/ *adj* **1a** chosen or filled by popular election **b** of election **2** permitting a choice; optional

elector /ɪ'lektəʳ/ *n* **1** sby qualified to vote in an election **2** sby entitled to participate in an election: e g **a** *often cap* any of the German princes entitled to elect the Holy Roman Emperor **b** a member of the electoral college in the USA

electoral /ɪ'lektərəl/ *adj* of (an) election or electors

electorate /ɪ'lektərɪ̣t/ *n* **1** *often cap* the territory, jurisdiction, etc of a German elector **2** *sing or pl in constr* a body of electors

electric /ɪ'lektrɪk/ *adj* **1a** of, being, supplying, producing, or produced by electricity **b** operated by or using electricity **2** producing an intensely stimulating effect; thrilling **3** *of a musical instrument* electronically producing or amplifying sound

electrical /ɪ'lektrɪkəl/ *adj* **1** of or connected with electricity **2** producing, produced, or operated by electricity – **~ly** *adv*

electric chair *n* **1** a chair used in legal electrocution **2** *the* penalty of death by electrocution

electricity /ɪˌlekˈtrɪsʒti/ *n* **1** (the study of) the phenomena due to (the flow or accumulation of) positively and negatively charged particles (e g protons and electrons) **2** electric current; *also* electric charge

electrify /ɪˈlektrʒfaɪ/ *v* **1a** to charge (a body) with electricity **b** to equip for use of or supply with electric power **2** to excite, thrill – **-fication** *n*

electrocardiogram /ɪˌlektrəʊˈkɑːdɪəgræm/ *n* the tracing made by an electrocardiograph

electrocardiograph /ɪˌlektrəʊˈkɑːdɪəgrɑːf/ *n* an instrument for recording the changes of electrical potential difference occurring during the heartbeat

electrocute /ɪˈlektrəkjuːt/ *v* to execute or kill by electricity – **-cution** *n*

electrode /ɪˈlektrəʊd/ *n* a conductor used to establish electrical contact with a nonmetallic part of a circuit (e g the acid in a car battery)

electroencephalogram /ɪˌlektrəʊɪnˈsefələgræm, -trəʊen-/ *n* the tracing made by an electroencephalograph

electroencephalograph /ɪˌlektrəʊɪnˈsefələgrɑːf, -trəʊen-/ *n* an instrument for detecting and recording brain waves

electrolysis /ɪˌlekˈtrɒlʒsʒs, ˌelek-/ *n* **1** the passage of an electric current through an electrolyte to generate a gas, deposit a metal on (an object serving as) an electrode, etc **2** the destruction of hair roots, warts, moles etc by means of an electric current

electrolyte /ɪˈlektrəlaɪt/ *n* a nonmetallic electric conductor (e g a salt solution) in which current is carried by the movement of ions

electromagnetic *adj* of or relating to magnetic effects produced by the flowing of an electric current

electron /ɪˈlektrɒn/ *n* a negatively charged elementary particle that occurs in atoms outside the nucleus and the mass movement of which constitutes an electric current in a metal

electronic /ɪˌlekˈtrɒnɪk, elek-/ *adj* of, being, or using devices constructed or working by the methods or principles of electronics – **~ally** *adv*

electronics /ɪˌlekˈtrɒnɪks/ *n pl but sing in constr* physics or technology dealing with the emission, behaviour, and effects of electrons in valves, transistors, or other electronic devices

electron microscope *n* an instrument in which a beam of electrons is used to produce an enormously enlarged image of a minute object

electroplate /ɪˌlektrəʊˈpleɪt/ *v* to plate with a continuous metallic coating by electrolysis

elegant /ˈelɪgənt/ *adj* **1** gracefully refined or dignified (e g in manners, taste, or style) **2** tastefully rich or luxurious, esp in design or ornamentation **3** *of ideas* neat and simple – **~ly** *adv* – **-ance** *n*

elegy /ˈelʒdʒi/ *n* **1** a song, poem, or other work expressing sorrow or lamentation, esp for one who is dead **2** a pensive or reflective poem that is usu nostalgic or melancholy – **-giac** *adj* – **-giacally** *adv*

element /ˈelʒmənt/ *n* **1a** any of the 4 substances air, water, fire, and earth formerly believed to constitute the physical universe **b** *pl* forces of nature; *esp* violent or severe weather **c** the state or sphere natural or suited to sby or sthg **2** a constituent part: e g **a** *pl* the simplest principles of a subject of study; the rudiments **b** a constituent of a mathematical set **c** any of the factors determining an outcome **d** a distinct part of a composite device; *esp* a resistor in an electric heater, kettle, etc **3** any of more than 100 fundamental substances that consist of atoms of only one kind

elemental /ˌelʒˈmentəl/ *adj* of or resembling a great force of nature

elementary /ˌelʒˈmentəri/ *adj* of or dealing with the basic elements or principles of sthg; simple

elementary particle *n* any of the constituents of matter and energy (e g the electron, proton, or photon) whose nature has not yet been proved to be due to the combination of other more fundamental entities

elephant /ˈelʒfənt/ *n* a very large

nearly hairless mammal having the snout prolonged into a muscular trunk and 2 upper incisors developed into long tusks which provide ivory

elephantine /ˌelɨ'fæntaɪn/ *adj* **1a** huge, massive **b** clumsy, ponderous **2** of an elephant

elevate /'elɨveɪt/ *v* **1** to lift up; raise **2** to raise in rank or status; exalt **3** to improve morally, intellectually, or culturally **4** to raise the spirits of; elate

elevated /'elɨveɪtɨd/ *adj* **1** raised, esp above a surface (e g the ground) **2** morally or intellectually on a high plane; lofty **3** exhilarated in mood or feeling **4** slightly tipsy – not now in vogue

elevation /ˌelɨ'veɪʃən/ *n* **1** the height to which sthg is elevated: e g **a** the angle to which a gun is aimed above the horizon **b** the height above sea level **2** (the ability to achieve) a ballet dancer's or a skater's leap and seeming suspension in the air **3** an elevated place **4** being elevated **5** a geometrical projection (e g of a building) on a vertical plane

elevator /'elɨveɪtəʳ/ *n* **1** sby or sthg that raises or lifts sthg up: e g **a** an endless belt or chain conveyer for raising grain, liquids, etc **b** *chiefly NAm* a lift **2** a movable horizontal control surface, usu attached to the tailplane of an aircraft for controlling climb and descent

eleven /ɪ'levən/ *n* **1** the number 11 **2** the eleventh in a set or series **3** *sing or pl in constr* sthg having 11 parts or members or a denomination of 11; *esp* a cricket, soccer, or hockey team – **~th** *adj, n, pron, adv*

eleven-plus *n* an examination taken, esp formerly, at the age of 10-11 to determine which type of British state secondary education a child should receive

elevenses /ɪ'levənzɨz/ *n pl but sometimes sing in constr, Br* light refreshment taken in the middle of the morning

eleventh hour *n* *the* latest possible time

elf /elf/ *n, pl* **elves** a (mischievous) fairy – **~in, ~ish** *adj*

elicit /ɪ'lɪsɨt/ *v* **1** to draw forth or bring out (sthg latent or potential) **2** to call forth or draw out (a response or reaction); evoke – **~ation** *n*

eligible /'elɨdʒəbəl/ *adj* **1** qualified to be chosen; *also* entitled **2** worthy or desirable, esp as a marriage partner – **-bility** *n* – **-bly** *adv*

eliminate /ɪ'lɪmɨneɪt/ *v* **1a** to cast out or get rid of completely; eradicate **b** to set aside as unimportant; ignore **2** to expel (e g waste) from the living body **3a** to kill (a person), esp so as to remove as an obstacle **b** to remove (a competitor, team, etc) from a competition, usu by defeat – **-nation** *n*

élite /eɪ'liːt, ɪ-/ *n sing or pl in constr* a small superior group; *esp* one that has a power out of proportion to its size

élitism /eɪ'liːtɪzəm, ɪ-/ *n* (advocacy of) leadership by an élite

elixir /ɪ'lɪksəʳ/ *n* **1** an alchemist's substance supposedly capable of changing base metals into gold **2a elixir, elixir of life** a substance held to be capable of prolonging life indefinitely **b** a cure-all **3** a sweetened liquid (e g a syrup) containing a drug or medicine

Elizabethan /ɪˌlɪzə'biːθə n/ *adj* (characteristic) of (the age of) Elizabeth I

elk /elk/ *n* **1** the largest existing deer of Europe and Asia **2** *NAm* a large N American deer

ellipse *n* a curve generated by a point that moves in such a way that the sum of its distances from 2 fixed points is constant – **elliptical** *adj*

elm /elm/ *n* (the wood of) any of a genus of large graceful trees

elocution /ˌelə'kjuːʃən/ *n* the art of effective public speaking, esp of good diction – **~ary** *adj* – **~ist** *n*

[1]**elongate** /'iːlɒŋgeɪt/ *v* **1** to extend the length of **2** to grow in length

[2]**elongate, elongated** *adj* long in proportion to width – used esp in botany and zoology

elongation /ˌiːlɒŋ'geɪʃən/ *n* the angular distance of one celestial body from another round which it revolves or from a particular point in the sky as viewed from earth

elope /ɪ'ləʊp/ *v* to run away secretly with the intention of getting married or cohabiting, usu without parental consent – ~**ment** *n*

eloquent /'eləkwənt/ *adj* **1** characterized by fluent, forceful, and persuasive use of language **2** vividly or movingly expressive or revealing – **-quence** *n* – ~**ly** *adv*

else /els/ *adv* **1** apart from the person, place, manner, or time mentioned or understood (e g how *else* could he have acted) **2** also, besides **3** if not, otherwise – used absolutely to express a threat (e g do what I tell you or *else*)

elsewhere /els'weəʳ, 'elsweəʳ/ *adv* in or to another place

elucidate /ɪ'luːsɨdeɪt/ *v* to make (sthg) lucid, esp by explanation – **-dation** *n*

elude /ɪ'luːd/ *v* **1** to avoid cunningly or adroitly **2** to escape the memory, understanding, or notice of

elusive /ɪ'luːsɪv/ *adj* tending to elude – ~**ly** *adv* – ~**ness** *n*

elver /'elvəʳ/ *n* a young eel

elves /elvz/ *pl of* elf

elvish /'elvɪʃ/ *adj* elfish

Elysium /ɪ'lɪzɪəm/ *n, pl* **Elysiums, Elysia** **1** the home of the blessed after death in Greek mythology **2** paradise – **-sian** *adj*

emaciate /ɪ'meɪʃiːeɪt/ *v* to make or become excessively thin or feeble – **-ation** *n*

emanate /'eməneɪt/ *v* to come out *from* a source – **-ation** *n*

emancipate /ɪ'mænsɨpeɪt/ *v* to free from restraint, control, or esp slavery – **-pator** *n* – **-pation** *n*

emasculate /ɪ'mæskjʊleɪt/ *v* **1** to castrate **2** to deprive of strength, vigour, or spirit; weaken – **-lation** *n*

embalm /ɪm'bɑːm/ *v* **1** to treat (a dead body) so as to give protection against decay **2** to preserve from oblivion – ~**er** *n*

embankment /ɪm'bæŋkmənt/ *n* a raised structure to hold back water or to carry a roadway or railway

embargo /ɪm'bɑːgəʊ/ *n, pl* **embargoes** **1** an order of a government prohibiting the departure or entry of commercial ships **2** a legal prohibition on commerce **3** a stoppage, impediment; *esp* a prohibition

embark /ɪm'bɑːk/ *v* **1** to go on board a boat or aircraft **2** to make a start; commence – usu + *on* or *upon* – ~**ation** *n*

embarrass /ɪm'bærəs/ *v* **1** to involve in financial difficulties, esp debt **2** to cause to experience a state of self-conscious distress; disconcert – ~**ingly** *adv* – ~**ment** *n*

embassy /'embəsi/ *n* **1a** the position of an ambassador **b** an ambassador's official mission abroad **2** (the residence of) a diplomatic body headed by an ambassador

embattled /ɪm'bætəld/ *adj* involved in battle or conflict

embed /ɪm'bed/ *v* to place or fix firmly (as if) in surrounding matter

embellish /ɪm'belɪʃ/ *v* **1** to make beautiful by adding ornaments; decorate **2** to make (speech or writing) more interesting by adding fictitious or exaggerated detail – ~**ment** *n*

ember /'embəʳ/ *n* **1** a glowing fragment (e g of coal or wood) in a (dying) fire **2** *pl* the smouldering remains of a fire **3** *pl* slowly fading emotions, memories, ideas, or responses

embezzle /ɪm'bezəl/ *v* to appropriate (e g property entrusted to one's care) fraudulently to one's own use – ~**ment** *n* – **-zler** *n*

embitter /ɪm'bɪtəʳ/ *v* **1** to make bitter **2** to excite bitter feelings in – ~**ment** *n*

emblazon /ɪm'bleɪzən/ *v* **1** to display conspicuously **2** to inscribe, adorn, or embellish (as if) with heraldic bearings or devices

emblem /'embləm/ *n* **1** an object or a typical representation of an object symbolizing another object or idea **2** a device, symbol, or figure adopted and used as an identifying mark – ~**atic** *adj* – ~**atically** *adv*

embody /ɪm'bɒdi/ *v* **1** to give a body to (a spirit); incarnate **2** to make (e g ideas or concepts) concrete and perceptible **3** to make (e g connected ideas or principles) a part of a body or system; incorporate, include – usu + *in* **4** to represent in human or animal form; personify – **-diment** *n*

embolden /ɪm'bəʊldən/ *v* to make bold or courageous

embolism /'embəlɪzəm/ *n* (the sudden obstruction of a blood vessel by) a clot, air bubble, or other particle

emboss /ɪm'bɒs/ *v* **1** to ornament with raised work **2** to raise in relief from a surface

[1]**embrace** /ɪm'breɪs/ *v* **1** to take and hold closely in the arms as a sign of affection; hug **2** to encircle, enclose **3a** to take up, esp readily or eagerly; adopt **b** to avail oneself of; welcome **4** to include as a part or element of a more inclusive whole **5** to join in an embrace; hug one another

[2]**embrace** *n* an act of embracing or gripping

embrocation /,embrə'keɪʃən/ *n* a liniment

embroider /ɪm'brɔɪdə^r/ *v* **1** to ornament (e g cloth or a garment) with decorative stitches made by hand or machine **2** to elaborate on (a narrative); embellish with exaggerated or fictitious details – **~y** *n*

embroil /ɪm'brɔɪl/ *v* **1** to throw (e g a person or affairs) into disorder or confusion **2** to involve in conflict or difficulties

embryo /'embriəʊ/ *n* **1** an animal in the early stages of growth before birth or hatching **2** a rudimentary plant within a seed **3a** sthg as yet undeveloped **b** a beginning or undeveloped state of sthg – esp in *in embryo* – **~nic** *adj*

emend /ɪ'mend/ *v* to correct, usu by textual alterations – **~ation** *n*

emerald /'emərəld/ *adj or n* (of the bright green colour of) a beryl used as a gemstone

emerge /ɪ'mɜːdʒ/ *v* **1** to rise (as if) from an enveloping fluid; come out into view **2** to become manifest or known **3** to rise from an obscure or inferior condition – **-gence** *n*

emergency /ɪ'mɜːdʒənsi/ *n* an unforeseen occurrence or combination of circumstances that calls for immediate action

emergent /ɪ'mɜːdʒənt/ *adj* emerging; *esp* in the early stages of formation or development

emery /'eməri/ *n* a dark granular mineral used for grinding and polishing

emetic /ɪ'metɪk/ *n or adj* (sthg) that induces vomiting

emigrant /'emɪgrənt/ *n* one who emigrates

emigrate /'emɪ̣greɪt/ *v* to leave one's home or country for life or residence elsewhere – **-tion** *n*

émigré /'emɪgreɪ/ *n* a (political) emigrant

eminence /'emɪnəns/ *n* **1** a position of prominence or superiority – used as a title for a cardinal **2** sby or sthg high, prominent, or lofty: e g **a** a person of high rank or attainments **b** a natural geographical elevation; a height

eminent /'emɪnənt/ *adj* **1** standing out so as to be readily seen or noted; conspicuous, notable **2** exhibiting eminence, esp in position, fame, or achievement

emir /e'mɪə^r/ *n* **1** a ruler of any of various Muslim states **2** a high-ranking Turkish official of former times **3** a male descendant of Muhammad

emirate /e'mɪəreɪt, -rɪ̣t/ *n* the position, state, power, etc of an emir

emissary /'emɪ̣səri/ *n* one sent on an often secret mission as the agent of another

emission /ɪ'mɪʃən/ *n* **1** an act or instance of emitting **2** an unpleasant discharge of waste

emit /ɪ'mɪt/ *v* **1a** to throw or give off or out (e g light) **b** to send out; eject **2** to give utterance or voice to

Emmenthal, Emmental /'eməntɑːl/ *n* a pale yellow Swiss cheese with many holes that form during ripening

emollient /ɪ'mɒlɪənt/ *n or adj* (a substance) that makes soft or gives relief

emolument /ɪ'mɒljʊmənt/ *n* the returns arising from office or employment; a salary

emotion /ɪ'məʊʃən/ *n* **1** excitement **2** a mental and physical reaction (e g anger, fear, or joy) marked by strong feeling and often physiological changes that prepare the body for immediate vigorous action – **~less** *adj*

emotional /ɪ'məʊʃənəl/ *adj* **1** of the emotions **2** inclined to show (excessive) emotion **3** emotive – **~ly** *adv*

emotive /ɪ'məʊtɪv/ *adj* **1** emotional

2 appealing to, expressing, or arousing emotion rather than reason – ~ly *adv*

empathy /'empəθi/ *n* **1** the imaginative projection of a subjective state into an object, esp a work of art, so allowing it to be better understood and appreciated **2** the capacity for participation in another's feelings or ideas – **-thize** *v* – **-thic** *adj*

emperor /'empərəʳ/ *n* the supreme ruler of an empire

emphasis /'emfəsɪ̈s/ *n, pl* **emphases** special consideration of or stress on sthg – **-atic** *adj* – **-atically** *adv* – **-asize** *v*

empire /'empaɪəʳ/ *n* **1a** (the territory of) a large group of countries or peoples under 1 authority **b** sthg resembling a political empire; *esp* an extensive territory or enterprise under single domination or control **2** imperial sovereignty

Empire *adj* (characteristic) of a style (e g of furniture or interior decoration) popular during the first French Empire (1804-14); *specif* of a style of women's dress having a high waistline

empirical /ɪm'pɪrɪkəl/ *also* **empiric** *adj* originating in, based, or relying on observation or experiment rather than theory – ~**ly** *adv* – **-cism** *n*

¹**employ** /ɪm'plɔɪ/ *v* **1a** to use in a specified way or for a specific purpose **b** to spend (time) **c** to use **2a** to engage the services of **b** to provide with a job that pays wages or a salary – ~**er** *n*

²**employ** *n* the state of being employed, esp for wages or a salary – fml

employee /ɪm'plɔɪ-iː, ˌemplɔɪ'iː/ *n* one employed by another, esp for wages or a salary and in a position below executive level

employment /ɪm'plɔɪmənt/ *n* (an) activity in which one engages or is employed

employment exchange *n* a labour exchange

emporium /ɪm'pɔːrɪəm/ *n, pl* **emporiums, emporia** a place of trade; *esp* a commercial centre or large shop

empower /ɪm'paʊəʳ/ *v* to give official authority or legal power to

empress /'emprɪ̈s/ *n* **1** the wife or widow of an emperor **2** a woman having in her own right the rank of emperor

¹**empty** /'empti/ *adj* **1a** containing nothing; *esp* lacking typical or expected contents **b** not occupied, inhabited, or frequented **2a** lacking reality or substance; hollow **b** lacking effect, value, or sincerity **c** lacking sense; foolish **3** hungry – infml – **emptily** *adv* – **emptiness** *n*

²**empty** *v* **1a** to make empty; remove the contents of **b** to deprive, divest **c** to discharge (itself) of contents **2** to remove from what holds, encloses, or contains **3** to transfer by emptying **4** to become empty

³**empty** *n* a bottle, container, vehicle, etc that has been emptied

empty-handed *adj* having or bringing nothing, esp because nothing has been gained or obtained

empty-headed *adj* foolish, silly

emu /'iːmjuː/ *n* a swift-running Australian flightless bird

emulate /'emjʊleɪt/ *v* **1** to rival **2** to imitate closely; approach equality with – **-tion** *n*

¹**emulsion** /ɪ'mʌlʃən/ *n* **1** (the state of) a substance (e g fat in milk) consisting of one liquid dispersed in droplets throughout another liquid **2** a suspension; *esp* a suspension of a silver compound in a gelatin solution or other solid medium for coating photographic plates, film, etc

²**emulsion** *v* to paint (e g a wall) with emulsion paint

enable /ɪ'neɪbəl/ *v* **1** to provide with the means or opportunity **2** to make possible, practical, or easy

enact /ɪ'nækt/ *v* **1** to make into law **2** to act out, play – ~**ment** *n*

enamel *n* **1** a usu opaque glassy coating applied to the surface of metal, glass, or pottery **2** a substance composed of calcium phosphate that forms a thin hard layer capping the teeth **3** a paint that dries with a glossy appearance

encamp /ɪn'kæmp/ *v* to place or establish (in) a camp – ~**ment** *n*

encapsulate /ɪn'kæpsjʊleɪt/ *v* **1** to enclose (as if) in a capsule **2** to epitomize, condense – **-ation** *n*

encase /ɪn'keɪs/ *v* to enclose (as if) in a case

enchant /ɪn'tʃɑːnt/ *v* **1** to bewitch **2** to attract and move deeply; delight – **~ment** *n*

enchanter /ɪn'tʃɑːntəʳ/ *n* a sorcerer

enchanting /ɪn'tʃɑːntɪŋ/ *adj* charming – **~ly** *adv*

encircle /ɪn'sɜːkəl/ *v* **1** to form a circle round; surround **2** to move or pass completely round – **~ment** *n*

enclave /'enkleɪv, 'eŋ-/ *n* a territorial or culturally distinct unit enclosed within foreign territory

enclose *also* **inclose** /ɪn'kləʊz/ *v* **1a(1)** to close in completely; surround **(2)** to fence off (common land) for individual use **b** to hold in; confine **2** to include in a package or envelope, esp along with sthg else – **-sure** *n*

encomium /ɪn'kəʊmɪəm/ *n, pl* **encomiums, encomia** a usu formal expression of warm or high praise; a eulogy

encompass /ɪn'kʌmpəs/ *v* **1** to form a circle about; enclose **2** to include

encore /'ɒŋkɔːʳ/ *n* (an audience's appreciative demand for) a performer's reappearance to give an additional or repeated performance – **encore** *interj*

¹encounter /ɪn'kaʊntəʳ/ *v* **1a** to meet as an adversary or enemy **b** to engage in conflict with **2** to meet or come across, esp unexpectedly

²encounter *n* **1** a meeting or clash between hostile factions or people **2** a chance meeting

encounter group *n* a group of people who meet to try and develop greater sensitivity to their own and one another's feelings

encourage /ɪn'kʌrɪdʒ/ *v* **1** to inspire with courage, spirit, or hope **2** to spur on **3** to give help or patronage to (e g a process or action); promote – **-agingly** *adv* – **~ment** *n*

encroach /ɪn'krəʊtʃ/ *v* **1** to enter gradually or by stealth into the possessions or rights of another; intrude, trespass **2** to advance beyond the usual or proper limits *USE* usu + *on* or *upon* – **~ment** *n*

encrust *also* **incrust** /ɪn'krʌst/ *v* **1** to cover, line, or overlay with a crust, esp of jewels or precious metal **2** to form a crust

encumber /ɪn'kʌmbəʳ/ *v* **1** to weigh down, burden **2** to impede or hamper the function or activity of **3** to burden with a legal claim – **-brance** *n*

encyclical /ɪn'sɪklɪkəl/ *n* a papal letter to the bishops of the church as a whole or to those in 1 country

encyclopedia, encyclopaedia /ɪnˌsaɪklə'piːdiə/ *n* a reference book containing information on all branches of knowledge or comprehensive information on 1 branch, usu in articles arranged alphabetically by subject

encyclopedic, encyclopaedic /inˌsaɪklə'piːdɪk/ *adj* very comprehensive

¹end /end/ *n* **1a** the part of an area that lies at the boundary; *also* the farthest point from where one is **b(1)** the point that marks the extent of sthg in space or time; the limit **(2)** the point where sthg ceases to exist **c** either of the extreme or last parts lengthways of an object that is appreciably longer than it is broad **2a** (the events, sections, etc immediately preceding) the cessation of action, activity, or existence **b** the final condition; *esp* death **3** sthg left over; remnant **4** an aim or purpose **5** sthg or sby extreme of a kind; *the* ultimate **6a** either half of a games pitch, court, etc **b** a period of action or turn to play in bowls, curling, etc **7** a particular part of an undertaking or organization *USE* (*5 & 7*) infml

²end *v* **1** to bring or come to an end **2** to destroy **3** to reach a specified ultimate situation, condition, or rank – often + *up*

³end *adj* final, ultimate

endanger /ɪn'deɪndʒəʳ/ *v* to bring into or expose to danger or peril

endear /ɪn'dɪəʳ/ *v* to cause to become beloved or admired – usu + *to*

endearment /ɪn'dɪəmənt/ *n* a word or act (e g a caress) expressing affection

¹endeavour /ɪn'devəʳ/ *v* to attempt by exertion or effort; try – usu + infin; fml

²endeavour *n* serious determined effort ; *also* an instance of this – fml

endemic /en'demɪk, ɪn-/ *adj* **1**

belonging or native to a particular people or region; not introduced or naturalized 2 regularly occurring in or associated with a particular topic or sphere of activity

ending /ˈendɪŋ/ *n* **1** the last part of a book, film, etc **2** one or more letters or syllables added to a word base, esp as an inflection

endless /ˈendlɪ̥s/ *adj* **1** (seeming) without end **2** extremely numerous **3** *of a belt, chain, etc* that is joined to itself at its ends – **~ly** *adv*

[1]**endocrine** /ˈendəʊkrɪn, -kraɪn/ *adj* **1** producing secretions that are discharged directly into the bloodstream **2** of or being an endocrine gland or its secretions

[2]**endocrine** *n* the thyroid, pituitary, or other gland that produces an endocrine secretion

endorse /ɪnˈdɔːs/ *v* **1a** to write on the back of **b** to write (one's signature) on a cheque, bill, or note **2** to express approval of; support; *specif, chiefly NAm* to express support for (e g a political candidate) publicly **3** *Br* to record on (e g a driving licence) particulars of an offence committed by the holder – **~ment** *n*

endow /ɪnˈdaʊ/ *v* **1** to provide with a continuing source of income **2** to provide *with* an ability or attribute – **~ment** *n*

endurance /ɪnˈdjʊərəns/ *n* the ability to withstand hardship, adversity, or stress

endure /ɪnˈdjʊəʳ/ *v* **1** to continue in the same state; last **2** to undergo (e g a hardship), esp without giving in **3** to tolerate, permit – **-durable** *adj* – **-ring** *adj* – **-ringly** *adv*

endways /ˈendweɪz/, **endwise** *adv or adj* **1** with the end forwards (e g towards the observer) **2** in or towards the direction of the ends; lengthways **3** upright; on end **4** end to end

enema /ˈenɪ̥mə/ *n, pl* **enemas** *also* **enemata** **1** injection of liquid into the intestine by way of the anus (e g to ease constipation) **2** material for injection as an enema

enemy /ˈenəmi/ *n* **1** one who is antagonistic to another; *esp* one seeking to injure, overthrow, or confound an opponent **2** sthg harmful or deadly **3** a hostile military unit or force

energetic /ˌenəˈdʒetɪk/ *adj* **1** marked by energy, activity, or vigour **2** operating with power or effect; forceful – **~ally** *adv*

energy /ˈenədʒi/ *n* **1** the capacity of acting or being active **2** natural power vigorously exerted **3** the capacity for doing work

enervate /ˈenəveɪt/ *v* to lessen the mental or physical strength or vitality of; weaken – **-ation** *n*

en famille /ˌɒn fæˈmiː/ *adv* all together as a family

enfeeble /ɪnˈfiːbəl/ *v* to make feeble – **~ment** *n*

enfold /ɪnˈfəʊld/ *v* **1** to wrap up; envelop **2** to clasp in the arms; embrace

enforce /ɪnˈfɔːs/ *v* **1** to give greater force to (e g an argument); reinforce **2** to impose, compel **3** to cause (a rule or law) to be carried out effectively – **~able** *adj* – **~ment** *n*

enfranchise /ɪnˈfræntʃaɪz/ *v* **1** to set free (e g from slavery) **2a** to admit to the right of voting **b** to admit (a municipality) to political privileges, esp the right of Parliamentary representation – **~ment** *n*

engage *v* **1a** to attract and hold (sby's thoughts, attention, etc) **b** to interlock or become interlocked with; cause to mesh **2a** to arrange to employ (sby) **b** to arrange to obtain the services of **c** to order (a room, seat, etc) to be kept for one; reserve **3a** to hold the attention of; engross **b** to induce to participate, esp in conversation **4a** to enter into contest with **b** to bring together or interlock (e g weapons) **5** to pledge oneself; promise **6** to occupy one's time; participate **7** to enter into conflict

engagé /ˌɒŋgæˈʒeɪ/ *adj* actively involved or committed (politically)

engaged /ɪnˈgeɪdʒd/ *adj* **1** involved in activity; occupied **2** pledged to be married **3** *chiefly Br* **a** in use **b** reserved, booked

engagement /ɪnˈgeɪdʒmənt/ *n* **1** an agreement to marry; a betrothal **2** a pledge **3a** a promise to be present at a certain time and place **b** employment, esp for a stated time **4** a hostile encounter between military forces

engaging /ɪn'geɪdʒɪŋ/ *adj* attractive, pleasing – **~ly** *adv*

engender /ɪn'dʒendəʳ/ *v* to cause to exist or develop; produce

engine /'endʒɪ̈n/ *n* **1** a mechanical tool **2** a machine for converting any of various forms of energy into mechanical force and motion **3** a railway locomotive

[1]**engineer** /,endʒɪ̈'nɪəʳ/ *n* **1a** a designer or builder of engines **b** a person who is trained in or follows as a profession a branch of engineering **c** a person who starts or carries through an enterprise, esp by skilful or artful contrivance **2** a person who runs or supervises an engine or apparatus

[2]**engineer** *v* **1** to lay out, construct, or manage as an engineer **2** to contrive, plan, or guide, usu with subtle skill and craft

engineering /,endʒɪ̈'nɪərɪŋ/ *n* **1** the art of managing engines **2** the application of science and mathematics by which the properties of matter and the sources of energy in nature are made useful to human beings

[1]**English** /'ɪŋglɪʃ/ *adj* (characteristic) of England

[2]**English** *n* **1a** the Germanic language of the people of Britain, the USA, and most Commonwealth countries **b** English language, literature, or composition as an academic subject **2** *pl in constr* the people of England

engrave /ɪn'greɪv/ *v* **1a** to cut (a design or lettering) on a hard surface (e g metal or stone) with a sharp tool **b** to impress deeply, as if by engraving **2a** to cut a design or lettering on (a hard surface) for printing; *also* to print from an engraved plate **b** to produce a plate for printing by photographic methods, photoengrave – **~r** *n*

engraving /ɪŋ'greɪvɪŋ/ *n* (a print made from) an engraved printing surface

engross /ɪŋ'grəʊs/ *v* to occupy fully the time and attention of; absorb

engulf /ɪn'gʌlf/ *v* to flow over and enclose; overwhelm

enhance /ɪn'hɑːns/ *v* to improve (e g in value, desirability, or attractiveness); heighten – **~ment** *n*

enjoin /ɪn'dʒɔɪn/ *v* **1** to order (sby) to do sthg; command **2** to impose (a condition or course of action) on sby **3** to forbid by law; prohibit ***USE*** fml

enjoy /ɪn'dʒɔɪ/ *v* **1** to take pleasure or satisfaction in **2a** to have the use or benefit of **b** to experience – **~ment** *n*

enlarge /ɪn'lɑːdʒ/ *v* **1** to make larger **2** to reproduce in a larger form; *specif* to make a photographic enlargement of **3** to grow larger **4** to speak or write at length; elaborate – often + *on* or *upon*

enlargement /ɪn'lɑːdʒmənt/ *n* a photographic print that is larger than the negative

enlighten /ɪn'laɪtn/ *v* to cause to understand; free from false beliefs

enlightenment /ɪn'laɪtənmənt/ *n* **1** *cap* an 18th-c movement marked by a belief in universal human progress and the importance of reason and the sciences – + *the* **2** nirvana

enlist /ɪn'lɪst/ *v* **1** to engage (a person) for duty in the armed forces **2** to secure the support and aid of – **~ment** *n*

enliven /ɪn'laɪvən/ *v* to give life, action, spirit, or interest to; animate

en masse /,ɒn 'mæs/ *adv* in a body; as a whole

enmesh /ɪn'meʃ/ *v* to catch or entangle (as if) in a net or mesh

enmity /'enmɪ̈ti/ *n* (a state of) hatred or ill will

ennoble /ɪ'nəʊbəl/ *v* to make noble; elevate to the rank of the nobility – **~ment** *n*

ennui /ɒn'wiː/ *n* weariness and dissatisfaction resulting from lack of interest or boredom

enormity /ɪ'nɔːmɪ̈ti/ *n* **1** great wickedness **2** a terribly wicked or evil act **3** the quality or state of being enormous

enormous /ɪ'nɔːməs/ *adj* marked by extraordinarily great size, number, or degree – **~ness** *n*

[1]**enough** /ɪ'nʌf/ *adj* fully adequate in quantity, number, or degree

[2]**enough** *adv* **1** to a fully adequate degree; sufficiently **2** to a tolerable degree

[3]enough *pron, pl* **enough** a sufficient quantity or number

en passant /ˌɒn pæ'sã *adv* in passing

enquire /ɪn'kwaɪə'/ *v* to inquire

enquiry /ɪŋ'kwaɪəri/ *n* an inquiry

enrage /ɪn'reɪdʒ/ *v* to fill with rage; anger – **~d** *adj*

enrapture /ɪn'ræptʃə'/ *v* to fill with delight – **~d** *adj*

enrich /ɪn'rɪtʃ/ *v* **1** to make rich or richer, esp in some desirable quality **2** to adorn, ornament – **~ment** *n*

enrol, enroll /ɪn'rəʊl/ *v* to enter (oneself) on a list (e g for a course of study)

en route /ˌɒn 'ruːt/ *adv or adj* on or along the way

ensconce /ɪn'skɒns/ *v* to settle (e g oneself) comfortably or snugly – **~d** *adj*

ensemble /ɒn'sɒmbəl/ *n* **1a** concerted music of 2 or more parts **b** a complete outfit of matching garments **c** the musicians engaged in the performance of a musical ensemble **2** the quality of togetherness in performance

enshrine /ɪn'ʃraɪn/ *v* **1** to enclose (as if) in a shrine **2** to preserve or cherish, esp as sacred – **~d** *adj*

enshroud /ɪn'ʃraʊd/ *v* to shroud – **~d** *adj*

ensign /'ensaɪn, -sən/ *n* **1** a flag that is flown (e g by a ship) as the symbol of nationality **2a** a standard-bearer **b** (in Britain before 1871) an officer of the lowest rank in the army **c** an officer of the lowest rank in the US navy

enslave /ɪn'sleɪv/ *v* to reduce (as if) to slavery; subjugate – **~ment** *n*

ensnare /ɪn'sneə'/ *v* to take (as if) in a snare

ensue /ɪn'sjuː/ *v* to take place afterwards or as a result

ensure /ɪn'ʃʊə'/ *v* to make sure, certain, or safe; guarantee

entail /ɪn'teɪl/ **1** to settle (property) so that sale or gift is not permitted and inheritance is limited to (a specified class of) the owner's lineal descendants **2** to involve or imply as a necessary accompaniment or result – **entail** *n*

entangle /ɪn'tæŋgəl/ *v* **1** to make tangled, complicated, or confused **2** to involve in a tangle

entanglement /ɪn'tæŋgəlmənt/ *n* **1** sthg that entangles, confuses, or ensnares **2** the condition of being deeply involved

entente /ɒn'tɒnt/ *n* **1** a friendly relationship between 2 or more countries **2** *sing or pl in constr* the countries having an entente

enter /'entə'/ *v* **1** to go or come in or into **2** to register as candidate in a competition **3** to make a beginning **4** to inscribe, register **5** to cause to be received, admitted, or considered – often + *for* **6** to put in; insert **7** to become a member of or an active participant in **8** to put on record **9a** to make oneself a party to – + *into* **b** to participate or share in – + *into*

enteritis /ˌentə'raɪtɪ̣s/ *n* inflammation of the intestines usu marked by diarrhoea

enterprise /'entəpraɪz/ *n* **1** a (difficult or complicated) project or undertaking **2** a unit of economic organization or activity; *esp* a business organization **3** readiness to engage in enterprises

enterprising /'entəpraɪzɪŋ/ *adj* marked by initiative and readiness to engage in enterprises – **~ly** *adv*

entertain /ˌentə'teɪn/ *v* **1** to show hospitality to **2** to be ready and willing to think about (an idea, doubt, suggestion, etc) **3** to hold the attention of, usu pleasantly or enjoyably; divert **4** to invite guests to esp one's home – **~er** *n*

entertainment /ˌentə'teɪnmənt/ *n* **1** sthg entertaining, diverting, or engaging **2** a public performance

enthral, enthrall /ɪn'θrɔːl/ *v* to captivate

enthrone /ɪn'θrəʊn/ *v* to seat, esp ceremonially, (as if) on a throne – **~ment** *n*

enthuse /ɪn'θjuːz/ *v* **1** to make enthusiastic **2** to show enthusiasm

enthusiasm /ɪn'θjuːziæzəm/ *n* **1** keen and eager interest and admiration – usu + *for* or *about* **2** an object of enthusiasm – **-ast** *n* – **-astic** *adj*

entice /ɪn'taɪs/ *v* to tempt or persuade by arousing hope or desire – **~ment** *n* – **-ticing** *adj*

entire /ɪn'taɪəʳ/ *adj* **1** having no element or part left out **2** complete in degree; total **3a** consisting of 1 piece; homogeneous **b** intact – **~ly** *adv*

entirety /ɪn'taɪərḷti/ *n* **1** the state of being entire or complete **2** the whole or total

entitle /ɪn'taɪtl/ *v* **1** to title **2** to give (sby) the right *to* (do or have) sthg – **~ment** *n*

entity /'entḷti/ *n* **1a** being, existence; *esp* independent, separate, or self-contained existence **b** the existence of a thing as contrasted with its attributes **2** sthg that has separate and distinct existence

entomb /ɪn'tuːm/ *v* to deposit (as if) in a tomb; bury – **~ment** *n*

entomology /ˌentə'mɒlədʒi/ *n* zoology that deals with insects – **-gist** *n* – **-gical** *adj*

entourage /'ɒntʊrɑːʒ/ *n sing or pl in constr* a group of attendants or associates, esp of sby of high rank

entr'act /'ɒntrækt/ *n* (sthg performed during) the interval between 2 acts of a play

entrails /'entreɪlz/ *n pl* internal parts; *esp* the intestines

[1]**entrance** /'entrəns/ *n* **1** the act of entering **2** the means or place of entry **3** power or permission to enter; admission **4** an arrival of a performer onto the stage or before the cameras

[2]**entrance** /ɪn'trɑːns/ *v* to fill with delight, wonder, or rapture – **~d** *adj*

entrant /'entrənt/ *n* sby or sthg that enters or is entered; *esp* one who enters a contest

entrap /ɪn'træp/ *v* **1** to catch (as if) in a trap **2** to lure into a compromising statement or act – **~ment** *n*

entreat /ɪn'triːt/ *v* to ask urgently or plead with (sby) *for* (sthg); beg – **~ingly** *adv*

entreaty /ɪn'triːti/ *n* an act of entreating; a plea

entrée, entree /'ɒntreɪ/ *n* **1** freedom of entry or access **2a** *chiefly Br* a dish served between the usual (fish and meat) courses of a dinner **b** *chiefly NAm* the principal dish of a meal

entrench /ɪn'trentʃ/ *v* to establish solidly, esp so as to make dislodgement difficult – **~ed** *adj*

entrepreneur /ˌɒntrəprə'nɜːʳ/ *n* one who organizes, manages, and assumes the risks of a business or enterprise

entropy /'entrəpi/ *n* **1** a measure of the unavailable energy in a closed thermodynamic system **2** the degradation of the matter and energy in the universe to an ultimate state of inert uniformity

entrust /ɪn'trʌst/ *v* to commit *to* the trust of another; to confer another *with* the trust of

entry /'entri/ *n* **1** the act of entering; entrance **2** the right or privilege of entering **3** a door, gate, hall, vestibule, or other place of entrance **4a** a record made in a diary, account book, index, etc **b** a dictionary headword, often with its definition **5** a person, thing, or group entered in a contest; an entrant **6** the total of those entered or admitted

entwine /ɪn'twaɪn/ *v* to twine together or round

enumerate /ɪ'njuːməreɪt/ *v* **1** to count **2** to specify one after another; list – **-ration** *n*

enunciate /ɪ'nʌnsieɪt/ *v* **1a** to make a definite or systematic statement of; formulate **b** to announce, proclaim **2** to articulate, pronounce – **-tion** *n*

envelop /ɪn'veləp/ *v* **1** to enclose or enfold completely (as if) with a covering **2** to surround so as to cut off communication or retreat – **~ment** *n*

envelope /'envələʊp, 'ɒn-/ *n* **1** sthg that envelops; a wrapper, covering **2** a flat container, usu of folded and gummed paper (e g for a letter) **3** a membrane or other natural covering that encloses

enviable /'envɪəbəl/ *adj* highly desirable – **-bly** *adv*

envious /'envɪəs/ *adj* feeling or showing envy – **~ly** *adv*

environment /ɪn'vaɪərənmənt/ *n* **1** the circumstances, objects, or conditions by which one is surrounded **2** the complex of climatic, soil, and biological factors that acts upon an organism or an ecological community – **~al** *adj* – **~ally** *adv*

environmentalist /ɪnˌvaɪərən'mentəlḷst/ *n* sby concerned about the quality of the human environment – **-ism** *n*

environs /ɪn'vaɪərənz/ *n pl* the neighbourhood surrounding sthg, esp a town

envisage /ɪn'vɪzɪdʒ/ *v* to have a mental picture of; visualize, esp in advance of an expected or hoped-for realization

envoy /'envɔɪ/ *n* **1** a diplomatic agent, esp one who ranks immediately below an ambassador **2** a messenger, representative

[1]**envy** /'envi/ *n* painful, resentful, or admiring awareness of an advantage enjoyed by another, accompanied by a desire to possess the same advantage; *also* an object of such a feeling

[2]**envy** *v* to feel envy towards or on account of

enzyme /'enzaɪm/ *n* any of numerous complex proteins that are produced by living cells and catalyse specific biochemical reactions at body temperatures

eon /'iːən/ *n* an aeon

epaulette /ˌepə'let/ *n* an ornamental (fringed) pad or strip attached to the shoulder of a uniform

épée /'epeɪ/ *n* (the sport of fencing with) a sword having a bowl-shaped guard and a rigid tapering blade of triangular cross-section with no cutting edge

ephemeral /ɪ'femərəl/ *adj* **1** lasting 1 day only **2** lasting a very short time – **~ly** *adv* – **~ity** *n*

[1]**epic** /'epɪk/ *adj* **1** (having the characteristics) of an epic **2a** extending beyond the usual or ordinary, esp in size or scope **b** heroic – **~ally** *adv*

[2]**epic** *n* **1** a long narrative poem recounting the deeds of a legendary or historical hero **2** a series of events or body of legend or tradition fit to form the subject of an epic

epicentre /'epɪˌsentəʳ/ *n* the centre from which an earthquake spreads

epicure /'epɪkjʊəʳ/ *n* sby with sensitive and discriminating tastes, esp in food or wine – **~an** *adj, n*

epidemic /ˌepɪ̣'demɪk/ *n or adj* (an outbreak of a disease) affecting many individuals within a population, community, or region at the same time

epidermis /ˌepɪ̣'dɜːmɪ̣s/ *n* **1** the thin outer layer of the skin of the animal body **2** a thin surface layer of tissue in higher plants

epigram /'epɪ̣græm/ *n* **1** a short often satirical poem **2** a neat, witty, and often paradoxical remark or saying – **~matic** *adj*

epilepsy /'epɪ̣lepsi/ *n* any of various disorders marked by disturbed electrical rhythms of the brain and spinal chord and typically manifested by convulsive attacks often with clouding of consciousness – **-ptic** *adj, n*

epilogue /'epɪ̣lɒg/ *n* **1** a concluding section of a literary or dramatic work that comments on or summarizes the main action or plot **2** a speech or poem addressed to the audience by an actor at the end of a play

epiphany /ɪ'pɪfəni/ *n* **1** *cap* (January 6 observed as a church festival in commemoration of) the coming of the Magi **2** a usu sudden manifestation or perception of the essential nature or meaning of sthg

episcopal /ɪ'pɪskəpəl/ *adj* **1** of a bishop **2** of, having, or constituting government by bishops **3** *cap* Anglican; *esp* of an Anglican church that is not established (e g in the USA or Scotland)

episode /'epɪ̣səʊd/ *n* **1a** a developed situation or incident that is integral to but separable from a continuous narrative (e g a play or novel) **b** the part of a serial presented at 1 performance **2** an event that is distinctive and separate although part of a larger series (e g in history or in sby's life)

epistle /ɪ'pɪsəl/ *n* **1** *cap* (a liturgical reading from) any of the letters (e g of St Paul) adopted as books of the New Testament **2** an esp formal letter

epitaph /'epɪ̣tɑːf/ *n* **1** a commemorative inscription on a tombstone or monument **2** a brief statement commemorating a deceased person or past event

epithet /'epɪ̣θet/ *n* **1** a descriptive word or phrase accompanying or occurring in place of the name of a person or thing **2** a disparaging or abusive word or phrase

epitome /ɪ'pɪtəmi/ *n* **1** a condensed account or summary, esp of a literary work **2** a typical or ideal example; an embodiment

epoch /ˈiːpɒk/ *n* **1** a memorable event or date; *esp* a turning point **2** an extended period of time, usu characterized by a distinctive development or by a memorable series of events

equable /ˈekwəbəl/ *adj* uniform, even; *esp* free from extremes or sudden changes – **-bly** *adv*

[1]**equal** /ˈiːkwəl/ *adj* **1a** of the same quantity, amount, or number as another **b** identical in value; equivalent **2a** like in quality, nature, or status **b** like for each member of a group, class, or society **3** evenly balanced or matched **4** capable of meeting the requirements of sthg (e g a situation or task) – + *to* – **~ity** *n* – **~ize** *v*

[2]**equal** *v* **1** to be equal to; *esp* to be identical in value to **2** to make or produce sthg equal to

equalitarian /ɪˌkwɒlɪ̣ˈteərɪən/ *n or adj* (an) egalitarian

equanimity /ˌiːkwəˈnɪmɪ̣ti, ˌekwə-/ *n* evenness of mind or temper, esp under stress

equate /ɪˈkweɪt/ *v* **1** to make or set equal **2** to treat, represent, or regard as equal, equivalent, or comparable

equation /ɪˈkweɪʒən/ *n* a statement of the equality of 2 mathematical expressions

equator /ɪˈkweɪtəʳ/ *n* **1** the great circle of the celestial sphere whose plane is perpendicular to the rotational axis of the earth **2** a great circle; *specif* the one that is equidistant from the 2 poles of the earth and divides the earth's surface into the northern and southern hemispheres – **~ial** *adj* – **~ially** *adv*

equerry /ˈekwəri, ɪˈkweri/ *n* **1** an officer of a prince or noble charged with the care of horses **2** an officer of the British royal household in personal attendance on a member of the royal family

equestrian /ɪˈkwestrɪən/ *adj* **1a** of or featuring horses, horsemen, or horsemanship **b** representing a person on horseback **2** (composed) of knights

equidistant /ˌiːkwɪ̣ˈdɪstənt, ˌekwɪ̣-/ *adj* equally distant

equilateral /ˌiːkwɪ̣ˈlætərəl/ *adj* having all sides equal

equilibrium /ˌiːkwɪ̣ˈlɪbrɪəm/ *n* **1** a state of balance between opposing forces, actions, or processes (e g in a reversible chemical reaction) **2a** a state of adjustment between opposing or divergent influences or elements **b** a state of intellectual or emotional balance **3** the normal state of the animal body in respect to its environment that involves adjustment to changing conditions

equine /ˈekwaɪn, ˈiː-/ *adj* of or resembling the horse (family)

equinox /ˈiːkwɪ̣nɒks, ˈe-/ *n* **1** either of the 2 times each year that occur about March 21st and September 23rd when the sun crosses the equator and day and night are of equal length everywhere on earth **2** either of the 2 points on the celestial sphere where the celestial equator intersects the ecliptic – **-noctial** *adj*

equip /ɪˈkwɪp/ *v* **1** to make ready for service, action, or use; provide with appropriate supplies **2** to dress, array

equipage /ˈekwɪ̣pɪdʒ/ *n* **1** material or articles used in equipment **2** trappings **3** a horse-drawn carriage (with its servants)

equipment /ɪˈkwɪpmənt/ *n* **1** the set of articles, apparatus, or physical resources serving to equip a person, thing, enterprise, expedition, etc **2** mental or emotional resources

equipoise /ˈekwɪ̣pɔɪz/ *n* **1** a state of equilibrium **2** a counterbalance

equitable /ˈekwɪ̣təbəl/ *adj* **1** fair and just **2** valid in equity as distinguished from law – **-bly** *adv*

equity /ˈekwɪ̣ti/ *n* **1** justice according to natural law or right; fairness **2** a system of justice originally developed in the Chancery courts on the basis of conscience and fairness to supplement or override the more rigid common law **3a** a right, claim, or interest existing or valid in equity **b** the money value of a property or of an interest in a property in excess of claims against it **4** a share that does not bear fixed interest – usu pl

equivalent /ɪˈkwɪvələnt/ *adj* **1** equal in force, amount, or value **2** corresponding or virtually identical, esp in effect, function, or meaning

equivocal /ɪ'kwɪvəkəl/ *adj* **1** subject to 2 or more interpretations; ambiguous **2** questionable, suspicious – **~ly** *adv*

equivocate /ɪ'kwɪvəkeɪt/ *v* to use equivocal language, esp with intent to deceive or avoid committing oneself – **-tion** *n*

era /'ɪərə/ *n* **1** a system of chronological notation computed from a given date as a basis **2** an epoch **3** a usu historical period set off or typified by some distinctive figure or characteristic feature

eradicate /ɪ'rædɟkeɪt/ *v* **1** to pull up by the roots **2** to eliminate; do away with – **-cation** *n*

erase /ɪ'reɪz/ *v* **1** to obliterate or rub out (e g written, painted, or engraved letters) **2** to remove from existence or memory as if by erasing – **~r** *n*

[1]**erect** /ɪ'rekt/ *adj* **1a** vertical in position; upright **b** standing up or out from the body **c** characterized by firm or rigid straightness (e g in bodily posture) **2** in a state of physiological erection – **~ly** *adv* – **~ness** *n*

[2]**erect** *v* **1a** to put up by the fitting together of materials or parts; build **b** to fix in an upright position **2** to elevate in status **3** to establish; set up

erectile /ɪ'rektaɪl/ *adj, of animal tissue* capable of becoming swollen with blood to bring about the erection of a body part esp the penis

erection /ɪ'rekʃən/ *n* **1** (an occurrence in the penis or clitoris of) the filling with blood and resulting firmness of a previously flaccid body part **2** sthg erected

erg /ɜːg/ *n* the cgs unit of work or energy; 10^{-7} J

ergo /'ɜːgəʊ/ *adv* therefore, hence

ergonomics /,ɜːgə'nɒmɪks/ *n pl but sing or pl in constr* a science concerned with the relationship between human beings, the machines they use, and the working environment

ermine /'ɜːmɟn/ *n* (the winter fur of) a stoat or related weasel that has a white winter coat usu with black on the tail

erode /ɪ'rəʊd/ *v* **1** to diminish or destroy by degrees **2** to eat into or away by slow destruction of substance; corrode **3** to wear away by the action of water, wind, glacial ice, etc – **erosion** *n*

erogenous /ɪ'rɒdʒɟnəs/ *also* **erogenic** *adj* of or producing sexual excitement (when stimulated)

erotic /ɪ'rɒtɪk/ *adj* **1** of, concerned with, or tending to arouse sexual desire **2** strongly affected by sexual desire – **~ism** *n* – **~ally** *adv*

err /ɜːʳ/ *v* **1a** to make a mistake **b** to do wrong; sin **2** to be inaccurate or incorrect

errand /'erənd/ *n* (the object or purpose of) a short trip taken to attend to some business, often for another

errant /'erənt/ *adj* **1** (given to) travelling, esp in search of adventure **2** going astray ; *esp* doing wrong; erring

erratic /ɪ'rætɪk/ *adj* **1** having no fixed course **2** characterized by lack of consistency, regularity, or uniformity, esp in behaviour – **~ally** *adv*

erratum /e'rɑːtəm/ *n, pl* **errata** a corrigendum

erroneous /ɪ'rəʊnɪəs/ *adj* containing or characterized by error; incorrect – **~ly** *adv*

error /'erəʳ/ *n* **1** a mistake or inaccuracy in speech, opinion, or action **2** the state of being wrong in behaviour or beliefs **3** an act that fails to achieve what was intended

ersatz /'eəzæts/ *adj* being a usu artificial and inferior substitute; imitation

erudite /'erʊdaɪt/ *adj* possessing or displaying extensive or profound knowledge; learned – **~ly** *adv* – **-dition** *n*

erupt /ɪ'rʌpt/ *v* **1a** *esp of a volcano* to release lava, steam, etc suddenly and usu violently **b** to burst violently from limits or restraint **c** to become suddenly active or violent; explode **2** to break out (e g in a rash) – **~ion** *n*

escalate /'eskəleɪt/ *v* **1** to expand **2** to rise – **-lation** *n*

escalator /'eskəleɪtəʳ/ *n* a power-driven set of stairs arranged like an endless belt that ascend or descend continuously

escalope /'eskə,lɒp/ *n* a thin boneless slice of meat; *esp* a slice of veal from the leg

escapade /ˈeskəpeɪd/ *n* a wild, reckless, and often mischievous adventure, esp one that flouts rules or convention

[1]**escape** /ɪˈskeɪp/ *v* **1a** to get away, esp from confinement or restraint **b** to leak out gradually; seep **2** to avoid a threatening evil **3** to get or stay out of the way of; avoid **4** to fail to be noticed or recallable by **5** to be produced or made by (esp a person), usu involuntarily

[2]**escape** *n* **1** an act or instance of escaping **2** a means of escape **3** a cultivated plant run wild

[3]**escape** *adj* **1** providing a means of escape **2** providing a means of evading a regulation, claim, or commitment

escapism /ɪˈskeɪpɪzəm/ *n* habitual diversion of the mind to purely imaginative activity or entertainment as an escape from reality or routine – **escapist** *adj, n*

escarpment /ɪˈskɑːpmənt/ *n* a long cliff or steep slope separating 2 more gently sloping surfaces

eschew /ɪsˈtʃuː/ *v* to avoid habitually, esp on moral or practical grounds; shun – fml

[1]**escort** /ˈeskɔːt/ *n* **1** a person, group of people, ship, aircraft, etc accompanying sby or sthg to give protection or show courtesy **2** one who accompanies another socially

[2]**escort** /ɪˈskɔːt/ *v* to accompany as an escort

escutcheon /ɪˈskʌtʃən/ *n* a protective or ornamental shield or plate (e g round a keyhole)

Eskimo /ˈeskɪ̣məʊ/ *n* (a member or the language of) any of a group of peoples of N Canada, Greenland, Alaska, and E Siberia

esoteric /ˌesəˈterɪk, ˌiːsə-/ *adj* **1** designed for, understood by, or restricted to a small group, esp of the specially initiated **2** private, confidential – **~ally** *adv*

ESP *n* awareness or perception taking place without the use of any of the known senses

espadrille /ˌespəˈdrɪl/ *n* a flat sandal that usu has a canvas upper and a rope sole and is tied round the ankle or leg with laces

especial /ɪˈspeʃəl/ *adj* (distinctively or particularly) special

Esperanto /ˌespəˈræntəʊ/ *n* an artificial international language largely based on words common to the chief European languages

espionage /ˈespɪənɑːʒ/ *n* spying or the use of spies to obtain information

esplanade /ˈespləneɪd/ *n* a level open stretch of paved or grassy ground, esp along a shore

espouse /ɪˈspaʊz/ *v* **1** to marry – fml **2** to take up and support as a cause; become attached to

espresso /ɪˈspresəʊ/ *n* (an apparatus for making) coffee brewed by forcing steam through finely ground coffee beans

esprit de corps /eˌspriː də ˈkɔːʳ/ *n* the common spirit and loyalty existing among the members of a group

espy /ɪˈspaɪ/ *v* to catch sight of

esquire, Esq /ɪˈskwaɪəʳ/ *n* – used as a title equivalent to Mr and placed after the surname

[1]**essay** /eˈseɪ/ *v* to attempt – fml

[2]**essay** /ˈeseɪ/ *n* **1** a usu short piece of prose writing on a specific topic **2** an (initial tentative) effort or attempt – fml – **~ist** *n*

essence /ˈesəns/ *n* **1a** the real or ultimate nature of an individual being or thing, esp as opposed to its existence or its accidental qualities **b** the properties or attributes by means of which sthg can be categorized or identified **2** sthg that exists, esp in an abstract form; an entity **3a** (an alcoholic solution or other preparation of) an extract, essential oil, etc possessing the special qualities of a plant, drug, etc in concentrated form **b** an odour, perfume **c** one who or that which resembles an extract in possessing a quality in concentrated form

[1]**essential** /ɪˈsenʃəl/ *adj* **1** of or being (an) essence; inherent **2** of the utmost importance; basic, necessary – **~ly** *adv*

[2]**essential** *n* sthg basic, indispensable, or fundamental

establish /ɪˈstæblɪʃ/ *v* **1** to make firm or stable **2** to enact permanently **3** to bring into existence; found **4a** to set on a firm basis; place (e g oneself) in a permanent or firm usu favourable position **b** to gain full recognition or acceptance of **5** to make (a church or religion) a national institution supported by civil authority **6** to put beyond doubt; prove **7** to cause (a plant) to grow and multiply in a place where previously absent

establishment /ɪ'stæblɪʃmənt/ *n* **1** sthg established: e g **a** a usu large organization or institution **b** a place of business or residence with its furnishings and staff **2** an established order of society: e g **a** *sing or pl in constr, often cap the* entrenched social, economic, and political leaders of a nation **b** *often cap* a controlling group

estate /ɪ'steɪt/ *n* **1** a social or political class (e g the nobility, clergy, or commons) **2a(1)** the whole of sby's real or personal property **(2)** the assets and liabilities left by sby at death **b** a large landed property, esp in the country, usu with a large house on it **3** *Br* a part of an urban area devoted to a particular type of development; *specif* one devoted to housing

estate agent *n, Br* **1** an agent who is involved in the buying and selling of land and property (e g houses) **2** one who manages an estate; a steward – **estate agency** *n*

estate car *n, Br* a relatively large motor car with a nearly vertical rear door and 1 compartment in which both passengers and bulky luggage can be carried

[1]**esteem** /ɪ'stiːm/ *n* favourable regard

[2]**esteem** *v* **1** to consider, deem **2** to set a high value on; regard highly and prize accordingly

ester /'estə/ *n* a (fragrant) compound formed by the relation between an acid and an alcohol

estimable /'estɪ̈məbəl/ *adj* worthy of esteem

[1]**estimate** /'estɪ̈meɪt/ *v* **1a** to judge approximately the value, worth, or significance of **b** to determine roughly the size, extent, or nature of **c** to produce a statement of the approximate cost of **2** to judge, conclude – **-tor** *n*

[2]**estimate** /'estɪ̈mɪ̈t/ *n* **1** the act of appraising or valuing; a calculation **2** an opinion or judgment of the nature, character, or quality of sby or sthg **3** a statement of the expected cost of a job

estimation /ˌestɪ̈'meɪʃən/ *n* **1** an opinion of the worth or character of sby or sthg **2** esteem

estrange /ɪ'streɪndʒ/ *v* to arouse enmity or indifference in (sby) in place of affection; alienate – usu + *from* – **~ment** *n*

estuary /'estʃʊəri/ *n* a water passage where the tide meets a river; *esp* a sea inlet at the mouth of a river

et al /ˌet 'æl/ *adv* and others

et cetera, etc /ˌet 'setərə/ *adv* and other things, esp of the same kind; *broadly* and so forth

[1]**etch** /etʃ/ *v* **1** to produce (e g a picture or letters), esp on a plate of metal or glass, by the corrosive action of an acid **2** to delineate or impress clearly – **~er** *n*

etching /'etʃɪŋ/ *n* **1** the art of producing pictures or designs by printing from an etched metal plate **2** an impression from an etched plate

eternal /ɪ'tɜːnəl/ *adj* **1** having infinite duration; everlasting **2** incessant, interminable **3** timeless

eternal triangle *n* a conflict that results from the sexual attraction between 2 people of one sex and 1 person of the other

eternity /ɪ'tɜːnɪ̈ti/ *n* **1** the quality or state of being eternal **2** infinite time **3** the eternal life after death **4** a (seemingly) endless or immeasurable time

ether /'iːθəʳ/ *n* **1** a medium formerly held to permeate all space and transmit electromagnetic waves (e g light and radio waves) **2** a volatile inflammable liquid used esp as a solvent and formerly as a general anaesthetic

ethereal /ɪ'θɪərɪəl/ *adj* **1** lacking material substance; light, delicate **2** of, resembling, or containing chemical ether – **~ly** *adv*

ethic /'eθɪk/ *n* **1** *pl but sing or pl in constr* inquiry into the nature and basis of moral principles and judgments **2** a set of moral principles or values **3** *pl but sing or pl in constr* the principles of conduct governing an individual or a group

ethical /'eθɪkəl/ *adj* conforming to accepted, esp professional, standards of conduct or morality – ~**ly** *adv*

[1]**ethnic** /'eθnɪk/ *adj* **1** of or being human races or large groups classed according to common traits **2** of an exotic, esp peasant, culture

[2]**ethnic** *n, chiefly NAm* a member of an ethnic (minority) group

ethnography /eθ'nɒgrəfi/ *n* ethnology; *specif* descriptive anthropology – **-pher** *n* – **-phic** *adj*

ethnology /eθ'nɒlədʒi/ *n* a science that deals with the various forms of social relationships (e g kinship, law, religion, etc) found in esp preliterate human societies – **-gist** *n* – **-gical** *adj*

ethyl alcohol /'iːθaɪl, 'eθəl/ *n* the main alcoholic component of beers, wines, spirits, etc

ethylene /'eθɪ,liːn/ *n* an inflammable gaseous unsaturated hydrocarbon, found in coal gas and used esp in organic chemical synthesis

etiolate /'ɪːtɪəleɪt/ *v* **1** to bleach and alter the natural development of (a green plant) by excluding sunlight **2** to make weak, pale, or sickly – **-lation** *n*

etiquette /'etɪket/ *n* the conventionally accepted standards of proper social or professional behaviour

etymology /,etɨ'mɒlədʒi/ *n* the history of the origin and development of a word or other linguistic form – **-gical** *adj* – **-gically** *adv* – **-gist** *n*

eucalyptus /juːkə'lɪptəs/ *n, pl* **eucalyptuses, eucalypti** any of a genus of mostly Australian evergreen trees of the myrtle family that are widely cultivated for their gums, resins, oils, and wood

Eucharist /'juːkərɨst/ *n* (the bread and wine consecrated in) the Christian sacrament in which bread and wine, being or representing the body and blood of Christ, are ritually consumed in accordance with Christ's injunctions at the Last Supper – ~**ic** *adj*

eugenics /juː'dʒenɪks/ *n pl but sing in constr* a science dealing with the improvement (e g by control of human mating) of the hereditary qualities of a race or breed – **eugenic** *adj* – **-ically** *adv*

eulogy /'juːlədʒi/ *n* **1** a (formal) speech or piece of writing in praise of a person or thing **2** high praise – **-gist** *n* – **-gistic** *adj* – **-gize** *v*

eunuch /'juːnək/ *n* **1** a castrated man employed, esp formerly, in a harem or as a chamberlain in a palace **2** a man or boy deprived of the testes or external genitals

euphemism /'juːfɨmɪzəm/ *n* the substitution of a mild, indirect, or vague expression for an offensive or unpleasant one; *also* the expression so substituted – **-istic** *adj* – **-istically** *adv*

euphonious /juː'fəʊnɪəs/ *adj* pleasing to the ear

euphonium /juː'fəʊnɪəm/ *n* a brass instrument smaller than but resembling a tuba

euphony /'juːfəni/ *n* a pleasing or sweet sound, esp in speech

euphoria /juː'fɔːrɪə/ *n* an (inappropriate) feeling of well-being or elation – **euphoric** *adj* – **-ically** *adv*

euphuism /'juːfjuːɪzəm/ *n* an artificial and ornate style of writing or speaking

Eurasian /jʊə'reɪʒən, -ʃən/ *adj* **1** of, growing in, or living in Europe and Asia **2** of mixed European and Asian origin

eureka /jʊə'riːkə/ *interj* – used to express triumph at a discovery

Eurocrat /'jʊərəʊkræt/ *n* a staff member of the administrative commission of the European Economic Community – infml

Eurodollar /'jʊərəʊ,dɒlə^r/ *n* a US dollar held (e g by a bank) outside the USA, esp in Europe

[1]**European** /jʊərə'pɪən/ *adj* **1** native to Europe **2** of European descent or origin **3** concerned with or affecting (the whole of) Europe

[2]**European** *n* a native or inhabitant of (the mainland of) Europe

eustachian tube /juː,steɪʃən 'tjuːb/ *n, often cap E* a tube connecting the middle ear with the pharynx that equalizes air pressure on both sides of the eardrum

euthanasia /juːθə'neɪzɪə/ *n* the act or practice of killing (hopelessly sick or injured) individuals for reasons of mercy

evacuate /ɪ'vækjʊeɪt/ *v* **1** to empty **2a** to remove, esp from a dangerous area **b** to vacate **3** to withdraw from a place in an organized way, esp for protection **4** to pass urine or faeces from the body – **-ation** *n*

evacuee /ɪ,vækjʊ'iː/ *n* a person evacuated from a dangerous place

evade /ɪ'veɪd/ *v* **1** to get away from or avoid, esp by deception **2a** to avoid facing up to **b** to fail to pay **3** to baffle, foil

evaluate /ɪ'væljʊeɪt/ *v* to determine the amount, value, or significance of, esp by careful appraisal and study – **-ation** *n*

evanescent /,evə'nesənt/ *adj* tending to dissipate or vanish like vapour – **-cence** *n*

evangelical /,iːvæn'dʒelɪkəl/ *also* **evangelic** *adj* **1** of or in agreement with the Christian message as presented in the 4 Gospels **2** *often cap* Protestant; *specif* of the German Protestant church **3** *often cap* (of or being a usu Protestant denomination) emphasizing salvation by faith in the atoning death of Jesus Christ, personal conversion, and the authority of Scripture **4a** of, adhering to, or marked by fundamentalism **b** low church **5** evangelistic, zealous

evangelist /ɪ'vændʒɮɮst/ *n* **1** *often cap* a writer of any of the 4 Gospels **2** one who evangelizes; *specif* a Protestant minister or layman who preaches at special services – **-lism** *n* – **-listic** *adj*

evangel·ize, -ise /ɪ'vændʒɮlaɪz/ *v* to preach the Christian gospel, esp in order to make converts to Christianity

evaporate /ɪ'væpəreɪt/ *v* **1a** to pass off in vapour **b** to pass off or away; disappear, fade **2** to give out vapour **3** to convert into vapour – **-ration** *n*

evasion /ɪ'veɪʒən/ *n* an act, instance, or means of evading

evasive /ɪ'veɪsɪv/ *adj* tending or intended to evade; equivocal – **~ly** *adv* – **~ness** *n*

eve /iːv/ *n* **1** the evening or the day before a special day, esp a religious holiday **2** the period immediately preceding an event **3** the evening – chiefly poetic

¹even /'iːvən/ *n, archaic* the evening – poetic

²even *adj* **1a** having a horizontal surface; flat, level **b** without break or irregularity; smooth **c** in the same plane or line – + *with* **2a** without variation; uniform **b** level **3a** equal; *also* fair **b** being in equilibrium **4** exactly divisible by 2 **5** exact, precise **6** fifty-fifty – **~ly** *adv* – **~ness** *n*

³even *adv* **1** at the very time – + *as* **2a** – used as an intensive to emphasize the contrast with a less strong possibility (e g can't *even* walk, let alone run) **b** – used as an intensive to emphasize the comparative degree

⁴even *v* to make or become even – often + *up* or *out*

evenhanded /,iːvən'hændɮd/ *adj* fair, impartial

evening /'iːvnɪŋ/ *n* **1** the latter part of the day and the early part of the night; the time between sunset and bedtime **2** a late period (e g of time or life); the end **3** (the period of) an evening's entertainment

evening dress *n* clothes for formal or semiformal evening occasions

evensong /'iːvənsɒŋ/ *n, often cap* **1** vespers **2** an evening service of worship esp in the Church of England

event /ɪ'vent/ *n* **1a** a (noteworthy or important) happening or occurrence **b** a social occasion or activity **2** a contingency, case – esp in *in the event of* and *in the event that* **3** any of the contests in a sporting programme or tournament

eventual /ɪ'ventʃʊəl/ *adj* taking place at an unspecified later time; ultimately resulting

eventuality /ɪ,ventʃʊ'ælɮti/ *n* a possible, esp unwelcome, event or outcome

ever /'evəʳ/ *adv* **1** always – now chiefly in certain phrases and in combination (e g an *ever*-growing need) **2** at any time – chiefly in negatives and questions (e g he won't *ever* do it) **3** – used as an intensive (e g looks *ever* so angry)

¹evergreen /'evəgriːn/ *adj* **1** having leaves that remain green and functional through more than 1 growing season 2 always retaining freshness, interest, or popularity

[2]**evergreen** *n* an evergreen plant; *also* a conifer

everlasting /ˌevəˈlɑːstɪŋ/ *adj* **1** lasting or enduring through all time **2a** continuing long or indefinitely; perpetual **b** *of a plant* retaining its form or colour for a long time when dried **3** lasting or wearing for a long time; durable

evermore /ˌevəˈmɔːʳ/ *adv* **1** always, forever **2** in the future

every /ˈevri/ *adj* **1** being each member without exception, of a group larger than 2 (e g *every* word counts) **2** being each or all possible (e g was given *every* chance) **3** being once in each (e g go *every* third day)

everybody /ˈevribɒdi/ *pron* every person

everyday /ˈevrideɪ/ *adj* encountered or used routinely or typically; ordinary

everything /ˈevriθɪŋ/ *pron* **1a** all that exists **b** all that is necessary or that relates to the subject **2** sthg of the greatest importance; all that counts

everywhere /ˈevriweəʳ/ *adv or n* (in, at, or to) every place or the whole place

evict /ɪˈvɪkt/ *v* **1a** to recover (property) from a person by a legal process **b** to remove (a tenant) from rented accommodation or land by a legal process **2** to force out – **~ion** *n*

[1]**evidence** /ˈevɪ̣dəns/ *n* **1** an outward sign; an indication **2** sthg, esp a fact, that gives proof or reasons for believing or agreeing with sthg; *specif* information used (by a tribunal) to arrive at the truth

[2]**evidence** *v* to offer evidence of; show

evident /ˈevɪ̣dənt/ *adj* clear to the vision or understanding – **~ly** *adv*

[1]**evil** /ˈiːvəl/ *adj* **1a** not good morally; sinful, wicked **b** arising from bad character or conduct **2a** causing discomfort or repulsion; offensive **b** disagreeable **3a** pernicious, harmful **b** marked by misfortune – **evilly** *adv*

[2]**evil** *n* **1** sthg evil; sthg that brings sorrow, distress, or calamity **2a** the fact of suffering, misfortune, or wrongdoing **b** wickedness, sin

evil eye *n* (a spell put on sby with) a look believed to be capable of inflicting harm

evince /ɪˈvɪns/ *v* to show clearly; reveal – fml

eviscerate /ɪˈvɪsəreɪt/ *v* **1** to disembowel **2** to deprive of vital content or force – fml – **-ation** *n*

evoke /ɪˈvəʊk/ *v* to call forth or up: e g **a** to conjure **b** to cite, esp with approval or for support; invoke **c** to bring to mind or recollection, esp imaginatively or poignantly – **evocation** *n*

evolution /ˌiːvəˈluːʃən, ˌevə-/ *n* **1a** a process of change and development, esp from a lower or simpler state to a higher or more complex state **b** a process of gradual and relatively peaceful social, political, economic, etc advance **2** the process of working out or developing **3a** the historical development of a biological group (e g a race or species) **b** a theory that the various types of animals and plants derived from preexisting types and that the distinguishable differences are due to natural selection – **~ary** *adj*

evolve /iˈvɒlv/ *v* **1a** to work out, develop **b** to produce by natural evolutionary processes **2** to undergo evolutionary change

ewe /juː/ *n* the female of the (mature) sheep or a related animal

ewer /ˈjuːəʳ/ *n* a wide-mouthed pitcher or jug; *esp* one used to hold water for washing or shaving

exacerbate /ɪgˈzæsəbeɪt/ *v* to make (sthg bad) worse; aggravate – **-bation** *n*

[1]**exact** /ɪgˈzækt/ *v* to demand and obtain by force, threats, etc; require – **~ion** *n*

[2]**exact** *adj* **1** exhibiting or marked by complete accordance with fact **2** marked by thorough consideration or minute measurement of small factual details – **~ness, ~itude** *n*

exacting /ɪgˈzæktɪŋ/ *adj* making rigorous demands; *esp* requiring careful attention and precise accuracy – **~ly** *adv*

exactly /ɪgˈzæktli/ *adv* **1** altogether, entirely **2** quite so – used to express agreement

exaggerate /ɪgˈzædʒəreɪt/ *v* **1** to say

or believe more than the truth about **2** to make greater or more pronounced than normal; overemphasize – **~d** *adj* – **~dly** *adv* – **-ation** *n*

exalt /ɪg'zɔːlt/ *v* **1** to raise high, esp in rank, power, or character **2** to praise highly; glorify

exaltation /ˌegzɔːl'teɪʃən, ˌeksɔːl-/ *n* an excessively intensified sense of well-being, power, or importance

examination /ɪgˌzæmɪ̣'neɪʃən/ *n* **1** (an) examining **2** (the taking by a candidate for a university degree, Advanced level, Ordinary level, etc of) a set of questions designed to test knowledge **3** a formal interrogation (in a law court)

examine /ɪg'zæmɪ̣n/ *v* **1** to inspect closely; investigate **2a** to interrogate closely **b** to test (e g a candidate for a university degree) by an examination in order to determine knowledge – **-iner** *n*

example /ɪg'zɑːmpəl/ *n* **1** sthg representative of all of the group or type to which it belongs **2** sby or sthg that may be copied by other people **3** (the recipient of) a punishment inflicted as a warning to others

exasperate /ɪg'zɑːspəreɪt/ *v* to anger or irritate (sby) – **-ration** *n* – **-ratedly** *adv* – **-ratingly** *adv*

excavate /'ekskəveɪt/ *v* **1** to form by hollowing **2** to dig out and remove – **-vation** *n*

exceed /ɪk'siːd/ *v* **1** to extend beyond **2** to be greater than or superior to **3** to act or go beyond the limits of

exceedingly /ɪk'siːdɪŋli/, **exceeding** *adv* very, extremely

excel /ɪk'sel/ *v* to be superior (to); surpass (others) in accomplishment or achievement – often + *at* or *in*

excellent /'eksələnt/ *adj* outstandingly good – **-ence** *n* – **~ly** *adv*

[1]**except** /ɪk'sept/ *v* to take or leave out from a number or a whole; exclude

[2]**except** *also* **excepting** *prep* with the exclusion or exception of

[3]**except** *also* **excepting** *conj* **1** only, but (e g would go *except* it's too far) **2** unless (e g *except* you repent) – fml

exception /ɪk'sepʃən/ *n* **1** excepting or excluding **2** sby or sthg excepted; *esp* a case to which a rule does not apply **3** question, objection

exceptionable /ɪk'sepʃənəbəl/ *adj* likely to cause objection; objectionable

exceptional /ɪk'sepʃənəl/ *adj* **1** forming an exception; unusual **2** not average; *esp* superior – **~ly** *adv*

[1]**excerpt** /ek'sɜːpt/ *v* **1** to select (a passage) for quoting, copying, or performing **2** to take excerpts from (e g a book)

[2]**excerpt** /'eksɜːpt/ *n* a passage taken from a book, musical composition, etc

[1]**excess** /ɪk'ses, 'ekses/ *n* **1a** the exceeding of usual, proper, or specified limits **b** the amount or degree by which one thing or quantity exceeds another **2** (an instance of) undue or immoderate indulgence; intemperance – **~ive** *adj* – **~ively** *adv*

[2]**excess** /'ekses/ *adj* more than the usual, proper, or specified amount; extra

[1]**exchange** /ɪks'tʃeɪndʒ/ *n* **1a** the act of exchanging one thing for another; a trade **b** a usu brief interchange of words or blows **2** sthg offered, given, or received in an exchange **3a** (the system of settling, usu by bills of exchange rather than money) debts payable currently, esp in a foreign country **b(1)** change or conversion of one currency into another **(2)** **exchange, exchange rate** the value of one currency in terms of another **4** a place where things or services are exchanged: e g **a** an organized market for trading in securities or commodities **b** a centre or device controlling the connection of telephone calls between many different lines

[2]**exchange** *v* **1a** to part with, give, or transfer in return for sthg received as an equivalent **b** *of 2 parties* to give and receive (things of the same type) **2** to replace by other goods **3** to engage in an exchange – **~able** *adj*

exchequer /ɪks'tʃekəʳ/ *n* **1** *cap* a former civil court having jurisdiction primarily over revenue and now merged with the Queen's Bench Division **2** *often cap* the department of state in charge of the national revenue **3** the (national or royal) treasury

[1]**excise** /'eksaɪz/ *n* **1** an internal tax levied on the manufacture, sale, or

consumption of a commodity within a country **2** any of various taxes on privileges, often levied in the form of a licence that must be bought

[2]**excise** /ɪk'saɪz/ *v* to impose an excise on

[3]**excise** /ɪk'saɪz/ *v* to remove (as if) by cutting out – **-sion** *n*

excitable /ɪk'saɪtəbəl/ *adj* capable of being readily activated or roused into a state of excitement or irritability; *specif* capable of being activated by and reacting to stimuli – **-bility** *n*

excite /ɪk'saɪt/ *v* **1** to provoke or stir up (action) **2** to rouse to strong, esp pleasurable, feeling **3** to arouse (e g an emotional response) – **~ment** *n*

exclaim /ɪk'skleɪm/ *v* to cry out or speak in strong or sudden emotion

exclamation /ˌekskləˈmeɪʃən/ *n* exclaiming or the words exclaimed

exclamation mark *n* a punctuation mark ! used esp after an interjection or exclamation

exclude /ɪk'sklu:d/ *v* **1a** to shut out **b** to bar from participation, consideration, or inclusion **2** to expel, esp from a place or position previously occupied – **-usion** *n*

[1]**exclusive** /ɪk'sklu:sɪv/ *adj* **1a** excluding or having power to exclude **b** limiting or limited to possession, control, use, etc by a single individual, group, etc **2a** excluding others (considered to be inferior) from participation, membership, or entry **b** snobbishly aloof **3** stylish and expensive **4a** sole **b** whole, undivided **5** not inclusive – **~ly** *adv* – **~ness** *n*

[2]**exclusive** *n* **1** a newspaper story printed by only 1 newspaper **2** an exclusive right (e g to sell a particular product in a certain area)

excommunicate /ˌekskəˈmju:nɟ̊keɪt/ *v* **1** to deprive officially of the rights of church membership **2** to exclude from fellowship of a group or community – **excommunicate** *n, adj* – **-ation** *n*

excoriate /ɪks'kɔ:rieɪt/ *v* **1** to wear away the skin of; abrade **2** to censure scathingly – fml – **-ation** *n*

excrement /'ekskrɟ̊mənt/ *n* faeces or other waste matter discharged from the body

excrescence /ɪk'skresəns/ *n* an excessive or abnormal outgrowth or enlargement

excreta /ɪk'skri:tə/ *n pl* excrement

excrete /ɪk'skri:t/ *v* to separate and eliminate or discharge (waste) from blood or living tissue – **-tion** *n*

excruciating /ɪk'skru:ʃieɪtɪŋ/ *adj* **1** causing great pain or anguish; agonizing, tormenting **2** very intense; extreme – **~ly** *adv*

exculpate /'ekskʌlpeɪt/ *v* to clear from alleged fault, blame, or guilt – **-pation** *n*

excursion /ɪk'skɜ:ʃən/ *n* **1** a (brief) pleasure trip, usu at reduced rates **2** a deviation from a direct, definite, or proper course; *esp* a digression

[1]**excuse** /ɪk'skju:z/ *v* **1a** to make apology for **b** to try to remove blame from **2** to forgive entirely or overlook as unimportant **3** to allow to leave; dismiss **4** to be an acceptable reason for; justify – usu neg **5** *Br* to free from (a duty) – usu pass

[2]**excuse** /ɪk'skju:s/ *n* **1** sthg offered as grounds for being excused **2** *pl* an expression of regret for failure to do sthg or esp for one's absence

ex-directory /ˌeks dɟ̊'rektəri/ *adj, Br* intentionally not listed in a telephone directory

execrable /'eksɟ̊krəbəl/ *adj* detestable, appalling – chiefly fml – **-bly** *adv*

execrate /'eksɟ̊kreɪt/ *v* **1** to declare to be evil or detestable; denounce **2** to detest utterly; abhor *USE* chiefly fml – **-cration** *n*

execute /'eksɟ̊kju:t/ *v* **1** to carry out fully; put completely into effect **2** to put to death (legally) as a punishment **3** to make or produce (e g a work of art), esp by carrying out a design **4** to (do what is required to) make valid **5** to play, perform

execution /ˌeksɟ̊'kju:ʃən/ *n* **1** a putting to death as a punishment **2** a judicial writ directing the enforcement of a judgment **3** the act, mode, or result of performance

executioner /ˌeksɟ̊'kju:ʃənə^r/ *n* one who puts to death; *specif* one legally appointed to perform capital punishment

[1]**executive** /ɪg'zekjʊtɪv/ *adj* **1** concerned with making and carrying out

laws, decisions, etc; *specif, Br* of or concerned with the detailed application of policy or law rather than its formulation **2** of, for, or being an executive

[2]**executive** *n* **1** the executive branch of a government **2** an individual or group that controls or directs an organization **3** one who holds a position of administrative or managerial responsibility

executor /ɪgˈzekjʊtəʳ/, *fem* **executrix** /-trɪks/ *n* one appointed to carry out the provisions of a will

exemplary /ɪgˈzemplәri/ *adj* **1** deserving imitation; commendable **2** serving as a warning **3** serving as an example, instance, or illustration

exemplify /ɪgˈzemplɟfaɪ/ *v* **1** to show or illustrate by example **2** to be an instance of or serve as an example of; typify, embody – **-fication** *n*

[1]**exempt** /ɪgˈzempt/ *adj* freed from some liability or requirement to which others are subject – **~ion** *n*

[2]**exempt** *v* to make exempt; excuse

[1]**exercise** /ˈeksəsaɪz/ *n* **1** the use of a specified power or right **2** bodily exertion for the sake of developing and maintaining physical fitness **3** sthg performed or practised in order to develop, improve, or display a specific power or skill

[2]**exercise** *v* **1** to make effective in action; use, exert **2a** to use repeatedly in order to strengthen or develop **b** to train (e g troops) by drills and manoeuvres **3** to engage the attention and effort of

exert /ɪgˈzɜːt/ *v* **1** to bring (e g strength or authority) to bear **2** to take upon (oneself) the effort of doing sthg – **~ion** *n*

exeunt /ˈeksiʊnt/ – used as a stage direction to specify that all or certain named characters leave the stage

ex gratia /ˌeks ˈgreɪʃə/ *adj or adv* as a favour; not compelled by legal right

exhale /eksˈheɪl/ *v* to breathe out – **-lation** *n*

[1]**exhaust** /ɪgˈzɔːst/ *v* **1** to empty by drawing off the contents; *specif* to create a vacuum in **2a** to consume entirely; use up **b** to tire out **3** to develop or deal with to the fullest possible extent

[2]**exhaust** *n* **1** (the escape of) used gas or vapour from an engine **2** the conduit or pipe through which used gases escape

exhaustion /ɪgˈzɔːstʃən/ *n* extreme tiredness

exhaustive /ɪgˈzɔːstɪv/ *adj* comprehensive, thorough – **~ly** *adv* – **~ness** *n*

[1]**exhibit** /ɪgˈzɪbɟt/ *v* **1** to reveal, manifest **2** to show publicly, esp for purposes of competition or demonstration – **~or** *n*

[2]**exhibit** *n* **1** sthg exhibited **2** sthg produced as evidence in a lawcourt

exhibition /ˌeksɟˈbɪʃən/ *n* **1** a public showing (e g of works of art or objects of manufacture) **2** *Br* a grant drawn from the funds of a school or university to help to maintain a student

exhibitionism /ˌeksɟˈbɪʃənɪzəm/ *n* **1** a perversion marked by a tendency to indecent exposure **2** behaving so as to attract attention to oneself – **-ist** *n* – **-istic** *adj*

exhilarate /ɪgˈzɪləreɪt/ *v* **1** to make cheerful **2** to enliven, invigorate – **-ration** *n*

exhort /ɪgˈzɔːt/ *v* to urge or advise strongly – **~ation** *n*

exhume /ɪgˈzjuːm, eksˈhjuːm/ *v* **1** to dig up again after burial **2** to bring back from neglect or obscurity – **exhumation** *n*

exigency /ˈeksɟdʒənsi, ɪgˈzɪ-/, **exigence** *n* such need or necessity as belongs to the occasion; a requirement – usu pl with sing. meaning *USE* fml – **exigent** *adj* – **exigently** *n*

exiguous /ɪgˈzigʊəs/ *adj* excessively scanty; inadequate, meagre – fml – **~ly** *adv* – **~ness** *n*

exile /ˈeksaɪl, ˈegzaɪl/ *n* **1** enforced or voluntary absence from one's country or home **2** one who is exiled voluntarily or by authority – **exile** *v*

exist /ɪgˈzɪst/ *v* **1** to have being esp in specified conditions **2** to continue to be **3a** to have life **b** to live at an inferior level or under adverse circumstances

existence /ɪgˈzɪstəns/ *n* **1a** the totality of existent things **b** the state or fact of existing; life **2** manner of living or being

existent /ɪg'zɪstənt/ *adj* **1** having being; existing **2** extant

existential /ˌegzɪ'stenʃəl/ *adj* **1** of or grounded in existence **2** existentialist

existentialism /ˌegzɪ'stenʃəlɪzəm/ *n* a philosophical movement characterized by inquiry into human beings' experience of themselves in relation to the world, esp with reference to their freedom, responsibility, and isolation and the experiences (e g of anxiety and despair) in which these are revealed – **-list** *adj, n*

[1]**exit** /'egzɪ̠t, 'eksɪ̠t/ – used as a stage direction to specify who goes off stage

[2]**exit** *n* **1** a departure of a performer from a scene **2** the act of going out or away **3** a way out of an enclosed place or space

exodus /'eksədəs/ *n* a mass departure; an emigration

exonerate /ɪg'zɒnəreɪt/ *v* to free from blame USE usu + *from* – **-ration** *n*

exorbitant /ɪg'zɔːbɪ̠tənt/ *adj, of prices, demands, etc* much greater than is reasonable; excessive – **-tance** *n* – **~ly** *adv*

exorcise /'eksɔːsaɪz/ *v* to free a place, person , etc from an evil spirit; *also* to expel an evil spirit – **-ism** *n* – **-ist** *n*

exoskeleton /ˌeksəʊ'skelɪ̠tn/ *n* an external supportive (hard or bony) covering of an animal

exotic /ɪg'zɒtɪk/ *adj* **1** introduced from another country; not native to the place where found **2** strikingly or excitingly different or unusual – **~ally** *adv* – **~ism** *n*

expand /ɪk'spænd/ *v* **1** to increase the size, extent, number, volume, or scope of **2** to express in detail or in full **3** to grow genial; become more sociable – **~able** *adj* – **expansion** *n*

expanse /ɪk'spæns/ *n* **1** sthg spread out, esp over a wide area **2** the extent to which sthg is spread out

expansive /ɪk'spænsɪv/ *adj* **1** having a capacity or tendency to expand or cause expansion **2** genial, effusive **3** having wide expanse or extent – **~ly** *adv* – **~ness** *n*

[1]**expatriate** /eks'pætrieɪt/ *v* **1** to exile, banish **2** to withdraw (oneself) from residence in or allegiance to one's native country

[2]**expatriate** /eks'pætrɪət, -trieɪt/ *n* one who lives in a foreign country

expect /ɪk'spekt/ *v* **1** to anticipate or look forward to **2** to be pregnant **3a** to consider an event probable or certain **b** to consider reasonable, due, or necessary **4** to suppose, think

expectant /ɪk'spektənt/ *adj* **1** characterized by expectation **2** *of a pregnant woman* expecting the birth of a child

expectation /ˌekspek'teɪʃən/ *n* **1** expecting or sthg expected **2** prospects of inheritance – usu pl with sing. meaning

expectorate /ɪk'spektəreɪt/ *v* to spit (e g saliva) – **-ation** *n* – **-ant** *n or adj*

expediency /ɪk'spiːdɪənsi/ *n* **1** **expediency, expedience** suitability, fitness **2** use of expedient means and methods **3** an expedient

[1]**expedient** /ɪk'spiːdɪənt/ *adj* **1** suitable for achieving a particular end **2** concerned with what is opportune rather than with what is moral – **~ly** *adv*

[2]**expedient** *n* a means to an end; *esp* one devised or used in case of urgent need

expedite /'ekspɪ̠daɪt/ *v* to hasten the process or progress of; facilitate

expedition /ˌekspɪ̠'dɪʃən/ *n* **1** a journey or excursion undertaken for a specific purpose (e g for war or exploration) **2** efficient promptness; speed

expeditionary /ˌekspɪ̠'dɪʃənəri/ *adj* sent on military service abroad

expeditious /ˌekspɪ̠'dɪʃəs/ *adj* speedy – **~ly** *adv*

expel /ɪk'spel/ *v* **1** to drive or force out **2** to drive away; *esp* to deport **3** to cut off from membership

expend /ɪk'spend/ *v* **1** to pay out **2** to consume (e g time, care, or attention)

expendable /ɪk'spendəbəl/ *adj* **1** normally used up in service; not intended to be kept or reused **2** regarded as available for sacrifice or destruction in order to accomplish an objective

expenditure /ɪk'spendɪtʃəʳ/ *n* **1** the

act or process of expending **2** the amount expended

expense /ɪk'spens/ *n* **1a** financial burden or outlay **b** *pl* the charges incurred by an employee in performing his/her duties **c** an item of business outlay chargeable against revenue in a specific period **2** a cause or occasion of usu high expenditure

expensive /ɪk'spensɪv/ *adj* **1** involving great expense **2** commanding a high price; dear – **~ly** *adv*

experience /ɪk'spɪərɪəns/ *n* **1** the usu conscious perception or apprehension of reality or of an external, bodily, or mental event **2** (the knowledge, skill, or practice derived from) direct participation or observation **3** sthg personally encountered or undergone – **experience** *v*

experienced /ɪk'spɪərɪənst/ *adj* skilful or wise as a result of experience

experiment /ɪk'sperǰmənt/ *n* **1** a tentative procedure or policy that is on trial **2** an operation carried out under controlled conditions in order to test or establish a hypothesis or to illustrate a known law – **~al** *adj*

expert /'ekspɜːt/ *n or adj* (sby or sthg) having or showing special skill or knowledge derived from training or experience – **~ly** *adv* – **~ness** *n*

expertise /ˌekspɜː'tiːz/ *n* skill in or knowledge of a particular field; know-how

expiate /'ekspieɪt/ *v* **1** to eradicate the guilt incurred by (e g a sin) **2** to make amends for – **-ation** *n*

expiration /ˌekspǰ'reɪʃən/ *n* **1** the release of air from the lungs through the nose or mouth **2** expiry, termination

expire /ɪk'spaɪəʳ/ *v* **1** to come to an end **2** to emit the breath **3** to die – **expiry** *n*

explain /ɪk'spleɪn/ *v* **1** to make sthg plain or understandable **2** to give the reason for or cause of – **~er** *n*

explanation /ˌekspla'neɪʃən/ *n* the act or process of explaining; sthg, esp a statement, that explains

explanatory /ɪk'splænətəri/ *adj* serving to explain

expletive /ɪk'spliːtɪv/ *n* a usu meaningless exclamatory word or phrase; *specif* one that is obscene or profane

explicable /'eksplɪkəbəl/ *adj* capable of being explained – **-bly** *adv*

explicate /'eksplǰkeɪt/ *v* **1** to give a detailed explanation of **2** to analyse logically – **-ation** *n* – **-atory, -ative** *adj*

explicit /ɪk'splɪsǰt/ *adj* clear, unambiguous ; *also* graphically frank – **~ly** *adv* – **~ness** *n*

explode /ɪk'spləʊd/ *v* **1** to give expression to sudden, violent, and usu noisy emotion **2** to burst or expand violently as a result of pressure, or a rapid chemical reaction **3** to bring (e g a belief or theory) into discredit by demonstrating falsity

[1]**exploit** /'eksplɔɪt/ *n* a deed, act; *esp* a notable or heroic one

[2]**exploit** /ɪk'splɔɪt/ *v* **1** to turn to economic account ; *also* to utilize **2** to take unfair advantage of for financial or other gain – **~ation** *n* – **~er** *n*

explore /ɪk'splɔːʳ/ **1** to make or conduct a search **2** to travel into or through for purposes of geographical discovery – **~r** *n* – **-ration** *n*

explosion /ɪk'spləʊʒən/ *n* **1** (a noise caused by something) exploding **2** a rapid large-scale expansion, increase, or upheaval **3** a sudden violent outburst of emotion

[1]**explosive** /ɪk'spləʊsɪv/ *adj* **1** threatening to burst forth with sudden violence or noise **2** tending to arouse strong reactions – **~ly** *adv* – **~ness** *n*

[2]**explosive** *n* an explosive substance

exponent /ɪk'spəʊnənt/ *n* **1** a symbol written above and to the right of a mathematical expression to indicate the operation of raising to a power **2a** sby or sthg that expounds or interprets **b** sby who advocates or exemplifies *USE* (*2*) usu + *of*

[1]**export** /ɪk'spɔːt/ *v* to carry or send a commodity to another country for purposes of trade – **~able** *adj* – **~ation** *n* – **~er** *n* – **export** *n*

expose /ɪk'spəʊz/ *v* **1** to submit or subject to an action or influence; *specif* to subject (a photographic film, plate, or paper) to the action of radiant energy **2a** to exhibit for public veneration **b** to engage in indecent exposure of (oneself) **3** to bring (sthg shameful) to light

exposé, expose /ek'spəʊzeɪ/ *n* **1** a formal recital or exposition of facts; a statement **2** an exposure of sthg discreditable

exposition /ˌekspə'zɪʃən/ *n* **1a** a detailed explanation or elucidation, esp of sthg difficult to understand **b** the first part of a musical composition in which the theme is presented **2** a usu international public exhibition or show (e g of industrial products)

expostulate /ɪk'spɒstʃʊleɪt/ *v* to reason earnestly *with* sby in order to dissuade or remonstrate – **-lation** *n*

exposure /ɪk'spəʊʒəʳ/ *n* **1a** a disclosure, esp of a weakness or sthg shameful or criminal **b(1)** the act of exposing a sensitized photographic film, plate, or paper; *also* the duration of such an exposure **(2)** a section of a film with 1 picture on it **2a** being exposed, specif to the elements **b** the specified direction in which a building, room, etc faces

expound /ɪk'spaʊnd/ *v* to set forth, esp in careful or elaborate detail

¹express /ɪk'spres/ *adj* **1** firmly and explicitly stated **2a** travelling at high speed **b** to be delivered without delay by special messenger

²express *n* **1** an express vehicle **2** express mail

³express *v* **1** to state **2** to make known the opinions, feelings, etc of (oneself) **3** to represent by a sign or symbol

expression /ɪk'spreʃən/ *n* **1a** expressing, esp in words **b** a significant word or phrase **2a** a means or manner of expressing sthg; *esp* sensitivity and feeling in communicating or performing **b** facial aspect or vocal intonation indicative of feeling – **~less** *adj*

expressionism /ɪk'spreʃənɪzən/ *n* a mode of artistic expression that attempts to depict the artist's subjective emotions and responses to objects and events – **expressionist** *n, adj*

expressive /ɪk'spresɪv/ *adj* **1** of expression **2** serving to express or represent **3** full of expression; significant – **~ly** *adv* – **~ness** *n*

expressly /ɪk'spresli/ *adv* **1** explicitly **2** for the express purpose; specially

expropriate /ɪk'sprəʊprieɪt/ *v* **1** to dispossess **2** to transfer to one's own possession – **-ation** *n* – **-ator** *n*

expulsion /ɪk'spʌlʃən/ *n* expelling or being expelled

expunge /ɪk'spʌndʒ/ *v* to strike out; obliterate, erase

expurgate /'ekspəgeɪt/ *v* to remove objectionable parts from, before publication or presentation – **-gation** *n*

exquisite /ɪk'skwɪzɪ̣t, 'ekskwɪ-/ *adj* **1a** marked by flawless delicate craftsmanship **b** keenly sensitive, esp in feeling **2a** extremely beautiful; delightful **b** acute, intense – **~ly** *adv* – **~ness** *n*

extant /ɪk'stænt/ *adj* still or currently existing

extemporaneous /ɪkˌstempə'reɪnɪəs/ *adj* **1** done, spoken, performed, etc on the spur of the moment **2** makeshift – **~ly** *adv* – **~ness** *n*

extempore /ɪk'stempəri/ *adj or adv* (spoken or done) in an extemporaneous manner

extempor·ize, -ise /ɪk'stempəraiz/ *v* to speak, perform, etc without prior preparation; improvise

extend /ɪk'stend/ *v* **1** to stretch out in distance, space, or time **2** to exert (e g a horse or oneself) to full capacity **3** to give or offer, usu in response to need; proffer **4a** to reach in scope or application **b** to prolong in time **c** to advance, further **5** to increase the scope, meaning, or application of

extended family *n* a family unit that includes 3 or more generations of near relatives in addition to a nuclear family in 1 household

extension /ɪk'stenʃən/ *n* **1a** extending or being extended **b** sthg extended **2** extent, scope **3** a straightening of (a joint between the bones of) a limb **4** an increase in length of time **5a** a part added (e g to a building) **b** an extra telephone connected to the principal line

extensive /ɪk'stensɪv/ *adj* having wide or considerable extent – **~ly** *adv* – **~ness** *n*

extent /ɪk'stent/ *n* **1** the range or distance over which sthg extends **2** the point or limit to which sthg extends

extenuate /ɪk'stenjʊeɪt/ *v* to (try to)

lessen the seriousness or extent of (e g a crime) by giving excuses – **-tion** *n*

[1]**exterior** /ɪk'stɪərɪə^r/ *adj* **1** on the outside or an outside surface; external **2** suitable for use on outside surfaces

[2]**exterior** *n* **1** an exterior part or surface; outside **2** an outward manner or appearance

exterminate /ɪk'stɜːmɨneɪt/ *v* to destroy completely; *esp* to kill all of – **-nation** *n*

[1]**external** /ɪk'stɜːnəl/ *adj* **1a** superficial **b** not intrinsic or essential **2** of, connected with, or intended for the outside or an outer part **3a(1)** situated outside, apart, or beyond **(2)** arising or acting from outside **b** of dealings with foreign countries **c** having existence independent of the mind – **~ly** *adj*

[2]**external** *n* an external feature or aspect – usu pl

extinct /ɪk'stɪŋkt/ *adj* no longer active, alive, or in operation

extinction /ɪk'stɪŋkʃən/ *n* making or being extinct or (causing to be) extinguished

extinguish /ɪk'stɪŋgwɪʃ/ *v* **1a** to cause to cease burning; quench **b** to bring to an end **2** to make void

extirpate /'ekstɜːpeɪt/ *v* to destroy completely (as if) by uprooting; annihilate – **-pation** *n*

extol /ɪk'stəʊl/ *v* to praise highly; glorify

extort /ɪk'stɔːt/ *v* to obtain from sby by force or threats

extortion /ɪk'stɔːʃən/ *n* the unlawful extorting of money – **~er, ~ist** *n*

extortionate /ɪk'stɔːʃənɨt/ *adj* excessive, exorbitant – **~ly** *adv*

[1]**extra** /'ekstrə/ *adj* **1** more than is due, usual, or necessary; additional **2** subject to an additional charge

[2]**extra** *n* sthg or sby extra or additional: e g **a** an added charge **b** a specified edition of a newspaper **c** a run in cricket (e g a bye, leg bye, no-ball, or wide) that is not credited to a batsman's score **d** an additional worker; *specif* one hired to act in a group scene in a film or stage production

[3]**extra** *adv* beyond or above the usual size, extent, or amount

[1]**extract** /ɪk'strækt/ *v* **1** to draw forth or pull out, esp with effort **2** to withdraw (e g a juice or fraction) by physical or chemical process **3** to separate (a metal) from an ore **4** to excerpt

[2]**extract** /'ekstrækt/ *n* an excerpt

extraction /ɪk'strækʃən/ *n* **1** ancestry, origin **2** sthg extracted

extracurricular /ˌekstrəkə'rɪkjʊlə^r/ *adj* **1** not falling within the scope of a regular curriculum **2** lying outside one's normal activities

extradite /'ekstrədaɪt/ *v* to return (someone accused of a crime) to the country in which the crime took place for trial – **-dition** *n*

extramural /ˌekstrə'mjʊərəl/ *adj* **1** outside (the walls or boundaries of) a place or organization **2** *chiefly Br* of courses or facilities offered by a university or college to those who are not regular full-time students

extraneous /ɪk'streɪnɪəs/ *adj* **1** on or coming from the outside **2** not forming an essential or vital part; irrelevant – **~ly** *adv*

extraordinary /ɪk'strɔːdənəri/ *adj* **1** exceptional; remarkable **2** on or for a special function or service – **-rily** *adv*

extrapolate /ɪk'stræpəleɪt/ *v* to use or extend (known data or experience) in order to surmise or work out sthg unknown – **-ation** *n*

extraterrestrial /ˌekstrətə'restrɪəl/ *adj* originating, existing, or occurring outside the earth or its atmosphere

extravagant /ɪk'strævəgənt/ *adj* **1** excessive **2a** wasteful, esp of money **b** profuse – **-ance** *n* – **~ly** *adv*

extravaganza /ɪkˌstrævə'gænzə/ *n* a lavish or spectacular show or event

extravert /'ekstrəvɜːt/ *n or adj* (an) extrovert

[1]**extreme** /ɪk'striːm/ *adj* **1a** existing in a very high degree **b** not moderate **c** exceeding the usual or expected **2** situated at the farthest possible point from a centre or the nearest to an end **3** most advanced or thoroughgoing – **~ly** *adv*

[2]**extreme** *n* **1** sthg situated at or marking one or other extreme point of a range **2** a very pronounced or extreme degree **3** an extreme measure or expedient

extremism /ɪk'striːmɪzəm/ *n* advocacy of extreme political measures; radicalism – **extremist** *n, adj*

extremity /ɪk'stremɟti/ *n* **1a** the most extreme part, point, or degree **b** a (human) hand, foot, or other limb **2** a drastic or desperate act or measure

extricate /'ekstrɟkeɪt/ *v* to disentangle, esp with considerable effort – **-cable** *adj* – **-cation** *n*

extrinsic /ek'strɪnzɪk, -sɪk/ *adj* **1** not forming part of or belonging to a thing; extraneous **2** originating from or on the outside – **~ally** *adv*

extrovert, extravert /'ekstrəvɜːt/ *n* one whose interests are directed outside the self; *broadly* an outgoing boisterous person

extrude /ɪk'struːd/ *v* **1** to force or push out **2** to shape (e g metal or plastic) by forcing through a die – **extrusion** *n*

exuberant /ɪg'zjuːbərənt/ *adj* **1** joyously unrestrained; flamboyant **2** abundant, luxuriant – **-ance** *n* – **~ly** *adv*

exude /ɪg'zjuːd/ *v* **1** to ooze out **2** to radiate an air of

exult /ɪg'zʌlt/ *v* to be extremely joyful; rejoice openly – usu + *at, in,* or *over* – **~ant** *adj* – **~antly** *adv* – **~ation** *n*

[1]**eye** /aɪ/ *n* **1a** any of various usu paired organs of sight **b** the faculty of seeing **c** a gaze, glance **2a** the hole through the head of a needle **b** a loop; *esp* one of metal or thread into which a hook is inserted **c** an undeveloped bud (e g on a potato) **d** a calm area in the centre of a tropical cyclone **e** the (differently coloured or marked) centre of a flower **3** the direction from which the wind is blowing – **~less** *adj*

[2]**eye** *v* to watch closely

eyeball /'aɪbɔːl/ *n* the capsule of the eye of a vertebrate together with the structures it contains

eyebrow /'aɪbraʊ/ *n* (hair growing on) the ridge over the eye

eyelash /'aɪlæʃ/ *n* (a single hair of) the fringe of hair edging the eyelid

eyelet /'aɪlɟt/ *n* a small usu reinforced hole designed so that a cord, lace, etc may be passed through it

eyelid /'aɪˌlɪd/ *n* a movable lid of skin and muscle that can be closed over the eyeball

eyeliner /'aɪlaɪnəʳ/ *n* a cosmetic for emphasizing the contours of the eyes

eye-opener *n* sthg surprising and esp revelatory – infml

eyepiece /'aɪpiːs/ *n* the lens or combination of lenses at the eye end of an optical instrument

eye shadow *n* a coloured cream or powder applied to the eyelids to accentuate the eyes

eyesore /'aɪsɔːʳ/ *n* sthg offensive to the sight

eyetooth /ˌaɪ'tuːθ/ *n* a canine tooth of the upper jaw

eyewash /'aɪwɒʃ/ *n* deceptive statements or actions; rubbish, claptrap – infml

eyewitness /'aɪˌwɪtnɟs/ *n* one who sees an occurrence and can bear witness to it (e g in court)

eyrie /'ɪəri, 'eəri, 'aɪəri/ *n* the nest of a bird of prey on a cliff or mountain top

F

f /ef/ *n, pl* **f's, fs** *often cap* **1** (a graphic representation of or device for reproducing) the 6th letter of the English alphabet **2** the 4th note of a C-major scale

fa, fah /fɑː/ *n* the 4th note of the diatonic scale in solmization

Fabian /'feɪbɪən/ *adj* of or being a society founded in England in 1884 to work for the gradual establishment of socialism

fable /'feɪbəl/ *n* **1** a legendary story of supernatural happenings **2** a fictitious account **3** a story conveying a moral; *esp* one in which animals speak and act like human beings

fabric /'fæbrɪk/ *n* **1a** the basic structure of a building **b** an underlying structure; a framework **2** cloth

fabricate /'fæbrɪkeɪt/ *v* **1** to construct or manufacture from many parts **2** to invent or create, esp in order to deceive – **-tion** *n*

fabulous /'fæbjʊləs/ *adj* **1** extraordinary, incredible **2** told in or based on fable **3** marvellous, great – infml

facade *also* **façade** /fə'sɑːd, fæ-/ *n* **1** a face, esp the front or principal face, of a building given special architectural treatment **2** a false or superficial appearance

[1]**face** /feɪs/ *n* **1** the front part of the (human) head including the chin, mouth, nose, eyes, etc and usu the forehead **2** a facial expression; *specif* a grimace **3a** an outward appearance **b** effrontery, impudence **c** dignity, reputation **4a** a front, upper, or outer surface **b** an exposed surface of rock **c** the right side (e g of cloth or leather) **5** the exposed working surface of a mine or excavation

[2]**face** *v* **1** to meet or deal with firmly and without evasion **2** to cover the front or surface of **3** to have the face towards ; *also* to turn the face in a specified direction

facecloth /'feɪsklɒθ/ *n* a flannel

faceless /'feɪslɨs/ *adj* lacking identity; anonymous

face-lift *n* **1** plastic surgery to remove facial defects (e g wrinkles) typical of aging **2** an alteration intended to improve appearance or utility

face out *v* to confront defiantly or impudently

face-pack *n* a cream, paste, etc applied to the face to improve the complexion and remove impurities

facet /'fæsɨt/ *n* **1** a small plane surface (e g of a cut gem or an insect's eye) **2** any of the aspects from which sthg specified may be considered

facetious /fə'siːʃəs/ *adj* inappropriately lacking seriousness in manner; flippant – **~ly** *adv* – **~ness** *n*

[1]**facial** /'feɪʃəl/ *adj* of the face – **~ly** *adv*

[2]**facial** *n* a facial beauty treatment

facile /'fæsaɪl/ *adj* **1** easily or readily accomplished or performed **2** specious, superficial – **~ly** *adv* – **~ness** *n*

facilitate /fə'sɪlɨteɪt/ *v* to make easier – fml – **-tation** *n*

facility /fə'sɪlɨti/ *n* **1** the ability to perform sthg easily; aptitude **2** sthg (e g equipment) that promotes the ease of an action or operation – usu pl

facing /'feɪsɪŋ/ *n* **1a** a lining at the edge of sthg, esp a garment, for stiffening or ornament **b** *pl* the collar, cuffs, and trimmings of a uniform coat **2** an ornamental or protective layer

facsimile /fæk'sɪmɨli/ *n* **1** an exact copy, esp of printed material **2** the transmission and reproduction of graphic material (e g typescript or pictures) by wire or radio

fact /fækt/ *n* **1** a thing done; *esp* a criminal act **2** the quality of having actual existence in the real world; *also* sthg having such existence **3** an event, esp as distinguished from its legal effect **4** a piece of information presented as having objective reality

faction /ˈfækʃən/ *n* **1** a party or minority group within a party **2** dissension with a party or group

fact of life *n, pl* **facts of life** *pl* the processes and behaviour involved in (human) sex and reproduction

factor /ˈfæktəʳ/ *n* **1** one who acts for another; an agent **2** a condition, force, or fact that actively contributes to a result **3** any of the numbers or symbols that when multiplied together form a product – **~ize** *v*

factory /ˈfæktəri/ *n* a building or set of buildings with facilities for manufacturing

factotum /fækˈtəʊtəm/ *n* a servant employed to carry out many types of work

factual /ˈfæktʃʊəl/ *adj* **1** of facts **2** restricted to or based on fact – **~ly** *adv*

faculty /ˈfækəlti/ *n* **1** an inherent capability, power, or function of the body **2** a group of related subject departments in a university

fad /fæd/ *n* **1** a usu short-lived but enthusiastically pursued practice or interest; a craze **2** an personal or eccentric taste or habit – **~dish** *adj* – **~dishly** *adv*

fade /feɪd/ *v* **1** to lose freshness or vigour; wither **2** *of a brake* to lose braking power gradually, esp owing to prolonged use **3** to lose freshness or brilliance of colour **4** to disappear gradually; vanish – often + *away*

faeces, *NAm chiefly* **feces** /ˈfiːsiːz/ *n pl* bodily waste discharged through the anus – **faecal** *adj*

faerie, faery /ˈfeəri/ *n* **1** fairyland **2** a fairy

[1]**fag** /fæg/ *n* **1** a British public-school pupil who acts as servant to an older schoolmate **2** *chiefly Br* a tiring or boring task – infml

[2]**fag** *n* a cigarette – infml

fag end *n* **1** a poor or worn-out end; a remnant **2** the extreme end USE infml

faggot /ˈfægət/ *n* **1** *NAm chiefly* **fagot a** a bundle of sticks **b** a round mass of minced meat (e g pig's liver) mixed with herbs and usu breadcrumbs **2** *chiefly NAm* a usu male homosexual – derog

Fahrenheit /ˈfærənhaɪt/ *adj* relating to, conforming to, or being a scale of temperature on which water freezes at 32° and boils at 212° under standard conditions

faience, faïence /faɪˈɒns, -ˈɑːns/ *n* tin-glazed decorated earthenware

[1]**fail** /feɪl/ *v* **1a** to lose strength; weaken **b** to fade or die away **c** to stop functioning **2a** to fall short **b** to be unsuccessful (e g in passing a test) **c** to become bankrupt or insolvent **3a** to disappoint the expectations or trust of **b** to prove inadequate for or incapable of carrying out an expected service or function for **4** to leave undone; neglect

[2]**fail** *n* **1** failure – chiefly in *without fail* **2** an examination failure

[1]**failing** /ˈfeɪlɪŋ/ *n* a usu slight or insignificant defect in character; *broadly* a fault, imperfection

[2]**failing** *prep* in absence or default of

failsafe /ˈfeɪlseɪf/ *adj* designed so as to counteract automatically the effect of an anticipated possible source of failure

failure /ˈfeɪljəʳ/ *n* **1** a failing to perform a duty or expected action **2** lack of success **3a** a falling short; a deficiency **b** deterioration, decay **4** sby or sthg unsuccessful

[1]**faint** /feɪnt/ *adj* **1** cowardly, timid – chiefly in *faint heart* **2** weak, dizzy, and likely to faint **3** feeble **4** lacking distinctness; *esp* dim – **~ly** *adv* – **~ness** *n*

[2]**faint** *v* to lose consciousness because of a temporary decrease in the blood supply to the brain (e g through exhaustion or shock) – **faint** *n*

[1]**fair** /feəʳ/ *adj* **1** attractive, beautiful **2** superficially pleasing **3** clean, clear **4** not stormy or foul; fine **5a** free from self-interest or prejudice; honest **b** conforming with the established rules; allowed **6** light in colour; blond **7** moderately good or large; adequate – **~ness** *n*

[2]**fair** *n* **1** a periodic gathering of buyers and sellers at a particular place and time for trade or a competitive exhibition, usu accompanied by entertainment and amusements **2** *Br* a fun fair

fair game *n* sby or sthg open to legitimate pursuit, attack, or ridicule

fairground /ˈfeəgraʊnd/ *n* an area where outdoor fairs, circuses, or exhibitions are held

fairly /ˈfeəli/ *adv* **1** completely, quite **2** properly, impartially, or honestly **3** to a full degree or extent **4** for the most part

fairway /ˈfeəweɪ/ *n* **1** a navigable channel in a river, bay, or harbour **2** the mowed part of a golf course between a tee and a green

fair-weather *adj* present or loyal only in untroubled times – chiefly in *fair-weather friend*

fairy /ˈfeəri/ *n* a small mythical being having magic powers and usu human form

fairy-tale *adj* marked by **a** unusual grace or beauty **b** apparently magical success or good fortune

fairy tale *n* **1** a story which features supernatural or imaginary forces and beings **2** a made-up story, usu designed to mislead – **fairy-tale** *adj*

fait accompli /ˌfeɪt əˈkɒmpli/ *n, pl* **faits accomplis** sthg already accomplished and considered irreversible

faith /feɪθ/ *n* **1a** allegiance to duty or a person; loyalty – chiefly in *good/ bad faith* **b** fidelity to one's promises – chiefly in *keep/ break faith* **2a** belief and trust in and loyalty to God or the doctrines of a religion **b** complete confidence **3** sthg believed with strong conviction; *esp* a system of religious beliefs

¹faithful /ˈfeɪθfəl/ *adj* **1** showing faith; loyal; *specif* loyal to one's spouse in having no sexual relations outside marriage **2** firm in adherence to promises or in observance of duty **3** true to the facts; accurate – **~ness** *n* – **~ly** *adv*

²faithful *n pl* **1** *the* full church members **2** *the* body of adherents of a religion (e g Islam) **3** loyal followers or members

faithless /ˈfeɪθlɪ̵s/ *adj* **1a** lacking esp religious faith **b** disloyal **2** untrustworthy – **~ly** *adv* – **~ness** *n*

¹fake /feɪk/ *n* any of the loops of a coiled rope or cable

²fake *v* **1** to alter or treat so as to impart a false character or appearance; falsify **2a** to counterfeit, simulate **b** to feign

³fake *n* **1** a worthless imitation passed off as genuine **2** an impostor, charlatan

⁴fake *adj* counterfeit, phoney

fakir /ˈfeɪkɪəʳ, ˈfækɪəʳ, fæˈkɪəʳ/ *n* **1** a Muslim mendicant **2** a wandering Hindu ascetic holy man

falcon /ˈfɔːlkən/ *n* any of various hawks distinguished by long wings

falconer /ˈfɔːlkənəʳ/ *n* one who hunts with hawks or who breeds or trains hawks for hunting – **falconry** *n*

¹fall /fɔːl/ *v* **fell; fallen** **1a** to descend freely (as if) by the force of gravity **b** to hang freely **2a** to become less or lower in degree, level, pitch, or volume **b** to be uttered; issue **c** to look down **3a** to come down from an erect to a usu prostrate position suddenly and esp involuntarily **b** to enter an undesirable state, esp unavoidably or unwittingly **c** to drop because wounded or dead; *esp* to die in battle – euph **d** to lose office **4a** to yield to temptation; sin **b** *of a woman* to lose one's virginity, esp outside marriage **5a** to move or extend in a downward direction – often + *off* or *away* **b** to decline in quality or quantity; abate, subside – often + *off* or *away* **c** to assume a look of disappointment or dismay **d** to decline in financial value **6a** to occur at a specified time or place **b** to come (as if) by chance – + *in* or *into* **c** to come or pass by lot, assignment, or inheritance; devolve – usu + *on, to,* or *upon* **7** to come within the limits, scope, or jurisdiction of sthg **8** to begin heartily or actively – usu + *to* **9** to fall in love with – + *for* **10** to be deceived by – + *for*

²fall *n* **1** the act of falling by the force of gravity **2a** a falling out, off, or away; a dropping **b** sthg or a quantity that falls or has fallen **3a** a loss of greatness or power; a collapse **b** the surrender or capture of a besieged place **c** *often cap* mankind's loss of innocence through the disobedience of Adam and Eve **4a** a downward slope **b** a cataract – usu pl with sing. meaning but sing. or pl in constr **5** a decrease in size, quantity, degree, or value **6** *chiefly NAm* autumn

fallacy /ˈfæləsi/ *n* **1** deceptive appearance or nature; deception, delusiveness **2** a false idea **3** an argument failing to satisfy the conditions of valid inference

fallible /ˈfæləbəl/ *adj* capable of being or likely to be wrong – **-bility** *n*

fall in *v* **1** to sink or collapse inwards **2** to take one's proper place in a military formation **3** to concur *with*

fallopian tube /fəˌləupɪən ˈtjuːb/ *n, often cap F* either of the pair of tubes conducting the egg from the ovary to the uterus in mammals

fallout /ˈfɔːlaut/ *n* **1** (the fall of) polluting particles, esp radioactive particles resulting from a nuclear explosion **2** secondary results or products

fall out *v* **1** to have a disagreement; quarrel **2** to leave one's place in the ranks of a military formation **3** to happen; come about – fml or poetic

[1]**fallow** /ˈfæləu/ *adj* light yellowish brown

[2]**fallow** *n* (ploughed and harrowed) land that is allowed to lie idle during the growing season

[3]**fallow** *v* to plough, harrow, etc (land) without seeding, esp so as to destroy weeds

[4]**fallow** *adj* **1** *of land* left unsown after ploughing **2** dormant, inactive – chiefly in *to lie fallow*

fallow deer *n* a small European deer with broad antlers and a pale yellow coat spotted with white in the summer

fall through *v* to fail to be carried out

fall to *v* to begin doing sthg (e g working or eating), esp vigorously – often imper

false /fɔːls/ *adj* **1** not genuine **2a** intentionally untrue; lying **b** adjusted or made so as to deceive **3** not based on reality; untrue **4** disloyal, treacherous **5** resembling or related to a more widely known kind **6** imprudent, unwise – **~ly** *adv* – **~ness** *n* – **falsity** *n*

falsehood /ˈfɔːlshud/ *n* **1** an untrue statement; a lie **2** absence of truth or accuracy; falsity

falsetto /fɔːlˈsetəu/ *n, pl* **falsettos** (a singer who uses) an artificially high voice, specif an artificially produced male singing voice that extends above the range of the singer's full voice

falsify /ˈfɔːlsɪ̣faɪ/ *v* **1** to prove or declare false **2a** to make false by alteration **b** to represent falsely; misrepresent – **-fication** *n*

falter /ˈfɔːltəʳ/ **1** to walk or move unsteadily or hesitatingly; stumble **2** to speak brokenly or weakly; stammer **3** to lose strength, purpose, or effectiveness; waver – **~ingly** *adv*

fame /feɪm/ *n* **1** public estimation; reputation **2** popular acclaim; renown – **~d** *adj*

familial /fəˈmɪlɪəl/ *adj* (characteristic) of a family or its members

[1]**familiar** /fəˈmɪlɪəʳ/ *n* an intimate associate; a companion

[2]**familiar** *adj* **1** closely acquainted; intimate **2a** casual, informal **b** too intimate and unrestrained; presumptuous **3** frequently seen or experienced; common – **~ize** *v* – **~ly** *adv*

familiarity /fəˌmɪliˈærɪ̣ti/ *n* **1a** absence of ceremony; informality **b** an unduly informal act or expression **2** close acquaintance *with* or knowledge of sthg

[1]**family** /ˈfæməli/ *n sing or pl in constr* **1** a group of people of common ancestry or common convictions **2** a group of people living under 1 roof; *esp* a set of 2 or more adults living together and rearing their children **3** a group of related languages descended from a single ancestral language **4** a category in the biological classification of living things ranking above a genus and below an order

[2]**family** *adj* of or suitable for a family or all of its members

family allowance *n* child benefit

family planning *n* a system of achieving planned parenthood by contraception

family tree *n* (a diagram of) a genealogy

famine /ˈfæmɪ̣n/ *n* an extreme scarcity of food; *broadly* any great shortage

famish /ˈfæmɪʃ/ *v* to cause to suffer severely from hunger – usu pass – **~ed** *adj*

famous /ˈfeɪməs/ *adj* well-known

[1]**fan** /fæn/ *n* **1** a folding circular or semicircular device that consists of material (e g paper or silk) mounted on thin slats that is waved to and fro

by hand to produce a cooling current of air **2** a device, usu a series of vanes radiating from a hub rotated by a motor, for producing a current of air

[2]**fan** *v* **1** to eliminate (e g chaff) by winnowing **2** to move or impel (air) with a fan **3** to stir up to activity as if by fanning a fire; stimulate **4** to spread *out* like a fan

[3]**fan** *n* an enthusiastic supporter or admirer (e g of a sport, pursuit, or celebrity)

fanatic /fə'nætɪk/ *n or adj* (one who is) excessively and often uncritically enthusiastic, esp in religion or politics – **~al** *adj* – **~ally** *adv* – **~ism** *n*

fan belt *n* an endless belt driving a cooling fan for a car radiator

fancier /'fænsɪəʳ/ *n* one who breeds or grows a usu specified animal or plant for points of excellence

fanciful /'fænsifəl/ *adj* **1** given to or guided by fancy or imagination rather than by reason and experience **2** existing in fancy only; imaginary **3** marked by fancy or whim – **~ly** *adv*

[1]**fancy** /'fænsi/ *n* **1** an inclination **2** a notion, whim **3a** imagination, esp of a capricious or misleading sort **b** the power of mental conception and representation, used in artistic expression (e g by a poet) **4** *sing or pl in constr the* group of fanciers of a particular animal or devotees of a particular sport

[2]**fancy** *v* **1** to believe without knowledge or evidence **2a** to have a fancy for; like, desire **b** to consider likely to do well **3** to form a conception of; imagine

[3]**fancy** *adj* **1** based on fancy or the imagination; whimsical **2a** not plain or ordinary; *esp* fine, quality **b** ornamental – **fancily** *adv*

fancy dress *n* unusual or amusing dress (e g representing a historical or fictional character) worn for a party or other special occasion

fanfare /'fænfeəʳ/ *n* **1** a flourish of trumpets **2** a showy outward display

fang /fæŋ/ *n* a projecting tooth or prong: e g **a** a tooth by which an animal's prey is seized and held or torn **b** any of the long hollow or grooved teeth of a venomous snake

fanlight /'fænlaɪt/ *n* an esp semicircular window with radiating divisions over a door or window

fanny /'fæni/ *n* **1** *Br* the female genitals – vulg **2** *NAm* the buttocks – infml

fantasia /fæn'teɪʒə, -'teɪzɪə, ˌfæntə'zɪə/ *n* a free instrumental or literary composition not in strict form (comprising familiar tunes)

fantastic /fæn'tæstɪk/ *adj* **1a** unreal, imaginary **b** so extreme as to challenge belief; *specif* exceedingly large or great **2** marked by extravagant fantasy or eccentricity **3** – used as a generalized term of approval – **~ally** *adv*

[1]**fantasy** /'fæntəsi/ *n* **1** unrestricted creative imagination; fancy **2** imaginative fiction or drama characterized esp by strange, unrealistic, or grotesque elements **3** (the power or process of creating) a usu extravagant mental image or daydream

[1]**far** /fɑːʳ/ *adv* **farther, further; farthest, furthest** **1** to or at a considerable distance in space (e g wandered *far* into the woods) **2b** in total contrast (e g *far* from criticizing you, I'm delighted) – + *from* **3** to or at an extent or degree (e g as *far* as I know **4a** to or at a considerable distance or degree (e g a bright student will go *far*) **b** much (e g *far* too hot) **5** to or at a considerable distance in time (e g worked *far* into the night)

[2]**far** *adj* **farther, further; farthest, furthest** **1** remote in space, time, or degree (e g in the *far* distance) **2** long **3** being the more distant of 2 (e g the *far* side of the lake) **4** *of a political position* extreme

faraway /'fɑːrəweɪ/ *adj* **1** lying at a great distance; remote **2** dreamy, abstracted

farce /fɑːs/ *n* **1** forcemeat **2** a comedy with an improbable plot that is concerned more with situation than characterization **3** a ridiculous or meaningless situation or event – **farcical** *adj* – **farcically** *adv*

[1]**fare** /feəʳ/ *v* to get along; succeed, do

[2]**fare** *n* **1a** the price charged to trans-

port sby **b** a paying passenger **2** food provided for a meal

[1]**farewell** /feə'wel/ *interj* goodbye

[2]**farewell** *n* an act of departure or leave-taking

farfetched /ˌfɑː'fetʃt/ *adj* not easily or naturally deduced; improbable

far-flung *adj* **1** widely spread or distributed **2** remote

[1]**farm** /fɑːm/ *n* an area of land devoted to growing crops or raising (domestic) animals

[2]**farm** *v* **1** to collect and take the proceeds of (e g taxation or a business) on payment of a fixed sum **2** to produce crops or livestock

farmer /'fɑːməʳ/ *n* **1** sby who pays a fixed sum for some privilege or source of income **2** sby who cultivates land or crops or raises livestock

farmhand /'fɑːmhænd/ *n* a farm worker

farmhouse /'fɑːmhaʊs/ *n* a dwelling house on a farm

farm out *v* **1** to turn over for performance or use, usu on contract **2** to put (e g children) into sby's care in return for a fee

farmyard /'fɑːmjɑːd/ *n* the area round or enclosed by farm buildings

far-out *adj* extremely unconventional; weird

farrago /fə'rɑːgəʊ, fə'reɪ-/ *n, pl* **farragoes** a confused collection; a hotchpotch

farrier /'færɪəʳ/ *n* a blacksmith who shoes horses

[1]**farrow** /'færəʊ/ *v* to give birth to (pigs) – often + *down*

[2]**farrow** *n* (farrowing) a litter of pigs

farsighted /ˌfɑː'saɪtɨd/ *adj* **1a** seeing or able to see to a great distance **b** having foresight or good judgment; sagacious **2** long-sighted – **~ness** *n*

[1]**farther** /'fɑːðəʳ/ *adv* **1** at or to a greater distance or more advanced point (e g *farther* down the corridor) **2** to a greater degree or extent

[2]**farther** *adj* **1a** more distant; remoter **b** far (e g the *farther* side) **2** additional

[1]**farthest** /'fɑːðɨst/ *adj* most distant in space or time

[2]**farthest** *adv* **1** to or at the greatest distance in space, time, or degree **2** by the greatest degree or extent; most

farthing /'fɑːðɪŋ/ *n* **1** (a coin representing) a former British money unit worth ¼ of an old penny **2** sthg of small value

fascia /'feɪʃə/ *n, pl* **fasciae, fascias** **1** a flat horizontal piece (e g of stone or board) under projecting eaves **2** *Br* the dashboard of a motor car

fascinate /'fæsɨneɪt/ *v* **1** to transfix by an irresistible mental power **2** to attract strongly, esp by arousing interest; captivate – **-ting** *adj* – **-tingly** *adv*

fascism /'fæʃɪzəm/ *n* **1** a political philosophy, movement, or regime that is usu hostile to socialism, exalts nation and race, and stands for a centralized government headed by a dictatorial leader **2** brutal dictatorial control – **fascist** *n, adj*

[1]**fashion** /'fæʃən/ *n* **1** a manner, way **2a** a prevailing and often short-lived custom or style **b** the prevailing style or custom, esp in dress

[2]**fashion** *v* **1** to give shape or form to, esp by using ingenuity; mould, construct **2** to mould into a particular character by influence or training; transform, adapt

fashionable /'fæʃənəbəl/ *adj* **1** conforming to the latest custom or fashion **2** used or patronized by people of fashion – **-ably** *adv*

[1]**fast** /fɑːst/ *adj* **1a** firmly fixed or attached **b** tightly closed or shut **2a(1)** moving or able to move rapidly; swift **(2)** taking a comparatively short time **(3)** accomplished quickly **(4)** quick to learn **b** conducive to rapidity of play or action or quickness of motion **c** *of a clock* indicating in advance of what is correct **3** *of a colour* permanently dyed; not liable to fade **4** dissipated, wild; *also* promiscuous

[2]**fast** *adv* **1** in a firm or fixed manner **2** sound, deeply **3a** in a rapid manner; quickly **b** in quick succession **4** in a reckless or dissipated manner **5** ahead of a correct time or posted schedule

[3]**fast** *v* to abstain from some or all foods or meals

[4]**fast** *n* an act or time of fasting

fasten /'fɑːsən/ *v* **1** to attach or secure, esp by pinning, tying, or nailing **2** to fix or direct steadily **3** to attach, impose *on* – **~er** *n*

fastening /ˈfɑːsənɪŋ/ *n* a fastener

fastidious /fæˈstɪdɪəs/ *adj* **1** excessively difficult to satisfy or please **2** showing or demanding great delicacy or care – **~ly** *adv* – **~ness** *n*

fastness /ˈfɑːstnɪ̈s/ *n* **1a** the quality of being fixed **b** colourfast quality **2** a fortified, secure, or remote place

¹fat /fæt/ *adj* **1a** plump **b** obese **2a** well filled out; thick, big **b** prosperous, wealthy **3** richly rewarding or profitable; substantial **4** productive, fertile **5** practically nonexistent – infml – **~ness** *n*

²fat *n* **1** (animal tissue consisting chiefly of cells distended with) greasy or oily matter **2** the best or richest part

fatal /ˈfeɪtl/ *adj* **1** fateful, decisive **2a** of fate **b** like fate in proceeding according to a fixed sequence; inevitable **3a** causing death **b** bringing ruin

fatalism /ˈfeɪtl-ɪzəm/ *n* the belief that all events are predetermined and outside the control of human beings – **-ist** *n* – **-istic** *adj*

fatality /fəˈtælɪ̈ti/ *n* **1a** the quality or state of causing death or destruction **b** the quality or condition of being destined for disaster **2** death resulting from a disaster

fatally /ˈfeɪtəli/ *adv* **1** mortally **2** as is or was fatal

¹fate /feɪt/ *n* **1** the power beyond human control that determines events; destiny **2a** a destiny **b** a disaster; *esp* death **3** an outcome, end; *esp* one that is adverse and inevitable

²fate *v* to destine; *also* to doom – usu pass

fateful /ˈfeɪtfəl/ *adj* **1** having an ominous quality **2a** having momentous and often unpleasant consequences **b** deadly, catastrophic – **~ly** *adv*

Fates /feɪts/ *n pl* the 3 goddesses of classical mythology who determine the course of human life

fathead /ˈfæthed/ *n* a slow-witted or stupid person; a fool – infml

¹father /ˈfɑːðəʳ/ *n* **1a** a male parent of a child; *also* a sire **b** *cap* God; the first person of the Trinity **2** a man receiving filial respect from another **3** *often cap* an early Christian writer accepted by the church as authoritative **4** a source, origin **5** a priest of the regular clergy – used esp as a title in the Roman Catholic church

²father *v* **1a** to beget **b** to give rise to; initiate **2** to fix the paternity of *on*

father-in-law *n, pl* **fathers-in-law** the father of one's spouse

¹fathom /ˈfæðəm/ *n* a unit of length equal to 6ft used esp for measuring the depth of water

²fathom *v* to penetrate and come to understand – often + *out*

fathomless /ˈfæðəmlɪ̈s/ *adj* incapable of being fathomed

¹fatigue /fəˈtiːg/ *n* **1** physical or nervous exhaustion **2a** manual or menial military work **b** *pl* the uniform or work clothing worn on fatigue **3** the tendency of a material to break under repeated stress

²fatigue *v* to weary, exhaust

fatten /ˈfætn/ *v* to make fat, fleshy, or plump; *esp* to feed (e g a stock animal) for slaughter – often + *up*

¹fatty /ˈfæti/ *adj* **1** containing (large amounts of) fat; *also* corpulent **2** greasy – **-tiness** *n*

²fatty *n* a fat person – infml

fatuous /ˈfætʃʊəs/ *adj* complacently or inanely foolish; idiotic – **-tuity** *n* – **~ly** *adv* – **~ness** *n*

¹fault /fɔːlt/ *n* **1a** a failing; a defect **b** a service that does not land in the prescribed area in tennis, squash, etc **2a** a misdemeanour **b** a mistake **3** responsibility for wrongdoing or failure **4** a fracture in the earth's crust accompanied by displacement (e g of the strata) along the fracture line – **~y** *adj* – **~ily** *adv* – **~iness** *n*

²fault *v* **1** to commit a fault; err **2** to produce a geological fault (in)

fauna /ˈfɔːnə/ *n* the animals or animal life of a region, period, or special environment

faux pas /ˌfəʊ ˈpɑː, ˈfəʊ pɑː/ *n, pl* **faux pas** an esp social blunder

¹favour, *NAm chiefly* **favor** /ˈfeɪvəʳ/ *n* **1a** friendly or approving regard shown towards another; approbation **b** popularity **2** (an act of) kindness beyond what is expected or due **3** a token of allegiance or love (e g a ribbon or badge), usu worn conspicuously **4** consent to sexual activities, esp given by a woman – usu pl with sing. meaning; euph

[2]**favour,** *NAm chiefly* **favor** *v* **1a** to regard or treat with favour **b** to do a favour or kindness for; oblige – usu + *by* or *with* **2** to show partiality towards; prefer **3** to sustain; facilitate

favourable /ˈfeɪvərəbəl/ *adj* **1a** disposed to favour; partial **b** giving a result in one's favour **2a** helpful, advantageous **b** successful – **-rably** *adv*

favoured /ˈfeɪvəd/ *adj* **1** endowed with special advantages or gifts **2** having an appearance or features of a specified kind – usu in combination **3** receiving preferential treatment

[1]**favourite** /ˈfeɪvərɪ̵t/ *n* **1** sby or sthg favoured or preferred above others; *specif* one unduly favoured **2** the competitor judged most likely to win, esp by a bookmaker

[2]**favourite** *adj* constituting a favourite

favouritism /ˈfeɪvərɪ̵tɪzəm/ *n* the showing of unfair favour; partiality

[1]**fawn** /fɔːn/ *v* to court favour by acting in a servilely flattering manner *USE* usu + *on* or *upon*

[2]**fawn** *n* **1** a young (unweaned) deer **2** a light greyish brown colour

fealty /ˈfiːəlti/ *n* fidelity or allegiance, esp to a feudal lord

[1]**fear** /fɪəʳ/ *n* **1** (an instance of) an unpleasant often strong emotion caused by anticipation or awareness of (a specified) danger **2** anxiety, solicitude **3** profound reverence and awe, esp towards God **4** reason for alarm; danger – **~less** *adj* – **~lessly** *adv* – **~lessness** *n*

[2]**fear** *v* **1** to have a reverential awe of **2** to be afraid of; consider or expect with alarm

fearful /ˈfɪəfəl/ *adj* **1** causing or likely to cause fear **2a** showing or arising from fear **b** timid, timorous **3** extremely bad, large, or intense – infml – **~ly** *adv* – **~ness** *n*

fearsome /ˈfɪəsəm/ *adj* fearful – **~ly** *adv* – **~ness** *n*

feasible /ˈfiːzɪ̵bəl/ *adj* **1** capable of being done or carried out **2** reasonable, likely; *also* suitable – **-sibility** *n* – **-sibly** *adv*

[1]**feast** /fiːst/ *n* **1a** an elaborate often public meal; a banquet **b** sthg that gives abundant pleasure **2** a periodic religious observance commemorating an event or honouring a deity, person, or thing

[2]**feast** *v* **1** to take part in a feast; give a feast for **2** to delight, gratify

feat /fiːt/ *n* **1** a notable and esp courageous act or deed **2** an act or product of skill, endurance, or ingenuity

[1]**feather** /ˈfeðəʳ/ *n* **1a** any of the light outgrowths forming the external covering of a bird's body **b** the vane of an arrow **2** plumage **3** the act of feathering an oar

[2]**feather** *v* **1** to cover, clothe, adorn, etc with feathers **2a** to turn (an oar blade) almost horizontal when lifting from the water **b** to change the angle at which (a propeller blade) meets the air so as to have the minimum wind resistance

featherbed /ˈfeðəbed/ *v* **1** to cushion or protect from hardship, worry, etc; to pamper **2** to assist (e g an industry) with government subsidies

featherweight /ˈfeðəweɪt/ *n* **1** a boxer weighing not more than 9st **2** sby or sthg of limited importance or effectiveness

[1]**feature** /ˈfiːtʃəʳ/ *n* **1** a part of the face ; *also, pl* the face **2** a prominent or distinctive part or characteristic **3a** a full-length film **b** a distinctive article or story, in a newspaper, magazine, or on radio

[2]**feature** *v* **1** to give special prominence to (e g in a performance or newspaper) **2** to play an important part; be a feature – usu + *in*

febrile /ˈfiːbraɪl/ *adj* of fever; feverish

February /ˈfebrʊəri/ *n* the 2nd month of the Gregorian calendar

feckless /ˈfeklɪ̵s/ *adj* worthless, irresponsible – **~ly** *adv* – **~ness** *n*

fecund /ˈfekənd, ˈfiːkənd/ *adj* **1** fruitful in offspring or vegetation; prolific **2** very intellectually productive or inventive to a marked degree *USE* fml – **~ity** *n*

federal /ˈfedərəl/ *adj* **1** formed by agreement between political units that surrender their individual sovereignty to a central authority but retain limited powers of government; *also* of or constituting a government so formed **2** of or loyal to the federal government of the USA in the American Civil War

Federal *n* a supporter or soldier of the North in the American Civil War

federation /ˌfedəˈreɪʃən/ *n* sthg formed by federating: e g **a** a country formed by the federation of separate states **b** a union of organizations

fed up *adj* discontented, bored – infml

fee /fiː/ *n* **1** a sum of money paid esp for entrance or for a professional service **2** money paid for education – usu pl with sing. meaning

feeble /ˈfiːbəl/ *adj* **1** lacking in strength or endurance; weak **2** deficient in authority, force, or effect – **feebly** *adv* – **~ness** *n*

[1]**feed** /fiːd/ *v* **fed** **1a** to give food to **b** to give as food **2** to provide sthg essential to the growth, sustenance, maintenance, or operation of **3** to produce or provide food for **4** to supply for use, consumption, or processing, esp in a continuous manner

[2]**feed** *n* **1** an act of eating **2** (a mixture or preparation of) food for livestock **3** a mechanism by which the action of feeding is effected **4** one who supplies cues for another esp comic performer's lines or actions

feedback /ˈfiːdbæk/ *n* **1** the return to the input of a part of the output of a machine, system, or process **2** (the return to a source of) information about the results of an action or process, usu in response to a request

feeder /ˈfiːdəʳ/ *n* a device feeding material into or through a machine

feed up *v* to fatten by plentiful feeding

[1]**feel** /fiːl/ *v* **felt** **1a** to handle or touch in order to examine or explore **b** to perceive by a physical sensation coming from discrete end organs (e g of the skin or muscles) **2** to experience actively or passively; be affected by **3** to ascertain or explore by cautious trial – often + *out* **4a** to be aware of by instinct or by drawing conclusions from the evidence available **b** to believe, think **5** to have sympathy or pity *for*

[2]**feel** *n* **1** the sense of feeling; touch **2a** the quality of a thing as imparted through touch **b** typical or peculiar quality or atmosphere **3** intuitive skill, knowledge, or ability – usu + *for*

feeler /ˈfiːləʳ/ *n* **1** a tactile appendage (e g a tentacle) of an animal **2** sthg (e g a proposal) ventured to ascertain the views of others

feeling /ˈfiːlɪŋ/ *n* **1** (a sensation experienced through) the one of the 5 basic physical senses **2a** an emotional state or reaction **b** *pl* susceptibility to impression; sensibility **3** a conscious recognition; a sense **4a** an opinion or belief, esp when unreasoned **b** a presentiment **5** capacity to respond emotionally, esp with the higher emotions – **feeling** *adj*

feign /feɪn/ *v* to deliberately give a false appearance or impression of; *also* to pretend

[1]**feint** /feɪnt/ *n* a mock blow or attack directed away from the point one really intends to attack

[2]**feint** *adj, of rulings on paper* faint, pale

feldspar /ˈfeldspɑːʳ/ , **felspar** /ˈfelspɑːʳ/ *n* any of a group of minerals that are an essential constituent of nearly all crystalline rocks

felicitate /fɪ̈ˈlɪsɪ̈teɪt/ *v* to offer congratulations or compliments to – usu + *on* or *upon*; fml – **-tation** *n*

felicitous /fɪ̈ˈlɪsɪ̈təs/ *adj* **1** very well suited or expressed; apt; *also* marked by or given to such expression **2** pleasant, delightful *USE* fml – **~ly** *adv*

felicity /fɪ̈ˈlɪsɪ̈ti/ *n* **1** (sthg causing) great happiness **2** a felicitous faculty or quality, esp in art or language; aptness **3** a felicitous expression *USE* fml

feline /ˈfiːlaɪn/ *adj* **1** of cats or the cat family **2** resembling a cat; having the characteristics generally attributed to cats, esp grace, stealth, or slyness

[1]**fell** /fel/ *v* **1** to cut, beat, or knock down **2** to kill

[2]**fell** *past of* **fall**

[3]**fell** *n* a steep rugged stretch of high moorland, esp in northern England – often pl with sing. meaning

[4]**fell** *adj* **1** fierce, cruel **2** very destructive; deadly *USE* poetic

[1]**fellow** /'feləʊ/ *n* **1** a comrade, associate – usu pl **2a** an equal in rank, power, or character; a peer **b** either of a pair; a mate **3** a member of an incorporated literary or scientific society **4** a man; *also* a boy **5** an incorporated member of a collegiate foundation **6** a person appointed to a salaried position allowing for advanced research

[2]**fellow** *adj* being a companion or associate; belonging to the same group – used before a noun

fellow feeling *n* a feeling of mutual understanding; *specif* sympathy

fellowship /'feləʊʃɪp/ *n* **1** the condition of friendly relations between people; companionship **2a** community of interest, activity, feeling, or experience **b** the state of being a fellow or associate **3** *sing or pl in constr* a group of people with similar interests; an association **4** the position of a fellow (e g of a university)

fellow traveller *n* a nonmember who sympathizes with and often furthers the ideals and programme of an organized group, esp the Communist party – chiefly derog

felon /'felən/ *n* sby who has committed a felony

felony /'feləni/ *n* a grave crime (e g murder or arson) that was formerly regarded in law as more serious than a misdemeanour and involved forfeiture of property in addition to any other punishment – **-nious** *adj*

felspar /'felspɑːʳ/ *n* feldspar

[1]**felt** /felt/ *n* a nonwoven cloth made by compressing wool or fur often mixed with natural or synthetic fibres

[2]**felt** *v* **1** to make into or cover with felt **2** to cause to stick and mat together

[3]**felt** *past of* **feel**

[1]**female** /'fiːmeɪl/ *n* **1** an individual that bears young or produces eggs; *esp* a woman or girl as distinguished from a man or boy **2** a plant or flower with an ovary but no stamens – **female** *adj*

[2]**female** *adj* designed with a hole or hollow into which a corresponding male part fits

[1]**feminine** /'femɪ̣nɪ̣n/ *adj* **1** of or being a female person **2** characteristic of, appropriate to, or peculiar to women; womanly **3** of or belonging to the gender that normally includes most words or grammatical forms referring to females – **-nity** *n*

[2]**feminine** *n* **1** the feminine principle in human nature – esp in *eternal feminine* **2** (a word of) the feminine gender

feminism /'femɪ̣nɪzəm/ *n* the advocacy or pursuit of women's rights, interests, and equality with men in political, economic, and social spheres – **-ist** *n*

femme fatale /ˌfæm fæ'tɑːl/ *n, pl* **femmes fatales** a seductive and usu mysterious woman

femur /'fiːməʳ/ *n, pl* **femurs, femora** **1** the bone of the hind or lower limb nearest the body; the thighbone **2** the third segment of an insect's leg counting from the base – **femoral** *adj*

fen /fen/ *n* an area of low wet or flooded land

[1]**fence** /fens/ *n* **1** a barrier (e g of wire or boards) intended to prevent escape or intrusion or to mark a boundary **2** a receiver of stolen goods

[2]**fence** *v* **1a** to enclose with a fence – usu + *in* **b** to separate *off* or keep *out* (as if) with a fence **2a** to practise fencing **b** to use tactics of attack and defence (e g thrusting and parrying) resembling those of fencing **3** to receive or sell stolen goods

fencing /'fensɪŋ/ *n* **1** the art of attack and defence with a sword (e g the foil, épeé, or sabre) **2** (material used for building) fences

fender /'fendəʳ/ *n* a device that protects: e g **a** a cushion (e g of rope or wood) hung over the side of a ship to absorb impact **b** a low metal guard for a fire used to confine the coals

fend off *v* to keep or ward off; repel

fennel /'fenəl/ *n* a European plant of the carrot family cultivated for its aromatic seeds, bulbous root, and foliage

feral /'fɪərəl/ *adj* **1** (suggestive) of a wild beast; savage **2a** not domesticated or cultivated; wild **b** having escaped from domestication and become wild

[1]**ferment** /fəˈment/ *v* **1** to (cause to) undergo fermentation **2** to (cause to) be in a state of agitation or intense activity

[2]**ferment** /ˈfɜːment/ *n* a state of unrest or upheaval; agitation, tumult

fermentation /ˌfɜːmenˈteɪʃən/ *n* **1** a chemical change with effervescence **2** a transformation of an organic compound that is controlled by an enzyme (e g a carbohydrate to carbon dioxide and alcohol)

fern /fɜːn/ *n* any of a class of flowerless seedless lower plants; *esp* any of an order resembling flowering plants in having a root, stem, and leaflike fronds but differing in reproducing by spores – **ferny** *adj*

ferocious /fəˈrəʊʃəs/ *adj* extremely fierce or violent – **~ly** *adv* – **~ness** *n*

ferocity /fəˈrɒsʒti/ *n* the quality or state of being ferocious

[1]**ferret** /ˈferʒt/ *n* **1** a partially domesticated usu albino European polecat used esp for hunting small rodents (e g rats) **2** an active and persistent searcher

[2]**ferret** *v* **1** to hunt with ferrets **2** to search *about, around* or *out* – infml

ferrite /ˈferaɪt/ *n* any of several highly magnetic substances consisting mainly of an iron oxide

ferrous /ˈferəs/ *adj* of, containing, or being (bivalent) iron

ferrule /ˈferʊl/ *n* **1** a ring or cap, usu of metal, strengthening a cane, tool handle, etc **2** a short tube or bush for making a tight joint (e g between pipes)

[1]**ferry** /ˈferi/ *v* **1** to carry by boat over a body of water **2** to convey (e g by car) from one place to another

[2]**ferry** *n* (a boat used at) a place where people or things are carried across a body of water (e g a river)

fertile /ˈfɜːtaɪl/ *adj* **1a** (capable of) producing or bearing fruit (in great quantities); productive **b** characterized by great resourcefulness and activity; inventive **2a** capable of sustaining abundant plant growth **b** affording abundant possibilities for development **c** capable of breeding or reproducing – **-lity** *n* – **-lize** *v*

fertil·izer, -iser /ˈfɜːtʒlaɪzəʳ/ *n* a substance (e g manure) used to make soil more fertile

fervent /ˈfɜːvənt/ *adj* exhibiting deep sincere emotion; ardent – **-vency** *n* – **~ly** *adv*

fervid /ˈfɜːvʒd/ *adj* passionately intense; ardent – **~ly** *adv*

fervour, *NAm chiefly* **fervor** /ˈfɜːvəʳ/ *n* the quality or state of being fervent or fervid

fester /ˈfestəʳ/ *v* **1** to generate pus **2** to putrefy, rot **3** to rankle

[1]**festival** /ˈfestʒvəl/ *adj* of, appropriate to, or set apart as a festival

[2]**festival** *n* **1a** a time marked by special (e g customary) celebration **b** a religious feast **2** a usu periodic programme or season of cultural events or entertainment **3** gaiety, conviviality

festive /ˈfestɪv/ *adj* **1** of or suitable for a feast or festival **2** joyous, gay

festivity /feˈstɪvʒti/ *n* festive activity – often pl with sing. meaning

[1]**festoon** /feˈstuːn/ *n* a decorative chain or strip hanging between 2 points; *also* a carved, moulded, or painted ornament representing this

[2]**festoon** *v* **1** to hang or form festoons on **2** to cover profusely and usu gaily

fetch /fetʃ/ *v* **1** to go or come after and bring or take back **2a** to cause to come; bring **b** to produce as profit or return; realize **3** to reach by sailing, esp against the wind or tide and without having to tack **4** to strike or deal (a blow, slap, etc) – infml

fetch up *v* to come to a specified standstill, stopping place, or result; arrive

[1]**fete, fête** /feɪt/ *n* **1** a festival **2** *Br* a usu outdoor bazaar or other entertainment held esp to raise money for a particular purpose

[2]**fete, fête** *v* to honour or commemorate (sby or sthg) with a fete or other ceremony

fetid, foetid /ˈfiːtʒd/ *adj* having a heavy offensive smell; stinking

fetish /ˈfetɪʃ, ˈfiː-/ *n* **1** an object believed among a primitive people to have magical power **2** an object of irrational reverence or obsessive devotion **3** an object or bodily part whose presence in reality or fantasy is psychologically necessary for sexual gratification

fetishism /'fetɪʃɪzəm/ *n* **1** belief in magical fetishes **2** the displacement of erotic interest and satisfaction to a fetish – **-ist** *n*

fetlock /'fetlɒk/ *n* **1** a projection bearing a tuft of hair on the back of the leg above the hoof of an animal of the horse family **2** the joint of the limb or tuft of hair at the fetlock

[1]**fetter** /'fetəʳ/ *n* **1** a shackle for the feet **2** sthg that confines; a restraint – usu pl with sing. meaning

[2]**fetter** *v* **1** to put fetters on **2** to bind (as if) with fetters; shackle, restrain

fettle /'fetl/ *n* a state of physical or mental fitness or order; condition

feud /fjuːd/ *n* a lasting state of hostilities, esp between families or clans, marked by violent attacks for the purpose of revenge – **feud** *v*

feudal /'fjuːdl/ *adj* of or resembling the system of social relations (e g lord to vassal) characteristic of the Middle Ages – **~ism** *n*

fever /'fiːvəʳ/ *n* **1** a rise of body temperature above the normal; *also* a disease marked by this **2a** a state of intense emotion or activity **b** a contagious usu transient enthusiasm; a craze

feverish /'fiːvərɪʃ/ *also* **feverous** *adj* **1a** having the symptoms of a fever **b** indicating, relating to, or caused by (a) fever **2** marked by intense emotion, activity, or instability

[1]**few** /fjuː/ *adj* **1** amounting to only a small number (e g one of his *few* pleasures) **2** at least some though not many – + *a* (e g caught a *few* more fish)

[2]**few** *n pl in constr* **1** not many (e g *few* of his stories were true) **2** at least some though not many – + *a* (e g a *few* of them) **3** a select or exclusive group of people; an élite

fey /feɪ/ *adj* **1** marked by an otherworldly and irresponsible air **2** *chiefly Scot* **a** fated to die; doomed **b** marked by an excited or elated state

fez /fez/ *n, pl* **-zz-** *also* **-z-** a brimless hat shaped like a truncated cone, usu red and with a tassel, which is worn by men in southern and eastern Mediterranean countries

fiancé, *fem* **fiancée** /fi'ɒnseɪ/ *n* sby engaged to be married

fiasco /fi'æskəʊ/ *n* a complete and ignominious failure

fiat /'faɪæt, 'fiːæt/ *n* an authoritative and often arbitrary order; a decree

fib /fɪb/ *v or n* (to tell) a trivial or childish lie – infml – **~ber** *n*

fibre, *NAm chiefly* **fiber** /'faɪbəʳ/ *n* **1** a slender natural or man-made thread or filament (e g of wool, cotton, or asbestos) **2** material made of fibres **3** essential structure or character; *also* strength, fortitude

fibreglass /'faɪbəglɑːs/ *n* **1** glass in fibrous form used in making various products (e g textiles and insulation materials) **2** a combination of synthetic resins and fibreglass

fibrous /'faɪbrəs/ *adj* **1a** containing, consisting of, or resembling fibres **b** capable of being separated into fibres **2** tough, stringy

fibula /'fɪbjʊlə/ *n, pl* **fibulae, fibulas** the (smaller) outer of the 2 bones of the hind limb of higher vertebrates between the knee and ankle

fickle /'fɪkəl/ *adj* lacking steadfastness or constancy; capricious – **~ness** *n*

fiction /'fɪkʃən/ *n* **1** an invented story **2** literature (e g novels or short stories) describing imaginary people and events – **~al** *adj* – **~alize** *v* – **~alization** *n*

fictitious /fɪk'tɪʃəs/ *adj* **1** (characteristic) of fiction **2** *of a name* false, assumed **3** not genuinely felt; feigned – **~ly** *adv* – **~ness** *n*

[1]**fiddle** /'fɪdl/ *n* **1** a violin **2** a device to keep objects from sliding off a table on board ship **3** a dishonest practice; a swindle – infml **4** an activity involving intricate manipulation – infml

[2]**fiddle** *v* **1** to play on a fiddle **2a** to move the hands or fingers restlessly **b** to spend time in aimless or fruitless activity – often + *about* or *around* **3** to falsify (e g accounts), esp so as to gain financial advantage **4** to get or contrive by cheating or deception – **~r** *n*

fiddle-faddle /'fɪdl ˌfædl/ *n* nonsense – often used as an interjection; infml

fiddlesticks /'fɪdlˌstɪks/ *n pl* nonsense – used as an interjection; infml

fiddling /'fɪdlɪŋ/ *adj* trifling, petty

fidelity /fɪ'delɪ̈ti/ *n* **1a** the quality or state of being faithful; loyalty **b** accuracy in details; exactness **2** the degree of similarity between some reproduced (e g recorded) material and its original source

[1]**fidget** /'fɪdʒɪ̈t/ *n* **1** uneasiness or restlessness shown by nervous movements – usu pl with sing. meaning **2** sby who fidgets *USE* infml

[2]**fidget** *v* to move or act restlessly or nervously –~**y** *adj*

fief /fiːf/ *n* **1** a feudal estate **2** sthg over which one has rights or exercises control

[1]**field** /fiːld/ *n* **1a** an (enclosed) area of land free of woods and buildings (used for cultivation or pasture) **b** an area of land containing a natural resource **c** (the place where) a battle is fought; *also* a battle **2a** an area or division of an activity **b** the sphere of practical operation outside a place of work (e g a laboratory) **c** an area in which troops are operating (e g in an exercise or theatre of war) **3** the participants in a sports activity, esp with the exception of the favourite or winner **4** a region or space in which a given effect (e g magnetism) exists **5** *also* **field of view** the area visible through the lens of an optical instrument

[2]**field** *v* **1a** to stop and pick up a hit ball **b** to deal with by giving an impromptu answer **2** to put into the field of play or battle

field day *n* a day for military exercises or manoeuvres

fielder /'fiːldəʳ/ *n* any of the players whose job is to field the ball (e g in cricket)

field event *n* an athletic event (e g discus, javelin, or jumping) other than a race

field glasses *n pl* an optical instrument usu consisting of 2 telescopes on a single frame with a focussing device

field marshal *n* the top-ranking officer in the British army

fieldwork /'fiːldwɜːk/ *n* **1** a temporary fortification **2** work done in the field (e g by students) to gain practical experience through firsthand observation **3** the gathering of data in anthropology, sociology, etc through the observation or interviewing of subjects in the field

fiend /fiːnd/ *n* **1a** *the* devil **b** a demon **c** a person of great wickedness or cruelty **2** sby excessively devoted to a specified activity or thing; a fanatic, devotee

fiendish /'fiːndɪʃ/ *adj* **1** perversely diabolical **2** extremely cruel or wicked **3** excessively bad, unpleasant, or difficult – ~**ness** *n* – ~**ly** *adv*

fierce /fɪəs/ *adj* **1** violently hostile or aggressive; combative, pugnacious **2a** lacking restraint or control; violent, heated **b** extremely intense or severe **3** furiously active or determined **4** wild or menacing in appearance – ~**ly** *adv* – ~**ness** *n*

fiery /'faɪəri/ *adj* **1a** consisting of fire **b** burning, blazing **2** very hot **3** of the colour of fire; *esp* red **4a** full of or exuding strong emotion or spirit; passionate **b** easily provoked; irascible

fiesta /fi'estə/ *n* a saint's day in Spain and Latin America, often celebrated with processions and dances

fife /faɪf/ *n* a small flute used chiefly to accompany the drum

fifteen /fɪf'tiːn/ *n* **1** the number 15 **2** the fifteenth in a set or series **3** *sing or pl in constr* sthg having 15 parts or members or a denomination of 15; *esp* a Rugby Union football team – ~**th** *adj, n, pron, adv*

15 *n or adj* (a film that is) certified in Britain as suitable for people of 15 or over

fifth /fɪfθ, fɪθ/ *n* **1** number five in a countable series **2** (the combination of 2 notes at) a musical interval of 5 diatonic degrees – **fifth** *adj* – **ly** *adv*

fifth column *n* a group within a nation or faction that sympathizes with and works secretly for an enemy or rival – ~**ist** *n*

fifty /'fɪfti/ *n* **1** the number 50 **2** *pl* the numbers 50 to 59; *specif* a range of temperatures, ages, or dates within a century characterized by those numbers – **-tieth** *adj, n, pron, adv*

[1]**fifty-fifty** *adv* evenly, equally

[2]**fifty-fifty** *adj* half favourable and half unfavourable; even

[1]**fig** /fɪg/ *n* **1** (any of a genus of trees that bear) a many-seeded fleshy usu

pear-shaped or oblong edible fruit **2** a contemptibly worthless trifle

[2]**fig** *n* dress, array

[1]**fight** /faɪt/ *v* **fought** **1a** to contend in battle or physical combat **b** to attempt to prevent the success, effectiveness, or development of **2** to stand as a candidate for (e g a constituency) in an election **3** to struggle to endure or surmount **4** to resolve or control by fighting – + *out* or *down*

[2]**fight** *n* **1a** a battle, combat **b** a boxing match **c** an argument **2** a usu protracted struggle for an objective **3** strength or disposition for fighting; pugnacity

fighter /'faɪtəʳ/ *n* **1** a pugnacious or boldly determined individual **2** a fast manoeuvrable aeroplane designed to destroy enemy aircraft

figment /'fɪgmənt/ *n* sthg fabricated or imagined

figurative /'fɪgjʊrətɪv, -gə-/ *adj* **1a** representing by a figure or likeness **b** representational **2** characterized by or using figures of speech, esp metaphor – ~ly *adv*

[1]**figure** /'fɪgəʳ/ *n* **1a** an (Arabic) number symbol **b** *pl* arithmetical calculations **c** value, esp as expressed in numbers **2** bodily shape or form, esp of a person **3** a diagram or pictorial illustration **4** an intentional deviation from the usual form or syntactic relation of words **5** an often repetitive pattern in a manufactured article (e g cloth) or natural substance (e g wood) **6a** a series of movements in a dance **b** an outline representation of a form traced by a series of evolutions (e g by a skater on an ice surface) **7** a personage, personality **8** a short musical phrase

[2]**figure** *v* **1** to decorate with a pattern **2** to take an esp important or conspicuous part – often + *in* **3** to seem reasonable or expected – infml; esp in *that figures* **4a** *chiefly NAm* to conclude, decide **b** *chiefly NAm* to regard, consider

figured /'fɪgəd/ *adj* **1** represented, portrayed **2** adorned with or formed into a figure

figurehead /'fɪgəhed/ *n* **1** an ornamental carved figure on a ship's bow **2** a head or chief in name only

figure of speech *n* a form of expression (e g a hyperbole or metaphor) used to convey meaning or heighten effect

figure out *v* **1** to discover, determine **2** to solve, fathom

figurine /,fɪgjʊ'riːn/ *n* an ornament in the form of a small figure or statue

filament /'fɪləmənt/ *n* a single thread or a thin flexible threadlike object or part: e g **a** a slender conductor (e g in an electric light bulb) made incandescent by the passage of an electric current **b** the anther-bearing stalk of a stamen

filch /fɪltʃ/ *v* to steal (sthg of small value); pilfer

[1]**file** /faɪl/ *n* a tool, usu of hardened steel, with many cutting ridges for shaping or smoothing objects or surfaces

[2]**file** *v* to rub, smooth, or cut away (as if) with a file

[3]**file** *v* **1** to arrange in order (e g alphabetically) for preservation and reference **2** to submit or record officially

[4]**file** *n* **1** a folder, cabinet, etc in which papers are kept in order **2** a collection of papers or publications on a subject, usu arranged or classified

[5]**file** *n* **1** a row of people, animals, or things arranged one behind the other **2** any of the rows of squares that extend across a chessboard from white's side to black's side

[6]**file** *v* to march or proceed in file

filial /'fɪlɪəl/ *adj* **1** of or befitting a son or daughter, esp in his/her relationship to a parent **2** having or assuming the relation of a child or offspring

filibuster /'fɪlɪ̣bʌstəʳ/ *v or n, chiefly NAm* (to engage in) the use of extreme delaying tactics in a legislative assembly

filigree /'fɪlɪ̣griː/ *v or n* (to decorate with) **a** ornamental openwork of delicate or intricate design **b** a pattern or design resembling such openwork

[1]**fill** /fɪl/ *v* **1a** to put into as much as can be held or conveniently contained **b** to supply with a full complement **c** to repair the cavities of (a tooth) **d** to stop up; obstruct, plug **2a** to feed, satiate **b** to satisfy, fulfil **3a** to occupy the whole of **b** to spread through **4** to

possess and perform the duties of; hold

[2]**fill** *n* **1** as much as one can eat or drink **2** as much as one can bear

[1]**fillet,** *chiefly NAm* **filet** /ˈfɪlɪ̣t, ˈfɪleɪ, fɪˈleɪ/ *n* **1** a ribbon or narrow strip of material used esp as a headband **2a** a fleshy boneless piece of meat cut from the hind loin or upper hind leg **b** a long slice of boneless fish **3a** a junction in which the interior angle is rounded off or partly filled in **b** a usu triangular piece that partly fills such an interior

[2]**fillet** *v* **1a** to cut (meat or fish) into fillets **b** to remove the bones from (esp fish) **2** to remove inessential parts from

fill in *v* **1** to give necessary or recently acquired information to **2** to add what is necessary to complete **3** to take sby's place, usu temporarily; substitute

filling /ˈfɪlɪŋ/ *n* **1** sthg used to fill a cavity, container, or depression **2** a food mixture used to fill cakes, sandwiches, etc

filling station *n* a retail establishment for selling fuel, oil, etc to motorists

[1]**fillip** /ˈfɪlɪ̣p/ *n* sthg that arouses or boosts; a stimulus

[2]**fillip** *v* to stimulate

fill out *v* to put on flesh

filly /ˈfɪli/ *n* **1** a young female horse, usu of less than 4 years **2** a young woman; a girl – infml

[1]**film** /fɪlm/ *n* **1a** a thin skin or membranous covering **b** an abnormal growth on or in the eye **2a** a thin layer or covering **b** a roll or strip of cellulose acetate or cellulose nitrate coated with a light-sensitive emulsion for taking photographs **3a** a series of pictures recorded on film for the cinema and projected rapidly onto a screen so as to create the illusion of movement **b** a representation (e g of an incident or story) on film **c** cinema – often pl with sing. meaning

[2]**film** *v* to make a film of or from

filmstrip /ˈfɪlm,strɪp/ *n* a strip of film containing photographs, diagrams, or graphic matter for still projection

[1]**filter** /ˈfɪltəʳ/ *n* **1** a porous article or mass (e g of paper, sand, etc) through which a gas or liquid is passed to separate out matter in suspension **2** an apparatus containing a filter medium

[2]**filter** *v* **1** to remove by means of a filter **2** to move gradually **3** to become known over a period of time **4** *Br, of traffic* to turn left or right in the direction of the green arrow while the main lights are still red

filter tip *n* (a cigar or cigarette with) a tip of porous material that filters the smoke before it enters the smoker's mouth – **filter-tipped** *adj*

filth /fɪlθ/ *n* **1** foul or putrid matter, esp dirt or refuse **2** sthg loathsome or vile; *esp* obscene or pornographic material – **~y** *adj* – **~ily** *adv* – **~iness** *n*

fin /fɪn/ *n* **1** an external membranous part of an aquatic animal (e g a fish or whale) used in propelling or guiding the body **2a** an appendage of a boat (e g a submarine) **b** a vertical control surface attached to an aircraft for directional stability

[1]**final** /ˈfaɪnəl/ *adj* **1** not to be altered or undone; conclusive **2** being the last; occurring at the end **3** of or relating to the ultimate purpose or result of a process – **~ize** *v* – **~ly** *adv*

[2]**final** *n* **1** a deciding match, game, trial, etc in a sport or competition; *also, pl* a round made up of these **2** the last examination in a course – usu pl

finalist /ˈfaɪnəl-ɪ̣st/ *n* a contestant in the finals of a competition

finality /faɪˈnælɪ̣ti, fɪ-/ *n* **1** the condition of being at an ultimate point, esp of development or authority **2** a fundamental fact, action, or belief

[1]**finance** /ˈfaɪnæns, fɪ̣ˈnæns/ *n* **1** *pl* resources of money **2** the system that includes the circulation of money and involves banking, credit, and investment **3** the science of the management of funds **4** the obtaining of funds – **-cial** *adj* – **-cially** *adv*

[2]**finance** *v* to raise or provide money for

financier /fɪ̣ˈnænsɪəʳ, faɪˈnæn-/ *n* one skilled in dealing with finance or investment

finch /fɪntʃ/ *n* any of numerous songbirds with a short stout beak adapted for crushing seeds

[1]**find** /faɪnd/ *v* **found** **1a** to come upon, esp accidentally; encounter **b** to meet with (a specified reception) **2a** to come upon or discover by searching, effort, or experiment; obtain **b** to obtain by effort or management **3a** to experience, feel **b** to perceive (oneself) to be in a specified place or condition **c** to gain or regain the use or power of **d** to bring (oneself) to a realization of one's powers or of one's true vocation **4** to provide, supply **5** to determine and announce

[2]**find** *n* **1** an act or instance of finding sthg, esp sthg valuable **2** sby or sthg found; *esp* a valuable object or talented person discovered

fin de siècle /ˌfæn də 'sjeklə/ *adj* (characteristic) of the close of the 19th c and esp its literary and artistic climate of sophisticated decadence and world-weariness

finding /'faɪndɪŋ/ *n* **1** the result of a judicial inquiry **2** the result of an investigation – usu pl with sing. meaning

find out *v* **1** to learn by study, observation, or search; discover **2a** to detect in an offence **b** to ascertain the true character or identity of; unmask

[1]**fine** /faɪn/ *n* **1** a sum payable as punishment for an offence **2** a forfeiture or penalty paid to an injured party in a civil action

[2]**fine** *v* to punish by a fine – **finable, fineable** *adj*

[3]**fine** *adj* **1** free from impurity **2a** very thin in gauge or texture **b** consisting of relatively small particles **c** very small **d** keen, sharp **3a** subtle or sensitive in perception or discrimination **b** performed with extreme care and accuracy **4a** superior in quality, conception, or appearance; excellent **b** bright and sunny **5** marked by or affecting often excessive elegance or refinement **6** very well **7** awful – used as an intensive – **~ly** *adv* – **~ness** *n*

[4]**fine** *v* **1** to purify, clarify – often + *down* **2** to make finer in quality or size – often + *down*

finery /'faɪnəri/ *n* dressy or showy clothing and jewels

fines herbes /ˌfiːn 'eəb/ *n pl* a mixture of finely chopped herbs used esp as a seasoning

[1]**finesse** /fɨ'nes/ *n* **1** skilful handling of a situation; adroitness **2** the withholding of one's highest card in the hope that a lower card will take the trick because the only opposing higher card is in the hand of an opponent who has already played

[2]**finesse** *v* to make a finesse in playing cards

[1]**finger** /'fɪŋgəʳ/ *n* **1** any of the 5 parts at the end of the hand or forelimb; *esp* one other than the thumb **2a** sthg that resembles a finger, esp in being long, narrow, and often tapering in shape **b** a part of a glove into which a finger is inserted

[2]**finger** *v* **1** to play (a musical instrument) with the fingers **2** to touch or feel with the fingers; handle

fingerboard /'fɪŋgəbɔːd/ *n* the part of a stringed instrument against which the fingers press the strings to vary the pitch

fingering /'fɪŋgərɪŋ/ *n* (the marking indicating) the use or position of the fingers in sounding notes on an instrument

fingerplate /'fɪŋgəpleɪt/ *n* a protective plate fastened to a door usu near the handle to protect the door surface from finger marks

fingerprint /'fɪŋgəˌprɪnt/ *n* **1** the impression of a fingertip on any surface; *esp* an ink impression of the lines upon the fingertip taken for purposes of identification **2** unique distinguishing characteristics (e g of a recording machine or infrared spectrum)

fingerstall /'fɪŋgəstɔːl/ *n* a protective cover for an injured finger

fingertip /'fɪŋgəˌtɪp/ *adj* readily accessible; being in close proximity

finicky /'fɪnɪki/ *adj* **1** excessively exacting or meticulous in taste or standards; fussy **2** requiring delicate attention to detail

finis /'fɪnɨs/ *n* the end, conclusion – used esp to mark the end of a book or film

[1]**finish** /'fɪnɪʃ/ *v* **1a** to end, terminate; *also* to end a relationship *with* **b** to

eat, drink, or use entirely – often + *off* or *up* **2a** to bring to completion or issue; complete, perfect – often + *off* **b** to complete the schooling of (a girl), esp in the social graces **3a** to bring to an end the significance or effectiveness of **b** to bring about the death of **4** to arrive, end, or come to rest in a specified position or manner – often + *up*

[2]**finish** *n* **1a** the final stage; the end **b** the cause of one's ruin; downfall **2** the texture or appearance of a surface, esp after a coating has been applied **3** the result or product of a finishing process **4** the quality or state of being perfected, esp in the social graces

finishing school *n* a private school for girls that prepares its students esp for social activities

finite /'faınaıt/ *adj* **1a** having definite or definable limits **b** subject to limitations, esp those imposed by the laws of nature **2** completely determinable in theory or in fact by counting, measurement, or thought – **~ly** *adv*

finnan haddock /,fınən 'hædək/ *n* a haddock that is split and smoked until pale yellow

[1]**Finnish** /'fınıʃ/ *adj* (characteristic) of Finland

[2]**Finnish** *n* a Finno-Ugric language of Finland, Karelia, and parts of Sweden and Norway

fiord, fjord /'fiːɔːd, fjɔːd/ *n* a narrow inlet of the sea between cliffs (e g in Norway)

fir /fɜːʳ/ *n* (the wood of) any of various related evergreen trees of the pine family that have flattish leaves and erect cones

[1]**fire** /faıəʳ/ *n* **1a** the phenomenon of combustion manifested in light, flame, and heat **b(1)** burning passion or emotion **(2)** inspiration **2** fuel in a state of combustion (e g in a fireplace or furnace) **3a** a destructive burning (e g of a building or forest) **b** a severe trial or ordeal **4** brilliance, luminosity **5** the discharge of firearms **6** *Br* a small usu gas or electric domestic heater

[2]**fire** *v* **1a** to ignite **b(1)** to inspire **(2)** to inflame **2** to dismiss from a position **3** to discharge a firearm

firearm /'faıərɑːm/ *n* a weapon from which a shot is discharged by gunpowder – usu used only with reference to small arms

fireball /'faıəbɔːl/ *n* **1** a large brilliant meteor **2** ball lightning **3** a highly energetic person – infml

firebrand /'faıəbrænd/ *n* **1** a piece of burning material, esp wood **2** one who creates unrest or strife; an agitator, troublemaker

firebreak /'faıəbreık/ *n* a strip of cleared or unplanted land intended to check a forest or grass fire

firebrick /'faıə,brık/ *n* a brick that is resistant to high temperatures and is used in furnaces, fireplaces, etc

fire brigade *n* an organization for preventing or extinguishing fires; *esp* one maintained in Britain by local government

firebug /'faıəbʌg/ *n* a pyromaniac, fire-raiser – infml

fireclay /'faıəkleı/ *n* clay that is resistant to high temperatures and is used esp for firebricks and crucibles

firedamp /'faıədæmp/ *n* (the explosive mixture of air with) a combustible mine gas that consists chiefly of methane

firedog /'faıədɒg/ *n* either of a pair of metal stands used on a hearth to support burning wood

firefly /'faıəflaı/ *n* any of various night-flying beetles that produce a bright intermittent light

fireguard /'faıəgɑːd/ *n* a protective metal framework placed in front of an open fire

fire irons *n pl* utensils (e g tongs, poker, and shovel) for tending a household fire

firelight /'faıəlaıt/ *n* the light of a fire, esp of one in a fireplace

fire lighter *n* a piece of inflammable material used to help light a fire (e g in a grate)

fireman /'faıəmən/ *n, pl* **firemen** **1** sby employed to extinguish fires **2** sby who tends or feeds fires or furnaces

fireplace /'faıəpleıs/ *n* a usu framed opening made in a chimney to hold a fire; a hearth

fireproof /'faıəpruːf/ *v or adj* (to make) proof against or resistant to fire; *also* heatproof

fire-raising *n, Br* arson – **fire-raiser** *n*

fireside /'faɪəsaɪd/ *n* **1** a place near the fire or hearth **2** home

fire station *n* a building housing fire apparatus and usu firemen

fire storm *n* a huge uncontrollable fire that is started typically by bombs and that causes and is kept in being by the high winds that it sucks into itself

firetrap /'faɪətræp/ *n* a building difficult to escape from in case of fire

fire-watcher *n* sby who watches for the outbreak of fire (e g during an air raid)

firewater /'faɪəwɔːtəʳ/ *n* strong alcoholic drink – infml

firework /'faɪəwɜːk/ *n* **1** a device for producing a striking display (e g of light or noise) by the combustion of explosive or inflammable mixtures **2** *pl* **a** a display of temper or intense conflict **b** pyrotechnics

firing line *n* the forefront of an activity, esp one involving risk or difficulty – esp in *in the firing line*

firing squad /'faɪərɪŋ skwɒd/ *n* a detachment detailed to fire a salute at a military burial or carry out an execution

firkin /'fɜːkɪn/ *n* a small wooden vessel or cask of usu 9 gall capacity

[1]**firm** /fɜːm/ *adj* **1a** securely or solidly fixed in place **b** not weak or uncertain; vigorous **c** having a solid or compact structure that resists stress or pressure **2** not subject to change, unsteadiness, or disturbance; steadfast **3** indicating firmness or resolution – **~ly** *adv* – **~ness** *n*

[2]**firm** *v* **1** to make solid, compact, or firm **2** to put into final form; settle **3** to support, strengthen *USE* often + *up*

[3]**firm** *n* a business partnership not usu recognized as a legal person distinct from the members composing it; *broadly* any business unit or enterprise

firmament /'fɜːməmənt/ *n* the vault or arch of the sky; the heavens

[1]**first** /fɜːst/ *adj* **1** preceding all others in time, order, or importance: e g **a** earliest **b** being the lowest forward gear or speed of a motor vehicle **c** relating to or having the (most prominent and) usu highest part among a group of instruments or voices **2** least, slightest (e g hasn't the *first* idea what to do)

[2]**first** *adv* **1** before anything else; at the beginning **2** for the first time **3** in preference to sthg else

[3]**first** *n* sthg or sby that is first: e g **a** the first occurrence or item of a kind **b** the first and lowest forward gear or speed of a motor vehicle **c** the winning place in a contest **d first, first class** *often cap* the highest level of an honours degree

first aid *n* emergency care or treatment given to an ill or injured person before proper medical aid can be obtained

firstborn /'fɜːstbɔːn/ *adj* born before all others; eldest

first class *n* the first or highest group in a classification: e g **a** the highest of usu 3 classes of travel accommodation **b** the highest level of an honours degree – **first-class** *adj*

firstfruits /ˌfɜːst'fruːts/ *n pl* **1** agricultural produce offered to God in thanksgiving **2** the earliest products or results of an enterprise

firsthand /ˌfɜːst'hænd/ *adj* of or coming directly from the original source

firstly /'fɜːstli/ *adv* in the first place; first

first person *n* (a member of) a set of linguistic forms (e g verb forms and pronouns) referring to the speaker or writer of the utterance in which they occur

first-rate *adj* of the first or greatest order of size, importance, or quality

[1]**fiscal** /'fɪskəl/ *adj* of taxation, public revenues, or public debt

[2]**fiscal** *n* a procurator-fiscal

[1]**fish** /fɪʃ/ *n, pl* **fish, fishes 1a** an aquatic animal – usu in combination **b** (the edible flesh of) any of numerous cold-blooded aquatic vertebrates that typically have gills and an elongated scaly body **2** a person; *esp* a fellow – usu derog

[2]**fish** *v* **1** to try to catch fish **2** to seek sthg by roundabout means **3a** to search for sthg underwater **b** to search (as if) by groping or feeling

[3]**fish** *n* a piece of wood or iron fastened alongside another member to strengthen it

fisherman /ˈfɪʃəmən/ *n* **1** *fem* **fisherwoman** one who engages in fishing as an occupation or for pleasure **2** a ship used in commercial fishing

fishery /ˈfɪʃəri/ *n* **1** the activity or business of catching fish and other sea animals **2** a place or establishment for catching fish and other sea animals

fish finger *n* a small oblong of fish coated with breadcrumbs

fishing /ˈfɪʃɪŋ/ *n* the sport or business of or a place for catching fish

fishmonger /ˈfɪʃmʌŋgəʳ/ *n, chiefly Br* a retail fish dealer

fish slice *n* **1** a broad-bladed knife for cutting and serving fish at table **2** a kitchen implement with a broad blade and long handle used esp for turning or lifting food in frying

fishwife /ˈfɪʃwaɪf/ *n* **1** a woman who sells or guts fish **2** a vulgar abusive woman

fishy /ˈfɪʃi/ *adj* **1** of or like fish, esp in taste or smell **2** creating doubt or suspicion; questionable – infml

fission /ˈfɪʃən/ *n* **1** a splitting or breaking up into parts **2** reproduction by spontaneous division into 2 or more parts each of which grows into a complete organism **3** the splitting of an atomic nucleus with the release of large amounts of energy

fissure /ˈfɪʃəʳ/ *n* a narrow, long, and deep opening, usu caused by breaking or parting

fist /fɪst/ *n* the hand clenched with the fingers doubled into the palm and the thumb across the fingers

fisticuffs /ˈfɪstɪkʌfs/ *n pl* the act or practice of fighting with the fists – no longer in vogue; humor

¹fit /fɪt/ *n* **1a** a sudden violent attack of a disease (e g epilepsy), esp when marked by convulsions or unconsciousness **b** a sudden but transient attack of a specified physical disturbance **2** a sudden outburst or flurry, esp of a specified activity or emotion

²fit *adj* **1a** adapted or suited to an end or purpose **b** acceptable from a particular viewpoint (e g of competence, morality, or qualifications) **2a** in a suitable state; ready **b** in such a distressing state as to be ready to do or suffer sthg specified **3** healthy – ~**ness** *n*

³fit *v* **fitted** *also* **fit** **1** to be suitable for or to; harmonize with **2a** to be of the correct size or shape for **b** to insert or adjust until correctly in place **c** to try on (clothes) in order to make adjustments in size **d** to make a place or room for **3** to be in agreement or accord with **4** to cause to conform to or suit sthg **5** to supply, equip –often + *out*

⁴fit *n* **1** the manner in which clothing fits the wearer **2** the degree of closeness with which surfaces are brought together in an assembly of parts

fitful /ˈfɪtfəl/ *adj* having a spasmodic or intermittent character; irregular – ~**ly** *adv*

fitment /ˈfɪtmənt/ *n* **1** a piece of equipment; *esp* an item of built-in furniture **2** *pl* fittings

fitter /ˈfɪtəʳ/ *n* sby who assembles or repairs machinery or appliances

¹fitting /ˈfɪtɪŋ/ *adj* appropriate to the situation

²fitting *n* **1** a trying on of clothes which are in the process of being made or altered **2** a small often standardized part

fit up *v* **1** to fix up **2** *Br* to frame (e g for a crime) – slang

five /faɪv/ *n* **1** the number 5 **2** the fifth in a set or series **3** sthg having 5 parts or members or a denomination of 5 **4** *pl but sing in constr* any of several games in which players hit a ball with their hands against the front wall of a 3- or 4-walled court

five o'clock shadow *n* a just visible beard-growth

fiver /ˈfaɪvəʳ/ *n* a £5 or $5 note; *also* the sum of £5 – infml

¹fix /fɪks/ *v* **1a** to make firm, stable, or stationary **b(1)** to kill, harden, and preserve for microscopic study **(2)** to make the image of (a photographic film) permanent by removing unused sensitive chemicals **c** to fasten, attach **2** to hold or direct steadily **3a** to set or place definitely; establish **b** to assign **4** to set in order; adjust **5** to repair, mend **6** *chiefly NAm* to get ready or prepare (esp food or drink) **7a** to get even with – infml **b** to influence by illicit means – infml

²fix *n* **1** a position of difficulty or embarrassment; a trying predicament

2 (a determination of) the position (e g of a ship) found by bearings, radio, etc **3** a shot of a narcotic – slang

fixation /fɪk'seɪʃən/ *n* an (obsessive or unhealthy) attachment or preoccupation

fixative /'fɪksətɪv/ *n* sthg that fixes or sets: e g **a** a substance added to a perfume, esp to prevent too rapid evaporation **b** a varnish used esp to protect crayon drawings **c** a substance used to fix living tissue

fixed /fɪkst/ *adj* **1a** securely placed or fastened; stationary **b** not subject to or capable of change or fluctuation **c** intent **2** supplied with sthg needed or desirable (e g money) – infml

fixed star *n* any of the stars so distant that they appear to remain fixed relative to one another

fixity /'fɪksɪ̵ti/ *n* the quality or state of being fixed or stable

fixture /'fɪkstʃə^r/ *n* **1** fixing or being fixed **2** sthg fixed (e g to a building) as a permanent appendage or as a structural part **3** (an esp sporting event held on) a settled date or time

fix up *v* to provide *with*; make the arrangements for – infml

¹fizz /fɪz/ *v* to make a hissing or sputtering sound

²fizz *n* **1a** a fizzing sound **b** spirit, liveliness **2** an effervescent beverage (e g champagne) – infml – **~y** *adj*

fizzle /'fɪzəl/ *v or n* (to make) a weak fizzing sound

fizzle out *v* to fail or end feebly, esp after a promising start – infml

fjord /'fiːɔːd, fjɔːd/ *n* a fiord

flabbergast /'flæbəgɑːst/ *v* to overwhelm with shock or astonishment – infml

flabby /'flæbi/ *adj* **1** (having flesh) lacking resilience or firmness **2** ineffective, feeble – **-bily** *adv* – **-biness** *n*

flaccid /'flæksɪ̵d/ *adj* **1a** lacking normal or youthful firmness; flabby **b** limp **2** lacking vigour or force – **~ity** *n*

¹flag /flæg/ *n* a (wild) iris or similar plant of damp ground with long leaves

²flag *n* a (slab of) hard evenly stratified stone that splits into flat pieces suitable for paving – **flag** *v*

³flag *n* **1** a usu rectangular piece of fabric of distinctive design that is used as a symbol (e g of a nation) or as a signalling device **2** the nationality of registration of a ship, aircraft, etc

⁴flag *v* **1** to put a flag on (e g for identification) **2a** to signal to (as if) with a flag **b** to signal to stop – usu + *down*

⁵flag *v* to become feeble, less interesting, or less active; decline

¹flagellate /'flædʒɪ̵leɪt/ *v* to whip or flog, esp as a religious punishment or for sexual gratification – **-lation** *n*

²flagellate /'flædʒɪ̵lət/, **flagellated** *adj* **1** having flagella **2** shaped like a flagellum

flagellum /flə'dʒeləm/ *n, pl* **flagella** /-lə/ *also* **flagellums** any of various elongated filament-shaped appendages of plants or animals; *esp* one that projects singly or in groups and powers the motion of a microorganism

¹flageolet /ˌflædʒə'let/ *n* a small flute

²flageolet *n* a French bean

flag of convenience *n* the flag of a country in which a ship is registered in order to avoid the taxes and regulations of the ship-owner's home country

flagon /'flægən/ *n* a large squat short-necked bottle, often with 1 or 2 ear-shaped handles, in which cider, wine, etc are sold

flagrant /'fleɪgrənt/ *adj* conspicuously scandalous; outrageous – **-ancy** *n* – **~ly** *adv*

flagship /'flægˌʃɪp/ *n* **1** the ship that carries the commander of a fleet or subdivision of a fleet and flies his flag **2** the finest, largest, or most important one of a set

flag-waving *n* passionate appeal to patriotic or partisan sentiment; jingoism

¹flail /fleɪl/ *n* a threshing implement consisting of a stout short free-swinging stick attached to a wooden handle

²flail *v* **1** to strike (as if) with a flail **2** to wave, thrash – often + *about*

flair /fleə^r/ *n* **1** intuitive discernment, esp in a specified field **2** natural aptitude; talent **3** sophistication or smartness *USE* (*1 & 2*) usu + *for*

flak /flæk/ *n* **1** the fire from antiaircraft guns **2** heavy criticism or opposition – infml

[1]flake /fleɪk/ *n* a platform, tray, etc for drying fish or produce

[2]flake *n* **1** a small loose mass or particle **2** a thin flattened piece or layer; a chip **3** a pipe tobacco of small irregularly cut pieces

[3]flake *v* to form or separate into flakes; chip

flake out *v* to collapse or fall asleep from exhaustion – infml

flaky /ˈfleɪki/ *adj* **1** consisting of flakes **2** tending to flake – **flakiness** *n*

flamboyant /flæmˈbɔɪənt/ *adj* **1** ornate, florid; *also* resplendent **2** given to dashing display; ostentatious – **-boyance** *n*

[1]flame /fleɪm/ *n* **1** (a tongue of) the glowing gaseous part of a fire **2a** a state of blazing usu destructive combustion – often pl with sing. meaning **b** a condition or appearance suggesting a flame, esp in having red, orange, or yellow colour **c** a bright reddish orange colour **3** a sweetheart – usu in *old flame*

[2]flame *v* **1** to burn with a flame; blaze **2** to break out violently or passionately **3** to shine brightly like flame; glow

flamenco /fləˈmeŋkəʊ/ *n, pl* **flamencos** (music suitable for) a vigorous rhythmic dance (style) of the Andalusian gypsies

flamethrower /ˈfleɪmθrəʊəʳ/ *n* a weapon that expels a burning stream of liquid

flaming /ˈfleɪmɪŋ/ *adj* **1** being in flames or on fire; blazing **2** resembling or suggesting a flame in colour, brilliance, or shape **3** ardent, passionate **4** bloody, blooming – slang

flamingo /fləˈmɪŋgəʊ/ *n, pl* **flamingos** *also* **flamingoes** any of several web-footed broad-billed aquatic birds with long legs and neck and rosy-white plumage with scarlet and black markings

flan /flæn/ *n* a pastry or cake case containing a sweet or savoury filling

flange /flændʒ/ *n* a rib or rim for strength, for guiding, or for attachment to another object

[1]flank /flæŋk/ *n* **1** the (fleshy part of the) side, esp of a quadruped, between the ribs and the hip **2a** a side **b** the right or left of a formation

[2]flank *v* to be situated at the side of; border

[1]flannel /ˈflænl/ *n* **1a** a twilled loosely woven wool or worsted fabric with a slightly napped surface **b** a stout cotton fabric usu napped on 1 side **2** *pl* garments of flannel; *esp* men's trousers **3** *Br* a cloth used for washing the skin, esp of the face **4** *chiefly Br* flattering talk; *also* nonsense – infml

[2]flannel *v, chiefly Br* to speak or write flannel, esp with intent to deceive *USE* infml

flannelette /ˌflænəˈlet/ *n* a napped cotton flannel

[1]flap /flæp/ *n* **1** sthg broad or flat, flexible or hinged, and usu thin, that hangs loose or projects freely: e g **a** an extended part forming a closure (e g of an envelope or carton) **b** a movable control surface on an aircraft wing for increasing lift or lift and drag **2** the motion of sthg broad and flexible (e g a sail); *also* an instance of the up-and-down motion of a wing (e g of a bird) **3** a state of excitement or panicky confusion; an uproar – infml

[2]flap *v* **1** to sway loosely, usu with a noise of striking and esp when moved by the wind **2** to beat (sthg suggesting) wings **3** to be in a flap or panic – infml

flapjack /ˈflæpdʒæk/ *n* **1** a thick pancake **2** a biscuit made with oats and syrup

[1]flare /fleəʳ/ *v* **1a** to shine or blaze with a sudden flame – usu + *up* **b** to become suddenly and often violently excited, angry, or active – usu + *up* **2** to open or spread outwards; *esp* to widen gradually towards the lower edge

[2]flare *n* **1a** (a device or substance used to produce) a fire or blaze of light used to signal, illuminate, or attract attention **b** a temporary outburst of energy from a small area of the sun's surface **3** a sudden outburst (e g of sound, excitement, or anger) **4** a spreading outwards; *also* a place or part that spreads

flare-up *n* an instance of sudden activity, emotion, etc

[1]**flash** /flæʃ/ *v* **1a** to cause the sudden appearance or reflection of (esp light) **b(1)** to cause (e g a mirror) to reflect light **(2)** to cause (a light) to flash **c** to convey by means of flashes of light **2a** to make known or cause to appear with great speed **b** to display ostentatiously **c** to expose to view suddenly and briefly

[2]**flash** *n* **1** a sudden burst of light **2** a sudden burst of perception, emotion, etc **3** a short time **4** an esp vulgar or ostentatious display **5a** a brief look; a glimpse **b** a brief news report, esp on radio or television **c** flashlight photography **6** a thin ridge on a cast or forged article, resulting from the hot metal, plastic, etc penetrating between the 2 parts of the mould **7** an indecent exposure of the genitals – slang

[3]**flash** *adj* **1** of sudden origin or onset and usu short duration ; *also* carried out very quickly **2** flashy, showy – infml

flashback /ˈflæʃbæk/ *n* **1** (an) interruption of chronological sequence in a book, play, or film by the evocation of earlier events **2** a burst of flame back or out to an unwanted position (e g in a furnace)

flashbulb /ˈflæʃbʌlb/ *n* an electric flash lamp in which metal foil or wire is burned

flasher /ˈflæfəʳ/ *n* **1** a device for automatically flashing a light **2** one who commits the offence of indecent exposure – slang

flashgun /ˈflæʃgʌn/ *n* a device for holding and operating a photographic flashlight

flashlight /ˈflæʃlaɪt/ *n* **1** a usu regularly flashing light used for signalling (e g in a lighthouse) **2** (a photograph taken with) a sudden bright artificial light used in taking photographic pictures **3** an electric torch

flash point *n* the temperature at which vapour from a volatile substance ignites

flashy /ˈflæʃi/ *adj* **1** superficially attractive; temporarily brilliant or bright **2** ostentatious or showy, esp beyond the bounds of good taste – **-hily** *adv* – **-hiness** *n*

flask /flɑːsk/ *n* **1** a broad flat bottle, usu of metal or leather-covered glass, used to carry alcohol or other drinks on the person **2** any of several conical, spherical, etc narrow-necked usu glass containers used in a laboratory **3** a vacuum flask

[1]**flat** /flæt/ *adj* **1** having a continuous horizontal surface **2a** lying at full length or spread out on a surface; prostrate **b** resting with a surface against sthg **3** having a broad smooth surface and little thickness; *also* shallow **4a** clearly unmistakable; downright **b(1)** fixed, absolute **(2)** exact **5a** lacking animation; dull, monotonous; *also* inactive **b** having lost effervescence or sparkle **6a** *of a tyre* lacking air; deflated **b** *of a battery* completely or partially discharged **7a** *of a musical note* lowered a semitone in pitch **b** lower than the proper musical pitch **8** having a low trajectory **9a** uniform in colour **b** *of a painting* lacking illusion of depth **c** *esp of paint* having a matt finish – **~ness** *n*

[2]**flat** *n* **1** a flat part or surface **2** (a character indicating) a musical note 1 semitone lower than a specified or particular note **3** a flat piece of theatrical scenery **4** a flat tyre **5** *often cap* horse racing over courses without jumps; *also the* season for this

[3]**flat** *adv* **1** positively, uncompromisingly **2a** on or against a flat surface **b** so as to be spread out; at full length **3** below the proper musical pitch **4** wholly, completely – infml

[4]**flat** *n* a self-contained set of rooms used as a dwelling

flatfish /ˈflæt,fɪʃ/ *n* any of an order of marine fishes (e g the flounders and soles) that swim on one side of the flattened body and have both eyes on the upper side

flat out *adv* at maximum speed, capacity, or performance

flat spin *n* **1** an aerial manoeuvre or flight condition consisting of a spin in which the aircraft is roughly horizontal **2** a state of extreme agitation – infml

flatten /ˈflætn/ *v* **1** to lower in pitch, esp by a semitone **2** to beat or overcome utterly – infml **3** to become flat or flatter: e g **a** to extend in or into a flat position or form – often + *out* **b** to become uniform or stabilized, often at a new lower level – usu + *out*

flatter /ˈflætəʳ/ *v* **1** to praise excessively, esp from motives of self-interest or in order to gratify another's vanity **2** to raise the hope of or gratify, often groundlessly or with intent to deceive **3** to portray or represent (too) favourably – **~er** *n* – **~y** *n*

flaunt /flɔːnt/ *v* **1** to display ostentatiously or impudently; parade **2** to flout – nonstandard

flautist /ˈflɔːtɪ̧st/ *n* one who plays a flute

[1]**flavour,** *NAm chiefly* **flavor** /ˈfleɪvəʳ/ *n* **1** the blend of taste and smell sensations evoked by a substance in the mouth; *also* a distinctive flavour **2** characteristic or predominant quality – **~less** *adj*

[2]**flavour,** *NAm chiefly* **flavor** *v* to give or add flavour to

flaw /flɔː/ *n* **1** a blemish, imperfection **2** a usu hidden defect (e g a crack) that may cause failure under stress **3** a weakness in sthg immaterial (e g an argument or piece of reasoning) –**flaw** *v*

flax /flæks/ *n* **1** (a plant related to or resembling) a slender erect blue-flowered plant cultivated for its strong woody fibre and seed **2** the fibre of the flax plant, esp when prepared for spinning into linen

flaxen /ˈflæksən/ *adj* **1** made of flax **2** resembling flax, esp in being a pale soft straw colour

flay /fleɪ/ *v* **1** to strip off the skin or surface of; *also* to whip savagely **2** to criticize or censure harshly

flea /fliː/ *n* any of an order of wingless bloodsucking jumping insects that feed on warm-blooded animals

fleabite /ˈfliːbaɪt/ *n* a trifling problem or expense – infml

fleapit /ˈfliːˌpɪt/ *n, chiefly Br* a shabby cinema or theatre – infml or humor

[1]**fleck** /flek/ *v* to mark or cover with flecks; streak

[2]**fleck** *n* **1** a small spot or mark, esp of colour **2** a grain, particle

fledgling, fledgeling /ˈfledʒlɪŋ/ *n* **1** a young bird just fledged **2** an inexperienced person

flee /fliː/ *v* **fled** /**fled**/ **1** to run away from danger, evil, etc **2** to pass away swiftly; vanish

[1]**fleece** /fliːs/ *n* **1a** the coat of wool covering a sheep or similar animal **b** the wool obtained from a sheep at 1 shearing **2** a soft bulky deep-piled fabric used chiefly for lining coats

[2]**fleece** *v* to strip of money or property, usu by fraud or extortion; *esp* to overcharge – infml

[1]**fleet** /fliːt/ *n* **1** a number of warships under a single command **2** *often cap* a country's navy – usu + *the* **3** a group of ships, aircraft, lorries, etc owned or operated under one management

[2]**fleet** *adj* swift in motion; nimble – **~ly** *adv* – **~ness** *n*

fleeting /ˈfliːtɪŋ/ *adj* passing swiftly; transitory – **~ly** *adv*

Fleet Street *n* the national London-based press

[1]**flesh** /fleʃ/ *n* **1a** the soft, esp muscular, parts of the body of a (vertebrate) animal as distinguished from visceral structures, bone, hide, etc **b** excess weight; fat **2** the edible parts of an animal **3a** the physical being of humans **b** the physical or sensual aspect of human nature **4a** human beings; humankind – esp in *all flesh* **b** kindred, stock **5** a fleshy (edible) part of a plant or fruit – **~y** *adj*

[2]**flesh** *v* to clothe or cover (as if) with flesh; *broadly* to give substance to – usu + *out*

flesh wound *n* an injury involving penetration of body muscle without damage to bones or internal organs

fleur-de-lis, fleur-de-lys /ˌflɜː də liː/ *n, pl* **fleurs-de-lis** a conventionalized iris in heraldry usu associated with France

flew /fluː/ *past of* **fly**

[1]**flex** /fleks/ *v* **1** to bend **2** to move (a muscle or muscles) so as to flex a limb or joint

[2]**flex** *n* a length of flexible insulated electrical cable used in connecting a portable electrical appliance to a socket

flexible /ˈfleksɪ̧bəl/ *adj* **1** capable of being bent; pliant **2** yielding to influence; tractable **3** capable of changing in response to new conditions; versatile – **-ibly** *adv* – **-ibility** *n*

flibbertigibbet /ˌflɪbəti'dʒɪbɪ̈t/ *n* a flighty or garrulous woman – infml

¹flick /flɪk/ *n* a light jerky movement or blow

²flick *v* **1a** to strike lightly with a quick sharp motion **b** to remove with flicks – usu + *away* or *off* **2** to cause to move with a flick

³flick *n* **1** a film, movie **2** (a showing of a film at) a cinema – + *the*; usu pl *USE* infml

¹flicker /'flɪkəʳ/ *v* **1** to move irregularly or unsteadily; quiver **2a** to burn fitfully or with a fluctuating light **b** *of a light* to fluctuate in intensity

²flicker *n* **1** a flickering (movement or light) **2** a momentary quickening or stirring

flick-knife *n* a pocket knife with a blade that flicks open when required

flier, flyer /'flaɪəʳ/ *n* **1** sby or sthg that moves very fast **2** an airman

¹flight /flaɪt/ *n* **1** a passage through the air using wings **2a** a passage or journey through air or space; *specif* any such flight scheduled by an airline **b** swift movement **3** a group of similar creatures or objects flying through the air **4** a brilliant, imaginative, or unrestrained exercise or display **5** (a series of locks, hurdles, etc resembling) a continuous series of stairs from one landing or floor to another **6** any of the vanes or feathers at the tail of a dart, arrow, etc that provide stability **7** a small unit of (military) aircraft or personnel in the Royal Air Force

²flight *n* an act or instance of fleeing

flight deck *n* **1** the deck of a ship used for the takeoff and landing of aircraft **2** the compartment housing the controls and those crew who operate them in an aircraft

flighty /'flaɪti/ *adj* **1** easily excited or upset; skittish **2** irresponsible, silly; *also* flirtatious – **-tiness** *n*

¹flimsy /'flɪmzi/ *adj* **1a** lacking in strength or substance **b** of inferior materials or workmanship; easily destroyed or broken **2** having little worth or plausibility – **-sily** *adv* – **-siness** *n*

²flimsy *n* (a document printed on) a lightweight paper used esp for multiple copies

flinch /flɪntʃ/ *v* to shrink (as if) from physical pain; *esp* to tense the muscles involuntarily in fear

¹fling /flɪŋ/ *v* **flung 1** to throw or cast (aside), esp with force or recklessness **2** to place or send suddenly and unceremoniously **3** to cast or direct (oneself or one's efforts) vigorously or unrestrainedly

²fling *n* **1** a period devoted to self-indulgence **2** a casual attempt – chiefly infml

flint /flɪnt/ *n* **1** a hard quartz found esp in chalk or limestone **2** a flint implement used by primitive human beings **3** a material used for producing a spark (e g in a cigarette lighter) – **~y** *adj*

flintlock /'flɪntlɒk/ *n* (a gun having) a gunlock used in the 17th and 18th c, in which the charge is ignited by sparks struck from flint

¹flip /flɪp/ *v* **1** to toss or cause to move with a sharp movement, esp so as to be turned over in the air **2** to flick **3** to turn *over* **4** to lose one's sanity or self-control

²flip *n* **1** a (motion used in) flipping or a flick **2** a somersault, esp when performed in the air **3** a mixed drink usu consisting of a sweetened spiced alcoholic drink to which beaten eggs have been added

³flip *adj* flippant, impertinent – infml

flip-flop /'flɪp flɒp/ *n* **1** a backward handspring **2** a rubber sandal consisting of a sole and a strap fixed between the toes

flippant /'flɪpənt/ *adj* lacking proper respect or seriousness, esp in the consideration of grave matters – **-pancy** *n* – **~ly** *adv*

flipper /'flɪpəʳ/ *n* **1** a broad flat limb (e g of a seal) adapted for swimming **2** a flat rubber shoe with the front expanded into a paddle used for underwater swimming

flipping /'flɪpɪŋ/ *adj or adv, Br* damned, bloody – euph

flip side *n* the side of a gramophone record which is not the principal marketing attraction

¹flirt /flɜːt/ *v* **1** to behave amorously without serious intent **2** to slow superficial interest in – + *with* – **~ation** *n* – **~atious** *adj* – **~atiously** *adv*

²flirt *n* **1** an act or instance of flirting **2** one, esp a woman, who flirts

flit /flɪt/ *v* **1** to pass lightly and quickly or irregularly from one place or condition to another; *esp* to fly in this manner **2** to move house, esp rapidly and secretly – **flit** *n*

¹float /fləʊt/ *n* **1a** a cork or other device used to keep the baited end of a fishing line afloat **b** sthg (e g a hollow ball) that floats at the end of a lever in a cistern, tank, or boiler and regulates the liquid level **c** a watertight structure enabling an aircraft to float on water **2** a tool for smoothing a surface of plaster, concrete, etc **3** (a vehicle with) a platform supporting an exhibit in a parade **4** a sum of money available for day-to-day use (e g for expenses or for giving change)

²float *v* **1** to rest on the surface of or be suspended in a fluid **2a** to drift (as if) on or through a liquid **b** to wander aimlessly **3** to lack firmness of purpose; vacillate **4** *of a currency* to find a level in the international exchange market in response to the law of supply and demand and without artificial support or control **5** to present (e g an idea) for acceptance or rejection – **~er** *n*

floating /ˈfləʊtɪŋ/ *adj* **1** located out of the normal position **2a** continually changing position or abode **b** not presently committed or invested

floating dock *n* a floating dry dock that can be partly submerged under a ship and then raised

¹flock /flɒk/ *n sing or pl in constr* **1** a group of birds or mammals assembled or herded together **2** a church congregation, considered in relation to its pastor **3** a large group

²flock *v* to gather or move in a crowd

³flock *n* **1** a tuft of wool or cotton fibre **2** woollen or cotton refuse used for stuffing furniture, mattresses, etc **3** very short or pulverized fibre used esp to form a velvety pattern on cloth or paper or a protective covering on metal

floe /fləʊ/ *n* (a sheet of) floating ice, esp on the sea

flog /flɒg/ *v* **1** to beat severely with a rod, whip, etc **2** to force into action; drive **3** to repeat (sthg) so frequently as to make uninteresting – esp in *flog something to death*; infml **4** *Br* to sell – slang

¹flood /flʌd/ *n* **1** an overflowing of a body of water, esp onto normally dry land **2** an overwhelming quantity or volume **3** a floodlight

²flood *v* **1** to cover with a flood; inundate **2** to fill abundantly or excessively **3** to drive *out* of a house, village, etc by flooding

floodgate /ˈflʌdgeɪt/ *n* sthg serving to restrain an outburst

floodlight /ˈflʌdlaɪt/ *n* (a source of) a broad beam of light for artificial illumination – **floodlight** *v*

¹floor /flɔːr/ *n* **1** the level base of a room **2a** the lower inside surface of a hollow structure (e g a cave or bodily part) **b** a ground surface **3** a structure between 2 storeys of a building; *also* a storey **4a** the part of an assembly in which members sit and speak **b** the members of an assembly **c** the right to address an assembly **5** a lower limit

²floor *v* **1** to knock to the floor or ground **2** to reduce to silence or defeat; nonplus

floor show *n* a series of acts presented in a nightclub

¹flop /flɒp/ *v* **1** to swing or hang loosely but heavily **2** to fall, move, or drop in a heavy, clumsy, or relaxed manner **3** to relax completely; slump **4** to fail completely

²flop *n* **1** (the dull sound of) a flopping motion **2** a complete failure – infml

³flop *adv* with a flop

floppy /ˈflɒpi/ *adj* tending to hang loosely; *esp* being both soft and flexible – **floppily** *adv* – **floppiness** *n*

floppy disk *n* a flexible disk that is coated with a magnetic substance and is used to store data for a computer

flora /ˈflɔːrə/ *n* **1** a treatise on, or a work used to identify, the plants of a region **2** plant life (of a region, period, or special environment)

floral /ˈflɔːrəl/ *adj* of flowers or a flora

florid /ˈflɒrɨd/ *adj* **1** excessively flowery or ornate in style **2** tinged with red; ruddy – **~ly** *adv*

florin /ˈflɒrɨn/ *n* **1** any of various former gold coins of European countries 2 a former British or Commonwealth silver coin worth 2 shillings 3 the major unit of currency of the Netherlands and Surinam

florist /ˈflɒrɪ̵st/ *n* one who deals in or grows flowers and ornamental plants for sale

floss /flɒs/ *n* **1** waste or short silk or silky fibres, esp from the outer part of a silkworm's cocoon **2** soft thread of silk or cotton for embroidery

flotilla /fləˈtɪlə/ *n* a small fleet of ships, esp warships

flotsam and jetsam /ˌflɒtsəm ən ˈdʒetsəm/ *n* **1** vagrants **2** unimportant miscellaneous material

¹flounce /flaʊns/ *v* **1** to move in a violent or exaggerated fashion **2** to go in such a way as to attract attention, esp when angry

²flounce *n* a wide gathered strip of fabric attached by the gathered edge (e g to the hem of a skirt or dress) – **~d** *adj*

¹flounder /ˈflaʊndəʳ/ *n, pl* **flounder,** *esp for different types* **flounders** any of various flatfishes including some marine food fishes

²flounder *v* **1** to struggle to move or obtain footing **2** to proceed or act clumsily or feebly

flour /ˈflaʊəʳ/ *n* **1** finely ground meal, esp of wheat **2** a fine soft powder – **~y** *adj*

¹flourish /ˈflʌrɪʃ/ *v* **1** to grow luxuriantly; thrive **2a** to prosper **b** to be in good health **3** to wave or wield with dramatic gestures; brandish – **~ingly** *adv*

²flourish *n* **1** a showy or flowery embellishment (e g in literature or handwriting) or passage (e g in music) **2a** an act of brandishing **b** an ostentatious or dramatic action

flout /flaʊt/ *v* to treat with contemptuous disregard; scorn

¹flow /fləʊ/ *v* **1a** to issue or move (as if) in a stream **b** to circulate **2** *of the tide* to rise **3** to abound **4a** to proceed smoothly and readily **b** to have a smooth graceful continuity **5** to hang loose or freely

²flow *n* **1** a flowing **2a** a smooth uninterrupted movement or supply; the motion characteristic of fluids **b** a stream or gush of fluid **c** the direction of (apparent) movement **3** the quantity that flows in a certain time

¹flower /ˈflaʊəʳ/ *n* **1a** a blossom **b** a plant cultivated for its blossoms **2a** the finest or most perfect part or example **b** the finest most vigorous period; prime **c** a state of blooming or flourishing – esp in *in flower* – **~less** *adj*

²flower *v* **1** to produce flowers; blossom **2** to reach a peak condition; flourish

flowerpot /ˈflaʊəpɒt/ *n* a pot, typically the shape of a small bucket, in which to grow plants

flowery /ˈflaʊəri/ *adj* **1** of or resembling flowers **2** containing or using highly ornate language

flown /fləʊn/ *past part of* **fly**

flu /fluː/ *n* influenza

fluctuate /ˈflʌktʃʊeɪt/ *v* **1** to rise and fall; swing back and forth **2** to change continually and irregularly; waver – **-ation** *n*

flue /fluː/ *n* **1** a channel in a chimney for flame and smoke **2** a pipe for conveying heat (e g to water in a steam boiler)

fluent /ˈfluːənt/ *adj* **1** able to speak or write with facility; *also* spoken or written in this way **2** effortlessly smooth and rapid; polished – **-ency** *n* – **~ly** *adv*

¹fluff /flʌf/ *n* **1a** small loose bits of waste material (e g hairs and threads) that stick to clothes, carpets, etc **b** soft light fur, down, etc **2** a blunder; *esp* an actor's lapse of memory – chiefly infml – **~y** *adj* – **~iness** *n*

²fluff *v* **1** to make or become fluffy – often + *out* or *up* **2** to make a mistake, esp in a performance

¹fluid /ˈfluːɪ̵d/ *adj* **1a** able to flow **b** likely or tending to change or move; not fixed **2** characterized by or employing a smooth easy style **3** easily converted into cash – **~ity** *n*

²fluid *n* sthg capable of flowing to conform to the outline of its container; *specif* a liquid or gas

fluid ounce *n* a British unit of liquid capacity equal to 1/20 imperial pt (about 28.41cm³)

¹fluke /fluːk/ *n* **1** a flatfish **2** a liver fluke or related parasitic worm

²fluke *n* **1** the part of an anchor that

digs into the sea, river, etc bottom **2** a barbed end (e g of a harpoon)

[3]**fluke** *n* **1** an accidentally successful stroke or action **2** a stroke of luck – **-ky, -key** *adj*

flummery /ˈflʌməri/ *n* **1** a sweet dish typically made with flour or oatmeal, eggs, honey, and cream **2** pretentious humbug

flummox /ˈflʌməks/ *v* to bewilder or confuse completely

flung /flʌŋ/ *past of* **fling**

flunk /flʌŋk/ *v, chiefly NAm* **1** to fail, esp in an examination or course **2** to be turned *out* of a school or college for failure

flunky, flunkey /ˈflʌŋki/ *n* **1** a liveried servant **2** a person performing menial duties

fluorescent /flʊəˈresənt/ *adj* **1** emitting light when subjected to electromagnetic radiation **2** bright and glowing – **-escence** *n*

fluoridate /ˈflʊərɪdeɪt, ˈflɔːrɪ-/ *v* to add a fluoride to (e g drinking water)

fluoride /ˈflʊəraɪd, ˈflɔː-/ *n* a compound of fluorine

fluorine /ˈflʊəriːn, ˈflɔː-/ *n* a nonmetallic element that is normally a pale yellowish toxic gas

[1]**flurry** /ˈflʌri/ *n* **1a** a gust of wind **b** a brief light fall of snow **2** a state of nervous excitement or bustle **3** a short-lived outburst of trading activity

[2]**flurry** *v* to (cause to) become agitated and confused

[1]**flush** /flʌʃ/ *v* to expose or chase from a place of concealment – often + *out*

[2]**flush** *n* **1** (a cleansing with) a sudden flow, esp of water **2** a surge of emotion **3a** a tinge of red, esp in the cheeks; a blush **b** a fresh and vigorous state **4** a transitory sensation of extreme heat

[3]**flush** *v* **1a** to glow brightly with a ruddy colour **b** to blush **2** to inflame, excite – usu pass **3** to pour liquid over or through; *esp* to cleanse or dispose of (the contents of a toilet) with a rush of liquid

[4]**flush** *adj* **1a** having or forming a continuous edge or plane surface; not indented, recessed, or projecting **b** arranged edge to edge so as to fit snugly **2** having a plentiful supply of money – infml

[5]**flush** *adv* **1** so as to form a level or even surface or edge **2** squarely

[6]**flush** *n* a hand of playing cards, esp in a gambling game, all of the same suit

fluster /ˈflʌstəʳ/ *v* to make or become agitated, nervous, or confused – **fluster** *n*

flute /fluːt/ *n* **1** a keyed woodwind instrument consisting of a cylindrical tube stopped at one end that is played by blowing air across a side hole **2a** a grooved pleat **b** any of the vertical parallel grooves on the shaft of a classical column

[1]**flutter** /ˈflʌtəʳ/ *v* **1** to flap the wings rapidly **2a** to move with quick wavering or flapping motions **b** to beat or vibrate in irregular spasms **3** to move about or behave in an agitated aimless manner

[2]**flutter** *n* **1** a state of (nervous) confusion, excitement, or commotion **2** *chiefly Br* a small gamble or bet

flux /flʌks/ *n* **1** a continuous flow or flowing **2a** an influx **b** continual change; fluctuation **3** a substance used to promote fusion of metals (e g in soldering)

[1]**fly** /flaɪ/ *v* **flew; flown** **1a** to move in or through the air by means of wings **b** to float, wave, or soar in the air **2** to take flight; flee **3a** to move, act, or pass swiftly **b** to move or pass suddenly and violently into a specified state **4** to operate or travel in an aircraft or spacecraft **5** to depart in haste; dash – chiefly infml

[2]**fly** *n* **1** *pl* the space over a stage where scenery and equipment can be hung **2** a (garment) opening concealed by a fold of cloth extending over the fastener; *esp, pl* such an opening in the front of a pair of trousers

[3]**fly** *adj, chiefly Br* keen, artful – infml

[4]**fly** *n* **1** a winged insect – often in combination (e g *may*fly) **2** a natural or artificial fly attached to a fishhook for use as bait

flyaway /ˈflaɪəweɪ/ *adj* **1** lacking practical sense; flighty **2** *esp of the hair* tending not to stay in place

flyblown /ˈflaɪbləʊn/ *adj* **1** infested with maggots **2** impure, tainted; *also* not new; used

[1]**fly-by-night** *n* **1** one who seeks to evade responsibilities or debts by flight **2** a shaky business enterprise *USE* chiefly infml

[2]**fly-by-night** *adj* **1** given to making a quick profit, usu by disreputable or irresponsible acts; *broadly* untrustworthy **2** transitory, passing *USE* chiefly infml

flyer /ˈflaɪəʳ/ *n* a flier

fly-fishing *n* fishing (e g for salmon or trout) using artificial flies as bait

fly-half *n* a position in rugby between the scrum and the three-quarters

flying /ˈflaɪ-ɪŋ/ *adj* **1a** (capable of) moving in the air **b** rapidly moving **c** very brief; hasty **2** intended for ready movement or action **3** of (the operation of) or using an aircraft **4** (to be) traversed after a flying start

flying buttress *n* a projecting arched structure that supports a wall or building

flying saucer *n* any of various unidentified flying objects reported as being saucer- or disc-shaped

flying squad *n, often cap F&S* a standby group of people, esp police, ready to move or act swiftly in an emergency

flying start *n* a privileged or successful beginning

flyover /ˈflaɪ-əʊvəʳ/ *n, Br* (the upper level of) a crossing of 2 roads, railways, etc at different levels

flypaper /ˈflaɪpeɪpəʳ/ *n* paper coated with a sticky, often poisonous, substance for killing flies

flypast /ˈflaɪpɑːst/ *n, Br* a ceremonial usu low-altitude flight by (an) aircraft over a person or public gathering

fly sheet *n* **1** a small pamphlet or circular **2** an outer protective sheet covering a tent

flyswatter /ˈflaɪswɒtəʳ/ *n* a implement for killing insects that consists of a flat piece of usu rubber or plastic attached to a handle

flyweight /ˈflaɪweɪt/ *n* a boxer who weighs not more than 8st (50.8kg) if professional or more than 48kg (about 7st 7lb) but not more than 51kg (about 8st) if amateur

flywheel /ˈflaɪwiːl/ *n* a wheel with a heavy rim that when revolving can either reduce speed fluctuations in the rotation of an engine or store energy

FM *adj* of or being a broadcasting or receiving system using frequency modulation and usu noted for lack of interference

[1]**foal** /fəʊl/ *n* a young animal of the horse family

[2]**foal** *v* to give birth to (a foal)

[1]**foam** /fəʊm/ *n* **1a** (a substance in the form of) a light frothy mass of fine bubbles formed in or on the surface of a liquid (e g by agitation or fermentation) **b** a frothy mass formed in salivating or sweating **c** a chemical froth discharged from fire extinguishers **2** a material in a lightweight cellular form resulting from introduction of gas bubbles during manufacture **3** *the* sea – poetic – **foamy** *adj*

[2]**foam** *v* **1a** to produce or form foam **b** to froth at the mouth, esp in anger; *broadly* to be angry **2** to gush out in foam **3** to become covered (as if) with foam **4** to cause air bubbles to form in

fob /fɒb/ *n* **1** a small pocket on or near the waistband of a man's trousers, orig for holding a watch **2** a short strap or chain attached to a watch carried in a fob or a waistcoat pocket

fob off *v* **1** to put off with a trick or excuse – usu + *with* **2** to pass or offer (sthg spurious or inferior) as genuine or perfect – usu + *on*

focal length *n* the distance between the optical centre of a lens or mirror and the focal point

fo'c'sle /ˈfəʊksəl/ *n* a forecastle

[1]**focus** /ˈfəʊkəs/ *n, pl* **focuses, foci** **1a** a point at which rays (e g of light, heat, or sound) converge or from which they (appear to) diverge after reflection or refraction **b** the point at which an object must be placed for an image formed by a lens or mirror to be sharp **2a** the distance between a lens and the point at which it forms a focus **b** adjustment (e g of the eye) necessary for distinct vision **c** a state in which sthg must be placed in order to be clearly perceived **3** a centre of activity

or attention **4** the place of origin of an earthquake – **focal** *adj*

[2]**focus** *v* **1** to bring or come to a focus; converge **2** to cause to be concentrated **3** to adjust the focus of **4** to bring one's eyes or a camera to a focus

fodder /ˈfɒdəʳ/ *n* **1** (coarse) food for cattle, horses, sheep, or other domestic animals **2** sthg used to supply a constant demand

foe /fəʊ/ *n* an enemy, adversary

foetus, fetus /ˈfiːtəs/ *n* an unborn or unhatched vertebrate; *specif* a developing human from usu 3 months after conception to birth – **foetal** *adj*

[1]**fog** /fɒg/ *n* **1** (a murky condition of the atmosphere caused esp by) fine particles, specif of water, suspended in the lower atmosphere **2a** a state of confusion or bewilderment **b** sthg that confuses or obscures

[2]**fog** *v* **1** to envelop or suffuse (as if) with fog **2** to make confused or confusing **3** to produce fog on (e g a photographic film) during development

fogbound /ˈfɒgbaʊnd/ *adj* **1** covered with or surrounded by fog **2** unable to move because of fog

fogey, fogy /ˈfəʊgi/ *n* a person with old-fashioned ideas

foggy /ˈfɒgi/ *adj* **1a** thick with fog **b** covered or made opaque by moisture or grime **2** blurred, obscured – **-ggily** *adv* – **-gginess** *n*

foghorn /ˈfɒghɔːn/ *n* **1** a horn (e g on a ship) sounded in a fog to give warning **2** a loud hoarse voice – infml

foible /ˈfɔɪbəl/ *n* a minor weakness or shortcoming in personal character or behaviour; *also* a quirk

[1]**foil** /fɔɪl/ *v* to prevent from attaining an end; frustrate, defeat

[2]**foil** *n* (fencing with) a light fencing sword with a circular guard and a flexible blade tapering to a blunted point

[3]**foil** *n* **1** any of several arcs that enclose a complex design **2** very thin sheet metal **3** sby or sthg that serves as a contrast to another **4** a hydrofoil

[4]**foil** *v* to back or cover with foil

foist /fɔɪst/ *v* **1a** to introduce or insert surreptitiously or without warrant – + *in* or *into* **b** to force another to accept or tolerate, esp by stealth or deceit **2** to pass off as genuine or worthy *USE* (*1b&2*) usu + *off on, on*, or *upon*

[1]**fold** /fəʊld/ *n* **1** an enclosure for sheep; *also* a flock of sheep **2** *sing or pl in constr* a group of people adhering to a common faith, belief, or enthusiasm

[2]**fold** *v* to pen (e g sheep) in a fold

[3]**fold** *v* **1** to lay one part of over another part **2** to reduce the length or bulk of by doubling over – often + *up* **3a** to clasp together; entwine **b** to bring (limbs) to rest close to the body **4a** to clasp closely; embrace **b** to wrap, envelop **5** to gently incorporate (a food ingredient) into a mixture without thorough stirring or beating – usu + *in* **6** to become or be capable of being folded **7** to fail completely; *esp* to stop production or operation because of lack of business or capital – often + *up*; chiefly infml

[4]**fold** *n* **1** (a crease made by) a doubling or folding over **2** a part doubled or laid over another part; a pleat **3** (a hollow inside) sthg that is folded or that enfolds **4** *chiefly Br* an undulation in the landscape

foldaway /ˈfəʊldəweɪ/ *adj* designed to fold out of the way or out of sight

folder /ˈfəʊldəʳ/ *n* a folded cover or large envelope for holding or filing loose papers

foliage /ˈfəʊli-ɪdʒ/ *n* **1** the leaves of a plant or clump of plants **2** (an ornamental representation of) a cluster of leaves, branches, etc

[1]**folk** /fəʊk/ *n* **1** *pl in constr* the great proportion of a people that tends to preserve its customs, superstitions, etc **2** *pl in constr* a specified kind or class of people – often pl with sing. meaning **3** simple music, usu song, of traditional origin or style **4** *pl in constr* people generally – infml; often pl with sing. meaning **5** *pl* the members of one's own family; relatives – infml

[2]**folk** *adj* **1** originating or traditional with the common people **2** of (the study of) the common people

folklore /ˈfəʊklɔːʳ/ *n* **1** traditional customs and beliefs of a people preserved by oral tradition **2** the study of the life and spirit of a people through their folklore – **-lorist** *n*

follicle /'fɒlɪkəl/ *n* **1** a small anatomical cavity or deep narrow depression **2** a dry 1-celled many-seeded fruit

follow /'fɒləʊ/ *v* **1** to go, proceed, or come after **2** to pursue, esp in an effort to overtake **3a** to accept as a guide or leader **b** to obey or act in accordance with **4** to copy, imitate **5a** to walk or proceed along **b** to engage in as a calling or way of life; pursue (e g a course of action) **6** to come or take place after in time or order **7** to come into existence or take place as a result or consequence of **8a** to attend closely to; keep abreast of **b** to understand the logic of (e g an argument) **9** to go or come after sby or sthg in place, time, or sequence **10** to result or occur as a consequence or inference

follower /'fɒləʊəʳ/ *n* **1a** one who follows the opinions or teachings of another **b** one who imitates another **2** a fan

¹following /'fɒləʊɪŋ/ *adj* **1** next after; succeeding **2** now to be stated **3** *of a wind* blowing in the direction in which sthg is travelling

²following *n* **1** sthg that comes immediately after or below in writing or speech **2** *sing or pl in constr* a group of followers, adherents, or partisans

³following *prep* subsequent to

follow on *v, of a side in cricket* to bat a second time immediately after making a score that is less, by more than a predetermined limit, than that of the opposing team in its first innings – **follow-on** *n*

follow through *v* **1** to pursue (an activity or process), esp to a conclusion **2** to continue the movement of a stroke after a cricket, golf, etc ball has been struck

follow up *v* **1a** to follow with sthg similar, related, or supplementary **b** to take appropriate action about **2** to maintain contact with or reexamine (a person) at usu prescribed intervals in order to evaluate a diagnosis or treatment – **follow-up** *n, adj*

folly /'fɒli/ *n* **1** lack of good sense or prudence **2** a foolish act or idea **3** (criminally or tragically) foolish actions or conduct **4** a usu fanciful structure (e g a summerhouse) built esp for scenic effect or to satisfy a whim

foment /fəʊ'ment/ *v* to promote the growth or development of; incite – **~ation** *n*

fond /fɒnd/ *adj* **1** foolish, silly **2** having an affection or liking for sthg specified – + *of* **3a** foolishly tender; indulgent **b** affectionate, loving **4** doted on; cherished – **~ly** *adv* – **~ness** *n*

fondant /'fɒndənt/ *n* (a sweet made from) a soft creamy preparation of flavoured sugar and water

fondle /'fɒndl/ *v* to handle tenderly, affectionately, or lingeringly

fondue /'fɒndjuː/ *n* a dish consisting of a hot liquid (e g oil or a thick sauce) into which pieces of food are dipped for cooking or coating; *esp* one made with melted cheese and white wine

font /fɒnt/ *n* **1** a receptacle for holy water; *esp* one used in baptism **2** a receptacle for oil in a lamp

food /fuːd/ *n* **1a** (minerals, vitamins, etc together with) material consisting essentially of protein, carbohydrate, and fat taken into the body of a living organism and used to provide energy and sustain processes (e g growth and repair) essential for life **b** inorganic substances absorbed (e g in gaseous form or in solution) by plants **2** nutriment in solid form **3** sthg that sustains or supplies

food chain *n* a series of organisms ordered according to each organism's use of the next as a food source

foodstuff /'fuːdstʌf/ *n* a substance with food value; *esp* the raw material of food before or after processing

¹fool /fuːl/ *n* **1** a person lacking in prudence, common sense, or understanding **2a** a jester **b** a person who is victimized or made to appear foolish; a dupe **3** a cold dessert of fruit puree mixed with whipped cream or custard

²fool *v* **1a** to act or spend time idly or aimlessly **b** to meddle, play, or trifle *with* **2** to play or improvise a comic role; *specif* to joke **3** to make a fool of; deceive

³fool *adj* foolish, silly – infml

foolhardy /ˈfuːlhɑːdi/ *adj* foolishly adventurous and bold; rash – **-diness** *n*

foolish /ˈfuːlɪʃ/ *adj* **1** marked by or proceeding from folly **2** absurd, ridiculous – **~ly** *adv* – **~ness** *n*

foolproof /ˈfuːlpruːf/ *adj* so simple or reliable as to leave no opportunity for error, misuse, or failure

foolscap /ˈfuːlskæp/ *n* a size of paper usu 17 × 13½in (432 × 343mm)

fool's errand *n* a needless or fruitless errand

fool's paradise *n* a state of illusory happiness

[1]**foot** /fʊt/ *n, pl* **feet** **1** the end part of the vertebrate leg on which an animal stands **2** an organ of locomotion or attachment of an invertebrate animal, esp a mollusc **3** a unit of length equal to ⅓yd (0.305m) **4** the basic unit of verse metre consisting of any of various fixed combinations of stressed and unstressed or long and short syllables **5** manner or motion of walking or running; step **6a** the lower end of the leg of a chair, table, etc **b** the piece on a sewing machine that presses the cloth against the feed **7** the lower edge or lowest part; the bottom **8a** the end that is opposite the head or top or nearest to the human feet **b** the part (e g of a stocking) that covers the human foot

[2]**foot** *v* **1** to walk, run, or dance on, over, or through **2** to pay or stand credit for

footage /ˈfʊtɪdʒ/ *n* **1** length or quantity expressed in feet **2** (the length in feet of) exposed film

football /ˈfʊtbɔːl/ *n* (the inflated round or oval ball used in) any of several games, esp soccer, that are played between 2 teams on a usu rectangular field having goalposts at each end and whose object is to get the ball over a goal line or between goalposts by running, passing, or kicking

football pools *n* a form of organized gambling based on forecasting the results of football matches

footboard /ˈfʊtbɔːd/ *n* **1** a narrow platform on which to stand or brace the feet **2** a board forming the foot of a bed

footbridge /ˈfʊt,brɪdʒ/ *n* a bridge for pedestrians

footfall /ˈfʊtfɔːl/ *n* the sound of a footstep

foothill /ˈfʊt,hɪl/ *n* a hill at the foot of mountains

foothold /ˈfʊthəʊld/ *n* **1** a footing **2** an (established) position or basis from which to progress

footing /ˈfʊtɪŋ/ *n* **1** a stable position or placing of or for the feet **2** a (condition of a) surface with respect to its suitability for walking or running on **3a** an established position **b** a position or rank in relation to others

footle /ˈfuːtl/ *v* to mess or potter *around* or *about*; *also* to waste time – infml

footlights /ˈfʊtlaɪts/ *n pl* a row of lights set across the front of a stage floor

footling /ˈfuːtlɪŋ/ *adj* **1** bungling, inept **2** unimportant, trivial; *also* pettily fussy ***USE*** infml

footloose /ˈfʊtluːs/ *adj* having no ties; free to go or do as one pleases

footman /ˈfʊtmən/ *n* a servant in livery hired chiefly to wait, receive visitors, etc

footnote /ˈfʊtnəʊt/ *n* **1** a note of reference, explanation, or comment typically placed at the bottom of a printed page **2** sthg subordinately related to a larger event or work

footpath /ˈfʊtpɑːθ/ *n* a narrow path for pedestrians; *also* a pavement

footplate /ˈfʊtpleɪt/ *n, Br* the platform on which the crew stand in a locomotive

footprint /ˈfʊt,prɪnt/ *n* an impression left by the foot

footslog /ˈfʊtslɒg/ *v* to march or tramp laboriously – infml – **~ger** *n* – **~ging** *n*

footstep /ˈfʊtstep/ *n* **1** the sound of a step or tread **2** distance covered by a step

footwear /ˈfʊtweəʳ/ *n* articles (e g shoes or boots) worn on the feet

footwork /ˈfʊtwɜːk/ *n* **1** the control and placing of the feet, esp in sport (e g in boxing or batting) **2** the activity of moving from place to place on foot

fop /fɒp/ *n* a dandy – **~pish** *adj*

[1]**for** /fəʳ; *strong* fɔːʳ/ *prep* **1a** – used to

indicate purpose (e g a grant *for* studying medicine) goal or direction (e g left *for* home) or that which is to be had or gained (e g run *for* your life) **b** to belong to (e g the flowers are *for* you) **2** as being or constituting (e g ate it *for* breakfast) **3** because of (e g cried *for* joy) **4a** in place of (e g change *for* a pound) **b** on behalf of; representing (e g acting *for* my client) **c** in support of; in favour of (e g he played *for* England) **5** considered as; considering (e g tall *for* her age) **6** with respect to; concerning (e g famous *for* its scenery) **7** – used to indicate cost, payment, equivalence, or correlation (e g £7 *for* a hat) **8** – used to indicate duration of time or extent of space (e g *for* 10 miles; gone *for* months) **9** on the occasion or at the time of (e g came home *for* Christmas)

[2]**for** *conj* **1** and the reason is that **2** because

[3]**for** *adj* being in favour of a motion or measure

[1]**forage** /'fɒrɪdʒ/ *n* **1** food for animals, esp when taken by browsing or grazing **2** a foraging for provisions; *broadly* a search

[2]**forage** *v* **1** to collect or take provisions or forage from **2** to wander in search of forage or food **3** to make a search *for*, rummage

[1]**foray** /'fɒreɪ/ *v* to make a raid or incursion

[2]**foray** *n* **1** a sudden invasion, attack, or raid **2** a brief excursion or attempt, esp outside one's accustomed sphere

[1]**forbear** /fɔː'beəʳ, fə-/ *v* **forbore; forborne** to hold oneself back from, esp with an effort of self-restraint

[2]**forbear** *n* a forebear

forbearance /fɔː'beərəns/ *n* **1** a refraining from the enforcement of sthg (e g a debt, right, or obligation) that is due **2** patience **3** leniency, mercifulness

forbid /fə'bɪd/ *v* **forbidding; forbade, forbad; forbidden 1a** to refuse (e g by authority) to allow; command against **b** to refuse access to or use of **2** to make impracticable; hinder, prevent – **-bidden** *adj*

forbidding /fə'bɪdɪŋ/ *adj* **1** having a menacing or dangerous appearance **2** unfriendly – **~ly** *adv*

[1]**force** /fɔːs/ *n* **1a** strength or energy exerted or brought to bear; active power **b** moral or mental strength **c** capacity to persuade or convince **d** (legal) validity; operative effect **2a** *pl* the armed services of a nation or commander **b** a body of people or things fulfilling an often specified function **c** an individual or group having the power of effective action **3** violence, compulsion, or constraint exerted on or against a person or thing **4a** (the intensity of) an agency that if applied to a free body results chiefly in an acceleration of the body and sometimes in elastic deformation and other effects **b** an agency or influence analogous to a physical force **5** *cap* a measure of wind strength as expressed by a number on the Beaufort scale

[2]**force** *v* **1** to compel by physical, moral, or intellectual means **2** to make or cause through natural or logical necessity **3a** to press, drive, or effect against resistance or inertia **b** to impose or thrust urgently, importunately, or inexorably **4** to break open or through **5a** to raise or accelerate to the utmost **b** to produce only with unnatural or unwilling effort **6** to hasten the growth, onset of maturity, or rate of progress of

forceful /'fɔːsfəl/ *adj* possessing or filled with force; effective – **~ly** *adv* – **~ness** *n*

force majeure /ˌfɔːs mæ'ʒɜːʳ/ *n* a disruptive event (e g war) that cannot be reasonably anticipated

forcemeat /'fɔːsmiːt/ *n* a savoury highly seasoned stuffing, esp of breadcrumbs and meat

forceps /'fɔːseps, -sɨps/ *n, pl* **forceps** an instrument used (e g in surgery and watchmaking) for grasping, holding firmly, or pulling – usu pl with sing. meaning

forcible /'fɔːsəbəl/ *adj* **1** effected by force used against opposition or resistance **2** powerful, forceful – **-bly** *adv*

[1]**ford** /fɔːd/ *n* a shallow part of a river or other body of water that can be crossed by wading, in a vehicle, etc

[2]**ford** *v* to cross (a river, stream, etc) at a ford

[1]**fore** /fɔːʳ/ *adj or adv* (situated) in, towards, or adjacent to the front

[2]**fore** *n* sthg that occupies a forward position

[3]**fore** *interj* – used by a golfer to warn anyone in the probable line of flight of his/her ball

fore-and-aft *adj* lying, running, or acting in the general line of the length of a ship or other construction

fore and aft *adv* from stem to stern

[1]**forearm** /ˌfɔːrˈɑːm/ *v* to arm in advance; prepare

[2]**forearm** /ˈfɔːrɑːm/ *n* (the part in other vertebrates corresponding to) the human arm between the elbow and the wrist

forebear, forbear /ˈfɔːbeəʳ/ *n* an ancestor, forefather

forebode /fɔːbəʊd/ *v* **1** to foretell, portend **2** to have a premonition of (evil, misfortune, etc)

foreboding /fɔːˈbəʊdɪŋ/ *n* an omen, prediction, or presentiment, esp of coming evil

[1]**forecast** /ˈfɔːkɑːst/ *v* **1** to estimate or predict (some future event or condition), esp as a result of rational study and analysis of available pertinent data **2** to serve as a forecast of; presage **3** to calculate or predict the future

[2]**forecast** /ˈfɔːkɑːst/ *n* a prophecy, estimate, or prediction of a future happening or condition; *esp* a weather forecast

forecastle, fo'c'sle /ˈfəʊksəl/ *n* **1** a short raised deck at the bow of a ship **2** a forward part of a merchant ship having the living quarters

foreclose /fɔːˈkləʊz/ *v* to take away the right to redeem (e g a mortgage), usu because of nonpayment – **-closure** *n*

forecourt /ˈfɔːkɔːt/ *n* an open or paved area in front of a building; *esp* that part of a petrol station where the petrol pumps are situated

forefather /ˈfɔːˌfɑːðəʳ/ *n* **1** an ancestor **2** a person of an earlier period and common heritage

forefinger /ˈfɔːˌfɪŋgəʳ/ *n* the finger next to the thumb

forefront /ˈfɔːfrʌnt/ *n* the foremost part or place; the vanguard

forego /fɔːˈgəʊ/ *v* **foregoes; foregoing; forewent; foregone** to forgo

foregoing /ˈfɔːgəʊɪŋ/ *adj* going before; that immediately precedes

foreground /ˈfɔːgraʊnd/ *n* **1** the part of a picture or view nearest to and in front of the spectator **2** a position of prominence; the forefront

[1]**forehand** /ˈfɔːhænd/ *n* a forehand stroke in tennis, squash, etc; *also* the side or part of the court on which such strokes are made

[2]**forehand** *adj or adv* (made) with the palm of the hand turned in the direction of movement

forehead /ˈfɒrɪ̥d, ˈfɔːhed/ *n* the part of the face above the eyes

foreign /ˈfɒrɪ̥n/ *adj* **1** (situated) outside a place or country; *esp* (situated) outside one's own country **2** born in, belonging to, or characteristic of some place or country other than the one under consideration **3** alien in character; not connected or pertinent *to* **4** of, concerned with, or dealing with other nations **5** occurring in an abnormal situation in the living body and commonly introduced from outside

foreigner /ˈfɒrɪ̥nəʳ/ *n* **1** a person belonging to or owing allegiance to a foreign country; an alien **2** *chiefly dial* a stranger; *esp* a person not native to a community

forelimb /ˈfɔːlɪm/ *n* a front leg or similar limb

forelock /ˈfɔːlɒk/ *n* a lock of hair growing just above the forehead

foreman /ˈfɔːmən/, *fem* **forewoman** *n* **1** the chairman and spokesman of a jury **2** a person, often a chief worker, who supervises a group of workers, a particular operation, or a section of a plant

[1]**foremost** /ˈfɔːməʊst/ *adj* **1** first in a series or progression **2** of first rank or position; preeminent

[2]**foremost** *adv* most importantly

forename /ˈfɔːneɪm/ *n* a name that precedes a person's surname

forenoon /ˈfɔːnuːn/ *n* *the* morning – fml

forensic /fəˈrensɪk, -zɪk/ *adj* of or being the scientific investigation of crime

foreordain /ˌfɔːrɔːˈdeɪn/ *v* to settle, arrange, or appoint in advance; predestine

forepart /'fɔːpɑːt/ *n* the front part of sthg

forerunner /'fɔːˌrʌnəʳ/ *n* **1** a warning sign or symptom **2a** a predecessor, forefather **b** a prototype

foresail /'fɔːsəl, -seɪl/ *n* **1** the lowest square sail on the foremast of a square-rigged ship **2** the principal fore-and-aft sail set on a schooner's foremast

foresee /fɔː'siː/ *v* **foreseeing; foresaw; foreseen** to be aware of (e g a development) beforehand – **~able** *adj*

foreshadow /fɔː'ʃædəʊ/ *v* to represent or typify beforehand; suggest

foreshore /'fɔːʃɔːʳ/ *n* the part of a seashore between high-tide and low-tide marks

foreshorten /fɔː'ʃɔːtn/ *v* **1** to shorten (a detail in a drawing or painting) so as to create an illusion of depth **2** to make more compact

foresight /'fɔːsaɪt/ *n* **1** foreseeing; insight into the future **2** provident care; prudence **3** the sight nearest the muzzle on a firearm

foreskin /'fɔːˌskɪn/ *n* a fold of skin that covers the head of the penis

[1]**forest** /'fɒrɨst/ *n* **1** a tract of wooded land in Britain formerly owned by the sovereign and used for hunting game **2** a dense growth of trees and underbrush covering a large tract of land **3** sthg resembling a profusion of trees

[2]**forest** *v* to cover with trees or forest

forestall /fɔː'stɔːl/ *v* **1** to exclude, hinder, or prevent by prior measures **2** to get ahead of; anticipate

forester /'fɒrɨstəʳ/ *n* **1** a person trained in forestry **2** a person, animal, etc that inhabits forest land

forestry /'fɒrɨstri/ *n* **1** forest land **2** the scientific cultivation or management of forests

foretaste /'fɔːteɪst/ *n* **1** an advance indication or warning **2** a small anticipatory sample

foretell /fɔː'tel/ *v* **foretold** to tell beforehand; predict

forethought /'fɔːθɔːt/ *n* **1** a thinking or planning out in advance; premeditation **2** consideration for the future

forever /fə'revəʳ/ *adv* **1** for all future time; indefinitely **2** persistently, incessantly

forewarn /fɔː'wɔːn/ *v* to warn in advance

foreword /'fɔːwɜːd/ *n* a preface; *esp* one written by sby other than the author of the text

[1]**forfeit** /'fɔːfɨt/ *n* **1** sthg lost, taken away, or imposed as a penalty **2** the loss or forfeiting of sthg, esp of civil rights **3a** an article deposited or a task performed in the game of forfeits **b** *pl but sing or pl in constr* a game in which articles are deposited (e g for making a mistake) and then redeemed by performing a silly task – **forfeit** *adj*

[2]**forfeit** *v* **1** to lose the right to by some error, offence, or crime **2** to subject to confiscation as a forfeit – **~ure** *n*

[1]**forge** /fɔːdʒ/ *n* (a workshop with) an open furnace where metal, esp iron, is heated and wrought

[2]**forge** *v* **1** to shape (metal or a metal object) by heating and hammering or with a press **2** to form or bring into being, esp by an expenditure of effort **3** to counterfeit (esp a signature, document, or bank note) **4** to commit forgery – **~r** *n*

[3]**forge** *v* **1** to move forwards slowly and steadily but with effort **2** to move with a sudden increase of speed and power

forgery /'fɔːdʒəri/ *n* **1** (the crime of) forging **2** a forged document, bank note, etc

forget /fə'get/ *v* **forgetting; forgot; forgotten** **1** to fail to remember **2** to fail to give attention to; disregard **3** to disregard intentionally

forgetful /fə'getfəl/ *adj* **1** likely or apt to forget **2** characterized by negligent failure to remember; neglectful – usu + *of* – **~ly** *adv* – **~ness** *n*

forget-me-not *n* any of a genus of small plants of the borage family with white or bright blue flowers usu arranged in a spike

forgive /fə'gɪv/ *v* **forgave; forgiven** **1** to cease to resent **2** to pardon – **-vable** *adj* – **-ving** *adj*

forgiveness /fə'gɪvnɨs/ *n* forgiving or being forgiven; pardon

forgo, forego /fɔː'gəʊ/ *v* to abstain or refrain from

[1]**fork** /fɔːk/ *n* **1** a tool or implement with 2 or more prongs set on the end of a handle: e g **a** an agricultural or gardening tool for digging, carrying, etc **b** a small implement for eating or serving food **2a** a forked part, or piece of equipment **b** a forked support for a cycle wheel – often pl with sing. meaning **3** (a part containing) a division into branches **4** any of the branches into which sthg forks

[2]**fork** *v* **1** to divide into 2 or more branches **2** to make a turn into one of the branches of a fork **3** to pay, contribute – + *out, over,* or *up*

forked /fɔːkt/ *adj* having one end divided into 2 or more branches or points

forklift /ˈfɔːk,lɪft/, **forklift truck** *n* a vehicle for hoisting and transporting heavy objects by means of steel prongs inserted under the load

forlorn /fəˈlɔːn/ *adj* **1a** bereft or forsaken *of* **b** sad and lonely because of isolation or desertion; desolate **2** in poor condition; miserable, wretched **3** nearly hopeless – **~ly** *adv* – **~ness** *n*

[1]**form** /fɔːm/ *n* **1** the shape and structure of sthg as distinguished from its material **2** the essential nature of a thing as distinguished from the matter in which it is embodied **3a** established or correct method of proceeding or behaving **b** a prescribed and set order of words **4** a printed or typed document; *esp* one with blank spaces for insertion of required or requested information **5** conduct regulated by external controls (e g custom or etiquette); ceremony **6a** the bed or nest of a hare **b** a long seat; a bench **7** sthg (e g shuttering) that holds, supports, and determines shape **8a** the way in which sthg is arranged, exists, or shows itself **b** a kind, variety **9** the structural element, plan, or design of a work of art **10** *sing or pl in constr* a class organized for the work of a particular year, esp in a British school **11a** the past performances of a competitor considered as a guide to its future performance **b** known ability to perform **c** condition suitable for performing, esp in sports – often + *in, out of,* or *off* **12** *Br* a criminal record – slang – **~less** *adj*

[2]**form** *v* **1** to give form, shape, or existence to **2a** to give a particular shape to; shape or mould into a certain state or after a particular model **b** to model or train by instruction and discipline **3** to develop, acquire **4** to serve to make up or constitute; be a usu essential or basic element of

formal /ˈfɔːməl/ *adj* **1a** determining or being the essential constitution or structure **b** of, concerned with, or being the (outward) form of sthg as distinguished from its content **2a** following or based on conventional forms and rules **b** characterized by punctilious respect for correct procedure **3** having the appearance without the substance; ostensible – **~ly** *adv*

formaldehyde /fɔːˈmældɪ̣haɪd/ *n* a pungent irritating gas used chiefly as a disinfectant and preservative and in chemical synthesis

formality /fɔːˈmælɪ̣ti/ *n* **1** compliance with or observance of formal or conventional rules **2** an established form that is required or conventional

format /ˈfɔːmæt/ *n* **1** the shape, size, and general make-up (e g of a book) **2** the general plan of organization or arrangement

formation /fɔːˈmeɪʃən/ *n* **1** giving form or shape to sthg or taking form; development **2** sthg formed **3** the manner in which a thing is formed; structure **4** an arrangement of a group of people or things in some prescribed manner or for a particular purpose

formative /ˈfɔːmətɪv/ *adj* **1** (capable of) giving form; constructive **2** capable of alteration by growth and development **3** of or characterized by formative effects or formation

[1]**former** /ˈfɔːməʳ/ *adj* **1** of or occurring in the past **2** preceding in time or order **3** first of 2 things (understood to have been) mentioned

[2]**former** *n, pl* **former** the first mentioned; first

formerly /ˈfɔːməli/ *adv* at an earlier time; previously

Formica /fɔːˈmaɪkə, fə-/ *trademark* –

used for any of various laminated plastics used for surfaces, esp on wood

formidable /'fɔːmɪ̣dəbəl, fə'mɪd-/ *adj* **1** difficult to overcome; discouraging approach **2** tending to inspire respect or awe – **-bly** *adv*

formula /'fɔːmjʊlə/ *n, pl* **formulas, formulae** **1a** a set form of words for use in a ceremony or ritual **b** (a conventionalized statement intended to express) a truth, principle, or procedure, esp as a basis for negotiation or action **2** (a list of ingredients used in) a recipe **3a** a fact, rule, or principle expressed in symbols **b** a symbolic expression of the chemical composition of a substance **4** a prescribed or set form or method (e g of writing); an established rule or custom **5** a classification of racing cars specifying esp size, weight, and engine capacity

formulate /'fɔːmjʊleɪt/ *v* **1** to state in or reduce to a formula **2** to devise or develop – **-ation** *n*

fornicate /'fɔːnɪ̣keɪt/ *v* to have sexual relations outside marriage – **-cation** *n*

forsake /fə'seɪk/ *v* **forsook; forsaken** **1** to renounce (e g sthg once cherished) without intent to recover or resume **2** to desert, abandon

forswear /fɔː'sweəʳ/ *v* to (solemnly) renounce

forsythia /fə'saɪθɪə/ *n* any of a genus of ornamental shrubs with bright yellow bell-shaped flowers which appear in early spring before the leaves

fort /fɔːt/ *n* a strong or fortified place

[1]**forte** /'fɔːteɪ/ *n* the area or skill in which a person excels

[2]**forte** /'fɔːteɪ/ *n, adv, or adj* (a note or passage played) in a loud and often forceful manner

forth /fɔːθ/ *adv* **1** onwards in time, place, or order; forwards (e g from this day *forth*) **2** out into notice or view (e g put *forth* leaves) **3** away from a centre; abroad (e g went *forth* to preach)

forthcoming /ˌfɔːθ'kʌmɪŋ/ *adj* **1** approaching **2a** made available **b** willing to give information; responsive

forthright /'fɔːθraɪt/ *adj* going straight to the point without ambiguity or hesitation – **~ness** *n*

forthwith /fɔːθ'wɪð, -'wɪθ/ *adv* immediately

fortification /ˌfɔːtɪ̣fɪ̣'keɪʃən/ *n* sthg that fortifies, defends, or strengthens; *esp* works erected to defend a place or position

fortified wine /ˌfɔːtɪ̣faɪd 'waɪn/ *n* a wine to which alcohol has been added during or after fermentation

fortify /'fɔːtɪ̣faɪ/ *v* **1** to give strength, courage, or endurance to; strengthen **2** to erect fortifications – **-fiable** *adj* – **-fier** *n*

fortissimo /fɔː'tɪsɪ̣məʊ/ *adv or adj* very loud

fortitude /'fɔːtɪ̣tjuːd/ *n* patient courage in pain or adversity

fortnight /'fɔːtnaɪt/ *n, chiefly Br* two weeks

[1]**fortnightly** /'fɔːtnaɪtli/ *adj* occurring or appearing once a fortnight – **fortnightly** *adv*

[2]**fortnightly** *n* a publication issued fortnightly

fortress /'fɔːtrɪ̣s/ *n* a fortified place; *esp* a large and permanent fortification, sometimes including a town

fortuitous /fɔː'tjuːɪ̣təs/ *adj* **1** occurring by chance **2** fortunate, lucky – **~ly** *adv* – **~ness** *n*

fortunate /'fɔːtʃənət/ *adj* **1** unexpectedly bringing some good; auspicious **2** lucky

fortune /'fɔːtʃən/ *n* **1** *often cap* a supposed (personified) power that unpredictably determines events and issues **2a** (prosperity attained partly through) luck **b** *pl* the favourable or unfavourable events that accompany the progress of an individual or thing **3** destiny, fate **4** material possessions or wealth

fortune hunter *n* a person who seeks wealth, esp by marriage

fortune-teller *n* a person who claims to foretell future events

forty /'fɔːti/ *n* **1** the number 40 **2** *pl* the numbers 40 to 49; *specif* a range of temperatures, ages, or dates in a century characterized by those numbers – **-tieth** *adj, n, pron, adv*

forty-five *n* a gramophone record that plays at 45 revolutions per minute – usu written 45

forum /'fɔːrəm/ *n, pl* **forums** *also* **fora** **1** the marketplace or public place of an ancient Roman city forming the public centre **2** a public meeting place or medium for open discussion (e g on radio or television)

[1]**forward** /'fɔːwəd/ *adj* **1a** located at or directed towards the front **b** situated in advance **2a** eager, ready **b** lacking modesty or reserve; pert **3** advanced in development; precocious **4** moving, tending, or leading towards a position in (or at the) front **5** of or getting ready for the future (e g *forward* planning) – **~ly** *adv* – **~ness** *n*

[2]**forward** *adv* **1** to or towards what is ahead or in front **2** to or towards an earlier time (e g bring *forward* the date of the meeting) **3** into prominence

[3]**forward** *n* a mainly attacking player in hockey, soccer, etc stationed at or near the front of his/her side or team

[4]**forward** *v* **1** to help onwards; promote **2a** to send (forwards) **b** to send onwards from an intermediate point in transit – **~ing** *n*

[1]**fossil** /'fɒsəl/ *n* **1** a relic of an animal or plant of a past geological age, preserved in the earth's crust **2a** a person with outmoded views **b** sthg that has become rigidly fixed – **~ize** *v*

[2]**fossil** *adj* **1** preserved in a petrified form from a past geological age **2** outmoded

[1]**foster** /'fɒstəʳ/ *adj* giving, receiving, or sharing parental care though not related by blood

[2]**foster** *v* **1** to give parental care to; nurture **2** to promote the growth or development of

fought /fɔːt/ *past of* **fight**

[1]**foul** /faʊl/ *adj* **1** dirty, stained **2** notably offensive, unpleasant, or distressing **3** obscene, abusive **4a** treacherous, dishonourable **b** constituting a foul in a game or sport **5** polluted **6** entangled – **~ly** *adv* – **~ness** *n*

[2]**foul** *n* **1** an entanglement or collision in angling, sailing, etc **2** an infringement of the rules in a game or sport

[3]**foul** *v* **1** to commit a foul in a sport or game **2** to pollute **3** to become entangled with **4** to obstruct, block **5** to dishonour, discredit

foul play *n* violence; *esp* murder

[1]**found** /faʊnd/ *past of* **find**

[2]**found** *adj* having all usual, standard, or reasonably expected equipment

[3]**found** *v* **1** to set or ground on sthg solid – often + *on* or *upon* **2** to establish (e g a city or institution)

foundation /faʊn'deɪʃən/ *n* **1** the act of founding **2** the basis on which sthg stands or is supported **3** an organization or institution established by endowment with provision for future maintenance **4** an underlying natural or prepared base or support; *esp* the whole masonry substructure on which a building rests **5** a cream, lotion, etc applied as a base for other facial make-up

foundation stone *n* a stone in the foundation of a building, esp when laid with public ceremony

founder /'faʊndəʳ/ *v* **1** to go lame **2** to collapse; give way **3** to sink **4** to come to grief; fail

foundry /'faʊndri/ *n* (a place for) casting metals

[1]**fountain** /'faʊntɪ̣n/ *n* **1** a spring of water issuing from the earth **2** a source **3** (the structure providing) an artificially produced jet of water

[2]**fountain** *v* to (cause to) flow or spout like a fountain

fountainhead /'faʊntɪ̣nhed/ *n* a principal source

fountain pen *n* a pen containing a reservoir that automatically feeds the nib with ink

four /fɔːʳ/ *n* **1** the number 4 **2** the fourth in a set or series **3** sthg having 4 parts or members or a denomination of 4; *esp* (the crew of) a 4-person racing rowing boat **4** a shot in cricket that crosses the boundary after having hit the ground and scores 4 runs

four-letter word *n* any of a group of vulgar or obscene words typically made up of 4 letters

four-poster *n* a bed with 4 tall often carved corner posts designed to support curtains or a canopy

[1]**foursquare** /,fɔːskweəʳ/ *adj* forthright

[2]**foursquare** *adv* **1** in a solidly based and steady way **2** resolutely

fourteen /,fɔːtiːn/ *n* the number 14 – **~th** *adj, n, pron, adv*

fourth /fɔːθ/ *n* **1** number four in a countable series **2** (the combination of 2 notes at) a musical interval of 4 diatonic degrees **3** the 4th and usu highest forward gear or speed of a motor vehicle – **fourth** *adj* – **fourthly** *adv*

fourth dimension *n* sthg outside the range of ordinary experience

fowl /faʊl/ *n* **1** a bird **2** a domestic fowl; *esp* an adult hen **3** the flesh of birds used as food

[1]**fox** /fɒks/ *n* **1** (the fur of) a red fox or related flesh-eating mammal of the dog family with a pointed muzzle, large erect ears, and a long bushy tail **2** a clever crafty person

[2]**fox** *v* **1** to outwit **2** to baffle

foxglove /'fɒksglʌv/ *n* a common tall European plant that has showy white or purple tubular flowers and is a source of a drug used to stimulate the heart

foxhole /'fɒkshəʊl/ *n* a pit dug, usu hastily, for individual cover against enemy fire

foxhound /'fɒkshaʊnd/ *n* any of various large swift powerful hounds of great endurance used in hunting foxes

fox-trot *v or n* (to dance) a ballroom dance that includes slow walking and quick running steps

foxy /'fɒksi/ *adj* **1** cunningly shrewd in conniving and contriving **2** warmly reddish brown **3** *NAm* physically attractive

foyer /'fɔɪeɪ/ *n* a lobby (e g of a theatre); *also* an entrance hallway

fracas /'frækɑː/ *n, pl* **fracas** a noisy quarrel; a brawl

fraction /'frækʃən/ *n* **1a** a number (e g ¾, ⅝, 0.234) that is expressed as the quotient of 2 numbers **b** a (small) portion or section **2** an act of breaking up **3** a tiny bit; a little **4** any of several separate portions separable by distillation

fractional /'frækʃənəl/ *adj* **1** of or being a fraction **2** relatively tiny or brief **3** of or being a process for separating components of a mixture through differences in physical or chemical properties

fractionally /'frækʃənəli/ *adv* to a very small extent

fractious /'frækʃəs/ *adj* irritable and restless; hard to control – **~ly** *adv* – **~ness** *n*

[1]**fracture** /'fræktʃəʳ/ *n* a break or breaking, esp of hard tissue (e g bone)

[2]**fracture** *v* **1** to cause or undergo fracture **2** to damage or destroy as if by breaking apart; break up

fragile /'frædʒaɪl/ *adj* **1** easily shattered **2** lacking in strength; delicate – **-gility** *n*

[1]**fragment** /'frægmənt/ *n* an incomplete, broken off, or detached part

[2]**fragment** /fræg'ment/ *v* to break up or apart into fragments

fragmentary /'frægməntəri/ *adj* consisting of fragments; incomplete

fragrant /'freɪgrənt/ *adj* sweet or pleasant smelling – **-ance** *n* – **~ly** *adv*

frail /freɪl/ *adj* **1** morally or physically weak **2** easily broken or destroyed **3** slight, insubstantial

frailty /'freɪlti/ *n* a (moral) fault due to weakness

[1]**frame** /freɪm/ *v* **1** to plan, shape **2** to fit or adjust for a purpose **3a** to contrive evidence against (an innocent person) **b** to prearrange the outcome of (e g a contest)

[2]**frame** *n* **1** the physical structure of a human body **2** a structure that gives shape or strength (e g to a building) **3a** an open case or structure made for admitting, enclosing, or supporting sthg **b** the rigid part of a bicycle **c** the outer structure of a pair of glasses that holds the lenses **4a** an enclosing border **b** the matter or area enclosed in such a border: e g **(1)** a single picture of the series on a length of film **(2)** a single complete television picture made up of lines **c** a limiting, typical, or esp appropriate set of circumstances; a framework **5** one round of play in snooker, bowling, etc

frame of mind *n* a particular mental or emotional state

frame of reference *n* a set or system of facts, ideas, etc serving to orient or give particular meaning to a statement, a point of view, etc

frame-up *n* a conspiracy to frame sby or sthg – infml

framework /'freɪmwɜːk/ *n* **1** a skeletal, openwork, or structural frame **2** a basic structure (e g of ideas)

franc /fræŋk/ *n* (a note or coin representing) the basic money unit of France, Belgium, Switzerland, and certain other French-speaking countries

[1]**franchise** /ˈfræntʃaɪz/ *n* **1** a right or privilege; *specif* the right to vote **2** the right granted to an individual or group to market a company's goods or services in a particular territory; *also* the territory involved in such a right

[2]**franchise** *v* to grant a franchise to

Franciscan /frænˈsɪskən/ *n* a member of the Order of missionary friars founded by St Francis of Assisi in 1209

frangipani /ˌfrændʒɪˈpɑːni/ *n* **1** a perfume derived from or imitating the odour of the flower of the red jasmine **2** any of several tropical American shrubs or small trees

[1]**frank** /fræŋk/ *adj* marked by free, forthright, and sincere expression *also* undisguised – **~ness** *n* – **~ly** *adv*

[2]**frank** *n* a mark or stamp on a piece of mail indicating postage paid – **frank** *v*

Frank *n* a member of a W Germanic people that established themselves in the Netherlands and Gaul and on the Rhine in the 3rd and 4th c

frankfurter /ˈfræŋkfɜːtəʳ/ *n* a cured cooked, usu beef and pork, sausage

frankincense /ˈfræŋkɨnsens/ *n* a fragrant gum resin chiefly from E African or Arabian trees that is burnt as incense

franklin /ˈfræŋklɨn/ *n* a medieval English landowner of free but not noble birth

frantic /ˈfræntɪk/ *adj* **1** emotionally out of control **2** marked by fast and nervous, disordered, or anxiety-driven activity – **~ally** *adv*

fraternal /frəˈtɜːnəl/ *adj* **1a** of or involving brothers **b** of or being a fraternity or society **2** friendly, brotherly – **~ly** *adv* – **-nize** *v*

fraternity /frəˈtɜːnɨti/ *n* **1** *sing or pl in constr* a group of people associated or formally organized for a common purpose, interest, or pleasure **2** brotherliness **3** *sing or pl in constr* men of the same usu specified class, profession, character, or tastes

fratricide /ˈfrætrɨsaɪd/ *n* (the act of) sby who kills his/her brother or sister – **-cidal** *adj*

fraud /frɔːd/ *n* **1a** deception, esp for unlawful gain **b** a trick **2a** a person who is not what he/she pretends to be **b** sthg that is not what it seems or is represented to be

fraught /frɔːt/ *adj* **1** filled or charged *with* sthg specified **2** *Br* characterized by anxieties and tensions

[1]**fray** /freɪ/ *n* a brawl, fight

[2]**fray** *v* to wear out or into shreds

[1]**freak** /friːk/ *n* **1** a person or animal with a physical oddity who appears in a circus, funfair, etc **2** a person seen as being highly unconventional, esp in dress or ideas **3** an ardent enthusiast **4a** a sexual pervert **b** someone addicted to a specified drug – slang – **freak** *adj*

[2]**freak** *v* to freak out – slang

freakish /ˈfriːkɪʃ/ *adj* whimsical, capricious – **~ly** *adv* – **~ness** *n*

freak out *v* **1** to experience hallucinations or withdraw from reality, esp by taking drugs **2** to behave in an irrational, uncontrolled, or unconventional manner (as if) under the influence of drugs *USE* slang – **freak-out** *n*

freckle /ˈfrekəl/ *n* any of the small brownish spots on the skin, esp of white people, that increase in number and intensity on exposure to sunlight – **freckle** *v*

[1]**free** /friː/ *adj* **1a** enjoying civil and political liberty **b** not subject to the control or domination of another **2a** not determined by external influences **b** voluntary, spontaneous **3a** exempt, relieved, or released, esp from an unpleasant or unwanted condition or obligation – often in combination **b** not bound, confined, or detained by force **4a** having no trade restrictions **b** not subject to government regulation **5** having or taken up with no obligations or commitments **6** having an unrestricted scope **7a** not obstructed or impeded **b** not being used or occupied **8** not fastened **9a** lavish, unrestrained **b** outspoken **c** too familiar or forward **10** not costing or charging

anything **11** not (permanently) united with, attached to, or combined with sthg else; separate **12a** not literal or exact **b** not restricted by or conforming to conventional forms – **~ly** *adv*

[2]**free** *adv* **1** in a free manner **2** without charge

[3]**free** *v* **1** to cause to be free **2** to relieve or rid of sthg that restrains, confines, restricts, or embarrasses **3** to disentangle, clear

freeboard /ˈfriːbɔːd/ *n* the vertical distance between the waterline and the deck of a ship

freebooter /ˈfriːbuːtəʳ/ *n* a pirate, plunderer

freeborn /ˈfriːbɔːn/ *adj* not born in slavery

Free Church *n, chiefly Br* a British Nonconformist church

freedman /ˈfriːdmæn, -mən/, *fem* **freedwoman** *n* sby freed from slavery

freedom /ˈfriːdəm/ *n* **1a** the absence of necessity or constraint in choice or action **b** liberation from slavery or restraint **c** being exempt or released *from* sthg (onerous) **2a** ease, facility **b** being frank, open, or outspoken **c** improper familiarity **3** boldness of conception or execution **4** unrestricted use *of*

free enterprise *n* an economic system based on private business operating competitively for profit

free-fall *n* **1** (the condition of) unrestrained motion in a gravitational field **2** the part of a parachute jump before the parachute opens

free-for-all *n* **1** a fight or competition open to all comers and usu with no rules **2** an often vociferous quarrel or argument involving several participants

freehand /ˈfriːhænd/ *adj* done without the aid of drawing or measuring instruments – **freehand** *adv*

free hand *n* freedom of action or decision

freehanded /ˌfriːˈhændɨd/ *adj* openhanded, generous

freehold /ˈfriːhəʊld/ *n* a tenure in absolute possession; *also* a property held by such tenure – **~er** *n*

free house *n* a public house in Britain that is entitled to sell drinks supplied by more than 1 brewery

free kick *n* an unhindered kick in soccer, rugby, etc awarded because of a breach of the rules by an opponent

[1]**freelance** /ˈfriːlɑːns/ *n* a person who pursues a profession without long-term contractual commitments to any one employer – **freelance** *adj*

[2]**freelance** *v* to act as a freelance – **-lancer** *n*

free-living *adj, of a living organism* neither parasitic nor symbiotic – **free-liver** *n*

freeman /ˈfriːmən/ *n* **1** sby enjoying civil or political liberty **2** sby who has the full rights of a citizen

Freemason /ˈfriːmeɪsən/ *n* a member of an ancient and widespread secret fraternity called Free and Accepted Masons

freemasonry /ˈfriːmeɪsənri, -ˈ---/ *n* **1** *cap* the principles, institutions, or practices of Freemasons **2** natural or instinctive fellowship or sympathy

free-range *adj* of, being, or produced by poultry reared in the open air rather than in a battery

freestanding /ˌfriːˈstændɪŋ/ *adj* standing without lateral support or attachment

freestyle /ˈfriːstaɪl/ *n* **1** (a style used in) a competition in which a contestant uses a style (e g of swimming) of his/her choice **2** a style of wrestling in which any kind of hold is allowed

freethinker /ˌfriːˈθɪŋkəʳ/ *n* a person who forms opinions on the basis of reason; *esp* one who rejects religious dogma – **-thinking** *adj*

free verse *n* verse without fixed metrical form

free will *n* the power of choosing without the constraint of divine necessity or causal law

[1]**freeze** /friːz/ *v* **froze; frozen 1** to convert from a liquid to a solid by cold **2a** to make extremely cold **b** to anaesthetize (as if) by cold **3a** to become clogged with ice **b** to become fixed or motionless; *esp* to abruptly cease acting or speaking **4** to immobilize the expenditure, withdrawal, or exchange of (foreign-owned bank balances) by

government regulation **5** to preserve (e g food) by freezing

[2]**freeze** *n* **1** freezing cold weather **2** an act or period of freezing sthg, esp wages or prices at a certain level

freeze-dry *v* to dehydrate (sthg) while in a frozen state in a vacuum, esp for preservation

freezer /ˈfriːzəʳ/ *n* an apparatus that freezes or keeps cool; *esp* an insulated cabinet or room for storing frozen food or for freezing food rapidly

freight /freɪt/ *n* **1** the charge made for transporting goods **2** a cargo **3** a goods train

freighter /ˈfreɪtəʳ/ *n* a ship or aircraft used chiefly to carry freight

freightliner /ˈfreɪtlaɪnəʳ/ *n, Br* a train designed for carrying containerized cargo

[1]**French** /frentʃ/ *adj* of France, its people, or their language

[2]**French** *n* **1** the Romance language of the people of France and of parts of Belgium, Switzerland, and Canada **2** *pl in constr* the people of France

French bean *n* (the seed or pod of) a common bean often cultivated for its slender edible green pods

French dressing *n* a salad dressing of oil, vinegar, and seasonings

french fry *n, chiefly NAm* a chip – usu pl

French horn *n* a circular valved brass instrument with a usual range from B below the bass staff upwards for more than 3 octaves

French kiss *n* a kiss made with open mouths and usu with tongue-to-tongue contact

French leave *n* leave taken without permission

French letter *n, Br* a condom – infml

French polish *n* a solution of shellac used as a wood polish – **French-polish** *v*

French windows *n pl* a pair of doors with full length glazing

frenetic /frʲ̈ˈnetɪk/ *adj* frenzied, frantic – **~ally** *adv*

frenzy /ˈfrenzi/ *n* **1** a temporary madness **2** (a spell of) wild, compulsive, or agitated behaviour – **-zied** *adj* – **-ziedly** *adv*

frequency /ˈfriːkwənsi/ *n* **1** the fact or condition of occurring frequently **2a** the number of complete alternations per second of an alternating current **b** the number of sound waves per second produced by a sounding body **c** the number of complete oscillations per second of an electromagnetic wave

[1]**frequent** /ˈfriːkwənt/ *adj* **1** often repeated or occurring **2** habitual, persistent – **~ly** *adv*

[2]**frequent** /friˈkwent/ *v* to be in or visit often or habitually

fresco /ˈfreskəʊ/ *n, pl* **frescoes, frescos** (a painting made by) the application of water colours to moist plaster

[1]**fresh** /freʃ/ *adj* **1a** not salt **b** free from taint; clean **c** *of weather* cool and windy **2a** *of food* not preserved **b** not stale, sour, or decayed **3a** (different or alternative and) new **b** newly or just come or arrived **4** too forward with a person of the opposite sex – infml – **~ness** *n* – **~ly** *adv* – **~en** *v*

[2]**fresh** *adv* **1** just recently; newly **2** *chiefly NAm* as of a very short time ago

freshen up *v* to make (oneself) fresher or more comfortable, esp by washing, changing one's clothes, etc

[1]**fret** /fret/ *v* **1** to torment with anxiety or worry; vex **2a** to eat or gnaw into; corrode **b** to rub, chafe **3** to agitate, ripple

[2]**fret** *n* a state of (querulous) mental agitation or irritation

[3]**fret** *v* **1** to decorate with interlaced designs **2** to decorate (e g a ceiling) with embossed or carved patterns

[4]**fret** *n* any of a series of ridges fixed across the fingerboard of a stringed musical instrument (e g a guitar)

fretful /ˈfretfəl/ *adj* **1** tending to fret; in a fret **2** *of water* having the surface agitated – **~ly** *adv* – **~ness** *n*

fretsaw /ˈfretsɔː/ *n* a narrow-bladed fine-toothed saw held under tension in a frame and used for cutting intricate patterns in thin wood

fretwork /ˈfretwɜːk/ *n* ornamental openwork, esp in thin wood; *also* ornamental work in relief

Freudian /ˈfrɔɪdɪən/ *adj* of or con-

forming to orthodox psychoanalytic theories or practices
Freudian slip *n* a slip of the tongue that is held to reveal some unconscious aspect of the speaker's mind
friar /'fraɪəʳ/ *n* a member of a religious order combining monastic life with outside religious activity and orig owning neither personal nor community property
friary /'fraɪəri/ *n* (a building housing) a community of friars
fricassee /,frɪkə'siː, '---/ *n* a dish of small pieces of stewed chicken, rabbit, etc served in a white sauce
friction /'frɪkʃən/ *n* **1a** the rubbing of one body against another **b** resistance to relative motion between 2 bodies in contact **2** disagreement between 2 people or parties of opposing views
Friday /'fraɪdi/ *n* the day of the week following Thursday
fridge /frɪdʒ/ *n, chiefly Br* a refrigerator
friend /frend/ *n* **1a** a person whose company, interests, and attitudes one finds sympathetic and to whom one is not closely related **b** an acquaintance **2a** sby or sthg not hostile **b** sby or sthg that favours or encourages sthg (e g a charity) **3** *cap* a Quaker
[1]**friendly** /'frendli/ *adj* **1a** having the relationship of friends **b** not hostile **c** inclined to be favourable – usu + *to* **2** cheerful, comforting – **-liness** *n*
[2]**friendly** *n, chiefly Br* a match played for practice or pleasure and not as part of a competition
friendly society *n, often cap F&S, Br* a mutual insurance association providing its subscribers with benefits during sickness, unemployment, and old age
friendship /'frendʃɪp/ *n* being friends or being friendly
frieze /friːz/ *n* a sculptured or ornamented band (e g on a building)
frigate /'frɪgɪ̵̆t/ *n* **1** a square-rigged 3-masted warship next in size below a ship of the line **2** a general-purpose naval escort vessel between a corvette and a cruiser in size
fright /fraɪt/ *n* **1** fear excited by sudden danger or shock **2** sthg unsightly, strange, ugly, or shocking – infml – **fright** *v*
frighten /'fraɪtn/ *v* **1** to make afraid; scare **2** to force by frightening – **~ingly** *adv*
frightful /'fraɪtfəl/ *adj* **1** causing intense fear, shock, or horror **2** unpleasant, difficult – infml – **~ness** *n* – **~ly** *adv*
frigid /'frɪdʒɪ̵̆d/ *adj* **1a** intensely cold **b** lacking warmth or intensity of feeling **2** *esp of a woman* abnormally averse to sexual contact, esp intercourse – **~ly** *adv* – **~ity** *n*
frill /frɪl/ *n* **1** a gathered or pleated fabric edging used on clothing **2** a ruff of hair or feathers round the neck of an animal **3a** an affectation, air **b** sthg decorative but not essential *USE* (*3*) usu pl
[1]**fringe** /frɪndʒ/ *n* **1** an ornamental border (e g on a curtain or garment) consisting of straight or twisted threads or tassels **2** the hair that falls over the forehead **3a** sthg marginal, additional, or secondary **b** *sing or pl in constr* a group with marginal or extremist views **c** *often cap* theatre featuring small-scale avant-garde productions
[2]**fringe** *v* **1** to provide or decorate with a fringe **2** to serve as a fringe for
fringe benefit *n* a benefit (e g a pension) granted by an employer to an employee that involves a money cost without affecting basic wage rates
frippery /'frɪpəri/ *n* **1** nonessential ornamentation, esp of a showy or tawdry kind **2** affected elegance – **frippery** *adj*
Frisbee /'frɪzbi/ *trademark* – used for a plastic disc thrown between players by a flip of the wrist
Frisian /'friːʒən, -zɪən/ *n* **1** a member of a Germanic people inhabiting Friesland and the Frisian islands **2** the language of the Frisian people
[1]**frisk** /frɪsk/ *v* **1** to leap, skip, or dance in a lively or playful way **2** to search (a person) for sthg, esp a hidden weapon, by passing the hands over his/her body – infml
[2]**frisk** *n* **1** a gambol, romp **2** an act of frisking
frisky /'frɪski/ *adj* lively, playful – **-kily** *adv* – **-kiness** *n*
fritter /'frɪtəʳ/ *n* a piece of fried batter often containing fruit, meat, etc

fritter away *v* to waste bit by bit

frivolous /ˈfrɪvələs/ *adj* **1** lacking in seriousness; irresponsibly self-indulgent **2** lacking practicality or serious purpose; unimportant – ~**ly** *adv* – ~**ness** *n* – **-volity** *n*

frizz /frɪz/ *n* (hair in) a mass of small tight curls

frizzle /ˈfrɪzəl/ *v* **1** to fry (e g bacon) until crisp and curled **2** to burn, scorch

fro /frəʊ/ *prep, dial* from

frock /frɒk/ *n* a woman's dress

frock coat *n* a usu double-breasted coat with knee-length skirts worn by men, esp in the 19th c

frog /frɒg/ *n* **1** any of various tailless smooth-skinned web-footed largely aquatic leaping amphibians **2** the triangular horny pad in the middle of the sole of a horse's foot **3** a usu ornamental fastening for the front of a garment consisting of a button and a loop **4** *often cap* a French person – chiefly derog; infml **5** the hollow in either or both faces of a brick to take mortar

frogman /ˈfrɒgmən/ *n* a person equipped with face mask, flippers, rubber suit, etc and an air supply for swimming underwater for extended periods

frogmarch /ˈfrɒgmɑːtʃ/ *v* **1** to carry (a person) face downwards by the arms and legs **2** to force (a person) to move forwards with the arms held firmly behind

frogspawn /ˈfrɒgspɔːn/ *n* (a gelatinous mass of) frog's eggs

[1]**frolic** /ˈfrɒlɪk/ *v* **1** to play and run about happily **2** to make merry

[2]**frolic** *n* **1** (a) playful expression of high spirits; gaiety **2** a lighthearted entertainment or game

from /frəm; *strong* frɒm/ *prep* **1** – used to indicate a starting point: e g **a** a place where a physical movement, or an action or condition suggestive of movement, begins (e g came here *from* the city) **b** a starting point in measuring or reckoning or in a statement of extent or limits (e g lives 5 miles *from* the coast) **c** a point in time after which a period is reckoned (e g a week *from* today) **d** a viewpoint **2** – used to indicate separation: e g **a** physical separation (e g absent *from* school) **b** removal, refraining, exclusion, release, or differentiation (e g relief *from* pain; don't know one *from* the other) **3** – used to indicate the source, cause, agent, or basis (e g a call *from* my lawyer; made *from* flour)

frond /frɒnd/ *n* (a shoot resembling) a leaf, esp of a palm or fern

[1]**front** /frʌnt/ *n* **1** (feigned) demeanour or bearing, esp in the face of a challenge, danger, etc **2** *often cap* a zone of conflict between armies **3a** a sphere of activity **b** a movement linking divergent elements to achieve certain common objectives; *esp* a political coalition **4a** the (main) face of a building **b** the forward part or surface: e g **(1)** the part of the human body opposite to the back **(2)** the part of a garment covering the chest **c** *the* beach promenade at a seaside resort **5** the boundary between 2 dissimilar air masses **6a** a position ahead of a person or of the foremost part of a thing **b** a position of importance, leadership, or advantage **7** a person, group, or thing used to mask the identity or true character of the actual controlling agent; *also* a poorly nominal head

[2]**front** *v* **1** to face – often + *on* or *onto* **2** to serve as a front – often + *for*

[3]**front** *adj* of or situated at the front

frontage /ˈfrʌntɪdʒ/ *n* **1** the land between the front of a building and the street **2** (the width of) the front face of a building

frontal /ˈfrʌntl/ *adj* **1** of or adjacent to the forehead **2a** of, situated at, or showing the front **b** direct **3** of a meteorological front

front bench *n* either of 2 rows of benches in Parliament on which party leaders sit

frontier /ˈfrʌntɪəʳ/ *n* **1** a border between 2 countries **2** the boundary between the known and the unknown – often pl with sing. meaning **3** *NAm* a region that forms the margin of settled or developed territory

frontispiece /ˈfrʌntɪ̥spiːs/ *n* an illustration preceding and usu facing the title page of a book or magazine

front-page *adj* very newsworthy

front-runner *n* **1** a contestant who runs best when in the lead **2** a leading contestant in a competition

[1]**frost** /frɒst/ *n* **1a** (the temperature that causes) freezing **b** a covering of minute ice crystals on a cold surface **2** coldness of attitude or manner

[2]**frost** *v* **1** to freeze – often + *over* **2a** to produce a fine-grained slightly roughened surface on (metal, glass, etc) **b** to cover (e g a cake or grapes) with sugar; *also, chiefly NAm* to ice (a cake)

frostbite /ˈfrɒstbaɪt/ *n* (gangrene or other local effect of a partial) freezing of some part of the body – **-bitten** *adj*

frosty /ˈfrɒsti/ *adj* **1** marked by or producing frost **2** (appearing as if) covered with frost **3** marked by coolness or extreme reserve in manner – **-tily** *adv* – **-tiness** *n*

[1]**froth** /frɒθ/ *n* **1a** a mass of bubbles formed on or in a liquid **b** a foamy saliva sometimes accompanying disease or exhaustion **2** sthg insubstantial or of little value – **~y** *adj* – **~ily** *adv* – **~iness** *n*

[2]**froth** *v* to cause to foam – often + *up*

[1]**frown** /fraʊn/ *v* **1** to contract the brow **2** to give evidence of displeasure or disapproval – often + *on* or *upon* – **~ingly** *adv*

[2]**frown** *n* **1** a wrinkling of the brow in displeasure, concentration, or puzzlement **2** an expression of displeasure

frowsy, frowzy /ˈfraʊzi/ *adj* **1** having a slovenly uncared-for appearance **2** musty, stale

froze /frəʊz/ *past of* **freeze**

frozen /ˈfrəʊzən/ *adj* **1a** treated, affected, solidified, or crusted over by freezing **b** subject to long and severe cold **2a** drained or incapable of emotion **b** incapable of being changed, moved, or undone **c** not available for present use

frugal /ˈfruːgəl/ *adj* economical in the expenditure of resources; sparing – **~ly** *adv* – **~ity** *n*

fruit /fruːt/ *n* **1a** a product of plant growth (e g grain or vegetables) **b** a succulent edible plant part used chiefly in a dessert or sweet dish **c** the ripened fertilized ovary of a flowering plant together with its contents **2** offspring, progeny **3** a (favourable) product or result – often pl with sing. meaning – **fruit** *v*

fruiterer /ˈfruːtərəʳ/ *n* one who deals in fruit

fruit fly *n* any of various small flies whose larvae feed on fruit or decaying vegetable matter

fruitful /ˈfruːtfəl/ *adj* **1** (conducive to) yielding or producing (abundant) fruit **2** abundantly productive – **~ly** *adv* – **~ness** *n*

fruition /fruːˈɪʃən/ *n* **1** bearing fruit **2** realization, fulfilment

fruitless /ˈfruːtlǝ̵s/ *adj* **1** lacking or not bearing fruit **2** useless, unsuccessful – **~ly** *adv* – **~ness** *n*

fruit machine *n, Br* a coin-operated gambling machine that pays out according to different combinations of symbols (e g different types of fruit) visible on wheels

fruity /ˈfruːti/ *adj* **1** having the flavour of the unfermented fruit **2** *of a voice* marked by richness and depth **3** amusing in a sexually suggestive way – infml

frump /frʌmp/ *n* **1** a dowdy unattractive girl or woman **2** a staid drab old-fashioned person *USE* chiefly infml – **~ish** *adj* – **~y** *adj*

frustrate /frʌˈstreɪt/ *v* **1a** to balk or defeat in an endeavour; foil **b** to induce feelings of discouragement and vexation in **2** to make ineffectual; nullify – **-ation** *n*

[1]**fry** /fraɪ/ *v* to cook in hot fat

[2]**fry** *n, pl* **fry** **1a** recently hatched or very small (adult) fishes **b** the young of other animals, esp when occurring in large numbers **2** a member of a group or class; *esp* a person

frying pan *n* a shallow metal pan with a handle that is used for frying foods

fry-up *n, Br* (a dish prepared by) the frying of food for a simple impromptu meal – chiefly infml

fuchsia /ˈfjuːʃə/ *n* any of a genus of decorative shrubs with showy nodding flowers usu in deep pinks, reds, and purples

fuck /fʌk/ *v* **1** to have sexual intercourse (with) **2** to mess *about* or *around* *USE* vulg – **fuck** *n*

fuddle /ˈfʌdl/ *v* **1** to make drunk **2** to make confused – **fuddle** *n*

fuddy-duddy /ˈfʌdi ˌdʌdi/ *n* a person who is old-fashioned, pompous, unimaginative, or concerned about trifles – infml

[1]**fudge** /fʌdʒ/ *v* **1** to devise or put together roughly or without adequate basis **2** to fail to come to grips with; dodge

[2]**fudge** *n* a soft (creamy) sweet made typically of sugar, milk, butter, and flavouring

[1]**fuel** /fjʊəl/ *n* **1a** a material used to produce heat or power by combustion **b** nutritive material **2** a source of sustenance, strength, or encouragement

[2]**fuel** *v* **1** to provide with fuel **2** to support, stimulate

fug /fʌg/ *n* the stuffy atmosphere of a poorly ventilated space – chiefly infml – **~gy** *adj*

[1]**fugitive** /ˈfjuːdʒɪtɪv/ *adj* **1** running away or trying to escape **2a** elusive **b** likely to change, fade, or disappear

[2]**fugitive** *n* a person who flees or tries to escape, esp from danger, justice, or oppression

fugue /fjuːg/ *n* **1** a musical composition in which 1 or 2 themes are repeated or imitated by successively entering voices and are developed in a continuous interweaving of the voice parts **2** a disturbed state in which a person performs acts of which on recovery he/she has no recollection and which usu involves disappearance from his/her usual environment

führer /ˈfjʊərəʳ/ *n* the leader of a totalitarian party or state

fulcrum /ˈfʊlkrəm, ˈfʌl-/ *n, pl* **fulcrums, fulcra** the support about which a lever turns

fulfil, *NAm chiefly* **fulfill** /fʊlˈfil/ *v* **1a** to cause to happen as appointed or predicted – usu pass **b** to put into effect **c** to measure up to; satisfy **2** to develop the full potential of – **~ment** *n*

[1]**full** /fʊl/ *adj* **1** possessing or containing a great amount or as much or as many as is possible or normal **2a** complete, esp in detail, number, or duration **b** lacking restraint, check, or qualification **3** at the highest or greatest degree; maximum **4** rounded in outline; *also* well filled out or plump **5a** having an abundance of material (e g in the form of gathers or folds) **b** rich in experience **6** satisfied, esp with food or drink, often to the point of discomfort – usu + *up* **7** filled with excited anticipation or pleasure **8** possessing a rich or pronounced quality – **~ness, fulness** *n*

[2]**full** *adv* exactly, squarely

[3]**full** *n* **1** the highest or fullest state, extent, or degree **2** the requisite or complete amount – chiefly in *in full*

[4]**full** *v* to cleanse and finish (woollen cloth) by moistening, heating, and pressing – **~er** *n*

fullback /ˈfʊlbæk/ *n* a primarily defensive player in soccer, rugby, etc, usu stationed nearest the defended goal

full-blooded *adj* **1** of unmixed ancestry; purebred **2** forceful, vigorous – **~ness** *n*

full-blown *adj* **1** at the height of bloom **2** fully developed or mature

fuller's earth *n* a clayey substance used in fulling cloth and as a catalyst

full house *n* a poker hand containing 3 of a kind and a pair

full-length *adj* **1** showing or adapted to the entire length, esp of the human figure **2** having a normal or standard length; unabridged

full-scale *adj* **1** identical to an original in proportion and size **2** involving full use of available resources

full stop *n* a punctuation mark . used to mark the end (e g of a sentence or abbreviation)

full-time *adj* employed for or involving full time

full time *n* **1** the amount of time considered the normal or standard amount for working during a given period, esp a week **2** the end of a sports, esp soccer, match

full toss *n* a throw, esp a bowled ball in cricket, that has not hit the ground by the time it arrives at the point at which it was aimed

fully /ˈfʊli/ *adv* **1** completely **2** at least

fully-fashioned *adj* employing or produced by a knitting process for shaping to body lines

fully-fledged *adj* having attained complete status

fulminate /ˈfʊlmɪ̈neɪt/ *v* **1** to thunder forth censure or invective – usu + *against* or *at* **2** to be agitated or enraged (by feelings of indignation) – **-ation** *n*

fulsome /ˈfʊlsəm/ *adj* **1** overabundant, copious **2a** unnecessarily effusive **b** obsequious – **~ly** *adv* – **~ness** *n*

fumble /ˈfʌmbəl/ *v* **1a** to grope for or handle sthg clumsily or awkwardly **b** to make awkward attempts to do or find sthg **2** to feel one's way or move awkwardly – **~r** *n* – **fumble** *n* – **-lingly** *adv*

[1]**fume** /fjuːm/ *n* **1** an (irritating or offensive) smoke, vapour, or gas – often pl with sing. meaning **2** a state of unreasonable excited irritation or anger

[2]**fume** *v* **1** to emit fumes **2** to be in a state of excited irritation or anger

fumigate /ˈfjuːmɪ̈geɪt/ *v* to apply smoke, vapour, or gas to, esp in order to disinfect or destroy pests – **-gation** *n*

[1]**fun** /fʌn/ *n* **1** (a cause of) amusement or enjoyment **2** derisive jest; ridicule **3** violent or excited activity or argument

[2]**fun** *adj* providing entertainment, amusement, or enjoyment – infml

[1]**function** /ˈfʌŋkʃən/ *n* **1** an occupational duty **2** the action characteristic of a person or thing or for which a thing exists **3** an impressive, elaborate, or formal ceremony or social gathering **4** a quality, trait, or fact dependent on and varying with another

[2]**function** *v* **1** to have a function; serve **2** to operate

functional /ˈfʌŋkʃənəl/ *adj* **1** of, connected with, or being a function **2** designed or developed for practical use without ornamentation – **~ly** *adv*

functionary /ˈfʌŋkʃənəri/ *n* **1** sby who serves in a certain function **2** sby holding office

[1]**fund** /fʌnd/ *n* **1** an available quantity of material or intangible resources **2** (an organization administering) a resource, esp a sum of money, whose principal or interest is set apart for a specific objective **3** *pl* an available supply of money

[2]**fund** *v* **1** to make provision of resources for discharging the interest or principal of **2** to provide funds for

[1]**fundamental** /ˌfʌndəˈmentl/ *adj* **1** serving as a basis to support existence or to determine essential structure or function – often + *to* **2** of essential structure, function, or facts **3** of, being, or produced by the lowest component of a complex vibration **4** of central importance; principal

[2]**fundamental** *n* **1** a minimum constituent without which a thing or system would not be what it is **2** the prime tone of a harmonic series **3** the harmonic component of a complex wave that has the lowest frequency

fundamentalism /ˌfʌndəˈmentəlɪzəm/ *n* (adherence to) a belief in the literal truth of the Bible – **-ist** *n, adj*

funeral /ˈfjuːnərəl/ *n* (a procession connected with) a formal and ceremonial disposing of dead body, esp by burial or cremation

funerary /ˈfjuːnərəri/ *adj* of, used for, or associated with burial

funereal /fjʊˈnɪərɪəl/ *adj* **1** of a funeral **2** gloomy, solemn – **~ly** *adv*

fun fair *n, chiefly Br* a usu outdoor show offering amusements (e g sideshows, rides, or games of skill)

fungicide /ˈfʌndʒɪ̈saɪd/ *n* a substance used for destroying or preventing fungus

fungous /ˈfʌŋgəs/ *adj* of, like, or caused by a fungus or fungi

fungus /ˈfʌŋgəs/ *n, pl* **fungi** *also* **funguses** any of a major group of often parasitic organisms lacking chlorophyll and including moulds, rusts, mildews, smuts, mushrooms, and toadstools – **-goid** *adj* – **-gal** *adj*

[1]**funicular** /fjʊˈnɪkjʊləʳ/ *adj* dependent on the tension of a cord or cable

[2]**funicular** *n* a cable railway in which an ascending carriage counterbalances a descending carriage

[1]**funk** /fʌŋk/ *n* **1a** a state of paralysing fear **b** a fit of inability to face difficulty **2** a coward *USE* infml

[2]funk *v* to avoid doing or facing (sthg) because of lack of determination *USE* infml

[3]funk *n* funky music – slang

funky /ˈfʌŋki/ *adj* **1** having an earthy unsophisticated style and feeling (as in the blues) **2** – used to approve sthg or sby, esp in pop culture *USE* slang

[1]funnel /ˈfʌnəl/ *n* **1** a utensil usu having the shape of a hollow cone with a tube extending from the smaller end, designed to direct liquids or powders into a small opening **2** a shaft, stack, or flue for ventilation or the escape of smoke or steam

[2]funnel *v* **1** to pass (as if) through a funnel **2** to move to a focal point or into a central channel

funny /ˈfʌni/ *adj* **1** causing mirth and laughter; seeking or intended to amuse **2** peculiar, strange, or odd **3** involving trickery, deception, or dishonesty **4** unwilling to be helpful; difficult **5a** slightly unwell **b** slightly mad **6** pleasantly amusing; nice – esp in *funny old* *USE* (*3, 4, 5, & 6*) infml – **funnily** *adv* – **funniness** *n*

funny bone *n* the place at the back of the elbow where the nerve supplying the hand and forearm rests against the bone

[1]fur /fɜːʳ/ *v* to (cause to) become coated or clogged (as if) with fur – often + *up*

[2]fur *n* **1** the hairy coat of a mammal, esp when fine, soft, and thick; *also* such a coat with the skin **2** an article of clothing made of or with fur **3** a coating resembling fur: **e g a** a coating of dead cells on the tongue of sby who is unwell **b** the thick pile of a fabric **c** a coating formed in vessels (e g kettles or pipes) by deposition of scale from hard water

furbish /ˈfɜːbɪʃ/ *v* **1** to polish **2** to renovate – often + *up*

furious /ˈfjʊərɪəs/ *adj* **1** exhibiting or goaded by uncontrollable anger **2** giving a stormy or turbulent appearance **3** marked by (violent) noise, excitement, or activity – **~ness** *n* – **~ly** *adv*

furl /fɜːl/ *v* to fold or roll (e g a sail or umbrella) close to or round sthg

furlong /ˈfɜːlɒŋ/ *n* a unit of length equal to 220yd (about 0.201km)

furlough /ˈfɜːləʊ/ *n* a leave of absence from duty granted esp to a soldier

furnace /ˈfɜːnɪ̈s/ *n* an enclosed apparatus in which heat is produced (e g for heating a building or reducing ore)

furnish /ˈfɜːnɪʃ/ *v* to provide or supply (with what is needed); *esp* to equip with furniture – **~ings** *n pl*

furniture /ˈfɜːnɪtʃəʳ/ *n* necessary, useful, or desirable equipment: e g **a** the movable articles (e g tables, chairs, and beds) that make an area suitable for living in or use **b** accessories **c** the whole movable equipment of a ship (e g rigging, sails, anchors, and boats)

furore /fjʊˈrɔːri, ˈfjʊərɔːʳ/ *n* an outburst of general excitement or indignation

furrier /ˈfʌrɪəʳ/ *n* a fur dealer

[1]furrow /ˈfʌrəʊ/ *n* **1** a trench in the earth made by a plough **2** a groove

[2]furrow *v* to make or form furrows, grooves, lines, etc (in)

furry /ˈfɜːri/ *adj* like, made of, or covered with fur

[1]further /ˈfɜːðəʳ/ *adv* **1** farther **2** moreover **3** to a greater degree or extent (e g *further* annoyed by a second interruption)

[2]further *adj* **1** farther **2** extending beyond what exists or has happened; additional (e g *further* volumes) **3** coming after the one referred to

[3]further *v* to help forward

furthermore /ˌfɜːðəˈmɔːʳ/ *adv* in addition to what precedes; moreover – used esp when introducing fresh matter for consideration

furthermost /ˈfɜːðəməʊst/ *adj* most distant

further to *prep* following up

furthest /ˈfɜːðɪ̈st/ *adv or adj* farthest

furtive /ˈfɜːtɪv/ *adj* expressing or done by stealth – **~ly** *adv* – **~ness** *n*

fury /ˈfjʊəri/ *n* **1** intense, disordered, and often destructive rage **2** *cap* any of the 3 avenging deities who in Greek mythology punished crimes **3** wild disordered force or activity

furze /fɜːz/ *n* gorse

[1]fuse /fjuːz/ *n* the detonating device

for setting off the charge in a projectile, bomb, etc

[2]**fuse** *v* **1** to become fluid with heat **2** to become blended (as if) by melting together **3** to fail because of the melting of a fuse

[3]**fuse** *n* (a device that includes) a wire or strip of fusible metal that melts and interrupts the circuit when the current exceeds a particular value

fuselage /ˈfjuːzəlɑːʒ/ *n* the central body portion of an aeroplane designed to accommodate the crew and the passengers or cargo

fusillade /ˌfjuːzlˈleɪd/ *n* **1** a number of shots fired simultaneously or in rapid succession **2** a spirited outburst, esp of criticism

fusion /ˈfjuːʒən/ *n* **1** fusing or rendering plastic by heat **2** a union (as if) by melting: e g **a** a merging of diverse elements into a unified whole **b** the union of light atomic nuclei to form heavier nuclei resulting in the release of enormous quantities of energy

[1]**fuss** /fʌs/ *n* **1a** needless or useless bustle or excitement **b** a show of (affectionate) attention – often in *make a fuss of* **2a** a state of agitation, esp over a trivial matter **b** an objection, protest

[2]**fuss** *v* **1a** to create or be in a state of restless activity; *specif* to shower affectionate attentions **b** to pay close or undue attention to small details **2** to become upset; worry

fusspot /ˈfʌspɒt/ *n* a person who fusses about trifles – infml

fussy /ˈfʌsi/ *adj* **1** nervous and excitable (about small matters) **2a** showing too much concern over details **b** fastidious **3** having too much or too detailed ornamentation – **-ssily** *adv* – **-ssiness** *n*

fustian /ˈfʌstɪən/ *n* **1** a strong cotton or linen fabric (e g corduroy or velveteen), usu having a pile face and twill weave **2** pretentious and banal writing or speech

fusty /ˈfʌsti/ *adj* **1** stale or musty from being left undisturbed for a long time **2** out-of-date **3** rigidly old-fashioned or reactionary – **-tiness** *n*

futile /ˈfjuːtaɪl/ *adj* **1** completely ineffective **2** *of a person* ineffectual – **-lity** *n*

[1]**future** /ˈfjuːtʃəʳ/ *adj* **1** that is to be; *specif* existing after death **2** of or constituting the future tense

[2]**future** *n* **1a** time that is to come **b** that which is going to occur **2** sthg (e g a bulk commodity) bought for future acceptance or sold for future delivery – usu pl **3** (a verb form in) a tense indicating the future

futuristic /ˌfjuːtʃəˈrɪstɪk/ *adj* bearing no relation to known or traditional forms; ultramodern – **~ally** *adv*

[1]**fuzz** /fʌz/ *n* fine light particles or fibres (e g of down or fluff)

[2]**fuzz** *n sing or pl in constr* the police – slang

fuzzy /ˈfʌzi/ *adj* **1** marked by or giving a suggestion of fuzz **2** not clear; indistinct – **-zzily** *adv* – **-zziness** *n*

G

g /dʒiː/ *n, pl* **g's, gs** *often cap* **1** (a graphic representation of or device for reproducing) the 7th letter of the English alphabet **2** the 5th note of a C-major scale

gabardine /'gæbədiːn/ *n* **1** gaberdine **2** a firm durable fabric (e g of wool or rayon) with diagonal ribs on the right side; *also* a waterproof coat made of this

gabble /'gæbəl/ *v* to talk or utter rapidly or unintelligibly

gaberdine /'gæbədiːn/ *n* **1** a coarse long coat or smock worn chiefly by Jews in medieval times **2** gabardine

gable /'geɪbəl/ *n* the vertical triangular section of wall between 2 slopes of a pitched roof – **~d** *adj*

gad /'gæd/ *v* to go or travel in an aimless or restless manner or in search of pleasure – usu + *about* – **gadabout** *n*

gadget /'gædʒɪt/ *n* a usu small and often novel device, esp on a piece of machinery – **~ry** *n*

Gaelic /'geɪlɪk, 'gælɪk/ *adj* of or being the Celts in Ireland, the Isle of Man, and the Scottish highlands

[1]gaff /gæf/ *n* **1a** a spear or spearhead for killing fish or turtles **b** a pole with a hook for holding or landing heavy fish **2** a spar on which the head of a fore-and-aft sail is extended

[2]gaff *v* to strike or secure (e g a fish) with a gaff

gaffe /gæf/ *n* a social blunder

gaffer /'gæfəʳ/ *n* **1** the chief lighting electrician in a film or television studio **2** *Br* a foreman or overseer **3** *dial* an old man

[1]gag /gæg/ *v* **1** to apply a gag to or put a gag in the mouth of (to prevent speech) **2** to (cause to) retch **3** to prevent from having free speech or expression – chiefly journ

[2]gag *n* **1** sthg thrust into the mouth to keep it open or prevent speech or outcry **2** a joke or trick

gaggle /'gægəl/ *n* **1** a flock of geese **2** *sing or pl in constr* a typically noisy or talkative group or cluster – chiefly infml

gaiety /'geɪəti/ *n* **1** merrymaking; *also* festive activity **2** gay quality, spirits, manner, or appearance

[1]gain /'geɪn/ *n* **1** resources or advantage acquired or increased; a profit **2** the obtaining of profit or possessions **3** an increase in amount, magnitude, or degree

[2]gain *v* **1a(1)** to get possession of or win, usu by industry, merit, or craft **(2)** to increase a lead over or catch up a rival by (esp time or distance) **b** to acquire **2** to increase, specif in weight **3** *of a timepiece* to run fast

gainful /'geɪnfəl/ *adj* profitable – **~ly** *adv*

gait /geɪt/ *n* **1** a manner of walking or moving on foot **2** a sequence of foot movements (e g a walk, trot, or canter) by which a horse moves forwards

gaiter /'geɪtəʳ/ *n* a cloth or leather covering reaching from the instep to ankle, mid-calf, or knee

gala /'gɑːlə/ *n* a festive gathering (that constitutes or marks a special occasion)

galactic /gə'læktɪk/ *adj* of a galaxy, esp the Milky Way

galantine /'gæləntiːn/ *n* a cold dish of boned and usu stuffed cooked meat glazed with aspic

galaxy /'gæləksi/ *n* **1** *often cap* the Milky Way **2** any of many independent systems composed chiefly of stars, dust, and gases and separated from each other in the universe by vast distances

gale /geɪl/ *n* **1** a strong wind **2** a noisy outburst

[1]gall /gɔːl/ *n* **1a** bile **b** sthg bitter to endure **c** rancour **2** brazen and insolent audacity or cheek

[2]gall *n* a skin sore caused by rubbing

[3]gall *v* **1** to become sore or worn by

rubbing **2** to cause feelings of dismay and irritation in; vex acutely

[4]**gall** *n* a diseased swelling of plant tissue produced by infection with fungi, insect parasites, etc

[1]**gallant** /'gælənt, gə'lænt/ *n* a (young) man of fashion (who is particularly attentive to women)

[2]**gallant** /'gælənt/ *adj* **1a** splendid, stately **b** nobly chivalrous and brave **2** courteously and elaborately attentive, esp to ladies

gallantry /'gæləntri/ **1** (an act of) courteous attention, esp to a lady **2** spirited and conspicuous bravery

gall bladder *n* a muscular sac in which bile from the liver is stored

galleon /'gælıən/ *n* a heavy square-rigged sailing ship of the 15th to early 18th c used (by the Spanish) for war or commerce

gallery /'gæləri/ *n* **1** a covered passage for walking; a colonnade **2** an outdoor balcony **3a** a long and narrow passage, room, or corridor **b** a horizontal subterranean passage in a cave or (military) mining system **4a** a room or building devoted to the exhibition of works of art **b** an institution or business exhibiting or dealing in works of art **5** *sing or pl in constr* **a** (the occupants of) a balcony projecting from 1 or more interior walls of a hall, auditorium, or church, to accommodate additional people, or reserved for musicians, singers, etc **b** the undiscriminating general public **c** the spectators at a tennis, golf, etc match

galley /'gæli/ *n* **1** a large low usu single-decked ship propelled by oars and sails and used esp in the Mediterranean in the Middle Ages and in classical antiquity **2** a kitchen on a ship or aircraft **3a** a long oblong tray with upright sides for holding set type **b galley, galley proof** a proof in the form of a long sheet (taken from type on a galley)

Gallic /'gælık/ *adj* (characteristic) of Gaul or France

gallicism /'gæl$\frac{1}{3}$sızəm/ *n, often cap* a characteristic French word or expression (occurring in another language)

gallivant /'gæl$\frac{1}{3}$vænt/ *v* to travel energetically or roam about for pleasure

gallon /'gælən/ *n* a unit of liquid capacity equal to 8pt

[1]**gallop** /'gæləp/ *n* **1** a fast bounding gait of a quadruped; *specif* the fastest natural 4-beat gait of the horse **2** a ride or run at a gallop **3** a rapid or hasty progression

[2]**gallop** *v* to progress or ride at a gallop

gallows /'gæləυz/ *v* **1** a frame, usu of 2 upright posts and a crosspiece, for hanging criminals **2** *the* punishment of hanging

gallows humour *n* grim humour that makes fun of a very serious or terrifying situation

gallstone /'gɔːlstəυn/ *n* a stone formed in the gall bladder or bile ducts

Gallup poll /'gæləp pəυl/ *n* a survey of public opinion frequently used as a means of forecasting sthg (e g an election result)

galore /gə'lɔːʳ/ *adj* abundant, plentiful – used after a noun

galosh /gə'lɒʃ/ a rubber overshoe

galvanism /'gælvənızəm/ *n* **1** (the therapeutic use of) direct electric current produced by chemical action **2** vital or forceful activity

galvan·ize, -ise /gælvənaız/ *v* **1** to subject to or stimulate, rouse, or excite (as if) by the action of an electric current **2** to coat (iron or steel) with zinc as a protection from rust

galvanometer /,gælvə'nɒm$\frac{1}{3}$təʳ/ *n* an instrument for measuring a small electric current

gambit /'gæmb$\frac{1}{3}$t/ *n* **1** a chess opening, esp in which a player risks (several) minor pieces to gain an advantage **2a** a remark intended to start a conversation or make a telling point **b** a calculated move; a stratagem

[1]**gamble** /'gæmbəl/ *v* **1a** to play a game (of chance) for money or property **b** to bet or risk sthg on an uncertain outcome **2** to speculate in business – **-bler** *n*

gamble 2 *n* (sthg involving) an element of risk

gamboge /gæm'bəυdʒ, -'buːʒ/ *n* **1** a gum resin from some SE Asian trees that is used as a yellow pigment **2** a strong yellow

gambol /'gæmbəl/ *v or n* (to engage in) skipping or leaping about in play

[1]**game** /geɪm/ *n* **1a** activity engaged in for diversion or amusement; play **b** often derisive or mocking jesting **2a** a course or plan consisting of (secret) manoeuvres directed towards some end **b** a specified type of activity seen as competitive or governed by rules (and pursued for financial gain) **3a(1)** a physical or mental competition conducted according to rules with the participants in direct opposition to each other; a match **(2)** a division of a larger contest **b** *pl* organized sports, esp athletics **4a** animals under pursuit or taken in hunting; *specif* (the edible flesh of) certain wild mammals, birds, and fish (e g deer and pheasant), hunted for sport or food **b** an object of ridicule or attack – often in *fair game* **5** prostitution – slang; often in *on the game*

[2]**game** *adj* **1** having a resolute unyielding spirit **2** ready to take risks or try sthg new – **~ly** *adv*

[3]**game** *adj* injured, crippled, or lame

game keeper /'geɪm,kiːpəʳ/ *n* one who has charge of the breeding and protection of game animals or birds on a private preserve

gamesmanship /'geɪmzmənʃɪp/ *n* the art or practice of winning games by means other than superior skill without actually violating the rules

gamete /'gæmiːt, gə'miːt/ *n* a mature cell with a single set of chromosomes capable of fusing with another gamete of the other sex to form a zygote from which a new organism develops

gamma /'gæmə/ *n* **1** the 3rd letter of the Greek alphabet **2** a mediocre mark or rating

gamma ray *n* electromagnetic radiation of shorter wavelength than X rays emitted in some radioactive decay processes

gammon /'gæmən/ *n* (the meat of) the lower end including the hind leg of a side of bacon removed from the carcass after curing with salt

gammy /'gæmi/ *adj, of a limb* game, lame

gamp /gæmp/ *n* a large, esp loosely tied, umbrella

gamut /'gæmət/ *n* **1** the whole series of recognized musical notes **2** an entire range or series

gamy, gamey /'geɪmi/ *adj* having the strong flavour or smell of game (that has been hung until high) – **-miness** *n*

[1]**gander** /'gændəʳ/ *n* an adult male goose

[2]**gander** *n* a look, glance

gang /gæŋ/ *n* **1** a combination of similar implements or devices arranged to act together **2** *sing or pl in constr* a group of people **a** associating for criminal, disreputable, etc ends; *esp* a group of adolescents who (disreputably) spend leisure time together **b** that have informal and usu close social relations **c** that have informal and usu close social relations

gangling /'gæŋglɪŋ/, **gangly** /'gæŋgli/ *adj* tall, thin, and awkward in movement

ganglion /'gæŋgliən/ *n, pl* **ganglia** *also* **ganglions** a mass of nerve cells outside the brain or spinal cord

gangplank /'gæŋplæŋk/ *n* a movable board, plank, etc used to board a ship from a quay or another ship

gangrene /'gæŋgriːn/ *n* **1** local death of the body's soft tissues due to loss of blood supply **2** a pervasive moral evil – **-grenous** *adj*

gangster /'gæŋstəʳ/ *n* a member of a criminal gang

gang up *v* **1** to combine as a group for a specific (disreputable) purpose **2** to make a joint assault *on*

gangway /'gæŋweɪ/ *n* **1** a (temporary) passageway (constructed of planks) **2a** the opening in a ship's side or rail through which it is boarded **b** a gangplank **3** a clear passage through a crowd – often used interjectionally **4** *Br* a narrow passage between sections of seats in a theatre, storage bays in a warehouse, etc

gannet /'gænɪt/ *n* any of several related large fish-eating seabirds that breed in large colonies chiefly on offshore islands

gantry /'gæntri/ *n* **1** a frame for supporting barrels **2** a frame structure raised on side supports that spans over or round sthg and is used for railway signals, as a travelling crane, for servicing a rocket before launching, etc

gaol /dʒeɪl/ *v or n, chiefly Br* (to) jail – **~er** *n*

gap /gæp/ *n* **1** a break in a barrier (e g a wall or hedge) **2a** a mountain pass **b** a ravine **3** an empty space between 2 objects or 2 parts of an object **4** a break in continuity **5** a disparity or difference

gape /geɪp/ *v* **1a** to open the mouth wide **b** to open or part widely **2** to gaze stupidly or in openmouthed surprise or wonder

garage /'gærɑːʒ, 'gærɪdʒ/ *n* **1** a building for the shelter of motor vehicles **2** an establishment for providing essential services (e g the supply of petrol or repair work) to motor vehicles

garb /gɑːb/ *n* **1** a style of clothing; dress **2** an outward form; appearance – **garb** *v*

garbage /'gɑːbɪdʒ/ *n* **1** worthless writing or speech **2** *chiefly NAm* domestic rubbish

garble /'gɑːbəl/ *v* to distort or confuse, giving a false impression of the facts

[1]**garden** /'gɑːdn/ *n* **1** a plot of ground where herbs, fruits, vegetables, or typically flowers are cultivated **2a** a public recreation area or park **b** an open-air eating or drinking place

[2]**garden** *v* to work in, cultivate, or lay out a garden – **~er** *n* – **~ing** *n*

[3]**garden** *adj* of a cultivated as distinguished from a wild kind grown in the open

garden city *n* a planned town with spacious residential areas including public parks and considerable garden space

gargantuan /gɑːgæntʃuən/ *adj* gigantic, colossal

[1]**gargle** /'gɑːgəl/ *v* **1** to blow air from the lungs through (a liquid) held in the mouth or throat **2** to cleanse (the mouth or throat) in this manner

[2]**gargle** *n* **1** a liquid used in gargling **2** a bubbling liquid sound produced by gargling

gargoyle /'gɑːgɔɪl/ *n* a spout in the form of a grotesque human or animal figure projecting from a roof gutter to throw rainwater clear of a building

garish /'geərɪʃ/ *adj* **1** excessively and gaudily bright or vivid **2** tastelessly showy – **~ly** *adv,* **~ness** *n*

[1]**garland** /'gɑːlənd/ *n* a wreath of flowers or leaves worn as an ornament or sign of distinction

[2]**garland** *v* to form into or deck with a garland

garlic /'gɑːlik/ *n* (the pungent compound bulb, much used as a flavouring in cookery, of) a plant of the onion family

garment /'gɑːmənt/ *n* an article of clothing

garnet /'gɑːn$_{\frac{1}{2}}$t/ *n* **1** a hard brittle mineral used as an abrasive and in its transparent deep red form as a gem **2** a dark red

[1]**garnish** /'gɑːnɪʃ/ *v* **1** to decorate, embellish **2** to add decorative or savoury touches to (food)

[2]**garnish** *n* **1** an embellishment, ornament **2** an edible savoury or decorative addition (e g watercress) to a dish

garret /'gær$_{\frac{1}{2}}$t/ *n* a small room just under the roof of a house

garrison /'gær$_{\frac{1}{2}}$sən/ *n* **1** a (fortified) town or place in which troops are stationed **2** *sing or pl in constr* the troops stationed at a garrison – **garrison** *v*

[1]**garrotte, garotte** /gə'rɒt/ *n* (a Spanish method of execution using) an iron collar for strangling sby

[2]**garrotte** *v* **1** to execute with a garrotte **2** to strangle and rob

garrulous /'gærələs/ *adj* excessively talkative, esp about trivial things – **~ly** *adv adv* – **-lity** *n* – **~ness** *n*

garter /'gɑːtəʳ/ **1** a band, usu of elastic, worn to hold up a stocking or sock **2** *cap* (the blue velvet garter that is the badge of) the Order of the Garter; *also* membership of the Order

[1]**gas** /gæs/ *n* **1** a fluid (e g air) that has neither independent shape nor volume and tends to expand indefinitely **2a** a gas or gaseous mixture used to produce general anaesthesia, as a fuel, etc **b** a substance (e g tear gas or mustard gas) that can be used to produce a poisonous, choking, or irritant atmos-

phere 3 *NAm* petrol 4 empty talk – chiefly infml – ~**eous** *adj*

²**gas** *v* 1 to poison or otherwise affect adversely with gas 2 to talk idly – chiefly infml

gas chamber *n* a chamber in which prisoners are executed by poison gas

gash /gæʃ/ *vt or n* (to injure with) a deep long cut or cleft, esp in flesh

gasholder /ˈgæˌshəʊldəʳ/ *n* a gasometer

gasify /ˈgæsɪ̥faɪ/ *v* to change into gas – **-fication** *n*

gasket /ˈgæskɪ̥t/ *v* (a specially shaped piece of) sealing material for ensuring that a joint, esp between metal surfaces, does not leak liquid or gas

gasoline /ˈgæsəliːn/ *n, NAm* petrol

gasometer /gæˈsɒmɪtə/ a (large cylindrical storage) container for gas

gasp /gɑːsp/ *v* 1 to catch the breath suddenly and audibly (e g with shock) 2 to utter with gasps – usu + *out* – **gasp** *n*

gas ring *n* a hollow metal perforated ring through which jets of gas issue and over which food is cooked

gassy /ˈgæsi/ *adj* full of, containing, or like gas – **gassiness** *n*

gastric /ˈgæstrɪk/ *adj* of the stomach

gastroenteritis /ˌgæstrəʊ-entəˈraɪtɪ̥s/ inflammation of the lining of the stomach and the intestines, usu causing painful diarrhoea

gastronomy /gæˈstrɒnəmi/ *n* the art of science of good eating – **-nomic** *adj*, **-nomically** *adv*

gasworks /ˈgæswɜːks/ *n* a plant for manufacturing gas

¹**gate** /geɪt/ *n* 1 (the usu hinged frame or door that closes) an opening in a wall, fence, etc **2a** a space between 2 markers through which a skier, canoeist, etc must pass in a slalom race **b** a mechanically operated barrier used as a starting device for a race **c** either of a pair of barriers that **(1)** let water in and out of a lock **(2)** close a road at a level crossing 3 an (electronic) device (e g in a computer) that produces a signal when specified input conditions are met 4 the total admission receipts or the number of spectators at a sporting event

²**gate** *v, Br* to punish by confinement to the premises of a school or college

gateau /ˈgætəʊ/ *n, pl* **gateaux** any of various rich often filled elaborate (cream) cakes

gate-crash *v* to enter, attend, or participate without a ticket or invitation – ~**er** *n*

gatepost /ˈgeɪtpəʊst/ *n* the post on which a gate is hung or against which it closes

¹**gather** /ˈgæðəʳ/ *v* 1 to bring together; collect (*up*) 2 to pick, harvest **3a** to summon up **b** to accumulate **4a** to bring together the parts of **b** to draw about or close to sthg **c** to pull (fabric) together, esp along a line of stitching, to create small tucks 5 to reach a conclusion (intuitively from hints or through inferences)

²**gather** *n* a tuck in cloth made by gathering

gathering /ˈgæðərɪŋ/ *n* 1 an assembly, meeting 2 an abscess 3 a gather or series of gathers in cloth

gauche /gəʊʃ/ *adj* lacking social experience or grace – ~**rie** *n*

¹**gaudy** /ˈgɔːdi/ *adj* ostentatiously or tastelessly (and brightly) ornamented – **-dily** *adv*, **-diness** *n*

²**gaudy** *n* a feast, esp a dinner for ex-students, in some British universities

¹**gauge** /geɪdʒ/ *n* 1 measurement according to some standard or system 2 an instrument for or a means of measuring or testing sthg (e g a dimension or quantity) 3 relative position of a ship with reference to another ship and the wind 4 the distance between the rails of a railway, wheels on an axle, etc **5a** the thickness of a thin sheet of metal, plastic,etc **b** the diameter of wire, a screw, etc **c** (a measure of) the fineness of a knitted fabric

²**gauge** *v* 1 to measure (exactly) the size, dimensions, capacity, or contents of 2 to estimate, judge

gaunt /gɔːnt/ *adj* 1 excessively thin and angular as if from suffering 2 barren, desolate – ~**ness** *n*

¹**gauntlet** /ˈgɔːntlɪ̥t/ *n* 1 a glove to protect the hand, worn with medieval armour 2 a strong protective glove with a wide extension above the wrist, used esp for sports and in industry 3

a challenge to combat – esp in *take up/throw down the gauntlet*

[2]**gauntlet** *n* a double file of men armed with weapons with which to strike at sby made to run between them; *broadly* criticism or an ordeal or test – usu in *run the gauntlet*

gauze /gɔːz/ *n* **1a** a thin often transparent fabric used chiefly for clothing or draperies **b** a loosely woven cotton surgical dressing **c** a fine mesh of metal or plastic filaments **2** a thin haze or mist – **-zy** *adj*

gave /geɪv/ *past of* **give**

gavel /'gævəl/ *n* a small mallet with which a chairman, judge, or auctioneer commands attention or confirms a vote, sale, etc

gavial /'geɪvɪəl/ *n* a large Indian crocodile

gavotte /gə'vɒt/ *n* **1** an 18th-c dance in which the feet are raised rather than slid **2** a composition or movement of music in moderately quick $\frac{4}{4}$ time

[1]**gawk** /gɔːk/ *v* to gawp – infml

[2]**gawk** *n* a clumsy awkward person

gawky /'gɔːki/ *adj* awkward and lanky – **-kiness** *n*

gawp /gɔːp/ to gape or stare stupidly – infml

gay /geɪ/ *adj* **1** happily excited **2** bright, attractive **3** given to social pleasures **4** homosexual

gaze /geɪz/ *v or n* (to fix the eyes in) a steady and intent look – **-er** *n*

gazebo /gə'ziːbəʊ/ *n* a freestanding structure placed to command a view; *also* a summer house

gazelle /gə'zel/ *n* any of numerous small, graceful, and swift African and Asian antelopes noted for their soft lustrous eyes

[1]**gazette** /gə'zet/ *n* **1** a newspaper – usu in newspaper titles **2** an official journal containing announcements of honours and government appointments

[2]**gazette** *v* to announce (the appointment or status of) in an official gazette

gazetteer /,gæzɪ̣'tɪəʳ/ *n* a dictionary of place names

gazump /gə'zʌmp/ *v* to thwart (a would-be house purchaser) by raising the price after agreeing to sell at a certain price

G clef /dʒiː/ *n* the treble clef

[1]**gear** /gɪəʳ/ *n* **1a** clothing, garments **b** movable property; goods **2** a set of equipment usu for a particular purpose **3a(1)** a mechanism that performs a specific function in a complete machine **(2)** a toothed wheel (that is one of a set of interlocking wheels) **b** any of 2 or more adjustments of a transmission (e g of a bicycle or motor vehicle) that determine direction of travel or ratio of engine speed to vehicle speed

[2]**gear** *v* **1a** to provide with or connect by gearing **b** to put into gear **2** to adjust *to* so as to match, blend with, or satisfy sthg

gearbox /'gɪəbɒks/ *n* (a protective casing enclosing) a set of (car) gears

gear up *v* to make ready for effective operation; *also* to put (e g oneself) into a state of anxious excitement or nervous anticipation

gecko /'gekəʊ/ *n, pl* **geckos, geckoes** any of numerous small chiefly tropical lizards able to walk on vertical or overhanging surfaces

gee-gee /'dʒiːdʒiː/ *n* a horse – used esp by or to children or in racing slang

geese /giːs/ *pl of* **goose**

geezer /'giːzəʳ/ *n* a man (who is thought a little odd or peculiar)

Geiger counter /'gaɪgə,kaʊntəʳ/ *n* an electronic instrument for detecting the presence and intensity of radiation from a radioactive substance

geisha /'geɪʃə/ *n* a Japanese girl who is trained to provide entertaining and lighthearted company, esp for a man or a group of men

[1]**gel** /dʒel/ *n* a substance in a state between solid and liquid; a jelly

[2]**gel** *v* **1** to change (from a sol) into a gel **2** to (cause to) take shape or become definite

gelatin, gelatine /'dʒelətiːn/ *n* **1** a glutinous material obtained from animal tissues by boiling; *esp* a protein used esp in food (e g to set jellies) and photography **2** a thin coloured transparent sheet used to colour a stage light – **-nous** *adj*

geld /geld/ *v* to castrate (a male animal)

gelding /ˈgeldɪŋ/ *n* a castrated male horse

gelignite /ˈdʒelɪgnaɪt/ *n* a dynamite in which the adsorbent base is a mixture of potassium or sodium nitrate usu with wood pulp

gem /dʒem/ *n* **1** a precious stone, esp when cut and polished for use in jewellery **2** sby or sthg highly prized or much beloved

Gemini /ˈdʒemɨ̥naɪ/ *n* (sby born under) the 3rd sign of the zodiac in astrology, which is pictured as twins

gen /dʒen/ *n* the correct or complete information – infml

gendarme /ˈʒɒndɑːm/ *n* a member of a corps of armed police, esp in France

gender /ˈdʒendəʳ/ *n* **1** sex **2** a system of subdivision within a grammatical class of a language (e g noun or verb), partly based on sexual characteristics, that determines agreement with and selection of other words or grammatical forms

gene /dʒiːn/ *n* a unit of inheritance that is carried on a chromosome and controls the transmission of hereditary characteristics

genealogy /ˌdʒiːniˈælədʒi/ *n* **1** (an account of) the descent of a person, family, or group from an ancestor or from older forms **2** the study of family pedigrees – **-gist** *n,* **-logical** *adj*

genera /ˈdʒenərə/ *pl of* **genus**

¹general /ˈdʒenərəl/ *adj* **1** involving or applicable to the whole **2** of, involving, or applicable to (what is common to) every member of a class, kind, or group **3a** applicable to or characteristic of the majority of individuals involved; prevalent **b** concerned or dealing with universal rather than particular aspects **4** approximate rather than strictly accurate **5** holding superior rank or taking precedence over others similarly titled

²general *n* a high-ranking officer in the armed forces; *esp* one in command of an army

general election *n* an election in which candidates are elected in all constituencies of a nation or state

generality /ˌdʒenəˈrælɨ̥ti/ *n* **1** total applicability **2** generalization **3** *the* greatest part; *the* bulk

general·ize, -ise /ˈdʒenərəlaɪz/ *v* **1** to give a general form to **2** to derive or induce (a general conception or principle) from particulars **3** to give general applicability to **4** to make vague or indefinite statements – **-ization** *n*

generally /ˈdʒenərəli/ *adv* **1** without regard to specific instances **2** usually; as a rule **3** collectively; as a whole

general practitioner *n* a medical doctor who treats all types of disease and is usu the first doctor consulted by a patient

general staff *n* a group of officers who aid a commander in administration, training, supply, etc

general strike *n* a strike in all or many of the industries of a region or country

generate /ˈdʒenəreɪt/ *v* **1** to bring into existence or originate produce **2** to define (a linguistic, mathematical, etc structure (e g a curve or surface)) by the application of 1 or more rules or operations to given quantities

generation /ˌdʒenəˈreɪʃən/ *n* **1** *sing or pl in constr* **a** a group of living organisms constituting a single step in the line of descent from an ancestor **b** a group of individuals born and living at the same time **c** a type or class of objects usu developed from an earlier type **2** the average time between the birth of parents and that of their offspring **3** the process of coming or bringing into being

generative /ˈdʒenərətɪv/ *adj* having the power or function of generating, originating, producing, reproducing, etc

generator /ˈdʒenəreɪtəʳ/ *n* **1** an apparatus for producing a vapour or gas **2** a machine for generating electricity; *esp* a dynamo

generic /dʒɨ̥ˈnerɪk/ *adj* **1** (characteristic) of or applied to (members of) a whole group or class **2** (having the rank) of a biological genus – **~ally** *adv*

generous /ˈdʒen(ə)rəs/ *adj* **1** magnanimous, kindly **2** liberal in giving (e g of money or help) **3** marked by abundance, ample proportions, or richness – **-rosity** n – **~ly** *adv*

genesis /ˈdʒenɨ̥sɨ̥s/ *n* the origin or coming into being of sthg

genetic /dʒʲ̣ˈnetɪk/ *adj* **1** of or determined by the origin or development of sthg **2** of or involving genes or genetics – **~ally** *adv*

genetics /dʒʲ̣ˈnetɪks/ *n pl but sing in constr* **1** the biology of (the mechanisms and structures involved in) the heredity and variation of organisms **2** the genetic make-up of an organism, type, group, or condition – **-icist** *n*

genial /dʒiːnɪal/ **1** favourable to growth or comfort; mild **2** cheerfully good-tempered; kindly – **-ally** *adv*, **~ity** *n*

genie /ˈdʒiːni/ *n* a spirit, often in human form, which in Muslim legends serves whoever summons it

genitals /ˈdʒenʲ̣tlz/ *n pl* the (external) reproductive and sexual organs – **genital** *adj*

genitive /ˈdʒenʲ̣tɪv/ *adj or n* (of or in) a grammatical case expressing typically a relationship of possessor or source; *also* sthg in this case

genius /ˈdʒiːnɪəs/ *n* **1** an attendant spirit of a person or place **2a** a peculiar, distinctive, or identifying character or spirit **b** the associations and traditions of a place **3** a spirit or genie **4a** a single strongly marked capacity or aptitude **b** (a person endowed with) extraordinary intellectual power (as manifested in creative activity)

genocide /ˈdʒenəsaɪd/ *n* the deliberate murder of a racial or cultural group

genre /ˈʒɒnrə/ *n* **1** a sort, type **2** a category of artistic, musical, or literary composition characterized by a particular style, form, or content

genteel /dʒenˈtiːl/ *adj* **1** free from vulgarity or rudeness; polite **2a** maintaining or striving to maintain the appearance of superior social status or respectability **b** marked by false delicacy, prudery, or affectation – **-teelly** *adv*, **-tility** *n*

gentian /ˈdʒenʃən/ *n* any of several related esp mountain plants with showy usu blue flowers

gentile /ˈdʒentaɪl/ *adj or n, often cap* (of) a non-Jewish person

[1]**gentle** /ˈdʒentl/ *adj* **1a** honourable, distinguished; *specif* of or belonging to a gentleman **b** kind, amiable **2** free from harshness, sternness, or violence; mild, soft; *also* tractable **3** soft, moderate – **~ness** *n*, **-ly** *adj*

[2]**gentle** *n* a maggot, esp when used as bait for fish

gentlefolk /ˈdʒentlfəʊk/ *also* **gentlefolks** *n pl* people of good family and breeding

gentleman /ˈdʒentlmən/ *n* **1a** a man belonging to the landed gentry or nobility; *also* a man of independent wealth **b** a man who is chivalrous, well-mannered, and honourable **2** a valet – usu in *gentleman's gentleman* **3** a man of social class or condition – **~ly** *adj*

gentleman's agreement, gentlemen's agreement *n* an unwritten agreement secured only by the honour of the participants

gentle sex *n* the female sex

gentry /ˈdʒentri/ *n, sing or pl in constr* **1** the upper class **2** a class whose members are (landed proprietors) entitled to bear a coat of arms though not of noble rank

gents /dʒents/ *n, pl* **gents** *often cap, Br* a public lavatory for men – chiefly infml

genuflect /ˈdʒenjʊflekt/ *v* to bend the knee, esp in worship or as a gesture of respect (to sacred objects) – **-tion** *n*

genuine /ˈdʒenjʊʲ̣n/ *adj* **1** actually produced by or proceeding from the alleged source or author or having the reputed qualities of character **2** free from pretence; sincere **~ly** *adv*, **~ness** *n*

genus /ˈdʒiːnəs/ *n*, **1** a category in the classification of living things ranking between the family and the species **2** a class divided into several subordinate classes

geocentric /ˌdʒiːəʊˈsentrɪk/ *adj* **1** measured from or observed as if from the earth's centre **2** having or relating to the earth as centre

geography /dʒiˈɒgrəfi, ˈdʒɒgrəfi/ *n* **1** a science that deals with the earth and its life; *esp* the description of land, sea, air, and the distribution of plant and animal life including human beings and their industries **2** the geographical features of an area – **-pher** *n*, **-phical** *adj*

geology /dʒiˈɒlədʒi/ *n* **1** a science

that deals with the history of the earth's crust, esp as recorded in rocks 2 the geological features of an area – **-gical** *adj*

geometric /ˌdʒɪəˈmetrɪk/, **geometrical** *adj* **1a** of or according to (the laws of) geometry **b** increasing in a geometric progression **2** using, being, or decorated with patterns formed from straight and curved lines

geometric progression *n* a sequence (e g 1.½.½.¼) in which the ratio of any term to its predecessor is constant

geometry /dʒɪˈɒmɪ̣tri/ *n* **1** a branch of mathematics that deals with the measurement, properties, and relationships of points, lines, angles, surfaces, and solids **2** (surface) shape **3** an arrangement of objects or parts that suggests geometrical figures

geophysics /ˌdʒiːəʊˈfɪzɪks/ *n pl but sing or pl in constr* the physics of the earth including meteorology, oceanography, seismology, etc – **-ical** *adj*

georgette /ˈdʒɔːdʒet/ *n* a thin strong clothing crepe of silk or of other material with a dull pebbly surface

[1]**Georgian** /ˈdʒɔːdʒən, -dʒɪən/ *n or adj* (a native or inhabitant or the language) of Georgia

[2]**Georgian** *adj* **1** (characteristic) of (the time of) the reigns of the first 4 Georges (1714 to 1830) **2** (characteristic) of the reign of George V (1910 to 1936)

geotropism /dʒiːəˈtrəʊˌpizəm/ *n* tropism (e g in the downward growth of roots) in which gravity is the orienting factor

geranium /dʒəˈreɪnɪəm/ *n* any of a widely distributed genus of plants having radially symmetrical flowers with glands that alternate with the petals; *esp* a garden variety with showy red flowers

gerbil /ˈdʒɜːbɪl/ *n* any of numerous Old World mouselike desert rodents with long hind legs adapted for leaping

geriatrics /ˌdʒeriˈætrɪks/ *n pl but sing in constr* a branch of medicine that deals with (the diseases of) old age – **geriatric** *adj*

germ /dʒɜːm/ *n* **1a** a small mass of cells capable of developing into (a part of) an organism **b** the embryo of a cereal grain that is usu separated from the starchy parts during milling **2** sthg that serves as an origin **3** a (disease-causing) microorganism

german /ˈdʒɜːmən/ *adj* having the same parents, or the same grandparents, on either the maternal or paternal side –usu in comb

[1]**German** *n* **1a** a native or inhabitant of Germany **b** one (e g a Swiss German) who speaks German as his/her native language outside Germany **2** the language of the people of Germany, Austria, and parts of Switzerland – **~ic** *adj*

[2]**German** *adj* (characteristic) of Germany, the Germans, or German

germane /dʒɜːˈmeɪn/ *adj* both relevant and appropriate

German measles *n pl but sing or pl in constr* a virus disease that is milder than typical measles but is damaging to the foetus when occurring early in pregnancy

germicide /ˈdʒɜːmɪ̣saɪd/ *n* sthg that kills germs

germinal /ˈdʒɜːmɪ̣nəl/ *adj* **1** in the earliest stage of development **2** creative, seminal

germinate /ˈdʒɜːmɪ̣neɪt/ *v* **1** to begin to grow; sprout **2** to come into being

gerrymander /ˈdʒerimændəʳ/ *v* to divide (an area) into election districts to give one political party an electoral advantage

gerund /ˈdʒerənd/ a verbal noun esp in Latin

gestapo /geˈstaːpəʊ/ *n* a secret-police organization operating esp against suspected traitors; *specif, cap* that of Nazi Germany

gestation /dʒeˈsteɪʃən/ *n* **1** the carrying of young in the uterus; pregnancy **2** conception and development, esp in the mind

gesticulate /dʒeˈstɪkjʊleɪt/ *v* to make expressive gestures, esp when speaking – **-lation** *n*

[1]**gesture** /ˈdʒestʃəʳ/ *n* **1** a movement, usu of the body or limbs, that expresses or emphasizes an idea, sentiment, or attitude **2** sthg said or done for its effect on the attitudes of others

or to convey a feeling (e g friendliness)

[2]**gesture** *v* to make or express (by) a gesture

get /get/ *v* **got; geting** **1** to gain possession of **2a** to receive as a return; earn **b** to become affected by; catch **c** to be subjected to **3a** to cause to come, go, or move **b** to prevail on; induce **4** to make ready; prepare **5a** to have – used in the present perfect tense form with present meaning **b** to have as an obligation or necessity –used in the present perfect tense form with present meaning; + *to* and an understood or expressed infinitive (e g in he's *got* to go) **6a** to puzzle **b** to irritate **7** to affect emotionally **8** to reach or enter into the specified condition or activity (e g in *get* drunk) **9** to contrive by effort, luck, or permission – + *to* and an infinitive

get across *v* to make or become clear or convincing

get along *v* **1** to move away; leave for another destination **2** to manage **3** to be or remain on congenial terms

getaway /ˈgetəweɪ/ *n* a departure, escape

get by *v* **1** to manage, survive **2** to succeed by a narrow margin; be just about acceptable

get down *v* **1** to leave (the table) or descend (from a vehicle) **2** to depress **3** to swallow **4** to record in writing **5** to apply serious attention or consideration

get off *v* **1** to start, leave **2** to escape from a dangerous situation or from punishment **3** to leave work with permission **4** *Br* to start an amorous or sexual relationship – often + *with*

get on *v* **1** to be friends **2** to become late or old **3** to come near; approach – + *for* **4** to hurry

get out *v* **1** to emerge, escape **2a** to become known **b** to bring before the public; *esp* to publish

get over *v* **1** to recover from **2** to accept calmly

get round *v* **1** to circumvent, evade **2** to cajole, persuade

get-together *n* an (informal social) gathering or meeting

get together *v* **1** to come together; assemble **2** to unite in discussion or promotion of a project

getup /ˈgetʌp/ *n* an outfit, clothing

get up *v* **1a** to arise from bed **b** to rise to one's feet **2** to go ahead or faster – used in the imperative as a command, esp to driven animals **3** to organize **4** to arrange the external appearance of; dress **5** to acquire a knowledge of **6** to create in oneself

geyser /ˈgiːzəʳ/ *n* **1** a spring that intermittently throws out jets of heated water and steam **2** *Br* an apparatus with a boiler in which water (e g for a bath) is rapidly heated by a gas flame

ghastly /ˈgɑːstli/ **1a** (terrifyingly) horrible **b** intensely unpleasant, disagreeable, or objectionable **2** pale, wan – **-liness** *n*

ghee /giː/ *n* a form of butter made in India from esp buffalo milk

gherkin /ˈgɜːkln̩/ *n* (a slender annual climbing plant of the cucumber family that bears) a small prickly fruit used for pickling

ghetto /ˈgetəʊ/ *n* **1** part of a city in which Jews formerly lived **2** an often slum area of a city in which a minority group live, esp because of social, legal, or economic pressures

[1]**ghost** /gəʊst/ *n* **1** a disembodied soul; *esp* the soul of a dead person haunting the living **2a** a faint shadowy trace **b** the least bit **3** a false image in a photographic negative or on a television screen – **~ly** *adj* – **~liness** *n*

[2]**ghost, ghostwrite** *v* to write something to appear under another person's name

ghoul /guːl/ *n* **1** a evil being of Arabic legend that robs graves and feeds on corpses **2** one who enjoys the macabre – **~ish** *adj* – **~ishness** *n*

[1]**GI** *adj* (characteristic) of US military personnel or equipment

[2]**GI** *n, pl* **GI's, GIs** a member of the US army, esp a private

[1]**giant** /ˈdʒaɪənt/ *n* **1** *fem* **giantess** a legendary human being of great stature and strength **2** sby or sthg extraordinarily large **3** a person of extraordinary powers

[2]**giant** *adj* extremely large

giant panda *n* the black and white Chinese panda

gibber /ˈdʒɪbəʳ/ *v* to make rapid, inarticulate, and usu incomprehensible utterances

gibbet /ˈdʒɪbɮt/ *v or n* (to execute or expose on) an upright post with an arm for hanging the bodies of executed criminals

gibbon /ˈgɪbən/ *n* any of several tailless Asian anthropoid tree-dwelling apes

gibe, jibe /dʒaɪb/ *v* to jeer *at* – **gibe** *n*

giblets /ˈdʒɪblɮts/ *n pl* a fowl's heart, liver, or other edible internal organs

giddy /ˈgɪdi/ *adj* **1** lightheartedly frivolous **2a** feeling, or causing to feel, a sensation of unsteadiness and lack of balance as if everything is whirling round **b** whirling rapidly

gift /gɪft/ *n* **1** a natural capacity or talent **2** sthg freely given by one person to another **3** the act, right, or power of giving

gifted /ˈgɪftɮd/ *adj* **1** having or revealing great natural ability **2** highly intelligent

[1]**gig** /gɪg/ *n* **1** a long light ship's boat propelled by oars, sails, etc **2** a light 2-wheeled one-horse carriage

[2]**gig** *n* a musician's engagement for a specified time; *esp* such an engagement for 1 performance

gigantic /dʒaɪˈgæntɪk/ *adj* unusually great or enormous – **~ally** *adv*

[1]**giggle** /ˈgɪgəl/ *v* to laugh with repeated short catches of the breath (and in a silly manner)

[2]**giggle** *n* **1** an act or instance of giggling **2** *chiefly Br* sthg that amuses or diverts

gigolo /ˈʒɪgələʊ, ˈdʒɪ-/ *n* **1** a man paid by a usu older woman for companionship or sex **2** a professional dancing partner or male escort

[1]**gild** /gɪld/ *v* **gilded, gilt** **1** to overlay (as if) with a thin covering of gold **2** to give an attractive but often deceptive appearance to

[2]**gild** *n* a guild

[1]**gill** /dʒɪl/ *n* a measure equal to ¼ pint or 0.142 litre

[2]**gill** /gɪl/ *n* **1** an organ, esp of a fish, for oxygenating blood using the oxygen dissolved in water **2** the flesh under or about the chin or jaws – usu pl with sing. meaning **3** any of the radiating plates forming the undersurface of the cap of some fungi (e g mushrooms)

[3]**gill, ghyll** /gɪl/ *n, Br* **1** a ravine **2** a narrow mountain stream

gillie, ghillie /ˈgɪli/ *n* an attendant to sby who is hunting or fishing in Scotland

[1]**gilt** /gɪlt/ *adj* covered with gold or gilt; of the colour of gold

[2]**gilt** *n* **1** (sthg that resembles) gold laid on a surface **2** superficial brilliance; surface attraction **3** a gilt-edged security – usu pl

gilt-edged, gilt-edge *adj* **1** of the highest quality or reliability **2** *of government securities* having a guaranteed fixed interest rate and redeemable at face value

[1]**gimlet** /ˈgɪmlɮt/ *n* a tool for boring small holes in wood, usu consisting of a crosswise handle fitted to a tapered screw

[2]**gimlet** *adj, of eyes* piercing, penetrating

gimmick /ˈgɪmɪk/ *n* a scheme, device, or object devised to gain attention or publicity – **~y** *adj*

[1]**gin** /dʒɪn/ *n* any of various tools or mechanical devices: e g **a** a snare or trap for game **b** a device for removing the seeds from cotton

[2]**gin** *n* a spirit made by distilling a mash of grain with juniper berries

ginger /ˈdʒɪndʒəʳ/ *n* **1a** (any of several cultivated tropical plants with) a thickened pungent aromatic underground stem used (dried and ground) as a spice, or candied as a sweet **b** the spice usu prepared by drying and grinding ginger **2** a strong brown colour

ginger ale *n* a sweet yellowish carbonated nonalcoholic drink flavoured with ginger

gingerbread /ˈdʒɪndʒəbred/ *n* a thick biscuit or cake made with treacle or syrup and flavoured with ginger

gingerly /ˈdʒɪndʒəli/ *adj* very cautious or careful

ginger nut *n* a hard brittle biscuit flavoured with ginger

ginger up *v* to stir to activity; vitalize

gingham /ˈgɪŋəm/ *n* a plain-weave often checked clothing fabric usu of yarn-dyed cotton

gipsy, *chiefly NAm* **gypsy** /'dʒɪpsi/ **1** *often cap* a member of a dark Caucasian people coming orig from India to Europe in the 14th or 15th c and leading a migratory way of life **2** a person who moves from place to place; a wanderer

giraffe /dʒʒ̍'rɑːf/ *n* a large African ruminant mammal with a very long neck and a beige coat marked with brown or black patches

gird /gɜːd/ *v* **girded, girt** **1a** to encircle or bind with a flexible band (e g a belt) **b** to surround **2** to prepare (oneself) for action

girder /'gɜːdəʳ/ *n* a horizontal main supporting beam

¹girdle /'gɜːdl/ *n* **1a** a belt or cord encircling the body, usu at the waist **b** a woman's tightly fitting undergarment that extends from the waist to below the hips **2** a ring made by the removal of the bark and cambium round a plant stem or tree trunk

²girdle *v* **1** to encircle (as if) with a girdle **2** to cut a girdle round (esp a tree), usu in order to kill

³girdle *n, Scot & dial Eng* a griddle

girl /gɜːl/ *n* **1a** a female child **b** a young unmarried woman **2a** a sweetheart, girlfriend **b** a daughter **3** a woman – chiefly infml

girl Friday *n* a female general assistant, esp in an office

girlfriend /'gɜːlfrend/ *n* **1** a frequent or regular female companion of a boy or man; *esp* one with whom he is romantically involved **2** a female friend

girlie /'gɜːli/ *adj, of a magazine* featuring nude or semi-nude photos of women

giro /'dʒaɪərəʊ/ *n* a computerized low-cost system of money transfer comparable to a current account that is one of the national post office services in many European countries

girt /gɜːt/ *v* to gird

girth /gɜːθ/ *n* **1** a strap that passes under the body of a horse or other animal to fasten esp a saddle on its back **2** a measurement of thickness round a body

gist /dʒɪst/ *n* *the* main point of a matter; *the* essence

¹give /gɪv/ *v* **gave; given** **1** to make a present of **2** to grant, bestow, or allot (by formal action) **3a** to administer **b** to commit to another as a trust or responsibility **c** to convey or express to another **4a** to proffer, present (for another to use or act on) **b** to surrender (oneself) to a partner in sexual intercourse **5** to present to view or observation **6a** to present for, or provide by way of, entertainment **b** to present, perform, or deliver in public **7** to attribute, ascribe **8** to yield as a product or effect **9** to yield possession of by way of exchange; pay **10** to make, execute, or deliver (e g by some bodily action) **11** to cause to undergo; impose **12** to award by formal verdict **13** to offer for consideration, acceptance, or use **14a** to cause to have or receive **b** to cause to catch or contract **15** to apply freely or fully; devote **16** to allow, concede **17** to care to the extent of **18** to yield or collapse in response to pressure **19** to impart information; talk – infml **20** to happen – slang – **giver** *n*

²give *n* the capacity or tendency to yield to pressure; resilience, elasticity

give-and-take *n* **1** the practice of making mutual concessions **2** the good-natured exchange of ideas or words

giveaway /'gɪvəweɪ/ *n* **1** an unintentional revelation or betrayal **2** sthg given free or at a reduced price

give away *v* **1** to make a present of **2** to hand over (a bride) to the bridegroom at a wedding **3a** to betray **b** to disclose, reveal – esp in **give the game/show away**

given /gɪvən/ *adj* **1** prone, disposed **2a** fixed, specified **b** assumed as actual or hypothetical

give off *v* to emit

give out *v* **1** to declare, publish **2** to emit **3** to issue, distribute **4** to come to an end; fail

give over *v* **1** to set apart for a particular purpose or use **2** to deliver to sby's care **3** to bring an activity to an end – infml

give up *v* **1** to surrender, esp as a prisoner **2** to stop trying **3** to renounce **4** to abandon (oneself) *to* sthg **5** to declare incurable or insoluble **6** to stop having a relationship with

gizzard /ˈgɪzəd/ *n* a muscular enlargement of the alimentary canal of birds that immediately follows the crop and has a tough horny lining for grinding food; *also* a similar anatomical part in other animals

glacé /ˈglæseɪ/ *adj* **1** made or finished so as to have a smooth glossy surface **2** coated with a glaze; candied

glacial /ˈgleɪʃəl/ *adj* **1** extremely cold **2** of or produced by glaciers **3** resembling ice in appearance, esp when frozen

glacier /ˈglæsɪəʳ/ *n* a large body of ice moving slowly down a slope or spreading outwards on a land surface

glad /glæd/ *adj* **1** expressing or experiencing pleasure, joy, or delight **2** very willing **3** causing happiness and joy

glade /gleɪd/ *n* an open space within a wood or forest

gladiator /ˈglædieɪtəʳ/ *n* **1** sby trained to fight in the arena for the entertainment of ancient Romans **2** sby engaging in a public fight or controversy – **~ial** *adj*

gladiolus /ˌglædiˈəʊləs/ *n, pl* **gladioli** any of a genus of (African) plants of the iris family with spikes of brilliantly coloured irregular flowers

glad rags *n pl* smart clothes – infml

glamour /ˈglæməʳ/ *n* a romantic, exciting, and often illusory attractiveness; *esp* alluring or fascinating personal attraction – **-orize** *v* – **-orous** *adj*

¹glance /glɑːns/ *v* **1** to strike a surface obliquely so as to go off at an angle – often + *off* **2** to touch on a subject or refer to it briefly or indirectly **3a** *of the eyes* to move swiftly from one thing to another **b** to take a quick look at sthg

²glance *n* **1** a quick intermittent flash or gleam **2** a deflected impact or blow **3a** a swift movement of the eyes **b** a quick or cursory look

glancing /ˈglɑːnsɪŋ/ *adj* having a slanting direction – **~ly** *adv*

gland /glænd/ *n* **1** an organ that selectively removes materials from the blood, alters them, and secretes them esp for further use in the body or for elimination **2** any of various secreting organs of plants

¹glare /gleəʳ/ *v* **1** to shine with a harsh uncomfortably brilliant light **2** to express hostility by staring fiercely

²glare *n* **1** a harsh uncomfortably bright light; *specif* painfully bright sunlight **2** an angry or fierce stare

glaring /ˈgleərɪŋ/ *adj* painfully and obtrusively evident – **~ly** *adv*

glass /glɑːs/ *n* **1a** a hard brittle usu transparent substance formed by fusing silica sand and other ingredients **b** a substance resembling glass, esp in hardness and transparency **2a** sthg made of glass: e g **(1)** a glass drinking vessel (e g a tumbler or wineglass) **(2)** a mirror **(3)** a barometer **b(1)** an optical instrument (e g a magnifying glass) for viewing objects not readily seen **(2)** *pl* a pair of lenses together with a frame to hold them in place for correcting defects of vision or protecting the eyes

glass fibre *n* fibreglass

glasshouse /ˈglɑːshaʊs/ *n, chiefly Br* **1** a greenhouse **2** a military prison – slang

glasspaper /ˈglɑːspeɪpəʳ/ *n* paper to which a thin layer of powdered glass has been glued for use as an abrasive

glassware /ˈglɑːsweəʳ/ *n* articles made of glass

glassy /ˈglɑːsi/ *adj* dull, lifeless

¹glaze /gleɪz/ *v* **1** to provide or fit with glass **2** to coat (as if) with a glaze **3** to give a smooth glossy surface to

²glaze *n* **1a** a liquid preparation that gives a glossy coating to food **b** a preparation applied to the surface of ceramic wares as decoration and to make them nonporous **2** a glassy film (e g of ice)

glazier /ˈgleɪzɪəʳ/ *n* one who fits glass, esp into windows, as an occupation

¹gleam /gliːm/ *n* **1a** a transient appearance of subdued or partly obscured light **b** a glint **2** a brief or faint appearance or occurrence

²gleam *v* **1** to shine with subdued steady light or moderate brightness **2** to appear briefly or faintly

glean /gliːn/ *v* **1** to gather produce, esp grain, left by reapers **2** to gather material (e g information) bit by bit – ~er *n*

gleanings /'gli'nɪŋz/ *n pl* things acquired by gleaning

glee /gliː/ *n* **1** a feeling of merry high-spirited joy or delight **2** an unaccompanied song for 3 or more usu male solo voices – ~**ful** *adj*

glen /glen/ *n* a secluded narrow valley

glib /glɪb/ *adj* **1** showing little forethought or preparation; lacking depth and substance **2** marked by (superficial or dishonest) ease and fluency in speaking or writing – ~**ly** *adv* – ~**ness** *n*

glide /glaɪd/ **1** to move noiselessly in a smooth, continuous, and effortless manner **2** to pass gradually and imperceptibly **3** *of an aircraft* to fly without the use of engines

glider /'glaɪdəʳ/ *n* an aircraft similar to an aeroplane but without an engine

¹glimmer /'glɪməʳ/ *v* **1** to shine faintly or unsteadily **2** to appear indistinctly with a faintly luminous quality

²glimmer *n* **1** a feeble or unsteady light **2a** a dim perception or faint idea **b** a small sign or amount

¹glimpse /glɪmps/ *v* to get a brief look at

²glimpse *n* a brief fleeting view or look

¹glint /glɪnt/ *v* to shine with tiny bright flashes; sparkle or glitter, esp by reflection

²glint *n* **1** a tiny bright flash of light; a sparkle **2** a brief or faint manifestation

glissando /glɪ'sændəʊ/ *n, pl* **glissandi, glissandos** a rapid sliding up or down the musical scale

glisten /'glɪsən/ *v* to shine, usu by reflection, with a sparkling radiance or with the lustre of a wet or oiled surface – ~**ing** *adj* – ~**ingly** *adv*

¹glitter /'glɪtəʳ/ *v* **1** to shine by reflection with a brilliant or metallic lustre **2** to be brilliantly attractive in a superficial or deceptive way

²glitter *n* **1** sparkling brilliance, showiness, or attractiveness **2** small glittering particles used for ornamentation

gloat /gləʊt/ *v* to observe or think about sthg with great and often malicious satisfaction, gratification, or relish

global /'gləʊbəl/ *adj* **1** spherical **2** of or involving the entire world **3** general, comprehensive – **globally** *adv*

globe /gləʊb/ *n* sthg spherical or rounded: e g **a** a spherical representation of the earth, a heavenly body, or the heavens **b** the earth

globe artichoke *n* an artichoke with an edible flower-head

globe-trotter *n* one who travels widely

globular /'glɒbjʊləʳ/ *adj* **1** globe- or globule-shaped **2** having or consisting of globules

globule /'glɒbjuːl/ *n* a tiny globe or ball (e g of liquid or melted solid)

glockenspiel /'glɒkənspiːl/ *n* a percussion instrument consisting of a series of graduated metal bars played with 2 hammers

gloom /'gluːm/ *n* **1** partial or total darkness **2a** lowness of spirits **b** an atmosphere of despondency – ~**y** *adj*

glorify /'glɔːrɪ̥faɪ/ *v* **1** to make glorious by bestowing honour, praise, or admiration **2** to shed radiance or splendour on **3** to cause to appear better, more appealing, or more important than in reality **4** to give glory to (e g in worship) – **-fication** *n*

glorious /'glɔːrɪəs/ *adj* **1a** possessing or deserving glory **b** conferring glory **2** marked by great beauty or splendour **3** delightful, wonderful – ~**ly** *adv*

¹glory /'glɔːri/ *n* **1** (sthg that secures) praise or renown **2** a (most) commendable asset **3a** (sthg marked by) resplendence or magnificence **b** the splendour, blessedness, and happiness of heaven; eternity **4** a state of great gratification or exaltation

²glory *v* to rejoice proudly

¹gloss /glɒs/ *n* **1** (sthg that gives) surface lustre or brightness **2** a deceptively attractive outer appearance **3** paint to which varnish has been added to give a gloss finish

²gloss *n* **1** a brief explanation (e g in the margin of a text) of a difficult word or expression **2a** a glossary **b** an interlinear translation **c** a continuous commentary accompanying a text – **gloss** *v*

glossary /ˈglɒsəri/ *n* a list of terms (e g those used in a particular text or in a specialized field), usu with their meanings

gloss over *v* **1** to make appear right and acceptable **2** to veil or hide by treating rapidly or superficially

¹**glossy** /ˈglɒsi/ *adj* **1** having a surface lustre or brightness **2** attractive in an artificially opulent, sophisticated, or smoothly captivating manner

²**glossy** *n, chiefly Br* a magazine expensively produced on glossy paper and often having a fashionable or sophisticated content

glottal stop /ˈglɒtl/ *n* a speech sound produced by sudden closure of the glottis

glottis /ˈglɒtɨs/ *n, pl* **glottises, glottides** (the structures surrounding) the elongated space between the vocal cords

glove /glʌv/ *n* a covering for the hand having separate sections for each of the fingers and the thumb and often extending part way up the arm

glove compartment *n* a small storage compartment in the dashboard of a motor vehicle

¹**glow** /gləʊ/ *v* **1** to shine (as if) with an intense heat **2a** to experience a sensation (as if) of heat; show a ruddy colour (as if) from being too warm **b** to show satisfaction or elation

²**glow** *n* **1** brightness or warmth of colour **2a** warmth of feeling or emotion **b** a sensation of warmth **3** light (as if) from sthg burning without flames or smoke

glower /ˈglaʊəʳ/ *v* to look or stare with sullen annoyance or anger – **~ingly** *adv*

glowworm /ˈgləʊwɜːm/ *n* a larva or wingless female of a firefly that emits light from the abdomen

glucose /ˈgluːkəʊs, -kəʊz/ *n* a sugar that occurs widely in nature and is the usual form in which carbohydrate is assimilated by animals

¹**glue** /gluː/ *n* any of various strong adhesives; *also* a solution of glue used for sticking things together – **~y** *adj*

²**glue** *v* **1** to cause to stick tightly with glue **2** to fix (e g the eyes) on an object steadily or with deep concentration

glum /glʌm/ *adj* **1** broodingly morose **2** dreary, gloomy – **~ly** *adv* – **~ness** *n*

¹**glut** /glʌt/ *v* **1** to fill, esp with food, to beyond capacity **2** to flood (the market) with goods so that supply exceeds demand

²**glut** *n* an excessive supply (e g of a harvested crop) which exceeds market demand

gluten /ˈgluːtn/ *n* a protein, esp of wheat flour, that gives cohesiveness to dough

glutinous /ˈgluːtɨnəs/ *adj* (thick and) sticky; gummy

glutton /ˈglʌtn/ *n* **1** one given habitually to greedy and voracious eating and drinking **2** one who has a great capacity for accepting or enduring sthg – **~ous** *adj* – **~ously** *adv* – **~y** *n*

glycerine, glycerin /ˈglɪsərɪn/ *n* a sticky colourless liquid, made from fats, used in the manufacture of soap and explosives

gnarled /nɑːld/ *adj* **1** full of or covered with knots or protuberances **2** crabbed in disposition, aspect, or character

gnash /næʃ/ *v* to strike or grind (esp the teeth) together

gnat /næt/ *n* any of various small usu biting 2-winged flies

gnaw /nɔː/ *v* **1** to bite or chew on with the teeth; *esp* to wear away by persistent biting or nibbling **2** to affect as if by continuous eating away; plague **3** to erode, corrode

gneiss /naɪs/ *n* a rock usu composed of light bands of feldspar and quartz and dark bands of mica

gnome /nəʊm/ *n* a dwarf of folklore who lives under the earth and guards treasure

gnu /nuː/ *n* any of several large horned African antelopes with an oxlike head, a short mane, and a long tail

¹**go** /gəʊ/ *v* **went; gone** **1** to proceed on a course **2a** to move out of or away from a place; leave – sometimes used with a further verb to express purpose **b** to make an expedition for a specified activity **3a** to pass by means of a

specified process or according to a specified procedure **b(1)** to proceed in a thoughtless or reckless manner – used to intensify a complementary verb **(2)** to proceed to do sthg surprising – used with *and* to intensify a complementary verb **c(1)** to extend **(2)** to speak, proceed, or develop in a specified direction or up to a specified limit **4** to travel on foot or by moving the feet **5** to be, esp habitually **6a** to become lost, consumed, or spent **b** to die **c** to elapse **d** to be got rid of (e g by sale or removal) **e** to fail **f** to succumb; give way **7a** to happen, progress – often + *on* **b** to be in general or on an average **c** to turn out (well) **8** to put or subject oneself **9a** to begin an action, motion, or process **b** to maintain or perform an action or motion **c** to function in a proper or specified way **d** to make a characteristic noise **e** to perform a demonstrated action **10a** to be known or identified as specified **b** to be performed or delivered in a specified manner **11a** to act or occur in accordance or harmony **b** to contribute to a total or result **12** to be about, intending, or destined – + *to* and an infinitive (e g is it *going* to rain) **13a** to come or arrive at a specified state or condition **b** to join a specified institution professionally or attend it habitually **c** to come to be; turn **d(1)** to become voluntarily **(2)** to change to a specified system or tendency **e** to continue to be; remain **14** to be compatible *with*, harmonize **15a** to be capable of passing, extending, or being contained or inserted **b** to belong **16a** to carry authority **b** to be acceptable, satisfactory, or adequate **c** to be the case; be valid **17** to empty the bladder or bowels – euph

[2]**go** *n, pl* **goes** **1** energy, vigour **2a** a turn in an activity (e g a game) **b** an attempt, try **3** a spell of activity **4** a success

[3]**go** *adj* functioning properly

[4]**go** *n* an Oriental game of capture and territorial domination played by 2 players with counters on a board covered in a grid

go about *v* to change tack when sailing

[1]**goad** /gəʊd/ *n* **1** a pointed rod used to urge on an animal **2** sthg that pricks, urges, or stimulates (into action)

[2]**goad** *v* to incite or rouse by nagging or persistent annoyance

[1]**go-ahead** *adj* energetic and progressive

[2]**go-ahead** *n* a sign, signal, or authority to proceed

goal /gəʊl/ *n* **1** an end towards which effort is directed **2a** an area or object through or into which players in various games attempt to put a ball or puck against the defence of the opposing side **b** (the points gained by) the act of putting a ball or puck through or into a goal

goalkeeper /ˈgəʊlˌkiːpəʳ/ *n* a player who defends the goal in soccer, hockey, lacrosse, etc

goal line *n* a line at either end and usu running the width of a playing area on which a goal or goal post is situated

goalmouth /ˈgəʊlmaʊθ/ *n* the area of a playing field directly in front of the goal

go along *v* **1** to move along; proceed **2** to go or travel as a companion **3** to agree, cooperate

goalpost /ˈgəʊlpəʊst/ *n* either of usu 2 vertical posts that with or without a crossbar constitute the goal in soccer, rugby, etc

goat /gəʊt/ *n* **1** any of various long-legged (horned) ruminant mammals smaller than cattle and related to the sheep **2** a lecherous man **3** a foolish person

go at *v* **1** to attack **2** to undertake energetically

goatee /gəʊˈtiː/ *n* a small pointed beard

[1]**gob** /gɒb/ *n* a shapeless or sticky lump

[2]**gob** *n, Br* a mouth – slang

[1]**gobble** /ˈgɒbəl/ *v* **1** to swallow or eat greedily or noisily **2** to take, accept, or read eagerly – often + *up*

[2]**gobble** *v* to make the guttural sound of a male turkey or a similar sound

gobbledygook, gobbledegook /ˈgɒbəldiguːk/ *n* wordy unintelligible jargon

go-between *n* an intermediate agent

goblet /ˈgɒblɨt/ *n* a drinking vessel

that has a usu rounded bowl, a foot, and a stem and is used esp for wine

goblin /ˈgɒblᵻn/ *n* a grotesque mischievous elf

go-by *n* an act of avoidance; a miss

go by *v* to pass

god /gɒd/ *n* **1** *cap* the being perfect in power, wisdom, and goodness whom human beings worship as creator and ruler of the universe **2** a being or object believed to have more than natural attributes and powers (e g the control of a particular aspect of reality) and to require human beings' worship **3** *pl* the highest gallery in a theatre, usu with the cheapest seats

godchild /ˈgɒdtʃaɪld/ *n* sby for whom sby else becomes sponsor at baptism

godforsaken /ˈgɒdfəseɪkən/ *adj* **1** remote, desolate **2** neglected, dismal

godless /ˈgɒdlᵻs/ *adj* not acknowledging a deity; impious – **~ly** *adv* – **~ness** *n*

godly /ˈgɒdli/ *adj* pious, devout

godown /ˈgəʊdaʊn/ *n* a warehouse in an Asian country, esp India

go down *v* **1a** to fall (as if) to the ground **b** to sink (below the horizon) **2** to be capable of being swallowed **3** to undergo defeat **4a** to find acceptance **b** to come to be remembered, esp by posterity **5a** to undergo a decline or decrease **b** *esp of a computer system or program* to crash **6** to become ill – usu + *with* **7** *Br* to leave a university **8** to be sent to prison – slang

godparent /ˈgɒd,peərənt/ *n* a sponsor at baptism

godsend /ˈgɒdsend/ *n* a desirable or needed thing or event that comes unexpectedly

go-getter *n* an aggressively enterprising person

goggle /ˈgɒgəl/ *v* to stare with wide or protuberant eyes

goggle-box *n, Br* a television set – infml

goggles /ˈgɒgəlz/ *n pl* protective glasses set in a flexible frame that fits snugly against the face

go-go *adj* of or being the music or a style of dance performed or a dancer performing at a disco

go in *n* **1** to enter **2** *of the sun, moon, etc* to be hidden by cloud **3** to form a union *with* **4** to enter *for* (a competition, exam, etc) **5** to have as a hobby – + *for*

¹going /ˈgəʊɪŋ/ *n* **1** an act or instance of going – often in combination **2** the condition of the ground (e g for horse racing) **3** advance, progress

²going *adj* **1** current, prevailing **2** profitable, thriving

going-over *n* **1** a thorough examination or investigation **2** a severe scolding; *also* a beating

goings-on *n pl* **1** actions, events **2** reprehensible happenings or conduct

go-kart /ˈgəʊ kɑːt/ *n* a tiny racing car with small wheels

gold /gəʊld/ *n* **1** a heavy ductile yellow metallic element that occurs chiefly free and is used esp in coins and jewellery **2** a gold medal **3** a deep metallic yellow colour **4** (a shot hitting) the golden or yellow centre spot of an archery target

golden /ˈgəʊldən/ *adj* **1** consisting of, relating to, or containing gold **2** of the colour of gold **3** prosperous, flourishing **4** favourable, advantageous **5** of or marking a 50th anniversary

golden age *n* a period of great happiness, prosperity, and achievement

golden handshake *n* a large money payment given by a company to an employee, esp on retirement

golden syrup *n* the pale yellow syrup derived from cane sugar refining and used in cooking

goldfinch /ˈgəʊld,fɪntʃ/ *n* a small red, black, yellow, and white European finch

goldfish /ˈgəʊld,fɪʃ/ *n* a small (golden yellow) fish related to the carps and widely kept in aquariums and ponds

gold mine *n* a rich source of sthg desired (e g information)

gold rush *n* a rush to newly discovered goldfields in pursuit of riches

goldsmith /ˈgəʊld,smɪθ/ *n* one who works in gold or deals in articles of gold

golf /gɒlf/ *n* a game in which a player using special clubs attempts to hit a ball into each of the 9 or 18 successive holes on a course with as few strokes as possible – **~er** *n*

gollywog, **golliwog** *also* **golly**

/'gɒliwɒg/ *n* a black-faced child's doll, usu made of fabric

gonad /'gəʊnæd/ *n* any of the primary sex glands (e g the ovaries or testes)

gondola /'gɒndələ/ *n* **1** a long narrow flat-bottomed boat used on the canals of Venice **2** a cabin suspended from a cable and used for transporting passengers (e g up a ski slope)

gondolier /,gɒndə'lɪəʳ/ *n* a boatman who propels a gondola

¹gone /gɒn/ *adj* **1a** involved, absorbed **b** pregnant by a specified length of time **c** infatuated – often + *on*; infml **2** dead – euph

²gone *adv, Br* past, turned (a certain age)

goner /'gɒnəʳ/ *n* one whose case or state is hopeless or lost – infml

gong /gɒŋ/ *n* **1** a disc-shaped percussion instrument that produces a resounding tone when struck with a usu padded hammer **2** a flat saucer-shaped bell **3** a medal or decoration – slang

gonorrhoea /,gɒnə'rɪə/ *n* a venereal disease characterized by bacterial infection of the mucous membranes of the genital tracts

goo /guː/ *n* **1** sticky matter **2** cloying sentimentality *USE* infml

¹good /gʊd/ *adj* **better; best 1a(1)** of a favourable character or tendency **(2)** bountiful, fertile **(3)** handsome, attractive **b(1)** suitable, fit **(2)** free from injury or disease; whole **c(1)** agreeable, pleasant; *specif* amusing **(2)** beneficial to the health or character **(3)** not rotten; fresh **d** ample, full **e(1)** well-founded, true **(2)** deserving of respect; honourable **(3)** legally valid **2a(1)** morally commendable; virtuous **(2)** correct; *specif* well-behaved **(3)** kind, benevolent **b** reputable; *specif* wellborn **c** competent, skilful **d** loyal

²good *n* **1** prosperity, benefit **2a** sthg that has economic utility or satisfies an economic want – usu pl **b** *pl* personal property having intrinsic value but usu excluding money, securities, and negotiable instruments **c** *pl* wares, merchandise **3** *pl but sing or pl in constr* the desired or necessary article – infml

³good *adv* well – infml

good book *n, often cap G&B the* Bible

good-for-nothing *adj* of no value; worthless; *also* idle

Good Friday *n* the Friday before Easter, observed in churches as the anniversary of the crucifixion of Christ

good-humoured *adj* good-natured, cheerful – **~ly** *adv*

good-natured *adj* of a cheerful and cooperative disposition – **~ly** *adv*

goodness /'gʊdnɪ̥s/ *n* the nutritious or beneficial part of sthg

good offices *n pl* power or action that helps sby out of a difficulty – often in *through the good offices of*

goodwill /,gʊd'wɪl/ *n* **1** a kindly feeling of approval and support; benevolent interest or concern **2** the favour or prestige that a business has acquired beyond the mere value of what it sells

goody, goodie /'gʊdi/ *n* **1** sthg particularly attractive, pleasurable, or desirable **2** a good person or hero *USE* infml

goody-goody *n or adj* (sby) affectedly or ingratiatingly prim or virtuous – infml

¹goof /guːf/ *n* **1** a ridiculous stupid person **2** *chiefly NAm* a blunder *USE* infml

²goof *v* to make a mess of; bungle – often + *up*

go off *v* **1** to explode **2** to go forth or away; depart **3** *of food or drink* to become rotten or sour **4** to follow a specified course; proceed **5** to make a characteristic noise; sound

goofy /'guːfi/ *adj* silly, daft – infml – **goofiness** *n*

googly /'guːgli/ *n* a delivery by a right-handed bowler in cricket that is an off break as viewed by a right-handed batsman although apparently delivered with a leg-break action

goon /guːn/ *n* **1** *NAm* a man hired to terrorize opponents **2** an idiot, dope – slang

go on *v* **1** to continue **2a** to proceed (as if) by a logical step **b** *of time* to pass **3** to take place; happen **4a** to talk, esp in an effusive manner **b** to criticize constantly; nag **5** to come into operation, action, or production

¹goose /guːs/ *n, pl* **geese** **1** (the female of) any of numerous large long-necked web-footed waterfowl **2** a simpleton, dolt

²goose *v* to poke between the buttocks

gooseberry /ˈgʊzbəri, ˈguːz-, ˈguːs-/ *n* **1** (the shrub that bears) an edible acid usu prickly green or yellow fruit **2** an unwanted companion to 2 lovers – chiefly in *to play gooseberry*

gooseflesh /ˈguːsfleʃ/ *n* a bristling roughness of the skin usu from cold or fear

goose step *n* a straight-legged marching step

go out *v* **1** to leave a room, house, country, etc **2a** to become extinguished **b** to become obsolete or unfashionable **3** to spend time regularly *with* sby of esp the opposite sex **4** to be broadcast

go over *v* **1** to become converted (e g to a religion or political party) **2** to receive approval; succeed

gopher /ˈgəʊfəʳ/ *n* any of several American burrowing rodents or ground squirrels

¹gore /gɔːʳ/ *n* (clotted) blood

²gore *n* a tapering or triangular piece of material (e g cloth) used to give shape to sthg (e g a garment or sail) – **gored** *adj*

³gore *v* to pierce or wound with a horn or tusk

¹gorge /gɔːdʒ/ *n* **1** the throat **2** a narrow steep-walled valley, often with a stream flowing through it

²gorge *v* **1** to eat greedily or until full **2** to fill completely or to the point of making distended

gorgeous /ˈgɔːdʒəs/ *adj* **1** splendidly beautiful or magnificent **2** very fine; pleasant – **~ly** *adv* – **~ness** *n*

gorgon /ˈgɔːgən/ *n* **1** *cap* any of 3 sisters in Greek mythology who had live snakes in place of hair and whose glance turned the beholder to stone **2** an ugly or repulsive woman

Gorgonzola /ˌgɔːgənˈzəʊlə/ *n* a blue-veined strongly flavoured cheese of Italian origin

gorilla /gəˈrɪlə/ *n* an anthropoid ape of western equatorial Africa related to but much larger than the chimpanzee

gormless /ˈgɔːmlɪ̈s/ *adj, Br* lacking understanding and intelligence; stupid – infml – **~ly** *adv*

go round *v* **1** to spread, circulate **2** to satisfy demand; meet the need

gorse /gɔːs/ *n* a spiny yellow-flowered evergreen leguminous European shrub

gory /ˈgɔːri/ *adj* **1** covered with gore; bloodstained **2** full of violence; bloodcurdling

gosling /ˈgɒzlɪŋ/ *n* a young goose

go-slow *n, Br* a deliberate slowing down of production by workers as a form of industrial action

¹gospel /ˈgɒspəl/ *n* **1** *often cap* the message of the life, death, and resurrection of Jesus Christ; *esp* any of the first 4 books of the New Testament **2** the message or teachings of a usu religious teacher or movement

²gospel *adj* **1** of the Christian gospel; evangelical **2** of or being usu evangelistic religious songs of American origin

gossamer /ˈgɒsəməʳ/ *n* **1** a film of cobwebs floating in air in calm clear weather **2** sthg light, insubstantial, or tenuous

gossip /ˈgɒsɪ̈p/ *n* **1** sby who habitually reveals usu sensational facts concerning other people's actions or lives **2a** (rumour or report of) the facts related by a gossip **b** a chatty talk – **gossip** *v*

got /gɒt/ **1** *past of* **get** **2** *pres pl & 1&2 sing of* **get** – nonstandard

¹Gothic /ˈgɒθɪk/ *adj* **1** of the Goths, their culture, or Gothic **2** of a style of architecture prevalent from the middle of the 12th c to the early 16th c characterized by vaulting and pointed arches **3** *often not cap* of or like a class of novels of the late 18th and early 19th c dealing with macabre or mysterious events

²Gothic *n* **1** the E Germanic language of the Goths **2** Gothic architectural style

go through *v* **1** to continue firmly or obstinately to the end – often + *with* **2** to receive approval or sanction

gouache /gʊˈɑːʃ, gwɑːʃ/ *n* a method of painting with opaque watercolours that have been ground in water and mixed with a gum preparation

Gouda /ˈgaʊdə, ˈguːdə/ *n* a mild cheese of Dutch origin that is similar to Edam but contains more fat

[1]**gouge** /gaʊdʒ/ *n* a chisel with a curved cross section and bevel on the concave side of the blade

[2]**gouge** *v* **1** to scoop out (as if) with a gouge **2** to force *out* (an eye), esp with the thumb

goulash /ˈguːlæʃ/ *n* **1** a meat stew made usu with veal or beef and highly seasoned with paprika **2** a round in bridge played with hands dealt in lots of 5, 5, and 3 cards consecutively from a pack formed by the unshuffled arranged hands from a previous deal

go under *v* to be destroyed or defeated; fail

go up *v, Br* to enter or return to a university

gourmand /ˈgʊəmənd, ˈgɔː-/ *n* one who is excessively fond of or heartily interested in food and drink

gourmet /ˈgʊəmeɪ/ / *n* a connoisseur of food and drink

gout /gaʊt/ *n* **1** painful inflammation of the joints, esp that of the big toe, resulting from a disorder of the blood **2** a sticky blob – **~y** *adj*

govern /ˈgʌvən/ *v* **1** to exercise continuous sovereign authority over **2a** to control, determine, or strongly influence **b** to hold in check; restrain

governess /ˈgʌvənɨs/ *n* a woman entrusted with the private teaching and often supervision of a child

government /ˈgʌvəmənt, ˈgʌvənmənt/ *n* **1** the office, authority, or function of governing **2** policy making as distinguished from administration **3** the machinery through which political authority is exercised **4** *sing or pl in constr* the body of people that constitutes a governing authority – **~al** *adj*

governor /ˈgʌvənəʳ/ *n* **1a** a ruler, chief executive, or nominal head of a political unit **b** the managing director and usu the principal officer of an institution or organization **c** a member of a group (e g the governing body of a school) that controls an institution **2** sby (e g a father, guardian, or employer) looked on as governing – slang – **~ship** *n*

governor-general *n, pl* **governors-general, governor-generals** a governor of high rank; *esp* one representing the Crown in a Commonwealth country

go with *v* **1** to match or suit **2** to accompany, be found with

gown /gaʊn/ *n* **1** a loose flowing robe worn esp by a professional or academic person when acting in an official capacity **2** a woman's dress, esp one that is elegant or for formal wear

grab /græb/ *v* **-bb- 1** to take or seize hastily; snatch **2** to obtain unscrupulously **3** to forcefully engage the attention of – infml – **grab** *n*

[1]**grace** /greɪs/ *n* **1a** divine assistance given to human beings **b** a state of being pleasing to God **2** a short prayer at a meal asking a blessing or giving thanks **3** disposition to or an act or instance of kindness or clemency **4a** a charming trait or accomplishment **b** an elegant appearance or effect; charm **c** ease and suppleness of movement or bearing **5** – used as a title for a duke, duchess, or archbishop **6** consideration, decency

[2]**grace** *v* **1** to confer dignity or honour on **2** to adorn, embellish

graceful /ˈgreɪsfəl/ *adj* displaying grace in form, action, or movement – **-fully** *adv*

grace note *n* a musical note added as an ornament

Graces /ˈgreɪsɨz/ *n pl* the 3 beautiful sister goddesses in Greek mythology who are the givers of charm and beauty

gracious /ˈgreɪʃəs/ *adj* **1a** marked by kindness and courtesy **b** having those qualities (e g comfort, elegance, and freedom from hard work) made possible by wealth **2** merciful, compassionate – used conventionally of royalty and high nobility – **~ly** *adv* – **~ness** *n*

gradation /grəˈdeɪʃən/ *n* **1** (a step or place in) a series forming successive stages **2** a gradual passing from one tint or shade to another (e g in a painting)

[1]**grade** /greɪd/ *n* **1** a position in a scale of ranks or qualities **2** a class of things

of the same stage or degree **3** *NAm* a school form; a class **4** *NAm* a mark indicating a degree of accomplishment at school

²grade *v* **1** to arrange in grades; sort **2** to arrange in a scale or series **3** *NAm* to assign a mark to

gradient /'greɪdɪənt/ *n* **1** the degree of inclination of a road or slope; *also* a sloping road or railway **2** change in the value of a (specified) quantity with change in a given variable, esp distance

gradual /'grædʒʊəl/ *adj* proceeding or happening by steps or degrees – **-ually** *adv* – **~ness** *n*

¹graduate /'grædʒʊə̇t/ *n* **1** the holder of an academic degree **2** *chiefly NAm* one who has completed a course of study

²graduate /'grædʒʊeɪt/ *v* **1** to mark with degrees of measurement **2** to divide into grades or intervals **3** to receive an academic degree **4** to move up to a usu higher stage of experience, proficiency, or prestige

graduation /ˌgrædʒʊ'eɪʃən/ *n* **1** a mark (e g on an instrument or vessel) indicating degrees or quantity **2** the award of an academic degree

¹graft /grɑːft/ *v* **1** to cause (a plant scion) to unite with a stock; *also* to unite (plants or scion and stock) to form a graft **2** to attach, add **3** to implant (living tissue) surgically **4** *NAm* to practise graft

²graft *n* **1a** a grafted plant **b** (the point of insertion upon a stock of) a scion **2** (living tissue used in) grafting **3** the improper use of one's position (e g public office) to one's private, esp financial, advantage

³graft *v, Br* to work hard – slang

¹grain /greɪn/ *n* **1** a seed or fruit of a cereal grass; *also* (the seeds or fruits collectively of) the cereal grasses or similar food plants **2a** a discrete (small hard) particle or crystal (e g of sand, salt, or a metal) **b** the least amount possible **3** a granular surface, nature, or appearance **4** a small unit of weight, used for medicines ($^{1}/_{7000}$ of a pound or 0.0648 gram) **5a** the arrangement of the fibres in wood **b** the direction, alignment, or texture of the constituent particles, fibres, or threads **6** natural disposition or character; temper

²grain *v* to paint in imitation of the grain of wood or stone

gram, gramme /græm/ *n* a metric unit of weight equal to about 0.04 oz

¹grammar /'græməʳ/ *n* **1** the study of the classes of words, their inflections, and their functions and relations in the sentence; *broadly* this study when taken to include that of phonology and sometimes of usage **2** the characteristic system of inflections and syntax of a language **3** a grammar textbook **4** the principles or rules of an art, science, or technique

²grammar *adj* of the type of education provided at a grammar school

grammar school *n, Br* a secondary school providing an academic type of education from the age of 11 to 18

grammatical /grə'mætɪkəl/ *adj* (conforming to the rules) of grammar – **~ly** *adv*

gramophone /'græməfəʊn/ *n* a device for reproducing sounds from the vibrations of a stylus resting in a spiral groove on a rotating disc; a record player

gran /græn/ *n, chiefly Br* a grandmother – infml

granary /'grænəri/ *n* **1** a storehouse for threshed grain **2** a region producing grain in abundance

¹grand /grænd/ *adj* **1** having more importance than others; foremost **2** complete, comprehensive **3** main, principal **4** large and striking in size, extent, or conception **5a** lavish, sumptuous **b** marked by regal form and dignity; imposing **c** lofty, sublime **6** intended to impress **7** very good; wonderful – infml – **~ly** *adv* – **~ness** *n*

²grand *n* **1** a grand piano **2a** *Br* a thousand pounds **b** *NAm* a thousand dollars *USE* (*2*) slang

grandad, granddad /'grændæd/ *n* a grandfather – infml

grandchild /'græntʃaɪld/ *n* a child of one's son or daughter

granddaughter /'grænˌdɔːtəʳ/ *n* a daughter of one's son or daughter

grandeur /'grændʒəʳ/ *n* **1** the quality of being large or impressive; magnificence **2** personal greatness marked by nobility, dignity, or power

grandfather /ˈɡræn,fɑːðəʳ/ *n* the father of one's father or mother; *broadly* a male ancestor

grandfather clock *n* a tall pendulum clock standing directly on the floor

grandiose /ˈɡrændiəʊs/ *adj* **1** impressive because of uncommon largeness, scope, or grandeur **2** characterized by affectation of grandeur or by absurd exaggeration

grand master *n* a chess player who has consistently scored higher than a standardized score in international competition

grandmother /ˈɡræn,mʌðəʳ/ *n* the mother of one's father or mother; *broadly* a female ancestor

grandparent /ˈɡræn,peərənt/ *n* the parent of one's father or mother

grand piano *n* a piano with horizontal frame and strings

grand slam *n* the winning of all the tricks in 1 hand of a card game, specif bridge

grandson /ˈɡrænsʌn/ *n* a son of one's son or daughter

grandstand /ˈɡrændstænd/ *n* a usu roofed stand for spectators at a racecourse, stadium, etc in an advantageous position for viewing the contest

grand tour *n* an extended tour of the Continent, formerly a usual part of the education of young British gentlemen – usu + *the*

grange /ɡreɪndʒ/ *n* a farm; *esp* a farmhouse with outbuildings

granite /ˈɡrænɪ̣t/ *n* **1** a very hard granular igneous rock formed of quartz, feldspar, and mica and used esp for building **2** unyielding firmness or endurance

granny, grannie /ˈɡræni/ a grandmother – infml

[1]grant /ɡrɑːnt/ *v* **1a** to consent to carry out or fulfil (e g a wish or request) **b** to permit as a right, privilege, or favour **2** to bestow or transfer formally **3a** to be willing to concede **b** to assume to be true

[2]grant *n* **1** sthg granted; *esp* a gift for a particular purpose **2** a transfer of property; *also* the property so transferred

granulate /ˈɡrænjʊleɪt/ *v* to form or crystallize into grains or granules

granule /ˈɡrænjuːl/ *n* a small grain – **-lar** *adj*

grape /ɡreɪp/ *n* (any of a genus of widely cultivated woody vines that bear, in clusters,) a smooth-skinned juicy greenish white to deep red or purple berry eaten as a fruit or fermented to produce wine

grapefruit /ˈɡreɪpfruːt/ *n* (a small tree that bears) a large round citrus fruit with a bitter yellow rind and a somewhat acid juicy pulp

grapevine /ˈɡreɪpvaɪn/ *n* a secret or unofficial means of circulating information or gossip

graph /ɡrɑːf/ *n* a diagram (e g a series of points, a line, a curve, or an area) expressing a relation between quantities or variables

[1]graphic /ˈɡræfɪk/ *also* **graphical** *adj* **1** formed by writing, drawing, or engraving **2** marked by clear and vivid description; sharply outlined **3a** of the pictorial arts **b** of or employing engraving, etching, lithography, photography, or other methods of reproducing material in the graphic arts **4** of or represented by a graph **5** of writing

[2]graphic *n* **1** a product of graphic art **2** a picture, map, or graph used for illustration or demonstration **3** a graphic representation displayed by a computer (e g on a VDU)

graphite /ˈɡræfaɪt/ *n* a soft black lustrous form of carbon that conducts electricity and is used esp in lead pencils and as a lubricant

grapnel /ˈɡræpnəl/ *n* an instrument with several claws that is hurled with a line attached in order to hook onto a ship, the top of a wall, etc

[1]grapple /ˈɡræpəl/ *n* **1** a grapnel **2** a hand-to-hand struggle

[2]grapple *v* to come to grips *with*

[1]grasp /ɡrɑːsp/ *v* **1** to take, seize, or clasp eagerly (as if) with the fingers or arms **2** to succeed in understanding; comprehend

[2]grasp *n* **1** a firm hold **2** control, power **3** the power of seizing and holding or attaining **4** comprehension

grasping /ˈɡrɑːspɪŋ/ *adj* eager for material possessions; avaricious – **~ly** *adv*

¹grass /grɑːs/ *n* **1** herbage suitable or used for grazing animals **2** any of a large family of plants with slender leaves and flowers in small spikes or clusters, that includes bamboo, wheat, rye, corn, etc **3** land on which grass is grown; *esp* a lawn **4** cannabis; *specif* marijuana – slang **5** *Br* a police informer – slang

²grass *v* **1** to cover or seed with grass – often + *down* **2** , Br to inform the police; *esp* to betray sby to the police – slang

grasshopper /ˈgrɑːsˌhɒpəʳ/ *n* any of numerous plant-eating insects with hind legs adapted for leaping

grass roots *n pl but sing or pl in constr* **1** society at the local level as distinguished from the centres of political leadership **2** the fundamental level or source

grassy /ˈgrɑːsi/ *adj* **1** consisting of or covered with grass **2** (having a smell) like grass

¹grate /greɪt/ *n* **1** a frame or bed of metal bars to hold the fuel in a fireplace, stove, or furnace **2** a fireplace

²grate *v* **1** to reduce to small particles by rubbing on sthg rough **2a** to gnash or grind noisily **b** to cause to make a rasping sound **3** to cause irritation; jar

grateful /ˈgreɪtfəl/ *adj* **1** feeling or expressing thanks **2** pleasing, comforting – **~ly** *adv* – **~ness** *n*

gratify /ˈgrætɪ̇faɪ/ *v* **1** to be a source of or give pleasure or satisfaction to **2** to give in to; satisfy – **-fication** *n* – **~ing** *adj* – **~ingly** *adv*

grating /ˈgreɪtɪŋ/ *n* **1** a partition, covering, or frame of parallel bars or crossbars **2** a lattice used to close or floor any of various openings

gratis /ˈgrætɪ̇s, ˈgrɑːtɪ̇s/ *adv or adj* without charge or recompense; free

gratitude /ˈgrætɪ̇tjuːd/ *n* the state or feeling of being grateful; thankfulness

gratuitous /grəˈtjuːɪ̇təs/ *adj* **1a** costing nothing; free **b** not involving a return benefit or compensation **2** not called for by the circumstances; unwarranted – **~ly** *adv* – **~ness** *n*

gratuity /grəˈtjuːɪ̇ti/ *n* sthg given voluntarily, usu in return for or in anticipation of some service; *esp* a tip

¹grave /greɪv/ *n* an excavation for burial of a body; *broadly* a tomb

²grave *adj* **1a** requiring serious consideration; important **b** likely to produce great harm or danger **2** serious, dignified **3** drab in colour; sombre – **~ly** *adv*

³grave /grɑːv/ *adj or n* (being or marked with) an accent ` used to show that a vowel is pronounced with a fall of pitch (e g in ancient Greek) or has a certain quality (e g *è* in French)

gravel /ˈgrævəl/ *n* **1** (a stratum or surface of) loose rounded fragments of rock mixed with sand **2** a sandy deposit of small stones in the kidneys and urinary bladder

gravelly /ˈgrævəli/ *adj* **1** of, containing, or covered with gravel **2** harsh, grating

gravestone /ˈgreɪvstəʊn/ *n* a stone over or at one end of a grave, usu inscribed with the name and details of the dead person

graveyard /ˈgreɪvjɑːd/ *n* a cemetery

gravitate /ˈgrævɪ̇teɪt/ *v* to move or be drawn *towards*

gravitation /ˌgrævɪ̇ˈteɪʃən/ *n* (movement resulting from) the natural force of mutual attraction between bodies or particles – **~al** *adj*

gravity /ˈgrævɪ̇ti/ *n* **1a** dignity or sobriety of bearing **b** significance; *esp* seriousness **2** (the quality of having) weight **3** (the attraction of a celestial body for bodies at or near its surface resulting from) gravitation

gravy /ˈgreɪvi/ *n* the (thickened and seasoned) fat and juices from cooked meat used as a sauce

¹graze /greɪz/ *v* **1** to feed on the grass of (e g a pasture) **2** to put to graze

²graze *v* **1** to touch (sthg) lightly in passing **2** to abrade, scratch

³graze *n* (an abrasion, esp of the skin, made by) a scraping along a surface

¹grease /griːs/ *n* **1** melted down animal fat **2** oily matter **3** a thick lubricant

²grease /griːs, griːz/ *v* **1** to smear, lubricate, or soil with grease **2** to hasten or ease the process or progress of

greasepaint /'griːspeɪnt/ *n* theatrical make-up

greasy /'griːsi, -zi/ *adj* **1a** smeared or soiled with grease **b** oily in appearance, texture, or manner **c** slippery **2** containing an unusual amount of grease – **-sily** *adv* – **-siness** *n*

¹**great** /greɪt/ *adj* **1a** notably large in size or number **b** of a relatively large kind – in plant and animal names **c** elaborate, ample **2a** extreme in amount, degree, or effectiveness **b** of importance; significant **3** eminent, distinguished **4** main, principal **5** removed in a family relationship by at least 3 stages directly or 2 stages indirectly – chiefly in combination **6** markedly superior in character or quality; *esp* noble **7a** remarkably skilled **b** enthusiastic, keen **8** – used as a generalized term of approval ; infml – **~ly** *adv* – **~ness** *n*

²**great** *n* one who is great – usu pl

greatcoat /'greɪtkəʊt/ *n* a heavy overcoat

Great Dane *n* any of a breed of massive powerful smooth-coated dogs

greater /'greɪtəʳ/ *adj, often cap* consisting of a central city together with adjacent areas that are geographically or administratively connected with it

grebe /griːb/ *n* any of a family of swimming and diving birds that have unwebbed feet

Grecian /'griːʃən/ *adj* Greek

greed /griːd/ *n* **1** excessive acquisitiveness; avarice **2** excessive desire for or consumption of food – **~y** *adj* – **~ily** *adv* – **~iness** *n*

¹**Greek** /griːk/ *n* **1** a native or inhabitant of Greece **2** the Indo-European language used by the Greeks **3** *not cap* sthg unintelligible – infml

²**Greek** *adj* **1** of Greece, the Greeks, or Greek **2 Greek, Greek Orthodox** of an Eastern church, esp the established Orthodox church of Greece using the Byzantine rite in Greek

¹**green** /griːn/ *adj* **1** of the colour green **2a** covered by green growth or foliage **b** consisting of green (edible) plants **3a** youthful, vigorous **b** not ripened or matured; immature **c** fresh, new **4** appearing pale, sickly, or nauseated **5** affected by intense envy or jealousy **6** not aged; unseasoned **7** deficient in training, knowledge, or experience – **~ness** *n* **~ish** *adj*

²**green** *n* **1** a colour whose hue resembles that of growing fresh grass or the emerald and lies between blue and yellow in the spectrum **2** sthg of a green colour **3** *pl* green leafy vegetables (e g spinach and cabbage) the leaves and stems of which are often cooked **4a** a common or park in the centre of a town or village **b** a smooth area of grass for a special purpose (e g bowling or putting)

green belt *n* a belt of parks, farmland, etc encircling an urban area and usu subject to restrictions on new building

greenery /'griːnəri/ *n* green foliage or plants

green fingers *n pl* an unusual ability to make plants grow

greenfly *n, Br* (an infestation by) any of various green aphids that are destructive to plants

greengage /'griːngeɪdʒ/ *n* any of several small rounded greenish cultivated plums

greengrocer /'griːn,grəʊsəʳ/ *n, chiefly Br* a retailer of fresh vegetables and fruit

greenhorn /'griːnhɔːn/ *n* **1** an inexperienced or unsophisticated (easily cheated) person **2** *chiefly NAm* a newcomer (e g to a country) unacquainted with local manners and customs

greenhouse /'griːnhaʊs/ *n* a glassed enclosure for the cultivation or protection of tender plants

green pepper *n* a sweet pepper

greenroom /'griːnrʊm, -ruːm/ *n* a room in a theatre or concert hall where performers can relax when not on stage

Greenwich Mean Time /,grɪnɪdʒ 'miːn taɪm, ,gre-, -nɪtʃ/ *n* the mean solar time of the meridian of Greenwich used as the primary point of reference for standard time throughout the world

¹**greet** /griːt/ *v,* **1** to welcome with gestures or words **2** to meet or react to in a specified manner

²**greet** *v Scot* to weep, lament

greeting /'griːtɪŋ/ *n* **1** a salutation at meeting **2** an expression of good wishes; regards – usu pl with sing. meaning

gregarious /grɪ'geərɪəs/ *adj* **1a** tending to associate with others of the same kind **b** marked by or indicating a liking for companionship; sociable **c** of a crowd, flock, or other group of people, animals, etc **2** *of a plant* growing in a cluster or a colony – **~ly** *adv* – **~ness** *n*

Gregorian calendar /grʒ̍,gɔːrɪən 'kælʒ̍ndəʳ/ *n* a revision of the Julian Calendar now in general use, that was introduced in 1582 by Pope Gregory XIII and adopted in Britain and the American colonies in 1752

Gregorian chant *n* a rhythmically free liturgical chant in unison practised in the Roman Catholic church

gremlin /'gremlʒ̍n/ *n* a mischievous creature said to cause malfunctioning of machinery or equipment

grenade /grʒ̍'neɪd/ *n* **1** a small missile that contains explosive, gas, incendiary chemicals, etc and is thrown by hand or launcher **2** a glass container of chemicals that bursts when thrown, releasing a fire extinguishing agent, tear gas, etc

grenadier /,grenə'dɪəʳ/ *n* a member of a regiment or corps formerly specially trained in the use of grenades

grenadine /'grenədiːn, --'-/ *n* a syrup flavoured with pomegranates and used in mixed drinks

grew /gruː/ *past of* **grow**

[1]**grey,** *NAm chiefly* **gray** /greɪ/ *adj* **1** of the colour grey **2** dull in colour **3a** lacking cheer or brightness; dismal **b** intermediate or unclear in position, condition, or character – **~ness** *n* – **~ish** *adj*

[2]**grey,** *NAm chiefly* **gray** *n* **1** any of a series of neutral colours ranging between black and white **2** sthg grey; *esp* grey clothes, paint, or horses

greyhound /'greɪhaʊnd/ *n* (any of) a tall slender smooth-coated breed of dogs characterized by swiftness and keen sight and used for coursing game and racing

grey matter *n* **1** brownish-grey nerve tissue, esp in the brain and spinal cord, containing nerve-cell bodies as well as nerve fibres **2** brains, intellect – infml

grid /grɪd/ *n* **1** a grating **2a** a network of conductors for distribution of electric power **b** (sthg resembling) a network of uniformly spaced horizontal and perpendicular lines for locating points on a map **3** the starting positions of vehicles on a racetrack

griddle /'grɪdl/ *n* a flat metal surface on which food is cooked by dry heat

grief /griːf/ *n* (a cause of) deep and poignant distress (e g due to bereavement)

grievance /'griːvəns/ *n* **1** a cause of distress (e g unsatisfactory working conditions) felt to afford reason for complaint or resistance **2** the formal expression of a grievance; a complaint

[1]**grieve** /griːv/ *v* to (cause to) suffer grief

[2]**grieve** *n, Scot* a farm or estate manager

grievous /'griːvəs/ *adj* **1** causing or characterized by severe pain, suffering, or sorrow **2** serious, grave – **~ly** *adv* – **~ness** *n*

griffin, gryphon /'grʒ̍fən/ *n* a mythical animal with the head and wings of an eagle and the body of a lion

[1]**grill** /grɪl/ *v* **1** to cook on or under a grill by radiant heat **2** to subject to intense and usu long periods of questioning – infml

[2]**grill** *n* **1** a cooking utensil of parallel bars on which food is exposed to heat (e g from burning charcoal) **2** an article or dish of grilled food **3 grill, grillroom** a usu informal restaurant or dining room, esp in a hotel **4** *Br* an apparatus on a cooker under which food is cooked or browned by radiant heat

grille, grill /grɪl/ *n* (an opening covered with) a grating forming a barrier or screen; *specif* an ornamental metal one at the front end of a motor vehicle

grim /grɪm/ *adj* **1** fierce or forbidding in disposition, action, or appearance **2** unflinching, unyielding **3** ghastly or sinister in character **4** unpleasant, nasty – infml – **~ly** *adv* – **~ness** *n*

grimace /grɪ'meɪs, 'grɪməs/ *n* a distorted facial expression, usu of disgust, anger, or pain – **grimace** *v*

grime /graɪm/ *n* soot or dirt, esp when

sticking to or embedded in a surface – **grimy** *adj*

grin /grɪn/ *v* to smile so as to show the teeth

[1]**grind** /graɪnd/ *v* **ground** **1** to reduce to powder or small fragments by crushing between hard surfaces **2** to wear down, polish, or sharpen by friction; whet **3a** to rub, press, or twist harshly **b** to press together with a rotating motion **4** to operate or produce by turning a crank **5** to become pulverized, polished, or sharpened by friction **6** to move with difficulty or friction, esp so as to make a grating noise **7** to work monotonously; *esp* to study hard **8** to rotate the hips in an erotic manner

[2]**grind** *n* **1** dreary monotonous labour or routine **2** the result of grinding; *esp* material obtained by grinding to a particular degree of fineness **3a** the act of rotating the hips in an erotic manner **b** *Br* an act of sexual intercourse – vulg

grind down *v* to oppress, harass

grindstone /ˈgraɪndstəʊn/ *n* **1** a millstone **2** a flat circular stone that revolves on an axle and is used for grinding, shaping, etc

[1]**grip** /grɪp/ *v* **1** to seize or hold firmly **2** to attract and hold the interest of

[2]**grip** *n* **1a** a strong or tenacious grasp **b** manner or style of gripping **2a** control, mastery, power **b** (power of) understanding or doing **3** a part or device that grips **4** a part by which sthg is grasped; *esp* a handle **5** one who handles scenery, properties, lighting, or camera equipment in a theatre or film or television studio **6** a travelling bag

[1]**gripe** /graɪp/ *v* **1** to cause or experience intestinal gripes (in) **2** to complain persistently – infml

[2]**gripe** *n* **1** a stabbing spasmodic intestinal pain – usu pl **2** a grievance, complaint – infml

grisly /ˈgrɪzli/ *adj* inspiring horror, intense fear, or disgust; forbidding

grist /grɪst/ *n* **1** (a batch of) grain for grinding **2** the product obtained from grinding grain

gristle /ˈgrɪsəl/ *n* cartilage; *broadly* tough cartilaginous or fibrous matter, esp in cooked meat – **-tly** *adj*

[1]**grit** /grɪt/ *n* **1** a hard sharp granule (e g of sand or stone); *also* material composed of such granules **2** the structure or texture of a stone that adapts it to grinding **3** firmness of mind or spirit; unyielding courage – infml – **gritty** *adj*

[2]**grit** *v* **1** to cover or spread with grit **2** to cause (esp one's teeth) to grind or grate

grizzle /ˈgrɪzəl/ *v, Br* **1** *of a child* to cry quietly and fretfully **2** to complain in a self-pitying way – often + *about* USE infml

grizzled /ˈgrɪzəld/ *adj* sprinkled or streaked with grey

[1]**grizzly** /ˈgrɪzli/ *adj* grizzled

[2]**grizzly, grizzly bear** *n* a very large typically brownish yellow bear that lives in the highlands of Western N America

groan /grəʊn/ *v* **1** to utter a deep moan **2** to creak under strain

[1]**groat** /grəʊt/ *n* hulled grain (broken into fragments larger than grits) – usu pl with sing. meaning but sing. or pl in constr

[2]**groat** *n* a former British coin worth 4 old pence

grocer /ˈgrəʊsəʳ/ *n* a dealer in (packaged or tinned) staple foodstuffs, household supplies, and usu fruit, vegetables, and dairy products

grocery /ˈgrəʊsəri/ *n* **1** *pl* commodities sold by a grocer **2** a grocer's shop

grog /grɒg/ *n* alcoholic drink; *specif* spirits (e g rum) mixed with water

groggy /ˈgrɒgi/ *adj* weak and dazed, esp owing to illness or tiredness – **-ggily** *adv*

groin /grɔɪn/ *n* **1a** the fold marking the join between the lower abdomen and the inner part of the thigh **b** the male genitals – euph **2** the line along which 2 intersecting vaults meet

[1]**groom** /gruːm, grʊm/ *n* **1** one who is in charge of the feeding, care, and stabling of horses **2** a bridegroom

[2]**groom** /gruːm/ *v* **1** to clean and care for (e g a horse) **2** to make neat or attractive **3** to get into readiness for a specific objective; prepare

[1]**groove** /gruːv/ *n* **1a** a long narrow channel or depression **b** the continuous spiral track on a gramophone

record whose irregularities correspond to the recorded sounds **2** a fixed routine; a rut **3** top form – infml **4** an enjoyable or exciting experience – infml; no longer in vogue

²**groove** *v* **1** to make or form a groove (in) **2** to excite pleasurably – infml; no longer in vogue **3** to enjoy oneself intensely; *also* to get on well – infml; no longer in vogue

groovy /ˈgruːvi/ *adj* fashionably attractive or exciting – infml; no longer in vogue

grope /grəʊp/ *v* **1** to feel about or search blindly or uncertainly *for* **2** to touch or fondle the body of (a person) for sexual pleasure – **grope** *n* – **-pingly** *adv*

¹**gross** /grəʊs/ *adj* **1** glaringly noticeable, usu because excessively bad or objectionable; flagrant **2a** big, bulky; *esp* excessively fat **b** *of vegetation* dense, luxuriant **3** consisting of an overall total before deductions (e g for taxes) are made **4** made up of material or perceptible elements; corporal **5** coarse in nature or behaviour; *specif* crudely vulgar – **~ly** *adv* – **~ness** *n*

²**gross** *n* an overall total exclusive of deductions

³**gross** *v* to earn or bring in (an overall total) exclusive of deductions

⁴**gross** *n, pl* **gross** a group of 12 dozen things

¹**grotesque** /grəʊˈtesk/ *n* a style of decorative art in which incongruous or fantastic human and animal forms are interwoven with natural motifs (e g foliage)

²**grotesque** *adj* (having the characteristics) of the grotesque: e g **a** fanciful, bizarre **b** absurdly incongruous **c** departing markedly from the natural, expected, or typical

grotto /ˈgrɒtəʊ/ *n, pl* **grottoes** *also* **grottos** **1** an esp picturesque cave **2** an excavation or structure made to resemble a natural cave

grotty /ˈgrɒti/ *adj, Br* nasty, unpleasant – slang – **-ttiness** *n*

grouch /graʊtʃ/ *n* **1** a bad-tempered complaint **2** a habitually irritable or complaining person; a grumbler – **grouch** *v*

¹**ground** /graʊnd/ *n* **1a** the bottom of a body of water **b** *pl* **(1)** sediment **(2)** ground coffee beans after brewing **2** a basis for belief, action, or argument – often pl with sing. meaning **3a** a surrounding area; a background **b** (material that serves as) a substratum or foundation **4a** the surface of the earth **b** an area used for a particular purpose **c** *pl* the area round and belonging to a house or other building **d** an area to be won or defended (as if) in battle **5** soil

²**ground** *v* **1** to bring to or place on the ground **2a** to provide a reason or justification for **b** to instruct in fundamentals (e g of a subject) **3** to restrict (e g a pilot or aircraft) to the ground **4** to run aground

³**ground** *past of* **grind**

groundbait /ˈgraʊndbeɪt/ *n* bait scattered on the water so as to attract fish

grounding /ˈgraʊndɪŋ/ *n* fundamental training in a field of knowledge

groundless /ˈgraʊndlɪs/ *adj* having no foundation – **~ly** *adv* – **~ness** *n*

groundnut /ˈgraʊndnʌt/ *n* **1** (a N American leguminous plant with) an edible root **2** *chiefly Br* the peanut

groundsel /ˈgraʊnsəl/ *n* a (plant related to a) European composite plant that is a common weed and has small yellow flower heads

groundsheet /ˈgraʊndʃiːt/ *n* a waterproof sheet placed on the ground (e g in a tent)

groundsman /ˈgraʊndzmən/ *n* sby who tends a playing field, esp a cricket pitch

groundwork /ˈgraʊndwɜːk/ *n* (work done to provide) a foundation or basis

¹**group** /gruːp/ *n* **1** two or more figures or objects forming a complete unit in a composition **2** *sing or pl in constr* **a** a number of individuals or objects assembled together or having some unifying relationship **b** an operational and administrative unit belonging to a command of an air force

²**group** *v* **1** to combine in a group **2** to assign to a group; classify **3** to form or belong to a group

group captain *n* a middle-ranking officer in the Royal Air Force, equal to a captain in the navy or a colonel in the army

grouping /ˈgruːpɪŋ/ *n* a set of individuals or objects combined in a group

[1]**grouse** /graʊs/ *n, pl* **grouse** any of several (important game) birds with a plump body and strong feathered legs

[2]**grouse** *v or n* (to) grumble – infml

grove /grəʊv/ *n* a small wood, group, or planting of trees

grovel /ˈgrɒvəl/ *v* **1** to lie or creep with the body prostrate in token of submission or abasement **2** to abase or humble oneself – **~ler** *n*

grow /grəʊ/ *v* **grew; grown** **1a** to spring up and develop to maturity (in a specified place or situation) **b** to assume some relation (as if) through a process of natural growth **2a** to increase in size by addition of material (e g by assimilation into a living organism or by crystallization) **b** to increase, expand **3** to develop from a parent source **4** to become gradually **5** to cause to grow; produce **6** to develop

growing pains *n pl* the early problems attending a new project or development

[1]**growl** /graʊl/ *v* **1** to rumble **2** to utter a growl

[2]**growl** *n* a deep guttural inarticulate sound

grown /grəʊn/ *adj* **1** fully grown; mature **2** overgrown or covered (*with*)

grown-up *n or adj* (an) adult

growth /grəʊθ/ *n* **1a** (a stage in the process of) growing **b** progressive development **c** an increase, expansion **2a** sthg that grows or has grown **b** a tumour or other abnormal growth of tissue **3** the result of growth; a product

grow up *v* **1** *of a person* to develop towards or arrive at a mature state **2** to arise and develop

groyne, groin /grɔɪn/ *n* a structure built out from the shore to prevent the erosion of a beach

[1]**grub** /grʌb/ *v* **1** to clear by digging up roots and stumps **2** to dig *up* or *out* (as if) by the roots **3** to dig in the ground, esp for sthg that is difficult to find or extract **4** to search about; rummage

[2]**grub** *n* **1** a soft thick wormlike larva of an insect **2** food – infml

grubby /ˈgrʌbi/ *adj* dirty, grimy

[1]**grudge** /grʌdʒ/ *v* to be unwilling or reluctant to give or admit; begrudge

[2]**grudge** *n* a feeling of deep-seated resentment or ill will

grudging /ˈgrʌdʒɪŋ/ *adj* unwilling, reluctant – **~ly** *adv*

gruel /ˈgruːəl/ *n* a thin porridge

gruelling /ˈgruːəlɪŋ/ *adj* trying or taxing to the point of causing exhaustion; punishing – **~ly** *adv*

gruesome /ˈgruːsəm/ *adj* inspiring horror or repulsion; – **~ly** *adv* – **~ness** *n*

gruff /grʌf/ *adj* **1** brusque or stern in manner, speech, or aspect **2** deep and harsh – **~ly** *adv* – **~ness** *n*

grumble /ˈgrʌmbəl/ *v* **1** to mutter in discontent **2** to rumble

grumbling /ˈgrʌmblɪŋ/ *adj* causing intermittent pain or discomfort

grumpy /ˈgrʌmpi/ *adj* moodily cross; surly – **-pily** *adv* – **-piness** *n*

[1]**grunt** /grʌnt/ *v* to utter (with) a grunt

[2]**grunt** *n* the deep short guttural sound of a pig; *also* a similar sound

Gruyère /ˈgruːjeəʳ/ *n* a Swiss cheese with smaller holes and a slightly fuller flavour than Emmenthal

gryphon /ˈgrɪfən/ *n* a griffin

G-string *n* a small piece of cloth covering the genitals and held in place by thongs, elastic, etc that is passed round the hips and between the buttocks

guano /ˈgwɑːnəʊ/ *n* (an artificial fertilizer similar to) a phosphate-rich substance consisting chiefly of the excrement of seabirds and used as a fertilizer

[1]**guarantee** /ˌgærənˈtiː/ *n* **1** one who guarantees **2** a (written) undertaking to answer for the payment of a debt or the performance of a duty of another in case of the other's default **3** an assurance of the quality of or of the length of use to be expected from a product offered for sale, accompanied by a promise to replace it or pay the customer back **4** sthg given as security; a pledge

²guarantee *v* **1** to undertake to answer for the debt or default of **2a** to undertake to do or secure (sthg) **b** to engage for the existence, permanence, or nature of **3** to give security to

guarantor /ˌgærən'tɔːʳ/ *n* **1** one who guarantees **2** one who makes or gives a guarantee

guaranty /'gærənti/ *n* a guarantee

¹guard /gɑːd/ *n* **1** a defensive position in boxing, fencing, etc **2** the act or duty of protecting or defending **3a** a person or group whose duty is to protect a place, people, etc **b** *pl* troops part of whose duties are to guard a sovereign **4** a protective or safety device; *esp* a device on a machine for protecting against injury **5** *Br* the person in charge of a railway train

²guard *v* **1** to protect from danger, esp by watchful attention; make secure **2** to watch over so as to prevent escape, entry, theft, etc; *also* to keep in check

guarded /'gɑːdɪ̵d/ *adj* marked by caution – **~ly** *adv*

guardian /'gɑːdɪən/ *n* **1** one who or that which guards or protects **2** sby who has the care of the person or property of another; *specif* sby entrusted by law with the care of sby who is of unsound mind, not of age, etc – **~ship** *n*

guardrail /'gɑːd-reɪl/ *n* a railing for guarding against danger or trespass

guardsman /'gɑːdzmən/ *n* a member of a military body called *guard* or *guards*

guard's van *n, Br* a railway wagon or carriage attached usu at the rear of a train for the use of the guard

guava /'gwɑːvə/ *n* (the sweet acid yellow edible fruit of) a shrubby tropical American tree

gudgeon /'gʌdʒən/ *n* a small European freshwater fish used esp for food or bait

guerilla, guerrilla /gə'rɪlə/ *n* a member of an irregular, usu politically motivated fighting unit often engaged in harassing stronger regular units

¹guess /ges/ *v* **1** to form an opinion of with little or no consideration of the facts **2** to arrive at a correct conclusion about by conjecture, chance, or intuition **3** *chiefly NAm* to believe, suppose – infml **4** to make a guess

²guess *n* a surmise, estimate

guesswork /'geswɜːk/ *n* (judgment based on) the act of guessing

guest /gest/ *n* **1a** a person entertained in one's home **b** a person taken out, entertained, and paid for by another **c** a person who pays for the services of an establishment (e g a hotel) **2** one who is present by invitation

guesthouse /'gesthaʊs/ *n* a private house used to accommodate paying guests

guffaw /gə'fɔː, 'gʌfɔː/ *v or n* (to utter) a loud or boisterous laugh

guidance /'gaɪdəns/ *n* help, advice

¹guide /gaɪd/ *n* **1a** one who leads or directs another **b** one who shows and explains places of interest to travellers, tourists, etc **c** sthg, esp a guidebook, that provides sby with information about a place, activity, etc **d** sthg or sby that directs a person in his/her conduct or course of life **2** a bar, rod, etc for steadying or directing the motion of sthg **3** *often cap, chiefly Br* a member of a worldwide movement of girls and young women founded with the aim of forming character and teaching good citizenship through outdoor activities and domestic skills

²guide *v* **1** to act as a guide (to); direct in a way or course **2** to direct or supervise, usu to a particular end; *also* to supervise the training of

guild /gɪld/ *n sing or pl in constr* an association of people with similar interests or pursuits; *esp* a medieval association of merchants or craftsmen

guilder /'gɪldəʳ/ *n* a gulden

guildhall /ˌgɪld'hɔːl, '--/ *n* a hall where a guild or corporation usu assembles; *esp* a town hall

guile /gaɪl/ *n* deceitful cunning; duplicity – **~ful** *adj* – **~fully** *adv* – **~fulness** *n*

guillemot /'gɪlɪ̵mɒt/ *n* any of several narrow-billed auks of northern seas

guillotine /'gɪlətiːn/ *n* **1** a machine for beheading consisting of a heavy blade that slides down between grooved posts **2** an instrument (e g a paper cutter) that works like a guillotine **3** the placing of a time limit on the discussion of legislative business

guilt /gɪlt/ *n* **1** the fact of having committed a breach of conduct, esp one that violates law **2a** responsibility for a criminal or other offence **b** feelings of being at fault or to blame, esp for imagined offences or from a sense of inadequacy – **~less** *adj* – **~lessly** *adv* – **~lessness** *n*

guilty /ˈgɪlti/ *adj* **1** justly answerable for an offence **2a** suggesting or involving guilt **b** feeling guilt – **-tily** *adv* – **-tiness** *n*

guinea /ˈgɪni/ *n* **1** a former British gold coin worth 21 shillings **2** a money unit worth £1 and 5 new pence

guinea fowl *n* a W African bird with white-speckled slate-grey plumage that is related to the pheasants and is widely kept for food

guinea pig *n* **1** a small stout-bodied short-eared nearly tailless rodent often kept as a pet **2** sby or sthg used as a subject of (scientific) research or experimentation

guise /gaɪz/ *n* **1** external appearance; aspect **2** assumed appearance; semblance

guitar /gɪˈtɑːʳ/ *n* a flat-bodied stringed instrument with a long fretted neck, plucked with a plectrum or the fingers

gulden /ˈgʊldən/ *n, pl* **guldens, gulden** the major unit of currency of the Netherlands, Netherlands Antilles, and Surinam

gulf /gʌlf/ *n* **1** a partially landlocked part of the sea, usu larger than a bay **2** a deep chasm; an abyss **3** an unbridgeable gap

[1]**gull** /gʌl/ *n* any of numerous related long-winged web-footed largely white, grey, or black aquatic birds

[2]**gull** *v* to trick, cheat, or deceive

gullet /ˈgʌlʒt/ *n* the throat; the windpipe

gullible /ˈgʌlʒbəl/ *adj* easily deceived or cheated – **-bility** *n* – **-bly** *adv*

gully, gulley /ˈgʌli/ *n* **1** a deep trench worn by running water **2** a deep gutter or drain

gulp /gʌlp/ **1** to swallow hurriedly, greedily, or in 1 swallow – often + *down* **2** to make a sudden swallowing movement as if surprised or nervous

[1]**gum** /gʌm/ *n* (the tissue that surrounds the teeth and covers) the parts of the jaws from which the teeth grow

[2]**gum** *n* **1** any of various substances (e g a mucilage or gum resin) that exude from plants **2** a substance or deposit resembling a plant gum (e g in adhesive quality)

[3]**gum** *v* **1** to smear or stick (as if) with gum **2** to exude or form gum

gumboil /ˈgʌmbɔɪl/ *n* an abscess in the gum

gumboot /ˈgʌmbuːt/ *n* a strong waterproof rubber boot reaching usu to the knee

gumption /ˈgʌmpʃən/ *n* **1** shrewd practical common sense **2** initiative; *specif* boldness

[1]**gun** /gʌn/ *n* **1a** a rifle, pistol, etc **b** a device that throws a projectile **2** a discharge of a gun **3** sby who carries a gun in a shooting party

[2]**gun** **1** to shoot – often + *down* **2** to search *for* to attack

gunboat /ˈgʌnbəʊt/ *n* a relatively heavily armed ship of shallow draught

gundog /ˈgʌndɒg/ *n* a dog trained to locate or retrieve game for hunters

gunfire /ˈgʌnfaɪəʳ/ *n* the (noise of) firing of guns

gunge /gʌndʒ/ *n, Br* an unpleasant, dirty, or sticky substance – slang

gunman /ˈgʌnmən/ *n* a man armed with a gun; *esp* a professional killer

gunmetal /ˈgʌn,metl/ *n* (a metal treated to imitate) a bronze formerly used for cannon

gunner /ˈgʌnəʳ/ *n* **1** a soldier or airman who operates a gun; *specif* a private in the Royal Artillery **2** sby who hunts with a gun **3** a warrant officer who supervises naval ordnance and ordnance stores

gunpowder /ˈgʌn,paʊdəʳ/ *n* an explosive mixture of potassium nitrate, charcoal, and sulphur used in gunnery and blasting

gunrunner /ˈgʌn,rʌnəʳ/ *n* one who carries or deals in contraband arms and ammunition – **-running** *n*

gunshot /ˈgʌnʃɒt/ *n* **1** a shot or projectile fired from a gun **2** the range of a gun

gunsmith /'gʌn,smɪθ/ *n* sby who designs, makes, or repairs firearms

gunwale, gunnel /'gʌnl/ *n* the upper edge of a boat's side

guppy /'gʌpi/ *n* a small (aquarium) fish native to the W Indies and S America

gurgle /'gɜːgəl/ *v* to make the sound (as if) of unevenly flowing water; *also* to flow or move with such a sound – **gurgle** *n*

guru /'gʊruː/ *n* **1** a personal religious teacher and spiritual guide (e g in Hinduism) **2** an acknowledged leader or chief proponent (e g of a cult or idea) – infml

[1]**gush** /gʌʃ/ *v* **1** to issue copiously or violently **2** to emit (in) a sudden copious flow **3** to make an effusive often affected display of sentiment or enthusiasm – **~ing** *adj* – **~ingly** *adv*

[2]**gush** *n* **1** (sthg emitted in) a sudden outpouring **2** an effusive and usu affected display of sentiment or enthusiasm

gusset /'gʌsɨ̣t/ *n* **1** a piece of material inserted in a seam (e g the crotch of an undergarment) to provide expansion or reinforcement **2** a plate or bracket for strengthening an angle in framework

[1]**gust** /gʌst/ *n* **1** a sudden brief rush of (rain carried by the) wind **2** a sudden outburst; a surge

[2]**gust** *v* to blow in gusts

gusto /'gʌstəʊ/ *n* enthusiastic and vigorous enjoyment or vitality

[1]**gut** /gʌt/ *n* **1a** the basic emotionally or instinctively responding part of a person **b** (a part of) the alimentary canal **c** the belly or abdomen **d** catgut **2** *pl* the inner essential parts – infml **3** *pl* courage, determination – infml

[2]**gut** *v* **1** to eviscerate, disembowel **2** to destroy the inside of **3** to extract the essentials of

[3]**gut** *adj* arising from or concerning one's strongest emotions or instincts

gutless /'gʌtlɨ̣s/ *adj* lacking courage; cowardly – infml – **~ness** *n*

gutta-percha /,gʌtə 'pɜːtʃə/ *n* a tough plastic substance obtained from the latex of several Malaysian trees and used esp for electrical insulation

[1]**gutter** /'gʌtə^r/ *n* **1** a trough just below the eaves or at the side of a street to catch and carry off rainwater, surface water, etc **2** *the* lowest or most vulgar level or condition of human life

[2]**gutter** *v, of a flame* to burn fitfully or feebly; be on the point of going out

[3]**gutter** *adj* (characteristic) of the gutter; *esp* marked by extreme vulgarity or cheapness

guttersnipe /'gʌtəsnaɪp/ *n* a deprived child living in poverty and usu dressed in ragged clothes

guttural /'gʌtərəl/ *adj* **1** of the throat **2** formed or pronounced in the throat

[1]**guy** /gaɪ/ *v or n* (to steady or reinforce with) a rope, chain, rod, etc attached to sthg as a brace or guide

[2]**guy** *n* **1** *often cap* a humorous effigy of a man burnt in Britain on Guy Fawkes Night **2** a man, fellow – infml

[3]**guy** *v* to make fun of; ridicule

Guy Fawkes Night /'gaɪ ,fɔːks ,naɪt/ *n* November 5 observed in Britain with fireworks and bonfires in commemoration of the arrest of Guy Fawkes in 1605 for attempting to blow up the Houses of Parliament

guzzle /'gʌzəl/ *v* to consume (sthg) greedily, continually, or habitually

gym /dʒɪm/ *n* **1** a gymnasium **2** development of the body by games, exercises, etc, esp in school

gymkhana /dʒɪm'kɑːnə/ *n* a sporting event featuring competitions and displays; *specif* a meeting involving competition in horse riding and carriage driving

gymnasium /dʒɪm'neɪzɪəm/ *n, pl* **gymnasiums, gymnasia** a large room or separate building used for indoor sports and gymnastic activities

gymnast /'dʒɪmnæst, -nəst/ *n* sby trained in gymnastics – **~ic** *adj* – **~ically** *adv*

gymnastics /dʒɪm'næstɪks/ *n pl but sing or pl in constr* **1** physical exercises developing or displaying bodily strength and coordination, often performed in competition **2** an exercise in intellectual or physical dexterity

[1]**gymslip** /'dʒɪm,slɪp/ *n, chiefly Br* a girl's tunic or pinafore dress that is

worn usu with a belt as part of a school uniform

²**gymslip** *adj, chiefly Br* of a schoolgirl or a girl of school age – infml

gynaecology /ˌgaɪnɪ̯ˈkɒlədʒi/ *n* a branch of medicine that deals with diseases and disorders (of the reproductive system) of women – **-logical** *adj* – **-logist** *n*

¹**gyp** /dʒɪp/ *n* a fraud, swindle

²**gyp** *v* to cheat – infml

³**gyp** *n* sharp pain – chiefly in *give one gyp*; infml

gypsum /ˈdʒɪpsəm/ *n* a mineral used to make plaster of paris

gypsy /ˈdʒɪpsi/ *n, chiefly NAm* a gipsy

gyrate /dʒaɪˈreɪt/ *v* **1** to revolve round a point or axis **2** to (cause to) move with a circular or spiral motion – **-tion** *n*

gyroscope /ˈdʒaɪərəskəʊp/ *n* a wheel that is mounted to spin rapidly about an axis and is free to turn in various directions but that maintains constant orientation while spinning in the absence of applied forces – **-scopic** *adj*

h /eɪtʃ/ *n, pl* **h's, hs** *often cap* **1** (a graphic representation of or device for reproducing) the 8th letter of the English alphabet **2** a speech counterpart of written *h*

habeas corpus /ˌheɪbɪəs 'kɔːpəs/ *n* a judicial writ requiring a detained person to be brought before a court so that the legality of his/her detention may be examined

haberdasher /'hæbədæʃəʳ/ *n, Br* a dealer in buttons, thread, ribbon, etc used in making clothes

haberdashery /'hæbədæʃəri/ *n* **1** goods sold by a haberdasher **2** a haberdasher's shop

habit /'hæbʲ̥t/ *n* **1** a costume characteristic of a calling, rank, or function **2** bodily or mental make-up **3a** a settled tendency or usual manner of behaviour **b** an acquired pattern or mode of behaviour **4** addiction

habitable /'hæbʲ̥təbəl/ *adj* capable of being lived in

habitat /'hæbʲ̥tæt/ *n* the (type of) place where a plant or animal naturally grows or lives

habitation /ˌhæbʲ̥'teɪʃən/ *n* **1** the act of inhabiting; occupancy **2** a dwelling place; a residence, home

habitual /hə'bɪtʃʊəl/ *adj* **1** having the nature of a habit **2** by force of habit **3** in accordance with habit; customary – **~ly** *adv*

habituate /hə'bɪtʃʊeɪt/ *v* to make used *to*

hacienda /ˌhæsi'endə/ *n* (the main house of) a large estate or plantation, esp in a Spanish-speaking country

¹hack /hæk/ *v* **1** to cut or sever (as if) with repeated (irregular or unskilful) blows **2** to clear by cutting away vegetation **3** to kick (an opposing player or the ball in football) **4** to cough in a short dry manner

²hack *n* **1** a mattock, pick, etc **2** a hacking blow

³hack *n* **1** a light easy saddle horse **2** an act of hacking; a ride **3** one who produces mediocre work for financial gain; *esp* a commercial writer

⁴hack *adj* **1** performed by, suited to, or characteristic of a hack **2** hackneyed, trite

⁵hack *v* to ride (a horse) at an ordinary pace, esp over roads

¹hackney /'hækni/ *n* any of an English breed of rather compact English horses with a conspicuously high leg action

²hackney *adj* kept for public hire

hackneyed /'hæknid/ *adj* lacking in freshness or originality; meaningless because used or done too often

hacksaw /'hæksɔː/ *n* a fine-toothed saw, esp for cutting metal

had /d, əd, həd; *strong* hæd/ *past of* **have**

haddock /'hædək/ *n* an important Atlantic food fish, usu smaller than the related common cod

Hades /'heɪdiːz/ *n* **1** the underground abode of the dead in Greek mythology **2** *often not cap* hell – euph

haemoglobin /ˌhiːmə'gləʊbɪn/ *n* an iron-containing protein that occurs in the red blood cells of vertebrates and is the means of oxygen transport from the lungs to the body tissues

haemophilia /ˌhiːmə'fɪlɪə/ *n* delayed clotting of the blood with consequent difficulty in controlling bleeding even after minor injuries, occurring as a hereditary defect, usu in males – **-philiac** *n, adj*

haemorrhage /'hemərɪdʒ/ *n* a (copious) loss of blood from the blood vessels

haemorrhoid /'hemərɔɪd/ *n* a mass of swollen veins round or near the anus – usu pl with sing. meaning

haft /hɑːft/ *n* the handle of a weapon or tool

¹hag /hæg/ *n* **1** a witch **2** an ugly and usu ill-natured old woman

²hag *n, Scot & NEng* (a firm spot in) a bog

haggard /'hægəd/ *adj* having a worn

or emaciated appearance, esp through anxiety or lack of sleep

haggis /ˈhægɪ̵s/ *n* a traditionally Scottish dish that consists of the heart, liver, and lungs of a sheep, calf, etc minced with suet, oatmeal, and seasonings

haggle /ˈhægəl/ *v* to bargain, wrangle

¹ha-ha /hɑː ˈhɑː/ *interj* – used to express or represent laughter or derision

²ha-ha /ˈhɑː hɑː/ *n* a fence or retaining wall sunk into a ditch and used as a boundary (e g of a park or grounds) so as to give an uninterrupted view

¹hail /heɪl/ *n* **1** (precipitation in the form of) small particles of clear ice or compacted snow **2** a group of things directed at sby or sthg and intended to cause pain, damage, or distress

²hail *v* **1** to precipitate hail **2** to pour down or strike like hail

³hail *interj* **1** – used to express acclamation **2** *archaic* – used as a salutation

⁴hail *v* **1a** to salute, greet **b** to greet with enthusiastic approval; acclaim *as* **2** to greet or summon by calling **3** to come *from,* be a native of

⁵hail *n* **1** a call to attract attention **2** hearing distance

hailstone /ˈheɪlstəʊn/ *n* a pellet of hail

hair /heəʳ/ *n* **1** (a structure resembling) a slender threadlike outgrowth on the surface of an animal; *esp* (any of) the many usu coloured hairs that form the characteristic coat of a mammal **2** the coating of hairs, esp on the human head or other body part

haircut /ˈheəkʌt/ *n* (the result of) cutting and shaping of the hair

hairdo /ˈheəduː/ *n* a hairstyle

hairdresser /ˈheəˌdresəʳ/ *n* sby whose occupation is cutting, dressing, and styling the hair – **-sing** *n*

hairgrip /ˈheəgrɪp/ *n, Br* a flat hairpin with prongs that close together

hairline /ˈheəlaɪn/ *n* **1** a very slender line; *esp* a tiny line or crack on a surface **2** the line above the forehead beyond which hair grows

hairpiece /ˈheəpiːs/ *n* a section of false hair worn to enhance a hairstyle or make a person's natural hair seem thicker or more plentiful

¹hairpin /ˈheəˌpɪn/ *n* **1** a 2-pronged U-shaped pin of thin wire for holding the hair in place **2** a sharp bend in a road

²hairpin *adj* having the shape of a hairpin

hair-raising *adj* causing terror or astonishment

hair's breadth *n* a very small distance or margin

hair-slide *n, Br* a (decorative) clip for the hair

hairsplitting /ˈheəˌsplɪtɪŋ/ *n* argument over unimportant differences and points of detail; quibbling

hairspring /ˈheəˌsprɪŋ/ *n* a slender spiral spring that regulates the motion of the balance wheel of a timepiece

hairstyle /ˈheəˌstaɪl/ *n* a way of wearing or arranging the hair – **-styling** *n* – **-stylist** *n*

hairy /ˈheəri/ *adj* **1** covered with (material like) hair **2** made of or resembling hair **3** frighteningly dangerous – infml – **-riness** *n*

hake /heɪk/ *n* any of several marine food fishes related to the common Atlantic cod

halberd /ˈhælbəd/ *n* a long-handled weapon combining a spear and battle-axe, used esp in the 15th and 16th c

halcyon /ˈhælsɪən/ *adj* calm, peaceful – esp in *halcyon days*

hale /heɪl/ *adj* free from defect, disease, or infirmity; sound

¹half /hɑːf/ *n, pl* **halves** /hɑːvz/ **1a** either of 2 equal parts into which sthg is divisible; *also* a part of a thing approximately equal to a half **b** half an hour – used in designation of time **2** either of a pair: e g **a** a partner **b** a school term – used esp at some British public schools **3** sthg of (approximately) half the value or quantity: e g **a** half a pint **b** a child's ticket

²half *adj* **1a** being one of 2 equal parts **b(1)** amounting to approximately half **(2)** falling short of the full or complete thing (e g a *half* smile) **2** extending over or covering only half (e g *half* sleeves) **3** *Br* half past

³half *adv* **1** in an equal part or degree (e g she was *half* laughing, *half* crying) **2** nearly but not completely (e g *half* cooked)

halfback /ˈhɑːfbæk/ *n* a player in

rugby, soccer, hockey, etc positioned immediately behind the forward line
half-baked *adj* marked by or showing a lack of forethought or judgment; foolish
half-breed *n* the offspring of parents of different races
half brother *n* a brother related through 1 parent only
half cock *n* **1** the position of the hammer of a firearm when about half retracted and held by the safety catch so that it cannot be operated by a pull on the trigger **2** a state of inadequate preparation – esp in *go off at half cock*
halfhearted /ˌhɑːfˈhɑːtɨ̣d/ *adj* lacking enthusiasm or effort
half-holiday *n* a holiday of half a day, esp an afternoon
half-mast *n* the position of a flag lowered halfway down the staff as a mark of mourning
halfpenny /ˈheɪpni/ *n* **1** (a British bronze coin representing) one half of a penny **2** a small amount
half sister *n* a sister related through 1 parent only
half term *n, chiefly Br* (a short holiday taken at) a period about halfway through a school term
half-timbered *adj* constructed of timber framework with spaces filled in by brickwork or plaster
halftime /ˌhɑːfˈtaɪm/ *n* (an intermission marking) the completion of half of a game or contest
halftone /ˈhɑːftəʊn/ *n* any of the shades of grey between the darkest and the lightest parts of a photographic image
half-volley *n* **1** a shot in tennis made at a ball just after it has bounced **2** an easily-hit delivery of the ball in cricket that bounces closer than intended to the batsman
halfway /ˌhɑːfˈweɪ/ *adj or adv* **1** midway between 2 points **2** (done or formed) partially
half-wit *n* a foolish or mentally deficient person – derog – **~ted** *adj* – **~tedly** *adv*
halibut /ˈhælɨ̣bət/ *n* a large marine food flatfish
halitosis /ˌhælɨ̣ˈtəʊsɨ̣s/ *n* (a condition of having) offensively smelling breath
hall /hɔːl/ *n* **1** the house of a medieval king or noble **2** the manor house of a landed proprietor **3** the entrance room or passage of a building **4** a large room for public assembly or entertainment
¹hallmark /ˈhɔːlmɑːk/ *n* **1** an official mark stamped on gold and silver articles in Britain after an assay test to testify to their purity **2** a distinguishing characteristic or object
²hallmark *v* to stamp with a hallmark
hallow /ˈhæləʊ/ *v* **1** to make holy or set apart for holy use **2** to respect and honour greatly; venerate
Halloween, Hallowe'en /ˌhæləʊˈiːn/ *n* October 31, the eve of All Saints' Day, observed by dressing up in disguise, party turns, etc
hallstand /ˈhɔːlstænd/ *n* a piece of furniture with pegs for holding coats, hats, and umbrellas
hallucinate /həˈluːsɨ̣neɪt/ *v* **1** to perceive or experience as a hallucination **2** to have hallucinations
hallucination /həˌluːsɨ̣ˈneɪʃən/ *n* **1** the perception of sthg apparently real to the perceiver but which has no objective reality, *also* the image, object, etc perceived **2** a completely unfounded or mistaken impression or belief – **-atory** *adj*
¹halo /ˈheɪləʊ/ *n, pl* **halos, haloes** **1** a circle of light appearing to surround the sun or moon and resulting from refraction or reflection of light by ice particles in the earth's atmosphere **2** a nimbus **3** the aura of glory or veneration surrounding an idealized person or thing
²halo *v* to form into or surround with a halo
¹halt /hɒlt/ *v* **1** to hesitate between alternative courses; waver **2** to display weakness or imperfection (e g in speech or reasoning); falter
²halt *n* **1** a (temporary) stop or interruption **2** *Br* a railway stopping place, without normal station facilities, for local trains
³halt *v* **1** to come to a halt **2** to bring to a stop **3** to cause to stop; end
halter /ˈhɔːltəʳ/ *n* **1** a rope or strap for

leading or tying an animal **2** a noose for hanging criminals

halter neck *n* (a garment having) a neckline formed by a strap passing from the front of a garment round the neck and leaving the shoulders and upper back bare

halting /ˈhɔːltɪŋ/ *adj* hesitant, faltering – ~**ly** *adv*

halve /hɑːv/ *v* **1a** to divide into 2 equal parts **b** to reduce to a half **2** to play (e g a hole or match in golf) in the same number of strokes as one's opponent

¹halves /hɑːvz/ *pl of* **half**

²halves *adv* with equal half shares

halyard, halliard /ˈhæljəd/ *n* a rope or tackle for hoisting or lowering

¹ham /hæm/ *n* **1** a buttock with its associated thigh – usu pl **2** (the meat of) the rear end of a bacon pig, esp the thigh, when removed from the carcass before curing with salt **3a** an inexpert but showy performer; *also* an actor performing in an exaggerated theatrical style **b** an operator of an amateur radio station

²ham *v* to execute with exaggerated speech or gestures; overact

hamburger /ˈhæmbɜːgəʳ/ *n* a round flat cake of minced beef; *also* a sandwich of a fried hamburger in a bread roll

ham-fisted *adj, chiefly Br* lacking dexterity with the hands; clumsy – infml

hamlet /ˈhæmlɪ̇t/ *n* a small village

¹hammer /ˈhæməʳ/ *n* **1a** a hand tool that consists of a solid head set crosswise on a handle and is used to strike a blow (e g to drive in a nail) **b** a power tool that substitutes a metal block or a drill for the hammerhead **2a** a lever with a striking head for ringing a bell or striking a gong **b** the part of the mechanism of a modern gun whose action ignites the cartridge **c** one of the three bones of the middle ear **d** a gavel **e(1)** a padded mallet in a piano action for striking a string **(2)** a hand mallet for playing various percussion instruments **3** (an athletic field event using) a metal sphere weighing 16lb (about 7.3kg) attached by a wire to a handle and thrown for distance

²hammer *v* **1** to strike blows, esp repeatedly, (as if) with a hammer; pound **2** to make repeated efforts *at*; *esp* to reiterate an opinion or attitude **3** to beat, drive, or shape (as if) with repeated blows of a hammer **4** to force as if by hitting repeatedly **5** to beat decisively – infml

hammer and sickle *n* an emblem consisting of a crossed hammer and sickle used chiefly as a symbol of Communism

hammer out *v* to produce or bring about through lengthy discussion

hammock /ˈhæmək/ *n* a hanging bed, usu made of netting or canvas and suspended by cords at each end

¹hamper /ˈhæmpəʳ/ *v* **1** to restrict the movement or operation of by bonds or obstacles; hinder **2** to interfere with; encumber

²hamper *n* a large basket with a cover for packing, storing, or transporting crockery, food, etc

hamster /ˈhæmstəʳ/ *n* any of numerous small Old World rodents with very large cheek pouches

¹hamstring /ˈhæm,strɪŋ/ *n* **1** either of 2 groups of tendons at the back of the human knee **2** a large tendon above and behind the hock of a quadruped

²hamstring /ˈhæm,strɪŋ/ *v* **1** to cripple by cutting the leg tendons **2** to make ineffective or powerless; cripple

¹hand /hænd/ *n* **1a** (the segment of the forelimb of vertebrate animals corresponding to) the end of the forelimb of human beings, monkeys, etc when modified as a grasping organ **b** a stylized figure of a hand used as a pointer or marker **c** a forehock of pork **d** an indicator or pointer on a dial **2** either of 2 sides or aspects of an issue or argument **3** a pledge, esp of betrothal or marriage **4** handwriting **5** a unit of measure equal to 4in (about 102mm) used esp for the height of a horse **6a** assistance or aid, esp when involving physical effort **b** a round of applause **7a** (the cards or pieces held by) a player in a card or board game **b** a single round in a game **c** the force or solidity of one's position (e g in negotiations) **d** a turn to serve in a game (e g squash) in which only the server may score points and which lasts as long as the server can win points **8a** a worker, employee ; *esp* one employed at manual labour or general tasks **b** a member of a ship's crew **c** one skilled in a particular action or pursuit **9a** handiwork **b** style of execution; workmanship

²**hand** *v* **1** to lead or assist with the hand **2** to give or pass (as if) with the hand

handbag /'hændbæg/ *n* a bag designed for carrying small personal articles and money, carried usu by women

handball /'hændbɔːl/ *n* **1** (the small rubber ball used in) a game resembling fives and played in a walled court or against a single wall **2** an amateur indoor or outdoor game between 2 teams of 7 or 11 players whose object is to direct a soccer ball into the opponent's goal by throwing and catching

handbarrow /'hændbærəʊ/ *n* a flat rectangular frame with handles at both ends for carrying loads

handbill /'hænd,bɪl/ *n* a small printed sheet to be distributed (e g for advertising) by hand

handbook /'hændbʊk/ *n* a short reference book, esp on a particular subject

handcuff /'hændkʌf/ *v* to apply handcuffs to; manacle

handcuffs /'hændkʌfs/ *n pl* a pair of metal rings, usu connected by a chain or bar, for locking round prisoners' wrists

hand down *v* **1** to transmit in succession (e g from father to son); bequeath **2** to give (an outgrown article of clothing) to a younger member of one's family **3** to deliver in court

handful /'hændfʊl/ *n, pl* **handfuls** *also* **handsful** **1** as much or as many as the hand will grasp **2** a small quantity or number **3** sby or sthg (e g a child or animal) that is difficult to control – infml

¹**handicap** /'hændikæp/ *n* **1** (a race or contest with) an artificial advantage or disadvantage given to contestants so that all have an equal chance of winning **2** a (physical) disability or disadvantage that makes achievement unusually difficult

²**handicap** *v* **1** to assign handicaps to; impose handicaps on **2** to put at a disadvantage

handicraft /'hændikrɑːft/ *n* **1** (an occupation requiring) manual skill **2** articles fashioned by handicraft

handiwork /'hændiwɜːk/ *n* **1** (the product of) work done by the hands **2** work done personally

handkerchief /'hæŋkətʃɪf/ *n* a small piece of cloth used for various usu personal purposes (e g blowing the nose or wiping the eyes) or as a clothing accessory

¹**handle** /'hændl/ *n* **1** a part that is designed to be grasped by the hand **2** the feel of a textile **3** a title; *also* an esp aristocratic or double-barrelled name – infml

²**handle** *v* **1a** to try or examine (e g by touching or moving) with the hand **b** to manage with the hands **2a** to deal with (e g a subject or idea) in speech or writing, or as a work of art **b** to manage, direct **3** to deal with, act on, or dispose of **4** to engage in the buying, selling, or distributing of (a commodity) **5** to respond to controlling movements in a specified way – **~able** *adj*

handler /'hændlə'/ *n* one who is in immediate physical charge of an animal

handmade /hænd'meɪd/ *adj* made by hand rather than by machine

handmaiden /'hænd,meɪdn/ *n* a personal maid or female servant

handout /'hændaʊt/ *n* **1** sthg (e g food, clothing, or money) distributed free, esp to people in need **2** a folder or circular of information for free distribution

hand out *v* **1** to give freely or without charge **2** to administer

hand over *v* to yield control or possession (of)

handpick /hænd'pɪk/ *v* **1** to pick by hand rather than by machine **2** to select personally and carefully

handrail /'hænd-reɪl/ *n* a narrow rail for grasping with the hand as a support, esp near stairs

handshake /'hændʃeɪk/ *n* a clasping and shaking of each other's usu right hand by 2 people (e g in greeting or farewell)

handsome /ˈhænsəm/ *adj* **1** considerable, sizable **2** marked by graciousness or generosity; liberal **3a** *of a man* having a pleasing appearance; good-looking **b** *of a woman* attractive in a dignified statuesque way – ~**ly** *adv*

hand-to-hand *adj* involving physical contact; very close – **hand to hand** *adv*

hand-to-mouth *adj* having or providing only just enough to live on; precarious – **hand to mouth** *adv*

handwork /ˈhændwɜːk/ *n* work done with the hands and not by machine

handwriting /ˈhændˌraɪtɪŋ/ *n* writing done by hand; *esp* the style of writing peculiar to a particular person

handy /ˈhændi/ *adj* **1** convenient for use; useful **2** clever in using the hands, esp in a variety of practical ways **3** conveniently near – infml – **-dily** *adv* – **-diness** *n*

handyman /ˈhændimæn/ *n* **1** sby who does odd jobs **2** sby competent in a variety of skills or repair work

[1]**hang** /hæŋ/ *v* **hung, hanged 1a** to fasten to some elevated point by the top so that the lower part is free; suspend **b** to suspend by the neck until dead **c** to fasten on a point of suspension so as to allow free motion within given limits **d** to suspend (meat, esp game) before cooking to make the flesh tender and develop the flavour **2** to decorate, furnish, or cover by hanging sthg up (e g flags or bunting) **3** to hold or bear in a suspended or inclined position **4** to fasten (sthg, esp wallpaper) to a wall (e g with paste) **5** to display (pictures) in a gallery **6** to remain fastened at the top so that the lower part is free; dangle **7** to remain poised or stationary in the air **8** to stay on; persist **9** to fall or droop from a usu tense or taut position **10** to depend **11** to lean, incline, or jut over or downwards **12** to fall in flowing lines

[2]**hang** *n* **1** the manner in which a thing hangs **2** a downward slope; *also* a droop **3** the special method of doing, using, or dealing with sthg; the knack – chiefly in *get the hang of*

hang about *v, Br* **1** to wait or stay, usu without purpose or activity **2** to delay or move slowly *USE* infml

hangar /ˈhæŋəʳ/ *n* a shed; *esp* a large shed for housing aircraft

hang back *v* to be reluctant to move or act; hesitate

hangdog /ˈhæŋdɒg/ *adj* ashamed; *also* abject

hanger /ˈhæŋəʳ/ *n* a device (e g a loop or strap) by which or to which sthg is hung or hangs; *esp* a hook and crosspiece to fit inside the shoulders of a dress, coat, etc to keep the shape of the garment when hung up

hanger-on *n* one who attempts to associate with a person, group, etc, esp for personal gain; a dependant

hang-glider *n* (sby who flies) a glider resembling a kite that is controlled by the body movements of the person harnessed beneath it – **hang-glide** *v* – **hang-gliding** *n*

[1]**hanging** /ˈhæŋɪŋ/ *n* **1** (an) execution by suspension from a noose **2a** a curtain **b** a covering (e g a tapestry) for a wall

[2]**hanging** *adj* **1** situated or lying on steeply sloping ground **2** jutting out; overhanging **3** adapted for sustaining a hanging object **4** deserving or liable to inflict hanging

hangman /ˈhæŋmən/ *n* one who hangs a condemned person; a public executioner

hangnail /ˈhæŋneɪl/ *n* a bit of skin hanging loose at the side or root of a fingernail

hang on *v* **1** to keep hold; hold onto sthg **2** to persist tenaciously **3** to wait for a short time **4** to remain on the telephone

hangout /ˈhæŋaʊt/ *n* a place where one is often to be seen – slang

hang out *v* **1** to protrude, esp downwards **2** to live or spend much time – slang

hangover /ˈhæŋəʊvəʳ/ *n* **1** sthg (e g a custom) that remains from the past **2** the disagreeable physical effects following heavy consumption of alcohol or use of other drugs

hang-up *n* a source of mental or emotional difficulty – infml

hang up *v* to terminate a telephone conversation, often abruptly

hank /hæŋk/ *n* **1** a coil, loop; *specif* a coiled or looped bundle (e g of yarn, rope, or wire) usu containing a definite length **2** a ring attaching a jib or staysail to a stay

hanker /ˈhæŋkəʳ/ *v* to desire strongly or persistently – usu + *after* or *for* – **~ing** *n*

hankie, hanky /ˈhæŋki/ *n* a handkerchief

hanky-panky /ˌhæŋki ˈpæŋki/ *n* mildly improper or deceitful behaviour – infml

Hansard /ˈhænsɑːd/ *n* the official report of Parliamentary proceedings

hansom /ˈhænsəm/, **hansom cab** *n* a light 2-wheeled covered carriage with the driver's seat high up at the back

haphazard /ˌhæpˈhæzəd/ *adj* marked by lack of plan or order; aimless – **~ly** *adv*

hapless /ˈhæplɪ̵s/ *adj* having no luck; unfortunate

happen /ˈhæpən/ *v* **1** to occur by chance; come *on* or *upon* by chance **2** to come into being as an event; occur **3** to have the luck or fortune *to*; chance

happening /ˈhæpənɪŋ/ *n* **1** sthg that happens; an occurrence **2a** the creation or presentation of a nonobjective work of art (e g an action painting) **b** a usu unscripted or improvised public performance in which the audience participates

happy /ˈhæpi/ *adj* **1** favoured by luck or fortune; fortunate **2** well adapted or fitting; felicitous **3a** enjoying or expressing pleasure and contentment **b** glad, pleased **4** characterized by a dazed irresponsible state – usu in combination **5** impulsively quick or overinclined to use sthg – usu in combination **6** having or marked by an atmosphere of good fellowship; friendly **7** satisfied as to the fact; confident, sure **8** tipsy – euph – **-pily** *adv* – **-piness** *n*

happy-go-lucky *adj* blithely unconcerned; carefree

hara-kiri /ˌhærə ˈkɪri/ *n* suicide by ritual disembowelment practised by the Japanese samurai, esp when disgraced or found guilty of a crime carrying the death penalty for commoners

[1]**harangue** /həˈræŋ/ *n* **1** a speech addressed to a public assembly **2** a lengthy, ranting, speech or piece of writing

[2]**harangue** *v* to make or address in a harangue

harass /ˈhærəs/ *v* **1** to worry and impede by repeated raids **2** to annoy or worry persistently – **harasser** *n* – **harassment** *n*

harbinger /ˈhɑːbɪndʒəʳ/ *n* **1** one who pioneers or initiates a major change; a precursor **2** sthg that presages or foreshadows what is to come

[1]**harbour,** *NAm chiefly* **harbor** /ˈhɑːbəʳ/ *n* **1** a place of security and comfort; a refuge **2** a part of a body of water providing protection and anchorage for ships

[2]**harbour** *v* **1** to give shelter or refuge to **2** to be the home or habitat of; contain **3** to have or keep (e g thoughts or feelings) in the mind – **~er** *n*

[1]**hard** /hɑːd/ *adj* **1** not easily penetrated or yielding to pressure; firm **2a** *of alcoholic drink* having a high percentage of alcohol **b** *of water* containing salts of calcium, magnesium, etc that inhibit lathering with soap **3** having or producing relatively great photographic contrast **4** *of currency* stable in value; *also* soundly backed and readily convertible into foreign currencies without large discounts **5** firmly and closely twisted **6** physically fit or resistant to stress **7a** not speculative or conjectural; factual **b** close, searching **8a(1)** difficult to endure **(2)** oppressive, inequitable **b** lacking consideration or compassion **c(1)** harsh, severe **(2)** resentful **d** not warm or mild **e(1)** forceful, violent **(2)** demanding energy or stamina **(3)** using or performing with great energy or effort **9** sharply defined; stark **10a** difficult to do, understand, or explain **b** having difficulty in doing sthg **11a** *of a drug* addictive and gravely detrimental to health **b** *of pornography* hard-core – **~ness** *n*

[2]**hard** *adv* **1a** with great or maximum effort or energy; strenuously **b** in a violent manner; fiercely **c** to the full

extent – used in nautical directions **d** in a searching or concentrated manner **2a** in such a manner as to cause hardship, difficulty, or pain; severely **b** with bitterness or grief **3** in a firm manner; tightly **4** to the point of hardness **5** close in time or space

[3]**hard** *n, chiefly Br* a firm usu artificial foreshore or landing place

hard-and-fast *adj* fixed, strict

hardback /ˈhaːdbæk/ *n* a book bound in stiff covers

hard-bitten *adj* steeled by difficult experience; tough

hardboard /ˈhaːdbɔːd/ *n* (a) composition board made by compressing shredded wood chips

hard-boiled *adj* devoid of sentimentality; tough

hardcore /ˈhaːdkɔːʳ/ *n, Br* compacted rubble or clinker used esp as a foundation for roads, paving, or floors

hard-core *adj* **1** of or constituting a hard core **2** *of pornography* extremely explicit

hard core *n sing or pl in constr* the unyielding or uncompromising members that form the nucleus of a group

harden /ˈhaːdn/ *v* **1** to make or become hard or harder **2** to confirm or become confirmed in disposition, feelings, or action; *esp* to make callous **3a** to toughen, inure *to* **b** to inure (e g plants) to cold or other unfavourable environmental conditions – often + *off* **4** to assume an appearance of harshness **5** *of currency, prices, etc* to become higher or less subject to fluctuations downwards

hardheaded /ˌhaːdˈhedɨd/ *adj* **1** stubborn **2** sober, realistic

hardhearted /ˌhaːdˈhaːtɨd/ *adj* lacking in sympathetic understanding; unfeeling

hardly /ˈhaːdli/ *adv* **1** in a severe manner; harshly **2** with difficulty; painfully **3** only just; barely **4** scarcely

hard-of-hearing *adj* partially deaf

hardship /ˈhaːdʃɪp/ *n* (an instance of) suffering, privation

hard shoulder *n* either of 2 surfaced strips of land along a road, esp a motorway, on which stopping is allowed only in an emergency

hard up *adj* short of sthg, esp money – infml

hardware /ˈhaːdweəʳ/ *n* **1** items sold by an ironmonger **2** the physical components (e g electronic and electrical devices) of a vehicle (e g a spacecraft) or an apparatus (e g a computer) **3** tape recorders, closed-circuit television, etc used as instructional equipment

hardwearing /haːdˈweərɪŋ/ *adj* durable

hardwood /ˈhaːdwʊd/ *n* (the wood of) a broad-leaved as distinguished from a coniferous tree

hardy /ˈhaːdi/ *adj* **1** bold, audacious **2a** inured to fatigue or hardships; robust **b** capable of withstanding adverse conditions; *esp* capable of living outdoors over winter without artificial protection – **-diness** *n*

[1]**hare** /heəʳ/ *n* **1** any of various swift timid long-eared mammals like large rabbits with long hind legs **2** a figure of a hare moved mechanically along a dog track for the dogs to chase

[2]**hare** *v* to run fast – infml

harebell /ˈheəbel/ *n* a slender plant with blue bell-shaped flowers that grows on heaths or in open woodland

harebrained /ˈheəbreɪnd/ *adj* flighty, foolish

harelip /ˌheəˈlɪp/ *n* a split in the upper lip like that of a hare occurring as a congenital deformity – **-lipped** *adj*

harem /ˈheərəm, haːˈriːm/ *n* **1a** a usu secluded (part of a) house allotted to women in a Muslim household **b** *sing or pl in constr* the women occupying a harem **2** a group of females associated with 1 male – used with reference to polygamous animals

haricot /ˈhærɪkəʊ/, **haricot bean** *n* a French bean

hark /haːk/ *v* to listen closely

hark back /haːk/ *v* to return *to* an earlier topic or circumstance

harlequin /ˈhaːlɨkwɨn/ *n* **1** *cap* a stock character in comedy and pantomime **2** a buffoon

harlot /ˈhaːlət/ *n, archaic* a woman prostitute – **~ry** *n*

[1]**harm** /haːm/ *n* **1** physical or mental

damage; injury **2** mischief, wrong – ~**ful** *adj* – ~**fully** *adv* – ~**fulness** *n*

²**harm** *v* to cause harm to

harmless /ˈhaːmlɨs/ *adj* **1** free from harm, liability, or loss **2** lacking capacity or intent to injure – ~**ly** *adv* – ~**ness** *n*

¹**harmonic** /haːˈmɒnɪk/ *adj* **1** of musical harmony, a harmonic, or harmonics **2** pleasing to the ear; harmonious

²**harmonic** *n* a tone in a harmonic series

harmonica /haːˈmɒnɪkə/ *n* a small rectangular wind instrument with free reeds recessed in air slots from which notes are sounded by breathing out and in

harmonium /haːˈməʊnɪəm/ *n* a reed organ in which pedals operate a bellows that forces air through free reeds

harmony /ˈhaːməni/ *n* **1a** the (pleasant-sounding) combination of simultaneous musical notes in a chord **b** (the science of) the structure of music with respect to the composition and progression of chords **2a** pleasing or congruent arrangement of parts **b** agreement, accord – **-nious** *adj* – **-niously** *adv* – **-niousness** *n* – **-nize** *v*

¹**harness** /ˈhaːnɨs/ *n* **1** the gear of a draught animal other than a yoke **2** sthg that resembles a harness (e g in holding or fastening sthg)

²**harness** *v* **1a** to put a harness on (e g a horse) **b** to attach (e g a wagon) by means of a harness **2** to tie together; yoke **3** to utilize; *esp* to convert (a natural force) into energy

harp /haːp/ *n* a musical instrument that has strings stretched across an open triangular frame, plucked with the fingers

harp on *v* to dwell on or return to (a subject) tediously or repeatedly

harpoon /haːˈpuːn/ *n* a barbed spear used esp in hunting large fish or whales

harpsichord /ˈhaːpsɪkɔːd/ *n* a keyboard instrument having a horizontal frame and strings and producing notes by the action of quills or leather points plucking the strings

harpy /ˈhaːpi/ *n* **1** *cap* a rapacious creature of Greek mythology with the head of a woman and the body of a bird **2** a predatory person; *esp* a rapacious woman – derog

harridan /ˈhærɪdn/ *n* an ill-tempered unpleasant woman

¹**harrier** /ˈhærɪəʳ/ *n* **1** a hunting dog resembling a small foxhound and used esp for hunting hares **2** a runner in a cross-country team

²**harrier** *n* any of various slender hawks with long angled wings

Harris tweed /ˌhærɨs ˈtwiːd/ *trademark* – used for a loosely woven tweed made in the Outer Hebrides

¹**harrow** /ˈhærəʊ/ *n* a cultivating implement set with spikes, spring teeth, or discs and drawn over the ground esp to pulverize and smooth the soil

²**harrow** *v* **1** to cultivate (ground or land) with a harrow **2** to cause distress to; agonize

harry /ˈhæri/ *v* **1** to make a destructive raid on; ravage **2** to torment (as if) by constant attack; harass

harsh /haːʃ/ *adj* **1** having a coarse uneven surface; rough **2** disagreeable or painful to the senses **3** unduly exacting; severe – ~**ly** *adv* – ~**ness** *n*

hart /haːt/ *n, chiefly Br* the male of the (red) deer, esp when over 5 years old

harum-scarum /ˌheərəm ˈskeərəm/ *adj* reckless, irresponsible – infml

¹**harvest** /ˈhaːvɨst/ *n* **1** (the season for) the gathering in of agricultural crops **2** (the yield of) a mature crop of grain, fruit, etc **3** the product or reward of exertion

²**harvest** *v* to gather in (a crop); reap

has /s, z, əz, həz; *strong* hæz/ *pres 3rd sing of* **have**

has-been *n* sby or sthg that has passed the peak of effectiveness, success, or popularity – infml

¹**hash** /hæʃ/ *n* **1** (a dish consisting chiefly of reheated cooked) chopped food, esp meat **2** a rehash **3** a muddle, mess *USE*(2 & 3) infml

²**hash** *n* hashish – infml

hashish /ˈhæʃiːʃ, -ɪʃ/ *n* the resin from the flowering tops of the female hemp plant that is smoked, chewed, etc for its intoxicating effect

hasp /hɑːsp/ *n* a device for fastening; *esp* a hinged metal strap that fits over a staple and is secured by a pin or padlock

[1]**hassle** /ˈhæsəl/ *n* **1** a heated often protracted argument; a wrangle **2** a trying problem; a struggle *USE* infml

[2]**hassle** *v* **1** to argue, fight **2** to subject to usu persistent harassment *USE* infml

hast /hæst/ *archaic pres 2 sing of* **have**

[1]**haste** /heɪst/ *n* **1** rapidity of motion; swiftness **2** rash or headlong action; precipitateness

[2]**haste** *v* to move or act swiftly – fml

hasten /ˈheɪsən/ *v* **1** to cause to hurry **2** to accelerate **3** to move or act quickly; hurry

hasty /ˈheɪsti/ *adj* **1** done or made in a hurry **2** precipitate, rash – **-tily** *adv* – **-tiness** *n*

hat /hæt/ *n* a covering for the head usu having a shaped crown and brim

[1]**hatch** /hætʃ/ *n* **1** a small door or opening (e g in a wall or aircraft) **2a** (the covering for) an opening in the deck of a ship or in the floor or roof of a building **b** a hatchway

[2]**hatch** *v* **1** to emerge from an egg or pupa **2** to incubate eggs; brood **3** to give forth young **4** to produce (young) from an egg by applying heat **5** to devise, esp secretly; originate

[3]**hatch** *v* to mark (e g a drawing, map, or engraving) with fine closely spaced parallel lines

hatchback /ˈhætʃbæk/ *n* (a usu small motor car with) an upward-opening hatch giving entry to the luggage and passenger compartment

hatchery /ˈhætʃəri/ *n* a place for hatching (esp fish) eggs

hatchet /ˈhætʃɪ̣t/ *n* a short-handled axe

[1]**hate** /heɪt/ *n* **1** intense hostility or dislike; loathing **2** an object of hatred – infml

[2]**hate** *v* to feel extreme enmity or aversion (towards)

hateful /ˈheɪtfəl/ *adj* **1** full of hate; malicious **2** deserving of or arousing hate – **~ly** *adv* – **~ness** *n*

hath /hæθ/ *archaic pres 3 sing of* **have**

hatred /ˈheɪtrɪ̣d/ *n* hate

hat trick *n* three successes by 1 person or side in a usu sporting activity

hauberk /ˈhɔːbɜːk/ *n* a tunic of chain mail worn as defensive armour, esp from the 12th to the 14th c

haughty /ˈhɔːti/ *adj* disdainfully proud; arrogant – **-tily** *adv* – **-tiness** *n*

[1]**haul** /hɔːl/ *v* **1a** to pull with effort; drag **b** to transport in a vehicle, esp a cart **2** to bring *up* (e g before an authority for judgment) – infml

[2]**haul** *n* **1** the act or process of hauling **2** an amount gathered or acquired; a take **3a** transport by hauling or the load transported **b** the distance or route over which a load is transported

haulier /ˈhɔːlɪəʳ/ *n* a person or commercial establishment whose business is transport by lorry

haulm /hɔːm/ *n* **1** the stems or tops of potatoes, peas, beans, etc (after the crop has been gathered) **2** *Br* an individual plant stem

haunch /hɔːntʃ/ *n* **1** a hip **2** the hind legs (and adjoining parts) of a quadruped – usu pl **3** the lower half of either of the sides of an arch

[1]**haunt** /hɔːnt/ *v* **1** to visit often; frequent **2a** to recur constantly and spontaneously to **b** to reappear continually in; pervade **3** to visit or inhabit as a ghost **4** to stay around or persist; linger

[2]**haunt** *n* a place habitually frequented

hauteur /əʊˈtɜːr/ *n* arrogance, haughtiness

Havana /həˈvænə/ *n* (a cigar made in Cuba or from) tobacco (of the type) grown in Cuba

[1]**have** /əv, həv; *strong* hæv/ *v* **has; had** **1a** to hold in one's possession or at one's disposal **b** to contain as a constituent or be characterized by **2** to own as an obligation or necessity – + *to* and an expressed or understood infinitive (e g you don't *have* to if you don't want to) **3** to stand in relationship to (e g *have* 2 sisters) **4a** to get,

obtain **b** to receive (e g *had* news) **c** to accept; *specif* to accept in marriage **d** to have sexual intercourse with (a woman or passive partner) **5a** to experience, esp by undergoing or suffering (e g *have* a cold) **b** to undertake and make or perform (e g *have* a look at that) **c** to entertain in the mind (e g *have* an opinion) **d** to engage in; carry on **6a** to cause to by persuasive or forceful means (e g so he would *have* us believe) **b** to cause to be (brought into a specified condition) (e g *have* it finished) **c** to invite as a guest **7** to allow, permit **8a** to hold in a position of disadvantage or certain defeat (e g we *have* him now) **b** to perplex, floor (e g you *have* me there) **9a** to be pregnant with or be the prospective parents of **b** to give birth to **10** to partake of; consume **11** to take advantage of; fool (e g been *had* by his partner) – infml **12** – used with the past participle to form perfect tenses (e g we *have* had); used with *got* to express obligation or necessity (e g *have* got to go) **13** would (e g I *had* as soon not) *USE* British speakers in particular often express the idea of momentary as opposed to habitual possession or experience with *have got*

[2]**have** *n* a wealthy person – usu pl; esp in *the haves and have-nots*

haven /ˈheɪvən/ *n* **1** a harbour, port **2** a place of safety or refuge

have on *v* **1** to be wearing **2** to have plans for **3** *chiefly Br* to deceive, tease – infml

haversack /ˈhævəsæk/ *n* a knapsack

have up *v* to bring before the authorities – infml

havoc /ˈhævək/ *n* **1** widespread destruction; devastation **2** great confusion and disorder

haw /hɔː/ *n* (a berry of) hawthorn

[1]**hawk** /hɔːk/ *n* **1** any of numerous medium-sized birds of prey that have (short) rounded wings and long tails and that hunt during the day **2** one who takes a militant attitude; a supporter of a warlike policy – **~ish** *adj* – **~ishness** *n*

[2]**hawk** *v* to hunt game with a trained hawk – **~er** *n*

[3]**hawk** *v* to offer for sale in the street

[4]**hawk** *v* to utter a harsh guttural sound (as if) in clearing the throat

hawser /ˈhɔːzəʳ/ *n* a large rope

hawthorn /ˈhɔːθɔːn/ *n* any of a genus of spring-flowering spiny shrubs of the rose family with white or pink flowers and small red fruits

hay /heɪ/ *n* herbage, esp grass, mowed and cured for fodder

hay fever *n* nasal catarrh and swollen eyes occurring usu in the spring and summer through allergy to pollen

haystack /ˈheɪstæk/ *n* a relatively large sometimes thatched outdoor pile of hay

haywire /ˈheɪwaɪəʳ/ *adj* **1** out of order **2** emotionally or mentally upset; crazy *USE* infml

[1]**hazard** /ˈhæzəd/ *n* **1** a game of chance played with 2 dice **2a** a risk, peril **b** a source of danger **3** a golf-course obstacle (e g a bunker)

[2]**hazard** *v* **1** to expose to danger **2** to venture, risk

hazardous /ˈhæzədəs/ *adj* **1** depending on hazard or chance **2** involving or exposing one to risk (e g of loss or harm) – **~ly** *adv* – **~ness** *n*

haze /heɪz/ *n* **1** vapour, dust, smoke, etc causing a slight decrease in the air's transparency **2** vagueness or confusion of mental perception

hazel /ˈheɪzəl/ *n* **1** (the wood or nut of) any of a genus of shrubs or small trees bearing nuts **2** a yellowish light to strong brown colour

hazy /ˈheɪzi/ *adj* **1** obscured, cloudy **2** vague, indefinite – **-zily** *adv* – **-ziness** *n*

H-bomb /ˈeɪtʃ bɒm/ *n* a hydrogen bomb

[1]**he** /i, hi; *strong* hiː/ *pron* **1** that male person or creature who is neither speaker nor hearer – + cap in reference to God **2** – used in a generic sense or when the sex of the person is unspecified

[2]**he** /hiː/ *n* **1** a male person or creature **2** the player in a children's game who must catch others; it

[1]**head** /hed/ *n* **1** the upper or foremost division of the body containing the brain, the chief sense organs, and the mouth **2a** the seat of the intellect; the mind **b** natural aptitude or talent **c** mental or emotional control; compo-

sure **3** the obverse of a coin – usu pl with sing. meaning **4a** a person, individual **b** a single individual (domestic animal) out of a number – usu pl **5a** the end that is upper, higher, or opposite the foot **b** the source of a stream, river, etc **6** a director, leader **a** a school principal **b** one in charge of a department in an institution **7** the part of a plant bearing a compact mass of leaves, fruits, flowers, etc **8** the leading part of a military column, procession, etc **9a** the uppermost extremity or projecting part of an object; the top **b** the striking part of a weapon, tool, implement, etc **10** a mass of water in motion **11** (the pressure resulting from) the difference in height between 2 points in a body of liquid **12a** (parts adjacent to) the bow of a ship **b** a (ship's) toilet – usu pl with sing. meaning in British English **13** a measure of length equivalent to a head **14** the place of leadership, honour, or command **15a** a word often in larger letters placed above a passage in order to introduce or categorize **b** a separate part or topic **16** the foam or froth that rises on a fermenting or effervescing liquid **17a** the part of a boil, pimple, etc at which it is likely to break **b** a culminating point; a crisis – esp in *come to a head* **18a** a part of a machine or machine tool containing a device (e g a cutter or drill); *also* the part of an apparatus that performs the chief or a particular function **b** any of at least 2 electromagnetic components which bear on the magnetic tape in a tape recorder, such that one can erase recorded material if desired and another may either record or play back **19** one who uses LSD, cannabis, etc habitually or excessively – often in combination; slang

[2]**head** *adj* **1** principal, chief **2** situated at the head

[3]**head** *v* **1** to cut back or off the upper growth of (a plant) **2a** to provide with or form a head **b** to form the head or top of **3** to be at the head of; lead **4a** to put sthg at the head of (e g a list); *also* to provide with a heading **b** to stand as the first or leading member of **5** to drive (e g a soccer ball) with the head **6** to point or proceed in a specified direction

headache /ˈhedeɪk/ *n* **1** pain in the head **2** a difficult situation or problem – **-achy** *adj*

headband /ˈhedbænd/ *n* a band worn round the head, esp to keep hair out of the eyes

headboard /ˈhedbɔːd/ *n* a board forming the head (e g of a bed)

headdress /ˈhed-dres/ *n* an often elaborate covering for the head

header /ˈhedəʳ/ *n* **1** a brick or stone laid in a wall with its end towards the face of the wall **2** a headfirst fall or dive **3** a shot or pass in soccer made by heading the ball

headfirst /hedˈfɜːst/ *adv* with the head foremost; headlong

heading /ˈhedɪŋ/ *n* **1** the compass direction in which a ship or aircraft points **2** an inscription, headline, or title standing at the top or beginning (e g of a letter or chapter)

headland /ˈhedlənd/ *n* **1** unploughed land near an edge of a field **2** a point of usu high land jutting out into a body of water

headlight /ˈhedlaɪt/ *n* (the beam cast by) the main light mounted on the front of a motor vehicle

headline /ˈhedlaɪn/ *n* a title printed in large type above a newspaper story or article; *also, pl, Br* a summary given at the beginning or end of a news broadcast

headlong /ˈhedlɒŋ/ *adv or adj* **1** headfirst **2** without thought or deliberation **3** without pause or delay

headman /ˈhedmən/ *n* a chief of a primitive community

headmaster /ˌhedˈmɑːstəʳ/, *fem* **headmistress** *n* one who heads the staff of a school

head off *v* to stop the progress of or turn aside by taking preventive action; block

head-on *adv or adj* **1** with the head or front making the initial contact **2** in direct opposition

headphone /ˈhedfəʊn/ *n* an earphone held over the ear by a band worn on the head – usu pl

headquarters /ˈhedˌkwɔːtəz, ˌhedˈkwɔːtəz/ *n, pl* **headquarters** **1** a place from which a commander exercises command **2** the administrative centre of an enterprise ***USE*** often pl with sing. meaning

headrest /'hed-rest/ *n* a support for the head; *esp* a cushioned pad supporting the head in a vehicle

headroom /'hed-rʊm, -ruːm/ *n* vertical space (e g beneath a bridge) sufficient to allow passage or unrestricted movement

headship /'hedʃɪp/ *n* the position or office of a head (e g a headmaster); leadership

headstrong /'hedstrɒŋ/ *adj* wilful, obstinate

headway /'hedweɪ/ *n* **1a** (rate of) motion in a forward direction **b** advance, progress **2** headroom

headwind /'hed,wɪnd, ,hed'wɪnd/ *n* a wind blowing in a direction opposite to a course, esp of a ship or aircraft

heady /'hedi/ *adj* **1** violent, impetuous **2** (tending to make) giddy or exhilarated; intoxicating

heal /hiːl/ *v* **1a** to make sound or whole **b** to restore to health **2** to restore to a sound or normal state; mend – ~**er** *n*

health /helθ/ *n* **1a** soundness of body, mind, or spirit **b** the general condition of the body **2** condition ; *esp* a sound or flourishing condition; well-being

healthful /'helθfəl/ *adj* beneficial to health of body or mind

healthy /'helθi/ *adj* **1** enjoying or showing health and vigour of body, mind, or spirit **2** conducive to good health **3** prosperous, flourishing – **healthily** *adv* – **healthiness** *n*

[1]**heap** /hiːp/ *n* **1** a collection of things lying one on top of another; a pile **2** a great number or large quantity; a lot – infml; often pl with sing. meaning

[2]**heap** *v* **1a** to throw or lay in a heap; pile *up* **b** to form or round into a heap **2** to supply abundantly *with*; *also* to bestow lavishly or in large quantities *upon*

hear /hɪəʳ/ *v* **heard** **1** to perceive or have the capacity of perceiving (sound) with the ear **2** to learn or gain information (by hearing) **3** to listen to with attention; heed **4** to give a legal hearing to **5** to receive a communication *from*

hearing /'hɪərɪŋ/ *n* **1a** the one of the 5 basic physical senses by which waves received by the ear are interpreted by the brain as sounds varying in pitch, intensity, and timbre **b** earshot **2a** an opportunity to be heard **b** a trial in court

hearken /'hɑːkən/ *v* to listen *to*; *also* to heed – poetic

hearsay /'hɪəseɪ/ *n* sthg heard from another; rumour

hearse /hɜːs/ *n* a vehicle for transporting a dead body in its coffin

heart /hɑːt/ *n* **1a** a hollow muscular organ that by its rhythmic contraction acts as a force pump maintaining the circulation of the blood **b** the breast, bosom **c** sthg resembling a heart in shape; *specif* a conventionalized representation of a heart **2a** a playing card marked with 1 or more red heart-shaped figures **b** *pl but sing or pl in constr* the suit comprising cards identified by this figure **3a** humane disposition; compassion **b** love, affections **c** courage, spirit **4** one's innermost character or feelings **5a** the central or innermost part (of a lettuce, cabbage, etc) **b** the essential or most vital part

heartache /'hɑːteɪk/ *n* mental anguish; sorrow

heart attack *n* an instance of abnormal functioning of the heart; *esp* coronary thrombosis

heartbeat /'hɑːtbiːt/ *n* a single complete pulse of the heart

heartbreak /'hɑːtbreɪk/ *n* intense grief or distress

heartbreaking /'hɑːt,breɪkɪŋ/ *adj* **1** causing intense sorrow or distress **2** extremely trying or difficult – ~**ly** *adv*

heartbroken /'hɑːt,brəʊkən/ *adj* overcome by sorrow

heartburn /'hɑːtbɜːn/ *n* a burning pain behind the lower part of the breastbone usu resulting from spasm of the stomach or throat muscles

hearten /'hɑːtn/ *v* to cheer, encourage

heartfelt /'hɑːtfelt/ *adj* deeply felt; earnest

hearth /hɑːθ/ *n* **1** a brick, stone, or cement area in front of the floor of a fireplace **2** home, fireside

heartless /ˈhɑːtlɪ̵s/ *adj* unfeeling, cruel – ~**ly** *adv* – ~**ness** *n*

heartrending /ˈhɑːtˌrendɪŋ/ *adj* heartbreaking – ~**ly** *adv*

heartsick /ˈhɑːtˌsɪk/ *adj* very despondent; depressed

heartstrings /ˈhɑːtˌstrɪŋz/ *n pl* the deepest emotions or affections

heartthrob /ˈhɑːtθrɒb/ *n* one who is the object of or arouses infatuation

[1]**heart-to-heart** *adj* sincere and intimate

[2]**heart-to-heart** *n* a frank or intimate talk – infml

heartwarming /ˈhɑːtwɔːmɪŋ/ *adj* inspiring sympathetic feeling; cheering – ~**ly** *adv*

heartwood /ˈhɑːtwʊd/ *n* the older harder nonliving central wood in a tree, usu darker and denser than the surrounding sapwood

hearty /ˈhɑːti/ *adj* **1a** enthusiastically or exuberantly friendly; jovial **b** unrestrained, vigorous **2a** robustly healthy **b** substantial, abundant

[1]**heat** /hiːt/ *v* to make or become warm or hot – often + *up*

[2]**heat** *n* **1a** the condition of being hot; warmth; *also* a marked degree of this **b** excessively high bodily temperature **c** any of a series of degrees of heating **2a** intensity of feeling or reaction **b** the height or stress of an action or condition **c** readiness for sexual intercourse in a female mammal – usu in *on heat* or (*chiefly NAm*) *in heat* **3** pungency of flavour **4a** a single round of a contest that has 2 or more rounds for each contestant **b** any of several preliminary contests whose winners go into the final **5** pressure, coercion – slang

heated /ˈhiːtɪ̵d/ *adj* marked by anger – ~**ly** *adv*

heater /ˈhiːtəʳ/ *n* a device that gives off heat or holds sthg to be heated

heath /hiːθ/ *n* **1** any of various related evergreen plants that thrive on barren usu acid soil, with whorls of needlelike leaves and clusters of small flowers **2a** a tract of wasteland **b** a large area of level uncultivated land usu with poor peaty soil and bad drainage

heathen /ˈhiːðən/ *n* **1** an unconverted member of a people or nation that does not acknowledge the God of the Bible – often pl + *the* **2** an uncivilized or irreligious person – ~**ish** *adj* – ~**dom** *n*

heather /ˈheðəʳ/ *n* a (common usu purplish-pink flowered northern) heath

heat rash *n* prickly heat

heat wave *n* a period of unusually hot weather

[1]**heave** /hiːv/ *v* **heaved, hove** **1** to lift upwards or forwards, esp with effort **2** to throw, cast **3** to utter with obvious effort **4** to cause to swell or rise **5** to haul, draw **6** to rise and fall rhythmically **7** to vomit **8** to pull

[2]**heave** *n* **1a** an effort to heave or raise **b** a throw, cast **2** an upward motion; *esp* a rhythmical rising

heaven /ˈhevən/ *n* **1** (any of the spheres of) the expanse of space that surrounds the earth like a dome; the firmament – usu pl with sing. meaning **2** *often cap* the dwelling place of God, his angels, and the spirits of those who have received salvation; Paradise **3** a place or condition of utmost happiness

heavenly /ˈhevənli/ *adj* **1** of heaven or the heavens; celestial **2a** suggesting the blessed state of heaven; divine **b** delightful – infml

heaven-sent *adj* providential

heave to *v* to bring (a ship) to a stop with head to wind

[1]**heavy** /ˈhevi/ *adj* **1** having great weight in proportion to size **2** hard to bear; *specif* grievous **3** of weighty import; serious **4** emotionally intense; profound **5** oppressed; burdened **6** lacking sparkle or vivacity; slow, dull **7** dulled with weariness; drowsy **8a** of an unusually large amount **b** of great force **c** overcast **d** *of ground or soil* full of clay and inclined to hold water; impeding motion **e** loud and deep **f** laborious, difficult **g** of large capacity or output **h** consuming in large quantities – usu + *on* **9a** digested with difficulty, usu because of excessive richness **b** *esp of bread* not sufficiently raised or leavened **10** producing heavy usu large goods (e g coal, steel, or machinery) often used in the production of other goods **11a** of the larger variety **b** heavily armoured,

armed, or equipped **12** *of rock music* loud and strongly rhythmic – slang **13** *chiefly NAm* frighteningly serious; *specif* threatening – slang; often used as an interjection – **-vily** *adv* – **-viness** *n*

²**heavy** *adv* in a heavy manner; heavily

³**heavy** *n* **1** *pl* units (e g of bombers, artillery, or cavalry) of the heavy sort **2a** (an actor playing) a villain **b** sby of importance or significance – infml **3** one hired to compel or deter by means of threats or physical violence – slang

heavy-duty *adj* able or designed to withstand unusual strain or wear

heavy-handed *adj* **1** clumsy, awkward **2** oppressive, harsh – **~ly** *adv* – **~ness** *n*

heavyhearted /ˌheviˈhɑːtɪ̣d/ *adj* despondent, melancholy

heavyweight /ˈheviweɪt/ *n* **1** sby or sthg above average weight **2** one in the usu heaviest class of contestants; *specif* a boxer whose weight is not limited if he is professional or is more than 81kg (about 12st 10lb) if he is amateur **3** an important or influential person

Hebraic /hɪˈbreɪ-ɪk/, **Hebraistic** *adj* of the Hebrews, their culture, or Hebrew

Hebrew /ˈhiːbruː/ *n* **1** a member or descendant of any of a group of N Semitic peoples including the Israelites; *esp* an Israelite **2** the Semitic language of the ancient Hebrews; *also* a later form of Hebrew

hecatomb /ˈhekətuːm, -təʊm/ *n* **1** an ancient Greek and Roman sacrifice of 100 oxen or cattle **2** the sacrifice or slaughter of many victims

heck /hek/ *n* hell – used as an interjection or intensive

heckle /ˈhekəl/ *v* to harass and try to disconcert (e g a speaker) with questions, challenges, or gibes – **~r** *n*

hectare /ˈhektɑːʳ, -teəʳ/ *n* (a measure of land which equals) 10,000 square metres

hectic /ˈhektɪk/ *adj* filled with excitement or feverish activity – **~ally** *adv*

¹**hedge** /hedʒ/ *n* **1a** a boundary formed by a dense row of shrubs or low trees **b** a barrier, limit **2** a means of protection or defence (e g against financial loss) **3** a calculatedly noncommittal or evasive statement

²**hedge** *v* **1** to enclose or protect (as if) with a hedge **2** to hem in or obstruct (as if) with a barrier; hinder **3** to protect oneself against losing (e g a bet), esp by making counterbalancing transactions **4** to plant, form, or trim a hedge **5** to avoid committing oneself to a definite course of action, esp by making evasive statements

hedgehog /ˈhedʒhɒg/ *n* any of a genus of small Old World spine-covered insect-eating mammals that are active at night

hedgehop /ˈhedʒhɒp/ *v* to fly an aircraft close to the ground and rise over obstacles as they appear – **~per** *n*

hedgerow /ˈhedʒrəʊ/ *n* a row of shrubs or trees surrounding a field

hedonism /ˈhiːdənɪzəm/ *n* (conduct based on) the doctrine that personal pleasure is the sole or chief good – **-ist** *n* – **-istic** *adj*

heebie-jeebies /ˌhiːbi ˈdʒiːbɪz/ *n pl* *the* jitters, willies – infml

¹**heed** /hiːd/ *v* to pay attention (to)

²**heed** *n* attention, notice – **~ful(ly)** *adj (adv)* – **~fulness** *n* – **~less(ly)** *adj (adv)*

¹**heel** /hiːl/ *n* **1** (the back part of the hind limb of a vertebrate corresponding to) the back of the human foot below the ankle and behind the arch or an anatomical structure resembling this **2** either of the crusty ends of a loaf of bread **3** the part of a garment or an article of footwear that covers or supports the human heel **4a** the lower end of a mast **b** the base of a tuber or cutting of a plant used for propagation **5** a backward kick with the heel in rugby, esp from a set scrum **6** a contemptible person – slang

²**heel** *v* **1** to supply with a heel; *esp* to renew the heel of **2** to exert pressure on, propel, or strike (as if) with the heel; *specif* to kick (a rugby ball) with the heel, esp out of a scrum

³**heel** *v* to tilt to one side

⁴**heel** *n* (the extent of) a tilt to one side

heelball /ˈhiːlbɔːl/ *n* a mixture of wax and lampblack used to polish the heels of footwear and to take brass or stone rubbings

hefty /ˈhefti/ *adj* **1** large or bulky and usu heavy **2** powerful, mighty **3** impressively large – **heftily** *adv*

hegemony /hɪˈgeməni, ˈhedʒɪ̆məni/ *n* domination by one nation, group, etc over others

Hegira, Hejira /ˈhedʒɪ̆rə, hɪˈdʒaɪərə/ the flight of Muhammad from Mecca in 622 AD, the event marking the beginning of the Islamic era

heifer /ˈhefəʳ/ *n* a young cow (that has at most 1 calf)

heigh-ho /ˈheɪ ˌhəʊ, ˌ- ˈ-/ *interj* – used to express boredom, weariness, or sadness

height /haɪt/ *n* **1** the highest or most extreme point; the zenith **2a** the distance from the bottom to the top of sthg standing upright **b** the elevation above a level **3** the condition of being tall or high **4a** a piece of land (e g a hill or plateau) rising to a considerable degree above the surrounding country – usu pl with sing. meaning **b** a high point or position

heighten /ˈhaɪtn/ *v* **1a** to increase the amount or degree of; augment **b** to deepen, intensify **2** to raise high or higher; elevate **3** to become great or greater in amount, degree, or extent

heinous /ˈheɪnəs, ˈhiːnəs/ *adj* hatefully or shockingly evil; abominable – **~ly** *adj* – **~ness** *n*

heir /eəʳ/ *n* **1** sby who inherits or is entitled to succeed to an estate or rank **2** sby who receives or is entitled to receive some position, role, or quality passed on from a parent or predecessor

heir apparent *n, pl* **heirs apparent** one whose succession, esp to a position or role, appears certain under existing circumstances

heirloom /ˈeəluːm/ *n* **1** a piece of valuable property handed down within a family for generations **2** sthg of special value handed on from one generation to another

held /held/ *past of* **hold**

helicopter /ˈhelɪ̆kɒptəʳ/ *n* an aircraft which derives both lift and propulsive power from a set of horizontally rotating rotors or vanes and is capable of vertical takeoff and landing

heliograph /ˈhiːlɪəgrɑːf/ *n* an apparatus for signalling using the sun's rays reflected from a mirror

heliotrope /ˈhiːlɪətrəʊp/ *n* **1** any of a genus of plants of the borage family **2** a light purple colour

heliport /ˈhelɪ̆pɔːt/ *n* a place for helicopters to take off and land

helium /ˈhiːlɪəm/ *n* a noble gaseous element found in natural gases and used esp for inflating balloons and in low-temperature research

helix /ˈhiːlɪks/ *n, pl* **helices** *also* **helixes** **1** sthg spiral in form (e g a coil formed by winding wire round a uniform tube) **2** the rim curved inwards of the external ear

hell /hel/ *n* **1a** a nether world (e g Hades or Sheol) inhabited by the spirits of the dead **b** the nether realm of the devil in which the souls of those excluded from Paradise undergo perpetual torment **2a** a place or state of torment, misery, or wickedness – often as an interjection, an intensive, or as a generalized term of abuse **b** a place or state of chaos or destruction **c** a severe scolding

hell-bent *adj* stubbornly and often recklessly determined

Hellene /ˈheliːn/ *n* Greek

Hellenic /heˈlenɪk/ *adj* of Greece, its people, or its language

Hellenistic /ˌhelɪ̆ˈnɪstɪk/ *adj* of Greek history, culture, or art after Alexander the Great

[1]**hellish** /ˈhelɪʃ/ *adj* of, resembling, or befitting hell; diabolical

[2]**hellish** *adv* extremely, damnably

hello /həˈləʊ, he-/ *n,* an expression or gesture of greeting – used interjectionally in greeting, in answering the telephone, to express surprise, or to attract attention

[1]**helm** /helm/ *n* **1** a tiller or wheel controlling the steering of a ship **2** the position of control; the head

[2]**helm** *v* to steer (as if) with a helm

helmet /ˈhelmɪ̆t/ *n* **1** a covering or enclosing headpiece of ancient or medieval armour **2** any of various protective head coverings, esp made of a hard material to resist impact **3** sthg, esp a hood-shaped petal or sepal, resembling a helmet

helmsman /'helmzmən/ *n* the person at the helm

helot /'helət/ *n* **1** *cap* a serf in ancient Sparta **2** a serf, slave

[1]**help** /help/ *v* **1** to give assistance or support to **2** to remedy, relieve **3a** to be of use to; benefit **b** to further the advancement of; promote **4a** to keep from occurring; prevent **b** to restrain (oneself) from taking action **5** to serve with food or drink, esp at a meal **6** to appropriate sthg for (oneself), esp dishonestly **7** to be of use or benefit

[2]**help** *n* **1** aid, assistance **2** remedy, relief **3a** sby, esp a woman, hired to do work, esp housework **b** the services of a paid worker; *also, chiefly NAm* the workers providing such services

helpful /'helpfəl/ *adj* of service or assistance; useful – **~ly** *adv* – **~ness** *n*

helping /'helpɪŋ/ *n* a serving of food

helpless /'helpl$\frac{1}{3}$s/ *adj* **1** lacking protection or support; defenceless **2** lacking strength or effectiveness; powerless – **~ly** *adv* – **~ness** *n*

helpmate /'helpmeɪt/ *n* one who is a companion and helper; *esp* a spouse

help out *v* to give assistance or aid (to), esp when in great difficulty

[1]**helter-skelter** /ˌheltəʳ 'skeltəʳ/ *adj or adv* (done) in a hurried and disorderly manner

[2]**helter-skelter** /ˌheltəʳ 'skeltəʳ/ *n* a spiral slide at a fairground

[1]**hem** /hem/ *n* **1** the border of a cloth article when turned back and stitched down; *esp* the bottom edge of a garment finished in this manner **2** a similar border on an article of plastic, leather, etc

[2]**hem** *v* **1a** to finish (e g a skirt) with a hem **b** to border, edge **2** to enclose, confine – usu + *in* or *about* **3** to make a hem in sewing

he-man *n* a strong virile man – infml

hemisphere /'hem$\frac{1}{3}$sfɪəʳ/ *n* **1a** a half of the celestial sphere when divided into 2 halves by the horizon, the celestial equator, or the ecliptic **b** the northern or southern half of the earth divided by the equator or the eastern or western half divided by a meridian **2** either of the 2 half spheres formed by a plane that passes through the sphere's centre

hemline /'hemlaɪn/ *n* the line formed by the lower hemmed edge of a garment, esp a dress

hemlock /'hemlɒk/ *n* **1** (a poison obtained from) a very tall plant of the carrot family or a related very poisonous plant **2** (the soft light wood of) any of a genus of evergreen coniferous trees of the pine family

hemp /hemp/ *n* **1** (marijuana, hashish, or a similar drug obtained from) a tall widely cultivated plant from which a tough fibre used esp for making rope is prepared **2** the fibre of hemp or (a plant yielding) a similar fibre (e g jute)

[1]**hen** /hen/ *n* **1a** a female bird, specif a domestic fowl (over a year old) **b** a female lobster, crab, fish, or other aquatic animal **2** an esp fussy woman – infml **3** *chiefly Scot* dear – used to girls and women

[2]**hen** *adj* relating to or intended for women only

henbane /'henbeɪn/ *n* a poisonous fetid Old World plant of the nightshade family

hence /hens/ *adv* **1** from this time; later than now **2** because of a preceding fact or premise **3** from here; away – fml; sometimes + *from;* sometimes used as an interjection

henceforth /ˌhens'fɔːθ, 'hensfɔːθ/ *adv* from this time or point on

henchman /'hentʃmən/ *n* **1** a trusted follower; a right-hand man **2** a follower whose support is chiefly for personal advantage

[1]**henna** /'henə/ *n* **1** an Old World tropical shrub or small tree with fragrant white flowers **2** a reddish brown dye obtained from the leaves of the henna plant and used esp on hair

henpecked /'henpekt/ *adj* cowed by persistent nagging

hepatic /hɪ'pætɪk/ *adj* of or resembling the liver

hepatitis /ˌhepə'taɪt$\frac{1}{3}$s/ *n* (a condition marked by) inflammation of the liver

Hepplewhite /'hepəlwaɪt/ *adj* of or being a late 18th-c English furniture style characterized by lightness, elegance, and graceful curves

¹her /əʳ, həʳ; *strong* hɜːʳ/ *adj* of her or herself, esp as possessor, agent, or object of an action – used in titles of females (e g *her* Majesty)

²her *pron, objective case of* **she** (e g older than *her*; that's *her*)

herald /ˈherəld/ *n* **1a** an officer whose original duties of officiating at tournaments gave rise to other duties (e g recording names, pedigrees, and coats of arms or tracing genealogies) **b** an official messenger between leaders, esp in war **2a** an official crier or messenger **b** sby or sthg that conveys news or proclaims **3** a harbinger, forerunner

heraldry /ˈherəldri/ *n* **1** the system, originating in medieval times, of identifying individuals by hereditary insignia; *also* the practice of granting, classifying, and creating these **2** the study of the history, display, and description of heraldry and heraldic insignia **3** pageantry – **-dic** *adj*

herb /hɜːb/ *n* **1** a seed plant that does not develop permanent woody tissue and dies down at the end of a growing season **2** a plant (part) valued for its medicinal, savoury, or aromatic qualities

herbaceous /həˈbeɪʃəs/ *adj* of, being, or having the characteristics of a (part of a) herb

herbalist /ˈhɜːbəlɨ̣st/ *n* sby who grows or sells herbs, esp for medicines

herbivore /ˈhɜːbɪvɔːʳ/ *n* a plant-eating animal – **-vorous** *adj*

herculean /ˌhɜːkjʊˈliːən, hɜːˈkjuːlɪən/ *adj* of extraordinary strength, size, or difficulty

¹herd /hɜːd/ *n* **1** a number of animals of 1 kind kept together or living as a group **2a** *sing or pl in constr* a group of people usu having a common bond – often derog **b** *the* masses – derog

²herd *v* **1** to keep or move (animals) together **2** to gather, lead, or drive as if in a herd

herdsman /ˈhɜːdzmən/ *n* a manager, breeder, or tender of livestock

¹here /hɪəʳ/ *adv* **1** in or at this place – often interjectional, esp in answering a roll call **2** at or in this point or particular (e g *here* we agree) **3** to this place or position (e g come *here*) **4** – used when introducing, offering, or drawing attention (e g *here* she comes) **5** – used interjectionally to attract attention

²here *adj* **1** – used for emphasis, esp after a demonstrative (e g this book *here*) **2** – used for emphasis between a demonstrative and the following noun; substandard (e g this *here* book)

³here *n* this place or point

hereabouts /ˌhɪərəˈbaʊts, ˈhɪərəbaʊts/ *adv* in this vicinity

¹hereafter /ˌhɪərˈɑːftəʳ/ *adv* **1** after this **2** in some future time or state

²hereafter /hɪərˈɑːftəʳ/ *n, often cap* **1** *the* future **2** an existence beyond earthly life

hereby /ˌhɪəˈbaɪ, ˈhɪəbaɪ/ *adv* by this means or pronouncement

hereditary /hɨ̣ˈredɨ̣təri/ *adj* **1a** genetically transmitted or transmissible from parent to offspring **b** characteristic of one's predecessors; ancestral **2a** received or passing by inheritance **b** having title through inheritance **3** traditional **4** of inheritance or heredity – **-rily** *adv*

heredity /hɨ̣ˈredɨ̣ti/ *n* **1** the sum of the qualities and potentialities genetically derived from one's ancestors **2** the transmission of qualities from ancestor to descendant through a mechanism lying primarily in the chromosomes

heresy /ˈherɨ̣si/ *n* **1** (adherence to) a religious belief or doctrine contrary to or incompatible with an explicit church dogma **2** an opinion or doctrine contrary to generally accepted belief

heretic /ˈherɨ̣tɪk/ *n* **1** a dissenter from established church dogma; *esp* a baptized member of the Roman Catholic church who disavows a revealed truth **2** one who dissents from an accepted belief or doctrine – **~al** *adj* – **~ally** *adv*

herewith /ˌhɪəˈwɪð/ *adv* **1** hereby **2** with this; enclosed in this – fml

heritable /ˈherɨ̣təbl/ *adj* **1** capable of being inherited **2** hereditary

heritage /ˈherɨ̣tɪdʒ/ *n* **1** sthg transmitted by or acquired from a predecessor; a legacy **2** a birthright

hermaphrodite /hɜːˈmæfrədaɪt/ *n* **1**

an animal or plant having both male and female reproductive organs **2** sthg that is a combination of 2 usu opposing elements – **-ditic** *adj*

hermetic /hɜːˈmetɪk/ *also* **hermetical** *adj* **1** *often cap* of or relating to the Gnostic and alchemical writings attributed to Hermes Trismegistus **2a** airtight **b** impervious to external influences **3** *often cap* abstruse, obscure – infml – **~ally** *adv*

hermit /ˈhɜːmɪ̥t/ *n* **1** one who retires from society and lives in solitude, esp for religious reasons **2** a recluse

hermitage /ˈhɜːmɪ̥tɪdʒ/ *n* **1** the habitation of one or more hermits **2** a secluded residence or private retreat; a hideaway

hernia /ˈhɜːnɪə/ *n, pl* **hernias, herniae** a protrusion of (part of) an organ through a wall of its enclosing cavity (e g the abdomen)

hero /ˈhɪərəʊ/ *fem* **heroine** /ˈherəʊɪn/ *n, pl* **heroes** **1a** a mythological or legendary figure often of divine descent endowed with great strength or ability **b** an illustrious warrior **c** a person, esp a man, admired for noble achievements and qualities (e g courage) **2** the principal (male) character in a literary or dramatic work

heroic /hɪˈrəʊɪk/ *also* **heroical** *adj* **1** of or befitting heroes **2a** showing or marked by courage **b** grand, noble – **~ally** *adv*

heroics /hɪˈrəʊɪks/ *n pl* extravagantly grand behaviour or language

heroin /ˈherəʊɪn/ *n* a strongly physiologically addictive narcotic made from, but more potent than, morphine

heroism /ˈherəʊɪzəm/ *n* heroic conduct or qualities; *esp* extreme courage

heron /ˈherən/ *n* any of various long-necked long-legged wading birds with a long tapering bill, large wings, and soft plumage

herpes /ˈhɜːpiːz/ *n* an inflammatory virus disease of the skin and esp the genitals

herring /ˈherɪŋ/ *n, pl* **herring,** *esp for different types* **herrings** a N Atlantic food fish that is preserved in the adult state by smoking or salting

¹herringbone /ˈherɪŋbəʊn/ *n* (sthg arranged in) a pattern made up of rows of parallel lines with any 2 adjacent rows slanting in opposite directions; *esp* a twilled fabric decorated with this pattern

²herringbone *v* **1** to make a herringbone pattern on **2** to ascend a (snow) slope by pointing the toes of the skis out

hers /hɜːz/ *pron, pl* **hers** that which or the one who belongs to her – used without a following noun as a pronoun equivalent in meaning to the adjective *her* (e g the car is *hers*)

herself /əˈself, hə-; *strong* hɜː-/ *pron* **1** that identical female person or creature used reflexively, for emphasis, or in absolute constructions (e g *herself* an orphan, she understood the situation) **2** her normal self (e g isn't quite *herself*)

hertz /hɜːts/ *n, pl* **hertz** the SI unit of frequency equal to 1 cycle per second

hesitant /ˈhezɪ̥tənt/ *adj* tending to hesitate; irresolute – **~ly** *adv*

hesitate /ˈhezɪ̥teɪt/ *v* **1** to hold back, esp in doubt or indecision **2** to be reluctant or unwilling *to* **3** to stammer – **-tating** *adj* – **-tion** *n*

hessian /ˈhesɪən/ *n* **1** a coarse heavy plain-weave fabric, usu of jute or hemp, used esp for sacking **2** a lightweight material resembling hessian and used chiefly in interior decoration

heterogeneous /ˌhetərəʊˈdʒiːnɪəs/ *adj* consisting of dissimilar ingredients or constituents; disparate – **~ly** *adv* – **-neity** *n*

heterosexual /ˌhetərəˈsekʃʊəl/ *adj or n* (of or being) sby having a sexual preference for members of the opposite sex – **~ly** *adv* – **~ity** *n*

het up /ˌhet ˈʌp/ *adj* highly excited; upset – infml

hew /hjuː/ *v* **hewed; hewed, hewn** **1** to strike, chop, or esp fell with blows of a heavy cutting instrument **2** to give form or shape to (as if) with heavy cutting blows – often + *out*

hexagon /ˈheksəgən/ *n* a polygon of 6 angles and 6 sides – **~al** *adj*

hexagram /ˈheksəgræm/ *n* a 6-pointed star drawn by extending the sides of a regular hexagon

hey /heɪ/ *interj* – used esp to call attention or to express inquiry, surprise, or exultation

heyday /ˈheɪdeɪ/ *n* the period of one's greatest vigour, prosperity, or fame

hey presto /heɪ ˈprestəʊ/ *interj* – used as an expression of triumph or satisfaction on completing or demonstrating sthg; *esp* used by conjurers about to reveal the outcome of a trick

hi /haɪ/ *interj* – used esp to attract attention or, esp in the USA, as a greeting

[1]**hiatus** /haɪˈeɪtəs/ *n* **1a** a break, gap **b** an (abnormal) anatomical gap or passage **2** a lapse in continuity

[2]**hiatus** *adj* **1** involving a hiatus **2** *of a hernia* protruding upwards through the diaphragm

hibernate /ˈhaɪbəneɪt/ *v* **1** to pass the winter in a torpid or resting state **2** to be or become inactive or dormant – **-nation** *n*

hibiscus /haɪˈbɪskəs, hɪ-/ *n* any of a genus of herbaceous plants, shrubs, or small trees of the mallow family with large showy flowers

hiccup, hiccough /ˈhɪkʌp, -kəp/ *n* **1** an involuntary spasmodic intake of breath with a characteristic sound **2** a snag, hitch – **hiccup** *v*

hickory /ˈhɪkəri/ *n* (the usu tough pale wood of) any of a genus of N American hardwood trees of the walnut family that often have sweet edible nuts

[1]**hide** /haɪd/ *v* **hid; hidden, hid 1** to put out of sight; conceal **2** to keep secret **3** to screen from view **4** to conceal oneself **5** to remain out of sight – often + *out*

[2]**hide** *n, chiefly Br* a camouflaged hut or other shelter used for observation, esp of wildlife or game

[3]**hide** *n* the raw or dressed skin of an animal – used esp with reference to large heavy skins

hide-and-seek *n* a children's game in which one player covers his/her eyes and then hunts for the other players who have hidden themselves

hidebound /ˈhaɪdbaʊnd/ *adj* narrow or inflexible in character

hideous /ˈhɪdɪəs/ *adj* **1** offensive to the senses, esp the sight; exceedingly ugly **2** morally offensive; shocking – **~ly** *adv* – **~ness** *n*

[1]**hiding** /ˈhaɪdɪŋ/ *n* a state or place of concealment

[2]**hiding** *n* a beating, thrashing; *also* a severe defeat – infml

hie /haɪ/ *v* **hying, hieing** *archaic* to hurry

hierarchy /ˈhaɪərɑːki/ *n* **1** (church government by) a body of clergy organized according to rank, specif the bishops of a province or nation **2** a graded or ranked series – **-chical** *adj* – **-chically** *adv*

hieroglyph /ˈhaɪərəˌglɪf/ *n* a pictorial character used in some writing systems (e g by the ancient Egyptians) – **~ic** *adj* – **~ics** *n*

hi-fi /ˈhaɪ faɪ, ˌhaɪ ˈfaɪ/ *n* **1** high fidelity **2** equipment for the high-fidelity reproduction of sound *USE* infml

higgledy-piggledy /ˌhɪgəldi ˈpɪgəldi/ *adv* in confusion; topsy-turvy – infml

[1]**high** /haɪ/ *adj* **1a** extending upwards for a considerable or above average distance **b** situated at a considerable height above a base (e g the ground) **c** *of physical activity* extending to or from, or taking place at a considerable height above, a base (e g the ground or water) **d** having a specified elevation; tall – often in combination **2** at the period of culmination or fullest development **3** elevated in pitch **4** relatively far from the equator **5** *of meat, esp game* slightly decomposed or tainted **6a** exalted in character; noble **b** good, favourable **7** of greater degree, amount, cost, value, or content than average **8a** foremost in rank, dignity, or standing **b** critical, climactic **c** marked by sublime or heroic events or subject matter **9** forcible, strong **10a** showing elation or excitement **b** intoxicated by alcohol or a drug **11** advanced in complexity, development, or elaboration **13** *of a gear* designed for fast speed

[2]**high** *adv* at or to a high place, altitude, or degree

[3]**high** *n* **1** a region of high atmospheric pressure **2** a high point or level; a height

high-and-mighty *adj* arrogant, imperious

highborn /'haɪbɔːn/ *adj* of noble birth

highbrow /'haɪbraʊ/ *adj* dealing with, possessing, or having pretensions to superior intellectual and cultural interests or activities

high chair *n* a child's chair with long legs, a footrest, and usu a feeding tray

high-class *adj* superior, first-class

high commissioner *n* a principal commissioner; *esp* an ambassadorial representative of one Commonwealth country stationed in another

High Court *n* the lower branch of the Supreme Court of Judicature of England and Wales

higher education *n* education beyond the secondary level, at a college or university

highfalutin /ˌhaɪfə'luːtɪn/ *adj* pretentious, pompous – infml

high fidelity *n* the faithful reproduction of sound

high-flier, high-flyer *n* a person of extreme ambition or outstanding promise

high-handed *adj* overbearingly arbitrary – **~ly** *adv* – **~ness** *n*

high jump *n* (an athletic field event consisting of) a jump for height over a bar suspended between uprights

highland /'haɪlənd/ *n* high or mountainous land – usu pl with sing. meaning

Highland /'haɪlənd/ *adj* relating to or being a member of a shaggy long-haired breed of hardy beef cattle

Highland fling *n* a lively solo Scottish folk dance

high-level *adj* **1** occurring, done, or placed at a high level **2** of high importance or rank

high life *n* luxurious living associated with the rich

[1]**highlight** /'haɪlaɪt/ *n* **1** the lightest spot or area (e g in a painting or photograph) **2** an event or detail of special significance or interest **3** a contrasting brighter part in the hair or on the face that reflects or gives the appearance of reflecting light

[2]**highlight** *v* **1** to focus attention on; emphasize **2** to emphasize (e g a figure) with light tones in painting, photography, etc

highly /'haɪli/ *adv* **1** to a high degree; extremely **2** with approval; favourably

highly-strung, high-strung *adj* extremely nervous or sensitive

high-minded *adj* having or marked by elevated principles and feelings – **~ly** *adv* – **~ness** *n*

Highness /'haɪnɪ̈s/ *n* – used as a title for a person of exalted rank (e g a king or prince)

high-powered *adj* having great drive, energy, or capacity; dynamic

high-pressure *adj* **1** having or involving a (comparatively) high pressure, esp greatly exceeding that of the atmosphere **2a** using, involving, or being aggressive and insistent sales techniques **b** imposing or involving severe strain or tension

high priest *n* **1** a chief priest, esp of the ancient Jewish priesthood **2** the head or chief exponent of a movement

high-rise *adj* (situated in a building) constructed with a large number of storeys

highroad /'haɪrəʊd/ *n, chiefly Br* a main road

high school *n, chiefly Br* a secondary school; *esp* a grammar school – now chiefly in names

high-spirited *adj* characterized by a bold or lively spirit; *also* highly-strung

high street *n, Br* a main or principal street, esp containing shops

high tea *n, Br* a fairly substantial early evening meal (at which tea is served)

high-tension *adj* having a high voltage; *also* relating to apparatus to be used at high voltage

high-water mark *n* **1** a mark showing the highest level reached by the surface of a body of water **2** the highest point or stage

highway /'haɪweɪ/ *n* a public way; *esp* a main direct road

highway code *n, often cap H&C, Br* the official code of rules and advice for the safe use of roads

highwayman /'haɪweɪmən/ *n* a

(mounted) robber of travellers on a road, esp in former times

hijack /'haɪdʒæk/ *v* **1a** to stop and steal from (a vehicle in transit) **b** to seize control of, and often divert, (a means of transport) by force **2** to steal, rob, or kidnap as if by hijacking – **hijack** *n* – **~er** *n* – **~ing** *n*

[1]**hike** /haɪk/ *v* to go on a hike – **hiker** *n* – **hiking** *n*

[2]**hike** *n* **1** a long walk in the country, esp for pleasure or exercise **2** *chiefly NAm* an increase or rise

hilarious /hɪ'leərɪəs/ *adj* marked by or causing hilarity – **~ly** *adv* – **~ness** *n*

hilarity /hɪ'lærəti/ *n* mirth, merriment

[1]**hill** /hɪl/ *n* **1** a usu rounded natural rise of land lower than a mountain **2** an artificial heap or mound (e g of earth) **3** an esp steep slope

[2]**hill** *v* to draw earth round the roots or base of (plants)

hillbilly /'hɪl,bɪli/ *n, chiefly NAm* a person from a remote or culturally unsophisticated area

hillock /'hɪlək/ *n* a small hill

hilt /hɪlt/ *n* a handle, esp of a sword or dagger

him /ɪm; *strong* hɪm/ *pron, objective case of* **he** (e g threw it at *him*, it's *him*)

himself /ɪm'self; *strong* hɪm-/ *pron* **1a** that identical male person or creature used reflexively, for emphasis, or in absolute constructions (e g *himself* a rich man, he knew the pitfalls) **b** – used reflexively when the sex of the antecedent is unspecified (e g everyone must fend for *himself*) **2** his normal self (e g isn't quite *himself*)

[1]**hind** /haɪnd/ *n, pl* **hinds** *also* **hind** a female (red) deer

[2]**hind** *adj* situated at the back or behind; rear

[1]**hinder** /'hɪndəʳ/ *vt* **1** to retard or obstruct the progress of; hamper **2** to restrain, prevent – often + *from*

[2]**hinder** *adj* situated behind or at the rear; posterior

hindmost /'haɪndməʊst/ *adj* furthest to the rear; last

hindrance /'hɪndrəns/ *n* **1** the action of hindering **2** an impediment, obstacle

hindsight /'haɪndsaɪt/ *n* the grasp or picture of a situation that one has after it has occurred

Hindu /'hɪnduː, hɪn'duː/ *n* an adherent of Hinduism

Hinduism *n* the dominant religion of India which involves belief in the illusory nature of the physical universe and in cycles of reincarnation, and is associated with a caste system of social organization

[1]**hinge** /hɪndʒ/ *n* **1a** a jointed or flexible device on which a swinging part (e g a door or lid) turns **b** a flexible joint in which bones are held together by ligaments **c** a small piece of thin gummed paper used in fastening a postage stamp in an album **2** a point or principle on which sthg turns or depends

[2]**hinge** *v* **1** to attach by or provide with hinges **2** to hang or turn (as if) on a hinge **3** to depend or turn *on* a single consideration or point

[1]**hint** /hɪnt/ *n* **1** a brief practical suggestion or piece of advice **2** an indirect or veiled statement; an insinuation **3** a slight indication or trace; a suggestion – usu + *of*

[2]**hint** *v* **1** to indicate indirectly or by allusion **2** to give a hint

hinterland /'hɪntəlænd/ *n* **1** a region lying inland from a coast **2** a region remote from urban or cultural centres

[1]**hip** /hɪp/ *n* the ripened fruit of a rose

[2]**hip** *n* **1** the projecting region at each side of the lower or rear part of the mammalian trunk formed by the pelvis and upper part of the thigh; *also* the joint or socket where the thighbone articulates with the pelvis **2** an external angle between 2 adjacent sloping sides of a roof

[3]**hip** *adj* keenly aware of or interested in the newest developments; *broadly* trendy – infml

hip flask *n* a flat flask, usu for holding spirits, carried in a hip pocket

hippie, hippy /'hɪpi/ *n* a usu long-haired unconventionally dressed young person esp of anti-establishment and non violent views

Hippocratic oath /,hɪpəkrætɪk əʊθ/

n an oath embodying a code of medical ethics

hippodrome /ˈhɪpədrəʊm/ *n* **1** an arena for equestrian performances or circuses **2** a music hall, theatre, etc – esp in names

hippopotamus /ˌhɪpəˈpɒtəməs/ *n, pl* **hippopotamuses, hippopotami** any of several large plant-eating 4-toed chiefly aquatic mammals, with an extremely large head and mouth, very thick hairless skin, and short legs

hipster /ˈhɪpstəʳ/ *n* **1** sby who is unusually aware of and interested in new and unconventional patterns, esp in jazz **2** *pl* trousers that start from the hips rather than the waist

¹hire /haɪəʳ/ *n* **1** payment for the temporary use of sthg **2** hiring or being hired

²hire *v* **1a** to engage the services of for a set sum **b** to engage the temporary use of for an agreed sum **2** to grant the services of or temporary use of for a fixed sum

hireling /ˈhaɪəlɪŋ/ *n* a person who works for payment, esp for purely mercenary motives – derog

hire purchase *n, chiefly Br* a system of paying for goods by instalments

hirsute /ˈhɜːsjuːt, -ˈ-/ *adj* covered with (coarse stiff) hairs

¹his /ɪz; *strong* hɪz/ *adj* **1** of him or himself, esp as possessor, agent, or object of an action – used in titles of females (e g *her* Majesty)

²his /hɪz/ *pron, pl* **his** that which or the one who belongs to him – used without a following noun as a pronoun equivalent in meaning to the adjective *his* (e g the house is *his*)

hiss /hɪs/ *v* **1** to make a sharp voiceless sound like a prolonged *s*, esp in disapproval **2** to show disapproval of by hissing – **hiss** *n*

histogram /ˈhɪstəgræm/ *n* a diagram consisting of a series of adjacent rectangles, the height and width of each rectangle being varied to represent each of 2 variables

histology /hɪˈstɒlədʒi/ *n* (anatomy that deals with) the organization and microscopic structure of animal and plant tissues

historian /hɪˈstɔːrɪən/ *n* a student or writer of history

historic /hɪˈstɒrɪk/ *adj* **1** (likely to be) famous or important in history **2** *of a tense* expressive of past time

historic present *n* the present tense used to relate past events

history /ˈhɪstəri/ *n* **1** (a chronological record of) significant past events **2a** a treatise presenting systematically related natural phenomena **b** an account of sby's medical, sociological, etc background **3** a branch of knowledge that records the past **4a** past events **b** an unusual or interesting past **c** previous treatment, handling, or experience – **-rical** *adj* – **-rically** *adv*

histrionic /ˌhɪstriˈɒnɪk/ *adj* **1** of actors, acting, or the theatre **2** deliberately affected; theatrical – **-ics** *n* – **~ally** *adv*

¹hit /hit/ *v* **hit** **1a** to reach (as if) with a blow; strike (a blow) **b** to make sudden forceful contact with **2a** to bring or come into contact (with) **b** to deliver, inflict **3** to have a usu detrimental effect or impact on **4** to discover or meet, esp by chance **5a** to reach, attain **b** to cause a propelled object to strike (e g a target), esp for a score in a contest **c** *of a batsman* to score (runs) in cricket; *also* to score runs off a ball bowled by (a bowler) **6** to indulge in, esp excessively **7** to arrive at or in **8** to rob – infml **9** *chiefly NAm* to kill – slang **10a** to attack **b** to happen or arrive, esp with sudden or destructive force **11** to come, esp by chance; arrive at or find sthg – + *on* or *upon*

²hit *n* **1** a blow; *esp* one that strikes its target **2a** a stroke of luck **b** sthg (e g a popular tune) that enjoys great success **3** a telling remark **4** a robbery **5** *chiefly NAm* an act of murder *USE* (*4 & 5*) slang

hit-and-run *adj* **1** being or involving a driver who does not stop after causing damage or injury **2** involving rapid action and immediate withdrawal

¹hitch /hɪtʃ/ *v* **1** to move by jerks **2** to catch or fasten (as if) by a hook or knot – often + *up* **3** to solicit and obtain (a free lift) in a passing vehicle

²hitch *n* **1** a sudden movement or pull;

a jerk **2** a sudden halt or obstruction; a stoppage **3** a knot used for a temporary fastening

hitchhike /'hɪtʃhaɪk/ *v* to travel by obtaining free lifts in passing vehicles – **-hiker** *n*

¹hither /'hɪðəʳ/ *adv* to or towards this place – fml

²hither *adj* being the closer of 2 or the left-hand member of a pair – fml

hitherto /ˌhɪðə'tuː/ *adv* up to this time; until now – fml

hit off *v* to represent or imitate accurately

hit-or-miss *adj* showing a lack of planning or forethought; haphazard

hit parade *n* a group or listing of popular songs ranked in order of the number of records of each sold

¹hive /haɪv/ *n* **1** (a structure for housing) a colony of bees **2** a place full of busy occupants

²hive *v* **1** to collect into a hive **2** *of bees* to enter and take possession of a hive

hive off *v* to separate or become separated from a group; form a separate or subsidiary unit

¹hoard /hɔːd/ *n* **1** an often secret supply (e g of money or food) stored up for preservation or future use **2** a cache of valuable archaeological remains

²hoard *v* to lay up a hoard (of) – **~er** *n*

hoarding /'hɔːdɪŋ/ *n* **1** a temporary fence put round a building site **2** *Br* a large board designed to carry outdoor advertising

hoarfrost /'hɔːfrɒst/ *n* a white frost

hoarse /hɔːs/ *adj* **1** rough or harsh in sound; grating **2** having a hoarse voice – **~ly** *adv* – **~ness** *n*

hoary /'hɔːri/ *adj* **1a** grey or white with age; *also* grey-haired **b** having greyish or whitish hair, down, or leaves **2** impressively or venerably old; ancient **3** hackneyed – **hoariness** *n*

¹hoax /həʊks/ *v* to play a trick on; deceive

²hoax *n* an act of deception; a trick – **~er** *n*

¹hob /hɒb/ *n, dial Br* a goblin, elf

²hob *n* **1** a ledge near a fireplace on which sthg may be kept warm **2** a horizontal surface either on a cooker or installed as a separate unit that contains heating areas on which pans are placed

¹hobble /'hɒbəl/ *v* **1** to move along unsteadily or with difficulty; *esp* to limp **2** to fasten together the legs of (e g a horse) to prevent straying; fetter

²hobble *n* sthg (e g a rope) used to hobble an animal

¹hobby /'hɒbi/ *n* a leisure activity or pastime engaged in for interest or recreation

²hobby *n* a small Old World falcon that catches small birds while in flight

hobbyhorse /'hɒbihɔːs/ *n* **1** a figure of a horse fastened round the waist of a performer in a morris dance **2a** a toy consisting of an imitation horse's head attached to one end of a stick on which a child can pretend to ride **b** a rocking horse **3** a topic to which one constantly returns

hobgoblin /hɒb'gɒblɪn, '---/ *n* **1** a goblin **2** a bugbear or bogey

hobnail /'hɒbneɪl/ *n* a short large-headed nail for studding shoe soles – **~ed** *adj*

hobnob /'hɒbnɒb/ *v* **1** to associate familiarly **2** to talk informally *USE* usu + *with*; infml

hobo /'həʊbəʊ/ *n, pl* **hoboes** *also* **hobos** **1** *chiefly NAm* a migratory worker **2** *NAm* a tramp

Hobson's choice /ˌhɒbsənz 'tʃɔɪs/ *n* an apparently free choice which offers no real alternative

¹hock /hɒk/ *n* the joint of the hind limb of a horse or related quadruped that corresponds to the ankle in human beings

²hock *n, often cap, chiefly Br* a dry to medium-dry or sometimes sweet white table wine produced in the Rhine valley

³hock *n* **1** pawn **2** debt **USE** infml; usu + *in*

⁴hock *v* to pawn – infml

hockey /'hɒki/ *n* **1** a game played on grass between 2 teams of usu 11 players whose object is to direct a ball into the opponents' goal with a stick that has a flat-faced blade **2** *NAm* ice hockey

hocus-pocus /ˌhəʊkəs 'pəʊkəs/ *n* **1**

sleight of hand **2** pointless activity or words, usu intended to obscure or deceive

hod /hɒd/ *n* **1** a trough mounted on a pole handle for carrying mortar, bricks, etc **2** a coal scuttle; *specif* a tall one used to shovel fuel directly onto a fire

[1]hoe /həʊ/ *n* any of various implements, esp one with a long handle and flat blade, used for tilling, weeding, etc

[2]hoe *v* **1** to weed or cultivate (land or a crop) with a hoe **2** to remove (weeds) by hoeing

[1]hog /hɒg/ *n* **1** a young unshorn sheep **2** a warthog or other wild pig **3** *Br* a castrated male pig raised for slaughter **4** a selfish, gluttonous, or filthy person – slang

[2]hog *v* to appropriate a selfish or excessive share of; monopolize – infml

Hogmanay /'hɒgmәneɪ/ *n, Scot* the eve of New Year's Day

hogshead /'hɒgzhed/ *n* **1** a large cask or barrel **2** any of several measures of capacity; *esp* a measure of 52½ imperial gallons (about 238l)

hogwash /'hɒgwɒʃ/ *n* **1** swill, slop **2** sthg worthless; *specif* meaningless talk – slang

hoi polloi /,hɔɪ pә'lɔɪ/ *n pl* *the* common people; *the* masses

[1]hoist /hɔɪst/ *v* to raise into position (as if) by means of tackle; *broadly* to raise

[2]hoist *n* an apparatus for hoisting

hoity-toity /,hɔɪti 'tɔɪti/ *adj* having an air of assumed importance; haughty – infml

[1]hold /həʊld/ *v* **held** **1a** to have in one's keeping; possess **b** to retain by force **c** to keep by way of threat or coercion **2a** to keep under control; check **b** to stop the action of temporarily; delay **c** to keep from advancing or from attacking successfully **d** to restrict, limit **e** to bind legally or morally **3a** to have, keep, or support in the hands or arms; grasp **b** to keep in a specified situation, position, or state **c** to support, sustain **d** to retain **e** to keep in custody **f** to set aside; reserve **4** to bear, carry **5a** to keep up without interruption; continue **b** to keep the uninterrupted interest or attention of **6a** to contain or be capable of containing **b** to have in store **7a** to consider to be true; believe **b** to have in regard **8a** to engage in with sby else or with others **b** to cause to be conducted; convene **9a** to occupy as a result of appointment or election **b** to have earned or been awarded **10a** to maintain position **b** to continue unchanged; last **11** to withstand strain without breaking or giving way **12** to bear or carry oneself **13** to be or remain valid; apply **14** to maintain a course; continue

[2]hold *n* **1a** a manner of grasping an opponent in wrestling **b** influence, control **c** possession **2** sthg that may be grasped as a support

[3]hold *n* **1** a space below a ship's deck in which cargo is stored **2** the cargo compartment of a plane

holdall /'həʊld-ɔːl/ *n* a bag or case for miscellaneous articles

hold back *v* **1** to hinder the progress of; restrain **2** to keep oneself in check

hold down *v* to hold and keep (a position of responsibility)

holder /'həʊldәʳ/ *n* **1** a device that holds an often specified object **2a** an owner **b** a tenant **c** a person in possession of and legally entitled to receive payment of a bill, note, or cheque

holding /'həʊldɪŋ/ *n* **1** land held **2** property (e g land or securities) owned – usu pl with sing. meaning

holding company *n* a company whose primary business is holding a controlling interest in the shares of other companies

hold off *v* **1** to resist successfully; withstand **2** to defer action; delay

hold on *v* **1** to persevere in difficult circumstances **2** to wait; hang on

hold out *v* **1** to last **2** to refuse to yield or give way

hold over *v* **1** to postpone **2** to prolong the engagement or tenure of

hold to *v* to (cause to) abide by

holdup /'həʊld-ʌp/ *n* **1** an armed robbery **2** a delay

hold up *v* **1** to delay, impede **2** to rob at gunpoint **3** to present, esp as an example **4** to endure a test

hold with *v* to agree with or approve of

[1]**hole** /həʊl/ *n* **1** an opening into or through a thing **2a** a hollow place; *esp* a pit or cavity **b** a deep place in a body of water **3** an animal's burrow **4** a serious flaw (e g in an argument) **5a** the unit of play from the tee to the hole in golf **b** a cavity in a putting green into which the ball is to be played in golf **6** a dirty or dingy place **7** an awkward position; a fix *USE* (*6 & 7*) infml

[2]**hole** *v* **1** to make a hole in **2** to drive into a hole **3** to make a hole in sthg

hole up *v* to take refuge or shelter *in USE* infml

[1]**holiday** /ˈhɒlɪ̈di/ *n* **1** a day, often in commemoration of some event, on which no paid employment is carried out **2** a period of relaxation or recreation spent away from home or work – often pl with sing. meaning

[2]**holiday** *v* to take or spend a holiday

holidaymaker /ˈhɒlɪ̈diˌmeɪkəʳ/ *n* a person who is on holiday

holiness /ˈhəʊlinɪ̈s/ *n* **1** *cap* – used as a title for various high religious dignitaries **2** sacredness

holler /ˈhɒləʳ/ *v, chiefly NAm* to call out or shout (sthg) – **holler** *n*

[1]**hollow** /ˈhɒləʊ/ *adj* **1a** having a recessed surface; sunken **b** curved inwards; concave **2** having a cavity within **3** echoing like a sound made in or by beating on an empty container; muffled **4a** deceptively lacking in real value or significance **b** lacking in truth or substance; deceitful – **~ly** *adv* – **~ness** *n*

[2]**hollow** *v* to make or become hollow

[3]**hollow** *n* **1** a depressed or hollow part of a surface; *esp* a small valley or basin **2** an unfilled space; a cavity

[4]**hollow** *adv* **1** in a hollow manner **2** completely, totally – infml

holly /ˈhɒli/ *n* (the foliage of) any of a genus of trees and shrubs with thick glossy spiny-edged leaves and usu bright red berries

hollyhock /ˈhɒlihɒk/ *n* a tall orig Chinese plant of the mallow family with large coarse rounded leaves and tall spikes of showy flowers

holocaust /ˈhɒləkɔːst/ *n* **1** a sacrificial offering consumed by fire **2** an instance of wholesale destruction or loss of life **3** *often cap the* genocidal persecution of the European Jews by Hitler and the Nazi party during WW II

holster /ˈhəʊlstəʳ/ *n* a usu leather holder for a pistol

holy /ˈhəʊli/ *adj* **1** set apart to the service of God or a god; sacred **2a** characterized by perfection and transcendence; commanding absolute adoration and reverence **b** spiritually pure; godly **3** terrible, awful – used as an intensive

Holy Communion *n* the sacrament of Communion

Holy Spirit *n the* 3rd person of the Trinity

Holy Week *n* the week before Easter during which the last days of Christ's life are commemorated

homage /ˈhɒmɪdʒ/ *n* **1a** a ceremony by which a man acknowledges himself the vassal of a lord **b** an act done or payment made by a vassal **2a** reverential regard; deference **b** flattering attention; tribute

homburg /ˈhɒmbɜːg/ *n* a felt hat with a stiff curled brim and a high crown creased lengthways

[1]**home** /həʊm/ *n* **1a** a family's place of residence; a domicile **b** a house **2** the social unit formed by a family living together **3a** a congenial environment **b** a habitat **4a** a place of origin; *also* one's native country **b** the place where sthg originates or is based **5** an establishment providing residence and often care for children, convalescents, etc – **~less** *adj* – **~lessness** *n*

[2]**home** *adv* **1** to or at home **2** to a final, closed, or standard position (e g drive a nail *home*) **3** to an ultimate objective (e g a finishing line) **4** to a vital sensitive core (e g the truth struck *home*)

[3]**home** *adj* **1** of or being a home, place of origin, or base of operations **2** prepared, carried out, or designed for use in the home **3** operating or occurring in a home area

[4]**home** *v* **1** to go or return home **2** *of an animal* to return accurately to one's home or birthplace from a distance **3** to be directed *in on* a target

home brew *n* an alcoholic drink (e g beer) made at home – **~ed** *adj*

homecoming /ˈhəʊm,kʌmɪŋ/ *n* a returning home

homegrown /,həʊmˈgrəʊn/ *adj* produced in, coming from, or characteristic of the home country or region

homeland /ˈhəʊmlænd, -lənd/ *n* **1** one's native land **2** a tribal state in South Africa

homely /ˈhəʊmli/ *adj* **1** commonplace, familiar **2** of a sympathetic character; kindly **3** simple, unpretentious **4** not good-looking; plain – **-liness** *n*

homemade /,həʊmˈmeɪd/ *adj* made in the home, on the premises, or by one's own efforts

home office *n, often cap H&O the* government office concerned with internal affairs

Homeric /həʊˈmerɪk/ *adj* **1** (characteristic) of Homer, his age, or his writings **2** of epic proportions; heroic

home rule *n* limited self-government by the people of a dependent political unit

homesick /ˈhəʊm,sɪk/ *adj* longing for home and family while absent from them – **~ness** *n*

homespun *adj* lacking sophistication; simple

homestead /ˈhəʊmsted, -stɪ̈d/ *n* a house and adjoining land occupied by a family

home truth *n* an unpleasant but true fact about a person's character or situation – often pl

homeward /ˈhəʊmwəd/ *adj* being or going towards home

homewards /ˈhəʊmwədz/ *adv* towards home

homework /ˈhəʊmwɜːk/ *n* **1** work done in one's own home for pay **2** an assignment given to a pupil to be completed esp away from school **3** preparatory reading or research (e g for a discussion)

homicide /ˈhɒmɪ̈saɪd/ *n* (the act of) sby who kills another

homing pigeon *n* a domesticated pigeon trained to return home

homoeopathy /,həʊmiˈɒpəθi/ *n* a system of disease treatment relying on the administration of minute doses of a substance that in larger doses produces symptoms like those of the disease – **-path** *n*

homogeneous /,həʊməˈdʒiːnɪəs/ *adj* **1** of the same or a similar kind or nature **2** of uniform structure or composition throughout – **-neity** *n* – **~ly** *adv* – **-nize** *v*

Homo sapiens /,hɒməʊ ˈsæpienz/ *n* mankind

homosexual /,heʊməˈsekʃʊəl/ *adj or n* (of, for, or being) sby having a sexual preference for members of his/her own sex

hone /həʊn/ *v or n* (to sharpen or make more keen or effective with or as if with) a stone for sharpening a cutting tool

honest /ˈɒnɪ̈st/ *adj* **1** free from fraud or deception; legitimate, truthful **2** respectable or worthy **3a** marked by integrity **b** frank, sincere – **~y** *n*

honestly /ˈɒnɪ̈stli/ *adv* to speak in an honest way

honey /ˈhʌni/ *n* **1** (a pale golden colour like that typical of) a sweet viscous sticky liquid formed from the nectar of flowers in the honey sac of various bees **2** sthg sweet or agreeable; sweetness **3** a superlative example – chiefly infml

honeybee /ˈhʌnibiː/ *n* (a social honey-producing bee related to) a European bee kept for its honey and wax

¹honeycomb /ˈhʌnikəʊm/ *n* (sthg resembling in shape or structure) a mass of 6-sided wax cells built by honeybees in their nest to contain their brood and stores of honey

²honeycomb *v* **1** to cause to be chequered or full of cavities like a honeycomb **2** to penetrate into every part; riddle

honeydew /ˈhʌnidjuː/ *n* a sweet deposit secreted on the leaves of plants usu by aphids

honeyed *also* **honied** /ˈhʌnid/ *adj* sweetened (as if) with honey

honeymoon /ˈhʌnimuːn/ *n* **1** the period immediately following marriage, esp when taken as a holiday by the married couple **2** a period of unusual harmony following the establishment of a new relationship

honeysuckle /ˈhʌni,sʌkəl/ *n* any of a genus of (climbing) shrubs usu with showy sweet-smelling flowers rich in nectar

[1]**honk** /hɒŋk/ *n* (a sound made by a car's electric horn like) the short loud unmusical tone that is the characteristic cry of the goose

[2]**honk** *v* to (cause to) make a honk

honorary /ˈɒnərəri/ *adj* **1a** conferred or elected in recognition of achievement, without the usual obligations **b** unpaid, voluntary **2** depending on honour for fulfilment

[1]**honour** /ˈɒnəʳ/ *n* **1a** good name or public esteem **b** outward respect; recognition **2** a privilege **3** *cap* a person of superior social standing – now used esp as a title for a holder of high office (e g a judge in court) **4** one who brings respect or fame **5** a mark or symbol of distinction: e g **a** an exalted title or rank **b** a ceremonial rite or observance – usu pl **6** *pl* a course of study for a university degree more exacting and specialized than that leading to a pass degree **7** (a woman's) chastity or purity **8a** a high standard of ethical conduct; integrity **b** one's word given as a pledge

[2]**honour** *v* **1a** to regard or treat with honour or respect **b** to confer honour on **2a** to live up to or fulfil the terms of **b** to accept and pay when due

honourable /ˈɒnərəbl/ *adj* **1** worthy of honour **2** performed or accompanied with marks of honour or respect **3** entitled to honour – used as a title for the children of certain British noblemen and for various government officials **4a** bringing credit to the possessor or doer **b** consistent with blameless reputation **5** characterized by (moral) integrity – **-bly** *adv*

hooch /huːtʃ/ *n* spirits, esp when inferior or illicitly made or obtained – slang

[1]**hood** /hʊd/ *n* **1a** a loose often protective covering for the top and back of the head and neck that is usu attached to the neckline of a garment **b** a usu leather covering for a hawk's head and eyes **2a** an ornamental scarf worn over an academic gown that indicates by its colour the wearer's university and degree **b** a hoodlike marking, crest, or expansion on the head of an animal (e g a cobra or seal) **3a** a folding waterproof top cover for an open car, pram, etc **b** a cover or canopy for carrying off fumes, smoke, etc

[2]**hood** *n* a hoodlum or gangster – infml

hooded /ˈhʊdɪ̣d/ *adj* **1** covered (as if) by a hood **2** shaped like a hood

hoodlum /ˈhuːdləm/ *n* **1** a (violent) thug **2** a young rowdy

hoodwink /ˈhʊd,wɪŋk/ *v* to deceive, delude – chiefly infml

hooey /ˈhuːi/ *n* nonsense – slang

[1]**hoof** /huːf/ *n, pl* **hooves, hoofs** (a foot with) a curved horny casing that protects the ends of the digits of a horse, cow, or similar mammal and that corresponds to a nail or claw

[2]**hoof** *v* **1** to kick **2** to go on foot – usu + *it* ***USE*** infml

hoo-ha /ˈhuː hɑː/ *n* a fuss, to-do – chiefly infml

[1]**hook** /hʊk/ *n* **1** (sthg shaped like) a curved or bent device for catching, holding, or pulling **2a** (a flight of) a ball in golf that deviates from a straight course in a direction opposite to the dominant hand of the player propelling it **b** an attacking stroke in cricket played with a horizontal bat aimed at a ball of higher than waist height and intended to send the ball on the leg side **3** a short blow delivered in boxing with a circular motion while the elbow remains bent and rigid

[2]**hook** *v* **1** to form (into a) hook (shape) **2** to seize, make fast, or connect (as if) by a hook **3** to hit or throw (a ball) so that a hook results **4** to become hooked

hookah /ˈhʊkə/ *n* a water pipe (with a single flexible tube by which smoke is drawn through water and into the mouth)

hooked /hʊkt/ *adj* **1** (shaped) like or provided with a hook **2a** addicted to drugs – slang **b** very enthusiastic or compulsively attached (to sthg specified) – infml

hooker /ˈhʊkəʳ/ *n* **1** (the position of) a player in rugby stationed in the middle of the front row of the scrum **2** a woman prostitute – slang

hookup /ˈhʊkʌp/ *n* (the plan of) a combination (e g of electronic circuits) used for a specific often temporary purpose (e g radio transmission)

hooky, hookey /ˈhʊki/ *n* truant – usu in *play hooky*

hooligan /ˈhuːlɪ̈gən/ *n* a young ruffian or hoodlum – **~ism** *n*

[1]**hoop** /huːp/ *n* **1** a large (rigid) circular strip used esp for holding together the staves of containers, as a child's toy, or to expand a woman's skirt **2** a circular figure or object **3** an arch through which balls must be hit in croquet

[2]**hoop** *v* to bind or fasten (as if) with a hoop

hoop-la /ˈhuːp lɑː/ *n* a (fairground) game in which prizes are won by tossing rings over them

hooray /hʊˈreɪ/ *interj* hurray

[1]**hoot** /huːt/ *v* **1** to utter a loud shout, usu in contempt **2a** to make (a sound similar to) the long-drawn-out throat noise of an owl **b** to sound the horn, whistle, etc of a motor car or other vehicle **3** to laugh loudly – infml

[2]**hoot** *n* **1** a sound of hooting **2** a damn **3** a source of laughter or amusement *USE* (*2, 3*) infml

hooter /ˈhuːtəʳ/ *n, chiefly Br* **1** a device (e g the horn of a car) for producing a loud hooting noise **2** the nose – infml

hoover /ˈhuːvəʳ/ *v* to clean using a vacuum cleaner

Hoover /ˈhuːvəʳ/ *trademark* – used for a vacuum cleaner

[1]**hop** /hɒp/ *v* **1** to move by a quick springy leap or in a series of leaps; *esp* to jump on 1 foot **2** to make a quick trip, esp by air **3** to board or leave a vehicle **4** to jump over

[2]**hop** *n* **1a** a short leap, esp on 1 leg **b** a bounce, a rebound **2** a short or long flight between 2 landings **3** a dance – infml

[3]**hop** *n* **1** a climbing plant of the hemp family with inconspicuous green flowers of which the female ones are in cone-shaped catkins **2** *pl* the ripe dried catkins of a hop used esp to impart a bitter flavour to beer

[1]**hope** /həʊp/ *v* **1** to wish or long for with expectation of fulfilment **2** to expect with desire; trust

[2]**hope** *n* **1** trust, reliance **2a** desire accompanied by expectation of or belief in fulfilment **b** sby or sthg on which hopes are centred **c** sthg hoped for

[1]**hopeful** /ˈhəʊpfəl/ *adj* **1** full of hope **2** inspiring hope – **~ness** *n*

[2]**hopeful** *n* a person who aspires to or is likely to succeed

hopefully /ˈhəʊpfəli/ *adv* **1** in a hopeful manner **2** it is hoped – disapproved of by some speakers

hopeless /ˈhəʊplɪ̈s/ *adj* **1** having no expectation of success **2a** giving no grounds for hope **b** incapable of solution, management, or accomplishment **3** incompetent, useless – chiefly infml – **~ly** *adv* – **~ness** *n*

hopper /ˈhɒpəʳ/ *n* **1** a (funnel-shaped) receptacle for the discharging or temporary storage of grain, coal, etc **2** a goods wagon with a floor through which bulk materials may be discharged

hopscotch /ˈhɒpskɒtʃ/ *n* a children's game in which a player tosses an object (e g a stone) into areas of a figure outlined on the ground and hops through the figure and back to regain the object

horde /hɔːd/ *n* **1** a (Mongolian) nomadic people or tribe **2** a crowd, swarm

horizon /həˈraɪzən/ *n* **1a** the apparent junction of earth and sky **b(1)** the plane that is tangent to the earth's surface at an observer's position **(2)** (the great circle formed by the intersection with the celestial sphere of) the plane parallel to such a plane but passing through the earth's centre **2** range of perception, experience, or knowledge

horizontal /ˌhɒrɪ̈ˈzɒntl/ *adj* **1a** near the horizon **b** in the plane of or (operating in a plane) parallel to the horizon or a base line; level **2** of or concerning relationships between people of the same rank in different hierarchies – **~ly** *adv*

hormone /ˈhɔːməʊn/ *n* (a synthetic substance with the action of) a product of living cells that usu circulates in body liquids (e g the blood or sap) and produces a specific effect on the activity of cells remote from its point of origin

horn /hɔːn/ *n* **1a(1)** any of the usu paired bony projecting parts on the head of cattle, giraffes, deer, and similar hoofed mammals and some extinct mammals and reptiles (2) a permanent solid pointed part attached to the nasal bone of a rhinoceros **b** a natural projection from an animal (e g a snail or owl) resembling or suggestive of a horn **c** the tough fibrous material consisting chiefly of keratin that covers or forms the horns and hooves of cattle and related animals, or other hard parts (e g claws or nails) **d** a hollow horn used as a container **2** sthg resembling or suggestive of a horn; *esp* either of the curved ends of a crescent **3a** an animal's horn used as a wind instrument **b(1)** a hunting horn **(2)** a French horn **c** a wind instrument used in a jazz band; *esp* a trumpet **d** a device (e g on a motor car) for making loud warning noises – **~like, ~ed** *adj*

hornet /'hɔːnɨt/ *n* a large wasp with a black and yellow banded abdomen and a powerful sting

hornet's nest *n* an angry or hostile reaction – esp in *stir up a hornet's nest*

hornpipe /'hɔːnpaɪp/ *n* (a piece of music for) a lively British folk dance typically associated with sailors

horny /'hɔːni/ *adj* **1** (made) of horn **2** sexually aroused – slang

horology /hɒ'rɒlədʒi/ *n* **1** the science of measuring time **2** the art of constructing instruments for indicating time

horoscope /'hɒrəskəʊp/ *n* (an astrological forecast based on) a diagram of the relative positions of planets and signs of the zodiac at a specific time, esp sby's birth, used by astrologers to infer individual character and personality traits and to foretell events in a person's life

horrendous /hə'rendəs/ *adj* dreadful, horrible – **~ly** *adv*

horrible /'hɒrəbəl/ *adj* **1** marked by or arousing horror **2** extremely unpleasant or disagreeable – chiefly infml – **-bly** *adv*

horrid /'hɒrɨd/ *adj* **1** horrible, shocking **2** repulsive, nasty – **~ly** *adv* – **~ness** *n*

horrify /'hɒrɨfaɪ/ *v* **1** to cause to feel horror **2** to fill with distaste; shock – **~ingly, -fically** *adv* – **-fic** *adj*

horror /'hɒrəʳ/ *n* **1a** intense fear, dread, or dismay **b** intense aversion or repugnance **2** (sby or sthg that has) the quality of inspiring horror

hors de combat /,ɔː də 'kɒmbɑː/ *adv or adj* out of the fight; disabled

hors d'oeuvre /,ɔː 'dɜːv/ *n, pl* **hors d'oeuvres** *also* **hors d'oeuvre** any of various savoury foods usu served as appetizers

horse /hɔːs/ *n* **1a(1)** a large solid-hoofed plant-eating quadruped mammal domesticated by humans since prehistoric times and used as a beast of burden, a draught animal, or for riding **(2)** a racehorse **b** a male horse; a stallion or gelding **2a** a usu 4-legged frame for supporting sthg (e g planks) **b** a padded obstacle for vaulting over **3** *sing or pl in constr* the cavalry **4** heroin – slang

horsebox /'hɔːsbɒks/ *n* a lorry or closed trailer for transporting horses

horse chestnut *n* (the large glossy brown seed of) a large tree with 5-lobed leaves and erect conical clusters of showy flowers

horsefly /'hɔːsflaɪ/ *n* any of a family of swift usu large flies with bloodsucking females

horselaugh /'hɔːslɑːf/ *n* a loud boisterous laugh

horseman /'hɔːsmən/, *fem* **horsewoman** *n* **1** a rider on horseback **2** a (skilled) breeder, tender, or manager of horses – **~ship** *n*

horseplay /'hɔːspleɪ/ *n* rough or boisterous play

horsepower /'hɔːs,paʊəʳ/ *n* an imperial unit of power equal to about 746W

horseradish /'hɔːs,rædɪʃ/ *n* **1** a tall coarse white-flowered plant of the mustard family **2** (a condiment prepared from) the pungent root of the horseradish

horseshoe /'hɔːʃ-ʃuː, 'hɔːs-/ *n* (sthg with a shape resembling) a shoe for horses, usu consisting of a narrow U-shaped plate of iron fitting the rim of the hoof

horse-trading *n* negotiation accompanied by hard bargaining and reciprocal concessions – **horse trader** *n*

horsewhip /ˈhɔːs,wɪp/ *v* to flog (as if) with a whip for horses

hortative /ˈhɔːtətɪv/, **hortatory** /ˈhɔːtətəri/ *adj* giving encouragement – fml

horticulture /ˈhɔːtɨ̧,kʌltʃəʳ/ *n* the science and art of growing fruits, vegetables, and flowers – **-tural** *adj* – **-turalist** *n*

hosanna /həʊˈzænə/ *interj or n* (used as) a cry of acclamation and adoration

[1]**hose** /həʊz/ *n* **1** a leg covering that sometimes covers the foot **2** a flexible tube for conveying fluids (e g from a tap or in a car engine)

[2]**hose** *v* to spray, water, or wash with a hose

hosiery /ˈhəʊzɪəri/ *n* socks, stockings, and tights in general

hospice /ˈhɒspɨ̧s/ *n* **1** a place of shelter for travellers or the destitute (run by a religious order) **2** *Br* a nursing home, esp for terminally ill patients

hospitable /ˈhɒspɪtəbəl, hɒˈspɪ-/ *adj* **1a** offering a generous and cordial welcome (to guests or strangers) **b** offering a pleasant or sustaining environment **2** readily receptive – **-bly** *adv*

hospital /ˈhɒspɪtl/ *n* **1** an institution where the sick or injured are given medical care – often used in British English without an article **2** a repair shop for specified small objects – **~ize** *v*

hospitality /,hɒspɨ̧ˈtælɨ̧ti/ *n* hospitable treatment or reception

[1]**host** /həʊst/ *n* **1** a very large number; a multitude **2** an army – chiefly poetic or archaic

[2]**host** *n* **1a** an innkeeper **b** one who receives or entertains guests socially or officially **c** sby or sthg that provides facilities for an event or function **2a** a living animal or plant on or in which a parasite or smaller organism lives **b** an individual into which a tissue or part is transplanted from another

[3]**host** *v* to act as host at or of

[4]**host** *n, often cap* the bread consecrated in the Eucharist

hostage /ˈhɒstɪdʒ/ *n* a person held by one party as a pledge that promises will be kept or terms met by another party

hostel /ˈhɒstl/ *n* **1** *chiefly Br* a supervised residential home: e g **a** an establishment providing accommodation for nurses, students, etc **b** an institution for junior offenders, ex-offenders, etc, encouraging social adaptation **2** a Youth Hostel **3** an inn – chiefly poetic or archaic

hostelry /ˈhɒstəlri/ *n* an inn, hotel

hostess /ˈhəʊstɨ̧s/ *n* **1** a woman who entertains socially or acts as host **2a** a female employee on a ship, aeroplane, etc who manages the provisioning of food and attends to the needs of passengers **b** a woman who acts as a companion to male patrons, esp in a nightclub; *also* a prostitute

hostile /ˈhɒstaɪl/ *adj* **1** of or constituting an enemy **2** antagonistic, unfriendly **3** not hospitable

hostility /hɒˈstɪlɨ̧ti/ *n* **1** *pl* overt acts of warfare **2** antagonism, opposition, or resistance

[1]**hot** /hɒt/ *adj* **1a** having a relatively high temperature **b** capable of giving a sensation of heat or of burning, searing, or scalding **c** having a temperature higher than normal body temperature **2a** vehement, fiery **b** sexually excited; *also* sexually arousing **c** eager, enthusiastic **d** of or being an exciting style of jazz with strong rhythms **3** severe, stringent – usu + *on* **4** having or causing the sensation of an uncomfortable degree of body heat **5a** very recent; fresh **b** close to sthg sought **6a** suggestive of heat or of burning objects **b** pungent, peppery **7a** of intense and immediate interest; sensational **b** performing well or strongly fancied to win (e g in a sport) **c** currently popular; selling very well **d** very good – used as a generalized term of approval **9a** recently and illegally obtained **b** wanted by the police *USE* (*2b, 2c, & 7d*) infml, (*9*) slang

[2]**hot** *adv* hotly

hot air *n* empty talk – chiefly infml

hotbed /ˈhɒtbed/ *n* **1** a bed of soil heated esp by fermenting manure and used for forcing or raising seedlings **2** an environment that favours rapid growth or development, esp of sthg specified

hot-blooded *adj* excitable, ardent

hotchpotch /'hɒtʃpɒtʃ/ *n* a mixture composed of many usu unrelated parts; a jumble

hot cross bun *n* a yeast-leavened spicy bun marked with a cross and eaten esp on Good Friday

hot dog *n* a frankfurter or other sausage (heated and served in a bread roll)

hotel /həʊ'tel/ *n* a usu large establishment that provides meals and (temporary) accommodation for the public, esp for people travelling away from home

hotelier /həʊ'telieɪ, -lɪə^r/ *n* a proprietor or manager of a hotel

hotfoot /ˌhɒt'fʊt/ *v or adv* (to go) in haste – **hotfoot** *adv*

hothead /'hɒthed/ *n* a fiery and impetuous person – **~ed** *adj* – **~edly** *adv*

¹hothouse /'hɒthaʊs/ *n* a heated greenhouse, esp for tropical plants

²hothouse *adj* delicate, overprotected

hot line *n* a direct telephone line kept in constant readiness for immediate communication (e g between heads of state)

hotly /'hɒtli/ *adv* in a hot or fiery manner

hot plate *n* a metal plate or spiral, usu on an electric cooker, on which food can be heated and cooked

hot pot *n* a (mutton, lamb, or beef and potato) stew cooked esp in a covered pot

hot rod *n* a motor vehicle rebuilt or modified for high speed and fast acceleration

hot seat *n* a position involving risk, embarrassment, or responsibility for decision-making – infml

hot stuff *n* sby or sthg of outstanding ability or quality

Hottentot /'hɒtəntɒt/ *n* a member, or the language, of a people of southern Africa apparently of mixed Bushman and Bantu origin

hot water *n* a distressing predicament (likely to lead to punishment); trouble – infml

hot-water bottle *n* a usu flat rubber container that is filled with hot water and used esp to warm a (person in) bed

¹hound /haʊnd/ *n* **1** a dog; *esp* one of any of various hunting breeds typically with large drooping ears and a deep bark that track their prey by scent **2** a mean or despicable person **3** one who is devoted to the pursuit of sthg specified

²hound *v* **1** to pursue (as if) with hounds **2** to harass persistently

hour /aʊə^r/ *n* **1** (any of the 7 times of day set aside for) a daily liturgical devotion **2** the 24th part of a day; a period of 60 minutes **3a** *the* time of day reckoned in hours and minutes by the clock; *esp* the beginning of each full hour measured by the clock **b** *pl* the time reckoned in one 24-hour period from midnight to midnight **4a** a fixed or customary period of time set aside for a usu specified purpose – often pl **b** a particular, usu momentous, period or point of time **c** *the* present **5** the work done or distance travelled at normal rate in an hour

¹hourglass /'aʊəglɑːs/ *n* a glass or perspex instrument for measuring time consisting of 2 bulbs joined by a narrow neck from the uppermost of which a quantity of sand, water, etc runs into the lower in the space of an hour

²hourglass *adj* shapely with a narrow waist

¹hourly /aʊəli/ *adv* **1** at or during every hour; *also* continually **2** by the hour

²hourly *adj* **1** occurring or done every hour; *also* continual **2** reckoned by the hour

¹house /haʊs/ *n* **1** a building designed for people to live in **2a** an animal's shelter or refuge (e g a nest or den) **b** a building in which sthg is housed or stored **c** a building used for a particular purpose, esp eating, drinking, or entertainment **3** any of the 12 equal sectors into which the celestial sphere is divided in astrology **4a** *sing or pl in constr* the occupants of a house **b** a family including ancestors, descendants, and kindred **5a** (a residence of) a religious community **b** any of several groups into which a British school may be divided for social purposes or games **6** (the chamber of) a legislative or deliberative assembly; *esp* a division of a body consisting of 2 chambers **7** a business organization or establishment **8** (the audience in) a theatre or concert hall

[2]**house** /haʊz/ *v* **1** to provide with accommodation or storage space **2** to serve as shelter for; contain

house arrest *n* confinement to one's place of residence instead of prison

houseboat /ˈhaʊsbəʊt/ *n* an often permanently moored boat that is fitted out as a home

housebound /ˈhaʊsbaʊnd/ *adj* confined to the house (e g because of illness)

housecoat /ˈhaʊskəʊt/ *n* a woman's light dressing gown for wear round the house; *also* a short overall

housecraft /ˈhaʊskrɑːft/ *n* **1** domestic science **2** skill in running a household

housefather /ˈhaʊsfɑːðəʳ/, *fem* **housemother** *n* sby in charge of a group of young people living in care (e g in a children's home)

housefly /ˈhaʊsflaɪ/ *n* a fly found in most parts of the world that frequents houses and carries disease

[1]**household** /ˈhaʊshəʊld/ *n sing or pl in constr* all the people who live together in a dwelling

[2]**household** *adj* **1** domestic **2** familiar, common

householder /ˈhaʊsˌhəʊldəʳ/ *n* a person who occupies a dwelling as owner or tenant

housekeeper /ˈhaʊsˌkiːpəʳ/ *n* sby, esp a woman, employed to take charge of the running of a house

housekeeping /ˈhaʊsˌkiːpɪŋ/ *n* **1** (money used for) the day-to-day running of a house and household affairs **2** the general management of an organization which ensures its smooth running (e g the provision of equipment, keeping of records, etc)

housemaid /ˈhaʊsmeɪd/ *n* a female servant employed to do housework

housemaid's knee *n* a swelling over the knee due to an enlargement of the tissues between the kneecap and the knee

houseman /ˈhaʊsmən/ *n* (one holding) the most junior grade of British hospital doctor

house martin *n* a European martin with blue-black plumage and white rump that nests on cliffs and under the eaves of houses

housemaster /ˈhaʊsˌmɑːstəʳ/, *fem* **housemistress** *n* a teacher in charge of a school house

housemother /ˈhaʊsmʌðəʳ/, *masc* **housefather** *n* sby in charge of a group of young people living in care (e g in a children's home)

House of Commons *n* the lower house of the British and Canadian parliaments

House of Lords *n* **1** the upper house of Parliament **2** the body of Law Lords that constitutes the highest British court of appeal

house party *n* a party lasting for a day or more held at a large, usu country, house

house-proud *adj* (excessively) careful about the management and appearance of one's house

house sparrow *n* a brown Eurasian sparrow that lives esp in or near human settlements

house-to-house *adj* door-to-door

housewarming /ˈhaʊsˌwɔːmɪŋ/ *n* a party to celebrate moving into a new house or premises

housewife /ˈhaʊs-waɪf; *sense 2* ˈhʌzɪf/ *n* **1** a usu married woman who runs a house **2** a small container for needlework articles (e g thread) – **~ly** *adj*

housework /ˈhaʊswɜːk/ *n* the work (e g cleaning) involved in maintaining a house

housing /ˈhaʊzɪŋ/ *n* **1** (the provision of) houses or dwelling-places collectively **2** a protective cover for machinery, sensitive instruments, etc

hove /həʊv/ *past of* **heave**

hovel /ˈhɒvəl/ *n* a small, wretched, and often dirty house or abode

hover /ˈhɒvəʳ/ *v* **1** to hang in the air or on the wing **2a** to linger or wait restlessly around a place **b** to be in a state of uncertainty, indecision, or suspense

hovercraft /ˈhɒvəkrɑːft/ *n, pl* **hovercraft** a vehicle supported on a cushion of air provided by fans and designed to travel over both land and sea

[1]**how** /haʊ/ *adv* **1a** in what manner or way (e g *how* do you spell it?) **b** with what meaning; to what effect (e g *how* can you explain it?) **c** for what reason; why (e g *how* could you do it?) **2** by what measure or quantity (e g *how* much does it cost) – often used in an exclamation as an intensive (e g *how* nice of you!) **3** in what state or condition (e g of health) (e g *how* are you?)

[2]**how** *conj* **1a** the way, manner, or state in which (e g remember *how* they fought?) **b** that (e g do you remember *how* he arrived right at the end?) **2** however, as (e g do it *how* you like)

[3]**how** *n* the manner in which sthg is done

howdah /ˈhaʊdə/ *n* a usu canopied seat on the back of an elephant or camel

how-do-you-do, how d'ye do *n* a confused or embarrassing situation – infml

[1]**however** /haʊˈevəʳ/ *conj* in whatever manner or way (e g can go *however* he likes)

[2]**however** *adv* **1** to whatever degree or extent; no matter how (e g *however* hard I try) **2** in spite of that; nevertheless (e g would like to; *however*, I'd better not) **3** how in the world (e g *however* did you manage it?) – infml

howitzer /ˈhaʊɪtsəʳ/ *n* a short cannon usu with a medium muzzle velocity and a relatively high trajectory

howl /haʊl/ *v* **1a** *esp of dogs, wolves, etc* to make a loud sustained doleful cry **b** *of wind* to make a sustained wailing sound **2** to cry loudly and without restraint (e g with pain or laughter) **3** to utter with a loud sustained cry – **howl** *n*

howl down *v* to express one's disapproval of (e g a speaker or his/her views), esp by shouting in order to prevent from being heard

howler /ˈhaʊləʳ/ *n* a stupid and comic blunder – infml

howling /ˈhaʊlɪŋ/ *adj* very great, extreme, or severe – infml

hoyden /ˈhɔɪdn/ *n* a boisterous girl – ~**ish** *adj*

hub /hʌb/ *n* **1** the central part of a wheel, propeller, or fan through which the axle passes **2** the centre of activity or importance

hubbub /ˈhʌbʌb/ *n* a noisy confusion; uproar

hubby /ˈhʌbi/ *n* a husband – infml

hubcap /ˈhʌbkæp/ *n* a removable metal cap placed over the hub of a wheel

hubris /ˈhjuːbrɨs/ *n* overweening pride, usu leading to retribution

[1]**huddle** /ˈhʌdl/ *v* **1** to crowd together **2** to draw or curl (oneself) up

[2]**huddle** *n* **1** a closely-packed group; a bunch **2** a secretive or conspiratorial meeting

hue /hjuː/ *n* **1** a complexion, aspect **2** the attribute of colours that permits them to be classed as red, yellow, green, blue, or an intermediate between any adjacent pair of these colours; *also* a colour having this attribute

hue and cry *n* a clamour of alarm or protest

huff /hʌf/ *v* **1** to emit loud puffs (e g of breath or steam) **2** to make empty threats

[1]**hug** /hʌg/ *v* **1** to hold or press tightly, esp in the arms **2a** to feel very pleased with (oneself) **b** to cling to; cherish **3** to stay close to

[2]**hug** *n* a tight clasp or embrace

huge /hjuːdʒ/ *adj* great in size, scale, degree, or scope; enormous – ~**ness** *n*

hugely /ˈhjuːdʒli/ *adv* very much; enormously

hugger-mugger *n* **1** secrecy **2** confusion, muddle

hulk /hʌlk/ *n* **1a** the hull of a ship that is no longer seaworthy and is used as a storehouse or, esp formerly, as a prison **b** an abandoned wreck or shell, esp of a vessel **2** a person, creature, or thing that is bulky or unwieldy

hulking /ˈhʌlkɪŋ/ *adj* bulky, massive

[1]**hull** /hʌl/ *n* **1a** the outer covering of a fruit or seed **b** the calyx that surrounds some fruits (e g the strawberry) **2** the main frame or body of a ship, flying boat, airship, etc **3** a covering, casing

[2]**hull** *v* to remove the hulls of

hullabaloo /ˈhʌləbəluː, ˌhʌləbəˈluː/ *n* a confused noise; uproar – infml

hullo /hʌˈləʊ/ *interj or n, chiefly Br* hello

hum /hʌm/ *v* **1a** to utter a prolonged /m/ sound **b** to make the characteristic droning noise of an insect in motion or a similar sound **2** to be lively or active – infml **3** to have an offensive smell – slang **4** to sing with the lips closed and without articulation – **hum** *n*

¹human /ˈhjuːmən/ *adj* **1** (characteristic) of humans **2** consisting of men and women **3a** having the esp good attributes (e g kindness and compassion) thought to be characteristic of humans **b** having, showing, or concerned with qualities or feelings characteristic of mankind – **~ize** *v*

²human, human being *n* a man, woman, or child; a person

humane /hjuːˈmeɪn/ *adj* **1a** marked by compassion or consideration for other human beings or animals **b** causing the minimum pain possible **2** characterized by broad humanistic culture; liberal

humanism /ˈhjuːmənɪzəm/ *n* **1** a cultural movement dominant during the Renaissance that was characterized by a revival of classical learning and a shift of emphasis from religious to secular concerns; *broadly* literary culture **2** humanitarianism **3** a doctrine, attitude, or way of life based on human interests or values; *esp* a philosophy that asserts the intrinsic worth of man and that usu rejects religious belief – **-ist** *n, adj* – **-istic** *adj*

humanitarian /hjuːˌmænɪ̈ˈteərɪən/ *n* one who promotes human welfare and social reform; a philanthropist

humanity /hjuːˈmænɪ̈ti/ *n* **1** the quality of being humane **2** the quality or state of being human **3** *pl the* cultural branches of learning **4** mankind

humankind /ˌhjuːmənˈkaɪnd/ *n sing or pl in constr* human beings collectively

humanly /ˈhjuːmənli/ *adv* **1a** from a human viewpoint **b** within the range of human capacity **2a** in a manner characteristic of humans, esp in showing emotion or weakness **b** with humaneness

¹humble /ˈhʌmbəl/ *adj* **1** having a low opinion of oneself; unassertive **2** marked by deference or submission **3a** ranking low in a hierarchy or scale **b** modest, unpretentious – **-bly** *adv*

²humble *v* **1** to make humble in spirit or manner; humiliate **2** to destroy the power, independence, or prestige of

¹humbug /ˈhʌmbʌg/ *n* **1a** sthg designed to deceive and mislead **b** an impostor, sham **2** drivel, nonsense **3** a hard usu peppermint-flavoured striped sweet made from boiled sugar

²humbug *v* to deceive with a hoax

humdinger /hʌmˈdɪŋəʳ/ *n* an excellent or remarkable person or thing – infml

humdrum /ˈhʌmdrʌm/ *adj* monotonous, dull

humerus /ˈhjuːmərəs/ *n, pl* **humeri** the long bone of the upper arm or forelimb extending from the shoulder to the elbow

humid /ˈhjuːmɪ̈d/ *adj* containing or characterized by perceptible moisture

humidity /hjuːˈmɪdɪ̈ti/ *n* (the degree of) moisture or dampness, esp in the atmosphere

humiliate /hjuːˈmɪlieɪt/ *v* to cause to feel humble; lower the dignity or self-respect of – **-ation** *n*

humility /hjuːˈmɪlɪ̈ti/ *n* the quality or state of being humble

hummingbird /ˈhʌmɪŋbɜːd/ *n* any of numerous tiny brightly coloured usu tropical American birds related to the swifts, having a slender bill and narrow wings that beat rapidly making a humming sound

humorist /ˈhjuːmərɪ̈st/ *n* a person specializing in or noted for humour in speech, writing, or acting

humorous /ˈhjuːmərəs/ *adj* full of, characterized by, or expressing humour – **~ly** *adv*

¹humour /ˈhjuːməʳ/ *n* **1** any of the 4 fluids of the body (blood, phlegm, and yellow and black bile) formerly held to determine, by their relative proportions, a person's health and temperament **2** characteristic or habitual disposition **3** a state of mind; a mood **4**

a sudden inclination; a caprice **5a** (sthg having) the quality of causing amusement **b** the faculty of expressing or appreciating what is comic or amusing

²humour *v* to comply with the mood or wishes of; indulge

¹hump /hʌmp/ *n* **1** a rounded protuberance: e g **a** a humped or crooked back **b** a fleshy protuberance on the back of a camel, bison, etc **2** a difficult, trying, or critical phase **3** *Br* a fit of depression or sulking – infml; + *the*

²hump *v* **1** to form or curve into a hump **2** *chiefly Br* to carry with difficulty **3** to have sexual intercourse (with) – slang

humpback /ˈhʌmpbæk/ *n* **1** a hunchback **2** *also* **humpback whale** a large whale with very long flippers – **~ed** *adj*

humph /hʌmf/ *interj* a grunt used to express doubt or contempt

humus /ˈhjuːməs/ *n* a brown or black organic soil material resulting from partial decomposition of plant or animal matter

Hun /hʌn/ *n* **1** a member of a nomadic Mongolian people who overran a large part of central and E Europe under Attila during the 4th and 5th c AD **2a** *often not cap* a person who is wantonly destructive **b** a German; *esp* a German soldier in WW I or II – derog

¹hunch /hʌntʃ/ *v* **1** to assume a bent or crooked posture **2** to bend into a hump or arch

²hunch *n* a strong intuitive feeling

hunchback /ˈhʌntʃbæk/ *n* (sby with) a humped back – **~ed** *adj*

hundred /ˈhʌndrɪ̣d/ *n, pl* **hundreds, hundred** **1** the number 100 **2** the number occupying the position 3 to the left of the decimal point in Arabic notation; *also, pl* this position **3** 100 units or digits; *specif* £100 **4** *pl the* numbers 100 to 999 **5** a score of 100 or more runs made by a batsman in cricket **6** *pl the* 100 years of a specified century **7** a historical subdivision of a county **8** an indefinitely large number – infml; often pl with sing. meaning – **~th** *adj, n, pron, adv*

hundredweight /ˈhʌndrɪ̣dweɪt/ *n, pl* **hundredweight, hundredweights** a British unit of weight equal to 112lb (about 50.80kg)

hung /hʌŋ/ *past of* **hang**

¹hunger /ˈhʌŋgəʳ/ *n* **1** (a weakened condition or unpleasant sensation arising from) a craving or urgent need for food **2** a strong desire; a craving

²hunger *v* to have an eager desire – usu + *for* or *after* *n*

hungry /ˈhʌŋgri/ *adj* **1a** feeling hunger **b** characterized by or indicating hunger or appetite **2** eager, avid – **-grily** *adv*

hunk /hʌŋk/ *n* **1** a large lump or piece **2** a usu muscular sexually attractive man – infml

¹hunt /hʌnt/ *v* **1a** to pursue for food or enjoyment **b** to use (e g hounds) in the search for game **2a** to pursue with intent to capture **b** to search out; seek **3** to persecute or chase, esp by harrying **4** to take part in a hunt, esp regularly **5** to attempt to find sthg

²hunt *n* **1** the act, the practice, or an instance of hunting **2** *sing or pl in constr* a group of usu mounted hunters and their hounds

hunter /ˈhʌntəʳ/, *fem* (*1a&2*) **huntress** *n* **1a** sby who hunts game, esp with hounds **b** a usu fast strong horse used in hunting **2** a person who hunts or seeks sthg, esp overeagerly **3** a watch with a hinged metal cover to protect it

hunting /ˈhʌntɪŋ/ *n* the pursuit of game on horseback with hounds

hunting pink *adj or n* (of) the red colour of the coats worn by fox-hunters

huntsman /ˈhʌntsmən/ *n* someone who hunts with hounds; *also* sby who looks after the hounds belonging to a hunt

¹hurdle /ˈhɜːdl/ *n* **1a** a portable framework, usu of interlaced branches and stakes, used esp for enclosing land or livestock **b** a frame formerly used for dragging traitors to execution **2a** a light barrier jumped by men, horses, dogs, etc in certain races **b** *pl* any of various races over hurdles **3** a barrier, obstacle

²hurdle *v* **1** to jump over, esp while running **2** to overcome, surmount **3** to run in hurdle races – **~r** *n*

hurdy-gurdy /ˈhɜːdi ˌgɜːdi/ *n* a musical instrument in which the sound is produced by turning a crank; *esp* a barrel organ

hurl /hɜːl/ *v* **1** to drive or thrust violently **2** to throw forcefully **3** to utter or shout violently

hurly-burly /ˈhɜːli ˌbɜːli/ *n* (an) uproar, commotion

hurray /hʊˈreɪ/ , **hurrah** /hʊˈrɑː/ *interj* – used to express joy, approval, etc

hurricane /ˈhʌrɨkən/ *n* (a usu tropical cyclone with) a wind of a velocity greater than 117km/h (73 to 136mph)

hurricane lamp *n* a candlestick or oil lamp equipped with a glass chimney to protect the flame

hurried /ˈhʌrid/ *adj* done in a hurry – **~ly** *adv*

¹hurry /ˈhʌri/ *v* **1a** to transport or cause to go with haste; rush **b** to cause to move or act with (greater) haste **2** to hasten the progress or completion of **3** to move or act with haste – often + *up*

²hurry *n* **1** flurried and often bustling haste **2** a need for haste; urgency

¹hurt /hɜːt/ *v* **1a** to afflict with physical pain; wound **b** to cause mental distress to; offend **2** to be detrimental to **3** to feel pain; suffer **4** to cause damage, distress, or pain

²hurt *n* **1** (a cause of) mental distress **2** wrong, harm

hurtle /ˈhɜːtl/ *v* **1** to move rapidly or precipitately **2** to hurl, fling

¹husband /ˈhʌzbənd/ *n* a married man, esp in relation to his wife

²husband *v* to make the most economical use of; conserve

husbandry /ˈhʌzbəndri/ *n* **1** the judicious management of resources **2** farming, esp of domestic animals

¹hush /hʌʃ/ *v* to make or become quiet or calm

²hush *n* a silence or calm, esp following noise

hush-hush *adj* secret, confidential – infml

hush money *n* money paid secretly to prevent disclosure of damaging information

hush up *v* to keep secret; suppress – **hush-up** *n*

¹husk /hʌsk/ *n* **1** a dry or membranous outer covering (e g a shell or pod) of a seed or fruit **2** a useless outer layer of sthg

²husk *v* to strip the husk from

¹husky /ˈhʌski/ *adj* of, resembling, or containing husks

²husky *adj* hoarse, breathy – **-kily** *adv* – **-kiness** *n*

³husky *adj* burly, hefty – infml

⁴husky *n* (any of) a breed of sledge dogs native to Greenland

hussar /hʊˈzɑːʳ/ *n* **1** a Hungarian horseman of the 15th c **2** *often cap* a member of any of various European cavalry regiments

hussy /ˈhʌsi, ˈhʌzi/ *n* an impudent or promiscuous woman or girl

hustings /ˈhʌstɪŋz/ *n pl but sing or pl in constr* **1** a raised platform used until 1872 for the nomination of candidates for Parliament and for election speeches **2** a place where election speeches are made **3** the proceedings of an election campaign

hustle /ˈhʌsəl/ *v* **1a** to push or convey roughly, forcibly, or hurriedly **b** to impel, force **2** to swindle, cheat *out of* – infml **3** *chiefly NAm* to make strenuous, often dishonest, efforts to secure money or business **4** *chiefly NAm* to engage in prostitution; solicit – **hustle** *n*

hut /hʌt/ *n* a small often temporary dwelling of simple construction

hutch /hʌtʃ/ *n* **1** a pen or cage for a small animal (e g a rabbit) **2** a shack, shanty – infml; derog

hyacinth /ˈhaɪəsɨnθ/ *n* **1** a common garden plant with fragrant usu blue, pink, or white flowers that grow in spikes; *also* any of various related bulbous plants of the lily family **2** a colour varying from light violet to mid-purple

hyaena /haɪˈiːnə/ *n* a hyena

hybrid /ˈhaɪbrɨd/ *n* **1** an offspring of 2 animals or plants of different races, breeds, varieties, etc **2** a person of mixed cultural background **3** sthg heterogeneous in origin or composition – **~ize** *v*

hydra /ˈhaɪdrə/ *n* any of numerous small tubular freshwater polyps having a mouth surrounded by tentacles

hydrangea /haɪ'dreɪndʒə/ *n* any of a genus of shrubs which produce large clusters of white, pink, or pale blue flowers

hydrant /'haɪdrənt/ *n* a discharge pipe with a valve and nozzle from which water may be drawn from a main

hydraulic /haɪ'drɒlɪk, -'drɔː-/ *adj* **1** operated, moved, or effected by means of liquid, esp liquid moving through pipes **2** of hydraulics **3** hardening or setting under water – **~ally** *adv*

hydraulics /haɪ'drɒlɪks, -'drɔː-/ *n pl but sing in constr* a branch of physics that deals with the practical applications of liquid in motion

hydrocarbon /,haɪdrə'kɑːbən/ *n* an organic compound (e g benzene) containing only carbon and hydrogen

hydroelectric /,haɪdrəʊ-ɪ'lektrɪk/ *adj* of or being the production of electricity by waterpower – **~ally** *adv*

hydrofoil /'haɪdrəfɔɪl/ *n* (a ship or boat fitted with) a device that, when attached to a ship, lifts the hull out of the water at speed

hydrogen /'haɪdrədʒən/ *n* the simplest and lightest of the elements that is normally a highly inflammable gas

hydrogen bomb *n* a bomb whose violent explosive power is due to the sudden release of atomic energy resulting from the nuclear fusion of hydrogen initiated by the explosion of an atom bomb

hydrolysis /haɪ'drɒlɪ̈sɪ̈s/ *n* chemical breakdown involving splitting of a bond and addition of the elements of water

hydrophobia /,haɪdrə'fəʊbɪə/ *n* **1** abnormal dread of water **2** rabies

hydroplane /'haɪdrəpleɪn/ *n* **1** a speedboat fitted with hydrofoils or a stepped bottom so that the hull is raised wholly or partly out of the water when moving at speed **2** a horizontal surface on a submarine's hull, used to control movement upwards or downwards

hydroponics /,haɪdrə'pɒnɪks/ *n pl but sing in constr* the growing of plants in (a mechanically supporting medium containing) nutrient solutions rather than soil – **-ponic** *adj*

hyena, hyaena /haɪ'iːnə/ *n* any of several large nocturnal Old World mammals that usu feed as scavengers

hygiene /'haɪdʒiːn/ *n* (conditions or practices, esp cleanliness, conducive to) the establishment and maintenance of health

hymen /'haɪmən/ *n* a fold of mucous membrane partly closing the opening of the vagina in virgins

hymn /hɪm/ *n* **1** a song of praise to God; *esp* a metrical composition that can be included in a religious service **2** a song of praise or joy

hyperbole /haɪ'pɜːbəli/ *n* a figure of speech based on extravagant exaggeration

hyperbolic /,haɪpə'bɒlɪk/ *also* **hyperbolical** *adj* of, characterized by, or given to hyperbole

hypermarket /'haɪpəmɑːkɪ̈t/ *n* a very large self-service retail store selling a wide range of household and consumer goods

hypersensitive /,haɪpə'sensɪ̈tɪv/ *adj* abnormally susceptible (e g to a drug or antigen) – **-tivity** *n*

hypha /'haɪfə/ *n, pl* **hyphae** any of the threads that make up the mycelium of a fungus

[1]**hyphen** /'haɪfən/ *n* a punctuation mark - used to divide or to join together words, word elements, or numbers

hypnosis /hɪp'nəʊsɪ̈s/ *n* any of various conditions that (superficially) resemble sleep; *specif* one induced by a person to whose suggestions the subject is then markedly susceptible – **-notic** *adj* – **-notically** *adv*

hypnotism /'hɪpnətɪzəm/ *n* **1** the induction of hypnosis **2** hypnosis – **-tist** *n* – **-ize** *v*

hypochondria /,haɪpə'kɒndrɪə/ *n* morbid concern about one's health – **~c** *n, adj*

hypocrisy /hɪ'pɒkrɪ̈si/ *n* the feigning of virtues, beliefs, or standards, esp in matters of religion or morality

hypocrite /'hɪpəkrɪt/ *n* one given to hypocrisy – **-critical** *adj*

[1]**hypodermic** /,haɪpə'dɜːmɪk/ *adj* of the parts beneath the skin – **~ally** *adv*

[2]**hypodermic** *n* **1** a hypodermic injection **2** a hypodermic syringe

hypodermic syringe *n* a small syringe used with a hollow needle for injection or withdrawal of material beneath the skin

hypotenuse /haɪ'pɒtɪnjuːz/ *n* the side of a right-angled triangle that is opposite the right angle

hypothermia /ˌhaɪpə'θɜːmɪə/ *n* abnormally low body temperature

hypothesis /haɪ'pɒθɪsɪs/ *n, pl* **hypotheses** **1** a provisional assumption made in order to investigate its logical or empirical consequences **2** a proposition assumed for the sake of argument

hypothetical /ˌhaɪpə'θetɪkəl/ *adj* **1** involving logical hypothesis **2** of or depending on supposition; conjectural

hyrax /'haɪəræks/ *n, pl* **hyraxes** *also* **hyraces** any of several small thickset short-legged mammals with feet with soft pads and broad nails

hysterectomy /ˌhɪstə'rektəmi/ *n* surgical removal of the uterus

hysteria /hɪ'stɪərɪə/ *n* **1** a mental disorder marked by emotional excitability and disturbances (e g paralysis) of the normal bodily processes **2** unmanageable emotional excess – **-ric** *n* – **-rical** *adj*

hysterics /hɪ'sterɪks/ *n pl but sing or pl in constr* a fit of uncontrollable laughter or crying; hysteria

I

i /aɪ/ *n, pl* **i's, is** *often cap* **1** (a graphic representation of or device for reproducing) the 9th letter of the English alphabet **2** one

I /aɪ/ *pron* the one who is speaking or writing

iamb /ˈaɪæm/ *n* a metrical foot consisting of 1 short or unstressed syllable followed by 1 long or stressed syllable – **~ic** *adj, n*

Iberian /aɪˈbɪərɪən/ *n* **1a** a member of any of the Caucasian peoples that in ancient times inhabited Spain and Portugal **b** a native or inhabitant of Spain or Portugal **2** any of the languages of the ancient Iberians

ibidem /ˈɪbɪdem, ɪˈbaɪdem/ *adv* in the same book, chapter, passage, etc as previously mentioned

ibis /ˈaɪbɪ̵s/ *n* any of several wading birds related to the herons but distinguished by a long slender downward-curving bill

[1]ice /aɪs/ *n* **1a** frozen water **b** a sheet or stretch of ice **2** a substance reduced to the solid state by cold **3** (a serving of) a frozen dessert: e g **a** an ice cream **b** a water ice **4** *NAm* diamonds – slang

[2]ice *v* **1a** to coat with or convert into ice **b** to supply or chill with ice **2** to cover (as if) with icing **3** to become ice-cold **4** to become covered or clogged with ice

ice age *n* a time of widespread glaciation; *esp* that ocurring in the Pleistocene epoch

iceberg /ˈaɪsbɜːg/ *n* **1** a large floating mass of ice detached from a glacier **2** an emotionally cold person

ice cap *n* a lasting (extensive) cover of ice

ice cream *n* a sweet flavoured frozen food containing cream (substitute) and often eggs

ice hockey *n* a game played on an ice rink by 2 teams of 6 players on skates whose object is to drive a puck into the opponent's goal with a hockey stick

[1]Icelandic /əɪsˈlændɪk/ *adj* (characteristic) of Iceland

[2]Icelandic *n* the N Germanic language of the Icelandic people

ice lolly *n* an ice cream or esp a flavoured piece of ice on a stick

icicle /ˈaɪsɪkəl/ *n* a hanging tapering mass of ice formed by the freezing of dripping water

icing /ˈaɪsɪŋ/ *n* a sweet (creamy) coating for cakes or other baked goods

icon, ikon /ˈaɪkɒn/ *n* **1** a usu pictorial image **2** a conventional religious image, usu painted on a small wooden panel, used in worship in the Eastern Church

iconoclast /aɪˈkɒnəklast/ *n* **1** a person who destroys religious images or opposes their veneration **2** one who attacks established beliefs or institutions – **~ic** *adj*

icy /ˈaɪsi/ *adj* **1a** covered with, full of, or consisting of ice **b** intensely cold **2** characterized by personal coldness – **icily** *adv* – **iciness** *n*

id /ɪd/ *n* the one of the 3 divisions of the mind in psychoanalytic theory that is completely unconscious and is the source of psychic energy derived from instinctual needs and drives

idea /aɪˈdɪə/ *n* **1a** a transcendent entity of which existing things are imperfect representations **b** a plan of action **2a** an indefinite or vague impression **b** sthg (e g a thought, concept, or image) actually or potentially present in the mind **3** a formulated thought or opinion **4** whatever is known or supposed about sthg **5** an individual's conception of the perfect or typical example of sthg specified **6** the central meaning or aim of a particular action or situation

[1]ideal /aɪˈdɪəl/ *adj* **1a** existing only in the mind; *broadly* lacking practicality **b** relating to or constituting mental images, ideas, or conceptions **2** of or embodying an ideal; perfect – **~ly** *adv*

²ideal *n* **1** a standard of perfection, beauty, or excellence **2** one looked up to as embodying an ideal or as a model for imitation **3** an ultimate object or aim – **~ize** *v*

idealism /aɪ'dɪəlɪzəm/ *n* **1a** a theory that the essential nature of reality lies in consciousness or reason **b** a theory that only what is immediately perceived (e g sensations or ideas) is real **2** the practice of living according to one's ideals **3** a literary or artistic theory or practice that affirms the preeminent value of imagination and representation of ideal types as compared with faithful copying of nature

idealist /aɪ'dɪəl̩ɪst/ *n* **1** one who advocates or practises idealism in art or writing **2** sby guided by ideals; *esp* one who places ideals before practical considerations – **~ic** *adj* – **~ically** *adv*

idem /'ɪdem, 'aɪdem/ *pron* the same as previously mentioned

identical /aɪ'dentɪkəl/ *adj* **1** being the same **2** being very similar or exactly alike **3** *of twins, triplets, etc* derived from a single egg

identification /aɪ,dentɪfɪ'keɪʃən/ *n* **1a** identifying or being identified **b** evidence of identity **2a** the putting of oneself mentally in the position of another

identification parade *n, chiefly Br* a line-up of people arranged by the police to allow a witness to identify a suspect

identify /aɪ'dentɪfaɪ/ *v* **1a** to cause to be or become identical **b** to associate or link closely **2** to establish the identity of

¹identikit /aɪ'dentɪ,kɪt/ *n, often cap* a set of alternative facial characteristics used by the police to build up a likeness, esp of a suspect; *also* a likeness constructed in this way

²identikit *adj, often cap* **1** of or produced by identikit **2** like many others of the same type

identity /aɪ'dentɪti/ *n* **1** the condition of being exactly alike **2** the distinguishing character or personality of an individual **3** the condition of being the same as sthg or sby known or supposed to exist **4** *Austr & NZ* a person, character

ideogram /'ɪdɪəgræm/ *n* a stylized picture or symbol used instead of a word or sound to represent a thing or idea

ideology /,aɪdi'ɒlədʒi/ *n* **1** a systematic body of concepts **2** a manner of thinking characteristic of an individual, group, or culture **3** the ideas behind a social, political, or cultural programme – **-ogical** *adj* – **-ogist** *n*

ides /aɪdz/ *n pl but sing or pl in constr* (the week preceding) the 15th day of March, May, July, or October or the 13th day of any other month in the ancient Roman calendar

idiocy /'ɪdɪəsi/ *n* **1** extreme mental deficiency **2** sthg notably stupid or foolish

idiom /'ɪdɪəm/ *n* **1a** the language peculiar to a people or to a district, community, or class **b** the syntactic, grammatical, or structural form peculiar to a language **2** an expression in the usage of a language that has a meaning that cannot be derived from the sum of the meanings of its elements **3** a characteristic style or form of artistic expression

idiomatic /,ɪdɪə'mætɪk/ *adj* of or conforming to idiom – **~ally** *adv*

idiosyncrasy /,ɪdɪə'sɪŋkrəsi/ *n* **1** characteristic peculiarity of habit or structure **2** a characteristic of thought or behaviour peculiar to an individual or group; *esp* an eccentricity

idiot /'ɪdɪət/ *n* **1** a person suffering from accute mental deficiency, esp from birth **2** a silly or foolish person – **~ic** *adj* – **~ically** *adv*

¹idle /'aɪdl/ *adj* **1** having no particular purpose or value **2** groundless **3** not occupied or employed: e g **a** not in use or operation **b** not turned to appropriate use **4** lazy – **~ness** *n* – **idly** *adv*

²idle *v* **1a** to spend time in idleness **b** to move idly **2** *esp of an engine* to run without being connected to the part (e g the wheels of a car) that is driven, so that no useful work is done

idol /'aɪdl/ *n* **1** an image or symbol used as an object of worship; *broadly* a false god **2** an object of passionate or excessive devotion – **~ize** *v*

idolater /aɪ'dɒlətəʳ/ *n* **1** a worshipper

of idols **2** a passionate and often uncritical admirer – **-trous** *adj* – **-trously** *adv* – **-try** *n*

idyll, idyl /ˈɪdl/ *n* (a work in poetry or prose describing) a scene or episode of peaceful country life – **~ic** *adj*

[1]**if** /ɪf/ *conj* **1a** in the event that (e g *if* she should call, let me know) **b** supposing (e g *if* you'd listened, you'd know) **c** on condition that **2** whether (e g asked *if* the mail had come) **3** – used to introduce an exclamation expressing a wish (e g *if* only it would rain) **4** even if; although (e g an interesting *if* irrelevant point) **5** that – used after expressions of emotion (e g I don't care *if* she's cross) **6** – used with a negative when an expletive introduces startling news (e g blow me *if* he didn't hit her)

[2]**if** *n* **1** a condition, stipulation **2** a supposition

igloo /ˈɪgluː/ *n* an Eskimo dwelling, usu made of snow blocks and in the shape of a dome

igneous /ˈɪgnɪəs/ *adj* **1** fiery **2** relating to or formed by the flow or solidification of molten rock from the earth's core

ignite /ɪgˈnaɪt/ *v* **1a** to set fire to; *also* to kindle **b** to cause (a fuel mixture) to burn **c** to catch fire **2** to spark off; excite, esp suddenly

ignition /ɪgˈnɪʃən/ *n* **1** the act or action of igniting **2** the process or means (e g an electric spark) of igniting a fuel mixture

ignoble /ɪgˈnəʊbəl/ *adj* **1** of low birth or humble origin **2** base, dishonourable

ignominious /ˌɪgnəˈmɪnɪəs/ *adj* **1** marked by or causing disgrace or discredit **2** humiliating, degrading

ignominy /ˈɪgnəmɪni/ *n* **1** deep personal humiliation and disgrace **2** disgraceful or dishonourable conduct or quality

ignoramus /ˌɪgnəˈreɪməs/ *n* an ignorant person

ignorance /ˈɪgnərəns/ *n* the state of being ignorant

ignorant /ˈɪgnərənt/ *adj* **1** lacking knowledge, education, or comprehension (of sthg specified) **2** caused by or showing lack of knowledge **3** lacking social training; impolite – chiefly infml

ignore /ɪgˈnɔːʳ/ *v* to refuse to take notice of; disregard

iguana /ɪˈgwɑːnə/ *n* any of various large lizards; *esp* a plant-eating (dark-coloured) tropical American lizard with a serrated crest on its back

ikon /ˈaɪkɒn/ *n* an icon

[1]**ilk** /ɪlk/ *pron, chiefly Scot* *that* same – esp in the names of landed families

[2]**ilk** *n* sort, kind

[1]**ill** /ɪl/ *adj* **worse; worst** **1** bad: e g **a** morally evil **b** malevolent, hostile **c** attributing evil or an objectionable quality **2a** causing discomfort or inconvenience; disagreeable **b(1)** not normal or sound **(2)** not in good health; *also* nauseated **3** unlucky, disadvantageous **4** socially improper **5a** unfriendly, hostile **b** harsh

[2]**ill** *adv* **worse; worst** **1a** with displeasure or hostility **b** in a harsh manner **c** so as to reflect unfavourably **2** in a reprehensible, harsh, or deficient manner **3** hardly, scarcely (e g can *ill* afford it) **4a** in an unfortunate manner; badly, unluckily **b** in a faulty, imperfect, or unpleasant manner *USE* often in combination

[3]**ill** *n* **1** the opposite of good; evil **2a** (a) misfortune, trouble **b(1)** an ailment **(2)** sthg that disturbs or afflicts **3** sthg that reflects unfavourably

ill-advised *adj* showing lack of proper consideration or sound advice

ill-bred *adj* having or showing bad upbringing; impolite

illegal /ɪˈliːgəl/ *adj* not authorized by law – **~ity** *n* – **~ly** *adv*

illegible /ɪˈledʒəbəl/ *adj* not legible – **-bility** *n* – **-bly** *adv*

illegitimate /ˌɪlɨ̣ˈdʒɪtɨ̣mɨ̣t/ *adj* **1** not recognized as lawful offspring; *specif* born out of wedlock **2** wrongly deduced or inferred **3** departing from the regular; abnormal **4** illegal – **-macy** *n*

ill-favoured *adj* **1** unattractive in physical appearance **2** offensive, objectionable

ill-gotten *adj* acquired by illicit or improper means – esp in *ill-gotten gains*

illiberal /ɪˈlɪbərəl/ *adj* not liberal: e g

a lacking culture and refinement **b** not broad-minded; bigoted **c** opposed to liberalism – ~**ity** *n*

illicit /ɪ'lɪsɟt/ *adj* not permitted; unlawful

illiterate /ɪ'lɪtərɟt/ *adj* **1** unable to read or write **2** showing lack of education – **-racy** *n*

ill-natured *adj* having a disagreeable disposition; surly

illness /'ɪlnɟs/ *n* an unhealthy condition of body or mind

illogical /ɪ'lɒdʒɪkəl/ *adj* **1** contrary to the principles of logic **2** devoid of logic; senseless

ill-timed *adj* badly timed; *esp* inopportune

ill-treat *v* to treat cruelly or improperly – ~**ment** *n*

illuminate /ɪ'luːmɟneɪt, ɪ'ljuː-/ *v* **1a(1)** to cast light on; fill with light **(2)** to brighten **b** to enlighten spiritually or intellectually **2** to elucidate **3** to decorate (a manuscript) with elaborate initial letters or marginal designs in gold, silver, and brilliant colours – **-ation** *n*

illusion /ɪ'luː·ʒən/ *n* **1** a false impression or notion **2a(1)** a misleading image presented to the vision **(2)** sthg that deceives or misleads intellectually **b** perception of an object in such a way that it presents a misleading image

illusory /ɪ'luːzəri/ *adj* deceptive, unreal

illustrate /'ɪləstreɪt/ *v* **1a** to clarify (by giving or serving as an example or instance) **b** to provide (e g a book) with visual material **2** to show clearly; demonstrate – **-tive** *adj* – **-tively** *adv*

illustration /ˌɪlə'streɪʃən/ *n* **1** illustrating or being illustrated **2** sthg that serves to illustrate: e g **a** an example that explains or clarifies sthg **b** a picture or diagram that helps to make sthg clear or attractive

illustrious /ɪ'lʌstrɪəs/ *adj* marked by distinction or renown

image /'ɪmɪdʒ/ *n* **1** a reproduction (e g a portrait or statue) of the form of a person or thing **2a** the optical counterpart of an object produced by a lens, mirror, etc or an electronic device **b** a likeness of an object produced on a photographic material **3a** exact likeness **b** a person who strikingly resembles another specified person **4** a typical example or embodiment (e g of a quality) **5a** a mental picture of sthg (not actually present) **b** an idea, concept **6** a figure of speech, esp a metaphor or simile

imagery /'ɪmɟdʒəri/ *n* **1** (the art of making) images **2** figurative language **3** mental images; *esp* the products of imagination

imaginable /ɪ'mædʒənəbəl/ *adj* capable of being imagined

imaginary /ɪ'mædʒənəri/ *adj* existing only in imagination; lacking factual reality

imagination /ɪˌmædʒɟ'neɪʃən/ *n* **1** the act or power of forming a mental image of sthg not present to the senses or never before wholly perceived in reality **2** creative ability **3** a fanciful or empty notion

imaginative /ɪ'mædʒənətɪv/ *adj* **1** of or characterized by imagination **2** given to imagining; having a lively imagination **3** of images; *esp* showing a command of imagery

imagine /ɪ'mædʒɟn/ *v* **1** to form a mental image of (sthg not present) **2** to suppose, think **3** to believe without sufficient basis **4** to use the imagination

imam /'ɪmɑːm, 'ɪmæm/ *n* **1** the leader of prayer in a mosque **2** *cap* a Shiite leader held to be the divinely appointed successor of Muhammad **3** a caliph; *also* any of various Islamic doctors of law or theology

imbalance /ɪm'bæləns/ *n* lack of balance: e g **a** lack of balance between segments of a country's economy **b** numerical disproportion

imbecile /'ɪmbəsiːl/ *n* **1** a mental defective **2** a fool, idiot – **-ility** *n*

imbibe /ɪm'baɪb/ *v* **1** to drink (habitually or to excess) **2** to take in or up; absorb, assimilate

imbroglio /ɪm'brəʊliəʊ/ *n* **1** a confused mass **2a** an intricate or complicated situation (e g in a drama) **b** a confused or complicated misunderstanding or disagreement

imbue /ɪm'bjuː/ *v* to cause to become permeated *with*

imitate /'ɪmɟteɪt/ *v* **1** to follow as a pattern, model, or example **2** to reproduce 3 to resemble 4 to mimic – **-ation, -ativeness** *n* – **-ative** *adj*

immaculate /ɪ'mækjʊlɟt/ *adj* 1 without blemish; pure 2 free from flaw or error 3 spotlessly clean

immaterial /ˌɪmə'tɪərɪəl/ *adj* 1 not consisting of matter; incorporeal 2 unimportant

immature /ˌɪmə'tʃʊəʳ/ *adj* 1 lacking complete growth, differentiation, or development 2a not having arrived at a definitive form or state b exhibiting less than an expected degree of maturity – **-turity** *n*

immeasurable /ɪ'meʒərəbəl/ *adj* indefinitely extensive – **-bly** *adv*

immediacy /ɪ'miːdɪəsi/ *n* 1 the quality or state of being immediate 2 sthg requiring immediate attention – usu pl

immediate /ɪ'miːdɪət/ *adj* 1a acting or being without any intervening agency or factor b involving or derived from a single premise 2 next in line or relationship 3 occurring at once or very shortly 4 in close or direct physical proximity 5 directly touching or concerning a person or thing

¹**immediately** /ɪ'miːdɪətli/ *adv* 1 in direct relation or proximity; directly 2 without delay

²**immediately** *conj* as soon as

immemorial /ˌɪmɟ'mɔːrɪəl/ *adj* extending beyond the reach of memory, record, or tradition

immense /ɪ'mens/ *adj* very great, esp in size, degree, or extent – **-ensity** *n*

immerse /ɪ'mɜːs/ *v* 1 to plunge into sthg, esp a fluid, that surrounds or covers 2 to baptize by complete submergence 3 to engross, absorb – **-sion** *n*

immigrate /'ɪmɟgreɪt/ *v* to come into a country of which one is not a native for permanent residence – **-gration** *n* – **-grant** *n*

imminent /'ɪmɟnənt/ *adj* about to take place; *esp* impending, threatening – **-ence, -ency** *n*

immobile /ɪ'məʊbaɪl/ *adj* 1 incapable of being moved 2 motionless – **-bility** *n*, **-bilize** *v*

immoderate /ɪ'mɒdərɟt/ *adj* lacking in moderation; excessive – **-racy** *n*

immodest /ɪ'mɒdɟst/ *adj* not conforming to standards of sexual propriety – **~y** *n*

immolate /'ɪməleɪt/ *v* to kill (as a sacrificial victim) – **-lation** *n*

immoral /ɪ'mɒrəl/ *adj* not conforming to conventional moral standards, esp in sexual matters – **~ity** *n*

¹**immortal** /ɪ'mɔːtəl/ *adj* 1 exempt from death 2 enduring forever; imperishable – **~ity** *n* – **~ize** *v*

²**immortal** *n* 1a one exempt from death b *pl, often cap* the gods of classical antiquity 2 a person of lasting fame

immovable /ɪ'muːvəbəl/ *adj* 1 not moving or not intended to be moved 2a steadfast, unyielding b incapable of being moved emotionally

immune /ɪ'mjuːn/ *adj* 1 free, exempt 2 having a high degree of resistance to a disease 3a having or producing antibodies to a corresponding antigen b concerned with or involving immunity – **immunity** *n* – **immunize** *v*

immure /ɪ'mjʊəʳ/ *v* 1 to enclose (as if) within walls; imprison 2 to build into, or esp entomb in, a wall

immutable /ɪ'mjuːtəbəl/ *adj* not capable of or susceptible to change – **-bility** *n*

imp /ɪmp/ *n* 1 a small demon 2 a mischievous child; a scamp

¹**impact** /ɪm'pækt/ *v* 1 to fix or press firmly (as if) by packing or wedging 2 to impinge or make contact, esp forcefully

²**impact** /'ɪmpækt/ *n* 1a an impinging or striking, esp of one body against another b (the impetus produced by or as if by) a violent contact or collision 2 a strong or powerful effect or impression

impacted /ɪm'pæktɟd/ *adj, of a tooth* not erupted as a result of lack of space in the jaw or of obstruction by bone or other teeth

impair /ɪm'peəʳ/ *v* to diminish in quality, strength, or amount – **~ment** *n*

impala /ɪm'pɑːlə/ *n* a large brownish African antelope

impale /ɪm'peɪl/ *v* to pierce (as if) with sthg pointed; *esp* to torture or kill by fixing on a stake

impalpable /ɪm'pælpəbəl/ *adj* 1 incapable of being sensed by the touch; intangible **2** not easily discerned or grasped by the mind

impart /ɪm'pɑːt/ *v* **1** to convey, transmit **2** to make known; disclose

impartial /ɪm'pɑːʃəl/ *adj* not biased – **~ity** *n*

impassable /ɪm'pɑːsəbəl/ *adj* incapable of being passed, traversed, or surmounted

impasse /æm'pɑːs/ *n* **1** a predicament from which there is no obvious escape **2** a deadlock

impassive /ɪm'pæsɪv/ *adj* **1** incapable of or not susceptible to emotion **2** showing no feeling or emotion – **-sivity** *n* – **~ly** *adv*

impatient /ɪm'peɪʃənt/ *adj* **1a** restless or quickly roused to anger or exasperation **b** intolerant **2** showing or caused by a lack of patience **3** eagerly desirous; anxious – **-ience** *n* – **~ly** *adv*

impeach /ɪm'piːtʃ/ *v* **1a** to bring an accusation against **b** to charge with a usu serious crime; *specif, chiefly NAm* to charge (a public official) with misconduct in office **2** to cast doubt on; *esp* to challenge the credibility or validity of – **~ment** *n* – **~able** *adj*

impeccable /ɪm'pekəbəl/ *adj* **1** incapable of sinning **2** free from fault or blame; flawless

impecunious /ˌɪmpɪ'kjuːnɪəs/ *adj* having very little or no money – chiefly fml – **~ness** *n*

impedance /ɪm'piːdəns/ *n* sthg that impedes; *esp* the opposition in an electrical circuit to the flow of an alternating current that is analogous to the opposition of an electrical resistance to the flow of a direct current

impede /ɪm'piːd/ *v* to interfere with or retard the progress of – **-diment** *n*

impel /ɪm'pel/ *v* **1** to urge forward or force into action **2** to propel

impenetrable /ɪm'penə̥trəbəl/ *adj* **1a** incapable of being penetrated or pierced **b** inaccessible to intellectual influences or ideas **2** incapable of being comprehended

¹imperative /ɪm'perətɪv/ *adj* **1a** of or being the grammatical mood that expresses command **b** expressive of a command, entreaty, or exhortation **c** having power to restrain, control, and direct **2** urgent

²imperative *n* **1** (a verb form expressing) the imperative mood **2** sthg imperative: e g **a** a command, order **b** an obligatory act or duty **c** an imperative judgment or proposition

imperceptible /ˌɪmpə'septəbəl/ *adj* **1** not perceptible by the mind or senses **2** extremely slight, gradual, or subtle – **-bility** *n* – **-bly** *adv*

¹imperfect /ɪm'pɜːfɪkt/ *adj* **1** not perfect: e g **a** defective **b** not having the stamens and carpels in the same flower **2** of or being a verb tense expressing a continuing state or an incomplete action, esp in the past – **~ion** *n* – **~ly** *adv*

²imperfect *n* (a verb form expressing) the imperfect tense

¹imperial /ɪm'pɪərɪəl/ *adj* **1a** of or befitting an empire, emperor, or empress **b** of the British Empire **2a** sovereign, royal **b** regal, imperious **3** belonging to an official nonmetric British series of weights and measures

²imperial *n* a size of paper usu 30 × 22in (762 × 559mm)

imperialism /ɪm'pɪərɪəlɪzəm/ *n* **1** government by an emperor **2** the policy, practice, or advocacy of extending the power and dominion of a nation, esp by territorial acquisition – **-ist** *adj, n* – **-istic** *adj*

imperil /ɪm'perə̥l/ *v* to endanger

imperious /ɪm'pɪərɪəs/ *adj* marked by arrogant assurance; domineering – **~ness** *n*

imperishable /ɪm'perɪʃəbl/ *adj* **1** not perishable or subject to decay **2** enduring permanently

impermanent /ɪm'pɜːmənənt/ *adj* transient – **-nence** *n*

impermeable /ɪm'pɜːmɪəbl/ *adj* not permitting passage, esp of a fluid

impersonal /ɪm'pɜːsənəl/ *adj* **1a** denoting verbal action with no expressed subject (e g *methinks*) or with a merely formal subject (e g *rained* in *it rained*) **b** *of a pronoun* indefinite **2a** having no personal reference or connection; objective **b** not involving or reflecting the human personality or emotions **c** not having personality

impersonate /ɪm'pɜːsəneɪt/ *v* to assume or act the character of – **-nation** *n* – **-nator** *n*

impertinent /ɪm'pɜːtɨnənt/ *adj* **1** not restrained within due or proper bounds; *also* rude, insolent **2** irrelevant – chiefly fml – **-nence** *n*

imperturbable /ˌɪmpə'tɜːbəbəl/ *adj* marked by extreme calm and composure – **-bility** *n*

impervious /ɪm'pɜːvɪəs/ *adj* **1** impenetrable **2** not capable of being affected or disturbed *USE* usu + *to*

impetuous /ɪm'petʃʊəs/ *adj* **1** marked by impulsive vehemence **2** marked by forceful and violent movement – chiefly poetic – **-osity** *n*

impetus /'ɪmpɨtəs/ *n* **1a** a driving force **b** an incentive, stimulus **2** the energy possessed by a moving body

impiety /ɪm'paɪɨti/ *n* (an act showing) a lack of reverence – **impious** *adj*

impinge /ɪm'pɪndʒ/ *v* **1** to make an impression **2** to encroach, infringe *USE* usu + *on* or *upon*

impish /'ɪmpɪʃ/ *adj* mischievous – **~ness** *n*

implacable /ɪm'plækəbəl/ *adj* not capable of being appeased or pacified

[1]**implant** /ɪm'plɑːnt/ *v* **1** to fix or set securely or deeply **2** to insert in the tissue of a living organism

[2]**implant** /'ɪmplɑːnt/ *n* sthg (e g a graft or hormone pellet) implanted in tissue

[1]**implement** /'ɪmplɨmənt/ *n* **1** an article serving to equip **2** (sby or sthg that serves as) a utensil or tool

[2]**implement** /'ɪmplɨment/ *v* to carry out; *esp* to give practical effect to

implicate /'ɪmplɨkeɪt/ *v* **1** to involve as a consequence, corollary, or inference; imply **2a** to bring into (incriminating) connection **b** to involve in the nature or operation of sthg; affect

implication /ˌɪmplɨ'keɪʃən/ *n* **1a** implicating or being implicated **b** incriminating involvement **2a** implying or being implied **b** a logical relation between 2 propositions such that if the first is true the second must be true **3** sthg implied

implicit /ɪm'plɪsɨt/ *adj* **1a** implied rather than directly stated **b** potentially present though not realized or visible **2** unquestioning, absolute

implore /ɪm'plɔːʳ/ *v* **1** to call on in supplication; beseech **2** to call or beg for earnestly; entreat

implosion /ɪm'pləʊʒən/ *n* **1** imploding **2** the act or action of coming (as if) to a centre

imply /ɪm'plaɪ/ *v* **1** to involve or indicate as a necessary or potential though not expressly stated consequence **2** to express indirectly; hint at

impolite /ˌɪmpə'laɪt/ *adj* not polite; rude – **~ness** *n*

impolitic /ɪm'pɒlɨtɪk/ *adj* unwise, ill-advised – chiefly fml

imponderable /ɪm'pɒndərəbəl/ *n or adj* (sthg) incapable of being precisely weighed or evaluated

[1]**import** /ɪm'pɔːt/ *v* **1** to bring from a foreign or external source; *esp* to bring (e g merchandise) into a place or country from another country **2** to convey as meaning or portent; signify – chiefly fml – **~er** *n*

[2]**import** /'ɪmpɔːt/ *n* **1** sthg imported **2** importing, esp of merchandise **3** purport, meaning **4** (relative) importance *USE* (*3 & 4*) fml

important /ɪm'pɔːtənt/ *adj* of considerable significance or consequence – **-ance** *n* – **~ly** *adv*

importunate /ɪm'pɔːtʃʊnɨt/ *adj* troublesomely urgent; extremely persistent in request or demand – chiefly fml – **-nity** *n*

importune /ˌɪmpə'tjuːn/ *v* **1** to press or urge with repeated requests; solicit with troublesome persistence **2** to solicit for purposes of prostitution *USE* chiefly fml

impose /ɪm'pəʊz/ *v* **1a** to establish or apply as compulsory **b** to establish or make prevail by force **2** to force into the company or on the attention of another **3** to take unwarranted advantage; *also* to be an excessive requirement or burden – **-sition** *n*

imposing /ɪm'pəʊzɪŋ/ *adj* impressive because of size, bearing, dignity, or grandeur

impossible /ɪm'pɒsɨbl/ *adj* **1a** incapable of being or occurring; not possible **b** seemingly incapable of being done, attained, or fulfilled; insuperably difficult **c** difficult to believe 2 extremely undesirable or difficult to put up with – **-bility** *n*

impostor, imposter /ɪm'pɒstəʳ/ *n* one who assumes a false identity or title for fraudulent purposes

impotent /'ɪmpətənt/ *adj* **1** lacking in efficacy, strength, or vigour **2a** unable to copulate through an inability to maintain an erection of the penis **b** *of a male* sterile – not used technically – **-tence** *n*

impound /ɪm'paʊnd/ *v* **1a** to shut up (as if) in a pound; confine **b** to take and hold in legal custody **2** to collect and confine (water) (as if) in a reservoir

impoverish /ɪm'pɒvərɪʃ/ *v* **1** to make poor **2** to deprive of strength, richness, or fertility

impracticable /ɪm'præktɪkəbəl/ *adj* **1** incapable of being put into effect or carried out **2** impassable – **-bility** *n*

impractical /ɪm'præktɪkəl/ *adj* not practical: e g **a** incapable of dealing sensibly with practical matters **b** impracticable – **~ity** *n*

impregnable /ɪm'pregnəbəl/ *adj* **1** incapable of being taken by assault **2** beyond criticism or question – **-bility** *n*

impregnate /ɪm'pregneɪt/ *v* **1a** to introduce sperm cells into **b** to make pregnant; fertilize **2a** to cause to be imbued, permeated, or saturated **b** to permeate thoroughly

impresario /,ɪmprɪ̍'sɑːriəʊ/ *n* one who organizes, puts on, or sponsors a public entertainment (e g a sports event); *esp* the manager or conductor of an opera or concert company

¹**impress** /ɪm'pres/ *v* **1a** to apply with pressure so as to imprint **b** to mark (as if) by pressure or stamping **2a** to fix strongly or deeply (e g in the mind or memory) **b** to produce a deep and usu favourable impression (on) **3** to transmit (force or motion) by pressure

²**impress** /'ɪmpres/ *n* **1** the act of impressing **2** a mark made by pressure **3** an impression, effect

³**impress** /ɪm'pres/ *v* to procure or enlist by forcible persuasion

impression /ɪm'preʃən/ *n* **1** the act or process of impressing **2** the effect produced by impressing: e g **a** a stamp, form, or figure produced by physical contact **b** a (marked) influence or effect on the mind or senses; *esp* a favourable impression **3a** an effect of alteration or improvement **b** a telling image impressed on the mind or senses **4a** (a print or copy made from) the contact of a printing surface and the material being printed **b** all the copies of a publication (e g a book) printed in 1 continuous operation **5** a usu indistinct or imprecise notion or recollection **6** an imitation or representation of salient features in an artistic or theatrical medium; *esp* an imitation in caricature of a noted personality as a form of theatrical entertainment

impressionable /ɪm'preʃənəbəl/ *adj* **1** easily influenced **2** easily moulded – **-bly** *adv* – **-bility** *n*

impressionism /ɪm'preʃənɪzəm/ *n* **1** *often cap* an art movement, esp in late 19th-c France, that tries to convey the effects of actual reflected light on natural usu outdoor subjects **2** literary depiction that seeks to convey a general subjective impression rather than a detailed re-creation of reality – **-ist** *adj, n*

impressionistic /ɪm,preʃə'nɪstɪk/ *adj* **1** of or being impressionism **2** based on or involving subjective impression as distinct from knowledge, fact, or systematic thought – **~ally** *adv*

impressive /ɪm'presɪv/ *adj* making a marked impression; stirring deep feelings, esp of awe or admiration – **~ly** *adv* – **~ness** *n*

¹**imprint** /ɪm'prɪnt/ *v* **1** to mark (as if) by pressure **2** to fix indelibly or permanently (e g on the memory)

²**imprint** /'ɪmprɪnt/ *n* **1** a mark or depression made by pressure **2** a publisher's name printed at the foot of a title-page **3** an indelible distinguishing effect or influence

imprison /ɪm'prɪzən/ *v* to put (as if) in prison – **~ment** *n*

improbable /ɪm'prɒbəbəl/ *adj* unlikely to be true or to occur – **-bility** *n* – **-bly** *adv*

¹**impromptu** /ɪm'prɒmptjuː/ *adj* made, done, composed, or uttered (as if) on the spur of the moment

²**impromptu** *n* **1** sthg impromptu **2** a

musical composition suggesting improvisation

improper /ɪm'prɒpəʳ/ *adj* **1** not in accordance with fact, truth, or correct procedure **2** not suitable or appropriate **3** not in accordance with propriety or modesty; indecent – **-priety** *n*

improve /ɪm'pruːv/ *v* **1** to enhance in value or quality; make better **2** to use to good purpose **3** to advance or make progress in what is desirable **4** to make useful additions or amendments – **~ment** *n*

improvident /ɪm'prɒvɨdənt/ *adj* lacking foresight; not providing for the future – **-dence** *n*

improvise /'ɪmprəvaɪz/ *v* **1** to compose, recite, or perform impromptu or without a set script, musical score, etc **2** to make, devise, or provide (sthg) without preparation (from what is conveniently to hand) – **-visation** *n*

imprudent /ɪm'pruːdənt/ *adj* lacking discretion or caution – **-dence** *n*

impudent /'ɪmpjʊdənt/ *adj* marked by contemptuous or cocky boldness or disregard of others – **-dence** *n*

impugn /ɪm'pjuːn/ *v* to assail by words or arguments; call into question the validity or integrity of

impulse /'ɪmpʌls/ *n* **1a** (motion produced by) the act of driving onwards with sudden force **b** a wave of excitation transmitted through a nerve that results in physiological (e g muscular) activity or inhibition **2a** a force so communicated as to produce motion suddenly **b** inspiration, stimulus **3a** a sudden spontaneous inclination or incitement to some usu unpremeditated action **b** a propensity or natural tendency, usu other than rational

impulsion /ɪm'pʌlʃən/ *n* **1** impelling or being impelled **2** an impelling force **3** an impetus

impulsive /ɪm'pʌlsɪv/ *adj* **1** having the power of driving or impelling **2** actuated by or prone to act on impulse – **~ness** *n*

impunity /ɪm'pjuːnɨti/ *n* exemption or freedom from punishment, harm, or loss

impure /ɪm'pjʊəʳ/ *adj* not pure: e g **a** not chaste **b** containing sthg unclean **c** ritually unclean **d** mixed; *esp* adulterated – **-rity** *n*

impute /ɪm'pjuːt/ *v* to attribute unjustly *to;* blame

¹in /ɪn/ *prep* **1a(1)** – used to indicate location within or inside sthg three-dimensional (e g swimming *in* the lake) **(2)** – used to indicate location within or not beyond limits (e g *in* sight) **(3)** at – used with the names of cities, countries, and seas (e g *in* London) **(4)** during (e g *in* the summer) **(5)** by or before the end of (e g will come *in* an hour) **b** into (e g come *in* the kitchen and get warm) **2a** – used to indicate means, instrumentality, or medium of expression (e g written *in* French) **b** – used to describe costume (e g a girl *in* red) **3a** – used to indicate qualification, manner, circumstance, or condition (e g *in* fun; *in* a hurry) **b** so as to be **c** – used to indicate occupation or membership (e g a job *in* insurance) **4a** as regards (e g equal *in* distance) **b** by way of (e g said *in* reply) **5a** – used to indicate division, arrangement, or quantity (e g standing *in* a circle) **b** – used to indicate the larger member of a ratio (e g one *in* six is eligible) **6** *of an animal* pregnant with (e g *in* calf) **7** – used to introduce indirect objects (e g rejoice *in*) or to form adverbial phrases

²in *adv* **1a** to or towards the inside or centre (e g come *in* out of the rain) **b** so as to incorporate (e g mix *in* the flour) **c** to or towards home, the shore, or one's destination (e g 3 ships came sailing *in*) **d** at a particular place, esp at one's home or business (e g be *in* for lunch) **e** into concealment (e g the sun went *in*) **2a** so as to be added or included (e g fit a piece *in*) **b** in or into political power (e g voted them *in*) **c(1)** on good terms (e g *in* with the boss) **(2)** in a position of assured success **(3)** into a state of efficiency or proficiency (e g work a horse *in*) **d** in or into vogue or fashion **e** in or into a centre, esp a central point of control (e g letters pouring *in*)

³in *adj* **1a** located inside **b** being in operation or power (e g the fire's still *in*) **c** shared by a select group (e g an *in* joke) **2** directed or serving to direct inwards (e g the *in* tray) **3** extremely fashionable

inability /ˌɪnəˈbɪlɪ̣ti/ *n* lack of sufficient power, resources, or capacity
inaccurate /ɪnˈækjʊrɪ̣t/ *adj* faulty – **-racy** *n*
inaction /ɪnˈækʃən/ *n* lack of action or activity – **-tive** *adj* – **-tivity** *n*
inadequate /ɪnˈædɪ̣kwɪ̣t/ *adj* not adequate: e g **a** insufficient **b** characteristically unable to cope – **-acy** *n*
inadvertent /ˌɪnədˈvɜːtənt/ *adj* **1** heedless, inattentive **2** unintentional – **-tence** *n*
inalienable /ɪnˈeɪlɪənəbəl/ *adj* incapable of being alienated
inane /ɪˈneɪn/ *adj* lacking significance, meaning, or point – **-nity** *n*
inanimate /ɪnˈænɪ̣mɪ̣t/ *adj* **1** not endowed with life or spirit **2** lacking consciousness or power of motion – **~ness** *n*
inappropriate /ɪnəˈprəʊprɪ̣ɪ̣t/ *adj* not suitable or fitting
inapt /ɪnˈæpt/ *adj* not suitable or appropriate – **~ness** *n*
inaptitude /ɪnˈæptɪ̣tjuːd/ *n* lack of aptitude
inarticulate /ˌɪnɑːˈtɪkjʊlɪ̣t/ *adj* **1a** not understandable as spoken words **b** incapable of (being expressed by) speech, esp under stress of emotion **2a** not giving or not able to give coherent, clear, or effective expression to one's ideas or feelings **b** not coherently, clearly, or effectively expressed **3** not jointed or hinged – **~ness** *n*
inasmuch as /ˌɪnəzˈmʌtʃ əz/ *conj* **1** insofar as **2** in view of the fact that; because
inattention /ˌɪnəˈtenʃən/ *n* failure to pay attention; disregard – **-tive** *adj* – **-tiveness** *n*
inaugurate /ɪˈnɔːgjʊreɪt/ *v* **1** to induct ceremonially into office **2** to observe formally, or bring about, the beginning of – **-tion** *n* – **-ral** *adj*
inboard /ɪnˈbɔːd/ *adv* towards the centre line of a vessel
inborn /ˌɪnˈbɔːn/ *adj* **1** born in or with one; forming part of one's natural make-up **2** hereditary, inherited
inbred /ˌɪnˈbred/ *adj* **1** rooted and deeply ingrained in one's nature **2** subjected to or produced by inbreeding
inbreeding /ˈɪnbriːdɪŋ/ *n* **1** the interbreeding of closely related individuals, esp to preserve and fix desirable characters **2** confinement to a narrow range or a local or limited field of choice
incalculable /ɪnˈkælkjʊləbəl/ *adj* **1** too large or numerous to be calculated **2** unpredictable, uncertain – **-bly** *adv*
incandescent /ˌɪnkænˈdesənt/ *adj* **1a** white, glowing, or luminous with intense heat **b** strikingly bright, radiant, or clear **2** of or being visible light produced by a (white) hot body – **-cence** *n*
incantation /ˌɪnkænˈteɪʃən/ *n* the use of spoken or sung spells in magic ritual; *also* a formula so used
incapable /ɪnˈkeɪpəbəl/ *adj* lacking capacity, ability, or qualification for the purpose or end in view: e g **a** not in a state or of a kind to admit *of* **b** not able or fit for the doing or performance *of* – **-bility** *n* – **-bly** *adv*
incapacitate /ˌɪnkəˈpæsɪ̣teɪt/ *v* **1** to deprive of capacity or natural power; disable **2** to disqualify legally – **-pacity** *n*
incarcerate /ɪnˈkɑːsəreɪt/ *v* to imprison, confine – **-ration** *n*
[1]**incarnate** /ɪnˈkɑːnɪ̣t/ *adj* **1** invested with bodily, esp human, nature and form **2** that is the essence of; typified
[2]**incarnate** /ɪnˈkɑːneɪt/ *v* to make incarnate
incarnation /ˌɪnkɑːˈneɪʃən/ *n* **1** making or being incarnate **2a(1)** the embodiment of a deity or spirit in an earthly form **(2)** *cap* Christ's human manifestation **b** a quality or concept typified or made concrete, esp in a person **3** any of several successive bodily manifestations or lives
[1]**incendiary** /ɪnˈsendɪəri/ *n* **1a** one who deliberately sets fire to property **b** an incendiary agent (e g a bomb) **2** one who inflames or stirs up factions, quarrels, or sedition
[2]**incendiary** *adj* **1** of the deliberate burning of property **2** tending to inflame or stir up trouble **3** (of, being, or involving the use of a missile containing a chemical) that ignites spontaneously on contact
[1]**incense** /ˈɪnsens/ *n* **1** material used to produce a fragrant smell when burned

2 the perfume given off by some spices and gums when burned; *broadly* a pleasing scent

²**incense** /ɪn'sens/ *v* to arouse the extreme anger or indignation of

incentive /ɪn'sentɪv/ *n* sthg that motivates or spurs one on (e g to action or effort)

inception /ɪn'sepʃən/ *n* an act, process, or instance of beginning

incessant /ɪn'sesənt/ *adj* continuing without interruption – **~ly** *adv*

incest /'ɪnsest/ *n* sexual intercourse between people so closely related that they are forbidden by law to marry – **~uous** *adj*

¹**inch** /ɪntʃ/ *n* **1** a unit of length equal to ¹⁄₃₆ yd (about 25.4mm) **2** a small amount, distance, or degree **3** *pl* stature, height **4** a fall of rain, snow, etc enough to cover a surface to the depth of 1in

²**inch** *v* to move by small degrees

inchoate /ɪn'kəʊɪ̣t/ *adj* only partly in existence or operation; *esp* imperfectly formed or formulated – fml

incidence /'ɪnsɪ̣dəns/ *n* **1** an occurrence **2** the rate of occurrence or influence

¹**incident** /'ɪnsɪ̣dənt/ *n* **1** an occurrence of an action or situation that is a separate unit of experience **2** an occurrence that is a cause of conflict or disagreement **3** an event occurring as part of a series or as dependent on or subordinate to sthg else

²**incident** *adj* **1** that is a usual accompaniment or consequence **2** dependent on another thing in law

¹**incidental** /ˌɪnsɪ̣'dentl/ *adj* **1** occurring merely by chance **2** likely to ensue as a chance or minor consequence

²**incidental** /ˌɪnsɪ̣'dentl/ *n* **1** sthg incidental **2** *pl* minor items (e g of expenses)

incidentally /ˌɪnsɪ̣'dentəli/ *adv* **1** by chance **2** by the way

incinerate /ɪn'sɪnəreɪt/ *v* to cause to burn to ashes – **-ration** *n*

incinerator /ɪn'sɪnəreɪtəʳ/ *n* a furnace or container for incinerating waste materials

incipient /ɪn'sɪpɪənt/ *adj* beginning to come into being or to become apparent – **-ience, -iency** *n*

incise /ɪn'saɪz/ *v* **1** to cut into **2** to carve (letters, figures, etc) into; engrave – **-cision** *n*

incisive /ɪn'saɪsɪv/ *adj* impressively direct and decisive (e g in manner or presentation)

incisor /ɪn'saɪzəʳ/ *n* a cutting tooth; *specif* any of the cutting teeth in mammals in front of the canines

incite /ɪn'saɪt/ *v* to move to action; stir up – **~ment** *n*

¹**incline** /ɪn'klaɪn/ *v* **1** to (cause to) lean, tend, or become drawn towards an opinion or course of conduct **2** to (cause to) deviate or move from a line, direction, or course, esp from the vertical or horizontal – **-nation** *n*

²**incline** /'ɪnklaɪn/ *n* an inclined surface; a slope

inclose /ɪn'kləʊz/ *v* to enclose

include /ɪn'kluːd/ *v* **1** to contain, enclose **2** to take in or comprise as a part of a larger group, set, or principle – **-ding** *prep* – **~d** *adj* – **-usion** *n*

inclusive /ɪn'kluːsɪv/ *adj* **1a** broad in orientation or scope **b** covering or intended to cover all or the specified items, costs, or services **2** including the stated limits or extremes

¹**incognito** /ˌɪnkɒg'niːtəʊ, ɪn'kɒgnɪtəʊ/ *adv or adj* with one's identity concealed

²**incognito** *n* the state or disguise of one who is incognito

incoherent /ˌɪnkəʊ'hɪərənt/ *adj* lacking in logical connection or clarity of expression; unintelligible – **-ence** *n*

incombustible /ˌɪnkəm'bʌstɪ̣bəl/ *adj* incapable of being ignited or burned

income /'ɪŋkʌm, 'ɪn-/ *n* (the amount of) a usu periodic gain or recurrent benefit usu measured in money that derives from one's work, property, or investment

income tax *n* a tax on income

¹**incoming** /'ɪnkʌmɪŋ/ *n* **1** a coming in, arrival **2** *pl* income

²**incoming** *adj* **1** arriving or coming in **2** just starting, beginning, or succeeding

incommensurable /ˌɪnkə'menʃərəbl/ *adj* lacking a common basis of comparison in respect to a quality normally subject to comparison; incapable of being compared

incommensurate /ˌɪnkəˈmenʃərɪ̣t/ *adj* not adequate (in proportion)

incommode /ˌɪnkəˈməʊd/ *v* to inconvenience, trouble – fml – **-dious** *adj*

incommunicado /ˌɪnkəmjuːnɪˈkɑːdəʊ/ *adv or adj* without means of communication; *also* in solitary confinement

incomparable /ɪnˈkɒmpərəbəl/ *adj* **1** matchless **2** not suitable for comparison – **-bility** *n* – **-bly** *adv*

incompatible /ˌɪnkəmˈpætəbəl/ *adj* **1** (incapable of association because) incongruous, discordant, or disagreeing **2** unsuitable for use together because of undesirable chemical or physiological effects – **-bility** *n* – **-bly** *adv*

incompetent /ɪnˈkɒmpɪ̣tənt/ *adj* **1** lacking the qualities needed for effective action **2** not legally qualified **3** inadequate to or unsuitable for a particular purpose – **-ence, -ency** *n*

incomplete /ˌɪnkəmˈpliːt/ *adj* **1** unfinished **2** lacking a part – **~ness** *n*

incomprehensible /ɪnˌkɒmprɪˈhensəbəl/ *adj* impossible to comprehend or understand – **-bility** *n* – **-bly** *adv*

incomprehension /ɪnˌkɒmprɪˈhenʃən/ *n* lack of comprehension or understanding

inconceivable /ˌɪnkənˈsiːvəbəl/ *adj* **1** beyond comprehension; unimaginable **2** unbelievable – **-bility** *n*

inconclusive /ˌɪnkənˈkluːsɪv/ *adj* leading to no conclusion or definite result – **~ness** *n*

incongruous /ɪnˈkɒŋgrʊəs/ *adj* out of place; discordant or disagreeing – **~ness** *n* – **-uity** *n*

inconsequential /ɪnˌkɒnsɪ̣ˈkwenʃəl/ *adj* **1** irrelevant **2** of no significance – **~ity** *n*

inconsiderable /ˌɪnkənˈsɪdərəbəl/ *adj* trivial

inconsiderate /ˌɪnkənˈsɪdərɪ̣t/ *adj* careless of the rights or feelings of others; thoughtless – **~ness** *n*

inconsistent /ˌɪnkənˈsɪstənt/ *adj* **1** not compatible; containing incompatible elements **2** not consistent or logical in thought or actions – **-ency** *n*

inconsolable /ˌɪnkənˈsəʊləbəl/ *adj* incapable of being consoled; brokenhearted – **-bly** *adv*

inconspicuous /ˌɪnkənˈspɪkjʊəs/ *adj* not readily noticeable – **~ly** *adv* – **~ness** *n*

inconstant /ɪnˈkɒnstənt/ *adj* **1** likely to change frequently without apparent reason **2** unfaithful – **-stancy** *n*

incontestable /ˌɪnkənˈtestəbəl/ *adj* not contestable; indisputable – **-bility** *n* – **-bly** *adv*

incontinent /ɪnˈkɒntɪ̣nənt/ *adj* **1** lacking self-restraint (e g in sexual appetite) **2** suffering from lack of control of urination or defecation **3** not under control or restraint – **-nence** *n*

incontrovertible /ɪnˌkɒntrəˈvɜːtəbəl/ *adj* indisputable – **-bly** *adv*

inconvenience /ˌɪnkənˈviːnɪəns/ *v or n* (to subject to) difficulty or discomfort or sthg that is inconvenient

inconvenient /ˌɪnkənˈviːnɪənt/ *adj* not convenient, esp in causing difficulty, discomfort, or annoyance – **~ly** *adv* – **-ence** *n*

incorporate /ɪnˈkɔːpəreɪt/ *v* **1a** to unite thoroughly with or work indistinguishably into sthg **b** to admit to membership in a corporate body **2a** to combine thoroughly to form a consistent whole **b** to form into a legal corporation **3** to unite in or as 1 body – **-ration** *n*

incorporated /ɪnˈkɔːpəreɪtɪ̣d/ *also* **incorporate** *adj* **1** united in 1 body **2** formed into a legal corporation

incorrect /ˌɪnkəˈrekt/ *adj* **1** inaccurate; factually wrong **2** not in accordance with an established norm; improper – **~ly** *adv* – **~ness** *n*

incorrigible /ɪnˈkɒrɪ̣dʒəbəl/ *adj* **1** incapable of being corrected or amended; *esp* incurably bad **2** unwilling or unlikely to change – **-bility** *n* – **-bly** *adv*

incorruptible /ˌɪnkəˈrʌptəbəl/ *adj* **1** not subject to decay or dissolution **2** incapable of being bribed or morally corrupted – **-bility** *n* – **-bly** *adv*

¹increase /ɪnˈkriːs/ *v* **1** to make or become (progressively) greater (e g in size, amount, quality, number, or intensity) **2** to multiply by the production of young

[2]**increase** /'ɪŋkriːs/ *n* **1** (an) addition or enlargement in size, extent, quantity, etc **2** sthg (e g offspring, produce, or profit) added to an original stock by addition or growth – **-singly** *adv*

incredible /ɪn'kredəbəl/ *adj* **1** too extraordinary and improbable to be believed; *also* hard to believe **2** – used as a generalized term of approval – **-bility** *n* – **-bly** *adv*

incredulous /ɪn'kredjʊləs/ *adj* **1** unwilling to admit or accept what is offered as true **2** expressing disbelief – **-ulity** *n* – **~ly** *adv*

increment /'ɪŋkrɨmənt/ *n* **1** (the amount of) an increase, esp in quantity or value **2** any of a series of regular consecutive additions **3** a regular increase in pay resulting from an additional year's service – **~al** *adj* – **~ally** *adv*

incriminate /ɪn'krɪmɨneɪt/ *v* to involve in or demonstrate involvement in a crime or fault – **-nation** *n*

incrustation /ˌɪnkrʌ'steɪʃən/ *n* **1** encrusting or being encrusted **2** (a growth or accumulation resembling) a crust or hard coating

incubate /'ɪŋkjʊbeɪt/ *v* **1** to sit on so as to hatch (eggs) by the warmth of the body; *also* to maintain (e g an embryo or a chemically active system) under conditions favourable for hatching, development, or reaction **2** to cause (e g an idea) to develop **3** to undergo incubation

incubation /ˌɪŋkjʊ'beɪʃən/ *n* **1** incubating **2** the period between infection by a disease-causing agent and the manifestation of the disease

incubator /'ɪŋkjʊbeɪtəʳ/ *n* **1** an apparatus in which eggs are hatched artificially **2** an apparatus that maintains controlled conditions, esp for the housing of premature or sick babies or the cultivation of microorganisms

incubus /'ɪŋkjʊbəs/ *n, pl* **incubuses, incubi** **1** a male demon believed to have sexual intercourse with women in their sleep **2** (one who or that which oppresses or burdens like) a nightmare

incumbency /ɪn'kʌmbənsi/ *n* the sphere of action or period of office of an incumbent

[1]**incumbent** /ɪn'kʌmbənt/ *n* the holder of an office or Anglican benefice

[2]**incumbent** *adj* **1** imposed as a duty or obligation – usu + *on* or *upon* **2** occupying a specified office

incur /ɪn'kɜːʳ/ *v* to become liable or subject to; bring upon oneself

incursion /ɪn'kɜːʃən, -ʒən/ *n* an unexpected or sudden usu brief invasion or entrance, esp into another's territory

indebted /ɪn'detɨd/ *adj* **1** owing money **2** owing gratitude or recognition to another – **~ness** *n*

indecent /ɪn'diːsənt/ *adj* **1** hardly suitable; unseemly **2** morally offensive – **~ly** *adv* – **-cency** *n*

indecent assault *n* a sexual assault exclusive of rape

indecent exposure *n* intentional public exposure of part of one's body (e g the genitals) in violation of generally accepted standards of decency

indecision /ˌɪndɪ'sɪʒən/ *n* a wavering between 2 or more possible courses of action

indecisive /ˌɪndɪ'saɪsɪv/ *adj* **1** giving an uncertain result **2** marked by or prone to indecision – **~ly** *adv* – **~ness** *n*

indeed /ɪn'diːd/ *adv* **1** without any question; truly – often used in agreement **2** – used for emphasis after *very* and an adjective or adverb **3** in point of fact; actually **4** – expressing irony, disbelief, or surprise

indefatigable /ˌɪndɪ'fætɪgəbəl/ *adj* tireless

indefensible /ˌɪndɪ'fensəbəl/ *adj* incapable of being defended or justified

indefinite /ɪn'defənɨt/ *adj* **1** designating an unidentified or not immediately identifiable person or thing **2** not precise; vague **3** having no exact limits – **~ness** *n* – **~ly** *adv*

indelible /ɪn'deləbəl/ *adj* (making marks difficult to remove or) incapable of being removed or erased – **-bly** *adv*

indelicate /ɪn'delɨkɨt/ *adj* offensive to good manners or refined taste – **~ly** *adv* – **-cacy** *n*

indemnify /ɪn'demnɨfaɪ/ *v* **1** to secure against harm, loss, or damage **2** to make compensation to for incurred harm, loss, or damage – **-fication** *n*

indemnity /ɪn'demnɪ̣ti/ *n* security against harm, loss, or damage

[1]indent /ɪn'dent/ *v* **1a** to cut or divide (a document) to produce sections with edges that can be matched for authentication **b** to draw up (e g a deed) in 2 or more exact copies **2** to notch the edge of **3** to set (e g a line of a paragraph) in from the margin **4** *chiefly Br* to requisition officially **5** to form an indentation

[2]indent /'ɪndent/ *n* **1** an indenture **2** an indention **3** *chiefly Br* an official requisition

[3]indent /ɪn'dent/ *v* (to force inwards so as) to form a depression in

indentation /,ɪnden'teɪʃən/ *n* **1a** an angular cut in an edge **b** a usu deep recess (e g in a coastline) **2** indention

indention /ɪn'denʃən/ *n* **1** indenting or being indented **2** the blank space produced by indenting

[1]indenture /ɪn'dentʃə'/ *n* **1a** an indented document **b** a contract binding sby to work for another – usu pl with sing. meaning **2a** a formal certificate (e g an inventory or voucher) prepared for purposes of control **b** a document stating the terms under which a security (e g a bond) is issued

[2]indenture *v* to bind (e g an apprentice) by indentures

[1]independent /,ɪndɪ̣'pendənt/ *adj* **1** not dependent: e g **a(1)** self-governing (2) not affiliated with a larger controlling unit **b(1)** not relying on sthg else (2) not committed to a political party **c(1)** not requiring or relying on, or allowing oneself to be controlled by, others (e g for guidance or care) (2) having or providing enough money to live on, esp without working **2a** *of a clause* able to stand alone as a complete statement – **-ence** *n* – **~ly** *adv*

[2]independent /,ɪndɪ̣'pendənt/ *n, often cap* sby not bound by a political party

indescribable /,ɪndɪs'kraɪbəbəl/ *adj* **1** that cannot be described **2** surpassing description – **-bly** *adv*

indeterminable /,ɪndɪ't3ːmɪ̣nəbəl/ *adj* incapable of being definitely decided or ascertained – **-bly** *adv*

indeterminate /,ɪndɪ't3ːmɪ̣nɪ̣t/ *adj* not definitely or precisely determined or fixed – **-nacy** *n*

[1]index /'ɪndeks/ *n, pl* **indexes, indices** **1** a guide or list to aid reference; e g *esp* an alphabetical list of items (e g topics or names) treated in a printed work that gives with each item the page number where it appears **2** sthg that points towards or demonstrates a particular state of affairs **3** a list of restricted or prohibited material; *specif, cap the* the list of books banned by the Roman Catholic church **4** a character ☞ used to direct attention (e g to a note or paragraph)

[2]index *v* **1** to provide with or list in an index **2** to serve as an index of **3** to cause to be index-linked **4** to prepare an index

index finger *n* the forefinger

Indian /'ɪndɪən/ *n* **1** a native or inhabitant of India **2a** a member of any of the indigenous peoples of N, Central, or S America excluding the Eskimos **b** any of the native languages of American Indians

Indian file *n* single file

indian ink *n, often cap 1st I, Br* (an ink made from) a solid black pigment used in drawing and lettering

Indian summer *n* **1** a period of warm weather in late autumn or early winter **2** a happy or flourishing period occurring towards the end of sthg, esp of a person's life

india rubber *n, often cap I* a rubber; an eraser

indicate /'ɪndɪ̣keɪt/ *v* **1a(1)** to point to; point out (2) to show or demonstrate as or by means of a sign or pointer **b** to be a sign or symptom of **c** to demonstrate or suggest the necessity or advisability of – chiefly pass **2** to state or express briefly; suggest – **-ation** *n*

indicative /ɪn'dɪkətɪv/ *adj* serving to indicate – **~ly** *adv*

indicator /'ɪndɪ̣keɪtə'/ *n* **1a** a hand or needle on an instrument (e g a dial) **b** an instrument for giving visual readings attached to a machine or apparatus **c** a device (e g a flashing light) on a vehicle that indicates an intention to change direction **2a** a substance (e g litmus) that shows, esp by change of colour, the condition (e g acidity or alkalinity) of a solution **b** a chemical tracer (e g an isotope) **3** a statistic (e g the level of industrial production) that gives an indication of the state of a national economy

indices /ˈɪndɨsiːz/ *pl of* **index**

indict /ɪnˈdaɪt/ *v* **1** to charge with an offence **2** to charge with a crime – **~ment** *n* – **~able** *adj*

indifferent /ɪnˈdɪfərənt/ *adj* **1** that does not matter one way or the other **2** not interested in or concerned about sthg **3a** neither good nor bad; mediocre **b** not very good; inferior – **~ly** *adv* – **-ence** *n*

indigenous /ɪnˈdɪdʒənəs/ *adj* **1** originating, growing, or living naturally in a particular region or environment **2** innate, inborn – **~ly** *adv*

indigent /ˈɪndɪdʒənt/ *adj* needy, poor – fml – **-gence** *n*

indigestible /ɪn,dɪˈʒestəbəl/ *adj* not (easily) digested – **-bility** *n*, **-bly** *adv*

indigestion /ˌɪndɪˈdʒestʃən/ *n* (pain in the digestive system usu resulting from) difficulty in digesting sthg

indignant /ɪnˈdɪgnənt/ *adj* angry because of sthg judged unjust, mean, etc – **-ation** *n* – **~ly** *adv*

indignity /ɪnˈdɪgnɨti/ *n* **1** an act that offends against a person's dignity or self-respect **2** humiliating treatment

indigo /ˈɪndɪgəʊ/ *n* **1** (any of several dyes related to) a blue dye with a coppery lustre formerly obtained from a plant and now made artificially **2** a dark greyish blue colour whose hue lies between violet and blue in the spectrum **3** a (leguminous) plant that yields indigo

indirect /ˌɪndɨˈrekt/ *adj* **1a** deviating from a direct line or course **b** not going straight to the point **2** not straightforward or open **3** not directly aimed at **4** stating what a real or supposed original speaker said but with changes of tense, person, etc – **~ly** *adv* – **~ness** *n*

indirect object *n* a grammatical object representing the secondary goal of the action of its verb (e g *her* in *I gave her the book*)

indiscernible /ˌɪndɪˈsɜːnəbəl/ *adj* **1** that cannot be perceived or recognized **2** not recognizable as separate or distinct

indiscipline /ɪnˈdɪsɨplɨn/ *n* lack of discipline

indiscreet /ˌɪndɪˈskriːt/ *adj* not discreet; imprudent – **-cretion** *n* – **~ly** *adv*

indiscriminate /ˌɪndɪˈskrɪmɨnɨt/ *adj* **1** not marked by careful distinction; lacking in discrimination and discernment **2** not differentiated; confused – **~ly** *adv*

indispensable /ˌɪndɪˈspensəbəl/ *adj* that cannot be done without – **-bility** *n* – **-bly** *adv*

indisposed /ˌɪndɪˈspəʊzd/ *adj* **1** slightly ill **2** averse – **-position** *n*

indisputable /ˌɪndɪˈspjuːtəbəl/ *adj* incontestable – **-bly** *adv*

indistinct /ˌɪndɪˈstɪŋkt/ *adj* not distinct: e g **a** not sharply outlined or separable; not clearly seen **b** not clearly recognizable or understandable – **~ly** *adv* – **~ness** *n*

indistinguishable /ˌɪndɪˈstɪŋgwɪʃəbəl/ *adj* incapable of being **a** clearly perceived **b** discriminated – **-bly** *adv*

[1]**individual** /ˌɪndɨˈvɪdʒʊəl/ *adj* **1a** of or being an individual **b** intended for 1 person **2** existing as a distinct entity; separate **3** having marked individuality – **~ly** *adv*

[2]**individual** *n* **1** a particular person, being, or thing (as distinguished from a class, species, or collection) **2** a person

individualism /ˌɪndɪˈvɪdʒʊəlɪzəm/ *n* (conduct guided by) **a** a doctrine that bases morality on the interests of the individual **b** a theory maintaining the independence of the individual and stressing individual initiative – **-ist** *n, adj* – **-istic** *adj*

individuality /ˌɪndɨˌvɪdʒʊˈælɨti/ *n* **1** the total character peculiar to and distinguishing an individual from others **2** the tendency to pursue one's course with marked independence or self-reliance

individual·ize, -ise /ˌɪndɨˈvɪdʒʊəlaɪz/ *v* **1** to make individual in character **2** to treat individually **3** to adapt to suit a particular individual – **-ization** *n*

indoctrinate /ɪn'dɒktrɪ̥neɪt/ *v* to imbue with a usu partisan or sectarian opinion, point of view, or ideology – **-nation** *n*

Indo-European *adj or n* (of or belonging to) a family of languages spoken in most of Europe, Asia as far east as N India, and N and S America

indolent /'ɪndələnt/ *adj* **1** averse to activity, effort, or movement **b** conducive to or exhibiting laziness – **~ly** *adv* – **-lence** *n*

indomitable /ɪn'dɒmɪ̥təbəl/ *adj* incapable of being subdued – **-bly** *adv*

indoor /'ɪndɔːʳ/ *adj* **1** of the interior of a building **2** done, living, or belonging indoors

indoors /ˌɪn'dɔːz/ *adv* in or into a building

indrawn /ˌɪn'drɔːn/ *adj* **1** drawn in **2** aloof, reserved

indubitable /ɪn'djuːbɪ̥təbəl/ *adj* too evident to be doubted – **-bly** *adv*

induce /ɪn'djuːs/ *v* **1** to lead on to do sthg; move by persuasion or influence **2a** to cause to appear or to happen; bring on; *specif* to cause (labour) to begin by the use of drugs **b** to cause the formation of **3** to establish by logical induction; *specif* to infer from particulars

inducement /ɪn'djuːsmənt/ *n* sthg that induces; *esp* a motive or consideration that encourages one to do sthg

inductance /ɪn'dʌktəns/ *n* a property of an electric circuit by which an electromotive force is induced in it by a variation of current either in the circuit itself or in a neighbouring circuit

induction /ɪn'dʌkʃən/ *n* **1a** the act or process of inducting (e g into office) **b** an initial experience; an initiation **2** the act or an instance of reasoning from particular premises to a general conclusion; *also* a conclusion reached by such reasoning **3a** the act of causing or bringing on or about **b** the drawing of the fuel-air mixture from the carburettor into the combustion chamber of an internal-combustion engine

inductive /ɪn'dʌktɪv/ *adj* **1** of or employing mathematical or logical induction **2** of inductance or electrical induction **3** introductory – **~ly** *adv*

inductor /ɪn'dʌktəʳ/ *n* a component that is included in an electrical circuit to provide inductance and that usu consists of a coiled conductor

indulge /ɪn'dʌldʒ/ *v* **1a** to give free rein to (e g a taste) **b** to allow (oneself) to do sthg pleasurable or gratifying **2** to treat with great or excessive leniency, generosity, or consideration – **~nt** *adj* – **~ntly** *adv*

indulgence /ɪn'dʌldʒəns/ *n* **1** a remission of (part of) the purgatorial atonement for confessed sin in the Roman Catholic church **2** indulging or being indulgent **3** an indulgent act **4** sthg indulged in

industrial /ɪn'dʌstrɪəl/ *adj* **1** of, involved in, or derived from industry **2** characterized by highly developed industries **3** used in industry

industrialism /ɪn'dʌstrɪəlɪzəm/ *n* social organization in which industries, esp large-scale industries, are dominant

industrialist /ɪn'dʌstrɪəlɪ̥st/ *n* one who is engaged in the management of an industry

industrial revolution *n* a rapid major development of an economy (e g in England in the late 18th c) marked by the general introduction of mechanized techniques and large-scale production

industrious /ɪn'dʌstrɪəs/ *adj* **1** persistently diligent **2** constantly, regularly, or habitually occupied – **~ly** *adv* – **~ness** *n*

industry /'ɪndəstri/ *n* **1** diligence in an employment or pursuit **2a** systematic work, esp for the creation of value **b(1)** a usu specified group of productive or profit-making enterprises **(2)** an organized field of activity regarded in its commercial aspects **c** manufacturing activity as a whole – **-rialize** *v*

inebriate /ɪ'niːbrieɪt/ *v* to exhilarate or stupefy (as if) by liquor; intoxicate

inedible /ɪn'edəbəl/ *adj* not fit to be eaten – **-bility** *n* – **-bly** *adv*

ineffable /ɪn'efəbəl/ *adj* **1** unutterable **2** not to be uttered; taboo – **-bility** *n* – **-bly** *adv*

ineffective /ˌɪnǰ'fektɪv/ *adj* **1** not producing an intended effect **2** not capable of performing efficiently or achieving results – **~ly** *adv* – **~ness** *n*

ineffectual /ˌɪnɪ'fektʃʊəl/ *adj* **1** not producing or not able to give the proper or intended effect **2** unable to get things done; weak in character

inefficient /ˌɪnǰ'fɪʃənt/ *adj* not producing the effect intended or desired, esp in a capable or economical way – **~ly** *adv* – **-ciency** *n*

inelegant /ɪn'elɪgənt/ *adj* lacking in refinement, grace, or good taste – **~ly** *adv* – **-gance** *n*

ineligible /ɪn'elǰdʒəbəl/ *adj* not qualified or not worthy to be chosen or preferred – **-bility** *n*

inept /ɪ'nept/ *adj* **1** not suitable or apt to the time, place, or occasion **2** lacking sense or reason **3** generally incompetent – **~ly** *adv* – **~itude, ~ness** *n*

inequality /ˌɪnɪ'kwɒlǰti/ *n* **1a** social disparity **b** disparity of distribution or opportunity **2** an instance of being unequal

inequitable /ɪn'ekwǰtəbəl/ *adj* unfair – **-bly** *adv*

inequity /ɪn'ekwǰti/ *n* (an instance of) injustice or unfairness

ineradicable /ˌɪnɪ'rædɪkəbəl/ *adj* incapable of being eradicated – **-bly** *adv*

inert /ɪ'nɜːt/ *adj* **1** lacking the power to move **2** deficient in active (chemical or biological) properties **3** not moving; inactive, indolent – **~ly** *adv* – **~ness** *n*

inertia /ɪ'nɜːʃə/ *n* **1** a property of matter by which it remains at rest or in uniform motion in the same straight line unless acted on by some external force **2** indisposition to motion, exertion, or change

inescapable /ˌɪnɪs'keɪpəbəl/ *adj* unavoidable

inessential /ˌɪnǰ'senʃəl/ *n or adj* (sthg) that is not essential

inestimable /ɪn'estǰməbəl/ *adj* **1** too great to be estimated **2** too valuable or excellent to be measured – **-bly** *adv*

inevitable /ɪ'nevǰtəbəl/ *adj* incapable of being avoided or evaded; bound to happen or to confront one – **-bility** *n* – **-bly** *adv*

inexact /ˌɪnɪg'zækt/ *adj* not precisely correct or true – **~itude, ~ness** *n*

inexcusable /ˌɪnɪk'skjuːzəbəl/ *adj* without excuse or justification – **-bly** *adv*

inexhaustible /ˌɪnɪg'zɔːstəbəl/ *adj* incapable of being used up or worn out – **-bly** *adv*

inexorable /ɪn'eksərəbəl/ *adj* **1** not to be persuaded or moved by entreaty **2** continuing inevitably; that cannot be averted – **-bly** *adv* – **-bility** *n*

inexpensive /ˌɪnɪk'spensɪv/ *adj* reasonable in price; cheap – **~ly** *adv*

inexperience /ˌɪnɪk'spɪərɪəns/ *n* **1** lack of (the skill gained from) experience **2** lack of knowledge of the ways of the world – **~d** *adj*

inexpert /ɪn'ekspɜːt/ *adj* unskilled – **~ly** *adv*

inexplicable /ˌɪnɪk'splɪkəbəl/ *adj* incapable of being explained, interpreted, or accounted for – **-bility** *n* – **-bly** *adv*

inexpressible /ˌɪnɪk'spresəbəl/ *adj* beyond one's power to express – **-bly** *adv*

inextinguishable /ˌɪnɪk'stɪŋgwɪʃəbəl/ *adj* unquenchable

inextricable /ɪn'ekstrɪkəbəl,ˌɪnɪk'strɪ-/ *adj* **1** from which one cannot extricate oneself **2** incapable of being disentangled or untied – **-bly** *adv*

infallible /ɪn'fæləbəl/ *adj* **1** incapable of error; *esp, of the Pope* incapable of error in defining dogma **2** not liable to fail – **-bility** *n*

infamy /'ɪnfəmi/ *n* **1** evil reputation brought about by sthg grossly criminal, shocking, or brutal **2** an extreme and publicly known criminal or evil act – **-mous** *adj*

infancy /'ɪnfənsi/ *n* **1** early childhood **2** a beginning or early period of existence **3** the legal status of an infant

[1]**infant** /'ɪnfənt/ *n* **1** a child in the first period of life **2** a minor

[2]**infant** *adj* **1** in an early stage of development **2** concerned with or intended for young children, esp those aged from 5 to 7 or 8

infanticide /ɪn'fæntǰsaɪd/ *n* (the act of) sby who kills an infant

infantile /'ɪnfəntaɪl/ *adj* (suggestive) of infants or infancy

infantry /'ɪnfəntri/ *n sing or pl in constr* (a branch of an army containing) soldiers trained, armed, and equipped to fight on foot – **~man** *n*

infant school *n, Br* a school for children aged from 5 to 7 or 8

infect /ɪn'fekt/ *v* **1** to contaminate (e g air or food) with a disease-causing agent **2a** to pass on a disease or a disease-causing agent to **b** to invade (an individual or organ), usu by penetration – used with reference to a disease-causing organism **3** to transmit or pass on sthg (e g an emotion) to

infection /ɪn'fekʃən/ *n* **1** infecting **2** (an agent that causes) a contagious or infectious disease **3** the communication of emotions or qualities through example or contact

infectious /ɪn'fekʃəs/ *adj* **1a infectious, infective** capable of causing infection **b** communicable by infection **2** readily spread or communicated to others – **~ly** *adj* – **~ness** *n*

infelicitous /,ɪnfɪ̣'lɪsɪ̣təs/ *adj* not apt; not suitably chosen for the occasion – **-licity** *n*

infer /ɪn'fɜːʳ/ *v* **1** to derive as a conclusion from facts or premises **2** to suggest, imply – disapproved of by some speakers – **~ence** *n* – **~ential** *adj* – **~entially** *adv*

inferior /ɪn'fɪərɪəʳ/ *adj* **1** situated lower down **2** of low or lower degree or rank **3** of little or less importance, value, or merit **4** *of a planet* nearer the sun than the earth is – **~ity** *n*

inferiority complex *n* a sense of personal inferiority often resulting either in timidity or, through overcompensation, in exaggerated aggressiveness

infernal /ɪn'fɜːnəl/ *adj* **1** of hell **2** hellish, diabolical **3** damned – infml – **~ly** *adv*

inferno /ɪn'fɜːnəʊ/ *n* a place or a state that resembles or suggests hell, esp in intense heat or raging fire

infertile /ɪn'fɜːtaɪl/ *adj* not fertile or productive – **-tility** *n*

infest /ɪn'fest/ *v* **1** to spread or swarm in or over in a troublesome manner **2** to live in or on as a parasite – **~ation** *n*

infidel /'ɪnfɪ̣dl/ *n* **1a** an unbeliever in or opponent of a particular religion, esp of Christianity or Islam **b** sby who acknowledges no religious belief **2** a disbeliever in sthg specified or understood

infidelity /,ɪnfɪ̣'delɪ̣ti/ *n* **1** lack of belief in a religion **2a** unfaithfulness, disloyalty **b** marital unfaithfulness

infighting /'ɪnfaɪtɪŋ/ *n* **1** fighting or boxing at close quarters **2** prolonged and often bitter dissension among members of a group or organization

infiltrate /'ɪnfɪltreɪt/ *v* **1** to cause (e g a liquid) to permeate sthg (e g by penetrating its pores or interstices) **2** to pass into or through (a substance) by filtering or permeating **3** to enter or become established in gradually or unobtrusively – **-trator** *n* – **-tion** *n*

[1]**infinite** /'ɪnfɪ̣nɪ̣t/ *adj* **1** subject to no limitation or external determination **2** extending indefinitely **3** immeasurably or inconceivably great or extensive **4a** extending beyond, lying beyond, or being greater than any arbitrarily chosen finite value, however large **b** extending to infinity – **~ly** *adv*

[2]**infinite** *n* **1** divineness, sublimity – + *the* **2** an infinite quantity or magnitude

infinitesimal *adj* immeasurably or incalculably small – **~ly** *adv*

infinitive /ɪn'fɪnɪ̣tɪv/ *adj or n* (using) a verb form that performs some functions of a noun and that in English is used with *to* (e g *go* in *I asked him to go*) except with auxiliary and various other verbs (e g *go* in *I must go*)

infinity /ɪn'fɪnɪ̣ti/ *n* **1a** the quality of being infinite **b** unlimited extent of time, space, or quantity **2** an indefinitely great number or amount

infirm /ɪn'fɜːm/ *adj* **1** physically feeble, esp from age **2** weak in mind, will, or character – **~ity** *n*

infirmary /ɪn'fɜːməri/ *n* a hospital

inflame /ɪn'fleɪm/ *v* **1** to set on fire **2a** to excite or arouse passion or excessive action or feeling in **b** to make more heated or violent **3** to cause to redden or grow hot **4** to cause or become affected with inflammation in (bodily tissue) **5** to burst into flame

inflammable /ɪnˈflæməbəl/ *adj* **1** capable of being easily ignited and of burning rapidly **2** easily inflamed, excited, or angered

inflammation /ɪnfləˈmeɪʃən/ *n* swelling, soreness, etc in a body part

inflammatory /ɪnˈflæmətəri/ *adj* **1** tending to inflame **2** accompanied by or tending to cause inflammation

inflate /ɪnˈfleɪt/ *v* **1** to swell or distend (with air or gas) **2** to increase (a price level) or cause (a volume of credit or the economy) to expand **3** to become inflated – **-atable** *adj*

inflated /ɪnˈfleɪtɪ̣d/ *adj* **1** bombastic, exaggerated **2** expanded to an abnormal or unjustifiable volume or level **3** swelled out; distended

inflation /ɪnˈfleɪʃən/ *n* inflating or being inflated; *esp* a substantial and continuing rise in the general level of prices, caused by or causing an increase in the volume of money and credit or an expansion of the economy

inflect /ɪnˈflekt/ *v* **1** to vary (a word) by inflection **2** to change or vary the pitch of (a voice or note) **3** to become modified by inflection

inflection, inflexion /ɪnˈflekʃən/ *n* **1** change in pitch or loudness of the voice **2** (an element showing) the change in the form of a word to mark case, gender, number, tense, etc

inflexible /ɪnˈfleksəbəl/ *adj* rigidly firm: e g **a** lacking or deficient in suppleness **b** unyielding **c** incapable of change – **-bility** *n* – **-bly** *adv*

inflict /ɪnˈflɪkt/ *v* to force or impose (sthg damaging or painful) *on* sby – **~er, ~or** *n* – **~ion** *n*

[1]**influence** /ˈɪnflʊəns/ *n* **1** the power to achieve sthg desired by using wealth or position **2** the act, power, or capacity of causing or producing an effect in indirect or intangible ways **3** sby or sthg that exerts influence; *esp* sby or sthg that tends to produce a moral or immoral effect on another – **-ential** *adj* **-entially** *adv*

[2]**influence** *v* to affect, alter, or modify by indirect or intangible means

influenza /ˌɪnflʊˈenzə/ *n* **1** a highly infectious virus disease characterized by sudden onset, fever, severe aches and pains, and inflammation of the respiratory mucous membranes **2** any of numerous feverish usu virus diseases of domestic animals marked by respiratory symptoms

influx /ˈɪnflʌks/ *n* a usu sudden increase in flowing in; the arrival of large amounts

info /ˈɪnfəʊ/ *n* information – infml

inform /ɪnˈfɔːm/ *v* **1** to impart an essential quality or character to **2** to communicate knowledge to **3** to give information or knowledge **4** to act as an informer *against* or *on* – **~ant** *n* – **~ative** *adj* – **~atively** *adv*

informal /ɪnˈfɔːməl/ *adj* marked by an absence of formality or ceremony; everyday – **~ity** *n* – **~ly** *adv*

information /ˌɪnfəˈmeɪʃən/ *n* **1** the communication or reception of facts or ideas **2a** knowledge obtained from investigation, study, or instruction **b** news **c** (significant) facts or data **3** a formal accusation presented to a magistrate

informed /ɪnˈfɔːmd/ *adj* **1** possessing or based on possession of information **2** knowledgeable about matters of contemporary interest

informer /ɪnˈfɔːməʳ/ *n* one who informs against another, esp to the police for a financial reward

infraction /ɪnˈfrækʃən/ *n* a violation, infringement

infra dig *adj* /ˌɪnfrə ˈdɪg/ beneath one's dignity – infml

infrared /ˌɪnfrəˈred/ *adj or n* (being, using, producing, or sensitive to) electromagnetic radiation with a wavelength between the red end of the visible spectrum and microwaves, that is commonly perceived as heat

infrastructure /ˈɪnfrəˌstrʌktʃəʳ/ *n* **1** an underlying foundation or basic framework **2** the permanent installations required for military purposes

infrequent /ɪnˈfriːkwənt/ *adj* **1** rare **2** not habitual or persistent – **~ly** *adv* – **-quency** *n*

infringe /ɪnˈfrɪndʒ/ *v* to encroach on; violate – **~ment** *n*

infuriate /ɪnˈfjʊərieɪt/ *v* to make furious

infuse /ɪnˈfjuːz/ *v* **1** to inspire, imbue **2** to steep in liquid without boiling so as to extract the soluble properties or constituents

infusion /ɪn'fjuːʒən/ *n* **1** infusing **2** the continuous slow introduction of a solution, esp into a vein **3** an extract obtained by infusing

ingenious /ɪn'dʒiːnɪəs/ *adj* marked by originality, resourcefulness, and cleverness – **~ly** *adv* – **ingenuity** *n*

ingenuous /ɪn'dʒenjʊəs/ *adj* showing innocent or childlike simplicity; frank, candid – **~ly** *adv* – **~ness** *n*

ingest /ɪn,dʒest/ *v* to take in (as if) for digestion; absorb – **~ion** *n*

inglenook /'ɪŋgəlnʊk/ *n* (a seat in) an alcove by a large open fireplace

inglorious /ɪn'glɔːrɪəs/ *adj* shameful, ignominious – **~ly** *adv*

ingot /'ɪŋgət/ *n* a (bar-shaped) mass of cast metal

ingrained /ɪn'greɪnd/ *adj* firmly and deeply implanted; deep-rooted

ingratiate /ɪn'greɪʃieɪt/ *v* to gain favour for (e g oneself) by deliberate effort – **-ting** *adj* – **-tingly** *adv*

ingratitude /ɪn'grætɪ̥tjuːd/ *n* forgetfulness or scant recognition of kindness received

ingredient /ɪn'griːdɪənt/ *n* sthg that forms a component part of a compound, combination, or mixture

inhabit /ɪn'hæbɪ̥t/ *v* to occupy or be present in – **~able** *adj* – **-ant** *n*

inhale /ɪn'heɪl/ *v* to breathe in – **-lation** *n*

inhaler /ɪn'heɪləʳ/ *n* a device used for inhaling a medication

inharmonious /,ɪnhɑː'məʊnɪəs/ *adj* **1** not harmonious **2** not congenial or compatible – **~ly** *adv* – **~ness** *n*

inherent /ɪn'hɪərənt, -'he-/ *adj* intrinsic to the constitution or essence of sthg – **~ly** *adv* – **-ence** *n*

inherit /ɪn'herɪ̥t/ *v* **1** to receive, either by right or from an ancestor at his/her death **2** to receive by genetic transmission – **~ance** *n*

inhibit /ɪn'hɪbɪ̥t/ *v* **1** to prohibit *from* doing sthg **2a** to restrain **b** to discourage from free or spontaneous activity, esp by psychological or social controls – **~ion** *n*

inhospitable /,ɪnhɒ'spɪtəbəl/ *adj* **1** not friendly or welcoming **2** providing no shelter or means of support – **-bly** *adv*

inhuman /ɪn'hjuːmən/ *adj* **1a** inhumane **b** failing to conform to basic human needs **2** being other than human

inhumane /,ɪnhjuː'meɪn/ *adj* lacking in kindness or compassion – **~ly** *adv*

inhumanity /,ɪnhjuː'mænɪ̥ti/ *n* **1** being pitiless or cruel **2** a cruel or barbarous act

inimical /ɪ'nɪmɪkəl/ *adj* **1** hostile or indicating hostility **2** adverse in tendency, influence, or effects

inimitable /ɪ'nɪmɪ̥təbəl/ *adj* defying imitation – **-bly** *adv*

iniquity /ɪ'nɪkwɪ̥ti/ *n* **1** gross injustice **2** a sin – **-tous** *adj* – **-tously** *adv*

[1]initial /ɪ'nɪʃəl/ *adj* **1** of the beginning **2** first

[2]initial *n* **1** the first letter of a name **2** *pl* the first letter of each word in a full name

[3]initial *v* to put initials (indicating ownership or authorization) on

[1]initiate /ɪ'nɪʃieɪt/ *v* **1** to cause or enable the beginning of; start **2** to instil with rudiments or principles (of sthg complex or obscure) **3** to induct into membership (as if) by formal rites

[2]initiate /ɪ'nɪʃiɪ̥t/ *n* **1** sby who is undergoing or has undergone initiation **2** sby who is instructed or proficient in a complex or specialized field

initiation /ɪ,nɪʃi'eɪʃən/ *n* **1** initiating or being initiated **2** the ceremony or formal procedure with which sby is made a member of a sect or society

[1]initiative /ɪ'nɪʃətɪv/ *adj* introductory, preliminary

[2]initiative *n* **1** a first step, esp in the attainment of an end or goal **2** energy or resourcefulness displayed in initiation of action **3** a procedure enabling voters to propose a law by petition

inject /ɪn'dʒekt/ *v* **1a** to throw, drive, or force into sthg **b** to force a fluid into **2** to introduce as an element or factor

injection /ɪn'dʒekʃən/ *n* **1** injecting **2** sthg (e g a medication) that is injected

injudicious /,ɪndʒʊ'dɪʃəs/ *adj* indiscreet, unwise – **~ly** *adv* – **~ness** *n*

injunction /ɪn'dʒʌŋkʃən/ *n* **1** an order, warning **2** a writ requiring sby to do or refrain from doing a particular act

injure /'ɪndʒəʳ/ *v* **1** to do injustice to **2a** to inflict bodily hurt on **b** to impair the soundness of **c** to inflict damage or loss on – **-rious** *adj* – **-riously** *adv*

injury /'ɪndʒəri/ *n* **1** a wrong **2** hurt, damage, or loss sustained

injustice /ɪn'dʒʌstɪ̀s/ *n* (an act or state of) unfairness

[1]**ink** /ɪŋk/ *n* **1** a coloured liquid used for writing and printing **2** the black secretion of a squid, octopus, etc that hides it from a predator or prey

[2]**ink** *v* to apply ink to

inkling /'ɪŋklɪŋ/ *n* **1** a faint indication **2** a slight knowledge or vague idea

inkstand /'ɪŋkstænd/ *n* a stand with fittings for holding ink and often pens

inkwell /'ɪŋkwel/ *n* a container (e g in a school desk) for ink

inlaid /,ɪn'leɪd/ *adj* **1** set into a surface in a decorative design **2** decorated with a design or material set into a surface

[1]**inland** /'ɪnlənd/ *adv or n* (into or towards) the interior part of a country

[2]**inland** /ɪn'lænd/ *adj* **1** of the interior of a country **2** *chiefly Br* not foreign; domestic

Inland Revenue *n* the government department responsible for collecting taxes in Britain

[1]**inlay** /ɪn'leɪ/ *v* **inlaid** **1** to set into a surface or ground material for decoration or reinforcement **2** to decorate with inlaid material

[2]**inlay** /'ɪnleɪ/ *n* inlaid work or a decorative inlaid pattern

inlet /'ɪnlet, 'ɪnlɪ̀t/ *n* **1** a (long and narrow) recess in a shoreline or a water passage between 2 land areas **2** a means of entry; *esp* an opening for intake

in loco parentis /ɪn ,ləʊkəʊ pə'rentɪs/ *adv* in the place of and esp having the responsibilities of a parent

inmate /'ɪnmeɪt/ *n* any of a group occupying a place of residence, esp a prison or hospital

in memoriam /ɪn mɪ̀'mɔːrɪəm/ *prep* in memory of

inmost /'ɪnməʊst/ *adj* **1** furthest within **2** most intimate

inn /ɪn/ *n* **1a** an establishment (e g a small hotel) providing lodging and food, esp for travellers **b** a public house **2** a residence formerly provided for students in London

innards /'ɪnədz/ *n pl* **1** the internal organs of a human being or animal; *esp* the viscera **2** the internal parts of a structure or mechanism ***USE*** infml

innate /,ɪ'neɪt/ *adj* **1** existing in or belonging to an individual from birth **2** inherent **3** originating in the intellect – **~ly** *adv*

inner /'ɪnəʳ/ *adj* **1a** situated within; internal **b** situated near to a centre, esp of influence **2** of the mind or soul

innings /'ɪnɪŋz/ *n* **1a** any of the alternating divisions of a cricket match during which one side bats and the other bowls **b** the (runs scored in or quality of the) turn of 1 player to bat **2a** a period in which sby has opportunity for action or achievements **b** *chiefly Br* the duration of sby's life

innocent /'ɪnəsənt/ *adj* **1a** free from guilt or sin; pure **b** harmless in effect or intention **c** free from legal guilt **2** lacking or deprived of sthg **3a** artless, ingenuous **b** ignorant, unaware – **-ence, -ency** *n* – **innocent** *n* – **~ly** *adv*

innocuous /ɪ'nɒkjʊəs/ *adj* **1** having no harmful effects **2** inoffensive, insipid – **~ly** *adv* – **~ness** *n*

innovate /'ɪnəveɪt/ *v* to make changes; introduce sthg new – **-vator** *n* – **-vatory** *adj* – **-vation** *n*

Inns of Court *n pl* (4 buildings housing) 4 societies of students and barristers in London which have the exclusive right of admission to the English Bar

innuendo /,ɪnjʊ'endəʊ/ *n* an oblique allusion; *esp* a veiled slight on sby's character or reputation

innumerable /ɪ'njuːmərəbəl/ *adj* countless – **-bly** *adv*

inoculate /ɪ'nɒkjʊleɪt/ *v* **1a** to introduce a microorganism into **b** to introduce (e g a microorganism) into a culture, animal, etc for growth **2** to vaccinate – **-lation** *n*

inoffensive /ˌɪnəˈfensɪv/ *adj* **1** not causing any harm; innocuous **2** not objectionable to the senses – **~ly** *adv* – **~ness** *n*

inoperable /ɪnˈɒpərəbəl/ *adj* impracticable

inoperative /ɪnˈɒpərətɪv/ *adj* not functioning; having no effect

inopportune /ɪnˈɒpətjuːn/ *adj* inconvenient, unseasonable – **~ly** *adv* – **~ness** *n*

inordinate /ɪˈnɔːdənɟt/ *adj* exceeding reasonable limits – **~ly** *adv*

inorganic /ˌɪnɔːˈgænɪk/ *adj* **1a** being or composed of matter other than plant or animal; mineral **b** of, being, or dealt with by a branch of chemistry concerned with inorganic substances **2** not arising through natural growth – **~ally** *adv*

input /ˈɪnpʊt/ *n* **1a** an amount coming or put in **b** sthg (e g energy, material, or data) supplied to a machine or system **c** a component of production (e g land, labour, or raw materials) **2** the point at which an input (e g of energy, material, or data) is made

inquest /ˈɪŋkwest/ *n* **1** a judicial inquiry, esp by a coroner, into the cause of a death **2** an inquiry or investigation, esp into sthg that has failed

inquietude /ɪnˈkwaɪɟtjuːd/ *n* uneasiness, restlessness

inquire, enquire /ɪnˈkwaɪəʳ/ *v* to seek information; ask about

inquiry, enquiry /ɪnˈkwaɪəri/ *n* **1** a request for information **2** a thorough or systematic investigation

inquisition /ˌɪŋkwɟˈzɪʃən/ *n* **1** the act of inquiring **2** a judicial or official inquiry **3a** *cap* a former Roman Catholic tribunal for the discovery and punishment of heresy **b** a ruthless investigation or examination – **-tor** *n* – **-torial** *adj* – **-torially** *adv*

inquisitive /ɪnˈkwɪzɟtɪv/ *adj* **1** eager for knowledge or understanding **2** fond of making inquiries; *esp* unduly curious about the affairs of others – **~ly** *adv* – **~ness** *n*

inroad /ˈɪnrəʊd/ *n* **1** a raid **2** a serious or forcible encroachment or advance

insalubrious /ˌɪnsəˈluːbrɪəs/ *adj* unhealthy

insane /ɪnˈseɪn/ *adj* **1** mentally disordered; exhibiting insanity **2** typical of or intended for insane people **3** utterly absurd – **~ly** *adv* – **-anity** *n*

insanitary /ɪnˈsænɟtəri/ *adj* unclean enough to endanger health; filthy, contaminated

insatiable /ɪnˈseɪʃəbəl/ *adj* incapable of being satisfied – **-bly** *adv*

inscribe /ɪnˈskraɪb/ *v* **1a** to write, engrave, or print (as a lasting record) **b** to enter on a list; enrol **2** to address or dedicate to sby, esp by a handwritten note

inscription /ɪnˈskrɪpʃən/ *n* **1a** a title, superscription **b** words engraved or stamped (e g on a coin) **2** a handwritten dedication in a book or on a work of art **3a** the act of inscribing **b** the enrolment of a name (as if) on a list

inscrutable /ɪnˈskruːtəbəl/ *adj* hard to interpret or understand; enigmatic – **-bility** *n* – **-bly** *adv*

insect /ˈɪnsekt/ *n* **1** any of a class of arthropods with a well-defined head, thorax, and abdomen, only 3 pairs of legs, and typically 1 or 2 pairs of wings **2** any of various small invertebrate animals (e g woodlice and spiders) – not used technically

insecticide /ɪnˈsektɟsaɪd/ *n* sthg that destroys insects – **-cidal** *adj*

insecure /ˌɪnsɪˈkjʊəʳ/ *adj* **1** lacking adequate protection or guarantee **2** not firmly fixed or supported **3a** not stable or well-adjusted **b** deficient in assurance; beset by fear and anxiety – **-curity** *n* – **~ly** *adv*

inseminate /ɪnˈsemɟneɪt/ *v* to introduce semen into the genital tract of (a female) – **-ation** *n*

insensible /ɪnˈsensəbəl/ *adj* **1** incapable or bereft of feeling or sensation: e g **a** having lost consciousness **b** lacking or deprived of sensory perception **2** incapable of being felt or sensed **3** lacking concern or awareness

insensitive /ɪnˈsensɟtɪv/ *adj* **1** lacking the ability to respond to or sympathize with the needs or feelings of others **2** not physically or chemically sensitive – **-tivity** *n* – **~ly** *adv*

inseparable /ɪnˈsepərəbəl/ *adj* incapable of being separated – **-bility** *n* – **-bly** *adv*

[1]**insert** /ɪnˈsɜːt/, ɪnˈzɜːt/ *v* **1** to put or thrust in **2** to put or introduce into the

body of sthg **3** to set in and make fast; *esp* to insert by sewing between 2 cut edges – **~ion** *n*

[2]**insert** /ˈɪnzɜːt, -sɜːt/ *n* sthg (esp written or printed) inserted

inset /ˈɪnset/ *n* sthg set in; *esp* a piece of cloth set into a garment for decoration, shaping, etc

inshore /ˌɪnˈʃɔːʳ/ *adj or adv* (near or moving) towards the shore

[1]**inside** /ɪnˈsaɪd/ *n* **1** an inner side or surface **2a** an interior or internal part **b** inward nature, thoughts, or feeling **c** viscera, entrails – usu pl with sing. meaning **3** a position of confidence or of access to confidential information **4** the middle portion of a playing area

[2]**inside** /ˈɪnsaɪd/ *adj* **1** of, on, near, or towards the inside **2** of or being the inner side of a curve or being near the side of the road nearest the kerb or hard shoulder

[3]**inside** *prep* **1a** in or into the interior of **b** on the inner side of **2** within (e g *inside* an hour)

[4]**inside** *adv* **1** to or on the inner side **2** in or into the interior **3** indoors **4** *chiefly Br* in or into prison – slang

insidious /ɪnˈsɪdɪəs/ *adj* **1** harmful but enticing **2a** acting gradually and imperceptibly but with grave consequences – **~ly** *adv* – **~ness** *n*

insight /ˈɪnsaɪt/ *n* the power of or an act or result of discerning the true or underlying nature of sthg

insignia /ɪnˈsɪgnɪə/ *n pl in constr* badges of authority or honour – sometimes treated as sing. in American English

insignificant /ˌɪnsɪgˈnɪfɪkənt/ *adj* **1** lacking meaning or import; inconsequential **2** very small in size, amount, or number – **-cance** *n* – **~ly** *adv*

insincere /ˌɪnsɪnˈsɪəʳ/ *adj* hypocritical – **~ly** *adv* – **-cerity** *n*

insinuate /ɪnˈsɪnjʊeɪt/ *v* **1** to introduce (an idea) or suggest (sthg unpleasant) in a subtle or oblique manner **2** to gain acceptance for (e g oneself) by craft or stealth – **-ation** *n*

insipid /ɪnˈsɪpɪ̣d/ *adj* **1** devoid of any definite flavour **2** devoid of interesting or stimulating qualities – **~ly** *adv* – **~ness** *n* – **~ity** *n*

insist /ɪnˈsɪst/ *v* **1** to take a resolute stand **2** to place great emphasis or importance *on* sthg **3** to maintain persistently – **~ence, ~ency** *n*

insistent /ɪnˈsɪstənt/ *adj* **1** insisting forcefully or repeatedly; emphatic **2** demanding attention – **~ly** *adv*

in situ /ɪn ˈsɪtjuː/ *adv or adj* in the natural or original position

insofar as *conj* to the extent or degree that

insolent /ˈɪnsələnt/ *adj* showing disrespectful rudeness; impudent – **~ly** *adv* – **-solence** *n*

insoluble /ɪnˈsɒljʊbəl/ *adj* **1** having or admitting of no solution or explanation **2** (practically) incapable of being dissolved in liquid – **-bly** *adv* – **-bility** *n*

insolvent /ɪnˈsɒlvənt/ *adj* **1** unable to pay debts as they fall due; *specif* having liabilities in excess of the value of assets held **2** relating to or for the relief of insolvents – **-vency** *n*

insomnia /ɪnˈsɒmnɪə/ *n* prolonged (abnormal) inability to obtain adequate sleep – **~c** *n, adj*

insouciance /ɪnˈsuːsɪəns/ *n* lighthearted unconcern – **-ant** *adj*

inspect /ɪnˈspekt/ *v* **1** to examine closely and critically; scrutinize **2** to view or examine officially – **~ion** *n*

inspector /ɪnˈspektəʳ/ *n* a police officer ranking immediately above a sergeant; *also,* an official who inspects – **~ate, ~ship** *n*

inspiration /ˌɪnspɪ̣ˈreɪʃən/ *n* **1a** a divine influence or action on a person which qualifies him/her to receive and communicate sacred revelation **b** the action or power of stimulating the intellect or emotions **2** an inspired idea **3** an inspiring agent or influence – **~al** *adj*

inspire /ɪnˈspaɪəʳ/ *v* **1** to influence or guide by divine inspiration **2** to exert an animating or exalting influence on **3** to act as a stimulus for **4** to affect – usu + *with*

inspired /ɪnˈspaɪəd/ *adj* outstanding or brilliant in a way that suggests divine inspiration

instability /ˌɪnstəˈbɪlɪ̣ti/ *n* lack of (emotional or mental) stability

install /ɪnˈstɔːl/ *v* **1** to induct into an office, rank, or order, esp with ceremonies or formalities **2** to establish in a specified place, condition, or status **3** to place in usu permanent position for use or service

installation /ˌɪnstəˈleɪʃən/ *n* **1** a device, apparatus, or piece of machinery fixed or fitted in place to perform some specified function **2** a military base or establishment

instalment /ɪnˈstɔːlmənt/ *n* **1** any of the parts into which a debt is divided when payment is made at intervals **2** any of several parts (e g of a publication) presented at intervals

[1]**instance** /ˈɪnstəns/ *n* **1** an example cited as an illustration or proof **2** the institution of a legal action **3** a situation viewed as 1 stage in a process or series of events

[2]**instance** *v* to put forward as a case or example; cite

[1]**instant** /ˈɪnstənt/ *n* **1** an infinitesimal space of time; *esp* a point in time separating 2 states **2** the present or current month

[2]**instant** *adj* **1a** present, current **b** of or occurring in the present month – used in commercial communications **2** immediate **3a(1)** premixed or precooked for easy final preparation **(2)** appearing (as if) in ready-to-use form **b** immediately soluble in water **4** demanding, urgent – fml – **~ly** *adv* – **~aneous** *adj* – **~aneously** *adv* – **~aneousness** *n*

instead /ɪnˈsted/ *adv* as a substitute or alternative (e g sent his son *instead*)

instep /ˈɪnstep/ *n* **1** (the upper surface of) the arched middle portion of the human foot **2** the part of a shoe or stocking over the instep

instigate /ˈɪnstɨgeɪt/ *v* **1** to goad or urge forwards; provoke, incite **2** to initiate (a course of action or procedure, e g a legal investigation) – **-gation** *n* – **-gator** *n*

instil /ɪnˈstɪl/ *v* **1** to cause to enter drop by drop **2** to impart gradually – + *in* or *into* – **~lation** *n*

instinct /ˈɪnstɪŋkt/ *n* **1** a natural or inherent aptitude, impulse, or capacity **2** (a largely inheritable tendency of an organism to make a complex and specific) response to environmental stimuli without involving reason – **~ive** *adj* – **~ively** *adv* – **~ual** *adj*

[1]**institute** /ˈɪnstɨtjuːt/ *v* to originate and establish; inaugurate

[2]**institute** *n* **1** (the premises used by) an organization for the promotion of a cause **2** an educational institution

institution /ˌɪnstɨˈtjuːʃən/ *n* **1** an established practice in a culture; *also* a familiar object **2** an established organization or (public) body (e g a university or hospital) – **~al** *adj*

instruct /ɪnˈstrʌkt/ *v* **1** to teach **2a** to direct authoritatively **b** to command **3** to engage (a lawyer, specif a barrister) for a case – **~or** *n*

instruction /ɪnˈstrʌkʃən/ *n* **1a** an order, a command – often pl with sing. meaning **b** *pl* an outline or manual of technical procedure **2** teaching – **~al** *adj*

instructive /ɪnˈstrʌktɪv/ *adj* carrying a lesson; enlightening – **~ly** *adv*

[1]**instrument** /ˈɪnstrəmənt/ *n* **1a** a means whereby sthg is achieved, performed, or furthered **b** a dupe; a tool of another **2** an implement, tool, or device designed esp for delicate work or measurement **3** a device used to produce music **4** a formal legal document **5** an electrical or mechanical device used in navigating an aircraft

[2]**instrument** *v* to orchestrate

[1]**instrumental** /ˌɪnstrəˈmentəl/ *adj* **1a** serving as an instrument, means, agent, or tool **b** of or done with an instrument or tool **2** relating to, composed for, or performed on a musical instrument

[2]**instrumental** *n* a musical composition or passage for instruments but not voice

instrumentalist /ˌɪnstrəˈmentəlɨst/ *n* a player on a musical instrument

instrumentation /ˌɪnstrəmenˈteɪʃən/ *n* the arrangement or composition of music for instruments

insubordinate /ˌɪnsəˈbɔːdənɨt/ *adj* unwilling to submit to authority – **-nation** *n*

insubstantial /ˌɪnsəbˈstænʃəl/ *adj* **1** lacking substance or material nature; unreal **2** lacking firmness or solidity; flimsy

insufferable /ɪnˈsʌfərəbəl/ *adj* intolerable – **-bly** *adv*

insufficient /ˌɪnsəˈfɪʃənt/ *adj* deficient in power, capacity, or competence – ~**ly** *adv* – **-ciency** *n*

insular /ˈɪnsjʊləʳ/ *adj* **1** of or being an island **2a** of island people **b** that results (as if) from lack of contact with other peoples or cultures; narrow-minded – ~**ity** *n*

insulate /ˈɪnsjʊleɪt/ *v* to place in a detached situation; *esp* to separate from conducting bodies by means of nonconductors so as to prevent transfer of electricity, heat, or sound

insulation /ˌɪnsjʊˈleɪʃən/ *n* **1** insulating or being insulated **2** material used in insulating

insulator /ˈɪnsjʊleɪtəʳ/ *n* (a device made from) a material that is a poor conductor of electricity and is used for separating or supporting conductors to prevent undesired flow of electricity

insulin /ˈɪnsjʊl̥ɪn/ *n* a hormone produced in the pancreas that is essential esp for the metabolism of carbohydrates and is used in the treatment of diabetes

[1]**insult** /ɪnˈsʌlt/ *v* to treat with insolence, indignity, or contempt; *also* to cause offence or damage to

[2]**insult** /ˈɪnsʌlt/ *n* an act of insulting; sthg that insults

insuperable /ɪnˈsjuːpərəbəl/ *adj* incapable of being surmounted, overcome, or passed over – **-bly** *adv*

insupportable /ˌɪnsəˈpɔːtəbəl/ *adj* **1** unendurable **2** incapable of being sustained

insurance /ɪnˈʃʊərəns/ *n* **1** insuring or being insured **2a** the business of insuring people or property **b** (the protection offered by) a contract whereby one party undertakes to indemnify or guarantee another against loss by a particular contingency or risk **c(1)** the premium demanded under such a contract **(2)** the sum for which sthg is insured

insure /ɪnˈʃʊəʳ/ *v* **1** to give, take, or procure insurance on or for **2** to contract to give or take insurance; *specif* to underwrite

insured /ɪnˈʃʊəd, ɪnˈʃɔːd/ *n* sby whose life or property is insured

insurgent /ɪnˈsɜːdʒənt/ *n* a rebel – **-ence, ency** *n* – **insurgent** *adj*

insurmountable /ˌɪnsəˈmaʊntəbəl/ *adj* insuperable

insurrection /ˌɪnsəˈrekʃən/ *n* (a) revolt against civil authority or established government – ~**ist** *n*

intact /ɪnˈtækt/ *adj* untouched, esp by anything that harms or diminishes; whole, uninjured – ~**ness** *n*

intaglio /ɪnˈtɑːlɪəʊ/ *n* **1a** (the act or process of producing) an incised or engraved design made in hard material, esp stone, and sunk below the surface of the material **b** printing done from a plate engraved in intaglio **2** sthg (e g a gem) carved in intaglio

intake /ˈɪnteɪk/ *n* **1** an opening through which liquid or gas enters an enclosure or system **2a** a taking in **b(1)** *sing or pl in constr* an amount or number taken in **(2)** sthg taken in

intangible /ɪnˈtændʒəbəl/ *n or adj* (sthg) not tangible – **-bility** *n* – **-bly** *adv*

integer /ˈɪnt̥ɪdʒəʳ/ *n* the number 1 or any number (e g 6, 0, -23) obtainable by once or repeatedly adding 1 to or subtracting 1 from the number 1

integral /ˈɪnt̥ɪgrəl/ *adj* **1a** essential to completeness; constituent – chiefly in *integral part* **b** formed as a unit with another part **2** composed of integral parts **3** lacking nothing essential; whole

integral calculus *n* a branch of mathematics dealing with the solutions of differential equations

integrate /ˈɪnt̥ɪgreɪt/ *v* **1** to form or blend into a whole **2a** to combine together or with sthg else **b** to incorporate into a larger unit – usu + *into* **3** to end the segregation of or in **4** to become integrated – **-gration** *n* – ~**d** *adj*

integrated circuit *n* an electronic circuit formed in or on a single tiny slice of semiconductor material (e g silicon)

integrity /ɪnˈtegr̥ɪti/ *n* **1** an unimpaired condition **2** uncompromising adherence to a code of esp moral or artistic values **3** the quality or state of being complete or undivided

intellect /ˈɪnt̥ɪlekt/ *n* the capacity for intelligent thought, esp when highly developed

[1]**intellectual** /ˌɪnt̥ɪˈlektʃʊəl/ *adj* **1a** of

the intellect **b** developed or chiefly guided by the intellect rather than by emotion or experience **2** given to or requiring the use of the intellect – **~ly** *adv*

[2]**intellectual** *n* an intellectual person

intelligence /ɪn'telɨdʒəns/ *n* **1** the ability to learn, apply knowledge, or think abstractly, esp in allowing one to deal with new or trying situations; *also* the skilled use of intelligence or reason **2** the act of understanding **3a** news; information **b** (a group of people who gather) information concerning an enemy – **-gent** *adj* – **-gently** *adv*

intelligence quotient *n* a number expressing the ratio of sby's intelligence as determined by a test to the average for his/her age

intelligible /ɪn'telɨdʒəbəl/ *adj* **1** capable of being understood **2** able to be apprehended by the intellect only – **-bility** *n* – **-bly** *adv*

intemperate /ɪn'tempərɨt/ *adj* not temperate; *esp* going beyond the bounds of reasonable behaviour – **-ance** *n* – **~ly** *adv*

intend /ɪn'tend/ *v* **1** to mean, signify **2a** to have in mind as a purpose or goal **b** to design for a specified use or future

intense /ɪn'tens/ *adj* **1a** existing or occurring in an extreme degree **b** having or showing a usual characteristic in extreme degree **2** intensive **3a** feeling emotion deeply, esp by nature or temperament **b** deeply felt – **~ly** *adv* – **-sity** *n*

intensifier /ɪn'tensɨfaɪəʳ/ *n* a linguistic element (e g *very*) that gives force or emphasis

intensify /ɪn'tensɨfaɪ/ *v* to make or become (more) intense – **-fication** *n*

[1]**intensive** /ɪn'tensɪv/ *adj* of or marked by intensity or intensification: e g **a** highly concentrated **b** constituting or relating to a method designed to increase productivity by the expenditure of more capital and labour rather than by increase in the land or raw materials used

[2]**intensive** *n* an intensifier

[1]**intent** /ɪn'tent/ *n* **1a** the act or fact of intending **b** the state of mind with which an act is done **2** criminal intention **3** meaning, significance

[2]**intent** *adj* **1** directed with strained or eager attention; concentrated **2** having the mind, attention, or will concentrated *on* sthg or some end or purpose – **~ly** *adv* – **~ness** *n*

intention /ɪn'tenʃən/ *n* **1** a determination to act in a certain way; a resolve **2** *pl* purpose with respect to proposal of marriage **3a** what one intends to do or bring about; an aim **b** the object for which religious devotion is offered **4** a concept

intentional /ɪn'tenʃənəl/ *adj* done by intention or design – **~ly** *adv*

interact /ˌɪntə'rækt/ *v* to act upon each other – **~ion** *n* – **~ive** *adj*

interbreed /ˌɪntə'briːd/ *v* **1** to crossbreed **2** to breed within a closed population **3** to cause to interbreed

intercalate /ɪn'tɜːkəleɪt/ *v* to insert between or among existing items, elements, or layers – **-ation** *n*

intercede /ˌɪntə'siːd/ *v* to beg or plead on behalf of another with a view to reconciling differences – **-cession** *n*

[1]**intercept** /ˌɪntə'sept/ *v* to stop, seize, or interrupt in progress, course, or movement, esp from one place to another – **~ion** *n*

[2]**intercept** /'ɪntəsept/ *n* an interception

interceptor, intercepter /'ɪntəseptəʳ/ *n* a high-speed fast-climbing fighter plane or missile designed for defence against raiding bombers or missiles

[1]**interchange** /ˌɪntə'tʃeɪndʒ/ *v* **1** to put each of (2 things) in the place of the other **2** to exchange **3** to change places reciprocally

[2]**interchange** /'ɪntətʃeɪndʒ/ *n* **1** (an) interchanging **2** a junction of 2 or more roads having a system of separate levels that permit traffic to pass from one to another without the crossing of traffic streams

intercom /'ɪntəkɒm/ *n* a local communication system (e g in a ship or building) with a microphone and loudspeaker at each station

intercontinental /ˌɪntəkɒntɨ'nentəl/ *adj* extending among continents; *also* carried on or (capable of) travelling between continents

intercourse /'ɪntəkɔːs/ *n* **1** connection or dealings between people or groups 2 exchange, esp of thoughts or feelings 3 physical sexual contact between individuals; *esp* sexual intercourse

¹interdict /ˈɪntədɪkt/ *n* **1** a Roman Catholic disciplinary measure withdrawing most sacraments and Christian burial from a person or district **2** a prohibition

²interdict /ˌɪntəˈdɪkt/ *v* to forbid in a usu formal or authoritative manner – **~ion** *n* – **~ory** *adj*

¹interest /ˈɪntrɪ̣st/ *n* **1a(1)** right, title, or legal share in sthg **(2)** participation in advantage and responsibility **b** a business in which one has an interest **2** benefit; advantage; *specif* self-interest **3a** a charge for borrowed money, generally a percentage of the amount borrowed **b** sthg added above what is due **4** a financially interested group **5a** readiness to be concerned with, moved by, or have one's attention attracted by sthg; curiosity **b** (the quality in) a thing that arouses interest

²interest *v* **1** to induce or persuade to participate or engage, esp in an enterprise **2** to concern or engage (sby, esp oneself) *in* an activity or cause **3** to engage the attention or arouse the interest of – **~ing** *adj* – **~ingly** *adv*

interested /ˈɪntrɪ̣stɪ̣d/ *adj* **1** having the interest aroused or attention engaged **2** affected or involved; not impartial

interface /ˈɪntəfeɪs/ *n* **1** a surface forming a common boundary of 2 bodies, regions, or phases **2** the place at which independent systems meet and act on or communicate with each other – **interface** *v*

interfacing /ˈɪntəfeɪsɪŋ/ *n* stiffening material attached between 2 layers of fabric

interfere /ˌɪntəˈfɪəʳ/ *v* **1** to get in the way of, hinder, or impede another – + *with* **2** to enter into or take a part in matters that do not concern one **3** to hinder illegally an attempt of a player to catch or hit a ball or puck – usu + *with*

interference /ˌɪntəˈfɪərəns/ *n* **1** the phenomenon resulting from the meeting of 2 wave trains (e g of light or sound) with an increase in intensity at some points and a decrease at others **2** the illegal hindering of an opponent in hockey, ice hockey, etc **3** (sthg that produces) the confusion of received radio signals by unwanted signals or noise

¹interim /ˈɪntərɪm/ *n* an intervening time

²interim *adj* temporary, provisional

¹interior /ɪnˌtɪərɪəʳ/ *adj* **1** lying, occurring, or functioning within the limits or interior **2** away from the border or shore **3** of the mind or soul

²interior *n* **1** the internal or inner part of a thing; *also* *the* inland **2** internal affairs **3** a representation of the interior of a building or room

interject /ɪntəˈdʒekt/ *v* to throw in (e g a remark) abruptly among or between other things

interjection /ˌɪntəˈdʒekʃən/ *n* an ejaculatory word (e g *Wonderful*) or utterance (e g *ah* or *good heavens*) usu expressing emotion – **~ally** *adv*

interlace /ˌɪntəˈleɪs/ *v* **1** to unite (as if) by lacing together **2** to mingle, blend, or intersperse **3** to cross one another intricately

interlock /ˌɪntəˈlɒk/ *v* **1** to become engaged, interrelated, or interlocked **2** to lock together

interloper /ˈɪntələupəʳ/ *n* sby who interferes or encroaches; an intruder

interlude /ˈɪntəluːd/ *n* **1** an intervening or interruptive period, space, or event, esp of a contrasting character; an interval **2** a musical composition inserted between the parts of a longer composition, a drama, or a religious service

intermarry /ˌɪntəˈmæri/ *v* **1** to marry each other or sby from the the same group **2** to become connected by marriage with another group or with each other – **-riage** *n*

intermediary /ˌɪntəˈmiːdɪəri/ *n or adj* (sby or sthg) acting as a mediator or go-between

intermediate /ˌɪntəˈmiːdɪət/ *adj* being or occurring at or near the middle place, stage, or degree or between 2 others or extremes

intermezzo /ˌɪntəˈmetsəu/ *n pl* **intermezzi, intermezzos** **1** a movement coming between the major sections of an extended musical work (e g an opera) **2** a short independent instrumental composition

interminable /ɪn'tɜːmɪ̣nəbəl/ *adj* having or seeming to have no end; *esp* wearisomely long – **-bly** *adv*

intermingle /ˌɪntə'mɪŋgəl/ *v* to mix or mingle together or with sthg else

intermission /ˌɪntə'mɪʃən/ *n* **1** intermitting or being intermitted **2** an intervening period of time (e g between acts of a performance or attacks of a disease)

intermit /ˌɪntə'mɪt/ *v* **-tt-** to (cause to) cease for a time or at intervals

intermittent /ˌɪntə'mɪtənt/ *adj* coming and going at intervals; not continuous – **~ly** *adv*

intern /ɪn'tɜːn/ *v* to confine, esp during a war

internal /ɪn'tɜːnl/ *adj* **1** existing or situated within the limits or surface of sthg **2** of or existing within the mind **3** depending only on the properties of the thing under consideration without reference to things outside it **4** (present or arising) within (a part of) the body or an organism **5** within a state – **~ize** *v* – **~ly** *adv*

internal-combustion engine *n* a heat engine in which the combustion that generates the heat energy takes place inside the engine (e g in a cylinder)

[1]**international** /ˌɪntə'næʃənəl/ *adj* **1** affecting or involving 2 or more nations **2** known, recognized, or renowned in more than 1 country – **~ize** *v*

[2]**international** *n* **1** (sby who plays or has played in) a sports, games, etc match between 2 national teams **2** *also* **internationale** *often cap* any of several socialist or communist organizations of international scope

internationalism /ˌɪntə'næʃənəlɪzəm/ *n* **1** international character, interests, or outlook **2** (an attitude favouring) cooperation among nations – **-ist** *n*

internecine /ˌɪntə'niːsaɪn/ *adj* **1** mutually destructive **2** of or involving conflict within a group

interplanetary /ˌɪntə'plænɪ̣təri/ *adj* existing, carried on, or operating between planets

interplay /'ɪntəpleɪ/ *n* interaction

Interpol /'ɪntəpɒl/ *n* an international police organization for liaison between national police forces

interpolate /ɪn'tɜːpəleɪt/ *v* **1** to alter or corrupt (e g a text) by inserting new or foreign matter **2** to insert between other things or parts; *esp* to insert (words) into a text or conversation – **-lation** *n*

interpose /ˌɪntə'pəʊz/ *v* **1** to place between 2 things or in an intervening position **2** to put forth by way of interference or intervention **3** to interrupt **4** to be or come in an intervening position – **-position** *n*

interpret /ɪn'tɜːprɪ̣t/ *v* **1** to expound the meaning of **2** to conceive of in the light of one's beliefs, judgments, or circumstances; construe **3** to represent by means of art; bring to realization by performance **4** to act as an interpreter – **~er** *n* – **~ative, ~ive** *adj*

interpretation /ɪnˌtɜːprɪ̣'teɪʃən/ *n* an instance of artistic interpreting in performance or adaptation

interregnum /ˌɪntə'regnəm/ *n, pl* **interregnums, interregna** **1** the time during which **a** a throne is vacant between reigns **b** the normal functions of government are suspended **2** a lapse or pause in a continuous series

interrelate /ˌɪntərɪ'leɪt/ *v* to bring into or be in a relationship where each one depends upon or is acting upon the other – **-lation, -lationship** *n*

interrogate /ɪn'terəgeɪt/ *v* to question formally – **-gation** *n* – **-gator** *n*

[1]**interrogative** /ˌɪntə'rɒgətɪv/, **interrogatory** *adj* **1a** of or being the grammatical mood that expresses a question **b** used in a question **2** questioning – **~ly** *adv*

[2]**interrogative** *n* **1** an interrogative utterance **2** a word, esp a pronoun, used in asking questions **3** the interrogative mood of a language

interrupt /ˌɪntə'rʌpt/ *v* **1** to break the flow or action of (a speaker or speech) **2** to break the uniformity or continuity of (sthg) **3** to interrupt an action; *esp* to interrupt another's utterance with one's own – **~ion** *n*

intersect /ˌɪntə'sekt/ *v* **1** to pierce or divide (e g a line or area) by passing through or across **2** to meet and cross at a point

intersection /ˌɪntəˈsekʃən/ *n* a place where 2 or more things (e g streets) intersect

intersperse /ˌɪntəˈspɜːs/ *v* **1** to insert at intervals among other things **2** to diversify or vary with scattered things

interstellar /ˌɪntəˈsteləʳ/ *adj* located or taking place among the stars

interstice /ɪnˈtɜːstɨs/ *n* a small space between adjacent things – fml

intertwine /ˌɪntəˈtwaɪn/ *v* to twine together

interval /ˈɪntəvəl/ *n* **1** an intervening space: e g **a** a time between events or states; a pause **b** a distance or gap between objects, units, or states **c** the difference in pitch between 2 notes **2** *Br* a break in the presentation of an entertainment (e g a play)

intervene /ˌɪntəˈviːn/ *v* **1** to enter or appear as sthg irrelevant or extraneous **2** to occur or come between 2 things, esp points of time or events **3** to come in or between so as to hinder or modify **4a** to enter a lawsuit as a third party **b** to interfere in another nation's internal affairs – **-vention** *n*

interview /ˈɪntəvjuː/ *n* **1** a formal consultation usu to evaluate qualifications (e g of a prospective student or employee) **2** (a report of) a meeting at which information is obtained (e g by a journalist) from sby – **interview** *v* – **~er** *n* – **~ee** *n*

interweave /ˌɪntəˈwiːv/ *v* **interwove, interwoven** **1** to weave together **2** to intermingle, blend

intestate /ɪnˈtesteɪt, -stɨt/ *adj* having made no valid will

intestine /ɪnˈtestɨn/ *n* the tubular part of the alimentary canal that extends from the stomach to the anus – **-inal** *adj*

¹intimate /ˈɪntɨmeɪt/ *v* to make known: e g **a** to announce **b** to hint; imply – **-mation** *n*

²intimate /ˈɪntɨmɨt/ *adj* **1a** intrinsic, essential **b** belonging to or characterizing one's deepest nature **2** marked by very close association, contact, or familiarity **3** suggesting informal warmth or privacy **4** of a very personal or private nature **5** involved in a sexual relationship; *specif* engaging in an act of sexual intercourse – euph – **~ly** *adv* – **-macy** *n*

³intimate /ˈɪntɨmɨt/ *n* a close friend or confidant

intimidate /ɪnˈtɪmɨdeɪt/ *v* to frighten; *esp* to compel or deter (as if) by threats – **-dation** *n*

into /ˈɪntə; *before consonants* ˈɪntʊ; *strong* ˈɪntuː/ *prep* **1a** so as to be inside (e g come *into* the house) **b** so as to be (e g grow *into* a woman) **c** so as to be in (a state) (e g shocked *into* silence) **d** so as to be expressed in, dressed in, engaged in, or a member of (e g translate *into* French; enter *into* an alliance) **e** – used in division as the inverse of *by* or *divided by* (e g divide 35 *into* 70) **2** – used to indicate a partly elapsed period of time or a partly traversed extent of space (e g far *into* the night; deep *into* the jungle) **3** in the direction of; *esp* towards the centre of (e g look *into* the sun) **4** to a position of contact with; against (e g ran *into* the wall) **5** involved with; *esp* keen on (e g are you *into* meditation?) – infml

intolerable /ɪnˈtɒlərəbəl/ *adj* unbearable – **-bly** *adv*

intolerant /ɪnˈtɒlərənt/ *adj* **1** unable or unwilling to endure **2** unwilling to grant or share social, professional, political, or religious rights; bigoted – **~ly** *adv* – **-rance** *n*

intonation /ˌɪntəˈneɪʃən/ *n* **1** performance of music with respect to correctness of pitch and harmony **2** the rise and fall in pitch of the voice in speech

intone /ɪnˈtəʊn/ *v* to utter (sthg) in musical or prolonged tones; recite in singing tones or in a monotone

in toto /ɪn ˈtəʊtəʊ/ *adv* totally, entirely

intoxicate /ɪnˈtɒksɨkeɪt/ *v* **1** to poison **2a** to excite or stupefy by alcohol or a drug, esp to the point where physical and mental control is markedly diminished **b** to cause to lose self-control through excitement or elation – **-cant** *adj, n* – **-cation** *n*

intractable /ɪnˈtræktəbəl/ *adj* **1** not easily managed or directed; obstinate

2 not easily manipulated, wrought, or solved – **-bility** *n* – **-bly** *adv*

intramural /ˌɪntrəˈmjʊərəl/ *adj* within the limits of a community or institution (e g a university)

intransigent /ɪnˈtrænsɨdʒənt/ *adj* refusing to compromise or to abandon an extreme position or attitude, esp in politics; uncompromising – **-gence** *n* – **~ly** *adv*

intransitive /ɪnˈtrænsɨtɪv/ *adj* characterized by not having a direct object – **~ly** *adv*

intrauterine device /ˌɪntrəˈjuːtərɪn dɪvaɪs, -raɪn/ *n* a device inserted and left in the uterus to prevent conception

intravenous /ˌɪntrəˈviːnəs/ *adj* situated or occurring in, or entering by way of a vein; *also* used in intravenous procedures – **~ly** *adv*

intrench /ɪnˈtrench/ *v* to entrench

intrepid /ɪnˈtrepɨd/ *adj* fearless, bold, and resolute – **~ly** *adv* – **~ity** *n*

intricate /ˈɪntrɪkɨt/ *adj* **1** having many complexly interrelating parts or elements **2** difficult to resolve or analyse – **~ly** *adv* – **-cacy** *n*

[1]**intrigue** /ɪnˈtriːg/ *v* **1** to arouse the interest or curiosity of **2** to captivate; fascinate **3** to carry on an intrigue; *esp* to plot, scheme

[2]**intrigue** /ˈɪntriːg, ɪnˈtriːg/ *n* **1** a secret scheme or plot **2** a clandestine love affair

intrinsic /ɪnˈtrɪnsɪk, -zɪk/ *adj* **1** belonging to the essential nature or constitution of sthg **2** originating or situated within the body – **~ally** *adv*

introduce /ˌɪntrəˈdjuːs/ *v* **1** to lead or bring in, esp for the first time **2a** to bring into play **b** to bring into practice or use; institute **3** to lead to or make known by a formal act, announcement, or recommendation **a** to cause to be acquainted; make (oneself or sby) known to another **b** to make preliminary explanatory or laudatory remarks about (e g a speaker) **4** to place, insert **5** to bring to a knowledge or discovery of sthg – **-ductory** *adj*

introduction /ˌɪntrəˈdʌkʃən/ *n* **1a** a preliminary treatise or course of study **b** a short introductory musical passage **2** sthg introduced; *specif* a plant or animal new to an area

[1]**introvert** /ˌɪntrəˈvɜːt/ *v* to turn inwards or in on itself or oneself

[2]**introvert** /ˈɪntrəvɜːt/ *n* one whose attention and interests are directed towards his/her own mental life

intrude /ɪnˈtruːd/ *v* to thrust or force in or on, esp without permission, welcome, or suitable reason – **~r, -usion** *n*

intrusive /ɪnˈtruːsɪv/ *adj* characterized by (a tendency to) intrusion

intuition /ˌɪntjʊˈɪʃən/ *n* **1a** (knowledge gained by) immediate apprehension or cognition **b** the power of attaining direct knowledge without evident rational thought and the drawing of conclusions from evidence available **2** quick and ready insight – **-tive** *adj* – **-tively** *adv*

inundate /ˈɪnəndeɪt/ *v* to cover or overwhelm (as if) with a flood – **-dation** *n*

inure /ɪˈnjʊəʳ/ *v* to accustom *to* sthg undesirable

invade /ɪnˈveɪd/ *v* **1** to enter (e g a country) for hostile purposes **2** to encroach on **3** to spread over or into as if invading – **~r** *n*

[1]**invalid** /ɪnˈvælɨd/ *adj* **1** without legal force **2** logically inconsistent – **~ly** *adv* – **~ity** *n*

[2]**invalid** /ˈɪnvəliːd, -lɨd/ *adj* **1** suffering from disease or disability **2** of or suited to an invalid – **~ism** *n*

[3]**invalid** /ˈɪnvəlɨd/ *n* one who is sickly or disabled

[4]**invalid** /ˈɪnvəlɨd, ˌɪnvəˈliːd/ *v* to remove from active duty by reason of sickness or disability

invalidate /ɪnˈvælɨdeɪt/ *v* to make invalid; *esp* to weaken or destroy the convincingness of (e g an argument or claim) – **-dation** *n*

invaluable /ɪnˈvæljʊbəl/ *adj* valuable beyond estimation; priceless

invariable /ɪnˈveərɪəbəl/ *adj* not (capable of) changing; constant – **-bly** *adv* – **-bility** *n*

invasion /ɪnˈveɪʒən/ *n* **1** an invading, esp by an army **2** the incoming or spread of sthg usu harmful – **-ive** *adj*

invective /ɪnˈvektɪv/ *n* abusive or

insulting (use of) language; denunciation

inveigh /ɪn'veɪ/ *v* to speak or protest bitterly *against*

inveigle /ɪn'veɪgəl, ɪn'viː-/ *v* to talk sby *into* sthg by ingenuity or flattery

invent /ɪn'vent/ *v* **1** to think up **2** to produce (e g sthg useful) for the first time – **~or** *n*

invention /ɪn'venʃən/ *n* **1** productive imagination; inventiveness **2a** a (misleading) product of the imagination **b** a contrivance or process devised after study and experiment

inventive /ɪn'ventɪv/ *adj* **1** creative **2** characterized by invention – **~ly** *adv* – **~ness** *n*

1**inventory** /'ɪnvəntri/ *n* **1** an itemized list (e g of the property of an individual or estate) **2** the items listed in an inventory **3** the taking of an inventory

2**inventory** *v* to make an inventory of; catalogue

1**inverse** /ɪn'vɜːs/ *adj* **1** opposite in order, direction, nature, or effect **2** *of a mathematical function* expressing the same relationship as another function but from the opposite viewpoint

2**inverse** /'ɪnvɜːs/ *n* a direct opposite – **~ly** *adv*

invert /ɪn'vɜːt/ *v* **1a** to turn inside out or upside down **b** to turn (e g a foot) inwards **2a** to reverse in position, order, or relationship **b** to subject to musical inversion

invertebrate /ɪn'vɜːtɪ̣brɪ̣t, -breɪt/ *n or adj* (an animal) lacking a spinal column

inverted comma *n, chiefly Br* a quotation mark

1**invest** /ɪn'vest/ *v* **1** to confer (the symbols of) authority, office, or rank on **2** to clothe, endow, or cover (as if) *with* sthg

2**invest** *v* **1** to commit (money) to a particular use (e g buying shares or new capital outlay) in order to earn a financial return **2** to devote (e g time or effort) to sthg for future advantages **3** to make an investment

investigate /ɪn'vestɪ̣geɪt/ *v* **1** to make a systematic examination or study (of) **2** to conduct an official inquiry (into) – **-gator** *n* – **-gation** *n*

investiture /ɪn'vestɪ̣tʃəʳ/ *n* a formal ceremony conferring an office or honour on sby

investment /ɪn'vestmənt/ *n* (a sum of) money invested for income or profit; *also* the asset (e g property) purchased

inveterate /ɪn'vetərɪ̣t/ *adj* **1** firmly, obstinately, and persistently established **2** habitual

invidious /ɪn'vɪdɪəs/ *adj* **1** tending to cause discontent, ill will, or envy **2** of an unpleasant or objectionable nature; of a kind causing or likely to cause harm or resentment – **~ly** *adv* – **~ness** *n*

invigilate /ɪn'vɪdʒɪ̣leɪt/ *v* to keep watch (over); *specif, Br* to supervise (candidates) at (an examination) – **-lator** *n* – **-lation** *n*

invigorate /ɪn'vɪgəreɪt/ *v* to give fresh life and energy to

invincible /ɪn'vɪnsəbəl/ *adj* incapable of being conquered or subdued – **-bility** *n* – **-bly** *adj*

inviolable /ɪn'vaɪələbəl/ *adj* (to be kept) secure from violation, profanation, or assault – **-bility** *n*

invisible /ɪn'vɪzəbəl/ *adj* **1** incapable (by nature or circumstances) of being seen **2a** not appearing in published financial statements **b** not reflected in statistics **3** too small or unobtrusive to be seen or noticed; inconspicuous – **-bility** *n* – **-bly** *adv*

invitation /,ɪnvɪ̣'teɪʃən/ *n* **1** an often formal request to be present or participate **2** an incentive, inducement

invite /ɪn'vaɪt/ *v* **1a** to offer an incentive or inducement to **b** to (unintentionally) increase the likelihood of **2** to request (the presence of) formally or politely

inviting /ɪn'vaɪtɪŋ/ *adj* attractive, tempting – **~ly** *adv*

1**invoice** /'ɪnvɔɪs/ *n* **1** a bill; *specif* an itemized list of goods shipped, usu specifying the price and the terms of sale **2** a consignment of merchandise

2**invoice** *v* to submit an invoice for or to

invoke /ɪn'vəʊk/ *v* **1** to appeal to or cite as an authority **2** to call forth (e g a spirit) by uttering a spell or magical formula **3** to put into effect – **-vocation** *n*

involuntary /ɪn'vɒləntəri/ *adj* **1** done contrary to or without choice **2** not subject to conscious control; reflex – **-tarily** *adv* – **-tariness** *n*

involve /ɪn'vɒlv/ *v* **1a** to cause to be associated or take part **b** to occupy (oneself) absorbingly; *esp* to commit (oneself) emotionally **2** to relate closely **3a** to have within or as part of itself **b** to require as a necessary accompaniment – **~ment** *n*

involved /ɪn'vɒlvd/ *adj* **1** (needlessly or excessively) complex **2** taking part *in*

invulnerable /ɪn'vʌlnərəbəl/ *adj* **1** incapable of being injured or harmed **2** immune to or proof against attack – **-bility** *n* – **-bly** *adv*

inward /'ɪnwəd/ *adj* **1** situated within or directed towards the inside **2** of or relating to the mind or spirit (e g struggled to achieve *inward* peace) – **~ly** *adv*

inwards /'ɪnwədz/ *adv* **1** towards the inside, centre, or interior **2** towards the inner being

iodine /'aɪədiːn/ *n* a chemical element used in photography, and in solution as a disinfectant for wounds, grazes, etc

ion /'aɪən/ *n* **1** an atom or group of atoms that carries a positive or negative electric charge as a result of having lost or gained 1 or more electrons **2** a free electron or other charged subatomic particle – **~ize** *v*

ionic /aɪ'ɒnɪk/ *adj* **1** of, existing as, or characterized by ions **2** functioning by means of ions

Ionic /aɪ'ɒnɪk/ *adj* of that 1 of the 3 Greek orders of architecture that is characterized esp by the scroll-shaped ornament of its capital

ionosphere /aɪ'ɒnəsfɪəʳ/ *n* the part of the earth's atmosphere that extends from an altitude above that of the stratosphere out to at least 480km (about 300mi) and consists of several distinct regions containing free ions; *also* a comparable region surrounding another planet

iota /aɪ'əʊtə/ *n* **1** the 9th letter of the Greek alphabet **2** an infinitesimal amount

IOU *n* (a written acknowledgment of) a debt

IPA *n* the International Phonetic Alphabet (the system of recording pronunciation used in this dictionary)

IQ *n* intelligence quotient

irascible /ɪ'ræsəbəl/ *adj* having an easily provoked temper – **-bility** *n* – **-bly** *adv*

irate /aɪ'reɪt/ *adj* roused to or arising from anger – **~ly** *adv* – **~ness** *n*

ire /aiəʳ/ *n* intense anger – **~ful** *adj*

iridium /ɪ'rɪdɪəm/ *n* a silver-white hard brittle very heavy metallic element of the platinum group

iris /'aɪərɪ̣s/ *n, pl* (*1*) **irises, irides** **1** the opaque contractile diaphragm perforated by the pupil that forms the coloured portion of the eye **2** any of a large genus of plants with long straight leaves and large showy flowers

¹Irish /'aɪərɪʃ/ *adj* **1** of Ireland or the Irish (language) **2** amusingly illogical

²Irish *n* **1** *pl in constr* the people of Ireland **2 Irish, Irish Gaelic** the Celtic language of Ireland, esp as used since the end of the medieval period

irk /ɜːk/ *v* to make weary, irritated, or bored

irksome /'ɜːksəm/ *adj* troublesome, annoying

¹iron /'aɪən/ *n* **1** a heavy malleable ductile magnetic silver-white metallic element that readily rusts in moist air, occurs in most igneous rocks, and is vital to biological processes **2a** sthg used to bind or restrain – usu pl **b** a heated metal implement used for branding or cauterizing **c** a metal implement with a smooth flat typically triangular base that is heated (e g by electricity) and used to smooth or press clothing **d** a stirrup **e** any of a numbered series of usu 9 golf clubs with metal heads of varying angles for hitting the ball to various heights and lengths

²iron *adj* **1** (made) of iron **2** resembling iron (e g in appearance, strength, solidity, or durability)

³iron *v* to smooth (as if) with a heated iron

Iron Age *n* the period of human culture characterized by the widespread use of iron for making tools and weapons and dating from before 1000 BC

iron curtain *n, often cap I&C* an esp political and ideological barrier between the Communist countries of E Europe and the non-Communist countries of (and those friendly to) W Europe

ironic /aɪˈrɒnɪk/, **ironical** *adj* **1** of, containing, or constituting irony **2** given to irony – **~ally** *adv*

ironmonger /ˈaɪən,mʌŋgəʳ/ *n, Br* a dealer in esp household hardware – **~y** *n*

iron out *v* to put right or correct (e g a problem or defect); resolve (e g difficulties)

ironworks /ˈaɪənwɜːks/ *n* a mill or building where iron or steel is smelted or heavy iron or steel products are made – often pl with sing. meaning

irony /ˈaɪərəni/ *n* **1** the use of words to express a meaning other than and esp the opposite of the literal meaning **2** (an event or situation showing) incongruity between actual circumstances and the normal, appropriate, or expected result **3** an attitude of detached awareness of incongruity

irradiate /ɪˈreɪdieɪt/ *v* **1a** to cast rays (of light) upon **b** to give intellectual or spiritual insight to **c** to affect or treat by (exposure to) radiant energy (e g heat) **2** to emit like rays (of light); radiate – **-ation** *n*

¹**irrational** /ɪˈræʃənəl/ *adj* not rational; not governed by or according to reason – **~ly** *adv* – **~ity** *n*

²**irrational, irrational number** *n* a number (e g π) that cannot be expressed as the result of dividing 1 integer by another

¹**irreconcilable** /ɪ,rekənˈsaɪləbəl/ *adj* impossible to reconcile: e g **a** resolutely opposed **b** incompatible – **-bly** *adv*

²**irreconcilable** *n* an opponent of compromise or collaboration

irrecoverable /,ɪrɪˈkʌvərəbəl/ *adj* not capable of being recovered or retrieved – **-bly** *adv*

irredeemable /,ɪrɪˈdiːməbəl/ *adj* not redeemable; *esp* beyond remedy; hopeless – **-bly** *adv*

irreducible /,ɪrɪˈdjuːsəbəl/ *adj* impossible to bring into a desired, normal, or simpler state – **-bly** *adv*

irrefutable /,ɪrɪˈfjuːtəbəl/ *adj* incontrovertible – **-bly** *adv*

irregular /ɪˈregjʊləʳ/ *adj* **1a** contrary to rule, custom, or moral principles **b** not inflected in the normal manner **c** inadequate because of failure to conform **2** lacking symmetry or evenness **3** lacking continuity or regularity, esp of occurrence or activity – **~ly** *adv*

irregularity /ɪ,regjʊˈlærɪ̣ti/ *n* sthg irregular (e g contrary to accepted professional or ethical standards)

irrelevant /ɪˈrelɪ̣vənt/ *adj* not relevant; inapplicable – **~ly** *adv* – **-vance, -vancy** *n*

irreparable /ɪˈrepərəbəl/ *adj* not able to be restored to a previous condition – **-bly** *adv*

irreplaceable /,ɪrɪˈpleɪsəbəl/ *adj* having no adequate substitute

irrepressible /,ɪrɪˈpresəbəl/ *adj* impossible to restrain or control – **-bly** *adv*

irreproachable /,ɪrɪˈprəʊtʃəbəl/ *adj* offering no foundation for blame or criticism – **-bly** *adv*

irresistible /,ɪrɪˈzɪstəbəl/ *adj* impossible to resist successfully; highly attractive or enticing – **-bly** *adv*

irresolute /ɪˈrezəluːt/ *adj* lacking decision or a firm aim and purpose – **-lution** *n*

irrespective of /,ɪrɪˈspektɪv əv/ *prep* without regard or reference to; in spite of

irresponsible /,ɪrɪˈspɒnsəbəl/ **1** showing no regard for the consequences of one's actions **2** unable to bear responsibility – **-bility** *n* – **-bly** *adv*

irreversible /,ɪrɪˈvɜːsəbəl/ *adj* unable to be changed back into a previous state or condition – **-bly** *adv*

irrevocable /ɪˈrevəkəbəl/ *adj* incapable of being revoked or altered – **-bly** *adv*

irrigate /ˈɪrɪ̣geɪt/ *v* **1** to supply (e g land) with water by artificial means **2** to flush (e g an eye or wound) with a stream of liquid – **-gable** *adj* – **-gation** *n*

irritable /ˈɪrɪ̣təbəl/ *adj* capable of being irritated: e g **a** easily exasperated or excited **b** (excessively) responsive to stimuli – **-bility** *n* – **-bly** *adv*

irritate /'ɪrʒteɪt/ *v* **1** to excite impatience, anger, or displeasure (in) **2** to induce a response to a stimulus in or of – **-tant** *n* – **-tation** *n*

is /s, z, əz; *strong* ɪz/ *v pres 3 sing of* **be,** *dial pres 1&2 sing of* **be,** *substandard pres pl of* **be**

Islam /'ɪslɑːm, 'ɪz-, ɪs'lɑːm/ *n* **1** the religious faith of Muslims including belief in Allah as the sole deity and in Muhammad as his prophet **2** the civilization or culture accompanying Islamic faith – **~ic** *adj*

island /'aɪlənd/ *n* **1** an area of land surrounded by water and smaller than a continent **2** sthg like an island (e g in being isolated or surrounded) **3** a traffic island **4** an isolated superstructure on the deck of a ship, esp an aircraft carrier

isle /aɪl/ *n* a (small) island – used in some names

islet /'aɪlʒt/ *n* a little island

isobar /'aɪsəbɑːʳ/ *n* a line on a chart connecting places where the atmospheric pressure is the same

isolate /'aɪsəleɪt/ *v* **1** to set apart from others; *also* to quarantine **2** to separate from another substance so as to obtain in a pure form **3** to insulate – **-lation** *n*

isolationism /,aɪsə'leɪʃənɪzəm/ *n* a policy of national isolation by refraining from engaging in international relations – **-ist** *n, adj*

isotope /'aɪsətəʊp/ *n* any of 2 or more species of atoms of a chemical element that have the same atomic number and nearly identical chemical behaviour but differ in atomic mass or mass number and physical properties

Israeli /ɪz'reɪli/ *adj* (characteristic) of modern Israel

Israelite /'ɪzrəlaɪt/ *n* any of the descendants of the Hebrew patriarch Jacob; *specif* a member of any of the 10 Hebrew tribes occupying northern Palestine in biblical times

¹issue /'ɪʃuː, 'ɪsjuː/ *n* **1** the action of going, coming, or flowing out **2** a means or place of going out **3** offspring **4** an outcome that usu resolves or decides a problem **5** a matter that is in dispute between 2 or more parties; a controversial topic **6** sthg coming out from a usu specified source **7a** the act of publishing, giving out, or making available **b** the thing or the whole quantity of things given out, published, or distributed at 1 time

²issue *v* **1a** to go, come, or flow out **b** to emerge **2** to appear or become available through being given out, published, or distributed **3a** to give out, distribute, or provide officially **b** to send out for sale or circulation

isthmus /'ɪsməs, 'ɪsθməs/ *n* a narrow strip of land connecting 2 larger land areas

¹it /ɪt/ *pron* **1a** that thing, creature, or group – used as subject or object; (e g noticed that *it* was old; had a baby but lost *it*) **b** the person in question **2** – used as subject of an impersonal verb (e g *it's* raining) **3a** – used to highlight part of a sentence (e g *it* was yesterday that he arrived) **b** – used with many verbs and prepositions as a meaningless object (e g run for *it*) **4** – used to refer to an explicit or implicit state of affairs (e g how's *it* going?) **5** that which is available, important, or appropriate (e g one boiled egg and that's *it*; a bit brighter, that's *it*)

²it *n* **1** the player in a usu children's game who performs a unique role (e g trying to catch others in a game of tag) **2** sex appeal; *also* sexual intercourse – infml

Italian /ɪ'tælɪən/ *n* **1** a native or inhabitant of Italy **2** the Romance language of the Italians

¹itch /ɪtʃ/ *v* **1** to have or produce an itch **2** to have a restless desire – infml

²itch *n* **1a** an irritating sensation in the upper surface of the skin that makes one want to scratch **b** a skin disorder characterized by such a sensation **2** a restless desire – infml

item /'aɪtəm/ *n* **1** a separate unit in an account or series **2** a separate piece of news or information – **~ize** *v*

itinerary /aɪ'tɪnərəri/ *n* **1** the (proposed) route of a journey **2** a travel diary **3** a traveller's guidebook

its /ɪts/ *adj* relating to it or itself, esp as possessor, agent, or object of an action

itself /ɪt'self/ *pron* **1** that identical thing, creature, or group **2** its normal self

IUD *n* an intrauterine device

ivory /'aɪvəri/ *n* **1** the hard creamy-white form of dentine of which the tusks of elephants and other tusked mammals are made **2** a creamy slightly yellowish white colour **3** *pl* things (e g dice or piano keys) made of (sthg resembling) ivory – infml

ivory tower *n* aloofness from practical concerns; *also* a place encouraging such an attitude

ivy /'aɪvi/ *n* a very common and widely cultivated Eurasian woody climbing plant with evergreen leaves, small yellowish flowers, and black berries

J

j /dʒeɪ/ *n, pl* **j's, js** *often cap* (a graphic representation of or device for reproducing) the 10th letter of the English alphabet

¹jab /dʒæb/ *v* **1a** to pierce (as if) with a sharp object **b** to poke quickly or abruptly **2** to strike (sby) with a short straight blow **3** to make quick or abrupt thrusts (as if) with a sharp or pointed object

²jab *n* a hypodermic injection – infml

jabber /ˈdʒæbəʳ/ *v or n* (to engage in) rapid or unintelligible talk or chatter

¹jack /dʒæk/ *n* **1** any of various portable mechanisms for exerting pressure or lifting a heavy object a short distance **2a** a small white target ball in lawn bowling **b(1)** *pl but sing in constr* a game in which players toss and pick up small bone or metal objects in a variety of shapes in between throws of a ball **(2)** a small 6-pointed metal object used in the game of jacks **3** a playing card carrying the figure of a soldier or servant and ranking usu below the queen **4** a single-pronged electric plug

²jack *v* **1** to move or lift (as if) by a jack **2** to raise the level or quality of **3** give up – usu + *in*; infml *USE* (*1&2*) usu + *up*

jackal /ˈdʒækɔːl, -kəl/ *n* **1** any of several Old World wild dogs smaller than the related wolves **2** sby who collaborates with another in committing immoral acts

jackass /ˈdʒækæs/ *n* **1** a male ass **2** a stupid person; a fool

jackboot /ˈdʒækbuːt/ *n* a laceless military boot reaching to the calf

jackdaw /ˈdʒækdɔː/ *n* a common black and grey Eurasian bird that is related to but smaller than the common crow

¹jacket /ˈdʒækɨ̠t/ *n* **1** an outer garment for the upper body opening down the full length of the centre front **2** the skin of a (baked) potato **3a** a thermally insulating cover (e g for a hot water tank) **b(1)** a dust jacket **(2)** the cover of a paperback book

²jacket *v* to put a jacket on; enclose in or with a jacket

Jack Frost *n* frost or frosty weather personified

jack-in-the-box *n, pl* **jack-in-the-boxes, jacks-in-the-box** a toy consisting of a small box out of which a figure springs when the lid is raised

¹jackknife /ˈdʒæknaɪf/ *n* **1** a large clasp knife for the pocket **2** a dive in which the diver bends from the waist, touches the ankles with straight knees, and straightens out before hitting the water

²jackknife **1** to (cause to) double up like a jackknife **2** *esp of an articulated lorry* to turn or rise and form an angle of 90 degrees or less

jack-of-all-trades *n* a handy versatile person – sometimes derog

jack-o'-lantern /ˌdʒæk ə ˈlæntən/ *n* **1** a will-o'-the-wisp **2** a lantern made from a hollowed-out pumpkin cut to look like a human face

jackpot /ˈdʒækpɒt/ *n* **1** (a combination that wins) a top prize on a fruit machine **2** a large prize (e g in a lottery), often made up of several accumulated prizes that have not been previously won

Jacobean /ˌdʒækəˈbɪən/ *adj* of (the age of) James I

Jacobite /ˈdʒækəbaɪt/ *n* a supporter of James II or of the Stuarts after 1688

¹jade /dʒeɪd/ *n* **1** a vicious or worn-out old horse **2** *archaic* a flirtatious or disreputable woman

²jade *n* either of 2 typically green hard gemstones

jaded /ˈdʒeɪdɨ̠d/ *adj* fatigued (as if) by overwork or dissipation

¹jag /dʒæg/ *v* **1** to cut or tear unevenly or raggedly **2** to cut indentations into

²jag *n* a sharp projecting part

[3]**jag** *n* a period of indulgence; *esp* a drinking bout – slang

jagged /ˈdʒægɪ̵d/ *adj* having a sharply uneven edge or surface – **~ly** *adv*

jaguar /ˈdʒægjʊəʳ/ *n* a big cat of tropical America that is typically brownish yellow or buff with black spots

[1]**jail,** *Br also* **gaol** /dʒeɪl/ *n* a prison

[2]**jail,** *Br also* **gaol** *v* to confine (as if) in a jail

jailbird /ˈdʒeɪlbɜːd/ *n* a person who has been (habitually) confined in jail

jailbreak /ˈdʒeɪlbreɪk/ *n* an escape from jail

jailer, *Br also* **gaoler** /ˈdʒeɪləʳ/ *n* **1** a keeper of a jail **2** sby or sthg that restricts another's liberty (as if) by imprisonment

jalopy /dʒəˈlɒpi/ *n* a dilapidated old vehicle or aircraft – infml

[1]**jam** /dʒæm/ *v* **1a** to press, squeeze, or crush into a close or tight position **b** to (cause to) become wedged or blocked so as to be unworkable **c** to block passage of or along **d** to fill (to excess) **2** to crush; *also* to bruise by crushing **3** to send out interfering signals or cause reflections so as to make unintelligible **4** to become blocked or wedged **5** to take part in a jam session – slang

[2]**jam** *n* **1** a crowded mass that impedes or blocks **2** the pressure or congestion of a crowd **3** a difficult state of affairs – infml

[3]**jam** *n* a preserve made by boiling fruit and sugar to a thick consistency

jamb /dʒæm/ *n* a straight vertical member or surface forming the side of an opening for a door, window, etc

jamboree /ˌdʒæmbəˈriː/ *n* **1** a large festive gathering **2** a large gathering of scouts or guides in a camp

jammy /ˈdʒæmi/ *adj, Br* **1** lucky **2** easy *USE* infml

jam session *n* an impromptu jazz performance that features group improvisation

jangle /ˈdʒæŋgəl/ *v* **1** *of the nerves* to be in a state of tense irritation **2** to make a harsh or discordant often ringing noise

janissary /ˈdʒænɪ̵səri/ *n* **1** *often cap* a soldier of an élite corps of Turkish troops organized in the 14th c and abolished in 1826 **2** a loyal or subservient official or supporter

janitor /ˈdʒænɪ̵təʳ/ *n* **1** a doorkeeper; a porter **2** a caretaker

January /ˈdʒænjʊəri/ *n* the 1st month of the Gregorian calendar

japan /dʒəˈpæn/ *n* **1** a varnish giving a hard brilliant finish **2** work (e g lacquer ware) finished and decorated in the Japanese manner

Japanese /ˈdʒæpəniːz/ *n* **1** a native or inhabitant of Japan **2** the language of the Japanese – **Japanese** *adj*

japonica /dʒəˈpɒnɪkə/ *n* a hardy ornamental shrub of the rose family with clusters of scarlet, white, or pink flowers

[1]**jar** /dʒɑːʳ/ *v* **1a** to make a harsh or discordant noise **b** to have a harshly disagreeable effect – + *on* or *upon* **2** to vibrate **3** to cause to jar, esp by shaking or causing a shock to

[2]**jar** *n* **1** a jarring noise **2a** a sudden or unexpected shake **b** an unsettling shock (e g to nerves or feelings)

[3]**jar** *n* **1a** a usu cylindrical short-necked and wide-mouthed container, made esp of glass **b** the contents of or quantity contained in a jar **2** a glass of an alcoholic drink, esp beer – infml

jargon /ˈdʒɑːgən/ *n* **1** the terminology or idiom of a particular activity or group **2** obscure and often pretentious language

jasmine /ˈdʒæzmɪ̵n/ *n* **1** any of numerous often climbing shrubs that usu have extremely fragrant flowers; *esp* a high-climbing half-evergreen Asian shrub with fragrant white flowers **2** a light yellow colour

jaundice /ˈdʒɔːndɪ̵s/ *n* **1** an abnormal condition marked by yellowish pigmentation of the skin, tissues, and body fluids caused by the deposition of bile pigments **2** a state of prejudice inspired by bitterness, envy, or disillusionment

jaundiced /ˈdʒɔːndɪ̵st/ *adj* mistrustful or prejudiced, esp because of bitterness, envy, or disillusionment

jaunt /dʒɔːnt/ *v or n* (to make) a short journey for pleasure

jaunty /ˈdʒɔːnti/ *adj* having or showing airy self-confidence; sprightly – **-tily** *adv* – **-tiness** *n*

javelin /ˈdʒævəlɪ̵n/ *n* a light spear

thrown as a weapon or in an athletic field event; *also* the sport of throwing the javelin

[1]**jaw** /dʒɔː/ *n* **1** either of 2 cartilaginous or bony structures that in most vertebrates form a framework above and below the mouth in which the teeth are set **2** *pl* **a** the entrance of a narrow pass or channel **b** the 2 parts of a machine, tool, etc between which sthg may be clamped or crushed **c** a position or situation of imminent danger

[2]**jaw** *v* to talk or gossip for a long time or long-windedly – infml

jay /dʒeɪ/ *n* an Old World bird of the crow family with a dull pink body, black, white, and blue wings, and a black-and-white crest

jaywalk /ˈdʒeɪwɔːk/ *v* to cross a street carelessly so as to be endangered by traffic

jazz /dʒæz/ *n* **1** music developed esp from ragtime and blues and characterized by syncopated rhythms and individual or group improvisation around a basic theme or melody **2** similar but unspecified things – infml

jazz up *v* to enliven *USE* infml

jazzy /ˈdʒæzi/ *adj* **1** having the characteristics of jazz **2** garish, gaudy – infml – **jazzily** *adv*

jealous /ˈdʒeləs/ *adj* **1a** intolerant of rivalry or unfaithfulness **b** apprehensive of and hostile towards a (supposed) rival **2** resentful, envious *of* **3** vigilant in guarding a possession, right, etc **4** distrustfully watchful – **~ly** *adv* – **~y** *n*

jeans /dʒiːnz/ *n pl in constr, pl* **jeans** casual usu close-fitting trousers, made esp of blue denim

jeep /dʒiːp/ *n* a small rugged general-purpose motor vehicle with 4-wheel drive, used esp by the armed forces

jeer /dʒɪəʳ/ *v* to laugh mockingly or scoff (at) – **jeer** *n*

Jehovah /dʒɪ̥ˈhəʊvə/ *n* God; *esp* the God of the Old Testament

Jehovah's Witness *n* a member of a fundamentalist sect practising personal evangelism, rejecting the authority of the secular state, and preaching that the end of the present world is imminent

[1]**jelly** /ˈdʒeli/ *n* **1a** a soft fruit-flavoured transparent dessert set with gelatin **b** a savoury food product of similar consistency, made esp from meat stock and gelatin **2** a clear fruit preserve made by boiling sugar and the juice of fruit **3** a substance resembling jelly in consistency

[2]**jelly** **1** to bring to the consistency of jelly; cause to set **2** to set in a jelly

jellyfish /ˈdʒelifɪʃ/ *n* a free-swimming marine animal that has a nearly transparent saucer-shaped body and extendable tentacles covered with stinging cells

jemmy /ˈdʒemi/ *v or n, Br* (to force open with) a steel crowbar, used esp by burglars

jeopardy /ˈdʒepədi/ *n* exposure to or risk of death, loss, injury, etc; danger – **-dize** *v*

[1]**jerk** /dʒɜːk/ *v* **1** to give a quick suddenly arrested push, pull, twist, or jolt to **2** to propel with short abrupt motions **3** to utter in an abrupt or snappy manner **4** to make a sudden spasmodic motion **5** to move in short abrupt motions

[2]**jerk** *n* **1** a single quick motion (e g a pull, twist, or jolt) **2** an involuntary spasmodic muscular movement due to reflex action **3** *chiefly NAm* a stupid, foolish, or naive person – infml

jerkin /ˈdʒɜːkɪ̥n/ *n* **1** a close-fitting hip-length sleeveless jacket, made esp of leather and worn by men in the 16th and 17th c **2** a man's or woman's sleeveless jacket

jerky /ˈdʒɜːki/ *adj* **1** marked by irregular or spasmodic movements **2** marked by abrupt or awkward changes – **-kily** *adv* – **-kiness** *n*

jeroboam /ˌdʒerəˈbəʊəm/ *n* a wine bottle holding 4 to 6 times the usual amount

Jerry /ˈdʒeri/ *n, chiefly Br* a German; *esp* a German soldier or the German armed forces in WW II

jersey /ˈdʒɜːzi/ *n* **1** a plain weft-knitted fabric made of wool, nylon, etc and used esp for clothing **2** a jumper **3** *often cap* any of a breed of small short-horned cattle noted for their rich milk

Jerusalem artichoke /dʒəˌruːsələm ˈɑːtɪ̥ tʃəʊk/ *n* (an edible sweet-tasting tuber of) a perennial N American sunflower

jess /dʒes/ *n* a short strap made esp of leather which is secured to the leg of a hawk and usu has a ring on the other end for attaching a leash

[1]**jest** /dʒest/ *n* **1** an amusing or mocking act or utterance; a joke **2** a frivolous mood or manner

[2]**jest** *v* **1** to speak or act without seriousness **2** to make a witty remark

jester /ˈdʒestəʳ/ *n* a retainer formerly kept in great households to provide casual amusement and commonly dressed in a brightly coloured costume

Jesuit /ˈdʒezjʊɪ̠t/ *n* a member of the Society of Jesus, a Roman Catholic order founded by St Ignatius Loyola in 1534 which is devoted to missionary and educational work

[1]**jet** /dʒet/ *n* **1** a hard black form of coal that is often polished and used for jewellery **2** an intense black

[2]**jet** *v* **1** to emit in a jet or jets **2** to direct a jet of liquid or gas at

[3]**jet** *n* **1a** a forceful stream of fluid discharged from a narrow opening or a nozzle **b** a nozzle or other narrow opening for emitting a jet of fluid **2** (an aircraft powered by) a jet engine

[4]**jet** *v* to travel by jet aircraft

jet-black *adj* of a very dark black

jet engine *n* an engine that produces motion in one direction as a result of the discharge of a jet of fluid in the opposite direction; *specif* an aircraft engine that discharges the hot air and gases produced by the combustion of a fuel to produce propulsion or lift

jet lag *n* a temporary disruption of normal bodily rhythms after a long flight, esp due to differences in local time

jetsam /ˈdʒetsəm/ *n* **1** goods thrown overboard to lighten a ship in distress; *esp* such goods when washed ashore **2** odds and ends; rubbish

jet set *n sing or pl in constr* an international wealthy élite who frequent fashionable resorts

[1]**jettison** /ˈdʒetɪ̠sən/ *n* **1** the act of jettisoning cargo **2** abandonment

[2]**jettison** *v* **1** to throw (e g goods or cargo) overboard to lighten the load of a ship in distress **2** to cast off as superfluous or encumbering; abandon **3** to drop (e g unwanted material) from an aircraft or spacecraft in flight

jetty /ˈdʒeti/ *n* **1** a structure (e g a pier or breakwater) extending into a sea, lake, or river to influence the current or tide or to protect a harbour **2** a small landing pier

jew /dʒuː/ *v* to get the better of financially, esp by hard bargaining – often + *out of*; derog

Jew /dʒuː/, *fem* **Jewess** *n* **1** a member of a Semitic people existing as a nation in Palestine from the 6th c BC to the 1st c AD, some of whom now live in Israel and others in various countries throughout the world **2** a person whose religion is Judaism **3** sby given to hard financial bargaining – derog – **~ish** *adj*

jewel /ˈdʒuːəl/ *n* **1** an ornament of precious metal often set with stones and worn as an accessory **2** sby or sthg highly esteemed **3** a precious stone **4** a bearing for a pivot (e g in a watch or compass) made of crystal, precious stone, or glass

jeweller /ˈdʒuːələʳ/ *n* sby who deals in, makes, or repairs jewellery and often watches, silverware, etc

jewellery /ˈdʒuːəlri/ *n* jewels, esp as worn for personal adornment

[1]**jib** /dʒɪb/ *n* a triangular sail set on a stay extending from the top of the foremast to the bow or the bowsprit

[2]**jib** *n* the projecting arm of a crane

[3]**jib** *v, esp of a horse* to refuse to proceed further

jibe /dʒaɪb/ *v* to gibe

jiffy /ˈdʒɪfi/ *n* a moment, instant – infml

[1]**jig** /dʒɪg/ *n* **1** (a piece of music for) any of several lively springy dances in triple time **2a** any of several fishing lures that jerk up and down in the water **b** a device used to hold a piece of work in position (e g during machining or assembly) and to guide the tools working on it **c** a device in which crushed ore or coal is separated from waste by agitating in water

[2]**jig** *v* **1** to dance (in the rapid lively manner of) a jig **2a** to (cause to) make a rapid jerky movement **b** to separate (a mineral from waste) with a jig **3** to

catch (a fish) with a jig **4** to work with or machine by using a jig

jiggered /ˈdʒɪgəd/ *adj* **1** blowed, damned – infml **2** *N Eng* tired out; exhausted

jiggery-pokery /ˌdʒɪgəri ˈpəʊkəri/ *n, Br* dishonest underhand dealings or scheming – infml

jiggle /ˈdʒɪgəl/ *v* to (cause to) move with quick short jerks – infml – **jiggle** *n* – **-gly** *adj*

jigsaw /ˈdʒɪgsɔː/ *n* **1** a power-driven fretsaw **2 jigsaw, jigsaw puzzle** a puzzle consisting of small irregularly cut pieces, esp of wood or card, that are fitted together to form a picture for amusement; *broadly* sthg composed of many disparate parts or elements

jihad /dʒɪˈhɑːd, dʒɪˈhæd/ *n* **1** a holy war waged on behalf of Islam as a religious duty **2** a crusade for a principle or belief

jilt /dʒɪlt/ *v* to cast off (e g one's lover) capriciously or unfeelingly

¹jingle /ˈdʒɪŋgəl/ *v* to (cause to) make a light clinking or tinkling sound

²jingle *n* **1** a light, esp metallic clinking or tinkling sound **2** a short catchy song or rhyme characterized by repetition of phrases and used esp in advertising

jingoism /ˈdʒɪŋgəʊɪzəm/ *n* belligerent patriotism; chauvinism – **-ist(ic)** *adj*

jinx /dʒɪŋks/ *n* sby or sthg (e g a force or curse) which brings bad luck – infml

jitter /dʒɪtə/ *v* to be nervous or anxious – **~s** *n pl* **~y** *adj*

¹jive /dʒaɪv/ *n* (dancing or *the* energetic dance performed to) swing music

²jive to dance to or play jive

¹job /dʒɒb/ *n* **1a** a piece of work; *esp* a small piece of work undertaken at a stated rate **b** sthg produced by work **2a(1)** a task **(2)** sthg requiring unusual exertion **b** a specific duty, role, or function **c** a regular paid position or occupation **d** *chiefly Br* a state of affairs – + *bad* or *good* **3** an object of a usu specified type **4a** a plan or scheme designed or carried out for private advantage **b** a crime; *specif* a robbery *USE* (*3&4*) infml

²job *v* **1** to do odd or occasional pieces of work, usu at a stated rate **2** to carry on public business for private gain **3a** to carry on the business of a middleman or wholesaler **b** to work as a stockjobber **4** to buy and sell (e g shares) for profit **5** to hire or let for a definite job or period of service **6** to get, deal with, or effect by jobbery **7** to subcontract – usu + *out*

Job /dʒəʊb/ *n* (a narrative and poetic book of the Old Testament which tells of) a Jewish patriarch who endured afflictions with fortitude and faith – usu in *the patience of Job*

jobber /ˈdʒɒbəʳ/ *n* a stockjobber

job lot *n* a miscellaneous collection of goods sold as a lot; *broadly* any miscellaneous collection of articles

¹jockey /ˈdʒɒki/ *n* sby who rides a horse, esp as a professional in races

²jockey *v* **1** to manoeuvre or manipulate by adroit or devious means **2** to act as a jockey

jockstrap /ˈdʒɒkstræp/ *n* a support for the genitals worn by men taking part in strenuous esp sporting activities

jocular /ˈdʒɒkjʊləʳ/ *adj* **1** habitually jolly **2** characterized by joking – **~ly** *adv* – **~ity** *n*

jodhpurs /ˈdʒɒdpəz/ *n pl in constr, pl* **jodhpurs** riding trousers cut full at the hips and close-fitting from knee to ankle

¹jog /dʒɒg/ *v* **1** to give a slight shake or push to; nudge **2** to rouse (the memory) **3** to move up and down or about with a short heavy motion **4** to run or ride at a slow trot – **~ger** *n*

²jog *n* **1** a slight shake **2a** a jogging movement or pace **b** a slow trot

John Bull *n* a typical Englishman, esp regarded as truculently insular

johnny /ˈdʒɒni/ *n, often cap* a fellow, guy – infml

¹join /dʒɔɪn/ *v* **1a** to put or bring together so as to form a unit **b** to connect (e g points) by a line **c** to adjoin; meet **2** to put, bring, or come into close association or relationship **3a** to come into the company of **b** to become a member of (a group) **4** to come together so as to be connected **5** to take part in a collective activity – usu + *in*

²join *n* a joint

joiner /ˈdʒɔɪnəʳ/ *n* **1** one who constructs or repairs wooden articles, esp furniture or fittings **2** a gregarious person who joins many organizations – infml

joinery /ˈdʒɔɪnəri/ *n* **1** the craft or trade of a joiner **2** woodwork done or made by a joiner

[1]**joint** /dʒɔɪnt/ *n* **1a(1)** a point of contact between 2 or more bones of an animal skeleton together with the parts that surround and support it **b** a part or space included between 2 articulations, knots, or nodes **c** a large piece of meat (for roasting) cut from a carcass **2a** a place where 2 things or parts are joined **b** an area at which 2 ends, surfaces, or edges are attached **c** the hinge of the binding of a book along the back edge of each cover **3** a shabby or disreputable place of entertainment – infml **4** a marijuana cigarette – slang

[2]**joint** *adj* **1** united, combined **2** common to 2 or more: e g **a** involving the united activity of 2 or more **b** held by, shared by, or affecting 2 or more **3** sharing with another – **~ly** *adv*

[3]**joint** *v* **1** to fit together **2** to provide with a joint **3** to prepare (e g a board) for joining by planing the edge **4** to separate the joints of (e g meat)

join up *v* to enlist in an armed service

joist /dʒɔɪst/ *n* any of the parallel small timbers or metal beams that support a floor or ceiling

[1]**joke** /dʒəʊk/ *n* **1a** sthg said or done to provoke laughter; *esp* a brief oral narrative with a humorous twist **b** the humorous or ridiculous element in sthg **c** an instance of joking or making fun **d** a laughingstock

[2]**joke** *v* to make jokes – **jokingly** *adv*

joker /ˈdʒəʊkəʳ/ *n* **1** sby given to joking **2** a playing card added to a pack usu as a wild card **3** sthg (e g an expedient or stratagem) held in reserve to gain an end or escape from a predicament **4** a fellow; *esp* an insignificant, obnoxious, or incompetent person – infml

[1]**jolly** /ˈdʒɒli/ *adj* **1a** full of high spirits **b** given to conviviality **c** expressing, suggesting, or inspiring gaiety **2** extremely pleasant or agreeable – infml **3** *Br* slightly drunk – euph – **jollity, jolliness** *n*

[2]**jolly** *adv* very – infml

[3]**jolly** *v* **1** to (try to) put in good humour, esp to gain an end – usu + *along* **2** to make cheerful or bright – + *up*; infml

Jolly Roger /ˌdʒɒli ˈrɒdʒəʳ/ *n* a pirate's black flag with a white skull and crossbones

[1]**jolt** /dʒəʊlt/ *v* **1** to (cause to) move with a sudden jerky motion **2** to give a (sudden) knock or blow to **3** to abruptly disturb the composure of

[2]**jolt** *n* an unsettling blow, movement, or shock

Jonah /ˈdʒəʊnə/ *n* (a narrative book of the Old Testament telling of) an Israelite prophet who resisted a divine call to preach repentance to the people of Nineveh, was swallowed and vomited by a great fish, and eventually carried out his mission

joss stick /ˈdʒɒs ˌstɪk/ *n* a slender stick of incense (e g for burning in front of a joss)

jostle /ˈdʒɒsəl/ *v* **1a** to come in contact or into collision (with) **b** to make (one's way) by pushing **2** to vie (with) in gaining an objective

[1]**jot** /dʒɒt/ *n* the least bit

[2]**jot** *v* to write briefly or hurriedly

joule /dʒuːl/ *n* the SI unit of work or energy equal to the work done when a force of 1N moves its point of application through a distance of 1m

journal /ˈdʒɜːnəl/ *n* **1a** an account of day-to-day events **b** a private record of experiences, ideas, or reflections kept regularly **c** a record of the transactions of a public body, learned society, etc **2a** a daily newspaper **b** a periodical dealing esp with matters of current interest or specialist subjects

journalism /ˈdʒɜːnəl-ɪzəm/ *n* **1** (the profession of) the collecting and editing of material of current interest for presentation through news media **2a** writing designed for publication in a newspaper or popular magazine **b** writing characterized by a direct presentation of facts or description of events without an attempt at interpretation – **-ist** *n* – **-istic** *adj*

journey /ˈdʒɜːni/ *n* **1** travel from one place to another, esp by land and over a considerable distance **2** the distance involved in a journey, or the time taken to cover it

journeyman /'dʒɜːnimən/ *n* **1** a worker who has learned a trade and is employed by another person, usu by the day **2** an experienced reliable worker or performer, as distinguished from one who is outstanding

[1]**joust** /dʒaʊst/ *v* to fight in a joust or tournament

[2]**joust** *n* a combat on horseback between 2 knights or men-at-arms with lances

jovial /'dʒəʊvɪəl/ *adj* markedly good-humoured – ~**ity** *n*

[1]**jowl** /dʒaʊl/ *n* **1** the jaw; *esp* a mandible **2** a cheek

[2]**jowl** *n* usu slack flesh associated with the lower jaw or throat – often pl with sing. meaning

joy /dʒɔɪ/ *n* **1** (the expression of) an emotion or state of great happiness, pleasure, or delight **2** a source or cause of delight **3** *Br* success, satisfaction – infml

joyful /'dʒɔɪfəl/ *adj* filled with, causing, or expressing joy – ~**ness** *n*

joyous /'dʒɔɪəs/ *adj* joyful – ~**ly** *adv* – ~**ness** *n*

joyride /'dʒɔɪraɪd/ *n* **1** a ride in a motor car taken for pleasure and often without the owner's consent **2** a short pleasure flight in an aircraft

joystick /'dʒɔɪˌstɪk/ *n* **1** a hand-operated lever that controls an aeroplane's elevators and ailerons **2** a control for any of various devices that resembles an aeroplane's joystick

jubilant /'dʒuːbɩ̣lənt/ *adj* filled with or expressing great joy – ~**ly** *adv*

jubilation /ˌdʒuːbɩ̣'leɪʃən/ *n* being jubilant; rejoicing

jubilee /'dʒuːbɩ̣liː, ˌdʒuːbɩ̣'liː/ *n* **1** (a celebration of) a special anniversary (e g of a sovereign's accession) **2** a season or occasion of celebration

Judaism /'dʒuːdeɪ-ɪzəm, 'dʒuːdə-/ *n* **1** a religion developed among the ancient Hebrews and characterized by belief in one transcendent God and by a religious life in accordance with Scriptures and traditions **2** (conformity with) the cultural, social, and religious beliefs and practices of the Jews

Judas /'dʒuːdəs/ *n* **1** one who betrays, esp under the guise of friendship **2 judas, judas hole** a peephole in a door

judder /'dʒʌdəʳ/ *v, chiefly Br* to vibrate jerkily

[1]**judge** /dʒʌdʒ/ *v* **1** to form an opinion about through careful weighing of evidence **2** to sit in judgment on **3** to determine or pronounce after deliberation **4** to decide the result of (a competition or contest) **5** to form an estimate or evaluation of **6** to hold as an opinion **7** to act as a judge

[2]**judge** *n* sby who judges: e g **a** a public official authorized to decide questions brought before a court **b** sby appointed to decide in a competition or (sporting) contest (e g diving) **c** sby who gives an (authoritative) opinion

judgment, judgement /'dʒʌdʒmənt/ *n* **1** a formal decision by a court **2** (the process of forming) an opinion or evaluation based on discerning and comparing **3** the capacity for judging **4 Judgment, Judgment Day** *the* final judging of mankind by God

judicature /'dʒuːdɩ̣kətʃəʳ/ *n* **1** the administration of justice **2** the judiciary

judicial /dʒuː'dɪʃəl/ *adj* **1** of a judgment, judging, justice, or the judiciary **2** ordered by a court **3** of, characterized by, or expressing judgment; critical – ~**ly** *adv*

judiciary /dʒuː'dɪʃəri/ *n* **1a** a system of courts of law **b** the judges of these courts **2** a judicial branch of the US government

judicious /dʒuː'dɪʃəs/ *adj* having, exercising, or characterized by sound judgment – ~**ly** *adv* – ~**ness** *n*

judo /'dʒuːdəʊ/ *n* a Japanese martial art emphasizing the use of quick movement and leverage to throw an opponent

[1]**jug** /dʒʌg/ *n* **1a** *chiefly Br* a vessel for holding and pouring liquids that typically has a handle and a lip or spout **b** the contents of or quantity contained in a jug; a jugful **2** prison – infml

[2]**jug** *v* to stew (e g a hare) in an earthenware vessel

juggernaut /'dʒʌgənɔːt/ *n* **1** an inexorable force or object that crushes anything in its path **2** *chiefly Br* a very large, usu articulated, lorry

juggle /'dʒʌgəl/ *v* **1** to perform the tricks of a juggler **2** to manipulate, esp in order to achieve a desired end **3** to hold or balance precariously

juggler /'dʒʌgələʳ/ *n* one skilled in keeping several objects in motion in the air at the same time by alternately tossing and catching them

jugular vein, jugular /'dʒʌgjʊlə/ *n* any of several veins of each side of the neck that return blood from the head

juice /dʒuːs/ *n* **1** the extractable fluid contents of cells or tissues **2a** *pl* the natural fluids of an animal body **b** the liquid or moisture contained in sthg **3** the inherent quality of sthg; *esp* the basic force or strength of sthg **4** a medium (e g electricity or petrol) that supplies power – infml

juicy /'dʒuːsi/ *adj* **1** succulent **2** financially rewarding or profitable – infml **3** rich in interest; *esp* interesting because of titillating content – infml – **-ciness** *n*

jujitsu /ˌdʒuː'dʒɪtsuː/ *n* a Japanese martial art employing holds, throws and paralysing blows to subdue an opponent

jukebox /'dʒuːkbɒks/ *n* a coin-operated record player that automatically plays records chosen from a restricted list

julep /'dʒuːlᵻp/ *n, chiefly NAm* a drink consisting of a spirit and sugar poured over crushed ice and garnished with mint

Julian calendar /ˌdʒuːlɪən 'kælᵻn-dəʳ/ *n* a calendar introduced in Rome in 46 BC establishing the 12-month year of 365 days with an extra day every fourth year

July /dʒʊ'laɪ/ *n* the 7th month of the Gregorian calendar

[1]**jumble** /'dʒʌmbəl/ *v* to mix *up* in a confused or disordered mass

[2]**jumble** *n* **1** a mass of things mingled together without order or plan **2** *Br* articles for a jumble sale

jumble sale *n, Br* a sale of donated secondhand articles, usu conducted to raise money for some charitable purpose

jumbo /'dʒʌmbəʊ/ *n* a very large specimen of its kind

[1]**jump** /dʒʌmp/ *v* **1a** to spring into the air, esp using the muscular power of feet and legs **b** to move suddenly or involuntarily from shock, surprise, etc **c** to move quickly or energetically (as if) with a jump; *also* to act with alacrity **2** to pass rapidly, suddenly, or abruptly (as if) over some intervening thing: e g **a** to skip **b** to rise suddenly in rank or status **c** to make a mental leap **d** to come to or arrive at a position or judgment without due deliberation **e** to undergo a sudden sharp increase **3** to make a sudden verbal or physical attack – usu + *on* or *upon* **4a** to (cause to) leap over **b** to pass over, esp to a point beyond; skip, bypass **c** to act, move, or begin before (e g a signal) **5a** to escape or run away from **b** to leave hastily or in violation of an undertaking **c** to depart from (a normal course) **6** to make a sudden or surprise attack on

[2]**jump** *n* **1a(1)** an act of jumping; a leap **(2)** a sports contest (e g the long jump) including a jump **(3)** a space, height, or distance cleared by a jump **(4)** an obstacle to be jumped over (e g in a horse race) **b** a sudden involuntary movement; a start **2a** a sharp sudden increase (e g in amount, price, or value) **b** a sudden change or transition; *esp* one that leaves a break in continuity **c** any of a series of moves from one place or position to another; a move

jumped-up *adj* recently risen in wealth, rank, or status – derog

[1]**jumper** /'dʒʌmpəʳ/ *n* a jumping animal; *esp* a horse trained to jump obstacles

[2]**jumper** *n, Br* a knitted or crocheted garment worn on the upper body

jumpy /'dʒʌmpi/ *adj* **1** having jumps or sudden variations **2** nervous, jittery – **-pily** *adv* – **-piness** *n*

junction /'dʒʌŋkʃən/ *n* **1** joining or being joined **2a** a place of meeting **b** an intersection of roads, esp where 1 terminates **3** sthg that joins

juncture /'dʒʌŋktʃəʳ/ *n* **1** an instance or place of joining; a connection or joining part **2** a point of time (made critical by a concurrence of circumstances)

June /dʒuːn/ *n* the 6th month of the Gregorian calendar

jungle /'dʒʌŋgəl/ *n* **1** an area overgrown with thickets or masses of (tropical) trees and other vegetation **2a** a confused, disordered, or complex mass **b** a place of ruthless struggle for survival

[1]**junior** /'dʒuːnɪə'/ *n* **1** a person who is younger than another **2a** a person holding a lower or subordinate position in a hierarchy of ranks **b** a member of a younger form in a school **3** *NAm* a male child; a son – infml

[2]**junior** *adj* **1** younger – used, esp in the USA, to distinguish a son with the same name as his father **2** lower in standing or rank **3** for children aged from 7 to 11

juniper /'dʒuːnɪ̣pə'/ *n* any of several evergreen shrubs or trees of the cypress family

[1]**junk** /dʒʌŋk/ *n* **1a** secondhand or discarded articles or material; *broadly* rubbish **b** sthg of little value or inferior quality **2** narcotics; *esp* heroin – slang

[2]**junk** *n* a sailing ship used in the Far East with a high poop and overhanging stem, little or no keel, and sails that are often stiffened with horizontal battens

[1]**junket** /'dʒʌŋkɪ̣t/ *n* **1** a dessert of sweetened flavoured milk curdled with rennet **2** a festive social affair (at public or a firm's expense) – chiefly infml

[2]**junket** *v* to feast, banquet – infml

junkie, junky /'dʒʌŋki/ *n* a drug addict – infml

Junoesque /,dʒuːnəʊ'esk/ *adj, of a woman* having stately beauty

junta /'dʒʌntə, 'hʊntə/ *n sing or pl in constr* a political council or committee; *esp* a group controlling a government after a revolution

Jupiter /'dʒuːpɪ̣tə'/ *n* the largest of the planets and 5th in order from the sun

juridical /dʒʊə'rɪdɪkəl/ *also* **juridic** *adj* **1** judicial **2** of or being jurisprudence; legal

jurisdiction /,dʒʊərɪ̣s'dɪkʃən/ *n* **1** the power, right, or authority to apply the law **2** the authority of a sovereign power **3** the limits within which authority may be exercised

jurisprudence /,dʒʊərɪ̣s'pruːdəns/ *n* (the science or philosophy of) a body or branch of law

jurist /'dʒʊərɪ̣st/ *n* sby with a thorough knowledge of law

juror /'dʒʊərə'/ *n* **1** a member of a jury **2** one who takes an oath

jury /'dʒʊəri/ *n* **1** a body of usu 12 people who hear evidence in court and are sworn to give an honest verdict, esp of guilty or not guilty, based on this evidence **2** a committee for judging a contest or exhibition

[1]**just** /dʒʌst/ *adj* **1a** conforming (rigidly) to fact or reason **b** conforming to a standard of correctness; proper **2a(1)** acting or being in conformity with what is morally upright or equitable **(2)** being what is merited; deserved **b** legally correct – **~ly** *adv* – **~ness** *n*

[2]**just** /dʒəst; *strong* dʒʌst/ *adv* **1a** exactly, precisely – not following *not* (e g *just* right) **b** at this moment and not sooner (e g he's only *just* arrived) – sometimes used with the past tense **c** only at this moment and not later (e g I'm *just* coming) **2a** by a very small margin; immediately, barely (e g only *just* possible) **b** only, simply (e g *just* a short note) **3** quite (e g not *just* yet) **4** perhaps, possibly (e g it might *just* snow) **5** very, completely (e g *just* wonderful) **6** indeed – sometimes expressing irony (e g didn't he *just*!) *USE (5, 6)* infml

justice /'dʒʌstɪ̣s/ *n* **1a** the maintenance or administration of what is just **b** the administration of law **2a** the quality of being just, impartial, or fair **b** (conformity to) the principle or ideal of just dealing or right action **3** conformity to truth, fact, or reason **4** *Br* – used as a title for a judge

justice of the peace *n* a lay magistrate empowered chiefly to administer summary justice in minor cases and to commit for trial

justify /'dʒʌstɪ̣faɪ/ *v* **1** to prove or show to be just, right, or reasonable **2** to space out (e g a line of printed text) so as to be flush with a margin – **-fiable** *adj* – **-fiably** *adv* – **-fication** *n*

jut /dʒʌt/ *v* to stick *out;* project

jute /dʒuːt/ *n* the glossy fibre of either of 2 E Indian plants of the linden family used chiefly for sacking, twine, etc

Jute *n* a member of a Germanic people that invaded England and esp Kent along with the Angles and Saxons in the 5th c AD

[1]**juvenile** /'dʒuːvənaɪl/ *adj* **1** physiologically immature or undeveloped **2** (characteristic) of or suitable for children or young people

[2]**juvenile** *n* **1** a young person **2** a young individual resembling an adult of its kind except in size and reproductive activity **3** an actor who plays youthful parts

juxtapose /ˌdʒʌkstə'pəʊz/ *v* to place side by side – **-position** *n*

K

k /keɪ/ *n, pl* **k's, ks,** *often cap* (a graphic representation of or device for reproducing) the 11th letter of the English alphabet

kaftan /'kæftæn/ *n* a caftan

kaiser /'kaɪzəʳ/ *n* an emperor of Germany during the period 1871 to 1918

kaleidoscope /kə'laɪdəskəʊp/ *n* **1** a tubular instrument containing loose chips of coloured glass between mirrors so placed that an endless variety of symmetrical patterns is produced as the instrument is rotated and the chips of glass change position **2** sthg that is continually changing; *esp* a variegated changing pattern, scene, or succession of events **– -scopic** *adj* **– -scopically** *adv*

kangaroo /ˌkæŋgə'ruː/ *n* any of various plant-eating marsupial mammals of Australia, New Guinea, and adjacent islands that hop on their long powerful hind legs

kaolin /'keɪəlɪ̈n/ *n* a fine usu white clay formed from decomposed feldspar and used esp in ceramics

kapok /'keɪpɒk/ *n* a mass of silky fibres that surround the seeds of a tropical tree and are used esp as a soft (insulating) filling for mattresses, cushions, sleeping bags, etc

kaput /kə'pʊt/ *adj* no longer able to function; broken, exhausted – infml

karakul, caracul /'kærəkl/ **1** any of a breed of hardy sheep from central Asia **2** the tightly curled glossy black coat of karakul lambs, valued as fur

karate /kə'rɑːti/ *n* a martial art in which opponents use their hands and feet to deliver crippling blows

karma /'kɑːmə/ *n, often cap* the force generated by a person's actions, held in Hinduism and Buddhism to determine his/her destiny in his/her next existence

kayak /'kaɪæk/ *n* an Eskimo canoe made of a frame covered with skins; *also* a similar canvas-covered or fibreglass canoe

kebab /kɪ̈'bæb/ *n* (cubes of) meat cooked on a skewer

kedgeree /'kedʒəriː, --'-/ *n* a dish containing rice, flaked fish, and chopped hard-boiled eggs

[1]**keel** /kiːl/ *n* a flat-bottomed ship; *esp* a barge used on the river Tyne to carry coal

[2]**keel** *n* **1a** a timber or plate which extends along the centre of the bottom of a vessel and usu projects somewhat from the bottom **b** the main load-bearing member (e g in an airship) **2** a projection (e g the breastbone of a bird) suggesting a keel

[3]**keel 1** to (cause to) turn over **2** to fall *over* (as if) in a faint

keelhaul /'kiːlhɔːl/ *v* **1** to drag (a person) under the keel of a ship as punishment **2** to rebuke severely

[1]**keen** /kiːn/ *adj* **1a** having or being a fine edge or point; sharp **b** affecting one as if by cutting or piercing **2a** enthusiastic, eager **b** *of emotion or feeling* intense **3a** intellectually alert; *also* shrewdly astute **b** sharply contested; competitive; *specif, Br, of prices* low in order to be competitive **c** extremely sensitive in perception – **~ly** *adv* – **keenness** *n*

[2]**keen** *v or n* (to utter) a loud wailing lamentation for the dead, typically at Irish funerals

[1]**keep** /kiːp/ *v* **kept 1a** to take notice of by appropriate conduct; fulfil (the obligations of) **b** to act fittingly in relation to (a feast or ceremony) **c** to conform to in habits or conduct **d** to stay in accord with (a beat) **2a** to watch over and defend; guard **b(1)** to take care of, esp as an owner; tend **(2)** to support **(3)** to maintain in a specified condition – often in combination **c** to continue to maintain **d(1)** to cause to remain in a specified place, situation, or condition **(2)** to store habitually for use **(3)** to preserve

(food) in an unspoilt condition **e** to have or maintain in one's service, employment, or possession or at one's disposal – often + *on* **f** to record by entries in a book **g** to have customarily in stock for sale **3a** to delay, detain **b** to hold back; restrain **c** to save, reserve **d** to refrain from revealing or releasing **4** to retain possession or control of **5a** to continue to follow **b** to stay or remain on or in, often against opposition **6** to manage, run **7a** to maintain a course **b** to continue, usu without interruption **c** to persist in a practice **8a** to stay or remain in a specified desired place, situation, or condition **b** to remain in good condition **c** to be or remain with regard to health **d** to call for no immediate action **9** to act as wicketkeeper or goalkeeper – infml

[2]**keep** *n* **1** a castle, fortress, or fortified tower **2** the means (e g food) by which one is kept – infml

keeper /'kiːpəʳ/ *n* **1a** a protector, guardian, or custodian **b** a gamekeeper **c** a curator **2** any of various devices (e g a latch or guard ring) for keeping sthg in position **3a** a goalkeeper **b** a wicketkeeper

keeping /'kiːpɪŋ/ *n* custody, care

keep on *v* to talk continuously; *esp* to nag

keepsake /'kiːpseɪk/ *n* sthg (given, to be) kept as a memento, esp of the giver

keep up *v* **1** to persist or persevere in; continue **2** to preserve from decline **3** to maintain an equal pace or level of activity, progress, or knowledge (e g with another) **4** to continue without interruption

keg /keg/ *n, Br* a small barrel having a capacity of (less than) 10gal (about 45.5l); *specif* a metal beer barrel from which beer is pumped by pressurized gas

kelvin /'kelvɪ̆n/ *n* the SI unit of temperature defined by the Kelvin scale

Kelvin *adj* of, conforming to, or being a scale of temperature on which absolute zero is at 0 and water freezes at 273.16K under standard conditions

[1]**ken** /ken/ *v, chiefly Scot* to have knowledge (of); know

[2]**ken** *n* the range of perception, understanding, or knowledge – usu + *beyond, outside*

[1]**kennel** /'kenl/ *n* **1** a shelter for a dog **2** an establishment for the breeding or boarding of dogs – often pl with sing. meaning but sing. or pl in constr

[2]**kennel** *v* to put or keep (as if) in a kennel

kept /kept/ *past of* **keep**

kerb /kɜːb/ *n, Br* the edging, esp of stone, to a pavement, path, etc

kerchief /'kɜːtʃɪ̆f/ *n, pl* **kerchiefs** *also* **kerchieves** **1** a square or triangle of cloth used as a head covering or worn as a scarf around the neck **2** a handkerchief

kerfuffle /kə'fʌfəl/ *n, chiefly Br* a fuss, commotion – infml

kernel /'kɜːnl/ *n* **1** the inner softer often edible part of a seed, fruit stone, or nut **2** a whole seed of a cereal **3** a central or essential part; core

kestrel /'kestrəl/ *n* a small common Eurasian and N African falcon that is noted for its habit of hovering

ketch /ketʃ/ *n* a fore-and-aft rigged ship with the mizzenmast stepped forward of the rudder

ketchup /'ketʃəp/ *n* any of several sauces made with vinegar and seasonings and used as a relish; *esp* a sauce made from seasoned tomato puree

kettle /'ketl/ *n* a metal vessel used esp for boiling liquids; *esp* one with a lid, handle, and spout that is placed on top of a stove or cooker or contains an electric heating-element and is used to boil water

kettledrum /'ketldrʌm/ *n* a percussion instrument that consists of a hollow brass or copper hemisphere with a parchment head whose tension can be changed to vary the pitch

[1]**key** /kiː/ *n* **1a** a usu metal instrument by which the bolt of a lock is turned **b** sthg having the form or function of such a key **2a** a means of gaining or preventing entrance, possession, or control **b** an instrumental or deciding factor **3a** sthg that gives an explanation or identification or provides a solution **b** a list of words or phrases explaining symbols or abbreviations **c** an arrangement of the important characteristics of a group of plants or animals used for identification **4a** any of

the levers of a keyboard musical instrument that is pressed by a finger or foot to actuate the mechanism and produce the notes **b** a lever that controls a vent in the side of a woodwind instrument or a valve in a brass instrument **c** a small button or knob on a keyboard (e g of a typewriter) designed to be pushed down by the fingers **5** a dry usu single-seeded fruit (e g of an ash or elm tree) **6** a particular system of 7 musical notes forming a scale

[2]**key** *v* **1** to roughen (a surface) to improve adhesion of plaster, paint, etc **2** to bring into harmony or conformity; make appropriate **3** to make nervous, tense, or excited – usu + *up* **4** to keyboard

[3]**key** *adj* of basic importance; fundamental

[4]**key** *n* a low island or reef, esp in the Caribbean area

[1]**keyboard** /ˈkiːbɔːd/ *n* **1a** a bank of keys on a musical instrument (e g a piano) typically having 7 usu white and 5 raised usu black keys to the octave **b** any instrument having such a keyboard, esp when forming part of a pop or jazz ensemble **2** a set of systematically arranged keys by which a machine is operated

[2]**keyboard** *v* **1** to operate a machine (e g for typesetting) by means of a keyboard **2** to capture or set (e g data or text) by means of a keyboard

key money *n* a payment made by a tenant to secure occupancy of a rented property

[1]**keynote** /ˈkiːnəʊt/ *n* **1** the first and harmonically fundamental note of a scale **2** the fundamental or central fact, principle, idea, or mood

[2]**keynote** *adj* being or delivered by a speaker who presents the issues of primary interest to an assembly

key signature *n* the sharps or flats placed on the musical staff to indicate the key

keystone /ˈkiːstəʊn/ *n* **1** the wedge-shaped piece at the apex of an arch that locks the other pieces in place **2** sthg on which associated things depend for support

khaki /ˈkɑːki/ *n* **1** a dull yellowish brown colour **2** a khaki-coloured cloth made usu of cotton or wool and used esp for military uniforms

khan /kɑːn/ *n* a medieval supreme ruler over the Turkish, Tartar, and Mongol tribes

kibbutz /kɪˈbʊts/ *n, pl* **kibbutzim** a collective farm or settlement in Israel

[1]**kick** /kɪk/ *v* **1a** to strike (out) with the foot or feet **b** to make a kick in football **2** to show opposition; rebel **3** *of a firearm* to recoil when fired **4** to free oneself of (a drug or drug habit) – infml

[2]**kick** *n* **1a** a blow or sudden forceful thrust with the foot; *specif* one causing the propulsion of an object **b** the power to kick **c** a repeated motion of the legs used in swimming **d** a sudden burst of speed, esp in a footrace **2** the recoil of a gun **3a** a stimulating effect or quality **b** a stimulating or pleasurable experience or feeling – often pl **c** an absorbing or obsessive new interest

kickback /ˈkɪkbæk/ *n* **1** a sharp violent reaction **2** a money return received usu because of help or favours given or sometimes because of confidential agreement or coercion

kickoff /ˈkɪk-ɒf/ *n* **1** a kick that puts the ball into play in soccer, rugby, etc **2** an act or instance of starting or beginning

kick off *v* **1** to start or resume play with a kickoff **2** to start or begin proceedings – infml

[1]**kid** /kɪd/ *n* **1** the young of a goat or related animal **2** the flesh, fur, or skin of a kid **3** a child; *also* a young person (e g a teenager) – infml

[2]**kid** *v* **1a** to mislead as a joke **b** to convince (oneself) of sthg untrue or improbable **2** to make fun of **3** to engage in good-humoured fooling

kiddie, kiddy /ˈkɪdi/ a small child – infml

kid-glove *adj* using or involving extreme tact

kidnap /ˈkɪdnæp/ *v* to seize and detain (a person) by force and often for ransom – **kidnap** *n* – **-napper** *n*

kidney /ˈkɪdni/ *n* **1a** either of a pair of organs situated in the body cavity near the spinal column that excrete waste products of metabolism in the form of urine **b** an excretory organ of an invertebrate **2** the kidney of an animal eaten as food **3** sort, kind, or type, esp with regard to temperament

kidney bean *n* (any of the kidney-shaped seeds of) the French bean

[1]kill /kɪl/ *v* **1** to deprive of or destroy life **2a** to put an end to **b** to defeat, veto **3a** to destroy the vital, active, or essential quality of **b** to spoil, subdue, or neutralize the effect of **4** to cause (time) to pass (e g while waiting) **5** to cause (e g an engine) to stop **6** to cause extreme pain to **7** to overwhelm with admiration or amusement **8** to discard or abandon further investigation of (a story) – journ

[2]kill *n* **1** a killing or being killed **2** sthg killed: e g **a** animals killed in a shoot, hunt, season, or particular period of time **b** an enemy aircraft, submarine, etc destroyed by military action

killer whale *n* a flesh-eating gregarious black-and-white toothed whale found in most seas of the world

[1]killing /ˈkɪlɪŋ/ *n* a sudden notable gain or profit – infml

[2]killing *adj* **1** extremely exhausting or difficult to endure **2** highly amusing *USE* infml

killjoy /ˈkɪldʒɔɪ/ *n* one who spoils the pleasure of others

kiln /kɪln/ *n* an oven, furnace, or heated enclosure used for processing a substance by burning, firing, or drying

kilocalorie /ˈkɪlə,kæləri/ *n* the quantity of heat required to raise the temperature of 1kg of water 1°C under standard conditions

kilogram /ˈkɪləgræm/ *n* **1** the SI unit of mass and weight equal to the mass of a platinum-iridium cylinder kept near Paris, and approximately equal to the weight of a litre of water (about 2.205lb) **2** a unit of force equal to the weight of a kilogram mass under the earth's gravitational attraction

kilohertz /ˈkɪləhɜːts/ *n* a unit of frequency equal to 1000 hertz

kilometre /ˈkɪlə,miːtəʳ, kɪˈlɒmɪ̵təʳ/ *n* 1000 metres

kilowatt /ˈkɪləwɒt/ *n* 1000 watts

kilt /kɪlt/ *n* a skirt traditionally worn by Scotsmen that is formed usu from a length of tartan, is pleated at the back and sides, and is wrapped round the body and fastened at the front

kimono /kɪˈməʊnəʊ/ *n* a loose robe with wide sleeves and a broad sash traditionally worn by the Japanese

[1]kin /kɪn/ *n* **1** a group of people of common ancestry **2** *sing or pl in constr* one's relatives **3** *archaic* kinship

[2]kin *adj* kindred, related

[1]kind /kaɪnd/ *n* **1** fundamental nature or quality **2a** a group united by common traits or interests **b** a specific or recognized variety – often in combination

[2]kind *adj* **1** disposed to be helpful and benevolent **2** forbearing, considerate, or compassionate **3** cordial, friendly **4** not harmful; mild, gentle – **~ness** *n*

kindergarten /ˈkɪndəgɑːtn/ *n* a school or class for small children

kindle /ˈkɪndl/ *v* **1** to set (a fire, wood, etc) burning **2** to stir up (e g emotion) **3** to catch fire

kindling /ˈkɪndlɪŋ/ *n* material (e g dry wood and leaves) for starting a fire

[1]kindly /ˈkaɪndli/ *adj* **1** agreeable, beneficial **2** sympathetic, generous – **-liness** *n*

[2]kindly *adv* **1** in an appreciative or sincere manner **2** – used (1) to add politeness or emphasis to a request (2) to convey irritation or anger in a command

[1]kindred /ˈkɪndrɪ̵d/ *n* **1** *sing or pl in constr* (one's) relatives **2** family relationship

[2]kindred *adj* similar in nature or character

kinetic /kɪˈnetɪk, kaɪ-/ *adj* of motion – **~ally** *adv*

kinetic art *n* art (e g sculpture) depending for its effect on the movement of surfaces or volumes

kinetic energy *n* energy that a body or system has by virtue of its motion

kinetics /kɪˈnetɪks, kaɪ-/ *n pl but sing or pl in constr* science that deals with the effects of forces on the motions of material bodies or with changes in a physical or chemical system

king /kɪŋ/ *n* **1** a male monarch of a major territorial unit; *esp* one who inherits his position and rules for life **2** the holder of a preeminent position **3** the principal piece of each colour in a set of chessmen that has the power to move 1 square in any direction and must be protected against check **4** a playing card marked with a stylized figure of a king and ranking usu below the ace **5** a draughtsman that has reached the opposite side of the board and is empowered to move both forwards and backwards – **~ly** *adj* – **~ship** *n*

kingdom /'kɪŋdəm/ *n* **1** a territorial unit with a monarchical form of government **2** *often cap* the eternal kingship of God **3** an area or sphere in which sby or sthg holds a preeminent position

kingfisher /'kɪŋ,fɪʃəʳ/ *n* any of numerous small brightly-coloured fish-eating birds with a short tail and a long stout sharp bill

kingmaker /'kɪŋmeɪkəʳ/ *n* sby having influence over the choice of candidates for office

kingpin /'kɪŋ,pɪn/ *n* the key person or thing in a group or undertaking

Kings /kɪŋz/ *n pl but sing in constr* any of 2 or, in the Roman Catholic canon, 4 narrative and historical books of the Old Testament

King's English *n* standard or correct S British English speech or usage – used when the monarch is a man

kink /kɪŋk/ *n* **1** a short tight twist or curl caused by sthg doubling or winding on itself **2** an eccentricity or mental peculiarity; *esp* such eccentricity in sexual behaviour or preferences – **~y** *adj*

kinsfolk /'kɪnzfəʊk/ *n pl* relatives

kinship /'kɪnʃɪp/ *n* **1** blood relationship **2** similarity

kiosk /'kiːɒsk/ *n* **1** an open summerhouse or pavilion common in Turkey or Iran **2** a small stall or stand used esp for the sale of newspapers, cigarettes, and sweets **3** *Br* a public telephone box

[1]**kip** *n, chiefly Br* **1** a place to sleep **2** a period of sleep *USE* infml

[2]**kip** *v, chiefly Br* to (lie down to) sleep *USE* infml

[1]**kipper** /'kɪpəʳ/ *n* a kippered fish, esp a herring

[2]**kipper** *v* to cure (split dressed fish) by salting and drying, usu by smoking

kirk /kɜːk/ *n* **1** *cap the* national Church of Scotland as distinguished from the Church of England or the Episcopal Church in Scotland **2** *chiefly Scot* a church

kirtle /'kɜːtl/ *n* a man's tunic or coat or a woman's dress worn esp in the Middle Ages

[1]**kiss** /kɪs/ *v* **1** to touch with the lips, esp as a mark of affection or greeting **2** to touch one another with the lips, esp as a mark of love or sexual desire **3** to touch gently or lightly – **~able** *adj*

[2]**kiss** *n* an act or instance of kissing

kisser /'kɪsəʳ/ *n* the mouth or face – slang

[1]**kit** /kɪt/ *n* **1** a set of tools or implements **2** a set of parts ready to be assembled **3** a set of clothes and equipment for use in a specified situation; *esp* the equipment carried by a member of the armed forces

[2]**kit** *v, chiefly Br* to equip, outfit; *esp* to clothe – usu + *out* or *up*

kitchen /'kɪtʃɪ̣n/ *n* a place (e g a room in a house or hotel) where food is prepared

kitchenette /,kɪtʃɪ̣'net/ *n* a small kitchen or alcove containing cooking facilities

kite /kaɪt/ *n* **1** any of various hawks with long narrow wings, a deeply forked tail, and feet adapted for taking insects and small reptiles as prey **2** a light frame covered with thin material (e g paper or cloth), designed to be flown in the air at the end of a long string

kitsch /kɪtʃ/ *n* artistic or literary material that is pretentious or inferior and is usu designed to appeal to popular or sentimental taste – **~y** *adj*

[1]**kitten** /'kɪtn/ *n* the young of a cat or other small mammal

[2]**kitten** *v* to give birth to kittens

kittiwake /'kɪtiweɪk/ *n* any of various gulls that have a short or rudimentary hind toe

kitty /'kɪti/ *n* a jointly held fund of money (e g for household expenses)

kiwi /'kiːwiː/ *n* **1** a flightless New Zealand bird with hairlike plumage **2** *cap* a New Zealander

Klaxon /ˈklæksən/ *trademark* – used for a powerful electrically operated horn or warning signal

Kleenex /ˈkliːneks/ *trademark* – used for a paper handkerchief

kleptomania /ˌkleptəˈmeɪnɪə/ *n* an irresistible desire to steal, esp when not accompanied by economic motives or desire for financial gain – **~c** *n*

knack /næk/ *n* a special ability, capacity, or skill that enables sthg, esp of a difficult or unusual nature, to be done with ease

[1]**knacker** /ˈnækəʳ/ *n, Br* **1** sby who buys and slaughters worn-out horses for use esp as animal food or fertilizer **2** a buyer of old ships, houses, or other structures for their constituent materials

[2]**knacker** *v, chiefly Br* to exhaust – infml

knave /neɪv/ *n* **1** an unprincipled deceitful fellow **2** a jack in a pack of cards – **knavish** *adj* – **knavishly** *adv* – **knavishness, knavery** *n*

knead /niːd/ *v* to work and press into a mass (as if) with the hands

[1]**knee** /niː/ *n* **a** (the part of the leg that includes) a joint in the middle part of the human leg that is the articulation between the femur, tibia, and kneecap **b** a corresponding joint in an animal, bird, or insect

[2]**knee** *v* to strike with the knee

[1]**kneecap** /ˈniːkæp/ *n* a thick flat triangular movable bone that forms the front point of the knee and protects the front of the joint

[2]**kneecap** *v* to smash the kneecap of, as a punishment or torture

kneel /niːl/ *v* **knelt, kneeled** to fall or rest on the knee or knees

knell /nel/ *n* **1** (the sound of) a bell rung slowly (e g for a funeral or disaster) **2** an indication of the end or failure of sthg

knew /njuː/ *past of* **know**

knickerbockers /ˈnɪkəbɒkəz/ *n pl* short baggy trousers gathered on a band at the knee

knickers /ˈnɪkəz/ *n pl, Br* women's pants

knick-knack /ˈnɪk næk/ *n* a trivial ornament or trinket

[1]**knife** /naɪf/ *n, pl* **knives** **1a** a cutting implement consisting of a more or less sharp blade fastened to a handle **b** such an instrument used as a weapon **2** a sharp cutting blade or tool in a machine

[2]**knife** *v* **1** to cut, slash, or wound with a knife **2** to cut, mark, or spread with a knife

knife-edge *n* **1** sthg sharp and narrow (e g a ridge of rock) resembling the edge of a knife **2** an uncertain or precarious position or condition

[1]**knight** /naɪt/ *n* **1a(1)** a mounted man-at-arms serving a feudal superior **(2)** a man honoured by a sovereign for merit, ranking below a baronet **b** a man devoted to the service of a lady (e g as her champion) **2** either of 2 pieces of each colour in a set of chessmen that move from 1 corner to the diagonally opposite corner of a rectangle of 3 by 2 squares over squares that may be occupied – **~hood** *n* – **~ly** *adj*

[2]**knight** *v* to make a knight of

[1]**knit** /nɪt/ *v* **1a** to link firmly or closely **b** to unite intimately **2a** to (cause to) grow together **b** to contract into wrinkles **3** to form (e g a fabric, garment, or design) by working 1 or more yarns into a series of interlocking loops using 2 or more needles or a knitting machine **4** to make knitted fabrics or articles

[2]**knit, knit stitch** *n* a basic knitting stitch that produces a raised pattern on the front of the work

knitting /ˈnɪtɪŋ/ *n* work that has been or is being knitted

knob /nɒb/ *n* **1a** a rounded protuberance **b** a small rounded ornament, handle, or control (for pushing, pulling, or turning) **2** a small piece or lump (e g of coal or butter) – **~bly** *adj*

[1]**knock** /nɒk/ *v* **1** to strike sthg with a sharp (audible) blow; *esp* to strike a door seeking admittance **2** to (cause to) collide with sthg **3** to be in a place, often without any clearly defined aim or purpose – usu + *about* or *around* **4a** to make a sharp pounding noise **b** *of an internal-combustion engine* to make a series of sharp popping noises because of faulty combustion of the fuel-air mixture **5** to find fault (with)

6a(1) to strike sharply (2) to drive, force, make, or take (as if) by so striking 7 to set forcibly in motion with a blow

²knock *n* **1a** (the sound of) a knocking or a sharp blow or rap **b** a piece of bad luck or misfortune **2** a harsh and often petty criticism

knockabout /'nɒkəbaʊt/ *adj* **1** suitable for rough use **2** (characterized by antics that are) boisterous

knock back *v, chiefly Br* **1** to drink (an alcoholic beverage) rapidly **2** to cost; set back **3** to surprise, disconcert *USE* infml

knockdown /'nɒkdaʊn/ *adj* **1** having such force as to strike down or overwhelm **2** easily assembled or dismantled **3** *of a price* very low or substantially reduced; *esp* being the lowest acceptable to the seller

knock down *v* **1** to dispose of (an item for sale at an auction) *to* a bidder **2** to take apart; disassemble

knocker /'nɒkəʳ/ *n* a metal ring, bar, or hammer hinged to a door for use in knocking

knock off **1** to stop doing sthg, esp one's work **2** to do hurriedly or routinely **3** to deduct **4** to kill; *esp* to murder **5** to steal **6** *Br* to have sexual intercourse with *USE* (*4&5*) infml, (*6*) slang

knock-on *n* (an instance of) the knocking of the ball forwards on the ground with the hand or arm in rugby in violation of the rules

knockout /'nɒk-aʊt/ *n* **1** a blow that knocks out an opponent (or knocks him down for longer than a particular time, usu 10s, and results in the termination of a boxing match) **2** a competition or tournament with successive rounds in which losing competitors are eliminated until a winner emerges in the final **3** sby or sthg that is sensationally striking or attractive – infml

knock out *v* **1a** to defeat (a boxing opponent) by a knockout **b** to make unconscious **2** to tire out; exhaust **3** to eliminate (an opponent) from a knockout competition **4** to overwhelm with amazement or pleasure – infml

knock up *v* **1** to make, prepare, or arrange hastily **2** to achieve a total of **3** *Br* to rouse, awaken **4** to make pregnant – infml **5** to practise informally before a tennis, squash, etc match

¹knot /nɒt/ *n* **1a** an interlacing of (parts of) 1 or more strings, threads, etc that forms a lump or knob **b** a piece of ribbon, braid etc tied as an ornament **c** a (sense of) tight constriction **2** sthg hard to solve **3** a bond of union; *esp* the marriage bond **4a** a protuberant lump or swelling in tissue **b** (a rounded cross-section in timber of) the base of a woody branch enclosed in the stem from which it arises **5** a cluster of people or things **6** a speed of 1 nautical mile per hour

²knot *v* **1** to tie in or with a knot **2** to unite closely or intricately **3** to form a knot or knots

knotty /'nɒti/ *adj* complicated or difficult (to solve)

¹know /nəʊ/ *v* **knew, known** **1a(1)** to perceive directly; have direct cognition of **(2)** to have understanding of **(3)** to recognize or identify **b(1)** to be acquainted or familiar with **(2)** to have experience of **2a** to be aware of the truth or factual nature of; be convinced or certain of **b** to have a practical understanding of **3** to (come to) have knowledge (of sthg)

know-all *n* one who behaves as if he knows everything

know-how *n* (practical) expertise

knowing /'nəʊɪŋ/ *adj* **1** having or reflecting knowledge, information, or intelligence **2** shrewd or astute; *esp* implying (that one has) knowledge of a secret **3** deliberate, conscious

knowledge /'nɒlɪdʒ/ *n* **1a** the fact or condition of knowing sthg or sby through experience or association **b** acquaintance with, or understanding or awareness of, sthg **2** the range of a person's information, perception, or understanding **3** the sum of what is known; the body of truth, information, and principles acquired by mankind (on some subject)

knowledgeable /'nɒlɪdʒəbəl/ *adj* having or exhibiting knowledge or intelligence; well-informed – **-bly** *adv*

known /nəʊn/ *adj* generally recognized

knuckle /ˈnʌkəl/ *n* **1** the rounded prominence formed by the ends of the 2 bones at a joint; *specif* any of the joints between the hand and the fingers or the finger joints closest to these **2** a cut of meat consisting of the lowest leg joint of a pig, sheep, etc with the adjoining flesh

knuckle down *v* to apply oneself earnestly

knuckle-duster *n* a metal device worn over the front of the doubled fist for protection and use as a weapon

knuckle under *v* to give in, submit

koala /kəʊˈɑːlə/, **koala bear** *n* an Australian tree-dwelling marsupial mammal that has large hairy ears, grey fur, and sharp claws and feeds on eucalyptus leaves

kohl /kəʊl/ *n* (a cosmetic preparation made with) a black powder used, orig chiefly by Asian women, to darken the eyelids

kookaburra /ˈkʊkəbʌrə/ *n* a large Australian kingfisher that has a call resembling loud laughter

kopeck, copeck /ˈkəʊpek/ *n* (a Russian coin worth) $^1/_{100}$ of a rouble

Koran, Qur'an /kɔːˈrɑːn, kəˈrɑːn, ˈkɔːræn/ *n* the book composed of writings accepted by Muslims as revelations made to Muhammad by Allah through the angel Gabriel – ~**ic** *adj*

kosher /ˈkəʊʃəʳ/ *adj* **1a** *of food* prepared according to Jewish law **b** selling kosher food **2** proper, legitimate – infml

¹kowtow /ˌkaʊˈtaʊ/ *n* a (Chinese) gesture of deep respect in which one kneels and touches the ground with one's forehead

²kowtow *v* **1** to make a kowtow **2** to show obsequious deference

kraal /krɑːl/ *n* **1** a village of S African tribesmen **2** an enclosure for domestic animals in S Africa

kremlin /ˈkremlɨn/ *n* **1** a citadel within a Russian town or city **2** *cap the* government of the USSR

krona /ˈkrəʊnə/ *n* the major unit of currency of Sweden

kudos /ˈkjuːdɒs/ *n* fame and renown, esp resulting from an act or achievement

Ku Klux Klan /ˌkuː klʌks ˈklæn/ *n* a secret political organization in the USA that confines its membership to American-born Protestant whites and is hostile to blacks

kung fu /ˌkʌŋ ˈfuː/ *n* a Chinese martial art resembling karate

kwashiorkor /ˌkwɒʃiˈɔːkəʳ/ *n* severe malnutrition in infants and children that is caused by a diet high in carbohydrate and low in protein

L

l /el/ *n, pl* **l's, ls** *often cap* **1a** (a graphic representation of or device for reproducing) the 12th letter of the English alphabet **b** sthg shaped like the letter L **2** fifty

la /lɑː/ *n* the 6th note of the diatonic scale in solmization

lab /læb/ *n* a laboratory

¹label /'leɪbəl/ *n* **1** a slip (e g of paper or cloth), inscribed and fastened to sthg to give information (e g identification or directions) **2** a descriptive or identifying word or phrase: e g **a** an epithet **b** a word or phrase used with a dictionary definition to provide additional information (e g level of usage) **3** an adhesive stamp **4** a trade name; *specif* a name used by a company producing commercial recordings

²label *v* **1** to fasten a label to **2** to describe or categorize (as if) with a label

laboratory /lə'bɒrətri/ *n* a place equipped for scientific experiment, testing, or analysis; *broadly* a place providing opportunity for research in a field of study

laborious /lə'bɔːrɪəs/ *adj* involving or characterized by effort – **~ly** *adv* – **~ness** *n*

¹labour /'leɪbəʳ/ *n* **1a** expenditure of effort, esp when difficult or compulsory; toil **b** human activity that provides the goods or services in an economy **c** (the period of) the physical activities involved in the birth of young **2** an act or process requiring labour; a task **3** workers **4** *sing or pl in constr, cap* the Labour party

²labour *v* **1** to exert one's powers of body or mind, esp with great effort; work, strive **2** to move with great effort **3** to be in labour when giving birth **4** to suffer from some disadvantage or distress **5** to treat in laborious detail

Labour *adj* of or being a political party, specif one in the UK, advocating a planned socialist economy and associated with working-class interests – **~ite** *n*

labourer /'leɪbərəʳ/ *n* one who does unskilled manual work, esp outdoors

labour exchange *n, often cap L&E* a government office that seeks to match unemployed people and vacant jobs and that is responsible for paying out unemployment benefit

labrador /'læbrədɔːʳ/ *n, often cap* a dog used esp for retrieving game, characterized by a dense black or golden coat

laburnum /lə'bɜːnəm/ *n* any of a small genus of Eurasian leguminous shrubs and trees with bright yellow flowers and poisonous seeds

labyrinth /'læbərɪnθ/ *n* **1** a place that is a network of intricate passageways, tunnels, blind alleys, etc **2** sthg perplexingly complex or tortuous in structure, arrangement, or character **3** (the tortuous anatomical structure in) the ear or its bony or membranous part – **~ine** *n*

¹lace /leɪs/ *n* **1** a cord or string used for drawing together 2 edges (e g of a garment or shoe) **2** an ornamental braid for trimming coats or uniforms **3** an openwork usu figured fabric made of thread, yarn, etc, used for trimmings, household furnishings, garments, etc

²lace *v* **1** to draw together the edges of (as if) by means of a lace passed through eyelets **2** to draw or pass (e g a lace) through sthg **3** to confine or compress by tightening laces, esp of a corset **4a** to add a dash of an alcoholic drink to **b** to give savour or variety to

lacerate /'læsəreɪt/ *v* **1** to tear or rend roughly **2** to cause sharp mental or emotional pain to – **-ration** *n*

lachrymal, lacrimal /'lækrɪ̥məl/ *adj* **1** of or constituting the glands that produce tears **2** of or marked by tears

[1]**lack** /læk/ *v* **1** to be deficient or missing **2** to be short or have need of sthg – usu + *for*

[2]**lack** *n* **1** the fact or state of being wanting or deficient **2** sthg lacking

lackadaisical /ˌlækəˈdeɪzɪkəl/ *adj* lacking life or zest; *also* (reprehensibly) casual or negligent – ~**ly** *adv*

lackey /ˈlæki/ *n* **1** a usu liveried retainer **2** a servile follower

lacklustre /ˈlækˌlʌstəʳ/ *adj* lacking in sheen, radiance, or vitality; dull

laconic /ləˈkɒnɪk/ *adj* using, or involving the use of, a minimum of words; terse – ~**ally** *adv*

[1]**lacquer** /ˈlækəʳ/ *n* **1** a clear or coloured varnish obtained by dissolving a substance (e g shellac) in a solvent (e g alcohol) **2** a durable natural varnish; *esp* one obtained from an Asian shrub of the sumach family

[2]**lacquer** *v* to coat with lacquer

lacrosse /ləˈkrɒs/ *n* a game played on grass by 2 teams of 10 players, whose object is to throw a ball into the opponents' goal, using a long-handled stick that has a triangular head with a loose mesh pouch for catching and carrying the ball

lactose /ˈlæktəʊs/ *n* a sugar that is present in milk

lacy /ˈleɪsi/ *adj* resembling or consisting of lace

lad /læd/ *n* **1** a male person between early boyhood and maturity **2** a fellow, chap **3** *Br* a stable lad

ladder /ˈlædəʳ/ *n* **1** a structure for climbing up or down that has 2 long sidepieces of metal, wood, rope, etc joined at intervals by crosspieces on which one may step **2a** sthg that resembles or suggests a ladder in form or use **b** *chiefly Br* a vertical line in hosiery or knitting caused by stitches becoming unravelled **3** a series of ascending steps or stages

laddie /ˈlædi/ *n* a (young) lad

laden /ˈleɪdn/ *adj* **1** heavily loaded **2** weighed down; deeply troubled

la-di-da, lah-di-dah /ˌlɑː di ˈdɑː/ *adj* affectedly refined in voice or manner

ladies *n* a public lavatory for women – infml

ladies' man, lady's man *n* a man who seeks women's company – derog

[1]**ladle** /ˈleɪdl/ *n* a deep-bowled long-handled spoon used esp for taking up and conveying liquids or semiliquid foods (e g soup)

[2]**ladle** *v* to take up and convey (as if) in a ladle

lady /ˈleɪdi/ *n* **1a** a woman with authority, esp as a feudal superior **b** a woman receiving the homage or devotion of a knight or lover **2a** a woman of refinement or superior social position **b** a woman – often in courteous reference or usu pl in address **3** a wife **4a** *cap* any of various titled women in Britain – used as a title **b** *cap* a female member of an order of knighthood

ladybird /ˈleɪdibɜːd/ *n* any of numerous small beetles of temperate and tropical regions; *esp* any of several ladybirds that have red wing cases with black spots

lady-in-waiting *n, pl* **ladies-in-waiting** a lady of a queen's or princess's household appointed to wait on her

lady-killer *n* a man who captivates women

ladylike /ˈleɪdilaɪk/ *adj* **1** resembling a lady, esp in manners; well-bred **2** becoming or suitable to a lady

ladyship /ˈleɪdiʃɪp/ *n* – used as a title for a woman having the rank of lady

[1]**lag** /læg/ *v* to stay or fall behind; fail to keep pace – often + *behind*

[2]**lag** *n* **1** the act or an instance of lagging **2** an interval between related events; *specif* a time lag

[3]**lag** *n* a convict or an ex-convict

[4]**lag** *v* to cover or provide with lagging

lager /ˈlɑːgəʳ/ *n* a light beer brewed by slow fermentation

lagging /ˈlægɪŋ/ *n* material for thermal insulation (e g wrapped round a boiler or laid in a roof)

lagoon /ləˈguːn/ *n* a shallow channel or pool usu separated from a larger body of water by a sand bank, reef, etc

laid /leɪd/ *past of* **lay**

lain /leɪn/ *past part of* **lie**

lair /leəʳ/ *n* **1** the resting or living place of a wild animal **2** a refuge or place for hiding

laird /leəd/ *n, Scot* a member of the landed gentry

laissez-faire /ˌleɪseɪ 'feəʳ/ *n* a doctrine opposing government regulation of economic affairs – **laissez-faire** *adj*

laity /'leɪʒti/ *n sing or pl in constr* **1** the people of a religion other than its clergy **2** the mass of the people as distinguished from those of a particular profession

[1]**lake** /leɪk/ *n* a large inland body of water; *also* a pool of oil, pitch, or other liquid

[2]**lake** *n* **1** a deep purplish red pigment orig prepared from cochineal **2** any of numerous usu bright pigments composed essentially of a soluble dye absorbed in or combined with an inorganic carrier

lam /læm/ *v* to beat soundly

lama /'lɑːmə/ *n* a Buddhist monk of Tibet

[1]**lamb** /læm/ *n* **1a** a young sheep, esp one that is less than a year old **b** the young of various animals (e g the smaller antelopes) other than sheep **2** a gentle, meek, or innocent person **3** the flesh of a lamb used as food

[2]**lamb** *v* to give birth to a lamb

lambaste, lambast /'læmbeɪst/ *v* **1** to beat, thrash **2** to attack verbally; censure

lambskin /'læmˌskɪn/ *n* **1** (leather made from) the skin of a lamb or small sheep **2** the skin of a lamb dressed with the wool on

[1]**lame** /leɪm/ *adj* **1** having a body part, esp a leg, so disabled as to impair freedom of movement; *esp* having a limp caused by a disabled leg **2** weak, unconvincing – **~ly** *adv* – **~ness** *n*

[2]**lame** *v* to make lame

lamé /'lɑːmeɪ/ *n* a brocaded clothing fabric made from any of various fibres combined with tinsel weft threads often of gold or silver

lame duck *n* sby or sthg (e g a person or business) that is weak or incapable

[1]**lament** /lə'ment/ *v* to feel or express grief or deep regret; mourn aloud – often + *for* or *over* – **~ation** *n*

[2]**lament** *n* **1** an expression of grief **2** a dirge, elegy

lamentable /'læməntəbəl, lə'mentəbəl/ *adj* that is to be regretted; deplorable – **-bly** *adv*

[1]**laminate** /'læmʒneɪt/ *v* **1** to roll or compress (e g metal) into a thin plate or plates **2** to separate into thin layers **3** to make by uniting superimposed layers of 1 or more materials **4** to overlay with a thin sheet or sheets of material (e g metal or plastic)

[2]**laminate** /'læmʒnʒt, -neɪt/ *adj* covered with or consisting of thin layers

lamp /læmp/ *n* **1** any of various devices for producing visible light: e g **a** a vessel containing an inflammable substance (e g oil or gas) that is burnt to give out artificial light **b** a usu portable electric device containing a light bulb **2** any of various light-emitting devices (e g a sunlamp) which produce electromagnetic radiation (e g heat radiation)

lampblack /'læmpˌblæk/ *n* a pigment made from finely powdered black soot

lampoon /læm'puːn/ *v or n* (to make the subject of) a harsh satire – **~ist** *n*

lamprey /'læmpri/ *n* any of several eel-like aquatic vertebrates that have a large sucking mouth with no jaws

lampshade /'læmpʃeɪd/ *n* a decorative translucent cover placed round an electric light bulb to reduce glare

[1]**lance** /lɑːns/ *n* **1** a weapon having a long shaft with a sharp steel head carried by horsemen for use when charging **2** a lancet

[2]**lance** *v* **1** to pierce (as if) with a lance **2** to open (as if) with a lancet

lance corporal *n* a noncommissioned officer of the lowest rank in the British army or US marines

lancer /'lɑːnsəʳ/ *n* **1** a member of a light-cavalry unit (formerly) armed with lances **2** *pl but sing in constr* (the music for) a set of 5 quadrilles each in a different metre

lancet /'lɑːnsʒt/ *n* a small surgical knife

[1]**land** /lænd/ *n* **1a** the solid part of the surface of a celestial body, esp the earth **b** ground or soil of a specified situation, nature, or quality **2** (*the* way of life in) *the* rural and esp agricultural regions of a country **3** (the people of) a country, region, etc **4** a realm, domain **5** ground owned as

property – often pl with sing. meaning

[2]**land** *v* **1** to set or put on shore from a ship **2a** to set down (e g passengers or goods) after conveying **b** to bring to or cause to reach a specified place, position, or condition **c** to bring (e g an aeroplane) to a surface from the air **3a** to catch and bring in (e g a fish) **b** to gain, secure – infml **4** to strike, hit – infml **5** to present or burden *with* sthg unwanted – infml **6a** to go ashore from a ship; disembark **b** *of a boat, ship, etc* to come to shore; *also* to arrive on shore in a boat, ship, etc **7a** to end up – usu + *up* **b** to strike or come to rest on a surface (e g after a fall) **c** *of an aircraft, spacecraft, etc* to alight on a surface; *also* to arrive in an aircraft, spacecraft, etc which has alighted on a surface

landau /ˈlændɔː/ *n* a 4-wheeled carriage with a folding top divided into 2 sections

land breeze *n* a breeze blowing seawards from the land, generally at night

landed /ˈlændᵻd/ *adj* **1** owning land **2** consisting of land

landfall /ˈlændfɔːl/ *n* an act or instance of sighting or reaching land after a voyage or flight

landing /ˈlændɪŋ/ *n* **1** the act of going or bringing to a surface from the air or to shore from the water **2** a place for discharging and taking on passengers and cargo **3** a level space at the end of a flight of stairs or between 2 flights of stairs

landing stage *n* a sometimes floating platform for landing passengers or cargo

landlady /ˈlænd,leɪdi/ *n* **1** a female landlord **2** the female proprietor of a guesthouse or lodging house

landlocked /ˈlændlɒkt/ *adj* (nearly) enclosed by land

landlord /ˈlændlɔːd/ *n* **1** sby who owns land, buildings, or accommodation for lease or rent **2** sby who owns or keeps an inn; an innkeeper

landlubber /ˈlænd,lʌbəʳ/ *n* a person unacquainted with the sea or seamanship

landmark /ˈlændmɑːk/ *n* **1a** an object (e g a stone) that marks a boundary **b** a conspicuous object that can be used to identify a locality **2** an event that marks a turning point or new development

[1]**landscape** /ˈlændskeɪp/ *n* **1** natural, esp inland scenery **2a** a picture, drawing, etc of landscape **b** the art of depicting landscape

[2]**landscape** *v* to improve or modify the natural beauties of

landslide /ˈlændslaɪd/ *n* **1** a usu rapid movement of rock, earth, etc down a slope; *also* the moving mass **2** an overwhelming victory, esp in an election

lane /leɪn/ *n* **1** a narrow passageway, road, or street **2a** a fixed ocean route used by ships **b** a strip of road for a single line of vehicles **c** any of several marked parallel courses to which a competitor must keep during a race (e g in running or swimming) **d** a narrow hardwood surface down which the ball is sent towards the pins in tenpin bowling

language /ˈlæŋgwɪdʒ/ *n* **1a** those words, their pronunciation, and the methods of combining them used by a particular people, nation, etc **b(1)** (the faculty of making and using) audible articulate meaningful sound **(2)** a systematic means of communicating using conventionalized signs, sounds, gestures, or marks **(3)** the suggestion by objects, actions, or conditions of associated ideas or feelings **2a** a particular style or manner of verbal expression **b** the specialized vocabulary and phraseology belonging to a particular group or profession

language laboratory *n* a room, usu divided into booths each equipped with a tape recorder, where foreign languages are learnt by listening and speaking

languid /ˈlæŋgwɪd/ *adj* **1** drooping or flagging (as if) from exhaustion; weak **2** spiritless or apathetic in character **3** lacking force or quickness, esp of movement; sluggish – **~ly** *adv*

languish /ˈlæŋgwɪʃ/ *v* **1** to be or become feeble or enervated **2a** to become dispirited or depressed; pine – often + *for* **b** to lose intensity or urgency **c** to suffer hardship or neglect **3** to assume an expression of emotion appealing for sympathy

languor /'læŋgəʳ/ *n* **1** weakness or weariness of body or mind **2** a feeling or mood of wistfulness or dreaminess **3** heavy or soporific stillness – ~**ous** *adj* – ~**ously** *adv*

lank /læŋk/ *adj* **1** lean, gaunt **2** straight, limp, and usu greasy – ~**ly** *adv* – ~**ness** *n*

lanky /'læŋki/ *adj* ungracefully tall and thin – **lankily** *adv* – **lankiness** *n*

lanolin /'lænəl$\frac{1}{2}$n/ *n* wool grease, esp when refined for use in ointments and cosmetics

lantern /'læntən/ *n* **1** a portable protective case with transparent windows that houses a light (e g a candle) **2a** the chamber in a lighthouse containing the light **b** a structure above an opening in a roof which has glazed or open sides for light or ventilation

lanyard /'lænjəd/ *n* **1** a piece of rope or line for fastening sthg on board ship **2** a cord worn round the neck as a decoration or to hold sthg (e g a knife) **3** a cord used in firing certain types of cannon

¹lap /læp/ *n* (the clothing covering) the front part of the lower trunk and thighs of a seated person

²lap *v* **1** to fold or wrap over or round **2a** to place or lie so as to (partly) cover (one another) **b** to unite (e g beams or timbers) so as to preserve the same breadth and depth throughout **3a** to overtake and thereby lead or increase the lead over (another contestant) by a full circuit of a racetrack **b** to complete a circuit of (a racetrack)

³lap *n* **1** the amount by which one object overlaps another **2a** (the distance covered during) the act or an instance of moving once round a closed course or track **b** one stage or segment of a larger unit (e g a journey) **c** one complete turn (e g of a rope round a drum)

⁴lap *v* **1** to take in (liquid) with the tongue **2** to move in little waves, usu making a gentle splashing sound **3** to take in eagerly or quickly – usu + *up*

⁵lap *n* **1** an act or instance of lapping **2** a gentle splashing sound

lapdog /'læpdɒg/ *n* a small dog that may be held in the lap

lapel /lə'pel/ *n* a fold of the top front edge of a coat or jacket that is continuous with the collar

lapidary /læp$\frac{1}{2}$dəri/ *adj* **1** sculptured in or engraved on stone **2** of or relating to (the cutting of) gems

lapis lazuli /ˌlæpɪs 'læzjʊli/ *n* (the colour of) a rich blue semiprecious stone

¹lapse /læps/ *n* **1** a slight error (e g of memory or in manners) **2a** a drop; *specif* a drop in temperature, humidity, or pressure with increasing height **b** an esp moral fall or decline **3a(1)** the legal termination of a right or privilege through failure to exercise it **(2)** the termination of insurance coverage for nonpayment of premiums **b** a decline into disuse **4** an abandonment of religious faith **5** a continuous passage or elapsed period

²lapse *v* **1a** to fall or depart from an attained or accepted standard or level (e g of morals) – usu + *from* **b** to sink or slip gradually **2** to go out of existence or use **3** to pass to another proprietor by omission or negligence **4** *of time* to run its course; pass

lapwing /'læpˌwɪŋ/ *n* a crested Old World plover noted for its shrill wailing cry

larceny /'lɑːsəni/ *n* theft

larch /lɑːtʃ/ *n* (the wood of) any of a genus of trees of the pine family with short deciduous leaves

¹lard /lɑːd/ *v* **1** to dress (e g meat) for cooking by inserting or covering with fat, bacon, etc **2** to intersperse or embellish (e g speech or writing) *with* sthg

²lard *n* a soft white solid fat obtained by rendering the esp abdominal fat of a pig

larder /'lɑːdəʳ/ *n* a place where food is stored; a pantry

¹large /lɑːdʒ/ *adj* **1** having more than usual power, capacity, or scope **2** exceeding most other things of like kind (in quantity or size) **3** dealing in great numbers or quantities; operating on an extensive scale

large intestine *n* the rear division of the vertebrate intestine that is divided into caecum, colon, and rectum, and concerned esp with the resorption of water and formation of faeces

largely /ˈlɑːdʒli/ *adv* to a large extent

largo /ˈlɑːgəʊ/ *n, adv, or adj* (a movement to be) played in a very slow and broad manner – used in music

[1]**lark** /lɑːk/ *n* any of numerous brown singing birds mostly of Europe, Asia, and northern Africa; *esp* a skylark

[2]**lark** *v* to have fun – usu + *about* or *around*

[3]**lark** *n* **1** a lighthearted adventure; *also* a prank **2** *Br* a type of activity; *esp* a business, job *USE* infml

larva /ˈlɑːvə/ *n, pl* **larvae** **1** the immature, wingless, and often wormlike feeding form that hatches from the egg of many insects and is transformed into a pupa or chrysalis from which the adult emerges **2** the early form (e g a tadpole) of an animal (e g a frog) that undergoes metamorphosis before becoming an adult – **~l** *adj*

laryngitis /ˌlærɪ̣nˈdʒaɪtɪ̣s/ *n* inflammation of the larynx

larynx /ˈlærɪŋks/ *n, pl* **larynges, larynxes** the modified upper part of the trachea of air-breathing vertebrates that contains the vocal cords in human beings, most other mammals, and a few lower forms – **laryngeal** *adj*

lascivious /ləˈsɪvɪəs/ *adj* inclined or inciting to lechery or lewdness – **~ly** *adv* – **~ness** *n*

laser /ˈleɪzəʳ/ *n* a device that generates an intense beam of light or other electromagnetic radiation of a single wavelength by using the natural oscillations of atoms or molecules

[1]**lash** /læʃ/ *v* **1** to move violently or suddenly **2** to beat, pour **3** to attack physically or verbally, (as if) with a whip – often + *at, against,* or *out* **4** to strike quickly and forcibly (as if) with a lash **5** to drive (as if) with a whip; rouse

[2]**lash** *n* **1a(1)** a stroke (as if) with a whip **(2)** (the flexible part of) a whip **b** a sudden swinging movement or blow **2** violent beating **3** an eyelash

[3]**lash** *v* to bind or fasten with a cord, rope, etc

[1]**lashing** /ˈlæʃɪŋ/ *n* a physical or verbal beating

[2]**lashing** *n* sthg used for binding, wrapping, or fastening

lashings /ˈlæʃɪŋz/ *n pl* an abundance – usu + *of*; infml

lash out *v* **1** to make a sudden violent physical or verbal attack – usu + *at* or *against* **2** *Br* to spend unrestrainedly – often + *on*; infml

lass /læs/, **lassie** *n* a young woman; a girl

[1]**lasso** /ləˈsuː, ˈlæsəʊ/ *n, pl* **lassos, lassoes** a rope or long thong of leather with a running noose that is used esp for catching horses and cattle

[2]**lasso** *v* to catch (as if) with a lasso

[1]**last** /lɑːst/ *v* **1** to continue in time **2a** to remain in good or adequate condition, use, or effectiveness **b** to manage to continue (e g in a course of action) **3** to continue in existence or action as long as or longer than – often + *out* **4** to be enough for the needs of

[2]**last** *adj* **1** following all the rest: e g **a** final, latest **b** being the only remaining **2** of the final stage of life (e g *last* rites) **3** next before the present; most recent **4a** lowest in rank or standing; *also* worst **b** least suitable or likely (e g the *last* person you'd think of) **5a** conclusive, definitive (e g the *last* word) **b** single – used as an intensive (e g ate every *last* scrap)

[3]**last** *adv* **1** after all others; at the end **2** on the most recent occasion **3** in conclusion; lastly

[4]**last** *n* sby or sthg last

[5]**last** *n* a form (e g of metal) shaped like the human foot, over which a shoe is shaped or repaired

last straw *n* *the* last of a series (e g of events or indignities) stretching one's patience beyond its limit

last word *n* the most up-to-date or fashionable example of its kind

[1]**latch** /lætʃ/ *v* **1** to attach oneself **2** to gain understanding or comprehension *USE* + *on* or *onto*

[2]**latch** *n* a fastener (e g for a door)

[1]**late** /leɪt/ *adj* **1a** occurring or arriving after the expected time **b** of the end of a specified time span **2a** (recently) deceased – used with reference to names, positions or specified relationships **b** just prior to the present, esp as the most recent of a succession **3** far on in the day or night

[2]late *adv* **1a** after the usual or proper time **b** at or near the end of a period of time or of a process – often + *on* **2** until lately – **~ness** *n*

lately /'leɪtli/ *adv* recently; of late

latent /'leɪtənt/ *adj* present but not manifest – **-tency** *n*

latent heat *n* heat given off or absorbed in a change of phase without a change in temperature

lateral /'lætərəl/ *adj* of the side; situated on, directed towards, or coming from the side

latest /'leɪtǰst/ *n* **1** *the* most recent or currently fashionable style or development **2** *the* latest acceptable time

latex /'leɪteks/ *n* **1** a milky usu white fluid that is produced by various flowering plants (e g of the spurge and poppy families) and is the source of rubber, gutta-percha, etc **2** a water emulsion of a synthetic rubber or plastic

lath /lɑːθ/ *n, pl* **laths, lath** a thin narrow strip of wood, esp for nailing to woodwork (e g rafters or studding) as a support (e g for tiles or plaster)

lathe /leɪð/ *n* a machine in which work is rotated about a horizontal axis and shaped by a fixed tool

[1]lather /'lɑːðəʳ/ *n* **1a** a foam or froth formed when a detergent (e g soap) is agitated in water **b** foam or froth from profuse sweating (e g on a horse) **2** an agitated or overwrought state – **~y** *adj*

[2]lather *v* **1** to spread lather over **2** to form a (froth like) lather

[1]Latin /'lætɪn/ *adj* **1** of Latium or the Latins **2a** of or composed in Latin **b** Romance **3** of the part of the Christian church using a Latin liturgy; *broadly* Roman Catholic **4** of the peoples or countries using Romance languages **5** *chiefly NAm* of the peoples or countries of Latin America

[2]Latin *n* **1** the language of ancient Latium and of Rome **2** a member of the people of ancient Latium **3** a member of any of the Latin peoples **4** *chiefly NAm* a native or inhabitant of Latin America

latitude /'lætǰtjuːd/ *n* **1a** the angular distance of a point on the surface of a celestial body, esp the earth, measured N or S from the equator **b** the angular distance of a celestial body from the ecliptic **2** a region as marked by its latitude – often pl with sing. meaning **3** (permitted) freedom of action or choice

latrine /lə'triːn/ *n* a small pit used as a toilet, esp in a military camp, barracks, etc; *broadly* a toilet

[1]latter /'lætəʳ/ *adj* **1** of the end; later, final **2** recent, present (e g in *latter* years) **3** second of 2 things, or last of several things mentioned or understood

[2]latter *n, pl* **latter** the second or last mentioned

latterly /'lætəli/ *adv* **1** towards the end or latter part of a period **2** lately

lattice /'lætǰs/ *n* **1** (a window, door, etc having) a framework or structure of crossed wooden or metal strips with open spaces between **2** a network or design like a lattice **3** a regular geometrical arrangement of points or objects over an area or in space

laudable /'lɔːdəbəl/ *adj* worthy of praise; commendable – **-bility** *n* – **-bly** *adv*

laudatory /'lɔːdətəri/, **laudative** *adj* of or expressing praise

[1]laugh /lɑːf/ *v* **1a** to make the explosive vocal sounds characteristically expressing amusement, mirth, joy, or derision **b** to experience amusement, mirth, joy, or derision **2** to dismiss as trivial – + *off* or *away*

[2]laugh *n* **1** the act or sound of laughing **2** an expression of mirth or scorn **3** a means of entertainment; a diversion – often pl with sing. meaning **4** a cause for derision or merriment; a joke – infml

laughable /'lɑːfəbəl/ *adj* of a kind to provoke laughter or derision; ridiculous – **-bly** *adv*

laughing gas *n* nitrous oxide

laughingstock /'lɑːfɪŋstɒk/ *n* an object of ridicule

laughter /'lɑːftəʳ/ *n* **1** a sound (as if) of laughing **2** the action of laughing

[1]launch /lɔːntʃ/ *v* **1a** to throw forward; hurl **b** to release or send off (e g a self-propelled object) **2a** to set (an esp newly built boat or ship) afloat **b** to start or set in motion (e g on a course or career) **c** to introduce (a new product) onto the market **3** to throw oneself energetically – + *into* or *out into* **4** to make a start – usu + *out* or *forth*

[2]**launch** *n* an act or instance of launching

[3]**launch** *n* **1** the largest boat carried by a warship **2** a large open or half-decked motorboat

launder /ˈlɔːndəʳ/ *v* **1** to wash (e g clothes) in water **2** to give (sthg, esp money, obtained illegally) the appearance of being respectable or legal

launderette /lɔːnˈdret/ *n* a self-service laundry

laundry /ˈlɔːndri/ *n* **1** clothes or cloth articles that have been or are to be laundered, esp by being sent to a laundry **2** a place where laundering is done; *esp* a commercial laundering establishment

laurel /ˈlɒrəl/ *n* **1** any of a genus of trees or shrubs that have alternate entire leaves, small flowers, and fruits that are ovoid berries **2** a tree or shrub that resembles the true laurel **3** a crown of laurel awarded as a token of victory or preeminence; distinction, honour – usu pl with sing. meaning

lava /ˈlɑːvə/ *n* (solidified) molten rock that issues from a volcano

lavatory /ˈlævətəri/ *n* a toilet

lavender /ˈlævɪ̣ndəʳ/ *n* **1** a Mediterranean plant of the mint family widely cultivated for its narrow aromatic leaves and spikes of lilac-purple flowers which are dried and used in perfume sachets **2** a pale purple colour

[1]**lavish** /ˈlævɪʃ/ *adj* **1** expending or bestowing profusely **2** expended, bestowed, or produced in abundance – **~ly** *adv*

[2]**lavish** *v* to expend or bestow *on* with profusion

law /lɔː/ *n* **1a(1)** a rule of conduct formally recognized as binding or enforced by authority **(2)** the whole body of such rules **(3)** common law **b** the control brought about by such law – esp in *law and order* **c** litigation **2a** a rule one should observe **b** control, authority **3** *often cap* the revelation of the will of God set out in the Old Testament **4** a rule of action, construction, or procedure **5** the law relating to one subject **6** *often cap the* legal profession **7a** a statement of an order or relation of natural phenomena **b** a necessary relation between mathematical or logical expressions **8** *sing or pl in constr, often cap the* police – infml

lawbreaker /ˈlɔːbreɪkəʳ/ *n* one who violates the law

lawful /ˈlɔːfəl/ *adj* **1** allowed by law **2** rightful – **~ly** *adv* – **~ness** *n*

lawless /ˈlɔːlɪ̣s/ *adj* **1** not regulated by or based on law **2** not restrained or controlled by law – **~ly** *adv* – **~ness** *n*

[1]**lawn** /lɔːn/ *n* a fine sheer linen or cotton fabric of plain weave that is thinner than cambric

[2]**lawn** *n* an area of ground (e g around a house or in a garden or park) that is covered with grass and is kept mowed

lawn tennis *n* tennis played on a grass court

lawsuit /ˈlɔːsjuːt, -suːt/ *n* a noncriminal case in a court of law

lawyer /ˈlɔːjəʳ/ *n* sby whose profession is to conduct lawsuits or to advise on legal matters

lax /læks/ *adj* **1** not strict or stringent; negligent; *also* deficient in firmness or precision **2a** not tense, firm, or rigid; slack **b** not compact or exhibiting close cohesion; loose – **~ly** *adv* – **~ness, ~ity** *n*

laxative /ˈlæksətɪv/ *n or adj* (a usu mild purgative) having a tendency to loosen or relax the bowels (to relieve constipation)

[1]**lay** /leɪ/ *v* **laid** **1** to beat or strike down with force **2a** to put or set down **b** to place for rest or sleep; *esp* to bury **3** *of a bird* to produce (an egg) **4** to calm, allay **5** to bet, wager **6a** to dispose or spread over or on a surface **b** to set in order or position **7** to put or impose as a duty, burden, or punishment – esp + *on* or *upon* **8** to prepare, contrive **9a** to bring into position or against or into contact with sthg **b** to prepare or position for action or operation **10** to bring to a specified condition **11a** to assert, allege **b** to submit for examination and judgment **12** to put aside for

future use; store, reserve – + *aside, by, in,* or *up* **13** to put out of use or consideration – + *aside* or *by* **14** to copulate with – slang

[2]**lay** *past of* **lie**

[3]**lay** *n* a simple narrative poem intended to be sung; a ballad

[4]**lay** *adj* **1** of or performed by the laity **2** of domestic or manual workers in a religious community **3** not belonging to a particular profession

layabout /ˈleɪəbaʊt/ *n, chiefly Br* a lazy shiftless person

lay-by *n, pl* **lay-bys** *Br* a branch from or widening of a road to permit vehicles to stop without obstructing traffic

[1]**layer** /ˈleɪəʳ/ *n* **1a** a single thickness of some substance spread or lying over or under another **b** any of a series of gradations or depths **2** a branch or shoot of a plant treated to induce rooting while still attached to the parent plant

[2]**layer** *v* **1** to propagate (a plant) by means of layers **2** to arrange or form (as if) in layers **3** to form out of or with layers

layman /ˈleɪmən/, *fem* **laywoman** *n* **1** a person not of the clergy **2** a person without special (e g professional) knowledge of some field

layoff /ˈleɪˌɒf/ *n* **1** the laying off of an employee or work force **2** a period of unemployment, inactivity, or idleness

lay off *v* **1** to cease to employ (a worker), usu temporarily **2** to stop or desist, specif from an activity causing annoyance – infml

lay on *v* to supply; organize

layout /ˈleɪaʊt/ *n* the plan, design, or arrangement of sthg (e g rooms in a building or matter to be printed) laid out

lay out *v* **1** to prepare (a corpse) for a funeral **2** to arrange according to a plan **3** to knock flat or unconscious

lay up *v* **1** to store up; have or keep for future use **2** to disable or confine with illness or injury **3** to take out of active service

laze /leɪz/ *v* to pass (time) *away* in idleness or relaxation

lazy /ˈleɪzi/ *adj* **1a** disinclined or averse to activity; indolent; *also* not energetic or vigorous **b** encouraging inactivity or indolence **2** moving slowly – **-zily** *adv* – **-ziness** *n*

leach /liːtʃ/ *v* to separate the soluble components from (a mixture) or remove (sthg soluble) by the action of a percolating liquid

[1]**lead** /liːd/ *v* **led** **1a(1)** to guide on a way, esp by going in advance **(2)** to cause to go with one (under duress) **b** to direct or guide on a course or to a state or condition; influence **c** to serve as a channel or route for **d(1)** to lie or run in a specified place or direction **(2)** to serve as an entrance or passage **2** to go through; live **3a** to direct the operations, activity, or performance of; have charge of **b** to go or be at the head or ahead of **c** to be first or ahead **4a** to begin, open – usu + *off* **b** to play the first card of a trick, round, or game **5** to tend or be directed towards a specified result **6** to direct the first of a series of blows at an opponent in boxing (*with* the right or left hand)

[2]**lead** /liːd/ *n* **1a(1)** position at the front or ahead **(2)** the act or privilege of leading in cards; *also* the card or suit led **b** guidance, direction; (an) example **c** a margin or position of advantage or superiority **2a** an indication, clue **b** (one who plays) a principal role in a dramatic production **c** a line or strap for leading or restraining an animal (e g a dog) **d** a news story of chief importance **3** an insulated electrical conductor

[3]**lead** /led/ *n* **1** a heavy soft malleable bluish-white metallic element used esp in pipes, cable sheaths, batteries, solder, type metal, and shields against radioactivity **2** the (lead) weight on a sounding line **3** a thin stick of graphite or crayon in or for a pencil **4** *pl, Br* (a usu flat roof covered with) thin lead sheets

leaden /ˈledn/ *adj* **1a** made of lead **b** dull grey **2a** oppressively heavy **b** lacking spirit or animation; sluggish

leader /ˈliːdəʳ/ *n* **1a** a main or end shoot of a plant **b** a blank section at the beginning or end of a reel of film or recorded tape **2** sby or sthg that ranks first, precedes others, or holds a principal position **3** *chiefly Br* a newspaper editorial **4** *Br* the principal first violinist and usu assistant conductor of an orchestra – ~**ship** *n*

leading /ˈliːdɪŋ/ *adj* coming or ranking first; foremost, principal

leading question *n* a question so phrased as to suggest the expected answer

lead on *v* **1** to entice or induce to proceed in a (mistaken or unwise) course **2** to cause to believe sthg that is untrue

[1]**leaf** /liːf/ *n, pl* **leaves** **1a** any of the usu green flat and typically broad-bladed outgrowths from the stem of a plant that function primarily in food manufacture by photosynthesis **b** (the state of having) foliage **2a** a part of a book or folded sheet of paper containing a page on each side **b** a part (e g of a window shutter, folding door, or table) that slides or is hinged **c** metal (e g gold or silver) in sheets, usu thinner than foil

[2]**leaf** *v* **1** to shoot out or produce leaves **2** to glance quickly *through* a book, magazine, etc

leaflet /ˈliːflɨt/ *n* **1** a small or young foliage leaf **2** a single sheet of paper or small loose-leaf pamphlet containing printed matter (e g advertising)

leaf mould *n* a compost or soil layer composed chiefly of decayed vegetable matter

leafy /ˈliːfi/ *adj* **1** having or thick with leaves **2** consisting chiefly of leaves

[1]**league** /liːg/ *n* any of various units of distance of about 3mi (5km)

[2]**league** *n* **1a** an association of nations, groups, or people for a common purpose or to promote a common interest **b** (a competition for an overall title, in which each person or team plays all the others at least once, held by) an association of people or sports clubs **2** a class, category

[1]**leak** /liːk/ *v* **1** to (let a substance) enter or escape through a crack or hole **2** to become known despite efforts at concealment – often + *out* **3** to give out (information) surreptitiously

[2]**leak** *n* **1a** a crack or hole through which sthg (e g a fluid) is admitted or escapes, usu by mistake **b** a means by which sthg (e g secret information) is admitted or escapes, usu with prejudicial effect **2** a leaking or that which is leaked; *esp* a disclosure **3** an act of urinating – slang

leaky /ˈliːki/ *adj* permitting fluid, information, etc to leak in or out; *broadly* not watertight – **-kily** *adv* – **-kiness** *n*

[1]**lean** /liːn/ *v* **leant, leaned** **1a** to incline or bend from a vertical position **b** to rest supported *on/against* sthg **2** to rely for support or inspiration – + *on* or *upon* **3** to incline in opinion, taste, etc **4** to exert pressure; use coercion – + *on*; infml

[2]**lean** *adj* **1a** lacking or deficient in flesh or bulk **b** *of meat* containing little or no fat **2** *esp of a fuel mixture* low in the combustible component – ~**ness** *n*

[3]**lean** *n* the part of meat that consists principally of fat-free muscular tissue

leaning /ˈliːnɪŋ/ *n* a definite but weak attraction, tendency, or partiality

lean-to *n* a small building having a roof that rests on the side of a larger building or wall

[1]**leap** /liːp/ *v* **leapt, leaped** **1** to jump **2a** to pass abruptly from one state or topic to another; *esp* to rise quickly **b** to seize eagerly *at* an opportunity, offer, etc

[2]**leap** *n* **1a** (the distance covered by) a jump **b** a place leapt over or from **2** a sudden transition, esp a rise or increase

[1]**leapfrog** /ˈliːpfrɒg/ *n* a game in which one player bends down and another leaps over him/her

[2]**leapfrog** *v* **1** to leap (over) (as if) in leapfrog **2** to go ahead of (each other) in turn

leap year *n* a year with an extra day added to make it coincide with the solar year

learn /lɜːn/ *v* **learnt, learned** **1a** to gain knowledge of or skill in **b** to memorize **2** to come to be able – + infinitive **3** to come to realize or know – ~**er** *n*

learned /ˈlɜːnɨd/ *adj* characterized by or associated with learning; erudite – ~**ly** *adv*

learning /ˈlɜːnɪŋ/ *n* **1** acquired knowledge or skill **2** modification of a behavioural tendency by experience (e g exposure to conditioning)

[1]**lease** /liːs/ *n* **1** a contract putting the land or property of one party at the disposal of another, usu for a stated period and rent **2** a (prospect of) continuance – chiefly in *lease of life*

[2]**lease** *v* to grant by or hold under lease

leasehold /ˈliːshəʊld/ *n* tenure by or property held by lease – **~er** *n*

leash /liːʃ/ *n* **1a** a (dog's) lead **b** a restraint, check **2** a set of 3 animals (e g greyhounds, foxes, or hares)

[1]**least** /liːst/ *adj* **1** lowest in rank, degree, or importance **2a** smallest in quantity or extent **b** smallest possible; slightest

[2]**least** *n* the smallest quantity, number, or amount

[3]**least** *adv* to the smallest degree or extent

[1]**leather** /ˈleðəʳ/ *n* **1** animal skin dressed for use **2** sthg wholly or partly made of leather; *esp* a piece of chamois, used esp for polishing metal or glass

[2]**leather** *v* to beat with a strap; thrash

leathery /ˈleðəri/ *adj* resembling leather in appearance or consistency; *esp* tough

[1]**leave** /liːv/ *v* **left** **1a** to bequeath **b** to cause to remain as an aftereffect **2a** to cause or allow to be or remain in a specified or unaltered condition **b** to fail to include, use, or take along – sometimes + *off* or *out* **c** to have remaining or as a remainder **d** to allow to do or continue sthg without interference **3a** to go away from; *also* set out *for* **b** to desert, abandon **c** to withdraw from **4** to put, station, deposit, or deliver, esp before departing

[2]**leave** *n* **1** permission to do sthg **2** authorized (extended) absence (e g from employment)

[1]**leaven** /ˈlevən/ *n* a substance (e g yeast) used to produce fermentation or a gas in dough, batter, etc to lighten it; *esp* a mass of fermenting dough reserved for this purpose

[2]**leaven** *v* to raise or make lighter (as if) with a leaven

leaves /liːvz/ *pl of* leaf

leave-taking *n* a departure, farewell

lecher /ˈletʃəʳ/ *n* a sexually promiscuous man – **~ous** *adj* – **~ously** *adv* – **~y**, **~ousness** *n*

lectern /ˈlektən/ *n* a reading desk; *esp* one from which the Bible is read in church

[1]**lecture** /ˈlektʃəʳ/ *n* **1** a discourse given to an audience, esp for instruction **2** a reproof delivered at length; a reprimand

[2]**lecture** *v* to deliver a lecture or series of lectures; *specif* to work as a teacher at a university or college – **~r** *n*

led /led/ *past of* **lead**

LED *n* a diode that emits light when an electric current is passed through it and that is used esp to display numbers, symbols, etc on a screen (e g in a pocket calculator)

ledge /ledʒ/ *n* **1** a (narrow) horizontal surface that projects from a vertical or steep surface (e g a wall or rock face) **2** an underwater ridge or reef

ledger /ˈledʒəʳ/ *n* **1** a book containing (the complete record of all) accounts **2** a horizontal piece of timber secured to the uprights of scaffolding

lee /liː/ *n* **1** protecting shelter **2** **lee, lee side** the side (e g of a ship) sheltered from the wind

[1]**leech** /liːtʃ/ *n* **1** any of numerous flesh-eating or bloodsucking usu freshwater worms **2** one who gains or seeks to gain profit or advantage from another, esp by clinging persistently

[2]**leech** *n* **1** either vertical edge of a square sail **2** the rear edge of a fore-and-aft sail

leek /liːk/ *n* an onion-like vegetable with a white cylindrical edible bulb

leer /lɪəʳ/ *v or n* (to give) a lascivious, knowing, or sly look

lees /liːz/ *n pl* the sediment of a liquor (e g wine) during fermentation and aging

leeward /ˈliːwəd; *tech* ˈluːəd/ *adj or adv* in or facing the direction towards which the wind is blowing

leeway /ˈliːweɪ/ *n* **1** off-course sideways movement of a ship in the direction of the wind **2** an allowable margin of freedom or variation; tolerance

[1]**left** /left/ *adj* **1a** of, situated on, or being the side of the body in which

most of the heart is located **b** located nearer to the left hand than to the right; *esp* located on the left hand when facing in the same direction as an observer **2** *often cap* of the Left in politics

[2]**left** *n* **1a** (a blow struck with) the left hand **b** the location or direction of the left side **c** the part on the left side **2** *sing or pl in constr, cap* those professing socialist or radical political views

[3]**left** *past of* **leave**

left-hand *adj* **1** situated on the left **2** left-handed

left-handed *adj* **1** using the left hand habitually or more easily than the right **2** of, designed for, or done with the left hand **3** clumsy, awkward **4** ambiguous, double-edged – **~ly** *adv* – **~ness** *n*

left wing *n sing or pl in constr, often cap L&W* the more socialist division of a group or party – **left-winger** *n*

[1]**leg** /leg/ *n* **1** a limb of an animal used esp for supporting the body and for walking: e g **a** (an artificial replacement for) either of the lower limbs of a human **b** a (hind) leg of a meat animal, esp above the hock **c** any of the appendages on each segment of an arthropod (e g an insect or spider) used in walking and crawling **3** the part of a garment that covers (part of) the leg **4** the side of a cricket pitch to the left of a right-handed batsmen or to the right of a left-handed one **5a** the course and distance sailed on a single tack **b** a portion of a trip; a stage **c** the part of a relay race run by 1 competitor **d** any of a set of events or games that must all be won to decide a competition

[2]**leg** *adj* in, on, through, or towards the leg side of a cricket field

legacy /'legəsi/ *n* **1** a gift by will; a bequest **2** sthg passed on or remaining from an ancestor or predecessor or from the past

legal /'li:gəl/ *adj* **1** of law **2a** deriving authority from law **b** established by or having a formal status derived from law **3** permitted by law – **~ly** *adv* – **~ity** *n* – **~ize** *v*

legal aid *n* payments from public funds to those who cannot afford legal advice or representation

legal tender *n* currency which a creditor is bound by law to accept as payment of a money debt

legate /'legɨ̣t/ *n* an official delegate or representative

legation /lɪ'geɪʃən/ *n* (the official residence of) a diplomatic mission in a foreign country headed by a minister

legato /lɪ'gɑ:təʊ/ *n, adv, or adj, pl* **legatos** (a manner of performing or passage of music performed) in a smooth and connected manner

leg bye *n* a run scored in cricket after the ball has touched a part of the batsman's body but not his bat or hands

legend /'ledʒənd/ *n* **1a** a story coming down from the past; *esp* one popularly regarded as historical **b** a person, act, or thing that inspires legends **2a** an inscription or title on an object (e g a coin) **b** a caption **c** the key to a map, chart, etc – **~ary** *adj*

leggings /'legɪŋs/ *n pl* closely-fitting coverings (e g of leather) reaching from the ankle to the knee or thigh

legible /'ledʒəbəl/ *adj* capable of being read or deciphered – **-bility** *n* – **-bly** *adv*

[1]**legion** /'li:dʒən/ *n sing or pl in constr.* **1** the principal unit of the ancient Roman army comprising 3000 to 6000 foot soldiers with cavalry **2** a very large number; a multitude **3** a national association of ex-servicemen

[2]**legion** *adj* many, numerous

legislate /'ledʒɨ̣sleɪt/ *v* to make or enact laws – **-tor** *n* – **-ture** *n*

legislation /,ledʒɨ̣s'leɪʃən/ *n* (the making of) laws – **-tive** *adj*

[1]**legitimate** /lɪ'dʒɪtɨ̣mɨ̣t/ *adj* **1** lawfully begotten; *specif* born in wedlock **2** neither spurious nor false; genuine **3a** in accordance with law **b** ruling by or based on the strict principle of hereditary right **4** conforming to recognized principles or accepted rules and standards

[2]**legitimate** /lɪ'dʒɪtɨ̣meɪt/, **legitimatize, legitimize** *v* **1a** to give legal status to **b** to justify **2** to give (an illegitimate child) the legal status of one legitimately born

legume /ˈlegjuːm, lɪˈgjuːm/ *n* **1** the (edible) pod or seed of a leguminous plant **2** any of a large family of plants, shrubs, and trees having pods containing 1 or many seeds and including important food and forage plants (e g peas, beans, or clovers) – **-minous** *adj*

leisure /ˈleʒəʳ/ *n* **1** freedom provided by the cessation of activities; *esp* time free from work or duties **2** unhurried ease – **~d** *adj*

[1]**leisurely** /ˈleʒəli/ *adv* without haste; deliberately

[2]**leisurely** *adj* characterized by leisure; unhurried

lemming /ˈlemɪŋ/ *n* any of several small short-tailed furry-footed northern voles; *esp* one of northern mountains that undergoes recurrent mass migrations

lemon /ˈlemən/ *n* **1** (a stout thorny tree that bears) an oval yellow acid citrus fruit **2** a pale yellow colour **3** one who or that which is unsatisfactory or worthless; a dud – infml

lemonade /ˌleməˈneɪd/ *n* a (carbonated) soft drink made or flavoured with lemon

lemur /ˈliːməʳ/ *n* any of numerous tree-dwelling chiefly nocturnal mammals, esp of Madagascar, typically having a muzzle like a fox, large eyes, very soft woolly fur, and a long furry tail

lend /lend/ *v* **lent** **1a** to give for temporary use on condition that the same or its equivalent be returned **b** to let out (money) for temporary use on condition of repayment with interest **2** to give the assistance or support of; afford, contribute – **~er** *n*

length /leŋθ/ *n* **1a(1)** the longer or longest dimension of an object **(2)** the extent from end to end **b** a measured distance or dimension **c** the quality or state of being long **2** duration or extent in or with regard to time **3** distance or extent in space **4** the degree to which sthg (e g a course of action or a line of thought) is carried; a limit, extreme – often pl with sing. meaning **5a** a long expanse or stretch **b** a piece, esp of a certain length (being or usable as part of a whole or of a connected series) **6** the vertical extent of sthg (e g an article of clothing), esp with reference to the position it reaches on the body – usu in combination

lengthen /ˈleŋθən/ *v* to make or become longer

lengthways /ˈleŋθweɪz/ *adv* in the direction of the length

lengthy /ˈleŋθi/ *adj* of great or unusual length; long; *also* excessively or tediously protracted – **-thily** *adv* – **-thiness** *n*

lenient /ˈliːnɪənt/ *adj* of a mild or merciful nature; not severe – **-ience** *n* – **~ly** *adv*

lens /lenz/ *n* **1** a piece of glass or other transparent material with 2 opposite regular surfaces, at least 1 of which is curved, that is used either singly or combined in an optical instrument to form an image by focussing rays of light **2** a device for directing or focussing radiation other than light (e g sound waves or electrons)

Lent /lent/ *n* the 40 weekdays from Ash Wednesday to Easter observed by Christians as a period of penitence and fasting

lentil /ˈlentl/ *n* (the small round edible seed of) a widely cultivated Eurasian leguminous plant

lento /ˈlentəʊ/ *adv or adj* in a slow manner – used in music

Leo /ˈliːəʊ/ *n* (sby born under) the 5th sign of the zodiac in astrology, pictured as a lion

leopard /ˈlepəd/, *fem* **leopardess** *n* **1** a big cat of southern Asia and Africa that is usu tawny or buff with black spots arranged in broken rings or rosettes **2** a heraldic figure of a lion with the farther forepaw raised and its head turned towards the observer

leotard /ˈliːətɑːd/ *n* a close-fitting one-piece garment worn by dancers or others performing physical exercises

leper /ˈlepəʳ/ *n* **1** sby suffering from leprosy **2** a person shunned for moral or social reasons; an outcast

leprechaun /ˈleprɪ̥kɔːn/ *n* a mischievous elf of Irish folklore

leprosy /ˈleprəsi/ *n* a long-lasting bacterial disease characterized by loss of sensation with eventual paralysis, wasting of muscle, and production of deformities and mutilations

lesbian /'lezbɪən/ *n, often cap* a female homosexual – ~**ism** *n*

lese majesty, lèse majesté /ˌliːz 'mædʒ̩sti/ *n* **1a** a crime (e g treason) committed against a sovereign power **b** an offence violating the dignity of a ruler **2** an affront to dignity or importance

lesion /'liːʒən/ *n* **1** injury, harm **2** abnormal change in the structure of an organ or part due to injury or disease

¹less /les/ *adj* **1** fewer (e g *less* than 3) – disapproved of by some speakers **2** lower in rank, degree, or importance (e g no *less* a person than the President himself(**3** smaller in quantity or extent (e g of *less* importance)

²less *adv* to a lesser degree or extent

³less *prep* diminished by; minus (e g £100 *less* tax)

⁴less *n, pl* **less** a smaller portion or quantity

lessee /le'siː/ *n* sby who holds property under a lease

lessen /'lesən/ *v* to reduce in size, extent, etc; diminish, decrease

lesser /'lesəʳ/ *adj or adv* less in size, quality, or significance

lesson /'lesən/ *n* **1** a passage from sacred writings read in a service of worship **2a** a reading or exercise to be studied **b** a period of instruction **3** sthg, esp a piece of wisdom, learned by study or experience

lessor /le'sɔːʳ/ *n* sby who conveys property by lease

lest /lest/ *conj* so that not; for fear that (e g obeyed her *lest* she should be angry)

¹let /let/ *n* **1** a serve or rally in tennis, squash, etc that does not count and must be replayed **2** sthg that impedes; an obstruction – fml

²let *v* **let; -tt- 1** to offer or grant for rent or lease **2** to give opportunity to, whether by positive action or by failure to prevent; allow to **3** – used in the imperative to introduce a request or proposal, a challenge, or a command

³let *n, Br* **1** an act or period of letting premises (e g a flat or bed-sitter) **2** premises rented or for rent

letdown /'letdaʊn/ *n* a disappointment, disillusionment – infml

let down *v* **1** to make (a garment) longer **2** to fail in loyalty or support; disappoint

lethal /'liːθəl/ *adj* relating to or (capable of) causing death

lethargy /'leθədʒi/ *n* **1** abnormal drowsiness **2** lack of energy or interest – **-gic** *adj*

let off *v* **1** to cause to explode **2** to excuse from punishment

let on *v* to reveal or admit sthg; *esp* to divulge secret information

let-out *n* sthg (e g an exclusion clause in a contract) that provides an opportunity to escape or be released from an obligation – infml

let out *v* **1** to make (a garment) wider (e g by inserting an inset) **2** *chiefly Br* to express publicly; *esp* to blab

letter /'letəʳ/ *n* **1** a symbol, usu written or printed, representing a speech sound and constituting a unit of an alphabet **2** a written or printed message addressed to a person or organization and usu sent through the post **3** *pl but sing or pl in constr* **a** literature; writing **b** learning; *esp* scholarly knowledge of or achievement in literature **4** the precise wording; the strict or literal meaning

letter box *n* a hole or box (e g in a door) to receive material delivered by post

letterhead /'letəhed/ *n* stationery printed with a heading; *also* the heading itself

lettering /'letərɪŋ/ *n* the letters used in an inscription, esp as regards their style or quality

lettuce /'let̩s/ *n* a common garden vegetable whose succulent edible leaves are used esp in salads

leucocyte /'luːkəsaɪt/ *n* a white blood cell

leukaemia /luː'kiːmɪə/ *n* any of several usu fatal types of cancer that are characterized by an abnormal increase in the number of white blood cells in the blood

¹level /'levəl/ *n* **1** a device (e g a spirit level) for establishing a horizontal line or plane **2a** a horizontal state or condition **b** an (approximately) horizontal line, plane, or surface **3a** a position of height in relation to the ground; height **b** a practically horizontal or flat area, esp of land **4** a position or place in a scale or rank (e g of value or importance) **5** the (often measurable) size or amount of sthg specified

²**level** *v* **1a** to make (a line or surface) horizontal; make level, even, or uniform **b** to raise or lower to the same height – often + *up* **c** to attain or come to a level – usu + *out* or *off* **2** to aim, direct – + *at* or *against* **3** to bring to a common level, plane, or standard; equalize **4** to lay level with the ground; raze

³**level** *adj* **1a** having no part higher than another **b** parallel with the plane of the horizon **2a** even, unvarying **b** equal in advantage, progression, or standing **c** steady, unwavering

level crossing *n* the crossing of railway and road or 2 railways on the same level

¹**lever** /ˈliːvəʳ/ *n* **1** a bar used for prizing up or dislodging sthg **2a** a rigid bar used to exert a pressure or sustain a weight at one end by applying force at the other and turning it on a fulcrum **b** a projecting part by which a mechanism is operated or adjusted

²**lever** *v* to prize, raise, or move *up* (as if) with a lever – **~age** *n*

leveret /ˈlevərɟt/ *n* a hare in its first year

leviathan /lɟˈvaɪəθən/ *n* **1** *often cap* a biblical sea monster **2** sthg large or formidable

levitate /ˈlevɟteɪt/ *v* to (cause to) rise or float in the air, esp in apparent defiance of gravity – **-ation** *n*

levity /ˈlevɟti/ *n* lack of seriousness; *esp* excessive or unseemly frivolity

¹**levy** /ˈlevi/ *n* **1** the imposing or collection of a tax, fine, etc **2a** the enlistment or conscription of men for military service **b** *sing or pl in constr* troops raised by levy

²**levy** *v* **1** to impose, collect, or demand by legal authority **2** to enlist or conscript for military service

lewd /luːd/ *adj* **1** sexually coarse or suggestive **2** obscene, salacious – **~ly** *adv* – **~ness** *n*

lexical /ˈleksɪkəl/ *adj* **1** of words or the vocabulary of a language as distinguished from its grammar and construction **2** of a lexicon – **~ly** *adv*

lexicography /ˌleksɪˈkɒgrəfi/ *n* (the principles of) the editing or making of a dictionary

lexicon /ˈleksɪkən/ *n, pl* **lexica, lexicons** **1** a dictionary, esp of Greek, Latin, or Hebrew **2** the vocabulary of a language, individual, or subject

liable /ˈlaɪəbəl/ *adj* **1** legally responsible **2** exposed or subject *to* **3** habitually likely *to* – **-bility** *n*

liaise /liˈeɪz/ *v* to establish a connection and cooperate *with* – **-son** *n*

liar /ˈlaɪəʳ/ *n* one who (habitually) tells lies

lib /lɪb/ *n, often cap* liberation – infml – **~ber** *n*

libation /laɪˈbeɪʃən/ *n* **1** (an act of pouring) a liquid used in a sacrifice to a god **2** an act or instance of drinking

¹**libel** /ˈlaɪbəl/ *n* **1** (a) defamation of sby by published writing or pictorial representation as distinguished from spoken words or gestures **2** a false insulting statement

²**libel** *v* to make or publish a libel (against) – **~lous** *adj* – **~lously** *adv*

¹**liberal** /ˈlɪbərəl/ *adj* **1a** generous, openhanded **b** abundant, ample **2** broad-minded, tolerant; *esp* not bound by authoritarianism, orthodoxy, or tradition **3** *cap* of a political party in the UK advocating economic freedom and moderate reform – **~ize** *v,* **~ly** *adv*

²**liberal** *n* **1** one who is not strict in the observance of orthodox ways (e g in politics or religion) **2** *cap* a supporter of a Liberal party – **~ism** *n*

liberate /ˈlɪbəreɪt/ *v* **1** to set free; *specif* to free (e g a country) from foreign domination **2** to steal – euph or humor – **-rator** *n*

liberation /ˌlɪbəˈreɪʃən/ *n* the seeking of equal rights and status; *also* a movement dedicated to seeking these for a specified group

liberty /ˈlɪbəti/ *n* **1a** freedom from physical restraint or dictatorial control **b** the power of choice **2** a right or immunity awarded or granted; a privilege **3** a breach of etiquette or propriety

Libra /ˈliːbrə/ *n* (sby born under) the 7th sign of the zodiac in astrology, pictured as a pair of scales

librarian /laɪˈbreərɪən/ *n* sby who

manages or assists in a library – ~**ship** *n*

library /'laɪbrəri/ *n* **1** a place in which books, recordings, films, etc are kept for reference or for borrowing by the public **2** a collection of such books, recordings, etc

libretto /lɪ'bretəʊ/ *n, pl* **librettos, libretti** (the book containing) the text of a work (e g an opera) that is both theatrical and musical

lice /laɪs/ *pl of* **louse**

licence, *NAm chiefly* **license** /'laɪsəns/ *n* **1** (a certificate giving evidence of) permission granted by authority to engage in an otherwise unlawful activity, esp the sale of alcoholic drink **2a** freedom that allows or is used with irresponsibility **b** disregard for rules of propriety or personal conduct

license, licence *v* to give official permission to or for

licensed *adj* permitted to sell alcoholic drinks

licensee /,laɪsən'siː/ *n* a publican

licentiate /laɪ'senʒʃɪət/ *n* **1** one licensed to practise a profession **2** an academic degree awarded by some European universities

lichen /'laɪkən, 'lɪtʃən/ *n* any of numerous complex plants made up of an alga and a fungus growing in symbiotic association on a solid surface (e g a rock or tree trunk)

[1]**lick** /lɪk/ *v* **1** to lap up (as if) with the tongue; *also* to dart like a tongue **2** to get the better of; overcome – ~**ing** *n*

[2]**lick** *n* **1** a small amount; a touch **2** a stroke or blow **3** a place to which animals regularly go to lick a salt deposit **4** speed, pace – infml

licorice /'lɪkərɪs, -rɪʃ/ *n* liquorice

lid /lɪd/ *n* a hinged or detachable cover (for a receptacle)

lido /'liːdəʊ, 'laɪ-/ *n* **1** a fashionable beach resort **2** a public open-air swimming pool

[1]**lie** /laɪ/ *v* **lying; lay; lain 1a** to be or to stay at rest in a horizontal position; rest, recline **b** to assume a horizontal position – often + *down* **2a** *of sthg inanimate* to be or remain in a flat or horizontal position on a surface **b** *of snow* to remain on the ground without melting **3** to have as a direction **4a** to occupy a specified place or position **b** *of an action, claim, etc in a court of law* to be sustainable or admissible

[2]**lie** *n* **1** the way, position, or situation in which sthg lies **2** a haunt of an animal or fish

[3]**lie** *v* **lying 1** to make an untrue statement with intent to deceive; speak falsely **2** to create a false or misleading impression

[4]**lie** *n* **1** an untrue or false statement, esp when made with intent to deceive **2** sthg that misleads or deceives

liege *n* **1a** a feudal vassal **b** a loyal subject **2** a feudal superior

lieutenant /lef'tenənt/ *n* **1** an official empowered to act for a higher official; a deputy or representative **2** a low-ranking officer in the navy, British army, etc

[1]**life** /laɪf/ *n, pl* **lives 1** the quality that distinguishes a vital and functional being from a dead body **b** a state of matter (e g a cell or an organism) characterized by capacity for metabolism, growth, reaction to stimuli, and reproduction **2** an aspect of the process of living **3** a biography **4** a state or condition of existence; a manner of living **5a** the period from birth to death or to the present time **b** the period from an event or the present time until death **c** a sentence of imprisonment for life **6** the period of usefulness, effectiveness, or functioning of sthg inanimate **7** living beings (e g of a specified kind or environment) **8** any of several chances to participate given to a contestant in some games, 1 of which is forfeited each time he/she loses

[2]**life** *adj* **1** using a living model **2** of, being, or provided by life insurance

life belt *n* a buoyant belt for keeping a person afloat

lifeboat /'laɪfbəʊt/ *n* a robust buoyant boat for use in saving lives at sea

life buoy *n* a buoyant often ring-shaped float to which a person may cling in the water

life cycle *n* the series of stages in form and functional activity through which an organism, group, culture, etc passes during its lifetime

lifeguard /'laɪfgɑːd/ *n* a usu expert

swimmer employed to safeguard other swimmers

life history *n* the changes through which an organism passes in its development from the primary stage to its natural death

life jacket *n* a buoyant device that is designed to keep a person afloat and can be worn continuously as a precaution against drowning

lifeless /ˈlaɪfləs/ *adj* **1a** dead **b** inanimate **2** having no living beings **3** lacking qualities expressive of life and vigour; dull – **~ly** *adv* – **~ness** *n*

lifelike /ˈlaɪflaɪk/ *adj* accurately representing or imitating (the appearance of objects in) real life

lifeline /ˈlaɪflaɪn/ *n* **1a** a rope for saving or safeguarding life: e g **(1)** one stretched along the deck of a ship in rough weather **(2)** one fired to a ship in distress by means of a rocket **b** the line by which a diver is lowered and raised **2** sthg, esp the sole means of communication, regarded as indispensable for the maintenance or protection of life

lifelong /ˈlaɪflɒŋ/ *adj* lasting or continuing throughout life

life peer, *fem* **life peeress** *n* a British peer whose title is not hereditary

lifer /ˈlaɪfəʳ/ *n* one sentenced to life imprisonment – infml

¹lift /lɪft/ *v* **1** to raise from a lower to a higher position; elevate **2** to put an end to (a blockade or siege) by withdrawing the surrounding forces **3** to revoke, rescind **4a** to copy without ackowledgement **b** to take out of normal setting **5** *of bad weather* to cease temporarily **6** to steal – infml

²lift *n* **1** (a device for) lifting or (the amount) being lifted **2** a usu free ride as a passenger in a motor vehicle **3** a slight rise or elevation of ground **4** the distance or extent to which sthg (e g water in a canal lock) rises **5** a usu temporary feeling of cheerfulness, pleasure, or encouragement **6** any of the ropes by which the yard is suspended from the mast on a square-rigged ship **7** *chiefly Br* a device for conveying people or objects from one level to another, esp in a building

lift-off *n* a vertical takeoff by an aircraft, rocket vehicle, or missile

ligament /ˈlɪgəmənt/ *n* a tough band of connective tissue forming the capsule round a joint or supporting an organ (e g the womb)

¹light /laɪt/ *n* **1** an electromagnetic radiation in the wavelength range including infrared, visible, ultraviolet, and X rays; *specif* the part of this range that is visible to the human eye **2** daylight **3** an electric light **4a** spiritual illumination **b** understanding, knowledge **c** *the* truth **5a** public knowledge **b** a particular aspect or appearance in which sthg is viewed **6** a medium (e g a window) through which light is admitted **7** *pl* a set of principles, standards, or opinions **8** the representation in art of the effect of light on objects or scenes **9** a flame or spark for lighting sthg (e g a cigarette)

²light *adj* **1** having plenty of light; bright **2a** pale in colour or colouring **b** *of colours* medium in saturation and high in lightness

³light *v* **lit, lighted** **1** to set fire to **2** to conduct (sby) with a light; guide

⁴light *adj* **1a** having little weight; not heavy **b** designed to carry a comparatively small load **c** (made of materials) having relatively little weight in proportion to bulk **d** containing less than the legal, standard, or usual weight **2a** of little importance; trivial **b** not abundant **3a** *of sleep or a sleeper* easily disturbed **b** exerting a minimum of force or pressure; gentle, soft **c** faint **4a** easily endurable **b** requiring little effort **5** nimble **6** lacking seriousness; frivolous **7** free from care; cheerful **8** intending or intended chiefly to entertain **9** *of a drink* having a comparatively low alcoholic content or a mild flavour **10** easily digested **11** producing light usu small goods often for direct consumption – **~ness** *n* – **~ly** *adv*

⁵light *adv* **1** lightly **2** with the minimum of luggage

⁶light *v* **lighted, lit** **1** to settle, alight **2** to arrive by chance; happen

¹lighten /ˈlaɪtn/ *v* **1** to make (more) light or clear; illuminate **2** to make (e g a colour) lighter **3** to discharge flashes of lightning

[2]**lighten** *v* **1** to reduce the weight of **2** to relieve (partly) of a burden **3** to make less wearisome; alleviate; *broadly* to cheer, gladden

[1]**lighter** /'laɪtəʳ/ *n* a large usu flat-bottomed barge used esp in unloading or loading ships

[2]**lighter** *n* a device for lighting (a cigar, cigarette, etc)

lighthearted /laɪt'hɑːtɨ̣d/ *adj* free from care or worry; cheerful

lighthouse /'laɪthaʊs/ *n* a tower, mast, etc equipped with a powerful light to warn or guide shipping at sea

lighting /'laɪtɪŋ/ *n* (the apparatus providing) an artificial supply of light

[1]**lightning** /'laɪtnɪŋ/ *n* (the brilliant light flash resulting from) an electric discharge between 2 clouds or between a cloud and the earth

[2]**lightning** *adj* very quick, short, or sudden

lightning conductor *n* a metal rod fixed to the highest point of a building or mast and connected to the earth or water below as a protection against lightning

lights /laɪts/ *n pl* the lungs, esp of a slaughtered sheep, pig, etc

lightship /'laɪt,ʃɪp/ *n* a moored vessel equipped with a powerful light to warn or guide shipping at sea

lightweight /'laɪt-weɪt/ *n or adj* **1** (a boxer) weighing not more than about 9½st **2** (sby) of little ability or importance

light-year *n* a unit of length in astronomy equal to the distance that light travels in 1 year in a vacuum; 9,460 thousand million km (about 5,878 thousand million mi)

[1]**like** /laɪk/ *v* **1a** to find agreeable, acceptable, or pleasant; enjoy **b** to feel towards; regard **2** to wish or choose to have, be, or do; want – **-kable** *adj* – **-king** *n*

[2]**like** *adj* **1a** alike in appearance, character, or quantity (e g suits of *like* design) **b** bearing a close resemblance; *esp* faithful (e g his portrait is very *like*) **2** likely

[3]**like** *prep* **1a** having the characteristics of; similar to **b** typical of **2a** in the manner of; similarly to **b** to the same degree as (e g fits *like* a glove) **c** close to (e g cost something *like* £5) **3** appearing to be, threaten, or promise (e g you seem *like* a sensible man) **4** – used to introduce an example (e g a subject *like* physics)

[4]**like** *n* one who or that which is like another, esp in high value; a counterpart

[5]**like** *adv* **1** likely, probably (e g he'll come *like* as not) **2** so to speak (e g went up to her casually, *like*) – nonstandard

[6]**like** *conj* **1** in the same way as (e g if she can sing *like* she can dance) **2** *chiefly NAm* as if (e g acts *like* he knows what he's doing)

likelihood /'laɪklihʊd/ *n* probability

[1]**likely** /'laɪkli/ *adj* **1** having a high probability of being or occurring **2** reliable, credible **3** seeming appropriate; suitable **4** promising

[2]**likely** *adv* probably – often in *most/very/more/quite likely*

likeness /'laɪknɨ̣s/ *n* **1** resemblance **2** a copy, portrait

likewise /'laɪk-waɪz/ *adv* **1** in like manner; similarly **2** moreover; in addition **3** similarly so with me

lilac /'laɪlək/ *n* **1** a shrub with large clusters of fragrant white or (pale pinkish) purple flowers **2** a pale pinkish purple colour

[1]**lilt** /lɪlt/ *v* to sing or speak rhythmically and with varying pitch

[2]**lilt** *n* **1** (a song or tune with) a rhythmic swing, flow, or rising and falling inflection **2** a light springy motion

lily /'lɪli/ *n* **1** any of a genus of plants that grow from bulbs and are widely cultivated for their variously coloured showy flowers **2** a water lily

lily of the valley *n* a low perennial plant of the lily family that has usu 2 large leaves and a stalk of fragrant drooping bell-shaped white flowers

[1]**limb** /lɪm/ *n* **1** any of the projecting paired appendages of an animal body used esp for movement and grasping but sometimes modified into sensory or sexual organs; *esp* a leg or arm of a human being **2** a large primary branch of a tree **3** an extension,

branch; *specif* any of the 4 branches or arms of a cross

²**limb** *n* **1** the outer edge of the apparent disc of a celestial body **2** the broad flat part of a petal or sepal furthest from its base

limber up /ˈlɪmbəʳ/ *v* to (cause to) become supple, flexible, or prepared for physical action

¹**limbo** /ˈlɪmbəʊ/ *n* **1** *often cap* an abode of souls that are according to Roman Catholic theology barred from heaven because of not having received Christian baptism **2a** a place or state of restraint or confinement, or of neglect or oblivion **b** an intermediate or transitional place or state

²**limbo** *n, pl* **limbos** a W Indian acrobatic dance that involves bending over backwards and passing under a low horizontal pole

¹**lime** /laɪm/ *n* **1** a caustic solid consisting of calcium (and some magnesium) oxide, obtained by heating calcium carbonate (e g in the form of shells or limestone) to a high temperature, and used in building (e g in plaster) and in agriculture **2** calcium hydroxide (occurring as a dry white powder), made by treating caustic lime with water

²**lime** *v* to treat or cover with lime

³**lime** *n* (the light fine-grained wood of) any of a genus of widely planted (ornamental) trees that usu have heart-shaped leaves

⁴**lime** *n* a (spiny tropical citrus tree cultivated for its) small spherical greenish-yellow fruit

limelight /ˈlaɪmlaɪt/ *n* **1** (the white light produced by) a stage lighting instrument producing illumination by means of an intense flame directed on a cylinder of lime **2** *the* centre of public attention

limerick /ˈlɪmərɪk/ *n* a humorous and often epigrammatic or indecent verse form of 5 lines with a rhyme scheme of aabba

limestone /ˈlaɪmstəʊn/ *n* a widely-occurring rock consisting mainly of calcium carbonate

limey /ˈlaɪmi/ *n, often cap, NAm* a British person, esp a sailor – slang

¹**limit** /ˈlɪmɨ̥t/ *n* **1a** a boundary **b** *pl* the place enclosed within a boundary **2a** sthg that bounds, restrains, or confines **b** a line or point that cannot or should not be passed **3** a prescribed maximum or minimum amount, quantity, or number **4** sby or sthg exasperating or intolerable – + *the*; infml

²**limit** *v* **1** to restrict to specific bounds or limits **2** to curtail or reduce in quantity or extent; curb – **~ation** *n*

limited /ˈlɪmɨ̥tɨ̥d/ *adj* **1** confined within limits; restricted **2** restricted as to the scope of powers **3** lacking the ability to grow or do better

limousine /ˈlɪməziːn, ˌlɪməˈziːn/ *n* a luxurious motor car (with a glass partition separating the driver from the passengers)

¹**limp** /lɪmp/ *v* **1** to walk in a manner that avoids putting the full weight of the body on 1 (injured) leg **2** to proceed slowly or with difficulty – **limp** *n*

²**limp** *adj* **1a** lacking firmness and body; drooping or shapeless **b** not stiff or rigid **2** lacking energy – **~ly** *adv*, **~ness** *n*

limpet /ˈlɪmpɨ̥t/ *n* **1** a shellfish with a low conical shell broadly open beneath, that clings very tightly to rock when disturbed **2** sby or sthg that clings tenaciously **3** an explosive device designed to cling to the hull of a ship, tank, etc

limpid /ˈlɪmpɨ̥d/ *adj* **1** transparent, pellucid **2** clear and simple in style – **~ly** *adv* – **~ity** *n*

linctus /ˈlɪŋktəs/ *n* any of various syrupy usu medicated liquids used to relieve throat irritation and coughing

linden /ˈlɪndən/ *n* a lime tree

¹**line** /laɪn/ *v* **1** to cover the inner surface of; provide with a lining **2** to fill

²**line** *n* **1a** a cord or rope; *esp* one on a ship **b** a device for catching fish consisting of a usu single-filament cord with hooks, floats, a reel, etc **c** a length of material (e g cord) used in measuring and levelling **d** piping for conveying a fluid (e g steam or compressed air) **e(1)** (a connection for communication by means of) a set of wires connecting one telephone or telegraph (exchange) with another **(2)**

the principal circuits of an electric power distribution system **2a** a horizontal row of written or printed characters **b** a single row of words in a poem **c** a short letter; a note **d** a short sequence of words spoken by an actor playing a particular role; *also, pl* all of the sequences making up a particular role **3a** sthg (e g a ridge, seam, or crease) that is distinct, elongated, and narrow **b** a wrinkle (e g on the face) **c** the course or direction of sthg in motion **d** (a single set of rails forming) a railway track **4a** a course of conduct, action, or thought **b** a field of activity or interest **5a** a related series of people or things coming one after the other in time; a family, lineage **b** a linked series of trenches and fortifications, esp facing the enemy – usu pl with sing. meaning **c** the regular and numbered infantry regiments of the army as opposed to auxiliary forces or household troops **d** a rank of objects of 1 kind; a row **e** (the company owning or operating) a group of vehicles, ships, aeroplanes, etc carrying passengers or goods regularly over a route **f** an arrangement of operations in manufacturing allowing ordered occurrence of various stages of production **6** a narrow elongated mark drawn, projected, or imagined (e g on a map): e g **a** a boundary, contour, circle of latitude or longitude, etc **b** *the* equator **c** a mark (e g in pencil) that forms part of the formal design of a picture; *also* an artist's use of such lines **d** a limit or farthest edge with reference to which the playing of some game or sport is regulated – usu in combination **7** a straight or curved geometric element, generated by a moving point (continually satisfying a particular condition), that has length but no breadth **8** merchandise or services of the same general class for sale or regularly available **9** *pl, Br* a (specified) number of lines of writing, esp to be copied as a school punishment

[3]**line** *v* **1** to mark or cover with a line or lines **2** to place or form a line along **3** to form *up* into a line or lines

lineage /ˈlɪniɪdʒ/ *n* a line of descent from a common ancestor or source – **lineal** *adj* – **lineally** *adv*

linear /ˈlɪnɪəʳ/ *adj* **1a** of, being, or resembling a line **b** involving a single dimension **2** characterized by an emphasis on line; *esp* having clearly defined outlines

linen /ˈlɪnɨn/ *n* **1** cloth or yarn made from flax **2** clothing or household articles (e g sheets and tablecloths) made of a usu washable cloth, esp linen

line-out *n* (a method in Rugby Union of returning the ball to play after it has crossed a touchline which involves throwing it in between) a line of forwards from each team

line printer *n* a high-speed printing device (e g for a computer) that prints each line as a unit rather than character by character

[1]**liner** /ˈlaɪnəʳ/ *n* a passenger ship belonging to a shipping company and usu sailing scheduled routes

[2]**liner** *n* a replaceable (metal) lining (for reducing the wear of a mechanism)

linesman /ˈlaɪnzmən/ *n* an official who assists the referee or umpire in various games, esp in determining if a ball or player is out of the prescribed playing area

lineup /ˈlaɪn-ʌp/ *n* (a list of) the players playing for usu 1 side in a game

line-up *n* **1** a line of people arranged esp for inspection or as a means of identifying a suspect **2** a group of people or items assembled for a particular purpose

line up 1 to put into alignment **2** to assemble or organize **3** to assume an orderly arrangement in a line

[1]**ling** /lɪŋ/ *n* a large food fish of shallow seas off Greenland and Europe

[2]**ling** *n* the commonest British heather

linger /ˈlɪŋgəʳ/ *v* **1a** to delay going; tarry **b** to dwell on a subject – usu + *over, on*, or *upon* **2** to continue unduly or unhappily in a failing or moribund state – often + *on* **3** to be slow to act; procrastinate **4** to be slow in disappearing – **~er** *n* – **~ing** *adj* – **~ingly** *adv*

lingerie /ˈlænʒəriː/ *n* women's underwear and nightclothes

lingo /ˈlɪŋgəʊ/ *n, pl* **lingoes 1** a foreign language **2** jargon

lingua franca /ˌlɪŋgwə ˈfræŋkə/ *n, pl*

lingua francas, linguae francae a language used as a common or commercial tongue among people not speaking the same native language

linguist /ˈlɪŋgwɨst/ *n* **1** sby accomplished in languages; *esp* a polyglot **2** sby who specializes in linguistics

linguistic /lɪŋˈgwɪstɪk/ *adj* of language or linguistics – **~ally** *adv*

linguistics /lɪŋˈgwɪstɪks/ *n pl but sing in constr* the study of human language with regard to its nature, structure, and modification

liniment /ˈlɪnɨmənt/ *n* a liquid preparation that is applied to the skin, esp to allay pain or irritation

lining /ˈlaɪnɪŋ/ *n* **1** (a piece of) material used to line sthg (e g a garment) **2** providing sthg with a lining

¹link /lɪŋk/ *n* **1** a connecting structure: e g **a** a single ring or division of a chain **b** the fusible part of an electrical fuse **2** sthg analogous to a link of chain; a connecting element

²link *v* **1** to join, connect **2** to become connected by a link – often + *up* – **~age** *n*

links /lɪŋks/ *n pl* **1** a golf course – often pl with sing. meaning **2** *Scot* sand hills, esp along the seashore

linnet /ˈlɪnɨt/ *n* a common small Old World finch having variable reddish brown plumage

linoleum /lɨˈnəʊlɪəm/ *n* a floor covering with a canvas back and a coloured or patterned surface of hardened linseed oil and a filler (e g cork dust)

linseed /ˈlɪnsiːd/ *n* the seed of flax used esp as a source of linseed oil

linseed oil /ˈlɪnsiːd ˌɔɪl/ *n* a yellowish drying oil obtained from flaxseed and used esp in paint, varnish, printing ink, and linoleum and for conditioning wood

lint /lɪnt/ *n* a soft absorbent material with a fleecy surface that is made from linen and is used chiefly for surgical dressings

lintel /ˈlɪntl/ *n* a horizontal architectural member spanning and usu carrying the load above an opening

lion /ˈlaɪən/, *fem* **lioness** *n* **1a** a flesh-eating big cat of open or rocky areas of Africa and formerly southern Asia that has a tawny body with a tufted tail and in the male a shaggy blackish or dark brown mane **b** *cap* Leo **2** a person of interest or importance

lionhearted /ˌlaɪənˈhɑːtɨd/ *adj* courageous, brave

lion·ize, -ise /ˈlaɪənaɪz/ *v* to treat as an object of great interest or importance

lip /lɪp/ *n* **1** either of the 2 fleshy folds that surround the mouth **2** a fleshy fold surrounding some other body opening (e g the vagina) **3** the edge of a hollow vessel or cavity; *esp* one shaped to make pouring easy **4** impudent or insolent talk, esp in reply – slang

lip gloss *n* a cosmetic for giving a gloss to the lips

lip service *n* support in words but not in deeds

lipstick /ˈlɪpˌstɪk/ *n* (a cased stick of) a waxy solid cosmetic for colouring the lips

liquefy *also* **liquify** /ˈlɪkwɨfaɪ/ *v* **1** to reduce to a liquid state **2** to become liquid

liqueur /lɪˈkjʊəʳ/ *n* any of several usu sweetened alcoholic drinks variously flavoured (e g with fruit or aromatic herbs)

liquid /ˈlɪkwɨd/ *adj* **1** flowing freely like water **2** neither solid nor gaseous **3a** shining and clear **b** *of a sound* flowing, pure, and free of harshness **c** smooth and unconstrained in movement **4** consisting of or capable of ready conversion into cash – **liquid** *n*

liquidate /ˈlɪkwɨdeɪt/ *v* **1a** to settle (a debt), esp by payment **b** to settle the accounts of (e g a business) and use the assets towards paying off the debts **2** to get rid of; *specif* to kill **3** to convert (assets) into cash – **-ation** *n*

liquidator /ˈlɪkwɨdeɪtəʳ/ *n* a person appointed by law to liquidate a company

liquid·ize, -ise /ˈlɪkwɨdaɪz/ *v* to cause to be liquid; *esp* to pulverize (e g fruit or vegetables) into a liquid

liquid·izer, -iser /ˈlɪkwɨdaɪzəʳ/ *n, chiefly Br* a domestic electric appliance for grinding, puréeing, liquidizing, or blending foods

liquor /ˈlɪkəʳ/ *n* a liquid substance: e g

a a solution of a drug in water **b** a liquid, esp water, in which food has been cooked **c** *chiefly NAm* a usu distilled rather than fermented alcoholic drink

liquorice /ˈlɪkərɪs, -rɪʃ/ *n* a sweet, black highly-flavoured plant-extract used in brewing, medicine and confectionery

lira /ˈlɪərə/ *n, pl (1)* **lire** *also* **liras,** *(2)* **liras** *also* **lire** **1** the major unit of currency of Italy **2** the major unit of currency of Turkey

[1]**lisp** /lɪsp/ *v* to pronounce /s/ and /z/ imperfectly, esp by giving them the sounds of /θ/ and /ð/ – **lisp** *n* – **-ingly** *adv*

[1]**list** /lɪst/ *n, pl but sing or pl in constr* **1** (the fence surrounding) a court or yard for jousting **2** a scene of competition

[2]**list** *n* a roll or catalogue of words or numbers (e g representing people or objects belonging to a class), usu arranged in order so as to be easily found

[3]**list** *v* **1** to make a list of **2** to include on a list; *specif, Br* to include (a building) in an official list as being of architectural or historical importance and hence protected from demolition

[4]**list** *v* to (cause to) lean to one side

listen /ˈlɪsən/ *v* **1** to pay attention to sound **2** to hear or consider with thoughtful attention; heed **3** to be alert to catch an expected sound

listen in *v* to tune in to or monitor a broadcast

listless /ˈlɪstl̥ɪs/ *adj* characterized by indifference, lack of energy, and disinclination for exertion; languid – **~ly** *adv* – **~ness** *n*

lit /lɪt/ *past of* **light**

literacy /ˈlɪtərəsi/ *n* the quality or state of being literate

[1]**literal** /ˈlɪtərəl/ *adj* **1a** according with the exact letter of a written text **b** having the factual or ordinary construction or primary meaning of a term or expression **c** characterized by a lack of imagination **2** of or expressed in letters **3** reproduced word for word; exact, verbatim – **~ly** *adv*

[2]**literal** *n* a misprint involving a single letter

literary /ˈlɪtərəri/ *adj* **1a** of, being, or concerning literature **b** characteristic of or being in a formal, rather than colloquial, style **2a** well-read **b** producing, well versed in, or connected with literature

literate /ˈlɪtərɪ̥t/ *adj* **1a** educated, cultured **b** able to read and write **2** versed in literature or creative writing

literature /ˈlɪtərətʃəʳ/ *n* **1** writings in prose or verse; *esp* writings having artistic value or expression and expressing ideas of permanent or universal interest **2** the body of writings on a particular subject **3** printed matter (e g leaflets or circulars)

lithe /laɪð/ *adj* flexible, supple – **~ly** *adv*

lithium /ˈlɪθɪəm/ *n* a soft silver-white element of the alkali metal group that is the lightest metal known

lithograph /ˈlɪθəgrɑːf/ *v or n* (to produce or copy in the form of) a print made on a prepared stone slab or metal plate – **~ic** *adj* – **~y** *n*

litigate /ˈlɪtɪ̥geɪt/ *v* to carry on a lawsuit – **-gant** *n* – **-gation** *n*

litmus /ˈlɪtməs/ *n* a colouring matter from lichens that turns red in acid solutions and blue in alkaline solutions and is used as an acid-alkali indicator

litre, *NAm chiefly* **liter** /ˈliːtəʳ/ *n* a metric unit of capacity equal to 1.000 028dm³ (about 0.220gal)

[1]**litter** /ˈlɪtəʳ/ *n* **1a** a covered and curtained couch carried by people or animals **b** a stretcher or other device for carrying a sick or injured person **2a** material used as bedding for animals **b** the uppermost slightly decayed layer of organic matter on the forest floor **3** a group of offspring of an animal, born at 1 birth **4a** rubbish or waste products, esp in a public place **b** an untidy accumulation of objects (e g papers)

[2]**litter** *v* **1** to give birth to a litter **2** to strew with litter **3** to scatter about in disorder

[1]**little** /ˈlɪtl/ *adj* **littler, less, lesser; littlest, least** **1a** amounting to only a small quantity **b** *of a plant or animal* small in comparison with related forms – used in vernacular names **c** small in condition, distinction, or

scope **2** not much: e g **a** existing only in a small amount or to a slight degree **b** short in duration; brief **c** existing to an appreciable though not extensive degree or amount – + *a* **3** small in importance or interest; trivial

[2]**little** *adv* **less; least** **1** to no great degree or extent; not much (e g *little*-known) **2** not at all (e g cared *little* for his neighbours)

[3]**little** *n* **1a** only a small portion or quantity; not much **b** at least some, though not much – + *a* (e g have a *little* of this cake) **2** a short time or distance

little finger *n* the fourth and smallest finger of the hand counting the index finger as the first

little people *n pl* imaginary beings (e g fairies, elves, etc) of folklore – + *the*

[1]**littoral** /ˈlɪtərəl/ *adj* of or occurring on or near a (sea) shore

[2]**littoral** *n* a coastal region; *esp* the region between high and low tides

liturgy /ˈlɪtədʒi/ *n* **1** *often cap* the form of service used in the celebration of Communion, esp in the Orthodox church **2** a prescribed form of public worship – **-gical** *adj* – **-gically** *adv*

livable *adj* **1** suitable for living in or with **2** endurable

[1]**live** /lɪv/ *v* **1** to be alive; have the life of an animal or plant **2** to continue alive **3** to maintain oneself; subsist **4** to conduct or pass one's life **5** to occupy a home; dwell **6** to have a life rich in experience **7** to cohabit – + *together* or *with* **8** *chiefly Br, of a thing* to be found in a specified place – infml

[2]**live** /laɪv/ *adj* **1** having life **2** containing living organisms **3** exerting force or containing energy: e g **a** glowing **b** connected to electric power **c** *of ammunition, bombs, etc* unexploded, unfired **4** of continuing or current interest

[3]**live** *adv* during, from, or at a live production

livelihood /ˈlaɪvlihʊd/ *n* a means of support or sustenance

livelong /ˈlɪvlɒŋ/ *adj* whole, entire – chiefly poetic

lively /ˈlaɪvli/ *adj* **1** briskly alert and energetic; vigorous, animated **2** quick to rebound; resilient **3** full of life, movement, or incident – **-liness** *n*

[1]**liver** /ˈlɪvəʳ/ *n* **1a** a large organ of vertebrates that secretes bile and causes changes in the blood (e g by acting upon blood sugar) **b** any of various large digestive glands of invertebrates **2** the liver of an animal (e g a calf or pig) eaten as food **3** a greyish reddish brown colour

[2]**liver** *n* one who lives, esp in a specified way

liverish /ˈlɪvərɪʃ/ *adj* **1** suffering from liver disorder; bilious **2** peevish, irascible; *also* glum

livery /ˈlɪvəri/ *n* **1** the uniform of servants employed by an individual or a single household **2** distinctive colouring or marking; *also* distinctive dress **3** a distinctive colour scheme (e g on aircraft) distinguishing an organization or group

livery stable *n* an establishment where horses are stabled and fed for their owners

lives /laɪvz/ *pl of* **life**

livestock /ˈlaɪvstɒk/ *n* farm animals

livid /ˈlɪvɨ̣d/ *adj* **1** discoloured by bruising **2** ashen, pallid **3** reddish **4** very angry; enraged – **~ly** *adv*

[1]**living** /ˈlɪvɪŋ/ *adj* **1a** having life; alive **b** existing in use **2** true to life; exact – esp in *the living image of* **3** – used as an intensive **4** *of feelings, ideas, etc* full of power and force

[2]**living** *n* **1** the condition of being alive **2** a manner of life **3** means of subsistence; a livelihood

living room *n* a room in a residence used for everyday activities

lizard /ˈlɪzəd/ *n* any of a suborder of reptiles distinguished from the snakes by 2 pairs of well differentiated functional limbs (which may be lacking in burrowing forms), external ears, and eyes with movable lids

llama /ˈlɑːmə/ *n* any of several wild and domesticated S American ruminant mammals related to the camels but smaller and without a hump

[1]**load** /ləʊd/ *n* **1a** an amount, esp large or heavy, that is (to be) carried, supported, or borne **b** the quantity that can be carried at 1 time by a specified means – often in combination **2** the forces to which a structure is subjected

3 a burden of responsibility, anxiety, etc 4 external resistance overcome by a machine or other source of power 5 power output (e g of a power plant) 6 the amount of work to be performed by a person, machine, etc 7 a large quantity or amount; a lot – usu pl with sing. meaning; infml

[2]**load** *v* **1a** to put a load in or on **b** to place in or on a means of conveyance **2** to encumber or oppress with sthg heavy, laborious, or disheartening; burden **3a** to weight or shape (dice) to fall unfairly **b** to charge with hidden implications; *also* to bias **4** to put a load or charge in a device or piece of equipment; esp to insert the charge in a firearm

loaded /ˈləʊdɪ̣d/ *adj* having a large amount of money – infml

loadstone /ˈləʊdstəʊn/ *n* (a) lodestone

[1]**loaf** /ləʊf/ *n, pl* **loaves** **1** a mass of bread often having a regular shape and standard weight **2** a shaped or moulded often symmetrical mass of food (e g sugar or chopped cooked meat) **3** *Br* head, brains – slang; esp in *use one's loaf*

[2]**loaf** *v* to spend time in idleness – **~er** *n*

loam /ləʊm/ *n* crumbly soil consisting of a mixture of clay, silt, and sand – **~y** *adj*

[1]**loan** /ləʊn/ *n* **1a** money lent at interest **b** sthg lent, usu for the borrower's temporary use **2** the grant of temporary use

[2]**loan** *v* to lend

loanword /ˈləʊnwɜːd/ *n* a word taken from another language and at least partly naturalized

loath, loth /ləʊθ/ unwilling, reluctant

loathe /ləʊð/ *v* to dislike greatly, often with disgust or intolerance – **-thing** *n*

loathsome /ˈləʊðsəm/ *adj* giving rise to loathing; disgusting – **~ly** *adv* – **~ness** *n*

loaves /ləʊvz/ *pl of* **loaf**

[1]**lob** /lɒb/ *v* to hit a ball easily in a high arc, esp in tennis, squash, etc

[2]**lob** *n* a lobbed ball

[1]**lobby** /ˈlɒbi/ *n* **1** a porch or small entrance hall **2** an anteroom of a legislative chamber to which members go to vote during a division **3** *sing or pl in constr* a group of people engaged in lobbying

[2]**lobby** *v* to try to influence (e g a member of a legislative body) towards an action

lobe /ləʊb/ *n* a curved or rounded projection or division; *esp* such a projection or division of a bodily organ or part – **~d** *adj*

lobster /ˈlɒbstəʳ/ *n* any of a family of large edible 10-legged marine crustaceans that have stalked eyes, a pair of large claws, and a long abdomen

lobster pot *n* (a basket used as) a trap for catching lobsters

[1]**local** /ˈləʊkəl/ *adj* **1** (characteristic) of or belonging to a particular place; not general or widespread **2a** primarily serving the needs of a particular limited district **b** *of a public conveyance* making all the stops on a route – **~ize** *v* – **~ly** *adv*

[2]**local** *n, Br* *the* neighbourhood pub

locality /ləʊˈkælɪ̣ti/ *n* **1** the fact or condition of having a location in space or time **2** a particular place, situation, or location

locate /ləʊˈkeɪt/ *v* **1** to determine or indicate the place, site, or limits of **2** to set or establish in a particular spot – **~d** *adj*

location /ləʊˈkeɪʃən/ *n* **1** a particular place or position **2** a place outside a studio where a (part of a) picture is filmed

loch /lɒx, lɒk/ *n* a lake or (nearly landlocked) arm of the sea in Scotland

loci /ˈləʊsaɪ, ˈləʊki/ *pl of* **locus**

[1]**lock** /lɒk/ *n* a curl, tuft, etc of hair

[2]**lock** *n* **1** a fastening that can be opened and often closed only by means of a particular key or combination **2** an enclosed section of waterway (e g a canal) which has gates at each end and in which the water level can be raised or lowered to move boats from one level to another **3** a hold in wrestling secured on a usu specified body part **4** *chiefly Br* the maximum extent to which the front wheels of a vehicle can be turned

[3]**lock** *v* **1a** to fasten the lock of **b** to make fast (as if) with a lock **2a** to shut

in or out or make secure or inaccessible (as if) by means of locks **b** to hold fast or inactive; fix in a particular situation or method of operation **3a** to make fast by the interlacing or interlocking of parts **b** to grapple in combat; *also* to bind closely – often pass – **~able** *adj*

locker /'lɒkəʳ/ *n* **1** a cupboard or compartment that may be closed with a lock; *esp* one for individual storage use **2** a chest or compartment on board ship

locket /'lɒkɨt/ *n* a small case usu of precious metal that has space for a memento (e g a small picture) and is usu worn on a chain round the neck

lockjaw /'lɒkdʒɔː/ *n* an early symptom of tetanus characterized by spasm of the jaw muscles and inability to open the jaws

locknut /'lɒknʌt/ *n* **1** a nut screwed hard up against another to prevent either of them from moving **2** a nut so constructed that it locks itself when screwed up tight

lockout /'lɒk-aʊt/ *n* a whole or partial closing of a business by an employer in order to gain concessions from or resist demands of employees

locksmith /'lɒk,smɪθ/ *n* sby who makes or mends locks as an occupation

lockstitch /'lɒk,stɪtʃ/ *n* a sewing machine stitch formed by the looping together of 2 threads, 1 on each side of the material being sewn

locomotion /,ləʊkə'məʊʃən/ *n* **1** an act or the power of moving from place to place **2** travel

locomotive /,ləʊkə'məʊtɪv/ *n* an engine that moves under its own power; *esp* one that moves railway carriages and wagons

locum /'ləʊkəm/ *n* sby filling an office for a time or temporarily taking the place of another

locus /'ləʊkəs/ *n, pl* **loci** *also* **locuses** **1** a place, locality **2** the set of all points whose location is determined by stated conditions

locust /'ləʊkəst/ *n* **1** a migratory grasshopper that often travels in vast swarms stripping the areas passed of all vegetation **2** any of various hard-wooded leguminous trees

lode /ləʊd/ *n* an ore deposit

lodestar, loadstar /'ləʊdstɑːʳ/ *n* **1** a star that guides; *esp* the pole star **2** sthg that serves as a guiding star

lodestone, loadstone /'ləʊdstəʊn/ a piece of magnetized rock; *broadly* a magnet

¹lodge /lɒdʒ/ *v* **1a** to provide temporary, esp rented, accommodation for **b** to establish or settle in a place **2** to serve as a receptacle for; contain, house **3** to fix in place **4** to deposit for safeguard or preservation **5** to place or vest (e g power), esp in a source, means, or agent **6** to lay (e g a complaint) before authority

²lodge *n* **1** the meeting place of a branch of an esp fraternal organization **2** a house set apart for residence in a particular season (e g the hunting season) **3a** a house orig for the use of a gamekeeper, caretaker, porter, etc **b** a porter's room (e g at the entrance to a college, block of flats, etc) **c** the house where the head of a university college lives, esp in Cambridge **4** a den or lair of an animal or a group of animals (e g beavers or otters)

lodger /'lɒdʒəʳ/ *n* one who occupies a rented room in another's house

lodging /'lɒdʒɪŋ/ *n* **1** a place to live; a dwelling **2a** a temporary place to stay **b** a rented room or rooms for residing in, usu in a private house rather than a hotel – usu pl with sing. meaning

loess /'ləʊes, -ɨs/ *n* a usu yellowish brown loamy deposit found in Europe, Asia, and N America and believed to be chiefly deposited by the wind

¹loft /lɒft/ *n* **1** an attic **2a** a gallery in a church or hall **b** an upper floor in a barn or warehouse used for storage – sometimes in combination

²loft *v* to propel through the air or into space – **~ed** *adj*

lofty /'lɒfti/ *adj* **1** having a haughty overbearing manner; supercilious **2a** elevated in character and spirit; noble **b** elevated in position; superior **3** impressively high – **-tily** *adv* – **-tiness** *n*

¹log /lɒg/ *n* **1** a usu bulky piece or length of unshaped timber (ready for sawing or for use as firewood) **2** an apparatus for measuring the rate of a ship's motion through the water **3a** the full nautical record of a ship's voyage **b** the full record of a flight by an aircraft

²log *v* **1** to cut trees for timber **2** to enter details of or about in a log **3a** to move or attain (e g an indicated distance, speed, or time) as noted in a log **b** to have (an indicated record) to one's credit; achieve

³log *n* a logarithm

loganberry /'ləʊgənbəri/ *n* (the red sweet edible berry of) an upright-growing raspberry hybrid

logarithm /'lɒgərɪðəm/ *n* the exponent that indicates the power to which a number is raised to produce a given number – **~ic** *adj* – **~ically** *adv*

logbook /'lɒgbʊk/ *n Br* a document held with a motor vehicle that gives the vehicle's registration number, make, engine size, etc and a list of its owners – not now used technically

logger /'lɒgəʳ/ *n, NAm* a lumberjack

logic /'lɒdʒɪk/ *n* **1a** a science that deals with the formal principles and structure of thought and reasoning **b** a particular mode of reasoning viewed as valid or faulty **2** the interrelation or sequence of facts or events when seen as inevitable or predictable – **~al** *adj* – **~ally** *adv*

logistics /lə'dʒɪstɪks/ *n pl but sing or pl in constr* **1** the aspect of military science dealing with the transportation, quartering, and supplying of troops in military operations **2** the handling of the details of an operation – **logistic** *adj* – **-cally** *adv*

loin /lɔɪn/ *n* **1a** the part of a human being or quadruped on each side of the spinal column between the hipbone and the lower ribs **b** a cut of meat comprising this part of one or both sides of a carcass with the adjoining half of the vertebrae included **2** *pl* the pubic region; *also* the genitals

loincloth /'lɔɪnklɒθ/ *n* a cloth worn about the hips and covering the genitals

loiter /'lɔɪtəʳ/ *v* **1** to remain in an area for no obvious reason **2** to dawdle – **~er** *n*

loll /lɒl/ *v* **1** to hang down loosely **2** to recline, lean, or move in a lazy or excessively relaxed manner; lounge

lollipop, lollypop /'lɒlipɒp/ *n* a large often round flat sweet of boiled sugar on the end of a stick

lollipop man, *fem* **lollipop lady** *n, Br* sby controlling traffic to allow (school) children to cross busy roads

lollop /'lɒləp/ *v* to move or proceed with an ungainly loping motion

lolly /'lɒli/ *n* **1** a lollipop or ice lolly **2** *Br* money – infml

lone /ləʊn/ *adj* **1** only, sole **2** situated alone or separately; isolated **3** having no company; solitary – fml

lonely /'ləʊnli/ *adj* **1** cut off from others; solitary **2** not frequented by people; desolate **3** sad from being alone or without friends – **-liness** *n*

loner /'ləʊnəʳ/ *n* a person or animal that prefers solitude

lonesome /'ləʊnsəm/ *adj* **1** lonely **2** isolated

¹long /lɒŋ/ *adj* **1a** extending for a considerable distance **b** having greater length than usual **2** having a specified length **3** extending over a considerable or specified time **4** containing a large or specified number of items or units **5** reaching or extending a considerable distance **6** *of betting odds* greatly differing in the amounts wagered on each side

²long *adv* **1** for or during a long or specified time **2** at a point of time far before or after a specified moment or event **3** after or beyond a specified time

³long *v* to feel a strong desire or craving, esp *for* sthg not likely to be attained – **~ing** *n, adj* – **~ingly** *adv*

longboat /'lɒŋbəʊt/ *n* the largest boat carried by a sailing vessel

longbow /'lɒŋbəʊ/ *n* a long wooden bow for shooting arrows, specif that used in medieval England that was about 6ft (1.8m) long, was made of yew or ash, and was drawn by hand

long division *n* arithmetical division in which the calculations corresponding to the division of parts of the dividend by the divisor are written out

longevity /lɒn'dʒevɪ̈ti/ *n* (great) length of life

longhand /ˈlɒŋhænd/ *n* ordinary writing; handwriting

long hop *n* an easily hit short-pitched delivery of a cricket ball

longitude /ˈlɒndʒɪ̇tjuːd/ *n* the (time difference corresponding to) angular distance of a point on the surface of a celestial body, esp the earth, measured E or W from a prime meridian (e g that of Greenwich)

longitudinal /ˌlɒndʒɪ̇ˈtjuːdənəl/ *adj* **1** of length or the lengthways dimension **2** placed or running lengthways – ~**ly** *adv*

long johns *n pl* underpants with legs extending usu down to the ankles – infml

long jump *n* (an athletic field event consisting of) a jump for distance from a running start

long-range *adj* involving or taking into account a long period of time

longship /ˈlɒŋˌʃɪp/ *n* a long open ship propelled by oars and a sail and used by the Vikings principally to carry warriors

long shot *n* **1** (a bet at long odds on) a competitor given little chance of winning **2** a venture that involves considerable risk and has little chance of success

longsighted /ˌlɒŋˈsaɪtɪ̇d/ *adj* able to see distant objects better than close ones

long-standing *adj* of long duration

long-suffering *n or adj* (the quality of) patiently enduring pain, difficulty, or provocation

long-term *adj* occurring over or involving a relatively long period of time

long wave *n* a band of radio waves typically used for sound broadcasting and covering wavelengths of 1000m or more

long-winded *adj* tediously long in speaking or writing

¹loo /luː/ *n* (money staked at) an old card game in which the winner of each trick takes a portion of the pool while losing players have to contribute to the next pool

²loo *n, chiefly Br* a toilet – infml

loofah /ˈluːfə/ *n* a dried seed-pod of any of several plants of the cucumber family, used as a rough bath sponge

¹look /lʊk/ *v* **1a** to use the power of sight; *esp* to make a visual search *for* **b** to direct one's attention **c** to direct the eyes **2** to have the appearance of being; appear, seem **3** to have a specified outlook

²look *n* **1a** the act of looking **b** a glance **2a** a facial expression **b** (attractive) physical appearance – usu pl with sing. meaning **3** the state or form in which sthg appears

look after *v* to take care of

look back *v* **1** to remember – often + *to, on* **2** to fail to make successful progress – in *never look back*

look-in *n* a chance to take part; *also* a chance of success – infml

look in *v, Br* to pay a short visit

looking glass *n* a mirror

lookout /ˈlʊk-aʊt/ *n* **1** one engaged in keeping watch **2** a place or structure affording a wide view for observation **3** a careful looking or watching **4** a matter of care or concern **5** *chiefly Br* a future possibility; a prospect

look out *v* **1** to take care – often imper **2** to keep watching

look up *v* **1** to search for (as if) in a reference work **2** to pay a usu short visit to **3** to improve in prospects or conditions

¹loom /luːm/ *n* a frame or machine for weaving together yarns or threads into cloth

²loom *v* **1** to come into sight indistinctly, in enlarged or distorted and menacing form, often as a result of atmospheric conditions **2** to appear in an impressively great or exaggerated form

loony, looney /ˈluːni/ *adj* crazy, foolish – infml

loony bin *n* a mental hospital – humor

¹loop /luːp/ *n* **1** a (partially) closed figure that has a curved outline surrounding a central opening **2** a zigzag-shaped intrauterine contraceptive device **3** a ring or curved piece used to form a fastening or handle **4** a piece of film or magnetic tape whose ends are spliced together so as to reproduce the same material continuously

²loop *v* **1a** to make a loop in, on, or about **b** to fasten with a loop **2** to form a loop with

loophole /ˈluːphəʊl/ *n* **1** a small opening through which missiles, firearms, etc may be discharged or light and air admitted **2** a means of escape; *esp* an ambiguity or omission in a text through which its intent may be evaded

[1]**loose** /luːs/ *adj* **1a** not rigidly fastened or securely attached **b** having worked partly free from attachments **c** not tight-fitting **2a** free from a state of confinement, restraint, or obligation **b** not brought together in a bundle, container, or binding **3** not dense, close, or compact in structure or arrangement **4a** lacking in (power of) restraint **b** dissolute, promiscuous **5** not tightly drawn or stretched; slack **6a** lacking in precision, exactness, or care **b** permitting freedom of interpretation – **~ly** *adv* – **~n** *v* – **~ness** *n*

[2]**loose** *v* **1a** to let loose; release **b** to free from restraint **2** to make loose; untie **3** to cast loose; detach **4** to let fly; discharge (e g a bullet)

[3]**loose** *adv* in a loose manner; loosely

loose box *n, Br* an individual enclosure within a barn or stable in which an animal may move about freely

[1]**loot** /luːt/ *n* **1** goods, usu of considerable value, taken in war; spoils **2** sthg taken illegally (e g by force or deception)

[2]**loot** *v* to seize and carry away (sthg) by force or illegally, esp in war or public disturbance – **~er** *n*

[1]**lop** /lɒp/ *n* small branches and twigs cut from a tree

[2]**lop** *v* **1** to cut off branches or twigs from **2** to remove or do away with as unnecessary or undesirable – usu + *off* or *away*

lope /ləʊp/ *n* an easy bounding gait capable of being sustained for a long time – **lope** *v*

lopsided /lɒpˈsaɪdɪ̯d/ *adj* **1** having one side heavier or lower than the other **2** lacking in balance, symmetry, or proportion

loquacious /ləʊˈkweɪʃəs/ *adj* talkative – fml – **~ly** *adv* – **-city** *n*

[1]**lord** /lɔːd/ *n* **1** one having power and authority over others **2** *cap* **a** God **b** Jesus – often + *Our* **3** a man of rank or high position: e g **a** a feudal tenant holding land directly from the king **b** a British nobleman **4** *pl* the House of Lords

[2]**lord** *v* to act like a lord; *esp* to put on airs – usu + *it*

lord chancellor *n, often cap L & C* an officer of state who presides over the House of Lords, serves as head of the judiciary, and is usu a member of the cabinet

lordly /ˈlɔːdli/ *adj* **1a** dignified **b** grand, noble **2** disdainful and arrogant – **-liness** *n*

Lord's Prayer *n the* prayer taught by Jesus beginning 'Our Father'

lore /lɔːʳ/ *n* a specified body of knowledge or tradition

lorgnette /lɔːˈnjet/ *n* a pair of glasses or opera glasses with a handle

lorry /ˈlɒri/ *n, Br* a large motor vehicle for carrying loads by road

lose /luːz/ *v* **lost** **1** to miss from one's possession or from a customary or supposed place; *also* to fail to find **2** to suffer deprivation of; part with, esp in an unforeseen or accidental manner **3** to suffer loss through the death of or final separation from (sby) **4a** to fail to use; let slip by **b** to be defeated in (a contest for) **c** to fail to catch with the senses or the mind **5** to fail to keep or maintain **6** to fail to keep in sight or in mind **7** to free oneself from; get rid of **8** to run slow by the amount of – used with reference to a timepiece

lose out *v* **1** to make a loss **2** to be the loser, esp unluckily *USE* often + *on*

loser /ˈluːzəʳ/ *n* **1** one who loses, esp consistently **2** one who does poorly; a failure

loss /lɒs/ *n* **1a** the act or an instance of losing possession **b** the harm or privation resulting from loss or separation **2** a person, thing, or amount lost; *esp, pl* killed, wounded, or captured soldiers **3a** failure to gain, win, obtain, or use sthg **b** an amount by which cost exceeds revenue **4** decrease in amount, size, or degree **5** destruction, ruin

loss leader *n* an article sold at a loss in order to draw customers

lost /lɒst/ *adj* **1a** unable to find the way **b** bewildered, helpless **2** ruined or destroyed physically or morally **3a**

no longer possessed **b** no longer known **4** rapt, absorbed

lot /lɒt/ *n* **1** an object used as a counter in deciding a question by chance **2** (the use of lots as a means of making) a choice **3a** sthg that falls to sby by lot; a share **b** one's way of life or worldly fate; fortune **4** a film studio and its adjoining property **5** an article or a number of articles offered as 1 item (e g in an auction sale) **6a** *sing or pl in constr* a number of associated people; a set (e g you *lot*) **b** a kind, sort – chiefly in *a bad lot* **7** a considerable amount or number – often pl with sing. meaning **8** *chiefly Br* the whole amount or number (e g ate up the whole *lot*) *USE* (*6a&8*) infml

lotion /ˈləʊʃən/ *n* a medicinal or cosmetic liquid for external use

lottery /ˈlɒtəri/ *n* **1** (a way of raising money by the sale or) the distribution of numbered tickets some of which are later randomly selected to entitle the holder to a prize **2** an event or affair whose outcome is (apparently) decided by chance

lotus /ˈləʊtəs/ *n* **1** a fruit considered in Greek legend to cause indolence and dreamy contentment **2** any of various water lilies including several represented in ancient Egyptian and Hindu art and religious symbolism

lotus-eater *n* sby who lives in dreamy indolence

loud /laʊd/ *adj* **1** marked by or producing a high volume of sound **2** clamorous, noisy **3** obtrusive or offensive in appearance; flashy – **~ly** *adv*

loud-hailer *n* a megaphone

loudmouth /ˈlaʊdmaʊθ/ *n* a person given to much loud offensive talk – infml – **~ed** *adj*

loudspeaker /ˌlaʊdˈspiːkəʳ, ˈlaʊdˌspiːkəʳ/ *n* an electromechanical device that converts electrical energy into acoustic energy and that is used to reproduce audible sounds

¹lounge /laʊndʒ/ *v* to act or move idly or lazily; loll – **~r** *n*

²lounge *n* **1** a room in a private house for sitting in **2** a room in a public building providing comfortable seating; *also* a waiting room (e g at an airport)

lounge suit *n* a man's suit for wear during the day

lour *also* **lower** /ˈlaʊəʳ/ *v* **1** to look sullen; frown **2** to become dark, gloomy and threatening – **lour** *n*

louse /laʊs/ *n, pl* **lice** **1** any of various small wingless insects parasitic on warm-blooded animals **2** a contemptible person – infml

lousy /ˈlaʊzi/ *adj* **1** infested with lice **2a** very mean; despicable **b** very bad, unpleasant, useless, etc

lout /laʊt/ *n* a rough ill-mannered man or youth – **~ish** *adj*

louvre, louver /ˈluːvəʳ/ *n* an opening provided with 1 or more slanted fixed or movable strips of metal, wood, glass, etc to allow flow of air but to exclude rain or sun

¹love /lʌv/ *n* **1a** strong affection for another **b** attraction based on sexual desire **2** warm interest in, enjoyment of, or attraction to sthg **3a** the object of interest and enjoyment **b** a person who is loved; a dear (one) **4** unselfish loyal and benevolent concern for the good of another **5** a god or personification of love **6** an amorous episode; a love affair **7** a score of zero in tennis, squash, etc **8** sexual intercourse – euph

²love *v* **1** to hold dear; cherish **2a** to feel a lover's passion, devotion, or tenderness for **b** to have sexual intercourse with **3** to like or desire actively; take pleasure in **4** to thrive in – **-vable** *adj*

loveless /ˈlʌvlɪ̵s/ *adj* **1** without love **2** unloving **3** unloved

lovelorn /ˈlʌvlɔːn/ *adj* sad because of unrequited love

¹lovely /ˈlʌvli/ *adj* **1** delicately or delightfully beautiful **2** very pleasing; fine – **-liness** *n*

²lovely *n* a beautiful woman – infml

lover /ˈlʌvəʳ/ *n* **1a** a person in love **b** a man with whom a woman has sexual relations, esp outside marriage **c** *pl* 2 people in love with each other; *esp* 2 people who habitually have sexual relations **2** a devotee

lovesick /ˈlʌvˌsɪk/ *adj* languishing with love

loving /ˈlʌvɪŋ/ *adj* feeling or showing love; affectionate – **~ly** *adv*

loving cup *n* a large ornamental

drinking vessel with 2 or more handles that is passed among a group of people for all to drink from

¹**low** /ləʊ/ *v or n* (to make) the deep sustained throat sound characteristic of esp a cow

²**low** *adj* **1** not measuring much from the base to the top; not high **2a** situated or passing below the normal level or below the base of measurement **b** marking a nadir or bottom **3** *of sound* not shrill or loud; soft **4** near the horizon **5** humble in character or status **6a** weak **b** depressed **7** of less than usual degree, size, amount, or value **8a** lacking dignity or formality **b** morally reprehensible **c** coarse, vulgar **9** unfavourable, disparaging **10** *of a gear* designed for slow speed – **~ness** *n*

³**low** *n* sthg low: e g **a** a depth, nadir **b** a region of low atmospheric pressure

⁴**low** *adv* at or to a low place, altitude, or degree

lowborn /ləʊ'bɔːn/ *adj* born to parents of low social rank

lowbrow /'ləʊbraʊ/ *adj* dealing with or having unsophisticated or unintellectual tastes, esp in the arts – often derog

lowdown /'ləʊdaʊn/ *n* inside information – usu + *the*; infml

low-down *adj* contemptible, base – infml

¹**lower** /'ləʊəʳ/ *adj* **1** relatively low in position, rank, or order **2** less advanced in the scale of evolutionary development **3** constituting the popular, more representative, and often (e g in Britain) more powerful branch of a legislative body consisting of 2 houses **4a** beneath the earth's surface **b** *often cap* being an earlier division of the named geological period or series

²**lower** /'ləʊəʳ/ *v* **1a** to cause to descend **b** to reduce the height of **2a** to reduce in value, amount, degree, strength, or pitch **b** to degrade; *also* to humble

lower-case *adj, of a letter* of or conforming to the series (e g a, b, c rather than A, B, C) typically used elsewhere than at the beginning of sentences or proper names

low-key *also* **low-keyed** *adj* of low intensity; restrained

Lowland /'ləʊlənd/ *adj* of the Lowlands of Scotland

¹**lowly** /'ləʊli/ *adv* **1** in a humble or meek manner **2** in a low position, manner, or degree

²**lowly** *adj* **1** humble and modest in manner or spirit **2** low in the scale of biological or cultural evolution **3** ranking low in a social or economic hierarchy – **-liness** *n*

low profile *n* an inconspicuous mode of operation or behaviour (intended to attract little attention)

loyal /'lɔɪəl/ *adj* unswerving in allegiance (e g to a person, country, or cause) – **~ly** *adv*, *adv*, n **~ty** *n*

loyalist /'lɔɪəlɪ̣st/ *n* sby loyal to a government or sovereign, esp in time of revolt

lozenge /'lɒzɪ̣ndʒ/ *n* **1** (sthg shaped like) a figure with 4 equal sides and 2 acute and 2 obtuse angles **2** a small often medicated sweet

LP *n* a gramophone record designed to be played at 33⅓ revolutions per minute and typically having a diameter of 12in (30.5cm) and a playing time of 20–25min

LSD *n* a drug taken illegally for its potent action in producing hallucinations and altered perceptions

lubricant /'luːbrɪkənt/ *n* **1** a substance (e g oil) capable of reducing friction and wear when introduced as a film between solid surfaces **2** sthg that lessens or prevents difficulty

lubricate /'luːbrɪkeɪt/ *v* **1** to make smooth or slippery **2** to act as a lubricant – **-cation** *n* – **-cator** *n*

lucerne *also* **lucern** /luː'sɜːn/ *n, chiefly Br* a deep-rooted European leguminous plant widely grown for fodder

lucid /'luːsɪ̣d/ *adj* **1** having full use of one's faculties; sane **2** clear to the understanding; plain – **~ly** *adv* – **~ity** *n*

luck /lʌk/ *n* **1** whatever good or bad events happen to a person by chance **2** the tendency for a person to be consistently fortunate or unfortunate **3** success as a result of good fortune

lucky /'lʌki/ *adj* having, resulting from, or bringing good luck – **-kily** *adv* – **-kiness** *n*

lucky dip *n* an attraction (e g at a fair)

in which articles can be drawn unseen from a receptacle

lucrative /'luːkrətɪv/ *adj* producing wealth; profitable – **~ly** *adv*

lucre /'luːkəʳ/ *n* financial gain; profit; *also* money – esp in *filthy lucre*

ludicrous /'luːdɨkrəs/ *adj* **1** amusing because of obvious absurdity or incongruity **2** meriting derision – **~ly** *adv* – **~ness** *n*

¹luff /lʌf/ *n* the forward edge of a fore-and-aft sail

²luff *v* to sail nearer the wind – often + *up*

¹lug /lʌg/ *v* to drag, pull, or carry with great effort – infml

²lug *n* **1** sthg (e g a handle) that projects like an ear **2** an ear – chiefly dial or humor

luggage /'lʌgɪdʒ/ *n* (cases, bags, etc containing) the belongings that accompany a traveller

lugger /'lʌgəʳ/ *n* a small fishing or coasting boat that carries 1 or more lugsails

lugsail *n* a 4-sided fore-and-aft sail set to an obliquely hanging yard

lugubrious /luː'guːbrɪəs/ *adj* (exaggeratedly or affectedly) mournful – **~ly** *adv* – **~ness** *n*

lugworm /'lʌgwɜːm/ *n* any of a genus of marine worms that are used for bait

lukewarm /ˌluːk'wɔːm/ *adj* **1** moderately warm; tepid **2** lacking conviction; indifferent

¹lull /lʌl/ *v* **1** to cause to sleep or rest; soothe **2** to cause to relax vigilance, esp by deception

²lull *n* a temporary pause or decline in activity

lullaby /'lʌləbaɪ/ *n* a song to quieten children or lull them to sleep

lumbago /lʌm'beɪgəʊ/ *n* muscular pain of the lumbar region of the back

lumbar /'lʌmbəʳ/ *adj* of or constituting the loins or the vertebrae to lower back

¹lumber /'lʌmbəʳ/ *v* to move heavily or clumsily

²lumber /'lʌmbəʳ/ *n* **1** surplus or disused articles (e g furniture) that are stored away **2** *NAm* timber or logs, esp when dressed for use

³lumber *v* to clutter, encumber

lumberjack /'lʌmbədʒæk/ *n* a person engaged in logging

luminous /'luːmɨnəs/ *adj* **1** emitting or full of light; bright **2** easily understood; *also* explaining clearly – **~ly** *adv* – **-nosity** *n*

¹lump /lʌmp/ *n* **1** a usu compact piece or mass of indefinite size and shape **2** an abnormal swelling **3** a heavy thickset person **4** *Br the* whole group of casual nonunion building workers

²lump *v* to group without discrimination

³lump *adj* not divided into parts; entire

⁴lump *v* to put up with – chiefly in *like it or lump it*

lumpy /'lʌmpi/ *adj* **1a** filled or covered with lumps **b** characterized by choppy waves **2** having a thickset clumsy appearance

lunacy /'luːnəsi/ *n* **1** insanity (amounting to lack of capability or responsibility in law) **2** wild foolishness; extravagant folly

lunar /'luːnəʳ/ *adj* **1a** of the moon **b** designed for use on the moon **2 lunar, lunate** shaped like a crescent **3** measured by the moon's revolution

lunar month *n* the period of time, averaging 29½ days, between 2 successive new moons

lunatic /'luːnətɪk/ *adj* **1a** insane **b** of or designed for the care of insane people **2** wildly foolish

lunch /lʌntʃ/ , **luncheon** /'lʌntʃən/ *n* a midday meal – **lunch** *v*

luncheon meat *n* a precooked mixture of meat (e g pork) and cereal shaped in a loaf

lung /lʌŋ/ *n* **1** either of the usu paired organs in the chest that constitute the basic respiratory organ of air-breathing vertebrates **2** any of various respiratory organs of invertebrates

¹lunge /lʌndʒ/ *v* to make a lunge (with)

²lunge *n* **1** a sudden thrust or forceful forward movement **2** the act of plunging forward

³lunge *n* a long rein used to hold and guide a horse in breaking and training

lungfish /'lʌŋˌfɪʃ/ *n* any of various

fishes that breathe by a modified air bladder as well as gills

lupin *also* **lupine** /'luːpɨn/ *n* any of a genus of leguminous plants some of which are cultivated for fertilizer, fodder, their edible seeds, or their long spikes of variously coloured flowers

lurch /lɜːtʃ/ *v* **1** to roll or tip abruptly; pitch **2** to stagger

[1]**lure** /lʊəʳ, ljʊəʳ/ *n* **1** a bunch of feathers and often meat attached to a long cord and used by a falconer to recall his/her bird **2a** sby or sthg used to entice or decoy **b** the power to appeal or attract **3** a decoy for attracting animals to capture

[2]**lure** *v* to tempt with a promise of pleasure or gain

lurid /'lʊərɨd, 'ljʊərɨd/ *adj* **1** wan and ghastly pale in appearance **2a** causing horror or revulsion; gruesome **b** sensational **c** highly coloured; gaudy – **~ly** *adv* – **~ness** *n*

lurk /lɜːk/ *v* **1** to lie hidden, esp with evil intent **2** to move furtively or inconspicuously

luscious /'lʌʃəs/ *adj* **1** having a delicious taste or smell **2** richly luxurious or appealing to the senses; *also* excessively ornate – **~ly** *adv* – **~ness** *n*

[1]**lush** /lʌʃ/ *adj* **1** producing or covered by luxuriant growth **2** opulent, sumptuous

[2]**lush** *n, chiefly NAm* a heavy drinker; an alcoholic

[1]**lust** /lʌst/ *n* **1** strong sexual desire, esp as opposed to love **2** an intense longing; a craving

[2]**lust** *v* to have an intense (sexual) desire or craving

lustre, *NAm chiefly* **luster** /'lʌstəʳ/ *n* **1** (the quality of) the glow of reflected light from a surface (e g of a mineral) **2a** a glow of light (as if) from within **b** radiant beauty **3** glory, distinction **4** a glass pendant used esp to ornament a chandelier

lustrous /'lʌstrəs/ *adj* evenly shining – **~ly** *adv*

lusty /'lʌsti/ *adj* **1** full of vitality; healthy **2** full of strength; vigorous – **-tily** *adv* – **-tiness** *n*

lute /luːt/ *n* a stringed instrument with a large pear-shaped body, a neck with a fretted fingerboard, and pairs of strings tuned in unison – **-tanist, -tenist** *n*

luxuriant /lʌg'zjʊərɪənt, ləg'ʒʊərɪənt/ *adj* **1** characterized by abundant growth **2a** exuberantly rich and varied; prolific **b** richly or excessively ornamented – **~ly** *adv* – **-ance** *n*

luxuriate /lʌg'zjʊəreɪt/ *v* to revel *in*

luxurious /lʌg'zjʊərɪəs, ləg'ʒʊərɪəs/ *adj* **1** fond of luxury or self-indulgence; *also* voluptuous **2** characterized by opulence and rich abundance – **~ly** *adv*

luxury /'lʌkʃəri/ *n* **1** great ease or comfort based on habitual or liberal use of expensive items without regard to cost **2a** sthg desirable but costly or difficult to obtain **b** sthg relatively expensive adding to pleasure or comfort but not indispensable

lycée /'liːseɪ/ *n* a French public secondary school

lychee, litchi /'laɪtʃiː/ *n* (a Chinese tree that bears) an oval fruit that has a hard scaly outer covering, sweet white perfumed flesh, and a small hard seed

lych-gate /'lɪtʃ 'geɪt/ *n* a roofed gate in a churchyard

lymph /lɪmf/ *n* a pale fluid resembling blood plasma – **~atic** *adj*

lynch /lɪntʃ/ *v* to put to death illegally by mob action

lynx /lɪŋks/ *n* any of various wildcats with relatively long legs, a short stubby tail, mottled coat, and often tufted ears

lyre /laɪəʳ/ *n* a stringed instrument of the harp family used by the ancient Greeks esp to accompany song and recitation

[1]**lyric** /'lɪrɪk/ *adj* **1** suitable for being set to music and sung **2** expressing direct personal emotion

[2]**lyric** *n* **1** a lyric poem **2** *pl* the words of a popular song

lyrical /'lɪrɪkəl/ *adj* **1** lyric **2** full of admiration or enthusiasm – esp in *wax lyrical* – **~ly** *adv*

lyricism /'lɪrɨsɪzəm/ *n* **1** a directly personal and intense style or quality in an art **2** great enthusiasm or exuberance

M

m /em/ *n, pl* **m's, ms** *often cap* **1** (a graphic representation of or device for reproducing) the 13th letter of the English alphabet **2** one thousand

ma /mɑː/ *n* mother – chiefly as a term of address; infml

ma'am /mæm, mɑːm, məm/ *n* madam – used widely in the USA and in Britain, esp by servants and when addressing the Queen or a royal princess

mac, mack /mæk/ *n, Br* a raincoat – infml

macabre /mə'kɑːbrə, -bə'/ *adj* **1** dwelling on the gruesome **2** tending to produce horror in an onlooker

macadam /mə'kædəm/ *n* small broken stones compacted into a solid layer as a method of road construction – **~ize** *v*

macaroni /ˌmækə'rəuni/ *n* **1** pasta made from hard wheat and shaped in hollow tubes that are wider in diameter than spaghetti **2** an English dandy of the late 18th and early 19th c who affected continental ways

macaroon /ˌmækə'ruːn/ *n* a small cake or biscuit composed chiefly of egg whites, sugar, and ground almonds or occasionally coconut

macaw /mə'kɔː/ *n* any of numerous parrots including some of the largest and showiest

[1]**mace** /meɪs/ *n* an ornamental staff used as a symbol of authority

[2]**mace** *n* an aromatic spice consisting of the dried external fibrous covering of a nutmeg

macerate /'mæsəreɪt/ *v* to cause to become soft or separated into constituent elements (as if) by steeping in fluid – **-ation** *n*

machete /mə'tʃeɪti/ *n* a large heavy knife used for cutting vegetation and as a weapon

Machiavellian /'mækɪə'velɪən/ *adj* cunning and deceitful

machination /ˌmækɪ̯'neɪʃən/ *n* a scheming or crafty action or plan intended to accomplish some usu evil end

[1]**machine** /mə'ʃiːn/ *n* **1a** a combination of parts that transmit forces, motion, and energy one to another in a predetermined manner **b** an instrument (e g a lever or pulley) designed to transmit or modify the application of power, force, or motion **c** a combination of mechanically, electrically, or electronically operated parts for performing a task **2** a person or organization that acts like a machine

[2]**machine** *v* **1** to shape, finish, or operate on by a machine **2** to act on, produce, or perform a particular operation or activity on, using a machine; *esp* to sew using a sewing machine

machine gun *n* an automatic gun for rapid continuous fire

machinery /mə'ʃiːnəri/ *n* **1a** machines in general or as a functioning unit **b** the working parts of a machine **2** the means by which sthg is kept in action or a desired result is obtained **3** the system or organization by which an activity or process is controlled

machine tool *n* a usu power-driven machine designed for cutting or shaping wood, metal, etc

machinist /mə'ʃiːnist/ *n* **1** a craftsman skilled in the use of machine tools **2** one who operates a machine, esp a sewing machine

mackerel /'mækərəl/ *n* a fish of the N Atlantic that is green with dark blue bars above and silvery below and is one of the most important food fishes

mackintosh *also* **macintosh** /'mækɪ̯ntɒʃ/ *n, chiefly Br* a raincoat

macrame, macramé /mə'krɑːmi/ *n* (the act of making) a coarse lace or fringe made by knotting threads or cords in a geometrical pattern

macrobiotic /ˌmækrəbaɪ'ɒtɪk/ *adj* of or being a diet consisting chiefly of whole grains or whole grains and vegetables

macrocosm /'mækrəukɒzəm/ *n* **1** the universe **2** a complex that is a large-scale reproduction of 1 of its constituents

mad /mæd/ *adj* **1** mentally disordered; insane **2** utterly foolish; senseless **3** carried away by intense anger **4** carried away by enthusiasm or desire **5** intensely excited or distraught; frantic **6** marked by intense and often chaotic hectic activity

madam /'mædəm/ *n* **1** a lady – used without a name as a form of respectful or polite address to a woman **2** a female brothel keeper **3** a conceited pert young lady or girl

madame /mə'dɑːm, -'dæm/ *n, pl* **mesdames** – used as a title equivalent to *Mrs* preceding the name of a married woman not of English-speaking nationality or used without a name as a generalized term of direct address

madcap /'mædkæp/ *adj* marked by impulsiveness or recklessness – **madcap** *n*

madden /'mædn/ *v* **1** to drive mad; craze **2** to exasperate, enrage

madder /'mædəʳ/ *n* **1** a Eurasian plant with small yellowish flowers **2** (a dye prepared from) the root of the madder

made /meɪd/ *adj* **1** assembled or prepared, esp by putting together various ingredients **2** assured of success – infml

Madeira /mə'dɪərə/ *n* any of several fortified wines from Madeira

madeira cake *n* a very rich sponge cake

mademoiselle /ˌmædəmw'zel/ *n, pl* **mademoiselles, mesdemoiselles** **1** an unmarried French-speaking girl or woman – used as a title equivalent to *Miss* for an unmarried woman not of English-speaking nationality **2** a French governess or female language teacher

made-to-measure *adj, of a garment* made according to an individual's measurements in order to achieve a good fit

madhouse /'mædhaʊs/ *n* **1** a lunatic asylum **2** a place of uproar or confusion

madly /'mædli/ *adv* to a degree suggestive of madness: e g **a** with great energy; frantically **b** without restraint; passionately

madness /'mædnɨs/ *n* **1** insanity **2** extreme folly

Madonna /mə'dɒnə/ *n the* Virgin Mary

madrigal /'mædrɪgəl/ *n* an unaccompanied and often complex song for several voices

maelstrom /'meɪlstrəm/ *n* **1** a powerful whirlpool **2** sthg resembling a maelstrom in turbulence and violence

maestro /'maɪstrəʊ/ *n* a master in an art; *esp* an eminent composer, conductor, or teacher of music

Mafia /'mæfɪə/ *n sing or pl in constr* **1** a secret society of Sicilian political terrorists **2** an organized secret body originating in Sicily and prevalent esp in the USA that controls illicit activities (e g vice and narcotics) **3** *often not cap* an excessively influential group or clique of a usu specified kind

magazine /ˌmægə'ziːn/ *n* **1** a storeroom for arms, ammunition, or explosives **2a** a usu illustrated periodical, bound in paper covers, containing miscellaneous pieces by different authors **b** a television or radio programme containing a number of usu topical items, often without a common theme **3** a supply chamber: e g **a** a holder from which cartridges can be fed into a gun chamber automatically **b** a lightproof chamber for films or plates in a camera or for film in a film projector

magenta /mə'dʒentə/ *n* a deep purplish red (dye)

maggot /'mægət/ *n* a soft-bodied legless grub that is the larva of a 2-winged fly (e g the housefly) – **~y** *adj*

magi /'meɪdʒaɪ/ *pl of* **magus**

¹magic /'mædʒɪk/ *n* **1** (rites, incantations, etc used in) the art of invoking supernatural powers to control natural forces by means of charms, spells, etc **2a** an extraordinary power or influence producing results which defy explanation **b** sthg that seems to cast a spell **3** the art of producing illusions by sleight of hand – ~**al** *adj*

²**magic** *adj* **1** of, being, or used in magic **2** having seemingly supernatural qualities **3** – used as a general term of approval; infml

³**magic** *v* **-ck-** to affect, influence, or take *away* (as if) by magic

magician /mə'dʒɪʃən/ *n* **1** one skilled in magic **2** a conjurer

magisterial /ˌmædʒʒ̍'stɪərɪəl/ *adj* **1a** of, being, or like a master or teacher **b** having masterly skill **2** of a magistrate

magistrate /'mædʒʒ̍streɪt, -strʒ̍t/ *n* a civil legislative or executive official: e g **a** a principal official exercising governmental powers **b** a paid or unpaid local judicial officer who presides in a magistrates' court – **-acy** *n* – **-ature** *n*

maglev /'mæglev/ *n* a railway system in which an electrically-driven train is levitated above the track by powerful magnets

magma /'mægmə/ *n* molten rock material within the earth from which an igneous rock results by cooling

magnate /'mægneɪt, -nʒ̍t/ *n* a person of wealth or influence, often in a specified area of business or industry

magnesium /mæg'niːzɪəm/ *n* a silver-white bivalent metallic element that burns with an intense white light, is lighter than aluminium, and is used in making light alloys

magnet /'mægnʒ̍t/ *n* **1** a body (of iron, steel, etc) that has an (artificially imparted) magnetic field external to itself and attracts iron **2** sthg that attracts – ~**ic** *adj* – ~**ically** *adv* – ~**ism** *n* – ~**ize** *v*

magnetic pole *n* either of 2 small nonstationary regions in the N and S geographical polar areas of the earth towards which a magnetic needle points from any direction

magnetic tape *n* a ribbon of thin paper or plastic with a magnetizable coating for use in recording sound, video, etc signals

Magnificat /mæg'nɪfɪkæt/ *n* (a musical setting of) the works of the Virgin Mary in Luke 1:46–55 used in Christian worship

magnification /ˌmægnʒ̍fʒ̍'keɪʃən/ *n* **1** a magnifying or being magnified **2** the apparent enlargement of an object by a microscope, telescope, etc

magnificent /mæg'nɪfʒ̍sənt/ *adj* **1** marked by stately grandeur and splendour **2a** sumptuous in structure and adornment **b** strikingly beautiful or impressive **3** sublime **4** exceptionally fine or excellent – **-cence** *n* – ~**ly** *adv*

magnify /'mægnʒ̍faɪ/ *v* **1** to have the power of causing objects to appear larger than they are **2** to enlarge in fact or in appearance – **-fier** *n*

magnifying glass *n* a single optical lens for magnifying

magnitude /'mægnʒ̍tjuːd/ *n* **1a** (great) size or extent **b** a quantity, number **2** the importance or quality of sthg

magnolia /mæg'nəʊlɪə/ *n* any of a genus of shrubs and trees with evergreen or deciduous leaves and usu large white, yellow, rose, or purple flowers

magnum /'mægnʌm/ *n* a wine bottle holding twice the usual amount (about 1.5l)

magpie /'mægpaɪ/ *n* **1** any of numerous birds of the crow family with a very long tail and black-and-white plumage **2** one who chatters noisily **3** one who collects objects in a random fashion

magus /'meɪgəs/ *n, pl* **magi** **1a** a member of a Zoroastrian hereditary priestly class in ancient Persia **b** *often cap* any of the traditionally 3 wise men from the East who paid homage to the infant Jesus **2** a magician, sorcerer

maharajah, **maharaja** /ˌmɑːhə'rɑːdʒə/, *fem* **maharani** /ˌmɑːhə'rɑːniː/ *n* an Indian prince ranking above a rajah

mahogany /mə'hɒgəni/ *n* **1** (any of various tropical, esp W Indian, trees that yield) a durable usu reddish-brown moderately hard and heavy wood, widely used for fine cabinetwork **2** the reddish-brown colour of mahogany

maid /meɪd/ *n* **1** an unmarried girl or woman; *also* a female virgin **2** a female servant

¹**maiden** /'meɪdn/ *n* **1** an unmarried girl or woman **2 maiden, maiden over**

an over in cricket in which no runs are credited to the batsman

[2]**maiden** *adj* **1a**(1) not married (2) virgin **b** *of a female animal* never having borne young or been mated **c** that has not been altered from its original state **2** being the first or earliest of its kind

maidenhead /'meɪdənhed/ *n* **1** virginity **2** the hymen

maiden name *n* the surname of a woman prior to marriage

maid of honour *n* **1** a bride's principal unmarried wedding attendant **2** a small puff pastry tart filled with custard

[1]**mail** /meɪl/ *n* **1** the postal matter that makes up 1 particular consignment **2** a conveyance that transports mail **3** a postal system

[2]**mail** *v* to post

[3]**mail** *n* **1** armour made of interlocking metal rings, chains, or sometimes plates **2** a hard enclosing covering of an animal

[4]**mail** *v* to clothe (as if) with mail

mail order *n* an order for goods that is received and fulfilled by post

maim /meɪm/ *v* to mutilate, disfigure, or wound seriously; cripple

[1]**main** /meɪn/ *n* **1** physical strength – in *with might and main* **2** the chief or essential part – chiefly in *in the main* **3** the chief pipe, duct, or cable of a public service (e g gas, electricity, or water) – often pl with sing. meaning **4** the high sea

[2]**main** *adj* **1** chief, principal **2** fully exerted **3** connected with or located near the mainmast or mainsail

mainframe /'meɪn,freɪm/ *n* a large computer that can run several independent programs independently or is connected to other smaller computers

mainland /'meɪnlənd/ *n* the largest land area of a continent, country, etc, considered in relation to smaller offshore islands

mainline /'meɪnlaɪn/ *v* to inject (a narcotic or other drug of abuse) into a vein – slang

mainly /'meɪnli/ *adv* in most cases or for the most part; chiefly

mainmast /'meɪnmaːst, -məst/ *n* (the lowest section of) a sailing vessel's principal mast

mains /meɪnz/ *adj* of or (suitable to be) powered by electricity from the mains

mainsail /'meɪnsəl/ *n* **1** the lowest square sail on the mainmast of a square-rigged ship **2** the principal fore-and-aft sail on the mainmast of a fore-and-aft rigged ship

mainspring /'meɪn,sprɪŋ/ *n* the chief motive, agent, or cause

mainstay /'meɪnsteɪ/ *n* **1** a rope that stretches forwards from the top of a sailing ship's mainmast, usu to the foot of the foremast, and provides the chief support of the mainmast **2** a chief support

mainstream /'meɪnstriːm/ *n* a prevailing current or direction of activity or influence

maintain /meɪn'teɪn, mən-/ *v* **1** to keep in an existing state (e g of operation, repair, efficiency, or validity) **2** to sustain against opposition or danger **3** to continue or persevere in **4** to support, sustain, or provide for **5** to affirm (as if) in argument – **~able** *adj*

maintenance /'meɪntənəns/ *n* **1** maintaining or being maintained **2** (payment for) the upkeep of property or equipment **3** payments for the support of one spouse by another, esp of a woman by a man, pending or following legal separation or divorce

maisonette /,meɪzə'net/ *n* a part of a house, usu on two floors, let or sold separately

maize /meɪz/ *n* (the ears or edible seeds of) a tall widely cultivated cereal grass bearing seeds on elongated ears

majesty /'mædʒəsti/ *n* **1** sovereign power **2a** impressive bearing or aspect **b** greatness or splendour of quality or character – **-tic** *adj* – **-tically** *adv*

[1]**major** /'meɪdʒəʳ/ *adj* **1a** greater in importance, size, rank, or degree **b** of considerable importance **2** notable or conspicuous in effect or scope **3** involving serious risk to life; serious **4** *esp of a scale* having semitones between the third and fourth and the seventh and eighth notes

[2]**major** *n* **1** a major musical interval,

scale, key, or mode **2** a middle-ranking officer in the army

majority /mə'dʒɒrəti/ *n* **1** the (status of one who has attained the) age at which full legal rights and responsibilities are acquired **2** a number greater than half of a total **3** the greatest in number of 2 or more groups constituting a whole; *specif* (the excess of votes over its rival obtained by) a group having sufficient votes to obtain control **4** the military office, rank, or commission of a major

[1]**make** /meɪk/ *v* **made** **1a** to create or produce (for someone) by work or action **b** to cause; bring about **2** to formulate in the mind **3** to put together from ingredients or components – often + *up* **4** to compute or estimate to be **5a** to assemble and set alight the materials for (a fire) **b** to renew or straighten the bedclothes on (a bed) **6a** to cause to be or become **b** to cause (sthg) to appear or seem to; represent as **c(1)** to change, transform **(2)** to produce as an end product **7a** to enact, establish **b** to draft or produce a version of **8** to perform; carry out **9** to put forward for acceptance **10** to cause to act in a specified way; compel **11a** to amount to; count as **b** to combine to form **12** to be capable of becoming or of serving as **13** to reach, attain – often + *it* **14** to gain (e g money) by working, trading, dealing, etc **15a** to act so as to acquire **b** to score (points, runs, etc) in a game or sport

[2]**make** *n* **1a** the manner or style in which sthg is constructed **b** a place or origin of manufacture; a brand **2** the physical, mental, or moral constitution of a person

make-believe *n or adj* (sthg) imaginary or pretended

make off *v* to leave in haste

make out *v* **1** to complete (e g a printed form or document) by writing information in appropriate spaces **2** to find or grasp the meaning of **3** to claim or pretend to be true **4** to identify (e g by sight or hearing) with difficulty or effort

make over *v* to transfer the title of (property)

makeshift /'meɪk,ʃɪft/ *adj or n* (being) a crude and temporary expedient

make-up *n* **1** the way in which the parts of sthg are put together **2a** cosmetics (e g lipstick and mascara) applied, esp to the face, to give colour or emphasis **b** materials (e g wigs and cosmetics) used for special costuming (e g for a play)

make up *v* **1** to invent (e g a story), esp in order to deceive **2** to arrange typeset matter into (columns or pages) for printing **3** to wrap or fasten up **4** to become reconciled; *also* to attempt to ingratiate **5** to compensate *for* **6** to put on costumes or make-up (e g for a play)

making /'meɪkɪŋ/ *n* **1** a process or means of advancement or success **2** the essential qualities for becoming – often pl with sing. meaning

maladjusted /,mælə'dʒʌstəd/ *adj* poorly or inadequately adjusted, specif to one's social environment and conditions of life – **-justment** *n*

maladministration /,mæləd,mɪnə'streɪʃən/ *n* incompetent or corrupt administration, esp in public office

maladroit /,mælə'drɔɪt/ *adj* clumsy, inept – **~ly** *adv* – **~ness** *n*

malady /'mælədi/ *n* a disease or disorder

malaise /mə'leɪz/ *n* **1** an indeterminate feeling of debility or lack of health, often accompanying the start of an illness **2** a vague sense of mental or moral unease

malapropism /'mæləprɒpɪzəm/ *n* (an instance of) an incongruous misapplication of a word (e g in 'a table with contemptible legs')

malaria /mə'leərɪə/ *n* a disease transmitted by the bite of mosquitoes, and characterized by periodic attacks of chills and fever – **~l** *adj*

[1]**malcontent** /'mælkəntent/ *n* a discontented person; *esp* sby violently opposed to a government or regime

[2]**malcontent** /,mælkən'tent/, **malcontented** *adj* dissatisfied with the existing state of affairs

[1]**male** /meɪl/ *adj* **1a(1)** of or being the sex that produces sperm or spermatozoa by which the eggs of a female are made fertile **(2)** *of a plant or flower*

having stamens but no ovaries **b(1)** (characteristic) of the male sex **(2)** made up of male individuals **2** designed for fitting into a corresponding hollow part

²**male** *n* a male person, animal, or plant

malediction /ˌmælʒ'dɪkʃən/ *n* a curse – fml

malefactor /'mælʒfæktəʳ/ *n* **1** a criminal; *esp* a felon **2** one who does evil – fml

malevolent /mə'levələnt/ *adj* having, showing, or arising from an often intense desire to do harm – **-lence** *n* – **~ly** *adv*

malfunction /mæl'fʌŋkʃən/ *v* to fail to operate in the normal manner

malice /'mælʒs/ *n* conscious desire to harm; *esp* a premeditated desire to commit a crime – **-cious** *adj*

¹**malign** /mə'laɪn/ *adj* **1** harmful in nature, influence, or effect **2** bearing or showing (vicious) ill will or hostility – **~ity** *n*

²**malign** *v* to utter injuriously (false) reports about; speak ill of

malignant /mə'lɪgnənt/ *adj* **1** harmful in nature, influence, or effect **2** *of a disease* very severe or deadly; *specif, of a tumour* tending to cause death – **-nancy** *n* – **~ly** *adv*

malinger /mə'lɪŋgəʳ/ *v* to pretend illness or incapacity so as to avoid duty or work – **~er** *n*

mall /mɔːl, mæl/ *n* **1** a public promenade, often bordered by trees **2** *NAm* a shopping precinct, usu with associated parking space

mallard /'mæləd/ *n* a common large wild duck that is the ancestor of the domestic ducks

malleable /'mælɪəbəl/ *adj* **1** *esp of metals* capable of being beaten or rolled into a desired shape **2** easily shaped by outside forces or influences – **-bility** *n*

mallet /'mælʒt/ *n* **1** a hammer with a usu large head of wood, plastic, etc **2** an implement with a large usu cylindrical wooden head for striking the ball in croquet, polo, etc **3** a light hammer with a small rounded or spherical usu padded head used in playing certain musical instruments (e g a vibraphone)

mallow /'mæləʊ/ *n* any of various related plants with usu deeply cut lobed leaves and showy flowers

malmsey /'mɑːmzi/ *n, often cap* the sweetest variety of Madeira

malnutrition /ˌmælnjʊ'trɪʃən/ *n* faulty or inadequate nutrition

malodorous /mæl'əʊdərəs/ *adj* smelling bad – fml

malpractice /ˌmæl'præktʒs/ *n* failure to exercise due professional skill or care

¹**malt** /mɔːlt, mɒlt/ *n* **1** grain softened in water, allowed to germinate, then roasted and used esp in brewing and distilling **2** unblended malt whisky produced in a particular area

Maltese /mɔːl'tiːz/ *n, pl* **Maltese** (the language of) a native or inhabitant of Malta

Maltese cross *n* a cross consisting of 4 equal arms that widen out from the centre and have their outer ends indented by a V

Malthusian /mæl'θjuːzɪən/ *adj* of Malthus or his theory that population tends to increase faster than its means of subsistence and that widespread poverty inevitably results unless population growth is checked

maltreat /mæl'triːt/ *v* to treat cruelly or roughly – **~ment** *n*

mama, mamma /mə'mɑː/ *n* mummy – used informally and by children

mamba /'mæmbə/ *n* any of several (tropical) African venomous snakes related to the cobras but with no hood

mammal /'mæməl/ *n* any of a class of higher vertebrates comprising humans and all other animals that have mammary glands and nourish their young with milk

mammary /'mæməri/ *adj* of, lying near, or affecting the breasts

¹**mammoth** /'mæməθ/ *n* any of numerous extinct large hairy elephants

²**mammoth** *adj* of very great size

¹**man** /mæn/ *n, pl* **men** **1a(1)** a human being; *esp* an adult male as distinguished from a woman or child **(2)** a husband – esp in *man and wife* **b** the human race **c** any ancestor of modern man **d** one possessing the qualities associated with manhood (e g courage

and strength) **e** a fellow, chap – used interjectionally **2a** *pl* the members of (the ranks of) a military force **b** *pl* the working force as distinguished from the employer and usu the management **3** any of the pieces moved by each player in chess, draughts, etc – **~like** *adj* – **~ly** *adj* – **~liness** *n*

[2]**man** *v* **1** to supply with the man or men necessary **2** to take up station by (e g in '*man* the pumps!')

manacle /'mænəkəl/ *n* **1** a shackle or handcuff **2** a restraint *USE* usu pl – **manacle** *v*

manage /'mænɪdʒ/ *v* **1a** to make and keep submissive **b** to use (e g money) economically **2** to succeed in handling (e g a difficult situation or person) **3** to succeed in accomplishing **4** to conduct the running of (esp a business); *also* to have charge of (e g a sports team or athlete)

management /'mænɪdʒmənt/ *n* **1** the act or art of managing **2** *sing or pl in constr* the collective body of those who manage or direct an enterprise

manager /'mænɪdʒəʳ/, *fem* **manageress** *n* **1** one who conducts business affairs **2** sby who directs a sports team, player, entertainer, etc

man-at-arms *n, pl* **men-at-arms** a (heavily armed and usu mounted) soldier

manatee /,mænə'tiː/ *n* any of several (tropical) aquatic plant-eating mammals with broad tails

mandarin /'mændərɪn/ *n* **1a** a public official in the Chinese Empire **b** a person of position and influence, esp in literary or bureaucratic circles; *esp* an elder and often reactionary member of such a circle **2** *cap* the chief dialect of Chinese that has a standard variety spoken in the Peking area **3** **mandarin, mandarin orange** (a small spiny Chinese orange tree that bears) a yellow to reddish orange fruit

mandate /'mændeɪt/ *n* **1** an authorization to act on the behalf of another; *specif* the political authority given by electors to parliament **2** an order granted by the League of Nations to a member nation for the establishment of a responsible government over a conquered territory

mandatory /'mændətəri/ *adj* **1** containing or constituting a command **2** compulsory, obligatory

mandible /'mændəbəl/ *n* **1a** a lower jaw together with its surrounding soft parts **b** the upper or lower part of a bird's bill **2** any of various mouth parts in insects or other invertebrates for holding or biting food

mandolin *also* **mandoline** /,mændə'lɪn/ *n* a musical instrument of the lute family with a fretted neck

mandrill /'mændrɪl/ *n* a large gregarious baboon found in W Africa, the male of which has red and blue striped cheeks

mane /meɪn/ *n* **1** long thick hair growing about the neck of a horse, male lion, etc **2** long thick hair on a person's head

man-eater *n* a person or animal that eats human flesh – **man-eating** *adj*

manful /'mænfəl/ *adj* having courage and resolution – **~ly** *adv*

manganese /'mæŋgəniːz/ *n* a hard greyish white metallic element

mange /meɪndʒ/ *n* any of various contagious skin diseases affecting domestic animals or sometimes human beings, marked by inflammation and loss of hair and caused by a minute parasitic mite

mangel-wurzel /'mæŋgəl ,wɜːzəl/, **mangel** *n* a large yellow to orange type of beet grown as food for livestock

manger /'meɪndʒəʳ/ *n* a trough or open box in a stable for holding feed

[1]**mangle** /'mæŋgəl/ *v* **1** to hack or crush (as if) by repeated blows **2** to spoil by poor work, errors, etc

[2]**mangle** *v or n* (to pass through) a machine with rollers for squeezing water from and pressing laundry

mango /'mæŋgəʊ/ *n, pl* **mangoes, mangos** (a tropical evergreen tree that bears) a yellowish red fruit with a firm skin, large stone, and juicy edible slightly acid pulp

mangrove /'mæŋgrəʊv/ *n* any of a genus of tropical maritime trees or shrubs with prop roots that form dense masses

mangy /'meɪndʒi, 'mændʒi/ *adj* **1** suffering or resulting from mange **2** having many worn or bare spots – **-gily** *adv*

manhandle /'mænhændl/ *v* **1** to move or manage by human force **2** to handle roughly

manhole /'mænhəʊl/ *n* a covered opening through which a person may go, esp to gain access to an underground or enclosed structure (e g a sewer)

manhood /'mænhʊd/ *n* **1** manly qualities **2** the condition of being an adult male as distinguished from a child or female

man-hour *n* a unit of 1 hour's work by 1 person, used esp as a basis for cost accounting and wage calculation

mania /'meɪnɪə/ *n* **1** abnormal excitement and euphoria marked by mental and physical hyperactivity and disorganization of behaviour **2** excessive or unreasonable enthusiasm – often in combination

maniac /'meɪniæk/ *n* one who is or acts as if (violently) insane; a lunatic – **~al** *adj* – **~ally** *adv*

manic /'mænɪk/ *adj* affected by, relating to, or resembling mania

manic-depressive *adj* of or affected by a mental disorder characterized by alternating mania and (extreme) depression

[1]**manicure** /'mænɪ̵kjʊəʳ/ *n* (a) treatment for the care of the hands and fingernails

[2]**manicure** *v* to trim closely and evenly

[1]**manifest** /'mænɪ̵fest/ *adj* readily perceived by the senses (e g sight) or mind; obvious – **~ly** *adv*

[2]**manifest** *v* **1** to make evident by showing **2** *of a spirit, ghost, etc* to appear in visible form

[3]**manifest** *n* a list of passengers or an invoice of cargo, esp for a ship

manifestation /,mænɪ̵fe'steɪʃən/ *n* a sign (e g materialization) of the presence of a spirit

manifesto /,mænɪ̵'festəʊ/ *n* a public declaration of intentions, esp by a political party before an election

[1]**manifold** /'mænɪ̵fəʊld/ *adj* many and varied

[2]**manifold** *n* **1** a whole that unites or consists of many diverse elements **2** a hollow fitting (e g connecting the cylinders of an internal combustion engine with the exhaust pipe) with several outlets or inlets for connecting 1 pipe with several other pipes

manikin, mannikin /'mænɪkɪ̵n/ *n* **1** a mannequin **2** a little man

manipulate /mə'nɪpjʊleɪt/ *v* **1** to handle or operate, esp skilfully **2a** to manage or use skilfully **b** to control or influence by artful, unfair, or insidious means, esp to one's own advantage **3** to examine and treat (a fracture, sprain, etc) by moving bones into the proper position manually – **-lative** *adj* – **-lation** *n*

mankind /,mæn'kaɪnd/ *n sing but sing or pl in constr* the human race

manky /'mæŋki/ *adj* nasty, unpleasant – slang

man-made *adj* made or produced by human beings rather than nature; *also* synthetic

manna /'mænə/ *n* **1** food miraculously supplied to the Israelites in their journey through the wilderness **2** a sudden source of benefit

manned /mænd/ *adj* equipped or carrying men

mannequin /'mænɪkɪ̵n/ *n* **1** an artist's, tailor's, or dressmaker's model of the human figure; *also* such a model used esp for displaying clothes **2** a woman who models clothing

manner /'mænəʳ/ *n* **1** a kind, sort; *also* sorts **2a** the mode or method in which sthg is done or happens **b** a method of artistic execution; a style **3** *pl* social behaviour evaluated as to politeness; *esp* conduct indicating good background **4** characteristic or distinctive bearing, air, or deportment

mannered /'mænəd/ *adj* **1** having manners of a specified kind – usu in combination **2** having an artificial or stilted character

mannerism /'mænərɪzəm/ *n* **1a** exaggerated or affected adherence to a particular style in art or literature **b** *often cap* a style of art in late 16th-c Europe characterized by distortion of the human figure **2** a characteristic (unconscious) gesture or trait; an idiosyncrasy

mannish /'mænɪʃ/ *adj* resembling, befitting, or typical of a man rather than a woman – **~ly** *adv* – **~ness** *n*

[1]**manoeuvre** /mə'nuːvə^r/ *n* **1a** a military or naval movement **b** a (large-scale) training exercise for the armed forces **2** an intended and controlled deviation from a straight and level flight path in the operation of an aircraft **3** a skilful or dexterous movement **4** an adroit and clever management of affairs, often using deception

[2]**manoeuvre** *v* **1** to perform a military or naval manoeuvre (to secure an advantage) **2** to perform a manoeuvre **3** to cause (e g troops) to execute manoeuvres **4** to manipulate with adroitness – **-vrer** *n*

man-of-war *n, pl* **men-of-war** a warship (of the days of sail)

manor /'mænə^r/ *n* **1** a landed estate **2a** a medieval estate under a lord who held a variety of rights over land and tenants, including the right to hold court **b manor, manor house** the house of the lord of a manor **3** a district of police administration – slang – **~ial** *adj*

manpower /'mæn,paʊə^r/ *n* the total supply of people available for work or service

manse /mɑns/ *n* the residence of an esp Presbyterian or Baptist clergyman

manservant /'mæn,sɜːvənt/ *n* a male servant, esp a valet

mansion /'mænʃən/ *n* **1a** the house of the lord of a manor **b** a large imposing residence **2** a separate apartment in a large structure

manslaughter /'mæn,slɔːtə^r/ *n* the unlawful killing of sby without malicious intent

mantelpiece /'mæntlpiːs/, **mantel** *n* an ornamental structure round a fireplace

mantilla /mæn'tɪlə/ *n* a light scarf worn over the head and shoulders esp by Spanish and Latin-American women

mantle /'mæntl/ *n* **1** a loose sleeveless garment worn over other clothes; a cloak **2** sthg that covers, envelops, or conceals **3** a lacelike sheath of some material that gives light by becoming white-hot when placed over a flame **4** the part of the earth or a similar planet that lies between the crust and central core

man-to-man *adj* **1** characterized by frankness and honesty **2** of or being a defensive system in soccer, basketball, etc in which each player marks 1 specific opponent

[1]**manual** /'mænjʊəl/ *adj* **1** of or involving the hands **2** requiring or using physical skill and energy **3** worked or done by hand and not by machine or automatically – **~ly** *adv*

[2]**manual** *n* **1** a book of instructions; a handbook **2** a keyboard for the hands; *specif* any of the several keyboards of an organ that control separate divisions of the instrument

[1]**manufacture** /,mænjʊ'fæktʃə^r/ *n* **1** the esp large-scale making of wares by hand or by machinery **2** the act or process of producing sthg

[2]**manufacture** *v* **1** to make (materials) into a product suitable for use **2** to make (wares) from raw materials by hand or by machinery, esp on a large scale **3** to invent, fabricate

manure /mə'njʊə^r/ *n* material that fertilizes land; *esp* the faeces of domestic animals

manuscript /'mænjʊskrɪpt/ *n or adj* (a composition or document) written by hand or typed as distinguished from a printed copy

[1]**Manx** /'mæŋks/ *adj* (characteristic) of the Isle of Man

[2]**Manx** *n pl in constr* the people of the Isle of Man

Manx cat *n* (any of) a breed of short-haired domestic cats some of which have no external tail

[1]**many** /'meni/ *adj* **more** /mɔː^r/; **most** /məʊst/ **1** consisting of or amounting to a large but unspecified number **2** being one of a large number (e g *many* a man)

[2]**many** *pron pl in constr* a large number of people or things

[3]**many** *n pl in constr* **1** a large but indefinite number **2** *the* great majority

[4]**many** *adv* to a considerable degree or amount; far – with plurals

many-sided *adj* **1** having many sides

or aspects 2 having many interests or aptitudes – ~**ness** *n*

Maoism /'maʊɪzəm/ *n* Marxism-Leninism as developed in China chiefly by Mao Zedong – **-ist** *adj, n*

Maori /'maʊri/ *n* **1** a member of the indigenous people of New Zealand **2** the Austronesian language of the Maori

¹map /mæp/ *n* **1** a representation, usu on a flat surface, of (part of) the earth's surface, the celestial sphere, etc **2** sthg that represents with a clarity suggestive of a map

²map *v* **1** to make a map of **2** to survey in order to make a map **3** to plan in detail – often + *out*

maple /'meɪpəl/ *n* (the hard light-coloured close-grained wood, used esp for furniture, of) any of a genus of widely planted trees or shrubs

mar /mɑːʳ/ *v* to detract from the perfection or wholeness of

maraca /mə'rækə/ *n* a dried gourd or a rattle like a gourd that is used as a rhythm instrument and is usu played as one of a pair

maraschino /,mærə'ʃiːnəʊ, -'skiːnəʊ/ *n often cap* **1** a sweet liqueur distilled from the fermented juice of a bitter wild cherry **2** a usu large cherry preserved in true or imitation maraschino

marathon /'mærəθən/ *n* **1** a long-distance race; *specif* a foot race of 26mi 385yd (about 42.2km) that is contested on an open course in major athletics championships **2a** an endurance contest **b** an event or activity characterized by great length or concentrated effort

maraud /mə'rɔːd/ *v* to roam about in search of plunder

¹marble /'mɑːbəl/ *n* **1a** (more or less) crystallized limestone that can be highly polished and is used esp in building and sculpture **b** a sculpture or carving made of marble **2** a little ball made of a hard substance, esp glass, and used in children's games **3** *pl* elements of common sense; *esp* sanity – infml

²marble *v* to give a veined or mottled appearance to (e g the edges of a book)

marbled /'mɑːbəld/ *adj* **1** made of or veneered with marble **2** *of meat* marked by a mixture of fat and lean

¹march /mɑːtʃ/ *n, often cap* a border region; *esp* a tract of land between 2 countries whose ownership is disputed – usu pl

²march *v* **1** to move along steadily, usu in step with others **2a** to move in a direct purposeful manner **b** to make steady progress **3** to cause to march **4** to cover by marching – ~**er** *n*

³march *n* **1a** the action of marching **b** the distance covered within a specified period of time by marching **c** a regular measured stride or rhythmic step used in marching **d** steady forward movement **2** a musical composition with a strongly accentuated beat and is designed or suitable to accompany marching

March *n* the 3rd month of the Gregorian calendar

marching orders *n pl* notice of dismissal

marchioness /,mɑːʃə'nes/ *n* **1** the wife or widow of a marquess **2** a woman having in her own right the rank of a marquess

Mardi Gras /,mɑːdi 'grɑː/ *n* (a carnival period culminating on) Shrove Tuesday often observed (e g in New Orleans) with parades and festivities

mare /meəʳ/ *n* a female equine animal, esp when fully mature or of breeding age; *esp* a female horse

margarine /,mɑːdʒə'riːn, ,mɑːgə-/ *n* a substitute for butter made usu from vegetable oils churned with ripened skimmed milk to a smooth emulsion

¹margin /'mɑːdʒɪn/ *n* **1** the part of a page outside the main body of printed or written text **2** the outside limit and adjoining surface of sthg **3a** a spare amount or measure or degree allowed (e g in case of error) **b(1)** a bare minimum below which or an extreme limit beyond which sthg becomes impossible or is no longer desirable **(2)** the limit below which economic activity cannot be continued under normal conditions **4** the difference between net sales and the cost of merchandise sold **5** measure or degree of difference

²margin *v* to provide with a border

marginal /ˈmɑːdʒɪ̵nl/ *adj* **1** written or printed in the margin **2** of or situated at a margin or border **3** close to the lower limit of qualification, acceptability, or function **4** of or providing a nominal profit margin **5** being a constituency where the Member of Parliament was elected with only a small majority

marigold /ˈmærɪ̵gəʊld/ *n* any of a genus of composite plants with showy yellow or red flower heads

marijuana, marihuana /ˌmærɪ̵ˈwɑːnə, -ˈhwɑːnə/ *n* a usu mild form of cannabis

marimba /məˈrɪmbə/ *n* a percussion instrument resembling a large xylophone

marina /məˈriːnə/ *n* a dock or basin providing secure moorings for motorboats, yachts, etc

marinade /ˌmærɪ̵ˈneɪd/ *v or n* (to soak in) a blend of oil, wine or vinegar, herbs, and spices in which meat, fish, etc is soaked, esp to enrich its flavour

marinate /ˈmærɪ̵neɪt/ *v* to marinade

[1]**marine** /məˈriːn/ *adj* **1** of or (living) in the sea **2** of or used in the navigation or commerce of the sea

[2]**marine** *n* **1** seagoing ships (of a specified nationality or class) **2a** any of a class of soldiers serving on shipboard or in close association with a naval force **b** a soldier who serves on a naval ship or in the navy

mariner /ˈmærɪ̵nəʳ/ *n* a seaman, sailor

marionette /ˌmærɪəˈnet/ *n* a small-scale usu wooden figure with jointed limbs that is moved from above by attached strings or wires

marital /ˈmærɪ̵tl/ *adj* of marriage – **~ly** *adv*

maritime /ˈmærɪ̵taɪm/ *adj* **1** marine **2** of or bordering on the sea

marjoram /ˈmɑːdʒərəm/ *n* any of various plants of the mint family used as herbs; *also* oregano

[1]**mark** /mɑːk/ *n* **1a** sthg (e g a line, notch, or fixed object) designed to record position **b** a target **c** the starting line or position in a track event **d** a goal or desired object **2a(1)** a sign or token **(2)** an impression on the surface of sthg; *esp* a scratch, stain, etc that spoils the appearance of a surface **(3)** a distinguishing characteristic **b** a symbol used for identification or indication of ownership **c** a written or printed symbol **d** *cap* – used with a numeral to designate a particular model of a weapon or machine **e** a point or level (reached) **3** an assessment of (educational) merits **4** an object of attack; *specif* a victim of a swindle – infml

[2]**mark** *v* **1a(1)** to fix or trace *out* the limits of **(2)** to plot the course of **b** to set apart (as if) by a line or boundary – usu + *off* **2a(1)** to designate, identify or indicate (as if) by a mark **(2)** to make or leave a mark on **(3)** to add appropriate symbols, characters, or other marks to or on – usu + *up* **b(1)** to register, record **(2)** to evaluate by marks **c(1)** to characterize, distinguish **(2)** to be the occasion of (sthg notable); to indicate as a particular time **3** to take notice of **4** *Br* to stay close to (an opposing player) in hockey, soccer, etc so as to hinder the getting or play of the ball **5** to become or make sthg stained, scratched, etc **6** to evaluate sthg by marks – **~er** *n*

[3]**mark** *n often cap* (a note or coin representing) the basic money unit of either East or West Germany

Mark *n* the 2nd Gospel in the New Testament

markdown *n* (the amount of) a reduction in price

marked /mɑːkt/ *adj* **1a** having natural marks (of a specified type) **b** made identifiable by marking **2** having a distinctive or emphasized character **3** being an object of attack, suspicion, or vengeance – **~ly** *adv*

[1]**market** /ˈmɑːkɪ̵t/ *n* **1a** a meeting together of people for the purpose of trade, by private purchase and sale **b** an open space, building, etc where a market (e g for trading in provisions or livestock) is held **2a** (a geographical area or section of the community in which there is) demand for commodities **b** commercial activity; extent of trading **c** an opportunity for selling **d** the area of economic activity in which the forces of supply and demand affect prices

[2]**market** *v* **1** to deal in a market **2** to sell – **~able** *adj* – **~ability** *n* – **~er, ~eer** *n*

market garden *n* a plot in which vegetables are grown for market – **~er** *n* – **~ing** *n*

marketing /ˈmaːkɪ̣tɪŋ/ *n* the skills and functions, including packaging, promotion, and distribution, involved in selling goods

marketplace /ˈmaːkɪ̣tpleɪs/ *n* **1** an open place in a town where markets are held **2** somewhere where there is a demand of commodities

market research *n* research (e g the collection and analysis of information about consumer preferences) dealing with the patterns or state of demand (for a particular product) in a market

marking /ˈmaːkɪŋ/ *n* **1** (the giving of) a mark or marks **2** arrangement, pattern, or disposition of marks

marksman /ˈmaːksmən/, *fem* **markswoman** *n* a person skilled in hitting a mark or target – **~ship** *n*

markup /ˈmaːk-ʌp/ *n* (the amount of) an increase in price

marl /maːl/ *v or n* (to fertilize with) a crumbly earthy deposit (e g of silt or clay) that contains calcium carbonate and is used esp as a fertilizer for lime-deficient soils

marlinespike /ˈmaːlɪ̣nspaɪk/ *n* a pointed steel tool used to separate strands of rope or wire

[1]**marmalade** /ˈmaːməleɪd/ *n* a clear sweetened preserve made from oranges, lemons, etc and usu containing pieces of fruit peel

[2]**marmalade** *adj, esp of cats* brownish orange

marmoreal /maːˈmɔːrɪəl/ *adj* of or like marble or a marble statue – chiefly poetic

marmoset /ˈmaːməzet/ *n* any of numerous soft-furred S and Central American monkeys

[1]**maroon** /məˈruːn/ *v* **1** to abandon on a desolate island or coast **2** to isolate in a helpless state

[2]**maroon** *n* **1** a dark brownish red colour **2** an explosive rocket used esp as a distress signal

Maroon *n* (a descendant of) a fugitive Negro slave of the W Indies and Guiana in the 17th and 18th c

marquee /maːˈkiː/ *n* a large tent (e g for an outdoor party or exhibition)

marquetry *also* **marqueterie** /ˈmaːkɪ̣tri/ *n* decorative work of pieces of wood, ivory, etc inlaid in a wood veneer that is then applied to a surface (e g of a piece of furniture)

marquis, marquess /ˈmaːkwɪ̣s/ *n* a member of the British peerage ranking below a duke and above an earl

marriage /ˈmærɪdʒ/ *n* **1a** the state of being or mutual relation of husband and wife **b** the institution whereby a man and a woman are joined in a special kind of social and legal dependence **2** an act or the rite of marrying; *esp* the wedding ceremony **3** an intimate or close union

married /ˈmærɪd/ *adj* **1a** joined in marriage **b** of married people **2** united, joined

marrow /ˈmærəʊ/ *n* **1a** a soft tissue that fills the cavities and porous part of most bones and contains many blood vessels **b** the substance of the spinal cord **2** the inmost, best, or essential part; the core **3** *chiefly Br* a vegetable marrow

marry /ˈmæri/ *v* **1a** to give in marriage **b** to take as spouse **c** to perform the ceremony of marriage for **d** to obtain by marriage **2** to bring together closely, harmoniously, and usu permanently **3a** to take a spouse **b** to become husband and wife

Mars /maːz/ *n* the planet 4th in order from the sun and conspicuous for its red colour

marsh /maːʃ/ *n* (an area of) soft wet land usu covered with sedges, rushes, etc

[1]**marshal** /ˈmaːʃəl/ *n* **1a** one who arranges and directs a ceremony **b** one who arranges the procedure at races **2a** a field marshal **b** an officer of the highest military rank **3** a chief officer in the USA responsible for court processes in a district

[2]**marshal** *v* **1** to place in proper rank or position **2** to bring together and order in an effective way **3** to lead ceremoniously or solicitously; usher

marshalling yard *n, chiefly Br* a

place where railway vehicles are shunted and assembled into trains

marsh gas *n* methane

marshmallow /ˌmɑːʃˈmæləʊ/ *n* **1** a pink-flowered Eurasian marsh plant of the mallow family **2** a light spongy confection made from the root of the marshmallow or from sugar, albumen, and gelatin

marsupial /mɑːˈsjuːpɪəl/ *n* any of an order of lower mammals including the kangaroos, wombats, and opossums that have a pouch on the abdomen of the female for carrying young, and do not develop a placenta

mart /mɑːt/ *n* a place of trade (e g an auction room or market)

marten /ˈmɑːtɨn, -tn/ *n* any of several slender-bodied flesh-eating tree-dwelling mammals larger than the related weasels

martial /ˈmɑːʃəl/ *adj* of or suited to war or a warrior; *also* warlike

martial law *n* the law administered by military forces in occupied territory or in an emergency

Martian /ˈmɑːʃən/ *adj* of or coming from the planet Mars

martin /ˈmɑːtɨn, -tn/ *n* any of various birds of the swallow family

martinet /ˌmɑːtɨˈnet/ *n* a strict disciplinarian

martini /mɑːˌtiːni/ *n* a cocktail made of gin and dry vermouth

¹martyr /ˈmɑːtəʳ/ *n* **1** one who is put to death for adherence to a cause, esp a religion **2** a victim, esp of constant (self-inflicted) suffering

²martyr *v* **1** to put to death as a martyr **2** to inflict agonizing pain on

¹marvel /ˈmɑːvəl/ *n* one who or that which is marvellous

²marvel *v* to become filled with surprise, wonder, or amazed curiosity

marvellous /ˈmɑːvələs/ *adj* **1** causing wonder **2** of the highest kind or quality – **~ly** *adv*

Marxism /ˈmɑːksɪzəm/ *n* the political and economic principles and policies advocated by Karl Marx, that stress the importance of human labour in determining economic value, the struggle between classes as an instrument of social change, and dictatorship of the proletariat – **-ist** *n, adj*

Marxism-Leninism *n* a theory and practice of communism developed by Lenin from the doctrines of Marx – **Marxist-Leninist** *n, adj*

marzipan /ˈmɑːzɨpæn/ *n* a paste made from ground almonds, sugar, and egg whites, used for coating cakes or shaped into small sweets

mascara /mæˈskɑːrə/ *n* a cosmetic for colouring, esp darkening, the eyelashes

mascot /ˈmæskət/ *n* a person, animal, or object adopted as a (good luck) symbol

masculine /ˈmæskjʊlɨn/ *adj* **1a** male **b** having qualities appropriate to a man **2** of, belonging to, or being the gender that normally includes most words or grammatical forms referring to males **3** having or occurring in a stressed final syllable

¹mash /mæʃ/ *n* **1** crushed malt or grain meal steeped and stirred in hot water to ferment **2** a mixture of bran or similar feeds and usu hot water for livestock **3** a soft pulpy mass **4** *Br* mashed potatoes – infml

²mash *v* to crush, pound, etc to a soft pulpy state

¹mask /mɑːsk/ *n* **1a** a (partial) cover for the face used for disguise or protection **b(1)** a figure of a head worn on the stage in ancient times to identify the character **(2)** a grotesque false face worn at carnivals or in rituals **c** a copy of a face made by sculpting or by means of a mould **2a** sthg that disguises or conceals; *esp* a pretence, facade **b** a translucent or opaque screen to cover part of the sensitive surface in taking or printing a photograph **3** a device covering the mouth and nose used **a** to promote breathing (e g by connection to an oxygen supply) **b** to remove noxious gas from air **c** to prevent breathing out of infective material (e g during surgery) **4** the head or face of a fox, dog, etc – **~ed** *adj*

²mask *v* **1** to provide, cover, or conceal (as if) with a mask: e g **a** to make indistinct or imperceptible **b** to cover up **2** to cover for protection **3** to modify the shape of (e g a photograph) by means of a mask

masochism /ˈmæsəkɪzəm/ *n* **1** a sexual perversion in which pleasure is experienced from being physically or mentally abused **2** pleasure from sthg tiresome or painful – not used technically – **-chist** *n* – **-chistic** *adj*

mason /'meɪsən/ *n* **1** a skilled worker with stone **2** *cap* a freemason – **~ic** *adj*

masonry /'meɪsənri/ *n* **1** work done with or sthg constructed of stone; *also* a brick construction **2** *cap* freemasonry

masque /mɑːsk/ *n* **1** a masquerade **2** a short allegorical dramatic entertainment of the 16th and 17th c performed by masked actors

[1]**masquerade** /,mæskə'reɪd/ *n* a social gathering of people wearing masks and often fantastic costumes

[2]**masquerade** *v* **1** to disguise oneself; *also* to wear a disguise **2** to assume the appearance of sthg that one is not – usu + *as* – **-rader** *n*

[1]**mass** /mæs, mɑːs/ *n* **1** *cap* the liturgy or a celebration of the Eucharist, esp in Roman Catholic and Anglo-Catholic churches **2** a musical setting of the Mass

[2]**mass** /mæs/ *n* **1a** a quantity of matter or the form of matter that holds together in 1 body **b(1)** an (unbroken) expanse **(2)** the principal part or main body **c** the property of a body that is a measure of its inertia, causes it to have weight in a gravitational field, and is commonly taken as a measure of the amount of material it contains **2** a large quantity, amount, or number – often pl with sing. meaning **3** *pl* the body of ordinary people as contrasted with the élite

[3]**mass** /mæs/ *v* to assemble in or collect into a mass

[4]**mass** /mæs/ *adj* **1a** of, designed for, or consisting of the mass of the people **b** participated in by or affecting a large number of individuals **c** large scale **2** viewed as a whole; total

[1]**massacre** /'mæsəkəʳ/ *v* **1** to kill (as if) in a massacre **2** to defeat severely – infml

[2]**massacre** *n* **1** the ruthless and indiscriminate killing of large numbers **2** complete defeat or destruction

massage /'mæsɑːʒ/ *n* (an act of) kneading, rubbing, etc of the body in order to relieve aches, tone muscles, give relaxation, etc – **massage** *v*

masseur /mæ'sɜːʳ, mə-/ , *fem* **masseuse** /mœ'sɜːz/ *n* one who practises massage and physiotherapy

massive /'mæsɪv/ *adj* **1a** large, solid, or heavy **b** impressively large or ponderous **2** large or impressive in scope or degree – **~ly** *adv* – **~ness** *n*

mass media *n pl* broadcasting, newspapers, and other means of communication designed to reach large numbers of people

mass-produce *v* to produce (goods) in large quantities by standardized mechanical processes – **-duction** *n*

[1]**mast** /mɑːst/ *n* **1** a tall pole or structure rising from the keel or deck of a ship, esp for carrying sails **2** a vertical pole or lattice supporting a radio or television aerial

[2]**mast** *n* beechnuts, acorns, etc accumulated on the forest floor and often serving as food for animals (e g pigs)

mastectomy /mæ'stektəmi/ *n* amputation of a breast

[1]**master** /'mɑːstəʳ/ *n* **1a(1)** a male teacher **(2)** a person holding an academic degree higher than a bachelor's but lower than a doctor's **b** a workman qualified to teach apprentices **c** an artist, performer, player, etc of consummate skill **2a** one having control or authority over another **b** one who or that which conquers or masters **c** a person qualified to command a merchant ship **d** an owner, esp of a slave or animal **e** an employer **3** *cap* a youth or boy too young to be called *mister* – used as a title **4** a presiding officer in an institution or society (e g a Masonic lodge) or at a function **5** an original from which copies (e g of film or gramophone records) can be made – **~y** *n*

[2]**master** *v* **1** to become master of; overcome **2a** to become skilled or proficient in the use of **b** to gain a thorough understanding of

[3]**master** *adj* **1** having chief authority; controlling **2** principal, main

masterful /'mɑːstəfəl/ *adj* **1** inclined to take control and dominate **2** having or showing the technical, artistic, or intellectual skill of a master – ~**ly** *adv*

masterly /'mɑːstəli/ *adj* showing superior knowledge or skill – **-liness** *n*

mastermind /'mɑːstəmaɪnd/ *v* to be the intellectual force behind (a project) – **mastermind** *n*

master of ceremonies *n* **1** one who determines the procedure to be observed on a state or public occasion **2** one who acts as host, esp by introducing speakers, performers, etc, at an event

masterpiece /'mɑːstəpiːs/ *n* a work done with extraordinary skill; *esp* the supreme creation of a type, period, or person

masterstroke /'mɑːstəstrəuk/ *n* a masterly performance or move

masthead /'mɑːsthed/ *n* **1** the top of a mast **2** the name of a newspaper displayed on the top of the first page

mastic /'mæstɪk/ *n* **1** an aromatic resin that exudes from mastic trees and is used esp in varnishes **2** a pasty substance used as a protective coating or cement

masticate /'mæstɨkeɪt/ *v* to chew – **-cation** *n*

mastiff /'mæstɨf/ *n* any of a breed of very large powerful deep-chested smooth-coated dogs used chiefly as guard dogs

mastitis /mæ'staɪtɨs/ *n* inflammation of the breast or udder, usu caused by infection

mastodon /'mæstədɒn/ *n* any of numerous extinct mammals similar to the related mammoths and elephants

mastoid /'mæstɔɪd/ *adj or n* (of, near, or being) a somewhat conical part of the temporal bone lying behind the ear

[1]**mat** /mæt/ *n* **1a** a piece of coarse usu woven, felted, or plaited fabric (e g of rushes or rope) used esp as a floor covering **b** a doormat **c** an often decorative piece of material used to protect a surface from heat, moisture, etc caused by an object placed on it **2** sthg made up of many intertwined or tangled strands

[2]**mat** *v* to become tangled or intertwined

[3]**mat** *v, adj, or n* (to) matt

matador /'mætədɔːʳ/ *n* one who has the principal role and who kills the bull in a bullfight

[1]**match** /mætʃ/ *n* **1a** one who or that which is equal to or able to contend with another **b** a person or thing exactly like another **2** two people, animals, or things that go well together **3** a contest between 2 or more teams or individuals **4a** a marriage union **b** a prospective partner in marriage

[2]**match** *v* **1** to be a counterpart or equal **2** to harmonize

[3]**match** *n* a short slender piece of wood, cardboard, etc tipped with a mixture that ignites when subjected to friction

matchless /'mætʃlɨs/ *adj* having no equal – ~**ly** *adv*

matchmaker /'mætʃ,meɪkəʳ/ *n* one who arranges marriages; *also* one who derives vicarious pleasure from contriving to arrange marriages – **making** *n*

match point *n* a situation in tennis, badminton, etc in which a player will win the match by winning the next point

matchwood /'mætʃwʊd/ *n* wood suitable for matches; *also* wood splinters

[1]**mate** /meɪt/ *v or n* (to) checkmate

[2]**mate** *n* **1a** an associate, companion – usu in combination **b** an assistant to a more skilled workman **2** a deck officer on a merchant ship ranking below the captain **3a** either of a pair: e g **(1)** either member of a breeding pair of animals **(2)** either of 2 matched objects **b** a marriage partner

[3]**mate** *v* **1** to join or fit together **2** to copulate

maté, mate /'mɑːteɪ/ *n* **1** a tealike aromatic beverage used chiefly in S America **2** (the leaves and shoots, used in making maté, of) a S American holly

[1]**material** /mə'tɪərɪəl/ *adj* **1a(1)** of, derived from, or consisting of matter; *esp* physical **(2)** bodily **b** of matter rather than form **2** important, significant **3** of or concerned with physical rather than spiritual things – ~**ly** *adv*

[2]**material** *n* **1a** the elements, constituents, or substances of which sthg is composed or can be made **b(1)** data that may be worked into a more finished form (2) a person considered with a view to his/her potential for successful training **c** cloth **2** *pl* apparatus necessary for doing or making sthg

materialism /mə'tɪərɪəlɪzəm/ *n* **1a** a theory that only physical matter is real and that all processes and phenomena can be explained by reference to matter **b** a doctrine that the highest values lie in material well-being and material progress **2** a preoccupation with or stress on material rather than spiritual things – **-ist** *n, adj* – **-istic** *adj* – **-istically** *adv*

material·ize, -ise /mə'tɪərɪəlaiz/ *v* **1** to (cause to) have existence **2** to (cause to) appear in or assume bodily form

maternal /mə'tɜːnəl/ *adj* **1** (characteristic) of a mother **2** related through a mother – **~ly** *adv*

[1]**maternity** /mə'tɜːnɪ̧ti/ *n* **1a** motherhood **b** motherliness **2** a hospital department for the care of women before and during childbirth

[2]**maternity** *adj* designed for wear during pregnancy

[1]**matey** /'meɪti/ *n, chiefly Br* mate – chiefly in familiar address

[2]**matey** *adj, chiefly Br* friendly – infml

mathematics /,mæθɪ̧'mætɪks/ *n pl but sing or pl in constr* the science of numbers and their operations, interrelations, and combinations and of space configurations and their structure, measurement, etc – **-ical** *adj* – **-ically** *adv* – **-ician** *n*

matinée, matinee /'mætɪ̧neɪ/ *n* a musical or dramatic performance during the day, esp the afternoon

matins /'mætɪ̧nz/ *n pl but sing or pl in constr, often cap* morning prayer

matriarchy /'meɪtriɑːki/ *n* a (system of) social organization in which the female is the head of the family, and descent and inheritance are traced through the female line – **matriarch** *n* – **-archal** *adj*

matricide /'mætrɪ̧saɪd/ *n* (the act of) one who kills his/her mother

matriculate /mə'trɪkjʊleɪt/ *v* to enrol as a member of a body, esp a college or university – **-lation** *n*

matrilineal /,mætrɪ'lɪnɪəl, ,meɪtrɪ-/ *adj* of or tracing descent through the maternal line

matrimony /'mætrɪ̧məni/ *n* marriage – **-monial** *adj*

matrix /'meɪtrɪks/ *n, pl* **matrices, matrixes** **1** a substance, environment, etc within which sthg else originates or develops **2** a mould in which sthg is cast or from which a surface in relief (e g a piece of type) is made by pouring or pressing

matron /'meɪtrən/ *n* **1a** a (dignified mature) married woman **b** a woman in charge of living arrangements in a school, residential home, etc **2** *Br* a woman in charge of the nursing in a hospital – not now used technically

[1]**matt, mat, matte** /mæt/ *v* to make (e g metal or colour) matt

[2]**matt, mat, matte** *adj* lacking lustre or gloss; *esp* having an even surface free from shine or highlights

[3]**matt, mat, matte** *n* **1** a border round a picture between the picture and frame or serving as the frame **2** a dull or roughened finish (e g on gilt or paint)

[1]**matter** /'mætə^r/ *n* **1a** a subject of interest or concern or which merits attention **b** an affair, concern **c** material (for treatment) in thought, discourse, or writing **d** a condition (unfavourably) affecting a person or thing **2a** the substance of which a physical object is composed **b** material substance that occupies space and has mass **c** sthg of a specified kind or for a specified purpose **d** material discharged by suppuration; pus

[2]**matter** *v* to be of importance

matter of course *n* sthg routine or to be expected as a natural consequence – **matter-of-course** *adj*

matter-of-fact *adj* keeping to or concerned with fact; *esp* not fanciful or imaginative

matting /'mætɪŋ/ *n* material (e g hemp) for mats

mattock /'mætək/ *n* a digging tool with a head like that of a pick and often a blade like that of an axe or adze

mattress /'mætrɨs/ *n* a fabric casing filled with resilient material (e g foam rubber or an arrangement of coiled springs) used esp on a bed

[1]**mature** /mə'tʃʊə'/ *adj* **1** based on careful consideration **2a** having completed natural growth and development; adult **b** having attained a final or desired state **3** older or more experienced than others of his/her kind – **-rity** *n* – **~ly** *adv*

[2]**mature** *v* **1** to bring to full development or completion **2** to become due for payment – **-ration** *n*

maudlin /'mɔːdlɪn/ *adj* **1** weakly and effusively sentimental **2** drunk enough to be emotionally silly

[1]**maul** /mɔːl/ *v* **1** *esp of an animal* to attack and tear the flesh of **2** to handle roughly

[2]**maul** *n* **1** a situation in Rugby Union in which 1 or more players from each team close round the player carrying the ball who tries to get the ball out to his own team **2** a confused and noisy struggle

maunder /'mɔːndə/ *v* **1** to act or wander idly **2** to speak in a rambling or indistinct manner; *also, Br* to grumble

Maundy Thursday /,mɔːndi 'θɜːzdi, -deɪ/ *n* the Thursday before Easter observed in commemoration of the Last Supper

mausoleum /,mɔːsə'lɪəm/ *n, pl* **mausoleums** *also* **mausolea** a large and elaborate tomb

mauve /məʊv/ *n or adj* bluish purple

maverick /'mævərɪk/ *n* **1** an independent and nonconformist individual **2** *NAm* an unbranded range animal; *esp* a motherless calf

mawkish /'mɔːkɪʃ/ *adj* sickly or feebly sentimental – **~ly** *adv* – **~ness** *n*

maxi /'mæksi/ *n, pl* **maxis** a floor-length woman's coat, skirt, etc

maxim /'mæksɨm/ *n* (a succinct expression of) a general truth, fundamental principle, or rule of conduct

maximal /'mæksɨməl/ *adj* greatest; most comprehensive – **~ly** *adv*

maximum /'mæksɨməm/ *n, pl* **maxima, maximums** **1** the greatest quantity or value attainable or attained **2** the period of highest or most extreme development – **-mize** *v*

may /meɪ/ *verbal auxiliary, pres sing & pl* **may**; *past* **might** **1a** have permission to; have liberty to **b** be in some degree likely to **2** – used to express a wish or desire, esp in prayer, curse, or benediction (e g long *may* he reign) **3** – used to express purpose or expectation (e g sit here so I *may* you better) contingency (e g he'll do his duty come what *may*); or concession (e g he *may* be slow, but he's thorough); used in questions to emphasize ironic uncertainty (e g and who *may* you be?)

May *n* **1** the 5th month of the Gregorian calendar **2** *not cap* (the blossom of) hawthorn

maybe /'meɪbi/ *adv* perhaps

May Day *n* May 1 celebrated as a springtime festival and in many countries as a public holiday in honour of working people

mayfly /'meɪflaɪ/ *n* any of an order of insects with an aquatic nymph and a short-lived fragile adult with membranous wings

mayhem /'meɪhem/ *n* **1** needless or wilful damage **2** a state of great confusion or disorder

mayonnaise /,meɪə'neɪz/ *n* a thick dressing (e g for salad) made with egg yolks, vegetable oil, and vinegar or lemon juice

mayor /meə'/ *n* the chief executive or nominal head of a city or borough – **~al** *adj*

mayoress /'meərɨs/ *n* **1** the wife or hostess of a mayor **2** a female mayor

maypole /'meɪpəʊl/ *n* a tall ribbon-wreathed pole forming a centre for dances, esp on May Day

maze *n* **1** (a drawn representation of) a network of paths designed to confuse and puzzle those who attempt to walk through it **2** sthg intricately or confusingly complicated

mazurka /mə'zɜːkə/ *n* (music for, or in the rhythm of) a Polish folk dance in moderate triple time

[1]**me** /mi; *strong* miː/ *pron, objective case of* **I** (e g fatter than *me*; it's *me*)

[2]**me** *n* sthg suitable for me (e g that dress isn't really *me*)

[3]**me** *n* the 3rd note of the diatonic scale in solmization

[1]**mead** /miːd/ *n* a fermented alcoholic drink made of water, honey, malt, and yeast

[2]**mead** *n* a meadow – archaic or poetic

meadow /ˈmedəʊ/ *n* (an area of moist low-lying usu level) grassland

meadowsweet /ˈmedəʊswiːt/ *n* a tall plant with creamy-white fragrant flowers

meagre /ˈmiːgəʳ/ *adj* **1** having little flesh **2** deficient in quality or quantity – **~ly** *adv* – **~ness** *n*

[1]**meal** /miːl/ *n* **1** the portion of food taken or provided at 1 time to satisfy appetite **2** (the time of) eating a meal

[2]**meal** *n* (a product resembling, esp in texture) the usu coarsely ground seeds of a cereal grass or pulse

mealy /ˈmiːli/ *adj* **1** soft, dry, and crumbly **2** containing meal **3** covered with meal or fine granules

mealy-mouthed /ˌmiːli ˈmaʊðd/ *adj* unwilling to speak plainly or directly, esp when this may offend

[1]**mean** /miːn/ *adj* **1** lacking distinction or eminence; merely ordinary or inferior **2** of poor shabby inferior quality or status **3** not honourable or worthy; base; *esp* small-minded **4a** not generous **b** characterized by petty malice; spiteful **c** *chiefly NAm* particularly bad-tempered, unpleasant, or disagreeable – **~ly** *adv* – **~ness** *n*

[2]**mean** *v* **meant** **1** to have in mind as a purpose; intend **2** to serve or intend to convey, produce, or indicate; signify **3** to intend for a particular use or purpose **4** to have significance or importance to the extent or degree of

[3]**mean** *n* **1a** a middle point between extremes **b** a value that lies within a range of values and is computed according to a prescribed law; *esp* an average **2** *pl but sing or pl in constr* that which enables a desired purpose to be achieved; *also* the method used to attain an end **3** *pl* resources available for disposal; *esp* wealth

[4]**mean** *adj* **1** occupying a middle position; intermediate in space, order, time, kind, or degree **2** being the mean of a set of values

[1]**meander** /miˈændəʳ/ *n* a turn or winding of a stream – usu pl

[2]**meander** *v* to wander aimlessly without urgent destination

[1]**meaning** /ˈmiːnɪŋ/ *n* **1** that which is conveyed or which one intends to convey, esp by language **2** significant quality; value **3** implication of a hidden or special significance – **~less** *adj*

[2]**meaning** *adj* significant, expressive

means test *n* an examination into sby's financial state to determine whether he/she should receive public assistance, a student grant, etc

meant /ment/ *adj, past of* **mean** *Br* expected, supposed

[1]**meantime** /ˈmiːntaɪm/ *n* the intervening time

[2]**meantime** *adv* meanwhile

mean time *n* time that is based on the motion of the mean sun and that has the mean solar second as its unit

[1]**meanwhile** /ˈmiːnwaɪl/ *n* the meantime

[2]**meanwhile** *adv* **1** during the intervening time **2** during the same period (e g *meanwhile,* down on the farm)

measles /ˈmiːzəlz/ *n pl but sing or pl in constr* an infectious virus disease marked by a rash of distinct red circular spots

measly /ˈmiːzli/ *adj* contemptibly small; *also* worthless – infml – **-liness** *n*

[1]**measure** /ˈmeʒəʳ/ *n* **1a(1)** an appropriate or due portion **(2)** a (moderate) extent, amount, or degree **(3)** a fixed, suitable, or conceivable limit **b(1)** the dimensions, capacity, or amount of sthg ascertained by measuring **(2)** the character, nature, or capacity of sby or sthg ascertained by assessment – esp in *get the measure of* **c** a measured quantity **2a** an instrument or utensil for measuring **b** a standard or unit of measurement **3a** a (slow and stately) dance **b(1)** poetic rhythm measured by quantity or accent **(2)** musical time **c(1)** the notes and rests that form a bar of music **(2)** a metrical unit; a foot **4** a basis or standard of comparison **5a** a step planned or taken to achieve an end **b** a proposed legislative act

[2]measure *v* **1** to take or allot in measured amounts – usu + *out* **2** to mark off by making measurements – often + *off* **3** to ascertain the measurements of **4** to estimate or appraise by a criterion – usu + *against* or *by*

measured /'meʒəd/ *adj* **1** rhythmical; *esp* slow and regular **2** carefully thought out

measureless /'meʒəlɨs/ *adj* having no observable limit; immeasurable

measurement /'meʒəmənt/ *n* **1** measuring **2** a figure, extent, or amount obtained by measuring

measure up *v* to have necessary or fitting qualifications – often + *to*

meat /miːt/ *n* **1** food; *esp* solid food as distinguished from drink **2** animal tissue used as food **3** the core or essence of sthg

meaty /'miːty/ *adj* **1** full of meat; fleshy **2** rich in matter for thought **3** of or like meat – **meatiness** *n*

mecca /'mekə/ *n, often cap* a place regarded as a goal (by a specified group of people)

mechanic /mɪ'kænɪk/ *n* a skilled worker who repairs or maintains machinery

mechanical /mɪ'kænɪkəl/ *adj* **1a** of or using machinery **b** made, operated by, or being a machine or machinery **2** done as if by machine; lacking in spontaneity **3** of, dealing with, or in accordance with (the principles of) mechanics – **~ly** *adv*

mechanics /mɪ'kænɪks/ *n pl but sing or pl in constr* **1** the physics and mathematics of (the effect on moving and stationary bodies of) energy and forces **2** the practical application of mechanics to the design, construction, or operation of machines or tools

mechanism /'mekənɪzəm/ *n* **1** a piece of machinery **2** mechanical operation or action **3** a theory that all natural processes are mechanically determined and can be explained by the laws of physics and chemistry – **-istic** *adj* – **-istically** *adv* – **-ize** *v*

medal /'medl/ *n* a piece of metal with a (stamped) design, emblem, inscription, etc that commemorates a person or event or is awarded for excellence or achievement

medallion /mɨ'dælɪən/ *n* **1** a large medal **2** a decorative tablet, panel, etc, often bearing a figure or portrait in relief

meddle /'medl/ *v* to interest oneself in what is not one's concern; interfere unduly – usu + *in* or *with* – **~r** *n* – **~some** *adj*

media /'miːdɪə/ *pl of* **medium**

medial /'miːdɪəl/ *adj* being, occurring in, or extending towards the middle; median – **~ly** *adv*

[1]median /'miːdɪən/ *n* a value in a series above and below which there are an equal number of values

[2]median *adj* **1** in the middle or in an intermediate position **2** lying in the plane that divides an animal into right and left halves

[1]mediate /'miːdɪət/ *adj* acting through an intervening agent or agency

[2]mediate /'miːdieɪt/ *v* **1** to intervene between parties in order to reconcile them **2** to transmit or effect by acting as an intermediate mechanism or agency

medic /'medɪk/ *n* a medical doctor or student – infml

[1]medical /'medɪkəl/ *adj* **1** of or concerned with physicians or the practice of medicine **2** requiring or devoted to medical treatment – **~ly** *adv*

[2]medical *n* an examination to determine sby's physical fitness

medicament /mɨ'dɪkəmənt, 'medɪ-/ *n* a medicine

medicate /'medɨkeɪt/ *v* to impregnate with a medicinal substance – **-tion** *n*

medicinal /mɨ'dɪsənəl/ *n or adj* (a substance) tending or used to cure disease or relieve pain – **~ly** *adv*

medicine /'medsən, 'medɨsən/ *n* **1** a substance or preparation used (as if) in treating disease **2** the science and art of the maintenance of health and the prevention and treatment of disease (using nonsurgical methods)

medicine ball *n* a heavy ball that is usu thrown between people for exercise

medicine man *n* a healer or sorcerer, esp among the N American Indians

medieval, mediaeval /,medi'iːvəl/ *adj* of or like the Middle Ages

mediocre /,miːdi'əʊkər/ *adj* **1** neither good nor bad; indifferent; *esp* conspicuously lacking distinction or imagination 2 not good enough; fairly bad – -**crity** *n*

meditate /'medɟteɪt/ *v* **1** to engage in deep or serious reflection **2** to empty the mind of thoughts and fix the attention on 1 matter, esp as a religious exercise – -**tion** *n* – -**tive** *adj* – -**tively** *adv*

Mediterranean /,medɟtə'reɪnɪən/ *adj* **1** of or characteristic of (the region round) the Mediterranean sea **2** of or resembling a physical type of the Caucasian race characterized by medium or short stature, slender build, and dark complexion

¹medium /'miːdɪəm/ *n, pl* **mediums, media 1** (sthg in) a middle position or state **2** a means of effecting or conveying sthg: e g **a(1)** a substance regarded as the means of transmission of a force or effect **(2)** a surrounding or enveloping substance **b** a mode of artistic expression or communication **c** one through whom others seek to communicate with the spirits of the dead **3a** a condition or environment in which sthg may function or flourish **b** a nutrient for the artificial cultivation of bacteria and other (single-celled) organisms **c** a liquid with which dry pigment can be mixed

²medium *adj* intermediate in amount, quality, position, or degree

medium wave *n* a band of radio waves, typically used for sound broadcasting, covering wavelengths between about 180m and 600m – sometimes pl with sing. meaning

medley /'medli/ *n* **1** a (confused) mixture **2** a musical composition made up of a series of songs or short musical pieces

meek /miːk/ *adj* **1** patient and without resentment **2** lacking spirit and courage; timid – ~**ly** *adv* – ~**ness** *n*

¹meet /miːt/ *v* **met 1a** to come into the presence of by accident or design **b** to be present to greet the arrival of **c** to come into contact or conjunction with **2** to encounter as antagonist or foe **3** to answer, esp in opposition **4** to conform to, esp exactly and precisely; satisfy **5** to pay fully **6** to become acquainted with **7** to experience during the course of sthg

²meet *n* the assembling of participants for a hunt or for competitive sports

³meet *adj* suitable, proper – fml

meeting /'miːtɪŋ/ *n* **1** a coming together: e g **a** an assembly of people for a common purpose **b** a session of horse or greyhound racing **2** a permanent organizational unit of the Quakers **3** an intersection, junction

megahertz /'megəhɜːts/ *n* a unit of frequency equal to 1,000,000 hertz

megalith /'megə,lɪθ/ *n* a huge undressed block of stone used in prehistoric monuments

megalomania /,megələ'meɪnɪə/ *n* **1** a mania for grandiose things **2** feelings of personal omnipotence and grandeur occurring as a delusional mental disorder – ~**c** *n*

megaphone /'megəfəʊn/ *n* a hand-held device used to amplify or direct the voice

megaton /'megətʌn/ *n* an explosive force (of an atom or hydrogen bomb) equivalent to that of 1,000,000 tons of TNT

meiosis /maɪ'əʊsɟs/ *n, pl* **meioses 1** understatement **2** a specialized process of cell division in gamete-producing cells by which 1 of each pair of chromosomes passes to each resulting gamete cell which thus has half the number of chromosomes of the original cell

¹melancholy /'melənkəli/ *n* **1** (a tendency to) bad temper or depression; melancholia **2a** depression of mind or spirits **b** a sad pensive mood – -**olic** *adj*

²melancholy *adj* **1** depressed in spirits; dejected **2** causing, tending to cause, or expressing sadness or depression

mélange /'meɪlɒnʒ/ *n* a mixture (of incongruous elements)

mêlée /'meleɪ/ *n* a confused or riotous struggle; *esp* a general hand-to-hand fight

mellifluous /mɟ'lɪfluəs/ *adj* smoothly or sweetly flowing

mellow /'meləʊ/ *adj* **1** *of a fruit* tender and sweet because ripe **2a** made gentle by age or experience **b** rich and full but free from harshness **c** pleasantly intoxicated

melodious /mʝ'ləʊdɪəs/ *adj* of or producing (a pleasing) melody – **~ly** *adv* – **~ness** *n*

melodrama /'melədrɑːmə/ *n* **1a** a work (e g a film or play) characterized by crude emotional appeal and by the predominance of plot and action over characterization **b** the dramatic genre comprising such works **2** sensational or sensationalized events or behaviour

melody /'melədi/ *n* **1** an agreeable succession or arrangement of sounds **2a** a rhythmic succession of single notes organized as an aesthetic whole **b** the chief part in a harmonic composition – **-dic** *adj*

melon /'melən/ *n* (any of various plants of the cucumber family having) a fruit (e g a watermelon) containing sweet edible flesh and usu eaten raw

[1]**melt** /melt/ *v* **1** to become altered from a solid to a liquid state, usu by heating **2a** to dissolve, disintegrate **b** to disappear as if by dissolving **3** to be or become mild, tender, or gentle

[2]**melt** *n* the spleen, esp when used as food

member /'membəʳ/ *n* **1** a part or organ of the body: e g **a** a limb **b** the penis – euph **2a** an individual or unit belonging to or forming part of a group or organization **b** *often cap* one who is entitled to sit in a legislative body; *esp* a member of Parliament **3a** a constituent part of a whole **b** a beam or similar (load-bearing) structure, esp in a building

membership /'membəʃɪp/ *n sing or pl in constr* the body of members

membrane /'membreɪn/ *n* a thin pliable sheet or layer, esp in an animal or plant – **-anous** *adj*

memento /mʝ'mentəʊ/ *n* sthg (e g a souvenir) that serves as a reminder of past events, people, etc

memo /'meməʊ/ *n* a memorandum

memoir /'memwɑːʳ/ *n* **1a** a narrative written from personal experience **b** an autobiography – usu pl with sing. meaning **c** a biography **2** a learned essay on a particular topic *USE* (*1a&1c*) often pl with sing. meaning

memorable /'memərəbəl/ *adj* worth remembering; notable – **-bly** *adv*

memorandum /,memə'rændəm/ *n, pl* **memorandums, memoranda** **1** an often unsigned informal record or communication; *also* a written reminder **2** a document recording the terms of an agreement, the formation of a company, etc **3** a usu brief communication for internal circulation (e g within an office)

[1]**memorial** /mʝ'mɔːrɪəl/ *adj* serving to commemorate a person or event

[2]**memorial** *n* sthg, esp a monument, that commemorates a person or event

memory /'meməri/ *n* **1** (the power or process of recalling or realizing) the store of things learned and retained from an organism's experience **2** commemorative remembrance **3a** (the object of) recall or recollection **b** the time within which past events can be or are remembered **4** (the capacity of) a device in which information, esp for a computer, can be inserted and stored, and from which it may be extracted when wanted – **-orize** *v*

men /men/ *pl of* **man**

[1]**menace** /'menʝs/ *n* **1** a show of intention to inflict harm; a threat **2a** a source of danger **b** a person who causes annoyance

[2]**menace** *v* to threaten or show intent to harm – **-acingly** *adv*

ménage à trois /,menɑːʒ ɑː 'trwɑː/ *n* a relationship in which 3 people, esp a married couple and the lover of 1, live together

menagerie /mʝ'nædʒəri/ *n* a place where animals are kept and trained, esp for exhibition; *also* a zoo

[1]**mend** /mend/ *v* **1** to improve or rectify **2** to restore to sound condition or working order; repair – **~er** *n*

[2]**mend** *n* a mended place or part

Mendelian /men'diːlɪən/ *adj* of or according with the genetic principle that genes occur in pairs, each gamete receives 1 member of each pair, and that an organism thus has 1 gene of each pair randomly selected from each of its parents

mendicant /'mendʝkənt/ *n* a beggar

menfolk /'menfəʊk/ *n pl in constr* **1**

men in general **2** the men of a family or community

[1]**menial** /ˈmiːnɪəl/ *adj* **1** of servants; lowly **2a** degrading; *also* servile **b** lacking in interest or status – **~ly** *adv*

[2]**menial** *n* a domestic servant or retainer

meningitis /ˌmenɨ̥nˈdʒaɪtɨ̥s/ *n* inflammation of the membrane enclosing the brain and spinal cord

meniscus /mɨ̥ˈnɪskəs/ *n, pl* **menisci** the curved concave or convex upper surface of a column of liquid

menopause /ˈmenəpɔːz/ *n* (the time of) the natural cessation of menstruation occurring usu between the ages of 45 and 50

menses /ˈmensiːz/ *n pl but sing or pl in constr* the menstrual flow

menstruation /ˌmenstrʊˈeɪʃən/ *n* the monthly discharging of blood and tissue debris from the uterus in nonpregnant females – **-truate** *v* – **-trual** *adj*

mensuration /ˌmenʃəˈreɪʃən/ *n* geometry applied to the computation of lengths, areas, or volumes

mental /ˈmentl/ *adj* **1a** of the mind or its activity **b** of intellectual as contrasted with emotional or physical activity **c** (performed or experienced) in the mind **2** of, being, or (intended for the care of people) suffering from a psychiatric disorder **3** crazy; *also* stupid – infml – **~ly** *adv*

mentality /menˈtælɨ̥ti/ *n* **1** mental power or capacity; intelligence **2** a mode of thought; mental disposition or outlook

menthol /ˈmenθɒl/ *n* an alcohol that occurs esp in mint oils and has the smell and cooling properties of peppermint – **~ated** *adj*

[1]**mention** /ˈmenʃən/ *n* **1** a brief reference to sthg; a passing remark **2** a formal citation for outstanding achievement

[2]**mention** *v* to make mention of; refer to

mentor /ˈmentəʳ/ *n* a wise and trusted adviser

menu /ˈmenjuː/ *n* (a list of) the dishes that may be ordered (e g in a restaurant) or that are to be served (e g at a banquet)

Mephistopheles /ˌmefɨ̥ˈstɒfɨ̥liːz/ *n* a devilish or fiendish person – **~lean** *adj*

mercantile /ˈmɜːkəntaɪl/ *adj* of or concerned with merchants or trading

Mercator's projection /məˌkeɪtəz prəˈdʒekʃən/ *n* a map projection showing the lines of longitude as parallel evenly-spaced straight lines and the lines of latitude as parallel straight lines whose distance from each other increases with their distance from the equator

[1]**mercenary** /ˈmɜːsənəri/ *n* a hired soldier in foreign service

[2]**mercenary** *adj* **1** serving merely for (financial) reward **2** hired for service in the army of a foreign country

merchandise /ˈmɜːtʃəndaɪs, -daɪz/ *n* **1** the commodities that are bought and sold in commerce **2** wares for sale

[1]**merchant** /ˈmɜːtʃənt/ *n* **1** a wholesaler; *also, chiefly NAm* a shopkeeper **2** a person who is given to a specified activity – chiefly derog

[2]**merchant** *adj* of or used in commerce; *esp* of a merchant navy

merchantman /ˈmɜːtʃəntmən/ *n* a ship used in commerce

merchant navy *n, Br* (the personnel of) the privately or publicly owned commercial ships of a nation

mercury /ˈmɜːkjʊri/ *n* **1** a heavy silver-white poisonous univalent or bivalent metallic element that is liquid at ordinary temperatures and used in thermometers, barometers, etc **2** *cap* the planet nearest the sun

mercy /ˈmɜːsi/ *n* **1** compassion or forbearance shown esp to an offender **2a** an act of divine compassion; a blessing **b** a fortunate circumstance **3** compassionate treatment of those in distress – **merciful** *adj*

[1]**mere** /mɪəʳ/ *n* a (small) lake

[2]**mere** *adj* being what is specified and nothing else; nothing more than – **~ly** *adv*

meretricious /ˌmerɨ̥ˈtrɪʃəs/ *adj* **1** tawdrily and falsely attractive **2** based on pretence or insincerity; specious – **~ly** *adv* – **~ness** *n*

merge /mɜːdʒ/ *v* **1** to (cause to) combine or unite **2** to blend or (cause to) come together gradually without abrupt change

merger /ˈmɜːdʒəʳ/ *n* a combining or combination, esp of 2 organizations (e g business concerns)

meridian /məˈrɪdɪən/ *n* **1** a great circle passing through the poles of the celestial sphere and the zenith of a given place **2** a high point, esp of success or greatness

meringue /məˈræŋ/ *n* (a small cake, cream-filled shell, etc made with) a mixture of stiffly beaten egg whites and sugar baked until crisp

merino /məˈriːnəʊ/ *n* **1** (any of) a breed of fine-woolled white orig Spanish sheep **3** a fine wool and cotton yarn used for hosiery and knitwear

¹merit /ˈmerɨt/ *n* **1a** the quality of deserving well or ill **b** a praiseworthy quality; virtue **c** worth, excellence **2** *pl* the intrinsic rights and wrongs of a (legal) case

²merit *v* to be worthy of or entitled to

meritocracy /ˌmerɨˈtɒkrəsi/ *n* (a social system based on) leadership by the talented

meritorious /ˌmerɨˈtɔːrɪəs/ *adj* deserving of reward or honour – **~ly** *adv*

mermaid /ˈmɜːmeɪd/ *n* a mythical sea creature usu represented with a woman's body to the waist and a fish's tail

merriment /ˈmerɪmənt/ *n* light-hearted gaiety or fun

merry /ˈmeri/ *adj* **1** full of gaiety or high spirits **2** marked by festivity **3** slightly drunk; tipsy – infml – **-rily** *adv* – **-riness** *n*

merry-go-round *n* a fairground machine with seats, often shaped like horses, that revolve about a fixed centre

merrymaking /ˈmeriˌmeɪkɪŋ/ *n* gay or festive activity – **-maker** *n*

mescal /meˈskæl/ *n* **1** a small cactus with rounded stems covered with protuberances containing a hallucinogenic substance **2** a usu colourless Mexican spirit made from various plants

¹mesh /meʃ/ *n* **1** an open space in a net, network, etc **2a** the cords, wires, etc that make up a net **b** a woven, knitted, or knotted fabric with evenly spaced small holes **3a** an interlocking or intertwining arrangement or construction **b** a web, snare – usu pl with sing. meaning **4** working contact (e g of the teeth of gears)

²mesh *v* **1** to catch or entangle (as if) in the openings of a net **2** to cause to engage **3** to fit or work together properly or successfully

mesmer·ize, -ise /ˈmezməraɪz/ *v* **1** to hypnotize **2** to fascinate

¹mess /mes/ *n* **1** a prepared dish of soft or liquid food; *also* a usu unappetizing mixture of ingredients eaten together **2** *sing or pl in constr* a group of people (e g servicemen or servicewomen) who regularly take their meals together **3a** a confused, dirty, or offensive state or condition **b** a disordered situation resulting from misunderstanding, blundering, or misconduct

²mess *v* **1** to take meals with a mess **2** to make a mess **3a** to dabble, potter **b** to handle or play *with* sthg, esp carelessly **c** to interfere, meddle *USE* (*3*) often + *about* or *around*

mess about *v* **1** to waste time **2a** to conduct an affair *with* **b** to treat roughly or without due consideration

message /ˈmesɪdʒ/ *n* **1** a communication in writing, in speech, or by signals **2** a central theme or idea intended to inspire, urge, warn, enlighten, advise, etc

messenger /ˈmesəndʒəʳ/ *n* one who bears a message or does an errand: e g **a** a dispatch bearer in government or military service **b** an employee who carries messages

messiah /mɨˈsaɪə/ *n* **1** *often cap* **a** *the* expected king and deliverer of the Jews **b** Jesus **2** a professed leader of some cause – **-ianic** *adj*

Messrs /ˈmesəz/ *pl of* **Mr**

messy /ˈmesi/ *adj* **1** marked by confusion, disorder, or dirt **2** lacking neatness or precision; slovenly **3** unpleasantly or tryingly difficult to conclude – **messily** *adv* – **messiness** *n*

¹met /met/ *past of* **meet**

²met *adj* meteorological

metabolism /mɨˈtæbəlɪzəm/ *n* the chemical changes in living cells by which energy is provided and new material is assimilated – **-ic** *adj*

metacarpal /,metə'kɑːpəl/ *n* a bone of the hand or forefoot between the wrist and fingers

metal /'metl/ *n* any of various opaque, fusible, ductile, and typically lustrous substances (e g iron, copper, or mercury), esp chemical elements, that are good conductors of electricity and heat

metallic /mɪ̣'tælɪk/ *adj* **1** of, containing, like, or being (a) metal **2** yielding metal **3** having an acrid quality

metallurgy /'metəlɜːdʒi, mɪ̣'tælədʒi/ *n* the science and technology of metals – **-gical** *adj* – **-gist** *n*

metalwork /'metlwɜːk/ *n* the craft or product of shaping things out of metal – **~er** *n*

metamorphosis /,metə'mɔːfəsɪ̣s/ *n, pl* **metamorphoses** **1a** change of form, structure, or substance, esp by supernatural means **b** a striking alteration (e g in appearance or character) **2** a marked (abrupt) change in the form or structure of a butterfly, frog, etc occurring in the course of development

metaphor /'metəfəʳ, -fɔːʳ/ *n* (an instance of) a figure of speech in which a word or phrase literally denoting one kind of object or idea is applied to another to suggest a likeness or analogy between them (e g in *the ship ploughs the sea*) – **~ical** *adj*

metaphysical /,metə'fɪzɪkəl/ *adj* **1** of metaphysics **2** *often cap* of or being poetry, esp of the early 17th c, marked by elaborate subtleties of thought and expression – **~ly** *adv*

metaphysics /,metə'fɪzɪks/ *n pl but sing in constr* **1** a division of philosophy concerned with ultimate causes and the underlying nature of things **2** pure or speculative philosophy

metatarsal /,metə'tɑːsəl/ *n* a bone of the foot between the ankle and the toes

meteor /'miːtɪəʳ/ *n* (the streak of light produced by the passage of) any of many small particles of matter in the solar system observable only when heated by friction so that they glow as they fall into the earth's atmosphere

meteoric /,miːti'ɒrɪk/ *adj* resembling a meteor in speed or in sudden and temporary brilliance – **~ally** *adv*

meteorite /'miːtɪəraɪt/ *n* a meteor that reaches the surface of the earth without being completely vaporized

meteoroid /'miːtɪərɔɪd/ *n* a particle in orbit round the sun that becomes a meteor when it meets the earth's atmosphere

meteorology /,miːtɪə'rɒlədʒi/ *n* the science of the atmosphere and its phenomena, esp weather and weather forecasting – **-gical** *adj* – **-gist** *n*

[1]**meter** /'miːtəʳ/ *n, NAm* a metre

[2]**meter** *n* an instrument for measuring (and recording) the amount of sthg (e g gas, electricity, or parking time) used

[3]**meter** *v* **1** to measure by means of a meter **2** to supply in a measured or regulated amount

methane /'miːθeɪn/ *n* an inflammable hydrocarbon gas used as a fuel and as a raw material in chemical synthesis

method /'meθəd/ *n* **1a** a systematic procedure for doing sthg **b** a regular way of doing sthg **2a** an orderly arrangement or system **b** the habitual practice of orderliness and regularity

methodical /mɪ̣'θɒdɪkəl/ *adj* **1** arranged, characterized by, or performed with method or order **2** habitually proceeding according to method; systematic – **~ly** *adv*

Methodism /'meθədɪzəm/ *n* (the doctrines and practice of) the churches derived from the teachings of John Wesley – **-dist** *adj, n*

methodology /,meθə'dɒlədʒi/ *n* (the analysis of) the body of methods and rules employed by a science or discipline – **-gical** *adj* – **-gically** *adv*

meths /meθs/ *n pl but sing in constr, Br* methylated spirits – infml

methylated spirits /,meθɪ̣leɪtɪ̣d 'spɪrɪ̣ts/ *n pl but sing or pl in constr* alcohol mixed with a substance that makes it undrinkable so that it can be sold exempt from duty

meticulous /mɪ̣'tɪkjʊləs/ *adj* marked by extreme or excessive care over detail – **~ly** *adv* – **~ness** *n*

métier /'metieɪ, 'meɪ-/ *n* one's trade; *also* sthg (e g an activity) in which one is expert or successful

[1]**metre,** *NAm chiefly* **meter** /'mi:tə^r/ *n* the SI unit of length equal to a certain number of wavelengths of a specific radiation of the krypton isotope $_{36}Kr^{86}$ (about 1.094yd)

[2]**metre,** *NAm chiefly* **meter** *n* **1** systematically arranged and measured rhythm in verse **2** a basic recurrent rhythmical pattern of accents and beats per bar in music

metric /'metrɪk/ *adj* (using or being units) based on the metre, litre, and kilogram as standard of measurement – **~ize** *v*

metrical /'metrɪkəl/, **metric** *adj* **1** of or composed in metre **2** of measurement – **~ly** *adv*

metric ton *n* a tonne

metro /'metrəʊ/ *n* an underground railway system in a city

metronome /'metrənəʊm/ *n* an instrument designed to mark exact time by a regularly repeated tick

metropolis /mɪ̱'trɒpəlɪ̱s/ *n* **1** the chief city of a country, state, or region **2** a centre of a usu specified activity – **-itan** *adj*

mettle /'metl/ *n* **1** strength of spirit or temperament **2** staying quality; stamina

mettlesome /'metlsəm/ *adj* spirited

mews /mju:z/ *n pl but sing or pl in constr, pl* **mews** *chiefly Br* (living accommodation adapted from) stables built round an open courtyard

mezzanine /'mezəni:n, 'metsə-/ *n* a low-ceilinged storey between 2 main storeys, esp the ground and first floors, of a building

mezzo /'metsəʊ/, **mezzo-soprano** *n* a woman's voice with a range between that of the soprano and contralto

mezzotint /,metsəʊ,tɪnt, 'medzəʊ-/ *n* (a print produced by) a method of engraving on copper or steel by scraping or burnishing a roughened surface to produce light and shade

mi /mi:/ *n* the 3rd note of the diatonic scale in solmization

miaow, meow /mi'aʊ/ *v or n* (to make) the characteristic cry of a cat

miasma /mi'æzmə, maɪ-/ *n, pl* **miasmas** *also* **miasmata** **1** a heavy vapour (e g from a swamp) formerly believed to cause disease; *broadly* any heavy or malodorous vapour **2** a pervasive influence that tends to weaken or corrupt – **~l** *adj*

mica /'maɪkə/ *n* any of various coloured or transparent silicate materials occurring as crystals that readily separate into very thin flexible leaves

mice /maɪs/ *pl of* **mouse**

Michaelmas /'mɪkəlməs/ *n* September 29 celebrated as the feast of St Michael the Archangel

Michaelmas daisy *n* any of several (Autumn-blooming) asters widely grown as garden plants

micro /'maɪkrəʊ/ *n* a microprocessor

microbe /'maɪkrəʊb/ *n* a microorganism, germ

microbiology /,maɪkrəʊbaɪ'ɒlədʒi/ *n* the biology of bacteria and other microscopic forms of life – **-gical** *adj* – **-gist** *n*

microcomputer /,maɪkrəʊkəm'pju:tə^r/ *n* a microprocessor

microcosm /'maɪkrəkɒzəm/ *n* **1** a little world; *esp* an individual human being or human nature seen as an epitome of the world or universe **2** a whole (e g a community) that is an epitome of a larger whole

microfilm /'maɪkrəʊ,fɪlm/ *n* a film bearing a photographic record on a reduced scale of graphic matter (e g printing)

micrometer /maɪ'krɒmɪ̱tə^r/ *n* a gauge for making precise measurements of length by means of a spindle moved by a finely threaded screw

microorganism /,maɪkrəʊ'ɔ:gənɪzəm/ *n* a very small, usu single celled, living creature

microphone /'maɪkrəfəʊn/ *n* a device that converts sounds into electrical signals, esp for transmission or recording

microprocessor /,maɪkrəʊ'prəʊsesə^r/ *n* a very small computer composed of 1 or more integrated circuits functioning as a unit

microscope /'maɪkrəskəʊp/ *n* an instrument consisting of (a combination of) lenses for making enlarged images of minute objects using light or other radiations – **-py** *n*

microscopic /,maɪkrə'skɒpɪk/ *adj* **1** of or conducted with the microscope or microscopy **2a** invisible or indistinguishable without the use of a microscope **b** very small, fine, or precise – **~ally** *adv*

microwave /'maɪkrəweɪv/ *n* a band of very short electromagnetic waves of between 1m and 0.1m in wavelength

[1]**mid** /mɪd/ *adj* **1** being the part in the middle or midst – often in combination **2** occupying a middle position

[2]**mid** *prep* amid – poetic

midday /ˌmɪd'deɪ/ *n* the middle part of the day; noon

midden /'mɪdn/ *n* **1** a dunghill **2** a heap or stratum of domestic rubbish found on the site of an ancient settlement

[1]**middle** /'mɪdl/ *adj* **1** equally distant from the extremes; central **2** at neither extreme

[2]**middle** *n* **1** a middle part, point, or position **2** the waist **3** the position of being among or in the midst of sthg **4** sthg intermediate between extremes; a mean

middle age *n* the period of life from about 40 to about 60

Middle Ages *n pl* the period of European history from about AD 500 to about 1500

middlebrow /'mɪdlbraʊ/ *adj* dealing with or having conventional intellectual and cultural interests and activities – often derog

middle class *n* a class occupying a position between upper and lower; *esp* a fluid heterogeneous grouping of business and professional people, bureaucrats, and some farmers and skilled workers – often pl with sing. meaning

middle ear *n* a cavity through which sound waves are transmitted by a chain of tiny bones from the eardrum to the inner ear

middleman /'mɪdlmæn/ *n* an intermediary between 2 parties; *esp* a dealer intermediate between the producer of goods and the retailer or consumer

middle school *n* (part of) a school for pupils aged 8–12 or 9–13

middleweight /'mɪdlweɪt/ *n* a boxer who weighs not more than about 11st 6lb

middling /'mɪdəlɪŋ/ *adj* **1** of middle or moderate size, degree, or quality **2** mediocre, second-rate

midfield /'mɪdfiːld/ *n* (the players who normally play in) the part of a pitch or playing field midway between the goals

midge /mɪdʒ/ *n* a tiny two-winged fly

midget /'mɪdʒɨt/ *n* **1** a very small person; a dwarf **2** sthg (e g an animal) much smaller than usual

midi /'mɪdi/ *n* a woman's garment that extends to the mid-calf

midland /'mɪdlənd/ *n, often cap* the central region of a country – usu pl with sing. meaning

midnight /'mɪdnaɪt/ *n* the middle of the night; *specif* 12 o'clock at night

mid-off *n* a fielding position in cricket near the bowler on the off side of the pitch

mid-on *n* a fielding position in cricket near the bowler on the leg side of the pitch

midriff /'mɪdrɪf/ *n* **1** the diaphragm **2** the middle part of the human torso

midshipman /'mɪdʃɪpmən/ *n* (the rank of) a young person training to become a naval officer

midst /mɪdst/ *n* **1** the inner or central part or point; the middle **2** a position near to the members of a group **3** the condition of being surrounded or beset (e g by problems) **4** a period of time about the middle of a continuing act or state

midsummer /ˌmɪd'sʌmə'/ *n* the summer solstice

midway /ˌmɪd'weɪ/ *adv* halfway

midweek /ˌmɪd'wiːk/ *n* the middle of the week

mid-wicket *n* a fielding position in cricket on the leg side equidistant from each wicket

midwife /'mɪdwaɪf/ *n* **1** a woman who assists other women in childbirth **2** sby or sthg that helps to produce or bring forth sthg – **~ry** *n*

mien /miːn/ *n* air or bearing, esp as expressive of mood or personality – fml

[1]**might** /maɪt/ *past of* **may** – used to express permission or liberty in the past (e g asked whether he *might* come), a past or present possibility

contrary to fact (e g I *might* well have been killed) purpose or expectation in the past (e g wrote it down so that I *might* not forget it), less probability or possibility than may (e g *might* get there before it rains), a polite request (e g you *might* post this letter for me), or as a polite or ironic alternative to *may* (e g who *might* you be?) or to *ought* or *should* (e g you *might* at least apologize)

²**might** *n* **1** power, authority, or resources wielded individually or collectively **2a** physical strength **b** all the power or effort one is capable of

mightily /ˈmaɪtʒli/ *adv* very much

¹**mighty** /ˈmaɪti/ *adj* **1** powerful **2** accomplished or characterized by might **3** imposingly great

²**mighty** *adv* to a great degree; extremely

migraine /ˈmiːgreɪn, ˈmaɪ-/ *n* recurrent severe headache usu associated with disturbances of vision, sensation, and movement often on only 1 side of the body

migrant /ˈmaɪgrənt/ *n* **1** a person who moves regularly in order to find work, esp in harvesting crops **2** an animal that moves from one habitat to another

migrate /maɪˈgreɪt/ *v* **1** to move from one country or locality to another **2** *of an animal* to pass usu periodically from one region or climate to another for feeding or breeding – **-ory** *adj*

mikado /mʒˈkɑːdəʊ/ *n, pl* **mikados** – formerly used as a title for the emperor of Japan

mike /maɪk/ *n* a microphone – infml

¹**mild** /maɪld/ *adj* **1** gentle in nature or manner **2a** not strong in flavour or effect **b** not being or involving what is extreme **3** not severe; temperate – **~ly** *adv* – **~ness** *n*

²**mild** *n, Br* a dark-coloured beer not flavoured with hops

¹**mildew** /ˈmɪldjuː/ *n* (a fungus producing) a usu whitish growth on the surface of organic matter (e g paper or leather) or living plants – **~y** *adj*

²**mildew** *v* to affect or become affected (as if) with mildew

mile /maɪl/ *n* **1** any of various units of distance: e g **a** a unit equal to 1760yd (about 1.61km) **b** a nautical mile **2 a** large distance or amount – often pl with sing. meaning

mileage /ˈmaɪlɪdʒ/ *n* **1** an allowance for travelling expenses at a certain rate per mile **2** total length or distance in miles: e g **a** the number of miles travelled (over a period of time) **b** the average distance in miles a vehicle will travel for an amount of fuel

milestone /ˈmaɪlstəʊn/ *n* **1** a stone serving as a milepost **2** a crucial stage in sthg's development

milieu /ˈmiːljɜː/ *n, pl* **milieus, milieux** an environment, setting

militant /ˈmɪlʒtənt/ *adj* **1** engaged in warfare or combat **2** aggressively active (e g in a cause); combative

militarism /ˈmɪlʒtərɪzəm/ *n* **1** exaltation of military virtues and ideals **2** a policy of aggressive military preparedness – **-rist** *n* – **-ristic** *adj* – **-ristically** *adv*

¹**military** /ˈmɪlʒtəri/ *adj* **1** (characteristic) of soldiers, arms, or war **2** carried on or supported by armed force **3** of the army or armed forces

²**military** *n* **1** *pl in constr* soldiers **2** *sing or pl in constr the* army (as opposed to civilians or police)

militate /ˈmɪlʒteɪt/ *v* to have significant weight or effect – usu + *against*

militia /mʒˈlɪʃə/ *n sing or pl in constr* a body of citizens with some military training who are called on to fight only in an emergency

¹**milk** /mɪlk/ *n* **1** a (white or creamy) liquid secreted by the mammary glands of females for the nourishment of their young (and used as a food by humans) **2** a milklike liquid: e g **a** the latex of a plant **b** the juice of a coconut **c** a cosmetic lotion, esp a cleanser

²**milk** *v* **1** to draw milk from the breasts or udder of **2** to draw sthg from as if by milking: e g **a** to induce (a snake) to eject venom **b** to compel or persuade to yield illicit or excessive profit or advantage

milk float *n, Br* a light usu electrically-propelled vehicle for carrying esp milk for domestic delivery

milkmaid /ˈmɪlkmeɪd/ *n* a female who works in a dairy

milkman /ˈmɪlkmən/ *n* one who sells or delivers milk

milk run *n* a regular journey or course

milk shake *n* a thoroughly shaken or blended beverage made of milk and a flavouring syrup

milk tooth *n* a tooth of a mammal, esp a child, that is replaced later in life

Milky Way *n* a broad irregular band of faint light that stretches completely round the celestial sphere and is caused by the light of the many stars forming the galaxy of which the sun and the solar system are a part

[1]**mill** /mɪl/ *n* **1** a building provided with machinery for grinding grain into flour **2a** a machine or apparatus for grinding grain **b** a machine or hand-operated device for crushing or grinding a solid substance (e g coffee beans or peppercorns) **3** a building or collection of buildings with machinery for manufacturing

[2]**mill** *v* **1a** to grind into flour, meal, or powder **b** to shape or dress by means of a rotary cutter **2** to give a raised rim or a ridged edge to (a coin) **3** to move in a confused swirling mass – usu + *about* or *around*

millennium /mɪˈlenɪəm/ *n, pl* **millennia** **1** a period of 1000 years **2a** *the* thousand years mentioned in Revelation 20 during which holiness is to prevail and Christ is to reign on earth **b** a (future) golden age

miller /ˈmɪləʳ/ *n* sby who owns or works a mill, esp for corn

millet /ˈmɪlʒt/ *n* (the seed of) any of various small-seeded annual cereal and forage grasses cultivated for their grain, used as food

milligram /ˈmɪlʒgræm/ *n* one thousandth of a gram (about 0.015 grain)

millilitre /ˈmɪlʒ,liːtəʳ/ *n* a thousandth of a litre (.002pt)

millimetre /ˈmɪlʒmiːtəʳ/ *n* one thousandth of a metre (about 0.039in)

milliner /ˈmɪlʒnəʳ/ *n* sby who designs, makes, trims, or sells women's hats – **~y** *n*

million /ˈmɪljən/ *n* **1** the number 1,000,000 **2** an indefinitely large number – infml; often pl with sing. meaning – **~th** *adj, n, pron, adv*

millionaire /,mɪljəˈneəʳ/ *n* sby whose wealth is estimated at a million or more money units

millipede, millepede /ˈmɪlʒpiːd/ *n* an insect-like creature with a many-segmented body and 2 pairs of legs on each segment

millrace /ˈmɪlreɪs/ *n* (the current in) a channel in which water flows to and from a mill wheel

millstone /ˈmɪlstəʊn/ *n* **1** either of a pair of circular stones that rotate against each other and are used for grinding (grain) **2** a heavy or crushing burden

millwright /ˈmɪlraɪt/ *n* sby who plans, builds, or maintains mills

milt /mɪlt/ *n* the male reproductive glands of fishes when filled with secretion

[1]**mime** /maɪm/ *n* **1** an ancient dramatic entertainment representing scenes from life usu in a ridiculous manner **2** the art of portraying a character or telling a story by body movement **3** sby who performs the art of mime

[2]**mime** *v* to act a part with mimic gesture and action, usu without words

mimetic /mʒˈmetɪk/ *adj* **1** imitative **2** relating to, characterized by, or exhibiting mimicry

[1]**mimic** /ˈmɪmɪk/ *adj* **1** imitation, mock **2** of mime or mimicry

[2]**mimic** *v* **-ck-** **1** to imitate slavishly; ape **2** to ridicule by imitation **3** to simulate

mimicry /ˈmɪmɪkri/ *n* **1** the act or an instance of mimicking **2** resemblance of one organism to another that secures it an advantage (e g protection from predation)

minaret /,mɪnəˈret, ˈmɪnəret/ *n* a slender tower attached to a mosque and surrounded by 1 or more projecting balconies from which the summons to prayer is made

[1]**mince** /mɪns/ *v* **1** to cut or chop into very small pieces **2** to walk with short affected steps

[2]**mince** *n* minced meat

mincemeat /ˈmɪns-miːt/ *n* a finely chopped mixture of raisins, apples, suet, spices, etc (with brandy) which traditionally used to contain meat

mince pie *n* a sweet usu small and round pie filled with mincemeat

[1]**mind** /maɪnd/ *n* **1** the (capabilities of the) organized conscious and unconscious mental processes of an organism that result in reasoning, thinking, perceiving, etc **2a** recollection, memory **b** attention, concentration **3** the normal condition of the mental faculties **4** a disposition, mood **5** the mental attributes of a usu specified group **6a** the intellect and rational faculties as contrasted with the emotions **b** the human spirit and intellect as opposed to the body and the material world

[2]**mind** *v* **1** to pay attention to or follow (advice, instructions, or orders) **2a** to be concerned about; care **b** to object to **3a** to be careful **b** to be attentive or wary – often + *out* **4** to give protective care to; look after

mind-blowing *adj* **1** of or causing a psychic state similar to that produced by a psychedelic drug **2** mentally or emotionally exhilarating *USE* infml

minded /ˈmaɪndʒd/ *adj* having a (specified kind of) mind – usu in combination

mindful /ˈmaɪndfəl/ *adj* keeping in mind; aware *of* – **~ness** *n*

mindless /ˈmaɪndlʒs/ *adj* **1** devoid of thought or intelligence; senseless **2** involving or requiring little thought or concentration **3** inattentive, heedless – usu + *of* – **~ly** *adv* – **~ness** *n*

mind's eye *n* the faculty of visual memory or imagination

[1]**mine** *pron, pl* **mine** that which or the one who belongs to me – used without a following noun as a pronoun equivalent in meaning to the adjective *my* (e g children younger than *mine*; that brother of *mine*)

[2]**mine** *n* **1** an excavation from which mineral substances are taken **2** an encased explosive designed to destroy enemy personnel, vehicles, or ships **3** a rich source *of*

[3]**mine** *v* **1** to dig an underground passage to gain access to or cause the collapse of (an enemy position) **2** to place military mines in, on, or under **3** to dig into for ore, coal, etc

minelayer /ˈmaɪnleɪəʳ/ *n* a vessel or aircraft for laying mines – **-laying** *n*

mineral /ˈmɪnərəl/ *n* **1** any of various naturally occurring substances (e g stone, coal, and petroleum) obtained by drilling, mining, etc **2** sthg neither animal nor vegetable

mineral water *n* water naturally or artificially impregnated with mineral salts or gases (e g carbon dioxide); *broadly* any effervescent nonalcoholic beverage

minestrone /ˌmɪnʒˈstrəʊni/ *n* a rich thick vegetable soup usu containing pasta (e g macaroni)

minesweeper /ˈmaɪnswiːpəʳ/ *n* a ship designed for removing or neutralizing mines – **-sweeping** *n*

mingle /ˈmɪŋgəl/ *v* **1** to bring or mix together or with sthg else **2** to mix with or go among a group of people

mingy /ˈmɪndʒi/ *adv* mean, stingy – infml

mini /mɪni/ *n, pl* **minis** **1** sthg small of its kind (e g a motor car) **2** a woman's skirt or dress with the hemline several inches above the knee

[1]**miniature** /ˈmɪnɪətʃəʳ, ˈmɪnʒtʃəʳ/ *n* **1a** a copy or representation on a much reduced scale **b** sthg small of its kind **2** a very small painting (e g a portrait on ivory or metal)

[2]**miniature** *adj* (represented) on a small or reduced scale

minibus /ˈmɪnibʌs/ *n* a small bus for carrying usu between 5 and 10 passengers

minim /ˈmɪnʒm/ *n* a musical note with the time value of 2 crotchets or ½ of a semibreve

minimal /ˈmɪnʒməl/ *adj* of or being a minimum; constituting the least possible – **~ly** *adv*

minimum /ˈmɪnʒməm/ *n, pl* **minima, minimums** **1** the least quantity or value assignable, admissible, or possible **2** the lowest degree or amount reached or recorded – **-mize** *v*

minion /ˈmɪnɪən/ *n* **1** a servile attendant **2** a minor official – derog

[1]**minister** /ˈmɪnʒstəʳ/ *n* **1** an agent **2** a clergyman, esp of a Protestant or nonconformist church **3** a high officer of state managing a division of government **4** a diplomatic representative

accredited to a foreign state – ~**ial** *adj* – ~**ially** *adv*

[2]**minister** *v* **1** to perform the functions of a minister of religion **2** to give aid or service

ministration /ˌmɪnɨ'streɪʃən/ *n* the act or process of ministering, esp in religious matters – **-trant** *n*

ministry /'mɪnɨstri/ *n* **1** service, ministration **2** the office, duties, or functions of a minister **3** the body of ministers of religion or government **4** the period of service or office of a minister or ministry **5** a government department presided over by a minister

mink /mɪŋk/ *n* **1** any of several semiaquatic flesh-eating mammals that resemble weasels and have partially webbed feet and a soft thick coat **2** the soft fur or pelt of the mink

minnow /'mɪnəʊ/ *n* **1** a small dark-coloured freshwater fish or any of various small fishes **2** sthg small or insignificant of its kind

[1]**minor** /'maɪnəʳ/ *adj* **1a** inferior in importance, size, rank, or degree **b** comparatively unimportant **2** not having attained majority **3a** *esp of a scale or mode* having semitones between the second and third, fifth and sixth, and sometimes seventh and eighth steps **b** being or based on a (specified) minor scale **4** not serious or involving risk to life

[2]**minor** *n* **1** sby who has not attained majority **2** a minor musical interval, scale, key, or mode

minority /maɪ'nɒrɨti/ *n* **1a** the period before attainment of majority **b** the state of being a legal minor **2** the smaller of 2 groups constituting a whole; *specif* a group with less than the number of votes necessary for control **3** *sing or pl in constr* a group of people who share common characteristics or interests differing from those of the majority of a population

Minotaur /'maɪnətɔːʳ/ *n* a mythological monster shaped half like a man and half like a bull and confined in the labyrinth at Crete

minster /'mɪnstəʳ/ *n* a large or important church often having cathedral status

minstrel /'mɪnstrəl/ *n* **1** a medieval singer, poet, or musical entertainer **2** any of a troupe of performers usu with blackened faces giving a performance of supposedly Negro singing, jokes, dancing, etc

[1]**mint** /mɪnt/ *n* **1** a place where money is made **2** a vast sum or amount – infml

[2]**mint** *v* **1** to make (e g coins) by stamping metal **2** to fabricate, invent

[3]**mint** *adj* unspoilt as if fresh from a mint; pristine

[4]**mint** *n* **1** any of a genus of plants that have leaves with a characteristic strong taste and smell, used esp as a flavouring **2** a sweet, chocolate, etc flavoured with mint

minuet /ˌmɪnjʊ'et/ *n* (music for or in the rhythm of) a slow graceful dance in $\frac{3}{4}$ time

[1]**minus** /'maɪnəs/ *prep* **1** diminished by **2** without

[2]**minus** *n* **1** a negative quantity **2** a deficiency, defect

[3]**minus** *adj* **1** negative **2** having negative qualities; *esp* involving a disadvantage

minuscule /'mɪnəskjuːl/ *adj* very small

[1]**minute** /'mɪnɨt/ *n* **1** the 60th part of an hour of time or of a degree **2** a short space of time; a moment **3a** a memorandum **b** *pl* the official record of the proceedings of a meeting

[2]**minute** *v* to make notes or a brief summary (of)

[3]**minute** /maɪ'njuːt/ *adj* **1** extremely small **2** of minor importance; petty **3** marked by painstaking attention to detail – ~**ness** *n*

minuteman /'mɪnɨtmæn/ *n* a member of a group of armed men pledged to take the field at a minute's notice during and immediately before the American Revolution

minutia /maɪ'njuːʃɪə, mɨ-/ *n, pl* **minutiae** a minor detail – usu pl

minx /mɪŋks/ *n* a flirtatious girl

miracle /'mɪrəkəl/ *n* **1** an extraordinary event manifesting divine intervention in human affairs **2** an astonishing or unusual event, thing, or accomplishment **3** a person or thing that is a remarkable example or instance of sthg

miracle play *n* a medieval drama

based on episodes from the Bible or the life of a saint

miraculous /mɪ̈'rækjʊləs/ *adj* **1** of the nature of a miracle; supernatural **2** evoking wonder like a miracle; marvellous – **~ly** *adv*

mirage /'mɪraːʒ/ *n* **1** an optical illusion appearing esp as a pool of water or as the reflection of distant objects caused by the reflection of rays of light by a layer of heated air (near the ground) **2** sthg illusory and unattainable

[1]**mire** /maɪəʳ/ *n* **1** a tract of soft waterlogged ground; a marsh, bog **2** (deep) mud or slush

[2]**mire** *v* to cause to stick fast (as if) in mire

[1]**mirror** /'mɪrəʳ/ *n* **1** a smooth surface (e g of metal or silvered glass) that forms images by reflection **2** sthg that gives a true representation

[2]**mirror** *v* to reflect (as if) in a mirror

mirth /mɜːθ/ *n* happiness or amusement accompanied with laughter – **~ful** *adj* – **~fully** *adv* – **~less** *adj*

misadventure /ˌmɪsəd'ventʃəʳ/ *n* a misfortune, mishap

misalliance /ˌmɪsə'laɪəns/ *n* an improper or unsuitable alliance

misanthrope /'mɪsənθrəʊp/ *n* one who hates or distrusts people – **-thropy** *n* – **-thropic** *adj* – **-thropically** *adv*

misapply /ˌmɪsə'plaɪ/ *v* to apply wrongly – **-lication** *n*

misapprehend /ˌmɪsæprɪ'hend/ *v* to misunderstand

misappropriate /ˌmɪsə'prəʊprieɪt/ *v* to appropriate wrongly (e g by theft or embezzlement) – **-ation** *n*

misbegotten /ˌmɪsbɪ'gɒtn/ *adj* **1** having a disreputable or improper origin **2** wretched, contemptible

misbehave /ˌmɪsbɪ'heɪv/ *v* to behave badly – **~d** *adj* – **-viour** *n*

miscalculate /ˌmɪs'kælkjʊleɪt/ *v* to calculate wrongly – **-lation** *n*

miscarriage /ˌmɪs'kærɪdʒ, 'mɪskærɪdʒ/ *n* **1** a failure in administration **2** the expulsion of a human foetus before it is viable, esp after the 12th week of gestation

miscarry /mɪs'kæri/ *v* **1** to suffer miscarriage of a foetus **2** to fail to achieve an intended purpose

miscast /ˌmɪs'kaːst/ *v* to cast in an unsuitable role

miscellaneous /ˌmɪsə'leɪnɪəs/ *adj* **1** consisting of diverse items or members **2** having various characteristics or capabilities – **~ly** *adv* – **~ness** *n*

miscellany /mɪ'seləni/ *n* a mixture of various things

mischance /ˌmɪs'tʃaːns/ *n* (a piece of) bad luck

mischief /'mɪstʃɪ̈f/ *n* **1** sthg or esp sby that causes harm or annoyance **2** often playful action that annoys or irritates, usu without causing or intending serious harm

mischievous /'mɪstʃɪ̈vəs/ *adj* **1** harmful, malicious **2** able or tending to cause annoyance, unrest, or minor injury **3a** playfully provocative; arch **b** disruptively playful – **~ly** *adv* – **~ness** *n*

misconceive /ˌmɪskən'siːv/ *v* to interpret wrongly; misunderstand – **-ception** *n*

misconduct /ˌmɪs'kɒndʌkt/ *n* **1** mismanagement of responsibilities **2** adultery

misconstrue /ˌmɪskən'struː/ *v* to construe wrongly; misinterpret

miscount /ˌmɪs'kaʊnt/ *v* to count wrongly; *esp* to make a wrong count – **miscount** *n*

miscreant /'mɪskrɪənt/ *adj or n* (of) one who behaves criminally or maliciously

misdate /ˌmɪs'deɪt/ *v* to date (e g a letter) wrongly

misdeal /ˌmɪs'diːl/ *v* to deal (cards) incorrectly – **misdeal** *n*

misdeed /ˌmɪs'diːd/ *n* a wrong deed; an offence

misdemeanour /ˌmɪsdɪ'miːnəʳ/ *n* **1** a minor crime **2** a misdeed

misdirect /ˌmɪsdɪ̈'rekt/ *v* **1** to give a wrong direction to **2** to address (mail) wrongly – **~ion** *n*

miser /'maɪzəʳ/ *n* a mean grasping person; *esp* one who hoards wealth – **~ly** *adj* – **~liness** *n*

miserable /'mɪzərəbəl/ *adj* **1a** wretchedly inadequate or meagre **b** causing extreme discomfort or unhappiness **2** in a pitiable state of distress or unhappiness **3** shameful, contemptible – **-bly** *adv*

misery /'mɪzəri/ *n* **1** (a cause of)

physical or mental suffering or discomfort **2** great unhappiness and distress **3** *chiefly Br* a grumpy or querulous person; *esp* a killjoy – infml

misfire /ˌmɪsˈfaɪəʳ/ *v* **1** *of an engine, rocket etc* to have the explosive or propulsive charge fail to ignite at the proper time **2** *esp of a firearm* to fail to fire **3** to fail to have an intended effect – **misfire** *n*

misfit /ˈmɪsˌfɪt/ *n* **1** sthg that fits badly **2** a person poorly adjusted to his/her environment

misfortune /mɪsˈfɔːtʃən/ *n* **1** bad luck **2** a distressing or unfortunate incident or event

misgiving /ˌmɪsˈgɪvɪŋ/ *n* a feeling of doubt, suspicion, or apprehension, esp concerning a future event

misgovern /ˌmɪsˈgʌvən/ *v* to govern badly – **~ment** *n*

misguide /ˌmɪsˈgaɪd/ *v* to lead astray – **~d** *adj* – **~dly** *adv*

mishandle /ˌmɪsˈhændl/ *v* **1** to treat roughly; maltreat **2** to mismanage (a situation, crisis, etc)

mishap /ˈmɪshæp/ *n* an unfortunate accident

mishear /ˌmɪsˈhɪəʳ/ *v* to hear wrongly

mishmash /ˈmɪʃmæʃ/ *n* a hotchpotch, jumble – infml

misinform /ˌmɪsɪnˈfɔːm/ *v* to give untrue or misleading information to

misinterpret /ˌmɪsɪnˈtɜːprɪ̣t/ *v* to understand or explain wrongly – **~ation** *n*

misjudge /ˌmɪsˈdʒʌdʒ/ *v* **1** to estimate wrongly **2** to have an unjust opinion of – **~ment** *n*

mislay /mɪsˈleɪ/ *v* to leave in an unremembered place

mislead /mɪsˈliːd/ *v* to lead in a wrong direction or into a mistaken action or belief – **~ingly** *adv*

mismanage /ˌmɪsˈmænɪdʒ/ *v* to manage wrongly or incompetently – **~ment** *n*

mismatch /ˌmɪsˈmætʃ/ *v* to match incorrectly or unsuitably, esp in marriage – **mismatch** *n*

misnomer /mɪsˈnəʊməʳ/ *n* (a use of) a wrong name or designation

misogynist /mɪ̣ˈsɒdʒɪ̣nɪ̣st/ *n* one who hates women – **-gyny** *n*

misplace /ˌmɪsˈpleɪs/ *v* **1a** to put in the wrong place **b** to mislay **2** to fail to suit to the occasion – **~ment** *n*

misprint /ˈmɪs-prɪnt/ *v* to print wrongly

mispronounce /ˌmɪs-prəˈnaʊns/ *v* to pronounce wrongly – **-nunciation** *n*

misquote /ˌmɪsˈkwəʊt/ *v* to quote incorrectly – **-quotation** *n*

misread /ˌmɪsˈriːd/ *v* to read or interpret incorrectly

misreport /ˌmɪsrɪˈpɔːt/ *v* to report falsely

misrepresent /ˌmɪsreprɪˈzent/ *v* to represent falsely; give an untrue or misleading account of – **~ation** *n*

[1]**misrule** /ˌmɪsˈruːl/ *v* to rule incompetently

[2]**misrule** *n* disorder, anarchy

[1]**miss** /mɪs/ *v* **1** to fail to hit, reach, contact, or attain **2** to discover or feel the absence of, esp with regret **3** to escape, avoid **4** to leave out; omit – often + *out* **5** to fail to perform or attend **6** to fail to take advantage of

[2]**miss** *n* **1** a failure to hit **2** a failure to attain a desired result **3** a deliberate avoidance or omission of sthg

[3]**miss** *n* **1** – used as a title preceding the name of an unmarried woman or girl **2** a young unmarried woman or girl – chiefly infml

missal /ˈmɪsəl/ *n* a book containing the order of service of the mass for the whole year

missile /ˈmɪsaɪl/ *n* an object thrown or projected, usu so as to strike sthg at a distance; *also* a self-propelled weapon that travels through the air

missing /ˈmɪsɪŋ/ *adj* absent; *also* lost

missing link *n* a supposed intermediate form between man and his anthropoid ancestors

mission /ˈmɪʃən/ *n* **1a** a ministry commissioned by a religious organization to propagate its faith or carry on humanitarian work, usu abroad **b** a mission establishment **c** a campaign to increase church membership or strengthen Christian faith **2a** a group sent to a foreign country to negotiate, advise, etc **b** a permanent embassy or legation **3** a specific task with which a person or group is charged **4** a definite military, naval, or aerospace task

[1]**missionary** /ˈmɪʃənəri/ *adj* **1** relating to, engaged in, or devoted to missions **2** characteristic of a missionary

[2]**missionary** *n* a person undertaking a mission; *esp* one in charge of a religious mission in some remote part of the world

missive /ˈmɪsɪv/ *n* a written communication; a letter – fml

misspell /ˌmɪsˈspel/ *v* to spell incorrectly – **~ing** *n*

misspend /ˌmɪsˈspend/ *v* to spend wrongly or foolishly; squander

misstate /ˌmɪsˈsteɪt/ *v* to state incorrectly; give a false account of – **~ment** *n*

mist /mɪst/ *n* **1** water in the form of diffuse particles in the atmosphere, esp near the earth's surface **2** sthg that dims or obscures **3** a film, esp of tears, before the eyes

[1]**mistake** /mɪ̸ˈsteɪk/ *v* **mistook; mistaken** **1** to choose wrongly **2a** to misunderstand the meaning, intention, or significance of **b** to estimate wrongly **3** to identify wrongly; confuse with another

[2]**mistake** *n* **1** a misunderstanding of the meaning or significance of sthg **2** a wrong action or statement arising from faulty judgment, inadequate knowledge, or carelessness

mistaken /mɪ̸ˈsteɪkən/ *adj* **1** *of a person* wrong in opinion **2** *of an action, idea, etc* based on wrong thinking; incorrect – **~ly** *adv*

mister /ˈmɪstəʳ/ *n* **1** – used sometimes in writing instead of the usual *Mr* **2** a man not entitled to a title of rank or an honorific or professional title

mistime /ˌmɪsˈtaɪm/ *v* to time badly

mistletoe /ˈmɪsəltəʊ/ *n* a European shrub that grows as a parasite on the branches of trees and has thick leaves and waxy white glutinous berries

mistress /ˈmɪstrɪ̸s/ *n* **1a** a woman in a position of power or authority **b** the female head of a household **2** a woman who has achieved mastery of a subject or skill **3** a woman with whom a man has a continuing sexual relationship outside marriage **4** *chiefly Br* a schoolmistress

mistrust /mɪsˈtrʌst/ *v* **1** to have little trust in; be suspicious of **2** to doubt the reliability or effectiveness of – **mistrust** *n*

misty /ˈmɪsti/ *adj* **1** obscured by mist **2** not clear to the mind or understanding; indistinct – **-tily** *adv* – **-tiness** *n*

misunderstand /ˌmɪsʌndəˈstænd/ *v* **1** to fail to understand **2** to interpret incorrectly

misunderstanding /ˌmɪsʌndəˈstændɪŋ/ *n* **1** a failure to understand; a misinterpretation **2** a disagreement, dispute

misuse /ˌmɪsˈjuːz/ *v* **1** to put to wrong or improper use **2** to abuse or maltreat – **misuse** *n*

mite /maɪt/ *n* **1** any of numerous (extremely) small arachnids that often infest animals, plants, and stored foods **2** a small coin or sum of money **3** a very small object or creature; *esp* a small child

mitigate /ˈmɪtɪ̸geɪt/ *v* **1** to cause to become less harsh or hostile **2a** to make less severe or painful; alleviate **b** to extenuate – **-gation** *n*

mitosis /maɪˈtəʊsɪ̸s/ *n, pl* **mitoses** the formation of 2 new nuclei from an original nucleus, each having the same number of chromosomes as the original nucleus, during cell division

[1]**mitre,** *NAm chiefly* **miter** /ˈmaɪtəʳ/ *n* **1** a tall pointed divided headdress with 2 bands hanging down at the back worn by bishops and abbots on ceremonial occasions **2 mitre, mitre joint** a joint made by cutting the ends of 2 pieces of wood at an oblique angle so that they form a right angle when fitted together **3** a seam joining 2 parts of a sail whose fabric runs in different directions

[2]**mitre,** *NAm chiefly* **miter** *v* **1** to bevel the ends of to make a mitre joint **2** to match or fit together in a mitre joint

mitt /mɪt/ *n* **1a** a glove that leaves the (ends of the) fingers uncovered **b** a mitten **2** a hand or paw; *specif* a person's hand – infml

mitten /ˈmɪtn/ *n* a glove that is divided into one part covering the fingers and another part covering the thumb

[1]**mix** /mɪks/ *v* **1a(1)** to combine or blend into a mass **(2)** to combine with another – often + *in* **b** to bring into close association **2** to prepare by mix-

ing different components or ingredients **3** to control the balance of (various sounds), esp during the recording of a film, broadcast, record, etc **4** to seek or enjoy the society of others

²mix *n* **1** an act or process of mixing **2** a product of mixing; *specif* a commercially prepared mixture of food ingredients **3** a combination **4** a combination in definite proportions of 2 or more recordings (e g of a singer and an accompaniment)

mixed /mɪkst/ *adj* **1** combining diverse elements **2** made up of or involving people of different races, national origins, religions, classes, or sexes **3** including or accompanied by conflicting or dissimilar elements

mixed bag *n* a miscellaneous collection; an assortment

mixed farming *n* the growing of food crops and the rearing of livestock on the same farm

mixed metaphor *n* a combination of incongruous metaphors (e g in *iron out bottlenecks*)

mixed-up *adj* marked by perplexity, uncertainty, or disorder; confused – infml

mixer /'mɪksəʳ/ *n* a person considered with respect to his/her ability to mix well in company

mixture /'mɪkstʃəʳ/ *n* **1a** mixing or being mixed **b** the relative proportions of constituents; *specif* the proportion of fuel to air produced in a carburettor **2a** (a portion of) matter consisting of 2 or more components in varying proportions that retain their own properties **b** a combination of several different kinds; a blend

mix-up *n* a state or instance of confusion

mix up *v* **1** to make untidy or disordered **2** to mistake or confuse – **mix-up** *n*

mizzen, mizen /'mɪzən/ *n* (the sail set on) the mast behind the mainsail

mnemonic /nɪ'mɒnɪk/ *adj* **1** assisting or intended to assist the memory **2** of memory – **mnemonic** *n*

mo, mo' /məʊ/ *n, chiefly Br* a very short space of time; a moment – infml; often in *half a mo*

¹moan /məʊn/ *n* a low prolonged sound of pain or grief

²moan *v* **1** to produce (a sound like) a moan **2** to complain, grumble – **~er** *n*

moat /məʊt/ *n* a deep wide trench round a castle, fortified home, etc that is usu filled with water

¹mob /mɒb/ *n* **1** *the* masses, populace **2** a disorderly riotous crowd **3** a criminal gang **4** *chiefly Austr* a flock, drove, or herd of animals **5** *sing or pl in constr, chiefly Br* a crowd, bunch – infml – **mob** *adj*

²mob *v* **1** to attack in a large crowd or group **2** to crowd round, esp out of curiosity or admiration

¹mobile /'məʊbaɪl/ *adj* **1** capable of moving or being moved **2** changing quickly in expression or mood **3** (capable of) undergoing movement into a different social class – **-ility** *n*

²mobile /'məʊbaɪl/ *n* a structure (e g of cardboard or metal) with usu suspended parts that are moved in different planes by air currents or machinery

mobil·ize, -ise /'məʊbḽlaɪz/ *v* **1** to put into movement or circulation **2a** to call up troops for active service **b** to marshal resources ready for action – **-ization** *n*

mobster /'mɒbstəʳ/ *n, chiefly NAm* a member of a criminal gang

moccasin /'mɒkəsɪn/ *n* a soft leather heelless shoe with the sole brought up the sides of the foot and joined to the upper by a puckered seam

mocha /'mɒkə, 'məʊkə/ *n* **1** a coffee of superior quality, specif grown in Arabia **2** a flavouring obtained from a (mixture of cocoa or chocolate with a) strong coffee infusion

¹mock /mɒk/ *v* **1** to treat with contempt or ridicule **2** to disappoint the hopes of **3** to mimic in fun or derision – **~er** *n* – **~ingly** *adv*

²mock *n* a school examination used as a rehearsal for an official one

³mock *adj* (having the character) of an imitation or simulation

⁴mock *adv* in an insincere or pretended manner – usu in combination

mockery /'mɒkəri/ *n* **1** jeering or contemptuous behaviour or words **2** an object of laughter or derision **3** a deceitful or contemptible imitation; a travesty

mockingbird /'mɒkɪŋbɜːd/ *n* a common bird of esp the southern USA that imitates the calls of other birds

mock-up *n* a full-sized structural model built accurately to scale

modal /'məʊdl/ *adj* **1** of or being (in) a mode (e g in music); *specif* being in one of the church modes rather than a major or minor key **2** of general form or structure as opposed to particular substance or content – **~ly** *adv*

modal auxiliary *n* an auxiliary verb (e g *can, must, may*) expressing a distinction of mood

mod con /,mɒd 'kɒn/ *n, Br* a modern convenience; *esp* a household fitting or device designed to increase comfort or save time – infml; often in *all mod cons*

[1]**mode** /məʊd/ *n* **1** an arrangement of the 8 diatonic musical notes of an octave in any of several fixed schemes which use different patterns of whole tones and semitones between successive notes **2a** a particular form or variety of sthg **b** a form or manner of expression; a style **3** a way of doing or carrying out sthg

[2]**mode** *n* a prevailing fashion or style (e g of dress or behaviour) – fml

[1]**model** /'mɒdl/ *n* **1** structural design **2** a replica of sthg in relief or 3 dimensions; *also* a representation of sthg to be constructed **3** an example worthy of imitation or emulation **4** sby or sthg that serves as a pattern for an artist; *esp* one who poses for an artist **5** one who is employed to wear merchandise, esp clothing, in order to display it **6** a type or design of an article or product (e g a garment or car)

[2]**model** *v* **1** to plan or form after a pattern **2** to shape in a mouldable material; *broadly* to produce a representation or simulation of **3** to construct or fashion in imitation of a particular model **4** to display, esp by wearing

[3]**model** *adj* **1** (worthy of) being a pattern for others **2** being a miniature representation of sthg

[1]**moderate** /'mɒdərʒt/ *adj* **1a** avoiding extremes of behaviour or expression **b** not violent; temperate **2** being (somewhat less than) average in quality, amount, or degree – **-tion** *n* – **~ly** *adv*

[2]**moderate** /'mɒdəreɪt/ *v* **1** to lessen the intensity or extremeness of **2** to preside over

[3]**moderate** /'mɒdərʒt/ *n* one who holds moderate views or favours a moderate course

moderato /,mɒdə'rɑːtəʊ/ *adv or adj* in a moderate tempo – used in music

moderator /'mɒdəreɪtə'/ *n* **1** a mediator **2** the presiding officer of a Presbyterian governing body

modern /'mɒdn/ *adj* **1a** (characteristic) of a period extending from a particular point in the past to the present time **b** (characteristic) of the present or the immediate past; contemporary **2** involving recent techniques, styles, or ideas – **~ize** *v*

modernism /'mɒdənɪzəm/ *n* **1** a practice, usage, or expression characteristic of modern times **2** the theory and practices of modern art; *esp* a search for new forms of expression involving a deliberate break with the past – **-ist** *adj, n*

modest /'mɒdʒst/ *adj* **1** having a moderate estimate of one's abilities or worth; not boastful or self-assertive **2** (characteristic) of a modest nature **3** carefully observant of proprieties of dress and behaviour **4** small or limited in size, amount, or aim – **~ly** *adv* – **~y** *n*

modicum /'mɒdɪkəm/ *n* a small or limited amount

modify /'mɒdʒfaɪ/ *v* **1** to make less extreme **2** to undergo change **3a** to make minor changes in **b** to make basic changes in, often for a specific purpose – **-fication** *n*

modish /'məʊdɪʃ/ *adj* fashionable, stylish – **~ly** *adv*

modulate /'mɒdjʊleɪt/ *v* **1** to vary in tone; make tuneful **2** to adjust to or keep in proper measure or proportion **3** to vary the amplitude, frequency, or phase of (a carrier wave or signal) by combining with a wave of a different frequency, so as to transmit a radio, television, etc signal **4** to pass by regular chord or melodic progression from one musical key or tonality into another – **-ation** *n*

module /ˈmɒdjuːl/ *n* a standardized or independent unit used in construction (e g of buildings, electronic systems, or spacecraft) – **modular** *adj*

mogul /ˈməʊgəl/ *n* **1 Mogul, Moghul** a member of a Muslim dynasty of Turkish and Mongolian origin ruling India from the 16th to the 18th c **2** a great or prominent (business) person

mohair /ˈməʊheəʳ/ *n* a fabric or yarn made (partly) from the long silky hair of the Angora goat

Mohammedan /məʊˈhæmɪdn, mə-/ *adj* Muhammadan – **~ism** *n*

moiré, moire /ˈmwɑːreɪ/ *n* an irregular wavy sheen on a fabric or metal

moist /mɔɪst/ *adj* **1** slightly wet; damp **2** highly humid – **~en** *v* – **~ly** *adv* – **~ness** *n*

moisture /ˈmɔɪstʃəʳ/ *n* liquid diffused, condensed, or absorbed in relatively small amounts

¹**molar** /ˈməʊləʳ/ *n* a grinding tooth with a rounded or flattened surface; *specif* one lying behind the incisors and canines of a mammal

²**molar** *adj* **1** of a mass of matter as distinguished from the properties of individual molecules or atoms **2** of or containing 1 gram molecule (of dissolved substance) in 1 litre of solution

molasses /məˈlæsɪz/ *n* the darkest most viscous syrup remaining after all sugar that can be separated by crystallization has been removed during the refining of raw sugar

¹**mole** /məʊl/ *n* a dark spot, mark, or lump on the human body

²**mole** *n* **1** any of numerous small burrowing insect-eating mammals with minute eyes, concealed ears, and soft fur **2** one who works subversively within an organization, esp to secretly further the interests of a rival organization or government

³**mole** *n* (a harbour formed by) a massive work of masonry, large stones, etc laid in the sea as a pier or breakwater

⁴**mole** *also* **mol** *n* the basic SI unit of substance; the amount of substance that contains the same number of atoms, molecules, ions, etc as there are atoms in 0.012kg of carbon-12

molecule /ˈmɒlɪkjuːl/ *n* the smallest particle of a substance that retains its characteristic properties, consisting of 1 or more atoms – **-ular** *adj*

molehill /ˈməʊl,hɪl/ *n* a mound of earth thrown up by a burrowing mole

molest /məˈlest/ *v* to annoy, disturb, or attack; *specif* to annoy or attack (esp a child or woman) sexually – **~ation** *n* – **~er** *n*

moll /mɒl/ *n* a gangster's girl friend *USE* infml

mollify /ˈmɒlɪfaɪ/ *v* **1** to lessen the anger or hostility of **2** to reduce in intensity – **-fication** *n*

mollusc, *NAm chiefly* **mollusk** /ˈmɒləsk/ *n* any of a large phylum of invertebrate animals with soft bodies not divided into segments and usu enclosed in a shell, including the snails, shellfish, octopuses, and squids

mollycoddle /ˈmɒlikɒdl/ *v* to treat with excessive indulgence and attention – **mollycoddle** *n*

Molotov cocktail /,mɒlətɒf ˈkɒkteɪl/ *n* a crude hand grenade made from a bottle filled with petrol or other inflammable liquid with usu a saturated rag for a wick

molten /ˈməʊltn/ *adj* melted by heat

molto /ˈmɒltəʊ/ *adv* much, very – used in music

molybdenum /məˈlɪbdənəm/ *n* a metallic element resembling chromium and tungsten and used esp in strengthening and hardening steel

moment /ˈməʊmənt/ *n* **1** a very brief interval or point of time **2a** present time **b** a time of excellence or prominence **3** importance in influence or effect **4** a stage in historical or logical development **5** (a measure of) the tendency of a force to produce turning motion

momentary /ˈməʊməntəri/ *adj* lasting a very short time – **-rily** *adv*

momentous /məʊˈmentəs, mə-/ *adj* of great consequence or significance

momentum /məʊˈmentəm, mə-/ *n* the product of the mass of a body and its velocity

monarch /ˈmɒnək/ *n* **1** sby who reigns over a kingdom or empire **2** sby or sthg occupying a commanding or preeminent position – ~**ic**, ~**ical** *adj*

monarchism /ˈmɒnəkɪzəm/ *n* government by or the principles of monarchy – -**chist** *n, adj*

monarchy /ˈmɒnəki/ *n* (a government or state with) undivided rule by a monarch

monastery /ˈmɒnəstri/ *n* a residence occupied by a religious community, esp of monks

monastic /məˈnæstɪk/ *adj* of or being monasteries, monks, or nuns – ~**ism** *n* – ~**ally** *adv*

Monday /ˈmʌndi, -deɪ/ *n* the day of the week following Sunday

monetary /ˈmʌnɪtəri/ *adj* of money or its behaviour in an economy

money /ˈmʌni/ *n* **1** sthg generally accepted as a means of payment; *esp* officially printed, coined, or stamped currency **2** a form or denomination of coin or paper money **3** the first, second, and third places in a race on whose result money is betted – usu in *in/out of the money* – ~**less** *adj*

money grubber *n* a person sordidly bent on accumulating money – infml

moneylender /ˈmʌnilendəʳ/ *n* one whose business is lending money and charging interest on it

money-maker *n* a product or enterprise that produces much profit

money-spinner *n, chiefly Br* a money-maker – infml

Mongol /ˈmɒŋgəl/ *n* **1** a member of any of the chiefly pastoral peoples of Mongolia **2** *often not cap* a sufferer from Down's syndrome

mongolism /ˈmɒŋəlɪzəm/ *n* Down's syndrome

mongoose /ˈmɒŋguːs/ *n* an agile ferret-sized Indian mammal that feeds on snakes and rodents

mongrel /ˈmʌŋgrəl/ *n* a dog or other individual (of unknown ancestry) resulting from the interbreeding of diverse breeds

[1]**monitor** /ˈmɒnɪtəʳ/ *n* **1** a pupil appointed to help a teacher **2** any of various large tropical Old World lizards closely related to the iguanas

[2]**monitor** *v* **1** to keep (a broadcast) under surveillance by means of a receiver, in order to check the quality or fidelity to a frequency or to investigate the content (e g for political significance) **2** to observe or inspect, esp for a special purpose **3** to regulate or control the operation of (e g a machine or process)

monk /mʌŋk/ *n* a male member of a religious order, living apart from the world under vows of poverty, chastity, etc – ~**ish** *adj*

[1]**monkey** /ˈmʌŋki/ *n* **1** any small long-tailed primate mammal **2a** a mischievous child; a scamp **b** a ludicrous figure; a fool *USE* (*2*) infml

[2]**monkey** *v* **1** to act in an absurd or mischievous manner **2** to mess around *with USE* infml; often + *about* or *around*

monkey business *n* mischievous or underhand activity – infml

monkey nut *n* a peanut

monkey wrench *n* a large spanner with one fixed and one adjustable jaw

mono /ˈmɒnəʊ/ *adj or n* monophonic (sound reproduction)

monochrome /ˈmɒnəkrəʊm/ *adj or n* (of, using, or being) reproduction or execution in 1 colour, black and white, or shades of grey

monocle /ˈmɒnəkəl/ *n* an eyeglass for 1 eye

monogamy /məˈnɒgəmi/ *n* the state or custom of being married to 1 person at a time – -**mous** *adj* – -**mously** *adv*

monogram /ˈmɒnəgræm/ *v or n* (to mark with) a character usu formed of the interwoven initials of a name – ~**med** *adj*

monograph /ˈmɒnəgrɑːf/ *n* a treatise on a small area of learning

monolith /ˈmɒnəlɪθ/ *n* **1** a single large block of stone, often in the form of an obelisk or column **2** a massive structure **3** an organized whole that acts as a single powerful force

monolithic /ˌmɒnəˈlɪθɪk/ *adj* constituting a massive uniform whole – ~**ally** *adv*

monologue /ˈmɒnəlɒg/ *n* **1** a dramatic or literary soliloquy; *also* a dramatic sketch performed by 1 speaker **2** a long speech monopolizing conversation

monomania /ˌmɒnəˈmeɪnɪə/ *n* obsessional concentration on a single object or idea – ~**c** *n*

monophonic /ˌmɒnəˈfɒnɪk/ *adj* of or being a system for sound reproduction in which the sound signal is not split into 2 or more different channels between the source and the point of use

monoplane /ˈmɒnəpleɪn/ *n* an aeroplane with only 1 main pair of wings

monopol·ize, -ise /məˈnɒpəlaɪz/ *v* to assume complete possession or control of

monopoly /məˈnɒpəli/ *n* **1** (a person or group having) exclusive ownership or control (through legal privilege, command of the supply of a commodity, concerted action, etc) **2** sthg, esp a commodity, controlled by one party

monorail /ˈmɒnəʊreɪl, -nə-/ *n* (a vehicle running on) a single rail serving as a track for a wheeled vehicle

monosodium glutamate /mɒnəˌsəʊdɪəm ˈgluːtəmeɪt/ *n* an artificially produced white powder used for seasoning foods

monosyllable /ˈmɒnəˌsɪləbəl/ *n* a word of 1 syllable; *specif* one used by sby intending to be pointedly brief in answering or commenting – **-syllabic** *adj*

monotheism /ˈmɒnəʊθiːɪzəm, mɒnə-/ *n* the doctrine or belief that there is only 1 God – **-ist** *n*

¹monotone /mɒnətəʊn/ *n* **1** a succession of speech sounds in 1 unvarying pitch **2** a single unvaried musical note **3** a tedious sameness or repetition

²monotone *adj* having a uniform colour

monotonous /məˈnɒtənəs/ *adj* **1** uttered or sounded in 1 unvarying tone **2** tediously uniform or repetitive – **-ny, ~ness** *n* – **~ly** *adv*

monsieur /məˈsjɜːʳ/ *n, pl* **messieurs** /meɪˈsjɜːz/ – used by or to a French-speaking man as a title equivalent to Mr or without a name as a term of direct address

monsignor /ˌmɒnsiːˈnjɔːʳ/ *n, pl* **monsignors, monsignori** – used as a title for certain Roman Catholic prelates and officers of the papal court

monsoon /mɒnˈsuːn/ *n* **1** a seasonal wind of S Asia blowing from the SW in summer and the NE in winter **2** the season of the SW monsoon, marked by very heavy rains

monster /ˈmɒnstəʳ/ *n* **1a** an animal or plant of (grotesquely) abnormal form or structure **b** an (imaginary) animal of incredible shape or form that is usu dangerous or horrifying **2** one exceptionally large for its kind **3** sthg monstrous; *esp* a person of appalling ugliness, wickedness, or cruelty

monstrosity /mɒnˈstrɒsəti/ *n* **1** a monstrous plant or animal **2** (the quality or state of being) sthg monstrous

monstrous /ˈmɒnstrəs/ *adj* **1** having the qualities or appearance of a monster; extraordinarily large **2a** extraordinarily ugly or vicious **b** outrageously wrong or ridiculous – **~ly** *adv*

montage /ˈmɒntɑːʒ/ *n* **1** a picture made by combining or overlapping several separate pictures **2** (a film sequence using) a method of film editing in which the chronological sequence of events is interrupted by juxtaposed or rapidly succeeding shots

month /mʌnθ/ *n* **1a** any of the 12 divisions of the year in the Julian or Gregorian calendars corresponding roughly with the period of the moon's rotation; *also* any similar division of the year in other calendars **b** 28 days or 4 weeks; *also* the interval between the same date in adjacent months **2** *pl* an indefinite usu protracted period of time – **~ly** *adj or adv*

monthly /ˈmʌnθli/ *n* **1** a monthly periodical **2** *pl* a menstrual period – infml

monument /ˈmɒnjʊmənt/ *n* **1a** a lasting evidence or reminder of sby or sthg notable or influential **b** a memorial stone, sculpture, or structure erected to commemorate a person or event **2** a structure or site of historical or archaeological importance

monumental /ˌmɒnjʊˈmentl/ *adj* **1a** of, serving as, or resembling a monument **b** occurring or used on a monument **2** very great in degree; imposing, outstanding

moo /muː/ *v or n* (to) low

¹mood /muːd/ *n* **1a** (the evocation, esp

in art or literature, of) a predominant emotion, feeling, or frame of mind **b** the right frame of mind **2** a fit of often silent anger or bad temper

[2]**mood** *n* a distinct form or set of inflectional forms of a verb indicating whether the action or state it denotes is considered a fact, wish, possibility, etc

moody /ˈmuːdi/ *adj* **1** sullen or gloomy **2** temperamental – **moodily** *adv* – **moodiness** *n*

[1]**moon** /muːn/ *n* **1** the earth's natural satellite that shines by reflecting the sun's light **2** a satellite

[2]**moon** *v* **1** to move about listlessly **2** to spend time in idle gazing or daydreaming *USE* often + *around* or *about*; infml

moonbeam /ˈmuːnbiːm/ *n* a ray of light from the moon

moonlight /ˈmuːnlaɪt/ *v* to hold a second job in addition to a regular one

moonshine /ˈmuːnʃaɪn/ *n* **1** the light of the moon **2** empty talk; nonsense **3** (illegally distilled) spirits, esp whisky – infml

moonstone /ˈmuːnstəʊn/ *n* a transparent or translucent opalescent feldspar used as a gem

moonstruck /ˈmuːnstrʌk/ *adj* affected (as if) by the moon; *specif* mentally unbalanced

[1]**moor** /mʊəʳ/ *n, chiefly Br* an expanse of open peaty infertile usu heath-covered upland

[2]**moor** *v* to make (e g a boat or buoy) fast with cables, lines, or anchors

Moor *n* a member of the mixed Arab and Berber people that conquered Spain in the 8th c AD

moorhen /ˈmʊəhen, ˈmɔː-/ *n* a common red-billed blackish bird of the rail family that nests near fresh water

moose /muːs/ *n, pl* **moose** a large N American ruminant mammal of the deer family with very large flattened antlers

[1]**moot** /muːt/ *n* **1** an early English assembly to decide points of community and political interest **2** a mock court in which law students argue hypothetical cases

[2]**moot** *v* to put forward for discussion

[3]**moot** *adj* open to question; debatable – usu in *moot point*

[1]**mop** /mɒp/ *n* **1** an implement consisting of a head made of absorbent material fastened to a long handle and used esp for cleaning floors **2** a shock of untidy hair

[2]**mop** *v* **1** to clean (a floor or other surface) with a mop **2** to wipe (as if) with a mop

mope /məʊp/ *v* to give oneself up to brooding; become listless or dejected

moped /ˈməʊped/ *n* a low-powered motorcycle whose engine can be pedal-assisted (e g for starting)

moppet /ˈmɒpɪ̣t/ *n* a young child; *esp* a little girl – chiefly infml; apprec

moraine /məˈreɪn/ *n* an accumulation of earth and stones carried and deposited by a glacier

[1]**moral** /ˈmɒrəl/ *adj* **1a** of or being principles of right and wrong in conduct; ethical **b** conforming to a standard of right conduct **c** capable of distinguishing right and wrong **2** of, occurring in, or acting on the mind, emotions, or will – ~**ly** *adv*

[2]**moral** *n* **1** (a concluding passage pointing out) the moral significance or practical lesson **2** *pl* **a** standards of esp sexual conduct **b** ethics

morale /məˈrɑːl/ *n* the mental and emotional condition (e g of enthusiasm or loyalty) of an individual or group with regard to the function or tasks at hand

moralist /ˈmɒrəlɪ̣st/ *n* one concerned with regulating the morals of others – often derog

morality /məˈrælɪ̣ti/ *n* **1** a system or sphere of moral conduct **2** (degree of conformity to standards of) right conduct or moral correctness

morality play *n* a form of allegorical drama popular esp in the 15th and 16th c in which the characters personify moral or abstract qualities (e g pride or youth)

moral·ize, -ise /ˈmɒrəlaɪz/ *v* to make (unnecessary) moral judgments or reflections

morass /məˈræs/ *n* **1** a marsh, swamp **2** sthg that ensnares, confuses, or impedes

moratorium /ˌmɒrəˈtɔːrɪəm/ *n, pl*

moratoriums, moratoria a suspension of (a specified) activity – usu + *on*

morbid /ˈmɔːbɪ̈d/ *adj* **1** of, affected with, induced by, or characteristic of disease **2** abnormally susceptible to or characterized by gloomy feelings; *esp* having an unnatural preoccupation with death **3** grisly, gruesome – **~ity** *n* – **~ly** *adv*

[1]**mordant** /ˈmɔːdənt/ *adj* **1** caustic or sharply critical in thought, manner, or style **2** burning, pungent

[2]**mordant** *n* a chemical that fixes a dye by combining with it to form an insoluble compound

mordent /ˈmɔːdənt/ *n* a musical ornament made by a quick alternation of a principal note with either of the immediately adjacent notes

[1]**more** /mɔːr/ *adj* **1** greater in quantity or number **2** additional, further

[2]**more** *adv* **1a** as an additional amount **b** moreover, again **2** to a greater degree or extent – often used with an adjective or adverb to form the comparative (e g much *more* even)

[3]**more** *n, pl* **more** **1** a greater or additional quantity, amount, or part **2** *pl* additional ones

moreover /mɔːˈrəʊvəʳ/ *adv* in addition to what has been said – used to introduce new matter

mores /ˈmɔːriːz/ *n pl* the (morally binding) customs or conventions of a particular group

morgue /mɔːg/ *n* **1** a mortuary **2** a collection of reference works and files in a newspaper office

moribund /ˈmɒrɪ̈bʌnd/ *adj* dying

Mormon /ˈmɔːmən/ *n* a member of the Church of Jesus Christ of Latter-Day Saints, founded in 1830 in the USA by Joseph Smith, and following precepts contained in the Book of Mormon, a sacred text that he discovered – **~ism** *n*

morn /mɔːn/ *n* the morning – chiefly poetic

morning /ˈmɔːnɪŋ/ *n* **1a** the dawn **b** the time from midnight or sunrise to noon **2** an early period (e g of time or life); the beginning

morning dress *n* men's dress for formal occasions (e g a wedding) during the day

morning sickness *n* nausea and vomiting occurring esp in the morning during the earlier months of a woman's pregnancy

morocco /məˈrɒkəʊ/ *n* a fine leather made from goatskin

moron /ˈmɔːrɒn/ *n* **1** a mental defective **2** a very stupid person – infml – **~ic** *adj*

morose /məˈrəʊs/ *adj* (having a disposition) marked by or expressive of gloom – **~ly** *adv* – **~ness** *n*

morphine /ˈmɔːfiːn/ *n* the principal alkaloid of opium that is an addictive narcotic drug used esp as a powerful painkiller

morris dance /ˈmɒrɪ̈s dɑːns/ *n* any of several traditional English dances that are performed by groups of people wearing costumes to which small bells are attached

morrow /ˈmɒrəʊ/ *n* the next day – fml

morsel /ˈmɔːsəl/ *n* **1** a small piece of food **2** a small quantity; a scrap

[1]**mortal** /ˈmɔːtl/ *adj* **1** causing or about to cause death; fatal **2** not living forever; subject to death **3** marked by relentless hostility **4** of or connected with death – infml

[2]**mortal** *n* **1** a human being **2** a person of a specified kind

mortality /mɔːˈtælɪ̈ti/ *n* **1** being mortal **2** the death of large numbers of people, animals, etc; *also* the number of deaths in a given time or place **3** the human race

mortally /ˈmɔːtəli/ *adv* **1** in a deadly or fatal manner **2** to an extreme degree; intensely

[1]**mortar** /ˈmɔːtəʳ/ *n* **1** a strong usu bowl-shaped vessel (e g of stone) in which substances are pounded or ground with a pestle **2** a usu muzzle-loading artillery gun having a tube short in relation to its calibre, a low muzzle velocity, and a high trajectory

[2]**mortar** *n* a mixture of cement, lime, gypsum plaster, etc with sand and water, that hardens and is used to join bricks, stones, etc or for plastering

mortarboard /ˈmɔːtəbɔːd/ *n* an academic cap consisting of a close-fitting crown with a stiff flat square attached on top

[1]**mortgage** /ˈmɔːgɪdʒ/ *n* a transfer of

the ownership of property (e g for security on a loan) on condition that the transfer becomes void on payment

[2]**mortgage** *v* **1** to transfer the ownership of (property) by a mortgage **2** to make subject to a claim or obligation

mortify /'mɔːtɪ̬faɪ/ *v* **1** to subdue (e g bodily needs and desires), esp by abstinence or self-inflicted suffering **2** to subject to feelings of shame or acute embarrassment **3** to become decaying infected with gangrene – **-fication** *n*

mortise *also* **mortice** /'mɔːtɪ̬s/ *n* a usu rectangular cavity cut into a piece of material (e g wood) to receive a protrusion, esp a tenon, of another piece – **mortise** *v*

mortise lock *n* a lock that is designed to be fitted into a mortise in the edge of a door

[1]**mortuary** /'mɔːtʃʊəri/ *n* a room or building in which dead bodies are kept before burial or cremation

[2]**mortuary** *adj* of death or the burial of the dead

mosaic /məʊ'zeɪ-ɪk/ *n* **1** (a piece of) decorative work made from small pieces of different coloured material (e g glass or stone) inlaid to form pictures or patterns **2** a virus disease of plants (e g tobacco) characterized esp by diffuse yellow and green mottling of the foliage

Mosaic *adj* of Moses or the institutions or writings attributed to him

Moselle, Mosel /məʊ'zel/ *n* a typically light-bodied white table wine made in the valley of the Moselle

Moslem /'mɒzlɪ̬m/ *n or adj* (a) Muslim

mosque /mɒsk/ *n* a building used for public worship by Muslims

mosquito /mə'skiːtəʊ/ *n* any of numerous 2-winged flies with females that suck the blood of animals and often transmit diseases (e g malaria) to them

moss /mɒs/ *n* **1** any of a class of primitive plants with small leafy stems bearing sex organs at the tip; *also* many of these plants growing together and covering a surface **2** *chiefly Scot* a (peat) bog – **~y** *adj*

[1]**most** /məʊst/ *adj* **1** the majority of **2** greatest in quantity or extent

[2]**most** *adv* **1** to the greatest degree or extent – often used with an adjective or adverb to form the superlative (e g the *most* challenging job he ever had) **2** very (e g shall *most* certainly come)

[3]**most** *n, pl* **most** the greatest quantity, number, or amount

[4]**most** *adv, archaic, dial, or NAm* almost

mostly /'məʊstli/ *adv* for the greatest part; mainly; *also* in most cases; usually

mot /məʊ/ *n, pl* **mots** a pithy or witty saying

MOT *also* **MoT** *n* a compulsory annual roadworthiness test in Britain for motor vehicles older than a certain age

mote /məʊt/ *n* a small particle; *esp* a particle of dust suspended in the air

motel /məʊ'tel/ *n* an establishment which provides accommodation and parking and in which the rooms are usu accessible from an outdoor parking area

motet /məʊ'tet/ *n* a choral composition on a sacred text

moth /mɒθ/ *n* **1** a clothes moth **2** a usu night-flying insect with feathery antennae and a stouter body and duller colouring than the butterflies

mothball /'mɒθbɔːl/ *n* **1** a naphthalene or (formerly) camphor ball used to keep moths from clothing **2** *pl* a state of indefinitely long protective storage; *also* a state of having been rejected as of no further use or interest

moth-eaten *adj* **1** very worn-out or shabby in appearance **2** antiquated, outmoded

[1]**mother** /'mʌðə^r/ *n* **1a** a female parent **b** an old or elderly woman **2** a source, origin – **~less** *adj*

[2]**mother** *adj* **1a** of or being a mother **b** bearing the relation of a mother **2** derived (as if) from one's mother **3** acting as or providing a parental stock – used without reference to sex

[3]**mother** *v* **1a** to give birth to **b** to give rise to; initiate, produce **2** to care for or protect like a mother – often derog

mother-in-law *n, pl* **mothers-in-law** the mother of one's spouse

motherly /ˈmʌðəli/ *adj* **1** (characteristic) of a mother **2** like a mother; maternal – **-liness** *n*

mother-of-pearl *n* the hard pearly iridescent substance forming the inner layer of a mollusc shell

mother superior *n, often cap M&S* the head of a religious community of women

motif /məʊˈtiːf/ *n* **1** a recurring element forming a theme in a work of art or literature; *esp* a dominant idea or central theme **2** a single or repeated design or colour

[1]motion /ˈməʊʃən/ *n* **1a** a formal proposal made in a deliberative assembly **b** an application to a court or judge for an order, ruling, or direction **2a** an act, process, or instance of changing position; movement **b** an active or functioning state or condition **3a** an act or instance of moving the body or its parts; a gesture **b** *pl* actions, movements; *esp* merely simulated or mechanical actions – often in *go through the motions* **4** an evacuation of the bowels – usu pl with sing. meaning – **~less** *adj*

[2]motion *v* to direct by a gesture

motion picture *n, chiefly NAm* a film, movie

motivate /ˈməʊtəveɪt/ *v* to provide with a motive or incentive; impel – **-ation** *n*

[1]motive /ˈməʊtɪv/ *n* **1** a need, desire, etc that causes sby to act **2** a recurrent phrase or figure that is developed through the course of a musical composition – **~less** *adj*

[2]motive *adj* **1** moving or tending to move to action **2** of (the causing of) motion

[1]motley /ˈmɒtli/ *adj* **1** multicoloured **2** composed of varied (disreputable or unsightly) elements

[2]motley *n* a haphazard mixture (of incompatible elements)

moto-cross /ˈməʊtəʊ ˌkrɒs/ *n* the sport of racing motorcycles across country on a rugged usu hilly closed course

[1]motor /ˈməʊtəʳ/ *n* **1** sthg or sby that imparts motion **2a** an internal-combustion engine **b** a rotating machine that transforms electrical energy into mechanical energy **3** a motor vehicle; *esp* a motor car

[2]motor *adj* **1a** causing or imparting motion **b** of or involving muscular movement **2a** equipped with or driven by a motor **b** of or involving motor vehicles

[3]motor *v* to travel by motor car; *esp* to drive – **~ist** *n*

motor bike *n* a motorcycle – infml

motorboat /ˈməʊtəbəʊt/ *n* a usu small boat propelled by a motor

motorcade /ˈməʊtəkeɪd/ *n* a procession of motor vehicles

motor car *n* a usu 4-wheeled motor vehicle designed for transporting a small number of people and typically propelled by an internal-combustion engine

motorcycle /ˈməʊtəˌsaɪkəl/ *n* a 2-wheeled motor vehicle that can carry 1 or sometimes 2 people astride the engine – **-clist** *n*

motor scooter *n* a usu 2-wheeled motor vehicle having a seat so that the driver sits in front of rather than astride the engine

motor vehicle *n* a self-propelled vehicle not operated on rails; *esp* one with rubber tyres for use on roads

motorway /ˈməʊtəweɪ/ *n, Br* a major road designed for high-speed traffic that has separate carriageways for different directions and certain restrictions on the types of vehicle and driver allowed on it

mottled /ˈmɒtld/ *adj* having irregular spots or markings; dappled

motto /ˈmɒtəʊ/ *n, pl* **mottoes** **1** a sentence, phrase, or word inscribed on sthg as appropriate to or indicative of its character or use **2** a short expression of a guiding principle; a maxim **3** (a piece of paper printed with) a usu humorous or sentimental saying

[1]mould, *NAm chiefly* **mold** /məʊld/ *n* crumbling soft (humus-rich) soil suited to plant growth

[2]mould, *NAm chiefly* **mold** *n* **1** the frame on or round which an object is constructed **2** a cavity or form in which a substance (e g a jelly or a metal casting) is shaped **3** a fixed pattern or form

[3]**mould,** *NAm chiefly* **mold** *v* **1** to give shape to **2** to form in a mould **3** to exert a steady formative influence on **4** to fit closely to the contours of

[4]**mould,** *NAm chiefly* **mold** *n* (a fungus producing) an often woolly growth on the surface of damp or decaying organic matter

moulder, *NAm chiefly* **molder** /'məʊldəʳ/ *v* to crumble into dust or decayed fragments, esp gradually

moulding /'məʊldɪŋ/ *n* a decorative band or strip used for ornamentation or finishing (e g on a cornice)

mouldy /'məʊldi/ *adj* **1** of, resembling, or covered with a mould-producing fungus **2** old and mouldering; fusty, crumbling **3a** miserable, nasty **b** stingy *USE* (*3*) infml – **mouldiness** *n*

moult, *NAm chiefly* **molt** /məʊlt/ *v* to shed or cast off (hair, feathers, shell, horns, or an outer layer) periodically – **moult** *n*

mound /maʊnd/ *n* **1a** an artificial bank of earth or stones **b** a small hill **2** a heap, pile

[1]**mount** /maʊnt/ *n* a high hill; a mountain – usu before a name

[2]**mount** *v* **1** to increase in amount, extent, or degree **2** to rise, ascend **3a** to get up on or into sthg above ground level; *esp* to seat oneself (e g on a horse) for riding **b** to go up; climb **c** *of a male animal* to copulate with (a female animal) **4** to initiate and carry out (e g an assault or strike) **5** to station for defence or observation or as an escort **6a** to attach to a support **b** to arrange or assemble for use or display **7a** to prepare (e g a specimen) for examination or display **b** to organize and present for public viewing or performance; stage

[3]**mount** *n* **1a** the material (e g cardboard) on which a picture is mounted **b** a jewellery setting **c** a hinge, card, etc for mounting a stamp in a stamp collection **2** a horse for riding

mountain /'maʊntɪ̣n/ *n* **1** a landmass that projects conspicuously above its surroundings and is higher than a hill **2a** a vast amount or quantity – often pl with sing. meaning **b** a supply, esp of a specified usu agricultural commodity, in excess of demand

mountain ash *n* a rowan or related tree usu with small red fruits

mountaineering /ˌmaʊntɪ̣'nɪərɪŋ/ *n* the pastime or technique of climbing mountains and rock faces – **mountaineer** *n*

mountainous /'maʊntɪ̣nəs/ *adj* **1** containing many mountains **2** resembling a mountain; huge

mountebank /ˌmaʊntɪbæŋk/ *n* **1** sby who sells quack medicines from a platform **2** a charlatan

Mountie /'maʊnti/ *n* a member of the Royal Canadian Mounted Police

mourn /mɔːn/ *v* to feel or express (e g in a conventional manner) grief or sorrow, esp for a death – **mourner** *n*

mournful /'mɔːnfəl/ *adj* expressing, causing, or filled with sorrow – **~ly** *adv* – **~ness** *n*

mourning /'mɔːnɪŋ/ *n* **1** the act or state of one who mourns **2a** an outward sign (e g black clothes or an armband) of grief for a person's death **b** a period of time during which signs of grief are shown

[1]**mouse** /maʊs/ *n, pl* **mice** /maɪs/ **1** any of numerous small rodents with a pointed snout, rather small ears, and slender tail **2** a timid person

[2]**mouse** *v* **1** to hunt for mice **2** *chiefly NAm* to search for carefully – usu + *out*

mousetrap /'maʊstræp/ *n* a trap for mice

moussaka, mousaka /muː'sɑːkə/ *n* a Greek dish consisting of layers of minced meat (e g lamb), aubergine or potato, tomato, and cheese with cheese or savoury custard topping

mousse /muːs/ *n* a light sweet or savoury cold dish usu containing cream, gelatin, and whipped egg whites

moustache, *NAm chiefly* **mustache** /mə'stɑːʃ/ *n* the hair growing or allowed to grow on sby's upper lip

mousy, mousey /'maʊsi/ *adj* **1** of or resembling a mouse: e g **a** quiet, stealthy **b** timid; *also* colourless **2** *of hair* light greyish brown – **mousiness** *n*

[1]**mouth** /maʊθ/ *n* **1a** the opening through which food passes into an

animal's body; *also* the cavity in the head of the typical vertebrate animal bounded externally by the lips that encloses the tongue, gums, and teeth **b** an individual, esp a child, requiring food **2** sthg like a mouth, esp in affording entrance or exit: e g **a** the place where a river enters a sea, lake, etc **b** the opening of a cave, volcano, etc **c** the opening of a container **3** a tendency to talk too much

[2]**mouth** /maʊð/ *v* **1** to utter pompously **2** to repeat without comprehension or sincerity **3** to form (words) soundlessly with the lips

mouthful /'maʊθfʊl/ *n* **1** a quantity that fills the mouth **2** a small quantity **3** a word or phrase that is very long or difficult to pronounce

mouth organ *n* a harmonica

mouthpiece /'maʊθpiːs/ *n* **1** sthg placed at or forming a mouth **2** a part (e g of a musical instrument or a telephone) that goes in the mouth or is put next to the mouth **3** sby or sthg that expresses or interprets another's views

mouth-watering *adj* stimulating or appealing to the appetite; appetizing

movable, moveable /'muːvəbəl/ *n or adj* (property) able to be removed – often used to distinguish personal property from land, buildings, etc; usu pl

[1]**move** /muːv/ *v* **1a(1)** to go or pass with a continuous motion **(2)** to proceed or progress towards a (specified) place or condition – often + *on* **b** to change the place or position of **c(1)** to transfer a piece in a board game (e g in chess) from one position to another **(2)** *of a piece in board games* to travel or be capable of travelling to another position **d** to change one's residence **2** to pass one's life in a specified environment **3** to (cause to) change position or posture **4a** to take action; act **b** to prompt to action **5a** to make a formal request, application, or appeal **b** to propose formally in a deliberative assembly **6** to affect in such a way as to lead to a show of emotion or of a specified emotion **7** *of the bowels* to evacuate **8a** to (cause to) operate or function, esp mechanically **b** to show marked activity or speed – infml – ~**r** *n*

[2]**move** *n* **1a** the act of moving a piece (e g in chess) **b** the turn of a player to move **2a** a step taken so as to gain an objective **b** a movement **c** a change of residence or official location

movement /'muːvmənt/ *n* **1a** the act or process of moving; *esp* change of place, position, or posture **b** an action, activity – usu pl with sing. meaning **2a** a trend, specif in prices **b** an organized effort to promote an end **3** the moving parts of a mechanism that transmit motion **4** a unit or division having its own key, rhythmic structure, and themes and forming a separate part of an extended musical composition

movie /'muːvi/ *n* a film

moving /'muːvɪŋ/ *adj* **1a** marked by or capable of movement **b** of a change of residence **2a** producing or transferring motion or action **b** evoking a deep emotional response – ~**ly** *adv*

[1]**mow** /maʊ/ *n* the part of a barn where hay or straw is stored

[2]**mow** /məʊ/ *v* **mowed; mowed, mown** **1** to cut down a crop, esp grass **2** to cut down the standing herbage, esp grass, of (e g a field) – ~**er** *n*

Mr /'mɪstəʳ/ *n* **1** – used as a conventional title of courtesy before a man's surname where no other title is appropriate **2** – used in direct address before a man's title of office

Mrs /'mɪsɨ̥z/ *n* **1** – used as a conventional title of courtesy before a married woman's surname where no other title is appropriate **2** a wife – infml

Ms /mɪz, məz/ *n* – used instead of Mrs or Miss, esp when marital status is unknown or irrelevant

[1]**much** /mʌtʃ/ *adj* **more** /mɔːʳ/; **most** /məʊst/ **1** great in quantity or extent (e g how *much* milk is there?) **2** excessive, immoderate (e g it's a bit *much*)

[2]**much** *adv* **more; most** **1a(1)** to a great degree or extent; considerably (e g was *much* happier) **(2)** very – with verbal adjectives (e g was *much* amused) **b** frequently, often (e g *much* married) **c** by far (e g *much* the fatter) **2** nearly, approximately (e g looks *much* the same)

[3]**much** *n* **1** a great quantity, amount, or part **2** sthg considerable or impressive (e g wasn't *much* to look at) **3** a relative quantity or part (e g I'll say this *much* for him)

muck /mʌk/ *n* **1** soft moist farmyard manure **2** slimy dirt or filth **3** mire, mud **4a** a worthless or useless thing; rubbish – infml **b** *Br* – used in *Lord Muck* and *Lady Muck* to designate an arrogantly patronizing person

muck about *v, chiefly Br* to mess about

muck in *v, Br* to share or join in esp a task; *also* to share sleeping accommodation

muck out *v* to remove manure or filth, esp from an animal's quarters

muckrake /ˈmʌkreɪk/ *v* to search out and publicly expose real or apparent misconduct of prominent individuals – **~r** *n* – **-raking** *n*

muck up *v, chiefly Br* to bungle, spoil

mucous /ˈmjuːkəs/ *adj* of, like, secreting, or covered (as if) with mucus

mucous membrane *n* a membrane rich in mucous glands, specif lining body passages and cavities (e g the mouth) with openings to the exterior

mucus /ˈmjuːkəs/ *n* a thick slippery secretion produced by mucous membranes (e g in the nose) which it moistens and protects

mud /mʌd/ *n* **1** (a sticky mixture of a solid and a liquid resembling) soft wet earth **2** abusive and malicious remarks or charges

[1]**muddle** /ˈmʌdl/ *v* **1** to stupefy, esp with alcohol **2** to mix confusedly in one's mind – often + *up* **3** to proceed or get along in a confused aimless way – + *along* or *on*

[2]**muddle** *n* **1** a state of (mental) confusion **2** a confused mess

muddleheaded /ˌmʌdlˈhedɨd/ *adj* **1** mentally confused **2** inept, bungling

[1]**muddy** /ˈmʌdi/ *adj* **1** lacking in clarity or brightness **2** obscure in meaning; muddled, confused

[2]**muddy** *v* to make cloudy, dull, or confused

mudguard /ˈmʌdgɑːd/ *n* a metal or plastic guard over the wheel of a bicycle, motorcycle, etc to deflect or catch mud

muesli /ˈmjuːzli/ *n* a (breakfast) dish of Swiss origin consisting of rolled oats, dried fruit, nuts, grated apple, etc

muezzin /muːˈezɨn, ˈmwezɨn/ *n* a mosque official who calls the faithful to prayer at fixed daily times, usu from a minaret

[1]**muff** /mʌf/ *n* a warm cylindrical wrap in which both hands are placed

[2]**muff** *n* **1** a failure to hold a ball in attempting a catch **2** a timid awkward person, esp in sports – infml

[3]**muff** *v* **1** to handle awkwardly; bungle **2** to fail to hold (a ball) when attempting a catch

muffin /ˈmʌfɨn/ *n* a light round yeast-leavened bun usu served hot

[1]**muffle** /ˈmʌfəl/ *v* **1** to wrap up so as to conceal or protect **2a** to wrap or pad with sthg to dull the sound **b** to deaden the sound of **3** to keep down; suppress

[2]**muffle** *n* a chamber in a furnace or kiln where articles can be heated without direct contact with flames or combustion products

muffler /ˈmʌfləʳ/ *n* a warm scarf worn round the neck

mufti /ˈmʌfti/ *n* civilian or ordinary clothes worn by one who is usually in uniform

[1]**mug** /mʌg/ *n* **1** a large usu cylindrical drinking cup **2** the face or mouth of sby **3** *Br* sby easily deceived; a sucker *USE* (*2 & 3*) infml

[2]**mug** *v* to assault, esp in the street with intent to rob – **mugger** *n* – **mugging** *n*

muggins /ˈmʌgɪnz/ *n, pl* **mugginses, muggins** a fool, simpleton – slang; often used in address

muggy /ˈmʌgi/ *adj, of weather* warm, damp, and close – **-giness** *n*

mug's game *n, chiefly Br* a profitless activity – infml

mug up *v, Br* to study hard – infml

mulatto /mjuːˌlætəʊ/ *n* the first-generation offspring of a Negro and a white person

mulberry /ˈmʌlbəri/ *n* (any of a genus of trees of the fig family bearing) an edible usu purple multiple fruit

mulch /mʌltʃ/ *v or n* (to spread) a protective covering (e g of compost) spread on the ground to control weeds, enrich the soil, etc

[1]**mule** /mjuːl/ *n* **1** the offspring of a mating between a (female) horse and an ass **2** a very stubborn person **3** a machine for simultaneously drawing and twisting fibre into yarn or thread and winding it onto spindles

[2]**mule** *n* a backless shoe or slipper

muleteer /ˌmjuːlɪ̈ˈtɪəʳ/ *n* sby who drives mules

mulish /ˈmjuːlɪʃ/ *adj* unreasonably and inflexibly obstinate – **~ly** *adv* – **~ness** *n*

[1]**mull** /mʌl/ *v* to heat, sweeten, and flavour (e g wine or beer) with spices

[2]**mull** *n* a headland or peninsula in Scotland

mullah /ˈmʌlə, ˈmʊlə/ *n* a Muslim trained in traditional law and doctrine

mullet /ˈmʌlɪ̈t/ *n* any of a family of **a** food fishes with elongated bodies **b** red or golden fishes with 2 barbels on the chin

mulligatawny /ˌmʌlɪgəˈtɔːni/ *n* a rich meat soup of Indian origin seasoned with curry

mullion /ˈmʌlɪən/ *n* a slender vertical bar placed esp between panes or panels (e g of windows or doors) – **~ed** *adj*

mull over *v* to consider at length

multifarious /ˌmʌltɪ̈ˈfeərɪəs/ *adj* having or occurring in great variety; diverse – **~ly** *adv* – **~ness** *n*

multiform /ˈmʌltɪfɔːm/ *adj* having many forms or appearances

multilateral /ˌmʌltɪˈlætərəl/ *adj* **1** having many sides **2** participated in by more than 2 parties – **~ly** *adv*

multilingual /ˌmʌltɪˈlɪŋgwəl/ *adj* using or able to use several languages

[1]**multiple** /ˈmʌltɪ̈pəl/ *adj* **1** consisting of, including, or involving more than 1 **2** many, manifold **3** shared by many

[2]**multiple** *n* **1** the product of a quantity by an integer **2 multiple, multiple store** a chain store

multiple sclerosis *n* progressively developing paralysis and jerking muscle tremor resulting from the formation of patches of hardened nerve tissue in nerves of the brain and spinal cord

multiplex /ˈmʌltɪ̈pleks/ *adj* manifold, multiple

multiplication /ˌmʌltɪ̈plɪ̈ˈkeɪʃən/ *n* **1** multiplying or being multiplied **2** a mathematical operation that at its simplest is an abbreviated process of adding an integer to itself a specified number of times

multiplicity /ˌmʌltɪ̈ˈplɪsɪ̈ti/ *n* **1** the quality or state of being multiple or various **2** a great number

multiply /ˈmʌltɪ̈plaɪ/ *v* **1a** to become greater in number; spread **b** to breed or propagate **2** to perform multiplication

multiracial /ˌmʌltɪˈreɪʃəl/ *adj* composed of, involving, or representing various races

multi-storey *n or adj* (a building, esp a car park) having several storeys

multitude /ˈmʌltɪ̈tjuːd/ *n* **1** a great number; a host **2** a crowd – chiefly fml **3** *the* populace, masses

multitudinous /ˌmʌltɪ̈ˈtjuːdɪ̈nəs/ *adj* **1** comprising a multitude of individuals; populous **2** existing in or consisting of innumerable elements or aspects ***USE*** fml – **~ly** *adv* – **~ness** *n*

[1]**mum** /mʌm/ *adj* silent – infml

[2]**mum** *n, chiefly Br* mother

mumble /ˈmʌmbəl/ *v* to say (words) in an inarticulate usu subdued voice

mumbo jumbo /ˌmʌmbəʊ ˈdʒʌmbəʊ/ *n* **1** elaborate but meaningless ritual **2** involved activity or language that obscures and confuses

mummify /ˈmʌmɪfaɪ/ *v* to embalm and dry (the body of an animal or human being) – **-fication** *n*

mumming /ˈmʌmɪŋ/ *n* **1** the practice of performing in a traditional pantomime **2** the custom of going about merrymaking in disguise during festivals – **mummer** *n*

[1]**mummy** /ˈmʌmi/ *n* a body embalmed for burial in the manner of the ancient Egyptians

[2]**mummy** *n* mother

mumps /mʌmps/ *n pl but sing or pl in constr* an infectious virus disease marked by gross swelling of esp the glands of the neck and face

munch /mʌntʃ/ *v* to chew (food) with

a crunching sound and visible movement of the jaws

mundane /mʌn'deɪn/ *adj* **1** (characteristic) of this world in contrast to heaven **2** practical and ordinary, esp to the point of dull familiarity – **~ly** *adv*

municipal /mjuː'nɪsʲpəl/ *adj* **1a** of a municipality **b** having local self-government **2** restricted to 1 locality – **~ly** *adv*

municipality /mjuːˌnɪsʲ'pælʲti/ *n* (the governing body of) a primarily urban political unit having corporate status and some self-government

¹mural /'mjʊərəl/ *adj* of, resembling, or applied to a wall

²mural *n* a mural work of art (e g a painting)

¹murder /'mɜːdəʳ/ *n* the crime of unlawfully and intentionally killing sby

²murder *v* **1** to kill (sby) unlawfully and intentionally **2** to slaughter brutally **3** to mutilate, mangle – **~er** *n* – **~ess** *n*

murderous /'mɜːdərəs/ *adj* **1** having the purpose or capability of murder **2** characterized by or causing murder or bloodshed – **~ly** *adv* – **~ness** *n*

murk /mɜːk/ *n* gloom, darkness; *also* fog

murky /'mɜːki/ *adj* dark and gloomy – **murkily** *adv*

¹murmur /'mɜːməʳ/ *n* **1** a half-suppressed or muttered complaint **2a** a low indistinct (continuous) sound **b** a subdued or gentle utterance

²murmur *v* **1** to make a murmur **2** to complain, grumble – **~ing** *n*

muscle /'mʌsəl/ *n* **1** (an organ that moves a body part, consisting of) a tissue made of modified elongated cells that contract when stimulated to produce motion **2** muscular strength; brawn – **~d** *adj*

muscle-bound *adj* **1** having enlarged muscles with impaired elasticity, often as a result of excessive exercise **2** lacking flexibility; rigid

muscle in *v* to interfere forcibly – infml; often + *on*

muscular /'mʌskjʊləʳ/ *adj* **1a** of, constituting, or performed by muscle or the muscles **b** having well-developed muscles **2** having strength of expression or character; vigorous – **~ly** *adv*

muscular dystrophy /ˌmʌskjʊlə 'dɪstrəfi/ *n* progressive wasting of muscles occurring as a hereditary disease

¹muse /mjuːz/ *v* to become absorbed in thought; *esp* to engage in daydreaming – **musingly** *adv*

²muse *n* **1** *cap* any of the 9 sister goddesses in Greek mythology who were the patrons of the arts and sciences **2** a source of inspiration; *esp* a woman who influences a creative artist

museum /mjuː'zɪəm/ *n* an institution devoted to the acquiring, care, study, and display of objects of interest or value; *also* a place exhibiting such objects

mush /mʌʃ/ *n* **1** a soft mass of semiliquid material **2** mawkish sentimentality

¹mushroom /'mʌʃruːm, -rʊm/ *n* the enlarged, esp edible, fleshy fruiting body of a fungus, consisting typically of a stem bearing a flattened cap

²mushroom *v* **1** to spring up suddenly or multiply rapidly **2** to flatten at the end on impact **3** to pick wild mushrooms

mushy /'mʌʃi/ *adj* **1** having the consistency of mush **2** mawkishly sentimental

music /'mjuːzɪk/ *n* **1** vocal, instrumental, or mechanical sounds having rhythm, melody, or harmony **2** an agreeable sound **3** the score of a musical composition set down on paper

¹musical /'mjuːzɪkəl/ *adj* **1** having the pleasing harmonious qualities of music **2** having an interest in or talent for music **3** set to or accompanied by music **4** of music, musicians, or music lovers – **-ly** *adv*

²musical *n* a film or theatrical production containing songs, dances, and dialogue

musical box *n* a container enclosing an apparatus that reproduces music mechanically when activated

musical chairs *n pl but sing in constr* a game in which players march to music round a row of chairs numbering 1 less than the players and scramble for seats when the music stops

music centre *n, Br* a record player, a radio, and a cassette tape recorder in a single unit

music hall *n* (a theatre formerly presenting) entertainments consisting of a variety of unrelated acts (e g acrobats, comedians, or singers)

musician /mjuːˈzɪʃən/ *n* a composer, conductor, or performer of music; *esp* an instrumentalist

musk /mʌsk/ *n* **1** a substance with a penetrating persistent smell that is obtained from a gland of the male musk deer and used as a perfume fixative **2** any of various plants with musky smells – **~y** *adj*

musket /ˈmʌskʲ̣t/ *n* a heavy large-calibre shoulder firearm with a smooth bore

musketeer /ˌmʌskʲ̣ˈtɪəʳ/ *n* a soldier armed with a musket

muskrat /ˈmʌskˌræt/ *n* an aquatic rodent of N America with a long scaly tail and webbed hind feet

Muslim /ˈmʌzlʲ̣m, ˈmʊz-, ˈmʊs-/ *n* an adherent of Islam

muslin /ˈmʌzlʲ̣n/ *n* a plain-woven sheer to coarse cotton fabric

musquash /ˈmʌskwɒʃ/ *n* (the dark glossy brown fur or pelt of) the muskrat

mussel /ˈmʌsəl/ *n* **1** a marine bivalve mollusc with a dark elongated shell **2** a freshwater bivalve mollusc whose shell has a lustrous mother-of-pearl lining

[1]**must** /məst; *strong* mʌst/ *verbal auxiliary, pres & past all persons* **must** **1a** be commanded or requested to (e g you *must* stop) **b** certainly should; ought by all means to (e g I *must* read that book) **2** be compelled by physical, social, or legal necessity to (e g man *must* eat to live); be required by need or purpose to (e g we *must* hurry if we want to catch the bus) – past often replaced by *had to* except in reported speech; used in the negative to express the idea of prohibition (e g we *must* not park here) **3** be unreasonably or perversely compelled to (e g why *must* you be so stubborn?) **4** be logically inferred or supposed to (e g it *must* be time) **5** was presumably certain to; was or were bound to (e g if he really was there, I *must* have seen him)

[2]**must** *n* an essential or prerequisite

[3]**must** *n* grape juice before and during fermentation

mustang /ˈmʌstæŋ/ *n* the small hardy naturalized horse of the western plains of the USA

mustard /ˈmʌstəd/ *n* a pungent yellow powder used as a condiment or in medicine, esp as an emetic; *also* any of several related plants with lobed leaves, yellow flowers, and straight pods that product seeds from which mustard is prepared

[1]**muster** /ˈmʌstəʳ/ *v* **1** to assemble, convene **2** to summon in response to a need

[2]**muster** *n* **1a** assembling (for military inspection) **b** an assembled group; a collection **2** a critical examination

musty /ˈmʌsti/ *adj* **1** affected by mould, damp, or mildew **2** tasting or smelling of damp and decay – **mustiness** *n*

mutable /ˈmjuːtəbəl/ *adj* **1** capable of or liable to change or alteration **2** capable of or subject to mutation – **-bility** *n*

mutation /mjuːˈteɪʃən/ *n* **1** (a) significant and fundamental alteration **2** (an individual or strain differing from others of its type and resulting from) a relatively permanent change in an organism's hereditary material

[1]**mute** /mjuːt/ *adj* **1** unable to speak; dumb **2** felt but not expressed – **~ly** *adv* – **~ness** *n*

[2]**mute** *n* **1** one who cannot or does not speak **2** a device attached to a musical instrument to reduce, soften, or muffle its tone

[3]**mute** *v* **1** to muffle or reduce the sound of **2** to tone down (a colour) – **muted** *adj*

mutilate /ˈmjuːtʲ̣leɪt/ *v* **1** to cut off or permanently destroy or damage a limb or essential part of **2** to damage or deface – **-tion** *n*

mutiny /ˈmjuːtʲ̣ni, -təni/ *n* concerted revolt (e g of a naval crew) against discipline or a superior officer – **-inous** *adj* – **-inously** *adv* – **mutiny** *v*

mutt /mʌt/ *n* **1** a dull or stupid person **2** a (mongrel) dog

mutter /'mʌtəʳ/ *v* to utter, esp in a low or indistinct voice – **mutter** *n* – **~er** *n*

mutton /'mʌtn/ *n* the flesh of a mature sheep used as food

mutual /'mjuːtʃʊəl/ *adj* **1a** directed by each towards the other **b** having the same specified feeling for each other **2** shared by 2 or more in common – **~ity** *n* – **~ly** *adv*

[1]**muzzle** /'mʌzəl/ *n* **1a** the projecting jaws and nose of a dog or other animal **b** a covering for the mouth of an animal used to prevent biting, barking, etc **2** the discharging end of a pistol, rifle, etc

[2]**muzzle** *v* to restrain from free expression; gag

muzzy /'mʌzi/ *adj* mentally confused; befuddled – **-zily** *adv* – **-ziness** *n*

my /maɪ/ *adj* **1** of me or myself, esp as possessor, agent, or object of an action – sometimes used with vocatives (e g *my* lord) **2** – used interjectionally to express surprise, in certain fixed exclamations (e g *my* God!), and with names of certain parts of the body to express doubt or disapproval (e g *my* foot!)

mycelium /maɪ'siːlɪəm/ *n, pl* **mycelia** the mass of interwoven threads that forms the body of a fungus

mycology /maɪ'kɒlədʒi/ *n* (the biology of) fungal life or fungi

myopia /maɪ'əʊpɪə/ *n* defective vision of distant objects resulting from the focussing of the visual images in front of the retina; shortsightedness – **-pic** *adj* – **-pically** *adv*

[1]**myriad** /'mɪrɪəd/ *n* an indefinitely large number – often pl with sing. meaning

[2]**myriad** *adj* innumerable, countless

myrrh /mɜːʳ/ *n* a brown bitter aromatic gum resin obtained from any of several African and Asian trees

myself /maɪ'self/ *pron* **1** that identical one that is I – used reflexively, for emphasis, or in absolute constructions (e g *myself* a tourist, I nevertheless avoided other tourists) **2** my normal self (e g I'm not quite *myself* today)

mysterious /mɪ'stɪərɪəs/ *adj* **1** difficult to comprehend **2** containing, suggesting, or implying mystery – **~ly** *adv* – **~ness** *n*

mystery /'mɪstəri/ *n* **1a** a religious truth disclosed by revelation alone **b** a secret religious rite **2a** sthg not understood or beyond understanding **b** a fictional work dealing usu with the solution of a mysterious crime **3** an enigmatic or secretive quality

mystery play, mystery *n* a medieval religious drama based on episodes from the Scriptures

mystic /'mɪstɪk/ *n* a person who believes that God or ultimate reality can only be apprehended by direct personal experience

mystical /'mɪstɪkəl/, **mystic** *adj* **1** having a sacred or spiritual meaning not given by normal modes of thought or feeling **2** of mysteries or esoteric rites **3** of mysticism or mystics **4a** mysterious, incomprehensible **b** obscure, esoteric

mystify /'mɪstʒfaɪ/ *v* **1** to perplex, bewilder **2** to cause to appear mysterious or obscure – **-fication** *n*

mystique /mɪ'stiːk/ *n* **1** a mystical reverential atmosphere or quality associated with a person or thing **2** an esoteric skill peculiar to an occupation or activity

myth /mɪθ/ *n* **1** a traditional story that embodies popular beliefs or explains a practice, belief, or natural phenomenon **2** a parable, allegory **3a** a person or thing having a fictitious existence **b** a belief subscribed to uncritically by an (interested) group – **~ical** *adj*

mythological /,mɪθə'lɒdʒɪkəl/ *adj* **1** of or dealt with in mythology or myths **2** lacking factual or historical basis

mythology /mɪ'θɒlədʒi/ *n* **1** a body of myths, esp those dealing with the gods and heroes of a particular people **2** a body of beliefs, usu with little factual foundation, lending glamour or mystique to sby or sthg

myxomatosis /,mɪksəmə'təʊsʒs/ *n* a severe flea-transmitted virus disease of rabbits that has been used in their biological control

N

n /en/ *n, pl* **n's, ns** *often cap* **1** (a graphic representation of or device for reproducing) the 14th letter of the English alphabet **2** an indefinite number

'n' *also* **'n** /n/ *conj* and

Naafi /ˈnæfi/ *n* the organization which runs shops and canteens in British military establishments

nab /næb/ *v* **-bb-** **1** to arrest; apprehend **2** to catch hold of; grab *USE* infml

nabob /ˈneɪbɒb/ *n* **1** a provincial governor of the Mogul empire in India **2** a man of great wealth – used orig of an Englishman grown rich in India

nacelle /næˈsel, nə-/ *n* a housing for an aircraft engine

nadir /ˈneɪdɪəʳ/ *n* **1** the point of the celestial sphere that is directly opposite the zenith and vertically downwards from the observer **2** the lowest point

¹nag /næg/ *n* a horse; *esp* one that is old or in poor condition

²nag *v* **1** to subject to constant scolding or urging **2** to be a persistent source of annoyance or discomfort – **~ger** *n*

³nag *n* a person, esp a woman, who nags habitually

naiad /ˈnaɪæd/ *n* **1** *often cap* a nymph in classical mythology living in lakes, rivers, etc **2** the aquatic larva of a mayfly, dragonfly, etc

¹nail /neɪl/ *n* **1** a horny sheath protecting the upper end of each finger and toe of human beings and other primates **2** a slender usu pointed and headed spike designed to be driven in, esp with a hammer, to join materials, act as a support, etc

²nail *v* **1** to fasten (as if) with a nail **2** to fix steadily **3** to catch, trap **4** to detect and expose (e g a lie or scandal) so as to discredit

naive, naïve /naɪˈiːv/ *adj* **1** ingenuous, unsophisticated **2** lacking worldly wisdom or experience; *esp* credulous – **~ty** *n*

naked /ˈneɪkɨd/ *adj* **1** having no clothes on **2a** *of a knife or sword* not enclosed in a sheath or scabbard **b** exposed to the air or to full view **3** without furnishings or ornamentation **4** unarmed, defenceless **5** not concealed or disguised **6** unaided by any optical device – **~ly** *adv* – **~ness** *n*

¹name /neɪm/ *n* **1** a word or phrase designating an individual person or thing **2** a descriptive usu disparaging epithet **3a** reputation **b** a famous or notorious person or thing

²name *v* **1** to give a name to; call **2** to identify by name **3** to nominate, appoint **4** to decide on; choose **5** to mention explicitly; specify

nameless /ˈneɪmlɨs/ *adj* **1** obscure, undistinguished **2** not known by name; anonymous **3** having no legal right to a name; illegitimate **4a** having no name **b** left purposely unnamed **5** too terrible or distressing to describe

namely /ˈneɪmli/ *adv* that is to say

namesake /ˈneɪmseɪk/ *n* sby or sthg that has the same name as another

nanny *also* **nannie** /ˈnæni/ *n* a child's nurse; a nursemaid

nanny goat *n* a female domestic goat – infml

¹nap /næp/ *v* **1** to take a short sleep, esp during the day **2** to be off one's guard

²nap *n* a short sleep, esp during the day

³nap *n* a hairy or downy surface (e g on a woven fabric); a pile – **~ped** *adj*

⁴nap *v* to recommend (a horse) as a possible winner – **nap** *n*

¹napalm /ˈneɪpɑːm/ *n* petrol thickened with a jelly and used esp in incendiary bombs and flamethrowers

²napalm *v* to attack with napalm

nape /neɪp/ *n* the back of the neck

napkin /ˈnæpkɨn/ *n* **1** a usu square piece of material (e g linen or paper) used at table to wipe the lips or fingers and protect the clothes **2** a nappy

nappy /ˈnæpi/ *n, chiefly Br* a square

piece of cloth or paper worn by babies to absorb and retain excreta and usu drawn up between the legs and fastened at the waist

narcissism /'nɑːsɪ̀sɪzəm/ *n* love of or sexual desire for one's self or one's own body – **-sist** *n* – **-sistic** *adj* – **-sistically** *adv*

narcissus /nɑː'sɪsəs/ *n* a daffodil; *esp* one whose flowers are borne separately and have a short corona

[1]**narcotic** /nɑː'kɒtɪk/ *n* a usu addictive drug, esp (a derivative of) morphine, that dulls the senses, induces prolonged sleep, and relieves pain

[2]**narcotic** *adj* **1** like, being, or yielding a narcotic **2** inducing mental lethargy; soporific

[1]**nark** /nɑːk/ *n, Br* a police informer

[2]**nark** *v* **1** to act as an informer – slang; often + *on* **2** to offend, affront – infml

narrate /nə'reɪt/ *v* to recite the details of (a story) – **-ator** *n*

narration /nə'reɪʃən/ *n* **1** (a) narrating **2** a story, narrative

narrative /'nærətɪv/ *n* **1** sthg (e g a story) that is narrated **2** the art or practice of narration

[1]**narrow** /'nærəʊ/ *adj* **1** of little width, esp in comparison with height or length **2** limited in size or scope; restricted **3** inflexible, hidebound **4** only just sufficient or successful – **~ness** *n* – **~ly** *adv*

[2]**narrow** *n* a narrow part or (water) passage – usu pl with sing. meaning

[3]**narrow** *v* to make or become narrow or narrower

narrow boat *n* a canal barge

narrow-minded *adj* lacking tolerance or breadth of vision; bigoted – **~ness** *n*

narwhal *also* **narwal** /'nɑːwəl/ *n* a small arctic whale, the male of which has a long twisted ivory tusk

nasal /'neɪzəl/ *adj* **1** of the nose **2a** uttered through the nose with the mouth passage closed (as in English /m, n, N/) **b** characterized by resonance produced through the nose

nascent /'næsənt/ *adj* in the process of being born; just beginning to develop – fml

nasturtium /nə'stɜːʃəm/ *n* (any of a genus of plants related to) a widely cultivated plant with showy spurred flowers and pungent seeds

nasty /'nɑːsti/ *adj* **1** repugnant, esp to smell or taste **2** obscene, indecent **3** mean, tawdry **4a** harmful, dangerous **b** disagreeable, dirty **5** giving cause for concern or anxiety **6** spiteful, vicious – **-tily** *adv* – **-tiness** *n*

natal /'neɪtl/ *adj* of, present at, or associated with (one's) birth

nation /'neɪʃən/ *n* **1** a people with a common origin, tradition, and language (capable of) constituting a nation-state **2** a community of people possessing a more or less defined territory and government

[1]**national** /'næʃənəl/ *adj* **1** of a nation **2** belonging to or maintained by the central government **3** of or being a coalition government – **~ally** *adv*

[2]**national** *n* **1** a citizen of a specified nation **2** a competition that is national in scope – usu pl

national debt *n* the amount of money owed by the government of a country

National Front *n* an extreme right-wing political party of Britain asserting the racial superiority of the indigenous British population over immigrants (e g blacks)

National Health Service, National Health *n* the British system of medical care, started in 1948, by which every person receives free or subsidized medical treatment paid for by taxation

national insurance *n, often cap N&I* a compulsory social-security scheme in Britain funded by contributions from employers, employees, and the government which insures the individual against sickness, retirement, and unemployment

nationalism /'næʃənəlɪzəm/ *n* loyalty and devotion to a nation; *esp* the exalting of one nation above all others – **-list** *n, adj* – **-listic** *adj* – **-listically** *adv*

nationality /ˌnæʃə'nælɪ̀ti/ *n* **1** national character **2** national status **3** citizenship of a particular nation **4** existence as a separate nation

national·ize, -ise /'næʃənəlaɪz/ *v* to invest control or ownership of in the national government

national service *n* conscripted service in the British armed forces

national socialism *n* Nazism

nation-state *n* a sovereign state inhabited by a relatively homogeneous people as opposed to several nationalities

[1]**native** /ˈneɪtɪv/ *adj* **1** inborn, innate **2** belonging to a particular place by birth **3a** belonging to or being the place of one's birth **b** of or being one's first language or sby using his/her first language **4** living (naturally), grown, or produced in a particular place; indigenous **5** found in nature, esp in a pure form

[2]**native** *n* **1** one born or reared in a particular place **2a** an original or indigenous (non-European) inhabitant **b** a plant, animal, etc indigenous to a particular locality **3** a local resident

nativity /nəˈtɪvɪ̣ti/ *n* **1** birth; *specif, cap* the birth of Jesus **2** a horoscope

natter /ˈnætəʳ/ *v or n* (to) chatter, gossip – infml

natty /ˈnæti/ *adj* neat and trim; spruce – **-tily** *adv*

[1]**natural** /ˈnætʃərəl/ *adj* **1** based on an inherent moral sense **2** in accordance with or determined by nature **3** related by blood rather than by adoption **4** innate, inherent **5** of nature as an object of study **6** having a specified character or attribute by nature **7** happening in accordance with the ordinary course of nature **8** normal or expected **9** of the physical as opposed to the spiritual world **10a** true to nature; lifelike **b** free from affectation or constraint **c** not disguised or altered in appearance or form **11** (containing only notes that are) neither sharp nor flat – **~ness** *n*

[2]**natural** *n* **1** (a note affected by) a sign placed on the musical staff to nullify the effect of a preceding sharp or flat **2** one having natural skills or talents

natural history *n* the usu amateur study, esp in the field, of natural objects (e g plants and animals), often in a particular area

naturalist /ˈnætʃərəlɪ̣st/ *n* a student of natural history

natural·ize, -ise /ˈnætʃərəlaɪz/ *v* **1** to cause a plant to become established as if native **2** to grant citizenship to

naturally /ˈnætʃərəli/ *adv* **1** by nature **2** as might be expected **3** in a natural manner

natural resources *n pl* industrial materials and capacities (e g mineral deposits and waterpower) supplied by nature

natural selection *n* a natural process that tends to result in the survival of organisms best adapted to their environment and the elimination of organisms carrying undesirable traits

nature /ˈneɪtʃəʳ/ *n* **1** the inherent character or constitution of a person or thing **2** a creative and controlling force in the universe **3** the physical constitution of an organism **4** the external world in its entirety **5** natural scenery

naturism /ˈneɪtʃərɪzəm/ *n* nudism – **-ist** *n*

naught /nɔːt/ *n* **1** nothing **2** nought

naughty /ˈnɔːti/ *adj* **1** badly behaved; wicked **2** slightly improper – euph or humor – **-tily** *adv* – **-tiness** *n*

nausea /ˈnɔːzɪə, -sɪə/ *n* **1** a feeling of discomfort in the stomach accompanied by a distaste for food and an urge to vomit **2** extreme disgust

nauseate /ˈnɔːzieɪt, -si-/ *v* to (cause to) become affected with nausea or disgust

nauseous /ˈnɔːzɪəs, -sɪəs/ *adj* causing or affected with nausea or disgust – **~ly** *adv* – **~ness** *n*

nautical /ˈnɔːtɪkəl/ *adj* of or associated with seamen, navigation, or ships – **~ly** *adv*

nautical mile *n* any of various units of distance used for sea and air navigation based on the length of a minute of arc of a great circle of the earth; *esp* a British unit equal to 6080ft (about 1853.18m)

nautilus /ˈnɔːtɪ̣ləs/ *n* any of a genus of molluscs related to the octopuses and squids that live in the Pacific and Indian oceans and have a spiral shell

naval /ˈneɪvəl/ *adj* **1** of a navy **2** consisting of or involving warships

[1]**nave** /neɪv/ *n* the hub of a wheel

[2]**nave** *n* the main body of a church lying to the west of the chancel; *esp*

the long central space flanked by aisles

navel /'neɪvəl/ *n* **1** a depression in the middle of the abdomen marking the point of former attachment of the umbilical cord **2** the central point

navigable /'nævɨgəbəl/ *adj* **1** suitable for ships to pass through or along **2** capable of being steered – **-gability** *n*

navigate /'nævɨgeɪt/ *v* **1** to steer a course through a medium (e g water) **2** to perform the activities (e g taking sightings and making calculations) involved in navigation **3a** to steer or manage (a boat) in sailing **b** to operate or direct the course of (e g an aircraft) – **-ation** *n* – **-ational** *adj* – **-ator** *n*

navvy /'nævi/ *n, Br* an unskilled labourer

navy /'neɪvi/ *n* **1** a nation's ships of war and support vessels together with the organization needed for maintenance **2** *sing or pl in constr* the personnel manning a navy **3** navy blue

navy blue *adj or n* deep dark blue

[1]**nay** /neɪ/ *adv* **1** not merely this but also **2** *N Eng or archaic* no

[2]**nay** *n* **1** denial, refusal **2** a vote or voter against

nazi /'nɑːtsi/ *n, often cap* a member of the German fascist party controlling Germany from 1933 to 1945

NCO *n* a noncommissioned officer

Neanderthal man /ni'ændətɑːl/ *n* a form of early man known from fossil remains in Europe, N Africa, and W Asia

Neapolitan *n or adj* (a native or inhabitant) of Naples

neap tide /niːp taɪd/ *n* a tide of minimum height occurring at the 1st and the 3rd quarters of the moon

[1]**near** /nɪəʳ/ *adv* **1** in or into a near position or manner (e g came *near* to tears) **2** closely approximating; nearly (e g a *near*-perfect performance)

[2]**near** *prep* near to (e g went too *near* the edge)

[3]**near** *adj* **1** intimately connected or associated **2a** not far distant in time, space, or degree **b** close, narrow (e g a *near* miss) **3a** being the closer of 2 (e g the *near* side) **b** being the left-hand one of a pair (e g the *near* wheel of a cart) – **~ness** *n*

[4]**near** *v* to approach

nearby /nɪə'baɪ/ *adv or adj* close at hand

nearly /'nɪəli/ *adv* **1** in a close manner or relationship (e g *nearly* related) **2** almost but not quite

nearside /'nɪəsaɪd/ *n, Br* the left-hand side (e g of a vehicle or road)

[1]**neat** /niːt/ *adj* **1** without addition or dilution **2** elegantly simple **3a** precise, well-defined **b** skilful, adroit **4** (habitually) tidy and orderly **5** *chiefly NAm* fine, excellent – infml

[2]**neat** *adv* without addition or dilution; straight

nebula /'nebjʊlə/ *n* **1** any of many immense bodies of highly rarefied gas or dust in interstellar space **2** a galaxy – **~r** *adj*

nebulous /'nebjʊləs/ *adj* **1** indistinct, vague **2** of or resembling a nebula; nebular – **-losity** *n* – **~ly** *adv* – **~ness** *n*

necessarily /'nesɨsərɨli, ˌnesɨ'serɨli/ *adv* as a necessary consequence; inevitably

[1]**necessary** /'nesəsəri/ *n* an indispensable item; an essential

[2]**necessary** *adj* **1a** inevitable, inescapable **b** logically unavoidable **2** essential, indispensable

necessitate /nɨ'sesɨteɪt/ *v* to make necessary or unavoidable

necessitous /nɨ'sesɨtəs/ *adj* needy, impoverished – fml – **~ly** *adv*

necessity /nɨ'sesɨti/ *n* **1** the quality of being necessary, indispensable, or unavoidable **2** impossibility of a contrary order or condition **3** poverty, want **4a** sthg necessary or indispensable **b** a pressing need or desire

[1]**neck** /nek/ *n* **1a** the part of an animal that connects the head with the body; *also* a cut of meat taken from this part **b** the part of a garment that covers the neck; *also* the neckline **2a** a narrow part, esp shaped like a neck **b** the part of a stringed musical instrument extending from the body and supporting the fingerboard and strings

[2]**neck** *v* to kiss and caress in sexual play – infml

neckerchief /'nekətʃɨf/ *n, pl* **neckerchiefs** *also* **neckerchieves** a square of fabric folded and worn round the neck

necklace /'nek-lɨs/ *n* a string of jewels, beads, etc worn round the neck as an ornament

neckline /'nek-laɪn/ *n* the upper edge of a garment that forms the opening for the neck and head

necromancy /,nekrəmænsi/ *n* **1** the conjuring up of the spirits of the dead in order to predict or influence the future **2** magic, sorcery – **-ancer** *n*

nectar /'nektəʳ/ *n* **1** the drink of the gods in classical mythology; *broadly* a delicious drink **2** a sweet liquid secreted by the flowers of many plants that is the chief raw material of honey

nectarine /'nektəri:n/ *n* (a tree that bears) a smooth-skinned peach

née, nee /neɪ/ *adj* – used to identify a woman by her maiden name

[1]**need** /ni:d/ *n* **1a** a lack of sthg necessary, desirable, or useful **b** a physiological or psychological requirement for the well-being of an organism **2** a condition requiring supply or relief **3** poverty, want

[2]**need** *v* **1** to be in need of; require **2** to be constrained (e g I'll *need* to work hard) **3** be under necessity or obligation to

needful /'ni:dfəl/ *adj* necessary, requisite – **~ly** *adv*

[1]**needle** /'ni:dl/ *n* **1a** a small slender usu steel instrument with an eye for thread at one end and a sharp point at the other, used for sewing **b** any of various similar larger instruments without an eye, used for carrying thread and making stitches (e g in crocheting or knitting) **c** the slender hollow pointed end of a hypodermic syringe for injecting or removing material **2** a slender, usu sharp-pointed, indicator on a dial; *esp* a magnetic needle **3** a needle-shaped leaf, esp of a conifer **4** *Br* a feeling of enmity or ill will – infml

[2]**needle** *v* to provoke by persistent teasing or gibes

needless /'ni:dlɨs/ *adj* not needed; unnecessary – **~ly** *adv*

needlewoman /'ni:dl,wʊmən/ *n* a woman who does needlework

needlework /'ni:dlwɜ:k/ *n* sewing; *esp* fancy work (e g embroidery)

needs /ni:dz/ *adv* necessarily (e g must *needs* be recognized)

needy /'ni:di/ *adj* in want, impoverished – **neediness** *n*

ne'er-do-well /'neə du: ,wel/ *n* an idle worthless person

nefarious /nɪ'feərɪəs/ *adj* evil, wicked – **~ly** *adv* – **~ness** *n*

negate /nɪ'geɪt/ *v* **1** to deny the existence or truth of **2** to make ineffective or invalid – **-gation** *n*

[1]**negative** /'negətɪv/ *adj* **1a** marked by denial, prohibition, or refusal **b** expressing negation **2** lacking positive or agreeable features **3** less than zero and opposite in sign to a positive number that when added to the given number yields zero **4** having lower electric potential and constituting the part towards which the current flows from the external circuit **5** having the light and dark parts in approximately inverse order to those of the original photographic subject – **~ly** *adv*

[2]**negative** *n* **1** a negative reply **2** sthg that is the negation or opposite of sthg else **3** an expression (e g the word *no*) of negation or denial **4** the side that upholds the contradictory proposition in a debate **5** the plate of an electric cell that is at the lower potential **6** a negative photographic image on transparent material used for printing positive pictures

[1]**neglect** /nɪ'glekt/ *v* **1** to pay insufficient attention to; disregard **2** to leave undone or unattended to

[2]**neglect** *n* neglecting or being neglected

neglectful /nɪ'glektfəl/ *adj* careless, forgetful – **~ly** *adv* – **~ness** *n*

negligee, negligé /'neglɨʒeɪ/ *n* a woman's light decorative housecoat, often designed to be worn with a matching nightdress

negligent /'neglɪdʒənt/ *adj* **1** (habitually or culpably) neglectful **2** pleasantly casual in manner – **~ly** *adv* – **-gence** *n*

negligible /'neglɪdʒəbəl/ *adj* trifling, insignificant – **-bly** *adv*

negotiable /nɪ'gəʊʃɪəbəl, -ʃə-/ *adj* **1** capable of being passed along or through 2 capable of being dealt with or settled through discussion

negotiate /nɪˈɡəʊʃieɪt/ *v* **1** to confer with another in order to reach an agreement **2a** to transfer (e g a bill of exchange) to another by delivery or endorsement **b** to convert into cash or the equivalent value **3a** to travel successfully along or over **b** to complete or deal with successfully – **-ation** *n* – **-ator** *n*

Negress /ˈniːɡrɪ̵s/ *n* a female Negro – chiefly derog

Negro /ˈniːɡrəʊ/ *n* a member of the esp African branch of the black race of mankind

neigh /neɪ/ *v* to make the loud prolonged cry characteristic of a horse

¹neighbour /ˈneɪbəʳ/ *n* **1** one living or situated near another **2** a fellow human being

²neighbour *v* to adjoin or lie near to

neighbourhood /ˈneɪbəhʊd/ *n* **1** an adjacent or surrounding region **2** an approximate amount, extent, or degree **3** (the inhabitants of) a district of a town, city etc, forming a distinct community

neighbouring /ˈneɪbərɪŋ/ *adj* nearby, adjacent

neighbourly /ˈneɪbəli/ *adj* characteristic of congenial neighbours; *esp* friendly – **-liness** *n*

¹neither /ˈnaɪðəʳ/ *pron* not the one or the other (e g *neither* of us)

²neither *conj* **1** not either (e g *neither* here nor there) **2** also not; nor (e g he didn't go and *neither* did I)

³neither *adj* not either (e g *neither* hand)

⁴neither *adv* **1** similarly not; also not (e g I can't swim. *Neither* can I) **2** *chiefly dial* either

nemesis /ˈnemɪ̵sɪ̵s/ *n* **1** (an agent of) retribution or vengeance **2** downfall, undoing

neocolonialism /ˌniːəʊkəˈləʊnɪəlɪzəm/ *n* the economic and political policies by which a great power indirectly extends its influence over other areas

Neolithic /ˌniːəˈlɪθɪk/ *adj* of the last period of the Stone Age characterized by polished stone implements

neologism /niːˈɒlədʒɪzəm/ *n* (the use of) a new word, usage, or expression

neon /ˈniːɒn/ *n* a gaseous element used esp in electric lamps

neophyte /ˈnɪəfaɪt/ *n* **1** a new convert **2** a beginner

nephew /ˈnevjuː, ˈnef-/ *n* a son of one's brother or sister or of one's brother-in-law or sister-in-law

ne plus ultra /ˌniː plʌs ˈʌltrə, neɪ-/ *n* **1** the highest point or stage **2** the greatest degree of a quality or state

nepotism /ˈnepətɪzəm/ *n* favouritism shown to a relative (e g by appointment to office)

Neptune /ˈneptjuːn/ *n* **1** the ocean personified **2** the planet 8th in order from the sun

¹nerve /nɜːv/ *n* **1** any of the filaments of nervous tissue that conduct nervous impulses to and from the nervous system and are made up of axons and dendrites **2** fortitude, tenacity **3** (disrespectful) assurance or boldness **4a** a sore or sensitive subject – esp in *hit/touch a nerve* **b** *pl* acute nervousness or anxiety

²nerve *v* **1** to give strength and courage to **2** to prepare (oneself) psychologically *for* – often + *up*

nerveless /ˈnɜːvlɪ̵s/ *adj* **1** lacking strength or vigour **2** not agitated or afraid; cool – **~ly** *adv* – **~ness** *n*

nerve-racking, nerve-wracking *adj* placing great strain on the nerves

nervous /ˈnɜːvəs/ *adj* **1** of, affected by, or composed of (the) nerves or neurons **2a** easily excited or agitated **b** timid, apprehensive – **~ly** *adv* – **~ness** *n*

nervous breakdown *n* (an occurrence of) a disorder in which worrying, depression, severe tiredness, etc prevent one from coping with one's responsibilities

nervous system *n* the brain, spinal cord, or other nerves and nervous tissue together forming a system for interpreting stimuli from the sense organs and transmitting impulses to muscles, glands, etc

nervy /ˈnɜːvi/ *adj* **1** suffering from nervousness or anxiety **2** brash, imprudent – infml

¹nest /nest/ *n* **1a** a bed or receptacle prepared by a bird for its eggs and young **b** a place or structure in which animals live, esp in their immature stages **2a** a place of rest, retreat, or lodging **b** a den or haunt **3** a series of objects made to fit close together or one inside another

[2]**nest** *v* **1** to build or occupy a nest **2** to fit compactly together

nest egg *n* an amount of money saved up as a reserve

nestle /ˈnesəl/ *v* **1** to settle snugly or comfortably together **2** to lie in a sheltered position

nestling /ˈnestlɪŋ, ˈneslɪŋ/ *n* a young bird that has not abandoned the nest

[1]**net** /net/ *n* **1** an open meshed fabric twisted, knotted, or woven together at regular intervals and used for a variety of purposes, e g fishing or as a barrier in various games **2** (the fabric that encloses the sides and back of) a soccer, hockey, etc goal **3a** a practice cricket pitch surrounded by nets – usu pl **b** a period of practice in such a net

[2]**net** *v* **1** to cover or enclose (as if) with a net **2** to hit (a ball) into the net for the loss of a point in a game

[3]**net** *adj* **1** remaining after all deductions (e g for taxes, outlay, or loss) **2** final, ultimate

[4]**net** *v* **1** to make by way of profit **2** to get possession of

netball /ˈnetbɔːl/ *n* a game, usu for women, between 2 sides of 7 players each who score goals by tossing an inflated ball through a high horizontal ring on a post at each end of a hard court

nether /ˈneðəʳ/ *adj* lower, under – fml

netting /ˈnetɪŋ/ *n* network

[1]**nettle** /ˈnetl/ *n* any of a genus of widely distributed green-flowered plants covered with (stinging) hairs

[2]**nettle** *v* **1** to strike or sting (as if) with nettles **2** to arouse to annoyance or anger

nettle rash *n* a skin rash resembling nettle stings

network /ˈnetwɜːk/ *n* **1** a fabric or structure of cords or wires that cross at regular intervals and are knotted or secured at the crossings **2** a system of crisscrossing lines or channels **3** an interconnected chain, group, or system **4a** a group of radio or television stations linked together so that they can broadcast the same programmes if desired **b** a radio or television company that produces programmes for broadcast over such a network

neural /ˈnjʊərəl/ *adj* **1** of or affecting a nerve or the nervous system **2** dorsal

neuralgia /njʊˈrældʒə/ *n* intense paroxysms of pain radiating along the course of a nerve without apparent cause – **-gic** *adj*

neurology /njʊˈrɒlədʒi/ *n* the study of (diseases of) the nervous system – **-gist** *n*

neuron /ˈnjʊərɒn/ *n* any of the many specialized cells that form the impulse-transmitting units of the nervous system – **~al** *adj*

neurosis /njʊˈrəʊsɪ̈s/ *n, pl* **neuroses** a nervous disorder in which phobias, compulsions, anxiety, and obsessions make normal life difficult

neurotic /njʊˈrɒtɪk/ *n* one who is emotionally unstable or is affected with a neurosis

[1]**neuter** /ˈnjuːtəʳ/ *adj* **1** of or belonging to the gender that is neither masculine nor feminine **2** lacking generative organs or having nonfunctional ones – **neuter** *n*

[2]**neuter** *v* to castrate

[1]**neutral** /ˈnjuːtrəl/ *adj* **1** (of or being a country, person, etc) not engaged on either side of a war, dispute, etc **2a** indifferent, indefinite **b** without colour **c** neither acid nor alkaline **d** not electrically charged or positive or negative; not live – **~ity** *n* – **~ly** *adv*

[2]**neutral** *n* **1** a neutral country, person, etc **2** a neutral colour **3** a position (of a gear lever) in which gears are disengaged

neutral·ize, -ise /ˈnjuːtrəlaɪz/ *v* **1** to make (chemically, politically, etc) neutral **2** to nullify or counteract the effect of sthg with an opposing action, force, etc – **~r** *n*

neutron /ˈnjuːtrɒn/ *n* an uncharged elementary particle with a mass about that of the proton, present in the nuclei of all atoms except those of normal hydrogen

never /ˈnevəʳ/ *adv* **1** not ever; at no time **2** not in any degree; not under any condition (e g this will *never* do) **3** surely not (e g you're *never* 18!) – chiefly infml

nevermore /ˌnevəˈmɔːʳ/ *adv* never again

never-never *n, Br* hire purchase – + *the*; infml

never-never land *n* an ideal or imaginary place

nevertheless /ˌnevəðəˈles/ *adv* in spite of that; yet

¹new /njuː/ *adj* **1** not old; not used previously; recent **2a** only recently discovered, recognized, or in use; novel **b** different from or replacing a former one of the same kind **3** having been in the specified condition or relationship for only a short time; unaccustomed **4** *cap* modern; *esp* in use after medieval times

²new *adv* newly, recently – usu in combination

newcomer /ˈnjuːkʌməʳ/ *n* **1** a recent arrival **2** a beginner, novice

newel /ˈnjuːəl/ *n* **1** an upright post about which the steps of a spiral staircase wind **2** *also* **newel post** a principal post supporting either end of a staircase handrail

newfangled /ˌnjuːˈfæŋgəld/ *adj* modern and unnecessarily complicated or gimmicky – derog or humor – **~ness** *n*

newly /ˈnjuːli/ *adv* **1** lately, recently **2** anew

newlywed /ˈnjuːliwed/ *n or adj* (one who is) recently married

news /njuːz/ *n pl but sing in constr* **1** (a report or series of reports of) recent (notable) events; new information about sthg **2a** news reported in a newspaper, a periodical, or a broadcast **b** material that is newsworthy **3** a radio or television broadcast of news

newsagent /ˈnjuːzˌeɪdʒənt/ *n, chiefly Br* a retailer of newspapers and magazines

newsboy /ˈnjuːzbɔɪ/, *fem* **newsgirl** *n* a paperboy

newscast /ˈnjuːzkɑːst/ *n* a news broadcast

newsletter /ˈnjuːzˌletəʳ/ *n* a printed pamphlet containing news or information of interest chiefly to a special group

newspaper /ˈnjuːsˌpeɪpəʳ/ *n* (an organization that publishes) a paper printed and distributed usu daily or weekly and containing news, articles of opinion, features, and advertising

newsprint /ˈnjuːzˌprɪnt/ *n* cheap paper made chiefly from wood pulp and used mostly for newspapers

newsreel /ˈnjuːzriːl/ *n* a short film dealing with current events

newsroom /ˈnjuːzrʊm, -ruːm/ *n* a place (e g an office) where news is prepared for publication or broadcast

newsstand /ˈnjuːzstænd/ *n* a stall where newspapers and periodicals are sold

newsworthy /ˈnjuːzˌwɜːði/ *adj* sufficiently interesting to warrant reporting

newt /njuːt/ *n* any of various small semiaquatic salamanders

New Testament *n* the second part of the Christian Bible comprising the canonical Gospels and Epistles, the books of Acts, and the book of Revelation

new wave *n, often cap N&W* a style of rock music that developed from punk rock and is usu more complex musically while retaining an emphasis on social comment

New World *n* the W hemisphere; *esp* the continental landmass of N and S America

New Year *n* the first day or days of a year

New Year's Day *n* January 1 observed as a public holiday in many countries

¹next /nekst/ *adj* **1** immediately adjacent or following (e g in place or order) **2** immediately after the present or a specified time

²next *adv* **1** in the time, place, or order nearest or immediately succeeding **2** on the first occasion to come (e g when we *next* meet)

³next *prep* nearest or adjacent to (e g wear wool *next* to the skin)

⁴next *n* the next occurrence, item, or issue of a kind

next-door *adj* situated or living in the next building, room, etc

next door *adv* in or to the next building, room, etc – **next-door** *adj*

next of kin *n, pl* **next of kin** the person most closely related to another person

nexus /ˈneksəs/ *n, pl* **nexuses, nexus** **1** a connection or link **2** a connected group or series

nib /nɪb/ *n* **1** a bill or beak **2** the writing point of a pen **3** a small pointed or projecting part or article

[1]**nibble** /ˈnɪbəl/ *v* **1** to take gentle, small, or cautious bites **2** to show cautious or qualified interest *USE* often + *at*

[2]**nibble** *n* **1** an act of nibbling **2** a very small amount (e g of food) *USE* infml

nice /naɪs/ *adj* **1** showing or requiring fine discrimination or treatment **2a** pleasant, agreeable **b** well done; well-executed **3** inappropriate or unpleasant – usu ironic **4a** socially acceptable; well-bred **b** decent, proper – **~ly** *adv* – **~ness** *n*

nicety /ˈnaɪsəti/ *n* **1** an elegant or refined feature **2** a fine point or distinction **3** (the showing or requiring of) delicacy, discernment, or careful attention to details

niche /nɪtʃ, niːʃ/ *n* **1** a recess in a wall, esp for a statue **2a** a place or activity for which a person is best suited **b** the ecological role of an organism in a community, esp in regard to food consumption

[1]**nick** /nɪk/ *n* **1** a small notch or groove **2** *Br* state of health or repair – infml; esp in *in good/bad nick* **3** *Br* a prison or police station – slang

[2]**nick** *v* **1** to cut into or wound slightly **2** *Br* **a** to steal **b** to arrest

nickel /ˈnɪkəl/ *n* **1** a hard bivalent metallic transition element with magnetic properties like those of iron **2** (a US coin containing 1 part of nickel to 3 of copper and worth) the sum of 5 cents

[1]**nicker** /ˈnɪkəʳ/ *n, pl* **nicker** *Br* the sum of £1 – slang

[2]**nicker** *v* to whinny

nickname /ˈnɪkneɪm/ *n* **1** a name used in place of or in addition to a proper name **2** a familiar form of a proper name, esp of a person

nicotine /ˈnɪkətiːn/ *n* an alkaloid that is the chief drug in tobacco

niece /niːs/ *n* a daughter of one's brother or sister or of one's brother-in-law or sister-in-law

nifty /ˈnɪfti/ *adj* very good or effective; *esp* cleverly conceived or executed – infml

niggard /ˈnɪgəd/ *n* a mean and stingy person – **~ly** *adj* – **~liness** *n*

niggle /ˈnɪgəl/ *v* **1** to waste time or effort on minor details **2** to find fault constantly in a petty way **3** to cause slight irritation to; bother – **~r** *n*

niggling /ˈnɪgəlɪŋ/ *adj* **1** petty **2** persistently annoying

nigh /naɪ/ *adv, adj, or prep* near (in place, time, or relation)

night /naɪt/ *n* **1** the period of darkness from dusk to dawn caused by the earth's daily rotation **2** an evening characterized by a specified event or activity **3a** darkness **b** a state of affliction, ignorance, or obscurity

nightcap /ˈnaɪtkæp/ *n* **1** a cloth cap worn in bed **2** a drink taken at bedtime

nightclub /ˈnaɪtklʌb/ *n* a place of entertainment open at night that has a floor show, provides music and space for dancing, and usu serves drinks and food

nightdress /ˈnaɪtdres/ *n* a woman's or girl's nightgown

nightfall /ˈnaɪtfɔːl/ *n* dusk

nightingale /ˈnaɪtɪŋgeɪl/ *n* any of several Old World thrushes noted for the sweet usu nocturnal song of the male

night-light *n* a dim light kept burning all night long, esp in sby's bedroom

nightly /ˈnaɪtli/ *adj or adv* (of, occurring, taken, or done) at or by night or every night

nightmare /ˈnaɪtmeəʳ/ *n* **1** a frightening dream that usu awakens the sleeper **2** an experience, situation, or object that causes acute anxiety or terror – **-marish** *adj* – **-marishly** *adv* – **-marishness** *n*

nightshade /ˈnaɪt·ʃeɪd/ *n* any of various related usu poisonous plants: e g **a** bittersweet **b** deadly nightshade

nightshirt /ˈnaɪt·ʃɜːt/ *n* a long loose shirt for sleeping in

nihilism /ˈnaɪəlɪzəm/ *n* **1** a view that rejects all values and beliefs as meaningless or unfounded **2a** *often cap* the doctrine that social conditions are so bad as to make destruction desirable for its own sake, adhered to specif by a 19th-c Russian terrorist revolutionary party **b** terrorism – **-ist** *n* – **-istic** *adj*

nil /nɪl/ *n* nothing, zero

nimble /ˈnɪmbəl/ *adj* **1** quick, light, and easy in movement **2** quick and clever in thought and understanding – **~ness** *n* – **-bly** *adv*

nimbus /ˈnɪmbəs/ *n, pl* **nimbi, nimbuses** **1** a luminous circle about the head of a representation of a god, saint, or sovereign **2** a cloud from which rain is falling

nincompoop /ˈnɪŋkəmpuːp/ *n* a silly or foolish person

nine /naɪn/ *n* **1** the number 9 **2** the ninth in a set or series **3** sthg having 9 parts or members or a denomination of 9 **4** the first or last 9 holes of an 18-hole golf course **5** *pl in constr, cap the* Common Market countries between 1973 and 1981

nineteen /ˌnaɪnˈtiːn/ *n* the number 19 – **~th** *adj, adv, n, pron*

ninety /ˈnaɪnti/ *n* **1** the number 90 **2** *pl* (a range of temperatures, ages, or dates within a century characterized by) the numbers 90 to 99 – **-tieth** *adj, n, adv, pron*

ninny /ˈnɪni/ *n* a silly or foolish person – humor; infml

ninth /naɪnθ/ *n* **1** number nine in a countable series **2a** (a chord containing) a musical interval of an octave and a second **b** the note separated by this interval from a lower note – **ninth** *adj* – **~ly** *adv*

¹nip /nɪp/ *v* **1** to catch hold of and squeeze sharply; pinch **2** to sever (as if) by pinching sharply – often + *off* **3** to injure or make numb with cold **4** to go quickly or briefly; hurry – infml

²nip *n* **1** a sharp stinging cold **2** (an instance of) nipping; a pinch

³nip *n* a small measure or drink of spirits

Nip *n* a Japanese – derog

nipper /ˈnɪpəʳ/ *n* **1** any of various devices (e g pincers) for gripping or cutting – usu pl with sing. meaning **2** *chiefly Br* a child; *esp* a small boy – infml

nipple /ˈnɪpəl/ *n* **1** the small protuberance of a breast from which milk is drawn in the female **2** an artificial teat through which a bottle-fed infant feeds **3** a small projection through which oil or grease is injected into machinery

nippy /ˈnɪpi/ *adj* **1** nimble and lively; snappy **2** chilly – **-piness** *n*

nirvana /nɪəˈvɑːnə, nɜː-/ *n, often cap* **1** a Hindu and Buddhist state of final bliss and freedom from the cycle of rebirth, attainable through the extinction of desire and individual consciousness **2** a place or state of relief from pain or anxiety

nisi /naɪsaɪ/ *adj* taking effect at a specified time unless previously modified or avoided

¹nit /nɪt/ *n* (the egg of) a parasitic insect (e g a louse)

²nit *n, chiefly Br* a nitwit – infml

nit-picking *n* petty and usu unjustified criticism

¹nitrate /ˈnaɪtreɪt, -trɪ̠t/ *n* **1** a salt or ester of nitric acid **2** sodium or potassium nitrate used as a fertilizer

²nitrate *v* to treat or combine with nitric acid or a nitrate

nitric /ˈnaɪtrɪk/ *adj* of or containing nitrogen (with a relatively high valency)

nitric acid /ˌnaɪtrɪk ˈæsɪ̠d/ *n* a corrosive inorganic liquid acid used esp as an oxidizing agent and in making fertilizers, dyes, etc

nitrogen /ˈnaɪtrədʒən/ *n* a trivalent gaseous chemical element that constitutes about 78 per cent by volume of the atmosphere and is found in combined form as a constituent of all living things

nitroglycerine /ˌnaɪtrəʊˈglɪsərɪ̠n, -riːn/ *n* an oily highly explosive liquid used chiefly to make dynamite

nitrous /ˈnaɪtrəs/ *adj* of or containing **a** potassium nitrate **b** nitrogen (with a relatively low valency)

nitwit /ˈnɪtˌwɪt/ *n* a scatterbrained or stupid person – infml

¹no /nəʊ/ *adv* **1** – used to negate an alternative choice **2** in no respect or degree – in comparisons **3** – used in answers expressing negation, dissent, denial, or refusal; contrasted with *yes* **4** – used like a question demanding assent to the preceding statement **5** nay **6** – used as an interjection to express incredulity **7** *chiefly Scot* not

[2]**no** *adj* **1a** not any (e g *no* money) **b** hardly any; very little (e g I'll be finished in *no* time) **2a** not a; quite other than a (e g he's *no* expert) **b** – used before a noun phrase to give force to an opposite meaning (e g in *no* uncertain terms)

[3]**no** *n, pl* **noes, nos** a negative reply or vote

No, Noh *n* a classic Japanese (form of) dance-drama

[1]**nob** /nɒb/ *n* a person's head – infml

[2]**nob** *n* a wealthy or influential person – infml

[1]**no-ball** *interj or n* – (used as a call by an umpire to indicate) an illegal delivery of the ball in cricket which cannot take a wicket and counts 1 run to the batsman's side if the batsman does not score a run off it

[2]**no-ball** **1** to bowl a no-ball **2** , of an umpire in cricket to declare (a bowler) to have delivered or (a delivery) to be a no-ball

nobble /ˈnɒbəl/ *v* **1** to incapacitate (esp a racehorse), esp by drugging **2a** to win over to one's side, esp by dishonest means **b** to get hold of, esp dishonestly **c** to swindle, cheat *USE* infml

Nobel prize /nəʊˌbel ˈpraɪz, ˌ-- ˈ-/ *n* any of various annual prizes established by the will of Alfred Nobel for the encouragement of people who work for the interests of humanity (e g in the fields of peace, literature, medicine, and physics)

nobility /nəʊˈbɪlʒti, nə-/ *n* **1** being noble **2** *sing or pl in constr* the people making up a noble class

[1]**noble** /ˈnəʊbəl/ *adj* **1a** gracious and dignified in character or bearing **b** famous, notable **2** of or being high birth or exalted rank **3** imposing, stately **4** having or showing a magnanimous character or high ideals – **nobly** *adv*

[2]**noble** *n* a person of noble rank or birth

noblesse oblige /nəʊˌbles ɒˈbliːʒ/ *n* the obligation of honourable and responsible behaviour associated with high rank

[1]**nobody** /ˈnəʊbədi/ *pron* not anybody

[2]**nobody** *n* a person of no influence or consequence

nocturnal /nɒkˈtɜːnl/ *adj* **1** of or occurring in the night **2** active at night – **~ly** *adv*

nocturne /ˈnɒktɜːn/ *n* a work of art dealing with evening or night; *esp* a dreamy pensive composition for the piano

[1]**nod** /nɒd/ *v* **1** to make a short downward movement of the head (e g in assent or greeting) **2** to become drowsy or sleepy **3** to make a slip or error in a moment of inattention

[2]**nod** *n* **1** (an instance of) nodding **2** an unconsidered indication of agreement, approval, etc – infml

node /nəʊd/ *n* a point on a stem at which 1 or more leaves are attached – **-dal** *adj*

nodule /ˈnɒdjuːl/ *n* **1** a small rounded mass **2** a swelling on the root of a leguminous plant (e g clover) containing bacteria that convert atmospheric nitrogen into a form in which it can be used by the plant

Noel, Noël /nəʊˈel/ *n* the Christmas season

noes /nəʊz/ *pl of* no

noggin /ˈnɒgʒn/ *n* **1** a small mug or cup **2** a small measure of spirits, usu 0.142 litres (¼pt) **3** a person's head – infml

[1]**noise** /nɔɪz/ *n* **1** loud confused shouting or outcry **2a** a (harsh or unwanted) sound **b** unwanted signals or fluctuations in an electrical circuit

[2]**noise** *v* to spread by gossip or hearsay – usu + *about* or *abroad*

noisome /ˈnɔɪsəm/ *adj* repellent, offensive – fml

noisy /ˈnɔɪzi/ *adj* **1** making noise **2** full of or characterized by noise – **noisily** *adv* – **noisiness** *n*

nomad /ˈnəʊmæd/ *n* **1** a member of a people that wanders from place to place, usu seasonally **2** one who wanders aimlessly from place to place – **~ic** *adj* – **~ically** *adv*

no-man's-land *n* **1a** an area of waste or unclaimed land **b** an unoccupied area between opposing armies **2** an area of anomalous, ambiguous, or indefinite character

nom de plume /ˌnɒm də ˈpluːm/ *n* a pseudonym under which an author writes

nomenclature /nəʊˈmenklətʃəʳ/ *n* **1** a name, designation **2** (an instance of) naming, esp within a particular system **3** a system of terms used in a particular science, discipline, or art

nominal /ˈnɒmɪ̣nl/ *adj* **1** of or constituting a name **2a** being sthg in name only **b** negligible, insignificant – ~**ly** *adv*

nominate /ˈnɒmɪ̣neɪt/ *v* **1** to designate, specify **2a** to appoint or recommend for appointment **b** to propose for an honour, award, or as a candidate – -**tion** *n*

nominative /ˈnɒmɪ̣nətɪv/ *adj* of or being the grammatical case expressing the subject of a verb

nonagenarian /ˌnəʊnədʒɪ̣ˈneərɪən/ *n* a person between 90 and 99 years old

nonaligned /ˌnɒn-əˈlaɪnd/ *adj* not allied with other nations, esp any of the great powers – -**lignment** *n*

nonce /nɒns/ *n* the present occasion, time, or purpose

nonchalant /ˈnɒnʃələnt/ *adj* giving an impression of easy unconcern or indifference – -**lance** *n* – ~**ly** *adv*

noncombatant /ˌnɒnˈkɒmbətənt/ *n* a civilian, army chaplain, etc who does not engage in combat

noncommissioned officer /ˌnɒnkəˌmɪʃənd ˈɒfɪsəʳ/ *n* a subordinate officer (e g a sergeant) in the armed forces appointed from among the personnel who do not hold a commission

noncommittal /ˌnɒnkəˈmɪtl/ *adj* giving no clear indication of attitude or feeling – ~**ly** *adv*

nonconformist /ˌnɒnkənˈfɔːmɪ̣st/ *n* **1** *often cap* a member of a Protestant body separated from the Church of England **2** one who does not conform to a generally accepted pattern of thought or behaviour

nonconformity /ˌnɒnkənˈfɔːmɪ̣ti/ *n* **1** refusal to conform to an established creed, rule, or practice **2** absence of correspondence or agreement

nondescript /ˈnɒndɪ̣ˌskrɪpt/ *adj* **1** (apparently) belonging to no particular class or kind **2** lacking distinctive or interesting qualities; dull

[1]none /nʌn/ *pron, pl* **none** **1** not any; no part or thing **2** not one person; nobody (e g it's *none* other than Tom) **3** not any such thing or person

[2]none *adv* **1** by no means; not at all **2** in no way; to no extent

nonentity /nɒˈnentɪ̣ti/ *n* sby or sthg of little importance or interest

nonesuch *also* **nonsuch** /ˈnʌnsʌtʃ/ *n* a person or thing without an equal; a paragon

nonetheless /ˌnʌnðəˈles/ *adv* nevertheless

nonflammable /ˌnɒnˈflæməbəl/ *adj* difficult or impossible to set alight

nonpareil /ˈnɒnpərəl, -pəreɪl/ *n or adj* (sby or sthg) having no equal

nonplus /ˌnɒnˈplʌs/ *v* to perplex or disconcert

nonsense /ˈnɒnsəns/ *n* **1a** meaningless words or language **b** foolish or absurd language, conduct, or thought **2** frivolous or insolent behaviour **3** – used interjectionally to express forceful disagreement

non sequitur /ˌnɒn ˈsekwɪ̣təʳ/ *n* **1** a conclusion that does not follow from the premises **2** a statement that does not follow logically from anything previously said

nonstandard /ˌnɒnˈstændəd/ *adj* not conforming in pronunciation, grammatical construction, idiom, or word choice to accepted usage

nonstarter /ˌnɒnˈstɑːtəʳ/ *n* sby or sthg that is sure to fail or prove impracticable

nonstick /ˌnɒnˈstɪk/ *adj* having or being a surface that prevents adherence of food during cooking

nonstop /ˌnɒnˈstɒp/ *adj* done or made without a stop – **nonstop** *adv*

non-U /ˌnɒn ˈjuː/ *adj* not characteristic of the upper classes

nonunion /ˌnɒnˈjuːnɪən/ *adj* not belonging to or connected with a trade union

nonviolence /ˌnɒnˈvaɪələns/ *n* **1** refraining from violence on moral grounds **2** passive resistance or peaceful demonstration for political ends – -**nt** *adj*

nonwhite /ˌnɒnˈwaɪt/ *n or adj* (one who is) not Caucasian

¹noodle /ˈnuːdl/ *n* a silly or foolish person – humor

²noodle *n* a narrow flat ribbon of pasta made with egg

nook /nʊk/ *n* a small secluded or sheltered place or part

noon /nuːn/ *n* **1 noon, noonday** the middle of the day; midday **2** the highest or culminating point

no one *pron* nobody

noose /nuːs/ *n* a loop with a running knot that tightens as the rope is pulled – **noose** *v*

nor /nɔːʳ/ *conj* **1** – used to join 2 sentence elements of the same class or function (e g not done by you *nor* me) **2** also not; neither (e g it didn't seem hard, *nor* was it)

Nordic /ˈnɔːdɪk/ *adj* **1** of a tall, fair, longheaded, blue-eyed physical type characteristic of the Germanic peoples of N Europe, esp Scandinavia **2** of competitive ski events consisting of ski jumping and cross-country racing

Norfolk jacket /ˌnɔːfək ˈdʒækɪ̡t/ *n* a man's semifitted belted single-breasted jacket with box pleats

norm /nɔːm/ *n* **1** an authoritative standard; a model **2** a principle of correctness that is binding upon the members of a group, and serves to regulate action and judgment **3** a pattern typical of a social group

normal /ˈnɔːməl/ *adj* **1** conforming to or constituting a norm, rule, or principle; not odd or unusual **2** occurring naturally **3a** having average intelligence or development **b** free from mental disorder – **~ize** *v* – **~ly** *adv* – **~ity** *n*

Norman /ˈnɔːmən/ *n* **1** a (former) native or inhabitant of Normandy; *esp* any of the Norman-French conquerors of England in 1066 **2** a style of architecture characterized, esp in its English form, by semicircular arches and heavy pillars

¹north /nɔːθ/ *adj or adv* towards, at, belonging to, or coming from the north

²north *n* **1** (the compass point corresponding to) the direction of the north terrestrial pole **2** *often cap* regions or countries lying to the north of a specified or implied point of orientation

¹northeast /ˌnɔːθˈiːst/ *adj or adv* towards, at, belonging to, or coming from the northeast

²northeast /ˌnɔːθˈiːst/ *n* **1** (the general direction corresponding to) the compass point midway between north and east **2** *often cap* regions or countries lying to the northeast of a specified or implied point of orientation

¹northeasterly /ˌnɔːθˈiːstəli/ *adj or adv* northeast

²northeasterly, northeaster *n* a wind from the northeast

northeastern /ˌnɔːθˈiːstən/ *adj* **1** *often cap* (characteristic) of a region conventionally designated Northeast **2** northeast

¹northerly /ˈnɔːðəli/ *adj or adv* north

²northerly *n* a wind from the north

northern /ˈnɔːðən/ *adj* **1** *often cap* (characteristic) of a region conventionally designated North **2** north

Northerner /ˈnɔːðənəʳ/ *n* a native or inhabitant of the North

north pole *n* **1a** *often cap N&P* the northernmost point of the rotational axis of the earth **b** the northernmost point on the celestial sphere, about which the stars seem to revolve **2** the northward-pointing pole of a magnet

¹northwest /ˌnɔːθˈwest/ *adj or adv* towards, at, belonging to, or coming from the northwest

²northwest *n* **1** (the general direction corresponding to) the compass point midway between north and west **2** *often cap* regions or countries lying to the northwest of a specified or implied point of orientation

¹northwesterly /ˌnɔːθˈwestəli/ *adj or adv* northwest

²northwesterly, northwester *n* a wind from the northwest

northwestern /ˌnɔːθˈwestən/ *adj* **1** *often cap* (characteristic) of a region conventionally designated Northwest **2** northwest

Norwegian /nɔːˈwiːdʒən/ *n or adj* (a native or inhabitant or the language) of Norway

¹nose /nəʊz/ *n* **1a** the part of the face that bears the nostrils and covers the front part of the nasal cavity **b** a snout, muzzle **2a** the sense or (vertebrate) organ of smell **b** aroma, bouquet **3** the projecting part or front end of sthg **4a** the nose as a symbol of undue curiosity or interference **b** a knack for detecting what is latent or concealed

[2]**nose** *v* **1** to use the nose in examining, smelling, etc; to sniff or nuzzle **2a** to pry – often + *into* **b** to search or look inquisitively – usu + *about* or *around* **3** to move ahead slowly or cautiously

nose dive *n* a sudden dramatic drop

nosegay /ˈnəʊzgeɪ/ *n* a small bunch of flowers; a posy

[1]**nosh** /nɒʃ/ *v* to eat – infml – ~**er** *n*

[2]**nosh** *n* food; a meal – infml

nosh-up *n,* a large meal – infml

nostalgia /nɒˈstældʒə/ *n* **1** homesickness **2** a wistful or excessively sentimental yearning for sthg past or irrecoverable – **-gic** *adj* – **-gically** *adv*

nostril /ˈnɒstrɨ̥l/ *n* the opening of the nose to the outside

nostrum /ˈnɒstrəm/ *n* a facile or questionable remedy

nosy, nosey /ˈnəʊzi/ *adj* prying, snooping – infml

nosy parker *n, Br* a busybody – infml

not /nɒt/ *adv* **1** – used to negate a (preceding) word or word group (e g *not* thirsty; will it rain? I hope *not*) **2** – used to give force to an opposite meaning (e g *not* without – reason)

[1]**notable** /ˈnəʊtəbəl/ *adj* **1** worthy of note; remarkable **2** distinguished, prominent – **-bly** *adv* – **-bility** *n*

[2]**notable** *n* **1** a prominent person **2** *pl, often cap* a group of people summoned, esp in France when it was a monarchy, to act as a deliberative body

notary /ˈnəʊtəri/, **notary public** *n* a public officer appointed to administer oaths and draw up and authenticate documents

notation /nəʊˈteɪʃən/ *n* (a representation of sthg by) a system or set of marks, signs, symbols, figures, characters, or abbreviated expressions (e g to express technical facts or quantities)

[1]**notch** /nɒtʃ/ *n* **1** a V-shaped indentation **2** a degree, step

[2]**notch** *v* **1** to make a notch in **2** to score or achieve – usu + *up*

[1]**note** /nəʊt/ *v* **1a** to take due or special notice of **b** to record in writing **2** to make special mention of; remark

[2]**note** *n* **1a(1)** a sound having a definite pitch **(2)** a call, esp of a bird **b** a written symbol used to indicate duration and pitch of a tone by its shape and position on the staff **2a** a characteristic feature of smell, flavour, etc **b** a mood or quality **3a** a memorandum **b** a brief comment or explanation **c** a piece of paper money **d(1)** a short informal letter **(2)** a formal diplomatic communication **4a** distinction, reputation **b** observation, notice

notebook /ˈnəʊtbʊk/ *n* a book for notes or memoranda

noted /ˈnəʊtɨ̥d/ *adj* well-known, famous

noteworthy /ˈnəʊtˌwɜːði/ *adj* worthy of or attracting attention; notable

[1]**nothing** /ˈnʌθɪŋ/ *pron* **1** not any thing; no thing **2** sthg of no consequence **3** no truth or value (e g there's *nothing* in this rumour)

[2]**nothing** *adv* not at all; in no degree

[3]**nothing** *n* **1** sthg that does not exist **2** sby or sthg of no or slight value or size

nothingness /ˈnʌθɪŋnɨ̥s/ *n* **1a** nonexistence **b** utter insignificance **2** a void, emptiness

[1]**notice** /ˈnəʊtɨ̥s/ *n* **1a** warning of a future occurrence **b** notification of intention of terminating an agreement at a particular time **2** attention, heed **3** a written or printed announcement **4** a review (e g of a play)

[2]**notice** *v* **1** to comment upon; refer to **2** to take notice of; mark

noticeable /ˈnəʊtɨ̥səbəl/ *adj* **1** worthy of notice **2** capable of being noticed; perceptible – **-ably** *adv*

notification /ˌnəʊtɨ̥fɨ̥ˈkeɪʃən/ *n* **1** (an instance of) notifying **2** sthg written that gives notice

notify /ˈnəʊtɨ̥faɪ/ *v* **1** to give (official) notice to **2** to make known

notion /ˈnəʊʃən/ *n* **1a** a broad general concept **b** a conception, impression **2** a whim or fancy

notional /ˈnəʊʃənəl/ *adj* **1** theoretical, speculative **2** existing only in the mind; imaginary

notoriety /ˌnəʊtəˈraɪəti/ *n* the quality or state of being notorious

notorious /nəʊˈtɔːrɪəs, nə-/ *adj* well-known, esp for a specified (unfavourable) quality or trait – **~ly** *adv*

[1]**notwithstanding** /ˌnɒtwɪθˈstændɪŋ, -wɪð-/ *prep* in spite of

[2]**notwithstanding** *adv* nevertheless

[3]**notwithstanding** *conj* although

nougat /ˈnuːgɑː, ˈnʌgət/ *n* a sweetmeat of nuts or fruit pieces in a semisolid sugar paste

nought /nɔːt/ *n* **1** naught; nothing **2** the arithmetical symbol 0; zero

noun /naʊn/ *n* a word that is the name of a person, place, thing, substance, or state and that belongs to 1 of the major form classes in grammar

nourish /ˈnʌrɪʃ/ *v* **1** to nurture, rear **2** to encourage the growth of; foster **3** to provide or sustain with nutriment; feed – **~ment** *n*

nouveau riche /ˌnuːvəʊ ˈriːʃ/ *n, pl* **nouveaux riches** sby who has recently become rich (and shows it)

nova /ˈnəʊvə/ *n, pl* **novas, novae** a previously faint star that becomes suddenly very bright and then fades away

[1]**novel** /ˈnɒvəl/ *adj* **1** new and unlike anything previously known **2** original and striking, esp in conception or style

[2]**novel** *n* an invented prose narrative that deals esp with human experience and social behaviour – **~ist** *n*

novelette /ˌnɒvəˈlet/ *n* a short novel or long short story, often of a sentimental nature

novelty /ˈnɒvəlti/ *n* **1** sthg new and unusual **2** a small manufactured often cheap article for personal or household adornment

November /nəʊˈvembəʳ, nə-/ *n* the 11th month of the Gregorian calendar

novice /ˈnɒvɪ̈s/ *n* **1** a person admitted to probationary membership of a religious community **2** a beginner

[1]**now** /naʊ/ *adv* **1a** at the present time **b** in the immediate past **c** in the time immediately to follow; forthwith **2** – used with the sense of present time weakened or lost **a** to introduce an important point or indicate a transition (e g *now* if we turn to the next aspect of the problem) **b** to express command, request, or warning (e g *now*, don't squabble) **3** sometimes – linking 2 or more coordinate words or phrases (e g *now* one and *now* another) **4** under the changed or unchanged circumstances (e g he'll never believe me *now*) **5** at the time referred to (e g *now* the trouble began) **6** up to the present or to the time referred to (e g haven't been for years *now*)

[2]**now** *conj* in view of the fact that; since

[3]**now** *n* **1** the present time **2** the time referred to

nowadays /ˈnaʊədeɪz/ *adv* in these modern times; today

noway /ˈnəʊweɪ/, **noways** *adv* in no way whatever; not at all – fml

[1]**nowhere** /ˈnəʊweəʳ/ *adv* **1** not anywhere **2** to no purpose or result

[2]**nowhere** *n* a nonexistent place

noxious /ˈnɒkʃəs/ *adj* **1** harmful to living things **2** having a harmful moral influence; unwholesome – **~ly** *adv* – **~ness** *n*

nozzle /ˈnɒzəl/ *n* a projecting part with an opening that usu serves as an outlet; *esp* a short tube with a taper or constriction used on a hose, pipe, etc to speed up or direct a flow of fluid

nth /enth/ *adj* **1** of or having an unspecified or indefinitely large number **2** extreme, utmost

nuance /ˈnjuːɒns/ *n* a subtle distinction or gradation; a shade

nub /nʌb/ *n* **1** a knob, lump **2** *the* gist or crux

nubile /ˈnjuːbaɪl/ *adj, of a girl* of marriageable age; *esp* young and sexually attractive – often humor

nuclear /ˈnjuːklɪəʳ/ *adj* **1** of or constituting a nucleus **2** of, using, or being the atomic nucleus, atomic energy, the atom bomb, or atomic power

nuclear family *n* a family unit that consists of husband, wife, and children

nuclear-free zone *n* an area in which

the use, storage, and transport of all nuclear materials are officially declared probihited

nucleus /'nju:klɪəs/ *n, pl* **nuclei** a central point, mass, etc about which gathering, concentration, etc takes place: e g **a** a usu round membrane-surrounded cell part that contains the chromosomes **b** the positively charged central part of an atom that accounts for nearly all of the atomic mass and consists of protons and usu neutrons

[1]**nude** /nju:d/ *adj* without clothing or covering; naked, bare – **nudity** *n*

[2]**nude** *n* **1a** a representation of a nude human figure **b** a nude person **2** the state of being nude

nudge /nʌdʒ/ *v* **1** to touch or push gently; *esp* to catch the attention of by a push of the elbow **2** to move (as if) by pushing gently or slowly – **nudge** *n*

nudism /'nju:dɪzəm/ *n* the cult or practice of going nude as much as possible – **-ist** *adj, n*

nugatory /'nju:gətəri/ *adj* **1** trifling, inconsequential **2** inoperative *USE* fml

nugget /'nʌgɨt/ *n* a solid lump, esp of a precious metal in its natural state

nuisance /'nju:səns/ *n* **1** (legally actionable) harm or injury **2** an annoying or troublesome person or thing

[1]**null** /nʌl/ *adj* amounting to nothing; nil

[2]**null** *n* zero, nought

null and void *adj* completely invalid

nullify /'nʌlɨfaɪ/ *v* **1** to make (legally) null or invalid **2** to make worthless, unimportant, or ineffective – **-ification** *n*

numb /nʌm/ *adj* **1** devoid of sensation, esp as a result of cold or anaesthesia **2** devoid of emotion

[1]**number** /'nʌmbəʳ/ *n* **1a(1)** *sing or pl in constr* an indefinite, usu large, total **(2)** *pl* a numerous group; many; *also* an instance of numerical superiority **b(1)** any of an ordered set of standard names or symbols (e g 2, 5, 27th) used in counting or in assigning a position in an order **(2)** an element (e g 6, -3, ⅝, √7) belonging to an arithmetical system based on or analogous to the numbers used in counting and subject to specific rules of addition, subtraction, and multiplication **2a** a word, symbol, letter, or combination of symbols representing a number **b** one or more numerals or digits used to identify or designate **3** a group of individuals **4a** sthg viewed in terms of the advantage or enjoyment obtained from it **b** an article of esp women's clothing **c** a person or individual, esp an attractive girl **5** insight into a person's motives or character

[2]**number** *v* **1** to include as part of a whole or total **2** to assign a number to **3** to comprise in number; total

number one *n* **1** sthg that is first in rank, order, or importance **2** one's own interests or welfare – infml

numberplate /'nʌmbəpleɪt/ *n, chiefly Br* a rectangular identifying plate fastened to a vehicle and bearing the vehicle's registration number

Numbers *n pl but sing in constr* the mainly narrative 4th book of the Old Testament

numeral /'nju:mərəl/ *n* a conventional symbol that represents a natural number or zero

numerate /'nju:mərɨt/ *adj* having an understanding of mathematics, esp arithmetic – **-racy** *n*

numerator /'nju:məreɪtəʳ/ *n* the part of a fraction that is above the line and signifies the number of parts of the denominator that is shown by the fraction

numerical /nju:'merɪkəl/, **numeric** *adj* of, expressed in, or involving numbers or a number system ~**ly** *adv*

numerology /,nju:mə'rɒlədʒi/ *n* the study of the occult significance of numbers

numerous /'nju:mərəs/ *adj* consisting of many units or individuals – ~**ly** *adv* – ~**ness** *n*

numismatics /,nju:mɨz'mætɪks/ *n pl but sing in constr* the study or collection of coinage, coins, paper money, medals, tokens, etc – **numismatic** *adj* – **-tist** *n*

numskull, numbskull /'nʌmskʌl/ *n* a dull or stupid person

nun /nʌn/ *n* a female member of a religious order living in a convent and often engaged in educational or nursing work

nunnery /ˈnʌnəri/ *n* a convent of nuns

[1]nuptial /ˈnʌpʃəl/ *adj* **1** of marriage **2** characteristic of or occurring in the breeding season

[2]nuptial *n* a wedding – usu pl

[1]nurse /nɜːs/ *n* **1** a woman employed to take care of a young child **2** sby skilled or trained in caring for the sick or infirm, esp under the supervision of a physician

[2]nurse *v* **1** to suckle an offspring **2** to encourage the development of; nurture **3a** to attempt to cure (e g an illness or injury) by appropriate treatment **b** to care for and wait on (e g a sick person) **4** to hold in one's mind; harbour **5** to hold (e g a baby) lovingly or caressingly

nursery /ˈnɜːsəri/ *n* **1** a child's bedroom or playroom **2** a place where small children are looked after in their parents' absence **3** an area where plants, trees, etc are grown for propagation, sale, or transplanting

nurseryman /ˈnɜːsərimən/ *n* one whose occupation is the cultivation of plants, usu for sale

nursery rhyme *n* a short traditional story in rhyme for children

nursery school *n* a school for children aged usu from 2 to 5

[1]nurture /ˈnɜːtʃəʳ/ *n* **1** training, upbringing **2** food, nourishment **3** all the environmental influences that affect the innate genetic potentialities of an organism

[2]nurture *v* **1** to give care and nourishment to **2** to educate or develop

nut /nʌt/ *n* **1** (the often edible kernel of) a dry fruit or seed with a hard separable rind or shell **2** a difficult person, problem, or undertaking **3** a typically hexagonal usu metal block with an internal screw thread cut on it that can be screwed onto a bolt to tighten or secure sthg **4** a small piece or lump **5** a person's head **6a** an insane or wildly eccentric person **b** an ardent enthusiast

nutcase /ˈnʌtkeɪs/ *n* a lunatic – infml

nuthouse /ˈnʌt-haʊs/ *n* a madhouse – slang

nutmeg /ˈnʌtmeg/ *n* (an Indonesian tree that produces) an aromatic seed used as a spice

nutria /ˈnjuːtrɪə/ *n* the fur of the coypu

nutrient /ˈnjuːtrɪənt/ *n or adj* (sthg) that provides nourishment

nutriment /ˈnjuːtrʒmənt/ *n* sthg that nourishes or promotes growth

nutrition /njuːˈtrɪʃən/ *n* all the processes by which an organism takes in and uses food

nutritious /njuːˈtrɪʃəs/ *adj* nourishing – **~ly** *adv* – **-tive** *adj*

nuts /nʌts/ *adj* **1** passionately keen or enthusiastic **2** crazy, mad *USE* infml

nutshell /ˈnʌt·ʃel/ *n* the hard outside covering enclosing the kernel of a nut

nutty /ˈnʌti/ *adj* **1** having a flavour like that of nuts **2** eccentric, silly; *also* nuts – infml – **-tiness** *n*

nuzzle /ˈnʌzəl/ *v* **1** to push or rub sthg with the nose **2** to lie close or snug; nestle

nylon /ˈnaɪlɒn/ *n* **1** any of numerous strong tough elastic synthetic fibres used esp in textiles and plastics **2** *pl* stockings made of nylon

nymph /nɪmf/ *n* **1** any of the minor female divinities of nature in classical mythology **2** any of various immature insects; *esp* a larva of a dragonfly or other insect with incomplete metamorphosis

O

o /əʊ/ *n, pl* **o's, os** *often cap* **1** (a graphic representation of or device for reproducing) the 15th letter of the English alphabet **2** sthg shaped like the letter O; *esp* zero

O /əʊ/ *interj or n* oh

o' /ə/ *prep* **1** of **2** *chiefly dial* on

oaf /əʊf/ *n* a clumsy slow-witted person – **~ish** *adj* – **~ishly** *adv* – **~ishness** *n*

oak /əʊk/ *n, pl* **oaks, oak** (the tough hard durable wood of) any of various trees or shrubs of the beech family, usu having lobed leaves and producing acorns as fruits

oak apple *n* a large round gall produced on oak stems or leaves by a gall wasp

oakum /'əʊkəm/ *n* hemp or jute fibre impregnated with tar and used in packing joints and stopping up gaps between the planks of a ship

oar /ɔːʳ/ *n* a long usu wooden shaft with a broad blade at one end used for propelling or steering a boat

oarsman /'ɔːzmən/ *n* one who rows a boat, esp in a racing crew

oasis /əʊ'eɪsʒs/ *n, pl* **oases** a fertile or green area in a dry region

oast house /'əʊst haʊs/ *n* a usu circular building housing a kiln for drying hops or making malt from barley

oath /əʊθ/ *n* **1** a solemn calling upon God or a revered person or thing to witness to the true or binding nature of one's declaration **2** an irreverent use of a sacred name; *broadly* a swear-word

oatmeal /'əʊtmiːl/ *n* **1** meal made from oats, used esp in porridge **2** a greyish beige colour

oats /əʊts/ *n pl* a widely cultivated cereal grass that does not form a tight head like wheat or barley

¹obbligato /ˌɒblʒ'gɑːtəʊ/ *adj* not to be omitted – used in music

²obbligato *n, pl* **obbligatos** *also* **obbligati** an elaborate, esp melodic, accompaniment, usu played by a single instrument

obdurate /'ɒbdʒʊrʒt/ *adj* **1** stubbornly persistent in wrong doing **2** inflexible, unyielding – **~ly** *adv* – **-racy** *n*

obedient /ə'biːdɪənt/ *adj* submissive to the will or authority of a superior; willing to obey – **~ly** *adv* – **-ence** *n*

obeisance /əʊ'beɪsəns/ *n* **1** a movement or gesture made as a sign of respect or submission **2** deference, homage

obelisk /'ɒbəlɪsk/ *n* an upright 4-sided usu monolithic pillar that gradually tapers towards the top and terminates in a pyramid

obese /əʊ'biːs/ *adj* excessively fat – **obesity** *n*

obey /əʊ'beɪ, ə-/ *v* **1** to submit to the commands or guidance of **2** to comply with; execute

obfuscate /'ɒbfəskeɪt/ *v* **1** to make obscure or difficult to understand **2** to confuse, bewilder – **-cation** *n*

obituary /ə'bɪtʃʊəri/ *n* a notice of a person's death, usu with a short biography

¹object /'ɒbdʒɪkt/ *n* **1** sthg that is (capable of) being sensed physically or examined mentally **2** sthg or sby that arouses an emotion or provokes a reaction or response **3** an end towards which effort, action, etc is directed; a goal **4** a noun or noun equivalent appearing in a prepositional phrase or representing the goal or the result of the action of its verb (e g *house* in *we built a house*)

²object /əb'dʒekt/ *v* **1** to oppose sthg with words or arguments **2** to feel dislike or disapproval – **~ion** *n* – **~or** *n*

objectionable /əb'dʒekʃənəbəl/ *adj* unpleasant or offensive – **-bly** *adv*

¹objective /əb'dʒektɪv/ *adj* **1a** constituting an object; *specif* belonging to the external world and observable or verifiable **b** concerned with or expressing the nature of external reality rather than personal feelings or beliefs **2** dealing with facts without distortion by personal feelings or prejudices – **~ly** *adv* – **-tivity** *n*

[2]**objective** *n* **1** sthg towards which efforts are directed; a goal **2** sthg to be attained or achieved by a military operation **3** a lens or system of lenses that forms an image of an object

objet d'art /ˌɒbʒeɪ 'dɑːʳ/ *n, pl* **objets d'art** a usu small article of some artistic value

[1]**obligate** /'ɒblɪ̣gɪ̣t, -geɪt/ *adj* always happening irrespective of environmental conditions

[2]**obligate** /'ɒblɪ̣geɪt/ *v* to constrain legally or morally

obligation /ˌɒblɪ̣'geɪʃən/ *n* **1** sthg (e g a contract or promise) that binds one to a course of action **2** (the amount of) a financial commitment **3** sthg one is bound to do; a duty

obligatory /ə'blɪgətəri/ *adj* **1** binding in law or conscience **2** relating to or enforcing an obligation **3** mandatory, compulsory

oblige /ə'blaɪdʒ/ *v* **1** to constrain by force or circumstance **2** to do sthg as a favour; be of service to

obliging /ə'blaɪdʒɪŋ/ *adj* eager to help; accommodating – **~ly** *adv*

oblique /ə'bliːk/ *adj* **1a** neither perpendicular nor parallel; inclined **b** *of an angle* greater than but not a multiple of 90° **2** not straightforward or explicit; indirect – **~ly** *adv*

obliterate /ə'blɪtəreɪt/ *v* **1** to make illegible or imperceptible **2** to destroy all trace or indication of – **-ation** *n*

oblivion /ə'blɪvɪən/ *n* **1** the state of forgetting or being oblivious **2** the state of being forgotten

oblivious /ə'blɪvɪəs/ *adj* lacking conscious knowledge; completely unaware – usu + *of* or *to* – **~ly** *adv* – **~ness** *n*

oblong /'ɒblɒŋ/ *adj* rectangular with adjacent sides unequal

obnoxious /əb'nɒkʃəs/ *adj* highly offensive or repugnant – **~ly** *adv* – **~ness** *n*

oboe /'əʊbəʊ/ *n* a double-reed woodwind instrument with a range from B flat below middle C upwards for about 2½ octaves – **oboist** *n*

obscene /əb'siːn/ *adj* **1** offending standards of sexual propriety or decency **2** (morally) repugnant – **~ly** *adv* – **-nity** *n*

[1]**obscure** /əb'skjʊəʳ/ *adj* **1** hard to understand; abstruse **2** not well-known or widely acclaimed **3** faint, indistinct – **~ly** *adv* – **-rity** *n*

[2]**obscure** *v* **1** to conceal (as if) by covering **2** to make indistinct or unintelligible

obsequious /əb'siːkwɪəs/ *adj* showing a servile willingness to oblige

observance /əb'zɜːvəns/ *n* **1** a customary practice, rite, or ceremony – often pl **2** an act of complying with a custom, rule, or law

observatory /əb'zɜːvətəri/ *n* a building or institution for (the interpretation of) astronomical observation

observe /əb'zɜːv/ *v* **1a** to act in due conformity with **b** to celebrate or perform (e g a ceremony or festival) **2** to perceive or take note of, esp for scientific purposes **3** to utter as a comment – **-vable** *adj* – **-vably** *adv* – **-vant** *adj* – **-vation** *n* – **~r** *n*

obsess /əb'ses/ *v* to preoccupy intensely or abnormally

obsession /əb'seʃən/ *n* a persistent (disturbing) preoccupation with an often unreasonable idea – **-ive** *adj*

obsolescent /ˌɒbsə'lesənt/ *adj* going out of use; becoming obsolete – **-cence** *n*

obsolete /'ɒbsəliːt/ *adj* **1** no longer in use **2** outdated, outmoded

obstacle /'ɒbstəkəl/ *n* sthg that hinders or obstructs

obstetrics /əb'stetrɪks/ *n pl but sing or pl in constr* a branch of medicine dealing with the care and treatment of women before, during, and after childbirth – **-ric(al)** *adj* – **-rician** *n*

obstinate /'ɒbstɪ̣nɪ̣t/ *adj* clinging stubbornly to an opinion or course of action; not yielding to arguments or persuasion – **~ly** *adv* – **-nacy** *n*

obstreperous /əb'strepərəs/ *adj* **1** aggressively noisy; clamorous **2** vociferously defiant; unruly – **~ly** *adv* – **~ness** *n*

obstruct /əb'strʌkt/ *v* **1** to block or close up by an obstacle **2** to hinder, impede – **~ion** *n* – **~ive** *adj* – **~ively** *adv*

obtain /əb'teɪn/ *v* **1** to acquire or attain **2** to be generally accepted or practised – fml – **~able** *adj*

obtrude /əb'truːd/ *v* **1** to thrust out **2** to assert without warrant or request – **-usion** *n*

obtrusive /əb'truːsɪv/ *adj* **1** forward in manner; pushing **2** unduly noticeable – **~ly** *adv* – **~ness** *n*

obtuse /əb'tjuːs/ *adj* **1** lacking sensitivity or mental alertness **2a** being or forming an angle greater than 90° but less than 180° **b** not pointed or acute – **~ly** *adv* – **~ness** *n*

[1]**obverse** /'ɒbvɜːs/ *adj* **1** facing the observer or opponent **2** constituting a counterpart or complement

[2]**obverse** *n* **1a** the side of a coin, medal, or currency note that bears the principal device and lettering **b** the more conspicuous of 2 possible sides or aspects **2** a counterpart to a fact or truth

obviate /'ɒbvieɪt/ *v* **1** to anticipate and dispose of in advance **2** to make unnecessary

obvious /'ɒbvɪəs/ *adj* **1** evident to the senses or understanding **2** unsubtle – **~ly** *adv* – **~ness** *n*

ocarina /,ɒkə'riːnə/ *n* a simple wind instrument with an oval body

[1]**occasion** /ə'keɪʒən/ *n* **1** a suitable opportunity or circumstance **2** a state of affairs that provides a reason or grounds **3** the immediate or incidental cause **4** a time at which sthg occurs **5** a special event or ceremony

[2]**occasion** *v* to bring about; cause – fml

occasional /ə'keɪʒənəl/ *adj* **1** of a particular occasion **2** composed for a particular occasion **3** occurring at irregular or infrequent intervals **4** acting in a specified capacity from time to time **5** designed for use as the occasion demands – **~ly** *adv*

Occident /'ɒksɮdənt/ *n* the west – **~al** *n, adj*

occult /'ɒkʌlt, ə'kʌlt/ *adj* **1** secret; *esp* esoteric **2** not easily understood; abstruse **3** involving (secret knowledge of) supernatural powers

occupation /,ɒkjʊ'peɪʃən/ *n* **1** an activity in which one engages, esp to earn a living **2a** the occupancy of land **b** tenure **3** taking possession or the holding and control of a place or area, esp by a foreign military force – **~al** *adj*

occupational therapy *n* creative activity used as therapy for promoting recovery or rehabilitation – **-pist** *n*

occupy /'ɒkjʊpaɪ/ *v* **1** to engage the attention or energies of **2** to fill up (a portion of space or time) **3** to take or maintain possession of **4** to reside in or use as an owner or tenant – **-pant** *n* – **-pancy** *n*

occur /ə'kɜːʳ/ *v* **-rr- 1** to be found; exist **2** to become the case; happen **3** to come to mind

occurrence /ə'kʌrəns/ *n* sthg that takes place; an event

ocean /'əʊʃən/ *n* **1** (any of the large expanses that together constitute) the whole body of salt water that covers nearly ¾ of the surface of the globe **2** *pl* a huge amount – infml – **~ic** *adj*

oceanography /,əʊʃən'ɒgrəfi/ *n* the science dealing with oceans and their form, biology, and resources – **-pher** *n*

ocelot /'ɒsɮlɒt/ *n* a medium-sized American wildcat with a yellow or greyish coat dotted and striped with black

oche /'ɒki/ *n* the line on the floor behind which a player must stand when throwing darts at a dartboard

ochre, *NAm chiefly* **ocher** /'əʊkəʳ/ *n* **1** the colour of esp yellow ochre **2** an earthy usu red or yellow (impure) iron ore used as a pigment

ocker /'ɒkəʳ/ *n, Austr & NZ* an Australian; *specif* one who boorishly asserts Australian nationality

o'clock /ə'klɒk/ *adv* according to the clock – used in specifying the exact hour

octagon /'ɒktəgən/ *n* a polygon of 8 angles and 8 sides – **~al** *adj*

octave /'ɒktɮv, -teɪv/ *n* **1** a group of 8 lines of verse, esp the first 8 of a sonnet **2a** (the combination of 2 notes at) a musical interval of 8 diatonic degrees **b** a note separated from a lower note by this interval **c** the whole series of notes or piano, organ, etc keys within this interval that form the unit of the modern scale

octet /ɒk'tet/ *n* (a musical composition for) 8 instruments, voices, or performers

October /ɒk'təʊbəʳ/ *n* the 10th month of the Gregorian calendar

octogenarian /ˌɒktədʒɪ̇'neərɪən/ *n* a person between 80 and 89 years old

octopus /'ɒktəpəs/ *n, pl* **octopuses, octopi** any of a genus of molluscs related to the squids and cuttlefishes with 8 muscular arms equipped with 2 rows of suckers

ocular /'ɒkjʊləʳ/ *adj* **1** performed or perceived with the eyes **2** of the eye

oculist /'ɒkjʊlɪ̇st/ *n* an ophthalmologist or optician

odd /ɒd/ *adj* **1a** left over when others are paired or grouped **b** not matching **2** not divisible by 2 without leaving a remainder **3** somewhat more than the specified number – usu in combination **4** not regular or planned; casual, occasional **5** different from the usual or conventional; strange – **~ly** *adv* – **~ness** *n*

oddball /'ɒdbɔːl/ *n* an eccentric or peculiar person – infml

oddity /'ɒdɪ̇ti/ *n* **1** an odd person, thing, event, or trait **2** oddness, strangeness

oddment /'ɒdmənt/ *n* **1** sthg left over; a remnant **2** *pl* odds and ends

odds /ɒdz/ *n pl but sing or pl in constr* **1** the probability (expressed as a ratio) that one thing will happen rather than another **2** disagreement, variance **3** the ratio between the amount to be paid off for a winning bet and the amount of the bet

odds and ends *n pl* miscellaneous items or remnants

odds-on *adj* **1** (viewed as) having a better than even chance to win **2** not involving much risk

ode /əʊd/ *n* a lyric poem, often addressed to a particular subject, marked by a usu exalted tone

odious /'əʊdɪəs/ *adj* arousing hatred or revulsion – **~ly** *adv*

odium /'əʊdɪəm/ *n* general condemnation or disgrace associated with a despicable act – fml

odour, *NAm chiefly* **odor** /'əʊdəʳ/ *n* **1** (the sensation resulting from) a quality of sthg that stimulates the sense of smell **2** repute, favour – fml **3** a characteristic quality; a savour – chiefly derog – **~less** *adj* – **odorous** *adj*

odyssey /'ɒdɪ̇si/ *n* a long wandering or quest

o'er /əʊəʳ/ *adv or prep* over – poetic

oesophagus /ə'sɒfəgəs/ *n* the muscular tube leading from the back of the mouth to the stomach

oestrogen /'iːstrədʒən/ *n* a sex hormone that stimulates the development of female secondary sex characteristics

oestrus cycle /'iːstrəsˌsaɪkəl/ *n* the series of changes in the female mammal corresponding to her degree of sexual nuptivity and ability to conceive

of /əv, ə; *strong* ɒv/ *prep* **1a** – used to indicate origin or derivation (e g a man *of* noble birth) **b** – used to indicate cause, motive, or reason (e g died *of* pneumonia) **c** proceeding from; on the part of (e g very kind *of* him) **d** by (e g the plays *of* Shaw) **2a(1)** composed or made from (e g a crown *of* gold) **b** containing (e g a cup *of* water) **c** – used to indicate the mass noun or class that includes the part denoted by the previous word (e g an inch *of* rain; a blade *of* grass) **d** from among (e g one *of* his poems) **3a** belonging to; related to (e g the leg *of* the chair) **b** that is or are – used before possessive forms (e g a friend *of* John's) **c** characterized by; with, having (e g a man *of* courage) **d** connected with (e g a teacher *of* French) **e** existing or happening in or on (e g the battle *of* Blenheim; my letter *of* the 19th) **4a** relating to (a topic); concerning (e g stories *of* his travels) **b** in respect to (e g slow *of* speech) **c** directed towards (e g love *of* nature) **d** – used to show separation or removal (e g eased *of* pain) **e** – used as a function word to indicate a whole or quantity from which a part is removed or expended **5** – used to indicate apposition (e g the art *of* painting) **6** in, during (e g go there *of* an evening) – infml

¹off /ɒf/ *adv* **1a(1)** from a place or position; *specif* away from land (e g the ship stood *off* to sea) **(2)** away in space or ahead in time (e g Christmas is a week *off*) **b** from a course; aside; (e g turned *off* into a lay-by) *specif*

away from the wind **c** into sleep or unconsciousness (e g dozed *off*) **2a** so as to be not supported, not in close contact, or not attached (e g the hands came *off*; took his coat *off*) **b** so as to be divided (e g a corner screened *off*) **3a** to or in a state of discontinuance or suspension (e g the radio is *off*) **b** so as to be completely finished or no longer existent (e g kill them *off*) **c** in or into a state of putrefaction (e g the cream's gone *off*) **d** (as if) by heart (e g knew it *off* pat) **4** away from an activity or function (e g the night shift went *off*) **5** offstage (e g noises *off*) **6** to a sexual climax (e g brought him *off*) – slang

[2]**off** *prep* **1a** – used to indicate physical separation or distance from (e g take it *off* the table) **b** to seaward of (e g 2 miles *off* shore) **c** lying or turning aside from; adjacent to (e g a shop just *off* the high street) **d** (slightly) away from – often in combination (e g a week *off* work; *off*-target) **2** – used to indicate the source from which sthg derives or is obtained (e g bought it *off* a friend) **3a** not occupied in (e g *off* duty) **b** tired of; no longer interested in or using (e g he's *off* drugs) **c** below the usual standard or level of (e g *off* his game)

[3]**off** *adj* **1a** being the most distant of 2 **b** seaward **c** being the right-hand one of a pair (e g the *off* wheel of a cart) **d** situated to one side; adjoining (e g bedroom with dressing room *off*) **2a** started on the way (e g *off* on a spree) **b** not taking place or staying in effect; cancelled (e g the match is *off*) **c** *of a dish on a menu* no longer being served **3a** not up to standard; unsatisfactory in terms of achievement (e g an *off* day) **b** slack (e g *off* season) **4** affected (as if) with putrefaction **5** provided (e g how are you *off* for socks?) **6a** in, on, through, or towards the off side of a cricket field **b** *esp of a ball bowled in cricket* moving or tending to move in the direction of the leg side **7** *of behaviour* not what one has a right to expect; *esp* rather unkind or dishonest – infml

[4]**off** *n* the start or outset; *also* a starting signal

offal /ˈɒfəl/ *n* **1** the liver, heart, kidney, etc of a butchered animal used as food **2** refuse

offbeat /ˌɒfˈbiːt/ *adj* unusual; *esp* unconventional – infml

off-colour *adj* **1** unwell **2** somewhat indecent; risqué

offence, *NAm chiefly* **offense** /əˈfens/ *n* **1** sthg that occasions a sense of outrage **2** (an) attack, assault **3** displeasure, resentment **4a** a sin or misdeed **b** an illegal act; a crime

offend /əˈfend/ *v* **1** to break a moral or divine law – often + *against* **2** to cause displeasure, difficulty, or discomfort to – **~er** *n*

[1]**offensive** /əˈfensɪv/ *adj* **1** of or designed for aggression or attack **2** arousing physical disgust; repellent **3** causing indignation or outrage – **~ly** *adv* – **~ness** *n*

[2]**offensive** *n* **1** *the* position or attitude of an attacking party **2** an esp military attack on a large scale

[1]**offer** /ˈɒfəʳ/ *v* **1** to present (e g a prayer or sacrifice) in an act of worship – often + *up* **2** to present (e g for acceptance, rejection, or consideration) **3** to declare one's willingness **4** to make available **5** to present (goods) for sale **6** to tender as payment; bid

[2]**offer** *n* **1a** a proposal; *specif* a proposal of marriage **b** an undertaking to do or give sthg on a specific condition **2** a price named by a prospective buyer

offering /ˈɒfərɪŋ/ *n* **1** the act of one who offers **2** sthg offered; *esp* a sacrifice ceremonially offered as a part of worship **3** a contribution to the support of a church or other religious organization

offhand /ˌɒfˈhænd/ *adv or adj* **1** without forethought or preparation **2** without proper attention or respect – **~edly** *adv* – **~edness** *n*

office /ˈɒfɪ̣s/ *n* **1** an esp beneficial service or action carried out for another **2** a position with special (public) duties or responsibilities **3** a prescribed form or service of worship **4a** a place, esp a large building, where the business of a particular organization is carried out **b** (a group of people sharing) a room in which the administrative, clerical, or professional work of an organization is performed

officer /'ɒfɪ̣sə^r/ *n* **1** a policeman **2** one who holds a position with special duties or responsibilities (e g in a government or business) **3a** one who holds a position of authority or command in the armed forces; *specif* a commissioned officer **b** a master or any of the mates of a merchant or passenger ship – **officer** *v*

[1]**official** /ə'fɪʃəl/ *n* one who holds an esp public office – **~dom** *n*

[2]**official** *adj* **1** of an office and its duties **2** holding an office **3** authoritative, authorized **4** suitable for or characteristic of a person in office; formal – **~ly** *adv*

officiate /ə'fɪʃieɪt/ *v* **1** to perform an esp religious ceremony, function, or duty **2** to act as an official or in an official capacity

officious /ə'fɪʃəs/ *adj* given to or marked by overzealousness in exercising authority or carrying out duties – **~ly** *adv* – **~ness** *n*

off-licence *n, Br* a shop, part of a public house, etc licensed to sell alcoholic drinks to be consumed off the premises

off-load *v* to unload

off-peak *adj* (used) at a time of less than the maximum demand or activity

offprint /'ɒf,print/ *n* a separately printed excerpt (e g an article from a magazine)

off-putting *adj* disagreeable, disconcerting – infml

[1]**offset** /'ɒfset/ *n* **1** an abrupt bend in an object by which one part is turned aside out of line **2** sthg that serves to compensate for sthg else **3** a printing process in which an inked impression from a plate is first made on a rubber surface and then transferred to paper

[2]**offset** /ɒf'set/ *v* **1** to balance **2** to compensate or make up for

offside /,ɒf'saɪd/ *adv or adj* illegally in advance of the ball or puck in a team game

off side *n* **1** the part of a cricket field on the opposite side of a line joining the middle stumps to that in which the batsman stands when playing a ball **2** *chiefly Br* the right side of a horse, vehicle, etc

offspring /'ɒf,sprɪŋ/ *n* the progeny of a person, animal, or plant; young

off-the-record *adj or adv* (given or made) unofficially or in confidence

off-white *n or adj* (a) yellowish or greyish white

oft /ɒft/ *adv* often – poetic

often /'ɒfən, 'ɒftən/ *adv* **1** (at) many times **2** in many cases

ogle /'əʊgəl/ *v* to glance or stare with esp sexual interest (at) – **ogle** *n* – **~r** *n*

ogre /'əʊgə^r/, *fem* **ogress** *n* **1** a hideous giant of folklore believed to feed on human beings **2** a dreaded person or thing – **ogreish** *adj* – **ogreishly** *adv*

[1]**oh, O** /əʊ/ *interj* – used to express surprise, pain, disappointment, etc

[2]**oh, O** *n* nought

ohm /əʊm/ *n* the derived SI unit of electrical resistance equal to the resistance between 2 points of a conductor when a constant potential difference of 1 volt applied to these points produces a current of 1 ampere

[1]**oil** /ɔɪl/ *n* **1** any of numerous smooth greasy combustible liquids or low melting-point solids that are insoluble in water but dissolve in organic solvents **2a** *pl* oil paint **b** an oil painting **3** petroleum – **oily** *adj*

[2]**oil** *v* to treat or lubricate with oil

oil cake *n* the solid residue left after extracting the oil from seeds (e g of cotton)

oilcloth /'ɔɪlklɒθ/ *n* cloth treated with oil or paint and used for table and shelf coverings

oil paint *n* paint consisting of ground pigment mixed with oil

oilskin /'ɔɪl,skɪn/ *n* **1** an oiled waterproof cloth used for coverings and garments **2** an oilskin or plastic raincoat **3** *pl* an oilskin or plastic suit of coat and trousers

oil slick *n* a film of oil floating on water

ointment /'ɔɪntmənt/ *n* a soothing or healing salve for application to the skin

[1]**OK, okay** /əʊ'keɪ/ *adv, adj, or interj* all right

[2]**OK, okay** *v or n* (to give) approval or authorization (of), sanction

okapi /əʊ'kɑːpi/ *n* an African mammal closely related to the giraffe but with a shorter neck and black and cream rings on the upper parts of the legs

[1]**old** /əʊld/ *adj* **1a** dating from the esp remote past **b** persisting from an earlier time **c** of long standing **2** having existed for a specified period of time **3** advanced in years or age **4** former **5a** made long ago; *esp* worn with time or use **b** no longer in use; discarded **6** long familiar

[2]**old** *n* **1** old or earlier time **2** one of a specified age – usu in combination

old boy, *fem* **old girl** *n, chiefly Br* **1** a former pupil of a particular, esp public, school **2** a fellow or friend – often used as an informal term of address

old boy network *n, chiefly Br the* system of favouritism operating among people of a similar privileged background, esp among former pupils of public schools

olden /ˈəʊldən/ *adj* of a bygone era

olde-worlde /ˌəʊldi ˈwɜːldi/ *adj* (excessively) of an old or mock old style

old-fashioned *adj* **1** (characteristic) of a past era; outdated **2** clinging to customs of a past era

old guard *n sing or pl in constr, often cap O&G* the (original) conservative members of a group or party

old hand *n* a very experienced person

old hat *adj* **1** old-fashioned **2** hackneyed, trite

old lady *n* one's wife or mother – infml

old maid *n* **1** a spinster **2** a prim fussy person – infml

old man *n* **1** one's husband or father **2** one in authority (e g one's employer, manager, or commander) – + *the USE* infml

old master *n* (a work by) a distinguished European painter of the 16th to early 18th c

old school *n* adherents of traditional ideas and practices

old school tie *n* the conservatism and upper-class solidarity traditionally attributed to former members of British public schools

old stager *n* a veteran

Old Testament *n* a collection of writings forming the Jewish canon of Scripture and the first part of the Christian Bible

old-timer *n* **1** an old hand **2** *chiefly NAm* an old man

old wives' tale *n* a traditional superstitious notion

old woman *n* **1** one's wife or mother **2** a timid, prim, or fussy person, esp a man – derog *USE* infml

old-world *adj* **1** of the E hemisphere **2** reminiscent of a past age; *esp* quaintly charming

Old World *n* the E Hemisphere; *specif* Europe, Asia, and Africa

oleaginous /ˌəʊliˈædʒɪnəs/ *adj* resembling, containing, or producing oil; oily

oligarchy /ˈɒlɪgɑːki/ *n* **1** government by a small group **2** a state or organization in which a small group exercises control, esp for its own interests **3** a small group exercising such control

oligopoly /ˌɒlɪˈgɒpəli/ *n* a market situation in which each of a few producers affects but does not control the market

[1]**olive** /ˈɒlɪv/ *n* **1** (an Old World evergreen tree that grows esp around the Mediterranean and bears) a small stone fruit used as a food and a source of oil **2 olive, olive green** a dull yellowish green colour resembling that of an unripe olive

[2]**olive, olive green** *adj* of the colour olive

olive branch *n* an offer or gesture of peace or goodwill

olympiad /əˈlɪmpiæd/ *n, often cap* an olympic games

[1]**Olympian** /əˈlɪmpɪən/ *adj* of the ancient Greek region of Olympia

[2]**Olympian** *adj* lofty, detached

[3]**Olympian** *n* **1** an inhabitant of the ancient Greek region of Olympia **2** any of the ancient Greek deities dwelling on Olympus **3** a loftily detached or superior person

Olympic /əˈlɪmpɪk/ *adj* of or executed in the Olympic Games

Olympic Games /əˌlɪmpɪk ˈgeɪmz/ *n pl* an international sports meeting held once every 4 years in a different host country

ombudsman /ˈɒmbədzmən/ *n* a government official appointed to investigate complaints made by individuals against government or public bodies

omega /'əumɬgə/ *n* **1** the 24th and last letter of the Greek alphabet **2** the last one in a series, order, etc

omelet, omelette /'ɒmlɬt/ *n* a mixture of beaten eggs cooked until set in a shallow pan

omen /'əumən/ *n* an event or phenomenon believed to be a sign of some future occurrence

ominous /'ɒmɬnəs/ *adj* portentous; *esp* foreboding evil or disaster – **~ly** *adv*

omit /əu'mɪt, ə-/ *v* **1** to leave out or unmentioned **2** to fail to do or perform – **omission** *n*

[1]**omnibus** /'ɒmnɪbəs/ *n* **1** a book containing reprints of a number of works, usu by 1 author **2** a bus

[2]**omnibus** *adj* of, containing, or providing for many things at once

omnipotent /ɒm'nɪpətənt/ *adj* having unlimited or very great power or influence – **-ence** *n*

omnipresent /,ɒmnɪ'prezənt/ *adj* present in all places at all times – **-ence** *n*

omniscient /ɒm'nɪʃənt, -'nɪsɪənt/ *adj* **1** having infinite awareness or understanding **2** possessed of complete knowledge; all-knowing – **-ence** *n*

omnivorous /ɒm'nɪvərəs/ *adj* **1** feeding on both animal and vegetable substances **2** avidly taking in, and esp reading, everything – **~ly** *adv* – **~ness** *n*

[1]**on** /ɒn/ *prep* **1a(1)** in contact with or supported from below by (e g *on* the table) **(2)** attached or fastened to (e g a dog *on* a lead) **(3)** carried on the person of (e g have you a match *on* you?) **(4)** very near to, esp along an edge or border (e g towns *on* the frontier) **(5)** within the limits of a usu specified area (e g *on* page 17) **b** at the usual standard or level of (e g *on* form) **c(1)** in the direction of (e g *on* the right) **(2)** into contact with (e g jumped *on* the horse) **(3)** with regard to; concerning (e g keen *on* sports) **(4)** with a specified person or thing as object (e g try it out *on* her) **(5)** having as a topic; about (e g a book *on* India) **(6)** staked on the success of (e g put £5 *on* a horse) **(7)** doing or carrying out a specified action or activity (e g here *on* business) **(8)** working for, supporting, or belonging to (e g *on* a committee) **(9)** working at; in charge of (e g the man *on* the gate) **2a** having as a basis or source (e g of knowledge or comparison) (e g have it *on* good authority) **b** at the expense of (e g drinks are *on* the house) **3a** in the state or process of (e g *on* strike) **b** in the specified manner (e g *on* the cheap) **c** using as a medium (e g played it *on* the clarinet); *esp* over 4b (e g talking *on* the telephone) **d** using by way of transport (e g arrived *on* foot) **e** sustained or powered by (e g car runs *on* petrol) **f** regularly taking (e g *on* valium) **4** through contact with (e g cut himself *on* a piece of glass) **5a** at the time of (e g every hour *on* the hour) **b** on the occasion of or immediately after and usu in consequence of (e g fainted *on* hearing the news) **c** in the course of (e g *on* a journey) **d** after (e g blow *on* blow)

[2]**on** *adv* **1** so as to be supported from below, in close contact, or attached (e g put the top *on*) **2a** ahead or forwards in space or time (e g do it later *on*) **b** with the specified part forward (e g cars crashed head *on*) **c** without interruption (e g chattered *on*) **d** in continuance or succession **3a** in or into (a state permitting) operation (e g put a record *on*) **b** in or into an activity or function (e g the night shift came *on*)

[3]**on** *adj* **1a** *cricket* leg (e g *on* drive) **b** taking place (e g the game is *on*) **c** performing or broadcasting (e g we're *on* in 10 minutes) **d** intended, planned (e g has nothing *on* for tonight) **e** worn as clothing (e g just a cardigan *on*) **2a** committed to a bet **b** in favour of a win (e g the odds are 2 to 1 *on*) **3** *chiefly Br* possible, practicable – usu neg (e g it's just not *on*) **4a** *chiefly Br* nagging (e g always *on* at him) **b** talking dully, excessively, or incomprehensibly (e g what's he *on* about) *USE* *(3&4)* infml

[1]**once** /wʌns/ *adv* **1** one time and no more **2** even 1 time; ever (e g if *once* we lose the key) **3** at some indefinite time in the past; formerly **4** by 1

degree of relationship (e g second cousin *once* removed)

²once *n* one single time

³once *conj* from the moment when; as soon as

once-over *n* a swift appraising glance – infml

oncoming /'ɒn,kʌmɪŋ/ *adj* coming nearer in time or space; advancing

¹one /wʌn/ *adj* **1a** being a single unit or thing **b** being the first – used after the noun modified (e g on page *one*) **2** being a particular but unspecified instance (e g saw her *one* morning) **3a(1)** the same; identical (e g both of *one* mind) **(2)** constituting a unified entity (e g all shouted with *one* voice) **b** being in a state of agreement; united **4** being some unspecified instance – used esp of future time (e g we might try it *one* weekend) **5a** being a particular object or person (e g close first *one* eye, then the other) **b** being the only individual of an indicated or implied kind (e g the *one* and only person she wanted)

²one *pron, pl* **ones** **1** a single member or specimen of a usu specified class or group **2** an indefinitely indicated person; anybody at all (e g has a duty to one's public) **3** – used to refer to a noun or noun phrase previously mentioned or understood (e g 2 grey shirts and 3 red *ones*) *USE* used as a subject or object; no pl for sense 2

³one *n* **1** the number 1 **2** the number denoting unity **3** the first in a set or series (e g takes a *one* in shoes) **4a** a single person or thing **b** a unified entity (e g is secretary and treasurer in *one*) **c** a particular example or instance (e g *one* of the coldest nights this year) **d** a certain specified person (e g *one* George Hopkins) **5a** a person with a liking or interest for a specified thing; an enthusiast (e g he's rather a *one* for bikes) **b** a bold, amusing, or remarkable character (e g oh! you are a *one*) **6a** a blow, stroke **7** sthg having a denomination of 1 (e g I'll take the money in *ones*)

one another *pron* each other

one-armed bandit *n* a fruit machine

one-horse *adj* of little importance or interest – infml

one-piece *adj* consisting of or made in a single undivided piece

onerous /'ɒnərəs, 'əʊ-/ *adj* burdensome, troublesome **~ly** *adv* – **~ness** *n*

oneself /wʌn'self/ *pron* **1** a person's self; one's own self – used reflexively (e g one should wash *oneself*) or for emphasis (e g to do it *oneself*) **2** one's normal self (e g not feeling quite *oneself*)

one-sided *adj* **1a** having or occurring on 1 side only **b** having 1 side prominent or more developed **2** partial, biased – **~ly** *adv* – **~ness** *n*

onetime /'wʌntaɪm/ *adj* former, sometime

one-upmanship /wʌn'ʌpmənʃɪp/ *n* the art of gaining a psychological advantage over others by professing social or professional superiority

one-way *adj* **1** that moves in or allows movement in only 1 direction **2** one-sided, unilateral

onion /'ʌnjən/ *n* (a plant with) a pungent usu white bulb much used in cooking

onlooker /'ɒn,lʊkəʳ/ *n* a passive spectator

¹only /'əʊnli/ *adj* **1** unquestionably the best **2** alone in its class or kind; sole

²only *adv* **1a** nothing more than; merely **b** solely, exclusively **2** nothing other than (e g it was *only* too true) **3a** in the final outcome (e g will *only* make you sick) **b** with nevertheless the final result (e g won the battle, *only* to lose the war) **4** no earlier than (e g *only* last week)

³only *conj* **1** but, however (e g they look very nice, *only* we can't use them) **2** were it not for the fact that *USE* infml

onomatopoeia /,ɒnəmætə'piːə/ *n* the formation or use of words intended to be a vocal imitation of the sound associated with the thing or action designated (e g in *buzz, cuckoo*) – **-poeic** *adj*

onrush /'ɒnrʌʃ/ *n* a forceful rushing forwards – **~ing** *adj*

onset /'ɒnset/ *n* **1** an attack, assault **2** a beginning, commencement

onside /,ɒn'saɪd/ *adv or adj* not offside

onslaught /ˈɒnslɔːt/ *n* a fierce attack

onto, on to /ˈɒntʊ, -tə/ *prep* **1** to a position on **2** in or into a state of awareness about (e g put the police *onto* him) **3** *chiefly Br* in or into contact with (e g been *onto* him about the drains); *esp* on at; nagging

onus /ˈəʊnəs/ *n* **1a** duty, responsibility **b** blame **2** burden of proof

onward /ˈɒnwəd/ *adj* directed or moving onwards; forward

onwards /ˈɒnwədz/, **onward** *adv* towards or at a point lying ahead in space or time; forwards

onyx /ˈɒnɪks/ *n* a translucent variety of quartz with layers of different colours, typically green and white or black or brown and white

oodles /ˈuːdlz/ *n pl but sing or pl in constr* a great quantity; a lot – infml

oomph /ʊmf/ *n* vitality, enthusiasm – humor

oops /ʊps/ *interj* – used to express apology or surprise

[1]**ooze** /uːz/ *n* a soft deposit of mud, slime, debris, etc on the bottom of a body of water – **oozy** *adj*

[2]**ooze** *v* **1a** to pass or flow slowly through small openings **b** to diminish gradually; dwindle *away* **2** to display in abundance

op /ɒp/ *n* an operation – infml

opal /ˈəʊpəl/ *n* a transparent to translucent mineral used in its opalescent forms as a gem

opalescent /ˌəʊpəˈlesənt/ *adj* reflecting a warm milky light – **-cence** *n*

opaque /əʊˈpeɪk/ *adj* **1** not transmitting radiant energy, esp light; not transparent **2** hard to understand; unintelligible – **-acity** *n* – **~ly** *adv* – **~ness** *n*

[1]**open** /ˈəʊpən/ *adj* **1** having no enclosing or confining barrier **2** allowing passage; not shut or locked **3a** exposed to general view or knowledge; public **b** vulnerable to attack or question **4a** not covered or protected **b** not fastened or sealed **5** not restricted to a particular category of participants; *specif* contested by both amateurs and professionals **6** presenting no obstacle to passage or view **7** having the parts or surfaces spread out or unfolded **8a** not finally decided or settled **b** available for a qualified applicant; vacant **c** remaining available for use or filling until cancelled **9** willing to consider new ideas; unprejudiced **10** candid, frank **11** having relatively wide spacing between words or lines **12a** *of a string on a musical instrument* not stopped by the finger **b** *of a note* produced on a musical instrument without fingering the strings, valves, slides, or keys **13** in operation; *esp* ready for business or use **14** free from checks or restraints **15** *Br, of a cheque* payable in cash to the person, organization, etc named on it; not crossed – **~ly** *adv* – **~ness** *n*

[2]**open** *v* **1a** to change or move from a closed position **b** to permit entry *into* or *onto* **c** to gain access to the contents of **2a** to make available for or active in a particular use or function; *specif* to establish **b** to declare available for use, esp ceremonially **c** to make the necessary arrangements for (e g a bank account), esp by depositing money **3** to disclose, reveal – often + *up* **4** to make 1 or more openings in **5** to unfold; spread *out* **6** to begin, commence

[3]**open** *n* **1** outdoors **2** *often cap* an open contest, competition, or tournament

open-air *adj* outdoor

opencast /ˌəʊpənˈkɑːst/ *adj, of a mine or mining* worked from or carried out on the earth's surface by removing material covering the mineral mined for

open-ended *adj* without any definite limits or restrictions (e g of time or purpose) set in advance

opener /ˈəʊpənəʳ/ *n* **1a** an instrument that opens sthg – usu in combination **b** one who opens; *specif* an opening batsman **2** the first item or event in a series

openhanded /ˌəʊpənˈhændɪ̣d/ *adj* generous in giving

openhearted /ˌəʊpənˈhɑːtɪ̣d/ *adj* **1** candidly straightforward **2** kind, generous – **~ly** *adv* – **~ness** *n*

opening /ˈəʊpənɪŋ/ *n* **1** an act of making or becoming open **2** a breach, aperture **3a** an often standard series of moves made at the beginning of a game of chess or draughts **b** a first performance **4a** a favourable opportunity; a chance **b** an opportunity for employment; a vacancy

open out *v* to speak more freely and confidently

open season *n* a period during which it is legal to kill or catch game or fish protected at other times by law

Open University *n* the nonresidential British university that caters mainly for adults studying part-time, has no formal entrance requirements, and operates mainly through correspondence and broadcasting

open verdict *n* a verdict at an inquest that records a death but does not state its cause

[1]**opera** /'ɒpərə/ *pl of* **opus**

[2]**opera** *n* **1** (the performance of or score for) a drama set to music and made up of vocal pieces with orchestral accompaniment and usu other orchestral music (e g an overture) **2** the branch of the arts concerned with such works **3** a company performing operas – **~tic** *adj*

operable /'ɒpərəbl/ *adj* suitable for surgical treatment – **-bly** *adv*

operate /'ɒpəreɪt/ *v* **1** to exert power or influence; act **2** to produce a desired effect **3a** to work; (cause to) function **b** to perform surgery – usu + *on* **c** to carry on a military or naval action or mission **4** to be in action; *specif* to carry out trade or business

operation /,ɒpə'reɪʃən/ *n* **1a** the act, method, or process of operating **b** sthg (to be) done; an activity **2** the state of being functional or operative **3** a surgical procedure carried out on a living body for the repair of damage or the restoration of health **4** any of various mathematical or logical processes (e g addition) carried out to derive one expression from others according to a rule **5** a usu military action, mission, or manoeuvre and its planning **6** a business or financiai transaction

operational /,ɒpə'reɪʃənəl/ *adj* **1** of or based on operations **2a** of, involved in, or used for the execution of commercial, military, or naval operations **b** (capable of) functioning – **~ly** *adv*

[1]**operative** /'ɒpərətɪv/ *adj* **1a** producing an appropriate effect; efficacious **b** significant, relevant **2** in force or operation

[2]**operative** *n* an operator; *esp* a workman

operator /'ɒpəreɪtə'/ *n* **1a** one who operates a machine or device **b** one who owns or runs a business, organization, etc **c** one who is in charge of a telephone switchboard **2** a shrewd and skilful manipulator – infml

operetta /,ɒpə'retə/ *n* a usu romantic comic opera that often includes dancing

ophthalmic /ɒf'θælmɪk; *also* ɒp-/ *adj* of (the medical treatment of the eye)

ophthalmology /,ɒfθæl'mɒlədʒi; *also* ɒp-/ *n* the branch of medical science dealing with the structure, functions, diseases of the eye – **-ogist** *n*

opiate /'əʊpieɪt/ *n* **1** a preparation or derivative of opium; *broadly* a narcotic **2** sthg that induces inaction or calm

opine /əʊ'paɪn/ *v* to state as an opinion – fml

opinion /ə'pɪnjən/ *n* **1** a view or judgment formed about a particular matter **2** a generally held view **3** a formal expression by an expert of his/her professional judgment or advice; *esp* a barrister's written advice to a client

opinionated /ə'pinjəneɪtɨd/ *adj* stubbornly sticking to one's own opinions

opium /'əʊpɪəm/ *n* the dried juice of the unripe seed capsules of the opium poppy, containing morphine and other addictive narcotics

opossum /ə'pɒsəm/ *n* any of various American or Australian marsupial mammals often tree-dwelling

opponent /ə'pəʊnənt/ *n* one who takes the opposite side in a contest, conflict, etc

opportune /'ɒpətjuːn/ *adj* **1** suitable or convenient for a particular occurrence **2** occurring at an appropriate time – **~ly** *adv*

opportunism /'ɑpətjuːnɪzəm/ *n* the taking advantage of opportunities or circumstances, esp with little regard for principles or consequences – **-ist** *n or adj*

opportunity /ˌɒpəˈtjuːnɪti/ *n* **1** a favourable set of circumstances **2** a chance for advancement or progress

oppose /əˈpəʊz/ *v* **1** to place opposite or against sthg so as to provide counterbalance, contrast, etc **2** to offer resistance to

[1]**opposite** /ˈɒpəzɨt/ *n* sthg or sby opposed or contrary

[2]**opposite** *adj* **1** set over against sthg that is at the other end or side of an intervening line or space **2a** occupying an opposing position **b** diametrically different; contrary **3** being the other of a matching or contrasting pair

[3]**opposite** *adv* on or to an opposite side

[4]**opposite** *prep* **1** across from and usu facing **2** in a role complementary to

opposition /ˌɒpəˈzɪʃən/ *n* **1** placing opposite or being so placed **2** hostile or contrary action **3** *sing of pl in constr* **a** the body of people opposing sthg **b** *often cap* a political party opposing the party in power

oppress /əˈpres/ *v* **1** to crush by harsh or authoritarian rule **2** to weigh heavily on the mind or spirit of – **~ion** *n* – **~ive** *adj* – **~ively** *adv* – **~iveness** *n* – **~or** *n*

opt /ɒpt/ *v* to decide in favour of sthg

optic /ˈɒptɪk/, **optical** *adj* of vision or the eye

optician /ɒpˈtɪʃən/ *n* one who prescribes spectacles for eye defects or supplies lenses for spectacles on prescription

optics /ˈɒptɪks/ *n pl but sing or pl in constr* **1** the science of the nature, properties, and uses of (radiation or particles that behave like) light **2** optical properties or components

optimism /ˈɒptɨmɪzəm/ *n* a tendency to emphasize favourable aspects of situations or events or to expect the best possible outcome – **-mist** *n* – **-mistic** *adj* – **-mistically** *adv*

optimum /ˈɒptɨməm/ *n, pl* **optima** *also* **optimums** (the amount or degree of) sthg that is most favourable to a particular end

option /ˈɒpʃən/ *n* **1** an act of choosing **2** (a contract conveying) a right to buy or sell designated securities or commodities at a specified price during a stipulated period **3a** an alternative course of action **b** an item offered in addition to or in place of standard equipment

optional /ˈɒpʃənəl/ *adj* not compulsory; available as a choice – **~ly** *adv*

opt out *v* to choose not to participate in sthg – often + *of*

opulent /ˈɒpjʊlənt/ *adj* **1** wealthy, rich **2** abundant, profuse – **-ence** *n* – **~ly** *adv*

opus /ˈəʊpəs/ *n, pl* **opera** a musical composition or set of compositions, usu numbered in the order of issue

[1]**or** /əʳ; *strong* ɔːʳ/ *conj* **1a** – used to join 2 sentence elements of the same class or function and often introduced by *either* to indicate that what immediately follows is another or a final alternative **b** – used before the second and later of several suggestions to indicate approximation or uncertainty (e g 5 *or* 6 days) **2** and not – used after a neg (e g never drinks *or* smokes) **3** that is – used to indicate equivalence or elucidate meaning (e g a heifer *or* a young cow) **4** – used to indicate the result of rejecting a preceding choice (e g hurry *or* you'll be late)

[2]**or** *n* a gold colour; *also* yellow – used in heraldry

oracle /ˈɒrəkəl/ *n* **1** an often cryptic answer to some question, usu regarding the future, purporting to come from a deity **2** (a shrine housing) a priest or priestess who delivers oracles – **-cular** *adj*

[1]**oral** /ˈɔːrəl/ *adj* **1** uttered in words; spoken **2a** of, given through, or affecting the mouth **b** of or characterized by (passive dependency, aggressiveness, or other personality traits typical of) the first stage of sexual development in which gratification is derived from eating, sucking, and later by biting

[2]**oral** *n* an oral examination

[1]**orange** /ˈɒrɨndʒ/ *n* **1** a spherical fruit with a reddish yellow leathery aromatic rind and sweet juicy edible pulp; *also* the tree that bears this **2** a colour whose hue resembles that of the orange and lies between red and yellow in the spectrum

[2]**orange** *adj* of the colour orange
Orange *adj* of Orangemen
Orangeman /ˈɒrɨndʒmən/ *n* a member of a Protestant loyalist society in the north of Ireland; *broadly* an Ulsterman
oration /əˈreɪʃən, ɔː-/ *n* a speech delivered in a formal and dignified manner
orator /ˈɒrətəʳ/ *n* a skilled public speaker
oratorio /ˌɒrəˈtɔːriəʊ/ *n, pl* **oratorios** a choral work based usu on a religious subject and composed chiefly of recitatives, arias, and choruses without action or scenery
[1]**oratory** /ˈɒrətri/ *n* a place of prayer; *esp* a private or institutional chapel
[2]**oratory** *n* **1** the art of public speaking **2** public speaking characterized by (excessive) eloquence – **-orical** *adj* – **-orically** *adv*
orb /ɔːb/ *n* **1** a spherical body; *esp* a celestial sphere **2** a sphere surmounted by a cross symbolizing royal power and justice
[1]**orbit** /ˈɔːbɨt/ *n* **1** the bony socket of the eye **2** a path described by one body in its revolution round another (e g that of the earth round the sun) **3** a sphere of influence – **~al** *adj*
[2]**orbit** *v* to revolve in an orbit round
orchard /ˈɔːtʃəd/ *n* a usu enclosed area in which fruit trees are planted
orchestra /ˈɔːkɨstrə/ *n* **1** the space in front of the stage in a modern theatre that is used by an orchestra **2** a group of musicians including esp string players organized to perform ensemble music – **~l** *adj*
orchestrate /ˈɔːkɨstreɪt/ *v* to compose or arrange (music) for an orchestra – **-tration** *n*
orchid /ˈɔːkɨd/ *n* a plant or flower of a large family of plants related to the lilies usu having striking 3-petalled flowers with an enlarged liplike middle petal
ordain /ɔːˈdeɪn/ *v* **1** to make a priest of **2** to order by appointment, decree, or law **b** to destine, foreordain
ordeal /ɔːˈdiːl, ˈɔːdiːl/ *n* a severe or testing experience
[1]**order** /ˈɔːdəʳ/ *n* **1a** a religious body or community often required to take vows of renunciation of earthly things **b** a military decoration **2** *pl* the office of a person in the Christian ministry **3a** a rank or group in a community **b** a category in the classification of living things ranking above the family and below the class **4a** a rank, level, or category **b** arrangement of objects or events according to sequence in space, time, value, etc **5a** (a rank in) a social or political system **b** regular or harmonious arrangement **6** customary procedure, esp in debate **7** the rule of law or proper authority **8** a proper, orderly, or functioning condition **9a** a direction to purchase, sell, or supply goods or to carry out work **b** goods bought or sold
[2]**order** *v* **1** to put in order; arrange **2a** to give an order to; command **b** to place an order for
ordered /ˈɔːdəd/ *adj* **1** well regulated or ordered **2a** having elements succeeding or arranged according to rule
[1]**orderly** /ˈɔːdəli/ *adj* **1a** arranged in order; neat, tidy **b** liking or exhibiting order; methodical **2** well behaved; peaceful – **-liness** *n*
[2]**orderly** *n* **1** a soldier assigned to carry messages, relay orders, etc for a superior officer **2** a hospital attendant who does routine or heavy work (e g carrying supplies or moving patients)
order paper *n* a programme of the day's business in a legislative assembly
ordinal /ˈɔːdɨnəl/ *adj* of a specified order or rank in a series
ordinance /ˈɔːdɨnəns/ *n* **1** an authoritative decree; *esp* a municipal regulation **2** a prescribed usage, practice, or ceremony
ordinary /ˈɔːdənri/ *adj* **1** routine, usual **2** not exceptional; commonplace – **-rily** *adv* – **-riness** *n*
ordinary seaman *n* (a sailor with) the lowest rank on a ship
ordination /ˌɔːdɨˈneɪʃən/ *n* (an) ordaining; being ordained
ordnance /ˈɔːdnəns/ *n* **1** (a branch of government service dealing with) military supplies **2** cannon, artillery
Ordnance Survey *n* (a British or Irish government organization that produces) a survey of Great Britain or

Ireland published as a series of detailed maps

ordure /ˈɔːdjʊəʳ/ *n* excrement

ore /ɔːʳ/ *n* a mineral containing a metal or other valuable constituent for which it is mined

öre /ˈɜːrə/ *n, pl* **öre** a unit of currency of Denmark, Norway, and Sweden

oregano /əˈregənəʊ, ˌɒrɪ̵ˈgɒːnəʊ/ *n* a bushy plant of the mint family whose leaves are used as a herb in cooking

organ /ˈɔːgən/ *n* **1** a wind instrument consisting of sets of pipes made to sound by compressed air and controlled by keyboards; *also* an electronic keyboard instrument producing a sound approximating to that of an organ **2** a differentiated structure (e g the heart or a leaf) consisting of cells and tissues and performing some specific function in an organism **3** a periodical

organdie, organdy /ˈɔːgəndi/ *n* a very fine transparent muslin with a stiff finish

organ-grinder *n* a street musician who operates a barrel organ

organic /ɔːˈgænɪk/ *adj* **1a** of or arising in a bodily organ **b** affecting the structure of the organism **2a** of or derived from living organisms **b** of or being food produced using fertilizer solely of plant or animal origin without the aid of chemical fertilizers, pesticides, etc **3a** forming an integral element of a whole **b** having systematic coordination of parts **c** containing carbon compounds, esp those occurring in living organisms; *also* of or being the branch of chemistry dealing with these – **~ally** *adv*

organism /ˈɔːgənɪzəm/ *n* **1** a complex structure of interdependent and subordinate elements **2** a living being

organization, -isation /ˌɔːgənaɪˈzeɪʃən/ *n* **1** the arrangement of parts so as to form an effective whole **2a** an association, society **b** an administrative and functional body

organ·ize, -ise /ˈɔːgənaɪz/ *v* **1** to arrange into a functioning whole **2a** to set up an administrative structure for **b** to cause to form an association, esp a trade union **3** to arrange by systematic planning and effort

orgasm /ˈɔːgæzəm/ *n* (an instance of) the climax of sexual excitement, occurring as the culmination of sexual intercourse – **~ic** *adj*

orgy /ˈɔːdʒi/ *n* **1a** drunken revelry **b** an instance (e g a party) of wild sexual activity **2** an excessive or frantic indulgence in a specified activity – **-giastic** *adj*

oriel window /ˈɔːrɪəl ˌwɪndəʊ/ *n* a bay window projecting from an upper storey

[1]**orient** /ˈɔːrɪənt, ˈɒrɪ-/ *n cap* the East

[2]**orient** /ˈɔːrient, ˈɒri-/ *v* **1** to set in a definite position, esp in relation to the points of the compass **2a** to adjust to an environment or a situation **b** to acquaint (oneself) with the existing situation or environment

orientate /ˈɔrɪənteɪt, ˈɒ-/ *v*, *chiefly Br* to orient – **-ation** *n*

orifice /ˈɒrɪ̵fɪ̵s/ *n* an opening (e g a vent or mouth) through which sthg may pass

origin /ˈɒrɪ̵dʒɪ̵n/ *n* **1** ancestry, parentage **2** a source or starting-point

[1]**original** /əˈrɪdʒɪ̵nəl, -dʒənəl/ *n* **1** that from which a copy, reproduction, or translation is made **2** an eccentric person

[2]**original** *adj* **1** initial, earliest; not secondary or derivative **2** being the first instance or source of a copy, reproduction, or translation **3** inventive, creative – **~ly** *adv* – **~ity** *n*

original sin *n* (the doctrine of) man's innate sinfulness resulting from Adam's fall

originate /əˈrɪdʒɪ̵neɪt/ *v* to (cause to) begin or come into existence – **-nator** *n*

oriole /ˈɔːriəʊl/ *n* any of a family of birds with black and either orange or yellow plumage

[1]**ornament** /ˈɔːnəmənt/ *n* **1** sthg that lends grace or beauty; (a) decoration or embellishment **2** an embellishing note not belonging to the essential harmony or melody – **~al** *adj* – **~ally** *adv*

[2]**ornament** /ˈɔːnəment/ *v* to add ornament to; embellish – **~ation** *n*

ornate /ɔːˈneɪt/ *adj* **1** rhetorical or florid in style **2** elaborately or excessively decorated – **~ly** *adv* – **~ness** *n*

ornithology /ˌɔːnɪ̵ˈθɒlədʒi/ *n* a branch of zoology dealing with birds – **-gist** *n* – **-gical** *adj*

orotund /ˈɒrəʊtʌnd/ *adj* **1** sonorous **2** pompous, bombastic

[1]**orphan** /ˈɔːfən/ *n* a child 1 or both of whose parents are dead

[2]**orphan** *v* to cause to be an orphan

orphanage /ˈɔːfənɪdʒ/ *n* an institution for the care of orphans

orrisroot /ˈɒrɪ̵sruːt/ *n* the fragrant root of an iris used in perfumes

orthodox /ˈɔːθədɒks/ *adj* **1a** conforming to established, dominant, or official doctrine (e g in religion) **b** conventional **2** *cap* (consisting) of the Eastern churches headed by the patriarch of Constantinople which separated from the Western church in the 9th c – **~y** *n*

orthography /ɔːˈθɒgrəfi/ *n* correct spelling – **-phic(al)** *adj* – **-phically** *adv*

orthopaedics /ˌɔːθəˈpiːdɪks/ *n pl* the prevention or correction of skeletal and muscular deformities, esp by surgery

Oscar /ˈɒskəʳ/ *n* an award made annually by a US professional organization for outstanding achievement in the cinema

oscillate /ˈɒsɪ̵leɪt/ *v* to swing backwards and forwards like a pendulum – **-ation** *n*

oscillator /ˈɒsɪ̵leɪtəʳ/ *n* a device for producing alternating current; *esp* a radio-frequency or audio-frequency signal generator

osier /ˈəʊzɪəʳ/ *n* **1** any of various willows whose pliable twigs are used for furniture and basketry **2** a willow rod used in basketry

osmosis /ɒzˈməʊsɪ̵s/ *n* movement of a solvent through a membrane (e g of a living cell) into a solution of higher concentration that tends to equalize the concentrations on the 2 sides of the membrane

osprey /ˈɒspri, -preɪ/ *n* **1** a large fish-eating hawk with dark brown and white plumage **2** a feather trimming used for millinery

ossify /ˈɒsɪ̵faɪ/ *v* **1** to become bone **2** to become unfeeling, unimaginative, or rigid

ostensible /ɒˈstensɪ̵bəl/ *adj* being such in appearance rather than reality; professed, declared – **-bly** *adv*

ostentation /ˌɒstənˈteɪʃən, -ten-/ *n* unnecessary display of wealth, knowledge, etc designed to impress or attract attention – **-tious** *adj* – **-tiously** *adv*

osteopathy /ˌɒstiˈɒpəθi/ *n* a system of treatment of diseases based on the theory that they can be cured by manipulation of bones – **osteopath** *n*

ostler, *chiefly NAm* **hostler** /ˈɒsləʳ/ *n* a groom or stableman at an inn

ostrac·ize, -ise /ˈɒstrəsaɪz/ *v* to refuse to have social contact with; exclude from membership of a group – **-cism** *n*

ostrich /ˈɒstrɪtʃ/ *n* **1** a swift-footed 2-toed flightless bird that has valuable wing and tail plumes and is the largest of existing birds **2** one who refuses to face up to unpleasant realities

[1]**other** /ˈʌðəʳ/ *adj* **1a** being the 1 left of 2 or more (e g held on with one hand and waved with the *other*) **b** being the ones distinct from that or those first mentioned (e g taller than the *other* boys) **c** second (e g every *other* day) **2a** not the same; different (e g schools *other* than hers) **b** far, opposite (e g lives on the *other* side of town) **3** additional, further (e g John and 2 *other* boys) **4** recently past (e g the *other* evening)

[2]**other** *pron, pl* **others** *also* **other** **1** the remaining or opposite one (e g went from one side to the *other*) **2** a different or additional one (e g some film or *other*)

[3]**other** *adv* otherwise – + *than*

[1]**otherwise** /ˈʌðəwaɪz/ *adv* **1** in a different way **2** in different circumstances **3** in other respects **4** if not; or else **5** not – used to express the opposite (e g mothers, whether married or *otherwise*) **6** alias

[2]**otherwise** *adj* of a different kind (e g how can I be *otherwise* than grateful?)

otherworldly /ˌʌðəˈwɜːldli/ *adj* concerned with spiritual or intellectual matters rather than the material world

otter /ˈɒtəʳ/ *n* (the dark brown fur or pelt of) any of several aquatic fish-eating mammals with webbed and clawed feet, related to the weasels

ottoman /ˈɒtəmən/ *n* **1** *cap* a Turk **2a** a usu heavily upholstered box or seat without a back or arms **b** a cushioned stool for the feet

Ottoman /ˈɒtəmən/ *adj* Turkish

ouch /aʊtʃ/ *interj* – used esp to express sudden sharp pain

¹ought /ɔːt/ *verbal auxiliary* – used to express moral obligation (e g *ought* to pay our debts), advisability (e g *ought* to be boiled for 10 minutes), enthusiastic recommendation (e g you *ought* to hear her *sing*), natural expectation (e g *ought* to have arrived by now) or logical consequence (e g the result *ought* to be infinity) used in the negative to express moral condemnation of an action (e g you *ought* not to treat him like that); often used with the perfect infinitive to express unfulfilled obligation (e g *ought* never to have been allowed)

¹ounce /aʊns/ *n* $^{1}/_{16}$ of a pound avoidupois or $^{1}/_{12}$ of a pound troy weight

²ounce *n* a snow leopard

our /ɑːʳ; *strong* aʊəʳ/ *adj* of us, ourself, or ourselves, esp as possessors or possessor, agents or agent, or objects or object of an action; of everybody

ours /aʊəz/ *pron, pl* **ours** that which or the one who belongs to us – used without a following noun as a pronoun equivalent in meaning to the adjective *our*

ourselves /aʊəˈselvz/ *pron, pl in constr* **1** those identical people that are we – used reflexively (e g we're doing it for *ourselves*) or for emphasis (e g we *ourselves* will never go) **2** our normal selves (e g not feeling quite *ourselves*)

oust /aʊst/ *v* **1** to remove from or dispossess of property or position **2** to take the place of; supplant

¹out /aʊt/ *adv* **1a** away from the inside or centre (e g went *out* into the garden) **b** from among other things (e g separate *out* the bad apples) **c** away from the shore, the city, or one's homeland (e g live *out* in the country) **d** away from a particular place, esp of one's home or business (e g move *out* into lodgings) **e(1)** clearly in or into view (e g when the sun's *out*) **(2)** *of a flower* in or into full bloom **2a(1)** out of the proper place (e g left a word *out*) **(2)** amiss in reckoning **b** in all directions from a central point of control (e g lent *out* money) **c** from political power (e g voted them *out*) **d** into shares or portions **e** out of vogue or fashion **3a** to or in a state of extinction or exhaustion (e g before the year is *out*) **b** to the fullest extent or degree; completely (e g hear me *out*) **c** in or into a state of determined effort (e g *out* to fight pollution) **4a** aloud **b** in existence; ever – with a superlative; infml (e g the funniest thing *out*) **5** so as to be put out of a game **6** – used on a 2-way radio circuit to indicate that a message is complete and no reply is expected

²out *v* to become publicly known

³out *adj* **1** located outside; external **2** located at a distance; outlying **3** not being in operation or power **4** directed or serving to direct outwards (e g the *out* tray) **5** not allowed to continue batting **6** out of the question

⁴out *n* a way of escaping from an embarrassing or difficult situation

outback /ˈaʊtbæk/ *n* isolated rural (Australian) country

outbalance /aʊtˈbæləns/ *v* to outweigh in value or importance

outbid /aʊtˈbɪd/ *v* to make a higher bid than

outbreak /ˈaʊtbreɪk/ *n* **1a** a sudden or violent breaking out **b** a sudden increase in numbers of a harmful organism or in sufferers from a disease within a particular area **2** an insurrection, revolt

outbuilding /ˈaʊtbɪldɪŋ/ *n* a smaller building (e g a stable or a woodshed) separate from but belonging to a main building

outburst /ˈaʊtbɜːst/ *n* **1** a violent expression of feeling **2** a surge of activity or growth

outcast /ˈaʊtkɑːst/ *n* one who is cast out by society

outcaste /ˈaʊtkɑːst/ *n* a Hindu who has been ejected from his/her caste

outclass /aʊtˈklɑːs/ *v* to excel, surpass

outcome /ˈaʊtkʌm/ *n* a result, consequence

[1]**outcrop** /'aʊtkrɒp/ *n* **1** (the emergence of) the part of a rock formation that appears at the surface of the ground **2** an outbreak – **outcrop** *v*

outcry /'aʊtkraɪ/ *n* **1** a loud cry; a clamour **2** a public expression of anger or disapproval

outdated /ˌaʊt'deɪtɪ̈d/ *adj* outmoded

outdistance /aʊt'dɪstəns/ *v* to go far ahead of (e g in a race)

outdo /aʊt'duː/ *v* to surpass in action or performance

outdoor /ˌaʊt'dɔːʳ/ *adj* **1** of or performed outdoors **2** not enclosed; without a roof

[1]**outdoors** /ˌaʊt'dɔːz/ *adv* outside a building; in or into the open air

[2]**outdoors** *n pl but sing in constr* **1** *the* open air **2** *the* world remote from human habitation

outer /'aʊtəʳ/ *adj* **1** existing independently of the mind; objective **2a** situated farther out **b** away from a centre **c** situated or belonging on the outside

outface /aʊt'feɪs/ *v* **1** to cause to waver or submit (as if) by staring **2** to confront unflinchingly; defy

outfield /'aʊtfiːld/ *n* the part of a cricket field beyond the prepared section on which wickets are laid out – **~er** *n*

outfit /'aʊtˌfɪt/ *n* **1a** a complete set of equipment needed for a particular purpose **b** a set of garments worn together, often for a specified occasion or activity **2** *sing or pl in constr* a group that works as a team – infml – **outfit** *v*

outflank /aʊt'flæŋk/ *v* **1** to go round or extend beyond the flank of (an opposing force) **2** to gain an advantage over by doing sthg unexpected

outgoing /ˌaʊt'gəʊɪŋ/ *adj* **1a** going away; departing **b** retiring or withdrawing from a position **2** friendly, sociable

outgoings /'aʊtˌgəʊɪŋz/ *n pl* expenditures; *esp* overheads

outgrow /aʊt'grəʊ/ *v* **1** to grow or increase faster than **2** to grow too large or too old for

outhouse /'aʊthaʊs/ *n* an outbuilding

outing /'aʊtɪŋ/ *n* a short pleasure trip

outlandish /aʊt'lændɪʃ/ *adj* strikingly unusual; bizarre – **~ly** *adv* – **~ness** *n*

outlast /aʊt'lɑːst/ *v* to last longer than

[1]**outlaw** /'aʊtlɔː/ *n* a fugitive from the law

[2]**outlaw** *v* **1** to deprive of the protection of law **2** to make illegal

outlay /'aʊtleɪ/ *n* expenditure, payment

outlet /'aʊtlet, -lɪ̈t/ *n* **1a** an exit or vent **b** a means of release or satisfaction for an emotion or drive **2** an agency (e g a shop or dealer) through which a product is marketed

[1]**outline** /'aʊtlaɪn/ *n* **1** a line bounding the outer limits of sthg; shape **2** (a) drawing with no shading **3** a condensed treatment or summary **4** a preliminary account of a project

[2]**outline** *v* **1** to draw the outline of **2** to indicate the principal features of

outlive /aʊt'lɪv/ *v* **1** to live longer than **2** to survive the effects of

outlook /'aʊtlʊk/ *n* **1** an attitude; point of view **2** a prospect for the future

outlying /'aʊtˌlaɪ-ɪŋ/ *adj* remote from a centre or main point

outmanoeuvre /ˌaʊtmə'nuːvəʳ/ *v* to defeat by more skilful manoeuvring

outmatch /aʊt'mætʃ/ *v* to surpass, outdo

outmoded /aʊt'məʊdɪ̈d/ *adj* **1** no longer in fashion **2** no longer acceptable or usable; obsolete

outplay /aʊt'pleɪ/ *v* to defeat or play better than in a game

outpost /'aʊtpəʊst/ *n* **1** a post or detachment established at a distance from a main body of troops, esp to protect it from surprise attack **2** an outlying or frontier settlement

output /'aʊtpʊt/ *n* **1** mineral, agricultural, or industrial production **2** mental or artistic production **3** the amount produced by sby in a given time **4** sthg (e g energy, material, or data) produced by a machine or system

[1]**outrage** /'aʊtreɪdʒ/ *n* **1** an act of violence or brutality **2** an act that

violates accepted standards of behaviour or taste

²**outrage** /aʊt'reɪdʒ/ *v* to violate the standards or principles of

outrageous /aʊt'reɪdʒəs/ *adj* **1** not conventional or moderate; extravagant **2** going beyond all standards of propriety, decency, or taste; shocking, offensive – ~**ly** *adv*

outré /uːtreɪ/ *adj* violating convention or propriety; bizarre

outrider /'aʊt,raɪdəʳ/ *n* a mounted attendant or motorcyclist who rides ahead of or beside a carriage or car as an escort

outrigger /'aʊt,rɪgəʳ/ *n* **1** a spar, beam, or framework run out or projecting from a ship's side (e g to help secure a mast or support a float or rowlock) **2** a member projecting from a main structure to provide additional stability or support sthg

¹**outright** /aʊt'raɪt/ *adv* **1** completely **2** instantaneously

²**outright** /'aʊtraɪt/ *adj* being completely or exactly what is stated

outrun /,aʊt'rʌn/ *v* **1** to run faster than **2** to exceed, surpass

outsell /,aʊt'sel/ *v* to surpass in selling, salesmanship, or numbers sold

outset /'aʊtset/ *n* *the* beginning, start

¹**outside** /aʊt'saɪd, 'aʊtsaɪd/ *n* **1a** an external part; the region beyond a boundary **b** the area farthest from a point of reference: e g **(1)** the section of a playing area towards the sidelines; *also* a corner **(2)** the side of a pavement nearer the traffic **2** an outer side or surface **3** an outer manifestation; an appearance **4** the extreme limit of an estimation or guess; a maximum

²**outside** /'aʊtsaɪd/ *adj* **1a** of or being on, near, or towards the outside **b** of or being the outer side of a curve or near the middle of the road **2** maximum **3a** originating elsewhere (e g an *outside* broadcast) **b** not belonging to one's regular occupation or duties **4** barely possible; remote

³**outside** /aʊt'saɪd/ *adv* **1** on or to the outside **2** outdoors **3** *chiefly Br* not in prison – slang

⁴**outside** /'aʊtsaɪd, -'-/ *prep* **1** on or to the outside of **2** beyond the limits of **3** except, besides (e g few interests *outside* her children)

outsider /aʊt'saɪdəʳ/ *n* **1** sby who does not belong to a particular group **2** a competitor who has only an outside chance of winning

outsize /'aʊtsaɪz/ *adj or n* (of) an unusual or above standard size

outsmart /aʊt'smɑːt/ *v* to get the better of; outwit

outspoken /aʊt'spəʊkən/ *adj* direct and open in speech or expression; frank – ~**ly** *adv* – ~**ness** *n*

outstanding /aʊt'stændɪŋ/ *adj* **1a** unpaid **b** continuing, unresolved **2a** standing out from a group; conspicuous **b** marked by eminence and distinction – ~**ly** *adv*

outstay /,aʊt'steɪ/ *v* **1** to overstay **2** to surpass in staying power

outstrip /aʊt'strɪp/ *v* **1** to go faster or farther than **2** to get ahead of; leave behind

¹**outward** /,aʊtwəd/ *adj* **1a** situated at or directed towards the outside **b** being or going away from home **2** of the body or external appearances

outwardly /'aʊtwədli/ *adv* in outward appearance; superficially

outwards /'aʊtwədz/ *adv* towards the outside

outweigh /aʊt'weɪ/ *v* to exceed in weight, value, or importance

outwit /aʊt'wɪt/ *v* to get the better of by superior cleverness

outwork /'aʊtwɜːk/ *n* **1** a minor defensive position constructed outside a fortified area **2** work done for a business or organization off its premises usu by employees based at home – ~**er** *n*

ova /'əʊvə/ *pl of* **ovum**

¹**oval** /'əʊvəl/ *adj* having the shape of an egg; *also* elliptical

²**oval** *n* an oval figure or object

ovary /'əʊvəri/ *n* **1** the typically paired female reproductive organ that produces eggs and female sex hormones **2** the enlarged rounded female part of a flowering plant that bears the ovules and consists of 1 or more carpels – **-arian** *adj*

ovation /əʊ'veɪʃən/ *n* an expression of popular acclaim

oven /'ʌvən/ *n* a chamber used for baking, heating, or drying

ovenware /ˈʌvənweəʳ/ *n* heat-resistant dishes (e g casseroles) in which food can be cooked in an oven

[1]**over** /ˈəʊvəʳ/ *adv* **1a** across a barrier **b** across an intervening space **c** downwards from an upright position (e g fell *over*) **d** across the brim or brink (e g the soup boiled *over*) **e** so as to bring the underside up **f** so as to be reversed or folded **g** from one person or side to another **h** across (e g got his point *over*) **2a(1)** beyond some quantity or limit **(2)** excessively, inordinately – often in combination **(3)** in excess; remaining **b** till a later time (e g stay *over* till Monday) **3** so as to cover the whole surface (e g windows boarded *over*) **4a** at an end **b** – used on a two-way radio circuit to indicate that a message is complete and a reply is expected **5** – used to show repetition (e g told you *over* and *over*)

[2]**over** *prep* **1a** higher than; above **b** vertically above but not touching **c** – used to indicate movement down upon (e g hit him *over* the head) or down across the edge of (e g fell *over* the cliff) **d** across (e g climbed *over* the gate) **e** so as to cover **f** divided by (e g 6 *over* 2 is 3) **2a** with authority, power, or jurisdiction in relation to **b** – used to indicate superiority, advantage, or preference (e g a big lead *over* the others) **3** more than **4a** all through or throughout (e g showed me all *over* the house) **b** by means of (a medium or channel of communication) (e g *over* the radio) **5a** in the course of; during **b** until the end of (stay *over* Sunday) **c** past, beyond **6** – used to indicate an object of occupation or activity or reference (e g sitting *over* their wine, laughed *over* the incident)

[3]**over** *adj* **1** upper, higher (e g *over*lord) **2** outer, covering (e g *over*coat) **3** excessive (e g *over*confident) *USE* often in combination

[4]**over** *n* any of the divisions of an innings in cricket during which 1 bowler bowls 6 or 8 balls from the same end of the pitch

overact /ˌəʊvərˈækt/ *v* to perform (a part) with undue exaggeration

[1]**overall** /ˌəʊvərˈɔːl/ *adv* **1** as a whole **2** from end to end, esp of a ship

[2]**overall** *n* **1** *pl* a protective garment resembling a boiler suit or dungarees **2** *chiefly Br* a usu loose-fitting protective coat worn over other clothing

[3]**overall** *adj* including everything

overarm /ˈəʊvərɑːm/ *adj or adv* overhand

overawe /ˌəʊvərˈɔː/ *v* to fill with respect or fear

overbalance /ˌəʊvəˈbæləns/ *v* (to cause) to lose one's balance

overbearing /ˌəʊvəˈbeərɪŋ/ *adj* harshly masterful or domineering – **~ly** *adv*

[1]**overblown** /ˌəʊvəˈbləʊn/ *adj* inflated, pretentious

[2]**overblown** *adj* past the prime of bloom

overboard /ˈəʊvəbɔːd/ *adv* **1** over the side of a ship or boat into the water **2** to extremes of enthusiasm

overcast /ˌəʊvəˈkɑːst/ *adj* being, having, or characterized by a cloudy sky

overcharge /ˌəʊvəˈtʃɑːdʒ/ *v* to make an excessive charge – **overcharge** *n*

overcoat /ˈəʊvəkəʊt/ *n* **1** a warm usu thick coat for wearing outdoors over other clothing **2** a protective coat (e g of paint)

overcome /ˌəʊvəˈkʌm/ *v* **1** to get the better of; surmount **2** to overpower, overwhelm

overcrowd /ˌəʊvəˈkraʊd/ *v* to (cause to) be too crowded

overdo /ˌəʊvəˈduː/ *v* **1a** to do or use in excess **b** to exaggerate **2** to cook too much

overdose /ˈəʊvədəʊs/ *v or n* (to give or take) too great a dose of drugs, medicine, etc

overdraft /ˈəʊvədrɑːft/ *n* an act of overdrawing at a bank; the state of being overdrawn; *also* the sum overdrawn

overdraw /ˌəʊvəˈdrɔː/ *v* to draw cheques on (a bank account) for more than the balance – **~n** *adj*

overdrive /ˈəʊvədraɪv/ *n* a transmission gear in a motor vehicle that provides a ratio higher than the normal top gear

overdue /ˌəʊvəˈdjuː/ *adj* **1a** unpaid when due **b** delayed beyond an appointed time **2** more than ready or ripe

overestimate /ˌəʊvər'estɪmeɪt/ *v* **1** to estimate as being more than the actual amount or size **2** to place too high a value on; overrate

[1]**overflow** /ˌəʊvə'fləʊ/ *v* to flow over or beyond a brim, edge, or limit

[2]**overflow** /'əʊvəfləʊ/ *n* **1** a flowing over; an inundation **2** sthg that flows over; *also, sing or pl in constr* the excess members of a group **3** an outlet or receptacle for surplus liquid

overgrown /ˌəʊvə'grəʊn/ *adj* **1** grown over or choked with vegetation **2** grown too large – **-growth** *n*

[1]**overhang** /ˌəʊvə'hæŋ/ *v* **1** to project over **2** to threaten

[2]**overhang** /'əʊvəhæŋ/ *n* **1** sthg that overhangs; *also* the extent by which sthg overhangs **2** a projection of the roof or upper storey of a building beyond the wall of the lower part

overhaul /ˌəʊvə'hɔːl/ *v* **1** to examine thoroughly and carry out necessary repairs **2** to overtake

[1]**overhead** /ˌəʊvə'hed/ *adv* above one's head

[2]**overhead** /'əʊvəhed/ *adj* **1** operating, lying, or coming from above **2** of overhead expenses

[3]**overhead** /'əʊvəhed/ *n* **1** a business expense (e g rent, insurance, or heating) not chargeable to a particular part of the work or product **2** a stroke in squash, tennis, etc made above head height

overhear /ˌəʊvə'hɪəʳ/ *v* to hear (sby or sthg) without the speaker's knowledge or intention

overjoyed /ˌəʊvə'dʒɔɪd/ *adj* extremely pleased; elated

[1]**overkill** /ˌəʊvə'kɪl/ *v* to obliterate (a target) with more (nuclear) force than required

[2]**overkill** /'əʊvəˌkɪl/ *n* **1** the capability of destroying an enemy or target with a force, esp nuclear, larger than is required **2** an excess of sthg beyond what is required or suitable for a particular purpose

overland /ˌəʊvə'lænd/ *adv or adj* by, upon, or across land rather than sea or air

overlap /ˌəʊvə'læp/ *v* to extend over and cover a part of; partly coincide

overlay /ˌəʊvə'leɪ/ *v* to cover usu thinly

overleaf /ˌəʊvə'liːf/ *adv* on the other side of the page

overlook /ˌəʊvə'lʊk/ *v* **1** to have or provide a view of from above **2a** to fail to notice; miss **b** to ignore **c** to excuse

overly /'əʊvəli/ *adv* to an excessive degree

overman /ˌəʊvə'mæn/ *v* to have or provide too many workers for – **~ning** *n*

overmaster /ˌəʊvə'mɑːstəʳ/ *v* to overpower, subdue

overmuch /ˌəʊvə'mʌtʃ/ *adj or adv* too much

overnight /ˌəʊvə'naɪt/ *adv* **1** during or throughout the evening or night **2** suddenly – **overnight** *adj*

overpass /'əʊvəpɑːs/ *n* a flyover

overplay /ˌəʊvə'pleɪ/ *v* **1** to exaggerate (e g a dramatic role) **2** to give too much emphasis to

overpower /ˌəʊvə'paʊəʳ/ *v* **1** to overcome by superior force **2** to overwhelm – **~ing** *adj* – **~ingly** *adv*

overrate /ˌəʊvə'reɪt/ *v* to rate too highly

overreach /ˌəʊvə'riːtʃ/ *v* to defeat (oneself) by trying to do or gain too much

[1]**override** /ˌəʊvə'raɪd/ *v* **1a** to prevail over; dominate **b** to set aside or annul; *also* to neutralize the action of (e g an automatic control) **2** to overlap

[2]**override** /'əʊvəraɪd/ *n* a device or system used to override a control

overrule /ˌəʊvə'ruːl/ *v* to rule against or set aside, esp by virtue of superior authority

overrun /ˌəʊvə'rʌn/ *v* **1a** to defeat decisively and occupy the positions of **b** to swarm over; infest **2** to run or go beyond or past **3** to flow over

[1]**overseas** /ˌəʊvə'siːz/, oversea *adv* beyond or across the seas

[2]**overseas** /'əʊvəsiːz/, **oversea** *adj* **1** of transport across the seas **2** of, from, or in (foreign) places across the seas

oversee /ˌəʊvə'siː/ *v* to supervise – **-seer** *n*

oversell /ˌəʊvə'sel/ *v* **1** to sell too much of **2** to make excessive claims for

oversexed /ˌəʊvə'sekst/ *adj* with an abnormally strong sexual drive
overshadow /ˌəʊvə'ʃædəʊ/ *v* **1** to cast a shadow over **2** to exceed in importance; outweigh
overshoe /'əʊvəʃuː/ *n* a usu rubber shoe worn over another as protection (e g from rain or snow)
overshoot /ˌəʊvə'ʃuːt/ *v* to shoot or pass over or beyond, esp so as to miss
oversight /'əʊvəsaɪt/ *n* **1** supervision **2** an inadvertent omission or error
oversimplify /ˌəʊvə'sɪmplɪ̵faɪ/ *v* to simplify (sthg) to such an extent as to cause distortion or error – **-fication** *n*
oversleep /ˌəʊvə'sliːp/ *v* to sleep beyond the intended time
overspill /'əʊvəˌspɪl/ *n* people who have moved away from crowded urban areas
overstate /ˌəʊvə'steɪt/ *v* to state in too strong terms; exaggerate – **~ment** *n*
oversteer /'əʊvəˌstɪəʳ/ *n* the tendency of a motor vehicle to steer into a sharper turn than the driver intends
overstep /ˌəʊvə'step/ *v* to exceed, transgress – esp in *overstep the mark*
overstrung /ˌəʊvə'strʌŋ/ *adj* too highly strung; too sensitive
overt /'əʊvɜːt, əʊ'vɜːt/ *adj* public, manifest – **~ly** *adv*
overtake /ˌəʊvə'teɪk/ *v* **1** to catch up with (and pass beyond), esp a motor vehicle **2** to come upon suddenly
overtax /ˌəʊvə'tæks/ *v* **1** to tax too heavily **2** to put too great a burden or strain on
[1]**overthrow** /ˌəʊvə'θrəʊ/ *v* **1** to overturn, upset **2** to cause the downfall of; defeat
[2]**overthrow** /'əʊvəθrəʊ/ *n* (a run scored from) a return of the ball from a fielder in cricket that goes past the wicket
overtime /'əʊvətaɪm/ *n* **1** time in excess of a set limit; *esp* working time in excess of a standard working day or week **2** the wage paid for overtime
overture /'əʊvətjʊəʳ, -tʃəʳ/ *n* **1** an initiative towards agreement or action – often pl with sing. meaning **2a** the orchestral introduction to a musical dramatic work **b** an orchestral concert piece written esp as a single movement
overturn /ˌəʊvə'tɜːn/ *v* **1** to cause to turn over; upset **2** to overthrow
overweening /ˌəʊvə'wiːnɪŋ/ *adj* **1** arrogant, presumptuous **2** immoderate, exaggerated – **~ly** *adv*
overweight /ˌəʊvə'weɪt/ *adj* exceeding the expected, normal, or proper (bodily) weight
overwhelm /ˌəʊvə'welm/ *v* **1** to cover over completely; submerge **2** to overcome by superior force or numbers **3** to overpower with emotion – **~ing** *adj* – **~ingly** *adv*
overwork /ˌəʊvə'wɜːk/ *v* **1** (to cause) to work too hard or too long **2** to make excessive use of – **overwork** *n*
overwrought /ˌəʊvə'rɔːt/ *adj* extremely excited; agitated
oviduct /'əʊvɪ̵dʌkt/ *n* the tube that serves for the passage of eggs from an ovary, esp before laying
ovoid /'əʊvɔɪd/, **ovoidal** *adj* shaped like an egg
ovulate /'ɒvjʊleɪt/ *v* to produce eggs or discharge them from an ovary – **-ation** *n*
ovule /'ɒvjuːl/ *n* an outgrowth of the ovary of a seed plant that develops into a seed after fertilization of the egg cell it contains
ovum /'əʊvəm/ *n, pl* **ova** /'əʊvə/ an animal's female gamete that when fertilized can develop into a new individual
owe /əʊ/ *v* **1a** to be under obligation to pay or render **b** to be indebted to **2** to have or enjoy as a result of the action or existence of sthg or sby else
owing to *prep* because of
owl /aʊl/ *n* any of an order of chiefly nocturnal birds of prey with large head and eyes and a short hooked bill – **~ish** *adj* – **~ishly** *adv*
[1]**own** /əʊn/ *adj* belonging to, for, or relating to oneself or itself – usu after a possessive pronoun (e g cooked his *own* dinner)
[2]**own** *v* **1** to have or hold as property; possess **2** to acknowledge, admit – often + *to* – **~er** *n* – **~ership** *n*
[3]**own** *pron, pl* **own** one belonging to

oneself or itself – usu after a possessive pronoun

own up *v* to confess a fault frankly

ox /ɒks/ *n, pl* **oxen** **1** a (domestic species of) bovine mammal **2** an adult castrated male domestic ox

Oxbridge /'ɒks,brɪdʒ/ *adj or n* (of) the universities of Oxford and Cambridge

oxide /'ɒksaɪd/ *n* a compound of oxygen with an element or radical

oxid·ize, -ise /'ɒksɪ̥daɪz/ *v* **1** to combine with oxygen **2** to remove hydrogen or 1 or more electrons from an atom, ion, or molecule

Oxonian /ɒk'səʊnɪən/ *n* a student or graduate of Oxford University

oxtail /'ɒksteɪl/ *n* the tail of cattle (skinned and used for food, esp in soup)

oxyacetylene /,ɒksɪə'setɪ̥liːn/ *adj* of or using a mixture of oxygen and acetylene, esp for producing a hot flame

oxygen /'ɒksɪdʒən/ *n* a bivalent gaseous chemical element that forms about 21 per cent by volume of the atmosphere and is essential for the life of all plants and animals

oxygen tent *n* a canopy placed over sby in bed to maintain a flow of oxygen-enriched air

oyez /əʊ'jeɪ, əʊ'jez/ *v imper* – uttered by a court official or public crier to gain attention

oyster /'ɔɪstəʳ/ *n* **1** any of various (edible) marine bivalve molluscs with a rough irregular shell **2** a small mass of muscle on each side of the back of a fowl

oystercatcher /'ɔɪstə,kætʃəʳ/ *n* any of a genus of usu black-and-white stout-legged wading birds

ozone /'əʊzəʊn/ *n* **1** a form of oxygen with 3 atoms in each molecule **2** pure and refreshing air

P

p /piː/ *n, pl* **p's, ps** *often cap* (a graphic representation of or device for reproducing) the 16th letter of the English alphabet

pa /pɑː/ *n* father – infml

[1]**pace** /peɪs/ *n* **1** rate of movement or activity **2** a manner of walking **3** the distance covered by a single step in walking, usu taken to be about 0.75m (about 30in) **4a** a gait; *esp* a fast 2-beat gait of a horse in which the legs move in lateral pairs **b** *pl* an exhibition of skills or abilities

[2]**pace** *v* **1** to walk with a slow or measured tread **2** to measure by pacing – often + *out* or *off* **3** to set or regulate the pace of; *specif* to go ahead of (e g a runner) as a pacemaker

[3]**pace** /ˈpeɪsiː, ˈpɑːkeɪ/ *prep* with due respect to

pacemaker /ˈpeɪs,meɪkəʳ/ *n* **1** sby or sthg that sets the pace for another (e g in a race) **2** (a device for applying regular electric shocks to the heart that reproduces the function of) a part of the heart that maintains rhythmic (coordinated) contractions

pachyderm /ˈpækɪdɜːm/ *n* an elephant, rhinoceros, pig, or other usu thick-skinned (hoofed) mammal that does not chew the cud

pacific /pəˈsɪfɪk/ *adj* **1** having a mild peaceable nature **2** *cap* of (the region round) the Pacific ocean – **~ally** *adv*

pacifism /ˈpæsɨfɪzəm/ *n* opposition to war as a means of settling disputes; *specif* refusal to bear arms on moral or religious grounds

pacify /ˈpæsɨfaɪ/ *v* **1** to allay the anger or agitation of **2a** to restore to a peaceful state; subdue **b** to reduce to submission – **-fication, -fier** *n*

[1]**pack** /pæk/ *n* **1** a bundle or bag of things carried on the shoulders or back **2a** a large amount or number **b** a full set of playing cards **3** an organized troop (e g of cub scouts) **4** *sing or pl in constr the* forwards in a rugby team, esp when acting together **5** *sing or pl in constr* **a** a group of domesticated animals trained to hunt or run together **b** a group of (predatory) animals of the same kind **6** wet absorbent material for application to the body as treatment (e g for a bruise)

[2]**pack** *v* **1a** to stow (as if) in a container, esp for transport or storage – often + *up* **b** to cover, fill, or surround with protective material **2a** to crowd together so as to fill; cram **b** to force into a smaller volume; compress **3** to bring to an end; finish – + *up* or *in* **4** to gather into a pack **5** to cover or surround with a pack

[3]**pack** *v* to influence the composition of (e g a jury) so as to bring about a desired result

package /ˈpækɪdʒ/ *n* **1a** a small or medium-sized pack; a parcel **b** sthg wrapped or sealed **2** a wrapper or container in which sthg is packed **3** **package, package holiday** a holiday, booked through a single agent, including transport, accommodation and (some) meals at an all-in price – **package** *v*

package deal *n* an offer or agreement involving a number of related items and making acceptance of one item dependent on the acceptance of all

packed /pækt/ *adj* **1a** that is crowded or stuffed – often in combination **b** compressed **2** filled to capacity

packet /ˈpækɨt/ *n* **1** a small pack or parcel **2** a passenger boat carrying mail and cargo on a regular schedule **3** *Br* a large sum of money – infml

pack ice *n* sea ice crushed together into a large floating mass

pack up *v* **1** to finish work **2** to cease to function

pact /pækt/ *n* an agreement, treaty

[1]**pad** /pæd/ *n* **1** a thin flat mat or cushion: e g **a** padding used to shape an article of clothing **b** a padded

guard worn to shield body parts, esp the legs of a batsman, against impact **c** a piece of absorbent material used as a surgical dressing or protective covering **2** (the cushioned thickening of the underside of) the foot of an animal **3** a number of sheets of paper (e g for writing or drawing on) fastened together at 1 edge **4** a flat surface for a vertical takeoff or landing **5** living quarters – infml

[2]**pad** *v* **1** to provide with a pad or padding **2** to expand or fill out (speech or writing) with superfluous matter – often + *out*

[3]**pad** *v* to walk with a muffled step

padding /ˈpædɪŋ/ *n* material used to pad

[1]**paddle** /ˈpædl/ *n* **1a** a usu wooden implement similar to but smaller than an oar, used to propel and steer a small craft (e g a canoe) **b** an implement with a short handle and broad flat blade used for stirring, mixing, hitting, etc **2** any of the broad boards at the circumference of a paddle wheel or waterwheel

[2]**paddle** *v* to go on or through water (as if) by means of paddling a craft

[3]**paddle** *v* to walk, play, or wade in shallow water

paddle wheel *n* a power-driven wheel with paddles, floats, or boards round its circumference used to propel a boat

paddock /ˈpædək/ *n* **1** a small usu enclosed field, esp for pasturing or exercising animals **2** an area at a motor-racing track where cars, motorcycles, etc are parked and worked on before a race

paddy /ˈpædi/ *n* **1** (threshed unmilled) rice **2** a paddyfield

Paddy *n* an Irishman – chiefly derog

paddyfield /ˈpædifiːld/ *n* a field of wet land in which rice is grown

padlock /ˈpædlɒk/ *n* a portable lock with a shackle that can be passed through a staple or link and then secured

padre /ˈpɑːdri, -reɪ/ *n* **1** a Christian priest **2** a military chaplain

paediatrics /ˌpiːdiˈætrɪks/ *n pl but sing or pl in constr* medicine dealing with the development, care, and diseases of children – **-trician** *n*

paella /paɪˈelə/ *n* a saffron-flavoured Spanish dish containing rice, meat, seafood, and vegetables

pagan /ˈpeɪgən/ *n* **1** sby worshipping several gods **2** an irreligious person – **pagan** *adj* – **~ism** *n*

[1]**page** /peɪdʒ/ *n* **1a** a youth attending on a person of rank; *esp* one in the personal service of a knight **b** a boy serving as an honorary attendant at a formal function (e g a wedding) **2** sby employed to deliver messages or run errands

[2]**page** *v* to summon esp by repeatedly calling out the name of (e g over a public-address system)

[3]**page** *n* (a single side of) a leaf of a book, magazine, etc

pageant /ˈpædʒənt/ *n* **1** an ostentatious display **2** a show, exhibition; *esp* a colourful spectacle with a series of tableaux, dramatic presentations, or a procession, expressing a common theme

pageantry /ˈpædʒəntri/ *n* **1** pageants and the presentation of pageants **2** colourful or splendid display; spectacle

pagoda /pəˈgəʊdə/ *n* a many-storied usu polygonal tower erected as a temple or memorial in the Far East

paid /peɪd/ *past of* **pay**

paid-up *adj* having paid the necessary fees to be a full member of a group or organization; *broadly* showing the characteristic attitudes and behaviour of a specified group to a marked degree

pail /peɪl/ *n* (the contents of or quantity contained in) an esp wooden or metal bucket

[1]**pain** /peɪn/ *n* **1a** a basic bodily sensation induced by a noxious stimulus or physical disorder and characterized by physical discomfort (e g pricking, throbbing, or aching) **b** acute mental or emotional distress **2** *pl* trouble or care taken **3** sby or sthg that annoys or is a nuisance – infml

[2]**pain** *v* to make suffer or cause distress to; hurt

painful /ˈpeɪnfəl/ *adj* **1a** feeling or giving pain **b** irksome, annoying **2**

requiring effort or exertion – ~**ly** *adv* – ~**ness** *n*

painstaking /ˈpeɪnzˌteɪkɪŋ/ *adj* showing diligent care and effort – ~**ly** *adv*

[1]**paint** /peɪnt/ *v* **1** to apply colour, pigment, etc to **2a** to represent in colours on a surface by applying pigments **b** to decorate by painting **3** to depict as having specified or implied characteristics

[2]**paint** *n* a mixture of a pigment and a suitable liquid which forms a closely adherent coating when spread on a surface

paintbrush /ˈpeɪntbrʌʃ/ *n* a brush for applying paint

[1]**painter** /ˈpeɪntəʳ/ *n* **1** an artist who paints **2** sby who applies paint (e g to a building), esp as an occupation

[2]**painter** *n* a line used for securing or towing a boat

painting /ˈpeɪntɪŋ/ *n* **1** a product of painting; *esp* a painted work of art **2** the art or occupation of painting

paintwork /ˈpeɪntwɜːk/ *n* paint that has been applied to a surface

[1]**pair** /peəʳ/ *n sing or pl in constr* **1a(1)** two corresponding things usu used together **(2)** two corresponding bodily parts **b** a single thing made up of 2 connected corresponding pieces **2a** two similar or associated things: e g **(1)** a couple in love, engaged, or married **(2)** two playing cards of the same value in a hand **(3)** two horses harnessed side by side **(4)** two mated animals **b** a partnership between 2 people, esp in a contest against another partnership

[2]**pair** *v* to arrange in pairs

paisley /ˈpeɪzli/ *adj, often cap* of a fabric or garment made usu of soft wool and woven or printed with colourful abstract teardrop-shaped figures

Pakistani /ˌpækɪˈstɑːni/ *n* **1** a native or inhabitant of Pakistan **2** a descendant of Pakistanis

pal /pæl/ *n* **1** a close friend **2** – used as a familiar form of address, esp to a stranger *USE* infml – ~**ly** *adj*

[1]**palace** /ˈpælɨs/ *n* **1** the official residence of a ruler (e g a sovereign or bishop) **2a** a large public building **b** a large and often ornate place of public entertainment

[2]**palace** *adj* **1** of a palace **2** of or involving the intimates of a chief executive

palais /ˈpæleɪ; *infml* ˈpæli/, **palais de dance** *n* a public dance hall – chiefly infml

palatable /ˈpælətəbəl/ *adj* **1** pleasant to the taste **2** acceptable to the mind – **-bly** *adv*

palate /ˈpælɨt/ *n* **1** the roof of the mouth, separating it from the nasal cavity **2a** the sense of taste **b** a usu intellectual taste or liking – **palatal** *adj*

palatial /pəˈleɪʃəl/ *adj* **1** of or being a palace **2** suitable to a palace; magnificent – ~**ly** *adv*

palaver /pəˈlɑːvəʳ/ *n* **1** a long parley or discussion **2** idle talk

[1]**pale** /peɪl/ *adj* **1** deficient in (intensity of) colour **2** not bright or brilliant; dim **3** feeble, faint – ~**ly** *adv* – ~**ness** *n*

[2]**pale** *n* **1** a slat in a fence **2** a territory under a particular jurisdiction

paleface /ˈpeɪlfeɪs/ *n* a white person, esp as distinguished from an American Indian

palette /ˈpælɨt/ *n* **1** a thin board held in the hand on which an artist mixes pigments **2** a particular range, quality, or use of colour; *esp* that of an individual artist

palette knife *n* a knife with a flexible steel blade and no cutting edge, used esp in cooking or by artists for mixing and applying paints

palindrome /ˈpælɨndrəʊm/ *n* a word, sentence, etc that reads the same backwards or forwards

[1]**palisade** /ˌpælɨˈseɪd/ *n* a long strong stake pointed at the top and set close with others as a defence

[2]**palisade** *v* to surround or fortify with palisades

[1]**pall** /pɔːl/ *n* **1** a square of linen used to cover the chalice containing the wine used at Communion **2** a heavy cloth draped over a coffin or tomb **3** sthg heavy or dark that covers or conceals

[2]**pall** *v* to cease to be interesting or attractive

pallbearer /ˈpɔːlˌbeərəʳ/ *n* a person

who helps to carry the coffin at a funeral or is part of its immediate escort

[1]**pallet** /ˈpælɨ̣t/ *n* **1** a straw-filled mattress **2** a small hard often makeshift bed

[2]**pallet** *n* **1** a flat-bladed wooden tool used esp by potters for shaping clay **2** a portable platform intended for handling, storing, or moving materials and packages

palliate /ˈpælieɪt/ *v* **1** to lessen the unpleasantness of (e g a disease) without removing the cause **2** to disguise the gravity of (a fault or offence) by excuses or apologies; extenuate **3** to moderate the intensity of – **-ation** *n* – **-ative** *n, adj*

pallid /ˈpælɨ̣d/ *adj* **1** lacking colour; wan **2** lacking sparkle or liveliness; dull – **~ly** *adv* – **~ness** *n*

pallor /ˈpæləʳ/ *n* deficiency of (facial) colour; paleness

[1]**palm** /pɑːm/ *n* **1** any of a family of tropical or subtropical trees, shrubs, etc usu having a simple stem and a crown of large leaves **2** (a leaf of the palm as) a symbol of victory, distinction, or rejoicing

[2]**palm** *n* the concave part of the human hand between the bases of the fingers and the wrist

[3]**palm** *v* **1a** to conceal in or with the hand **b** to pick up stealthily **2** to impose by fraud

palm off *v* to get rid of (sthg unwanted or inferior) by deceiving sby into taking it – often + *on*

Palm Sunday *n* the Sunday before Easter celebrated in commemoration of Christ's triumphal entry into Jerusalem

palmy /ˈpɑːmi/ *adj* marked by prosperity; flourishing

palomino /ˌpæləˌmiːnəʊ/ *n* a light tan or cream usu slender-legged horse

palpable /ˈpælpəbəl/ *adj* **1** capable of being touched or felt; tangible **2** easily perceptible by the mind; manifest – **-bly** *adv*

palpitate /ˈpælpɨ̣teɪt/ *v* to beat rapidly and strongly; throb – **-tation** *n*

palsy /ˈpɔːlzi/ *n* paralysis or uncontrollable tremor of (a part of) the body

paltry /ˈpɔːltri/ *adj* **1** mean, despicable **2** trivial

pamper /ˈpæmpəʳ/ *v* to treat with extreme or excessive care and attention

pamphlet /ˈpæmflɨ̣t/ *n* a usu small unbound printed publication with a paper cover, often dealing with topical matters

pamphleteer /ˌpæmflɨ̣ˈtɪəʳ/ *n* a writer of (political) pamphlets attacking sthg or urging a cause

[1]**pan** /pæn/ *n* **1a** any of various usu broad shallow open receptacles: e g **(1)** a dustpan **(2)** a round metal container or vessel usu with a long handle, used to heat or cook food **2** a hollow or depression in land **3** *chiefly Br* the bowl of a toilet **4** *chiefly NAm* a baking tin

[2]**pan** *v* **1** to wash earth, gravel, etc in search of metal (e g gold) **2** to separate (e g gold) by panning **3** to criticize severely – infml

[3]**pan** *n* (a substance for chewing consisting of betel nut and various spices etc wrapped in) a betel leaf

[4]**pan** *v* to rotate a film or television camera so as to keep a moving object in view

[5]**pan** *n* the act or process of panning a camera; the movement of the camera in a panning shot

panacea /ˌpænəˈsɪə/ *n* a remedy for all ills or difficulties

panache /pəˈnæʃ, pæ-/ *n* dash or flamboyance in style and action; verve

panama /ˈpænəmə, ˌpænəˈmɑː/ *n, often cap* a lightweight hat of plaited straw

panatela /ˌpænəˈtelə/ *n* a long thin cigar

pancake /ˈpæŋkeɪk/ *n* **1** a flat cake made from thin batter and cooked on both sides usu in a frying pan **2** make-up compressed into a flat cake or stick form

panchromatic /ˌpæŋkrəʊˈmætɪk/ *adj* sensitive to light of all colours in the visible spectrum

pancreas /ˈpæŋkrɪəs/ *n* a large compound gland in vertebrates that secretes digestive enzymes into the intestines and hormones (e g insulin) into the blood

panda /'pændə/ *n* **1** a long-tailed Himalayan flesh-eating mammal resembling the American racoon and having long chestnut fur spotted with black **2** a large black-and-white plant-eating mammal of western China resembling a bear but related to the racoons

panda car *n, Br* a small car used by police patrols, esp in urban areas

pandemonium /,pændɪ̈'məʊnɪəm/ *n* a wild uproar; a tumult

pander /pændəʳ/ *v* to provide gratification for other's desires – usu + *to*

pane /peɪn/ *n* **1** a framed sheet of glass in a window or door **2** any of the sections into which a sheet of postage stamps is cut for distribution

panegyric /,pænɪ̈'dʒɪrɪk/ *n* a oration or piece of writing in praise of sby

¹panel /'pænl/ *n* **1a** a list of people summoned for jury service **b** a group of people selected to perform some service (e g investigation or arbitration), or to discuss or compete on radio or television programme **2** a separate or distinct part of a surface: e g **a** a thin usu rectangular board set in a frame (e g in a door) **b** a vertical section of fabric **3** a thin flat piece of wood on which a picture is painted **4a** a flat often insulated support (e g for parts of an electrical device) usu with controls on 1 face **b** a usu vertical mount for controls or dials (e g in a car or aircraft)

²panel *v* to furnish or decorate with panels

panellist /'pænəlɪ̈st/ *n* a member of a discussion or advisory panel or of a radio or television panel

pang /pæŋ/ *n* **1** a brief piercing spasm of pain **2** a sharp attack of mental anguish

¹panic /'pænɪk/ *n* **1** a sudden overpowering fright; *esp* a sudden unreasoning terror that spreads rapidly through a group **2** a sudden widespread fright concerning financial affairs and resulting in a depression in values – **~ky** *adj*

²panic *v* to (cause to) be affected with panic

panic-stricken *adj* overcome with panic

pannier, panier /'pænɪəʳ/ *n* **1** a large basket; *esp* either of a pair carried on the back of an animal **2** a hoop petticoat or overskirt that gives extra width to the sides of a skirt at hip level **3** *chiefly Br* either of a pair of bags or boxes fixed on either side of the rear wheel of a bicycle or motorcycle

panoply /'pænəpli/ *n* **1** ceremonial dress **2** a magnificent or impressive array – **-plied** *adj*

panorama /,pænə'rɑːmə/ *n* **1a** a large pictorial representation encircling the spectator **b** a picture exhibited by being unrolled before the spectator **2a** an unobstructed or complete view of a landscape or area **b** a comprehensive presentation or survey of a series of events – **-mic** *adj* – **-mically** *adv*

pansy /'pænzi/ *n* **1** (a flower of) a garden plant derived from wild violets **2** an effeminate male or male homosexual – derog

¹pant /pænt/ *v* **1a** to breathe quickly, spasmodically, or in a laboured manner **b** to make a puffing sound **2** to long eagerly; yearn – **~ingly** *adv*

²pant *n* **1** a panting breath **2** a puffing sound

pantaloon /,pæntə'luːn/ *n* **1** a stock character in the commedia dell'arte who is usu a skinny old man wearing pantaloons **2** *pl* any of several kinds of men's breeches or trousers; *esp* close-fitting trousers fastened under the calf or instep and worn in the 18th and 19th c

pantheism /'pænθi-ɪzəm/ *n* **1** a doctrine that equates God with the forces and laws of nature **2** the indiscriminate worship of all the gods of different religions and cults – **-ist** *n* – **-istic** *adj*

pantheon /'pænθɪən, pæn'θiːən/ *n* **1** a building serving as the burial place of or containing memorials to famous dead **2** the gods of a people; *esp* the officially recognized gods

panther /'pænθəʳ/ *n* **1** a leopard, esp of the black colour phase **2** *NAm* a puma

panties /'pæntiz/ *n pl* pants for women or children; *also* knickers

pantile /'pæntaɪl/ *n* a roofing tile whose transverse section is a flattened S-shape

pantomime /'pæntəmaɪm/ *n* **1a** any of various dramatic or dancing performances in which a story is told by bodily or facial movements **b** a British theatrical and musical entertainment of the Christmas season based on a nursery tale with stock roles and topical jokes **2** mime

pantry /'pæntri/ *n* **1** a room or cupboard used for storing provisions or tableware **2** a room (e g in a hotel or hospital) for preparation of cold foods to order

pants /pænts/ *n pl* **1** *chiefly Br* an undergarment that covers the crotch and hips and that may extend to the waist and partly down each leg **2** *chiefly NAm* trousers

[1]**panzer** /'pænzəʳ/ *adj* of, carried out by, or being a (WW II German) armoured unit

[2]**panzer** *n* a German tank of WW II

pap /pæp/ *n* **1** a soft food for infants or invalids **2** sthg lacking solid value or substance

[1]**papa** /pə'pɑː/ *n, chiefly Br* father – formerly used formally, esp in address

[2]**papa** /'papə/ *n* daddy – used informally and by children

papacy /'peɪpəsi/ *n* the (term of) office of pope

papal /'peɪpəl/ *adj* of a pope or the Roman Catholic church

[1]**paper** /'peɪpəʳ/ *n* **1** a sheet of closely compacted vegetable fibres (e g of wood or cloth) **2a** a piece of paper containing a written or printed statement; a document; *specif* a document carried as proof of identity or status – often pl **b** a piece of paper containing writing or print **c** the question set or answers written in an examination in 1 subject **3** a paper container or wrapper **4** a newspaper **5** wallpaper

[2]**paper** *v* to cover or line with paper; *esp* to apply wallpaper to

[3]**paper** *adj* **1a** made of paper, thin cardboard, or papier-mâché **b** papery **2** of clerical work or written communication **3** existing only in theory; nominal

paperback /'peɪpəbæk/ *n* a book with a flexible paper binding

paperboy /'peɪpəbɔɪ/, *fem* **papergirl** *n* a boy who delivers or sells newspapers

paperweight /'peɪpəweɪt/ *n* a usu small heavy object used to hold down loose papers (e g on a desk)

paperwork /'peɪpəwɜːk/ *n* routine clerical or record-keeping work, often incidental to a more important task

papery /'peɪpəri/ *adj* resembling paper in thinness or consistency

papier-mâché /ˌpæpieɪ 'mæʃeɪ, ˌpeɪpə'mæʃeɪ/ *n* a light strong moulding material made of paper pulped with glue that is used for making boxes, trays, etc

papist /'peɪpəst/ *n, often cap* a Roman Catholic – chiefly derog

papoose /pə'puːs/ *n* a young N American Indian child

paprika /'pæprɪkə/ *n* (a mild to hot red condiment consisting of the finely ground dried pods of) any of various cultivated sweet peppers

papyrus /pə'paɪərəs/ *n, pl* **papyruses, papyri** **1** a tall sedge of the Nile valley **2** the pith of the papyrus plant, esp when made into a material for writing on **3** a usu ancient manuscript written on papyrus

par /pɑːʳ/ *n* **1** the money value assigned to each share of stock in the charter of a company **2** a common level; equality – esp in *on a par with* **3a** an amount taken as an average or norm **b** an accepted standard; *specif* a usual standard of physical condition or health **4** the standard score (of a good player) for each hole of a golf course

parable /'pærəbəl/ *n* a usu short allegorical story illustrating a moral or religious principle

parachute /'pærəʃuːt/ *n* a folding device of light fabric used esp for ensuring a safe descent of a person or object from a great height (e g from a aeroplane) – **-chutist** *n*

[1]**parade** /pə'reɪd/ *n* **1** an ostentatious show **2** the (ceremonial) ordered assembly of a body of troops before a superior officer **3** a public procession **4** *chiefly Br* a row of shops, esp with a service road

[2]**parade** *v* **1** to march in a procession **2** to promenade **3** to show off

paradise /'pærədaɪs/ *n* **1** *often cap* **a**

the garden of Eden **b** Heaven **2** a place of bliss, felicity, or delight

paradox /'pærədɒks/ *n* **1** a tenet contrary to received opinion **2** a statement that is apparently contradictory or absurd and yet might be true **3** sthg (e g a person, condition, or act) with seemingly contradictory qualities or phases – **~ical** *adj* – **~ically** *adv*

paraffin /,pærə'fɪn, 'pærəfɪ̥n/ *n* **1** a usu waxy inflammable mixture of hydrocarbons used chiefly in candles, cosmetics, and in making other chemicals **2** an inflammable liquid hydrocarbon obtained by distillation of petroleum and used esp as a fuel

paragon /'pærəgən/ *n* a model of excellence or perfection

paragraph /'pærəgrɑːf/ *n* a usu indented division of a written composition that develops a single point or idea

parakeet /'pærəkiːt/ *n* any of numerous usu small slender long-tailed parrots

[1]**parallel** /'pærəlel/ *adj* **1a** extending in the same direction, everywhere equidistant, and not meeting **b** everywhere equally distant **2** analogous, comparable

[2]**parallel** *n* **1** a parallel line, curve, or surface **2** sby or sthg equal or similar in all essential particulars; a counterpart, analogue **3** a comparison to show resemblance **4** the arrangement of 2-terminal electrical devices in which one terminal of each device is joined to one conductor and the others are joined to another conductor

[3]**parallel** *v* **1** to compare **2a** to equal, match **b** to correspond to

parallel bars *n pl* (a men's gymnastic event using) a pair of bars supported horizontally 1.7m (5ft 7in) above the floor usu by a common base

parallelogram /,pærə'leləgræm/ *n* a quadrilateral with opposite sides parallel and equal

paralysis /pə'ræləsɪs/ *n* loss of function or the ability to move – **-yse** *v*

[1]**paralytic** /'pærə'lɪtɪk/ *adj* **1** of, resembling, or affected with paralysis **2** *chiefly Br* very drunk – infml

[2]**paralytic** *n* one suffering from paralysis

parameter /pə'ræmɪ̥tə'/ *n* a characteristic, factor

paramilitary /,pærə'mɪlɪ̥tri/ *adj* formed on a military pattern (as a potential auxiliary military force)

paramount /'pærəmaʊnt/ *adj* superior to all others; supreme – **~cy** *n*

paramour /'pærəmʊə', -mɔː'/ *n* an illicit lover; *esp* a mistress

paranoia /,pærə'nɔɪə/ *n* **1** a mental disorder characterized by delusions of persecution or grandeur **2** a tendency towards excessive or irrational suspiciousness and distrustfulness of others

parapet /'pærəpɪ̥t, -pet/ *n* **1** a wall, rampart, or elevation of earth or stone to protect soldiers **2** a low wall or balustrade to protect the edge of a platform, roof, or bridge

paraphernalia /,pærəfə'neɪlɪə/ *n* **1** personal belongings **2a** articles of equipment **b** accessory items

[1]**paraphrase** /'pærəfreɪz/ *n* a restatement of a text, passage, or work giving the meaning in another form

[2]**paraphrase** *v* to make a paraphrase (of)

paraplegia /,pærə'pliːdʒə/ *n* paralysis of the lower half of the body including the legs – **-gic** *adj, n* – **-gically** *adv*

parasite /'pærəsaɪt/ *n* **1** an organism living in or on another organism to its own benefit **2** sthg or sby depending on sthg or sby else for existence or support without making a useful or adequate return – **-sitic, -sitical** *adj* – **-sitically** *adv* – **-sitism** *n*

parasol /'pærəsɒl/ *n* a lightweight umbrella used, esp by women, as a protection from the sun

paratroops /'pærətruːps/ *n pl* troops trained and equipped to parachute from an aeroplane – **-trooper** *n*

parboil /'pɑːbɔɪl/ *v* to boil briefly as a preliminary or incomplete cooking procedure

[1]**parcel** /'pɑːsəl/ *n* a wrapped bundle; a package

[2]**parcel** *v* **1** to divide into parts; distribute – often + *out* **2** to make up into a parcel; wrap – often + *up*

parch /pɑːtʃ/ *v* to make or become dry or scorched

parchment /ˈpɑːtʃmənt/ *n* **1** the skin of an animal, esp of a sheep or goat, prepared for writing on **2** a parchment manuscript

[1]**pardon** /ˈpɑːdn/ *n* **1** a release from legal penalties **2** excuse or forgiveness for a fault, offence, or discourtesy

[2]**pardon** *v* **1** to absolve from the consequences of a fault or crime **2** to allow (an offence) to pass without punishment

pare /peəʳ/ *v* **1** to cut or shave off (an outer surface) **2** to diminish gradually (as if) by paring – **parer** *n*

[1]**parent** /ˈpeərənt/ *n* **1** sby who begets or brings forth offspring; a father or mother **2a** an animal or plant regarded in relation to its offspring **b** the material or source from which sthg is derived – **~al** *adj*

[2]**parent** *v* to be or act as the parent of

parentage /ˈpeərəntɪdʒ/ *n* descent from parents or ancestors; lineage

parenthesis /pəˈrenθɪ̣sɪ̣s/ *n, pl* **parentheses** **1** an amplifying or explanatory word or phrase inserted in a passage from which, in writing, it is usu set off by punctuation **2** an interlude, interval

parent-teacher association *n sing or pl in constr* an organization of teachers at a school and the parents of their pupils, that works for the improvement of the school

par excellence /ˌpɑːr ˈeksəlɒns/ *adj* being the best example of a kind; without equal – used after the noun qualified

pariah /pəˈraɪə/ *n* **1** a member of a low caste of S India and Burma **2** an outcast

parish /ˈpærɪʃ/ *n* **1** the subdivision of a diocese served by a single church or clergyman **2** a unit of local government in rural England

parishioner /pəˈrɪʃənəʳ/ *n* a member or inhabitant of a parish

parity /ˈpærəti/ *n* the quality or state of being equal or equivalent

[1]**park** /pɑːk/ *n* **1** an area of land for recreation in or near a city or town **2** an area maintained in its natural state as a public property **3** an assigned space for military animals, vehicles, or materials

[2]**park** *v* **1** to leave or place (a vehicle) for a time, esp at the roadside or in a car park or garage **2** to set and leave temporarily

parka /ˈpɑːkə/ *n* **1** a hooded fur garment for wearing in the arctic **2** an anorak

parkin /ˈpɑːkɪ̣n/ *n* a thick heavy ginger cake made with oatmeal and treacle

parking meter *n* a coin-operated device which registers the payment and shows the time allowed for parking a motor vehicle

Parkinson's disease /ˈpɑːkɪ̣nsənz dɪˌziːz/ *n* tremor, weakness of resting muscles, and a peculiar gait occurring in later life as a progressive nervous disease

Parkinson's Law *n* an observation in office organization: work expands so as to fill the time available for its completion

parky /ˈpɑːki/ *adj, Br* chilly – infml

parlance /ˈpɑːləns/ *n* manner of speech and esp choice of words

[1]**parley** /ˈpɑːli/ *v* to speak with another; confer; *specif* to discuss terms with an enemy

[2]**parley** *n* a conference for discussion of points in dispute; *specif* a conference under truce to discuss terms with an enemy

parliament /ˈpɑːləmənt/ *n* **1** a formal conference for the discussion of public affairs **2** *often cap* the supreme legislative body of the UK that consists of the House of Commons and the House of Lords; *also* a similar body in another nation or state – **~ary** *adj*

parliamentarian /ˌpɑːləmənˈteərɪən/ *n* **1** *often cap* an adherent of the parliament during the Civil War **2** an expert in parliamentary rules and practice

[1]**parlour** /ˈpɑːləʳ/ *n* **1a** a room in a private house for the entertainment of guests **b** a room in an inn, hotel, or club for conversation or semiprivate uses **2** any of various business places **3** a place for milking cows

[2]**parlour** *adj* fostered or advocated in comfortable seclusion without consequent action or application to affairs

parlour game *n* an indoor word game, board game, etc

parlous /ˈpɑːləs/ *adj* full of uncertainty and danger – fml or humor

Parmesan /ˌpɑːmɪ̣ˈzæn/ *n* a very hard dry strongly flavoured cheese that is often used grated

parochial /pəˈrəʊkɪəl/ *adj* **1** of a (church) parish **2** limited in range or scope (e g to a narrow area or region); provincial, narrow – **~ly** *adv* – **~ism** *n*

[1]**parody** /ˈpærədi/ *n* **1** a literary or musical work in which the style of an author is imitated for comic or satirical effect **2** a feeble or ridiculous imitation

[2]**parody** *v* to compose a parody on – **-dist** *n*

[1]**parole** /pəˈrəʊl/ *n* **1** a pledge of one's honour; *esp* the promise of a prisoner of war to fulfil stated conditions in consideration of release or the granting of privileges **2** a password given only to officers of the guard and of the day **3** a conditional release of a prisoner

[2]**parole** *v* to put on parole

paroxysm /ˈpærəksɪzəm/ *n* **1** a fit, attack, or sudden increase or recurrence of (disease) symptoms; a convulsion **2** a sudden violent emotion or action

parquet /ˈpɑːkeɪ, pɑːki/ *n* a floor made of wooden blocks

parr /pɑːr/ *n* a young salmon actively feeding in fresh water

parricide /ˈpærɪ̣saɪd/ *n* (the act of) sby who murders his/her father, mother, or a close relative

[1]**parrot** /ˈpærət/ *n* **1** any of numerous chiefly tropical birds that have a distinctive stout hooked bill, are often crested and brightly coloured, and are excellent mimics **2** a person who parrots another's words

[2]**parrot** *v* to repeat or imitate (e g another's words) without understanding or thought

parry /ˈpæri/ *v* **1** to ward off a weapon or blow **2** to evade, esp by an adroit answer – **parry** *n*

parse /pɑːs/ *v* to resolve (e g a sentence) into component parts of speech and describe them grammatically

parsec /ˈpɑːsek/ *n* a unit of distance for use in astronomy equal to about 3¼ light-years

Parsi, Parsee /pɑːˈsiː/ *n* an Indian member of an ancient Persian religious group

parsimonious /ˌpɑːsɪ̣ˈməʊnɪəs/ *adj* frugal to the point of stinginess; niggardly – **~ly** *adv* – **~ness** *n*

parsimony /ˈpɑːsɪ̣məni/ *n* thrift; *also* stinginess

parsley /ˈpɑːsli/ *n* an orig S European plant of the carrot family widely cultivated for its leaves used as a herb or garnish in cooking

parsnip /ˈpɑːsnɪp/ *n* (the long edible tapering root of) a European plant of the carrot family with large leaves and yellow flowers

parson /ˈpɑːsən/ *n* **1** the incumbent of a parish **2** a clergyman

parsonage /ˈpɑːsənɪdʒ/ *n* the house provided by a church for its parson

parson's nose *n* the fatty extension of the rump of a cooked fowl

[1]**part** /pɑːt/ *n* **1a** any of the often indefinite or unequal subdivisions into which sthg is (regarded as) divided and which together constitute the whole **b** an amount equal to another amount **c** an organ, member, or other constituent element of a plant or animal body **d** a division of a literary work **e** a vocal or instrumental line or melody in music or harmony **f** a constituent member of an apparatus (e g a machine); *also* a spare part **2** sthg falling to one in a division or apportionment; a share **3** any of the opposing sides in a conflict or dispute **4** a function or course of action performed **5a** an actor's lines in a play **b** a role

[2]**part** *v* **1** to separate from or take leave of sby **2** to become separated, detached, or broken **3** to separate (the hair) by combing on each side of a line

[3]**part** *adv* partly

[4]**part** *adj* partial

partake /pɑːˈteɪk/ *v* to take a part or share; participate – usu + *in* or *of*; fml

parthenogenesis /ˌpɑːθənəʊˈdʒenɪ̣sɪ̣s/ *n* reproduction by development of an unfertilized gamete that occurs esp among lower plants and invertebrate animals

partial /ˈpɑːʃəl/ *adj* **1** inclined to favour one party more than the other; biased **2** markedly fond of sby or sthg – + *to* **3** of a part rather than the whole; not general or total – **~ly** *adv*

partiality /ˌpɑːʃiˈælәti/ *n* **1** a bias **2** a special taste or liking

participate /pɑːˈtɪsәpeɪt/ *v* **1** to take part **2** to have a part or share in sthg – **-pant** *n* – **-pation** *n*

participle /ˈpɑːtәsɪpəl/ *n* a verbal form (e g *singing* or *sung*) that has the function of an adjective and at the same time can be used in compound verb forms

particle /ˈpɑːtɪkəl/ *n* **1** a minute subdivision of matter (e g an electron, atom or molecule) **2** a minute quantity or fragment **3** a minor unit of speech including all uninflected words or all words except nouns and verbs; *esp* a function word

[1]**particular** /pəˈtɪkjʊləʳ/ *adj* **1** of or being a single person or thing; specific **2** detailed, exact **3** worthy of notice; special, unusual **4a** concerned over or attentive to details; meticulous **b** hard to please; exacting – **~ity** *n* – **~ly** *adv*

[2]**particular** *n* an individual fact, point, circumstance, or detail

particular·ize, -ise /pəˈtɪkjʊləraɪz/ *v* to go into details; specify

[1]**parting** /ˈpɑːtɪŋ/ *n* **1** a place or point where a division or separation occurs **2** the line where the hair is parted

[2]**parting** *adj* given, taken, or performed at parting

partisan /ˌpɑːtәˈzæn/ *n* **1** an over-zealous adherent to a party, faction, or cause **2** a guerrilla

partita /pɑːˈtiːtə/ *n* a musical suite

[1]**partition** /pɑːˈtɪʃən/ *n* **1** division into parts **2** sthg that divides; *esp* a light interior dividing wall

[2]**partition** *v* **1** to divide into parts or shares **2** to divide or separate *off* by a partition

partly /ˈpɑːtli/ *adv* in some measure or degree; partially

[1]**partner** /ˈpɑːtnəʳ/ *n* **1a** either of a couple who dance together **b** sby who plays with 1 or more others in a game against an opposing side **c** a person with whom one is having a sexual relationship; a spouse, lover, etc **2** any of the principal members of a joint business – **~ship** *n*

[2]**partner** *v* to act as a partner to

part of speech *n* a class of words distinguished according to the kind of idea denoted and the function performed in a sentence

partridge /ˈpɑːtrɪdʒ/ *n* any of various typically medium-sized stout-bodied Old World game birds

part-time *adj* involving or working less than customary or standard hours

parturition /ˌpɑːtjʊˈrɪʃən/ *n* the action or process of giving birth to offspring

party /ˈpɑːti/ *n* **1a** a person or group taking 1 side of a question, dispute, or contest **b** *sing or pl constr* a group of people organized to carry out an activity or fulfil a function together **2** *sing or pl in constr* a group organized for political involvement **3** one who is involved; a participant – usu + *to* **4** a (festive) social gathering

party line *n* **1** a single telephone line connecting 2 or more subscribers with an exchange **2** the official principles of a political party

paschal /ˈpæskəl/ *adj* **1** of the Passover **2** of or appropriate to Easter

pasha /ˈpæʃə/ *n* a man of high rank or office (e g in Turkey or N Africa)

[1]**pass** /pɑːs/ *v* **1** to move, proceed **2a** to go away – often + *off* **b** to die – often + *on* or *away*; euph **3a** to go by; move past; *also* surpass **b** *of time* to elapse **c** to overtake another vehicle **4a** to go across, over, or through **b** to emit or discharge from a bodily part, esp the bowels or bladder **c** to go uncensured or unchallenged **5** to go from one quality, state, or form to another **6a** to pronounce a judgment **b** to utter – esp in *pass a comment, pass a remark* **7** to go from the control or possession of one person or group to that of another **8** to take place as a mutual exchange or transaction **9a** to become approved by a body (e g a legislature) **b** to undergo an inspection, test, or examination successfully **10a** to be accepted or regarded as adequate or fitting **b** to resemble or act the part of so well as to be accepted – usu + *for* **11** to kick, throw, or hit

a ball or puck to a teammate **12** to decline to bid, bet, or play in a card game

[2]**pass** *n* a narrow passage over low ground in a mountain range

[3]**pass** *n* **1** a usu distressing or bad state of affairs – often in *come to a pretty pass* **2a** a written leave of absence from a military post or station for a brief period **b** a permit or ticket allowing free transport or free admission **3** the passing of an examination **4a** an act of passing in cards, soccer, rugby, etc; *also* a ball or puck passed **b** a ball hit to the side and out of reach of an opponent, esp in tennis **5** a sexually inviting gesture or approach – usu in *make a pass at*

passable /ˈpɑːsəbəl/ *adj* **1** capable of being passed, crossed, or travelled on **2** barely good enough; tolerable

passage /ˈpæsɪdʒ/ *n* **1** the action or process of passing from one place or condition to another **2a** a way of exit or entrance; a road, path, channel, or course by which sthg passes **b passage, passageway** a corridor or lobby giving access to the different rooms or parts of a building or apartment **3a** a specified act of travelling or passing, esp by sea or air **b** the passing of a legislative measure **4** a right, liberty, or permission to pass **5a** a brief noteworthy portion of a written work or speech **b** a phrase or short section of a musical composition

pass away *v* **1** to go out of existence **2** to die – euph

passé /ˈpɑːseɪ, ˈpæseɪ/ *adj* **1** outmoded **2** behind the times

passenger /ˈpæsɪ̣ndʒəʳ, -sən-/ *n* **1** sby who travels in, but does not operate, a public or private conveyance **2** *chiefly Br* a member of a group who contributes little or nothing to the functioning or productivity of the group

passerby /ˌpɑːsəˈbaɪ/ *n* a person who happens by chance to pass by a particular place

passing /ˈpɑːsɪŋ/ *adj* **1** going by or past **2** having a brief duration **3** superficial

passion /ˈpæʃən/ *n* **1** *often cap* **a** the sufferings of Christ between the night of the Last Supper and his death **b** a musical setting of a gospel account of the Passion story **2a** intense, driving, or uncontrollable feeling **b** an outbreak of anger **3** ardent affection; *also* strong sexual desire **b** (the object of) a strong liking, devotion, or interest – **~less** *adj* – **~lessly** *adv*

passionate /ˈpæʃənɪ̣t/ *adj* **1** easily aroused to anger **2a** capable of, affected by, or expressing intense feeling, esp love, hatred, or anger **b** extremely enthusiastic; keen – **~ly** *adv*

passionflower /ˈpæʃənˌflaʊəʳ/ *n* any of a genus of chiefly tropical plants with usu showy flowers and pulpy often edible berries

passion play *n, often cap 1st P* a dramatic representation of the passion and crucifixion of Christ

passive /ˈpæsɪv/ *adj* **1a** acted on, receptive to, or influenced by external forces or impressions **b** *of a verb form or voice* expressing an action that is done to the grammatical subject of a sentence (e g *was hit* in 'the ball was hit') **c** *of a person* lacking in energy, will, or initiative; meekly accepting **2a** not active or operative; inert **b** of or characterized by chemical inactivity **3** offering no resistance; submissive – **~ly** *adv*

passive resistance *n* resistance characterized by nonviolent noncooperation

pass off *v* **1** to present with intent to deceive **2** to give a false identity or character to **3** to take place and be completed

pass out *v* **1** to lose consciousness **2** *chiefly Br* to finish a period of (military) training

Passover /ˈpɑːsəʊvəʳ/ *n* the Jewish celebration of the liberation of the Hebrews from slavery in Egypt

pass over *v* **1** to ignore in passing **2** to pay no attention to the claims of; disregard

passport /ˈpɑːspɔːt/ *n* **1** an official document issued by a government as proof of identity and nationality to one of its citizens for use when leaving or reentering the country **2a** a permission or authorization to go somewhere **b** sthg that secures admission or acceptance

pass up *v* to decline, reject

password /'pɑːswɜːd/ *n* **1** a word or phrase that must be spoken by a person before being allowed to pass a guard **2** a watchword

[1]**past** /pɑːst/ *adj* **1a** just gone or elapsed **b** having gone by; earlier **2** finished, ended **3** of or constituting the past tense expressing elapsed time **4** preceding, former

[2]**past** *prep* **1a** beyond the age of or for **b** subsequent to in time (e g half *past* 2) **2a** at the farther side of; beyond **b** up to and then beyond (e g drove *past* the house) **3** beyond the capacity, range, or sphere of

[3]**past** *n* **1a** time gone by **b** sthg that happened or was done in the past **2** a past life, history, or course of action; *esp* one that is kept secret

[4]**past** *adv* so as to pass by the speaker (e g children ran *past*)

pasta /'pæstə/ *n* any of several (egg or oil enriched) flour and water doughs that are usu shaped and used fresh or dried (e g as spaghetti)

[1]**paste** /peɪst/ *n* **1a** a fat-enriched dough used esp for pastry **b** a usu sweet doughy confection **c** a smooth preparation of meat, fish, etc used as a spread **2a** a preparation of flour or starch and water used as an adhesive **b** clay or a clay mixture used in making pottery or porcelain **3** a brilliant glass used in making imitation gems

[2]**paste** *v* **1** to stick with paste **2** to cover with sthg pasted on

[1]**pasteboard** /'peɪstbɔːd/ *n* board made by pasting together sheets of paper

[2]**pasteboard** *adj* **1** made of pasteboard **2** sham, insubstantial

[1]**pastel** /'pæstl/ *n* **1** (a crayon made of) a paste of powdered pigment mixed with gum **2** a drawing in pastel

[2]**pastel** *adj* pale and light in colour

pastern /'pæstɜːn/ *n* a part of a horse's foot extending from the fetlock to the hoof

pasteur·ize, -ise /'pɑːstʃəraɪz/ *v* to sterilize a liquid by heating for a short period

pastiche /pæ'stiːʃ/ *n* **1** a literary, artistic, or musical work that imitates the style of a previous work **2** a musical, literary, or artistic composition made up of elements borrowed from various sources

pastille *also* **pastil** /pæ'stiːl/ *n* **1** a small cone of aromatic paste, burned to fumigate or scent a room **2** an aromatic or medicated lozenge

pastime /'pɑːstaɪm/ *n* sthg (e g a hobby, game, etc) that amuses and serves to make time pass agreeably

past master *n* one who is expert or experienced (in a particular activity)

pastor /'pɑːstə^r/ *n* one having responsibility for the spiritual welfare of a group (e g a congregation)

pastoral /'pɑːstərəl/ *adj* **1a(1)** (composed) of shepherds or herdsmen **(2)** used for or based on livestock rearing **b** of the countryside; not urban **c** portraying rural life, esp in an idealized and conventionalized manner; *also* idyllic **2** of or providing spiritual care or guidance, esp of a church congregation

pastorale /ˌpæstə'rɑːli, -'rɑːl/ *n* an instrumental composition or opera with a pastoral theme

past participle *n* a participle with past, perfect, or passive meaning

past perfect *adj* of or being a verb tense (e g *had finished*) that expresses completion of an action at or before a past time

pastry /'peɪstri/ *n* **1** a dough containing fat esp when baked (e g for piecrust) **2** (an article of) usu sweet food made with pastry

pasturage /'pɑːstʃərɪdʒ/ *n* pasture

pasture /'pɑːstʃə^r/ *n* **1** plants (e g grass) grown for feeding (grazing) animals **2** (a plot of) land used for grazing **3** the feeding of livestock; grazing – **pasture** *v*

[1]**pasty** /'pæsti/ *n* a small filled usu savoury pie or pastry case baked without a container

[2]**pasty** /'peɪsti/ *adj* resembling paste; *esp* pallid and unhealthy in appearance

[1]**pat** /pæt/ *n* **1** a light tap, esp with the hand or a flat instrument **2** a small mass of sthg (e g butter) shaped (as if) by patting

[2]**pat** *v* **1** to strike lightly with the open hand or some other flat surface **2** to flatten, smooth, or put into place or shape with light blows **3** to tap or

stroke gently with the hand to soothe, caress, or show approval

[3]**pat** *adv* in a pat manner; aptly, promptly

[4]**pat** *adj* **1** prompt, immediate **2** suspiciously appropriate; contrived **3** learned, mastered, or memorized exactly

[1]**patch** /pætʃ/ *n* **1** a piece of material used to mend or cover a hole or reinforce a weak spot **2** a tiny piece of black silk worn on the face, esp by women in the 17th and 18th c, to set off the complexion **3a** a small piece; a scrap **b** a small piece of land usu used for growing vegetables **4** *chiefly Br* a usu specified period **5** *chiefly Br* an area for which a particular individual or unit (e g of police) has responsibility

[2]**patch** *v* **1** to mend or cover (a hole) with a patch **2** to mend or put together, esp in a hasty or shabby fashion – usu + *up*

patchouli, patchouly /pəˈtʃuːli, ˈpætʃʊli/ *n* **1** an E Indian shrubby plant of the mint family that yields a fragrant essential oil **2** a heavy perfume made from patchouli

patch pocket *n* a flat pocket attached to the outside of a garment

patch up *v* to bring (a quarrel, dispute, etc) to an end

patchwork /ˈpætʃwɜːk/ *n* **1** sthg composed of miscellaneous or incongruous parts **2** work consisting of pieces of cloth of various colours and shapes sewn together

patchy /ˈpætʃi/ *adj* **1** uneven in quality; incomplete **2** *of certain types of weather* appearing in patches – **-chily** *adv* – **-chiness** *n*

pate /peɪt/ *n* (the crown of) the head

pâté /ˈpæteɪ/ *n* a rich savoury paste of seasoned and spiced meat, fish, etc

patella /pəˈtelə/ *n, pl* **patellae** the kneecap

[1]**patent** /ˈpeɪtnt, ˈpæ-/ *adj* **1a** secured by or made under a patent **b** proprietary **2** made of patent leather **3** readily visible or intelligible; not hidden or obscure

[2]**patent** *n* **1** (a formal document securing to an inventor) the exclusive right to make or sell an invention **2** a patented invention **3** a privilege, licence

[3]**patent** *v* to obtain a patent for (an invention)

patent leather /ˌpeɪtnt ˈleðəʳ/ *n* a leather with a hard smooth glossy surface

pater /ˈpeɪtəʳ/ *n, chiefly Br* a father – now usu humor

paternal /pəˈtɜːnl/ *adj* **1** fatherly **2** received or inherited from one's male parent **3** related through one's father – **~ly** *adv*

paternalism /pəˈtɜːnəl-ɪzəm/ *n* a system under which a government or organization deals with its subjects or employees in an authoritarian but benevolent way – **-ist** *n* – **-istic** *adj* – **-istically** *adv*

paternity /pəˈtɜːnəti/ *n* **1** being a father **2** origin or descent from a father

path /pɑːθ/ *n* **1** a track formed by the frequent passage of people or animals **2** a course, route **3** a way of life, conduct, or thought – **~less** *adj*

pathetic /pəˈθetɪk/ *adj* **1** pitiful **2** marked by sorrow or melancholy; sad – **-ically** *adv*

pathfinder /ˈpɑːθˌfaɪndəʳ/ *n* **1** sby or sthg that explores unexplored regions to mark out a new route **2** sby who discovers new ways of doing things

pathology /pəˈθɒlədʒi/ *n* **1** the study of (the structure and functional changes produced by) diseases **2** the anatomical and physiological abnormalities that constitute or characterize (a particular) disease – **-gist** *n* – **-gical** *adj* – **-gically** *adv*

pathos /ˈpeɪθɒs/ *n* **1** a quality in experience or in artistic representation evoking pity or compassion **2** an emotion of sympathetic pity

patience /ˈpeɪʃəns/ *n* **1** the capacity, habit, or fact of being patient **2** *chiefly Br* any of various card games that can be played by 1 person and usu involve the arranging of cards into a prescribed pattern

[1]**patient** /ˈpeɪʃənt/ *adj* **1** bearing pains or trials calmly or without complaint **2** not hasty or impetuous **3** steadfast despite opposition, difficulty, or adversity – **~ly** *adv*

[2]**patient** *n* an individual awaiting or under medical care

patina /ˈpætɨ̠nə/ *n* **1** a usu green film formed on copper and bronze by weathering **2** a surface appearance of sthg (e g polished wood) that has grown more beautiful esp with age or use

patio /ˈpætiəʊ/ *n* a usu paved area adjoining a dwelling

patisserie /pəˈtɪsəri/ *n* **1** sweet cakes and pastry **2** an establishment where patisserie is made and sold

patois /ˈpætwɑː/ *n, pl* **patois** a provincial dialect other than the standard or literary dialect

patrial /ˈpeɪtrɪəl, ˈpæt-/ *n* sby who has a legal right to reside in the UK because one of his/her parents or grandparents was born there

patriarch /ˈpeɪtriɑːk/ *n* **1a** any of the biblical fathers of the human race or of the Hebrew people **b** a man who is father or founder (e g of a race, science, religion, or class of people) **c** a venerable old man **2** the head or bishop of any of various Eastern churches – **~al** *adj*

patriarchy /ˈpeɪtriɑːki/ *n* social organization marked by the supremacy of the father in the clan or family and the reckoning of descent and inheritance in the male line

patrician /pəˈtrɪʃən/ *n* **1** a member of any of the original citizen families of ancient Rome **2** sby of high birth; an aristocrat – **patrician** *adj*

patricide /ˈpætrɨ̠saɪd/ *n* (the act of) sby who kills his/her father

patrilineal /ˌpætrɪˈlɪnɪəl/ *adj* relating to or tracing descent through the paternal line

patriot /ˈpætrɪət, -triɒt, ˈpeɪ-/ *n* one who loves and zealously supports his/her country – **~ism** *n* – **~ic** *adj* – **~ically** *adv*

[1]**patrol** /pəˈtrəʊl/ *n* **1a** traversing a district or beat or going the rounds of a garrison or camp for observation or the maintenance of security **b** *sing or pl in constr* a detachment of men employed for reconnaissance, security, or combat **2** *sing or pl in constr* a subdivision of a scout troop or guide company that has 6 to 8 members

[2]**patrol** *v* to carry out a patrol (of)

patron /ˈpeɪtrən/, *fem* **patroness** *n* **1** a wealthy or influential supporter of an artist or writer **2** sby who uses his/her wealth or influence to help an individual, institution, or cause **3** a customer **4** the proprietor of an establishment (e g an inn), esp in France

patronage /ˈpætrənɪdʒ/ *n* **1** the support or influence of a patron **2** the granting of favours in a condescending way **3** business or activity provided by patrons **4** the power to appoint to government jobs

patron·ize, -ise /ˈpætrənaɪz/ *v* **1** to be or act as a patron of **2** to adopt an air of condescension towards

patron saint *n* a saint regarded as having a particular person, group, church, etc under his/her special care and protection

[1]**patter** /ˈpætəʳ/ *n* **1** the sales talk of a street hawker **2** empty chattering talk **3** the talk with which an entertainer accompanies his/her routine

[2]**patter** *v* **1** to strike or tap rapidly and repeatedly **2** to run with quick light-sounding steps

[1]**pattern** /ˈpætn/ *n* **1** a form or model proposed for imitation; an example **2** a design, model, or set of instructions for making things **3** a specimen, sample **4** a usu repeated decorative design (e g on fabric) **5** a (natural or chance) configuration

[2]**pattern** *v* **1** to make or model according to a pattern **2** to decorate with a design

paunch /pɔːntʃ/ *n* **1** the belly **2** a potbelly – **~y** *adj* – **~iness** *n*

pauper /ˈpɔːpəʳ/ *n* a very poor person

[1]**pause** /pɔːz/ *n* **1** a temporary stop **2** temporary inaction, esp as caused by uncertainty; hesitation

[2]**pause** *v* **1** to stop temporarily **2** to linger for a time

pave /peɪv/ *v* **1** to lay or cover with material (e g stone or concrete) to form a firm level surface for walking or travelling on **2** to serve as a covering or pavement of

pavement /ˈpeɪvmənt/ *n* a paved surface for pedestrians at the side of a road

pavilion /pəˈvɪljən/ *n* **1** a large often

sumptuous tent **2** a light sometimes ornamental structure in a garden, park, etc **3** *chiefly Br* a permanent building on a sports ground, specif a cricket ground, containing changing rooms and often also seats for spectators

[1]**paw** /pɔː/ *n* **1** the (clawed) foot of a lion, dog, or other (quadruped) animal **2** a human hand – infml; chiefly humor

[2]**paw** *v* **1** to feel or touch clumsily, rudely, or indecently **2** to touch or strike at with a paw **3** to scrape or strike (as if) with a hoof

pawky /ˈpɔːki/ *adj, chiefly Br* artfully shrewd, esp in a humorous way; canny – **-kily** *adv* – **-kiness** *n*

[1]**pawn** /pɔːn/ *n* **1** sthg delivered to or deposited with another as a pledge or security (e g for a loan) **2** the state of being pledged – usu + *in*

[2]**pawn** *v* to deposit in pledge or as security

[3]**pawn** *n* **1** any of the 8 chessmen of each colour of least value that have the power to move only forwards usu 1 square at a time **2** sby or sthg that can be used to further the purposes of another

pawnbroker /ˈpɔːnˌbrəʊkəʳ/ *n* one who lends money on the security of personal property pledged in his/her keeping

pawnshop /ˈpɔːnʃɒp/ *n* a pawnbroker's shop

pawpaw /ˈpɔːpɔː/ *n* an edible yellow tropical fruit

[1]**pay** /peɪ/ *v* **paid** **1** to make due return to for services done or property received **2a** to give in return for goods or service **b** to discharge indebtedness for **3** to give or forfeit in reparation or retribution **4** to requite according to what is deserved **5** to give, offer, or make willingly or as fitting **6** to be profitable to; be worth the expense or effort to **7** to slacken (e g a rope) and allow to run out – usu + *out* – **~er** *n*

[2]**pay** *n* **1** the status of being paid by an employer; employ **2** sthg paid as a salary or wage

[3]**pay** *adj* **1** equipped with a coin slot for receiving a fee for use **2** requiring payment

payable /ˈpeɪəbəl/ *adj* that may, can, or must be paid

payday /ˈpeɪdeɪ/ *n* a regular day on which wages are paid

payload /ˈpeɪləʊd/ *n* **1** the revenue-producing load that a vehicle of transport can carry **2** the explosive charge carried in the warhead of a missile **3** the load (e g instruments) carried in a spacecraft relating directly to the purpose of the flight as opposed to the load (e g fuel) necessary for operation

paymaster /ˈpeɪmɑːstəʳ/ *n* an officer or agent whose duty it is to pay salaries or wages

paymaster general *n, often cap P&G* a British government minister who is often made a member of the cabinet and entrusted with special functions

payment /ˈpeɪmənt/ *n* **1** the act of paying **2** sthg that is paid **3** a recompense (e g a reward or punishment)

payoff /ˈpeɪɒf/ *n* **1** a profit or reward, esp received by a player in a game **2** a decisive fact or factor resolving a situation or bringing about a definitive conclusion **3** the climax of an incident or chain of events; the denouement – infml

pay off *v* **1** to pay in full and discharge (an employee) **2** to pay (a debt or a creditor) in full **3** to yield returns

pay-out *n* (the act of making) a usu large payment of money – infml

pay-packet *n, Br* (an envelope containing) sby's wages

payroll /ˈpeɪrəʊl/ *n* **1** a list of those entitled to be paid and of the amounts due to each **2** the sum necessary to pay those on a payroll

pay up *v* to pay in full

pea /piː/ *n* **1** (a leguminous climbing plant that bears) an edible rounded protein-rich green seed **2** any of various leguminous plants related to or resembling the pea – usu with a qualifying term

peace /piːs/ *n* **1** a state of tranquillity or quiet **2** freedom from disquieting or oppressive thoughts or emotions **3** harmony in personal relations **4a** mutual concord between countries **b** an agreement to end hostilities

peaceable /ˈpiːsəbəl/ *adj* **1a** disposed to peace; not inclined to dispute or quarrel **b** quietly behaved **2** free from strife or disorder – **-bly** *adv*

peaceful /ˈpiːsfəl/ *adj* **1** peaceable **2** untroubled by conflict, agitation, or commotion; quiet, tranquil **3** of a state or time of peace – **~ly** *adv* – **~ness** *n*

peacetime /ˈpiːstaɪm/ *n* a time when a nation is not at war

[1]**peach** /piːtʃ/ *n* **1** (a low spreading tree that bears) an edible fruit with a large stone, thin downy skin, and sweet white or yellow flesh **2** a light yellowish pink colour **3** a particularly excellent person or thing; *specif* an unusually attractive girl or young woman – infml

[2]**peach** *v* to turn informer *on*

peacock /ˈpiːkɒk/ *n* a bird the male of which has very large tail feathers that are usu tipped with eyelike spots and can be erected and spread in a fan shimmering with iridescent colour

peacock blue *n* lustrous greenish blue

[1]**peak** /piːk/ *v* to grow thin or sickly

[2]**peak** *n* **1** a projecting part on the front of a cap or hood **2** a sharp or pointed end **3** (the top of) a hill or mountain ending in a point **4** the upper aftermost corner of a 4-cornered fore-and-aft sail **5** the highest level or greatest degree, esp as represented on a graph

[3]**peak** *v* to reach a maximum

[4]**peak** *adj* at or reaching the maximum of capacity, value, or activity

[1]**peaked** /piːkt/ *adj* having a peak; pointed

[2]**peaked** *adj* peaky

peaky /ˈpiːki/ *adj* looking pale and wan; sickly

peal /piːl/ *n* **1a** a complete set of changes on a given number of bells **b** a set of bells tuned to the notes of the major scale for change ringing **2** a loud prolonged sound – **peal** *v*

peanut /ˈpiːnʌt/ *n* **1** (the pod or oily edible seed of) a low-branching widely cultivated leguminous plant with showy yellow flowers and pods containing 1 to 3 seeds that ripen in the earth **2** *pl* a trifling amount – infml

pear /peəʳ/ *n* (a tree that bears) a large fleshy edible fruit wider at the end furthest from the stalk

[1]**pearl** /pɜːl/ *n* **1** a dense usu milky white lustrous mass of mother-of-pearl layers, formed as an abnormal growth in the shell of some molluscs, esp oysters, and used as a gem **2** sby or sthg very rare or precious

[2]**pearl** *adj* **1a** of or resembling pearl **b** made of or adorned with pearls **2** having medium-sized grains

[1]**pearly** /ˈpɜːli/ *adj* resembling, containing, or decorated with pearls or mother-of-pearl

[2]**pearly** *n, Br* **1** a button made of mother-of-pearl **2** a member of certain cockney families who are traditionally costermongers and entitled to wear a special costume covered with pearlies

peasant /ˈpezənt/ *n* **1** a small landowner or farm labourer **2** a usu uneducated person of low social status

peashooter /ˈpiːʃuːtəʳ/ *n* a toy blowpipe for shooting peas

pea-souper *n* a heavy fog

peat /piːt/ *n* partially carbonized vegetable tissue found in large bogs and used esp as a fuel for domestic heating and as a fertilizer – **~y** *adj*

pebble /ˈpebəl/ *n* a small usu rounded stone, often worn smooth by the action of water

pebbledash /ˈpebəldæʃ/ *n* a finish for exterior walls consisting of small pebbles embedded in a stucco base

pecan /pɪˈkæn/ *n* (the smooth oblong thin-shelled edible nut of) a large hickory tree with roughish bark and hard but brittle wood

peccadillo /ˌpekəˈdɪləʊ/ *n, pl* **peccadilloes, peccadillos** a slight or trifling offence

[1]**peck** /pek/ *n* a unit of volume or capacity equal to 2gall (about 9.1l)

[2]**peck** *v* **1** to strike or pierce (repeatedly) with the beak or a pointed tool **b** to kiss perfunctorily **2** to eat reluctantly and in small bites

[3]**peck** *v, of a horse* to stumble on landing from a jump

pecker /ˈpekəʳ/ *n* **1** *chiefly Br* courage – in *keep one's pecker up*; infml **2** *NAm* a penis – vulg

pecking order *n* the natural hierarchy within a flock of birds, esp poultry, in which each bird pecks another lower in the scale without fear of retaliation

peckish /'pekɪʃ/ *adj, chiefly Br* agreeably hungry – infml

pectin /'pektɪn/ *n* any of various water-soluble substances that yield a gel which acts as a setting agent in jams and fruit jellies

pectoral /'pektərəl/ *adj* of, situated in or on, or worn on the chest

peculate /'pekjʊleɪt/ *v* to embezzle – **-lation** *n*

peculiar /pɪ'kjuːlɪə^r/ *adj* **1** belonging exclusively to 1 person or group **2** distinctive **3** different from the usual or normal; strange, curious

peculiarity /pɪˌkjuːli'ærɪ̣ti/ *n* a distinguishing characteristic

pecuniary /pɪ'kjuːnɪəri/ *adj* of or measured in money – fml – **-rily** *adv*

pedagogue /'pedəgɒg/ *n* a teacher, schoolmaster – now chiefly derog

pedagogy /'pedəgɒdʒi/ *n* the science of teaching – **-gic** *adj* – **-gical** *adj* – **-gically** *adv*

[1]**pedal** /'pedl/ *n* **1** a lever pressed by the foot in playing a musical instrument **2** a foot lever or treadle by which a part is activated in a mechanism

[2]**pedal** *adj* of the foot

[3]**pedal** *v* **1** to use or work a pedal or pedals **2** to ride a bicycle

pedant /'pednt/ *n* one who is unimaginative or unnecessarily concerned with detail, esp in academic matters – **~ic** *adj* – **~ically** *adv*

peddle /'pedl/ *v* **1** to sell goods as a pedlar **2** to deal out or seek to disseminate (e g ideas or opinions)

pedestal /'pedɪ̣stl/ *n* **1** a base supporting a column, statue, etc **2** a position of esteem or idealized respect

[1]**pedestrian** /pɪ̣'destrɪən/ *adj* **1** commonplace, unimaginative **2a** going or performed on foot **b** of or designed for walking

[2]**pedestrian** *n* sby going on foot; a walker

pedicure /'pedɪkjʊə^r/ *n* (a) treatment for the care of the feet and toenails – **-curist** *n*

pedigree /'pedɪ̣griː/ *n* **1** a register recording a line of ancestors **2a** an esp distinguished ancestral line; a lineage **b** the origin and history of sthg **3** the recorded purity of breed of an individual or strain – **pedigree** *adj*

pedlar /'pedlə^r/ *n* **1** one who travels about offering small wares for sale **2** one who deals in or promotes sthg intangible

[1]**pee** /piː/ *v* to urinate – euph – infml

[2]**pee** *n* **1** an act of urinating **2** urine *USE* infml

peek /piːk/ *v* **1** to look furtively – often + *in* or *out* **2** to take a brief look; glance – **peek** *n*

[1]**peel** /piːl/ *v* **1** to strip off an outer layer **2a** to come off in sheets or scales **b** to lose an outer layer (e g of skin) **3** to take off one's clothes – usu + *off*; infml

[2]**peel** *n* the skin or rind of a fruit

[3]**peel** *also* **pele** *n* a small fortified tower built in the 16th c along the Scottish-English border

[4]**peel** *n* a usu long-handled (baker's) shovel for getting bread, pies, etc into or out of an oven

peeler /'piːlə^r/ *n, archaic Br* a policeman

peel off *v* **1** to veer away from an aircraft formation, esp when diving or landing **2** to break away from a group or formation (e g of marchers or ships in a convoy)

[1]**peep** /piːp/ *v* **1** to utter a feeble shrill sound characteristic of a newly hatched bird; cheep **2** to utter a slight sound

[2]**peep** *n* **1** a cheep **2** a slight sound, esp spoken – infml

[3]**peep** *v* **1** to look cautiously or slyly, esp through an aperture **2** to begin to emerge (as if) from concealment; show slightly

[4]**peep** *n* **1** the first faint appearance **2** a brief or furtive look; a glance

peephole /'piːphəʊl/ *n* a hole or crevice to peep through

[1]**peer** /pɪə^r/ *n* **1** sby who is of equal standing with another **2** a duke, marquess, earl, viscount, or baron of the British peerage

[2]**peer** *adj* belonging to the same age, grade, or status group

[3]**peer** *v* to look narrowly or curiously; *esp* to look searchingly at sthg difficult to discern

peerage /ˈpɪərɪdʒ/ *n* **1** *sing or pl in constr* the body of peers **2** the rank or dignity of a peer

peeress /ˈpɪərɨ̣s/ *n* **1** the wife or widow of a peer **2** a woman having in her own right the rank of a peer

peerless /ˈpɪəlɨ̣s/ *adj* matchless, incomparable

peevish /ˈpiːvɪʃ/ *adj* querulous in temperament or mood; fretful – **~ly** *adv* – **~ness** *n*

peewit, pewit /ˈpiːˌwɪt/ *n* a lapwing

[1]**peg** /peg/ *n* **1** a small usu cylindrical pointed or tapered piece of wood, metal, or plastic used to pin down or fasten things or to fit into or close holes; a pin **2a** a projecting piece used to hold or support **b** sthg (e g a fact or opinion) used as a support, pretext, or reason **3a** any of the wooden pins set in the head of a stringed instrument and turned to regulate the pitch of the strings **b** a step or degree, esp in estimation – esp in *take sby down a peg (or two)*

[2]**peg** *v* **1** to put a peg into **2** to pin down; restrict **3** to fix or hold (e g prices) at a predetermined level **4** *Br* to fasten (e g washing) to a clothesline with a clothes peg – often + *out*

peg away *v* to work hard and steadily – often + *at*

peg out *v* **1** to mark by pegs **2** *chiefly Br* to die – infml

pejorative /pɨ̣ˈdʒɒrətɪv/ *adj* rude or belittling, disparaging **~ly** *adv*

pekinese, pekingese /ˌpiːkɨ̣ˈniːz/ *n* (any of) a breed of small short-legged dogs with a broad flat face and a long coat

pekoe /ˈpiːkəʊ/ *n* a black tea of superior quality

pelf /pelf/ *n* money, riches

pelican /ˈpelɪkən/ *n* any of a genus of large web-footed birds with a very large bill containing a pouch in which fish are kept

pelican crossing *n* a crossing in the UK at which the movement of vehicles and pedestrians is controlled by pedestrian-operated traffic lights

pellet /ˈpelɨ̣t/ *n* **1** a usu small rounded or spherical body (e g of food or medicine) **2** a piece of small shot

pell-mell /ˌpel ˈmel/ *adv* **1** in confusion or disorder **2** in confused haste – **pell-mell** *adj*

pellucid /pɨ̣ˈluːsɨ̣d/ *adj* **1** transparent **2** easy to understand *USE* fml or poetic – **~ly** *adv*

pelmet /ˈpelmɨ̣t/ *n, chiefly Br* a length of board or fabric placed above a window to conceal curtain fixtures

[1]**pelt** /pelt/ *n* **1** a usu undressed skin with its hair, wool, or fur **2** a skin stripped of hair or wool before tanning

[2]**pelt** *v* **1** *of rain* to fall heavily and continuously **2** to move rapidly and vigorously; hurry **3** to hurl, throw **4** to strike with a succession of blows or missiles

pelvis /ˈpelvɨ̣s/ *n, pl* **pelvises, pelves** (the cavity of) a basin-shaped structure in the skeleton of many vertebrates that is formed by the pelvic girdle and adjoining bones of the spine – **pelvic** *adj*

pemmican, pemican /ˈpemɪkən/ *n* a concentrated food of lean dried meat traditionally made by N American Indians

[1]**pen** /pen/ *n* **1** a small enclosure for animals **2** a small place of confinement or storage

[2]**pen** *v* to shut in a pen

[3]**pen** *n* **1** an implement for writing or drawing with fluid (e g ink) **2a** a writing instrument as a means of expression **b** a writer – fml

[4]**pen** *v* to write – fml

[5]**pen** *n* a female swan

penal /ˈpiːnl/ *adj* **1** of punishment **2** liable to punishment – **penally** *adv*

penal·ize, -ise /ˈpiːnəlaɪz/ *v* **1** to inflict a penalty on **2** to put at a serious disadvantage

penalty /ˈpenlti/ *n* **1** a punishment legally imposed or incurred **2** a forfeiture to which a person agrees to be subject if conditions are not fulfilled **3a** disadvantage, loss, or suffering due to some action **b** a disadvantage imposed for violation of the rules of a sport

penalty area *n* a rectangular area 44yd (about 40m) wide and 18yd (about 16m) deep in front of each goal on a soccer pitch

penance /ˈpenəns/ *n* an act of self-abasement or devotion performed to show repentance for sin

pence /pens/ *pl of* **penny**

penchant /ˈpɒnʃɒn, ˈpentʃənt/ *n* a strong leaning; a liking

[1]**pencil** /ˈpensəl/ *n* **1** an implement for writing, drawing, or marking consisting of or containing a slender cylinder or strip of a solid marking substance (e g graphite) **2** a set of light rays, esp when diverging from or converging to a point **3** sthg long and thin like a pencil

[2]**pencil** *v* to draw, write, or mark with a pencil

pendant, pendent /ˈpendənt/ *n* a hanging ornament; *esp* one worn round the neck

pendent, pendant /ˈpendənt/ *adj* **1** suspended **2** jutting or leaning over; overhanging **3** remaining undetermined; pending

[1]**pending** /ˈpendɪŋ/ *prep* until – fml

[2]**pending** *adj* **1** not yet decided or dealt with **2** imminent, impending

pendulous /ˈpendjʊləs/ *adj* suspended, inclined, or hanging downwards – **~ly** *adv*

pendulum /ˈpendjʊləm/ *n* a body suspended from a fixed point so as to swing freely periodically under the action of gravity and commonly used to regulate movements (e g of clockwork)

penetrate /ˈpenɪ̥treɪt/ *v* **1a** to pass into or through **b** to enter, esp by overcoming resistance; pierce **2** to see into or through; discern **3** to be absorbed by the mind; be understood – **-tration** *n* – **-trable, -trative** *adj* – **-trability** *n*

penetrating /ˈpenɪ̥treɪtɪŋ/ *adj* **1** having the power of entering, piercing, or pervading **2** acute, discerning – **~ly** *adv*

pen-friend *n* a person, esp one in another country, with whom a friendship is made through correspondence

penguin /ˈpeŋgwɪ̥n/ *n* any of various erect short-legged flightless aquatic birds of the southern hemisphere

penicillin /ˌpenɪ̥ˈsɪlɪ̥n/ *n* any of several antibiotics or antibacterial drugs orig obtained from moulds

peninsula /pɪ̥ˈnɪnsjʊlə/ *n* a piece of land jutting out into or almost surrounded by water; *esp* one connected to the mainland by an isthmus – **~r** *adj*

penis /ˈpiːnɪ̥s/ *n, pl* **penes, penises** the male sexual organ by means of which semen is introduced into the female during coitus

penitent /ˈpenɪ̥tənt/ *adj* feeling or expressing sorrow for sins or offences – **penitent** *n* – **~ly** *adv* – **-tence** *n*

penitential /ˌpenɪ̥ˈtenʃəl/ *adj* of penitence or penance – **~ly** *adv*

penitentiary /ˌpenɪ̥ˈtenʃəri/ *n* a prison in the USA

penknife /ˈpen-naɪf/ *n* a small pocketknife

pen name *n* an author's pseudonym

pennant /ˈpenənt/ *n* a flag that tapers to a point or has a swallowtail

penniless /ˈpenɪlɪ̥s/ *adj* lacking money; poor

pennon /ˈpenən/ *n* a long usu triangular or swallow-tailed streamer typically attached to the head of a lance as a knight's personal flag

penny /ˈpeni/ *n, pl* **pennies, pence 1a** (a usu bronze coin representing) (1) a former British money unit worth £1/240 (2) a British money unit in use since 1971 that is worth £1/100 **b** a unit of currency of the Irish Republic, Gibraltar and the Falkland Islands **2** *NAm* a cent

penny-farthing *n, Br* an early type of bicycle having 1 small and 1 large wheel

penology /piːˈnɒlədʒi/ *n* criminology dealing with prison management and the treatment of offenders

pen pusher *n* one whose work involves usu boring or repetitive writing at a desk

[1]**pension** /ˈpenʃən/ *n* a fixed sum paid regularly to a person (e g following retirement or as compensation for a wage-earner's death) – **~able** *adj*

[2]**pension** /ˈpɒnsiɒn/ *n* (bed and board provided by) a hotel or boarding-house, esp in continental Europe

pensioner /ˈpenʃənəʳ/ *n* one who receives or lives on an esp old-age pension

pension off *v* **1** to dismiss or retire from service with a pension **2** to set aside or dispense with after long use – infml

pensive /ˈpensɪv/ *adj* sadly or dreamily thoughtful – **~ly** *adv* – **~ness** *n*

pentagon /ˈpentəgən/ *n* a polygon of 5 angles and 5 sides – **~al** *adj*

Pentagon *n sing or pl in constr the* US military establishment

pentagram /ˈpentəgræm/ *n* a 5-pointed star used as a magical symbol

pentathlon /penˈtæθlən/ *n* **1** a (women's) contest in which all contestants compete in the 100m hurdles, shot put, high jump, long jump, and 200m sprint **2 pentathlon, modern pentathlon** a contest in which all contestants compete in 300m free style swimming, 4000m cross-country running, 5000m equestrian steeplechaser, fencing and target shooting

Pentecost /ˈpentɪkɒst/ *n* (a Christian festival on the 7th Sunday after Easter commemorating the descent of the Holy Spirit on the apostles at) the Jewish festival of Shabuoth

penthouse /ˈpenthaʊs/ *n* **1** a structure (e g a shed or roof) attached to and sloping from a wall or building **2** a structure or dwelling built on the roof of a (tall) building

pent-up *adj* confined, held in check

penultimate /penˈʌltɪ̵mɪ̵t/ *adj* next to the last

penumbra /pɪ̵ˈnʌmbrə/ *n, pl* **penumbrae, penumbras 1** a region of partial darkness (e g in an eclipse) in a shadow surrounding the umbra **2** a less dark region surrounding the dark centre of a sunspot

penury /ˈpenjʊri/ *n* severe poverty – fml – **-rious** *adj*

peony, paeony /ˈpiːəni/ *n* any of various garden plants with large usu double red, pink, or white flowers

[1]**people** /ˈpiːpəl/ *n* **1** human beings in general **2** a group of persons considered collectively **3** the members of a family or kinship **4** the mass of a community **5** a body of persons that are united by a common culture and that often constitute a politically organized group

[2]**people** *v* **1** to supply or fill with people **2** to dwell in; inhabit

pep /pep/ *v or n* **-pp-** (to liven up or instil with) brisk energy or initiative and high spirits

[1]**pepper** /ˈpepəʳ/ *n* **1a** any of a genus of tropical mostly climbing shrubs with aromatic leaves; *esp* one with red berries from which black pepper and white pepper are prepared **b** a condiment made from ground dried pepper berries **2** any of various products similar to pepper; *esp* a pungent condiment obtained from capsicums – used with a qualifying term **3** (the usu red or green fruit of) a capsicum whose fruits are hot peppers or sweet peppers

[2]**pepper** *v* **1a** to sprinkle, season, or cover (as if) with pepper **b** to shower with shot or other missiles **2** to sprinkle

pepper-and-salt *adj, of a fabric or garment* having black and white or dark and light colour intermingled in small flecks

peppercorn /ˈpepəkɔːn/ *n* a dried berry of the pepper plant

peppermint /ˈpepəˌmɪnt/ *n* **1** (an aromatic essential oil obtained from) a mint with dark green tapering leaves and whorls of small pink flowers **2** a sweet flavoured with peppermint oil

peppery /ˈpepəri/ *adj* **1** hot, pungent **2** hot-tempered, touchy **3** fiery, stinging

pep pill *n* a tablet of a stimulant drug

pep talk *n* a usu brief, high-pressure, and emotional talk designed esp to encourage

peptic /ˈpeptɪk/ *adj* connected with or resulting from the action of digestive juices

per /pəʳ; *strong* pɜːʳ/ *prep* **1** by the means or agency of; through **2** with respect to every; for each **3** according to (e g *per* list price)

peradventure /ˌperədˈventʃəʳ/ *adv, archaic* perhaps, possibly

perambulate /pəˈræmbjʊleɪt/ *v* to stroll (through) ***USE*** fml – **-lation** *n*

perambulator /pəˈræmbjʊleɪtəʳ/ *n* a pram

per annum /pər ˈænəm/ *adv* in or for each year

per capita /pə 'kæpɟtə/ *adv or adj* per unit of population; by or for each person

perceive /pə'siːv/ *v* **1** to understand, realize **2** to become aware of through the senses; *esp* to see, observe – **-ceivable** *adj*

[1]**per cent** /pə 'sent/ *adv* in or for each 100

[2]**per cent** *n, pl* **per cent** **1** one part in a 100 **2** a percentage

[3]**per cent** *adj* reckoned on the basis of a whole divided into 100 parts

percentage /pə'sentɪdʒ/ *n* **1** a proportion (expressed as per cent of a whole) **2** a share of winnings or profits **3** an advantage, profit – infml

perceptible /pə'septəbəl/ *adj* capable of being perceived, esp by the senses – **-bly** *adv* – **-bility** *n*

perception /pə'sepʃən/ *n* **1a** a result of perceiving; an observation **b** a mental image; a concept **2** the mental interpretation of physical sensations produced by stimuli from the external world **3** intuitive discernment; insight, understanding

perceptive /pə'septɪv/ *adj* **1** capable of or exhibiting (keen) perception; observant, discerning **2** characterized by sympathetic understanding or insight – **~ly** *adv* – **~ness** *n* – **-tivity** *n*

[1]**perch** /pɜːtʃ/ *n* **1** a roost for a bird **2** *chiefly Br* a unit of length equal to 5½ yds; a rod **3a** a resting place or vantage point; a seat **b** a prominent position *USE* (*3*) infml

[2]**perch** *v* to alight, settle, or rest, esp briefly or precariously

[3]**perch** *n* a small European freshwater spiny-finned fish

perchance /pə'tʃɑːns/ *adv* perhaps, possibly – usu poetic or humor

percipient /pə'sɪpɪənt/ *adj* perceptive, discerning – fml – **-ence** *n*

percolate /'pɜːkəleɪt/ *v* **1a** to ooze or filter through a substance; seep **b** to prepare coffee in a percolator **2** to become diffused – **-lation** *n*

percolator /'pɜːkəleɪtə^r/ *n* a coffee pot in which boiling water rising through a tube is repeatedly deflected downwards through a perforated basket containing ground coffee beans

percussion /pə'kʌʃən/ *n* **1a** the beating or striking of a musical instrument **b** the tapping of the surface of a body part (e g the chest) to learn the condition of the parts beneath (e g the lungs) by the resultant sound **3** *sing or pl in constr* percussion instruments that form a section of a band or orchestra – **-sive** *adj*

percussionist /pə'kʌʃənɟst/ *n* one who plays percussion instruments

perdition /pə'dɪʃən/ *n* eternal damnation; Hell

peregrination /ˌperəgrɟ'neɪʃən/ *n* a long and wandering journey, esp in a foreign country – humor

peremptory /pə'remptəri/ *adj* **1** admitting no contradiction or refusal **2** expressive of urgency or command **3** (having an attitude or nature) characterized by imperious or arrogant self-assurance – **-rily** *adv*

perennial /pə'renɪəl/ *adj* **1** present at all seasons of the year **2** *of a plant* living for several years, usu with new herbaceous growth each year **3** lasting for a long time or forever; constant – **~ly** *adv*

[1]**perfect** /'pɜːfɪkt/ *adj* **1a** entirely without fault or defect; flawless **b** corresponding to an ideal standard or abstract concept **2a** accurate, exact **b** lacking in no essential detail; complete **c** absolute, utter **3** of or constituting a verb tense or form that expresses an action or state completed at the time of speaking or at a time spoken of

[2]**perfect** /pə'fekt/ *v* **1** to make perfect; improve, refine **2** to bring to final form – **~ible** *adj* – **~ibility** *n*

perfection /pə'fekʃən/ *n* **1a** making or being perfect **b** freedom from (moral) fault or defect **c** full development; maturity **2** (an example of) unsurpassable accuracy or excellence

perfectly /'pɜːfɪktli/ *adv* to an adequate extent; quite

perfidy /'pɜːfɟdi/ *n* being faithless or disloyal; treachery – **-dious** *adj* – **-diously** *adv*

perforate /'pɜːfəreɪt/ *v* to make a hole through; *specif* to make a line of holes in or between (e g rows of postage stamps in a sheet) to make separation easier

perforce /pə'fɔːs/ *adv* by force of circumstances – fml

perform /pə'fɔːm/ *v* **1** to do; carry out **2a** to do in a formal manner or according to prescribed ritual **b** to give a rendering of; present – **~er** *n*

performance /pə'fɔːməns/ *n* **1a** the execution of an action **b** sthg accomplished; a deed, feat **2** the fulfilment of a claim, promise, etc **3** a presentation to an audience of a (character in a) play, a piece of music, etc **4** the ability to perform or work (efficiently or well) **5a** a lengthy or troublesome process or activity **b** a display of bad behaviour

[1]**perfume** /'pɜːfjuːm/ *n* **1** a sweet or pleasant smell; a fragrance **2** a pleasant-smelling (liquid) preparation (e g of floral essences)

[2]**perfume** /pə'fjuːm/ *v* to fill or imbue with a sweet smell

perfunctory /pə'fʌŋktəri/ *adj* mechanical, cursory – **-rily** *adv* – **-riness** *n*

pergola /'pɜːgələ/ *n* (an arbour made by training plants over) a support for climbing plants

perhaps /pə'hæps/ *adv* possibly but not certainly; maybe

perihelion /ˌperḷ'hiːlɪən/ *n, pl* **perihelia** the point in the path of a planet, comet, etc that is nearest to the sun

peril /'perḷl/ *n* **1** exposure to the risk of being injured, destroyed, or lost; danger **2** sthg that imperils; a risk

perimeter /pə'rɪmḷtəʳ/ *n* **1** (the length of) the boundary of a closed plane figure **2** a line, strip, fence, etc bounding or protecting an area **3** the outer edge or limits of sthg

[1]**period** /'pɪərɪəd/ *n* **1a** the full pause at the end of a sentence; *also, chiefly NAm* a full stop **b** a stop, end **2a** a portion of time **b** the (interval of) time that elapses before a cyclic motion or phenomenon begins to repeat itself; the reciprocal of the frequency **c** (a single cyclic occurrence of) menstruation **3** a chronological division; a stage (of history) **4** any of the divisions of the school day

[2]**period** *adj* of, representing, or typical of a particular historical period

periodic /ˌpɪəri'ɒdɪk/ *adj* **1** recurring at regular intervals **2** consisting of or containing a series of repeated stages – **~ally** *adv*

[1]**periodical** /ˌpɪəri'ɒdɪkəl/ *adj* **1** periodic **2** *of a magazine or journal* published at fixed intervals (e g weekly or quarterly)

[2]**periodical** *n* a periodical publication

periodic table *n* an arrangement of chemical elements in the order of their atomic numbers, that shows a periodic variation in their properties

period piece *n* a piece (e g of fiction, art, furniture, or music) whose special value lies in its evocation of a historical period

[1]**peripatetic** /ˌperḷpə'tetɪk/ *n* sby, esp a teacher unattached to a particular school, or sthg that travels about from place to place (on business)

[2]**peripatetic** *adj* itinerant

peripheral /pə'rɪfərəl/ *adj* **1** of, involving, or forming a periphery; *also* of minor significance **2** located away from a centre or central portion; external **3** of, using, or being the outer part of the field of vision

periphery /pə'rɪfəri/ *n* the perimeter of a closed curve (e g a circle or polygon)

periphrasis /pə'rɪfrəsəs/ *n, pl* **periphrases** (a) circumlocution

periscope /'perḷskəʊp/ *n* a tubular optical instrument containing lenses, mirrors, or prisms for seeing objects not in the direct line of sight

perish /'perɪʃ/ *v* **1a** to be destroyed or ruined **b** to die, esp in a terrible or sudden way – poetic or journ **2** *chiefly Br* to deteriorate, spoil

perishable /'perɪʃəbəl/ *n or adj* (sthg, esp food) liable to spoil or decay

perisher /'perɪʃəʳ/ *n, Br* an annoying or troublesome person or thing – infml

perishing /'perɪʃɪŋ/ *adj* **1** freezingly cold **2** damnable, confounded

peritonitis /ˌperḷtə'naɪtḷs/ *n* inflammation of the inside wall of the abdomen

perjure /'pɜːdʒəʳ/ *v* to make (oneself) guilty of perjury – **~r** *n*

perjury /'pɜːdʒəri/ *n* the voluntary violation of an oath, esp by a witness

perk up *v* to (cause to) recover one's vigour or cheerfulness, esp after a period of weakness or depression

perky /'pɜːki/ *adj* **1** briskly

self-assured; cocky **2** jaunty **– -kily** *adv* **– -kiness** *n*

[1]**perm** /pɜːm/ *n* a long-lasting wave set in the hair by chemicals

[2]**perm** *v* to give a perm to

[3]**perm** *v, Br* to permute; *specif* to pick out and combine (a specified number of teams in a football pool) in all the possible permutations

permafrost /'pɜːməfrɒst/ *n* a layer of permanently frozen ground in frigid regions

permanent /'pɜːmənənt/ *adj* **1** continuing or enduring without fundamental or marked change; lasting, stable **2** not subject to replacement according to political circumstances **– ~ly** *adv* **– -ence, -ency** *n*

permeate /'pɜːmieɪt/ *v* to diffuse through or penetrate sthg **– -ation, -ability** *n*

permissible /pə'mɪsəbəl/ *adj* allowable **– -bly** *adv*

permission /pə'mɪʃən/ *n* formal consent; authorization

permissive /pə'mɪsɪv/ *adj* **1** tolerant; *esp* accepting a relaxed social or sexual morality **2** allowing (but not enforcing) **– ~ly** *adv* **– ~ness** *n*

[1]**permit** /pə'mɪt/ *v* **1** to consent to, usu expressly or formally **2** to give leave; authorize **3** to make possible

[2]**permit** /'pɜːmɪt/ *n* a written warrant allowing the holder to do or keep sthg

permutation /ˌpɜːmjʊ'teɪʃən/ *n* **1** a variation or change (e g in character or condition) brought about by rearrangement of existing elements **2** (the changing from one to another of) any of the various possible ordered arrangements of a set of objects, numbers, letters, etc

permute /pə'mjuːt/ *v* to change the order or arrangement of; *esp* to arrange successively in all possible ways

pernicious /pə'nɪʃəs/ *adj* highly injurious or destructive; deadly **– ~ly** *adv* **– ~ness** *n*

pernickety /pə'nɪkɮti/ *adj* **1** fussy about small details; fastidious **2** requiring precision and care

peroration /ˌperə'reɪʃən/ *n* **1** the concluding part of a discourse, in which the main points are summed up **2** a highly rhetorical speech

peroxide /pə'rɒksaɪd/ *v* to bleach (hair) with the chemical compound hydrogen peroxide

[1]**perpendicular** /ˌpɜːpən'dɪkjʊləʳ/ *adj* **1** being or standing at right angles to the plane of the horizon or a given line or plane **2** *cap* of, being, or built in a late Gothic style of architecture prevalent in England from the 15th to the 16th c characterized by large windows, fan vaults, and an emphasis on vertical lines **– ~ly** *adv*

[2]**perpendicular** *n* a line, plane, or surface at right angles to the plane of the horizon or to another line or surface

perpetrate /'pɜːpɮtreɪt/ *v* to be guilty of performing or doing; commit **– -tration** *n* **– -trator** *n*

perpetual /pə'petʃʊəl/ *adj* **1a** everlasting **b** holding sthg (e g an office) for life or for an unlimited time **2** occurring continually; constant **3** *of a plant* blooming continuously throughout the season **– ~ly** *adv*

perpetuate /pə'petʃʊeɪt/ *v* to make perpetual; cause to last indefinitely **– -ation** *n*

perpetuity /ˌpɜːpɮ'tjuːɮti/ *n* (the quality or state of) sthg that is perpetual; eternity

perplex /pə'pleks/ *v* **1** to puzzle, confuse **2** to complicate

perplexity /pə'pleksɮti/ *n* (sthg that causes) the state of being perplexed or bewildered

perquisite /'pɜːkwɮzɪt/ *n* **1** sthg held or claimed as an exclusive right or possession **2** a perk – fml

perry /'peri/ *n* an alcoholic drink made from fermented pear juice

per se /ˌpɜː 'seɪ/ *adv* by, of, or in itself; intrinsically

persecute /'pɜːsɪkjuːt/ *v* **1** to cause to suffer because of race, religion, political beliefs, etc **2** to pester **– -cution** *n* **– -cutor** *n*

persevere /ˌpɜːsɮ'vɪəʳ/ *v* to persist in a state, enterprise, or undertaking in spite of adverse influences, opposition, or discouragement **– -verance** *n*

Persian /'pɜːʃən, -ʒən/ *n or adj* (a native, inhabitant, or language) of ancient Persia or modern Iran

persimmon /pə'sɪmən/ *n* (the globular orange fruit of) any of a genus of American and Asian trees with hard fine wood

persist /pəˈsɪst/ *v* **1** to go on resolutely or stubbornly in spite of opposition or warning **2** to be insistent in the repetition or pressing of an utterance (e g a question or opinion) **3** to continue to exist, esp past a usual, expected, or normal time

persistent /pəˈsɪstənt/ *adj* **1** continuing to exist in spite of interference or treatment **2** remaining **a** beyond the usual period **b** without change in function or structure – **~ly** *adv* – **-tence** *n*

person /ˈpɜːsən/ *n* **1** a human being (considered as being different from all others) **2** any of the 3 modes of being in the Trinity as understood by Christians **3** a living human body or its outward appearance

personable /ˈpɜːsənəbəl/ *adj* pleasing in person; attractive – **-bly** *adv*

personage /ˈpɜːsənɪdʒ/ *n* **1** a person of rank, note, or distinction **2** a dramatic, fictional, or historical character

personal /ˈpɜːsənəl/ *adj* **1** of or affecting a person; private **2a** done in person without the intervention of another **b** carried on between individuals directly **3** of the person or body **4** of or referring to (the character, conduct, motives, or private affairs of) an individual, often in an offensive manner

personality /ˌpɜːsəˈnælʒti/ *n* **1** the totality of an individual's behavioural and emotional tendencies; *broadly* a distinguishing complex of individual or group characteristics **2a** (sby having) distinction or excellence of personal and social traits **b** a person of importance, prominence, renown, or notoriety

personally /ˈpɜːsənəli/ *adv* **1** in person **2** as a person; in personality **3** for oneself; as far as oneself is concerned **4** as directed against oneself in a personal way

personal pronoun *n* a pronoun (e g *I, you,* or *they*) that expresses a distinction of person

persona non grata /pəˌsəunə nɒn ˈgrɑːtə/ *adj* personally unacceptable or unwelcome

personification /pəˌsɒnʒfʒˈkeɪʃən/ *n* **1** the personifying of an abstract quality or thing **2** an embodiment, incarnation

personify /pəˈsɒnʒfaɪ/ *v* **1** to conceive of or represent as having human qualities or form **2** to be the embodiment of in human form

personnel /ˌpɜːsəˈnel/ *n* **1** *sing or pl in constr* a body of people employed (e g in a factory, office, or organization) or engaged on a project **2** a division of an organization concerned with the employees and their welfare at work

[1]**perspective** /pəˈspektɪv/ *adj* of, using, or seen in perspective

[2]**perspective** *n* **1a** the visual appearance of solid objects with respect to their relative distance and position **b** a technique for representing this, esp by showing parallel lines as converging **2** the aspect of an object of thought from a particular standpoint

Perspex /ˈpɜːspeks/ *trademark* – used for a transparent plastic

perspicacious /ˌpɜːspɪˈkeɪʃəs/ *adj* of acute mental vision or discernment – fml – **~ly** *adv* – **-city** *n*

perspiration /ˌpɜːspəˈreɪʃən/ *n* **1** sweating **2** sweat

perspire /pəˈspaɪəʳ/ *v* to sweat

persuade /pəˈsweɪd/ *v* **1** to move by argument, reasoning, or entreaty to a belief, position, or course of action **2** to get (sthg) with difficulty *out of* or *from*

persuasion /pəˈsweɪʒən/ *n* **1a** persuading or being persuaded **b** persuasiveness **2a** an opinion held with complete assurance **b** (a group adhering to) a particular system of religious beliefs

persuasive /pəˈsweɪsɪv/ *adj* tending or able to persuade – **~ly** *adv* – **~ness** *n*

pert /pɜːt/ *adj* **1** impudent and forward; saucy **2** trim and chic; jaunty – **~ly** *adv* – **~ness** *n*

pertain /pəˈteɪn/ *v* to belong *to;* be about, or appropriate *to*

pertinacious /ˌpɜːtʒˈneɪʃəs/ *adj* clinging resolutely or stubbornly to an opinion, purpose, or design – fml – ~**ly** *adv* – **-city** *n*

pertinent /'pɜːtɪ̣nənt/ *adj* clearly relevant (to the matter in hand) – ~**ly** *adv* – **-nence** *n*

perturb /pə'tɜːb/ *v* **1** to disturb greatly in mind; disquiet **2** to throw into confusion; disorder – ~**ation** *n*

peruse /pə'ruːz/ *v* **1** to study – fml **2** to look over the contents of (e g a book) – **perusal** *n*

pervade /pə'veɪd/ *v* to become diffused throughout every part of

perverse /pə'vɜːs/ *adj* **1a** obstinate in opposing what is right, reasonable, or accepted; wrongheaded **b** arising from or indicative of stubbornness or obstinacy **2** unreasonably opposed to the wishes of others; uncooperative, contrary – ~**ly** *adv* – ~**ness** *n* – **-sity** *n*

perversion /pə'vɜːʃən, -ʒən/ *n* **1** perverting or being perverted **2** abnormal sexual behaviour

[1]**pervert** /pə'vɜːt/ *v* **1** to cause to turn aside or away from what is good, true, or morally right; corrupt **2a** to divert to a wrong end or purpose; misuse **b** to twist the meaning or sense of; misinterpret

[2]**pervert** /'pɜːvɜːt/ *n* a person given to some form of sexual perversion

peseta /pə'seɪtə/ *n* the basic unit of currency of Spain

pessary /'pesəri/ *n* **1** a vaginal suppository **2** a device worn in the vagina to support the uterus or prevent conception

pessimism /'pesɪ̣mɪzəm/ *n* a tendency to stress the adverse aspects of a situation or event or to expect the worst possible outcome – **-mist** *n* – **-mistic** *adj* – **-mistically** *adv*

pest /pest/ *n* **1** a plant or animal capable of causing damage or carrying disease **2** sby or sthg that pesters or annoys; a nuisance

pester /'pestəʳ/ *v* to harass with petty irritations; annoy

pesticide /'pestɪ̣saɪd/ *n* a chemical used to destroy insects and other pests of crops, domestic animals, etc

pestilence /'pestɪ̣ləns/ *n* a virulent and devastating epidemic disease

pestilent /'pestɪ̣lənt/ *adj* **1** destructive of life; deadly **2** morally harmful; pernicious

pestle /'pesəl, 'pestl/ *n* **1** a usu club-shaped implement for pounding substances in a mortar **2** any of various devices for pounding, stamping, or pressing

[1]**pet** /pet/ *n* **1** a domesticated animal kept for companionship rather than work or food **2** sby who is treated with unusual kindness or consideration; a favourite **3** *chiefly Br* darling – used chiefly by women as an affectionate form of address

[2]**pet** *adj* **1a** kept or treated as a pet **b** for pet animals **2** expressing fondness or endearment **3** favourite

[3]**pet** *v* **1** to treat with unusual kindness and consideration; pamper **2** to engage in amorous embracing, caressing, etc

[4]**pet** *n* a fit of peevishness, sulkiness, or anger

petal /'petl/ *n* any of the modified often brightly coloured leaves making up the flower head of a plant

petard /pɪ̣'tɑːd/ *n* a case containing an explosive for military demolitions

petiole /'piːtiəʊl/ *n* the usu slender stalk by which a leaf is attached to a stem

petit bourgeois /,pətiː 'bʊəʒwɑː, ,peti-/ *n, pl* **petits bourgeois** a member of the lower middle class

petite /pə'tiːt/ *adj, esp of a woman* having a small trim figure

[1]**petition** /pɪ̣'tɪʃən/ *n* **1** an earnest request; an entreaty **2** (a document embodying) a formal written request to a superior – ~**er** *n*

[2]**petition** *v* to make an esp formal written request (to or for)

petrel /'petrəl/ *n* any of the smaller long-winged seabirds (e g a storm petrel) that fly far from land

petrify /'petrɪ̣faɪ/ *v* **1** to convert (as if) into stone or a stony substance **2** to confound with fear, amazement, or awe; paralyse – **-faction** *n*

petrochemical /,petrə'kemɪkəl/ *n* a chemical obtained from petroleum or natural gas

petrol /'petrəl/ *n, chiefly Br* a volatile inflammable liquid used as a fuel for internal-combustion engines

petroleum /pɪ̣'trəʊlɪəm/ *n* an oily

inflammable usu dark liquid widely occurring in the upper strata of the earth that is refined to produce petrol and other products

petroleum jelly *n* a semisolid obtained from petroleum and used esp as the basis of ointments

petrology /pɮ'trɒlədʒi/ *n* a science that deals with the origin, structure, composition, etc of rocks – **-gist** *n*

[1]**petticoat** /'petikəʊt/ *n* a skirt designed to be worn as an undergarment

[2]**petticoat** *adj* of or exercised by women; female – chiefly humor or derog

petty /'peti/ *adj* **1** having secondary rank or importance; *also* trivial **2** small-minded – **-tily** *adv* – **-tiness** *n*

petty cash *n* cash kept on hand for payment of minor items

petty officer *n* a non-commissioned naval officer

petulant /'petʃʊlənt/ *adj* ill humoured; peevish – **~ly** *adv* – **-lance** *n*

petunia /pɮ'tjuːnɪə/ *n* any of a genus of plants with large brightly coloured funnel-shaped flowers

pew /pjuː/ *n* **1** a bench fixed in a row for the use of the congregation in a church **2** *Br* a seat – infml

pewter /'pjuːtəʳ/ *n* (utensils, vessels, etc made of) an alloy of tin and lead

peyote /peɪ'əʊti/ *n* any of several American cacti

pfennig /'fenɪg/ *n, pl* **pfennigs, pfennige** *often cap* a unit of currency of the Federal Republic of Germany and the German Democratic Republic

PG *n or adj* (a film that is) certified in Britain as suitable for all ages although parental guidance is recommended for children under 15

pH *n* a measure of the acidity or alkalinity of a solution, on a scale of 0 to 14 with 7 representing neutrality, equal to the negative logarithm of the hydrogen-ion concentration in moles per litre

phaeton /'feɪtn/ *n* a light open 4-wheeled carriage

phagocyte /'fægəsaɪt/ *n* a cell, esp white blood cell, that engulfs foreign material (e g bacteria) and consumes debris (e g from tissue injury)

phalanx /'fælæŋks/ *n, pl* **phalanges** *sing or pl in constr* **1** a body of troops, esp those of ancient Greece, in close array **2** a massed arrangement of people, animals, or things

phallus /'fæləs/ *n, pl* **phalli, phalluses** (a symbol or representation of) the penis – **phallic** *adj*

phantasmagoria /fæn,tæzmə'gɔːrɪə/ *n* a constantly shifting, confused succession of things seen or imagined (e g in a dreaming or feverish state) – **-goric** *adj* – **-gorical** *adj*

phantasy /'fæntəsi/ *v or n* (to) fantasy

[1]**phantom** /'fæntəm/ *n* **1** sthg (e g a ghost) apparent to the senses but with no substantial existence **2** sthg existing only in the imagination

[2]**phantom** *adj* **1** of or being a phantom **2** fictitious, dummy

pharaoh /'feərəʊ/ *n, often cap* a ruler of ancient Egypt

pharisaic /,færɮ'seɪ-ɪk/ *adj* **1** *cap* of the Pharisees **2** marked by hypocritical self-righteousness – **-ism** *n*

pharisee /'færɮsiː/ *n* **1** *cap* a member of a Jewish party noted for strict adherence to (their own oral traditions interpreting) the Torah **2** a pharisaic person

[1]**pharmaceutical** /,fɑːmə'sjuːtɪkəl/ *adj* of or engaged in pharmacy or in the manufacture of medicinal substances

[2]**pharmaceutical** *n* a medicinal drug

pharmacist /fɑːməsɮst/ *n* sby who prepares and sells drugs – **-cy** *n*

pharmacology /,fɑːmə'kɒlədʒi/ *n* the science of drugs and their effect on living things – **-gist** *n*

pharmacopoeia /,fɑːməkə'piːə/ *n* an (official) book describing drugs, chemicals, and medicinal preparations

pharmacy /'fɑːməsi/ *n* **1** the preparation, compounding, and dispensing of drugs **2** a place where medicines are compounded or dispensed

[1]**phase** /feɪz/ *n* **1a** a discernible part or stage in a course, development, or cycle **b** an aspect or part (e g of a problem) under consideration **2** a stage of a regularly recurring motion

or cyclic process (e g an alternating electric current) with respect to a starting point or standard position

²**phase** *v* **1** to conduct or carry out by planned phases **2** to schedule (e g operations) or contract for (e g goods or services) to be performed or supplied as required

pheasant /'fezənt/ *n* any of numerous large often long-tailed and brightly coloured Old World (game) birds

phenomenal /fı'nɒmı̣nəl/ *adj* extraordinary, remarkable – ~**ly** *adv*

phenomenon /fı'nɒmı̣nən/ *n, pl* **phenomena** **1** an object of sense perception rather than of thought or intuition **2** a fact or event that can be scientifically described and explained **3** a rare, exceptional, unusual, or abnormal person, thing, or event

phial /'faıəl/ *n* a small closed or closable vessel, esp for holding liquid medicine

philander /fı̣'lændəʳ/ *v* to have many casual love affairs – ~**er** *n*

philanthropy /fı̣'lænθrəpi/ *n* **1** active effort to promote the welfare of others **2** a philanthropic act or gift – **-pic** *adj* – **-pically** *adv*

philately /fı̣'lætəli/ *n* the study and collection of (postage) stamps – **-list** *n* – **-lic** *adj*

philistine /'fılı̣staın/ *n* **1** *cap* a native or inhabitant of ancient Philistia **2** *often cap* a person who professes indifference or opposition to intellectual or aesthetic values – **-tinism** *n*

philology /fı̣'lɒlədʒi/ *n* (historical and comparative) linguistics – **-logical** *adj* – **-logist** *n*

philosopher /fı̣'lɒsəfəʳ/ *n* **1** a specialist in philosophy **2** a person whose philosophical viewpoint enables him/her to meet trouble with equanimity

philosophers' stone *n* a substance believed by alchemists to have the power of transmuting base metals into gold

philosophical /,fılə'sɒfıkəl/ *adj* **1** of philosophers or philosophy **2** calm in the face of trouble – ~**ly** *adv*

philosoph·ize, -ise /fı̣'lɒsəfaız/ *v* **1** to engage in philosophical reasoning **2** to expound a trite philosophy

philosophy /fı̣'lɒsəfi/ *n* **1** the study of the nature of knowledge and existence and the principles of moral and aesthetic value **2** the philosophical principles, teachings, or beliefs of a specified individual, group, or period **3** equanimity in the face of trouble or stress

philtre, *NAm chiefly* **philter** /'fıltəʳ/ *n* a potion or drug reputed to have the power to arouse sexual passion

phlegm /flem/ *n* **1** thick mucus secreted in abnormal quantities in the respiratory passages **2a** dull or apathetic coldness or indifference **b** intrepid coolness; composure

phlegmatic /fleg'mætık/ *adj* having or showing a slow and stolid temperament – ~**ally** *adv*

phloem /'fləυem/ *n* a complex vascular tissue of higher plants that functions chiefly in the conduction of soluble food substances (e g sugars)

phlox /flɒks/ *n* any of a genus of American plants with red, purple, white, or variegated flowers

phobia /'fəυbıə/ *n* an exaggerated and illogical fear of sthg – **phobic** *n, adj*

phoenix /'fi:nıks/ *n* a mythical bird believed to live for 500 years, burn itself on a pyre, and rise alive from the ashes to live another cycle

¹**phone** /fəυn/ *n* a telephone

²**phone** *v* to telephone – often + *up*

phone-in *n* a broadcast programme in which viewers or listeners can participate by telephone

phonetic /fə'netık/ *adj* **1a** of spoken language or speech sounds **b** of the study of phonetics **2** representing speech sounds by symbols that each have 1 value only – ~**ally** *adv*

phonetics /fə'netıks/ *n pl* **1** *sing in constr* the study and classification of speech sounds **2** *sing or pl in constr* the system of speech sounds of a language

phoney, phony /'fəυni/ *adj* not genuine or real: e g **a** counterfeit; false, sham **b** *of a person* pretentious – **phoney** *n*

phonics /'fɒnıks/ *n pl but sing in constr* a method of teaching reading and pronunciation through the phonetic value of letters, syllables, etc

phosphate /'fɒsfeıt/ *n* a salt or ester

of a phosphoric acid; esp one used as a fertilizer

phosphorescence /ˌfɒsfəˈresəns/ *n* emission of light without noticeable heat – **-cent** *adj*

phosphorus /ˈfɒsfərəs/ *n* a nonmetallic element of the nitrogen family that occurs widely, esp as phosphates, 1 form of which ignites readily in warm moist air – **-ric** *adj*

[1]**photo** /ˈfəʊtəʊ/ *v or n* (to) photograph

[2]**photo** *adj* photographic

[1]**photocopy** /ˈfəʊtəʊkɒpi/ *n* a photographic reproduction of graphic matter

[2]**photocopy** *v* to make a photocopy (of) – **-pier** *n*

photoelectric /ˌfəʊtəʊ-ɪˈlektrɪk/ *adj* involving, relating to, or using any of various electrical effects caused by the interaction of radiation (e g light) with matter

photoelectric cell *n* a cell whose electrical properties are modified by the action of light

photo finish *n* **1** a race finish so close that the winner is only revealed (as if) by a photograph of the contestants as they cross the finishing line **2** a close contest

photogenic /ˌfəʊtəʊˈdʒenɪk, ˌfəʊtə-/ *adj* suitable for being photographed

[1]**photograph** /ˈfəʊtəgrɑːf/ *n* a picture or likeness obtained by photography

[2]**photograph** *v* to take a photograph – **~er** *n* – **~ic** *adj* – **~ically** *adv*

photography /fəˈtɒgrəfi/ *n* the art or process of producing images on a sensitized surface (e g a film) by the action of radiant energy, esp light

photosynthesis /ˌfəʊtəʊˈsɪnθɨsɨs/ *n* the formation of carbohydrates from carbon dioxide in the chlorophyll-containing tissues of plants exposed to light

phototropism /fəʊˈtɒtrəpɪzəm, ˌfəʊtəʊˈtrəʊpɪzəm/ *n* a tropism in which light is the orienting factor

[1]**phrase** /freɪz/ *n* **1** a brief usu idiomatic or pithy expression; *esp* a catchphrase **2** a group of musical notes forming a natural unit of melody **3** a group of 2 or more grammatically related words that do not form a clause

[2]**phrase** *v* **1** to express in words or in appropriate or telling terms **2** to divide into melodic phrases

phrenology /frɪˈnɒlədʒi/ *n* the study of the shape and esp irregularities of the skull as a supposed indicator of mental faculties and character

phylloxera /fɪˈlɒksərə, ˌfɪlɒkˈsɪərə/ *n* any of various plant lice that are destructive to many plants (e g grapevines)

phylum /ˈfaɪləm/ *n, pl* **phyla** a major group of related species in the classification of plants and animals

physical /ˈfɪzɪkəl/ *adj* **1** having material existence; perceptible, esp through the senses, and subject to the laws of nature **2** of natural science or physics **3** of the body, esp as opposed to the spirit – **~ly** *adv*

physical jerks *n* bodily exercises – infml

physician /fɨˈzɪʃən/ *n* a person skilled in the art of healing

physics /ˈfɪzɪks/ *n pl but sing or pl in constr* **1** a science that deals with (the properties and interactions of) matter and energy in such fields as mechanics, heat, electricity, magnetism, atomic structure, etc **2** the physical properties and phenomena of a particular system

physiology /ˌfɪziˈɒlədʒi/ *n* **1** biology that deals with the functions and activities of life or of living matter (e g organs, tissues, or cells) and the physical and chemical phenomena involved **2** the physiological activities of (part of) an organism or a particular bodily function – **-gist** *n* – **-gical** *adj*

physiotherapy /ˌfɪziəʊˈθerəpi/ *n* the treatment of disease by physical and mechanical means (e g massage and regulated exercise) – **-pist** *n*

physique /fɨˈziːk/ *n* the form or structure of a person's body

[1]**pi** /paɪ/ *n, pl* **pis** **1** the 16th letter of the Greek alphabet **2** (the symbol π denoting) the ratio of the circumference of a circle to its diameter with a value, to 8 decimal places, of 3.14159265

[2]**pi** *adj, Br* pious – derog

pianissimo /pɪəˈnɪsɨməʊ/ *adv or adj* very soft

pianist /'pɪənʝst, 'pjɑː-/ *n* a performer on the piano

[1]**piano** /'pjɑːnəʊ, pi'ænəʊ/ *adv or adj* in a soft or quiet manner

[2]**piano** *n, pl* **pianos** a stringed instrument having steel wire strings that sound when struck by felt-covered hammers operated from a keyboard

picador /'pɪkədɔːʳ/ *n, pl* **picadors, picadores** a horseman who in a bullfight prods the bull with a lance to weaken its neck and shoulder muscles

picaresque /,pɪkə'resk/ *adj* of or being fiction narrating in loosely linked episodes the adventures of a rogue

piccalilli /,pɪkə'lɪli/ *n* a hot relish of chopped vegetables, mustard, and spices

piccolo /'pɪkələʊ/ *n* a flute with a range an octave higher than an ordinary flute's

[1]**pick** /pɪk/ *v* **1a** to remove bit by bit **b** to remove covering or clinging matter from **2a** to gather by plucking **b** to choose, select **3** to provoke **4a** to dig into, esp in order to remove unwanted matter; probe **b** to pluck with a plectrum or with the fingers **5** to unlock with a device (e g a wire) other than the key **6** to make (one's way) carefully on foot

[2]**pick** *n* **1** the act or privilege of choosing or selecting; a choice **2** *sing or pl in constr* the best or choicest

[3]**pick** *n* **1 pick, pickaxe** a heavy wooden-handled tool with a head that is pointed at one or both ends **2** a plectrum

picker /'pɪkəʳ/ *n* a person or machine that picks crops

[1]**picket** /'pɪkʝt/ *n* **1** a pointed or sharpened stake, post, or pale **2** *sing or pl in constr* a small body of troops detached to guard an army from surprise attack **3** a person posted by a trade union at a place of work to enforce a strike

[2]**picket** *v* **1** to enclose, fence, or fortify with pickets **2** to tether **3a** to post pickets at **b** to walk or stand in front of as a picket – **~er** *n*

pickle /'pɪkəl/ *n* **1** a brine or vinegar solution in which meat, fish, vegetables, etc are preserved **2** (an article of) food preserved in a pickle; *also* chutney – often pl **3** a difficult situation – infml – **pickle** *v*

pickpocket /'pɪk,pɒkʝt/ *n* one who steals from pockets or bags

pickup /'pɪkʌp/ *n* **1** sby or sthg picked up: e g **a** a hitchhiker who is given a lift **b** a casual acquaintance made with the intention of having sex **2** a device (e g on a record player) that converts mechanical movements into electrical signals **3** a light motor truck having an open body with low sides and tailboard

pick up *v* **1b** to gather together; collect; *also* tidy **2** to take (passengers or freight) into a vehicle **3a** to acquire casually or by chance **b** to acquire by study or experience; learn **4** to enter informally into conversation or companionship with (a previously unknown person), usu with the intention of having sex **5** to bring within range of sight, hearing, or a sensor **6** to revive or improve **7** to resume after a break; continue

[1]**picnic** /'pɪknɪk/ *n* **1** (the food eaten at) an outing that includes an informal meal, usu lunch, eaten in the open **2** a pleasant or amusingly carefree experience; *also* an easily accomplished task or feat – infml

[2]**picnic** *v* **-ck-** to go on a picnic – **picnicker** *n*

pictorial /pɪk'tɔːrɪəl/ *adj* **1** of (a) painting or drawing **2** consisting of or illustrated by pictures – **~ly** *adv*

[1]**picture** /'pɪktʃəʳ/ *n* **1** a design or representation made by painting, drawing, etc **2a** a description so vivid or graphic as to suggest a mental image or give an accurate idea of sthg **b** a presentation of the relevant or characteristic facts concerning a problem or situation **3a** a film **b** *pl, chiefly Br* the cinema

[2]**picture** *v* **1** to paint or draw a representation, image, or visual conception of; depict **2** to describe graphically in words **3** to form a mental image of; imagine

picturesque /,pɪktʃə'resk/ *adj* **1** pleasing to the eye **2** quaint, charming **3** vivid – **~ly** *adv* – **~ness** *n*

[1]**piddle** /'pɪdl/ *v* **1** to act or work in an

idle or trifling manner **2** to urinate *USE* infml

[2]**piddle** *n* **1** urine **2** an act of urinating *USE* infml

pidgin /ˈpɪdʒɪ̣n/ *n* a language based on 2 or more languages and used esp for trade between people with different native languages

[1]**pie** /paɪ/ *n* **1** a magpie **2** a variegated animal

[2]**pie** *n* a dish consisting of a sweet or savoury filling covered or encased by pastry and baked in a container

piebald /ˈpaɪbɔːld/ *adj* **1** *esp of a horse* of different colours; *specif* spotted or blotched with different colours, esp black and white **2** composed of incongruous parts; heterogeneous

[1]**piece** /piːs/ *n* **1** a part of a whole; *esp* a part detached, cut, etc from a whole **2** an object or individual regarded as a unit of a kind or class **3** a standard quantity (e g of length, weight, or size) in which sthg is made or sold **4a** a literary, artistic, dramatic, or musical work **b** a passage to be recited **5** a man used in playing a board game; *esp* a chessman of rank superior to a pawn

[2]**piece** *v* **1** to repair, renew, or complete by adding pieces; patch – often + *up* **2** to join into a whole – often + *together*

[1]**piecemeal** /ˈpiːsmiːl/ *adv* **1** one piece at a time; gradually **2** in pieces or fragments; apart

[2]**piecemeal** *adj* done, made, or accomplished piece by piece or in a fragmentary way

piecework /ˈpiːswɜːk/ *n* work that is paid for at a set rate per unit

pied /paɪd/ *adj* having patches of 2 or more colours

pie-eyed *adj* drunk – infml

pier /pɪəʳ/ *n* **1** an intermediate support for the adjacent ends of 2 bridge spans **2** a structure extending into navigable water for use as a landing place, promenade, etc

pierce /pɪəs/ *v* **1** to enter or thrust into sharply or painfully **2** to make a hole in or through **3** to penetrate with the eye or mind **4** to move or affect the emotions of, esp sharply or painfully

piercing /ˈpɪəsɪŋ/ *adj* penetrating: e g **a** loud, shrill **b** perceptive **c** penetratingly cold; biting **d** cutting, incisive – **~ly** *adv*

Pierrot /ˈpɪərəʊ/ *n* a stock comic character of old French pantomime usu having a whitened face

piety /ˈpaɪəti/ *n* **1** devoutness **2** dutifulness, esp to parents

[1]**pig** /pɪg/ *n* **1** *chiefly Br* any of various (domesticated) stout-bodied short-legged omnivorous mammals with a thick bristly skin and a long mobile snout **2** sby like or suggestive of a pig in habits or behaviour (e g in dirtiness, greed, or selfishness) **3** a policeman – slang; derog

[2]**pig** *v* **1** to live like a pig – + *it* **2a** to eat (food) greedily **b** to overindulge (oneself)

pigeon /ˈpɪdʒɪ̣n/ *n* any of a family of birds with a stout body and smooth and compact plumage, many of which are domesticated or live in urban areas

[1]**pigeonhole** /ˈpɪdʒɪ̣nhəʊl/ *n* **1** a small open compartment (e g in a desk or cabinet) for letters or documents **2** a neat category which usu fails to reflect actual complexities

[2]**pigeonhole** *v* **1a** to place (as if) in the pigeonhole of a desk **b** to lay aside; shelve **2** to assign to a category; classify

[1]**piggyback** /ˈpɪgibæk/ *adv* up on the back and shoulders

[2]**piggyback** *n* a ride on the back and shoulders of another

pigheaded /ˌpɪgˈhedɪ̣d/ *adj* obstinate, stubborn – **~ly** *adv* – **~ness** *n*

pig iron *n* crude iron from the blast furnace before refining

pigment /ˈpɪgmənt/ *n* **1** a substance that colours other materials **2** any of various colouring matters in animals and plants – **pigment** *v*

pigmentation /ˌpɪgmənˈteɪʃən/ *n* (excessive) coloration with, or deposition of, (bodily) pigment

pigmy, pygmy /ˈpɪgmi/ *n* **1** a member of a people of equatorial Africa who are under 5ft in height **2** a dwarf; *also* sby markedly inferior or insignificant in a particular area

pignut /ˈpɪgnʌt/ *n* a common plant of the carrot family

pigsty /ˈpɪgstaɪ/ *n* **1** an enclosure

with a covered shed for pigs **2** a dirty, untidy, or neglected place

pigtail /'pɪgteɪl/ *n* **1** a tight plait of hair, esp at the back of the head **2** either of 2 bunches of hair worn loose or plaited at either side of the head by young girls – **~ed** *adj*

pike /paɪk/ *n* a large long-snouted fish-eating bony fish widely distributed in cooler parts of the N hemisphere

[2]**pike** *n* a weapon consisting of a long wooden shaft with a pointed steel head that was used by foot soldiers until superseded by the bayonet

pilaster /pɪ̧'læstəʳ/ *n* an upright rectangular column that is usu embedded in a wall

pilau /'pɪlaʊ/ *n* (a dish of) seasoned rice often with meat or vegetables

pilchard /'pɪltʃəd/ *n* a fish of the herring family that occurs in great schools along the coasts of Europe

[1]**pile** /paɪl/ *n* a beam of timber, steel, reinforced concrete, etc driven into the ground to carry a vertical load

[2]**pile** *n* **1a** a quantity of things heaped together **b** a large quantity, number, or amount **2** a large building or group of buildings **3** a great amount of money; a fortune **4** an atomic reactor

[3]**pile** *v* **1** to lay or place in a pile; stack – often + *up* **2** to move or press forwards (as if) in a mass; crowd

[4]**pile** *n* a soft raised surface on a fabric or carpet consisting of cut threads or loops

[5]**pile** *n* a haemorrhoid – usu pl

pileup /'paɪlʌp/ *n* a collision involving usu several motor vehicles and causing damage or injury

pile up *v* to accumulate

pilfer /'pɪlfəʳ/ *v* to steal stealthily in small amounts or to small value – **~er** *n* – **~age** *n*

pilgrim /'pɪlgrɪ̧m/ *n* a person making a pilgrimage

pilgrimage /'pɪlgrɪ̧mɪdʒ/ *n* a journey to a shrine or sacred place as an act of devotion, in order to acquire spiritual merit, or as a penance

Pilgrim Fathers *n pl* the English colonists who settled at Plymouth, Massachusetts, in 1620

pill /pɪl/ *n* **1a** a small rounded solid mass of medicine to be swallowed whole **b** an oral contraceptive taken daily by a woman over a monthly cycle – + *the* **2** sthg repugnant or unpleasant that must be accepted or endured

pillage *v* to plunder ruthlessly; loot – **pillage** *n*

pillar /'pɪləʳ/ *n* **1a** a firm upright support for a superstructure **b** a usu ornamental column or shaft **2** a chief supporter; a prop

pillar box *n* a red pillar-shaped public letter box

pillbox /'pɪlbɒks/ *n* **1** a box for pills; *esp* a shallow round box made of pasteboard **2** a small low concrete weapon emplacement **3** a small round brimless hat with a flat crown and straight sides

[1]**pillion** /'pɪlɪən/ *n* a saddle or seat for a passenger on a motorcycle or motor scooter

[2]**pillion** *adv* (as if) on a pillion

pillory /'pɪləri/ *n* **1** a device for publicly punishing offenders consisting of a wooden frame with holes for the head and hands **2** a means for exposing one to public scorn or ridicule – **pillory** *v*

[1]**pillow** /'pɪləʊ/ *n* a usu rectangular cloth bag (e g of cotton) filled with soft material (e g down) and used to support the head of a reclining person

[2]**pillow** *v* **1** to rest or lay (as if) on a pillow **2** to serve as a pillow for

pillowcase /'pɪləʊkeɪs/ *n* a removable washable cover for a pillow

[1]**pilot** /'paɪlət/ *n* **1** sby qualified and usu licensed to conduct a ship into and out of a port or in specified waters **2** a guide, leader **3** sby who handles or is qualified to handle the controls of an aircraft or spacecraft

[2]**pilot** *v* **1** to act as a guide to; lead or conduct over a usu difficult course **2a** to direct the course of **b** to act as pilot of

[3]**pilot** *adj* serving as a guide, activator, or trial

pilot light *n* a small permanent flame used to ignite gas at a burner

pimento /pɪ̧'mentəʊ/ *n pl* **pimentos, pimento** **1** a mild-flavoured sweet pepper **2** allspice

pimp /pɪmp/ *n* a man who solicits clients for a prostitute or brothel

pimpernel /ˈpɪmpənel/ *n* any of several plants of the primrose family: e g **a** the scarlet pimpernel, having usu red flowers that close in cloudy weather **b** the yellow pimpernel, having bright yellow flowers

pimple /ˈpɪmpəl/ *n* a small solid inflamed (pus-containing) swelling – **-ply** *adj* – **~d** *adj*

[1]**pin** /pɪn/ *n* **1** a piece of solid material (e g wood or metal) used esp for fastening separate articles together or as a support **2a** a small thin pointed piece of metal with a head used esp for fastening cloth, paper, etc **b** sthg of small value; a trifle **3** a projecting metal bar on a plug which is inserted into a socket **4** a leg – infml; usu pl

[2]**pin** *v* **1a** to fasten, join, or secure with a pin **b** to hold fast or immobile **2a** to attach, hang **b** to assign the blame or responsibility for

pinafore /ˈpɪnəfɔːʳ/ *n* **1** an apron, usu with a bib **2** *also* **pinafore dress** a sleeveless usu low-necked dress designed to be worn over another garment (e g a blouse)

pinball /ˈpɪnbɔːl/ *n* a game in which a ball is propelled across a sloping surface at pins and targets that score points if hit

pince-nez /ˌpæns ˈneɪ, pɪns-/ *n, pl* **pince-nez** glasses clipped to the nose by a spring

pincer /ˈpɪnsəʳ/ *n* **1a** *pl* an instrument having 2 short handles and 2 grasping jaws working on a pivot and used for gripping things **b** a claw (e g of a lobster) resembling a pair of pincers **2** either part of a double military envelopment of an enemy position

[1]**pinch** /pɪntʃ/ *v* **1a** to squeeze or compress painfully (e g between the finger and thumb) **b** to prune the tip of (a plant or shoot), usu to induce branching – + *out* or *back* **2** to subject to strict economy or want **3a** to steal – slang **b** to arrest – slang – **~ed** *adj*

[2]**pinch** *n* **1a** a critical juncture; an emergency **b(1)** pressure, stress **(2)** hardship, privation **2a** an act of pinching **b** as much as may be taken between the finger and thumb

pincushion /ˈpɪnˌkʊʃən/ *n* a small cushion in which pins are stuck ready for use, esp in sewing

pin down *v* **1** to force (sby) to state his/her position or make a decision **2** to define precisely **3** to fasten down; prevent from moving

[1]**pine** /paɪn/ *v* **1** to lose vigour or health (e g through grief) – often + *away* **2** to yearn intensely and persistently, esp for sthg unattainable

[2]**pine** *n* **1** (any of various trees related to) any of a genus of coniferous evergreen trees which have slender elongated needles **2** the straight-grained white or yellow usu durable and resinous wood of a pine

pineapple /ˈpaɪnæpəl/ *n* **1** (the large oval edible succulent yellow-fleshed fruit of) a tropical plant with rigid spiny leaves and a dense head of small flowers

pine marten *n* a slender Eurasian marten with a yellow patch on the chest and throat

ping /pɪŋ/ *v or n* (to make) a sharp ringing sound

Ping-Pong /ˈpɪŋ pɒŋ/ *n* table tennis

[1]**pinion** /ˈpɪnɪən/ *n* **1** (the end section of) a bird's wing **2** a bird's feather

[2]**pinion** *v* **1** to restrain (a bird) from flight, esp by cutting off the pinion of a wing **2** to disable or restrain by binding the arms

[3]**pinion** *n* a gear with a small number of teeth designed to mesh with a larger gear wheel or rack

[1]**pink** /pɪŋk/ *v* to cut a zigzag or saw-toothed edge on

[2]**pink** *n* any of a genus of plants related to the carnation and widely grown for their white, pink, red, or variegated flowers

[3]**pink** *adj* **1** of the colour pink **2** holding moderately radical political views

[4]**pink** *n* **1** any of various shades of pale red **2** (the scarlet colour of) a fox hunter's coat

[5]**pink** *v, Br, of an internal-combustion engine* to make a series of sharp popping noises because of faulty combustion of the fuel-air mixture

pink gin *n* gin flavoured with angostura bitters

pinking shears *n pl* shears with a saw-toothed inner edge on the blades, used in sewing for making a zigzag cut in cloth to prevent fraying

pin money *n* **1a** extra money earned by sby, esp a married woman (e g in a part-time job) **b** money set aside for the purchase of incidentals **2** a trivial amount of money

pinnacle /'pɪnəkəl/ *n* **1** an architectural ornament resembling a small spire and used esp to crown a buttress **2** a lofty mountain **3** the highest point of development or achievement

pinnate /'pɪneɪt/ *adj* resembling a feather, esp in having similar parts arranged on opposite sides of an axis like the barbs on the shaft of a feather

pinny /'pɪni/ *n* a pinafore – infml

¹pinpoint /'pɪnpɔɪnt/ *v* **1** to fix, determine, or identify with precision **2** to cause to stand out conspicuously; highlight

²pinpoint *adj* **1** extremely small, fine, or precise **2** located, fixed, or directed with extreme precision

³pinpoint *n* a very small point or area

pins and needles *n pl* a pricking tingling sensation in a limb recovering from numbness

pinstripe /'pɪnstraɪp/ *n* **1** a very thin stripe, esp on a fabric **2** a suit or trousers with pinstripes – often pl with sing. meaning

pint /paɪnt/ *n* **1** a unit of liquid capacity equal to ⅛gal **2** a pint of liquid, esp milk or beer

pinup /'pɪnʌp/ *n* (a person whose glamorous qualities make him/her a suitable subject of) a photograph pinned up on an admirer's wall

¹pioneer /,paɪə'nɪəʳ/ *n* **1** a member of a military unit (e g engineers) engaging in light construction and defensive works **2a** a person or group that originates or helps open up a new line of thought or activity or a new method or technical development **b** any of the first people to settle in a territory

²pioneer *adj* **1** original, earliest **2** (characteristic) of early settlers or their time

³pioneer *v* **1** to open or prepare for others to follow; *esp* to settle **2** to originate or take part in the development of

pious /'paɪəs/ *adj* **1** devout **2** sacred or devotional as distinct from the profane or secular **3** dutiful **4** sanctimonious – **~ly** *adv* – **~ness** *n*

¹pip /pɪp/ *n* a fit of irritation, low spirits, or disgust – chiefly infml; esp in *to give one the pip*

²pip *n* **1** any of the dots on dice and dominoes that indicate numerical value **2** a star worn, esp on the shoulder, to indicate an army officer's rank

³pip *v* to beat by a narrow margin – infml

⁴pip *n* a small fruit seed of an apple, orange, etc

⁵pip *n* a short high-pitched tone, esp broadcast in a series as a time signal

¹pipe /paɪp/ *n* **1a** a tubular wind instrument **b** a bagpipe – usu pl with sing. meaning **2** a long tube or hollow body for conducting a liquid, gas, etc **3a** a tubular or cylindrical object, part, or passage **4** a large cask used esp for wine (e g port) **5** a wood, clay, etc tube with a mouthpiece at one end, and at the other a small bowl in which tobacco is burned for smoking

²pipe *v* **1** to play on a pipe **2a** to speak in a high or shrill voice **b** to make a shrill sound **3a** to trim with piping **b** to force (e g cream or icing) through a piping tube or nozzle in order to achieve a decorative effect

pipe dream *n* an illusory or fantastic plan, hope, or story

pipeline /'paɪp-laɪn/ *n* **1** the processes through which supplies pass from source to user **2** sthg considered as a continuous set of processes which the individual must go through or be subjected to

piper /'paɪpəʳ/ *n* one who plays on a pipe

pipette /pɪ'pet/ *n* a narrow tube into which fluid is drawn (e g for dispensing or measuring) by suction and retained by closing the upper end

piping /'paɪpɪŋ/ *n* **1a** the music of a pipe **b** a sound, note, or call like that of a pipe **2** a quantity or system of pipes **3a** a narrow trimming consisting of a folded strip of cloth often enclosing a cord, used to decorate upholstery, garments, etc **b** a thin cordlike line of icing piped onto a cake

pipit /'pɪpɪt/ *n* any of various small birds resembling larks

pip-squeak *n* a small or insignificant person – infml

piquant /'piːkənt/ *adj* **1** agreeably stimulating to the palate; savoury **2** pleasantly stimulating to the mind – **~ly** *adv* – **-quancy** *n*

[1]**pique** /piːk/ *n* resentment resulting from wounded vanity

[2]**pique** *v* **1** to offend by slighting **2** to excite or arouse by a provocation, challenge, or rebuff

piqué, pique /'piːkeɪ/ *n* a durable ribbed fabric of cotton, rayon, or silk

piracy /'paɪrəsi/ *n* **1** robbery or illegal violence at sea; *also* a similar act against an aircraft in flight **2** the infringement of a copyright, patent, etc

piranha /pɪ̈'rɑːnjə, -nə/ *n* a small S American fish capable of attacking and (fatally) wounding human beings and large animals

[1]**pirate** /'paɪərət/ *n* **1** sby who commits piracy **2** an unauthorized radio station; *esp* one located on a ship in international waters – **-ratical** *adj* – **-ratically** *adv*

[2]**pirate** *v* **1** to commit piracy on **2** to take or appropriate by piracy **3** to reproduce without authorization

pirouette /,pɪrʊ'et/ *n* a rapid whirling about of the body; *specif* a full turn on the toe or ball of one foot in ballet

Pisces /'paɪsiːz/ *n pl but sing in constr* (sby born under) the 12th sign of the zodiac in astrology, which is pictured as 2 fishes

[1]**piss** /pɪs/ *v* **1** to urinate **2** to discharge (as if) as urine **3** to rain heavily *USE* vulg

[2]**piss** *n* **1** urine **2** an act of urinating *USE* vulg

pissed /pɪst/ *adj, Br* drunk – slang

piss off *v, Br* **1** to go away **2** to cause to be annoyed or fed up *USE* vulg

pistachio /pɪ̈'stɑːʃiəʊ/ *n* **1** a small green much-prized nut; *also* the tree on which it grows **2** the vivid green colour of the pistachio nut

pistil /'pɪstl/ *n* a carpel

pistol /'pɪstl/ *n* a short firearm intended to be aimed and fired with 1 hand

piston /'pɪstn/ *n* **1** a sliding disc or short cylinder fitting within a cylindrical vessel along which it moves back and forth by or against fluid pressure **2** a sliding valve in a cylinder in a brass instrument that is used to lower its pitch

[1]**pit** /pɪt/ *n* **1a** a hole, shaft, or cavity in the ground **b** a mine **2** an area often sunken or depressed below the adjacent floor area; *esp* one in a theatre housing an orchestra **3** a hollow or indentation, esp in the surface of a living plant or animal; *esp* a natural hollow in the surface of the body **4** any of the areas alongside a motor-racing track used for refuelling and repairing the vehicles during a race – usu pl with sing. meaning; + *the*

[2]**pit** *v* **1** to make pits in; *esp* to scar or mark with pits **2** to set into opposition or rivalry; oppose – often + *against*

[3]**pit** *n, NAm* a fruit stone

[1]**pitch** /pɪtʃ/ *n* **1** a black or dark viscous substance obtained as a residue in the distillation of tar **2** resin obtained from various conifers

[2]**pitch** *v* **1** to erect and fix firmly in place **2** to throw, fling **3a(1)** to cause to be at a particular level or of a particular quality **(2)** to set in a particular musical pitch or key **b** to cause to be set at a particular angle; slope **4a** to fall precipitately or headlong **b** *of a ship* to move so that the bow is alternately rising and falling **5** *of a ball* to bounce

[3]**pitch** *n* **1** pitching; *esp* an up-and-down movement **2a** a slope; *also* the degree of slope **b** distance from any point on the thread of a screw to the corresponding point on an adjacent thread measured parallel to the axis **c** the distance advanced by a propeller in 1 revolution **d** the number of teeth on a gear or of threads on a screw per unit distance **3a** the relative level, intensity, or extent of some quality or state **b(1)** the property of a sound, esp a musical note, that is determined by the frequency of the waves producing it; highness or lowness of sound **(2)** a standard fre-

quency for tuning instruments **4** an often high-pressure sales talk or advertisement **5** a wicket **6** *chiefly Br* **a** a usu specially marked area used for playing soccer, rugby, hockey, etc **b** an area or place, esp in a street, to which a person lays unofficial claim for carrying out business or activities

pitch-black *adj* intensely dark or black – ~**ness** *n*

pitchblende /ˈpɪtʃblend/ *n* a radium-containing uranium oxide occurring as a brown to black lustrous mineral

pitched battle *n* an intense battle; *specif* one fought on previously chosen ground

pitcher /ˈpɪtʃəʳ/ *n* a large deep usu earthenware vessel with a wide lip and a handle or 2 ear-shaped handles, for holding and pouring liquids; *broadly* a large jug

¹pitchfork /ˈpɪtʃfɔːk/ *n* a long-handled fork with 2 or 3 long curved prongs used esp for hay

²pitchfork *v* **1** to lift and toss (as if) with a pitchfork **2** to thrust (sby) into a position, office, etc suddenly or without preparation

piteous /ˈpɪtɪəs/ *adj* causing or deserving pity or compassion – ~**ly** *adv* – ~**ness** *n*

pitfall /ˈpɪtfɔːl/ *n* **1** a trap or snare; *specif* a camouflaged pit used to capture animals **2** a hidden or not easily recognized danger or difficulty

¹pith /pɪθ/ *n* **1a** a (continuous) central area of spongy tissue in the stems of most vascular plants **b** the white tissue surrounding the flesh and directly below the skin of a citrus fruit **2** the essential part; the core

²pith *v* to remove the pith from (a plant part)

pithy /ˈpɪθi/ *adj* **1** consisting of or having much pith **2** tersely cogent – **-thily** *adv* – **-thiness** *n*

pitiable /ˈpɪtɪəbəl/ *adj* deserving or exciting pity or contempt, esp because of inadequacy – **-bly** *adv*

pitiful /ˈpɪtɪfəl/ *adj* **1** deserving or arousing pity or sympathy **2** exciting pitying contempt (e g by meanness or inadequacy) – ~**ly** *adv* – ~**ness** *n*

pitiless /ˈpɪtɪlɨ̥s/ *adj* devoid of pity; merciless – ~**ly** *adv* – ~**ness** *n*

piton /ˈpiːtɒn/ *n* a spike or peg that is driven into a rock or ice surface as a support, esp for a rope, in mountaineering

pittance /ˈpɪtəns/ *n* a small amount or allowance; *specif* a meagre wage or remuneration

pituitary /pɨ̥ˈtjuːɨ̥təri/ *adj or n* (of) the gland attached to the brain that secretes hormones regulating growth, metabolism, etc

¹pity /ˈpɪti/ *n* **1a** (the capacity to feel) sympathetic sorrow for one suffering, distressed, or unhappy **b** a contemptuous feeling of regret aroused by the inferiority or inadequacy of another **2** sthg to be regretted

²pity *v* to feel pity (for)

¹pivot /ˈpɪvət/ *n* **1** a shaft or pin on which sthg turns **2a** a person, thing, or factor having a major or central role, function, or effect **b** a key player or position – ~**al** *adj*

²pivot *v* to turn (as if) on a pivot

pixie, pixy /ˈpɪksi/ *n* a (mischievous) fairy

pizza /ˈpiːtsə/ *n* a round thin cake of baked bread dough spread with a mixture of tomatoes, cheese, herbs, etc

pizzicato /ˌpɪtsɪˈkɑːtəʊ/ *n, adv, or adj, pl* **pizzicati** (a note or passage played) by means of plucking instead of bowing

placard /ˈplækɑːd/ *n* a notice for display or advertising purposes, usu printed on or fixed to a stiff backing material

placate /pləˈkeɪt/ *v* to soothe or mollify, esp by concessions – **-catory** *adj*

¹place /pleɪs/ *n* **1a** physical environment; a space **b** physical surroundings; atmosphere **2** an indefinite region or expanse; an area **3** a particular region or centre of population **4** a particular part of a surface or body; a spot **5** relative position in a scale or series: e g **a** a particular part in a piece of writing; *esp* the point at which a reader has temporarily stopped **b** an important or valued position **c** degree of prestige **6** a leading place, esp second or third, in a competition **7a** a proper or designated niche **b** an appropriate moment or point **8** an available seat or accommodation **9a** employment; a job; *esp* public office **b** prestige accorded to one of high rank; status **10** a public square

[2]**place** *v* **1** to distribute in an orderly manner **2a** to put in, direct to, or assign to a particular place **b** to put in a particular state **3** to appoint to a position **4** to find employment or a home for **5a** to assign to a position in a series or category **b** to identify by connecting with an associated context **c** to put, lay **6** to give (an order) to a supplier

placebo /plə'siːbəʊ/ *n* **1a** a medication that has no physiological effect and is prescribed more for the mental relief of the patient **b** an inert substance against which an active substance (e g a drug) is tested in a controlled trial **2** sthg tending to soothe or gratify

placed /pleɪst/ *adj* in a leading place, esp second or third, at the end of a competition, horse race, etc

placekick /'pleɪs,kɪk/ *v or n* (to kick or score by means of) a kick at a ball (e g in rugby) placed or held in a stationary position on the ground

placenta /plə'sentə/ *n, pl* **placentas, placentae** the organ in all higher mammals that unites the foetus to the maternal uterus and provides for the nourishment of the foetus and the elimination of waste

placid /'plæsɨd/ *adj* serenely free of interruption or disturbance – **~ly** *adv* – **~ity** *n*

plagiar·ize, -ise /'pleɪdʒəraɪz/ *v* to copy the ideas or words of another and pass them off as one's own – **-izer, -ist** *n* – **-ism** *n*

[1]**plague** /pleɪg/ *n* **1a** a disastrous evil or affliction; a calamity **b** a large destructive influx **2** any of several epidemic virulent diseases that cause many deaths **3** a cause of irritation; a nuisance

[2]**plague** *v* **1** to cause worry or distress to **2** to disturb or annoy persistently

plaice /pleɪs/ *n, pl* **plaice** any of various flatfishes; a flounder

plaid /plæd/ *n* **1** a rectangular length of tartan worn over the left shoulder as part of Highland dress **2** a usu twilled woollen fabric with a tartan pattern

[1]**plain** /pleɪn/ *n* **1** an extensive area of level or rolling treeless country **2** a broad unbroken expanse

[2]**plain** *adj* **1** lacking ornament; undecorated **2** free of added substances; pure **3a** evident to the mind or senses; obvious **b** clear **4** free from deceitfulness or subtlety; candid **5** lacking special distinction; ordinary **6a** not complicated **b** not rich or elaborately prepared or decorated **7** unremarkable either for physical beauty or for ugliness **8** *of flour* not containing a raising agent

[3]**plain, plainly** *adv* in a plain manner; clearly, simply; *also* totally, utterly

plain clothes *n* ordinary civilian dress as opposed to (police) uniform

plainsong /'pleɪnsɒŋ/ *n* **1** the music of the medieval church **2** a liturgical chant of any of various Christian rites

plaint /pleɪnt/ *n* a protest

plaintiff /'pleɪntɨf/ *n* sby who commences a civil legal action

plaintive /'pleɪntɪv/ *adj* expressive of suffering or woe; melancholy, mournful – **~ly** *adv* – **~ness** *n*

[1]**plait** /plæt/ *n* a length of plaited material, esp hair

[2]**plait** *v* **1** to interweave the strands of **2** to make by plaiting

[1]**plan** /plæn/ *n* **1** a drawing or diagram: e g **a** a top or horizontal view of an object **b** a large-scale map of a small area **2a** a method for achieving an end **b** a customary method of doing sthg **c** a detailed formulation of a programme of action

[2]**plan** *v* **1** to design **2** to arrange in advance **3** to have in mind; intend – **~ner** *n*

[1]**plane** /pleɪn/ *v* **1** to make flat or even with a plane **2** to remove by planing – often + *away* or *down*

[2]**plane, plane tree** *n* any of a genus of trees with large deeply cut lobed leaves and flowers in spherical heads

[3]**plane** *n* a tool with a sharp blade protruding from the base of a flat metal or wooden stock for smoothing or shaping a wood surface

[4]**plane** *n* **1** a surface such that any 2 included points can be joined by a

straight line lying wholly within the surface **2** a level of existence, consciousness, or development **3** an aeroplane; *also* any of the surfaces that support it in flight

[5]**plane** *adj* **1** having no elevations or depressions; flat **2a** of or dealing with geometric planes **b** lying in a plane

planet /ˈplænɨt/ *n* **1** any of the bodies, except a comet, meteor, or satellite, that revolve round a star, esp the sun in our solar system **2** a star held to have astrological significance – **~ary** *adj*

planetarium /ˌplænɨˈteərɪəm/ *n* **1** a model of the solar system **2** (a building or room housing) an optical projector for projecting images of celestial bodies and effects as seen in the night sky

[1]**plank** /plæŋk/ *n* **1** a long flat piece of wood **2** a (principal) item of a political policy or programme

[2]**plank** *v* to cover or floor with planks

plankton /ˈplæŋktən/ *n* the floating or weakly swimming minute animal and plant organisms of a body of water

[1]**plant** /plɑːnt/ *v* **1a** to put in the ground, soil, etc for growth **b** to set or sow (land) with seeds or plants **2** to establish, institute **3** to place firmly or forcibly **4** to position secretly; *specif* to conceal in order to observe or deceive

[2]**plant** *n* **1** any of a kingdom of living things (e g a green alga, moss, fern, conifer, or flowering plant) typically lacking locomotive movement or obvious nervous or sensory organs **2a** the buildings, machinery, etc employed in carrying on a trade or an industrial business **b** a factory or workshop for the manufacture of a particular product

[1]**plantain** /ˈplæntɨn/ *n* any of a genus of short-stemmed plants bearing dense spikes of minute greenish or brownish flowers

[2]**plantain** *n* (the angular greenish starchy fruit of) a type of banana plant

plantation /plænˈteɪʃən, plɑːn-/ *n* **1** (a place with) a usu large group of plants, esp trees, under cultivation **2** a settlement in a new country or region; a colony **3** an agricultural estate, usu worked by resident labour

planter /ˈplɑːntəʳ/ *n* **1** one who owns or operates a plantation **2** one who settles or founds a new colony

plaque /plæk/ *n* **1** a commemorative or decorative inscribed tablet of ceramic, wood, metal, etc **2** a film of mucus on a tooth that harbours bacteria

plasma /ˈplæzmə/ *n* the fluid part of blood, lymph, or milk as distinguished from suspended material

[1]**plaster** /ˈplɑːstəʳ/ *n* **1** a medicated or protective dressing **2** a pastelike mixture (e g of lime, water, and sand) that hardens on drying and is used esp for coating walls, ceilings, and partitions **3 plaster, plaster cast** a rigid dressing of gauze impregnated with plaster of paris for immobilizing a diseased or broken body part

[2]**plaster** *v* **1** to overlay or cover with (a) plaster **2a** to cover over or conceal as if with a coat of plaster **b** to smear (sthg) thickly (on); coat **3** to fasten (sthg) (to) or place (sthg) (on), esp conspicuously or in quantity **4** to inflict heavy damage, injury, or casualties on, esp by a concentrated or unremitting attack – infml

plasterboard /ˈplɑːstəbɔːd/ *n* a board with a plaster core used esp as a substitute for plaster on walls

plastered /ˈplɑːstəd/ *adj* drunk – infml

plaster of paris *n, often cap 2nd P* a white powdery plaster made from gypsum that when mixed with water forms a quicksetting paste used chiefly for casts and moulds

[1]**plastic** /ˈplæstɪk/ *adj* **1** capable of being moulded or modelled **2** supple, pliant **3** sculptural **4** made or consisting of a plastic **5** formed by or adapted to an artificial or conventional standard; synthetic – chiefly derog – **~ally** *adv* – **~ity** *n*

[2]**plastic** *n* any of numerous (synthetic) organic polymers that can be moulded, cast, extruded, etc into objects, films, or filaments

Plasticine /ˈplæstɨsiːn/ *trademark* – used for a modelling substance that remains plastic for a long period

plastic surgery *n* surgery concerned with the repair or cosmetic improvement of parts of the body chiefly by the grafting of tissue

[1]**plate** /pleɪt/ *n* **1a** a smooth flat thin usu rigid piece of material **b** an (external) scale or rigid layer of bone, horn, etc forming part of an animal body **2a** domestic utensils and tableware made of or plated with gold, silver, or base metals **b** a shallow usu circular vessel, made esp of china, from which food is eaten or served **3a** a prepared surface from which printing is done **b** a sheet of material (e g glass) coated with a light-sensitive photographic emulsion **c** an electrode in an accumulator **4** a horizontal structural member (e g a timber) that provides bearing and anchorage, esp for rafters or joists **5** the part of a denture that fits to the mouth **6** a full-page book illustration

[2]**plate** *v* to cover permanently with an adherent layer, esp of metal; *also* to deposit (e g a layer) on a surface – **plating** *n*

plateau /ˈplætəʊ/ *n, pl* **plateaux** **1** a usu extensive relatively flat land area raised sharply above adjacent land on at least 1 side **2** a relatively stable level, period, or condition

plate glass *n* rolled, ground, and polished sheet glass – **plate-glass** *adj*

platelayer /ˈpleɪtˌleɪəʳ/ *n, Br* a person who lays and maintains railway track

platform /ˈplætfɔːm/ *n* **1** a declaration of (political) principles and policies **2a** a raised surface at a railway station to facilitate access to trains **b** a raised flooring (e g for speakers) **3** a place or opportunity for public discussion **4** *chiefly Br* the area next to the entrance or exit of a bus

platinum /ˈplætɪ̣nəm/ *n* a heavy precious greyish white noncorroding metallic element used esp as a catalyst and for jewellery

platinum blonde *n* (sby having hair of) a pale silvery blond colour usu produced in human hair by bleach and bluish rinse

platitude /ˈplætɪ̣tjuːd/ *n* a banal, trite, or stale remark, esp when presented as if it were original and significant – **-tudinous** *adj*

platonic /pləˈtɒnɪk/ *adj* of or being a close relationship between 2 people in which sexual desire is absent or has been repressed or sublimated – **~ally** *adv*

platoon /pləˈtuːn/ *n* a subdivision of a military company normally consisting of 2 or more sections or squads

platter /ˈplætəʳ/ *n* a large often oval plate used esp for serving meat

platypus /ˈplætɪ̣pəs/ *n* a small aquatic Australian and Tasmanian primitive mammal that lays eggs and has a fleshy bill resembling that of a duck, webbed feet, and a broad flattened tail

plausible /ˈplɔːzəbəl/ *adj* **1** apparently fair, reasonable, or valid but often specious **2** *of a person* persuasive but deceptive – **-bly** *adv* – **-bility** *n*

[1]**play** /pleɪ/ *n* **1** the conduct, course, or (a particular) action in or of a game **2a** (children's spontaneous) recreational activity **b** the absence of serious or harmful intent; jest **3a** operation, activity **b** light, quick, transitory, or fitful movement **c** free or unimpeded motion **4a** the dramatized representation of an action or story on stage **b** a dramatic composition (for presentation in a theatre)

[2]**play** *v* **1a** to engage in sport or recreation **b(1)** to deal or behave frivolously, mockingly, or playfully – often + *around* or *about* **(2)** to make use of double meaning or of the similarity of sound of 2 words for stylistic or humorous effect – usu in *play on words* **c(1)** to deal with, handle, or manage – often + *it* **(2)** to exploit, manipulate **d** to pretend to engage in **e(1)** to perform or execute for amusement or to deceive or mock **(2)** to wreak **2a** to take advantage **b** to move or operate in a lively, irregular, or intermittent manner **c** to move or function freely within prescribed limits **d** to discharge repeatedly or in a stream **3** to act with special consideration so as to gain favour, approval, or sympathy – usu + *up to* **4a** to put on a performance of (a play) **b** to act or perform in or as **5a(1)** to

contend against in a game (2) to perform the duties associated with (a certain position) **b(1)** to make bets on (2) to operate on the basis of **c** to put into action in a game **d** to direct the course of (e g a ball); hit **6a** to perform music on an instrument **b** to perform music on **c** to perform music of a specified composer **d** to reproduce sounds, esp music, on (an apparatus) **7** to have (promiscuous or illicit) sexual relations – euph; usu in *play around* – **~er** *n*

playback /ˈpleɪbæk/ *n* (a device that provides for) the reproduction of recorded sound or pictures

play back *v* to listen to or look at material on (a usu recently recorded disc or tape)

playboy /ˈpleɪbɔɪ/ *n* a man who lives a life devoted chiefly to the pursuit of pleasure

play down *v* to cause to seem less important; minimize

playful /ˈpleɪfəl/ *adj* **1** full of fun; frolicsome **2** humorous, lighthearted – **~fully** *adv* – **~ness** *n*

playground /ˈpleɪgraʊnd/ *n* a piece of land for children to play on

playgroup /ˈpleɪgruːp/ *n, chiefly Br* a supervised group of children below school age who play together regularly

playhouse /ˈpleɪhaʊs/ *n* a theatre

playmate /ˈpleɪmeɪt/ *n* a companion in play

play-off *n* a final contest to determine a winner

play off *v* **1** to decide the winner of (a competition) or break (a tie) by a play-off **2** to set in opposition for one's own gain

playpen /ˈpleɪpen/ *n* a portable usu collapsible enclosure in which a baby or young child may play

plaything /ˈpleɪˌθɪŋ/ *n* a toy

play up *v* **1** to give special emphasis or prominence to **2** to cause pain or distress to **3** to behave in a disobedient or annoying manner

playwright /ˈpleɪraɪt/ *n* one who writes plays

plaza /ˈplɑːzə/ *n* a public square in a city or town

plea /pliː/ *n* **1** an accused person's answer to an indictment **2** sthg offered by way of excuse or justification **3** an earnest entreaty; an appeal

plea bargaining *n* pleading guilty to a lesser charge in order to avoid standing trial for a more serious one

plead /pliːd/ *v* **1** to make or answer an allegation in a legal proceeding **2** to make a specified plea **3a** to urge reasons for or against sthg **b** to entreat or appeal earnestly; implore – **~ing** *n*

pleasant /ˈplezənt/ *adj* **1** having qualities that tend to give pleasure; agreeable **2** *of a person* likable, friendly – **~ly** *adv*

pleasantry /ˈplezəntri/ *n* **1** an agreeable remark (made in order to be polite) **2** a humorous act or remark; a joke

please /pliːz/ *v* **1** to afford or give pleasure or satisfaction **2** to like, wish **3** to be willing – usu used in the imperative (1) to express a polite request (e g *please* come in) (2) to turn an apparent question into a request (e g can you shut it, *please*?) **4** to be the will or pleasure of – fml

pleasure /ˈpleʒəʳ/ *n* **1** (a state of) gratification **2** enjoyment, recreation **3** a source of delight or joy **4** a wish, desire – fml – **pleasure** *v* – **-rable** *adj* – **-rably** *adv*

[1]**pleat** /pliːt/ *v* to fold; *esp* to arrange in pleats

[2]**pleat** *n* a fold in cloth made by doubling material over on itself

[1]**plebeian** /plɪˈbiːən/ *n* a member of the (Roman) common people

[2]**plebeian** *adj* **1** of plebeians **2** crude or coarse in manner or style; common

plebiscite /ˈplebɪ̵sɪ̵t/ *n* a vote by the people of an entire country or district for or against a proposal

plectrum /ˈplektrəm/ *n, pl* **plectra** a small thin piece of plastic, metal, etc used to pluck the strings of a musical instrument

[1]**pledge** /pledʒ/ *n* **1** sthg delivered as security for an obligation (e g a debt) **2** the state of being held as a security **3** a token, sign, or earnest of sthg else **4** a binding promise to do or forbear

[2]**pledge** *v* **1** to deposit as security for fulfilment of a contract or obligation

2 to drink the health of **3** to bind by a pledge **4** to give a promise of

plenary /ˈpliːnəri/ *adj* **1** absolute, unqualified **2** attended by all entitled to be present

plenipotentiary /ˌplenɪ̣pəˈtenʃəri/ *n or adj* (sby, esp a diplomatic agent) invested with full power to transact business

¹plenty /ˈplenti/ *n* **1a** *sing or pl in constr* a full or more than adequate amount or supply **b** a large number or amount **2** copiousness, plentifulness – **-tiful** *adj*

²plenty *adv* **1** quite, abundantly **2** *chiefly NAm* to a considerable or extreme degree; very (e g *plenty* hungry) *USE* infml

pleurisy /ˈpluərɪ̣si/ *n* inflammation of the membrane surrounding the lungs, usu with fever and painful breathing

pliable /ˈplaɪəbəl/ *adj* **1** easily bent without breaking; flexible **2** yielding readily to others; compliant – **-bility** *n*

pliant /ˈplaɪənt/ *adj* pliable

pliers /ˈplaɪəz/ *n pl* a pair of pincers with long jaws for holding small objects or for bending and cutting wire

¹plight /plaɪt/ *v* to put or give in pledge; engage

²plight *n* an (unpleasant or difficult) state; a predicament

plimsoll /ˈplɪmsəl, -səul/ *n, Br* a shoe with a rubber sole and canvas top worn esp for sports

Plimsoll line *n* a set of markings indicating the draught levels to which a vessel may legally be loaded in various seasons and waters

plod /plɒd/ *v* **1** to tread slowly or heavily along or over **2** to work laboriously and monotonously

¹plonk /plɒŋk/ *v* to set down suddenly

²plonk *n, chiefly Br* cheap or inferior wine – infml

plop /plɒp/ *v* **1** to drop or move suddenly with a sound suggestive of sthg dropping into water **2** to allow (the body) to drop heavily –**plop** *n*

¹plot /plɒt/ *n* **1** a small piece of land, esp one used or designated for a specific purpose **2** the plan or main story of a literary work **3** a secret plan for accomplishing a usu evil or unlawful end; an intrigue

²plot *v* **1** to make a plot, map, or plan of **2** to draw (a curve) by means of plotted points **3** to plan or contrive, esp secretly **4** to invent or devise the plot of (a literary work) – **~ter** *n*

¹plough, *NAm* **plow** /plau/ *n* **1** an implement used to cut, lift, and turn over soil, esp in preparing ground for sowing **2** ploughed land

²plough *v* **1** to make or work with a plough **2** to cut into, open, or make furrows or ridges in (as if) with a plough – often + *up* **3** to force a way, esp violently **4** to proceed steadily and laboriously; plod **5** to fail an exam

plough back *v* to reinvest (profits) in an industry

ploughman's lunch *n* a cold lunch of bread, cheese, and usu pickled onions often served in a public house

ploughshare /ˈplauʃeəʳ/ *n* the part of a plough that cuts the furrow

plover /ˈplʌvəʳ/ *n* any of numerous wading birds with a short beak and usu a stout compact build

ploy /plɔɪ/ *n* sthg devised or contrived, esp to embarrass or frustrate an opponent

¹pluck /plʌk/ *v* **1** to pull or pick off or out **2** to pick, pull, or grasp at; *also* to play (an instrument) in this manner

²pluck *n* **1** an act or instance of plucking or pulling **2** courage and determination

plucky /ˈplʌki/ *adj* marked by courage; spirited – **-kily** *adv* – **-kiness** *n*

¹plug /plʌg/ *n* **1** a stopper **2** a flat compressed cake of (chewing) tobacco **3** a small core or segment removed from a larger object **4** a device having usu 3 pins projecting from an insulated case for making electrical connection with a suitable socket; *also* the electrical socket **5** a piece of favourable publicity (e g for a commercial product) usu incorporated in general matter – infml

²plug *v* **1** to block, close, etc (as if) by inserting a plug **2** to hit with a bullet **3** to advertise or publicize insistently **4** to work doggedly and persistently *on*

plug in *v* to attach or connect to a power point

plum /plʌm/ *n* **1** (any of numerous trees that bear) an edible globular to oval smooth-skinned fruit with an oblong seed **2** sthg excellent or superior; *esp* an opportunity or position offering exceptional advantages **3** a dark reddish purple colour

plumage /'pluːmɪdʒ/ *n* the entire covering of feathers of a bird

¹plumb /plʌm/ *n* **1** a lead weight attached to a cord and used to indicate a vertical line **2** any of various weights (e g a sinker for a fishing line or a lead for sounding)

²plumb *adv* **1** straight down or up; vertically **2** exactly, precisely

³plumb *v* **1** to examine minutely and critically, esp so as to achieve complete understanding **2** to adjust, measure, or test by a plumb line **3** to supply with or install as plumbing – often + *in*

⁴plumb *adj* **1** exactly vertical or true **2** downright, complete – infml

plumber /'plʌmə^r/ *n* sby who installs, repairs, and maintains water piping and fittings

plumbing /'plʌmɪŋ/ *n* the apparatus (e g pipes and fixtures) concerned in the distribution and use of water in a building

plume /pluːm/ *n* **1** a usu large feather or cluster of feathers esp worn as an ornament **2** sthg resembling a feather (e g in shape, appearance, or lightness): e g **a** a feathery or feather-like animal or plant part; *esp* a full bushy tail **b** a trail of smoke, blowing snow, etc – **~d** *adj*

plummet /'plʌmɪ̣t/ *v* to fall sharply and abruptly

¹plump /plʌmp/ *v* to drop or sink suddenly or heavily

²plump *adj* having a full rounded form; slightly fat

plump up *v* to cause to fill or swell out

plumule /'pluːmjuːl/ *n* the primary bud of a plant embryo

¹plunder /'plʌndə^r/ *v* **1** to pillage, sack **2** to take, esp by force (e g in war); steal – **~er** *n*

²plunder *n* sthg taken by force, theft, or fraud; loot

¹plunge /plʌndʒ/ *v* **1** to thrust or cast oneself (as if) into water **2** to cause to penetrate quickly and forcibly **3a** to be thrown headlong or violently forwards and downwards; *also* to move oneself in such a manner **b** to act with reckless haste; enter suddenly or unexpectedly **4** to descend or dip suddenly

²plunge *n* a dive; *also* a swim

plunger /'plʌndʒə^r/ *n* **1** a device (e g a piston in a pump) that acts with a plunging or thrusting motion **2** a rubber suction cup on a handle used to free plumbing from blockages

pluperfect /pluː'pɜːfɪkt/ *adj* past perfect

plural /'plʊərəl/ *adj* **1** of or being a word form (e g *we, houses, cattle*) denoting more than 1, or in some languages more than 2 or 3, persons, things, or instances **2** consisting of or containing more than 1 (kind or class) – **~ly** *adv* – **~ize** *v* – **~ism** *n* – **~ity** *n*

¹plus /plʌs/ *prep* **1** increased by; with the addition of **2** and also

²plus *n* **1** an added quantity **2** a positive factor, quantity, or quality

³plus *adj* **1** algebraically or electrically positive **2** additional and welcome **3** greater than that specified

⁴plus *conj* and moreover

plus fours *n pl* loose wide trousers gathered on a band and finishing just below the knee

¹plush /plʌʃ/ *n* a fabric with an even pile longer and less dense than that of velvet

²plush, plushy *adj* luxurious, showy

Pluto /'pluːtəʊ/ *n* the planet furthest from the sun

plutocracy /pluː'tɒkrəsi/ *n* (government by) a controlling class of wealthy people

plutonium /pluː'təʊnɪəm/ *n* a radioactive metallic element similar to uranium that is formed in atomic reactors

¹ply /plaɪ/ *n* **1a** a strand in a yarn, wool, etc **b** any of several layers (e g of cloth) usu sewn or laminated together **2** (any of the veneer sheets forming) plywood

²ply **1** to apply oneself steadily **2** *of a boatman, taxi driver, etc* to wait regularly in a particular place for custom – esp in *ply for hire* **3** to go or travel regularly

plywood /ˈplaɪwʊd/ *n* a light structural material of thin sheets of wood glued or cemented together

pneumatic /njuːˈmætɪk/ *adj* **1** moved or worked by air pressure **2** adapted for holding or inflated with compressed air – **~ally** *adv*

pneumoconiosis /ˌnjuːməʊkəʊniˈəʊsɪ̈s/ *n* a crippling disease of the lungs, esp of miners, caused by the habitual inhalation of irritant particles

pneumonia /njuːˈməʊnɪə/ *n* localized or widespread inflammation of the lungs with change from an air-filled to a solid consistency, caused by infection or irritants

[1]**poach** /pəʊtʃ/ *v* to cook (e g fish or an egg) in simmering liquid

[2]**poach** *v* **1** to take game or fish illegally **2** to trespass *on* or *upon* – **~er** *n*

pock /pɒk/ *n* a spot or blister caused by a disease (e g smallpox)

[1]**pocket** /ˈpɒkɪ̈t/ *n* **1** a small bag that is sewn or inserted in a garment so that it is open at the top or side **2** any of several openings at the corners or sides of a billiard table into which balls are propelled **3** a small isolated area or group

[2]**pocket** *v* **1** to appropriate to one's own use; steal **2** to accept; put up with **3** to drive (a ball) into a pocket of a billiard table

[3]**pocket** *adj* small, miniature

pocketknife /ˈpɒkɪ̈tnaɪf/ *n* a knife that has 1 or more blades that fold into the handle so that it can be carried in the pocket

pocket money *n* money for small personal expenses, esp as given to a child

pockmark /ˈpɒkmɑːk/ *n* a mark or pit (like that) caused by smallpox – **~ed** *adj*

[1]**pod** /pɒd/ *n* **1** a long seed vessel or fruit, esp of the pea, bean, or other leguminous plant **2** an egg case of a locust or similar insect

[2]**pod** *v* to remove (e g peas) from the pod

podgy /ˈpɒdʒi/ *adj* short and plump; chubby – **-giness** *n*

poem /ˈpəʊɪ̈m/ *n* **1** an individual work of poetry **2** a creation, experience, or object suggesting a poem

poet /ˈpəʊɪ̈t/, *fem* **poetess** *n* **1** one who writes poetry **2** a creative artist with special sensitivity to his/her medium – **~ical** *adj* – **~ic** *adj* – **~ically** *adv*

poetic justice *n* an outcome in which vice is punished and virtue rewarded in an (ironically) appropriate manner

poet laureate *n* a poet appointed for life by the sovereign as a member of the British royal household and expected to compose poems for state occasions

poetry /ˈpəʊɪ̈tri/ *n* **1a** metrical writing; verse **b** a poet's compositions; poems **2** writing that is arranged to formulate a concentrated imaginative awareness of experience through meaning, sound, and rhythm **3** a quality of beauty, grace, and great feeling

pogo stick /ˈpəʊgəʊ ˌstɪk/ *n* a pole with a spring at the bottom and 2 footrests on which sby stands and can move along with a series of jumps

pogrom /ˈpɒgrəm/ *n* an organized massacre, esp of Jews

poignant /ˈpɔɪnjənt/ *adj* **1a** painfully affecting the feelings; distressing **b** deeply affecting; touching **2** designed to make an impression; cutting – **~ly** *adv* – **-nancy** *n*

[1]**point** /pɔɪnt/ *n* **1a** an individual detail; an item **b** the most important essential in a discussion or matter **2** an end or object to be achieved; a purpose **3a** a geometric element that has a position but no extent or magnitude **b** a precisely indicated position **c** an exact moment; *esp the* moment before sthg **d** a particular step, stage, or degree in development **4a** the sharp or narrowly rounded end of sthg; a tip **b** the tip of the toes – used in ballet; usu pl **5a** a projecting usu tapering piece of land **b(1)** the tip of a projecting body part **(2)** a tine **6a** a very small mark **b(1)** a punctuation mark; *esp* full stop **(2)** a decimal point **7** any of the 32 evenly spaced compass direc-

tions; *also* the 11° 15′ interval between 2 successive points **8** a unit of counting in the scoring of a game or contest **9** a fielding position in cricket near to the batsman on the off side **10** *pl, Br* a device made of usu 2 movable rails and necessary connections and designed to turn a locomotive or train from one track to another

[2]**point** *v* **1** to give added force, emphasis, or piquancy to **2** to scratch out the old mortar from the joints of (e g a brick wall) and fill in with new material **3a** to indicate the position or direction of sthg, esp by extending a finger **b** *of a gundog* to indicate the presence and place of (game) for a hunter **4** to lie extended, aimed, or turned in a particular direction

point-blank *adj* **1** so close to a target that a missile fired will travel in a straight line to the mark **2** direct, blunt

point-duty *n* traffic regulation carried out usu by a policeman stationed at a particular point

pointed /ˈpɔɪntɪ̣d/ *adj* **1** having a point **2a** pertinent **b** aimed at a particular person or group **3** conspicuous, marked – **~ly** *adv*

pointer /ˈpɔɪntəʳ/ *n* **1** a rod used to direct attention **2** a large strong slender smooth-haired gundog that hunts by scent and indicates the presence of game by pointing **3** a useful suggestion or hint; a tip

pointless /ˈpɔɪntlɪ̣s/ *adj* devoid of meaning, relevance, or purpose; senseless – **~ly** *adv* – **~ness** *n*

point of order *n* a question relating to procedure in an official meeting

point of view *n* a position from which sthg is considered or evaluated

point out *v* to direct sby's attention to

pointsman /ˈpɔɪntsmən/ *n* a person in charge of railway points

point-to-point *n* a usu cross-country steeplechase for amateur riders

[1]**poise** /pɔɪz/ *v* **1** to hold supported or suspended without motion in a steady position **2** to put into readiness; brace

[2]**poise** *n* **1** easy self-possessed assurance of manner **2** a particular way of carrying oneself

poised /pɔɪzd/ *adj* **1** marked by balance or equilibrium or by easy composure of manner **2** in readiness

[1]**poison** /ˈpɔɪzən/ *n* a substance that through its chemical action kills, injures, or impairs an organism

[2]**poison** *v* **1** to injure, kill, treat, etc with poison **2** to exert a harmful influence on; corrupt – **~er** *n*

poisonous /ˈpɔɪzənəs/ *adj* having the properties or effects of poison – **~ly** *adv*

[1]**poke** /pəʊk/ *n, chiefly dial NAm* a bag, sack

[2]**poke** *v* **1a** to prod, jab **b** to stir the coals or logs of (a fire) so as to promote burning **2a** to look *about* or *through* sthg without system; rummage **b** to meddle **3** to become stuck out or forwards; protrude **4** *of a man* to have sexual intercourse with – vulg

[3]**poke** *n* **1** a quick thrust; a jab **2** a punch – infml **3** an act of sexual intercourse – vulg

[1]**poker** /ˈpəʊkəʳ/ *n* a metal rod for poking a fire

[2]**poker** *n* any of several card games in which a player bets that the value of his/her hand is greater than that of the hands held by others

poker face *n* an inscrutable face that reveals no hint of a person's thoughts or feelings – **-faced** *adj*

pokerwork /ˈpəʊkəwɜːk/ *n* (the art of doing) decorative work burnt into a material by a heated instrument

poky *also* **pokey** /ˈpəʊki/ *adj* small and cramped – infml – **pokiness** *n*

polar /ˈpəʊləʳ/ *adj* **1a** of, coming from, or characteristic of (the region round) a geographical pole **b** *esp of an orbit* passing over a planet's N and S poles **2** of 1 or more poles (e g of a magnet) **3** resembling a pole or axis round which all else revolves; pivotal

polar bear *n* a large creamy-white bear that inhabits arctic regions

polarity /pəˈlærɪ̣ti/ *n* **1** the quality or condition of a body that has opposite or contrasted properties or powers in opposite directions **2** attraction towards a particular object or in a specific direction **3** the particular electrical state of being either positive or negative **4** (an instance of) total opposition – **-ize** *v*

polder /ˈpəʊldəʳ/ *n* an area of low land reclaimed from a body of water, esp in the Netherlands.

¹pole /pəʊl/ *n* **1a** a long slender usu cylindrical object (e g a length of wood) **b** a shaft which extends from the front axle of a wagon between the draught animals **2** a unit of length equal to 5½ yd (about 5m) **3** the most favourable front-row position on the starting line of a (motor) race

²pole *v* to push or propel (e g a boat) with poles

³pole *n* **1** either extremity of an axis of (a body, esp the earth, resembling) a sphere **2a** either of 2 related opposites **b** a point of guidance or attraction **3a** either of the 2 terminals of an electric cell, battery, or dynamo **b** any of 2 or more regions in a magnetized body at which the magnetic flux density is concentrated

Pole *n* a native or inhabitant of Poland

¹poleaxe /pəʊlæks/ *n* **1** a battle-axe with a short handle and often a hook or spike opposite the blade **2** an axe used, esp formerly, in slaughtering cattle

²poleaxe *v* to attack, strike, or fell (as if) with a poleaxe

polecat /ˈpəʊlkæt/ *n* **1** a European flesh-eating mammal of which the ferret is considered a domesticated variety **2** *NAm* a skunk

polestar /ˈpəʊlstɑːʳ/ *n* **1** a directing principle; a guide **2** a centre of attraction

Pole Star *n* the star in the constellation Ursa Minor that lies very close to the N celestial pole

pole vault *n* (an athletic field event consisting of) a jump for height over a crossbar with the aid of a pole

police /pəˈliːs/ *n* **1** the department of government concerned with maintenance of public order and enforcement of laws **2a** *sing or pl in constr* a police force **b** *pl in constr* policemen – **police** *v*

policeman /pəˈliːsmən/, *fem* **policewoman** *n* a member of a police force

police state *n* a political unit characterized by repressive governmental control of political, economic, and social life, usu enforced by (secret) police

¹policy /ˈpɒlɪ̤si/ *n* **1** a definite course of action selected from among alternatives to guide and determine present and future decisions **2** an overall plan embracing general goals and procedures, esp of a governmental body

²policy *n* (a document embodying) a contract of insurance

polio /ˈpəʊliəʊ/, **poliomyelitis** /ˌpəʊliəʊmaɪəˈlaɪtɪ̤s/ *n* an infectious virus disease, esp of children, characterized by motor paralysis and atrophy of skeletal muscles often leading to permanent disability or deformity

¹polish /ˈpɒlɪʃ/ *v* **1** to make smooth and glossy, usu by friction **2** to refine in manners or condition **3** to bring to a highly developed, finished, or refined state; perfect – often + *up* – **~er** *n*

²polish *n* **1a** a smooth glossy surface **b** freedom from rudeness or coarseness **2** a preparation used to produce a gloss and often a colour for the protection and decoration of a surface

¹Polish /ˈpəʊlɪʃ/ *adj* (characteristic) of Poland

²Polish *n* the language of the Poles

polish off *v* to dispose of rapidly or completely

politburo /ˈpɒlitˌbjʊərəu, pəˈlɪt-/ *n* the principal committee of a Communist party

polite /pəˈlaɪt/ *adj* **1** showing or characterized by correct social usage; refined **2** marked by consideration and deference; courteous – **~ly** *adv* – **~ness** *n*

politic /ˈpɒlɪtɪ̤k/ *adj* **1** *of a person* shrewd and sagacious in managing, contriving, or dealing **2** *of a policy* expedient

political /pəˈlɪtɪkəl/ *adj* **1** of government **2a** of (party) politics **b** sensitive to politics – **~ly** *adv*

political economy *n* a social science dealing with the interrelationship of political and economic processes – **-mist** *n*

politician /ˌpɒlɪ̤ˈtɪʃən/ *n* a person experienced or engaged in politics

politics /'pɒlətɪks/ *n pl but sing or pl in constr* **1** the art or science of government **2a** political affairs; *specif* competition between interest groups in a government **b** political life as a profession **3** sby's political sympathies

polka /'pɒlkə, 'pəʊlkə/ *n* (music for or in the rhythm of) a vivacious dance of Bohemian origin in duple time

polka dot *n* any of many regularly distributed dots in a textile design

[1]**poll** /pəʊl/ *n* **1** (the hairy top or back of) the head **2** the broad or flat end of the head of a striking tool (e g a hammer) **3a** the casting of votes **b** the place where votes are cast – usu pl with sing. meaning **c** the number of votes recorded **4** a survey conducted by the questioning of people selected at random or by quota

[2]**poll** *v* **1** to cut off or cut short the horns of (a cow) **2** to pollard (a tree) **3** to receive and record the votes of; *also* to cast one's vote **4** to question in a poll

[3]**poll** *n* a polled animal

pollard /'pɒləd/ *n* a tree cut back to the main stem to promote the growth of a dense head of foliage – **pollard** *v*

pollen /'pɒlən/ *n* (a fine dust of) the minute granular spores discharged from the anther of the flower of a flowering plant that serve to fertilize the ovules

pollinate /'pɒləneɪt/ *v* to fertilize with pollen – **-nation** *n*

pollute /pə'luːt/ *v* **1** to make morally impure; defile **2** to make physically impure or unclean; *esp* to contaminate (an environment), esp with man-made waste – **-tion** *n*

polo /'pəʊləʊ/ *n* a game played by teams of usu 4 players on ponies using mallets with long flexible handles to drive a wooden ball into the opponent's goal

polonaise /,pɒlə'neɪz/ *n* (music in moderate 3/4 time for) a stately Polish processional dance

polo neck *n, chiefly Br* (a jumper with) a very high closely fitting collar worn folded over

polony /pə'ləʊni/ *n* a dry sausage of partly cooked meat, esp pork

poltergeist /'pɒltəgaɪst/ *n* a noisy mischievous ghost believed to be responsible for unexplained noises and physical damage

poly /'pɒli/ *n, pl* **polys** *Br* a polytechnic – infml

polyandry /,pɒli'ændri/ *n* having more than 1 husband at a time – **-rous** *adj*

polyester /'pɒliestəʳ, ,pɒli'estəʳ/ *n* a polymer containing ester groups used esp in making fibres, resins, or plastics

polyethylene /,pɒli'eθəliːn/ *n* polythene

polygamy /pə'lɪgəmi/ *n* being married to more than 1 person at a time; *esp* marriage to more than 1 wife – **-mous** *adj*

[1]**polyglot** /'pɒliglɒt/ *n* **1** one who is polyglot **2** a mixture or confusion of languages

[2]**polyglot** *adj* **1** multilingual **2** containing matter in several languages

polygon /'pɒlɪgən/ *n* a closed plane figure bounded by straight lines – **~al** *adj*

polyhedron /,pɒli'hiːdrən/ *n, pl* **polyhedra** a solid formed by plane faces – **-ral** *adj*

polymer /'pɒləməʳ/ *n* a chemical compound or mixture of compounds containing repeating structural units and formed by chemical combination of many small molecules

polyp /'pɒləp/ *n* **1** a primitive animal with a hollow cylindrical body attached at one end and having a central mouth surrounded by tentacles at the other **2** a projecting mass of tissue (e g a tumour) – **~ous** *adj*

polyphony /pə'lɪfəni/ *n* a style of musical composition in which 2 or more independent but organically related voice parts sound against one another – **-nic** *adj*

polystyrene /,pɒlɪ'staɪəriːn/ *n* a rigid plastic used esp in moulded products, foams, and sheet materials

[1]**polytechnic** /,pɒlɪ'teknɪk/ *adj* relating to or devoted to instruction in many technical arts or applied sciences

[2]**polytechnic** *n* any of a number of British institutions offering full-time, sandwich, and part-time courses in

various subjects but with a bias towards the vocational

polytheism /'pɒlɪθiːɪzəm/ *n* belief in or worship of 2 or more gods

polythene /'pɒlɨθiːn/ *n* any of various lightweight plastics used esp for packaging and bowls, buckets, etc

pomander /pə'mændəʳ/ *n* a mixture of aromatic substances enclosed in a perforated bag or box and used to scent clothes or linen

pomegranate /'pɒmɨgrænɨt/ *n* (an Old World tree that bears) a thick-skinned reddish fruit about the size of an orange that contains many seeds each surrounded by a tart edible crimson pulp

pommel /'pʌməl/ *n* **1** the knob on the hilt of a sword **2** the protuberance at the front and top of a saddle

pommel horse *n* a leather-covered horizontal rectangular or cylindrical piece of gymnastic apparatus with 2 handles on the top used for swinging and balancing exercises

Pommy, Pommie /'pɒmi/ *n, often not cap, Austr & NZ* a British person; *esp* a British immigrant

pomp /pɒmp/ *n* **1** a show of magnificence; splendour **2** ostentatious or specious display

[1]**pom-pom** /'pɒm ˌpɒm/ *n* an automatic gun mounted on ships in pairs, fours, or eights

[2]**pom-pom** *n* an ornamental ball or tuft used esp on clothing, hats, etc

pompous /'pɒmpəs/ *adj* **1** self-important, pretentious **2** excessively elevated or ornate – **~ly** *adv* – **-posity, ~ness** *n*

[1]**ponce** /pɒns/ *n, Br* **1** a pimp **2** a man who behaves in an effeminate manner – infml

[2]**ponce** *v* **1** to pimp **2** to act in a frivolous, showy, or effeminate manner – usu + *around* or *about*

poncho /'pɒntʃəʊ/ *n* a cloak resembling a blanket with a slit in the middle for the head

pond /pɒnd/ *n* a body of (fresh) water usu smaller than a lake

ponder /'pɒndəʳ/ *v* **1** to weigh in the mind; assess **2** to review mentally; think over

ponderous /'pɒndərəs/ *adj* **1** unwieldy or clumsy because of weight and size **2** oppressively or unpleasantly dull; pedestrian – **~ly** *adv* – **~ness** *n*

pong /pɒŋ/ *v or n, Br* (to emit) an unpleasant smell; stink – infml – **~y** *adj*

poniard /'pɒnjəd/ *n* a small dagger

pontiff /'pɒntɨf/ *n* a bishop; *specif* the pope

pontifical /pɒn'tɪfɪkəl/ *adj* **1** of a pontiff **2** pretentiously dogmatic

[1]**pontificate** /pɒn'tɪfɪkɨt/ *n* the state, office, or term of office of the pope

[2]**pontificate** /pɒn'tɪfɨkeɪt/ *v* to deliver dogmatic opinions

[1]**pontoon** /pɒn'tuːn/ *n* a flat-bottomed boat or portable float (used in building a floating temporary bridge)

[2]**pontoon** *n* a gambling card game in which the object is to be dealt cards scoring more than those of the dealer up to but not exceeding 21

pony /'pəʊni/ *n* a small horse; *esp* a member of any of several breeds of very small stocky horses under 14.2 hands in height

ponytail /'pəʊniteɪl/ *n* a hairstyle in which the hair is drawn back tightly and tied high at the back of the head

poodle /'puːdl/ *n* (any of) a breed of active intelligent dogs with a thick curly coat which is of 1 colour only

poof, pouf /puːf/ *n* an effeminate or homosexual man

pooh-pooh /ˌpuː'puː/ *v* to express contempt (for)

[1]**pool** /puːl/ *n* **1** a small and relatively deep body of usu fresh water (e g a still place in a stream or river) **2** a small body of standing liquid; a puddle

[2]**pool** *n* **1** an aggregate stake to which each player of a game has contributed **2** any of various games played on a billiard table with 6 pockets and often 15 numbered balls **3** a facility, service, or group of people providing a service for a number of people (e g the members of a business organization) **4** *pl the* football pools

[3]**pool** *v* to contribute to a common stock (e g of resources or effort)

[1]**poop** /puːp/ *n* an enclosed superstructure at the stern of a ship above the main deck

[2]poop *v, chiefly NAm* to put out of breath; *also* to tire out

poor /pʊəʳ/ *adj* **1** lacking material possessions **2** less than adequate; meagre **3** exciting pity **4** inferior in quality, value, or workmanship **5** humble, unpretentious – **~ly** *adv* – **~ness** *n*

poor law *n* a law that in former times provided for the relief of the poor

poorly /ˈpʊəli, ˈpɔːli/ *adj* somewhat ill

[1]pop /pɒp/ *v* **1** to push, put, or thrust *out* suddenly **2** to cause to explode or burst open **3** to protrude from the sockets **4** *Br* to pawn

[2]pop *n* **1** a popping sound **2** a flavoured fizzy drink

[3]pop *adv* like or with a pop; suddenly – infml

[4]pop *n, chiefly NAm* a father – infml

[5]pop *adj* popular: e g **a** of pop music **b** of or constituting a mass culture widely disseminated through the mass media

[6]pop *n* pop music

pop art *n, often cap P&A* art that incorporates everyday objects from popular culture and the mass media (e g comic strips)

popcorn /ˈpɒpkɔːn/ *n* (the popped kernels of) a maize whose kernels burst open when heated to form a white starchy mass

pope /pəʊp/ *n* **1** *often cap* the prelate who as bishop of Rome is the head of the Roman Catholic church **2** a priest of an Eastern church

pop-eyed *adj* having staring or bulging eyes (e g as a result of surprise or excitement)

popgun /ˈpɒpgʌn/ *n* a toy gun that shoots a cork or pellet and produces a popping sound; *also* an inadequate or inefficient firearm

poplar /ˈpɒplər/ *n* (the wood of) any of a genus of slender quick-growing trees (e g an aspen) of the willow family

poplin /ˈpɒpl̥ɪn/ *n* a strong usu cotton fabric in plain weave with crosswise ribs

pop music *n* modern commercially promoted popular music that is usu short and simple and has a strong beat

pop off *v* **1** to leave suddenly **2** to die unexpectedly **USE** infml

popper /ˈpɒpəʳ/ *n, chiefly Br* a press-stud

poppet /ˈpɒpɪ̈t/ *n* a lovable or enchanting person or animal – infml

popping crease *n* either of the lines behind which the foot or bat of a batsman must be grounded in cricket to avoid being run out or stumped

poppy /ˈpɒpi/ *n* any of several genera of plants with showy flowers and capsular fruits including the opium poppy and several other plants cultivated for their ornamental value

poppycock /ˈpɒpikɒk/ *n* empty talk; nonsense – infml

populace /ˈpɒpjʊləs/ *n sing or pl in constr* the (common) people; the masses

popular /ˈpɒpjʊləʳ/ *adj* **1** (suited to the needs, means, tastes, or understanding) of the general public **2** having general currency **3** commonly liked or approved – **~ity** *n* – **~ize** *v* – **~ly** *adv*

populate /ˈpɒpjʊleɪt/ *v* **1** to have a place in; occupy, inhabit **2** to supply or provide with inhabitants; people

population /ˌpɒpjʊˈleɪʃən/ *n* **1** *sing or pl in constr* the whole number of people or inhabitants in a country or region **2** *sing or pl in constr* a body of people or individuals having a quality or characteristic in common **3** a set (e g of individual people or items) from which samples are taken for statistical measurement

populist /ˈpɒpjʊlɪ̈st/ *n* **1** a member of a political party claiming to represent the common people **2** a believer in the rights, wisdom, or virtues of the common people

populous /ˈpɒpjʊləs/ *adj* densely populated – **~ness** *n*

porcelain /ˈpɔːslɪ̈n/ *n* **1** a type of hard translucent white ceramic ware made from a mixture of kaolin, quartz, and feldspar fired at a high temperature **2** a type of translucent ceramic ware made from a mixture of refined clay and ground glass fired at a low temperature

porch /pɔːtʃ/ *n* **1** a covered usu projecting entrance to a building **2** *NAm* a veranda

porcupine /ˈpɔːkjʊpaɪn/ *n* any of various large rodents with stiff sharp erectile bristles mingled with the hair

[1]**pore** /pɔːʳ/ *v* **1** to study closely or attentively **2** to reflect or meditate steadily ***USE*** usu + *on, over,* or *upon*

[2]**pore** *n* a minute opening; *esp* one (e g in a membrane, esp the skin, or between soil particles) through which fluids pass or are absorbed

pork /pɔːk/ *n* the flesh of a pig used as food

porker /ˈpɔːkəʳ/ *n* a young pig fattened for food

porky /ˈpɔːki/ *adj* fat, fleshy – infml

porn /pɔːn/ *n* pornography – infml

pornography /pɔːˈnɒgrəfi/ *n* (books, photographs, films, etc containing) the depiction of erotic behaviour intended to cause sexual excitement – **-pher** *n* – **-phic** *adj* – **-phically** *adv*

porous /ˈpɔːrəs/ *adj* **1** having or full of pores or spaces **2** allowing liquids to pass through – **~ness** *n*

porpoise /ˈpɔːpəs/ *n* a blunt-snouted usu largely black whale about 2m (6ft) long

porridge /ˈpɒrɪdʒ/ *n* **1** a soft food made by boiling oatmeal in milk or water until thick **2** *Br* time spent in prison – slang

porringer /ˈpɒrɪ̣ndʒəʳ/ *n* a small bowl from which esp soft or liquid foods (e g porridge) are eaten

[1]**port** /pɔːt/ *n* a town or city with a harbour where ships may take on or discharge cargo or passengers

[2]**port** *n* **1** an opening (e g in machinery) for intake or exhaust of a fluid **2** an opening in a ship's side to admit light or air or to load cargo **3** a hole in an armoured vehicle or fortification through which guns may be fired

[3]**port** *adj or n* (of or at) the left side of a ship or aircraft looking forwards

[4]**port** *v* to turn or put (a helm) to the left – used chiefly as a command

[5]**port** *n* a fortified sweet wine of rich taste and aroma made in Portugal

portable /ˈpɔːtəbəl/ *n or adj* (sthg) capable of being carried or moved about – **-bility** *n*

portage /ˈpɔːtɪdʒ/ *n* **1** the carrying of boats or goods overland from one body of water to another **2** the route followed in portage; *also* a place where such a transfer is necessary – **portage** *v*

portal /ˈpɔːtl/ *n* a (grand or imposing) door or entrance

portcullis /pɔːtˈkʌlɪ̣s/ *n* a usu iron or wood grating that can prevent entry to a fortified place by being lowered into a gateway

portend /pɔːˈtend/ *v* **1** to give an omen or fore warning sign of; bode **2** to indicate, signify

portent /ˈpɔːtent/ *n* **1** sthg foreshadowing a coming event; an omen **2** prophetic indication or significance

portentous /pɔːˈtentəs/ *adj* **1** eliciting amazement or wonder; prodigious **2** self-consciously weighty; pompous – **~ly** *adv*

[1]**porter** /ˈpɔːtəʳ/ *n* a gatekeeper or doorkeeper, esp of a large building, who usu regulates entry and answers enquiries

[2]**porter** *n* **1** sby who carries burdens; *specif* sby employed to carry luggage **2** a heavy dark brown beer – **~age** *n*

porterhouse /ˈpɔːtəhaʊs/ *n* a large steak cut from the back end of the sirloin above the ribs and containing part of the fillet

portfolio /pɔːtˈfəʊliəʊ/ *n* **1** a hinged cover or flexible case for carrying loose papers, pictures, etc **2** the office of a government minister or member of a cabinet **3** the securities held by an investor

porthole /ˈpɔːthəʊl/ *n* a usu glazed opening, esp in the side of a ship or aircraft

portico /ˈpɔːtɪkəʊ/ *n* a colonnade or covered veranda, usu at the entrance of a building and characteristic of classical architecture

[1]**portion** /ˈpɔːʃən/ *n* **1** a part or share of sthg; *esp* a helping of food **2** an individual's lot or fate

[2]**portion** *v* to divide into portions; distribute – often + *out*

portly /ˈpɔːtli/ *adj* rotund, stout – **-liness** *n*

[1]**portmanteau** /pɔːtˈmæntəʊ/ *n, pl* **portmanteaus, portmanteaux** a trunk for a traveller's belongings that opens into 2 equal parts

[2]portmanteau *adj* combining more than 1 use or quality

portmanteau word *n* a word (e g *brunch*) formed by combining other (parts of) words

port of call *n* **1** a port where ships customarily stop during a voyage **2** a stop included in an itinerary

portrait /'pɔːtrɨt/ *n* **1** a pictorial likeness of a person **2** a verbal portrayal or representation

portray /pɔː'treɪ/ *v* **1** to make a picture of; depict **2a** to describe in words **b** to play the role of – **~al** *n*

Portuguese /ˌpɔːtʃʊ'giːz/ *n* **1** a native or inhabitant of Portugal **2** the language of esp Portugal and Brazil

Portuguese man-of-war *n* any of several large floating jellyfishes with very long stinging tentacles

[1]pose /pəʊz/ *v* **1** to assume a posture or attitude, usu for artistic purposes **2** to affect an attitude or character; posture – usu + *as* **3** to present for attention or consideration

[2]pose *n* **1** a sustained posture; *esp* one assumed for artistic purposes **2** an assumed attitude of mind or mode of behaviour

[1]poser /'pəʊzəʳ/ *n* a puzzling or baffling question

[2]poser, poseur *n* an affected or insincere person

posh /pɒʃ/ *adj* **1** very fine; splendid **2** socially exclusive or fashionable – often derog *USE* infml

[1]position /pə'zɪʃən/ *n* **1** an opinion; point of view **2** a market commitment in securities or commodities **3** the place occupied by sby or sthg; *also* the proper place **4a** a condition, situation **b** social or official rank or status **5** a post, job – fml

[2]position *v* to put in a proper or specified position

positional /pə'zɪʃənəl/ *adj* of or fixed by position

positive /'pɒzɨtɪv/ *adj* **1** fully assured; confident **2** incontestable **3** utter **4** real, active **5a** capable of being constructively applied; helpful **b** concentrating on what is good or beneficial **6** having or expressing actual existence or quality as distinguished from deficiency **7** having the light and dark parts similar in tone to those of the original photographic subject **8** in a direction arbitrarily or customarily taken as that of increase or progression **9** numerically greater than zero **10a** charged with electricity **b** having higher electric potential and constituting the part from which the current flows to the external circuit **11** marked by or indicating acceptance, approval, or affirmation – **positive** *n* – **~ly** *adv*

positron /'pɒzɪtrɒn/ *n* an elementary particle that has the same mass as the electron but the opposite electrical charge

posse /'pɒsi/ *n sing or pl in constr* a body of people summoned by a sheriff, esp in N America, to assist in preserving the public peace, usu in an emergency

possess /pə'zes/ *v* **1** to make the owner or holder – + *of* or *with* **2a** to have and hold as property; own **b** to have as an attribute, knowledge, or skill **3** to influence so strongly as to direct the actions; *also, of a demon, evil spirit, etc* to enter into and control – **~or** *n*

possessed /pə'zest/ *adj* **1** influenced or controlled by sthg (e g an evil spirit or a passion) **2** mad, crazed

possession /pə'zeʃən/ *n* **1a** having or taking into control **b** ownership **2a** sthg owned, occupied, or controlled **b** *pl* wealth, property **3** domination by sthg (e g an evil spirit or passion)

[1]possessive /pə'zesɪv/ *adj* **1** manifesting possession or the desire to own or dominate **2** of or being the grammatical possessive – **~ly** *adv* – **~ness** *n*

[2]possessive *n* (a form in) a grammatical case expressing ownership or a similar relation

possibility /ˌpɒsɨ'bɪlɨti/ *n* **1** the condition or fact of being possible **2** sthg possible **3** potential or prospective value – usu pl with sing. meaning

possible /'pɒsɨbəl/ *adj* **1** within the limits of ability, capacity, or realization **2** capable of being done or occurring according to nature, custom, or manners **3** that may or may not occur – **possible** *n*

possibly /'pɒsɨbli/ *adv* **1** it is possible

that; maybe **2** – used as an intensifier with *can* or *could*

possum /ˈpɒsəm/ *n* an opossum

[1]post /pəʊst/ *n* **1** a piece of timber, metal, etc fixed firmly in an upright position, esp as a stay or support **2** a pole marking the starting or finishing point of a horse race **3** a goalpost

[2]post *v* **1** to fasten to a wall, board, etc in order to make public – often + *up* **2** to publish, announce, or advertise (as if) by use of a placard

[3]post *n* **1** (a single despatch or delivery of) the mail handled by a postal system **2** *chiefly Br* a postal system or means of posting

[4]post *v* **1** to send by post **2** to provide with the latest news; inform

[5]post *n* **1a** the place at which a soldier or body of troops is stationed **b** a station or task to which one is assigned **2** an office or position to which a person is appointed **3** a trading post, settlement **4** *Br* either of 2 bugle calls giving notice of the hour for retiring at night

[6]post *v* to station

postage /ˈpəʊstɪdʒ/ *n* (markings or stamps representing) the fee for a postal service

postal /ˈpəʊstl/ *adj* **1** of or being a system for the conveyance of written material, parcels, etc between a large number of users **2** conducted by post

postal order *n, Br* an order issued by a post office for payment of a specified sum of money usu at another post office

postbox /ˈpəʊstbɒks/ *n* a secure receptacle for the posting of outgoing mail

postcard /ˈpəʊstkɑːd/ *n* a card that can be posted without an enclosing envelope

postcode /ˈpəʊstkəʊd/ *n* a combination of letters and numbers that is used in the postal address of a place in the UK to assist sorting

postdate /ˌpəʊstˈdeɪt/ *v* **1** to date with a date later than that of execution **2** to assign (an event) to a date subsequent to that of actual occurrence

poster /ˈpəʊstəʳ/ *n* a (decorative) bill or placard for display often in a public place

poste restante /ˌpəʊst ˈrestɒnt/ *n, chiefly Br* mail that is intended for collection from a post office

[1]posterior /pɒˈstɪərɪəʳ/ *adj* **1** situated behind or towards the back: e g **2a** *of an animal part* near the tail **b** *of the human body or its parts* dorsal **3** *of a plant part* (on the side) facing towards the stem or axis

[2]posterior *n* the buttocks

posterity /pɒˈsterɪ̥ti/ *n* all future generations

postern /ˈpɒstən/ *n* a back door or gate

poster paint *n* an opaque watercolour paint containing gum

postgraduate /ˌpəʊstˈgrædjʊɪ̥t/ *n* a student continuing higher education after completing a first degree

posthaste /ˌpəʊstˈheɪst/ *adv* with all possible speed

post horn *n* a simple wind instrument with cupped mouthpiece used esp in the 18th and 19th c by stage coaches

posthumous /ˈpɒstjʊməs/ *adj* following, occurring, published, etc after death – **~ly** *adv*

postman /ˈpəʊstmən/ *n* sby who delivers the post

postmark /ˈpəʊstmɑːk/ *v or n* (to mark with) a cancellation mark showing the post office and date of posting of a piece of mail

postmaster /ˈpəʊstˌmɑːstəʳ/ *n* sby who has charge of a post office

postmaster general *n* an official in charge of a national post office

post meridiem /ˌpəʊst məˈrɪdɪəm/ *adj* being after noon – abbr **pm**

[1]postmortem /ˌpəʊstˈmɔːtəm/ *adj* occurring after death

[2]postmortem *n* **1** an examination of a body after death for determining the cause of death or the character and extent of changes produced by disease **2** an examination of a plan or event that failed, in order to discover the cause of failure

post office *n* **1** a national usu governmental organization that runs a postal system **2** a local branch of a national post office

postpone /pəʊsˈpəʊn/ *v* to hold back to a later time; defer – **~ment** *n*

postscript /ˈpəʊstˌskrɪpt/ *n* **1** a note

or series of notes appended to a completed article, a book, or esp a letter **2** a subordinate or supplementary part

[1]**postulate** /'pɒstjʊleɪt/ *v* **1** to assume or claim as true **2** to assume as a postulate or axiom

[2]**postulate** /'pɒstjʊlət/ *n* **1** a hypothesis advanced as a premise in a train of reasoning **2** an axiom

[1]**posture** /'pɒstʃəʳ/ *n* **1** the position or bearing of (relative parts of) the body **2** a frame of mind; an attitude

[2]**posture** *v* **1** to assume a posture; *esp* to strike a pose for effect **2** to assume an artificial or insincere attitude; attitudinize

posy /'pəʊzi/ *n* a small bouquet of flowers; a nosegay

[1]**pot** /pɒt/ *n* **1** any of various usu rounded vessels (e g of metal or earthenware) used for holding liquids or solids, esp in cooking **2** an enclosed framework for catching fish or lobsters **3** a drinking vessel (e g of pewter) used esp for beer **4** the total of the bets at stake at 1 time **5** *Br* a shot in billiards or snooker in which an object ball is pocketed **6** *NAm* the common fund of a group **7** a large amount (of money) – usu pl with sing. meaning; infml **8** a potbelly – infml **9** cannabis; *specif* marijuana – slang

[2]**pot** *v* **1** to preserve in a sealed pot, jar, or can **2** to make or shape (earthenware) as a potter

potash /'pɒtæʃ/ *n* potassium or a potassium compound, esp as used in agriculture or industry

potassium /pə'tæsɪəm/ *n* a soft light metallic element of the alkali metal group

potation /pəʊ'teɪʃən/ *n* an act or instance of drinking; *also* a usu alcoholic drink – fml or humor

potato /pə'teɪtəʊ/ *n, pl* **potatoes** **1** a sweet potato, yam **2** a plant widely cultivated in temperate regions for its edible starchy tubers; *also* a potato tuber eaten as a vegetable

potbelly /'pɒt,beli/ *n* an enlarged, swollen, or protruding abdomen

potboiler /pɒt,bɔɪləʳ/ *n* a usu inferior work (e g of art or literature) produced chiefly to make money

pot-bound *adj, of a potted plant* having roots so densely matted as to allow little or no space for further growth

poteen, potheen /pɒ'tʃiːn, -'tiːn/ *n* Irish whiskey illicitly distilled

potent /'pəʊtənt/ *adj* **1** having or wielding force, authority, or influence; powerful **2** achieving or bringing about a particular result; effective **3** producing an esp unexpectedly powerful reaction; strong **4** *esp of a male* able to have sexual intercourse – **potency** *n* – ~**ly** *adv*

potentate /'peʊtənteɪt/ *n* one who wields controlling power

[1]**potential** /pə'tenʃəl/ *adj* existing in possibility; capable of being made real – ~**ly** *adv*

[2]**potential** *n* **1** sthg that can develop or become actual; possible capacity or value **2** the difference between the voltages at 2 points (e g in an electrical circuit or in an electrical field)

potential energy *n* the energy that sthg has because of its position or because of the arrangement of parts

potentiality /pə,tenʃi'æləti/ *n* potential

pother /'pɒðəʳ/ *n* needless agitation over a trivial matter; fuss

[1]**pothole** /'pɒthəʊl/ *n* **1** a circular hole worn in the rocky bed of a river by stones or gravel whirled round by the water **2** a natural vertically descending hole in the ground or in the floor of a cave; *also* a system of these usu linked by caves **3** an unwanted hole in a road surface

[2]**pothole** *v* to explore pothole systems – ~**er** *n*

potion /'pəʊʃən/ *n* a mixed drink, esp of medicine, often intended to produce a specified effect

potluck /pɒt'lʌk/ *n* **1** food that is available without special preparations being made **2** whatever luck or chance brings – esp in *take potluck*

potpourri /pəʊ'pʊəri, ,pəʊpə'riː/ *n* **1** a mixture of dried flowers, herbs, and spices, usu kept in a jar for its fragrance **2** a miscellaneous collection; a medley

pot roast *n* a joint of meat cooked by braising, usu on the top of a cooker

potsherd /'pɒt,ʃɜːd/ *n* a pottery fragment

potshot /'pɒt-ʃɒt/ *n* **1** a shot taken in

a casual manner or at an easy target 2 a critical remark made in a careless manner

potted /ˈpɒtɨd/ *adj* 1 planted or grown in a pot 2 *chiefly Br* abridged or summarized, usu in a simplified or popular form

[1]**potter** /ˈpɒtəʳ/ *n* one who makes pottery

[2]**potter** *v* 1 to spend time in aimless or unproductive activity – often + *around* or *about* 2 to move or travel in a leisurely or random fashion – **potter** *n*

pottery /ˈpɒtəri/ *n* 1 a place where ceramic ware is made and fired 2 articles of fired clay; *esp* coarse or hand-made ceramic ware

[1]**potty** /ˈpɒti/ *adj, chiefly Br* 1 slightly crazy 2 foolish, silly *USE* infml – **pottiness** *n*

[2]**potty** *n* a chamber pot, esp for a small child

pouch /paʊtʃ/ *n* 1 a small drawstring bag carried on the person 2 a lockable bag for mail or diplomatic dispatches 3 an anatomical structure resembling a pouch: e g **a** a pocket of skin in the abdomen of marsupials for carrying their young **b** a pocket of skin in the cheeks of some rodents used for storing food

poulterer /ˈpəʊltərəʳ/ *n* one who deals in poultry, poultry products, or game

poultice /ˈpəʊltɨs/ *n* a soft usu heated and sometimes medicated mass spread on cloth and applied to inflamed or injured parts (e g sores)

poultry /ˈpəʊltri/ *n* domesticated birds (e g chickens) kept for eggs or meat

pounce /paʊns/ *v* 1 to swoop on and seize sthg (as if) with talons 2 to make a sudden assault or approach – **pounce** *n*

[1]**pound** /paʊnd/ *n* 1 a unit of mass and weight equal to 16oz avoirdupois (about 0.453kg) 2 the basic money unit of the UK and many other countries

[2]**pound** *v* 1 to reduce to powder or pulp by beating or crushing 2 to strike heavily or repeatedly 3 to move or run along with heavy steps

[3]**pound** *n* 1 an enclosure for animals; *esp* a public enclosure for stray or unlicensed animals 2 a place for holding personal property until redeemed by the owner

pour /pɔːʳ/ *v* 1 (to cause) to flow in a stream 2 to dispense (a drink) into a container 3 to supply or produce freely or copiously 4 to rain hard – often + *down*

pout /paʊt/ *v* **1a** to show displeasure by thrusting out the lips or wearing a sullen expression **b** to sulk 2 *of lips* to protrude – **pout** *n*

poverty /ˈpɒvəti/ *n* **1a** the lack of sufficient money or material possessions **b** the renunciation of individual property by a person entering a religious order 2 the condition of lacking desirable elements; deficiency, death

poverty-stricken *adj* very poor; destitute

[1]**powder** /ˈpaʊdəʳ/ *n* 1 matter reduced to a state of dry loose particles (e g by crushing or grinding) 2 a preparation in the form of fine particles, esp for medicinal or cosmetic use 3 any of various solid explosives used chiefly in gunnery and blasting

[2]**powder** *v* 1 to sprinkle or cover (as if) with powder 2 to reduce or convert to powder

powder keg *n* an explosive place or situation

powder room *n* a public toilet for women in a hotel, department store, etc

[1]**power** /ˈpaʊəʳ/ *n* **1a** possession of control, authority, or influence over others **b** a sovereign state **c** a controlling group – often in *the powers that be* 2 ability to act or produce or undergo an effect **3a** physical might **b** mental or moral efficacy; vigour **c** political control or influence 4 the number of times, as indicated by an exponent, that a number has to be multiplied by itself **5a** electricity **b** the rate at which work is done or energy emitted or transferred 6 magnification 7 a large amount *of* – infml

[2]**power** *v* 1 to supply with esp motive power 2 to make (one's way) in a powerful and vigorous manner

[3]**power** *adj* driven by a motor

powerful /'paʊəfəl/ *adj* having great power, prestige, or influence – ~**ly** *adv*

powerless /'paʊəlɨ̥s/ *adj* **1** devoid of strength or resources; helpless **2** lacking the authority or capacity to act – ~**ly** *adv* – ~**ness** *n*

power of attorney *n* a legal document authorizing one to act as sby's agent

power station *n* an electricity generating station

[1]**powwow** /'paʊ,waʊ/ *n* **1** a N American Indian ceremony **2** a meeting for discussion – infml

[2]**powwow** *v* to hold a powwow

practicable /'præktɪkəbəl/ *adj* **1** capable of being carried out; feasible **2** usable – **-bly** *adv* – **-bility** *n*

[1]**practical** /'præktɪkəl/ *adj* **1a** of or manifested in practice or action **b** being such in practice or effect; virtual **2** capable of being put to use or account; useful **3** suitable for use **4** disposed to or capable of positive action as opposed to speculation; *also* prosaic – ~**ity** *n*

[2]**practical** *n* a practical examination or lesson

practical joke *n* a trick or prank played on sby to derive amusement from his/her discomfiture

practically /'præktɪkəli/ *adv* almost, nearly

practice, *NAm also* **practise** /'præktɨ̥s/ *n* **1a** actual performance or application **b** a repeated or customary action; a habit **c** the usual way of doing sthg **d** dealings, conduct – esp in *sharp practice* **2** (an instance of) regular or repeated exercise in order to acquire proficiency; *also* proficiency or experience gained in this way **3** a professional business

practise, *NAm chiefly* **practice** /'præktɨ̥s/ *v* **1** to perform or work at repeatedly so as to become proficient **2** to be professionally engaged in

practised, *NAm chiefly* **practiced** /'præktɨ̥st/ *adj* **1** experienced, skilled **2** learned by practice – often derog

practitioner /præk'tɪʃənəʳ/ *n* **1** one who practises a profession, esp law or medicine **2** one who practises a skill or art

praetor, *chiefly NAm* **pretor** /'priːtəʳ/ *n* an ancient Roman magistrate ranking below a consul

praetorian /prɪ'tɔːrɪən/ *adj, often cap* of the Roman imperial bodyguard

pragmatic /præg'mætɪk/ *adj* concerned with practicalities or expediency rather than theory or dogma; realistic – ~**ally** *adv*

pragmatism /'prægmətɪzəm/ *n* **1** a practical approach to problems and affairs **2** an American philosophical movement asserting that the meaning or truth of a concept depends on its practical consequences – **-tist** *n*

prairie /'preəri/ *n* an extensive area of level or rolling (practically) treeless grassland, esp in N America

[1]**praise** /preɪz/ *v* **1** to express a favourable judgment of; commend **2** to glorify or extol (e g God or a god)

[2]**praise** *n* **1** expression of approval; commendation **2** worship

praiseworthy /'preɪzwɜːði/ *adj* laudable, commendable – **-thily** *adv* – **-thiness** *n*

praline /'prɑːliːn/ *n* (sthg, esp a powder or paste, made from) a confection of nuts, esp almonds, caramelized in boiling sugar

[1]**pram** /præm/ *n* a small lightweight nearly flat-bottomed boat with a broad transom and usu squared-off bow

[2]**pram** *n* a usu 4-wheeled carriage for babies that is pushed by a person on foot

prance /prɑːns/ *v* to walk or move in a gay, lively, or haughty manner – **prance** *n*

prank /præŋk/ *n* a mildly mischievous act; a trick

prankster /'præŋkstəʳ/ *n* one who plays pranks

prate /preɪt/ *v* to talk foolishly and excessively *about*; chatter

[1]**prattle** /'prætl/ *v* to chatter in an artless or childish manner – ~**r** *n*

[2]**prattle** *n* idle or childish talk

prawn /prɔːn/ *n* any of numerous widely distributed edible 10-legged crustaceans that resemble large shrimps

pray /preɪ/ *v* **1** to request earnestly or humbly **2** to address prayers to God or a god

prayer /preəʳ/ *n* **1a** an address to God or a god in word or thought, with a petition, confession, thanksgiving, etc **b** an earnest request **2** the act or practice of praying **3** a religious service consisting chiefly of prayers – often pl with sing. meaning

praying mantis *n* a (large green) mantis

preach /priːtʃ/ *v* **1** to deliver a sermon **2** to urge acceptance or abandonment of an idea or course of action, esp in an officious manner – **~er** *n*

preamble /ˈpriːæmbəl/ *n* **1** an introductory statement; *specif* that of a constitution or statute **2** an introductory or preliminary fact or circumstance

prearrange /ˌpriːəˈreɪndʒ/ *v* to arrange beforehand – **~ment** *n*

precarious /prɪˈkeərɪəs/ *adj* **1** dependent on chance or uncertain circumstances; doubtful **2** characterized by a lack of security or stability; dangerous – **~ly** *adv* – **~ness** *n*

precast /ˌpriːˈkɑːst/ *adj* being concrete that is cast in the form of a panel, beam, etc before being placed in final position

precaution /prɪˈkɔːʃən/ *n* **1** care taken in advance; foresight **2** a measure taken beforehand to avoid possible harmful consequences; a safeguard – **~ary** *adj*

precede /prɪˈsiːd/ *v* **1** to surpass in rank, dignity, or importance **2** to be, go, or come before, ahead, or in front of

precedence /ˈpresᵻdəns/ *n* **1** the right to superior honour on a ceremonial or formal occasion **2** priority of importance; preference

[2]precedent /ˈpresᵻdənt/ *n* **1** an earlier occurrence of sthg similar **2** a judicial decision that serves as a rule for subsequent similar cases

precept /ˈpriːsept/ *n* a command or principle intended as a general rule of conduct – **~ive** *adj*

precinct /ˈpriːsɪŋkt/ *n* **1** *pl* the region immediately surrounding a place; environs **2** an area of a town or city containing a shopping centre and not allowing access to traffic **3** *NAm* an administrative district for election purposes or police control

[1]precious /ˈpreʃəs/ *adj* **1** of great value or high price **2** highly esteemed or cherished; dear **3** excessively refined; affected – **~ly** *adv* – **~ness** *n*

[2]precious *adv* very, extremely

[3]precious *n* a dear one; darling

precipice /ˈpresᵻpᵻs/ *n* **1** a very steep, perpendicular, or overhanging surface (e g of a rock or mountain) **2** the brink of disaster

[1]precipitate /prᵻˈsɪpᵻteɪt/ *v* **1** to throw violently; hurl **2** to bring about suddenly, unexpectedly, or too soon **3a** to separate from solution or suspension **b** to fall as rain, snow, etc

[2]precipitate /prᵻˈsɪpᵻtᵻt/ *n* a substance separated from a solution or suspension by chemical or physical change, often as crystals

[3]precipitate /prᵻˈsɪpᵻtᵻt/ *adj* **1** exhibiting violent or undue haste **2** lacking due care or consideration; rash – **~ly** *adv*

precipitation /prᵻˌsɪpᵻˈteɪʃən/ *n* (the amount of) a deposit of rain, snow, hail, etc on the earth

precipitous /prᵻˈsɪpᵻtəs/ *adj* **1** precipitate **2** dangerously steep or perpendicular – **~ly** *adv* – **~ness** *n*

précis /ˈpreɪsiː/ *n, pl* **précis** a concise summary of essential points, facts, etc – **précis** *v*

precise /prɪˈsaɪs/ *adj* **1** exactly or sharply defined or stated **2** highly exact **3** strictly conforming to a rule, convention, etc; punctilious **4** distinguished from every other; very – **~ly** *adv* – **~ness** *n*

[1]precision /prɪˈsɪʒən/ *n* **1** being precise; exactness **2** the degree of refinement with which an operation is performed or a measurement stated

[2]precision *adj* **1** adapted for extremely accurate measurement or operation **2** marked by precision of execution

preclude /prɪˈkluːd/ *v* **1** to exclude **2** to prevent – **-clusion** *n*

precocious /prɪˈkəʊʃəs/ *adj* exhibiting mature qualities at an unusually early age – **~ly** *adv* – **~ness** *n* – **-city** *n*

precognition /ˌpriːkɒgˈnɪʃən/ *n* clairvoyance of a future event

precursor /prɪ'kɜːsəʳ/ *n* **1** sby or sthg that precedes and signals the approach of sby or sthg else **2** a predecessor

predatory /'predətəri/ *adj* **1a** of or carrying out plunder or robbery **b** injuring or exploiting others for one's own gain **2** feeding by killing and eating other animals – **-ation** *n* – **-ator** *n*

predecessor /'priːdɨsesəʳ/ *n* **1** the previous occupant of a position or office to which another has succeeded **2** an ancestor

predestination /prɪ,destɨ'neɪʃən, ,priːdes-/ *n* the doctrine that salvation or damnation is foreordained

predestine /prɪ'destɨn/ *v* to destine or determine (e g damnation or salvation) beforehand

predetermine /,priːdɪ'tɜːmɨn/ *v* **1** to determine or arrange beforehand **2** to impose a direction or tendency on beforehand – **-mination** *n*

predicament /prɪ'dɪkəmənt/ *n* a (difficult, perplexing, or trying) situation

[1]**predicate** /'predɨkɨt/ *n* **1** sthg that is stated or denied of the subject in a logical proposition **2** the part of a sentence or clause that expresses what is said of the subject

[2]**predicate** /'predɨkeɪt/ *v* **1** to affirm, declare **2** to assert to be a quality or property **3** *chiefly NAm* to base – usu + *on* or *upon* *USE* chiefly fml

predicative /prɪ'dɪkətɪv/ *adj* **1** of a predicate **2** joined to a modified noun by a copula (e g *red* in *the dress is red*) – ~**ly** *adv*

predict /prɪ'dɪkt/ *v* to foretell (sthg) on the basis of observation, experience, or scientific reason

prediction /prɪ'dɪkʃən/ *n* sthg that is predicted; a forecast – **-tive** *adj* – **-tively** *adv*

predilection /,priːdɪ'lekʃən/ *n* a liking, preference

predispose /,priːdɪ'spəʊz/ *v* **1** to incline, esp in advance **2** to make susceptible *to* – **-sition** *n*

predominate /prɪ'dɒmɨneɪt/ *v* **1** to exert controlling power or influence; prevail **2** to hold advantage in numbers or quantity – **-ance** *n* – **-ant** *adj* – **-antly** *adv*

preeminent /priː'emɨnənt/ *adj* excelling all others; paramount – **-nence** *n*

preempt /priː'empt/ *v* to invalidate or render useless by taking action or appearing in advance – ~**or** *n*

preemption /priː'empʃən/ *n* **1** the right of purchasing before others **2** a prior seizure or appropriation

preemptive /priː'emptɪv/ *adj* **1** (capable) of preemption **2** of or being a bid in bridge high enough to shut out bids by the opponents **3** carried out in order to forestall intended action by others

preen /priːn/ *v* **1** to smarten oneself, esp in a vain way **2** to pride or congratulate oneself *on*; gloat **3** *of a bird* to trim and arrange the feathers

prefab /'priːfæb/ *n* a prefabricated structure or building

prefabricate /priː'fæbrɪkeɪt/ *v* to fabricate the parts of (e g a building) at a factory ready for assembly elsewhere – **-cation** *n* – ~**d** *adj*

[1]**preface** /'prefɨs/ *n* **1** an introduction to a book, speech, etc **2** sthg that precedes or heralds; a preliminary

[2]**preface** *v* to introduce *by* or provide *with* a preface – **-atory** *adj*

prefect /'priːfekt/ *n* **1** a chief officer or chief magistrate (e g in France or Italy) **2** a monitor in a secondary school, usu with some authority over other pupils

prefecture /'priːfektʃəʳ/ *n* the office or official residence of a prefect – **-tural** *adj*

prefer /prɪ'fɜːʳ/ *v* **1** to choose or esteem above another; like better **2** to bring (a charge) against sby

preference /'prefərəns/ *n* **1** the power or opportunity of choosing **2** sby or sthg preferred; a choice **3** priority in the settlement of an obligation – **-ential** *adj* – **-entially** *adv*

[1]**prefix** /'priːfɪks/ *v* to add to the beginning

[2]**prefix** *n* **1** an affix (e g *un* in *unhappy*) placed at the beginning of a word or before a root **2** a title used before a person's name

pregnancy /'pregnənsi/ *n* **1** the condition or quality of being pregnant **2** fertility of mind; inventiveness

pregnant /'pregnənt/ *adj* **1** full of ideas or resourcefulness; inventive **2**

containing unborn young within the body **3** showing signs of the future; portentous **4** full, teeming – usu + *with* – ~**ly** *adv*

prehensile /prɪ'hensaɪl/ *adj* adapted for seizing or grasping, esp by wrapping round

prehistoric /ˌpriːhɪ'stɒrɪk/ *adj* of or existing in times antedating written history – ~**ally** *adv*

prehistory /ˌpriː'hɪstəri/ *n* (the study of) the prehistoric period of human beings' evolution

prejudge /ˌpriː'dʒʌdʒ/ *v* to pass judgment on prematurely or before a full and proper examination – **-judgment, -judgement** *n*

[1]**prejudice** /'predʒədʒ̍s/ *n* **1** (an instance of) a preconceived judgment or opinion; *esp* a biased and unfavourable one formed without sufficient reason or knowledge **2** an irrational attitude of hostility directed against an individual, group, or race

[2]**prejudice** *v* **1** to injure by some judgment or action **2** to cause (sby) to have an unreasonable bias

prejudiced /'predʒədʒ̍st/ *adj* having a prejudice or bias esp against

prejudicial /ˌpredʒʊ'dɪʃəl, -dʒə-/, **prejudicious** *adj* **1** detrimental **2** leading to prejudiced judgments – ~**ly** *adv*

prelate /'prelʒ̍t/ *n* a clergyman (e g a bishop or abbot) of high rank

prelim /'priːlɪm/ *n* a preliminary

[1]**preliminary** /prɪ'lɪmʒ̍nəri/ *n* sthg that precedes or is introductory or preparatory: e g **a** a preliminary scholastic examination **b** *pl, Br* matter (e g a list of contents) preceding the main text of a book

[2]**preliminary** *adj* preceding and preparing for what is to follow

preliterate /ˌpriː'lɪtərʒ̍t/ *adj* not yet employing writing

prelude /'preljuːd/ *n* **1** an introductory or preliminary performance, action, or event; an introduction **2a** a musical section or movement introducing the theme or chief subject or serving as an introduction (e g to an opera) **b** a short separate concert piece, usu for piano or orchestra – **prelude** *v*

premature /'premətʃə^r, -tʃʊə^r, ˌpremə'tʃʊə^r/ *adj* happening, arriving, existing, or performed before the proper or usual time; *esp, of a human* born after a gestation period of less than 37 weeks – ~ **ly** *adj*

premeditate /priː'medʒ̍teɪt/ *v* to think over and plan beforehand – **-tation** *n* – ~**d** *adj*

[1]**premier** /'premɪə^r/ *adj* **1** first in position, rank, or importance; principal **2** first in time; earliest

[2]**premier** *n* a prime minister – ~**ship** *n*

premiere /'premieə^r/ *n* a first public showing (e g of a play or film)

premise /'premʒ̍s/ *n* a proposition taken as the basis for argument or inference

premises /'premʒ̍sʒ̍z/ *n pl* a piece of land with the buildings on it; *also* (part of) a building

[1]**premium** /'priːmɪəm/ *n* **1a** a sum above a fixed price or wage, paid chiefly as an incentive **b** a sum in advance of or in addition to the nominal value of sthg **2** the sum paid for a contract of insurance **3** a high value or a value in excess of that normally expected

[2]**premium** *adj* of exceptional quality

premium bond *n* a government bond that is issued in units of £1 and which instead of earning interest is entered into a monthly draw for money prizes

premolar /'priːməʊlə^r/ *n or adj* (a tooth) situated in front of the true molar teeth

premonition /ˌpremə'nɪʃən, ˌpriː-/ *n* an anticipation of an event without conscious reason – **-tory** *adj*

preoccupation /priːˌɒkjʊ'peɪʃən/ *n* (sthg that causes) complete mental absorption

preoccupy /priː'ɒkjʊpaɪ/ *v* to engage or engross the attention of to the exclusion of other things – **-pied** *adj*

preordain /ˌpriːɔː'deɪn/ *v* to decree or determine in advance – **-dination** *n* – ~**ment** *n*

prep /prep/ *n* homework done at or away from school

preparation /ˌprepə'reɪʃən/ *n* **1** preparing **2** a state of being prepared; readiness **3** a preparatory act or measure – usu pl **4** sthg prepared; *esp* a medicine

[1]**preparatory** /prɪ'pærətəri/, **preparative** *adj* preparing or serving to prepare for sthg; introductory

[2]**preparatory** *adv* by way of preparation; in a preparatory manner – usu + *to*

preparatory school *n* a private school preparing pupils for public schools

prepare /prɪ'peə'/ *v* **1a** to make ready beforehand for some purpose, use, or activity **b** to put into a suitable frame of mind for sthg **2** to work out the details of; plan in advance **3** to draw up in written form

prepared /prɪ'peəd/ *adj* subjected to a special process or treatment

preparedness /prɪ'peədnɨs, -'peərɨd-/ *n* adequate preparation (in case of war)

preponderant /prɪ'pɒndərənt/ *adj* **1** having superior weight, force, or influence **2** occurring in greater number or quantity – **-ance** *n* – **~ly** *adv*

preponderate /prɪ'pɒndəreɪt/ *v* to predominate

preposition /,prepə'zɪʃən/ *n* a linguistic form (e g *by, of, for*) that combines with a noun, pronoun, etc to form a phrase – **~al** *adj* – **~ally** *adv*

prepossessing /,priːpə'zesɪŋ/ *adj* tending to create a favourable impression; attractive

prepossession /,priːpə'zeʃən/ *n* **1** an opinion or impression formed beforehand; a prejudice **2** a preoccupation

preposterous /prɪ'pɒstərəs/ *adj* contrary to nature or reason; absurd; *also* ridiculous – **~ly** *adv* – **~ness** *n*

prep school *n* a preparatory school

prepuce /'priːpjuːs/ *n* the foreskin; *also* a similar fold surrounding the clitoris

prerequisite /priː'rekwɨzɨt/ *n* a requirement that must be satisfied in advance

prerogative /prɪ'rɒgətɪv/ *n* **1** an exclusive or special right or privilege belonging esp to a person or group of people by virtue of rank or status **2** the discretionary power of the Crown

presage /'presɪdʒ, prɨ'seɪdʒ/ *v* **1** to portend **2** to forecast, predict **3** to have a presentiment of – **presage** *n*

presbyter /'prezbɨtə'/ *n* a member of the governing body of an early Christian or nonconformist church

Presbyterian /,prezbɨ'tɪərɪən/ *adj* of or constituting a Christian church governed by elected representative bodies and traditionally Calvinistic in doctrine – **Presbyterian** *n*

presbytery /'prezbɨtəri/ *n* **1** the part of a church (e g the E end of the chancel) reserved for the officiating clergy **2** a local ruling body in Presbyterian churches **3** the house of a Roman Catholic parish priest

preschool /,priː'skuːl/ *adj* of the period from infancy to first attendance at primary school

prescribe /prɪ'skraɪb/ *v* **1** to lay down a rule; dictate **2** to designate or order the use of as a remedy

prescription /prɪ'skrɪpʃən/ *n* **1** the action of laying down authoritative rules or directions **2** a written direction or order for the preparation and use of a medicine; *also* the medicine prescribed

presence /'prezəns/ *n* **1** the fact or condition of being present **2** the immediate vicinity of a (specified) person **3** sby or sthg present; *also* a spirit felt to be present **4** a quality of poise or distinction that enables a person, esp a performer, to impress, or have a strong effect on, others

presence of mind *n* the ability to retain one's self-possession and act calmly in emergencies or difficult situations

[1]**present** /'prezənt/ *n* sthg presented; a gift

[2]**present** /prɪ'zent/ *v* **1a** to introduce (sby) esp to another of higher rank **b** to bring (e g a play) before the public **2** to make a gift (to) **3** to give or bestow formally **4** to lay (e g a charge) before a court **5a** to offer for show; exhibit **b** to offer for approval or consideration

[3]**present** /'prezənt/ *adj* **1** now existing or in progress **2a** in or at a usu specified place **b** existing in sthg mentioned or understood **c** vividly felt, remembered, or imagined – usu + *to* or *in* **3**

of or being a verb tense that expresses present time or the time of speaking

[4]**present** *n* **1** (a verb form in) the present tense of a language **2** the present time

presentable /prɪ'zentəbəl/ *adj* **1** fit to be seen or inspected **2** fit (e g in dress or manners) to appear in company – **-bly** *adv*

presentation /,prezən'teɪʃən/ *n* **1a** sthg offered or given; a gift **b** a descriptive or persuasive account (e g by a salesman of a product) **2** the manner in which sthg is set forth, laid out, or presented

present-day /,prezənt 'deɪ/ *adj* now existing or occurring

presentiment /prɪ'zentɟmənt/ *n* a feeling that sthg will or is about to happen; a premonition

presently /'prezəntli/ *adv* **1** before long; soon **2** *chiefly NAm & Scot* at the present time; now

present participle *n* a participle (e g *dancing, being*) with present or active meaning

preservative /prɪ'zɜːvətɪv/ *n or adj* (sthg) that preserves or has the power to preserve; *specif* (sthg) used to protect esp food against decay, discoloration, etc

[1]**preserve** /prɪ'zɜːv/ *v* **1** to keep safe from harm or destruction; protect **2a** to keep alive, intact, or free from decay **b** to maintain **3a** to keep or save from decomposition **b** to can, pickle, or similarly prepare (a perishable food) for future use **c** to make a preserve of (fruit) – **-servable** *adj*

[2]**preserve** *n* **1** a preparation (e g a jam or jelly) consisting of fruit preserved by cooking with sugar **2** an area restricted for the preservation of natural resources (e g animals or trees); *esp* one used for regulated hunting or fishing **3** sthg (e g a sphere of activity) reserved for certain people

preset /,priː'set/ *v* to set beforehand

preshrunk /,priː'ʃrʌŋk/ *adj* of or being material subjected to a process during manufacture designed to reduce later shrinking

preside /prɪ'zaɪd/ *v* **1** to occupy the place of authority **2** to exercise guidance, authority, or control *over*

presidency /'prezɟdənsi/ *n* **1** the office of president **2** the term during which a president holds office

president /'prezɟdənt/ *n* **1** an elected head of state in a republic **2** *chiefly NAm* the chief officer of an organization (e g a business corporation or university) – **~ial** *adj*

[1]**press** /pres/ *n* **1** a crowd of people; a throng; *also* crowding **2** an apparatus or machine by which pressure is applied (e g for shaping material, extracting liquid, or compressing sthg) **3** a cupboard; *esp* one for books or clothes **4** an action of pressing or pushing; pressure **5a** a printing press; *also* a publishing house **b** the act or process of printing **6a** *sing or pl in constr, often cap* **(1)** *the* newspapers and magazines collectively **(2)** *the* journalists collectively **b** comment or notice in newspapers and magazines

[2]**press** *v* **1** to push firmly and steadily against **2a** to squeeze out the juice or contents of (e g citrus fruits) **b** to iron (clothes) **3a** to exert influence on; constrain **b** to try hard to persuade; entreat **4** to follow through (a course of action) **5** to clasp in affection or courtesy **6** to require haste or speed in action

[3]**press** *v* **1** to force into military service, esp in an army or navy **2** to take by authority, esp for public use; commandeer

press cutting *n* a paragraph or article cut from a newspaper or magazine

press-gang *n sing or pl in constr* a detachment empowered to press men into military or naval service

press gang *v* to force into service (as if) by a press-gang

[1]**pressing** /'presɪŋ/ *adj* **1** very important; critical **2** earnest, insistent – **~ly** *adv*

[2]**pressing** *n* one or more gramophone records produced from a single matrix

press on *v* **1** to continue on one's way **2** to proceed in an urgent or resolute manner

press-stud *n, Br* a metal fastener consisting of 2 parts joined by pressing

press-up *n* an exercise performed in a prone position by raising and lowering the body with the arms while supporting it only on the hands and toes

[1]**pressure** /'preʃəʳ/ *n* **1** the burden of physical or mental distress **2** the application of force to sthg by sthg else in direct contact with it; compression **3** the force or thrust exerted over a surface divided by its area **4** the stress of urgent matters **5a** influence or compulsion directed towards achieving a particular end **b** repeated persistent attack; harassment – **-rize** *v*

[2]**pressure** *v* **1** to apply pressure to **2** *chiefly NAm* to cook in a pressure cooker

pressure cooker *n* a metal vessel with an airtight lid in which steam under pressure produces a very high temperature so that food can be cooked very quickly

pressure group *n* an interest group organized to influence public, esp governmental, policy

prestige /pre'stiːʒ/ *n* **1** high standing or esteem in the eyes of others **2** superiority or desirability in the eyes of society resulting from associations of social rank or material success

prestigious /pre'stɪdʒəs/ *adj* having or conferring prestige

presto /'prestəʊ/ *n, adv, or adj* (a musical passage or movement played) at a rapid tempo – used in music

presume /prɪ'zjuːm/ *v* **1** to suppose or assume, esp with some degree of certainty **2** to take sthg for granted **3** to take liberties **4** to take advantage, esp in an unscrupulous manner – usu + *on* or *upon* – **-mable** *adj* – **-mably** *adv*

presumption /prɪ'zʌmpʃən/ *n* **1** presumptuous attitude or conduct; effrontery **2** an attitude or belief based on reasonable evidence or grounds; an assumption

presumptive /prɪ'zʌmptɪv/ *adj* **1** giving grounds for reasonable opinion or belief **2** based on probability or presumption – **~ly** *adv*

presumptuous /prɪ'zʌmptʃʊəs/ *adj* overstepping due bounds; forward – **~ly** *adv*

presuppose /ˌpriːsə'pəʊz/ *v* **1** to suppose beforehand **2** to require as an antecedent in logic or fact – **-position** *n*

pretence, *NAm chiefly* **pretense** /prɪ'tens/ *n* **1** a claim made or implied; *esp* one not supported by fact **2** a false or feigning act or assertion **3** an outward and often insincere or inadequate show; a semblance **4** a professed rather than a real intention or purpose; a pretext – esp in *false pretences*

[1]**pretend** /prɪ'tend/ *v* **1** to give a false appearance of; feign **2** to claim or assert falsely; profess

[2]**pretend** *adj* make-believe – used esp by children

pretender /prɪ'tendəʳ/ *n* **1** sby who lays claim to sthg; *specif* a (false) claimant to a throne **2** sby who makes a false or hypocritical show

pretension /prɪ'tenʃən/ *n* vanity, pretentiousness

pretentious /prɪ'tenʃəs/ *adj* making usu unjustified or excessive claims (e g of value or standing) – **~ness** *n* – **~ly** *adv*

preternatural /ˌpriːtə'nætʃərəl/ *adj* **1** exceeding what is natural or regular; extraordinary **2** lying beyond or outside normal experience *USE* fml – **~ly** *adv*

pretext /'priːtekst/ *n* a false reason given to disguise the real one; an excuse

[1]**pretty** /'prɪti/ *adj* **1a** attractive or aesthetically pleasing, esp because of delicacy or grace, but less than beautiful **b** outwardly pleasant but lacking strength, purpose, or intensity **2** miserable, terrible **3** moderately large; considerable – **-tily** *adv* – **-tiness** *n*

[2]**pretty** *adv* **1a** in some degree; *esp* somewhat excessively **b** very – used to emphasize *much* or *nearly* **2** in a pretty manner; prettily – infml

pretty-pretty *adj* excessively pretty, esp in an insipid or inappropriate way

pretzel /'pretsəl/ *n* a brittle glazed and salted biscuit typically having the form of a loose knot

prevail /prɪ'veɪl/ *v* **1** to gain ascendancy through strength or superiority; triumph – often + *against* or *over* **2** to persuade successfully – + *on, upon,* or *with* **3** to be frequent; *also* to persist

prevalent /'prevələnt/ *adj* generally

or widely occurring or existing; widespread – ~**ly** *adv* – **-lence** *n*

prevaricate /prɪ'værɪ̈keɪt/ *v* to speak or act evasively so as to hide the truth – **-cation** *n* – **-cator** *n*

prevent /prɪ'vent/ *v* **1** to keep from happening or existing **2** to hold or keep back; stop – often + *from* – ~**able** *adj* – ~**ion** *n*

preventive /prɪ'ventɪv/, **preventative** *adj* **1** intended or serving to prevent; precautionary **2** undertaken to forestall anticipated hostile action

[1]**preview** /'priːvjuː/ *v* to see beforehand; *specif* to view or show in advance of public presentation

[2]**preview** *n* **1** an advance showing or performance (e g of a film or play) **2** a brief view or foretaste of sthg that is to come

previous /'priːvɪəs/ *adj* **1** going before in time or order **2** acting too soon; premature – ~**ly** *adv*

prevision /ˌpriː'vɪʒən/ *n* **1** foreknowledge, prescience **2** a forecast, prophecy

[1]**prey** /preɪ/ *n* **1** an animal taken by a predator as food **2** sby or sthg helpless or unable to resist attack; a victim

[2]**prey** *v* **1** to seize and devour prey – often + *on* or *upon* **2** to live by extortion, deceit, or exerting undue influence **3** to have continuously oppressive or distressing effect

price /praɪs/ *n* **1** the money, or amount of goods or services, that is exchanged or demanded in barter or sale **2** the terms for the sake of which sthg is done or undertaken: e g **a** an amount sufficient to bribe sby **b** a reward for the catching or killing of sby **3** the cost at which sthg is done or obtained – **price** *v* – ~**y** *adj*

priceless /'praɪslɪ̈s/ *adj* **1** having a worth beyond any price; invaluable **2** particularly amusing or absurd – infml

[1]**prick** /prɪk/ *n* **1** a mark or shallow hole made by a pointed instrument **2a** a nagging or sharp feeling of sorrow or remorse **b** a sharp localized pain **3** the penis – infml **4** a disagreeable person – infml

[2]**prick** *v* **1** to pierce slightly with a sharp point **2** to trace or outline with punctures **3** to cause to be or stand erect – often + *up*

[1]**prickle** /'prɪkəl/ *n* **1** a sharp pointed spike arising from the skin or bark of a plant **2** a prickling sensation

[2]**prickle** *v* to cause or feel a stinging sensation; tingle

prickly /'prɪkli/ *adj* **1** full of or covered with prickles **2** prickling, stinging **3a** troublesome, vexatious **b** easily irritated – **-liness** *n*

prickly heat *n* a skin eruption of red spots with intense itching and tingling caused by inflammation round the sweat ducts

prickly pear *n* any of a genus of cacti having yellow flowers and bearing spines or prickly hairs

prick out *v* to transplant (seedlings) from the place of germination to a more permanent position (e g in a flower bed)

[1]**pride** /praɪd/ *n* **1a** inordinate self-esteem; conceit **b** a reasonable or justifiable self-respect **c** delight or satisfaction arising from some act, possession, or relationship **2** *sing or pl in constr* a group of lions

[2]**pride** *v* to be proud of (oneself) – + *on* or *upon*

priest /priːst/ *n* a person authorized to perform the sacred rites of a religion – ~**hood** *n* – ~**ly** *adj* – ~**liness** *n*

prig /prɪg/ *n* one who is excessively self-righteous or affectedly precise about the observance of proprieties (e g of speech or manners) – ~**gish** *adj* – ~**gishly** *adv* – ~**gishness** *n*

prim /prɪm/ *adj* **1** stiffly formal and proper; decorous **2** prudish – ~**ly** *adv* – ~**ness** *n*

prima ballerina /ˌpriːmə bælə'riːnə/ *n* the principal female dancer in a ballet company

primacy /'praɪməsi/ *n* **1** the office or rank of an ecclesiastical primate **2** the state of being first (e g in importance, order, or rank); preeminence – fml

prima donna /ˌpriːmə 'dɒnə/ *n, pl* **prima donnas** **1** a principal female singer (e g in an opera company) **2** an extremely sensitive or temperamental person

primaeval /praɪ'miːvəl/ *adj, chiefly Br* primeval

[1]**prima facie** /ˌpraɪmə ˈfeɪʃi/ *adv* at first view; on the first appearance

[2]**prima facie** *adj* true, valid, or sufficient at first impression; apparent

primal /ˈpraɪməl/ *adj* **1** original, primitive **2** first in importance; fundamental

primarily /ˈpraɪmərəli/ *adv* **1** for the most part, chiefly **2** in the first place; originally

[1]**primary** /ˈpraɪməri/ *adj* **1a** of first rank, importance, or value; principal **b** basic, fundamental **2a** direct, first-hand **b** not derivable from other colours, odours, or tastes **c** of or at a primary school **3** of or being an industry that produces raw materials

[2]**primary** *n* **1** sthg that stands first in rank, importance, or value; a fundamental – usu pl **2** any of the usu 9 or 10 strong feathers on the joint of a bird's wing furthest from the body **3** a primary colour **4** a caucus **5** a primary school

primary colour *n* **1** any of the 3 bands of the spectrum: red, green, and bluish violet, from which all other colours can be obtained by suitable combinations **2** any of the 3 coloured pigments red, yellow, and blue that cannot be matched by mixing other pigments

primary school *n* a school for pupils from 5 to 11

primate /ˈpraɪmɨ̍t/ *n* **1** *often cap* a bishop having precedence (e g in a nation) **2** any of an order of mammals including human beings, the apes, monkeys, etc

[1]**prime** /praɪm/ *n* **1** the most active, thriving, or successful stage or period **2** the chief or best individual or part; the pick **3** **prime, prime number** a positive integer that has no factor except itself and 1

[2]**prime** *adj* **1** having no factor except itself and 1 **2** first in rank, authority, or significance; principal **3** *of meat* of the highest grade or best quality **4** not deriving from sthg else; primary

[3]**prime** *v* **1** to fill, load; *esp* to fill or ply (a person) *with* liquor **2** to prepare (a firearm or charge) for firing by supplying with priming or a primer **3** to apply a first coat (e g of paint or oil) to (a surface) **4** to put into working order by filling or charging with sthg, esp a liquid **5** to instruct beforehand; prepare

prime minister *n* the chief executive of a parliamentary government – **~ship** *n*

prime mover *n* **1** God as the creator of (motion in) the physical universe **2** the original or most influential force in a development or undertaking

[1]**primer** /ˈpraɪməʳ/ *n* a small book for teaching children to read

[2]**primer** *n* **1** a device (e g a percussion cap) used for igniting a charge **2** material used in priming a surface

primeval /praɪˈmiːvəl/ *adj* **1** of the earliest age or period **2** existing in or persisting from the begining (e g of the universe)

priming /ˈpraɪmɪŋ/ *n* the explosive used for igniting a charge

[1]**primitive** /ˈprɪmɨ̍tɪv/ *adj* **1** original, primary **2a** of the earliest age or period; primeval **b** belonging to or characteristic of an early stage of development or evolution **3a** of or produced by a relatively simple people or culture **b** lacking in sophistication or subtlety; crude; *also* uncivilized – **~ly** *adv* – **~ness** *n*

[2]**primitive** *n* **1a** a primitive concept, term, or proposition **2a** an artist of an early, esp pre-Renaissance, period **b** an artist, esp self-taught, whose work is marked by directness and naiveté **3** a member of a primitive people

primordial /praɪˈmɔːdɪəl/ *adj* **1** existing from or at the beginning; primeval **2** fundamental, primary – **~ly** *adv*

primrose /ˈprɪmrəʊz/ *n* **1** any of a genus of perennial plants with showy, esp yellow, flowers **2** a pale yellow colour

primula /ˈprɪmjʊlə/ *n* a primrose

Primus /ˈpraɪməs/ *trademark* – used for a portable oil-burning stove used chiefly for cooking (e g when camping)

prince /prɪns/ *n* **1** a sovereign ruler, esp of a principality **2** a foreign nobleman of varying rank and status

prince consort *n* the husband of a reigning female sovereign

princely /ˈprɪnsli/ *adj* **1** befitting a prince; noble **2** magnificent, lavish

[1]**princess** /prɪnˈses/ *n* **1** a female

member of a royal family; *esp* a daughter of a sovereign **2** the wife or widow of a prince **3** a woman having in her own right the rank of a prince

[2]**princess** *adj* closely fitting at the top, flared from the hips to the hemline, and having gores or panels

[1]**principal** /ˈprɪnsəpəl/ *adj* most important, consequential, or influential; chief – **~ly** *adv*

[2]**principal** *n* **1** a person who has controlling authority or is in a leading position: e g **a** the head of an educational institution **b** one who employs another to act for him/her **c** a leading performer **2** a capital sum placed at interest, due as a debt, or used as a fund

principal boy *n* the role of the hero in British pantomime traditionally played by a girl

principality /ˌprɪnsəˈpæləti/ *n* the office or territory of a prince

principle /ˈprɪnsəpəl/ *n* **1a** a universal and fundamental law, doctrine, or assumption **b** a rule or code of conduct **c** the laws or facts of nature underlying the working of an artificial device **2** a primary source; a fundamental element **3** an underlying faculty or endowment

principled /ˈprɪnsɪpəld/ *adj* exhibiting, based on, or characterized by principle – often used in combination

[1]**print** /prɪnt/ *n* **1a** a mark made by pressure **b** sthg impressed with a print or formed in a mould **2** printed state or form **3** printed matter or letters **4a(1)** a copy made by printing (e g from a photographic negative) **(2)** a reproduction of an original work of art (e g a painting) **(3)** an original work of art (e g a woodcut or lithograph) intended for graphic reproduction **b** (an article made from) cloth with a pattern applied by printing **c** a photographic copy, esp from a negative

[2]**print** *v* **1** to stamp (e g a mark or design) in or on sthg **2a** to make a copy of by impressing paper against an inked printing surface **b** to impress with a design or pattern **c** to publish in print **3** to write each letter of separately, not joined together **4** to make (a positive picture) on sensitized photographic surface from a negative or a positive

printable /ˈprɪntəbl/ *adj* **1** capable of being printed or of being printed from or on **2** considered fit to publish

printed circuit *n* a circuit for electronic apparatus consisting of conductive material in thin continuous paths from terminal to terminal on an insulating surface

printer /ˈprɪntəʳ/ *n* **1** a person engaged in printing **2** a machine for printing from photographic negatives **3** a device (e g a line printer) that produces printout

printing /ˈprɪntɪŋ/ *n* **1** reproduction in printed form **2** the art, practice, or business of a printer

printout /ˈprɪntˌaʊt/ *n* a printed record produced automatically (e g by a computer)

[1]**prior** /ˈpraɪəʳ/ *n* the head (of a house) of any of various religious communities

[2]**prior** *adj* **1** earlier in time or order **2** taking precedence (e g in importance)

priority /praɪˈɒrəti/ *n* **1a** being prior **b** superiority in rank **2** sthg meriting prior attention

prior to *prep* before in time; in advance of – fml

priory /ˈpraɪəri/ *n* (the church of) a religious house under a prior or prioress

prise /praɪz/ *vt, chiefly Br* to prize up or open

prism /ˈprɪzəm/ *n* a transparent body that is bounded in part by 2 nonparallel plane faces and is used to deviate or disperse a beam of light

prismatic /prɪzˈmætɪk/ *adj* **1** of, like, or being a prism **2** formed, dispersed, or refracted (as if) by a prism

prison /ˈprɪzən/ *n* a place of enforced confinement; *specif* a building in which people are confined for safe custody while on trial or for punishment after conviction

prisoner /ˈprɪzənəʳ/ *n* sby kept under involuntary confinement; *esp* sby on trial or in prison

prissy /ˈprɪsi/ *adj* prim and over-precise; finicky – **prissily** *adv* – **prissiness** *n*

pristine /ˈprɪstiːn/ *adj* **1** belonging to the earliest period or state **2** free from impurity or decay; fresh and clean as if new

privacy /ˈprɪvəsi, ˈpraɪ-/ *n* **1** seclusion **2** freedom from undesirable intrusions and esp publicity

[1]**private** /ˈpraɪvɪ̈t/ *adj* **1a** intended for or restricted to the use of a particular person, group, etc **b** belonging to or concerning an individual person, company, or interest **c** of or receiving medical treatment in Britain outside the National Health Service and paying fees for it **2** not related to one's official position; personal **3a** withdrawn from company or observation **b** not (intended to be) known publicly; secret – **~ly** *adv*

[2]**private** *n* a soldier of the lowest rank

private enterprise *n* an economic system based on private businesses operating competetively for profit

privateer /ˌpraɪvəˈtɪəʳ/ *n* an armed private ship commissioned to cruise against the commerce or warships of an enemy

private school *n* an independent school that is not a British public school

privation /praɪˈveɪʃən/ *n* **1** an act or instance of depriving; deprivation **2** being deprived; *esp* lack of the usual necessities of life

privet /ˈprɪvɪ̈t/ *n* an ornamental shrub with half-evergreen leaves widely planted for hedges

privilege /ˈprɪvɪ̈lɪdʒ/ *n* a right, immunity, or advantage granted exclusively to a particular person, class, or group; a prerogative; *esp* such an advantage attached to a position or office

[1]**privy** /ˈprɪvi/ *adj* **1** sharing in a secret – + *to* **2** secret, private

[2]**privy** *n* (a small building containing a bench with a hole in it used as) a toilet

Privy Council *n* an advisory council nominally chosen by the British monarch and usu functioning through its committees – **-cillor** *n*

[1]**prize** /praɪz/ *n* **1** sthg offered or striven for in competition or in a contest of chance **2** sthg exceptionally desirable or precious

[2]**prize** *adj* **1a** awarded or worthy of a prize **b** awarded as a prize **2** outstanding of a kind

[3]**prize** *v* **1** to estimate the value of; rate **2** to value highly; esteem

[4]**prize** *n* property or shipping lawfully captured at sea in time of war

[5]**prize,** *Br also* **prise** *v* **1** to press, force, or move with a lever **2** to open, obtain, or remove with difficulty

[1]**pro** /prəʊ/ *n, pl* **pros** an argument or piece of evidence in favour of a particular proposition or view

[2]**pro** *adv* in favour or affirmation

[3]**pro** *prep* for; in favour of

[4]**pro** *n or adj, pl* **pros** (a) professional – infml

pro-am /ˌprəʊ ˈæm/ *n* an esp golf competition in which amateurs play professionals

probability /ˌprɒbəˈbɪlɪ̈ti/ *n* **1** being probable **2** sthg (e g an occurrence or circumstance) probable **3** a measure of the likelihood that a given event will occur, usu expressed as the ratio of the number of times it occurs in a test series to the total number of trials in the series

[1]**probable** /ˈprɒbəbəl/ *adj* **1** supported by evidence strong enough to establish likelihood but not proof **2** likely to be or become true or real

[2]**probable** *n* sby or sthg probable; *esp* sby who will probably be selected

probate /ˈprəʊbeɪt, -bɪ̈t/ *n* the judicial determination of the validity of a will

probation /prəˈbeɪʃən/ *n* **1** subjection of an individual to a period of testing to ascertain fitness **2** a method of dealing with (young) offenders by which sentence is suspended subject to regular supervision by a probation officer – **~ary** *adj*

probationer /prəˈbeɪʃənəʳ/ *n* **1** one (e g a newly admitted student nurse) whose fitness for a post is being tested during a trial period **2** an offender on probation

[1]**probe** /prəʊb/ *n* **1** a slender surgical instrument for examining a cavity **2** a device used to investigate or send back information, esp from interplanetary space **3a** a tentative exploratory sur-

vey **b** a penetrating or critical investigation; an inquiry – journ

[2]**probe** *v* **1** to investigate thoroughly – journ **2** to make an exploratory investigation – **probing** *adj* – **probingly** *adv*

probity /ˈprəʊbɪ̈ti/ *n* adherence to the highest principles and ideals; uprightness – fml

[1]**problem** /ˈprɒbləm/ *n* **1a** a question raised for inquiry, consideration, or solution **b** a proposition in mathematics or physics stating sthg to be done **2a** a situation or question that is difficult to understand or resolve **b** sby who is difficult to deal with or understand

[2]**problem** *adj* difficult to deal with; presenting a problem

problematic /ˌprɒblɪ̈ˈmætɪk/ *adj* **1** difficult to solve or decide; puzzling **2** open to question or debate; questionable – **~ally** *adv*

proboscis /prəˈbɒsɪ̈s/ *n, pl* **proboscises** *also* **proboscides** **1** a long flexible snout (e g the trunk of an elephant) **2** any of various elongated or extendable tubular parts (e g the sucking organ of a mosquito) of an invertebrate

procedural /prəˈsiːdʒərəl/ *adj* of procedure

procedure /prəˈsiːdʒəʳ/ *n* **1** a particular way of acting or accomplishing sthg **2** an established method of doing things

proceed /prəˈsiːd/ *v* **1** to arise from a source; originate **2** to continue after a pause or interruption **3** to begin and carry on an action, process, or movement **4** to move along a course; advance

proceeding /prəˈsiːdɪŋ/ *n* **1** a procedure **2** *pl* events, goings-on **3** *pl* legal action **4** *pl* an official record of things said or done

proceeds /ˈprəʊsiːdz/ *n pl* **1** the total amount brought in **2** the net amount received

[1]**process** /ˈprəʊses/ *n* **1** sthg going on; a proceeding **2a** a natural phenomenon marked by gradual changes that lead towards a particular result **b** a series of actions or operations designed to achieve an end; *esp* a continuous operation or treatment (e g in manufacture) **3** a whole course of legal proceedings **4** a prominent or projecting part of a living organism or an anatomical structure

[2]**process** *v* **1** to subject to a special process or treatment (e g in the course of manufacture) **2** to take appropriate action on

[3]**process** *v* to move in a procession

procession /prəˈseʃən/ *n* **1** a group of individuals moving along in an orderly way, esp as part of a ceremony or demonstration **2** a succession, sequence

[1]**processional** /prəˈseʃənəl/ *n* a musical composition (e g a hymn) designed for a procession

[2]**processional** *adj* of or moving in a procession

proclaim /prəˈkleɪm/ *v* **1** to declare publicly and usu officially; announce **2** to give outward indication of; show

proclamation /ˌprɒkləˈmeɪʃən/ *n* **1** proclaiming or being proclaimed **2** an official public announcement

proclivity /prəˈklɪvɪ̈ti/ *n* an inclination or predisposition towards sthg, esp sthg reprehensible – often pl with sing. meaning

proconsul /prəʊˈkɒnsəl/ *n* a governor or military commander of an ancient Roman province – **~ar** *adj* – **~ate** *n*

procrastinate /prəˈkræstɪ̈neɪt/ *v* to delay intentionally and reprehensibly in doing sthg necessary – fml – **-nation** *n*

procreate /ˈprəʊkrieɪt/ *v* to beget or bring forth (young) – **-ation** *n*

procurator-fiscal /ˌprɒkjʊreɪtə ˈfɪskəl/ *n, often cap P&F* a local public prosecutor in Scotland

procure /prəˈkjʊəʳ/ *v* **1** to get and provide (esp women) to act as prostitutes **2** to obtain, esp by particular care and effort **3** to achieve – **-curable** *adj* – **~ment** *n* – **~r** *n*

[1]**prod** /prɒd/ *v* **1** to poke or jab (as if) with a pointed instrument, esp repeatedly **2** to incite to action; stir

[2]**prod** *n* **1** a prodding action; a jab **2** an incitement to act

[1]**prodigal** /ˈprɒdɪgəl/ *adj* **1** recklessly extravagant or wasteful **2** yielding abundantly; lavish – fml

[2]**prodigal** *n* **1** a repentant sinner or

reformed wastrel **2** one who spends or gives lavishly and foolishly

prodigious /prə'dɪdʒəs/ *adj* **1** exciting amazement or wonder **2** extraordinary in bulk, quantity, or degree; enormous – ~**ly** *adv*

prodigy /'prɒdɪdʒi/ *n* **1** sthg extraordinary, inexplicable, or marvellous **2** a person, esp a child, with extraordinary talents

[1]**produce** /prə'djuːs/ *v* **1** to give birth or rise to **2** to act as a producer of **3** to give being, form, or shape to; make; *esp* to manufacture **4** to (cause to) accumulate

[2]**produce** /'prɒdjuːs/ *n* agricultural products; *esp* fresh fruits and vegetables as distinguished from grain and other staple crops

producer /prə'djuːsəʳ/ *n* **1** an individual or entity that grows agricultural products or manufactures articles **2a** sby who has responsibility for the administrative aspects of the production of a film (e g casting, schedules, and esp finance) **b** *Br* a theatre director

product /'prɒdʌkt/ *n* **1** the result of the multiplying together of 2 or more numbers or expressions **2** sthg produced by a natural or artificial process; *esp* a marketable commodity

production /prə'dʌkʃən/ *n* **1a** a literary or artistic work **b** a work presented on the stage or screen or over the air **2** the making of goods available for human wants **3** total output, esp of a commodity or an industry

productive /prə'dʌktɪv/ *adj* **1** having the quality or power of producing, esp in abundance **2** effective in bringing about; being the cause *of* **3a** yielding or furnishing results or benefits **b** yielding or devoted to the satisfaction of wants or the creation of utilities – ~**ly** *adv* – ~**ness** *n*

prof *n* a professor – slang

[1]**profane** /prə'feɪn/ *v* **1** to treat (sthg sacred) with abuse, irreverence, or contempt; desecrate **2** to debase by an unworthy or improper use – **-fanation** *n*

[2]**profane** *adj* **1** not concerned with religion or religious purposes **2** debasing or defiling what is holy; irreverent **3** not possessing esoteric or expert knowledge – ~**ly** *adv* – **-fanity** *n*

profess /prə'fes/ *v* **1** to declare or admit openly or freely; affirm **2** to declare falsely; pretend **3** to confess one's faith in or allegiance to

professed /prə'fest/ *adj* **1** openly and freely admitted or declared **2** pretended, feigned

profession /prə'feʃən/ *n* **1** an act of openly declaring or claiming a faith, opinion, etc **2** an avowed religious faith **3** a calling requiring specialized knowledge and often long and intensive academic preparation

[1]**professional** /prə'feʃənəl/ *adj* **1a** (characteristic) of a profession **b** engaged in 1 of the learned professions **c(1)** characterized by or conforming to the technical or ethical standards of a profession **(2)** characterized by conscientious workmanship **2** engaging for gain or livelihood in an activity or field of endeavour often engaged in by amateurs **3** following a line of conduct as though it were a profession – derog **4** *of a breaking of rules, esp in sport* intentional – euph – ~**ly** *adv*

[2]**professional** *n* **1** one who engages in a pursuit or activity professionally **2** one with sufficient experience or skill in an occupation or activity to resemble a professional – infml

professionalism /prə'feʃənəlɪzəm/ *n* **1** the esp high and consistent conduct, aims, or qualities that characterize a profession or a professional person **2** the following for gain or livelihood of an activity often engaged in by amateurs

professor /prə'fesəʳ/ *n* a staff member of the highest academic rank at a university; *esp* the head of a university department – ~**ial** *adj* – ~**ially** *adv* – ~**ship** *n*

proffer /'prɒfəʳ/ *v* to present for acceptance; tender

proficient /prə'fɪʃənt/ *adj* well advanced or expert in an art, skill, branch of knowledge, etc – ~**ly** *adv* – **-ciency** *n*

profile /'prəʊfaɪl/ *n* **1** a side view, esp of the human face **2** an outline seen or represented in sharp relief; a contour **3** a side or sectional elevation **4** a concise written or spoken biographical sketch – **profile** *v*

[1]**profit** /ˈprɒfɪ̣t/ *n* **1** a valuable return; a gain **2** the excess of returns over expenditure – **~able** *adj* – **~ably** *adv* – **~less** *adj* – **~lessly** *adv*

[2]**profit** *v* to derive benefit; gain – usu + *from* or *by*

profiteer /ˌprɒfɪ̣ˈtɪəʳ/ *n* one who makes an unreasonable profit, esp on the sale of scarce and essential goods – **profiteer** *v*

[1]**profligate** /ˈprɒflɪ̣gɪ̣t/ *adj* **1** utterly dissolute; immoral **2** wildly extravagant; prodigal – **-gacy** *n*

[2]**profligate** *n* a person given to wildly extravagant and usu grossly self-indulgent expenditure

profound /prəˈfaʊnd/ *adj* **1a** having intellectual depth and insight **b** difficult to fathom or understand **2** coming from, reaching to, or situated at a depth; deep-seated **3a** characterized by intensity of feeling or quality **b** all encompassing; complete – **~ly** *adv*

profundity /prəˈfʌndɪ̣ti/ *n* **1a** intellectual depth **b** sthg profound or abstruse **2** being profound or deep

profuse /prəˈfjuːs/ *adj* **1** liberal, extravagant **2** greatly abundant; bountiful – **~ly** *adv* – **~ness** *n*

profusion /prəˈfjuːʒən/ *n* **1** being profuse **2** a large or lavish amount

progenitor /prəʊˈdʒenɪ̣təʳ/ *n* **1a** a direct ancestor; a forefather **b** a biologically ancestral form **2** a precursor, originator

progeny /ˈprɒdʒɪ̣ni/ *n* **1** descendants, children **2** offspring of animals or plants

prognosis /prɒgˈnəʊsɪ̣s/ *n, pl* **prognoses** **1** the prospect of recovery as anticipated from the usual course of disease or peculiarities of a particular case **2** a forecast, prognostication – fml

prognostic /prɒgˈnɒstɪk/ *n* **1** sthg that foretells; a portent **2** prognostication, prophecy *USE* fml

prognosticate /prɒgˈnɒstɪ̣keɪt/ *v* to foretell from signs or symptoms; predict – **-cation** *n* – **-cator** *n*

[1]**program** /ˈprəʊgræm/ *n* **1** a sequence of coded instructions that can be inserted into a mechanism (e g a computer) or that is part of an organism **2** *chiefly NAm* a programme

[2]**program** *v* to work out a sequence of operations to be performed by (a computer or similar mechanism); provide with a program

[1]**programme,** *NAm chiefly* **program** /ˈprəʊgræm/ *n* **1a** a brief usu printed (pamphlet containing a) list of the features to be presented, the people participating, etc (e g in a public performance or entertainment) **b** a radio or television broadcast characterized by some feature (e g a presenter, a purpose, or a theme) giving it coherence and continuity **2** a systematic plan of action **3** a curriculum **4** a prospectus, syllabus

[2]**programme,** *NAm chiefly* **program** *v* to cause to conform to a pattern (e g of thought or behaviour); condition

programme music *n* music intended to suggest a sequence of images or incidents

[1]**progress** /ˈprəʊgres/ *n* **1** a ceremonial journey; *esp* a monarch's tour of his/her dominions **2** a forward or onward movement (e g to an objective or goal); an advance **3** gradual improvement; *esp* the progressive development of mankind

[2]**progress** /prəˈgres/ *v* **1** to move forwards; proceed **2** to develop to a higher, better, or more advanced stage

progression /prəˈgreʃən/ *n* **1a** progressing, advance **b** a continuous and connected series; a sequence **2** succession of musical notes or chords

[1]**progressive** /prəˈgresɪv/ *adj* **1a** making use of or interested in new ideas, findings, or opportunities **b** of or being an educational theory marked by emphasis on the individual, informality, and self-expression **2** moving forwards continuously or in stages; advancing – **~ly** *adv*

[2]**progressive** *n* **1** sby or sthg progressive **2** sby believing in moderate political change, esp social improvement

prohibit /prəˈhɪbɪ̣t/ *v* **1** to forbid by authority **2** to prevent from doing sthg

prohibition /ˌprəʊhɪ̣ˈbɪʃən/ *n* **1** the act of prohibiting by authority **2** an order to restrain or stop **3** *often cap* the forbidding by law of the manufacture and sale of alcohol

prohibitive /prəˈhɪbɪ̣tɪv/ *adj* **1** tending to prohibit or restrain **2** tending to preclude the use or acquisition of sthg – **~ly** *adv*

[1]**project** /ˈprɒdʒekt/ *n* **1** a specific plan or design; a scheme **2a** a large undertaking, esp a public works scheme **b** a task or problem engaged in usu by a group of pupils, esp to supplement and apply classroom studies

[2]**project** /prəˈdʒekt/ *v* **1** to plan, figure, or estimate for the future **2** to throw forwards or upwards, esp by mechanical means **3** to present or transport in imagination **4** to cause to protrude **5** to cause (light or an image) to fall into space or on a surface **6a** to cause (one's voice) to be heard at a distance **b** to communicate vividly, esp to an audience **7** to attribute (sthg in one's own mind) to a person, group, or object

projectile /prəˈdʒektaɪl/ *n* a body projected by external force and continuing in motion by its own inertia; *esp* a missile (e g a bullet, shell, or grenade) fired from a weapon

projection /prəˈdʒekʃən/ *n* **1** a systematic representation on a flat surface of latitude and longitude from the curved surface of the earth, celestial sphere, etc **2** the act of throwing or shooting forward; ejection **3** a part that juts out **4** the attribution of one's own ideas, feelings, or attitudes to other people or to objects, esp as a defence against feelings of guilt or inadequacy **5** the display of films or slides by projecting an image from them onto a screen **6** an estimate of future possibilities based on a current trend

projectionist /prəˈdʒekʃənɪ̣st/ *n* the operator of a film projector

projector /prəˈdʒektəʳ/ *n* an apparatus for projecting films or pictures onto a surface

proletarian /ˌprəʊlɪ̣ˈteərɪən/ *n or adj* (a member) of the proletariat

proletariat /ˌprəʊlɪ̣ˈteərɪət/ *n* **1** the lowest class of a community **2** those workers who lack their own means of production and hence sell their labour to live

proliferate /prəˈlɪfəreɪt/ *v* to grow or increase (as if) by rapid production of new parts, cells, buds, etc – **-ation** *n*

prolific /prəˈlɪfɪk/ *adj* **1** producing young or fruit (freely) **2** marked by abundant inventiveness or productivity – **~ally** *adv*

prologue /ˈprəʊlɒg/ *n* **1** the preface or introduction to a literary work **2** (the actor delivering) a speech, often in verse, addressed to the audience at the beginning of a play **3** an introductory or preceding event or development

prolong /prəˈlɒŋ/ *v* to lengthen – **~ation** *n*

prom /prɒm/ *n* **1** a promenade concert **2** *Br* a seaside promenade

[1]**promenade** /ˌprɒməˈnɑːd, ˈprɒmənɑːd/ *n* **1** a leisurely stroll or ride taken for pleasure, usu in a public place and often as a social custom **2** a paved walk along the seafront at a resort

[2]**promenade** *v* **1** to walk about in or on **2** to display (as if) by promenading around

promenade concert *n* a concert at which some of the audience stand or can walk about

prominence /ˈprɒmɪ̣nəns/ *n* **1** being prominent or conspicuous **2** sthg prominent; a projection

prominent /ˈprɒmɪ̣nənt/ *adj* **1** projecting beyond a surface or line; protuberant **2a** readily noticeable; conspicuous **b** widely and popularly known; leading – **~ly** *adv*

promiscuous /prəˈmɪskjʊəs/ *adj* **1** not restricted to 1 class or person; indiscriminate; *esp* not restricted to 1 sexual partner **2** casual, irregular – **-cuity**, **~ness** *n* – **~ly** *adv*

[1]**promise** /ˈprɒmɪ̣s/ *n* **1** a declaration that one will do or refrain from doing sthg specified **2** grounds for expectation usu of success, improvement, or excellence **3** sthg promised

[2]**promise** *v* **1** to pledge oneself to do, bring about, or provide (sthg for) **2** to assure **3** to suggest beforehand; indicate

promised land *n* a place or condition

believed to promise final satisfaction or realization of hopes

promising /'prɒmɪ̈sɪŋ/ *adj* likely to succeed or to yield good results – **~ly** *adv*

promissory note *n* a written promise to pay, either on demand or at a fixed future time, a sum of money to a specified individual or to the bearer

promontory /'prɒməntəri/ *n* a headland

promote /prə'məʊt/ *v* **1** to advance in station, rank, or honour; raise **2a** to contribute to the growth or prosperity of; further **b** to help bring (e g an enterprise) into being; launch **c** to present (e g merchandise) for public acceptance through advertising and publicity – **~r** *n*

promotion /prə'məʊʃən/ *n* **1** being raised in position or rank **2a** the act of furthering the growth or development of sthg, esp sales or public awareness **b** sthg (e g a price reduction or free sample) intended to promote esp sales of merchandise – **~al** *adj*

[1]**prompt** /prɒmpt/ *v* **1** to move to action; incite **2** to assist (sby acting or reciting) by saying the next words of sthg forgotten or imperfectly learnt

[2]**prompt** *adj* of or for prompting actors – **~ly** *adv* – **~ness** *n*

[3]**prompt** *adj* **1a** ready and quick to act as occasion demands **b** punctual **2** performed readily or immediately

[4]**prompt** *n* the act or an instance of prompting; a reminder

promulgate /'prɒməlgeɪt/ *v* to make known by open declaration – fml – **-gation** *n* – **-gator** *n*

prone /prəʊn/ *adj* **1** having a tendency or inclination; disposed *to* **2** having the front or ventral surface downwards; prostrate – **~ness** *n*

prong /prɒŋ/ *n* **1** any of the slender sharp-pointed parts of a fork **2** a subdivision of an argument, attacking force, etc

pronoun /'prəʊnaʊn/ *n* a word used as a substitute for a noun or noun equivalent and referring to a previously named or understood person or thing

pronounce /prə'naʊns/ *v* **1** to pass judgment; declare one's opinion definitely or authoritatively – often + *on* or *upon* **2** to produce speech sounds; *also* to say correctly

pronounced /prə'naʊnst/ *adj* strongly marked; decided – **~ly** *adv*

pronouncement /prə'naʊnsmənt/ *n* **1** a usu formal declaration of opinion **2** an authoritative announcement

pronto /'prɒntəʊ/ *adv* without delay; quickly – infml

pronunciation /prə,nʌnsi'eɪʃən/ *n* the act or manner of pronouncing sthg

[1]**proof** /pruːf/ *n* **1** the cogency of evidence that compels acceptance of a truth or a fact **2** an act, effort, or operation designed to establish or discover a fact or the truth; a test **3a** an impression (e g from type) taken for examination or correction **b** a proof impression of an engraving, lithograph, etc **4** the alcoholic content of a beverage compared with the standard for proof spirit

[2]**proof** *adj* **1** designed for or successful in resisting or repelling; impervious – often in combination **2** used in proving or testing or as a standard of comparison **3** of standard strength or quality or alcoholic content

[3]**proof** *v* **1** to make or take a proof of **2** to give a resistant quality to; make (sthg) proof *against*

proofread /'pruːf,riːd/ *v* to read and mark corrections on (a proof) – **~er** *n*

proof spirit *n* a mixture of alcohol and water containing a standard amount of alcohol, in Britain 57.1% by volume

[1]**prop** /prɒp/ *n* **1** a rigid usu auxiliary vertical support (e g a pole) **2** a source of strength or support

[2]**prop** *v* **1** to support by placing sthg under or against **2** to support by placing against sthg *USE* often + *up*

[3]**prop** *n* any article or object used in a play or film other than painted scenery or costumes

propaganda /,prɒpə'gændə/ *n* (the usu organized spreading of) ideas, information, or rumour designed to promote or damage an institution, movement, person, etc

propagate /'prɒpəgeɪt/ *v* **1** to reproduce or increase by sexual or asexual reproduction 2 to increase, extend – **-gation** *n* – **-gator** *n*

propane /ˈprəʊpeɪn/ *n* a hydrocarbon used as a fuel

propel /prəˈpel/ *v* **1** to drive forwards by means of a force that imparts motion **2** to urge on; motivate – **~lant** *adj or n*

propeller /prəˈpeləʳ/ *n* a device consisting of a central hub with radiating blades that is used to propel a ship, aeroplane, etc

propeller shaft *n* a shaft that transmits mechanical power, esp from an engine

propelling pencil *n, Br* a usu metal or plastic pencil whose lead can be extended by a screw device

propensity /prəˈpensɪ̈ti/ *n* a natural inclination or tendency

[1]**proper** /ˈprɒpəʳ/ *adj* **1** suitable, appropriate **2** belonging to one; own **3** belonging characteristically *to* a species or individual; peculiar **4** being strictly so-called **5** strictly decorous; genteel **6** *chiefly Br* thorough, complete

[2]**proper** *adv, chiefly dial* in a thorough manner; completely

proper fraction *n* a fraction in which the numerator is less or of lower degree than the denominator

properly /ˈprɒpəli/ *adv* **1** in a fit manner; suitably **2** strictly in accordance with fact; correctly **3** *chiefly Br* to the full extent; completely

proper noun *n* a noun that designates a particular being or thing and is usu capitalized (e g *Janet, London*)

propertied /ˈprɒpətid/ *adj* possessing property, esp land

property /ˈprɒpəti/ *n* **1a** a quality, attribute, or power inherent in sthg **b** an attribute common to all members of a class **2a** sthg owned or possessed; *specif* a piece of real estate **b** sthg to which a person has a legal title **3** a prop

prophecy /ˈprɒfɪ̈si/ *n* **1** (the capacity to utter) an inspired declaration of divine will and purpose **2** a prediction of an event

prophesy /ˈprɒfɪ̈saɪ/ *v* **1** to speak as if divinely inspired **2** to make a prediction

prophet /ˈprɒfɪ̈t/ *n* **1** a person who utters divinely inspired revelations **2** one who foretells future events; a predictor **3** a spokesman for a doctrine, movement, etc – **~ic, ~ical** *adj* – **~ically** *adv*

Prophets *n pl* the second part of the Jewish scriptures

prophylactic /ˌprɒfɪ̈ˈlæktɪk/ *adj* **1** guarding or protecting from or preventing disease **2** tending to prevent or ward off; preventive – fml – **prophylactic** *n* – **~ally** *adv*

prophylaxis /ˌprɒfɪ̈ˈlæksɪ̈s/ *n* measures designed to preserve health and prevent the spread of disease

propinquity /prəˈpɪŋkwɪ̈ti/ *n* **1** nearness of blood; kinship **2** nearness in place or time; proximity *USE* fml

propitiate /prəˈpɪʃieɪt/ *v* to gain or regain the favour or goodwill of; appease – **-ation** *n* – **-atory** *adj*

propitious /prəˈpɪʃəs/ *adj* **1** boding well; auspicious **2** tending to favour; opportune – **~ly** *adv*

proponent /prəˈpəʊnənt/ *n* one who argues in favour of sthg; an advocate

[1]**proportion** /prəˈpɔːʃən/ *n* **1** the relation of one part to another or to the whole with respect to magnitude, quantity, or degree **2** harmonious relation of parts to each other or to the whole; balance **3a** proper or equal share **b** a quota, percentage **4** *pl* size, dimension

[2]**proportion** *v* **1** to adjust (a part or thing) in proportion to other parts or things **2** to make the parts of harmonious or symmetrical

proportional /prəˈpɔːʃənəl/ *adj* **1a** proportionate – usu + *to* **b** having the same or a constant ratio **2** regulated or determined in proportionate amount or degree

proportional representation *n* an electoral system designed to represent in a legislative body each political group in proportion to its voting strength in the electorate

proportionate /prəˈpɔːʃənɪ̈t/ *adj* being in due proportion – **proportionate** *v*

proposal /prəˈpəʊzəl/ *n* **1** an act of putting forward or stating sthg for consideration **2a** a proposed idea or plan of action; a suggestion **b** an offer of marriage **3** an application for insurance

propose /prəˈpəʊz/ *v* **1** to present for consideration or adoption **2** to make an offer of marriage **3a** to recommend to fill a place or vacancy; nominate **b** to offer as a toast – **~r** *n*

[1]**proposition** /ˌprɒpəˈzɪʃən/ *n* **1** sthg offered for consideration or acceptance; *specif* a proposal of sexual intercourse **2** an expression, in language or signs, of sthg that can be either true or false **3** a project, situation, or individual requiring to be dealt with

[2]**proposition** *v* to make a proposal to; *specif* to propose sexual intercourse to

propound /prəˈpaʊnd/ *v* to offer for discussion or consideration – fml

proprietary /prəˈpraɪətəri/ *adj* **1** (characteristic) of a proprietor **2** made and marketed under a patent, trademark, etc **3** privately owned and managed

proprietor /prəˈpraɪətəʳ/ *n* an owner

propriety /prəˈpraɪəti/ *n* **1** the quality or state of being proper; fitness **2** the standard of what is socially or morally acceptable in conduct or speech, esp between the sexes; decorum

propulsion /prəˈpʌlʃən/ *n* the action or process of propelling – **-sive** *adj*

pro rata /ˌprəʊ ˈrɑːtə/ *adv* proportionately according to an exactly calculable factor

prorogue /prəʊˈrəʊg, prə-/ *v* to suspend a legislative session of – **-gation** *n*

prosaic /prəʊˈzeɪ-ɪk, prə-/ *adj* **1a** characteristic of prose as distinguished from poetry **b** dull, unimaginative **2** belonging to the everyday world; commonplace – **~ally** *adv*

proscenium /prəˈsiːnɪəm, prəʊ-/ *n* **1** the stage of an ancient Greek or Roman theatre **2 proscenium arch, proscenium** the space occupied by a theatre curtain when lowered

proscribe /prəʊˈskraɪb/ *v* **1** to outlaw, exile **2** to condemn or forbid as harmful; prohibit – **-scription** *n*

prose /prəʊz/ *n* **1** ordinary unrhymed language **2** a literary medium distinguished from poetry esp by its closer correspondence to the patterns of everyday speech

prosecute /ˈprɒsɪkjuːt/ *v* **1** to institute legal proceedings **2** to follow through, pursue

prosecution /ˌprɒsɪˈkjuːʃən/ *n* **1** prosecuting; *specif* the formal institution of a criminal charge **2** *sing or pl in constr* the party by whom criminal proceedings are instituted or conducted

prosecutor /ˈprɒsɪkjuːtəʳ/ *n* sby who institutes or conducts an official prosecution

proselyte /ˈprɒsɪ̈laɪt/ *n* a new convert, esp to Judaism – **-tize** *v*

prose poem *n* a work in prose that has some of the qualities of a poem

prosody /ˈprɒsədi/ *n* the study of verse forms and esp of metrical structure – **-dic** *adj* – **-dically** *adv*

[1]**prospect** /ˈprɒspekt/ *n* **1** an extensive view; a scene **2** *pl* **a** financial and social expectations **b** chances, esp of success **3** a potential client, candidate, etc

[2]**prospect** /prəˈspekt/ *v* to explore (an area), esp for mineral deposits – **~or** *n*

prospective /prəˈspektɪv/ *adj* **1** likely to come about; expected **2** likely to be or become

prospectus /prəˈspektəs/ *n* a printed statement, brochure, etc describing an organization or enterprise and distributed to prospective buyers, investors, or participants

prosper /ˈprɒspəʳ/ *v* to succeed, thrive; *specif* to achieve economic success

prosperous /ˈprɒspərəs/ *adj* marked by esp financial success – **~ly** *adv* – **-rity** *n*

prostate /ˈprɒsteɪt/, **prostate gland** *n* a partly muscular, partly glandular body situated around the base of the male mammalian urethra that secretes a major constituent of the ejaculatory fluid

prosthesis /prɒsˈθiːsɪ̈s/ *n, pl* **prostheses** an artificial device to replace a missing part of the body

[1]**prostitute** /ˈprɒstɪ̈tjuːt/ *v* to devote to corrupt or unworthy purposes; debase

[2]**prostitute** *n* a person, esp a woman,

who engages in sex for money – -tion *n*

¹**prostrate** /ˈprɒstreɪt/ *adj* **1** lying full-length face downwards **2a** physically and emotionally weak; overcome **b** physically exhausted **3** *of a plant* trailing on the ground – -**tration** *n*

²**prostrate** /prɒˈstreɪt/ *v* **1** to put (oneself) in a humble and submissive posture **2** to reduce to submission, helplessness, or exhaustion

prosy /ˈprəʊzi/ *adj* dull, commonplace; *esp* tedious in speech or manner – -**sily** *adv* – -**siness** *n*

protagonist /prəʊˈtægənɪ̣st/ *n* **1** one who takes the leading part in a drama, novel, or story **2** a leader or notable supporter of a cause

protect /prəˈtekt/ *v* **1** to cover or shield *from* injury or destruction; guard *against* **2** to shield or foster (a home industry) by a protective tariff – ~**ive** *adj*

protection /prəˈtekʃən/ *n* **1** protecting or being protected **2** sthg that protects **3** the shielding of the producers of a country from foreign competition by import tariffs **4a** immunity from threatened violence, often purchased under duress **b** money extorted by racketeers posing as a protective association

protector /prəˈtektəʳ/ *n* **1a** a guardian **b** a device used to prevent injury; a guard **2** *often cap* the executive head of the Commonwealth from 1653 to 1659

protectorate /prəˈtektərɪ̣t/ *n* **1a** government by a protector **b** *often cap* the government of the Commonwealth from 1653 to 1659 **2** the relationship of one state over another dependent state which it partly controls but has not annexed **b** the dependent political unit in such a relationship

protégé, *fem* **protégée** /ˈprɒtɪ̣ʒeɪ/ *n* a person under the protection, guidance, or patronage of sby influential

protein /ˈprəʊtiːn/ *n* any of numerous extremely complex combinations of amino acids that are essential constituents of all living cells and are an essential part of the diet of animals and humans

¹**protest** /ˈprəʊtest/ *n* **1** a formal declaration of disapproval **2** protesting; *esp* an organized public demonstration of disapproval **3** an objection or display of unwillingness

²**protest** /prəˈtest/ *v* **1** to make formal or solemn declaration or affirmation of **2** to enter a protest – ~**er,** ~**or** *n*

protestant /ˈprɒtɪ̣stənt/ *n cap* a Christian who denies the universal authority of the pope and affirms the principles of the Reformation – **protestant** *adj* – ~**ism** *n*

protestation /ˌprɒtɪ̣ˈsteɪʃən ˌprəʊ-/ *n* **1** an act of protesting **2** a solemn declaration or avowal

protocol /ˈprəʊtəkɒl/ *n* **1** an original draft or record of a document or transaction **2** a code of correct etiquette and precedence

proton /ˈprəʊtɒn/ *n* an elementary particle identical with the nucleus of the hydrogen atom, that carries a positive charge numerically equal to the charge of an electron and has a mass of 1.672×10^{-27}kg

protoplasm /ˈprəʊtəplæzəm/ *n* **1** the organized complex of organic and inorganic substances (e g proteins and salts in solution) that constitutes the living nucleus and contents of the cell **2** cytoplasm

prototype /ˈprəʊtətaɪp/ *n* **1** sby or sthg that exemplifies the essential or typical features of a type **2** a first full-scale and usu operational form of a new type or design of a construction (e g an aeroplane)

protozoan /ˈprəʊtəˈzəʊən/ *n* any of a subkingdom of minute single-celled animals which have varied structure and physiology and often complex life cycles

protozoon /ˈprəʊtəˈzəʊən/ *n, pl* **protozoa** a protozoan

protract /prəˈtrækt/ *v* to prolong in time or space – ~**ion** *n*

protractor /prəˈtræktəʳ/ *n* **1** a muscle that extends a body part **2** an instrument that is used for marking out or measuring angles in drawing

protrude /prəˈtruːd/ *v* to (cause to) jut out – -**trusion** *n*

protuberant /prəˈtjuːbərənt/ *adj* thrusting or projecting out from a surrounding or adjacent surface – **-nce** *n* – **~ly** *adv*

proud /praʊd/ *adj* **1a** having or displaying excessive self-esteem **b** much pleased; exultant **2a** stately, magnificent **b** giving reason for pride; glorious **3** projecting slightly from a surrounding surface

prove /pruːv/ *v* **proved, proven 1a** to test the quality of; try out **b** to subject to a testing process **2** to establish the truth or validity of by evidence or demonstration **3** to turn out, esp after trial **4** to allow (bread dough) to rise and become light before baking – **-vable** *adj* – **-vably** *adv*

proverb /'prɒvɜːb/ *n* a brief popular epigram or maxim; an adage

proverbial /prə'vɜːbɪəl/ *adj* **1** of or like a proverb **2** that has become a proverb or byword; commonly spoken of – **~ly** *adv*

Proverbs /'prɒvɜːbz/ *n pl but sing in constr* a collection of moral sayings forming a book of the Old Testament

provide /prə'vaɪd/ *v* **1** to furnish, equip *with* **2** to supply what is needed for sustenance or support **3** to stipulate

provided /prə'vaɪdɨd/ *conj* on condition; if and only if

providence /'prɒvɨdəns/ *n often cap* God conceived as the power sustaining and guiding human destiny

provident /'prɒvɨdənt/ *adj* making provision for the future, esp by saving – **~ly** *adv*

providential /,prɒvɨ'denʃəl/ *adj* of or determined (as if) by Providence; lucky – **~ly** *adv*

provider /prə'vaɪdəʳ/ *n* one who provides for his/her family

province /'prɒvɨns/ *n* **1a** an administrative district of a country **b** *pl* all of a country except the metropolis – usu + *the* **2** a field of knowledge or activity; sphere

[1]**provincial** /prə'vɪnʃəl/ *n* **1** one living in or coming from a province **2** a person with a narrow or unrefined outlook

[2]**provincial** *adj* **1** of or coming from a province **2a** limited in outlook; narrow **b** lacking polish; unsophisticated

proving ground *n* a place where sthg new is tried out

[1]**provision** /prə'vɪʒən/ *n* **1a** providing **b** a measure taken beforehand; a preparation **2** *pl* a stock of food or other necessary goods **3** a proviso, stipulation

[2]**provision** *v* to supply with provisions

provisional /prə'vɪʒənəl/ *adj* serving for the time being; *specif* requiring later confirmation – **~ly** *adv*

Provisional *adj* of or being the secret terrorist wing of the IRA

proviso /prə'vaɪzəʊ/ *n* **1** a clause that introduces a condition **2** a conditional stipulation

provocation /,prɒvə'keɪʃən/ *n* **1** an act of provoking; incitement **2** sthg that provokes or arouses

provocative /prə'vɒkətɪv/ *adj* serving or tending to provoke or arouse to indignation, sexual desire, etc – **~ly** *adv*

provoke /prə'vəʊk/ *v* **1** to incite to anger; incense **2a** to call forth; evoke **b** to stir up on purpose; induce

provoking /prə'vəʊkɪŋ/ *adj* causing mild anger; annoying – **~ly** *adv*

provost /'prɒvəst/ *n* **1** the head of a collegiate or cathedral chapter **2** the chief magistrate of a Scottish burgh **3** the head of certain colleges at Oxford, Cambridge, etc

prow /praʊ/ *n* **1** the bow of a ship **2** a pointed projecting front part

prowess /'praʊɨs/ *n* **1** outstanding (military) valour and skill **2** outstanding ability

[1]**prowl** /praʊl/ *v* to move about (in) or roam (over) in a stealthy or predatory manner

[2]**prowl** *n* an act or instance of prowling

proximal /'prɒksɨməl/ *adj, esp of an anatomical part* next to or nearest the point of attachment or origin – **~ly** *adv*

proximate /'prɒksɨmɨt/ *adj* **1a** very near; close **b** forthcoming; imminent **2** next preceding or following *USE* fml – **~ly** *adv*

proximity /prɒk'sɪmɨti/ *n* being close in space, time, or association; *esp* nearness

proxy /'prɒksi/ *n* **1** (the agency, function, or office of) a deputy authorized to act as a substitute for another 2 (a document giving) authority to act or vote for another

prude /pruːd/ *n* one who shows or affects extreme modesty or propriety, esp in sexual matters – **-dish** *adj* – **-dishly** *adv* – **-dishness** *n*

prudence /ˈpruːdəns/ *n* **1** discretion or shrewdness **2** caution or circumspection with regard to danger – **-ent** *adj* – **-ently** *adv*

prudential /pruːˈdenʃəl/ *adj* **1** of or proceeding from prudence **2** exercising prudence, esp in business matters – **~ly** *adv*

prudery /ˈpruːdəri/ *n* **1** the quality of being a prude **2** a prudish act or remark

¹prune /pruːn/ *n* a plum dried or capable of drying without fermentation

²prune *v* to cut off the dead or unwanted parts of (a usu woody plant or shrub)

prurient /ˈprʊərɪənt/ *adj* inclined to, having, or arousing an excessive or unhealthy interest in sexual matters – **-ence** *n* – **~ly** *adv*

Prussian blue /ˌprʌʃən ˈbluː/ *n* **1** any of numerous blue iron pigments **2** a strong greenish blue colour

pry /praɪ/ *v* **1** to inquire in an overinquisitive or impertinent manner *into* **2** to look closely or inquisitively at sby's possessions, actions, etc

psalm /sɑːm/ *n, often cap* any of the sacred songs attributed to King David and collected in the Book of Psalms of the Old Testament

Psalter /ˈsɔːltəʳ/ *n* a book containing a collection of Psalms for liturgical or devotional use

pseudonym /ˈsjuːdənɪm/ *n* a fictitious name; *esp* one used by an author – **~ous** *adj*

psyche /ˈsaɪki/ *n* **1** the soul, self **2** the mind

psychedelic /ˌsaɪkɨˈdelɪk/ *adj* **1** *of drugs* capable of producing altered states of consciousness that involve changed mental and sensory awareness, hallucinations, etc **2** *of colours* fluorescent

psychiatry /saɪˈkaɪətri/ *n* a branch of medicine that deals with mental, emotional, or behavioural disorders – **-trist** *n* – **-tric** *adj* – **-trically** *adv*

¹psychic /ˈsaɪkɪk/ *adj* **1** lying outside the sphere of physical science or knowledge **2** *of a person* sensitive to nonphysical or supernatural forces and influences – **~ally** *adv*

²psychic *n* **1** a psychic person **2** a medium

psycho /ˈsaɪkəʊ/ *n* a psychopath, psychotic – infml

psychoanalysis /ˌsaɪkəʊ-əˈnælɨsɨs/ *n* a method of analysing unconscious mental processes and treating mental disorders, esp by allowing the patient to talk freely about early childhood experiences, dreams, etc – **-lyst** *n* – **-lytic** *adj* – **-lytically** *adv*

psychokinesis /ˌsaɪkəʊkaɪˈniːsɨs, -kɪn-/ *n* apparent movement in physical objects produced by the power of the mind – **-netic** *adj* – **-netically** *adv*

psychological /ˌsaɪkəˈlɒdʒɪkəl/ *adj* **1a** of psychology **b** mental **2** directed towards or intended to affect the will or mind – **~ly** *adv*

psychology /saɪˈkɒlədʒi/ *n* the science or study of mind and behaviour – **-logist** *n*

psychopath /ˈsaɪkəpæθ/ *n* a person suffering from a severe emotional and behavioural disorder characterized by the pursuit of immediate gratification through often violent acts; *broadly* a dangerously violent mentally ill person – **~ic** *adj* – **~ically** *adv*

psychosis /saɪˈkəʊsɨs/ *n, pl* **psychoses** severe mental derangement (e g schizophrenia) that results in the impairment or loss of contact with reality – **-otic** *adj*

psychosomatic /ˌsaɪkəʊsəˈmætɪk/ *adj* of or resulting from the interaction of psychological and bodily factors, esp the production of physical symptoms by mental processes – **~ally** *adv*

psychotherapy /ˌsaɪkəʊˈθerəpi/ *n* treatment by psychological methods for mental, emotional, or psychosomatic disorders – **-pist** *n*

ptarmigan /ˈtaːmɪgən/ *n* any of various grouse of northern regions whose plumage turns white in winter

pterodactyl /ˌterəˈdæktɪl/ *n* any of an

order of extinct flying reptiles without feathers

Ptolemaic system /ˌtɒlǥ'meɪ-ɪk/ *n* the system of planetary motions according to which the sun, moon, and planets revolve round a stationary earth

pub /pʌb/ *n* an establishment where alcoholic beverages are sold and consumed

puberty /'pjuːbəti/ *n* the condition of being or the period of becoming capable of reproducing sexually

pubic /'pjuːbɪk/ *adj* of or situated in or near the region of the bone above the genitals

[1]**public** /'pʌblɪk/ *adj* **1** of or being in the service of the community **2** general, popular **3** of national or community concerns as opposed to private affairs **4** accessible to or shared by all members of the community **5a** exposed to general view; open **b** well-known, prominent – ~**ly** *adv*

[2]**public** *n* **1** *the* people as a whole; *the* populace **2** a group or section of people having common interests or characteristics

publican /'pʌblɪkən/ *n, chiefly Br* the licensee of a public house

publication /ˌpʌblǥ'keɪʃən/ *n* **1** the act or process of publishing **2** a published work

public bar *n, Br* a plainly furnished and often relatively cheap bar in a public house

public company *n* a company whose shares are offered to the general public

public convenience *n, Br* public toilet facilities provided by local government

public house *n, chiefly Br* an establishment where alcoholic beverages are sold to be drunk on the premises

publicist /'pʌblǥsǥst/ *n* an expert or commentator on public affairs

publicity /pʌ'blɪsǥti/ *n* **1a** paid advertising **b** the dissemination of information or promotional material **2** public attention or acclaim – **-cize** *v*

public prosecutor *n* an official who conducts criminal prosecutions on behalf of the state

public relations *n pl but usu sing in constr* the business of inducing the public to have understanding for and goodwill towards a person, organization, or institution

public school *n* an endowed independent usu single-sex school in Britain, typically a large boarding school preparing pupils for higher education

public servant *n* a government employee

publish /'pʌblɪʃ/ *v* **1** to make generally known **2a** to produce or release for publication; *specif* to print **b** to issue the work of (an author) – ~**er** *n*

puce /pjuːs/ *adj or n* brownish purple

puck /pʌk/ *n* a hard rubber disc used in ice hockey

[1]**pucker** /'pʌkəʳ/ *v* to (cause to) become wrinkled or irregularly creased

[2]**pucker** *n* a crease or wrinkle in a normally even surface

puckish /'pʌkɪʃ/ *adj* impish, whimsical – ~**ly** *adv*

pud /pʊd/ *n, Br* a pudding – infml

pudding /'pʊdɪŋ/ *n* **1** a sausage **2** any of various sweet or savoury dishes of a soft to spongy or fairly firm consistency that are made from rice, tapioca, flour, etc and are cooked by boiling, steaming, or baking **3** dessert

pudding stone *n* (a) conglomerate rock

[1]**puddle** /'pʌdl/ *n* a small pool of liquid; *esp* one of usu muddy rainwater

[2]**puddle** *v* to work (a wet mixture of earth or concrete) into a dense impervious mass

pudendum /pjuː'dendəm/ *n, pl* **pudenda** the external genital organs of a (female) human being – usu pl with sing. meaning

puerile /'pjʊəraɪl/ *adj* **1** juvenile **2** not befitting an adult; childish – **-ility** *n*

puerperal /pjuː'ɜːpərəl/ *adj* of or occurring during (the period immediately following) childbirth

[1]**puff** /pʌf/ *v* **1a(1)** to blow in short gusts **(2)** to exhale or blow forcibly **b** to breathe hard and quickly; pant **c** to draw on (a pipe, cigarette, etc) with intermittent exhalations of smoke **2a**

to become distended; swell **b** to distend (as if) with air or gas; inflate **c** to make proud or conceited *USE (2)* usu + *up*

²puff *n* **1a** an act or instance of puffing **b** a small cloud (e g of smoke) emitted in a puff **2** a light round hollow pastry made of puff paste **3** a highly favourable notice or review, esp one that publicizes sthg or sby **4** *chiefly Br* a breath of wind – infml

puff adder *n* a large venomous African viper that inflates its body and hisses loudly when disturbed

puffball /ˈpʌfbɔːl/ *n* any of various spherical and often edible fungi

puffin /ˈpʌfɨn/ *n* any of several seabirds that have a short neck and a deep grooved multicoloured bill

puff out *v* **1** to extinguish by blowing **2** to cause to enlarge, esp by filling or inflating with air

puff pastry *n* a light flaky pastry made with a rich dough containing a large quantity of butter

pug /pʌg/ *n* a small sturdy compact dog with a tightly curled tail and broad wrinkled face

pugilism /ˈpjuːdzɨlɪzəm/ *n* boxing – fml – **pugilist** *n* – **-istic** *adj*

pugnacious /pʌgˈneɪʃəs/ *adj* inclined to fight or quarrel; belligerent – **-ity,** **~ness** *n* – **~ly** *adv*

puissance /ˈpwiːsɑːns, -əns/ *n* **1** a showjumping competition which tests the horse's power to jump high obstacles **2** strength, power – fml or poetic

puke /pjuːk/ *v* to vomit – infml – **puke** *n*

pukka /pʌkə/ *adj* **1** genuine, authentic; *also* first-class **2** *chiefly Br* stiffly formal or proper

pulchritude /ˈpʌlkrɨtjuːd/ *n* physical beauty – fml – **-dinous** *adj*

pule /pjuːl/ *v* to whine, whimper

¹pull /pʊl/ *v* **1a** to exert force upon so as to (tend to) cause motion towards the force; tug at **b** to move, esp through the exercise of mechanical energy **2** to strain (a muscle) **3** to hit (e g a ball in cricket or golf) towards the left from a right-handed swing or towards the right from a left-handed swing **4** to draw apart; tear **5** to print (e g a proof) by impression **6** to bring out (a weapon) ready for use **7** to draw from the barrel, esp by pulling a pump handle **8a** to carry out, esp with daring and imagination – usu + *off* **b** to do, perform, or say with a deceptive intent **9** to draw or inhale hard in smoking

²pull *n* **1a** the act or an instance of pulling **b(1)** a draught of liquid **(2)** an inhalation of smoke (e g from a cigarette) **2** (special influence exerted to obtain) an advantage **3** a force that attracts, compels, or influences

pull away *v* **1** to draw oneself back or away; withdraw **2** to move off or ahead

pull down *v* to demolish, destroy

pullet /ˈpʊlɨt/ *n* a young female domestic fowl less than a year old

pulley /ˈpʊli/ *n* **1** a wheel with a grooved rim that is used with a rope or chain to change the direction and point of application of a pulling force **2** a wheel used to transmit power or motion by means of a belt, rope, or chain passing over its rim

pull-in *n, chiefly Br* a place where vehicles may pull in and stop; *also* a roadside café

pull in *v* **1** to arrest **2** to acquire as payment or profit – infml **3** *of a vehicle or driver* to move to the side of or off the road in order to stop

Pullman /ˈpʊlmən/ *n* a railway passenger carriage with extra-comfortable furnishings, esp for night travel

pull off *v* to carry out or accomplish despite difficulties

pullout *n* **1** a larger leaf in a book or magazine that when folded is the same size as the ordinary pages **2** a removable section of a magazine, newspaper, or book

pull out *v* **1** *esp of a train or road vehicle* to leave, depart **2a** to withdraw from a military position **b** to withdraw from a joint enterprise or agreement **3** *of a motor vehicle* **a** to move into a stream of traffic **b** to move out from behind a vehicle (e g when preparing to overtake)

pullover /ˈpʊl,əʊvəʳ/ *n* a garment for the upper body, esp a jumper, put on by being pulled over the head

pull over *v, of a driver or vehicle* to

move towards the side of the road, esp in order to stop

pull through *v* to (cause to) survive a dangerous or difficult situation (e g illness)

pull up *v* **1** to bring to a stop; halt **2** to reprimand, rebuke **3** to draw even with or gain on others (e g in a race)

pulmonary /ˈpʌlmənəri/, **pulmonic** *adj* of, associated with, or carried on by the lungs

[1]**pulp** /pʌlp/ *n* **1a** the soft juicy or fleshy part of a fruit or vegetable **b** a material prepared by chemical or mechanical means from rags, wood, etc that is used in making paper **2** a soft shapeless mass, esp produced by crushing or beating **3** a magazine or book cheaply produced on rough paper and containing sensational material – **~y** *adj*

[2]**pulp** *v* **1** to reduce to pulp **2** to remove the pulp from

pulpit /ˈpʊlpɪt/ *n* a raised platform or high reading desk in church from which a sermon is preached

pulsar /ˈpʌlsɑːʳ/ *n* a celestial source, prob a rotating neutron star, of uniformly pulsating radio waves

pulsate /pʌlˈseɪt/ *v* **1** to beat with a pulse **2** to throb or move rhythmically; vibrate – **-sation** *n*

[1]**pulse** /pʌls/ *n* the edible seeds of any of various leguminous crops (e g peas, beans, or lentils); *also* the plant yielding these

[2]**pulse** *n* **1** a regular throbbing caused in the arteries by the contractions of the heart; *also* a single movement of such throbbing **2a** (an indication of) underlying sentiment or opinion **b** a feeling of liveliness; vitality **3a** rhythmical vibrating or sounding **b** a single beat or throb

[3]**pulse** *v* to pulsate, throb

pulver·ize, -ise /ˈpʌlvəraɪz/ *v* **1** to reduce (e g by crushing or grinding) to very small particles **2** to annihilate, demolish

puma /ˈpjuːmə/ *n* a powerful tawny big cat formerly widespread in the Americas but now extinct in many areas

pumice /ˈpʌmɨs/ *n* a light porous volcanic rock used esp as an abrasive and for polishing

pummel /ˈpʌməl/ *v* to pound or strike repeatedly, esp with the fists

[1]**pump** /pʌmp/ *n* a device that raises, transfers, or compresses fluids or that reduces the density of gases, esp by suction or pressure or both

[2]**pump** *v* **1a** to raise (e g water) with a pump **b** to draw fluid from with a pump – often + *out* **2** to question persistently **3** to move (sthg) rapidly up and down as if working a pump handle **4** to inflate by means of a pump or bellows – usu + *up*

[3]**pump** *n* **1** a low shoe without fastenings that grips the foot chiefly at the toe and heel **2** *Br* a plimsoll

pumpernickel /ˈpʌmpənɪkəl/ *n* a dark coarse slightly sour-tasting bread made from wholemeal rye

pumpkin /ˈpʌmpkɨn/ *n* (a usu hairy prickly plant that bears) a very large usu round fruit with a deep yellow to orange rind and edible flesh

pump room *n* a room at a spa in which the water is distributed and drunk

[1]**pun** /pʌn/ *n* a humorous use of a word with more than 1 meaning or of words with (nearly) the same sound but different meanings

[2]**pun** *v* to make puns

[1]**punch** /pʌntʃ/ *v* **1** to strike, esp with a hard and quick thrust of the fist **2** to drive or push forcibly (as if) by a punch **3** to emboss, cut, or make (as if) with a punch – **~er** *n*

[2]**punch** *n* **1** a blow (as if) with the fist **2** effective energy or forcefulness

[3]**punch** *n* **1** a tool, usu in the form of a short steel rod, used esp for perforating, embossing, cutting, or driving the heads of nails below a surface **2** a device for cutting holes or notches in paper or cardboard

[4]**punch** *n* a hot or cold drink usu made from wine or spirits mixed with fruit, spices, water, and occas tea

punch-drunk *adj* **1** suffering brain damage as a result of repeated punches or blows to the head **2** behaving as if punch-drunk; dazed

punched card, punch card *n* a card used in data processing in which a pattern of holes or notches has been cut to represent information or instructions

punch line *n* a sentence or phrase, esp a joke, that forms the climax to a speech or dialogue

punch-up *n, chiefly Br* a usu spontaneous fight, esp with the bare fists – infml

punctilious /pʌŋk'tɪlɪəs/ *adj* strict or precise in observing codes of conduct or conventions – **~ly** *adv* – **~ness** *adv*

punctual /'pʌŋktʃʊəl/ *adj* (habitually) arriving, happening, performing, etc at the exact or agreed time – **~ity** *n* – **~ly** *adv*

punctuate /'pʌŋktʃʊeɪt/ *v* **1** to mark or divide with punctuation marks **2** to break into or interrupt at intervals

punctuation /ˌpʌŋktʊ'eɪʃən/ *n* the dividing of writing with marks to clarify meaning; *also* a system of punctuation

[1]**puncture** /'pʌŋktʃə'/ *n* a hole, narrow wound, etc made by puncturing; *esp* a small hole made accidentally in a pneumatic tyre

[2]**puncture** *v* **1** to pierce with a pointed instrument or object **2** to make useless or deflate as if by a puncture

pundit /'pʌndɪ̈t/ *n* **1** a learned man or teacher **2** one who gives opinions in an authoritative manner; an authority

pungent /'pʌndʒənt/ *adj* **1** marked by a sharp incisive quality; caustic **2** to the point; highly expressive **3** having a strong sharp smell or taste; *esp* acrid – **~ly** *adv* – **-gency** *n*

Punic /'pjuːnɪk/ *n or adj* (the dialect) of Carthage or the Carthaginians

punish /'pʌnɪʃ/ *v* **1** to impose a penalty on (an offender) or for (an offence) **2** to treat roughly or damagingly – infml

punishment /'pʌnɪʃmənt/ *n* **1a** punishing or being punished **b** a judicial penalty **2** rough or damaging treatment – infml

punitive /'pjuːnɪ̈tɪv/ *adj* inflicting or intended to inflict punishment – **~ly** *adv*

[1]**punk** /pʌŋk/ *n* **1** sby following punk styles in music, dress, etc **2** *chiefly NAm* sby considered worthless or inferior; *esp* a petty criminal

[2]**punk** *adj* **1** of or being a movement among young people of the 1970s and 1980s in Britain characterized by a violent rejection of established society and expressed through punk rock and the wearing of aggressively outlandish clothes and hairstyles **2** *chiefly NAm* of very poor quality; inferior – slang

[3]**punk** *n* a dry spongy substance prepared from fungi and used to ignite fuses

punnet /'pʌnɪ̈t/ *n, chiefly Br* a small basket of wood, plastic, etc, esp for soft fruit or vegetables

[1]**punt** /pʌnt/ *n* a long narrow flat-bottomed boat with square ends, usu propelled with a pole

[2]**punt** *v* to propel (e g a punt) with a pole – **~er** *n*

[3]**punt** *v, Br* to gamble – **~er** *n*

[4]**punt** *n* kicking a football with the top or tip of the foot after it is dropped from the hands and before it hits the ground – **punt** *v*

[5]**punt** *n* the basic currency unit of the Irish Republic

puny /'pjuːni/ *adj* slight or inferior in power, size, or importance; weak – **-nily** *adv* – **-niness** *n*

[1]**pup** /pʌp/ *n* a young dog; *also* a young seal, rat, etc

[2]**pup** *v* to give birth to pups

pupa /'pjuːpə/ *n, pl* **pupae** the intermediate usu inactive form of an insect (e g a bee, moth, or beetle) that occurs between the larva and the final adult stage – **~l** *adj*

pupate /pjuː'peɪt/ *v* to become a pupa – **-pation** *n*

[1]**pupil** /'pjuːpəl/ *n* **1** a child or young person at school or receiving tuition **2** one who has been taught or influenced by a distinguished person

[2]**pupil** *n* the contractile usu round dark opening in the iris of the eye

puppet /'pʌpɪ̈t/ *n* **1a** a small-scale toy figure (e g of a person or animal) usu with a cloth body and hollow head that fits over and is moved by the hand **b** a marionette **2** one whose acts are controlled by an outside force or influence

puppy /'pʌpi/ *n* **1** a young dog (less than a year old) **2** a conceited or ill-mannered young man

puppy fat *n* temporary plumpness in children and adolescents

puppy love *n* short-lived romantic affection felt by an adolescent for sby of the opposite sex

[1]**purchase** /ˈpɜːtʃɨs/ *v* **1** to obtain by paying money or its equivalent; buy **2** to obtain by labour, danger, or sacrifice – **-chasable** *adj* – **~r** *n*

[2]**purchase** *n* **1** sthg obtained by payment of money or its equivalent **2a** a mechanical hold or advantage (e g that applied through a pulley or lever); *broadly* an advantage used in applying power or influence **b** a means, esp a mechanical device, by which one gains such an advantage

pure /pjʊəʳ/ *adj* **1a(1)** unmixed with any other matter **(2)** free from contamination **(3)** free from moral fault **b** *of a musical sound* being in tune and free from harshness **2a** sheer, unmitigated **b** abstract, theoretical **3a** free from anything that vitiates or weakens **b** containing nothing that does not properly belong **4a** chaste **b** ritually clean

[1]**puree, purée** /ˈpjʊəreɪ/ *n* a thick pulp (e g of fruit or vegetable) usu produced by rubbing cooked food through a sieve or blending in a liquidizer

[2]**puree, purée** *v* to reduce to a puree

purely /ˈpjʊəli/ *adv* **1** simply, merely **2** in a chaste or innocent manner **3** wholly, completely

purgative /ˈpɜːgətɪv/ *n or adj* (a medicine) causing evacuation of the bowels

purgatory /ˈpɜːgətəri/ *n* **1** a place or state of punishment in which, according to Roman Catholic doctrine, souls may make amends for past sins and so become fit for heaven **2** a place or state of temporary suffering or misery – infml – **-rial** *adj*

[1]**purge** /pɜːdʒ/ *v* **1a** to clear of guilt **b** to free from moral or physical impurity **2a** to cause evacuation from (e g the bowels) **b** to rid (e g a nation or party) of unwanted or undesirable members, often summarily or by force – **-gation** *n*

[2]**purge** *n* **1** an (esp political) act of purging **2** a purgative

purify /ˈpjʊərɨfaɪ/ *v* **1** to free of physical or moral impurity or imperfection **2** to free from undesirable elements – **-fication** *n*

purist /ˈpjʊərɨst/ *n* one who keeps strictly and often excessively to established or traditional usage, esp in language – **-ism** *n*

puritan /ˈpjʊərɨtn/ *n* **1** *cap* a member of a 16th- and 17th-c mainly Calvinist Protestant group in England and New England **2** one who practises or preaches a rigorous or severe moral code – **~ism** *n* – **~ical** *adj* – **~ically** *adv*

purity /ˈpjʊərɨti/ *n* **1** pureness **2** saturation of a colour

[1]**purl** /pɜːl/ *n* **1** a thread of twisted gold or silver wire used for embroidering or edging **2 purl, purl stitch** a basic knitting stitch made by inserting the needle into the back of a stitch that produces a raised pattern on the back of the work

[2]**purl** *v* to knit in purl stitch

purlieus /ˈpɜːljuːz/ *n pl* **1** environs, neighbourhood **2** confines, bounds – fml

purloin /pɜːˈlɔɪn, ˈpɜːlɔɪn/ *v* to take dishonestly; steal – fml

[1]**purple** /ˈpɜːpəl/ *adj* **1** of the colour purple **2** highly rhetorical; ornate – **purplish** *adj*

[2]**purple** *n* **1** a colour falling about midway between red and blue in hue **2** imperial, regal, or very high rank

purple heart *n* a light blue tablet containing the drug phenobarbitone and formerly prescribed as a hypnotic or sedative

[1]**purport** /ˈpɜːpɔːt/ *n* professed or implied meaning; import; *also* substance – fml

[2]**purport** /pɜːˈpɔːt/ *v* to (be intended to) seem; profess

[1]**purpose** /ˈpɜːpəs/ *n* **1** the object for which sthg exists or is done; the intention **2** resolution, determination

[2]**purpose** *v* to have as one's intention – fml

purpose-built *n* designed to meet a specific need

purposeful /ˈpɜːpəsfəl/ *adj* **1** full of determination **2** having a purpose or aim – **~ly** *adv*

purposely /ˈpɜːpəsli/ *adv* with a deliberate or express purpose

purr /pɜːʳ/ *v* to make the low vibratory murmur of a contented cat – **purr** *n*

[1]**purse** /pɜːs/ *n* **1** a small flattish bag for money; *esp* a wallet with a compartment for holding change **2** a sum of money offered as a prize or present; *also* the total amount of money offered in prizes for a given event **3** *NAm* a handbag

[2]**purse** *v* to pucker, knit

purser /ˈpɜːsəʳ/ *n* an officer on a ship responsible for documents and accounts and on a passenger ship also for the comfort and welfare of passengers

purse strings *n pl* control over expenditure

pursuance /pəˈsjuːəns/ *n* a carrying out or into effect (e g of a plan or order)

pursue /pəˈsjuː/ *v* **1** to follow in order to overtake, capture, kill, or defeat **2** to find or employ measures to obtain or accomplish **3a** to engage in **b** to follow up **4** to continue to afflict; haunt – **~r** *n*

pursuit /pəˈsjuːt/ *n* **1** an act of pursuing **2** an activity that one regularly engages in (e g as a pastime or profession)

purulent /ˈpjʊərələnt/ *adj* **1** containing, consisting of, or being pus **2** accompanied by suppuration – **-lence** *n* – **~ly** *adv*

purvey /pɜːˈveɪ/ *v* to supply (e g provisions), esp in the course of business – **~ance,** **~or** *n*

pus /pʌs/ *n* thick opaque usu yellowish white fluid matter formed by suppuration (e g in an abscess)

[1]**push** /pʊʃ/ *v* **1** to apply a force to (sthg) in order to cause movement away from the person or thing applying the force **2a** to develop (e g an idea or argument), esp to an extreme degree **b** to urge or press the advancement, adoption, or practice of; *specif* to make aggressive efforts to sell **c** to press or urge (sby) to sthg; pressurize **3** to press forwards energetically against obstacles or opposition **4** to exert oneself continuously or vigorously to achieve an end **5** to approach in age or number – infml **6** to engage in the illicit sale of (drugs) – slang **7** to press against sthg with steady force (as if) in order to move it away

[2]**push** *n* **1** a vigorous effort to attain an end; a drive **2a** an act or action of pushing **b** vigorous enterprise or energy **3a** an exertion of influence to promote another's interests **b** stimulation to activity; an impetus **4** *Br* dismissal – esp in *get/give the push*

push around *v* to order about; bully

push-bike *n* a pedal bicycle

push-button *adj* **1** operated by means of a push button **2** characterized by the use of long-range weapons rather than physical combat

pushchair /ˈpʊʃ-tʃeəʳ/ *n, Br* a light folding chair on wheels in which young children may be pushed

pushed /pʊʃt/ *adj* having difficulty in finding enough time, money, etc – infml

pusher /ˈpʊʃəʳ/ *n* **1** a utensil used by a child for pushing food onto a spoon or fork **2** one who sells drugs illegally – slang

push in *v* to join a queue at a point in front of others already waiting, esp by pushing or jostling

push off *v* to go away, esp hastily or abruptly – infml

push on *v* to continue on one's way, esp despite obstacles or difficulties

pushover /ˈpʊʃˌəʊvəʳ/ *n* **1** an opponent who is easy to defeat or a victim who is incapable of effective resistance **2** sby unable to resist a usu specified attraction; a sucker **3** sthg accomplished without difficulty *USE* infml

pushy /ˈpʊʃi/ *adj* self-assertive often to an objectionable degree; forward – infml – **-hily** *adv* – **-hiness** *n*

pusillanimous /ˌpjuːsɪ̈ˈlænɪ̈mɪ̈s/ *adj* lacking courage and resolution; contemptibly timid – fml – **~ly** *adv* – **-mity** *n*

puss /pʊs/ *n* a cat – used chiefly as a pet name or calling name *USE* infml

pussy /ˈpʊsi/ *n* **1** a catkin of the pussy willow **2** a cat – infml; used chiefly as a pet name

pussyfoot /ˈpʊsifʊt/ *v* **1** to tread or move warily or stealthily **2** to avoid committing oneself (e g to a course of action)

pussy willow *n* any of various willows having grey silky catkins

pustule /'pʌstjuːl/ *n* a small raised spot on the skin filled with pus; *also* a blister, pimple

[1]**put** /pʊt/ *v* **1a** to place in or move into a specified position or relationship **b** to bring into a specified condition **2a** to cause to endure or undergo; subject **b** to impose, establish **3a** to formulate for judgment or decision **b** to express, state **4a** to turn into language or literary form **b** to adapt, set **5a** to devote, apply **b** to impel, incite **6a** to repose, rest **b** to invest **7** to give as an estimate; *also* to imagine as being **8** to write, inscribe **9** to bet, wager

[2]**put** *n* a throw made with an overhand pushing motion; *specif* the act or an instance of putting the shot

[3]**put** *adj* in the same position, condition, or situation – in *stay put*

put about *v* , *of a ship* to change direction

put across *v* to convey (the meaning or significance of sthg) effectively

putative /'pjuːtətɪv/ *adj* **1** commonly accepted or supposed **2** assumed to exist or to have existed *USE* fml

put away *v* **1** to discard, renounce **2a** to place for storage when not in use **b** to save (money) for future use **3** to confine, esp in an asylum

put by *v* to save or store up

put-down *n* a humiliating remark; a snub

put down *v* **1** to bring to an end; suppress **2** to kill (e g a sick or injured animal) painlessly **3a** to put in writing **b** to enter in a list (e g of subscribers) **4** to pay as a deposit **5** to attribute **6** to store or set aside (e g bottles of wine) for future use **7** to disparage, humiliate **8** , *of an aircraft* to land

put forward *v* **1** to propose (e g a theory) **2** to bring into prominence

put in *v* **1** to spend (time) at an occupation or job **2** to make an application, request, or offer *for*

put off *v* **1** to disconcert, distract **2a** to postpone **b** to get rid of or persuade to wait, esp by means of excuses or evasions

[1]**put-on** *adj* pretended, assumed

[2]**put-on** *n* an instance of deliberately misleading sby; *also, chiefly NAm* a parody, spoof

put on *v* **1a** to dress oneself in; don **b** to feign, assume **2** to cause to act or operate; apply **3** to come to have an increased amount of **4** to stage, produce (e g a play) **5** to bet (a sum of money)

put out *v* **1** to extinguish **2** to publish, issue **3** to produce for sale **4a** to disconcert, confuse **b** to annoy, irritate **c** to inconvenience **5** to give or offer (a job of work) to be done by another outside the premises **6** to set out from shore

put over *v* to put across

putrefaction /ˌpjuːtrɪ̈'fækʃən/ *n* the decomposition of organic matter; *esp* the breakdown of proteins by bacteria and fungi, typically in the absence of oxygen, with the formation of foul-smelling products

putrefy /'pjuːtrɪ̈faɪ/ *v* to make or become putrid – **-rescent** *adj* – **-rescence** *n*

putrid /pjuːtrɪ̈d/ *adj* **1** in a state of putrefaction **2** foul-smelling – **~ity** *n*

putsch /pʊtʃ/ *n* a secretly plotted and suddenly executed attempt to overthrow a government

putt /pʌt/ *n* a gentle golf stroke made to roll the ball towards or into the hole on a putting green

puttee /'pʌtiː, -'-/ *n* a long cloth strip wrapped spirally round the leg from ankle to knee, esp as part of an army uniform

putter /'pʌtəʳ/ *n* a golf club used for putting

put through *v* **1** to carry into effect or to a successful conclusion **2** to obtain a connection for (a telephone call)

putto /'pʊtəʊ/ *n, pl* **putti** a figure of a Cupid-like boy, esp in Renaissance painting

[1]**putty** /'pʌti/ *n* a dough-like cement, usu made of whiting and boiled linseed oil, used esp in fixing glass in sashes and stopping crevices in woodwork

[2]**putty** *v* to use putty on or apply putty to

put-up *adj* contrived secretly beforehand – infml

put up *v* **1** to nominate for election – often + *for* **2** to offer for public sale **3** to give food and shelter to; accommodate **4** to build, erect **5** to offer as a prize or stake **6** to increase the amount of; raise

put-upon *adj* imposed upon; taken advantage of

[1]**puzzle** /'pʌzəl/ *v* to offer or represent a problem difficult to solve or a situation difficult to resolve; perplex; *also* to exert (e g oneself) *over* or *about* such a problem or situation – **puzzled** *adj* – **puzzler** *n*

[2]**puzzle** *n* a problem, contrivance, etc designed for testing one's ingenuity – **~ment** *n*

PVC *n* polyvinyl chloride

pygmy /pɪgmi/ *n* **1** a member of a very small people of equatorial Africa **2** an insignificant or worthless person in a specified sphere

pyjamas, *NAm chiefly* **pajamas** /pə'dʒɑːməz/ *n pl* **1** loose lightweight trousers traditionally worn in the East **2** a suit of loose lightweight jacket and trousers for sleeping in

pylon /'paɪlən/ *n* a tower for supporting either end of a wire, esp electricity power cables, over a long span

pyorrhoea /,paɪə'riə/ *n* an inflammation of the tooth sockets

pyramid /'pɪrəmɪd/ *n* **1** an ancient massive structure having typically a square ground plan and tapering smooth or stepped walls that meet at the top **2** a polyhedron having for its base a polygon and for faces triangles with a common vertex **3** a nonphysical structure or system (e g a social or organizational hierarchy) having a broad supporting base and narrowing gradually to an apex

pyre /paɪəʳ/ *n* a heap of combustible material for burning a dead body as part of a funeral rite

Pyrex /'paɪəreks/ *trademark* – used for glass and glassware that is resistant to heat, chemicals, and electricity

pyromania /,paɪərə'meɪnɪə, ,paɪərəʊ-/ *n* a compulsive urge to start fires – **~c** *n*

pyrotechnics /paɪərəʊ'teknɪks/ *n pl* **1** fireworks **2** a brilliant or spectacular display (e g of oratory)

Pyrrhic victory /,pɪrɪk 'vɪktəri/ *n* a victory won at excessive cost

python /'paɪθən/ *n* a large boa or other constrictor; *esp* any of a genus that includes the largest living snakes

Q

q /kjuː/ *n, pl* **q's, qs** *often cap* (a graphic representation of or device for reproducing) the 17th letter of the English alphabet

qua /kwaː, kweɪ/ *prep* in the capacity or character of; as

[1]**quack** /kwæk/ *v or n* (to make) the characteristic cry of a duck

[2]**quack** *n* **1** one who has or pretends to have medical skill **2** a charlatan *USE* infml – **~ery** *n*

[1]**quad** /kwɒd/ *n* a quadrangle

[2]**quad** *n* a quadruplet

Quadragesima /ˌkwɒdrəˈdʒesɨmə/ *n* the first Sunday in Lent

quadrant /ˈkwɒdrənt/ *n* **1** an instrument for measuring angles, consisting commonly of a graduated arc of 90° **2** (the area of 1 quarter of a circle that is bounded by) an arc of a circle containing an angle of 90° **3** any of the 4 quarters into which sthg is divided by 2 real or imaginary lines that intersect each other at right angles

quadrilateral /ˌkwɒdrɨˈlætərəl/ *n or adj* (a polygon) having 4 sides

quadrille /kwəˈdrɪl/ *n* (the music for) a square dance for 4 couples made up of 5 or 6 figures

quadruped /ˈkwɒdrʊped/ *n* an animal having 4 feet

[1]**quadruple** /ˈkwɒdrʊpəl, kwɒˈdruː-/ *v* to make or become 4 times as great or as many

[2]**quadruple** *n* a sum 4 times as great as another – **-ply** *adv*

[3]**quadruple** *adj* **1** having 4 units or members **2** being 4 times as great or as many **3** marked by 4 beats per bar

quadruplet /ˈkwɒdrʊplɨt/ *n* **1** any of 4 offspring born at 1 birth **2** a combination of 4 of a kind **3** a group of 4 musical notes performed in the time of 3 notes of the same value

quaff /kwɒf, kwɑːf/ *v* to drink (a beverage) deeply in long draughts

quagmire /ˈkwægmaɪəʳ, ˈkwɒg-/ *n* **1** soft miry land that shakes or yields under the foot **2** a predicament from which it is difficult to extricate oneself

[1]**quail** /kweɪl/ *n* **1** a migratory Old World game bird **2** any of various small American game birds

[2]**quail** *v* to shrink back in fear; cower

quaint /kweɪnt/ *adj* **1** unusual or different in character or appearance; odd **2** pleasingly or strikingly old-fashioned or unfamiliar – **~ly** *adv* – **~ness** *n*

[1]**quake** /kweɪk/ *v* **1** to shake or vibrate, usu from shock or instability **2** to tremble or shudder, esp inwardly from fear

[2]**quake** *n* **1** a quaking **2** an earthquake – infml

Quaker /ˈkweɪkəʳ/ *n* a member of a pacifist Christian sect that stresses Inner Light and rejects sacraments and an ordained ministry

qualification /ˌkwɒlɨfɨˈkeɪʃən/ *n* **1** a restriction in meaning or application **2a** a quality or skill that fits a person (e g for a particular task or appointment) **b** a condition that must be complied with (e g for the attainment of a privilege)

qualified /ˈkwɒlɨfaɪd/ *adj* **1a** fitted (e g by training or experience) for a usu specified purpose; competent **b** complying with the specific requirements or conditions (e g for appointment to an office); eligible **2** limited or modified in some way

qualify /ˈkwɒlɨfaɪ/ *v* **1a** to reduce from a general to a particular or restricted form; modify **b** to make less harsh or strict; moderate **2** to reach an accredited level of competence **3** to exhibit a required degree of ability or achievement in a preliminary contest

qualitative /ˈkwɒlɨtətɪv/ *adj* of or involving quality or kind – **~ly** *adv*

[1]**quality** /ˈkwɒlɨti/ *n* **1a** peculiar and essential character; nature **b** an inherent feature; a property **2a** degree of excellence; grade **b** superiority in

kind **3** a distinguishing attribute; a characteristic

[2]**quality** *adj* **1** concerned with or displaying excellence **2** *of a newspaper* aiming to appeal to an educated readership

qualm /kwɑːm/ *n* **1** a sudden and brief attack of illness, faintness, or nausea **2** a sudden feeling of anxiety or apprehension **3** a scruple or feeling of uneasiness, esp about a point of conscience or honour

quandary /'kwɒndəri/ *n* a state of perplexity or doubt

quango /'kwæŋgəʊ/ *n, pl* **quangos** ***Br*** an autonomous body (e g the Race Relations Board) set up by the British government and having statutory powers in a specific field

quantify /'kwɒntɪ̣faɪ/ *v* to determine, express, or measure the quantity of – **-fiable** *adj* – **-fication** *n*

quantitative /'kwɒntɪ̣tətɪv/ *adj* **1** (expressible in terms) of quantity **2** of or involving the measurement of quantity or amount – **~ly** *adv*

quantity /'kwɒntɪ̣ti/ *n* **1a** an indefinite amount or number **b** a known, measured or estimated amount **c** the total amount or number **d** a considerable amount or number – often pl with sing. meaning **2** the character of a logical proposition as universal, particular, or singular

quantity surveyor *n* sby who estimates or measures quantities (e g for builders)

quantum /'kwɒntəm/ *n, pl* **quanta** **1a** a quantity, amount **b** a portion, part **2** any of the very small parcels or parts into which many forms of energy are subdivided and which cannot be further subdivided

[1]**quarantine** /'kwɒrəntiːn/ *n* **1** (the period of) a restraint on the activities or communication of people or the transport of goods or animals, designed to prevent the spread of disease or pests **2** a state of enforced isolation

[2]**quarantine** *v* **1** to detain in or exclude by quarantine **2** to isolate from normal relations or communication

quark /kwɑːk, kwɔːk/ *n* a hypothetical particle that carries a fractional electric charge and is held to be a constituent of known elementary particles

[1]**quarrel** /'kwɒrəl/ *n* **1** a reason for dispute or complaint **2** a usu verbal conflict between antagonists; a dispute

[2]**quarrel** *v* **1** to find fault *with* **2** to contend or dispute actively; argue

quarrelsome /'kwɒrəlsəm/ *adj* inclined or quick to quarrel, esp in a petty manner

[1]**quarry** /'kwɒri/ *n* the prey or game of a predator, esp a hawk, or of a hunter

[2]**quarry** *n* **1** an open excavation from which building materials (e g stone, slate, and sand) are obtained **2** a source from which useful material, esp information, may be extracted – **quarry** *v*

quart /kwɔːt/ *n* a unit of liquid capacity equal to 2pt

[1]**quarter** /'kwɔːtə^r/ *n* **1** any of 4 equal parts into which sthg is divisible **2** any of various units equal to or derived from a fourth of some larger unit **3** a fourth of a measure of time: e g **a** any of 4 3-month divisions of a year **b** a quarter of an hour – used in designation of time **4** (a coin worth) a quarter of a (US) dollar **5** a hindquarter, rump **6** (the direction of or region round) a (cardinal) compass point **7** *pl* living accommodation; lodgings; *esp* accommodation for military personnel or their families **8** merciful consideration of an opponent; *specif* the clemency of not killing a defeated enemy **9** the part of a ship's side towards the stern

[2]**quarter** *v* **1** to divide into 4 (almost) equal parts **2** to provide with lodgings or shelter; *esp* to assign (a member of the armed forces) to accommodation **3** to crisscross (an area) in many directions

[3]**quarter** *adj* consisting of or equal to a quarter

quarter day *n* a day which begins a quarter of the year and on which a quarterly payment often falls due

quarterdeck /'kwɔːtədek/ *n* **1** the stern area of a ship's upper deck **2** *chiefly Br* the officers of a ship or navy

quarterfinal /ˌkwɔːtəˈfaɪnl/ *n* a match whose winner goes through to the semifinals of a knockout tournament

quartering /ˈkwɔːtərɪŋ/ *n* any of the divisions of a heraldic shield or the coat of arms borne on it

[1]**quarterly** /ˈkwɔːtəli/ *n* a periodical published at 3-monthly intervals

[2]**quarterly** *adj* **1** computed for or payable at 3-monthly intervals **2** recurring, issued, or spaced at 3-monthly intervals

quartermaster /ˈkwɔːtəˌmɑːstəʳ/ *n* **1** a petty officer or seaman who attends to a ship's compass, tiller or wheel, and signals **2** an army officer who provides clothing, subsistence, and quarters for a body of troops

quarterstaff /ˈkwɔːtəstɑːf/ *n, pl* **quarterstaves** a long stout staff formerly used as a weapon

quartet /kwɔːˈtet/ *n* (a musical composition for) a group of four performers

[1]**quartz** /kwɔːts/ *n* a mineral occurring in transparent hexagonal crystals or in crystalline masses

[2]**quartz** *adj* controlled by the oscillations of a quartz crystal

quasar /ˈkweɪzɑːʳ/ *n* any of various unusually bright very distant star-like celestial objects that have spectra with large red shifts

quash /kwɒʃ/ *v* **1a** to nullify (by judicial action) **b** to reject (a legal document) as invalid **2** to suppress or extinguish summarily and completely

quatrain /ˈkwɒtreɪn/ *n* a stanza of 4 lines

[1]**quaver** /ˈkweɪvəʳ/ *v* **1** *esp of the voice* to tremble, shake **2** to speak or sing in a trembling voice – **~y** *adj*

[2]**quaver** *n* **1** a musical note with the time value of ½ that of a crotchet **2** a tremulous sound

quay /kiː/ *n* an artificial landing place beside navigable water for loading and unloading ships

queasy *also* **queazy** /ˈkwiːzi/ *adj* **1** causing or suffering from nausea **2** causing or feeling anxiety or uneasiness – **-sily** *adv* – **-siness** *n*

queen /kwiːn/ *n* **1** the wife or widow of a king **2** a female monarch **3** the most powerful piece of each colour in a set of chessmen, which has the power to move any number of squares in any direction **4** a playing card marked with a stylized figure of a queen and ranking usu below the king **5** the fertile fully developed female in a colony of bees, ants, or termites

queen mother *n* a woman who is the widow of a king and the mother of the reigning sovereign

Queen's Counsel *n* a barrister who has been appointed by the Crown to a senior rank with special privileges – used when the British monarch is a queen

[1]**queer** /kwɪəʳ/ *adj* **1a** eccentric, unconventional **b** mildly insane **2** questionable, suspicious **3** not quite well; queasy – infml **4** homosexual – derog

[2]**queer** *v* to spoil the effect or success of

quell /kwel/ *v* **1** to overwhelm thoroughly and reduce to submission or passivity **2** to quiet, pacify

quench /kwentʃ/ *v* **1** to put out (the light or fire of) **2a** to terminate (as if) by destroying; eliminate **b** to relieve or satisfy with liquid

querulous /ˈkwərʊləs/ *adj* habitually complaining; fretful, peevish – **~ly** *adv* – **~ness** *n*

[1]**query** /ˈkwɪəri/ *n* a question, esp expressing doubt or uncertainty

[2]**query** *v* **1** to put as a question **2** to question the accuracy of (e g a statement)

[1]**quest** /kwest/ *n* **1** (the object of) a pursuit or search **2** an adventurous journey undertaken by a knight in medieval romance

[2]**quest** *v* to search for – chiefly poetic

[1]**question** /ˈkwestʃən/ *n* **1a** an interrogative expression used to elicit information or test knowledge **b** an interrogative sentence or clause **2** an act or instance of asking; an inquiry **3a** a subject or concern that is uncertain or in dispute **b** the specific point at issue **4a** (room for) doubt or objection **b** chance, possibility

[2]**question** *v* **1a** to ask a question of **b** to interrogate **2** to doubt, dispute – **~ing** *adj* – **~ingly** *adv* – **~er** *n*

questionable /'kwestʃənəbəl/ *adj* **1** open to doubt or challenge; not certain or exact **2** of doubtful morality or propriety; shady – **-bly** *adv*

question mark *n* a punctuation mark ? used in writing and printing at the end of a sentence to indicate a direct question

questionnaire /ˌkwestʃə'neəʳ, ˌkes-/ *n* (a form having) a set of questions to be asked of a number of people to obtain statistically useful information

¹**queue** /kjuː/ *n* **1** a pigtail **2** a waiting line, esp of people or vehicles

²**queue** *v* to line up or wait in a queue

¹**quibble** /'kwɪbəl/ *n* a minor objection or criticism

²**quibble** *v* **1** to equivocate **2** to bicker – **~r** *n* – **-ling** *adj*

quiche /kiːʃ/ *n* a pastry shell filled with a rich savoury egg and cream custard and various other ingredients (e g ham, cheese, or vegetables)

¹**quick** /kwɪk/ *adj* **1a** fast in understanding, thinking, or learning; mentally agile **b** reacting with speed and keen sensitivity **2a** fast in development or occurrence **b** done or taking place with rapidity **c** inclined to hastiness (e g in action or response) **d** capable of being easily and speedily prepared – **~ly** *adv* – **~ness** *n*

²**quick** *adv* in a quick manner

³**quick** *n* **1** painfully sensitive flesh, esp under a fingernail, toenail, etc **2** the inmost sensibilities

quicken /'kwɪkən/ *v* **1** to enliven, stimulate **2** to make more rapid; accelerate **3** to come to life

quickie /'kwɪki/ *n* sthg done or made in a hurry – infml

quicksand /'kwɪksænd/ *n* (a deep mass of) loose sand, esp mixed with water, into which heavy objects readily sink

quicksilver /'kwɪkˌsɪlvəʳ/ *n* mercury

quickstep /'kwɪkstep/ *n* a fast fox-trot characterized by a combination of short rapid steps

quick-witted *adj* quick in understanding; mentally alert

¹**quid** /kwɪd/ *n, Br* the sum of £1 – infml

²**quid** *n* a wad of sthg, esp tobacco, for chewing

quid pro quo /ˌkwɪd prəʊ 'kwəʊ/ *n* sthg given or received in exchange for sthg else

quiescent /kwaɪ'esənt/ *adj* **1** causing no trouble **2** at rest; inactive – **-cence** *n* – **~ly** *adv*

¹**quiet** /'kwaɪət/ *n* being quiet; tranquillity

²**quiet** *adj* **1a** marked by little or no motion or activity; calm **b** free from noise or uproar; still **c** secluded **2a** gentle, reserved **b** unobtrusive, conservative **3** private, discreet – **~ly** *adv* – **~ness** *n*

³**quiet** *adv* in a quiet manner

⁴**quiet** *v* to calm, soothe

quieten /'kwaɪətn/ *v* to make or become quiet – often + *down*

quietude /'kwaɪətjuːd/ *n* being quiet; repose – fml

quietus /kwaɪ'itəs, -'eɪtəs/ *n* removal from activity; *esp* death

quiff /kwɪf/ *n, Br* a lock of hair brushed so as to stand up over the forehead

quill /kwɪl/ *n* **1a** the hollow horny barrel of a feather **b** any of the large stiff feathers of a bird's wing or tail **c** any of the hollow sharp spines of a porcupine, hedgehog, etc **2** sthg made from or resembling the quill of a feather; *esp* a pen for writing

¹**quilt** /kwɪlt/ *n* **1** a thick warm top cover for a bed consisting of padding held in place between 2 layers of cloth by lines of stitching **2** a bedspread

²**quilt** *v* to stitch or sew together in layers with padding in between

quin /kwɪn/ *n, Br* a quintuplet

quince /kwɪns/ *n* (a central Asian tree that bears) a fruit resembling a hard-fleshed yellow apple, used for marmalade, jelly, and preserves

quinine /'kwɪniːn/ *n* a drug obtained from cinchona bark formerly used as the major treatment of malaria

quintessence /kwɪn'tesəns/ *n* **1** the pure and concentrated essence of sthg; the most significant or typical element in a whole **2** the most typical example or representative (e g of a quality or class) – **-sential** *adj* – **-sentially** *adv*

quintet /kwɪn'tet/ *n* (a musical composition for) a group of 5 performers

quintuplet /ˈkwɪntjʊplɪ̧t, kwɪnˈtjuːp-/ *n* **1** a combination of 5 of a kind **2** any of 5 offspring born at 1 birth

quip /kwɪp/ *v or n* (to make) a clever, witty, or sarcastic observation or response

quire /kwaɪəʳ/ *n* **1** twenty-four sheets of paper of the same size and quality **2** a set of folded sheets (e g of a book) fitting one within another

quirk /kwɜːk/ *n* **1** an odd or peculiar trait; an idiosyncrasy **2** an accident, vagary

quisling /ˈkwɪzlɪŋ/ *n* a traitor who collaborates with invaders

¹quit /kwɪt/ *adj* released from obligation, charge, or penalty – + *of*

²quit *v* **1** to cease doing sthg; *specif* to give up one's job **2** *of a tenant* to vacate occupied premises **3** to admit defeat; give up

quite /kwaɪt/ *adv or adj* **1a** wholly, completely **b** positively, certainly **2** more than usually; rather **3** *chiefly Br* to only a moderate degree

quits /kwɪts/ *adj* on even terms as a result of repaying a debt or retaliating for an injury

quitter /ˈkwɪtəʳ/ *n* one who gives up too easily; a defeatist

¹quiver /ˈkwɪvəʳ/ *n* a case for carrying or holding arrows

²quiver *v* to shake or move with a slight trembling motion

quixotic /kwɪkˈsɒtɪk/ *adj* idealistic or chivalrous in a rash or impractical way – **~ally** *adv*

¹quiz /kwɪz/ *n* **-zz-** a public test of (general) knowledge, esp as a television or radio entertainment

²quiz *v* to question closely – journ

quizzical /ˈkwɪzɪkəl/ *adj* **1** gently mocking; teasing **2** indicating a state of puzzlement; questioning – **~ly** *adv*

quorum /ˈkwɔːrəm/ *n* the number of members of a body that when duly assembled is constitutionally competent to transact business

quota /ˈkwəʊtə/ *n* **1** a proportional part or share; *esp* the share or proportion to be either contributed or received by an individual or body **2** a numerical limit set on some class of people or things

quotable /ˈkwəʊtəbəl/ *adj* **1** fit for or worth quoting **2** made with permission for publication (e g in a newspaper) – **-bility** *n*

quotation /kwəʊˈteɪʃən/ *n* **1** sthg quoted; *esp* a passage or phrase quoted from printed literature **2** quoting **3a** current bids and offers for or prices of shares, securities, commodities, etc **b** an estimate

quotation mark *n* either of a pair of punctuation marks ' " or ' ' used to indicate the beginning and end of a direct quotation

¹quote /kwəʊt/ *v* **1** to repeat a passage or phrase previously said or written, esp by another in writing or speech, esp in substantiation or illustration and usu with an acknowledgment **2** to cite in illustration **3** to make an estimate of or give exact information on (e g the price of a commodity or service)

²quote *n* **1** a quotation **2** quotation mark

quoth /kwəʊθ/ *v past, archaic* said – chiefly in the 1st and 3rd persons with a subject following

quotient /ˈkwəʊʃənt/ *n* **1** the result of the division of one number or expression by another **2** the ratio, usu multiplied by 100, between a test score and a measurement on which that score might be expected to depend

R

r /ɑːʳ/ *n, pl* **r's, rs** *often cap* (a graphic representation of or device for reproducing) the 18th letter of the English alphabet

rabbi /ˈræbaɪ/ *n* a Jew trained and ordained for professional religious leadership; *specif* the official leader of a Jewish congregation – **~nical** *adj*

[1]**rabbit** /ˈræbɨt/ *n* **1** (the fur of) a small long-eared mammal that is related to the hares but differs from them in producing naked young and in its burrowing habits **2** *Br* an unskilful player (e g in golf, cricket, or tennis)

[2]**rabbit** *v, Br* to talk aimlessly or inconsequentially – infml; often + *on*

rabble /ˈræbəl/ *n* a disorganized or disorderly crowd of people; *also the* mob

Rabelaisian /ˌræbəˈleɪzɪən, -ʒən/ *adj* marked by the robust humour, extravagant caricature, or bold naturalism characteristic of Rabelais or his works

rabid /ˈræbɨd/ *adj* **1** unreasoning or fanatical in an opinion or feeling **2** affected with rabies

rabies /ˈreɪbiːz/ *n* a fatal short-lasting disease of the nervous system transmitted esp through the bite of an affected animal and characterized by extreme fear of water and convulsions

[1]**race** /reɪs/ *n* **1a** a strong or rapid current of water in the sea, a river, etc **b** a watercourse used to turn the wheel of a mill **2a** a contest of speed (e g in running or riding) **b** *pl* a meeting in which several races (e g for horses) are run

[2]**race** *v* **1** to compete in a race **2** to go or move at top speed or out of control **3** *of a motor, engine, etc* to revolve too fast under a diminished load – **~r** *n*

[3]**race** *n* **1** a family, tribe, people, or nation belonging to the same stock **2** an actually or potentially interbreeding group within a species **3a** a division of mankind having traits that are sufficient to characterize it as a distinct human type **b** human beings collectively – **race, racial** *adj* – **racially** *adv*

racecourse /ˈreɪs-kɔːs/ *n* a place where or the track on which races, esp horse races, are held

racialism /ˈreɪʃəlɪzəm/ , **racism** /ˈreɪsɪzəm/ *n* **1** racial prejudice or discrimination **2** the belief that racial differences produce an inherent superiority for a particular race – **racialist, racist** *adj, n*

[1]**rack** /ræk/ *n* **1** an instrument of torture on which the victim's body is stretched – usu + *the* **2** a framework, stand, or grating on or in which articles are placed

[2]**rack** *v* **1** to torture on the rack **2** to cause to suffer torture, pain, or anguish **3** to raise (rents) oppressively **4** to place in a rack

[3]**rack** *v* to draw off (e g wine) from the lees

[4]**rack** *n* the front rib section of lamb used for chops or as a roast

[5]**rack** *n* destruction – chiefly in *rack and ruin*

[1]**racket, racquet** /ˈrækɨt/ *n* **1** a lightweight implement consisting of netting stretched in an open frame with a handle attached that is used for striking the ball, shuttle, etc in various games **2** *pl, but sing in constr* a game for 2 or 4 players play on a 4-walled court

[2]**racket** *n* **1** a loud and confused noise **2a** a fraudulent enterprise made workable by bribery or intimidation **b** an easy and lucrative occupation or line of business – infml

racketeer /rækɨˈtɪəʳ/ *n* one who extorts money or advantages by threats, blackmail, etc

raconteur /ˌrækɒnˈtɜːʳ/ *n* one who excels in telling anecdotes

racoon, raccoon /rəˈkuːn, ræ-/ *n* (the

fur of) a small flesh-eating mammal of N America that has a bushy ringed tail

racy /'reɪsi/ *adj* **1** full of zest or vigour **2** having a strongly marked quality; piquant **3** risqué, suggestive – **racily** *adv* – **raciness** *n*

radar /'reɪdɑːʳ/ *n* an electronic device that generates high-frequency radio waves and locates objects in the vicinity by analysis of the radio waves reflected back from them

[1]**radial** /'reɪdɪəl/ *adj* **1** (having parts) arranged like rays or radii from a central point or axis **2** characterized by divergence from a centre – ~**ly** *adv*

[2]**radial** *n* **1** any line in a system of radial lines **2** **radial, radial tyre** a pneumatic tyre in which the ply cords are laid at a right angle to the centre line of the tread

radiant /'reɪdɪənt/ *adj* **1a** radiating rays or reflecting beams of light **b** vividly bright and shining; glowing **2** of or emitting radiant heat

radiate /'reɪdieɪt/ *v* **1** to send out rays of light, heat, or any other form of radiation **2** to proceed in a direct line from or towards a centre **3** to show or display clearly

radiation /,reɪdi'eɪʃən/ *n* **1** the action or process of radiating; *esp* the process of emitting radiant energy in the form of waves or particles **2** electromagnetic radiation (e g light) or emission from radioactive sources (e g alpha rays)

radiator /'reɪdieɪtəʳ/ *n* **1** a room heater through which hot water or steam circulates as part of a central-heating system **2** a device with a large surface area used for cooling an internal-combustion engine by means of water circulating through it

[1]**radical** /'rædɪkəl/ *adj* **1a** of or growing from the root or the base of a stem **b** designed to remove the root of a disease or all diseased tissue **2** essential, fundamental **3a** departing from the usual or traditional; extreme **b** of or constituting a political group advocating extreme measures – ~**ly** *adv*

[2]**radical** *n* sby who is a member of a radical party or who holds radical views

radicle /'rædɪkəl/ *n* **1** the lower part of the axis of a plant embryo or seedling, including the embryonic root **2** the rootlike beginning of an anatomical vessel or part

radii /'reɪdiaɪ/ *pl of* **radius**

[1]**radio** /'reɪdiəʊ/ *n* **1** the system of wireless transmission and reception of signals by means of electromagnetic waves **2** a radio receiver **3a** a radio transmitter (e g in an aircraft) **b** a radio broadcasting organization or station **c** the radio broadcasting industry

[2]**radio** *v* to send or communicate sthg by radio

radioactivity /,reɪdiəʊæk'tɪvɨti/ *n* the property possessed by some elements (e g uranium) of spontaneously emitting alpha or beta rays and sometimes also gamma rays by the disintegration of the nuclei of atoms – **-tive** *adj*

radiogram /'reɪdiəʊgræm/ *n* **1** a radiograph **2** *Br* a combined radio receiver and record player

radiograph /'reɪdiəʊgrɑːf/ *n* a picture produced on a sensitive surface by a form of radiation other than light; *specif* an X-ray or gamma-ray photograph

radiology /,reɪdi'ɒlədʒi/ *n* the use of radiant energy (e g X rays and gamma rays) in the diagnosis and treatment of disease – **-gist** *n*

radiotelegraphy /,reɪdiəʊtə'legrəfi/ *n* telegraphy carried out by means of radio waves – **-graphic** *adj*

radiotelephone /,reɪdiəʊ'telɨfəʊn/ *n* an apparatus for enabling telephone messages to be sent by radio (e g from a moving vehicle) – **-phony** *n*

radio telescope *n* a radio receiver connected to a large often dish-shaped aerial for recording and measuring radio waves from celestial bodies

radish /'rædɪʃ/ *n* (a plant of the mustard family with) a pungent fleshy typically dark red root, eaten raw as a salad vegetable

radium /'reɪdiəm/ *n* an intensely radioactive metallic element that occurs naturally and is used chiefly in luminous materials and in the treatment of cancer

radius /ˈreɪdɪəs/ *n, pl* **radii** **1** a straight line extending from the centre of a circle or sphere to the circumference or surface **2** a bounded or circumscribed area

raffia, raphia /ˈræfɪə/ *n* the fibre of a palm tree used esp for making baskets, hats, and table mats

raffish /ˈræfɪʃ/ *adj* marked by careless unconventionality; rakish – **~ly** *adv* – **~ness** *n*

raffle /ˈræfəl/ *v or n* (to dispose of by means of) a lottery in which the prizes are usually goods

raft /rɑːft/ *n* **1** a flat usu wooden structure designed to float on water and used as a platform or vessel **2** a foundation slab for a building, usu made of reinforced concrete – **raft** *v*

rafter /ˈrɑːftəʳ/ *n* any of the parallel beams that form the framework of a roof

¹rag /ræg/ *n* **1a** (a waste piece of) worn cloth **b** *pl* clothes, esp when in poor or ragged condition **2** a usu sensational or poorly written newspaper

²rag *v* to torment, tease; *also* to engage in horseplay

³rag *n, chiefly Br* **1** an outburst of boisterous fun; a prank **2** a series of processions and stunts organized by students to raise money for charity

⁴rag *n* (a composition or dance in) ragtime

raga /ˈrɑːgə/ *n* (an improvisation based on) any of the ancient traditional melodic patterns or modes in Indian music

ragamuffin /ˈrægəˌmʌfɪ̲n/ *n* a ragged often disreputable person, esp a child

ragbag /ˈrægbæg/ *n* **1** a dishevelled or slovenly person **2** a miscellaneous collection *USE* infml

¹rage /reɪdʒ/ *n* **1** (a fit or bout of) violent and uncontrolled anger **2** (an object of) fashionable and temporary enthusiasm

²rage *v* **1** to be in a rage **2** to be unchecked in violence or effect

ragged /ˈrægɪ̲d/ *adj* **1** having an irregular edge or outline **2** torn or worn to tatters **3** straggly – **~ly** *adv* – **~ness** *n*

raglan /ˈræglən/ *adj* having sleeves that extend to the neckline with slanted seams from the underarm to the neck

ragout /ˈræguː, -ˈ-/ *n* a well-seasoned stew, esp of meat and vegetables, cooked in a thick sauce

ragtime /ˈrægtaɪm/ *n* (music having) rhythm characterized by strong syncopation in the melody with a regularly accented accompaniment

rag trade *n* *the* clothing trade – infml

¹raid /reɪd/ *n* **1a** a usu hostile incursion made in order to seize sby or sthg **b** a surprise attack by a small force **2** a sudden invasion by the police (e g in search of criminals or stolen goods)

²raid *v* to make or take part in a raid

¹rail /reɪl/ *n* **1** an esp horizontal bar, usu supported by posts, which may serve as a barrier (e g across a balcony) or as a support on or from which sthg (e g a curtain) may be hung **2a** a railing **b** either of the fences on each side of a horse-racing track – usu pl with sing. meaning **3a** either of a pair of lengths of rolled steel forming a guide and running surface (e g a railway) for wheeled vehicles **b** the railway

²rail *v* to enclose or separate with a rail or rails – often + *off*

³rail *n* any of numerous wading birds of small or medium size, usu having very long toes which enable them to run on soft wet ground

⁴rail *v* to utter angry complaints or abuse – often + *against* or *at*

railhead /ˈreɪlhed/ *n* the farthest point reached by a railway

railing /ˈreɪlɪŋ/ *n* **1** a usu vertical rail in a fence or similar barrier **2** (material for making) rails

raillery /ˈreɪləri/ *n* (a piece of) good-humoured teasing

¹railroad /ˈreɪlrəʊd/ *n, NAm* (a) railway

²railroad *v* **1** to push through hastily or without due consideration **2** to hustle into taking action or making a decision

railway /ˈreɪlweɪ/ *n, chiefly Br* **1** a line of track usu having 2 parallel lines or rails fixed to sleepers on which vehicles run to transport goods and passengers **2** an organization which runs a railway network

raiment /ˈreɪmənt/ *n* garments, clothing – poetic

[1]**rain** /reɪn/ *n* **1** (a descent of) water falling in drops condensed from vapour in the atmosphere **2** *pl* the rainy season **3** a dense flow or fall of sthg – **~less** *adj*

[2]**rain** *v* **1** *of rain* to fall in drops from the clouds **2** to cause to fall; pour or send down **3** to bestow abundantly

rainbow /ˈreɪnbəʊ/ *n* **1** an arch in the sky consisting of a series of concentric arcs of the colours red, orange, yellow, green, blue, indigo, and violet, formed esp opposite the sun by the refraction, reflection, and interference of light rays in raindrops, spray, etc **2** an array of bright colours

rainbow trout *n* a large stout-bodied trout of Europe and western N America

raincoat /ˈreɪnkəʊt/ *n* a coat made from waterproof or water-resistant material

rainfall /ˈreɪnfɔːl/ *n* **1** a fall of rain; a shower **2** the amount of rain that has fallen in a given area during a given time, usu measured by depth

rain forest *n* a dense tropical woodland with an annual rainfall of at least 2500mm (about 100in) and containing lofty broad-leaved evergreen trees forming a continuous canopy

rain off *v* to interrupt or prevent (e g a sporting fixture) by rain

rainy /ˈreɪni/ *adj* **1** having or characterized by heavy rainfall **2** wet with rain

[1]**raise** /reɪz/ *v* **1** to cause or help to rise to an upright or standing position **2** to stir up; incite **3** to lift up **4a** to levy, obtain **b** to assemble, collect **5a** to grow, cultivate **b** to rear (e g a child) **6** to give rise to; provoke **7** to bring up for consideration or debate **8** to increase the strength, intensity, degree, or pitch of

[2]**raise** *n* **1** an act of raising or lifting **2** an increase of a bet or bid

raisin /ˈreɪzən/ *n* a dried grape

raison d'être /ˌrezɔ̃ ˈdetrə, ˌreɪzɒn-/ *n* a reason or justification for existence

raj /rɑːdʒ/ *n* rule; *specif, cap* British rule in India

rajah, raja /rɑːdʒə/ *n* an Indian, esp Hindu, prince or ruler

[1]**rake** /reɪk/ *n* **1** a long-handled implement with a head on which a row of projecting prongs is fixed for gathering hay, grass, etc or for loosening or levelling the surface of the ground **2** a mechanical implement, usu with rotating pronged wheels, used for gathering hay

[2]**rake** *v* **1** to gather, loosen, or level (as if) with a rake **2** to search through, esp in a haphazard manner – often + *through* or *among* **3** to sweep the length of, esp with gunfire

[3]**rake** *v* to (cause to) incline from the perpendicular

[4]**rake** *n* **1** the overhang of a ship's bow or stern **2** the angle of inclination or slope, esp of a stage in a theatre

[5]**rake** *n* a dissolute man, esp in fashionable society – **rakish** *adj* – **rakishly** *adv*

rake-off *n* a share of usu dishonestly gained profits – infml

rake up *v* **1** to uncover, revive **2** to find or collect, esp with difficulty

rallentando /ˌrælənˈtændəʊ/ *n, adj, or adv, pl* **rallentandi** (a passage performed) with a gradual decrease in tempo

[1]**rally** /ˈræli/ *v* **1** to bring together for a common cause **2a** to come together again to renew an effort **b** to arouse for or recall to order or action **3** to recover, revive

[2]**rally** *n* **1a** a mustering of scattered forces to renew an effort **b** a recovery of strength or courage after weakness or dejection **c** an increase in price after a decline **2** a mass meeting of people sharing a common interest or supporting a common, usu political, cause **3** a series of strokes interchanged between players (e g in tennis) before a point is won **4** *also* **rallye** a motor race, usu over public roads, designed to test both speed and navigational skills

[1]**ram** /ræm/ *n* **1** an uncastrated male sheep **2a** a battering ram **b** a heavy beak on the prow of a warship for piercing enemy vessels

²**ram** *v* to strike against violently and usu head-on

Ramadan, Ramadhan /ˈræmədæn/ *n* the 9th month of the Muslim year, during which fasting is practised daily from dawn to sunset

¹**ramble** /ˈræmbəl/ *v* **1** to walk for pleasure, esp without a planned route **2** to talk or write in a disconnected long-winded fashion **3** to grow or extend irregularly

²**ramble** *n* a leisurely walk taken for pleasure and often without a planned route – **~r** *n*

rambunctious /ræmˈbʌŋkʃəs/ *adj, NAm* rumbustious, unruly – infml – **~ly** *adv* – **~ness** *n*

ramification /ˌræmɨ̣fɨ̣ˈkeɪʃən/ *n* **1** a branching out **2** a branched structure **3** a usu extended or complicated consequence

ramify /ˈræmɨ̣faɪ/ *v* to (cause to) separate or split up into branches, divisions, or constituent parts

ramp /ræmp/ *n* **1** a sloping floor, walk, or roadway leading from one level to another **2** a stairway for entering or leaving an aircraft

rampage /ˈræmpeɪdʒ, -ˈ-/ *v* to rush about wildly or violently – **rampage** *n*

rampant /ˈræmpənt/ *adj* **1** *of a heraldic animal* rearing upon the hind legs with forelegs extended – used after a noun **2** characterized by wildness or absence of restraint – **~ly** *adv*

rampart /ˈræmpɑːt/ *n* **1** a broad embankment raised as a fortification (e g around a fort or city) and usu surmounted by a parapet **2** a protective barrier; a bulwark

ramrod /ˈræmrɒd/ *n* **1** a rod for ramming home the charge in a muzzle-loading firearm **2** a rod for cleaning the barrels of rifles and other small arms

ramshackle /ˈræmʃækəl/ *adj* badly constructed or needing repair; rickety

ran /ræn/ *past of* **run**

ranch /rɑːntʃ/ *n* **1** a large farm for raising livestock esp in N America and Australia **2** *chiefly NAm* a farm or area devoted to raising a particular crop or animal

rancid /ˈrænsɨ̣d/ *adj* (smelling or tasting) rank – **~ity** *n*

rancour, *NAm* **rancor** /ˈræŋkəʳ/ *n* bitter and deep-seated ill will or hatred

rand /rænd/ *n, pl* **rand** the basic unit of currency of South Africa

random *adj* **1** lacking a definite plan, purpose, or pattern **2** (of, consisting of, or being events, parts, etc) having or relating to a probability of occurring equal to that of all similar parts, events, etc – **~ly** *adv* – **~ness** *n*

randy /ˈrændi/ *adj* sexually aroused; lustful – infml – **randiness** *n*

rang /ræŋ/ *past of* **ring**

¹**range** /reɪndʒ/ *n* **1a** a series of mountains **b** a number of objects or products forming a distinct class or series **c** a variety, cross-section **2** a usu solid-fuel fired cooking stove with 1 or more ovens, a flat metal top, and 1 or more areas for heating pans **3a** an open region over which livestock may roam and feed, esp in N America **b** the region throughout which a kind of living organism or ecological community naturally lives or occurs **4a(1)** the distance to which a projectile can be propelled **(2)** the distance between a weapon and the target **b** the maximum distance a vehicle can travel without refuelling **c** a place where shooting (e g with guns or missiles) is practised **5a** the space or extent included, covered, or used **b** the extent of pitch within a melody or within the capacity of a voice or instrument **6a** a sequence, series, or scale between limits **b** (the difference between) the least and greatest values of an attribute or series

²**range** *v* **1** to set in a row or in the proper order **2** to roam over or through **3** to determine or give the elevation necessary for (a gun) to propel a projectile to a given distance **4** to extend in a usu specified direction **5** to change or differ within limits

range finder *n* a device for indicating or measuring the distance between a gun and a target or a camera and an object

ranger /ˈreɪndʒəʳ/ *n* **1** the keeper of a park or forest **2** a soldier in the US army specially trained in close-range fighting and raiding tactics **3** *often cap* a private in an Irish line regiment **4** *cap* a senior member of the British Guide movement aged from 14 to 19

rani, ranee /rɑːni/ *n* a Hindu queen or princess; *esp* the wife of a rajah

[1]**rank** /ræŋk/ *adj* **1** excessively vigorous and often coarse in growth **2** offensively gross or coarse **3a** shockingly conspicuous; flagrant **b** complete – used as an intensive **4** offensive in odour or flavour – **~ly** *adv* – **~ness** *n*

[2]**rank** *n* **1a** a row, line, or series of people or things **b(1)** *sing or pl in constr* a line of soldiers ranged side by side in close order **(2)** *pl* rank and file **c** any of the 8 rows of squares that extend across a chessboard perpendicular to the files **2** an esp military formation – often pl with sing. meaning **3a** a degree or position in a hierarchy or order; *specif* an official position in the armed forces **b** (high) social position **4** *Br* a place where taxis wait to pick up passengers

[3]**rank** *v* **1** to take or have a position in relation to others **2** to determine the relative position of; rate

rank and file *n sing or pl in constr* **1** the body of members of an armed force as distinguished from the officers **2** the individuals constituting the body of an organization as distinguished from the leading or principal members

ranking /ˈræŋkɪŋ/ *adj* having a high or the highest position

rankle /ˈræŋkəl/ *v* to cause continuing anger, irritation, or bitterness

ransack /ˈrænsæk/ *v* **1** to search in a disordered but thorough manner **2** to rob, plunder

[1]**ransom** /ˈrænsəm/ *n* a price paid or demanded for the release of a captured or kidnapped person

[2]**ransom** *v* to free from captivity or punishment by paying a ransom – **~er** *n*

[1]**rant** /rænt/ *v* to talk in a noisy, excited, or declamatory manner

[2]**rant** *n* (a) bombastic extravagant speech

[1]**rap** /ræp/ *n* **1** (the sound made by) a sharp blow or knock **2** blame, punishment – infml

[2]**rap** *v* **1** to strike with a sharp blow **2** to utter (e g a command) abruptly and forcibly – usu + *out* **3** to criticize sharply – journ

[3]**rap** *n* the least bit (e g of care or consideration) – infml

[4]**rap** *n, chiefly NAm* talk, conversation – slang – **rap** *v*

rapacious /rəˈpeɪʃəs/ *adj* **1** excessively grasping or covetous **2** *of an animal* living on prey – **-city** *n* – **~ly** *adv* – **~ness** *n*

[1]**rape** /reɪp/ *n* a European plant of the mustard family grown as a forage crop and for its oil-producing seeds

[2]**rape** *v* **1** to despoil **2** to commit rape on – **rapist** *n*

[3]**rape** *n* **1** an act or instance of robbing, despoiling, or violating **2** the crime of forcing a woman to have sexual intercourse against her will **3** an outrageous violation

[1]**rapid** /ˈræpɨd/ *adj* moving, acting, or occurring with speed; swift – **~ity** *n* – **~ly** *adv*

[2]**rapid** *n* a part of a river where the water flows swiftly over a steep usu rocky slope in the river bed – usu pl with sing. meaning

rapier /ˈreɪpɪəʳ/ *n* a straight 2-edged sword with a narrow pointed blade

rapine /ˈræpaɪn/ *n* pillage, plunder

rapport /ræˈpɔː/ *n* a sympathetic or harmonious relationship

rapprochement /ræˈprɒʃmɑ̃, ræˈprəʊʃ-/ *n* the reestablishment of cordial relations, esp between nations

rapscallion /ræpˈskælɪən/ *n* a rascal

rapt /ræpt/ *adj* **1** enraptured **2** wholly absorbed – **~ly** *adv* – **~ness** *n*

rapture /ˈræptʃəʳ/ *n* **1** a state or experience of being carried away by overwhelming emotion **2** an expression or manifestation of ecstasy or extreme delight – **-rous** *adj* – **-rously** *adv*

[1]**rare** /reəʳ/ *adj, of meat* cooked so that the inside is still red

[2]**rare** *adj* **1** lacking in density; thin **2** marked by unusual quality, merit, or

appeal 3 seldom occurring or found – ~**ness** *n*

rarefied *also* **rarified** /ˈreərǰfaɪd/ *adj* esoteric, abstruse

rarefy *also* **rarify** /ˈreərǰfaɪ/ *v* **1** to make or become rare, porous, or less dense **2** to make more spiritual, refined, or abstruse

rarity /ˈreərǰti/ *n* **1** the quality, state, or fact of being rare **2** sby or sthg rare

rascal /ˈrɑːskəl/ *n* **1** an unprincipled or dishonest person **2** a mischievous person or animal – usu humor or affectionate

[1]**rash** /ræʃ/ *adj* acting with, characterized by, or proceeding from undue haste or impetuosity – ~**ly** *adv* – ~**ness** *n*

[2]**rash** *n* **1** an outbreak of spots on the body **2** a large number of instances of a specified thing during a short period

rasher /ˈræʃəʳ/ *n* a thin slice of bacon or ham

[1]**rasp** /rɑːsp/ *v* **1** to rub with sthg rough **2** to grate upon; irritate **3** to utter in a grating tone – ~**ingly** *adv*

[2]**rasp** *n* a coarse file with rows of cutting teeth

raspberry /ˈrɑːzbəri/ *n* **1** (a widely grown shrub that bears) any of various usu red edible berries **2** a rude sound made by sticking the tongue out and blowing noisily – slang

[1]**rat** /ræt/ *n* **1** any of numerous rodents that are considerably larger than the related mice **2** a contemptible or wretched person; *specif* one who betrays or deserts his party, friends, or associates

[2]**rat** *v* to betray, desert, or inform on one's associates – usu + *on*

ratatouille /ˌrætəˈtuːi/ *n* a dish containing vegetables (e g tomatoes, aubergines, etc) stewed slowly in a vegetable stock

ratchet /ˈrætʃǰt/ *n* a mechanism that consists of a bar or wheel having inclined teeth into which a bar or lever drops so that motion is allowed in 1 direction only

[1]**rate** /reɪt/ *n* **1** valuation **2a** a fixed ratio between 2 things **b** a charge, payment, or price fixed according to a ratio, scale, or standard **c** *Br* a tax levied by a local authority – usu pl with sing. meaning **3** a quantity, amount, or degree of sthg measured per unit of sthg else

[2]**rate** *v* **1** to consider to be; value as **2** to determine or assign the relative rank or class of **3** to be worthy of; deserve **4** to think highly of; consider to be good – infml

rate-capping *n, Br* restriction by central government legislation of the level of rates which a local authority can levy

rather /ˈrɑːðəʳ/ *adv or adj* **1** more readily or willingly; sooner **2** more properly, reasonably, or truly **3** to some degree; somewhat; *esp* somewhat excessively **4** on the contrary

ratify /ˈrætǰfaɪ/ *v* to approve or confirm formally

rating /ˈreɪtɪŋ/ *n* **1** a classification according to grade **2** relative estimate or evaluation **3** *pl* any of various indexes which list television programmes, new records, etc in order of popularity – usu + *the* **4** *chiefly Br* an ordinary seaman

ratio /ˈreɪʃiəʊ/ *n* **1** the indicated division of one mathematical expression by another **2** the relationship in quantity, number, or degree between things or between one thing and another thing

[1]**ration** /ˈræʃən/ *n* a share or amount (e g of food) which one permits oneself or which one is permitted

[2]**ration** *v* **1** to distribute or divide (e g commodities in short supply) in fixed quantities – often + *out* **2** to use sparingly

rational /ˈræʃənəl/ *adj* **1** having, based on, or compatible with reason; reasonable **2** of, involving, or being (a mathematical expression containing) 1 or more rational numbers – ~**ly** *adv* – ~**ity** *n*

rationale /ˌræʃəˈnɑːl/ *n* an underlying reason; basis

rationalism /ˈræʃənlɪzəm/ *n* a theory that reason is a source of knowledge superior to and independent of sense perception – **-list** *n*

rational·ize, -ise /ˈræʃənlaɪz/ *v* **1** to provide plausible reasons for one's behaviour, opinions, etc **2** to increase the efficiency of (e g an industry) by more effective organization – -zation *n*

rational number *n* a number (e g 2, 5/2, - ½) that can be expressed as the result of dividing one integer by another

rat race *n the* struggle to maintain one's position in a career or survive the pressures of modern urban life

¹rattle /'rætl/ *v* **1** to (cause to) make a rapid succession of short sharp sounds **2** to chatter incessantly and aimlessly – often + *on* **3** to say or perform in a brisk lively fashion – often + *off* **4** to upset to the point of loss of poise and composure

²rattle *n* **1** a rattling sound **2a** a child's toy consisting of loose pellets in a hollow container that rattles when shaken **b** a device that consists of a springy tongue in contact with a revolving ratchet wheel which is rotated or shaken to produce a loud noise **3** a throat noise caused by air passing through mucus and heard esp at the approach of death

rattlesnake /'rætlsneɪk/ *n* any of various American poisonous snakes with horny interlocking joints at the end of the tail that rattle when shaken

ratty /'ræti/ *adj* irritable – infml

raucous /'rɔːkəs/ *adj* disagreeably harsh or strident; noisy – **~ly** *adv* – **~ness** *n*

¹ravage /'rævɪdʒ/ *n* damage resulting from ravaging – usu pl

²ravage *v* to wreak havoc (on); cause (violent) destruction (to)

¹rave /reɪv/ *v* **1** to talk irrationally (as if) in delirium; *broadly* to rage, storm **2** to talk with extreme or passionate enthusiasm

²rave *n* **1** a raving **2** an extravagantly favourable review

¹ravel /'rævəl/ *v* **1** to unravel, disentangle – usu + *out* **2** to entangle, confuse

²ravel *n* a tangle or tangled mass

raven /'reɪvən/ *n* a very large glossy black bird of the crow family

ravenous /'rævənəs/ *adj* **1** urgently seeking satisfaction, gratification, etc; grasping, insatiable **2** fiercely eager for food; famished – **~ly** *adv*

raver /'reɪvəʳ/ *n, chiefly Br* an energetic and uninhibited person who enjoys a hectic social life; *also* a sexually uninhibited or promiscuous person – slang

rave-up *n, chiefly Br* a wild party – slang

ravine /rə'viːn/ *n* a narrow steep-sided valley smaller than a canyon and usu worn by running water

¹raving /'reɪvɪŋ/ *n* irrational, incoherent, wild, or extravagant utterance or declamation – usu pl with sing. meaning

²raving *adj* extreme, marked – infml

ravioli /ˌrævi'əʊli/ *n* little cases of pasta containing meat, cheese, etc

ravish /'rævɪʃ/ *v* **1** to overcome with joy, delight, etc **2** to rape, violate

ravishing /'rævɪʃɪŋ/ *adj* unusually attractive or pleasing – **~ly** *adv*

raw /rɔː/ *adj* **1** not cooked **2** not processed or purified **3** having the surface abraded or chafed **4** lacking experience, training, etc; new **5** disagreeably damp or cold – **~ness** *n*

rawhide /'rɔːhaɪd/ *n* (a whip of) untanned hide

¹ray /reɪ/ *n* any of numerous fishes having the eyes on the upper surface of a flattened body and a long narrow tail

²ray *n* **1a** any of the lines of light that appear to radiate from a bright object **b** a narrow beam of radiant energy (e g light or X rays) **c** a stream of (radioactive) particles travelling in the same line **2** any of a group of lines diverging from a common centre **3a** any of the bony rods that support the fin of a fish **b** any of the radiating parts of the body of a radially symmetrical animal (e g a starfish) **4** a slight manifestation or trace (e g of intelligence or hope)

rayon /'reɪɒn/ *n* (a fabric made from) a yarn or fibre produced by forcing and drawing cellulose through minute holes

raze, rase /reɪz/ *v* to lay (e g a town or building) level with the ground

razor /'reɪzəʳ/ *n* a sharp-edged cutting implement for shaving or cutting (facial) hair

razzle /'ræzəl/ *n* a spree, binge

¹re /reɪ, riː/ *n* the 2nd note of the diatonic scale in solmization

²re /riː/ *prep* with regard to; concerning

¹reach /riːtʃ/ *v* **1** to stretch out **2a** to touch or grasp by extending a part of the body (e g a hand) or an object **b** to pick up and draw towards one; pass **c(1)** to extend to **(2)** to get up to or as far as; arrive at **d** to contact or communicate with

²reach *n* **1a** the action or an act of reaching **b** the distance or extent of reaching or of ability to reach **c** a range; *specif* comprehension **2** a straight uninterrupted portion of a river or canal **3** the tack sailed by a vessel with the wind blowing more or less from the side

react /ri'ækt/ *v* **1** to exert a reciprocal or counteracting force or influence – often + *on* or *upon* **2** to respond to a stimulus **3** to act in opposition to a force or influence – usu + *against* **4** to undergo chemical reaction

reaction /ri'ækʃən/ *n* **1a** a reacting **b** tendency towards a former and usu outmoded (political or social) order or policy **2** bodily response to or activity aroused by a stimulus: e g **a** the response of tissues to a foreign substance (e g an antigen or infective agent) **b** a mental or emotional response to circumstances **3** the force that sthg subjected to the action of a force exerts equally in the opposite direction **4a** a chemical transformation or change; an action between atoms, molecules, etc to form new substances **b** a process involving change in atomic nuclei resulting from interaction with a particle or another nucleus

reactionary /ri'ækʃənəri/ *n or adj* (a person) opposing radical social change or favouring a return to a former (political) order

reactivate /ri'æktɪ̣veɪt/ *v* to make or become active again

reactive /ri'æktɪv/ *adj* **1** of or marked by reaction or reacting **2** tending to or liable to react – **~ly** *adv* – **~ness** *n*

reactor /ri'æktəʳ/ *n* an apparatus in which a chain reaction of fissile material (e g uranium or plutonium) is started and controlled, esp for the production of nuclear power or elementary particles

¹read /riːd/ *v* **read** /red/ **1a(1)** to look at or otherwise sense (e g letters, symbols, or words) with mental assimilation of the communication represented **(2)** to utter aloud (interpretatively) the printed or written words of – often + *out* **b** to study (a subject), esp for a degree **2a** to understand, comprehend **b** to interpret the meaning or significance of

²read /riːd/ *n* **1** sthg to read with reference to the interest, enjoyment, etc it provides **2** *chiefly Br* a period of reading

³read /red/ *adj* instructed by or informed through reading

readable /'riːdəbəl/ *adj* **1** legible **2** pleasurable or interesting to read – **-bility** *n*

reader /'riːdəʳ/ *n* **1a** one who reads and corrects proofs **b** one who evaluates manuscripts **2** a member of a British university staff between the ranks of lecturer and professor **3** a usu instructive (introductory) book or anthology

readership /'riːdəʃɪp/ *n, sing or pl in constr* a collective body of readers; *esp* the readers of a particular publication or author

readily /'redɪ̣li/ *adv* **1** without hesitating **2** without much difficulty

reading /'riːdɪŋ/ *n* **1a** material read or for reading **b** the extent to which a person has read **c** an event at which a play, poetry, etc is read to an audience **d** an act of formally reading a bill that constitutes any of 3 successive stages of approval by a legislature, specif Parliament **2a** a form or version of a particular (passage in a) text **b** the value indicated or data produced by an instrument **3** a particular interpretation

readout /'riːd-aʊt/ *n* the removal of information from storage (e g in a computer memory or on magnetic tape) for display in an understandable form (e g as a printout)

¹ready /'redi/ *adj* **1a** prepared mentally or physically for some experience or action **b** prepared or available for immediate use **2a(1)** willingly disposed (2) likely or about to do the specified thing **b** spontaneously prompt – **ready** *adv* – **-diness** *n*

[2]**ready** *v* to make ready

[3]**ready** *n* (ready) money

[4]**ready** *adv* in advance

ready-made *adj* **1** made beforehand, esp for general sale or use rather than to individual specifications **2** lacking originality or individuality

reafforest /ˌriːəˈfɒrəst/ *v* to renew the forest cover of by seeding or planting – **~ation** *n*

reagent /riˈeɪdʒənt/ *n* a substance that takes part in or brings about a particular chemical reaction, used esp to detect sthg

[1]**real** /rɪəl/ *adj* **1a** not artificial, fraudulent, illusory, fictional, etc; *also* being precisely what the name implies; genuine **b** of practical or everyday concerns or activities **2** measured by purchasing power rather than the paper value of money **3** complete, great – used chiefly for emphasis

real estate *n* property in buildings and land

realign /ˌriːəˈlaɪn/ *v* to reorganize or make new groupings of – **~ment** *n*

realism /ˈrɪəlɪzəm/ *n* **1** concern for fact or reality and rejection of the impractical and visionary **2** the belief that objects of sense perception have real existence independent of the mind **3** fidelity in art, literature, etc to nature and to accurate representation without idealization – **-list** *n*

realistic /rɪəˈlɪstɪk/ *adj* **1** not impractical or over optimistic; sober **2** of realism

reality /riˈæləti/ *n* **1** being real **2a** a real event, entity, or state of affairs **b** the totality of real things and events

real·ize, -ise /ˈrɪəlaɪz/ *v* **1** to accomplish **2** to bring or get by sale, investment or effort **3** to be fully aware of – **-zation** *n*

really /ˈrɪəli/ *adv* **1a** in reality, actually **b** without question; thoroughly **2** more correctly – used to give force to an injunction (e g you *really* should have asked me first) **3** – expressing surprise or indignation

realm /relm/ *n* **1** a kingdom **2** a sphere, domain – often pl with sing. meaning

realpolitik /reɪˈɑːlpɒlɪtiːk/ *n* politics based on practical factors rather than on moral objectives

real tennis *n* a game played with a racket and ball in an irregularly-shaped indoor court divided by a net

[1]**ream** /riːm/ *n* **1** a quantity of paper equal to 20 quires or variously 480, 500, or 516 sheets **2** a great amount (e g of sthg written or printed) – usu pl with sing. meaning

[2]**ream** *v* to enlarge or widen a hole – **~er** *n*

reap /riːp/ *v* **1** to cut a crop; *also* to harvest **2** to obtain or win, esp as the reward for effort – **~er** *n*

[1]**rear** /rɪəʳ/ *v* **1a** to breed and tend (an animal) or grow (e g a crop) for use or sale **b** to bring up **2** to rise to a height **3** *of a horse* to rise up on the hind legs

[2]**rear** *n* **1** the back part of sthg: e g **a** the part (e g of an army) away from the enemy **b** the part of sthg located opposite its front **c** the buttocks **2** the space or position at the back

[3]**rear** *adj* at the back

rearguard /ˈrɪəgɑːd/ *adj* of vigorous resistance in the face of defeat

rearm /riːˈɑːm/ *v* to arm (e g a nation or military force) again, esp with new or better weapons – **~ament** *n*

[1]**rearward** /ˈrɪəwəd/ *n* the rear; *esp* the rear division (e g of an army)

[2]**rearward** *adj* located at or directed towards the rear

[1]**reason** /ˈriːzən/ *n* **1a** (a statement offered as) an explanation or justification **b** a rational ground or motive **2a** proper exercise of the mind; *also* the intelligence **b** sanity

[2]**reason** *v* **1** to use the faculty of reason so as to arrive at conclusions **2** to talk or argue *with* another so as to influence his/her actions or opinions **3** to formulate, assume, analyse, or conclude by the use of reason – often + *out* – **~er** *n*

reasonable /ˈriːzənəbəl/ *adj* **1a** in accord with reason **b** not extreme or excessive **c** moderate, fair **d** inexpensive **2a** having the faculty of reason; rational **b** sensible – **-bleness** *n* – **-bly** *adv*

reasoning /ˈriːzənɪŋ/ *n* the drawing

of inferences or conclusions through the use of reason

reassure /ˌriːəˈʃʊəʳ/ *v* to restore confidence to – **-surance** *n* – **-suringly** *adv*

rebate /ˈriːbeɪt/ *n* **1** a return of part of a payment **2** a deduction from a sum before payment; a discount

[1]**rebel** /ˈrebəl/ *adj* **1** in rebellion **2** of rebels

[2]**rebel** *n* one who rebels against a government, authority, convention, etc

[3]**rebel** /rɪˈbel/ *v* **1** to oppose or disobey (one in) authority or control, esp a government **2** to act in or show opposition

rebellion /rɪˈbeljən/ *n* **1** opposition to (one in) authority or dominance **2** (an instance of) open armed resistance to an established government

rebellious /rɪˈbeljəs/ *adj* **1a** in rebellion **b** (characteristic) of or inclined towards rebellion **2** refractory – **~ly** *adv* – **~ness** *n*

rebirth /ˌriːˈbɜːθ/ *n* **1a** a new or second birth **b** spiritual regeneration **2** a renaissance, revival

reborn /ˌriːˈbɔːn/ *adj* born again; regenerated

[1]**rebound** /rɪˈbaʊnd/ *v* **1** to spring back (as if) on collision or impact with another body **2** to return with an adverse effect to a source or starting point

[2]**rebound** /ˈriːbaʊnd/ *n* **1** a rebounding, recoil **2** a recovery

rebuff /rɪˈbʌf/ *v or n* (to) snub

rebuke /rɪˈbjuːk/ *v or n* (to) reprimand

rebus /ˈriːbəs/ *n* (a riddle using) a representation of words or syllables by pictures that suggest the same sound

rebut /rɪˈbʌt/ *v* **1** to drive back; repel **2** to disprove or expose the falsity of; refute – **rebuttal** *n*

recalcitrant /rɪˈkælsɨtrənt/ *adj* **1** obstinately defiant of authority or restraint **2** difficult to handle or control – **-trance** *n*

[1]**recall** /rɪˈkɔːl/ *v* **1a** to call or summon back **b** to bring back to mind **2** to cancel, revoke – **~able** *adj*

[2]**recall** /rɪˈkɔːl, ˈriːkɔːl/ *n* **1** a call or summons to return **2** remembrance of what has been learned or experienced **3** the act of revoking or the possibility of being revoked

recant /rɪˈkænt/ *v* to make an open confession of error; *esp* to disavow a religious belief or withdraw a statement – **~ation** *n*

recap /ˈriːkæp, rɪˈkæp/ *v* to recapitulate

recapitulate /ˌriːkəˈpɪtʃʊleɪt/ *v* to repeat the principal points or stages of (e g an argument or discourse) in summing up – **-lation** *n*

recapture /riːˈkæptʃəʳ/ *v* **1** to capture again **2** to experience again

recede /rɪˈsiːd/ *v* **1a** to move back or away; withdraw **b** to slant backwards **2** to grow less, smaller, or more distant; diminish

receipt /rɪˈsiːt/ *n* **1** the act or process of receiving **2** sthg (e g goods or money) received – usu pl with sing. meaning **3** a written acknowledgment of having received goods or money

receive /rɪˈsiːv/ *v* **1** to (willingly) come into possession of or be provided with **2a** to act as a receptacle or container for; *also* to take (an impression, mark, etc) **b** to assimilate through the mind or senses **3** to welcome, greet; *also* to entertain **4a** to take the force or pressure of **b** to suffer the hurt or injury of

receiver /rɪˈsiːvəʳ/ *n* **1** a person appointed to hold in trust and administer property of a bankrupt or insane person or property under litigation **2** one who receives stolen goods **3a** a radio, television, or other part of a communications system that receives the signal **b** the part of a telephone that contains the mouthpiece and earpiece

recent /ˈriːsənt/ *adj* **1** of a time not long past **2** having lately come into existence – **~ly** *adv*

receptacle /rɪˈseptəkəl/ *n* **1** an object that receives and contains sthg **2** the end of the flower stalk of a flowering plant upon which the floral organs are borne

reception /rɪˈsepʃən/ *n* **1** receiving or being received: e g **a** an admission **b** a response, reaction **c** the receiving of a radio or television broadcast **2** a formal social gathering during which guests are received **3** *Br* an office or desk where visitors or clients (e g to an office, factory, or hotel) are received on arrival

receptionist /rɪ'sepʃənɨst/ *n* one employed to greet and assist callers or clients

receptive /rɪ'septɪv/ *adj* open and responsive to ideas, impressions, or suggestions – **~ly** *adv* – **~ness** *n* – **-tivity** *n*

[1]**recess** /rɪ'ses, 'riːses/ *n* **1** a hidden, secret, or secluded place – usu pl **2** an alcove **3** a suspension of business or activity, usu for a period of rest or relaxation

[2]**recess** /rɪ'ses/ *v* **1** to put in a recess **2** to make a recess in **3** to interrupt for a recess

recession /rɪ'seʃən/ *n* **1** a withdrawal **2** a period of reduced economic activity

recessional /rɪ'seʃənəl/ *n* a hymn or musical piece at the conclusion of a church service

recessive /rɪ'sesɪv/ *adj* **1** receding or tending to recede **2** being the one of a pair of (genes determining) contrasting inherited characteristics that is suppressed if a dominant gene is present

recharge /ˌriː'tʃɑːdʒ/ *v* to charge again; *esp* to renew the active materials in (a storage battery)

recherché /rə'ʃeəʃeɪ/ *adj* **1** exotic, rare **2** precious, affected

recidivist /rɪ'sɪdɨvɨst/ *n* one who relapses, specif into criminal behaviour – **-vism** *n*

recipe /'resɨpi/ *n* **1** a list of ingredients and instructions for making sthg, specif a food dish **2** a procedure for doing or attaining sthg

recipient /rɪ'sɪpɪənt/ *n* sby who or sthg that receives

[1]**reciprocal** /rɪ'sɪprəkəl/ *adj* **1** shared, felt, or shown by both sides **2** consisting of or functioning as a return in kind **3** mutually corresponding; equivalent

[2]**reciprocal** *n* **1** either of a pair of numbers (e g ⅔, $^3/_2$) that when multiplied together equal 1 **2** the inverse of a number under multiplication – **~ly** *adv*

reciprocate /rɪ'sɪprəkeɪt/ *v* **1** to give and take mutually **2** to return in kind or degree – **-cation** *n*

recital /rɪ'saɪtl/ *n* **1** a reciting **2** a concert or public performance given by a musician, small group of musicians, or dancer

recitative /ˌresɨtə'tiːv/ *n* (a passage delivered in) a rhythmically free declamatory style for singing a narrative text

recite /rɪ'saɪt/ *v* **1** to repeat from memory or read aloud, esp before an audience **2** to relate in detail; enumerate – **-tation** *n* – **~r** *n*

reckless /'reklɨs/ *adj* marked by lack of proper caution; careless of consequences – **~ly** *adv* – **~ness** *n*

reckon /'rekən/ *v* **1a** to count – usu + *up* **b** to estimate, compute **2** to consider or think of in a specified way **3** to suppose, think **4** to esteem highly – infml **5** to place reliance *on* **6** to take into account – + *with* – **~er** *n*

reckoning /'rekənɪŋ/ *n* **1a** a calculation or counting **b** an account, bill **2** a settling of accounts **3** an appraisal

reclaim /rɪ'kleɪm/ *v* **1** to rescue or convert from an undesirable state; reform **2** to make available for human use by changing natural conditions **3** to obtain from a waste product – **reclamation** *n*

recline /rɪ'klaɪn/ *v* **1** (to cause or permit) to incline backwards **2** to place or be in a recumbent position; lean, repose

recluse /rɪ'kluːs/ *n or adj* (sby) leading a secluded or solitary life

recognition /ˌrekəg'nɪʃən/ *n* **1** recognizing or being recognized **2** special notice or attention

recogn·ize, -ise /'rekəgnaɪz/ *v* **1** to perceive to be something already known **2** to show appreciation of **3** to admit as being of a particular status or having validity

[1]**recoil** /rɪ'kɔɪl/ *v* **1** to shrink back physically or emotionally (e g in horror, fear, or disgust) **2** to spring back; rebound

[2]**recoil** /'riːkɔɪl, rɪ'kɔɪl/ *n* recoiling; *esp* the backwards movement of a gun on firing

recollect /ˌrekə'lekt/ *v* **1** to bring back to the level of conscious awareness; remember, recall **2** to bring (oneself) back to a state of composure or concentration – ~**ion** *n*

recommend /ˌrekəˈmend/ *v* **1** to endorse as fit, worthy, or competent **2** to advise – ~**ation** *n*

[1]**recompense** /ˈrekəmpens/ *v* **1** to give sthg to by way of compensation **2** to make or amount to an equivalent or compensation for

[2]**recompense** *n* an equivalent or a return for sthg done, suffered, or given

reconcile /ˈrekənsaɪl/ *v* **1** to restore to friendship or harmony **2** to make consistent or congruous **3** to cause to submit to or accept – **-cilable** *adj*

recondition /ˌriːkənˈdɪʃən/ *v* to restore to good (working) condition (e g by replacing parts)

reconnaissance /rɪˈkɒnɪ̣səns/ *n* a preliminary survey to gain information; *esp* an exploratory military survey of enemy territory or positions

reconnoitre /ˌrekəˈnɔɪtəʳ/ *v* to make a reconnaissance (of)

reconsider /ˌriːkənˈsɪdəʳ/ *v* to consider (sthg) again with a view to change, revision, or revocation – ~**ation** *n*

reconstitute /riːˈkɒnstɪ̣tjuːt/ *v* to constitute again or anew; *esp* to restore to a former condition by adding water

reconstruct /ˌriːkənˈstrʌkt/ *v* **1a** to restore to a previous condition **b** to recreate **2** to build up a mental image or physical representation of (e g a crime or a battle) from the available evidence – ~**ion** *n*

[1]**record** /rɪˈkɔːd/ *v* **1a** to commit to writing so as to supply written evidence **b** to register by mechanical or other means **2** to give evidence of; show **3** to convert (e g sound) into a permanent form fit for reproduction

[2]**record** /ˈrekɔːd/ *n* **1a** sthg recorded or on which information, evidence, etc has been registered **b** sthg that recalls, relates, or commemorates past events or feats **c** an authentic official document **2a(1)** a body of known or recorded facts regarding sthg or sby **(2)** a list of previous criminal convictions **b** the best recorded performance in a competitive sport **3** a flat usu plastic disc with a spiral groove whose undulations represent recorded sound for reproduction on a gramophone

recorder /rɪˈkɔːdəʳ/ *n* **1** *often cap* a magistrate formerly presiding over the court of quarter sessions **2** any of a group of wind instruments consisting of a slightly tapering tube with usu 8 finger holes and a mouthpiece like a whistle

recording /rɪˈkɔːdɪŋ/ *n* sthg (e g sound or a television programme) that has been recorded electronically

[1]**recount** /rɪˈkaʊnt/ *v* to relate in detail

[2]**recount** /ˈriːkaʊnt/ *n* a recounting, esp of votes

recoup /rɪˈkuːp/ *v* **1** to get an equivalent for (e g losses) **2** to regain

recourse /rɪˈkɔːs/ *n* (a turning or resorting to) a source of help, strength, or protection

recover /rɪˈkʌvəʳ/ *v* **1a** to get back **b** to regain a normal or stable position or condition (e g of health) **2** to obtain by legal action – ~**able** *adj*

recovery /rɪˈkʌvəri/ *n* a recovering: e g **a** a return to normal health **b** a regaining of balance or control (e g after a stumble or mistake) **c** an economic upturn (e g after a depression)

recreate /ˌriːkriˈeɪt/ *v* to create again: e g **a** to reproduce so as to resemble exactly **b** to visualize or create again in the imagination

recreation /ˌrekriˈeɪʃən/ *n* (a means of) pleasurable activity, diversion, etc

recriminate /rɪˈkrɪmɪ̣neɪt/ *v* to indulge in bitter mutual accusations – **-natory** *adj*

[1]**recruit** /rɪˈkruːt/ *n* a newcomer to a field or activity; *specif* a newly enlisted member of the armed forces

[2]**recruit** *v* **1** to enlist recruits **2** to secure the services of; hire – ~**ment** *n*

rectangle /ˈrektæŋgəl/ *n* a parallelogram all of whose angles are right angles; *esp* one that is not a square – **-gular** *adj*

rectify /ˈrektɪ̣faɪ/ *v* **1** to set right; remedy **2** to correct by removing errors

rectilinear /ˌrektɪ̣ˈlɪnɪəʳ/ *adj* **1** (moving) in or forming a straight line **2** characterized by straight lines

rectitude /'rektɪ̯tjuːd/ *n* **1** moral integrity **2** correctness in judgment or procedure

rector /'rektəʳ/ *n* **1** a clergyman in charge of a parish **2** the head of a university or college

rectory /'rektəri/ *n* a rector's residence or benefice

rectum /'rektəm/ *n* the last part of the intestine of a vertebrate, ending at the anus – **-tal** *adj*

recumbent /rɪ'kʌmbənt/ *adj* **1** in an attitude suggestive of repose **2** lying down

recuperate /rɪ'kjuːpəreɪt, -'kuː-/ *v* to regain a former (healthy) state or condition – **-ration** *n*

recur /rɪ'kɜːʳ/ *v* to occur again, esp repeatedly or after an interval: e g **a** to come up again for consideration **b** to come again to mind – **~rence** *n*

recurrent /rɪ'kʌrənt/ *adj* returning or happening repeatedly or periodically – **~ly** *adv*

recycle /ˌriː'saɪkəl/ *v* to process (sewage, waste paper, glass, etc) for conversion back into a useful product

[1]**red** /red/ *adj* **1** of the colour red **2a** flushed, esp with anger or embarrassment **b** tinged with or rather red **3** failing to show a profit **4** *often cap* communist – infml – **~ness** *n* – **~dish** *adj*

[2]**red** *n* **1** a colour whose hue resembles that of blood or of the ruby or is that of the long-wave extreme of the visible spectrum **2** the condition of being financially in debt or of showing a loss – usu in *in/out of the red* **3** a red traffic light meaning 'stop' **4** *cap* a communist *USE* (*4*) chiefly derog

red admiral *n* a common N American and European butterfly that has broad orange-red bands on the fore wings and feeds on nettles in the larval stage

red-blooded *adj* full of vigour; virile

redbrick /'redˌbrɪk/ *n or adj* (an English university) founded between 1800 and WW II

redcurrant /ˌred'kʌrənt/ *n* (the small red edible fruit of) a widely cultivated European currant bush

redden /'redn/ *v* to make or become red; *esp* to blush

redeem /rɪ'diːm/ *v* **1** to release from blame or debt **2** to free from the consequences of sin **3a** to eliminate another's right to (sthg) by payment of a debt; *esp* to repurchase a pawned item **b** to convert (trading stamps, tokens, etc) into money or goods **c** to make good; fulfil **4a** to atone for **b** to make worthwhile; retrieve – **~able** *adj* – **~er** *n*

redemption /rɪ'dempʃən/ *n* redeeming or being redeemed; *also* sthg that redeems

redeploy /ˌriːdɪ'plɔɪ/ *v* to transfer (e g troops or workers) from one area or activity to another – **~ment** *n*

red giant *n* a star that has a low surface temperature and a large diameter relative to the sun

red-handed *adv or adj* in the act of committing a crime or misdeed

redhead /'redhed/ *n* a person with red hair

red-hot *adj* **1** glowing with heat; extremely hot **2a** ardent, passionate **b** sensational; *specif* salacious **3** new, topical

Red Indian *n* a N American Indian

red-light district *n* a district having many brothels

red meat *n* dark-coloured meat (e g beef or lamb)

redo /riː'duː/ *v* **1** to do over again **2** to decorate (a room or interior of a building) anew

redolent /'redələnt/ *adj* **1** full of a specified fragrance **2** evocative, suggestive – **-lence** *n*

redouble /riː'dʌbəl/ *v* to make or become greater, more numerous, or more intense

redoubtable /rɪ'daʊtəbəl/ *adj* **1** formidable **2** inspiring or worthy of awe or reverence

[1]**redress** /rɪ'dres/ *v* **1** to set right **2** to make or exact reparation for

[2]**redress** *n* **1** compensation for wrong or loss **2** the (means or possibility of) putting right what is wrong

red shift *n* a displacement of the spectrum of a celestial body towards longer wavelengths, that is a consequence of the Doppler effect or the gravitational field of the source

redskin /'red,skɪn/ *n* a N American Indian– chiefly derog

red squirrel *n* a reddish brown Eurasian squirrel native to British woodlands

red tape *n* excessively complex bureaucratic routine that results in delay

reduce /rɪ'djuːs/ *v* **1** to diminish in size, amount, extent, or number; *also* to lose weight by dieting **2** to bring or force to a specified state or condition **3** to force to capitulate **4** to bring to a systematic form or character **5** to lower in grade, rank, status, or condition **6a** to diminish in strength, density, or value **b** to lower the price of – **reducible** *adj*

reductio ad absurdum /rɪ,dʌktiəʊ æd əb'sɜːdəm/ *n* proof of the falsity of a proposition by revealing the absurdity of its logical consequences

reduction /rɪ'dʌkʃən/ *n* **1** a reducing or being reduced **2a** sthg made by reducing; *esp* a reproduction (e g of a picture) in a smaller size **b** the amount by which sthg is reduced

redundancy /rɪ'dʌndənsi/ *n* dismissal from a job

redundant /rɪ'dʌndənt/ *adj* **1a** superfluous **b** excessively verbose **2** *chiefly Br* unnecessary, unfit, or no longer required for a job – ~**ly** *adv*

redwing /'red,wɪŋ/ *n* a Eurasian thrush with red patches beneath its wings

redwood /'redwʊd/ *n* (the wood of) a commercially important Californian timber tree of the pine family that often reaches a height of 100m (about 300ft)

reed /riːd/ *n* **1** (the slender, often prominently jointed, stem of) any of various tall grasses that grow esp in wet areas **2** a growth or mass of reeds; *specif* reeds for thatching **3a** a thin elastic tongue or flattened tube (e g of cane) fastened over an air opening in a musical instrument (e g an organ or clarinet) and set in vibration by an air current **b** a woodwind instrument having a reed

reeducate /riː'edʒʊkeɪt/ *v* to rehabilitate through education – **-cation** *n*

reedy /'riːdi/ *adj* **1** full of, covered with, or made of reeds **2** slender, frail **3** having the tonal quality of a reed instrument; *esp* thin and high – **reediness** *n*

[1]**reef** /riːf/ *n* a part of a sail taken in or let out to regulate the area exposed to the wind

[2]**reef** *v* to reduce the area of (a sail) exposed to the wind by rolling up or taking in a portion

[3]**reef** *n* a ridge of rocks or sand at or near the surface of water

[1]**reefer, reefer jacket** /'riːfəʳ/ *n* a close-fitting usu double-breasted jacket of thick cloth

[2]**reefer** *n* a cigarette containing cannabis

reef knot *n* a symmetrical knot made of 2 half-knots tied in opposite directions and commonly used for joining 2 pieces of material

[1]**reek** /riːk/ *n* **1** a strong or disagreeable smell **2** *chiefly Scot & N Eng* smoke, vapour

[2]**reek** *v* **1** to give off or become permeated with a strong or offensive smell **2** to give a strong impression (of some usu undesirable quality or feature) – + *of* or *with*

[1]**reel** /riːl/ *n* a revolvable device on which sthg flexible is wound: e g **a** a small wheel at the butt of a fishing rod for winding the line **b** a flanged spool for photographic film, magnetic tape, etc **c** *chiefly Br* a small spool for sewing thread – **reel** *v*

[2]**reel** *v* **1** to be giddy; be in a whirl **2** to waver or fall back (e g from a blow) **3** to walk or (appear to) move unsteadily (e g from dizziness or intoxication)

[4]**reel** *n* (the music for) a lively esp Scottish-Highland or Irish dance in which 2 or more couples perform a series of circular figures and winding movements

reel off *v* **1** to tell or repeat readily and without pause **2** to chalk up, usu as a series

reentry /riː'entri/ *n* **1** the retaking of possession **2** the return to and entry of the earth's atmosphere by a space vehicle

[1]**reeve** /riːv/ *n* a medieval English manor officer

[2]**reeve** *v* **rove, reeved 1** to pass a rope

through a hole or opening **2** to fasten by passing through a hole or round sthg

ref /ref/ *n* a referee – infml

refectory /rɪ'fektəri/ *n* a dining hall in an institution (e g a monastery or college)

refer /rɪ'fɜːʳ/ *v* **1** to explain in terms of a general cause **2** to send or direct for information, aid, treatment, etc **3** to relate *to* sthg; *also* allude *to* **4** to have recourse; glance briefly for information

[1]**referee** /ˌrefə'riː/ *n* **1a** one to whom a legal matter is referred for investigation or settlement **b** a (character) reference **2** an official who supervises the play and enforces the laws in any of several sports (e g football and boxing)

[2]**referee** *v* to act as a referee (in or for)

[1]**reference** /'refərəns/ *n* **1** referring or consulting **2** (a) bearing on or connection with a matter – often in *in/with reference to* **3a** an allusion, mention **b** sthg that refers a reader to another source of information (e g a book or passage); *also* the other source of information **4a** a person to whom inquiries as to character or ability can be made **b** a statement of the qualifications of a person seeking employment or appointment given by sby familiar with him/her **c** a standard for measuring, evaluating, etc

[2]**reference** *v* to provide (e g a book) with references to authorities and sources of information

reference book *n* a book (e g a dictionary, encyclopedia, or atlas) intended primarily for consultation rather than for consecutive reading

referendum /ˌrefə'rendəm/ *n, pl* **referendums** *also* **referenda** the submitting to popular vote of a measure proposed by a legislative body or by popular initiative

refill /'riːˌfɪl/ *n* a fresh or replacement supply (for a device)

refine /rɪ'faɪn/ *v* **1** to free from impurities **2** to improve or perfect by pruning or polishing **3** to free from imperfection, esp from what is coarse, vulgar, or uncouth

refined /rɪ'faɪnd/ *adj* **1** fastidious, cultivated **2** *esp of food* processed to the extent that desirable ingredients may be lost in addition to impurities or imperfections

refinement /rɪ'faɪnmənt/ *n* **1** refining or being refined **2a** a (highly) refined feature, method, or distinction **b** a contrivance or device intended to improve or perfect

refinery /rɪ'faɪnəri/ *n* a plant where raw materials (e g oil or sugar) are refined or purified

refit /ˌriː'fɪt/ *v* to fit out or supply again; *esp* to renovate and modernize (e g a ship)

reflation /ri'fleɪʃən/ *n* an expansion in the volume of available money and credit or in the economy, esp as a result of government policy

reflect /rɪ'flekt/ *v* **1** to send or throw (light, sound, etc) back or at an angle **2** to show as an image or likeness; mirror **3** to make manifest or apparent **4** to consider **5** to tend to bring reproach or discredit – usu + *on* or *upon*

reflection /rɪ'flekʃən/ *n* **1** a reflecting of light, sound, etc **2a** an image given back (as if) by a reflecting surface **b** an effect produced by or related to a specified influence or cause **3** an often obscure or indirect criticism **4** consideration of some subject matter, idea, or purpose

reflective /rɪ'flektɪv/ *adj* **1** capable of reflecting light, images, or sound waves **2** thoughtful, deliberative **3** of or caused by reflection

reflector /rɪ'flektəʳ/ *n* **1** a polished surface for reflecting radiation, esp light **2** a telescope in which the principal focussing element is a mirror

[1]**reflex** /'riːfleks/ *n* **1** an automatic response to a stimulus that does not reach the level of consciousness **2** *pl* the power of acting or responding with adequate speed **3** an (automatic) way of behaving or responding

[2]**reflex** *adj* **1** bent, turned, or directed back **2** occurring as an (automatic) response **3** *of an angle* greater than 180° but less than 360°

reflex camera *n* a camera in which the image formed by the lens is reflected onto a ground-glass screen or is seen through the viewfinder for focussing and composition

reflexive /rɪ'fleksɪv/ *adj* **1** directed or turned back on itself **2** of, denoting, or being an action (e g in *he perjured himself*) directed back upon the agent or the grammatical subject – **-ly** *adv*

[1]**reform** /rɪ'fɔːm/ *v* **1** to amend or alter for the better **2** to put an end to (an evil) by enforcing or introducing a better method or course of action **3** to induce or cause to abandon evil ways – **~er** *n*

[2]**reform** *n* **1** amendment of what is defective or corrupt **2** (a measure intended to effect) a removal or correction of an abuse, a wrong, or errors

reformation /,refə'meɪʃən/ *n* **1** reforming or being reformed **2** *cap the* 16th-c religious movement marked by the rejection of papal authority and the establishment of the Protestant churches

reformatory /rɪ'fɔːmətəri/ *n, chiefly NAm* a penal institution to which young or first offenders or women are sent for reform

refract /rɪ'frækt/ *v* to deflect (light or another wave motion) from one straight path to another when passing from one medium (e g glass) to another (e g air) in which the velocity is different – **~ion** *n*

refracting telescope *n* a telescope in which the focussing elements are lenses

refractory /rɪ'fræktəri/ *adj* **1** resisting control or authority; stubborn, unmanageable **2** resistant to treatment or cure **3** difficult to fuse, corrode, or draw out; *esp* capable of enduring high temperatures

[1]**refrain** /rɪ'freɪn/ *v* to keep oneself from doing, feeling, or indulging in sthg, esp from following a passing impulse – usu + *from*

[2]**refrain** *n* (the musical setting of) a regularly recurring phrase or verse, esp at the end of each stanza or division of a poem or song; a chorus

refresh /rɪ'freʃ/ *v* **1** to restore strength or vigour to; revive (e g by food or rest) **2** to arouse, stimulate (e g the memory)

refreshing /rɪ'freʃɪŋ/ *adj* agreeably stimulating because of freshness or newness – **~ly** *adv*

refreshment /rɪ'freʃmənt/ *n* **1** refreshing or being refreshed **2** assorted foods, esp for a light meal – usu pl with sing. meaning

refrigerate /rɪ'frɪdʒəreɪt/ *v* to freeze or chill (e g food) or remain frozen for preservation – **-rant** *n* – **-ration** *n*

refrigerator /rɪ'frɪdʒəreɪtə^r/ *n* an insulated cabinet or room for keeping food, drink, etc cool

refuge /'refjuːdʒ/ *n* **1** (a place that provides) shelter or protection from danger or distress **2** a person, thing, or course of action that offers protection or is resorted to in difficulties

refugee /,refjʊ'dʒiː/ *n* one who flees for safety, esp to a foreign country to escape danger or persecution

[1]**refund** /rɪ'fʌnd/ *v* to return (money) in restitution, repayment, or balancing of accounts

[2]**refund** /'riːfʌnd/ *n* **1** a refunding **2** a sum refunded

[3]**refund** /,riː'fʌnd/ *v* to fund (a debt) again

refurbish /,riː'fɜːbɪʃ/ *v* to renovate

refusal /rɪ'fjuːzəl/ *n* **1** a refusing, denying, or being refused **2** the right or option of refusing or accepting sthg before others

[1]**refuse** /rɪ'fjuːz/ *v* **1** to express oneself as unwilling to accept **2a** to show or express unwillingness to do or comply with **b** *of a horse* to decline to jump a fence, wall, etc

[2]**refuse** /'refjuːs/ *n* worthless or useless stuff; rubbish, garbage

refute /rɪ'fjuːt/ *v* **1** to prove wrong by argument or evidence **2** to deny the truth or accuracy of

regain /rɪ'geɪn/ *v* to gain or reach again; recover

regal /'riːgəl/ *adj* **1** of or suitable for a king or queen **2** stately, splendid – **~ly** *adv*

regalia /rɪ'geɪlɪə/ *n pl but sing or pl in constr* **1** (the) ceremonial emblems or symbols indicative of royalty **2** special dress; *esp* official finery

[1]**regard** /rɪ'gɑːd/ *n* **1** a gaze, look **2** attention, consideration **3a** a feeling of respect and affection **b** *pl* friendly greetings

[2]**regard** *v* **1** to pay attention to; take

into consideration or account **2** to look steadily at **3** to consider and appraise in a specified way or from a specified point of view

regarding /rɪ'gɑːdɪŋ/ *prep* with regard to

1**regardless** /rɪ'gɑːdlɨs/ *adj* heedless, careless

2**regardless** *adv* despite everything

regatta /rɪ'gætə/ *n* a series of rowing, speedboat, or sailing races

regency /'riːdʒənsi/ *n* the office, period of rule, or government of a regent or regents

Regency /'riːdʒənsi/ *adj* of or resembling the styles (e g of furniture or dress) prevalent during the time of the Prince Regent (c 1810–1830)

1**regenerate** /rɪ'dzenərɨt/ *adj* **1** spiritually reborn or converted **2** restored to a better, higher, or more worthy state

2**regenerate** /rɪ'dzenəreɪt/ *v* **1** to change radically and for the better **2** to generate or produce anew; *esp* to replace (a body part) by a new growth of tissue

regent /'riːdʒənt/ *n* one who governs a kingdom in the minority, absence, or disability of the sovereign

reggae /'regeɪ/ *n* popular music of West Indian origin that is characterized by a strongly accented subsidiary beat

regicide /'redzɨsaɪd/ *n* (the act of) one who kills a king

regime *also* **régime** /reɪ'ʒiːm/ *n* **1** a regimen **2a** a form of management or government **b** a government in power

regimen /'redzɨmɨn/ *n* a systematic plan (e g of diet, exercise, or medical treatment) adopted esp to achieve some end

1**regiment** /'redʒɨmənt/ *n sing or pl in constr* **1** a permanent military unit consisting usu of a number of companies, troops, batteries, or sometimes battalions **2** a large number or group – **~al** *adj*

2**regiment** /'redʒɨment/ *v* to subject to strict and stultifying organization or control – **~ation** *n*

regimentals /ˌredzɨ'mentlz/ *n pl* **1** the uniform of a regiment **2** military dress

Regina /rɪ'dzaɪnə/ *n* the Queen as head of state

region /'riːdʒən/ *n* **1** an administrative area **2** an indefinite area of the world or universe; *esp* an area with broadly uniform features **3** an indefinite area surrounding a specified body part **4** a sphere of activity or interest – **~al** *adj* – **~ally** *adv*

1**register** /'redʒɨstəʳ/ *n* **1** a written record containing (official) entries of items, names, transactions, etc **2a** a roster of qualified or available individuals **b** a school attendance record **3** (a part of) the range of a human voice or a musical instrument **4** a device registering a number or a quantity **5** a condition of correct alignment or proper relative position (e g of the plates used in colour printing) – often in *in/out of register*

2**register** *v* **1a** to enrol formally **b** to record automatically; indicate **c** to make a (mental) record of; note **2** to secure special protection for (a piece of mail) by prepayment of a fee **3** to convey an impression of **4** to achieve, win

registrar /ˌredʒɨ'strɑːʳ/ *n* **1** an official recorder or keeper of records: e g **a** a senior administrative officer of a university **b** an official responsible for recording births, marriages and deaths in an area and for conducting civil marriages **2** a British hospital doctor in training

registration /ˌredʒɨ'streɪʃən/ *n* **1** registering or being registered **2** an entry in a register

registry /'redʒɨstri/, **registry office** *n* a place where births, marriages and deaths are recorded and civil marriages conducted

regnant /'regnənt/ *adj* reigning

1**regress** /'riːgres/ *n* **1** a trend to a lower, less perfect, or earlier condition **2** an act of going or coming back

2**regress** /rɪ'gres/ *v* to undergo or exhibit backwards movement, esp to an earlier state – **~ion** *n*

1**regret** /rɪ'gret/ *v* to be very sorry about

2**regret** *n* **1** grief or sorrow tinged esp with disappointment, longing, or remorse **2** *pl* a conventional expression of disappointment, esp on declining an invitation – ~**ful** *adj* – ~**fully** *adv* – ~**fulness** *n*

[1]**regular** /'regjʊləʳ/ *adj* **1a** formed, built, arranged, or ordered according to some rule, principle, or type **b(1)** both equilateral and equiangular **(2)** having faces that are identical regular polygons with identical angles between them **c** perfectly (radially) symmetrical or even **2a** steady or uniform in course, practice, or occurrence; habitual, usual, or constant **b** recurring or functioning at fixed or uniform intervals **3** constituted, conducted, or done in conformity with established or prescribed usages, rules, or discipline **4** of or being a permanent standing army – infml – ~**ity** *n* – ~**ize** *v* – ~**ly** *adv*

[2]**regular** *n* **1** a soldier in a regular army **2** one who is usu present or participating; *esp* one who habitually visits a particular place

regulate /'regjʊleɪt/ *v* **1** to govern or direct according to rule **2** to bring order, method, or uniformity to **3** to fix or adjust the time, amount, degree, or rate of

[1]**regulation** /ˌregjʊ'leɪʃən/ *n* **1** regulating or being regulated **2** an authoritative rule or order

[2]**regulation** *adj* conforming to regulations; official

regulo /'regjʊləʊ/ *n, chiefly Br* the temperature in a gas oven expressed as a specified number

regurgitate /rɪ'gɜːdʒ̩teɪt/ *v* to vomit or pour back or out (as if) from a cavity – **-tation** *n*

rehabilitate /ˌriːhə'bɪl̩teɪt/ *v* **1** to reestablish the good name of **2** to restore to a condition of health or useful and constructive activity (e g after illness or imprisonment) – **-tation** *n*

[1]**rehash** /ˌriː'hæʃ/ *v* to present or use again in another form without substantial change or improvement

[2]**rehash** /'riːhæʃ/ *n* sthg presented in a new form without change of substance

rehearsal /rɪ'hɜːsəl/ *n* a practice session, esp of a play, concert, etc preparatory to a public appearance

rehearse /rɪ'hɜːs/ *v* **1** to present an account of (again) **2** to give a rehearsal of; practise

rehouse /ˌriː'haʊz/ *v* to establish in new or better-quality housing

[1]**reign** /reɪn/ *n* the time during which sby or sthg reigns

[2]**reign** *v* **1** to hold office as head of state; rule **2** to be predominant or prevalent

reimburse /ˌriː̩m'bɜːs/ *v* to pay back – ~**ment** *n*

[1]**rein** /reɪn/ *n* **1** a long line fastened usu to both sides of a bit, by which a rider or driver controls an animal **2** controlling or guiding power – usu pl

[2]**rein** *v* to check or stop (as if) by pulling on reins – often + *in*

reincarnate /ˌriːɪn'kaːneɪt/ *v* to give a new form or fresh embodiment to – **-nation** *n*

reindeer /'reɪndɪəʳ/ *n* any of several deer that inhabit N Europe, Asia, and America, have antlers in both sexes, and are often domesticated

reinforce /ˌriː̩n'fɔːs/ *v* **1** to make stronger or more pronounced **2** to strengthen or increase (e g an army) by fresh additions **3** to stimulate (an experimental subject) with a reward following a correct or desired performance – ~**ment** *n*

reinforced concrete *n* concrete in which metal is embedded for strengthening

reinstate /ˌriː̩n'steɪt/ *v* to restore to a previous state or condition – ~**ment** *n*

reiterate /riː'ɪtəreɪt/ *v* to say or do over again or repeatedly – **-ration** *n*

[1]**reject** /rɪ'dʒekt/ *v* **1a** to refuse to accept, consider, submit to, or use **b** to refuse to accept or admit **2** to fail to accept (e g a skin graft or transplanted organ) as part of the organism because of immunological differences – ~**ion** *n*

[2]**reject** /'riːdʒekt/ *n* a rejected person or thing; *esp* a substandard article of merchandise

rejoice /rɪ'dʒɔɪs/ *v* to feel or express joy or great delight

rejoin /rɪ'dʒɔɪn/ *v* to say (sharply or critically) in response

rejoinder /rɪ'dʒɔɪndəʳ/ *n* (an answer to) a reply

rejuvenate /rɪ'dʒuːvəneɪt/ *v* to make young or youthful again – **-nation** *n*

[1]**relapse** /rɪ'læps, 'riːlæps/ *n* a relapsing or backsliding; *esp* a recurrence of symptoms of a disease after a period of improvement

[2]**relapse** /rɪ'læps/ *v* **1** to slip or fall back into a former worse state **2** to sink, subside

relate /rɪ'leɪt/ *v* **1** to give an account of; tell **2** to show or establish logical or causal connection between **3** to respond, esp favourably – often + *to*

related /rɪ'leɪtɨd/ *adj* **1** connected by reason of an established or discoverable relation **2** connected by common ancestry or sometimes by marriage – **~ness** *n*

relation /rɪ'leɪʃən/ *n* **1** the act of telling or recounting **2** an aspect or quality (e g resemblance) that connects 2 or more things as belonging or working together or as being of the same kind **3** a relative **4** reference, respect, or connection **5** the interaction between 2 or more people or groups – usu pl with sing. meaning **6** *pl* **a** dealings, affairs **b** communication, contact

relationship /rɪ'leɪʃənʃɪp/ *n* **1** the state or character of being related or interrelated **2** (a specific instance or type of) kinship **3** a state of affairs existing between those having relations or dealings

[1]**relative** /'relətɪv/ *n* **1** a word referring grammatically to an antecedent **2a** a person connected with another by blood relationship or marriage **b** an animal or plant related to another by common descent

[2]**relative** *adj* **1** introducing a subordinate clause qualifying an expressed or implied antecedent; *also* introduced by such a connective **2a** not absolute or independent; comparative **b** expressing, having, or existing in connection with or with reference to sthg else (e g a standard) *adv*

relativity /,relə'tɪvɨti/ *n* **1** being relative **2a** *also* **special theory of relativity** a theory (based on the 2 postulates (1) that the speed of light in a vacuum is constant and independent of the source or observer and (2) that all motion is relative) that leads to the assertion that mass and energy are equivalent and that mass, dimension, and time will change with increased velocity **b** *also* **general theory of relativity** an extension of this theory to include gravitation and related acceleration phenomena

relax /rɪ'læks/ *v* **1** to make less tense, rigid or severe **2** to cast off inhibition, nervous tension, or anxiety **3** to seek rest or recreation

relaxation /,riːlæk'seɪʃən/ *n* **1** relaxing or being relaxed **2** a relaxing or recreational state, activity, or pastime

[1]**relay** /'riːleɪ/ *n* **1** a number of people who relieve others in some work **2** a race between teams in which each team member successively covers a specified portion of the course **3** the act of passing sthg along by stages; *also* such a stage

[2]**relay** *v* **1** to provide with relays **2** to pass along by relays

[1]**release** /rɪ'liːs/ *v* **1** to set free from restraint, confinement, or servitude **2** to relieve from sthg that confines, burdens, or oppresses **3** to relinquish (e g a claim or right) in favour of another **4** to give permission for publication, performance, exhibition, or sale of, on but not before a specified date; *also* to publish, issue

[2]**release** *n* **1** relief or deliverance from sorrow, suffering, or trouble **2** discharge from obligation or responsibility **3** freeing or being freed; liberation (e g from jail) **4a** (the act of permitting) performance or publication **b(1)** a statement prepared for the press **(2)** a (newly issued) gramophone record

relegate /'relɨgeɪt/ *v* **1** to assign to a place of insignificance or oblivion; put out of sight or mind; *specif* to demote to a lower division of a sporting competition (e g a football league) **2** to submit or refer to sby or sthg for appropriate action – **-gation** *n*

relent /rɪ'lent/ *v* **1** to become less severe, harsh, or strict, usu from reasons of humanity **2** to slacken; let up

relentless /rɪ'lentlɨs/ *adj* persistent, unrelenting – **~ly** *adv* – **~ness** *n*

relevant /'relɨvənt/ *adj* **1** having significant and demonstrable bearing on the matter at hand **2** having practical application, esp to the real world – ~**ly** *adv* – **-vance, -vancy** *n*

reliable /rɪˈlaɪəbəl/ *adj* suitable or fit to be relied on; dependable – **-bly** *adv*

reliance /rɪˈlaɪəns/ *n* the act of relying; the condition or attitude of one who relies

relic /ˈrelɪk/ *n* **1** a part of the body of or some object associated with a saint or martyr, that is preserved as an object of reverence **2** sthg left behind after decay, disintegration, or disappearance; *also* an outmoded custom, belief, or practice

relict /ˈrelɪkt/ *n* **1** a (type of) plant or animal that is a remnant of an otherwise extinct flora, fauna, or kind of organism **2** a geological or geographical feature (e g a lake or mountain) or a rock remaining after other parts have disappeared or substantially altered

relief /rɪˈliːf/ *n* **1a** removal or lightening of sthg oppressive, painful, or distressing **b** aid in the form of money or necessities, esp for the poor **c** military assistance to an endangered or surrounded post or force **d** a means of breaking or avoiding monotony or boredom **2** (release from a post or duty by) one who takes over the post or duty of another **3** (a method of) sculpture in which the design stands out from the surrounding surface **4** sharpness of outline due to contrast **5** the differences in elevation of a land surface

relieve /rɪˈliːv/ *v* **1a** to free from a burden; give aid or help to **b** to set free from an obligation, condition, or restriction – often + *of* **2** to bring about the removal or alleviation of **3** to release from a post, station, or duty **4** to remove or lessen the monotony of **5** to give relief to (oneself) by urinating or defecating

relieved /rɪˈliːvd/ *adj* experiencing or showing relief, esp from anxiety or pent-up emotions

religion /rɪˈlɪdʒən/ *n* **1a** the (organized) service and worship of a god, gods, or the supernatural **b** personal commitment or devotion to religious faith or observance **2** a cause, principle, or system of beliefs held to with ardour and faith; sthg considered to be of supreme importance

religious /rɪˈlɪdʒəs/ *adj* **1** of or manifesting faithful devotion to an acknowledged ultimate reality or deity **2** of, being, or devoted to the beliefs or observances of a religion **3** scrupulously and conscientiously faithful

relinquish /rɪˈlɪŋkwɪʃ/ *v* **1** to renounce or abandon **2** to give over possession or control of

[1]**relish** /ˈrelɪʃ/ *n* **1** characteristic, pleasing, or piquant flavour or quality **2** enjoyment of or delight in sthg (that satisfies one's tastes, inclinations, or desires) **3** sthg that adds an appetizing or savoury flavour; *esp* a highly seasoned sauce (e g of pickles or mustard) eaten with plainer food

[2]**relish** *v* to enjoy; have pleasure from

relive /ˌriːˈlɪv/ *v* to live over again; *esp* to experience again in the imagination

reluctance /rɪˈlʌktəns/ *n* being reluctant

reluctant /rɪˈlʌktənt/ *adj* holding back; unwilling – ~**ly** *adv*

rely /ˈrilaɪ/ *v* **1** to have confidence based on experience **2** to be dependent *USE* + *on* or *upon*

remain /rɪˈmeɪn/ *v* **1** to be sthg or a part not destroyed, taken, or used up **2** to stay behind (with) **3** to continue to be

remainder /rɪˈmeɪndəʳ/ *n* **1a** a remaining group, part, or trace **b(1)** the number left after a subtraction **(2)** the final undivided part after division, that is less than the divisor **2** a book sold at a reduced price by the publisher after sales have fallen off

remains /rɪˈmeɪnz/ *n* **1** a remaining part or trace **2** a dead body

[1]**remake** /ˌriːˈmeɪk/ *v* to make anew or in a different form

[2]**remake** /ˈriːmeɪk/ *n* a new version of a film

remand /rɪˈmɑːnd/ *v* to return to custody, esp pending further enquiries – **remand** *n*

remand home *n, Br* a temporary centre for (juvenile) offenders

[1]**remark** /rɪˈmɑːk/ *v* to notice sthg and make a comment or observation *on* or *upon*

[2]**remark** *n* **1** mention or notice of that which deserves attention **2** a casual expression of an opinion or judgment

remarkable /rɪ'mɑːkəbəl/ *adj* worthy of being or likely to be noticed, esp as being uncommon or extraordinary – **-bly** *adv*

remedial /rɪ'miːdɪəl/ *adj* **1** intended as a remedy **2** concerned with the correction of faulty study habits – **~ly** *adv*

[1]**remedy** /'remʒdi/ *n* **1** a medicine, application, or treatment that relieves or cures a disease **2** sthg that corrects or counteracts an evil or deficiency

[2]**remedy** *v* to provide or serve as a remedy for

remember /rɪ'membəʳ/ *v* **1** to bring to mind or think of again (for attention or consideration) **2** to retain in the memory **3** to convey greetings from

remembrance /rɪ'membrəns/ *n* **1** the period over which one's memory extends **2** an act of recalling to mind **3** a memory of a person, thing, or event **4** sthg that serves to keep in or bring to mind

remind /rɪ'maɪnd/ *v* to cause to remember – **~er** *n*

reminisce /,remʒ'nɪs/ *v* to indulge in reminiscence

reminiscence /,remʒ'nɪsəns/ *n* **1** the process or practice of thinking or telling about past experiences **2** an account of a memorable experience – often pl

reminiscent /,remʒ'nɪsənt/ *adj* tending to remind one (e g of sthg seen or known before)

remiss /rɪ'mɪs/ *adj* **1** negligent in the performance of work or duty **2** showing neglect or inattention – **~ness** *n*

remission /rɪ'mɪʃən/ *n* **1** the act or process of remitting **2** reduction of a prison sentence

[1]**remit** /rɪ'mɪt/ *v* **1** to refer for consideration; *specif* to return (a case) to a lower court **2** to postpone, defer **3** to send (money) to a person or place **4** to moderate

[2]**remit** /'riːmɪt, rɪ'mɪt/ *n* **1** an act of remitting **2** sthg remitted to another person or authority for consideration or judgment

remittance /rɪ'mɪtəns/ *n* a transmittal of money

remittent /rɪ'mɪtənt/ *adj, of a disease* marked by alternating periods of abatement and increase of symptoms

remnant /'remnənt/ *n* **1a** a usu small part or trace remaining **b** a small surviving group – often pl **2** an unsold or unused end of fabric

remodel /,riː'mɒdl/ *v* to reconstruct

remonstrate /'remənstreɪt/ *v* to present and urge reasons in opposition – often + *with* – **-strance** *n*

remorse /rɪ'mɔːs/ *n* a deep and bitter distress arising from a sense of guilt for past wrongs – **~ful** *adj* – **~fully** *adv* – **~fulness** *n* – **~less** *adj* – **~lessly** *adv* – **~lessness** *n*

remote /rɪ'məʊt/ *adj* **1** far removed in space, time, or relation **2** out-of-the-way, secluded **3** small in degree **4** distant in manner – **~ly** *adv* – **~ness** *n*

remote control *n* control over an operation (e g of a machine or weapon) exercised from a distance usu by means of an electrical circuit or radio waves

[1]**remould** /,riː'məʊld/ *v* to refashion the tread of (a worn tyre)

[2]**remould** /'riːməʊld/ *n* a remoulded tyre

remount /,riː'maʊnt/ *v* **1** to mount again **2** to provide (e g a unit of cavalry) with remounts

removal /rɪ'muːvəl/ *n* **1** *Br* the moving of household goods from one residence to another **2** removing or being removed

[1]**remove** /rɪ'muːv/ *v* **1** to change the location, position, station, or residence of **2** to move by lifting, pushing aside, or taking away or off **3** to get rid of – **removable** *adj*

[2]**remove** *n* **1a** a distance or interval separating one person or thing from another **b** a degree or stage of separation **2** a form intermediate between 2 others in some British schools

remunerate /rɪ'mjuːnəreɪt/ *v* **1** to pay an equivalent for **2** to recompense – **-ration** *n*

remunerative /rɪ'mjuːnərətɪv/ *adj* profitable, well-paid

renaissance /rɪ'nesəns, -'neɪ-/ *n* **1** *cap the* (period of the) humanistic revival of classical influence in Europe from the 14th c to the 17th c, expressed in a flowering of the arts and literature and by the beginnings of modern science 2 a rebirth, revival, esp of artistic or intellectual activity

renal /'riːnl/ *adj* relating to or located in the region of the kidneys

rend /rend/ *v* **rent** **1** to wrest, split, or tear apart or in pieces (as if) by violence **2** to tear (the hair or clothing) as a sign of anger, grief, or despair **3** to pierce with sound

render /'rendəʳ/ *v* **1** to melt down; extract by melting **2a** to yield; give up **b** to deliver for consideration, approval, or information **3a** to give in return or retribution **b** to restore; give back **4a** to cause to be or become **b** to reproduce or represent by artistic or verbal means **5** to apply a coat of plaster or cement directly to

rendering /'rendərɪŋ/ *n* a covering material, usu of cement, sand, and a small percentage of lime, applied to exterior walls

rendezvous /'rɒndɮvuː, -deɪ-/ *n, pl* **rendezvous** **1** a place (appointed) for assembling or meeting **2** a meeting at an appointed place and time

rendition /ren'dɪʃən/ *n* **1** a translation **2** a performance, interpretation

renegade /'renɮgeɪd/ *n* **1** a deserter from one faith, cause, or allegiance to another **2** an individual who rejects lawful or conventional behaviour

renew /rɪ'njuː/ *v* **1** to restore to freshness, vigour, or perfection **2** to revive **3** to make changes in; rebuild **4** to make or do again **5** to begin again; resume **6** to replace, replenish **7** to grant or obtain an extension of or on (e g a subscription, lease, or licence) – **~able** *adj* – **~al** *n*

rennet /'renɮt/ *n* a preparation used for curdling milk

renounce /rɪ'naʊns/ *v* **1** to give up, refuse, or resign, usu by formal declaration **2** to refuse to follow, obey, or recognize any further – **renunciation** *n*

renovate /'renəveɪt/ *v* to restore to a former or improved state (e g by cleaning, repairing, or rebuilding) – **-vation** *n*

renown /rɪ'naʊn/ *n* a state of being widely acclaimed; fame – **~ed** *adj*

[1]**rent** /rent/ *n* **1** a usu fixed periodical payment made by a tenant or occupant of property or user of goods to the owner for the possession and use thereof **2** the portion of the income of an economy (e g of a nation) attributable to land as a factor of production in addition to capital and labour

[2]**rent** *v* **1** to take and hold under an agreement to pay rent **2** to grant the possession and use of for rent – **~able** *adj*

[3]**rent** *past of* **rend**

[4]**rent** *n* **1** an opening or split made (as if) by rending **2** an act or instance of rending

[1]**rental** /'rentl/ *n* **1** an amount paid or collected as rent **2** an act of renting

[2]**rental** *adj* of or relating to rent or renting

[1]**rep, repp** /rep/ *n* a plain-weave fabric with raised crosswise ribs

[2]**rep** *n* a (sales) representative – infml

[3]**rep** *n* repertory

[1]**repair** /rɪ'peəʳ/ *v* to go; take oneself off *to* – fml

[2]**repair** *v* **1** to restore by replacing a part or putting together what is torn or broken **2** to restore to a sound or healthy state – **~able** *adj* – **~er** *n*

[3]**repair** *n* **1** an instance or the act or process of repairing **2** relative condition with respect to soundness or need of repairing

reparable /'repərəbl/ *adj* capable of being repaired

reparation /ˌrepə'reɪʃən/ *n* **1** the act of making amends, offering expiation, or giving satisfaction for a wrong or injury **2** damages; *specif* compensation payable by a defeated nation for war damages – usu pl with sing. meaning

repartee /ˌrepɑː'tiː/ *n* **1** a quick and witty reply **2** (skill in) amusing and usu light sparring with words

repast /rɪ'pɑːst/ *n* a meal – fml

repatriate /riː'pætrieɪt/ *v* to restore to the country of origin – **-ation** *n*

repay /rɪ'peɪ/ *v* **1a** to pay back **b** to give or inflict in return or requital **2** to compensate, requite **3** to recompense – **~able** *adj* – **~ment** *n*

repeal /rɪ'piːl/ *v* to revoke (a law) – **repeal** *n*

[1]**repeat** /rɪ'piːt/ *v* **1a** to say or state again **b** to say through from memory **c** to say after another **2** to make, do, perform, present, or broadcast again **3** to express or present (oneself or itself) again in the same words, terms, or form – **~ed** *adj* – **~edly** *adv*

[2]**repeat** *n* **1** the act of repeating **2a** a television or radio programme that has previously been broadcast at least once **b** (a sign placed before or after) a musical passage to be repeated in performance

repeater /rɪ'piːtəʳ/ *n* **1** a watch that strikes the time when a catch is pressed **2** a firearm that fires several times without having to be reloaded

repel /rɪ'pel/ *v* **1** to drive back; repulse **2a** to be incapable of sticking to, mixing with, taking up, or holding **b** to (tend to) force away or apart by mutual action at a distance **3** to cause aversion in; disgust

[1]**repellent** *also* **repellant** /rɪ'pelənt/ *adj* **1** serving or tending to drive away or ward off **2** repulsive

[2]**repellent** *also* **repellant** *n* sthg that repels; *esp* a substance used to prevent insect attacks

repent /rɪ'pent/ *v* to feel sorrow, regret, or contrition for – **~ance** *n* – **~ant** *adj*

repercussion /ˌriːpə'kʌʃən/ *n* **1** an echo, reverberation **2** a widespread, indirect, or unforeseen effect of an act, action, or event

repertoire /'repətwɑːʳ/ *n* **1a** a list or supply of dramas, operas, pieces, or parts that a company or person is prepared to perform **b** a range of skills, techniques, or expedients **2** a list or stock of capabilities

repertory /'repətəri/ *n* **1** a repertoire **2** (a theatre housing) a company that presents several different plays in the course of a season at one theatre

repetition /ˌrepȷ̇'tɪʃən/ *n* **1** repeating or being repeated **2** a reproduction, copy – **-tive** *adj* – **-tively** *adv*

repetitious /ˌrepȷ̇'tɪʃəs/ *adj* tediously repeating – **~ness** *n* – **~ly** *adv*

replace /rɪ'pleɪs/ *v* **1** to restore to a former place or position **2** to take the place of, esp as a substitute or successor **3** to put sthg new in the place of – **~able** *adj*

replacement /rɪ'pleɪsmənt/ *n* **1** replacing or being replaced **2** sthg or sby that replaces another

[1]**replay** /ˌriː'pleɪ/ *v* to play again

[2]**replay** /'riːpleɪ/ *n* **1a** an act or instance of replaying **b** the playing of a tape (e g a videotape) **2** a match played to resolve a tie in an earlier match

replenish /rɪ'plenɪʃ/ *v* to stock or fill up again – **~ment** *n*

replete /rɪ'pliːt/ *adj* **1** fully or abundantly provided or filled **2** abundantly fed; sated – **repletion** *n*

replica /'replɪkə/ *n* a copy, duplicate

replicate /'replȷ̇keɪt/ *v* to duplicate, repeat

[1]**reply** /rɪ'plaɪ/ *v* **1** to respond in words or writing **2** to do sthg in response **3** to give as an answer

[2]**reply** *n* sthg said, written, or done in answer or response

[1]**report** /rɪ'pɔːt/ *n* **1** (an account spread by) common talk **2a** a usu detailed account or statement **b** a usu formal record of the proceedings of a meeting or inquiry **c** a statement of a pupil's performance at school usu issued every term to the pupil's parents or guardian **3** a loud explosive noise

[2]**report** *v* **1** to give information about; relate **2a** to convey news of **b** to make a written record or summary of **c** to present the newsworthy aspects or developments of in writing or for broadcasting **3a** to make known to the relevant authorities **b** to make a charge of misconduct against

reportedly /rɪ'pɔːtȷ̇dli/ *adv* reputedly

reporter /rɪ'pɔːtəʳ/ *n* sby who or sthg that reports: e g **a** one who makes a shorthand record of a proceeding **b** a journalist who writes news stories **c** one who gathers and broadcasts news

[1]**repose** /rɪ'pəʊz/ *v* **1a** to lie resting **b** to lie dead **2** to take rest **3** to rest for support – chiefly fml

[2]**repose** *n* **1** a place or state of rest or resting; *esp* rest in sleep **2a** calm, tranquillity **b** a restful effect (e g of a

painting or colour scheme) **3** cessation of activity, movement, or animation – **~ful** *adj*

repository /rɪ'pɒzɪ̣təri/ *n* **1** a place, room, or container where sthg is deposited or stored **2** sby who or sthg that holds or stores sthg nonmaterial (e g knowledge)

repossess /ˌriːpə'zes/ *v* **1** to regain possession of **2** to resume possession of in default of the payment of instalments due – **~ion** *n*

reprehend /ˌreprɪ'hend/ *v* to voice disapproval of; censure

reprehensible /ˌreprɪ'hensəbəl/ *adj* deserving censure; culpable – **-bly** *adv*

represent /ˌreprɪ'zent/ *v* **1** to convey a mental impression of **2** to serve as a sign or symbol of **3** to portray or exhibit in art; depict **4a** to take the place of in some respect; stand in for **b** to serve, esp in a legislative body, by delegated authority **5** to serve as a specimen, exemplar, or instance of

representation /ˌreprɪzen'teɪʃən/ *n* **1a** an artistic likeness or image **b** a usu formal protest **2** representing or being represented on or in some formal, esp legislative, body

representational /ˌreprɪzen'teɪʃənəl/ *adj* **1** of representation **2** of realistic depiction of esp physical objects or appearances in the graphic or plastic arts

[1]**representative** /ˌreprɪ'zentətɪv/ *adj* **1** serving to represent **2a** standing or acting for another, esp through delegated authority **b** of or based on representation of the people in government by election **3** serving as a typical or characteristic example

[2]**representative** *n* **1** a typical example of a group, class, or quality **2a(1)** one who represents a constituency **(2)** a member of a House of Representatives or of a US state legislature **b** a deputy, delegate **c** one who represents a business organization

repress /rɪ'pres/ *v* **1a** to curb **b** to put down by force **2a** to hold in or prevent the expression of, by self-control **b** to exclude (e g a feeling) from consciousness – **~ive** *adj* – **~ively** *adv*

repression /rɪ'preʃən/ *n* **1** repressing or being repressed **2** an instance of repressing

[1]**reprieve** /rɪ'priːv/ *v* **1** to delay or remit the punishment of (e g a condemned prisoner) **2** to give temporary relief or rest to

[2]**reprieve** *n* **1a** reprieving or being reprieved **b** (a warrant for) a suspension or remission of a (death) sentence **2** a temporary remission (e g from pain or trouble)

[1]**reprimand** /'reprɪ̣mɑːnd/ *n* a severe (and formal) reproof

[2]**reprimand** *v* to criticize sharply or formally censure, usu from a position of authority

reprint /'riːprɪnt/ *n* **1** a subsequent impression of a book previously published in the same form **2** matter (e g an article) that has appeared in print before

reprisal /rɪ'praɪzəl/ *n* **1** (a) retaliation by force short of war **2** a retaliatory act

reprise /rɪ'priːz/ *n* a repetition of a musical passage, theme, or performance

[1]**reproach** /rɪ'prəʊtʃ/ *n* **1** (a cause or occasion of) discredit or disgrace **3** an expression of rebuke or disapproval – **~ful** *adj* – **~fully** *adv*

[2]**reproach** *v* to express disappointment and displeasure with (a person) for conduct that is blameworthy or in need of amendment

[1]**reprobate** /'reprəbeɪt/ *v* to condemn strongly as unworthy, unacceptable, or evil

[2]**reprobate** *adj* morally dissolute; unprincipled

reproduce /ˌriːprə'djuːs/ *v* **1** to produce (new living things of the same kind) by a sexual or asexual process **2** to imitate closely **3** to make an image or copy of – **-ducible** *adj*

reproduction /ˌriːprə'dʌkʃən/ *n* **1** the sexual or asexual process by which plants and animals give rise to offspring **2** sthg (e g a painting) that is reproduced – **-tive** *adj*

reproof /rɪ'pruːf/ *n* criticism for a fault

reprove /rɪ'pruːv/ *v* **1** to call attention to the remissness of **2** to express disapproval of; censure

reptile /'reptaɪl/ *n* **1** any of a class of

vertebrates that include the alligators and crocodiles, lizards, snakes, turtles, and extinct related forms (e g the dinosaurs) and have a bony skeleton and a body usu covered with scales or bony plates **2** a grovelling or despicable person – **-tilian** *adj, n*

republic /rɪ'pʌblɪk/ *n* **1** a state in which supreme power resides in the people and is exercised by their elected representatives governing according to law **2** a body of people freely and equally engaged in a common activity

¹republican /rɪ'pʌblɪkən/ *adj* **1a** of or like a republic **b** advocating a republic **2** *cap* of or constituting a political party of the USA that is usu primarily associated with business, financial, and some agricultural interests and is held to favour a restricted governmental role in social and economic life

²republican *n* **1** one who favours republican government **2** *cap* a member of the US Republican party

repudiate /rɪ'pjuːdieɪt/ *v* **1** to refuse to have anything to do with **2a** to refuse to accept **b** to reject as untrue or unjust – **-ation** *n*

repugnance /rɪ'pʌgnəns/ *n* **1** the quality or fact or an instance of being contradictory or incompatible **2** strong dislike, aversion, or antipathy – **-nant** *adj*

¹repulse /rɪ'pʌls/ *v* **1** to drive or beat back **2** to repel by discourtesy, coldness, or denial

²repulse *n* **1** a rebuff, rejection **2** repelling an assailant or being repelled

repulsion /rɪ'pʌlʃən/ *n* **1** repulsing or being repulsed **2** a force (e g between like electric charges or like magnetic poles) tending to produce separation **3** a feeling of strong aversion – **-sive** *adj* – **-sively** *adv* – **-siveness** *n*

reputable /'repjʊtəbəl/ *adj* held in good repute; well regarded – **-bly** *adv*

reputation /repjʊ'teɪʃən/ *n* **1** overall quality or character as seen or judged by others **2** a place in public esteem or regard; good name

repute /rɪ'pjuːt/ *n* **1** the character, quality, or status commonly ascribed **2** the state of being favourably known or spoken of

reputed /rɪ'pjuːtɨ̣d/ *adj* being such according to general or popular belief – **~ly** *adv*

¹request /rɪ'kwest/ *n* **1** the act or an instance of asking for sthg **2** sthg asked for

²request *v* **1** to make a request to or of **2** to ask as a favour or privilege **3** to ask for

requiem /'rekwɪəm, 'rekwiem/ *n, often cap* (a musical setting of) the mass for the dead

require /rɪ'kwaɪə^r/ *v* **1a** to call for as suitable or appropriate **b** to call for as necessary or essential; have a compelling need for **2** to impose an obligation or command on; compel – **~ment** *n*

requisite /'rekwɨ̣zɨ̣t/ *adj* necessary, required

requisition /ˌrekwɨ̣'zɪʃən/ *n* **1** the act of requiring sthg to be supplied **2** a formal and authoritative (written) demand or application

requite /rɪ'kwaɪt/ *v* **1** to make suitable return to (for a benefit or service) **2** to compensate sufficiently for (an injury) – **requital** *n*

reredos /'rɪədɒs/ *n* a usu ornamental wood or stone screen or partition wall behind an altar

rerun /'riːrʌn/ *n* a presentation of a film or television programme after its first run

rescind /rɪ'sɪnd/ *v* **1** to annul **2** to repeal, revoke (e g a law, custom, etc)

rescue /'reskjuː/ *v* to free from confinement, danger, or evil – **rescue** *n* – **~r** *n*

¹research /rɪ'sɜːtʃ, 'riːsɜːtʃ/ *n* scientific or scholarly inquiry; *esp* study or experiment aimed at the discovery, interpretation, reinterpretation, or application of (new) facts, theories, or laws

²research *v* **1** to search or investigate thoroughly **2** to engage in research on or for – **~er** *n*

resemble /rɪ'zembəl/ *v* to be like or similar to – **-blance** *n*

resent /rɪ'zent/ *v* to harbour or express ill will or bitterness at – **~ful** *adj* – **~fully** *adv* – **~fulness** *n* – **~ment** *n*

reservation /ˌrezəˈveɪʃən/ *n* **1** an act of reserving sthg; *esp* (a promise, guarantee, or record of) an arrangement to have sthg (e g a hotel room) held for one's use **2** a tract of land set aside; *specif* one designated for the use of American Indians by treaty **3** a specific doubt or objection **4** a strip of land separating carriageways **5** *chiefly NAm* an area in which hunting is not permitted; *esp* one set aside as a secure breeding place

[1]**reserve** /rɪˈzɜːv/ *v* to hold in reserve; keep back

[2]**reserve** *n* **1** sthg retained for future use or need **2** sthg reserved or set aside for a particular use or reason: e g **a(1)** a military force withheld from action for later use – usu pl with sing. meaning (2) the military forces of a country not part of the regular services; *also* a reservist **b** *chiefly Br* a tract (e g of public land) set apart for the conservation of natural resources or (rare) flora and fauna **3** restraint, closeness, or caution in one's words and actions **4** money, gold, foreign exchange, etc kept in hand or set apart usu to meet liabilities – often pl with sing. meaning **5** a player or participant who has been selected to substitute for another if the need should arise

reserved /rɪˈzɜːvd/ *adj* **1** restrained in speech and behaviour **2** kept or set apart or aside for future or special use

reservoir /ˈrezəvwɑːʳ/ *n* **1a** an artificial lake where water is collected and kept in quantity for use **b** a part of an apparatus in which a liquid is held **2** an available but unused extra source or supply

reshuffle /riːʃʌfəl/ *v* to reorganize by the redistribution of (existing) elements – **reshuffle** *n*

reside /rɪˈzaɪd/ *v* **1a** to dwell permanently or continuously; occupy a place as one's legal domicile **b** to make one's home for a time **2** to be present as an element or quality

residence /ˈrezɪ̣dəns/ *n* **1** the act or fact of dwelling in a place **2** a (large or impressive) dwelling **3** the period of abode in a place

[1]**resident** /ˈrezɪ̣dənt/ *adj* **1** living in a place, esp for some length of time **2** *of an animal* not migratory

[2]**resident** *n* one who resides in a place

residential /ˌrezɪ̣ˈdenʃəl/ *adj* **1a** used as a residence or by residents **b** entailing residence **2** given over to private housing as distinct from industry or commerce

residual /rɪˈzɪdʒʊəl/ *adj* of or constituting a residue

residue /ˈrezɪ̣djuː/ *n* sthg that remains after a part is taken, separated, or designated; a remnant, remainder

resign /rɪˈzaɪn/ *v* **1** to give up one's office or position **2** to reconcile, consign; *esp* to give (oneself) over without resistance

resignation /ˌrezɪgˈneɪʃən/ *n* **1a** an act or instance of resigning sthg **b** a formal notification of resigning **2** the quality or state of being resigned

resigned /rɪˈzaɪnd/ *adj* marked by or expressing submission to sthg regarded as inevitable – **~ly** *adv*

resilient /rɪˈzɪlɪənt/ *adj* **1** capable of withstanding shock without permanent deformation or rupture **2** able to recover quickly from or adjust easily to misfortune, change, etc – **~ly** *adv* – **-ence, -ency** *n*

resin /ˈrezɪ̣n/ *n* (a synthetic plastic with some of the characteristics of) any of various solid or semisolid yellowish to brown inflammable natural plant secretions (e g amber) that are insoluble in water and are used esp in varnishes, sizes, inks, and plastics – **~ous** *adj*

resist /rɪˈzɪst/ *v* **1a** to withstand the force or effect of **b** to exert force in opposition **2** to refrain from

resistance /rɪˈzɪstəns/ *n* **1** an act or instance of resisting **2** the ability to resist **3** an opposing or retarding force **4** the opposition offered to the passage of a steady electric current through a substance, usu measured in ohms **5** *often cap* an underground organization of a conquered country engaging in sabotage – **-tant** *adj*

resistor /rɪˈzɪstəʳ/ *n* a component included in an electrical circuit to provide resistance

resolute /ˈrezəluːt/ *adj* **1** firmly

resolved; determined **2** bold, unwavering – **~ly** *adv* – **~ness** *n*

resolution /ˌrezəˈluːʃən/ *n* **1a** the act of making a firm decision **b** the act of finding out sthg (e g the answer to a problem); solving **c** the process or capability (e g of a microscope) of making individual parts or closely adjacent images distinguishable **2a** sthg that is resolved **b** firmness of resolve **3** a formal expression of opinion, will, or intent voted by a body or group

[1]**resolve** /rɪˈzɒlv/ *v* **1** to break up or separate into constituent parts **2** to cause or produce the resolution of **3a** to deal with successfully **b** to find an answer to **4** to reach a firm decision about

[2]**resolve** *n* **1** sthg that is resolved **2** fixity of purpose

resonance /rezənəns/ *n* **1** strong vibration caused by the stimulus of a relatively small vibration of (nearly) the same frequency as the natural frequency of the system **2** the enrichment of musical tone resulting from supplementary vibration **3** the possession by a molecule, radical, etc of two or more possible structures

resonant /ˈrezənənt/ *adj* **1** continuing to sound **2a** capable of inducing resonance **b** relating to or exhibiting resonance **3** intensified and enriched by resonance – **~ly** *adv*

resonate /ˈrezəneɪt/ *v* to produce or exhibit resonance (in)

[1]**resort** /rɪˈzɔːt/ *n* **1** sby who or sthg that is looked to for help **2** a frequently visited place (e g a village or town), esp providing accommodation and recreation for holidaymakers

[2]**resort** *v* **1** to go, esp frequently or in large numbers **2** to have recourse *to*

resound /rɪˈzaʊnd/ *v* **1** to become filled with sound **2** to produce a sonorous or echoing sound **3** to become renowned

resounding /rɪˈzaʊndɪŋ/ *adj* **1a** resonating **b** impressively sonorous **2** vigorously emphatic; unequivocal – **~ly** *adv*

resource /rɪˈzɔːs, -ˈsɔːs/ *n* **1a** a natural source of wealth or revenue **b** a source of information or expertise **2** a means of occupying one's spare time **3** the ability to deal with a difficult situation

resourceful /rɪˈzɔːsfəl, -ˈsɔːs-/ *adj* skilful in handling situations; capable of devising expedients – **~ly** *adv* – **~ness** *n*

[1]**respect** /rɪˈspekt/ *n* **1** a relation to or concern with sthg usu specified; reference – in *with/in respect to* **2a** high or special regard; esteem **b** *pl* expressions of respect or deference **3** an aspect; detail

[2]**respect** *v* **1a** to consider worthy of high regard **b** to refrain from interfering with **2** to have reference to

respectable /rɪˈspektəbəl/ *adj* **1** decent or conventional in character or conduct **2a** acceptable in size or quantity **b** fairly good; tolerable **3** presentable – **-bly** *adv* – **~ness** *n* – **-ability** *n*

respectful /rɪˈspektfəl/ *adj* marked by or showing respect or deference – **~ly** *adv* – **~ness** *n*

respecting /rɪˈspektɪŋ/ *prep* with regard to; concerning

respective /rɪˈspektɪv/ *adj* of or relating to each; particular, separate

respectively /rɪˈspektɪvli/ *adv* **1** in particular; separately **2** in the order given

respiration /ˌrespɨˈreɪʃən/ *n* the processes by which an organism supplies its cells with the oxygen needed for and removes the carbon dioxide formed in energy-producing reactions; breathing – **respire** *v* – **-tory** *adj*

respirator /ˈrespɨreɪtəʳ/ *n* **1** a device worn over the mouth or nose to prevent the breathing of poisonous gases, harmful dusts, etc **2** a device for maintaining artificial respiration

respite /ˈrespɪt, -paɪt/ *n* **1** a period of temporary delay **2** an interval of rest or relief

resplendent /rɪˈsplendənt/ *adj* characterized by splendour – **~ly** *adv* – **-dence, -dency** *n*

respond /rɪˈspɒnd/ *v* **1** to write or speak in reply; make an answer **2** to show a (favourable) reaction

[1]**respondent** /rɪˈspɒndənt/ *n* **1** a defendant, esp in an appeal or divorce case **2** a person who replies to a poll

[2]**respondent** *adj* making response

response /rɪ'spɒns/ *n* **1** an act of responding **2a** sthg (e g a verse) sung or said by the people or choir after or in reply to the officiant in a liturgical service **b** a change in the behaviour of an organism resulting from stimulation

responsibility /rɪ,spɒnsə'bɪlʒti/ *n* **1a** moral or legal obligation **b** reliability, trustworthiness **2** sthg or sby that one is responsible for

responsible /rɪ'spɒnsəbəl/ *adj* **1a** liable to be required to justify **b** being the reason or cause **2a** able to answer for one's own conduct **b** able to discriminate between right and wrong – **-ibly** *adv*

responsive /rɪ'spɒnsɪv/ *adj* **1** giving response; constituting a response **2** quick to respond or react appropriately or sympathetically – **~ly** *adv* – **~ness** *n*

[1]**rest** /rest/ *n* **1** repose, sleep **2a** freedom or a break from activity or labour **b** a state of motionlessness or inactivity **3** peace of mind or spirit **4** a silence in music of a specified duration **5** sthg (e g an armrest) used for support

[2]**rest** *v* **1a** to relax by lying down; *esp* to sleep **b** to lie dead **2** to cease from action or motion; desist from labour or exertion **3** to be free from anxiety or disturbance **4** to be set or lie fixed or supported **5** to be based or founded **6** to depend for action or accomplishment **7** to stop introducing evidence in a law case

[3]**rest** *n* a collection or quantity that remains over

restate /,riː'steɪt/ *v* to state again or in a different way (e g more emphatically) – **~ment** *n*

restaurant /'restərɔ̃, -rɒnt/ *n* a place where refreshments, esp meals, are sold usu to be eaten on the premises

restaurateur /,restərə'tɜː'/ *n* the manager or proprietor of a restaurant

restful /'restfəl/ *adj* **1** marked by, affording, or suggesting rest and repose **2** quiet, tranquil – **~ly** *adv* – **~ness** *n*

restitution /,restʒ'tjuːʃən/ *n* **1a** the returning of sthg (e g property) to its rightful owner **b** the making good of or giving a compensation for an injury **2** a legal action serving to cause restoration of a previous state

restive /'restɪv/ *adj* **1** stubbornly resisting control **2** restless, uneasy – **~ly** *adv* – **~ness** *n*

restless /'restləs/ *adj* **1** affording no rest **2** continuously agitated **3** characterized by or manifesting unrest, esp of mind; *also* changeful, discontented – **~ly** *adv* – **~ness** *n*

restoration /,restə'reɪʃən/ *n* **1** restoring or being restored: e g **a** a reinstatement **b** a handing back of sthg **2** a representation or reconstruction of the original form (e g of a fossil or building) **3** *cap* the reestablishment of the monarchy in England in 1660 under Charles II; *also* the reign of Charles II

restorative /rɪ'stɔːrətɪv/ *n or adj* (sthg capable of) restoring esp health or vigour

restore /rɪ'stɔː'/ *v* **1** to give back **2** to bring back into existence or use **3** to bring back to or put back into a former or original (unimpaired) state

restrain /rɪ'streɪn/ *v* **1** to prevent *from* doing sthg **2** to limit, repress, or keep under control

restrained /rɪ'streɪnd/ *adj* characterized by restraint; being without excess or extravagance

restraint /rɪ'streɪnt/ *n* **1a** restraining or being restrained **b** a means of restraining; a restraining force or influence **2** moderation of one's behaviour; self-restraint

restrict /rɪ'strɪkt/ *v* to regulate or limit as to use or distribution – **~ed** *adj* – **~ion** *n*

restrictive /rɪ'strɪktɪv/ *adj* restricting or tending to restrict – **~ly** *adv* – **~ness** *n*

restructure /,riː'strʌktʃə'/ *v* to change the make-up, organization, or pattern of

[1]**result** /rɪ'zʌlt/ *v* **1** to proceed or arise as a consequence, effect, or conclusion **2** to have a usu specified outcome or end

[2]**result** *n* **1** sthg that results as a (hoped for or required) consequence, outcome, or conclusion **2** sthg obtained by calculation or investigation

resultant /rɪ'zʌltənt/ *adj* derived or

resulting from sthg else, esp as the total effect of many causes

resume /rɪ'zjuːm/ *v* **1** to take or assume again **2** to return to or begin again after interruption – **resumption** *n*

résumé, resumé /'rezjʊmeɪ, 'reɪ-/ *n* a summing up of sthg (e g a speech or narrative)

resurgence /rɪ'sɜːdʒəns/ *n* a rising again into life, activity, or influence – **-gent** *adj*

resurrect /ˌrezə'rekt/ *v* **1** to bring back to life from the dead **2** to bring back into use or view

resurrection /ˌrezə'rekʃən/ *n* **1a** *cap* the rising of Christ from the dead **b** *often cap* the rising again to life of all the human dead before the last judgment **2** a resurgence, revival, or restoration

resuscitate /rɪ'sʌsɟteɪt/ *v* to revive from apparent death or from unconsciousness; *also* to revitalize – **-tation** *n*

[1]**retail** /'riːteɪl/ *v* to sell (goods) in carrying on a retail business

[2]**retail** *adj, adv, or n* (of, being, or concerned with) the sale of commodities or goods in small quantities to final consumers who will not resell them

retain /rɪ'teɪn/ *v* **1a** to keep in possession or use **b** to engage by paying a retainer **c** to keep in mind or memory **2** to hold secure or intact; contain in place – **retention** *n* – **retentive** *adj* – **retentively** *adv*

[1]**retainer** /rɪ'teɪnəʳ/ *n* a fee paid to a lawyer or professional adviser for services

[2]**retainer** *n* an old and trusted domestic servant

retaliate /rɪ'tælieɪt/ *v* to return like for like; *esp* to get revenge – **-ation** *n* – **-atory, -ative** *adj*

retard /rɪ'tɑːd/ *v* to slow down or delay, esp by preventing or hindering advance or accomplishment – **~ation** *n*

retarded /rɪ'tɑːdɟd/ *adj* slow in intellectual or emotional development or academic progress

retch /retʃ/ *v* to (make an effort to) vomit

rethink /ˌriː'θɪŋk/ *v* to think (about) again; *esp* to reconsider (a plan, attitude, etc) with a view to changing

reticent /'retɟsənt/ *adj* **1** inclined to be silent or reluctant to speak **2** restrained in expression, presentation, or appearance – **~ly** *adv* – **-cence** *n*

reticule /'retɪkjuːl/ *n* a decorative drawstring bag used as a handbag by women in the 18th and 19th c

retina /'retɟnə/ *n* the sensory membrane at the back of the eye that receives the image formed by the lens and is connected with the brain by the optic nerve

retinue /'retɪnjuː/ *n* a group of retainers or attendants accompanying an important personage (e g a head of state)

retire /rɪ'taɪəʳ/ *v* **1** to withdraw **a** from action or danger **b** for rest or seclusion; go to bed **2** to recede; fall back **3** to give up one's position or occupation; conclude one's working or professional career

retired /rɪ'taɪəd/ *adj* **1** remote from the world; secluded **2** having concluded one's career **3** received or due in retirement – **-rement** *n*

retiring /rɪ'taɪərɪŋ/ *adj* reserved, shy

[1]**retort** /rɪ'tɔːt/ *v* **1** to say or exclaim in reply or as a counter argument **2** to answer (e g an argument) by a counter argument

[2]**retort** *n* a terse, witty, or cutting reply; *esp* one that turns the first speaker's words against him/her

[3]**retort** *v or n* (to treat by heating in) a vessel in which substances are distilled or decomposed by heat

retouch /ˌriː'tʌtʃ/ *v* **1** to touch up a painting **2** to alter (e g a photographic negative) to produce a more acceptable appearance

retrace /rɪ'treɪs, riː-/ *v* to trace again or back

retract /rɪ'trækt/ *v* **1** to draw back or in **2** to withdraw; take back – **~ion** *n* – **~able** *adj*

retractile /rɪ'træktaɪl/ *adj* capable of being retracted

[1]**retread** /ˌriː'tred/ *v* to replace the tread of (a worn tyre)

[2]**retread** /'riːtred/ *n* (a tyre with) a new tread

[1]**retreat** /rɪ'triːt/ *n* **1** an act or process of withdrawing, esp from what is diffi-

cult, dangerous, or disagreeable; *specif* (a signal for) the forced withdrawal of troops from an enemy or position **2** a place of privacy or safety; a refuge **3** a period of usu group withdrawal for prayer, meditation, and study

[2]**retreat** *v* **1** to make a retreat; withdraw **2** to recede

retrench /rɪ'trentʃ/ *v* to make reductions, esp in expenses; economize – **~ment** *n*

retribution /ˌretrɪ'bjuːʃən/ *n* **1** requital for an insult or injury **2** (the dispensing or receiving of reward or) punishment – used esp with reference to divine judgment – **-tive** *adj*

retrieve /rɪ'triːv/ *v* **1a** to get back again; recover (and bring back) **b** to rescue, save **2** to remedy the ill effects of **3** to recover (e g information) from storage, esp in a computer memory **4** *esp of a dog* to retrieve game; *also* to bring back an object thrown by a person – **-vable** *adj* – **-val** *n*

retriever /rɪ'triːvəʳ/ *n* a medium-sized dog with water-resistant coat used esp for retrieving game

retroactive /ˌretrəʊ'æktɪv/ *adj* extending in scope or effect to a prior time – **~ly** *adv*

retrogress /ˌretrə'gres/ *v* to regress, or decline from a better to a worse state – **~ion** *n* – **~ive** *adj* – **~ively** *adv*

retrospect /'retrəspekt/ *n* a survey or consideration of past events

retrospection /ˌretrə'spekʃən/ *n* the act or process or an instance of surveying the past

[1]**retrospective** /ˌretrə'spektɪv/ *adj* **1** of, being, or given to retrospection **2** relating to or affecting things past; retroactive

[2]**retrospective** *n* an exhibition showing the evolution of an artist's work over a period of years

retsina /ret'sɪːnə/ *n* a white resin-flavoured Greek wine

[1]**return** /rɪ'tɜːn/ *v* **1a** to go back or come back again **b** to go back *to* in thought, conversation, or practice **2** to pass back to an earlier possessor **3** to reply, retort – fml **4a** to elect a candidate **b** to bring in (a verdict) **5** to restore to a former or proper place, position, or state **6** to bring in (e g a profit) **7** to give or send back, esp to an owner

[2]**return** *n* **1** the act or process of coming back to or from a place or condition **2a** a (financial) account or formal report **b** a report or declaration of the results of an election – usu pl with sing. meaning **3** the profit from labour, investment, or business – often pl with sing. meaning **4** the act of returning sthg, esp to a former place, condition, or owner **5** *Br* a ticket bought for a trip to a place and back again

[3]**return** *adj* **1** doubled back on itself **2** played, delivered, or given in return; taking place for the second time **3** used or followed on returning **4** permitting return **5** of or causing a return to a place or condition

returning officer *n, Br* an official who presides over an election count and declares the result

reunion /riː'juːnɪən/ *n* **1** reuniting or being reunited **2** a gathering of people (e g relatives or associates) after a period of separation

reunite /ˌriːjuː'naɪt/ *v* to come or bring together again

reuse /ˌriː'juːz/ *v* to use again, esp after reclaiming or reprocessing – **reusable** *adj*

[1]**rev** /rev/ *n* a revolution of a motor

[2]**rev** *v* to increase the number of revolutions per minute of (esp an engine) – often + *up*

revalue /riː'væljuː/ *v* **1** to change, specif to increase, the exchange rate of (a currency) **2** to reappraise – **-uation** *n*

revamp /ˌriː'væmp/ *v* **1** to renovate, reconstruct **2** to revise without fundamental alteration

[1]**reveal** /rɪ'viːl/ *v* **1** to make known (sthg secret or hidden) **2** to open up to view

[2]**reveal** *n* the side of an opening (e g for a window) between a frame and the outer surface of a wall; *also* a jamb

reveille /rɪ'væli/ *n* a call or signal to get up in the morning; *specif* a military bugle call

[1]**revel** /'revəl/ *v* **1** to take part in a revel **2** to take intense satisfaction *in*

[2]**revel** *n* a usu riotous party or celebration – often pl with sing. meaning

revelation /ˌrevəˈleɪʃən/ *n* **1** *cap* a prophetic book of the New Testament – often pl with sing. meaning but sing. in constr **2** a revealing or sthg revealed; *esp* a sudden and illuminating disclosure

revelry /ˈrevəlri/ *n* exuberant festivity or merrymaking

[1]**revenge** /rɪˈvendʒ/ *v* **1** to inflict injury in return for (an insult, slight, etc) **2** to avenge (e g oneself) usu by retaliating in kind or degree

[2]**revenge** *n* **1** (a desire for) retaliating in order to get even **2** an opportunity for getting satisfaction or requital – **~ful** *adj* – **~fully** *adv* – **~fulness** *n*

revenue /ˈrevɪ̣njuː/ *n* **1** the total yield of income; *esp* the income of a national treasury **2** a government department concerned with the collection of revenue

reverberate /rɪˈvɜːbəreɪt/ *v* **1a** to be reflected **b** to continue (as if) in a series of echoes **2** to produce a continuing strong effect – **-ration** *n* – **-rant** *adj*

revere /rɪˈvɪəʳ/ *v* to regard with deep and devoted or esp religious respect

[1]**reverence** /ˈrevərəns/ *n* **1** honour or respect felt or shown; *esp* profound respect accorded to sthg sacred **2** a gesture (e g a bow) denoting respect **3** being revered **4** – used as a title for a clergyman

[2]**reverence** *v* to regard or treat with reverence

reverend /ˈrevərənd/ *adj* **1** revered **2** *cap* being a member of the clergy – used as a title, usu preceded by *the*

reverie, revery /ˈrevəri/ *n* **1** a daydream **2** the condition of being lost in thought or dreamlike fantasy

revers /rɪˈvɪəʳ/ *n, pl* **revers** a wide turned-back or applied facing along each of the front edges of a garment

[1]**reverse** /rɪˈvɜːs/ *adj* **1a** (acting, operating, or arranged in a manner) opposite or contrary to a previous, normal, or usual condition **b** having the front turned away from an observer or opponent **2** effecting reverse movement

[2]**reverse** *v* **1a** to turn or change completely about in position or direction **b** to turn upside down **2a** to overthrow (a legal decision) **b** to change (e g a policy) to the contrary **3** to cause (e g a motor car) to go backwards or in the opposite direction – **reversal** *n* – **reversible** *adj* – **reversibility** *n*

[3]**reverse** *n* **1** the opposite of sthg **2** reversing or being reversed **3** a misfortune **4a** the side of a coin, medal, or currency note that does not bear the principal device **b** the back part of sthg; *esp* the back cover of a book **5** a gear that reverses sthg

reversion /rɪˌvɜːʃən/ *n* **1** the right of future possession or enjoyment **2** (an organism showing) a return to an ancestral type or reappearance of an ancestral character

revert /rɪˈvɜːt/ *v* **1** to return, esp to a lower, worse or more primitive condition or ancestral type **2** to go back in thought or conversation

[1]**review** /rɪˈvjuː/ *n* **1** a revision **2** a formal military or naval inspection **3** a general survey (e g of current affairs) **4** an act of inspecting or examining **5** judicial reexamination of a case **6a** a critical evaluation of a book, play, etc **b** (a part of) a magazine or newspaper devoted chiefly to reviews and essays

[2]**review** *v* **1a** to go over (again) or examine critically or thoughtfully **b** to give a review of (a book, play, etc) **2** to hold a review of (troops, ships, etc)

reviewer /rɪˈvjuːəʳ/ *n* a writer of critical reviews

revile /rɪˈvaɪl/ *v* to subject to harsh verbal abuse – **reviler** *n*

revise /rɪˈvaɪz/ *v* **1** to look over again in order to correct or improve **2** to make an amended, improved, or up-to-date version of **3** *Br* to refresh knowledge of (e g a subject), esp before an exam – **reviser** *n* – **revision** *n*

revisionism /rɪˈvɪʒənɪzəm/ *n* **1** advocacy of revision (e g of a doctrine) **2** a movement in Marxist socialism favouring an evolutionary rather than a revolutionary transition to socialism – chiefly derog – **-ist** *adj, n*

revital·ize, -ise /riː'vaɪtəlaɪz/ *v* to impart new life or vigour to

revival /rɪ'vaɪvəl/ *n* **1** renewed attention to or interest in sthg **2** a new presentation or production (e g of a play) **3** an often emotional evangelistic meeting or series of meetings **4** restoration of an earlier fashion, style, or practice

revive /rɪ'vaɪv/ *v* to return to consciousness, life, health, (vigorous) activity, or current use

revoke /rɪ'vəʊk/ *v* to annul, rescind, or withdraw

[1]**revolt** /rɪ'vəʊlt/ *v* **1** to renounce allegiance or subjection to a government; rebel **2** to experience or recoil from disgust or abhorrence

[2]**revolt** *n* **1** a (determined armed) rebellion **2** a movement or expression of vigorous opposition

revolting /rɪ'vəʊltɪŋ/ *adj* extremely offensive; nauseating – **~ly** *adv*

revolution /,revə'luːʃən/ *n* **1a** the action of or time taken by a celestial body in going round in an orbit **b** the motion of a figure or object about a centre or axis **2a** a sudden or far-reaching change **b** the overthrow of one government and the substitution of another by the governed

[1]**revolutionary** /,revə'luːʃənəri/ *adj* **1a** of or being a revolution **b** promoting or engaging in revolution; *also* extremist **2** completely new and different

[2]**revolutionary** *n* sby who advocates or is engaged in a revolution

revolution·ize, -ise /,revə'luːʃənaɪz/ *v* to cause a revolution in; change utterly or fundamentally

revolve /rɪ'vɒlv/ *v* **1** to move in a curved path round (and round) a centre or axis; turn round (as if) on an axis **2** to be centred on a specified theme or main point

revolver /rɪ'vɒlvəʳ/ *n* a handgun with a revolving cylinder of several chambers each holding 1 cartridge and allowing several shots to be fired without reloading

revue /rɪ'vjuː/ *n* a theatrical production consisting typically of brief loosely connected often satirical sketches, songs, and dances

revulsion /rɪ'vʌlʃən/ *n* a feeling of utter distaste or repugnance

[1]**reward** /rɪ'wɔːd/ *v* **1** to give a reward to or for **2** to recompense

[2]**reward** *n* sthg that is given in return for good or evil done or received; *esp* sthg offered or given for some service, effort, or achievement

rewarding /rɪ'wɔːdɪŋ/ *adj* yielding a reward; personally satisfying

rewire /,riː'waɪəʳ/ *v* to provide (e g a house) with new electric wiring

reword /,riː'wɜːd/ *v* to alter the wording of; *also* to restate in different words

rewrite /,riː'raɪt/ *v* to revise (sthg previously written)

rhapsod·ize, -ise /'ræpsədaɪz/ *v* to over-enthuse

rhapsody /'ræpsədi/ *n* **1** a highly rapturous or emotional utterance or literary composition **2** a musical composition of irregular form suggesting improvisation

rhea /rɪə/ *n* any of several large tall flightless S American birds like but smaller than the ostrich

rheostat /'rɪəstæt/ *n* an adjustable resistor for regulating an electric current

rhesus factor /'riːsəs/ *n* any of several substances in red blood cells that can induce intense allergic reactions

rhetoric /'retərɪk/ *n* **1** the art of speaking or writing effectively; *specif* (the study of) the principles and rules of composition **2** insincere or exaggerated language (that is calculated to produce an effect) – **~al** *adj* – **~ally** *adv* – **~ian** *n*

rhetorical question *n* a question asked merely for effect with no answer expected

rheumatic /ruː'mætɪk/ *adj* of, being, characteristic of, or suffering from rheumatism

rheumatic fever *n* rheumatism – not used technically

rheumatism /'ruːmətɪzəm/ *n* any of various conditions characterized by inflammation and pain in muscles, joints, or fibrous tissue

rheumatoid /'ruːmətɔɪd/ *adj* characteristic of or affected with rheumatism

rhinestone /'raɪnstəʊn/ *n* a lustrous

imitation gem made of glass, paste, quartz, etc

rhinoceros /raɪ'nɒsərəs/ *n* any of various large plant-eating very thick-skinned hoofed African or Asian mammals with 1 or 2 horns on the snout

rhizome /'raɪzəʊm/ *n* an elongated (thickened and horizontal) underground plant stem distinguished from a true root in having buds and usu scalelike leaves

rhododendron /,rəʊdə'dendrən/ *n* any of a genus of showy-flowered shrubs and trees of the heath family; *esp* one with leathery evergreen leaves

rhomboid /'rɒmbɔɪd/ *n* a parallelogram that is neither a rhombus nor a square – **rhomboid, ~al** *adj*

rhombus /'rɒmbəs/ *n* a parallelogram with equal sides but unequal angles; a diamond-shaped figure

rhubarb /'ruːbɑːb/ *n* **1** (the thick succulent stems, edible when cooked, of) any of several plants of the dock family **2** *chiefly Br* – used by actors to suggest the sound of (many) people talking in the background

[1]**rhyme** /raɪm/ *n* **1a** correspondence in the sound of (the last syllable of) words, esp those at the end of lines of verse **b** a word that provides a rhyme for another **2** (a) rhyming verse

[2]**rhyme** *v* **1** to compose rhyming verse **2a** *of a word or (line of) verse* to end in syllables that rhyme

rhyming slang *n* slang in which the word actually meant is replaced by a rhyming phrase of which only the first element is usu pronounced (e g 'head' becomes 'loaf of bread' and then 'loaf')

rhythm /'rɪðəm/ *n* **1** the pattern of recurrent alternation of strong and weak elements in the flow of sound and silence in speech **2a** (the aspect of music concerning) the regular recurrence of a pattern of stress and length of notes **b** a characteristic rhythmic pattern **c rhythm, rhythm section** *sing or pl in constr* the group of instruments in a band (e g the drums, piano, and bass) supplying the rhythm **3** movement or fluctuation marked by a regular recurrence of elements (e g pauses or emphases) **4** a regularly recurrent change in a biological process or state (e g with night and day) **5 rhythm, rhythm method** birth control by abstinence from sexual intercourse during the period when ovulation is most likely to occur – **~ic, ~ical** *adj* – **~ically** *adv*

[1]**rib** /rɪb/ *n* **1** any of the paired curved rods of bone or cartilage that stiffen the body walls of most vertebrates and protect the heart, lungs, etc **2a** a transverse member of the frame of a ship that runs from keel to deck **b** any of the stiff strips supporting an umbrella's fabric **c** an arched support or ornamental band in Romanesque and Gothic vaulting **3a** a vein of a leaf or insect's wing **b** any of the ridges in a knitted or woven fabric; *also* ribbing – **~bed** *adj*

[2]**rib** *v* to form a pattern of vertical ridges in by alternating knit stitches and purl stitches

[3]**rib** *v* to tease – infml

ribald /'rɪbəld/ *adj* **1** crude, offensive **2** characterized by coarse or indecent humour – **~ry** *n*

ribbing /'rɪbɪŋ/ *n* an arrangement of ribs; *esp* a knitted pattern of ribs

ribbon /'rɪbən/ *n* **1a** a (length of a) narrow band of decorative fabric used for ornamentation (e g of hair), fastening, tying parcels, etc **b** a piece of usu multicoloured ribbon worn as a military decoration or in place of a medal **2** *pl* tatters, shreds

rib cage *n* the enclosing wall of the chest consisting chiefly of the ribs and their connections

rice /raɪs/ *n* (the seed, important as a food, of) a cereal grass widely cultivated in warm climates

rice paper *n* a very thin edible paper made from the pith of an oriental tree

rich /rɪtʃ/ *adj* **1** having abundant possessions, esp material and financial wealth **2** well supplied or endowed – often + *in* **3** sumptuous **4a** vivid and deep in colour **b** full and mellow in tone and quality **5** highly productive or remunerative; giving a high yield **6a** (of food that is) highly seasoned, fatty, oily, or sweet **b** *esp of mixtures of fuel with air* containing more petrol than normal 7 highly amusing; *also* laughable – infml – ~**ly** *adv* – ~**ness** *n*

riches /ˈrɪtʃɪ̣z/ *n pl* (great) wealth

[1]**rick** /rɪk/ *n* a stack (e g of hay) in the open air

[2]**rick** *v* to wrench or sprain (e g one's neck)

rickets /ˈrɪkɪ̣ts/ *n pl but sing in constr* soft and deformed bones in children normally due to a lack of sunlight or vitamin D

rickety /ˈrɪkɪ̣ti/ *adj* **1** suffering from rickets **2** shaky, unsound

rickshaw /ˈrɪkʃɔː/ *n* a small covered 2-wheeled vehicle pulled by usu 1 person

[1]**ricochet** /ˈrɪkəʃeɪ/ *n* the glancing rebound of a projectile (e g a bullet) off a hard or flat surface

[2]**ricochet** *v* to proceed (as if) with glancing rebounds

rid /rɪd/ *v* to relieve, disencumber

riddance /ˈrɪdəns/ *n* deliverance, relief – often in *good riddance*

[1]**riddle** /ˈrɪdl/ *n* **1** a short and esp humorous verbal puzzle **2** sthg or sby mystifying or difficult to understand

[2]**riddle** *v* to speak in or propound riddles

[3]**riddle** *n* a coarse sieve (e g for sifting grain or gravel)

[4]**riddle** *v* **1** to separate (e g grain from chaff) with a riddle; sift **2** to cover *with* holes **3** to spread through, esp as an affliction

[1]**ride** /raɪd/ *v* **rode, ridden 1a** to sit and travel mounted on and usu controlling an animal **b** to travel on or in a vehicle **2a** to lie moored or anchored **b** to appear to float **3** to be contingent; depend *on* **4** to work *up* or *down* the body **5** to survive without great damage or loss; last *out* **6** to obsess, oppress **7** to give with (a punch) to soften the impact

[2]**ride** *n* **1** a trip on horseback or by vehicle **2** a usu straight road or path in a wood, forest, etc used for riding, access, or as a firebreak **3** *chiefly NAm* a trip on which gangsters take a victim to murder him/her – euph

rider /ˈraɪdəʳ/ *n* **1** sby who rides; *specif* sby who rides a horse **2** sthg added by way of qualification or amendment **3** sthg used to overlie another or to move along on another piece

ridge /rɪdʒ/ *n* **1a** a range of hills or mountains **b** an elongated elevation of land **2** the line along which 2 upward-sloping surfaces meet; *specif* the top of a roof **3** an elongated part that is raised above a surrounding surface (e g the raised part between furrows on ploughed ground)

[1]**ridicule** /ˈrɪdɪ̣kjuːl/ *n* exposure to laughter

[2]**ridicule** *v* to mock; make fun of

ridiculous /rɪˈdɪkjʊləs/ *adj* arousing or deserving ridicule – ~**ly** *adv* – ~**ness** *n*

riding /ˈraɪdɪŋ/ *n* any of the 3 former administrative jurisdictions of Yorkshire

rife /raɪf/ *adj* **1** prevalent, esp to a rapidly increasing degree **2** abundant, common **3** abundantly supplied – usu + *with*

riff /rɪf/ *n* (a piece based on) a constantly repeated phrase in jazz or rock music, typically played as a background to a solo improvisation

riffraff /ˈrɪfræf/ *n sing or pl in constr* **1** disreputable people **2** rabble

[1]**rifle** /ˈraɪfəl/ *v* to search through, esp in order to steal and carry away sthg

[2]**rifle** *v* to cut spiral grooves into the bore of (a rifle, cannon, etc)

[3]**rifle** *n* **1** a shoulder weapon with a rifled bore **2** *pl* a body of soldiers armed with rifles

[1]**rift** /rɪft/ *n* **1** a fissure or crack, esp in the earth **2** an estrangement

[2]**rift** *v* to tear apart; split

rift valley *n* a valley formed by the subsidence of the earth's crust between at least 2 faults

[1]**rig** /rɪg/ *v* **1** to fit out (e g a ship) with rigging **2** to clothe, dress up – usu + *out* **3** to supply with special gear **4** to put together, esp for temporary use – usu + *up*

[2]**rig** *n* **1** the distinctive shape, number, and arrangement of sails and masts of a ship **2** an outfit of clothing worn for an often specified occasion or activity **3** tackle, equipment, or machinery fitted for a specified purpose

[3]**rig** *v* to manipulate, influence, or control for dishonest purposes

rigging /ˈrɪgɪŋ/ *n* lines and chains used aboard a ship, esp for controlling sails and supporting masts and spars

[1]**right** /raɪt/ *adj* **1** in accordance with what is morally good, just, or proper **2** conforming to facts or truth **3** suitable, appropriate **4** straight **5a** of, situated on, or being the side of the body that is away from the heart **b** located on the right hand when facing in the same direction as an observer **c** being the side of a fabric that should show or be seen when made up **6** having its axis perpendicular to the base **7** acting or judging in accordance with truth or fact; not mistaken **8** in a correct, proper, or healthy state **9** *often cap* of the Right, esp in politics **10** *chiefly Br* real, utter – infml

[2]**right** *n* **1** qualities (e g adherence to duty) that together constitute the ideal of moral conduct or merit moral approval **2a** a power, privilege, interest, etc to which one has a just claim **b** a property interest in sthg – often pl with sing. meaning **3** sthg one may legitimately claim as due **4** the cause of truth or justice **5** the quality or state of being factually or morally correct **6a** *sing or pl in constr, cap* those professing conservative political views **b** *often cap* a conservative position

[3]**right** *adv* **1** in a right, proper, or correct manner **2** in the exact location or position **3** in a direct line or course; straight **4** all the way; completely **5a** without delay; straight **b** immediately **6** to the full (e g entertained *right* royally) – often in British titles **7** on or to the right – **~ness** *n*

[4]**right** *v* **1** to avenge **2a** to adjust or restore to the proper state or condition; correct **b** to bring or restore (e g a boat) to an upright position

right angle *n* the angle bounded by 2 lines perpendicular to each other; an angle of 90° – **right-angled** *adj*

right away *adv* without delay or hesitation

righteous /ˈraɪtʃəs/ *adj* **1** acting in accord with divine or moral law; free from guilt or sin **2a** morally right or justified **b** arising from an outraged sense of justice – **~ly** *adv* – **~ness** *n*

rightful /ˈraɪtfəl/ *adj* **1** just, equitable **2a** having a just claim **b** held by right – **~ly** *adv* – **~ness** *n*

right-hand *adj* **1** situated on the right **2** chiefly or constantly relied on

right hand *n* **1** a reliable or indispensable person **2a** the right side **b** a place of honour

right-handed *adj* **1** using the right hand habitually or more easily than the left **2** relating to, designed for, or done with the right hand **3** clockwise – used of a twist, rotary motion, or spiral curve as viewed from a given direction with respect to the axis of rotation – **~ly** *adv* – **~ness** *n*

rightly /ˈraɪtli/ *adv* **1** in accordance with right conduct; fairly **2** in the right manner; properly **3** according to truth or fact **4** with certainty

right-minded *adj* thinking and acting by just or honest principles – **~ness** *n*

right of way *n* **1** a legal right of passage over another person's property **2** the strip of land over which a public road is built **3** a precedence in passing accorded to one vehicle over another by custom, decision, or statute

rightward /ˈraɪtwəd/ *adj* being towards or on the right – **~s** *adv*

right wing *n often cap R&W* the more conservative division of a group or party – **~er** *n*

rigid /ˈrɪdʒɨ̇d/ *adj* **1** deficient in or devoid of flexibility **2a** inflexibly set in opinions or habits **b** strictly maintained **3** precise and accurate in procedure – **~ly** *adv* – **~ity** *n*

rigmarole /ˈrɪgmərəʊl/ *n* **1** confused or nonsensical talk **2** an absurd and complex procedure

rigor mortis /ˌrɪgə ˈmɔːtɨ̇s, ˌraɪgɔː-/ *n* the temporary rigidity of muscles that occurs after death

rigour /ˈrɪgəʳ/ *n* **1a(1)** harsh inflexibility **(2)** severity of life; austerity **b** an act or instance of strictness or severity – often pl **2** a condition that makes life difficult, challenging, or painful; *esp* extremity of cold – often pl **3** strict precision – **rigorous** *adj*

rigout /ˈrɪgaʊt/ *n* a complete outfit of clothing – infml

rile /raɪl/ *v* to make angry or resentful

rim /rɪm/ *n* **1** an outer usu curved edge or border **2** the outer ring of a wheel not including the tyre – **~less** *adj*

[1]**rime** /raɪm/ *n* **1** frost **2** an accumulation of granular ice tufts on the windward sides of exposed objects at low temperatures

[2]**rime** *v* to cover (as if) with rime

rind /raɪnd/ *n* **1** the bark of a tree **2** a usu hard or tough outer layer of fruit, cheese, bacon, etc

[1]**ring** /rɪŋ/ *n* **1** a circular band for holding, connecting, hanging, moving, fastening, etc or for identification **2** a circlet usu of precious metal, worn on the finger **3a** a circular line, figure, or object **b** an encircling arrangement **4a** an often circular space, esp for exhibitions or competitions; *esp* such a space at a circus **b** a square enclosure in which boxers or wrestlers contest **5** any of the concentric bands that revolve round some planets (e g Saturn or Uranus) **6** an electric element or gas burner in the shape of a circle, set into the top of a cooker, stove, etc, which provides a source of heat for cooking

[2]**ring** *v* **1** to place or form a ring round; encircle **2** to attach a ring to

[3]**ring** *v* **rang; rung** **1** to sound resonantly **2a** to sound a bell as a summons **b** to announce (as if) by ringing – often + *in* or *out* **3a** to be filled with talk or report **b** to sound repeatedly **4** *chiefly Br* to telephone – often + *up*

[4]**ring** *n* **1** a set of bells **2** a clear resonant sound made by vibrating metal **3** resonant tone **4** a loud sound continued, repeated, or reverberated **5** a sound or character suggestive of a particular quality or feeling **6** a telephone call – usu in *give somebody a ring*

ringleader /ˈrɪŋ,liːdəʳ/ *n* a leader of a group that engages in objectionable activities

ringlet /ˈrɪŋlɪ̣t/ *n* a long lock of hair curled in a spiral

ringmaster /ˈrɪŋ,mɑːstəʳ/ *n* one in charge of performances in a ring (e g of a circus)

ring road *n, Br* a road round a town or town centre designed to relieve traffic congestion

ring up *v* **1** to record by means of a cash register **2** to record, achieve **3** to telephone

ringworm /ˈrɪŋwɜːm/ *n* any of several fungous diseases of the skin or hair in which ring-shaped blistered patches form on the skin

rink /rɪŋk/ *n* **1a** (a building containing) a surface of ice for ice-skating **b** an enclosure for roller-skating **2** part of a bowling green being used for a match

[1]**rinse** /rɪns/ *v* **1** to cleanse (e g from soap) with liquid (e g clean water) – often + *out* **2** to remove (dirt or impurities) by washing lightly

[2]**rinse** *n* **1** (a) rinsing **2a** liquid used for rinsing **b** a solution that temporarily tints the hair

riot /ˈraɪət/ *n* **1** unrestrained revelry **2** (a) violent public disorder **3** a profuse and random display **4** sby or sthg wildly funny – **riot** *v* – **~er** *n*

riotous /ˈraɪətəs/ *adj* **1** participating in a riot **2a** wild and disorderly **b** exciting, exuberant – **~ly** *adv* – **~ness** *n*

[1]**rip** /rɪp/ *v* **1a** to tear or split apart, esp in a violent manner **b** to saw or split (wood) along the grain **2** to rush along **3** to remove by force – + *out* or *off*

[2]**rip** *n* a rough or violent tear

[3]**rip** *n* a body of rough water formed **a** by the meeting of opposing currents, winds, etc **b** by passing over ridges

[4]**rip** *n* a mischievous usu young person

rip cord *n* a cord or wire for releasing a parachute from its pack

ripe /raɪp/ *adj* **1** fully grown and developed; mature **2** mature in knowledge, understanding, or judgment **3** of advanced years **4** fully prepared; ready *for* **5** brought by aging to full flavour or the best state; mellow – **~ly** *adv* – **~n** *v* – **~ness** *n*

rip-off *n* **1** an act or instance of stealing **2** an instance of financial exploitation; *esp* the charging of an exorbitant price *USE* infml

rip off *v* **1** to rob; *also* to steal **2** to defraud *USE* infml

riposte /rɪˈpɒst, rɪˈpəʊst/ *n* **1** a piece

of retaliatory banter **2** a usu rapid retaliatory manoeuvre or measure

[1]**ripple** /'rɪpəl/ *v* **1** to cover with small waves **2a** to proceed with an undulating motion (so as to cause ripples) **b** to impart a wavy motion or appearance to **3** to spread irregularly outwards, esp from a central point

[2]**ripple** *n* **1** a small wave or succession of small waves **2** a sound like that of rippling water

rip-roaring *adj* noisily excited or exciting; exuberant

ripsaw /'rɪpsɔː/ *n* a coarse-toothed saw having teeth only slightly bent to alternate sides that is designed to cut wood in the direction of the grain

riptide /'rɪptaɪd/ *n* a strong surface current flowing outwards from a shore

[1]**rise** /raɪz/ *v* **rose; risen 1a** to assume an upright position, esp from lying, kneeling, or sitting **b** to get up from sleep or from one's bed **2** to take up arms **3** to respond warmly or readily; applaud – usu + *to* **4** to respond to nasty words or behaviour, esp by annoyance or anger **5** to appear above the horizon **6a** to move upwards; ascend **b** to increase in height or volume **7** to extend above other objects or people **8** to increase in fervour or intensity **9** to attain a higher office or rank **10** to increase in amount or number **11** to come into being; originate **12** to show oneself equal to a challenge

[2]**rise** *n* **1a** a movement upwards **b** emergence (e g of the sun) above the horizon **c** the upward movement of a fish to seize food or bait **2** origin **3** the vertical height of sthg, esp a step **4a** an increase, esp in amount, number, or intensity **b** an increase in pay **5a** an upward slope or gradient **b** a spot higher than surrounding ground

riser /'raɪzəʳ/ *n* the upright part between 2 consecutive stair treads

risible /'rɪzəbəl/ *adj* arousing or provoking laughter

[1]**rising** /'raɪzɪŋ/ *n* an insurrection, uprising

[2]**rising** *adv* approaching a specified age

[1]**risk** /rɪsk/ *n* **1** possibility of loss, injury, or damage **2** a dangerous element or factor; hazard **3** the chance of loss or the dangers to that which is insured in an insurance contract – **~y** *adj* – **~iness** *n*

[2]**risk** *v* **1** to expose to hazard or danger **2** to incur the risk or danger of

risotto /rɪ'zɒtəʊ/ *n* an Italian dish of rice cooked in meat stock

risqué /'rɪskeɪ/ *adj* verging on impropriety or indecency

rissole /'rɪsəʊl/ *n* a small fried cake or ball of cooked minced food, esp meat

rite /raɪt/ *n* **1** (a prescribed form of words or actions for) a ceremonial act or action **2** the characteristic liturgy of a church or group of churches

[1]**ritual** /'ritʃʊəl/ *adj* according to religious law or social custom – **~ly** *adv*

[2]**ritual** *n* **1** the form or order of words prescribed for a religious ceremony **2** (a) ritual observance; *broadly* any formal and customary act or series of acts

[1]**rival** /'raɪvəl/ *n* **1a** any of 2 or more competing for a single goal **b** sby who tries to compete with and be superior to another **2** sby who or sthg that equals another in desirable qualities – **~ry** *n*

[2]**rival** *adj* having comparable pretensions or claims

[3]**rival** *v* **1** to be in competition with; contend with **2** to strive to equal or excel **3** to possess qualities that approach or equal (those of another)

river /'rɪvəʳ/ *n* **1** a natural stream of water of considerable volume **2** a copious or overwhelming quality – often pl

[1]**rivet** /'rɪvɪ̣t/ *n* a headed metal pin used to unite 2 or more pieces by passing the shank through a hole in each piece and then beating or pressing down the plain end so as to make a second head – **~er** *n*

[2]**rivet** *v* **1** to hammer or flatten the end or point of (e g a metal pin, rod, or bolt) so as to form a head **2** to fix firmly **3** to attract and hold (e g the attention) completely

RNA *n* any of various acids in the nuclei of cells similar to DNA that are associated with the control of cellular chemical activities

[1]**roach** /rəʊtʃ/ *n* a silver-white European freshwater fish of the carp family

[2]**roach** *n, NAm* **1** a cockroach **2** the butt of a marijuana cigarette – slang

road /rəʊd/ *n* **1** a relatively sheltered stretch of water near the shore where ships may ride at anchor – often pl with sing. meaning **2** an open usu paved way for the passage of vehicles, people, and animals **3** a route or path – **~less** *adj*

roadbed /ˈrəʊdbed/ *n* **1** the bed on which the sleepers, rails, and ballast of a railway rest **2** the earth foundation of a road prepared for surfacing

roadblock /ˈrəʊdblɒk/ *n* **1** a road barricade set up by an army, the police, etc **2** an obstruction in a road

road hog *n* a driver of a motor vehicle who obstructs or intimidates others

roadhouse /ˈrəʊdhaʊs/ *n* an inn situated usu on a main road in a country area

roadworthy /ˈrəʊd,wɜːði/ *adj, of a vehicle* in a fit condition to be used on the roads; in proper working order – **-thiness** *n*

roam /rəʊm/ *v* **1** to go aimlessly from place to place; wander **2** to travel unhindered through a wide area – **~er** *n*

roan /rəʊn/ *adj, esp of horses and cattle* having a coat of a usu reddish brown base colour that is muted and lightened by some white hairs – **roan** *n*

[1]**roar** /rɔːʳ/ *v* **1** to give a roar **2** to laugh loudly and deeply **3** to be boisterous or disorderly – usu + *about*

[2]**roar** *n* **1** the deep prolonged cry characteristic of a wild animal **2** a loud cry, call, etc (e g of pain, anger, or laughter) **3** a loud continuous confused sound

[1]**roaring** *adj* **1** making or characterized by a sound resembling a roar **2** marked by energetic or successful activity

[2]**roaring** *adv* extremely, thoroughly – infml

roaring forties *n pl* either of 2 areas of stormy westerly winds between latitudes 40° and 50° N and S

[1]**roast** /rəʊst/ *v* **1a** to cook by exposing to dry heat (e g in an oven) **b** to dry and brown slightly by exposure to heat **2** to heat to excess **3** *chiefly NAm* to criticize severely

[2]**roast** *n* a piece of meat roasted or suitable for roasting

[3]**roast** *adj* roasted

rob /rɒb/ *v* **1** to steal sthg from (a person or place), esp by violence or threat **2** to deprive of sthg due, expected, or desired – **~ber** *n*

robbery /ˈrɒbəri/ *n* theft accompanied by violence or threat

robe /rəʊb/ *n* **1** a long flowing outer garment; *esp* one used for ceremonial occasions or as a symbol of office or profession **2** *NAm* a woman's dressing gown – **robe** *v*

robin /ˈrɒbɪn/, **robin redbreast** *n* a small brownish European thrush resembling a warbler and having an orange red throat and breast; *also* a larger but similarly coloured N American bird

robot /ˈrəʊbɒt/ *n* **1a** a (fictional) humanoid machine that walks and talks **b** sby efficient or clever who lacks human warmth or sensitivity **2** an automatic apparatus or device that performs functions ordinarily performed by human beings **3** sthg guided by automatic controls

robust /rəˈbʌst, ˈrəʊbʌst/ *adj* **1a** having or exhibiting vigorous health or stamina **b** firm in purpose or outlook **c** strongly formed or constructed **2** earthy, rude – **~ly** *adv* – **~ness** *n*

[1]**rock** /rɒk/ *v* **1** to become moved rapidly or violently backwards and forwards (e g under impact) **2a** to move rhythmically back and forth **b(1)** to daze or stun **(2)** to disturb, upset

[2]**rock, rock and roll, rock 'n' roll** *n* music usu played on electronically amplified instruments, with a persistent heavily accented beat and often country, folk, and blues elements

[3]**rock** *n* **1** a large mass of stone forming a cliff, promontory, or peak **2** a large mass of stony material **3** a firm or solid foundation or support **4** a coloured and flavoured sweet produced in the form of a usu cylindrical stick

rock-bottom *adj* being the lowest possible

rock bottom *n* the lowest or most fundamental part or level

rock crystal *n* transparent colourless quartz

rocker /ˈrɒkəʳ/ *n* **1a** either of the 2 curved pieces of wood or metal on which an object (e g a cradle) rocks **b** sthg mounted on rockers **2** a device that works with a rocking motion **3** a member of a group of aggressive leather-jacketed young British motorcyclists in the 1960s

rockery /ˈrɒkəri/ *n* a bank of rocks and earth where rock plants are grown

¹rocket /ˈrɒkɪ̯t/ *n* any of numerous plants of the mustard family

²rocket *n* **1a** a firework consisting of a long case filled with a combustible material fastened to a guiding stick and projected through the air by the rearward discharge of gases released in combustion **b** such a device used as an incendiary weapon or as a propelling unit (e g for a lifesaving line or whaling harpoon) **2** a jet engine that carries with it everything necessary for its operation and is thus independent of the oxygen in the air **3** a rocket-propelled bomb, missile, or projectile **4** *chiefly Br* a sharp reprimand – infml

³rocket *v* **1** to rise or increase rapidly or spectacularly **2** to travel with the speed of a rocket

rocketry /ˈrɒkɪ̯tri/ *n* the study of, experimentation with, or use of rockets

rocking horse *n* a toy horse mounted on rockers

rock 'n' roll /ˌrɒk ən ˈrəʊl/ *n* rock music

rock salt *n* common salt occurring as a solid mineral

¹rocky /ˈrɒki/ *adj* **1** full of or consisting of rocks **2** filled with obstacles; difficult

²rocky *adj* unsteady, tottering

rococo /rəˈkəʊkəʊ/ *adj* **1a** (typical) of a style of architecture and decoration in 18th-c Europe characterized by elaborate curved forms and shell motifs **b** of an 18th-c musical style marked by light gay ornamentation **2** excessively ornate or florid

²rococo *n* rococo work or style

rod /rɒd/ *n* **1a(1)** a straight slender stick **(2)** (a stick or bundle of twigs used for) punishment **(3)** a pole with a line for fishing **b** a slender bar (e g of wood or metal) **2** a unit of length equal to 5½yd (about 5m) **3** any of the relatively long rod-shaped light receptors in the retina that are sensitive to faint light

rode /rəʊd/ *past of* **ride**

rodent /ˈrəʊdənt/ *n* any of an order of relatively small gnawing mammals including the mice, rats, and squirrels

rodeo /rəʊˈdeɪ-əʊ, ˈrəʊdi-əʊ/ *n* **1** a roundup **2** a public performance featuring the riding skills of cowboys

roe /rəʊ/ *n* **1** the eggs of a female fish, esp when still enclosed in a membrane, or the corresponding part of a male fish **2** the eggs or ovaries of an invertebrate (e g a lobster)

roe deer *n* a small Eurasian deer with erect cylindrical antlers that is noted for its nimbleness and grace

¹rogue /rəʊg/ *n* **1** a wilfully dishonest or corrupt person **2** a mischievous person; a scamp

²rogue *adj, of an animal* (roaming alone and) vicious and destructive

roguery /ˈrəʊgəri/ *n* an act characteristic of a rogue

roister /ˈrɔɪstəʳ/ *v* to engage in noisy revelry

role, rôle /rəʊl/ *n* **1a** a socially expected behaviour pattern, usu determined by an individual's status in a particular society **b** a part played by an actor or singer **2** a function

¹roll /rəʊl/ *n* **1a** a written document that may be rolled up; *specif* one bearing an official or formal record **b** a list of names or related items; a catalogue **c** an official list of people (e g members of a school or of a legislative body) **2a** a quantity (e g of fabric or paper) rolled up to form a single package **b** any of various food preparations rolled up for cooking or serving; *esp* a small piece of baked yeast dough

²roll *v* **1a** to propel forwards by causing to turn over and over on a surface **b** to cause to move in a circular manner;

turn over and over **c** to form into a mass by revolving and compressing **d** to carry forwards with an easy continuous motion **2** to move onwards in a regular cycle or succession **3** to flow with an undulating motion **4a** to become carried on a stream **b** to move on wheels **5a** to take the form of a cylinder or ball – often + *up* **b** to wrap round on itself; shape into a ball or roll – often + *up* **6** to press, spread, or level with a roller; make thin, even, or compact **7** to luxuriate *in* an abundant supply; wallow **8a** to make a deep reverberating sound **b** to utter with a trill **9a** to rock from side to side **b** to walk with a swinging gait **c** to move so as to reduce the impact of a blow – + *with* **10a** to begin to move or operate **b** to move forwards; develop and maintain impetus **11** *NAm* to rob (sby sleeping or unconscious) – infml

[3]**roll** *n* **1a** a sound produced by rapid strokes on a drum **b** a reverberating sound **2a** a swaying movement of the body (e g in walking or dancing) **b** a side-to-side movement (e g of a ship) **c** a flight manoeuvre in which a complete revolution about the longitudinal axis of an aircraft is made with the horizontal direction of flight being approximately maintained

roll call *n* the calling out of a list of names (e g for checking attendance)

[1]**roller** /ˈrəʊlə^r/ *n* **1a(1)** a revolving cylinder over or on which sthg is moved or which is used to press, shape, or apply sthg **(2)** a hair curler **b** a cylinder or rod on which sthg (e g a blind) is rolled up **2** a long heavy wave

[2]**roller** *n* **1** any of a group of mostly brightly coloured Old World birds noted for performing aerial rolls in their nuptial display **2** a canary that has a song in which the notes are soft and run together

roller coaster *n* an elevated railway (e g in a funfair) constructed with curves and inclines on which the cars roll

roller skate *n* (a shoe fitted with) a metal frame holding usu 4 small wheels that allows the wearer to glide over hard surfaces

rollicking /ˈrɒlɪkɪŋ/ *adj* boisterously carefree

rolling pin *n* a long usu wooden cylinder for rolling out dough

rolling stock *n* the vehicles owned and used by a railway

rolling stone *n* one who leads a wandering or unsettled life

rolltop desk /ˈrəʊltɒp ˈdesk/ *n* a writing desk with a sliding cover often of parallel slats fastened to a flexible backing

roll-up *n, Br* a hand-rolled cigarette – infml

roll up *v* **1** to arrive in a vehicle **2** to turn up at a destination, esp unhurriedly

[1]**roly-poly** /ˌrəʊliˈpəʊli/ *n* a dish, esp a pudding, consisting of pastry spread with a filling (e g jam), rolled, and baked or steamed

[2]**roly-poly** *adj* short and plump – infml

[1]**Roman** *n* **1** a native or inhabitant of (ancient) Rome **2** a Roman Catholic **3** *not cap* roman letters or type

[2]**Roman** *adj* **1** (characteristic) of Rome or the (ancient) Romans **2** *not cap, of numbers and letters* not slanted; perpendicular **3** of the see of Rome or the Roman Catholic church

[1]**Roman Catholic** *n* a member of the Roman Catholic church

[2]**Roman Catholic** *adj* of the body of Christians headed by the pope, with a liturgy centred on the Mass and a body of dogma formulated by the church as the infallible interpreter of revealed truth

[1]**romance** /rəʊˈmæns, rə-/ *n* **1a** a medieval usu verse tale dealing with courtly love and adventure **b** a prose narrative dealing with imaginary characters involved in usu heroic, adventurous, or mysterious events that are remote in time or place; *broadly* a love story **2** sthg lacking any basis in fact **3** an emotional aura attaching to an enthralling era, adventure, or pursuit **4** a love affair

[2]**romance** *v* **1** to exaggerate or invent detail or incident **2** to entertain romantic thoughts or ideas

[3]**romance** *n* a short instrumental piece of music in ballad style

Romance *adj* of or constituting the languages developed from Latin

Romanesque /ˌrəʊməˈnesk/ *adj* of a style of architecture developed in Italy and western Europe after 1000 AD and using typically the round arch and vault and elaborate mouldings

Roman numeral *n* a numeral in a system of notation based on the ancient Roman system using the symbols I, V, X, L, C, D, M

[1]**romantic** /rəʊˈmæntɪk, rə-/ *adj* **1** consisting of or like a romance **2** having no basis in real life **3** impractical or fantastic in conception or plan **4a** marked by the imaginative appeal of the heroic, remote, or mysterious **b** *often cap* of romanticism **c** of or being (a composer of) 19th-c music characterized by an emphasis on subjective emotional qualities and freedom of form **5a** having an inclination for romance **b** marked by or constituting strong feeling, esp love – **~ally** *adv* – **~ize** *v*

[2]**romantic** *n* **1** a romantic person **2** *cap* a romantic writer, artist, or composer

romanticism /rəʊˈmæntɪsɪzəm/ *n, often cap* a chiefly late 18th- and early 19th-c literary, artistic, and philosophical movement that reacted against neoclassicism by emphasizing individual aspirations, nature, the emotions, and the remote and exotic – **-cist** *n*

Romany /ˈrəʊməni/ *n* **1** a gipsy **2** the Indic language of the Gipsies

[1]**romp** /rɒmp/ *n* **1** boisterous or bawdy entertainment or play **2** an effortless winning pace

[2]**romp** *v* **1** to play in a boisterous manner **2** to win easily

rondo /ˈrɒndəʊ/ *n, pl* **rondos** an instrumental composition, esp a movement in a concerto or sonata, typically having a recurring theme

[1]**roof** /ruːf/ *n* **1a** the upper usu rigid cover of a building **b** a dwelling, home **2** the highest point or level **3** the vaulted or covering part of the mouth, skull, etc

[2]**roof** *v* **1** to cover (as if) with a roof **2** to serve as a roof over

[1]**rook** /rʊk/ *n* a common Old World social bird similar to the related carrion crow but having a bare grey face

[2]**rook** *n* either of 2 pieces of each colour in a set of chessmen having the power to move along the ranks or files across any number of consecutive unoccupied squares

rookery /ˈrʊkəri/ *n* **1a** (the nests, usu built in the upper branches of trees, of) a colony of rooks **b** (a breeding ground or haunt of) a colony of penguins, seals, etc **2** a crowded dilapidated tenement or maze of dwellings

rookie /ˈrʊki/ *n* a recruit; *also* a novice

room /ruːm, rʊm/ *n* **1** an extent of space occupied by, or sufficient or available for, sthg **2a** a partitioned part of the inside of a building **b** such a part used as a separate lodging – often pl **3** suitable or fit occasion; opportunity + *for*

roommate /ˈruːmˌmeɪt, ˈrʊm-/ *n* any of 2 or more people sharing the same room (e g in a university hall)

room service *n* the facility by which a hotel guest can have food, drinks, etc brought to his/her room

roomy /ˈruːmi/ *adj* spacious – **roominess** *n*

[1]**roost** /ruːst/ *n* **1** a support or place where birds roost **2** a group of birds roosting together

[2]**roost** *v, esp of a bird* to settle down for rest or sleep; perch

rooster /ˈruːstəʳ/ *n, chiefly NAm* a cock

[1]**root** /ruːt/ *n* **1a** the (underground) part of a flowering plant that usu anchors and supports it and absorbs and stores food **b** a (fleshy and edible) root, bulb, tuber, or other underground plant part **2** the part of a tooth, hair, the tongue, etc by which it is attached to the body **3a** sthg that is an underlying cause or basis **b** *pl* a feeling of belonging established through close familiarity or family ties with a particular place **4** a number which produces a given number when taken an indicated number of times as a factor **5** the basis from which a word is derived

[2]**root** *v* **1** to grow roots or take root **2** to have an origin or base

[3]**root** *v* **1** *esp of a pig* to dig with the

snout **2** to poke or dig about *in*; search (unsystematically) for sthg

[4]**root** *v* to lend vociferous or enthusiastic support to sby or sthg – + *for*

root crop *n* a crop (e g turnips or sugar beet) grown for its enlarged roots

root out *v* **1** to discover or cause to emerge by rooting **2** to get rid of or destroy completely

[1]**rope** /rəup/ *n* **1** a strong thick cord composed of strands of fibres or wire twisted or braided together **2** a row or string consisting of things united (as if) by braiding, twining, or threading **3** *pl* special methods or procedures

[2]**rope** *v* **1** to bind, fasten, or tie with a rope **2** to enlist (sby reluctant) *in* a group or activity

ropeway /ˈrəupweɪ/ *n* an endless aerial cable moved by a stationary engine and used to transport goods (e g logs and ore)

ropy, ropey /ˈrəupi/ *adj* **1** like rope, esp in being able to be drawn out in a thread **2a** of poor quality; shoddy **b** somewhat unwell

Roquefort /ˈrɒkfɔːʳ/ *trademark* – used for a strong-flavoured crumbly French cheese with bluish green veins, made from the curds of ewes' milk

rosary /ˈrəuzəri/ *n* a string of beads used in counting prayers

[1]**rose** /rəuz/ *past of* **rise**

[2]**rose** *n* **1** (the showy often double flower of) any of a genus of widely cultivated usu prickly shrubs **2a** a compass card **b** a perforated outlet for water (e g from a shower or watering can) **c** an electrical fitting that anchors the flex of a suspended light bulb to a ceiling **3** a pale to dark pinkish colour – **rose** *adj*

rosé /ˈrəuzeɪ/ *n* a light pink table wine made from red grapes by removing the skins after fermentation has begun

rosebud /ˈrəuzbʌd/ *n* the bud of a rose

rosemary /ˈrəuzməri/ *n* a fragrant shrubby Eurasian plant used as a cooking herb

rosette /rəuˈzet/ *n* **1** an ornament usu made of material gathered so as to resemble a rose and worn as a badge, trophy, or trimming **2** a cluster of leaves in crowded circles or spirals (e g in the dandelion)

rose window *n* a circular window filled with tracery radiating from its centre

rosewood /ˈrəuzwud/ *n* (in any of various esp leguminous tropical trees yielding) a valuable dark red or purplish wood, streaked and variegated with black

roster /ˈrɒstəʳ/ *n* **1** a list or register giving the order in which personnel are to perform a duty, go on leave, etc **2** an itemized list

rostrum /ˈrɒstrəm/ *n* **1** a stage for public speaking **2** a raised platform (on a stage)

rosy /ˈrəuzi/ *adj* **1a** rose **b** having a rosy complexion – often in combination **2** characterized by or encouraging optimism – **rosiness** *n*

[1]**rot** /rɒt/ *v* **1a** to undergo decomposition, esp from the action of bacteria or fungi – often + *down* **b** to become unsound or weak (e g from chemical or water action) **2** to go to ruin

[2]**rot** *n* **1** (sthg) rotting or being rotten; decay **2** any of several plant or animal diseases, esp of sheep, with breakdown and death of tissues **3** nonsense, rubbish – often used interjectionally

rota /ˈrəutə/ *n* a list specifying a fixed order of rotation (e g of people or duties)

rotary /ˈrəutəri/ *adj* **1a** turning on an axis like a wheel **b** proceeding about an axis **2** having a principal part that turns on an axis **3** characterized by rotation

rotate /rəuˈteɪt/ *v* **1** to turn about an axis or a centre; revolve **2a** to take turns at performing an act or operation **b** to perform an ordered series of actions or functions

rotation /rəuˈteɪʃən/ *n* **1a** a rotating or being rotated (as if) on an axis or centre **b** one complete turn **2a** recurrence in a regular series **b** the growing of different crops in succession in 1 field, usu in a regular sequence

rote /rəut/ *n* the mechanical use of the memory

rotgut /ˈrɒtgʌt/ *n* spirits of low quality – infml

rotisserie /rəuˈtɪsəri/ *n* **1** a restaurant specializing in roast and barbecued meats **2** an appliance fitted with a spit on which food is cooked

rotor /ˈrəʊtəʳ/ *n* **1** a part that revolves in a machine **2** a complete system of more or less horizontal blades that supplies (nearly) all the force supporting an aircraft (e g a helicopter) in flight

rotten /ˈrɒtn/ *adj* **1** having rotted; putrid **2** morally or politically corrupt **3** extremely unpleasant or inferior **4** marked by illness, discomfort, or unsoundness *USE* (*3, 4*) infml – **~ly** *adv* – **~ness** *n*

rotter /ˈrɒtəʳ/ *n* a thoroughly objectionable person – often humor

rotund /rəʊˈtʌnd/ *adj* **1** rounded **2** high-flown or sonorous **3** markedly plump – **~ity** *n* – **~ly** *adv*

rotunda /rəʊˈtʌndə/ *n* a round building covered by a dome

rouble, ruble /ˈruːbəl/ *n* **1** the major monitary unit of the USSR

rouge /ruːʒ/ *n* a red cosmetic, esp for the cheeks

¹rough /rʌf/ *adj* **1a** not smooth **b** covered with or made up of coarse hair **c** covered with boulders, bushes, etc **2a** turbulent, stormy **b(1)** harsh, violent **(2)** requiring strenuous effort **(3)** unfortunate and hard to bear – often + *on* **3a** harsh to the ear **b** crude in style or expression **c** ill-mannered, uncouth **4a** crude, unfinished **b** executed hastily or approximately **5** *Br* poorly or exhausted, esp through lack of sleep or heavy drinking – infml

²rough *n* **1** uneven ground bordering a golf fairway **2** the rugged or disagreeable side or aspect **3a** sthg, esp written or illustrated, in a crude or preliminary state **b** broad outline **c** a quick preliminary drawing or layout

³rough *adv, chiefly Br* in want of material comforts; without proper lodging – esp in *live/sleep rough*

roughage /ˈrʌfɪdʒ/ *n* coarse bulky food (e g bran) that is relatively high in fibre and low in digestible nutrients and that by its bulk stimulates the passage of matter through the intestines

rough-and-tumble *n* disorderly unrestrained fighting or struggling

roughcast /ˈrʌfkɑːst/ *n* a plaster of lime mixed with shells or pebbles used for covering buildings – **roughcast** *v*

roughen /ˈrʌfən/ *v* to make or become (more) rough

rough-hewn *adj* **1** in a rough or unfinished state **2** lacking refinement

roughhouse /ˈrʌfhaʊs/ *n* an instance of brawling or excessively boisterous play – infml

roughly /ˈrʌfli/ *adv* **1a** with insolence or violence **b** in primitive fashion; crudely **2** without claim to completeness or exactness

rough out *v* **1** to shape or plan in a preliminary way **2** to outline

roughshod /ˈrʌfʃɒd/ *adv* forcefully and without justice or consideration

rough stuff *n* violent behaviour; violence – infml

rouleau /ˈruːləʊ/ *n, pl* **rouleaux** a decorative piping or rolled strip used esp as a trimming

roulette /ruːˈlet/ *n* a gambling game in which players bet on which compartment of a revolving wheel a small ball will come to rest in

¹round /raʊnd/ *adj* **1a** having every part of the surface or circumference equidistant from the centre **b** cylindrical **2** well filled out; plump **3a** complete, full **b** approximately correct; *esp* exact only to a specific decimal **c** substantial in amount **4** direct in expression **5a** moving in or forming a ring or circle **b** following a roughly circular route **6** presented with lifelike fullness **7** having full resonance or tone – **~ness** *n*

²round *adv* **1a** in a circular or curved path **b** with revolving or rotating motion **c** in circumference **d** in, along, or through a circuitous or indirect route **e** in an encircling position **2a** in close from all sides so as to surround (e g the children crowded *round*) **b** near, about **c** here and there in various places **3a** in rotation or recurrence **b** from beginning to end; through (e g all year *round*) **c(1)** in or to the other or a specified direction (e g turn *round*) **(2)** to (e g came *round* after fainting) **(3)** in the specified order or relationship (e g got the story the wrong way *round*) **4** about, approximately **5** to a particular person or place (e g invite them *round* for drinks)

[3]round *prep* **1a** so as to revolve or progress about (a centre) **b** so as to encircle or enclose **c** so as to avoid or get past; beyond the obstacle of **d** near to; about **2a** in all directions outwards from (e g looked *round* her) **b** here and there in or throughout (e g travel *round* Europe) **3** so as to have a centre or basis in (e g a movement organized *round* the idea of service) **4** continuously during; throughout

[4]round *n* **1a** sthg round (e g a circle, curve, or ring) **b** a circle of people or things **2** a musical canon sung in unison in which each part is continuously repeated **3a** a circling or circuitous path or course **b** a route or assigned territory habitually traversed (e g by a milkman or policeman) **c** a series of visits made by **(1)** a general practitioner to patients in their homes **(2)** a hospital doctor to the patients under his/her care **4** a set of usu alcoholic drinks served at 1 time to each person in a group **5** a unit of ammunition consisting of the parts necessary to fire 1 shot **6** a division of a tournament in which each contestant plays 1 other **7** a prolonged burst (e g of applause) **8** a single slice of bread or toast; *also* a sandwich made with 2 whole slices of bread

[5]round *v* **1** to make round or rounded **2** to go round (e g a bend, corner) **3** to bring to completion or perfection – often + *off* or *out* **4** to express as a round number – often + *off, up*, or *down* **5** to turn *on* suddenly and attack

[1]roundabout /ˈraʊndəbaʊt/ *n, Br* **1** a merry-go-round **2** a road junction formed round a central island about which traffic moves in 1 direction only

[2]roundabout *adj* circuitous, indirect

roundel /ˈraʊndl/ *n* **1** a circular panel, window, etc **2** a circular mark identifying the nationality of an aircraft, esp a warplane

roundelay /ˈraʊndl̩leɪ/ *n* **1** a simple song with a refrain poem with a refrain recurring frequently or at fixed intervals

Roundhead /ˈraʊndhed/ *n* an adherent of Parliament in its contest with Charles I

roundhouse /ˈraʊndhaʊs/ *n* **1** a cabin or apartment on the after part of a quarterdeck **2** a circular building for housing and repairing locomotives

roundly /ˈraʊndli/ *adv* **1** in a round or circular form or manner **2** in a blunt or severe manner

round-shouldered *adj* having stooping or rounded shoulders

roundsman /ˈraʊndzmən/ *n* sby (e g a milkman) who takes, orders, sells, or delivers goods on an assigned route

round table *n* a meeting or conference of several people on equal terms

round-the-clock *adj* lasting or continuing 24 hours a day; constant

roundup /ˈraʊndʌp/ *n* **1a** the collecting in of cattle by riding round them and driving them **b** a gathering in of scattered people or things **2** a summary of information (e g from news bulletins)

round up *v* **1** to collect (cattle) by a roundup **2** to gather in or bring together from various quarters

rouse /raʊz/ *v* **1** to stir up; provoke **2** to arouse from sleep or apathy

rousing /ˈraʊzɪŋ/ *adj* giving rise to enthusiasm; stirring

[1]rout /raʊt/ *n* a disorderly crowd of people; a mob

[2]rout *n* **1** a state of wild confusion; *specif* a confused retreat; headlong flight **2** a disastrous defeat

[3]rout *v* **1** to disorganize completely; wreak havoc among **2** to put to headlong flight **3** to defeat decisively or disastrously

[1]route /ruːt/ *n* **1a** a regularly travelled way **b** a means of access **2** a line of travel **3** an itinerary

[2]route *v* to send by a selected route; direct

route march *n* a usu long and tiring march, esp as military training

[1]routine /ruːˈtiːn/ *n* **1a** a regular course of procedure **b** habitual or mechanical performance of an established procedure **2** a fixed piece of entertainment often repeated

[2]routine *adj* **1** commonplace or repetitious in character **2** of or in accordance with established procedure – ~ly *adv*

roux /ruː/ *n, pl* **roux** a cooked mixture of fat and flour used as a thickening agent in a sauce

[1]**rove** /rəʊv/ *v* to wander aimlessly or idly (through or over) – ~ **r** *n*

[2]**rove** *past of* **reeve**

[3]**rove** *v* to join (textile fibres) with a slight twist and draw out

[1]**row** /rəʊ/ *v* **1** to propel a boat by means of oars **2** to occupy a specified position in a rowing crew – ~**er** *n* – ~**ing** *adj*

[2]**row** /rəʊ/ *n* an act of rowing a boat

[3]**row** *n* **1** a number of objects arranged in a (straight) line; *also* the line along which such objects are arranged **2** a way, street

[4]**row** /raʊ/ *n* **1** a noisy quarrel or stormy dispute **2** excessive or unpleasant noise

[5]**row** /raʊ/ *v* to engage in quarrelling

rowan /ˈrəʊən, ˈraʊən/ *n* (the red berry of) a small Eurasian tree that bears flat clusters of white flowers and red berries; a mountain ash

rowdy /ˈraʊdi/ *n or adj* (sby) coarse or boisterous – **rowdily** *adv* – **rowdiness, rowdyism** *n*

rowlock /ˈrɒlək; *not tech* ˈrəʊlɒk/ *n* a device for holding a oar in place and providing a fulcrum for its action

[1]**royal** /ˈrɔɪəl/ *adj* **1a** of monarchical ancestry **b** of the crown **c** in the crown's service **2** of superior size, magnitude, or quality **3** of or being a part of the rigging of a sailing ship next above the topgallant – ~**ly** *adv*

[2]**royal** *n* **1** a royal sail or mast **2** a size of paper usu 25 x 20in (635 × 508mm)

royalist /ˈrɔɪəlɪst/ *n, often cap* a supporter of a king or of monarchical government (e g a Cavalier)

royal jelly *n* a highly nutritious secretion of the honeybee that is fed to the very young larvae and to all larvae that will develop into queens

royal prerogative *n* the constitutional rights of the monarch

royalty /ˈrɔɪəlti/ *n* **1** royal sovereignty **2** people of royal blood **3** a share of the product or profit reserved by one who grants esp an oil or mining lease **4** a payment made to an author, composer, or inventor for each copy or example of his/her work sold

[1]**rub** /rʌb/ *v* **1** to subject to pressure and friction, esp with a back-and-forth motion **2a** to cause (a body) to move with pressure and friction along a surface **b** to treat in any of various ways by rubbing

[2]**rub** *n* **1a** an obstacle, difficulty – usu + *the* **b** sthg grating to the feelings (e g a gibe or harsh criticism) **2** the application of friction and pressure

rub along *v* **1** to continue coping in a trying situation **2** to remain on friendly terms

[1]**rubber** /ˈrʌbəʳ/ *n* **1a** an instrument or object used in rubbing, polishing, or cleaning **b** *Br* a small piece of rubber or plastic used for rubbing out esp pencil marks on paper, card, etc **2** (any of various synthetic substances like) an elastic substance obtained by coagulating the milky juice of the rubber tree or other plant that is used, esp when toughened by chemical treatment, in car tyres, waterproof materials, etc

[2]**rubber** /ˈrʌbəʳ/ *n* a contest consisting of an odd number of games won by the side that takes a majority

rubber plant *n* a tall Asian tree of the fig family frequently dwarfed and grown as an ornamental plant

rubber-stamp *v* **1** to imprint with a rubber stamp **2** to approve, endorse, or dispose of as a matter of routine or at the dictate of another

rubber stamp *n* **1** a stamp of rubber for making imprints **2** sby who unthinkingly assents to the actions or policies of others **3** a routine endorsement or approval

rubber tree *n* a S American tree that is cultivated in plantations and is the chief source of rubber

rubbing /ˈrʌbɪŋ/ *n* an image of a raised surface obtained by placing paper over it and rubbing the paper with charcoal, chalk, etc

[1]**rubbish** /ˈrʌbɪʃ/ *n* **1** worthless or rejected articles; trash **2** sthg worthless; nonsense – often used interjectionally – ~**y** *adj*

[2]**rubbish** *v* **1** to condemn as rubbish **2** to litter with rubbish

rubble /ˈrʌbəl/ *n* **1** broken fragments of building material (e g brick, stone, etc) **2** rough broken stones or bricks used in coarse masonry or in filling courses of walls **3** rough stone from the quarry

rubella /ruːˈbelə/ *n* German measles

Rubicon /ˈruːbɪkən, -kɒn/ *n* a bounding or limiting line; *esp* one that when crossed commits sby irrevocably

rub in *v* to harp on (e g sthg unpleasant or embarrassing)

rubric /ˈruːbrɪk/ *n* **1** a heading under which sthg is classed **2** an authoritative rule; *esp* a rule for the conduct of church ceremonial **3** an explanatory or introductory commentary

rub up *v* to revive or refresh knowledge of; revise – **rub-up** *n*

[1]**ruby** /ˈruːbi/ *n* **1** a red corundum used as a gem **2** the dark red colour of the ruby

[2]**ruby** *adj* of or marking a 40th anniversary

[1]**ruck** /rʌk/ *n* **1a** an indistinguishable mass **b** *the* usual run of people or things **2** a situation in Rugby Union in which 1 or more players from each team close round the ball when it is on the ground and try to kick the ball out to their own team

[2]**ruck** *v* to wrinkle, crease – often + *up*

rucksack /ˈrʌksæk/ *n* a lightweight bag carried on the back and fastened by straps over the shoulders, used esp by walkers and climbers

rudder /ˈrʌdəʳ/ *n* **1** a flat piece or structure of wood or metal hinged vertically to a ship's stern for changing course with **2** a movable auxiliary aerofoil, usu attached to the fin, that serves to control direction of flight of an aircraft in the horizontal plane – **~less** *adj*

ruddy /ˈrʌdi/ *adj* **1** having a healthy reddish colour **2** red, reddish **3** *Br* bloody

rude /ruːd/ *adj* **1a** in a rough or unfinished state **b** primitive, undeveloped **2a** discourteous **b** vulgar, indecent **c** ignorant, unlearned **3** showing or suggesting lack of training or skill **4** robust, vigorous – esp in *rude health* **5** sudden and unpleasant; abrupt – **~ly** *adv* – **~ness** *n*

rudiment /ˈruːdʒ̍mənt/ *n* **1** a basic principle or element or a fundamental skill **2a** sthg as yet unformed or undeveloped **b** a deficiently developed body part or organ

rudimentary /ˌruːdʒ̍ˈmentəri/ *adj* **1** basic, fundamental **2** of a primitive kind; crude **3** very poorly developed or represented only by a vestige

[1]**rue** /ruː/ *v* to feel penitence or bitter regret for – **~ful** *adj* – **~fully** *adv*

[2]**rue** *n* a strong-scented woody plant with bitter leaves formerly used in medicine

[1]**ruff, ruffe** /rʌf/ *n* a small freshwater European perch

[2]**ruff** *n* **1** a broad starched collar of fluted linen or muslin worn in the late 16th and early 17th c **2** a fringe or frill of long hairs or feathers growing round the neck **3** *fem* **reeve** a Eurasian sandpiper the male of which has a large ruff of erectable feathers during the breeding season

[3]**ruff** *v* to trump

ruffian /ˈrʌfɪən/ *n* a brutal and lawless person – **~ly** *adj*

[1]**ruffle** /ˈrʌfəl/ *v* **1a** to disturb the smoothness of **b** to trouble, vex **2** to erect (e g feathers) (as if) in a ruff **3** to make into a ruffle

[2]**ruffle** *n* **1** a disturbance of surface evenness (e g a ripple or crumple) **2a** a strip of fabric gathered or pleated on 1 edge **b** a ruff

rug /rʌg/ *n* **1** a heavy mat, usu smaller than a carpet and with a thick pile, which is used as a floor covering **2a** a woollen blanket, often with fringes on 2 opposite edges, used as a wrap esp when travelling **b** a blanket for an animal (e g a horse)

rugby /ˈrʌgbi/ *n, often cap* a football game that is played with an oval football, that features kicking, lateral hand-to-hand passing, and tackling, and in which forward passing is prohibited

rugged /ˈrʌgʒ̍d/ *adj* **1** having a rough uneven surface or outline **2** seamed with wrinkles and furrows **3** austere, stern; *also* uncompromising **4** strongly built or constituted; sturdy – **~ly** *adv* – **~ness** *n*

[1]**ruin** /ˈruːʒ̍n/ *n* **1** physical, moral, economic, or social collapse **2a** the state

of being wrecked or decayed **b** the remains of sthg destroyed – usu pl with sing. meaning **3** (a cause of) destruction or downfall **4** a ruined person or structure – **~ation** *n*

[2]**ruin** *v* **1** to reduce to ruins **2a** to damage irreparably; spoil **b** to reduce to financial ruin

ruinous /ˈruːɨ̥nəs/ *adj* **1** dilapidated, ruined **2** causing (the likelihood of) ruin – **~ly** *adv*

[1]**rule** /ruːl/ *n* **1a** a prescriptive specification of conduct or action **b** an established procedure, custom, or habit **2a** a usu valid generalization **b** a standard of judgment **c** a regulating principle, esp of a system **3** the exercise or a period of dominion **4** a strip or set of jointed strips of material marked off in units and used for measuring or marking off lengths

[2]**rule** *v* **1a** to exercise power or firm authority over **b** to be preeminent in; dominate **2** to lay down authoritatively, esp judicially **3** to mark with lines drawn (as if) along the straight edge of a ruler

rule out *v* **1a** to exclude, eliminate **b** to deny the possibility of **2** to make impossible; prevent

ruler /ˈruːləʳ/ *n* **1** sby, specif a sovereign, who rules **2** a smooth-edged strip of material that is usu marked off in units (e g centimetres) and is used for guiding a pen or pencil in drawing lines, for measuring, or for marking off lengths

[1]**ruling** /ˈruːlɪŋ/ *n* an official or authoritative decision

[2]**ruling** *adj* **1** exerting power or authority **2** chief, predominant

[1]**rum** /rʌm/ *adj, chiefly Br* queer, strange – infml

[2]**rum** *n* a spirit distilled from a fermented cane product (e g molasses)

rumba, rhumba /ˈrʌmbə/ *n* (the music for) a ballroom dance of Cuban Negro origin marked by steps with a delayed transfer of weight and pronounced hip movements

[1]**rumble** /ˈrʌmbəl/ *v* **1** to make a low heavy rolling sound **2** to reveal or discover the true character of – infml

[2]**rumble** *n* **1** a rumbling sound **2** *NAm* a street fight, esp between gangs – infml

rumbustious /rʌmˈbʌstʃəs/ *adj, chiefly Br* irrepressibly or coarsely exuberant

[1]**ruminant** /ˈruːmɨ̥nənt/ *n* a ruminant mammal

[2]**ruminant** *adj* **1** of or being (a member of) a group of hoofed mammals including the cattle, sheep, giraffes, and camels that chew the cud and have a complex 3- or 4-chambered stomach **2** meditative

ruminate /ˈruːmɨ̥neɪt/ *v* **1** to chew again (what has been chewed slightly and swallowed) **2** to engage in contemplation (of) – **-nation** *n*

[1]**rummage** /ˈrʌmɪdʒ/ *n* a thorough search, esp among a jumbled assortment of objects

[2]**rummage** *v* **1** to make a thorough search of (an untidy or congested place) **2** to uncover by searching – usu + *out*

rummy /ˈrʌmi/ *n* any of several card games for 2 or more players in which each player tries to assemble combinations of 3 or more related cards and to be the first to turn all his/her cards into such combinations

[1]**rumour** /ˈruːməʳ/ *n* **1** a statement or report circulated without confirmation of its truth **2** talk or opinion widely disseminated but with no identifiable source

[2]**rumour** *v* to tell or spread by rumour

rump /rʌmp/ *n* **1** the rear part of a quadruped mammal, bird, etc; the buttocks **2** a cut of beef between the loin and round **3** a small or inferior remnant of a larger group (e g a parliament)

[1]**rumple** /ˈrʌmpəl/ *n* a fold, wrinkle

[2]**rumple** *v* **1** to wrinkle, crumple **2** to make unkempt; tousle

rumpus /ˈrʌmpəs/ *n* a usu noisy commotion

[1]**run** /rʌn/ *v* **ran; run 1a** to go faster than a walk; *specif* to go steadily by springing steps so that both feet leave the ground for an instant in each step **b** to flee, escape **2a** to contend in a race; *also* to finish a race in the specified place **b** to put forward as a candidate for office **3a** to move (as if) on

wheels **b** to pass or slide freely or cursorily **4a** to slip through or past **b** to smuggle **5** to sing or play quickly **6a** to go back and forth; ply **b** *of fish* to ascend a river to spawn **7a** to function, operate **b** to carry on, manage, or control **8** to own and drive **9** to continue in force **10** to pass, esp by negligence or indulgence, into a specified state **11a(1)** to flow **(2)** to be full of; flow with **b** to discharge liquid **c** to melt **d** to spread, dissolve **12** to have a tendency; be prone **13a** to lie or extend in a specified position, direction, or relation to sthg **b** to extend in a continuous range **14** to occur persistently **15** to make oneself liable to **16** to carry in a printed medium; print **17** to spread quickly from point to point **18** to ladder

[2]**run** *n* **1a** an act or the activity of running; continued rapid movement **b** the gait of a runner **c** (a school of fish) migrating or ascending a river to spawn **2a** the direction in which sthg (e g a vein of ore or the grain of wood) lies **b** general tendency or direction **3** a continuous series or unbroken course, esp of identical or similar things: e g **a** a rapid passage up or down a musical scale **b** an unbroken course of performances or showings **c** a persistent and heavy commercial or financial demand **4** the quantity of work turned out in a continuous operation **5** the average or prevailing kind or class **6a** the distance covered in a period of continuous journeying **b** a short excursion in a car **c** freedom of movement in or access to a place **7** an enclosure for domestic animals where they may feed or exercise **8a** an inclined course (e g for skiing) **b** a support or channel (e g a track, pipe, or trough) along which sthg runs **9** a unit of scoring in cricket made typically by each batsman running the full length of the wicket **10** a ladder (e g in a stocking)

runaround /'rʌnəraʊnd/ *n* delaying action, esp in response to a request

[1]**runaway** /'rʌnaweɪ/ *n* a fugitive

[2]**runaway** *adj* **1** fugitive **2** won by a long lead; decisive **3** out of control

run away *v* **1** to take to flight **2** to flee from home; *esp* to elope

rundown /'rʌndaʊn/ *n* an item-by-item report; a résumé

run-down *adj* **1** in a state of disrepair **2** in poor health

run down *v* **1** to knock down, esp with a motor vehicle **2a** to chase to exhaustion or until captured **b** to find by searching **3** to disparage **4** to allow the gradual decline or closure of **5** to cease to operate because of the exhaustion of motive power **6** to decline in physical condition

rune /ruːn/ *n* **1** any of the characters of an alphabet prob derived from Latin and Greek and used in medieval times, esp in carved inscriptions, by the Germanic peoples **2** a magical or cryptic utterance or inscription – **runic** *adj*

[1]**rung** /rʌŋ/ *past part of* **ring**

[2]**rung** *n* **1a** a rounded part placed as a crosspiece between the legs of a chair **b** any of the crosspieces of a ladder **2** a level or stage in sthg that can be ascended

run in *v* **1** to use (e g a motor car) cautiously for an initial period **2** to arrest, esp for a minor offence – infml

runnel /,rʌnl/ *n* a small stream; a brook

runner /'rʌnəʳ/ *n* **1** an entrant for a race who actually competes in it **2** sby who smuggles or distributes illicit or contraband goods – usu in combination **3** a straight piece on which sthg slides: e g **a** a longitudinal piece on which a sledge or ice skate slides **b** a groove or bar along which sthg (e g a drawer or sliding door) slides **4a** a long narrow carpet (e g for a hall or staircase) **b** a narrow decorative cloth for a table or dresser top

runner bean *n, chiefly Br* (the long green edible pod of) a widely cultivated orig tropical American high-climbing bean with large usu bright red flowers

runner-up *n* a competitor other than the outright winner whose attainment still merits a prize

[1]**running** /'rʌnɪŋ/ *n* **1** the state of competing, esp with a good chance of winning – in *in/out of the running* **2** management, operation

[2]**running** *adj* **1** runny **2a** having stages

that follow in rapid succession **b** made during the course of a process or activity **3** being part of a continuous length **4** cursive, flowing

[3]**running** *adv* in succession

runny /'rʌni/ *adj* tending to run

runoff /'rʌnɒf/ *n* a final decisive race, contest, or election

run off *v* **1a** to compose rapidly or glibly **b** to produce with a printing press or copier **c** to decide (e g a race) by a runoff **2** to drain off (a liquid) **3** to run away; elope

run-of-the-mill *adj* average, commonplace

run out *v* **1a** to come to an end **b** to become exhausted or used up **2** to dismiss a batsman who is outside his crease and attempting a run by breaking the wicket with the ball **3** *chiefly NAm* to compel to leave

runt /rʌnt/ *n* **1** an animal unusually small of its kind; *esp* the smallest of a litter of pigs **2** a puny person

run-through *n* **1** a cursory reading, summary, or rehearsal **2** a sequence of actions performed for practice

run through *v* **1** to pierce with a weapon (e g a sword) **2** to perform, esp for practice or instruction

run-up *n* **1** (the track or area provided for) an approach run to provide momentum (e g for a jump or throw) **2** *Br* a period that immediately precedes an action or event

run up *v* **1** to make (esp a garment) quickly **2a** to erect hastily **b** to hoist (a flag) **3** to accumulate or incur (debts)

runway /'rʌnweɪ/ *n* an artificially surfaced strip of ground on an airfield for the landing and takeoff of aeroplanes

rupee /ruː'piː/ *n* (a note or coin representing) the basic money unit of various countries of the Indian subcontinent and the Indian Ocean (e g India, Pakistan, Seychelles, and Sri Lanka)

[1]**rupture** /'rʌptʃəʳ/ *n* **1** breach of peace or concord; *specif* open hostility between nations **2a** the tearing apart of a tissue, esp muscle **b** a hernia **3** a breaking apart or bursting

[2]**rupture** *v* **1a** to part by violence; break, burst **b** to create a breach of **2** to produce a rupture in

rural /'rʊərəl/ *adj* of the country, country people or life, or agriculture – **~ly** *adv*

Ruritanian /,rʊərɪ̣'teɪnɪən/ *adj* (characteristic) of an imaginary Central European country used as a setting for contemporary cloak-and-dagger court intrigues

ruse /ruːz/ *n* a wily subterfuge

[1]**rush** /rʌʃ/ *n* any of various often tufted marsh plants with cylindrical (hollow) leaves, used for the seats of chairs and for plaiting mats – **rushy** *adj*

[2]**rush** *v* **1** to push or impel forwards with speed or violence **2** to perform or finish in a short time or without adequate preparation **3** to run against in attack, often with an element of surprise

[3]**rush** *n* **1a** a rapid and violent forward motion **b** a sudden onset of emotion **2** a surge of activity; *also* busy or hurried activity **3** a great movement of people, esp in search of wealth **4** the unedited print of a film scene processed directly after shooting – usu pl

[4]**rush** *adj* requiring or marked by special speed or urgency

rush hour *n* a period of the day when traffic is at a peak

rusk /rʌsk/ *n* (a light dry biscuit similar to) a piece of sliced bread baked again until dry and crisp

russet /'rʌsɪ̣t/ *n* **1** a reddish to yellowish brown colour **2** any of various russet-coloured winter eating apples

Russian /'rʌʃən/ *n* **1** a native or inhabitant of Russia; *broadly* a native or inhabitant of the USSR **2** a Slavonic language of the Russians

Russian roulette *n* an act of bravado consisting of spinning the cylinder of a revolver loaded with 1 cartridge, pointing the muzzle at one's own head, and pulling the trigger

[1]**rust** /rʌst/ *n* **1** a brittle reddish coating on iron, esp iron chemically attacked by moist air **2** corrosive or injurious influence or effect **3** (a fungus causing) any of numerous destructive diseases of plants in which reddish

brown blisters form **4** a reddish brown to orange colour

²**rust** *v* **1** to form rust; become oxidized **2** to degenerate, esp through lack of use or advancing age **3** to become reddish brown as if with rust

¹**rustic** /ˈrʌstɪk/ *adj* **1** of or suitable for the country **2** made of the rough limbs of trees **3** characteristic of country people – **~ity** *n*

²**rustic** *n* an unsophisticated rural person

rusticate /ˈrʌstɪkeɪt/ *v* **1** to suspend (a student) from college or university **2** to bevel or cut a groove, channel etc in (e g the edges of stone blocks) to make the joints conspicuous **3** to impart a rustic character to

¹**rustle** /ˈrʌsəl/ *v* **1a** to make or cause a rustle **b** to move with a rustling sound **2** *chiefly NAm* to steal cattle or horses – **~r** *n*

²**rustle** *n* a quick succession or confusion of faint sounds

rusty /ˈrʌsti/ *adj* **1** affected (as if) by rust; *esp* stiff (as if) with rust **2** inept and slow through lack of practice or advanced age **3a** of the colour rust **b** dulled in colour by age and use; shabby – **rustiness** *n*

¹**rut** /rʌt/ *n* an annually recurrent state of readiness to copulate, in the male deer or other mammal; *also* oestrus, heat

²**rut** *n* **1** a track worn by habitual passage, esp of wheels on soft or uneven ground **2** an established practice; *esp* a tedious routine

ruthless /ˈruːθlɪ̵s/ *adj* showing no pity or compassion – **~ly** *adv* – **~ness** *n*

rye /raɪ/ *n* (the seeds, from which a wholemeal flour is made, of) a hardy grass widely grown for grain

S

s /es/ *n, pl* **s's, ss** *often cap* (a graphic representation of or device for reproducing) the 19th letter of the English alphabet

sabbath /'sæbəθ/ *n* **1** *often cap* the 7th day of the week observed from Friday evening to Saturday evening as a day of rest and worship by Jews **2** *often cap* Sunday observed among Christians as a day of rest and worship

[1]**sabbatical** /sə'bætɪkəl/, **sabbatic** *adj* **1** of the sabbath **2** of or being a sabbatical

[2]**sabbatical** *n* a leave, often with pay, granted usu every 7th year (e g to a university teacher)

sable /'seɪbəl/ *n* **1** (the valuable dark brown fur of) a N Asian and European flesh-eating mammal related to the martens **2** black – poetic or used technically in heraldry

sabot /'sæbəʊ/ *n* a wooden shoe worn in various European countries

[1]**sabotage** /'sæbətɑːʒ/ *n* **1** destructive or obstructive action carried on by a civilian or enemy agent, intended to hinder military activity **2** deliberate subversion (e g of a plan or project)

[2]**sabotage** *v* to practise sabotage on – **-teur** *n*

sabre /'seɪbəʳ/ *n* **1** a cavalry sword with a curved blade, thick back, and guard **2** a light fencing or duelling sword having an arched guard that covers the back of the hand and a tapering flexible blade with a full cutting edge along one side

sabre-toothed tiger *n* an extinct big cat with long curved upper canines

sac /sæk/ *n* a (fluid-filled) pouch within an animal or plant

saccharin /'sækərɨn/ *n* a compound containing no calories that is several hundred times sweeter than cane sugar and is used as a sugar substitute (e g in low-calorie diets)

saccharine /'sækəriːn/ *adj* **1** of, like, or containing sugar **2** excessively sweet; mawkish

sachet /'sæʃeɪ/ *n* **1** a small usu plastic bag or packet; *esp* one holding just enough of sthg (e g shampoo or sugar) for use at 1 time **2** a small bag containing a perfumed powder used to scent clothes and linens

[1]**sack** /sæk/ *n* **1** a usu rectangular large bag (e g of paper or canvas) **2** a garment without shaping; *esp* a loosely fitting dress **3** dismissal from employment – usu + *get* or *give* + *the*; infml

[2]**sack** *v* to dismiss from a job – infml

[3]**sack** *n* any of various dry white wines formerly imported to England from S Europe

[4]**sack** *n* the plundering of a place captured in war

[5]**sack** *v* **1** to plunder (e g a town) after capture **2** to strip (a place) of valuables

sackbut /'sækbʌt/ *n* the renaissance trombone

sacrament /'sækrəmənt/ *n* **1** a formal religious act (e g baptism) functioning as a sign or symbol of a spiritual reality **2** *cap* the bread and wine used at Communion; *specif* the consecrated Host – **~al** *adj*

sacred /'seɪkrɨd/ *adj* **1** dedicated or set apart for the service or worship of a god or gods **2a** worthy of religious veneration **b** commanding reverence and respect **3** of religion; not secular or profane – **~ly** *adv* – **~ness** *n*

sacred cow *n* sby or sthg granted unreasonable immunity from criticism

[1]**sacrifice** /'sækrɨfaɪs/ *n* **1** an act of offering to a deity; *esp* the killing of a victim on an altar **2a** destruction or surrender of one thing for the sake of another of greater worth or importance **b** sthg given up or lost – **-ficial** *adj*

[2]**sacrifice** *v* **1** to offer as a sacrifice **2**

to give up or lose for the sake of an ideal or end

sacrilege /ˈsækrɪ̣lɪdʒ/ *n* **1** a violation of what is sacred **2** gross irreverence toward sby or sthg sacred – **-legious** *adj* – **-legiously** *adv*

sacristy /ˈsækrɪ̣sti/ *n* a room in a church where sacred vessels and vestments are kept and where the clergy put on their vestments

sacrosanct /ˈsækrəsæŋkt/ *adj* accorded the highest reverence and respect; *also* regarded with unwarranted reverence

sad /sæd/ *adj* **1a** affected with or expressing unhappiness **b** deplorable, regrettable **2** of a dull sombre colour **3** *of baked goods* heavy – **~ly** *adv* – **~ness** *n*

sadden /ˈsædn/ *v* to make or become sad

[1]**saddle** /ˈsædl/ *n* **1a** a usu padded and leather-covered seat secured to the back of a horse, donkey, etc for the rider to sit on **b** a seat in certain types of vehicles (e g a bicycle or agricultural tractor) **2** a ridge connecting 2 peaks **3** a large cut of meat from a sheep, hare, rabbit, deer, etc consisting of both sides of the unsplit back including both loins

[2]**saddle** *v* to encumber

saddler /ˈsædləʳ/ *n* one who makes, repairs, or sells furnishings (e g saddles) for horses

saddlery /ˈsædləri/ *n* **1** the trade, articles of trade, or shop of a saddler **2** a set of the equipment used for sitting on and controlling a riding horse

sadism /ˈseɪdɪzəm/ *n* a sexual perversion in which pleasure is obtained by inflicting physical or mental pain on others; broadly delight in inflicting pain – **sadist** *n* – **sadistic** *adj* – **sadistically** *adv*

sae /ˌes eɪ ˈiː/ *n* a stamped addressed envelope

[1]**safari** /səˈfɑːri/ *n* (the caravan and equipment of) a hunting or scientific expedition, esp in E Africa

[2]**safari** *adj* made of lightweight material, esp cotton, and typically having 2 breast pockets and a belt

safari park *n* a park stocked with usu big game animals (e g lions) so that visitors can observe them in natural-appearing surroundings

[1]**safe** /seɪf/ *adj* **1** freed from harm or risk **2** secure from threat of danger, harm, or loss **3** affording safety from danger **4a** not threatening or entailing danger **b** unlikely to cause controversy **5a** not liable to take risks **b** trustworthy, reliable – **~ly** *adv* – **~ness** *n*

[2]**safe** *n* **1** a room or receptacle for the safe storage of valuables **2** a receptacle, esp a cupboard, for the temporary storage of fresh and cooked foods that typically has at least 1 side of wire mesh to allow ventilation while preventing flies from entering

safe-conduct *n* (a document authorizing) protection given to a person passing through a military zone or occupied area

[1]**safeguard** /ˈseɪfgɑːd/ *n* a precautionary measure or stipulation

[2]**safeguard** *v* to make safe; protect

safekeeping /ˌseɪfˈkiːpɪŋ/ *n* keeping safe or being kept safe

safety /ˈseɪfti/ *n* the condition of being safe from causing or suffering hurt, injury, or loss

safety glass *n* glass strengthened by tempering so that when broken, it shatters into relatively safe rounded granules

safety match *n* a match capable of being ignited only on a specially prepared surface

safety pin *n* a pin in the form of a clasp with a guard covering its point when fastened

safety valve *n* **1** an automatic escape or relief valve (e g for a steam boiler) **2** an outlet for pent-up energy or emotion

saffron /ˈsæfrən/ *n* **1** (the deep orange aromatic pungent dried stigmas, used to colour and flavour foods, of) a purple-flowered crocus **2** an orange-yellow colour

[1]**sag** /sæg/ *v* **1** to droop, sink, or settle (as if) from weight, pressure, or loss of tautness **2** to lose firmness or vigour **3** to fail to stimulate or retain interest

[2]**sag** *n* **1** a sagging part **2** an instance or amount of sagging

saga /ˈsɑːgə/ *n* **1** a medieval Icelandic narrative dealing with historic or legendary figures and events **2** a long detailed account

sagacious /sə'geɪʃəs/ *adj* **1** of keen and farsighted judgment **2** prompted by or indicating acute discernment – **-city** *n* – **~ly** *adv*

[1]**sage** /seɪdʒ/ *adj* **1** wise on account of reflection and experience **2** proceeding from or indicating wisdom and sound judgment – **~ly** *adv*

[2]**sage** *n* **1** sby (e g a great philosopher) renowned for wise teachings **2** a venerable man of sound judgment

[3]**sage** *n* a plant of the mint family whose greyish green aromatic leaves are used esp in flavouring meat

Sagittarius /ˌsædʒɪ'teərɪəs/ *n* (sby born under) the 9th sign of the zodiac in astrology, pictured as a centaur shooting an arrow

sago /'seɪgəʊ/ *n, pl* **sagos** a dry powdered starch prepared from the pith of a palmtree and used esp as a food (e g in a milk pudding)

sahib /sɑːb, sɑːɪb/ *n* sir, master – used, esp among Hindus and Muslims in colonial India, when addressing or speaking of a European of some social or official status

said /sed/ *adj* aforementioned

[1]**sail** /seɪl/ *n* **1** an expanse of fabric which is spread to catch or deflect the wind as a means of propelling a ship, sand yacht, etc **2** a voyage by ship

[2]**sail** *v* **1** to travel in a boat or ship **2a** to travel on water, esp by the action of wind on sails **b** to move without visible effort or in a stately manner **3** to begin a journey by water

sailor /'seɪləʳ/ *n* **1a** a seaman, mariner **b** a member of a ship's crew other than an officer **2** a traveller by water; *esp* one considered with reference to any tendency to seasickness

saint /seɪnt/ *n* **1** a person officially recognized through canonization as being outstandingly holy and so worthy of veneration **2** any of the spirits of the departed in heaven **b** an angel **3** a person of outstanding piety or virtue – **~ly** *adj* – **~liness** *n*

saint's day *n* a day in a church calendar on which a saint is commemorated

[1]**sake** /seɪk/ *n* **1** the purpose *of* – in *for the sake of* **2** interest, benefit or advantage – in *for someone's/something's sake*

[2]**sake, saki** /'sɑːki/ *n* a Japanese alcoholic drink of fermented rice

salaam /sə'lɑːm/ *n* **1** a ceremonial greeting in E countries **2** an obeisance made by bowing low and placing the right palm on the forehead – **salaam** *v*

salacious /sə'leɪʃəs/ *adj* **1** arousing or appealing to sexual desire **2** lecherous, lustful – **~ly** *adv* – **~ness** *n*

salad /'sæləd/ *n* **1a** (mixed) raw vegetables (e g lettuce, watercress, or tomato) often served with a dressing **b** a dish of raw or (cold) cooked foods often cut into small pieces and combined with a dressing **2** a vegetable or herb eaten raw (in salad); *esp* lettuce

salad days *n pl* time of youthful inexperience or indiscretion

salamander /'sæləmændəʳ/ *n* **1** a mythical animal with the power to endure fire without harm **2** any of numerous scaleless amphibians superficially resembling lizards

salami /sə'lɑːmi/ *n* a highly seasoned, esp pork, sausage often containing garlic

salary /'sæləri/ *n* a fixed usu monthly payment for regular services, esp of a nonmanual kind

sale /seɪl/ *n* **1** the act or an instance of selling **2** quantity sold – often pl with sing. meaning **3** an event at which goods are offered for sale **4** public disposal to the highest bidder **5** a selling of goods at bargain prices **6a** *pl* operations and activities involved in promoting and selling goods or services **b** gross receipts obtained from selling

saleroom /'seɪlrʊm, -ruːm/ *n, chiefly Br* a place where goods are displayed for sale, esp by auction

sales /seɪlz/ *adj* of, engaged in, or used in selling

[1]**salient** /'seɪlɪənt/ *adj* **1** pointing upwards or outwards **2a** projecting beyond a line or level **b** standing out conspicuously

[2]**salient** *n* an outwardly projecting part of a fortification, trench system, or line of defence

saline /ˈseɪlaɪn/ *adj* (consisting) of, containing, or resembling (a) salt

saliva /səˈlaɪvə/ *n* a liquid secreted into the mouth by glands that lubricates ingested food and often begins the breakdown of starches – **-vary** *adj*

salivate /ˈsælɨveɪt/ *v* to have an (excessive) flow of saliva – **-vation** *n*

¹sallow /ˈsæləʊ/ *n* any of various Old World broad-leaved willows some of which are important sources of charcoal

²sallow *adj* of a sickly yellowish colour

¹sally *n* **1** a rushing forth; *esp* a sortie of troops from a besieged position **2** a witty or penetrating remark **3** a short excursion; a jaunt

²sally *v* **1** to rush out or issue forth suddenly **2** to set out (e g on a journey) – usu + *forth*

salmon /ˈsæmən/ *n* **1** (any of various fishes related to) a large soft-finned game and food fish of the N Atlantic that is highly valued for its pink flesh **2** an orangy-pink colour

salmonella /ˌsælməˈnelə/ *n* any of a genus of bacteria that cause food poisoning

salon /ˈsælɒn/ *n* **1** an elegant reception room or living room **2** a gathering of literary figures, statesmen, etc held at the home of a prominent person and common in the 17th and 18th c **3** *cap* an exhibition, esp in France, of works of art by living artists

saloon /səˈluːn/ *n* **1** a public apartment or hall (e g a ballroom, exhibition room, or shipboard social area) **2** *Br* an enclosed motor car having no partition between the driver and passengers **3** *NAm* a room or establishment in which alcoholic beverages are sold and consumed

saloon bar *n, Br* a comfortable, well-furnished, and often relatively expensive bar in a public house

salsify /ˈsælsɨfaɪ/ *n* a long tapering root-vegetable

¹salt /sɔːlt/ *n* **1a** sodium chloride, occurring naturally esp as a mineral deposit and dissolved in sea water, and used esp for seasoning or preserving **b** any of numerous compounds resulting from replacement of (part of) the hydrogen ion of an acid by a (radical acting like a) metal **c** *pl* **(1)** a mixture of the salts of alkali metals or magnesium (e g Epsom salts) used as a purgative **(2)** smelling salts **2a** an ingredient that imparts savour, piquancy, or zest **b** sharpness of wit **3** an experienced sailor

²salt *v* **1** to treat, provide, season, or preserve with common salt or brine **2** to give flavour or piquancy to (e g a story)

³salt *adj* **1a** saline, salty **b** being or inducing a taste similar to that of common salt that is one of the 4 basic taste sensations **2** cured or seasoned with salt; salted **3** containing, overflowed by, or growing in salt water **4** sharp, pungent – **~ness** *n*

salt away *v* to put by in reserve; save

saltcellar /ˈsɔːltˌseləʳ/ *n* a cruet for salt

saltpan /ˈsɔːltpæn, ˈsɒlt-/ *n* a depression (e g made in rock) or vessel for evaporating brine

saltpetre, *NAm* **saltpeter** /ˌsɔːltˈpiːtəʳ, ˌsɒlt-/ *n* potassium nitrate, esp as used in gunpowder and in curing meat

salty /ˈsɔːlti/ *adj* **1** of, seasoned with, or containing salt **2** having a taste of (too much) salt **3a** piquant, witty **b** earthy, coarse – **saltiness** *n*

salubrious /səˈluːbrɪəs/ *adj* **1** favourable to health or well-being **2** respectable – **~ness, -brity** *n*

salutary /ˈsæljʊtəri/ *adj* having a beneficial or edifying effect

salutation /ˌsæljʊˈteɪʃən/ *n* **1** an expression of greeting or courtesy by word or gesture **2** *pl* regards

¹salute /səˈluːt/ *v* **1** to address with expressions of greeting, goodwill, or respect **2a** to honour by a conventional military or naval ceremony **b** to show respect and recognition to (a military superior) by assuming a prescribed position

²salute *n* **1** a greeting, salutation **2a** a sign or ceremony expressing goodwill or respect **b** an act of saluting a military superior; *also* the position (e g of the hand or weapon) or the entire attitude of a person saluting a superior

[1]**salvage** /'sælvɪdʒ/ *n* **1a** compensation paid to those who save property from loss or damage; *esp* compensation paid for saving a ship from wreckage or capture **b** the act of saving or rescuing a ship or its cargo **c** the act of saving or rescuing property in danger (e g from fire) **2a** property saved from a calamity (e g a wreck or fire) **b** sthg of use or value extracted from waste material

[2]**salvage** *v* to rescue or save (e g from wreckage or ruin)

salvation /sæl'veɪʃən/ *n* **1** deliverance from the power and effects of sin **2** deliverance from danger, difficulty, or destruction

Salvation Army *n* an international Christian group organized on military lines and founded in 1865 by William Booth for evangelizing and performing social work among the poor – **salvationist** *n*

[1]**salve** /sɑːv, sælv/ *n* **1** an ointment for application to wounds or sores **2** a soothing influence or agency

[2]**salve** *v* to ease

salver /'sælvəʳ/ *n* a tray; *esp* an ornamental tray (e g of silver) on which food or beverages are served or letters and visiting cards are presented

salvo /'sælvəʊ/ *n* **1a** a simultaneous discharge of 2 or more guns or missiles in military or naval action or as a salute **b** the release at one moment of several bombs or missiles from an aircraft **2** a sudden or emphatic burst (e g of cheering or approbation)

Samaritan /sə'mærɨtn/ *n* **1** a native or inhabitant of ancient Samaria **2a** *often not cap* one who selflessly gives aid to those in distress **b** a member of an organization that offers help to those in despair

samba /'sæmbə/ *n* (the music for) a Brazilian dance of African origin characterized by a dip and spring upwards at each beat of the music

[1]**same** /seɪm/ *adj* **1** being 1 single thing, person, or group; identical – often as an intensive (e g born in this very *same* house) **2** being the specified one or ones – + *as* or *that* **3** corresponding so closely as to be indistinguishable

[2]**same** *pron, pl* **same** **1** *the* same thing, person, or group (e g do the *same* for you) **2** sthg previously mentioned (e g ordered a drink and refused to pay for *same*)

[3]**same** *adv* in the same manner – + *the*

sameness /'seɪmnɨs/ *n* **1** identity, similarity **2** monotony, uniformity

samovar /'sæməvɑːʳ/ *n* a metal urn with a tap at its base and an interior heating tube, that is used, esp in Russia, to boil water for tea

sampan /'sæmpæn/ *n* a small flat-bottomed boat used in rivers and harbours in the Far East

[1]**sample** /'sɑːmpəl/ *n* **1** an item serving to show the character or quality of a larger whole or group **2** a part of a statistical population whose properties are studied to gain information about the whole

[2]**sample** *v* to take a sample of or from; *esp* to test the quality of by a sample

[3]**sample** *adj* intended as an example

sampler /'sɑːmpləʳ/ *n* a decorative piece of needlework typically having letters or verses embroidered on it in various stitches as an example of skill

samurai /'sæmʊraɪ/ *n, pl* **samurai** **1** a military retainer of a Japanese feudal baron **2** the warrior aristocracy of Japan

sanatorium /,sænə'tɔːrɪəm/ *n* an establishment that provides therapy, rest, or recuperation for convalescents, the chronically ill, etc

sanctify /'sæŋktɨfaɪ/ *v* **1** to set apart for a sacred purpose or for religious use **2** to give moral or social sanction to – **-fication** *n*

sanctimonious /,sæŋktɨ'məʊnɪəs/ *adj* self-righteous – **~ly** *adv* – **~ness** *n*

[1]**sanction** /'sæŋkʃən/ *n* **1** a penalty annexed to an offence **2a** a consideration that determines moral action or judgment **b** a mechanism of social control (e g shame) for enforcing a society's standards **c** official permission or authoritative ratification **3** an economic or military coercive measure adopted to force a nation to conform to international law

[2]**sanction** *v* **1** to make valid; ratify **2** to give authoritative consent to

sanctity /'sæŋktəti/ *n* **1** holiness of life and character **2** the quality or state of being holy or sacred

sanctuary /'sæŋktʃʊəri/ *n* **1** a consecrated place: e g **a** the ancient temple at Jerusalem or its holy of holies **b** the part of a Christian church in which the altar is placed **2a** a place of refuge and protection **b** a refuge for (endangered) wildlife where predators are controlled and hunting is illegal

sanctum /'sæŋktəm/ *n* a place of total privacy and security (e g a study)

[1]**sand** /sænd/ *n* **1** loose granular particles smaller than gravel and coarser than silt that result from the disintegration of (silica-rich) rocks **2** an area of sand; a beach – usu pl with sing. meaning **3** moments of time measured (as if) with an hourglass – usu pl with sing. meaning **4** a yellowish grey colour

[2]**sand** *v* **1** to sprinkle (as if) with sand **2** to cover or choke with sand – usu + *up* **3** to smooth or dress by grinding or rubbing with an abrasive (e g sandpaper) – often + *down*

sandal /'sændl/ *n* a shoe consisting of a sole held on to the foot by straps or thongs

sandalwood /'sændlwʊd/ *n* (the compact close-grained fragrant yellowish heartwood, used in ornamental carving and cabinetwork, of) an Indo-Malayan tree

sandbag /'sændbæg/ *n* a bag filled with sand and used in usu temporary fortifications or constructions, as ballast, or as a weapon

sandbank /'sændbæŋk/ *n* a large deposit of sand, esp in a river or coastal waters

sandbar /'sændbɑːʳ/ *n* a sandbank

sandblast /'sændblɑːst/ *v or n* (to treat with) a high-speed jet of sand propelled by air or steam (e g for cutting or cleaning glass or stone)

sandcastle /'sænd,kɑːsəl/ *n* a model of a castle made in damp sand, esp at the seaside

[1]**sandpaper** /'sænd,peɪpəʳ/ *n* paper to which a thin layer of sand has been glued for use as an abrasive; *broadly* any abrasive paper (e g glasspaper)

[2]**sandpaper** *v* to rub (as if) with sandpaper

sandpiper /'sænd,paɪpəʳ/ *n* any of numerous small wading birds with longer bills than the plovers

sandpit /'sænd,pɪt/ *n* an enclosure containing sand for children to play in

sandstone /'sændstəʊn/ *n* a sedimentary rock consisting of cemented (quartz) sand

sandstorm /'sændstɔːm/ *n* a storm driving clouds of sand, esp in a desert

[1]**sandwich** /'sænwɪdʒ/ *n* **1a** two slices of usu buttered bread containing a layer of filling **b** a sponge cake containing a filling **2** sthg like a sandwich in having a layered or banded arrangement

[2]**sandwich** *v* **1** to insert *between* 2 things of a different quality or character **2** to create room or time for – often + *in* or *between*

[3]**sandwich** *adj* **1** of or used for sandwiches **2** *Br* of a sandwich course

sandwich board *n* either of 2 boards hung at the front of and behind the body by straps from the shoulders and used esp for advertising

sandwich course *n* a British vocational course consisting of alternate periods of some months' duration in college and in employment

sandy /'sændi/ *adj* **1** consisting of, containing, or sprinkled with sand **2** resembling sand in colour or texture – **sandiness** *n*

sane /seɪn/ *adj* mentally sound; able to anticipate and appraise the effect of one's actions – **~ly** *adv* – **-nity** *n*

sang /sæŋ/ *past of* **sing**

sangfroid /,sɒŋ'frwɑː/ *n* imperturbability, esp under strain

sanguine /'sæŋgwəɪn/ *adj* **1** confident, optimistic **2** ruddy – **-guinity** *n*

sanitary /'sænətəri/ *adj* **1** of or promoting health **2** free from danger to health

sanitary towel *n* a disposable absorbent pad worn after childbirth or during menstruation to absorb the flow from the womb

sanitation /ˌsænḭˈteɪʃən/ *n* (the promotion of hygiene and prevention of disease by) maintenance or improvement of sanitary conditions

sank /sæŋk/ *past of* **sink**

Sanskrit /ˈsænskrɪt/ *n* an ancient sacred Indic language of India and of Hinduism

Santa Claus /ˈsæntə klɔːz/ *n* Father Christmas

[1]**sap** /sæp/ *n* **1a** a watery solution that circulates through a plant's vascular system **b** (a fluid essential to life or) bodily health and vigour **2** a foolish gullible person – infml

[2]**sap** *n* the extension of a trench from within the trench itself to a point near an enemy's fortifications

[3]**sap** *v* **1** to destroy (as if) by undermining **2** to weaken or exhaust gradually **3** to operate against or pierce by a sap

sapling /ˈsæplɪŋ/ *n* **1** a young tree **2** a youth

sapper /ˈsæpəʳ/ *n* a (private) soldier of the Royal Engineers

sapphire /ˈsæfaɪəʳ/ *n* **1** a semitransparent corundum of a colour other than red, used as a gem; *esp* a transparent rich blue sapphire **2** a deep purplish blue colour

sapwood /ˈsæpwʊd/ *n* the younger softer usu lighter-coloured living outer part of wood that lies between the bark and the heartwood

sarcasm /ˈsɑːkæzəm/ *n* (the use of) caustic and often ironic language to express contempt or bitterness, esp towards an individual – **-castic** *adj* – **-castically** *adv*

sarcophagus /sɑːˈkɒfəgəs/ *n, pl* **sarcophagi** a stone coffin

sardine /sɑːˈdiːn/ *n* the young of the European pilchard, or another small or immature fish, when of a size suitable for preserving for food

sardonic /sɑːˈdɒnɪk/ *adj* disdainfully or cynically humorous; derisively mocking – **~ally** *adv*

sarge /sɑːdʒ/ *n* a sergeant – infml

sari *also* **saree** /ˈsɑːri/ *n* a garment worn by Hindu women that consists of a length of lightweight cloth draped so that one end forms a skirt and the other a head or shoulder covering

sarong /səˈrɒŋ/ *n* a loose skirt made of a long strip of cloth wrapped round the body and traditionally worn by men and women in Malaysia and the Pacific islands

sartorial /sɑːˈtɔːrɪəl/ *adj* with regard to clothing – fml; used esp with reference to men – **~ly** *adv*

[1]**sash** /sæʃ/ *n* a band of cloth worn round the waist or over 1 shoulder as a dress accessory or as the emblem of an honorary or military order

[2]**sash** *n, pl* **sash** *also* **sashes** the framework in which panes of glass are set in a window or door; *also* such a framework forming a sliding part of a window

sat /sæt/ *past of* **sit**

Satan /ˈseɪtn/ *n* the adversary of God and lord of evil in Judaism and Christianity

satanic /səˈtænɪk/ *adj* **1** (characteristic) of Satan or satanism **2** extremely cruel or malevolent – **~ally** *adv*

satanism /ˈseɪtənɪzəm/ *n, often cap* **1** diabolism **2** the worship of Satan marked by the travesty of Christian rites

satchel /ˈsætʃəl/ *n* a usu stiff bag often with a shoulder strap; *esp* one carried by schoolchildren

sate /seɪt/ *v* **1** to surfeit with sthg **2** to satisfy (e g a thirst) by indulging to the full

satellite /ˈsætḭlaɪt/ *n* **1** an obsequious follower **2a** a celestial body orbiting another of larger size **b** a man-made object or vehicle intended to orbit a celestial body **3** a country subject to another more powerful country **4** an urban community that is physically separate from an adjacent city but dependent on it

satiate /ˈseɪʃieɪt/ *v* to satisfy (e g a need or desire) to the point of excess – **-iety** *n* – **-iable** *adj* – **-iation** *n*

[1]**satin** /ˈsætḭn/ *n* a fabric (e g of silk) with lustrous face and dull back

[2]**satin** *adj* **1** made of satin **2** like satin, esp in lustrous appearance or smoothness

satinwood /ˈsætḭnwʊd/ *n* (the lustrous yellowish brown wood of) an E Indian tree of the mahogany family or any of various trees with similar wood

satire /ˈsætaɪəʳ/ *n* **1** a literary work

holding up human vices and follies to ridicule or scorn **2** biting wit, irony, or sarcasm intended to expose foolishness or vice – **-ric, -rical** *adj* – **-rize** *v*

satisfaction /ˌsætɟsˈfækʃən/ *n* **1a** fulfilment of a need or want **b** being satisfied **c** a source of pleasure or fulfilment **2a** compensation for a loss, insult, or injury **b** vindication of one's honour, esp through a duel **3** full assurance or certainty

satisfactory /ˌsætɟsˈfæktəri/ *adj* satisfying needs or requirements; adequate – **-rily** *adv*

satisfy /ˈsætɟsfaɪ/ *v* **1a** to discharge; carry out **2a** to make content **b** to meet the requirements of **3** to convince **4** to conform to (e g criteria) – **~ing** *adj*

satsuma /sætˈsuːmə/ *n* a sweet seedless type of mandarin orange

saturate /ˈsætʃəreɪt/ *v* **1** to treat or provide with sthg to the point where no more can be absorbed, dissolved, or retained **2** to cause to combine chemically until there is no further tendency to combine

saturation /ˌsætʃəˈreɪʃən/ *n* **1** the chromatic purity of a colour; freedom from dilution with white **2** the point at which a market is supplied with all the goods it will absorb **3** an overwhelming concentration of military forces or firepower

Saturday /ˈsætədi, -deɪ/ *n* the day of the week following Friday

Saturn /ˈsætən/ *n* the planet 6th in order from the sun and conspicuous for its rings

saturnine /ˈsætənaɪn/ *adj* **1** gloomy **2** sullen

satyr /ˈsætəʳ/ *n* a Greek minor woodland deity having certain characteristics of a horse or goat and associated with revelry

¹sauce /sɔːs/ *n* **1** a liquid or soft preparation used as a relish, dressing, or accompaniment to food **2** sthg adding zest or piquancy **3** cheek – infml

²sauce *v* to be impudent to – infml

saucepan /ˈsɔːspən/ *n* a deep usu cylindrical cooking pan typically having a long handle and a lid

saucer /ˈsɔːsəʳ/ *n* **1** a small usu circular shallow dish with a central depression in which a cup is set **2** a flying saucer

saucy /ˈsɔːsi/ *adj* **1a** disrespectfully bold and impudent **b** engagingly forward and flippant **2** smart, trim – **saucily** *adv* – **sauciness** *n*

sauerkraut /ˈsaʊəkraʊt/ *n* finely cut cabbage fermented in a brine made from its juice

sauna /ˈsɔːnə/ *n* a Finnish steam bath in which water is thrown on hot stones

saunter /ˈsɔːntəʳ/ *v* to walk about in a casual manner

saurian /ˈsɔːrɪən/ *n* any of a group of reptiles including the lizards and formerly the crocodiles and dinosaurs

sausage /ˈsɒsɪdʒ/ *n* (sthg shaped like) a fresh, precooked, or dried cylindrical mass of seasoned minced pork or other meat often mixed with a filler (e g bread) and enclosed in a casing usu of prepared animal intestine

sauté /ˈsəʊteɪ/ *v* to fry in a small amount of fat – **sauté** *adj*

¹savage /ˈsævɪdʒ/ *adj* **1** not domesticated or under human control; untamed **2** rugged, rough **3** boorish, rude **4** lacking a developed culture – now usu taken to be offensive – **~ly** *adv* – **~ness, ~ry** *n*

²savage *n* **1** a member of a primitive society **2** a brutal, rude, or unmannerly person

³savage *v* to attack or treat brutally; *esp* to maul

savant /ˈsævənt/ *n* one who has exceptional knowledge of a particular field (e g science or literature)

¹save /seɪv/ *v* **1** to rescue from danger or harm **2a** to put aside as a store or for a particular use – usu + *up* **b** to economize in the use of; conserve **3a** to make unnecessary **b** to prevent an opponent from scoring, winning, or scoring with – **~r** *n*

²save *prep* except – chiefly fml

³save *conj* were it not; only – chiefly fml

saveloy /ˈsævəlɔɪ/ *n* a precooked highly seasoned dry sausage

¹saving /ˈseɪvɪŋ/ *n* **1** preservation from danger or destruction **2** sthg saved **3a** *pl* money put by over a period of time **b** the excess of income over expenditures – often pl

[2]**saving** *prep* **1** except, save **2** without disrespect to

saviour, *NAm chiefly* **savior** /ˈseɪvɪəʳ/ *n* **1** one who brings salvation; *specif, cap* Jesus **2** one who saves sby or sthg from danger or destruction

savoir faire /ˌsævwɑː ˈfeəʳ/ *n* polished self-assurance in social behaviour

savory /ˈseɪvəri/ *n* any of several aromatic plants of the mint family used as herbs in cooking

[1]**savour,** *NAm chiefly* **savor** /ˈseɪvəʳ/ *n* **1** the characteristic taste or smell of sthg **2** a particular flavour or smell **3** a (pleasantly stimulating) distinctive quality

[2]**savour,** *NAm chiefly* **savor** *v* **1** to taste or smell with pleasure; relish **2** to delight in; enjoy

[1]**savoury,** *NAm chiefly* **savory** /ˈseɪvəri/ *adj* salty, spicy, meaty, etc, rather than sweet

[2]**savoury,** *NAm chiefly* **savory** *n* a dish of piquant or stimulating flavour served usu at the end of a main meal but sometimes as an appetizer

[1]**savvy** /ˈsævi/ *v* to know, understand – slang

[2]**savvy** *n* practical know-how; shrewd judgment – slang

[1]**saw** /sɔː/ *past of* **see**

[2]**saw** *n* a hand or power tool with a toothed part (e g a blade or disc) used to cut wood, metal, bone, etc

[3]**saw** *v* **sawed, sawn** **1** to cut or shape with a saw **2** to make motions as though using a saw

[4]**saw** *n* a maxim, proverb

sawdust /ˈsɔːdʌst/ *n* fine particles of wood produced in sawing

sawmill /ˈsɔːˌmɪl/ *n* a factory or machine that cuts wood

saxifrage /ˈsæksɨfrɪdʒ/ *n* any of a genus of usu showy-flowered plants often with tufted leaves, many of which are grown in rock gardens

Saxon /ˈsæksən/ *n* **1a** a member of a Germanic people that invaded England along with the Angles and Jutes in the 5th c AD and merged with them to form the Anglo-Saxon people **b** a native or inhabitant of Saxony **2** the Germanic language or dialect of any of the Saxon peoples

saxophone /ˈsæksəfəʊn/ *n* any of a group of single-reed woodwind instruments having a conical metal tube and finger keys and used esp in jazz and popular music – **-nist** *n*

[1]**say** /seɪ/ *v* **says; said** **1a** to state in spoken words **b** to form an opinion as to **2** to utter, pronounce **3a** to indicate, show **b** to give expression to; communicate **4a** to suppose, assume **b** to allege – usu pass

[2]**say** *n* **1** an expression of opinion – esp in *have one's say* **2** a right or power to influence action or decisions; *esp* the authority to make final decisions

[3]**say** *adv* **1** at a rough estimate **2** for example

saying /ˈseɪ-ɪŋ/ *n* a maxim, proverb

say-so *n* **1** one's unsupported assertion **2** the right of final decision

[1]**scab** /skæb/ *n* **1** scabies of domestic animals **2** a crust of hardened blood and serum over a wound **3** a blackleg **4** any of various plant diseases characterized by crusted spots; *also* any of these spots

[2]**scab** *v* to act as a scab

scabbard /ˈskæbəd/ *n* a sheath for a sword, dagger, or bayonet

scabies /ˈskeɪbiz/ *n, pl* **scabies** a skin disease, esp contagious itch or mange, caused by a parasitic mite and usu characterized by oozing scabs

scabious /ˈskeɪbɪəs/ *n* any of a genus of plants with flowers in dense heads at the end of usu long stalks

scabrous /ˈskeɪbrəs/ *adj* **1** rough to the touch with scales, scabs, raised patches, etc **2** dealing with indecent or offensive themes – fml

scaffold /ˈskæfəld, -fəʊld/ *n* a platform on which a criminal is executed

scaffolding /ˈskæfəldɪŋ/ *n* **1** a supporting framework **2** a temporary platform for workmen working above the ground

[1]**scalar** /ˈskeɪləʳ/ *adj* **1** having a continuous series of steps **2** capable of being represented by a point on a scale

[2]**scalar** *n* **1** a real number rather than a vector **2** a quantity (e g mass or

time) that has a magnitude describable by a real number, and no direction

[1]**scald** /skɔːld/ *v* **1** to burn (as if) with hot liquid or steam **2a** to subject to boiling water or steam **b** to heat to just short of boiling

[2]**scald** *n* an injury to the body caused by scalding

scalding /ˈskɔːldɪŋ/ *adj* **1** boiling hot **2** biting, scathing

[1]**scale** /skeɪl/ *n* **1a** either pan of a balance **b** a beam that is supported freely in the centre and has 2 pans of equal weight suspended from its ends **2** an instrument or machine for weighing *USE* (*1b, 2*) usu pl with sing. meaning

[2]**scale** *n* **1** (a small thin plate resembling) a small flattened rigid plate forming part of the external body covering of a fish, reptile, etc **2** a small thin dry flake shed from the skin **3** a thin coating, layer, or incrustation; *esp* a hard incrustation usu of calcium sulphate or carbonate that is deposited on the inside of a kettle, boiler, etc by the evaporation or constant passage of hard water **4** a usu thin, membranous, chaffy, or woody modified leaf

[3]**scale** *v* **1** to cover with scale **2** to shed or separate or come off in scales; flake

[4]**scale** *n* **1** a graduated series of musical notes ascending or descending in order of pitch according to a specified scheme of their intervals **2** sthg graduated, esp when used as a measure or rule: e g **a** a linear region divided by lines into a series of spaces and used to register or record sthg (e g the height of mercury in a barometer) **b** a graduated line on a map or chart indicating the length used to represent a larger unit of measure **c** an instrument having a scale for measuring or marking off distances or dimensions **3** a graduated system **4** a proportion between 2 sets of dimensions (e g between those of a drawing and its original) **5** a graded series of tests

[5]**scale** *v* **1** to climb up or reach (as if) by means of a ladder **2a** to change the scale of **b** to pattern, make, regulate, set, or estimate according to some rate or standard *USE* (*2*) often + *up* or *down*

scalene /ˈskeɪliːn/ *adj, of a triangle* having the 3 sides of unequal length

scallion /ˈskælɪən/ *n* **1** a leek **2** a spring onion **3** *chiefly NAm* a shallot

scallop /ˈskɒləp/ *n* **1** a shellfish having 2 wavy-edged halves **2** one of a row of small curves forming a patterned edge

scallywag /ˈskæliwæg/ *n* a trouble-making or dishonest person; a rascal

[1]**scalp** /skælp/ *n* **1** the skin of the human head, usu covered with hair in both sexes **2a** a part of the human scalp with attached hair cut or torn from an enemy as a trophy, esp formerly by N American Indian warriors **b** a trophy of victory

[2]**scalp** *v* **1** to remove the scalp of **2** *NAm* **a** to buy and sell to make small quick profits **b** to obtain speculatively and resell at greatly increased prices USE (*2*) infml

scalpel /ˈskælpəl/ *n* a small very sharp straight thin-bladed knife used esp in surgery

scaly /ˈskeɪli/ *adj* flaky – **scaliness** *n*

[1]**scamp** /skæmp/ *n* an impish or playful young person

[2]**scamp** *v* to perform in a hasty, careless, or haphazard manner

[1]**scamper** /ˈskæmpəʳ/ *v* to run about nimbly and playfully

[2]**scamper** *n* a playful scurry

scampi /ˈskæmpi/ *n, pl* **scampi** a (large) prawn (often prepared with a batter coating)

[1]**scan** /skæn/ *v* **1** to check or read hastily or casually **2a** to traverse (a region) with a controlled beam (e g radar) **b** to make a detailed examination of (e g the human body) using any of a variety of sensing devices (e g ones using ultrasonics, thermal radiation, X-rays, or radiation from radioactive materials) **3** *of verse* to conform to a metrical pattern

[2]**scan** *n* **1** a scanning **2** a radar or television trace

scandal /ˈskændl/ *n* **1** a circumstance or action that causes general offence or indignation or that disgraces those associated with it **2** malicious or defamatory gossip **3** indignation, chagrin, or bewilderment brought about by a flagrant violation of propriety or religious opinion – ~**ize** *v*

scandalous /ˈskændələs/ *adj* **1** libellous, defamatory **2** offensive to propriety – ~**ly** *adv*

Scandinavian /ˌskændɪˈneɪvɪən/ *n* (a language of) a native or inhabitant of Scandinavia **Scandinavian** *adj*

scanner /ˈskænəʳ/ *n* **1** a device that automatically monitors a system or process **2** a device for sensing recorded data **3** the rotating aerial of a radar set

scansion /ˈskænʃən/ *n* the way in which a piece of verse scans

[1]**scant** /skænt/ *adj* **1a** barely sufficient; inadequate **b** lacking in quantity **2** having a small or insufficient supply

[2]**scant** *v* to restrict or withhold the supply of

scanty /ˈskænti/ *adj* scant; *esp* deficient in coverage – **-tily** *adv* – **-tiness** *n*

scapegoat /ˈskeɪpgəʊt/ *n* sby or sthg made to bear the blame for others' faults

scapula /ˈskæpjʊlə/ *n, pl* **scapulae** a large flat triangular bone at the upper part of each side of the back forming most of each half of the shoulder girdle; the shoulder blade

[1]**scar** /skɑːʳ/ *n* a steep rocky place on a mountainside

[2]**scar** *n* **1** a mark left (e g on the skin) by the healing of injured tissue **2** a mark left on a stem after the fall of a leaf **3** a mark of damage or wear **4** a lasting moral or emotional injury

[3]**scar** *v* **1** to mark with or form a scar **2** to do lasting injury to

scarab /ˈskærəb/ *n* a representation of a beetle, usu made of stone or glazed earthenware, used in ancient Egypt esp as a talisman

scarce /skeəs/ *adj* **1** not plentiful or abundant **2** few in number; rare – ~**ness, scarcity** *n*

scarcely /ˈskeəsli/ *adv* **1a** by a narrow margin; only just **b** almost not **2** not without unpleasantness or discourtesy

[1]**scare** /skeəʳ/ *v* **1** to frighten suddenly **2** to drive off by frightening – ~**d** *adj*

[2]**scare** *n* **1** a sudden or unwarranted fright **2** a widespread state of alarm or panic

scarecrow /ˈskeəkrəʊ/ *n* **1** an object usu suggesting a human figure, set up to frighten birds away from crops **2** a skinny or ragged person – infml

[1]**scarf** /skɑːf/ *n, pl* **scarves** a strip or square of cloth worn round the shoulders or neck or over the head for decoration or warmth

[2]**scarf** *n, pl* **scarfs** **1** either of the chamfered or cut away ends that fit together to form a scarf joint **2** **scarf, scarf joint** a joint made by chamfering, halving, or notching 2 pieces to correspond and lapping and bolting them

[3]**scarf, scarph** *v* **1** to unite by a scarf joint **2** to form a scarf on

scarify /ˈskærɪ̣faɪ, ˈskeə-/ *v* **1** to make scratches or small cuts in (e g the skin) **2** to wound the feelings of (e g by harsh criticism) **3** to break up and loosen the surface of (e g a field or road)

scarlet /ˈskɑːlɪ̣t/ *adj or n* (of) a vivid red colour tinged with orange

scarlet fever *n* an infectious fever caused by a bacterium in which there is a red rash and inflammation of the nose, throat, and mouth

scarlet woman *n* a prostitute – euph

scarp /skɑːp/ *n* **1** the inner side of a ditch below the parapet of a fortification **2** a steep slope, esp a cliff face, produced by faulting or erosion

scarper /ˈskɑːpəʳ/ *v, Br* to run away (e g from creditors) – infml

[1]**scat** /skæt/ *v* to depart rapidly – infml

[2]**scat** *n* jazz singing with nonsense syllables

scathing /ˈskeɪðɪŋ/ *adj* bitterly severe – ~**ly** *adv*

scatter /ˈskætəʳ/ *v* **1** to cause (a group or collection) to separate widely **2a** to distribute at irregular intervals **b** to distribute recklessly and at random **3** to sow (seed) by casting in all directions **4** to reflect or disperse (e g a beam of radiation or particles) irregularly and diffusely – **scatter** *n*

scatterbrain /ˈskætəbreɪn/ *n* sby incapable of concentration – ~**ed** *adj*

scatty /'skæti/ *adj, Br* scatterbrained – infml – **-tiness** *n*

scavenge /'skævǐndʒ/ **1** to salvage from discarded or refuse material; *also* to salvage usable material from **2** to feed on (carrion or refuse) – **~r** *n*

scenario /sǐ'nɑːriəʊ/ *n* **1** an outline or synopsis of a dramatic work **2a** a screenplay **b** a shooting script **3** an account or synopsis of a projected course of action

scene /siːn/ *n* **1** any of the smaller subdivisions of a dramatic work: e g **a** a division of an act presenting continuous action in 1 place **b** an episode, sequence, or unit of dialogue in a play, film, or television programme **2** a vista suggesting a stage setting **3** the place of an occurrence or action **4** an exhibition of unrestrained feeling **5** a sphere of activity or interest – slang

scenery /'siːnəri/ *n* **1** the painted scenes or hangings and accessories used on a theatre stage **2** landscape, esp when considered attractive

scenic /'siːnɪk/ *also* **scenical** *adj* **1** of the stage, a stage setting, or stage representation **2** of or displaying (fine) natural scenery – **~ally** *adv*

¹scent /sent/ *v* **1** to get or have an inkling of **2** to fill with a usu pleasant smell

²scent *n* **1** odour: e g **a** a smell left by an animal on a surface it passes over **b** a characteristic or particular, esp agreeable, smell **c** a perfume **2a** power of smelling; the sense of smell **b** power of detection; a nose **3** a course of pursuit or discovery **4** a hint, suggestion – **~less** *adj*

sceptic /'skeptɪk/ *n* a person disposed to scepticism, esp regarding religion or religious principles

sceptical /'skeptɪkəl/ *adj* relating to, characteristic of, or marked by scepticism – **~ly** *adv*

scepticism /'skeptǐsɪzəm/ *n* **1** doubt concerning basic religious principles (e g immortality, providence, or revelation) **2** the doctrine that certain knowledge is unattainable either generally or in a particular sphere **3** an attitude of doubt, esp associated with implied criticism

sceptre, *NAm chiefly* **scepter** /'septəʳ/ *n* **1** a staff borne by a ruler as an emblem of sovereignty **2** royal or imperial authority

¹schedule /'ʃedjuːl/ *n* **1** a statement of supplementary details appended to a document **2** a list, catalogue, or inventory **3** (the times fixed in) a timetable **4** a programme, proposal **5** a body of items to be dealt with

²schedule *v* **1a** to place on a schedule **b** to make a schedule of **2** to appoint or designate for a fixed time **3** *Br* to place on a list of buildings or historical remains protected by state legislation

schema /'skiːmə/ *n, pl* **schemata** a diagrammatic representation; a plan

schematic /skɪ'mætɪk, skiː-/ *adj* of a scheme or schema; diagrammatic – **~ally** *adv*

schemat·ize, -ise /'skiːmətaɪz/ *v* **1** to form into a systematic arrangement **2** to express or depict schematically

¹scheme /skiːm/ *n* **1** a concise statement or table **2** a plan or programme of action; a project **3** a crafty or secret strategy **4** a systematic arrangement of parts or elements

²scheme *v* to make plans; *also* to plot, intrigue – **schemer** *n*

scherzo /'skeətsəʊ/ *n, pl* **scherzos, scherzi** a lively instrumental musical composition or movement in quick usu triple time

schism /'sɪzəm, 'skɪzəm/ *n* **1** separation into opposed factions **2** formal division in or separation from a religious body

¹schismatic /sɪz'mætɪk, skɪz-/ *n* a person who creates or takes part in schism

²schismatic *also* **schismatical** *adj* **1** (having the character) of schism **2** guilty of schism

schist /ʃɪst/ *n* a metamorphic crystalline rock composed of thin layers of minerals and splitting along approx parallel planes

schizoid /'skɪtsɔɪd/ *adj* characterized by, resulting from, tending towards, or suggestive of schizophrenia

schizophrenia /ˌskɪtsəʊ'friːnɪə, -sə-/ *n* a mental disorder characterized by loss of contact with reality and disintegration of personality, usu with hallucinations and disorder of feeling, behaviour, etc – **-nic** *n, adj* – **-nically** *adv*

schnapps /ʃnæps/ *n* strong gin as orig made in the Netherlands

schnitzel /'ʃnɪtsəl/ *n* a veal escalope

scholar /'skɒləʳ/ *n* **1** one who attends a school or studies under a teacher **2** one who has done advanced study **3** the holder of a scholarship

scholarly /'skɒləli/ *adj* learned, academic

scholarship /'skɒləʃɪp/ *n* **1** a grant of money to a student **2** the character, methods, or attainments of a scholar; learning **3** a fund of knowledge and learning

scholastic /skə'læstɪk/ *adj* **1** suggestive or characteristic of a scholar or pedant, esp in specious subtlety or dryness **2** of schools or scholars

[1]**school** /skuːl/ *n* **1a** an institution for the teaching of children **b** a part of a university **c** an establishment offering specialized instruction **d** *NAm* a college, university **2a** a session of a school **b** a school building **3a** people with a common doctrine or teacher (e g in philosophy or theology) **b** a group of artists under a common stylistic influence **4** a body of people with similar opinions

[2]**school** *v* **1** to educate in an institution of learning **2a** to teach or drill in a specific knowledge or skill **b** to discipline or habituate to sthg

[3]**school** *n* a large number of fish or aquatic animals of 1 kind swimming together

[4]**school** *v* to swim or feed in a school

schoolboy /'skuːlbɔɪ/, *fem* **schoolgirl** *n* a child still at school

schoolhouse /'skuːlhaʊs/ *n* a building used as a school; *esp* a country primary school

schooling /'skuːlɪŋ/ *n* **1a** instruction in school **b** training or guidance from practical experience **2** the cost of instruction and maintenance at school **3** the training of a horse to service

schoolmarm, schoolma'am /'skuːlmɑːm/ *n* **1** a prim censorious woman **2** *chiefly NAm* a female schoolteacher; *esp* a rural or small-town schoolmistress

schoolmaster /'skuːl,mɑːstəʳ/, *fem* **schoolmistress** *n* a schoolteacher

schoolwork /'skuːlwɜːk/ *n* lessons

schooner /'skuːnəʳ/ *n* **1** a fore-and-aft rigged sailing vessel having 2 or more masts **2** a relatively tall narrow glass used esp for a large measure of sherry or port

sciatic /saɪ'ætɪk/ *adj* **1** of or situated near the hip **2** of or caused by sciatica

sciatica /saɪ'ætɪkə/ *n* pain in the back of the thigh, buttocks, and lower back

science /'saɪəns/ *n* **1a** a department of systematized knowledge **b** sthg (e g a skill) that may be learned systematically **c** any of the natural sciences **2a** coordinated knowledge of the operation of general laws, esp as obtained and tested through scientific method **b** such knowledge of the physical world and its phenomena; natural science **3** a system or method (purporting to be) based on scientific principles – **scientist** *n*

science fiction *n* fiction of a type orig set in the future and dealing principally with the impact of science on society or individuals, but now including also works of literary fantasy

scientific /,saɪən'tɪfɪk/ *adj* of or exhibiting the methods of science – **~ally** *adv*

scimitar /'sɪmɪ̈təʳ/ *n* a chiefly Middle Eastern sword having a curved blade which narrows towards the hilt and is sharpened on the convex side

scintillate /'sɪntɪ̈leɪt/ *v* **1** to emit sparks **2** to emit flashes as if throwing off sparks; *also* to sparkle, twinkle **3** to be brilliant or animated – **-lation** *n*

scion /'saɪən/ *n* **1** a detached living part of a plant joined to a stock in grafting and usu supplying parts above ground of the resulting graft **2** a (male) descendant or offspring

scissors /'sɪzəz/ *n pl* a cutting instrument with 2 blades pivoted so that their cutting edges slide past each other

sclerosis /sklɪ̈'rəʊsɪ̈s/ *n* (a disease characterized by) abnormal hardening of tissue, esp from overgrowth of fibrous tissue

[1]**scoff** /skɒf/ *n* an expression of scorn, derision, or contempt – **~er** *n*

[2]**scoff** *v* to show contempt by derisive acts or language – often + *at*

[3]**scoff** *v, chiefly Br* to eat, esp greedily, rapidly, or in an ill-mannered way – infml

[1]**scold** /skəʊld/ *n* a woman who habitually nags or quarrels

[2]**scold** *v* **1** to find fault noisily and at length **2** to reprove sharply – **~ing** *n*

scollop /ˈskɒləp/ *n* a scallop

scone /skɒn, skəʊn/ *n* any of several small light cakes made from a dough or batter containing a raising agent and baked in a hot oven or on a griddle

[1]**scoop** /skuːp/ *n* **1a** a large ladle for taking up or skimming liquids **b** a deep shovel for lifting and moving granular material (e g corn or sand) **c** a handled utensil of shovel shape or with a hemispherical bowl for spooning out soft food (e g ice cream) **2a** an act or the action of scooping **b** the amount held by a scoop **3** a cavity **4** material for publication or broadcast, esp when obtained ahead or to the exclusion of competitors

[2]**scoop** *v* **1** to take out or up (as if) with a scoop **2** to empty by scooping **3** to make hollow; dig out **4** to obtain a news story in advance or to the exclusion of (a competitor)

scoot /skuːt/ *v* to go suddenly and swiftly – infml

scooter /ˈskuːtəʳ/ *n* **1** a child's foot-operated vehicle consisting of a narrow board with usu 1 wheel at each end and an upright steering handle **2** a motor scooter

[1]**scope** /skəʊp/ *n* **1** space or opportunity for unhampered action, thought, or development **2a** extent of treatment, activity, or influence **b** extent of understanding or perception

[2]**scope** *n* a periscope, telescope, or other optical instrument – infml

[1]**scorch** /skɔːtʃ/ *v* **1** to burn so as to produce a change in colour and texture **2a** to parch (as if) with intense heat **b** to criticize or deride bitterly **3** to devastate completely, esp before abandoning – used in *scorched earth,* of property of possible use to an enemy **4** to travel at (excessive) speed

[2]**scorch** *n* a mark resulting from scorching

scorcher /ˈskɔːtʃəʳ/ *n* a very hot day – infml

[1]**score** /skɔːʳ/ *n* **1a** twenty **b** a group of 20 things – used in combination with a cardinal number **c** *pl* an indefinite large number **2** a line (e g a scratch or incision) made (as if) with a sharp instrument **3** an account of debts **4** a grudge **5a** a reason, ground **b** a subject, topic **6a** the copy of a musical composition in written or printed notation **b** the music for a film or theatrical production **7a** a number that expresses accomplishment (e g in a game or test) **b** an act (e g a goal, run, or try) in any of various games or contests that increases such a number **8** the inescapable facts of a situation

[2]**score** *v* **1a** to enter (a debt) in an account – usu + *to* or *against* **b** to cancel or strike out (e g record of a debt) with a line or notch – often + *out* **2** to mark with grooves, scratches, or notches **3a(1)** to gain (e g points) in a game or contest **(2)** to have as a value in a game or contest **b** to gain, win **c** to gain or have an advantage or a success **d** to obtain illicit drugs – slang **e** to achieve a sexual success – slang **4** to write or arrange (music) for specific voice or instrumental parts

scoreboard /ˈskɔːbɔːd/ *n* a usu large board for displaying the state of play (e g the score) in a game or match

[1]**scorn** /skɔːn/ *n* **1** vigorous contempt; disdain **2** an object of extreme disdain or derision – **~ful** *adj* – **~fully** *adv*

[2]**scorn** *v* to reject with outspoken contempt

Scorpio /ˈskɔːpiəʊ/ *n* (sby born under) the 8th sign of the zodiac in astrology, which is pictured as a scorpion

scorpion /ˈskɔːpɪən/ *n* any of an order of arachnids having an elongated body and a narrow tail bearing a venomous sting at the tip

scotch /skɒtʃ/ *v* **1** to stamp out; crush **2** to hinder, thwart

[1]**Scotch** *adj* Scottish

[2]**Scotch** *n* **1** *pl in constr the* Scots **2** *often not cap* scotch whisky

Scotch broth *n* soup made from beef or mutton, vegetables, and barley

Scotch egg *n* a hard-boiled egg covered with sausage meat, coated with breadcrumbs, and deep-fried

scot-free *adj* without any penalty, payment, or injury

Scotland Yard /ˌskɒtlənd ˈjɑːd/ *n sing or pl in constr* the criminal investigation department of the London metropolitan police force

Scottish /ˈskɒtɪʃ/ *adj* (characteristic) of Scotland

Scottish terrier *n* (any of) a Scottish breed of terrier with short legs and a very wiry coat of usu black hair

scoundrel /ˈskaʊndrəl/ *n* a wicked or dishonest fellow

[1]**scour** /skaʊəʳ/ *v* **1** to move through or range over usu swiftly **2** to make a rapid but thorough search of

[2]**scour** *v* **1** to rub vigorously in order to cleanse **2** to clear, excavate, or remove (as if) by a powerful current of water

[3]**scour** *n* diarrhoea or dysentery, esp in cattle – usu pl with sing. meaning but sing. or pl in constr

[1]**scourge** /skɜːdʒ/ *n* **1** a means of vengeance or criticism **2** a cause of affliction

[2]**scourge** *v* **1** to punish severely **2** to subject to affliction; devastate

[1]**scout** /skaʊt/ *v* **1** to observe or explore in order to obtain information **2** to find by making a search – often + *out* or *up*

[2]**scout** *n* **1** sby or sthg sent to obtain (military) information **2** *often cap* a member of a worldwide movement of boys and young men that was founded with the aim of developing leadership and comradeship and that lays stress on outdoor activities

scoutmaster /ˈskaʊtˌmɑːstəʳ/ *n* the adult leader of a troop of scouts – no longer used technically

[1]**scowl** /skaʊl/ *v* **1** to frown or wrinkle the brows in expression of displeasure **2** to exhibit a gloomy or threatening aspect

[2]**scowl** *n* an angry frown

[1]**scrabble** /ˈskræbəl/ *v* **1** to scratch or scrape about **2a** to scramble, clamber **b** to struggle frantically *USE* infml

[2]**scrabble** *n* **1** a persistent scratching or clawing **2** a scramble *USE* infml

Scrabble *trademark* – used for a board game of word-building from individual letters

[1]**scrag** /skræg/ *n* **1** a scraggy person or animal **2** a neck of mutton or veal

[2]**scrag** *v* **1** to kill or execute by hanging, garrotting, or wringing the neck of **2** to attack in anger – infml

scraggy /ˈskrægi/ *adj* lean and lanky in growth or build

scram /skræm/ *v* to go away at once – infml

[1]**scramble** /ˈskræmbəl/ *v* **1a** to move or climb using hands and feet, esp hastily **b** to move with urgency or panic **2** to struggle eagerly or chaotically for possession of sthg **3a** to toss or mix together **b** to prepare (eggs) in a pan by stirring during cooking **4** *esp of an aircraft or its crew* to take off quickly in response to an alert **5** to collect by scrambling – + *up* or *together* **6** to encode (the elements of a telecommunications transmission) in order to make unintelligible on unmodified receivers

[2]**scramble** *n* **1** a scrambling movement or struggle **2** a disordered mess; a jumble **3** a rapid emergency takeoff of aircraft **4** a motorcycle race over very rough ground

[1]**scrap** /skræp/ *n* **1** *pl* fragments of leftover food **2a** a small detached fragment **b** the smallest piece **3a** the residue from a manufacturing process **b** manufactured articles or parts, esp of metal, rejected or discarded and useful only for reprocessing

[2]**scrap** *v* **1** to convert into scrap **2** to abandon or get rid of, as without further use

[3]**scrap** *v or n* (to engage in) a minor fight or dispute – infml

scrapbook /ˈskræpbʊk/ *n* a blank book in which miscellaneous items (e g newspaper cuttings or postcards) may be pasted

[1]**scrape** /skreɪp/ *v* **1a** to remove (clinging matter) from a surface by usu repeated strokes of an edged instrument **b** to make (a surface) smooth or clean with strokes of an edged or rough instrument **2** to grate harshly over or against **3** to collect or

procure (as if) by scraping – often + *up* or *together* **4** to get by with difficulty or succeed by a narrow margin – often + *in, through*, or *by*

[2]**scrape** *n* **1a** an act, process, or result of scraping **b** the sound of scraping **2** a disagreeable predicament, esp as a result of foolish behaviour – infml

scrappy /ˈskræpi/ *adj* consisting of scraps

[1]**scratch** /skrætʃ/ *v* **1** to use the claws or nails in digging, tearing, or wounding **2** to scrape or rub oneself (e g to relieve itching) **3** to acquire money by hard work and saving **4** to make a thin grating sound **5** to withdraw (an entry) from competition

[2]**scratch** *n* **1** a mark, injury, or slight wound (produced by scratching) **2** the sound of scratching **3** the most rudimentary beginning – in *from scratch* **4** standard or satisfactory condition or performance

[3]**scratch** *adj* **1** arranged or put together haphazardly or hastily **2** without handicap or allowance

scratchy /ˈskrætʃi/ *adj* **1** tending to scratch or irritate **2** making a scratching noise **3** uneven in quality **4** irritable, fractious – **scratchiness** *n*

scrawl /skrɔːl/ *v* to write or draw awkwardly, hastily, or carelessly – **scrawl** *n*

scrawny /ˈskrɔːni/ *adj* exceptionally thin and slight

[1]**scream** /skriːm/ *v* **1a** to voice a sudden piercing cry, esp in alarm or pain **b** to move with or make a shrill noise like a scream **2** to produce a vivid or startling effect

[2]**scream** *n* **1** a shrill penetrating cry or noise **2** sby or sthg that provokes screams of laughter – infml

screamingly /ˈskriːmɪŋli/ *adv* extremely

scree /skriː/ *n* (a mountain slope covered with) loose stones or rocky debris

[1]**screech** /skriːtʃ/ *v* **1** to utter a shrill piercing cry; cry out, esp in terror or pain **2** to make a sound like a screech

[2]**screech** *n* a shrill sound or cry

screed /skriːd/ *n* **1** an overlong usu dull piece of writing **2** a strip (e g of plaster) serving as a guide to the thickness of a subsequent coat

[1]**screen** /skriːn/ *n* **1** a usu movable piece of furniture that gives protection from heat or draughts or is used as an ornament **2a** sthg that shelters, protects, or conceals **b** a shield for secret usu illicit practices **3** a frame holding a netting used esp in a window or door to exclude mosquitoes and other pests **4a** a surface on which images are projected or reflected **b** the surface on which the image appears in a television or radar receiver **5a** *the* film industry; films

[2]**screen** *v* **1** to guard from injury, danger, or punishment **2** to examine systematically so as to separate into different groups **3** to show or broadcast a film or television programme

screenplay /ˈskriːnpleɪ/ *n* the script of a film including description of characters, details of scenes and settings, dialogue, and stage directions

[1]**screw** /skruː/ *n* **1a** a usu pointed tapering metal rod having a raised thread along all or part of its length and a usu slotted head which may be driven into a body by rotating (e g with a screwdriver) **b** a screw-bolt that can be turned by a screwdriver **2** sthg like a screw in form or function; a spiral **3** a propeller **4** *chiefly Br* a small twisted paper packet (e g of tobacco) **5** sby who drives a hard bargain – slang **6** a prison guard – slang **7** an act of sexual intercourse – vulg

[2]**screw** *v* **1a** to attach, close, operate, adjust, etc by means of a screw **b** to unite or separate by means of a screw or a twisting motion **2a** to contort (the face) or narrow (the eyes) (e g with effort or an emotion) – often + *up* **b** to crush into irregular folds – usu + *up* **3** to increase the intensity, quantity, or effectiveness of – usu + *up* **4a** to make oppressive demands on **b** to extract by pressure or threat – usu + *from* or *out of* **5** to copulate with – vulg

screwdriver /ˈskruːˌdraɪvəʳ/ *n* a tool for turning screws

screw top *n* (an opening designed to take) a cover secured by twisting

screw up *v* **1** to bungle, botch **2** to

cause to become anxious or neurotic *USE* slang

screwy /ˈskruːi/ *adj* crazily absurd, eccentric, or unusual; *also* mad – infml

scribble /ˈskrɪbəl/ *v* to write or draw without regard for legibility or coherence – **scribble** *n*

scribbler /ˈskrɪbləʳ/ *n* a minor or worthless author

[1]scribe /skraɪb/ *n* **1** a member of a learned class of lay jurists in ancient Israel up to New Testament times **2** a copier of manuscripts **3** an author; *specif* a journalist – chiefly humor

[2]scribe *v* **1** to mark a line on by scoring with a pointed instrument **2** to make (e g a line) by scratching or gouging

scrimmage /ˈskrɪmɪdʒ/ *v or n* (to take part in) a confused fight or minor battle; a mêlée

scrimp /skrɪmp/ *v* to be frugal or niggardly – esp in *scrimp and save*

[1]script /skrɪpt/ *n* **1a** sthg written; text **b** an original document **c** the written text of a stage play, film, or broadcast (used in production or performance) **2a** (printed lettering resembling) handwriting **b** the characters used in the alphabet of a particular language

[2]script *v* to prepare a script for or from

scripture /ˈskrɪptʃəʳ/ *n* **1a** *often cap* the sacred writings of a religion; *esp* the Bible – often pl with sing. meaning **b** a passage from the Bible **2** an authoritative body of writings – **-ral** *adj*

scroll /skrəʊl/ *n* **1** a written document in the form of a roll **2** a stylized ornamental design imitating the spiral curves of a scroll

scrooge /skruːdʒ/ *n, often cap* a miserly person – infml

scrotum /ˈskrəʊtəm/ *n, pl* **scrota** the external pouch of most male mammals that contains the testes

[1]scrounge /skraʊndʒ/ *v* **1** to hunt *around* **2** to wheedle, beg

[1]scrub /skrʌb/ *n* (an area covered with) vegetation consisting chiefly of stunted trees or shrubs

[2]scrub *v* **1** to clean by rubbing, esp with a stiff brush **2** to abolish; do away with; *also* to cancel – infml

scrubber /ˈskrʌbəʳ/ *n* **1** *Br* a girl who is readily available for casual sex; *also* a prostitute **2** *Br* a coarse or unattractive person *USE* slang

scrubby /ˈskrʌbi/ *adj* **1** inferior in size or quality; stunted **2** lacking distinction; trashy – infml

[1]scruff /skrʌf/ *n* the back of the neck; the nape

[2]scruff *n* an untidily dressed or grubby person – infml

scruffy /ˈskrʌfi/ *adj* **1** seedy, disreputable **2** slovenly and untidy, esp in appearance

scrum /skrʌm/ *n* **1** a set piece in rugby in which the forwards of each side crouch in a tight formation with the 2 front rows of each team meeting shoulder to shoulder so that the ball can be put in play between them **2** a disorderly struggle

scrum-half *n* the player in rugby who puts the ball into the scrum

scrummage /ˈskrʌmɪdʒ/ *v or n* (to take part in) a scrum

scrumptious /ˈskrʌmpʃəs/ *adj, esp of food* delicious – infml

scrumpy /ˈskrʌmpi/ *n, Br* dry rough cider

scrunch /skrʌntʃ/ *v* **1** to crunch, crush **2** to crumple – often + *up* – **scrunch** *n*

[1]scruple /ˈskruːpəl/ *n* a unit of weight equal to 20 grains, ⅓ drachm, or 1/24 ounce, usu used by apothecaries

[2]scruple *n* a moral consideration that inhibits action

[3]scruple *v* to be reluctant on grounds of conscience

scrupulous /ˈskruːpjʊləs/ *adj* **1** inclined to have moral scruples **2** painstakingly exact – **~ly** *adv* – **~ness** *n*

scrutineer /ˌskruːtɪ̬ˈnɪəʳ/ *n, Br* sby who examines or observes sthg, esp the counting of votes at an election

scrutiny /ˈskruːtɪ̬ni/ *n* **1** a searching study, inquiry, or inspection **2** a searching or critical look **3** close watch – **-nize** *v*

scuba /ˈskuːbə, ˈskjuːbə/ *n* an aqualung

[1]scud /skʌd/ *v* **1** to move or run swiftly, esp as if swept along **2** *of a ship* to run before a gale

[2]scud *n* **1** ocean spray or loose vaporizing clouds driven swiftly by the wind **2** a gust of wind

scuff /skʌf/ *v* **1** to slouch along without lifting the feet **2** to become scratched or roughened by wear – **scuff** *n*

[1]**scuffle** /ˈskʌfəl/ *v* **1** to struggle confusedly and at close quarters **2** to move (hurriedly) about with a shuffling gait

[2]**scuffle** *n* a confused impromptu usu brief fight

[1]**scull** /skʌl/ *n* **1** an oar worked to and fro over the stern of a boat as a means of propulsion **2** either of a pair of light oars used by a single rower

[2]**scull** *v* to propel a boat by sculls or by a large oar worked to and fro over the stern – **~er** *n*

scullery /ˈskʌləri/ *n* a room for menial kitchen work (e g washing dishes and preparing vegetables)

scullion /ˈskʌliən/ *n, archaic* a kitchen servant

sculptor /ˈskʌlptəʳ/, *fem* **sculptress** *n* an artist who sculptures

[1]**sculpture** /ˈskʌlptʃəʳ/ *n* **1** the art of creating three-dimensional works of art out of mouldable or hard materials by carving, modelling, casting, etc **2** (a piece of) work produced by sculpture – **-ral** *adj*

[2]**sculpture** *v* **1a** to represent in sculpture **b** to form (e g wood or stone) into a sculpture **2** to shape (as if) by carving or moulding

scum /skʌm/ *n* **1** pollutants or impurities risen to or collected on the surface of a liquid **2** *pl in constr* the lowest class; the dregs

[1]**scupper** /ˈskʌpəʳ/ *n* an opening in a ship's side for draining water from the deck

[2]**scupper** *v, Br* to wreck; put paid to – infml

scurf /skɜːf/ *n* dandruff – **~y** *adj*

scurrilous /ˈskʌrᵻləs/ *adj* **1** wicked and unscrupulous in behaviour **2** containing obscenities or coarse abuse – **~ly** *adv* – **~ness, -ility** *n*

scurry /ˈskʌri/ *v* to move briskly, esp with short hurried steps, and often in some agitation or confusion; scamper

[1]**scurvy** /ˈskɜːvi/ *adj* disgustingly mean or contemptible – **scurvily** *adv*

[2]**scurvy** *n* a disease caused by lack of vitamin C and marked by loosening of the teeth, and bleeding under the skin

scut /skʌt/ *n* a short erect tail (e g of a hare)

[1]**scuttle** /ˈskʌtl/ *n* a vessel that resembles a bucket and is used for storing and carrying coal

[2]**scuttle** *v* **1** to sink (a ship) by making holes in the hull or opening the sea-cocks **2** to destroy, wreck

[3]**scuttle** *v* to scurry, scamper

[4]**scuttle** *n* **1** a quick shuffling pace **2** a short swift dash; *esp* a swift departure

scythe /saɪð/ *n* a long curving blade fastened at an angle to a long handle for cutting standing plants, esp grass – **scythe** *v*

sea /siː/ *n* **1** an ocean; *broadly* the waters of the earth as distinguished from the land and air **2** sthg vast or overwhelming likened to the sea **3** the seafaring life **4** any of several dark areas on the surface of the moon or Mars

sea anemone *n* any of numerous brightly coloured polyps with a cluster of tentacles superficially resembling a flower

seaboard /ˈsiːbɔːd/ *n* (the land near) a seashore

seaborne /ˈsiːbɔːn/ *adj* conveyed on or over the sea

sea change *n* a complete transformation

seafaring /ˈsiːˌfeərɪŋ/ *n* travel by sea; *esp* the occupation of a sailor

seafood /ˈsiːfuːd/ *n* edible marine fish, shellfish, crustaceans, etc

seafront /ˈsiːfrʌnt/ *n* the waterfront of a seaside town

seagirt /ˈsiːgɜːt/ *adj* surrounded by the sea – poetic

sea gull *n* any of various sea birds

sea horse *n* any of numerous small fishes whose head and body are shaped like the head and neck of a horse

[1]**seal** /siːl/ *n* **1** any of numerous marine flesh-eating mammals chiefly of cold regions with limbs modified

into webbed flippers for swimming **2** sealskin

[2]**seal** *n* **1a** an emblem or word impressed or stamped on a document as a mark of authenticity **b** an article used to impress such a word or emblem (e g on wax); *also* a disc, esp of wax, bearing such an impression **2a** a closure (e g a wax seal on a document or a strip of paper over the cork of a bottle) that must be broken in order to give access, and so guarantees that the item so closed has not been tampered with **b** a tight and effective closure (e g against gas or liquid)

[4]**seal** *v* **1** to confirm or make secure (as if) by a seal **2** to attach an authenticating seal to; *also* to authenticate, ratify **3** to close or make secure against access, leakage, or passage by a fastening or coating; *esp* to make airtight **4** to determine irrevocably

sea legs *n pl* bodily adjustment to the motion of a ship, indicated esp by ability to walk steadily and by freedom from seasickness

sealer /ˈsiːləʳ/ *n* a coat (e g of size) applied to prevent subsequent coats of paint or varnish from being too readily absorbed

sealing wax *n* a resinous composition that becomes soft when heated and is used for sealing letters, parcels, etc

sea lion *n* any of several large Pacific seals

[1]**seam** /siːm/ *n* **1** a line of stitching joining 2 separate pieces of fabric, esp along their edges **2** a line, groove, or ridge formed at the meeting of 2 edges **3** a layer or stratum of coal, rock, etc – **~less** *adj*

[2]**seam** *v* **1** to join (as if) by sewing **2** to mark with a seam, furrow, or scar

seaman /ˈsiːmən/ *n* **1** a sailor, mariner **2** a member of the navy holdng any of the lowest group of ranks below Petty Officer

seamstress /ˈsiːmstrɨs/ *n* a woman whose occupation is sewing

seamy /ˈsiːmi/ *adj* unpleasant, sordid – **seaminess** *n*

séance /ˈseɪɑ̃s, ˈseɪɒns/ *n* a meeting at which spiritualists attempt to communicate with the dead

[1]**sear, sere** /sɪəʳ/ *adj* shrivelled, withered

[2]**sear** *v* **1** to make withered and dried up **2** to burn, scorch, or injure (as if) with a sudden application of intense heat

[3]**sear** *n* a mark or scar left by searing

[1]**search** /sɜːtʃ/ *v* **1a** to look through or over carefully or thoroughly in order to find or discover sthg **b** to examine (a person) for concealed articles (e g weapons or drugs) **c** to scrutinize, esp in order to discover intention or nature **2** to uncover or ascertain by investigation – usu + *out* – **~er** *n*

[2]**search** *n* **1** an act or process of searching; *esp* an organized act of searching **2** an exercise of the right of search

searching /ˈsɜːtʃɪŋ/ *adj* piercing, penetrating – **~ly** *adv*

searchlight /ˈsɜːtʃlaɪt/ *n* (an apparatus for projecting) a movable beam of light

seashell /ˈsiːʃel/ *n* the shell of a sea animal, esp a mollusc

seashore /ˈsiːʃɔː/ *n* land (between high and low water marks) next to the sea

seasick /ˈsiːˌsɪk/ *adj* suffering from the motion sickness associated with travelling by boat or hovercraft – **~ness** *n*

seaside /ˈsiːsaɪd/ *n* (a holiday resort or beach on) land bordering the sea

[1]**season** /ˈsiːzən/ *n* **1** any of the 4 quarters into which the year is commonly divided **2** a period characterized by a particular kind of weather **3** the time of year when a place is most frequented

[2]**season** *v* **1** to give (food) more flavour by adding seasoning or savoury ingredients **2a** to treat or expose (e g timber) over a period so as to prepare for use **b** to make fit or expert by experience

seasonable /ˈsiːzənəbəl/ *adj* **1** occurring in good or proper time; opportune **2** suitable to the season or circumstances – **-bly** *adv*

seasonal /ˈsiːzənəl/ *adj* **1** of, occurring, or produced at a particular season **2** determined by seasonal need or availability

seasoning /'siːzənɪŋ/ *n* a condiment, spice, herb, etc added to food primarily for the savour that it imparts

season ticket *n, Br* a ticket sold, usu at a reduced price, for an unlimited number of trips over the same route during a limited period

[1]**seat** /siːt/ *n* **1a** a piece of furniture (e g a chair, stool, or bench) for sitting in or on **b** the part of sthg on which one rests when sitting; *also* the buttocks **2a** a special chair (e g a throne) of sby in authority; *also* the status symbolized by it **b** a large country mansion **3a** a place where sthg is established or practised **b** a place from which authority is exercised **4** a bodily part in which a particular function, disease, etc is centred **5** posture in or a way of sitting on horseback

[2]**seat** *v* **1a** to cause to sit or assist in finding a seat **b** to put (e g oneself) in a sitting position **2** to fit to or with a seat **3** , *of a garment* to become baggy in the area covering the buttocks

seat belt *n* an arrangement of straps designed to secure a person in a seat in an aeroplane, vehicle, etc

seating /'siːtɪŋ/ *n* **1a** the act of providing with seats **b** the arrangement of seats (e g in a theatre) **2a** material for upholstering seats **b** a base on or in which sthg rests

sea urchin *n* any of a class of echinoderms usu with a thin shell covered with movable spines

seaway /'siːweɪ/ *n* **1** a ship's headway **2** the sea as a route for travel **3** a deep inland waterway that admits ocean shipping

seaweed /'siːwiːd/ *n* (an abundant growth of) a plant, specif an alga, growing in the sea, typically having thick slimy fronds

seaworthy /'siːwɜːði/ *adj* fit or safe for a sea voyage

sebaceous /sɪ'beɪʃəs/ *adj* of, producing, or being fatty material secreted from the skin

sec /sek/ *n, Br* a second, moment – infml

secede /sɪ'siːd/ *v* to withdraw from an organization (e g a church or federation) – **secession, secessionist** *n*

seclude /sɪ'kluːd/ *v* to remove or separate from contact with others

secluded /sɪ'kluːdɪ̣d/ *adj* **1** screened or hidden from view **2** living in isolation – **-usion** *n*

[1]**second** /'sekənd/ *adj* **1a** next to the first in place or time **b(1)** next to the first in value, quality, or degree **(2)** inferior, subordinate **c** standing next below the top in authority or importance **2** alternate, other **3** resembling or suggesting a prototype **4** being the forward gear or speed 1 higher than first in a motor vehicle

[2]**second** *n* **1a** number two in a countable series **b** sthg that is next after the first in rank, position, authority, or precedence **2** sby who aids, supports, or stands in for another; *esp* the assistant of a duellist or boxer **3** a slightly flawed or inferior article (e g of merchandise) **4a** a place next below the first in a contest **b** *also* **second class** *often cap* the second level of British honours degree **5** the second forward gear or speed of a motor vehicle **6** *pl* a second helping of food – infml

[3]**second** *n* **1** a 60th part of a minute of time or of a minute of angular measure **2** a moment

[4]**second** *v* **1** to give support or encouragement to **2** to endorse (a motion or nomination) – **~er** *n* – **~ment** *n*

[5]**second** /sɪ'kɒnd/ *v* to release (e g a teacher, businessman, or military officer) from a regularly assigned position for temporary duty with another organization

secondary /'sekəndəri/ *adj* **1** of second rank or importance **2** immediately derived from sthg primary or basic; derivative **3a** not first in order of occurrence or development **b** of the second order or stage in a series or sequence

secondary modern *n* a secondary school formerly providing a practical rather than academic type of education

second-best *adj* next after the best

second childhood *n* dotage

[1]**second-class** *adj* **1** of a second class **2** inferior, mediocre; *also* socially, politically, or economically deprived

[2]**second-class** *adv* **1** in accommoda-

tion next below the best **2** by second-class mail

Second Coming *n* the return of Christ to judge the world on the last day

[1]**secondhand** /ˌsekənd'hænd/ *adj* **1** not original; derivative **2** acquired after being owned by another

[2]**secondhand** *adv* indirectly; at second hand

second lieutenant *n* an army officer of the lowest rank

second nature *n* an action or ability that practice has made instinctive

second person *n* (any of) a set of linguistic forms referring to the person or thing addressed (e g 'you")

second-rate *adj* of inferior quality or value

second sight *n* clairvoyance, precognition

secrecy /'siːkrɪ̈si/ *n* **1** the habit or practice of keeping secrets or maintaining privacy or concealment **2** the condition of being hidden or concealed

[1]**secret** /'siːkrɪ̈t/ *adj* **1a** kept or hidden from knowledge or view **b** conducted in secret **2** revealed only to the initiated; esoteric **3** containing information whose unauthorized disclosure could endanger national security – **~ly** *adv*

[2]**secret** *n* **1** sthg kept hidden or unexplained **2** a fact concealed from others or shared confidentially with a few

secret agent *n* a spy

secretariat /ˌsekrə'teərɪət/ *n* **1** the office of secretary **2** the clerical staff of an organization **3** a government administrative department

secretary /'sekretəri/ *n* **1** sby employed to handle correspondence and manage routine work for a superior **2** an officer of an organization or society responsible for its records and correspondence **3** an officer of state who superintends a government administrative department – **-rial** *adj*

secretary bird *n* a large long-legged African bird of prey that feeds largely on reptiles

secretary-general *n* a principal administrative officer (e g of the United Nations)

[1]**secrete** /sɪ'kriːt/ *v* to form and give off (a secretion)

[2]**secrete** *v* to deposit in a hidden place

secretion /sɪ'kriːʃən/ *n* **1** (a product formed by) the bodily process of making and releasing some material either functionally specialized (e g a hormone, saliva, latex, or resin) or isolated for excretion (e g urine) **2** the act of hiding sthg

secretive /'siːkrɪ̈tɪv, sɪ'kriːtɪv/ *adj* inclined to secrecy; not open or outgoing in speech or behaviour – **~ly** *adv* – **~ness** *n*

secret service *n* a (secret) governmental agency concerned with national security or intelligence gathering

sect /sekt/ *n* **1** a (heretical) dissenting or schismatic religious body **2a** a group maintaining strict allegiance to a doctrine or leader **b** a party; *esp* a faction

[1]**sectarian** /sek'teərɪən/ *n* **1** a (fanatical) adherent of a sect **2** a bigoted person

[2]**sectarian** *adj* **1** (characteristic) of a sect or sectarian **2** limited in character or scope; parochial

[1]**section** /'sekʃən/ *n* **1** the action or an instance of (separating by) cutting; *esp* the action of dividing sthg (e g tissues) surgically **2** a distinct part or portion of sthg written; *esp* a subdivision of a chapter **3** the profile of sthg as it would appear if cut through by an intersecting plane **4** a distinct part of an area, community, or group **5** *sing or pl in constr* a subdivision of a platoon, troop, or battery that is the smallest tactical military unit **6** any of several component parts that may be separated and reassembled **7** a division of an orchestra composed of 1 class of instruments

[2]**section** *v* **1** to cut or separate into sections **2** to represent in sections (e g by a drawing)

sectional /'sekʃənəl/ *adj* **1** restricted to a particular group or locality **2** composed of or divided into sections

sectionalism /'sekʃənəlɪzəm/ *n* an excessive concern for the interests of a region or group

sector /'sektəʳ/ *n* **1** a portion of a

military area of operation 2 a part of a field of activity, esp of business, trade, etc

secular /ˈsekjʊləʳ/ *adj* **1a** of this world rather than the heavenly or spiritual **b** not overtly or specifically religious **2** taking place once in an age or a century

secularism /ˈsekjʊlərɪzəm/ *n* disregard for or rejection of religious beliefs and practices – **-ist** *n, adj*

¹**secure** /sɪˈkjʊəʳ/ *adj* **1a** free from danger **b** free from risk of loss **c** firm, dependable; *esp* firmly fastened **2** assured, certain – **~ly** *adv*

²**secure** *v* **1a** to make safe from risk or danger **b** to guarantee against loss **c** to give pledge of payment to (a creditor) or of (an obligation) **2** to make fast; shut tightly **3** to obtain or bring about, esp as the result of effort

security /sɪˈkjʊərətɪ/ *n* **1a** freedom from danger, fear, or anxiety **b** stability, dependability **2** sthg pledged to guarantee the fulfilment of an obligation **3** an evidence of debt or of ownership (e g a stock certificate) **4a** protection **b** measures taken to protect against esp espionage or sabotage

Security Council *n* a permanent council of the United Nations responsible for the maintenance of peace and security

sedan chair /sɪˈdæn/ *n* a portable often enclosed chair, esp of the 17th and 18th c, designed to seat 1 person and be carried on poles by 2 people

¹**sedate** /sɪˈdeɪt/ *adj* calm and even in temper or pace – **~ly** *adv* – **~ness** *n*

²**sedate** *v* to give a sedative to – **-ation** *n*

sedative /ˈsedətɪv/ *n or adj* (sthg, esp a drug) tending to calm or to tranquillize nervousness or excitement

sedentary /ˈsedəntərɪ/ *adj* **1** *esp of birds* not migratory **2** doing or involving much sitting

sedge /sedʒ/ *n* any of a family of usu tufted marsh plants differing from grasses in having solid stems – **sedgy** *adj*

sediment /ˈsedəmənt/ *n* **1** the matter that settles to the bottom of a liquid **2** material deposited by water, wind, or glaciers

sedimentary /ˌsedəˈmentərɪ/ *adj* **1** of or containing sediment **2** formed by or from deposits of sediment

sedimentation /ˌsedəmənˈteɪʃən/ *n* the forming or depositing of sediment

sedition /sɪˈdɪʃən/ *n* incitement to defy or rise up against lawful authority – **-ious** *adj* – **-iously** *adv* – **-iousness** *n*

seduce /sɪˈdjuːs/ *v* **1** to incite to disobedience or disloyalty **2** to lead astray, esp by false promises **3** to effect the physical seduction of – **seducer** *n*

seduction /sɪˈdʌkʃən/ *n* **1** the act of seducing to wrong; *specif* enticement to sexual intercourse **2** a thing or quality that attracts by its charm

seductive /sɪˈdʌktɪv/ *adj* tending to seduce; alluring – **~ly** *adv* – **~ness** *n*

sedulous /ˈsedjʊləs/ *adj* **1** involving or accomplished with steady perseverance **2** diligent in application or pursuit *USE* fml – **~ly** *adv*

¹**see** /siː/ *v* **saw; seen 1a** to perceive by the eye **b** to look at; inspect **2a** to have experience of; undergo **b** to (try to) find out or determine **3** to form a mental picture of; imagine, envisage **4** to perceive the meaning or importance of; understand **5a** to observe, watch **b** to be a witness of **6** to ensure; make certain **7** *of a period of time* to be marked by **8a** to call on; visit **b** to keep company with **c** to grant an interview to **9** to meet (a bet) in poker or equal the bet of (a player)

²**see** *n* a bishopric

¹**seed** /siːd/ *n* **1a** the grains or ripened ovules of plants used for sowing **b** the fertilized ripened ovule of a (flowering) plant that contains an embryo and is capable of germination to produce a new plant **c** semen or milt **2** a source of development or growth **3** a competitor who has been seeded in a tournament – **~less** *adj*

²**seed** *v* **1** to sow seed **2** *of a plant* to produce or shed seeds **3** to extract the seeds from (e g raisins) **4** to schedule (tournament players or teams) so that superior ones will not meet in early rounds

seedbed /'siːdbed/ *n* a place where sthg specified develops

seedling /'siːdlɪŋ/ *n* **1** a plant grown from seed rather than from a cutting **2** a young plant; *esp* a nursery plant before permanent transplantation

seedy /'siːdi/ *adj* **1** containing or full of seeds **2a** shabby, grubby **b** somewhat disreputable; run-down **c** slightly unwell – infml – **seedily** *adv* – **seediness** *n*

seek /siːk/ *v* **sought** **1a** to go in search of – often + *out* **b** to try to discover **2** to ask for **3** to try to acquire or gain **4** to make an effort; aim – + infinitive – **~er** *n*

seem /siːm/ *v* **1** to give the impression of being **2** to appear to the observation or understanding **3** to give evidence of existing

seeming /'siːmɪŋ/ *adj* apparent rather than real

seemingly /'siːmɪŋli/ *adv* **1** so far as can be seen or judged **2** to outward appearance only

seemly /'siːmli/ *adj* in accord with good taste or propriety – **seemliness** *n*

see off *v* **1** to be present at the departure of **2** to avert, repel

see out *v* **1** to escort to the outside (e g of a room, office, or house) **2** to last until the end of

seep /siːp/ *v* to pass slowly (as if) through fine pores or small openings – **~age** *n*

seer /sɪəʳ/ *n* **1** sby who predicts future events **2** sby credited with exceptional moral and spiritual insight

seersucker /'sɪə,sʌkəʳ/ *n* a light slightly puckered fabric of linen, cotton, or rayon

[1]**seesaw** /'siːsɔː/ *n* **1** an alternating up-and-down or backwards-and-forwards movement; *also* anything (e g a process or movement) that alternates **2** (a game in which 2 or more children ride on opposite ends of) a plank balanced in the middle so that one end goes up as the other goes down

[2]**seesaw** *v* **1a** to move backwards and forwards or up and down **b** to play at seesaw **2a** to alternate **b** to vacillate

seethe /siːð/ *v* **1** to be in a state of agitated usu confused movement **2** to churn or foam as if boiling

see-through *adj* transparent

see through *v* to undergo or endure to the end

[1]**segment** /'segmənt/ *n* **1a** a separated piece of sthg **b** any of the constituent parts into which a body, entity, or quantity is divided or marked off **2** a portion cut off from a geometrical figure by 1 or more points, lines, or planes

[2]**segment** /seg'ment/ *v* to separate into segments

segregate /'segrɪgeɪt/ *v* **1** to separate or set apart **2** to cause or force separation of (e g criminals from society) or in (e g a community) – **~d** *adj*

segregation /,segrɪ'geɪʃən/ *n* the separation or isolation of a race, class, or ethnic group

seigneur /se'njɜːʳ/ *n* a feudal lord

seismic /'saɪzmɪk/, **seismal** *adj* of or caused by an earth vibration, specif an earthquake

seismograph /'saɪzməgrɑːf/ *n* an apparatus to measure and record earth tremors

seismology /saɪz'mɒlədʒi/ *n* a science that deals with earth vibrations, esp earthquakes – **-gist** *n*

seize /siːz/ *v* **1a** to confiscate, esp by legal authority **b** to lay hold of sthg suddenly, forcibly, or eagerly – usu + *on* or *upon* **2a** to take possession of by force **b** to take prisoner **3** to take hold of abruptly or eagerly **4** to attack or afflict physically or mentally **5** *of brakes, pistons, etc* to become jammed through excessive pressure, temperature, or friction – often + *up*

seizure /'siːʒəʳ/ *n* **1** the taking possession of sby or sthg by legal process **2** a sudden attack (e g of disease)

[1]**seldom** /'seldəm/ *adv* in few instances; rarely, infrequently

[2]**seldom** *adj* rare, infrequent

[1]**select** /sə̇'lekt/ *adj* **1** picked out in preference to others **2a** of special value or quality **b** exclusively or fastidiously chosen, esp on the basis of social characteristics **3** judicious in choice

[2]**select** *v* to take according to preference from among a number; pick out – **~or** *n*

select committee *n* a temporary committee of a legislative body, established to examine 1 particular matter

selection /sɪ̣'lekʃən/ *n* **1** sby or sthg selected; *also* a collection of selected items **2** a range of things from which to choose

selective /sɪ̣'lektɪv/ *adj* of or characterized by selection; selecting or tending to select – **~ly** *adv* – **~ness** *n* – **-tivity** *n*

[1]**self** /self/ *pron* myself, himself, herself

[2]**self** *adj* identical throughout, esp in colour

[3]**self** *n, pl* **selves** **1** the entire being of an individual **2** a (part or aspect of a) person's individual character **3** the body, emotions, thoughts, sensations, etc that constitute the individuality and identity of a person **4** personal interest, advantage, or welfare

self-addressed *adj* addressed for return to the sender

self-assertion *n* the act of asserting oneself or one's own rights, claims, or opinions, esp aggressively or conceitedly – **-tive** *adj* – **-tiveness** *n*

self-assurance *n* self-confidence – **-red** *adj*

self-centred *adj* concerned excessively with one's own desires or needs – **~ness** *n*

self-confessed *adj* openly acknowledged

self-confidence *n* confidence in oneself and one's powers and abilities – **-dent** *adj*

self-conscious *adj* **1a** conscious of oneself as a possessor of mental states and originator of actions **b** intensely aware of oneself **2** uncomfortably conscious of oneself as an object of notice; ill at ease – **~ly** *adv* – **~ness** *n*

self-contained *adj* **1** complete in itself **2a** showing self-possession **b** formal and reserved in manner

self-control *n* restraint of one's own impulses or emotions – **-trolled** *adj*

self-defence *n* **1** the act of defending or justifying oneself **2** the legal right to defend oneself with reasonable force

self-denial *n* the restraint or limitation of one's desires or their gratification – **self-denying** *adj*

self-determination *n* **1** free choice of one's own actions or states without outside influence **2** determination by a territorial unit of its own political status

self-discipline *n* the act of disciplining or power to discipline one's thoughts and actions, usu for the sake of improvement

self-drive *adj, of a hired vehicle* intended to be driven by the hirer

self-employed *adj* earning income directly from one's own business, trade, or profession rather than as salary or wages from an employer

self-esteem *n* **1** confidence and satisfaction in oneself; self-respect **2** vanity

self-evident *adj* requiring no proof; obvious

self-examination *n* the analysis of one's conduct, motives, etc

self-explanatory *adj* capable of being understood without explanation

self-government *n* control of one's own (political) affairs – **self-governing** *adj*

self-help *n* the bettering or helping of oneself without dependence on others

self-importance *n* **1** an exaggerated sense of one's own importance **2** arrogant or pompous behaviour – **-ant** *adj* – **-antly** *adv*

self-indulgence *n* excessive or unrestrained gratification of one's own appetites, desires, or whims – **-ent** *adj* – **-ently** *adv*

self-interest *n* (a concern for) one's own advantage and well-being – **~ed** *adj*

selfish /'selfɪʃ/ *adj* concerned with or directed towards one's own advantage, pleasure, or well-being without regard for others – **~ly** *adv* – **~ness** *n*

selfless /'selflɪ̣s/ *adj* having no concern for self; unselfish – **~ly** *adv* – **~ness** *n*

self-made *adj* raised from poverty or obscurity by one's own efforts

self-opinionated *adj* **1** conceited **2**

stubbornly holding to one's own opinion; opinionated

self-pity *n* a self-indulgent dwelling on one's own sorrows or misfortunes

self-possession *n* control of one's emotions or behaviour, esp when under stress; composure – **-sed** *adj*

self-preservation *n* an instinctive tendency to act so as to safeguard one's own existence

self-raising flour *n* a commercially prepared mixture of flour containing a raising agent

self-reliance *n* reliance on one's own efforts and abilities; independence – **-ant** *adj*

self-respect *n* a proper respect for one's human dignity

self-respecting *adj* having or characterized by self-respect or integrity

self-righteous *adj* assured of one's own righteousness, esp in contrast with the actions and beliefs of others; narrow-mindedly moralistic – **~ly** *adv* – **~ness** *n*

self-sacrifice *n* sacrifice of oneself or one's well-being for the sake of an ideal or for the benefit of others – **-icing** *adj*

selfsame /ˈselfseɪm/ *adj* precisely the same; identical

self-satisfaction *n* a smug satisfaction with oneself or one's position or achievements – **-fied** *adj*

self-seeking *adj* seeking only to safeguard or further one's own interests – **-seeker** *n*

self-service *n* the serving of oneself (e g in a cafeteria or supermarket) with things to be paid for at a cashier's desk, usu upon leaving

self-starter *n* an electric motor used to start an internal-combustion engine

self-styled *adj* called by oneself, esp without justification

self-sufficient *adj* **1** able to maintain oneself or itself without outside aid; capable of providing for one's own needs **2** having unwarranted assurance of one's own ability or worth – **-ency** *n*

self-supporting *adj* **1** meeting one's needs by one's own labour or income **2** supporting itself or its own weight

self-will *n* stubborn or wilful adherence to one's own desires or ideas; obstinacy – **~ed** *adj*

[1]**sell** /sel/ *v* **sold 1** to deliver or give up in violation of duty, trust, or loyalty; betray – often + *out* **2a** to give up (property) in exchange, esp for money **b** to give up or dispose of foolishly or dishonourably (in return for sthg else) **3** to cause or promote the sale of **4a** to make acceptable, believable, or desirable by persuasion **b** to persuade to accept or enjoy sthg – usu + *on*; infml

[2]**sell** *n* **1** the act or an instance of selling **2** a deliberate deception; a hoax – infml

seller /ˈseləʳ/ *n* a product offered for sale and selling well, to a specified extent, or in a specified manner

seller's market *n* a market in which demand exceeds supply

sellotape /ˈseləteɪp, ˈseləʊ-/ *v* to fix (as if) with Sellotape

Sellotape /ˈseləteɪp/ *trademark* – used for a usu transparent adhesive tape

sell-out *n* **1** a performance, exhibition, or contest for which all tickets or seats are sold **2** a betrayal – infml

sell out *v* to betray or be unfaithful to (e g one's cause or associates), esp for the sake of money

sell up *v* to sell (e g one's house or business) in a conclusive or forced transaction

selvage, selvedge /ˈselvɪdʒ/ *n* the edge on either side of a woven fabric

selves /selvz/ *pl of* **self**

semantics /sɪˈmæntɪks/ *n pl but sing or pl in constr* the branch of linguistics concerned with meaning; *also* the study of the relation between signs and the objects they refer to – **semantic** *adj*

semaphore /ˈseməfɔːʳ/ *n* **1** an apparatus for conveying information by visual signals (e g by the position of 1 or more pivoted arms) **2** a system of visual signalling by 2 flags held 1 in each hand – **semaphore** *v*

semblance /ˈsembləns/ *n* outward and often deceptive appearance; a show

semen /ˈsiːmən/ *n* a suspension of spermatozoa produced by the male reproductive glands that is conveyed to the female reproductive tract during coitus

semester /sʝ'mestəʳ/ *n* an academic term lasting half a year, esp in America and Germany

semibreve /'semibriːv/ *n* a musical note with the time value of 2 minims or 4 crotchets

semicircle /'semɪ,sɜːkəl/ *n* (an object or arrangement in the form of) a half circle – **-cular** *adj*

semicolon /,semɪ'kəʊlən/ *n* a punctuation mark ; used chiefly to coordinate major sentence elements where there is no conjunction

semiconductor /,semikən'dʌktəʳ/ *n* a substance (e g silicon) whose electrical conductivity at room temperature is between that of a conductor and that of an insulator

semidetached /,semɪdɪ'tætʃt/ *adj* forming 1 of a pair of residences joined into 1 building by a common wall – **semidetached** *n*

[1]**semifinal** /,semi'faɪnl/ *adj* **1** next to the last in a knockout competition **2** of or participating in a semifinal

[2]**semifinal** /'semifaɪnl,--'--/ *n* a semifinal match or round – often pl with sing. meaning

seminal /'semʝnəl/ *adj* **1** (consisting) of, storing, or conveying seed or semen **2** containing or contributing the seeds of future development; original and influential

seminar /'semʝnɑːʳ/ *n* **1** an advanced or graduate class often featuring informality and discussion **2** a meeting for exchanging and discussing information

seminary /'semʝnəri/ *n* an institution for the training of candidates for the (Roman Catholic) priesthood – **-rist** *n*

semiprecious /,semɪ'preʃəs/ *adj, of a gemstone* of less commercial value than a precious stone

semiquaver /'semikweɪvəʳ/ *n* a musical note with time value of ½ of a quaver

Semitic /sʝ'mɪtɪk/ *adj* **1** of or characteristic of the Semites; *specif* Jewish **2** of a branch of the Afro-Asiatic language family that includes Hebrew, Aramaic, Arabic, and Ethiopic

semitone /'semitəʊn/ *n* the musical interval (e g E–F or F–F #) equal to the interval between 2 adjacent keys on a keyboard instrument

semiweekly /,semi'wiːkli/ *adj or adv* appearing or taking place twice a week

semolina /,semə'liːnə/ *n* the purified hard parts left after milling of (hard) wheat used for pasta and in milk puddings

senate /'senʝt/ *n sing or pl in constr* **1a** the supreme council of the ancient Roman republic and empire **b** the 2nd chamber in some legislatures that consist of 2 houses **2** the governing body of some universities

senator /'senətəʳ/ *n* a member of a senate

send /send/ *v* **sent** **1** *of God, fate, etc* to cause to be; grant; bring about **2** to dispatch by a means of communication **3a** to cause, direct, order, or request to go **b** to dismiss **4** to cause to assume a specified state **5a** to pour out; discharge **b** to emit (e g radio signals) **c** to grow out (parts) in the course of development **6** to consign to a destination (e g death or a place of imprisonment)

send down *v, Br* **1** to suspend or expel from a university **2** to send to jail – infml

send-off *n* a usu enthusiastic demonstration of goodwill at the beginning of a venture (e g a trip)

send off *v* to attend to the departure of

send-up *n, Br* a satirical imitation, esp on stage or television; a parody

send up *v, chiefly Br* to make an object of mockery or laughter; ridicule

seneschal /'senʝʃəl/ *n* the agent or bailiff of a feudal lord's estate

senile /'siːnaɪl/ *adj* of, exhibiting, or characteristic of (the mental or physical weakness associated with) old age – **-lity** *n*

[1]**senior** /'siːnɪəʳ/ *n* **1** sby who is older than another **2** sby of higher standing or rank

[2]**senior** *adj* **1** elder – used, chiefly in the USA, to distinguish a father with the same name as his son **2** higher in standing or rank

senior citizen *n* sby beyond the usual age of retirement – euph

senor, señor /se'njɔːʳ/ *n*, *pl* **senors, señores** a Spanish-speaking man – used as a title equivalent to *Mr* or as a generalized term of direct address

senora, señora /se'njɔːrə/ *n* a married Spanish-speaking woman – used as a title equivalent to *Mrs* or as a generalized term of direct address

senorita, señorita /ˌsenjɔː'riːtə/ *n* an unmarried Spanish-speaking girl or woman – used as a title equivalent to *Miss*

sensation /sen'seɪʃən/ *n* **1a** a mental process (e g seeing or hearing) resulting from stimulation of a sense organ **b** a state of awareness of a usu specified type resulting from internal bodily conditions or external factors; a feeling or sense **2a** a surge of intense interest or excitement **b** a cause of such excitement; *esp* sby or sthg in some respect remarkable or outstanding

sensational /sen'seɪʃənəl/ *adj* **1** arousing an immediate, intense, and usu superficial interest or emotional reaction **2** exceptionally or unexpectedly excellent or impressive – infml – **~ly** *adv*

sensationalism /sen'seɪʃənəlɪzəm/ *n* the use of sensational subject matter or style, esp in journalism – **-ist** *n*

[1]**sense** /sens/ *n* **1** a meaning conveyed or intended; *esp* any of a range of meanings a word or phrase may bear, esp as isolated in a dictionary entry **2** any of the senses of feeling, hearing, sight, smell, taste, etc **3** soundness of mind or judgment – usu pl with sing. meaning **4a** an ability to use the senses for a specified purpose **b** a definite but often vague awareness or impression **c** an awareness that motivates action or judgment **d** a capacity for discernment and appreciation **5** an ability to put the mind to effective use; practical intelligence

[2]**sense** *v* **1a** to perceive by the senses **b** to be or become conscious of **2** to grasp, comprehend

senseless /'sensl̥ɨs/ *adj* deprived of, deficient in, or contrary to sense: e g **a** unconscious **b** foolish, stupid **c** meaningless, purposeless – **~ly** *adv* – **~ness** *n*

sensibility /ˌsensə'bɪlɨti/ *n* **1** heightened susceptibility to feelings of pleasure or pain (e g in response to praise or blame) – often pl with sing. meaning **2** the ability to discern and respond freely to sthg (e g emotion in another)

sensible /'sensəbəl/ *adj* **1** having, containing, or indicative of good sense or sound reason **2a** perceptible to the senses or to understanding **b** large enough to be observed or noticed; considerable – **-bly** *adv*

sensitive /'sensɨtɪv/ *adj* **1** capable of being stimulated or excited by external agents (e g light, gravity, or contact) **2** highly responsive or susceptible: e g **a(1)** easily provoked or hurt emotionally **(2)** finely aware of the attitudes and feelings of others or of the subtleties of a work of art **b** capable of registering minute differences; delicate **3** concerned with highly classified information – **~ly** *adv* – **-tivity** *n*

sensit·ize, -ise /'sensɨtaɪz/ *v* to make or become sensitive

sensor /'sensəʳ/ *n* a device that responds to heat, light, sound, pressure, magnetism, etc and transmits a resulting impulse (e g for measurement or operating a control)

sensory /'sensəri/ *adj* of sensation or the senses

sensual /'senʃʊəl/ *adj* **1** sensory **2** relating to or consisting in the gratification of the senses or the indulgence of appetites **3a** devoted to or preoccupied with the senses or appetites **b** voluptuous – **~ity** *n*

sensuous /'senʃʊəs/ *adj* **1a** of (objects perceived by) the senses **b** providing or characterized by gratification of the senses; appealing strongly to the senses **2** suggesting or producing rich imagery or sense impressions – **~ly** *adv* – **~ness** *n*

sent /sent/ *past of* **send**

[1]**sentence** /'sentəns/ *n* **1a** a judgment formally pronounced by a court and specifying a punishment **b** the punishment so imposed **2** a grammatically self-contained speech unit that expresses an assertion, a question, a

command, a wish, or an exclamation and is usu shown in writing with a capital letter at the beginning and with appropriate punctuation at the end

[2]**sentence** *v* **1** to impose a judicial sentence on **2** to consign to a usu unpleasant fate

sententious /sen'tenʃəs/ *adj* **1** terse, pithy **2a** full of terse or pithy sayings **b** pompous, moralizing – **~ly** *adv* – **~ness** *n*

sentient /'senʃənt/ *adj* **1** capable of perceiving through the senses; conscious **2** keenly sensitive in perception or feeling *USE* chiefly fml

sentiment /'sentɪ̣mənt/ *n* **1a** (an attitude, thought, or judgment prompted or coloured by) feeling or emotion **b** a specific view or attitude; an opinion – usu pl with sing. meaning **2** indulgently romantic or nostalgic feeling

sentimental /ˌsentɪ̣'mentl/ *adj* **1** resulting from feeling rather than reason **2** having an excess of superficial sentiment – **~ly** *adv* – **~ism, ~ity, ~ist** *n* – **~ize** *v*

sentry /'sentri/ *n* a guard, watch; *esp* a soldier standing guard at a gate, door, etc

sepal /'sepəl/ *n* any of the modified leaves comprising the calyx of a flower

separable /'sepərəbəl/ *adj* capable of being separated or dissociated – **-bly** *adv* – **-bility** *n*

[1]**separate** /'sepəreɪt/ *v* **1a** to set or keep apart; detach, divide **b** to make a distinction between; distinguish **c** to disperse in space or time; scatter **2a** to isolate from a mixture or compound – often + *out* **b** to divide into constituent parts or types **3** to cease to live together as man and wife, esp by formal arrangement **4** to go in different directions

[2]**separate** /'sepərɪ̣t/ *adj* **1** set or kept apart; detached, separated **2** not shared with another; individual **3a** existing independently; autonomous **b** different in kind; distinct – **~ness** *n* – **~ly** *adv*

separation /ˌsepə'reɪʃən/ *n* **1a** a point, line, or means of division **b** an intervening space; a gap, break **2** cessation of cohabitation between husband and wife by mutual agreement or judicial decree

separatism /'sepərətɪzəm/ *n* a belief or movement advocating separation (e g schism, secession, or segregation) – **-ist** *n*

[1]**sepia** /'siːpɪə/ *n* **1** the inky secretion of cuttlefishes; *also* a pigment prepared from this **2** a rich dark brown colour

[2]**sepia** *adj* **1** of the colour sepia **2** made of or done in sepia

sepoy /'siːpɔɪ/ *n* an Indian soldier employed by a European power, esp Britain

sepsis /'sepsɪ̣s/ *n, pl* **sepses** the spread of bacteria from a focus of infection

September /sep'tembəʳ/ *n* the 9th month of the Gregorian calendar

septet /sep'tet/ *n* **1** a musical composition for 7 instruments, voices, or performers **2** *sing or pl in constr* a group or set of 7; *esp* the performers of a septet

septic /'septɪk/ *adj* relating to, involving, or characteristic of sepsis

septic tank *n* a tank in which the solid matter of continuously flowing sewage is disintegrated by bacteria

septuagenarian /ˌseptʃʊədʒɪ̣'neərɪən/ *n* sby between 70 and 79 years old

septum /'septəm/ *n, pl* **septa** a dividing wall or membrane, esp between bodily spaces or masses of soft tissue

sepulchral /sɪ̣'pʌlkrəl/ *adj* **1** of the burial of the dead **2** suited to or suggestive of a tomb; funereal

sepulchre, *NAm chiefly* **sepulcher** /'sepəlkəʳ/ *n* **1** a place of burial; a tomb **2** a receptacle (in an altar) for religious relics

sequel /'siːkwəl/ *n* **1** a consequence, result **2a** subsequent development or course of events **b** a play, film, or literary work continuing the course of a narrative begun in a preceding one

sequence /'siːkwəns/ *n* **1** a continuous or connected series **2** an episode, esp in a film **3** order of succession **4** a continuous progression – **sequence** *v* – **-ential** *adj* – **-entially** *adv*

sequin /'siːkwɪ̣n/ *n* a very small disc of shining metal or plastic used for ornamentation, esp on clothing – ~**ed** *adj*

sequoia /sɪ'kwɔɪə/ *n* a huge coniferous Californian tree; *esp* a redwood

seraglio /sə̆'rɑːljəʊ/ *n, pl* **seraglios** a harem

[1]**serenade** /ˌserə̆'neɪd/ *n* **1** a complimentary vocal or instrumental performance (given outdoors at night for a woman) **2** an instrumental composition in several movements written for a small ensemble

[2]**serenade** *v* to perform a serenade (in honour of)

serendipity /ˌserən'dɪpə̆ti/ *n* the faculty of discovering pleasing or valuable things by chance

serene /sə̆'riːn/ *adj* **1** free of storms or adverse changes; clear, fine **2** having or showing tranquillity and peace of mind – ~**ly** *adv* – **serenity** *n*

serf /sɜːf/ *n* a member of a class of agricultural labourers in a feudal society, bound in service to a lord, and esp transferred with the land they worked if its ownership changed hands – ~**dom** *n*

serge /sɜːdʒ/ *n* a durable twilled fabric having a smooth clear face and a pronounced diagonal rib on the front and the back

sergeant /'sɑːdʒənt/ *n* **1** a police officer ranking in Britain between constable and inspector **2** a non-commissioned officer of upper rank in the army, airforce, or marines

sergeant major *n* a warrant officer in the British army or Royal Marines

[1]**serial** /'sɪərɪəl/ *adj* **1** of or constituting a series, rank, or row **2** appearing in successive instalments **3** of or being music based on a series of notes in an arbitrary but fixed order without regard for traditional tonality – ~**ly** *adv*

[2]**serial** *n* **1** a work appearing (e g in a magazine or on television) in parts at usu regular intervals **2** a publication issued as 1 of a consecutively numbered continuing series

series /'sɪəriːz/ *n* **1** a number of things or events of the same kind following one another in spatial or temporal succession **2** a usu infinite mathematical sequence whose terms are to be added together **3** a succession of issues of volumes published with continuous numbering or usu related subjects or authors and format **4** a division of rock formations that comprises the rocks deposited during an epoch **5** an arrangement of devices in an electrical circuit in which the whole current passes through each device

serious /'sɪərɪəs/ *adj* **1** grave or thoughtful in appearance or manner; sober **2a** requiring careful attention and concentration **b** of or relating to a weighty or important matter **3** not jesting or deceiving; in earnest **4** having important or dangerous consequences; critical – ~**ly** *adv* – ~**ness** *n*

sermon /'sɜːmən/ *n* **1** a religious discourse delivered in public, usu by a clergyman as a part of a religious service **2** a speech on conduct or duty; *esp* one that is unduly long or tedious

serpent /'sɜːpənt/ *n* **1** a (large) snake **2** *the* Devil **3** a wily treacherous person

[1]**serpentine** /'sɜːpəntaɪn/ *adj* **1** of or like a serpent (e g in form or movement) **2** subtly tempting; wily, artful **3** winding or turning one way and another

[2]**serpentine** *n* a usu dull green mottled mineral consisting mainly of hydrated magnesium silicate

serried /'serid/ *adj* crowded or pressed together; compact

serum /'sɪərəm/ *n, pl* **serums, sera** the watery part of an animal liquid (remaining after coagulation): **a** blood serum, esp when containing specific antibodies **b** whey

servant /'sɜːvənt/ *n* sby who or sthg that serves others; *specif* sby employed to perform personal or domestic duties for another

[1]**serve** /sɜːv/ *v* **1a** to act as a servant **b** to do military or naval service **c** to undergo a term of imprisonment **2a** to be of use; fulfil a specified purpose – often + *as* **b** to be favourable, opportune, or convenient **c** to hold a post or office; discharge a duty **3** to prove

adequate or satisfactory; suffice **4** to distribute drinks or helpings of food **5** to attend to customers in a shop **6** to put the ball or shuttle in play in any of various games (e g tennis or volleyball)

[2]**serve** *n* the act of putting the ball or shuttle in play in any of various games (e g volleyball, badminton, or tennis)

server /'sɜːvəʳ/ *n* **1** sby who serves food or drink **2** the player who serves (e g in tennis) **3** sthg (e g tongs) used in serving food or drink

[1]**service** /'sɜːvɨs/ *n* **1a** work or duty performed for sby **b** employment as a servant **2a** the function performed by sby who or sthg that serves **b** help, use, benefit **c** disposal for use or assistance **3a** a form followed in a religious ceremony **b** a meeting for worship **4a** a helpful act; a favour **b** a piece of useful work that does not produce a tangible commodity – usu pl with sing. meaning **c** a serve **5** a set of articles for a particular use; *specif* a set of matching tableware **6** any of a nation's military forces (e g the army or navy) **7a(1)** a facility supplying some public demand **(2)** *pl* utilities (e g gas, water sewage, or electricity) available or connected to a building **b** the usu routine repair and maintenance of a machine or motor vehicle **c** a facility providing broadcast programmes **8** the bringing of a legal writ, process, or summons to notice as prescribed

[2]**service** *adj* **1** of the armed services **2** used in serving or delivering **3** providing services

[3]**service** *v* to perform services for: e g **a** to repair or provide maintenance for **b** to meet interest and sinking fund payments on (e g government debt) **c** to perform any of the business functions auxiliary to production or distribution of **d** *of a male animal* to copulate with

[4]**service, service tree** *n* an Old World tree resembling the related mountain ashes but with larger flowers and larger edible fruits

serviceable /'sɜːvɨsəbəl/ *adj* **1** fit to use; suited for a purpose **2** wearing well in use; durable – **-bility** *n* – **~ness** *n* – **-bly** *adv*

service charge *n* a proportion of a bill added onto the total bill to pay for service, usu instead of tips

serviceman /'sɜːvɨsmən/ *n* a member of the armed forces

service station *n* a retail station for servicing motor vehicles, esp with oil and petrol

serviette /ˌsɜːvi'et/ *n, chiefly Br* a table napkin

servile /'sɜːvaɪl/ *adj* **1** of or befitting a slave or a menial position **2** slavishly or unctuously submissive; abject, obsequious – **-vility** *n* – **~ly** *adv*

serving /'sɜːvɪŋ/ *n* a single portion of food or drink; a helping

servitude /'sɜːvɨtjuːd/ *n* lack of liberty; bondage

servomechanism /'sɜːvəʊˌmekənɪzəm/ *n* an automatic device for controlling large amounts of power by means of very small amounts of power and automatically correcting performance of a mechanism

sesame /'sesəmi/ *n* (an E Indian plant with) small flattish seeds used as a source of oil and as a flavouring agent

session /'seʃən/ *n* **1** a meeting or series of meetings of a body (e g a court or council) for the transaction of business; a sitting **2** a period devoted to a particular activity, esp by a group of people

sestet /ses'tet/ *n* a poem or stanza of 6 lines; *specif* the last 6 lines of an Italian sonnet

[1]**set** /set/ *v* **-tt-; set** **1** to cause to sit; place in or on a seat **2a** to place with care or deliberate purpose and with relative stability **b** to transplant **3** to cause to assume a specified condition **4a** to appoint or assign to an office or duty **b** to post, station **5a** to place in a specified relation or position **b** to place in a specified setting **6a** to fasten **b** to apply **7** to fix or decide on as a time, limit, or regulation; prescribe **8a** to establish as the most extreme, esp the highest, level **b** to provide as a pattern or model **c** to allot as or compose for a task **9a** to adjust (a device, esp a measuring device) to a desired position **b** to restore to normal position or connection after disloca-

tion or fracturing **c** to spread to the wind **10** to divide (an age-group of pupils) into sets **11a** to make ready for use **b** to provide music or instrumentation for (a text) **c** to arrange (type) for printing **12a** to put a fine edge on by grinding or honing **b** to bend slightly the alternate teeth of (a saw) in opposite directions **13** to fix in a desired position **14** to fix (the hair) in a desired style by waving, curling, or arranging, usu while wet **15** to fix a gem in a metal setting **16a** to fix at a specified amount **b** to value, rate **17** to place in relation for comparison; *also* to offset **18a** to put into activity or motion **b** to incite to attack or antagonism **c** to make an attack – + *on* or *upon* **19** to fix firmly; give rigid form to **20** to cause to become firm or solid **21** to cause fruit to develop **22** to pass below the horizon; go down **23** – used as an interjection to command runners to put themselves into the starting position before a race

[2]**set** *adj* **1** intent, determined **2** fixed by authority or binding decision; prescribed, specified **3** *of a meal* consisting of a specified combination of dishes available at a fixed price **4** reluctant to change; fixed by habit **5** immovable, rigid **6** ready, prepared

[3]**set** *n* **1** setting or being set **2** a mental inclination, tendency, or habit **3** a number of things, usu of the same kind, that belong or are used together or that form a unit **4** the arrangement of the hair by curling or waving **5** a young plant, rooted cutting, etc ready for transplanting **6** an artificial setting for a scene of a theatrical or film production **7** a division of a tennis match won by the side that wins at least 6 games beating the opponent by 2 games or that wins a tie breaker **8** *sing or pl in constr* a group of people associated by common interests **9** a collection of mathematical elements (e g numbers or points) **10** an apparatus of electronic components assembled so as to function as a unit **11** *sing or pl in constr* a group of pupils of roughly equal ability in a particular subject who are taught together **12** a sett

set aside *v* **1** to reserve for a particular purpose; save **2** to reject from consideration **3** to annul or overrule (a sentence, verdict, etc)

setback /'setbæk/ *n* **1** an arresting of or hindrance in progress **2** a defeat, reverse

set back *v* **1** to prevent or hinder the progress of; impede, delay **2** to cost – infml

set down *v* **1** to cause or allow (a passenger) to alight from a vehicle **2** to land (an aircraft) on the ground or water **3** to put in writing **4** to attribute, ascribe

set-in *adj* cut separately and stitched in

set in *v* **1** to become established **2** to insert; *esp* to stitch (a small part) into a larger article

set-off *n* **1a** a decoration, adornment **b** a counterbalance, compensation **2** the discharge of a debt by setting against it a sum owed by the creditor to the debtor

set off *v* **1a** to put in relief; show up by contrast **b** to make distinct or outstanding; enhance **2** to treat as a compensating item **3a** to set in motion; cause to begin **b** to cause to explode; detonate **4** to start out on a course or journey

set piece *n* **1** (a part of) a work of art, literature, etc with a formal pattern or style **2** any of various moves in soccer or rugby (e g a corner kick or free kick) by which the ball is put back into play after a stoppage

setscrew /'set,skruː/ *n* a screw that serves to adjust a machine

set square *n, chiefly Br* a flat triangular instrument with 1 right angle and 2 other precisely known angles, used to mark out or test angles

sett, set /set/ *n* **1** the burrow of badger **2** a block of usu stone used for paving streets

settee /se'tiː/ *n* a long often upholstered seat with a back and usu arms for seating more than 1 person; *broadly* a sofa

setter /'setəʳ/ *n* a large gundog trained to point on finding game

setting /'setɪŋ/ *n* **1** the manner, position, or direction in which sthg (e g a dial) is set **2** the (style of) frame in which a gem is mounted **3a** the background, surroundings **b** the time and place of the action of a literary, dramatic, or cinematic work **4** the music composed for a text (e g a poem)

[1]settle /'setl/ *n* a wooden bench with arms, a high solid back, and an enclosed base which can be used as a chest

[2]settle *v* **1** to place firmly or comfortably **2a** to establish in residence **b** to supply with inhabitants; colonize **3a** to cause to sink and become compacted **b** to clarify by causing the sediment to sink **4** to come to rest **5** to free from pain, discomfort, disorder, or disturbance **6** to fix or resolve conclusively **7** to bestow legally for life – usu + *on* **8a** to become calm or orderly – often + *down* **b** to adopt an ordered or stable life-style – usu + *down* **9a** to adjust differences or accounts; pay – often + *with* or *up* **b** to end a legal dispute by the agreement of both parties, without court action

settlement /'setlmənt/ *n* **1** settling **2** an estate, income, etc legally bestowed on sby **3a** a newly settled place or region **b** a small, esp isolated, village **4** an agreement resolving differences

settler /'setləʳ/ *n* one who settles sthg (e g a new region)

set-to *n* a usu brief and vigorous conflict – chiefly infml

set to *v* **1** to make an eager or determined start on a job or activity **2** to begin fighting

set-up *n* **1** an arrangement; *also* an organization **2** a task or contest with a prearranged or artificially easy course – chiefly infml

set up *v* **1** to put forward (e g a theory) for acceptance; propound **2** to assemble and prepare for use or operation **3** to give voice to, esp loudly; raise **4** to claim (oneself) to be a specified thing **5** to found, institute **6** to provide with what is necessary or useful – usu + *with* or *for*

seven /'sevən/ *n* **1** the number 7 **2** the seventh in a set or series **3** sthg having 7 parts or members or a denomination of 7 – **~th** *adj, n, pron, adv*

seventeen /,sevən'tiːn/ *n* the number 17 – **~th** *adj, n, pron, adv*

seventh heaven *n* a state of supreme rapture or bliss

seventy /'sevənti/ *n* **1** the number 70 **2** *pl* the numbers 70 to 79; *specif* a range of temperatures, ages, or dates within a century characterized by those numbers – **-tieth** *adj, n, pron, adv*

seven-year itch *n* marital discontent allegedly leading to infidelity after about 7 years of marriage

sever /'sevəʳ/ *v* **1** to put or keep apart; separate; *esp* to remove (a major part or portion) (as if) by cutting **2** to break off; terminate – **~ance** *n*

[1]several /'sevərəl/ *adj* **1** more than 2 but fewer than many **2** separate or distinct from one another; respective – chiefly fml

[2]several *pron, pl in constr* an indefinite number more than 2 and fewer than many

severally /'sevərəli/ *adv* each by itself or him-/herself; separately – chiefly fml

severe /sɪ̈'vɪəʳ/ *adj* **1** having a stern expression or character; austere **2** rigorous in judgment, requirements, or punishment; stringent **3** strongly critical or condemnatory; censorious **4** sober or restrained in decoration or manner; plain **5** marked by harsh or extreme conditions **6** serious, grave – **~ly** *adv* – **-rity** *n*

sew /səʊ/ *v* **sewed; sewn 1** to unite, fasten, or attach by stitches made with a needle and thread **2** to close or enclose by sewing **3** to make or mend by sewing – **~er** *n*

sewage /'sjuːɪdʒ, 'suː-/ *n* waste matter carried off by sewers

sewer /'sjuːəʳ, 'suːəʳ/ *n* an artificial usu underground conduit used to carry off waste matter, esp excrement, from houses, schools, towns, etc and surface water from roads and paved areas

sewerage /'sjuːərɪdʒ, 'suː-/ *n* **1** sewage **2** the removal and disposal of surface water by sewers **3** a system of sewers

sewing /'səʊɪŋ/ *n* **1** the act, action, or work of one who sews **2** work that has been or is to be sewn

sew up *v* to bring to a successful or satisfactory conclusion – chiefly infml

sex /seks/ *n* **1** either of 2 divisions of organisms distinguished as male or female **2** the structural, functional, and behavioural characteristics that are involved in reproduction and that distinguish males and females **3** sexual intercourse – **sex, sexual** *adj* – **~ually** *adv*

sexagenarian /ˌseksədʒɪ̈ˈneərɪən/ *n* a person between 60 and 69 years old

sexism /ˈseksɪzəm/ *n* **1** a belief that sex determines intrinsic capacities and role in society and that sexual differences produce an inherent superiority of one sex, usu the male **2** discrimination on the basis of sex; *esp* prejudice against women on the part of men – **-ist** *adj, n*

sexless /ˈsekslɪ̈s/ *adj* **1** lacking sexuality or sexual intercourse **2** lacking sex appeal

sextant /ˈsekstənt/ *n* an instrument for measuring angles that is used, esp in navigation, to observe the altitudes of celestial bodies and so determine the observer's position on the earth's surface

sextet /seksˈtet/ *n* (a musical composition for) a group of 6 instruments, voices, or performers

sexton /ˈsekstən/ *n* a church officer who takes care of the church property and is often also the gravedigger

sextuplet /sekˈstjuːplɪ̈t/ *n* **1** a combination of 6 of a kind **2** a group of 6 equal musical notes performed in the time ordinarily given to 4 of the same value

sexual intercourse *n* intercourse with genital contact **a** involving penetration of the vagina by the penis; coitus **b** other than penetration of the vagina by the penis

sexy /ˈseksi/ *adj* sexually suggestive or stimulating; erotic – **sexily** *adv* – **sexiness** *n*

sforzando /sfɔːtˈsændəʊ/ *n, adj, or adv, pl* **sforzandos, sforzandi** (a note or chord played) with prominent stress or accent – used in music

sh /ʃ/ *interj* – used often in prolonged or reduplicated form to urge or command silence

shabby /ˈʃæbi/ *v* **1a** threadbare or faded from wear **b** dilapidated, run-down **2** dressed in worn or grubby clothes; seedy **3** shameful, despicable – **-bily** *adv* – **-biness** *n*

shack /ʃæk/ *n* a small crudely built dwelling or shelter

[1]**shackle** /ˈʃækəl/ *n* **1** (a metal ring like) a manacle or handcuff **2** sthg that restricts or prevents free action or expression – usu pl with sing. meaning **3** a U-shaped piece of metal with a pin or bolt to close the opening

[2]**shackle** *v* **1** to bind or make fast with shackles **2** to deprive of freedom of thought or action by means of restrictions or handicaps

shack up *v* to live with and have a sexual relationship with sby; *also* to spend the night as a partner in sexual intercourse – usu + *together* or *with*

[1]**shade** /ʃeɪd/ *n* **1a** partial darkness caused by the interception of rays of light **b** relative obscurity or insignificance **2a** a transistory or illusory appearance **b** a ghost **3** sthg that intercepts or diffuses light or heat; e g **a** a lampshade **b** *chiefly NAm pl* sunglasses – infml **4** a particular level of depth or brightness of a colour **5** a minute difference or amount

[2]**shade** *v* **1** to shelter or screen by intercepting radiated light or heat **2** to darken or obscure (as if) with a shadow **3** to mark with shading or gradations of colour **4** to pass by slight changes or inperceptible degrees – usu + *into* or *off into*

shading /ˈʃeɪdɪŋ/ *n* an area of filled-in outlines to suggest three-dimensionality, shadow, or degrees of light and dark in a picture

[1]**shadow** /ˈʃædəʊ/ *n* **1** partial darkness caused by an opaque body interposed so as to cut off rays from a light source **2** a faint representation or suggestion; an imitation **3** a dark figure cast on a surface by a body intercepting light rays **4** a phantom **5** *pl* darkness **6** a shaded or darker portion of a picture **7a** an inseparable companion or follower **b** one (e g a spy or detective) who shadows **8** a small

degree or portion; a trace **9** a source of gloom or disquiet

[2]**shadow** *v* **1** to cast a shadow over **2** to follow (a person) secretly; keep under surveillance **3** to shade

[3]**shadow** *adj* **1** identical with another in form but without the other's power or status; *specif* of or constituting the probable cabinet when the opposition party is returned to power **2** shown by throwing the shadows of performers or puppets on a screen

shadow-box *v* to box with an imaginary opponent, esp as a form of training

shadowy /ˈʃædəʊi/ *adj* **1a** of the nature of or resembling a shadow, insubstantial **b** scarcely perceptible; indistinct **2** lying in or obscured by shadow

shady /ˈʃeɪdi/ *adj* **1** sheltered from the direct heat or light of the sun **2** of doubtful integrity; disreputable – chiefly infml

shaft /ʃɑːft/ *n* **1a** (the long handle of) a spear, lance, or similar weapon **b** either of 2 poles between which a horse is hitched to a vehicle **2** a sharply delineated beam of light shining from an opening **3a** the trunk of a tree **b** the cylindrical pillar between the capital and the base of a column **c** the handle of a tool or implement (e g a hammer or golf club) **d** a usu cylindrical bar used to support rotating pieces or to transmit power or motion by rotation **e** a man-made vertical or inclined opening leading underground to a mine, well, etc **f** a vertical opening or passage through the floors of a building **4** a scornful, satirical, or pithily critical remark; a barb

[1]**shag** /ʃæg/ *n* **1a** an unkempt or uneven tangled mass or covering (e g of hair) **b** long coarse or matted fibre or nap **2** a strong coarse tobacco cut into fine shreds **3** a European bird smaller than the closely related cormorant – **~gy** *adj*

[2]**shag** *v* **1** to fuck, screw – vulg **2** *Br* to make utterly exhausted – usu + *out*; slang

[3]**shag** *n* an act of sexual intercourse – vulg

shaggy-dog story *n* a protracted and inconsequential funny story whose humour lies in the pointlessness or irrelevance of the conclusion

shagreen /ʃəˈgriːn, ʃæ-/ *n* **1** an untanned leather covered with small round granulations and usu dyed green **2** the rough skin of various sharks and rays

shah /ʃɑː/ *n, often cap* a sovereign of Iran

[1]**shake** /ʃeɪk/ *v* **shook; shaken 1a** to move to and fro with rapid usu irregular motion **b** to brandish, wave, or flourish, esp in a threatening manner **2** to vibrate, esp from the impact of a blow or shock **3a** to tremble as a result of physical or emotional disturbance **b** to cause to quake, quiver, or tremble **4** to cause to waver; weaken **5** to clasp (hands) in greeting or farewell or to convey goodwill or agreement **6** to agitate the feelings of; upset

[2]**shake** *n* **1** an act of shaking **2** *pl* a condition of trembling (e g from chill or fever); *specif* delirium tremens **3** a wavering, vibrating, or alternating motion caused by a blow or shock **4** a trill **5** *chiefly NAm* a milk shake **6** a moment – (*6*) infml

shake down *v* **1** to stay the night or sleep, esp in a makeshift bed **2** to become comfortably established, esp in a new place or occupation

shakedown 1 /ˈʃeɪkdaʊn/ *n* a makeshift bed (e g one made up on the floor)

shakedown 2 *adj* designed to test a new ship, aircraft, etc and allow the crew to become familiar with it

shaker /ˈʃeɪkəʳ/ *n* **1** a container or utensil used to sprinkle or mix a substance by shaking **2** *cap* a member of an American sect practising celibacy and a self-denying communal life, and looking forward to the millennium

shake-up *n* an act or instance of shaking up; *specif* an extensive and often drastic reorganization (e g of a company) – infml

shake up *v* **1** to jar (as if) by a physical shock **2** to reorganize by extensive and often drastic measures – infml

shaky /ˈʃeɪki/ *adj* **1a** lacking stability; precarious **b** lacking in firmness (e g of beliefs or principals) **2** unsound in health; poorly **3** likely to give way or break down; rickety – **shakily** *adv* – **shakiness** *n*

shale /ʃeɪl/ *n* a finely stratified or laminated rock formed by the consolidation of clay

shale oil *n* a crude dark oil obtained from oil shale by heating

shall /ʃəl; *strong* ʃæl/ *verbal auxiliary pres sing & pl* **shall;** *past should* **1** – used to urge or command or denote what is legally mandatory **2a** –used to express what is inevitable or seems likely to happen in the future **b** – used in the question form to express simple futurity or with the force of an offer or suggestion **3** – used to express determination

shallot /ʃə'lɒt/ *n* (any of the small clusters of bulbs, used esp for pickling and in seasoning, produced by) a plant that resembles an onion

[1]**shallow** /'ʃæləʊ/ *adj* **1** having little depth **2** superficial in knowledge, thought, or feeling **3** not marked or accentuated – ~**ly** *adv* – ~**ness** *n*

[2]**shallow** *n* a shallow place in a body of water – usu pl with sing. meaning but sing. or pl in constr

shalom /ʃæ'lɒm/ *interj* – used as a Jewish greeting and farewell

shalt /ʃəlt; *strong* ʃælt/ *archaic pres 2 sing of* **shall**

[1]**sham** /ʃæm/ *n* **1** cheap falseness; hypocrisy **2** an imitation or counterfeit purporting to be genuine **3** a person who shams

[2]**sham** *v* to act so as to counterfeit; *also* to give a deliberately false impression

[1]**shamble** /'ʃæmbəl/ *v* to walk awkwardly with dragging feet; shuffle

[2]**shamble** *n* a shambling gait

shambles /'ʃæmbəlz/ *n* **1** a slaughterhouse **2a** a place of carnage **b** a scene or a state of chaos or confusion; a mess

[1]**shame** /ʃeɪm/ *n* **1** a painful emotion caused by consciousness of guilt, shortcomings, impropriety, or disgrace **2** humiliating disgrace or disrepute; ignominy **3** sthg bringing regret or disgrace

[2]**shame** *v* **1** to bring shame to; disgrace **2** to put to shame by outdoing **3** to fill with a sense of shame **4** to compel by causing to feel guilty

shamefaced /ˌʃeɪm'feɪst/ *adj* **1** showing modesty; bashful **2** showing shame; ashamed

shameful /'ʃeɪmfəl/ *adj* **1** bringing disrepute or igonminy; disgraceful **2** arousing the feeling of shame – ~**ly** *adv* – ~**ness** *n*

shameless /'ʃeɪmləs/ *adj* **1** insensible to disgrace **2** showing lack of shame; disgraceful – ~**ly** *adv* – ~**ness** *n*

[1]**shampoo** /ʃæm'puː/ *v* **1** to clean (esp the hair or a carpet) with shampoo **2** to wash the hair of

[2]**shampoo** *n* **1** a washing of the hair esp by a hairdresser **2** a soap, detergent, etc used for shampooing

shamrock /'ʃæmrɒk/ *n* any of several plants (e g a wood sorrel or some clovers) whose leaves have 3 leaflets and are used as a floral emblem by the Irish

shandy /'ʃændi/ *n* a drink consisting of beer mixed with lemonade or ginger beer

shanghai /ʃæŋ'haɪ/ *n* **1** to compel to join a ship's crew, esp by the help of drink or drugs **2** to put into an awkward or unpleasant position by trickery

Shangri-la /ˌʃæŋgri 'lɑː/ *n* a remote imaginary place where life approaches perfection

shank /ʃæŋk/ *n* **1a** a leg; *specif* the part of the leg between the knee and the ankle **b** a cut of beef, veal, mutton, or lamb from the upper of the lower part of the leg **2** a straight narrow usu vital part of an object; e g **a** the straight part of a nail or pin **b** the part of an anchor between the ring and the crown **c** the part of a fishhook between the eye and the bend **d** the part of a key between the handle and the bit **3** a part of an object by which it can be attached to sthg else: e g **a** a projection on the back of a solid button **b** the end (e g of a drill bit) that is gripped in a chuck

shanks's pony *n* one's own feet or legs considered as a means of transport

shantung /ʃæn'tʌŋ/ *n* a silk fabric in

plain weave with a slightly irregular surface

[1]**shanty** /ˈʃænti/ *n* a small crudely built or dilapidated dwelling or shelter; a shack

[2]**shanty** *n* a song sung by sailors in rhythm with their work

shanty town /ˈʃæntitaʊn/ *n* (part of) a town consisting mainly of shanties

[1]**shape** /ʃeɪp/ *v* **1** to form, create; *esp* to give a particular form or shape to **2** to adapt in shape so as to fit neatly and closely **3** to guide or mould into a particular state or condition **4** to determine or direct the course of (e g a person's life)

[2]**shape** *n* **1a** the visible or tactile form of a particular (kind of) item **b** spatial form **2** the contour of the body, esp of the trunk; the figure **3** an assumed appearance; a guise **4** definite form (e g in thought or words) **5** a general structure or plan **6** sthg made in a particular form **7** the condition of a person or thing, esp at a particular time – **shapeless** *adj* – **~lessly** *adv* – **~lessness** *n*

shapely /ˈʃeɪpli/ *adj* having a pleasing shape; well-proportioned – **-liness** *n*

shape up *v* to (begin to) behave or perform satisfactorily

shard /ʃɑːd/ *n* a piece or fragment of sthg brittle (e g earthenware)

[1]**share** /ʃeəʳ/ *n* **1a** a portion belonging to, due to, or contributed by an individual **b** a full or fair portion **2a** the part allotted or belonging to any of a number owning property or interest together **b** any of the equal portions into which property or invested capital is divided **c** *pl, chiefly Br* the proprietorship element in a company, usu represented by transferable certificates

[2]**share** *v* **1** to divide and distribute in shares; apportion – usu + *out* **2** to partake of, use, experience, or enjoy with others **3** to have a share or part – often + *in*

[3]**share** *n* a ploughshare

sharecropper /ˈʃeə,krɒpəʳ/ *n, NAm* a tenant farmer, esp in southern USA, who lives on credit provided by the landlord and receives an agreed share of the value of the crop

shareholder /ˈʃeə,həʊldəʳ/ *n* the holder or owner of a share in property

shark /ʃɑːk/ *n* **1** any of numerous mostly large typically grey marine fishes that are mostly active, voracious, and predators and have gill slits at the sides and a mouth on the under part of the body **2** a greedy unscrupulous person who exploits others by usury, extortion, or trickery

[1]**sharp** /ʃɑːp/ *adj* **1** (adapted to) cutting or piercing: e g **a** having a thin keen edge or fine point **b** bitingly cold; icy **2a** keen in intellect, perception, attention, etc **b** paying shrewd usu selfish attention to personal gain **3a** brisk, vigorous **b** capable of acting or reacting strongly; *esp* caustic **4a** marked by irritability or anger; fiery **b** causing intense usu sudden anguish **5** affecting the senses or sense organs intensely; e g **a(1)** pungent, tart, or acid, esp in flavour **(2)** acrid **b** shrill, piercing **6a** characterized by hard lines and angles **b** involving an abrupt change in direction **c** clear in outline or detail; distinct **7** *of a musical note* raised a semitone in pitch **8** stylish, dressy – infml – **~ly** *adv* – **~ness** *n*

[2]**sharp** *adv* **1** in an abrupt manner **2** exactly, precisely **3** above the proper musical pitch

[3]**sharp** *n* **1** a musical note 1 semitone higher than another indicated or previously specified note **2** a relatively long needle with a sharp point and a small rounded eye for use in general sewing **3** *chiefly NAm* a swindler, sharper

sharpen /ˈʃɑːpən/ *v* to make or become sharp or sharper – **~er** *n*

sharpshooter /ˈʃɑːp,ʃuːtəʳ/ *n* a good marksman

shatter /ˈʃætəʳ/ *v* **1** to break suddenly apart; disintegrate **2** to have a forceful or violent effect on the feelings of **3** to cause to be utterly exhausted

[1]**shave** /ʃeɪv/ *v* **shaved, shaven 1a** to remove in thin layers or shreds – often + *off* **b** to cut or trim closely **2** to cut off (hair or beard) close to the skin **3** to come very close to or brush against in passing

[2]**shave** *n* **1** a tool or machine for shaving **2** an act or process of shaving

shaver /ˈʃeɪvəʳ/ *n* **1** an electric-powered razor **2** a boy, youngster

shaving /ˈʃeɪvɪŋ/ *n* sthg shaved off – usu pl

shawl /ʃɔːl/ *n* a usu decorative square, oblong, or triangular piece of fabric that is worn to cover the head or shoulders

[1]**she** /ʃi; *strong* ʃiː/ *pron* **1** that female person or creature who is neither speaker nor hearer **2** – used to refer to sthg (e g a ship) regarded as feminine

[2]**she** *n* a female person or creature – often in combination

sheaf /ʃiːf/ *n, pl* **sheaves** **1** a quantity of plant material, esp the stalks and ears of a cereal grass, bound together **2** a collection of items laid or tied together

[1]**shear** /ʃɪəʳ/ *v* **sheared, shorn** **1** to cut or clip (hair, wool, a fleece, etc) from sby or sthg; *also* to cut sthg from **2** to cut with sthg sharp **3** to deprive of sthg as if by cutting off – usu passive + *of* **4** to become divided or separated under the action of a shear force

[2]**shear** *n* **1a** a cutting implement similar to a pair of scissors but typically larger **b** any of various cutting tools or machines operating by the action of opposed cutting edges of metal **2** an action or force that causes or tends to cause 2 parts of a body to slide on each other in a direction parallel to their plane of contact – (*1a, b*) usu pl with sing. meaning

sheath /ʃiːθ/ *n* **1** a case or cover for a blade (e g of a knife or sword) **2** a cover or case of a (part of a) plant or animal body **3** a condom

sheathe /ʃiːð/ *v* **1** to put into or provide with a sheath **2** to withdraw (a claw) into a sheath **3** to encase or cover with sthg protective (e g thin boards or sheets of metal)

[1]**shed** /ʃed/ *v* **shed** **1** to be incapable of holding or absorbing; repel **2a** to cause (blood) to flow by wounding or killing **b** to pour forth; let flow **3** to cast off hairs, threads etc; moult

[2]**shed** *n* a usu single-storied building for shelter, storage, etc, esp with 1 or more sides open

she'd /ʃid; *strong* ʃiːd/ she had; she would

sheen /ʃiːn/ *n* **1** a bright or shining quality or condition; brightness, lustre **2** a subdued shininess or glitter of a surface **3** a lustrous surface imparted to textiles through finishing processes or use of shiny yarns

sheep /ʃiːp/ *n, pl* **sheep** **1** any of numerous ruminant mammals related to the goats but stockier and lacking a beard in the male; *specif* one domesticated, esp for its flesh and wool **2** an inane or docile person; *esp* one easily influenced or led

sheep-dip *n* a liquid preparation into which sheep are plunged, esp to destroy parasites

sheepdog /ˈʃiːpdɒg/ *n* a dog used to tend, drive, or guard sheep; *esp* a collie

sheepish /ˈʃiːpɪʃ/ *adj* embarrassed by consciousness of a fault – **~ly** *adv* – **~ness** *n*

sheepskin /ˈʃiːpˌskɪn/ *n* **1** (leather from) the skin of a sheep **2** the skin of a sheep dressed with the wool on

[1]**sheer** /ʃɪəʳ/ *adj* **1** transparently fine; diaphanous **2a** unqualified, utter **b** not mixed or mingled with anything else; pure, unadulterated **3** marked by great and unbroken steepness; precipitous

[2]**sheer** *adv* **1** altogether, completely **2** straight up or down without a break

[3]**sheer** *v* to (cause to) deviate from a course

[4]**sheer** *n* a turn, deviation, or change in a course (e g of a ship)

[1]**sheet** /ʃiːt/ *n* **1** a broad piece of cloth; *specif* a rectangle of cloth (e g of linen or cotton) used as an article of bed linen **2a** a usu rectangular piece of paper **b** a printed section for a book, esp before it has been folded, cut, or bound – usu pl **3** a broad usu flat expanse **4** a suspended or moving expanse **5** a piece of sthg that is thin in comparison to its length and breadth

[2]**sheet** *v* **1** to form into, provide with, or cover with a sheet or sheets **2** to come down in sheets

[3]**sheet** *adj* rolled into or spread out in a sheet

[4]**sheet** *n* **1** a rope that regulates the

angle at which a sail is set in relation to the wind **2** *pl* the spaces at either end of an open boat

sheet anchor *n* **1** an emergency anchor formerly carried in the broadest part of a ship **2** a principal support or dependence, esp in danger; a mainstay

sheeting /ˈʃiːtɪŋ/ *n* (material suitable for making into) sheets

sheet lightning *n* lightning in diffused or sheet form due to reflection and diffusion by clouds

sheikh, sheik /ʃeɪk/ **1** an Arab chief **2 sheik, sheikh** a romantically attractive or dashing man

sheila, sheilah /ˈʃiːlə/ *n, Austr, NZ, & SAfr* a young woman; a girl – infml

shekel /ˈʃekəl/ *n* **1** the standard currency of Israel **2** *pl* money – infml

shelduck /ˈʃeldʌk/ *n* a common mostly black and white duck slightly larger than the mallard

shelf /ʃelf/ *n, pl* **shelves** **1** a thin flat usu long and narrow piece of material (e g wood) fastened horizontally (e g on a wall or in a cupboard, bookcase, etc) at a distance from the floor to hold objects **2a** a (partially submerged) sandbank or ledge of rocks **b** a flat projecting layer of rock

[1]**shell** /ʃel/ *n* **1a** a hard rigid often largely calcium-containing covering of a (sea) animal **b** the hard or tough outer covering of an egg, esp a bird's egg **2** the covering or outside part of a fruit or seed, esp when hard or fibrous **3a** a framework or exterior structure; *esp* the outer frame of a building that is unfinished or has been destroyed (e g by fire) **b** a hollow form devoid of substance **c** an edible case for holding a filling **4** a cold and reserved attitude that conceals the presence or absence of feeling **5a** a projectile for a cannon containing an explosive bursting charge **b** a metal or paper case which holds the charge in cartridges, fireworks, etc

[2]**shell** *v* **1** to take out of a natural enclosing cover, esp a pod **2** to fire shells at, on, or into

she'll /ʃil; *strong* ʃiːl/ she will; she shall

shellac /ˈʃelæk/ *n* the purified form of a resin produced by various insects, usu obtained as yellow or orange flakes; *also* a solution of this in alcohol used esp in making varnish

shellfish /ˈʃel,fɪʃ/ *n* an aquatic invertebrate animal with a shell; *esp* an edible mollusc or crustacean

shell out *v* to pay (money) – infml

shell shock *n* a mental disorder characterized by neurotic and often hysterical symptoms that occurs under conditions (e g wartime combat) that cause intense stress

[1]**shelter** /ˈʃeltəʳ/ *n* **1** sthg. esp a structure, affording cover or protection **2** the state of being covered and protected; refuge

[2]**shelter** *v* **1** to take shelter **2** to keep concealed or protected

shelve /ʃelv/ *v* **1** to provide with shelves **2** to put off or aside **3** to slope gently

shelving /ˈʃelviŋ/ *n* (material for constructing) shelves

shenanigan /ʃə̇ˈnænɪgən/ *n* **1** deliberate deception; trickery **2** boisterous mischief; high jinks – usu pl with sing. meaning USE infml

[1]**shepherd** /ˈʃepəd/ *n* **1** *fem* **shepherdess** one who tends sheep **2** a pastor

[2]**shepherd** *v* **1** to tend as a shepherd **2** to guide, marshal, or conduct (people) like sheep

shepherd's pie *n* a hot dish of minced meat, esp lamb, with a mashed potato topping

Sheraton /ˈʃerətn/ *adj* of or being a style of furniture that originated in England around 1800 and is characterized by straight lines and graceful proportions

sherbet /ˈʃɜːbət/ *n* **1** (a drink made with) a sweet powder that effervesces in liquid and is eaten dry or used to make fizzy drinks **2** a water ice with egg white, gelatin, or sometimes milk added

sherd /ʃɜːd/ *n* **1** a shard **2** fragments of pottery vessels

sheriff /ˈʃerə̇f/ *n* **1** the honorary chief executive officer of the Crown in each English county who has mainly judicial and ceremonial duties **2** the chief judge of a Scottish county or district **3** a county law enforcement officer in the USA

Sherpa /ˈʃɜːpə/ *n* a member of a

Tibetan people living on the high southern slopes of the Himalayas

sherry /ˈʃeri/ *n* a blended fortified wine from S Spain that varies in colour from very light to dark brown

she's /ʃisz; *strong* ʃiːz/ she is; she has

Shetland pony *n* (any of) a breed of small stocky shaggy hardy ponies that originated in the Shetland islands of N Scotland

Shetland wool *n* (yarn spun from) fine wool from sheep raised in the Shetland islands

shibboleth /ˈʃibəleθ/ *n* **1a** a catchword, slogan **b** a use of language that distinguishes a group of people **c** a commonplace belief or saying **2** a custom that characterizes members of a particular group

¹shield /ʃiːld/ *n* **1** a piece of armour (e g of wood, metal, or leather) carried on the arm or in the hand and used esp for warding off blows **2** sby or sthg that protects or defends; a defence **3** a piece of material or a pad attached inside a garment (e g a dress) at the armpit to protect the garment from perspiration **4** sthg designed to protect people from injury from moving parts of machinery, live electrical conductors, etc **5** the Precambrian central rock mass of a continent

²shield *v* **1** to protect (as if) with a shield; provide with a protective cover or shelter **2** to cut off from observation; hide

¹shift /ʃɪft/ *v* **1** to exchange for or replace by another; change **2** to change the place, position, or direction of; move **3** to get rid of; dispose of **4** to assume responsibility for

²shift *n* **1** a loose unfitted slip or dress **2a** a change in direction **b** a change in emphasis, judgment, or attitude **3** *sing or pl in constr* a group who work (e g in a factory) in alternation with other groups **4** a change in place or position

shift key *n* a key on a keyboard (e g of a typewriter) that when held down permits a different set of characters, esp the capitals, to be printed

shiftless /ˈʃɪftləs/ *adj* **1** lacking resourcefulness; inefficient **2** lacking ambition or motivation; lazy

shifty /ˈʃɪfti/ *adj* **1** given to deception, evasion, or fraud; slippery **2** indicative of a fickle or devious nature – **-tily** *adv* – **-tiness** *n*

shilling /ˈʃɪlɪŋ/ *n* **1** (a coin representing) a former money unit of the UK worth 12 old pence or £1/20 **2** a money unit equal to £1/20 of any of various other countries (formerly) in the Commonwealth

shilly-shally /ˈʃɪli,ʃæli/ *v* to show hesitation or lack of decisiveness

¹shimmer /ˈʃɪməʳ/ *v* **1** to shine with a softly tremulous or wavering light; glimmer **2** to (cause sthg to) appear in a fluctuating wavy form

²shimmer *n* **1** a shimmering light **2** a wavering and distortion of the visual image of a far object usu resulting from heat-induced changes in atmospheric refraction

¹shin /ʃɪn/ the front part of the leg of a vertebrate animal below the knee; *also* a cut of meat from this part, esp from the front leg

²shin *v* to climb by gripping with the hands or arms and the legs and hauling oneself up or lowering oneself down

shinbone /ˈʃɪnbəʊn/ *n* the tibia

shindy /ˈʃɪndi/ *n* a quarrel, brawl – infml

¹shine /ʃaɪn/ *v* **shone** **1** to emit light **2** to be bright with reflected light **3** to be outstanding or distinguished **4** to make bright by polishing **5** to direct the light of

²shine *n* **1** brightness caused by the emission or reflection of light **2** brilliance, splendour **3** fine weather; sunshine **4** an act of polishing shoes **5** a fancy, crush –esp in *take a shine to;* infml

¹shingle /ˈʃɪŋgəl/ *n* **1** a small piece of building material for laying in overlapping rows as a covering for the roof or sides of a building **2** a woman's short haircut in which the hair is shaped into the nape of the neck

²shingle *v* **1** to cover (as if) with shingles **2** to cut (hair) in a shingle

³shingle *n* (a place, esp a seashore, strewn with) small rounded pebbles.

shingles /ˈʃɪŋgəlz/ *n pl but sing in constr* severe short-lasting inflammation of certain nerves that leave the brain and spinal cord, caused by a virus and associated with a rash of blisters and often intense neuralgic pain

Shinto /ˈʃɪntəʊ/ *n* the indigenous animistic religion of Japan, including the veneration of the Emperor as a descendant of the sun-goddess

shiny /ˈʃaɪni/ *adj* **1** bright or glossy in appearance; lustrous, polished **2** *of material, clothes, etc* rubbed or worn to a smooth surface that reflects light

[1]**ship** /ʃɪp/ *n* **1** a large seagoing vessel **2** a boat (propelled by power or sail) **3** *sing or pl in constr* a ship's crew **4** an airship, aircraft, or spacecraft

[2]**ship** *v* **1** to place or receive on board a ship for transportation **2** to put in place for use **3** to take into a ship or boat **4** to engage for service on a ship **5** to cause to be transported or sent

shipboard *adj* existing or taking place on board a ship

shipment /ˈʃɪpmənt/ *n* **1** the act or process of shipping **2** the quantity of goods shipped

shipper /ˈʃɪpəʳ/ *n* a person or company that ships goods

shipping /ˈʃɪpɪŋ/ *n* **1** ships (in 1 place or belonging to 1 port or country) **2** the act or business of a shipper

shipshape /ˈʃɪpʃeɪp/ trim, tidy

[1]**shipwreck** /ˈʃɪp-rek/ *n* **1** a wrecked ship or its remains **2** the destruction or loss of a ship **3** an irrevocable collapse or destruction

[2]**shipwreck** *v* **1** to cause to undergo shipwreck **2** to ruin

shipwright /ˈʃɪp-raɪt/ *n* a carpenter skilled in ship construction and repair

shire /ʃaɪəʳ/ *n* **1a** an administrative subdivision; *specif* an English county, esp with a name ending in *-shire* **b** *pl the* English fox-hunting district consisting chiefly of Leicestershire and Northamptonshire **2** any of a British breed of large heavy draught horses

shirk /ʃɜːk/ *v* to evade or dodge a duty, responsibility, etc

shirring /ˈʃɜːrɪŋ/ *n* a decorative gathering, esp in cloth, made by drawing up the material along 2 or more parallel lines of stitching or by stitching in rows of elastic thread or an elastic webbing

shirt /ʃɜːt/ *n* an (esp man's) garment for the upper body; *esp* one that opens the full length of the centre front and has sleeves and a collar

shirting /ˈʃɜːtɪŋ/ *n* fabric suitable for shirts

shirt-sleeve *also* **shirt-sleeves, shirt-sleeved** *adj* **1** (having members) without a jacket **2** marked by informality and directness

shirty /ˈʃɜːti/ bad-tempered, fractious

shish kebab /ˈʃɪʃ kə̩ˌbæb/ *n* kebab cooked on skewers

shit /ʃɪt/ *n* **1** faeces **2** an act of defecation **3a** nonsense, foolishness **b** a despicable person *USE* vulg

shitty /ˈʃɪti/ *adj* nasty, unpleasant – vulg

[1]**shiver** /ˈʃɪvəʳ/ *n* any of the small pieces that result from the shattering of sthg brittle

[2]**shiver** *v* to break into many small fragments; shatter

[3]**shiver** *v* to tremble, esp with cold or fever

[4]**shiver** *n* an instance of shivering; a tremor

[1]**shoal** /ʃəʊl/ *n* **1** a shallow **2** an underwater sandbank; *esp* one exposed at low tide

[2]**shoal** *v* to become shallow or less deep

[3]**shoal** *n* a large group (e g of fish)

[1]**shock** /ʃɒk/ *n* a pile of sheaves of grain or stalks of maize set upright in a field

[2]**shock** *n* **1** a violent shaking or jarring **2a** a disturbance in the equilibrium or permanence of sthg (e g a system) **b** a sudden or violent disturbance of thoughts or emotions **3** a state of serious depression of most bodily functions associated with reduced blood volume and pressure and caused usu by severe injuries, bleeding, or burns **4** sudden stimulation of the nerves and convulsive contraction of the muscles caused by the passage of electricity through the body

[3]**shock** *v* **1a** to cause to feel sudden surprise, terror, horror, or offence **b** to cause to undergo a physical or nerv-

ous shock **2** to cause (e g an animal) to experience an electric shock

[4]**shock** *n* a thick bushy mass, usu of hair

shock absorber *n* any of various devices for absorbing the energy of sudden impulses or shocks in machinery, vehicles, etc

shocking /ˈʃɒkɪŋ/ *adj* **1** giving cause for indignation or offence **2** very bad – infml

shockproof /ˈʃɒkpruːf/ *adj* resistant to shock; constructed so as to absorb shock without damage

shock troops *n pl* troops trained and selected for assault

shod /ʃɒd/ *adj* **1a** wearing shoes, boots, etc **b** equipped with (a specified type or) tyres **2** furnished or equipped with a shoe

[1]**shoddy** /ˈʃɒdi/ *n* a fabric often of inferior quality manufactured wholly or partly from reclaimed wool

[2]**shoddy** *adj* **1** made wholly or partly of shoddy **2a** cheaply imitative; vulgarly pretentious **b** hastily or poorly done; inferior **c** shabby

[1]**shoe** /ʃuː/ *n* **1a** an outer covering for the human foot that does not extend above the ankle and has a thick or stiff sole and often an attached heel **b** a metal plate or rim for the hoof of an animal **2** sthg resembling a shoe in shape or function **3** *pl* a situation, position; *also* a predicament **4** the part of a vehicle braking system that presses on the brake drum

[2]**shoe** *v* **shoeing; shod** **1** to fit (e g a horse) with a shoe **2** to protect or reinforce with a usu metal shoe

shoehorn /ˈʃuːhɔːn/ *n* a curved piece of metal, plastic, etc used to ease the heel into the back of a shoe

shoe-horn *v* to force into a limited space

shoelace /ˈʃuːleɪs/ *n* a lace or string for fastening a shoe

[1]**shoestring** /ˈʃuːˌstrɪŋ/ *n* **1** a shoelace **2** an amount of money inadequate or barely adequate to meet one's needs

[2]**shoestring** *adj* operating on, accomplished with, or consisting of a small amount of money

shone /ʃɒn/ *past of* **shine**

[1]**shoo** /ʃuː/ *interj* – used in frightening away an (esp domestic) animal

[2]**shoo** *v* to drive away (as if) by crying 'shoo''

shook /ʃʊk/ *past & chiefly dial past part of* **shake**

[1]**shoot** /ʃuːt/ *v* **shot** **1a** to eject or impel by a sudden release of tension (e g of a bowstring or by a flick of a finger) **b** to drive forth **(1)** by an explosion (e g of a powder charge in a firearm or of ignited fuel in a rocket) **(2)** by a sudden release of gas or air **c** to drive the ball or puck in football, hockey, etc towards a goal **d** to send forth with suddenness or intensity **2** to wound or kill with a bullet, arrow, shell, etc shot from a gun, bow, etc **3a** to push or slide (a bolt) in order to fasten or unfasten a door **b** to pass (a shuttle) through the warp threads in weaving **c** to push or thrust forwards; stick out –usu + *out* **d** to put forth in growing – usu + *out* **4** to score by shooting **5** to hunt over with a firearm or bow **6** to cause to move suddenly or swiftly forwards **7** to pass swiftly by, over, or along **8** to take a picture or series of pictures or television images of; film; *also* to make (a film, videotape, etc)

[2]**shoot** *n* **1** a stem or branch with its leaves, buds, etc, esp when not yet mature **2a** a shooting trip or party **b** (land over which is held) the right to shoot game **3** (a rush of water down) a descent in a stream

shooting match *n* an affair, matter – chiefly in *the whole shooting match*; infml

shooting star *n* a meteor appearing as a temporary streak of light in the night sky

shooting stick *n* a spiked stick with a handle that opens out into a seat

shoot-out *n* a usu decisive battle fought with handguns or rifles

[1]**shop** /ʃɒp/ *n* **1** a building or room for the retail sale of merchandise or for the sale of services **2** a place or part of a factory where a particular manufacturing or repair process takes place **3** the jargon or subject matter peculiar to an occupation or sphere of interest – chiefly in *talk shop*

[2]**shop** *v* **1** to visit a shop with intent to purchase goods **2** to make a search; hunt **3** to inform on; betray

shop around *v* to investigate a market or situation in search of the best buy or alternative

shop assistant *n, Br* one employed to sell goods in a retail shop

shopfloor /ˌ-ˈflɔː/ *n* the area in which machinery or workbenches are located in a factory or mill, esp considered as a place or work; *also, sing or pl in constr* the workers in an establishment as distinct from the management

shoplift /ˈ-ˌlɪft/ *v* to steal from a shop – **~ing** *n*

shopping centre *n* a group of retail shops and service establishments of different types, often designed to serve a community or neighbourhood

shopsoiled *adj, chiefly Br* **1** deteriorated (e g soiled or faded) through excessive handling or display in a shop **2** no longer fresh or effective; clichéd

shop steward *n* a union member elected to represent usu manual workers

[1]**shore** /ʃɔːʳ/ *n* **1** the land bordering the sea or another (large) body of water **2** land as distinguished from the sea

[2]**shore** *v* **1** to support with shores; prop **2** to give support to; brace, sustain – usu + *up*

[3]**shore** *n* a prop for preventing sinking or sagging

shorn /ʃɔːn/ *past part of* **shear**

[1]**short** /ʃɔːt/ *adj* **1** having little or insufficient length or height **2a** not extended in time; brief **b** *of the memory* not retentive **c** quick, expeditious **d** seeming to pass quickly **3a** *of a speech sound* having a relatively short duration **b** *of a syllable in prosody* unstressed **4** limited in distance **5a** not coming up to a measure or requirement **b** insufficiently supplied **6a** abrupt, curt **b** quickly provoked **7** *of pastry, biscuits, etc* crisp and easily broken owing to the presence of fat **8** made briefer; abbreviated **9** being or relating to a sale of securities or commodities that the seller does not possess at the time of the sale

[2]**short** *adv* **1** curtly **2** for or during a brief time **3** in an abrupt manner; suddenly **4** at a point or degree before a specified or intended goal or limit

[3]**short** **1** *pl* knee-length or less than knee-length trousers **2** *pl* short-term bonds **3** a short circuit **4** a brief often documentary or educational film **5** *Br* a drink of spirits

[4]**short** *v* to short-circuit

shortage /ˈʃɔːtɪdʒ/ *n* a lack, deficit

shortbread /ˈʃɔːtbred/ *n* a thick biscuit made from flour, sugar, and fat

shortchange /ˌʃɔːtˈtʃeɪndʒ/ *v* **1** to give less than the correct amount of change to **2** to cheat – infml

short-circuit *v* **1** to apply a short circuit to or cause a short circuit in (so as to render inoperative) **2** to bypass, circumvent

short circuit *n* the accidental or deliberate joining by a conductor of 2 parts of an electric circuit

shortcoming /ˈʃɔːtˌkʌmɪŋ/ *n* a deficiency, defect

shortcut /ˌʃɔːtˈkʌt, ˈ--/ *n* a route or procedure quicker and more direct than one customarily followed

shorten /ˈʃɔːtn/ *v* **1** to make short or shorter **2** to add fat to (e g pastry dough) **3** to reduce the area or amount of (sail that is set)

shortening /ˈʃɔːtnɪŋ/ *n* an edible fat (e g butter or lard) used to shorten pastry, biscuits, etc

shortfall /ˈʃɔːtfɔːl/ *n* (the degree or amount of) a deficit

shorthand /ˈʃɔːthænd/ *n* **1** a method of rapid writing that substitutes symbols and abbreviations for letters, words, or phrases **2** a system or instance of rapid or abbreviated communication

shorthanded /ˌʃɔːtˈhændɨd/ *adj* short of the usual or requisite number of staff; undermanned

shorthand typist *n* sby who takes shorthand notes, esp from dictation, then transcribes them using a typewriter

short list *n, Br* a list of selected candidates (e g for a job) from whom a final choice must be made

short-lived *adj* not living or lasting long

shortly /ˈʃɔːtli/ *adv* **1a** in a few words; briefly **b** in an abrupt manner

2a in a short time b at a short interval

short-range *adj* 1 short-term 2 relating to, suitable for, or capable of travelling (only) short distances

short shrift *n* 1 a brief respite for confession before execution 2 summary or inconsiderable treatment

shortsighted /ˌʃɔːtˈsaɪtɪ̣d/ *adj* 1 able to see near objects more clearly than distant objects 2 lacking foresight

short story *n* a piece of prose fiction usu dealing with a few characters and often concentrating on mood rather than plot

short-term *adj* 1 involving a relatively short period of time 2 of or constituting a financial operation or obligation based on a brief term, esp one of less than a year

shortwave /ˌʃɔːtˈweɪv/ *n* a band of radio waves having wavelengths between about 120m and 20m and typically used for amateur transmissions or long-range broadcasting – often pl with sing. meaning

short-winded *adj* 1 affected with or characterized by shortness of breath 2 brief or concise in speaking or writing

[1]**shot** /ʃɒt/ *n* 1a an action of shooting b a directed propelling of a missile; *specif* a directed discharge of a firearm c a stroke or throw in a game (e g tennis, cricket, or basketball); *also* an attempt to kick the ball into the goal in soccer d a hypodermic injection 2a(1) small lead or steel pellets (for a shotgun) (2) a single (nonexplosive) projectile for a gun or cannon b a metal sphere that is thrown for distance as an athletic field event 3 one who shoots; *esp* a marksman 4a an attempt, try b a guess, conjecture 5a a single photographic exposure b an image or series of images in a film or a television programme shot by a camera from 1 angle without interruption 6 a small amount applied at one time; a dose

[2]**shot** *adj* 1a *of a fabric* having contrasting and changeable colour effects; iridescent b infused or permeated *with* a quality or element 2 utterly exhausted or ruined

[1]**shotgun** /ˈʃɒtgʌn/ *n* an often double-barrelled smoothbore shoulder weapon for firing quantities of metal shot at short ranges

[2]**shotgun** *adj* enforced

shot put /ˈʃɒtpʊt/ *n* the athletic event of throwing the shot

should /ʃəd; *strong* ʃʊd/ *past of* **shall** 1 – used (e g in the main clause of a conditional sentence) to introduce a contingent fact, possibility, or presumption 2 ought to 3 used in reported speech to represent *shall* or *will* 4 will probably 5 –used to soften a direct statement

[1]**shoulder** /ˈʃəʊldəʳ/ *n* 1 the part of the human body formed of bones, joints, and muscles that connects the arm to the trunk; *also* a corresponding part of another animal 2 *pl* a the 2 shoulders and the upper part of the back b capacity for bearing a burden (e g of blame or responsibility) 3 a cut of meat including the upper joint of the foreleg and adjacent parts 4 an area adjacent to a higher, more prominent, or more important part; e g a(1) the slope of a mountain near the top (2) a lateral protrusion of a mountain b that part of a road to the side of the surface on which vehicles travel 5 a rounded or sloping part (e g of a stringed instrument or a bottle) where the neck joins the body

[2]**shoulder** *v* 1 to push or thrust (as if) with the shoulder 2a to place or carry on the shoulder b to assume the burden or responsibility of

shoulder blade *n* the scapula

shouldest /ˈʃʊdɪst/ , **shouldst** /ʃʊdst/ *archaic past 2 sing of* **shall**

[1]**shout** /ʃaʊt/ *v* 1 to utter a sudden loud cry or in a loud voice 2 to buy a round of drinks

shout 2 *n* 1 a loud cry or call 2 a round of drinks

shove /ʃʌv/ *v* 1 to push along with steady force 2 to push in a rough, careless, or hasty manner; thrust 3 to force a way forwards – **shove** *n*

[1]**shovel** /ˈʃʌvəl/ *n* 1a an implement consisting of a broad scoop or a dished blade with a handle, used to lift and throw loose material b (a similar part on) a digging or earth-moving machine 2 a shovelful

[2]**shovel** *v* 1 to dig, clear, or shift with

a shovel **2** to convey clumsily or in a mass as if with a shovel

shove off *v* to go away; leave – infml

[1]**show** /ʃəʊ/ *v* **shown, showed 1a** to cause or permit to be seen; exhibit **b** to be or come in view **c** to appear in a specified way **2** to present as a public spectacle **3** to reveal by one's condition **4** to demonstrate by one's achievements **5a** to point out to sby **b** to conduct, usher **6** to make evident; indicate **7a** to establish or make clear by argument or reasoning **b** to inform, instruct

[2]**show** *n* **1** a display – often + *on* **2a** a false semblance; a pretence **b** a more or less true appearance of sthg **c** an impressive display **d** ostentation **3a** a large display or exhibition arranged to arouse interest or stimulate sales **b** a competitive exhibition of animals, plants, etc to demonstrate quality in breeding, growing, etc **4a** a theatrical presentation **b** a radio or television programme **5** an enterprise, affair

show biz /ˈʃəʊbɪz/ *n* show business – infml

show business *n* the arts, occupations, and businesses (e g theatre, films, and television) that comprise the entertainment industry

showdown /ˈʃəʊdaʊn/ *n* the final settlement of a contested issue or the confrontation by which it is settled

[1]**shower** /ˈʃaʊəʳ/ *n* **1** a fall of rain, snow, etc of short duration **2** sthg like a rain shower **3** an apparatus that provides a stream of water for spraying on the body; *also* an act of washing oneself using such an apparatus **4** *sing or pl in constr, Br* a motley or inferior collection of people – infml

[2]**shower** *v* **1a** to wet copiously (e g with water) in a spray, fine stream, or drops **b** to descend (as if) in a shower **c** to cause to fall in a shower **2** to bestow or present in abundance **3** to take a shower

showing /ˈʃəʊɪŋ/ *n* **1** an act of putting sthg on view; a display, exhibition **2** performance in competition

showjumping /ˈʃəʊˌdʒʌmpɪŋ/ *n* the competitive riding of horses 1 at a time over a set course of obstacles in which the winner is judged according to ability and speed

showman /ˈʃəʊmən/ *n* **1** one who presents a theatrical show; *also* the manager of a circus or fairground **2** a person with a flair for dramatically effective presentation

show off *v* **1** to exhibit proudly **2** to seek attention or admiration by conspicuous behaviour – **show-off** *n*

showpiece /ˈʃəʊpiːs/ *n* a prime or outstanding example used for exhibition

showplace /ˈʃəʊpleɪs/ *n* a place (e g an estate or building) regarded as an example of beauty or excellence

showroom /ˈʃəʊrʊm, -ruːm/ *n* a room where (samples of) goods for sale are displayed

show up *v* **1a** to be plainly evident; stand out **b** to appear in a specified light or manner **2** to expose (e g a defect, deception, or impostor) **3** to embarrass **4** to arrive

showy /ˈʃəʊi/ *adj* **1** making an attractive show; striking **2** given to or marked by pretentious display; gaudy – **-wily** *adv* – **-winess** *n*

shrank /ʃræŋk/ *past of* **shrink**

shrapnel /ˈʃræpnəl/ *n* **1** a hollow projectile that contains bullets or pieces of metal and that is exploded by a bursting charge to produce a shower of fragments **2** bomb, mine, or shell fragments thrown out during explosion

[1]**shred** /ʃred/ *n* a narrow strip cut or torn off; *also* a fragment, scrap

[2]**shred** *v* to cut or tear into shreds – **~der** *n*

shrew /ʃruː/ *n* **1** any of numerous small chiefly nocturnal mammals having a long pointed snout, very small eyes, and velvety fur **2** an ill-tempered nagging woman; a scold

shrewd /ʃruːd/ *adj* **1** marked by keen discernment and hardheaded practicality **2** wily, artful – **~ly** *adv* – **~ness** *n*

shrewish /ˈʃruːɪʃ/ *adj* ill-tempered, intractable

[1]**shriek** /ʃriːk/ *v* **1** to utter or make a shrill piercing cry; screech **2** to utter with a shriek or sharply and shrilly – often + *out*

[2]**shriek** *n* (a sound similar to) a shrill usu wild cry

shrike /ʃraɪk/ *n* any of numerous usu largely grey or brownish birds that often impale their (insect) prey on thorns

[1]**shrill** /ʃrɪl/ *v* to utter or emit a high-pitched piercing sound

[2]**shrill** *adj* having, making, or being a sharp high-pitched sound

[1]**shrimp** /ʃrɪmp/ *n* **1** any of numerous mostly small marine 10-legged crustacean animals with a long slender body, compressed abdomen, and long legs **2** a very small or puny person – infml; humor

[2]**shrimp** *v* to fish for or catch shrimps – usu in *go shrimping*

shrine /ʃraɪn/ *n* **1a** a receptacle for sacred relics **b** a place in which devotion is paid to a saint or deity **2** a place or object hallowed by its history or associations

[1]**shrink** /ʃrɪŋk/ *v* **shrank** *also* **shrunk; shrunk, shrunken** **1** to draw back or cower away (e g from sthg painful or horrible) **2** to contract to a smaller volume or extent (e g as a result of heat or moisture) **3** to show reluctance (e g before a difficult or unpleasant duty); recoil

[2]**shrink** *n* **1** shrinkage **2** a psychoanalyst or psychiatrist – humor

shrivel /ˈʃrɪvəl/ *v* to (cause to) contract into wrinkles, esp through loss of moisture

[1]**shroud** /ʃraʊd/ *n* **1** a burial garment (e g a winding sheet) **2** sthg that covers, conceals, or guards **3** any of the ropes or wires giving support, usu in pairs, to a ship's mast

[2]**shroud** *v* **1** to envelop and conceal **2** to obscure, disguise

Shrove Tuesday /ˌʃrəʊv ˈtjuːzdi/ *n* the Tuesday before Ash Wednesday; pancake day

shrub /ʃrʌb/ *n* a low-growing usu several-stemmed woody plant – **~by** *adj*

shrubbery /ˈʃrʌbəri/ *n* a planting or growth of shrubs, esp in a garden

shrug /ʃrʌg/ *v* to lift and contract (the shoulders), esp to express aloofness, aversion, or doubt – **shrug** *n*

shrug off *v* to brush aside; disregard, belittle

shrunk /ʃrʌnk/ *past & past part of* **shrink**

shrunken /ˈʃrʌnkən/ *past part of* **shrink**

[1]**shuck** /ʃʌk/ *n* **1** a pod, husk **2** *pl* – used interjectionally to express mild annoyance or disappointment; infml

[2]**shuck** *v, NAm* to remove or dispose of like a shuck – often + *off*

shudder /ˈʃʌdəʳ/ *v* **1** to tremble with a sudden brief convulsive movement **2** to quiver, vibrate – **shudder** *n*

[1]**shuffle** /ˈʃʌfəl/ *v* **1** to rearrange (e g playing cards or dominoes) to produce a random order **2** to move or walk by sliding or dragging the feet – **~r** *n*

[2]**shuffle** /ˈʃʌfəl/ *n* **1a** shuffling (e g of cards) **b** a right or turn to shuffle **2** (a dance characterized by) a dragging sliding movement

shuffleboard /ˈʃʌfəlbɔːd/ *n* a game in which players use long-handled cues to shove wooden discs into scoring areas of a diagram marked on a smooth surface

shun /ʃʌn/ *v* to avoid deliberately, esp habitually

[1]**shunt** /ʃʌnt/ *v* **1** to move a train from one track to another **2** to travel back and forth

[2]**shunt** *n* **1** a means or mechanism for turning or thrusting aside **2** a usu minor collision of motor vehicles – infml

[1]**shush** /ʃ, ʃəʃ/ *n* **1** – used interjectionally to demand silence **2** peace and quiet; silence – infml

[2]**shush** /ʃəʃ, ʃʌʃ/ *v* to tell to be quiet, esp by saying 'Shush!" – infml

shut /ʃʌt/ *v* **shut** **1** to place in position to close an opening **2** to confine (as if) by enclosure **3** to fasten with a lock or bolt **4** to close by bringing enclosing or covering parts together **5** to cause to cease or suspend operation – usu + *down*

shutdown /ˈʃʌtdaʊn/ *n* the cessation or suspension of an activity (e g work in a mine or factory)

shut-eye *n* sleep – infml

[1]**shutter** /ˈʃʌtəʳ/ *n* **1** a usu hinged outside cover for a window, often fitted as one of a pair **2** a device that opens and closes the lens aperture of a camera

²shutter *v* to provide or close with shutters

¹shuttle /ˈʃʌtl/ *n* **1a** a usu spindle-shaped device that holds a bobbin and is used in weaving for passing the thread of the weft between the threads of the warp **b** a sliding thread holder that carries the lower thread in a sewing machine through a loop of the upper thread to make a stitch **2** a lightweight conical object with a rounded nose that is hit as the object of play in badminton and consists of (a moulded plastic imitation of) a cork with feathers stuck in it **3a** (a route or vehicle for) a regular going back and forth over a usu short route **b** a reusable space vehicle for use esp between earth and outer space

²shuttle *v* **1** to (cause to) move to and fro rapidly **2** to transport or be transported (as if) in or by a shuttle

shuttlecock /ˈʃʌtlkɒk/ *n* a badminton shuttle

shut up *v* to become silent; *esp* to stop talking *USE* infml

¹shy /ʃaɪ/ *adj* **1** easily alarmed; timid, distrustful – often in combination **2** wary *of* **3** sensitively reserved or retiring; bashful; *also* expressive of such a state or nature – **~ly** *adv* – **~ness** *n*

²shy *v* **1** to start suddenly aside in fright or alarm; recoil **2** to move or dodge to evade a person or thing – usu + *away* or *from*

³shy *v* to throw with a jerking movement; fling

⁴shy *n* **1** a toss, throw **2** a verbal sally **3** a stall (e g at a fairground) in which people throw balls at targets (e g coconuts) in order to knock them down **4** an attempt

shyster /ˈʃaɪstəʳ/ *n, chiefly NAm* sby (esp a lawyer) who is professionally unscrupulous

SI *n* a system of units whose basic units are the metre, kilogram, second, ampere, kelvin, candela, and mole and which uses prefixes (e g micro-, kilo-, and mega-) to indicate multiples or fractions of 10

Siamese twin /ˌsaɪəˈmiːz/ *n* either of a pair of congenitally joined twins

sibilant /ˈsɪbɨlənt/ *adj* having, containing, or producing a hissing sound (e g /S, J, s, z/) – **sibilant** *n*

sibling /ˈsɪblɪŋ/ *n* any of 2 or more individuals having common parents

sibyl /ˈsɪbɪl, -bəl/ *n, often cap* any of several female prophets credited to widely separate parts of the ancient world; *broadly* any female prophet – **~line** *adj*

sic /sɪk/ *adv* intentionally so written – used after a printed word or passage to indicate that it is intended exactly as printed or that it exactly reproduces an original

¹sick /sɪk/ *adj* **1a** ill, ailing **b** queasy, nauseated; likely to vomit – often in combination **2a** disgusted or weary, esp because of surfeit **b** distressed and longing for sthg that one has lost or been parted from **3** mentally or emotionally disturbed; *also* macabre – **~en** *v*

²sick *n, Br* vomit

sick bay *n* a compartment or room (e g in a ship) used as a dispensary and hospital

sicken /ˈsɪkən/ *v* **1** to become ill; show signs of illness **2** to drive to the point of despair or loathing

sickening /ˈsɪkənɪŋ/ *adj* very horrible or repugnant – **~ly** *adv*

¹sickle /ˈsɪkəl/ *n* **1** an agricultural implement for cutting plants or hedges, consisting of a curved metal blade with a short handle **2** a cutting mechanism (e g of a combine harvester) consisting of a bar with a series of cutting parts

²sickle *adj* having a curve resembling that of a sickle blade

sickly /ˈsɪkli/ *adj* **1** somewhat unwell; *also* habitually ailing **2** feeble, weak **3** mawkish, saccharine – **-liness** *n*

sickness /ˈsɪknɨs/ *n* **1** ill health **2** a specific disease **3** nausea, queasiness

¹side /saɪd/ *n* **1a** the right or left part of the wall or trunk of the body **b** the right or left half of the animal body or of a meat carcass **2** a location, region, or direction considered in relation to a centre or line of division **3** a surface forming a border or face of an object **4** a slope of a hill, ridge, etc **5** a bounding line or surface of a geometrical figure **6a** *sing or pl in constr* a person or group in competition or dispute with another **b** the attitude or activity of such a person or group; a part **7** a line of descent traced through a parent **8** an aspect or part of sthg viewed in contrast with some other aspect or part

[2]**side** *adj* **1** at, from, towards, etc the side **2a** incidental, subordinate **b** made on the side, esp in secret **c** additional to the main part or portion

[3]**side** *v* to take sides; join or form sides

side arm *n* a weapon (e g a sword, revolver, or bayonet) worn at the side or in the belt

sideboard /'saɪdbɔːd/ *n* **1** a usu flat-topped piece of dining-room furniture having compartments and shelves for holding articles of table service **2** *pl, Br* whiskers on the side of the face that extend from the hairline to below the ears

sidecar /'saɪdkɑːʳ/ *n* a car attached to the side of a motorcycle or motor scooter for 1 or more passengers

sidelight /'saɪdlaɪt/ *n* **1** incidental or additional information **2a** the red port light or the green starboard light carried by ships travelling at night **b** a light at the side of a (motor) vehicle

sideline /'saɪdlaɪn/ *n* **1** a line at right angles to a goal line or end line and marking a side of a court or field of play **2a** a line of goods manufactured or esp sold in addition to one's principal line **b** a business or activity pursued in addition to a full-time occupation

[1]**sidelong** /'saɪdlɒŋ/ *adv* towards the side; obliquely

[2]**sidelong** *adj* **1** inclining or directed to one side **2** indirect rather than straightforward

sidereal /saɪ'dɪərɪəl/ *adj* of or expressed in relation to stars or constellations

sidesaddle /'saɪd,sædl/ *n* a saddle for women in which the rider sits with both legs on the same side of the horse

sideshow /'saɪdʃəʊ/ *n* **1** a fairground booth or counter offering a game of luck or skill **2** an incidental diversion

sidesman /'saɪdzmən/ *n* any of a group of people in an Anglican church who assist the churchwardens, esp in taking the collection in services

sidesplitting /'saɪd,splɪtɪŋ/ *adj* causing raucous laughter

sidestep /'saɪdstep/ *v* **1** to step sideways or to one side **2** to evade an issue or decision

side street *n* a minor street branching off a main thoroughfare

[1]**sidetrack** /'saɪdtræk/ *n* an unimportant line of thinking that is followed instead of a more important one

[2]**sidetrack** *v* to divert from a course or purpose; distract

sidewards /'saɪdwədz/, *NAm chiefly* **sideward** *adv* towards one side

sideways /'saɪdweɪz/, *NAm also* **sideway** *adv or adj* **1** to or from the side; *also* askance **2** with 1 side forward (e g turn it *sideways*) **3** to a position of equivalent rank (e g he was promoted *sideways*)

siding /'saɪdɪŋ/ *n* a short railway track connected with the main track

sidle /'saɪdl/ *v* **1** to move obliquely **2** to walk timidly or hesitantly; edge along – usu + *up*

siege /siːdʒ/ *n* a military blockade of a city or fortified place to compel it to surrender

sienna /si'enə/ *n* an earthy substance containing oxides of iron and usu of manganese that is brownish yellow when raw and orange red or reddish brown when burnt and is used as a pigment

sierra /si'erə/ *n* a range of mountains, esp with a serrated or irregular outline

siesta /si'estə/ *n* an afternoon nap or rest

[1]**sieve** /sɪv/ *n* a device with a meshed or perforated bottom that will allow the passage of liquids or fine solids while retaining coarser material or solids

[2]**sieve** *v* to sift

sift /sɪft/ *v* **1a** to put through a sieve **b** to separate (out) (as if) by passing through a sieve **2** to scatter (as if) with a sieve

sifter /'sɪftəʳ/ *n* a castor for strewing sugar, flour, etc

[1]**sigh** /saɪ/ *v* **1** to take a long deep audible breath (e g in weariness or

grief) **2** *esp of the wind* to make a sound like sighing **3** to grieve, yearn – usu + *for*

²**sigh** *n* an act of sighing, esp when expressing an emotion or feeling (e g weariness or relief)

¹**sight** /saɪt/ *n* **1** sthg seen; *esp* a spectacle **2a** a thing (e g an impressive or historic building) regarded as worth seeing – often pl **b** sthg ridiculous or displeasing in appearance **3** the process, power, or function of seeing **4** a view, glimpse **5** the range of vision **6a** a device for guiding the eye (e g in aiming a firearm or bomb) **b** a device with a small aperture through which objects are to be seen and by which their direction is ascertained **7** a great deal; a lot – infml

²**sight** *v* **1** to get or catch sight of **2** to aim (e g a weapon) by means of sights – **~ing** *n*

sighted /ˈsaɪtɪ̣d/ *adj* having sight, esp of a specified kind – often in combination

sightly /ˈsaɪtli/ *adj* pleasing to the eye; attractive – **-liness** *n*

sight-read *v* to read at sight; *esp* to perform music at sight – **~er** *n* – **~ing** *n*

sight screen *n* a screen placed on the boundary of a cricket field behind the bowler to improve the batsman's view of the ball

sightseeing /ˈsaɪtsiːɪŋ/ *n* the act or pastime of touring interesting or attractive sights – often in *go sightseeing* – **-seer** *n*

¹**sign** /saɪn/ *n* **1a** a motion or gesture by which a thought, command, or wish is made known **b** a signal **2** a mark with a conventional meaning, used to replace or supplement words **3** a character (e g ÷) indicating a mathematical operation; *also* either of 2 characters + and – that form part of the symbol of a number and characterize it as positive or negative **4** a board or notice bearing information or advertising matter or giving warning, command, or identification **5a** sthg serving to indicate the presence or existence of sby or sthg **b** a presage, portent

²**sign** *v* **1** to indicate, represent, or express by a sign **2** to put one's signature to **3** to engage by securing the signature of on a contract of employment – often + *on* or *up*

¹**signal** /ˈsɪgnəl/ *n* **1** sthg that occasions action **2** a conventional sign (e g a siren or flashing light) made to give warning or command **3** an object used to transmit or convey information beyond the range of human voice **4** the sound or image conveyed in telegraphy, telephony, radio, radar, or television

²**signal** *v* **1** to warn, order, or request by a signal **2** to communicate by signals **3** to be a sign of; mark

³**signal** *adj* **1** used in signalling **2** distinguished from the ordinary; conspicuous – chiefly fml

signalbox /ˈsɪgnəlˌbɒks/ *n, Br* a raised building above a railway line from which signals and points are worked

signally /ˈsɪgnəli/ *adv* in a signal manner; remarkably – chiefly fml

signalman /ˈsɪgnəlmən/ *n* sby employed to operate signals (e g for a railway)

signatory /ˈsɪgnətəri/ *n* a signer with another or others; *esp* a government bound with others by a signed convention

signature /ˈsɪgnətʃəʳ/ *n* **1** the name of a person written with his/her own hand **2** a letter or figure placed usu at the bottom of the first page on each sheet of printed pages (e g of a book) as a direction to the binder in gathering the sheets

signature tune *n* a melody, passage, or song used to identify a programme, entertainer, etc

signet /ˈsɪgnɪ̣t/ *n* **1** a personal seal used officially in place of signature **2** a small intaglio seal (e g in a finger ring)

significance /sɪgˈnɪfɪkəns/ *n* **1** sthg conveyed as a meaning, often latently or indirectly **2** the quality of being important; consequence

significant /sɪgˈnɪfɪkənt/ *adj* **1** having meaning; *esp* expressive **2** suggesting or containing a veiled or special meaning **3a** having or likely to have influence or effect; important **b** probably caused by sthg other than chance – **~ly** *adv*

signify /ˈsɪgnɪ̇faɪ/ *v* **1** to mean, denote **2** to show, esp by a conventional token (e g a word, signal, or gesture)

sign off *v* **1** to announce the end of a message, programme, or broadcast and finish broadcasting **2** to end a letter (e g with a signature)

sign on *v* **1** to commit oneself to a job by signature or agreement **2** *Br* to register as unemployed, esp at an employment exchange

signor /siːˈnjɔːʳ/ *n, pl* **signors, signori** an Italian man – used as a title equivalent to *Mr*

signora /siːˈnjɔːra/ *n, pl* **signoras, signore** /-reɪ/ an Italian married woman – used as a title equivalent to *Mrs* or as a generalized term of direct address

signorina /ˌsiːnjɔːˈriːnə/ *n, pl* **signorinas, signorine** an unmarried Italian girl or woman – used as a title equivalent to *Miss*

[1]**signpost** /ˈsaɪnpəʊst/ *n* a post (e g at a road junction) with signs on it to direct travellers

[2]**signpost** *v* **1** to provide with signposts or guides **2** to indicate, mark, *esp* conspicuously

sign up *v* to join an organization or accept an obligation by signing a contract; *esp* to enlist in the armed services

Sikh /siːk/ *n or adj* (an adherent) of a monotheistic religion of India marked by rejection of idolatry and caste

silage /ˈsaɪlɪdʒ/ *n* fodder converted, esp in a silo, into succulent feed for livestock

[1]**silence** /ˈsaɪləns/ *n* **1** forbearance from speech or noise; muteness – often interjectional **2** absence of sound or noise; stillness **3** failure to mention a particular thing **4a** oblivion, obscurity **b** secrecy

[2]**silence** *v* **1** to put or reduce to silence; still **2** to restrain from expression; suppress **3** to cause (a gun, mortar, etc) to cease firing by return fire, bombing, etc

silencer /ˈsaɪlənsəʳ/ *n* **1** a silencing device for a small firearm **2** *chiefly Br* a device for deadening the noise of the exhaust gas release of an internal-combustion engine

silent /ˈsaɪlənt/ *adj* **1** mute, speechless; *also* not talkative **2** free from sound or noise; *also* without spoken dialogue **3a** endured without utterance **b** conveyed by refraining from reaction or comment; tacit – **~ly** *adv*

silhouette /ˌsɪluːˈet/ *n* **1** a portrait in profile cut from dark material and mounted on a light background **2** the shape of a body as it appears against a lighter background – **silhouette** *v*

silica /ˈsɪlɪkə/ *n* silicon dioxide occurring in many rocks and minerals (e g quartz, opal, and sand)

silicate /ˈsɪlɪkɪ̇t, -keɪt/ *n* any of numerous insoluble often complex compounds that contain silicon and oxygen, constitute the largest class of minerals, and are used in building materials (e g cement, bricks, and glass)

silicon /ˈsɪlɪkən/ *n* a tetravalent nonmetallic element that occurs, in combination with other elements, as the most abundant element next to oxygen in the earth's crust and is used esp in alloys

silicosis /ˌsɪlɪ̇ˈkəʊsɪ̇s/ *n* a disease of the lungs marked by hardening of the tissue and shortness of breath and caused by prolonged inhalation of silica dusts

silk /sɪlk/ *n* **1** a fibre produced by various insect larvae, usu for cocoons; *esp* a lustrous tough elastic fibre produced by silkworms and used for textiles **2** thread, yarn, or fabric made from silk filaments

silken /ˈsɪlkən/ *adj* **1** made of silk **2** resembling silk, esp in softness or lustre

silk screen *n* a stencil process in which paint or ink is forced onto the material to be printed, through the meshes of a prepared silk screen

silkworm /ˈsɪlkwɜːm/ *n* a moth whose larva spins a large amount of strong silk in constructing its cocoon

silky /ˈsɪlki/ *adj* **1** silken **2** having or covered with fine soft hairs, plumes, or scales – **silkiness** *n*

sill /sɪl/ *n* a horizontal piece (e g a timber) that forms the lowest member or one of the lowest members of a framework or supporting structure (e g a window frame or door frame)

silly /ˈsɪli/ *adj* **1a** showing a lack of common sense or sound judgment **b** trifling, frivolous **2** stunned, dazed – **silliness** *n*

silo /ˈsaɪləʊ/ *n* **1** a trench, pit, or esp a tall cylinder (e g of wood or concrete) usu sealed to exclude air and used for making and storing silage **2** an underground structure for housing a guided missile

[1]**silt** /sɪlt/ *n* a deposit of sediment (e g at the bottom of a river)

[2]**silt** *v* to make or become choked or obstructed with silt – often + *up*

[1]**silver** /ˈsɪlvəʳ/ *n* **1** a white ductile and malleable metallic element that takes a very high degree of polish and has the highest thermal and electrical conductivity of any substance **2** coins made of silver or cupro-nickel **3** articles, esp tableware, made of or plated with silver; *also* cutlery made of other metals **4** a whitish grey colour **5** a silver medal for second place in a competition

[2]**silver** *adj* **1** made of silver **2** resembling silver, esp in having a white lustrous sheen **3** consisting of or yielding silver **4** of or marking a 25th anniversary

silver birch *n* a common Eurasian birch with a silvery-white trunk

silverfish /ˈsɪlvəˌfɪʃ/ *n* any of various small wingless insects; *esp* one found in houses and sometimes injurious to sized paper (e g wallpaper) or starched fabrics

silverside /ˈsɪlvəsaɪd/ *n, Br* a boned and often salted cut of beef from the outer part of the top of the leg

silversmith /ˈsɪlvəˌsmɪθ/ *n* sby who works in silver

silvery /ˈsɪlvəri/ *adj* **1** having a soft clear musical tone **2** having the lustre or whiteness of silver

similar /ˈsɪmələʳ, ˈsɪmɪləʳ/ *adj* **1** marked by correspondence or resemblance, esp of a general kind **2** alike in 1 or more essential aspects – **~ity** *n* – **~ly** *adv*

simile /ˈsɪmɨli/ *n* a figure of speech explicitly comparing 2 unlike things (e g in *cheeks like roses*)

simmer /ˈsɪməʳ/ **1** to bubble gently below or just at the boiling point **2** to be agitated by suppressed emotion – **simmer** *n*

[1]**simper** /ˈsɪmpəʳ/ *v* to smile in a foolish self-conscious manner

[2]**simper** *n* a foolish self-conscious smile

simple /ˈsɪmpəl/ *adj* **1a** free from guile or vanity; unassuming **b** free from elaboration or showiness; unpretentious **2a** lacking intelligence; *esp* mentally retarded **b** naive **3a** sheer, unqualified **b** composed essentially of 1 substance **4** not subdivided **5** readily understood or performed; straightforward

simple interest *n* interest paid or calculated on only the original capital sum of a loan

simpleminded /ˌsɪmpəlˈmaɪndɨd/ *adj* devoid of subtlety; unsophisticated; *also* mentally retarded

simplicity /sɪmˈplɪsɨti/ *n* **1** the state or quality of being simple **2** naivety **3** freedom from affectation or guile **4a** directness of expression; clarity **b** restraint in ornamentation

simplify /ˈsɪmplɨfaɪ/ *v* to make or become simple or simpler – **-fication** *n*

simply /ˈsɪmpli/ *adv* **1a** without ambiguity; clearly **b** without ornamentation or show **c** without affectation or subterfuge; candidly **2a** solely, merely **b** without any question

simulate /ˈsɪmjʊleɪt/ *v* **1** to assume the outward qualities or appearance of, usu with the intent to deceive **2** to make a functioning model of (a system, device, or process) (e g by using a computer) – **~d** *adj* – **-ator** *n* – **-ation** *n*

simultaneous /ˌsɪməlˈteɪnɪəs/ *adj* existing, occurring, or functioning at the same time – **~ly** *adv* – **-neity, ~ness** *n*

[1]**sin** /sɪn/ *n* **1** an offence against moral or religious law or divine commandments **2** an action considered highly reprehensible

[2]**sin** *v* to commit a sin or an offence – often + *against* – **~ner** *n*

[1]**since** /sɪns/ *adv* **1** continuously from then until now (e g has stayed here ever *since*) **2** before now; ago (e g

should have done it long *since*) **3** between then and now; subsequently (e g has *since* become rich) *USE* + tenses formed with *to have*

[2]**since** *prep* in the period between (a specified past time) and now (e g haven't met *since* 1973); from (a specified past time) until now (e g it's a long time *since* breakfast) – + present tenses and tenses formed with *to have*

[3]**since** *conj* **1** between now and the past time when (e g has held 2 jobs *since* he left school); continuously from the past time when (e g ever *since* he was a child) **2** in view of the fact that; because (e g more interesting, *since* rarer)

sincere /sɪn'sɪəʳ/ *adj* free from deceit or hypocrisy; honest, genuine – **~ly** *adv* – **-rity** *n*

sine /saɪn/ *n* the trigonometric function that for an acute angle in a right-angled triangle is the ratio between the side opposite the angle and the hypotenuse

sinecure /'saɪnɪkjʊəʳ, 'sɪn-/ *n* an office or position that provides an income while requiring little or no work

sinew /'sɪnjuː/ *n* **1** a tendon **2a** solid resilient strength; vigour **b** the chief means of support; mainstay

sinful /'sɪnfəl/ *adj* tainted with, marked by, or full of sin; wicked – **~ly** *adv* – **~ness** *n*

sing /sɪŋ/ *v* **sang, sung 1a** to produce musical sounds by means of the voice **b** to utter words in musical notes and with musical inflections and modulations **2** to make a loud clear sound or utterance **3a** to relate or celebrate in verse **b** to express vividly or enthusiastically **4** to give information or evidence – slang – **~able** *adj* – **~er** *n*

singe *v* **singeing; singed** to burn superficially or slightly; scorch – **singe** *n*

[1]**single** /'sɪŋgəl/ *adj* **1** not married **2** not accompanied by others; sole **3** consisting of or having only 1 part or feature **4** consisting of a separate unique whole; individual **5** *of combat* involving only 2 people

[2]**single** *n* **1** a single person, thing or amount **2** a single run scored in cricket **3** a gramophone record, esp of popular music, with a single short track on each side **4** *Br* a ticket bought for a trip to a place but not back again

[3]**single** *v* to select or distinguish from a number or group – usu + *out*

single-breasted *adj* having a centre fastening with 1 row of buttons

single file *n* a line (e g of people) moving one behind the other

single-handed *adj* **1** performed or achieved by 1 person or with 1 on a side **2** working or managing alone or unassisted by others

single-minded *adj* having a single overriding purpose – **~ly** *adv* – **~ness** *n*

singles /'sɪŋgəlz/ *n* a game (e g of tennis) with 1 player on each side

singlet /'sɪŋglɪ̣t/ *n, chiefly Br* a vest; *also esp* one worn by athletes

singsong /'sɪŋsɒŋ/ *n* **1** a voice delivery characterized by a monotonous cadence or rhythm or rising and falling inflection **2** *Br* a session of group singing

[1]**singular** /'sɪŋgjʊləʳ/ *adj* **1a** of a separate person or thing; individual **b** of or being a word form denoting 1 person, thing, or instance **2** distinguished by superiority; exceptional **3** not general **4** very unusual or strange; peculiar

[2]**singular** *n* the singular number, the inflectional form denoting it, or a word in that form

Sinhalese /ˌsɪnhə'liːz/ *n, pl* **Sinhalese 1** a member of the predominant people that inhabit Sri Lanka **2** the Indic language of the Sinhalese

sinister /'sɪnɪ̣stəʳ/ *adj* **1** (darkly or insidiously) evil or productive of vice **2** threatening evil or ill fortune; ominous **3** of or situated on the left side or to the left of sthg, esp in heraldry

[1]**sink** /sɪŋk/ *v* **sank, sunk 1a** to go down below a surface (e g of water or a soft substance) **b** to cause sthg to penetrate **2a** to fall or drop to a lower place or level **b** to disappear from view **c** to take on a hollow appearance **3** to be or become deeply absorbed *in* **4** to dig or bore (a well or shaft) in the earth **5** to invest – **~able** *adj*

[2]**sink** *n* **1** a basin, esp in a kitchen, connected to a drain and usu a water supply for washing up **2** a place of vice or corruption **3** a depression in

which water (e g from a river) collects and becomes absorbed or evaporated

sink in *v* **1** to enter a solid through the surface **2** to become understood

sinuous /ˈsɪnjʊəs/ *adj* **1a** of or having a serpentine or wavy form; winding **b** lithe, supple **2** intricate, tortuous – **-osity,** ~**ness** *n*

sinus /ˈsaɪnəs/ *n* a cavity, hollow: *esp* any of several cavities in the skull that usu communicate with the nostrils and contain air

[1]**sip** /sɪp/ *v* to drink (sthg) delicately or a little at a time

[2]**sip** *n* (a small quantity imbibed by) sipping

[1]**siphon, syphon** /ˈsaɪfən/ *n* **1** a tube by which a liquid can be transferred up over the wall of a container to a lower level by using atmospheric pressure **2** a bottle for holding carbonated water in which the pressure of the gas is used to drive the contents out when a valve is opened

[2]**siphon, syphon** *v* to draw off, empty, etc, (as if) using a siphon

sir /səʳ; *strong* sɜːʳ/ *n* **1** a man entitled to be addressed as *sir* – used as a title before the Christian name of a knight or baronet **2a** – used as a usu respectful form of address to a male **b** *cap* – used as a conventional form of address at the beginning of a letter

[1]**sire** /ˈsaɪəʳ/ *n* **1** the male parent of a (domestic) animal **2** *archaic* **a** a father **b** a male ancestor **3** a man of rank or authority; *esp* a lord – used formerly as a title and form of address

[2]**sire** *v* **1** to beget – esp with reference to a male domestic animal **2** to bring into being; originate

siren /ˈsaɪərən/ *n* **1** *often cap* any of a group of mythological partly human female creatures that lured mariners to destruction by their singing **2** a dangerously alluring or seductive woman; a temptress **3** a usu electrically operated device for producing a penetrating warning sound

sirloin /ˈsɜːlɔɪn/ *n* a cut of beef from the upper part of the hind loin just in front of the rump

sirocco /sʒ̍ˈrɒkəʊ/ *n* **1** a hot dust-laden wind from the Libyan deserts that blows onto the N Mediterranean coast **2** a warm moist oppressive southeasterly wind in the same regions

sisal /ˈsaɪsəl, -zəl/ *n* (a W Indian plant whose leaves yield) a strong white fibre used esp for ropes and twine

[1]**sister** /ˈsɪstəʳ/ *n* **1a** a female having the same parents as another person **b** a half sister **2** *often cap* **a** (the title given to) a Roman Catholic nun **b** a female fellow member of a Christian church **3** a woman related to another person by a common tie or interest (e g adherence to feminist principles) **4** *chiefly Br* a female nurse; *esp* one who is next in rank below a nursing officer and is in charge of a ward or a small department – ~**hood** *n*

[2]**sister** *adj* related (as if) by sisterhood; essentially similar

sister-in-law *n, pl* **sisters-in-law** **1** the sister of one's spouse **2** the wife of one's brother

sit /sɪt/ *v* **sat** **1a** to rest on the buttocks or haunches **b** to perch, roost **2** to occupy a place as a member of an official body **3** to be in session for official business **4** to cover eggs for hatching **5a** to take up a position for being photographed or painted **b** to act as a model **6** to lie or hang relative to a wearer **7** to take an examination

sitar /ˈsɪtɑːʳ, sɪˈtɑːʳ/ *n* an Indian lute with a long neck and a varying number of strings

[1]**site** /saɪt/ *n* **1** an area of ground that was, is, or will be occupied by a structure or set of structures (e g a building, town, or monument) **2** the place, scene, or point of sthg

[2]**site** *v* to place on a site or in position; locate

sit-in *n* a continuous occupation of a building by a body of people as a protest and means towards forcing compliance with demands

sit in *v* to participate as a visitor or observer – usu + *on*

sit out *v* **1** to remain until the end of or the departure of **2** to refrain from participating in

sitter /ˈsɪtəʳ/ *n* **1** sby who sits (e g as an artist's model) **2** a baby-sitter

[1]**sitting** /ˈsɪtɪŋ/ *n* **1** a single occasion of

continuous sitting (e g for a portrait or meal) **2** a session

[2]**sitting** *adj* **1** that is sitting **2** in office or actual possession

sitting duck *n* an easy or defenceless target for attack, criticism, or exploitation

situated /ˈsɪtʃʊeɪtɨ̣d/ *adj* **1** located **2** supplied to the specified extent with money or possessions **3** being in the specified situation

situation /ˌsɪtʃʊˈeɪʃən/ *n* **1a** the way in which sthg is placed in relation to its surroundings **b** a locality **2** position with respect to conditions and circumstances **3** the circumstances at a particular moment; *esp* a critical or problematic state of affairs **4** a position of employment; a post – chiefly fml

sit up *v* **1** to show interest, alertness, or surprise **2** to stay up after the usual time for going to bed

six /sɪks/ *n* **1** the number 6 **2** the sixth in a set or series **3** sthg having 6 parts or members or a denomination of 6: e g **a** a shot in cricket that crosses the boundary before it bounces and so scores 6 runs **b** *pl in constr, cap the* Common Market countries before 1973 – ~**th** *adj, n, pron, adv*

six-shooter *n* a revolver holding six shots

sixteen /ˌsɪkˈstiːn/ *n* **1** the number 16 **2** *pl but sing in constr* a book format in which a folded sheet forms 16 leaves – ~**th** *adj, n, pron, adv*

sixth sense *n* a keen intuitive power viewed as analogous to the 5 physical senses

sixty /ˈsɪksti/ *n* **1** the number 60 **2** *pl* the numbers 60-69; *specif* a range of temperatures, ages, or dates in a century characterized by those numbers – **-tieth** *adj, n, pron, adv*

sizable, sizeable /ˈsaɪzəbəl/ *adj* of a good size, fairly large

[1]**size** /saɪz/ *n* **1a** physical magnitude, extent, or bulk **b** relative amount or number **c** bigness **2** any of a series of graduated measures, esp of manufactured articles (e g of clothing), conventionally identified by numbers or letters

[2]**size** *v* to arrange or grade according to size or bulk

[3]**size** *n* any of various thick and sticky materials used for filling the pores in surfaces (e g of paper, textiles, leather, or plaster) or for applying colour or metal leaf (e g to book edges or covers)

[4]**size** *v* to cover, stiffen, or glaze (as if) with size

size up *v* to form a judgment of

sizzle /ˈsɪzəl/ *v* to make a hissing sound (as if) in frying

[1]**skate** /skeɪt/ *n* any of numerous rays that have greatly developed pectoral fins and many of which are important food fishes

[2]**skate** *n* **1** a roller skate **2** an ice skate

[3]**skate** *v* **1** to glide along on skates propelled by the alternate action of the legs **2** to glide or slide as if on skates **3** to proceed in a superficial manner – ~**r** *n*

skateboard /ˈskeɪtbɔːd/ *n* a narrow board about 60cm (2ft) long mounted on roller-skate wheels

skedaddle /skɪˈdædl/ *v* to run away; *specif* to disperse rapidly – often imper; infml

skein /skeɪn/ *n* **1** a loosely coiled length of yarn or thread **2** a flock of geese in flight

skeleton /ˈskelɨ̣tn/ *n* **1** a supportive or protective usu rigid structure or framework of an organism; *esp* the bony or more or less cartilaginous framework supporting the soft tissues and protecting the internal organs of a fish or mammal **2** sthg reduced to its bare essentials **3** an emaciated person or animal **4** a secret cause of shame, esp in a family – often in *skeleton in the cupboard*

skeleton key *n* a key, esp one with most or all of the serrations absent, that is able to open many simple locks

[1]**sketch** /sketʃ/ *n* **1** a preliminary study or draft; *esp* a rough often preliminary drawing representing the chief features of an object or scene **2** a brief description or outline **3** a short theatrical piece having a single scene; *esp* a comic variety act

[2]**sketch** *v* to make a sketch, rough draft, or outline of – ~**er** *n*

sketchy /ˈsketʃi/ *adj* lacking completeness, clarity, or substance; superficial, scanty – **sketchily** *adv* – **sketchiness** *n*

[1]**skew** /skjuː/ *v* **1** to take an oblique course; twist **2** to distort from a true value or symmetrical curve

[2]**skew** *adj* **1** set, placed, or running obliquely **2** more developed on one side or in one direction than another; not symmetrical

[3]**skew** *n* a deviation from a straight line or symmetrical curve

skewbald /ˈskjuːbɔːld/ *n or adj* (an animal) marked with spots and patches of white and another colour, esp not black

[1]**skewer** /ˈskjuːəʳ/ *n* a long pin of wood or metal used chiefly to fasten a piece of meat together while roasting or to hold small pieces of food for grilling (e g for a kebab)

[2]**skewer** *v* to fasten or pierce (as if) with a skewer

[1]**ski** /skiː/ *n, pl* **skis** **1a** a long narrow strip usu of wood, metal, or plastic that curves upwards in front and is typically one of a pair used esp for gliding over snow **b** a water ski **2** a runner on a vehicle – **ski** *v* – **~er** *n*

[1]**skid** /skɪd/ *n* **1** a device placed under a wheel to prevent its turning or used as a drag **2** the act of skidding; a slide

[2]**skid** *v, of a vehicle, wheel, driver, etc* to slip or slide, esp out of control

skidpan /ˈskɪdpæn/ *n* a slippery surface on which vehicle drivers may practise the control of skids

skid row /ˌskɪd ˈrəʊ/ *n, chiefly NAm* a district frequented by down-and-outs and alcoholics

skiff /skɪf/ *n* a light rowing or sailing boat

skiffle /ˈskɪfəl/ *n* jazz or folk music played by a group and using nonstandard instruments or noisemakers (e g washboards or Jew's harps)

skilful, *NAm chiefly* **skillful** /ˈskɪlfəl/ *adj* possessing or displaying skill; expert – **~ly** *adv*

ski lift *n* a power-driven conveyor for transporting skiers or sightseers up and down a long slope or mountainside

skill /skɪl/ *n* **1** the ability to utilize one's knowledge effectively and readily **2** a developed aptitude or ability in a particular field – **~ed** *adj*

skillet /ˈskɪlɪ̣t/ *n* **1** *chiefly Br* a small saucepan usu having 3 or 4 legs and used for cooking on the hearth **2** *chiefly NAm* a frying pan

skim /skɪm/ *v* **1a** to remove (e g film or scum) from the surface of a liquid **b** to remove cream from (milk) **c** to remove (the choicest part or members) from sthg; cream **2** to glance through (e g a book) for the chief ideas or the plot **3** to glide lightly or smoothly along or just above a surface

skimp /skɪmp/ *v* **1** to give insufficient or barely sufficient attention or effort to or money for **2** to save (as if) by skimping sthg – **~y** *adj* – **~ily** *adv* – **~iness** *n*

[1]**skin** /skɪn/ *n* **1a** the external covering of an animal (e g a fur-bearing mammal or a bird) separated from the body, usu with its hair or feathers; pelt **b(1)** the pelt of an animal prepared for use as a trimming or in a garment **(2)** a container (e g for wine or water) made of animal skin **2a** the external limiting layer of an animal body, esp when forming a tough but flexible cover **b** any of various outer or surface layers (e g a rind, husk, or film) **3** the life or welfare of a person – esp in *save one's skin* **4** a sheathing or casing forming the outside surface of a ship, aircraft, etc – **~less** *adj*

[2]**skin** *v* **1a** to strip, scrape, or peel away an outer covering (e g the skin or rind) of **b** to cut, graze, or damage the surface of **2** to strip of money or property; fleece – infml

skin-deep *adj* **1** as deep as the skin **2** superficial

skinflint /ˈskɪnˌflɪnt/ *n* a miser, niggard

skinny /ˈskɪni/ *adj* very thin; lean, emaciated – infml

skint /skɪnt/ *adj, Br* penniless – infml

skintight /ˌskɪnˈtaɪt/ *adj* extremely closely fitted to the body

[1]**skip** /skɪp/ *v* **-pp-** **1a** to swing a rope round the body from head to toe, making a small jump each time it passes beneath the feet **b** to rebound from one point or thing after another; ricochet **2** to leave hurriedly or sec-

retly; abscond **3** to leave out (a step in a progression or series); omit **4** to fail to attend

[2]**skip** *n* **1** a light bounding step or gait **2** an act of omission (e g in reading)

[3]**skip** *n* **1** a bucket or cage for carrying men and materials (e g in mining or quarrying) **2** a large open container for waste or rubble

[1]**skipper** /ˈskɪpəʳ/ *n* any of numerous small butterflies that differ from the typical butterflies in the arrangement of the veins in the wings and the form of the antennae

[2]**skipper** *n* **1** the master of a fishing, small trading, or pleasure boat **2** the captain or first pilot of an aircraft **3** *Br* the captain of a sports team *USE* (*2&3*) infml

[1]**skirmish** /ˈskɜːmɪʃ/ *n* **1** a minor or irregular fight in war, usu between small outlying detachments **2** a brief preliminary conflict; *broadly* any minor or petty dispute

[2]**skirmish** *v* to engage in a skirmish – ~**er** *n*

[1]**skirt** /skɜːt/ *n* **1a(1)** a free-hanging part of a garment (e g a coat) extending from the waist down **(2)** a garment or undergarment worn by women and girls that hangs from and fits closely round the waist **b** either of 2 usu leather flaps on a saddle covering the bars on which the stirrups are hung **2** the borders or outer edge of an area or group – often pl with sing. meaning

[2]**skirt** *v* **1** to extend along or form the border or edge of; border **2** to go or pass round; *specif* to avoid through fear of difficulty, danger, or dispute

skirting board *n, Br* a board, esp with decorative moulding, that is fixed to the base of a wall and that covers the joint of the wall and floor

skit /skɪt/ *n* a satirical or humorous story or sketch

skitter /ˈskɪtəʳ/ *v* **1** to glide or skip lightly or swiftly **2** to skim along a surface

skittish /ˈskɪtɪʃ/ *adj* **1a** lively or frisky in behaviour; capricious **b** variable, fickle **2** easily frightened; restive – ~**ly** *adv* – ~**ness** *n*

skittle /ˈskɪtl/ *n* **1** *pl but sing in constr* any of various bowling games played with 9 pins and wooden balls or discs **2** a pin used in skittles

skive /skaɪv/ *v* , *Br* to evade one's work or duty, esp out of laziness; shirk – often + *off*; infml – ~**r** *n*

[1]**skivvy** /ˈskɪvi/ *n, Br* a female domestic servant

[2]**skivvy** *v, Br* to perform menial domestic tasks; act as a skivvy

skua /ˈskjuːə/ *n* any of several large dark-coloured seabirds of northern and southern seas that tend to harass weaker birds until they drop or disgorge the fish they have caught

skulk /skʌlk/ *v* **1** to move in a stealthy or furtive manner **2** to hide or conceal oneself, esp out of cowardice or fear or for a sinister purpose – ~**er** *n*

skull /skʌl/ *n* the skeleton of the head of a vertebrate animal forming a bony or cartilaginous case that encloses and protects the brain and chief sense organs and supports the jaws

skull and crossbones *n, pl* **skulls and crossbones** a representation of a human skull over crossbones, usu used as a warning of danger to life

skullcap /ˈskʌlkæp/ *n* a closely fitting cap; *esp* a light brimless cap for indoor wear

skunk /skʌŋk/ *n* **1a** any of various common black-and-white New World mammals that have a pair of anal glands from which a foul-smelling secretion is ejected **b** the fur of a skunk **2** a thoroughly obnoxious person – infml

[1]**sky** /skaɪ/ *n* **1** the upper atmosphere when seen as an apparent great vault over the earth; the firmament, heavens **2** weather as manifested by the condition of the sky

[2]**sky** *v, chiefly Br* to throw, toss, or hit (e g a ball) high in the air

sky blue *adj or n* (of) the light blue colour of the sky on a clear day

skydiving /ˈskaɪˌdaɪvɪŋ/ *n* jumping from an aeroplane and executing body manoeuvres while in free-fall before pulling the rip cord of a parachute – **skydiver** *n*

sky-high *adv or adj* **1a** very high **b** to a high level or degree **2** to bits; apart – in *blow sthg sky-high*

[1]**skylark** /ˈskaɪlɑːk/ *n* a common

largely brown Old World lark noted for its song, esp as uttered in vertical flight or while hovering

[2]**skylark** *v* to act in a high-spirited or mischievous manner; frolic

skylight /ˈskaɪlaɪt/ *n* a window or group of windows in a roof or ceiling

skyline /ˈskaɪlaɪn/ *n* **1** the apparent juncture of earth and sky; the horizon **2** an outline (e g of buildings or a mountain range) against the background of the sky

skyscraper /ˈskaɪˌskreɪpəʳ/ *n* a many-storeyed building

slab /slæb/ *n* a thick flat usu large plate or slice (e g of stone, wood, or bread)

[1]**slack** /slæk/ *adj* **1** insufficiently prompt, diligent, or careful; negligent **2a** characterized by slowness, indolence, or languor **b** *of tide* flowing slowly; sluggish **3a** not taut; relaxed **b** lacking in usual or normal firmness and steadiness – **~ly** *adv* – **~ness** *n*

[2]**slack** *v* **1** to be or become slack **2** to shirk or evade work or duty

[3]**slack** *n* **1** cessation in movement or flow **2** a part of sthg (e g a sail or a rope) that hangs loose without strain **3** *pl* trousers, esp for casual wear **4** a lull or decrease in activity; a dull season or period

[4]**slack** *n* the finest particles of coal produced at a mine

slacken /ˈslækən/ *v* **1** to make or become less active, rapid, or intense – often + *off* **2** to make or become slack

slack water *n* the period at the turn of the tide when there is no apparent tidal motion

slag /slæg/ *n* **1** waste matter from the smelting of metal ores **2** the rough cindery lava from a volcano **3** *Br* a dirty slovenly (immoral) woman – slang

slain /sleɪn/ *past part of* **slay**

slake /sleɪk/ *v* **1** to satisfy, quench **2** to cause (e g lime) to heat and crumble by treatment with water

slalom /ˈslɑːləm/ *n* a skiing or canoeing race against time on a zigzag or wavy course between obstacles

[1]**slam** /slæm/ *n* a banging noise; *esp* one made by a door

[2]**slam** *v* **1** to shut forcibly and noisily; bang **2** to put or throw down noisily and violently **3** to criticize harshly – infml

[1]**slander** /ˈslɑːndəʳ/ *n* the utterance of false charges which do damage to another's reputation

[2]**slander** *v* to utter slander against – **~er** *n* – **~ous** *adj* – **~ously** *adv*

slang /slæŋ/ *n* **1** language peculiar to a particular group **2** informal usu spoken vocabulary – **~y** *adj* – **~iness** *n*

[1]**slant** /slɑːnt/ *v* **1** to turn or incline from a horizontal or vertical line or a level **2** to take a diagonal course, direction, or path **3** to interpret or present in accord with a particular interest; bias – **~ingly** *adv*

[2]**slant** *n* **1** a slanting direction, line, or plane; a slope **2a** a particular or personal point of view, attitude, or opinion **b** an unfair bias or distortion (e g in a piece of writing)

[1]**slap** /slæp/ *n* a quick sharp blow, esp with the open hand

[2]**slap** *v* **1** to strike sharply (as if) with the open hand **2** to put, place, or throw with careless haste or force

[3]**slap** *adv* directly, smack

slap-bang *adv* **1** in a highly abrupt or forceful manner **2** precisely *USE* infml

slapdash /ˈslæpdæʃ/ *adj* haphazard, slipshod

slaphappy /ˈslæpˌhæpi/ *adj* **1** punch-drunk **2** irresponsibly casual; happy-go-lucky

slapstick /ˈslæpˌstɪk/ *n* comedy stressing farce and horseplay; knockabout comedy

slap-up *adj, chiefly Br* marked by lavish consumption or luxury – infml

[1]**slash** /slæʃ/ *v* **1** to cut with violent usu random sweeping strokes **2** *esp of rain* to fall hard and slantingly **3** to cut slits in (e g a garment) so as to reveal an underlying fabric or colour **4** to criticize cuttingly **5** to reduce drastically; cut

[2]**slash** *n* **1** the act of slashing; *also* a long cut or stroke made (as if) by slashing **2** an ornamental slit in a

garment 3 *chiefly Br* an act of urinating – vulg

slat /slæt/ *n* a thin narrow flat strip, esp of wood or metal (e g a lath, louvre, or stave)

¹slate /sleɪt/ *n* **1** a piece of slate rock used as roofing material **2** a fine-grained metamorphic rock consisting of compressed clay, shale, etc and easily split into (thin) layers **3** a tablet of material, esp slate, used for writing on **4** a dark bluish or greenish grey colour

²slate *v, chiefly Br* to criticize or censure severely – infml

slattern /ˈslætən/ *n* an untidy slovenly woman; a slut – **~ly** *adj*

¹slaughter /ˈslɔːtəʳ/ *n* **1** the act of killing; *specif* the butchering of livestock for market **2** killing of many people (e g in battle); carnage

²slaughter *v* **1** to kill (animals) for food **2** to kill violently or in large numbers

slaughterhouse /ˈslɔːtəhaʊs/ *n* an establishment where animals are killed for food

Slav /slɑːv/ *n* a speaker of a group of E European languages including Russian, Polish, Czech, and Serbo-Croat

¹slave /sleɪv/ *n* **1** sby held in servitude as the property of another **2** sby who is dominated by a specified thing or person **3** a drudge

²slave *v* to work like a slave; toil

slave driver *n* a harsh taskmaster

¹slaver /ˈslævəʳ/ *v* to drool, slobber

²slaver /ˈsleɪvəʳ/ *n* **1** sby engaged in the slave trade **2** a ship used in the slave trade

slavery /ˈsleɪvəri/ *n* **1** drudgery, toil **2a** being a slave **b** owning slaves

Slavic /ˈslɑːvɪk, ˈslæ-/, **Slavonic** *adj* of or related to the Slavs or their language – **Slavic, -vonic** *n*

slavish /ˈsleɪvɪʃ/ *adj* **1** abjectly servile **2** obsequiously imitative; devoid of originality – **~ly** *adv*

slay /sleɪ/ *v* **slew; slain** **1** to kill violently or with great bloodshed; slaughter **2** to affect overpoweringly (e g with awe or delight) – infml – **~er** *n*

sleazy /ˈsliːzi/ *adj* squalid and disreputable – **-ziness** *n*

¹sledge /sledʒ/ *n* a sledgehammer

²sledge *n* a vehicle with runners that is pulled by reindeer, horses, dogs, etc and is used esp over snow or ice; *also* a toboggan

sledgehammer /ˈsledʒˌhæməʳ/ *n* a large heavy hammer that is wielded with both hands

sledge-hammer *adj* clumsy, heavy-handed

¹sleek /sliːk/ *v* to slick

²sleek *adj* **1a** smooth and glossy as if polished **b** well-groomed **c** having a well fed or flourishing appearance **2** elegant, stylish – **~ly** *adv* – **~ness** *n*

¹sleep /sliːp/ *n* **1** the natural periodic suspension of consciousness that is essential for the physical and mental well-being of higher animals **2** a sleeplike state: e g **a** a state marked by a diminution of feeling followed by tingling **b** the state of an animal during hibernation **c** death – euph **3** a period spent sleeping

²sleep *v* **slept** **1** to rest in a state of sleep **2** to have sexual relations – + *with* or *together*

sleeper /ˈsliːpəʳ/ *n* **1** a timber, concrete, or steel transverse support to which railway rails are fixed **2** a railway carriage containing bunks or beds **3** a ring or stud worn in a pierced ear to keep the hole open

sleep in *v* to sleep late, either intentionally or accidentally

sleeping car *n* a railway carriage divided into compartments having berths for sleeping

sleeping partner *n* a partner who takes no active part or an unknown part in the running of a firm's business

sleeping sickness *n* a serious disease prevalent in much of tropical Africa that is transmitted by tsetse flies

sleepless /ˈsliːplɪ̈s/ *adj* **1** not able to sleep **2** unceasingly active – **~ly** *adv* – **~ness** *n*

sleepy /ˈsliːpi/ *adj* **1** ready to fall asleep **2** lacking alertness; sluggish, lethargic **3** sleep-inducing – **sleepily** *adv* – **sleepiness** *n*

sleepyhead /ˈsliːpihed/ *n* a sleepy person – humor

[1]**sleet** /sliːt/ *n* precipitation in the form of partly frozen rain, or snow and rain falling together – **~y** *adj*

[2]**sleet** *v* to send down sleet

sleeve /sliːv/ *n* **1** a part of a garment covering the arm **2** a paper or often highly distinctive cardboard covering that protects a gramophone record when not in use – **~less** *adj*

[1]**sleigh** /sleɪ/ *n* a sledge

[2]**sleigh** *v* to drive or travel in a sleigh

sleight of hand /ˌslaɪt əv ˈhænd/ *n* **1** manual skill and dexterity in conjuring or juggling **2** adroitness in deception

slender /ˈslendəʳ/ *adj* **1a** gracefully slim **b** small or narrow in circumference or width in proportion to length or height **2a** flimsy, tenuous **b** limited or inadequate in amount; meagre – **~ly** *adv* – **~ness** *n*

sleuth /sluːθ/ *v or n* (to act as) a detective – infml

[1]**slew** /sluː/ *past of* **slay**

[2]**slew** *v* **1** to turn, twist, or swing about **2** to skid

[1]**slice** /slaɪs/ *n* **1a** a thin broad flat piece cut from a usu larger whole **b** a wedge-shaped piece (e g of pie or cake) **2** an implement with a broad blade used for lifting, turning, or serving food **3** a portion, share

[2]**slice** *v* **1** to cut through (as if) with a knife **2** to cut into slices

[1]**slick** /slɪk/ *v* to make sleek or smooth

[2]**slick** *adj* **1** superficially plausible; glib **2a** characterized by suave or wily cleverness **b** deft, skilful **3** *of a tyre* having no tread – **~ly** *adv* – **~ness** *n*

[3]**slick** *n* (a patch of water covered with) a smooth film of crude oil

slicker /ˈslɪkəʳ/ *n, NAm* an artful crook; a swindler – infml

[1]**slide** /slaɪd/ *v* **slid** /slɪd/ **1a** to move in continuous contact with a smooth surface **b** to glide over snow or ice **2** to pass quietly and unobtrusively; steal **3** to pass by smooth or imperceptible gradations

[2]**slide** *n* **1** an act or instance of sliding **2** a sliding part or mechanism: e g **a** a U-shaped section of tube in the trombone that is pushed out and in to produce notes of different pitch **b** a moving piece of a mechanism that is guided by a part along which it slides **3a(1)** a track or slope suitable for sliding or tobogganing **(2)** a chute with a slippery surface down which children slide in play **b** a channel or track down or along which sthg is slid **4a** a flat piece of glass on which an object is mounted for examination using a light microscope **b** a photographic transparency on a small plate or film suitably mounted for projection **5** *Br* a hair-slide

slide rule *n* an instrument consisting in its simple form of a ruler with a central slide both of which are graduated in such a way that the addition of lengths corresponds to the multiplication of numbers

sliding scale *n* a flexible scale (e g of fees or subsidies) adjusted to the needs or income of individuals

[1]**slight** /slaɪt/ *adj* **1a** having a slim or frail build **b** lacking strength or bulk; flimsy **c** trivial; minor **2** scanty, meagre – **~ly** *adv* – **~ness** *n*

[2]**slight** *v* **1** to treat as slight or unimportant **2** to treat with disdain or pointed indifference; snub – **~ingly** *adv*

[3]**slight** *n* **1** an act of slighting **2** a humiliating affront

[1]**slim** /slɪm/ *adj* **1** of small or narrow circumference or width, esp in proportion to length or height **2** slender in build **3** scanty, slight – **~ly** *adv* – **~ness** *n*

[2]**slim** *v* to become thinner (e g by dieting) – **~mer** *n* – **~ming** *n*

slime /slaɪm/ *n* **1** soft moist soil or clay; *esp* viscous mud **2** mucus or a mucus-like substance secreted by slugs, catfish, etc

slimy /ˈslaɪmi/ *adj* **1** of or resembling slime; viscous; *also* covered with or yielding slime **2** characterized by obsequious flattery; offensively ingratiating – **sliminess** *n*

[1]**sling** /slɪŋ/ *v* **slung** **1** to cast with a careless and usu sweeping or swirling motion; fling **2** *Br* to cast forcibly and usu abruptly – infml – **~er** *n*

[2]**sling** *n* an act of slinging or hurling a stone or other missile

[3]**sling** *n* **1** a device that gives extra

force to a stone or other missile thrown by hand and usu consists of a short strap that is looped round the missile, whirled round, and then released at 1 end **2a** a usu looped line used to hoist, lower, or carry sthg (e g a rifle); *esp* a bandage suspended from the neck to support an arm or hand **b** a device (e g a rope net) for enclosing material to be hoisted by a tackle or crane

slink /slɪŋk/ *v* **slunk** **1** to go or move stealthily or furtively (e g in fear or shame); steal **2** to move in a graceful provocative manner

[1]**slip** /slɪp/ *v* **1a** to move with a smooth sliding motion **b** to move quietly and cautiously; steal **2** *of time* to elapse, pass **3a** to slide out of place or away from a support or one's grasp **b** to slide on or down a slippery surface **4** to get speedily *into* or *out of* clothing **5** to fall off from a standard or accustomed level by degrees **6** to escape from (one's memory or notice) **7a** to cause to slip open; release, undo **b** to let go of **8a** to insert, place, or pass quietly or secretly **b** to give or pay on the sly **9** to dislocate

[2]**slip** *n* **1** a sloping ramp extending out into the water to serve as a place for landing, repairing, or building ships **2** *the* act or an instance of eluding or evading **3a** a mistake in judgment, policy, or procedure; a blunder **b** an inadvertent and trivial fault or error **4** (a movement producing) a small geological fault **5** a fall from some level or standard **6** a women's sleeveless undergarment with shoulder straps that resembles a light dress **7** any of several fielding positions in cricket that are close to the batsman and just to the (off) side of the wicketkeeper

[3]**slip** *n* **1** a long narrow strip of material (e g paper or wood) **2** a young and slim person

[4]**slip** *n* a semifluid mixture of clay and water used by potters (e g for coating or decorating ware)

slipknot /ˈslɪpnɒt/ *n* a knot that can be untied by pulling

slipped disc *n* a protrusion of 1 of the cartilage discs that normally separate the spinal vertebrae, producing pressure on spinal nerves and usu resulting in intense pain, esp in the region of the lower back

slipper /ˈslɪpəʳ/ *n* a light shoe that is easily slipped on the foot; *esp* a flat-heeled shoe that is worn while resting at home

slippery /ˈslɪpəri/ *adj* **1a** causing or tending to cause sthg to slide or fall **b** tending to slip from the grasp **2** not to be trusted; shifty – **-eriness** *n*

slipshod /ˈslɪpʃɒd/ *adj* careless, slovenly

[1]**slipstream** /ˈslɪpstriːm/ *n* **1** an area of reduced air pressure and forward suction immediately behind a rapidly moving vehicle **2** sthg that sweeps one along in its course

[2]**slipstream** *v* to drive or ride in a slipstream and so gain the advantage of reduced air resistance (e g in a bicycle race)

slip-up *n* a mistake, oversight

slip up *v* to make a mistake; blunder

slipway /ˈslɪpweɪ/ *n* a slip on which ships are built

[1]**slit** /slɪt/ *v* **slit** **1** to make a slit in **2** to cut or tear into long narrow strips

[2]**slit** *n* a long narrow cut or opening

slither /ˈslɪðəʳ/ *v* **1** to slide unsteadily, esp (as if) on a slippery surface **2** to slip or slide like a snake – **~y** *adj*

[1]**sliver** /ˈslɪvəʳ/ *n* a small slender piece cut, torn, or broken; a splinter

[2]**sliver** *v* to become split into slivers; splinter

slob /slɒb/ *n* a slovenly or uncouth person – infml

[1]**slobber** /ˈslɒbəʳ/ *v* **1** to let saliva dribble from the mouth; drool **2** to express emotion effusively and esp oversentimentally – often + *over*

[2]**slobber** *n* **1** saliva drooled from the mouth **2** oversentimental language or conduct

sloe /sləʊ/ *n* (the small dark spherical astringent fruit of) the blackthorn

[1]**slog** /slɒg/ *v* **1** to hit (e g a cricket ball or an opponent in boxing) hard and often wildly **2** to plod (one's way) with determination, esp in the face of difficulty

[2]**slog** *n* **1** a hard and often wild blow **2**

persistent hard work 3 an arduous march or tramp

slogan /'sləʊgən/ *n* **1** a phrase used to express and esp make public a particular view, position, or aim **2** a brief catchy phrase used in advertising or promotion

sloop /sluːp/ *n* a fore-and-aft rigged sailing vessel with 1 mast and a single foresail

¹slop /slɒp/ *n* **1** thin tasteless drink or liquid food; *also, pl* waste food or a thin gruel fed to animals **2** *pl* liquid household refuse (e g dirty water or urine) **3** mawkish sentiment in speech or writing; gush

²slop *v* **1a** to cause (a liquid) to spill over the side of a container **b** to splash or spill liquid on **2** to serve messily **3** to slouch, flop

¹slope /sləʊp/ *v* to lie at a slant; incline

²slope *n* **1** a piece of inclined ground **2** upward or downward inclination or (degree of) slant

slope off *v* to go away, esp furtively; sneak off – infml

slop out *v, of a prisoner* to empty slops from a chamber pot

sloppy /'slɒpi/ *adj* **1a** wet so as to splash; slushy **b** wet or smeared (as if) with sthg slopped over **2** slovenly, careless **3** disagreeably effusive – **-pily** *adv* – **-piness** *n*

¹slosh /slɒʃ/ *n* **1** slush **2** the slap or splash of liquid **3** *chiefly Br* a heavy blow; a bash – infml

²slosh *v* **1** to flounder or splash through water, mud, etc **2** to splash (a liquid) about, on, or into sthg **3** *chiefly Br* to hit, beat – infml

sloshed /ʃlɒʃt/ *adj* drunk – infml

¹slot /slɒt/ *n* **1** a narrow opening, groove, or passage; a slit **2** a place or position in an organization or sequence; a niche

²slot *v* **1** to cut a slot in **2** to place in or assign to a slot – often + *in* or *into*

sloth /sləʊθ/ *n* **1** disinclination to action or work; indolence **2** any of several slow-moving tree-dwelling mammals that inhabit tropical forests of S and Central America, hang face upwards from the branches, and feed on leaves, shoots, and fruits

slot machine *n* a machine (e g for selling cigarettes, chocolate, etc or for gambling) whose operation is begun by dropping a coin or disc into a slot

¹slouch /slaʊtʃ/ *n* a gait or posture characterized by stooping or excessive relaxation of body muscles

²slouch *v* **1** to sit, stand, or walk with a slouch **2** to cause to droop; *specif* to turn down one side of (a hat brim) – **~ingly** *adv*

¹slough /slaʊ/ *n* **1a** a place of deep mud or mire **b** a swamp **2** a state of dejection

²slough *also* **sluff** /slʌf/ *n* the cast-off skin of a snake

³slough *also* **sluff** /slʌf/ *v* **1** to cast off (e g a skin or shell) **2** to get rid of or discard as irksome or objectionable – usu + *off*

sloven /'slʌvən/ *n* one habitually negligent of neatness or cleanliness, esp in personal appearance – **~ly** *adj* – **~liness** *n*

¹slow /sləʊ/ *adj* **1a** lacking in intelligence; dull **b** naturally inert or sluggish **2a** lacking in readiness, promptness, or willingness **b** not quickly aroused or excited **3a** flowing or proceeding with little or less than usual speed **b** exhibiting or marked by retarded speed **c** low, feeble **4** requiring a long time; gradual **5a** having qualities that hinder or prevent rapid movement **b** (designed) for slow movement **6** registering a time earlier than the correct one **7** lacking in liveliness or variety; boring – **~ly** *adj* – **~ness** *n*

²slow *adv* in a slow manner; slowly

³slow *v* to make or become slow or slower – often + *down* or *up*

slowcoach /'sləʊkəʊtʃ/ *n* one who thinks or acts slowly

slow motion *n* a technique in filming which allows an action to be shown as if it is taking place unnaturally slowly, which usu involves increasing the number of frames exposed in a given time and then projecting the film at the standard speed

slowworm /'sləʊwɜːm/ *n* a legless European lizard popularly believed to be blind

sludge /slʌdʒ/ *n* **1** (a deposit of) mud

or ooze **2a** a slimy or slushy mass, deposit, or sediment **b** precipitated solid matter produced by water and sewage treatment processes

[1]**slug** /slʌg/ *n* any of numerous slimy elongated chiefly ground-living gastropod molluscs that are found in most damp parts of the world and have no shell

[2]**slug** *n* **1** a lump, disc, or cylinder of material (e g plastic or metal): e g **a** a bullet – slang **b** *NAm* a disc for insertion in a slot machine; *esp* one used illegally instead of a coin **2** *chiefly NAm* a quantity of spirits that can be swallowed at a single gulp – slang

[3]**slug** *n* a heavy blow, esp with the fist – infml

[4]**slug** *v* to hit hard (as if) with the fist – infml

sluggish /ˈslʌgɪʃ/ *adj* **1** averse to activity or exertion; indolent **2** slow to respond (e g to stimulation or treatment) **3** markedly slow in movement, flow, or growth – **~ly** *adv* – **~ness** *n*

[1]**sluice** /sluːs/ *n* **1** an artificial passage for water (e g in a millstream) fitted with a gate for stopping or regulating flow **2** a dock gate **3** a long inclined trough (e g for washing ores or gold-bearing earth)

[2]**sluice** *v* **1** to wash with or in water running through or from a sluice **2** to drench with a sudden vigorous flow; flush

[1]**slum** /slʌm/ *n* **1** a poor overcrowded run-down area, esp in a city – often pl with sing. meaning **2** a squalid disagreeable place to live – **~my** *adj*

[2]**slum** *v* **1** to live in squalor or on very slender means – often + *it* **2** to amuse oneself by visiting a place on a much lower social level; *also* to affect the characteristics of a lower social class

[1]**slumber** /ˈslʌmbəʳ/ *v* **1** to sleep **2** to lie dormant or latent

[2]**slumber** *n* sleep – often pl with sing. meaning

[1]**slump** /slʌmp/ *v* **1a** to fall or sink abruptly **b** to drop down suddenly and heavily; collapse **2** to assume a drooping posture or carriage; slouch

[2]**slump** *n* a marked or sustained decline, esp in economic activity or prices

slung /slʌŋ/ *past of* **sling**

slunk /slʌŋk/ *past of* **slink**

[1]**slur** /slɜːʳ/ *v* **1** to pass *over* without due mention, consideration, or emphasis **2** to run together, omit, or pronounce unclearly (words, sounds, etc)

[2]**slur** *n* **1** (a curved line connecting) notes to be sung to the same syllable or performed without a break **2** a slurring manner of speech

[3]**slur** *v* to cast aspersions on; disparage

[4]**slur** *n* **1a** an insulting or disparaging remark **b** a shaming or degrading effect **2** a blurred spot in printed matter

slurp /slɜːp/ *v* to eat or drink noisily or with a sucking sound

slurry /ˈslʌri/ *n* a watery mixture of insoluble matter (e g mud, manure, or lime)

slush /slʌʃ/ *n* **1** partly melted or watery snow **2** liquid mud; mire **3** worthless and usu oversentimental material (e g literature) – **slushy** *adj*

slut /slʌt/ *n* **1** a dirty slovenly woman **2** an immoral woman; *esp* a prostitute – **~tish** *adj*

sly /slaɪ/ *adj* **slier** *also* **slyer; sliest** *also* **slyest** **1a** clever in concealing one's ends or intentions; furtive **b** lacking in integrity and candour; crafty **2** humorously mischievous; roguish – **~ly** *adv* – **~ness** *n*

[1]**smack** /smæk/ *n* (a slight hint of) a characteristic taste, flavour, or aura

[2]**smack** *v* **1** to slap smartly, esp in punishment **2** to open (the lips) with a sudden sharp sound, esp in anticipation of food or drink

[3]**smack** *n* **1** a sharp blow, esp from sthg flat; a slap **2** a noisy parting of the lips **3** a loud kiss **4** *chiefly NAm* heroin – slang

[4]**smack** *adv* squarely and with force; directly – infml

[5]**smack** *n* a small inshore fishing vessel

[1]**small** /smɔːl/ *adj* **1a** having relatively little size or dimensions **b** immature, young **2a** little in quantity, value, amount, etc **b** made up of few individuals or units **3** lower-case **4** lacking in strength **5a** operating on a limited scale **b** minor in power, influence, etc

c limited in degree **6** of little consequence; trivial **7a** mean, petty **b** reduced to a humiliating position – ~**ness** *n*

[2]**small** *adv* **1** in or into small pieces **2** in a small manner or size

[3]**small** *n* **1** a part smaller and esp narrower than the remainder; *specif* the narrowest part of the back **2** *pl, Br* small articles of underwear – infml

small ad *n, Br* a classified advertisement

small change *n* coins of low denomination

small fry *n pl in constr* young or insignificant people or things; *specif* children

smallholding /ˈsmɔːlˌhəʊldɪŋ/ *n, chiefly Br* a small agricultural farm – **smallholder** *n*

small intestine *n* the part of the intestine that lies between the stomach and colon

small-minded *adj* **1** having narrow interests or outlook; narrow-minded **2** characterized by petty meanness – ~**ness** *n*

smallpox /ˈsmɔːlpɒks/ *n* an acute infectious feverish virus disease characterized by skin eruption with pustules and scar formation

small talk *n* light or casual conversation; chitchat

small-time *adj* insignificant in operation and status; petty – **-timer** *n*

smarmy /ˈsmɑːmi/ *adj* marked by flattery or smugness; unctuous – infml

[1]**smart** /smɑːt/ *v* **1** to be (the cause or seat of) a sharp pain **2** to feel or endure mental distress

[2]**smart** *adj* **1** making one smart; causing a sharp stinging **2** forceful, vigorous **3** brisk, spirited **4a** mentally alert; bright **b** clever, shrewd **5** witty, persuasive **6a** neat or stylish in dress or appearance **b** characteristic of or frequented by fashionable society – ~**ly** *adv* – ~**ness** *n*

[3]**smart** *adv* in a smart manner; smartly

[4]**smart** *n* **1** a smarting pain; *esp* a stinging local pain **2** poignant grief or remorse

[1]**smash** /smæʃ/ *v* **1** to break in pieces by violence; shatter **2a** to drive, throw, or hit violently, esp causing breaking or shattering **b** to hit (e g a ball) with a forceful stroke, specif a smash **3** to destroy utterly; wreck – often + *up* **4** to crash *into*; collide

[2]**smash** *n* **1a(1)** a smashing blow, attack, or collision **(2)** the result of smashing; *esp* a wreck due to collision **b** a forceful overhand stroke (e g in tennis or badminton) **2** utter collapse; ruin; *esp* bankruptcy

[3]**smash** *adv* with a resounding crash

smash-and-grab *n or adj, chiefly Br* (a robbery) committed by smashing a shop window and snatching the goods on display

smashed /smæʃt/ *adj* extremely drunk – infml

smashing /ˈsmæʃɪŋ/ *adj* extremely good; excellent – infml

smash-up *n* a serious accident; a crash

smattering /ˈsmætərɪŋ/ *n* a piecemeal or superficial knowledge *of*

[1]**smear** /smɪəʳ/ *n* **1** a mark or blemish made (as if) by smearing a substance **2** material taken or prepared for microscopic examination by smearing on a slide **3** a usu unsubstantiated accusation

[2]**smear** *v* **1** to spread with sthg sticky, greasy, or viscous **2a** to stain or dirty (as if) by smearing **b** to sully, besmirch; *specif* to blacken the reputation of

[1]**smell** /smel/ *v* **smelled, smelt** **1a** to have a usu specified smell **b** to have a characteristic aura; be suggestive *of* **c** to have an offensive smell; stink **2** to perceive the odour of (as if) by use of the sense of smell **3** to detect or become aware of by instinct

[2]**smell** *n* **1** the one of the 5 basic physical senses by which the qualities of gaseous or volatile substances in contact with certain sensitive areas in the nose are interpreted by the brain as characteristic odours **2** an odour **3** a pervading quality; an aura

smelling salts *n pl but sing or pl in constr* a usu scented preparation of ammonium carbonate and ammonia water sniffed as a stimulant to relieve faintness

smelly /ˈsmeli/ *adj* having an esp unpleasant smell – **smelliness** *n*

[1]**smelt** /smelt/ *n* any of various small fishes that closely resemble the trouts and have delicate oily flesh with a distinctive smell and taste

[2]**smelt** *v* **1** to melt (ore) to separate the metal **2** to separate (metal) by smelting

[1]**smile** /smaɪl/ *v* **1** to have or assume a smile **2a** to look with amusement or scorn **b** to bestow approval **c** to appear pleasant or agreeable – **smilingly** *adv*

[2]**smile** *n* **1** a change of facial expression in which the corners of the mouth curve slightly upwards and which expresses esp amusement, pleasure, approval, or sometimes scorn **2** a pleasant or encouraging appearance

smirch /smɜːtʃ/ *v* **1** to make dirty or stained, esp by smearing **2** to bring discredit or disgrace on – **smirch** *n*

smirk /smɜːk/ *v* to smile in a fatuous or scornful manner – **smirk** *n*

smite /smaɪt/ *v* **smote; smitten, smote** **1** to strike sharply or heavily, esp with (an implement held in) the hand **2** to kill, injure, or damage by smiting **3** to have a sudden powerful effect on; afflict; *specif* to attract strongly

smith /smɪθ/ *n* **1** a worker in metals; *specif* a blacksmith **2** a maker – often in combination

smithereens /ˌsmɪðəˈriːnz/ *n pl* fragments, bits

smithy /ˈsmɪði/ *n* the workshop of a smith

[1]**smock** /smɒk/ *n* a light loose garment esp with a yoke

[2]**smock** *v* to ornament (e g a garment) with smocking

smocking /ˈsmɒkɪŋ/ *n* a decorative embroidery or shirring made by gathering cloth in regularly spaced round or diamond-shaped tucks held in place with ornamental stitching

smog /smɒg/ *n* a fog made heavier and darker by smoke and chemical fumes

[1]**smoke** /sməʊk/ *n* **1** the gaseous products of burning carbon-containing materials made visible by the presence of small particles of carbon **2** fumes or vapour resembling smoke **3** an act or spell of smoking esp tobacco – **~less** *adj*

[2]**smoke** *v* **1** to emit smoke **2** to (habitually) inhale and exhale the fumes of burning tobacco **3a** to fumigate **b** to drive *out* or away by smoke **4** to colour or darken (as if) with smoke **5** to cure (e g meat or fish) by exposure to smoke, traditionally from green wood or peat

smoker /ˈsməʊkəʳ/ *n* **1** sby who regularly or habitually smokes tobacco **2** a carriage or compartment in which smoking is allowed

smoke screen *n* **1** a screen of smoke to hinder observation **2** sthg designed to conceal, confuse, or deceive

smokestack /ˈsməʊkstæk/ *n* a chimney or funnel through which smoke and gases are discharged, esp from a locomotive or steamship

smoky *also* **smokey** /ˈsməʊki/ *adj* **1** emitting smoke, esp in large quantities **2** suggestive of smoke, esp in flavour, smell, or colour **3a** filled with smoke **b** made black or grimy by smoke – **smokiness** *n*

smooch /smuːtʃ/ *v* to kiss, caress – infml – **smooch** *n* – **~er** *n*

[1]**smooth** /smuːð/ *adj* **1a** having a continuous even surface **b** free from hair or hairlike projections **c** *of liquid* of an even consistency; free from lumps **d** giving no resistance to sliding; frictionless **2** free from difficulties or obstructions **3** even and uninterrupted in movement or flow **4a** urbane, courteous **b** excessively and often artfully suave; ingratiating **5** not sharp or acid – **~ly** *adv* – **~ness** *n*

[2]**smooth** *v* **1** to make smooth **2** to free from what is harsh or disagreeable **3** to dispel or alleviate (e g enmity or perplexity) – often + *away* or *over* **4** to free from obstruction or difficulty **5** to press flat – often + *out* **6** to cause to lie evenly and in order – often + *down*

smorgasbord /ˈsmɔːgəsbɔːd/ *n* a luncheon or supper buffet offering a variety of foods and dishes (e g hors d'oeuvres, hot and cold meats, smoked and pickled fish, cheeses, salads, and relishes)

smote /sməʊt/ *past of* **smite**

[1]**smother** /ˈsmʌðəʳ/ *n* a confused mass of things; a welter

[2]**smother** *v* **1** to overcome or kill with smoke or fumes **2** to overcome or

discomfort (as if) through lack of air **3a** to suppress expression or knowledge of; conceal **b** to prevent the growth or development of; suppress **4a** to cover thickly; blanket **b** to overwhelm

smoulder, *NAm chiefly* **smolder** /ˈsməʊldəʳ/ *v* **1** to burn feebly with little flame and often much smoke **2** to exist in a state of suppressed ferment

¹smudge /smʌdʒ/ *v* **1** to soil (as if) with a smudge **2a** to smear, daub **b** to make indistinct; blur

²smudge *n* **1** a blurry spot or streak **2** an indistinct mass; a blur

smug /smʌg/ *adj* highly self-satisfied and complacent – **~ly** *adv* – **~ness** *n*

smuggle /ˈsmʌgəl/ *v* **1** to import or export secretly contrary to the law, esp without paying duties **2** to convey or introduce surreptitiously – **-gler** *n* – **-gling** *n*

¹smut /smʌt/ *v* **1** to stain or taint with smut **2** to affect (a crop or plant) with smut

²smut *n* **1** matter, esp a particle of soot, that soils or blackens **2** any of various destructive fungous diseases, esp of cereal grasses, marked by transformation of plant organs into dark masses of spores **3** obscene language or matter

snack /snæk/ *n* a light meal; food eaten between regular meals

¹snaffle /ˈsnæfəl/ *n* a simple usu jointed bit for a bridle

²snaffle *v* to appropriate, esp by devious means; pinch – infml

snag /snæg/ *n* **1** a sharp or jagged projecting part **2** a concealed or unexpected difficulty or obstacle **3** an irregular tear or flaw made (as if) by catching on a snag

snail /sneɪl/ *n* **1** a gastropod mollusc; *esp* one that has an external enclosing spiral shell **2** a slow-moving or sluggish person or thing

¹snake /sneɪk/ *n* **1** any of numerous limbless scaly reptiles with a long tapering body and with salivary glands often modified to produce venom which is injected through grooved or tubular fangs **2** a sly treacherous person **3** *often cap* a system in which the values of the currencies of countries in the European Economic Community are allowed to vary against each other within narrow limits

²snake *v* to wind in the manner of a snake – **snaky** *adj*

¹snap /snæp/ *v* **1** to grasp or snatch at sthg eagerly **2** to utter sharp biting words; give an irritable retort **3a** to break suddenly, esp with a sharp cracking sound **b** to close or fit in place with an abrupt movement or sharp sound **4** to take possession or advantage of suddenly or eagerly – usu + *up* **5** to photograph

²snap *n* **1** an abrupt closing (e g of the mouth in biting or of scissors in cutting) **2** an act or instance of seizing abruptly; a sudden snatch or bite **3** a brief usu curt retort **4a** a sound made by snapping **b** a sudden sharp breaking of sthg thin or brittle **5** a sudden spell of harsh weather **6** a thin brittle biscuit **7** a snapshot **8** a card game in which each player tries to be the first to shout '*snap*'' when 2 cards of identical value are laid successively

³snap *interj, Br* – used to draw attention to an identity or similarity

⁴snap *adv* with (the sound of) a snap

⁵snap *adj* performed suddenly, unexpectedly, or without deliberation

snapdragon /ˈsnæpˌdrægən/ *n* any of several garden plants having showy white, red, or yellow 2-lipped flowers

snappish /ˈsnæpɪʃ/ *adj* **1a** given to curt irritable speech **b** bad-tempered, testy **2** inclined to snap or bite – **~ly** *adv* – **~ness** *n*

snappy /ˈsnæpi/ *adj* **1** snappish **2a** brisk, quick **b** lively, animated **c** stylish, smart – **-pily** *adv* – **-piness** *n*

snapshot /ˈsnæpʃɒt/ *n* a casual photograph made typically by an amateur with a small hand-held camera and without regard to technique

¹snare /sneəʳ/ *n* **1a** a trap often consisting of a noose for catching animals **b** sthg by which one is trapped or deceived **2** any of the catgut strings or metal spirals of a snare drum which produce a rattling sound

²snare *v* **1** to procure by artful or

skilful actions **2** to entangle or hold as if in a snare

snare drum *n* a small double-headed drum with 1 or more snares stretched across its lower head

¹snarl /snɑːl/ *n* **1** a tangle, esp of hair or thread; a knot **2** a confused or complicated situation

²snarl *v* **1** to cause to become knotted and intertwined; tangle **2** to make excessively confused or complicated *USE* often + *up*

³snarl *v* **1** to growl with bared teeth **2** to speak in a vicious or bad-tempered manner – **snarl** *n*

snarl-up *n* an instance of confusion, disorder, or obstruction; *specif* a traffic jam

¹snatch /snætʃ/ *v* to attempt to seize sthg suddenly – often + *at* – **~er** *n*

²snatch *n* **1** a snatching at or of sthg **2a** a brief period of time or activity **b** sthg fragmentary or hurried **3** a robbery – infml

snazzy /ˈsnæzi/ *adj* stylishly or flashily attractive – infml

¹sneak /sniːk/ *v* **1** to go or leave stealthily or furtively; slink **2** to behave in a furtive or servile manner **3** *Br* to tell tales – infml

²sneak *n* **1** a person who acts in a stealthy or furtive manner **2** the act or an instance of sneaking **3** *Br* a person, esp a schoolchild, who tells tales against others – infml

sneaker /ˈsniːkəʳ/ *n, chiefly NAm* a plimsoll – usu pl

sneaking /ˈsniːkɪŋ/ *adj* **1** furtive, underhand **2** mean, contemptible **3** instinctively felt but unverified

¹sneer /snɪəʳ/ *v* **1** to smile or laugh with a curl of the lips to express scorn or contempt **2** to speak or write in a scornfully jeering manner – **~er** *n* – **~ingly** *adv*

²sneer *n* a sneering expression or remark

sneeze /sniːz/ *v or n* (to make) a sudden violent involuntary audible expiration of breath

snick /snɪk/ *v* **1** to cut slightly; nick **2** to edge

snide /snaɪd/ *adj* **1** slyly disparaging; insinuating **2** *chiefly NAm* mean, low – **~ly** *adv* – **~ness** *n*

¹sniff /snɪf/ *v* **1** to draw air audibly up the nose, esp for smelling **2** to show or express disdain or scorn *at* **3** to detect or become aware of (as if) by smelling – **~er** *n*

²sniff *n* **1** an act or sound of sniffing **2** a quantity that is sniffed

¹sniffle /ˈsnɪfəl/ *v* to sniff repeatedly – **~r** *n*

²sniffle *n* **1** an act or sound of sniffling **2** *often pl* a head cold marked by nasal discharge

snifter /ˈsnɪftəʳ/ *n* a small drink of spirits – infml

snigger /ˈsnɪgəʳ/ *v* to laugh in a partly suppressed often derisive manner – **snigger** *n*

¹snip /snɪp/ *n* **1a** a small piece snipped off; *also* a fragment, bit **b** a cut or notch made by snipping **2** *pl but sing or pl in constr* shears used esp for cutting sheet metal by hand **3** *Br* a bargain

²snip *v* to cut (as if) with shears or scissors, esp with short rapid strokes

¹snipe /snaɪp/ *n* any of several game birds that occur esp in marshy areas and resemble woodcocks

²snipe *v* **1** to shoot *at* exposed individuals usu from in hiding at long range **2** to aim a snide or obliquely critical attack *at* – **sniper** *n*

snippet /ˈsnɪpɪ̣t/ *n* a small part, piece, or item; *esp* a fragment of writing or conversation

¹snitch /snɪtʃ/ *v* to pilfer, pinch – infml

²snitch *n* an esp petty theft – infml

snivel /ˈsnɪvəl/ *v* **1** to sniff mucus up the nose audibly **2** to whine, snuffle **3** to speak or act in a whining, tearful, cringing, or weakly emotional manner – **~ler** *n*

snob /snɒb/ *n* **1** one who blatantly attempts to cultivate or imitate those he/she admires as social superiors **2** one who has an air of smug superiority in matters of knowledge or taste – **~bish** *adj* – **~bishly** *adv* – **~bishness** *n*

snobbery /ˈsnɒbəri/ *n* (an instance of) snobbishness

snog /snɒg/ *v, Br* to kiss and cuddle – slang – **snog** *n*

snood /snuːd/ *n* a net or fabric bag, formerly worn at the back of the head by women, to hold the hair

¹snooker /ˈsnuːkəʳ/ *n* **1** a game played with a white ball, 15 red balls and 6 variously coloured balls on a table with side cushions and pockets in which the object is to use a cue to hit the white ball in such a manner as to drive a coloured ball into a pocket **2** a position of the balls in snooker in which a direct shot would lose points

²snooker *v* **1** to prevent (an opponent) from making a direct shot in snooker by playing the cue ball so that another ball rests between it and the object ball **2** to present an obstacle to; thwart – infml

snoop /snuːp/ *v* to look or pry in a sneaking or interfering manner – **~er** *n*

snooty /ˈsnuːti/ *adj* **1** haughty, disdainful **2** characterized by snobbish attitudes *USE* infml – **snootily** *adv* – **snootiness** *n*

snooze /snuːz/ *v or n* (to take) a nap – infml

snore /snɔːʳ/ *v or n* (to breathe with) a rough hoarse noise due to vibration of the soft palate during sleep

snorkel /ˈsnɔːkəl/ *n* **1** a tube housing an air intake and exhaust pipes that can be extended above the surface of the water from a submerged submarine **2** a J-shaped tube allowing a skin diver to breathe while face down in the water

¹snort /snɔːt/ *v* **1** to force air violently through the nose with a rough harsh sound **2** to express scorn, anger, or surprise by a snort **3** to take in (a drug) by inhalation – infml

²snort *n* **1** an act or sound of snorting **2** a snifter – infml

snot /snɒt/ *n* **1** nasal mucus **2** a snotty person – slang

snotty /ˈsnɒti/ *adj* **1** soiled with nasal mucus – infml **2** arrogantly or snobbishly unpleasant

snout /snaʊt/ *n* **1** a long projecting nose (e g of a pig) **2** a forward prolongation of the head of various animals

¹snow /snəʊ/ *n* **1a** (a descent of) water falling in the form of white flakes consisting of small ice crystals formed directly from vapour in the atmosphere **b** fallen snow **2** cocaine – slang

²snow *v* **1** to fall in or as snow **2** to cover, shut in, or block (as if) with snow – usu + *in* or *up*

¹snowball /ˈsnəʊbɔːl/ *n* a round mass of snow pressed or rolled together for throwing

²snowball *v* **1** to throw snowballs at **2** to increase or expand at a rapidly accelerating rate

snow blindness *n* inflammation and painful sensitiveness to light caused by exposure of the eyes to ultraviolet rays reflected from snow or ice – **snow-blind** *adj*

snowbound /ˈsnəʊbaʊnd/ *adj* confined or surrounded by snow

snowdrift /ˈsnəʊˌdrɪft/ *n* a bank of drifted snow

snowdrop /ˈsnəʊdrɒp/ *n* a bulbous European plant of the daffodil family bearing nodding white flowers in spring

snowfall /ˈsnəʊfɔːl/ *n* the amount of snow falling at one time or in a given period

snowflake /ˈsnəʊfleɪk/ *n* a flake or crystal of snow

snow line *n* the lower margin of a permanent expanse of snow

snowman /ˈsnəʊmæn/ *n* a pile of snow shaped to resemble a human figure

¹snowplough /ˈsnəʊplaʊ/ *n* **1** any of various vehicles or devices used for clearing snow **2** a turn in skiing with the skis in the snowploughing position

²snowplough *v* to force the heels of one's ski's outwards, keeping the tips together, in order to descend slowly or to stop

snowshoe /ˈsnəʊʃuː/ *n* a light oval wooden frame that is strung with thongs and attached to the foot to enable a person to walk on soft snow without sinking

snow under *v* to overwhelm, esp in excess of capacity to handle or absorb sthg

snowy /ˈsnəʊi/ *adj* **1a** composed of (melted) snow **b** characterized by or covered with snow **2** snow-white – **snowiness** *n*

¹snub /snʌb/ *v* **1** to check or interrupt

with a cutting retort; rebuke **2** to treat with contempt, esp by deliberately ignoring

[2]**snub** *n* an act or an instance of snubbing; *esp* a slight

[3]**snub** *adj* short and stubby

[1]**snuff** /snʌf/ *v* **1** to trim or put out a candle by pinching or by the use of snuffers **2** to make extinct; put an end to – usu + *out*

[2]**snuff** *n* a preparation of pulverized often scented tobacco inhaled usu through the nostrils

snuffer /ˈsnʌfəʳ/ *n* **1** an instrument resembling a pair of scissors for trimming the wick of a candle – usu pl but sing. or pl in constr **2** an instrument consisting of a small hollow cone attached to a handle, used to extinguish candles

snuffle /ˈsnʌfəl/ *v* **1a** to sniff, usu audibly and repeatedly **b** to draw air through an obstructed nose with a sniffing sound **2** to speak (as if) through the nose

[1]**snug** /snʌg/ *adj* **1** fitting closely and comfortably **2a** enjoying or affording warm secure comfortable shelter **b** marked by relaxation and cordiality **3** affording a degree of comfort and ease – **~ly** *adv*

[2]**snug** *v* to snuggle

[3]**snug** *n, Br* a small private room or compartment in a pub

snuggle /ˈsnʌgəl/ *v* to curl up comfortably or cosily; nestle – infml

[1]**so** /səʊ/ *adv* **1a(1)** in this way; thus – often used as a substitute for a preceding word or word group (e g do you really think *so*?) **(2)** most certainly; indeed (e g I hope to win and *so* I shall) **b(1)** in the same way; also – used after *as* to introduce a parallel (e g as the French drink wine, *so* the British love their beer) **(2)** as an accompaniment – after *as* **c** in such a way – used esp before *as* or *that*, to introduce a result or to introduce the idea of purpose **2a** to such an extreme degree – used before *as* to introduce a comparison, esp in the negative (e g not *so* fast as mine), or, esp before *as* or *that*, to introduce a result (e g *so* tired that I went to bed) **b** very **c** to a definite but unspecified extent or degree (e g can only do *so* much in a day) **3** therefore, consequently **4** then, subsequently **5** *chiefly dial & NAm* – used, esp by children, to counter a negative charge

[2]**so** *conj* **1** with the result that **2** in order that **3a** for that reason; therefore **b(1)** – used as an introductory particle (e g *so* here we are) often to belittle a point under discussion (e g *so* what?)

[3]**so** *adj* **1** conforming with actual facts; true **2** disposed in a definite order (e g his books were always exactly *so*)

[4]**so** *pron* such as has been specified or suggested; the same

[5]**so, soh** *n* the musical note sol

[1]**soak** /səʊk/ *v* **1** to lie immersed in liquid (e g water), esp so as to become saturated or softened **2** to become fully felt or appreciated – usu + *in* or *into* **3** to intoxicate (oneself) with alcohol – infml **4** to charge an excessive amount of money – infml – **~ed** *adj* – **~ing** *adj*

[2]**soak** *n* **1a** soaking or being soaked **b** that (e g liquid) in which sthg is soaked **2** a drunkard – infml

so-and-so *n, pl* **so-and-sos, so-and-so's** **1** an unnamed or unspecified person or thing **2** a disliked or unpleasant person – euph

[1]**soap** /səʊp/ *n* a cleansing and emulsifying agent that lathers when rubbed in water – **soapy** *adj*

[2]**soap** *v* **1** to rub soap over or into **2** to flatter – often + *up*; infml

soapbox /ˈsəʊpbɒks/ *n* an improvised platform used by an informal orator

soap opera *n* a radio or television drama characterized by stock domestic situations and melodramatic or sentimental treatment

soapstone /ˈsəʊpstəʊn/ *n* a soft greyish green or brown stone having a soapy feel and composed mainly of magnesium silicate

[1]**soar** /sɔːʳ/ *v* **1a** to fly high in the air **b** to sail or hover in the air, often at a great height **2** to rise rapidly or to a very high level **3** to be of imposing height or stature; tower

[2]**soar** *n* (the range, distance, or height attained in) soaring

[1]**sob** /sɒb/ *v* **1** to weep with convulsive catching of the breath **2** to make a sound like that of a sob or sobbing

[2]**sob** *n* an act or sound of sobbing; *also* a similar sound

[1]**sober** /'səʊbə^r/ *adj* **1** not drunk or addicted to drink **2** gravely or earnestly thoughtful **3** calmly self-controlled; sedate **4a** well balanced; realistic **b** sane, rational **5** subdued in tone or colour – **~ly** *adv*

[2]**sober** *v* to make or become sober – usu + *up*

sobriety /sə'braɪəti/ *n* being sober – fml

sob story *n* a sentimental story or account intended chiefly to elicit sympathy – infml

so-called *adj* **1** commonly named; popularly so termed **2** falsely or improperly so named

soccer /'sɒkə^r/ *n* a football game that is played with a round ball between teams of 11 players each, that features the kicking and heading of the ball, and in which use of the hands and arms is prohibited except to the goalkeepers

sociable /'səʊʃəbəl/ *adj* **1** inclined to seek or enjoy companionship; companionable **2** conducive to friendliness or cordial social relations – **-bility** *n* – **-bly** *adv*

[1]**social** /'səʊʃəl/ *adj* **1** of or promoting companionship or friendly relations **2a** tending to form cooperative relationships; gregarious **b** living and breeding in more or less organized communities **3** of human society – **~ly** *adv*

[2]**social** *n* a social gathering, usu connected with a church or club

social climber *n* one who strives to gain a higher social position or acceptance in fashionable society – derog

social democracy *n* a political movement advocating a gradual and democratic transition to socialism

socialism /'səʊʃəlɪzəm/ *n* **1** an economic and political theory advocating, or a system based on, collective or state ownership and administration of the means of production and distribution of goods **2** a transitional stage of society in Marxist theory distinguished by unequal distribution of goods according to work done

[1]**socialist** /'səʊʃələst/ *n* **1** one who advocates or practises socialism **2** *cap* a member of a socialist party or group

[2]**socialist** *adj* **1** of socialism **2** *cap* of or constituting a party advocating socialism

socialite /'səʊʃəlaɪt/ *n* a socially active or prominent person

social·ize, -ise /'səʊʃəlaɪz/ *v* **1** to fit or train for life in society; learn to get on with others **2** to adapt to the needs or take into the ownership of society **3** to act in a sociable manner

social science *n* **1** the scientific study of human society and the relationships between its members **2** a science (e g economics or politics) dealing with a particular aspect of human society

social security *n* **1** provision by the state through pensions, unemployment benefit, sickness benefit, etc for its citizens' economic security and social welfare **2** supplementary benefit

social service *n* activity designed to promote social welfare; *esp* an organized service (e g education or housing) provided by the state

social work *n* any of various professional activities concerned with the aid of the economically underprivileged and socially maladjusted – **~er** *n*

[1]**society** /sə'saɪəti/ *n* **1** companionship or association with others; company **2a** *often cap* the human race considered in terms of its structure of social institutions **b(1)** a community having common traditions, institutions, and collective interests **(2)** an organized group working together or periodically meeting because of common interests, beliefs, or profession **3** a fashionable leisure class

[2]**society** *adj* (characteristic) of fashionable society

sociology /ˌsəʊsi'ɒlədʒi, ˌsəʊʃi-/ *n* the science of social institutions and relationships; *specif* the study of the behaviour of organized human groups – **-gical** *adj* – **-gically** *adv* – **-gist** *n*

[1]**sock** /sɒk/ *n* a knitted or woven covering for the foot usu extending above the ankle and sometimes to the knee

[2]**sock** *v* to hit or apply forcefully – infml

[3]**sock** *n* a vigorous or forceful blow; a punch – infml

socket /ˈsɒkɨt/ *n* an opening or hollow that forms a holder for sthg; *also* an electrical plug

[1]**sod** /sɒd/ *n* **1** turf; *also* the grass-covered surface of the ground **2** one's native land – infml

[2]**sod** *n, Br* an objectionable person, esp male *USE* slang

[3]**sod** *v, Br* to damn – usu used as an oath or in the present participle as a meaningless intensive; slang

soda /səʊdə/ *n* **1** any of various compounds of sodium **2a** soda water **b** *chiefly NAm* a sweet drink consisting of soda water, flavouring, and often ice cream

soda water *n* a beverage consisting of water highly charged with carbonic acid gas

sodden /ˈsɒdn/ *adj* **1** full of moisture or water; saturated **2** heavy, damp, or doughy because of imperfect cooking **3** dull or expressionless, esp from habitual drunkenness

sodium /ˈsəʊdɪəm/ *n* a silver white soft ductile element of the alkali metal group that occurs abundantly in nature in combined form and is very active chemically

sodium chloride *n* common salt

sofa /ˈsəʊfə/ *n* a long upholstered seat with a back and 2 arms or raised ends that typically seats 2 to 4 people

[1]**soft** /sɒft/ *adj* **1a** yielding to physical pressure **b** of a consistency that may be shaped, moulded, spread, or easily cut **c** lacking in hardness **2a** pleasing or agreeable to the senses; bringing ease or quiet **b** having a bland or mellow taste **c** not bright or glaring; subdued **d(1)** quiet in pitch or volume; not harsh **(2)** *of c and g* pronounced /s/ and /j/ respectively (e g in *acid* and *age*) – not used technically **e(1)** *of the eyes* having a liquid or gentle appearance **(2)** having a gently curved outline **f** smooth or delicate in texture falling or blowing with slight force or impact **3a** marked by a kindness, lenience, or moderation: e g **b** mild, low-key; *specif* not of the most extreme or harmful kind **4a** lacking resilience or strength, esp as a result of having led a life of ease **b** mentally deficient; feebleminded **5** amorously attracted, esp covertly – + *on*

[2]**soft** *n* a soft object, material, or part

[3]**soft** *adv* in a soft or gentle manner; softly

soften /ˈsɒfən/ *v* **1** to make soft or softer **2a** to weaken the military resistance or the morale of **b** to impair the strength or resistance of *USE* (*2*) often + *up*

softhearted /ˌsɒftˈhɑːtɨd/ *adj* kind, compassionate – ~**ness** *n*

soft-pedal *v* to attempt to minimize the importance of (sthg), esp by talking cleverly or evasively

soft pedal *n* a foot pedal on a piano that reduces the volume of sound

soft-soap *v* to persuade or mollify with flattery or smooth talk – infml

soft soap *n* flattery – infml

soft spot *n* a sentimental weakness

software /ˈsɒftweəʳ/ *n* **1** the entire set of programs and procedures associated with a system, esp a computer system **2** sthg contrasted with hardware; *esp* materials for use with audiovisual equipment

softwood /ˈsɒftwʊd/ *n* the wood of a coniferous tree

soggy /ˈsɒgi/ *adj* **1a** waterlogged, soaked **b** sodden **2** heavily dull – **-gily** *adv* – **-giness** *n*

[1]**soil** /sɔɪl/ *v* **1** to stain or make unclean, esp superficially; dirty **2** to defile morally; corrupt **3** to blacken or tarnish (e g a person's reputation)

[2]**soil** *n* **1** firm land; earth **2** the upper layer of earth that may be dug or ploughed and in which plants grow **3** country, land **4** refuse or sewage **5** a medium in which sthg takes hold and develops

sojourn /ˈsɒdʒɜːn/ *v or n* (to make) a temporary stay – fml

[1]**sol** /sɒl/ *n* the 5th note of the diatonic scale in solmization

[2]**sol** *n, pl* **soles** the basic unit of currency of Peru

[1]**solace** /ˈsɒlɨs/ *n* (a source of) consolation or comfort in grief or anxiety

[2]**solace** *v* **1** to give solace to; console **2** to alleviate, relieve

solar /ˈsəʊləʳ/ *adj* **1** of or derived from

the sun, esp as affecting the earth **2** (of or reckoned by time) measured by the earth's course in relation to the sun **3** produced or operated by the action of the sun's light or heat; *also* using the sun's rays

solarium /sə'leərɪəm/ *n, pl* **solaria** a room exposed to the sun (e g for relaxation or treatment of illness); *also* an establishment offering facilities for producing a sun tan, usu artificially

solar plexus /ˌsəʊlə 'pleksəs/ *n* the pit of the stomach

solar system *n* the sun together with the group of celestial bodies that are held by its attraction and revolve round it

sold /səʊld/ *past of* **sell**

[1]**solder** /'səʊldəʳ, 'sɒl-/ *n* an alloy, esp of tin and lead, used when melted to join metallic surfaces

[2]**solder** *v* **1** to unite or make whole (as if) by solder **2** to hold or join together; unite

soldering iron *n* a usu electrically heated device that is used for melting and applying solder

[1]**soldier** /'səʊldʒəʳ/ *n* **1** sby engaged in military service, esp in the army **2** any of a caste of ants or wingless termites having a large head and jaws

[2]**soldier** *v* **1** to serve as a soldier **2** to press doggedly forward – usu + *on*

soldier of fortune *n* sby who seeks an adventurous, esp military, life wherever chance allows

[1]**sole** /səʊl/ *n* **1a** the undersurface of a foot **b** the part of a garment or article of footwear on which the sole rests **2** the usu flat bottom or lower part of sthg or the base on which sthg rests

[2]**sole** *v* to provide with a (new) sole

[3]**sole** *n* any of several flatfish including some valued as superior food fishes

[4]**sole** *adj* **1** being the only one; only **2** belonging or relating exclusively to 1 individual or group – **~ly** *adv*

solecism /'sɒlɪ̣sɪzəm/ *n* **1** a minor blunder in speech or writing **2** a breach of etiquette or decorum

solemn /'sɒləm/ *adj* **1** performed so as to be legally binding **2** celebrated with full liturgical ceremony **3a** conveying a deep sense of reverence or exaltation; sublime **b** marked by seriousness and sobriety **c** sombre, gloomy – **~ly** *adv* – **~ness** *n*

solemnity /sə'lemnɪ̣ti/ *n* **1** formal or ceremonious observance of an occasion or event **2** a solemn event or occasion **3** solemn character or state – **-nize** *v*

solenoid /'sɒlənɔɪd, 'səʊ-/ *n* a coil of wire commonly in the form of a long cylinder that when carrying a current produces a magnetic field and draws in a movable usu ferrous core

sol-fa /'sɒl ˌfɑː/ *n* the system of using syllables *do, re, mi,* etc for the notes of the scale

solicit /sə'lɪsɪ̣t/ *v* **1** to make a formal or earnest appeal or request to; entreat **2a** to attempt to lure or entice, esp into evil **b** *of a prostitute* to proposition publicly **3** to try to obtain by usu urgent requests or pleas – **~ation** *n*

solicitor /sə'lɪsɪ̣təʳ/ *n* a qualified lawyer who advises clients, represents them in the lower courts, and prepares cases for barristers to try in higher courts

solicitor general *n often cap S&G* a Crown law officer ranking after the attorney general in England

solicitous /sə'lɪsɪ̣təs/ *adj* **1** showing consideration or anxiety; concerned **2** desirous *of*; eager *to* – fml – **~ly** *adv* – **~ness** *n*

solicitude /sə'lɪsɪ̣tjuːd/ *n* being solicitous; concern; *also* excessive care or attention

[1]**solid** /'sɒlɪ̣d/ *adj* **1a** without an internal cavity **b** having no opening or division **2** of uniformly close and coherent texture; compact **3** of good substantial quality or kind: e g **a** well constructed from durable materials **b** sound, cogent **4a** having, involving, or dealing with 3 dimensions or with solids **b** neither gaseous nor liquid **5** without interruption; full **6** of a single substance or character: e g **a** (almost) entirely of 1 metal **b** of uniform colour or tone **7** reliable, reputable, or acceptable – **~ity** *n* – **~ly** *adv* – **~ness** *n* – **~ify** *v* – **~ification** *n*

[2]**solid** *adv* in a solid manner; *also* unanimously

[3]**solid** *n* **1** a substance that does not flow perceptibly under moderate

stress 2 sthg solid; *esp* a solid colour

solidarity /ˌsɒlɟˈdærɟti/ *n* unity based on shared interests and standards

solid-state *adj* using the electric, magnetic, or photic properties of solid materials; not using thermionic valves

soliloquy /səˈlɪləkwi/ *n* a dramatic monologue that gives the illusion of being a series of unspoken reflections – **-quize** *v*

solitaire /ˈsɒlɟteəʳ, ˌ--ˈ-/ *n* **1** a gem, esp a diamond, set by itself **2** a game played by 1 person in which a number of pieces are removed from a cross-shaped pattern according to certain rules **3** *chiefly NAm* (a card-game similar to) patience

¹**solitary** /ˈsɒlɟtəri/ *adj* **1a** (fond of) being or living alone or without companions **b** lonely **2** taken, spent, or performed without companions **3** being the only one; sole **4** unfrequented, remote

²**solitary** *n* one who habitually seeks solitude

solitude /ˈsɒlɟtjuːd/ *n* **1** being alone or remote from society; seclusion **2** a lonely place; a fastness

solmization /ˌsɒlmɪˈzeɪʃən/ *n* the use of sol-fa syllables in or for singing

¹**solo** /ˈsəʊləʊ/ *n* **1** a (musical composition for) performance by a single voice or instrument with or without accompaniment **2** a flight by 1 person alone in an aircraft; *esp* a person's first solo flight

²**solo** *adv* without a companion; alone

solstice /ˈsɒlstɟs/ *n* either of the times when the sun's distance from the celestial equator is greatest and which occurs about June 22nd and December 22nd each year

soluble /ˈsɒljʊbəl/ *adj* **1** capable of being dissolved (as if) in a liquid **2** capable of being solved or explained – **-bility** *n*

solution /səˈluːʃən/ *n* **1a** an act or the process by which a solid, liquid, or gaseous substance is uniformly mixed with a liquid or sometimes a gas or solid **b** a typically liquid uniform mixture formed by this process **c** a liquid containing a dissolved substance **2a** an action or process of solving a problem **b** an answer to a problem

solve /sɒlv/ *v* to find a solution for sthg – **solvable** *adj* – **solver** *n*

¹**solvent** /ˈsɒlvənt/ *adj* **1** able to pay all legal debts; *also* in credit **2** that dissolves or can dissolve – **-vency** *n*

²**solvent** *n* a usu liquid substance capable of dissolving or dispersing 1 or more other substances

sombre /ˈsɒmbəʳ/ *adj* **1** dark, gloomy **2** of a dull, dark, or heavy shade or colour **3a** serious, grave **b** depressing, melancholy – **~ly** *adv* – **~ness** *n*

sombrero /sɒmˈbreərəʊ/ *n* a high-crowned hat of felt or straw with a very wide brim, worn esp in Mexico

¹**some** /sʌm/ *adj* **1a** being an unknown, undetermined, or unspecified unit or thing (e g *some* film or other) **b** being an unspecified member of a group or part of a class (e g *some* gems are hard) **c** being an appreciable number, part, or amount of (e g have *some* consideration for others) **d** being of an unspecified amount or number (e g give me *some* water) – used as an indefinite pl of **a** (e g have *some* apples) **2a** important, striking, or excellent (e g that was *some* party) – chiefly infml **b** no kind of (e g *some* friend you are) – chiefly infml

²**some** /səm; *strong* sʌm/ *pron* **1** *sing or pl in constr* some part, quantity, or number but not all **2** *chiefly NAm* an indefinite additional amount (e g ran a mile and then *some*)

³**some** /sʌm/ *adv* **1** about (e g *some* 80 houses) **2** somewhat – used in Br English in *some more* and more widely in NAm

¹**somebody** /ˈsʌmbɒdi/ *pron* some indefinite or unspecified person

²**somebody** *n* a person of position or importance

somehow /ˈsʌmhaʊ/ *adv* **1a** by some means not known or designated **b** no matter how **2** for some mysterious reason

someone /ˈsʌmwʌn, -wən/ *pron* somebody

somersault /ˈsʌməsɔːlt/ *n* a leaping or rolling movement in which a person turns forwards or backwards in a complete revolution bringing the feet over the head and finally landing on the feet

[1]**something** /'sʌmθɪŋ/ *pron* **1a** some indeterminate or unspecified thing – used to replace forgotten matter or to express vagueness (e g he's *something* or other in the Foreign Office) **b** some part; a certain amount (e g seen *something* of her work) **2a** a person or thing of consequence (e g their daughter is quite *something*) **b** some truth or value (e g there's *something* in what you say)

[2]**something** *adv* **1** in some degree; somewhat – also used to suggest approximation (e g *something* like 1,000 people) **2** to an extreme degree (e g swears *something* awful) – infml

[1]**sometime** /'sʌmtaɪm/ *adv* **1** at some unspecified future time **2** at some point of time in a specified period

[2]**sometime** *adj* having been formerly; late (e g the *sometime* chairman)

sometimes /'sʌmtaɪmz/ *adv* at intervals; occasionally; now and again

somewhat /'sʌmwɒt/ *adv* to some degree; slightly

[1]**somewhere** /'sʌmweəʳ/ *adv* **1** in, at, or to some unknown or unspecified place **2** to a place or state symbolizing positive accomplishment or progress (e g at last we're getting *somewhere*) **3** in the vicinity of; approximately

[2]**somewhere** *n* an undetermined or unnamed place

somnolent /'sɒmnələnt/ *adj* **1** inclined to or heavy with sleep **2** tending to induce sleep – **~ly** *adv* – **-ence** *n*

son /sʌn/ *n* **1a** a male offspring, esp of human beings **b** a male adopted child **c** a male descendant – often pl **2** *cap* the second person of the Trinity; Christ

sonar /'səʊnɑːʳ, -nəʳ/ *n* an apparatus that detects the presence and location of a submerged object (by reflected sound waves)

sonata /sə'nɑːtə/ *n* an instrumental musical composition typically for 1 or 2 players and of 3 or 4 movements in contrasting forms and keys

son et lumière /ˌsɒn eɪ luː'mjeəʳ/ *n* an entertainment held at night at a historical site (e g a cathedral or stately home) that uses lighting and recorded sound to present the place's history

song /sɒŋ/ *n* **1** the act, art, or product of singing **2** poetry **3** (the melody of) a short musical composition usu with words **4** a very small sum

songster /'sɒŋstəʳ/ *n* a skilled singer

sonic /'sɒnɪk/ *adj* **1** *of waves and vibrations* having a frequency within the audibility range of the human ear **2** using, produced by, or relating to sound waves **3** of or being the speed of sound in air at sea level (about 340 m/s or 741 mph)

sonic boom *n* a sound resembling an explosion produced when a shock wave formed at the nose of an aircraft travelling at supersonic speed reaches the ground

son-in-law *n, pl* **sons-in-law** the husband of one's daughter

sonnet /'sɒnɨt/ *n* (a poem in) a fixed verse form with any of various rhyming schemes, consisting typically of 14 lines of 10 syllables each

sonny /'sʌni/ *n* a young boy – usu used in address; infml

sonorous /'sɒnərəs, sə'nɔːrəs/ *adj* **1** giving out sound (e g when struck) **2** pleasantly loud **3** impressive in effect or style – **~ly** *adv* – **-rity** *n*

[1]**soon** /suːn/ *adv* **1** before long; without undue time lapse **2** in a prompt manner; speedily **3** in agreement with one's preference; willingly – in comparisons (e g I'd *soon*er walk than drive)

[2]**soon** *adj* advanced in time; early

soot /sʊt/ *n* a fine black powder that consists chiefly of carbon and is formed by combustion, or separated from fuel during combustion – **~y** *adj* – **~iness** *n*

soothe /suːð/ *v* **1** to calm (as if) by showing attention or concern; placate **2** to relieve, alleviate **3** to bring comfort or reassurance to – **soothingly** *adv*

sop /sɒp/ *n* **1** a piece of food, esp bread, dipped, steeped, or for dipping in a liquid (e g soup) **2** sthg offered as a concession, appeasement, or bribe

sophisticated /sə'fɪstɨkeɪtɨd/ *adj* **1a** highly complicated or developed; complex **b** worldly-wise, knowing **2**

intellectually subtle or refined – -cation *n*

sophistry /ˈsɒfǝstri/ *n* speciously subtle reasoning or argument – **sophist** *n*

soporific /ˌsɒpəˈrɪfɪk/ *adj* **1** causing or tending to cause sleep **2** of or marked by sleepiness or lethargy – **~ally** *adv*

[1]**sopping** /ˈsɒpɪŋ/ *adj* wet through; soaking

[2]**sopping** *adv* to an extreme degree of wetness

soppy /ˈsɒpi/ *adj* **1** weakly sentimental; mawkish **2** *chiefly Br* silly, inane *USE* infml

soprano /səˈprɑːnəʊ/ *n* **1** the highest part in 4-part harmony **2** (a person with) the highest singing voice of women or boys **3** a member of a family of instruments having the highest range

sorbet /ˈsɔːbǝt, ˈsɔːbeɪ/ *n* a water ice; *also* a sherbet

sorcerer /ˈsɔːsərəʳ/ *n* a person who uses magical power, esp with the aid of evil spirits; a wizard

sorcery /ˈsɔːsəri/ *n* the arts and practices of a sorcerer

sordid /ˈsɔːdǝd/ *adj* **1a** dirty, filthy **b** wretched, squalid **2** base, vile **3** meanly avaricious; niggardly – **~ly** *adv* – **~ness** *n*

[1]**sore** /sɔːʳ/ *adj* **1a** causing pain or distress **b** painfully sensitive **c** hurt or inflamed so as to be or seem painful **2a** causing irritation or offence **b** causing great difficulty or anxiety; desperate **3** *chiefly NAm* angry, vexed – **~ness** *n*

[2]**sore** *n* **1** a localized sore spot on the body **2** a source of pain or vexation; an affliction

sorely /ˈsɔːli/ *adv* **1** painfully, grievously **2** much, extremely

[1]**sorrel** /ˈsɒrəl/ *n* **1** a brownish orange to light brown colour **2** a sorrel-coloured animal; *esp* a sorrel-coloured horse

[2]**sorrel** *n* any of various plants similar to the dock

[1]**sorrow** /ˈsɒrəʊ/ *n* **1** deep distress and regret (e g over the loss of sthg precious) **2** a cause or display of grief or sadness – **~ful** *adj* – **~fully** *adv* – **~fulness** *n*

[2]**sorrow** *v* to feel or express sorrow

sorry /ˈsɒri/ *adj* **1** feeling regret, penitence, or pity **2** inspiring sorrow, pity, or scorn

[1]**sort** /sɔːt/ *n* **1a** a group constituted on the basis of any common characteristic; a class, kind **b** an instance of a kind **2** nature, disposition **3** a person, individual – infml

[2]**sort** *v* **1** to put in a rank or particular place according to kind, class, or quality – often + *through* **2** *chiefly Scot* to put in working order; mend – **~er** *n*

sortie /ˈsɔːti/ *n* **1** a sudden issuing of troops from a defensive position **2** a single mission or attack by 1 aircraft

sort of *adv* **1** to a moderate degree; rather **2** kind of *USE* infml

SOS *n* **1** an internationally recognized signal of distress which is rendered in Morse code as · · · – – – · · · **2** a call or request for help or rescue

[1]**so-so** *adv* moderately well; tolerably

[2]**so-so** *adj* neither very good nor very bad; middling

sou /suː/ *n, pl* **sous** **1** any of various former French coins of low value **2** the smallest amount of money

[1]**soufflé** /ˈsuːfleɪ/ *n* a light fluffy baked or chilled dish made with a thick sauce into which stiffly beaten egg whites are incorporated

[2]**soufflé, souffléed** *adj* puffed or made light by or in cooking

sought /sɔːt/ *past of* **seek**

sought-after *adj* greatly desired or courted

[1]**soul** /səʊl/ *n* **1** the immaterial essence or animating principle of an individual life **2** all that constitutes a person's self **3a** an active or essential part **b** a moving spirit; a leader **4** a person **5** exemplification, personification **6a** a strong positive feeling esp of intense sensitivity and emotional fervour conveyed esp by American Negro performers **b** music that originated in American Negro gospel singing, is closely related to rhythm and blues, and is characterized by intensity of feeling and earthiness

[2]**soul** *adj* (characteristic) of American Negroes or their culture

soul-destroying *adj* giving no chance

for the mind to work; very uninteresting

soulful /'səʊlfəl/ *adj* full of or expressing esp intense or excessive feeling – ~**ly** *adv* – ~**ness** *n*

soulless /'səʊl-lɨs/ *adj* **1** having no soul or no warmth of feeling **2** bleak, uninviting – ~**ly** *adv* – ~**ness** *n*

soul-searching *n* scrutiny of one's mind and conscience, esp with regard to aims and motives

[1]**sound** /saʊnd/ *adj* **1a** healthy **b** free from defect or decay **2** solid, firm; *also* stable **3a** free from error, fallacy, or misapprehension **b** exhibiting or grounded in thorough knowledge and experience **c** conforming to accepted views; orthodox **4a** deep and undisturbed **b** thorough, severe – ~**ly** *adv* – ~**ness** *n*

[2]**sound** *adv* fully, thoroughly

[3]**sound** *n* **1a** the sensation perceived by the sense of hearing **b** energy that is transmitted by longitudinal pressure waves in a material medium (e g air) and is the objective cause of hearing **2** a speech sound **3** a characteristic musical style **4** radio broadcasting as opposed to television – ~**less** *adj* – ~**lessly** *adv*

[4]**sound** *v* **1a** to make a sound **b** to resound **c** to give a summons by sound **2** to have a specified import when heard; seem

[5]**sound** *n* **1** a long broad sea inlet **2** a long passage of water connecting 2 larger bodies or separating a mainland and an island

[6]**sound** *v* **1** to determine the depth of water, esp with a sounding line **2** *of a fish or whale* to dive down suddenly

sound barrier *n* a sudden large increase in aerodynamic drag that occurs as an aircraft nears the speed of sound

sounding board *n* **1a(1)** a structure behind or over a pulpit, rostrum, or platform to direct sound forwards **(2)** a thin board placed so as to increase the resonance of a musical instrument **b** a device or agency that helps disseminate opinions or ideas **2** sby or sthg used to test reaction to new ideas, plans, etc

sound out *v* to attempt to find out the views or intentions of

[1]**soundproof** /'saʊndpruːf/ *adj* impervious to sound

[2]**soundproof** *v* to insulate so as to obstruct the passage of sound

sound track *n* the area on a film that carries the sound recording; *also* the recorded music accompanying a film

soup /suːp/ *n* **1** a liquid food typically having a meat, fish, or vegetable stock as a base and often thickened and containing pieces of solid food **2** an awkward or embarrassing predicament – infml

soup kitchen *n* an establishment dispensing minimum food (e g soup and bread) to the needy

soup up *v* **1** to increase the power of (an engine or car) **2** to make more attractive, interesting, etc ***USE*** infml

[1]**sour** /saʊəʳ/ *adj* **1** being or inducing the one of the 4 basic taste sensations that is produced chiefly by acids **2a** having the acid taste or smell (as if) of fermentation **b** smelling or tasting of decay; rotten **c** wrong, awry **3a** unpleasant, distasteful **b** morose, bitter – ~**ly** *adv* – ~**ness** *n*

[2]**sour** *n* the primary taste sensation produced by sthg sour

source /sɔːs/ *n* **1** the point of origin of a stream of water **2a(1)** a generative force; a cause **(2)** a means of supply **b(1)** a place of origin; a beginning **(2)** sby or sthg that initiates **(3)** a person, publication, etc that supplies information, esp at firsthand

sourpuss /'saʊəpʊs/ *n* a habitually gloomy or bitter person – infml

sousaphone /'suːzəfəʊn/ *n* a large tuba that has a flared adjustable bell and is designed to encircle the player and rest on the left shoulder

souse /saʊs/ *v* **1** to pickle **2** to drench, saturate; *also* immerse **3** to make drunk; inebriate – infml

[1]**south** /saʊθ/ *adj or adv* towards, at, belonging to, or coming from the south

[2]**south** *n* **1** (the compass point corresponding to) the direction of the south terrestrial pole **2** *often cap* regions or countries lying to the south of a specified or implied point of orientation

[1]**southeast** /ˌsaʊθ'iːst/ *adj or adv*

towards, at, belonging to, or coming from the southeast

[2]**southeast** /ˌsaʊθ'iːst/ *n* **1** (the general direction corresponding to) the compass point midway between south and east **2** *often cap* regions or countries lying to the southeast of a specified or implied point of orientation

[1]**southeasterly** /ˌsaʊθ'iːstəli/ *adj or adv* southeast

[2]**southeasterly, southeaster** *n* a wind from the SE

southeastern /ˌsaʊθ'iːstən/ *adj* **1** *often cap* (characteristic) of a region conventionally designated Southeast **2** southeast

[1]**southerly** /'sʌðəli/ *adj or adv* south

[2]**southerly** *n* a wind from the S

southern /'sʌðən/ *adj* **1** *often cap* (characteristic) of a region conventionally designated South **2** south

Southerner /'sʌðənəʳ/ *n* a native or inhabitant of the South

southpaw /'saʊθpɔː/ *n* a left-hander; *specif* a boxer who leads with the right hand and guards with the left

south pole *n* **1a** *often cap S&P* the southernmost point of the rotational axis of the earth or another celestial body **b** the southernmost point on the celestial sphere, about which the stars seem to revolve **2** the southward-pointing pole of a magnet

[1]**southwest** /ˌsaʊθ'west/ *adj or adv* towards, at, belonging to, or coming from the southwest

[2]**southwest** /ˌsaʊθ'west/ *n* **1** (the general direction corresponding to) the compass point midway between south and west **2** *often cap* regions or countries lying to the southwest of a specified or implied point of orientation

[1]**southwesterly** /ˌsaʊθ'westəli/ *adj or adv* southwest

[2]**southwesterly, southwester** *n* a wind from the SW

southwestern /ˌsaʊθ'westən/ *adj* **1** *often cap* (characteristic) of a region conventionally designated Southwest **2** southwest

souvenir /ˌsuːvə'nɪəʳ, '---/ *n* sthg that serves as a reminder (e g of a place or past event); a memento

sou'wester /saʊ'westəʳ/ *n* **1** a southwesterly **2a** a long usu oilskin waterproof coat worn esp at sea during stormy weather **b** a waterproof hat with a wide slanting brim longer at the back than in front

[1]**sovereign** /'sɒvrɪn/ *n* **1** a ruler **2** a former British gold coin worth 1 pound

[2]**sovereign** *adj* **1a** possessing supreme (political) power **b** unlimited in extent; absolute **c** enjoying political autonomy **2a** of outstanding excellence or importance **b** of an unqualified nature; utmost **3** (characteristic) of or befitting a sovereign – **~ty** *n*

soviet /'səʊviɪt, 'sɒ-/ *n* **1** an elected council in a Communist country **2** *pl, cap* the people, esp the leaders, of the USSR

[1]**sow** /saʊ/ *n* an adult female pig; *also* the adult female of various other animals (e g the grizzly bear)

[2]**sow** /səʊ/ *v* **sowed; sown, sowed** **1a** to scatter (e g seed) on the earth for growth **b** to strew (as if) with seed **2** to implant, initiate – **~er** *n*

soya bean /'sɔɪə biːn/ *n* (the edible oil-rich and protein-rich seeds of) an annual Asiatic leguminous plant widely grown for its seed and soil improvement

sozzled /'sɒzəld/ *adj, chiefly Br* drunk – slang; often humor

spa /spɑː/ *n* **1** a usu fashionable resort with mineral springs **2** a spring of mineral water

[1]**space** /speɪs/ *n* **1** (the duration of) a period of time **2a** a limited extent in 1, 2, or 3 dimensions; distance, area, or volume **b** an amount of room set apart or available **3a** a boundless 3-dimensional extent in which objects and events occur and have relative position and direction **b** physical space independent of what occupies it **4** the region beyond the earth's atmosphere **5** (a piece of type giving) a blank area separating words or lines (e g on a page)

[2]**space** *v* to place at intervals or arrange with space between

spacecraft /'speɪs-krɑːft/ *n* a device designed to travel beyond the earth's atmosphere

spaced-out *adj* dazed or stupefied (as if) by a narcotic substance – slang

spaceship /'speɪsˌʃɪp/ *n* a manned spacecraft

space shuttle *n* a vehicle that has usu 2 stages and is designed to serve as a reusable transport between the earth and an orbiting space station

spacing /'speɪsɪŋ/ *n* **1a** the act of providing with spaces or placing at intervals **b** an arrangement in space **2** the distance between any 2 objects in a usu regularly arranged series

spacious /'speɪʃəs/ *adj* **1** containing ample space; roomy **2a** broad or vast in area **b** large in scale or space; expansive – **~ly** *adv* – **~ness** *n*

[1]**spade** /speɪd/ *n* a digging implement that can be pushed into the ground with the foot

[2]**spade** *n* **1a** a playing card marked with 1 or more black figures shaped like a spearhead **b** *pl but sing or pl in constr* the suit comprising cards identified by these figures **2** a Negro – derog

spadework /'speɪdwɜːk/ *n* the routine preparatory work for an undertaking

spaghetti /spə'geti/ *n* pasta in the form of thin often solid strings of varying widths smaller in diameter than macaroni

spake /speɪk/ *archaic past of* **speak**

Spam /spæm/ *trademark* – used for a tinned pork luncheon meat

[1]**span** /spæn/ *archaic past of* **spin**

[2]**span** *n* **1** the distance from the end of the thumb to the end of the little finger of a spread hand **2** an extent, distance, or spread between 2 limits: e g **a** a limited stretch (e g of time); *esp* an individual's lifetime **b** the full reach or extent **c** the distance or extent between supports (e g of a bridge); *also* a part of a bridge between supports **d** a wingspan

[3]**span** *v* **1** to extend across **2** to form an arch over

[1]**spangle** /'spæŋgəl/ *n* **1** a sequin **2** a small glittering object or particle

[2]**spangle** *v* to set or sprinkle (as if) with spangles

spaniel /'spænjəl/ *n* **1** any of several breeds of small or medium-sized mostly short-legged dogs usu having long wavy hair, feathered legs and tail, and large drooping ears **2** a fawning servile person

Spanish /'spænɪʃ/ *n* **1** the official Romance language of Spain and of the countries colonized by Spaniards **2** *pl in constr* the people of Spain

[1]**spank** /spæŋk/ *v* to strike, esp on the buttocks, (as if) with the open hand – **spank** *n* – **~ing** *n*

[2]**spank** *v* to move quickly or spiritedly

spanner /'spænəʳ/ *n, chiefly Br* a tool with 1 or 2 ends shaped for holding or turning nuts or bolts with nut-shaped heads

[1]**spar** /spɑːʳ/ *n* **1** a stout pole **2** a mast, boom, gaff, yard, etc used to support or control a sail

[2]**spar** *v* **1** to engage in (a practice bout of) boxing **2** to skirmish, wrangle

[1]**spare** /speəʳ/ *v* **1** to refrain from destroying, punishing, or harming **2** to relieve of the necessity of doing, undergoing, or learning sthg **3** to refrain from; avoid **4** to use or dispense frugally – chiefly neg **5** to give up as surplus to requirements

[2]**spare** *adj* **1** not in use; *esp* reserved for use in emergency **2a** in excess of what is required; surplus **b** not taken up with work or duties; free **3** healthily lean; wiry **4** not abundant; meagre – infml **5** *Br* extremely angry or distraught – infml

[3]**spare** *n* a spare or duplicate item or part; *specif* a spare part for a motor vehicle

spare tyre *n* a roll of fat at the waist – infml

sparing /'speərɪŋ/ *adj* **1** not wasteful; frugal **2** meagre, scant – **~ly** *adv*

[1]**spark** /spɑːk/ *n* **1a** a small particle of a burning substance thrown out by a body in combustion or remaining when combustion is nearly completed **b** a hot glowing particle struck from a larger mass **2** a luminous disruptive electrical discharge of very short duration between 2 conductors of opposite high potential separated by a gas (e g air) **3** a sparkle, flash **4** sthg that sets off or stimulates an event, development, etc

[2]**spark** *v* **1** to produce or give off sparks **2** to cause to be suddenly active; precipitate – usu + *off*

[3]**spark** *n* a lively and usu witty person – esp in *bright spark*

sparking plug *n* a part that fits into

the cylinder head of an internal-combustion engine and produces the spark which ignites the explosive mixture

[1]**sparkle** /ˈspɑːkəl/ *v* **1** to give off or reflect glittering points of light **2** to effervesce **3** to show brilliance or animation

[2]**sparkle** *n* **1** a little spark **2** sparkling **3a** vivacity, gaiety **b** effervescence

sparkler /ˈspɑːkləʳ/ *n* **1** a firework that throws off brilliant sparks on burning **2** a (cut and polished) diamond – infml

sparrow /ˈspærəʊ/ *n* any of several small dull-coloured songbirds related to the finches

sparse /spɑːs/ *adj* of few and scattered elements; *esp* not thickly grown or settled – **~ly** *adv* – **~ness, sparsity** *n*

[1]**Spartan** /ˈspɑːtən/ *n* **1** a native or inhabitant of ancient Sparta **2** a person of great courage and endurance

[2]**Spartan** *adj* **1** of Sparta in ancient Greece **2a** rigorously strict; austere **b** having or showing courage and endurance

spasm /ˈspæzəm/ *n* **1** an involuntary and abnormal muscular contraction **2** a sudden violent and brief effort or emotion

spasmodic /spæzˈmɒdɪk/ *adj* **1a** relating to, being, or affected or characterized by spasm **b** resembling a spasm, esp in sudden violence **2** acting or proceeding fitfully; intermittent – **~ally** *adv*

[1]**spastic** /ˈspæstɪk/ *adj* **1** of or characterized by spasm **2** suffering from a form of paralysis marked by involuntary jerks and twitches

[2]**spastic** *n* **1** one who is suffering from spastic paralysis **2** an ineffectual person – used esp by children

[1]**spat** /spæt/ *past of* **spit**

[2]**spat** *n* a cloth or leather gaiter covering the instep and ankle

[3]**spat** *n* **1** *NAm* a light splash **2** a petty argument – infml

spate /speɪt/ *n* **1** flood **2a** a large number or amount, esp occurring in a short space of time **b** a sudden or strong outburst; a rush

spatial /ˈspeɪʃəl/ *adj* relating to, occupying, or occurring in space – **~ly** *adv*

[1]**spatter** /ˈspætəʳ/ *v* to splash or sprinkle (as if) with drops of liquid; *also* to soil in this way

[2]**spatter** *n* **1** (the sound of) spattering **2** a drop spattered on sthg or a stain due to spattering

spatula /ˈspætjʊlə/ *n* a flat thin usu metal implement used esp for spreading, mixing, etc soft substances or powders

[1]**spawn** /spɔːn/ *v* **1** *of an aquatic animal* to produce or deposit (eggs) **2** to bring forth, esp abundantly

[2]**spawn** *n* **1** the large number of eggs of frogs, oysters, fish, etc **2** material for propagating mushrooms

spay /speɪ/ *v* to remove the ovaries of

speak /spiːk/ *v* **spoke; spoken 1a** to utter words with the ordinary voice; talk **b(1)** to give voice to thoughts or feelings **(2)** to be on speaking terms **c** to address a group **2** to act as spokesman *for* **3** to make a claim *for*; reserve **4** to make a characteristic or natural sound **5** to be indicative or suggestive

speakeasy /ˈspiːkˌiːzi/ *n* a place where alcoholic drinks were illegally sold during Prohibition in the USA in the 1920's and 30's

speaker /ˈspiːkəʳ/ *n* **1a** one who speaks, esp at public functions **b** one who speaks a specified language **2** the presiding officer of a deliberative or legislative assembly **3** a loudspeaker

speak out *v* **1** to speak loudly enough to be heard **2** to speak boldly; express an opinion frankly

speak up *v* **1** to speak more loudly – often imper **2** to express an opinion boldly

[1]**spear** /spɪəʳ/ *n* a thrusting or throwing weapon with long shaft and sharp head or blade used esp by hunters or foot soldiers

[2]**spear** *v* to pierce, strike, or take hold of (as if) with a spear

[3]**spear** *n* a usu young blade, shoot, or sprout (e g of asparagus or grass)

[1]**spearhead** /ˈspɪəhed/ *n* **1** the sharp-pointed head of a spear **2** a leading element or force in a development, course of action, etc

[2]**spearhead** *v* to serve as leader or leading force of

spearmint /'spɪə,mɪnt/ *n* a common mint grown esp for its aromatic oil

spec /spek/ *n* a speculation – infml

[1]**special** /'speʃəl/ *adj* **1** distinguished from others of the same category, esp because in some way superior **2** held in particular esteem **3** specific **4** other than or in addition to the usual **5** designed, undertaken, or used for a particular purpose or need – **~ly** *adv*

[2]**special** *n* **1** sthg that is not part of a series **2** sby or sthg reserved or produced for a particular use or occasion

specialist /'speʃəlɨst/ *n* **1** one who devotes him-/herself to a special occupation or branch of knowledge **2** a medical practitioner limiting his/her practice to a specific group of complaints – **-ist** *adj* – **-ism** *n*

speciality /,speʃi'ælɨti/ *n* **1** (the state of having) a distinctive mark or quality **2** a product or object of particular quality **3a** a special aptitude or skill **b** a particular occupation or branch of knowledge

special·ize, -ise /'speʃəlaɪz/ *v* to apply or direct to a specific end or use; *esp* to concentrate one's efforts in a special or limited activity or field

species /'spiːʃiːz/ *n* **1a** a class of individuals having common attributes and designated by a common name **b** a category in the biological classification of living things that ranks immediately below a genus, comprises related organisms or populations potentially capable of interbreeding, and is designated by a name (e g *Homo sapiens*) that consists of the name of a genus followed by a Latin or latinized uncapitalized noun or adjective **2** a kind, sort – chiefly derog

[1]**specific** /spɨ'sɪfɪk/ *adj* **1** being or relating to those properties of sthg that allow it to be assigned to a particular category **2** confined to a particular individual, group, or circumstance **3** free from ambiguity; explicit **4** of or constituting a (biological) species

[2]**specific** *n* **1** a characteristic quality or trait **2** *pl, chiefly NAm* particulars

specification /,spesɨfɨ'keɪʃən/ *n* **1** specifying **2a** a detailed description of sthg (e g a building or car), esp in the form of a plan – usu pl with sing. meaning **b** a written description of an invention for which a patent is sought

specific gravity *n* the ratio of the density of a substance to the density of a substance (e g pure water or hydrogen) taken as a standard when both densities are obtained by weighing in air

specify /'spesɨfaɪ/ *v* **1** to name or state explicitly or in detail **2** to include as an item in a specification

specimen /'spesɨmən/ *n* **1** an item, part, or individual typical of a group or category; an example **2** a person, individual – chiefly derog

specious /'spiːʃəs/ *adj* **1** having deceptive attraction or fascination **2** superficially sound or genuine but fallacious – **~ly** *adv* – **~ness** *n*

[1]**speck** /spek/ *n* **1** a small spot or blemish, esp from stain or decay **2** a small particle

[2]**speck** *v* to mark with specks

[1]**speckle** /'spekəl/ *n* a little speck (e g of colour)

[2]**speckle** *v* to mark (as if) with speckles

spectacle /'spektəkəl/ *n* **1a** sthg exhibited as unusual, noteworthy, or entertaining **b** an object of scorn or ridicule, esp due to odd appearance or behaviour **2** *pl* glasses

spectacled /'spektəkəld/ *adj* having (markings suggesting) a pair of spectacles

[1]**spectacular** /spek'tækjʊləʳ/ *adj* of or being a spectacle; sensational – **~ly** *adv*

[2]**spectacular** *n* sthg (e g a stage show) that is spectacular

spectator /spek'teɪtəʳ/ *n* **1** one who attends an event or activity in order to watch **2** one who looks on without participating; an onlooker

spectre, *NAm chiefly* **specter** /'spektəʳ/ *n* **1** a visible ghost **2** sthg that haunts or perturbs the mind; a phantasm – **-tral** *adj*

spectrum /'spektrəm/ *n, pl* **spectra**

1a a series of images formed when a beam of radiant energy is subjected to dispersion and brought to focus so that the component waves are arranged in the order of their wavelengths (e g when a beam of sunlight that is refracted and dispersed by a prism forms a display of colours) **b** the range of frequencies of electromagnetic or sound waves **2** a sequence, range

speculate /ˈspekjʊleɪt/ *v* **1** to meditate *on* or ponder *about* sthg; reflect **2** to buy or sell in expectation of profiting from market fluctuations – **-lation** *n* – **-lator** *n*

speculative /ˈspekjʊlətɪv/ *adj* **1** involving, based on, or constituting speculation; *also* theoretical rather than demonstrable **2** questioning, inquiring – **~ly** *adv*

speech /spiːtʃ/ *n* **1a** the communication or expression of thoughts in spoken words **b** conversation **2** a public discourse; an address **3** a language, dialect

speechless /ˈspiːtʃləs/ *adj* **1a** unable to speak; dumb **b** deprived of speech (e g through horror or rage) **2** refraining from speech; silent **3** incapable of being expressed in words – **~ly** *adv* – **~ness** *n*

[1]**speed** /spiːd/ *n* **1a** moving swiftly; swiftness **b** rate of motion **2** rate of performance or execution **3a** the sensitivity of a photographic film, plate, or paper expressed numerically **b** the duration of a photographic exposure **4** an amphetamine drug – slang

[2]**speed** *v* **sped, speeded** **1** to move or go quickly **2** to travel at excessive or illegal speed **3** to promote the success or development of

speedometer /spɪˈdɒmɪ̯tər, ˈspiːdɒ-/ *n* **1** an instrument for indicating speed **2** an instrument for indicating distance travelled as well as speed

speedway /ˈspiːdweɪ/ *n* **1** a usu oval racecourse for motorcycles **2** the sport of racing motorcycles usu belonging to professional teams on closed cinder or dirt tracks

speedwell /ˈspiːdwel/ *n* any of a genus of plants that mostly have slender stems and small blue or whitish flowers

speedy /ˈspiːdi/ *adj* swift, quick – **speedily** *adv* – **speediness** *n*

[1]**spell** /spel/ *n* **1a** a spoken word or form of words held to have magic power **b** a state of enchantment **2** a compelling influence or attraction

[2]**spell** *v* **spelt** **1** to name or write the letters of (e g a word) in order; *also, of letters* to form (e g a word) **2** to amount to; mean – chiefly journ – **~er** *n*

[3]**spell** *v* **1** to give a brief rest to **2** to relieve for a time; stand in for

[4]**spell** *n* **1** a period spent in a job or occupation **2** a short or indefinite period or phase

spelling /ˈspelɪŋ/ *n* **1** the forming of or ability to form words from letters **2** the sequence of letters that make up a particular word

spell out *v* **1** to read slowly and haltingly **2** to come to understand; discern **3** to explain clearly and in detail

spend /spend/ *v* **spent** **1** to use up or pay out; expend **2** to wear out, exhaust **3** to cause or permit to elapse; pass

spendthrift /ˈspend,θrɪft/ *n* one who spends carelessly or wastefully

spent /spent/ *adj* **1a** used up; consumed **b** exhausted of useful components or qualities **2** drained of energy; exhausted

sperm /spɜːm/ *n* **1a** the male fertilizing fluid; semen **b** a male gamete **2** oil and other products from the sperm whale

sperm whale *n* a large toothed whale that has a vast blunt head in the front part of which is a cavity containing a fluid mixture of oil and other waxy substances used in cosmetics

spew /spjuː/ *v* **1** to vomit **2** to come forth in a flood or gush

sphagnum /ˈspægnəm, ˈsfæg-/ *n* any of a large genus of atypical mosses that grow only in wet acid areas (e g bogs) where their remains become compacted with other plant debris to form peat

sphere /sfɪər/ *n* **1a** a globular body; a ball **b** (a space or solid enclosed by) a surface, all points of which are equidistant from the centre **2** natural or proper place; *esp* social position or class **3** a field of action, existence, or influence

spherical /ˈsferɪkəl/ *adj* **1** having the form of (a segment of) a sphere **2** relating to or dealing with (the properties of) a sphere

spheroid /ˈsfɪərɔɪd/ *n* a figure resembling a sphere

sphinx /sfɪŋks/ *n, pl* **sphinxes, sphinges** **1a** *cap* a female monster in Greek mythology, with a lion's body and a human head, that killed those who failed to answer a riddle she asked **b** an enigmatic or mysterious person **2** an ancient Egyptian image in the form of a recumbent lion, usu with a human head

[1]**spice** /spaɪs/ *n* **1** any of various aromatic vegetable products (e g pepper, ginger, or nutmeg) used to season or flavour foods **2** sthg that adds zest or relish **3** a pungent or aromatic smell

[2]**spice** *v* **1** to season with spice **2** to add zest or relish to

spick-and-span, spic-and-span /ˌspɪk ən ˈspæn/ *adj* spotlessly clean and tidy; spruce

spicy /ˈspaɪsi/ *adj* **1** lively, spirited **2** piquant, zestful **3** somewhat scandalous; risqué – **spicily** *adv* – **-ciness** *n*

spider /ˈspaɪdəʳ/ *n* any of an order of arachnids having a body with 2 main divisions, 4 pairs of walking legs, and 2 or more pairs of abdominal glands for spinning threads of silk used for cocoons, nests, or webs

spidery /ˈspaɪdəri/ *adj* resembling a spider in form or manner; *specif* long, thin, and sharply angular like the legs of a spider

[1]**spiel** /ʃpiːl, spiːl/ *v, chiefly NAm* to utter or express volubly or extravagantly – usu + *off* *USE* infml

[2]**spiel** *n, chiefly NAm* a voluble talk designed to influence or persuade; patter – infml

spigot /ˈspɪgət/ *n* **1** a small plug used to stop up the vent of a cask **2** the part of a tap, esp on a barrel, which controls the flow

[1]**spike** /spaɪk/ *n* **1** a very large nail **2a** any of a row of pointed iron pieces (e g on the top of a wall or fence) **b(1)** any of several metal projections set in the sole and heel of a shoe to improve traction **(2)** *pl* a pair of (athletics) shoes having spikes attached

[2]**spike** *v* **1** to fasten or provide with spikes **2** to disable (a muzzle-loading cannon) by driving a spike into the vent **3** to pierce with or impale on a spike; *specif* to reject (newspaper copy), orig by impaling on a spike **4** to add spirits to (a nonalcoholic drink)

[3]**spike** *n* **1** an ear of grain **2** an elongated plant inflorescence with the flowers stalkless on a single main axis

[1]**spill** /spɪl/ *v* **spilt** **1** to cause or allow to fall or flow out so as to be lost or wasted, esp accidentally **2** to spread profusely or beyond limits

[2]**spill** *n* **1** a fall from a horse or vehicle **2** a quantity spilt

[3]**spill** *n* a thin twist of paper or sliver of wood used esp for lighting a fire

[1]**spin** /spɪn/ *v* **spun** **1** to draw out and twist fibre into yarn or thread **2** *esp of a spider or insect* to form a thread by forcing out a sticky rapidly hardening fluid **3a** to revolve rapidly; whirl **b** to have the sensation of spinning; reel **4** to move swiftly, esp on wheels or in a vehicle **5** to compose and tell (a usu involved or fictitious story)

[2]**spin** *n* **1a** the act or an instance of spinning sthg **b** the whirling motion imparted (e g to a cricket ball) by spinning **c** a short excursion, esp in or on a motor vehicle **2** a state of mental confusion; a panic – infml

spina bifida /ˌspaɪnə ˈbɪfɟdə/ *n* a congenital condition in which there is a defect in the formation of the spine so that the spinal cord is uncovered

spinach /ˈspɪnɪdʒ, -ɪtʃ/ *n* a plant cultivated for its edible leaves

spinal /ˈspaɪnl/ *adj* **1** of or situated near the backbone **2** of or affecting the spinal cord

spinal cord *n* the cord of nervous tissue that extends from the brain lengthways along the back in the spinal canal, carries impulses to and from the brain, and serves as a centre for initiating and coordinating many reflex actions

spindle /ˈspɪndl/ *n* **1a** a round stick with tapered ends used to form and twist the yarn in hand spinning **b** the long slender pin by which the thread is twisted in a spinning wheel **c** any of various rods or pins holding a bobbin in a textile machine (e g a spinning frame) **2a** a turned often decorative piece (e g on a piece of furniture) **b** a newel **c** a pin or axis about which sthg turns

spindly /ˈspɪndli/ *adj* having an unnaturally tall or slender appearance, esp suggestive of physical weakness

spin-dry *v* to remove water from (wet laundry) by placing in a rapidly rotating drum

spine /spaɪn/ *n* **1a** the spinal column **b** the back of a book, usu lettered with the title and author's name **2** a stiff pointed plant part **3** a sharp rigid part of an animal or fish

spineless /ˈspaɪnlɨs/ *adj* **1** free from spines, thorns, or prickles **2a** having no spinal column; invertebrate **b** lacking strength of character – **~ly** *adv* – **~ness** *n*

spinet /spɪˈnet/ *n* a small harpsichord having the strings at an angle to the keyboard

spinnaker /ˈspɪnəkəʳ/ *n* a large triangular sail set forward of a yacht's mast on a long light pole and used when running before the wind

spinner /ˈspɪnəʳ/ *n* **1** a fisherman's lure consisting of a spoon, blade, or set of wings that revolves when drawn through the water **2** a bowler of spin bowling

spinney /ˈspɪni/ *n, Br* a small wood with undergrowth

spinning jenny *n* an early multiple-spindle machine for spinning wool or cotton

spinning wheel *n* a small domestic machine for spinning yarn or thread by means of a spindle driven by a hand- or foot-operated wheel

spin-off *n* a by-product; *also* sthg which is a further development of some idea or product

spinster /ˈspɪnstəʳ/ *n* an unmarried woman; *esp* a woman who is past the usual age for marrying or who seems unlikely to marry – **~hood** *n*

spiny /ˈspaɪni/ *adj* **1** covered or armed with spines; *broadly* bearing spines, prickles, or thorns **2** full of difficulties or annoyances; thorny

[1]**spiral** /ˈspaɪərəl/ *adj* **1a** winding round a centre or pole and gradually approaching or receding from it **b** helical **2** of the advancement to higher levels through a series of cyclical movements

[2]**spiral** *n* **1a** the path of a point in a plane moving round a central point while continuously receding from or approaching it **b** a 3-dimensional curve (e g a helix) with 1 or more turns about an axis **2** a single turn or coil in a spiral object **3** a continuously expanding and accelerating increase or decrease – **spiral** *v*

spire /spaɪəʳ/ *n* a tall tapering roof or other construction on top of a tower

[1]**spirit** /ˈspɪrɨt/ *n* **1** a supernatural being or essence: e g **a** *cap* the Holy Spirit **b** the soul **c** a ghost **d** a malevolent being that enters and possesses a human being **2** temper or state of mind – often pl with sing. meaning **3** the immaterial intelligent or conscious part of a person **4** the attitude or intention characterizing or influencing sthg **5** liveliness, energy; *also* courage **6** a person of a specified kind or character **7** distilled liquor of high alcoholic content – usu pl with sing. meaning **8a** prevailing characteristic **b** the true meaning of sthg (e g a rule or instruction) in contrast to its verbal expression

[2]**spirit** *v* to carry off, esp secretly or mysteriously – usu + *away* or *off*

spirited /ˈspɪrɨtɨd/ *adj* **1** full of energy, animation, or courage **2** having a specified frame of mind – often in combination

spirit level *n* a level that uses the position of a bubble in a curved transparent tube of liquid to indicate whether a surface is level

[1]**spiritual** /ˈspɪrɨtʃʊəl/ *adj* **1** (consisting) of spirit; incorporeal **2** ecclesiastical rather than lay or temporal **3** concerned with religious values **4** of supernatural beings or phenomena – **~ly** *adv*

[2]**spiritual** *n* a usu emotional religious song of a kind developed esp among Negroes in the southern USA

spiritualism /ˈspɪrɨtʃʊlɪzəm/ *n* a

belief that spirits of the dead communicate with the living, esp through a medium or at a séance – **-ist** *n* – **-istic** *adj*

spirituality /ˌspɪrɪ̈tʃʊˈælɪ̈ti/ *n* **1** sensitivity or attachment to religious values **2** a practice of personal devotion and prayer

¹spit /spɪt/ *n* **1** a slender pointed rod for holding meat over a source of heat (e g an open fire) **2** a small point of land, esp of sand or gravel, running into a river mouth, bay, etc

²spit *v* to fix (as if) on a spit; impale

³spit *v* **spat, spit 1** to eject saliva from the mouth (as an expression of aversion or contempt); *also* to get rid of something in the mouth by ejecting it with some force **2** to express (hostile or malicious feelings) (as if) by spitting **3** to rain or snow slightly or in flurries **4** to sputter

⁴spit *n* **1a** spittle, saliva **b** the act or an instance of spitting **2** a frothy secretion exuded by some insects

spit and polish *n* extreme attention to cleanliness, orderliness, and ceremonial

¹spite /spaɪt/ *n* petty ill will or malice – **~ful** *adj* – **~fully** *adv* – **~fulness** *n*

²spite *v* to treat vindictively or annoy out of spite

spitting image *n* perfect likeness

spittle /ˈspɪtl/ *n* saliva (ejected from the mouth)

spittoon /spɪˈtuːn/ *n* a receptacle for spit

¹splash /splæʃ/ *v* **1a** to strike and move about a liquid **b** to move through or into a liquid and cause it to spatter **2a** to dash a liquid or semiliquid substance on or against **b** to soil or stain with splashed liquid; spatter **3a** to spread or scatter in the manner of splashed liquid **b** to flow, fall, or strike with a splashing sound **4** *chiefly Br* to spend money liberally; splurge – usu + *out*

²splash *n* **1a** a spot or daub (as if) from splashed liquid **b** a usu vivid patch of colour or of sthg coloured **2a** (the sound of) splashing **b** a short plunge **3** (a vivid impression created esp by) an ostentatious display **4** a small amount, esp of a mixer added to an alcoholic drink; a dash

splashdown /ˈsplæʃdaʊn/ *n* the landing of a spacecraft in the ocean

splatter /ˈsplætəʳ/ *v* **1** to spatter **2** to scatter or fall (as if) in heavy drops

¹splay /spleɪ/ *v* **1** to spread out **2** to make (e g the edges of an opening) slanting

²splay *adj* turned outwards

spleen /spliːn/ *n* **1** an organ near the stomach or intestine of most vertebrates that is concerned with final destruction of blood cells, storage of blood, and production of white blood cells **2** bad temper; spite **3** *archaic* melancholy

splendid /ˈsplendɪ̈d/ *adj* **1** magnificent, sumptuous **2** illustrious, distinguished **3** of the best or most enjoyable kind; excellent – **~ly** *adv*

splendour /ˈsplendəʳ/ *n* **1a** great brightness or lustre; brilliance **b** grandeur, pomp **2** sthg splendid

¹splice /splaɪs/ *v* **1a** to join (e g ropes) by interweaving the strands **b** to unite (e g film, magnetic tape, or timber) by overlapping the ends or binding with adhesive tape **2** *Br* to unite in marriage; marry – infml

²splice *n* a joining or joint made by splicing

splint /splɪnt/ *n* material or a device used to protect and immobilize a body part (e g a broken arm)

¹splinter /ˈsplɪntəʳ/ *n* **1** a sharp thin piece, esp of wood or glass, split or broken off lengthways **2** a small group or faction broken away from a parent body

²splinter *v* **1** to split or rend into long thin pieces; shatter **2** to split into fragments, parts, or factions

¹split /splɪt/ *v* **split 1a** to divide, esp lengthways or into layers **b** to break apart; burst **2** to subject (an atom or atomic nucleus) to artificial disintegration, esp by fission **3** to divide into parts or portions: e g **a** to divide between people; share **b** to divide into opposing factions, parties, etc **4** to sever relations or connections – often + *up* **5** to share sthg (e g loot or profits) with others – often + *with* **6** to let out a secret; act as an informer

– often + *on* 7 to leave, esp hurriedly; depart – infml

[2]**split** *n* 1 a narrow break made (as if) by splitting 2 a piece broken off by splitting 3 a division into divergent groups or elements; a breach **4a** splitting **b** *pl but sing in constr* the act of lowering oneself to the floor or leaping into the air with legs extended at right angles to the trunk 5 a wine bottle holding a quarter of the usual amount; *also* a small bottle of mineral water, tonic water, etc 6 a sweet dish composed of sliced fruit, esp a banana, ice cream, syrup, and often nuts and whipped cream

[3]**split** *adj* 1 divided, fractured 2 prepared for use by splitting

split-level *adj* divided so that the floor level in one part is less than a full storey higher than an adjoining part

split pea *n* a dried pea in which the cotyledons are usu split apart

split personality *n* a personality composed of 2 or more internally consistent groups of behaviour tendencies and attitudes each acting more or less independently of the other

split second *n* a fractional part of a second; a flash – **split-second** *adj*

splitting /ˈsplɪtɪŋ/ *adj* causing a piercing sensation

splutter /ˈsplʌtəʳ/ *v* to utter hastily and confusedly

[1]**spoil** /spɔɪl/ *n* plunder taken from an enemy in war or a victim in robbery; loot – often pl with sing. meaning

[2]**spoil** *v* **spoilt, spoiled** **1a** to damage seriously; ruin **b** to impair the enjoyment of; mar **2a** to impair the character of by overindulgence or excessive praise **b** to treat indulgently; pamper 3 to lose good or useful qualities, usu as a result of decay 4 to have an eager desire *for* – esp in *spoiling for a fight* – ~**er** *n*

spoilsport /ˈspɔɪlspɔːt/ *n* one who spoils the fun of others – infml

[1]**spoke** /spəʊk/ *past & archaic past part of* **speak**

[2]**spoke** *n* 1 any of the small radiating bars inserted in the hub of a wheel to support the rim 2 a rung of a ladder

spoken /ˈspəʊkən/ *adj* **1a** delivered by word of mouth; oral **b** used in speaking or conversation; uttered 2 characterized by speaking in a specified manner – in combination

spokeshave /ˈspəʊkʃeɪv/ *n* a plane having a blade set between 2 handles and used for shaping curved surfaces

spokesman /ˈspəʊksmən/ *n* one who speaks on behalf of another or others

spoliation /ˌspəʊliˈeɪʃən/ *n* **1a** the act of plundering **b** the state of being plundered, esp in war 2 the act of damaging or injuring, esp irreparably

spondee /ˈspɒndiː/ *n* a metrical foot consisting of 2 long or stressed syllables – **-daic** *adj*

[1]**sponge** /spʌndʒ/ *n* **1a(1)** an elastic porous mass of interlacing horny fibres that forms the internal skeleton of various marine animals and is able when wetted to absorb water **(2)** a porous rubber or cellulose product used similarly to a sponge **b** any of a group of aquatic lower invertebrate animals that are essentially double-walled cell colonies and permanently attached as adults 2 a sponger 3 a cake or sweet steamed pudding made from a light-textured mixture

[2]**sponge** *v* 1 to cleanse, wipe, or moisten (as if) with a sponge 2 to obtain esp financial assistance by exploiting natural generosity or organized welfare facilities – usu + *on* – ~**r** *n*

sponge bag *n, Br* a small waterproof usu plastic bag for holding toilet articles

spongy /ˈspʌndʒi/ *adj* 1 resembling a sponge, esp in being soft, porous, absorbent, or moist – **-giness** *n*

[1]**sponsor** /ˈspɒnsəʳ/ *n* 1 sby who presents a candidate for baptism or confirmation and undertakes responsibility for his/her religious education or spiritual welfare 2 sby who assumes responsibility for some other person or thing 3 sby who or sthg that pays for a project or activity – ~**ship** *n*

[2]**sponsor** *v* to be or stand as sponsor for

spontaneous /spɒnˈteɪnɪəs/ *adj* 1 proceeding from natural feeling or innate tendency without external constraint **2** springing from a sudden impulse **3** controlled and directed internally **4** developing without apparent external influence, force, cause, or treatment – **~ly** *adv* – **~ness, -neity** *n*

[1]**spoof** /spuːf/ *v* **1** to deceive, hoax **2** to make good-natured fun of; lampoon *USE* infml

[2]**spoof** *n* **1** a hoax, deception **2** a light, humorous, but usu telling parody *USE* infml

spook /spuːk/ *n* a ghost, spectre – chiefly infml

spooky /ˈspuːki/ *adj* causing irrational fear, esp because suggestive of supernatural presences; eerie – chiefly infml

[1]**spool** /spuːl/ *n* **1** a cylindrical device on which wire, yarn, film, etc is wound **2** (the amount of) material wound on a spool

[2]**spool** *v* to wind on a spool

[1]**spoon** /spuːn/ *n* **1** an eating, cooking, or serving implement consisting of a small shallow round or oval bowl with a handle

[2]**spoon** *v* **1** to take up and usu transfer (as if) in a spoon **2** to propel (a ball) weakly upwards **3** to indulge in caressing and amorous talk – not now in vogue

spoonerism /ˈspuːnərɪzəm/ *n* a transposition of usu initial sounds of 2 or more words (e g in *tons of soil* for *sons of toil*)

spoon-feed *v* to present (e g information or entertainment) in an easily assimilable form that precludes independent thought or critical judgment

spoonful /ˈspuːnfʊl/ *n, pl* **spoonfuls** *also* **spoonsful** as much as a spoon will hold

spoor /spɔːʳ, spʊəʳ/ *n* a track, a trail, or droppings, esp of a wild animal

sporadic /spəˈrædɪk/ *adj* occurring occasionally or in scattered instances – **~ally** *adv*

spore /spɔːʳ/ *n* a primitive usu single-celled hardy reproductive body produced by plants, protozoans, bacteria, etc and capable of development into a new individual either on its own or after fusion with another spore

sporran /ˈspɒrən/ *n* a pouch of animal skin with the hair or fur on that is worn in front of the kilt with traditional Highland dress

[1]**sport** /spɔːt/ *v* **1** to exhibit for all to see; show off **2** to play about happily; frolic **3** to speak or act in jest; trifle

[2]**sport** *n* **1a** a source of diversion or recreation; a pastime **b** physical activity engaged in for recreation **2a** pleasantry, jest **b** mockery, derision **3** sby who is fair, generous, and esp a good loser **4** an individual exhibiting a sudden deviation from type beyond the normal limits of individual variation

sporting /ˈspɔːtɪŋ/ *adj* **1** concerned with, used for, or suitable for sport **2** marked by or calling for sportsmanship **3** involving such risk as a sports competitor might take or encounter **4** fond of or taking part in sports – **~ly** *adv*

sportive /ˈspɔːtɪv/ *adj* frolicsome, playful – **~ly** *adv* – **~ness** *n*

sports /spɔːts/ *adj* of or suitable for sports; *esp* styled in a manner suitable for casual or informal wear

sports car *n* a low fast usu 2-passenger motor car

sportsman /ˈspɔːtsmən/ *n* **1** sby who engages in sports, esp blood sports **2** sby who is fair, a good loser, and a gracious winner – **~like** *adj*

sportsmanship /ˈspɔːtsmənʃɪp/ *n* conduct becoming to a sportsman

sporty /ˈspɔːti/ *adj* **1** fond of sport **2a** notably loose or dissipated; fast **b** flashy, showy – **sportiness** *n*

[1]**spot** /spɒt/ *n* **1** a blemish on character or reputation; a stain **2a** a small usu round area different (e g in colour or texture) from the surrounding surface **b(1)** an area marred or marked (e g by dirt) **(2)** a pimple **c** a conventionalized design used on playing cards to distinguish suits and indicate values **3** a small amount; a bit **4** a particular place or area **5** a place on an entertainment programme **6** a spotlight **7** a usu difficult or embarrassing position; a fix

[2]**spot** *v* **1** to mark or mar (as if) with spots **2a** to single out; identify **b** to detect, notice **c** to watch for and record the sighting of **3** *chiefly Br* to fall lightly in scattered drops

[3]**spot** *adj* **1a** available for immediate delivery after sale **b** involving immediate cash payment **2** given on the spot or restricted to a few random places or instances; *also* selected at random or as a sample

spot-check *v* to make a quick or random sampling or investigation of

spotless /ˈspɒtlɪ̈s/ *adj* **1** free from dirt or stains; immaculate **2** pure, unblemished – **~ly** *adv* – **~ness** *n*

[1]**spotlight** /ˈspɒtlaɪt/ *n* **1a** a projected spot of light used for brilliant illumination of a person or object on a stage **b** a light designed to direct a narrow intense beam on a small area **2** full public attention – **spotlight** *v*

spot-on *adj, Br* **1** absolutely correct or accurate **2** exactly right *USE* infml

spotted /ˈspɒtɪ̈d/ *adj* **1** marked with spots **2** sullied, tarnished

spotted dick *n, Br* a steamed or boiled sweet suet pudding containing currants

spotter /ˈspɒtəʳ/ *n* sby or sthg that keeps watch or observes; *esp* a person who watches for and notes down vehicles (e g aircraft or trains)

spotty /ˈspɒti/ *adj* **1a** marked with spots **b** having spots, esp on the face **2** lacking evenness or regularity, esp in quality

spouse /spaʊs, spaʊz/ *n* a married person; a husband or wife

[1]**spout** /spaʊt/ *v* **1** to eject (e g liquid) in a copious stream **2** to speak or utter in a strident, pompous, or hackneyed manner; declaim – infml – **~er** *n*

[2]**spout** *n* **1** a projecting tube or lip through which liquid issues from a teapot, roof, kettle, etc **2** a discharge or jet of liquid (as if) from a pipe

sprain /spreɪn/ *n* a sudden or violent twist or wrench of a joint with stretching or tearing of ligaments – **sprain** *v*

sprang /spræŋ/ *past of* **spring**

sprat /spræt/ *n* a small or young herring

[1]**sprawl** /sprɔːl/ *v* **1** to lie or sit with arms and legs spread out carelessly or awkwardly **2** to spread or develop irregularly

[2]**sprawl** *n* **1** a sprawling position **2** an irregular spreading mass or group

[1]**spray** /spreɪ/ *n* **1** a usu flowering branch or shoot **2** a decorative arrangement of flowers and foliage (e g on a dress)

[2]**spray** *n* **1** fine droplets of water blown or falling through the air **2a** a jet of vapour or finely divided liquid **b** a device (e g an atomizer or sprayer) by which a spray is dispersed or applied

[3]**spray** *v* **1** to discharge, disperse, or apply as a spray **2** to direct a spray on – **~er** *n*

[1]**spread** /spred/ *v* **spread** **1a** to open or extend over a larger area – often + *out* **b** to stretch out; extend **2a** to distribute over an area **b** to distribute over a period or among a group **c** to apply as a layer or covering **3a** to make widely known **b** to extend the range or incidence of **4** to force apart – **~able** *adj*

[2]**spread** *n* **1** (extent of) spreading **2** sthg spread out: e g **a** a surface area; an expanse **b** (the matter occupying) 2 facing pages, usu with printed matter running across the fold **3a** a food product suitable for spreading **b** a sumptuous meal; a feast **c** a cloth cover; *esp* a bedspread

spread-eagle *v* to (cause to) stand or lie with arms and legs stretched out wide; (cause to) sprawl

spreadsheet /ˈspredˌʃiːt/ *n* a software system in which large groups of numerical data can be displayed on a VDU in a set format (e g in rows and columns) and rapid automatic calculations can be made

spree /spriː/ *n* a bout of unrestrained indulgence in an activity; *esp* a binge

[1]**sprig** /sprɪg/ *n* **1** a small shoot or twig **2** a small headless nail **3** a young offspring; *specif* a youth – infml

[2]**sprig** *v* to decorate with a representation of plant sprigs

sprightly /ˈspraɪtli/ *adj* marked by vitality and liveliness; spirited – **-liness** *n*

[1]**spring** /sprɪŋ/ *v* **sprang; sprung** **1a(1)** to dart, shoot **(2)** to be resilient or elastic; *also* to move by elastic force **b** to become warped **2** to issue suddenly and copiously; pour out **3a** to issue by birth or descent **b** to come into being;

arise **4a** to make a leap or leaps **b** to rise or jump up suddenly **5** to produce or disclose suddenly or unexpectedly **6** to release from prison – infml

[2]**spring** *n* **1a** a source of supply; *esp* an issue of water from the ground **b** an ultimate source, esp of thought or action **2** a time or season of growth or development; *specif* the season between winter and summer comprising, in the northern hemisphere, the months of March, April, and May **3** a mechanical part that recovers its original shape when released after deformation **4a** the act or an instance of leaping up or forward; a bound **b(1)** capacity for springing; resilience **(2)** bounce, energy – **~less** *adj*

springboard /ˈsprɪŋbɔːd/ *n* **1** a flexible board secured at one end that a diver or gymnast jumps off to gain extra height **2** sthg that provides an initial stimulus or impetus

springbok /ˈsprɪŋbɒk/ *n* **1** a swift and graceful southern African gazelle noted for its habit of springing lightly and suddenly into the air **2** *often cap* a sportsman or sportswoman representing S Africa in an international match or tour abroad

spring-clean *v* **1** to give a thorough cleaning to (e g a house or furnishings) **2** to put into a proper or more satisfactory order – **spring-clean, ~ing** *n*

spring onion *n* an onion with a small mild-flavoured thin-skinned bulb and long shoots that is chiefly eaten raw in salads

spring tide *n* a tide of maximum height occurring at new and full moon

springy /ˈsprɪŋi/ *adj* having an elastic or bouncy quality; resilient

[1]**sprinkle** /ˈsprɪŋkəl/ *v* **1** to scatter in fine drops or particles **2a** to distribute (sthg) at intervals (as if) by scattering **b** to occur at (random) intervals on; dot **c** to wet lightly

[2]**sprinkle** *n* **1** an instance of sprinkling; *specif* a light fall of rain **2** a sprinkling

sprinkler /ˈsprɪŋkləʳ/ *n* a device for spraying a liquid, esp water: e g **a** a fire extinguishing system that works automatically on detection of smoke or a high temperature **b** an apparatus for watering a lawn

sprinkling /ˈsprɪnklɪŋ/ *n* a small quantity or number, esp falling in scattered drops or particles or distributed randomly

[1]**sprint** /sprɪnt/ *v* to run or ride a bicycle at top speed, esp for a short distance – **~er** *n*

[2]**sprint** *n* **1** (an instance of) sprinting **2a** a short fast running, swimming, or bicycle race **b** a burst of speed

sprite /spraɪt/ *n* a (playful graceful) fairy

sprocket /ˈsprɒkʲ̥t/ *n* **1** a tooth or projection on the rim of a wheel, shaped so as to engage the links of a chain **2** *also* **sprocket wheel** a wheel or cylinder having sprockets (e g to engage a bicycle chain)

[1]**sprout** /spraʊt/ *v* **1** to grow, spring up, or come forth as (if) a shoot **2** to send out shoots or new growth

[2]**sprout** *n* **1** a (young) shoot (e g from a seed or root) **2** a Brussels sprout

[1]**spruce** /spruːs/ *n* any of a genus of evergreen coniferous trees with a conical head of dense foliage and soft light wood

[2]**spruce** *adj* neat or smart in dress or appearance; trim – **~ly** *adv* – **~ness** *n*

[3]**spruce** *v* to make (oneself) spruce *USE* usu + *up*

sprung /sprʌŋ/ *adj*, **1** *past of* **spring** **2** equipped with springs

spry /spraɪ/ *adj* vigorously active; nimble – **~ly** *adv* – **~ness** *n*

spud /spʌd/ *n* **1** a small narrow spade **2** a potato – infml

spume /spjuːm/ *v or n* (to) froth, foam

spun /spʌn/ *past of* **spin**

spunk /spʌŋk/ *n* **1** any of various fungi used to make tinder **2** spirit, pluck **3** *Br* semen – vulg – **~y** *adj*

[1]**spur** /spɜːʳ/ *n* **1a** a pointed device secured to a rider's heel and used to urge on a horse **b** *pl* recognition and reward for achievement **2** a goad to action; a stimulus **3a** a stiff sharp spine (e g on the wings or legs of a bird or insect); *esp* one on a cock's leg **b** a hollow projection from a plant's petals or sepals (e g in larkspur or colum-

bine) **4** a lateral projection (e g a ridge) of a mountain (range)

[2]**spur** *v* to incite to usu faster action or greater effort; stimulate – usu + *on*

spurious /'spjʊərɪəs/ *adj* **1** having a superficial usu deceptive resemblance or correspondence; false **2a** of deliberately falsified or mistakenly attributed origin; forged **b** based on mistaken ideas – **~ly** *adv* – **~ness** *n*

spurn /spɜːn/ *v* to reject with disdain or contempt; scorn

[1]**spurt** /spɜːt/ *v or n* (to make) a sudden brief burst of increased effort, activity, or speed

[2]**spurt** *v* to (cause to) gush out in a jet

[3]**spurt** *n* a sudden forceful gush; a jet

sputnik /'spʊtnɪk, 'spʌt-/ *n* a Russian artificial satellite

[1]**sputter** /'spʌtəʳ/ *v* **1** to utter hastily or explosively in confusion, anger, or excitement; splutter **2** to make explosive popping sounds

[2]**sputter** *n* **1** confused and excited speech **2** (the sound of) sputtering

sputum /'spjuːtəm/ *n* matter, made up of discharges from the respiratory passages and saliva, that is coughed up

[1]**spy** /spaɪ/ *v* **1** to catch sight of; see **2** to watch secretly; act as a spy – often + *on*

[2]**spy** *n* **1** one who keeps secret watch on sby or sthg **2** one who attempts to gain information secretly from a country, company, etc and communicate it to another

spyglass /'spaɪglɑːs/ *n* a small telescope

squabble /'skwɒbəl/ *v or n* (to engage in) a noisy or heated quarrel, esp over trifles

squad /skwɒd/ *n* **1** a small group of military personnel assembled for a purpose **2** a small group working as a team

squadron /'skwɒdrən/ *n* a unit of military organization: **a** a unit of cavalry or of an armoured regiment, usu consisting of 3 or more troops **b** a variable naval unit consisting of a number of warships on a particular operation **c** a unit of an air force consisting usu of between 10 and 18 aircraft

squalid /'skwɒlɪ̈d/ *adj* **1** filthy and degraded from neglect or poverty **2** sordid – **~ly** *adv*

[1]**squall** /skwɔːl/ *v* to cry out raucously; scream – **squall, ~er** *n*

[2]**squall** *n* **1** a sudden violent wind, often with rain or snow **2** a short-lived commotion – **squally** *adj*

squalor /'skwɒləʳ/ *n* the quality or state of being squalid

squander /'skwɒndəʳ/ *v* to spend extravagantly, foolishly, or wastefully; dissipate – **~er** *n*

[1]**square** /skweəʳ/ *n* **1** an instrument (e g a set square or T square) with at least 1 right angle and 2 straight edges, used to draw or test right angles or parallel lines **2** a rectangle with all 4 sides equal **3a** a square scarf **b** an area of ground for a particular purpose (e g military drill) **4** any of the rectangular, square, etc spaces marked out on a board used for playing games **5** the product of a number multiplied by itself **6** an open space in a town, city, etc formed at the meeting of 2 or more streets, and often laid out with grass and trees **7** one who is excessively conventional or conservative in tastes or outlook – infml; no longer in vogue

[2]**square** *adj* **1a** having 4 equal sides and 4 right angles **b** forming a right angle **2a** approximating to a cube **b** of a shape or build suggesting strength and solidity; broad in relation to length or height **c** square in cross section **3** *of a unit of length* denoting the area equal to that of a square whose edges are of the specified length **4a** exactly adjusted, arranged, or aligned; neat and orderly **b** fair, honest, or straightforward **c** leaving no balance; settled **d** even, tied **5** excessively conservative; dully conventional – infml; no longer in vogue – **~ly** *adv* – **~ness** *n*

[3]**square** *v* **1a** to make square or rectangular **b** to test for deviation from a right angle, straight line, or plane surface **2a** to multiply (a number) by the same number; to raise to the second power **3a** to balance, settle *up*; *esp* to pay the bill **b** to even the score of (a contest) **4** to mark *off* into squares or

rectangles **5a** to bring into agreement *with*; match **b** to bribe – infml

[4]**square** *adv* **1** in a straightforward or honest manner **2a** so as to face or be face to face **b** at right angles

square dance *n* a dance for 4 couples who form a hollow square

square-rigged *adj, of a ship* having square sails hanging from horizontal yards

square root *n* a (positive) number whose square is a usu specified number

[1]**squash** /skwɒʃ/ *v* **1a** to press or beat into a pulp or a flat mass; crush **b** to apply pressure to by pushing or squeezing **2** to reduce to silence or inactivity

[2]**squash** *n* **1** the act or soft dull sound of squashing **2** a crushed mass; *esp* a mass of people crowded into a restricted space **3** *also* **squash rackets** a game played in a 4-walled court with long-handled rackets and a rubber ball that can be played off any number of walls **4** *Br* a beverage made from sweetened and often concentrated citrus fruit juice, usu drunk diluted

[3]**squash** *n, pl* **squashes, squash** any of various (plants of the cucumber family bearing) fruits widely cultivated as vegetables

[1]**squat** /skwɒt/ *v* **1** to crouch close to the ground as if to escape detection **2** to assume or maintain a position in which the body is supported on the feet and the knees are bent, so that the haunches rest on or near the heels **3** to occupy property as a squatter

[2]**squat** *n* **1a** squatting **b** the posture of sby or sthg that squats **2** an empty building occupied by or available to squatters – infml

[3]**squat** *adj* **1** with the heels drawn up under the haunches **2** disproportionately short or low and broad

squatter /ˈskwɒtəʳ/ *n* **1** one who occupies usu otherwise empty property without rights of ownership or payment of rent **2** *Austr* one who owns large tracks of grazing land

squaw /skwɔː/ *n* a N American Indian (married) woman

squawk /skwɔːk/ *v or n* **1** (to utter) a harsh abrupt scream **2** (to make) a loud or vehement protest – ~**er** *n*

[1]**squeak** /skwiːk/ *v* to utter or make a squeak – ~**er** *n*

[2]**squeak** *n* **1** a short shrill cry or noise **2** an escape – usu in *a narrow squeak*; infml – ~**y** *adj*

[1]**squeal** /skwiːl/ *v* **1** to utter or make a squeal **2a** to turn informer – infml **b** to complain, protest – infml – ~**er** *n*

[2]**squeal** *n* a shrill sharp cry or noise

squeamish /ˈskwiːmɪʃ/ *adj* **1** easily nauseated **2a** excessively fastidious in manners, scruples, or convictions **b** easily shocked or offended – ~**ly** *adv* – ~**ness** *n*

[1]**squeeze** /skwiːz/ *v* **1a** to apply physical pressure to; compress the (opposite) sides of **b** to extract or discharge under pressure **c** to force one's way **2a** to obtain by force or extortion **b** to cause (economic) hardship to **3** to fit into a limited time span or schedule – usu + *in* or *into* **4** to pass, win, or get by narrowly

[2]**squeeze** *n* **1a** a squeezing or compressing **b** a handshake; *also* an embrace **2** a condition of being crowded together; a crush **3a** a financial pressure caused by narrowing margins or by shortages **b** pressure brought to bear on sby – chiefly in *put the squeeze on*; infml

squelch /skweltʃ/ *v* **1** to emit a sucking sound like that of an object being withdrawn from mud **2** to walk or move, esp through slush, mud, etc, making a squelching noise – **squelch** *n*

squib /skwɪb/ *n* **1** a small firework that burns with a fizz and finishes with a small explosion **2** a short witty or satirical speech or piece of writing

squid /skwɪd/ *n* any of numerous 10-armed marine creatures, related to the octopus and cuttlefish, that have a long tapered body and a tail fin on each side

squidgy /ˈskwɪdzi/ *adj, chiefly Br* soft and squashy – infml

squiffy /ˈskwɪfi/ *adj* slightly drunk, tipsy – infml

squiggle /ˈskwɪgəl/ *v or n* (to draw) a short wavy twist or line, esp in handwriting or drawing – **-gly** *adj*

[1]**squint** /skwɪnt/ *adj* having a squint; squinting

[2]**squint** *v* **1** to have or look with a squint **2** to look or peer with eyes partly closed

[3]**squint** *n* **1** an inability to direct both eyes to the same object because of imbalance of the muscles of the eyeball **2** a glance, look – esp in *have/take a squint at*; infml

[1]**squire** /skwaɪəʳ/ *n* **1** a shield-bearer or armour-bearer of a knight **2** an owner of a country estate; *esp* the principal local landowner

[2]**squire** *v* to attend on or escort (a woman)

squirearchy, **squirarchy** /ˈskwaɪərɑːki/ *n* the gentry or landed-proprietor class

squirm /skwɜːm/ *v* **1** to twist about like a worm; wriggle **2** to feel or show acute discomfort at sthg embarrassing, shameful, or unpleasant – **squirm** *n*

squirrel /ˈskwɪrəl/ *n* (the usu grey or red fur of) any of various New or Old World small to medium-sized tree-dwelling rodents that have a long bushy tail and strong hind legs

[1]**squirt** /skwɜːt/ *v* **1** to issue in a sudden forceful stream from a narrow opening **2** to direct a jet or stream of liquid at

[2]**squirt** *n* **1** a small rapid stream of liquid; a jet **2** a small or insignificant (impudent) person – infml

SS *n sing or pl in constr* Hitler's bodyguard and special police force

[1]**stab** /stæb/ *n* **1** a wound produced by a pointed weapon **2a** a thrust (as if) with a pointed weapon **b(1)** a sharp spasm of pain **(2)** a pang of intense emotion **3** an attempt, try – infml

[2]**stab** *v* **1** to pierce or wound (as if) with a pointed weapon **2** to thrust, jab – **~ber** *n*

stabilize /ˈsteɪbɪ̵laɪz/ *v* to make stable

[1]**stable** /ˈsteɪbəl/ *n* **1** a building in which domestic animals, esp horses, are sheltered and fed – often pl with sing. meaning **2** *sing or pl in constr* **a** the racehorses or racing cars owned by one person or organization **b** a group of athletes (e g boxers) or performers under one management

[2]**stable** *v* to put or keep in a stable

[3]**stable** *adj* **1a** securely established; fixed **b** not subject to change or fluctuation; unvarying **2** not subject to feelings of mental or emotional insecurity **3a** placed or constructed so as to resist forces tending to cause (change of) motion **b** able to resist alteration in chemical, physical, or biological properties – **-bility** *n* – **-bly** *adv*

stabling /ˈsteɪblɪŋ/ *n* indoor accommodation for animals

staccato /stəˈkɑːtəʊ/ *n, adv, or adj,* (a manner of speaking or performing, or a piece of music performed) in a sharp, disconnected, or abrupt way

[1]**stack** /stæk/ *n* **1** a large usu circular or square pile of hay, straw, etc **2** an (orderly) pile or heap **3** a chimney stack **4** a high pillar of rock rising out of the sea, that was detached from the mainland by the erosive action of waves **5** a large quantity or number – often pl with sing. meaning; infml

[2]**stack** *v* **1** to arrange in a stack; pile **2** to arrange (cards) secretly for cheating **3** to assign (an aircraft) to a particular altitude and position within a group of aircraft circling before landing

stadium /ˈsteɪdɪəm/ *n, pl* **stadiums** *also* **stadia** a sports ground surrounded by a large usu unroofed building with tiers of seats for spectators

[1]**staff** /stɑːf/ *n, pl* **staffs, staves,** (4) **staffs** **1a** a long stick carried in the hand for use in walking or as a weapon **b** sthg which gives strength or sustains **2** a rod carried as a symbol of office or authority **3** a set of usu 5 parallel horizontal lines on which music is written **4** *sing or pl in constr* **a** the body of people in charge of the internal operations of an institution, business, etc **b** a group of officers appointed to assist a military commander **c** the teachers at a school or university

[2]**staff** *v* **1** to supply with a staff or with workers **2** to serve as a staff member of

staff sergeant *n* a sergeant of the highest rank in the British army

[1]**stag** /stæg/ *n* an adult male red deer; *broadly* the male of any of various deer

[2]**stag** *adj* of or intended for men only

[1]**stage** /steɪdʒ/ *n* **1a** a raised platform **b(1)** the area of a theatre where the acting takes place, including the wings and storage space **(2)** *the* acting profession; *also* *the* theatre as an occupation or activity **2** a centre of attention or scene of action **3a** a place of rest formerly provided for those travelling by stagecoach **b** the distance between 2 stopping places on a road **c** a stagecoach **4** a period or step in a progress, activity, or development **5** any of the divisions (e g 1 day's riding or driving between predetermined points) of a race or rally that is spread over several days

[2]**stage** *v* **1** to produce (e g a play) on a stage **2** to produce and organize, esp for public view

stagecoach /ˈsteɪdʒkəʊtʃ/ *n* a horse-drawn passenger and mail coach that in former times ran on a regular schedule between established stops

stage direction *n* a description (e g of a character or setting) or direction (e g to indicate sound effects or the movement or positioning of actors) provided in the text of a play

stage-manage *v* to arrange or direct, esp from behind the scenes, so as to achieve a desired result

stage manager *n* one who is in charge of the stage during a performance and supervises related matters beforehand

stagestruck /ˈsteɪdzstrʌk/ *adj* fascinated by the stage; *esp* having an ardent desire to become an actor or actress

stage whisper *n* **1** a loud whisper by an actor, audible to the audience, but supposedly inaudible to others on stage **2** a whisper that is deliberately made audible

stagger /ˈstægəʳ/ *v* **1** to reel from side to side (while moving); totter **2** to dumbfound, astonish **3** to arrange in any of various alternating or overlapping positions or times – **stagger** *n*

staggering /ˈstægərɪŋ/ *adj* astonishing, overwhelming – **~ly** *adv*

stagnant /ˈstægnənt/ *adj* **1a** not flowing in a current or stream; motionless **b** stale **2** dull, inactive – **~ly** *adv*

stagnate /stægˈneɪt/ *v* to become or remain stagnant – **-nation** *n*

stagy, stagey /ˈsteɪdzi/ *adj* marked by showy pretence or artificiality; theatrical – **stagily** *adv* – **staginess** *n*

staid /steɪd/ *adj* sedate and often primly self-restrained; sober – **~ly** *adv* – **~ness** *n*

[1]**stain** /steɪn/ *v* **1** to discolour, soil **2** to taint with guilt, vice, corruption, etc; bring dishonour to

[2]**stain** *n* **1** a soiled or discoloured spot **2** a moral taint or blemish **3a** a preparation (e g of dye or pigment) used in staining; *esp* one capable of penetrating the pores of wood **b** a dye or mixture of dyes used in microscopy to make minute and transparent structures visible, to differentiate tissue elements, or to produce specific chemical reactions

stainless /ˈsteɪnlɪs/ *adj* **1** free from stain or stigma **2** (made from materials) resistant to stain, specif rust

stair /steəʳ/ *n* **1** a series of (flights of) steps for passing from one level to another – usu pl with sing. meaning **2** any step of a stairway

staircase /ˈsteəkeɪs/ *n* **1** the structure or part of a building containing a stairway **2** a flight of stairs with the supporting framework, casing, and balusters

stairwell /ˈsteəwel/ *n* a vertical shaft in which stairs are located

[1]**stake** /steɪk/ *n* **1** a pointed piece of material (e g wood) for driving into the ground as a marker or support **2a** a post to which sby was bound for execution by burning **b** execution by burning at a stake – + *the* **3a** sthg, esp money, staked for gain or loss **b** the prize in a contest, esp a horse race – often pl with sing. meaning **c** an interest or share in an undertaking (e g a commercial venture)

[2]**stake** *v* **1** to mark the limits of (as if) by stakes – often + *off* or *out* **2** to tether to a stake **3** to bet, hazard **4** to fasten up or support (e g plants) with stakes

stalactite /ˈstæləktaɪt/ *n* an icicle-like deposit of calcium carbonate hanging from the roof or sides of a cavern

stalagmite /'stæləgmaɪt/ *n* a deposit of calcium carbonate like an inverted stalactite formed on the floor of a cavern

stale /steɪl/ *adj* **1a** tasteless or unpalatable from age **b** *of air* musty, foul **2** tedious from familiarity **3** impaired in vigour or effectiveness, esp from overexertion – **stale** *v* – ~**ly** *adv* – ~**ness** *n*

stalemate /'steɪlmeɪt/ *v or n* (to bring into) **a** a drawing position in chess in which only the king can move and although not in check can move only into check **b** a deadlock

[1]**stalk** /stɔːk/ *v* **1** to pursue or approach quarry or prey stealthily **2** to walk stiffly or haughtily – ~**er** *n*

[2]**stalk** *n* **1** the stalking of quarry or prey **2** a stiff or haughty walk

[3]**stalk** *n* **1** the main stem of a herbaceous plant, often with its attached parts **2** a slender upright supporting or connecting (animal) structure

[1]**stall** /stɔːl/ *n* **1** any of usu several compartments for domestic animals in a stable or barn **2a** a wholly or partly enclosed seat in the chancel of a church **b** a church pew **3a** a booth, stand, or counter at which articles are displayed or offered for sale **b** a sideshow **4** *Br* a seat on the main floor of an auditorium (e g in a theatre)

[2]**stall** *v* **1** to put or keep in a stall **2a** to bring to a standstill; block **b** to cause (e g a car engine) to stop, usu inadvertently

[3]**stall** *n* the condition of an aerofoil or aircraft when the airflow is so obstructed (e g from moving forwards too slowly) that lift is lost

[4]**stall** *v* to play for time; delay

stallholder /'stɔːlhəʊldəʳ/ *n* one who runs a (market) stall

stallion /'stæliən/ *n* an uncastrated male horse; *esp* one kept for breeding

[1]**stalwart** /'stɔːlwət/ *adj* **1** strong in body, mind, or spirit **2** dependable, staunch – ~**ly** *adv* – ~**ness** *n*

[2]**stalwart** *n* a stalwart person; *specif* a staunch supporter

stamen /'steɪmən/ *n* the organ of a flower that produces pollen, and consists of an anther and a filament

stamina /'stæmɪ̣nə/ *n* (capacity for) endurance

stammer /'stæməʳ/ *v* to speak or utter with involuntary stops and repetitions

[1]**stamp** /stæmp/ *v* **1** to bring down the foot forcibly **2a** to impress, imprint **b(1)** to attach a (postage) stamp to **(2)** to mark with an (official) impression, device, etc **3** to provide with a distinctive character

[2]**stamp** *n* **1** a device or instrument for stamping **2** the impression or mark made by stamping or imprinting **3a** a distinctive feature, indication, or mark **b** a lasting imprint **4** a printed or stamped piece of paper that for some restricted purpose is used as a token of credit or occasionally of debit: e g **a** a postage stamp **b** a stamp used as evidence that tax has been paid

[1]**stampede** /stæm'piːd/ *n* **1** a wild headlong rush or flight of frightened animals **2** a sudden mass movement of people

[2]**stampede** *v* to (cause to) run away or rush in panic or on impulse

stamping ground *n* a favourite or habitual haunt

stamp out *v* to eradicate, destroy

stance /stɑːns, stæns/ *n* **1a** a way of standing or being placed **b** intellectual or emotional attitude **2** the position of body or feet from which a sportsman (e g a batsman or golfer) plays

stanchion /'stɑːntʃən, 'stæn-/ *v or n* (to provide with) an upright bar, post, or support (e g for a roof)

[1]**stand** /stænd/ *v* **stood** **1a** to support oneself on the feet in an erect position **b** to rise to or maintain an erect or upright position **2** to take up or maintain a specified position or posture **3** to be in a specified state or situation **4** to be in a position to gain or lose because of an action taken or a commitment made **5** to occupy a place or location **6** to remain stationary or inactive **7** to agree, accord – chiefly in *it stands to reason* **8a** to exist in a definite (written or printed) form **b** to remain valid or effective **9** *chiefly Br* to be a candidate in an election **10a** to endure or undergo **b** to tolerate, bear;

put up with **11** to remain firm in the face of **12** to pay the cost of; pay for – infml – ~**er** *n*

²**stand** *n* **1** an act, position, or place of standing **2a** a usu defensive effort of some length or success **b** a stop made by a touring theatrical company, rock group, etc to give a performance **3** a strongly or aggressively held position, esp on a debatable issue **4a** a structure of tiered seats for spectators – often pl with sing. meaning **b** a raised platform serving as a point of vantage or display (e g for a speaker or exhibit) **5** a small usu temporary and open-air stall where goods are sold or displayed **6** a place where a passenger vehicle awaits hire **7** a frame on or in which sthg may be placed for support **8** a group of plants or trees growing in a continuous area **9** *NAm the* witness-box

¹**standard** /ˈstændəd/ *n* **1** a (long narrow tapering) flag **2a** sthg established by authority, custom, or general consent as a model or example; a criterion **b** a (prescribed) degree of quality or worth **3** *pl* moral integrity; principles **4** sthg set up and established by authority as a rule for the measure of quantity, weight, value, or quality **5** the basis of value in a money system **6** a shrub or herbaceous plant grown with an erect main stem so that it forms or resembles a tree

²**standard** *adj* **1a** being or conforming to a standard, esp as established by law or custom **b** sound and usable but not of top quality **2a** regularly and widely used, available, or supplied **b** well established and familiar **3** having recognized and permanent value – ~**ize** *v*

standard lamp *n* a lamp with a tall support that stands on the floor

standard of living *n* a level of welfare or subsistence maintained by an individual, group, or community and shown esp by the level of consumption of necessities, comforts, and luxuries

standard time *n* the officially established time, with reference to Greenwich Mean Time, of a region or country

¹**standby** /ˈstændbaɪ/ *n* one who or that which is held in reserve and can be relied on, made, or used in case of necessity

²**standby** *adj* **1** held near at hand and ready for use **2** relating to the act or condition of standing by

stand by *v* **1** to be present but remain aloof or inactive **2** to wait in a state of readiness

stand down *v* **1** to leave the witness-box **2** *chiefly Br* to relinquish (candidature for) an office or position **3** *chiefly Br* to send (soldiers) off duty; *broadly* to dismiss (workers); lay off

stand-in *n* **1** one who is employed to occupy an actor's place while lights and camera are made ready **2** a substitute

¹**standing** /ˈstændɪŋ/ *adj* **1** used or designed for standing in **2** not yet cut or harvested **3** not flowing; stagnant **4** continuing in existence or use indefinitely **5** established by law or custom **6** done from a standing position

²**standing** *n* **1a** length of service or experience, esp as determining rank, pay, or privilege **b** position, status, or condition, esp in relation to a group or other individuals in a similar field; *esp* good reputation **2** maintenance of position or condition; duration

standing order *n* **1** a rule governing the procedure of an organization, which remains in force until specifically changed **2** an instruction (e g to a banker or newsagent) in force until specifically changed

standoffish /stændˈɒfɪʃ/ *adj* reserved, aloof – ~**ly** *adv* – ~**ness** *n*

stand out *v* **1a** to appear (as if) in relief; project **b** to be prominent or conspicuous **2** to be stubborn in resolution or resistance

standpipe /ˈstændpaɪp/ *n* a pipe fitted with a tap and used for outdoor water supply

standpoint /ˈstændpɔɪnt/ *n* a position from which objects or principles are viewed and according to which they are compared and judged

standstill /ˈstændˌstɪl/ *n* a state in which motion or progress is absent; a stop

stand-up *adj* **1** stiffened to stay upright without folding over **2** performed in or requiring a standing position **3** (having an act) consisting of jokes usu performed solo standing before an audience

stand up *v* **1** to remain sound and intact under stress, attack, or close scrutiny **2** to fail to keep an appointment with

stank /stæŋk/ *past of* **stink**

stanza /ˈstænzə/ *n* a division of a poem consisting of a series of lines arranged together in a usu recurring pattern of metre and rhyme

¹staple /ˈsteɪpəl/ *v or n* (to provide with or secure by) **a** a U-shaped metal loop both ends of which can be driven into a surface (e g to secure sthg) **b** a small piece of wire with ends bent at right angles which can be driven through thin sheets of material, esp paper, and clinched to secure the items

²staple *n* **1** a chief commodity or production of a place **2** a raw material

³staple *adj* **1** used, needed, or enjoyed constantly, usu by many individuals **2** produced regularly or in large quantities **3** principal, chief

stapler /ˈsteɪpləʳ/ *n* a small usu hand-operated device for inserting wire staples

¹star /stɑːʳ/ *n* **1** any natural luminous body visible in the sky, esp at night **2a** a planet or a configuration of the planets that is held in astrology to influence a person's destiny – often pl **b** a waxing or waning fortune or fame **3a** an often star-shaped ornament or medal worn as a badge of honour, authority, or rank or as the insignia of an order **b** any of a group of stylized stars used to place sthg in a scale of value or quality – often in combination **4a** a (highly publicized) performer in the cinema or theatre who plays leading roles **b** an outstandingly talented performer **~ry, ~less** *adj*

²star *v* to play the most prominent or important role

³star *adj* of, being, or appropriate to a star

¹starboard /ˈstɑːbəd/ *adj or n* (of or at) the right side of a ship or aircraft looking forwards

²starboard *v* to turn or put (a helm or rudder) to the right

¹starch /stɑːtʃ/ *v* to stiffen (as if) with starch

²starch *n* **1** an odourless tasteless complex carbohydrate that is the chief storage form of carbohydrate in plants, is an important foodstuff, and is used also in adhesives and sizes, in laundering, and in pharmacy and medicine **2** a stiff formal manner; formality

starchy /ˈstɑːtʃi/ *adj* marked by formality or stiffness

star-crossed *adj* not favoured by the stars; ill-fated

stardom /ˈstɑːdəm/ *n* the status or position of a celebrity or star

stardust /ˈstɑːdʌst/ *n* a feeling or impression of romance or magic

¹stare /steəʳ/ *v* to look fixedly, often with wide-open eyes

²stare *n* a staring look

starfish /ˈstɑːˌfɪʃ/ *n* any of a class of sea animals that have a body consisting of a central disc surrounded by 5 equally spaced arms

stargazer /ˈstɑːgeɪzəʳ/ *n* **1** an astrologer **2** an astronomer *USE* chiefly humor

¹stark /stɑːk/ *adj* **1** sheer, utter **2a(1)** barren, desolate **(2)** having few or no ornaments; bare **b** harsh, blunt **3** sharply delineated **– ~ly** *adv* **– ~ness** *n*

²stark *adv* to an absolute or complete degree; wholly

starkers /ˈstɑːkəz/ *adj, Br* completely naked – used predicatively; slang

starlet /ˈstɑːlɨt/ *n* a young film actress being coached and publicized for starring roles

starling /ˈstɑːlɪŋ/ *n* a dark brown (or in summer, glossy greenish black) European bird that lives in large social groups

starry-eyed *adj* given to thinking in a dreamy, impractical, or overoptimistic manner

Stars and Stripes *n pl but sing in constr* the flag of the USA

¹start /stɑːt/ *v* **1** to react with a sudden brief involuntary movement **2** to come into being, activity, or operation **3a** to begin a course or journey **b** to range from a specified initial point **4** to begin an activity or undertaking;

esp to begin work **5a** to cause to move, act, operate, or do sthg specified **b** to cause to enter or begin a game, contest, or business activity; *broadly* to put in a starting position **6** to perform or undergo the first stages or actions of; begin

[2]**start** *n* **1** a sudden involuntary bodily movement or reaction (e g from surprise or alarm) **2** a beginning of movement, activity, or development **3a** a lead conceded at the start of a race or competition **b** an advantage, lead; a head start **4** a place of beginning

starter /'stɑːtəʳ/ *n* **1** one who initiates or sets going; *esp* one who gives the signal to start a race **2a** one who is in the starting lineup of a race or competition **b** one who begins to engage in an activity or process **3** an electric motor used to start a petrol engine **4a** sthg that is the beginning of a process, activity, or series **b** *chiefly Br* the first course of a meal – often pl with sing. meaning

startle /'stɑːtl/ *v* to (cause to) be suddenly frightened or surprised and usu to (cause to) make a sudden brief movement – **-lingly** *adv*

starve /stɑːv/ *v* **1** to suffer or feel extreme hunger **2** to suffer or perish from deprivation

starveling /'stɑːvlɪŋ/ *n* a person or animal that is thin (as if) from lack of food

[1]**stash** /stæʃ/ *v* to store in a usu secret place for future use – often + *away*

[2]**stash** *n, chiefly NAm* **1** a hiding place; a cache **2** sthg stored or hidden away

[1]**state** /steɪt/ *n* **1a** a mode or condition of being (with regard to circumstances, health, temperament, etc) **b** a condition of abnormal tension or excitement **2** a condition or stage in the physical being of sthg **3a** luxurious style of living **b** formal dignity; pomp – usu + *in* **4** a politically organized (sovereign) body, usu occupying a definite territory; *also* its political organization **5** the operations of the government **6** *often cap* a constituent unit of a nation having a federal government

[2]**state** *v* **1** to set, esp by regulation or authority; specify **2** to express the particulars of, esp in words; *broadly* to express in words

stateless /'steɪtlɪ̵s/ *adj* having no nationality – **~ness** *n*

stately /'steɪtli/ *adj* **1** imposing, dignified **2** impressive in size or proportions – **-liness** *n*

statement /'steɪtmənt/ *n* **1** stating orally or on paper **2** sthg stated: e g **a** a report of facts or opinions **b** a single declaration or remark; an assertion **3** a proposition (e g in logic) **4** the presentation of a theme in a musical composition **5** a summary of a financial account **6** an outward expression of thought, feeling, etc made without words

stateroom /'steɪtrʊm, -ruːm/ *n* **1** a large room in a palace or similar building for use on ceremonial occasions **2** a (large and comfortable) private cabin in a ship

statesman /'steɪtsmən/ *n* **1** one versed in or esp engaged in the business of a government **2** one who exercises political leadership wisely and without narrow partisanship – **~ship** *n*

[1]**static** /'stætɪk/ *adj* **1** exerting force by reason of weight alone without motion **2** of or concerned with bodies at rest or forces in equilibrium **3** characterized by a lack of movement, animation, progression, or change **4** of, producing, or being stationary charges of electricity

[2]**static** *n* (the electrical disturbances causing) unwanted signals in a radio or television system; atmospherics

statics /'stætɪks/ *n pl but sing or pl in constr* a branch of mechanics dealing with the relations of forces that produce equilibrium among solid bodies

[1]**station** /'steɪʃən/ *n* **1** the place or position in which sthg or sby stands or is assigned to stand or remain **2** a stopping place; *esp* (the buildings at) a regular or major stopping place for trains, buses, etc **3a** a post or sphere of (naval or military) duty or occupation **b** a stock farm or ranch in Australia or New Zealand **4** standing, rank **5** a place for specialized observation and study of scientific phenomena **6** a place established to provide a public service; *esp* a police station **7** an

establishment equipped for radio or television transmission or reception

[2]**station** *v* to assign to or set in a station or position; post

stationary /ˈsteɪʃənəri/ *adj* **1a** having a fixed position; immobile **2** unchanging in condition

stationer /ˈsteɪʃənəʳ/ *n* one who deals in stationery

stationery /ˈsteɪʃənəri/ *n* materials (e g paper) for writing or typing; *specif* paper and envelopes for letter writing

stationmaster /ˈsteɪʃən,mɑːstəʳ/ *n* an official in charge of a railway station

statistics /stəˈtɪstɪks/ *n pl but sing or pl in constr* **1** a branch of mathematics dealing with the collection, analysis, interpretation, and presentation of masses of numerical data **2** a collection of quantitative data – **-tical** *adj* – **-tically** *adv* – **-tician** *n*

[1]**statuary** /ˈstæʃʊəri/ *n* statues collectively

[2]**statuary** *adj* of or suitable for statues

statue /ˈstætʃuː/ *n* a likeness (e g of a person or animal) sculptured, cast, or modelled in a solid material (e g bronze or stone)

statuesque /,stætʃʊˈesk/ *adj* resembling a statue, esp in dignity, shapeliness, or formal beauty

stature /ˈstætʃəʳ/ *n* **1** natural height (e g of a person) in an upright position **2** quality or status gained by growth, development, or achievement

status /ˈsteɪtəs/ *n* **1** the condition of sby or sthg (in the eyes of the law) **2** (high) position or rank in relation to others or in a hierarchy

status quo /,steɪtəs ˈkwəʊ/ *n* the existing state of affairs

statute /ˈstætʃuːt/ *n* **1** a law passed by a legislative body and recorded **2** a rule made by a corporation or its founder, intended as permanent

statute book *n* the whole body of legislation of a given jurisdiction

statutory /ˈstætʃʊtəri/ *adj* established, regulated, or imposed by or in conformity to statute

[1]**staunch** /stɔːntʃ/ *v* to stop the flow of, esp blood

[2]**staunch** *adj* steadfast in loyalty or principle – **~ly** *adv* – **~ness** *n*

[1]**stave** /steɪv/ *n* **1** the musical staff **2** any of the narrow strips of wood or iron placed edge to edge to form the sides, covering, or lining of a vessel (e g a barrel) or structure **3** a supporting bar **4** a stanza

[2]**stave** *v* **staved, stove** to crush or break inwards – usu + *in*

stave off *v* to ward or fend off, esp temporarily

staves /steɪvz/ *pl of* **staff**

[1]**stay** /steɪ/ *n* a strong rope, now usu of wire, used to support a ship's mast or similar tall structure (e g a flagstaff)

[2]**stay** *v* to support (e g a chimney) (as if) with stays

[3]**stay** *v* **1** to continue in a place or condition; remain **2** to take up temporary residence; lodge **3** *of a racehorse* to run well over long distances **4** to stop or delay the proceeding, advance, or course of; halt

[4]**stay** *n* **1a** stopping or being stopped **b** a suspension of judicial procedure **2** a residence or sojourn in a place

[5]**stay** *n* **1** sby who or sthg that serves as a prop; a support **2** a corset stiffened with bones – usu pl with sing. meaning

stay-at-home *n or adj* (one) preferring to remain in his/her own home, locality, or country

stayer /ˈsteɪəʳ/ *n* a racehorse that habitually stays the course

stead /sted/ *n* the office, place, or function ordinarily occupied or carried out by sby or sthg else

steadfast /ˈstedfɑːst/ *adj* **1a** firmly fixed in place or position **b** not subject to change **2** firm in belief, determination, or adherence; loyal – **~ly** *adv* – **~ness** *n*

[1]**steady** /ˈstedi/ *adj* **1a** firm in position; not shaking, rocking, etc **b** direct or sure; unfaltering **2** showing or continuing with little variation or fluctuation **3a** not easily moved or upset; calm **b** dependable, constant **c** not given to dissipation; sober – **steadily** *adv* – **steadiness** *n*

[2]**steady** *v* to make, keep, or become steady

[3]**steady** *adv* in a steady manner; steadily

[4]**steady** *n* a regular boy/girl friend

steady state theory *n* a theory in cosmology: the universe has always existed and has always been expanding with matter being created continuously

steak /steɪk/ *n* **1a** a slice of meat cut from a fleshy part (e g the rump) of a (beef) carcass and suitable for grilling or frying **b** a poorer-quality less tender beef cut, usu from the neck and shoulder, suitable for braising or stewing **2** a cross-sectional slice from between the centre and tail of a large fish

steal /stiːl/ *v* **stole; stolen 1** to take (the property of another) **2** to come or go secretly or unobtrusively

stealth /stelθ/ *n* **1** the act or action of proceeding furtively or unobtrusively **2** the state of being furtive or unobtrusive – **~y** *adj* – **~ily** *adv*

[1]**steam** /stiːm/ *n* **1** a vapour given off by a heated substance; *esp* the vapour into which water is converted when heated to its boiling point **2a** energy or power generated (as if) by steam under pressure **b** driving force; power – infml

[2]**steam** /stiːm/ *v* **1** to give off steam or vapour **2** to apply steam to; *esp* to expose to the action of steam (e g for softening or cooking) **3** to proceed quickly **4** to be angry; boil **5** to become covered *up* or *over* with steam or condensation

steamer /ˈstiːməʳ/ *n* **1** a device in which articles are steamed; *esp* a vessel in which food is cooked by steam **2a** a ship propelled by steam **b** an engine, machine, or vehicle operated or propelled by steam

[1]**steamroller** /ˈstiːmˌrəʊləʳ/ *n* **1** a machine equipped with wide heavy rollers for compacting the surfaces of roads, pavements, etc **2** a crushing force, esp when ruthlessly applied to overcome opposition

[2]**steamroller** *also* **steamroll** *v* to force to a specified state or condition by the use of overwhelming pressure

steam up *v* to make angry or excited; arouse

steed /stiːd/ *n* a horse; *esp* a spirited horse for state or war – chiefly poetic

[1]**steel** /stiːl/ *n* **1** commercial iron distinguished from cast iron by its malleability and lower carbon content **2a** a fluted round steel rod with a handle for sharpening knives **b** a piece of steel for striking sparks from flint **3** a quality (e g of mind or spirit) that suggests steel, esp in strength or hardness

[2]**steel** *v* **1** to make unfeeling; harden **2** to fill with resolution or determination

steel band *n* a band that plays tuned percussion instruments cut out of oil drums, developed orig in Trinidad

steely /ˈstiːli/ *adj* of or like (the hardness, strength, or colour of) steel

[1]**steep** /stiːp/ *adj* **1** making a large angle with the plane of the horizon; almost vertical **2** being or characterized by a rapid and severe decline or increase **3** difficult to accept, comply with, or carry out; excessive – infml – **~ly** *adv* – **~ness** *n*

[2]**steep** *v* **1** to cover with or plunge into a liquid (e g in rinsing, bleaching or soaking) **2** to imbue with or subject thoroughly to – usu + *in*

steeple /ˈstiːpəl/ *n* (a tower with) a tall spire on a church

steeplechase /ˈstiːpəltʃeɪs/ *n* **1** a horse race across country or over jumps; *specif* one over a course longer than 2mi (about 3.2km) containing fences higher than 4ft 6in (about 1.4m) **2** a middle-distance running race over obstacles

steeplejack /ˈstiːpəldʒæk/ *n* one who climbs chimneys, towers, etc to paint, repair, or demolish them

[1]**steer** /ˈstɪəʳ/ *n* a male bovine animal castrated before sexual maturity

[2]**steer** *v* **1** to direct the course of; *esp* to guide a ship by means of a rudder **2** to set and hold to (a course)

steerage /ˈstɪərɪdʒ/ *n* **1** the act or practice of steering; *broadly* direction **2** a large section in a passenger ship for passengers paying the lowest fares

steersman /ˈstɪəzmən/ *n* a helmsman

stegosaurus /ˌstegəˈsɔːrəs/ *n* any of a genus of large armoured dinosaurs

stele /ˈstiːli/ *n* **1** a usu carved or inscribed stone slab or pillar used esp as a gravestone **2** the (cylindrical) central vascular portion of the stem of a vascular plant

stellar /'steləʳ/ *adj* of or composed of (the) stars

[1]**stem** /stem/ *n* **1a** the main trunk of a plant **b** a branch or other plant part that supports a leaf, fruit, etc **2** the bow or prow of a vessel **3** a line of ancestry; *esp* a fundamental line from which others have arisen **4** that part of a word which has unchanged spelling when the word is inflected **5a** the tubular part of a tobacco pipe from the bowl outwards, through which smoke is drawn **b** the often slender and cylindrical upright support between the base and bowl of a wineglass

[2]**stem** *v* **1** to make headway against (e g an adverse tide, current, or wind) **2** to check or go counter to (sthg adverse)

[3]**stem** *v* to originate – usu + *from*

[4]**stem** *v* to stop or check (as if) by damming

stench /stentʃ/ *n* a stink

stencil /'stensəl/ *n* **1** (a printing process using, or a design, pattern, etc produced by means of) an impervious material perforated with a design or lettering through which ink or paint is forced onto the surface below **2** a sheet of strong tissue paper impregnated or coated (e g with paraffin or wax) for use esp in typing a stencil

stenography /stə̣'nɒgrəfi/ *n* the writing and transcription of shorthand – **-pher** *n*

stentorian /sten'tɔːrɪən/ *adj* extremely loud

[1]**step** /step/ *n* **1** a rest for the foot in ascending or descending: e g **a** a single tread and riser on a stairway; a stair **b** a ladder rung **2a(1)** an advance or movement made by raising the foot and bringing it down at another point (2) a combination of foot (and body) movements constituting a unit or a repeated pattern **b** the sound of a footstep **3** a short distance **4** *pl* a course, way **5a** a degree, grade, or rank in a scale **b** a stage in a process **c** an action, proceeding, or measure often occurring as 1 in a series – often pl with sing. meaning **6** *pl* a stepladder

[2]**step** *v* **1** to move by raising the foot and bringing it down at another point or by moving each foot in succession **2a** to go on foot; walk **b** to be on one's way; leave – often + *along* **3** to press down *on* sthg with the foot **4** to measure by steps – usu + *off* or *out*

stepbrother /'step,brʌðəʳ/ *n* a son of one's stepparent by a former marriage

stepchild /'steptʃaɪld/ *n* a child of one's wife or husband by a former marriage

step down *v* **1** to lower (the voltage at which an alternating current is operating) by means of a transformer **2** to retire, resign

stepladder /'step,lædəʳ/ *n* a portable set of steps with a hinged frame

stepparent /'step,peərənt/ *n* the husband or wife of one's parent by a subsequent marriage

steppe /step/ *n* a vast usu level and treeless plain, esp in SE Europe or Asia

stepping-stone *n* **1** a stone on which to step (e g in crossing a stream) **2** a means of progress or advancement

stepsister /'step,sɪstəʳ/ *n* a daughter of one's stepparent by a former marriage

stereo /'steriəʊ, 'stɪər-/ *n* a device (e g a record player) for reproducing sound in which the sound is split into and reproduced by 2 different channels to give a special effect – **stereo** *adj*

stereophonic /,sterɪə'fɒnɪk/ *adj* stereo

stereoscope /'sterɪəskəʊp/ *n* an optical instrument with 2 eyepieces through which the observer views 2 pictures taken from points of view a little way apart to get the effect of a single three-dimensional picture – **-pic** *adj*

[1]**stereotype** /'sterɪətaɪp/ *n* sby who or sthg that conforms to a fixed or general pattern; *esp* a standardized, usu oversimplified, mental picture or attitude held in common by members of a group

[2]**stereotype** *v* to repeat without variation; make hackneyed

sterile /'steraɪl/ *adj* **1** failing or not able to produce or bear fruit, crops, or offspring **2a** deficient in ideas or originality **b** free from living organisms, esp microorganisms **3** bringing no rewards or results; not productive – **-lization** *n* – **-lize** *v*

[1]**sterling** /'stɜːlɪŋ/ *n* British money

[2]**sterling** *adj* **1** of or calculated in terms of British sterling **2a** *of silver* having a fixed standard of purity; *specif* 92.5 per cent pure **3** conforming to the highest standard

sterling area *n* a group of countries whose currencies are tied to British sterling

[1]**stern** /stɜːn/ *adj* **1a** hard or severe in nature or manner; austere **b** expressive of severe displeasure; harsh **2** forbidding or gloomy in appearance **3** inexorable, relentless – **~ly** *adv* – **~ness** *n*

[2]**stern** *n* **1** the rear end of a ship or boat **2** a back or rear part; the last or latter part

sternum /'stɜːnəm/ *n* a bone or cartilage at the front of the body that connects the ribs, both sides of the shoulder girdle, or both; the breastbone

steroid /'stɪərɔɪd/ *n* any of numerous compounds of similar to fats which effect the body's metabolism in various ways

stertorous /'stɜːtərəs/ *adj* characterized by a harsh snoring or gasping sound – **~ly** *adv*

stet /stet/ *v* to direct retention of (a word or passage previously ordered to be deleted or omitted) by annotating, usu with the word *stet*

stethoscope /'steθəskəʊp/ *n* an instrument used to detect and study sounds produced in the body

stetson /'stetsən/ *n* a broad-brimmed high-crowned felt hat

stevedore /'stiːvɺdɔːʳ/ *n* a docker

[1]**stew** /stjuː/ *n* **1a** a savoury dish, usu of meat and vegetables stewed and served in the same liquid **b** a mixture composed of many usu unrelated parts **2** a state of excitement, worry, or confusion – infml

[2]**stew** *v* to cook (e g meat or fruit) slowly by boiling gently or simmering in liquid

[1]**steward** /'stjuːəd/ *n* **1** one employed to look after a large household or estate **2a** one who manages the provisioning of food and attends to the needs of passengers (e g on an airliner, ship, or train) **b** one who supervises the provision and distribution of food and drink in a club, college, etc **3** an official who actively directs affairs (e g at a race meeting)

[2]**steward** *v* to act as a steward (for)

stewardess /,stjuːə'des/ *n* a woman who performs the duties of a steward

stewed /stjuːd/ *adj* drunk – infml

[1]**stick** /stɪk/ *n* **1** a (dry and dead) cut or broken branch or twig **2a** a walking stick **b** an implement used for striking an object in a game (e g hockey) **3** sthg prepared (e g by cutting, moulding, or rolling) in a relatively long and slender often cylindrical form **4** a person of a specified type **5** a stick-shaped plant stalk (e g of rhubarb or celery) **6** several bombs, parachutists, etc released from an aircraft in quick succession **7** *pl the* wooded or rural and usu backward districts

[2]**stick** *v* **stuck** **1** to fasten in position (as if) by piercing **2** to push, thrust **3** to attach (as if) by causing to adhere to a surface **4** to become blocked, wedged, or jammed **5** to project, protrude – often + *out* or *up* **6a** to halt the movement or action of **b** to baffle, stump **7** to put or set in a specified place or position **8** to saddle with sthg disadvantageous or disagreeable **9** *chiefly Br* to bear, stand

[3]**stick** *n* adhesive quality or substance

stick around *v* to stay or wait about; linger – infml

sticker /'stɪkəʳ/ *n* **1** sby who or sthg that sticks or causes sticking **2** a slip of paper with gummed back that, when moistened, sticks to a surface

sticking plaster *n* an adhesive plaster, esp for covering superficial wounds

stick-in-the-mud *n* one who dislikes and avoids change

stickleback /'stɪkəlbæk/ *n* any of numerous small scaleless fishes that have 2 or more spines in front of the dorsal fin

stickler /'stɪkləʳ/ *n* one who insists on exactness or completeness in the observance of sthg

stick out *v* **1** to be prominent or

conspicuous – often in *stick out a mile, stick out like a sore thumb* **2** to be persistent (e g in a demand or an opinion) – usu + *for* **3** to endure to the end – often + *it*

stick up *v* to rob at gunpoint – infml – **stick-up** *n*

sticky /ˈstɪki/ *adj* **1a** adhesive **b** viscous, gluey **2** humid, muggy; *also* clammy **3a** disagreeable, unpleasant **b** awkward, stiff **c** difficult, problematic – **stickily** *adv* – **stickiness** *n*

sticky wicket *n* a difficult situation – infml

[1]**stiff** /stɪf/ *adj* **1a** not easily bent; rigid **b** lacking in suppleness and often painful **2a** firm, unyielding **b(1)** marked by reserve or decorum; formal **(2)** lacking in ease or grace; stilted **3** hard fought **4** exerting great force; forceful **5** of a dense or glutinous consistency; thick **6a** harsh, severe **b** arduous **7** expensive, steep – **~en** *v* – **~ly** *adv* – **~ness** *n*

[2]**stiff** *adv* in a stiff manner; stiffly

[3]**stiff** *n* a corpse – slang

stiff-necked *adj* haughty, stubborn

stifle /ˈstaɪfəl/ *v* **1a** to overcome or kill by depriving of oxygen; suffocate, smother **b** to muffle **2a** to cut off (e g the voice or breath) **b** to prevent the development or expression of; check, suppress

stigma /ˈstɪgmə/ *n, pl* **stigmata, stigmas** **1** a mark of shame or discredit **2** *pl* marks resembling the wounds of the crucified Christ, believed to be impressed on the bodies of holy or saintly people **3** the portion of the female part of a flower which receives the pollen grains and on which they germinate

stigmat·ize, -ise /ˈstɪgmətaɪz/ *v* to describe or identify in disparaging or abusive terms

stile /staɪl/ *n* **1** a step or set of steps for passing over a fence or wall **2** a turnstile

stiletto /stɪ̈ˈletəʊ/ *n* **1** a slender rodlike dagger **2** a pointed instrument for piercing holes (e g for eyelets) in leather, cloth, etc **3** *Br* an extremely narrow tapering high heel on a woman's shoe

[1]**still** /stɪl/ *adj* **1a** devoid of or abstaining from motion **b** having no effervescence; not carbonated **2** uttering no sound; quiet **3a** calm, tranquil **b** free from noise or turbulence – **~ness** *n*

[2]**still** *v* **1a** to allay, calm **b** to put an end to; settle **2** to arrest the motion or noise of; quiet

[3]**still** *adv* **1** as before; even at this or that time **2** in spite of that; nevertheless **3a** even (e g a *still* more difficult problem) **b** yet

[4]**still** *n* **1** a still photograph; *specif* a photograph of actors or of a scene from a film **2** quiet, silence – chiefly poetic

[5]**still** *n* an apparatus used in distillation, esp of spirits, consisting of either the chamber in which the vaporization is carried out or the entire equipment

stillbirth /ˈstɪlbɜːθ/ *n* the birth of a dead infant

stillborn /ˈstɪlbɔːn, ˌstɪlˈbɔːn/ *adj* **1** dead at birth **2** failing from the start; abortive

still life *n* a picture showing an arrangement of inanimate objects (e g fruit or flowers)

stilt /stɪlt/ *n* **1a** either of 2 poles each with a rest or strap for the foot, that enable the user to walk along above the ground **b** any of a set of piles, posts, etc that support a building above ground or water level **2** any of various notably long-legged 3-toed wading birds related to the avocets

stilted /ˈstɪltɪ̈d/ *adj* stiffly formal and often pompous – **~ly** *adv*

Stilton /ˈstɪltən/ *n* a cream-enriched white cheese that has a wrinkled rind and is often blue-veined

stimulant /ˈstɪmjʊlənt/ *n* sthg (e g a drug) that produces a temporary increase in the functional activity or efficiency of (a part of) an organism

stimulate /ˈstɪmjʊleɪt/ *v* to excite to (greater) activity – **-lation** *n*

stimulus /ˈstɪmjʊləs/ *n, pl* **stimuli** **1** sthg that rouses or incites to activity; an incentive **2** sthg (e g light) that directly influences the activity of living organisms (e g by exciting a sensory organ or evoking muscular contraction or glandular secretion)

[1]**sting** /stɪŋ/ *v* **stung** **1a** to give an irritating or poisonous wound to, esp with a sting **b** to affect with sharp

quick pain **2** to cause to suffer acute mental pain; *also* to incite or goad thus **3** to overcharge, cheat – infml

[2]**sting** *n* **1a** a stinging; *specif* the thrust of a sting into the flesh **b** a wound or pain caused (as if) by stinging **2** *also* **stinger** a sharp organ of a bee, scorpion, stingray, etc that is usu connected with a poison gland or otherwise adapted to wound by piercing and injecting a poisonous secretion

stingray /ˈstɪŋreɪ/ *n* any of numerous rays with a whiplike tail having 1 or more large sharp spines capable of inflicting severe wounds

stingy /ˈstɪndʒi/ *adj* **1** mean or ungenerous in giving or spending **2** meanly scanty or small – **-gily** *adv* – **-giness** *n*

[1]**stink** /stɪŋk/ *v* **stank; stunk** **1** to emit a strong offensive smell **2** to be offensive; *also* to be in bad repute or of bad quality **3** to possess sthg to an offensive degree – usu + *with USE* (*except l*) infml

[2]**stink** *n* **1** a strong offensive smell; a stench **2** a public outcry against sthg offensive – infml

[1]**stinking** /ˈstɪŋkɪŋ/ *adj* severe and unpleasant – infml

[2]**stinking** *adv* to an extreme degree – infml

[1]**stint** /stɪnt/ *v* to restrict to a small share or allowance; be frugal with

[2]**stint** *n* **1** restraint, limitation **2** a definite quantity or period of work assigned

stipend /ˈstaɪpend/ *n* a fixed sum of money paid periodically (e g to a clergyman) as a salary or to meet expenses – **~iary** *adj*

[1]**stipple** /ˈstɪpəl/ *v* to speckle, fleck

[2]**stipple** *n* (the effect produced by) a method of painting using small points, dots, or strokes to represent degrees of light and shade

stipulate /ˈstɪpjʊleɪt/ *v* **1** to specify as a condition or requirement of an agreement or offer **2** to give a guarantee of in making an agreement – **-ation** *n*

[1]**stir** /stɜːʳ/ *v* **1a** to make or cause a slight movement or change of position **b** to disturb the quiet of; agitate **2a** to disturb the relative position of the particles or parts of (a fluid or semifluid), esp by a continued circular movement in order to make the composition homogeneous **b** to mix (as if) by stirring **3** to bestir, exert **4a** to rouse to activity; produce strong feelings in **b** to provoke – often + *up*

[2]**stir** *n* **1a** a state of disturbance, agitation, or brisk activity **b** widespread notice and discussion **2** a slight movement **3** a stirring movement

stirring /ˈstɜːrɪŋ/ *adj* rousing, inspiring – **~ly** *adv*

stirrup /ˈstɪrəp/ *n* either of a pair of D-shaped metal frames attached by a strap to a saddle to support the feet of a rider

stirrup cup *n* a farewell usu alcoholic drink; *specif* one taken on horseback

[1]**stitch** /stɪtʃ/ *n* **1** a local sharp and sudden pain, esp in the side **2a** a single in-and-out movement of a threaded needle in sewing, embroidering, or closing (surgical) wounds **b** a portion of thread left in the material after 1 stitch **3** a single loop of thread or yarn round a stitching implement (e g a knitting needle) **4** the least scrap of clothing – usu neg; infml

[2]**stitch** *v* **1** to fasten, join, or close (as if) with stitches; sew **2** to work on or decorate (as if) with stitches

stoat /stəʊt/ *n* a European weasel with a long black-tipped tail

[1]**stock** /stɒk/ *n* **1a** *pl* a wooden frame with holes for the feet (and hands) in which offenders are held for public punishment **b** the part to which the barrel and firing mechanism of a gun are attached **2a** the main stem of a plant or tree **b(1)** a plant (part) consisting of roots and lower trunk onto which a graft is made **(2)** a plant from which cuttings are taken **3a** the original (e g a man, race, or language) from which others derive; a source **b** the descendants of an individual; family, lineage **4a** *sing or pl in constr* livestock **b** a store or supply accumulated (e g of raw materials or finished goods) **5a** a debt or fund due (e g from a government) for money loaned at interest; *also, Br* capital or a debt or fund which continues to bear interest but is not usually redeemable as far as the original sum is concerned **b** (preference) shares – often pl **6** any of a

genus of plants with usu sweet-scented flowers **7** a wide band or scarf worn round the neck, esp by some clergymen **8** the liquid in which meat, fish, or vegetables have been simmered that is used as a basis for soup, gravy, etc **9a** an estimate or appraisal of sthg **b** the estimation in which sby or sthg is held

²**stock** *v* **1** to provide with (a) stock; supply **2** to procure or keep a stock of **3** to take in a stock – often + *up*

³**stock** *adj* **1a** kept in stock regularly **b** regularly and widely available or supplied **2** used for (breeding and rearing) livestock **3** commonly used or brought forward; standard – chiefly derog

¹**stockade** /stɒˈkeɪd/ *n* **1** a line of stout posts set vertically to form a defence **2** an enclosure or pen made with posts and stakes

²**stockade** *v* to fortify or surround with a stockade

stockbreeder *n* one who breeds livestock

stockbroker /ˈstɒk,brəʊkəʳ/ *n* a broker who buys and sells securities

stock car *n* a racing car having the chassis of a commercially produced assembly-line model

stock exchange *n* (a building occupied by) an association of people organized to provide an auction market among themselves for the purchase and sale of securities

stocking /ˈstɒkɪŋ/ *n* a usu knitted close-fitting often nylon covering for the foot and leg

stock-in-trade *n* **1** the equipment necessary to or used in a trade or business **2** sthg like the standard equipment of a tradesman or business

stockist /ˈstɒkɪ̈st/ *n, Br* one (e g a retailer) who stocks goods, esp of a particular kind or brand

stockman /ˈstɒkmən/ *n* one who owns or takes care of livestock

stockpile /ˈstɒkpaɪl/ *n* an accumulated store; *esp* a reserve supply of sthg essential accumulated for use during a shortage – **stockpile** *v*

stock-still *adj* completely motionless

stocktaking /ˈstɒk,teɪkɪŋ/ *n* **1** the checking or taking of an inventory of goods or supplies on hand (e g in a shop) **2** estimating a situation at a given moment (e g by considering past progress and resources)

stocky /ˈstɒki/ *adj* short, sturdy, and relatively thick in build – **stockily** *adv* – **stockiness** *n*

stockyard /ˈstɒkjɑːd/ *n* a yard in which cattle, pigs, horses, etc are kept temporarily for slaughter, market, or shipping

stodge /stɒdʒ/ *n* **1** filling (starchy) food **2** turgid and unimaginative writing – infml

stodgy /ˈstɒdʒi/ *adj* **1** *of food* heavy and filling **2** dull, boring – infml – **stodginess** *n*

¹**stoic** /ˈstəʊɪk/ *n* **1** *cap* a member of an ancient Greek or Roman school of philosophy equating happiness with knowledge and holding that wisdom consists in self-mastery and submission to natural law **2** sby apparently or professedly indifferent to pleasure or pain

²**stoic, stoical** *adj* not affected by or showing passion or feeling; *esp* firmly restraining response to pain or distress

stoke /stəʊk/ *v* **1** to poke or stir up (e g a fire); *also* to supply with fuel **2** to feed abundantly

stoker /ˈstəʊkəʳ/ *n* one employed to tend a furnace, esp on a ship

¹**stole** /stəʊl/ *past of* **steal**

²**stole** *n* **1** a long usu silk band worn traditionally over both shoulders and hanging down in front by priests **2** a long wide strip of material worn by women usu across the shoulders, esp with evening dress

stolen /ˈstəʊlən/ *past part of* **steal**

stolid /ˈstɒlɪ̈d/ *adj* difficult to arouse emotionally or mentally; unemotional – **~ly** *adv* – **~ness, ~ity** *n*

¹**stomach** /ˈstʌmək/ *n* **1a** (a cavity in an invertebrate animal analogous to) a saclike organ formed by a widening of the alimentary canal of a vertebrate, that is between the oesophagus at the top and the duodenum at the bottom and in which the first stages of digestion occur **b** the part of the body that contains the stomach; belly, abdomen **2a** desire for food; appetite **b** inclination, desire – usu neg

[2]stomach *v* **1** to find palatable or digestible **2** to bear without protest or resentment *USE* usu neg

stomach pump *n* a suction pump with a flexible tube for removing liquids from the stomach or injecting liquids into it

[1]stomp /stɒmp/ *v* to walk or dance with a heavy step – infml

[2]stomp *n* a jazz dance characterized by heavy stamping

[1]stone /stəʊn/ *n* **1** a concretion of earthy or mineral matter: **a(1)** a piece of this, esp one smaller than a boulder **(2)** rock **b(1)** a building or paving block **(2)** a gem **(3)** a sharpening stone **2** the hard central portion of a fruit (e g a peach or date) **3** an imperial unit of weight equal to 14lb (about 6.35kg)

[2]stone *v* **1** to hurl stones at; *esp* to kill by pelting with stones **2** to face, pave, or fortify with stones **3** to remove the stones or seeds of (a fruit)

[3]stone *adj* (made) of stone

Stone Age *n* the first known period of prehistoric human culture characterized by the use of stone tools and weapons

stoned /stəʊnd/ *adj* intoxicated by alcohol or a drug (e g marijuana) – infml

stone's throw *n* a short distance

stony /ˈstəʊni/ *adj* **1** containing many stones or having the nature of stone **2a** insensitive to pity or human feeling **b** showing no movement or reaction; dumb, expressionless – **stonily** *adv*

stony-broke *adj, Br* completely without funds; broke – infml

stood /ˈstʊd/ *past of* **stand**

[1]stooge /stuːdz/ *n* **1** one who usu speaks the feed lines in a comedy duo **2** one who plays a subordinate or compliant role to another

[2]stooge *v* **1** to act as a stooge – usu + *for* **2** to move, esp fly, aimlessly to and fro or at leisure – usu + *around* or *about* *USE* infml

stool /stuːl/ *n* **1a** a seat usu without back or arms supported by 3 or 4 legs or a central pedestal **b** a low bench or portable support for the feet or for kneeling on **2** a discharge of faecal matter

stool pigeon *n, chiefly NAm* sby acting as a decoy; *esp* a police informer

[1]stoop /stuːp/ *v* **1a** to bend the body forwards and downwards, sometimes simultaneously bending the knees **b** to stand or walk with a temporary or habitual forward inclination of the head, body, or shoulders **2a** to condescend **b** to lower oneself morally **3** *of a bird* to fly or dive down swiftly, usu to attack prey

[2]stoop *n* **1a** an act of bending the body forwards **b** a temporary or habitual forward bend of the back and shoulders **2** the descent of a bird, esp on its prey

[3]stoop *n, chiefly NAm* a porch, platform, entrance stairway, or small veranda at a house door

[1]stop /stɒp/ *v* **1a** to close by filling or obstructing **b** to hinder or prevent the passage of **2a** to restrain, prevent **b** to withhold **3a** to cause to cease; check, suppress **b** to discontinue; come to an end **4** to instruct one's bank not to honour or pay **5a** to arrest the progress or motion of; cause to halt **b** to cease to move on; halt **c** to pause, hesitate **6a** to break one's journey – often + *off* **b** *chiefly Br* to remain **c** *chiefly NAm* to make a brief call; drop in – usu + *by* **7** to get in the way of, esp so as to be wounded or killed – infml – **~pable** *adj*

[2]stop *n* **1** a cessation, end **2** a graduated set of organ pipes of similar design and tone quality **3a** sthg that impedes, obstructs, or brings to a halt; an impediment, obstacle **b** (any of a series of markings, esp f-numbers, for setting the size of) the circular opening of an optical system (e g a camera lens) **4** a device for arresting or limiting motion **5** stopping or being stopped **6a** a halt in a journey **b** a stopping place **7** *chiefly Br* any of several punctuation marks; *specif* full stop

stopcock /ˈstɒpkɒk/ *n* a cock for stopping or regulating flow (e g of fluid through a pipe)

stopgap /ˈstɒpgæp/ *n* sthg that serves as a temporary expedient; a makeshift

stop-go *adj* alternately active and inactive

stop-off *n* a stopover

stopover /'stɒp,əʊvəʳ/ *n* a stop at an intermediate point in a journey

stoppage /'stɒpɪdʒ/ *n* **1** a deduction from pay **2** a concerted cessation of work by a group of employees that is usu more spontaneous and less serious than a strike

stopper /'stɒpəʳ/ *n* sby or sthg that closes, shuts, or fills up; *specif* sthg (e g a bung or cork) used to plug an opening

stop press *n* (space reserved for) late news added to a newspaper after printing has begun

stopwatch /'stɒpwɒtʃ/ *n* a watch that can be started and stopped at will for exact timing

storage /'stɔːrɪdʒ/ *n* **1** (a) space for storing **2a** storing or being stored (e g in a warehouse) **b** the price charged for keeping goods in storage

[1]**store** /stɔːʳ/ *v* **1** to collect as a reserve supply – often + *up* or *away* **2** to place or leave in a location (e g a warehouse, library, or computer memory) for preservation or later use or disposal **3** to provide storage room for; hold

[2]**store** *n* **1a** sthg stored or kept for future use **b** *pl* articles accumulated for some specific object and drawn on as needed **c** a source from which things may be drawn as needed; a reserve fund **2** storage – usu + *in* **3** a large quantity, supply, or number **4** a warehouse **5** a large shop

storehouse /'stɔːhaʊs/ *n* **1** a warehouse **2** an abundant supply or source

storeroom /'stɔːrʊm, -ruːm/ *n* a place for the storing of goods or supplies

storey /'stɔːri/ *n* (a set of rooms occupying) a horizontal division of a building

stork /stɔːk/ *n* any of various large mostly Old World wading birds that have long stout bills and are related to the ibises and herons

[1]**storm** /stɔːm/ *n* **1** a violent disturbance of the weather marked by high winds, thunder and lightning, rain or snow, etc **2** a disturbed or agitated state; a sudden or violent commotion **3** a tumultuous outburst **4** a violent assault on a defended position

[2]**storm** *v* **1a** *of wind* to blow with violence **b** to rain, hail, snow, or sleet **2** to be in or to exhibit a violent passion; rage **3** to rush about or move impetuously, violently, or angrily **4** to attack or take (e g a fortified place) by storm

stormbound /'stɔːmbaʊnd/ *adj* confined or delayed by a storm or its effects

storm trooper *n* **1** a member of a Nazi party militia **2** a member of a force of shock troops

stormy /'stɔːmi/ *adj* marked by turmoil or fury – **stormily** *adv* – **storminess** *n*

stormy petrel *n* **1** a small black and white sea bird of the N Atlantic **2** sby fond of strife

story /'stɔːri/ *n* **1a** an account of incidents or events **b** a statement of the facts of a situation in question **c** an anecdote; *esp* an amusing one **2a** a short fictional narrative **b** the plot of a literary work **3** a widely circulated rumour **4** a lie **5** a news article or broadcast

storybook *adj* fairy-tale

storyteller /'stɔːritelәʳ/ *n* **1** a teller of tales or anecdotes; a narrator **2** a liar

[1]**stout** /staʊt/ *adj* **1** firm, resolute **2** physically or materially strong: **a** sturdy, vigorous **b** staunch, enduring **3** corpulent, fat – **~ly** *adv* – **~ness** *n*

[2]**stout** *n* a dark sweet heavy-bodied beer

stouthearted /,staʊt'hɑːtɪ̣d/ *adj* courageous

[1]**stove** /stəʊv/ *n* **1** an enclosed appliance that burns fuel or uses electricity to provide heat chiefly for domestic purposes **2** a cooker

[2]**stove** *past of* **stave**

stow /stəʊ/ *v* **1a** to pack away in an orderly fashion in an enclosed space **b** to fill (e g a ship's hold) with cargo **2** to stop, desist – slang; esp in *stow it*

stowage /'stəʊɪdʒ/ *n* **1** goods in storage or to be stowed **2** storage capacity **3** the state of being stored

[1]**stowaway** /'stəʊəweɪ/ *n* sby who stows away

[2]**stowaway** *adj* designed to be dismantled or folded for storage

stow away *v* to hide oneself aboard a vehicle, esp a ship, as a means of travelling without payment or escaping from a place undetected

straddle /'strædl/ *v* **1** to stand or esp sit with the legs wide apart **2** to bracket (a target) with missiles (e g shells or bombs)

strafe /strɑːf, streɪf/ *v* to rake (e g ground troops) with fire at close range, esp with machine-gun fire from low-flying aircraft

straggle /'strægəl/ *v* **1** to lag behind or stray away from the main body of sthg, esp from a line of march **2** to move or spread untidily away from the main body of sthg – **-gler** *n*

straggly /'strægəli/ *adj* loosely spread out or scattered irregularly

[1]**straight** /streɪt/ *adj* **1a** free from curves, bends, angles, or irregularities **b** generated by a point moving continuously in the same direction **2** direct, uninterrupted: e g **a** holding to a direct or proper course or method **b** candid, frank **c** coming directly from a trustworthy source **3a** honest, fair **b** properly ordered or arranged (e g with regard to finance) **c** correct **4** unmixed **5a** not deviating from the general norm or prescribed pattern **b** accepted as usual, normal, or proper **6a** conventional in opinions, habits, appearance etc **b** heterosexual *USE* (6) infml – **~ness** *n*

[2]**straight** *adv* **1** in a straight manner **2** without delay or hesitation; immediately

[3]**straight** *n* **1** sthg straight: e g **a** a straight line or arrangement **b** a straight part of sthg; *esp* a home straight **2** a poker hand containing 5 cards in sequence but not of the same suit **3a** a conventional person **b** a heterosexual *USE* (*3*) infml

straightaway /,streɪtə'weɪ/ *adv* without hesitation or delay; immediately

straighten /'streɪtn/ *v* to make or become straight – usu + *up* or *out*

straightforward /,streɪt'fɔːwəd/ *adj* **1** free from evasiveness or ambiguity; direct, candid **2** presenting no hidden difficulties **3** clear-cut, precise – **~ly** *adv* – **~ness** *n*

straight up *adv, Br* truly, honestly – infml; used esp in asking or replying to a question

[1]**strain** /streɪn/ *n* **1a** a lineage, ancestry **b** a kind, sort **2** a passage of verbal or musical expression – usu pl with sing. meaning

[2]**strain** *v* **1** to stretch to maximum extension and tautness **2a** to exert (e g oneself) to the utmost **b** to injure by overuse, misuse, or excessive pressure **3** to cause to pass through a strainer; filter **4** to stretch beyond a proper limit

[3]**strain** *n* straining or being strained: e g **a** (a force, influence, or factor causing) physical or mental tension **b** excessive or difficult exertion or labour **c** a wrench, twist, or similar bodily injury resulting esp from excessive stretching of muscles or ligaments

strained /streɪnd/ *adj* **1** done or produced with excessive effort **2** subjected to considerable tension

strainer /'streɪnəʳ/ *n* a device (e g a sieve) to retain solid pieces while a liquid passes through

strait /streɪt/ *n* **1** a narrow passageway connecting 2 large bodies of water – often pl with sing. meaning but sing. or pl in constr **2** a situation of perplexity or distress – usu pl with sing. meaning

straitjacket, straightjacket /'streɪt,dʒækɨt/ *n* a cover or outer garment of strong material used to bind the body and esp the arms closely, in restraining a violent prisoner or patient

straitlaced, *NAm also* **straightlaced** /,streɪt'leɪst/ *adj* excessively strict in manners or morals

[1]**strand** /strænd/ *n* a shore, beach

[2]**strand** *v* to leave in a strange or unfavourable place, esp without funds or means to depart

[3]**strand** *n* **1** any of the threads, strings, or wires twisted or laid parallel to make a cord, rope, etc **2** an elongated or twisted and plaited body resembling a rope **3** any of the elements interwoven in a complex whole

strange /streɪndʒ/ *adj* **1** not native to or naturally belonging in a place; of external origin, kind, or character **2a** not known, heard, or seen before **b**

exciting wonder or surprise 3 lacking experience or acquaintance; unaccustomed *to* – ~**ly** *adv* – ~**ness** *n*

stranger /ˈstreɪndʒəʳ/ *n* **1a** a foreigner, alien **b** sby who is unknown or with whom one is unacquainted **2** one ignorant of or unacquainted with sby or sthg

strangle /ˈstræŋgəl/ *v* **1** to choke (to death) by compressing the throat; throttle **2** to suppress or hinder the rise, expression, or growth of

stranglehold /ˈstræŋgəlhəʊld/ *n* a force or influence that prevents free movement or expression

[1]**strap** /stræp/ *n* **1** a strip of metal or a flexible material, esp leather, for holding objects together or in position **2** (*the* use of, or punishment with) a strip of leather for flogging

[2]**strap** *v* **1a** to secure with or attach by means of a strap **b** to support (e g a sprained joint) with adhesive plaster **2** to beat with a strap

strapping /ˈstræpɪŋ/ *adj* big, strong, and sturdy in build

stratagem /ˈstrætədʒəm/ *n* **1** an artifice or trick for deceiving and outwitting the enemy **2** a cleverly contrived trick or scheme

strategy /ˈstrætɪ̈dʒi/ *n* **1** the science and art of military command exercised to meet the enemy in combat under advantageous conditions **2a** a clever plan or method **b** the art of employing plans towards achieving a goal – **-gic** *adj* – **-gically** *adv* – **-gist** *n*

stratify /ˈstrætɪ̈faɪ/ *v* to form, deposit, or arrange in layers – **-fication** *n*

stratosphere /ˈstrætəsfɪəʳ/ *n* the upper part of the atmosphere above about 11km (7mi) in which the temperature changes little and clouds are rare

stratum /ˈstrɑːtəm/ *n, pl* **strata** **1** a horizontal layer or series of layers of any homogeneous material: e g **a** a sheetlike mass of rock or earth deposited between beds of other rock **b** a layer of the sea or atmosphere **c** a layer in which archaeological remains are found on excavation **2** a socioeconomic level of society

[1]**straw** /strɔː/ *n* **1** dry stalky plant residue, specif stalks of grain after threshing, used for bedding, thatching, fodder, making hats, etc **2** a dry coarse stem, esp of a cereal grass **3** sthg of small value or importance **4** a tube of paper, plastic, etc for sucking up a drink

[2]**straw** *adj* of or resembling (the colour of) straw

strawberry /ˈstrɔːbəri/ *n* (the juicy edible usu red fruit of) any of several white-flowered creeping plants

strawberry mark *n* a usu red and elevated birthmark composed of small blood vessels

straw poll *n* an assessment made by an unofficial vote

[1]**stray** /streɪ/ *v* **1** to wander from a proper place, course, or line of conduct or argument **2** to roam about without fixed direction or purpose

[2]**stray** *n* a domestic animal wandering at large or lost

[3]**stray** *adj* **1** having strayed; wandering, lost **2** occurring at random or sporadically

[1]**streak** /striːk/ *n* **1** a line or band of a different colour from the background **2** an inherent quality; *esp* one which is only occasionally manifested

[2]**streak** *v* **1** to make streaks on or in **2** to move swiftly **3** to run through a public place while naked

streaky /ˈstriːki/ *adj* **1** marked with streaks **2** *of meat, esp bacon* having lines of fat and lean **3** *of a shot in cricket* hit off the edge of the bat – **-kily** *adv* – **-kiness** *n*

[1]**stream** /striːm/ *n* **1** a body of running water, esp one smaller than a river **2a** a steady succession of words, events, etc **b** a continuous moving procession **3** an unbroken flow (e g of gas or particles of matter) **4** a prevailing attitude or direction of opinion – esp in *go against/with the stream* **5** *Br* a group of pupils of the same general academic ability

[2]**stream** *v* **1** to flow (as if) in a stream **2** to run with a fluid **3** to trail out at full length **4** to pour in large numbers in the same direction **5** *Br* to practise the division of pupils into streams

streamer /ˈstriːməʳ/ *n* **1a** a pennant **b** a strip of coloured paper used as a party decoration **2** a long extension of the sun's corona visible only during a total eclipse

[1]**streamline** /'striːmlaɪn/ *n* a contour given to a car, aeroplane, etc so as to minimize resistance to motion through a fluid (e g air)

[2]**streamline** *v* to make simpler, more efficient, or better integrated

street /striːt/ *n* **1** a thoroughfare, esp in a town or village, with buildings on either side **2** the part of a street reserved for vehicles

streetwise /'striːtwaɪz/ *adj* familiar with the (disreputable or criminal) life of city streets; *broadly* able to survive and prosper in modern urban conditions

strength /streŋθ/ *n* **1** the quality of being strong; capacity for exertion or endurance **2** solidity, toughness **3a** legal, logical, or moral force **b** a strong quality or inherent asset **4a** degree of potency of effect or of concentration **b** intensity of light, colour, sound, or smell **5** force as measured in members **6** a basis – chiefly in *on the strength of*

strengthen /'streŋθən, 'strenθən/ *v* to make or become stronger

strenuous /'strenjuəs/ *adj* **1** vigorously active **2** requiring effort or stamina – **~ly** *adv* – **~ness** *n*

streptomycin /ˌstreptəʊ'maɪsɪ̍n/ *n* an antibiotic obtained from a soil bacterium and used esp in the treatment of tuberculosis

[1]**stress** /stres/ *n* **1a** the force per unit area producing or tending to produce deformation of a body; *also* the state of a body under such stress **b** (a physical or emotional factor that causes) bodily or mental tension **c** strain, pressure **2** emphasis, weight **3** intensity of utterance given to a speech sound, syllable, or word so as to produce relative loudness

[2]**stress** *v* **1** to subject to physical or mental stress **2** to lay stress on; emphasize

[1]**stretch** /stretʃ/ *v* **1** to extend in a reclining position – often + *out* **2** to extend to full length **3** to extend (oneself or one's limbs), esp so as to relieve muscular stiffness **4** to pull taut **5** to strain **6** to cause to reach (e g from one point to another or across a space) **7** to fell (as if) with a blow – often + *out*; infml – **~able** *adj*

[2]**stretch** *n* **1** the extent to which sthg may be stretched **2** stretching or being stretched **3** a continuous expanse of time or space **4** elasticity **5** a term of imprisonment – infml

stretcher /'stretʃəʳ/ *n* **1** a brick or stone laid with its length parallel to the face of the wall **2** a device, consisting of a sheet of canvas or other material stretched between 2 poles, for carrying a sick, injured, or dead person **3** a rod or bar extending between 2 legs of a chair or table

strew /struː/ *v* **strewed, strewn 1** to spread by scattering **2** to become dispersed over

stricken /'strɪkən/ *adj* afflicted or overwhelmed (as if) by disease, misfortune, or sorrow

strict /strɪkt/ *adj* **1a** stringent in requirement or control **b** severe in discipline **2a** inflexibly maintained or kept to; complete **b** rigorously conforming to rules or standards **3** exact, precise – **~ly** *adv* – **~ness** *n*

stricture /'strɪktʃəʳ/ *n* **1** an abnormal narrowing of a bodily passage **2** sthg that closely restrains or limits; a restriction **3** an unfavourable criticism; a censure ***USE*** *(2&3)* usu pl with sing. meaning

[1]**stride** /straɪd/ *v* **strode** to walk (as if) with long steps

[2]**stride** *n* **1** a long step **2** an advance – often pl with sing. meaning **3** (the distance covered in) an act of movement completed when the feet regain the initial relative positions **4** a striding gait

strident /'straɪdənt/ *adj* characterized by harsh and discordant sound; *also* loud and obtrusive – **~ly** *adv* – **-dency** *n*

stridulate /'strɪdjʊleɪt/ *v, esp of crickets, grasshoppers, etc* to make a shrill creaking noise by rubbing together special bodily structures – **-lation** *n*

strife /straɪf/ *n* bitter conflict or dissension

[1]**strike** /straɪk/ *v* **struck; struck** *also* **stricken 1a** to aim a blow at; hit **b** to make an attack **2a** to haul down **b** to

take down the tents of a camp **3a** to collide forcefully **b** to afflict suddenly **4** to delete, cancel **5** to penetrate painfully **6** *of the time* to be indicated by the sounding of a clock, bell, etc **7a** *of light* to fall on **b** *of a sound* to become audible to **8** to cause suddenly to become **9** to cause (a match) to ignite **10a** to make a mental impact on **b** to occur suddenly to **11** to make and ratify (a bargain) **12** *of a fish* to snatch at (bait) **13** to arrive at (a balance) by computation **14** to assume (a pose) **15** to place (a plant cutting) in a medium for rooting **16** to engage in a strike *against*

²strike *n* **1** a work stoppage by a body of workers, made as a protest or to force an employer to comply with demands **2** a success in finding or hitting sthg; *esp* a discovery of a valuable mineral deposit **3** the opportunity to receive the bowling by virtue of being the batsman at the wicket towards which the bowling is being directed **4** an (air) attack on a target

strikebreaker /ˈstraɪk,breɪkəʳ/ *n* one hired to replace a striking worker – **-king** *n*

strike out *v* **1** to delete **2** to set out vigorously

striker /ˈstraɪkəʳ/ *n* **1** a games player who strikes; *esp* a soccer player whose main duty is to score goals **2** a worker on strike

strike up *v* **1** to begin to sing or play **2** to cause to begin

striking /ˈstraɪkɪŋ/ *adj* attracting attention, esp because of unusual or impressive qualities – **~ly** *adv*

¹string /strɪŋ/ *n* **1** a narrow cord used to bind, fasten, or tie **2a** the gut or wire cord of a musical instrument **b** a stringed instrument of an orchestra – usu pl **3a** a group of objects threaded on a string **b** (a set of things arranged in) a sequence **c** a group of usu scattered business concerns **d** the animals, esp horses, belonging to or used by sby **4** *pl* conditions or obligations attached to sthg

²string *v* **strung** **1** to equip with strings **2a** to thread (as if) on a string **b** to tie, hang, or fasten with string **3** to remove the strings of

³string *adj* made with wide meshes and usu of string

string along *v* **1** to accompany sby, esp reluctantly **2** to agree; go along – usu + *with* **3** to deceive, fool *USE* infml

stringent /ˈstrɪndʒənt/ *adj* **1** rigorous or strict, esp with regard to rules or standards **2** marked by money scarcity and credit strictness – **~ly** *adv* – **-gency** *n*

string up *v* to hang; *specif* to kill by hanging

stringy /ˈstrɪŋi/ *adj* **1a** containing or resembling fibrous matter or string **b** sinewy, wiry **2** capable of being drawn out to form a string – **stringiness** *n*

¹strip /strɪp/ *v* **1a(1)** to remove clothing, covering, or surface or extraneous matter from; *esp* to undress **(2)** to perform a striptease **b** to deprive of possessions, privileges, or rank **2** to remove furniture, equipment, or accessories from **3** to damage the thread or teeth of (a screw, cog, etc)

²strip *n* **1a** a long narrow piece of material **b** a long narrow area of land or water **2** *Br* clothes worn by a rugby or soccer team

stripe /straɪp/ *n* **1** a line or narrow band differing in colour or texture from the adjoining parts **2** a bar, chevron, etc of braid or embroidery worn usu on the sleeve of a uniform to indicate rank or length of service

stripling /ˈstrɪplɪŋ/ *n* an adolescent boy

stripper /ˈstrɪpəʳ/ *n* **1** sby who performs a striptease **2** a tool or solvent for removing sthg, esp paint

striptease /ˈstrɪptiːz, ˌstrɪpˈtiːz/ *n* an act or entertainment in which a performer, esp a woman, undresses gradually in view of the audience

stripy /ˈstraɪpi/ *adj* striped

strive /straɪv/ *v* **strove; striven** /ˈstrɪvən/ **1** to struggle in opposition; contend **2** to endeavour; try hard – **~r** *n*

strode /strəʊd/ *past of* **stride**

¹stroke /strəʊk/ *v* to pass the hand over gently in 1 direction

²stroke *n* **1** the act of striking; *esp* a blow with a weapon or implement **2** a single unbroken movement; *esp* one that is repeated **3** a striking of the ball in a game (e g cricket or tennis); *specif* an (attempted) striking of the ball that constitutes the scoring unit in golf **4** an unexpected occurrence **5** (an attack of) sudden usu complete loss of consciousness, sensation, and voluntary motion caused by rupture, thrombosis, etc of a brain artery **6a** (the technique or mode used for) a propelling beat or movement against a resisting medium **b** an oarsman who sits at the stern of a racing rowing boat and sets the pace for the rest of the crew **7** (the distance of) the movement in either direction of a reciprocating mechanical part (e g a piston rod) **8** the sound of a striking clock **9** a mark or dash made by a single movement of an implement

stroll /strəʊl/ *v* to walk in a leisurely or idle manner – **stroll** *n* – **~er** *n*

strong /strɒŋ/ *adj* **1** having or marked by great physical power **2** having moral or intellectual power **3** of a specified number **4a** striking or superior of its kind **b** effective or efficient, esp in a specified area **5** forceful, cogent **6a** rich in some active agent (e g a flavour or extract) **b** *of a colour* intense **7** moving with vigour or force **8** ardent, zealous **9** well established; firm **10** having a pungent or offensive smell or flavour **11** of or being a verb that forms inflections by internal vowel change (e g *drink, drank, drunk*) – **~ly** *adv*

strongarm /ˈstrɒŋɑːm/ *adj* using or involving undue force

strongbox /ˈstrɒŋbɒks/ *n* a strongly made chest for money or valuables

stronghold /ˈstrɒŋhəʊld/ *n* **1** a fortified place **2a** a place of refuge or safety **b** a place dominated by a specified group

strong-minded *adj* marked by firmness and independence of judgment – **~ly** *adv* – **~ness** *n*

strong point *n* sthg in which one excels

strong room *n* a (fireproof and burglarproof) room for money and valuables

strontium /ˈstrɒntiəm/ *n* a soft bivalent metallic element of the alkaline-earth group chemically similar to calcium

strontium 90 *n* a radioactive isotope of strontium present in the fallout from nuclear explosions and hazardous because it can replace calcium in bone

strop /strɒp/ *n* sthg, esp a leather band, for sharpening a razor – **strop** *v*

stroppy /ˈstrɒpi/ *adj, Br* quarrelsome, obstreperous – infml

strove /strəʊv/ *past of* **strive**

[1]**structure** /ˈstrʌktʃəʳ/ *n* **1a** sthg (e g a building) that is constructed **b** sthg organized in a definite pattern **2a** the arrangement of particles or parts in a substance or body **b** arrangement or interrelation of elements – **-ral** *adj* – **-rally** *adv*

[2]**structure** *v* to form into a structure

strudel /ˈstruːdl/ *n* a pastry made from a thin sheet of dough rolled up with filling and baked

[1]**struggle** /ˈstrʌgəl/ *v* **1** to make violent or strenuous efforts against opposition **2** to proceed with difficulty or great effort

[2]**struggle** *n* **1** a violent effort; a determined attempt in adverse circumstances **2** a hard-fought contest

strum /strʌm/ *v* **1** to brush the fingers lightly over the strings of (a musical instrument) in playing **2** to play (music) on a guitar

strumpet /ˈstrʌmpi̥t/ *n* a prostitute

strung /strʌŋ/ *past of* **string**

[1]**strut** /strʌt/ *v* **1** to walk with a proud or erect gait **2** to walk with a pompous air; swagger

[2]**strut** *n* **1** a structural piece designed to resist pressure in the direction of its length **2** a pompous step or walk

strychnine /ˈstrɪkniːn/ *n* a plant product used as a poison (e g for rodents) and medicinally as a stimulant to the central nervous system

[1]**stub** /stʌb/ *n* **1** a short blunt part of a pencil, cigarette, etc left after a larger part has been broken off or used up **2a** a small part of a leaf or page (e g of a chequebook) left on the spine as a record of the contents of the part torn away **b** the part of a ticket returned to the user after inspection

[2]**stub** *v* **1** to extinguish (e g a cigarette) by crushing – usu + *out* **2** to strike (one's foot or toe) against an object

stubble /'stʌbəl/ *n* **1** the stalky remnants of plants, esp cereal grasses, which remain rooted in the soil after harvest **2** a rough growth (e g of beard) resembling stubble – **-bly** *adv*

stubborn /'stʌbən/ *adj* **1** (unreasonably) unyielding or determined **2** refractory, intractable – **~ly** *adv* – **~ness** *n*

stubby /'stʌbi/ *adj* short and thick like a stub

stucco /'stʌkəʊ/ *n* a cement or fine plaster used in the covering and decoration of walls – **stucco** *v*

stuck /stʌk/ *past of* **stick**

stuck-up *adj* superciliously self-important or conceited – infml

[1]stud /stʌd/ *n* **1** *sing or pl in constr* a group of animals, esp horses, kept primarily for breeding **2a** a male animal, esp a stallion, kept for breeding **b** a sexually active man – vulg

[2]stud *n* **1** any of the smaller upright posts in the walls of a building to which panelling or laths are fastened **2a** a rivet or nail with a large head used for ornament or protection **b** a solid button with a shank or eye on the back inserted through an eyelet in a garment as a fastener or ornament **3a** a piece (e g a rod or pin) projecting from a machine and serving chiefly as a support or axis **b** a projecting piece of metal inserted in a horseshoe or snow tyre to increase grip

[3]stud *v* to set thickly with a number of prominent objects

student /'stjuːdənt/ *n* **1** a scholar, learner; *esp* one who attends a college or university **2** an attentive and systematic observer

studied /'stʌdid/ *adj* **1** carefully considered or prepared **2** deliberate, premeditated

studio /'stjuːdiəʊ/ *n* **1a** the workroom of a painter, sculptor, or photographer **b** a place for the study of an art (e g dancing, singing, or acting) **2** a place where films are made; *also, sing or pl in constr* a film production company including its premises and employees **3** a room equipped for the production of radio or television programmes

studio couch *n* an upholstered usu backless couch that can be converted into a double bed by sliding from underneath it the frame of a single bed

studious /'stjuːdɪəs/ *adj* **1** of, concerned with, or given to study **2a** earnest **b** studied, deliberate – **~ly** *adv* – **~ness** *n*

[1]study /'stʌdi/ *n* **1a** the application of the mind to acquiring (specific) knowledge **b** a careful examination or analysis of a subject **2** a room devoted to study **3** a branch of learning **4** a literary or artistic work intended as a preliminary or experimental interpretation

[2]study *v* **1** to engage in the study of **2** to consider attentively or in detail

[1]stuff /stʌf/ *n* **1a** materials, supplies, or equipment used in various activities **b** personal property; possessions **2** a finished textile suitable for clothing; *esp* wool or worsted material **3** an unspecified material substance **4** the essence of a usu abstract thing **5** subject matter

[2]stuff *v* **1a** to fill (as if) by packing things in; cram **b** to gorge (oneself) with food **c** to fill (e g meat or vegetables) with a stuffing **d** to fill with stuffing or padding **e** to fill out the skin of (an animal) for mounting **2** to choke or block *up* (the nasal passages) **3** to force into a limited space; thrust

stuffed shirt *n* a smug, pompous, and usu reactionary person

stuffing /'stʌfɪŋ/ *n* material used to stuff sthg; *esp* a seasoned mixture used to stuff meat, eggs, etc

stuffy /'stʌfi/ *adj* **1a** badly ventilated; close **b** stuffed up **2** stodgy, dull **3** prim, straitlaced – **stuffily** *adv* – **stuffiness** *n*

stultify /'stʌltɪfaɪ/ *v* to make futile or absurd – **-fication** *n*

stumble /'stʌmbəl/ *v* **1** to trip in walking or running **2a** to walk unsteadily or clumsily **b** to speak or act in a hesitant or faltering manner **3** to come unexpectedly or by chance – + *upon, on,* or *across* – **stumble** *n*

stumbling block *n* an obstacle to progress or understanding

[1]stump /stʌmp/ *n* **1** the part of an arm, leg, etc remaining attached to the trunk after the rest is removed **2** the part of a plant, esp a tree, remaining in the ground attached to the root after the stem is cut **3** any of the 3 upright wooden rods that together with the bails form the wicket in cricket

[2]**stump** *v* **1** to walk heavily or noisily **2** *of a wicketkeeper* to dismiss (a batsman who is outside his popping crease but not attempting to run) by breaking the wicket with the ball before it has touched another fieldsman **3** to baffle, bewilder – infml

stumpy /'stʌmpi/ *adj* short and thick; stubby

stun /stʌn/ *v* **1** to make dazed or dizzy (as if) by a blow **2** to overcome, esp with astonishment or disbelief

stung /stʌŋ/ *past of* **sting**

stunk /stʌŋk/ *past of* **stink**

stunner /'stʌnəʳ/ *n* an unusually beautiful or attractive person or thing – infml

stunning /'stʌnɪŋ/ *adj* strikingly beautiful or attractive – infml – **~ly** *adv*

[1]**stunt** /stʌnt/ *v* to hinder or arrest the growth or development of

[2]**stunt** *n* an unusual or difficult feat performed to gain publicity

stunt man *n* sby employed, esp as a substitute for an actor, to perform dangerous feats

stupefy /'stjuːpɨ̥faɪ/ *v* **1** to make groggy or insensible **2** to astonish – **-faction** *n*

stupendous /stjuː'pendəs/ *adj* of astonishing size or greatness; amazing, astounding – **~ly** *adv*

stupid /'stjuːpɨ̥d/ *adj* **1** slow-witted, obtuse **2** dulled in feeling or perception; torpid **3** annoying, exasperating – infml – **~ity** *n* – **~ly** *adv*

stupor /'stjuːpəʳ/ *n* a state of extreme apathy, torpor, or reduced sense or feeling (e g resulting from shock or intoxication)

sturdy /'stɜːdi/ *adj* **1** strongly built or constituted; stout, hardy **2a** having physical strength or vigour; robust **b** firm, resolute – **sturdily** *adv* – **sturdiness** *n*

sturgeon /'stɜːdʒən/ *n* any of various usu large edible fishes whose roe is made into caviar

stutter /'stʌtəʳ/ *v* to speak with involuntary disruption or blocking of speech (e g by spasmodic repetition or prolongation of vocal sounds) – **stutter** *n*

[1]**sty** /staɪ/ *n, pl* **sties** a pigsty

[2]**sty, stye** *n, pl* **styes** an inflamed swelling of a sebaceous gland at the margin of an eyelid

stygian /'stɪdʒɪən/ *adj, often cap* extremely dark or gloomy – fml

[1]**style** /staɪl/ *n* **1** a prolongation of a plant ovary bearing a stigma at the top **2a** a manner of expressing thought in language, esp when characteristic of an individual, period, etc **b** the custom or plan followed in spelling, capitalization, punctuation, and typographic arrangement and display **3** mode of address; a title **4a** a distinctive or characteristic manner of doing sthg **b** excellence or distinction in social behaviour, manners, or appearance – **~less** *adj*

[2]**style** *v* **1** to designate by an identifying term; name **2** to fashion according to a particular mode

stylish /'staɪlɪʃ/ *adj* fashionably elegant – **~ly** *adv* – **~ness** *n*

stylistic /staɪ'lɪɪstɪk/ *adj* of esp literary or artistic style

styl·ize, -ise /'staɪlaɪz/ *v* to make (e g a work of art) conform to a conventional style rather than to nature

stylus /'staɪləs/ *n, pl* **styli, styluses** an instrument for writing, marking, incising, or following a groove: e g **a** an instrument used by ancients for writing on clay or waxed tablets **b** a tiny piece of material (e g diamond) with a rounded tip used in a gramophone to follow the groove on a record

stymie /'staɪmi/ *v* to present an obstacle to; thwart

styptic /'stɪptɪk/ *adj* tending to contract, bind, or check bleeding; astringent – **styptic** *n*

suave /swɑːv/ *adj* smoothly though often superficially affable and polite – **suavity** *n* – **~ly** *adv*

[1]**sub** /sʌb/ *n* a substitute – infml

[2]**sub** *v* **1** to act as a substitute **2** to subedit

[3]**sub** *n* a submarine – infml

[4]**sub** *n, Br* **1** a small loan or advance **2** a subscription *USE* infml

[5]**sub** *n* a subeditor – infml

subcommittee /'sʌbkə,mɪti/ *n* a subdivision of a committee usu organized for a specific purpose

subconscious /sʌb'kɒnʃəs/ *adj* existing in the mind but not immediately available to consciousness – ~**ly** *adv* – **subconscious,** ~**ness** *n*

subcontinent /ˌsʌb'kɒntɪ̇nənt/ *n* a vast subdivision of a continent; *specif, often cap the* Indian subcontinent

[1]**subcontract** /ˌsʌbkən'trækt/ *v* **1** to engage a third party to perform under a subcontract all or part of (work included in an original contract) **2** to undertake (work) under a subcontract

[2]**subcontract** /sʌb'kɒntrækt/ *n* a contract between a party to an original contract and a third party; *esp* one to provide all or a specified part of the work or materials required in the original contract

subcutaneous /ˌsʌbkjuː'teɪnɪəs/ *adj* being, living, used, or made under the skin – ~**ly** *adv*

subdue /səb'djuː/ *v* **1** to conquer and bring into subjection **2** to bring under control; curb **3** to reduce the intensity or degree of (e g colour)

subdued /səb'djuːd/ *adj* **1** brought under control (as if) by military conquest **2** reduced or lacking in force, intensity, or strength

subeditor /'sʌbˌedɪ̇təʳ/ *n* **1** an assistant editor **2** *chiefly Br* one who edits sthg (e g newspaper copy) in preparation for printing

subhuman /sʌb'hjuːmən/ *adj* less than human: e g **a** below the level expected of or suited to normal human beings **b** of animals lower than humans; *esp* anthropoid

[1]**subject** /'sʌbdʒɪkt/ *n* **1a** sby subject to a ruler and governed by his/her law **b** sby who enjoys the protection of and owes allegiance to a sovereign power or state **2a** that of which a quality, attribute, or relation may be stated **b** the entity (e g the mind or ego) that sustains or assumes the form of thought or consciousness **3a** a department of knowledge or learning **b** an individual whose reactions are studied **c(1)** sthg concerning which sthg is said or done **(2)** sby or sthg represented in a work of art **d(1)** the term of a logical proposition denoting that of which sthg is stated, denied, or predicated **(2)** the word or phrase in a sentence or clause denoting that of which sthg is predicated or asserted **e** the principal melodic phrase on which a musical composition or movement is based

[2]**subject** *adj* **1** owing obedience or allegiance to another **2a** liable or exposed to **b** having a tendency or inclination; prone to **3** dependent or conditional on sthg *USE* usu + *to*

[3]**subject** /səb'dʒekt/ *v* **1** to bring under control or rule **2** to make liable; expose **3** to cause to undergo sthg *USE* usu + *to* – ~**ion** *n*

subjective /səb'dʒektɪv/ *adj* **1** of or being a grammatical subject **2a** relating to, determined by, or arising from the mind or self **b** characteristic of or belonging to reality as perceived rather than as independent of mind; phenomenal **3a** peculiar to a particular individual; personal **b** lacking in reality or substance; illusory – ~**ly** *adv* – **-tivity** *n*

subject to *prep* depending on; conditionally upon

sub judice /ˌsʌb 'dʒuːdɪsi/ *adv* before a court; not yet judicially decided

subjugate /'sʌbdʒʊgeɪt/ *v* to conquer and hold in subjection – **-gation** *n*

subjunctive /səb'dʒʌŋktɪv/ *adj* of or being a grammatical mood that represents the denoted act or state not as fact but as contingent or possible or viewed emotionally (e g with doubt or desire)

sublet /ˌsʌb'let/ *v* to lease or rent (all or part of a property) to a subtenant

sublieutenant /ˌsʌb-lef'tenənt, -ləf-/ *n* an officer of the lowest rank in the British navy

sublimate /'sʌblɪ̇meɪt/ *v* **1** to sublime **2** to divert the expression of (an instinctual desire or impulse) from a primitive form to a socially or culturally acceptable one – **-ation** *n*

[1]**sublime** /sə'blaɪm/ *v* to pass directly from the solid to the vapour state

[2]**sublime** *adj* **1** lofty, noble, or exalted in thought, expression, or manner **2** tending to inspire awe, usu because of elevated quality

subliminal /sʌb'lɪmɪ̇nəl/ *adj* existing, functioning, or having effects below the level of conscious awareness – ~**ly** *adv*

[1]**submarine** /'sʌbməri:n, ˌsʌbmə'ri:n/ *adj* being, acting, or growing under water, esp in the sea

[2]**submarine** *n* a vessel designed for undersea operations; *esp* a submarine warship that is typically armed with torpedoes or missiles and uses electric, diesel, or nuclear propulsion

submerge /səb'mɜ:dʒ/ *v* **1** to go or put under water **2** to cover (as if) with water; inundate – ~**nce** *n*

[1]**submersible** /səb'mɜ:səbəl/ *adj* capable of going under water

[2]**submersible** *n* a vessel used for undersea exploration and construction work

submission /səb'mɪʃən/ *n* **1** an act of submitting sthg for consideration, inspection, etc **2** the state of being submissive, humble, or compliant **3** an act of submitting to the authority or control of another

submissive /səb'mɪsɪv/ *adj* willing to submit to others – ~**ly** *adv* – ~**ness** *n*

submit /səb'mɪt/ *v* **1a** to yield to the authority or will of another **b** to subject to a process or practice **2a** to send or commit to another for consideration, inspection, etc **b** to put forward as an opinion; suggest

subnormal /ˌsʌb'nɔ:məl/ *adj* **1** lower or smaller than normal **2** having less of sthg, esp intelligence, than is normal

[1]**subordinate** /sə'bɔ:dɪ̣nət/ *adj* **1** occupying a lower class or rank; inferior **2** subject to or controlled by authority **3** *of a clause* functioning as a noun, adjective, or adverb in a complex sentence (e g the clause *'when he heard"* in *'he laughed when he heard"*) – ~**ly** *adv*

[2]**subordinate** /sə'bɔ:dɪ̣neɪt/ *v* **1** to place in a lower order or class **2** to make subject or subservient; subdue – -**ation** *n* – -**ative** *adj*

suborn /sə'bɔ:n/ *v* to induce to commit perjury or another illegal act

subplot /'sʌbplɒt/ *n* a subordinate plot in fiction or drama

[1]**subpoena** /sə'pi:nə, səb-/ *n* a writ commanding sby to appear in court

[2]**subpoena** *v* **subpoenaing; subpoenaed** to serve with a subpoena

subscribe /səb'skraɪb/ *v* **1a** to give consent or approval to sthg written by signing **b** to give money (e g to charity) **c** to pay regularly in order to receive a periodical or service **2** to feel favourably disposed *USE* usu + *to*

subscriber /səb'skraɪbə[r]/ *n* sby who subscribes; *specif* the owner of a telephone who pays rental and call charges

subscription /səb'skrɪpʃən/ *n* **1** a sum subscribed **2a** a purchase by prepayment for a certain number of issues (e g of a periodical) **b** *Br* membership fees paid regularly

subsequent /'sʌbsɪ̣kwənt/ *adj* following in time or order; succeeding – ~**ly** *adv*

subservient /səb'sɜ:vɪənt/ *adj* obsequiously submissive – ~**ly** *adv* – -**ience** *n*

subside /səb'saɪd/ *v* **1** to sink or fall to the bottom; settle **2a** to descend; *esp* to sink so as to form a depression **b** *of ground* to cave in; collapse **3** to become quiet; abate – ~**nce** *n*

[1]**subsidiary** /səb'sɪdɪəri/ *adj* **1** serving to assist or supplement; auxiliary **2** of secondary importance

[2]**subsidiary** *n* sby or sthg subsidiary; *esp* a company wholly controlled by another

subsidy /'sʌbsɪ̣di/ *n* a grant or gift of money (e g by a government to a person or organization, to assist an enterprise deemed advantageous to the public) – -**dize** *v*

subsist /səb'sɪst/ *v* to have the bare necessities of life; be kept alive – ~**ence** *n*

subsoil /'sʌbsɔɪl/ *n* the layer of weathered material that underlies the surface soil

subsonic /ˌsʌb'sɒnɪk/ *adj* of or relating to (objects moving at) less than the speed of sound

substance /'sʌbstəns/ *n* **1a** a fundamental or essential part or import **b** correspondence with reality **2** ultimate underlying reality **3a** (a) physical material from which sthg is made **b** matter of particular or definite chemical constitution **4** material possessions; property

substandard /ˌsʌbˈstændəd/ *adj* deviating from or falling short of a standard or norm: e g **a** of a quality lower than that prescribed **b** in widespread use but not accepted as linguistically correct by some

substantial /səbˈstænʃəl/ *adj* **1a** having material existence; real **b** important, essential **2** ample to satisfy and nourish **3a** well-to-do, prosperous **b** considerable in quantity; significantly large **4** firmly constructed; solid

substantiate /səbˈstænʃieɪt/ *v* to establish (e g a statement or claim) by proof or evidence; verify **– -ation** *n* **– -ative** *adj*

[1]**substitute** /ˈsʌbstɪ̈tjuːt/ *n* sby or sthg that takes the place of another

[2]**substitute** *v* **1** to exchange for another **2** to take the place of; *also* to introduce a substitute for **– -tution** *n*

subtenant /ˌsʌbˈtenənt/ *n* sby who rents from a tenant

subtend /səbˈtend/ *v* to fix the angular extent of with respect to a fixed point

subterfuge /ˈsʌbtəfjuːdʒ/ *n* **1** deception or trickery used as a means of concealment or evasion **2** a trick or ruse

subterranean /ˌsʌbtəˈreɪnɪən/ *adj* **1** being or operating under the surface of the earth **2** hidden or out of sight

subtitle /ˈsʌbˌtaɪtl/ *n* **1** a secondary or explanatory title **2** a printed explanation (e g a fragment of dialogue or a translation) that appears on the screen during a film

subtle /ˈsʌtl/ *adj* **1** delicate, elusive **2** cleverly contrived; ingenious **3** artful, cunning **– -tly** *adv*

subtlety /ˈsʌtəlti/ *n* **1** the quality of being subtle **2** sthg subtle; *esp* a fine distinction

subtract /səbˈtrækt/ *v* to take away (a quantity or amount) from another **– ~ion** *n*

suburb /ˈsʌbɜːb/ *n* an outlying part of a city or large town

suburbia /səˈbɜːbɪə/ *n* (the inhabitants of) the suburbs of a city

subvert /səbˈvɜːt/ *v* to overthrow or undermine the power of **– -version** *n*

subway /ˈsʌbweɪ/ *n* an underground way: e g **a** a passage under a street (e g for pedestrians, power cables, or water or gas mains) **b** *chiefly NAm* an underground railway

succeed /səkˈsiːd/ *v* **1a** to inherit sthg, esp sovereignty, rank, or title **b** to follow after another in order **2** to have a favourable or desired result; turn out well

success /səkˈses/ *n* **1** a favourable outcome to an undertaking **2** the attainment of wealth or fame **3** sby or sthg that succeeds **– ~ful** *adj* **– ~fully** *adv*

succession /səkˈseʃən/ *n* **1** the order or right of succeeding to a property, title, or throne **2a** the act of following in order; a sequence **b** the act or process of becoming entitled to a deceased person's property or title

successive /səkˈsesɪv/ *adj* following one after the other in succession **– ~ly** *adv*

successor /səkˈsesəʳ/ *n* sby or sthg that follows another; *esp* a person who succeeds to throne, title, or office

succinct /səkˈsɪŋkt/ *adj* clearly expressed in few words; concise **– ~ly** *adv* **– ~ness** *n*

[1]**succour** /ˈsʌkəʳ/ *n* relief; *also* aid, help

[2]**succour** *v* to go to the aid of (sby in need or distress)

succubus /ˈsʌkjʊbəs/ *n, pl* **succubi** a female demon believed to have sexual intercourse with men in their sleep

[1]**succulent** /ˈsʌkjʊlənt/ *adj* **1** full of juice; juicy **2** *of a plant* having juicy fleshy tissues **– -lence** *n*

[2]**succulent** *n* a succulent plant (e g a cactus)

succumb /səˈkʌm/ *v* to yield or give in *to*

[1]**such** /sətʃ, sʌtʃ; *strong* sʌtʃ/ *adj or adv* **1a** of the kind, quality, or extent – used before *as* to introduce an example or comparison **b** of the same sort **2** of so extreme a degree or extraordinary a nature – used before *as* to suggest that a name is unmerited (e g we forced down the soup, *such* as it was)

[2]**such** /sʌtʃ/ *pron, pl* **such** **1** *pl* such people; those **2** that thing, fact, or action (e g *such* was the result) **3** *pl*

similar people or things (e g tin and glass and *such*)

¹suchlike /'sʌtʃlaɪk/ *adj* of like kind; similar

²suchlike *pron* a similar person or thing

¹suck /sʌk/ *v* **1** to draw sthg into esp the mouth by suction; *esp* to draw milk from a breast or udder with the mouth **2** to act in an obsequious manner – infml; usu + *up*

²suck *n* **1** the act of sucking **2** a sucking movement

sucker /'sʌkəʳ/ *n* **1a** a mouth (e g of a leech) or other animal organ adapted for sucking or sticking **b** a device, esp of rubber, that can cling to a surface by suction **2** a shoot from the roots or lower part of the stem of a plant **3a** a gullible person – infml **b** a person irresistibly attracted by sthg specified – infml

suckle /'sʌkəl/ *v* to give milk to from the breast or udder; *also* to receive milk from the udder or breast of

suckling /'sʌklɪŋ/ *n* a young unweaned animal

sucrose /'suːkrəʊz, 'sjuː-/ *n* the sugar obtained from sugarcane and sugar beet and occurring in most plants

suction /'sʌkʃən/ *n* **1** the act of sucking **2** the action of exerting a force on a solid, liquid, or gaseous body by means of reduced air pressure over part of its surface

¹sudden /'sʌdn/ *adj* **1a** happening or coming unexpectedly **b** abrupt, steep **2** marked by or showing haste – **~ly** *adv* – **~ness** *n*

suds /sʌdz/ *n pl but sing or pl in constr* (the lather on) soapy water – **sudsy** *adj*

sue /suː, sjuː/ *v* **1** to bring a legal action against **2** to make a request or application – usu + *for* or *to*

suede /sweɪd/ *n* leather with a napped surface

suet /'suːʝt, 'sjuːʝt/ *n* the hard fat round the kidneys in beef and mutton esp as used in cooking – **~y** *adj*

suffer /'sʌfəʳ/ *v* **1** to submit to or be forced to endure pain, distress, etc **2** to allow, permit **3** to sustain loss or damage **4** to be handicapped or at a disadvantage

sufferance /'sʌfərəns/ *n* tacit permission

suffering /'sʌfərɪŋ/ *n* the state of one who suffers

suffice /sə'faɪs/ *v* to be enough (for)

sufficiency /sə'fɪʃənsi/ *n* **1** sufficient means to meet one's needs **2** the quality of being sufficient; adequacy

sufficient /sə'fɪʃənt/ *adj* enough to meet the needs of a situation – **~ly** *adv*

suffix /'sʌfɪks/ *n* an affix (e g *-ness* in *happiness*) appearing at the end of a word or phrase or following a root

suffocate /'sʌfəkeɪt/ *v* **1** to stop the breathing of (e g by asphyxiation) **2** to make uncomfortable by want of cool fresh air – **-cation** *n*

suffrage /'sʌfrɪdʒ/ *n* the right of voting

suffragette /,sʌfrə'dʒet/ *n* a woman who advocates suffrage for her sex

suffuse /sə'fjuːz/ *v* to spread over or through, esp with a liquid or colour; permeate – **-fusion** *n*

¹sugar /'ʃʊgəʳ/ *n* any of a class of water-soluble carbohydrates that are of varying sweetness and include glucose, ribose, and sucrose; *specif* a sweet crystallizable material that consists of sucrose, is colourless or white when pure tending to brown when less refined, is obtained commercially esp from sugarcane or sugar beet, and is used as a sweetener and preservative of other foods – **~less** *adj*

²sugar *v* to make palatable or attractive

sugar beet *n* a white-rooted beet grown for the sugar in its root

sugar cane /'ʃʊgəkeɪn/ *n* a stout tall grass widely grown in warm regions as a source of sugar

sugar daddy *n* a usu elderly man who lavishes gifts and money on a young woman in return for sex or companionship

sugary /'ʃʊgəri/ *adj* **1** containing, resembling, or tasting of sugar **2** exaggeratedly or cloyingly sweet

suggest /sə'dʒest/ *v* **1** to put forward as a possibility or for consideration **2a** to call to mind by thought or association; evoke **b** to indicate the presence of

suggestible /sə'dʒestəbəl/ *adj* easily influenced by suggestion

suggestion /sə'dʒestʃən/ *n* **1** sthg suggested; a proposal **2a** indirect means (e g the natural association of ideas) to evoke ideas or feeling **b** the impressing of an idea, attitude, desired action, etc on the mind of another **3** a slight indication; a trace

suggestive /sə'dʒestɪv/ *adj* **1a** indicative **b** evocative **2** suggesting sthg improper or indecent – **~ly** *adv*

suicidal /ˌsuːɟ'saɪdl, ˌsjuː-/ *adj* **1** dangerous, esp to life **2** harmful to one's own interests – **~ly** *adv*

suicide /'suːɟsaɪd, 'sjuː-/ *n* **1a** (an) act of taking one's own life intentionally **b** ruin of one's own interests **2** one who commits or attempts suicide

[1]**suit** /suːt, sjuːt/ *n* **1** a legal action **2** a petition or appeal; *specif* courtship **3** a group of things forming a unit or constituting a collection – used chiefly with reference to sails **4a** an outer costume of 2 or more matching pieces that are designed to be worn together **b** a costume to be worn for a specified purpose **5** all the playing cards in a pack bearing the same symbol (i e hearts, clubs, diamonds, or spades)

[2]**suit** *v* **1** to be appropriate or satisfactory **2a** to be good for the health or well-being of **b** to be becoming to; look right with **3** to satisfy, please

suitable /'suːtəbəl, 'sjuː-/ *adj* appropriate, fitting – **-bility** *n* – **~ness** *n* – **-bly** *adv*

suitcase /'suːtkeɪs, 'sjuːt-/ *n* a rectangular usu rigid case with a hinged lid and a handle, used for carrying articles (e g clothes)

suite /swiːt/ *n* **1** *sing or pl in constr* a retinue; *esp* the personal staff accompanying an official or dignitary on business **2a** a group of rooms occupied as a unit **b** a musical work consisting of several loosely connected instrumental pieces **c** a set of matching furniture (e g a settee and 2 armchairs) for a room

suitor /'suːtəʳ, 'sjuː-/ *n* one who courts a woman with a view to marriage

[1]**sulk** /sʌlk/ *v* to be moodily silent

[2]**sulk** *n* a fit of sulking – usu pl with sing. meaning

sullen /'sʌlən/ *adj* **1** silently gloomy or resentful; ill-humoured and unsociable **2** dismal, gloomy – **~ly** *adv* – **~ness** *n*

sully /'sʌli/ *v* to mar the purity of; tarnish

sulphate /'sʌlfeɪt/ *n* a salt or ester of sulphuric acid

sulphide /'sʌlfaɪd/ *n* a compound of sulphur, usu with a more electropositive element

sulphur /'sʌlfəʳ/ *n* **1** a nonmetallic element chemically resembling oxygen that occurs esp as yellow crystals **2** a pale greenish yellow colour

sulphuric acid /sʌlˌfjʊərɪk 'æsɟd/ *n* a corrosive oily strong acid that is a vigorous oxidizing and dehydrating agent

sultan /'sʌltən/ *n* a sovereign of a Muslim state

sultana /sʊl'tɑːnə/ *n* **1** a sultan's wife **2** (the raisin of) a pale yellow seedless grape

sultry /'sʌltri/ *adj* **1** oppressively hot and humid **2** (capable of) exciting strong sexual desire; sensual – **-trily** *adv* – **-triness** *n*

sum /sʌm/ *n* **1** a (specified) amount of money **2** the whole amount; the total **3a** the result of adding numbers **b** numbers to be added; *broadly* a problem in arithmetic – **sum** *v*

[1]**summary** /'sʌməri/ *adj* **1** concise but comprehensive **2a** done quickly without delay or formality **b** of or using a summary proceeding; *specif* tried or triable in a magistrates' court – **-rily** *adv*

[2]**summary** *n* a brief account covering the main points of sthg – **-arize** *v*

summation /sə'meɪʃən/ *n* **1** the act or process of forming a sum **2** a total **3** (a) summing up of an argument

[1]**summer** /'sʌməʳ/ *n* **1** the season between spring and autumn comprising in the northern hemisphere the months of June, July, and August **2** a period of maturity **3** a year – chiefly poetic

[2]**summer** *adj* sown in the spring and harvested in the same year as sown

summerhouse /'sʌməhaʊs/ *n* a

small building in a garden designed to provide a shady place in summer

summer school *n* a course of teaching held during the summer vacation, esp on university premises

summer time *n* a system of having clock time behind solar time so as to make use of daylight hours in the summer

summery /'sʌməri/ *adj* of, suggesting, or suitable for summer

summing-up *n* **1** a concluding summary **2** a survey of evidence given by a judge to the jury before it considers its verdict

summit /'sʌmɨ̵t/ *n* **1** a top; *esp* the highest point or peak **2** the topmost level attainable; the pinnacle **3** a conference of highest-level officials

summon /'sʌmən/ *v* **1** to command by a summons to appear in court **2** to call upon to come; send for

summons /'sʌmənz/ *n, pl* **summonses** a written notification warning sby to appear in court

sump /sʌmp/ *n* **1a** a cesspool **b** *chiefly Br* the lower section of the crankcase used as a lubricating-oil reservoir in an internal-combustion engine **2** the lowest part of a mine shaft, into which water drains

sumptuous /'sʌmptʃʊəs/ *adj* lavishly rich, costly, or luxurious – **~ly** *adv* – **~ness** *n*

sum up *v* **1** to summarize **2** to form or express a rapid appraisal of

[1]**sun** /sʌn/ *n* **1a** the star nearest to the earth, round which the earth and other planets revolve **b** a star or other celestial body that emits its own light **2** the heat or light radiated from the sun

[2]**sun** *v* to expose oneself to the rays of the sun

sunbaked /'sʌnbeɪkt/ *adj* baked hard by exposure to sunshine

sunbathe /'sʌnbeɪð/ *v* to expose the body to the rays of the sun or a sunlamp – **~r** *n*

sunbeam /'sʌnbiːm/ *n* a ray of light from the sun

sunblind /'sʌnblaɪnd/ *n* an awning or a shade on a window (e g a venetian blind) that gives protection from the sun's rays

sunburn /'sʌnbɜːn/ *v* to burn or tan by exposure to sunlight – **sunburn** *n*

sundae /'sʌndeɪ/ *n* an ice cream served with a topping of fruit, nuts, syrup, etc

[1]**Sunday** /'sʌndeɪ, -di/ *n* **1** the day of the week falling between Saturday and Monday, observed by Christians as a day of worship **2** a newspaper published on Sundays

[2]**Sunday** *adj* **1** of or associated with Sunday **2** amateur – derog

Sunday best *n sing or pl in constr* one's best clothes – infml

Sunday school *n* a class usu of religious instruction held, esp for children, on Sundays

sunder /'sʌndəʳ/ *v* to break apart or in two; sever

sundew /'sʌndjuː/ *n* any of a genus of bog plants with long glistening hairs on the leaves that attract and trap insects

sundial /'sʌndaɪəl/ *n* an instrument to show the time of day by the shadow of a pointer on a graduated plate

sundown /'sʌndaʊn/ *n* sunset

sundrenched /'sʌndrentʃt/ *adj* exposed to much hot sunshine

[1]**sundry** /'sʌndri/ *adj* miscellaneous, various

[2]**sundry** *pron pl in constr* an indeterminate number – chiefly in *all and sundry*

[3]**sundry** *n* **1** *pl* miscellaneous small articles or items **2** *Austr* a run in cricket that is not credited to a batsman; an extra

sunflower /'sʌnˌflaʊəʳ/ *n* any of a genus of composite plants with large yellow-rayed flower heads bearing edible seeds that are often used as animal feed and yield an edible oil

sung /sʌŋ/ *past of* **sing**

sunglasses /'sʌnˌglɑːsɨ̵z/ *n pl* glasses to protect the eyes from the sun

sunk /sʌŋk/ *past of* **sink**

sunken /'sʌŋkən/ *adj* **1** submerged; *esp* lying at the bottom of a body of water **2a** hollow, recessed **b** lying or constructed below the surrounding or normal level

sunlight /'sʌnlaɪt/ *n* sunshine

sunlounge /'sʌnlaʊndʒ/ *n* a room

having a large glazed area placed to admit much sunlight

sunny /'sʌni/ *adj* **1** bright with sunshine **2** cheerful, optimistic **3** exposed to or warmed by the sun – **-nily** *adv* – **-niness** *n*

sunrise /'sʌnraɪz/ *n* (the time of) the rising of the topmost part of the sun above the horizon as a result of the rotation of the earth

sunroof /'sʌnruːf/ *n* a motor-car roof having an opening or removable panel

sunset /'sʌnset/ *n* (the time of) the descent of the topmost part of the sun below the horizon as a result of the rotation of the earth

sunshade /'sʌnʃeɪd/ *n* **1** a parasol **2** an awning

sunshine /'sʌnʃaɪn/ *n* the sun's light or direct rays

sunspot /'sʌnspɒt/ *n* a transient dark marking on the visible surface of the sun caused by a relatively cooler area

sunstroke /'sʌnstrəʊk/ *n* heatstroke caused by direct exposure to the sun

suntan /'sʌntæn/ *n* a browning of the skin from exposure to the sun – **~ned** *adj*

suntrap /'sʌntræp/ *n* a sheltered place that receives a large amount of sunshine

[1]**sup** /sʌp/ *v, chiefly dial* to drink (liquid) in small mouthfuls – **sup** *n*

[2]**sup** *v* **1** to eat the evening meal **2** to make one's supper – + *on* or *off*

[1]**super** /'suːpəʳ, 'sjuː-/ *n* **1** a superfine grade or extra large size **2** a police or other superintendent – infml

[2]**super** *adj* – used as a general term of approval; infml

superb /suː'pɜːb, sjuː-/ *adj* **1** marked by grandeur or magnificence **2** of excellent quality – **~ly** *adv*

supercharger /'suːpə,tʃɑːdʒəʳ/ *n* a device supplying fuel or air to an internal-combustion engine at a pressure higher than normal for greater efficiency

supercilious /,suːpə'sɪlɪəs/ *adj* coolly disdainful – **~ly** *adv* – **~ness** *n*

superconductivity /,suːpəkɒndʌk'tɪvɨti, ,sjuː-/ *n* a complete disappearance of electrical resistance in various metals and alloys at temperatures near absolute zero

superficial /,suːpə'fɪʃəl, ,sjuː-/ *adj* **1** not penetrating below the surface **2a** not thorough or profound; shallow **b** apparent rather than real – **~ity** *n* – **~ly** *adv*

superfluous /suː'pɜːflʊəs, sjuː-/ *adj* exceeding what is sufficient or necessary – **~ly** *adv* – **~ness, -fluity** *n*

superhuman /,suːpə'hjuːmən, ,sjuː-/ *adj* **1** being above the human; divine **2** exceeding normal human power, size, or capability

superimpose /,suːpərɪm'pəʊz, ,sjuː-/ *v* to place or lay over or above sthg

superintend /,suːpərɪn'tend, ,sjuː-/ *v* to be in charge of; direct

superintendent /,suːpərɪn'tendənt, ,sjuː-/ *n* **1** one who supervises or manages sthg **2** a British police officer ranking next above a chief inspector

[1]**superior** /suː'pɪərɪəʳ, sjuː-/ *adj* **1** situated higher up; upper **2** of higher rank or status **3a** greater in quality, amount, or worth **b** excellent of its kind **4** *of an animal or plant part* situated above or at the top of another (corresponding) part **5** thinking oneself better than others; supercilious – **~ity** *n*

[2]**superior** *n* **1** a person who is above another in rank or office **2** sby or sthg that surpasses another in quality or merit

[1]**superlative** /suː'pɜːlətɪv, sjuː-/ *adj* **1** of or constituting the degree of grammatical comparison expressing an extreme or unsurpassed level or extent **2** surpassing all others; of the highest degree

[2]**superlative** *n* an exaggerated expression, esp of praise

superman /'suːpəmæn, 'sjuː-/ *n* a person of extraordinary power or achievements – infml

supermarket /'suːpə,mɑːkɨt, 'sjuː-/ *n* a usu large self-service retail shop selling foods and household merchandise

supernatural /,suːpə'nætʃərəl, ,sjuː-/ *adj* **1** of an order of existence or an agency (e g a god or spirit) not bound by normal laws of cause and effect **2a** departing from what is usual or normal, esp in nature **b** attributed to an invisible agent (e g a ghost or spirit) – ~**ly** *adv*

supernova /ˌsuːpəˈnəʊvə, ˌsjuː-/ *n* any of the rarely observed nova outbursts in which the luminosity reaches 100 million times that of the sun

superscription /ˌsuːpəˈskrɪpʃən, ˌsjuː-/ *n* words written on the surface of, outside, or above sthg else; an inscription

supersede /ˌsuːpəˈsiːd, ˌsjuː-/ *v* **1** to take the place of (esp sthg inferior or outmoded) **2** to displace in favour of another; supplant – **-session** *n*

supersonic /ˌsuːpəˈsɒnɪk, ˌsjuː-/ *adj* **1** (using, produced by, or relating to waves or vibrations) having a frequency above the upper threshold of human hearing of about 20,000Hz **2** of, being, or using speeds from 1 to 5 times the speed of sound in air

superstition /ˌsuːpəˈstɪʃən, ˌsjuː-/ *n* **1** a belief or practice resulting from ignorance, fear of the unknown, trust in magic or chance, or a false conception of causation **2** an irrational abject attitude of mind towards the supernatural, nature, or God resulting from superstition – **-tious** *adj* – **-tiously** *adv*

superstructure /ˈsuːpəˌstrʌktʃəʳ, ˈsjuː-/ *n* **1a** the part of a building above the ground **b** the structural part of a ship above the main deck **2** an entity or complex based on a more fundamental one

supertax /ˈsuːpətæks, ˈsjuː-/ *n* a tax paid in addition to normal tax by people with high incomes

supervene /ˌsuːpəˈviːn, ˌsjuː-/ *v* to happen in a way that interrupts some plan or process – fml

supervise /ˈsuːpəvaɪz, ˈsjuː-/ *v* to superintend, oversee – **-vision** *n* – **-visor** *n* – **-visory** *adj*

supine /ˈsuːpaɪn, ˈsjuː-/ *adj* **1** lying on the back or with the face upwards **2** mentally or morally lazy; lethargic

supper /ˈsʌpəʳ/ *n* (the food for) a usu light evening meal or snack – ~**less** *n*

supplant /səˈplɑːnt/ *v* to take the place of (another), esp by force or treachery – ~**er** *n*

supple /ˈsʌpəl/ *adj* **1** capable of easily being bent or folded; pliant **2** able to perform bending or twisting movements with ease and grace; lithe

supplement /ˈsʌplʒmənt/ *n* **1** sthg that completes, adds, or makes good a deficiency, or makes an addition **2** a part issued to update or extend a book or periodical – **supplement** *v*

supplementary /ˌsʌplʒˈmentəri/ *adj* additional

supplementary benefit *n* British social-security benefit paid to those who do not qualify for unemployment benefit

supplicant /ˈsʌplɪkənt/ *adj* humbly imploring or entreating – **supplicant** *n*

[1]**supply** /səˈplaɪ/ *v* **1** to provide for; satisfy **2** to provide, furnish – **-lier** *n*

[2]**supply** *n* **1a** the quantity or amount needed or available **b** provisions, stores – usu pl with sing. meaning **2** the quantities of goods and services offered for sale at a particular time or at one price **3 supply, supply teacher** *Br* a teacher who fills a temporary vacancy

[1]**support** /səˈpɔːt/ *v* **1** to bear, tolerate **2a(1)** to promote the interests of; encourage **(2)** to argue or vote for **b** to assist, help **3** to provide livelihood or subsistence for **4** to hoid up or serve as a foundation or prop for – ~**ive** *adj*

[2]**support** *n* **1** supporting or being supported **2** maintenance, sustenance **3** a device that supports sthg **4** *sing or pl in constr* a body of supporters

supporter /səˈpɔːtəʳ/ *n* **1** an adherent or advocate **2** either of 2 figures (e g of men or animals) placed one on each side of a heraldic shield as if holding or guarding it

suppose /səˈpəʊz/ *v* **1a** to lay down tentatively as a hypothesis, assumption, or proposal **b(1)** to hold as an opinion; believe **(2)** to conjecture, think **2** to devise for a purpose; intend **3** to presuppose **4** to allow, permit – used negatively **5** to expect because of moral, legal, or other obligations *USE* (*2, 4, & 5*) chiefly in *be supposed to*

supposed /səˈpəʊzd/ *adj* believed or imagined to be such – ~**ly** *adv*

supposition /ˌsʌpəˈzɪʃən/ *n* a hypothesis

suppository /səˈpɒzɪ̈təri/ *n* a readily meltable cone or cylinder of medicated material for insertion into a bodily passage or cavity (e g the rectum)

suppress /səˈpres/ *v* **1** to put down by authority or force **2** to stop the publication or revelation of **3** to hold back, check **4** to inhibit the growth or development of – **~ion** *n*

suppressor /səˈpresəʳ/ *n* an electrical component (e g a capacitor) added to a circuit to suppress oscillations that would otherwise cause radio interference

suppurate /ˈsʌpjʊreɪt/ *v* to form or discharge pus – **-ration** *n*

supremacy /səˈpreməsi/ *n* the state of being supreme; supreme authority, power, or position

supreme /suːˈpriːm, sjuː-, sə-/ *adj* **1** highest in rank or authority **2** highest in degree or quality – **~ly** *adv*

Supreme Court *n* the highest judicial tribunal in a nation or state

¹surcharge /ˈsɜːtʃɑːdʒ/ *v* to subject to an additional or excessive charge

²surcharge *n* **1** an additional tax or cost **2** an extra fare

surd /sɜːd/ *n* an irrational root (e g $\sqrt{2}$); *also* an algebraic expression containing irrational roots

¹sure /ʃʊəʳ, ʃɔːʳ/ *adj* **1** firm, secure **2** reliable, trustworthy **3** assured, confident **4** bound, certain – **~ness** *n*

²sure *adv, chiefly NAm* surely, certainly – infml

surefire /ˈʃʊəfaɪəʳ, ˈʃɔː-/ *adj* certain to succeed – infml

surefooted /ˌʃʊəˈfʊtɪ̈d,ˌʃɔː-/ *adj* not liable to stumble or fall – **~ly** *adv* – **~ness** *n*

surely /ˈʃʊəli/ *adv* **1** without doubt; certainly **2** it is to be believed, hoped, or expected that

surety /ˈʃʊərɪ̈ti/ *n* **1** a guarantee **2** sby who assumes legal liability for the debt, default, or failure in duty (e g appearance in court) of another

surf /sɜːf/ *n* the foam and swell of waves breaking on the shore

¹surface /ˈsɜːfɪ̈s/ *n* **1** the external or upper boundary or layer of an object or body **2** (a portion of) the boundary of a three-dimensional object **3** the external or superficial aspect of sthg

²surface *v* **1** to come to the surface; emerge **2** to wake up; *also* get up – infml

³surface *adj* **1** situated or employed on the surface, esp of the earth or sea **2** lacking depth; superficial

surfboard /ˈsɜːfbɔːd/ *n* a usu long narrow buoyant board used in surfing

¹surfeit /ˈsɜːfɪ̈t/ *n* **1** an excessive amount **2** excessive indulgence in food, drink, etc

²surfeit *v* to fill to excess; satiate

¹surge /sɜːdʒ/ *v* to rise and move (as if) in waves or billows

²surge *n* the motion of swelling, rolling, or sweeping forwards like a wave

surgeon /ˈsɜːdʒən/ *n* a medical specialist who practises surgery

surgery /ˈsɜːdʒəri/ *n* **1** medicine that deals with diseases and conditions requiring or amenable to operative or manual procedures **2** a surgical operation **3** *Br* (the hours of opening of) a doctor's, dentist's, etc room where patients are advised or treated **4** *Br* a session at which an elected representative (e g an MP) is available for usu informal consultation

surgical /ˈsɜːdʒɪkəl/ *adj* of surgeons or surgery – **~ly** *adv*

surly /ˈsɜːli/ *adj* irritably sullen and churlish

¹surmise /səˈmaɪz/ *v* to infer on scanty evidence; guess

²surmise /səˈmaɪz, ˈsɜːmaɪz/ *n* a conjecture or guess – fml

surmount /səˈmaʊnt/ *v* **1** to overcome, conquer **2** to get over or above – **~able** *adj*

surname /ˈsɜːneɪm/ *n* the name shared in common by members of a family

surpass /səˈpɑːs/ *v* **1** to go beyond in quality, degree, or performance; exceed **2** to transcend the reach, capacity, or powers of – **~ing** *adj* – **~ingly** *adv*

surplice /ˈsɜːplɪ̈s/ *n* a loose white outer ecclesiastical vestment usu of knee length with large open sleeves – **~d** *adj*

surplus /ˈsɜːpləs/ *n* **1** the amount in

excess of what is used or needed **2** an excess of receipts over disbursements

[1]**surprise** /sə'praɪz/ *n* **1** an act of taking unawares **2** sthg unexpected or surprising **3** the feeling caused by an unexpected event; astonishment

[2]**surprise** *v* **1** to take unawares **2** to fill with wonder or amazement

surprising /sə'praɪzɪŋ/ *adj* causing surprise; unexpected – **~ly** *adv*

surrealism /sə'rɪəlɪzəm/ *n, often cap* a 20th-c movement in art and literature seeking to use the incongruous images formed by the unconscious to transcend reality as perceived by the conscious mind; *also* surrealistic practices or atmosphere – **-ist** *adj, n* – **-istic** *adj*

[1]**surrender** /sə'rendəʳ/ **1a** to give oneself up into the power of another; yield **b** to relinquish; give up **2** to abandon (oneself) to sthg unrestrainedly

[2]**surrender** *n* **1** the act or an instance of surrendering oneself or sthg **2** the voluntary cancellation of an insurance policy by the party insured in return for a payment

surreptitious /ˌsʌrəp'tɪʃəs/ *adj* done, made, or acquired by stealth; clandestine – **~ly** *adv* – **~ness** *n*

surrogate /'sʌrəgeɪt, -gɪt/ *n* **1** a deputy **2** sthg that serves as a substitute

[1]**surround** /sə'raʊnd/ *v* **1a** to enclose on all sides **b** to be part of the environment of; be present round **2** to form a ring round; encircle – **~ing** *adj*

[2]**surround** *n* a border or edging

surroundings /sə'raʊndɪŋz/ *n pl* the circumstances, conditions, or objects by which one is surrounded

surtax /'sɜːtæks/ *n* a graduated income tax formerly imposed in the UK in addition to the normal income tax if one's net income exceeded a specified sum

surveillance /sɜː'veɪləns/ *n* close watch kept over sby or sthg

[1]**survey** /sə'veɪ/ *v* **1a** to look over and examine closely **b** to examine the condition of and often give a value for (a building) **2** to determine and portray the form, extent, and position of (e g a tract of land) **3** to view as a whole or from a height

[2]**survey** /'sɜːveɪ/ *n* a surveying or being surveyed; *also* sthg surveyed

surveyor /sə'veɪəʳ/ *n* sby whose occupation is surveying land

survival /sə'vaɪvəl/ *n* **1a** the condition of living or continuing **b** the continuation of life or existence **2** sby or sthg that survives, esp after others of its kind have disappeared

survive /sə'vaɪv/ *v* to remain alive or in existence; live on – **-vivor** *n*

susceptible /sə'septəbəl/ *adj* **1** capable of submitting to an action, process, or operation **2** open, subject, or unresistant to some stimulus, influence, or agency **3** easily moved or emotionally affected; impressionable – **-bility** *n*

[1]**suspect** /'sʌspekt/ *adj* (deserving to be) regarded with suspicion

[2]**suspect** /'sʌspekt/ *n* sby who is suspected

[3]**suspect** /sə'spekt/ *v* **1** to be suspicious of; distrust **2** to believe to be guilty without conclusive proof **3** to imagine to be true, likely, or probable

suspend /sə'spend/ *v* **1** to debar temporarily from a privilege, office, membership, or employment **2** to make temporarily inoperative **3** to defer till later on certain conditions **4** to hang, esp so as to be free on all sides

suspender /sə'spendəʳ/ *n* **1** an elasticated band with a fastening device for holding up a sock **2** *Br* any of the fastening devices on a suspender belt **3** *pl, NAm* braces

suspender belt *n, Br* a garment consisting of 2 pairs of short straps hanging from a girdle to which are attached fastening devices for holding up a woman's stockings

suspense /sə'spens/ *n* a state of uncertain expectation as to a decision or outcome

suspension /sə'spenʃən/ *n* **1a** temporary removal from office or privileges **b** temporary withholding or postponement **c** temporary abolishing of a law or rule **2a** hanging or being hung **b** a solid that is dispersed, but not dissolved, in a solid, liquid, or gas **3** the system of devices supporting the upper part of a vehicle on the axles

suspicion /sə'spɪʃən/ *n* **1a** suspecting

or being suspected **b** a feeling of doubt or mistrust **2** a slight touch or trace

suspicious /sə'spɪʃəs/ *adj* **1** tending to arouse suspicion; dubious **2** inclined to suspect; distrustful – **~ly** *adv* – **~ness** *n*

sustain /sə'steɪn/ *v* **1** to give support or relief to **2** to cause to continue; prolong **3** to buoy up the spirits of **4** to suffer, undergo

sustenance /'sʌstənəns/ *n* **1** food, provisions; *also* nourishment **2** sustaining

suttee /'sʌtiː/ *n* the custom of a Hindu widow willingly being cremated on the funeral pile of her husband; *also* such a widow

suture /'suːtʃəʳ/ *n* **1a** the sewing together of parts of the living body **b** a stitch made in a suture **2** the solid join between 2 bones (e g of the skull)

suzerain /'suːzəreɪn/ *n* **1** a feudal overlord **2** a dominant state controlling the foreign relations of an internally autonomous vassal state – **~ty** *n*

svelte /svelt/ *adj* slender, lithe

[1]**swab** /swɒb/ *n* a wad of absorbent material used for applying medication, cleaning wounds, taking bacterial specimens, etc

[2]**swab** *v* **1** to clean (a wound) with a swab **2** to clean (a surface, esp a deck) by washing (e g with a mop) – often + *down*

swaddle /'swɒdl/ *v* **1** to wrap an infant tightly in narrow strips of cloth **2** to swathe, envelop

swag /swæg/ *n* **1a** an arrangement of fabric hanging in a heavy curve or fold **b** a suspended cluster (e g of flowers) **2** *chiefly Austr* a pack or roll of personal belongings **3** goods acquired, esp by unlawful means; loot – infml

[1]**swagger** /'swægəʳ/ *v* to behave or esp walk in an arrogant or pompous manner – **~er** *n* – **~ingly** *adv*

[2]**swagger** *n* **1** an act or instance of swaggering **2** arrogant or conceitedly self-assured behaviour

swain /sweɪn/ *n* **1** a male admirer or suitor **2** a peasant; *specif* a shepherd – chiefly poetic

[1]**swallow** /'swɒləʊ/ *n* any of numerous small long-winged migratory birds noted for their graceful flight, that have a short bill, a forked tail, and feed on insects caught while flying

[2]**swallow** *v* **1** to take through the mouth into the stomach **2** to envelop, engulf **3** to accept without question or protest; *also* to believe naively **4** to refrain from expressing or showing – **~er** *n*

[3]**swallow** *n* an amount that can be swallowed at one time

swam /swæm/ *past of* **swim**

[1]**swamp** /swɒmp/ *n* (an area of) wet spongy land sometimes covered with water – **~y** *adj*

[2]**swamp** *v* **1** to inundate, submerge **2** to overwhelm by an excess of work, difficulties, etc

[1]**swan** /swɒn/ *n* any of various heavy-bodied long-necked mostly pure white aquatic birds larger than geese

[2]**swan** *v* to wander or travel aimlessly – infml

[1]**swank** /swæŋk/ *v* to swagger; show off – infml

[2]**swank** *n* (one given to) pretentiousness or swagger – infml – **~y** *adj* – **~iness** *n*

swan song *n* a farewell appearance or final work or pronouncement

swap, swop /swɒp/ *n* **1** an act of exchanging one thing for another **2** sthg so exchanged – **swap, swop** *v*

[1]**swarm** /swɔːm/ *n* **1** a colony of honeybees, esp when emigrating from a hive with a queen bee to start a new colony elsewhere **2** *sing or pl in constr* a group of animate or inanimate things, esp when massing together

[2]**swarm** *v* **1** to collect together and depart from a hive **2** to move or assemble in a crowd **3** to contain a swarm; teem

[3]**swarm** *v* to climb, esp with the hands and feet – usu + *up*

swarthy /'swɔːði/ *adj* of a dark colour, complexion, or cast

swashbuckler /'swɒʃˌbʌkləʳ/ *n* a swaggering adventurer or daredevil – **-ling** *adj*

swastika /'swɒstɪkə/ *n* an ancient symbol in the shape of a cross with the ends of the arms extended at right angles in a clockwise or anticlockwise direction

[1]**swat** /swɒt/ *v* to hit with a sharp slapping blow; *esp* to kill (an insect) with such a blow – ~**ter** *n*

[2]**swat** *n* **1** a quick crushing blow **2** a swatter

swatch /swɒtʃ/ *n* a sample piece (e g of fabric)

swath /swɔːθ/ *n* **1a** a row of cut grain or grass left by a scythe or mowing machine **b** the path cut in 1 passage (e g of a mower) **2** a long broad strip

[1]**swathe** /sweɪð/ *v* **1** to bind or wrap (as if) with a bandage **2** to envelop

[2]**swathe** *n* a swath

[1]**sway** /sweɪ/ *v* **1** to swing slowly and rhythmically back and forth **2** to fluctuate or alternate between one attitude or position and another **3** to change the opinions of, esp by eloquence or argument

[2]**sway** *n* **1** swaying or being swayed **2a** controlling influence or power **b** rule, dominion

swear /sweəʳ/ *v* **swore; sworn 1** to utter or take (an oath) solemnly **2** to promise emphatically or earnestly **3** to use profane or obscene language – ~**er** *n*

swear in *v* to induct into office by administration of an oath

[1]**sweat** /swet/ *v* **1** to excrete sweat in visible quantities **2a** to emit or exude moisture **b** to gather surface moisture as a result of condensation **3** to undergo anxiety or tension **4** to exact work from under sweatshop conditions

[2]**sweat** *n* **1** the fluid excreted from the sweat glands of the skin; perspiration **2** moisture gathering in drops on a surface **3** hard work; drudgery **4** a state of anxiety or impatience *USE* (*3&4*) infml – ~**y** *adj*

sweatband /ˈswetbænd/ *n* a band of material worn round the head or wrist or inserted in a hat or cap to absorb sweat

sweater /ˈswetəʳ/ *n* a pullover

sweat out *v* to endure or wait through the course of

sweat shirt *n* a loose collarless pullover of heavy cotton jersey

sweat shop /ˈswet-ʃɒp/ *n* a place of work in which workers are employed for long hours at low wages and under unhealthy conditions

swede /swiːd/ *n* **1** *cap* a native or inhabitant of Sweden **2** a large type of turnip with edible yellow flesh

Swedish /ˈswiːdɪʃ/ *n* the N Germanic language spoken in Sweden and part of Finland

[1]**sweep** /swiːp/ *v* **swept 1a** to remove or clean (as if) by brushing **b** to destroy completely – usu + *away* **c** to drive or carry along with irresistible force **2** to move through or along with overwhelming speed or violence **3** to go with stately or sweeping movements **4** to cover the entire range of **5** to move or extend in a wide curve

[2]**sweep** *n* **1a** a long oar **b** a windmill sail **2** a clearing out or away (as if) with a broom **3a** a curving course or line **b** a broad extent **4** a sweepstake

sweeper /ˈswiːpəʳ/ *n* a defensive player in soccer who plays behind the backs as a last line of defence before the goalkeeper

sweeping /ˈswiːpɪŋ/ *adj* **1** extending in a wide curve or over a wide area **2a** extensive, wide-ranging **b** marked by wholesale and indiscriminate inclusion – ~**ly** *adv*

sweepstake /ˈswiːpsteɪk/ *n* a lottery *USE* often pl with sing. meaning but sing. or pl in constr

[1]**sweet** /swiːt/ *adj* **1a** being or inducing the one of the 4 basic taste sensations that is typically induced by sugar **b** *of a beverage* containing a sweetening ingredient; not dry **2a** delightful, charming **b** marked by gentle good humour or kindliness **c** fragrant **d** pleasing to the ear or eye **3** much loved **4a** not sour, rancid, decaying, or stale **b** not salt or salted; fresh – ~**ly** *adv* – ~**ness** *n* – ~**ish** *adj*

[2]**sweet** *n* **1** a darling or sweetheart **2** *Br* a dessert **b** a toffee, truffle, or other small piece of confectionery prepared with (flavoured or filled) chocolate or sugar; *esp* one made chiefly of (boiled and crystallized) sugar

sweet-and-sour *adj* seasoned with a sauce containing sugar and vinegar or lemon juice

sweetbread /ˈswiːtbred/ *n* the pancreas of a young animal (e g a calf) used for food

sweet corn *n* (the young kernels of) a maize with kernels that contain a high percentage of sugar and are eaten as a vegetable when young and milky

sweeten /ˈswiːtn/ *v* **1** to make (more) sweet **2** to soften the mood or attitude of **3** to make less painful or trying – ~**er** *n*

sweetheart /ˈswiːthɑːt/ *n* a darling, lover

sweetmeat /ˈswiːtmiːt/ *n* a crystallized fruit, sugar-coated nut, or other sweet or delicacy rich in sugar

sweet pea *n* a leguminous garden plant with slender climbing stems and large fragrant flowers

sweet pepper *n* a large mild thick-walled capsicum fruit

sweet tooth *n* a craving or fondness for sweet food

[1]**swell** /swel/ *v* **swollen, swelled** **1a** to expand gradually beyond a normal or original limit **b** to be distended or puffed up **c** to curve outwards or upwards; bulge **2** to become charged with emotion

[2]**swell** *n* **1** a rounded protuberance or bulge **2** a (massive) surge of water, often continuing beyond or after its cause (e g a gale) **3** a gradual increase and decrease of the loudness of a musical sound **4** a person of fashion or high social position – infml

[3]**swell** *adj, chiefly NAm* excellent

swelling /ˈswelɪŋ/ *n* an abnormal bodily protuberance or enlargement

[1]**swelter** /ˈsweltəʳ/ *v* to suffer, sweat, or be faint from heat

[2]**swelter** *n* a state of oppressive heat

sweltering /ˈsweltərɪŋ/ *adj* oppressively hot

swerve /swɜːv/ *v* to (cause to) turn aside abruptly from a straight line or course

[1]**swift** /swɪft/ *adj* **1** (capable of) moving at great speed **2** occurring suddenly or within a very short time **3** quick to respond; ready – ~**ly** *adv* – ~**ness** *n*

[2]**swift** *n* any of numerous dark-coloured birds that resemble swallows and are noted for their fast darting flight in pursuit of insects

[1]**swig** /swɪg/ *n* a quantity drunk in 1 draught – infml

[2]**swig** *v* to drink (sthg) in long draughts – infml

[1]**swill** /swɪl/ *v* **1** to wash, esp by flushing with water **2** to drink greedily

[2]**swill** *n* a semiliquid food for animals (e g pigs) composed of edible refuse mixed with water or skimmed or sour milk

[1]**swim** /swɪm/ *v* **swam; swum** **1** to propel oneself in water by bodily movements (e g of the limbs, fins, or tail) **2** to surmount difficulties; not go under **3** to have a floating or dizzy effect or sensation – ~**mer** *n*

[2]**swim** *n* **1** an act or period of swimming **2** the main current of events

swimming /ˈswɪmɪŋ/ *adj* capable of, adapted to, or used in or for swimming

swimmingly /ˈswɪmɪŋli/ *adv* very well; splendidly – infml

[1]**swindle** /ˈswɪndl/ *v* to obtain property or take property from by fraud – ~**r** *n*

[2]**swindle** *n* a fraud, deceit

swine /swaɪn/ *n, pl* **swine** **1** a pig – used esp technically or in literature **2** a contemptible person **3** sthg unpleasant *USE* (*2 & 3*) infml – -**nish** *adj*

swineherd /ˈswaɪnhɜːd/ *n* sby who tends pigs

[1]**swing** /swɪŋ/ *v* **swung** **1** to move freely to and fro, esp when hanging from an overhead support **2** to turn (as if) on a hinge or pivot **3a** to influence decisively **b** to manage; bring about **4** to play or sing with a lively compelling rhythm; *specif* to play swing music **5** to shift or fluctuate between 2 moods, opinions, etc **6a** to move along rhythmically **b** to start up in a smooth rapid manner **7** to engage freely in sex, specif wife-swapping – slang

[2]**swing** *n* **1a** a sweeping or rhythmic movement of the body or a bodily part **b** the regular movement of a freely suspended object to and fro along an arc **c** a steady vigorous rhythm or action **2** the progression of an activity; course **3** the arc or range through which sthg swings **4** a suspended seat on which one may swing to and fro **5** jazz played usu by a large dance band

and characterized by a steady lively rhythm, simple harmony, and a basic melody often submerged in improvisation

swingeing /ˈswɪndʒɪŋ/ *adj, chiefly Br* severe, drastic

swinging /ˈswɪŋɪŋ/ *adj* lively and up-to-date – infml – **~ly** *adv*

¹swipe /swaɪp/ *n* a strong sweeping blow – infml

²swipe *v* **1** to strike or hit out with a sweeping motion **2** to steal, pilfer *USE* infml

¹swirl /swɜːl/ *n* **1** a whirling mass or motion **2** a twisting shape, mark, or pattern

²swirl *v* to move in eddies or whirls

¹swish /swɪʃ/ *v* to move with (the sound of) a swish

²swish *n* **1a** a sound as of a whip cutting the air **b** a light sweeping or brushing sound **2** a swishing movement

³swish *adj* smart, fashionable – infml

Swiss /swɪs/ *n, pl* **Swiss** a native or inhabitant of Switzerland – **Swiss** *adj*

Swiss roll *n* a thin sheet of sponge cake spread with jam and rolled up

¹switch /swɪtʃ/ *n* **1** a slender flexible twig or rod **2** a shift or change from one to another **3** a tuft of long hairs at the end of the tail of an animal (e g a cow) **4** a device for making, breaking, or changing the connections in an electrical circuit

²switch *v* **1** to shift, change **2a** to shift to another electrical circuit by means of a switch **b** to operate an electrical switch so as to turn *off* or *on* **3** to lash from side to side – **~able** *adj*

switchback /ˈswɪtʃbæk/ *n* **1** a zigzag road or railway in a mountainous region **2** *chiefly Br* any of various amusement rides; *esp* a roller coaster

switchboard /ˈswɪtʃbɔːd/ *n* an apparatus consisting of a panel or frame on which switching devices are mounted; *specif* an arrangement for the manual switching of telephone calls

switched-on *adj* alive to experience; *also* swinging – infml

switchgear /ˈswɪtʃgɪəʳ/ *n* equipment used for the switching of esp large electrical currents

switchover /ˈswɪtʃ-əʊvəʳ/ *n* a conversion to a different system or method

¹swivel /ˈswɪvəl/ *n* a device joining 2 parts so that the moving part can pivot freely

²swivel *v* to turn (as if) on a swivel

swiz /swɪz/ *n, pl* **-zz-** *Br* sthg that does not live up to one's hopes or expectations – infml

swizzle stick /ˈswɪzəl stɪk/ *n* a thin rod used to stir mixed drinks

swollen /ˈswəʊlən/ *past part of* **swell**

swoon /swuːn/ *v* to faint – **swoon** *n*

¹swoop /swuːp/ *v* **1** to make a sudden attack or downward sweep **2** to carry off abruptly; snatch – **~er** *n*

²swoop *n* an act of swooping

swop /swɒp/ *n or v* (to) swap

sword /sɔːd/ *n* **1** a cutting or thrusting weapon having a long usu sharp-pointed and sharp-edged blade **2** death caused (as if) by a sword – usu + *the* – **~sman** *n* **~smanship** *n*

sword dance *n* a Scottish-Highland solo dance usu performed in the angles formed by 2 swords crossed on the ground – **sword dancer** *n*

swordfish /ˈsɔːd,fɪʃ/ *n* a very large oceanic food fish that has a long swordlike beak formed by the bones of the upper jaw

swordstick /ˈsɔːd,stɪk/ *n* a walking stick in which a sword blade is concealed

swore /swɔːʳ/ *past of* **swear**

sworn /swɔːn/ *past part of* **swear**

¹swot /swɒt/ *n, Br* one who studies hard or excessively – infml

²swot *v, Br* **1** to study hard **2** to study a subject intensively – usu + *up* *USE* infml – **~ter** *n*

swum /swʌm/ *past part of* **swim**

swung /swʌŋ/ *past of* **swing**

sybarite /ˈsɪbəraɪt/ *n, often cap* a voluptuary, sensualist – **-itic** *adj*

sycamore /ˈsɪkəmɔːʳ/ *n* a Eurasian maple widely planted as a shade tree

sycophant /ˈsɪkəfænt/ *n* a self-seeking flatterer; a toady – **~ic** *adj*

syllable /ˈsɪləbəl/ *n* (a letter or symbol representing) an uninterruptible unit of spoken language that usu consists of 1 vowel sound either alone or with a consonant sound preceding or following – **-abic** *adj*

syllabub, sillabub /'sɪləbʌb/ *n* a cold dessert usu made by curdling sweetened cream or milk with wine, cider, etc

syllabus /'sɪləbəs/ *n* a summary of a course of study or of examination requirements

sylph /sɪlf/ *n* a slender graceful woman or girl – **~like** *adj*

symbiosis /ˌsɪmbi'əʊsɪ̵s/ *n, pl* **symbioses** the living together of 2 dissimilar organisms in intimate association (to their mutual benefit) – **-otic** *adj*

symbol /'sɪmbəl/ *n* **1** sthg that stands for or suggests sthg else by reason of association, convention, etc **2** a sign used in writing or printing to represent operations, quantities, elements, relations, or qualities in a particular field (e g chemistry or music) – **~ic, ~ical** *adj* – **~ically** *adv* – **~ize** *v*

symbolism /'sɪmbəlɪzəm/ *n* **1** *often cap* an artistic movement, esp in 19th-c France, making much use of symbols rather than using direct expressions or representations **2** a system of symbols – **-list** *n*

symmetry /'sɪmɪ̵tri/ *n* **1** (beauty of form arising from) balanced proportions **2** the property of being symmetrical; *esp* correspondence in size, shape, and relative position of parts on opposite sides of a dividing line or about a centre or axis – **-trical, -tric** *adj* – **-trically** *adv*

sympathetic /ˌsɪmpə'θetɪk/ *adj* **1** appropriate to one's mood or temperament; congenial **2** given to or arising from compassion and sensitivity to others' feelings **3** favourably inclined – **~ally** *adv*

sympathy /'sɪmpəθi/ *n* **1a** relationship between people or things in which each is simultaneously affected in a similar way **b** unity or harmony in action or effect **2a** inclination to think or feel alike **b** tendency to favour or support – often pl with sing. meaning **3** (the expression of) pity or compassion – **-thize** *v*

symphony /'sɪmfəni/ *n* **1** a usu long and complex sonata for symphony orchestra **2** sthg of great harmonious complexity or variety – **-onic** *adj*

symposium /sɪm'pəʊzɪəm/ *n, pl* **symposia** **1** a party (e g after a banquet in ancient Greece) with music and conversation **2** a formal meeting at which several specialists deliver short addresses on a topic

symptom /'sɪmptəm/ *n* **1** sthg giving (subjective) evidence or indication of disease or physical disturbance **2** sthg that indicates the existence of sthg else – **~atic** *adj* – **~atically** *adv*

synagogue /'sɪnəgɒg/ *n* (the house of worship and communal centre of) a Jewish congregation

sync /sɪŋk/ *n* synchronization – infml

synchron·ize, -ise /'sɪŋkrənaɪz/ *v* **1** to happen at the same time; *esp* to make sound and image coincide (e g with a film) **2** to make synchronous in operation; *esp* to set clocks or watches to the same time – **-ization** *n*

syncopate /'sɪŋkəpeɪt/ *v* to change the rhythm of music by altering the note on which the beat falls – **-ation** *n*

syndic /'sɪndɪk/ *n* an agent who transacts business for a university or corporation

syndicalism /'sɪndɪkəlɪzəm/ *n* **1** a revolutionary doctrine according to which workers should seize control of the economy and the government by direct means (e g a general strike) **2** a system of economic organization in which industries are owned and managed by the workers – **-list** *adj, n*

[1]**syndicate** /'sɪndɪkɪ̵t/ *n* **1** *sing or pl in constr* a group of people or concerns who combine to carry out a particular transaction (e g buying or renting property) or to promote some common interest **2** a business concern that supplies material for simultaneous publication in many newspapers or periodicals

[2]**syndicate** /'sɪndɪ̵keɪt/ *v* **1** to form into or manage as a syndicate **2** to sell (e g a cartoon) to a syndicate for simultaneous publication in many newspapers or periodicals – **-cation** *n*

syndrome /'sɪndrəʊm/ *n* a group of signs and symptoms that occur together and characterize a particular (medical) abnormality

synod /'sɪnəd/ *n* **1** a formal meeting to decide ecclesiastical matters **2** a church governing or advisory council

synonym /'sɪnənɪm/ *n* any of 2 or more words or expressions in a language that are used with (nearly) the same meaning – **~ous** *adj* – **~ously** *adv*

synopsis /sɪ̵'nɒpsɪ̵s/ *n, pl* **synopses** a condensed statement or outline (e g of a narrative)

syntax /'sɪntæks/ *n* (the part of grammar dealing with) the way in which words are put together to form phrases, clauses, or sentences

synthes·ize, -ise /sɪnθɪ̵saɪz/ *v* to make, esp by combining parts or in imitation of a natural product

synthetic /sɪn'θetɪk/ *adj* **1** asserting of a subject a predicate that is not part of the meaning of that subject **2** produced artificially; man-made – **~ally** *adv*

syphilis /'sɪfəlɪ̵s/ *n* a contagious usu venereal and often congenital disease caused by a bacterium – **-itic** *adj*

syphon /'saɪfən/ *v or n* (to) siphon

syringe /sɪ̵'rɪndʒ/ *n* a device used to inject fluids into or withdraw them from sthg (e g the body or its cavities); *esp* one that consists of a hollow barrel fitted with a plunger and a hollow needle

syrup /'sɪrəp/ *n* **1a** a thick sticky solution of (flavoured, medicated, etc) sugar and water **b** the raw sugar juice obtained from crushed sugarcane after evaporation and before crystallization in sugar manufacture **2** cloying sweetness or sentimentality – **~y** *adj*

system /'sɪstɪ̵m/ *n* **1a** a group of body organs that together perform 1 or more usu specified functions **b** a group of interrelated and interdependent objects or units **c** a form of social, economic, or political organization **2** an organized set of doctrines or principles usu intended to explain the arrangement or working of a systematic whole **3** a manner of classifying, symbolizing, or formalizing **4** orderly methods

systematic /ˌsɪstɪ̵'mætɪk/ *adj* **1** relating to, consisting of, or presented as a system **2** methodical in procedure or plan; thorough **3** of or concerned with classification; *specif* taxonomic – **~ally** *adv* – **-tize** *v*

T

t /tiː/ *n, pl* *t's, ts often cap* (a graphic representation of or device for reproducing) the 20th letter of the English alphabet

t' /t/ *definite article, NEng dial* the

't /t/ *pron* it

[1]**tab** /tæb/ *n* **1** a flap, loop, etc fixed to or projecting from sthg and used for gripping or suspending or to aid identification **2** close surveillance; watch – usu pl with sing. meaning **3** *chiefly NAm* a statement of money owed; a bill – infml

[2]**tab** *v* to provide or decorate with tabs

tabard /ˈtæbəd, -ɑːd/ *n* a short loosely fitting sleeveless or short-sleeved coat or cape: e g **a** an emblazoned tunic worn by a knight over his armour **b** a herald's official cape or coat emblazoned with his lord's arms

Tabasco /təˈbæskəʊ/ *trademark* – used for a pungent condiment sauce made from hot peppers

tabby /ˈtæbi/ *n* **1** a domestic cat with a usu buff and black striped and mottled coat **2** a female domestic cat

tabernacle /ˈtæbənækəl/ *n* **1** a receptacle for the consecrated bread and wine used at Communion, often forming part of an altar **2** a support in which a mast is stepped and pivoted so that it can be lowered (e g to negotiate a bridge)

[1]**table** /ˈteɪbəl/ *n* **1** a piece of furniture consisting of a smooth flat slab (e g of wood) fixed on legs **2** a systematic arrangement of data usu in rows and columns **3** sthg having a flat level surface

tableau /ˈtæbləʊ/ *n, pl* **tableaux** **1** a graphic representation of a group or scene **2** a depiction of a scene usu presented on a stage by silent and motionless costumed participants

tablecloth /ˈteɪbəlklɒθ/ *n* an often decorative cloth spread over a dining table before the places are set

table d'hôte /ˌtɑːbəl ˈdəʊt/ *n* a meal often of several prearranged courses served to all guests at a fixed price

tableland /ˈteɪbəl-lænd/ *n* a broad level area elevated on all sides

tablemat /ˈteɪbəlmæt/ *n* a small often decorative mat placed under a hot dish to protect the surface of a table from heat

tablespoon /ˈteɪbəlspuːn/ *n* a large spoon used for serving – **~ful** *n*

tablet /ˈtæblɨt/ *n* **1** a flat slab or plaque suitable for or bearing an inscription **2a** a compressed block of a solid material **b** a small solid shaped mass or capsule of medicinal material

table tennis *n* a game resembling lawn tennis that is played on a tabletop with bats and a small hollow plastic ball

tableware /ˈteɪbəlweəʳ/ *n* utensils (e g glasses, dishes, plates, and cutlery) for table use

tabloid /ˈtæblɔɪd/ *n* a newspaper of which 2 pages make up 1 printing plate and which contains much photographic matter

[1]**taboo** *also* **tabu** /təˈbuː, tæˈbuː/ *adj* **1a** too sacred or evil to be touched, named, or used **b** set apart as unclean or accursed **2** forbidden, esp on grounds of morality, tradition, or social usage

[2]**taboo** *also* **tabu** *n* **1** a prohibition against touching, saying, or doing sthg for fear of harm from a supernatural force **2** a prohibition imposed by social custom

[3]**taboo** *also* **tabu** *v* **1** to set apart as taboo **2** to avoid or ban as taboo

tabor *also* **tabour** /ˈteɪbəʳ/ *n* a small drum with 1 head of soft calfskin used to accompany a pipe or fife played by the same person

tabular /ˈtæbjʊləʳ/ *adj* **1** having a

broad flat surface **2** arranged in the form of a table

tabulate /ˈtæbjʊleɪt/ *v* to arrange in tabular form – **-lation** *n*

tabulator /ˈtæbjʊleɪtəʳ/ *n* **1** a business machine that sorts and selects information from marked or perforated cards **2** an attachment to a typewriter that is used for arranging data in columns

tacit /ˈtæsɪ̆t/ *adj* implied or understood but not actually expressed – **~ly** *adv*

taciturn /ˈtæsɪ̆tɜːn/ *adj* not communicative or talkative – **~ity** *n* – **~ly** *adv*

[1]**tack** /tæk/ *n* **1** a small short sharp-pointed nail, usu with a broad flat head **2** the lower forward corner of a fore-and-aft sail **3a** the direction of a sailing vessel with respect to the direction of the wind **b** a change of course from one tack to another **c** a course of action **4** a long loose straight stitch usu used to hold 2 or more layers of fabric together temporarily **5** saddlery

[2]**tack** *v* **1a** to fasten or attach with tacks **b** to sew with long loose stitches in order to join or hold in place temporarily before fine or machine sewing **2** to add as a supplement **3a** to change the course of (a close-hauled sailing vessel) from one tack to the other by turning the bow to windward **b** to follow a zigzag course **c** to change one's policy or attitude abruptly

[1]**tackle** /ˈtækəl/ *n* **1** a set of equipment used in a particular activity **2** an assembly of ropes and pulleys arranged to gain mechanical advantage for hoisting and pulling **3** an act of tackling

[2]**tackle** *v* **1a** to take hold of or grapple with, esp in an attempt to stop or restrain **b(1)** to (attempt to) take the ball from (an opposing player) in hockey or soccer **(2)** to seize and pull down or stop (an opposing player with the ball) in rugby or American football **2** to set about dealing with

[1]**tacky** /ˈtæki/ *adj* slightly sticky to the touch

[2]**tacky** *adj, chiefly NAm* shabby, shoddy – slang

tact /tækt/ *n* a keen sense of how to handle people or affairs so as to avoid friction or giving offence – **~ful** *adj* – **~fully** *adv* – **~less** *adj* – **~lessly** *adv* – **~lessness** *n*

tactic /ˈtæktɪk/ *n* **1** a method of employing forces in combat **2** a device for achieving an end

tactician /tækˈtɪʃən/ *n* sby skilled in tactics

tactics /ˈtæktɪks/ *n pl but sing or pl in constr* **1** the science and art of disposing and manoeuvring forces in combat **2** the art or skill of employing available means to accomplish an end – **-tical** *adj* – **-tically** *adv*

tactile /ˈtæktaɪl/ *adj* of or perceptible by (the sense of) touch

tadpole /ˈtædpəʊl/ *n* a frog or toad larva with a rounded body, a long tail, and external gills

taffeta /ˈtæfɪ̆tə/ *n* a crisp plain-woven lustrous fabric of various fibres used esp for women's clothing

taffrail /ˈtæfˌreɪl/ *n* a rail round the stern of a ship

[1]**tag** /tæg/ *n* **1** a loose hanging piece of torn cloth **2** a rigid binding on an end of a shoelace **3** a piece of hanging or attached material; *specif* a flap on a garment that carries information (e g washing instructions) **4** a trite quotation used for rhetorical effect **5** a marker of plastic, metal, etc used for identification or classification

[2]**tag** *v* **1a** to provide with an identifying marker **b** to label, brand **2** to attach, append

[3]**tag** *n* a game in which one player chases others and tries to make one of them it by touching him/her

[1]**tail** /teɪl/ *n* **1** (an extension or prolongation of) the rear end of the body of an animal **2** sthg resembling an animal's tail in shape or position **3** *pl* a tailcoat; *broadly* formal evening dress for men including a tailcoat and a white bow tie **4** the last, rear, or lower part of sthg **5** the reverse of a coin – usu pl with sing. meaning **6** the stabilizing assembly (e g fin, rudder, and tailplane) at the rear of an aircraft **7** sby who follows or keeps watch on sby – infml – **~less** *adj*

[2]**tail** *v* **1** to remove the stalk of (e g a gooseberry) **2** to diminish gradually in strength, volume, quantity, etc –

usu + *off* or *away* **3a** to follow for purposes of surveillance – infml **b** to follow closely

tailback /'teɪlbæk/ *n* a long queue of motor vehicles, esp when caused by an obstruction that blocks the road

tailcoat /teɪl'kəʊt, 'teɪlkəʊt/ *n* a coat with tails; *esp* a man's formal evening coat with 2 long tapering skirts at the back

tail end *n* **1** the back or rear end **2** the concluding period

tailgate *v* to drive dangerously close behind another vehicle

[1]**tailor** /'teɪlə^r/ *n* sby whose occupation is making or altering esp men's garments

[2]**tailor** *v* **1** to make or fashion as the work of a tailor; *specif* to cut and stitch (a garment) so that it will hang and fit well **2** to make or adapt to suit a special need or purpose

tailor-made *adj* made or fitted for a particular use or purpose

[1]**taint** /teɪnt/ *v* **1** to touch or affect slightly with sthg bad **2** to affect with putrefaction; spoil **3** to contaminate morally; corrupt

[2]**taint** *n* a contaminating mark or influence

[1]**take** /teɪk/ *v* **took; taken** **1** to seize or capture physically **2** to grasp, grip **3a** to catch or attack through a sudden effect **b** to surprise; come upon suddenly **c** to attract, delight **4a** to receive into one's body, esp through the mouth **b** to eat or drink habitually **5** to bring or receive into a relationship or connection **6a** to acquire, borrow, or use without authority or right **b** to pay to have (e g by contract or subscription) **7a** to assume **b** to perform or conduct (e g a lesson) as a duty, task, or job **c** to commit oneself to **d** to involve oneself in **e** to consider or adopt as a point of view **f** to claim as rightfully one's own **8** to obtain by competition **9** to pick out; choose **10** to adopt or avail oneself of for use: e g **a** to have recourse to as an instrument for doing sthg **b** to use as a means of transport or progression **11a** to derive, draw **b(1)** to obtain or ascertain by testing, measuring, etc **(2)** to record in writing **(3)** to get or record by photography **12a** to receive or accept either willingly or reluctantly **b** to have the natural or intended effect or reaction **c** to begin to grow; strike root **13a** to accommodate **b** to be affected injuriously by (e g a disease) **14a** to apprehend, understand **b** to look upon; consider **c** to feel, experience **15a** to lead, carry, or remove with one to another place **b** to require or cause to go **16a** to obtain by removing **b** to subtract **17** to undertake and make, do, or perform **18a** to deal with **b** to consider or view in a specified relation **c** to apply oneself to the study of or undergo examination in – **~r** *n*

[2]**take** *n* **1** the uninterrupted recording, filming, or televising of sthg (e g a gramophone record or film sequence); *also* the recording or scene produced **2** proceeds, takings

takeaway /'teɪkəweɪ/ *n, Br* **1** a cooked meal that is eaten away from the premises from which it was bought **2** a shop or restaurant that sells takeaways

take back *v* to retract, withdraw

take in *v* **1a** to furl **b** to make (a garment) smaller (e g by altering the positions of the seams or making tucks) **2** to offer accommodation or shelter to **3** to include **4** to perceive, understand **5** to deceive, trick – infml

takeoff /'teɪk-ɒf/ *n* **1** an imitation; *esp* a caricature **2** an act of leaving or a rise from a surface (e g in making a jump, dive, or flight or in the launching of a rocket) **3** a starting point

take off *v* **1a** to deduct **b** to remove (e g clothing) **2** to take or spend (a period of time) as a holiday, rest, etc **3** to mimic **4** to start off or away **5** to begin a leap or spring **6** to leave the surface; begin flight

take on *v* **1a** to agree to undertake **b** to contend with as an opponent **2** to engage, hire **3** to assume or acquire (e g an appearance or quality) **4** to become emotional or distraught – infml

take out *v* **1a** to extract **b** to give vent to – usu + *on* **2** to escort or accompany in public **3a** to obtain officially or formally **b** to acquire (insurance) by making the necessary payment

takeover /ˈteɪk,əʊvəʳ/ *n* an act of gaining control of a business company by buying a majority of the shares

take over *v* to assume control or possession (of) or responsibility (for)

take up *v* **1** to remove by lifting or pulling up **2** to receive internally or on the surface and hold **3a** to begin to engage in or study **b** to raise (a matter) for consideration **4** to occupy (e g space or time) entirely or exclusively **5** to shorten (e g a garment) **6** to respond favourably to a bet, challenge, or proposal made by **7** to begin again; resume

taking /ˈteɪkɪŋ/ *adj* attractive, captivating

takings /ˈteɪkɪŋz/ *n pl* receipts, esp of money

talc /tælk/ *n* **1** a soft usu greenish or greyish mineral consisting of a magnesium silicate **2** talcum powder

talcum powder /ˈtælkəm ˌpaʊdəʳ/ *n* a powder for toilet use consisting of perfumed talc

tale /teɪl/ *n* **1** a series of events or facts told or presented; an account **2a** a usu fictitious narrative; a story **b** a lie, a falsehood

talebearer /ˈteɪlbeərəʳ/ *n* a telltale, gossip

talent /ˈtælənt/ *n* **1a** any of several ancient units of weight **b** a unit of money equal to the value of a talent of gold or silver **2a** a special often creative or artistic aptitude **b** general ability or intelligence **3** sexually attractive members of the opposite sex – slang – **~ed** *adj*

talisman /ˈtæl̥zmən/ *n, pl* **talismans** **1** an engraved object believed to act as a charm **2** sthg believed to produce magical or miraculous effects

¹talk /tɔːk/ *v* **1** to express or exchange ideas verbally or by other means **2** to use speech; speak **3** to use a particular, esp foreign language for conversing or communicating **4a** to gossip **b** to reveal secret or confidential information

²talk *n* **1** a verbal exchange of thoughts or opinions; a conversation **2** meaningless speech; verbiage **3** a formal discussion or exchange of views – often pl with sing. meaning **4** an often informal address or lecture

talkative /ˈtɔːkətɪv/ *adj* given to talking – **~ness** *n*

talk down *v* **1** to defeat or silence by argument or by loud talking **2** to radio instructions to (a pilot) to enable him/her to land when conditions are difficult **3** to speak in a condescending or oversimplified fashion *to*

talkie /ˈtɔːki/ *n* a film with a synchronized sound track

talking point *n* a subject of conversation or argument

talk out *v* to clarify or settle by discussion

talk over *v* to review or consider in conversation

tall /tɔːl/ *adj* **1a** of above average height **b** of a specified height **2** *of a plant* of a higher growing variety or species **3** highly exaggerated; incredible – **~ish** *adj* – **~ness** *n*

tallboy /ˈtɔːlbɔɪ/ *n* **1** a tall chest of drawers supported on a low legged base **2** a double chest of drawers usu with the upper section slightly smaller than the lower

tallow /ˈtæləʊ/ *n* the solid white rendered fat of cattle and sheep used chiefly in soap, candles, and lubricants

¹tally /ˈtæli/ *n* **1** a record or account (e g of items or charges) **2** a record of the score (e g in a game)

²tally *v* **1** to make a count of **2** to correspond, match

tally-ho /ˌtæliˈhəʊ/ *n* a call of a huntsman at the sight of a fox

tallyman /ˈtælimən/ *n* **1** one who checks or keeps an account or record (e g of receipt of goods) **2** *Br* one who sells goods on credit; *also* one who calls to collect hire purchase payments

Talmud /ˈtælmʊd/ *n* the authoritative body of Jewish traditional lore

talon /ˈtælən/ *n* a claw of an animal, esp a bird of prey

tamarisk /ˈtæmərɪsk/ *n* any of a genus of chiefly tropical or Mediterranean shrubs and trees having tiny narrow leaves and masses of minute flowers

tambourine /ˌtæmbəˈriːn/ *n* a shallow one-headed drum with loose metallic discs at the sides

¹tame /teɪm/ *adj* **1** changed from a

state of native wildness, esp so as to be trainable and useful to human beings 2 made docile and submissive 3 lacking spirit, zest, or interest – ~**ly** *adv* – ~**ness** *n*

[2]**tame** *v* **1** to make tame; domesticate **2** to deprive of spirit; subdue – **tamable** *or* **tameable** *adj* – **tamer** *n*

tam-o'-shanter /ˌtæm ə 'ʃæntəʳ/ *n* a round flat woollen or cloth cap of Scottish origin, with a tight headband, a full crown, and usu a pom-pom on top

tamp /tæmp/ *v* to drive in or down by a succession of light or medium blows – often + *down*

tamper /tæmpəʳ/ *v* to interfere or meddle *with* without permission

tampon /'tæmpɒn/ *v or n* (to plug with) an absorbent plug put into a cavity (e g the vagina) to absorb secretions, arrest bleeding, etc

[1]**tan** /tæn/ *v* **1** to convert (hide) into leather, esp by treatment with an infusion of tannin-rich bark **2** to make (skin) tan-coloured, esp by exposure to the sun **3** to thrash, beat – infml

[2]**tan** *n* **1** a brown colour given to the skin by exposure to sun or wind **2** (a) light yellowish brown colour – **tan** *adj*

[1]**tandem** /'tændəm/ *n* **1** (a 2-seat carriage drawn by) horses harnessed one before the other **2** a bicycle or tricycle having 2 or more seats one behind the other

[2]**tandem** *adv* one behind the other

[1]**tang** /tæŋ/ *n* **1** a projecting shank or tongue (e g on a knife, file, or sword) that connects with and is enclosed by a handle **2a** a sharp distinctive flavour **b** a pungent or distinctive smell

[2]**tang** *n* any of various large coarse seaweeds

Tang *n* a Chinese dynasty (AD 618 to 907) under which printing developed and poetry and art flourished

[1]**tangent** /'tændʒənt/ *adj* **1** touching a curve or surface at only 1 point **2** having a common tangent at a point

[2]**tangent** *n* **1** the trigonometric function that for an acute angle in a right-angled triangle is the ratio between the shorter sides opposite and adjacent to the angle **2** a straight line tangent to a curve

tangential /tæn'dʒenʃəl/ *adj* **1** divergent, digressive **2** incidental, peripheral

tangerine /ˌtændʒə'riːn/ *n* **1** (a tree that produces) any of various mandarin oranges with deep orange skin and pulp **2** (a) bright reddish orange colour

tangible /'tændʒəbəl/ *adj* **1a** capable of being perceived, esp by the sense of touch **b** substantially real; material **2** capable of being appraised at an actual or approximate value – **-bility** *n* – **-bly** *adv*

[1]**tangle** /'tæŋgəl/ *v* **1** to involve so as to be trapped or hampered **2** to bring together or intertwine in disordered confusion **3** to engage in conflict or argument – usu + *with*; infml

[2]**tangle** *n* **1** a confused twisted mass **2** a complicated or confused state

tango /'tæŋgəʊ/ *n, pl* **tangos** (the music for) a ballroom dance of Latin-American origin in $\frac{4}{4}$ time, characterized by long pauses and stylized body positions

tank /tæŋk/ *n* **1** a large receptacle for holding, transporting, or storing liquids or gas **2** an enclosed heavily armed and armoured combat vehicle that moves on caterpillar tracks

tankard /'tæŋkəd/ *n* a silver or pewter mug

tanker /'tæŋkəʳ/ *n* a ship, aircraft, or road or rail vehicle designed to carry fluid, esp liquid, in bulk (e g an aircraft used for transporting fuel and usu capable of refuelling other aircraft in flight)

tanner /'tænəʳ/ *n, Br* a coin worth 6 old pence – infml

tannin /'tænɪ̣n/ *n* any of various acidic substances of plant origin used esp in tanning, dyeing, and making ink

Tannoy /'tænɔɪ/ *trademark* – used for a loudspeaker apparatus that broadcasts to the public, esp throughout a large building

tansy /'tænzi/ *n* an aromatic composite plant sometimes used as a herb

tantal·ize, -ise /'tæntlaɪz/ *v* to tease or frustate by offering sthg just out of reach

tantamount /'tæntəmaʊnt/ *adj*

equivalent in value, significance, or effect *to*

tantrum /'tæntrəm/ *n* a fit of childish bad temper

Taoism /'taʊɪzəm, 'tɑːəʊ-/ *n* a Chinese philosophy traditionally founded by Lao-tzu in the 6th c BC that teaches action in conformity with nature rather than striving against it; *also* a religion developed from this philosophy together with folk and Buddhist religion and concerned with obtaining long life and good fortune often by magical means – **-ist** *adj, n*

[1]**tap** /tæp/ *n* **1a** a plug designed to fit an opening, esp in a barrel **b** a device consisting of a spout and valve attached to a pipe, bowl, etc to control the flow of a fluid **2** a tool for forming an internal screw thread **3** the act or an instance of tapping a telephone, telegraph, etc; *also* an electronic listening device used to do this

[2]**tap** *v* **1** to let out or cause to flow by piercing or by drawing a plug from the containing vessel **2a** to pierce so as to let out or draw off a fluid (e g from a body cavity) **b** to draw from or upon **c** to connect an electronic listening device to (e g a telegraph or telephone wire), esp in order to acquire secret information **3** to form an internal screw thread in (e g a nut) by means of a special tool **4** to get money from as a loan or gift – infml

[3]**tap** *v* **1** to strike lightly, esp with a slight sound **2** to produce by striking in this manner – often + *out*

[4]**tap** *n* (the sound of) a light blow

[1]**tape** /teɪp/ *n* **1** a narrow band of woven fabric **2** *the* string stretched above the finishing line of a race **3** a narrow flexible strip or band; *esp* magnetic tape **4** a tape recording

[2]**tape** *v* **1** to fasten, tie, or bind with tape **2** to record on tape, esp magnetic tape

tape deck *n* a mechanism or self-contained unit that causes magnetic tape to move past the heads of a magnetic recording device in order to generate electrical signals or to make a recording

tape measure *n* a narrow strip (e g of a limp cloth or steel tape) marked off in units (e g inches or centimetres) for measuring

[1]**taper** /'teɪpəʳ/ *n* **1a** a slender candle **b** a long waxed wick used esp for lighting candles, fires, etc **2** gradual diminution of thickness, diameter, or width

[2]**taper** *v* to decrease gradually in thickness, diameter, or width towards one end; *broadly* to diminish gradually

tape recorder *n* a device for recording on magnetic tape

tapestry /'tæpɨstri/ *n* **1** a heavy handwoven textile used for hangings, curtains, and upholstery, characterized by complicated pictorial designs **2** a machine-made imitation of tapestry used chiefly for upholstery – **-tried** *adj*

tapeworm /'teɪpwɜːm/ *n* any of numerous worms, which when adult are parasitic in the intestine of human beings or other vertebrates

tapioca /ˌtæpi'əʊkə/ *n* (a milk pudding made with) a usu granular preparation of starch produced from the cassava root

tapir /'teɪpəʳ/ *n* any of several large chiefly nocturnal hoofed mammals with long snouts found in tropical America and Asia that are related to the horses and rhinoceroses

tappet /'tæpɨt/ *n* a lever or projection moved by or moving some other piece (e g a cam)

taproot /'tæp-ruːt/ *n* a main root of a plant that grows vertically downwards and gives off small side roots

[1]**tar** /tɑːʳ/ *n* **1a** a dark bituminous usu strong-smelling viscous liquid obtained by heating and distilling wood, coal, peat, etc **b** a residue present in smoke from burning tobacco that contains resins, acids, phenols, etc **2** a sailor – infml

[2]**tar** *v* to smear with tar

tarantella /ˌtærən'telə/ *n* (music suitable for) a vivacious folk dance of southern Italy in $^6_8$ time

tarantula /tə'ræntjʊlə/ *n* any of various large hairy spiders

tardy /'tɑːdi/ *adj* **1** moving or progressing slowly; sluggish **2** delayed beyond the expected time; late – **tardily** *adv* – **tardiness** *n*

[1]**tare** /teəʳ/ *n* **1** any of several vetches

2 *pl* a weed found in cornfields – used in the Bible

[2]**tare** *n* **1** a deduction from the gross weight of a substance and its container made in allowance for the weight of the container **2** the weight of an unloaded goods vehicle

target /'tɑːgɪ̈t/ *n* **1** a small round shield **2a** an object to fire at in practice or competition; *esp* one consisting of a series of concentric circles with a bull's-eye at the centre **b** sthg (e g an aircraft or installation) fired at or attacked **3a** an object of ridicule, criticism, etc **b** a goal, objective

tariff /'tærɪ̈f/ *n* **1** a duty or schedule of duties imposed by a government on imported or in some countries exported goods **2** a schedule of rates or prices

tarmac /'tɑːmæk/ *n* **1** stone chippings bonded with tar to produce a road surface **2** a runway, apron, or road made of tarmac

tarn /'tɑːn/ *n* a small mountain lake

tarnish /'tɑːnɪʃ/ *v* **1** to dull the lustre of (as if) by dirt, air, etc **2a** to mar, spoil **b** to bring discredit on – **tarnish** *n*

tarot /'tærəʊ/ *n* any of a set of 78 pictorial playing cards used esp for fortune-telling

tarpaulin /tɑː'pɔːlɪ̈n/ *n* (a piece of) heavy waterproof usu tarred canvas material used for protecting objects or ground exposed to the elements

tarragon /'tærəgən/ *n* (a small European herb with) pungent aromatic leaves used as a flavouring (e g in chicken dishes and vinegar)

tarry /'tæri/ *v* **1** to delay or be slow in acting or doing **2** to stay in or at a place

tarsus /'tɑːsəs/ *n, pl* **tarsi** **1** (the small bones that support) the back part of the foot of a vertebrate that includes the ankle and heel **2** the part of the limb of an arthropod furthest from the body – **-sal** *adj*

[1]**tart** /tɑːt/ *adj* **1** agreeably sharp or acid to the taste **2** caustic, cutting – **~ly** *adv* – **~ness** *n*

[2]**tart** *n* **1** a pastry shell or shallow pie containing a usu sweet filling (e g jam or fruit) **2** a sexually promiscuous girl or woman; *also* a prostitute – infml

tartan /'tɑːtn/ *n* (a usu twilled woollen fabric with) a plaid textile design of Scottish origin consisting of checks of varying width and colour usu patterned to designate a distinctive clan

[1]**tartar** /'tɑːtə^r/ *n* **1** a substance derived from the juice of grapes deposited in wine casks as a reddish crust or sediment **2** an incrustation on the teeth consisting esp of calcium salts

[2]**tartar** *n* **1** *cap, NAm chiefly* **Tatar** a member of a group of people found mainly in the Tartar Republic of the USSR, the north Caucasus, Crimea, and parts of Siberia **2** an irritable, formidable, or exacting person

tartaric acid /tɑː,tærɪk 'æsɪ̈d/ *n* a strong acid from plants that is usu obtained from tartar, and is used esp in food and medicines

task /tɑːsk/ *n* **1** an assigned piece of work; a duty **2** sthg hard or unpleasant that has to be done; a chore

task force *n* a temporary grouping under 1 leader for the purpose of accomplishing a definite objective

taskmaster /'tɑːsk,mɑːstə^r/ *n* one who assigns tasks

tassel /'tæsəl/ *n* **1** a dangling ornament (e g for a curtain or bedspread) consisting of a bunch of cords or threads usu of even length fastened at 1 end **2** the tassel-like flower clusters of some plants, esp maize

[1]**taste** /teɪst/ *v* **1** to test the flavour of sthg by taking a little into the mouth **2** to have perception, experience, or enjoyment – usu + *of* **3** to eat or drink, esp in small quantities **4** to have a specified flavour – often + *of*

[2]**taste** *n* **1a** the act of tasting **b** a small amount tasted **c** a first acquaintance or experience of sthg **2** (the quality of a dissolved substance as perceived by) the basic physical sense by which the qualities of dissolved substances in contact with taste buds on the tongue are interpreted by the brain as a sensation of sweet, bitter, sour, or salt **3** individual preference; inclination **4** (a manner or quality indicative of) critical judgment or discernment esp in aesthetic or social matters

taste bud *n* any of the small organs, esp on the surface of the tongue, that receive and transmit the sensation of taste

tasteful /'teɪstfəl/ *adj* showing or conforming to good taste – **~ly** *adv* – **~ness** *n*

tasteless /'teɪstləs/ *adj* **1** having no taste; insipid **2** showing poor taste – **~ly** *adv* – **~ness** *n*

taster /'teɪstə^r/ *n* sby who tests food or drink by tasting, esp in order to assess quality

tasty /'teɪsti/ *adj* having an appetizing flavour – **tastily** *adv* – **tastiness** *n*

tatter /'tætə^r/ *n* **1** an irregular torn shred, esp of material **2** *pl* tattered clothing; rags

tattered /'tætəd/ *adj* (dressed in clothes which are) old and torn

tatting /'tætɪŋ/ *n* (the act or art of making) a delicate handmade lace formed usu by making loops and knots using a single cotton thread and a small shuttle

tattle /'tætl/ *v* to chatter, gossip – **tattle** *n*

[1]**tattoo** /tə'tuː, tæ'tuː/ *n* **1a** an evening drum or bugle call sounded as notice to soldiers to return to quarters **b** an outdoor military display given by troops as a usu evening entertainment **2** a rapid rhythmic beating or rapping

[2]**tattoo** *n* (an indelible mark made by) tattooing

[3]**tattoo** *v* to mark (the body) by inserting pigments under the skin – **~ist** *n*

tatty /'tæti/ *adj* shabby, dilapidated – infml – **-tily** *adv* – **-tiness** *n*

taught /tɔːt/ *past & past part of* **teach**

[1]**taunt** /tɔːnt/ *v* to provoke in a mocking way; jeer at – **~ingly** *adv*

[2]**taunt** *n* a sarcastic provocation or insult

Taurus /'tɔːrəs/ *n* (sby born under) the 2nd sign of the zodiac in astrology which is pictured as a bull

taut /tɔːt/ *adj* **1** tightly drawn; tensely stretched **2** showing anxiety; tense – **~ly** *adv* – **~ness** *n*

tautology /tɔː'tɒlədʒi/ *n* **1** (an instance of) needless repetition of an idea, statement, or word **2** a statement that is true by virtue of its logical form; an analytic proposition – **-gical** *adj*

tavern /'tævən/ *n* an inn

tawdry /'tɔːdri/ *adj* cheap and tastelessly showy in appearance – **-drily** *adv* – **-driness** *n*

tawny /'tɔːni/ *adj* of a warm sandy or brownish orange colour like that of well-tanned skin

[1]**tax** /tæks/ *v* **1** to levy a tax on **2** to charge, accuse *with* **3** to make strenuous demands on – **~ability** *n* – **~able** *adj*

[2]**tax** *n* a charge, usu of money, imposed by a government on individuals, organizations, or property, esp to raise revenue

taxation /tæk'seɪʃən/ *n* **1** the action of taxing; *esp* the imposition of taxes **2** revenue obtained from taxes **3** the amount assessed as a tax

tax haven *n* a country with a relatively low level of taxation, esp on incomes

[1]**taxi** /'tæksi/ *n, pl* **taxis** a motor car that may be hired to carry passengers short distances, esp in towns

[2]**taxi** *v, of an aircraft* to go at low speed along the surface of the ground or water

taxidermy /'tæksɪ̥dɜːmi/ *n* the art of preparing, stuffing, and mounting the skins of animals – **-mist** *n*

taxonomy /tæk'sɒnəmi/ *n* (the study of the principles of) classification, specif of plants and animals according to their presumed natural relationships

TB *n* tuberculosis

T-bone *n* a thick steak from the thin end of a beef sirloin containing a T-shaped bone

tea /tiː/ *n* **1a** a shrub cultivated esp in China, Japan, and the E Indies **b** the leaves of the tea plant prepared for the market, classed according to method of manufacture (e g green tea or oolong), and graded according to leaf size (e g pekoe) **2** an aromatic beverage prepared from tea leaves by infusion with boiling water **3a** refreshments including tea with sandwiches, cakes, etc served in the late afternoon **b** a late-afternoon or early-evening meal that is usu less substantial than the midday meal

tea cake *n* a round yeast-leavened (sweet) bread bun that often contains currants and is usu eaten toasted with butter

teach /tiːtʃ/ *v* **taught** **1** to provide instruction in **2** to guide the studies of **3** to impart the knowledge of **4** to instruct by precept, example, or experience

teacher /ˈtiːtʃəʳ/ *n* sby whose occupation is teaching

teach-in *n* **1** an informally structured conference on a usu topical issue **2** an extended meeting for lectures, demonstrations, and discussions on a topic

teaching /ˈtiːtʃɪŋ/ *n* **1** the profession of a teacher **2** sthg taught; *esp* a doctrine

teaching hospital *n* a hospital that is affiliated to a medical school and provides medical students with the opportunity of gaining practical experience under supervision

teahouse /ˈtiːhaʊs/ *n* a restaurant, esp in China or Japan, where tea and light refreshments are served

teak /tiːk/ *n* (a tall E Indian tree with) hard yellowish brown wood used for furniture and shipbuilding

teal /tiːl/ *n* (any of several ducks related to) a small Old World dabbling duck the male of which has a distinctive green and chestnut head

[1]team /tiːm/ *n* **1** two or more draught animals harnessed together **2** *sing or pl in constr* a group formed for work or activity: e g **a** a group on 1 side (e g in a sporting contest or debate) **b** a crew, gang

[2]team *v* **1** to come together (as if) in a team – often + *up* **2** to form a harmonizing combination

teamwork /ˈtiːmwɜːk/ *n* mutual cooperation in a group enterprise

teapot /ˈtiːpɒt/ *n* a usu round pot with a lid, spout, and handle in which tea is brewed and from which it is served

[1]tear /tɪəʳ/ *n* **1** a drop of clear salty fluid secreted by the lachrymal gland that lubricates the eye and eyelids and is often shed as a result of grief or other emotion **2** a transparent drop of (hardened) fluid (e g resin)

[2]tear /teəʳ/ *v* **tore; torn** **1a** to pull apart by force **b** to wound by tearing; lacerate **2** to move or act with violence, haste, or force

[3]tear /teəʳ/ *n* **1** damage from being torn – chiefly in *wear and tear* **2** a hole or flaw made by tearing

tearaway /ˈteərəweɪ/ *n, Br* an unruly and reckless young person – infml

tear away *v* to remove (oneself or another) reluctantly

teardrop /ˈtɪədrɒp/ *n* a tear

tearful /ˈtɪəfəl/ *adj* **1** flowing with or accompanied by tears **2** causing tears **3** inclined or about to cry – **~ly** *adv* – **~ness** *n*

tearoom /ˈtiːruːm, -rʊm/ *n* a restaurant where light refreshments are served

tear up /ˌteər ˈʌp/ *v* **1** to tear into pieces **2** to cancel or annul, usu unilaterally

[1]tease /tiːz/ *v* **1** to disentangle and straighten by combing or carding **2a** to (attempt to) disturb or annoy by persistently irritating or provoking **b** to persuade to acquiesce, esp by persistent small efforts; coax; *also* to obtain by repeated coaxing

[2]tease *n* sby or sthg that teases

teaser /ˈtiːzəʳ/ *n* **1** a frustratingly difficult problem **2** sby who derives malicious pleasure from teasing

teaspoon /ˈtiːspuːn/ *n* a small spoon used esp for eating soft foods and stirring beverages – **~ful** *n*

teat /tiːt/ *n* **1** a nipple **2** a small projection or a nib (e g on a mechanical part); *specif* a rubber mouthpiece with usu 2 or more holes in it, attached to the top of a baby's feeding bottle

tea towel *n* a cloth for drying the dishes

tech /tek/ *n, Br* a technical school or college – infml

technical /ˈteknɪkəl/ *adj* **1a** having special and usu practical knowledge, esp of a mechanical or scientific subject **b** marked by or characteristic of specialization **2** of a particular subject; *esp* of a practical subject organized on scientific principles – **~ly** *adv*

technicality /ˌteknʒˈkælʒti/ *n* sthg technical; *esp* a detail meaningful only to a specialist

technician /tekˈnɪʃən/ *n* **1** a specialist in the technical details of a subject or occupation **2** sby who has acquired the technique of an area of specialization (e g an art)

technique /tek'niːk/ *n* **1** the manner in which an artist, performer, or athlete displays or manages the formal aspect of his/her skill **2a** a body of technical methods (e g in a craft or in scientific research) **b** a method of accomplishing a desired aim

technocracy /tek'nɒkrəsi/ *n* (management of society by) a body of technical experts; *also* a society so managed – chiefly derog

technology /tek'nɒlədʒi/ *n* **1** (the theory and practice of) applied science **2** the totality of the means and knowledge used to provide objects necessary for human sustenance and comfort – **-gical** *adj* – **-gically** *adv* – **-gist** *n*

tectonics /tek'tɒnɪks/ *n pl but sing or pl in constr* **1** the science or art of construction (e g of a building) **2** (a branch of geology concerned with) structural features, esp those connected with folding and faulting

teddy bear /'tedi beəʳ/ *n* a stuffed toy bear

Te Deum /ˌteɪ 'deɪ-əm, ˌtiː 'diːəm/ *n* a liturgical Christian hymn of praise to God

tedious /'tiːdɪəs/ *adj* tiresome because of length or dullness – **~ly** *adv* – **~ness** *n*

tedium /'tiːdɪəm/ *n* tediousness; *also* boredom

[1]**tee** /tiː/ *n* **1** sthg shaped like a capital T **2** a mark aimed at in various games (e g curling)

[2]**tee** *n* **1** a peg or a small mound used to raise a golf ball into position for striking at the beginning of play on a hole **2** the area from which a golf ball is struck at the beginning of play on a hole

[3]**tee** *v* to place (a ball) on a tee – often + *up*

[1]**teem** /tiːm/ *v* **1** to abound **2** to be present in large quantities

[2]**teem** *v* to rain hard

teenage /'tiːneɪdʒ/, **teenaged** *adj* of or being people in their teens

teens /tiːnz/ *n pl* the numbers 13 to 19 inclusive; *specif* the years 13 to 19 in a lifetime

tee off *v* to drive a golf ball from a tee; *broadly* to start

tee shirt /'tiː ʃɜːt/ *n* a short-sleeved vest worn in place of a shirt

teeter /'tiːtəʳ/ *v* to move unsteadily; wobble, waver

teeth /tiːθ/ *pl of* **tooth**

teethe /tiːð/ *v* to cut one's teeth; grow teeth

teething troubles *n pl* temporary problems occurring with new machinery or during the initial stages of an activity

teetotal /ˌtiː'təʊtl/ *adj* practising complete abstinence from alcoholic drinks – **~ler** *n*

telegram /'teləgræm/ *n* a message sent by telegraph and delivered as a written or typed note

[1]**telegraph** /'teləgrɑːf/ *n* an apparatus or system for communicating at a distance, esp by making and breaking an electric circuit

[2]**telegraph** *v* **1** to send or communicate (as if) by telegraph **2** to make known by signs, esp unknowingly and in advance

telegraphese /ˌteləgrə'fiːz/ *n* the terse and abbreviated language characteristic of telegrams

telegraphic /ˌtelə'græfɪk/ *adj* concise, terse – **~ally** *adv*

telekinesis /ˌteləkɪ'niːsəs, -kaɪ-/ *n* movement of objects by the power of the mind carried out at an appreciable distance

telepathy /tə'lepəθi/ *n* communication directly from one mind to another without use of the known senses – **-thic** *adj* – **-thically** *adv*

[1]**telephone** /'teləfəʊn/ *n* **1** a device for reproducing sounds at a distance; *specif* one for converting sounds into electrical impulses for transmission, usu by wire, to a particular receiver **2** the system of communications that uses telephones

[2]**telephone** *v* to make a telephone call

telephonist /tə'lefənəst/ *n, Br* a telephone switchboard operator

telephoto /ˌtelə'fəʊtəʊ/ *adj* being a lens (system) designed to give enlarged images of distant objects

telephotography /ˌteləfə'tɒgrəfi/ *n*

the photography of distant objects – **-phic** *adj*

teleprinter /'telǰ,prɪntəʳ/ *n* a typewriter keyboard that transmits telegraphic signals, a typewriting device activated by telegraphic signals, or a machine that combines both these functions

¹telescope /'telǰskəʊp/ *n* **1** a usu tubular optical instrument for viewing distant objects by means of the refraction of light rays through a lens or the reflection of light rays by a concave mirror **2** a radio telescope

²telescope *v* **1** to slide one part within another like the cylindrical sections of a hand telescope **2** to become compressed under impact **3** to become condensed or shortened

telescopic /,telǰ'skɒpɪk/ *adj* **1** suitable for seeing or magnifying distant objects **2** able to discern objects at a distance **3** having parts that telescope

televise /'telǰvaɪz/ *v* to broadcast (an event or film) by television

television /'telǰ,vɪʒən, ,telǰ'vɪʒən/ *n* **1** an electronic system of transmitting changing images together with sound by converting the images and sounds into electrical signals **2** a television receiving set **3a** the television broadcasting industry **b** a television broadcasting organization or station

telex /'teleks/ *n* a communications service involving teleprinters connected by wire through automatic exchanges; *also* a message by telex

tell /tel/ *v* **told** **1a** to relate in detail; narrate **b** to give utterance to; express in words **2** to make known; divulge **3a** to report to; inform; *also* to inform *on* **b** to assure emphatically **4** to order **5a** to ascertain by observing **b** to distinguish, discriminate **6** to take effect **7** to serve as evidence or indication

teller /'teləʳ/ *n* **1** sby who relates or communicates **2** sby who counts: e g **a** sby appointed to count votes **b** a member of a bank's staff concerned with the direct handling of money received or paid out

telling /'telɪŋ/ *adj* carrying great weight and producing a marked effect – **~ly** *adv*

tell off *v* **1** to number and set apart; *esp* to assign to a special duty **2** to reprimand

telltale /'telteɪl/ *n* sby who spreads gossip or rumours; *esp* an informer

telly /'teli/ *n, chiefly Br* (a) television – infml

temerity /tǰ'merǰti/ *n* unreasonable disregard for danger or opposition; *broadly* cheek, nerve

temp /temp/ *n* sby (e g a typist or secretary) employed temporarily – infml – **temp** *v*

¹temper /'tempəʳ/ *v* **1** to moderate (sthg harsh) *with* the addition of sthg less severe **2** to bring (esp steel) to the right degree of hardness by reheating (and quenching) after cooling **3** to strengthen the character of through hardship

²temper *n* **1** the state of a substance with respect to certain desired qualities (e g the degree of hardness or resilience given to steel by tempering) **2a** a characteristic cast of mind or state of feeling **b** composure, equanimity **c** (proneness to displays of) an uncontrolled and often disproportionate rage

tempera /'tempərə/ *n* (a work produced by) a method of painting using pigment ground and mixed with an emulsion (e g of egg yolk and water)

temperament /'tempərəmənt/ *n* **1a** a person's peculiar or distinguishing mental or physical character **b** excessive sensitiveness or irritability **2** the modification of the musical intervals of the pure scale to produce a set of 12 fixed notes to the octave which enables a keyboard instrument to play in more than 1 key

temperamental /,tempərə'mentl/ *adj* **1** of or arising from individual character or constitution **2a** easily upset or irritated; liable to sudden changes of mood **b** unpredictable in behaviour or performance – **~ly** *adv*

temperance /'tempərəns/ *n* **1** moderation, self-restraint **2** abstinence from the use of alcoholic drink

temperate /'tempərǰt/ *adj* **1** moderate: e g **a** not extreme or excessive **b** abstemious in the consumption of alcohol **2a** having a moderate climate b found in or associated with a temperate climate

temperature /'tempərətʃə'/ *n* **1a** degree of hotness or coldness as measured on an arbitrary scale (e g in degrees Celsius) **b** the degree of heat natural to the body of a living being **2** an abnormally high body heat

tempest /'tempəst/ *n* **1** a violent storm **2** a tumult, uproar

tempestuous /tem'pestʃʊəs/ *adj* turbulent, stormy – ~**ly** *adv*

[1]**temple** /'tempəl/ *n* **1** a building dedicated to worship among any of various ancient civilizations (e g the Egyptians, the Greeks, and the Romans) and present-day non-Christian religions (e g Hinduism and Buddhism) **2** a place devoted or dedicated to a specified purpose

[2]**temple** *n* the flattened space on either side of the forehead of some mammals (e g human beings)

tempo /'tempəʊ/ *n, pl* **tempi** **1** the speed of a musical piece or passage indicated by any of a series of directions and often by an exact metronome marking **2** rate of motion or activity

temporal /'tempərəl/ *adj* **1** of time as opposed to eternity or space; *esp* transitory **2** of earthly life **3** of lay or secular concerns

[1]**temporary** /'tempərəri/ *adj* lasting for a limited time – **-arily** *adv* – **-ariness** *n*

[2]**temporary** *n* a temp

tempt /tempt/ *v* **1** to entice, esp to evil, by promise of pleasure or gain **2** to risk provoking the disfavour of **3a** to induce to do sthg **b** to cause to be strongly inclined **c** to appeal to; entice – ~**er** *n* – ~**ingly** *adv*

temptation /temp'teɪʃən/ *n* **1** tempting or being tempted, esp to evil **2** sthg tempting

ten /ten/ *n* **1** the number 10 **2** the tenth in a set or series **3** sthg having 10 parts or members or a denomination of 10 **4** the number occupying the position 2 to the left of the decimal point in the Arabic notation; *also, pl* this position – **tenth** *adj, n, pron, adv*

tenacious /tə'neɪʃəs/ *adj* **1** tending to stick or cling, esp to another substance **2a** persistent in maintaining or keeping to sthg valued as habitual **b** retentive – ~**ly** *adv* – ~**ness** *n* – **-city** *n*

tenant /'tenənt/ *n* **1** an occupant of lands or property of another; *specif* sby who rents or leases a house or flat from a landlord **2** an occupant, dweller – **tenant** *v*

[1]**tend** /tend/ *v* to have charge of; take care of

[2]**tend** *v* **1** to move, direct, or develop one's course in a specified direction **2** to show an inclination or tendency – + *to, towards,* or *to* and an infinitive

tendency /'tendənsi/ *n* **1** a general trend or movement **2** an inclination or predisposition to some particular end, or towards a particular kind of thought or action

[1]**tender** /'tendə'/ *adj* **1** having a soft or yielding texture; easily broken, cut, or damaged **2a** physically weak **b** immature, young **3** fond, loving **4a** showing care **b** highly susceptible to impressions or emotions **5** gentle, mild **6a** sensitive to touch **b** sensitive to injury or insult – ~**ly** *adv* – ~**ness** *n*

[2]**tender** *n* **1a** a ship employed to attend other ships (e g to supply provisions) **b** a boat or small steamer for communication between shore and a larger ship **2** a vehicle attached to a locomotive for carrying a supply of fuel and water

[3]**tender** *v* **1** to make a bid **2** to present for acceptance

[4]**tender** *n* **1a** a formal esp written offer or bid for a contract **b** a public expression of willingness to buy not less than a specified number of shares at a fixed price from shareholders **2** sthg that may be offered in payment; *specif* money

tenderfoot /'tendəfʊt/ *n* an inexperienced beginner

tenderhearted /,tendə'hɑːtəd/ *adj* easily moved to love, pity, or sorrow – ~**ly** *adv* – ~**ness** *n*

tenderloin /'tendəlɔɪn/ *n* a pork or beef fillet

tendon /'tendən/ *n* a tough cord or band of dense white fibrous connective tissue that connects a muscle with a bone or other part and transmits the force exerted by the muscle

tendril /ˈtendrɨl/ *n* a slender spirally coiling sensitive organ that attaches a plant to its support

tenement /ˈtenɨmənt/ *n* (a flat in) a large building; *esp* one meeting minimum standards and typically found in the poorer parts of a large city

tenet /ˈtenɨt/ *n* a principle, belief, or doctrine; *esp* one held in common by members of an organization or group

tenner /ˈtenəʳ/ *n, Br* a £10 note; *also* the sum of £10 – infml

tennis /ˈtenɨs/ *n* a singles or doubles game that is played with rackets and a light elastic ball on a flat court divided by a low net

tennis elbow *n* inflammation and pain of the elbow, usu resulting from excessive twisting movements of the hand

[1]**tenon** /ˈtenən/ *n* a projecting part of a piece of material (e g wood) for insertion into a mortise

[2]**tenon** *v* **1** to unite by a tenon **2** to cut or fit for insertion in a mortise

tenon saw *n* a woodworking saw that has a reinforced blade and is used for making fine cuts

tenor /ˈtenəʳ/ *n* **1** the course of thought of sthg spoken or written **2a** (sby with) the highest natural adult male singing voice **b** a member of a family of instruments having a range next lower than that of the alto **3** a continuance in a course or activity

tenpin bowling /ˌtenpɪnˈbəʊlɪŋ/ *n* an indoor bowling game using 10 pins and a large ball in which each player is allowed to bowl 2 balls in each of 10 frames

[1]**tense** /tens/ *n* (a member of) a set of inflectional forms of a verb that express distinctions of time

[2]**tense** *adj* **1** stretched tight; made taut **2a** feeling or showing nervous tension **b** marked by strain or suspense – **~ly** *adv* – **~ness** *n*

[3]**tense** *v* to make or become tense – often + *up*

tensile /ˈtensaɪl/ *adj* **1** ductile **2** of or involving tension

[1]**tension** /ˈtenʃən/ *n* **1a** stretching or being stretched to stiffness **b** stress **2** either of 2 balancing forces causing or tending to cause extension **3a** inner striving, unrest, or imbalance, often with physiological indication of emotion **b** latent hostility **c** a balance maintained in an artistic work between opposing forces or elements

[2]**tension** *v* to tighten to a desired or appropriate degree

tent /tent/ *n* **1** a collapsible shelter (e g of canvas) stretched and supported by poles **2** a canopy or enclosure placed over the head and shoulders to retain vapours or oxygen during medical treatment

tentacle /ˈtentɨkəl/ *n* any of various elongated flexible animal parts, chiefly on the head or about the mouth, used for feeling, grasping, etc

tentative /ˈtentətɪv/ *adj* **1** not fully worked out or developed **2** hesitant, uncertain – **~ly** *adv* – **~ness** *n*

tenuous /ˈtenjʊəs/ *adj* **1** not dense in consistency **2** not thick **3** having little substance or strength – **~ly** *adv* – **~ness** *n*

tenure /ˈtenjəʳ, -jʊəʳ/ *n* **1** the holding of property, an office, etc **2** freedom from summary dismissal, esp from a teaching post

tepee /ˈtiːpiː/ *n* a N American Indian conical tent, usu made of skins

tepid /ˈtepɨd/ *adj* **1** moderately warm **2** not enthusiastic – **~ity** *n* – **~ly** *adv* – **~ness** *n*

tequila /tɨˈkiːlə/ *n* **1** a Mexican plant cultivated as a source of mescal **2** a Mexican spirit made by redistilling mescal

[1]**term** /tɜːm/ *n* **1a** an end, termination; *also* a time assigned for sthg (e g payment) **b** the time at which a pregnancy of normal length ends **2a** a limited or definite extent of time; *esp* the time for which sthg lasts **b** any one of the periods of the year during which the courts are in session **c** any of the usu 3 periods of instruction into which an academic year is divided **3** an expression that forms part of a fraction or proportion or of a series or sequence **4** a word or expression with a precise meaning; *esp* one peculiar to a restricted field **5** *pl* provisions relating to an agreement; *also* agreement

on such provisions **6** *pl* mutual relationship

[2]**term** *v* to apply a term to; call

termagant /'tɜːməgənt/ *n* an overbearing or nagging woman

[1]**terminal** /'tɜːmɪ̣nəl/ *adj* **1a** of or being an end, extremity, boundary, or terminus **b** growing at the end of a branch or stem **2a** of or occurring in a term or each term **b** occurring at or causing the end of life **3** occurring at or being the end of a period or series – **~ly** *adv*

[2]**terminal** *n* **1** a device attached to the end of a wire or cable or to an electrical apparatus for convenience in making connections **2** the end of a carrier line (e g shipping line or airline) with its associated buildings and facilities **3** a device (e g a teleprinter) through which a user can communicate with a computer

terminate /'tɜːmɪ̣neɪt/ *v* **1** to bring to an end; form the conclusion of **2** to come to an end in time; form an ending or outcome – often + *in* or *with* – **-ation** *n*

terminology /,tɜːmɪ̣'nɒlədʒi/ *n* the technical terms used in a particular subject – **-ogical** *adj* – **-ogically** *adv*

terminus /'tɜːmɪ̣nəs/ *n, pl* **termini, terminuses** **1** a finishing point; an end **2** a post or stone marking a boundary **3** (the station, town, or city at) the end of a transport line or travel route

termite /'tɜːmaɪt/ *n* any of numerous often destructive pale-coloured soft-bodied insects that live in colonies and feed on wood

tern /tɜːn/ *n* any of numerous water birds that are smaller than the related gulls and have a black cap, a white body, and often forked tails

terrace /'terɪ̣s/ *n* **1** a relatively level paved or planted area adjoining a building **2** a raised embankment with a level top **3a** a row of houses or flats on raised ground or a sloping site **b** a row of similar houses joined into 1 building by common walls

terracotta /,terə'kɒtə/ *n* **1** an unglazed brownish red fired clay used esp for statuettes and vases and as a building material **2** brownish orange

terra firma /,terə 'fɜːmə/ *n* dry land; solid ground

terrain /te'reɪn, tɪ̣-/ *n* **1** (the physical features of) an area of land **2** an environment, milieu

terrapin /'terəpɪ̣n/ *n* any of several small edible freshwater reptiles of the same order as, and similar to, tortoises but adapted for swimming

terrestrial /tɪ̣'restrɪəl/ *adj* **1a** of the earth or its inhabitants **b** mundane, prosaic **2a** of land as distinct from air or water **b** *of organisms* living on or in land or soil – **~ly** *adv*

terrible /'terəbəl/ *adj* **1a** exciting intense fear; terrifying **b** formidable in nature **c** requiring great fortitude; *also* severe **2** extreme, great **3** of very poor quality; awful; *also* highly unpleasant *USE* (*2&3*) infml

terribly /'terəbli/ *adv* very – infml

terrier /'terɪə^r/ *n* (a member of) any of various breeds of usu small dogs, orig used by hunters to drive out small furred game from underground

terrific /tə'rɪfɪk/ *adj* **1** exciting fear or awe **2** extraordinarily great or intense **3** unusually fine – **~ally** *adv* *USE* (*2&3*) infml

terrify /'terɪ̣faɪ/ *v* **1** to fill with terror or apprehension **2** to drive or impel by menacing; scare, deter – **~ingly** *adv*

territorial /,terɪ̣'tɔːrɪəl/ *adj* **1a** of territory or land **b** of private property **2** of or restricted to a particular area or district

territorial army *n* a voluntary force organized by a locality to provide a trained army reserve that can be mobilized in an emergency

territorial waters *n pl* the waters under the sovereign jurisdiction of a nation

territory /'terɪ̣təri/ *n* **1a** a geographical area under the jurisdiction of a government **b** an administrative subdivision of a country **2a** a geographical area; *esp* one having a specified characteristic **b** a field of knowledge or interest **3a** an assigned area; *esp* one in which an agent or distributor operates **b** an area, often including a nesting site or den, occupied and defended by an animal or group of animals

terror /'terə^r/ *n* **1** a state of intense fear **2** sby or sthg that inspires fear **3** revolutionary violence (e g the planting of bombs) **4** an appalling person or thing; *esp* a brat – infml

terrorism /'terərɪzəm/ *n* the systematic use of terror, esp as a means of coercion – **-ist** *adj, n* – **-ize** *v*

terror-stricken *adj* overcome with an uncontrollable terror

terse /tɜːs/ *adj* concise; *also* brusque, curt – **~ly** *adv* – **~ness** *n*

tertiary /'tɜːʃəri/ *adj* **1a** of third rank, importance, or value **b** of higher education **c** of or being a service industry **2** *cap* of or being the first period of the Cainozoic era or the corresponding system of rocks **3** occurring in or being a third stage

tessellated /'tesɨleɪtɨd/ *adj* chequered

¹test /test/ *n* **1a** a critical examination, observation, or evaluation **b** a basis for evaluation **2a** a procedure used to identify a substance **b** a series of questions or exercises for measuring the knowledge, intelligence, etc of an individual or group **c** a test match

²test *v* **1** to put to the test; try **2** to apply a test as a means of analysis or diagnosis – often + *for* – **~er** *n*

³test *n* an external hard or firm covering (e g a shell) of an invertebrate (e g a mollusc)

testa /'testə/ *n, pl* **testae** the hard external coat of a seed

testament /'testəmənt/ *n* **1** *cap* either of the 2 main divisions of the Bible **2** a tangible proof or tribute **3** a will – **~ary** *adj*

testate /'testeɪt, -tɨt/ *adj* having made a valid will

testator /tes'teɪtəʳ/ , *fem* **testatrix** /tes'teɪtrɪks/ *n* sby who leaves a will

test ban *n* a self-imposed ban on the atmospheric testing of nuclear weapons

test case *n* a representative case whose outcome is likely to serve as a precedent

testicle /'testɪkəl/ *n* a testis, esp of a mammal and usu with its enclosing structures (e g the scrotum)

testify /'testɨfaɪ/ *v* **1a** to make a statement based on personal knowledge or belief **b** to serve as evidence or proof **2a** to make a solemn declaration under oath **b** to make known (a personal conviction)

¹testimonial /ˌtestɨ'məʊnɪəl/ *adj* **1** of or constituting testimony **2** expressive of appreciation, gratitude, or esteem

²testimonial *n* **1** a letter of recommendation **2** an expression of appreciation or esteem (e g in the form of a gift)

testimony /'testɨməni/ *n* **1a** firsthand authentication of a fact **b** an outward sign; evidence **c** a sworn statement by a witness **2** a public declaration of religious experience

testis /'testɨs/ *n, pl* **testes** a male reproductive gland

test match *n* any of a series of international (cricket) matches

test pilot *n* a pilot who specializes in putting new or experimental aircraft through manoeuvres designed to test them by producing strains in excess of normal

test-tube *adj, of a baby* conceived by artificial insemination, esp outside the mother's body

test tube *n* a thin glass tube closed at 1 end and used in chemistry, biology, etc

testy /'testi/ *adj* impatient, ill-humoured – **-tily** *adv* – **-tiness** *n*

tetanus /'tetənəs/ *n* (the bacterium, usu introduced through a wound, that causes) an infectious disease characterized by spasm of voluntary muscles, esp of the jaw

¹tête-à-tête /ˌtet ɑː 'tet/ *adv or adj* (in) private

²tête-à-tête *n* **1** a private conversation between 2 people **2** a seat (e g a sofa) designed for 2 people to sit facing each other

¹tether /'teðəʳ/ *n* **1** a rope, chain, etc by which an animal is fastened so that it can move only within a set radius **2** the limit of one's strength or resources – chiefly in *the end of one's tether*

²tether *v* to fasten or restrain (as if) by a tether

tetrahedron /ˌtetrə'hiːdrən/ *n, pl* **tetrahedrons, tetrahedra** a polyhedron of 4 faces

Teutonic /tjuː'tɒnɪk/ *n* Germanic

text /tekst/ *n* **1** (a work containing) the original written or printed words and form of a literary composition **2** the main body of printed or written matter, esp on a page or in a book **3a**

a passage of Scripture chosen esp for the subject of a sermon or in authoritative support of a doctrine **b** a passage from an authoritative source providing a theme (e g for a speech)

[1]**textbook** /'tekstbʊk/ *n* a book used in the study of a subject; *specif* one containing a presentation of the principles of a subject and used by students

[2]**textbook** *adj* conforming to the principles or descriptions in textbooks: e g **a** ideal **b** typical

textile /'tekstaɪl/ *n* **1** a (woven or knitted) cloth **2** a fibre, filament, or yarn used in making cloth

[1]**texture** /'tekstʃəʳ/ *n* **1** identifying quality; character **2a** the size or organization of the constituent particles of a body or substance **b** the visual or tactile surface characteristics of sthg, esp fabric **3** the distinctive or identifying part or quality

[2]**texture** *v* to give a particular texture to

thalidomide /θə'lɪdəmaɪd/ *adj or n* (of or affected by) a sedative and hypnotic drug found to cause malformation of infants born to mothers using it during pregnancy

[1]**than** /ðən; *strong* ðæn/ *conj* **1a** – used with comparatives to indicate the second member or the member taken as the point of departure in a comparison (e g older *than* I am) **b** – used to indicate difference of kind, manner, or degree (e g would starve rather *than* beg) **2** rather than – usu only after *prefer, preferable* **3** other than; but (e g no alternative *than* to sack) **4** *chiefly NAm* from – usu only after *different, differently*

[2]**than** *prep* in comparison with

thane *also* **thegn** /θeɪn/ *n* **1** a free retainer of an Anglo-Saxon lord; *esp* one holding lands in exchange for military service **2** a Scottish feudal lord

thank /θæŋk/ *v* **1** to express gratitude to – used in *thank you,* usu without a subject, to express gratitude politely; used in such phrases as *thank God, thank heaven,* usu without a subject, to express the speaker's or writer's pleasure or satisfaction in sthg **2** to hold responsible

thankful /'θæŋkfəl/ *adj* **1** conscious of benefit received; grateful **2** feeling or expressing thanks **3** well pleased; glad – **~ly** *adv* – **~ness** *n*

thankless /'θæŋklɪ̧s/ *adj* **1** not expressing or feeling gratitude **2** not likely to obtain thanks; unappreciated; *also* unprofitable, futile – **~ly** *adv* – **~ness** *n*

thanks /θæŋks/ *n pl* **1** kindly or grateful thoughts; gratitude **2** an expression of gratitude – often in an utterance containing no verb and serving as a courteous and somewhat informal expression of gratitude

thanksgiving /ˌθæŋks'gɪvɪŋ/ *n* an expression of gratefulness, esp to God

thank-you *n* a polite expression of one's gratitude

[1]**that** /ðæt/ *pron, pl* **those** **1a** the thing or idea just mentioned (e g after *that* we went to bed) **b** a relatively distant person or thing introduced for observation or discussion (e g who's *that?*) **c** the thing or state of affairs there (e g look at *that*) – sometimes used disparagingly of a person **d** the kind or thing specified as follows (e g the purest water is *that* produced by distillation) **e** what is understood from the context (e g take *that*!) **2** one of such a group; such (e g *that's* life) **3** – used to indicate emphatic repetition of an idea previously presented (e g is he capable? He is *that*) **4** *pl* the people; such (e g *those* who think the time has come)

[2]**that** /ðæt/ *adj, pl* **those** **1** being the person, thing, or idea specified, mentioned, or understood (e g *that* cake we bought) **2** the farther away or less immediately under observation (e g this chair or *that* one)

[3]**that** /ðət; *strong* ðæt/ *conj* **1** – used to introduce a noun clause as subject, object, or complement (e g said *that* he was afraid; the fact *that* you're here) **2** – used to introduce a subordinate clause expressing (1) purpose, (2) reason, or (3) result (e g worked harder *that* he might win; glad *that* you are free of it)

[4]**that** /ðət; *strong* ðæt/ *pron* **1** – used to introduce some relative clauses (e g it was George *that* told me; the house *that* Jack built) or as object of a verb

or of a following preposition **2a** at, in, on, by, with, for, or to which (e g the reason *that* he came; the way *that* he spoke) **b** according to what; to the extent of what – used after a negative (e g has never been there *that* I know of)

[5]**that** /ðæt/ *adv* **1** to the extent indicated or understood (e g a nail about *that* long) **2** very, extremely – usu with the negative (e g not really *that* expensive) **3** *dial Br* to such an extreme degree (e g I'm *that* hungry I could eat a horse)

[1]**thatch** /θætʃ/ *v* to cover (as if) with thatch

[2]**thatch** *n* **1** plant material (e g straw) used as a roof covering **2** the hair of one's head; *broadly* anything resembling the thatch of a house

[1]**thaw** /θɔː/ *v* **1a** to go from a frozen to a liquid state **b** to become free of the effect (e g stiffness, numbness, or hardness) of cold as a result of exposure to warmth – often + *out* **2** to be warm enough to melt ice and snow – used in reference to the weather **3** to become less hostile **4** to become less aloof, cold, or reserved

[2]**thaw** *n* **1** the action, fact, or process of thawing **2** a period of weather warm enough to thaw ice

[1]**the** /ðə, ði; *strong* ðiː/ *definite article* **1a** – used before nouns when the referent has been previously specified by context or circumstance (e g put *the* cat out; ordered bread and cheese, but didn't eat *the* cheese) **b** – indicating that a following noun is unique or universally recognized (e g *the* Pope; *the* south) **c** – used before certain proper names (e g *the* Rhine; *the* MacDonald) **d** – designating 1 of a class as the best or most worth singling out (e g you can't be *the* Elvis Presley) **e** – used before the pl form of a number that is a multiple of 10 to denote a particular decade of a century or of a person's life (e g life in *the* twenties) **2** – used before a singular noun to indicate generic use (e g a history of *the* novel) **3a** that which is (e g nothing but *the* best) **b** those who are (e g *the* élite) **c** he or she who is (e g *the* accused stands before you) **4** – used after *how, what, where, who,* and *why* to introduce various expletives (e g who *the* devil are you?)

[2]**the** *adv* **1** than before; than otherwise – with comparatives (e g so much *the* worse) **2a** to what extent (e g *the* sooner the better) **b** to that extent (e g the sooner *the* better) **3** beyond all others – with superlatives (e g likes this *the* best)

[3]**the** *prep* per (e g 50p *the* dozen)

theatre, *NAm chiefly* **theater** /ˈθɪətəʳ/ *n* **1** a building for dramatic performances **2** a room with rising tiers of seats (e g for lectures) **3** a place of enactment of significant events or action **4** *the* theatrical world **5** *Br* an operating theatre

theatrical /θiˈætrɪkəl/ *adj* **1** of the theatre or the presentation of plays **2** marked by artificiality (e g of emotion) **3** marked by exhibitionism; histrionic – **~ly** *adv*

theatricals /θiˈætrɪkəlz/ *n pl* the performance of plays

thee /ðiː/ *pron, archaic or dial* **1a** *objective case of* **thou** **2** thyself

theft /θeft/ *n* the act of stealing; *specif* dishonest appropriation of property with the intention of keeping it

their /ðəʳ; *strong* ðeəʳ/ *adj* **1** of them or themselves, esp as possessors, agents, or objects of an action **2** his or her; his, her, its *USE* used attributively

theirs /ðeəz/ *pron, pl* **theirs** **1** that which or the one who belongs to them – used without a following noun as a pronoun equivalent in meaning to the adjective *their* **2** his or hers; his, hers

theism /ˈθiːɪzəm/ *n* belief in the existence of a creator god everwhere in the universe but transcending it – **-ist** *n* – **-istic** *adj* – **-istically** *adv*

[1]**them** /ðəm; *strong* ðem/ *pron, objective case of* **they**

[2]**them** /ðem/ *adj* those – nonstandard

theme /θiːm/ *n* **1** a subject of artistic representation or a topic of discourse **2** a melodic subject of a musical composition or movement

themselves /ðəmˈselvz/ *pron pl in constr* **1a** those identical people, creatures, or things that are they – used reflexively or for emphasis **b** himself or herself; himself, herself (e g hoped nobody would hurt *themselves*) **2** their normal selves (e g soon be *themselves* again)

[1]**then** /ðen/ *adv* **1** at that time **2a** soon after that; next in order (of time) **b** besides; in addition **3a** in that case **b** as may be inferred (e g your mind is made up *then*?) **c** accordingly, so – indicating casual connection in speech or writing (e g our hero, *then*, was greatly relieved) **d** as a necessary consequence **e** – used after *but* to offset a preceding statement (e g he lost the race, but *then* he never expected to win)

[2]**then** *n* that time

[3]**then** *adj* existing or acting at that time (e g the *then* secretary of state)

thence /ðens/ *adv* **1** from there **2** from that preceding fact or premise – chiefly fml

thenceforth /ðens'fɔːθ/ *adv* from that time or point on – chiefly fml

theocracy /θi'ɒkrəsi/ *n* (a state having) government by immediate divine guidance or by officials regarded as divinely guided – **-cratic** *adj*

theodolite /θi'ɒdəlaɪt/ *n* a surveyor's instrument for measuring horizontal and usu also vertical angles

theology /θi'ɒlədʒi/ *n* **1** the study of God, esp by analysis of the origins and teachings of an organized religion **2** a theological theory, system, or body of opinion – **-ogical** *adj* – **-ogically** *adv* – **-ogian** *n*

theorem /'θɪərəm/ *n* **1** a proposition in mathematics or logic deducible from other more basic propositions **2** an idea proposed as a demonstrable truth, often as a part of a general theory; a proposition

theoretical /θɪə'retɪkəl/ *adj* **1a** relating to or having the character of theory; abstract **b** confined to theory or speculation; speculative **2** existing only in theory; hypothetical – **~ly** *adv*

theorist /'θɪərɪ̣st/ *n* a theoretician

theory /'θɪəri/ *n* **1a** a belief, policy, or procedure forming the basis for action **b** an ideal or supposed set of facts, principles, or circumstances – often in *in theory* **2** the general or abstract principles of a subject **3** a scientifically acceptable body of principles offered to explain a phenomenon **4a** a hypothesis assumed for the sake of argument or investigation **b** an unproved assumption; a conjecture – **-rize** *v*

therapeutic /ˌθerə'pjuːtɪk/ *adj* of the treatment of disease or disorders by remedial agents or methods – **~ally** *adv*

therapist /'θerəpɪ̣st/ *n* sby trained in methods of treatment and rehabilitation other than the use of drugs or surgery

therapy /'θerəpi/ *n* therapeutic treatment of bodily, mental, or social disorders

[1]**there** /ðeəʳ/ *adv* **1** in or at that place – often used to draw attention or to replace a name **2** thither **3a** now (e g *there* goes the hooter) **b** at or in that point or particular (e g *there* is where I disagree with you) **4** – used interjectionally to express satisfaction, approval, encouragement, or defiance

[2]**there** /ðeəʳ, ðəʳ/ *pron* – used to introduce a sentence or clause expressing the idea of existence (e g *there* shall come a time)

[3]**there** *n* that place or point

[4]**there** *adj* – used for emphasis, esp after a demonstrative (e g those men *there* can tell you)

thereabouts /ˌðeərə'baʊts/, *NAm also* **thereabout** *adv* **1** in that vicinity **2** near that time, number, degree, or quantity

thereafter /ðeə'rɑːftəʳ/ *adv* after that

thereby /ðeə'baɪ, 'ðeəbaɪ/ *adv* **1** by that means; resulting from which **2** in which connection (e g *thereby* hangs a tale)

therefore /'ðeəfɔːʳ/ *adv* **1** for that reason; to that end **2** by virtue of that; consequently (e g I was tired and *therefore* irritable) **3** as this proves (e g I think *therefore* I exist)

therein /ðeə'rɪn/ *adv* in that; *esp* in that respect – fml

therm /θɜːm/ *n* a quantity of heat equal to 100,000Btu (about 105,506MJ)

[1]thermal /ˈθɜːməl/ *adj* **1 thermal, thermic** of or caused by heat **2** designed (e g with insulating air spaces) to prevent the dissipation of body heat

[2]thermal *n* a rising body of warm air

thermodynamics /ˌθɜːməʊdaɪˈnæmɪks/ *n pl but sing or pl in constr* (physics that deals with) the mechanical action of, or relations between, heat and other forms of energy

thermometer /θəˈmɒmɪ̈təʳ/ *n* an instrument for determining temperature; *esp* a glass bulb attached to a fine graduated tube of glass and containing a liquid (e g mercury) that rises and falls with changes of temperature

thermonuclear /ˌθɜːməʊˈnjuːklɪəʳ/ *adj* of, using, or being (weapons using) transformations occurring in the nucleus of low atomic weight atoms (e g hydrogen) at very high temperatures

Thermos /ˈθɜːməs/ *trademark* – used for an insulated flask used for keeping liquids, etc hot or cold

thermostat /ˈθɜːməstæt/ *n* an automatic device for regulating temperature

thesaurus /θɪˈsɔːrəs, ˈθesərəs/ *n, pl* **thesauri, thesauruses** a book of words or of information about a particular field or set of concepts; *esp* a book of words and their synonyms

these /ðiːz/ *pl of* **this**

thesis /ˈθiːsɪ̈s/ *n, pl* **theses** **1** a proposition to be proved or one advanced without proof; a hypothesis **2** the first stage of a reasoned argument presenting the case **3** a dissertation embodying the results of original research; *specif* one submitted for a doctorate in Britain

they /ðeɪ/ *pron pl in constr* **1a** those people, creatures, or things; *also, chiefly Br* that group **b** he (e g if anyone has found it, *they* will hand it in) **2a** people (e g *they* say that there's no truth in it) **b** the authorities

they'd /ðeɪd/ they had; they would

[1]thick /θɪk/ *adj* **1a** having or being of relatively great depth or extent between opposite surfaces **b** of comparatively large diameter in relation to length **2a** closely-packed; dense **b** great in number **c** viscous in consistency **d** foggy or misty **3a** imperfectly articulated **b** plainly apparent; marked **4a** sluggish, dull **b** obtuse, stupid **5** on close terms; intimate **6** unreasonable, unfair *USE* (*4, 5, & 6*) infml – **~ly** *adv*

[2]thick *n* **1** the most crowded or active part **2** the part of greatest thickness

thicket /ˈθɪkɪ̈t/ *n* a dense growth of shrubbery or small trees

thickness /ˈθɪknɪ̈s/ *n* **1** the smallest of the 3 dimensions of a solid object **2** the thick part of sthg **3** a layer, ply

thickset /ˌθɪkˈset/ *adj* **1** closely placed; *also* growing thickly **2** heavily built; burly

thick-skinned *adj* callous, insensitive

thief /θiːf/ *n, pl* **thieves** sby who steals, esp secretly and without violence

thieve /θiːv/ *v* to steal, rob – **-ving** *n, adj* – **-vish** *adj* – **-vishly** *adv* – **-vishness** *n*

thigh /θaɪ/ *n* the segment of the vertebrate hind limb nearest the body that extends from the hip to the knee and is supported by a single large bone

thimble /ˈθɪmbəl/ *n* **1** a pitted metal or plastic cap or cover worn to protect the finger and to push the needle in sewing **2** a movable ring, tube, or lining in a hole

[1]thin /θɪn/ *adj* **1a** having little depth between opposite surfaces **b** measuring little in cross section **2** not dense or closely-packed **3** without much flesh; lean **4a** more rarefied than normal **b** few in number **5** lacking substance or strength **6** flimsy, unconvincing **7** somewhat feeble and lacking in resonance **8** lacking in intensity or brilliance **9** disappointingly poor or hard – **~ly** *adv* – **~ness** *n*

[2]thin *v* **1** to reduce in thickness or depth; attenuate **2** to reduce in strength or density **3** to reduce in number or bulk

[1]thine /ðaɪn/ *adj, archaic* thy – used esp before a vowel or *h*

[2]thine *pron, pl* **thine** *archaic or dial* that which belongs to thee – used without a following noun as a pronoun equivalent in meaning to the adjective *thy*

thing /θɪŋ/ *n* **1a** a matter, affair, concern **b** an event, circumstance **2a(1)** a deed, act, achievement **(2)** an activity, action **b** a product of work or activity **c** the aim of effort or activity **d** sthg necessary or desirable **3a** a separate and distinct object of thought (e g a quality, fact, or idea) **b** an inanimate object as distinguished from a living being **c** *pl* imaginary objects or entities **4a** *pl* possessions, effects **b** an article of clothing **c** *pl* equipment or utensils, esp for a particular purpose **5** an object or entity not (capable of being) precisely designated **6** *the* proper or fashionable way of behaving, talking, or dressing **7a** a preoccupation (e g a mild obsession or phobia) of a specified type **b** an intimate relationship; *esp* a love affair

[1]**think** /θɪŋk/ *v* **thought** **1a** to exercise the powers of judgment, conception, or inference **b** to have in mind or call to mind a thought or idea – usu + *of* **2** to have as an opinion; consider **3a** to reflect on – often + *over* **b** to determine by reflecting – often + *out* **c** to have the mind engaged in reflection – usu + *of* or *about* **4** to call to mind; remember **5** to devise by thinking – usu + *up* **6** to have as an expectation **7** to subject to the processes of logical thought – usu + *out* or *through* – ~**er** *n*

[2]**think** *n* an act of thinking – infml

[1]**thinking** /ˈθɪŋkɪŋ/ *n* **1** the action of using one's mind to produce thoughts **2** opinion that is characteristic (e g of a period, group, or individual)

[2]**thinking** *adj* marked by use of the intellect

think tank *n sing or pl in constr* a group of people formed as a consultative body to evolve new ideas and offer expert advice

thinner /ˈθɪnəʳ/ *n* liquid (e g turpentine) used esp to thin paint

thin-skinned *adj* unduly susceptible to criticism or insult

[1]**third** /θɜːd/ *adj* **1a** next after the second in place or time **b** ranking next to second in authority or precedence **2a** being any of 3 equal parts into which sthg is divisible **b** being the last in each group of 3 in a series

[2]**third** *n* **1a** number three in a countable series **b** sthg or sby that is next after second in rank, position, authority, or precedence **c third, third class** *often cap* the third and usu lowest level of British honours degree **2** any of 3 equal parts of sthg **3** (the combination of 2 notes at) a musical interval of 3 diatonic degrees

third degree *n* the subjection of a prisoner to torture to obtain information

third-party *adj* of insurance covering loss or damage sustained by sby other than the insured

third party *n* sby other than the principals

third person *n* a set of linguistic forms (e g verb forms or pronouns) referring neither to the speaker or writer of the utterance in which they occur nor to the one to whom that utterance is addressed

third-rate *adj* third in quality or value; *broadly* of extremely poor quality

third world *n, often cap T&W, sing or pl in constr* **1** a group of nations, esp in Africa and Asia, that are not aligned with either the communist or the capitalist blocs **2** the underdeveloped nations of the world

[1]**thirst** /θɜːst/ *n* **1** (the sensation of dryness in the mouth and throat associated with) a desire or need to drink **2** an ardent desire; a craving

[2]**thirst** *v* **1** to feel thirsty **2** to crave eagerly

thirsty /ˈθɜːsti/ *adj* **1a** feeling thirst **b** deficient in moisture; parched **2** having a strong desire; avid – **thirstily** *adv*

thirteen /ˌθɜːˈtiːn/ *n* the number 13 – ~**th** *adj, pron, adv*

thirty /ˈθɜːti/ *n* **1** the number 30 **2** *pl* the numbers 30 to 39; *specif* a range of temperatures, ages, or dates in a century characterized by these numbers – **-tieth** *adj, n, pron, adv*

[1]**this** /ðɪs/ *pron, pl* **these** **1a** the thing or idea that has just been mentioned **b** what is to be shown or stated (e g do it like *this*) **c** this time or place **2a** a nearby person or thing introduced for

observation or discussion **b** the thing or state of affairs here (e g what's all *this*?; please carry *this*)

[2]**this** *adj, pl* **these** **1a** being the person, thing, or idea that is present or near in time or thought (e g early *this* morning; who's *this* Mrs Fogg anyway?) **b** the nearer at hand or more immediately under observation (e g *this* chair or that one) **c** constituting the immediate past or future period (e g have lived here *these* 10 years) **d** constituting what is to be shown or stated (e g have you heard *this* one?) **2** a certain (e g there was *this* Irishman ...)

[3]**this** *adv* **1** to this extent (e g known her since she was *this* high) **2** to this extreme degree – usu + the negative (e g didn't expect to wait *this* long)

thistle /ˈθɪsəl/ *n* any of various prickly composite plants with (showy) heads of mostly tubular flowers – **thistly** *adv*

thistledown /ˈθɪsəldaʊn/ *n* the fluffy hairs from the ripe flower head of a thistle

thither /ˈðɪðəʳ/ *adv* to or towards that place – chiefly fml

thong /θɒŋ/ *n* a narrow strip, esp of leather

thorax /ˈθɔːræks/ *n, pl* **thoraxes, thoraces** (a division of the body of an insect, spider, etc corresponding to) the part of the mammalian body between the neck and the abdomen; *also* its cavity in which the heart and lungs lie

thorn /θɔːn/ *n* **1** a woody plant (of the rose family) bearing sharp prickles of thorns **2** a short hard sharp-pointed plant part, specif a leafless branch **3** sby or sthg that causes irritation

thorny /ˈθɔːni/ *adj* **1** full of or covered in thorns **2** full of difficulties or controversial points – **thorniness** *n*

thorough /ˈθʌrə/ *adj* **1** marked by full detail **2** painstaking **3** being fully and without qualification as specified – **~ly** *adv*

[1]**thoroughbred** /ˈθʌrəbred/ *adj* having the characteristics associated with good breeding or pedigree

[2]**thoroughbred** *n cap* any of an English breed of horses kept chiefly for racing that originated from crosses between English mares of uncertain ancestry and Arabian stallions

thoroughfare /ˈθʌrəfeəʳ/ *n* **1** a public way (e g a road, street, or path); *esp* a main road **2** passage, transit

thoroughgoing /ˈθʌrəgəʊɪŋ/ *adj* **1** extremely thorough or zealous **2** absolute, utter

those /ðəʊz/ *pl of* [1,2]**that**

[1]**thou** /ðaʊ/ *pron, archaic or dial* the one being addressed; you

[2]**thou** /θaʊ/ *n, pl* **thou, thous** **1** a thousand (of sthg, esp money) **2** a unit of length equal to $^{1}/_{1000}$in (about 25.4mm)

[1]**though** *also* **tho** /ðəʊ/ *adv* however, nevertheless

[2]**though** *also* **tho** *conj* **1** in spite of the fact that; while **2** in spite of the possibility that; even if **3** and yet; but

[1]**thought** /θɔːt/ *past of* **think**

[2]**thought** *n* **1a** thinking **b** serious consideration **2** reasoning or conceptual power **3a** an idea, opinion, concept, or intention **b** the intellectual product or the organized views of a period, place, group, or individual

thoughtful /ˈθɔːtfəl/ *adj* **1a** having thoughts; absorbed in thought **b** showing careful reasoned thinking **2** showing concern for others – **~ly** *adv* – **~ness** *n*

thoughtless /ˈθɔːtləs/ *adj* **1** lacking forethought; rash **2** lacking concern for others – **~ly** *adv* – **~ness** *n*

thousand /ˈθaʊzənd/ *n, pl* **thousands, thousand** **1** the number 1,000 **2** the number occupying the position 4 to the left of the decimal point in the Arabic notation; *also, pl* this position **3** an indefinitely large number – often pl with sing. meaning – **~th** *adj, n, pron, adv*

thrall /θrɔːl/ *n* a state of complete absorption or enslavement – **thraldom** *n*

[1]**thrash** /θræʃ/ *v* **1** to thresh **2a** to beat soundly (as if) with a stick or whip **b** to defeat heavily or decisively **3** to move or stir about violently; toss about – usu + *around* or *about*

[2]**thrash** *n* **1** an act of thrashing, esp in swimming **2** a wild party – infml

thrash out *v* to discuss (e g a problem) exhaustively with a view to finding a solution; *also* to arrive at (e g a decision) in this way

[1]**thread** /θred/ *n* **1** a filament, group of filaments twisted together, or continuous strand (formed by spinning and twisting together short textile fibres) **2a** sthg (e g a thin stream of liquid) like a thread in length and narrowness **b** a projecting spiral ridge (e g on a bolt or pipe) by which parts can be screwed together **3** sthg continuous or drawn out: e g **a** a train of thought **b** a pervasive recurring element **4** a precarious or weak support

[2]**thread** *v* **1a** to pass a thread through the eye of (a needle) **b** to arrange a thread, yarn, or lead-in piece in working position for use in (a machine) **2a(1)** to pass sthg through the entire length of **(2)** to pass (e g a tape or film) into or through sthg **b** to make one's way cautiously through or between **3** to string together (as if) on a thread

threadbare /'θredbeəʳ/ *adj* **1** having the nap worn off so that the threads show; worn, shabby **2** hackneyed

threat /θret/ *n* **1** an indication of sthg, usu unpleasant, to come **2** an expression of intention to inflict punishment, injury, or damage **3** sthg that is a source of imminent danger or harm

threaten /'θretn/ *v* **1** to utter threats against **2a** to give ominous signs of **b** to be a source of harm or danger to **3** to announce as intended or possible – **~ingly** *adv*

three /θriː/ *n* **1** the number 3 **2** the third in a set or series **3** sthg having 3 parts or members or a denomination of 3

three-dimensional *adj* **1** having 3 dimensions **2** giving the illusion of depth – used of an image or pictorial representation, esp when this illusion is enhanced by stereoscopic means

three-line whip *n* an instruction from a party to its Members of Parliament that they must attend a debate and vote in the specified way

three-quarter *adj* **1** consisting of 3 fourths of the whole **2** *esp of a view of a rectangular object* including 1 side and 1 end

three R's *n pl* *the* fundamentals taught in primary school; *esp* reading, writing, and arithmetic

threnody /'θrenədi/ *n* a song of lamentation, esp for the dead

thresh /θreʃ/ *v* **1** to separate the seeds from (a harvested plant) by (mechanical) beating **2** to strike repeatedly

thresher /'θreʃəʳ/ *n* a large shark reputed to thresh the water to round up fish on which it feeds using the greatly elongated curved upper lobe of its tail

threshold /'θreʃhəʊld, -ʃəʊld/ *n* **1a** the doorway or entrance to a building **b** the point of entering or beginning **2** a level, point, or value above which sthg is true or will take place

threw /θruː/ *past of* **throw**

thrice /θraɪs/ *adv* **1** three times **2** in a threefold manner or degree

thrift /θrɪft/ *n* **1** careful management, esp of money; frugality **2** any of a genus of tufted herbaceous plants; *esp* a sea-pink – **~y** *adj* **~ily** *adv*

thrill /θrɪl/ *v* **1** to (cause to) experience a sudden tremor of excitement or emotion **2** to tingle, throb

thriller /'θrɪləʳ/ *n* a work of fiction or drama characterized by a high degree of intrigue or suspense

thrive /θraɪv/ *v* **throve, thrived; thriven 1** to grow vigorously **2** to gain in wealth or possessions

throat /θrəʊt/ *n* **1a** the part of the neck in front of the spinal column **b** the passage through the neck to the stomach and lungs **2** sthg throatlike, esp in being a constricted passageway

throaty /'θrəʊti/ uttered or produced low in the throat; hoarse, guttural – **throatily** *adv* – **throatiness** *n*

[1]**throb** /θrɒb/ *v* **1** to pulsate with unusual force or rapidity **2** to (come in waves that seem to) beat or vibrate rhythmically

[2]**throb** *n* a beat, pulse

thrombosis /θrɒm'bəʊsɪ̍s/ *n, pl* **thromboses** the formation or presence of a blood clot within a blood vessel during life

throne /θrəʊn/ *n* **1** the chair of state of a sovereign or bishop **2** sovereignty

¹throng /θrɒŋ/ *n sing or pl in constr* **1** a multitude of assembled people, esp when crowded together **2** a large number

²throng *v* **1** to crowd upon (esp a person) **2** to crowd into

¹throttle /ˈθrɒtl/ *v* **1a** to compress the throat of; *also* to kill in this way **b** to suppress **2** to regulate, esp reduce the speed of (e g an engine), by means of a throttle – usu + *back* or *down*

²throttle *n* **1** the windpipe **2** (the lever or pedal controlling) a valve for regulating the supply of a fluid (e g fuel) to an engine

¹through *also* **thro,** *NAm also* **thru** /θruː/ *prep* **1a(1)** into at one side or point and out at the other **(2)** past (e g saw *through* the deception) **b** – used to indicate passage into and out of a treatment, handling, or process (e g flashed *through* my mind) **2** – used to indicate means, agency, or intermediacy: e g **a** by means of; by the agency of **b** because of (e g failed *through* ignorance) **c** by common descent from or relationship with (e g related *through* their grandfather) **3a** over the whole surface or extent of (e g homes scattered *through* the valley) **b** – used to indicate movement within a large expanse (e g flew *through* the air) **c** among or between the parts or single members of (e g search *through* my papers) **4** during the entire period of (e g all *through* her life) **5a** – used to indicate completion, exhaustion, or accomplishment (e g got *through* the book) **b** – used to indicate acceptance or approval, esp by an official body (e g got the bill *through* Parliament) **6** *chiefly NAm* up till and including (e g Saturday *through* Sunday)

²through, *NAm also* **thru** *adv* **1** from one end or side to the other **2a** all the way from beginning to end **b** to a favourable or successful conclusion (e g see it *through*) **3** to the core; completely (e g wet *through*) **4** into the open; out (e g break *through*) **5** *chiefly Br* in or into connection by telephone (e g put me *through* to him)

³through, *NAm also* **thru** *adj* **1a** extending from one surface to the other (e g a *through* beam) **b** direct (e g a *through* road) **2a** allowing a continuous journey from point of origin to destination without change or further payment (e g a *through* train) **b** starting at and destined for points outside a local zone (e g *through* traffic) **3** arrived at completion, cessation, or dismissal; finished (e g I'm *through* with man)

¹throughout /θruːˈaʊt/ *adv* **1** in or to every part; everywhere (e g of 1 colour *throughout*) **2** during the whole time or action; from beginning to end

²throughout *prep* **1** in or to every part of **2** during the entire period of

throughput /ˈθruːpʊt/ *n* the amount of material put through a process

¹throw /θrəʊ/ *v* **threw; thrown** **1** to propel through the air in some manner, esp by a forward motion of the hand and arm **2** to cause to fall **3a** to fling (oneself) abruptly **b** to hurl violently **4** to put *on* or *off* hastily or carelessly **5** to shape by hand on a potter's wheel **6** to deliver (a punch) **7** to send forth; cast, direct **8** to commit (oneself) for help, support, or protection **9** to bring forth; produce **10** to move (a lever or switch) so as to connect or disconnect parts of a mechanism **11** to project (the voice) **12** to give by way of entertainment **13** to disconcert – infml – **~er** *n*

²throw *n* **1a** an act of throwing **b** a method or instance of throwing an opponent in wrestling or judo **2** (the distance of) the extent of movement of a cam, crank, or other pivoted or reciprocating piece

¹throwaway /ˈθrəʊəweɪ/ *n* a line of dialogue (e g in a play) made to sound incidental by casual delivery

²throwaway *adj* written or spoken (e g in a play) with deliberate casualness

throw away *v* **1** to get rid of as worthless or unnecessary **2** to use in a foolish or wasteful manner

throwback /ˈθrəʊbæk/ *n* (an individual exhibiting) reversion to an earlier genetic type or phase

throw back *v* **1** to delay the progress or advance of **2** to cause to rely; make dependent – + *on* or *upon*; usu pass

throw-in *n* a throw made from the touchline in soccer to put the ball back in play after it has gone over the touchline

throw in *v* **1** to add as a gratuity or supplement **2** to introduce or interject in the course of sthg

throw out *v* **1** to remove from a place or from employment, usu in a sudden or unexpected manner **2** to refuse to accept or consider **3** to confuse, disconcert

throw over *v* to forsake or abandon (esp a lover)

throw up *v* **1** to raise quickly **2** to give up **3** to vomit

thrum /θrʌm/ *v* **1** to play or pluck a stringed instrument idly **2** to drum or tap idly **3** to sound with a monotonous hum

¹**thrush** /θrʌʃ/ *n* any of numerous small or medium-sized mostly drab-coloured birds many of which are excellent singers

²**thrush** *n* **1** a whitish intensely irritating fungal growth occurring on mucous membranes, esp in the mouth or vagina **2** a disorder of the feet in various animals, esp horses

¹**thrust** /θrʌst/ *v* **thrust** **1** to force an entrance or passage – often + *into* or *through* **2** to stab, pierce **3** to put (an unwilling person) into a course of action or position **4** to press, force, or impose the acceptance of *on* or *upon* sby

²**thrust** *n* **1a** a push or lunge with a pointed weapon **b(1)** a verbal attack **(2)** a concerted military attack **2a** a strong continued pressure **b** the force exerted by a propeller, jet engine, etc to give forward motion **3a** a forward or upward push **b** a movement (e g by a group of people) in a specified direction

¹**thud** /θʌd/ *v* to move or strike with a thud

²**thud** *n* **1** a blow **2** a dull thump

thug /θʌg/ *n* **1** *often cap* a member of a former religious sect in India given to robbery and murder **2** a violent criminal – **~gery** *n*

¹**thumb** /θʌm/ *n* the short thick digit of the hand that is next to the forefinger; *also* the part of a glove, etc that covers this

²**thumb** *v* **1** to leaf through pages **2** to request or obtain a lift in a passing vehicle; hitchhike

thumbscrew /ˈθʌmskruː/ *n* an instrument of torture for squeezing the thumb

¹**thump** /θʌmp/ *v* **1** to strike or knock with a thump **2** to thrash **3** to produce (music) mechanically or in a mechanical manner

²**thump** *n* (a sound of) a blow or knock (as if) with sthg blunt or heavy

³**thump** *adv* with a thump

thumping /ˈθʌmpɪŋ/ *adv, Br* very – chiefly in *thumping great* and *thumping good*; infml

¹**thunder** /ˈθʌndəʳ/ *n* **1** the low loud sound that follows a flash of lightning and is caused by sudden expansion of the air in the path of the electrical discharge **2** a loud reverberating noise

²**thunder** *v* **1a** to give forth thunder – usu impersonally **b** to make a sound like thunder **2** to roar, shout – **~er** *n*

thunderbolt /ˈθʌndəbəʊlt/ *n* **1** a single discharge of lightning with the accompanying thunder **2** sthg like lightning in suddenness, effectiveness, or destructive power

thunderclap /ˈθʌndəklæp/ *n* (sthg loud or sudden like) a clap of thunder

thundercloud /ˈθʌndəklaʊd/ *n* a cloud charged with electricity and producing lightning and thunder

thundering /ˈθʌndərɪŋ/ *adv, Br* very, thumping – infml

thunderstorm /ˈθʌndəstɔːm/ *n* a storm accompanied by lightning and thunder

thunderstruck /ˈθʌndəstrʌk/ *adj* dumbfounded, astonished

thundery /ˈθʌndəri/ *adj* producing or presaging thunder

Thursday /ˈθɜːzdi, -deɪ/ *n* the day of the week following Wednesday

thus /ðʌs/ *adv* **1** in the manner indicated; in this way **2** to this degree or extent; so **3** because of this preceding fact or premise; consequently **4** as an example

¹**thwart** /θwɔːt/ *v* to defeat the hopes or aspirations of

²**thwart** *n* a seat extending across a boat

thy /ðaɪ/ *adj, archaic or dial* of thee or thyself

thyme /taɪm/ *n* any of a genus of plants of the mint family with small pungent aromatic leaves; *esp* a garden plant used in cooking as a seasoning

[1]**thyroid** /'θaɪrɔɪd/ *adj* of or being (an artery, nerve, etc associated with) **a** the thyroid gland **b** the chief cartilage of the larynx

[2]**thyroid** *n* a large endocrine gland that lies at the base of the neck and produces hormones (e g thyroxine) that increase the metabolic rate and influence growth and development

thyself /ðaɪ'self/ *pron, archaic or dial* that identical person that is thou; yourself

ti /tiː/ *n* the 7th note of the diatonic scale in tonic sol-fa

tiara /ti'ɑːrə/ *n* **1** the 3-tiered crown worn by the pope **2** a decorative usu jewelled band worn on the head by women on formal occasions

tibia /'tɪbɪə/ *n, pl* **tibiae** **1** the inner and usu larger of the 2 bones of the vertebrate hind limb between the knee and ankle; the shinbone **2** the 4th joint of the leg of an insect between the femur and tarsus

tic /tɪk/ *n* **1** (a) local and habitual spasmodic motion of particular muscles, esp of the face; twitching **2** a persistent trait of character or behaviour

[1]**tick** /tɪk/ *n* **1** any of numerous related bloodsucking arachnids that feed on warm-blooded animals and often transmit infectious diseases **2** any of various usu wingless parasitic insects (e g the sheep ked)

[2]**tick** *n* **1** a light rhythmic audible tap or beat; *also* a series of such sounds **2** a small spot or mark, typically ✓; *esp* one used to mark sthg as correct, to draw attention to sthg, to check an item on a list, or to represent a point on a scale **3** *Br* a moment, second – infml

[3]**tick** /tɪk/ *v* **1** to make the sound of a tick **2** to function or behave characteristically **3** to mark or count (as if) by ticks – usu + *off*

[4]**tick** *n* credit, trust – infml

ticker /'tɪkəʳ/ *n* sthg that produces a ticking sound: e g **a** a watch **b** the heart – infml

ticker tape *n* a paper tape on which a certain type of telegraphic receiving instrument prints out its information

ticket /'tɪkɪ̵t/ *n* **1a** a mariner's or pilot's certificate **b** a tag, label **2** an official notification issued to sby who has violated a traffic regulation **3** a usu printed card or piece of paper entitling its holder to the use of certain services (e g a library), showing that a fare or admission has been paid, etc **4** *Br* a certificate of discharge from the armed forces **5** *chiefly NAm* a list of candidates for nomination or election **6** the correct, proper, or desirable thing – infml

ticking /'tɪkɪŋ/ *n* a strong linen or cotton fabric used esp for a case for a mattress or pillow

tickle /'tɪkəl/ *v* **1** to provoke to laughter **2** to touch (e g a body part) lightly and repeatedly so as to excite the surface nerves and cause uneasiness, laughter, or spasmodic movements – **tickle** *n*

ticklish /'tɪklɪʃ/ *adj* **1** sensitive to tickling **2** easily upset **3** requiring delicate handling – **~ly** *adv* – **~ness** *n*

tick off *v* to scold, rebuke

tick over *v* to operate at a normal or reduced rate of activity

tidal /'taɪdl/ *adj* of, caused by, or having tides

tidal wave *n* **1** an unusually high sea wave that sometimes follows an earthquake **2** an unexpected, intense, and often widespread reaction (e g a sweeping majority vote or an overwhelming impulse)

tiddler /'tɪdləʳ/ *n, Br* sby or sthg small in comparison to others of the same kind; *esp* a minnow, stickleback, or other small fish

tiddly, tiddley /tɪdəli/ *adj* **1** slightly drunk **2** very small

tide /taɪd/ *n* **1a** (a current of water resulting from) the periodic rise and fall of the surface of a body of water, specif the sea, that occurs twice a day and is caused by the gravitational attraction of the sun and moon **b** the level or position of water on a shore with respect to the tide; *also* the water at its highest level **2** a flowing stream; a current

tidemark /ˈtaɪdmɑːk/ *n* a mark left on a bath that shows the level reached by the water; *also* a mark left on the body showing the limit of washing – chiefly infml

tide over *v* to enable to surmount or withstand a difficulty

[1]**tidy** /ˈtaɪdi/ *adj* **1a** neat and orderly in appearance or habits; well ordered and cared for **b** methodical, precise **2** large, substantial – infml – **-dily** *adv* – **-diness** *n*

[2]**tidy** *v* to put (things) in order; make (things) neat or tidy

[3]**tidy** *n* a receptacle for odds and ends (e g kitchen scraps)

[1]**tie** /taɪ/ *n* **1a** a line, ribbon, or cord used for fastening or drawing sthg together **b** a structural element (e g a rod or angle iron) holding 2 pieces together **2a** a moral or legal obligation to sby or sthg that restricts freedom of action **b** a bond of kinship or affection **3** a curved line that joins 2 musical notes of the same pitch to denote a single sustained note with the time value of the 2 **4a** a match or game between 2 teams, players, etc **b** (a contest that ends in) a draw or dead heat **5** a narrow length of material designed to be worn round the neck and tied in a knot in the front

[2]**tie** *v* **1a** to fasten, attach, or close by knotting **b** to form a knot or bow in **2a** to unite in marriage **b** to unite (musical notes) by a tie **3** to restrain from independence or from freedom of action or choice; constrain (as if) by authority or obligation – often + *down* **4a** to even the score in a game or contest

tied cottage *n, Br* a house owned by an employer (e g a farmer) and reserved for occupancy by an employee

tied house *n* a public house in Britain that is bound to sell only the products of the brewery that owns or rents it out

[1]**tier** /tɪəʳ/ *n* any of a series of levels (e g in an administration)

[2]**tier** *v* to place, arrange, or rise in tiers

tie-up *n* a connection, association

tie up *v* **1** to attach, fasten, or bind securely; *also* to wrap up and fasten **2** to place or invest in such a manner as to make unavailable for other purposes **3** to keep busy **4** to dock

tiff /tɪf/ *v or n* (to have) a petty quarrel

tiffin /ˈtɪfɨn/ *n* a meal or snack taken at midday or in the middle of the morning, esp by the British in India

tiger /ˈtaɪgəʳ/ *n* **1** a very large Asiatic cat having a tawny coat transversely striped with black **2** a fierce and often bloodthirsty person

[1]**tight** /taɪt/ *adj* **1** so close or solid in structure as to prevent passage (e g of a liquid or gas) – often in combination **2a** fixed very firmly in place **b** firmly stretched, drawn, or set **c** fitting (too) closely **3** set close together **4** difficult to get through or out of **5** evenly contested **6** packed, compressed or condensed to (near) the limit **7** stingy, miserly **8** intoxicated, drunk *USE* (*7&8*) infml – **~en** *v* – **~ly** *adv* – **~ness** *n*

[2]**tight** *adv* **1** fast, tightly **2** in a sound manner

tighten /ˈtaɪtn/ *v* to make or become tight or tighter or more firm or severe – often + *up*

tighten up *v* to enforce regulations more stringently – usu + *on*

tightfisted /ˌtaɪtˈfɪstɨd/ *adj* reluctant to part with money – **~ness** *n*

tight-lipped *adj* **1** having the lips compressed (e g in determination) **2** reluctant to speak; taciturn

tightrope /ˈtaɪt-rəʊp/ *n* **1** a rope or wire stretched taut for acrobats to perform on **2** a dangerously precarious situation

tights /taɪts/ *n pl* a skintight garment covering each leg (and foot) and reaching to the waist

tigress /ˈtaɪgrɨs/ *n* a female tiger; *also* a tigerish woman

[1]**tile** /taɪl/ *n* **1** a thin slab of fired clay, stone, or concrete shaped according to use: e g **a** a flat or curved slab for use on roofs **b** a flat and often ornamented slab for floors, walls, or surrounds **2** a thin piece of resilient material (e g cork or linoleum) used esp for covering floors or walls

[2]**tile** *v* to cover with tiles – **tiler** *n*

[1]till /tɪl/ *prep* until

[2]till *conj* until

[3]till /tɪl/ *v* to work (e g land) by ploughing, sowing, and raising crops

[4]till *n* **1a** a receptacle (e g a drawer or tray) in which money is kept in a shop or bank **b** a cash register **2** the money contained in a till

tiller /'tɪləʳ/ *n* a lever used to turn the rudder of a boat from side to side

[1]tilt /tɪlt/ *v* **1** to cause to slope **2** to point or thrust (as if) in a joust

[2]tilt *n* **1** a military exercise in which a mounted person charges at an opponent or mark **2** speed – in *at full tilt* **3** a written or verbal attack – + *at* **4** a sloping surface

[1]timber /'tɪmbəʳ/ *n* **1** growing trees or their wood **2** wood suitable for carpentry or woodwork **3** material, stuff; *esp* personal character or quality

[2]timber *v* to frame, cover, or support with timbers

timbered /'tɪmbəd/ *adj* having walls framed by exposed timbers

timberline /'tɪmbəlaɪn/ *n* the tree line

timbre /'tæmbəʳ, 'tɪm-/ *n* the quality given to a sound by its overtones; *esp* the quality of tone distinctive of a particular singing voice or musical instrument

[1]time /taɪm/ *n* **1a** the measurable period during which an action, process, or condition exists or continues **b** a continuum in which events succeed one another **2a** the point or period when sthg occurs **b** the period required for an action **3a** a period set aside or suitable for an activity or event **b** an appointed, fixed, or customary moment for sthg to happen, begin, or end; *esp, Br* closing time in a public house as fixed by law **4a** a historical period – often pl with sing. meaning **b** conditions or circumstances prevalent during a period – usu pl with sing. meaning **5** a term of imprisonment – infml **6** a season **7a** a tempo **b** the grouping of the beats of music; a rhythm, metre **8** a moment, hour, day, or year as measured or indicated by a clock or calendar **9a** any of a series of recurring instances or repeated actions **b** *pl* (1) multiplied instances (2) equal fractional parts of which a specified number equal a comparatively greater quantity (e g 7 *times* smaller) **10** the end of the playing time of a (section of a) game – often used as an interjection

[2]time *v* **1** to arrange or set the time of **2** to regulate the moment, speed, or duration of, esp to achieve the desired effect **3** to determine or record the time, duration, or speed of

[3]time *adj* (able to be) set to function at a specific moment

time-honoured *adj* sanctioned by custom or tradition

timeless /'taɪmlɨs/ *adj* **1a** unending, eternal **b** not restricted to a particular time or date **2** not affected by time; ageless – **~ly** *adv* – **~ness** *n*

timely /'taɪmli/ *adv or adj* at an appropriate time – **-liness** *n*

times /taɪmz/ *prep* multiplied by

time-sharing *n* **1** simultaneous access to a computer by many users **2** a method of sharing holiday accommodation whereby each of a number of people buys a share of a lease on a property, entitling him/her to spend a proportionate amount of time there each year

time signature *n* a sign placed on a musical staff being usu a fraction whose denominator indicates the kind of note taken as the time unit for the beat (e g 4 for a crotchet or 8 for a quaver) and whose numerator indicates the number of beats per bar

[1]timetable /'taɪm,teɪbəl/ *n* **1** a table of departure and arrival times of public transport **2** a schedule showing a planned order or sequence of events, esp of classes (e g in a school)

[2]timetable *v* to arrange or provide for in a timetable

time zone *n* a geographical region within which the same standard time is used

timid /'tɪmɨd/ *adj* lacking in courage, boldness, or self-confidence – **~ity** *n* – **~ly** *adv* – **~ness** *n*

timing /'taɪmɪŋ/ *n* selection for maximum effect of the precise moment for doing sthg

timorous /'tɪmərəs/ *adj* timid – **~ly** *adv* – **~ness** *n*

timpani /'tɪmpəni/ *n pl but sing or pl in constr* a set of 2 or 3 kettledrums played by 1 performer (e g in an orchestra) – ~**st** *n*

[1]**tin** /tɪn/ *n* **1** a soft lustrous metallic element that is malleable and ductile at ordinary temperatures and is used as a protective coating, in tinfoil, and in soft solders and alloys **2** a box, can, pan, vessel, or sheet made of tinplate: e g **a** a hermetically sealed tinplate container for preserving foods **b** any of various usu tinplate or aluminium containers of different shapes and sizes in which food is cooked, esp in an oven

[2]**tin** *v, chiefly Br* to can

[1]**tincture** /ˈtɪŋktʃəʳ/ *n* **1a** a substance that colours or stains **b** a colour, hue **2** a slight addition; a trace **3** a solution of a substance in alcohol for medicinal use

[2]**tincture** *v* to tint or stain with a colour

tinder /ˈtɪndəʳ/ *n* any combustible substance suitable for use as kindling

tinderbox /ˈtɪndəbɒks/ *n* **1** a metal box for holding tinder and usu a flint and steel for striking a spark **2** a potentially unstable place, situation, or person

tine /taɪn/ *n* **1** a prong (e g of a fork) **2** a pointed branch of an antler

tinfoil /ˈtɪnfɔɪl/ *n* a thin metal sheeting of tin, aluminium, or a tin alloy

[1]**tinge** /tɪndʒ/ *v* **1** to colour with a slight shade **2** to impart a slight smell, taste, or other quality to

[2]**tinge** *n* **1** a slight staining or suffusing colour **2** a slight modifying quality; a trace

tingle /ˈtɪŋgəl/ *v or n* (to feel or cause) a stinging, prickling, or thrilling sensation

tin god *n* **1** a pompous and self-important person **2** sby unjustifiably esteemed or venerated *USE* infml

[1]**tinker** /ˈtɪŋkəʳ/ *n* **1** a usu itinerant mender of household utensils **2** *chiefly Scot & Irish* a gipsy

[2]**tinker** *v* to repair, adjust, or work with sthg in an unskilled or experimental manner – usu + *at* or *with*

[1]**tinkle** /ˈtɪŋkəl/ *v* to make (a sound suggestive of) a tinkle

[2]**tinkle** *n* **1** a series of short light ringing or clinking sounds **2** a jingling effect in verse or prose **3** *Br* a telephone call – infml

tinny /ˈtɪni/ *adj* **1** of, containing, or yielding tin **2a** having the taste, smell, or appearance of tin **b** not solid or durable; shoddy **3** having a thin metallic sound – **-niness** *n*

[1]**tinsel** /ˈtɪnsəl/ *n* **1** a thread, strip, or sheet of metal, plastic, or paper used to produce a glittering and sparkling effect (e g in fabrics or decorations) **2** sthg superficial, showy, or glamorous

[2]**tinsel** *adj* cheaply gaudy; tawdry

[1]**tint** /tɪnt/ *n* **1** a usu slight or pale coloration; a hue **2** any of various lighter or darker shades of a colour; *esp* one produced by adding white

[2]**tint** *v* to apply a tint to – ~**er** *n*

tiny /ˈtaɪni/ *adj* very small or diminutive

tip /tɪp/ *n* **1** the usu pointed end of sthg **2** a small piece or part serving as an end, cap, or point – **tip** *v*

[2]**tip** *v* **1** to overturn, upset – usu + *over* **2** to cant, tilt **3** to deposit or transfer by tilting

[3]**tip** *n* a place for tipping sthg (e g rubbish or coal); a dump – ~**per** *n*

[4]**tip** *v* to strike lightly

[5]**tip** *v or n* **-pp-** (to give or present with) a sum of money in appreciation of a service performed

[6]**tip** *n* **1** a piece of useful or expert information **2** a piece of inside information which, acted upon, may bring financial gain (e g by betting or investment) – **tip** *v*

tip-off *n* a tip given usu as a warning – **tip off** *v*

[1]**tipple** /ˈtɪpəl/ *v* to drink (esp spirits), esp continuously in small amounts

[2]**tipple** *n* a drink; *esp* the drink one usually takes – infml

tipstaff /ˈtɪpstɑːf/ *n* an officer in certain lawcourts

tipster /ˈtɪpstəʳ/ *n* one who gives or sells tips, esp for gambling or speculation

tipsy /ˈtɪpsi/ *adj* **1** unsteady, staggering, or foolish from the effects of alcoholic drink **2** askew – **-sily** *adv* – **-siness** *n*

[1]**tiptoe** /ˈtɪptəʊ/ *n* the tip of a toe; *also* the ends of the toes

[2]**tiptoe** *adv* (as if) on tiptoe

[3]**tiptoe** *adj* **1** standing or walking (as if) on tiptoe **2** cautious, stealthy

[4]**tiptoe** *v* **1** to stand, walk, or raise oneself on tiptoe **2** to walk silently or stealthily as if on tiptoe

tip-top *adj* excellent, first-rate – infml – **tip-top** *adv*

tirade /taɪˈreɪd, tɪ̇-/ *n* a long vehement speech or denunciation

[1]**tire** /taɪəʳ/ *v* **1** to fatigue **2** to wear out the patience of

[2]**tire** *n, chiefly NAm* a tyre

tired /taɪəd/ *adj* **1** weary, fatigued **2** exasperated; fed up **3a** trite, hackneyed **b** lacking freshness – **~ly** *adv* – **~ness** *n*

tireless /ˈtaɪəlɪ̇s/ *adj* indefatigable, untiring – **~ly** *adv*

tiresome /ˈtaɪəsəm/ *adj* wearisome, tedious – **~ly** *adv*

tissue /ˈtɪʃuː, -sjuː/ *n* **1a** a fine gauzy often sheer fabric **b** a mesh, web **2** a paper handkerchief **3** a cluster of cells, usu of a particular kind, together with their intercellular substance that form any of the structural materials of a plant or animal

[1]**tit** /tɪt/ *n* **1** a teat or nipple **2** a woman's breast – infml

[2]**tit** *n* any of various small tree-dwelling insect-eating birds (e g a blue tit)

titan /ˈtaɪtn/ *n* sby or sthg very large or strong; *also* sby notable for outstanding achievement – **~ic** *adj*

titanium /taɪˈteɪnɪəm/ *n* a light strong metallic element used esp in alloys and combined in refractory materials and in coatings

titbit /ˈtɪtˌbɪt/ , *chiefly NAm* **tidbit** /ˈtɪdˌbɪt/ *n* a choice or pleasing piece (e g of food or news)

tithe /taɪð/ *n* a tax or contribution of a 10th part of sthg (e g income) for the support of a religious establishment; *esp* such a tax formerly due in an English parish to support its church

titillate /ˈtɪtɪ̇leɪt/ *v* to excite pleasurably; arouse by stimulation – **-lation** *n*

titivate /ˈtɪtɪ̇veɪt/ *v* to smarten up (oneself or another)

[1]**title** /ˈtaɪtl/ *n* **1** (a document giving proof of) legal ownership **2** an alleged or recognized right **3a** a descriptive or general heading (e g of a chapter in a book) **b** a title page and the printed matter on it **c** written material introduced into a film or television programme to represent credits, dialogue, or fragments of narrative – usu pl with sing. meaning **4** the distinguishing name of a work of art (e g a book, picture or musical composition) **5** a descriptive name **6** designation as champion **7** a hereditary or acquired appellation given to a person or family as a mark of rank, office, or attainment

[2]**title** *v* **1** to provide a title for **2** to designate or call by a title

titled /ˈtaɪtld/ *adj* having a title, esp of nobility

title deed *n* the deed constituting evidence of ownership

titrate /ˈtaɪtreɪt/ *v* to determine the amount of a substance in (a solution) by reaction with another substance of known composition – **-tion** *n*

titter /ˈtɪtəʳ/ *v* to giggle, snigger – **titter** *n*

tittle-tattle /ˈtɪtl ˌtætl/ *v or n* (to) gossip, prattle

titular /ˈtɪtʃʊləʳ/ *adj* **1** in title only; nominal **2** of or constituting a title

tizzy /ˈtɪzi/ *n* a highly excited and confused state of mind – infml

TNT *n* trinitrotoluene: a type of powerful explosive

[1]**to** /tə, tʊ; *strong* tuː/ *prep* **1** – used to indicate a terminal point or destination: e g **a** a place where a physical movement or an action or condition suggestive of movement ends (e g drive *to* the city) **b** a direction (e g turned his back *to* the door) **c** a terminal point in measuring or reckoning or in a statement of extent or limits (e g 10 miles *to* the nearest town; not *to* my knowledge) **d** a point in time before which a period is reckoned (e g how long *to* dinner?) **e** a point of contact or proximity (e g pinned it *to* my coat) **f** a purpose, intention, tendency, result, or end (e g a temple *to* Mars; held them *to* ransom; broken *to* pieces) **g** the one to or for which sthg exists or is done or directed (e g kind *to* animals) **2** – used to indicate addition, attachment, connection, belonging, or possession (e g add 17 *to* 20; the key *to* the door) **3** – used to indicate

relationship or conformity: e g **a** relative position (e g next door *to* me) **b** proportion or composition (e g 400 *to* the box; won by 17 points *to* 11) **c** correspondence to a standard (e g second *to* none) **4a** – used to indicate that the following verb is an infinitive (e g wants *to* go); often used by itself at the end of a clause in place of an infinitive suggested by the preceding context (e g knows more than he seems *to*) **b** for the purpose of (e g did it *to* annoy)

²to *adv* **1a** – used to indicate direction towards; chiefly in *to and fro* **b** close to the wind (e g the ship hove *to*) **2** *of a door or window* into contact, esp with the frame **3** – used to indicate application or attention **4** back into consciousness or awareness **5** at hand (e g saw her close *to*)

toad /təʊd/ *n* **1** any of numerous tailless leaping amphibians that differ from the related frogs by living more on land and in having a shorter squatter body with a rough, dry, and warty skin **2** a loathsome and contemptible person or thing

toad-in-the-hole *n* a dish of sausages baked in a thick Yorkshire-pudding batter

toady /'təʊdi/ *v or n* (to behave as) a sycophant

to-and-fro *n or adj* (activity involving alternating movement) forwards and backwards

to and fro *adv* from one place to another; back and forth

¹toast /təʊst/ *v* **1** to make (e g bread) crisp, hot, and brown by heat **2** to warm thoroughly (e g at a fire)

²toast *n* **1** sliced bread browned on both sides by heat **2** sthg in honour of which people drink **3** an act of drinking in honour of sby or sthg

³toast *v* to drink to as a toast

toaster /'təʊstəʳ/ *n* an electrical appliance for toasting esp bread

toasting fork *n* a long-handled fork on which bread is held for toasting in front of or over a fire

toastmaster /'təʊst,mɑːstəʳ/ *n* sby who presides at a banquet, proposes toasts, and introduces after-dinner speakers

tobacco /tə'bækəʊ/ *n* **1** a tall erect annual S American herb cultivated for its leaves **2** the leaves of cultivated tobacco prepared for use in smoking or chewing or as snuff; *also* cigars, cigarettes, or other manufactured products of tobacco

tobacconist /tə'bækənɨst/ *n* a seller of tobacco, esp in a shop

toboggan /tə'bɒgən/ *v or n* (to ride on) a long light sledge, usu curved up at the front and used esp for gliding downhill over snow or ice

toccata /tə'kɑːtə/ *n* a musical composition in a free style and characterized by rapid runs, usu for organ or harpsichord

today /tə'deɪ/ *adv or n* **1** (on) this day **2** (at) the present time or age

toddle /'tɒdl/ *v* **1** to walk haltingly in the manner of a young child **2a** to take a stroll; saunter **b** *Br* to depart *USE* (*2*) infml

toddler /'tɒdləʳ/ *n* a young child

toddy /'tɒdi/ *n* a usu hot drink consisting of spirits mixed with water, sugar, and spices

to-do /tə 'duː/ *n, pl* **to-dos** bustle, fuss – infml

toe /təʊ/ *n* **1a** any of the digits at the end of a vertebrate's foot **b** the fore end of a foot or hoof **2** the front of sthg worn on the foot – **toe** *v*

toe cap *n* a piece of material (e g steel or leather) attached to the toe of a shoe or boot to reinforce or decorate it

toffee,toffy /'tɒfi/ *n* a sweet with a texture from chewy to brittle, made by boiling sugar, water, and often butter

toga /'təʊgə/ *n* a loose outer garment worn in public by citizens of ancient Rome

together /tə'geðəʳ/ *adv* **1a** in or into 1 place, mass, collection, or group **b** in joint agreement or cooperation; as a group **2a** in or into contact (e g connection, collision, or union) (e g mix the ingredients *together*) **b** in or into association, relationship, or harmony (e g colours that go well *together*) **3a** at one time; simultaneously **b** in succession; without intermission (e g was depressed for days *together*) **4** *of a single unit* in or into an integrated whole (e g pull yourself *together*) **5a**

to or with each other **b** considered as a unit; collectively (e g these arguments taken *together* make a convincing case)

togetherness /tə'geðən!s/ *n* the feeling of belonging together

toggle /'tɒgəl/ *n* a piece or device for holding or securing; *esp* a crosspiece attached to the end of or to a loop in a chain, rope, line, etc, usu to prevent slipping, to serve as a fastening, or as a grip for tightening

togs /tɒgz/ *n pl* clothes – infml

[1]**toil** /tɔɪl/ *n* long strenuous fatiguing labour

[2]**toil** *v* **1** to work hard and long **2** to proceed with laborious effort

[3]**toil** *n* sthg by or with which one is held fast or inextricably involved – usu pl with sing. meaning

toilet /'tɔɪl!t/ *n* **1** the act or process of dressing and grooming oneself **2a** a fixture or arrangement for receiving and disposing of faeces and urine **b** a room or compartment containing a toilet and sometimes a washbasin **3** formal or fashionable (style of) dress – fml

toilet paper *n* a thin usu absorbent paper for sanitary use after defecation or urination

toilet water *n* (a) liquid containing a high percentage of alcohol used esp as a light perfume

[1]**token** /'təʊkən/ *n* **1** an outward sign or expression (e g of an emotion) **2** a characteristic mark or feature **3a** a souvenir, keepsake **b** sthg given or shown as a guarantee (e g of authority, right, or identity) **4** a coinlike object used in place of money (e g to pay a milkman) **5** a certified statement redeemable for a usu specified form of merchandise to the amount stated thereon

[2]**token** *adj* **1** done or given as a token, esp in partial fulfilment of an obligation or engagement **2** done or given merely for show

told /təʊld/ *past of* **tell**

tolerable /'tɒlərəbəl/ *adj* **1** capable of being borne or endured **2** moderately good or agreeable

tolerance /'tɒlərəns/ *n* **1a** indulgence for beliefs or practices differing from one's own **b** the act of allowing sthg; toleration **2** an allowable variation from a standard dimension

tolerant /'tɒlərənt/ *adj* inclined to tolerate; *esp* marked by forbearance or endurance – **~ly** *adv*

tolerate /'tɒləreɪt/ *v* to allow to be (done) without prohibition, hindrance, or contradiction

toleration /ˌtɒlə'reɪʃən/ *n* a government policy of permitting forms of religious belief and worship not officially established

[1]**toll** /təʊl/ *n* **1** a fee paid for some right or privilege (e g of passing over a highway or bridge) or for services rendered **2** a grievous or ruinous price; *esp* cost in life or health

[2]**toll** *v* **1** to sound (a bell) by pulling the rope **2** to signal, announce, or summon (as if) by means of a tolled bell

tollgate /'təʊlgeɪt/ *n* a barrier across a road to prevent passage until a toll is paid

tomahawk /'tɒməhɔːk/ *n* a light axe used by N American Indians as a throwing or hand weapon

tomato /tə'mɑːtəʊ/ *n, pl* **tomatoes** **1** any of a genus of S American plants of the nightshade family; *esp* one widely cultivated for its edible fruits **2** the usu large and rounded red, yellow, or green pulpy fruit of a tomato

tomb /tuːm/ *n* **1** an excavation in which a corpse is buried **2** a chamber or vault for the dead, built either above or below ground and usu serving as a memorial

tombola /tɒm'bəʊlə/ *n* a lottery in which people buy tickets which may entitle them to a prize

tomboy /'tɒmbɔɪ/ *n* a girl who behaves in a manner conventionally thought of as typical of a boy – **~ish** *adj*

tombstone /'tuːmstəʊn/ *n* a gravestone

tomcat /'tɒmkæt/ *n* a male cat

tome /təʊm/ *n* a (large scholarly) book

tomfoolery /tɒm'fuːləri/ *n* foolish trifling; nonsense

tomorrow /tə'mɒrəʊ/ *adv or n* **1** (on) the day after today **2** (in) the future

tom-tom /'tɒm tɒm/ *n* a usu long and

narrow small-headed drum commonly beaten with the hands

ton /tʌn/ *n* **1** any of various units of weight; *esp* one equal to 2,240 lbs **2a** a great quantity – often pl with sing. meaning **b** a great weight **3** a group, score, or speed of 100 *USE* (*2&3*) infml

tonal /'təʊnl/ *adj* **1** of tone, tonality, or tonicity **2** having tonality

tonality /təʊ'nælǀ̧ti/ *n* **1** tonal quality **2a** musical key **b** the organization of all the notes and chords of a piece of music in relation to a tonic

¹tone /təʊn/ *n* **1** a vocal or musical sound; *esp* one of a specified quality **2** a sound of a definite frequency with relatively weak overtones **3** an accent or inflection of the voice expressive of a mood or emotion **4** (a change in) the pitch of a word often used to express differences of meaning **5** style or manner of verbal expression **6** the colour that appreciably modifies a hue or white or black **7** the general effect of light, shade, and colour in a picture **8** the state of (an organ or part of) a living body in which the functions are healthy and performed with due vigour **9** prevailing character, quality, or trend (e g of morals)

²tone *v* to blend or harmonize in colour

tone-deaf *adj* relatively insensitive to differences in musical pitch

tone language *n* a language (e g Chinese) in which variations in tone distinguish words of different meaning

toneless /'təʊnlǀ̧s/ *adj* lacking in expression – **~ly** *adv*

tongs /tɒŋz/ *n pl* any of various grasping devices consisting commonly of 2 pieces joined at 1 end by a pivot or hinged like scissors

¹tongue /tʌŋ/ *n* **1a** a fleshy muscular movable organ of the floor of the mouth in most vertebrates that bears sensory end organs and small glands and functions esp in tasting and swallowing food and in human beings as a speech organ **b** a part of various invertebrate animals that is analogous to the tongue of vertebrates **2** the tongue of an ox, sheep, etc used as food **3** the power of communication through speech **4a** a (spoken) language **b** the cry (as if) of a hound pursuing or in sight of game – esp in *give tongue* **6** sthg like an animal's tongue (e g elongated and fastened at 1 end only):e g **a** a piece of metal suspended inside a bell so as to strike against the sides as the bell is swung **b** the flap under the lacing or buckles on the front of a shoe or boot **7** the rib on one edge of a board that fits into a corresponding groove in an edge of another board to make a flush joint

²tongue *v* **1** to touch or lick (as if) with the tongue **2** to articulate notes on a wind instrument by successively interrupting the stream of wind with the action of the tongue

tongue-tied *adj* unable to speak freely (e g because of shyness)

tongue twister *n* a word or phrase difficult to articulate because of several similar consonantal sounds (e g 'she sells seashells on the seashore")

¹tonic /'tɒnɪk/ *adj* **1** increasing or restoring physical or mental tone **2** of or based on the first note of a scale

²tonic *n* **1a** sthg that invigorates, refreshes, or stimulates **b tonic, tonic water** a carbonated drink flavoured with a small amount of quinine, lemon, and lime **2** the first note of a diatonic scale

tonic sol-fa *n* a system of solmization that replaces the normal notation with sol-fa syllables

tonight /tə'naɪt/ *adv or n* (on) this night or the night following today

tonnage /'tʌnɪdʒ/ *n* **1** ships considered in terms of the total number of tons registered or carried or of their carrying capacity **2** the carrying capacity of a merchant ship in units of $100ft^3$ (about $2.83m^3$) **3** total weight in tons shipped, carried, or produced

tonne /tʌn/ *n* a metric unit of weight equal to 1000kg

tonsil /'tɒnsəl/ *n* either of a pair of prominent oval masses of spongy tissue that lie 1 on each side of the throat at the back of the mouth – **~litis** *n*

ton-up /'tʌn ˌʌp/ *adj, Br* of or being sby who has achieved a score, speed, etc of 100 – infml

too /tuː/ *adv* **1** also; in addition **2a** to a regrettable degree; excessively **b** to a higher degree than meets a standard

3 indeed, so – used to counter a negative charge (e g he did *too*!)

took /tʊk/ *past of* **take**

[1]**tool** /tuːl/ *n* **1a** an implement that is used, esp by hand, to carry out work of a mechanical nature (e g cutting, levering, or digging) – not usu used with reference to kitchen utensils or cutlery **b** (the cutting or shaping part in) a machine tool **2** sthg (e g an instrument or apparatus) used in performing an operation, or necessary for the practice of a vocation or profession **3** sby who is used or manipulated by another **4** a penis – vulg

[2]**tool** *v* **1** to work, shape, or finish with a tool; *esp* to letter or ornament (e g leather) by means of hand tools **2** to equip (e g a plant or industry) with tools, machines, and instruments for production – often + *up*

toot /tuːt/ *v* to produce a short blast or similar sound – **toot** *n*

tooth /tuːθ/ *n, pl* **teeth** **1a** any of the hard bony structures that are borne esp on the jaws of vertebrates and serve esp for the seizing and chewing of food and as weapons **b** any of various usu hard and sharp projecting parts about the mouth of an invertebrate **2** a taste, liking **3** any of the regular projections on the rim of a cogwheel **4** *pl* effective means of enforcement

toothache /ˈtuːθ-eɪk/ *n* pain in or about a tooth

toothy /ˈtuːθi/ *adj* having or showing prominent teeth

tootle /ˈtuːtl/ *v* **1** to toot gently or continuously **2** to drive or move along in a leisurely manner – infml – **tootle** *n*

[1]**top** /tɒp/ *n* **1a(1)** the highest point, level, or part of sthg **(2)** the (top of the) head – esp in *top to toe* **(3)** the head of a plant, esp one with edible roots **(4)** a garment worn on the upper body **b(1)** the highest or uppermost region or part **(2)** the upper end, edge, or surface **2** a fitted or attached part serving as an upper piece, lid, or covering **3** the highest degree or pitch conceivable or attained **4** (sby or sthg in) the highest position (e g in rank or achievement) **5** *Br* the transmission gear of a motor vehicle giving the highest ratio of propeller-shaft to engine-shaft speed and hence the highest speed of travel

[2]**top** *v* **1a** to cut the top off **b** to shorten or remove the top of (a plant); *also* to remove the calyx of (e g a strawberry) **2a** to cover with a top or on the top; provide, form, or serve as a top for **b** to complete the basic structure of (e g a high-rise building) by putting on a cap or uppermost section – usu + *out* or *off* **3** to be or become higher than; overtop **4** to go over the top of; clear, surmount

[3]**top** *adj* **1** of or at the top **2** foremost, leading **3** of the highest quality, amount, or degree

[4]**top** *n* a child's toy that has a tapering point on which it is made to spin

topaz /ˈtəʊpæz/ *n* a yellow sapphire or quartz

topcoat /ˈtɒpkəʊt/ *n* **1** a (lightweight) overcoat **2** a final coat of paint

top dog *n* a person in a position of authority, esp through victory in a hard-fought competition – infml

top-dress *v* to scatter fertilizer over (land) without working it in – **~ing** *n*

top-flight *adj* of the highest grade or quality; best

top hat *n* a man's tall-crowned hat

top-heavy *adj* **1** having the top part too heavy for or disproportionate to the lower part **2** capitalized beyond what is prudent

topiary /ˈtəʊpɪəri/ *adj or n* (of or being) the practice or art of training, cutting, and trimming trees or shrubs into odd or ornamental shapes

topic /ˈtɒpɪk/ *n* **1a** a heading in an outlined argument or exposition **b** the subject of a (section of a) discourse **2** a subject for discussion or consideration

topical /ˈtɒpɪkəl/ *adj* **1** of a place **2a** of or arranged by topics **b** referring to the topics of the day; of current interest – **~ly** *adv* – **~ity** *n*

topknot /ˈtɒpnɒt/ *n* an arrangement or growth of hair or feathers on top of the head

topless /ˈtɒplɪ̵s/ *adj* **1** nude above the waist; *esp* having the breasts exposed 2 featuring topless waitresses or entertainers

topmast /'tɒpmɑːst/ *n* a mast that is next above the lowest mast

topmost /'tɒpməʊst/ *adj* highest of all

top-notch *adj* of the highest quality – infml

topography /tə'pɒgrəfi/ *n* **1** (the mapping or charting of) the configuration of a land surface, including its relief and the position of its natural and man-made features **2** the physical or natural features of an object or entity and their structural relationships – **-phical** *adj* – **-phically** *adv*

topology /tɒ'pɒlədʒi/ *n* a branch of mathematics that deals with geometric properties which are unaltered by elastic deformation (e g stretching or twisting)

topper /'tɒpəʳ/ *n* **1** a top hat **2** sthg (e g a joke) that caps everything preceding – infml

[1]**topping** /'tɒpɪŋ/ *n* sthg that forms a top; *esp* a garnish or edible decoration on top of a food

[2]**topping** *adj, chiefly Br* excellent – not now in vogue

topple /'tɒpəl/ *v* **1** to fall (as if) from being top-heavy **2** to overthrow

topside /'tɒpsaɪd/ *n* **1** *pl* the sides of a ship above the waterline **2** a lean boneless cut of beef from the inner part of a round

topsoil /'tɒpsɔɪl/ *n* surface soil, usu including the organic layer in which plants form roots and which is turned over in ploughing

top spin *n* a rotary motion imparted to a ball that causes it to rotate forwards in the direction of its travel

topsy-turvy /ˌtɒpsi 'tɜːvi/ *adj or adv* **1** upside down **2** in utter confusion or disorder

top up *v* to make up to the full quantity, capacity, or amount

tor /tɔːʳ/ *n* a high rock or rocky mound

torch /tɔːtʃ/ *n* **1** a burning stick of resinous wood or twist of tow used to give light **2** *Br* a small portable electric lamp powered by batteries

tore /tɔːʳ/ *past of* **tear**

toreador /'tɒrɪədɔːʳ/ *n* a bullfighter

[1]**torment** /'tɔːment/ *n* **1** extreme pain or anguish of body or mind **2** a source of vexation or pain

[2]**torment** /tɔː'ment/ *v* to cause severe usu persistent distress of body or mind to – **~or** *n*

torn /tɔːn/ *past part of* **tear**

tornado /tɔː'neɪdəʊ/ *n* a violent or destructive whirlwind, usu progressing in a narrow path over the land and accompanied by a funnel-shaped cloud

[1]**torpedo** /tɔː'piːdəʊ/ *n, pl* **torpedoes** **1** an electric ray **2** a self-propelling cigar-shaped submarine explosive projectile used for attacking ships

[2]**torpedo** *v* **1** to hit or destroy by torpedo **2** to destroy or nullify (e g a plan) – infml

torpedo boat *n* a small fast warship armed primarily with torpedoes

torpid /'tɔːpɨd/ *adj* **1a** having temporarily lost the power of movement or feeling (e g in hibernation) **b** sluggish in functioning or acting **2** lacking in energy or vigour – **~ity, ~ness** *n* – **~ly** *adv*

torpor /'tɔːpəʳ/ *n* **1a** a state of mental and motor inactivity with partial or total insensibility **b** extreme sluggishness of action or function **2** apathy

[1]**torque** /tɔːk/ *n* a twisted metal collar or neck chain worn by the ancient Gauls, Germans, and Britons

[2]**torque** *n* a turning or twisting force

torrent /'tɒrənt/ *n* **1** a violent stream of water, lava, etc **2** a raging tumultuous flow – **~ial** *adj*

torrid /'tɒrɨd/ *adj* **1a** parched with heat, esp of the sun **b** giving off intense heat **2** ardent, passionate – **~ly** *adv*

torsion /'tɔːʃən/ *n* **1** the act or process of twisting or turning sthg, esp by forces exerted on one end while the other is fixed or twisted in the opposite direction **2** the state of being twisted

torso /'tɔːsəʊ/ *n, pl* **torsos, torsi** **1** (a sculptured representation of) the human trunk **2** sthg (e g a piece of writing) that is mutilated or left unfinished

tortilla /tɔː'tiːjə/ *n* a round thin cake of unleavened maize bread, usu eaten hot with a topping or filling of minced meat or cheese

tortoise /ˈtɔːtəs/ *n* **1** any of an order of land and freshwater (and marine) reptiles with a toothless horny beak and a bony shell which encloses the trunk and into which the head, limbs, and tail may be withdrawn **2** sby or sthg slow or laggard

[1]**tortoiseshell** /ˈtɔːtəsʃel/ *n* **1** the mottled horny substance of the shell of some marine turtles used in inlaying and in making various ornamental articles **2** any of several butterflies with striking orange, yellow, brown, and black coloration

[2]**tortoiseshell** *adj* mottled black, brown, and yellow

tortuous /ˈtɔːtʃʊəs/ *adj* **1** marked by repeated twists, bends, or turns **2a** marked by devious or indirect tactics **b** circuitous, involved – **~ly** *adv* – **~ness** *n*

[1]**torture** /ˈtɔːtʃəʳ/ *n* **1** the infliction of intense physical or mental suffering as a means of punishment, coercion, or sadistic gratification **2** (sthg causing) anguish of body or mind

[2]**torture** *v* **1** to subject to torture **2** to cause intense suffering to **3** to twist or wrench out of shape; *also* to pervert (e g the meaning of a word) – **~r** *n*

Tory /ˈtɔːri/ *n* **1** a member of a major British political group of the 18th and early 19th c favouring at first the Stuarts and later royal authority and the established church and seeking to preserve the traditional political structure and defeat parliamentary reform **2** a Conservative – **~ism** *n*

[1]**toss** /tɒs/ *v* **1** to fling or heave repeatedly about; *also* to bandy **2a** to throw with a quick, light, or careless motion **b** to throw up in the air **c** to flip (a coin) to decide an issue **3** to lift with a sudden jerking motion

[2]**toss** *n* **1** a fall, esp from a horse – chiefly in *take a toss* **2a** an abrupt tilting or upward fling **b** an act or instance of deciding by chance, esp by tossing a coin **c** a throw

toss off *v* **1** to perform or write quickly and easily **2** to consume quickly; *esp* to drink in a single draught **3** *Br* to masturbate – infml

toss-up *n* **1** a toss of a coin **2** an even chance or choice – infml

tot /tɒt/ *n* **1** a small child; a toddler **2** a small amount or allowance of alcoholic drink

[1]**total** /ˈtəʊtl/ *adj* **1** comprising or constituting a whole; entire **2** complete **3** concentrating all available personnel and resources on a single objective – **~ly** *adv*

[2]**total** *n* **1** a product of addition **2** an entire quantity

[3]**total** *v* to amount to

totalitarian /təʊˌtælɪ̈ˈteərɪən/ *adj* **1** authoritarian, dictatorial **2** of or constituting a political regime based on subordination of the individual to the state and strict control over all aspects of the life and productive capacity of the nation – **~ism** *n*

totality /təʊˈtælɪ̈ti/ *n* **1** an entire amount; a whole **2** wholeness

[1]**tote** /təʊt/ *v* **1** to carry by hand or on the person **2** to transport, convey *USE* infml

[2]**tote** *n* a system of horse-race betting

totem /ˈtəʊtəm/ *n* **1** a natural object serving as the emblem of a family or clan; *also* a carved or painted representation of this **2** sthg that serves as an emblem or revered symbol

[1]**totter** /ˈtɒtəʳ/ *v* **1a** to tremble or rock as if about to fall **b** to become unstable; threaten to collapse **2** to move unsteadily; stagger

[2]**totter** *n* an unsteady gait

tot up *v* to add together; *also* to increase by additions

toucan /ˈtuːkən, -kæn/ *n* any of a family of fruit-eating birds of tropical America with brilliant colouring and a very large but light beak

[1]**touch** /tʌtʃ/ *v* **1** to bring a bodily part into contact with, esp so as to perceive through the sense of feeling; feel **2** to strike or push lightly, esp with the hand or foot or an implement **3** to take into the hands or mouth **4** to put hands on in any way or degree; *esp* to commit violence against **5** to concern oneself with **6** to cause to be briefly in contact with sthg **7** to affect the interest of; concern **8** to move to esp sympathetic feeling **9** to speak or tell of, esp in passing **10** to rival **11** to induce to give or lend – **~able** *adj* – **~er** *n*

[2]**touch** *n* **1** a light stroke, tap, or push **2** the act or fact of touching **3** the

sense of feeling, esp as exercised deliberately with the hands, feet, or lips **4** mental or moral sensitivity, responsiveness, or tact **5** sthg slight of its kind: e g **a** a light attack **b** a small amount; a trace **6a** a manner or method of touching or striking esp the keys of a keyboard instrument **b** the relative resistance to pressure of the keys of a keyboard (e g of a piano or typewriter) **7** an effective and appropriate detail; *esp* one used in an artistic composition **8** a distinctive or characteristic manner, trait, or quality **9** the state or fact of being in contact or communication **10** the area outside the touchlines in soccer or outside and including the touchlines in rugby **11** sby who can be easily induced to part with money – chiefly in *a soft/easy touch*

touch and go *n* a highly uncertain or precarious situation

touchdown *n* **1** the act of touching down a football **2** (the moment of) touching down (e g of an aeroplane or spacecraft)

touch down *v* **1** to place (the ball in rugby) by hand on the ground either positioned on or over an opponent's goal line in scoring a try, or behind one's own goal line as a defensive measure **2** to reach the ground

touché /tuː'ʃeɪ/ *interj* – used to acknowledge a hit in fencing or the success of an argument, accusation, or witty point

touched /tʌtʃt/ *adj* **1** emotionally moved (e g with gratitude) **2** slightly unbalanced mentally – infml

touchline /'tʌtʃlaɪn/ *n* either of the lines that bound the sides of the field of play in rugby and soccer

touch off *v* to cause to explode (as if) by touching with a naked flame

touchstone /'tʌtʃstəʊn/ *n* **1** a black flintlike siliceous stone that when rubbed by gold or silver showed a streak of colour and was formerly used to test the purity of these metals **2** a test or criterion for determining the genuineness of sthg

touch up *v* **1** to improve or perfect by small alterations; make good the minor defects of **2** to make often unwelcome physical advances to; touch with a view to arousing sexually – slang

touchy /'tʌtʃi/ *adj* **1** ready to take offence on slight provocation **2** calling for tact, care, or caution – **touchily** *adv* – **touchiness** *n*

[1]**tough** /tʌf/ *adj* **1a** strong and flexible; not brittle or liable to cut, break, or tear **b** not easily chewed **2** capable of enduring great hardship or exertion **3** very hard to influence **4** extremely difficult or testing **5** aggressive or threatening in behaviour **6** without softness or sentimentality **7** unfortunate, unpleasant – infml – **~ly** *adv* – **~ness** *n*

[2]**tough** *n* a tough person; *esp* sby aggressively violent

[3]**tough** *adv* in a tough manner

toughen /'tʌfən/ *v* to make or become tough

toupee /'tuːpeɪ/ *n* a wig or hairpiece worn to cover a bald spot

[1]**tour** /tʊəʳ/ *n* **1** a period during which an individual or unit is engaged on a specific duty, esp in 1 place **2a** a journey (e g for business or pleasure) in which one returns to the starting point **b** a visit (e g to a historic site or factory) for pleasure or instruction **c** a series of professional engagements involving travel

[2]**tour** *v* **1** to make a tour of **2** to present (e g a theatrical production or concert) on a tour

tour de force /ˌtʊə də 'fɔːs/ *n, pl* **tours de force** a feat of strength, skill, or ingenuity

tourism /'tʊərɪzəm/ *n* **1** the practice of travelling for recreation **2** the organizing of tours for commercial purposes **3** the provision of services (e g accommodation) for tourists

tourist /'tʊərɪ̥st/ *n* **1** sby who makes a tour for recreation or culture **2** a member of a sports team that is visiting another country to play usu international matches

tournament /'tʊənəmənt, 'tɔː-/ *n* **1** a contest between 2 parties of mounted knights armed with usu blunted lances or swords **2** a series of games or contests for a championship

tourniquet /'tʊənɪkeɪ, 'tɔː-/ *n* a bandage or other device for applying pressure to check bleeding or blood flow

tousle /'taʊzəl/ *v* to dishevel, rumple

[1]**tout** /taʊt/ *v* to solicit for customers

[2]**tout** *n* **1** sby who solicits custom, usu importunately **2** *Br* sby who offers tickets for a sold-out entertainment (e g a concert or football match) at vastly inflated prices

[1]**tow** /təʊ/ *v* to draw or pull along behind, esp by a rope or chain

[2]**tow** *n* **1** a rope or chain for towing **2** towing or being towed **3** sthg towed (e g a boat or car)

[3]**tow** *n* short or broken fibre (e g of flax or hemp) prepared for spinning

towards /tə'wɔːdz/ *prep* **1** moving or situated in the direction of **2a** along a course leading to **b** in relation to (e g an attitude *towards* life) **3** turned in the direction of **4** not long before (e g *towards* evening) **5** for the partial financing of (e g gave her £5 *towards* a new dress)

[1]**towel** /'taʊəl/ *n* an absorbent cloth or paper for wiping or drying sthg (e g crockery or the body) after washing

[2]**towel** *v* to rub or dry (e g the body) with a towel

[1]**tower** /'taʊəʳ/ *n* **1** a building or structure typically higher than its diameter and high relative to its surroundings that may stand apart or be attached to a larger structure and that may be fully walled in or of skeleton framework **2 tower block, tower** a tall multi-storey building, often containing offices

[2]**tower** *v* to reach or rise to a great height

towering /'taʊərɪŋ/ *adj* **1** impressively high or great **2** reaching a high point of intensity **3** going beyond proper bounds

town /taʊn/ *n* **1a** a compactly settled area as distinguished from surrounding rural territory; *esp* one larger than a village but smaller than a city **b** a city **2** the city or urban life as contrasted with the country or rural life

town clerk *n* the chief official of a British town who until 1974 was appointed to administer municipal affairs and to act as secretary to the town council

town crier *n* a town officer who makes public proclamations

town hall *n* the chief administrative building of a town

township /'taʊnʃɪp/ *n* **1** an ancient unit of administration in England identical in area with or being a division of a parish **2** an urban area inhabited by nonwhite citizens in S Africa

townspeople /'taʊnz,piːpəl/ *n pl* the inhabitants of a town or city

toxic /'tɒksɪk/ *adj* **1** of or caused by a poison or toxin **2** poisonous – **~ity** *n*

toxin /'tɒksɪ̣n/ *n* an often extremely poisonous protein produced by a living organism (e g a bacterium), esp in the body of a host

[1]**toy** /tɔɪ/ *n* **1** a trinket, bauble **2a** sthg for a child to play with **b** sthg designed for amusement or diversion rather than practical use **3** an animal of a breed or variety of exceptionally small size

[2]**toy** *v* to act or deal *with* sthg without purpose or conviction

[3]**toy** *adj* **1** designed or made for use as a toy **2** toylike, esp in being small

[1]**trace** /treɪs/ *n* **1** a mark or line left by sthg that has passed **2** a vestige of some past thing **3** sthg traced or drawn (e g the graphic record made by a seismograph) **4** a minute and often barely detectable amount or indication, esp of a chemical

[2]**trace** *v* **1a** to delineate, sketch **b** to copy (e g a drawing) by following the lines or letters as seen through a semitransparent superimposed sheet **2a** to follow back or study in detail or step by step **b** to discover signs, evidence, or remains of – **~able** *adj*

[3]**trace** *n* either of 2 straps, chains, or lines of a harness for attaching a vehicle to a horse

tracery /'treɪsəri/ *n* ornamental stone openwork in architecture, esp in the head of a Gothic window

trachea /trə'kɪə/ *n, pl* **tracheae** *also* **tracheas** **1** the main trunk of the system of tubes by which air passes to and from the lungs in vertebrates; the windpipe **2** any of the small tubes carrying air in most insects and many other arthropods

tracing /ˈtreɪsɪŋ/ *n* a copy (e g of a design or map) made on a superimposed semitransparent sheet

¹track /træk/ *n* **1a** detectable evidence (e g a line of footprints or a wheel rut) that sthg has passed **b** a path beaten (as if) by feet **c** a specially laid-out course, esp for racing **d(1)** the parallel rails of a railway **(2)** a rail or length of railing along which sthg, esp a curtain, moves or is pulled **e** a more or less independent sequence of recording (e g a single song) visible as a distinct band on a gramophone record **2** a footprint **3** the course along which sthg moves **4** the condition of being aware of a fact or development **5a** the width of a wheeled vehicle from wheel to wheel, usu from the outside of the rims **b** either of 2 endless usu metal belts on which a tracklaying vehicle travels

²track *v* **1** to follow the tracks or traces of **2** to observe or plot the course of (e g a spacecraft) instrumentally **3** to move a film or television camera towards, beside, or away from a subject while shooting a scene – **~er** *n*

track suit *n* a warm loose-fitting suit worn by athletes when training

¹tract /trækt/ *n* a short practical treatise; *esp* a pamphlet of religious propaganda

²tract *n* **1** a region or area of land of indefinite extent **2** a system of body parts or organs that collectively serve some often specified purpose

tractable /ˈtræktəbəl/ *adj* **1** easily taught or controlled **2** easily handled or wrought – **-ability** *n*

traction /ˈtrækʃən/ *n* **1** pulling or being pulled; *also* the force exerted in pulling **2** the drawing of a vehicle by motive power **3a** the adhesive friction of a body on a surface on which it moves **b** a pulling force exerted on a skeletal structure (e g in treating a fracture) by means of a special device

traction engine *n* a large steam- or diesel-powered vehicle used to draw other vehicles or equipment over roads or fields and sometimes to provide power (e g for sawing or ploughing)

tractor /ˈtræktəʳ/ *n* **1** a 4-wheeled or tracklaying vehicle used esp for pulling or using farm machinery **2** a truck with a short chassis and no body except a driver's cab, used to haul a large trailer or trailers

¹trad /træd/ *adj, chiefly Br* traditional – infml

²trad *n* traditional jazz

¹trade /treɪd/ *n* **1a** the business or work in which one engages regularly **b** an occupation requiring manual or mechanical skill; a craft **c** the people engaged in an occupation, business, or industry **2a** the business of buying and selling or bartering commodities **b** business, market **3** *sing or pl in constr the* people or group of firms engaged in a particular business or industry

²trade *v* to give in exchange for another commodity; *also* to make an exchange of – **~r** *n*

³trade *adj* **1** of or used in trade **2** intended for or limited to people in a business or industry

trade gap *n* the value by which a country's imports exceed its exports

trade-in *n* an item of merchandise (e g a car or refrigerator) that is traded in

trade in *v* to give as payment or part payment for a purchase or bill

trademark /ˈtreɪdmɑːk/ *n* **1** a name or distinctive symbol or device attached to goods produced by a particular firm or individual and legally reserved to the exclusive use of the owner of the mark as maker or seller **2** a distinguishing feature firmly associated with sby or sthg

tradesman /ˈtreɪdzmən/ *n* **1** a shopkeeper **2** one who delivers goods to private houses

trade union *also* **trades union** *n* an organization of workers formed for the purpose of advancing its members' interests – **~ism** *n* – **~ist** *n*

trade wind *n* a wind blowing almost continually towards the equator from the NE in the belt between the N horse latitudes and the doldrums and from the SE in the belt between the S horse latitudes and the doldrums

tradition /trəˈdɪʃən/ *n* **1** the handing down of information, beliefs, and customs by word of mouth or by example from one generation to another **2a** an inherited practice or opinion **b** conventions associated with a group or period **3** cultural continuity in attitudes and institutions – **~al** *adj* – **~ally** *adv*

traduce /trə'djuːs/ *v* to (attempt to) damage the reputation or standing of, esp by misrepresentation – fml – **~r** *n*

traffic /'træfɪk/ *n* **1a** the business of bartering or buying and selling **b** illegal or disreputable trade **2a** the movement (e g of vehicles or pedestrians) through an area or along a route **b** the vehicles, pedestrians, ships, or aircraft moving along a route **3** dealings between individuals or groups – fml

tragedy /'trædʒɨdi/ *n* **1** (a) serious drama in which destructive circumstances result in adversity for and usu the deaths of the main characters **2** a disastrous event; a calamity **3** tragic quality or element

tragic /'trædʒɪk/ *also* **tragical** *adj* **1** (expressive) of tragedy **2** of, appropriate to, dealing with, or treated in tragedy **3** deplorable, lamentable – **~ally** *adv*

tragicomedy /ˌtrædʒɪ'kɒmɨdi/ *n* a literary work in which tragic and comic elements are mixed in a usu ironic way; *also* a situation or event of such a character

¹trail /treɪl/ *v* **1** to hang down so as to sweep the ground **2a** to walk or proceed draggingly or wearily – usu + *along* **b** to lag behind; do poorly in relation to others **3** to dwindle **4** to follow a trail; track game

²trail *n* **1a** sthg that follows as if being drawn behind **b** the streak of light produced by a meteor **2a** a trace or mark left by sby or sthg that has passed or is being followed **b(1)** a track made by passage, esp through a wilderness **(2)** a marked path through a forest or mountainous region

trailer /'treɪləʳ/ *n* **1** a trailing plant **2** a wheeled vehicle designed to be towed (e g by a lorry or car) **3** a set of short excerpts from a film shown in advance for publicity purposes

¹train /treɪn/ *n* **1** a part of a gown that trails behind the wearer **2a** a retinue, suite **b** a moving file of people, vehicles, or animals **3** the vehicles, men, and sometimes animals that accompany an army with baggage, supplies, ammunition, or siege artillery **4** a connected series of ideas, actions, or events **5** a connected line of railway carriages or wagons with or without a locomotive

²train *v* **1** to direct the growth of (a plant), usu by bending, pruning, etc **2a** to form by instruction, discipline, or drill **b** to teach so as to make fit or proficient **3** to prepare (e g by exercise) for a test of skill **4** to aim at an object or objective – **~able** *adj* – **~er** *n*

trainee /treɪ'niː/ *n* one who is being trained for a job

training /'treɪnɪŋ/ *n* **1** the bringing of a person or animal to a desired degree of proficiency in some activity or skill **2** the condition of being trained, esp for a contest

traipse, trapse /treɪps/ *v* to walk or trudge about, often to little purpose

trait /treɪt, treɪ/ *n* a distinguishing (personal) quality or characteristic

traitor /'treɪtəʳ/ *n* **1** sby who betrays another's trust **2** sby who commits treason

trajectory /trə'dʒektəri/ *n* **1** the curve that a planet, projectile, etc follows **2** a path, progression, or line of development like a physical trajectory

tram /træm/ *n, chiefly Br* a passenger vehicle running on rails and typically operating on urban streets

tramline /'træmlaɪn/ *n, Br pl* (the area between) either of the 2 pairs of sidelines on a tennis court that mark off the area used in doubles play

¹trammel /'træməl/ *n* sthg that impedes freedom of action – usu pl with sing. meaning

²trammel *v* to impede the free play of

¹tramp /træmp/ *v* **1** to walk or tread, esp heavily **2a** to travel about on foot **b** to journey as a tramp

²tramp *n* **1** a wandering vagrant who survives by taking the occasional job or by begging or stealing money and food **2** a usu long and tiring walk **3** the heavy rhythmic tread of feet **4** a merchant vessel that does not work a regular route but carries general cargo to any port as required

trample /træmpəl/ *v* **1** to tread heavily so as to bruise, crush, or injure **2** to treat destructively with ruthlessness or contempt – usu + *on, over,* or *upon*

trampoline /'træmpəliːn/ *n* a resilient sheet or web supported by springs in a frame and used as a springboard in tumbling

trance /trɑːns/ *n* **1** a state of semi-consciousness or unconsciousness with reduced or absent sensitivity to external stimulation **2** a state of profound abstraction or absorption

tranny /'træni/ *n, chiefly Br* a transistor radio – infml

tranquil /'træŋkwḷl/ *adj* free from mental agitation or from disturbance or commotion – **~lity** *n* – **~ly** *adv* – **~lize** *v*

tranquillizer *n* a drug used to reduce tension, anxiety, etc

transact /træn'zækt/ *v* to perform; carry out; *esp* to conduct – **~ion** *n*

transatlantic /ˌtrænzət'læntɪk/ *adj* **1** crossing or extending across the Atlantic ocean **2** situated beyond the Atlantic ocean **3** (characteristic) of people or places situated beyond the Atlantic ocean; *specif, chiefly Br* American

transcend /træn'send/ *v* to rise above or extend notably beyond ordinary limits

transcendent /træn'sendənt/ *adj* **1a** exceeding usual limits; surpassing **b** beyond the limits of ordinary experience **2** transcending the universe or material existence – **~ly** *adv* – **-ence, -ency** *n*

transcendental /ˌtrænsen'dentl/ *adj* **1** of or employing the basic categories (e g space and time) presupposed by knowledge and experience **2a** supernatural **b** abstruse, abstract – **~ly** *adv*

transcontinental /ˌtrænzkɒntḷ-'nentl, ˌtræns-/ *adj* crossing or extending across a continent

transcribe /træn'skraɪb/ *v* **1a** to make a written copy or version of (e g sthg written or printed) **b** to write in a different medium; transliterate **2** to make a musical transcription of – **-scription** *n*

transcript /'trænskrɪpt/ *n* **1** a written, printed, or typed copy, esp of dictated or recorded material **2** an official written copy

transept /'trænsept/ *n* (either of the projecting arms of) the part of a cross-shaped church that crosses the E end of the nave at right angles

[1]**transfer** /træns'fɜːʳ/ *v* **1a** to convey or cause to pass from one person, place, or situation to another **b** to move or send to another location; *specif* to move (a professional soccer player) to another football club **2** to make over the possession or control of – **~ability** *n* – **~able** *adj* – **~ence** *n*

[2]**transfer** /'trænsfɜːʳ/ *n* **1** conveyance of right, title, or interest in property **2** transferring

transfiguration /ˌtrænzfɪgə'reɪʃən, -fɪgjʊ-/ *n* **1a** a change in form or appearance; a metamorphosis **b** an exalting, glorifying, or spiritual change **2** *cap* August 6 observed as a Christian festival in commemoration of the transfiguration of Christ as described in Mt 17:2 and Mk 9:2–3

transfigure /træns'fɪgəʳ/ *v* to give a new appearance to; transform outwardly and usu for the better

transfix /træns'fɪks/ *v* **1** to pierce through (as if) with a pointed weapon **2** to hold motionless (as if) by piercing

transform /træns'fɔːm/ *v* **1** to change radically (e g in structure, appearance, or character) **2** to subject to mathematical transformation **3** to change (a current) in potential (e g from high voltage to low) or in type (e g from alternating to direct)

transformation /ˌtrænsfə'meɪʃən/ *n* the operation of changing one configuration or expression into another in accordance with a mathematical rule – **~al** *adj*

transformer /træns'fɔːməʳ/ *n* an electrical device making use of the principle of mutual induction to convert variations of current in a primary circuit into variations of voltage and current in a secondary circuit

transfuse /'træns'fjuːz/ *v* **1** to diffuse into or through; *broadly* to spread across **2** to transfer (e g blood) into a vein – **-fusion** *n*

transgress /trænz'gres/ *v* **1** to go beyond limits set or prescribed by **2** to violate a command or law – **~ion** *n* – **~or** *n*

[1]**transient** /'trænzıənt/ *adj* **1** passing quickly away; transitory **2** making only a brief stay

[2]**transient** *n* a transient guest or worker

transistor /træn'zıstəʳ, -'sıstəʳ/ *n* any of several semiconductor devices that have usu 3 electrodes and make use of a small current to control a larger one; *also* a radio using using such devices

transit /'trænzǰt, -sǰt/ *n* **1a** passing or conveying through or over **b** a change, transition **2** passage of a smaller celestial body across the disc of a larger one – **~ory** *adj*

transition /træn'zıʃən, -'sı-/ *n* **1a** passage from one state or stage to another **b** a movement, development, or evolution from one form, stage, or style to another **2** a musical passage leading from one section of a piece to another – **~al** *adj* – **~ally** *adv*

transitive /'trænsǰtıv, -zǰ-/ *adj* **1** having or containing a direct object **2** of or being a relation such that if the relation holds between a first element and a second and between the second element and a third, it holds between the first and third elements

translate /trænz'leıt, træns-/ *v* **1a** to bear, remove, or change from one place, state, form, or appearance to another **b** to transfer (a bishop) from one see to another **2a** to turn into another language **b** to express in different or more comprehensible terms – **-latable** *adj* – **-lator** *n*

translation /trænz'leıʃən, træns-/ *n* **1** (a version produced by) a rendering from one language into another **2** a change to a different substance or form

transliterate /trænz'lıtəreıt/ *v* to represent or spell in the characters of another alphabet – **-ation** *n*

translucent /trænz'luːsənt/ *adj* **1** transparent **2** transmitting and diffusing light so that objects beyond cannot be seen clearly – **-cence, -cency** *n*

transmission /trænz'mıʃən/ *n* **1** transmitting; *esp* transmitting by radio waves or over a wire **2** the assembly by which the power is transmitted from a motor vehicle engine to the axle

transmit /trænz'mıt/ *v* **1a** to send or transfer from one person or place to another **b** to convey (as if) by inheritance or heredity **2a** to cause (e g light or force) to pass or be conveyed through a medium **b** to send out (a signal) either by radio waves or over a wire

transmitter /trænz'mıtəʳ/ *n* **1** the portion of a telegraphic or telephonic instrument that sends the signals **2** a radio or television transmitting station or set

transmogrify /trænz'mɒgrǰfaı/ *v* to transform, often with grotesque or humorous effect – **-fication** *n*

transmute /trænz'mjuːt/ *v* to change in form, substance, or characteristics – **-mutable** *adj* – **-mutation** *n*

transom /'trænsəm/ *n* a transverse piece in a structure: e g **a** a lintel **b** a horizontal crossbar in a window, over a door, or between a door and a window or fanlight above it **c** any of several transverse timbers or beams secured to the sternpost of a boat

transparency /træn'spærənsi, -'speər-/ *n* **1** a picture or design on glass, film, etc viewed by a light shining through it from behind; *esp* a colour photograph for projecting onto a screen; a slide **2** a framework covered with thin cloth or paper bearing a device for public display (e g for advertisement) and lit from within

transparent /træn'spærənt, -'speər-/ *adj* **1a(1)** transmitting light without appreciable scattering so that bodies lying beyond are entirely visible **(2)** penetrable by a specified form of radiation (e g X rays or ultraviolet) **b** fine or sheer enough to be seen through **2a** free from pretence or deceit **b** easily detected or seen through **c** readily understood – **~ly** *adv*

transpire /træn'spaıəʳ/ *v* **1** to give off a vapour; *specif* to give off or exude water vapour, esp from the surfaces of leaves **2** to become known; come to light **3** to occur; take place – **-piration** *n*

¹transplant /træns'plɑːnt/ *v* **1** to lift and reset (a plant) in another soil or place **2** to remove from one place and settle or introduce elsewhere **3** to transfer (an organ or tissue) from one part or individual to another – **~ation** *n*

²transplant /'trænsplɑːnt/ *n* **1** transplanting **2** sthg transplanted

¹transport /træn'spɔːt/ *v* **1** to transfer or convey from one place to another **2** to carry away with strong and often pleasurable emotion **3** to send to a penal colony overseas – **~able** *adj*

²transport /'trænspɔːt/ *n* **1** the conveying of goods or people from one place to another **2** strong and often pleasurable emotion – often pl with sing. meaning **3** a ship or aircraft for carrying soldiers or military equipment **4** a mechanism for moving a tape, esp a magnetic tape, or disk past a sensing or recording head

transportation /ˌtrænspɔː'teɪʃən/ *n* **1** the act of transporting **2** banishment to a penal colony **3** means of conveyance or travel from one place to another

transport café *n, Br* an inexpensive roadside cafeteria catering mainly for long-distance lorry drivers

transporter /træn'spɔːtəʳ/ *n* a vehicle for transporting large or heavy loads

transpose /træn'spəʊz/ *v* **1** to transfer from one place or period to another **2** to change the relative position of; alter the sequence of **3** to write or perform (music) in a different key

transship, tranship /træns'ʃɪp/ *v* to transfer from one ship or conveyance to another for further transportation – **~ment** *n*

transubstantiation /ˌtrænsəbstænʃi'eɪʃən/ *n* the miraculous change by which, according to Roman Catholic and Eastern Orthodox dogma, bread and wine used at communion become the body and blood of Christ when they are consecrated, although their appearance remains unchanged

transverse /trænz'vɜːs/ *adj* lying or being across; set or made crosswise – **~ly** *adv*

¹trap /træp/ *n* **1** a device for taking animals; *esp* one that holds by springing shut suddenly **2a** sthg designed to catch sby unawares **b** a situation from which it is impossible to escape; *also* a plan to trick a person into such a situation **3a** a trapdoor **b** a device from which a greyhound is released at the start of a race **4** a light usu 1-horse carriage with springs **5** the mouth – slang

²trap *v* **1** to catch or take (as if) in a trap **2** to provide or set (a place) with traps **3** to stop, retain

trapdoor /'træpdɔːʳ/ *n* a lifting or sliding door covering an opening in a floor, ceiling, etc

trapeze /trə'piːz/ *n* a gymnastic or acrobatic apparatus consisting of a short horizontal bar suspended by 2 parallel ropes

trapezium /trə'piːzɪəm/ *n, pl* **trapeziums, trapezia** *Br* a quadrilateral having only 2 sides parallel

trappings /'træpɪŋz/ *n pl* outward decoration or dress; *also* outward signs and accessories

Trappist /'træpɨst/ *n* a member of a reformed branch of the Roman Catholic Cistercian Order established in 1664 at the monastery of La Trappe in Normandy and noted for its vow of silence

trash /træʃ/ *n* **1** sthg of little or no value: e g **a** junk, rubbish **b** inferior literary or artistic work **2** a worthless person; *also, sing or pl in constr* such people as a group – infml

trashy /'træʃi/ *adj* of inferior quality or worth – **-shiness** *n*

trauma /'trɔːmə, 'traʊmə/ *n, pl* **traumata, traumas** a disordered mental or behavioural state resulting from mental or emotional stress or shock – **~tic** *adj*

¹travel /'trævəl/ *v* **1a** to go (as if) on a tour **b** to go as if by travelling **c** to go from place to place as a sales representative **2a** to move or be transmitted from one place to another **b** *esp of machinery* to move along a specified direction or path **c** to move at high speed – infml

²travel *n* **1** a journey, esp to a distant or unfamiliar place – often pl **2** movement, progression

travel agent *n* sby engaged in selling

and arranging personal transport, tours, or trips for travellers

travelled, *NAm chiefly* **traveled** /'trævəld/ *adj* **1** experienced in travel **2** used by travellers

traveller, *NAm chiefly* **traveler** /'trævələʳ/ *n* **1** a sales representative **2** any of various devices for handling sthg that is being moved laterally **3** *dial Br* a gipsy

traveller's cheque *n* a cheque that is purchased from a bank and that may be exchanged abroad for foreign currency

travelogue /'trævəlɒg/ *n* **1** a film or illustrated talk or lecture on some usu exotic or remote place **2** a narrated documentary film about travel

[1]**traverse** /'trævɜːs, trə'vɜːs/ *n* **1** sthg that crosses or lies across **2** a route or way across or over: e g **a** a curving or zigzag way up a steep slope **b** the course followed in traversing **3** (a) traversing **4** the lateral movement of a gun to change direction of fire

[2]**traverse** /trə'vɜːs,'trævɜːs/ *v* **1** to pass or travel across, over, or through **2** to lie or extend across **3a** to move to and fro over or along **b** to ascend, descend, or cross (a slope or gap) at an angle **c** to move (a gun) to right or left

[3]**traverse** /'trævɜːs, trə'vɜːs/ *adj* lying across

[1]**travesty** /'trævɨ̣sti/ *n* **1** a crude or grotesque literary or artistic parody **2** a debased, distorted, or grossly inferior imitation

[2]**travesty** *v* to make a travesty of

[1]**trawl** /trɔːl/ *v* to fish (for or in) with a trawl

[2]**trawl** *n* a large conical net dragged along the sea bottom to catch fish

trawler /'trɔːləʳ/ *n* a boat used in trawling

tray /treɪ/ *n* an open receptacle with a flat bottom and a low rim for holding, carrying, or exhibiting articles

treacherous /'tretʃərəs/ *adj* **1** characterized by treachery; perfidious **2a** of uncertain reliability **b** marked by hidden dangers or hazards – **~ly** *adv*

treachery /'tretʃəri/ *n* (an act of) violation of allegiance; (a) betrayal of trust

treacle /'triːkəl/ *n, chiefly Br* **1** any of the edible grades of molasses that are obtained in the early stages of sugar refining **2** golden syrup

[1]**tread** /tred/ *v* **trod; trodden, trod 1a** to step or walk on or over **b** to walk along **2** to beat or press with the feet **3** *of a male bird* to copulate with **4** to execute by stepping or dancing

[2]**tread** *n* **1** an imprint made (as if) by treading **2** the sound or manner of treading **3a** the part of a wheel or tyre that makes contact with a road or rail **b** the pattern of ridges or grooves made or cut in the face of a tyre **4** (the width of) the upper horizontal part of a step

treadle /'tredl/ *n* a lever pressed by the foot to drive a machine (e g a sewing machine)

treadmill /'tred,mɪl/ *n* **1a** a mill used formerly in prison punishment that was worked by people treading on steps inside a wide wheel with a horizontal axis **b** a mill worked by an animal treading an endless belt **2** a wearisome or monotonous routine

treason /'triːzən/ *n* **1** the betrayal of a trust **2** the offence of violating the duty of allegiance owed to one's crown or government – **~able** *adj* – **~ably** *adv*

[1]**treasure** /'treʒəʳ/ *n* **1** wealth, esp in a form which can be accumulated or hoarded **2** sthg of great worth or value; *also* sby highly valued or prized

[2]**treasure** *v* to hold or preserve as precious

treasurer /'treʒərəʳ/ *n* the financial officer of an organization (e g a society)

treasure trove *n* treasure that anyone finds; *specif* gold or silver money, plate, or bullion which is found hidden and whose ownership is not known

treasury /'treʒəri/ *n* **1a** a place in which stores of wealth are kept **b** the place where esp public funds that have been collected are deposited and disbursed **2** *often cap* a government department in charge of finances, esp the collection, management, and expenditure of public revenues

[1]**treat** /triːt/ *v* **1** to deal with **2a** to behave oneself towards **b** to regard

and deal with in a specified manner – usu + *as* **3** to provide with free food, drink, entertainment, etc – usu + *to* **4** to care for or deal with medically or surgically **5** to act on with some agent, esp so as to improve or alter – **~able** *adj* – **~er** *n*

[2]**treat** *n* **1** an entertainment given free of charge to those invited **2** a source of pleasure or amusement; *esp* an unexpected one

treatise /'triːtɨs, -tɨz/ *n* a formal written exposition on a subject

treatment /'triːtmənt/ *n* **1a** treating sby or sthg **b** the actions customarily applied in a particular situation **2** a substance or technique used in treating

treaty /'triːti/ *n* (a document setting down) an agreement or contract made by negotiation (e g between states)

[1]**treble** /'trebəl/ *n* **1a** the highest voice part in harmonic music; *also* sby, esp a boy, who performs this part **b** a member of a family of instruments having the highest range **c** the upper half of the whole vocal or instrumental tonal range **2** sthg treble in construction, uses, amount, number, or value: e g **a** a type of bet in which the winnings and stake from a previous race are bet on the next of 3 races **b** (a throw landing on) the middle narrow ring on a dart board counting treble the stated score

[2]**treble** *adj* **1a** having 3 parts or uses **b** triple **2a** relating to or having the range or part of a treble **b** high-pitched, shrill

treble clef *n* a clef that places the note G above middle C on the second line of the staff

tree /triː/ *n* **1** a tall woody perennial plant having a single usu long and erect main stem, generally with few or no branches on its lower part **2** a device for inserting in a boot or shoe to preserve its shape when not being worn **3** a diagram or graph that branches, usu from a single stem

trefoil /'triːfɔɪl, 'tre-/ *n* **1a** (a) clover; *broadly* any of several leguminous plants having leaves of 3 leaflets **b** a leaf consisting of 3 leaflets **2** a stylized figure or ornament in the form of a 3-lobed leaf or flower

trek /trek/ *v or n* (to make) **1** a journey; *esp* an arduous one **2** *chiefly SAfr* a journey by ox wagon

[1]**trellis** /'trelɨs/ *n* a frame of latticework used as a screen or as a support for climbing plants

[2]**trellis** *v* to provide with a trellis; *esp* to train (e g a vine) on a trellis

[1]**tremble** /'trembəl/ *v* **1** to shake involuntarily (e g with fear or cold) **2** to be affected with fear or apprehension – **-blingly** *adv*

[2]**tremble** *n* **1** a fit or spell of involuntary shaking or quivering **2** a tremor or series of tremors

tremendous /trɪ'mendəs/ *adj* **1** such as to arouse awe or fear **2** of extraordinary size, degree, or excellence – **~ly** *adv*

tremolo /'treməlәʊ/ *n* **1a** the rapid reiteration of a musical note or of alternating notes to produce a tremulous effect **b** a perceptible rapid variation of pitch in the (singing) voice; vibrato **2** a mechanical device in an organ for causing a tremulous effect

tremor /'treməʳ/ *n* **1** a trembling or shaking, usu from physical weakness, emotional stress, or disease **2** a (slight) quivering or vibratory motion, esp of the earth **3** a thrill, quiver

tremulous /'tremjʊləs/ *adj* **1** characterized by or affected with trembling or tremors **2** uncertain, wavering – **~ly** *adv* – **~ness** *n*

[1]**trench** /trentʃ/ *n* a deep narrow excavation (e g for the laying of underground pipes); *esp* one used for military defence

[2]**trench** *v* to dig a trench (in)

trenchant /'trenʃənt/ *adj* **1** keen, sharp **2** vigorously effective and articulate **3a** incisive, penetrating **b** clear-cut, distinct – **~ly** *adv* – **-ancy** *n*

trench coat *n* a double-breasted raincoat with deep pockets, a belt, and epaulettes

[1]**trend** /trend/ *v* **1** to show a general tendency to move or extend in a specified direction **2** to deviate, shift

[2]**trend** *n* **1** a line of general direction **2a** a prevailing tendency or inclination **b** a general movement, esp in taste or fashion

[1]**trendy** /'trendi/ *adj, chiefly Br* char-

acterized by uncritical adherence to the latest fashions or progressive ideas – infml – **trendiness** *n*

²**trendy** *n, chiefly Br* sby trendy – chiefly derog

trepidation /ˌtrepȷ̇ˈdeɪʃən/ *n* nervous agitation or apprehension

¹**trespass** /ˈtrespəs, -pæs/ *n* **1** a violation of moral or social ethics; *esp* a sin **2** any unlawful act that causes harm to the person, property, or rights of another; *esp* wrongful entry on another's land

²**trespass** *v* **1a** to err, sin **b** to make an unwarranted or uninvited intrusion *on* **2** to commit a trespass; *esp* to enter sby's property unlawfully

trestle /ˈtresəl/ *n* **1** a (braced) frame serving as a support (e g for a table top) **2** a braced framework of timbers, piles, or girders for carrying a road or railway over a depression

trestle table *n* a table consisting of a board or boards supported on trestles

trews /truːz/ *n pl in constr, pl* **trews** trousers; *specif* tartan trousers

¹**trial** /ˈtraɪəl/ *n* **1** trying or testing **2** the formal examination and determination by a competent tribunal of the matter at issue in a civil or criminal cause **3** a test of faith, patience, or stamina by suffering or temptation; *broadly* a source of vexation or annoyance **4** an experiment to test quality, value, or usefulness **5** an attempt, effort

²**trial** *adj* **1** of a trial **2** made or done as, or used or tried out in, a test or experiment

triangle /ˈtraɪæŋgəl/ *n* **1** a polygon of 3 sides and 3 angles **2** a percussion instrument consisting of a steel rod bent into the form of a triangle open at 1 angle and sounded by striking with a small metal rod

triangular /traɪˈæŋgjʊləʳ/ *adj* **1** (having the form) of a triangle **2** between or involving 3 elements, things, or people

tribalism /ˈtraɪbəl-ɪzəm/ *n* **1** tribal consciousness and loyalty **2** strong loyalty or attachment to a group

tribe /traɪb/ *n sing or pl in constr* **1** a social group comprising numerous families, clans, or generations together with slaves, dependants, or adopted strangers **2** a group of people having a common character or interest **3** a category in the classification of living things ranking above a genus and below a family – **tribal** *adj*

tribesman /ˈtraɪbzmən/ *n* a member of a tribe

tribulation /ˌtrɪbjʊˈleɪʃən/ *n* distress or suffering resulting from oppression

tribunal /traɪˈbjuːnəl/ *n* a court of justice; *specif* a board appointed to decide disputes of a specified kind

tribune /ˈtrɪbjuːn/ *n* **1** an official of ancient Rome with the function of protecting the plebeian citizens from arbitrary action by the patrician magistrates **2** an unofficial defender of the rights of the individual

¹**tributary** /ˈtrɪbjʊtəri/ *adj* **1** paying tribute to another; subject **2** paid or owed as tribute **3** providing with material or supplies

²**tributary** *n* **1** a tributary ruler or state **2** a stream feeding a larger stream or a lake

tribute /ˈtrɪbjuːt/ *n* **1** a payment by one ruler or nation to another in acknowledgment of submission or as the price of protection **2a** sthg (e g a gift or formal declaration) given or spoken as a testimonial of respect, gratitude, or affection **b** evidence of the worth or effectiveness of sthg specified – chiefly in ***a tribute to***

trice /traɪs/ *n* a brief space of time – chiefly in *in a trice*

¹**trick** /trɪk/ *n* **1a** a crafty practice or stratagem meant to deceive or defraud **b** a mischievous act **c** a deceptive, dexterous, or ingenious feat designed to puzzle or amuse **2a** a habitual peculiarity of behaviour or manner **b** a deceptive appearance, esp when caused by art or sleight of hand **3a** a quick or effective way of getting a result **b** a technical device or contrivance (e g of an art or craft) **4** the cards played in 1 round of a card game, often used as a scoring unit – **~ery** *n*

²**trick** *adj* **1** of or involving tricks or trickery **2** skilled in or used for tricks

³**trick** *v* **1** to deceive by cunning or

artifice – often + *into, out of* **2** to dress or embellish showily – usu + *out* or *up*

[1]**trickle** /'trɪkəl/ *v* **1** to flow in drops or a thin slow stream **2** to move or go gradually or one by one

[2]**trickle** *n* a thin slow stream or movement

trickster /'trɪkstəʳ/ *n* a person who defrauds others by trickery

tricky /'trɪki/ *adj* **1** inclined to or marked by trickery **2** containing concealed difficulties or hazards **3** requiring skill, adroitness, or caution (e g in doing or handling) – **trickiness** *n*

[1]**tricolour,** *NAm* **tricolor** /'trɪkələʳ, 'traɪ,kʌləʳ/ *n* a flag of 3 colours

[2]**tricolour** /'traɪ,kʌləʳ/, **tricoloured** *adj* having or using 3 colours

tricycle /'traɪsɪkəl/ *n* a 3-wheeled pedal-driven vehicle

[1]**trident** /'traɪdənt/ *n* a 3-pronged (fish) spear **a** serving as the attribute of a sea god **b** used by ancient Roman gladiators

[2]**trident** *adj* having 3 prongs or points

tried /traɪd/ *adj* **1** found to be good or trustworthy through experience or testing **2** subjected to trials or severe provocation – often in combination

triennial /traɪ'enɪəl/ *adj* **1** consisting of or lasting for 3 years **2** occurring every 3 years

trier /'traɪəʳ/ *n* **1** sby who makes an effort or perseveres **2** an implement (e g a tapered hollow tube) used in obtaining samples of bulk material, esp foodstuffs, for examination and testing

[1]**trifle** /'traɪfəl/ *n* **1** sthg of little value or importance; *esp* an insignificant amount (e g of money) **2** *chiefly Br* a dessert typically consisting of sponge cake soaked in wine (e g sherry), spread with jam or jelly, and topped with custard and whipped cream

[2]**trifle** *v* **1** to act heedlessly or frivolously – often + *with* **2** to handle sthg idly **3** to spend or waste in trifling or on trifles

trifling /'traɪflɪŋ/ *adj* lacking in significance or solid worth: e g **a** frivolous **b** trivial, insignificant

[1]**trigger** /'trɪgəʳ/ *n* a device (e g a lever) connected with a catch as a means of release; *esp* the tongue of metal in a firearm which when pressed allows the gun to fire

[2]**trigger** *v* **1a** to release, activate, or fire by means of a trigger **b** to cause the explosion of **2** to initiate or set off as if by pulling a trigger – often + *off*

trigger-happy *adj* **1** irresponsible in the use of firearms **2a** aggressively belligerent **b** too prompt in one's response

trigonometry /,trɪgə'nɒmɪ̆tri/ *n* the study of the properties of triangles and trigonometric functions and of their applications – **-ric, -rical** *adj*

trilateral /,traɪ'lætərəl/ *adj* having 3 sides – **~ly** *adv*

trilby /'trɪlbi/ *n, chiefly Br* a soft felt hat with an indented crown

trilingual /,traɪ'lɪŋgwəl/ *adj* **1** of, containing, or expressed in 3 languages **2** using or able to use 3 languages, esp with the fluency of a native – **~ly** *adv*

trill /trɪl/ *n* **1** the alternation of 2 musical notes 2 semitones apart **2** a sound resembling a musical trill – **trill** *v*

trillion /'trɪljən/ *n* **1a** *Br* a million million millions (10^{18}) **b** *chiefly NAm* a million millions (10^{12})

trilobite /'traɪləbaɪt/ *n* any of numerous extinct Palaeozoic marine arthropods that had a 3-lobed body

trilogy /'trɪlədʒi/ *n* a group of 3 closely related works (e g novels)

[1]**trim** /trɪm/ *v* **1** to decorate (e g clothes) with ribbons, lace, or ornaments; adorn **2** to make trim and neat, esp by cutting or clipping **3a** to cause (e g a ship, aircraft, or submarine) to assume a desired position by arrangement of ballast, cargo, passengers, etc **b** to adjust (e g a sail) to a desired position **4** to maintain a neutral attitude towards opposing parties or favour each equally

[2]**trim** *adj* appearing neat or in good order; compact or clean-cut in outline or structure – **~ly** *adv*

[3]**trim** *n* **1** the readiness or fitness of a person or thing for action or use; *esp* physical fitness **2a** material used for decoration or trimming **b** the decorative accessories of a motor vehicle **3a** the position of a ship or boat, esp with

reference to the horizontal **b** the inclination of an aircraft or spacecraft in flight with reference to a fixed point (e g the horizon), esp with the controls in some neutral position

trimaran /ˈtraɪmərӕn/ *n* a sailing vessel used for cruising or racing that has 3 hulls side by side

trimming /ˈtrɪmɪŋ/ *n* **1** *pl* pieces cut off in trimming sthg; scraps **2a** a decorative accessory or additional item (e g on the border of a garment) that serves to finish or complete **b** an additional garnish or accompaniment to a main item – usu pl

Trinity /ˈtrɪnɪ̵ti/ *n* **1** the unity of Father, Son, and Holy Spirit as 3 persons in 1 Godhead according to Christian theology **2** the Sunday after Whitsunday observed as a festival in honour of the Trinity

trinket /ˈtrɪŋkɪ̵t/ *n* a small (trifling) article; *esp* an ornament or piece of (cheap) jewellery

trio /ˈtriːəʊ/ *n* **1a** (a musical composition for) 3 instruments, voices, or performers **b** the secondary division of a minuet, scherzo, etc **2** *sing or pl in constr* a group or set of 3

[1]**trip** /trɪp/ *v* **1a** to dance, skip, or walk with light quick steps **b** to proceed smoothly, lightly, and easily; flow **2a** to catch the foot against sthg so as to stumble **b** to detect in a fault or blunder; catch out – usu + *up* **3** to stumble in articulation when speaking **4** to make a journey **5** to release or operate (a device or mechanism), esp by releasing a catch or producing an electrical signal **6** to get high on a psychedelic drug (e g LSD) – slang

[2]**trip** *n* **1a** a voyage, journey, or excursion **b** a single round or tour (e g on a business errand) **2** an error, mistake **3** a quick light step **4** a faltering step caused by stumbling **5** a device (e g a catch) for tripping a mechanism **6** an intense, often visionary experience undergone by sby who has taken a psychedelic drug (e g LSD) **7** a self-indulgent or absorbing course of action, way of behaving, or frame of mind *USE* (*6&7*) infml

tripartite /traɪˈpɑːtaɪt/ *adj* made between or involving 3 parties

tripe /traɪp/ *n* **1** the stomach tissue of an ox, cow, etc for use as food **2** sthg inferior, worthless, or offensive – infml

[1]**triple** /ˈtrɪpəl/ *v* to make or become 3 times as great or as many

[2]**triple** *n* **1** a triple sum, quantity, or number **2** a combination, group, or series of 3

[3]**triple** *adj* **1** having 3 units or members **2** being 3 times as great or as many **3** marked by 3 beats per bar of music **4** having units of 3 components

triple jump *n* an athletic field event consisting of a jump for distance combining a hop, a step, and a jump in succession

triplet /ˈtrɪplɪ̵t/ *n* **1** a unit of 3 lines of verse **2** a combination, set, or group of 3 **3** any of 3 children or animals born at 1 birth

triplex /ˈtrɪpleks/ *adj* threefold, triple

triplicate /ˈtrɪplɪ̵kɪ̵t/ *n* **1** any of 3 things exactly alike; *specif* any of 3 identical copies **2** three copies all alike – + *in* – **triplicate** *v*

tripod /ˈtraɪpɒd/ *n* **1** a stool, table, or vessel (e g a cauldron) with 3 legs **2** a 3-legged stand (e g for a camera)

tripos /ˈtraɪpɒs/ *n* either part of the honours examination for the Cambridge BA degree

tripper /ˈtrɪpəʳ/ *n, chiefly Br* one who goes on an outing or pleasure trip, esp one lasting only 1 day – often used disparagingly

triptych /ˈtrɪptɪk/ *n* a picture or carving on 3 panels side by side; *esp* an altarpiece consisting of a central panel hinged to 2 flanking panels that fold over it

trireme /ˈtraɪriːm/ *n* a galley with 3 banks of oars

trite /traɪt/ *adj* hackneyed from much use – **~ly** *adv* – **~ness** *n*

[1]**triumph** /ˈtraɪəmf, -ʌmf/ *n* **1** the joy or exultation of victory or success **2** (a) notable success, victory, or achievement – **~al** *adj*

[2]**triumph** /ˈtraɪəmf/ *v* **1** to celebrate victory or success boastfully or exultantly **2** to obtain victory – often + *over*

triumphant /traɪˈʌmfənt/ *adj* **1** victorious, conquering **2** rejoicing in or celebrating victory – **~ly** *adv*

triumvirate /traɪ'ʌmvɪ̴rɪ̴t/ *n* a group of 3; *esp* a group of 3 ruling a country

trivet /'trɪvɪ̴t/ *n* **1** a three-legged (iron) stand for holding cooking vessels over or by a fire; *also* a bracket that hooks onto a grate for this purpose **2** a (metal) stand with 3 feet for holding a hot dish at table

trivia /'trɪvɪə/ *n pl but sing or pl in constr* unimportant matters or details

trivial /'trɪvɪəl/ *adj* **1** commonplace, ordinary **2** of little worth or importance; insignificant – **~ly** *adv* – **~ity** *n* – **~ize** *v*

trochee /'trəʊkiː/ *n* a metrical foot consisting of 1 long or stressed syllable followed by 1 short or unstressed syllable (e g in *apple*) – **trochaic** *adj*

trod /trɒd/ *past of* **tread**

trodden /'trɒdn/ *past part of* **tread**

troglodyte /'trɒglədaɪt/ *n* **1** a cave dweller **2** a person resembling a troglodyte, esp in being solitary or unsocial or in having primitive or outmoded ideas

Trojan /'trəʊdʒən/ *n* **1** a native of Troy **2** one who shows qualities (e g pluck or endurance) attributed to the defenders of ancient Troy – chiefly in *work like a Trojan*

[1]**troll** /trəʊl/ *v* **1** to sing or play an instrument in a jovial manner **2** to fish, esp by drawing a hook through the water

[2]**troll** *n* (a line with) a lure used in trolling

[3]**troll** /trəʊl, trɒl/ *n* a dwarf or giant of Germanic folklore inhabiting caves or hills

trolley /'trɒli/ *n* **1** a device (e g a grooved wheel or skid) attached to a pole that collects current from an overhead electric wire for powering an electric vehicle **2** *chiefly Br* **a** a shelved stand mounted on castors used for conveying sthg (e g food or books) **b** a basket on wheels that is pushed or pulled by hand and used for carrying goods (e g purchases in a supermarket)

trollop /'trɒləp/ *n* a slovenly or immoral woman

trombone /trɒm'bəʊn/ *n* a brass instrument consisting of a long cylindrical metal tube with a movable slide for varying the pitch and a usual range 1 octave lower than that of the trumpet – **-nist** *n*

[1]**troop** /truːp/ *n* **1** *sing or pl in constr* **a** a military subunit (e g of cavalry) corresponding to an infantry platoon **b** a collection of people or things **c** a unit of scouts under a leader **2** *pl* the armed forces

[2]**troop** *v* to move in a group, esp in a way that suggests regimentation

trooper /'truːpəʳ/ *n* **1a** a cavalry soldier; *esp* a private soldier in a cavalry or armoured regiment **b** the horse of a cavalry soldier **2** *chiefly NAm & Austr* a mounted policeman

trophy /'trəʊfi/ *n* sthg gained or awarded in victory or conquest, esp when preserved as a memorial

tropic /'trɒpɪk/ *n* **1** either of the 2 small circles of the celestial sphere on each side of and parallel to the equator at a distance of 23½ degrees, which the sun reaches at its greatest declination N or S **2** *pl, often cap* the region between the 2 terrestrial tropics

tropical /'trɒpɪkəl/ *adj* **1** *also* **tropic** of, occurring in, or characteristic of the tropics **2** *of a sign of the zodiac* beginning at either of the tropics – **~ly** *adv*

tropism /'trəʊpɪzəm/ *n* (an) involuntary orientation by (a part of) an organism, esp a plant, that involves turning or curving in response to a source of stimulation (e g light)

[1]**trot** /trɒt/ *n* **1** a moderately fast gait of a horse or other quadruped in which the legs move in diagonal pairs **2** *pl but sing or pl in constr* diarrhoea – usu + *the*; humor

[2]**trot** *v* **1** to ride, drive, or proceed at a trot **2** to proceed briskly

Trot *n* a Trotskyite; *broadly* any adherent of the extreme left – chiefly derog

troth /trəʊθ/ *n, archaic* one's pledged word; *also* betrothal – chiefly in *plight one's troth*

Trotskyism /'trɒtski-ɪzəm/ *n* the political, economic, and social principles advocated by Trotsky; *esp* adherence to the concept of permanent worldwide revolution – **-ist, -ite** *n, adj*

trotter /ˈtrɒtəʳ/ *n* the foot of an animal, esp a pig, used as food

troubadour /ˈtruːbədɔːr, -dʊəʳ/ *n* any of a class of lyric poets and poet-musicians, chiefly in France in the 11th to 13th c, whose major theme was courtly love

[1]**trouble** /ˈtrʌbəl/ *v* **1a** to agitate mentally or spiritually; worry **b** to produce physical disorder or discomfort in **c** to put to exertion or inconvenience **2** to make (e g the surface of water) turbulent

[2]**trouble** *n* **1a** being troubled **b** an instance of distress, annoyance, or disturbance **2** a cause of disturbance, annoyance, or distress: e g **a** public unrest or demonstrations of dissatisfaction – often pl with sing. meaning **b** effort made; exertion **3** a problem, snag

troubleshooter /ˈtrʌbəl,ʃuːtəʳ/ *n* **1** a skilled workman employed to locate faults and make repairs in machinery and technical equipment **2** one who specializes or is expert in resolving disputes

troublesome /ˈtrʌbəlsəm/ *adj* giving trouble or anxiety; annoying or burdensome

trough /trɒf/ *n* **1** a long shallow receptacle for the drinking water or feed of farm animals **2** a long narrow or shallow trench between waves, ridges, etc **3a** the (region round the) lowest point of a regularly recurring cycle of a varying quantity (e g a sine wave) **b** an elongated area of low atmospheric pressure

trounce /traʊns/ *v* **1** to thrash or punish severely **2** to defeat decisively

troupe /truːp/ *n* a company or troop (of theatrical performers)

trouper /ˈtruːpəʳ/ *n* a loyal or dependable person

trousers /ˈtraʊzəz/ *n pl, pl* **trousers** a 2-legged outer garment extending from the waist to the ankle or sometimes only to the knee – **trouser** *adj*

trousseau /ˈtruːsəʊ, truːˈsəʊ/ *n* the personal outfit of a bride including clothes, accessories, etc

trout /traʊt/ *n* **1** any of various food and sport fishes of the salmon family restricted to cool clear fresh waters; *esp* any of various Old World or New World fishes some of which ascend rivers from the sea to breed **2** an ugly unpleasant old woman – slang

trove /trəʊv/ *n* a treasure trove

trowel /ˈtraʊəl/ *n* any of various smooth-bladed hand tools used to apply, spread, shape, or smooth loose or soft material; *also* a scoop-shaped or flat-bladed garden tool for taking up and setting small plants

troy weight *n* the series of units of weight based on the pound of 12oz and the ounce of 20 pennyweights or 480 grains

truant /ˈtruːənt/ *n* one who shirks duty; *esp* one who stays away from school without permission – **-ancy** *n*

truce /truːs/ *n* a (temporary) suspension of fighting by agreement of opposing forces

[1]**truck** /trʌk/ *n* **1** close association; dealings – chiefly in *have no truck with* **2** payment of wages in goods instead of cash

[2]**truck** *n* **1a** a usu 4- or 6-wheeled vehicle for moving heavy loads; a lorry **b** a usu 2- or 4-wheeled cart for carrying heavy articles (e g luggage at railway stations) **2** *Br* an open railway goods wagon – **truck** *v*

truckle bed /ˈtrʌkəl bed/ *n* a low bed, usu on castors, that can be slid under a higher bed

truculent /ˈtrʌkjʊlənt/ *adj* aggressively self-assertive; belligerent – **~ly** *adv* – **-ence, -ency** *n*

[1]**trudge** /trʌdʒ/ *v* to walk steadily and laboriously (along or over)

[2]**trudge** *n* a long tiring walk

[1]**true** /truː/ *adj* **1** steadfast, loyal **2a** in accordance with fact or reality **b** being that which is the case rather than what is claimed or assumed **c** consistent, conforming **3** genuine, real **4a** accurately fitted, adjusted, balanced, or formed **b** exact, accurate

[2]**true** *n* the state of being accurate (e g in alignment or adjustment) – chiefly in *in/out of true*

[3]**true** *adv* **1** truly **2a** without deviation; straight **b** without variation from type

true-blue *adj* staunchly loyal; *specif,*

Br being a staunch supporter of the Conservative party

truffle /ˈtrʌfəl/ *n* **1** (any of several European fungi with) a usu dark and wrinkled edible fruiting body that grows under the ground and is eaten as a delicacy **2** a rich soft creamy sweet made with chocolate

trug /trʌg/ *n, Br* a shallow rectangular wooden basket for carrying garden produce

truism /ˈtruːɪzəm/ *n* an undoubted or self-evident truth

truly /ˈtruːli/ *adv* **1** in accordance with fact or reality; truthfully **2** accurately, exactly **3a** indeed **b** genuinely, sincerely **4** properly, duly

[1]**trump** /trʌmp/ *n* a trumpet (call) – chiefly poetic

[2]**trump** *n* **1a** a card of a suit any of whose cards will win over a card that is not of this suit **b** *pl* the suit whose cards are trumps for a particular hand **2** a worthy and dependable person – infml

[3]**trump** *v* to play a trump on (a card or trick) when another suit was led

trumpery /ˈtrʌmpəri/ *adj* **1** worthless, useless **2** cheap, tawdry

[1]**trumpet** /ˈtrʌmpɨt/ *n* **1** a wind instrument consisting of a usu metal tube, a cup-shaped mouthpiece, and a flared bell; *specif* a valved brass instrument having a cylindrical tube and a usual range from F sharp below middle C upwards for 2½ octaves **2** sthg that resembles (the flared bell or loud penetrating sound of) a trumpet; *esp* the loud cry of an elephant

[2]**trumpet** *v* to sound or proclaim loudly (as if) on a trumpet – **~er** *n*

trump up *v* to concoct, fabricate

[1]**truncate** /trʌŋˈkeɪt/ *v* to shorten (as if) by cutting off a part

[2]**truncate** /ˈtrʌŋkeɪt/ *adj* having the end square or even

truncheon /ˈtrʌntʃən/ *n* **1** a staff of office or authority **2** a short club carried esp by policemen

trundle /ˈtrʌndl/ *v* to move heavily or pull along (as if) on wheels

trunk /trʌŋk/ *n* **1a** the main stem of a tree as distinguished from branches and roots **b** the human or animal body apart from the head and limbs **2** a large rigid box used usu for transporting clothing and personal articles **3** the long muscular proboscis of the elephant **4** *pl* men's usu close-fitting shorts worn chiefly for swimming or sports

trunk call *n* a long distance telephone call

trunk road *n* a road of primary importance, esp for long distance travel

[1]**truss** /trʌs/ *v* **1** to secure tightly; bind – often + *up* **2** to bind the wings or legs of (a fowl) closely in preparation for cooking to support or stiffen (e g a bridge) with a truss

[2]**truss** *n* **1** a usu triangular assemblage of members (e g beams) forming a rigid framework (e g in a roof or bridge) **2** a device worn to reduce a hernia by pressure **3** a compact flower or fruit cluster (e g of tomatoes)

[1]**trust** /trʌst/ *n* **1** confident belief in or reliance on (the ability, character, honesty, etc of) sby or sthg **2a** a property interest held by one person for the benefit of another **b** a combination of companies formed by a legal agreement **3a** responsible charge or office **b** care, custody

[2]**trust** *v* **1** to place confidence in; rely on **2** to expect or hope, esp confidently

trustee /trʌsˈtiː/ *n* **1** a country charged with the supervision of a trust territory **2a** a natural or legal person appointed to administer property in trust for a beneficiary **b** any of a body of people administering the affairs of a company or institution and occupying a position of trust

trustworthy /ˈtrʌstˌwɜːði/ *adj* dependable, reliable – **-thiness** *n*

[1]**trusty** /ˈtrʌsti/ *adj* trustworthy

[2]**trusty** *n* a trusted person; *specif* a convict considered trustworthy and allowed special privileges

truth /truːθ/ *n* **1** sincerity, honesty **2a(1)** the state or quality of being true or factual **(2)** reality, actuality **b** a judgment, proposition, idea, or body of statements that is (accepted as) true **3** conformity to an original or to a standard

[1]**try** /traɪ/ *v* **1a** to investigate judicially **b** to conduct the trial of **2a** to test by experiment or trial – often + *out* **b** to

subject to sthg that tests the patience or endurance **3** to make an attempt at

²try *n* **1** an experimental trial; an attempt **2** a score in rugby that is made by touching down the ball behind the opponent's goal line

try on *v* **1** to put on (a garment) in order to examine the fit or appearance **2** *Br* to attempt to impose on sby – infml

tsar, czar /zɑːʳ, tsɑːʳ/ *fem* **tsarina** *n* a male ruler of Russia

tsetse fly /ˈtetsi flaɪ/ *n* an African fly responsible for the transmission of various diseases including sleeping sickness

T-shirt *n* a vest-like garment worn casually as a shirt

T square *n* a ruler with a crosspiece or head at 1 end used in making parallel lines

tub /tʌb/ *n* **1a** any of various wide low often round vessels typically made of wood, metal, or plastic, and used industrially or domestically (e g for washing clothes or holding soil for shrubs) **b** a small round (plastic) container in which cream, ice cream, etc may be bought **2** a bath **3** an old or slow boat – infml

tuba /ˈtjuːbə/ *n* a large brass instrument having valves, a conical tube, a cup-shaped mouthpiece, and a usual range an octave lower than that of the euphonium

tubby /ˈtʌbi/ *adj* podgy, fat

tube /tjuːb/ *n* **1** a hollow elongated cylinder; *esp* one to convey fluids **2** any of various usu cylindrical structures or devices: e g **a** a small cylindrical container of soft metal or plastic sealed at one end, and fitted with a cap at the other, from which a paste is dispensed by squeezing **b** the basically cylindrical section between the mouthpiece and bell of a wind instrument **3** *Br* (a train running in) an underground railway running through deep bored tunnels – **-bular** *adj*

tubeless /ˈtjuːbl̩ʒs/ *adj* being a pneumatic tyre that does not depend on an inner tube to be airtight

tuber /ˈtjuːbəʳ/ *n* (a root resembling) a short fleshy usu underground stem (e g a potato) that is potentially able to produce a new plant

tuberculosis /tjuːˌbɜːkjʊˈləʊsl̩ʒs/ *n* a serious infectious disease of human beings and other vertebrates caused by the tubercle bacillus and characterized by fever and the formation of abnormal lumps in the body – **-lar** *adj*

tubing /ˈtjuːbɪŋ/ *n* **1** (a length of) material in the form of a tube **2** a series or system of tubes

tub-thumper *n* an impassioned or ranting public speaker

¹tuck /tʌk/ *v* **1** to draw into a fold or folded position **2** to place in a snug often concealed or isolated spot **3a** to push in the loose end or ends of so as to make secure or tidy **b** to cover snugly by tucking in bedclothes **4a** to eat – usu + *away* **b** to eat heartily – usu + *in* or *into*

²tuck *n* **1** a (narrow) fold stitched into cloth to shorten, decorate, or reduce fullness **2** (an act of) tucking **3** *Br* food, esp chocolate, pastries, etc, as eaten by schoolchildren – infml

tuck-in *n, chiefly Br* a hearty meal – infml

Tuesday /ˈtjuːzdi, -deɪ/ *n* the day of the week following Monday

¹tuft /tʌft/ *n* **1** a small cluster of long flexible hairs, feathers, grasses, etc attached or close together at the base **2** a clump, cluster

²tuft *v* **1** to adorn with a tuft or tufts **2** to make (e g a mattress) firm by stitching at intervals and sewing on tufts

¹tug /tʌg/ *v* to pull hard (at)

²tug *n* **1a** a hard pull or jerk **b** a strong pulling force **2** a struggle between 2 people or opposite forces **3a tug, tugboat** a strongly built powerful boat used for towing or pushing large ships (e g in and out of dock) **b** an aircraft that tows a glider

tug-of-war *n* **1** a struggle for supremacy **2** a contest in which teams pulling at opposite ends of a rope attempt to pull each other across a line marked between them

tuition /tjuːˈɪʃən/ *n* teaching, instruction

tulip /ˈtjuːl̩ʒp/ *n* (the flower of) any of a genus of Eurasian bulbous plants widely grown for their showy flowers

tulle /tjuːl/ *n* a sheer, often silk, net used chiefly for veils and dresses

[1]**tumble** /'tʌmbəl/ *v* **1** to turn end over end in falling or flight **2a** to fall suddenly and helplessly **b** to suffer a sudden overthrow or defeat **c** to decline suddenly and sharply **3** to roll over and over, to and fro, or around **4** to realize suddenly – often + *to*; infml

[2]**tumble** *n* **1** a confused heap **2** an act of tumbling; *specif* a fall

tumbledown /'tʌmbəldaʊn/ *adj* dilapidated, ramshackle

tumbler /'tʌmbləʳ/ *n* **1a** an acrobat **b** any of various domestic pigeons that tumble or somersault backwards in flight or on the ground **2** a relatively large drinking glass without a foot, stem, or handle

tumbleweed /'tʌmbəlwiːd/ *n* a plant that breaks away from its roots in the autumn and is blown about by the wind

tumescent /tjuː'mesənt/ *adj* somewhat swollen; *esp, of the penis or clitoris* engorged with blood in response to sexual stimulation – **-cence** *n*

tummy /'tʌmi/ *n* the stomach – infml

tumour /'tjuːməʳ/ *n* an abnormal mass of tissue that arises without obvious cause from cells of existing tissue and possesses no physiological function

tumult /'tjuːmʌlt/ *n* **1a** commotion, uproar (e g of a crowd) **b** a turbulent uprising; a riot **2** violent mental or emotional agitation

tumultuous /tjuː'mʌltʃʊəs/ *adj* **1** marked by commotion; riotous **2** marked by violent turbulence or upheaval – **~ly** *adv*

tumulus /'tjuːmjʊləs/ *n, pl* **tumuli** an ancient grave; a barrow

tun /tʌn/ *n* a large cask, esp for wine

tuna /'tjuːnə/ *n* **1** any of numerous large vigorous food and sport fishes related to the mackerels **2** the flesh of a tuna, often canned for use as food

tundra /'tʌndrə/ *n* a level or undulating treeless plain with a permanently frozen subsoil that is characteristic of arctic and subarctic regions

[1]**tune** /tjuːn/ *n* **1a** a pleasing succession of musical notes; a melody **b** *the* dominant tune in a musical composition **2** correct musical pitch (with another instrument, voice, etc) **3a** accord, harmony **b** general attitude; approach

[2]**tune** *v* **1** to bring a musical instrument or instruments into tune, esp with a standard pitch – usu + *up* **2** to adjust for optimum performance – often + *up* **3** to adjust a receiver for the reception of a particular broadcast or station – + *in* or *to*

tungsten /'tʌŋstən/ *n* a hard metallic element with a high melting point that is used esp for electrical purposes and in hard alloys (e g steel)

tunic /'tjuːnɪk/ *n* **1** a simple (hip- or knee-length) slip-on garment usu belted or gathered at the waist **2** a close-fitting jacket with a high collar worn esp as part of a uniform

tuning fork *n* a 2-pronged metal implement that gives a fixed tone when struck and is useful for tuning musical instruments and setting pitches for singing

[1]**tunnel** /'tʌnl/ *n* **1** a hollow conduit or recess (e g for a propeller shaft) **2a** a man-made horizontal passageway through or under an obstruction **b** a subterranean passage (e g in a mine)

[2]**tunnel** *v* **1** to make a passage through or under **2** to make (e g one's way) by excavating a tunnel – **~ler** *n*

tunny /'tʌni/ *n* tuna

tuppence /'tʌpəns/ *n* (a) twopence

turban /'tɜːbən/ *n* (a headdress, esp for a lady, resembling) a headdress worn esp by Muslims and Sikhs and made of a long cloth wound round a cap or directly round the head – **~ed** *adj*

turbid /'tɜːbɨ̥d/ *adj* **1a** opaque (as if) with disturbed sediment; cloudy **b** thick with smoke or mist **2** (mentally or emotionally) confused – **~ness, ~ity** *n*

turbine /'tɜːbaɪn/ *n* a rotary engine whose central driving shaft is fitted with vanes whirled round by the pressure of water, steam, exhaust gases, etc

turboprop /ˈtɜːbəʊprɒp/ *n* (an aircraft powered by) an engine that has a turbine-driven propeller for providing the main thrust

turbot /ˈtɜːbɒt, -bət/ *n* a large European flatfish highly valued as food

turbulence /ˈtɜːbjʊləns/ *n* **1** wild commotion or agitation **2** irregular atmospheric motion, esp when characterized by strong currents of rising and falling air

turbulent /ˈtɜːbjʊlənt/ *adj* **1** causing unrest, violence, or disturbance **2** agitated, stormy, or tempestuous **3** exhibiting physical turbulence

turd /tɜːd/ *n* **1** a piece of excrement **2** a despicable person *USE* vulg

tureen /tjʊˈriːn/ *n* a deep (covered) dish from which a food, esp soup, is served at table

[1]**turf** /tɜːf/ *n, pl* **turfs, turves** **1** the upper layer of soil bound by grass and plant roots into a thick mat **2** (a piece of dried) peat **3** *the* sport or business of horse racing or the course on which horse races are run

[2]**turf** *v* to cover with turf

turf accountant *n, Br* a bookmaker

turf out *v* to dismiss or throw out forcibly – infml

turgid /ˈtɜːdʒɨd/ *adj* **1** distended, swollen **2** in a pompous inflated style; laboured – **~ity** *n* – **~ly** *adv*

turkey /ˈtɜːki/ *n* (the flesh of) a large orig American bird that is farmed for its meat in most parts of the world

[1]**Turkish** /ˈtɜːkɪʃ/ *adj* (characteristic) of Turkey or the Turks

[2]**Turkish** *n* the Turkic language of the Republic of Turkey

Turkish bath *n* a steam bath followed by a rubdown, massage, and cold shower

Turkish delight *n* a jellylike confection, usu cut in cubes and dusted with sugar

turmeric /ˈtɜːmərɪk/ *n* **1** an E Indian plant of the ginger family **2** the cleaned, boiled, dried, and usu powdered underground stem of the turmeric plant used as a colouring agent or condiment

turmoil /ˈtɜːmɔɪl/ *n* an extremely confused or agitated state

[1]**turn** /tɜːn/ *v* **1a(1)** to (make) rotate or revolve **(2)** to alter the functioning of (as if) by turning a knob **b** to perform by rotating or revolving **c(1)** to become giddy or dizzy **(2)** *of the stomach* to feel nauseated **d** to centre or hinge on sthg **2a(1)** to dig or plough so as to bring the lower soil to the surface **(2)** to renew (e g a garment) by reversing the material and resewing **b** to cause to change or reverse direction **c** to direct one's course **3a** to change position so as to face another way **b** to change one's attitude to one of hostility **c** to make a sudden violent physical or verbal assault – usu + *on* or *upon* **4a** to direct, present, or point (e g the face) in a specified direction **b** to aim, train **c** to direct, induce, or influence in a specified direction, esp towards or away from sby or sthg **d** to apply, devote; *also* resort, have recourse to **e** to direct into or out of a receptacle (as if) by inverting **5a** to become changed, altered, or transformed: e g **(1)** to change colour **(2)** to become acid or sour **b** to become by change **6a** to give a rounded form to **b** to fashion elegantly or neatly **7** to fold, bend **8** to gain in the course of business – esp in *turn an honest penny*

[2]**turn** *n* **1a** a turning about a centre or axis; (a) rotation **b** any of various rotating or pivoting movements (in dancing) **2a** a change or reversal of direction, stance, position, or course **b** a deflection, deviation **3** a short trip out and back or round about **4** an act or deed of a specified kind **5a** a place, time, or opportunity granted in succession or rotation **b** a period of duty, action, or activity **6a** an alteration, change **b** a point of change in time **7** a style of expression **8** a single coil (e g of rope wound round an object) **9** a bent, inclination **10a** a spell or attack of illness, faintness, etc **b** a nervous start or shock

turnabout /ˈtɜːnəbaʊt/ *n* a change or reversal of direction, trend, etc

turncoat /ˈtɜːnkəʊt/ *n* one who switches to an opposing side or party; a traitor

turndown /ˈtɜːndaʊn/ *adj* worn turned down

turn down *v* **1** to reduce the intensity, volume, etc of (as if) by turning a control **2** to decline to accept; reject

turner /ˈtɜːnəʳ/ *n* one who forms articles on a lathe

turn in *v* **1** to deliver, hand over; *esp* to deliver up to an authority **2** to give, execute **3** to go to bed – infml

turning /ˈtɜːnɪŋ/ *n* **1** a place of turning, turning off, or turning back, esp on a road **2a** a forming or being formed by use of a lathe **b** *pl* waste produced in turning sthg on a lathe **3** the width of cloth that is folded under for a seam or hem

turning point *n* a point at which a significant change occurs

turnip /ˈtɜːnɪ̣p/ *n* (a plant of the mustard family with) a thick white-fleshed root eaten as a vegetable or fed to stock

turnkey /ˈtɜːnkiː/ *n* a prison warden

turnoff /ˈtɜːnɒf/ *n* a turning off

turn off *v* **1** to stop the flow or operation of (as if) by turning a control **2** to deviate from a straight course or from a main road **3** to cause to lose (sexual) interest – infml

turn on *v* **1** to cause to flow or operate (as if) by turning a control **2** to excite or interest pleasurably and esp sexually – infml

turnout /ˈtɜːnaʊt/ *n* **1** people in attendance (e g at a meeting) **2** manner of dress; getup

turn out *v* **1** to empty the contents of, esp for cleaning **2** to produce often rapidly or regularly (as if) by machine **3** to equip or dress in a specified way **4** to put out (esp a light) by turning a switch **5** to leave one's home for a meeting, public event, etc **6** to get out of bed – infml

turnover /ˈtɜːn,əʊvəʳ/ *n* **1** a small semicircular filled pastry made by folding half of the crust over the other half **2a** the total sales revenue of a business **b** the ratio of sales to average stock for a stated period **3** (the rate of) movement (e g of goods or people) into, through, and out of a place

turn over *v* **1** to think over; meditate on **2** *of an internal combustion engine* to revolve at low speed **3** *of merchandise* to be stocked and disposed of

turnstile /ˈtɜːnstaɪl/ *n* a gate with arms pivoted on the top that turns to admit 1 person at a time

turntable /ˈtɜːn,teɪbəl/ *n* **1** a circular platform for turning wheeled vehicles, esp railway engines **2** the platform on which a gramophone record is rotated while being played

turn to *v* to apply oneself to work

turn-up *n* **1** *chiefly Br* a turned-up hem, esp on a pair of trousers **2** an unexpected or surprising event – esp in *turn-up for the book*; infml

turn up *v* **1** to increase the intensity, volume, etc of (as if) by turning a control **2** to find, discover **3** to come to light unexpectedly; *also* to happen unexpectedly **4** to appear, arrive

turpentine /ˈtɜːpəntaɪn/ *n* **1** a resinous substance obtained from various trees **2** an essential oil obtained from turpentines by distillation and used esp as a solvent and paint thinner

turquoise /ˈtɜːkwɔɪz, -kwɑːz/ *n* **1** a sky blue to greenish mineral consisting of a hydrated copper aluminium phosphate and used as a gem **2** a light greenish blue colour

turret /ˈtʌrɪ̣t/ *n* **1** a little tower, often at the corner of a larger building **2** a rotatable holder (e g for a tool or die) in a lathe, milling machine, etc **3** a usu revolving armoured structure on warships, forts, tanks, aircraft, etc in which guns are mounted

turtle /ˈtɜːtl/ *n* any of several marine reptiles of the same order as and similar to tortoises but adapted for swimming

turtledove /ˈtɜːtldʌv/ *n* any of several small wild pigeons noted for plaintive cooing

turtleneck /ˈtɜːtlnek/ *n* a high close-fitting neckline, esp of a sweater

tusk /tʌsk/ *n* a long greatly enlarged tooth of an elephant, boar, walrus, etc, that projects when the mouth is closed and serves for digging food or as a weapon

tussle /ˈtʌsəl/ *n* a (physical) contest or struggle – **tussle** *v*

tussock /ˈtʌsək/ *n* a compact tuft of grass, sedge, etc

tut /tʌt/, **tut-tut** *interj* – used to express disapproval or impatience – **tut** *v*

tutelage /'tjuːtǀlɪdʒ/ *n* **1** guardianship **2** the state or period of being under a guardian or tutor

[1]**tutor** /'tjuːtəʳ/ *n* **1** a private teacher **2** a British university teacher who **a** gives instruction to students, esp individually **b** is in charge of the social and moral welfare of a group of students **3** *Br* an instruction book

[2]**tutor** *v* to teach or guide usu individually; coach

[1]**tutorial** /tjuː'tɔːrɪəl/ *adj* of or involving (individual tuition by) a tutor

[2]**tutorial** *n* a class conducted by a tutor for 1 student or a small number of students

tutti-frutti /ˌtuːti 'fruːti/ *n* (a confection, esp an ice cream, containing) a mixture of chopped, dried, or candied fruits

tutu /'tuːtuː/ *n* a very short projecting stiff skirt worn by a ballerina

tuxedo /tʌk'siːdəʊ/ *n, NAm* a dinner jacket

TV *n* television

twaddle /'twɒdl/ *n* rubbish or drivel – **twaddle** *v*

twain /tweɪn/ *n, adj, or pron, archaic* two

[1]**twang** /twæŋ/ *n* a harsh quick ringing sound like that of a plucked bowstring

[2]**twang** *v* to pluck the string of

tweak /twiːk/ *v* to pinch and pull with a sudden jerk and twist – **tweak** *n*

twee /twiː/ *adj* excessively sentimental, pretty, or coy

tweed /twiːd/ *n* **1** a rough woollen fabric made usu in twill weaves and used esp for suits and coats **2** *pl* tweed clothing; *specif* a tweed suit

tweet /twiːt/ *v or n* (to) chirp

tweeter /'twiːtəʳ/ *n* a small loudspeaker that responds mainly to the higher frequencies

tweezers /'twiːzəz/ *n pl* a small metal instrument that is usu held between thumb and forefinger, is used for plucking, holding, or manipulating, and consists of 2 prongs joined at 1 end

twelfth /twelfθ, twelθ/ *n* **1** number twelve in a countable series **2** *often cap, Br the* twelfth of August on which the grouse-shooting season begins – **twelfth** *adj* – **~ly** *adv*

twelve /twelv/ *n* **1** the number 12 **2** the twelfth in a set or series **3** sthg having 12 parts or members or a denomination of 12

twenty /'twenti/ *n* **1** the number 20 **2** *pl the* numbers 20 to 29; *specif* a range of temperatures, ages, or dates in a century characterized by those numbers **3** sthg (e g a bank note) having a denomination of 20 – **-tieth** *n, adj, adv*

twenty-one *n* **1** the number 21 **2** pontoon

twerp, twirp /'twɜːp/ *n* a silly fool

twice /twaɪs/ *adv* **1** on 2 occasions **2** two times;in doubled quantity or degree

[1]**twiddle** /'twɪdl/ *v* to play negligently with sthg

[2]**twiddle** *n* a turn, twist

[1]**twig** /twɪg/ *n* a small woody shoot or branch, usu without its leaves – **twiggy** *adj*

[2]**twig** *v* to catch on; understand – infml

twilight /'twaɪlaɪt/ *n* **1a** the light from the sky between full night and sunrise or esp between sunset and full night **b** the period between sunset and full night **2a** a shadowy indeterminate state **b** a period or state of decline

twill /twɪl/ *n* (a fabric with) a textile weave in which the weft threads pass over 1 and under 2 or more warp threads to give an appearance of diagonal lines – **~ed** *adj*

[1]**twin** /twɪn/ *adj* **1** born with one other or as a pair at 1 birth **2** having or made up of 2 similar, related, or identical units or parts

[2]**twin** *n* **1** either of 2 offspring produced at 1 birth **2** either of 2 people or things closely related to or resembling each other

[3]**twin** *v* **1** to become paired or closely associated **2** to give birth to twins

twin bed *n* either of 2 matching single beds

[1]**twine** /twaɪn/ *n* a strong string of 2 or more strands twisted together

[2]**twine** *v* **1** to twist together **2** to twist or coil round sthg

twinge /twɪndʒ/ *v or n* (to feel) **1** a

sudden sharp stab of pain **2** an emotional pang

[1]twinkle /ˈtwɪŋkəl/ *v* **1** to shine with a flickering or sparkling light **2** to appear bright with gaiety or amusement

[2]twinkle *n* **1** an instant, twinkling **2** an (intermittent) sparkle or gleam

twinkling /ˈtwɪŋklɪŋ/ *n* a very short time; a moment

twin set *n* a jumper and cardigan designed to be worn together, usu by a woman

[1]twirl /twɜːl/ *v* to revolve rapidly – **~er** *n*

[2]twirl *n* **1** an act of twirling **2** a coil, whorl – **~y** *adj*

twirp /twɜːp/ *n* a twerp

[1]twist /twɪst/ *v* **1** to join together by winding; *also* to mingle by interlacing **2** to wind or coil round sthg **3a** to wring or wrench so as to dislocate or distort **b** to distort the meaning of; pervert **c** to pull off, turn, or break by a turning force **d** to warp **4** to follow a winding course; snake

[2]twist *n* **1** sthg formed by twisting: e g **a** a thread, yarn, or cord formed by twisting 2 or more strands together **b** a screw of paper used as a container **2a** a twisting or being twisted **b** a dance popular esp in the 1960s and performed with gyrations, esp of the hips **c** a spiral turn or curve **3a** a turning off a straight course; a bend **b** a distortion of meaning or sense **4** an unexpected turn or development – **twisty** *adj*

twister /ˈtwɪstəʳ/ *n* a dishonest person; a swindler – infml

[1]twit /twɪt/ *v* to tease, taunt

[2]twit *n, Br* an absurd or silly person

[1]twitch /twɪtʃ/ *v* **1** to pull, pluck **2** to move jerkily or involuntarily – **~er** *n*

[2]twitch *n* **1** a short sudden pull or jerk **2** a physical or mental pang **3** (the recurrence of) a short spasmodic contraction or jerk; a tic

[1]twitter /ˈtwɪtəʳ/ *v* **1** to utter twitters **2** to talk in a nervous chattering fashion **3** to tremble with agitation; flutter – **~er** *n*

[2]twitter *n* **1** a nervous agitation – esp in *all of a twitter* **2** a small tremulous intermittent sound characteristic of birds – **~y** *adj*

[1]two /tuː/ *pron, pl in constr* **1** two unspecified countable individuals **2** a small approximate number of indicated things

[2]two *n, pl* **twos** **1** the number 2 **2** the second in a set or series **3** sthg having 2 parts or members or a denomination of 2

two-edged *adj* double-edged

two-faced *adj* double-dealing, hypocritical

two-handed *adj* **1** used with both hands **2** requiring 2 people **3** ambidextrous

two-piece *n or adj* (a suit of clothes, swimming costume, etc) consisting of 2 matching pieces

twosome /ˈtuːsəm/ *n* a group of 2 people or things

two-step *n* (a piece of music for) a ballroom dance in either $\frac{2}{4}$ or $\frac{4}{4}$ time

two-time *v* to be unfaithful to (a spouse or lover) by having a secret relationship with another – **two-timer** *n*

two-tone *adj also* **two-toned** having 2 colours or shades

two-way *adj* **1** moving or allowing movement or use in 2 (opposite) directions **2** involving mutual responsibility or a reciprocal relationship **3** involving 2 participants

tycoon /taɪˈkuːn/ *n* a businessman of exceptional wealth and power

tying /taɪ-ɪŋ/ *pres part of* **tie**

tyke, tike /taɪk/ *n* **1** a (mongrel) dog **2** *Br* a boorish churlish person **3** a small child

tympanum /ˈtɪmpənəm/ *n, pl* **tympana, tympanums** **1a** the eardrum **b** a thin tense membrane covering the hearing-organ of an insect **2** the space within an arch and above a lintel (e g in a medieval doorway)

[1]type /taɪp/ *n* **1a** a model, exemplar, or characteristic specimen (possessing the distinguishable or essential qualities of a class) **b** a lower taxonomic category selected as reference for a higher category **2a** (any of) a collection of usu rectangular blocks or characters bearing a relief from which an inked print can be made **b** printed letters **3a** a person of a specified nature **b** a particular kind, class, or group with distinct characteristics **c** sthg distinguishable as a variety; a sort

²type *v* to write with a typewriter; *also* to keyboard

typecast /'taɪpkɑːst/ *v* to cast an actor repeatedly in the same type of role; *broadly* to stereotype

typeface /'taɪpfeɪs/ *n* (the appearance of) a single design of printing type

typescript /'taɪpˌskrɪpt/ *n* a typewritten manuscript (e g for use as printer's copy)

typewriter /'taɪpˌraɪtəʳ/ *n* a machine with a keyboard for writing in characters resembling type

typhoid, typhoid fever /'taɪfɔɪd/ *n* a serious communicable human disease caused by a bacterium and marked esp by fever, diarrhoea, headache, and intestinal inflammation

typhoon /taɪ'fuːn/ *n* a tropical cyclone occurring in the Philippines or the China sea

typhus /'taɪfəs/ *n* a serious human disease marked by high fever, stupor alternating with delirium, intense headache, and a dark red rash and transmitted esp by body lice

typical /'tɪpɪkəl/ *adj* **1** being or having the nature of a type; symbolic, representative **2a** having or showing the essential characteristics of a type **b** showing or according with the usual or expected (unfavourable) traits – **~ly** *adv*

typify /'tɪpɨ̣faɪ/ *v* **1** to constitute a typical instance of **2** to embody the essential characteristics of

typist /'taɪpɨ̣st/ *n* one who uses a typewriter, esp as an occupation

typography /taɪ'pɒgrəfi/ *n* the style, arrangement, or appearance of typeset matter – **-pher** *n* – **-phic** *adj* – **-phically** *adv*

tyranny /'tɪrəni/ *n* **1** a government in which absolute power is vested in a single ruler **2** oppressive power (exerted by a tyrant) **3** sthg severe, oppressive, or inexorable in effect – **-nical** *adj* – **-nically** *adv* – **-nize** *v*

tyrant /'taɪərənt/ *n* **1** a ruler who exercises absolute power, esp oppressively or brutally **2** one who exercises authority harshly or unjustly

tyre /taɪəʳ/ *n* a continuous solid or inflated hollow rubber cushion set round a wheel to absorb shock

U

u /juː/ *n, pl* **u's, us** *often cap* (a graphic representation of or device for reproducing) the 21st letter of the English alphabet

[1]**U** *adj, chiefly Br* upper-class

[2]**U** *n or adj* (a film that is) certified in Britain as suitable for all age groups

ubiquitous /juːˈbɪkwɨtəs/ *adj* existing or being everywhere at the same time; omnipresent

U-boat *n* a German submarine

udder /ˈʌdəʳ/ *n* a large pendulous organ consisting of 2 or more mammary glands enclosed in a common envelope and each having a single nipple

UFO /ˈjuːfəʊ, juː ef ˈəʊ/ *n, pl* **UFO's, UFOs** an unidentified flying object; *esp* a flying saucer

ugh /ʌg/ *interj* – used to express disgust or horror

ugly /ˈʌgli/ *adj* **1** frightful, horrible **2** offensive or displeasing to any of the senses, esp to the sight **3** morally offensive or objectionable **4a** ominous, threatening **b** surly, quarrelsome – **-liness** *n*

ugly duckling *n* sby who or sthg that appears unpromising but turns out successful

ukulele /juːkəˈleɪli/ *n* a small usu 4-stringed guitar

ulcer /ˈʌlsəʳ/ *n* **1** a persistent open sore in skin that often discharges pus **2** sthg that festers and corrupts – **~ous** *adj*

ulcerate /ˈʌlsəreɪt/ *v* to (cause to) become affected (as if) with an ulcer – **-ation** *n*

ulna /ˈʌlnə/ *n* the bone of the human forearm on the little-finger side

ulterior /ʌlˈtɪərɪəʳ/ *adj* going beyond what is openly said or shown; intentionally concealed

[1]**ultimate** /ˈʌltɨmɨt/ *adj* **1a** last in a progression or series **b** eventual **2a** fundamental, basic **b** incapable of further analysis, division, or separation **3** maximum, greatest

[2]**ultimate** *n* sthg ultimate; *the* highest point

ultimately /ˈʌltɨmɨtli/ *adv* finally; at last

ultimatum /ˌʌltɨˈmeɪtəm/ *n, pl* **ultimatums, ultimata** a final proposition or demand; *esp* one whose rejection will end negotiations and cause a resort to direct action

ultrahigh frequency *n* a radio frequency in the range between 300 megahertz and 3000 megahertz

ultramarine /ˌʌltrəməˈriːn/ *n* a deep blue (pigment)

ultrasonic /ˌʌltrəˈsɒnɪk/ *adj, of waves and vibrations* having a frequency above about 20,000Hz – **ultrasonic** *n*

ultraviolet /ˌʌltrəˈvaɪəlɨt/ *n* electromagnetic radiation having a wavelength between the violet end of the visible spectrum and X rays – **ultraviolet** *adj*

umber /ˈʌmbəʳ/ *n* **1** a brown earth used as a pigment **2** a dark or yellowish brown colour – **umber** *adj*

umbilical cord /ʌmˌbɪlɪkəl ˈkɔːd/ *n* a cord arising from the navel that connects the foetus with the placenta

umbra /ˈʌmbrə/ *n, pl* **umbras, umbrae** **1** a region of total shadow, esp in an eclipse **2** the central dark region of a sunspot

umbrage /ˈʌmbrɪdʒ/ *n* a feeling of pique or resentment

umbrella /ʌmˈbrelə/ *n* **1** a collapsible shade for protection against weather, consisting of fabric stretched over hinged ribs radiating from a central pole **2** the bell-shaped or saucer-shaped largely gelatinous structure that forms the chief part of the body of most jellyfishes

[1]**umpire** /ˈʌmpaɪəʳ/ *n* **1** one having authority to settle a controversy or question between parties **2** a referee in any of several sports (e g cricket, table tennis, badminton, and hockey)

[2]**umpire** *v* to act as or supervise (e g a match) as umpire

umpteen /ˌʌmpˈtiːn/ *adj* very many; indefinitely numerous – infml – **~th** *n, adj*

un /nn/ *pron, dial* one

unable /ʌnˈeɪbəl/ *adj* not able; incapable: **a** unqualified, incompetent **b** impotent, helpless

unaccountable /ˌʌnəˈkaʊntəbəl/ *adj* **1** inexplicable, strange **2** not to be called to account; not responsible – **-bly** *adv*

unaccustomed /ˌʌnəˈkʌstəmd/ *adj* **1** not customary; not usual or common **2** not used *to*

unadulterated /ˌʌnəˈdʌltəreɪtɪ̣d/ *adj* unmixed, esp with anything inferior; pure

unaffected /ˌʌnəˈfektɪ̣d/ *adj* **1** not influenced or changed mentally, physically, or chemically **2** free from affectation; genuine – **~ly** *adv*

unanimous /juːˈnænɪ̣məs/ *adj* **1** being of one mind; agreeing **2** characterized by the agreement and consent of all – **~ly** *adv* – **-mity** *n*

unarmed /ˌʌnˈɑːmd/ *adj* not armed or armoured

unassuming /ˌʌnəˈsjuːmɪŋ, -ˈsuː-/ *adj* not arrogant or presuming; modest – **~ly** *adv*

unawares /ˌʌnəˈweəz/ *adv* **1** without noticing or intending **2** suddenly, unexpectedly

unbalance /ˌʌnˈbæləns/ *v* to put out of balance; *esp* to derange mentally

unbearable /ʌnˈbeərəbəl/ *adj* not endurable; intolerable – **-ly** *adv*

unbeknown /ˌʌnbɪˈnəʊn/ *adj* happening without one's knowledge – usu + *to*

unbelievable /ˌʌnbɪ̣ˈliːvəbəl/ *adj* too improbable for belief; incredible – **-bly** *adv*

unbeliever /ˌʌnbɪ̣ˈliːvəʳ/ *n* one who does not believe, esp in a particular religion

unbend /ʌnˈbend/ *v* **unbent** **1** to become more relaxed, informal, or outgoing in manner **2** to become straight

unbending /ʌnˈbendɪŋ/ *adj* **1** unyielding, inflexible **2** aloof or unsociable in manner

unblushing /ˌʌnˈblʌʃɪŋ/ *adj* shameless, unabashed – **~ly** *adv*

unborn /ˌʌnˈbɔːn/ *adj* still to appear; future

unbosom /ˌʌnˈbʊzəm/ *v* to disclose the thoughts or feelings of (oneself)

unbounded /ʌnˈbaʊndɪ̣d/ *adj* having no limits or constraints

unbowed /ˌʌnˈbaʊd/ *adj* not bowed down; *esp* not subdued

unbridled /ʌnˈbraɪdld/ *adj* unrestrained, ungoverned

unbuckle /ˌʌnˈbʌkəl/ *v* to unfasten

unburden /ˌʌnˈbɜːdn/ *v* to free or relieve from anxiety, cares, etc

uncalled-for /ʌnˈkɔːld fɔːʳ/ *adj* **1** unnecessary **2** offered without provocation or justification; gratuitous

uncanny /ʌnˈkæni/ *adj* **1** eerie, mysterious **2** beyond what is normal or expected – **-nily** *adv*

unceremonious /ˌʌnserɪ̣ˈməʊnɪəs/ *adj* abrupt, rude – **~ly** *adv* – **~ness** *n*

uncertain /ʌnˈsɜːtn/ *adj* **1** not reliable or trustworthy **2a** not definitely known; undecided, unpredictable **b** not confident or sure; doubtful **3** variable, changeable – **~ly** *adv* – **~ness** *n* – **~ty** *n*

uncharitable /ʌnˈtʃærɪ̣təbəl/ *adj* severe in judging others; harsh – **-bly** *adv*

unchristian /ʌnˈkrɪstɪən/ *adj* barbarous, uncivilized

uncle /ˈʌŋkəl/ *n* **1a** the brother of one's father or mother **b** the husband of one's aunt **2** a man who is a very close friend of a young child or its parents

unclean /ˌʌnˈkliːn/ *adj* **1** morally or spiritually impure **2** ritually prohibited as food – **~ness** *n*

Uncle Sam *n* the American nation, people, or government

uncomfortable /ʌnˈkʌmftəbəl/ *adj* feeling discomfort; ill at ease – **-bly** *adv*

uncommitted /ˌʌnkəˈmɪtɪ̣d/ *adj* not pledged to a particular belief, allegiance, or course of action

uncompromising /ʌnˈkɒmprəmaɪzɪŋ/ *adj* not making or accepting a compromise; unyielding – **~ly** *adv*

unconcerned /ˌʌnkənˈsɜːnd/ *adj* **1**

not involved or interested **2** not anxious or worried – **~ly** *adv*

unconditional /ˌʌnkənˈdɪʃənəl/ *adj* absolute, unqualified – **~ly** *adv*

unconscionable /ʌnˈkɒnʃənəbəl/ *adj* **1** unscrupulous, unprincipled **2** excessive, unreasonable – **-bly** *adv*

[1]**unconscious** /ʌnˈkɒnʃəs/ *adj* **1** not knowing or perceiving **2a** not possessing mind or having lost consciousness **b** not marked by or resulting from conscious thought, sensation, or feeling **3** not intentional or deliberate – **~ly** *adv* – **~ness** *n*

[2]**unconscious** *n* the part of the mind that does not ordinarily enter a person's awareness but nevertheless influences behaviour and may be manifested in dreams or slips of the tongue

unconsidered /ˌʌnkənˈsɪdəd/ *adj* **1** disregarded, unnoticed **2** not carefully thought out

uncork /ʌnˈkɔːk/ *v* to release from a pent-up state; unleash

uncouple /ʌnˈkʌpəl/ *v* to detach, disconnect

uncouth /ʌnˈkuːθ/ *adj* awkward and uncultivated in speech or manner; boorish – **~ly** *adv* – **~ness** *n*

uncover /ʌnˈkʌvəʳ/ *v* to disclose, reveal

uncritical /ʌnˈkrɪtɪkəl/ *adj* lacking in discrimination or critical analysis

uncrowned /ˌʌnˈkraʊnd/ *adj* having a specified status in fact but not in name

unctuous /ˈʌŋktʃʊəs/ *adj* marked by ingratiating smoothness and false sincerity – **~ly** *adv* – **~ness** *n*

uncut /ˌʌnˈkʌt/ *adj* **1** not cut down or into **2** *of a book* not having the folds of the leaves trimmed off **3** not abridged or curtailed

undaunted /ʌnˈdɔːntʒd/ *adj* not discouraged by danger or difficulty

undecided /ˌʌndɪˈsaɪdʒd/ *adj* **1** in doubt **2** without a result – **~ly** *adv* – **~ness** *n*

undeniable /ˌʌndɪˈnaɪəbəl/ *adj* **1** plainly true; incontestable **2** unquestionably excellent or genuine – **-bly** *adv*

[1]**under** /ˈʌndəʳ/ *adv* **1** in or to a position below or beneath sthg **2a** in or to a lower rank or number (e g £10 or *under*) **b** to a subnormal degree; deficiently – often in combination (e g *under*-financed) **3** in or into a condition of subjection, subordination, or unconsciousness **4** so as to be covered, buried, or sheltered

[2]**under** *prep* **1a** below or beneath so as to be overhung, surmounted, covered, protected, or hidden **b** using as a pseudonym or alias **2a(1)** subject to the authority, control, guidance, or instruction of **(2)** during the rule or control of **b** receiving or undergoing the action or effect of (e g *under* treatment) **3** within the group or designation of (e g *under* this heading) **4** less than or inferior to; *esp* falling short of (a standard or required degree)

[3]**under** *adj* **1a** lying or placed below, beneath, or on the lower side **b** facing or pointing downwards **2** lower in rank or authority; subordinate **3** lower than usual, proper, or desired in amount or degree *USE* often in combination

underact /ˌʌndərˈækt/ *v* **1** to perform (a dramatic part) without adequate force or skill **2** to perform with restraint for greater dramatic impact or personal force

[1]**underarm** /ˈʌndərɑːm/ *adj* **1** under or on the underside of the arm **2** made with the hand brought forwards and up from below shoulder level

[2]**underarm** *v or adv* (to throw) with an underarm motion

undercarriage /ˈʌndəˌkærɪdʒ/ *n* the part of an aircraft's structure that supports its weight, when in contact with the land or water

undercharge /ˌʌndəˈtʃɑːdʒ/ *v* to charge (e g a person) too little

underclothes /ˈʌndəkləʊðz, -kləʊz/ *n pl* underwear

undercoat /ˈʌndəkəʊt/ *n* **1** a growth of short hair or fur partly concealed by a longer growth **2** a coat (e g of paint) applied as a base for another coat

undercover /ˌʌndəˈkʌvəʳ/ *adj* acting or done in secret; *specif* engaged in spying

undercurrent /ˈʌndəˌkʌrənt/ *n* a hidden opinion, feeling, or tendency

undercut /ˌʌndəˈkʌt/ *v* **1** to cut away material from the underside of so as to leave a portion overhanging **2** to offer sthg at lower prices than or work for lower wages than (a competitor)

underdog /ˈʌndədɒg/ *n* a victim of injustice or persecution

underdone /ˌʌndəˈdʌn/ *adj* not thoroughly cooked

underestimate /ˌʌndərˈestɪ̆meɪt/ *v* **1** to estimate as being less than the actual size, quantity, etc **2** to place too low a value on; underrate

underfelt /ˈʌndəfelt/ *n* a thick felt underlay placed under a carpet

underfoot /ˌʌndəˈfʊt/ *adv* under the feet, esp against the ground

undergarment /ˈʌndəgɑːmənt/ *n* a garment to be worn under another

undergo /ˌʌndəˈgəʊ/ *v* to be subjected to; experience

undergraduate /ˌʌndəˈgrædʒʊɪ̆t/ *n* a college or university student who has not taken a first degree

¹underground /ˈʌndəgraʊnd/ *adv* **1** beneath the surface of the earth **2** in or into hiding or secret operation

²underground *adj* **1** growing, operating, or situated below the surface of the ground **2a** conducted in hiding or in secret **b** existing or operated outside the establishment, esp by the avant-garde

³underground *n* **1** *sing or pl in constr* **a** a secret movement or group esp in an occupied country, for concerted resistive action **b** a usu avant-garde group or movement that functions outside the establishment **2** *Br* a usu electric underground urban railway; *also* a train running in an underground

undergrowth /ˈʌndəgrəʊθ/ *n* shrub, bushes, saplings, etc growing under larger trees in a wood or forest

¹underhand /ˌʌndəˈhænd/ *adv* **1** in an underhand manner; secretly **2** underarm

²underhand *adj* not honest and aboveboard; sly

¹underlay /ˌʌndəˈleɪ/ *v* to cover or line the bottom of; give support to on the underside or below

²underlay /ˈʌndəleɪ/ *n* sthg that is (designed to be) laid under sthg else

underlie /ˌʌndəˈlaɪ/ *v* **1** to lie or be situated under **2** to form the basis or foundation of **3** to be concealed beneath the exterior of

underline /ˌʌndəˈlaɪn/ *v* to emphasize, stress

underling /ˈʌndəlɪŋ/ *n* a subordinate or inferior

undermanned /ˌʌndəˈmænd/ *adj* inadequately staffed

undermentioned /ˌʌndəˈmenʃənd/ *adj, Br* referred to at a later point in a text

undermine /ˌʌndəˈmaɪn/ *v* to weaken or destroy gradually or insidiously

¹underneath /ˌʌndəˈniːθ/ *prep* directly below; close under

²underneath *adv* **1** under or below an object or a surface; beneath **2** on the lower side

underpants /ˈʌndəpænts/ *n pl* men's pants

underpass /ˈʌndəpɑːs/ *n* a tunnel or passage taking a road and pavement under another road or a railway

underpin /ˈʌndəˌpɪn/ *v* to form part of, strengthen, or replace the foundation of

underplay /ˌʌndəˈpleɪ/ *v* **1** to underact (a role) **2** to play down the importance of

underprivileged /ˌʌndəˈprɪvɪ̆lɪdʒd/ *adj* deprived of some of the fundamental social or economic rights of a civilized society

underrate /ˌʌndəˈreɪt/ *v* to rate too low; undervalue

underscore /ˌʌndəˈskɔːʳ/ *v* to underline

undersecretary /ˈʌndəˌsekrətəri/ *n* a secretary immediately subordinate to a principal secretary

undersell /ˌʌndəˈsel/ *v* **1** to be sold cheaper than **2** to make little of the merits of; *esp* to promote or publicize in a (deliberately) low-key manner

undersigned /ˈʌndəsaɪnd/ *n the* one who signs his/her name at the end of a document

undersized /ˌʌndəˈsaɪzd/ *adj* of less than average size

understaffed /ˌʌndəˈstɑːft/ *adj* undermanned

understand /ˌʌndəˈstænd/ *v* **1a** to grasp the meaning of; comprehend **b** to have a thorough knowledge of or expertise in **2** to assume, suppose **3** to interpret in one of a number of possible ways **4** to show a sympathetic or tolerant attitude – ~**able** *adj* – ~**ably** *adv*

[1]**understanding** /ˌʌndəˈstændɪŋ/ *n* **1** a mental grasp; comprehension **2** the power of comprehending; intelligence; *esp* the power to make experience intelligible by applying concepts **3a** a friendly or harmonious relationship **b** an informal mutual agreement

[2]**understanding** *adj* tolerant, sympathetic

understate /ˌʌndəˈsteɪt/ *v* **1** to state as being less than is the case **2** to present with restraint, esp for greater effect – ~**ment** *n*

[1]**understudy** /ˌʌndəˈstʌdi/ *v* to study another actor's part in order to take it over in an emergency

[2]**understudy** /ˈʌndəstʌdi/ *n* one who is prepared to act another's part or take over another's duties

undertake /ˌʌndəˈteɪk/ *v* **1** to take upon oneself as a task **2** to put oneself under obligation to do; contract **3** to guarantee, promise

undertaker /ˈʌndəteɪkəʳ/ *n* sby whose business is preparing the dead for burial and arranging and managing funerals

undertaking /ˌʌndəˈteɪkɪŋ/ *n* **1** an enterprise **2** a pledge, guarantee

undertone /ˈʌndətəʊn/ *n* **1** a subdued utterance **2** an underlying quality (e g of emotion)

undertow /ˈʌndətəʊ/ *n* **1** an undercurrent that flows in a different direction from the surface current, esp out to sea **2** a hidden tendency often contrary to the one that is publicly apparent

underwater /ˌʌndəˈwɔːtəʳ/ *adj* **1** situated, used, or designed to operate below the surface of the water **2** being below the waterline of a ship

underwear /ˈʌndəweəʳ/ *n* clothing worn next to the skin and under other clothing

underweight /ˌʌndəˈweɪt/ *adj or n* (of a) weight below average or normal

underworld /ˈʌndəwɜːld/ *n* **1** the place of departed souls; Hades **2** the world of organized crime

underwrite /ˌʌndəˈraɪt/ *v* **1** to set one's signature to (an insurance policy) thereby assuming liability in case of specified loss or damage; *also* to assume (a sum or risk) by way of insurance **2** to subscribe to; agree to **3** to guarantee financial support of

underwriter /ˈʌndəraɪtəʳ/ *n* **1** one who underwrites sthg, esp an insurance policy **2** one who selects risks to be solicited or rates the acceptability of risks solicited

undesirable /ˌʌndɪˈzaɪərəbəl/ *n or adj* (sby or sthg) unwanted or objectionable

undies /ˈʌndɪz/ *n pl* women's underwear – infml

undo /ʌnˈduː/ *v* **1** to open or loosen by releasing a fastening **2** to reverse or cancel out the effects of **3** to destroy the standing, reputation, hopes, etc of

undoing /ʌnˈduːɪŋ/ *n* (a cause of) ruin or downfall

[1]**undone** /ʌnˈdʌn/ *past part of* **undo**

[2]**undone** *adj* not performed or finished

undoubted /ʌnˈdaʊtɪ̣d/ *adj* not disputed; genuine – ~**ly** *adv*

[1]**undress** /ʌnˈdres/ *v* to take off (one's) clothes

[2]**undress** *n* a state of having little or no clothing on

undressed /ʌnˈdrest/ *adj* partially or completely unclothed

undue /ˌʌnˈdjuː/ *adj* **1** not yet due **2** excessive, immoderate

[1]**undulate** /ˈʌndjʊleɪt, -lɪ̣t/ *adj* having a wavy surface, edge, or markings

[2]**undulate** /ˈʌndjʊleɪt/ *v* **1** to rise and fall in waves; fluctuate **2** to have a wavy form or appearance

undulation /ˌʌndjʊˈleɪʃən/ *n* **1** a wavelike motion; *also* a single wave or gentle rise **2** a wavy appearance, outline, or form

unduly /ʌnˈdjuːli/ *adv* excessively

undying /ʌnˈdaɪ-ɪŋ/ *adj* eternal, perpetual

unearth /ʌnˈɜːθ/ *v* **1** to dig up out of the ground **2** to make known or public

unearthly /ʌnˈɜːθli/ *adj* **1** exceeding what is normal or natural; supernatural **2** weird, eerie **3** unreasonable, preposterous – **-liness** *n*

uneasy /ʌnˈiːzi/ *adj* **1** uncomfortable, awkward **2** apprehensive, worried **3** precarious, unstable – **-sily** *adv* – **-siness** *n*

uneconomic /ˌʌniːkəˈnɒmɪk, ˌʌnekə-/ *adj* not economically practicable – **~ally** *adv*

unemployed /ˌʌnɪmˈplɔɪd/ *adj* **1** not engaged in a job **2** not invested

unemployment /ˌʌnɪmˈplɔɪmənt/ *n* the state of being unemployed; lack of available employment

unequal /ʌnˈiːkwəl/ *adj* **1a** not of the same measurement, quantity, or number as another **b** not like in quality, nature, or status **c** not the same for every member of a group, class, or society **2** badly balanced or matched **3** incapable of meeting the requirements of sthg – + *to* – **~ly** *adv* – **~ness** *n*

unequalled /ʌnˈiːkwəld/ *adj* not equalled; unparalleled

unequivocal /ˌʌnɪˈkwɪvəkəl/ *adj* clear, unambiguous – **~ly** *adv*

unerring /ʌnˈɜːrɪŋ/ *adj* faultless, unfailing – **~ly** *adv*

uneven /ʌnˈiːvən/ *adj* **1a** not level, smooth, or uniform **b** irregular, inconsistent **c** varying in quality **2** unequal – **~ly** *adv* – **~ness** *n*

uneventful /ˌʌnɪˈventfəl/ *adj* without any noteworthy or untoward incidents – **~ly** *adv* – **~ness** *n*

unexceptionable /ˌʌnɪkˈsepʃənəbəl/ *adj* beyond reproach or criticism; unimpeachable – **-bly** *adv*

unfailing /ʌnˈfeɪlɪŋ/ *adj* that can be relied on; constant – **~ly** *adv*

unfaithful /ʌnˈfeɪθfəl/ *adj* **1** disloyal, faithless **2** not faithful to a marriage partner, lover, etc, esp in having sexual relations with another person – **~ly** *adv* – **~ness** *n*

unfaltering /ʌnˈfɔːltərɪŋ/ *adj* not wavering or hesitating; firm – **~ly** *adv*

unfavourable /ʌnˈfeɪvərəbəl/ *adj* **1** expressing disapproval; negative **2** disadvantageous, adverse – **-bly** *adv*

unfeeling /ʌnˈfiːlɪŋ/ *adj* not kind or sympathetic; hardhearted – **~ly** *adv*

unfit /ʌnˈfɪt/ *adj* **1** unsuitable, inappropriate **2** incapable, incompetent **3** physically or mentally unsound

unflagging /ʌnˈflægɪŋ/ *adj* never flagging; tireless – **~ly** *adv*

unflappable /ʌnˈflæpəbəl/ *adj* remaining calm and composed – **-bly** *adv*

unflinching /ʌnˈflɪntʃɪŋ/ *adj* steadfast – **~ly** *adv*

unfold /ʌnˈfəʊld/ *v* **1** to open from a folded state **2** to open out gradually to the mind or eye

unforgettable /ˌʌnfəˈgetəbəl/ *adj* incapable of being forgotten; memorable – **-bly** *adv*

[1]unfortunate /ʌnˈfɔːtʃʊnɪ̵t/ *adj* **1a** unsuccessful, unlucky **b** accompanied by or resulting in misfortune **2** unsuitable, inappropriate

[2]unfortunate *n* an unfortunate person

unfortunately /ʌnˈfɔːtʃʊnɪ̵tli/ *adv* **1** in an unfortunate manner **2** as is unfortunate

unfounded /ʌnˈfaʊndɪ̵d/ *adj* lacking a sound basis; groundless

unfrequented /ˌʌnfriˈkwentɪ̵d/ *adj* not often visited or travelled over

ungainly /ʌnˈgeɪnli/ *adj* lacking in grace; clumsy – **-liness** *n*

ungenerous /ʌnˈdʒenərəs/ *adj* **1** petty, uncharitable **2** stingy, mean – **~ly** *adv*

ungodly /ʌnˈgɒdli/ *adj* **1** sinful, wicked **2** indecent, outrageous

ungovernable /ʌnˈgʌvənəbəl/ *adj* not capable of being controlled or restrained

ungracious /ʌnˈgreɪʃəs/ *adj* rude, impolite – **~ly** *adv*

ungrateful /ʌnˈgreɪtfəl/ *adj* **1** showing no gratitude **2** disagreeable, unpleasant – **~ly** *adv* – **~ness** *n*

unguarded /ʌnˈgɑːdɪ̵d/ *adj* **1** vulnerable to attack **2** showing lack of forethought or calculation; imprudent

unguent /ˈʌŋgwənt/ *n* a soothing or healing salve; ointment

unhappy /ʌnˈhæpi/ *adj* **1** not fortunate; unlucky **2** sad, miserable **3** unsuitable, inappropriate – **-piness** *n* – **-pily** *adv*

unhealthy /ʌnˈhelθi/ *adj* **1** not in or conducive to good health **2** morbid – **-thily** *adv* – **-thiness** *n*

unheard /ˈʌnˈhɜːd/ *adj* **1** not perceived by the ear **2** not given a hearing

unheard-of *adj* previously unknown; unprecedented

unhinge /ʌn'hɪndʒ/ *v* to make (mentally) unstable; unsettle

unholy /ʌn'həʊli/ *adj* **1** wicked, reprehensible **2** terrible, awful – infml – **-liness** *n*

unicorn /'juːnɪ̈kɔːn/ *n* a mythical animal usu depicted as a white horse with a single horn in the middle of the forehead

[1]**uniform** /'juːnɪ̈fɔːm/ *adj* **1** not varying in character, appearance, quantity, etc **2** conforming to a rule, pattern, or practice; consonant – **~ity** *n* – **~ly** *adv*

[2]**uniform** *n* dress of a distinctive design or fashion worn by members of a particular group and serving as a means of identification – **~ed** *adj*

unify /'juːnɪ̈faɪ/ *v* to make into a unit or a coherent whole; unite – **-fication** *n*

unilateral /juːnɪ̈'lætərəl/ *adj* **1a** done or undertaken by 1 person or party **b** of or affecting 1 side **2** produced or arranged on or directed towards 1 side – **~ly** *adv*

unimpeachable /ˌʌnɪm'piːtʃəbəl/ *adj* **1** not to be doubted; beyond question **2** irreproachable, blameless – **-bly** *adv*

uninhibited /ˌʌnɪn'hɪbɪ̈tɪ̈d/ *adj* acting spontaneously without constraint or regard for what others might think – **~ly** *adv*

[1]**union** /'juːnɪən/ *n* **1a(1)** the formation of a single political unit from 2 or more separate and independent units **(2)** a uniting in marriage; *also* sexual intercourse **b** combination, junction **2a** an association of independent individuals (e g nations) for some common purpose **b** a trade union

[2]**union** *adj* of, dealing with, or constituting a union

unionism /'juːnɪənɪzəm/ *n* **1** adherence to the principles of trade unions **2** *cap* a political movement giving support for the continued union of Great Britain and Ireland – **-ist** *n, adj*

Union Jack *n* the national flag of the UK combining crosses representing England, Scotland, and N Ireland

unique /juː'niːk/ *adj* **1** sole, only **2** without a like or equal; unequalled **3** very rare or unusual – disapproved of by some speakers – **~ly** *adv* – **~ness** *n*

unisex /'juːnɪ̈seks/ *adj* able to be worn by both sexes

unison /'juːnɪ̈sən, -zən/ *n* **1** the writing, playing, or singing of parts in a musical passage at the same pitch or in octaves **2** harmonious agreement or union

unit /'juːnɪ̈t/ *n* **1a(1)** the first and lowest natural number; one **(2)** a single quantity regarded as a whole in calculation **b** the number occupying the position immediately to the left of the decimal point in the Arabic notation; *also, pl* this position **2** a determinate quantity (e g of length, time, heat, value, or housing) adopted as a standard of measurement **3** a part of a military establishment that has a prescribed organization (e g of personnel and supplies)

unite /juː'naɪt/ *v* **1** to join together to form a single unit **2** to link by a legal or moral bond **3** to act in concert

united /juː'naɪtɪ̈d/ *adj* **1** combined, joined **2** relating to or produced by joint action **3** in agreement; harmonious – **~ly** *adv*

unit trust *n* an investment company that minimizes the risk to investors by collective purchase of shares in many different enterprises

unity /'juːnɪ̈ti/ *n* **1a** the state of being 1 or united **b** a definite amount taken as 1 or for which 1 is made to stand in calculation **2a** concord, harmony **b** continuity and agreement in aims and interests

univalent /juːnɪ'veɪlənt/ *adj* having a valency of 1

[1]**universal** /juːnɪ̈'vɜːsəl/ *adj* **1** including or covering all or a whole without limit or exception **2** present or occurring everywhere or under all conditions

[2]**universal** *n* a general concept or term

universal joint *n* a shaft coupling capable of transmitting rotation from one shaft to another at an angle

universe /'juːnɪ̈vɜːs/ *n* **1a** all things that exist; the cosmos **b** a galaxy **2** the whole world; everyone

university /juːnɪ̈'vɜːsɪ̈ti/ *n* (the premises of) an institution of higher learning that provides facilities for full-time teaching and research and is authorized to grant academic degrees

unjust /ʌn'dʒʌst/ *adj* unfair; without showing, giving, etc justice

unkempt /ˌʌn'kempt/ *adj* **1** not combed; dishevelled **2** not neat or tidy

unkind /ˌʌn'kaɪnd/ *adj* **1** not pleasing or mild **2** lacking in kindness or sympathy; harsh – **~ly** *adv*

unknowing /ˌʌn'nəʊɪŋ/ *adj* not knowing – **~ly** *adv*

[1]**unknown** /ˌʌn'nəʊn/ *adj* not known; *also* having an unknown value

[2]**unknown** *n* a person who is little known (e g to the public)

unlawful /ʌn'lɔːfəl/ *adj* **1** illegal **2** not morally right or conventional – **~ly** *adv*

unleash /ʌn'liːʃ/ *v* to loose from restraint or control

unless /ʌn'les, ən-/ *conj* **1** except on the condition that **2** without the necessary accompaniment that; except when

[1]**unlike** /ʌn'laɪk/ *prep* **1** different from **2** not characteristic of **3** in a different manner from

[2]**unlike** /ʌn'laɪk/ *adj* **1** marked by dissimilarity; different **2** unequal

unlikely /ʌn'laɪkli/ *adj* **1** having a low probability of being or occurring **2** not believable; improbable **3** likely to fail; unpromising **4** not foreseen (e g the *unlikely* result) – **-liness, -lihood** *n*

unload /ʌn'ləʊd/ *v* **1a** to take (cargo) off or out **b** to give vent to; pour forth **2** to relieve of sthg burdensome **3** to draw the charge from – **~er** *n*

unlock /ʌn'lɒk/ *v* **1** to unfasten the lock of **2** to open, release

unmannerly /ʌn'mænəli/ *adj* discourteous, rude

unmask /ʌn'mɑːsk/ *v* to reveal the true nature of; expose

unmentionable /ʌn'menʃənəbəl/ *adj* not fit to be mentioned; unspeakable

unmistakable /ˌʌnmɪ̣'steɪkəbəl/ *adj* clear, obvious – **-bly** *adv*

unmitigated /ʌn'mɪtɪ̣geɪtɪ̣d/ *adj* **1** not diminished in severity, intensity, etc **2** out-and-out, downright – **~ly** *adv*

unnatural /ˌʌn'nætʃərəl/ *adj* **1** not in accordance with nature or a normal course of events **2a** not in accordance with normal feelings or behaviour; perverse **b** artificial or contrived in manner – **~ly** *adv*

unnerve /ˌʌn'nɜːv/ *v* to deprive of nerve, courage, or the power to act

unnumbered /ˌʌn'nʌmbəd/ *adj* innumerable

unobtrusive /ˌʌnəb'truːsɪv/ *adj* not too easily seen or noticed; inconspicuous – **~ly** *adv* – **~ness** *n*

unorthodox /ʌn'ɔːθədɒks/ *adj* not conventional in behaviour, beliefs, doctrine, etc

unpack /ʌn'pæk/ *v* **1** to remove the contents of **2** to remove or undo from packing or a container

unparalleled /ʌn'pærəleld/ *adj* having no equal or match; unique

unparliamentary /ˌʌnpɑːlə'mentəri, -pɑːljə-/ *adj* not in accordance with parliamentary practice

unpick /ʌn'pɪk/ *v* to undo (e g sewing) by taking out stitches

unpleasant /ʌn'plezənt/ *adj* not pleasant or agreeable; displeasing – **~ly** *adv* – **~ness** *n*

unprecedented /ʌn'presɪ̣dentɪ̣d/ *adj* having no precedent; novel – **~ly** *adv*

unprejudiced /ʌn'predʒədɪ̣st/ *adj* impartial, fair

unpretentious /ˌʌnprɪ'tenʃəs/ *adj* not seeking to impress others by means of wealth, standing, etc; not affected or ostentatious – **~ly** *adv* – **~ness** *n*

unprincipled /ʌn'prɪnsɪ̣pəld/ *adj* without moral principles; unscrupulous

unprintable /ʌn'prɪntəbəl/ *adj* unfit to be printed

unqualified /ʌn'kwɒlɪ̣faɪd/ *adj* **1** not having the necessary qualifications **2** not modified or restricted by reservations

unquestionable /ʌn'kwestʃənəbəl/ *adj* not able to be called in question; indisputable – **-bly** *adv*

unquestioning /ʌn'kwestʃənɪŋ/ *adj* not expressing doubt or hesitation

unquote /ˌʌn'kwəʊt/ *n* – used orally

to indicate the end of a direct quotation

unravel /ʌn'rævəl/ *v* **1** to disentangle **2** to clear up or solve (sthg intricate or obscure)

unreasonable /ʌn'riːzənəbəl/ *adj* **1** not governed by or acting according to reason **2** excessive, immoderate – **-bly** *adv* – **~ness** *n*

unreasoning /ʌn'riːzənɪŋ/ *adj* not moderated or controlled by reason

unrelenting /ˌʌnrɪ'lentɪŋ/ *adj* **1** not weakening in determination; stern **2** not letting up in vigour, pace, etc – **~ly** *adv*

unremitting /ˌʌnrɪ'mɪtɪŋ/ *adj* constant, incessant – **~ly** *adv*

unreserved /ˌʌnrɪ'zɜːvd/ *adj* **1** entire, unqualified **2** frank and open in manner – **~ly** *adv*

unrest /ʌn'rest/ *n* agitation, turmoil

unrestrained /ˌʌnrɪ'streɪnd/ *adj* not held in check; uncontrolled

unrivalled /ʌn'raɪvəld/ *adj* unequalled, unparalleled

unroll /ʌn'rəʊl/ *v* to open out; uncoil

unruffled /ʌn'rʌfəld/ *adj* **1** poised, serene **2** smooth, calm

unruly /ʌn'ruːli/ *adj* difficult to discipline or manage – **-liness** *n*

unsaid /ʌn'sed/ *adj* not said or spoken

unsavoury /ʌn'seɪvəri/ *adj* disagreeable, distasteful; *esp* morally offensive

unscathed /ʌn'skeɪðd/ *adj* entirely unharmed or uninjured

unschooled /ˌʌn'skuːld/ *adj* untaught, untrained

unscramble /ʌn'skræmbəl/ *v* **1** to separate into original components **2** to restore (scrambled communication) to intelligible form

unscrew /ʌn'skruː/ *v* to loosen or withdraw by turning

unscrupulous /ʌn'skruːpjʊləs/ *adj* without moral scruples; unprincipled – **~ly** *adv* – **~ness** *n*

unseat /ʌn'siːt/ *v* to remove from a (political) position

unseemly /ʌn'siːmli/ *adj* not conforming to established standards of good behaviour or taste – **-liness** *n*

¹unseen /ˌʌn'siːn/ *adj* done without previous preparation

²unseen /ˌʌn'siːn/ *n, chiefly Br* a passage of unprepared translation

unsettle /ʌn'setl/ *v* to perturb or agitate

unsettled /ˌʌn'setld/ *adj* **1a** not calm or tranquil; disturbed **b** variable, changeable **2** not resolved or worked out; undecided **3** not inhabited or populated **4** not paid or discharged

unsex /ʌn'seks/ *v* to deprive of sexual power or the typical qualities of one's sex

unshod /ˌʌn'ʃɒd/ *adj* wearing no (horse-) shoes

unsightly /ʌn'saɪtli/ *adj* not pleasing to the eye; ugly – **-liness** *n*

unskilled /ˌʌn'skɪld/ *adj* **1** of, being, or requiring workers who are not skilled in any particular branch of work **2** showing a lack of skill

unsociable /ʌn'səʊʃəbəl/ *adj* not liking social activity; reserved, solitary

unsocial /ʌn'səʊʃəl/ *adj* **1** marked by or showing a dislike for social interaction **2** *Br* worked at a time that falls outside the normal working day and precludes participation in normal social activities

unsound /ˌʌn'saʊnd/ *adj* **1** not healthy or whole **2** mentally abnormal **3** not firmly made, placed, or fixed **4** not valid or true; specious

unsparing /ʌn'speərɪŋ/ *adj* **1** not merciful; hard, ruthless **2** liberal, generous – **~ly** *adv*

unspeakable /ʌn'spiːkəbəl/ *adj* **1** incapable of being expressed in words **2** too terrible or shocking to be expressed – **-bly** *adv*

unstable /ʌn'steɪbəl/ *adj* not stable; not firm or fixed; not constant: e g **a** apt to move, sway, or fall; unsteady **b** characterized by inability to control the emotions

unstop /ˌʌn'stɒp/ *v* to free from an obstruction

unstudied /ˌʌn'stʌdʒd/ *adj* **1** not acquired by study **2** not done or planned for effect

unsung /ʌn'sʌŋ/ *adj* not celebrated or praised (e g in song or verse)

unswerving /ʌn'swɜːvɪŋ/ *adj* not deviating; constant

untangle /ˌʌn'tæŋgəl/ *v* to loose from tangles or entanglement; unravel

untapped /ˌʌn'tæpt/ *adj* **1** not yet tapped **2** not drawn on or exploited
untenable /ʌn'tenəbəl/ *adj* not able to be defended
unthinkable /ʌn'θɪŋkəbəl/ *adj* contrary to what is acceptable or probable; out of the question
unthinking /ʌn'θɪŋkɪŋ/ *adj* not taking thought; heedless, unmindful – **~ly** *adv*
untie /ʌn'taɪ/ *v* **1** to free from sthg that fastens or restrains **2a** to separate out the knotted parts of **b** to disentangle, resolve
¹until /ʌn'tɪl, ən-/ *prep* **1** up to as late as **2** up to as far as
²until *conj* up to the time that; until such time as
untimely /ʌn'taɪmli/ *adj* **1** occurring before the natural or proper time; premature **2** inopportune, unseasonable – **-liness** *n*
unto /'ʌntuː/ *prep, archaic* to
untold /ˌʌn'təʊld/ *adj* **1** incalculable, vast **2** not told or related
¹untouchable /ʌn'tʌtʃəbəl/ *adj* **1** that may not be touched **2** lying beyond reach
²untouchable *n* sby or sthg untouchable; *specif, often cap* a member of a large formerly segregated hereditary group in India who in traditional Hindu belief can defile a member of a higher caste by contact or proximity
untoward /ˌʌntə'wɔːd/ *adj* not favourable; adverse, unfortunate – **~ly** *adv* – **~ness** *n*
untruth /ʌn'truːθ, 'ʌntruːθ/ *n* **1** lack of truthfulness **2** sthg untrue; a falsehood
untruthful /ʌn'truːθfəl/ *adj* not telling the truth; false, lying – **~ly** *adv*
unused /ʌn'juːst; *sense* 2 ʌn'juːzd/ *adj* **1** unaccustomed – usu + *to* **2a** fresh, new **b** not used up
unusual /ʌn'juːʒʊəl, -ʒəl/ *adj* **1** uncommon, rare **2** different, unique – **~ly** *adv*
unutterable /ʌn'ʌtərəbəl/ *adj* **1** beyond the powers of description; inexpressible **2** out-and-out, downright – **-bly** *adv*
unvarnished /ˌʌn'vɑːnɪʃt/ *adj* not adorned or glossed; plain
unveil /ˌʌn'veɪl/ *v* to make public; divulge
unwarranted /ʌn'wɒrəntɪ̣d/ *adj* not justified; (done) without good reason
unwell /ʌn'wel/ *adj* in poor health
unwieldy /ʌn'wiːldi/ *adj* difficult to move or handle; cumbersome – **-diness** *n*
unwind /ʌn'waɪnd/ *v* **1** to uncoil; unroll **2** to become less tense; relax
unwitting /ˌʌn'wɪtɪŋ/ *adj* not intended; inadvertent – **~ly** *adv*
unzip /ˌʌn'zɪp/ *v* to open (as if) by means of a zip
¹up /ʌp/ *adv* **1a** at or towards a relatively high level **b** from beneath the ground or water to the surface **c** above the horizon **d** upstream **e** in or to a raised or upright position; *specif* out of bed **f** off or out of the ground or a surface (e g pull *up* a daisy) **g** to the top; *esp* so as to be full **2a** into a state of, or with, greater intensity or activity (e g speak *up*) **b** into a faster pace or higher gear **3a** in or into a relatively high condition or status – sometimes used interjectionally as an expression of approval (e g *up* BBC2!) **b** above a normal or former level: e g (1) upwards (2) higher in price **c** ahead of an opponent (e g we're 3 points *up*) **4a(1)** in or into existence, evidence, prominence, or prevalence (e g new houses haven't been *up* long) (2) in or into operation or full power (e g get *up* steam) **b** under consideration or attention; *esp* before a court **5** so as to be together (e g add *up* the figures) **6a** entirely, completely (e g eat *up* your spinach) **b** so as to be firmly closed, joined, or fastened **c** so as to be fully inflated **7** in or into storage **8** in a direction conventionally the opposite of down: **a(1)** to windward (2) with rudder to leeward – used with reference to a ship's helm **b** in or towards the north **c** so as to arrive or approach (e g walked *up* to her) **d** to or at the rear of a theatrical stage **e** *chiefly Br* to or in the capital of a country or a university city (e g *up* in London) **9** in or into parts (e g chop *up*) **10** to a stop – usu + *draw, bring, fetch,* or *pull*
²up *adj* **1** moving, inclining, bound, or directed upwards or up **2** ready, prepared (e g dinner's *up*) **3** going on, taking place; *esp* being the matter (e g

what's *up*?) **4** at an end; *esp* hopeless (e g it's all *up* with him now) **5** well informed **6** *of a road* being repaired; having a broken surface **7** ahead of an opponent **8** *of a ball in court games* having bounced only once on the ground or floor after being hit by one's opponent and therefore playable **9** *Br, of a train* travelling towards a large town; *specif* travelling towards London

³up *v* **1** – used with *and* and another verb to indicate that the action of the following verb is either surprisingly or abruptly initiated (e g he *upped* and married) **2** to increase

⁴up *prep* **1a** up along, round, through, towards, in, into, or on **b** at the top of (e g the office is *up* those stairs) **2** *Br* (up) to (e g going *up* the West End) – nonstandard

⁵up *n* **1** (sthg in) a high position or an upward incline **2** a period or state of prosperity or success

up-and-coming *adj* likely to advance or succeed

up-and-up *n, chiefly Br* a potentially or increasingly successful course – chiefly in *on the up-and-up*

¹upbeat /ˈʌpbiːt/ *n* an unaccented (e g the last) beat in a musical bar

²upbeat *adj, chiefly NAm* optimistic, cheerful – infml

upbraid /ˌʌpˈbreɪd/ *v* to scold or reproach severely

upbringing /ˈʌpbrɪŋɪŋ/ *n* a particular way of bringing up a child

up-country *adj* **1** (characteristic) of an inland, upland, or outlying region **2** not socially or culturally sophisticated

¹update /ˌʌpˈdeɪt/ *v* to bring up to date – **update** *n*

upend /ʌpˈend/ *v* **1** to cause to stand on end **2** to knock down

upgrade /ˌʌpˈgreɪd/ *v* to advance to a job requiring a higher level of skill, esp as part of a training programme

upheaval /ʌpˈhiːvəl/ *n* (an instance of) extreme agitation or radical change

¹uphill /ˌʌpˈhɪl/ *adv* upwards on a hill or incline

²uphill /ˌʌpˈhɪl/ *adj* **1** situated on elevated ground **2** going up; ascending **3** difficult, laborious

uphold /ˌʌpˈhəʊld/ *v* **1** to give support to; maintain **2** to support against an opponent or challenge – **~er** *n*

upholster /ʌpˈhəʊlstəʳ/ *v* to provide with upholstery – **~er** *n*

upholstery /ʌpˈhəʊlstəri/ *n* materials (e g fabric, padding, and springs) used to make a soft covering, esp for a seat

upkeep /ˈʌpkiːp/ *n* (the cost of) maintaining or being maintained in good condition

¹uplift /ʌpˈlɪft/ *v* **1** to raise, elevate **2** to improve the spiritual, social, or intellectual condition of

²uplift /ˈʌpˌlɪft/ *n* **1** a moral or social improvement **2** influences intended to uplift

upon /əˈpɒn/ *prep* on – chiefly fml

¹upper /ˈʌpəʳ/ *adj* **1a** higher in physical position, rank, or order **b** farther inland **2** being the branch of a legislature consisting of 2 houses that is usu more restricted in membership, is in many cases less powerful, and possesses greater traditional prestige than the lower house

²upper *n* the parts of a shoe or boot above the sole

³upper *n* a stimulant drug; *esp* amphetamine – infml

upper case *n* capital letters – **upper-case** *adj*

upper class *n* the class occupying the highest position in a society; *esp* the wealthy or the aristocracy

upper crust *n sing or pl in constr* the highest social class – infml

uppercut /ˈʌpəkʌt/ *n* a swinging blow directed upwards with a bent arm

upper hand *n* mastery, advantage – + *the*

uppermost /ˈʌpəməʊst/ *adv* in or into the highest or most prominent position

uppish /ˈʌpɪʃ/ *adj* **1** hit up and travelling far in the air **2** conceited – infml – **~ly** *adv* – **~ness** *n*

¹upright /ˈʌp-raɪt/ *adj* **1a** perpendicular, vertical **b** erect in carriage or posture **2** marked by strong moral rectitude – **~ly** *adv* – **~ness** *n*

²upright *adv* in an upright or vertical position

³upright *n* **1** sthg that stands upright

2 **upright, upright piano** a piano with vertical frame and strings

uprising /ˈʌp,raɪzɪŋ/ *n* a usu localized rebellion

uproar /ˈʌp-rɔːʳ/ *n* a state of commotion or violent disturbance

uproarious /ʌpˈrɔːrɪəs/ *adj* **1** marked by noise and disorder **2** extremely funny – **~ly** *adv*

uproot /,ʌpˈruːt/ *v* **1** to remove by pulling up by the roots **2** to displace from a country or traditional habitat or environment

[1]**upset** /ʌpˈset/ *v* **1** to overturn, knock over **2a** to trouble mentally or emotionally **b** to throw into disorder **3** to make somewhat ill

[2]**upset** /,ʌpˈset/ *n* **1** a minor physical disorder **2** an emotional disturbance **3** an unexpected defeat (e g in politics)

upshot /ˈʌpʃɒt/ *n* the final result; the outcome

upside down /,ʌpsaɪd ˈdaʊn/ *adv* **1** with the upper and·the lower parts reversed **2** in or into great disorder or confusion

[1]**upstage** /,ʌpˈsteɪdʒ/ *adv* at the rear of a theatrical stage; *also* away from the audience or film or television camera

[2]**upstage** /ʌpˈsteɪdʒ/ *adj* **1** of or at the rear of a stage **2** haughty, aloof

[3]**upstage** /ˈʌpsteɪdʒ/ *n* the part of a stage that is farthest from the audience or camera

[4]**upstage** /ʌpˈsteɪdʒ/ *v* to steal attention from

[1]**upstairs** /ʌpˈsteəz/ *adv* **1** up the stairs; to or on a higher floor **2** to or at a higher position

[2]**upstairs** *adj* situated above the stairs, esp on an upper floor

[3]**upstairs** *n pl but sing or pl in constr* the part of a building above the ground floor

upstanding /ʌpˈstændɪŋ/ *adj* **1** erect, upright **2** marked by integrity; honest

upstart /ˈʌpstɑːt/ *n* one who has risen suddenly (e g from a low position to wealth or power); *esp* one who claims more personal importance than he/she warrants

upstream /,ʌpˈstriːm/ *adv or adj* in the direction opposite to the flow of a stream

upsurge /ˈʌpsɜːdʒ/ *n* a rapid or sudden rise

upswing /ˈʌp,swɪŋ/ *n* **1** an upward swing **2** a marked increase or rise

uptake /ˈʌpteɪk/ *n* understanding, comprehension – infml

uptight /ˈʌptaɪt, ʌpˈtaɪt/ *adj* **1** tense, nervous, or uneasy **2** angry, indignant *USE* infml

up to *prep* **1** – used to indicate an upward limit or boundary **2** as far as; until **3a** equal to **b** good enough for **4** engaged in (a suspect activity) (e g what's he *up to*?) **5** being the responsibility of (e g it's *up to* me)

up-to-date *adj* **1** including the latest information **2** abreast of the times; modern

[1]**upturn** /,ʌpˈtɜːn/ *v* **1** to turn up or over **2** to direct upwards

[2]**upturn** /ˈʌptɜːn/ *n* an upward turn, esp towards better conditions or higher prices

upward /ˈʌpwəd/ *adj* moving or extending upwards; ascending

upwards /ˈʌpwədz/ *adv* **1a** from a lower to a higher place, condition, or level; in the opposite direction from down **b** so as to expose a particular surface (e g turned the cards *upwards*) **2** to an indefinitely greater amount, price, figure, age, or rank (e g from £5 *upwards*)

uranium /jʊˈreɪnɪəm/ *n* a heavy radioactive element found in pitchblende

Uranus /jʊˈreɪnəs, ˈjʊərənəs/ *n* the planet 7th in order from the sun

urban /ˈɜːbən/ *adj* (characteristic) of or constituting a city or town

urbane /ɜːˈbeɪn/ *adj* notably polite or smooth in manner; suave – **~ly** *adv* – **-banity** *n*

urchin /ˈɜːtʃɪ̣n/ *n* a mischievous and impudent young boy, esp one who is scruffy

[1]**urge** /ɜːdʒ/ *v* **1** to advocate or demand earnestly or pressingly **2** to try to persuade **3** to force or impel in a specified direction or to greater speed

[2]**urge** *n* a force or impulse that urges

urgent /ˈɜːdʒənt/ *adj* **1** calling for immediate attention; pressing **2** conveying a sense of urgency – ~**ly** *adv* – **-gency** *n*

urinal /jʊ'raɪnəl, 'jʊərɪ̣nəl/ *n* a fixture used for urinating into, esp by men; *also* a room, building, etc containing a urinal

urinary /'jʊərɪ̣nəri/ *adj* relating to (or occurring in or constituting the organs concerned with the formation and discharge of) urine

urinate /'jʊərɪ̣neɪt/ *v* to discharge urine – **-nation** *n*

urine /'jʊərɪ̣n/ *n* waste material that is secreted by the kidney in vertebrates and forms a clear amber and usu slightly acid fluid

urn /ɜːn/ *n* **1** an ornamental vase on a pedestal used esp for preserving the ashes of the dead after cremation **2** a large closed container, usu with a tap at its base, in which large quantities of tea, coffee, etc may be heated or served

us /əs, s; *strong* ʌs/ *pron* **1** *objective case of* **we** **2** *chiefly Br* me – nonstandard

usage /'juːzɪdʒ, 'juːsɪdʒ/ *n* **1** (an instance of) established and generally accepted practice or procedure **2** (an instance of) the way in which words and phrases are actually used in a language

[1]**use** /juːs/ *n* **1a** using or being used **b** a way of using sthg **2** habitual or customary usage **3a** the right or benefit of using sthg **b** the ability or power to use sthg (e g a limb) **4a** a purpose or end **b** practical worth or application

[2]**use** /juːz/ *v* **1** to put into action or service **2** to carry out sthg by means of **3** to expend or consume **4** to treat in a specified manner **5** – used in the past with *to* to indicate a former fact or state – **user** *n* – **usable** *adj*

used /juːzd; *sense* 3 juːst/ *adj* **1** employed in accomplishing sthg **2** that has endured use; *specif* secondhand **3** accustomed

useful /'juːsfəl/ *adj* **1** having utility, esp practical worth or applicability; *also* helpful **2** of highly satisfactory quality – ~**ly** *adv* – ~**ness** *n*

useless /'juːslɪ̣s/ *adj* **1** having or being of no use **2** inept – infml – ~**ly** *adv* – ~**ness** *n*

user-friendly *adj* **1** *of a computer system* designed for easy operation by guiding users along a series of simple steps **2** easy to operate or understand

[1]**usher** /'ʌʃəʳ/ *n* **1** an officer or servant who acts as a doorkeeper (e g in a court of law) **2** *fem* **usherette** one who shows people to their seats (e g in a theatre)

[2]**usher** *v* **1** to conduct to a place **2** to inaugurate, introduce – usu + *in*

usual /'juːʒʊəl, 'juːʒəl/ *adj* **1** in accordance with usage, custom, or habit; normal **2** commonly or ordinarily used – ~**ly** *adv*

usurer /'juːʒərəʳ/ *n* one who lends money, esp at an exorbitant rate

usurp /juː'zɜːp/ *v* to seize and possess by force or without right – ~**ation** *n* – ~**er** *n*

usury /'juːʒəri/ *n* **1** the lending of money at (exorbitant) interest **2** an exorbitant or illegal rate or amount of interest – **-rious** *adj* – **-riously** *adv* – **-riousness** *n*

utensil /juː'tensəl/ *n* **1** an implement, vessel, or device used in the household, esp the kitchen **2** a useful tool or implement

uterus /'juːtərəs/ *n, pl* **uteri** an organ of the female mammal for containing and usu for nourishing the young during development before birth – **-rine** *adj*

utilitarian /juːˌtɪlɪ̣'teərɪən/ *adj* **1** marked by utilitarian views or practices **2** made for or aiming at practical use rather than beautiful appearance – **utilitarian** *n*

utilitarianism /juːˌtɪlɪ̣'teərɪənɪzəm/ *n* a doctrine that the criterion for correct conduct should be the usefulness of its consequences; *specif* a theory that the aim of action should be the greatest happiness of the greatest number

[1]**utility** /juː'tɪlɪ̣ti/ *n* **1** fitness for some purpose; usefulness **2** sthg useful or designed for use **3** a business organization performing a public service

[2]**utility** *adj* **1** capable of serving as a substitute in various roles or positions **2** designed or adapted for general use – **-ize** *v*

[1]**utmost** /'ʌtməʊst/ *adj* **1** situated at

the farthest or most distant point; extreme **2** of the greatest or highest degree

²utmost *n* **1** the highest point or degree **2** the best of one's abilities, powers, etc

utopia /juːˈtəʊpɪə/ *n* **1** *often cap* a place or state of ideal (political and social) perfection **2** an impractical scheme for social or political improvement

utopian /juːˈtəʊpɪən/ *adj* **1** impossibly ideal, esp in social and political organization **2** proposing impractically ideal social and political schemes – **utopian** *n*

¹utter /ˈʌtəʳ/ *adj* absolute, total – **~ly** *adv*

²utter *v* **1** to emit as a sound **2** to give (verbal) expression to – **~ance** *n*

U-turn /ˈjuː tɜːn/ *n* **1** a turn executed by a motor vehicle without reversing that takes it back along the direction from which it has come **2** a total reversal of policy

V

v /viː/ *n, pl* **v's** *or* **vs** *often cap* **1** (a graphic representation of or device for reproducing) the 22nd letter of the English alphabet **2** five

vac /væk/ *n, Br* a vacation, esp from college or university – infml

vacancy /ˈveɪkənsi/ *n* **1** physical or mental inactivity; idleness **2** a vacant office, post, or room **3** an empty space

vacant /ˈveɪkənt/ *adj* **1** without an occupant **2** free from activity or work **3a** stupid, foolish **b** expressionless – **~ly** *adv*

vacate /vəˈkeɪt, veɪ-/ *v* to give up the possession or occupancy of

¹vacation /vəˈkeɪʃən/ *n* **1** a scheduled period during which activity (e g of a university) is suspended **2** *chiefly NAm* a holiday

²vacation *v, chiefly NAm* to take or spend a holiday

vaccinate /ˈvæksɨneɪt/ *v* to administer a vaccine to, usu by injection – **-ation** *n*

vaccine /ˈvæksiːn/ *n* material (e g a preparation of killed or modified virus or bacteria) used in vaccinating to produce an immunity

vacillate /ˈvæsɨleɪt/ *v* **1** to sway; *also* to fluctuate, oscillate **2** to hesitate or waver in choosing between opinions or courses of action – **-lation** *n*

vacuole /ˈvækjʊ-əʊl/ *n* a small cavity or space containing air or fluid in the tissues of an organism or in the protoplasm of an individual cell

vacuous /ˈvækjʊəs/ *adj* **1** empty **2** stupid, inane **3** idle, aimless – **~ly** *adv* – **~ness** *n*

¹vacuum /ˈvækjʊəm/ *n* **1a** a space absolutely devoid of matter **b** an air pressure below atmospheric pressure **2a** a vacant space; a void **b** a state of isolation from outside influences **3** a vacuum cleaner

²vacuum *v* to clean using a vacuum cleaner

vacuum cleaner *n* an (electrical) appliance for removing dust and dirt (e g from carpets or upholstery) by suction

vacuum-packed *adj* packed in a wrapping from which most of the air has been removed

¹vagabond /ˈvægəbɒnd/ *adj* **1** (characteristic) of a wanderer **2** leading an unsettled, irresponsible, or disreputable life

²vagabond *n* a wanderer; *esp* a tramp

vagary /ˈveɪgəri/ *n* an erratic, unpredictable, or extravagant idea, act, etc

vagina /vəˈdʒaɪnə/ *n* a canal in a female mammal that leads from the uterus to the external orifice of the genital canal – **~l** *adj*

¹vagrant /ˈveɪgrənt/ *n* **1** one who has no established residence or lawful means of support **2** a wanderer, vagabond – **-rancy** *n*

²vagrant *adj* **1** wandering about from place to place, usu with no means of support **2** having no fixed course; random

vague /veɪg/ *adj* **1a** not clearly defined, expressed, or understood; indistinct **b** not clearly felt or sensed **2** not thinking or expressing one's thoughts clearly – **~ly** *adv* – **~ness** *n*

vain /veɪn/ *adj* **1** unsuccessful, ineffectual **2** having or showing excessive pride in one's appearance, ability, etc; conceited – **~ly** *adv*

valance /ˈvæləns/ *n* **1** a piece of drapery hung as a border, esp along the edge of a bed, canopy, or shelf **2** a pelmet

vale /veɪl/ *n* a valley – poetic or in place-names

valediction /ˌvælɨˈdɪkʃən/ *n* **1** an act of bidding farewell **2** an address or statement of farewell or leave-taking *USE* fml – **-tory** *n*

valency /ˈveɪlənsi/ *n* the degree of combining power of an element or radical as shown by the number of atomic weights of a univalent element (e g hydrogen) with which the atomic weight of the element will combine or for which it can be substituted or with which it can be compared

valentine /ˈvæləntaɪn/ *n* **1** a sweetheart chosen on St Valentine's Day **2** a gift or greeting card sent or given, esp to a sweetheart, on St Valentine's Day

valerian /vəˈlɪərɪən/ *n* any of several usu perennial plants, many of which possess medicinal properties

valet /ˈvælɨt, ˈvæleɪ/ *n* a gentleman's male servant who performs personal services (e g taking care of clothing)

valiant /ˈvælɪənt/ *adj* characterized by or showing valour; courageous – **~ly** *adv*

valid /ˈvælɨd/ *adj* **1** having legal efficacy; *esp* executed according to the proper formalities **2** well-grounded or justifiable; relevant and meaningful – **~ity** *n* – **~ly** *adv*

valley /ˈvæli/ *n* **1** an elongated depression of the earth's surface, usu between hills or mountains **2** a hollow, depression

valour /ˈvæləʳ/ *n* strength of mind or spirit that enables sby to encounter danger with firmness; personal bravery

valse /væls/ *n* a (concert) waltz

[1]**valuable** /ˈvæljʊəbəl/ *adj* **1** having (high) money value **2** of great use or worth

[2]**valuable** *n* a usu personal possession of relatively great money value – usu pl

[1]**value** /ˈvæljuː/ *n* **1** a fair return or equivalent for sthg exchanged **2** the worth in money or commodities of sthg **3** relative worth, utility, or importance **4** a numerical quantity assigned or computed **5** sthg (e g a principle or quality) intrinsically valuable or desirable – **~less** *adj*

[2]**value** *v* **1a** to estimate the worth of in terms of money **b** to rate in terms of usefulness, importance, etc **2** to consider or rate highly; esteem – **-uation** *n*

value-added tax *n, often cap V, A, & T* a tax levied at each stage of the production and distribution of a commodity and passed on to the consumer as a form of purchase tax

valve /vælv/ *n* **1** a structure, esp in the heart or a vein, that closes temporarily to obstruct passage of material or permits movement of fluid in 1 direction only **2a** any of numerous mechanical devices by which the flow of liquid, gas, or loose material in bulk may be controlled, usu to allow movement in 1 direction only **b** a device in a brass musical instrument for quickly varying the tube length in order to change the fundamental tone by a definite interval **3** any of the separate joined pieces that make up the shell of an (invertebrate) animal; *specif* either of the 2 halves of the shell of a bivalve mollusc **4** *chiefly Br* a vacuum- or gas-filled device for the regulation of electric current by the control of free electrons or ions

valvular /ˈvælvjʊləʳ/ *adj* resembling or functioning as a valve; *also* opening by valves

vamoose /væˈmuːs, və-/ *v, chiefly NAm* to depart quickly – slang

[1]**vamp** /væmp/ *n* **1** the part of a shoe or boot covering the front of the foot **2** a simple improvised musical accompaniment – **vamp** *v*

[2]**vamp** *n* a woman who uses her charm to seduce and exploit men

vampire /ˈvæmpaɪəʳ/ *n* **1** a dead person believed to come from the grave at night and suck the blood of sleeping people **2** any of various S American bats that feed on blood and are dangerous to human beings and domestic animals, esp as transmitters of disease (e g rabies); *also* any of several other bats that do not feed on blood but are sometimes reputed to do so

[1]**van** *n* the vanguard

[2]**van** *n* **1** an enclosed motor vehicle used for transport of goods, animals, furniture, etc **2** *chiefly Br* an enclosed railway goods wagon

vanadium /vəˈneɪdɪəm/ *n* a metallic element found combined in minerals and used esp to form alloys

vandal /ˈvændl/ *n* **1** *cap* a member of a Germanic people who overran Gaul, Spain, and N Africa in the 4th and 5th C AD and in 455 sacked Rome **2** one who wilfully or ignorantly destroys or defaces (public) property

vandalism /ˈvændəl-ɪzəm/ *n* wilful destruction or defacement of property – **-ize** *v*

vane /veɪn/ *n* **1** a weather vane **2** a thin flat or curved object that is rotated about an axis by wind or water; *also* a device revolving in a similar manner and moving in water or air **3** the flat expanded part of a feather

vanguard /ˈvæŋgɑːd/ *n* **1** *sing or pl in constr* the troops moving at the head of an army **2** the forefront of an action or movement

vanilla /vəˈnɪlə/ *n* **1** any of a genus of tropical American climbing orchids whose long capsular fruit-pods yield an important flavouring **2** a commercially important extract of the vanilla pod that is used esp as a flavouring

vanish /ˈvænɪʃ/ **1** to pass quickly from sight; disappear **2** to cease to exist

vanishing cream *n* a light cosmetic cream used chiefly as a foundation for face powder

vanity /ˈvænɪ̈ti/ *n* **1** worthlessness **2** excessive pride in oneself; conceit

vanquish /ˈvæŋkwɪʃ/ *v* **1** to overcome, conquer **2** to gain mastery over (an emotion, passion, etc)

vapid /ˈvæpɪ̈d/ *adj* lacking liveliness, interest, or force; insipid – **~ly** *adv* – **~ness** *n* – **~ity** *n*

vapour /ˈveɪpəʳ/ *n* **1** smoke, fog, etc suspended floating in the air and impairing its transparency **2** a substance in the gaseous state; *esp* such a substance that is liquid under normal conditions – **vaporize** *v* – **vaporous** *adj*

[1]**variable** /ˈveərɪəbəl/ *adj* **1** subject to variation or changes **2** having the characteristics of a variable – **-bly** *adv* – **~ness** *n*

[2]**variable** *n* **1** sthg (e g a variable star) that is variable **2** (a symbol representing) a quantity that may assume any of a set of values

[1]**variant** /ˈveərɪənt/ *adj* varying (slightly) from the standard form

[2]**variant** *n* any of 2 or more people or things displaying usu slight differences; *esp* sthg that shows variation from a type or norm

variation /ˌveəriˈeɪʃən/ *n* **1a** varying or being varied **b** an instance of varying **c** the extent to which or the range in which a thing varies **2** the repetition of a musical theme with modifications in rhythm, tune, harmony, or key **3** divergence in characteristics of an organism or genotype from those typical or usual of its group **4** a solo dance in ballet

varicoloured /ˈveəriˌkʌləd/ *adj* having various colours

varicose /ˈværɪ̈kəʊs/ *also* **varicosed** *adj* abnormally swollen or dilated

varied /ˈveərid/ *adj* **1** having numerous forms or types; diverse **2** variegated

variegated /ˈveərɪəgeɪtɪ̈d/ *adj* having patches of different colours, dappled

variety /vəˈraɪəti/ *n* **1** the state of having different forms or types; diversity **2** an assortment of different things, esp of a particular class **3a** sthg differing from others of the same general kind; a sort **b** any of various groups of plants or animals ranking below a species **4** theatrical entertainment consisting of separate performances (e g of songs, skits, acrobatics, etc)

variform /ˈveərɪ̈fɔːm/ *adj* varied in form

various /ˈveərɪəs/ *adj* **1a** of differing kinds; diverse **b** dissimilar in nature or form; unlike **2** having a number of different aspects or characteristics **3** more than one; several

variously /ˈveərɪəsli/ *adv* in various ways; at various times

[1]**varnish** /ˈvɑːnɪʃ/ *n* **1** a liquid preparation that forms a hard shiny transparent coating on drying **2** outside show

[2]**varnish** *v* **1** to apply varnish to **2** to gloss *over*

varsity /ˈvɑːsɪ̈ti/ *n, Br* university – now chiefly humor

vary /ˈveəri/ *v* **1** to exhibit or undergo change **2** to deviate

vascular /ˈvæskjʊləʳ/ *adj* of or being a channel or system of channels conducting blood, sap, etc in a plant or animal; *also* supplied with or made up of such channels, esp blood vessels

vascular bundle *n* a single strand of the vascular system of a plant

vase /vɑːz/ *n* an ornamental vessel usu of greater depth than width, used esp for holding flowers

vasectomy /vəˈsektəmi/ *n* surgical cutting out of a section of the tube conducting sperm from the testes usu to induce permanent sterility

Vaseline /ˌvæsɪˈliːn, ˈ---/ *trademark* – used for petroleum jelly

vassal /ˈvæsəl/ *n* **1** sby under the protection of another who is his/her feudal lord **2** sby in a subservient or subordinate position

vast /vɑːst/ *adj* very great in amount, degree, intensity, or esp in extent or range

[1]**vat** /væt/ *n* a tub, barrel, or other large vessel, esp for holding liquids undergoing chemical change or preparations for dyeing or tanning

[2]**vat** *n, often cap* value-added tax

Vatican /ˈvætɪkən/ *n* the official residence of the Pope and the administrative centre of Roman Catholicism

vaudeville /ˈvɔːdəvɪl, ˈvəʊ-/ *n* a light often comic theatrical piece frequently combining pantomime, dialogue, dancing, and song

[1]**vault** /vɔːlt/ *n* **1** an arched structure of masonry, usu forming a ceiling or roof **2a** an underground passage, room, or storage compartment **b** a room or compartment for the safekeeping of valuables **3** a burial chamber, esp beneath a church or in a cemetery

[2]**vault** *v* to form or cover (as if) with a vault

[3]**vault** *v* to bound vigorously (over); *esp* to execute a leap (over) using the hands or a pole – **~er** *n*

[4]**vault** *n* an act of vaulting

VD *n* venereal disease

VDU *n* a screen for displaying information from a computer visually

veal /viːl/ *n* the flesh of a young calf used as food

[1]**vector** /ˈvektəʳ/ *n* a quantity (e g velocity or force) that has magnitude and direction and that is commonly represented by a directed line segment whose length represents the magnitude and whose orientation in space represents the direction

veer /vɪəʳ/ **1** to change direction, position, or inclination **2** *of the wind* to shift in a clockwise direction – **veer** *n*

veg /vedʒ/ *n, Br* a vegetable – infml

vegan /ˈviːgən/ *n* a strict vegetarian who avoids food or other products derived from animals

[1]**vegetable** /ˈvedʒtəbəl/ *adj* **1a** of, constituting, or growing like plants **b** consisting of plants **2** made or obtained from plants or plant products

[2]**vegetable** *n* **1** a plant **2** a plant (e g the cabbage, bean, or potato) grown for an edible part which is usu eaten with the principal course of a meal; *also* this part of the plant **3** a person whose physical and esp mental capacities are severely impaired by illness or injury

vegetable marrow *n* (any of various large smooth-skinned elongated fruits, used as a vegetable, of) a cultivated variety of a climbing plant of the cucumber family

[1]**vegetarian** /ˌvedʒɪˈteərɪən/ *n* one who practises vegetarianism

[2]**vegetarian** *adj* **1** of vegetarians or vegetarianism **2** consisting wholly of vegetables

vegetarianism /ˌvedʒɪˈteərɪənɪzəm/ *n* the often ethically based theory or practice of living on a diet that excludes the flesh of animals and often other animal products and that is made up of vegetables, fruits, cereals, and nuts

vegetate /ˈvedʒɪteɪt/ *v* **1** to grow in the manner of a plant **2** to lead a passive monotonous existence

vegetation /ˌvedʒɪˈteɪʃən/ *n* plant life or total plant cover (e g of an area)

vehement /ˈvɪəmənt/ *adj* **1** intensely felt; impassioned **2** forcibly expressed – **~ly** *adv* – **-mence** *n*

vehicle /ˈviːɪkəl/ *n* **1** any of various usu liquid media acting esp as solvents, carriers, or binders for active ingredients (e g drugs) or pigments **2** a means of transmission; a carrier **3** a medium through which sthg is expressed or communicated **4** a motor vehicle

vehicular /viːˈhɪkjʊləʳ/ *adj* of or

designed for vehicles, esp motor vehicles

[1]**veil** /veɪl/ *n* **1a** a length of cloth worn by women as a covering for the head and shoulders and often, esp in eastern countries, the face **b** a piece of sheer fabric attached for protection or ornament to a hat or headdress **2** *the* cloistered life of a nun **3** a concealing curtain or cover of cloth **4** a disguise, pretext – **~ed** *adj*

[2]**veil** *v* to cover, provide, or conceal (as if) with a veil

[1]**vein** /veɪn/ *n* **1** a deposit of ore, coal, etc, esp in a rock fissure **2** any of the tubular converging vessels that carry blood from the capillaries towards the heart **3a** any of the vascular bundles forming the framework of a leaf **b** any of the ribs that serve to stiffen the wings of an insect **4** a streak or marking suggesting a vein (e g in marble) **5** a distinctive element or quality; a strain

[2]**vein** *v* to pattern (as if) with veins

veld, veldt /velt/ *n* shrubby grassland, esp in S Africa

vellum /'veləm/ *n* a fine-grained skin (e g calf) prepared esp for writing on or binding books

velocity /vʃ'lɒsʃti/ *n* **1** speed, esp of inanimate things **2** speed in a given direction

velvet /'velvʃt/ *n* **1** a fabric (e g of silk, rayon, or cotton) characterized by a short soft dense pile **2** sthg suggesting velvet in softness, smoothness, etc – **~y** *adj*

velveteen /'velvʃtiːn/ *n* a fabric made with a short close weft pile in imitation of velvet

venal /'viːnl/ *adj* open to corrupt influence, esp bribery – **~ity** *n* – **~ly** *adv*

vend /vend/ *v* to sell, esp by means of a vending machine – **~or** *n*

vendetta /ven'detə/ *n* **1** a blood feud arising from the murder or injury of a member of one family by a member of another **2** a prolonged bitter feud

vending machine *n* a coin-operated machine for selling merchandise

[1]**veneer** /vʃ'nɪəʳ/ *n* **1** a thin layer of wood of superior appearance or hardness used esp to give a decorative finish (e g to joinery) **2** a protective or ornamental facing (e g of brick or stone) **3** a superficial or deceptively attractive appearance

[2]**veneer** *v* **1** to overlay (e g a common wood) with veneer; *broadly* to face with a material giving a superior surface **2** to conceal under a superficial and deceptive attractiveness

venerable /'venərəbəl/ *adj* **1** – used as a title for an Anglican archdeacon, or for a Roman Catholic who has been accorded the lowest of 3 degrees of recognition for sanctity **2** made sacred, esp by religious or historical association **3a** commanding respect through age, character, and attainments **b** impressive by reason of age

venerate /'venəreɪt/ *v* to regard with reverence or admiring deference – **-ration** *n*

venereal /vʃ'nɪərɪəl/ *adj* **1** of sexual desire or sexual intercourse **2** resulting from or contracted during sexual intercourse

venereal disease /vʃ'nɪərɪəl/ *n* a contagious disease (e g gonorrhoea or syphilis) that is typically acquired during sexual intercourse

venetian blind /vʃˌniːʃən 'blaɪnd/ *n* a blind (e g for a window) made of horizontal slats that may be adjusted so as to vary the amount of light admitted

vengeance /'vendʒəns/ *n* punishment inflicted in retaliation for injury or offence

venial /'viːnɪəl/ *adj* forgivable, pardonable

venison /'venʃsən/ *n* the flesh of a deer as food

venom /'venəm/ *n* **1** poisonous matter normally secreted by snakes, scorpions, bees, etc and transmitted chiefly by biting or stinging **2** ill will, malevolence

venomous /'venəməs/ *adj* **1a** poisonous **b** spiteful, malevolent **2** able to inflict a poisoned wound – **~ly** *adv*

venous /'viːnəs/ *adj, of blood* containing carbon dioxide rather than oxygen

[1]**vent** /vent/ *v* to give (vigorous) expression to

[2]**vent** *n* **1** a means of escape or release; an outlet – chiefly in *give vent to* **2a** the anus of a bird or reptile **b** an outlet

of a volcano **c** a hole at the breech of a gun through which the powder is ignited

[3]**vent** *n* a slit in a garment; *specif* an opening in the lower part of a seam (e g of a jacket or skirt)

ventilate /'ventɨleɪt/ *v* **1** to examine freely and openly; expose publicly **2** to cause fresh air to circulate through – **-lation** *n*

ventilator /'ventɨleɪtəʳ/ *n* an apparatus or aperture for introducing fresh air or expelling stagnant air

ventral /'ventrəl/ *adj* **1a** abdominal **b** relating to or situated near or on the front or lower surface of an animal or aircraft opposite the back **2** being or located on the lower or inner surface of a plant structure – **~ly** *adv*

ventricle /'ventrɪkəl/ *n* a chamber of the heart which receives blood from a corresponding atrium and from which blood is pumped into the arteries

ventriloquism /ven'trɪləkwɪzəm/ *n* the production of the voice in such a manner that the sound appears to come from a source other than the vocal organs of the speaker and esp from a dummy manipulated by the producer of the sound – **-ist** *n*

[1]**venture** /'ventʃəʳ/ *v* **1** to proceed despite danger; dare to go or do **2** to offer at the risk of opposition or censure

[2]**venture** *n* **1** an undertaking involving chance, risk, or danger, esp in business **2** sthg (e g money or property) at risk in a speculative venture – **~r** *n*

venturesome /'ventʃəsəm/ *adj* **1** ready to take risks; daring **2** involving risk; hazardous – **~ness** *n*

venue /'venjuː/ *n* the place where a gathering takes place

Venus /'viːnəs/ *n* the planet second in order from the sun

veracious /və'reɪʃəs/ *adj* true, accurate; *also* truthful – **-city** *n*

veranda, verandah /və'rændə/ *n* a usu roofed open structure attached to the outside of a building

verb /vɜːb/ *n* any of a class of words that characteristically are the grammatical centre of a predicate and express an act, occurrence, or mode of being

[1]**verbal** /'vɜːbəl/ *adj* **1** of, involving, or expressed in words **2** of or formed from a verb **3** spoken rather than written; oral **4** verbatim, word-for-word

[2]**verbal** *n, Br* a spoken statement; *esp* one made to the police admitting or implying guilt and used in evidence

verbatim /vɜː'beɪtɨm/ *adv or adj* in the exact words

verbiage /'vɜːbi-ɪdʒ/ *n* wordiness, verbosity

verbose /vɜː'bəʊs/ *adj* **1** containing more words than necessary **2** given to wordiness – **~ly** *adv* – **-sity, ~ness** *n*

verdant /'vɜːdənt/ *adj* green in tint or colour; *esp* green with growing plants – **-dancy** *n*

verdict /'vɜːdɪkt/ *n* **1** the decision of a jury on the matter submitted to them **2** an opinion, judgment

verdigris /'vɜːdɨgrɪs/ *n* a green or bluish deposit formed on copper, brass, or bronze surfaces

[1]**verge** /vɜːdʒ/ *n* **1** an outer margin of an object or structural part **2** the brink, threshold **3** *Br* a surfaced or planted strip of land at the side of a road

[2]**verge** *v* to move or extend *towards* a specified condition

verger /'vɜːdʒəʳ/ *n* a church official who keeps order during services or serves as an usher or sacristan

verify /'verɨfaɪ/ *v* **1** to ascertain the truth, accuracy, or reality of **2** to bear out, fulfil – **-fiable** *adj* – **-fication** *n*

verily /'verɨli/ *adv, archaic* **1** indeed, certainly **2** truly, confidently

veritable /'verɨtəbəl/ *adj* being in fact the thing named and not false or imaginary – often used to stress the aptness of a metaphor – **-bly** *adv*

verity /'verɨti/ *n* **1** the quality or state of being true or real **2** sthg (e g a statement) that is true; *esp* a permanently true value or principle

vermiform /'vɜːmɨfɔːm/ *adj* resembling a worm in shape

vermilion, vermillion /və'mɪlɪən/ *adj or n* (of the brilliant red colour of) mercuric sulphide used as a pigment

vermin /'vɜːmɨn/ *n* **1** *pl* lice, rats, or other common harmful or objectionable animals **2** an offensive person – **~ous** *adj*

vermouth /'vɜːməθ/ *n* a dry or sweet alcoholic drink that has a white wine base and is flavoured with aromatic herbs

[1]**vernacular** /və'nækjʊləʳ/ *adj* **1** expressed or written in a language or dialect native to a region or country rather than a literary, learned, or foreign language **2** of or being the common building style of a period or place

[2]**vernacular** *n* the mode of expression of a group or class

vernal /'vɜːnl/ *adj* **1** of or occurring in the spring **2** fresh, youthful

verruca /və'ruːkə/ *n* **1** a wart or warty skin growth **2** a warty prominence on a plant or animal

versatile /'vɜːsətaɪl/ *adj* **1** embracing a variety of subjects, fields, or skills; *also* turning with ease from one thing to another **2** having many uses or applications – **-tility** *n*

verse /vɜːs/ *n* **1** a line of metrical writing **2** poetry; *esp* undistinguished poetry **3** a stanza **4** any of the short divisions into which a chapter of the Bible is traditionally divided

versed /vɜːst/ *adj* possessing a thorough knowledge (cf) or skill *in*

versify /'vɜːsɪ̆faɪ/ *v* to compose verses – **-fier** *n* – **-fication** *n*

version /'vɜːʃən/ *n* **1** an account or description from a particular point of view, esp as contrasted with another account **2** an adaptation of a work of art into another medium **3** a form or variant of a type or original

versus /'vɜːsəs/ *prep* **1** against **2** in contrast to or as the alternative of

vertebra /'vɜːtɪ̆brə/ *n, pl* **vertebrae** any of the bony or cartilaginous segments composing the spinal column – **~l** *adj*

[1]**vertebrate** /'vɜːtɪ̆brɪ̆t, -breɪt/ *adj* **1** having a spinal column **2** of the vertebrates

[2]**vertebrate** *n* any of a large group of animals (e g mammals, birds, reptiles, amphibians, and fishes) with a segmented backbone

vertex /'vɜːteks/ *n, pl* **vertices** **1a** the point opposite to and farthest from the base in a figure **b** the zenith **2** the highest point; the summit

vertical /'vɜːtɪkəl/ *adj* **1** situated at the highest point; directly overhead or in the zenith **2** perpendicular to the plane of the horizon **3** of or concerning the relationships between people of different rank in a hierarchy – **~ly** *adv*

vertigo /'vɜːtɪgəʊ/ *n* a disordered state in which the individual loses balance and the surroundings seem to whirl dizzily – **-ginous** *adj*

verve /vɜːv/ *n* **1** the spirit and enthusiasm animating artistic work **2** energy, vitality

[1]**very** /'veri/ *adj* **1** properly so called; actual, genuine **2** absolute (e g the *very* thing for the purpose) **3** being no more than; mere (e g the *very* thought terrified me) *USE* used attributively

[2]**very** *adv* **1** to a high degree; exceedingly **2**. – used as an intensive to emphasize *same, own,* or the superlative degree

very high frequency *n* a radio frequency in the range between 30MHz and 300MHz

vesicle /'vesɪkəl/ *n* **1** a membranous usu fluid-filled pouch (e g a cyst, vacuole, or cell) in a plant or animal **2** a pocket of embryonic tissue from which an organ develops – **-cular** *adj*

vespers /'vespəz/ *n* a service of evening worship

vessel /'vesəl/ *n* **1** a hollow utensil (e g a jug, cup, or bowl) for holding esp liquid **2** a large hollow structure designed to float on and move through water carrying a crew, passengers, or cargo **3a** a tube or canal (e g an artery) in which a body fluid is contained and conveyed or circulated **b** a conducting tube in a plant

[1]**vest** /vest/ *v* **1** to endow with a particular authority, right, or property **2** to robe in ecclesiastical vestments

[2]**vest** *n* **1** *chiefly Br* a usu sleeveless undergarment for the upper body **2** *chiefly NAm* a waistcoat

vested interest *n* an interest (e g in an existing political or social arrangement) in which the holder has a strong personal commitment

vestibule /'vestɪ̆bjuːl/ *n* **1** a lobby or chamber between the outer door and the interior of a building **2** any of various bodily cavities, esp when serving as or resembling an entrance to some other cavity or space

vestige /ˈvestɪdʒ/ *n* **1a** a trace or visible sign left by sthg vanished or lost **b** a minute remaining amount **2** a small or imperfectly formed body part or organ that remains from one more fully developed in an earlier stage of the individual, in a past generation, or in closely related forms – **-gial** *adj*

vestment /ˈvestmənt/ *n* any of the ceremonial garments and insignia worn by ecclesiastical officiants and assistants as appropriate to their rank and to the rite being celebrated

vestry /ˈvestri/ *n* **1a** a sacristy **b** a room used for church meetings and classes **2** the business meeting of an English parish

¹vet /vet/ *n* sby qualified and authorized to treat diseases and injuries of animals

²vet *v, chiefly Br* to subject to careful and thorough appraisal

vetch /vetʃ/ *n* any of a genus of climbing or twining leguminous plants including valuable fodder and soil-improving plants

veteran /ˈvetərən/ *n* **1** sby who has had long experience of an occupation, skill, or (military) service **2 veteran, veteran car** *Br* an old motor car; *specif* one built before 1916 **3** *NAm* a former serviceman

veterinary /ˈvetərɪnəri/ *adj* of or being the medical care of animals, esp domestic animals

¹veto /ˈviːtəʊ/ *n* a right to declare inoperative decisions made by others; *esp* a power vested in a chief executive to prevent permanently or temporarily the enactment of measures passed by a legislature

²veto *v* to subject to a veto – **vetoer** *n*

vex /veks/ *v* **vexed** *also* **vext** **1a** to bring distress, discomfort, or agitation to **b** to irritate or annoy by petty provocations; harass **2** to puzzle, baffle – **~ation** *n* – **~atious** *adj* – **~atiously** *adv*

via /ˈvaɪə/ *prep* **1** passing through or calling at (a place) on the way **2** through the medium of; *also* by means of

viable /ˈvaɪəbəl/ *adj* **1** (born alive and developed enough to be) capable of living **2** capable of working; practicable – **-bility** *n* – **-bly** *adv*

viaduct /ˈvaɪədʌkt/ *n* a usu long bridge, esp on a series of arches, that carries a road, railway, canal, etc over a deep valley

vibrant /ˈvaɪbrənt/ *adj* **1a** oscillating or pulsating rapidly **b** pulsating with life, vigour, or activity **2** sounding as a result of vibration; resonant – **~ly** *adv* – **-ancy** *n*

vibraphone /ˈvaɪbrəfəʊn/ *n* a percussion instrument resembling the xylophone but having metal bars and motor-driven resonators for sustaining its sound and producing a vibrato

vibrate /vaɪˈbreɪt/ *v* **1** to move to and fro; oscillate **2** to have an effect as of vibration; throb **3** to be in a state of vibration; quiver **4** to emit (e g sound) (as if) with a vibratory motion

vibration /vaɪˈbreɪʃən/ *n* **1a** a periodic motion of the particles of an elastic body or medium in alternately opposite directions from a position of equilibrium **b** an oscillation or quivering **2** a distinctive usu emotional atmosphere capable of being sensed – usu pl with sing. meaning – **-tory** *adj*

vibrato /vɪˈbrɑːtəʊ/ *n* a slightly tremulous effect imparted to musical tone to add expressiveness, by slight and rapid variations in pitch

vicar /ˈvɪkəʳ/ *n* a Church of England incumbent receiving a stipend but formerly not the tithes of a parish

vicarage /ˈvɪkərɪdʒ/ *n* the benefice or house of a vicar

vicarious /vɪˈkeərɪəs/ *adj* **1** performed or suffered by one person as a substitute for, or to the benefit of, another **2** experienced through imaginative participation in the experience of another – **~ly** *adv* – **~ness** *n*

¹vice /vaɪs/ *n* **1a** moral depravity or corruption; wickedness **b** a habitual and usu minor fault or shortcoming **2** sexual immorality; *esp* prostitution

²vice, *NAm chiefly* **vise** *n* any of various tools, usu attached to a workbench, that have 2 jaws that close for holding work by operation of a screw, lever, or cam

vice-chancellor *n* an officer ranking next below a chancellor; *esp* the administrative head of a British university

viceroy /'vaɪsrɔɪ/ *n* the governor of a country or province who rules as the representative of his sovereign – **viceregal** *adj*

vice versa /ˌvaɪs 'vɜːsə, ˌvaɪsi-/ *adv* with the order changed and relations reversed; conversely

vicinity /vɨ'sɪnɨti/ *n* **1** a surrounding area or district **2** being near; proximity – fml

vicious /'vɪʃəs/ *adj* **1** having the nature or quality of vice; depraved **2** unpleasantly fierce, malignant, or severe **3** malicious, spiteful – **~ly** *adv* – **~ness** *n*

vicious circle *n* **1** a chain of events in which the apparent solution of 1 difficulty creates a new problem that makes the original difficulty worse **2** the logical fallacy of using 1 argument or definition to prove or define a second on which the first depends

victim /'vɪktɨm/ *n* sby or sthg that is adversely affected by a force or agent: e g **a** one who or that which is injured, destroyed, or subjected to oppression or mistreatment **b** a dupe, prey – **~ize** *v*

victor /'vɪktəʳ/ *n* a person, country, etc that defeats an enemy or opponent; a winner

Victoria Cross *n* a bronze Maltese cross that is the highest British military decoration

¹Victorian /vɪk'tɔːrɪən/ *adj* **1** (characteristic) of the reign of Queen Victoria or the art, letters, or taste of her time **2** typical of the moral standards or conduct of the age of Queen Victoria, esp in being prudish or hypocritical

²Victorian *n* sby living during Queen Victoria's reign

victorious /vɪk'tɔːrɪəs/ *adj* **1a** having won a victory **b** (characteristic) of victory **2** successful, triumphant – **~ly** *adv*

victory /'vɪktəri/ *n* **1** the overcoming of an enemy or antagonist **2** achievement of mastery or success in a struggle or endeavour

victualler, *NAm also* **victualer** /'vɪtələʳ/ *n* **1** a publican **2** sby who or sthg that provisions an army, a navy, or a ship with food

vide /'viːdi, 'vaɪdi/ *v imper* see – used to direct a reader to another item

¹video /'vɪdiəʊ/ *adj* of a form of magnetic recording for reproduction on a television screen

²video, videorecorder, videocassette recorder *n* a machine for videotaping

video nasty *n* a video film of (allegedly) sensational nature, usu including scenes of explicit sex, violence, and horror

videotape /'vɪdiəʊteɪp/ *v* to make a recording of (e g sthg that is televised) on magnetic tape

vie /vaɪ/ *v* **vying; vied** to strive for superiority; contend

¹view /vjuː/ *n* **1** the act of seeing or examining; inspection; *also* a survey **2** a way of regarding sthg; an opinion **3** a scene, prospect; *also* an aspect **4** extent or range of vision; sight **5** an intention, object **6** a pictorial representation

²view *v* **1a** to see, watch; *also* to watch television **b** to look on in a specified way; regard **2** to look at attentively; inspect

viewer /'vjuːəʳ/ *n* **1** an optical device used in viewing **2** sby who watches television

viewfinder /'vjuːfaɪndəʳ/ *n* a device on a camera for showing what will be included in the picture

viewpoint /'vjuːpɔɪnt/ *n* a standpoint; point of view

vigil /'vɪdʒɨl/ *n* **1** a devotional watch formerly kept on the night before a religious festival **2** the act of keeping awake at times when sleep is customary; *also* a period of wakefulness **3** an act or period of watching or surveillance; a watch

vigilant /'vɪdʒɨlənt/ *adj* alert and watchful, esp to avoid danger – **~ly** *adv* – **-ance** *n*

vigorous /'vɪgərəs/ *adj* **1** possessing or showing vigour; full of active strength **2** done with vigour; carried out forcefully and energetically – **~ly** *adv*

vigour /'vɪgəʳ/ *n* **1** active physical or

mental strength or force **2** active healthy well-balanced growth, esp of plants **3** intensity of action or effect; force

Viking /'vaɪkɪŋ/ *n* **1** a Norse trader and warrior of the 8th to 10th c **2** a Scandinavian

vile /vaɪl/ *adj* **1a** morally despicable or abhorrent **b** physically repulsive; foul **2** tending to degrade **3** disgustingly or utterly bad; contemptible – ~**ly** *adv* – ~**ness** *n*

vilify /'vɪlɨfaɪ/ *v* to utter slanderous and abusive statements against; defame – **-fication** *n*

villa /'vɪlə/ *n* **1** a country mansion **2** an ancient Roman mansion and the surrounding agricultural estate **3** *Br* a detached or semidetached suburban house, usu having a garden and built before WW I

village /'vɪlɪdʒ/ *n* a group of dwellings in the country, larger than a hamlet and smaller than a town

villain /'vɪlən/ *n* **1** a scoundrel, rascal; *also* a criminal **2** a character in a story or play whose evil actions affect the plot – ~**ous** *adj*

villainy /'vɪləni/ *n* **1** villainous conduct; *also* a villainous act **2** depravity

villein /'vɪlɨn, -leɪn/ *n* **1** a free village peasant **2** an unfree peasant standing as the slave of his feudal lord

vim /vɪm/ *n* robust energy and enthusiasm – infml

vinaigrette /,vɪnɨ'gret, ,vɪneɪ-/ *n* **1** a small ornamental box or bottle with a perforated top used for holding an aromatic preparation (e g smelling salts) **2** a sharp sauce of oil and vinegar flavoured with salt, pepper, mustard, herbs, etc and used esp on green salads

vindicate /'vɪndɨkeɪt/ *v* **1a** to exonerate, absolve **b** to provide justification for; justify **2** to maintain the existence of; uphold – **-cation** *n*

vindictive /vɪn'dɪktɪv/ *adj* **1a** disposed to seek revenge; vengeful **b** intended as revenge **2** intended to cause anguish; spiteful – ~**ly** *adv* – ~**ness** *n*

vine /vaɪn/ *n* **1** the climbing plant that bears grapes **2** (a plant with) a stem that requires support and that climbs by tendrils or twining

vinegar /'vɪnɪgə^r/ *n* a sour liquid obtained esp by acetic fermentation of wine, cider, etc and used as a condiment or preservative – ~**y** *adj*

vineyard /'vɪnjəd/ *n* a plantation of grapevines

vino /'viːnəʊ/ *n* wine – infml

vinous /'vaɪnəs/ *adj* **1** of or made with wine **2** (showing the effects of being) addicted to wine

[1]**vintage** /'vɪntɪdʒ/ *n* **1a** wine, specif one of a particular type, region, and year and usu of superior quality that is dated and allowed to mature **b** a collection of contemporaneous and similar people or things; a crop **2** the act or time of harvesting grapes or making wine

[2]**vintage** *adj* **1** of a vintage; *esp* being a product of 1 particular year rather than a blend of wines from different years **2** of the best and most characteristic; classic **3** *Br, of a motor vehicle* built between 1917 and 1930

vintner /'vɪntnə^r/ *n* a wine merchant

vinyl /'vaɪnɨl/ *n* a plastic derived from ethylene

viol /'vaɪəl/ *n* any of a family of bowed stringed instruments chiefly of the 16th and 17th c with usu 6 strings and a fretted fingerboard, played resting on or between the player's knees

[1]**viola** /'vaɪələ, vaɪ'əʊlə/ *n* a musical instrument of the violin family that is intermediate in size and range between the violin and cello and is tuned a 5th below the violin

[2]**viola** *n* a violet; *esp* any of various cultivated violets with (variegated) flowers resembling pansies

violate /'vaɪəleɪt/ *v* **1** to fail to comply with; infringe **2** to do harm to; *specif* to rape – **-lation** *n*

violence /'vaɪələns/ *n* **1** (an instance of) exertion of physical force so as to injure or abuse **2** unjust or unwarranted distortion; outrage **3a** intense or turbulent action or force **b** (an instance of) vehement feeling or expression; fervour

violent /'vaɪələnt/ *adj* **1** marked by extreme force or sudden intense activity **2** notably furious or vehement; *also* excited or mentally disordered to the point of loss of self-control – ~**ly** *adv*

violet /'vaɪələ̩t/ *n* **1** any of a genus of plants with often sweet-scented flowers, usu of all 1 colour, esp as distinguished from the usu larger-flowered violas and pansies **2** a bluish purple colour

violin /ˌvaɪə'lɪn/ *n* a bowed stringed instrument having a fingerboard with no frets, 4 strings, and a usual range from G below middle C upwards for more than 4½ octaves – ~**ist** *n*

violoncello /ˌvaɪələn'tʃeləʊ/ *n* a cello

VIP *n, pl* **VIPs** a person of great influence or prestige

viper /'vaɪpəʳ/ *n* **1** (any of various snakes related to) the adder **2** a malignant or treacherous person

virago /və̩'rɑːgəʊ/ *n* **1** a loud overbearing woman; a termagant **2** *archaic* a woman of great stature, strength, and courage

[1]**virgin** /'vɜːdʒə̩n/ *n* a person, esp a girl, who has not had sexual intercourse – ~**ity** *n*

[2]**virgin** *adj* **1** free of impurity or stain; unsullied **2** being a virgin **3** characteristic of or befitting a virgin; modest **4** untouched, unexploited; *specif* not altered by human activity

[1]**virginal** /'vɜːdʒə̩nl/ *adj* **1** (characteristic) of a virgin or virginity; *esp* pure, chaste **2** fresh, untouched, uncorrupted

[2]**virginal** *n* a small rectangular harpsichord popular in the 16th and 17th c – often pl with sing. meaning

Virgo /'vɜːgəʊ/ *n* (sby born under) the 6th sign of the zodiac in astrology, which is pictured as a woman holding an ear of corn

virile /'vɪraɪl/ *adj* **1** having the nature, properties, or qualities (often thought of as typical) of a man; *specif* capable of functioning as a male in copulation **2** vigorous, forceful – **-ility** *n*

virology /vaɪə'rɒlədʒi/ *n* a branch of science that deals with viruses – **-gist** *n*

virtual /'vɜːtʃʊəl/ *adj* that is such in essence or effect though not formally recognized or admitted

virtually /'vɜːtʃʊəli/ *adv* almost entirely; for all practical purposes

virtue /'vɜːtʃuː/ *n* **1a** conformity to a standard of right; morality **b** a particular moral excellence **2** a beneficial or commendable quality **3** a capacity to act; potency **4** chastity, esp in a woman

virtuoso /ˌvɜːtʃʊ'əʊzəʊ/ *n, pl* **virtuosos, virtuosi** one who excels in the technique of an art, esp in musical performance – **virtuoso** *adj*

virtuous /'vɜːtʃʊəs/ *adj* **1** having or exhibiting virtue; *esp* morally excellent; righteous **2** chaste – ~**ly** *adv*

virulent /'vɪrʊlənt/ *adj* **1** *of a disease* severe and developing rapidly **2** extremely poisonous or venomous **3** full of malice; malignant – ~**ly** *adv* – **-ence, -ency** *n*

virus /'vaɪərəs/ *n* (a disease caused by) any of a large group of submicroscopic often disease-causing agents that typically consist of a protein coat surrounding an RNA or DNA core and that multiply only in living cells

visa /'viːzə/ *n* an endorsement made on a passport by the proper authorities (e g of a country at entrance or exit) denoting that the bearer may proceed

visage /'vɪzɪdʒ/ *n* a face, countenance; *also* an aspect – fml or poetic

vis-à-vis /ˌviːz ɑː 'viː, ˌviːz ə 'viː/ *prep* **1** face to face with; opposite **2** in relation to

viscera /'vɪsərə/ *n pl* the internal body organs collectively – ~**l** *adj*

viscosity /vɪs'kɒsə̩ti/ *n* **1** being viscous **2** (a measure of the force needed to overcome) the property of a liquid, gas, or semifluid that enables it to offer resistance to flow

viscount /'vaɪkaʊnt/ *n* a member of the peerage in Britain ranking below an earl and above a baron – ~**cy** *n*

viscountess /'vaɪkaʊntə̩s/ *n* **1** the wife or widow of a viscount **2** a woman having the rank of a viscount

viscous /'vɪskəs/ *adj* **1** sticky, adhesive **2** having or characterized by (high) viscosity

visibility /ˌvɪzə'bɪlə̩ti/ *n* **1** being visible **2** the clearness of the atmosphere as revealed by the greatest distance at which prominent objects can be identified visually with the naked eye

visible /ˈvɪzəbəl/ *adj* **1** capable of being seen **2** exposed to view **3** capable of being perceived; noticeable **4** of or being trade in goods rather than services

vision /ˈvɪʒən/ *n* **1** sthg (revelatory) seen in a dream, trance, or ecstasy **2** discernment, foresight **3a** the act or power of seeing; sight **b** the sense by which the qualities of an object (e g colour, luminosity, shape, and size) constituting its appearance are perceived and which acts through the eye **4** a lovely or charming sight

¹visionary /ˈvɪʒənəri/ *adj* **1a** able or likely to see visions **b** disposed to daydreaming or imagining; dreamy **2** impracticable, utopian

²visionary *n* **1** one who sees visions; a seer **2** one whose ideas or projects are impractical; a dreamer

¹visit /ˈvɪzɪ̣t/ *v* **1a** to afflict **b** to inflict punishment for **2a** to pay a call on for reasons of kindness, friendship, ceremony, or business **b** to go or come to look at or stay at (e g for business or sightseeing)

²visit *n* **1a** an act of visiting; a call **b** an extended but temporary stay **2** an official or professional call; a visitation

visitation /ˌvɪzɪ̣ˈteɪʃən/ *n* **1** the act or an instance of visiting; *esp* an official visit (e g for inspection) **2a** a special dispensation of divine favour or wrath **b** a severe trial; an affliction

visiting card *n* a small card of introduction bearing the name and sometimes the address and profession of the owner

visitor /ˈvɪzɪ̣təʳ/ *n* sby who or sthg that makes (formal) visits

visor, vizor /ˈvaɪzəʳ/ *n* **1** the (movable) part of a helmet that covers the face **2** a usu movable flat sunshade attached at the top of a vehicle windscreen **3** *chiefly NAm* a peak on a cap

vista /ˈvɪstə/ *n* **1** a distant view esp through or along an avenue or opening; a prospect **2** an extensive mental view (e g over a stretch of time or a series of events)

visual /ˈvɪʒʊəl/ *adj* **1** visible **2** producing mental images; vivid **3** done or executed by sight only

visual display unit *n* a device that has a cathode ray tube on which information (held in a computer) may be displayed or updated; a VDU

visual·ize, -ise /ˈvɪʒʊəlaɪz/ *v* to see or form a mental picture of

vital /ˈvaɪtl/ *adj* **1** concerned with or necessary to the maintenance of life **2** full of life and vigour; animated **3** of the utmost importance; essential to continued worth or well-being – **~ly** *adv*

vitality /vaɪˈtælɪ̣ti/ *n* **1a** the quality which distinguishes the living from the dead or inanimate **b** capacity to live and develop; *also* physical or mental liveliness **2** power of enduring

vitals /ˈvaɪtlz/ *n pl* **1** the vital organs (e g the heart, liver, or brain) **2** essential parts

vital statistics *n pl* **1** statistics relating to births, deaths, health, etc **2** facts considered to be interesting or important; *specif* a woman's bust, waist, and hip measurements

vitamin /ˈvɪtəmɪ̣n, ˈvaɪ-/ *n* any of various organic compounds that are essential in minute quantities to the nutrition of most animals and regulate metabolic processes

vitiate /ˈvɪʃieɪt/ *v* **1** to make faulty or defective; debase **2** to invalidate – **-ation** *n*

vitreous /ˈvɪtrɪəs/ *adj* resembling glass in colour, composition, brittleness, etc

vituperate /vɪˈtjuːpəreɪt/ *v* to use harsh condemnatory language – **-ation** *n* – **-ative** *adj*

vivacious /vɪ̣ˈveɪʃəs/ *adj* lively in temper or conduct; sprightly – **~ly** *adv* – **vivacity** *n* – **~ness** *n*

vivarium /vaɪˈveərɪəm/ *n* an enclosure for keeping and observing plants or esp terrestrial animals indoors

viva voce /ˌviːvə ˈvəʊtʃi, ˌvaɪvə-, -ˈvəʊsi/ *n, adj, or adv* (an examination conducted) by word of mouth

vivid /ˈvɪvɪ̣d/ *adj* **1** *of a colour* very intense **2** producing a strong or clear impression on the senses; *specif* producing distinct mental images – **~ly** *adv* – **~ness** *n*

viviparous /vɪˈvɪpərəs/ *adj* producing

living young, instead of eggs, from within the body in the manner of nearly all mammals, many reptiles, and a few fishes

vivisect /ˈvɪvɪ̈sekt/ *v* to perform an operation on (a living animal), esp for experimental purposes – **~ion** *n* – **~ionist** *n*

vixen /ˈvɪksən/ *n* **1** a female fox **2** a scolding ill-tempered woman

vizier /vɪ̈ˈzɪəʳ/ *n* a high executive officer of various Muslim countries, esp of the former Ottoman Empire

vocabulary /vəˈkæbjʊləri, vəʊ-/ *n* **1** a list of words, and sometimes phrases, usu arranged alphabetically and defined or translated **2** the words employed by a language, group, or individual or in a field of work or knowledge **3** a supply of expressive techniques or devices (e g of an art form)

¹vocal /ˈvəʊkəl/ *adj* **1** uttered by the voice; oral **2** of, composed or arranged for, or sung by the human voice **3a** having or exercising the power of producing voice, speech, or sound **b** given to strident or insistent expression; outspoken – **~ly** *adv*

²vocal *n* **1** a vocal sound **2** a usu accompanied musical composition or passage for the voice

vocalist /ˈvəʊkəlɪ̈st/ *n* a singer

vocation /vəʊˈkeɪʃən/ *n* **1** a summons or strong inclination to a particular state or course of action; *esp* a divine call to the religious life **2** the work in which a person is regularly employed; a career

vocational /vəʊˈkeɪʃənəl/ *adj* of or being training in a skill or trade to be pursued as a career

vocative /ˈvɒkətɪv/ *n* (a form in) a grammatical case expressing the one addressed

vociferate /vəˈsɪfəreɪt, vəʊ-/ *v* to cry out or utter loudly; clamour, shout – **-ation** *n*

vociferous /vəˈsɪfərəs, vəʊ-/ *adj* marked by or given to vehement insistent outcry – **~ly** *adv* – **~ness** *n*

vodka /ˈvɒdkə/ *n* a colourless and unaged neutral spirit distilled from a mash (e g of rye or wheat)

vogue /vəʊg/ *n* **1** the prevailing, esp temporary, fashion **2** popular acceptance or favour; popularity

¹voice /vɔɪs/ *n* **1a** sound produced by humans, birds, etc by forcing air from the lungs through the larynx in mammals or syrinx in birds **b(1)** (the use, esp in singing or acting, of) musical sound produced by the vocal cords and resonated by the cavities of the head, throat, lungs, etc **(2)** any of the melodic parts in a vocal or instrumental composition **c** the faculty of utterance; speech **2a** the expressed wish or opinion **b** right of expression; say **3** distinction of form or a particular system of inflections of a verb to indicate whether it is the subject of the verb that acts

²voice *v* **1** to express (a feeling or opinion) in words; utter **2** to adjust (e g an organ pipe) in manufacture, for producing the proper musical sounds

voice box *n* the larynx

¹void /vɔɪd/ *adj* **1** containing nothing; unoccupied **2a** devoid **b** having no members or examples; *specif, of a suit* having no cards represented in a particular hand **3** vain, useless **4** of no legal effect

²void *n* **1a** empty space; vacuum **b** an opening, gap **2** a feeling of lack, want, or emptiness

³void *v* **1** to make empty or vacant; clear **2** to discharge or emit

voile /vɔɪl/ *n* a fine soft sheer fabric used esp for women's summer clothing or curtains

volatile /ˈvɒlətaɪl/ *adj* **1** capable of being readily vaporized at a relatively low temperature **2a** lighthearted, lively **b** dangerously unstable; explosive **3a** frivolously changeable; fickle **b** characterized by rapid change

vol-au-vent /ˌvɒl əʊ ˈvã/ *n* a round case of puff pastry filled with a mixture of meat, poultry, or fish in a thick sauce

volcanic /vɒlˈkænɪk/ *adj* explosively violent; volatile

volcano /vɒlˈkeɪnəʊ/ *n, pl* **volcanoes, volcanos** **1** (a hill or mountain surrounding) an outlet in a planet's crust from which molten or hot rock and steam issue **2** a dynamic or violently creative person; *also* a situation liable to become violent

vole /vəʊl/ *n* any of various small plant-eating rodents usu with a stout body, blunt nose, and short ears

volition /və'lɪʃən/ *n* **1** (an act of making) a free choice or decision **2** the power of choosing or determining; will – **~al** *adj*

[1]**volley** /'vɒli/ *n* **1a** simultaneous discharge of a number of missile weapons **b** a return or succession of returns made by hitting a ball, shuttle, etc before it touches the ground **2** a burst or emission of many things at once or in rapid succession

[2]**volley** *v* **1** to discharge (as if) in a volley **2** to propel (an object that has not yet hit the ground), esp with an implement or the hand or foot

volleyball /'vɒlibɔːl/ *n* a game between 2 teams of usu 6 players who volley a ball over a high net in the centre of a court

volt /vəʊlt/ *n* the derived SI unit of electrical potential difference and electromotive force equal to the difference of potential between 2 points in a conducting wire carrying a constant current of 1 ampere when the power dissipated between these 2 points is equal to 1 watt

voltage /'vəʊltɪdʒ/ *n* an electric potential difference; electromotive force

volte-face /ˌvɒlt 'fɑːs/ *n* a sudden reversal of attitude or policy; an about-face

voltmeter /'vəʊltˌmiːtəʳ/ *n* an instrument for measuring in volts the differences of potential between different points of an electrical circuit

voluble /'vɒljʊbəl/ *adj* characterized by ready or rapid speech; talkative – **-bility** *n* – **-bly** *adv*

volume /'vɒljuːm/ *n* **1a** a series of printed sheets bound typically in book form; a book **b** a series of issues of a periodical **2** space occupied as measured in cubic units (e g litres); cubic capacity **3a** an amount; *also* a bulk, mass **b** (the representation of) mass in art or architecture **c** a considerable quantity; a great deal – often pl with sing. meaning; esp in *speak volumes for* **4** the degree of loudness or the intensity of a sound

voluminous /və'luːmɪ̣nəs, və'ljuː-/ *adj* **1** having or containing a large volume; *specif, of a garment* very full **2** writing much or at great length – **~ly** *adv* – **~ness** *n*

[1]**voluntary** /'vɒləntəri/ *adj* **1** proceeding from free choice or consent **2** intentional **3** provided or supported by voluntary action – **-tarily** *adv*

[2]**voluntary** *n* an organ piece played before or after a religious service

[1]**volunteer** /ˌvɒlən'tɪəʳ/ *n* one who undertakes a service of his/her own free will; *esp* sby who enters into military service voluntarily

[2]**volunteer** *adj* being, consisting of, or engaged in by volunteers

[3]**volunteer** *v* **1** to communicate voluntarily; say **2** to offer oneself as a volunteer

voluptuary /və'lʌptʃʊəri/ *n* one whose chief interest is luxury and sensual pleasure

voluptuous /və'lʌptʃʊəs/ *adj* **1** causing delight or pleasure to the senses; conducive to, occupied with, or arising from sensual gratification **2** suggestive of sensual pleasure; *broadly* sexually attractive, esp owing to shapeliness – **~ly** *adv* – **~ness** *n*

[1]**vomit** /'vɒmɪt/ *n* a vomiting; *also* the vomited matter

[2]**vomit** /'vɒmɪ̣t/ *v* **1** to disgorge (the contents of the stomach) through the mouth **2** to eject (sthg) violently or abundantly; spew

[1]**voodoo** /'vuːduː/ *n* a set of magical beliefs and practices, mainly of W African origin, practised chiefly in Haiti and characterized by communication by trance with deities

[2]**voodoo** *v* to bewitch (as if) by means of voodoo

voracious /və'reɪʃəs, vɒ-/ *adj* **1** having a huge appetite; ravenous **2** excessively eager; insatiable – **~ly** *adv*

vortex /'vɔːteks/ *n, pl* **vortices** **1** a mass of whirling water, air, etc that tends to form a cavity or vacuum in the centre of the circle into which material is drawn; *esp* a whirlpool or whirlwind **2** sthg that resembles a whirlpool in violent activity or in engulfing or overwhelming

[1]**vote** /vəʊt/ *n* **1** a ballot **2** the collective verdict of a body of people expressed by voting **3** *the* franchise **4** a sum of money voted for a special use

[2]**vote** *v* **1** to cast one's vote; *esp* to exercise a political franchise **2a** to judge by general agreement; declare **b** to offer as a suggestion; propose

vouch /vaʊtʃ/ *v* **1** to give or act as a guarantee *for* **2** to supply supporting evidence or personal assurance *for*

voucher /ˈvaʊtʃəʳ/ *n, Br* a ticket that can be exchanged for specific goods or services

vouchsafe /vaʊtʃˈseɪf/ *v* **1** to grant as a special privilege or in a gracious or condescending manner **2** to condescend, deign *to* do sthg

[1]**vow** /vaʊ/ *n* a solemn and often religiously binding promise or assertion; *specif* one by which a person binds him-/herself to an act, service, or condition

[2]**vow** *v* **1** to promise solemnly; swear **2** to resolve to bring about

vowel /ˈvaʊəl/ *n* (a letter, in English usu *a, e, i, o, u,* and sometimes *y,* representing) any of a class of speech sounds (e g /iː, aː, ʌ/) characterized by lack of closure in the breath channel or lack of audible friction

vox populi /ˌvɒks ˈpɒpjʊli/ *n* the opinion of the general public

[1]**voyage** /ˈvɔɪ-ɪdʒ/ *n* a considerable course or period of travelling by other than land routes; *broadly* a journey

[2]**voyage** *v* to make a voyage (across) – ~r *n*

voyeur /vwɑːˈjɜːʳ/ *n* **1** one who gains sexual satisfaction by looking, esp at sexual acts, organs, etc **2** a prying observer who is usu seeking the sordid or scandalous

V sign *n* a gesture made by raising the index and middle fingers in a V **a** with the palm outwards signifying victory **b** with the palm inwards signifying insult or contempt

vulcan·ize, -ise /ˈvʌlkənaɪz/ *v* to treat rubber so as to make more suitable for certain purposes (e g making tyres)

vulgar /ˈvʌlgəʳ/ *adj* **1** generally used, applied, or accepted **2a** of or being the common people; plebeian **b** generally current; public **3a** lacking in cultivation, breeding, or taste; coarse **b** ostentatious or excessive in expenditure or display; pretentious **4** lewdly or profanely indecent; obscene – ~**ize** *v* – ~**ly** *adv* – ~**ity** *n*

vulgar fraction *n* a fraction in which both the denominator and numerator are explicitly present and are separated by a horizontal or slanted line

vulgarian /vʌlˈgeərɪən/ *n* a vulgar and esp rich person

vulgarism /ˈvʌlgərɪzəm/ *n* **1** a word or expression originated or used chiefly by illiterate people **2** vulgarity

vulnerable /ˈvʌlnərəbəl/ *adj* **1** capable of being physically or mentally wounded **2** open to attack or damage; assailable – **-bility** *n* – **-bly** *adv*

vulture /ˈvʌltʃəʳ/ *n* any of various large usu bald-headed birds of prey that are related to the hawks, eagles, and falcons and feed on carrion

vulva /ˈvʌlvə/ *n* the (opening between the projecting) external parts of the female genital organs

vying /ˈvaɪ-ɪŋ/ *pres part of* **vie**

W

w /'dʌbəljuː/ *n, pl* **w's, ws** *often cap* (a graphic representation of, or device for reproducing,) the 23rd letter of the English alphabet

wacky /'wæki/ *adj, chiefly NAm* absurdly or amusingly eccentric or irrational; crazy – infml – **wackiness** *n*

[1]**wad** /wɒd/ *n* **1a** a soft mass, esp of a loose fibrous material, variously used (e g to stop an aperture or pad a garment) **b** a soft plug used to retain a powder charge, esp in a muzzle-loading cannon or gun **2** a roll of paper money

[2]**wad** *v* **1** to form into a wad or wadding **2** to stuff, pad, or line with some soft substance

wadding /'wɒdɪŋ/ *n* stuffing or padding in the form of a soft mass or sheet of short loose fibres

[1]**waddle** /'wɒdl/ *v* **1** to walk with short steps swinging the forepart of the body from side to side **2** to move clumsily in a manner suggesting a waddle

[2]**waddle** *n* an awkward clumsy swaying gait

[1]**wade** /weɪd/ *v* **1** to walk through water **2** to proceed with difficulty or effort **3** to attack with determination or vigour – + *in* or *into*

[2]**wade** *n* an act of wading

wader /'weɪdəʳ/ *n* **1** *pl* high waterproof boots used for wading **2** any of many long-legged birds (e g sandpipers and snipes) that wade in water in search of food

wadge /wɒdʒ/ *n, Br* a thick bundle; a wad – infml

wadi /'wɒdi/ *n* a dry river bed in desert country, esp N Africa and Arabia

wafer /'weɪfəʳ/ *n* **1a** a thin crisp biscuit; *also* a biscuit consisting of layers of wafer sometimes sandwiched with a filling **b** a round piece of thin unleavened bread used in the celebration of the Eucharist **2** an adhesive disc of dried paste used, esp formerly, as a seal

[1]**waffle** /'wɒfəl/ *n* a cake of batter that is baked in a waffle iron and has a crisp dimpled surface

[2]**waffle** *v* to talk or write foolishly, inconsequentially, and usu at length; blather

[3]**waffle** *n* empty or pretentious words – infml

waffle iron *n* a cooking utensil with 2 hinged metal parts that shut on each other and impress surface projections on the waffle being cooked

[1]**waft** /wɒft/ *v* to convey or be conveyed lightly (as if) by the impulse of wind or waves

[2]**waft** *n* **1** sthg (e g a smell) that is wafted; a whiff **2** a slight breeze; a puff

[1]**wag** /wæg/ *v* **1** to move to and fro, esp with quick jerky motions **2** to move in chatter or gossip

[2]**wag** *n* an act of wagging; a shake

[3]**wag** *n* a wit, joker

[1]**wage** /weɪdʒ/ *v* to engage in or carry on (a war, conflict, etc)

[2]**wage** *n* **1a** a payment for services, esp of a manual kind, usu according to contract and on an hourly, daily, weekly, or piecework basis – usu pl with sing. meaning **b** *pl* the share of the national product attributable to labour as a factor in production **2** a recompense, reward

[1]**wager** /'weɪdʒəʳ/ *n* **1** sthg (e g a sum of money) risked on an uncertain event **2** sthg on which bets are laid

[2]**wager** *v* to lay as or make a bet

waggish /'wægɪʃ/ *adj* befitting or characteristic of a wag; humorous – ~**ly** *adv* – ~**ness** *n*

waggle /'wægəl/ *v* to (cause to) sway or move repeatedly from side to side; wag – **waggle** *n*

waggon, wagon /'wægən/ *n* **1** a usu 4-wheeled vehicle for carrying bulky or heavy loads; *esp* one drawn by horses **2** a railway goods vehicle

wagtail /'wægteɪl/ *n* any of numerous birds with trim slender bodies and very long tails that they habitually jerk up and down

waif /weɪf/ *n* a stray helpless person or animal; *esp* a homeless child

[1]**wail** /weɪl/ *v* **1** to express sorrow by uttering mournful cries; lament **2** to express dissatisfaction plaintively; complain

[2]**wail** *n* **1** a usu loud prolonged high-pitched cry expressing grief or pain **2** a sound suggestive of wailing

[1]**wainscot** /'weɪnskət/ *n* **1** a usu panelled wooden lining of an interior wall **2** the lower part of an interior wall when finished differently from the remainder of the wall

[2]**wainscot** *v* to line (as if) with boards or panelling

waist /weɪst/ *n* **1a** the (narrow) part of the body between the chest and hips **b** the greatly constricted part of the abdomen of a wasp, fly, etc **2** the part of sthg corresponding to or resembling the human waist; *esp* the middle part of a sailing ship between foremast and mainmast **3** the part of a garment covering the body at the waist or waistline

waistband /'weɪstbænd/ *n* a band (e g on trousers or a skirt) fitting round the waist

waistcoat /'weɪskəʊt, 'weskət/ *n, chiefly Br* a sleeveless upper garment that fastens down the centre front and usu has a V-neck; *esp* such a garment worn under a jacket as part of a man's suit

waistline /'weɪstlaɪn/ *n* **1** an imaginary line encircling the narrowest part of the waist; *also* the part of a garment corresponding to this line or to the place where fashion dictates this should be **2** body circumference at the waist

[1]**wait** /weɪt/ *v* **1a** to remain stationary in readiness or expectation **b** to pause for another to catch up **2a** to look forward expectantly **b** to hold back expectantly **3** to serve at meals – usu in *wait at table* **4** to be ready and available

[2]**wait** *n* **1** any of a group who serenade for gratuities, esp at the Christmas season **2** an act or period of waiting

waiter /'weɪtəʳ/, *fem* **waitress** /-trɨs/ *n* one who waits at table (e g in a restaurant), esp as a regular job

waive /weɪv/ *v* **1** to refrain from demanding or enforcing; relinquish, forgo **2** to put off from immediate consideration; postpone

waiver /'weɪvəʳ/ *n* (a document giving proof of) the relinquishing of a right

[1]**wake** /weɪk/ *v* **waked, woke; waked, woken, woke** **1** to rouse (as if) from sleep; awake – often + *up* **2** to arouse, evoke **3** to arouse conscious interest in; alert – usu + *to*

[2]**wake** *n* **1** a watch held over the body of a dead person prior to burial and sometimes accompanied by festivity; *broadly* any festive leavetaking **2** *Br* an annual holiday in northern England – usu pl but sing. or pl in constr

[3]**wake** *n* the track left by a ship

wakeful /'weɪkfəl/ *adj* **1** not sleeping or able to sleep **2** spent without sleep – **~ly** *adv* – **~ness** *n*

waken /'weɪkən/ *v* to awake – often + *up*

[1]**walk** /wɔːk/ **1a** to move along on foot; advance by steps, in such a way that at least 1 foot is always in contact with the ground **b** to go on foot for exercise or pleasure **2** to take (an animal) for a walk **3** to follow on foot for the purposes of examining, measuring, etc – **~er** *n*

[2]**walk** *n* **1** an act or instance of going on foot, esp for exercise or pleasure **2** a route for walking **3** a railed or colonnaded platform **4** distance to be walked **5a** the gait of a 2-legged animal in which the feet are lifted alternately with 1 foot always (partially) on the ground **b** the slow 4-beat gait of a quadruped, specif a horse, in which there are always at least 2 feet on the ground **c** a low rate of speed **6** a route regularly traversed by a person (e g a postman or policeman) in the performance of a particular activity **7** an occupation, calling – chiefly in *walk of life*

walkabout /'wɔːkəbaʊt/ *n* **1** a short period of wandering bush life engaged in occasionally by an Australian aborigine for ceremonial reasons **2** an informal walk among the crowds by a public figure

walkie-talkie /ˌwɔːki ˈtɔːki/ *n* a compact battery-operated transmitter/receiver

walk-in *adj* large enough for a person to enter and move around in

walking *adj* **1a** animate; *esp* human **b** able to walk **2a** used for or in walking **b** characterized by or consisting of walking

walk-on *n* (sby who has) a small usu nonspeaking part in a dramatic production

walkout /ˈwɔːkaʊt/ *n* **1** a strike **2** the action of leaving a meeting or organization as an expression of protest

walk out *v* **1** to go on strike **2** to depart suddenly, often as an expression of protest

walkover /ˈwɔːkˌəʊvəʳ/ *n* an easily won contest; *also* an advance from one round of a competition to the next without contest, due to the withdrawal or absence of other entrants

¹wall /wɔːl/ *n* **1** a usu upright and solid structure, esp of masonry or concrete, having considerable height and length in relation to width and serving esp to divide, enclose, retain, or support: e g **a** a structure bounding a garden, park, or estate **b** any of the upright enclosing structures of a room or house **2** a material layer enclosing space **3a** an almost vertical rock surface **b** sthg that acts as a barrier or defence

²wall *v* **1** to protect or surround (as if) with a wall **b** to separate or shut out (as if) by a wall **2a** to immure **b** to close (an opening) (as if) with a wall *USE* (*2*) usu + *up*

wallaby /ˈwɒləbi/ *n* any of various small or medium-sized kangaroos

wallet /ˈwɒlɪ̈t/ *n* **1** a holder for paper money, usu with compartments for other items (e g credit cards and stamps) **2** a flat case or folder

wallflower /ˈwɔːlflaʊəʳ/ *n* **1** any of several Old World perennial plants of the mustard family; *esp* a hardy erect plant with showy fragrant flowers **2** a woman who fails to get partners at a dance – infml

¹wallop /ˈwɒləp/ *n* **1** a powerful body blow – sometimes used interjectionally; infml **2** emotional or psychological force; impact – infml **3** *Br* beer – slang

²wallop *v* **1** to hit with force; thrash **2** to beat by a wide margin; trounce *USE* infml

¹wallow /ˈwɒləʊ/ *v* **1** to roll or lie around lazily or luxuriously **2** to indulge oneself immoderately; revel *in* **3** *of a ship* to struggle laboriously in or through rough water; *broadly* to pitch

²wallow *n* **1** an act or instance of wallowing **2** a muddy or dusty area used by animals for wallowing

¹wallpaper /ˈwɔːlpeɪpəʳ/ *n* decorative paper for the walls of a room

²wallpaper *v* to apply wallpaper to (the walls of a room)

Wall Street *n* the influential financial interests of the US economy

wall-to-wall *adj, of carpeting* covering the whole floor of a room

walnut /ˈwɔːlnʌt/ *n* (an edible nut or the wood of) any of a genus of trees with richly grained wood used for cabinetmaking and veneers

walrus /ˈwɔːlrəs/ *n* either of 2 large sea mammals of northern seas, related to the seals, and hunted for their tough heavy hide, ivory tusks, and the oil yielded by the blubber

¹waltz /wɔːls/ *n* (music for or in the tempo of) a ballroom dance in $\frac{3}{4}$ time with strong accent on the first beat

²waltz *v* **1** to dance a waltz **2** to move *along* in a lively or confident manner **3** to grab and lead (e g a person) unceremoniously; march

wampum /ˈwɒmpəm/ *n* beads of polished shells strung together and used by N American Indians as money and ornaments

wan /wɒn/ *adj* **1a** suggestive of poor health; pallid **b** lacking vitality; feeble **2** *of light* dim, faint – **~ly** *adv* – **~ness** *n*

wand /wɒnd/ *n* a slender rod **a** carried as a sign of office **b** used by conjurers and magicians

wander /ˈwɒndəʳ/ *v* **1** to go or travel idly or aimlessly **2** to follow or extend along a winding course; meander **3a** to deviate (as if) from a course; stray

b to lose concentration; stray in thought **c** to think or speak incoherently or illogically

[1]**wandering** /'wɒndərɪŋ/ *n* **1** a going about from place to place **2** movement away from the proper or usual course or place *USE* often pl with sing. meaning

[2]**wandering** *adj* **1** winding, meandering **2** not keeping a rational or sensible course **3** nomadic

wanderlust /'wɒndəlʌst/ *n* eager longing for or impulse towards travelling

[1]**wane** /weɪn/ *v* **1** to decrease in size or extent; dwindle **2** to fall gradually from power, prosperity, or influence; decline

[2]**wane** *n* **1** the act or process of waning **2** a time of waning; *specif* the period from full phase of the moon to the new moon

wangle /'wæŋgəl/ *v* **1** to adjust or manipulate for personal or fraudulent ends **2** to bring about or get by devious means *USE* infml

[1]**want** /wɒnt/ *v* **1** to fail to possess, esp in customary or required amount; lack **2a** to have a desire for **b** to have an inclination to; like **3a** to have need of; require **b** to suffer from the lack of; need **4** to wish or demand the presence of **5** ought – + *to* and infinitive

[2]**want** *n* **1a** the quality or state of lacking sthg required or usual **b** extreme poverty **2** sthg wanted; a need

wanting /'wɒntɪŋ/ *adj* **1** not present or in evidence; absent **2a** not up to the required standard or expectation **b** lacking in the specified ability or capacity; deficient

[1]**wanton** /'wɒntən/ *adj* **1** sexually unbridled; promiscuous **2** having no just foundation or provocation; malicious **3** uncontrolled, unbridled – ~**ly** *adv* – ~**ness** *n*

[2]**wanton** *n* a wanton person; *esp* a lewd or lascivious woman

[1]**war** /wɔːʳ/ *n* **1** a state or period of usu open and declared armed hostile conflict between states or nations **2** a struggle between opposing forces or for a particular end

[2]**war** *v* **1** to engage in warfare **2** to be in active or vigorous conflict

[1]**warble** /'wɔːbəl/ *v* to sing or sound in a trilling manner or with many turns and variations

[2]**warble** *n* (a swelling under the hide of cattle, horses, etc caused by) the maggot of a fly

warbler /'wɔːbləʳ/ *n* any of numerous small Old World birds (e g a whitethroat) which are related to the thrushes and many of which are noted songsters

ward /wɔːd/ *n* **1** a division of a prison or hospital **2** a division of a city or town for electoral or administrative purposes **3** a person under guard, protection, or surveillance; *esp* one under the care or control of a legal guardian

warden /'wɔːdn/ *n* **1** one having care or charge of sthg; a guardian **2** the governor of a town, district, or fortress **3** an official charged with special supervisory duties or with the enforcement of specified laws or regulations **4** any of various British college officials

warder /'wɔːdəʳ/ *n* a prison guard

ward off *v* to deflect, avert

wardrobe /'wɔːdrəʊb/ *n* **1** a room or (movable) cupboard, esp fitted with shelves and a rail or pegs, where clothes are kept **2a** a collection of clothes (e g belonging to 1 person) **b** a collection of stage costumes and accessories

ware /weəʳ/ *n* **1a** manufactured articles; goods – usu in combination **b** *pl* goods for sale **2** pottery or china, esp of a specified kind or make

warehouse /'weəhaʊs/ *v or n* (to deposit, store, or stock in) a structure or room for the storage of merchandise or commodities

warfare /'wɔːfeər/ *n* **1** hostilities, war **2** struggle, conflict

warhead /'wɔːhed/ *n* the section of a missile containing the explosive, chemical, or incendiary charge

warlike /'wɔːlaɪk/ *adj* **1** fond of war **2** of or useful in war **3** hostile

warlock /'wɔːlɒk/ *n* a man practising black magic

warlord /'wɔːlɔːd/ *n* a supreme military leader

[1]**warm** /wɔːm/ *adj* **1a** having or giving out heat to a moderate or adequate degree; *also* experiencing heat to this degree **b** feeling or causing sensations of heat brought about by strenuous exertion **2a** marked by enthusiasm; cordial **b** marked by excitement, disagreement, or anger **3** affectionate and outgoing in temperament **4** dangerous, hostile **5** *of a colour* producing an impression of being warm; *specif* in the range yellow to red **6** near to a goal, object, or solution sought – chiefly in children's games – **~ish** *adj* – **~ly** *adv* – **~ness** *n*

[2]**warm** *v* **1** to make warm **2** to become filled with interest, enthusiasm, or affection – + *to* or *towards* **3** to reheat (cooked food) for eating – often + *up*

warm-blooded *adj* **1** having a relatively high and constant body temperature more or less independent of the environment **2** fervent or ardent in spirit – **~ly** *adv* – **~ness** *n*

warming pan *n* a usu long-handled flat covered pan (e g of brass) filled with hot coals, formerly used to warm a bed

warmonger /ˈwɔːˌmʌŋgəʳ/ *n* one who attempts to stir up war

warmth /wɔːmθ/ *n* the quality or state of being warm **a** in temperature **b** in feeling

warm-up *n* the act or an instance of warming up; *also* a procedure (e g a set of exercises) used in warming up

warm up *v* **1** to engage in exercise or practice, esp before entering a game or contest; *broadly* to get ready **2** to put (an audience) into a receptive mood (e g before a show), esp by telling jokes, singing, etc

warn /wɔːn/ *v* **1a** to give notice to beforehand, esp of danger or evil **b** to give admonishing advice to; counsel **2** to order to go or stay away – often + *off* or *away*

warning /ˈwɔːnɪŋ/ *n* sthg that warns; *also* a notice

[1]**warp** /wɔːp/ *n* **1** a series of yarns extended lengthways in a loom and crossed by the weft **2** a rope for warping a ship or boat **3a** a twist or curve that has developed in sthg formerly flat or straight **b** a mental twist or aberration

[2]**warp** *v* **1a** to turn or twist (e g planks) out of shape, esp out of a plane **b** to cause to think or act wrongly; pervert **2** to manoeuvre (e g a ship) by hauling on a line attached to a fixed object

war paint *n* **1** paint put on the body by N American Indians as a sign of going to war **2** cosmetics – infml

warpath /ˈwɔːpɑːθ/ *n* the route taken by a war party of N American Indians

[1]**warrant** /ˈwɒrənt/ *n* **1a** a sanction, authorization; *also* evidence for or token of authorization **b** a guarantee, security **c** a ground, justification; *also* proof **2a** a document authorizing an officer to make an arrest, a search, etc **b** an official certificate of appointment issued to a noncommissioned officer

[2]**warrant** *v* **1** to declare or maintain with certainty **2** to guarantee to be as represented **3** to give sanction to **4a** to prove or declare the authenticity or truth of **b** to give assurance of the nature of or for the undertaking of; guarantee **5** to serve as or give adequate ground or reason for

warrant officer *n* a member of the British army, airforce, or Royal Marines with a rank between non-commissioned officer and commissioned officer

warranty /ˈwɒrənti/ *n* a usu written guarantee of the soundness of a product and of the maker's responsibility for repair or replacement

warren /ˈwɒrən/ *n* **1** an area of ground (or a structure) where rabbits breed **2** a crowded tenement or district

warrior /ˈwɒrɪəʳ/ *n* a man engaged or experienced in warfare

warship /ˈwɔːˌʃɪp/ *n* an (armed) ship for use in warfare

wart /wɔːt/ *n* **1** a horny projection on the skin, usu of the hands or feet, caused by a virus; *also* a protuberance, esp on a plant, resembling this **2** an ugly or objectionable man or boy – chiefly Br schoolboy slang – **~y** *adj*

warthog /ˈwɔːthɒg/ *n* any of a genus of African wild pigs with 2 pairs of rough warty lumps on the face and large protruding tusks

wartime /ˈwɔːtaɪm/ *n* a period during which a war is in progress

wary /ˈweəri/ *adj* marked by caution and watchful prudence in detecting and escaping danger – **warily** *adv* – **wariness** *n*

was /wəz; *strong* wɒz/ *past 1 & 3 sing of* **be**

[1]**wash** /wɒʃ/ *v* **1a** to cleanse (as if) by the action of liquid (e g water) **b** to remove (e g dirt) by applying liquid **c** to wash articles; do the washing **2** *of an animal* to cleanse (fur or a furry part) by licking or by rubbing with a paw moistened with saliva **3** to suffuse with light **4** to flow along, over, or against **5** to move, carry, or deposit (as if) by the force of water in motion **6** to cover or daub lightly with a thin coating (e g of paint or varnish) **7** to gain acceptance; inspire belief – infml

[2]**wash** *n* **1a** (an instance of) washing or being washed **b** articles for washing **2** the surging action of waves **3a** a thin coat of paint (e g watercolour) **4** a lotion

washable /ˈwɒʃəbəl/ *adj* capable of being washed without damage

washbasin /ˈwɒʃˌbeɪsən/ *n* a basin or sink usu connected to a water supply for washing the hands and face

washboard /ˈwɒʃbɔːd/ *n* a corrugated board for scrubbing clothes on when washing

wash down *v* **1** to facilitate the swallowing of (food) by taking gulps of liquid **2** to wash the whole surface of

wash drawing *n* (a) watercolour painting done (mainly) in washes, esp in black, white, and grey tones only

washed-out *adj* **1** faded in colour **2** listless, exhausted – infml

washed-up *adj* no longer successful or useful; finished – infml

washer /ˈwɒʃəʳ/ *n* **1** a washing machine **2** a thin flat ring (e g of metal or leather) used to ensure tightness or prevent friction in joints and assemblies

washerwoman /ˈwɒʃəwʊmən/ *n* a woman who takes in washing

washing /ˈwɒʃɪŋ/ *n* articles, esp clothes, that have been or are to be washed

washing soda *n* a transparent crystalline hydrated sodium carbonate

washing-up *n, chiefly Br* the act or process of washing dishes and kitchen utensils; *also* the dishes and utensils to be washed

wash-leather *n* a soft leather similar to chamois

washout /ˈwɒʃ-aʊt/ *n* **1** the washing out or away of a road, railway line, etc by a large amount of water **2** a failure, fiasco

wash out *v* to become depleted of colour or vitality; fade

washroom /ˈwɒʃrʊm, -ruːm/ *n, NAm* the toilet – euph

washstand /ˈwɒʃstænd/ *n* a piece of furniture used, esp formerly, to hold a basin, jug, etc needed for washing one's face and hands

wash up *v* **1** to bring into the shore **2** *Br* to wash (the dishes and utensils) after a meal

wasp /wɒsp/ *n* any of numerous largely flesh-eating slender narrow-waisted insects many of which have an extremely painful sting; *esp* one with black and yellow stripes

WASP, Wasp /wɒsp/ *n* an American of N European, esp British, stock and of Protestant background; *esp* one in North America considered to be a member of the dominant and most privileged class

waspish /ˈwɒspɪʃ/ *adj* resembling a wasp in behaviour; *esp* snappish – **~ly** *adv* – **~ness** *n*

[1]**wassail** /ˈwɒseɪl/ *n* **1** a toast to sby's health made in England in former times **2** *archaic* revelry, carousing

[2]**wassail** *v* **1** to carouse **2** *dial Eng* to sing carols from house to house at Christmas

wast /wəst; *strong* wɒst/ *archaic past 2 sing of* **be**

wastage /ˈweɪstɪdʒ/ *n* **1a** loss, decrease, or destruction of sthg (e g by use, decay, or leakage); *esp* wasteful or avoidable loss of sthg valuable **b** waste, refuse **2** reduction or loss in numbers (e g of employees or students), usu caused by individuals leaving or retiring voluntarily – esp in *natural wastage*

[1]**waste** /weɪst/ *n* **1a** uncultivated land **b** a broad and empty expanse (e g of

water) **2** wasting or being wasted **3** gradual loss or decrease by use, wear, or decay **4** material rejected during a textile manufacturing process and used usu for wiping away dirt and oil **5** human or animal refuse

²**waste** *v* **1** to lose weight, strength, or vitality – often + *away* **2** to spend or use carelessly or inefficiently; squander

³**waste** *adj* **1a** uninhabited, desolate **b** not cultivated or used; not productive **2** discarded as refuse **3** serving to conduct or hold refuse material; *specif* carrying off superfluous fluid

wasteful /ˈweɪstfəl/ *adj* given to or marked by waste; prodigal – ~**ly** *adv* – ~**ness** *n*

waste product *n* **1** debris resulting from a process (e g of manufacture) that is of no further use to the system producing it **2** material (e g faeces) discharged from, or stored in an inert form in, a living body as a by-product of metabolic processes

waster /ˈweɪstəʳ/ *n* **1** one who spends or consumes extravagantly without thought for the future **2** a good-for-nothing, idler

wastrel /ˈweɪstrəl/ *n* **1** a vagabond, waif **2** a waster

¹**watch** /wɒtʃ/ *v* **1** to remain awake during the night, esp in order to keep vigil **2a** to be attentive or vigilant; wait *for* **b** to keep guard **3a** to observe closely, esp in order to check on action or change **b** to look at (an event or moving scene) **4a** to take care of; tend **b** to be careful of **c** to take care that **5** to be on the alert for – ~**er** *n*

²**watch** *n* **1a** the act of keeping awake or alert to guard, protect, or attend **b** a state of alert and continuous attention; lookout **2** a watchman; *also, sing or pl in constr* a body of watchmen, specif those formerly assigned to patrol the streets of a town at night **3a** a period of keeping guard **b(1)** a period of time during which a part of a ship's company is on duty while another part rests **(2)** *sing or pl in constr* the part of a ship's company on duty during a particular watch **4** a small portable timepiece powered esp by a spring or battery and usu worn on a wrist

watchdog /ˈwɒtʃdɒg/ *n* **1** a dog kept to guard property **2** a person or group (e g a committee) that guards against inefficiency, undesirable practices, etc

watchful /ˈwɒtʃfəl/ *adj* carefully observant or attentive – ~**ly** *adv* – ~**ness** *n*

watchman /ˈwɒtʃmən/ *n* sby who keeps watch; a guard

watchtower /ˈwɒtʃˌtaʊəʳ/ *n* a tower from which a lookout can keep watch

watchword /ˈwɒtʃwɜːd/ *n* **1** a word or phrase used as a sign of recognition among members of the same group **2** a motto that embodies a guiding principle

¹**water** /ˈwɔːtəʳ/ *n* **1a** the colourless odourless liquid that descends from the clouds as rain, forms streams, lakes, and seas, is a major constituent of all living matter, and is an oxide of hydrogen which freezes at 0°C and boils at 100°C **2a(1)** *pl* the water occupying or flowing in a particular bed **(2)** *chiefly Br* a body of water (e g a river or lake) **b(1)** *pl* a stretch of sea surrounding and controlled by a country **(2)** the sea of a specified part of the earth – often pl with sing. meaning **c** a water supply **3** the level of water at a specified state of the tide **4** liquid containing or resembling water; *esp* a pharmaceutical or cosmetic preparation **5** a wavy lustrous pattern (e g of a textile)

²**water** *v* **1a** to moisten, sprinkle, or soak with water **b** to form or secrete water or watery matter (e g tears or saliva) **2a** to supply with water for drink **b** to supply water to **3** to be a source of water for **4** to impart a lustrous appearance and wavy pattern to (cloth) by calendering **5** to dilute (as if) by the addition of water – often + *down*

water closet *n* (a room or structure containing) a toilet with a bowl that can be flushed with water

watercolour /ˈwɔːtəˌkʌləʳ/ *n* **1** a paint made from pigment mixed with water rather than oil **2** (a work produced by) the art of painting with watercolours

watercourse /ˈwɔːtəkɔːs/ *n* (a natural or man-made channel for) a stream of water

watercress /ˈwɔːtəkres/ *n* any of several cresses of wet places widely grown for use in salads

waterfall /ˈwɔːtəfɔːl/ *n* a vertical or steep descent of the water of a river or stream

waterfront /ˈwɔːtəfrʌnt/ *n* land or a section of a town fronting or bordering on a body of water

water hen *n* any of various birds (e g a coot or moorhen) related to the rails

water ice *n* a frozen dessert of water, sugar, and flavouring

watering can *n* a vessel having a handle and a long spout often fitted with a rose, used for watering plants

watering place *n* a health or recreational resort featuring mineral springs or bathing; *esp* a spa

water lily *n* any of a family of aquatic plants with floating leaves and usu showy colourful flowers

waterline /ˈwɔːtəlaɪn/ *n* the level on the hull of a vessel to which the surface of the water comes when it is afloat; *also* any of several lines marked on the hull to correspond with this level

waterlogged /ˈwɔːtəlɒgd/ *adj* filled or soaked with water; *specif, of a vessel* so filled with water as to be (almost) unable to float

waterloo /ˌwɔːtəˈluː/ *n often cap* a decisive defeat

water main *n* a major pipe for conveying water

waterman /ˈwɔːtəmən/ *n* a man who works on or near water or who engages in water recreations; *esp* a boatman whose boat and services are available for hire

watermark /ˈwɔːtəmaːk/ *n* **1** a mark indicating the height to which water has risen **2** (the design or the metal pattern producing) a marking in paper visible when the paper is held up to the light

water meadow *n* a meadow kept fertile by a regular influx of water (e g from the flooding of a bordering river)

watermelon *n* (an African climbing plant of the cucumber family that bears) a large oblong or roundish fruit with a hard green often striped or variegated rind, a sweet watery pink pulp, and many seeds

water polo *n* a game played in water by teams of 7 swimmers using a ball that is thrown or dribbled with the object of putting it into a goal

[1]**waterproof** /ˈwɔːtəpruːf/ *adj* impervious to water; *esp* covered or treated with a material to prevent passage of water

[2]**waterproof** *n* (a garment made of) waterproof fabric

[3]**waterproof** *v* to make waterproof

watershed /ˈwɔːtəʃed/ *n* **1** a dividing ridge between 2 drainage areas **2** a crucial turning point

water-skiing *n* the sport of planing and jumping on water skis

water-softener *n* a substance or device for softening hard water

water table *n* the level below which the ground is wholly saturated with water

watertight /ˈwɔːtətaɪt/ *adj* **1** of such tight construction or fit as to be impermeable to water **2** *esp of an argument* impossible to disprove; without loopholes

water tower *n* a tower supporting a raised water tank to provide the necessary steady pressure to distribute water

water vole *n* a common large vole of W Europe that inhabits river banks and often digs extensive tunnels

waterwheel /ˈwɔːtəwiːl/ *n* **1** a wheel made to rotate by direct action of water, and used esp to drive machinery **2** a wheel for raising water

water wings *n pl* a pair of usu air-filled floats worn to give support to the body of sby learning to swim

waterworks /ˈwɔːtəwɜːks/ *n* **1** the reservoirs, mains, building, and pumping and purifying equipment by which a water supply is obtained and distributed (e g to a city) – often pl with sing. meaning **2** *chiefly Br* the urinary system – euph or humor **3** (the shedding of) tears – infml

watery /ˈwɔːtəri/ *adj* **1a** consisting of or filled with water **b** containing, sodden with, or yielding water or a thin liquid **c** containing too much water **2a** pale, faint **b** vapid, wishy-washy

watt /wɒt/ *n* the SI unit of power equal to the power that in 1s gives rise to an energy of 1J

wattage /ˈwɒtɪdʒ/ *n* amount of power expressed in watts

¹wattle /ˈwɒtl/ *n* **1** (material for) a framework of poles interwoven with slender branches or reeds and used, esp formerly, in building **2** a fleshy protuberance usu near or on the head or neck, esp of a bird

²wattle *v* **1** to form or build of or with wattle **2** to unite or make solid by interweaving light flexible material

¹wave /weɪv/ **1** to flutter or sway to and fro **2** to direct by waving; signal **3** to move (the hand or an object) to and fro in greeting, farewell, or homage **4** to brandish, flourish

²wave *n* **1** a moving ridge or swell on the surface of a liquid (e g the sea) **2a** a shape or outline having successive curves **b** a waviness of the hair **c** an undulating line or streak **3** sthg that swells and dies away: e g **a** a surge of sensation or emotion **b** a movement involving large numbers of people in a common activity **4** a sweep of the hand or arm or of some object held in the hand, used as a signal or greeting **5** a rolling or undulatory movement or any of a series of such movements passing along a surface or through the air **6** a movement like that of an ocean wave: e g **a** a surging movement; an influx **b** *sing or pl in constr* a line of attacking or advancing troops, aircraft, etc **7** (a complete cycle of) a periodic variation of pressure, electrical or magnetic intensity, electric potential, etc by which energy is transferred progressively from point to point without a corresponding transfer of a medium

wave band *n* a band of radio frequency waves

wavelength /ˈweɪvleŋθ/ *n* the distance in the line of advance of a wave from any 1 point to the next point of corresponding phase (e g from 1 peak to the next)

waver /ˈweɪvəʳ/ *v* **1** to vacillate between choices; fluctuate **2a** to sway unsteadily to and fro **b** to hesitate as if about to give way; falter **3** to make a tremulous sound; quaver – **~er** *n* – **~ingly** *adv*

wavy /ˈweɪvi/ *adj* **1** having waves **2** having a wavelike form or outline – **waviness** *n*

¹wax /wæks/ *n* **1** beeswax **2a** any of numerous plant or animal substances that are harder, more brittle, and less greasy than fats **b** a pliable or liquid composition used esp for sealing, taking impressions, or polishing

²wax *v* **1** to increase in size and strength **2** *archaic* to assume a specified quality or state; become

³wax *n* a fit of temper – infml

waxen /ˈwæksən/ *adj* **1** made of or covered with wax **2** resembling wax, esp in being pliable, smooth, or pallid

waxy /ˈwæksi/ *adj* **1** made of, full of, or covered with wax **2** resembling wax, esp in smooth whiteness or pliability – **waxiness** *n*

¹way /weɪ/ *n* **1a** a thoroughfare for travel or transport from place to place **b** an opening for passage **c** space or room, esp for forward movement **2** the course to be travelled from one place to another; a route **3a** a course leading in a direction or towards an objective **b** what one desires, or wants to do **4a** the manner in which sthg is done or happens **b** a method of doing or accomplishing; a means **c** a characteristic, regular, or habitual manner or mode of being, behaving, or happening **5** the distance to be travelled in order to reach a place or point **6a** a direction – often in combination **b** (the direction of) the area in which one lives **7** a state of affairs; a condition **8** motion or speed of a ship or boat through the water

²way *adv* **1** away **2** *chiefly NAm* all the way

waylay /weɪˈleɪ/ *v* **1** to attack from ambush **2** to accost

way-out *adj* far-out – infml

ways and means *n pl, often cap W&M* methods and resources for raising revenue for the use of government

wayside /ˈweɪsaɪd/ *n* the side of or land adjacent to a road

wayward /ˈweɪwəd/ *adj* **1** following

one's own capricious or wanton inclinations; ungovernable **2** following no clear principle or law; unpredictable

we /wi; *strong* wiː/ *pron pl in constr* **1** I and one or more other people **2** I – used, esp formerly, by sovereigns; used by writers to maintain an impersonal character

weak /wiːk/ *adj* **1a** deficient in physical vigour; feeble **b** not able to sustain or exert much weight, pressure, or strain **c** not able to resist external force or withstand attack **2a** lacking determination or decisiveness; ineffectual **b** unable to withstand temptation or persuasion **3** not factually grounded or logically presented **4a** unable to function properly **b** lacking skill or proficiency **5a** deficient in a specified quality or ingredient **b** lacking normal intensity or potency **c** mentally or intellectually deficient **d** deficient in strength or flavour; dilute **6** not having or exerting authority or political power **7** of or constituting a verb (conjugation) that in English forms inflections by adding the suffix *-ed* or *-d* or *-t* – **~ly** *adv* – **~en** *v*

weak-kneed *adj* lacking in resolution; easily intimidated

weakling /ˈwiːk-lɪŋ/ *n* a person or animal weak in body, character, or mind

weakness /ˈwiːknʝs/ *n* **1** a fault, defect **2** (an object of) a special desire or fondness

weal, wheal /wiːl/ *n* a welt, scar

wealth /welθ/ *n* **1** the state of being rich **2** abundance of money and valuable material possessions **3** abundant supply; a profusion – **~y** *adj*

wean /wiːn/ *v* **1** to accustom (a child or other young mammal) to take food other than mother's milk **2** to cause to abandon a state of usu unwholesome dependence or preoccupation **3** to cause to become acquainted with an idea, writer, etc at an early age; bring up *on*

weapon /ˈwepən/ *n* an instrument of offensive or defensive combat – **~less** *adj* – **~ry** *n*

[1]**wear** /weəʳ/ *v* **wore; worn** **1a** to have or carry on the body as clothing or adornment **b** to dress in (a particular manner, colour, or garment), esp habitually **2** to have or show on the face **3** to impair, damage, or diminish by use or friction **4** to produce gradually by friction or attrition **5** to exhaust or lessen the strength of; weary **8** *chiefly Br* to find (a claim, proposal etc) acceptable – infml – **~able** *adj* – **~er** *n*

[2]**wear** *n* **1** clothing, usu of a specified kind **2** capacity to withstand use; durability **3** minor damage or deterioration through use

wear and tear *n* the normal deterioration or depreciation which sthg suffers in the course of use

wearing /ˈweərɪŋ/ *adj* causing fatigue; tiring

wearisome /ˈwɪərisəm/ *adj* causing weariness; tiresome

[1]**weary** /ˈwɪəri/ *adj* **1** exhausted, tired **2** having one's patience, tolerance, or pleasure exhausted – + *of* **3** wearisome – **wearily** *adv* – **weariness** *n*

[2]**weary** *v* to make or become weary

weasel /ˈwiːzəl/ *n* any of various small slender flesh-eating mammals with reddish brown fur which, in northern forms, turns white in winter

[1]**weather** /ˈweðəʳ/ *n* the prevailing (bad) atmospheric conditions, esp with regard to heat or cold, wetness or dryness, calm or storm, and clearness or cloudiness

[2]**weather** *v* **1** to expose or subject to atmospheric conditions **2** to bear up against and come safely through

weather-beaten *adj* **1** worn or damaged by exposure to weather **2** toughened or tanned by the weather

weatherboard /ˈweðəbɔːd/ *n* **1** a board fixed horizontally and usu overlapping the board below to form a protective outdoor wall covering that will throw off water **2** a sloping board fixed to the bottom of a door for excluding rain, snow, etc

weathercock /ˈweðəkɒk/ *n* a weather vane; *esp* one in the figure of a cockerel

weatherglass /ˈweðəglɑːs/ *n* a barometer

weatherproof /ˈweðəpruːf/ *adj* able to withstand exposure to weather without damage or loss of function

weather station *n* a station for

taking, recording, and reporting meteorological observations

[1]**weave** /wiːv/ *v* **wove, weaved; woven, weaved** **1a** to form (cloth) by interlacing strands (e g of yarn), esp on a loom **b** to interlace (e g threads) into a fabric, design, etc **c** to make (e g a basket) by intertwining **2a** to produce by elaborately combining elements into a coherent whole **b** to introduce; work in – usu + *in* or *into* – **weave** *n*

[2]**weave** *v* **weaved** to direct (e g the body or one's way) in a winding or zigzag course, esp to avoid obstacles

weaver /ˈwiːvəʳ/ *n* **1** sby who weaves, esp as an occupation **2 weaver, weaverbird** any of numerous Old World birds that resemble finches and usu construct elaborate nests of interlaced vegetation

[1]**web** /web/ *n* **1** a woven fabric; *esp* a length of fabric still on the loom **2** a spider's web; *also* a similar network spun by various insects **3** a tissue or membrane; *esp* that uniting fingers or toes either at their bases (e g in human beings) or for most of their length (e g in many water birds) **4** an intricate structure suggestive of sthg woven; a network **5** a continuous sheet of paper for use in a printing press

[2]**web** *v* to entangle, ensnare

webbed *adj, of a water bird* having a web between the toes

webbing /ˈwebɪŋ/ *n* a strong narrow closely woven tape used esp for straps, upholstery, or harnesses

wed /wed/ *v* to marry

wedded /ˈwedɪ̣d/ *adj* **1** joined in marriage **2** conjugal, connubial **3** strongly emotionally attached; committed *to*

wedding /ˈwedɪŋ/ *n* **1** a marriage ceremony, usu with its accompanying festivities **2** a joining in close association **3** a wedding anniversary or its celebration – usu in combination

wedding breakfast *n* a celebratory meal that follows a marriage ceremony

wedding ring *n* a ring usu of plain metal (e g gold) given by 1 marriage partner to the other during the wedding ceremony and worn thereafter to signify marital status

[1]**wedge** /wedʒ/ *n* **1** a piece of wood, metal, etc tapered to a thin edge and used esp for splitting wood or raising heavy objects **2a** (a shoe with) a wedge-shaped sole raised at the heel and tapering towards the toe **b** an iron golf club with a broad face angled for maximum loft **3** sthg causing a breach or separation

[2]**wedge** *v* **1** to fasten or tighten by driving in a wedge **2** to force or press into a narrow space; cram – usu + *in* or *into*

Wedgwood /ˈwedʒwʊd/ *trademark* – used for pottery made by Josiah Wedgwood and his successors and typically decorated with a classical cameo-like design in white relief

wedlock /ˈwedlɒk/ *n* the state of being married; marriage

Wednesday /ˈwenzdi,-deɪ/ *n* the day of the week following Tuesday

[1]**wee** /wiː/ *adj* very small; diminutive

[2]**wee** *n* (an act of passing) urine – used esp by or to children

[1]**weed** /wiːd/ *n* **1** an unwanted wild plant which often overgrows or chokes out more desirable plants **2** an obnoxious growth or thing **3** *Br* a weedy person – infml

[2]**weed** *v* **1** to clear of weeds **2** to remove the undesirable parts of

weed out *v* to get rid of (sby or sthg harmful or unwanted); remove

weeds /wiːdz/ *n pl* mourning garments

weedy /ˈwiːdi/ *adj* **1** covered with or consisting of weeds **2** noticeably weak, thin, and ineffectual – infml – **weediness** *n*

week /wiːk/ *n* **1a** any of several 7-day cycles used in various calendars **b** a week beginning with a specified day or containing a specified event **2** a period of 7 consecutive days

weekday /ˈwiːkdeɪ/ *n* any day of the week except (Saturday and) Sunday

[1]**weekend** /wiːkˈend, ˈ--/ *n* the end of the week; *specif* the period from Friday night to Sunday night

[2]**weekend** *v* to spend the weekend (e g at a place)

[1]**weekly** /ˈwiːkli/ *adv* every week; once a week; by the week

[2]**weekly** *adj* **1** occurring, appearing, or

done weekly **2** calculated by the week

[3]**weekly** *n* a weekly newspaper or periodical

[1]**weep** /wiːp/ *v* **wept** **1a** to express deep sorrow for, usu by shedding tears; bewail **b** to mourn *for* sby or sthg **2** to pour forth (tears) from the eyes **3** to exude (a fluid) slowly; ooze

[2]**weep** *n* a fit of weeping

weeping /ˈwiːpɪŋ/ *adj, of a tree* (being a variety) having slender drooping branches

weevil /ˈwiːvəl/ *n* any of numerous usu small beetles with a long snout bearing jaws at the tip, many of which are injurious, esp as larvae, to grain, fruit, etc

weft /weft/ *n* the thread or yarn that interlaces the warp in a fabric; the crosswise yarn in weaving

weigh /weɪ/ *v* **1** to ascertain the weight of (as if) on a scale **2** to have weight or a specified weight **3** to consider carefully; evaluate – often + *up* **4** to measure (a definite quantity) (as if) on a scale – often + *out* **5** to be a burden or cause of anxiety to – often + *on* or *upon*

weigh down *v* **1** to make heavy **2** to oppress, burden

weigh in *v* to have oneself or one's possessions (e g luggage) weighed; *esp* to be weighed after a horse race or before a boxing or wrestling match

[1]**weight** /weɪt/ *n* **1a** the amount that a quantity or body weighs, esp as measured on a particular scale **b** any of the classes into which contestants in certain sports (e g boxing and wrestling) are divided according to body weight **2a** a quantity weighing a certain amount **b** a heavy object thrown or lifted as an athletic exercise or contest **3a** a system of units of weight **b** any of the units of weight used in such a system **c** a piece of material (e g metal) of known weight for use in weighing articles **4a** sthg heavy; a load **b** a heavy object to hold or press sthg down or to counterbalance **5a** a burden, pressure **b** corpulence **6** relative heaviness **7a** relative importance, authority, or influence **b** *the* main force or strength

[2]**weight** *v* **1** to load or make heavy (as if) with a weight **2** to oppress with a burden **3** to arrange in such a way as to create a bias

weighting /ˈweɪtɪŋ/ *n, Br* an additional sum paid on top of wages; *esp* one paid to offset the higher cost of living in a particular area

weightless /ˈweɪtlɨs/ *adj* having little weight; lacking apparent gravitational pull – **~ly** *adv* – **~ness** *n*

weighty /ˈweɪti/ *adj* **1** of much importance, influence, or consequence; momentous **2** heavy, esp in proportion to bulk **3** burdensome, onerous – **weightily** *adv* – **weightiness** *n*

weir /wɪəʳ/ *n* a dam in a stream to raise the water level or control its flow

weird /wɪəd/ *adj* of a strange or extraordinary character; odd – infml – **~ly** *adv* – **~ness** *n*

welch /welʃ/ *v* to welsh

Welch *adj* Welsh – now only in names

[1]**welcome** /ˈwelkəm/ *interj* – used to express a greeting to a guest or newcomer on his/her arrival

[2]**welcome** *v* **1** to greet hospitably and with courtesy **2** to greet or receive in the specified, esp unpleasant, way **3** to receive or accept with pleasure

[3]**welcome** *adj* **1** received gladly into one's presence or companionship **2** giving pleasure; received with gladness, esp because fulfilling a need

[4]**welcome** *n* **1** a greeting or reception on arrival or first appearance **2** the hospitable treatment that a guest may expect

[1]**weld** /weld/ *v* **1a** to fuse (metallic parts) together by heating and allowing the metals to flow together or by hammering or compressing with or without previous heating **b** to unite (plastics) in a similar manner by heating or by using a chemical solvent **2** to unite closely or inseparably – **~er** *n*

[2]**weld** *n* a welded joint

welfare /ˈwelfeəʳ/ *n* **1** well-being **2** organized efforts to improve the living conditions of the poor, elderly, etc

welfare state *n* (a country operating) a social system based on the assumption by the state of responsibility for the individual and social welfare of its citizens

welkin /'welkın/ *n the* sky, firmament –poetic

[1]**well** /wel/ *n* **1** (a pool fed by) a spring of water **2** a pit or hole sunk into the earth to reach a supply of water **3** a shaft or hole sunk in the earth to reach a natural deposit (e g oil or gas) **4** an open space extending vertically through floors of a structure **5** a source from which sthg springs **6** *Br* the open space in front of the judge in a law court

[2]**well** *v* **1** to rise to the surface and usu flow forth **2** to rise to the surface like a flood of liquid

[3]**well** *adv* **better; best** **1** in a good or proper manner; rightly **2** in a way appropriate to the circumstances; satisfactory, skilfully **3** in a kind or friendly manner; favourably **4** in a prosperous manner (e g he lives *well*) **5a** to an extent approaching completeness; thoroughly (e g after being *well* dried with a towel) **b** on a close personal level; intimately **6a** easily, fully (e g *well* worth the price) **b** much, considerably (e g *well* over a million) **c** in all likelihood; indeed (e g may *well* be true)

[4]**well** *interj* **1** – used to express surprise, indignation, or resignation **2** – used to indicate a pause in talking or to introduce a remark

[5]**well** *adj* **1** satisfactory, pleasing **2** advisable, desirable **3** prosperous, well-off **4** healthy **5** being a cause for thankfulness; fortunate (e g it is *well* that this has happened)

well-advised *adj* **1** acting with wisdom; prudent **2** resulting from or showing wisdom

well-appointed *adj* having good and complete facilities, furniture, etc

well-being *n* the state of being happy, healthy, or prosperous

well-bred *adj* **1** having or indicating good breeding; refined **2** of good pedigree

well-connected *adj* having useful social or family contacts

well-disposed *adj* having a favourable or sympathetic disposition

well-done *adj* cooked thoroughly

well-favoured *adj* good-looking; handsome – not now in vogue

well-founded *adj* based on good grounds or reasoning

well-groomed *adj* well dressed and scrupulously neat

well-grounded *adj* **1** having a good basic knowledge **2** well-founded

well-informed *adj* **1** having a good knowledge of a wide variety of subjects **2** having reliable information on a usu specified topic, event, etc

well-intentioned *adj* well-meaning

well-knit *adj* well constructed; *esp* having a compact usu muscular physique

well-known *adj* fully or widely known; *specif* famous

well-meaning *adj* having or based on good intentions though often failing

well-meant *adj* based on good intentions

well-nigh *adv* almost, nearly

well-off *adj* **1** well-to-do, rich **2** in a favourable or fortunate situation **3** well provided

well-read *adj* well-informed through much and varied reading

well-spoken *adj* **1** speaking clearly, courteously, and usu with a refined accent **2** spoken in a pleasing or fitting manner

well-timed *adj* said or done at an opportune moment; timely

well-to-do *adj* moderately rich; prosperous

well-wisher *n* one who feels goodwill towards a person, cause, etc

well-worn *adj* **1** having been much used or worn **2** made trite by overuse; hackneyed

welsh /welʃ/ *v* **1** to evade an obligation, esp payment of a debt **2** to break one's word – **~er** *n*

Welsh, Welch /welʃ/ *adj* of Wales, its people, or its language

[1]**welt** /welt/ *n* **1** a strip, usu of leather, between a shoe sole and upper through which they are fastened together **2** a doubled edge, strip, insert, or seam (e g on a garment) for ornament or reinforcement **3** (a ridge or lump raised on the body usu by) a heavy blow

[2]**welt** *v* to hit hard

[1]**welter** /'weltə[r]/ *v* **1** to writhe, toss;

also to wallow **2** to become soaked, sunk, or involved *in* sthg

[2]**welter** *n* **1** a state of wild disorder; a turmoil **2** a chaotic mass or jumble

welterweight /ˈweltəweɪt/ *n* a boxer who weighs not more than 10st 7lb

[1]**wench** /wentʃ/ *n* **1** a female servant or rustic working girl **2** a young woman; a girl – now chiefly humor or dial

[2]**wench** *v* to have sexual relations habitually with women, esp prostitutes

wend /wend/ *v* to proceed on (one's way)

Wensleydale /ˈwenzlideɪl/ *n* a crumbly mild-flavoured English cheese

went /went/ *past of* **go**

were /wəʳ; *strong* wɜːʳ/ *past 2 sing, past pl, substandard past 1 & 3 sing, or past subjunctive of* **be**

werewolf /ˈweəwʊlf, ˈwɪə-/ *n* a person transformed into a wolf or capable of assuming a wolf's form

[1]**west** /west/ *adj or adv* towards, at, belonging to, or coming from the west

[2]**west** *n* **1** (the compass point corresponding to) the direction 90° to the left of north that is the general direction of sunset **2** *often cap* regions or countries lying to the west of a specified or implied point of orientation; esp the non-Communist countries of Europe and America **3** European civilization in contrast with that of the Orient

West End *n* *the* western part of central London where the main shopping centres, theatres, etc are located

[1]**westerly** /ˈwestəli/ *adj or adv* west

[2]**westerly** *n* a wind from the west

[1]**western** /ˈwestən/ *adj* **1** *often cap* (characteristic) of a region conventionally designated West: e g **a** of or stemming from European traditions in contrast with those of the Orient **b** of the non-Communist countries of Europe and America **2** west

[2]**western** *n, often cap* a novel, film, etc dealing with cowboys, frontier life, etc in the W USA, esp during the latter half of the 19th c

West Indian *n* **1** a native or inhabitant of the W Indies **2** a descendant of W Indians

[1]**wet** /wet/ *adj* **1** consisting of, containing, or covered or soaked with liquid (e g water) **2** rainy **3** still moist enough to smudge or smear **4** involving the use or presence of liquid **5** *chiefly Br* feebly ineffectual or dull; *also, of a politician* moderate – infml – ~**ly** *adv* – ~**ness** *n*

[2]**wet** *n* **1** moisture, wetness **2** rainy weather; rain **3** *chiefly Br* a wet person; a drip – infml

[3]**wet** *v* **1** to make wet **2** to urinate in or on

wet blanket *n* one who quenches or dampens enthusiasm or pleasure

wet dream *n* an erotic dream culminating in orgasm

wet-nurse *v* **1** to act as wet nurse to **2** to give constant and often excessive care to

wet nurse *n* a woman who cares for and suckles another's children

wet suit *n* a close-fitting suit made of material, usu rubber, that admits water but retains body heat so as to insulate its wearer (e g a skin diver), esp in cold water

wetting agent *n* a substance that prevents a surface from being repellent to a wetting liquid

[1]**whack** /wæk/ *vt* **1** to strike with a smart or resounding blow **2** to get the better of; defeat *USE* infml

[2]**whack** *n* **1** (the sound of) a smart resounding blow **2** a portion, share **3** an attempt, go *USE* infml

whacked /wækt/ *adj* completely exhausted – infml

[1]**whacking** /ˈwækɪŋ/ *adj* extremely big; whopping – infml

[2]**whacking** *adv* very, extremely – infml

whale /weɪl/ *n* any of an order of often enormous aquatic mammals that superficially resemble large fish, have tails modified as paddles, and are frequently hunted for oil, flesh, or whalebone

whalebone /ˈweɪlbəʊn/ *n* a horny substance found in 2 rows of plates up to 4m (about 12ft) long attached along the upper jaw of whalebone whales and used for stiffening things

whaler /ˈweɪləʳ/ *n* a person or ship engaged in whaling

whaling /ˈweɪlɪŋ/ *n* the occupation of catching and processing whales for oil, food, etc

[1]**wham** /wæm/ *n* (the sound made by) a forceful blow – infml

[2]**wham** *interj* – used to express the noise of a forceful blow or impact; infml

[3]**wham** *v* to throw or strike with a loud impact – infml

wharf /wɔːf/ *n, pl* **wharves** a structure built along or out from the shore of navigable water so that ships may load and unload

[1]**what** /wɒt/ *pron* **1a(1)** – used as an interrogative expressing inquiry about the identity, nature, purpose, or value of sthg or sby (e g *what* is this?) **(2)** – used to ask for repetition of sthg not properly heard or understood **b** – used as an exclamation expressing surprise or excitement and frequently introducing a question **c** *chiefly Br* – used in demanding assent (e g a clever play, *what*?); not now in vogue **2** that which; the one that (e g no income but *what* he gets from his writing) **3a** anything or everything that; whatever **b** how much – used in exclamations (e g *what* it must cost!)

[2]**what** *adv* in what respect?; how much?

[3]**what** *adj* **1a** which **b** how remarkable or striking – used esp in exclamatory utterances and dependent clauses (e g *what* a suggestion!) **2** the . . . that; as much or as many . . . as (e g told him *what* little I knew)

[1]**whatever** /wɒˈtevəʳ/ *pron* **1a** anything or everything that **b** no matter what **2** what in the world? – infml

[2]**whatever** *adj* **1a** any . . . that; all . . . that (e g buy peace on *whatever* possible terms) **b** no matter what **2** of any kind at all – used after a noun with *any* or with a negative

whatnot /ˈwɒtnɒt/ *n* **1** a lightweight open set of shelves for bric-a-brac **2** other usu related goods, objects, etc **3** sthg whose name is unknown or (temporarily) forgotten *USE* (*2&3*) infml

wheat /wiːt/ *n* (any of various grasses cultivated in most temperate areas for) a cereal grain that yields a fine white flour and is used for making bread and pasta, and in animal feeds

wheaten /ˈwiːtn/ *adj* made of (the grain, meal, or flour of) wheat

wheat germ *n* the embryo of the wheat kernel separated in milling and used esp as a source of vitamins

wheedle /ˈwiːdl/ *v* **1** to influence or entice by soft words or flattery **2** to cause to part with sthg by wheedling – + *out of*

[1]**wheel** /wiːl/ *n* **1** a circular frame of hard material that may be (partly) solid or spoked and that is capable of turning on an axle **2** a contrivance or apparatus having as its principal part a wheel; *esp* a chiefly medieval instrument of torture to which the victim was tied while his/her limbs were broken by a metal bar **3** sthg resembling a wheel in shape or motion; *esp* a catherine wheel **4a** a curving or circular movement **b** a rotation or turn, usu about an axis or centre; *specif* a turning movement of troops or ships in line in which the units preserve alignment and relative positions **5** *pl* the workings or controlling forces of sthg **6** *pl* a motor vehicle, esp a motor car *USE* (*6*) infml

[2]**wheel** *v* **1** to turn (as if) on an axis; revolve **2** to change direction as if revolving on a pivot **3** to move or extend in a circle or curve **4** to alter or reverse one's opinion – often + *about* or *round* **5** to convey or move (as if) on wheels; *esp* to push (a wheeled vehicle or its occupant)

wheelbarrow /ˈwiːlˌbærəʊ/ *n* a load-carrying device that consists of a shallow box supported at 1 end by usu 1 wheel and at the other by a stand when at rest or by handles when being pushed

wheelbase /ˈwiːlbeɪs/ *n* the distance between the front and rear axles of a vehicle

wheelchair /ˈwiːltʃeəʳ/ *n* an invalid's chair mounted on wheels

wheelwright /ˈwiːlraɪt/ *n* sby who makes or repairs wheels, esp wooden ones for carts

[1]**wheeze** /wiːz/ *v* **1** to breathe with difficulty, usu with a whistling sound

2 to make a sound like that of wheezing – -zy *adj* – -zily *adv* – -ziness *n*

[2]**wheeze** *n* **1** a sound of wheezing **2** a cunning trick or expedient – infml

whelk /welk/ *n* any of numerous large marine snails; *esp* one much used as food in Europe

[1]**whelp** /welp/ *n* **1** any of the young of various flesh-eating mammals, esp a dog **2** a disagreeable or impudent child or youth

[2]**whelp** *v* to give birth to (esp a puppy)

[1]**when** /wen/ *adv* **1** at what time? **2a** at or during which time **b** and then; whereupon

[2]**when** *conj* **1a** at or during the time that **b** as soon as **c** whenever **2** in the event that; if **3a** considering that (e g why smoke *when* you know it's bad for you?) **b** in spite of the fact that; although (e g he gave up politics *when* he might have done well)

[3]**when** *pron* what or which time (e g since *when* have you known that?)

[4]**when** *n* a date, time

whence /wens/ *adv or conj* **1a** from where?; from which place, source, or cause? **b** from which place, source, or cause **2** to the place from which *USE* chiefly fml

[1]**whenever** /we'nevəʳ/ *conj* **1** at every or whatever time **2** in any circumstance

[2]**whenever** *adv* when in the world? – infml

[1]**where** /weəʳ/ *adv* **1a** at, in, or to what place? (e g *where* is the house?) **b** at, in, or to what situation, direction, circumstances, or respect? (e g *where* does this plan lead?) **2** at, in, or to which (place) (e g the town *where* he lives)

[2]**where** *conj* **1a** at, in, or to the place at which (e g stay *where* you are) **b** wherever **c** in a case, situation, or respect in which (e g outstanding *where* endurance is called for) **2** whereas, while

[3]**where** *n* **1** what place or point? **2** a place, point – infml

[1]**whereabouts** /,weərə'baʊts/ *also* **whereabout** *adv or conj* in what vicinity

[2]**whereabouts** /'weərəbaʊts/ *n pl but sing or pl in constr* the place or general locality where a person or thing is

whereas /weə'ræz/ *conj* **1** in view of the fact that; since – used, esp formally, to introduce a preamble **2** while on the contrary; although

whereby /weə'baɪ/ *conj* **1** in accordance with which (e g a law *whereby* children receive cheap milk) **2** by which means – chiefly fml

[1]**wherefore** /'weəfɔːʳ/ *adv* **1** for what reason; why **2** for that reason; therefore *USE* chiefly fml

[2]**wherefore** *n* a reason, cause – chiefly in *the whys and wherefores*

[1]**wherein** /weə'rɪn/ *adv* in what; how (e g showed him *wherein* he was wrong) – chiefly fml

[2]**wherein** *conj* in which; where – chiefly fml

whereupon /,weərə'pɒn/ *adv or conj* closely following and in consequence of which – chiefly fml

[1]**wherever** /weə'revəʳ/ *adv* where in the world? – chiefly infml

[2]**wherever** *conj* at, in, or to every or whatever place

wherewithal /'weəwɪðɔːl/ *n* means, resources; *specif* money

wherry /weri/ *n* **1** a long light rowing boat used to transport passengers on rivers and about harbours **2** a large light barge, lighter, or fishing boat used in Britain

whet /wet/ *v* **1** to sharpen by rubbing on or with sthg (e g a stone) **2** to make keen or more acute; stimulate

whether /'weðəʳ/ *conj* – used usu with correlative *or* or with *or whether* to indicate **a** an indirect question involving alternatives (e g decide *whether* he should protest) **b** indifference between alternatives (e g seated him next to her, *whether* by accident or design)

whetstone /'wetstəʊn/ *n* **1** a stone for sharpening an edge (e g of a chisel) **2** sthg that stimulates or makes keen

whey /weɪ/ *n* the watery part of milk separated from the curd, esp in cheese-making, and rich in lactose, minerals, and vitamins

[1]**which** /wɪtʃ/ *adj* **1** being what one or ones out of a known or limited group? (e g *which* tie should I wear?) **2** whichever **3** – used to introduce a

relative clause by modifying the noun which refers either to a preceding word or phrase or to a whole previous clause (e g he may come, in *which* case I'll ask him)

[2]**which** *pron, pl* **which** **1** what one out of a known or specified group? (e g *which* of those houses do you live in?) **2** whichever **3** – used to introduce a relative clause (e g the office in *which* I work)

[1]**whichever** /wɪ'tʃevəʳ/ *pron, pl* **whichever** **1** whatever one out of a group **2** no matter which **3** which in the world? – chiefly infml

[2]**whichever** *adj* being whatever one or ones out of a group; no matter which

[1]**whiff** /wɪf/ *n* **1** a quick puff, slight gust, or inhalation, esp of air, a smell, smoke, or gas **2** a slight trace

[2]**whiff** *v* to smell unpleasant – **~y** *adj*

Whig /wɪg/ *n or adj* (a member) of a major British political group of the 18th and early 19th c seeking to limit royal authority and increase parliamentary power

[1]**while** /waɪl/ *n* **1** a period of time, esp when short and marked by the occurrence of an action or condition; a time (e g stay here for a *while*) **2** the time and effort used; trouble (e g it's worth your *while*)

[2]**while** *conj* **1a** during the time that **b** providing that; as long as **2a** when on the other hand; whereas **b** in spite of the fact that; although (e g *while* respected, he is not liked)

[3]**while** *prep, archaic or dial* until

while away *v* to pass (time) in a leisurely, often pleasant manner

whim /wɪm/ *n* a sudden, capricious, or eccentric idea or impulse; a fancy

whimper /'wɪmpəʳ/ *v or n* **1** (to make) a low plaintive whining sound **2** (to make) a petulant complaint or protest

whi nsical /'wɪmzɪkəl/ *adj* **1** full of whims; capricious **2** resulting from or suggesting mild affectation; *esp* quizzical, playful – **~ly** *adv*

[1]**whine** /waɪn/ *v* to utter or make a whine

[2]**whine** *n* **1** (a sound like) a prolonged high-pitched cry, usu expressive of distress or pain **2** a querulous or peevish complaint

whinny /'wɪni/ *v or n* (to make or utter with or as if with) a low gentle neigh or similar sound

[1]**whip** /wɪp/ *v* **1** to take, pull, jerk, or move very quickly **2a** to strike with a whip or similar slender flexible implement, esp as a punishment; *also* to spank **b** to drive or urge on (as if) by using a whip **3** to bind or wrap (e g a rope or rod) with cord for protection and strength **4** to beat (e g eggs or cream) into a froth with a whisk, fork, etc **5** to overcome decisively; defeat – infml **6** to snatch suddenly; *esp* to steal – slang

[2]**whip** *n* **1** an instrument consisting usu of a lash attached to a handle, used for driving and controlling animals and for punishment **2** a dessert made by whipping some of the ingredients **3** a light hoisting apparatus consisting of a single pulley, a block, and a rope **4a** a member of Parliament or other legislative body appointed by a political party to enforce discipline and to secure the attendance and votes of party members **b** *often cap* an instruction (e g a three-line whip or a two-line whip) to each member of a political party in Parliament to be in attendance for voting **c** (the privileges and duties of) membership of the official parliamentary representation of a political party

whipcord /'wɪpkɔːd/ *n* a usu cotton or worsted cloth with fine diagonal cords or ribs

whip hand *n* a controlling position; *the* advantage

whiplash /'wɪplæʃ/ *n* **1** the lash of a whip **2** **whiplash, whiplash injury** injury to the neck resulting from a sudden sharp whipping movement of the neck and head (e g in a car collision)

whippersnapper /'wɪpəsnæpəʳ/ *n* an insignificant but impudent person, esp a child

whippet /'wɪpɪ̣t/ *n* (any of) a breed of small swift slender dogs related to greyhounds

whipping boy *n* a scapegoat

whippy /'wɪpi/ *adj* unusually resilient; springy

whip-round *n, chiefly Br* a collection of money made usu for a benevolent purpose – infml

whip up *v* **1** to stir up; stimulate **2** to produce in a hurry

[1]**whirl** /wɜːl/ *v* **1** to move along a curving or circling course, esp with force or speed **2** to turn abruptly or rapidly round (and round) on an axis; rotate, wheel **3** to pass, move, or go quickly **4** to become giddy or dizzy; reel

[2]**whirl** *n* **1** (sthg undergoing or having a form suggestive of) a rapid rotating or circling movement **2a** a confused tumult; a bustle **b** a confused or disturbed mental state; a turmoil **3** an experimental or brief attempt; a try – infml

whirlpool /'wɜːlpuːl/ *n* (sthg resembling, esp in attracting or engulfing power) a circular eddy of rapidly moving water with a central depression into which floating objects may be drawn

whirlwind /'wɜːl,wɪnd/ *n* **1** a small rapidly rotating windstorm of limited extent marked by an inward and upward spiral motion of the lower air round a core of low pressure **2** a confused rush; a whirl

whirr, whir /wɜːʳ/ *v or n* (to make or revolve or move with) a continuous buzzing or vibrating sound made by sthg in rapid motion

[1]**whisk** /wɪsk/ *n* **1** a quick light brushing or whipping motion **2a** any of various small usu hand-held kitchen utensils used for whisking food **b** a small bunch of flexible strands (e g twigs, feathers, or straw) attached to a handle for use as a brush

[2]**whisk** *v* **1** to convey briskly **2** to mix or fluff up (as if) by beating with a whisk **3** to brandish lightly; flick

whisker /'wɪskəʳ/ *n* **1a** a hair of the beard or sideboards **b** a hair's breadth **2** any of the long projecting hairs or bristles growing near the mouth of an animal (e g a cat)

whisky /'wɪski/ *n* a spirit distilled from fermented mash of rye, corn, wheat, or esp barley

[1]**whisper** /'wɪspəʳ/ *v* **1** to speak softly with little or no vibration of the vocal cords **2** to make a hissing or rustling sound like whispered speech **3** to report or suggest confidentially – **~er** *n*

[2]**whisper** *n* **1a** whispering; *esp* speech without vibration of the vocal cords **b** a hissing or rustling sound like whispered speech **2a** a rumour **b** a hint, trace

[1]**whist** /wɪst/ *v, dial Br* to be silent; hush – often used as an interjection to call for silence

[2]**whist** *n* (any of various card games similar to) a card game for 4 players in 2 partnerships in which each trick made in excess of 6 tricks scores 1 point

whist drive *n, Br* an evening of whist playing with a periodic change of partners, usu with prizes at the finish

[1]**whistle** /'wɪsəl/ *n* **1** a device (e g a small wind instrument) in which the forcible passage of air, steam, the breath, etc through a slit or against a thin edge in a short tube produces a loud sound **2** (a sound like) a shrill clear sound produced by whistling or by a whistle

[2]**whistle** *v* **1** to utter a (sound like a) whistle (by blowing or drawing air through the puckered lips) **2** to make a whistle by rapid movement; *also* to move rapidly (as if) with such a sound **3** to blow or sound a whistle

whit /wɪt/ *n* the smallest part imaginable; a bit

Whit /wɪt/ *n* Whitsuntide

[1]**white** /waɪt/ *adj* **1a** free from colour **b** of the colour white **c** light or pallid in colour **d** *of wine* light yellow or amber in colour **e** *Br, of coffee* served with milk or cream **2** of a group or race characterized by reduced pigmentation **3** *of magic* not intended to cause harm **4a** dressed in white **b** accompanied by snow **5** reactionary, counterrevolutionary – **~ness** *n*

[2]**white** *n* **1** the neutral colour that belongs to objects that reflect diffusely nearly all incident light **2** a white or light-coloured part of sthg: e g **a** the mass of albumin-containing material surrounding the yolk of an egg **b** the white part of the ball of the eye **c** (the player playing) the light-coloured pieces in a two-handed board game **3a** *pl* white (sports) clothing **b** a white

animal (e g a butterfly or pig) **4** sby belonging to a light-skinned race

whitebait /ˈwaɪtbeɪt/ *n* (any of various small food fishes similar to) the young of any of several European herrings (e g the common herring or the sprat) eaten whole

white-collar *adj* of or being the class of nonmanual employees whose duties do not call for the wearing of work clothes or protective clothing

white dwarf *n* a small whitish star of high surface temperature, low brightness, and high density

white elephant *n* **1** a property requiring much care and expense and yielding little profit **2** sthg that is no longer of value (to its owner)

white feather *n* a mark or symbol of cowardice

white flag *n* a flag of plain white used as a flag of truce or as a token of surrender

Whitehall /ˈwaɪthɔːl, ˌwaɪtˈhɔːl/ *n* the British government

white heat *n* a temperature higher than red heat, at which a body emits white light

white hope *n* a person expected to bring fame and glory to his/her group, country, etc

White House *n* *the* executive branch of the US government

white lead *n* any of several white lead-containing pigments

white magic *n* magic used for good purposes (e g to cure disease)

whiten /ˈwaɪtn/ *v* to make or become white or whiter; bleach

white paper *n, often cap W&P* a (British) government report

white pepper *n* a condiment prepared from the husked dried berries of an E Indian plant used either whole or ground

white sauce *n* a sauce made with milk, cream, or a chicken, veal, or fish stock

white spirit *n* an inflammable liquid distilled from petroleum and used esp as a solvent and thinner for paints

white-tie *adj* characterized by or requiring the wearing of formal evening dress by men

¹whitewash /ˈwaɪtwɒʃ/ *v* **1** to apply whitewash to **2a** to gloss over or cover up (e g vices or crimes) **b** to exonerate by concealment or through biased presentation of data **3** to defeat overwhelmingly in a contest or game – infml

²whitewash *n* **1** a liquid mixture (e g of lime and water or whiting, size, and water) for whitening outside walls or similar surfaces **2** a whitewashing

whither /ˈwɪðəʳ/ *adv or conj* **1** to or towards what place? – also used in rhetorical questions without a verb **2** to the place at, in, or to which **3** to which place *USE* chiefly fml

whiting /ˈwaɪtɪŋ/ *n* any of various marine food fishes; *esp* one related to the cod

Whitsun /ˈwɪtsən/ *adj or n* (of, being, or observed on or at) Whitsunday or Whitsuntide

Whitsunday /ˌwɪtˈsʌndi/ *n* a Christian feast on the 7th Sunday after Easter commemorating the descent of the Holy Spirit at Pentecost

Whitsuntide /ˈwɪtsəntaɪd/ *n* Whitsunday and the following Monday and/or the days of public holiday celebrated with or in place of these days

whittle *v* **1a** to pare or cut off chips from the surface of (wood) with a knife **b** to shape or form by so paring or cutting **2** to reduce, remove, or destroy gradually as if by cutting off bits with a knife; pare – usu + *down* or *away*

whiz, whizz /wɪz/ *v* **1** to move (through the air) with a buzz or whirr **2** to move swiftly

whiz kid *n* sby unusually successful or clever, esp at an early age

who /huː/ *pron, pl* **who** **1** what or which person or people? **2** – used to introduce a relative clause (e g my father, *who* was a lawyer) *USE* often used as object of a verb or of a following preposition though still disapproved of by some

whoa /wəʊ, həʊ/ *interj* – used as a command (e g to a draught animal) to stand still

whodunit *also* **whodunnit** /ˌhuːˈdʌnɪt/ *n* a play, film, or story dealing with the detection of crime or criminals

whoever /huːˈevəʳ/ *pron* **1** whatever person **2** no matter who **3** who in the world? – chiefly infml *USE* (*1&2*) used in any grammatical relation except that of a possessive

[1]**whole** /həʊl/ *adj* **1a** free of wound, injury, defect, or impairment; intact, unhurt, or healthy **b** restored **2** having all its proper constituents; unmodified **3** each or all of; entire **4a** constituting an undivided unit; unbroken **b** directed to (the accomplishment of) 1 end or aim **5** very great – in *a whole lot*

[2]**whole** *n* **1** a complete amount or sum; sthg lacking no part, member, or element **2** sthg constituting a complex unity; a coherent system or organization of parts

wholehearted /ˌhəʊlˈhɑːtɪ̣d/ *adj* earnestly committed or devoted; free from all reserve or hesitation

wholemeal /ˈhəʊlmiːl/ *adj* made with (flour from) ground entire wheat kernels

[1]**wholesale** /ˈhəʊlseɪl/ *n* the sale of commodities in large quantities usu for resale (by a retailer) – **~r** *n*

[2]**wholesale** *adj or adv* **1** (sold or selling) at wholesale **2** (performed) on a large scale, esp without discrimination

wholesome /ˈhəʊlsəm/ *adj* **1** promoting health or well-being of mind or spirit **2** promoting health of body; *also* healthy – **~ness** *n*

wholly /ˈhəʊl-li/ *adv* **1** to the full or entire extent; completely **2** to the exclusion of other things; solely

whom /huːm/ *pron, objective case of* **who** – used as an interrogative or relative; used as object of a preceding preposition (e g for *whom* the bell tolls); or less frequently as object of a verb or of a following preposition (e g the man *whom* you wrote to)

whoop /wuːp, huːp/ *n* **1** a loud yell expressive of eagerness, exuberance, or jubilation **2** the hoot of an owl, crane, etc – **whoop** *v*

[1]**whoopee** /wʊˈpiː/ *interj* – used to express exuberance

[2]**whoopee** *n* boisterous convivial fun – in *make whoopee*; infml

whooping cough /ˈhuːpɪŋ kɒf/ *n* an infectious bacterial disease, esp of children, marked by a convulsive spasmodic cough sometimes followed by a crowing intake of breath

whoosh /wʊʃ/ *v or n* (to move quickly with) a swift or explosive rushing sound

whop /wɒp/ *v* **1** to beat, strike **2** to defeat totally *USE* infml

whopper /ˈwɒpəʳ/ *n* **1** sthg unusually large or otherwise extreme of its kind **2** an extravagant or monstrous lie *USE* infml

[1]**whopping** /ˈwɒpɪŋ/ *adj* extremely big – infml

[2]**whopping** *adv* very, extremely – infml

[1]**whore** /hɔːʳ/ *n* a prostitute

[2]**whore** *v* **1** to have sexual intercourse outside marriage, esp with a prostitute **2** to pursue an unworthy or idolatrous desire

whorl /wɜːl, wɔːl/ *n* **1** an arrangement of similar anatomical parts (e g leaves) in a circle round a point on an axis (e g a stem) **2** sthg spiral in form or movement; a swirl **3** a single turn of a spiral (shape) **4** a fingerprint in which the central ridges turn through at least 1 complete circle

[1]**whose** /huːz/ *adj* of whom or which, esp as possessor agent or object of an action (e g *whose* hat is this; the factory in *whose* construction they were involved)

[2]**whose** *pron, pl* **whose** that which belongs to whom – used without a following noun as a pronoun equivalent in meaning to the adjective *whose* (e g tell me *whose* it was)

whosoever /ˌhuːsəʊˈevəʳ/ *pron, archaic* whoever

[1]**why** /waɪ/ *adv* for what cause, reason, or purpose?

[2]**why** *conj* **1** the cause, reason, or purpose for which **2** on which grounds

[3]**why** *n, pl* **whys** a reason, cause – chiefly in *the whys and wherefores*

[4]**why** *interj* – used to express mild surprise, hesitation, approval, disapproval, or impatience

wick /wɪk/ *n* a cord, strip, or cylinder of loosely woven material through which a liquid (e g paraffin, oil, or melted wax) is drawn by capillary action to the top in a candle, lamp, oil stove, etc for burning

wicked /ˈwɪkɪ̣d/ *adj* **1** morally bad;

evil **2** disposed to mischief; roguish **3** very unpleasant, vicious, or dangerous – infml – **~ly** *adv* – **~ness** *n*

wicker /ˈwɪkəʳ/ *adj or n* (made of) interlaced osiers, twigs, canes, or rods

wickerwork /ˈwɪkəwɜːk/ *n* (work consisting of) wicker

wicket /ˈwɪkɨt/ *n* **1** a small gate or door; *esp* one forming part of or placed near a larger one **2a** either of the 2 sets of stumps set 22yd (20.12m) apart, at which the ball is bowled and which the batsman defends in cricket **b** the area 12ft (3.66m) wide bounded by these wickets **c** a partnership between 2 batsmen who are in at the same time

wicketkeeper /ˈwɪkɨtkiːpəʳ/ *n* the fieldsman in cricket who is stationed behind the batsman's wicket and whose object is to catch balls missed or hit with the edge of the bat by the batsman and to stump him if possible

[1]**wide** /waɪd/ *adj* **1a** having great horizontal extent; vast **b** embracing much; comprehensive **2a** having a specified width **b** having much extent between the sides; broad **3a** extending or fluctuating over a considerable range **b** distant or deviating from sthg specified **4** *Br* shrewd, astute – slang – **~ly** *adv*

[2]**wide** *adv* **1** over a great distance or extent; widely **2a** so as to leave much space or distance between **b** so as to miss or clear a point by a considerable distance **3** to the fullest extent; completely – often as an intensive + *open*

[3]**wide** *n* a ball bowled in cricket that is out of reach of the batsman in his normal position and counts as 1 run to his side

wide-angle *adj* (having or using a camera with a lens) that has an angle of view wider than the ordinary

wide-awake *adj* **1** fully awake **2** alertly watchful, esp for advantages or opportunities

widespread /ˈwaɪdspred/ *adj* **1** widely extended or spread out **2** widely diffused or prevalent

widgeon /ˈwɪdʒən/ *n* an Old World freshwater dabbling duck the male of which has a chestnut head

[1]**widow** /ˈwɪdəʊ/ *n* **1** a woman whose husband has died (and who has not remarried) **2** a woman whose husband spends much time away from her pursuing a specified (sporting) activity

[2]**widow** *v* **1** to cause to become a widow **2** to deprive of sthg greatly valued or needed

widower /ˈwɪdəʊəʳ/ *n* a man whose wife has died (and who has not remarried)

width /wɪdθ/ *n* **1** the measurement taken at right angles to the length **2** largeness of extent or scope

wield /wiːld/ *v* **1** to handle (e g a tool) effectively **2** to exert, exercise – **~er** *n*

wife /waɪf/ *n, pl* **wives** a married woman, esp in relation to her husband

wig /wɪg/ *n* a manufactured covering of natural or synthetic hair for the (bald part of a) head

wigging /ˈwɪgɪŋ/ *n* a severe scolding – infml

[1]**wiggle** /ˈwɪgəl/ *v* to (cause to) move with quick jerky or turning motions or smoothly from side to side

[2]**wiggle** *n* **1** a wiggling movement **2** a wavy line; a squiggle

wigwam /ˈwɪgwæm/ *n* a N American Indian hut having a framework of poles covered with bark, rush mats, or hides

[1]**wild** /waɪld/ *adj* **1a** (of organisms) living in a natural state and not (ordinarily) tame, domesticated, or cultivated **b** growing or produced without the aid and care of humans **2** not (amenable to being) inhabited or cultivated **3a(1)** free from restraint or regulation; uncontrolled **(2)** emotionally overcome; *also* passionately eager or enthusiastic **(3)** very angry; infuriated **b** marked by great agitation; *also* stormy **c** going beyond reasonable or conventional bounds; fantastic **4** uncivilized, barbaric **5a** deviating from the intended or regular course **b** having no logical basis; random **6** *of a playing card* able to represent any card designated by the holder – **~ly** *adv* – **~ness** *n*

²wild *n* **1** the wilderness **2** a wild, free, or natural state or existence

³wild *adv* in a wild manner: e g **a** without regulation or control **b** off an intended or expected course

wild boar *n* an Old World wild pig from which most domestic pigs have derived

¹wildcat /ˈwaɪldkæt/ *n* **1a** either of 2 cats that resemble but are heavier in build than the domestic cat and are usu held to be among its ancestors **b** any of various small or medium-sized cats (e g the lynx or ocelot) **2** a savage quick-tempered person

²wildcat *adj* **1** operating, produced, or carried on outside the bounds of standard or legitimate business practices **2** of or being an oil or gas well drilled in territory not known to be productive **3** initiated by a group of workers without formal union approval or in violation of a contract

³wildcat *v* to prospect and drill an experimental oil or gas well

wildebeest /ˈwɪldɪ̵biːst/ *n* a gnu

wilderness /ˈwɪldənɪ̵s/ *n* **1a** a (barren) region or area that is (essentially) uncultivated and uninhabited by human beings **b** an empty or pathless area or region **c** a part of a garden or nature reserve devoted to wild growth **2** a confusing multitude or mass **3** *the* state of exclusion from office or power

wildfire /ˈwaɪldfaɪəʳ/ *n* sthg that spreads very rapidly – usu in *like wildfire*

wildfowl /ˈwaɪldfaʊl/ *n* a wild duck, goose, or other game bird, esp a waterfowl

wild-goose chase *n* a hopeless pursuit after sthg unattainable

wildlife /ˈwaɪldlaɪf/ *n* wild animals

wiles /waɪlz/ *n pl* deceitful or beguiling tricks, esp used to persuade

wilful /ˈwɪlfəl/ *adj* **1** obstinately and often perversely self-willed **2** done deliberately; intentional – **~ly** *adv* – **~ness** *n*

¹will /wɪl/ *v, pres sing & pl* **will**; *pres neg* **won't** /wəʊnt/; *past* **would** /wəd; *strong* wʊd/ **1** – used to express choice, willingness, or consent or in negative constructions refusal (e g can find no one who *will* take the job); used in the question form with the force of a request or of an offer or suggestion (e g *will* you have some tea) **2** – used to express custom or inevitable tendency (e g accidents *will* happen); used with emphatic stress to express exasperation (e g he *will* drink his tea from a saucer) **3** – used to express futurity (e g tomorrow I will get up early) **4** can (e g the back seat *will* hold 3 passengers) **5** – used to express logical probability (e g that *will* be the milkman) **6** – used to express determination or to command or urge (e g you *will* do as I say at once) **7** to wish, desire (e g whether we *will* or no)

²will *n* **1** a desire, wish: e g **a** a resolute intention **b** an inclination **c** a choice, wish **2** what is wished or ordained by the specified agent **3a** a mental power by which one (apparently) controls one's wishes, intentions, etc **b** an inclination to act according to principles or ends **c** a specified attitude towards others **4** willpower, self-control **5** a (written) legal declaration of the manner in which sby would have his/her property disposed of after his/her death

³will *v* **1** to bequeath **2a** to determine deliberately; purpose **b** to (attempt to) cause by exercise of the will

willies /ˈwɪliz/ *n pl* nervousness, jitters – + *the*; infml

¹willing /ˈwɪlɪŋ/ *adj* **1** inclined or favourably disposed in mind; ready **2** prompt to act or respond **3** done, borne, or given without reluctance – **~ly** *adv* – **~ness** *n*

²willing *n* cheerful alacrity – in *show willing*

will-o'-the-wisp /ˌwɪl ə ðə ˈwɪsp/ *n* **1** a phosphorescent light sometimes seen over marshy ground and often caused by the combustion of gas from decomposed organic matter **2** an enticing but elusive goal

willow /ˈwɪləʊ/ *n* **1** any of a genus of trees and shrubs bearing catkins of petal-less flowers **2** an object made of willow wood; *esp* a cricket bat – infml

willow pattern *n* china tableware decorated with a usu blue-and-white story-telling design of oriental style

willowy /'wɪləʊi/ *adj* **1** full of willows **2a** supple, pliant **b** gracefully tall and slender

willpower /'wɪl,paʊəʳ/ *n* self-control, resoluteness

willy-nilly /,wɪli 'nɪli/ *adv or adj* **1** by compulsion; without choice **2** (carried out or occurring) in a haphazard or random manner

[1]**wilt** /wɪlt/ *archaic pres 2 sing of* **will**

[2]**wilt** *v* **1** *of a plant* to lose freshness and become flaccid; droop **2** to grow weak or faint; languish

[3]**wilt** *n* a disease of plants marked by wilting

wily /'waɪli/ *adj* full of wiles; crafty

wimple /'wɪmpəl/ *n* a cloth covering worn over the head and round the neck and chin, esp by women in the late medieval period and by some nuns

[1]**win** /wɪn/ *v* **won** **1a** to gain the victory in a contest; succeed **b** to be right in an argument, dispute, etc; *also* to have one's way **2a** to get possession of by qualities or fortune **b** to obtain by effort; earn **3a** to solicit and gain the favour of; *also* to persuade – usu + *over* or *round* **b** to induce (a woman) to accept oneself in marriage **4** to reach by expenditure of effort

[2]**win** *n* **1** a victory or success, esp in a game or sporting contest **2** first place at the finish, esp of a horse race

wince /wɪns/ *v* to shrink back involuntarily (e g from pain); flinch

winceyette /,wɪnsi'et/ *n* a lightweight usu cotton fabric napped on 1 or both sides

winch /wɪntʃ/ *n* any of various machines or instruments for hoisting or pulling; a windlass – **winch** *v*

[1]**wind** /wɪnd/ *n* **1** a (natural) movement of air, esp horizontally **2** a force or agency that carries along or influences; a trend **3** breath **4** gas generated in the stomach or the intestines **5a** musical wind instruments collectively, esp as distinguished from stringed and percussion instruments **b** *sing or pl in constr* the group of players of such instruments

[2]**wind** /wɪnd/ *v* **1** to make short of breath **2** to rest (e g a horse) in order to allow the breath to be recovered

[3]**wind** /waɪnd/ *v* **winded, wound** to sound (e g a call or note) on a horn

[4]**wind** *v* **wound** **1** to have a curving course; extend or proceed in curves **2** to coil, twine **3a** to surround or wrap with sthg pliable **b** to tighten the spring of **4** to raise to a high level (e g of excitement or tension) – usu + *up*

[5]**wind** *n* a coil, turn

windbag /'wɪndbæg/ *n* an excessively talkative person – infml

windbreak /'wɪndbreɪk/ *n* sthg (e g a growth of trees or a fence) that breaks the force of the wind

windcheater /'wɪnd,tʃiːtəʳ/ *n, chiefly Br* a weatherproof or windproof coat or jacket; an anorak

windfall /'wɪndfɔːl/ *n* **1** sthg, esp a fruit, blown down by the wind **2** an unexpected gain or advantage; *esp* a legacy

winding-sheet *n* a sheet in which a corpse is wrapped for burial

wind instrument /'wɪnd ,ɪnstrʊmənt/ *n* a musical instrument (e g a trumpet, clarinet, or recorder) sounded by the player's breath

windjammer /'wɪnd,dʒæməʳ/ *n* **1** a large fast square-rigged sailing vessel **2** *Br* a windcheater

windlass /'wɪndləs/ *n* any of various machines for hoisting or hauling: e g **a** a horizontal drum supported on vertical posts and turned by a crank so that the hoisting rope is wound round the drum **b** a steam, electric, etc winch with a horizontal or vertical shaft and 2 drums, used to raise a ship's anchor

windmill /'wɪnd,mɪl/ *n* **1** a mill operated by vanes that are turned by the wind **2** a toy consisting of lightweight vanes that revolve at the end of a stick

window /'wɪndəʊ/ *n* **1** an opening, esp in the wall of a building, for admission of light and air that is usu fitted with a frame containing glass and capable of being opened and shut **2** a pane (e g of glass) in a window **3** an interval of time within which a rocket or spacecraft must be launched to accomplish a particular mission

window box *n* a box for growing plants on the (outside) sill of a window

window dressing *n* the display of merchandise in a shop window

windpipe /ˈwɪndpaɪp/ *n* the trachea – not used technically

windscreen /ˈwɪndskriːn/ *n, Br* a transparent screen, esp of glass, at the front of a (motor) vehicle

wind-sock *n* a truncated cloth cone that is open at both ends and mounted on a pole and is used to indicate the direction of the wind, esp at airfields

windswept /ˈwɪndswept/ *adj* dishevelled (as if) from being exposed to the wind

wind tunnel *n* a tunnel-like apparatus through which air is blown at a known velocity to determine the effects of wind pressure on an object placed in the apparatus

wind up *v* **1** to bring to a conclusion; *specif* to bring (a business) to an end by liquidation **2** to put in order; settle

windward /ˈwɪndwəd/ *adj, adv, or n* (in or facing) the direction from which the wind is blowing

windy /ˈwɪndi/ *adj* **1a** windswept **b** marked by strong or stormy wind **2** *chiefly Br* frightened, nervous – infml – **windily** *adv* – **windiness** *n*

¹wine /waɪn/ *n* **1** fermented grape juice containing varying percentages of alcohol together with ethers and esters that give it bouquet and flavour **2** the usu fermented juice of a plant or fruit used as a drink **3** the colour of red wine

²wine *v* to entertain with or drink wine – usu in *wine and dine*

wineglass /ˈwaɪnglɑːs/ *n* any of several variously shaped and sized drinking glasses for wine, that usu have a rounded bowl and are mounted on a stem and foot

¹wing /wɪŋ/ *n* **1a** (a part of a nonflying bird or insect corresponding to) any of the movable feathered or membranous paired appendages by means of which a bird, bat, or insect flies **b** any of various body parts (e g of a flying fish or flying lemur) providing means of limited flight **2** an appendage or part resembling a wing in shape, appearance, or position: e g **a** a sidepiece at the top of a high-backed armchair **b** any of the aerofoils that develop a major part of the lift which supports a heavier-than-air aircraft **c** *Br* a mudguard, esp when forming an integral part of the body of a motor vehicle **3** a means of flight – usu pl with sing. meaning **4** a part of a building projecting from the main or central part **5** *pl* the area at the side of the stage out of sight of the audience **6a** a left or right flank of an army or fleet **b** any of the attacking positions or players on either side of a centre position in certain team sports **7** *sing or pl in constr* a group or faction holding distinct opinions or policies within an organized body (e g a political party) **8** an operational and administrative unit of an air force – **~less** *adj*

²wing *v* **1** to (enable to) fly or move swiftly **2** to wound (e g with a bullet) without killing

wing commander *n* a middle-ranking officer in the Royal Air Force

winger /ˈwɪŋəʳ/ *n, chiefly Br* a player (e g in soccer) in a wing position

wing nut *n* a nut that has projecting wings or flanges so that it may be turned by finger and thumb

wingspan /ˈwɪŋspæn/ *n* the distance from the tip of one of a pair of wings to that of the other

¹wink /wɪŋk/ *v* **1** to shut 1 eye briefly as a signal or in teasing; *also, of an eye* to shut briefly **2** to avoid seeing or noting sthg – usu + *at* **3** to gleam or flash intermittently; twinkle

²wink *n* **1** a brief period of sleep; a nap **2** an act of winking **3** the time of a wink; an instant **4** a hint or sign given by winking

winkle /ˈwɪŋkəl/ *n* a small edible marine snail

winkle out *v, chiefly Br* to displace or extract from a position; *also* to discover or identify with difficulty

winner /ˈwɪnəʳ/ *n* sthg (expected to be) successful – infml

winnow /ˈwɪnəʊ/ *v* **1a** to get rid of (sthg undesirable or unwanted); remove – often + *out* **b** to separate, sift **2** to remove waste matter from (e g grain) by exposure to a current of air

winsome /ˈwɪnsəm/ *adj* pleasing and engaging, often because of a childlike charm and innocence – ~ly *adv* – ~ness *n*

[1]**winter** /ˈwɪntəʳ/ *n* **1** the season between autumn and spring comprising in the N hemisphere the months December, January, and February **2** the colder part of the year **3** a year – usu pl **4** a period of inactivity or decay – -try, ~y *adj*

[2]**winter** *adj* **1** of, during, or suitable for winter **2** sown in autumn and harvested the following spring or summer

[3]**winter** *v* to keep or feed (e g livestock) during the winter

win through *v* to reach a desired or satisfactory end, esp after overcoming difficulties

[1]**wipe** /waɪp/ *v* **1a** to clean or dry by rubbing, esp with or on sthg soft **b** to draw or pass for rubbing or cleaning **2a** to remove (as if) by rubbing **b** to erase completely; obliterate **3** to spread (as if) by wiping

[2]**wipe** *n* **1** an act or instance of wiping **2** power or capacity to wipe

wipeout /ˈwaɪpaʊt/ *n* a fall from a surfboard caused usu by loss of control

wipe out *v* to destroy completely; annihilate

[1]**wire** /waɪəʳ/ *n* **1** metal in the form of a usu very flexible thread or slender rod **2a** a line of wire for conducting electrical current **b** a telephone or telegraph wire or system **c** a telegram **3** a barrier or fence of usu barbed wire

[2]**wire** *v* to send or send word to by telegraph

[1]**wireless** /ˈwaɪələ̟s/ *adj, chiefly Br* of radiotelegraphy, radiotelephony, or radio

[2]**wireless** *n, chiefly Br* (a) radio

wire netting *n* a network of coarse woven wire

wire wool *n* an abrasive material consisting of fine wire strands woven into a mass and used for scouring esp kitchen utensils (e g pans)

wireworm /ˈwaɪəwɜːm/ *n* the slender hard-coated larva of various click beetles, destructive esp to plant roots

wiry /ˈwaɪəri/ *adj* **1** resembling wire, esp in form and flexibility **2** lean and vigorous; sinewy – **wiriness** *n*

wisdom /ˈwɪzdəm/ *n* **1a** accumulated learning; knowledge **b** the thoughtful application of learning; insight **2** good sense; judgment

wisdom tooth *n* any of the 4 molar teeth in humans which are the last to erupt on each side at the back of each jaw

[1]**wise** /waɪz/ *n* manner, way

[2]**wise** *adj* **1a** characterized by or showing wisdom; marked by understanding, discernment, and a capacity for sound judgment **b** judicious, prudent **2** well-informed **3** possessing inside knowledge; shrewdly cognizant – often + *to*

wisecrack /ˈwaɪzkræk/ *v or n* (to make) a sophisticated or knowing witticism – infml

wise guy *n* a conceited and self-assertive person – infml

[1]**wish** /wɪʃ/ *v* **1** to express the hope that sby will have or attain (sthg); *esp* to bid **2a** to give form to (a wish) **b** to feel or express a wish for; want **c** to request in the form of a wish; order **3** to make a wish

[2]**wish** *n* **1a** an act or instance of wishing or desire; a want **b** an object of desire; a goal **2a** an expressed will or desire **b** an expressed greeting – usu pl **3** a ritual act of wishing

wishbone /ˈwɪʃbəʊn/ *n* a forked bone in front of the breastbone of a bird consisting chiefly of the 2 clavicles fused at their lower ends

wishy-washy /ˈwɪʃi ˌwɒʃi/ *adj* **1** lacking in strength or flavour **2** lacking in character or determination; ineffectual *USE* infml

wisp /wɪsp/ *n* **1a** a thin separate streak or piece **b** sthg frail, slight, or fleeting **2** a flock of birds (e g snipe) – ~**y** *adj*

wisteria /wɪˈstɪərɪə/ , **wistaria** /wɪˈsteərɪə/ *n* any of a genus of chiefly Asiatic climbing plants with showy blue, white, purple, or rose flowers like those of the pea

wistful /ˈwɪstfəl/ *adj* **1** full of unfulfilled desire; yearning **2** musingly sad; pensive – ~**ly** *adv* – ~**ness** *n*

wit /wɪt/ *n* **1** reasoning power; intelligence **2a** mental soundness; sanity **b**

mental resourcefulness; ingenuity **3a** the ability to relate seemingly disparate things so as to illuminate or amuse **b** a talent for banter or raillery **4** a witty individual **5** *pl* senses

witch /wɪtʃ/ *n* **1** one who is credited with supernatural powers; *esp* a woman practising witchcraft **2** an ugly old woman; a hag – **~ery** *n*

witchcraft /ˈwɪtʃkrɑːft/ *n* (the use of) sorcery or magic

witch doctor *n* a professional sorcerer, esp in a primitive tribal society

witch-hunt *n* the searching out and harassment of those with unpopular views – **witch-hunting** *n*

with /wɪð, wɪθ/ *prep* **1a** in opposition to; against (e g had a fight *with* his brother) **b** so as to be separated or detached from (e g I disagree *with* you) **2a** in relation to (e g the frontier *with* Yugoslavia) **b** – used to indicate the object of attention, behaviour, or feeling (e g in love *with* her) **c** in respect to; so far as concerns (e g the trouble *with* this machine) – sometimes used redundantly (e g get it finished *with*) **3a** – used to indicate accompaniment or association **b** – used to indicate one to whom a usu reciprocal communication is made (e g talking *with* a friend) **c** – used to express agreement or sympathy (e g forced to conclude *with* him that it is a forgery) **d** able to follow the reasoning of **4a** on the side of; for **b** employed by **5a** – used to indicate the object of a statement of comparison, equality, or harmony (e g dress doesn't go *with* her shoes) **b** as well as **c** in addition to – used to indicate combination **d** inclusive of (e g costs £5 *with* tax) **6a** by means of; using **b** through the effect of (e g pale *with* anger) **7b** – used to indicate an attendant or contributory circumstance (e g stood there *with* his hat on) **c** in the possession or care of (e g the decision rests *with* you) **8a** – used to indicate a close association in time e g *with* the outbreak of war, they went home) **b** in proportion to (e g the pressure varies *with* the depth) **9a** notwithstanding; in spite of (e g love her *with* all her faults) **b** except for (e g similar, *with* 1 important difference)

withdraw /wɪðˈdrɔː, wɪθ-/ *v* **1a** to go back or away; retire from participation **b** to retreat **c** to remove money from a place of deposit **2** to become socially or emotionally detached **3** to retract – **~al** *n*

withdrawn /wɪðˈdrɔːn, wɪθ-/ *adj* **1** secluded, isolated **2** socially detached and unresponsive; *also* shy

wither /ˈwɪðəʳ/ *v* **1** to become dry and shrivel (as if) from loss of bodily moisture **2** to lose vitality, force, or freshness **3** to make speechless or incapable of action; stun – **~ing** *adj* – **~ingly** *adv*

withers /ˈwɪðəz/ *n pl* the ridge between the shoulder bones of a horse or other quadruped

withhold /wɪðˈhəʊld, wɪθ-/ *v* **1** to hold back from action; check **2** to refrain from granting or giving

¹within /wɪˈðɪn/ *adv* **1** in or into the interior; inside **2** in one's inner thought, mood, or character

²within *prep* **1** inside – used to indicate enclosure or containment, esp in sthg large **2** – used to indicate situation or circumstance in the limits or compass of: e g **a(1)** before the end of (e g gone *within* a week) **(2)** since the beginning of (e g been there *within* the last week) **b(1)** not beyond the quantity, degree, or limitations of (e g was *within* his income) **(2)** in or into the scope or sphere of (e g *within* his rights) **(3)** in or into the range of (e g *within* reach) **(4)** – used to indicate a specific difference or margin (e g *within* a mile of the town) **3** to the inside of; into

³within *n* an inner place or area

¹without /wɪˈðaʊt/ *prep* **1** – used to indicate the absence or lack of or freedom from sthg **2** outside – now chiefly poetic

²without *adv* **1** with sthg lacking or absent **2** on or to the exterior; outside – now chiefly poetic

³without *conj, chiefly dial* unless

⁴without *n* an outer place or area

withstand /wɪðˈstænd, wɪθ-/ *v* **1** to resist with determination; *esp* to stand up against successfully **2** to be proof against

witless /ˈwɪtlɨs/ *adj* **1** lacking wit or

understanding; foolish **2** crazy – **~ly** *adv* – **~ness** *n*

¹witness /ˈwɪtn̩ɪ̈s/ *n* **1** sby who gives evidence, specif before a tribunal **2** sby asked to be present at a transaction so as to be able to testify to its having taken place **3** sby who personally sees or hears an event take place **4** public affirmation by word or example of usu religious faith or conviction

²witness *v* **1** to testify to **2** to act as legal witness of (e g by signing one's name) **3** to give proof of; betoken – often in the subjunctive **4** to observe personally or directly; see for oneself **5** to be the scene or time of

witness-box *n, chiefly Br* an enclosure in which a witness testifies in court

witticism /ˈwɪtɪ̈sɪzəm/ *n* a witty and often ironic remark

witty /ˈwɪti/ *adj* **1** amusingly or ingeniously clever **2** having or showing wit **3** quick to see or express illuminating or amusing relationships or insights

wives /waɪvz/ *pl of* **wife**

¹wizard /ˈwɪzəd/ *n* **1** a man skilled in magic **2** one who is very clever or skilful, esp in a specified field – infml

²wizard *adj, chiefly Br* great, excellent – infml

woad /wəʊd/ *n* (a European plant of the mustard family formerly grown for) the blue dyestuff yielded by its leaves

¹wobble /ˈwɒbəl/ *v* **1a** to proceed with an irregular swerving or staggering motion **b** to rock unsteadily from side to side **2** to waver, vacillate

²wobble *n* **1** an unequal rocking motion **2** an act or instance of vacillating or fluctuating – **wobbly** *adj*

¹woe /wəʊ/ *interj* – used to express grief, regret, or distress

²woe *n* **1** great sorrow or suffering caused by misfortune, grief, etc **2** a calamity, affliction – usu pl

woebegone /ˈwəʊbɪgɒn/ *adj* expressive of great sorrow or misery

woeful *also* **woful** /ˈwəʊfəl/ *adj* **1** feeling or expressing woe **2** inspiring woe; grievous – **~ly** *adv*

woke /wəʊk/ *past of* **wake**

woken /ˈwəʊkən/ *past part of* **wake**

wold /wəʊld/ *n* an upland area of open country

¹wolf /wʊlf/ *n* **1** (the fur of) any of various large predatory flesh-eating mammals that resemble the related dogs, prey on livestock, and usu hunt in packs **2** a fiercely rapacious person **3** a man who pursues women in an aggressive way – infml – **~ish** *adj*

²wolf *v* to eat greedily; devour – often + *down*

wolf whistle *n* a distinctive whistle sounded by a man to express sexual admiration for a woman

woman /ˈwʊmən/ *n, pl* **women** /ˈwɪmɪ̈n/ **1a** an adult female human as distinguished from a man or child **b** a woman belonging to a particular category (e g by birth, residence, membership, or occupation) – usu in combination **2** womankind **3** distinctively feminine nature; womanliness **4** a personal maid, esp in former times – **~ly** *adj*

womanhood /ˈwʊmənhʊd/ *n* **1a** the condition of being an adult female as distinguished from a child or male **b** the distinguishing character or qualities of a woman or of womankind **2** women, womankind

womanish /ˈwʊmənɪʃ/ *adj* unsuitable to a man or to a strong character of either sex; effeminate

womanize /wʊmənaiz/ *v* to spend much time with, or chase after women, esp for sex

womankind /ˈwʊmənkaɪnd/ *n sing or pl in constr* female human beings; women as a whole, esp as distinguished from men

womb /wuːm/ *n* **1** the uterus **2** a place where sthg is generated

wombat /ˈwɒmbæt/ *n* any of several stocky Australian marsupial mammals resembling small bears

won /wʌn/ *past of* **win**

¹wonder /ˈwʌndəʳ/ *n* **1a** a cause of astonishment or admiration; a marvel **b** a miracle **2** rapt attention or astonishment at sthg unexpected, strange, new to one's experience, etc

²wonder *adj* noted for outstanding success or achievement

³wonder *v* **1a** to be in a state of wonder; marvel *at* **b** to feel surprise **2** to feel curiosity or doubt; speculate – ~**ingly** *adv*

wonderful /ˈwʌndəfəl/ *adj* **1** exciting wonder; astonishing **2** unusually good; admirable – ~**ly** *adv*

wonderland /ˈwʌndəlænd/ *n* **1** a fairylike imaginary place **2** a place that excites admiration or wonder

wonderment /ˈwʌndəmənt/ *n* **1** astonishment, marvelling **2** a cause of or occasion for wonder **3** curiosity

wondrous /ˈwʌndrəs/ *adj* wonderful – poetic

wonky /ˈwɒŋki/ *adj, Br* awry, crooked; *also* shaky, unsteady – infml

[1]**wont** /wəʊnt/ *adj* **1** accustomed, used **2** inclined, apt *USE* + *to* and infin; fml

[2]**wont** *n* customary practice – fml

woo /wuː/ *v* to try to win the affection of and a commitment of marriage from (a woman); court – ~**er** *n*

[1]**wood** /wʊd/ *n* **1** a dense growth of trees, usu greater in extent than a copse and smaller than a forest – often pl with sing. meaning **2a** a hard fibrous plant tissue that makes up the greater part of the stems and branches of trees or shrubs beneath the bark **b** wood suitable or prepared for some use (e g burning or building) **3a** a golf club with a wooden head **b** a wooden cask **c** any of the large wooden bowls used in the sport of bowling

[2]**wood** *adj* **1** wooden **2** suitable for cutting, storing, or carrying wood

[1]**woodblock** /ˈwʊdblɒk/ *n* a woodcut

[2]**woodblock** *adj, of a floor* made of parquet

woodcock /ˈwʊdkɒk/ *n* an Old World long-billed wading bird of wooded regions that is related to the sandpipers and shot as game

woodcraft /ˈwʊdkrɑːft/ *n* **1** skill and practice in anything relating to woods or forests, esp in surviving, travelling, and hunting **2** skill in shaping or making things from wood

woodcut /ˈwʊdkʌt/ *n* (a print taken from) a relief-printing surface consisting of a wooden block with a design cut esp in the direction of the grain

wooded /ˈwʊdɨd/ *adj* covered with growing trees

wooden /ˈwʊdən/ *adj* **1** made or consisting of or derived from wood **2** lacking ease or flexibility; awkwardly stiff

woodland /ˈwʊdlənd, -lænd/ *n* land covered with trees, scrub, etc – often pl with sing. meaning

woodlouse /ˈwʊdlaʊs/ *n* a small ground-living crustacean with a flattened elliptical body often capable of rolling into a ball in defence

woodpecker /ˈwʊd,pekəʳ/ *n* any of numerous usu multicoloured birds with very hard bills used to drill holes in the bark or wood of trees to find insect food or to dig out nesting cavities

woodshed /ˈwʊdʃed/ *n* a shed for storing wood, esp firewood

woodsman /ˈwʊdzmən/ *n* one who lives in, frequents, or works in the woods

woodwind /ˈwʊd,wɪnd/ *n* **1** any of a group of wind instruments (e g a clarinet, flute, or saxophone) that is characterized by a cylindrical or conical tube of wood or metal, usu with finger holes or keys, that produces notes by the vibration of a single or double reed or by the passing of air over a mouth hole **2** *sing or pl in constr* the woodwind section of a band or orchestra – often pl with sing. meaning

woodwork /ˈwʊdwɜːk/ *n* **1** wooden interior fittings (e g mouldings or stairways) **2** the craft of constructing things from wood

woodworm /ˈwʊdwɜːm/ *n* an insect larva, esp that of the furniture beetle, that bores in dead wood; *also* an infestation of woodworm

woody /ˈwʊdi/ *adj* **1** overgrown with or having many woods **2a** of or containing (much) wood or wood fibres **b** *of a plant stem* tough and fibrous

[1]**woof** /wuːf/ *n* **1** the weft **2** a basic or essential element or material

[2]**woof** /wʊf/ *v or n* (to make) the low gruff sound characteristic of a dog

woofer /ˈwuːfəʳ/ *n* a loudspeaker that responds mainly to low frequencies

wool /wʊl/ *n* **1** the soft wavy coat of various hairy mammals, esp the sheep **2** a dense felted hairy covering, esp on a plant **3** a wiry or fibrous mass (e g of steel or glass) – usu in combination – ~len *adj*

[1]**woolly,** *NAm also* **wooly** /'wʊli/ *adj* **1** (made) of or resembling wool; *also* bearing (sthg like) wool **2a** lacking in clearness or sharpness of outline **b** marked by mental vagueness or confusion **3** boisterously rough – chiefly in *wild and woolly* – **-liness** *n*

[2]**woolly, woolie,** *NAm also* **wooly** *n, chiefly Br* a woollen jumper or cardigan

woolsack /'wʊlsæk/ *n* *the* official seat of the Lord Chancellor in the House of Lords

woozy /'wuːzi/ *adj* **1** mentally unclear or hazy **2** dizzy or slightly nauseous *USE* infml

Worcester sauce /,wʊstə 'sɔːs/ *n* a pungent sauce containing soy sauce, vinegar, and spices

[1]**word** /wɜːd/ *n* **1a** sthg that is said **b** *pl* talk, discourse **c** a short remark, statement, or conversation **2** a meaningful unit of spoken language that can stand alone as an utterance and is not divisible into similar units; *also* a written or printed representation of a spoken word that is usu set off by spaces on either side **3** an order, command **4** the expressed or manifested mind and will of God; *esp the* Gospel **5a** news, information **b** rumour **6** the act of speaking or of making verbal communication **7** a promise **8** *pl* a quarrelsome utterance or conversation **9** a verbal signal; a password **10** *the* most appropriate description – **~less** *adj* – **~lessly** *adv* – **~lessness** *n*

[2]**word** *v* to express in words; phrase

word-for-word *adj, of a report or translation* in or following the exact words; verbatim

wording /'wɜːdɪŋ/ *n* the act or manner of expressing in words

word-perfect *adj* having memorized sthg perfectly

wordy /'wɜːdi/ *adj* using or containing (too) many words – **wordily** *adv* – **wordiness** *n*

wore /wɔːʳ/ *past of* **wear**

[1]**work** /wɜːk/ *n* **1a** sustained physical or mental effort to achieve a result **b** the activities that afford one's accustomed means of livelihood **c** a specific task, duty, function, or assignment **2a** the (result of) expenditure of energy by natural phenomena **b** the transference of energy that is produced by the motion of the point of application of a force and is measured by the product of the force and the distance moved along the line of action **3a** (the result of) a specified method of working – often in combination **b** sthg made from a specified material – often in combination **4b** *pl* structures in engineering (e g docks, bridges, or embankments) or mining (e g shafts or tunnels) **5** *pl but sing or pl in constr* a place where industrial activity is carried out; a factory – often in combination **6** *pl* the working or moving parts of a mechanism **7** an artistic production or creation **8a** effective operation; an effect, result **b** activity, behaviour, or experience of the specified kind **9** *pl* **a** everything possessed, available, or belonging – infml; + *the* **b** subjection to all possible abuse – infml; usu + *get* or *give*

[2]**work** *adj* **1** suitable for wear while working **2** used for work

[3]**work** *v* **worked, wrought 1** to bring to pass; effect **2a** to fashion or create sthg by expending labour on; forge, shape **b** to make or decorate with needlework; embroider **3** to prepare or form into a desired state for use by kneading, hammering, etc **4** to operate **5** to solve (a problem) by reasoning or calculation – usu + *out* **6** to carry on an operation in (a place or area) **7a** to manoeuvre (oneself or an object) gradually or with difficulty into or out of a specified condition or position **b** to contrive, arrange

workable /'wɜːkəbəl/ *adj* **1** capable of being worked **2** practicable, feasible – **~ness** *n*

workaday /'wɜːkədeɪ/ *adj* **1** of or suited for working days **2** prosaic, ordinary

workbasket /'wɜːkbɑːskɪ̈t/ *n* a basket for needlework implements and materials

workbench /'wɜːkbentʃ/ *n* a bench on which work, esp of mechanics or carpenters, is performed

workbook /'wɜːkbʊk/ *n* an exercise

book of problems to be solved directly on the pages

worked up *adj* emotionally aroused; excited

worker /'wɜːkəʳ/ *n* **1a** one who works, esp at manual or industrial work or with a particular material – often in combination **b** a member of the working class **2** any of the sexually underdeveloped usu sterile members of a colony of ants, bees, etc that perform most of the labour and protective duties of the colony

workforce /'wɜːkfɔːs/ *n sing or pl in constr* the workers engaged in a specific activity or potentially available

workhouse /'wɜːkhaʊs/ *n Br* an institution formerly maintained at public expense to house paupers

work-in *n* a continuous occupation of a place of employment by employees continuing to work normally as a protest, usu against the threat of factory closure

work in *v* **1** to cause to penetrate by persistent effort **2** to insinuate unobtrusively; *also* to find room for

[1]**working** /'wɜːkɪŋ/ *adj* **1a** that functions or performs labour **b** *of a domestic animal* trained or bred for useful work **2** adequate to permit effective work to be done **3** serving as a basis for further work **4** during which one works; *also* during which one discusses business or policy

[2]**working** *n* **1** (a part of) a mine, quarry, or similar excavation **2** the fact or manner of functioning or operating – usu pl with sing. meaning

working class *n sing or pl in constr* the class of people who work (manually) for wages – often pl with sing. meaning

working party *n, chiefly Br* a committee set up (e g by a government) to investigate and report on a particular problem

workman /'wɜːkmən/ *n* an artisan

workmanlike /'wɜːkmənlaɪk/ *adj* worthy of a good workman: **a** skilful **b** efficient in appearance

workmanship /'wɜːkmənʃɪp/ *n* the relative art or skill of a workman; craftsmanship; *also* the quality or finish exhibited by a thing

work off *v* to dispose of or get rid of by work or activity

workout /'wɜːkaʊt/ *n* a practice or exercise to test or improve fitness, ability, or performance, esp for sporting competition

work out *v* **1a** to find out by calculation **b** to amount to a total or calculated figure – often + *at* or *to* **2** to devise by resolving difficulties **3** to elaborate in detail

work over *v* **1** to subject to thorough examination, study, or treatment **2** to beat up thoroughly; manhandle – infml

works /wɜːks/ *adj* of a place of industrial labour

workshop /'wɜːkʃɒp/ *n* **1** a room or place (e g in a factory) in which manufacture or repair work is carried out **2** a brief intensive educational programme for a relatively small group of people in a given field that emphasizes participation

workshy /'wɜːkʃaɪ/ *adj* disliking work; lazy

worktop /'wɜːktɒp/ *n* a flat surface (e g of Formica) on a piece of esp kitchen furniture (e g a cupboard or dresser) suitable for working on

work-to-rule *n* an instance of industrial action designed to reduce output by deliberately keeping very rigidly to rules and regulations

[1]**world** /wɜːld/ *n* **1** the earth with its inhabitants and all things on it **2** the course of human affairs **3** the human race **4** the concerns of earthly existence or secular affairs as distinguished from heaven and the life to come or religious and ecclesiastical matters **5** the system of created things; the universe **6** a distinctive class of people or their sphere of interest **7a** human society as a whole; *also* the public **b** fashionable or respectable people; public opinion **8** a part or section of the earth that is a separate independent unit **9a** one's personal environment in the sphere of one's life or work **b** a particular aspect of one's life **10** an indefinite multitude or a great quantity or amount **11** a planet; *esp* one that is inhabited *USE* (*except 10 & 11*) + *the*

[2]**world** *adj* **1** of the whole world **2**

extending or found throughout the world; worldwide

worldly /ˈwɜːldli/ *adj* of or devoted to this world and its pursuits rather than to religion or spiritual affairs – **-liness** *n*

worldly-wise *adj* possessing a practical and often shrewd and materialistic understanding of human affairs; sophisticated

world war *n* a war engaged in by (most of) the principal nations of the world; *esp, cap both Ws* either of 2 such wars of the first half of the 20th c

world-weary *adj* bored with the life of the world and its material pleasures – **-riness** *n*

worldwide /ˌwɜːldˈwaɪd/ *adj* extended throughout or involving the entire world

[1]**worm** /wɜːm/ *n* **1a** an earthworm **b** any of numerous relatively small elongated soft-bodied invertebrate animals **2** a human being who is an object of contempt, loathing, or pity; a wretch **3** infestation with or disease caused by parasitic worms – usu pl with sing. meaning but sing. or pl in constr **4** the thread of a screw

[2]**worm** *v* **1a** to cause to move or proceed (as if) in the manner of a worm **b** to insinuate or introduce (oneself) by devious or subtle means **2** to obtain or extract by artful or insidious questioning or by pleading, asking, or persuading – usu + *out of*

worm-eaten *adj* **1** eaten or burrowed into (as if) by worms **2** worn-out, antiquated

worn /wɔːn/ *past part of* **wear**

worn-out *adj* exhausted or used up (as if) by wear

worrisome /ˈwʌrɪsəm/ *adj* **1** causing distress or worry **2** inclined to worry or fret

[1]**worry** /ˈwʌri/ *v* **1** to shake or pull at with the teeth **2** to work at sthg difficult **3a** to feel or experience concern or anxiety; fret **b** to subject to persistent or nagging attention or effort **4** to afflict with mental distress or agitation; make anxious – **~ingly** *adv*

[2]**worry** *n* **1** mental distress or agitation resulting from concern, usu for sthg impending or anticipated; anxiety **2** a cause of worry; a trouble, difficulty – **-ried** *adj* – **-riedly** *adv*

[1]**worse** /wɜːs/ *adj, comparative of* **bad** *or* **ill** **1** of lower quality **2** in poorer health

[2]**worse** *n, pl* **worse** sthg worse

[3]**worse** *adv, comparative of* **bad, badly,** *or* **ill** in a worse manner; to a worse extent or degree

[1]**worship** /ˈwɜːʃɪp/ *n* **1** (an act of) reverence offered to a divine being or supernatural power **2** a form of religious practice with its creed and ritual **3** extravagant admiration for or devotion to an object of esteem **4** *chiefly Br* a person of importance – used as a title for various officials (e g magistrates and some mayors)

[2]**worship** *v* **1** to honour or reverence as a divine being or supernatural power **2** to regard with great, even extravagant respect, honour, or devotion – **~per** *n*

[1]**worst** /wɜːst/ *adj, superlative of* **bad** *or* **ill** **1** most productive of evil **2** most wanting in quality

[2]**worst** *n, pl* **worst** **1** the worst state or part **2** sby or sthg that is worst **3** the utmost harm of which one is capable (e g do your *worst*)

[3]**worst** *adv, superlative of* **bad, badly,** *or* **ill** in the worst manner; to the worst extent or degree

[4]**worst** *v* to get the better of; defeat

worsted /ˈwʊstɪ̣d/ *n* a smooth compact yarn from long wool fibres used esp for firm napless fabrics, carpeting, or knitting

[1]**worth** /wɜːθ/ *prep* **1a** equal in value to **b** having property equal to (e g he's *worth* £1,000,000) **2** deserving of

[2]**worth** *n* **1a** (money) value **b** the equivalent of a specified amount or figure (e g 3 quids*worth* of petrol) **2** moral or personal merit, esp high merit – **~less** *adj* – **~lessly** *adv* – **~lessness** *n*

worthwhile /ˌwɜːθˈwaɪl/ *adj* worth the time or effort spent

[1]**worthy** /ˈwɜːði/ *adj* **1a** having moral worth or value **b** honourable, meritorious **2** important enough; deserving – **-thily** *adv* – **-thiness** *n*

[2]**worthy** *n* a worthy or prominent person – often humor

would /wʊd/ *past of* **will** **1a** to desire,

wish **b** – used in auxiliary function with *rather* or *soon, sooner* to express preference **2a** – used in auxiliary function to express wish, desire, or intent (e g those who *would* forbid gambling); used in the question form with the force of a polite request or of an offer or suggestion (e g *would* you like some tea?) **b** – used in auxiliary function in reported speech or writing to represent *shall* or *will* (e g said he *would* come) **3a** used to (e g we *would* meet often for lunch) – used with emphatic stress to express exasperation **b** – used in auxiliary function with emphatic stress as a comment on the annoyingly typical (e g you *would* say that) **4** – used in auxiliary function to introduce a contingent fact, possibility, or presumption (e g it *would* break if you dropped it) or after a verb expressing desire, request, or advice (e g wish he *would* go) **5** could (e g door *wouldn't* open) **6** – used in auxiliary function to soften direct statement (e g that *would* be the milkman)

would-be *adj* desiring or intended to be

[1]**wound** /wu:nd/ *n* **1** an injury to the body or to a plant (e g from violence or accident) that involves tearing or breaking of a membrane (e g the skin) and usu damage to underlying tissues **2** a mental or emotional hurt or blow

[2]**wound** /wu:nd/ *v* to cause a wound to or in

[3]**wound** /waʊnd/ *past of* **wind**

[1]**wove** /wəʊv/ *past of* **weave**

[2]**wove** *n* paper made in such a way that no fine lines run across the grain

woven /ˈwəʊvən/ *past part of* **weave**

[1]**wow** /waʊ/ *interj* – used to express strong feeling (e g pleasure or surprise); slang

[2]**wow** *n* a striking success; a hit – slang

[3]**wow** *v* to excite to enthusiastic admiration or approval – slang

[4]**wow** *n* a distortion in reproduced sound that is heard as a slow rise and fall in the pitch of the sound and is caused by variations in the speed of the reproducing system

[1]**wrack** /ræk/ *n* **1** destruction **2** (a remnant of) sthg destroyed

[2]**wrack** *n* (dried) marine vegetation

wraith /reɪθ/ *n* an apparition of a living person in his/her exact likeness seen before or after death

[1]**wrangle** /ˈræŋgəl/ *v* to dispute angrily or peevishly; bicker

[2]**wrangle** *n* an angry, noisy, or prolonged dispute or quarrel

wrangler /ˈræŋgləʳ/ *n* **1** a bickering disputant **2** the holder of a Cambridge first in mathematics

[1]**wrap** /ræp/ *v* **1a** to envelop, pack, or enfold in sthg flexible **b** to fold round sthg specified **2** to involve completely; engross – usu + *up*

[2]**wrap** *n* **1** a wrapping; *specif* a waterproof wrapping placed round food to be frozen, esp in a domestic freezer **2** an article of clothing that may be wrapped round a person; *esp* an outer garment (e g a shawl)

wrapper /ˈræpəʳ/ *n* that in which sthg is wrapped: e g **a** a fine quality tobacco leaf used for the covering of a cigar **b** a dust jacket on a book

wrapping /ˈræpɪŋ/ *n* material used to wrap an object

wrap up *v* **1** to bring to a usu successful conclusion; end – infml **2** to protect oneself with outer garments

wrath /rɒθ/ *n* **1** strong vengeful anger or indignation **2** retributory, esp divine, chastisement – **~ful** *adj* – **~fully** *adv*

wreak /ri:k/ *v* **1** to give free play to (malevolent feeling); inflict **2** to cause or create (havoc or destruction)

wreath /ri:θ/ *n* **1** sthg intertwined into a circular shape; *esp* a garland **2** a drifting and coiling whorl

wreathe /ri:ð/ *v* **1** to cause (the face) to take on a happy joyful expression – usu pass **2a** to shape (e g flowers) into a wreath **b** to coil about sthg

[1]**wreck** /rek/ *n* **1** sthg cast up on the land by the sea, esp after a shipwreck **2a** (a) shipwreck **b** destruction **3a** the broken remains of sthg (e g a building or vehicle) wrecked or ruined **b** a person or animal of broken constitution, health, or spirits

[2]**wreck** *v* **1** to cast ashore **2a** to reduce to a ruinous state by violence **b** to

cause (a vessel) to be shipwrecked **c** to involve in disaster or ruin

wreckage /'rekɪdʒ/ *n* **1** wrecking or being wrecked **2** broken and disordered parts or material from a wrecked structure

wrecker /'rekəʳ/ *n* **1** sby who wrecks ships (e g by false lights) for plunder **2** sby whose work is the demolition of buildings

wren /ren/ *n* a very small European bird that has a short erect tail and is noted for its loud song

Wren *n* a woman serving in the Women's Royal Naval Service

¹wrench /rentʃ/ *v* **1** to pull or twist violently **2** to injure or disable by a violent twisting or straining **3** to distort, pervert **4** to snatch forcibly; wrest

²wrench *n* **1a** a violent twisting or a sideways pull **b** (a sharp twist or sudden jerk causing) a strain to a muscle, ligament, etc (e g of a joint) **2** a spanner with jaws adjustable for holding nuts of different sizes

wrest /rest/ *v* **1** to obtain or take away by violent wringing or twisting **2** to obtain with difficulty by force or determined labour

wrestle /'resəl/ *v* **1** to fight hand-to-hand without hitting with the aim of throwing or immobilizing an apponent **2** to push, pull, or manhandle by force – **-tling** *n* – **~r** *n*

wretch /retʃ/ *n* **1** a profoundly unhappy or unfortunate person **2** a base, despicable, or vile person or animal – **~ed** *adj* – **~edly** *adv* – **~edness** *n*

¹wriggle /'rɪgəl/ *v* **1** to move the body or a bodily part to and fro with short writhing motions; squirm **2** to move or advance by twisting and turning **3** to extricate or insinuate oneself by manoeuvring, equivocation, evasion, etc

²wriggle *n* a short or quick writhing motion or contortion

wring /rɪŋ/ *v* **wrung** **1** to twist or compress, esp so as to extract liquid **2** to exact or extort by coercion or with difficulty **3** to twist together (one's clasped hands) as a sign of anguish **4** to distress, torment **5** to shake (sby's hand) vigorously in greeting

wringer /'rɪŋəʳ/ *n* a mangle

¹wrinkle /'rɪŋkəl/ *n* **1** a small ridge, crease, or furrow formed esp in the skin due to aging or stress or on a previously smooth surface (e g by shrinkage or contraction) **2** a valuable trick or dodge for effecting a result – infml – **-kly** *adj*

²wrinkle *v* to contract into wrinkles

wrist /rɪst/ *n* **1** (a part of a lower animal corresponding to) the (region of the) joint between the human hand and the arm **2** the part of a garment or glove covering the wrist

wristband /'rɪstbænd/ *n* a band (e g on the sleeve of a garment) encircling the wrist

wristwatch /'rɪstwɒtʃ/ *n* a small watch attached to a bracelet or strap and worn round the wrist

writ /rɪt/ *n* **1** an order in writing issued under seal in the name of the sovereign or of a court or judicial officer commanding or forbidding an act specified in it **2** a written order constituting a symbol of the power and authority of the issuer

write /raɪt/ *v* **wrote; written** **1a** to form (legible characters, symbols, or words) on a surface, esp with an instrument **b** to spell in writing **c** to cover, fill, or fill in by writing **2** to set down in writing: e g **a** to be the author of; compose **b** to use (a specific script or language) in writing

write-off *n* sthg written off as a total loss

write off *v* **1** to cancel **2** to concede to be irreparably lost, useless, or dead

writer /'raɪtəʳ/ *n* one who writes as an occupation; an author

writer's cramp *n* a painful spasmodic cramp of the hand or finger muscles brought on by excessive writing

write-up *n* a written, esp flattering, account

write up *v* **1** to put into finished written form **2** to bring up to date the writing of (e g a diary)

writhe /raɪð/ *v* **1** to proceed with twists and turns **2** to twist (as if) from pain or struggling **3** to suffer keenly

writing /'raɪtɪŋ/ *n* **1** the act, practice, or occupation of literary composition

2a written letters or words; *esp* handwriting **b** a written composition

[1]**wrong** /rɒŋ/ *n* **1** an injurious, unfair, or unjust act; action or conduct inflicting harm without due provocation or just cause **2** what is wrong, immoral, or unethical **3a** the state of being mistaken or incorrect **b** the state of being or appearing to be the offender

[2]**wrong** *adj* **1** against moral standards; evil **2** not right or proper according to a code, standard, or convention; improper **3** not according to truth or facts; incorrect; *also* in error; mistaken **4** not satisfactory (e g in condition, results, health, or temper) **5** not in accordance with one's needs, intent, or expectations **6** of or being the side of sthg not meant to be used or exposed or thought the less desirable – **~ly** *adv*

[3]**wrong** *adv* **1** without accuracy; incorrectly **2** without regard for what is proper **3** on a mistaken course; astray **4** out of proper working order

[4]**wrong** *v* **1** to do wrong to; injure, harm **2** to mistakenly impute a base motive to; misrepresent

wrongful /ˈrɒŋfəl/ *adj* **1** wrong, unjust **2** unlawful – **~ly** *n*

wrongheaded /ˌrɒŋˈhedɨd/ *adj* stubborn in adherence to wrong opinion or principles; perverse – **~ly** *adv* – **~ness** *n*

wrote /rəʊt/ *past of* **write**

wrought /rɔːt/ *adj* **1** worked into shape by artistry or effort **2** processed for use; manufactured **3** *of metals* beaten into shape by tools **4** deeply stirred; excited – usu + *up*

wrought iron *n* a tough malleable iron containing very little carbon and 1 or 2 per cent slag

wrung /rʌŋ/ *past of* **wring**

wry /raɪ/ *adj* **1** bent or twisted, esp to one side **2** ironically or grimly humorous – **~ly** *adv*

x /eks/ *n, pl* **x's, xs** *often cap* **1** (a graphic representation of or device for reproducing) the 24th letter of the English alphabet **2** ten **3** sby or sthg whose identity is unknown or withheld

X /eks/ *n or adj,* (a film that is) certified in Britain as suitable only for people over 18 – no longer used technically

X chromosome *n* a sex chromosome that in humans occurs paired in each female cell and single in each male cell

xerox /ˈzɪərɒks, ˈze-/ *v, often cap* to photocopy

Xmas /ˈkrɪsməs, ˈeksməs/ *n* Christmas

x-ray /ˈeks reɪ/ *v, often cap x* to examine, treat, or photograph with X rays

X ray *n* **1** an electromagnetic radiation of extremely short wavelength that has the properties of ionizing a gas when passing through it and of penetrating various thicknesses of all solids **2** an examination or photograph made by means of X rays

xylem /ˈzaɪləm, -lem/ *n* a complex vascular tissue of higher plants that functions chiefly in the conduction of water, gives support, and forms the woody part of many plants

xylophone /ˈzaɪləfəʊn/ *n* a percussion instrument that has a series of wooden bars graduated in length and sounded by striking with 2 small wooden hammers

Y

y /waɪ/ *n, pl* **y's, ys** *often cap* (a graphic representation of or device for reproducing) the 25th letter of the English alphabet

¹yacht /jɒt/ *n* any of various relatively small sailing or powered vessels that characteristically have a sharp prow and graceful lines and are used for pleasure cruising or racing

²yacht *v* to race or cruise in a yacht

¹yak /jæk/ *n* a large long-haired wild or domesticated ox of Tibet and nearby mountainous regions

²yak, yack *n* persistent or voluble talk – slang

³yak, yack *v* to talk persistently; chatter – slang

yam /jæm/ *n* **1** (any of various related plants with) an edible starchy tuberous root used as a staple food in tropical areas **2** *NAm* a moist-fleshed usu orange sweet potato

yank /jæŋk/ *v* to pull or extract (sthg) with a quick vigorous movement – infml

Yankee /'jæŋki/ *n* a native or inhabitant of **a** *chiefly Br* the USA **b** *chiefly NAm* the N USA **c** *NAm* New England

¹yap /jæp/ *v* **1** to bark snappishly; yelp **2** to talk in a shrill insistent querulous way; scold – infml

²yap *n* **1** a quick sharp bark; a yelp **2** (foolish) chatter – infml

¹yard /jɑːd/ *n* **1a** a unit of length equal to 3ft (about 0.914m) **b** a unit of volume equal to 1yd³ (about 0.765m³) **2** a long spar tapered towards the ends to support and spread a sail

²yard *n* **1a** a small usu walled and often paved area open to the sky and adjacent to a building; a courtyard **b** the grounds of a specified building or group of buildings – in combination **2a** an area with its buildings and facilities set aside for a specified business or activity – often in combination **b** a system of tracks for the storage and maintenance of railway carriages and wagons and the making up of trains **3** *cap, Br* Scotland Yard – + *the* **4** *NAm* a garden of a house

³yard *v* to drive into or confine in a restricted area; herd, pen

yardarm /'jɑːdɑːm/ *n* either end of the yard of a square-rigged ship

yardstick /'jɑːd,stɪk/ *n* a standard basis of calculation or judgment; a criterion

¹yarn /jɑːn/ *n* **1** thread; *esp* a spun thread (e g of wood, cotton, or hemp) as prepared and used for weaving, knitting, and rope-making **2a** a narrative of adventures; *esp* a tall tale **b** a conversation, chat *USE* (*2*) infml

²yarn *v* to tell a yarn; *also* to chat garrulously – infml

yarrow /'jærəʊ/ *n* a strong-scented Eurasian composite plant with dense heads of small usu white flowers

yashmak *also* **yasmak** /'jæʃmæk/ *n* a veil worn over the face by Muslim women, so that only the eyes remain exposed

yaw /jɔː/ *v* **1** to deviate erratically from a course **2** *of an aircraft, spacecraft, or projectile* to deviate from a straight course by esp side-to-side movement

yawl /jɔːl/ *n* a fore-and-aft rigged sailing vessel with sails set from a mainmast and a mizzenmast that is situated aft of the rudder

¹yawn /jɔːn/ *v* **1** to open wide; gape **2** to open the mouth wide and inhale, usu in reaction to fatigue or boredom

²yawn *n* **1** a deep usu involuntary intake of breath through the wide open mouth **2** a boring thing or person – slang

Y chromosome *n* a sex chromosome that in humans occurs paired with an X chromosome in each male cell and does not occur in female cells

¹ye /jiː/ *pron, archaic or dial* the ones being addressed; you

²ye *definite article, archaic* the

[1]yea /jeɪ/ *adv* **1** more than this; indeed **2** *archaic* yes

[2]yea *n* **1** affirmation, assent **2** *chiefly NAm* (a person casting) an affirmative vote

year /jɪəʳ, jɜːʳ/ *n* **1a** the period of about 365¼ solar days required for 1 revolution of the earth round the sun **b** the time required for the apparent sun to return to an arbitrary fixed or moving reference point in the sky **2a** a cycle in the Gregorian calendar of 365 or 366 days divided into 12 months beginning with January and ending with December **b** a period of time equal to 1 year of the Gregorian calendar but beginning at a different time **3** a calendar year specified usu by a number **4** *pl* age; *also* old age

yearbook /'jɪəbʊk/ *n* a book published yearly as a report or summary of statistics or facts

yearling /'jɪəlɪŋ, 'jɜː-/ *n* sby or sthg 1 year old: e g **a** an animal 1 year old or in its second year **b** a racehorse between January 1st of the year following its birth and the next January 1st

yearly /'jɪəli, 'jɜː-/ *adj* **1** reckoned by the year **2** done or occurring once every year; annual

yearn /jɜːn/ *v* **1** to long persistently, wistfully, or sadly **2** to feel tenderness or compassion – **~ing** *n*

yeast /jiːst/ *n* **1** a (commercial preparation of) yellowish surface froth or sediment that consists largely of fungal cells, occurs esp in sweet liquids in which it promotes alcoholic fermentation, and is used esp in making alcoholic drinks and as a leaven in baking **2** a minute fungus that is present and functionally active in yeast, usu has little or no mycelium, and reproduces by budding

yeasty /'jiːsti/ *adj* **1** of or resembling yeast **2** churning with growth and change; turbulent

[1]yell /jel/ *v* to utter a sharp loud cry, scream, or shout

[2]yell *n* a scream, shout

[1]yellow /'jeləʊ/ *adj* **1a** of the colour yellow **b** yellowish through age, disease, or discoloration; sallow **2a** featuring sensational or scandalous items or ordinary news sensationally distorted **b** dishonourable, cowardly – infml

[2]yellow *v* to make or become yellow – **~ish** *adj*

[3]yellow *n* **1** a colour whose hue resembles that of ripe lemons or dandelions and lies between green and orange in the spectrum **2** sthg yellow: *esp* the yolk of an egg

yellow fever *n* an often fatal infectious disease of warm regions caused by a mosquito-transmitted virus and marked by fever, jaundice, and often bleeding

yelp /jelp/ *v or n* (to utter) a sharp quick shrill cry

[1]yen /jen/ *n* the basic unit of currency of Japan

[2]yen *n* a strong desire or propensity; a longing – infml

yeoman /'jəʊmən/ *n* **1** a petty officer who carries out visual signalling in the British navy **2** a small farmer who cultivates his own land

yeomanry /'jəʊmənri/ *n sing or pl in constr* **1** the body of small landed proprietors **2** a British volunteer cavalry force created from yeomen in 1761 as a home defence force and reorganized in 1907 as part of the territorial force

[1]yes /jes/ *adv* **1** – used in answers expressing affirmation, agreement, or willingness; contrasted with *no* **2** – used in answers correcting or contradicting a negative assertion or direction

[2]yes *n* an affirmative reply or vote; an aye

yes-man /'jes mæn/ *n* one who endorses or supports everything said to him, esp by a superior; a sycophant – infml

[1]yesterday /'jestədi, -deɪ/ *adv* on the day before today

[2]yesterday *n* **1** the day before today **2** recent time; time not long past

[1]yet /jet/ *adv* **1a** again; in addition **b** – used to emphasize the comparative degree (e g a *yet* higher speed) **2a** up to this or that time; so far – not in affirmative statements **b** still (e g while it was *yet* dark) **c** at some future time and despite present appearances (e g we may win *yet*) **3** nevertheless (e g strange and *yet* true)

²yet *conj* but nevertheless

yeti /ˈjeti/ *n* an abominable snowman

yew /juː/ *n* (the wood of) any of a genus of evergreen coniferous trees and shrubs with stiff straight leaves and red fruits

Yiddish /ˈjɪdɪʃ/ *n* a High German language containing elements of Hebrew and Slavonic that is usu written in Hebrew characters and is spoken by Jews chiefly in or from E Europe

¹yield /jiːld/ *v* **1** to give or render as fitting, rightfully owed, or required **2** to give up possession of on claim or demand: e g **a** to surrender or submit (oneself) to another **b** to give (oneself) up to an inclination, temptation, or habit **3a** to bear or bring forth as a natural product **b** to give as a return or in result of expended effort **c** to produce as revenue **4** to give way under physical force (e g bending, stretching, or breaking) **5** to give place or precedence; acknowledge the superiority of another

²yield *n* the capacity of yielding produce; *also* the produce yielded

yielding /ˈjɪəldɪŋ/ *adj* lacking rigidity or stiffness; flexible

yobbo /ˈjɒbəʊ/, **yob** *n, Br* a rough idle youth; a slob

¹yodel /ˈjəʊdl/ *v* to sing, shout, or call (a tune) by suddenly changing from a natural voice to a falsetto and back

²yodel *n* a yodelled song, shout, or cry

yoga /ˈjəʊgə/ *n* **1** *cap* a Hindu philosophy teaching the suppression of all activity of body, mind, and will so that the self may attain liberation from them **2** a system of exercises for attaining bodily or mental control and well-being

yoghurt, yogurt /ˈjɒgət/ *n* a slightly acid semisolid preparation of fermented milk eaten as a dessert or used in cooking

yogi /ˈjəʊgi/ *n* **1** sby who practises or is a master of yoga **2** *cap* an adherent of Yoga philosophy

¹yoke /jəʊk/ *n* **1a** a bar or frame by which 2 draught animals (e g oxen) are joined at the heads or necks for working together **b** a frame fitted to sby's shoulders to carry a load in 2 equal portions **2** *sing or pl in constr* 2 animals yoked or worked together **3a** an oppressive agency **b** a tie, link; *esp* marriage **4** a fitted or shaped piece at the top of a garment from which the rest hangs

²yoke *v* **1** to attach (a draught animal) to (sthg) **2** to join (as if) by a yoke

yokel /ˈjəʊkəl/ *n* a naive or gullible rustic; a country bumpkin

yolk *also* **yoke** /jəʊk/ *n* the usu yellow round mass of stored food that forms the inner portion of the egg of a bird or reptile and is surrounded by the white

yonder /ˈjɒndəʳ/ *adj or adv* over there

yore /jɔːʳ/ *n* time (long) past – usu in *of yore*

yorker /ˈjɔːkəʳ/ *n* a ball bowled in cricket that is aimed to bounce on the popping crease and so pass under the bat

Yorkshire pudding /jɔːkʃə ˈpʊdɪŋ, -ʃɪəʳ/ *n* a savoury baked pudding made from a batter and usu eaten before or with roast beef

you /jə, jʊ; *strong* juː/ *pron, pl* **you** **1** the one being addressed – used as subject or object; **2** a person; one

¹young /jʌŋ/ *adj* **1** in the first or an early stage of life, growth, or development **2** recently come into being; new **3** of or having the characteristics (e g vigour or gaiety) of young people – **~ish** *adj*

²young *n pl* **1** young people; youth **2** immature offspring, esp of an animal

youngster /ˈjʌŋstəʳ/ *n* **1** a young person or creature **2** a child, baby

your /jəʳ; *strong* jɔːʳ/ *adj* **1** of you or yourself or yourselves, esp as possessor, agent or object of an action –used with certain titles in the vocative (e g *your* Eminence) **2** of one or oneself (e g when you face north, east is on *your* right) **3** – used for indicating sthg well-known and characteristic; infml (e g *your* typical commuter) ***USE*** used attributively

yours /jɔːz/ *pron, pl* **yours** that which or the one who belongs to you – used without a following noun as a pronoun equivalent in meaning to the adjective *your* in the

yourself /jə'self/ *pron, pl* **yourselves** **1a** that identical person or creature that is you – used reflexively, for emphasis, or in absolute constructions (e g *yourself* a man of learning, you will know what I mean) **b** your normal self (e g you'll soon be *yourself* again) **2** oneself

youth /juːθ/ *n* **1** the time of life when one is young; *esp* adolescence **2a** a young male adolescent **b** young people – often pl in constr **3** the quality of being youthful – **~ful** *adj* – **~fully** *adv* – **~fulness** *n*

youth hostel *n* a lodging typically providing inexpensive bed and breakfast accommodation for esp young travellers or hikers

yowl /jaʊl/ *v or n* (to utter) the loud long wail of a cat or dog in pain or distress

yo-yo /'jəʊ jəʊ/ *n, pl* **yo-yos** a toy that consists of 2 discs separated by a deep groove in which a string is attached and wound and that is made to fall and rise when held by the string

Z

z /zed/ *n, pl* **z's, zs** *often cap* (a graphic representation of or device for reproducing) the 26th letter of the English alphabet

[1]**zany** /'zeɪni/ *n* one who acts the buffoon to amuse others

[2]**zany** *adj* fantastically or absurdly ludicrous – **zanily** *adv* – **zaniness** *n*

zeal /ziːl/ *n* eagerness and ardent interest in pursuit of sthg; keenness

zealot /'zelət/ *n* a zealous person; *esp* a fanatical partisan

zealous /'zeləs/ *adj* filled with or characterized by zeal – **~ly** *adv* – **~ness** *n*

zebra /'ziːbrə, 'ze-/ *n* any of several black and white striped fast-running African mammals related to the horse

zebra crossing *n* a crossing in Britain marked by a series of broad white stripes to indicate that pedestrians have the right of way across a road

zed /zed/ *n, chiefly Br* the letter *z*

Zen /zen/ *n* a Japanese sect of Buddhism that aims at enlightenment by direct intuition through meditation (e g on paradoxes)

zenith /'zenɪ̣θ/ *n* **1** the point of the celestial sphere that is directly opposite the nadir and vertically above the observer **2** the highest point reached in the heavens by a celestial body **3** the culminating point or stage

zephyr /'zefəʳ/ *n* a gentle breeze, esp from the west

zeppelin /'zepəlɪn/ *n, often cap* a large rigid cigar-shaped airship of a type built in Germany in the early 20th c; *broadly* an airship

[1]**zero** /'zɪərəʊ/ *n, pl* **zeros** *also* **zeroes** **1** the arithmetical symbol 0 or ∅ denoting the absence of all magnitude or quantity **2** the number 0 **3** the point of departure in reckoning; *specif* the point from which the graduation of a scale begins **4a** nothing **b** the lowest point

[2]**zero** *adj* having no magnitude or quantity

[3]**zero** *v* to move near to or focus attention as if on a target; close – usu + *in on*

zero hour *n* the time at which an event is scheduled to take place

zest /zest/ *n* **1** the outer peel of a citrus fruit used as flavouring **2** piquancy, spice **3** keen enjoyment; gusto – **~ful, ~y** *adj*

ziggurat /'zɪgʊræt/ *n* a temple tower of ancient Mesopotamia in the form of a stepped pyramid

[1]**zigzag** /'zɪgzæg/ *n* a line, course, or pattern consisting of a series of sharp alternate turns or angles

[2]**zigzag** *adj* forming or going in a zigzag; consisting of zigzags

[3]**zigzag** *v* to proceed along or consist of a zigzag course

zinc /zɪŋk/ *n* a bluish white bivalent metallic element that occurs abundantly in minerals and is used esp as a protective coating for iron and steel

Zionism /'zaɪənɪzəm/ *n* a movement for setting up a Jewish homeland in Palestine – **-ist** *adj, n*

[1]**zip** /zɪp/ *v* **1** to move with speed and vigour **2** to become open, closed, or attached by means of a zip **3** to travel (as if) with a sharp hissing or humming sound **4** to add zest or life to – often + *up*

[2]**zip** *n* **1** a light sharp hissing sound **2** energy, liveliness **3** *chiefly Br* a fastener that joins 2 edges of fabric by means of 2 flexible spirals or rows of teeth brought together by a sliding clip

zither /'zɪðəʳ/ *n* a stringed instrument having usu 30 to 40 strings over a shallow horizontal soundboard and played with plectrum and fingers

zodiac /'zəʊdiæk/ *n* an imaginary belt in the heavens that encompasses the apparent paths of all the principal planets except Pluto, has the ecliptic as its central line, and is divided into

12 constellations or signs each taken for astrological purposes to extend 30 degrees of longitude – ~**al** *adj*

Zombie /'zɒmbi/ *n* **1** a human in W Indies voodooism who is held to have died and have been reanimated **2** a person resembling the walking dead; a shambling automaton

[1]**zone** /zəʊn/ *n* **1** any of 5 great divisions of the earth's surface with respect to latitude and temperature **2** a distinctive layer of rock or other earth materials **3** an area distinct from adjoining parts **4** any of the sections into which an area is divided for a particular purpose – **-nal** *adj*

[2]**zone** *v* **1** to arrange in, mark off, or partition into zones **2** to assign to a zone

zonked /zɒŋkt/ *adj* **1** highly intoxicated by alcohol, LSD, etc – often + *out* **2** completely exhausted *USE* slang

zoo /zuː/ *n, pl* **zoos** a collection of living animals usu open to the public

zoology /zəʊ'ɒlədʒi, zʊ'ɒ-/ *n* (biology that deals with) animals and animal life, usu excluding human beings – **-gical** *adj* – **-gist** *n*

[1]**zoom** /zuːm/ *v* **1** to move with a loud low hum or buzz **2** to rise sharply

[2]**zoom** *n* **1** an act or process of zooming **2** a photographic lens that can be used to move quickly from a distant shot into close-up

Zulu /'zuːluː/ *n* **1** a member of a Bantu-speaking people of Natal **2** a Bantu language of the Zulus

zygote /'zaɪgəʊt, 'zɪgəʊt/ *n* (the developing individual produced from) a cell formed by the union of 2 gametes

Common Abbreviations

A

a 1 acceleration 2 acre 3 answer 4 are – a metric unit of area 5 area

A 1 ampere 2 Associate

AA 1 Alcoholics Anonymous 2 antiaircraft 3 Automobile Association

AAA 1 Amateur Athletic Association 2 American Automobile Association

A and M ancient and modern – used of hymns

AB 1 able seaman; able-bodied seaman 2 *NAm* bachelor of arts

ABA Amateur Boxing Association

ABC 1 American Broadcasting Company 2 Australian Broadcasting Commission

ABM antiballistic missile

Abp archbishop

AC 1 alternating current 2 appellation contrôlée 3 athletic club

a/c account

ACA Associate of the Institute of Chartered Accountants

ACAS Advisory Conciliation and Arbitration Service

acc 1 according to 2 account 3 accusative

acct account; accountant

ACV air-cushion vehicle

ACW aircraftwoman

AD anno domini

ADAS Agricultural Development and Advisory Service

ADC 1 aide-de-camp 2 amateur dramatic club

ad inf ad infinitum

adj 1 adjective 2 adjustment – used in banking 3 adjutant

Adm admiral

adv 1 adverb; adverbial 2 against

AEA Atomic Energy Authority

AERE Atomic Energy Research Establishment

aet, aetat of the specified age; aged

AEU Amalgamated Engineering Union – now AUEW

AEW airborne early warning

AF 1 Anglo-French 2 audio frequency

AFM Air Force Medal

Afr Africa; African

AG 1 adjutant general 2 attorney general 3 joint-stock company

agcy agency

AGM *chiefly Br* annual general meeting

AGR advanced gas-cooled reactor

AI artificial insemination

AIA Associate of the Institute of Actuaries

AIB Associate of the Institute of Bankers

AID 1 Agency for International Development – a US agency 2 artificial insemination by donor

AIH artificial insemination by husband

AKA also known as

ALA Associate of the Library Association

ald alderman

alt 1 alternate 2 altitude 3 alto

am ante meridiem

AM 1 Albert Medal 2 amplitude modulation 3 associate member 4 *NAm* master of arts

AMDG to the greater glory of God

anon anonymous

A/O account of

aob any other business

AOC Air Officer Commanding

AP Associated Press

APEX Association of Professional, Executive, Clerical, and Computer Staff

app 1 apparent; apparently 2 appendix 3 appointed

approx approximate; approximately

Apr April

APT Advanced Passenger Train

ARA Associate of the Royal Academy

ARAM Associate of the Royal Academy of Music

ARC Agricultural Research Council

ARCA Associate of the Royal College of Art

Arch archbishop

ARCM Associate of the Royal College of Music

ARCS Associate of the Royal College of Science

ARIBA Associate of the Royal Institute of British Architects

ARP air-raid precautions

arr 1 arranged by – used in music 2 arrival; arrives

art 1 article 2 artificial 3 artillery

arty artillery

AS 1 airspeed 2 Anglo-Saxon 3 antisubmarine

asap as soon as possible

ASLEF Associated Society of Locomotive Engineers and Firemen

assoc association

ASSR Autonomous Soviet Socialist Republic

asst assistant
ASTMS Association of Scientific, Technical, and Managerial Staffs
ATC 1 air traffic control 2 Air Training Corps
attn for the attention of
ATV Associated Television
AUEW Amalgamated Union of Engineering Workers
Aug August
AUT Association of University Teachers
av 1 average 2 avoirdupois
Av avenue
AV 1 ad valorem 2 audiovisual 3 Authorized Version (of the Bible)
avdp avoirdupois
Ave avenue
AVM Air Vice Marshal

B

b 1 born 2 bowled by – used in cricket 3 breadth 4 bye – used in cricket
B 1 bachelor 2 bishop – used in chess 3 black – used esp on lead pencils
BA 1 Bachelor of Arts 2 British Academy 3 British Airways 4 British Association
b and b, *often cap B & B, Br* bed and breakfast
b and w black and white
BAOR British Army of the Rhine
Bart baronet
BB 1 Boys' Brigade 2 double black – used on lead pencils
BBBC British Boxing Board of Control
BBC British Broadcasting Corporation
BC 1 before Christ 2 British Columbia 3 British Council
BCh Bachelor of Surgery
BCom Bachelor of Commerce
BD 1 Bachelor of Divinity 2 bank draft 3 barrels per day
BDA British Dental Association
BDS Bachelor of Dental Surgery
BEA British European Airways – now BA
BEd Bachelor of Education
Beds Bedfordshire
BEF British Expeditionary Force
BEM British Empire Medal
BEng Bachelor of Engineering
Berks Berkshire
BeV billion electron volts
BFPO British Forces Post Office
bk book
BL 1 Bachelor of Law 2 bill of lading 3 British Legion 4 British Leyland 5 British Library
BLitt Bachelor of Letters
BM 1 Bachelor of Medicine 2 bench mark 3 British Medal 4 British Museum
BMA British Medical Association
BMC British Medical Council
BMJ British Medical Journal
BMus Bachelor of Music
BO body odour – euph
BOAC British Overseas Airways Corporation – now BA
BOC British Oxygen Company
BOSS Bureau of State Security – a SAfr organization
BOT Board of Trade
BOTB British Overseas Trade Board
Bp bishop
BP 1 boiling point 2 British Petroleum 3 British Pharmacopoeia
BPC British Pharmaceutical Codex
BPhil Bachelor of Philosophy
Br 1 British 2 brother
BR British Rail
Brig brigade; brigadier
Brig-Gen brigadier-general
Brit Britain; British
bros, Bros brothers
BRS British Road Services
BS 1 Bachelor of Surgery 2 balance sheet 3 bill of sale 4 British Standard 5 *NAm* Bachelor of Science
BSA Building Societies Association
BSc Bachelor of Science
BSC 1 British Steel Corporation 2 British Sugar Corporation
BSI 1 British Standards Institution 2 Building Societies Institute
BST British Standard Time; British Summer Time
Bt Baronet
BTh Bachelor of Theology
Btu British thermal unit
Bucks Buckinghamshire
BUPA British United Provident Association
BV Blessed Virgin
BVM Blessed Virgin Mary

C

c 1 canine – used in dentistry 2 carat 3 caught by – used in cricket 4 centi- 5 century 6 chapter 7 circa 8 cloudy 9 cold 10 college 11 colt 12 copyright 13 cubic
C 1 calorie 2 castle – used in chess 3 Catholic 4 Celsius 5 centigrade 6 *Br* Conservative 7 corps
ca circa
CA 1 California 2 chartered accountant 3 chief accountant 4 Consumers' Association 5 current account

CAA Civil Aviation Authority
CAB Citizens' Advice Bureau
cal 1 calibre 2 (small) calorie
Cal 1 California 2 (large) calorie
Cambs Cambridgeshire
Can Canada; Canadian
c and b caught and bowled by – used in cricket
C and G City and Guilds
C and W country and western
Cantab of Cambridge – used with academic awards <MA ~ >
Cantuar of Canterbury – used chiefly in the signature of the Archbishop of Canterbury
caps 1 capital letters 2 capsule
Capt captain
Card cardinal
CAT 1 College of Advanced Technology 2 computerized axial tomography
CB 1 Citizens' Band 2 Companion of the (Order of the) Bath
CBC Canadian Broadcasting Corporation
CBE Commander of the (Order of the) British Empire
CBI Confederation of British Industry
CBS Columbia Broadcasting System
cc 1 carbon copy 2 chapters 3 cubic centimetre
CC 1 Chamber of Commerce 2 County Council 3 Cricket Club
CD 1 civil defence 2 diplomatic corps
Cdr Commander
Cdre Commodore
CE 1 Church of England 2 civil engineer 3 Council of Europe
CEGB Central Electricity Generating Board
CENTO Central Treaty Organization
cf compare
CFE College of Further Education
cgs centimetre-gram-second (system)
ch 1 chain – a unit of length 2 central heating 3 chapter 4 check – used in chess 5 child; children 6 church
CH 1 clubhouse 2 Companion of Honour
chap 1 chaplain 2 chapter
ChB Bachelor of Surgery
Ches Cheshire
ChM Master of Surgery
CI Channel Islands
CIA Central Intelligence Agency
cia company
CID Criminal Investigation Department
cie company
C in C Commander in Chief
cl 1 centilitre 2 clerk
Cllr *Br* councillor
Clo close – used in street names
cm centimetre
Cmdr Commander
Cmdre Commodore
CMG Companion of (the Order of) St Michael and St George
CND Campaign for Nuclear Disarmament
CO 1 commanding officer 2 Commonwealth Office 3 conscientious objector
c/o 1 care of 2 carried over
COD 1 cash on delivery 2 Concise Oxford Dictionary
C of E 1 Church of England 2 Council of Europe
C of S Church of Scotland
COHSE Confederation of Health Service Employees
COI Central Office of Information
col 1 colour; coloured 2 column
Col 1 Colonel 2 Colorado
coll 1 college 2 colloquial
Com, Comm 1 Commander 2 Commodore 3 Commonwealth 4 Communist
Comdr Commander
Comdt Commandant
Con, Cons Conservative
cont 1 containing 2 contents 3 continent; continental 4 continued
contd continued
Corp 1 Corporal 2 corporation
coy company – used esp for a military company
cp 1 candlepower 2 compare
CP 1 Communist Party 2 Country Party – an Australian political party
Cpl Corporal
CPR Canadian Pacific Railway
CPRE Council for the Preservation of Rural England
cresc, cres 1 crescendo 2 *often cap* crescent – used esp in street names
CRO 1 cathode ray oscilloscope 2 Criminal Records Office
CRT cathode-ray tube
CS 1 chartered surveyor 2 Civil Service 3 Court of Session – the supreme civil court of Scotland
CSE Certificate of Secondary Education
CSM Company Sergeant Major
CSO 1 Central Statistical Office 2 Community Service Order
cu cubic
Cumb Cumbria
CV curriculum vitae
CVO Commander of the (Royal) Victorian Order
Cwlth Commonwealth
CWS Cooperative Wholesale Society
cwt hundredweight

D

d 1 date 2 daughter 3 day 4 deca- 5 deci- 6 delete 7 penny; pence – used before introduction of decimal currency 8 density 9 departs 10 diameter 11 died 12 dose 13 drizzle
DA 1 deposit account 2 *NAm* district attorney
D & C dilatation and curettage
dB decibel
DBE Dame Commander of the (Order of the) British Empire
DC 1 from the beginning 2 Detective Constable 3 direct current 4 District of Columbia 5 District Commissioner
DCB Dame Commander of the (Order of the) Bath
DCh Doctor of Surgery
DCL 1 Distillers Company Limited 2 Doctor of Civil Law
DCM Distinguished Conduct Medal
DCMG Dame Commander of (the Order of) St Michael and St George
DCVO Dame Commander of the (Royal) Victorian Order
DD 1 direct debit 2 Doctor of Divinity
DDS Doctor of Dental Surgery
DE 1 Delaware 2 Department of Employment
dec 1 deceased 2 declared – used esp in cricket 3 declension 4 declination 5 decrease 6 decrescendo
Dec December
dep 1 departs; departure 2 deposed 3 deposit 4 depot 5 deputy
dept department
DES Department of Education and Science
det detached; detachment
Det Detective
DF Defender of the Faith
DFC Distinguished Flying Cross
DFM Distinguished Flying Medal
DG 1 by the grace of God 2 director general
DHSS Department of Health and Social Security
DI Detective Inspector
Dip Diploma
Dip Ed Diploma in Education
Dip HE Diploma in Higher Education
dir director
div 1 divergence 2 divide; divided 3 dividend 4 division 5 divorced
DIY do-it-yourself
DLitt Doctor of Letters
DM Doctor of Medicine
DMus Doctor of Music
do ditto
DOA dead on arrival – used chiefly in hospitals
DOE Department of the Environment
DoT Department of Trade
doz dozen
DP 1 data processing 2 displaced person
dpc damp proof course
DPhil Doctor of Philosophy
DPP Director of Public Prosecutions
dpt department
dr 1 debtor 2 drachm 3 dram 4 drawer
Dr 1 doctor 2 Drive – used in street names
DS 1 from the sign 2 Detective Sergeant
DSc Doctor of Science
DSC Distinguished Service Cross
DSM Distinguished Service Medal
DSO Distinguished Service Order
dsp 1 died without issue 2 dessertspoon; dessertspoonful
DST daylight saving time
DTh, DTheol Doctor of Theology
DV God willing
DVLC Driver and Vehicle Licensing Centre
dz dozen

E

E 1 Earl 2 earth – used esp on electrical plugs 3 East; Easterly; Eastern 4 energy 5 English
E and OE errors and omissions excepted
EC East Central – a London postal district
ECG electrocardiogram; electrocardiograph
ECT electroconvulsive therapy
ed, edit edited; edition; editor
EDP electronic data processing
EEC European Economic Community
EEG electroencephalogram; electroencephalograph
EFL English as a foreign language
EFTA European Free Trade Association
eg for example
EHF extremely high frequency
EHT extremely high tension
ELF extremely low frequency
ELT English language teaching
EMI Electrical and Musical Industries
Emp Emperor; Empress
ENE east-northeast
ENEA European Nuclear Energy Agency
Eng England; English
ENSA Entertainments National Service Association
ENT ear, nose, and throat
EO Executive Officer
EOC Equal Opportunities Commission

ep en passant
EPNS electroplated nickel silver
eq equal
equiv equivalent
ER **1** Eastern Region **2** King Edward **3** Queen Elizabeth
ESA European Space Agency
ESE east-southeast
ESL English as a second language
ESN educationally subnormal
Esq *also* **Esqr** esquire
est **1** established **2** estate **3** estimate; estimated
EST **1** Eastern Standard Time **2** electroshock treatment
ETA estimated time of arrival
ETD estimated time of departure
et seq **1** and the following one **2** and the following ones
ETU Electrical Trades Union
EVA extravehicular activity
ex **1** examined **2** example **3** except **4** exchange

F

f **1** fathom **2** female **3** femto- **4** force **5** forte **6** frequency **7** focal length **8** folio **9** following (e g page) **10** foot
F **1** Fahrenheit **2** false **3** farad **4** Fellow **5** filial generation **6** fine – used esp on lead pencils **7** forward **8** French
FA Football Association
Fahr Fahrenheit
F and F fixtures and fittings
FBI Federal Bureau of Investigation
FBR fast breeder reactor
FC **1** Football Club **2** Forestry Commission
FCA Fellow of the (Institute of) Chartered Accountants
FCII Fellow of the Chartered Insurance Institute
FCIS Fellow of the Chartered Institute of Secretaries
FCO Foreign and Commonwealth Office
FCS Fellow of the Chemical Society
FD Defender of the Faith
Feb February
ff **1** folios **2** following (e g pages) **3** fortissimo
FIFA International Football Federation
fig **1** figurative; figuratively **2** figure
fl **1** floor **2** flourished – used to indicate a period of renown of sby whose dates of birth and death are unknown **3** fluid
FL **1** Florida **2** focal length
fl oz fluid ounce
Flt Lt Flight Lieutenant
Flt Off Flight Officer
Flt Sgt Flight Sergeant
fm fathom
FM Field Marshal
fo, fol folio
FO **1** Field Officer **2** Flying Officer **3** Foreign Office
FOC Father of the Chapel (in a Trade Union)
FOE Friends of the Earth
fpm feet per minute
fps **1** feet per second **2** foot-pound-second
Fr **1** Father **2** French **3** Friar
FRCM Fellow of the Royal College of Music
FRCOG Fellow of the Royal College of Obstetricians and Gynaecologists
FRCP Fellow of the Royal College of Physicians
FRCS Fellow of the Royal College of Surgeons
FRCVS Fellow of the Royal College of Veterinary Surgeons
Fri Friday
FRIBA Fellow of the Royal Institute of British Architects
FRIC Fellow of the Royal Institute of Chemistry
FRICS Fellow of the Royal Institution of Chartered Surveyors
FRS Fellow of the Royal Society
FSA Fellow of the Society of Actuaries
ft **1** feet; foot **2** fort
FT Financial Times
fth, fthm fathom
FWD **1** four-wheel drive **2** front-wheel drive

G

g **1** gauge **2** giga- **3** good **4** gram
G acceleration due to gravity
gal, gall gallon
GB Great Britain
GBE Knight/Dame Grand Cross of the (Order of the) British Empire
GBH *Br* grievous bodily harm
GC George Cross
GCB Knight/Dame Grand Cross of the (Order of the) Bath
GCE General Certificate of Education
GCHQ Government Communications Headquarters
GCMG Knight/Dame Grand Cross of (the Order of) St Michael and St George
GCVO Knight/Dame Grand Cross of the (Royal) Victorian Order
gd good
Gdns Gardens – used esp in street names
GDP gross domestic product

GDR German Democratic Republic
GHQ general headquarters
gi gill
Gib Gibraltar
Glam Glamorgan
GLC Greater London Council
Glos Gloucestershire
gm gram
GM **1** general manager **2** George Medal **3** guided missile
GMC **1** General Medical Council **2** general management committee
GMT Greenwich Mean Time
GMWU General and Municipal Workers Union
GNP gross national product
GOC General Officer Commanding
gov **1** government **2** governor
govt government
GP **1** general practitioner **2** Grand Prix
Gp Capt Group Captain
GPI general paralysis of the insane
GPO general post office
GQ general quarters
gr **1** grade **2** grain **3** gram **4** gravity **5** gross
GR King George
gro gross
Gro Grove – used in street names
gt great
GT grand tourer

H

h **1** hect-; hecto **2** height **3** high **4** hot **5** hour **6** husband
H **1** harbour **2** hard – used esp on lead pencils **3** hardness
ha hectare
h and c hot and cold (water)
Hants Hampshire
HB hard black – used on lead pencils
HBM His/Her Britannic Majesty
HCF highest common factor
HE **1** high explosive **2** His Eminence **3** His/Her Excellency
HEO Higher Executive Officer
Here, Heref Herefordshire
Herts Hertfordshire
HF high frequency
HG **1** His/Her Grace **2** Home Guard
HGV *Br* heavy goods vehicle
HH **1** double hard – used on lead pencils **2** His/Her Highness **3** His Holiness
HIH His/Her Imperial Highness
HIM His/Her Imperial Majesty
HM **1** headmaster **2** headmistress **3** His/Her Majesty
HMF His/Her Majesty's Forces
HMG His/Her Majesty's Government
HMI His/Her Majesty's Inspector (of Schools)
HMS His/Her Majesty's Ship
HMSO His/Her Majesty's Stationery Office
HMV His Master's Voice
HNC Higher National Certificate
HND Higher National Diploma
HO Home Office
Hon (the) Honourable
Hons *Br* honours
Hon Sec *Br* Honorary Secretary
HP **1** high pressure **2** hire purchase **3** horsepower **4** Houses of Parliament
HQ headquarters
hr hour
HRH His/Her Royal Highness
HSO Higher Scientific Officer
HST high speed train
ht height
HT **1** high-tension **2** under this title
HV **1** high velocity **2** high-voltage
HW **1** high water **2** hot water
Hz hertz

I

I **1** inductance **2** island; isle
IAEA International Atomic Energy Agency
IAM Institute of Advanced Motorists
IATA International Air Transport Association
ib ibidem
IBA Independent Broadcasting Authority
ibid ibidem
IBM International Business Machines
i/c in charge
IC integrated circuit
ICA Institute of Contemporary Arts
ICBM intercontinental ballistic missile
ICC International Cricket Conference
ICE **1** Institute of Civil Engineers **2** internal-combustion engine
ICI Imperial Chemical Industries
ICL International Computers Limited
id idem
ID **1** Idaho **2** (proof of) identification **3** inner diameter **4** intelligence department
IDA International Development Association
i e that is
IHS Jesus
ILEA Inner London Education Authority
ill, illus, illust illustrated; illustration
ILO **1** International Labour Organization **2** International Labour Office

ILP Independent Labour Party
IMF International Monetary Fund
imp **1** Emperor; Empress **2** imperative **3** imperfect **4** imperial
in inch
inc **1** increase **2** *chiefly NAm* incorporated
incl included; including; inclusive
ind **1** independent **2** indicative **3** industrial; industry
INRI Jesus of Nazareth, King of the Jews
insp inspector
inst **1** instant **2** institute; institution
int **1** integral **2** interior **3** intermediate **4** internal **5** international **6** interpreter **7** intransitive
intro introduction
I/O input/output
IOC International Olympic Committee
IOM Isle of Man
IOW Isle of Wight
IPA International Phonetic Alphabet
IPC International Publishing Corporation
IPM **1** inches per minute **2** Institute of Personnel Management
IPS inches per second
IR **1** information retrieval **2** infrared **3** Inland Revenue
IRA Irish Republican Army
IRBM intermediate range ballistic missile
IRO **1** Inland Revenue Office **2** International Refugee Organization
ISBN International Standard Book Number
ISD international subscriber dialling
ISO **1** Imperial Service Order **2** International Standardization Organization
ita initial teaching alphabet
ITA Independent Television Authority – now IBA
ital italic; italicized
ITN Independent Television News
ITT International Telephone and Telegraph (Corporation)
ITU International Telecommunications Union
ITV Independent Television
IU international unit
IUD intrauterine device
IVR International Vehicle Registration
IWW Industrial Workers of the World

J

J **1** joule **2** Judge **3** Justice
JA, J/A joint account
Jan January
JC **1** Jesus Christ **2** Julius Caesar
JCD **1** Doctor of Canon Law **2** Doctor of Civil Law
JCR Junior Common Room
jnr junior
JP Justice of the Peace
Jr junior
jt, jnt joint
Jul July
Jun June

K

k **1** carat **2** kilo- **3** kitchen **4** knot **5** kosher
K **1** kelvin **2** king – used in chess **3** knit
KB **1** King's Bench **2** Knight Bachelor
KBE Knight (Commander of the Order of the) British Empire
KC **1** Kennel Club **2** King's Counsel
KCB Knight Commander of the (Order of the) Bath
KCIE Knight Commander of the (Order of the) Indian Empire
KCMG Knight Commander of (the Order of) St Michael and St George
KCSI Knight Commander of the (Order of the) Star of India
KCVO Knight Commander of the (Royal) Victorian Order
kg **1** keg **2** kilogram
KG Knight of the (Order of the) Garter
KGB (Soviet) State Security Committee
kHz kilohertz
KKK Ku Klux Klan
kl kilolitre
km kilometre
kn knot
kph kilometres per hour
kt karat
KT **1** knight – used in chess **2** Knight Templar **3** Knight of the (Order of the) Thistle
kV kilovolt
kW kilowatt
kWh, kwh kilowatt-hour

L

l **1** Lady **2** lake **3** large **4** left **5** length **6** Liberal **7** pound **8** lightning **9** line **10** litre **11** little **12** long **13** last **14** lower
L **1** Latin **2** live – used esp on electrical plugs **3** *Br* learner (driver)
La **1** lane – used esp in street names **2** Louisiana
LA **1** law agent **2** Library Association **3** *Br* local authority **4** Los Angeles **5** Louisiana
Lab **1** Labour **2** Labrador
Lancs Lancashire
lat latitude
lb **1** pound **2** leg bye

LBC London Broadcasting Company
lbw leg before wicket
lc **1** letter of credit **2** in the place cited **3** lowercase
LCC London County Council
lcd **1** liquid crystal display **2** lowest (*or* least) common denominator
LCM lowest (*or* least) common multiple
LCpl lance corporal
Ld Lord
LDS Licentiate in Dental Surgery
LEA Local Education Authority
led light emitting diode
leg legato
Leics Leicestershire
LEM lunar excursion module
LF low frequency
lh left hand
LHA Local Health Authority
LHD Doctor of Letters; Doctor of Humanities
Lieut Lieutenant
Lincs Lincolnshire
lit **1** litre **2** literature
Litt D doctor of letters; doctor of literature
ll lines
LLB Bachelor of Laws
LLD Doctor of Laws
LLM Master of Laws
LOB Location of Offices Bureau
loc cit in the place cited
long longitude
LPG liquefied petroleum gas
LPO London Philharmonic Orchestra
LRAM Licentiate of the Royal Academy of Music
LSE London School of Economics
LSO London Symphony Orchestra
lt light
LT **1** lieutenant **2** low-tension
LTA Lawn Tennis Association
Lt Cdr Lieutenant Commander
Lt Col Lieutenant Colonel
Ltd limited
Lt Gen Lieutenant General
LV **1** low velocity **2** low voltage **3** *Br* luncheon voucher
LVT **1** landing vehicle, tracked **2** landing vehicle (tank)
LW **1** long wave **2** low water
LWR light water reactor
LWT London Weekend Television

M

m **1** maiden (over) – used in cricket **2** male **3** married **4** masculine **5** mass **6** metre **7** middle **8** mile **9** thousand **10** milli- **11** million **12** minute – used for the unit of time **13** molar **14** month
M **1** Mach **2** Master **3** mega- **4** Member **5** Monsieur **6** motorway
MA **1** Massachusetts **2** Master of Arts **3** Middle Ages **4** Military Academy
MAFF Ministry of Agriculture, Fisheries, and Food
Maj Major
Maj Gen Major General
M & S Marks and Spencer
Mar March
Marq Marquess; Marquis
MASH *NAm* mobile army surgical hospital
max maximum
MB Bachelor of Medicine
MBE Member of the (Order of the) British Empire
MC **1** Master of Ceremonies **2** Member of Congress **3** Military Cross
MCC Marylebone Cricket Club
mcg microgram
MCh, MChir Master of Surgery
MD **1** Managing Director **2** Doctor of Medicine **3** right hand – used in music
MDS Master of Dental Surgery
MEP Member of the European Parliament
met **1** meteorological; meteorology **2** metropolitan
mf **1** medium frequency **2** mezzo forte
MFH Master of Foxhounds
mg milligram
Mgr **1** Monseigneur **2** Monsignor
MHz megahertz
mi mile; mileage
MI **1** Michigan **2** military intelligence
Middx Middlesex
min **1** minimum **2** minor **3** minute – used for the unit of time
Min Minister; Ministry
misc miscellaneous; miscellany
ml **1** mile **2** millilitre
MLitt Master of Letters
Mlle mademoiselle
MLR minimum lending rate
mm millimetre
MM **1** Maelzel's metronome **2** messieurs **3** Military Medal
Mme madame
Mmes mesdames
MN **1** Merchant Navy **2** Minnesota
MO **1** Medical Officer **2** Missouri **3** modus operandi **4** money order
mod **1** moderate **2** moderato **3** modern **4** modulus
MoD Ministry of Defence
MOH Medical Officer of Health
mol **1** molecular; molecule **2** mole
Mon Monday

MP 1 Member of Parliament 2 Metropolitan Police 3 Military Police; Military Policeman
mpg miles per gallon
mph miles per hour
MPhil Master of Philosophy
Mr *see entry in main text*
MRCP Member of the Royal College of Physicians
MRCS Member of the Royal College of Surgeons
MRCVS Member of the Royal College of Veterinary Surgeons
Mrs *see entry in main text*
Ms *see entry in main text*
MS 1 left hand – used in music 2 manuscript 3 Mississippi 4 multiple sclerosis
MSc Master of Science
Msgr *chiefly NAm* Monseigneur; Monsignor
MSS manuscripts
Mt 1 Matthew 2 Mount
mth month
MW 1 medium wave 2 megawatt
mW milliwatt

N

n 1 name 2 nano- 3 born 4 net 5 new 6 neuter 7 nominative 8 noon 9 noun 10 numerical aperture
N 1 knight – used in chess 2 newton 3 North; Northerly; Northern 4 neutral – used esp on electric plugs
n/a no account – used in banking
NA 1 North America 2 not applicable
NAAFI Navy, Army, and Air Force Institutes
NALGO National and Local Government Officers Association
NAm North America; North American
NASA National Aeronautics and Space Administration – a US government organization
NATO North Atlantic Treaty Organization
NATSOPA National Society of Operative Printers, Graphical and Media Personnel
nb no ball – used in cricket
NB 1 Nebraska 2 New Brunswick 3 note well
NCB National Coal Board
NCC Nature Conservancy Council
NCO non-commissioned officer
NCP National Car Parks
NCR National Cash Register (Company)
nd no date
NE 1 modern English [*New English*] 2 New England 3 Northeast; Northeastern
NEB 1 National Enterprise Board 2 New English Bible
NEC National Executive Committee
NEDC National Economic Development Council
neg negative
NERC Natural Environment Research Council
NF 1 National Front 2 Newfoundland 3 no funds
NFU National Farmers' Union
NFWI National Federation of Women's Institutes
ng no good
NGA National Graphical Association
NHS National Health Service
NI 1 National Insurance 2 Northern Ireland
NLF National Liberation Front
NNE north-northeast
NNW north-northwest
no 1 not out – used in cricket 2 number 3 *NAm* north
Norf Norfolk
Northants Northamptonshire
Northumb Northumberland
nos numbers
Notts Nottinghamshire
Nov November
np new paragraph
nr near
NSB National Savings Bank
NSPCC National Society for the Prevention of Cruelty to Children
NSW New South Wales
NT 1 National Trust 2 New Testament 3 no trumps
NUJ National Union of Journalists
NUM National Union of Mineworkers
NUPE National Union of Public Employees
NUR National Union of Railwaymen
NUS 1 National Union of Seamen 2 National Union of Students
NUT National Union of Teachers
NW Northwest; Northwestern
NY New York
NYC New York City
NZ New Zealand

O

o 1 ohm 2 old
O & M organization and methods
OAP *Br* old-age pensioner
OB 1 outside broadcast 2 *Br* old boy
OBE Officer of the (Order of the) British Empire
OC *Br* Officer Commanding
Oct October

OCTU Officer Cadets Training Unit
OECD Organization for Economic Cooperation and Development
OG *Br* old girl
OHMS On His/Her Majesty's Service
OM Order of Merit
ONC Ordinary National Certificate
OND Ordinary National Diploma
ono or near offer – used with prices of goods for sale
op opus
op cit in the work cited
OPEC Organization of Petroleum Exporting Countries
orig original; originally; originator
OS **1** ordinary seaman **2** Ordnance Survey **3** out of stock **4** outsize
O/S outstanding
OT **1** occupational therapy; Occupational Therapist **2** Old Testament **3** overtime
OTC Officers' Training Corps
OU Open University
OXFAM Oxford Committee for Famine Relief
Oxon **1** Oxfordshire **2** of Oxford – used chiefly with academic awards <*MA* ~>
oz ounce; ounces

P

p **1** page **2** participle **3** past **4** pence; penny **5** per **6** piano – used as an instruction in music **7** pico- **8** pint **9** power **10** premolar **11** pressure
pa per annum
Pa **1** Pennsylvania **2** pascal
PA **1** Pennsylvania **2** personal assistant **3** press agent **4** public address (system) **5** purchasing agent
PABX *Br* private automatic branch (telephone) exchange
P & O Peninsular and Oriental (Steamship Company)
p & p *Br* postage and packing
par **1** paragraph **2** parallel **3** parish
PAX *Br* private automatic (telephone) exchange
PAYE pay as you earn
PBX private branch (telephone) exchange
pc **1** per cent **2** postcard
PC **1** police constable **2** Privy Councillor
Pde parade – used in street names
PDSA People's Dispensary for Sick Animals
PE physical education
PEP *Br* Political and Economic Planning
PER Professional Employment Register
per pro by the agency (of)
PGA Professional Golfers' Association
PhB Bachelor of Philosophy
PhD Doctor of Philosophy
pk **1** *often cap* park – used esp in street names **2** peck
pl **1** *often cap* place – used esp in street names **2** platoon **3** plural
plc public limited company
PLO Palestine Liberation Organization
PLP Parliamentary Labour Party
PLR Public Lending Right
pm **1** post meridiem **2** premium
PM **1** postmortem **2** Prime Minister **3** Provost Marshal
PO **1** Petty Officer **2** Pilot Officer **3** postal order **4** Post Office
POB Post Office box
POE **1** port of embarkation **2** port of entry
pop population
POP *Br* Post Office Preferred
POW prisoner of war
pp **1** pages **2** past participle **3** by proxy **4** pianissimo
PPE Philosophy, Politics, and Economics
PPS **1** Parliamentary Private Secretary **2** further postscript
Pr **1** Priest **2** Prince
PR **1** proportional representation **2** public relations **3** Puerto Rico
prec preceding
pref **1** preface **2** preferred **3** prefix
prelim preliminary
prep **1** preparation; preparatory **2** preposition
Pres President
PRO **1** Public Records Office **2** public relations officer
Prof Professor
PROM programmable read-only memory
PS **1** Police Sergeant **2** postscript **3** Private Secretary **4** prompt side – used to designate part of the theatrical stage
pseud pseudonym; pseudonymous
psf pounds per square foot
psi pounds per square inch
PSV *Br* public service vehicle
pt **1** part **2** pint **3** point **4** port
PT **1** Pacific time **2** physical training
PTA Parent-Teacher Association
Pte Private
PTO please turn over
Pty *chiefly Austr, NZ, & SAfr* Proprietary
PVC polyvinyl chloride
Pvt *chiefly NAm* Private
pw per week
PW *Br* policewoman
PX post exchange

Q

q **1** quarto **2** quintal **3** quire
Q queen – used in chess

QB Queen's Bench
QC Queen's Counsel
QED which was to be demonstrated
QM quartermaster
QMG Quartermaster General
QMS Quartermaster Sergeant
QPR Queen's Park Rangers
qqv which (*pl*) see
QSO quasi-stellar object
qt quart
qto quarto
qty quantity
qv which see

R

r **1** radius **2** railway **3** recto **4** resistance **5** right **6** runs – used in cricket
R **1** rabbi **2** radical – used in chemistry **3** rain **4** Réaumur **5** rector **6** queen **7** registered (as a trademark) **8** king **9** ring road **10** river **11** röntgen **12** rook – used in chess **13** Royal
RA **1** Rear Admiral **2** Royal Academician; Royal Academy **3** Royal Artillery
RAAF Royal Australian Air Force
RAC **1** Royal Armoured Corps **2** Royal Automobile Club
RADA Royal Academy of Dramatic Art
RAF Royal Air Force
RAM **1** random access memory **2** Royal Academy of Music
RAMC Royal Army Medical Corps
R and A Royal and Ancient – used as the title of St Andrews Golf Club
R & B rhythm and blues
R and D research and development
RAOC Royal Army Ordnance Corps
RC **1** Red Cross **2** reinforced concrete **3** Roman Catholic
RCAF Royal Canadian Air Force
RCM Royal College of Music
RCMP Royal Canadian Mounted Police
RCN **1** Royal Canadian Navy **2** Royal College of Nursing
rd *often cap R* road
RDC Rural District Council
RE **1** religious education **2** Royal Engineers
ref **1** reference **2** referred
reg **1** regiment **2** register; registered **3** registrar; registry **4** regulation **5** regulo
regd registered
regt regiment
rel relating; relation; relative
Rev **1** Revelation – used for the book of the Bible **2** Reverend
Revd Reverend
RF **1** radio frequency **2** Rugby Football
RFC **1** Royal Flying Corps **2** Rugby Football Club
RFU Rugby Football Union
rh **1** relative humidity **2** right hand
RH Royal Highness
RHS **1** Royal Historical Society **2** Royal Horticultural Society **3** Royal Humane Society
RI **1** refractive index **2** religious instruction **3** Rhode Island
RIBA Royal Institute of British Architects
RIC Royal Institute of Chemistry
RICS Royal Institution of Chartered Surveyors
RIP **1** may he rest in peace **2** may they rest in peace
RK religious knowledge
RL Rugby League
RM **1** Royal Mail **2** Royal Marines
RMA Royal Military Academy (Sandhurst)
RN Royal Navy
RNAS Royal Naval Air Service
RNIB Royal National Institute for the Blind
RNLI Royal National Lifeboat Institution
RNR Royal Naval Reserve
RNVR Royal Naval Volunteer Reserve
ROC Royal Observer Corps
RoSPA Royal Society for the Prevention of Accidents
RPI *Br* retail price index
rpm **1** *Br, often cap* retail price maintenance **2** revolutions per minute
rps revolutions per second
rpt **1** repeat **2** report
RS **1** right side **2** Royal Society
RSC Royal Shakespeare Company
RSM **1** Regimental Sergeant Major **2** Royal Society of Medicine
RSPB Royal Society for the Protection of Birds
RSPCA Royal Society for the Prevention of Cruelty to Animals
RSV Revised Standard Version (of the Bible)
RSVP please answer
Rt Hon Right Honourable
Rt Rev, Rt Revd Right Reverend
RU Rugby Union
RUC Royal Ulster Constabulary
RV Revised Version (of the Bible)

S

s **1** school **2** scruple **3** second **4** shilling **5** singular **6** sire **7** small **8** snow **9** son **10** succeeded

S **1** saint **2** sea **3** siemens **4** Signor **5** society **6** South; Southerly; Southern **7** sun

SA **1** Salvation Army **2** sex appeal **3** small arms **4** limited liability company **5** Society of Actuaries **6** South Africa **7** South America

sae stamped addressed envelope

SALT Strategic Arms Limitation Talks

SAM surface-to-air missile

SAS Special Air Service

Sat Saturday

SATB soprano, alto, tenor, bass

SAYE save-as-you-earn

SBN Standard Book Number

sc **1** scene **2** scilicet **3** small capitals

s/c self-contained

Sc Scots

ScD Doctor of Science

SCE Scottish Certificate of Education

SCF Save the Children Fund

SCR **1** senior common room **2** script **3** scripture

SDLP Social Democratic and Labour Party

SDP Social Democratic Party

SE southeast; southeastern

SEATO Southeast Asia Treaty Organization

sec **1** second; secondary **2** secretary **3** section **4** according to **5** secant

SEN State Enrolled Nurse

Sep, Sept September

seq the following

seqq the following

Serg, Sergt Sergeant

SF science fiction

SG **1** Solicitor General **2** *often not cap* specific gravity

sgd signed

Sgt Sergeant

Sgt Maj Sergeant Major

SHAPE Supreme Headquarters Allied Powers Europe

SI International System of Units

Sig Signor

SIS Secret Intelligence Service

SJ Society of Jesus

SLADE Society of Lithographic Artists, Designers and Etchers

SLP Scottish Labour Party

SM Sergeant Major

SNP Scottish National Party

snr senior

So south

soc society

SOGAT Society of Graphical and Allied Trades

Som Somerset

sop soprano

SP **1** without issue **2** starting price

SPCK Society for Promoting Christian Knowledge

SPQR the Senate and the people of Rome

sq square

Sqn Ldr Squadron Leader

Sr **1** senior **2** Senor **3** Sir **4** Sister

SRC Science Research Council

SRN State Registered Nurse

SS **1** saints **2** steamship **3** Sunday School

SSE south-southeast

SSgt staff sergeant

SSM surface-to-surface missile

SSR Soviet Socialist Republic

SSRC Social Science Research Council

SSW south-southwest

st **1** stanza **2** stitch **3** stone **4** stumped by

St **1** Saint **2** street

Staffs Staffordshire

STD **1** doctor of sacred theology **2** subscriber trunk dialling

sth south

STOL short takeoff and landing

STP standard temperature and pressure

STUC Scottish Trades Union Congress

Sun Sunday

supp, suppl supplement; supplementary

supt superintendent

SW **1** shortwave **2** southwest; southwestern

SWALK sealed with a loving kiss

SWAPO South-West Africa People's Organization

Sx Sussex

T

t **1** time **2** ton; tonne **3** transitive

T temperature

TA Territorial Army

T & AVR Territorial and Army Volunteer Reserve

TASS the official news agency of the Soviet Union

TB tubercle bacillus

tbs, tbsp tablespoon; tablespoonful

TCCB Test and County Cricket Board

Tce *Br* terrace – used esp in street names

tech **1** technical; technically; technician **2** technological; technology

temp **1** temperature **2** temporary **3** in the time of

Terr, Terr **1** terrace – used esp in street names **2** territory

TGWU Transport and General Workers' Union

Th Thursday

Thur, Thurs Thursday

TIR International Road Transport
TM **1** trademark **2** transcendental meditation
TOPS Training Opportunities Scheme
tot total
trans **1** transitive **2** translated; translation; translator
transl translated; translation
trs transpose
TSB Trustee Savings Bank
tsp teaspoon; teaspoonful
TT **1** teetotal; teetotaller **2** Tourist Trophy **3** tuberculin tested
Tue, Tues Tuesday
TU trade union
TUC Trades Union Congress
TV television
TVP textured vegetable protein
TWA Trans-World Airlines

U

u **1** unit **2** upper
UAE United Arab Emirates
UAR United Arab Republic
UAU Universities Athletic Union
uc upper case
UCCA Universities Central Council on Admissions
UCL University College, London
UDA Ulster Defence Association
UDI unilateral declaration of independence
UDR Ulster Defence Regiment
UEFA Union of European Football Associations
UHF ultrahigh frequency
UHT ultrahigh temperature
UK United Kingdom
UKAEA United Kingdom Atomic Energy Authority
ult **1** ultimate **2** ultimo
UN United Nations
UNA United Nations Association
UNESCO United Nations Educational, Scientific, and Cultural Organization
UNICEF United Nations Children's Fund
univ **1** universal **2** university
UNO United Nations Organization
US United States
USA **1** United States Army **2** United States of America
USAF United States Air Force
USN United States Navy
USS United States Ship
USSR Union of Soviet Socialist Republics
UU Ulster Unionist
UV ultraviolet
UVF Ulster Volunteer Force

V

v **1** vector **2** verb **3** verse **4** versus **5** very **6** verso **7** vice **8** vide **9** von – used in German personal names
V **1** velocity **2** volt; voltage **3** volume
V & A Victoria and Albert Museum
var **1** variable **2** variant **3** variation **4** variety **5** various
VAT value-added tax
VC **1** Vice Chairman **2** Vice Chancellor **3** Vice Consul **4** Victoria Cross
VCR video cassette recorder
VD venereal disease
VDT visual display terminal
VDU visual display unit
VE Victory in Europe
Ven Venerable
Vet MB Bachelor of Veterinary Medicine
VG **1** very good **2** Vicar General
VHF very high frequency
vi **1** verb intransitive **2** see below
viz videlicet
VLF very low frequency
vol **1** volume **2** volunteer
VR **1** Queen Victoria **2** Volunteer Reserve
VSO Voluntary Service Overseas
VSOP Very Special Old Pale – a type of brandy
vt verb transitive
VTOL vertical takeoff and landing
VTR video tape recorder
vv **1** verses **2** vice versa **3** volumes

W

w **1** week **2** weight **3** white **4** wicket **5** wide **6** width **7** wife **8** with
W **1** Watt **2** West; Westerly; Western
WAAC **1** Women's Army Auxiliary Corps – the women's component of the British army from 1914 to 1918 **2** Women's Army Auxiliary Corps – the women's component of the US army from 1942 to 1948
WAAF Women's Auxiliary Air Force – the women's component of the RAF
WAC Women's Army Corps – the women's component of the US army
WAF Women in the Air Force – the women's component of the USAF
War, Warw, Warwks Warwickshire
WBA World Boxing Association
WBC **1** white blood cells; white blood count **2** World Boxing Council
wf wrong fount
WHO World Health Organization
WI **1** West Indies **2** Wisconsin **3** Women's Institute

Wilts Wiltshire
wk **1** week **2** work
wkly weekly
wkt wicket
Wlk walk – used in street names
Wm William
WNP Welsh National Party
WNW west-northwest
w/o without
WO Warrant Officer
Worcs Worcestershire
WOW War on Want
wpb wastepaper basket
WPC Woman Police Constable
wpm words per minute
WPS Woman Police Sergeant
WR Western Region
WRAC Women's Royal Army Corps
WRAF Women's Royal Air Force
WRNS Women's Royal Naval Service
WRVS Women's Royal Voluntary Service
WSW west-southwest
wt weight
WW World War

X

x **1** ex **2** extra
X Christ
XL extra large
XT Christ

Y

y year
yd yard
YHA Youth Hostels Association
YMCA Young Men's Christian Association
YMHA Young Men's Hebrew Association
Yorks Yorkshire
yr **1** year **2** younger **3** your
YWCA Young Women's Christian Association
YWHA Young Women's Hebrew Association

Z

ZANU Zimbabwe African National Union
ZAPU Zimbabwe African People's Union

Tables

Periodic table of chemical elements

	IA	IIA	IIIA		IVA	VA	VIA	VIIA	VIII	
1	1 **H** Hydrogen 1.008									
2	3 **Li** Lithium 6.94	4 **Be** Beryllium 9.012								
3	11 **Na** Sodium 22.930	12 **Mg** Magnesium 24.305								
4	19 **K** Potassium 39.09	20 **Ca** Calcium 40.08	21 **Sc** Scandium 44.956		22 **Ti** Titanium 47.9	23 **V** Vanadium 50.941	24 **Cr** Chromium 51.996	25 **Mn** Manganese 54.938	26 **Fe** Iron 55.84	27 **Co** Cobalt 58.933
5	37 **Rb** Rubidium 85.467	38 **Sr** Strontium 87.62	39 **Y** Yttrium 88.906		40 **Zr** Zirconium 91.22	41 **Nb** Niobium 92.906	42 **Mo** Molyb- denum 95.9	43 **Tc** Technetium 97	44 **Ru** Ruthenium 101.0	45 **Rh** Rhodium 102.906
6	55 **Cs** Caesium 132.905	56 **Ba** Barium 137.34	57 **La** Lanthanum 138.905	*	72 **Hf** Hafnium 178.4	73 **Ta** Tantalum 180.947	74 **W** Tungsten 183.8	75 **Re** Rhenium 186.2	76 **Os** Osmium 190.2	77 **Ir** Iridium 192.2
7	87 **Fr** Francium 223	88 **Ra** Radium 226.025	89 **Ac** Actinium 227	†	104 **Rf** Rutherford- ium 261	105 **Hn** Hahnium 260	106 263			

Key

4 **Be** Beryllium 9.012	atomic number symbol element atomic weight

*Lanthanide Series	58 **Ce** Cerium 140.12	59 **Pr** Praseo- dymium 140.908	60 **Nd** Neodymium 144.2	61 **Pm** Promethium 147	62 **Sm** Samarium 150.4	63 **Eu** Europium 151.96
†Actinide Series	90 **Th** Thorium 232.038	91 **Pa** Protactin- ium 231.036	92 **U** Uranium 238.029	93 **Np** Neptunium 237.048	94 **Pu** Plutonium 244	95 **Am** Americium 243

	IB	IIB	IIIB	IVB	VB	VIB	VIIB	0
								2 **He** Helium 4.003
			5 **B** Boron 10.81	6 **C** Carbon 12.011	7 **N** Nitrogen 14.007	8 **O** Oxygen 15.999	9 **F** Fluorine 18.998	10 **Ne** Neon 20.17
			13 **Al** Aluminium 26.982	14 **Si** Silicon 28.08	15 **P** Phosphorus 30.974	16 **S** Sulphur 32.06	17 **Cl** Chlorine 35.453	18 **Ar** Argon 39.94
28 **Ni** Nickel 58.7	29 **Cu** Copper 63.54	30 **Zn** Zinc 65.38	31 **Ga** Gallium 69.72	32 **Ge** Germanium 72.5	33 **As** Arsenic 74.922	34 **Se** Selenium 78.9	35 **Br** Bromine 79.904	36 **Kr** Krypton 83.80
46 **Pd** Palladium 106.4	47 **Ag** Silver 107.868	48 **Cd** Cadmium 112.40	49 **In** Indium 114.82	50 **Sn** Tin 118.6	51 **Sb** Antimony 121.7	52 **Te** Tellurium 127.6	53 **I** Iodine 126.905	54 **Xe** Xenon 131.30
78 **Pt** Platinum 195.0	79 **Au** Gold 196.967	80 **Hg** Mercury 200.5	81 **Tl** Thallium 204.3	82 **Pb** Lead 207.2	83 **Bi** Bismuth 208.980	84 **Po** Polonium 209	85 **At** Astatine 210	86 **Rn** Radon 222

64 **Gd** Gadolinium 157.2	65 **Tb** Terbium 158.925	66 **Dy** Dysprosium 162.5	67 **Ho** Holmium 164.930	68 **Er** Erbium 167.2	69 **Tm** Thulium 168.934	70 **Yb** Ytterbium 173.0	71 **Lu** Lutetium 174.97

96 **Cm** Curium 247	97 **Bk** Berkelium 247	98 **Cf** Californium 251	99 **Es** Einsteinium 254	100 **Fm** Fermium 257	101 **Md** Mendel- evium 257	102 **No** Nobelium 255	103 **Lr** Lawrencium 256

Physical units table

Base SI units

unit	symbol	concept
ampere	A	electric current
candela	cd	luminous intensity
kelvin	K	thermodynamic temperature
kilogram	kg	mass
metre	m	length
mole	mol	amount of substance
second	s	time

Supplementary SI units

unit	symbol	concept
radian	rad	plane angle
steradian	sr	solid angle

Derived SI units with names

unit	symbol	concept
coulomb	C	electric charge
farad	F	capacitance
henry	H	inductance
hertz	Hz	frequency
joule	J	work or energy
lumen	lm	luminous flux
lux	lx	illumination
newton	N	force
ohm	Ω	electric resistance
pascal	Pa	pressure
tesla	T	magnetic flux density
volt	V	electric potential (difference)
watt	W	power
weber	Wb	magnetic flux

Fundamental constants

constant	symbol	value
velocity of light in a vacuum	c	2.998×10^{8} m s^{-1}
charge on electron	e	1.602×10^{-19} C
rest mass of an electron	m_e	9.110×10^{-31} kg
rest mass of a proton	m_p	1.673×10^{-27} kg
rest mass of a neutron	m_n	1.675×10^{-27} kg
Avogadro's constant	L,N_A	6.022×10^{23} mol^{-1}
standard atmospheric pressure		1.013 Pa
acceleration due to gravity	g	9.807 m s^{-2}
velocity of sound at sea level at 0°C		331.46 m s^{-1}
magnetic constant (permeability of free space)	μ_o	$4\pi \times 10^{-7}$ H m^{-1}
electric constant (permittivity of free space)	$\epsilon_o = \mu_o{}^{-1}c^{-2}$	8.854×10^{-12} F m^{-1}
Planck's constant	h	6.626×10^{-34} J s
Boltzmann's constant	$k = \frac{R}{L}$	1.381×10^{-23} J K^{-1}
universal gas constant	R = Lk	8.314 J K^{-1} mol^{-1}
Faraday constant	F = Ne	9.649×10^{4} C mol^{-1}
gravitational constant	G	6.673×10^{-11} N m^{2} kg^{-2}

Other units used with SI (in specialized fields)

unit	symbol	value	concept
ångstrom	Å	10^{-10} m	length
astronomical unit	AU	149,600,000 km	length
degree celcius	C	1 K	temperature
electron volt	eV	1.60219×10^{-19} J	energy
parsec	pc	30857×10^{12} m	length

Metric prefixes

exa	E	10^{18}	1 000 000 000 000 000 000
peta	P	10^{15}	1 000 000 000 000 000
tera	T	10^{12}	1000 000 000 000
giga	G	10^{9}	1000 000 000
mega	M	10^{6}	1000 000
kilo	k	10^{3}	1000
hecto	h	10^{2}	100
deca	da	10^{1}	10
deci	d	10^{-1}	0.1
centi	c	10^{-2}	0.01
milli	m	10^{-3}	0.001
micro	μ	10^{-6}	0.000 001
nano	n	10^{-9}	0.000 000 001
pico	p	10^{-12}	0.000 000 000 001
femto	f	10^{-15}	0.000 000 000 000 001
atto	a	10^{-18}	0.000 000 000 000 000 001

Spectrum of electromagnetic radiation

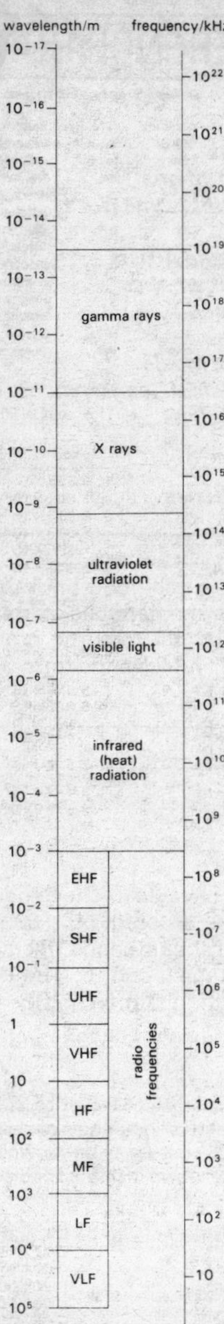

PENGUIN REFERENCE BOOKS

- ☐ *The Penguin English Thesaurus*
- ☐ *The Penguin Dictionary of Quotations*
- ☐ *The Penguin Dictionary of Troublesome Words*
- ☐ *A Dictionary of Literary Terms*
- ☐ *The Penguin Dictionary of Art and Artists*
- ☐ *The Penguin Dictionary of Mathematics*
- ☐ *The Penguin Medical Encyclopedia*
- ☐ *The Penguin Guide to the Law*
- ☐ *The New Penguin Dictionary of Music*
- ☐ *The Penguin Dictionary of Physical Geography*
- ☐ *The Penguin Dictionary of Religions*
- ☐ *The Penguin Map of the World*
- ☐ *The Penguin Map of Europe*
- ☐ *The Penguin Map of the British Isles*

These books should be available at all good bookshops or newsagents, but if you live in the UK or the Republic of Ireland and have difficulty in getting to a bookshop, they can be ordered by post. Please indicate the titles required and fill in the form below.

NAME ______________________________ BLOCK CAPITALS

ADDRESS ______________________________

____

____

Enclose a cheque or postal order payable to The Penguin Bookshop to cover the total price of books ordered, plus 50p for postage. Readers in the Republic of Ireland should send £1R equivalent to the sterling prices, plus 67p for postage. Send to: The Penguin Bookshop, 54/56 Bridlesmith Gate, Nottingham, NG1 2GP.

You can also order by phoning (0602) 599295, and quoting your Barclaycard or Access number.

Every effort is made to ensure the accuracy of the price and availability of books at the time of going to press, but it is sometimes necessary to increase prices and in these circumstances retail prices may be shown on the covers of books which may differ from the prices shown in this list or elsewhere. This list is not an offer to supply any book.

This order service is only available to residents in the UK and the Republic of Ireland.